GREAT BOOKS OF THE WESTERN WORLD

GREAT BOOKS
OF THE WESTERN WORLD

ROBERT MAYNARD HUTCHINS, *EDITOR IN CHIEF*

7.

PLATO

GREAT BOOKS
OF THE WESTERN WORLD

ROBERT MAYNARD HUTCHINS, EDITOR IN CHIEF

7

PLATO

MORTIMER J. ADLER, *Associate Editor*

Members of the Advisory Board: STRINGFELLOW BARR, SCOTT BUCHANAN, JOHN ERSKINE,
CLARENCE FAUST, ALEXANDER MEIKLEJOHN, JOSEPH J. SCHWAB, MARK VAN DOREN.

Editorial Consultants: A. F. B. CLARK, F. L. LUCAS, WALTER MURDOCH.

WALLACE BROCKWAY, *Executive Editor*

The Dialogues of
PLATO

TRANSLATED BY BENJAMIN JOWETT

The Seventh Letter

TRANSLATED BY J. HARWARD

WILLIAM BENTON, *Publisher*

ENCYCLOPÆDIA BRITANNICA, INC.

CHICAGO · LONDON · TORONTO · GENEVA

The Dialogues of Plato, translated by Benjamin Jowett, is reprinted by arrangement with OXFORD UNIVERSITY PRESS

The Seventh Epistle is reprinted from *The Platonic Epistles,* translated by J. Harward, by arrangement with CAMBRIDGE UNIVERSITY PRESS

THE UNIVERSITY OF CHICAGO

The Great Books
is published with the editorial advice of the faculties
of The University of Chicago

BIOGRAPHICAL NOTE

PLATO, c. 428 B.C.–c. 348 B.C.

PLATO, son of Ariston and Perictione, was born in 428 or 427 B.C. His family was, on both sides, one of the most distinguished of Athens. Ariston is said to have traced his descent through Codrus to the god Poseidon; on the mother's side, the family, which was related to Solon, goes back to Dropides, archon of the year 644 B.C. His mother apparently married as her second husband her uncle Pyrilampes, a prominent supporter of Pericles, and Plato was probably chiefly brought up in his house.

Plato's early life coincided with the disastrous years of the Peloponnesian War, the shattering of the Athenian Empire, and the fierce civil strife of oligarchs and democrats in the year of anarchy 404–403 B.C. He was too young to have learned anything by experience of the imperial democracy of Pericles, or of the full tide of the "sophistic" movement. He must have known Socrates from boyhood, for his relatives, Critias and Charmides, were old friends of the philosopher. Aristotle also ascribes to him an early familiarity with the Heracleitean, Cratylus. But Plato himself tells us in *The Seventh Letter* that his early ambitions were political. Following the establishment of the Tyranny of the Thirty in 404, in which his relatives were leaders, Plato was "invited to share in their doings as something to which I had a claim." He held back until their policy was revealed and then was repelled by their violence, particularly by their attempt to implicate Socrates in an illegal execution. He hoped for better things from the restored democracy until the condemnation of Socrates convinced him that he could no more collaborate with the democrats than with the oligarchs. Concluding that "public affairs at Athens were not carried on in accordance with the manners and practices of our fathers, nor was there any ready method by which I could make new friends," Plato abandoned his intention of devoting himself to politics.

After the execution of Socrates in 399 B.C., Plato went on a series of travels. It would seem that he then discovered his vocation to philosophy as he reflected on the life and teaching of Socrates. Hermodorus, an immediate disciple, is the authority for the statement that Plato and other Socratic men took temporary refuge at Megara with the philosopher Eucleides, who is said to have taught the doctrines of Socrates and of Parmenides. The Alexandrian *Lives* represent the next few years as spent in extensive travels in Greece, Egypt, and Italy. Plato's own statement is only that he visited Italy and Sicily at the age of forty, was disgusted by the gross sensuality of life there, but found a kindred spirit in Dion, brother-in-law of Dionysius I of Syracuse, who was to involve him again in politics twenty years later.

On his return to Athens about 387, Plato founded the Academy. He had presumably already completed some of his dialogues, in particular those celebrating the memory of Socrates. For the rest of his life he presided over the Academy, making it the intellectual center of Greek life; its only rival was the school of Isocrates. From the allusions of Aristotle it appears that Plato lectured without manuscript, and "problems" were propounded for solution by the joint researches of the students. In addition to philosophy, particular attention was given to science and law. The most important mathematical work of the fourth century was done by friends or pupils of Plato. Theatetus, the founder of solid geometry, was a member of the Academy, and Eudoxus of Cnidus is said to have removed his school from Cyzicus to Athens for the purpose of cooperation with Plato. The Academy was frequently called upon by various cities and colonies to furnish advisers on legislative matters; Plutarch records that among others "Plato sent Aristonymus to the Arcadians, Phormion to Elis, Menedemus to Pyrrha."

In 367, when Plato was in his sixtieth year and renowned as the head of the Academy, he was invited to intervene in the politics of Syracuse. Dionysius II had just assumed power, and Plato's friend, Dion, urged the philosopher to come and undertake the education of the young king and to strengthen him against the encroachment of Carthage in Sicily. Plato's reluctance to make such an attempt was overcome

v

only by his friendship for Dion and "a feeling of shame . . . lest I might someday appear to myself wholly and solely a mere man of words." Plato started Dionysius on a program of philosophical education, but in a few months found himself involved in the intrigues of the court against Dion, and when Dion was finally forced into virtual banishment, Plato returned to Athens. Dionysius, who prided himself on his philosophical accomplishments, kept in correspondence with Plato and prevailed upon him to visit Syracuse again in 361. Plato renewed his attempt to persuade Dionysius "not to enslave Sicily nor any other State to despots . . . but to put it under the rule of laws." But he again found that the tyrant refused "to act righteously" and allowed no opportunity for a rule in which "philosophy and power really met together." It was only after considerable personal danger that Plato reached Athens. He

never again attempted direct intervention in political affairs, although several members of the Academy joined Dion's expedition against Syracuse in 357, which resulted in the overthrow of the tyranny.

The Sicilian voyages are considered to mark a distinct break in Plato's literary activity. The work of his last years is now usually held to consist of a group of seven dialogues: *Theaetetus, Parmenides, Sophist, Statesman, Timaeus, Philebus,* and *Laws.* The Academy was presumably well organized by that time and made fewer administrative demands upon Plato. But we know from Aristotle, who became a student there in 367, that Plato still continued to lecture and to take a leading part in the research "problems." Legislation seems to have been given particular concern, and the *Laws* is said to have been in the process of publication when Plato died in 348 or 347 B.C.

CONTENTS

CONTENTS

CHARMIDES, or Temperance

PERSONS OF THE DIALOGUE: SOCRATES, *who is the narrator;* CHARMIDES; CHAEREPHON; CRITIAS. *Scene: The Palaestra of Taureas, which is near the Porch of the King Archon*

∞∞∞∞∞∞∞∞∞∞∞∞∞∞∞∞∞∞∞∞∞∞

[153] YESTERDAY evening I returned from the army at Potidaea, and having been a good while away, I thought that I should like to go and look at my old haunts. So I went into the palaestra of Taureas, which is over against the temple adjoining the porch of the King Archon, and there I found a number of persons, most of whom I knew, but not all. My visit was unexpected, and no sooner did they see me entering than they saluted me from afar on all sides; and Chaerephon, who is a kind of madman, started up and ran to me, seizing my hand, and saying, How did you escape, Socrates?—(I should explain that an engagement had taken place at Potidaea not long before we came away, of which the news had only just reached Athens.)

You see, I replied, that here I am.

There was a report, he said, that the engagement was very severe, and that many of our acquaintance had fallen.

That, I replied, was not far from the truth.

I suppose, he said, that you were present.

I was.

Then sit down, and tell us the whole story, which as yet we have only heard imperfectly.

I took the place which he assigned to me, by the side of Critias the son of Callaeschrus, and when I had saluted him and the rest of the company, I told them the news from the army, and answered their several enquiries.

Then, when there had been enough of this, I, in my turn, began to make enquiries about matters at home—about the present state of philosophy, and about the youth. I asked whether any of them were remarkable for wisdom or beauty, or both. Critias, glancing at the door, [154] invited my attention to some youths who were coming in, and talking noisily to one another, followed by a crowd. Of the beauties, Socrates, he said, I fancy that you will soon be able to form a judgment. For those who are just entering are the advanced guard of the great beauty, as he is thought to be, of the day, and he is likely to be not far off himself.

Who is he, I said; and who is his father?

Charmides, he replied, is his name; he is my cousin, and the son of my uncle Glaucon: I rather think that you know him too, although he was not grown up at the time of your departure.

Certainly, I know him, I said, for he was remarkable even then when he was still a child, and I should imagine that by this time he must be almost a young man.

You will see, he said, in a moment what progress he has made and what he is like. He had scarcely said the word, when Charmides entered.

Now you know, my friend, that I cannot measure anything, and of the beautiful, I am simply such a measure as a white line is of chalk; for almost all young persons appear to be beautiful in my eyes. But at that moment, when I saw him coming in, I confess that I was quite astonished at his beauty and stature; all the world seemed to be enamoured of him; amazement and confusion reigned when he entered; and a troop of lovers followed him. That grown-up men like ourselves should have been affected in this way was not surprising, but I observed that there was the same feeling among the boys; all of them, down to the very least child, turned and looked at him, as if he had been a statue.

Chaerephon called me and said: What do you think of him, Socrates? Has he not a beautiful face?

Most beautiful, I said.

But you would think nothing of his face, he replied, if you could see his naked form: he is absolutely perfect.

And to this they all agreed.

By Heracles, I said, there never was such a paragon, if he has only one other slight addition.

What is that? said Critias.

If he has a noble soul; and being of your house, Critias, he may be expected to have this.

He is as fair and good within, as he is without, replied Critias.

Then, before we see his body, should we not ask him to show us his soul, naked and undisguised? he is just of an age at which he will like to talk.

[155] That he will, said Critias, and I can tell you that he is a philosopher already, and also a considerable poet, not in his own opinion only, but in that of others.

That, my dear Critias, I replied, is a distinction which has long been in your family, and is inherited by you from Solon. But why do you not call him, and show him to us? for even if he were younger than he is, there could be no impropriety in his talking to us in the presence of you, who are his guardian and cousin.

Very well, he said; then I will call him; and turning to the attendant, he said, Call Charmides, and tell him that I want him to come and see a physician about the illness of which he spoke to me the day before yesterday. Then again addressing me, he added: He has been complaining lately of having a headache when he rises in the morning: now why should you not make him believe that you know a cure for the headache?

Why not, I said; but will he come?

He will be sure to come, he replied.

He came as he was bidden, and sat down between Critias and me. Great amusement was occasioned by every one pushing with might and main at his neighbour in order to make a place for him next to themselves, until at the two ends of the row one had to get up and the other was rolled over sideways. Now I, my friend, was beginning to feel awkward; my former bold belief in my powers of conversing with him had vanished. And when Critias told

him that I was the person who had the cure, he looked at me in such an indescribable manner, and was just going to ask a question. And at that moment all the people in the palaestra crowded about us, and, O rare! I caught a sight of the inwards of his garment, and took the flame. Then I could no longer contain myself. I thought how well Cydias understood the nature of love, when, in speaking of a fair youth, he warns some one "not to bring the fawn in the sight of the lion to be devoured by him," for I felt that I had been overcome by a sort of wild-beast appetite. But I controlled myself, and when he asked me if I knew the cure of the headache, I answered, but with an effort, that I did know.

And what is it? he said.

I replied that it was a kind of leaf, which required to be accompanied by a charm, and if a person would repeat the charm at the same time that he used the cure, he would be made whole; but that without the charm the leaf would be of no avail.

[156] Then I will write out the charm from your dictation, he said.

With my consent? I said, or without my consent?

With your consent, Socrates, he said, laughing.

Very good, I said; and are you quite sure that you know my name?

I ought to know you, he replied, for there is a great deal said about you among my companions; and I remember when I was a child seeing you in company with my cousin Critias.

I am glad to find that you remember me, I said; for I shall now be more at home with you and shall be better able to explain the nature of the charm, about which I felt a difficulty before. For the charm will do more, Charmides, than only cure the headache. I dare say that you have heard eminent physicians say to a patient who comes to them with bad eyes, that they cannot cure his eyes by themselves, but that if his eyes are to be cured, his head must be treated; and then again they say that to think of curing the head alone, and not the rest of the body also, is the height of folly. And arguing in this way they apply their methods to the whole body, and try to treat and heal the whole and the part together. Did you ever observe that this is what they say?

Yes, he said.

And they are right, and you would agree with them?

Yes, he said, certainly I should.

His approving answers reassured me, and I began by degrees to regain confidence, and the vital heat returned. Such, Charmides, I said, is the nature of the charm, which I learned when serving with the army from one of the physicians of the Thracian king Zamolxis, who are said to be so skilful that they can even give immortality. This Thracian told me that in these notions of theirs, which I was just now mentioning, the Greek physicians are quite right as far as they go; but Zamolxis, he added, our king, who is also a god, says further, "that as you ought not to attempt to cure the eyes without the head, or the head without the body, so neither ought you to attempt to cure the body without the soul; and this," he said, "is the reason why the cure of many diseases is unknown to the physicians of Hellas, because they are ignorant of the whole, which ought to be studied also; for the part can never be well unless the whole is well." For all good and evil, whether in the body or in human nature, originates, as he declared, in the soul, and overflows from thence, as if from the head into the eyes. [157] And therefore if the head and body are to be well, you must begin by curing the soul; that is the first thing. And the cure, my dear youth, has to be effected by the use of certain charms, and these charms are fair words; and by them temperance is implanted in the soul, and where temperance is, there health is speedily imparted, not only to the head, but to the whole body. And he who taught me the cure and the charm at the same time added a special direction: "Let no one," he said, "persuade you to cure the head, until he has first given you his soul to be cured by the charm. For this," he said, "is the great error of our day in the treatment of the human body, that physicians separate the soul from the body." And he added with emphasis, at the same time making me swear to his words, "Let no one, however rich, or noble, or fair, persuade you to give him the cure, without the charm." Now I have sworn, and I must keep my oath, and therefore if you will allow me to apply the Thracian charm first to your soul, as the stranger directed, I will afterwards proceed to apply the cure to your head. But if not, I do not know what I am to do with you, my dear Charmides.

Critias, when he heard this, said: The headache will be an unexpected gain to my young relation, if the pain in his head compels him to improve his mind: and I can tell you, Socrates, that Charmides is not only pre-eminent in beauty among his equals, but also in that quality which is given by the charm; and this, as you say, is temperance?

Yes, I said.

Then let me tell you that he is the most temperate of human beings, and for his age inferior to none in any quality.

Yes, I said, Charmides; and indeed I think that you ought to excel others in all good qualities; for if I am not mistaken there is no one present who could easily point out two Athenian houses, whose union would be likely to produce a better or nobler scion than the two from which you are sprung. There is your father's house, which is descended from Critias the son of Dropidas, whose family has been commemorated in the panegyrical verses of Anacreon, Solon, and many other poets, as famous for beauty and virtue and all other high fortune: [158] and your mother's house is equally distinguished; for your maternal uncle, Pyrilampes, is reputed never to have found his equal, in Persia at the court of the great king, or on the continent of Asia, in all the places to which he went as ambassador, for stature and beauty; that whole family is not a whit inferior to the other. Having such ancestors you ought to be first in all things, and, sweet son of Glaucon, your outward form is no dishonour to any of them. If to beauty you add temperance, and if in other respects you are what Critias declares you to be, then, dear Charmides, blessed art thou, in being the son of thy mother. And here lies the point; for if, as he declares, you have this gift of temperance already, and are temperate enough, in that case you have no need of any charms, whether of Zamolxis or of Abaris the Hyperborean, and I may as well let you have the cure of the head at once; but if you have not yet acquired this quality, I must use the charm before I give you the medicine. Please, therefore, to inform me whether you admit the truth of what Critias has been saying;—have you or have you not this quality of temperance?

Charmides blushed, and the blush heightened his beauty, for modesty is becoming in youth; he then said very ingenuously, that he really could not at once answer, either yes, or no, to the question which I had asked: For, said he, if I affirm that I am not temperate, that would be a strange thing for me to say of myself, and also I should give the lie to Critias, and many others who think as he tells you, that I am temperate: but, on the other hand, if I say that I am, I shall have to praise myself, which would be ill manners; and therefore I do not know how to answer you.

I said to him: That is a natural reply, Charmides, and I think that you and I ought together to enquire whether you have this quality about which I am asking or not; and then you will not be compelled to say what you do not like; neither shall I be a rash practitioner of medicine: therefore, if you please, I will share the enquiry with you, but I will not press you if you would rather not.

There is nothing which I should like better, he said; and as far as I am concerned you may proceed in the way which you think best.

[159] I think, I said, that I had better begin by asking you a question; for if temperance abides in you, you must have an opinion about her; she must give some intimation of her nature and qualities, which may enable you to form a notion of her. Is not that true?

Yes, he said, that I think is true.

You know your native language, I said, and therefore you must be able to tell what you feel about this.

Certainly, he said.

In order, then, that I may form a conjecture whether you have temperance abiding in you or not, tell me, I said, what, in your opinion, is Temperance?

At first he hesitated, and was very unwilling to answer: then he said that he thought temperance was doing things orderly and quietly, such things for example as walking in the streets, and talking, or anything else of that nature. In a word, he said, I should answer that, in my opinion, temperance is quietness.

Are you right, Charmides? I said. No doubt some would affirm that the quiet are the temperate; but let us see whether these words have any meaning; and first tell me whether you would not acknowledge temperance to be of the class of the noble and good?

Yes.

But which is best when you are at the writing-master's, to write the same letters quickly or quietly?

Quickly.

And to read quickly or slowly?

Quickly again.

And in playing the lyre, or wrestling, quickness or sharpness are far better than quietness and slowness?

Yes.

And the same holds in boxing and in the pancratium?

Certainly.

And in leaping and running and in bodily exercises generally, quickness and agility are good; slowness, and inactivity, and quietness, are bad?

That is evident.

Then, I said, in all bodily actions, not quietness, but the greatest agility and quickness, is noblest and best?

Yes, certainly.

And is temperance a good?

Yes.

Then, in reference to the body, not quietness, but quickness will be the higher degree of temperance, if temperance is a good?

True, he said.

And which, I said, is better—facility in learning, or difficulty in learning?

Facility.

Yes, I said; and facility in learning is learning quickly, and difficulty in learning is learning quietly and slowly?

True.

And is it not better to teach another quickly and energetically, rather than quietly and slowly?

Yes.

And which is better, to call to mind, and to remember, quickly and readily, or quietly and slowly?

The former.

[160] And is not shrewdness a quickness or cleverness of the soul, and not a quietness?

True.

And is it not best to understand what is said, whether at the writing-master's or the music-master's, or anywhere else, not as quietly as possible, but as quickly as possible?

Yes.

And in the searchings or deliberations of the soul, not the quietest, as I imagine, and he who with difficulty deliberates and discovers, is thought worthy of praise, but he who does so most easily and quickly?

Quite true, he said.

And in all that concerns either body or soul, swiftness and activity are clearly better than slowness and quietness?

Clearly they are.

Then temperance is not quietness, nor is the temperate life quiet,—certainly not upon this view; for the life which is temperate is supposed to be the good. And of two things, one is true,—either never, or very seldom, do the quiet actions in life appear to be better than the quick and energetic ones; or supposing that of the nobler actions, there are as many quiet, as quick and vehement: still, even if we grant this, temperance will not be acting quietly any more than acting quickly and energetically, either in walking or talking or in anything else; nor will the quiet life be more temperate than the unquiet, seeing that temperance is admitted by us to be a good and noble thing, and the quick have been shown to be as good as the quiet.

I think, he said, Socrates, that you are right.

Then once more, Charmides, I said, fix your attention, and look within; consider the effect which temperance has upon yourself, and the nature of that which has the effect. Think over all this, and, like a brave youth, tell me—What is temperance?

After a moment's pause, in which he made a real manly effort to think, he said: My opinion is, Socrates, that temperance makes a man ashamed or modest, and that temperance is the same as modesty.

Very good, I said; and did you not admit, just now, that temperance is noble?

Yes, certainly, he said.

And the temperate are also good?

Yes.

And can that be good which does not make men good?

Certainly not.

And you would infer that temperance is not only noble, but also good?

[161] That is my opinion.

Well, I said; but surely you would agree with Homer when he says,

Modesty is not good for a needy man?

Yes, he said; I agree.

Then I suppose that modesty is and is not good?

Clearly.

But temperance, whose presence makes men only good, and not bad, is always good?

That appears to me to be as you say.

And the inference is that temperance cannot be modesty—if temperance is a good, and if modesty is as much an evil as a good?

All that, Socrates, appears to me to be true; but I should like to know what you think about another definition of temperance, which I just now remember to have heard from some one, who said, "That temperance is doing our own business." Was he right who affirmed that?

You monster! I said; this is what Critias, or some philosopher has told you.

Some one else, then, said Critias; for certainly I have not.

But what matter, said Charmides, from whom I heard this?

No matter at all, I replied; for the point is not who said the words, but whether they are true or not.

There you are in the right, Socrates, he replied.

To be sure, I said; yet I doubt whether we shall ever be able to discover their truth or falsehood; for they are a kind of riddle.

What makes you think so? he said.

Because, I said, he who uttered them seems to me to have meant one thing, and said another. Is the scribe, for example, to be regarded as doing nothing when he reads or writes?

I should rather think that he was doing something.

And does the scribe write or read, or teach you boys to write or read, your own names only, or did you write your enemies' names as well as your own and your friends'?

As much one as the other.

And was there anything meddling or intemperate in this?

Certainly not.

And yet if reading and writing are the same as doing, you were doing what was not your own business?

But they are the same as doing.

And the healing art, my friend, and building, and weaving, and doing anything whatever which is done by art,—these all clearly come under the head of doing?

Certainly.

And do you think that a state would be well ordered by a law which compelled every man to weave and wash his own coat, and make his own shoes, and his own flask and strigil, and other implements, [162] on this principle of every one doing and performing his own, and abstaining from what is not his own?

I think not, he said.

But, I said, a temperate state will be a well-ordered state.

Of course, he replied.

Then temperance, I said, will not be doing one's own business; not at least in this way, or doing things of this sort?

Clearly not.

Then, as I was just now saying, he who declared that temperance is a man doing his own business had another and a hidden meaning; for I do not think that he could have been such a fool as to mean this. Was he a fool who told you, Charmides?

Nay, he replied, I certainly thought him a very wise man.

Then I am quite certain that he put forth his definition as a riddle, thinking that no one would know the meaning of the words "doing his own business."

I dare say, he replied.

And what is the meaning of a man doing his own business? Can you tell me?

Indeed, I cannot; and I should not wonder if the man himself who used this phrase did not understand what he was saying. Whereupon he laughed slyly, and looked at Critias.

Critias had long been showing uneasiness, for he felt that he had a reputation to maintain with Charmides and the rest of the company. He had, however, hitherto managed to restrain himself; but now he could no longer forbear, and I am convinced of the truth of the suspicion which I entertained at the time, that Charmides had heard this answer about temperance from Critias. And Charmides, who did not want to answer himself, but to make Critias answer, tried to stir him up. He went on pointing out that he had been refuted, at which Critias grew angry, and appeared, as I thought, inclined to quarrel with him; just as a poet might quarrel with an actor who spoiled his poems in repeating them; so he looked hard at him and said—

Do you imagine, Charmides, that the author of this definition of temperance did not understand the meaning of his own words, because you do not understand them?

Why, at his age, I said, most excellent Critias, he can hardly be expected to understand; but you, who are older, and have studied, may well be assumed to know the meaning of them; and therefore, if you agree with him, and accept his definition of temperance, I would much rather argue with you than with him about the truth or falsehood of the definition.

I entirely agree, said Critias, and accept the definition.

Very good, I said; and now let me repeat my question—Do you admit, as I was just now saying, that all craftsmen make or do something?

I do.

[163] And do they make or do their own business only, or that of others also?

They make or do that of others also.

And are they temperate, seeing that they make not for themselves or their own business only?

Why not? he said.

No objection on my part, I said, but there may be a difficulty on his who proposes as a definition of temperance, "doing one's own business," and then says that there is no reason why those who do the business of others should not be temperate.

Nay, said he; did I ever acknowledge that those who do the business of others are temperate? I said, those who make, not those who do.

What! I asked; do you mean to say that doing and making are not the same?

No more, he replied, than making or working are the same; thus much I have learned from Hesiod, who says that "work is no disgrace." Now do you imagine that if he had meant by working and doing such things as you were describing, he would have said that there was no disgrace in them—for example, in the manufacture of shoes, or in selling pickles, or sitting for hire in a house of ill-fame? That, Socrates, is not to be supposed: but I conceive him to have distinguished making from doing and work; and, while admitting that the making anything might sometimes become a disgrace, when the employment was not honourable, to have thought that work was never any disgrace at all. For things nobly and usefully made he called works; and such makings he called workings, and doings; and he must be supposed to have called such things only man's proper business, and what is hurtful, not his business: and in that sense Hesiod, and any other wise man, may be reasonably supposed to call him wise who does his own work.

O Critias, I said, no sooner had you opened your mouth, than I pretty well knew that you would call that which is proper to a man, and that which is his own, good; and that the markings of the good you would call doings, for I am no stranger to the endless distinctions which Prodicus draws about names. Now I have no objection to your giving names any signification which you please, if you will only tell me what you mean by them. Please then to begin again, and be a little plainer. Do you mean that this doing or making, or whatever is the word which you would use, of good actions, is temperance?

I do, he said.

Then not he who does evil, but he who does good, is temperate?

Yes, he said; and you, friend, would agree.

No matter whether I should or not; just now, not what I think, but what you are saying, is the point at issue.

Well, he answered; I mean to say, that he who does evil, and not good, is not temperate; and that he is temperate who does good, and not evil: for temperance I define in plain words to be the doing of good actions.

[164] And you may be very likely right in

what you are saying; but I am curious to know whether you imagine that temperate men are ignorant of their own temperance?

I do not think so, he said.

And yet were you not saying, just now, that craftsmen might be temperate in doing another's work, as well as in doing their own?

I was, he replied; but what is your drift?

I have no particular drift, but I wish that you would tell me whether a physician who cures a patient may do good to himself and good to another also?

I think that he may.

And he who does so does his duty?

Yes.

And does not he who does his duty act temperately or wisely?

Yes, he acts wisely.

But must the physician necessarily know when his treatment is likely to prove beneficial, and when not? or must the craftsman necessarily know when he is likely to be benefited, and when not to be benefited, by the work which he is doing?

I suppose not.

Then, I said, he may sometimes do good or harm, and not know what he is himself doing, and yet, in doing good, as you say, he has done temperately or wisely. Was not that your statement?

Yes.

Then, as would seem, in doing good, he may act wisely or temperately, and be wise or temperate, but not know his own wisdom or temperance?

But that, Socrates, he said, is impossible; and therefore if this is, as you imply, the necessary consequence of any of my previous admissions, I will withdraw them, rather than admit that a man can be temperate or wise who does not know himself; and I am not ashamed to confess that I was in error. For self-knowledge would certainly be maintained by me to be the very essence of knowledge, and in this I agree with him who dedicated the inscription, "Know thyself!" at Delphi. That word, if I am not mistaken, is put there as a sort of salutation which the god addresses to those who enter the temple; as much as to say that the ordinary salutation of "Hail!" is not right, and that the exhortation "Be temperate!" would be a far better way of saluting one another. The notion of him who dedicated the inscription was, as I believe, that the god speaks to those who enter his temple, not as men speak; but, when a worshipper enters, the first word which he hears is "Be temperate!" This, however, like a prophet he expresses in a sort of riddle, for "Know thyself!" and "Be temperate!" are the same, as I maintain, and as the letters imply, and yet they may be easily misunderstood; [165] and succeeding sages who added "Never too much," or, "Give a pledge, and evil is nigh at hand," would appear to have so misunderstood them; for they imagined that "Know thyself!" was a piece of advice which the god gave, and not his salutation of the worshippers at their first coming in; and they dedicated their own inscription under the idea that they too would give equally useful pieces of advice. Shall I tell you, Socrates, why I say all this? My object is to leave the previous discussion (in which I know not whether you or I are more right, but, at any rate, no clear result was attained), and to raise a new one in which I will attempt to prove, if you deny, that temperance is self-knowledge.

Yes, I said, Critias; but you come to me as though I professed to know about the questions which I ask, and as though I could, if I only would, agree with you. Whereas the fact is that I enquire with you into the truth of that which is advanced from time to time, just because I do not know; and when I have enquired, I will say whether I agree with you or not. Please then to allow me time to reflect.

Reflect, he said.

I am reflecting, I replied, and discover that temperance, or wisdom, if implying a knowledge of anything, must be a science, and a science of something.

Yes, he said; the science of itself.

Is not medicine, I said, the science of health?

True.

And suppose, I said, that I were asked by you what is the use or effect of medicine, which is this science of health, I should answer that medicine is of very great use in producing health, which, as you will admit, is an excellent effect.

Granted.

And if you were to ask me, what is the result or effect of architecture, which is the science of building, I should say houses, and so of other arts, which all have their different results. Now I want you, Critias, to answer a similar question about temperance, or wisdom, which, according to you, is the science of itself. Admitting this view, I ask of you, what good work, worthy of the name wise, does temperance or wisdom, which is the science of itself, effect? Answer me.

That is not the true way of pursuing the enquiry, Socrates, he said; for wisdom is not like the other sciences, any more than they are like one another: but you proceed as if they were alike. For tell me, he said, what result is there of computation or geometry, in the same sense as a house is the result of building, or a garment of weaving, [166] or any other work of any other art? Can you show me any such result of them? You cannot.

That is true, I said; but still each of these sciences has a subject which is different from the science. I can show you that the art of computation has to do with odd and even numbers in their numerical relations to themselves and to each other. Is not that true?

Yes, he said.

And the odd and even numbers are not the same with the art of computation?

They are not.

The art of weighing, again, has to do with lighter and heavier; but the art of weighing is one thing, and the heavy and the light another. Do you admit that?

Yes.

Now, I want to know, what is that which is not wisdom, and of which wisdom is the science?

You are just falling into the old error, Socrates, he said. You come asking in what wisdom or temperance differs from the other sciences, and then you try to discover some respect in which they are alike; but they are not, for all the other sciences are of something else, and not of themselves; wisdom alone is a science of other sciences, and of itself. And of this, as I believe, you are very well aware: and that you are only doing what you denied that you were doing just now, trying to refute me, instead of pursuing the argument.

And what if I am? How can you think that I have any other motive in refuting you but what I should have in examining into myself? which motive would be just a fear of my unconsciously fancying that I knew something of which I was ignorant. And at this moment I pursue the argument chiefly for my own sake, and perhaps in some degree also for the sake of my other friends. For is not the discovery of things as they truly are, a good common to all mankind?

Yes, certainly, Socrates, he said.

Then, I said, be cheerful, sweet sir, and give your opinion in answer to the question which I asked, never minding whether Critias or Socrates is the person refuted; attend only to the argument, and see what will come of the refutation.

I think that you are right, he replied; and I will do as you say.

Tell me, then, I said, what you mean to affirm about wisdom.

I mean to say that wisdom is the only science which is the science of itself as well as of the other sciences.

But the science of science, I said, will also be the science of the absence of science.

Very true, he said.

[167] Then the wise or temperate man, and he only, will know himself, and be able to examine what he knows or does not know, and to see what others know and think that they know and do really know; and what they do not know, and fancy that they know, when they do not. No other person will be able to do this. And this is wisdom and temperance and self-knowledge—for a man to know what he knows, and what he does not know. That is your meaning?

Yes, he said.

Now then, I said, making an offering of the third or last argument to Zeus the Saviour, let us begin again, and ask, in the first place, whether it is or is not possible for a person to know that he knows and does not know what he knows and does not know; and in the second place, whether, if perfectly possible, such knowledge is of any use.

That is what we have to consider, he said.

And here, Critias, I said, I hope that you will find a way out of a difficulty into which I have got myself. Shall I tell you the nature of the difficulty?

By all means, he replied.

Does not what you have been saying, if true, amount to this: that there must be a single science which is wholly a science of itself and of other sciences, and that the same is also the science of the absence of science?

Yes.

But consider how monstrous this proposition is, my friend: in any parallel case, the impossibility will be transparent to you.

How is that? and in what cases do you mean?

In such cases as this: Suppose that there is a kind of vision which is not like ordinary vision, but a vision of itself and of other sorts of vision, and of the defect of them, which in seeing sees no colour, but only itself and other sorts of vision: Do you think that there is such a kind of vision?

Certainly not.

Or is there a kind of hearing which hears no

sound at all, but only itself and other sorts of hearing, or the defects of them?

There is not.

Or take all the senses: can you imagine that there is any sense of itself and of other senses, but which is incapable of perceiving the objects of the senses?

I think not.

Could there be any desire which is not the desire of any pleasure, but of itself, and of all other desires?

Certainly not.

Or can you imagine a wish which wishes for no good, but only for itself and all other wishes?

I should answer, No.

Or would you say that there is a love which is not the love of beauty, but of itself and of other loves?

I should not.

[168] Or did you ever know of a fear which fears itself or other fears, but has no object of fear?

I never did, he said.

Or of an opinion which is an opinion of itself and of other opinions, and which has no opinion on the subjects of opinion in general?

Certainly not.

But surely we are assuming a science of this kind, which, having no subject-matter, is a science of itself and of the other sciences?

Yes, that is what is affirmed.

But how strange is this, if it be indeed true: we must not however as yet absolutely deny the possibility of such a science; let us rather consider the matter.

You are quite right.

Well then, this science of which we are speaking is a science of something, and is of a nature to be a science of something?

Yes.

Just as that which is greater is of a nature to be greater than something else?

Yes.

Which is less, if the other is conceived to be greater?

To be sure.

And if we could find something which is at once greater than itself, and greater than other great things, but not greater than those things in comparison of which the others are greater, then that thing would have the property of being greater and also less than itself?

That, Socrates, he said, is the inevitable inference.

Or if there be a double which is double of itself and of other doubles, these will be halves; for the double is relative to the half?

That is true.

And that which is greater than itself will also be less, and that which is heavier will also be lighter, and that which is older will also be younger: and the same of other things; that which has a nature relative to self will retain also the nature of its object: I mean to say, for example, that hearing is, as we say, of sound or voice. Is that true?

Yes.

Then if hearing hears itself, it must hear a voice; for there is no other way of hearing.

Certainly.

And sight also, my excellent friend, if it sees itself must see a colour, for sight cannot see that which has no colour.

No.

Do you remark, Critias, that in several of the examples which have been recited the notion of a relation to self is altogether inadmissible, and in other cases hardly credible—inadmissible, for example, in the case of magnitudes, numbers, and the like?

Very true.

But in the case of hearing and sight, or in the power of self-motion, and the power of heat to burn, this relation to self will be regarded as incredible by some, [169] but perhaps not by others. And some great man, my friend, is wanted, who will satisfactorily determine for us, whether there is nothing which has an inherent property of relation to self, or some things only and not others; and whether in this class of self-related things, if there be such a class, that science which is called wisdom or temperance is included. I altogether distrust my own power of determining these matters: I am not certain whether there is such a science of science at all; and even if there be, I should not acknowledge this to be wisdom or temperance, until I can also see whether such a science would or would not do us any good; for I have an impression that temperance is a benefit and a good. And therefore, O son of Callaeschrus, as you maintain that temperance or wisdom is a science of science, and also of the absence of science, I will request you to show in the first place, as I was saying before, the possibility, and in the second place, the advantage, of such a science; and then perhaps you may satisfy me that you are right in your view of temperance.

Critias heard me say this, and saw that I was in a difficulty; and as one person when another yawns in his presence catches the infection of yawning from him, so did he seem to be driven into a difficulty by my difficulty. But as he had a reputation to maintain, he was ashamed to admit before the company that he could not answer my challenge or determine the question at issue; and he made an unintelligible attempt to hide his perplexity. In order that the argument might proceed, I said to him, Well then, Critias, if you like, let us assume that there is this science of science; whether the assumption is right or wrong may hereafter be investigated. Admitting the existence of it, will you tell me how such a science enables us to distinguish what we know or do not know, which, as we were saying, is self-knowledge or wisdom: so we were saying?

Yes, Socrates, he said; and that I think is certainly true: for he who has this science or knowledge which knows itself will become like the knowledge which he has, in the same way that he who has swiftness will be swift, and he who has beauty will be beautiful, and he who has knowledge will know. In the same way he who has that knowledge which is self-knowing, will know himself.

I do not doubt, I said, that a man will know himself, when he possesses that which has self-knowledge: but what necessity is there that, having this, he should know what he knows and what he does not know?

[170] Because, Socrates, they are the same.

Very likely, I said; but I remain as stupid as ever; for still I fail to comprehend how this knowing what you know and do not know is the same as the knowledge of self.

What do you mean? he said.

This is what I mean, I replied: I will admit that there is a science of science;—can this do more than determine that of two things one is and the other is not science or knowledge?

No, just that.

But is knowledge or want of knowledge of health the same as knowledge or want of knowledge of justice?

Certainly not.

The one is medicine, and the other is politics; whereas that of which we are speaking is knowledge pure and simple.

Very true.

And if a man knows only, and has only knowledge of knowledge, and has no further knowledge of health and justice, the probability is that he will only know that he knows something, and has a certain knowledge, whether concerning himself or other men.

True.

Then how will this knowledge or science teach him to know what he knows? Say that he knows health;—not wisdom or temperance, but the art of medicine has taught it to him;—and he has learned harmony from the art of music, and building from the art of building,—neither, from wisdom or temperance: and the same of other things.

That is evident.

How will wisdom, regarded only as a knowledge of knowledge or science of science, ever teach him that he knows health, or that he knows building?

It is impossible.

Then he who is ignorant of these things will only know that he knows, but not what he knows?

True.

Then wisdom or being wise appears to be not the knowledge of the things which we do or do not know, but only the knowledge that we know or do not know?

That is the inference.

Then he who has this knowledge will not be able to examine whether a pretender knows or does not know that which he says that he knows: he will only know that he has a knowledge of some kind; but wisdom will not show him of what the knowledge is?

Plainly not.

Neither will he be able to distinguish the pretender in medicine from the true physician, nor between any other true and false professor of knowledge. Let us consider the matter in this way: If the wise man or any other man wants to distinguish the true physician from the false, how will he proceed? He will not talk to him about medicine; and that, as we were saying, is the only thing which the physician understands.

True.

And, on the other hand, the physician knows nothing of science, for this has been assumed to be the province of wisdom.

True.

[171] And further, since medicine is science, we must infer that he does not know anything of medicine.

Exactly.

Then the wise man may indeed know that the physician has some kind of science or knowledge; but when he wants to discover the nature of this he will ask, What is the subject-matter? For the several sciences are distinguished not by the mere fact that they are sciences, but by the nature of their subjects. Is not that true?

Quite true.

And medicine is distinguished from other sciences as having the subject-matter of health and disease?

Yes.

And he who would enquire into the nature of medicine must pursue the enquiry into health and disease, and not into what is extraneous?

True.

And he who judges rightly will judge of the physician as a physician in what relates to these?

He will.

He will consider whether what he says is true, and whether what he does is right, in relation to health and disease?

He will.

But can any one attain the knowledge of either unless he have a knowledge of medicine?

He cannot.

No one at all, it would seem, except the physician can have this knowledge; and therefore not the wise man; he would have to be a physician as well as a wise man.

Very true.

Then, assuredly, wisdom or temperance, if only a science of science, and of the absence of science or knowledge, will not be able to distinguish the physician who knows from one who does not know but pretends or thinks that he knows, or any other professor of anything at all; like any other artist, he will only know his fellow in art or wisdom, and no one else.

That is evident, he said.

But then what profit, Critias, I said, is there any longer in wisdom or temperance which yet remains, if this is wisdom? If, indeed, as we were supposing at first, the wise man had been able to distinguish what he knew and did not know, and that he knew the one and did not know the other, and to recognize a similar faculty of discernment in others, there would certainly have been a great advantage in being wise; for then we should never have made a mistake, but have passed through life the unerring guides of ourselves and of those who are under us; and we should not have attempted to do what we did not know, but we should have found out those who knew, and have handed the business over to them and trusted in them; nor should we have allowed those who were under us to do anything which they were not likely to do well and they would be likely to do well just that of which they had knowledge; and the house or state which was ordered or administered under the guidance of wisdom, and everything else of

which wisdom was the lord, would have been well ordered; for truth guiding, and error having been eliminated, [172] in all their doings, men would have done well, and would have been happy. Was not this, Critias, what we spoke of as the great advantage of wisdom—to know what is known and what is unknown to us?

Very true, he said.

And now you perceive, I said, that no such science is to be found anywhere.

I perceive, he said.

May we assume then, I said, that wisdom, viewed in this new light merely as a knowledge of knowledge and ignorance, has this advantage:—that he who possesses such knowledge will more easily learn anything which he learns; and that everything will be clearer to him, because, in addition to the knowledge of individuals, he sees the science, and this also will better enable him to test the knowledge which others have of what he knows himself; whereas the enquirer who is without this knowledge may be supposed to have a feebler and weaker insight? Are not these, my friend, the real advantages which are to be gained from wisdom? And are not we looking and seeking after something more than is to be found in her?

That is very likely, he said.

That is very likely, I said; and very likely, too, we have been enquiring to no purpose; as I am led to infer, because I observe that if this is wisdom, some strange consequences would follow. Let us, if you please, assume the possibility of this science of sciences, and further admit and allow, as was originally suggested, that wisdom is the knowledge of what we know and do not know. Assuming all this, still, upon further consideration, I am doubtful, Critias, whether wisdom, such as this, would do us much good. For we were wrong, I think, in supposing, as we were saying just now, that such wisdom ordering the government of house or state would be a great benefit.

How so? he said.

Why, I said, we were far too ready to admit the great benefits which mankind would obtain from their severally doing the things which they knew, and committing the things of which they are ignorant to those who were better acquainted with them.

Were we not right in making that admission?

I think not.

How very strange, Socrates!

By the dog of Egypt, I said, there I agree with you; and I was thinking as much just now when I said that strange consequences would follow, and that I was afraid we were on the wrong track; for however ready we may be to admit that this is wisdom, *[173]* I certainly cannot make out what good this sort of thing does to us.

What do you mean? he said; I wish that you could make me understand what you mean.

I dare say that what I am saying is nonsense, I replied; and yet if a man has any feeling of what is due to himself, he cannot let the thought which comes into his mind pass away unheeded and unexamined.

I like that, he said.

Hear, then, I said, my own dream; whether coming through the horn or the ivory gate, I cannot tell. The dream is this: Let us suppose that wisdom is such as we are now defining, and that she has absolute sway over us; then each action will be done according to the arts or sciences, and no one professing to be a pilot when he is not, or any physician or general, or any one else pretending to know matters of which he is ignorant, will deceive or elude us; our health will be improved; our safety at sea, and also in battle, will be assured; our coats and shoes, and all other instruments and implements will be skilfully made, because the workmen will be good and true. Aye, and if you please, you may suppose that prophecy, which is the knowledge of the future, will be under the control of wisdom, and that she will deter deceivers and set up the true prophets in their place as the revealers of the future. Now I quite agree that mankind, thus provided, would live and act according to knowledge, for wisdom would watch and prevent ignorance from intruding on us. But whether by acting according to knowledge we shall act well and be happy, my dear Critias,—this is a point which we have not yet been able to determine.

Yet I think, he replied, that if you discard knowledge, you will hardly find the crown of happiness in anything else.

But of what is this knowledge? I said. Just answer me that small question. Do you mean a knowledge of shoemaking?

God forbid.

Or of working in brass?

Certainly not.

Or in wool, or wood, or anything of that sort?

No, I do not.

Then, I said, we are giving up the doctrine that he who lives according to knowledge is happy, for these live according to knowledge, and yet they are not allowed by you to be happy; but I think that you mean to confine happiness to particular individuals who live according to knowledge, *[174]* such for example as the prophet, who, as I was saying, knows the future. Is it of him you are speaking or of some one else?

Yes, I mean him, but there are others as well.

Yes, I said, some one who knows the past and present as well as the future, and is ignorant of nothing. Let us suppose that there is such a person, and if there is, you will allow that he is the most knowing of all living men.

Certainly he is.

Yet I should like to know one thing more: which of the different kinds of knowledge makes him happy? or do all equally make him happy?

Not all equally, he replied.

But which most tends to make him happy? the knowledge of what past, present, or future thing? May I infer this to be the knowledge of the game of draughts?

Nonsense about the game of draughts.

Or of computation?

No.

Or of health?

That is nearer the truth, he said.

And that knowledge which is nearest of all, I said, is the knowledge of what?

The knowledge with which he discerns good and evil.

Monster! I said; you have been carrying me round in a circle, and all this time hiding from me the fact that the life according to knowledge is not that which makes men act rightly and be happy, not even if knowledge include all the sciences, but one science only, that of good and evil. For, let me ask you, Critias, whether, if you take away this, medicine will not equally give health, and shoemaking equally produce shoes, and the art of the weaver clothes?—whether the art of the pilot will not equally save our lives at sea, and the art of the general in war?

Quite so.

And yet, my dear Critias, none of these things will be well or beneficially done, if the science of the good be wanting.

True.

But that science is not wisdom or temperance, but a science of human advantage; not a science of other sciences, or of ignorance, but of good and evil: and if this be of use, then wisdom or temperance will not be of use.

And why, he replied, will not wisdom be of use? For, however much we assume that wisdom is a science of sciences, and has a sway over other sciences, surely she will have this particular science of the good under her control, and in this way will benefit us.

And will wisdom give health? I said; is not this rather the effect of medicine? Or does wisdom do the work of any of the other arts,— do they not each of them do their own work? Have we not long ago asseverated that wisdom is only the knowledge of knowledge and of ignorance, and of nothing else?

That is obvious.

Then wisdom will not be the producer of health.

Certainly not.

The art of health is different.

Yes, different.

[175] Nor does wisdom give advantage, my good friend; for that again we have just now been attributing to another art.

Very true.

How then can wisdom be advantageous, when giving no advantage?

That, Socrates, is certainly inconceivable.

You see then, Critias, that I was not far wrong in fearing that I could have no sound notion about wisdom; I was quite right in depreciating myself; for that which is admitted to be the best of all things would never have seemed to us useless, if I had been good for anything at an enquiry. But now I have been utterly defeated, and have failed to discover what that is to which the imposer of names gave this name of temperance or wisdom. And yet many more admissions were made by us than could be fairly granted; for we admitted that there was a science of science, although the argument said No, and protested against us; and we admitted further, that this science knew the works of the other sciences (although this too was denied by the argument), because we wanted to show that the wise man had knowledge of what he knew and did not know; also we nobly disregarded, and never even considered, the impossibility of a man knowing in a sort of way that which he does not know at all; for our assumption was, that he knows that which he does not know; than which nothing, as I think, can be more irrational. And yet, after finding us so easy and good-natured, the enquiry is still unable to discover the truth; but mocks us to a degree, and has gone out of its way to prove the inutility of that which we admitted only by a sort of supposition and fiction to be the true definition of temperance or wisdom: which result, as far as I am con-

cerned, is not so much to be lamented, I said. But for your sake, Charmides, I am very sorry —that you, having such beauty and such wisdom and temperance of soul, should have no profit or good in life from your wisdom and temperance. And still more am I grieved about the charm which I learned with so much pain, and to so little profit, from the Thracian, for the sake of a thing which is nothing worth. I think indeed that there is a mistake, and that I must be a bad enquirer, for wisdom or temperance I believe to be really a great good; and happy are you, Charmides, if you certainly possess it. Wherefore examine yourself, [176] and see whether you have this gift and can do without the charm; for if you can, I would rather advise you to regard me simply as a fool who is never able to reason out anything; and to rest assured that the more wise and temperate you are, the happier you will be.

Charmides said: I am sure that I do not know, Socrates, whether I have or have not this gift of wisdom and temperance; for how can I know whether I have a thing, of which even you and Critias are, as you say, unable to discover the nature?—(not that I believe you.) And further, I am sure, Socrates, that I do need the charm, and as far as I am concerned, I shall be willing to be charmed by you daily, until you say that I have had enough.

Very good, Charmides, said Critias; if you do this I shall have a proof of your temperance, that is, if you allow yourself to be charmed by Socrates, and never desert him at all.

You may depend on my following and not deserting him, said Charmides: if you who are my guardian command me, I should be very wrong not to obey you.

And I do command you, he said.

Then I will do as you say, and begin this very day.

You sirs, I said, what are you conspiring about?

We are not conspiring, said Charmides, we have conspired already.

And are you about to use violence, without even going through the forms of justice?

Yes, I shall use violence, he replied, since he orders me; and therefore you had better consider well.

But the time for consideration has passed, I said, when violence is employed; and you, when you are determined on anything, and in the mood of violence, are irresistible.

Do not you resist me then, he said.

I will not resist you, I replied.

LYSIS, or Friendship

PERSONS OF THE DIALOGUE: SOCRATES, *who is the narrator;* MENEXENUS; HIPPOTHALES; LYSIS; CTESIPPUS. *Scene: A newly-erected Palaestra outside the walls of Athens*

❧❧❧❧❧❧❧❧❧❧❧❧❧

[203] I WAS going from the Academy straight to the Lyceum, intending to take the outer road, which is close under the wall. When I came to the postern gate of the city, which is by the fountain of Panops, I fell in with Hippothales, the son of Hieronymus, and Ctesippus the Paeanian, and a company of young men who were standing with them. Hippothales, seeing me approach, asked whence I came and whither I was going.

I am going, I replied, from the Academy straight to the Lyceum.

Then come straight to us, he said, and put in here; you may as well.

Who are you, I said; and where am I to come?

He showed me an enclosed space and an open door over against the wall. And there, he said, is the building at which we all meet: and a goodly company we are.

And what is this building, I asked; and what sort of entertainment have you?

[204] The building, he replied, is a newly-erected Palaestra; and the entertainment is generally conversation, to which you are welcome.

Thank you, I said; and is there any teacher there?

Yes, he said, your old friend and admirer, Miccus.

Indeed, I replied; he is a very eminent professor.

Are you disposed, he said, to go with me and see them?

Yes, I said; but I should like to know first, what is expected of me, and who is the favourite among you?

Some persons have one favourite, Socrates, and some another, he said.

And who is yours? I asked: tell me that, Hippothales.

At this he blushed; and I said to him, O Hippothales, thou son of Hieronymus! do not say that you are, or that you are not, in love; the confession is too late; for I see that you are not only in love, but are already far gone in your love. Simple and foolish as I am, the Gods have given me the power of understanding affections of this kind.

Whereupon he blushed more and more.

Ctesippus said: I like to see you blushing, Hippothales, and hesitating to tell Socrates the name; when, if he were with you but for a very short time, you would have plagued him to death by talking about nothing else. Indeed, Socrates, he has literally deafened us, and stopped our ears with the praises of Lysis; and if he is a little intoxicated, there is every likelihood that we may have our sleep murdered with a cry of Lysis. His performances in prose are bad enough, but nothing at all in comparison with his verse; and when he drenches us with his poems and other compositions, it is really too bad; and worse still is his manner of singing them to his love; he has a voice which is truly appalling, and we cannot help hearing him: and now having a question put to him by you, behold he is blushing.

Who is Lysis? I said: I suppose that he must be young; for the name does not recall any one to me.

Why, he said, his father being a very well-known man, he retains his patronymic, and is not as yet commonly called by his own name; but, although you do not know his name, I am sure that you must know his face, for that is quite enough to distinguish him.

But tell me whose son he is, I said.

He is the eldest son of Democrates, of the deme of Aexonè.

Ah, Hippothales, I said; what a noble and really perfect love you have found! I wish that you would favour me with the exhibition which you have been making to the rest of the company, and then I shall be able to judge whether you know what a lover ought to say [205] about his love, either to the youth himself, or to others.

Nay, Socrates, he said; you surely do not attach any importance to what he is saying.

Do you mean, I said, that you disown the love of the person whom he says that you love?

No; but I deny that I make verses or address compositions to him.

He is not in his right mind, said Ctesippus; he is talking nonsense, and is stark mad.

O Hippothales, I said, if you have ever made any verses or songs in honour of your favourite, I do not want to hear them; but I want to know the purport of them, that I may be able to judge of your mode of approaching your fair one.

Ctesippus will be able to tell you, he said; for if, as he avers, the sound of my words is always dinning in his ears, he must have a very accurate knowledge and recollection of them.

Yes, indeed, said Ctesippus; I know only too well; and very ridiculous the tale is: for although he is a lover, and very devotedly in love, he has nothing particular to talk about to his beloved which a child might not say. Now is not that ridiculous? He can only speak of the wealth of Democrates, which the whole city celebrates, and grandfather Lysis, and the other ancestors of the youth, and their stud of horses, and their victory at the Pythian games, and at the Isthmus, and at Nemea with four horses and single horses—these are the tales which he composes and repeats. And there is greater twaddle still. Only the day before yesterday he made a poem in which he described the entertainment of Heracles, who was a connexion of the family, setting forth how in virtue of this relationship he was hospitably received by an ancestor of Lysis; this ancestor was himself begotten of Zeus by the daughter of the founder of the deme. And these are the sort of old wives' tales which he sings and recites to us, and we are obliged to listen to him.

When I heard this, I said: O ridiculous Hippothales! how can you be making and singing hymns in honour of yourself before you have won?

But my songs and verses, he said, are not in honour of myself, Socrates.

You think not? I said.

Nay, but what do you think? he replied.

Most assuredly, I said, those songs are all in your own honour; for if you win your beautiful love, your discourses and songs will be a glory to you, and may be truly regarded as hymns of praise composed in honour of you who have conquered and won such a love; but if he slips away from you, the more you have praised him, the more ridiculous you will look at having lost this fairest and best of blessings; [206] and therefore the wise lover does not praise his beloved until he has won him, because he is afraid of accidents. There is also another danger; the fair, when any one praises or magnifies them, are filled with the spirit of pride and vain-glory. Do you not agree with me?

Yes, he said.

And the more vain-glorious they are, the more difficult is the capture of them?

I believe you.

What should you say of a hunter who frightened away his prey, and made the capture of the animals which he is hunting more difficult?

He would be a bad hunter, undoubtedly.

Yes; and if, instead of soothing them, he were to infuriate them with words and songs, that would show a great want of wit: do you not agree.

Yes.

And now reflect, Hippothales, and see whether you are not guilty of all these errors in writing poetry. For I can hardly suppose that you will affirm a man to be a good poet who injures himself by his poetry.

Assuredly not, he said; such a poet would be a fool. And this is the reason why I take you into my counsels, Socrates, and I shall be glad of any further advice which you may have to offer. Will you tell me by what words or actions I may become endeared to my love?

That is not easy to determine, I said; but if you will bring your love to me, and will let me talk with him, I may perhaps be able to show you how to converse with him, instead of singing and reciting in the fashion of which you are accused.

There will be no difficulty in bringing him, he replied; if you will only go with Ctesippus into the Palaestra, and sit down and talk, I believe that he will come of his own accord; for he is fond of listening, Socrates. And as this is the festival of the Hermaea, the young men and boys are all together, and there is no separation between them. He will be sure to come: but if he does not, Ctesippus with whom he is familiar, and whose relation Menexenus is his great friend, shall call him.

That will be the way, I said. Thereupon I led Ctesippus into the Palaestra, and the rest followed.

Upon entering we found that the boys had just been sacrificing; and this part of the festival was nearly at an end. They were all in their white array, and games at dice were going on among them. Most of them were in the outer court amusing themselves; but some were in a corner of the Apodyterium playing at odd and even with a number of dice, which they took out of little wicker baskets. There was also a circle of lookers-on; among them was Lysis. He was standing with the other boys and youths, [207] having a crown upon his head, like a fair vision, and not less worthy of praise for his goodness than for his beauty. We left them, and went over to the opposite side of the room, where, finding a quiet place, we sat down; and then we began to talk. This attracted Lysis, who was constantly turning round to look at us— he was evidently wanting to come to us. For a time he hesitated and had not the courage to come alone; but first of all, his friend Menexenus, leaving his play, entered the Palaestra from the court, and when he saw Ctesippus and myself, was going to take a seat by us; and then Lysis, seeing him, followed, and sat down by his side; and the other boys joined. I should observe that Hippothales, when he saw the crowd, got behind them, where he thought that he would be out of sight of Lysis, lest he should anger him; and there he stood and listened.

I turned to Menexenus, and said: Son of Demophon, which of you two youths is the elder?

That is a matter of dispute between us, he said.

And which is the nobler? Is that also a matter of dispute?

Yes, certainly.

And another disputed point is, which is the fairer?

The two boys laughed.

I shall not ask which is the richer of the two, I said; for you are friends, are you not?

Certainly, they replied.

And friends have all things in common, so that one of you can be no richer than the other, if you say truly that you are friends.

They assented. I was about to ask which was the juster of the two, and which was the wiser of the two; but at this moment Menexenus was called away by some one who came and said that the gymnastic-master wanted him. I supposed that he had to offer sacrifice. So he went away, and I asked Lysis some more questions. I dare say, Lysis, I said, that your father and mother love you very much.

Certainly, he said.

And they would wish you to be perfectly happy.

Yes.

But do you think that any one is happy who is in the condition of a slave, and who cannot do what he likes?

I should think not indeed, he said.

And if your father and mother love you, and desire that you should be happy, no one can doubt that they are very ready to promote your happiness.

Certainly, he replied.

And do they then permit you to do what you like, and never rebuke you or hinder you from doing what you desire?

Yes, indeed, Socrates; there are a great many things which they hinder me from doing.

What do you mean? I said. Do they want you to be happy, and yet hinder you from doing what you like? [208] For example, if you want to mount one of your father's chariots, and take the reins at a race, they will not allow you to do so—they will prevent you?

Certainly, he said, they will not allow me to do so.

Whom then will they allow?

There is a charioteer, whom my father pays for driving.

And do they trust a hireling more than you? and may he do what he likes with the horses? and do they pay him for this?

They do.

But I dare say that you may take the whip and guide the mule-cart if you like;—they will permit that?

Permit me! indeed they will not.

Then, I said, may no one use the whip to the mules?

Yes, he said, the muleteer.

And is he a slave or a free man?

A slave, he said.

And do they esteem a slave of more value than you who are their son? And do they entrust their property to him rather than to you? and allow him to do what he likes, when they prohibit you? Answer me now: Are you your own master, or do they not even allow that?

Nay, he said; of course they do not allow it.

Then you have a master?

Yes, my tutor; there he is.

And is he a slave?

To be sure; he is our slave, he replied.

Surely, I said, this is a strange thing, that a free man should be governed by a slave. And what does he do with you?

He takes me to my teachers.

You do not mean to say that your teachers also rule over you?

Of course they do.

Then I must say that your father is pleased to inflict many lords and masters on you. But at any rate when you go home to your mother, she will let you have your own way, and will not interfere with your happiness; her wool, or the piece of cloth which she is weaving, are at your disposal: I am sure that there is nothing to hinder you from touching her wooden spathe, or her comb, or any other of her spinning implements.

Nay, Socrates, he replied, laughing; not only does she hinder me, but I should be beaten if I were to touch one of them.

Well, I said, this is amazing. And did you ever behave ill to your father or your mother?

No, indeed, he replied.

But why then are they so terribly anxious to prevent you from being happy, and doing as you like?—keeping you all day long in subjection to another, and, in a word, doing nothing which you desire; [209] so that you have no good, as would appear, out of their great possessions, which are under the control of anybody rather than of you, and have no use of your own fair person, which is tended and taken care of by another; while you, Lysis, are master of nobody, and can do nothing?

Why, he said, Socrates, the reason is that I am not of age.

I doubt whether that is the real reason, I said; for I should imagine that your father Democrates, and your mother, do permit you to do many things already, and do not wait until you are of age: for example, if they want anything read or written, you, I presume, would be the first person in the house who is summoned by them.

Very true.

And you would be allowed to write or read the letters in any order which you please, or to take up the lyre and tune the notes, and play with the fingers, or strike with the plectrum, exactly as you please, and neither father nor mother would interfere with you.

That is true, he said.

Then what can be the reason, Lysis, I said, why they allow you to do the one and not the other?

I suppose, he said, because I understand the one, and not the other.

Yes, my dear youth, I said, the reason is not any deficiency of years, but a deficiency of knowledge; and whenever your father thinks that you are wiser than he is, he will instantly commit himself and his possessions to you.

I think so.

Aye, I said; and about your neighbour, too, does not the same rule hold as about your father? If he is satisfied that you know more of housekeeping than he does, will he continue to administer his affairs himself, or will he commit them to you?

I think that he will commit them to me.

Will not the Athenian people, too, entrust their affairs to you when they see that you have wisdom enough to manage them?

Yes.

And oh! let me put another case, I said: There is the great king, and he has an eldest son, who is the Prince of Asia;—suppose that you and I go to him and establish to his satisfaction that we are better cooks than his son, will he not entrust to us the prerogative of making soup, and putting in anything that we like while the pot is boiling, rather than to the Prince of Asia, who is his son?

To us, clearly.

And we shall be allowed to throw in salt by handfuls, whereas the son will not be allowed to put in as much as he can take up between his fingers?

Of course.

Or suppose again that the son has bad eyes, will he allow him, or will he not allow him, to touch his own eyes if he thinks that he has no knowledge of medicine?

[210] He will not allow him.

Whereas, if he supposes us to have a knowledge of medicine, he will allow us to do what we like with him—even to open the eyes wide and sprinkle ashes upon them, because he supposes that we know what is best?

That is true.

And everything in which we appear to him to be wiser than himself or his son he will commit to us?

That is very true, Socrates, he replied.

Then now, my dear Lysis, I said, you perceive that in things which we know every one will trust us—Hellenes and barbarians, men and women—and we may do as we please about them, and no one will like to interfere with us; we shall be free, and masters of others; and these things will be really ours, for we shall be benefited by them. But in things of which we have no understanding, no one will trust us to do as seems good to us—they will hinder us as far as they can; and not only strangers, but father and mother, and the friend, if there be one, who is dearer still, will also hinder us; and we shall be subject to others; and these things will not be ours, for we shall not be benefited by them. Do you agree?

He assented.

And shall we be friends to others, and will any others love us, in as far as we are useless to them?

Certainly not.

Neither can your father or mother love you, nor can anybody love anybody else, in so far as they are useless to them?

No.

And therefore, my boy, if you are wise, all men will be your friends and kindred, for you will be useful and good; but if you are not wise, neither father, nor mother, nor kindred, nor any one else, will be your friends. And in matters of which you have as yet no knowledge, can you have any conceit of knowledge?

That is impossible, he replied.

And you, Lysis, if you require a teacher, have not yet attained to wisdom.

True.

And therefore you are not conceited, having nothing of which to be conceited.

Indeed, Socrates, I think not.

When I heard him say this, I turned to Hippothales, and was very nearly making a blunder, for I was going to say to him: That is the way, Hippothales, in which you should talk to your beloved, humbling and lowering him, and not as you do, puffing him up and spoiling him. But I saw that he was in great excitement and confusion at what had been said, and I remembered that, although he was in the neighbourhood, [211] he did not want to be seen by Lysis; so upon second thoughts I refrained.

In the meantime Menexenus came back and sat down in his place by Lysis; and Lysis, in a childish and affectionate manner, whispered privately in my ear, so that Menexenus should not hear: Do, Socrates, tell Menexenus what you have been telling me.

Suppose that you tell him yourself, Lysis, I replied; for I am sure that you were attending.

Certainly, he replied.

Try, then, to remember the words, and be as exact as you can in repeating them to him, and if you have forgotten anything, ask me again the next time that you see me.

I will be sure to do so, Socrates; but go on telling him something new, and let me hear, as long as I am allowed to stay.

I certainly cannot refuse, I said, since you ask me; but then, as you know, Menexenus is very pugnacious, and therefore you must come to the rescue if he attempts to upset me.

Yes, indeed, he said; he is very pugnacious, and that is the reason why I want you to argue with him.

That I may make a fool of myself?

No, indeed, he said; but I want you to put him down.

That is no easy matter, I replied; for he is a terrible fellow—a pupil of Ctesippus. And there is Ctesippus himself: do you see him?

Never mind, Socrates, you shall argue with him.

Well, I suppose that I must, I replied.

Hereupon Ctesippus complained that we were talking in secret, and keeping the feast to ourselves.

I shall be happy, I said, to let you have a share. Here is Lysis, who does not understand something that I was saying, and wants me to ask Menexenus, who, as he thinks, is likely to know.

And why do you not ask him? he said.

Very well, I said, I will; and do you, Menexenus, answer. But first I must tell you that I am one who from my childhood upward have set my heart upon a certain thing. All people have their fancies; some desire horses, and others dogs; and some are fond of gold, and others of honour. Now, I have no violent desire of any of these things; but I have a passion for friends; and I would rather have a good friend than the best cock or quail in the world: I would even go further, and say the best horse or dog. Yea, by the dog of Egypt, I should greatly prefer a real friend to all the gold of Darius, [212] or even to Darius himself: I am such a lover of friends as that. And when I see you and Lysis, at your early age, so easily possessed of this treasure, and so soon, he of you, and you of him, I am amazed and delighted, seeing that I myself, although I am now advanced in years, am so far from having made a similar acquisition, that I do not even know in what way a friend is acquired. But I want to ask you a question about this, for you have experience: tell me then, when one loves another, is the lover or the beloved the friend; or may either be the friend?

Either may, I should think, be the friend of either.

Do you mean, I said, that if only one of them loves the other, they are mutual friends?

Yes, he said; that is my meaning.

But what if the lover is not loved in return? which is a very possible case.

Yes.

Or is, perhaps, even hated? which is a fancy which sometimes is entertained by lovers respecting their beloved. Nothing can exceed their love; and yet they imagine either that they are not loved in return, or that they are hated. Is not that true?

Yes, he said, quite true.

In that case, the one loves, and the other is loved?

Yes.

Then which is the friend of which? Is the lover the friend of the beloved, whether he be loved in return, or hated; or is the beloved the friend; or is there no friendship at all on either side, unless they both love one another?

There would seem to be none at all.

Then this notion is not in accordance with our previous one. We were saying that both were friends, if one only loved; but now, unless they both love, neither is a friend.

That appears to be true.

Then nothing which does not love in return is beloved by a lover?

I think not.

Then they are not lovers of horses, whom the horses do not love in return; nor lovers of quails, nor of dogs, nor of wine, nor of gymnastic exercises, who have no return of love; no, nor of wisdom, unless wisdom loves them in return. Or shall we say that they do love them, although they are not beloved by them; and that the poet was wrong who sings—

Happy the man to whom his children are dear,
and steeds having single hoofs, and dogs of chase,
and the stranger of another land?

I do not think that he was wrong.

You think that he is right?

Yes.

Then, Menexenus, the conclusion is, that what is beloved, whether loving or hating, may be dear to the lover of it: for example, very young children, too young to love, or even hating their father or mother when they are punished by them, [213] are never dearer to them than at the time when they are being hated by them.

I think that what you say is true.

And, if so, not the lover, but the beloved, is the friend or dear one?

Yes.

And the hated one, and not the hater, is the enemy?

Clearly.

Then many men are loved by their enemies, and hated by their friends, and are the friends of their enemies, and the enemies of their friends. Yet how absurd, my dear friend, or indeed impossible is this paradox of a man being an enemy to his friend or a friend to his enemy.

I quite agree, Socrates, in what you say.

But if this cannot be, the lover will be the friend of that which is loved?

True.

And the hater will be the enemy of that which is hated?

Certainly.

Yet we must acknowledge in this, as in the preceding instance, that a man may be the friend of one who is not his friend, or who may be his enemy, when he loves that which does not love him or which even hates him. And he may be the enemy of one who is not his enemy, and is even his friend: for example, when he hates that which does not hate him, or which even loves him.

That appears to be true.

But if the lover is not a friend, nor the beloved a friend, nor both together, what are we to say? Whom are we to call friends to one another? Do any remain?

Indeed, Socrates, I cannot find any.

But, O Menexenus! I said, may we not have been altogether wrong in our conclusions?

I am sure that we have been wrong, Socrates, said Lysis. And he blushed as he spoke, the words seeming to come from his lips involuntarily, because his whole mind was taken up with the argument; there was no mistaking his attentive look while he was listening.

I was pleased at the interest which was shown by Lysis, and I wanted to give Menexenus a rest, so I turned to him and said, I think, Lysis, that what you say is true, and that, if we had been right, we should never have gone so far wrong; let us proceed no further in this direction (for the road seems to be getting troublesome), but take the other path into which we turned, and see what the poets have to say; [214] for they are to us in a manner the fathers and authors of wisdom, and they speak of friends in no light or trivial manner, but God himself, as they say, makes them and draws them to one another; and this they express, if I am not mistaken, in the following words:—

God is ever drawing like towards like, and making them acquainted.

I dare say that you have heard those words.

Yes, he said; I have.

And have you not also met with the treatises of philosophers who say that like must love like? they are the people who argue and write about nature and the universe.

Very true, he replied.

And are they right in saying this?

They may be.

Perhaps, I said, about half, or possibly, altogether, right, if their meaning were rightly apprehended by us. For the more a bad man has to do with a bad man, and the more nearly he is brought into contact with him, the more he will be likely to hate him, for he injures him; and injurer and injured cannot be friends. Is not that true?

Yes, he said.

Then one half of the saying is untrue, if the wicked are like one another?

That is true.

But the real meaning of the saying, as I imagine, is, that the good are like one another, and friends to one another; and that the bad, as is often said of them, are never at unity with one another or with themselves; for they are passionate and restless, and anything which is at variance and enmity with itself is not likely to be in union or harmony with any other thing. Do you not agree?

Yes, I do.

Then, my friend, those who say that the like is friendly to the like mean to intimate, if I rightly apprehend them, that the good only is the friend of the good, and of him only; but that the evil never attains to any real friendship, either with good or evil. Do you agree?

He nodded assent.

Then now we know how to answer the question "Who are friends?" for the argument declares "That the good are friends."

Yes, he said, that is true.

Yes, I replied; and yet I am not quite satisfied with this answer. By heaven, and shall I tell you what I suspect? I will. Assuming that like, inasmuch as he is like, is the friend of like, and useful to him—or rather let me try another way of putting the matter: Can like do any good or harm to like which he could not do to

himself, or suffer anything from his like which he would not suffer from himself? [215] And if neither can be of any use to the other, how can they be loved by one another? Can they now?

They cannot.

And can he who is not loved be a friend?

Certainly not.

But say that the like is not the friend of the like in so far as he is like; still the good may be the friend of the good in so far as he is good?

True.

But then again, will not the good, in so far as he is good, be sufficient for himself? Certainly he will. And he who is sufficient wants nothing—that is implied in the word sufficient.

Of course not.

And he who wants nothing will desire nothing?

He will not.

Neither can he love that which he does not desire?

He cannot.

And he who loves not is not a lover or friend?

Clearly not.

What place then is there for friendship, if, when absent, good men have no need of one another (for even when alone they are sufficient for themselves), and when present have no use of one another? How can such persons ever be induced to value one another?

They cannot.

And friends they cannot be, unless they value one another?

Very true.

But see now, Lysis, whether we are not being deceived in all this—are we not indeed entirely wrong?

How so? he replied.

Have I not heard some one say, as I just now recollect, that the like is the greatest enemy of the like, the good of the good?—Yes, and he quoted the authority of Hesiod, who says:

Potter quarrels with potter, bard with bard, Beggar with beggar;

and of all other things he affirmed, in like manner, "That of necessity the most like are most full of envy, strife, and hatred of one another, and the most unlike, of friendship. For the poor man is compelled to be the friend of the rich, and the weak requires the aid of the strong, and the sick man of the physician; and every one who is ignorant, has to love and court him who knows." And indeed he went on to say in grandiloquent language, that the idea of friendship existing between similars is not the truth, but the very reverse of the truth, and that the most opposed are the most friendly; for that everything desires not like but that which is most unlike: for example, the dry desires the moist, the cold the hot, the bitter the sweet, the sharp the blunt, the void the full, the full the void, and so of all other things; for the opposite is the food of the opposite, whereas like receives nothing from like. [216] And I thought that he who said this was a charming man, and that he spoke well. What do the rest of you say?

I should say, at first hearing, that he is right, said Menexenus.

Then we are to say that the greatest friendship is of opposites?

Exactly.

Yes, Menexenus; but will not that be a monstrous answer? and will not the all-wise eristics be down upon us in triumph, and ask, fairly enough, whether love is not the very opposite of hate; and what answer shall we make to them—must we not admit that they speak the truth?

We must.

They will then proceed to ask whether the enemy is the friend of the friend, or the friend the friend of the enemy?

Neither, he replied.

Well, but is a just man the friend of the unjust, or the temperate of the intemperate, or the good of the bad?

I do not see how that is possible.

And yet, I said, if friendship goes by contraries, the contraries must be friends.

They must.

Then neither like and like nor unlike and unlike are friends.

I suppose not.

And yet there is a further consideration: may not all these notions of friendship be erroneous? but may not that which is neither good nor evil still in some cases be the friend of the good?

How do you mean? he said.

Why really, I said, the truth is that I do not know; but my head is dizzy with thinking of the argument, and therefore I hazard the conjecture, that "the beautiful is the friend," as the old proverb says. Beauty is certainly a soft, smooth, slippery thing, and therefore of a nature which easily slips in and permeates our souls. For I affirm that the good is the beautiful. You will agree to that?

Yes.

This I say from a sort of notion that what is

neither good nor evil is the friend of the beautiful and the good, and I will tell you why I am inclined to think so: I assume that there are three principles—the good, the bad, and that which is neither good nor bad. You would agree—would you not?

I agree.

And neither is the good the friend of the good, nor the evil of the evil, nor the good of the evil;—these alternatives are excluded by the previous argument; and therefore, if there be such a thing as friendship or love at all, we must infer that what is neither good nor evil must be the friend, either of the good, or of that which is neither good nor evil, for nothing can be the friend of the bad.

True.

But neither can like be the friend of like, as we were just now saying.

True.

And if so, that which is neither good nor evil can have no friend which is neither good nor evil.

Clearly not.

Then the good alone is the friend of that only which is neither good nor evil.

[217] That may be assumed to be certain.

And does not this seem to put us in the right way? Just remark, that the body which is in health requires neither medical nor any other aid, but is well enough; and the healthy man has no love of the physician, because he is in health.

He has none.

But the sick loves him, because he is sick?

Certainly.

And sickness is an evil, and the art of medicine a good and useful thing?

Yes.

But the human body, regarded as a body, is neither good nor evil?

True.

And the body is compelled by reason of disease to court and make friends of the art of medicine?

Yes.

Then that which is neither good nor evil becomes the friend of good, by reason of the presence of evil?

So we may infer.

And clearly this must have happened before that which was neither good nor evil had become altogether corrupted with the element of evil—if itself had become evil it would not still desire and love the good; for, as we were saying, the evil cannot be the friend of the good.

Impossible.

Further, I must observe that some substances are assimilated when others are present with them; and there are some which are not assimilated: take, for example, the case of an ointment or colour which is put on another substance.

Very good.

In such a case, is the substance which is anointed the same as the colour or ointment?

What do you mean? he said.

This is what I mean: Suppose that I were to cover your auburn locks with white lead, would they be really white, or would they only appear to be white?

They would only appear to be white, he replied.

And yet whiteness would be present in them?

True.

But that would not make them at all the more white, notwithstanding the presence of white in them—they would not be white any more than black?

No.

But when old age infuses whiteness into them, then they become assimilated, and are white by the presence of white.

Certainly.

Now I want to know whether in all cases a substance is assimilated by the presence of another substance; or must the presence be after a peculiar sort?

The latter, he said.

Then that which is neither good nor evil may be in the presence of evil, but not as yet evil, and that has happened before now?

Yes.

And when anything is in the presence of evil, not being as yet evil, the presence of good arouses the desire of good in that thing; [218] but the presence of evil, which makes a thing evil, takes away the desire and friendship of the good; for that which was once both good and evil has now become evil only, and the good was supposed to have no friendship with the evil?

None.

And therefore we say that those who are already wise, whether Gods or men, are no longer lovers of wisdom; nor can they be lovers of wisdom who are ignorant to the extent of being evil, for no evil or ignorant person is a lover of wisdom. There remain those who have the misfortune to be ignorant, but are not yet hardened in their ignorance, or void of understanding, and do not as yet fancy that they know what they do not know: and therefore those who are the lovers of wisdom are as yet neither good nor bad. But the bad do not love wisdom any more than the good; for, as we have already seen, neither is unlike the friend of unlike, nor like of like. You remember that?

Yes, they both said.

And so, Lysis and Menexenus, we have discovered the nature of friendship—there can be no doubt of it: Friendship is the love which by reason of the presence of evil the neither good nor evil has of the good, either in the soul, or in the body, or anywhere.

They both agreed and entirely assented, and for a moment I rejoiced and was satisfied like a huntsman just holding fast his prey. But then a most unaccountable suspicion came across me, and I felt that the conclusion was untrue. I was pained, and said, Alas! Lysis and Menexenus, I am afraid that we have been grasping at a shadow only.

Why do you say so? said Menexenus.

I am afraid, I said, that the argument about friendship is false: arguments, like men, are often pretenders.

How do you mean? he asked.

Well, I said; look at the matter in this way: a friend is the friend of some one; is he not?

Certainly he is.

And has he a motive and object in being a friend, or has he no motive and object?

He has a motive and object.

And is the object which makes him a friend, dear to him, or neither dear nor hateful to him?

I do not quite follow you, he said.

I do not wonder at that, I said. But perhaps, if I put the matter in another way, you will be able to follow me, and my own meaning will be clearer to myself. The sick man, as I was just now saying, is the friend of the physician—is he not?

Yes.

And he is the friend of the physician because of disease, and for the sake of health?

Yes.

And disease is an evil?

Certainly.

And what of health? I said. Is that good or evil, or neither?

[219] Good, he replied.

And we were saying, I believe, that the body being neither good nor evil, because of disease, that is to say because of evil, is the friend of medicine, and medicine is a good: and medicine has entered into this friendship for the sake of health, and health is a good.

True.

And is health a friend, or not a friend?

A friend.

And disease is an enemy?

Yes.

Then that which is neither good nor evil is the friend of the good because of the evil and hateful, and for the sake of the good and the friend?

Clearly.

Then the friend is a friend for the sake of the friend, and because of the enemy?

That is to be inferred.

Then at this point, my boys, let us take heed, and be on our guard against deceptions. I will not again repeat that the friend is the friend of the friend, and the like of the like, which has been declared by us to be an impossibility; but, in order that this new statement may not delude us, let us attentively examine another point, which I will proceed to explain: Medicine, as we were saying, is a friend, or dear to us for the sake of health?

Yes.

And health is also dear?

Certainly.

And if dear, then dear for the sake of something?

Yes.

And surely this object must also be dear, as is implied in our previous admissions?

Yes.

And that something dear involves something else dear?

Yes.

But then, proceeding in this way, shall we not arrive at some first principle of friendship or dearness which is not capable of being referred to any other, for the sake of which, as we maintain, all other things are dear, and, having there arrived, we shall stop?

True.

My fear is that all those other things, which, as we say, are dear for the sake of another, are illusions and deceptions only, but where that first principle is, there is the true ideal of friendship. Let me put the matter thus: Suppose the case of a great treasure (this may be a son, who is more precious to his father than all his other treasures); would not the father, who values his son above all things, value other things also for the sake of his son? I mean, for instance, if he knew that his son had drunk hemlock, and the father thought that wine would save him, he would value the wine?

He would.

And also the vessel which contains the wine?

Certainly.

But does he therefore value the three measures of wine, or the earthen vessel which contains them, equally with his son? Is not this rather the true state of the case? All his anxiety has regard not to the means which are provided for the sake of an object, [220] but to the object for the sake of which they are provided. And although we may often say that gold and silver are highly valued by us, that is not the truth; for there is a further object, whatever it may be, which we value most of all, and for the sake of which gold and all our other possessions are acquired by us. Am I not right?

Yes, certainly.

And may not the same be said of the friend? That which is only dear to us for the sake of something else is improperly said to be dear, but the truly dear is that in which all these so-called dear friendships terminate.

That, he said, appears to be true.

And the truly dear or ultimate principle of friendship is not for the sake of any other or further dear.

True.

Then we have done with the notion that friendship has any further object. May we then infer that the good is the friend?

I think so.

And the good is loved for the sake of the evil? Let me put the case in this way: Suppose that of the three principles, good, evil, and that which is neither good nor evil, there remained only the good and the neutral, and that evil went far away, and in no way affected soul or body, nor ever at all that class of things which, as we say, are neither good nor evil in themselves;—would the good be of any use, or other than useless to us? For if there were nothing to hurt us any longer, we should have no need of anything that would do us good. Then would be clearly seen that we did but love and desire the good because of the evil, and as the remedy of the evil, which was the disease; but if there had been no disease, there would have been no need of a remedy. Is not this the nature of the good—to be loved by us who are placed between the two, because of the evil? but there is no use in the good for its own sake.

I suppose not.

Then the final principle of friendship, in which all other friendships terminated, those, I mean, which are relatively dear and for the sake of something else, is of another and a different nature from them. For they are called dear because of another dear or friend. But with the true friend or dear, the case is quite the reverse; for that is proved to be dear because of the hated, and if the hated were away it would be no longer dear.

Very true, he replied: at any rate not if our present view holds good.

But, oh! will you tell me, I said, whether if evil were to perish, we should hunger any more, or thirst any more, or have any similar desire? [221] Or may we suppose that hunger will remain while men and animals remain, but not so as to be hurtful? And the same of thirst and the other desires,—that they will remain, but will not be evil because evil has perished? Or rather shall I say, that to ask what either will be then or will not be is ridiculous, for who knows? This we do know, that in our present condition hunger may injure us, and may also benefit us:—Is not that true?

Yes.

And in like manner thirst or any similar desire may sometimes be a good and sometimes an evil to us, and sometimes neither one nor the other?

To be sure.

But is there any reason why, because evil perishes, that which is not evil should perish with it?

None.

Then, even if evil perishes, the desires which are neither good nor evil will remain?

Clearly they will.

And must not a man love that which he desires and affects?

He must.

Then, even if evil perishes, there may still remain some elements of love or friendship?

Yes.

But not if evil is the cause of friendship: for in that case nothing will be the friend of any other thing after the destruction of evil; for the effect cannot remain when the cause is destroyed.

True.

And have we not admitted already that the friend loves something for a reason? and at the time of making the admission we were of opinion that the neither good nor evil loves the good because of the evil?

Very true.

But now our view is changed, and we conceive that there must be some other cause of friendship?

I suppose so.

May not the truth be rather, as we were saying just now, that desire is the cause of friendship; for that which desires is dear to that which is desired at the time of desiring it? and may not the other theory have been only a long story about nothing?

Likely enough.

But surely, I said, he who desires, desires that of which he is in want?

Yes.

And that of which he is in want is dear to him?

True.

And he is in want of that of which he is deprived?

Certainly.

Then love, and desire, and friendship would appear to be of the natural or congenial. Such, Lysis and Menexenus, is the inference.

They assented.

Then if you are friends, you must have natures which are congenial to one another?

Certainly, they both said.

And I say, my boys, that no one who loves or desires another would ever have loved or desired or affected him, [222] if he had not been in some way congenial to him, either in his soul, or in his character, or in his manners, or in his form.

Yes, yes, said Menexenus. But Lysis was silent.

Then, I said, the conclusion is, that what is of a congenial nature must be loved.

It follows, he said.

Then the lover, who is true and no counterfeit, must of necessity be loved by his love.

Lysis and Menexenus gave a faint assent to this; and Hippothales changed into all manner of colours with delight.

Here, intending to revise the argument, I said: Can we point out any difference between the congenial and the like? For if that is possible, then I think, Lysis and Menexenus, there may be some sense in our argument about friendship. But if the congenial is only the like, how will you get rid of the other argument, of the uselessness of like to like in as far as they are like; for to say that what is useless is dear, would be absurd? Suppose, then, that we agree to distinguish between the congenial and the like—in the intoxication of argument, that may perhaps be allowed.

Very true.

And shall we further say that the good is congenial, and the evil uncongenial to every one? Or again that the evil is congenial to the evil, and the good to the good; and that which is neither good nor evil to that which is neither good nor evil?

They agreed to the latter alternative.

Then, my boys, we have again fallen into the old discarded error; for the unjust will be the friend of the unjust, and the bad of the bad, as well as the good of the good.

That appears to be the result.

But again, if we say that the congenial is the same as the good, in that case the good and he only will be the friend of the good.

True.

But that too was a position of ours which, as you will remember, has been already refuted by ourselves.

We remember.

Then what is to be done? Or rather is there anything to be done? I can only, like the wise men who argue in courts, sum up the arguments:—If neither the beloved, nor the lover, nor the like, nor the unlike, nor the good, nor the congenial, nor any other of whom we spoke —for there were such a number of them that I cannot remember all—if none of these are friends, I know not what remains to be said.

[223] Here I was going to invite the opinion of some older person, when suddenly we were interrupted by the tutors of Lysis and Menexenus, who came upon us like an evil apparition with their brothers, and bade them go home, as it was getting late. At first, we and the by-standers drove them off; but afterwards, as they would not mind, and only went on shouting in their barbarous dialect, and got angry, and kept calling the boys—they appeared to us to have been drinking rather too much at the Hermaea, which made them difficult to manage —we fairly gave way and broke up the company.

I said, however, a few words to the boys at parting: O Menexenus and Lysis, how ridiculous that you two boys, and I, an old boy, who would fain be one of you, should imagine ourselves to be friends—this is what the by-standers will go away and say—and as yet we have not been able to discover what is a friend!

LACHES, or Courage

PERSONS OF THE DIALOGUE: LYSIMACHUS, *son of Aristides;* MELESIAS, *son of Thucydides;* THEIR SONS; NICIAS; LACHES; SOCRATES

[178] Lys. You have seen the exhibition of the man fighting in armour, Nicias and Laches, but we did not tell you at the time the reason why my friend Melesias and I asked you to go with us and see him. I think that we may as well confess what this was, for we certainly ought not to have any reserve with you. The reason was, that we were intending to ask your advice. Some laugh at the very notion of advising others, and when they are asked will not say what they think. They guess at the wishes of the person who asks them, and answer according to his, and not according to their own, opinion. But as we know that you are good judges, and will say exactly what you think, we have taken you into our counsels. The matter about which I am making all this preface is as follows: Melesias and I have two sons; that is his son, and he is named Thucydides, after his grandfather; [179] and this is mine, who is also called after his grandfather, Aristides. Now, we are resolved to take the greatest care of the youths, and not to let them run about as they like, which is too often the way with the young, when they are no longer children, but to begin at once and do the utmost that we can for them. And knowing you to have sons of your own, we thought that you were most likely to have attended to their training and improvement, and, if perchance you have not attended to them, we may remind you that you ought to have done so, and would invite you to assist us in the fulfilment of a common duty. I will tell you, Nicias and Laches, even at the risk of being tedious, how we came to think of this. Melesias and I live together, and our sons live with us; and now, as I was saying at first, we are going to confess to you. Both of us often talk to the lads about the many noble deeds which our own fathers did in war and peace—in the management of the allies, and in the administration of the city; but neither of us has any deeds of his own which he can show. The truth is that we are ashamed of this contrast being seen by them, and we blame our fathers for letting us be spoiled in the days of our youth, while they were occupied with the concerns of others; and we urge all this upon the lads, pointing out to them that they will not grow up to honour if they are rebellious and take no pains about themselves; but that if they take pains they may, perhaps, become worthy of the names which they bear. They, on their part, promise to comply with our wishes; and our care is to discover what studies or pursuits are likely to be most improving to them. Some one commended to us the art of fighting in armour, which he thought an excellent accomplishment for a young man to learn; and he praised the man whose exhibition you have seen, and told us to go and see him. And we determined that we would go, and get you to accompany us; and we were intending at the same time, if you did not object, to take counsel with you about the education of our sons. That is the matter which we wanted to talk over with you; [180] and we hope that you will give us your opinion about this art of fighting in armour, and about any other studies or pursuits which may or may not be desirable for a young man to learn. Please to say whether you agree to our proposal.

Nic. As far as I am concerned, Lysimachus and Melesias, I applaud your purpose, and will gladly assist you; and I believe that you, Laches, will be equally glad.

La. Certainly, Nicias; and I quite approve of the remark which Lysimachus made about his own father and the father of Melesias, and which is applicable, not only to them, but to us, and to every one who is occupied with public affairs. As he says, such persons are too apt to be negligent and careless of their own children and their private concerns. There is much truth in that remark of yours, Lysimachus. But why, instead of consulting us, do you not consult our friend Socrates about the education of the youths? He is of the same deme with you, and is always passing his time in places where the youth have any noble study or pursuit, such as you are enquiring after.

Lys. Why, Laches, has Socrates ever attended to matters of this sort?

La. Certainly, Lysimachus.

Nic. That I have the means of knowing as well as Laches; for quite lately he supplied me with a teacher of music for my sons,—Damon, the disciple of Agathocles, who is a most accomplished man in every way, as well as a musician, and a companion of inestimable value for young men at their age.

Lys. Those who have reached my time of life, Socrates and Nicias and Laches, fall out of acquaintance with the young, because they are generally detained at home by old age; but you, O son of Sophroniscus, should let your fellow demesman have the benefits of any advice which you are able to give. Moreover I have a claim upon you as an old friend of your father; for I and he were always companions and friends, and to the hour of his death there never was a difference between us; and now it comes back to me, at the mention of your name, that I have heard these lads talking to one another at home, *[181]* and often speaking of Socrates in terms of the highest praise; but I have never thought to ask them whether the son of Sophroniscus was the person whom they meant. Tell me, my boys, whether this is the Socrates of whom you have often spoken?

Son. Certainly, father, this is he.

Lys. I am delighted to hear, Socrates, that you maintain the name of your father, who was a most excellent man; and I further rejoice at the prospect of our family ties being renewed.

La. Indeed, Lysimachus, you ought not to give him up; for I can assure you that I have seen him maintaining, not only his father's, but also his country's name. He was my companion in the retreat from Delium, and I can tell you that if others had only been like him, the honour of our country would have been upheld, and the great defeat would never have occurred.

Lys. That is very high praise which is accorded to you, Socrates, by faithful witnesses and for actions like those which they praise. Let me tell you the pleasure which I feel in hearing of your fame; and I hope that you will regard me as one of your warmest friends. You ought to have visited us long ago, and made yourself at home with us; but now, from this day forward, as we have at last found one another out, do as I say—come and make acquaintance with me, and with these young men, that I may continue your friend, as I was your father's. I shall expect you to do so, and shall venture at some future time to remind you of your duty. But what say you of the matter of which we were beginning to speak—the art of fighting in armour? Is that a practice in which the lads may be advantageously instructed?

Soc. I will endeavour to advise you, Lysimachus, as far as I can in this matter, and also in every way will comply with your wishes; but as I am younger and not so experienced, I think that I ought certainly to hear first what my elders have to say, and to learn of them, and if I have anything to add, then I may venture to give my opinion to them as well as to you. Suppose, Nicias, that one or other of you begin.

Nic. I have no objection, Socrates; and my opinion is that the acquirement of this art is in many ways useful to young men. It is an advantage to them that among the favourite amusements of their leisure hours they should have one which tends to improve and not to injure their bodily health. *[182]* No gymnastics could be better or harder exercise; and this, and the art of riding, are of all arts most befitting to a freeman; for they only who are thus trained in the use of arms are the athletes of our military profession, trained in that on which the conflict turns. Moreover in actual battle, when you have to fight in a line with a number of others, such an acquirement will be of some use, and will be of the greatest whenever the ranks are broken and you have to fight singly, either in pursuit, when you are attacking some one who is defending himself, or in flight, when you have to defend yourself against an assailant. Certainly he who possessed the art could not meet with any harm at the hands of a single person, or perhaps of several; and in any case he would have a great advantage. Further, this sort of skill inclines a man to the love of other noble lessons; for every man who has learned how to fight in armour will desire to learn the proper arrangement of an army, which is the sequel of the lesson: and when he has learned this, and his ambition is once fired, he will go on to learn the complete art of the general. There is no difficulty in seeing that the knowledge and practice of other military arts will be honourable and valuable to a man; and this lesson may be the beginning of them. Let me add a further advantage, which is by no means a slight one,—that this science will make any man a great deal more valiant and self-possessed in the field. And I will not disdain to mention, what by some may be thought to be a small matter;—he will make a better appearance at the right time; that is to say, at the time when his appearance will strike terror into his enemies. My opinion then, Lysimachus, is, as I say, that the youths should be instructed in this art, and for the reasons which I have given. But Laches may take a different view; and I shall be very glad to hear what he has to say.

La. I should not like to maintain, Nicias, that any kind of knowledge is not to be learned; for all knowledge appears to be a good: and if, as Nicias and as the teachers of the art affirm, this use of arms is really a species of knowledge, then it ought to be learned; but if not, and if those who profess to teach it are deceivers only; or if it be knowledge, but not of a valuable sort, then what is the use of learning it? *[183]* I say this, because I think that if it had been really valuable, the Lacedaemonians, whose whole life is passed in finding out and practising the arts which give them an advantage over other nations in war, would have discovered this one. And even if they had not, still these professors of the art would certainly not have failed to discover that of all the Hellenes the Lacedaemonians have the greatest interest in such matters, and that a master of the art who was honoured among them would be sure to make his fortune among other nations, just as a tragic poet would who is honoured among ourselves; which is the reason why he who fancies that he can write a tragedy does not go about itinerating in the neighbouring states, but rushes hither straight, and exhibits at Athens; and this is natural. Whereas I perceive that these fighters in armour regard Lacedaemon as a sacred inviolable territory, which they do not touch with the point of their foot; but they make a circuit of the neighbouring states, and would rather exhibit to any others than to the Spartans; and

particularly to those who would themselves acknowledge that they are by no means first-rate in the arts of war. Further, Lysimachus, I have encountered a good many of these gentlemen in actual service, and have taken their measure, which I can give you at once; for none of these masters of fence have ever been distinguished in war,—there has been a sort of fatality about them; while in all other arts the men of note have been always those who have practised the art, they appear to be a most unfortunate exception. For example, this very Stesilaus, whom you and I have just witnessed exhibiting in all that crowd and making such great professions of his powers, I have seen at another time making, in sober truth, an involuntary exhibition of himself, which was a far better spectacle. He was a marine on board a ship which struck a transport vessel, and was armed with a weapon, half spear, half scythe; the singularity of this weapon was worthy of the singularity of the man. To make a long story short, I will only tell you what happened to this notable invention of the scythe-spear. He was fighting, and the scythe was caught in the rigging of the other ship, and stuck fast; and he tugged, but was unable to get his weapon free. The two ships were passing one another. He first ran along his own ship holding on to the spear; but as the other ship passed by and drew him after as he was holding on, *[184]* he let the spear slip through his hand until he retained only the end of the handle. The people in the transport clapped their hands, and laughed at his ridiculous figure; and when some one threw a stone, which fell on the deck at his feet, and he quitted his hold of the scythe-spear, the crew of his own trireme also burst out laughing; they could not refrain when they beheld the weapon waving in the air, suspended from the transport. Now I do not deny that there may be something in such an art, as Nicias asserts, but I tell you my experience; and, as I said at first, whether this be an art of which the advantage is so slight, or not an art at all, but only an imposition, in either case such an acquirement is not worth having. For my opinion is, that if the professor of this art be a coward, he will be likely to become rash, and his character will be only more notorious; or if he be brave, and fail ever so little, other men will be on the watch, and he will be greatly traduced; for there is a jealousy of such pretenders; and unless a man be pre-eminent in valour, he cannot help being ridiculous, if he says that he has this sort of skill. Such is my judgment, Lysimachus, of the desirableness of this art; but, as I said at first, ask Socrates, and do not let him go until he has given you his opinion of the matter.

Lys. I am going to ask this favour of you, Socrates; as is the more necessary because the two councillors disagree, and some one is in a manner still needed who will decide between them. Had they agreed, no arbiter would have been required. But as Laches has voted one way and Nicias another, I should like to hear with which of our two friends you agree.

Soc. What, Lysimachus, are you going to accept the opinion of the majority?

Lys. Why, yes, Socrates; what else am I to do?

Soc. And would you do so too, Melesias? If you were deliberating about the gymnastic training of your son, would you follow the advice of the majority of us, or the opinion of the one who had been trained and exercised under a skilful master?

Mel. The latter, Socrates; as would surely be reasonable.

Soc. His one vote would be worth more than the vote of all us four?

Mel. Certainly.

Soc. And for this reason, as I imagine,—because a good decision is based on knowledge and not on numbers?

Mel. To be sure.

[185] Soc. Must we not then first of all ask, whether there is any one of us who has knowledge of that about which we are deliberating? If there is, let us take his advice, though he be one only, and not mind the rest; if there is not, let us seek further counsel. Is this a slight matter about which you and Lysimachus are deliberating? Are you not risking the greatest of your possessions? For children are your riches; and upon their turning out well or ill depends the whole order of their father's house.

Mel. That is true.

Soc. Great care, then, is required in this matter?

Mel. Certainly.

Soc. Suppose, as I was just now saying, that we were considering, or wanting to consider, who was the best trainer. Should we not select him who knew and had practised the art, and had the best teachers?

Mel. I think that we should.

Soc. But would there not arise a prior question about the nature of the art of which we want to find the masters?

Mel. I do not understand.

Soc. Let me try to make my meaning plainer then. I do not think that we have as yet decided what that is about which we are consulting, when we ask which of us is or is not skilled in the art, and has or has not had a teacher of the art.

Nic. Why, Socrates, is not the question whether young men ought or ought not to learn the art of fighting in armour?

Soc. Yes, Nicias; but there is also a prior question, which I may illustrate in this way: When a person considers about applying a medicine to the eyes, would you say that he is consulting about the medicine or about the eyes?

Nic. About the eyes.

Soc. And when he considers whether he shall set a bridle on a horse and at what time, he is thinking of the horse and not of the bridle?

Nic. True.

Soc. And in a word, when he considers anything for the sake of another thing, he thinks of the end and not of the means?

Nic. Certainly.

Soc. And when you call in an adviser, you should see whether he too is skilful in the accomplishment of the end which you have in view?

Nic. Most true.

Soc. And at present we have in view some knowledge, of which the end is the soul of youth?

Nic. Yes.

Soc. And we are enquiring, Which of us is skilful or successful in the treatment of the soul, and which of us has had good teachers?

La. Well but, Socrates; did you never observe that some persons, who have had no teachers, are more skilful than those who have, in some things?

Soc. Yes, Laches, I have observed that; but you would not be very willing to trust them if they only professed to be masters of their art, *[186]* unless they could show some proof of their skill or excellence in one or more works.

La. That is true.

Soc. And therefore, Laches and Nicias, as Lysimachus and Melesias, in their anxiety to improve the minds of their sons, have asked our advice about them, we too should tell them who our teachers were, if we say that we have had any, and prove them to be in the first place men of merit and experienced trainers of the minds of youth and also to have been really our teachers. Or if any of us says that he has no teacher, but that he has works of his own to show; then he should point out to them what

Athenians or strangers, bond or free, he is generally acknowledged to have improved. But if he can show neither teachers nor works, then he should tell them to look out for others; and not run the risk of spoiling the children of friends, and thereby incurring the most formidable accusation which can be brought against any one by those nearest to him. As for myself, Lysimachus and Melesias, I am the first to confess that I have never had a teacher of the art of virtue; although I have always from my earliest youth desired to have one. But I am too poor to give money to the Sophists, who are the only professors of moral improvement; and to this day I have never been able to discover the art myself, though I should not be surprised if Nicias or Laches may have discovered or learned it; for they are far wealthier than I am, and may therefore have learnt of others. And they are older too; so that they have had more time to make the discovery. And I really believe that they are able to educate a man; for unless they had been confident in their own knowledge, they would never have spoken thus decidedly of the pursuits which are advantageous or hurtful to a young man. I repose confidence in both of them; but I am surprised to find that they differ from one another. And therefore, Lysimachus, as Laches suggested that you should detain me, and not let me go until I answered, I in turn earnestly beseech and advise you to detain Laches and Nicias, and question them. I would have you say to them: Socrates avers that he has no knowledge of the matter—he is unable to decide which of you speaks truly; neither discoverer nor student is he of anything of the kind. But you, Laches and Nicias, should each of you tell us who is the most skilful educator whom you have ever known; and whether you invented the art yourselves, or learned of another; and if you learned, [187] who were your respective teachers, and who were their brothers in the art; and then, if you are too much occupied in politics to teach us yourselves, let us go to them, and present them with gifts, or make interest with them, or both, in the hope that they may be induced to take charge of our children and of yours; and then they will not grow up inferior, and disgrace their ancestors. But if you are yourselves original discoverers in that field, give us some proof of your skill. Who are they who, having been inferior persons, have become under your care good and noble? For if this is your first attempt at education, there is a danger that you may be trying the experiment, not on the "vile corpus"

of a Carian slave, but on your own sons, or the sons of your friend, and, as the proverb says, "break the large vessel in learning to make pots." Tell us then, what qualities you claim or do not claim. Make them tell you that, Lysimachus, and do not let them off.

Lys. I very much approve of the words of Socrates, my friends; but you, Nicias and Laches, must determine whether you will be questioned, and give an explanation about matters of this sort. Assuredly, I and Melesias would be greatly pleased to hear you answer the questions which Socrates asks, if you will: for I began by saying that we took you into our counsels because we thought that you would have attended to the subject, especially as you have children who, like our own, are nearly of an age to be educated. Well, then, if you have no objection, suppose that you take Socrates into partnership; and do you and he ask and answer one another's questions: for, as he has well said, we are deliberating about the most important of our concerns. I hope that you will see fit to comply with our request.

Nic. I see very clearly, Lysimachus, that you have only known Socrates' father, and have no acquaintance with Socrates himself: at least, you can only have known him when he was a child, and may have met him among his fellow-wardsmen, in company with his father, at a sacrifice, or at some other gathering. You clearly show that you have never known him since he arrived at manhood.

Lys. Why do you say that, Nicias?

Nic. Because you seem not to be aware that any one who has an intellectual affinity to Socrates and enters into conversation with him is liable to be drawn into an argument; and whatever subject he may start, he will be continually carried round and round by him, until at last he finds that he has to give an account both of his present [188] and past life; and when he is once entangled, Socrates will not let him go until he has completely and thoroughly sifted him. Now I am used to his ways; and I know that he will certainly do as I say, and also that I myself shall be the sufferer; for I am fond of his conversation, Lysimachus. And I think that there is no harm in being reminded of any wrong thing which we are, or have been, doing: he who does not fly from reproof will be sure to take more heed of his after-life; as Solon says, he will wish and desire to be learning so long as he lives, and will not think that old age of itself brings wisdom. To me, to be cross-examined by Socrates is neither unusual nor unpleasant; indeed, I knew all along that where Socrates was, the argument would soon pass from our sons to ourselves; and therefore, I say that for my part, I am quite willing to discourse with Socrates in his own manner; but you had better ask our friend Laches what his feeling may be.

La. I have but one feeling, Nicias, or (shall I say?) two feelings, about discussions. Some would think that I am a lover, and to others I may seem to be a hater of discourse; for when I hear a man discoursing of virtue, or of any sort of wisdom, who is a true man and worthy of his theme, I am delighted beyond measure: and I compare the man and his words, and note the harmony and correspondence of them. And such an one I deem to be the true musician, attuned to a fairer harmony than that of the lyre, or any pleasant instrument of music; for truly he has in his own life a harmony of words and deeds arranged, not in the Ionian, or in the Phrygian mode, nor yet in the Lydian, but in the true Hellenic mode, which is the Dorian, and no other. Such an one makes me merry with the sound of his voice; and when I hear him I am thought to be a lover of discourse; so eager am I in drinking in his words. But a man whose actions do not agree with his words is an annoyance to me; and the better he speaks the more I hate him, and then I seem to be a hater of discourse. As to Socrates, I have no knowledge of his words, but of old, as would seem, I have had experience of his deeds; and his deeds show that free and noble sentiments are natural to [189] him. And if his words accord, then I am of one mind with him, and shall be delighted to be interrogated by a man such as he is, and shall not be annoyed at having to learn of him: for I too agree with Solon, "that I would fain grow old, learning many things." But I must be allowed to add "of the good only." Socrates must be willing to allow that he is a good teacher, or I shall be a dull and uncongenial pupil: but that the teacher is younger, or not as yet in repute—anything of that sort is of no account with me. And therefore, Socrates, I give you notice that you may teach and confute me as much as ever you like, and also learn of me anything which I know. So high is the opinion which I have entertained of you ever since the day on which you were my companion in danger, and gave a proof of your valour such as only the man of merit can give. Therefore, say whatever you like, and do not mind about the difference of our ages.

Soc. I cannot say that either of you show any reluctance to take counsel and advise with me.

Lys. But this is our proper business; and yours as well as ours, for I reckon you as one of us. Please then to take my place, and find out from Nicias and Laches what we want to know, for the sake of the youths, and talk and consult with them: for I am old, and my memory is bad; and I do not remember the questions which I am going to ask, or the answers to them; and if there is any interruption I am quite lost. I will therefore beg of you to carry on the proposed discussion by yourselves; and I will listen, and Melesias and I will act upon your conclusions.

Soc. Let us, Nicias and Laches, comply with the request of Lysimachus and Melesias. There will be no harm in asking ourselves the question which was first proposed to us: "Who have been our own instructors in this sort of training, and whom have we made better?" But the other mode of carrying on the enquiry will bring us equally to the same point, and will be more like proceeding from first principles. For if we knew that the addition of something would improve some other thing, and were able to make the addition, then, clearly, we must know how that about which we are advising may be best and most easily attained. Perhaps you do not understand what I mean. [190] Then let me make my meaning plainer in this way. Suppose we knew that the addition of sight makes better the eyes which possess this gift, and also were able to impart sight to the eyes, then, clearly, we should know the nature of sight, and should be able to advise how this gift of sight may be best and most easily attained; but if we knew neither what sight is, nor what hearing is, we should not be very good medical advisers about the eyes or the ears, or about the best mode of giving sight and hearing to them.

La. That is true, Socrates.

Soc. And are not our two friends, Laches, at this very moment inviting us to consider in what way the gift of virtue may be imparted to their sons for the improvement of their minds?

La. Very true.

Soc. Then must we not first know the nature of virtue? For how can we advise any one about the best mode of attaining something of which we are wholly ignorant?

La. I do not think that we can, Socrates.

Soc. Then, Laches, we may presume that we know the nature of virtue?

La. Yes.

Soc. And that which we know we must surely be able to tell?

La. Certainly.

Soc. I would not have us begin, my friend, with enquiring about the whole of virtue; for that may be more than we can accomplish; let us first consider whether we have a sufficient knowledge of a part; the enquiry will thus probably be made easier to us.

La. Let us do as you say, Socrates.

Soc. Then which of the parts of virtue shall we select? Must we not select that to which the art of fighting in armour is supposed to conduce? And is not that generally thought to be courage?

La. Yes, certainly.

Soc. Then, Laches, suppose that we first set about determining the nature of courage, and in the second place proceed to enquire how the young men may attain this quality by the help of studies and pursuits. Tell me, if you can, what is courage.

La. Indeed, Socrates, I see no difficulty in answering; he is a man of courage who does not run away, but remains at his post and fights against the enemy; there can be no mistake about that.

Soc. Very good, Laches; and yet I fear that I did not express myself clearly; and therefore you have answered not the question which I intended to ask, but another.

[191] *La.* What do you mean, Socrates?

Soc. I will endeavour to explain; you would call a man courageous who remains at his post, and fights with the enemy?

La. Certainly I should.

Soc. And so should I; but what would you say of another man, who fights flying, instead of remaining?

La. How flying?

Soc. Why, as the Scythians are said to fight, flying as well as pursuing; and as Homer says in praise of the horses of Aeneas, that they knew "how to pursue, and fly quickly hither and thither"; and he passes an encomium on Aeneas himself, as having a knowledge of fear or flight, and calls him "an author of fear or flight."

La. Yes, Socrates, and there Homer is right: for he was speaking of chariots, as you were speaking of the Scythian cavalry, who have that way of fighting; but the heavy-armed Greek fights, as I say, remaining in his rank.

Soc. And yet, Laches, you must except the Lacedaemonians at Plataea, who, when they came upon the light shields of the Persians, are said not to have been willing to stand and fight, and to have fled; but when the ranks of the Persians were broken, they turned upon them like cavalry, and won the battle of Plataea.

La. That is true.

Soc. That was my meaning when I said that I was to blame in having put my question badly, and that this was the reason of your answering badly. For I meant to ask you not only about the courage of heavy-armed soldiers, but about the courage of cavalry and every other style of soldier; and not only who are courageous in war, but who are courageous in perils by sea, and who in disease, or in poverty, or again in politics, are courageous; and not only who are courageous against pain or fear, but mighty to contend against desires and pleasures, either fixed in their rank or turning upon their enemy. There is this sort of courage—is there not, Laches?

La. Certainly, Socrates.

Soc. And all these are courageous, but some have courage in pleasures, and some in pains: some in desires, and some in fears, and some are cowards under the same conditions, as I should imagine.

La. Very true.

Soc. Now I was asking about courage and cowardice in general. And I will begin with courage, and once more ask, What is that common quality, which is the same in all these cases, and which is called courage? Do you now understand what I mean?

La. Not over well.

[192] *Soc.* I mean this: As I might ask what is that quality which is called quickness, and which is found in running, in playing the lyre, in speaking, in learning, and in many other similar actions, or rather which we possess in nearly every action that is worth mentioning of arms, legs, mouth, voice, mind;—would you not apply the term quickness to all of them?

La. Quite true.

Soc. And suppose I were to be asked by some one: What is that common quality, Socrates, which, in all these uses of the word, you call quickness? I should say the quality which accomplishes much in a little time—whether in running, speaking, or in any other sort of action.

La. You would be quite correct.

Soc. And now, Laches, do you try and tell me in like manner, What is that common quality which is called courage, and which includes all the various uses of the term when applied both to pleasure and pain, and in all the cases to which I was just now referring?

La. I should say that courage is a sort of endurance of the soul, if I am to speak of the universal nature which pervades them all.

Soc. But that is what we must do if we are to answer the question. And yet I cannot say that every kind of endurance is, in my opinion, to be deemed courage. Hear my reason: I am sure, Laches, that you would consider courage to be a very noble quality.

La. Most noble, certainly.

Soc. And you would say that a wise endurance is also good and noble?

La. Very noble.

Soc. But what would you say of a foolish endurance? Is not that, on the other hand, to be regarded as evil and hurtful?

La. True.

Soc. And is anything noble which is evil and hurtful?

La. I ought not to say that, Socrates.

Soc. Then you would not admit that sort of endurance to be courage—for it is not noble, but courage is noble?

La. You are right.

Soc. Then, according to you, only the wise endurance is courage?

La. True.

Soc. But as to the epithet "wise,"—wise in what? In all things small as well as great? For example, if a man shows the quality of endurance in spending his money wisely, knowing that by spending he will acquire more in the end, do you call him courageous?

La. Assuredly not.

Soc. Or, for example, if a man is a physician, and his son, or some patient of his, has inflammation of the lungs, and begs that he may be allowed to eat or drink something, and the other is firm and refuses; is that courage?

[*193*] *La*. No; that is not courage at all, any more than the last.

Soc. Again, take the case of one who endures in war, and is willing to fight, and wisely calculates and knows that others will help him, and that there will be fewer and inferior men against him than there are with him; and suppose that he has also advantages of position;—would you say of such a one who endures with all this wisdom and preparation, that he, or some man in the opposing army who is in the opposite circumstances to these and yet endures and remains at his post, is the braver?

La. I should say that the latter, Socrates, was the braver.

Soc. But, surely, this is a foolish endurance in comparison with the other?

La. That is true.

Soc. Then you would say that he who in an engagement of cavalry endures, having the knowledge of horsemanship, is not so courageous as he who endures, having no such knowledge?

La. So I should say.

Soc. And he who endures, having a knowledge of the use of the sling, or the bow, or of any other art, is not so courageous as he who endures, not having such a knowledge?

La. True.

Soc. And he who descends into a well, and dives, and holds out in this or any similar action, having no knowledge of diving, or the like, is, as you would say, more courageous than those who have this knowledge?

La. Why, Socrates, what else can a man say?

Soc. Nothing, if that be what he thinks.

La. But that is what I do think.

Soc. And yet men who thus run risks and endure are foolish, Laches, in comparison of those who do the same things, having the skill to do them.

La. That is true.

Soc. But foolish boldness and endurance appeared before to be base and hurtful to us.

La. Quite true.

Soc. Whereas courage was acknowledged to be a noble quality.

La. True.

Soc. And now on the contrary we are saying that the foolish endurance, which was before held in dishonour, is courage.

La. Very true.

Soc. And are we right in saying so?

La. Indeed, Socrates, I am sure that we are not right.

Soc. Then according to your statement, you and I, Laches, are not attuned to the Dorian mode, which is a harmony of words and deeds; for our deeds are not in accordance with our words. Any one would say that we had courage who saw us in action, but not, I imagine, he who heard us talking about courage just now.

La. That is most true.

Soc. And is this condition of ours satisfactory?

La. Quite the reverse.

Soc. Suppose, however, that we admit the principle of which we are speaking to a certain extent.

[194] La. To what extent and what principle do you mean?

Soc. The principle of endurance. We too must endure and persevere in the enquiry, and then courage will not laugh at our faintheartedness in searching for courage; which after all may, very likely, be endurance.

La. I am ready to go on, Socrates; and yet I am unused to investigations of this sort. But the spirit of controversy has been aroused in me by what has been said; and I am really grieved at being thus unable to express my meaning. For I fancy that I do know the nature of courage; but, somehow or other, she has slipped away from me, and I cannot get hold of her and tell her nature.

Soc. But, my dear friend, should not the good sportsman follow the track, and not be lazy?

La. Certainly, he should.

Soc. And shall we invite Nicias to join us? he may be better at the sport than we are. What do you say?

La. I should like that.

Soc. Come then, Nicias, and do what you can to help your friends, who are tossing on the waves of argument, and at the last gasp: you see our extremity, and may save us and also settle your own opinion, if you will tell us what you think about courage.

Nic. I have been thinking, Socrates, that you and Laches are not defining courage in the right way; for you have forgotten an excellent saying which I have heard from your own lips.

Soc. What is it, Nicias?

Nic. I have often heard you say that "Every man is good in that in which he is wise, and bad in that in which he is unwise."

Soc. That is certainly true, Nicias.

Nic. And therefore if the brave man is good, he is also wise.

Soc. Do you hear him, Laches?

La. Yes, I hear him, but I do not very well understand him.

Soc. I think that I understand him; and he appears to me to mean that courage is a sort of wisdom.

La. What can he possibly mean, Socrates?

Soc. That is a question which you must ask of himself.

La. Yes.

Soc. Tell him then, Nicias, what you mean by this wisdom; for you surely do not mean the wisdom which plays the flute?

Nic. Certainly not.

Soc. Nor the wisdom which plays the lyre?

Nic. No.

Soc. But what is this knowledge then, and of what?

La. I think that you put the question to him very well, Socrates; and I would like him to say what is the nature of this knowledge or wisdom.

[195] Nic. I mean to say, Laches, that courage is the knowledge of that which inspires fear or confidence in war, or in anything.

La. How strangely he is talking, Socrates.

Soc. Why do you say so, Laches?

La. Why, surely courage is one thing, and wisdom another.

Soc. That is just what Nicias denies.

La. Yes, that is what he denies; but he is so silly.

Soc. Suppose that we instruct instead of abusing him?

Nic. Laches does not want to instruct me, Socrates; but having been proved to be talking nonsense himself, he wants to prove that I have been doing the same.

La. Very true, Nicias; and you are talking nonsense, as I shall endeavour to show. Let me ask you a question: Do not physicians know the dangers of disease? or do the courageous know them? or are the physicians the same as the courageous?

Nic. Not at all.

La. No more than the husbandmen who know the dangers of husbandry, or than other craftsmen, who have a knowledge of that which inspires them with fear or confidence in their own arts, and yet they are not courageous a whit the more for that.

Soc. What is Laches saying, Nicias? He appears to be saying something of importance.

Nic. Yes, he is saying something, but it is not true.

Soc. How so?

Nic. Why, because he does not see that the physician's knowledge only extends to the nature of health and disease: he can tell the sick man no more than this. Do you imagine, Laches, that the physician knows whether health or disease is the more terrible to a man? Had not many a man better never get up from a sick bed? I should like to know whether you think that life is always better than death. May not death often be the better of the two?

La. Yes certainly so in my opinion.

Nic. And do you think that the same things are terrible to those who had better die, and to those who had better live?

La. Certainly not.

Nic. And do you suppose that the physician

or any other artist knows this, or any one indeed, except he who is skilled in the grounds of fear and hope? And him I call the courageous.

Soc. Do you understand his meaning, Laches?

La. Yes; I suppose that, in his way of speaking, the soothsayers are courageous. For who but one of them can know to whom to die or to live is better? And yet, Nicias, would you allow that you are yourself a soothsayer, or are you neither a soothsayer nor courageous?

Nic. What! do you mean to say that the soothsayer ought to know the grounds of hope or fear?

La. Indeed I do: who but he?

Nic. Much rather I should say he of whom I speak; for the soothsayer ought to know only the signs of things that are about to come to pass, whether death or disease, or loss of property, or victory, or defeat in war, *[196]* or in any sort of contest; but to whom the suffering or not suffering of these things will be for the best, can no more be decided by the soothsayer than by one who is no soothsayer.

La. I cannot understand what Nicias would be at, Socrates; for he represents the courageous man as neither a soothsayer, nor a physician, nor in any other character, unless he means to say that he is a god. My opinion is that he does not like honestly to confess that he is talking nonsense, but that he shuffles up and down in order to conceal the difficulty into which he has got himself. You and I, Socrates, might have practised a similar shuffle just now, if we had only wanted to avoid the appearance of inconsistency. And if we had been arguing in a court of law there might have been reason in so doing; but why should a man deck himself out with vain words at a meeting of friends such as this?

Soc. I quite agree with you, Laches, that he should not. But perhaps Nicias is serious, and not merely talking for the sake of talking. Let us ask him just to explain what he means, and if he has reason on his side we will agree with him; if not, we will instruct him.

La. Do you, Socrates, if you like, ask him: I think that I have asked enough.

Soc. I do not see why I should not; and my question will do for both of us.

La. Very good.

Soc. Then tell me, Nicias, or rather tell us, for Laches and I are partners in the argument: Do you mean to affirm that courage is the knowledge of the grounds of hope and fear?

Nic. I do.

Soc. And not every man has this knowledge; the physician and the soothsayer have it not; and they will not be courageous unless they acquire it—that is what you were saying?

Nic. I was.

Soc. Then this is certainly not a thing which every pig would know, as the proverb says, and therefore he could not be courageous.

Nic. I think not.

Soc. Clearly not, Nicias; not even such a big pig as the Crommyonian sow would be called by you courageous. And this I say not as a joke, but because I think that he who assents to your doctrine, that courage is the knowledge of the grounds of fear and hope, cannot allow that any wild beast is courageous, unless he admits that a lion, or a leopard, or perhaps a boar, or any other animal, has such a degree of wisdom that he knows things which but a few human beings ever know by reason of their difficulty. He who takes your view of courage must affirm that a lion, and a stag, and a bull, and a monkey, have equally little pretensions to courage.

[197] La. Capital, Socrates; by the gods, that is truly good. And I hope, Nicias, that you will tell us whether these animals, which we all admit to be courageous, are really wiser than mankind; or whether you will have the boldness, in the face of universal opinion, to deny their courage.

Nic. Why, Laches, I do not call animals or any other things which have no fear of dangers, because they are ignorant of them, courageous, but only fearless and senseless. Do you imagine that I should call little children courageous, which fear no dangers because they know none? There is a difference, to my way of thinking, between fearlessness and courage. I am of opinion that thoughtful courage is a quality possessed by very few, but that rashness and boldness, and fearlessness, which has no forethought, are very common qualities possessed by many men, many women, many children, many animals. And you, and men in general, call by the term "courageous" actions which I call rash;—my courageous actions are wise actions.

La. Behold, Socrates, how admirably, as he thinks, he dresses himself out in words, while seeking to deprive of the honour of courage those whom all the world acknowledges to be courageous.

Nic. Not so, Laches, but do not be alarmed; for I am quite willing to say of you and also of Lamachus, and of many other Athenians, that you are courageous and therefore wise.

La. I could answer that; but I would not have you cast in my teeth that I am a haughty Aexonian.

Soc. Do not answer him, Laches; I rather fancy that you are not aware of the source from which his wisdom is derived. He has got all this from my friend Damon, and Damon is always with Prodicus, who, of all the Sophists, is considered to be the best puller to pieces of words of this sort.

La. Yes, Socrates; and the examination of such niceties is a much more suitable employment for a Sophist than for a great statesman whom the city chooses to preside over her.

Soc. Yes, my sweet friend, but a great statesman is likely to have a great intelligence. And I think that the view which is implied in Nicias' definition of courage is worthy of examination.

La. Then examine for yourself, Socrates.

Soc. That is what I am going to do, my dear friend. Do not, however, suppose I shall let you out of the partnership; for I shall expect you to apply your mind, and join with me in the consideration of the question.

La. I will if you think that I ought.

[198] Soc. Yes, I do; but I must beg of you, Nicias, to begin again. You remember that we originally considered courage to be a part of virtue.

Nic. Very true.

Soc. And you yourself said that it was a part; and there were many other parts, all of which taken together are called virtue.

Nic. Certainly.

Soc. Do you agree with me about the parts? For I say that justice, temperance, and the like, are all of them parts of virtue as well as courage. Would you not say the same?

Nic. Certainly.

Soc. Well then, so far we are agreed. And now let us proceed a step, and try to arrive at a similar agreement about the fearful and the hopeful: I do not want you to be thinking one thing and myself another. Let me then tell you my own opinion, and if I am wrong you shall set me right: in my opinion the terrible and the hopeful are the things which do or do not create fear, and fear is not of the present, nor of the past, but is of future and expected evil. Do you not agree to that, Laches?

La. Yes, Socrates, entirely.

Soc. That is my view, Nicias; the terrible things, as I should say, are the evils which are future; and the hopeful are the good or not

evil things which are future. Do you or do you not agree with me?

Nic. I agree.

Soc. And the knowledge of these things you call courage?

Nic. Precisely.

Soc. And now let me see whether you agree with Laches and myself as to a third point.

Nic. What is that?

Soc. I will tell you. He and I have a notion that there is not one knowledge or science of the past, another of the present, a third of what is likely to be best and what will be best in the future; but that of all three there is one science only: for example, there is one science of medicine which is concerned with the inspection of health equally in all times, present, past, and future; and one science of husbandry in like manner, which is concerned with the productions of the earth in all times. As to the art of the general, you yourselves will be my witnesses that he has an excellent foreknowledge of the future, and that he claims to be the master and not the servant of the soothsayer, because he knows better what is happening or is likely to happen in war: *[199]* and accordingly the law places the soothsayer under the general, and not the general under the soothsayer. Am I not correct in saying so, Laches?

La. Quite correct.

Soc. And do you, Nicias, also acknowledge that the same science has understanding of the same things, whether future, present, or past?

Nic. Yes, indeed Socrates; that is my opinion.

Soc. And courage, my friend, is, as you say, a knowledge of the fearful and of the hopeful?

Nic. Yes.

Soc. And the fearful, and the hopeful, are admitted to be future goods and future evils?

Nic. True.

Soc. And the same science has to do with the same things in the future or at any time?

Nic. That is true.

Soc. Then courage is not the science which is concerned with the fearful and hopeful, for they are future only; courage, like the other sciences, is concerned not only with good and evil of the future, but of the present and past, and of any time?

Nic. That, as I suppose, is true.

Soc. Then the answer which you have given, Nicias, includes only a third part of courage; but our question extended to the whole nature of courage: and according to your view, that is, according to your present view, courage is not only the knowledge of the hopeful and the fearful, but seems to include nearly every good and evil without reference to time. What do you say to that alteration in your statement?

Nic. I agree, Socrates.

Soc. But then, my dear friend, if a man knew all good and evil, and how they are, and have been, and will be produced, would he not be perfect, and wanting in no virtue, whether justice, or temperance, or holiness? He would possess them all, and he would know which were dangers and which were not, and guard against them whether they were supernatural or natural; and he would provide the good, as he would know how to deal both with gods or men.

Nic. I think, Socrates, that there is a great deal of truth in what you say.

Soc. But then, Nicias, courage, according to this new definition of yours, instead of being a part of virtue only, will be all virtue?

Nic. It would seem so.

Soc. But we were saying that courage is one of the parts of virtue?

Nic. Yes, that was what we were saying.

Soc. And that is in contradiction with our present view?

Nic. That appears to be the case.

Soc. Then, Nicias, we have not discovered what courage is.

Nic. We have not.

[200] *La.* And yet, friend Nicias, I imagined that you would have made the discovery, when you were so contemptuous of the answers which I made to Socrates. I had very great hopes that you would have been enlightened by the wisdom of Damon.

Nic. I perceive, Laches, that you think nothing of having displayed your ignorance of the nature of courage, but you look only to see whether I have not made a similar display; and if we are both equally ignorant of the things which a man who is good for anything should know, that, I suppose, will be of no consequence. You certainly appear to me very like the rest of the world, looking at your neighbour and not at yourself. I am of opinion that enough has been said on the subject which we have been discussing; and if anything has been imperfectly said, that may be hereafter corrected by the help of Damon, whom you think to laugh down, although you have never seen him, and with the help of others. And when I am satisfied myself, I will freely impart my satisfaction to you, for I think that you are very much in want of knowledge.

La. You are a philosopher, Nicias; of that I am aware: nevertheless I would recommend Lysimachus and Melesias not to take you and me as advisers about the education of their children; but, as I said at first, they should ask Socrates and not let him off; if my own sons were old enough, I would have asked him myself.

Nic. To that I quite agree, if Socrates is willing to take them under his charge. I should not wish for any one else to be the tutor of Niceratus. But I observe that when I mention the matter to him he recommends to me some other tutor and refuses himself. Perhaps he may be more ready to listen to you, Lysimachus.

Lys. He ought, Nicias: for certainly I would do things for him which I would not do for many others. What do you say, Socrates—will you comply? And are you ready to give assistance in the improvement of the youths?

Soc. Indeed, Lysimachus, I should be very wrong in refusing to aid in the improvement of anybody. And if I had shown in this conversation that I had a knowledge which Nicias and Laches have not, then I admit that you would be right in inviting me to perform this duty; but as we are all in the same perplexity, why should one of us be preferred to another? [201] I certainly think that no one should; and under these circumstances, let me offer you a piece of advice (and this need not go further than ourselves). I maintain, my friends, that every one of us should seek out the best teacher whom he can find, first for ourselves, who are greatly in need of one, and then for the youth, regardless of expense or anything. But I cannot advise that we remain as we are. And if any one laughs at us for going to school at our age, I would quote to them the authority of Homer, who says, that

Modesty is not good for a needy man.

Let us, then, regardless of what may be said of us, make the education of the youths our own education.

Lys. I like your proposal, Socrates; and as I am the oldest, I am also the most eager to go to school with the boys. Let me beg a favour of you: Come to my house to-morrow at dawn, and we will advise about these matters. For the present, let us make an end of the conversation.

Soc. I will come to you to-morrow, Lysimachus, as you propose, God willing.

PROTAGORAS

PERSONS OF THE DIALOGUE: SOCRATES, *who is the narrator of the Dialogue to his Companion;* HIPPOCRATES; ALCIBIADES; CRITIAS; PROTAGORAS, HIPPIAS, PRODICUS, *Sophists;* CALLIAS, *a wealthy Athenian. Scene: The House of Callias*

[309] *Com.* Where do you come from, Socrates? And yet I need hardly ask the question, for I know that you have been in chase of the fair Alcibiades. I saw him the day before yesterday; and he had got a beard like a man—and he is a man, as I may tell you in your ear. But I thought that he was still very charming.

Soc. What of his beard? Are you not of Homer's opinion, who says

Youth is most charming when the beard first appears?

And that is now the charm of Alcibiades.

Com. Well, and how do matters proceed? Have you been visiting him, and was he gracious to you?

Soc. Yes, I thought that he was very gracious; and especially to-day, for I have just come from him, and he has been helping me in an argument. But shall I tell you a strange thing? I paid no attention to him, and several times I quite forgot that he was present.

Com. What is the meaning of this? Has anything happened between you and him? For surely you cannot have discovered a fairer love than he is; certainly not in this city of Athens.

Soc. Yes, much fairer.

Com. What do you mean—a citizen or a foreigner?

Soc. A foreigner.

Com. Of what country?

Soc. Of Abdera.

Com. And is this stranger really in your opinion a fairer love than the son of Cleinias?

Soc. And is not the wiser always the fairer, sweet friend?

Com. But have you really met, Socrates, with some wise one?

Soc. Say rather, with the wisest of all living men, if you are willing to accord that title to Protagoras.

Com. What! Is Protagoras in Athens?

Soc. Yes; he has been here two days.

Com. And do you just come from an interview with him?

[310] *Soc.* Yes; and I have heard and said many things.

Com. Then, if you have no engagement, suppose that you sit down and tell me what passed, and my attendant here shall give up his place to you.

Soc. To be sure; and I shall be grateful to you for listening.

Com. Thank you, too, for telling us.

Soc. That is thank you twice over. Listen then:—

Last night, or rather very early this morning, Hippocrates, the son of Apollodorus and the brother of Phason, gave a tremendous thump with his staff at my door; some one opened to him, and he came rushing in and bawled out: Socrates, are you awake or asleep?

I knew his voice, and said: Hippocrates, is that you? and do you bring any news?

Good news, he said; nothing but good.

Delightful, I said; but what is the news? and why have you come hither at this unearthly hour?

38

He drew nearer to me and said: Protagoras is come.

Yes, I replied; he came two days ago: have you only just heard of his arrival?

Yes, by the gods, he said; but not until yesterday evening.

At the same time he felt for the truckle-bed, and sat down at my feet, and then he said: Yesterday quite late in the evening, on my return from Oenoe whither I had gone in pursuit of my runaway slave Satyrus, as I meant to have told you, if some other matter had not come in the way;—on my return, when we had done supper and were about to retire to rest, my brother said to me: Protagoras is come. I was going to you at once, and then I thought that the night was far spent. But the moment sleep left me after my fatigue, I got up and came hither direct.

I, who knew the very courageous madness of the man, said: What is the matter? Has Protagoras robbed you of anything?

He replied, laughing: Yes, indeed he has, Socrates, of the wisdom which he keeps from me.

But, surely, I said, if you give him money, and make friends with him, he will make you as wise as he is himself.

Would to heaven, he replied, that this were the case! He might take all that I have, and all that my friends have, if he pleased. But that is why I have come to you now, in order that you may speak to him on my behalf; for I am young, and also I have never seen nor heard him; [311] (when he visited Athens before I was but a child) and all men praise him, Socrates; he is reputed to be the most accomplished of speakers. There is no reason why we should not go to him at once, and then we shall find him at home. He lodges, as I hear, with Callias the son of Hipponicus: let us start.

I replied: Not yet, my good friend; the hour is too early. But let us rise and take a turn in the court and wait about there until daybreak; when the day breaks, then we will go. For Protagoras is generally at home, and we shall be sure to find him; never fear.

Upon this we got up and walked about in the court, and I thought that I would make trial of the strength of his resolution. So I examined him and put questions to him. Tell me, Hippocrates, I said, as you are going to Protagoras, and will be paying your money to him, what is he to whom you are going? and what will he make of you? If, for example, you had thought of going to Hippocrates of Cos, the Asclepiad, and were about to give him your money, and some one had said to you: You are paying money to your namesake Hippocrates, O Hippocrates; tell me, what is he that you give him money? how would you have answered?

I should say, he replied, that I gave money to him as a physician.

And what will he make of you?

A physician, he said.

And if you were resolved to go to Polycleitus the Argive, or Pheidias the Athenian, and were intending to give them money, and some one had asked you: What are Polycleitus and Pheidias? and why do you give them this money? —how would you have answered?

I should have answered, that they were statuaries.

And what will they make of you?

A statuary, of course.

Well now, I said, you and I are going to Protagoras, and we are ready to pay him money on your behalf. If our own means are sufficient, and we can gain him with these, we shall be only too glad; but if not, then we are to spend the money of your friends as well. Now suppose, that while we are thus enthusiastically pursuing our object some one were to say to us: Tell me, Socrates, and you Hippocrates, what is Protagoras, and why are you going to pay him money,—how should we answer? I know that Pheidias is a sculptor, and that Homer is a poet; but what appellation is given to Protagoras? how is he designated?

They call him a Sophist, Socrates, he replied.

Then we are going to pay our money to him in the character of a Sophist?

Certainly.

But suppose a person were to ask this further question: And how about yourself? [312] What will Protagoras make of you, if you go to see him?

He answered, with a blush upon his face (for the day was just beginning to dawn, so that I could see him): Unless this differs in some way from the former instances, I suppose that he will make a Sophist of me.

By the gods, I said, and are you not ashamed at having to appear before the Hellenes in the character of a Sophist?

Indeed, Socrates, to confess the truth, I am.

But you should not assume, Hippocrates, that the instruction of Protagoras is of this nature: may you not learn of him in the same way that you learned the arts of the grammarian, or musician, or trainer, not with the view of making any of them a profession, but only as a part of education, and because a private gentleman and freeman ought to know them?

Just so, he said; and that, in my opinion, is a far truer account of the teaching of Protagoras.

I said: I wonder whether you know what you are doing?

And what am I doing?

You are going to commit your soul to the care of a man whom you call a Sophist. And yet I hardly think that you know what a Sophist is; and if not, then you do not even know to whom you are committing your soul and whether the thing to which you commit yourself be good or evil.

I certainly think that I do know, he replied.

Then tell me, what do you imagine that he is?

I take him to be one who knows wise things, he replied, as his name implies.

And might you not, I said, affirm this of the painter and of the carpenter also: Do not they, too, know wise things? But suppose a person were to ask us: In what are the painters wise? We should answer: In what relates to the making of likenesses, and similarly of other things. And if he were further to ask: What is the wisdom of the Sophist, and what is the manufacture over which he presides?—how should we answer him?

How should we answer him, Socrates? What other answer could there be but that he presides over the art which makes men eloquent?

Yes, I replied, that is very likely true, but not enough; for in the answer a further question is involved: Of what does the Sophist make a man talk eloquently? The player on the lyre may be supposed to make a man talk eloquently about that which he makes him understand, that is about playing the lyre. Is not that true?

Yes.

Then about what does the Sophist make him eloquent? Must not he make him eloquent in that which he understands?

Yes, that may be assumed.

And what is that which the Sophist knows and makes his disciple know?

Indeed, he said, I cannot tell.

[313] Then I proceeded to say: Well, but are you aware of the danger which you are incurring? If you were going to commit your body to some one, who might do good or harm to it, would you not carefully consider and ask the opinion of your friends and kindred, and deliberate many days as to whether you should give him the care of your body? But when the soul is in question, which you hold to be of far more value than the body, and upon the good or evil of which depends the well-being of your all,—about this you never consulted either with your father or with your brother or with any one of us who are your companions. But no sooner does this foreigner appear, than you instantly commit your soul to his keeping. In the evening, as you say, you hear of him, and in the morning you go to him, never deliberating or taking the opinion of any one as to whether you ought to intrust yourself to him or not;—you have quite made up your mind that you will at all hazards be a pupil of Protagoras, and are prepared to expend all the property of yourself and of your friends in carrying out at any price this determination, although, as you admit, you do not know him, and have never spoken with him: and you call him a Sophist, but are manifestly ignorant of what a Sophist is; and yet you are going to commit yourself to his keeping.

When he heard me say this, he replied: No other inference, Socrates, can be drawn from your words.

I proceeded: Is not a Sophist, Hippocrates, one who deals wholesale or retail in the food of the soul? To me that appears to be his nature.

And what, Socrates, is the food of the soul?

Surely, I said, knowledge is the food of the soul; and we must take care, my friend, that the Sophist does not deceive us when he praises what he sells, like the dealers wholesale or retail who sell the food of the body; for they praise indiscriminately all their goods, without knowing what are really beneficial or hurtful: neither do their customers know, with the exception of any trainer or physician who may happen to buy of them. In like manner those who carry about the wares of knowledge, and make the round of the cities, and sell or retail them to any customer who is in want of them, praise them all alike; though I should not wonder, O my friend, if many of them were really ignorant of their effect upon the soul; and their customers equally ignorant, unless he who buys of them happens to be a physician of the soul. If, therefore, you have understanding of what is good and evil, you may safely buy knowledge of Protagoras or of any one; [314] but if not, then, O my friend, pause, and do not hazard your dearest interests at a game of chance. For there is far greater peril in buying knowledge than in buying meat and drink: the one you purchase of the wholesale or retail dealer, and carry them away in other vessels, and before you receive them into the body as food, you may deposit them at home and call in any experienced friend who knows what is good to be eaten or drunken, and what not, and how much, and when; and then the danger of purchasing them is not so great. But you cannot buy the wares of knowledge and carry them away in another vessel; when you have paid for them you must receive them into the soul and go your way, either greatly harmed or greatly benefited; and therefore we should deliberate and take counsel with our elders; for we are still young—too young to determine such a matter. And now let us go, as we were intending, and hear Protagoras; and when we have heard what he has to say, we may take counsel of others; for not only is Protagoras at the house of Callias, but there is Hippias of Elis, and, if I am not mistaken, Prodicus of Ceos, and several other wise men.

To this we agreed, and proceeded on our way until we reached the vestibule of the house; and there we stopped in order to conclude a discussion which had arisen between us as we were going along; and we stood talking in the vestibule until we had finished and come to an understanding. And I think that the doorkeeper, who was a eunuch, and who was probably annoyed at the great inroad of the Sophists, must have heard us talking. At any rate, when we knocked at the door, and he opened and saw us, he grumbled: They are Sophists—he is not at home; and instantly gave the door a hearty bang with both his hands. Again we knocked, and he answered without opening: Did you not hear me say that he is not at home, fellows? But, my friend, I said, you need not be alarmed; for we are not Sophists, and we are not come to see Callias, but we want to see Protagoras; and I must request you to announce us. At last, after a good deal of difficulty, the man was persuaded to open the door.

When we entered, we found Protagoras taking a walk in the cloister; and next to him, on one side, were walking Callias, the son of Hipponicus, and Paralus, the son of Pericles, who, by the mother's side, is his half-brother, and Charmides, the son of Glaucon. [315] On the other side of him were Xanthippus, the other son of Pericles, Philippides, the son of Philomelus; also Antimoerus of Mende, who of all the disciples of Protagoras is the most famous, and intends to make sophistry his profession. A train of listeners followed him; the greater part of them appeared to be foreigners, whom Protagoras had brought with him out of the various cities visited by him in his journeys, he, like Orpheus, attracting them by his voice, and they following.[1] I should mention also that there were some Athenians in the company. Nothing delighted me more than the precision of their movements: they never got into his way at all; but when he and those who were with him turned back, then the band of listeners parted regularly on either side; he was always in front, and they wheeled round and took their places behind him in perfect order.

After him, as Homer says, "I lifted up my eyes and saw" Hippias the Elean sitting in the opposite cloister on a chair of state, and around him were seated on benches Eryximachus, the son of Acumenus, and Phaedrus the Myrrhinusian, and Andron the son of Androtion, and there were strangers whom he had brought with him from his native city of Elis, and some others: they were putting to Hippias certain physical and astronomical questions, and he, *ex cathedra,* was determining their several questions to them, and discoursing of them.

Also, "my eyes beheld Tantalus"; for Prodicus the Cean was at Athens: he had been lodged in a room which, in the days of Hipponicus, was a storehouse; but, as the house was full, Callias had cleared this out and made the room into a guest-chamber. Now Prodicus was still in bed, wrapped up in sheepskins and bed-clothes, of which there seemed to be a great heap; and there was sitting by him on the couches near, Pausanias of the deme of Cerameis, and with Pausanias was a youth quite young, who is certainly remarkable for his good looks, and, if I am not mistaken, is also of a fair and gentle nature. I thought that I heard him called Agathon, and my suspicion is that he is the beloved of Pausanias. There was this youth, and also there were the two Adeimantuses, one the son of Cepis, and the other of Leucolophides, and some others. I was very anxious to hear what Prodicus was saying, for he seems to me to be an all-wise and inspired man; [316] but I was not able to get into the inner circle, and his fine deep voice made an echo in the room which rendered his words inaudible.

No sooner had we entered than there followed us Alcibiades the beautiful, as you say, and I believe you; and also Critias the son of Callaeschrus.

On entering we stopped a little, in order to look about us, and then walked up to Protagoras, and I said: Protagoras, my friend Hippocrates and I have come to see you.

[1] Cf. *Republic,* x. 600.

Do you wish, he said, to speak with me alone, or in the presence of the company?

Whichever you please, I said; you shall determine when you have heard the purpose of our visit.

And what is your purpose? he said.

I must explain, I said, that my friend Hippocrates is a native Athenian; he is the son of Apollodorus, and of a great and prosperous house, and he is himself in natural ability quite a match for anybody of his own age. I believe that he aspires to political eminence; and this he thinks that conversation with you is most likely to procure for him. And now you can determine whether you would wish to speak to him of your teaching alone or in the presence of the company.

Thank you, Socrates, for your consideration of me. For certainly a stranger finding his way into great cities, and persuading the flower of the youth in them to leave the company of their kinsmen or any other acquaintances, old or young, and live with him, under the idea that they will be improved by his conversation, ought to be very cautious; great jealousies are aroused by his proceedings, and he is the subject of many enmities and conspiracies. Now the art of the Sophist is, as I believe, of great antiquity; but in ancient times those who practised it, fearing this odium, veiled and disguised themselves under various names, some under that of poets, as Homer, Hesiod, and Simonides, some, of hierophants and prophets, as Orpheus and Musaeus, and some, as I observe, even under the name of gymnastic-masters, like Iccus of Tarentum, or the more recently celebrated Herodicus, now of Selymbria and formerly of Megara, who is a first-rate Sophist. Your own Agathocles pretended to be a musician, but was really an eminent Sophist; also Pythocleides the Cean; and there were many others; and all of them, as I was saying, adopted these arts as veils or disguises because they were afraid of the odium which they would incur. But that is not my way, *[317]* for I do not believe that they effected their purpose, which was to deceive the government, who were not blinded by them; and as to the people, they have no understanding, and only repeat what their rulers are pleased to tell them. Now to run away, and to be caught in running away, is the very height of folly, and also greatly increases the exasperation of mankind; for they regard him who runs away as a rogue, in addition to any other objections which they have to him; and therefore I take an entirely opposite

course, and acknowledge myself to be a Sophist and instructor of mankind; such an open acknowledgement appears to me to be a better sort of caution than concealment. Nor do I neglect other precautions, and therefore I hope, as I may say, by the favour of heaven that no harm will come of the acknowledgment that I am a Sophist. And I have been now many years in the profession—for all my years when added up are many: there is no one here present of whom I might not be the father. Wherefore I should much prefer conversing with you, if you want to speak with me, in the presence of the company.

As I suspected that he would like to have a little display and glorification in the presence of Prodicus and Hippias, and would gladly show us to them in the light of his admirers, I said: But why should we not summon Prodicus and Hippias and their friends to hear us?

Very good, he said.

Suppose, said Callias, that we hold a council in which you may sit and discuss.—This was agreed upon, and great delight was felt at the prospect of hearing wise men talk; we ourselves took the chairs and benches, and arranged them by Hippias, where the other benches had been already placed. Meanwhile Callias and Alcibiades got Prodicus out of bed and brought in him and his companions.

When we were all seated, Protagoras said: Now that the company are assembled, Socrates, tell me about the young man of whom you were just now speaking. *[318]*

I replied: I will begin again at the same point, Protagoras, and tell you once more the purport of my visit: this is my friend Hippocrates, who is desirous of making your acquaintance; he would like to know what will happen to him if he associates with you. I have no more to say.

Protagoras answered: Young man, if you associate with me, on the very first day you will return home a better man than you came, and better on the second day than on the first, and better every day than you were on the day before.

When I heard this, I said: Protagoras, I do not at all wonder at hearing you say this; even at your age, and with all your wisdom, if any one were to teach you what you did not know before, you would become better no doubt: but please to answer in a different way—I will explain how by an example. Let me suppose that Hippocrates, instead of desiring your acquaintance, wished to become acquainted with the young man Zeuxippus of Heraclea, who has lately been in Athens, and he had come to him as he has come to you, and had heard him say, as he has heard you say, that every day he would grow and become better if he associated with him: and then suppose that he were to ask him, "In what shall I become better, and in what shall I grow?"—Zeuxippus would answer, "In painting." And suppose that he went to Orthagoras the Theban, and heard him say the same thing, and asked him, "In what shall I become better day by day?" he would reply, "In flute-playing." Now I want you to make the same sort of answer to this young man and to me, who am asking questions on his account. When you say that on the first day on which he associates with you he will return home a better man, and on every day will grow in like manner,—in what, Protagoras, will he be better? and about what?

When Protagoras heard me say this, he replied: You ask questions fairly, and I like to answer a question which is fairly put. If Hippocrates comes to me he will not experience the sort of drudgery with which other Sophists are in the habit of insulting their pupils; who, when they have just escaped from the arts, are taken and driven back into them by these teachers, and made to learn calculation, and astronomy, and geometry, and music (he gave a look at Hippias as he said this); but if he comes to me, he will learn that which he comes to learn. And this is prudence in affairs private as well as public; he will learn to order his own house in the best manner, and he will be able to speak and act for the best in the affairs of the state.

[319] Do I understand you, I said; and is your meaning that you teach the art of politics, and that you promise to make men good citizens?

That, Socrates, is exactly the profession which I make.

Then, I said, you do indeed possess a noble art, if there is no mistake about this; for I will freely confess to you, Protagoras, that I have a doubt whether this art is capable of being taught, and yet I know not how to disbelieve your assertion. And I ought to tell you why I am of opinion that this art cannot be taught or communicated by man to man. I say that the Athenians are an understanding people, and indeed they are esteemed to be such by the other Hellenes. Now I observe that when we are met together in the assembly, and the matter in hand relates to building, the builders are summoned as advisers; when the question is one of ship-building, then the ship-wrights; and the like of other arts which they think capable of being taught and learned. And if some person offers to give them advice who is not supposed by them to have any skill in the art, even though he be good-looking, and rich, and noble, they will not listen to him, but laugh and hoot at him, until either he is clamoured down and retires of himself; or if he persist, he is dragged away or put out by the constables at the command of the prytanes. This is their way of behaving about professors of the arts. But when the question is an affair of state, then everybody is free to have a say—carpenter, tinker, cobbler, sailor, passenger; rich and poor, high and low —any one who likes gets up, and no one reproaches him, as in the former case, with not having learned, and having no teacher, and yet giving advice; evidently because they are under the impression that this sort of knowledge cannot be taught. And not only is this true of the state, but of individuals; the best and wisest of our citizens are unable to impart their political wisdom to others: [320] as for example, Pericles, the father of these young men, who gave them excellent instruction in all that could be learned from masters, in his own department of politics neither taught them, nor gave them teachers; but they were allowed to wander at their own free will in a sort of hope that they would light upon virtue of their own accord. Or take another example: there was Cleinias the younger brother of our friend Alcibiades, of whom this very same Pericles was the guardian; and he being in fact under the apprehension that Cleinias would be corrupted by Alcibiades, took him away, and placed him in the house of Ariphron to be educated; but before six months had elapsed, Ariphron sent him back, not knowing what to do with him. And I could mention numberless other instances of persons who were good themselves, and never yet made any one else good, whether friend or stranger. Now I, Protagoras, having these examples before me, am inclined to think that virtue cannot be taught. But then again, when I listen to your words, I waver; and am disposed to think that there must be something in what you say, because I know that you have great experience, and learning, and invention. And I wish that you would, if possible, show me a little more clearly that virtue can be taught. Will you be so good?

That I will, Socrates, and gladly. But what would you like? Shall I, as an elder, speak to you as younger men in an apologue or myth, or shall I argue out the question?

To this several of the company answered that he should choose for himself.

Well, then, he said, I think that the myth will be more interesting.

Once upon a time there were gods only, and no mortal creatures. But when the time came that these also should be created, the gods fashioned them out of earth and fire and various mixtures of both elements in the interior of the earth; and when they were about to bring them into the light of day, they ordered Prometheus and Epimetheus to equip them, and to distribute to them severally their proper qualities. Epimetheus said to Prometheus: "Let me distribute, and do you inspect." This was agreed, and Epimetheus made the distribution. There were some to whom he gave strength without swiftness, while he equipped the weaker with swiftness; some he armed, and others he left unarmed; and devised for the latter some other means of preservation, making some large, and having their size as a protection, and others small, whose nature was to fly in the air or burrow in the ground; [321] this was to be their way of escape. Thus did he compensate them with the view of preventing any race from becoming extinct. And when he had provided against their destruction by one another, he contrived also a means of protecting them against the seasons of heaven; clothing them with close hair and thick skins sufficient to defend them against the winter cold and able to resist the summer heat, so that they might have a natural bed of their own when they wanted to rest; also he furnished them with hoofs and hair and hard and callous skins under their feet. Then he gave them varieties of food—herb of the soil to some, to others fruits of trees, and to others roots, and to some again he gave other animals as food. And some he made to have few young ones, while those who were their prey were very prolific; and in this manner the race was preserved. Thus did Epimetheus, who, not being very wise, forgot that he had distributed among the brute animals all the qualities which he had to give—and when he came to man, who was still unprovided, he was terribly perplexed. Now while he was in this perplexity, Prometheus came to inspect the distribution, and he found that the other animals were suitably furnished, but that man alone was naked and shoeless, and had neither bed nor arms of defence. The appointed hour was approaching when man in his turn was to go forth into the light of day; and Prometheus, not knowing how he could devise his salvation, stole the mechanical arts of Hephaestus and Athene, and fire with them (they could neither have been acquired nor used without fire), and gave them to man. Thus man had the wisdom necessary to the support of life, but political wisdom he had not; for that was in the keeping of Zeus, and the power of Prometheus did not extend to entering into the citadel of heaven, where Zeus dwelt, who moreover had terrible sentinels; but he did enter by stealth into the common workshop of Athene and Hephaestus, in which they used to practise their favourite arts, and carried off Hephaestus' art of working by fire, and also the art of Athene, and gave them to man. And in this way man was supplied with the means of life. But Prometheus is said to have been afterwards prosecuted for theft, owing to the blunder of Epimetheus.

[322] Now man, having a share of the divine attributes, was at first the only one of the animals who had any gods, because he alone was of their kindred; and he would raise altars and images of them. He was not long in inventing articulate speech and names; and he also constructed houses and clothes and shoes and beds, and drew sustenance from the earth. Thus provided, mankind at first lived dispersed, and there were no cities. But the consequence was that they were destroyed by the wild beasts, for they were utterly weak in comparison of them, and their art was only sufficient to provide them with the means of life, and did not enable them to carry on war against the animals: food they had, but not as yet the art of government, of which the art of war is a part. After a while the desire of self-preservation gathered them into cities; but when they were gathered together, having no art of government, they evil intreated one another, and were again in process of dispersion and destruction. Zeus feared that the entire race would be exterminated, and so he sent Hermes to them, bearing reverence and justice to be the ordering principles of cities and the bonds of friendship and conciliation. Hermes asked Zeus how he should impart justice and reverence among men:— Should he distribute them as the arts are distributed; that is to say, to a favoured few only, one skilled individual having enough of medicine or of any other art for many unskilled ones? "Shall this be the manner in which I am to distribute justice and reverence among men, or shall I give them to all?" "To all," said

Zeus; "I should like them all to have a share; for cities cannot exist, if a few only share in the virtues, as in the arts. And further, make a law by my order, that he who has no part in reverence and justice shall be put to death, for he is a plague of the state."

And this is the reason, Socrates, why the Athenians and mankind in general, when the question relates to carpentering or any other mechanical art, allow but a few to share in their deliberations; and when any one else interferes, then, as you say, they object, if he be not of the favoured few; which, as I reply, is very natural. But when they meet to deliberate about political virtue, *[323]* which proceeds only by way of justice and wisdom, they are patient enough of any man who speaks of them, as is also natural, because they think that every man ought to share in this sort of virtue, and that states could not exist if this were otherwise. I have explained to you, Socrates, the reason of this phenomenon.

And that you may not suppose yourself to be deceived in thinking that all men regard every man as having a share of justice or honesty and of every other political virtue, let me give you a further proof, which is this. In other cases, as you are aware, if a man says that he is a good flute-player, or skilful in any other art in which he has no skill, people either laugh at him or are angry with him, and his relations think that he is mad and go and admonish him; but when honesty is in question, or some other political virtue, even if they know that he is dishonest, yet, if the man comes publicly forward and tells the truth about his dishonesty, then, what in the other case was held by them to be good sense, they now deem to be madness. They say that all men ought to profess honesty whether they are honest or not, and that a man is out of his mind who says anything else. Their notion is, that a man must have some degree of honesty; and that if he has none at all he ought not to be in the world.

I have been showing that they are right in admitting every man as a counsellor about this sort of virtue, as they are of opinion that every man is a partaker of it. And I will now endeavour to show further that they do not conceive this virtue to be given by nature, or to grow spontaneously, but to be a thing which may be taught; and which comes to a man by taking pains. No one would instruct, no one would rebuke, or be angry with those whose calamities they suppose to be due to nature or chance; they do not try to punish or to prevent them from being what they are; they do but pity them. Who is so foolish as to chastise or instruct the ugly, or the diminutive, or the feeble? And for this reason. Because he knows that good and evil of this kind is the work of nature and of chance; whereas if a man is wanting in those good qualities which are attained by study and exercise and teaching, and has only the contrary evil qualities, other men are angry with him, and punish and reprove him—of these evil qualities one is impiety, *[324]* another injustice, and they may be described generally as the very opposite of political virtue. In such cases any man will be angry with another, and reprimand him,—clearly because he thinks that by study and learning, the virtue in which the other is deficient may be acquired. If you will think, Socrates, of the nature of punishment, you will see at once that in the opinion of mankind virtue may be acquired; no one punishes the evil-doer under the notion, or for the reason, that he has done wrong,—only the unreasonable fury of a beast acts in that manner. But he who desires to inflict rational punishment does not retaliate for a past wrong which cannot be undone; he has regard to the future, and is desirous that the man who is punished, and he who sees him punished, may be deterred from doing wrong again. He punishes for the sake of prevention, thereby clearly implying that virtue is capable of being taught. This is the notion of all who retaliate upon others either privately or publicly. And the Athenians, too, your own citizens, like other men, punish and take vengeance on all whom they regard as evil doers; and hence, we may infer them to be of the number of those who think that virtue may be acquired and taught. Thus far, Socrates, I have shown you clearly enough, if I am not mistaken, that your countrymen are right in admitting the tinker and the cobbler to advise about politics, and also that they deem virtue to be capable of being taught and acquired.

There yet remains one difficulty which has been raised by you about the sons of good men. What is the reason why good men teach their sons the knowledge which is gained from teachers, and make them wise in that, but do nothing towards improving them in the virtues which distinguish themselves? And here, Socrates, I will leave the apologue and resume the argument. Please to consider: Is there or is there not some one quality of which all the citizens must be partakers, if there is to be a city at all? In the answer to this question is contained the only solution of your difficulty; there is no other. For if there be any such quality, and this quality or unity is not the art of the carpenter, [325] or the smith, or the potter, but justice and temperance and holiness and, in a word, manly virtue—if this is the quality of which all men must be partakers, and which is the very condition of their learning or doing anything else, and if he who is wanting in this, whether he be a child only or a grown-up man or woman, must be taught and punished, until by punishment he becomes better, and he who rebels against instruction and punishment is either exiled or condemned to death under the idea that he is incurable—if what I am saying be true, good men have their sons taught other things and not this, do consider how extraordinary their conduct would appear to be. For we have shown that they think virtue capable of being taught and cultivated both in private and public; and, notwithstanding, they have their sons taught lesser matters, ignorance of which does not involve the punishment of death: but greater things, of which the ignorance may cause death and exile to those who have no training or knowledge of them—aye, and confiscation as well as death, and, in a word, may be the ruin of families—those things, I say, they are supposed not to teach them—not to take the utmost care that they should learn. How improbable is this, Socrates!

Education and admonition commence in the first years of childhood, and last to the very end of life. Mother and nurse and father and tutor are vying with one another about the improvement of the child as soon as ever he is able to understand what is being said to him: he cannot say or do anything without their setting forth to him that this is just and that is unjust; this is honourable, that is dishonourable; this is holy, that is unholy; do this and abstain from that. And if he obeys, well and good; if not, he is straightened by threats and blows, like a piece of bent or warped wood. At a later stage they send him to teachers, and enjoin them to see to his manners even more than to his reading and music; and the teachers do as they are desired. And when the boy has learned his letters and is beginning to understand what is written, as before he understood only what was spoken, [326] they put into his hands the works of great poets, which he reads sitting on a bench at school; in these are contained many admonitions, and many tales, and praises, and encomia of ancient famous men, which he is required to learn by heart, in order that he may imitate or emulate them and desire to become like them. Then, again, the teachers of the lyre take similar care that their young disciple is temperate and gets into no mischief; and when they have taught him the use of the lyre, they introduce him to the poems of other excellent poets, who are the lyric poets; and these they set to music, and make their harmonies and rhythms quite familiar to the children's souls, in order that they may learn to be more gentle, and harmonious, and rhythmical, and so more fitted for speech and action; for the life of man in every part has need of harmony and rhythm. Then they send them to the master of gymnastic, in order that their bodies may better minister to the virtuous mind, and that they may not be compelled through bodily weakness to play the coward in war or on any other occasion. This is what is done by those who have the means, and those who have the means are the rich; their children begin to go to school soonest and leave off latest. When they have done with masters, the state again compels them to learn the laws, and live after the pattern which they furnish, and not after their own fancies; and just as in learning to write, the writing-master first draws lines with a style for the use of the young beginner, and gives him the tablet and makes him follow the lines, so the city draws the laws, which were the invention of good lawgivers living in the olden time; these are given to the young man, in order to guide him in his conduct whether he is commanding or obeying; and he who transgresses them is to be corrected, or, in other words, called to account, which is a term used not only in your country, but also in many others, seeing that justice calls men to account. Now when there is all this care about virtue private and public, why, Socrates, do you still wonder and doubt whether virtue can be taught? Cease to wonder, for the opposite would be far more surprising.

But why then do the sons of good fathers often turn out ill? There is nothing very wonderful in this; for, as I have been saying, the existence of a state implies that virtue is not any man's private possession. [327] If so—and nothing can be truer—then I will further ask you to imagine, as an illustration, some other pursuit or branch of knowledge which may be assumed equally to be the condition of the existence of a state. Suppose that there could be no state unless we were all flute-players, as far as each had the capacity, and everybody was freely teaching everybody the art, both in private and public, and reproving the bad player as freely and openly as every man now teaches justice and the laws, not concealing them as he would conceal the other arts, but imparting them—for all of us have a mutual interest in the justice and virtue of one another, and this is the reason why every one is so ready to teach justice and the laws;—suppose, I say, that there were the same readiness and liberality among us in teaching one another flute-playing, do you imagine, Socrates, that the sons of good flute-players would be more likely to be good than the sons of bad ones? I think not. Would not their sons grow up to be distinguished or undistinguished according to their own natural capacities as flute-players, and the son of a good player would often turn out to be a bad one, and the son of a bad player to be a good one, and all flute-players would be good enough in comparison of those who were ignorant and unacquainted with the art of flute-playing? In like manner I would have you consider that he who appears to you to be the worst of those who have been brought up in laws and humanities, would appear to be a just man and a master of justice if he were to be compared with men who had no education, or courts of justice, or laws, or any restraints upon them which compelled them to practise virtue—with the savages, for example, whom the poet Pherecrates exhibited on the stage at the last year's Lenaean festival. If you were living among men such as the man-haters in his Chorus, you would be only too glad to meet with Eurybates and Phrynondas, and you would sorrowfully long to revisit the rascality of this part of the world. And you, Socrates, are discontented, and why? Because all men are teachers of virtue, each one according to his ability; and you say, Where are the teachers? [328] You might as well ask, Who teaches Greek? For of that too there will not be any teachers found. Or you might ask, Who is to teach the sons of our artisans this same art which they have learned of their fathers? He and his fellow-workmen have taught them to the best of their ability,—but who will carry them further in their arts? And you would certainly have a difficulty, Socrates, in finding a teacher of them; but there would be no difficulty in finding a teacher of those who are wholly ignorant. And this is true of virtue or of anything else; if a man is better able than we are to promote virtue ever so little, we must be content with the result. A teacher of this sort I believe myself to be,

and above all other men to have the knowledge which makes a man noble and good; and I give my pupils their money's-worth, and even more, as they themselves confess. And therefore I have introduced the following mode of payment:— When a man has been my pupil, if he likes he pays my price, but there is no compulsion; and if he does not like, he has only to go into a temple and take an oath of the value of the instructions, and he pays no more than he declares to be their value.

Such is my Apologue, Socrates, and such is the argument by which I endeavour to show that virtue may be taught, and that this is the opinion of the Athenians. And I have also attempted to show that you are not to wonder at good fathers having bad sons, or at good sons having bad fathers, of which the sons of Polycleitus afford an example, who are the companions of our friends here, Paralus and Xanthippus, but are nothing in comparison with their father; and this is true of the sons of many other artists. As yet I ought not to say the same of Paralus and Xanthippus themselves, for they are young and there is still hope of them.

Protagoras ended, and in my ear

So charming left his voice, that I the while
Thought him still speaking; still stood fixed
   to hear.[1]

At length, when the truth dawned upon me, that he had really finished, not without difficulty I began to collect myself, and looking at Hippocrates, I said to him: O son of Apollodorus, how deeply grateful I am to you for having brought me hither; I would not have missed the speech of Protagoras for a great deal. For I used to imagine that no human care could make men good; but I know better now. Yet I have still one very small difficulty which I am sure that Protagoras will easily explain, as he has already explained so much. If a man were to go and consult Pericles or any of our great speakers [329] about these matters, he might perhaps hear as fine a discourse; but then when one has a question to ask of any of them, like books, they can neither answer nor ask; and if any one challenges the least particular of their speech, they go ringing on in a long harangue, like brazen pots, which when they are struck continue to sound unless some one puts his hand upon them; whereas our friend Protagoras can not only make a good speech, as he has already shown, but when he is asked a question he can answer briefly; and when he asks he will

[1] Borrowed by Milton, *Paradise Lost*, viii. 2, 3.

wait and hear the answer; and this is a very rare gift. Now I, Protagoras, want to ask of you a little question, which if you will only answer, I shall be quite satisfied. You were saying that virtue can be taught;—that I will take upon your authority, and there is no one to whom I am more ready to trust. But I marvel at one thing about which I should like to have my mind set at rest. You were speaking of Zeus sending justice and reverence to men; and several times while you were speaking, justice, and temperance, and holiness, and all these qualities, were described by you as if together they made up virtue. Now I want you to tell me truly whether virtue is one whole, of which justice and temperance and holiness are parts; or whether all these are only the names of one and the same thing: that is the doubt which still lingers in my mind.

There is no difficulty, Socrates, in answering that the qualities of which you are speaking are the parts of virtue which is one.

And are they parts, I said, in the same sense in which mouth, nose, and eyes, and ears, are the parts of a face; or are they like the parts of gold, which differ from the whole and from one another only in being larger or smaller?

I should say that they differed, Socrates, in the first way; they are related to one another as the parts of a face are related to the whole face.

And do men have some one part and some another part of virtue? Of if a man has one part, must he also have all the others?

By no means, he said; for many a man is brave and not just, or just and not wise.

You would not deny, then, that courage and wisdom are also parts of virtue?

[330] Most undoubtedly they are, he answered; and wisdom is the noblest of the parts.

And they are all different from one another? I said.

Yes.

And has each of them a distinct function like the parts of the face;—the eye, for example, is not like the ear, and has not the same functions; and the other parts are none of them like one another, either in their functions, or in any other way? I want to know whether the comparison holds concerning the parts of virtue. Do they also differ from one another in themselves and in their functions? For that is clearly what the simile would imply.

Yes, Socrates, you are right in supposing that they differ.

Then, I said, no other part of virtue is like knowledge, or like justice, or like courage, or like temperance, or like holiness?

No, he answered.

Well then, I said, suppose that you and I enquire into their natures. And first, you would agree with me that justice is of the nature of a thing, would you not? That is my opinion: would it not be yours also?

Mine also, he said.

And suppose that some one were to ask us, saying, "O Protagoras, and you, Socrates, what about this thing which you were calling justice, is it just or unjust?"—and I were to answer, just: would you vote with me or against me?

With you, he said.

Thereupon I should answer to him who asked me, that justice is of the nature of the just: would not you?

Yes, he said.

And suppose that he went on to say: "Well now, is there also such a thing as holiness?"— we should answer, "Yes," if I am not mistaken?

Yes, he said.

Which you would also acknowledge to be a thing—should we not say so?

He assented.

"And is this a sort of thing which is of the nature of the holy, or of the nature of the unholy?" I should be angry at his putting such a question, and should say, "Peace, man; nothing can be holy if holiness is not holy." What would you say? Would you not answer in the same way?

Certainly, he said.

And then after this suppose that he came and asked us, "What were you saying just now? Perhaps I may not have heard you rightly, but you seemed to me to be saying that the parts of virtue were not the same as one another." [331] I should reply, "You certainly heard that said, but not, as you imagine, by me; for I only asked the question; Protagoras gave the answer." And suppose that he turned to you and said, "Is this true, Protagoras? and do you maintain that one part of virtue is unlike another, and this your position?"—how would you answer him?

I could not help acknowledging the truth of what he said, Socrates.

Well then, Protagoras, we will assume this; and now supposing that he proceeded to say further, "Then holiness is not of the nature of justice, nor justice of the nature of holiness, but of the nature of unholiness; and holiness is of the nature of the not just, and therefore of the unjust, and the unjust is the unholy": how shall we answer him? I should certainly answer him on my own behalf that justice is holy, and that holiness is just; and I would say in like manner on your behalf also, if you would allow me, that justice is either the same with holiness, or very nearly the same; and above all I would assert that justice is like holiness and holiness is like justice; and I wish that you would tell me whether I may be permitted to give this answer on your behalf, and whether you would agree with me.

He replied, I cannot simply agree, Socrates, to the proposition that justice is holy and that holiness is just, for there appears to me to be a difference between them. But what matter? if you please I please; and let us assume, if you will, that justice is holy, and that holiness is just.

Pardon me, I replied; I do not want this "if you wish" or "if you will" sort of conclusion to be proven, but I want you and me to be proven: I mean to say that the conclusion will be best proven if there be no "if."

Well, he said, I admit that justice bears a resemblance to holiness, for there is always some point of view in which everything is like every other thing; white is in a certain way like black, and hard is like soft, and the most extreme opposites have some qualities in common; even the parts of the face which, as we were saying before, are distinct and have different functions, are still in a certain point of view similar, and one of them is like another of them. And you may prove that they are like one another on the same principle that all things are like one another; and yet things which are like in some particular ought not to be called alike, nor things which are unlike in some particular, however slight, unlike.

And do you think, I said in a tone of surprise, that justice and holiness have but a small degree of likeness?

Certainly not; any more than I agree with what I understand to be your view.

[332] Well, I said, as you appear to have a difficulty about this, let us take another of the examples which you mentioned instead. Do you admit the existence of folly?

I do.

And is not wisdom the very opposite of folly?

That is true, he said.

And when men act rightly and advantageously they seem to you to be temperate?

Yes, he said.

And temperance makes them temperate?

Certainly.

And they who do not act rightly act foolishly, and in acting thus are not temperate?

I agree, he said.

Then to act foolishly is the opposite of acting temperately?

He assented.

And foolish actions are done by folly, and temperate actions by temperance?

He agreed.

And that is done strongly which is done by strength, and that which is weakly done, by weakness?

He assented.

And that which is done with swiftness is done swiftly, and that which is done with slowness, slowly?

He assented again.

And that which is done in the same manner, is done by the same; and that which is done in an opposite manner by the opposite?

He agreed.

Once more, I said, is there anything beautiful?

Yes.

To which the only opposite is the ugly?

There is no other.

And is there anything good?

There is.

To which the only opposite is the evil?

There is no other.

And there is the acute in sound?

True.

To which the only opposite is the grave?

There is no other, he said, but that.

Then every opposite has one opposite only and no more?

He assented.

Then now, I said, let us recapitulate our admissions. First of all we admitted that everything has one opposite and not more than one?

We did so.

And we admitted also that what was done in opposite ways was done by opposites?

Yes.

And that which was done foolishly, as we further admitted, was done in the opposite way to that which was done temperately?

Yes.

And that which was done temperately was done by temperance, and that which was done foolishly by folly?

He agreed.

And that which is done in opposite ways is done by opposites?

Yes.

And one thing is done by temperance, and quite another thing by folly?

Yes.

And in opposite ways?

Certainly.

And therefore by opposites:—then folly is the opposite of temperance?

Clearly.

And do you remember that folly has already been acknowledged by us to be the opposite of wisdom?

He assented.

And we said that everything has only one opposite?

Yes.

[333] Then, Protagoras, which of the two assertions shall we renounce? One says that everything has but one opposite; the other that wisdom is distinct from temperance, and that both of them are parts of virtue; and that they are not only distinct, but dissimilar, both in themselves and in their functions, like the parts of a face. Which of these two assertions shall we renounce? For both of them together are certainly not in harmony; they do not accord or agree: for how can they be said to agree if everything is assumed to have only one opposite and not more than one, and yet folly, which is one, has clearly the two opposites—wisdom and temperance? Is not that true, Protagoras? What else would you say?

He assented, but with great reluctance.

Then temperance and wisdom are the same, as before justice and holiness appeared to us to be nearly the same. And now, Protagoras, I said, we must finish the enquiry, and not faint. Do you think that an unjust man can be temperate in his injustice?

I should be ashamed, Socrates, he said, to acknowledge this which nevertheless many may be found to assert.

And shall I argue with them or with you? I replied.

I would rather, he said, that you should argue with the many first, if you will.

Whichever you please, if you will only answer me and say whether you are of their opinion or not. My object is to test the validity of the argument; and yet the result may be that I who ask and you who answer may both be put on our trial.

Protagoras at first made a show of refusing, as he said that the argument was not encouraging; at length, he consented to answer.

Now then, I said, begin at the beginning and answer me. You think that some men are temperate, and yet unjust?

Yes, he said; let that be admitted.

And temperance is good sense?

Yes.

And good sense is good counsel in doing injustice?

Granted.

If they succeed, I said, or if they do not succeed?

If they succeed.

And you would admit the existence of goods?

Yes.

And is the good that which is expedient for man?

Yes, indeed, he said: and there are some things which may be inexpedient, and yet I call them good.

I thought that Protagoras was getting ruffled and excited; he seemed to be setting himself in an attitude of war. Seeing this, I minded my business, and gently said:—

[334] When you say, Protagoras, that things inexpedient are good, do you mean inexpedient for man only, or inexpedient altogether? and do you call the latter good?

Certainly not the last, he replied; for I know of many things—meats, drinks, medicines, and ten thousand other things, which are inexpedient for man, and some which are expedient; and some which are neither expedient nor inexpedient for man, but only for horses; and some for oxen only, and some for dogs; and some for no animals, but only for trees; and some for the roots of trees and not for their branches, as for example, manure, which is a good thing when laid about the roots of a tree, but utterly destructive if thrown upon the shoots and young branches; or I may instance olive oil, which is mischievous to all plants, and generally most injurious to the hair of every animal with the exception of man, but beneficial to human hair and to the human body generally; and even in this application (so various and changeable is the nature of the benefit), that which is the greatest good to the outward parts of a man, is a very great evil to his inward parts: and for this reason physicians always forbid their patients the use of oil in their food, except in very small quantities, just enough to extinguish the disagreeable sensation of smell in meats and sauces.

When he had given this answer, the company cheered him. And I said: Protagoras, I have a wretched memory, and when any one makes a long speech to me I never remember what he is talking about. As then, if I had been deaf, and you were going to converse with me, you would have had to raise your voice; so now, having such a bad memory, I will ask you to cut your answers shorter, if you would take me with you.

What do you mean? he said: how am I to shorten my answers? shall I make them too short?

Certainly not, I said.

But short enough?

Yes, I said.

Shall I answer what appears to me to be short enough, or what appears to you to be short enough?

I have heard, I said, that you can speak and teach others to speak about the same things at such length that words never seemed to fail, or with such brevity that no one could use fewer of them. Please therefore, [335] if you talk with me, to adopt the latter or more compendious method.

Socrates, he replied, many a battle of words have I fought, and if I had followed the method of disputation which my adversaries desired, as you want me to do, I should have been no better than another, and the name of Protagoras would have been nowhere.

I saw that he was not satisfied with his previous answers, and that he would not play the part of answerer any more if he could help; and I considered that there was no call upon me to continue the conversation; so I said: Protagoras, I do not wish to force the conversation upon you if you had rather not, but when you are willing to argue with me in such a way that I can follow you, then I will argue with you. Now you, as is said of you by others and as you say of yourself, are able to have discussions in shorter forms of speech as well as in longer, for you are a master of wisdom; but I cannot manage these long speeches: I only wish that I could. You, on the other hand, who are capable of either, ought to speak shorter as I beg you, and then we might converse. But I see that you are disinclined, and as I have an engagement which will prevent my staying to hear you at greater length (for I have to be in another place), I will depart; although I should have liked to have heard you.

Thus I spoke, and was rising from my seat, when Callias seized me by the right hand, and in his left hand caught hold of this old cloak of mine. He said: We cannot let you go, Socrates, for if you leave us there will be an end of our discussions: I must therefore beg you to remain, as there is nothing in the world that I should like better than to hear you and Protagoras discourse. Do not deny the company this pleasure.

Now I had got up, and was in the act of departure. Son of Hipponicus, I replied, I have always admired, and do now heartily applaud and love your philosophical spirit, and I would gladly comply with your request, if I could. But the truth is that I cannot. And what you ask is as great an impossibility to me, as if you bade me run a race with Crison of Himera, [336] when in his prime, or with some one of the long or day course runners. To such a request I should reply that I would fain ask the same of my own legs; but they refuse to comply. And therefore if you want to see Crison and me in the same stadium, you must bid him slacken his speed to mine, for I cannot run quickly, and he can run slowly. And in like manner if you want to hear me and Protagoras discoursing, you must ask him to shorten his answers, and keep to the point, as he did at first; if not, how can there be any discussion? For discussion is one thing, and making an oration is quite another, in my humble opinion.

But you see, Socrates, said Callias, that Protagoras may fairly claim to speak in his own way, just as you claim to speak in yours.

Here Alcibiades interposed, and said: That, Callias, is not a true statement of the case. For our friend Socrates admits that he cannot make a speech—in this he yields the palm to Protagoras: but I should be greatly surprised if he yielded to any living man in the power of holding and apprehending an argument. Now if Protagoras will make a similar admission, and confess that he is inferior to Socrates in argumentative skill, that is enough for Socrates; but if he claims a superiority in argument as well, let him ask and answer—not, when a question is asked, slipping away from the point, and instead of answering, making a speech at such length that most of his hearers forget the question at issue (not that Socrates is likely to forget—I will be bound for that, although he may pretend in fun that he has a bad memory). And Socrates appears to me to be more in the right than Protagoras; that is my view, and every man ought to say what he thinks.

When Alcibiades had done speaking, some one—Critias, I believe—went on to say: O Prodicus and Hippias, Callias appears to me to be a partisan of Protagoras: and this led Alcibiades, who loves opposition, to take the other side. But we should not be partisans either of

Socrates or of Protagoras; let us rather unite in entreating both of them not to break up the discussion.

[337] Prodicus added: That, Critias, seems to me to be well said, for those who are present at such discussions ought to be impartial hearers of both the speakers; remembering, however, that impartiality is not the same as equality, for both sides should be impartially heard, and yet an equal meed should not be assigned to both of them; but to the wiser a higher meed should be given, and a lower to the less wise. And I as well as Critias would beg you, Protagoras and Socrates, to grant our request, which is, that you will argue with one another and not wrangle; for friends argue with friends out of goodwill, but only adversaries and enemies wrangle. And then our meeting will be delightful; for in this way you, who are the speakers, will be most likely to win esteem, and not praise only, among us who are your audience; for esteem is a sincere conviction of the hearers' souls, but praise is often an insincere expression of men uttering falsehoods contrary to their conviction. And thus we who are the hearers will be gratified and not pleased; for gratification is of the mind when receiving wisdom and knowledge, but pleasure is of the body when eating or experiencing some other bodily delight. Thus spoke Prodicus, and many of the company applauded his words.

Hippias the sage spoke next. He said: All of you who are here present I reckon to be kinsmen and friends and fellow-citizens, by nature and not by law; for by nature like is akin to like, whereas law is the tyrant of mankind, and often compels us to do many things which are against nature. How great would be the disgrace then, if we, who know the nature of things, and are the wisest of the Hellenes, and as such are met together in this city, which is the metropolis of wisdom, and in the greatest and most glorious house of this city, should have nothing to show worthy of this height of dignity, but should only quarrel with one another like the meanest of mankind! I do pray and advise you, Protagoras, and you, Socrates, to agree upon a compromise. Let us be your peacemakers. And do not you, Socrates, aim at this precise and extreme brevity in discourse, if Protagoras objects, [338] but loosen and let go the reins of speech, that your words may be grander and more becoming to you. Neither do you, Protagoras, go forth on the gale with every sail set out of sight of land into an ocean of words, but let there be a mean observed by both of you. Do as I say. And let me also persuade you to choose an arbiter or overseer or president; he will keep watch over your words and will prescribe their proper length.

This proposal was received by the company with universal approval; Callias said that he would not let me off, and they begged me to choose an arbiter. But I said that to choose an umpire of discourse would be unseemly; for if the person chosen was inferior, then the inferior or worse ought not to preside over the better; or if he was equal, neither would that be well; for he who is our equal will do as we do, and what will be the use of choosing him? And if you say, "Let us have a better then,"—to that I answer that you cannot have any one who is wiser than Protagoras. And if you choose another who is not really better, and whom you only say is better, to put another over him as though he were an inferior person would be an unworthy reflection on him; not that, as far as I am concerned, any reflection is of much consequence to me. Let me tell you then what I will do in order that the conversation and discussion may go on as you desire. If Protagoras is not disposed to answer, let him ask and I will answer; and I will endeavour to show at the same time how, as I maintain, he ought to answer: and when I have answered as many questions as he likes to ask, let him in like manner answer me; and if he seems to be not very ready at answering the precise question asked of him, you and I will unite in entreating him, as you entreated me, not to spoil the discussion. And this will require no special arbiter—all of you shall be arbiters.

This was generally approved, and Protagoras, though very much against his will, was obliged to agree that he would ask questions; and when he had put a sufficient number of them, that he would answer in his turn those which he was asked in short replies. He began to put his questions as follows:—

I am of opinion, Socrates, he said, that skill in poetry is the principal part of education; [339] and this I conceive to be the power of knowing what compositions of the poets are correct, and what are not, and how they are to be distinguished, and of explaining when asked the reason of the difference. And I propose to transfer the question which you and I have been discussing to the domain of poetry; we will speak as before of virtue, but in reference to a passage of a poet. Now Simonides says to

Scopas the son of Creon the Thessalian:

Hardly on the one hand can a man become truly
good, built four-square in hands and feet and
mind, a work without a flaw.

Do you know the poem? or shall I repeat the
whole?

There is no need, I said; for I am perfectly
well acquainted with the ode—I have made a
careful study of it.

Very well, he said. And do you think that
the ode is a good composition, and true?

Yes, I said, both good and true.

But if there is a contradiction, can the composition be good or true?

No, not in that case, I replied.

And is there not a contradiction? he asked.
Reflect.

Well, my friend, I have reflected.

And does not the poet proceed to say, "I do
not agree with the word of Pittacus, albeit the
utterance of a wise man: Hardly can a man be
good"? Now you will observe that this is said
by the same poet.

I know it.

And do you think, he said, that the two sayings are consistent?

Yes, I said, I think so (at the same time I
could not help fearing that there might be
something in what he said). And you think
otherwise?

Why, he said, how can he be consistent in
both? First of all, premising as his own thought,
"Hardly can a man become truly good"; and
then a little further on in the poem, forgetting,
and blaming Pittacus and refusing to agree
with him, when he says, "Hardly can a man be
good," which is the very same thing. And yet
when he blames him who says the same with
himself, he blames himself; so that he must be
wrong either in his first or his second assertion.

Many of the audience cheered and applauded
this. And I felt at first giddy and faint, as if I
had received a blow from the hand of an expert
boxer, when I heard his words and the sound of
the cheering; and to confess the truth, I wanted
to get time to think what the meaning of the
poet really was. So I turned to Prodicus and
called him. Prodicus, I said, Simonides is a
countryman of yours, and you ought to come to
his aid. *[340]* I must appeal to you, like the
river Scamander in Homer, who, when be-
leaguered by Achilles, summons the Simoïs to
aid him, saying:

Brother dear, let us both together stay the force of
the hero.

And I summon you, for I am afraid that Protagoras will make an end of Simonides. Now is
the time to rehabilitate Simonides, by the application of your philosophy of synonyms,
which enables you to distinguish "will" and
"wish," and make other charming distinctions
like those which you drew just now. And I
should like to know whether you would agree
with me; for I am of opinion that there is no
contradiction in the words of Simonides. And
first of all I wish that you would say whether,
in your opinion, Prodicus, "being" is the same
as "becoming."

Not the same, certainly, replied Prodicus.

Did not Simonides first set forth, as his own
view, that "Hardly can a man become truly
good"?

Quite right, said Prodicus.

And then he blames Pittacus, not, as Protagoras imagines, for repeating that which he says
himself, but for saying something different
from himself. Pittacus does not say as Simonides says, that hardly can a man become good,
but hardly can a man be good: and our friend
Prodicus would maintain that being, Protagoras, is not the same as becoming; and if they
are not the same, then Simonides is not inconsistent with himself. I dare say that Prodicus
and many others would say, as Hesiod says,

On the one hand, hardly can a man become good,
For the gods have made virtue the reward of toil;
But on the other hand, when you have climbed the
height,
Then, to retain virtue, however difficult the acqui-
sition, is easy.

Prodicus heard and approved; but Protagoras said: Your correction, Socrates, involves a
greater error than is contained in the sentence
which you are correcting.

Alas! I said, Protagoras; then I am a sorry
physician, and do but aggravate a disorder
which I am seeking to cure.

Such is the fact, he said.

How so? I asked.

The poet, he replied, could never have made
such a mistake as to say that virtue, which in
the opinion of all men is the hardest of all
things, can be easily retained.

Well, I said, and how fortunate are we in
having Prodicus among us, at the right moment; for he has a wisdom, Protagoras, which,
as I imagine, is more than human and of very
ancient date, and may be as old as Simonides
or even older. *[341]* Learned as you are in
many things, you appear to know nothing of

this; but I know, for I am a disciple of his. And now, if I am not mistaken, you do not understand the word "hard" (χαλεπόν) in the sense which Simonides intended; and I must correct you, as Prodicus corrects me when I use the word "awful" (δεινόν) as a term of praise. If I say that Protagoras or any one else is an "awfully" wise man, he asks me if I am not ashamed of calling that which is good "awful"; and then he explains to me that the term "awful" is always taken in a bad sense, and that no one speaks of being "awfully" healthy or wealthy, or "awful" peace, but of "awful" disease, "awful" war, "awful" poverty, meaning by the term "awful," evil. And I think that Simonides and his countrymen the Ceans, when they spoke of "hard" meant "evil," or something which you do not understand. Let us ask Prodicus, for he ought to be able to answer questions about the dialect of Simonides. What did he mean, Prodicus, by the term "hard?"

Evil, said Prodicus.

And therefore, I said, Prodicus, he blames Pittacus for saying, "Hard is the good," just as if that were equivalent to saying, Evil is the good.

Yes, he said, that was certainly his meaning; and he is twitting Pittacus with ignorance of the use of terms, which in a Lesbian, who has been accustomed to speak a barbarous language, is natural.

Do you hear, Protagoras, I asked, what our friend Prodicus is saying? And have you an answer for him?

You are entirely mistaken, Prodicus, said Protagoras; and I know very well that Simonides in using the word "hard" meant what all of us mean, not evil, but that which is not easy—that which takes a great deal of trouble: of this I am positive.

I said: I also incline to believe, Protagoras, that this was the meaning of Simonides, of which our friend Prodicus was very well aware, but he thought that he would make fun, and try if you could maintain your thesis; for that Simonides could never have meant the other is clearly proved by the context, in which he says that God only has this gift. Now he cannot surely mean to say that to be good is evil, when he afterwards proceeds to say that God only has this gift, and that this is the attribute of him and of no other. For if this be his meaning, Prodicus would impute to Simonides a character of recklessness which is very unlike his countrymen. And I should like to tell you, *[342]* I said, what I imagine to be the real

meaning of Simonides in this poem, if you will test what, in your way of speaking, would be called my skill in poetry; or if you would rather, I will be the listener.

To this proposal Protagoras replied: As you please;—and Hippias, Prodicus, and the others told me by all means to do as I proposed.

Then now, I said, I will endeavour to explain to you my opinion about this poem of Simonides. There is a very ancient philosophy which is more cultivated in Crete and Lacedaemon than in any other part of Hellas, and there are more philosophers in those countries than anywhere else in the world. This, however, is a secret which the Lacedaemonians deny; and they pretend to be ignorant, just because they do not wish to have it thought that they rule the world by wisdom, like the Sophists of whom Protagoras was speaking, and not by valour of arms; considering that if the reason of their superiority were disclosed, all men would be practising their wisdom. And this secret of theirs has never been discovered by the imitators of Lacedaemonian fashions in other cities, who go about with their ears bruised in imitation of them, and have the caestus bound on their arms, and are always in training, and wear short cloaks; for they imagine that these are the practices which have enabled the Lacedaemonians to conquer the other Hellenes. Now when the Lacedaemonians want to unbend and hold free conversation with their wise men, and are no longer satisfied with mere secret intercourse, they drive out all these laconizers, and any other foreigners who may happen to be in their country, and they hold a philosophical *séance* unknown to strangers; and they themselves forbid their young men to go out into other cities—in this they are like the Cretans—in order that they may not unlearn the lessons which they have taught them. And in Lacedaemon and Crete not only men but also women have a pride in their high cultivation. And hereby you may know that I am right in attributing to the Lacedaemonians this excellence in philosophy and speculation: If a man converses with the most ordinary Lacedaemonian, he will find him seldom good for much in general conversation, but at any point in the discourse he will be darting out some notable saying, terse and full of meaning, with unerring aim; and the person with whom he is talking seems to be like a child in his hands. And many of our own age and of former ages have noted that the true Lacedaemonian type of character has the love of philosophy even stronger than the love of gymnastics; they are conscious that only a perfectly educated man is capable of uttering such expressions. [343] Such were Thales of Miletus, and Pittacus of Mitylene, and Bias of Priene, and our own Solon, and Cleobulus the Lindian, and Myson the Chenian; and seventh in the catalogue of wise men was the Lacedaemonian Chilo. All these were lovers and emulators and disciples of the culture of the Lacedaemonians, and any one may perceive that their wisdom was of this character; consisting of short memorable sentences, which they severally uttered. And they met together and dedicated in the temple of Apollo at Delphi, as the first-fruits of their wisdom, the far-famed inscriptions, which are in all men's mouths—"Know thyself," and "Nothing too much."

Why do I say all this? I am explaining that this Lacedaemonian brevity was the style of primitive philosophy. Now there was a saying of Pittacus which was privately circulated and received the approbation of the wise, "Hard is it to be good." And Simonides, who was ambitious of the fame of wisdom, was aware that if he could overthrow this saying, then, as if he had won a victory over some famous athlete, he would carry off the palm among his contemporaries. And if I am not mistaken, he composed the entire poem with the secret intention of damaging Pittacus and his saying.

Let us all unite in examining his words, and see whether I am speaking the truth. Simonides must have been a lunatic, if, in the very first words of the poem, wanting to say only that to become good is hard, he inserted μέν, "on the one hand" ["on the one hand to become good is hard"]; there would be no reason for the introduction of μέν, unless you suppose him to speak with a hostile reference to the words of Pittacus. Pittacus is saying "Hard is it to be good," and he, in refutation of this thesis, rejoins that the truly hard thing, Pittacus, is to become good, not joining "truly" with "good," but with "hard." Not, that the hard thing is to be truly good, as though there were some truly good men, and there were others who were good but not truly good (this would be a very simple observation, and quite unworthy of Simonides); but you must suppose him to make a trajection of the word "truly," construing the saying of Pittacus thus (and let us imagine Pittacus to be speaking and Simonides answering him): "O my friends," says Pittacus, "hard is it to be good," and Simonides answers, [344] "In that, Pittacus, you are mistaken; the difficulty is not to be good, but on the one hand, to become good, four-square in hands and feet and mind, without a flaw—that is hard truly." This way of reading the passage accounts for the insertion of μέν, "on the one hand," and for the position at the end of the clause of the word "truly," and all that follows shows this to be the meaning. A great deal might be said in praise of the details of the poem, which is a charming piece of workmanship, and very finished, but such minutiae would be tedious. I should like, however, to point out the general intention of the poem, which is certainly designed in every part to be a refutation of the saying of Pittacus. For he speaks in what follows a little further on as if he meant to argue that although there is a difficulty in becoming good, yet this is possible for a time, and only for a time. But having become good, to remain in a good state and be good, as you, Pittacus, affirm, is not possible, and is not granted to man; God only has this blessing; "but man cannot help being bad when the force of circumstances overpowers him." Now whom does the force of circumstance overpower in the command of a vessel?—not the private individual, for he is always overpowered; and as one who is already prostrate cannot be overthrown, and only he who is standing upright but not he who is prostrate can be laid prostrate, so the force of circumstances can only overpower him who, at some time or other, has resources, and not him who is at all times helpless. The descent of a great storm may make the pilot helpless, or the severity of the season the husbandman or the physician; for the good may become bad, as another poet witnesses:

The good are sometimes good and sometimes bad.

But the bad does not become bad; he is always bad. So that when the force of circumstances overpowers the man of resources and skill and virtue, then he cannot help being bad. And you, Pittacus, are saying, "Hard is it to be good." Now there is a difficulty in becoming good; and yet this is possible: but to be good is an impossibility—

For he who does well is the good man, and he who does ill is the bad.

But what sort of doing is good in letters? [345] and what sort of doing makes a man good in letters? Clearly the knowing of them. And what sort of well-doing makes a man a good physician? Clearly the knowledge of the art of healing the sick. "But he who does ill is the bad."

Now who becomes a bad physician? Clearly he who is in the first place a physician, and in the second place a good physician; for he may become a bad one also: but none of us unskilled individuals can by any amount of doing ill become physicians, any more than we can become carpenters or anything of that sort; and he who by doing ill cannot become a physician at all, clearly cannot become a bad physician. In like manner the good may become deteriorated by time, or toil, or disease, or other accident (the only real doing ill is to be deprived of knowledge), but the bad man will never become bad, for he is always bad; and if he were to become bad, he must previously have been good. Thus the words of the poem tend to show that on the one hand a man cannot be continuously good, but that he may become good and may also become bad; and again that

They are the best for the longest time whom the gods love.

All this relates to Pittacus, as is further proved by the sequel. For he adds:

Therefore I will not throw away my span of life to no purpose in searching after the impossible, hoping in vain to find a perfectly faultless man among those who partake of the fruit of the broad-bosomed earth: if I find him, I will send you word.

(this is the vehement way in which he pursues his attack upon Pittacus throughout the whole poem):

But him who does no evil, voluntarily I praise and love;—not even the gods war against necessity.

All this has a similar drift, for Simonides was not so ignorant as to say that he praised those who did no evil voluntarily, as though there were some who did evil voluntarily. For no wise man, as I believe, will allow that any human being errs voluntarily, or voluntarily does evil and dishonourable actions; but they are very well aware that all who do evil and dishonourable things do them against their will. And Simonides never says that he praises him who does no evil voluntarily; the word "voluntarily" applies to himself. For he was under the impression that a good man might often compel himself [346] to love and praise another, and to be the friend and approver of another; and that there might be an involuntary love, such as a man might feel to an unnatural father or mother, or country, or the like. Now bad men, when their parents or country have any defects, look on them with malignant joy, and

find fault with them and expose and denounce them to others, under the idea that the rest of mankind will be less likely to take themselves to task and accuse them of neglect; and they blame their defects far more than they deserve, in order that the odium which is necessarily incurred by them may be increased: but the good man dissembles his feelings, and constrains himself to praise them; and if they have wronged him and he is angry, he pacifies his anger and is reconciled, and compels himself to love and praise his own flesh and blood. And Simonides, as is probable, considered that he himself had often had to praise and magnify a tyrant or the like, much against his will, and he also wishes to imply to Pittacus that he does not censure him because he is censorious.

For I am satisfied [he says] when a man is neither bad nor very stupid; and when he knows justice (which is the health of states), and is of sound mind, I will find no fault with him, for I am not given to finding fault, and there are innumerable fools

(implying that if he delighted in censure he might have abundant opportunity of finding fault).

All things are good with which evil is unmingled.

In these latter words he does not mean to say that all things are good which have no evil in them, as you might say "All things are white which have no black in them," for that would be ridiculous; but he means to say that he accepts and finds no fault with the moderate or intermediate state. He says:

I do not hope to find a perfectly blameless man among those who partake of the fruits of the broad-bosomed earth (if I find him, I will send you word); in this sense I praise no man. But he who is moderately good, and does no evil, is good enough for me, who love and approve every one.

(and here observe that he uses a Lesbian word, ἐπαίνημι [approve], because he is addressing Pittacus—

Who love and approve every one voluntarily, who does no evil:

and that the stop should be put after "voluntarily"); "but there are some whom I involuntarily praise and love. And you, Pittacus, I would never have blamed, [347] if you had spoken what was moderately good and true; but I do blame you because, putting on the appearance of truth, you are speaking falsely about the highest matters."—And this, I said, Prodicus and Protagoras, I take to be the meaning of Simonides in this poem.

Hippias said: I think, Socrates, that you have given a very good explanation of the poem; but I have also an excellent interpretation of my own which I will propound to you, if you will allow me.

Nay, Hippias, said Alcibiades; not now, but at some other time. At present we must abide by the compact which was made between Socrates and Protagoras, to the effect that as long as Protagoras is willing to ask, Socrates should answer; or that if he would rather answer, then that Socrates should ask.

I said: I wish Protagoras either to ask or answer as he is inclined; but I would rather have done with poems and odes, if he does not object, and come back to the question about which I was asking you at first, Protagoras, and by your help make an end of that. The talk about the poets seems to me like a commonplace entertainment to which a vulgar company have recourse; who, because they are not able to converse or amuse one another, while they are drinking, with the sound of their own voices and conversation, by reason of their stupidity, raise the price of flute-girls in the market, hiring for a great sum the voice of a flute instead of their own breath, to be the medium of intercourse among them: but where the company are real gentlemen and men of education, you will see no flute-girls, nor dancing-girls, nor harp-girls; and they have no nonsense or games, but are contented with one another's conversation, of which their own voices are the medium, and which they carry on by turns and in an orderly manner, even though they are very liberal in their potations. And a company like this of ours, and men such as we profess to be, do not require the help of another's voice, or of the poets whom you cannot interrogate about the meaning of what they are saying; people who cite them declaring, some that the poet has one meaning, and others that he has another, and the point which is in dispute can never be decided. This sort of entertainment they decline, and prefer to talk with one another, and put one another to the proof in conversation. [348] And these are the models which I desire that you and I should imitate. Leaving the poets, and keeping to ourselves, let us try the mettle of one another and make proof of the truth in conversation. If you have a mind to ask, I am ready to answer; or if you would rather, do you answer, and give me

the opportunity of resuming and completing our unfinished argument.

I made these and some similar observations; but Protagoras would not distinctly say which he would do. Thereupon Alcibiades turned to Callias, and said:—Do you think, Callias, that Protagoras is fair in refusing to say whether he will or will not answer? for I certainly think that he is unfair; he ought either to proceed with the argument, or distinctly to refuse to proceed, that we may know his intention; and then Socrates will be able to discourse with some one else, and the rest of the company will be free to talk with one another.

I think that Protagoras was really made ashamed by these words of Alcibiades, and when the prayers of Callias and the company were superadded, he was at last induced to argue, and said that I might ask and he would answer.

So I said: Do not imagine, Protagoras, that I have any other interest in asking questions of you but that of clearing up my own difficulties. For I think that Homer was very right in saying that

When two go together, one sees before the other,

for all men who have a companion are readier in deed, word, or thought; but if a man

Sees a thing when he is alone,

he goes about straightway seeking until he finds some one to whom he may show his discoveries, and who may confirm him in them. And I would rather hold discourse with you than with any one, because I think that no man has a better understanding of most things which a good man may be expected to understand, and in particular of virtue. For who is there, but you?—who not only claim to be a good man and a gentleman, for many are this, and yet have not the power of making others good—whereas you are not only good yourself, but also the cause of goodness in others. Moreover such confidence have you in yourself, that although other Sophists conceal their profession, you proclaim in the face of Hellas that you are a Sophist or teacher of virtue and education, and are the first who demanded pay in return. [349] How then can I do otherwise than invite you to the examination of these subjects, and ask questions and consult with you? I must, indeed. And I should like once more to have my memory refreshed by you about the questions which I was asking you at first, and also to have your help in considering them.

If I am not mistaken the question was this: Are wisdom and temperance and courage and justice and holiness five names of the same thing? or has each of the names a separate underlying essence and corresponding thing having a peculiar function, no one of them being like any other of them? And you replied that the five names were not the names of the same thing, but that each of them had a separate object, and that all these objects were parts of virtue, not in the same way that the parts of gold are like each other and the whole of which they are parts, but as the parts of the face are unlike the whole of which they are parts and one another, and have each of them a distinct function. I should like to know whether this is still your opinion; or if not, I will ask you to define your meaning, and I shall not take you to task if you now make a different statement. For I dare say that you may have said what you did only in order to make trial of me.

I answer, Socrates, he said, that all these qualities are parts of virtue, and that four out of the five are to some extent similar, and that the fifth of them, which is courage, is very different from the other four, as I prove in this way: You may observe that many men are utterly unrighteous, unholy, intemperate, ignorant, who are nevertheless remarkable for their courage.

Stop, I said; I should like to think about that. When you speak of brave men, do you mean the confident, or another sort of nature?

Yes, he said; I mean the impetuous, ready to go at that which others are afraid to approach.

In the next place, you would affirm virtue to be a good thing, of which good thing you assert yourself to be a teacher.

Yes, he said; I should say the best of all things, if I am in my right mind.

And is it partly good and partly bad, I said, or wholly good?

Wholly good, and in the highest degree.

[350] Tell me then; who are they who have confidence when diving into a well?

I should say, the divers.

And the reason of this is that they have knowledge?

Yes, that is the reason.

And who have confidence when fighting on horseback—the skilled horseman or the unskilled?

The skilled.

And who when fighting with light shields—the peltasts or the nonpeltasts?

The peltasts. And that is true of all other things, he said, if that is your point: those who have knowledge are more confident than those who have no knowledge, and they are more confident after they have learned than before.

And have you not seen persons utterly ignorant, I said, of these things, and yet confident about them?

Yes, he said, I have seen such persons far too confident.

And are not these confident persons also courageous?

In that case, he replied, courage would be a base thing, for the men of whom we are speaking are surely madmen.

Then who are the courageous? Are they not the confident?

Yes, he said; to that statement I adhere.

And those, I said, who are thus confident without knowledge are really not courageous, but mad; and in that case the wisest are also the most confident, and being the most confident are also the bravest, and upon that view again wisdom will be courage.

Nay, Socrates, he replied, you are mistaken in your remembrance of what was said by me. When you asked me, I certainly did say that the courageous are the confident; but I was never asked whether the confident are the courageous; if you had asked me, I should have answered "Not all of them": and what I did answer you have not proved to be false, although you proceeded to show that those who have knowledge are more courageous than they were before they had knowledge, and more courageous than others who have no knowledge, and were then led on to think that courage is the same as wisdom. But in this way of arguing you might come to imagine that strength is wisdom. You might begin by asking whether the strong are able, and I should say "Yes"; and then whether those who know how to wrestle are not more able to wrestle than those who do not know how to wrestle, and more able after than before they had learned, and I should assent. And when I had admitted this, you might use my admissions in such a way as to prove that upon my view wisdom is strength; whereas in that case I should not have admitted, any more than in the other, that the able are strong, although I have admitted that the strong are able. [351] For there is a difference between ability and strength; the former is given by knowledge as well as by madness or rage, but strength comes from nature and a healthy state of the body. And in like manner I say of confidence and courage, that they are not the same; and I argue that the courageous are confident, but not all the confident courageous. For confidence may be given to men by art, and also, like ability, by madness and rage; but courage comes to them from nature and the healthy state of the soul.

I said: You would admit, Protagoras, that some men live well and others ill?

He assented.

And do you think that a man lives well who lives in pain and grief?

He does not.

But if he lives pleasantly to the end of his life, will he not in that case have lived well?

He will.

Then to live pleasantly is a good, and to live unpleasantly an evil?

Yes, he said, if the pleasure be good and honourable.

And do you, Protagoras, like the rest of the world, call some pleasant things evil and some painful things good?—for I am rather disposed to say that things are good in as far as they are pleasant, if they have no consequences of another sort, and in as far as they are painful they are bad.

I do not know, Socrates, he said, whether I can venture to assert in that unqualified manner that the pleasant is the good and the painful the evil. Having regard not only to my present answer, but also to the whole of my life, I shall be safer, if I am not mistaken, in saying that there are some pleasant things which are not good, and that there are some painful things which are good, and some which are not good, and that there are some which are neither good nor evil.

And you would call pleasant, I said, the things which participate in pleasure or create pleasure?

Certainly, he said.

Then my meaning is, that in as far as they are pleasant they are good; and my question would imply that pleasure is a good in itself.

According to your favourite mode of speech, Socrates, "let us reflect about this," he said; and if the reflection is to the point, and the result proves that pleasure and good are really the same, then we will agree; but if not, then we will argue.

And would you wish to begin the enquiry? I said; or shall I begin?

You ought to take the lead, he said; for you are the author of the discussion.

[352] May I employ an illustration? I said. Suppose some one who is enquiring into the health or some other bodily quality of another: —he looks at his face and at the tips of his fingers, and then he says, Uncover your chest and back to me that I may have a better view:— that is the sort of thing which I desire in this speculation. Having seen what your opinion is about good and pleasure, I am minded to say to you: Uncover your mind to me, Protagoras, and reveal your opinion about knowledge, that I may know whether you agree with the rest of the world. Now the rest of the world are of opinion that knowledge is a principle not of strength, or of rule, or of command: their notion is that a man may have knowledge, and yet that the knowledge which is in him may be overmastered by anger, or pleasure, or pain, or love, or perhaps by fear,—just as if knowledge were a slave, and might be dragged about anyhow. Now is that your view? or do you think that knowledge is a noble and commanding thing, which cannot be overcome, and will not allow a man, if he only knows the difference of good and evil, to do anything which is contrary to knowledge, but that wisdom will have strength to help him?

I agree with you, Socrates, said Protagoras; and not only so, but I, above all other men, am bound to say that wisdom and knowledge are the highest of human things.

Good, I said, and true. But are you aware that the majority of the world are of another mind; and that men are commonly supposed to know the things which are best, and not to do them when they might? And most persons whom I have asked the reason of this have said that when men act contrary to knowledge they are overcome by pain, or pleasure, or some of those affections which I was just now mentioning.

Yes, Socrates, he replied; and that is not the only point about which mankind are in error.

Suppose, then, that you and I endeavour to instruct and inform them what is the nature of this affection which they call "being overcome by pleasure," [353] and which they affirm to be the reason why they do not always do what is best. When we say to them: Friends, you are mistaken, and are saying what is not true, they would probably reply: Socrates and Protagoras, if this affection of the soul is not to be called "being overcome by pleasure," pray, what is it, and by what name would you describe it?

But why, Socrates, should we trouble ourselves about the opinion of the many, who just say anything that happens to occur to them?

I believe, I said, that they may be of use in

helping us to discover how courage is related to the other parts of virtue. If you are disposed to abide by our agreement, that I should show the way in which, as I think, our recent difficulty is most likely to be cleared up, do you follow; but if not, never mind.

You are quite right, he said; and I would have you proceed as you have begun.

Well then, I said, let me suppose that they repeat their question, What account do you give of that which, in our way of speaking, is termed being overcome by pleasure? I should answer thus: Listen, and Protagoras and I will endeavour to show you. When men are overcome by eating and drinking and other sensual desires which are pleasant, and they, knowing them to be evil, nevertheless indulge in them, would you not say that they were overcome by pleasure? They will not deny this. And suppose that you and I were to go on and ask them again: "In what way do you say that they are evil—in that they are pleasant and give pleasure at the moment, or because they cause disease and poverty and other like evils in the future? Would they still be evil, if they had no attendant evil consequences, simply because they give the consciousness of pleasure of whatever nature?"—Would they not answer that they are not evil on account of the pleasure which is immediately given by them, but on account of the after consequences—diseases and the like?

I believe, said Protagoras, that the world in general would answer as you do.

And in causing diseases do they not cause pain? and in causing poverty do they not cause pain;—they would agree to that also, if I am not mistaken?

Protagoras assented.

Then I should say to them, in my name and yours: Do you think them evil for any other reason, except because they end in pain and rob us of other pleasures:—there again they would agree?

[354] We both of us thought that they would.

And then I should take the question from the opposite point of view, and say: "Friends, when you speak of goods being painful, do you not mean remedial goods, such as gymnastic exercises, and military service, and the physician's use of burning, cutting, drugging, and starving? Are these the things which are good but painful?"—they would assent to me?

He agreed.

"And do you call them good because they

occasion the greatest immediate suffering and pain; or because, afterwards, they bring health and improvement of the bodily condition and the salvation of states and power over others and wealth?"—they would agree to the latter alternative, if I am not mistaken?

He assented.

"Are these things good for any other reason except that they end in pleasure, and get rid of and avert pain? Are you looking to any other standard but pleasure and pain when you call them good?"—they would acknowledge that they were not?

I think so, said Protagoras.

"And do you not pursue after pleasure as a good, and avoid pain as an evil?"

He assented.

"Then you think that pain is an evil and pleasure is a good: and even pleasure you deem an evil, when it robs you of greater pleasures than it gives, or causes pains greater than the pleasure. If, however, you call pleasure an evil in relation to some other end or standard, you will be able to show us that standard. But you have none to show."

I do not think that they have, said Protagoras.

"And have you not a similar way of speaking about pain? You call pain a good when it takes away greater pains than those which it has, or gives pleasures greater than the pains: then if you have some standard other than pleasure and pain to which you refer when you call actual pain a good, you can show what that is. But you cannot."

True, said Protagoras.

Suppose again, I said, that the world says to me: "Why do you spend many words and speak in many ways on this subject?" Excuse me, friends, I should reply; but in the first place there is a difficulty in explaining the meaning of the expression "overcome by pleasure"; and the whole argument turns upon this. And even now, if you see any possible way in which evil can be explained as other [355] than pain, or good as other than pleasure, you may still retract. Are you satisfied, then, at having a life of pleasure which is without pain? If you are, and if you are unable to show any good or evil which does not end in pleasure and pain, hear the consequences:—If what you say is true, then the argument is absurd which affirms that a man often does evil knowingly, when he might abstain, because he is seduced and overpowered by pleasure; or again, when you say that a man knowingly refuses to do what is good because he is overcome at the moment by pleasure. And that this is ridiculous will be evident if only we give up the use of various names, such as pleasant and painful, and good and evil. As there are two things, let us call them by two names—first, good and evil, and then pleasant and painful. Assuming this, let us go on to say that a man does evil knowing that he does evil. But some one will ask, Why? Because he is overcome, is the first answer. And by what is he overcome? the enquirer will proceed to ask. And we shall not be able to reply "By pleasure," for the name of pleasure has been exchanged for that of good. In our answer, then, we shall only say that he is overcome. "By what?" he will reiterate. By the good, we shall have to reply; indeed we shall. Nay, but our questioner will rejoin with a laugh, if he be one of the swaggering sort, "That is too ridiculous, that a man should do what he knows to be evil when he ought not, because he is overcome by good. Is that, he will ask, because the good was worthy or not worthy of conquering the evil?" And in answer to that we shall clearly reply, Because it was not worthy; for if it had been worthy, then he who, as we say, was overcome by pleasure, would not have been wrong. "But how," he will reply, "can the good be unworthy of the evil, or the evil of the good?" Is not the real explanation that they are out of proportion to one another, either as greater and smaller, or more and fewer? This we cannot deny. And when you speak of being overcome—"what do you mean," he will say, "but that you choose the greater evil in exchange for the lesser good?" Admitted. And now substitute the names of pleasure and pain for good and evil, and say, not as before, that a man does what is evil knowingly, but that he does what is painful knowingly, and because he is overcome by pleasure, [356] which is unworthy to overcome. What measure is there of the relations of pleasure to pain other than excess and defect, which means that they become greater and smaller, and more and fewer, and differ in degree? For if any one says: "Yes, Socrates, but immediate pleasure differs widely from future pleasure and pain"—To that I should reply: And do they differ in anything but in pleasure and pain? There can be no other measure of them. And do you, like a skilful weigher, put into the balance the pleasures and the pains, and their nearness and distance, and weigh them, and then say which outweighs the other. If you weigh pleasures against pleasures, you of course take the more

and greater; or if you weigh pains against pains, you take the fewer and the less; or if pleasures against pains, then you choose that course of action in which the painful is exceeded by the pleasant, whether the distant by the near or the near by the distant; and you avoid that course of action in which the pleasant is exceeded by the painful. Would you not admit, my friends, that this is true? I am confident that they cannot deny this.

He agreed with me.

Well then, I shall say, if you agree so far, be so good as to answer me a question: Do not the same magnitudes appear larger to your sight when near, and smaller when at a distance? They will acknowledge that. And the same holds of thickness and number; also sounds, which are in themselves equal, are greater when near, and lesser when at a distance. They will grant that also. Now suppose happiness to consist in doing or choosing the greater, and in not doing or in avoiding the less, what would be the saving principle of human life? Would not the art of measuring be the saving principle; or would the power of appearance? Is not the latter that deceiving art which makes us wander up and down and take the things at one time of which we repent at another, both in our actions and in our choice of things great and small? But the art of measurement would do away with the effect of appearances, and, showing the truth, would fain teach the soul at last to find rest in the truth, and would thus save our life. Would not mankind generally acknowledge that the art which accomplishes this result is the art of measurement?

Yes, he said, the art of measurement.

Suppose, again, the salvation of human life to depend on the choice of odd and even, and on the knowledge of when a man ought to choose the greater or less, either in reference to themselves or to each other, [357] and whether near or at a distance; what would be the saving principle of our lives? Would not knowledge? —a knowledge of measuring, when the question is one of excess and defect, and a knowledge of number, when the question is of odd and even? The world will assent, will they not?

Protagoras himself thought that they would.

Well then, my friends, I say to them; seeing that the salvation of human life has been found to consist in the right choice of pleasures and pains,—in the choice of the more and the fewer, and the greater and the less, and the nearer and remoter, must not this measuring be a consideration of their excess and defect and equality in relation to each other?

This is undeniably true.

And this, as possessing measure, must undeniably also be an art and science?

They will agree, he said.

The nature of that art or science will be a matter of future consideration; but the existence of such a science furnishes a demonstrative answer to the question which you asked of me and Protagoras. At the time when you asked the question, if you remember, both of us were agreeing that there was nothing mightier than knowledge, and that knowledge, in whatever existing, must have the advantage over pleasure and all other things; and then you said that pleasure often got the advantage even over a man who has knowledge; and we refused to allow this, and you rejoined: O Protagoras and Socrates, what is the meaning of being overcome by pleasure if not this?—tell us what you call such a state:—if we had immediately and at the time answered "Ignorance," you would have laughed at us. But now, in laughing at us, you will be laughing at yourselves: for you also admitted that men err in their choice of pleasures and pains; that is, in their choice of good and evil, from defect of knowledge; and you admitted further, that they err, not only from defect of knowledge in general, but of that particular knowledge which is called measuring. And you are also aware that the erring act which is done without knowledge is done in ignorance. This, therefore, is the meaning of being overcome by pleasure;—ignorance, and that the greatest. And our friends Protagoras and Prodicus and Hippias declare that they are the physicians of ignorance; but you, who are under the mistaken impression that ignorance is not the cause, and that the art of which I am speaking cannot be taught, neither go yourselves, nor send your children, to the Sophists, who are the teachers of these things—you take care of your money and give them none; and the result is, that you are the worse off both in public and private life:—Let us suppose this to be our answer to the world in general: And now I should like to ask you, [358] Hippias, and you, Prodicus, as well as Protagoras (for the argument is to be yours as well as ours), whether you think that I am speaking the truth or not?

They all thought that what I said was entirely true.

Then you agree, I said, that the pleasant is the good, and the painful evil. And here I would beg my friend Prodicus not to introduce his distinction of names, whether he is disposed to say pleasurable, delightful, joyful. However, by whatever name he prefers to call them, I will ask you, most excellent Prodicus, to answer in my sense of the words.

Prodicus laughed and assented, as did the others.

Then, my friends, what do you say to this? Are not all actions honourable and useful, of which the tendency is to make life painless and pleasant? The honourable work is also useful and good?

This was admitted.

Then, I said, if the pleasant is the good, nobody does anything under the idea or conviction that some other thing would be better and is also attainable, when he might do the better. And this inferiority of a man to himself is merely ignorance, as the superiority of a man to himself is wisdom.

They all assented.

And is not ignorance the having a false opinion and being deceived about important matters?

To this also they unanimously assented.

Then, I said, no man voluntarily pursues evil, or that which he thinks to be evil. To prefer evil to good is not in human nature; and when a man is compelled to choose one of two evils, no one will choose the greater when he may have the less.

All of us agreed to every word of this.

Well, I said, there is a certain thing called fear or terror; and here, Prodicus, I should particularly like to know whether you would agree with me in defining this fear or terror as expectation of evil.

Protagoras and Hippias agreed, but Prodicus said that this was fear and not terror.

Never mind, Prodicus, I said; but let me ask whether, if our former assertions are true, a man will pursue that which he fears when he is not compelled? Would not this be in flat contradiction to the admission which has been already made, that he thinks the things which he fears to be evil; and no one will pursue or voluntarily accept that which he thinks to be evil?

[359] That also was universally admitted.

Then, I said, these, Hippias and Prodicus, are our premisses; and I would beg Protagoras to explain to us how he can be right in what he said at first. I do not mean in what he said quite at first, for his first statement, as you may remember, was that whereas there were five parts of virtue none of them was like any other of them; each of them had a separate function. To this, however, I am not referring, but to the assertion which he afterwards made that of the five virtues four were nearly akin to each other, but that the fifth, which was courage, differed greatly from the others. And of this he gave me the following proof. He said: You will find, Socrates, that some of the most impious, and unrighteous, and intemperate, and ignorant of men are among the most courageous; which proves that courage is very different from the other parts of virtue. I was surprised at his saying this at the time, and I am still more surprised now that I have discussed the matter with you. So I asked him whether by the brave he meant the confident. Yes, he replied, and the impetuous or goers. (You may remember, Protagoras, that this was your answer.)

He assented.

Well then, I said, tell us against what are the courageous ready to go—against the same dangers as the cowards?

No, he answered.

Then against something different?

Yes, he said.

Then do cowards go where there is safety, and the courageous where there is danger?

Yes, Socrates, so men say.

Very true, I said. But I want to know against what do you say that the courageous are ready to go—against dangers, believing them to be dangers, or not against dangers?

No, said he; the former case has been proved by you in the previous argument to be impossible.

That, again, I replied, is quite true. And if this has been rightly proven, then no one goes to meet what he thinks to be dangers, since the want of self-control, which makes men rush into dangers, has been shown to be ignorance.

He assented.

And yet the courageous man and the coward alike go to meet that about which they are confident; so that, in this point of view, the cowardly and the courageous go to meet the same things.

And yet, Socrates, said Protagoras, that to which the coward goes is the opposite of that to which the courageous goes; the one, for example, is ready to go to battle, and the other is not ready.

And is going to battle honourable or disgraceful? I said.

Honourable, he replied.

And if honourable, then already admitted by us to be good; for all honourable actions we have admitted to be good.

That is true; and to that opinion I shall always adhere.

[360] True, I said. But which of the two are they who, as you say, are unwilling to go to war, which is a good and honourable thing?

The cowards, he replied.

And what is good and honourable, I said, is also pleasant?

It has certainly been acknowledged to be so, he replied.

And do the cowards knowingly refuse to go to the nobler, and pleasanter, and better?

The admission of that, he replied, would belie our former admissions.

But does not the courageous man also go to meet the better, and pleasanter, and nobler?

That must be admitted.

And the courageous man has no base fear or base confidence?

True, he replied.

And if not base, then honourable?

He admitted this.

And if honourable, then good?

Yes.

But the fear and confidence of the coward or foolhardy or madman, on the contrary, are base?

He assented.

And these base fears and confidences originate in ignorance and uninstructedness?

True, he said.

Then as to the motive from which the cowards act, do you call it cowardice or courage?

I should say cowardice, he replied.

And have they not been shown to be cowards through their ignorance of dangers?

Assuredly, he said.

And because of that ignorance they are cowards?

He assented.

And the reason why they are cowards is admitted by you to be cowardice?

He again assented.

Then the ignorance of what is and is not dangerous is cowardice?

He nodded assent.

But surely courage, I said, is opposed to cowardice?

Yes.

Then the wisdom which knows what are and are not dangers is opposed to the ignorance of them?

To that again he nodded assent.

And the ignorance of them is cowardice?

To that he very reluctantly nodded assent.

And the knowledge of that which is and is not dangerous is courage, and is opposed to the ignorance of these things?

At this point he would no longer nod assent, but was silent.

And why, I said, do you neither assent nor dissent, Protagoras?

Finish the argument by yourself, he said.

I only want to ask one more question, I said. I want to know whether you still think that there are men who are most ignorant and yet most courageous?

You seem to have a great ambition to make me answer, Socrates, and therefore I will gratify you, and say, that this appears to me to be impossible consistently with the argument.

My only object, I said, in continuing the discussion, has been the desire to ascertain the nature and relations of virtue; for if this were clear, [361] I am very sure that the other controversy which has been carried on at great length by both of us—you affirming and I denying that virtue can be taught—would also become clear. The result of our discussion appears to me to be singular. For if the argument had a human voice, that voice would be heard laughing at us and saying: "Protagoras and Socrates, you are strange beings; there are you, Socrates, who were saying that virtue cannot be taught, contradicting yourself now by your attempt to prove that all things are knowledge, including justice, and temperance, and courage,—which tends to show that virtue can certainly be taught; for if virtue were other than knowledge, as Protagoras attempted to prove, then clearly virtue cannot be taught; but if virtue is entirely knowledge, as you are seeking to show, then I cannot but suppose that virtue is capable of being taught. Protagoras, on the other hand, who started by saying that it might be taught, is now eager to prove it to be anything rather than knowledge; and if this is true, it must be quite incapable of being taught." Now I, Protagoras, perceiving this terrible confusion of our ideas, have a great desire that they should be cleared up. And I should like to carry on the discussion until we ascertain what virtue is, and whether capable of being taught or not, lest haply Epimetheus should trip us up and deceive us in the argument, as he forgot us in the story; I prefer your Prometheus to your Epimetheus, for of him I make use, whenever I am busy about these questions, in Promethean care of my own life. And if you have no objection, as I said at first, I should like to have your help in the enquiry.

Protagoras replied: Socrates, I am not of a base nature, and I am the last man in the world to be envious. I cannot but applaud your energy and your conduct of an argument. As I have often said, I admire you above all men whom I know, and far above all men of your age; and I believe that you will become very eminent in philosophy. Let us come back to the subject at some future time; at present we had better turn to something else.

By all means, I said, if that is your wish; for I too ought long since to have kept the engagement of which I spoke before, and only tarried because I could not refuse the request of the noble Callias. So the conversation ended, and we went our way.

EUTHYDEMUS

PERSONS OF THE DIALOGUE: SOCRATES, *who is the narrator;* CRITO; CLEINIAS;
EUTHYDEMUS; DIONYSODORUS; CTESIPPUS. *Scene: The Lyceum*

⫷⫸⫷⫸⫷⫸⫷⫸⫷⫸

[271] *Crito.* WHO was the person, Socrates, with whom you were talking yesterday at the Lyceum? There was such a crowd around you that I could not get within hearing, but I caught a sight of him over their heads, and I made out, as I thought, that he was a stranger with whom you were talking: who was he?

Socrates. There were two, Crito; which of them do you mean?

Cri. The one whom I mean was seated second from you on the right-hand side. In the middle was Cleinias the young son of Axiochus, who has wonderfully grown; he is only about the age of my own Critobulus, but he is much forwarder and very good-looking: the other is thin and looks younger than he is.

Soc. He whom you mean, Crito, is Euthydemus; and on my left hand there was his brother Dionysodorus, who also took part in the conversation.

Cri. Neither of them are known to me, Socrates; they are a new importation of Sophists, as I should imagine. Of what country are they, and what is their line of wisdom?

Soc. As to their origin, I believe that they are natives of this part of the world, and have migrated from Chios to Thurii; they were driven out of Thurii, and have been living for many years past in these regions. As to their wisdom, about which you ask, Crito, they are wonderful—consummate! I never knew what the true pancratiast was before; they are simply made up of fighting, not like the two Acarnanian brothers who fight with their bodies only, but this pair of heroes, besides being perfect in the use of their bodies, are invincible in every sort

of warfare; [272] for they are capital at fighting in armour, and will teach the art to any one who pays them; and also they are most skilful in legal warfare; they will plead themselves and teach others to speak and to compose speeches which will have an effect upon the courts. And this was only the beginning of their wisdom, but they have at last carried out the pancratiastic art to the very end, and have mastered the only mode of fighting which had been hitherto neglected by them; and now no one dares even to stand up against them: such is their skill in the war of words, that they can refute any proposition whether true or false. Now I am thinking, Crito, of placing myself in their hands; for they say that in a short time they can impart their skill to any one.

Cri. But, Socrates, are you not too old? there may be reason to fear that.

Soc. Certainly not, Crito; as I will prove to you, for I have the consolation of knowing that they began this art of disputation which I covet, quite, as I may say, in old age; last year, or the year before, they had none of their new wisdom. I am only apprehensive that I may bring the two strangers into disrepute, as I have done Connus the son of Metrobius, the harp-player, who is still my music-master; for when the boys who go to him see me going with them, they laugh at me and call him grandpapa's master. Now I should not like the strangers to experience similar treatment; the fear of ridicule may make them unwilling to receive me; and therefore, Crito, I shall try and persuade some old men to accompany me to them, as I persuaded them to go with me to

65

Connus, and I hope that you will make one: and perhaps we had better take your sons as a bait; they will want to have them as pupils, and for the sake of them will be willing to receive us.

Cri. I see no objection, Socrates, if you like; but first I wish that you would give me a description of their wisdom, that I may know beforehand what we are going to learn.

Soc. In less than no time you shall hear; for I cannot say that I did not attend—I paid great attention to them, and I remember and will endeavour to repeat the whole story. Providentially I was sitting alone in the dressing-room of the Lyceum where you saw me, and was about to depart; when I was getting up I recognized the familiar divine sign: *[273]* so I sat down again, and in a little while the two brothers Euthydemus and Dionysodorus came in, and several others with them, whom I believe to be their disciples, and they walked about in the covered court; they had not taken more than two or three turns when Cleinias entered, who, as you truly say, is very much improved: he was followed by a host of lovers, one of whom was Ctesippus the Paeanian, a well-bred youth, but also having the wildness of youth. Cleinias saw me from the entrance as I was sitting alone, and at once came and sat down on the right hand of me, as you describe; and Dionysodorus and Euthydemus, when they saw him, at first stopped and talked with one another, now and then glancing at us, for I particularly watched them; and then Euthydemus came and sat down by the youth, and the other by me on the left hand; the rest anywhere. I saluted the brothers, whom I had not seen for a long time; and then I said to Cleinias: Here are two wise men, Euthydemus and Dionysodorus, Cleinias, wise not in a small but in a large way of wisdom, for they know all about war,—all that a good general ought to know about the array and command of an army, and the whole art of fighting in armour: and they know about law too, and can teach a man how to use the weapons of the courts when he is injured.

They heard me say this, but only despised me. I observed that they looked at one another, and both of them laughed; and then Euthydemus said: Those, Socrates, are matters which we no longer pursue seriously; to us they are secondary occupations.

Indeed, I said, if such occupations are regarded by you as secondary, what must the principal one be; tell me, I beseech you, what that noble study is?

The teaching of virtue, Socrates, he replied, is our principal occupation; and we believe that we can impart it better and quicker than any man.

My God! I said, and where did you learn that? I always thought, as I was saying just now, that your chief accomplishment was the art of fighting in armour; and I used to say as much of you, for I remember that you professed this when you were here before. But now if you really have the other knowledge, O forgive me: I address you as I would superior beings, and ask you to pardon the impiety of my former expressions. *[274]* But are you quite sure about this, Dionysodorus and Euthydemus? the promise is so vast, that a feeling of incredulity steals over me.

You may take our word, Socrates, for the fact.

Then I think you happier in having such a treasure than the great king is in the possession of his kingdom. And please to tell me whether you intend to exhibit your wisdom; or what will you do?

That is why we have come hither, Socrates; and our purpose is not only to exhibit, but also to teach any one who likes to learn.

But I can promise you, I said, that every unvirtuous person will want to learn. I shall be the first; and there is the youth Cleinias, and Ctesippus: and here are several others, I said, pointing to the lovers of Cleinias, who were beginning to gather round us. Now Ctesippus was sitting at some distance from Cleinias; and when Euthydemus leaned forward in talking with me, he was prevented from seeing Cleinias, who was between us; and so, partly because he wanted to look at his love, and also because he was interested, he jumped up and stood opposite to us: and all the other admirers of Cleinias, as well as the disciples of Euthydemus and Dionysodorus, followed his example. And these were the persons whom I showed to Euthydemus, telling him that they were all eager to learn: to which Ctesippus and all of them with one voice vehemently assented, and bid him exhibit the power of his wisdom. Then I said: O Euthydemus and Dionysodorus, I earnestly request you to do myself and the company the favour to exhibit. There may be some trouble in giving the whole exhibition; but tell me one thing,—can you make a good man of him only who is already convinced that he ought to learn of you, or of him also who is not convinced, either because he imagines that virtue is a thing which cannot be taught at all, or that you are not the teachers of it? Has your art power to persuade him, who is of the latter temper of mind, that virtue can be taught; and that you are the men from whom he will best learn it?

Certainly, Socrates, said Dionysodorus; our art will do both.

And you and your brother, Dionysodorus, I said, of all men who are now living are the most likely to stimulate him to philosophy and to the study of virtue?

[275] Yes, Socrates, I rather think that we are.

Then I wish that you would be so good as to defer the other part of the exhibition, and only try to persuade the youth whom you see here that he ought to be a philosopher and study virtue. Exhibit that, and you will confer a great favour on me and on every one present; for the fact is I and all of us are extremely anxious that he should become truly good. His name is Cleinias, and he is the son of Axiochus, and grandson of the old Alcibiades, cousin of the Alcibiades that now is. He is quite young, and we are naturally afraid that some one may get the start of us, and turn his mind in a wrong direction, and he may be ruined. Your visit, therefore, is most happily timed; and I hope that you will make a trial of the young man, and converse with him in our presence, if you have no objection.

These were pretty nearly the expressions which I used; and Euthydemus, in a manly and at the same time encouraging tone, replied: There can be no objection, Socrates, if the young man is only willing to answer questions.

He is quite accustomed to do so, I replied; for his friends often come and ask him questions and argue with him; and therefore he is quite at home in answering.

What followed, Crito, how can I rightly narrate? For not slight is the task of rehearsing infinite wisdom, and therefore, like the poets, I ought to commence my relation with an invocation to Memory and the Muses. Now Euthydemus, if I remember rightly, began nearly as follows: O Cleinias, are those who learn the wise or the ignorant?

The youth, overpowered by the question, blushed, and in his perplexity looked at me for help; and I, knowing that he was disconcerted, said: Take courage, Cleinias, and answer like a man whichever you think; for my belief is that you will derive the greatest benefit from their questions.

Whichever he answers, said Dionysodorus, leaning forward so as to catch my ear, his face beaming with laughter, I prophesy that he will be refuted, Socrates.

While he was speaking to me, Cleinias gave his answer: and therefore I had no time to warn him of the predicament in which he was placed, [276] and he answered that those who learned were the wise.

Euthydemus proceeded: There are some whom you would call teachers, are there not?

The boy assented.

And they are the teachers of those who learn—the grammar-master and the lyre-master used to teach you and other boys; and you were the learners?

Yes.

And when you were learners you did not as yet know the things which you were learning?

No, he said.

And were you wise then?

No, indeed, he said.

But if you were not wise you were unlearned?

Certainly.

You then, learning what you did not know, were unlearned when you were learning?

The youth nodded assent.

Then the unlearned learn, and not the wise, Cleinias, as you imagine.

At these words the followers of Euthydemus, of whom I spoke, like a chorus at the bidding of their director, laughed and cheered. Then, before the youth had time to recover his breath, Dionysodorus cleverly took him in hand, and said: Yes, Cleinias; and when the grammar-master dictated anything to you, were they the wise boys or the unlearned who learned the dictation?

The wise, replied Cleinias.

Then after all the wise are the learners and not the unlearned; and your last answer to Euthydemus was wrong.

Then once more the admirers of the two heroes, in an ecstasy at their wisdom, gave vent to another peal of laughter, while the rest of us were silent and amazed. Euthydemus, observing this, determined to persevere with the youth; and in order to heighten the effect went on asking another similar question, which might be compared to the double turn of an expert dancer. Do those, said he, who learn, learn what they know, or what they do not know?

Again Dionysodorus whispered to me: That, Socrates, is just another of the same sort.

Good heavens, I said; and your last question was so good!

Like all our other questions, Socrates, he replied—inevitable.

I see the reason, I said, why you are in such reputation among your disciples.

Meanwhile Cleinias had answered Euthydemus that those who learned learn what they do not know; and he put him through a series of questions the same as before.

[277] Do you not know letters?

He assented.

All letters?

Yes.

But when the teacher dictates to you, does he not dictate letters?

To this also he assented.

Then if you know all letters, he dictates that which you know?

This again was admitted by him.

Then, said the other, you do not learn that which he dictates; but he only who does not know letters learns?

Nay, said Cleinias; but I do learn.

Then, said he, you learn what you know, if you know all the letters?

He admitted that.

Then, he said, you were wrong in your answer.

The word was hardly out of his mouth when Dionysodorus took up the argument, like a ball which he caught, and had another throw at the youth. Cleinias, he said, Euthydemus is deceiving you. For tell me now, is not learning acquiring knowledge of that which one learns?

Cleinias assented.

And knowing is having knowledge at the time?

He agreed.

And not knowing is not having knowledge at the time?

He admitted that.

And are those who acquire those who have or have not a thing?

Those who have not.

And have you not admitted that those who do not know are of the number of those who have not?

He nodded assent.

Then those who learn are of the class of those who acquire, and not of those who have?

He agreed.

Then, Cleinias, he said, those who do not know learn, and not those who know.

Euthydemus was proceeding to give the youth a third fall; but I knew that he was in deep water, and therefore, as I wanted to give him a respite lest he should be disheartened, I said to him consolingly: You must not be surprised, Cleinias, at the singularity of their mode of speech: this I say because you may not understand what the two strangers are doing with you; they are only initiating you after the manner of the Corybantes in the mysteries; and this answers to the enthronement, which, if you have ever been initiated, is, as you will know, accompanied by dancing and sport; and now they are just prancing and dancing about you, and will next proceed to initiate you; imagine then that you have gone through the first part of the sophistical ritual, which, as Prodicus says, begins with initiation into the correct use of terms. The two foreign gentlemen, perceiving that you did not know, wanted to explain to you that the word "to learn" has two meanings, [278] and is used, first, in the sense of acquiring knowledge of some matter of which you previously have no knowledge, and also, when you have the knowledge, in the sense of reviewing this matter, whether something done or spoken by the light of this newly-acquired knowledge; the latter is generally called "knowing" rather than "learning," but the word "learning" is also used; and you did not see, as they explained to you, that the term is employed of two opposite sorts of men, of those who know, and of those who do not know. There was a similar trick in the second question, when they asked you whether men learn what they know or what they do not know. These parts of learning are not serious, and therefore I say that the gentlemen are not serious, but are only playing with you. For if a man had all that sort of knowledge that ever was, he would not be at all the wiser; he would only be able to play with men, tripping them up and oversetting them with distinctions of words. He would be like a person who pulls away a stool from some one when he is about to sit down, and then laughs and makes merry at the sight of his friend overturned and laid on his back. And you must regard all that has hitherto passed between you and them as merely play. But in what is to follow I am certain that they will exhibit to you their serious purpose, and keep their promise (I will show them how); for they promised to give me a sample of the hortatory philosophy, but I suppose that they wanted to have a game with you first. And now, Euthydemus and Dionysodorus, I think that we have had enough of this. Will you let me see you explaining to the young man how he is to apply himself to the study of virtue and wisdom? And I will first show you what I conceive to be the nature of the task, and what sort of a discourse I desire to hear; and if I do this in a very inartistic and ridiculous manner, do not laugh at me, for I only venture to improvise before you because I am eager to hear your wisdom: and I must therefore ask you and your disciples to refrain from laughing. And now, O son of Axiochus, let me put a question to you: Do not all men desire happiness? And yet, perhaps, this is one of those ridiculous questions which I am afraid to ask, and which ought not to be asked by a sensible man: for what human being is there who does not desire happiness?

[279] There is no one, said Cleinias, who does not.

Well, then, I said, since we all of us desire happiness, how can we be happy?—that is the next question. Shall we not be happy if we have many good things? And this, perhaps, is even a more simple question than the first, for there can be no doubt of the answer.

He assented.

And what things do we esteem good? No solemn sage is required to tell us this, which may be easily answered; for every one will say that wealth is a good.

Certainly, he said.

And are not health and beauty goods, and other personal gifts?

He agreed.

Can there be any doubt that good birth, and power, and honours in one's own land, are goods?

He assented.

And what other goods are there? I said. What do you say of temperance, justice, courage: do you not verily and indeed think, Cleinias, that we shall be more right in ranking them as goods than in not ranking them as goods? For a dispute might possibly arise about this. What then do you say?

They are goods, said Cleinias.

Very well, I said; and where in the company shall we find a place for wisdom—among the goods or not?

Among the goods.

And now, I said, think whether we have left out any considerable goods.

I do not think that we have, said Cleinias.

Upon recollection, I said, indeed I am afraid that we have left out the greatest of them all.

What is that? he asked.

Fortune, Cleinias, I replied; which all, even the most foolish, admit to be the greatest of goods.

True, he said.

On second thoughts, I added, how narrowly, O son of Axiochus, have you and I escaped making a laughing-stock of ourselves to the strangers.

Why do you say so?

Why, because we have already spoken of good-fortune, and are but repeating ourselves.

What do you mean?

I mean that there is something ridiculous in again putting forward good-fortune, which has a place in the list already, and saying the same thing twice over.

He asked what was the meaning of this, and I replied: Surely wisdom is good-fortune; even a child may know that.

The simple-minded youth was amazed; and, observing his surprise, I said to him: Do you not know, Cleinias, that flute-players are most fortunate and successful in performing on the flute?

He assented.

And are not the scribes most fortunate in writing and reading letters?

Certainly.

Amid the dangers of the sea, again, are any more fortunate on the whole than wise pilots?

None, certainly.

And if you were engaged in war, in whose company would you rather take the risk—in company with a wise general, or with a foolish one?

With a wise one.

And if you were ill, whom would you rather have as a companion in a dangerous illness—a wise physician, or an ignorant one?

A wise one.

You think, I said, that to act with a wise man is more fortunate than to act with an ignorant one?

He assented.

[280] Then wisdom always makes men fortunate: for by wisdom no man would ever err, and therefore he must act rightly and succeed, or his wisdom would be wisdom no longer.

We contrived at last, somehow or other, to agree in a general conclusion, that he who had wisdom had no need of fortune. I then recalled to his mind the previous state of the question. You remember, I said, our making the admission that we should be happy and fortunate if many good things were present with us?

He assented.

And should we be happy by reason of the presence of good things, if they profited us not, or if they profited us?

If they profited us, he said.

And would they profit us, if we only had them and did not use them? For example, if we had a great deal of food and did not eat, or a great deal of drink and did not drink, should we be profited?

Certainly not, he said.

Or would an artisan, who had all the implements necessary for his work, and did not use them, be any the better for the possession of them? For example, would a carpenter be any the better for having all his tools and plenty of wood, if he never worked?

Certainly not, he said.

And if a person had wealth and all the goods of which we were just now speaking, and did not use them, would he be happy because he possessed them?

No indeed, Socrates.

Then, I said, a man who would be happy must not only have the good things, but he must also use them; there is no advantage in merely having them?

True.

Well, Cleinias, but if you have the use as well as the possession of good things, is that sufficient to confer happiness?

Yes, in my opinion.

And may a person use them either rightly or wrongly?

He must use them rightly.

That is quite true, I said. And the wrong use of a thing is far worse than the non-use; for the one is an evil, and the other is neither a good nor an evil. [281] You admit that?

He assented.

Now in the working and use of wood, is not that which gives the right use simply the knowledge of the carpenter?

Nothing else, he said.

And surely, in the manufacture of vessels, knowledge is that which gives the right way of making them?

He agreed.

And in the use of the goods of which we spoke at first—wealth and health and beauty, is not knowledge that which directs us to the right use of them, and regulates our practice about them?

He assented.

Then in every possession and every use of a thing, knowledge is that which gives a man not only good-fortune but success?

He again assented.

And tell me, I said, O tell me, what do possessions profit a man, if he have neither good sense nor wisdom? Would a man be better off, having and doing many things without wisdom, or a few things with wisdom? Look at the matter thus: If he did fewer things would he not make fewer mistakes? if he made fewer mistakes would he not have fewer misfortunes? and if he had fewer misfortunes would he not be less miserable?

Certainly, he said.

And who would do least—a poor man or a rich man?

A poor man.

A weak man or a strong man?

A weak man.

A noble man or a mean man?

A mean man.

And a coward would do less than a courageous and temperate man?

Yes.

And an indolent man less than an active man?

He assented.

And a slow man less than a quick; and one who had dull perceptions of seeing and hearing less than one who had keen ones?

All this was mutually allowed by us.

Then, I said, Cleinias, the sum of the matter appears to be that the goods of which we spoke before are not to be regarded as goods in themselves, but the degree of good and evil in them depends on whether they are or are not under the guidance of knowledge: under the guidance of ignorance, they are greater evils than their opposites, inasmuch as they are more able to minister to the evil principle which rules them; and when under the guidance of wisdom and prudence, they are greater goods: but in themselves they are nothing?

That, he replied, is obvious.

What then is the result of what has been said? Is not this the result—that other things are indifferent, and that wisdom is the only good, and ignorance the only evil?

He assented.

[282] Let us consider a further point, I said: Seeing that all men desire happiness, and happiness, as has been shown, is gained by a use, and a right use, of the things of life, and the right use of them, and good fortune in the use of them, is given by knowledge,—the inference is that everybody ought by all means to try and make himself as wise as he can?

Yes, he said.

And when a man thinks that he ought to obtain this treasure, far more than money, from a father or a guardian or a friend or a suitor, whether citizen or stranger—the eager desire and prayer to them that they would impart wisdom to you, is not at all dishonourable, Cleinias; nor is any one to be blamed for doing any honourable service or ministration to any man, whether a lover or not, if his aim is to get wisdom. Do you agree? I said.

Yes, he said, I quite agree, and think that you are right.

Yes, I said, Cleinias, if only wisdom can be taught, and does not come to man spontaneously; for this is a point which has still to be considered, and is not yet agreed upon by you and me—

But I think, Socrates, that wisdom can be taught, he said.

Best of men, I said, I am delighted to hear you say so; and I am also grateful to you for having saved me from a long and tiresome investigation as to whether wisdom can be taught or not. But now, as you think that wisdom can be taught, and that wisdom only can make a man happy and fortunate, will you not acknowledge that all of us ought to love wisdom, and you individually will try to love her?

Certainly, Socrates, he said; I will do my best.

I was pleased at hearing this; and I turned to Dionysodorus and Euthydemus and said: That is an example, clumsy and tedious I admit, of the sort of exhortations which I would have you give; and I hope that one of you will set forth what I have been saying in a more artistic style: or at least take up the enquiry where I left off, and proceed to show the youth whether he should have all knowledge; or whether there is one sort of knowledge only which will make him good and happy, and what that is. For, as I was saying at first, the improvement of this young man in virtue and wisdom is a matter which we have very much at heart.

[283] Thus I spoke, Crito, and was all attention to what was coming. I wanted to see how they would approach the question, and where they would start in their exhortation to the young man that he should practise wisdom and virtue. Dionysodorus, who was the elder, spoke first. Everybody's eyes were directed towards him, perceiving that something wonderful might shortly be expected. And certainly they were not far wrong; for the man, Crito, began a remarkable discourse well worth hearing, and wonderfully persuasive regarded as an exhortation to virtue.

Tell me, he said, Socrates and the rest of you who say that you want this young man to become wise, are you in jest or in real earnest?

I was led by this to imagine that they fancied us to have been jesting when we asked them to converse with the youth, and that this made them jest and play, and being under this impression, I was the more decided in saying that we were in profound earnest. Dionysodorus said:

Reflect, Socrates; you may have to deny your words.

I have reflected, I said; and I shall never deny my words.

Well, said he, and so you say that you wish Cleinias to become wise?

Undoubtedly.

And he is not wise as yet?

At least his modesty will not allow him to say that he is.

You wish him, he said, to become wise and not to be ignorant?

That we do.

You wish him to be what he is not, and no longer to be what he is?

I was thrown into consternation at this.

Taking advantage of my consternation he added: You wish him no longer to be what he is, which can only mean that you wish him to perish. Pretty lovers and friends they must be who want their favourite not to be, or to perish!

When Ctesippus heard this he got very angry (as a lover well might) and said: Stranger of Thurii—if politeness would allow me I should say, A plague upon you! What can make you tell such a lie about me and the others, which I hardly like to repeat, as that I wish Cleinias to perish?

Euthydemus replied: And do you think, Ctesippus, that it is possible to tell a lie?

Yes, said Ctesippus; I should be mad to say anything else.

[284] And in telling a lie, do you tell the thing of which you speak or not?

You tell the thing of which you speak.

And he who tells, tells that thing which he tells, and no other?

Yes, said Ctesippus.

And that is a distinct thing apart from other things?

Certainly.

And he who says that thing says that which is?

Yes.

And he who says that which is, says the truth. And therefore Dionysodorus, if he says that which is, says the truth of you and no lie.

Yes, Euthydemus, said Ctesippus; but in saying this, he says what is not.

Euthydemus answered: And that which is not is not?

True.

And that which is not is nowhere?

Nowhere.

And can any one do anything about that which has no existence, or do to Cleinias that which is not and is nowhere?

I think not, said Ctesippus.

Well, but do rhetoricians, when they speak in the assembly, do nothing?

Nay, he said, they do something.

And doing is making?

Yes.

And speaking is doing and making?

He agreed.

Then no one says that which is not, for in saying what is not he would be doing something; and you have already acknowledged that no one can do what is not. And therefore, upon your own showing, no one says what is false; but if Dionysodorus says anything, he says what is true and what is.

Yes, Euthydemus, said Ctesippus; but he speaks of things in a certain way and manner, and not as they really are.

Why, Ctesippus, said Dionysodorus, do you mean to say that any one speaks of things as they are?

Yes, he said—all gentlemen and truth-speaking persons.

And are not good things good, and evil things evil?

He assented.

And you say that gentlemen speak of things as they are?

Yes.

Then the good speak evil of evil things, if they speak of them as they are?

Yes, indeed, he said; and they speak evil of evil men. And if I may give you a piece of advice, you had better take care that they do not speak evil of you, since I can tell you that the good speak evil of the evil.

And do they speak great things of the great, rejoined Euthydemus, and warm things of the warm?

To be sure they do, said Ctesippus; and they speak coldly of the insipid and cold dialectician.

You are abusive, Ctesippus, said Dionysodo-

rus, you are abusive!

Indeed, I am not, Dionysodorus, he replied; for I love you and am giving you friendly advice, and, if I could, would persuade you not like a boor to say in my presence that I desire my beloved, [285] whom I value above all men, to perish.

I saw that they were getting exasperated with one another, so I made a joke with him and said: O Ctesippus, I think that we must allow the strangers to use language in their own way, and not quarrel with them about words, but be thankful for what they give us. If they know how to destroy men in such a way as to make good and sensible men out of bad and foolish ones—whether this is a discovery of their own, or whether they have learned from some one else this new sort of death and destruction which enables them to get rid of a bad man and turn him into a good one—if they know this (and they do know this—at any rate they said just now that this was the secret of their newly-discovered art)—let them, in their phraseology, destroy the youth and make him wise, and all of us with him. But if you young men do not like to trust yourselves with them, then *fiat experimentum in corpore senis;* I will be the Carian on whom they shall operate. And here I offer my old person to Dionysodorus; he may put me into the pot, like Medea the Colchian, kill me, boil me, if he will only make me good.

Ctesippus said: And I, Socrates, am ready to commit myself to the strangers; they may skin me alive, if they please (and I am pretty well skinned by them already), if only my skin is made at last, not like that of Marsyas, into a leathern bottle, but into a piece of virtue. And here is Dionysodorus fancying that I am angry with him, when really I am not angry at all; I do but contradict him when I think that he is speaking improperly to me: and you must not confound abuse and contradiction, O illustrious Dionysodorus; for they are quite different things.

Contradiction! said Dionysodorus; why, there never was such a thing.

Certainly there is, he replied; there can be no question of that. Do you, Dionysodorus, maintain that there is not?

You will never prove to me, he said, that you have heard any one contradicting any one else.

Indeed, said Ctesippus; then now you may hear me contradicting Dionysodorus.

Are you prepared to make that good?

Certainly, he said.

Well, have not all things words expressive of them?

Yes.

Of their existence or of their non-existence?

Of their existence.

[286] Yes, Ctesippus, and we just now proved, as you may remember, that no man could affirm a negative; for no one could affirm that which is not.

And what does that signify? said Ctesippus; you and I may contradict all the same for that.

But can we contradict one another, said Dionysodorus, when both of us are describing the same thing? Then we must surely be speaking the same thing?

He assented.

Or when neither of us is speaking of the same thing? For then neither of us says a word about the thing at all?

He granted that proposition also.

But when I describe something and you describe another thing, or I say something and you say nothing—is there any contradiction? How can he who speaks contradict him who speaks not?

Here Ctesippus was silent; and I in my astonishment said: What do you mean, Dionysodorus? I have often heard, and have been amazed to hear, this thesis of yours, which is maintained and employed by the disciples of Protagoras, and others before them, and which to me appears to be quite wonderful, and suicidal as well as destructive, and I think that I am most likely to hear the truth about it from you. The dictum is that there is no such thing as falsehood; a man must either say what is true or say nothing. Is not that your position?

He assented.

But if he cannot speak falsely, may he not think falsely?

No, he cannot, he said.

Then there is no such thing as false opinion?

No, he said.

Then there is no such thing as ignorance, or men who are ignorant; for is not ignorance, if there be such a thing, a mistake of fact?

Certainly, he said.

And that is impossible?

Impossible, he replied.

Are you saying this as a paradox, Dionysodorus; or do you seriously maintain no man to be ignorant?

Refute me, he said.

But how can I refute you, if, as you say, to tell a falsehood is impossible?

Very true, said Euthydemus.

Neither did I tell you just now to refute me, said Dionysodorus; for how can I tell you to do that which is not?

O Euthydemus, I said, I have but a dull conception of these subtleties and excellent devices of wisdom; I am afraid that I hardly understand them, and you must forgive me therefore if I ask a very stupid question: [287] if there be no falsehood or false opinion or ignorance, there can be no such thing as erroneous action, for a man cannot fail of acting as he is acting—that is what you mean?

Yes, he replied.

And now, I said, I will ask my stupid question: If there is no such thing as error in deed, word, or thought, then what, in the name of goodness, do you come hither to teach? And were you not just now saying that you could teach virtue best of all men, to any one who was willing to learn?

And are you such an old fool, Socrates, rejoined Dionysodorus, that you bring up now what I said at first—and if I had said anything last year, I suppose that you would bring that up too—but are non-plussed at the words which I have just uttered?

Why, I said, they are not easy to answer; for they are the words of wise men: and indeed I know not what to make of this word "nonplussed," which you used last: what do you mean by it, Dionysodorus? You must mean that I cannot refute your argument. Tell me if the words have any other sense.

No, he replied, they mean what you say. And now answer.

What, before you, Dionysodorus? I said.

Answer, said he.

And is that fair?

Yes, quite fair, he said.

Upon what principle? I said. I can only suppose that you are a very wise man who comes to us in the character of a great logician, and who knows when to answer and when not to answer—and now you will not open your mouth at all, because you know that you ought not.

You prate, he said, instead of answering. But if, my good sir, you admit that I am wise, answer as I tell you.

I suppose that I must obey, for you are master. Put the question.

Are the things which have sense alive or lifeless?

They are alive.

And do you know of any word which is alive?

I cannot say that I do.

Then why did you ask me what sense my words had?

Why, because I was stupid and made a mistake. And yet, perhaps, I was right after all in saying that words have a sense;—what do you say, wise man? If I was not in error, even you will not refute me, and all your wisdom will be non-plussed; but if I did fall into error, then again you are wrong in saying that there is no error,—and this remark was made by you not quite a year ago. [288] I am inclined to think, however, Dionysodorus and Euthydemus, that this argument lies where it was and is not very likely to advance: even your skill in the subtleties of logic, which is really amazing, has not found out the way of throwing another and not falling yourself, now any more than of old.

Ctesippus said: Men of Chios, Thurii, or however and whatever you call yourselves, I wonder at you, for you seem to have no objection to talking nonsense.

Fearing that there would be high words, I again endeavoured to soothe Ctesippus, and said to him: To you, Ctesippus, I must repeat what I said before to Cleinias—that you do not understand the ways of these philosophers from abroad. They are not serious, but, like the Egyptian wizard, Proteus, they take different forms and deceive us by their enchantments: and let us, like Menelaus, refuse to let them go until they show themselves to us in earnest. When they begin to be in earnest their full beauty will appear: let us then beg and entreat and beseech them to shine forth. And I think that I had better once more exhibit the form in which I pray to behold them; it might be a guide to them. I will go on therefore where I left off, as well as I can, in the hope that I may touch their hearts and move them to pity, and that when they see me deeply serious and interested, they also may be serious. You, Cleinias, I said, shall remind me at what point we left off. Did we not agree that philosophy should be studied? and was not that our conclusion?

Yes, he replied.

And philosophy is the acquisition of knowledge?

Yes, he said.

And what knowledge ought we to acquire? May we not answer with absolute truth—A knowledge which will do us good?

Certainly, he said.

And should we be any the better if we went about having a knowledge of the places where most gold was hidden in the earth?

Perhaps we should, he said.

But have we not already proved, I said, that we should be none the better off, even if without trouble and digging all the gold which there is in the earth were ours? And if we knew how to convert stones into gold, [289] the knowledge would be of no value to us, unless we also knew how to use the gold? Do you not remember? I said.

I quite remember, he said.

Nor would any other knowledge, whether of money-making, or of medicine, or of any other art which knows only how to make a thing, and not to use it when made, be of any good to us. Am I not right?

He agreed.

And if there were a knowledge which was able to make men immortal, without giving them the knowledge of the way to use the immortality, neither would there be any use in that, if we may argue from the analogy of the previous instances?

To all this he agreed.

Then, my dear boy, I said, the knowledge which we want is one that uses as well as makes?

True, he said.

And our desire is not to be skilful lyre-makers, or artists of that sort—far otherwise; for with them the art which makes is one, and the art which uses is another. Although they have to do with the same, they are divided: for the art which makes and the art which plays on the lyre differ widely from one another. Am I not right?

He agreed.

And clearly we do not want the art of the flute-maker; this is only another of the same sort?

He assented.

But suppose, I said, that we were to learn the art of making speeches—would that be the art which would make us happy?

I should say no, rejoined Cleinias.

And why should you say so? I asked.

I see, he replied, that there are some composers of speeches who do not know how to use the speeches which they make, just as the makers of lyres do not know how to use the lyres; and also some who are of themselves unable to compose speeches, but are able to use the speeches which the others make for them; and this proves that the art of making speeches is not the same as the art of using them.

Yes, I said; and I take your words to be a

sufficient proof that the art of making speeches is not one which will make a man happy. And yet I did think that the art which we have so long been seeking might be discovered in that direction; for the composers of speeches, whenever I meet them, always appear to me to be very extraordinary men, Cleinias, and their art is lofty and divine, and no wonder. For their art is a part of the great art of enchantment, [290] and hardly, if at all, inferior to it: and whereas the art of the enchanter is a mode of charming snakes and spiders and scorpions, and other monsters and pests, this art of theirs acts upon dicasts and ecclesiasts and bodies of men, for the charming and pacifying of them. Do you agree with me?

Yes, he said, I think that you are quite right.

Whither then shall we go, I said, and to what art shall we have recourse?

I do not see my way, he said.

But I think that I do, I replied.

And what is your notion? asked Cleinias.

I think that the art of the general is above all others the one of which the possession is most likely to make a man happy.

I do not think so, he said.

Why not? I said.

The art of the general is surely an art of hunting mankind.

What of that? I said.

Why, he said, no art of hunting extends beyond hunting and capturing; and when the prey is taken the huntsman or fisherman cannot use it; but they hand it over to the cook, and the geometricians and astronomers and calculators (who all belong to the hunting class, for they do not make their diagrams, but only find out that which was previously contained in them)—they, I say, not being able to use but only to catch their prey, hand over their inventions to the dialectician to be applied by him, if they have any sense in them.

Good, I said, fairest and wisest Cleinias. And is this true?

Certainly, he said; just as a general when he takes a city or a camp hands over his new acquisition to the statesman, for he does not know how to use them himself; or as the quail-taker transfers the quails to the keeper of them. If we are looking for the art which is to make us blessed, and which is able to use that which it makes or takes, the art of the general is not the one, and some other must be found.

Cri. And do you mean, Socrates, that the youngster said all this?

Soc. Are you incredulous, Crito?

Cri. Indeed, I am; for if he did say so, then in my opinion he needs neither Euthydemus nor any one else to be his instructor.

Soc. Perhaps I may have forgotten, and Ctesippus was the real answerer.

[291] Cri. Ctesippus! nonsense.

Soc. All I know is that I heard these words, and that they were not spoken either by Euthydemus or Dionysodorus. I dare say, my good Crito, that they may have been spoken by some superior person: that I heard them I am certain.

Cri. Yes, indeed, Socrates, by some one a good deal superior, as I should be disposed to think. But did you carry the search any further, and did you find the art which you were seeking?

Soc. Find! my dear sir, no indeed. And we cut a poor figure; we were like children after larks, always on the point of catching the art, which was always getting away from us. But why should I repeat the whole story? At last we came to the kingly art, and enquired whether that gave and caused happiness, and then we got into a labyrinth, and when we thought we were at the end, came out again at the beginning, having still to seek as much as ever.

Cri. How did that happen, Socrates?

Soc. I will tell you; the kingly art was identified by us with the political.

Cri. Well, and what came of that?

Soc. To this royal or political art all the arts, including the art of the general, seemed to render up the supremacy, that being the only one which knew how to use what they produce. Here obviously was the very art which we were seeking—the art which is the source of good government, and which may be described, in the language of Aeschylus, as alone sitting at the helm of the vessel of state, piloting and governing all things, and utilizing them.

Cri. And were you not right, Socrates?

Soc. You shall judge, Crito, if you are willing to hear what followed; for we resumed the enquiry, and a question of this sort was asked: Does the kingly art, having this supreme authority, do anything for us? To be sure, was the answer. And would not you, Crito, say the same?

Cri. Yes, I should.

Soc. And what would you say that the kingly art does? If medicine were supposed to have supreme authority over the subordinate arts, and I were to ask you a similar question about that, you would say—it produces health?

Cri. I should.

Soc. And what of your own art of husbandry, supposing that to have supreme authority over the subject arts—what does that do? Does it not supply us with the fruits of the earth? [292]

Cri. Yes.

Soc. And what does the kingly art do when invested with supreme power? Perhaps you may not be ready with an answer?

Cri. Indeed I am not, Socrates.

Soc. No more were we, Crito. But at any rate you know that if this is the art which we were seeking, it ought to be useful.

Cri. Certainly.

Soc. And surely it ought to do us some good?

Cri. Certainly, Socrates.

Soc. And Cleinias and I had arrived at the conclusion that knowledge of some kind is the only good.

Cri. Yes, that was what you were saying.

Soc. All the other results of politics, and they are many, as for example, wealth, freedom, tranquillity, were neither good nor evil in themselves; but the political science ought to make us wise, and impart knowledge to us, if that is the science which is likely to do us good, and make us happy.

Cri. Yes; that was the conclusion at which you had arrived, according to your report of the conversation.

Soc. And does the kingly art make men wise and good?

Cri. Why not, Socrates?

Soc. What, all men, and in every respect? and teach them all the arts,—carpentering, and cobbling, and the rest of them?

Cri. I think not, Socrates.

Soc. But then what is this knowledge, and what are we to do with it? For it is not the source of any works which are neither good nor evil, and gives no knowledge, but the knowledge of itself; what then can it be, and what are we to do with it? Shall we say, Crito, that it is the knowledge by which we are to make other men good?

Cri. By all means.

Soc. And in what will they be good and useful? Shall we repeat that they will make others good, and that these others will make others again, without ever determining in what they are to be good; for we have put aside the results of politics, as they are called. This is the old, old song over again; and we are just as far as ever, if not farther, from the knowledge of the art or science of happiness.

Cri. Indeed, Socrates, you do appear to have got into a great perplexity.

Soc. Thereupon, Crito, seeing that I was on the point of shipwreck, [293] I lifted up my voice, and earnestly entreated and called upon the strangers to save me and the youth from the whirlpool of the argument; they were our Castor and Pollux, I said, and they should be serious, and show us in sober earnest what that knowledge was which would enable us to pass the rest of our lives in happiness.

Cri. And did Euthydemus show you this knowledge?

Soc. Yes, indeed; he proceeded in a lofty strain to the following effect: Would you rather, Socrates, said he, that I should show you this knowledge about which you have been doubting, or shall I prove that you already have it?

What, I said, are you blessed with such a power as this?

Indeed I am.

Then I would much rather that you should prove me to have such a knowledge; at my time of life that will be more agreeable than having to learn.

Then tell me, he said, do you know anything?

Yes, I said, I know many things, but not anything of much importance.

That will do, he said: And would you admit that anything is what it is, and at the same time is not what it is?

Certainly not.

And did you not say that you knew something?

I did.

If you know, you are knowing.

Certainly, of the knowledge which I have.

That makes no difference;—and must you not, if you are knowing, know all things?

Certainly not, I said, for there are many other things which I do not know.

And if you do not know, you are not knowing.

Yes, friend, of that which I do not know.

Still you are not knowing, and you said just now that you were knowing; and therefore you are and are not at the same time, and in reference to the same things.

A pretty clatter, as men say, Euthydemus, this of yours! and will you explain how I possess that knowledge for which we were seeking? Do you mean to say that the same thing cannot be and also not be; and therefore, since I know one thing, that I know all, for I cannot be knowing and not knowing at the same time, and if I know all things, then I must have the knowledge for which we are seeking—May I assume this to be your ingenious notion?

Out of your own mouth, Socrates, you are convicted, he said.

Well, but, Euthydemus, I said, has that never happened to you? for if I am only in the same case with you and our beloved Dionysodorus, I cannot complain. Tell me, then, you two, do you not know some things, and not know others?

Certainly not, Socrates, said Dionysodorus.

What do you mean, I said; do you know nothing?

Nay, he replied, we do know something.

[294] Then, I said, you know all things, if you know anything?

Yes, all things, he said; and that is as true of you as of us.

O, indeed, I said, what a wonderful thing, and what a great blessing! And do all other men know all things or nothing?

Certainly, he replied; they cannot know some things, and not know others, and be at the same time knowing and not knowing.

Then what is the inference? I said.

They all know all things, he replied, if they know one thing.

O heavens, Dionysodorus, I said, I see now that you are in earnest; hardly have I got you to that point. And do you really and truly know all things, including carpentering and leather-cutting?

Certainly, he said.

And do you know stitching?

Yes, by the gods, we do, and cobbling, too.

And do you know things such as the numbers of the stars and of the sand?

Certainly; did you think we should say no to that?

By Zeus, said Ctesippus, interrupting, I only wish that you would give me some proof which would enable me to know whether you speak truly.

What proof shall I give you? he said.

Will you tell me how many teeth Euthydemus has? and Euthydemus shall tell how many teeth you have.

Will you not take our word that we know all things?

Certainly not, said Ctesippus: you must further tell us this one thing, and then we shall know that you are speaking the truth; if you tell us the number, and we count them, and you are found to be right, we will believe the rest. They fancied that Ctesippus was making game of them, and they refused, and they would only say in answer to each of his ques-

tions, that they knew all things. For at last Ctesippus began to throw off all restraint; no question in fact was too bad for him; he would ask them if they knew the foulest things, and they, like wild boars, came rushing on his blows, and fearlessly replied that they did. At last, Crito, I too was carried away by my incredulity, and asked Euthydemus whether Dionysodorus could dance.

Certainly, he replied.

And can he vault among swords, and turn upon a wheel, at his age? has he got to such a height of skill as that?

He can do anything, he said.

And did you always know this?

Always, he said.

When you were children, and at your birth?

[295] They both said that they did.

This we could not believe. And Euthydemus said: You are incredulous, Socrates.

Yes, I said, and I might well be incredulous, if I did not know you to be wise men.

But if you will answer, he said, I will make you confess to similar marvels.

Well, I said, there is nothing that I should like better than to be self-convicted of this, for if I am really a wise man, which I never knew before, and you will prove to me that I know and have always known all things, nothing in life would be a greater gain to me.

Answer then, he said.

Ask, I said, and I will answer.

Do you know something, Socrates, or nothing?

Something, I said.

And do you know with what you know, or with something else?

With what I know; and I suppose that you mean with my soul?

Are you not ashamed, Socrates, of asking a question when you are asked one?

Well, I said; but then what am I to do? for I will do whatever you bid; when I do not know what you are asking, you tell me to answer nevertheless, and not to ask again.

Why, you surely have some notion of my meaning, he said.

Yes, I replied.

Well, then, answer according to your notion of my meaning.

Yes, I said; but if the question which you ask in one sense is understood and answered by me in another, will that please you—if I answer what is not to the point?

That will please me very well; but will not please you equally well, as I imagine.

I certainly will not answer unless I understand you, I said.

You will not answer, he said, according to your view of the meaning, because you will be prating, and are an ancient.

Now I saw that he was getting angry with me for drawing distinctions, when he wanted to catch me in his springes of words. And I remembered that Connus was always angry with me when I opposed him, and then he neglected me, because he thought that I was stupid; and as I was intending to go to Euthydemus as a pupil, I reflected that I had better let him have his way, as he might think me a blockhead, and refuse to take me. So I said: You are a far better dialectician than myself, Euthydemus, for I have never made a profession of the art, and therefore do as you say; ask your questions once more, and I will answer.

Answer then, he said, again, whether you know what you know with something, or with nothing.

Yes, I said; I know with my soul.

[296] The man will answer more than the question; for I did not ask you, he said, with what you know, but whether you know with something.

Again I replied, Through ignorance I have answered too much, but I hope that you will forgive me. And now I will answer simply that I always know what I know with something.

And is that something, he rejoined, always the same, or sometimes one thing, and sometimes another thing?

Always, I replied, when I know, I know with this.

Will you not cease adding to your answers?

My fear is that this word "always" may get us into trouble.

You, perhaps, but certainly not us. And now answer: Do you always know with this?

Always; since I am required to withdraw the words "when I know."

You always know with this, or, always knowing, do you know some things with this, and some things with something else, or do you know all things with this?

All that I know, I replied, I know with this.

There again, Socrates, he said, the addition is superfluous.

Well, then, I said, I will take away the words "that I know."

Nay, take nothing away; I desire no favours of you; but let me ask: Would you be able to know all things, if you did not know all things?

Quite impossible.

And now, he said, you may add on whatever you like, for you confess that you know all things.

I suppose that is true, I said, if my qualification implied in the words "that I know" is not allowed to stand; and so I do know all things.

And have you not admitted that you always know all things with that which you know, whether you make the addition of "when you know them" or not? for you have acknowledged that you have always and at once known all things, that is to say, when you were a child, and at your birth, and when you were growing up, and before you were born, and before the heaven and earth existed, you knew all things, if you always know them; and I swear that you shall always continue to know all things, if I am of the mind to make you.

But I hope that you will be of that mind, reverend Euthydemus, I said, if you are really speaking the truth, and yet I a little doubt your power to make good your words unless you have the help of your brother Dionysodorus; then you may do it. Tell me now, both of you, for although in the main I cannot doubt that I really do know all things, when I am told so by men of your prodigious wisdom—how can I say that I know such things, Euthydemus, as that the good are unjust; come, do I know that or not?

Certainly, you know that.

What do I know?

That the good are not unjust.

[297] Quite true, I said; and that I have always known; but the question is, where did I learn that the good are unjust?

Nowhere, said Dionysodorus.

Then, I said, I do not know this.

You are ruining the argument, said Euthydemus to Dionysodorus; he will be proved not to know, and then after all he will be knowing and not knowing at the same time.

Dionysodorus blushed.

I turned to the other, and said, What do you think, Euthydemus? Does not your omniscient brother appear to you to have made a mistake?

What, replied Dionysodorus in a moment; am I the brother of Euthydemus?

Thereupon I said, Please not to interrupt, my good friend, or prevent Euthydemus from proving to me that I know the good to be unjust; such a lesson you might at least allow me to learn.

You are running away, Socrates, said Dionysodorus, and refusing to answer.

No wonder, I said, for I am not a match for

one of you, and *a fortiori* I must run away from two. I am no Heracles; and even Heracles could not fight against the Hydra, who was a she-Sophist, and had the wit to shoot up many new heads when one of them was cut off; especially when he saw a second monster of a sea-crab, who was also a Sophist, and appeared to have newly arrived from a sea-voyage, bearing down upon him from the left, opening his mouth and biting. When the monster was growing troublesome he called Iolaus, his nephew, to his help, who ably succoured him; but if my Iolaus, who is my brother Patrocles [the statuary], were to come, he would only make a bad business worse.

And now that you have delivered yourself of this strain, said Dionysodorus, will you inform me whether Iolaus was the nephew of Heracles any more than he is yours?

I suppose that I had best answer you, Dionysodorus, I said, for you will insist on asking—that I pretty well know—out of envy, in order to prevent me from learning the wisdom of Euthydemus.

Then answer me, he said.

Well then, I said, I can only reply that Iolaus was not my nephew at all, but the nephew of Heracles; and his father was not my brother Patrocles, but Iphicles, who has a name rather like his, and was the brother of Heracles.

And is Patrocles, he said, your brother?

Yes, I said, he is my half-brother, the son of my mother, but not of my father.

Then he is and is not your brother.

Not by the same father, my good man, I said, for Chaeredemus was his father, and mine was Sophroniscus.

And was Sophroniscus a father, and Chaeredemus also?

Yes, I said; the former was my father, and the latter his.

[298] Then, he said, Chaeredemus is not a father.

He is not my father, I said.

But can a father be other than a father? or are you the same as a stone?

I certainly do not think that I am a stone, I said, though I am afraid that you may prove me to be one.

Are you not other than a stone?

I am.

And being other than a stone, you are not a stone; and being other than gold, you are not gold?

Very true.

And so Chaeredemus, he said, being other than a father, is not a father?

I suppose that he is not a father, I replied.

For if, said Euthydemus, taking up the argument, Chaeredemus is a father, then Sophroniscus, being other than a father, is not a father; and you, Socrates, are without a father.

Ctesippus, here taking up the argument, said: And is not your father in the same case, for he is other than my father?

Assuredly not, said Euthydemus.

Then he is the same?

He is the same.

I cannot say that I like the connection; but is he only my father, Euthydemus, or is he the father of all other men?

Of all other men, he replied. Do you suppose the same person to be a father and not a father?

Certainly, I did so imagine, said Ctesippus.

And do you suppose that gold is not gold, or that a man is not a man?

They are not *"in pari materia,"* Euthydemus, said Ctesippus, and you had better take care, for it is monstrous to suppose that your father is the father of all.

But he is, he replied.

What, of men only, said Ctesippus, or of horses and of all other animals?

Of all, he said.

And your mother, too, is the mother of all?

Yes, our mother too.

Yes; and your mother has a progeny of sea-urchins then?

Yes; and yours, he said.

And gudgeons and puppies and pigs are your brothers?

And yours too.

And your papa is a dog?

And so is yours, he said.

If you will answer my questions, said Dionysodorus, I will soon extract the same admissions from you, Ctesippus. You say that you have a dog.

Yes, a villain of a one, said Ctesippus.

And he has puppies?

Yes, and they are very like himself.

And the dog is the father of them?

Yes, he said, I certainly saw him and the mother of the puppies come together.

And is he not yours?

To be sure he is.

Then he is a father, and he is yours; ergo, he is your father, and the puppies are your brothers.

Let me ask you one little question more, said Dionysodorus, quickly interposing, in order that Ctesippus might not get in his word: You beat this dog?

Ctesippus said, laughing, Indeed I do; and I only wish that I could beat you instead of him.

[299] Then you beat your father, he said.

I should have far more reason to beat yours, said Ctesippus; what could he have been thinking of when he begat such wise sons? much good has this father of you and your brethren the puppies got out of this wisdom of yours.

But neither he nor you, Ctesippus, have any need of much good.

And have you no need, Euthydemus? he said.

Neither I nor any other man; for tell me now, Ctesippus, if you think it good or evil for a man who is sick to drink medicine when he wants it; or to go to war armed rather than unarmed.

Good, I say. And yet I know that I am going to be caught in one of your charming puzzles.

That, he replied, you will discover, if you answer; since you admit medicine to be good for a man to drink, when wanted, must it not be good for him to drink as much as possible; when he takes his medicine, a cartload of hellebore will not be too much for him?

Ctesippus said: Quite so, Euthydemus, that is to say, if he who drinks is as big as the statue of Delphi.

And seeing that in war to have arms is a good thing, he ought to have as many spears and shields as possible?

Very true, said Ctesippus; and do you think, Euthydemus, that he ought to have one shield only, and one spear?

I do.

And would you arm Geryon and Briareus in that way? Considering that you and your companion fight in armour, I thought that you would have known better. . . . Here Euthydemus held his peace, but Dionysodorus returned to the previous answer of Ctesippus and said:—

Do you not think that the possession of gold is a good thing?

Yes, said Ctesippus, and the more the better.

And to have money everywhere and always is a good?

Certainly, a great good, he said.

And you admit gold to be a good?

Certainly, he replied.

And ought not a man then to have gold everywhere and always, and as much as possible in himself, and may he not be deemed the happiest of men who has three talents of gold in his belly, and a talent in his pate, and a stater of gold in either eye?

Yes, Euthydemus, said Ctesippus; and the Scythians reckon those who have gold in their own skulls to be the happiest and bravest of men (that is only another instance of your manner of speaking about the dog and father), and what is still more extraordinary, they drink out of their own skulls gilt, and see the inside of them, and hold their own head in their hands.

[300] And do the Scythians and others see that which has the quality of vision, or that which has not? said Euthydemus.

That which has the quality of vision clearly.

And [1] you also see that which has the quality of vision? he said.

Yes, I do.

Then do you see our garments?

Yes.

Then our garments have the quality of vision.

They can see to any extent, said Ctesippus.

What can they see?

Nothing; but you, my sweet man, may perhaps imagine that they do not see; and certainly, Euthydemus, you do seem to me to have been caught napping when you were not asleep, and that if it be possible to speak and say nothing—you are doing so.

And may there not be a silence of the speaker? said Dionysodorus.

Impossible, said Ctesippus.

Or a speaking of the silent?

That is still more impossible, he said.

But when you speak of stones, wood, iron bars, do you not speak of the silent?

Not when I pass a smithy; for then the iron bars make a tremendous noise and outcry if they are touched: so that here your wisdom is strangely mistaken, please, however, to tell me how you can be silent when speaking (I thought that Ctesippus was put upon his mettle because Cleinias was present).

When you are silent, said Euthydemus, is there not a silence of all things?

Yes, he said.

But if speaking things are included in all things, then the speaking are silent.

What, said Ctesippus; then all things are not silent?

Certainly not, said Euthydemus.

Then, my good friend, do they all speak?

[1] Note: the ambiguity of δυνατὰ ὁρᾶν, "things visible and able to see," σιγῶντα λέγειν, "the speaking of the silent," the silent denoting either the speaker or the subject of the speech, cannot be perfectly rendered in English. Compare Aristotle, *Sophistical Refutations*, iv. 166ᵃ 12-14.

Yes; those which speak.

Nay, said Ctesippus, but the question which I ask is whether all things are silent or speak?

Neither and both, said Dionysodorus, quickly interposing; I am sure that you will be "non-plussed" at that answer.

Here Ctesippus, as his manner was, burst into a roar of laughter; he said, That brother of yours, Euthydemus, has got into a dilemma; all is over with him. This delighted Cleinias, whose laughter made Ctesippus ten times as uproarious; but I cannot help thinking that the rogue must have picked up this answer from them; for there has been no wisdom like theirs in our time. Why do you laugh, Cleinias, I said, at such solemn and beautiful things?

Why, Socrates, said Dionysodorus, did you ever see a beautiful thing?

Yes, Dionysodorus, I replied, I have seen many.

[301] Were they other than the beautiful, or the same as the beautiful?

Now I was in a great quandary at having to answer this question, and I thought that I was rightly served for having opened my mouth at all: I said however, They are not the same as absolute beauty, but they have beauty present with each of them.

And are you an ox because an ox is present with you, or are you Dionysodorus, because Dionysodorus is present with you?

God forbid, I replied.

But how, he said, by reason of one thing being present with another, will one thing be another?

Is that your difficulty? I said. For I was beginning to imitate their skill, on which my heart was set.

Of course, he replied, I and all the world are in a difficulty about the non-existent.

What do you mean, Dionysodorus? I said. Is not the honourable honourable and the base base?

That, he said, is as I please.

And do you please?

Yes, he said.

And you will admit that the same is the same, and the other other; for surely the other is not the same; I should imagine that even a child will hardly deny the other to be other. But I think, Dionysodorus, that you must have intentionally missed the last question; for in general you and your brother seem to me to be good workmen in your own department, and to do the dialectician's business excellently well.

What, said he, is the business of a good work-

man? tell me, in the first place, whose business is hammering?

The smith's.

And whose the making of pots?

The potter's.

And who has to kill and skin and mince and boil and roast?

The cook, I said.

And if a man does his business he does rightly?

Certainly.

And the business of the cook is to cut up and skin; you have admitted that?

Yes, I have admitted that, but you must not be too hard upon me.

Then if some one were to kill, mince, boil, roast the cook, he would do his business, and if he were to hammer the smith, and make a pot of the potter, he would do their business.

Poseidon, I said, this is the crown of wisdom; can I ever hope to have such wisdom of my own?

And would you be able, Socrates, to recognize this wisdom when it has become your own?

Certainly, I said, if you will allow me.

What, he said, do you think that you know what is your own?

Yes, I do, subject to your correction; for you are the bottom, and Euthydemus is the top, of all my wisdom.

Is not that which you would deem your own, he said, that which you have in your own power, and which you are able to use as you would desire, [302] for example, an ox or a sheep—would you not think that which you could sell and give and sacrifice to any god whom you pleased, to be your own, and that which you could not give or sell or sacrifice you would think not to be in your own power?

Yes, I said (for I was certain that something good would come out of the questions, which I was impatient to hear); yes, such things, and such things only are mine.

Yes, he said, and you would mean by animals living beings?

Yes, I said.

You agree then, that those animals only are yours with which you have the power to do all these things which I was just naming?

I agree.

Then, after a pause, in which he seemed to be lost in the contemplation of something great, he said: Tell me, Socrates, have you an ancestral Zeus? Here, anticipating the final move, like a person caught in a net, who gives a desperate twist that he may get away, I said: No, Dionysodorus, I have not.

What a miserable man you must be then, he said; you are not an Athenian at all if you have no ancestral gods or temples, or any other mark of gentility.

Nay, Dionysodorus, I said, do not be rough; good words, if you please; in the way of religion I have altars and temples, domestic and ancestral, and all that other Athenians have.

And have not other Athenians, he said, an ancestral Zeus?

That name, I said, is not to be found among the Ionians, whether colonists or citizens of Athens; an ancestral Apollo there is, who is the father of Ion, and a family Zeus, and a Zeus guardian of the phratry, and an Athene guardian of the phratry. But the name of ancestral Zeus is unknown to us.

No matter, said Dionysodorus, for you admit that you have Apollo, Zeus, and Athene.

Certainly, I said.

And they are your gods, he said.

Yes, I said, my lords and ancestors.

At any rate they are yours, he said, did you not admit that?

I did, I said; what is going to happen to me?

And are not these gods animals? for you admit that all things which have life are animals; and have not these gods life?

They have life, I said.

Then are they not animals?

They are animals, I said.

And you admitted that of animals those are yours which you could give away or sell or offer in sacrifice, as you pleased?

I did admit that, Euthydemus, and I have no way of escape.

[303] Well then, said he, if you admit that Zeus and the other gods are yours, can you sell them or give them away or do what you will with them, as you would with other animals?

At this I was quite struck dumb, Crito, and lay prostrate. Ctesippus came to the rescue.

Bravo, Heracles, brave words, said he.

Bravo Heracles, or is Heracles a Bravo? said Dionysodorus.

Poseidon, said Ctesippus, what awful distinctions. I will have no more of them; the pair are invincible.

Then, my dear Crito, there was universal applause of the speakers and their words, and what with laughing and clapping of hands and rejoicings the two men were quite overpowered; for hitherto their partisans only had cheered at each successive hit, but now the whole company shouted with delight until the columns of the Lyceum returned the sound, seeming to sympathize in their joy. To such a pitch was I affected myself, that I made a speech, in which I acknowledged that I had never seen the like of their wisdom; I was their devoted servant, and fell to praising and admiring of them. What marvellous dexterity of wit, I said, enabled you to acquire this great perfection in such a short time? There is much, indeed, to admire in your words, Euthydemus and Dionysodorus, but there is nothing that I admire more than your magnanimous disregard of any opinion—whether of the many, or of the grave and reverend seigniors—you regard only those who are like yourselves. And I do verily believe that there are few who are like you, and who would approve of such arguments; the majority of mankind are so ignorant of their value, that they would be more ashamed of employing them in the refutation of others than of being refuted by them. I must further express my approval of your kind and public-spirited denial of all differences, whether of good and evil, white or black, or any other; the result of which is that, as you say, every mouth is sewn up, not excepting your own, which graciously follows the example of others; and thus all ground of offence is taken away. But what appears to me to be more than all is, that this art and invention of yours has been so admirably contrived by you, that in a very short time it can be imparted to any one. I observed that Ctesippus learned to imitate you in no time. [304] Now this quickness of attainment is an excellent thing; but at the same time I would advise you not to have any more public entertainments; there is a danger that men may undervalue an art which they have so easy an opportunity of acquiring; the exhibition would be best of all, if the discussion were confined to your two selves; but if there must be an audience, let him only be present who is willing to pay a handsome fee;—you should be careful of this;—and if you are wise, you will also bid your disciples discourse with no man but you and themselves. For only what is rare is valuable; and "water," which, as Pindar says, is the "best of all things," is also the cheapest. And now I have only to request that you will receive Cleinias and me among your pupils.

Such was the discussion, Crito; and after a few more words had passed between us we went away. I hope that you will come to them with me, since they say that they are able to teach any one who will give them money; no age or want of capacity is an impediment. And I must repeat one thing which they said, for your especial benefit,—that the learning of their art did not at all interfere with the business of money-making.

Cri. Truly, Socrates, though I am curious and ready to learn, yet I fear that I am not like-minded with Euthydemus, but one of the other sort, who, as you were saying, would rather be refuted by such arguments than use them in refutation of others. And though I may appear ridiculous in venturing to advise you, I think that you may as well hear what was said to me by a man of very considerable pretensions—he was a professor of legal oratory—who came away from you while I was walking up and down. "Crito," said he to me, "are you giving no attention to these wise men?" "No, indeed," I said to him; "I could not get within hearing of them—there was such a crowd." "You would have heard something worth hearing if you had." "What was that?" I said. "You would have heard the greatest masters of the art of rhetoric discoursing." "And what did you think of them?" I said. "What did I think of them?" he said:—"theirs was the sort of discourse which anybody might hear from men who were playing the fool, and making much ado about nothing." That was the expression which he used. "Surely," I said, "philosophy is a charming thing." *[305]* "Charming!" he said; "what simplicity! philosophy is nought; and I think that if you had been present you would have been ashamed of your friend—his conduct was so very strange in placing himself at the mercy of men who care not what they say, and fasten upon every word. And these, as I was telling you, are supposed to be the most eminent professors of their time. But the truth is, Crito, that the study itself and the men themselves are utterly mean and ridiculous." Now censure of the pursuit, Socrates, whether coming from him or from others, appears to me to be undeserved; but as to the impropriety of holding a public discussion with such men, there, I confess that, in my opinion, he was in the right.

Soc. O Crito, they are marvellous men; but what was I going to say? First of all let me know;—What manner of man was he who came up to you and censured philosophy; was he an orator who himself practises in the courts, or an instructor of orators, who makes the speeches with which they do battle?

Cri. He was certainly not an orator, and I doubt whether he had ever been into court; but they say that he knows the business, and is a clever man, and composes wonderful speeches.

Soc. Now I understand, Crito; he is one of an amphibious class, whom I was on the point of mentioning—one of those whom Prodicus describes as on the border-ground between philosophers and statesmen—they think that they are the wisest of all men, and that they are generally esteemed the wisest; nothing but the rivalry of the philosophers stands in their way; and they are of the opinion that if they can prove the philosophers to be good for nothing, no one will dispute their title to the palm of wisdom, for that they are themselves really the wisest, although they are apt to be mauled by Euthydemus and his friends, when they get hold of them in conversation. This opinion which they entertain of their own wisdom is very natural; for they have a certain amount of philosophy, and a certain amount of political wisdom; there is reason in what they say, for they argue that they have just enough of both, and so they keep out of the way of all risks and conflicts and reap the fruits of their wisdom.

Cri. What do you say of them, Socrates? There is certainly something specious in that notion of theirs.

Soc. Yes, Crito, there is more speciousness than truth; they cannot be made to understand the nature of intermediates. *[306]* For all persons or things, which are intermediate between two other things, and participate in both of them—if one of these two things is good and the other evil, are better than the one and worse than the other; but if they are in a mean between two good things which do not tend to the same end, they fall short of either of their component elements in the attainment of their ends. Only in the case when the two component elements which do not tend to the same end are evil is the participant better than either. Now, if philosophy and political action are both good, but tend to different ends, and they participate in both, and are in a mean between them, then they are talking nonsense, for they are worse than either; or, if the one be good and the other evil, they are better than the one and worse than the other; only on the supposition that they are both evil could there be any truth in what they say. I do not think that they will admit that their two pursuits are either wholly or partly evil; but the truth is, that these philosopher-politicians who aim at both fall short of both in the attainment of their respective ends, and are really third, although they would like to stand first. There is no need, however, to be angry at this ambition of theirs—which may be forgiven; for every man ought to be loved who says and manfully pursues and works out anything which is at all like wisdom: at the same time we shall do well to see them as they really are.

Cri. I have often told you, Socrates, that I am in a constant difficulty about my two sons. What am I to do with them? There is no hurry about the younger one, who is only a child; but the other, Critobulus, is getting on, and needs some one who will improve him. I cannot help thinking, when I hear you talk, that there is a sort of madness in many of our anxieties about our children:—in the first place, about marrying a wife of good family to be the mother of them, and then about heaping up money for them—and yet taking no care about their education. But then again, when I contemplate any of those who pretend to educate others, I am amazed. To me, if I am to confess the truth, *[307]* they all seem to be such outrageous beings: so that I do not know how I can advise the youth to study philosophy.

Soc. Dear Crito, do you not know that in every profession the inferior sort are numerous and good for nothing, and the good are few and beyond all price: for example, are not gymnastic and rhetoric and money-making and the art of the general, noble arts?

Cri. Certainly they are, in my judgment.

Soc. Well, and do you not see that in each of these arts the many are ridiculous performers?

Cri. Yes, indeed, that is very true.

Soc. And will you on this account shun all these pursuits yourself and refuse to allow them to your son?

Cri. That would not be reasonable, Socrates.

Soc. Do you then be reasonable, Crito, and do not mind whether the teachers of philosophy are good or bad, but think only of philosophy herself. Try and examine her well and truly, and if she be evil seek to turn away all men from her, and not your sons only; but if she be what I believe that she is, then follow her and serve her, you and your house, as the saying is, and be of good cheer.

CRATYLUS

PERSONS OF THE DIALOGUE: SOCRATES, HERMOGENES, CRATYLUS

[383] Hermogenes. SUPPOSE that we make Socrates a party to the argument?

Cratylus. If you please.

Her. I should explain to you, Socrates, that our friend Cratylus has been arguing about names; he says that they are natural and not conventional; not a portion of the human voice which men agree to use; but that there is a truth or correctness in them, which is the same for Hellenes as for barbarians. Whereupon I ask him, whether his own name of Cratylus is a true name or not, and he answers "Yes." And Socrates? "Yes." Then every man's name, as I tell him, is that which he is called. To this he replies—"If all the world were to call you Hermogenes, that would not be your name." And when I am anxious to have a further explanation he is ironical and mysterious, *[384]* and seems to imply that he has a notion of his own about the matter, if he would only tell, and could entirely convince me, if he chose to be intelligible. Tell me, Socrates, what this oracle means; or rather tell me, if you will be so good, what is your own view of the truth or correctness of names, which I would far sooner hear.

Socrates. Son of Hipponicus, there is an ancient saying, that "hard is the knowledge of the good." And the knowledge of names is a great part of knowledge. If I had not been poor, I might have heard the fifty-drachma course of the great Prodicus, which is a complete education in grammar and language—these are his own words—and then I should have been at once able to answer your question about the correctness of names. But, indeed, I have only heard the single-drachma course, and therefore, I do not know the truth about such mat-

ters; I will, however, gladly assist you and Cratylus in the investigation of them. When he declares that your name is not really Hermogenes, I suspect that he is only making fun of you;—he means to say that you are no true son of Hermes, because you are always looking after a fortune and never in luck. But, as I was saying, there is a good deal of difficulty in this sort of knowledge, and therefore we had better leave the question open until we have heard both sides.

Her. I have often talked over this matter, both with Cratylus and others, and cannot convince myself that there is any principle of correctness in names other than convention and agreement; any name which you give, in my opinion, is the right one, and if you change that and give another, the new name is as correct as the old—we frequently change the names of our slaves, and the newly-imposed name is as good as the old: for there is no name given to anything by nature; all is convention and habit of the users;—such is my view. But if I am mistaken I shall be happy to hear and learn of Cratylus, or of any one else.

[385] Soc. I dare say that you be right, Hermogenes: let us see;—Your meaning is, that the name of each thing is only that which anybody agrees to call it?

Her. That is my notion.

Soc. Whether the giver of the name be an individual or a city?

Her. Yes.

Soc. Well, now, let me take an instance;—suppose that I call a man a horse or a horse a man, you mean to say that a man will be rightly called a horse by me individually, and rightly called a man by the rest of the world; and a horse again would be rightly called a man by me and a horse by the world:—that is your meaning?

Her. He would, according to my view.

Soc. But how about truth, then? you would acknowledge that there is in words a true and a false?

Her. Certainly.

Soc. And there are true and false propositions?

Her. To be sure.

Soc. And a true proposition says that which is, and a false proposition says that which is not?

Her. Yes; what other answer is possible?

Soc. Then in a proposition there is a true and false?

Her. Certainly.

Soc. But is a proposition true as a whole only, and are the parts untrue?

Her. No; the parts are true as well as the whole.

Soc. Would you say the large parts and not the smaller ones, or every part?

Her. I should say that every part is true.

Soc. Is a proposition resolvable into any part smaller than a name?

Her. No; that is the smallest.

Soc. Then the name is a part of the true proposition?

Her. Yes.

Soc. Yes, and a true part, as you say.

Her. Yes.

Soc. And is not the part of a falsehood also a falsehood?

Her. Yes.

Soc. Then, if propositions may be true and false, names may be true and false?

Her. So we must infer.

Soc. And the name of anything is that which any one affirms to be the name?

Her. Yes.

Soc. And will there be so many names of each thing as everybody says that there are? and will they be true names at the time of uttering them?

Her. Yes, Socrates, I can conceive no correctness of names other than this; you give one name, and I another; and in different cities and countries there are different names for the same things; Hellenes differ from barbarians in their use of names, and the several Hellenic tribes from one another.

Soc. But would you say, Hermogenes, that the things differ as the names differ? [386]

and are they relative to individuals, as Protagoras tells us? For he says that man is the measure of all things, and that things are to me as they appear to me, and that they are to you as they appear to you. Do you agree with him, or would you say that things have a permanent essence of their own?

Her. There have been times, Socrates, when I have been driven in my perplexity to take refuge with Protagoras; not that I agree with him at all.

Soc. What! have you ever been driven to admit that there was no such thing as a bad man?

Her. No, indeed; but I have often had reason to think that there are very bad men, and a good many of them.

Soc. Well, and have you ever found any very good ones?

Her. Not many.

Soc. Still you have found them?

Her. Yes.

Soc. And would you hold that the very good were the very wise, and the very evil very foolish? Would that be your view?

Her. It would.

Soc. But if Protagoras is right, and the truth is that things are as they appear to any one, how can some of us be wise and some of us foolish?

Her. Impossible.

Soc. And if, on the other hand, wisdom and folly are really distinguishable, you will allow, I think, that the assertion of Protagoras can hardly be correct. For if what appears to each man is true to him, one man cannot in reality be wiser than another.

Her. He cannot.

Soc. Nor will you be disposed to say with Euthydemus, that all things equally belong to all men at the same moment and always; for neither on his view can there be some good and other bad, if virtue and vice are always equally to be attributed to all.

Her. There cannot.

Soc. But if neither is right, and things are not relative to individuals, and all things do not equally belong to all at the same moment and always, they must be supposed to have their own proper and permanent essence: they are not in relation to us, or influenced by us, fluctuating according to our fancy, but they are independent, and maintain to their own essence the relation prescribed by nature.

Her. I think, Socrates, that you have said the truth.

Soc. Does what I am saying apply only to the things themselves, or equally to the actions which proceed from them? Are not actions also a class of being?

Her. Yes, the actions are real as well as the things.

[387] *Soc.* Then the actions also are done according to their proper nature, and not according to our opinion of them? In cutting, for example, we do not cut as we please, and with any chance instrument; but we cut with the proper instrument only, and according to the natural process of cutting; and the natural process is right and will succeed, but any other will fail and be of no use at all.

Her. I should say that the natural way is the right way.

Soc. Again, in burning, not every way is the right way; but the right way is the natural way, and the right instrument the natural instrument.

Her. True.

Soc. And this holds good of all actions?

Her. Yes.

Soc. And speech is a kind of action?

Her. True.

Soc. And will a man speak correctly who speaks as he pleases? Will not the successful speaker rather be he who speaks in the natural way of speaking, and as things ought to be spoken, and with the natural instrument? Any other mode of speaking will result in error and failure.

Her. I quite agree with you.

Soc. And is not naming a part of speaking? for in giving names men speak.

Her. That is true.

Soc. And if speaking is a sort of action and has a relation to acts, is not naming also a sort of action?

Her. True.

Soc. And we saw that actions were not relative to ourselves, but had a special nature of their own?

Her. Precisely.

Soc. Then the argument would lead us to infer that names ought to be given according to a natural process, and with a proper instrument, and not at our pleasure: in this and no other way shall we name with success.

Her. I agree.

Soc. But again, that which has to be cut has to be cut with something?

Her. Yes.

Soc. And that which has to be woven or pierced has to be woven or pierced with something?

Her. Certainly.

Soc. And that which has to be named has to be named with something?

Her. True.

Soc. What is that with which we pierce?

Her. An awl.

[388] *Soc.* And with which we weave?

Her. A shuttle.

Soc. And with which we name?

Her. A name.

Soc. Very good: then a name is an instrument?

Her. Certainly.

Soc. Suppose that I ask, "What sort of instrument is a shuttle?" And you answer, "A weaving instrument."

Her. Well.

Soc. And I ask again, "What do we do when we weave?"—The answer is, that we separate or disengage the warp from the woof.

Her. Very true.

Soc. And may not a similar description be given of an awl, and of instruments in general?

Her. To be sure.

Soc. And now suppose that I ask a similar question about names: will you answer me? Regarding the name as an instrument, what do we do when we name?

Her. I cannot say.

Soc. Do we not give information to one another, and distinguish things according to their natures?

Her. Certainly we do.

Soc. Then a name is an instrument of teaching and of distinguishing natures, as the shuttle is of distinguishing the threads of the web.

Her. Yes.

Soc. And the shuttle is the instrument of the weaver?

Her. Assuredly.

Soc. Then the weaver will use the shuttle well—and well means like a weaver? and the teacher will use the name well—and well means like a teacher?

Her. Yes.

Soc. And when the weaver uses the shuttle, whose work will he be using well?

Her. That of the carpenter.

Soc. And is every man a carpenter, or the skilled only?

Her. Only the skilled.

Soc. And when the piercer uses the awl, whose work will he be using well?

Her. That of the smith.

Soc. And is every man a smith, or only the skilled?

Her. The skilled only.

Soc. And when the teacher uses the name, whose work will he be using?

Her. There again I am puzzled.

Soc. Cannot you at least say who gives us the names which we use?

Her. Indeed I cannot.

Soc. Does not the law seem to you to give us them?

Her. Yes, I suppose so.

Soc. Then the teacher, when he gives us a name, uses the work of the legislator?

Her. I agree.

Soc. And is every man a legislator, or the skilled only?

Her. The skilled only.

Soc. Then, Hermogenes, not every man is able to give a name, but only a maker of names; [389] and this is the legislator, who of all skilled artisans in the world is the rarest.

Her. True.

Soc. And how does the legislator make names? and to what does he look? Consider this in the light of the previous instances: to what does the carpenter look in making the shuttle? Does he not look to that which is naturally fitted to act as a shuttle?

Her. Certainly.

Soc. And suppose the shuttle to be broken in making, will he make another, looking to the broken one? or will he look to the form according to which he made the other?

Her. To the latter, I should imagine.

Soc. Might not that be justly called the true or ideal shuttle?

Her. I think so.

Soc. And whatever shuttles are wanted, for the manufacture of garments, thin or thick, of flaxen, woollen, or other material, ought all of them to have the true form of the shuttle; and whatever is the shuttle best adapted to each kind of work, that ought to be the form which the maker produces in each case.

Her. Yes.

Soc. And the same holds of other instruments: when a man has discovered the instrument which is naturally adapted to each work, he must express this natural form, and not others which he fancies, in the material, whatever it may be, which he employs; for example, he ought to know how to put into iron the forms of awls adapted by nature to their several uses?

Her. Certainly.

Soc. And how to put into wood forms of shuttles adapted by nature to their uses?

Her. True.

Soc. For the several forms of shuttles naturally answer to the several kinds of webs; and this is true of instruments in general.

Her. Yes.

Soc. Then, as to names: ought not our legislator also to know how to put the true natural names of each thing into sounds and syllables, and to make and give all names with a view to the ideal name, if he is to be a namer in any true sense? And we must remember that different legislators will not use the same syllables. For neither does every smith, although he may be making the same instrument for the same purpose, make them all of the same iron. The form must be the same, but the material may vary, and still the instrument may be equally good of whatever iron made, whether in Hellas or in a foreign country; [390]—there is no difference.

Her. Very true.

Soc. And the legislator, whether he be Hellene or barbarian, is not therefore to be deemed by you a worse legislator, provided he gives the true and proper form of the name in whatever syllables; this or that country makes no matter.

Her. Quite true.

Soc. But who then is to determine whether the proper form is given to the shuttle, whatever sort of wood may be used? the carpenter who makes, or the weaver who is to use them?

Her. I should say, he who is to use them, Socrates.

Soc. And who uses the work of the lyremaker? Will not he be the man who knows how to direct what is being done, and who will know also whether the work is being well done or not?

Her. Certainly.

Soc. And who is he?

Her. The player of the lyre.

Soc. And who will direct the shipwright?

Her. The pilot.

Soc. And who will be best able to direct the legislator in his work, and will know whether the work is well done, in this or any other country? Will not the user be the man?

Her. Yes.

Soc. And this is he who knows how to ask questions?

Her. Yes.

Soc. And how to answer them?

Her. Yes.

Soc. And him who knows how to ask and

answer you would call a dialectician?

Her. Yes; that would be his name.

Soc. Then the work of the carpenter is to make a rudder, and the pilot has to direct him, if the rudder is to be well made.

Her. True.

Soc. And the work of the legislator is to give names, and the dialectician must be his director if the names are to be rightly given?

Her. That is true.

Soc. Then, Hermogenes, I should say that this giving of names can be no such light matter as you fancy, or the work of light or chance persons; and Cratylus is right in saying that things have names by nature, and that not every man is an artificer of names, but he only who looks to the name which each thing by nature has, and is able to express the true forms of things in letters and syllables.

Her. I cannot answer you, Socrates; but I find a difficulty in changing my opinion all in a moment, [391] and I think that I should be more readily persuaded, if you would show me what this is which you term the natural fitness of names.

Soc. My good Hermogenes, I have none to show. Was I not telling you just now (but you have forgotten), that I knew nothing, and proposing to share the enquiry with you? But now that you and I have talked over the matter, a step has been gained; for we have discovered that names have by nature a truth, and that not every man knows how to give a thing a name.

Her. Very good.

Soc. And what is the nature of this truth or correctness of names? That, if you care to know, is the next question.

Her. Certainly, I care to know.

Soc. Then reflect.

Her. How shall I reflect?

Soc. The true way is to have the assistance of those who know, and you must pay them well both in money and in thanks; these are the Sophists, of whom your brother, Callias, has—rather dearly—bought the reputation of wisdom. But you have not yet come into your inheritance, and therefore you had better go to him, and beg and entreat him to tell you what he has learnt from Protagoras about the fitness of names.

Her. But how inconsistent should I be, if, whilst repudiating Protagoras and his *Truth*,[1] I were to attach any value to what he and his book affirm!

[1] *Truth* was the title of the book of Protagoras; cf. *Theaetetus*, 161.

Soc. Then if you despise him, you must learn of Homer and the poets.

Her. And where does Homer say anything about names, and what does he say?

Soc. He often speaks of them; notably and nobly in the places where he distinguishes the different names which Gods and men give to the same things. Does he not in these passages make a remarkable statement about the correctness of names? For the Gods must clearly be supposed to call things by their right and natural names; do you not think so?

Her. Why, of course they call them rightly, if they call them at all. But to what are you referring?

Soc. Do you not know what he says about the river in Troy who had a single combat with Hephaestus?

Whom the Gods call Xanthus, and men call Scamander.

[392] *Her.* I remember.

Soc. Well, and about this river—to know that he ought to be called Xanthus and not Scamander—is not that a solemn lesson? Or about the bird which, as he says,

The Gods call Chalcis, and men Cymindis:

to be taught how much more correct the name Chalcis is than the name Cymindis—do you deem that a light matter? Or about Batieia and Myrina? And there are many other observations of the same kind in Homer and other poets. Now, I think that this is beyond the understanding of you and me; but the names of Scamandrius and Astyanax, which he affirms to have been the names of Hector's son, are more within the range of human faculties, as I am disposed to think; and what the poet means by correctness may be more readily apprehended in that instance: you will remember I dare say the lines to which I refer.[2]

Her. I do.

Soc. Let me ask you, then, which did Homer think the more correct of the names given to Hector's son—Astyanax or Scamandrius?

Her. I do not know.

Soc. How would you answer, if you were asked whether the wise or the unwise are more likely to give correct names?

Her. I should say the wise, of course.

Soc. And are the men or the women of a city, taken as a class, the wiser?

Her. I should say, the men.

Soc. And Homer, as you know, says that the

[2] *Iliad,* vi. 402.

Trojan men called him Astyanax (king of the city); but if the men called him Astyanax, the other name of Scamandrius could only have been given to him by the women.

Her. That may be inferred.

Soc. And must not Homer have imagined the Trojans to be wiser than their wives?

Her. To be sure.

Soc. Then he must have thought Astyanax to be a more correct name for the boy than Scamandrius?

Her. Clearly.

Soc. And what is the reason of this? Let us consider:—does he not himself suggest a very good reason, when he says,

For he alone defended their city and long walls?

This appears to be a good reason for calling the son of the saviour king of the city which his father was saving, as Homer observes.

Her. I see.

Soc. Why, Hermogenes, I do not as yet see myself; and do you?

Her. No, indeed; not I.

[393] Soc. But tell me, friend, did not Homer himself also give Hector his name?

Her. What of that?

Soc. The name appears to me to be very nearly the same as the name of Astyanax—both are Hellenic; and a king (ἄναξ) and a holder (ἕκτωρ) have nearly the same meaning, and are both descriptive of a king; for a man is clearly the holder of that of which he is king; he rules, and owns, and holds it. But, perhaps, you may think that I am talking nonsense; and indeed I believe that I myself did not know what I meant when I imagined that I had found some indication of the opinion of Homer about the correctness of names.

Her. I assure you that I think otherwise, and I believe you to be on the right track.

Soc. There is reason, I think, in calling the lion's whelp a lion, and the foal of a horse a horse; I am speaking only of the ordinary course of nature, when an animal produces after his kind, and not of extraordinary births;—if contrary to nature a horse have a calf, then I should not call that a foal but a calf; nor do I call any inhuman birth a man, but only a natural birth. And the same may be said of trees and other things. Do you agree with me?

Her. Yes, I agree.

Soc. Very good. But you had better watch me and see that I do not play tricks with you. For on the same principle the son of a king is to be called a king. And whether the syllables.

of the name are the same or not the same, makes no difference, provided the meaning is retained; nor does the addition or subtraction of a letter make any difference so long as the essence of the thing remains in possession of the name and appears in it.

Her. What do you mean?

Soc. A very simple matter. I may illustrate my meaning by the names of letters, which you know are not the same as the letters themselves with the exception of the four ε, υ, ο, ω; the names of the rest, whether vowels or consonants, are made up of other letters which we add to them; but so long as we introduce the meaning, and there can be no mistake, the name of the letter is quite correct. Take, for example, the letter *beta*—the addition of η, τ, α, gives no offence, and does not prevent the whole name from having the value which the legislator intended—so well did he know how to give the letters names.

Her. I believe you are right.

Soc. And may not the same be said of a king? a king will often be the son of a king, *[394]* the good son or the noble son of a good or noble sire; and similarly the offspring of every kind, in the regular course of nature, is like the parent, and therefore has the same name. Yet the syllables may be disguised until they appear different to the ignorant person, and he may not recognize them, although they are the same, just as any one of us would not recognize the same drugs under different disguises of colour and smell, although to the physician, who regards the power of them, they are the same, and he is not put out by the addition; and in like manner the etymologist is not put out by the addition or transposition or subtraction of a letter or two, or indeed by the change of all the letters, for this need not interfere with the meaning. As was just now said, the names of Hector and Astyanax have only one letter alike, which is the τ, and yet they have the same meaning. And how little in common with the letters of their names has Archepolis (ruler of the city)—and yet the meaning is the same. And there are many other names which just mean "king." Again, there are several names for a general, as, for example, Agis (leader) and Polemarchus (chief in war) and Eupolemus (good warrior); and others which denote a physician, as Iatrocles (famous healer) and Acesimbrotus (curer of mortals); and there are many others which might be cited, differing in their syllables and letters, but having the same meaning. Would you not say so?

Her. Yes.

Soc. The same names, then, ought to be assigned to those who follow in the course of nature?

Her. Yes.

Soc. And what of those who follow out of the course of nature, and are prodigies? for example, when a good and religious man has an irreligious son, he ought to bear the name not of his father, but of the class to which he belongs, just as in the case which was before supposed of a horse foaling a calf.

Her. Quite true.

Soc. Then the irreligious son of a religious father should be called irreligious?

Her. Certainly.

Soc. He should not be called Theophilus (beloved of God) or Mnesitheus (mindful of God), or any of these names: if names are correctly given, his should have an opposite meaning.

Her. Certainly, Socrates.

Soc. Again, Hermogenes, there is Orestes (the man of the mountains) who appears to be rightly called; whether chance gave the name, or perhaps some poet who meant to express the brutality and fierceness and mountain wildness of his hero's nature.

[395] Her. That is very likely, Socrates.

Soc. And his father's name is also according to nature.

Her. Clearly.

Soc. Yes, for as his name, so also is his nature; Agamemnon (admirable for remaining) is one who is patient and persevering in the accomplishment of his resolves, and by his virtue crowns them; and his continuance at Troy with all the vast army is a proof of that admirable endurance in him which is signified by the name Agamemnon. I also think that Atreus is rightly called; for his murder of Chrysippus and his exceeding cruelty to Thyestes are damaging and destructive to his reputation—the name is a little altered and disguised so as not to be intelligible to every one, but to the etymologist there is no difficulty in seeing the meaning, for whether you think of him as ἀτειρὴς the stubborn, or as ἄτρεστος the fearless, or as ἀτηρὸς the destructive one, the name is perfectly correct in every point of view. And I think that Pelops is also named appropriately; for, as the name implies, he is rightly called Pelops who sees what is near only (ὁ τὰ πέλας ὁρῶν).

Her. How so?

Soc. Because, according to the tradition, he had no forethought or foresight of all the evil which the murder of Myrtilus would entail upon his whole race in remote ages; he saw only what was at hand and immediate,—or in other words, πέλας (near), in his eagerness to win Hippodamia by all means for his bride. Every one would agree that the name of Tantalus is rightly given and in accordance with nature, if the traditions about him are true.

Her. And what are the traditions?

Soc. Many terrible misfortunes are said to have happened to him in his life—last of all, came the utter ruin of his country; and after his death he had the stone suspended (ταλαντεία) over his head in the world below—all this agrees wonderfully well with his name. You might imagine that some person who wanted to call him ταλάντατος (the most weighted down by misfortune), disguised the name by altering it into Tantalus; and into this form, by some accident of tradition, it has actually been transmuted. The name of Zeus, who is his alleged father, *[396]* has also an excellent meaning, although hard to be understood, because really like a sentence, which is divided into two parts, for some call him Zena (Ζῆνα), and use the one half, and others who use the other half call him Dia (Δία); the two together signify the nature of the God, and the business of a name, as we were saying, is to express the nature. For there is none who is more the author of life to us and to all, than the lord and king of all. Wherefore we are right in calling him Zena and Dia, which are one name, although divided, meaning the God through whom all creatures always have life (δι' ὃν ζῆν ἀεὶ πᾶσι τοῖς ζῶσιν ὑπάρχει). There is an irreverence, at first sight, in calling him son of Cronos (who is a proverb for stupidity), and we might rather expect Zeus to be the child of a mighty intellect. Which is the fact; for this is the meaning of his father's name: Κρόνος quasi Κόρος (χορέω, to sweep), not in the sense of a youth, but signifying τὸ χαθαρὸν χαὶ ἀχήρατον τοῦ νοῦ, the pure and garnished mind (sc. ἀπὸ τοῦ χορεῖν). He, as we are informed by tradition, was begotten of Uranus, rightly so called (ἀπὸ τοῦ ὁρᾶν τὰ ἄνω) from looking upwards; which, as philosophers tell us, is the way to have a pure mind, and the name Uranus is therefore correct. If I could remember the genealogy of Hesiod, I would have gone on and tried more conclusions of the same sort on the remoter ancestors of the Gods,—then I might have seen whether this wisdom, which has come to me all in an instant, I know not whence, will or will not hold good to the end.

Her. You seem to me, Socrates, to be quite like a prophet newly inspired, and to be uttering oracles.

Soc. Yes, Hermogenes, and I believe that I caught the inspiration from the great Euthyphro of the Prospaltian deme, who gave me a long lecture which commenced at dawn: he talked and I listened, and his wisdom and enchanting ravishment has not only filled my ears but taken possession of my soul, and to-day I shall let his superhuman power work and finish the investigation of names—that will be the way; but to-morrow, if you are so disposed, we will conjure him away, and make a purgation of him, if we can only find some priest or sophist who is skilled in purifications of this [397] sort.

Her. With all my heart; for I am very curious to hear the rest of the enquiry about names.

Soc. Then let us proceed; and where would you have us begin, now that we have got a sort of outline of the enquiry? Are there any names which witness of themselves that they are not given arbitrarily, but have a natural fitness? The names of heroes and of men in general are apt to be deceptive because they are often called after ancestors with whose names, as we were saying, they may have no business; or they are the expression of a wish like Eutychides (the son of good fortune), or Sosias (the Saviour), or Theophilus (the beloved of God), and others. But I think that we had better leave these, for there will be more chance of finding correctness in the names of immutable essences;—there ought to have been more care taken about them when they were named, and perhaps there may have been some more than human power at work occasionally in giving them names.

Her. I think so, Socrates.

Soc. Ought we not to begin with the consideration of the Gods, and show that they are rightly named Gods?

Her. Yes, that will be well.

Soc. My notion would be something of this sort:—I suspect that the sun, moon, earth, stars, and heaven, which are still the Gods of many barbarians, were the only Gods known to the aboriginal Hellenes. Seeing that they were always moving and running, from their running nature they were called Gods or runners (θεοὺς, θέοντας); and when men became acquainted with the other Gods, they proceeded to apply the same name to them all. Do you think that likely?

Her. I think it very likely indeed.

Soc. What shall follow the Gods?

Her. Must not demons and heroes and men come next?

Soc. Demons! And what do you consider to be the meaning of this word? Tell me if my view is right.

Her. Let me hear.

Soc. You know how Hesiod uses the word?

Her. I do not.

Soc. Do you not remember that he speaks of a golden race of men who came first?

Her. Yes, I do.

Soc. He says of them—

But now that fate has closed over this race
They are holy demons upon the earth,
Beneficent, averters of ills, guardians of mortal
*   men.*

[398] *Her.* What is the inference?

Soc. What is the inference! Why, I suppose that he means by the golden men, not men literally made of gold, but good and noble; and I am convinced of this, because he further says that we are the iron race.

Her. That is true.

Soc. And do you not suppose that good men of our own day would by him be said to be of golden race?

Her. Very likely.

Soc. And are not the good wise?

Her. Yes, they are wise.

Soc. And therefore I have the most entire conviction that he called them demons, because they were δαήμονες (knowing or wise), and in our older Attic dialect the word itself occurs. Now he and other poets say truly, that when a good man dies he has honour and a mighty portion among the dead, and becomes a demon; which is a name given to him signifying wisdom. And I say too, that every wise man who happens to be a good man is more than human (δαιμόνιον) both in life and death, and is rightly called a demon.

Her. Then I rather think that I am of one mind with you; but what is the meaning of the word "hero"? (ἥρως, in the old writing ἔρως.)

Soc. I think that there is no difficulty in explaining, for the name is not much altered, and signifies that they were born of love.

Her. What do you mean?

Soc. Do you not know that the heroes are demigods?

Her. What then?

Soc. All of them sprang either from the love of a God for a mortal woman, or of a mortal man for a Goddess; think of the word in the old Attic, and you will see better that the name heros is only a slight alteration of Eros, from whom the heroes sprang: either this is the meaning, or, if not this, then they must have been skilful as rhetoricians and dialecticians, and able to put the question (ἐρωτᾶν), for εἴρειν is equivalent to λέγειν. And therefore, as I was saying, in the Attic dialect the heroes turn out to be rhetoricians and questioners. All this is easy enough; the noble breed of heroes are a tribe of sophists and rhetors. But can you tell me why men are called ἄνθρωποι?—that is more difficult.

Her. No, I cannot; and I would not try even if I could, because I think that you are the more likely to succeed.

[399] *Soc.* That is to say, you trust to the inspiration of Euthyphro.

Her. Of course.

Soc. Your faith is not vain; for at this very moment a new and ingenious thought strikes me, and, if I am not careful, before tomorrow's dawn I shall be wiser than I ought to be. Now, attend to me; and first, remember that we often put in and pull out letters in words, and give names as we please and change the accents. Take, for example, the word Δῐ Φίλος; in order to convert this from a sentence into a noun, we omit one of the iotas and sound the middle syllable grave instead of acute; as, on the other hand, letters are sometimes inserted in words instead of being omitted, and the acute takes the place of the grave.

Her. That is true.

Soc. The name ἄνθρωπος, which was once a sentence, and is now a noun, appears to be a case just of this sort, for one letter, which is the α, has been omitted, and the acute on the last syllable has been changed to a grave.

Her. What do you mean?

Soc. I mean to say that the word "man" implies that other animals never examine, or consider, or look up at what they see, but that man not only sees (ὄπωπε) but considers and looks up at that which he sees, and hence he alone of all animals is rightly called ἄνθρωπος, meaning ἀναθρῶν ἃ ὄπωπεν.

Her. May I ask you to examine another word about which I am curious?

Soc. Certainly.

Her. I will take that which appears to me to follow next in order. You know the distinction of soul and body?

Soc. Of course.

Her. Let us endeavour to analyze them like the previous words.

Soc. You want me first of all to examine the natural fitness of the word ψυχὴ (soul), and then of the word σῶμα (body)?

Her. Yes.

Soc. If I am to say what occurs to me at the moment, I should imagine that those who first use the name ψυχὴ meant to express that the soul when in the body is the source of life, and gives the power of breath and revival (ἀναψῦχον), and when this reviving power fails then the body perishes and dies, and this, if I am not mistaken, they called psyche. But please stay a moment; I fancy that I can discover something which will be more acceptable to the disciples of Euthyphro, [400] for I am afraid that they will scorn this explanation. What do you say to another?

Her. Let me hear.

Soc. What is that which holds and carries and gives life and motion to the entire nature of the body? What else but the soul?

Her. Just that.

Soc. And do you not believe with Anaxagoras, that mind or soul is the ordering and containing principle of all things?

Her. Yes; I do.

Soc. Then you may well call that power φυσέχη which carries and holds nature (ἡ φύσιν ὀκεῖ, καὶ ἔκει), and this may be refined away into ψυχή.

Her. Certainly; and this derivation is, I think, more scientific than the other.

Soc. It is so; but I cannot help laughing, if I am to suppose that this was the true meaning of the name.

Her. But what shall we say of the next word?

Soc. You mean σῶμα (the body).

Her. Yes.

Soc. That may be variously interpreted; and yet more variously if a little permutation is allowed. For some say that the body is the grave (σῆμα) of the soul which may be thought to be buried in our present life; or again the index of the soul, because the soul gives indications to (σημαίνει) the body; probably the Orphic poets were the inventors of the name, and they were under the impression that the soul is suffering the punishment of sin, and that the body is an enclosure or prison in which the soul is incarcerated, kept safe (σῶμα, σώζηται), as the name σῶμα implies, until the penalty is paid; according to this view, not even a letter of the word need be changed.

Her. I think, Socrates, that we have said enough of this class of words. But have we any more explanations of the names of the Gods, like that which you were giving of Zeus? I should like to know whether any similar principle of correctness is to be applied to them.

Soc. Yes, indeed, Hermogenes; and there is one excellent principle which, as men of sense, we must acknowledge,—that of the Gods we know nothing, either of their natures or of the names which they give themselves; but we are sure that the names by which they call themselves, whatever they may be, are true. And this is the best of all principles; and the next best is to say, as in prayers, that we will call them by any sort of kind of names or patronymics which they like, *[401]* because we do not know of any other. That also, I think, is a very good custom, and one which I should much wish to observe. Let us, then, if you please, in the first place announce to them that we are not enquiring about them; we do not presume that we are able to do so; but we are enquiring about the meaning of men in giving them these names,—in this there can be small blame.

Her. I think, Socrates, that you are quite right, and I would like to do as you say.

Soc. Shall we begin, then, with Hestia, according to custom?

Her. Yes, that will be very proper.

Soc. What may we suppose him to have meant who gave the name Hestia?

Her. That is another and certainly a most difficult question.

Soc. My dear Hermogenes, the first imposers of names must surely have been considerable persons; they were philosophers, and had a good deal to say.

Her. Well, and what of them?

Soc. They are the men to whom I should attribute the imposition of names. Even in foreign names, if you analyze them, a meaning is still discernible. For example, that which we term οὐσία is by some called ἐσία, and by others again ὠσία. Now that the essence of things should be called ἑστία, which is akin to the first of these (ἐσία = ἑστία), is rational enough. And there is reason in the Athenians calling that ἑστία which participates in οὐσία. For in ancient times we too seem to have said ἐσία for οὐσία, and this you may note to have been the idea of those who appointed that sacrifices should be first offered to ἑστία, which was natural enough if they meant that ἑστία was the essence of things. Those again who read ὠσία seem to have inclined to the opinion of Heracleitus, that all things flow and nothing stands; with them the pushing principle (ὠθοῦν) is the cause and ruling power of all things, and is

therefore rightly called ὠσία. Enough of this, which is all that we who know nothing can affirm. Next in order after Hestia we ought to consider Rhea and Cronos, although the name of Cronos has been already discussed. But I dare say that I am talking great nonsense.

Her. Why, Socrates?

Soc. My good friend, I have discovered a hive of wisdom.

Her. Of what nature?

[402] *Soc.* Well, rather ridiculous, and yet plausible.

Her. How plausible?

Soc. I fancy to myself Heracleitus repeating wise traditions of antiquity as old as the days of Cronos and Rhea, and of which Homer also spoke.

Her. How do you mean?

Soc. Heracleitus is supposed to say that all things are in motion and nothing at rest; he compares them to the stream of a river, and says that you cannot go into the same water twice.

Her. That is true.

Soc. Well, then, how can we avoid inferring that he who gave the names of Cronos and Rhea to the ancestors of the Gods, agreed pretty much in the doctrine of Heracleitus? Is the giving of the names of streams to both of them purely accidental? Compare the line in which Homer, and, as I believe, Hesiod also, tells of

Ocean, the origin of Gods, and mother Tethys.

And again, Orpheus says, that

The fair river of Ocean was the first to marry, and he espoused his sister Tethys, who was his mother's daughter.

You see that this is a remarkable coincidence, and all in the direction of Heracleitus.

Her. I think that there is something in what you say, Socrates; but I do not understand the meaning of the name Tethys.

Soc. Well, that is almost self-explained, being only the name of a spring, a little disguised; for that which is strained and filtered (διαττώμενον, ἠθούμενον) may be likened to a spring, and the name Tethys is made up of these two words.

Her. The idea is ingenious, Socrates.

Soc. To be sure. But what comes next?—of Zeus we have spoken.

Her. Yes.

Soc. Then let us next take his two brothers,

CRATYLUS

Poseidon and Pluto, whether the latter is called by that or by his other name.

Her. By all means.

Soc. Poseidon is ποσίδεσμος, the chain of the feet; the original inventor of the name had been stopped by the watery element in his walks, and not allowed to go on, and therefore he called the ruler of this element Poseidon; the ε was probably inserted as an ornament. Yet, perhaps, not so; but the name may have been originally written with a double λ and not with an σ, [403] meaning that the God knew many things (πολλὰ εἰδώς). And perhaps also he being the shaker of the earth, has been named from shaking (σείειν), and then π and δ have been added. Pluto gives wealth (πλοῦτος), and his name means the giver of wealth, which comes out of the earth beneath. People in general appear to imagine that the term Hades is connected with the invisible (ἀειδές); and so they are led by their fears to call the God Pluto instead.

Her. And what is the true derivation?

Soc. In spite of the mistakes which are made about the power of this deity, and the foolish fears which people have of him, such as the fear of always being with him after death, and of the soul denuded of the body going to him,[1] my belief is that all is quite consistent, and that the office and name of the God really correspond.

Her. Why, how is that?

Soc. I will tell you my own opinion; but first, I should like to ask you which chain does any animal feel to be the stronger? and which confines him more to the same spot,—desire or necessity?

Her. Desire, Socrates, is stronger far.

Soc. And do you not think that many a one would escape from Hades, if he did not bind those who depart to him by the strongest of chains?

Her. Assuredly they would.

Soc. And if by the greatest of chains, then by some desire, as I should certainly infer, and not by necessity?

Her. That is clear.

Soc. And there are many desires?

Her. Yes.

Soc. And therefore by the greatest desire, if the chain is to be the greatest?

Her. Yes.

Soc. And is any desire stronger than the thought that you will be made better by associating with another?

[1] Cf. *Republic,* iii. 386, 387.

Her. Certainly not.

Soc. And is not that the reason, Hermogenes, why no one, who has been to him, is willing to come back to us? Even the Sirens, like all the rest of the world, have been laid under his spells. Such a charm, as I imagine, is the God able to infuse into his words. And, according to this view, he is the perfect and accomplished Sophist, and the great benefactor of the inhabitants of the other world; and even to us who are upon earth he sends from below exceeding blessings. For he has much more than he wants down there; wherefore he is called Pluto (or the rich). Note also, that he will have nothing to do with men while they are in the body, but only when the soul is liberated from the desires and evils of the body. Now there is a great deal of philosophy and reflection in that; [404] for in their liberated state he can bind them with the desire of virtue, but while they are flustered and maddened by the body, not even father Cronos himself would suffice to keep them with him in his own far-famed chains.

Her. There is a deal of truth in what you say.

Soc. Yes, Hermogenes, and the legislator called him Hades, not from the unseen (ἀειδές) —far otherwise, but from his knowledge (εἰδέναι) of all noble things.

Her. Very good; and what do we say of Demeter, and Herè, and Apollo, and Athene, and Hephaestus, and Ares, and the other deities?

Soc. Demeter is ἡ διδοῦσα μήτηρ, who gives food like a mother; Herè is the lovely one (ἐρατή)—for Zeus, according to tradition, loved and married her; possibly also the name may have been given when the legislator was thinking of the heavens, and may be only a disguise of the air (ἀήρ), putting the end in the place of the beginning. You will recognize the truth of this if you repeat the letters of Herè several times over. People dread the name of Pherephatta as they dread the name of Apollo—and with as little reason; the fear, if I am not mistaken, only arises from their ignorance of the nature of names. But they go changing the name into Phersephone, and they are terrified at this; whereas the new name means only that the Goddess is wise (σοφή); for seeing that all things in the world are in motion (φερομένων), that principle which embraces and touches and is able to follow them, is wisdom. And therefore the Goddess may be truly called Pherepaphe (Φερεπάφα), or some name like it, because she touches that which is in motion (τοῦ φερομένου ἐφαπτομένη), herein showing her wisdom. And Hades, who is wise, consorts with her, because she is wise. They alter her name into Pherephatta now-a-days, because the present generation care for euphony more than truth. There is the other name, Apollo, which, as I was saying, is generally supposed to have some terrible signification. Have you remarked this fact?

Her. To be sure I have, and what you say is true.

Soc. But the name, in my opinion, is really most expressive of the power of the God.

Her. How so?

Soc. I will endeavour to explain, for I do not believe that any single name could have been better adapted to express the attributes [405] of the God, embracing and in a manner signifying all four of them,—music, and prophecy, and medicine, and archery.

Her. That must be a strange name, and I should like to hear the explanation.

Soc. Say rather an harmonious name, as beseems the God of Harmony. In the first place, the purgations and purifications which doctors and diviners use, and their fumigations with drugs magical or medicinal, as well as their washings and lustral sprinklings, have all one and the same object, which is to make a man pure both in body and soul.

Her. Very true.

Soc. And is not Apollo the purifier, and the washer, and the absolver from all impurities?

Her. Very true.

Soc. Then in reference to his ablutions and absolutions, as being the physician who orders them, he may be rightly called Ἀπολούων (purifier); or in respect of his powers of divination, and his truth and sincerity, which is the same as truth, he may be most fitly called Ἁπλῶς, from ἁπλοῦς (sincere), as in the Thessalian dialect, for all the Thessalians call him Ἁπλός; also he is ἀεὶ Βάλλων (always shooting), because he is a master archer who never misses; or again, the name may refer to his musical attributes, and then, as in ἀκόλουθος, and ἄκοιτις, and in many other words the a is supposed to mean "together," so the meaning of the name Apollo will be "moving together," whether in the poles of heaven as they are called, or in the harmony of song, which is termed concord, because he moves all together by an harmonious power, as astronomers and musicians ingeniously declare. And he is the God who presides over harmony, and makes all things move together, both among Gods and among men. And as in the words ἀκόλουθος and ἄκοιτις the a is substituted for an o, so the name Ἀπόλλων is equivalent to ὁμοπολῶν; only the second λ is added in order to avoid the ill-omened sound of destruction (ἀπολῶν). Now the suspicion of this destructive power still haunts the minds of some who do not consider the true value of the name, [406] which, as I was saying just now, has reference to all the powers of the God, who is the single one, the everdarting, the purifier, the mover together (ἁπλοῦς, ἀεὶ Βάλλων, ἀπολούων, ὁμοπολῶν). The name of the Muses and of music would seem to be derived from their making philosophical enquiries (μῶσθαι); and Leto is called by this name, because she is such a gentle Goddess, and so willing (ἐθελήμων) to grant our requests; or her name may be Letho, as she is often called by strangers—they seem to imply by it her amiability, and her smooth and easy-going way of behaving. Artemis is named from her healthy (ἀρτεμής), well-ordered nature, and because of her love of virginity, perhaps because she is a proficient in virtue (ἀρετή), and perhaps also as hating intercourse of the sexes (τὸν ἄροτον μισήσασα). He who gave the Goddess her name may have had any or all of these reasons.

Her. What is the meaning of Dionysus and Aphrodite?

Soc. Son of Hipponicus, you ask a solemn question; there is a serious and also a facetious explanation of both these names; the serious explanation is not to be had from me, but there is no objection to your hearing the facetious one; for the Gods too love a joke. Διόννσος is simply διδοὺς οἶνον (giver of wine), Διδοίννσος, as he might be called in fun,—and οἶνος is properly οἰόνους, because wine makes those who drink, think (οἴεσθαι) that they have a mind (νοῦν) when they have none. The derivation of Aphrodite, born of the foam (ἀφρός), may be fairly accepted on the authority of Hesiod.

Her. Still there remains Athene, whom you, Socrates, as an Athenian, will surely not forget; there are also Hephaestus and Ares.

Soc. I am not likely to forget them.

Her. No, indeed.

Soc. There is no difficulty in explaining the other appellation of Athene.

Her. What other appellation?

Soc. We call her Pallas.

Her. To be sure.

Soc. And we cannot be wrong in supposing that this is derived from armed dances. For the elevation of oneself or anything else above the earth, [407] or by the use of the hands, we call shaking (πάλλειν), or dancing.

Her. That is quite true.

Soc. Then that is the explanation of the name Pallas?

Her. Yes; but what do you say of the other name?

Soc. Athene?

Her. Yes.

Soc. That is a graver matter, and there, my friend, the modern interpreters of Homer may, I think, assist in explaining the view of the ancients. For most of these in their explanations of the poet, assert that he meant by Athene "mind" (νοῦς) and "intelligence" (διάνοια), and the maker of names appears to have had a singular notion about her; and indeed calls her by a still higher title, "divine intelligence" (θεοῦ νόησις), as though he would say: This is she who has the mind of God (θεονόα); —using *a* as a dialectical variety for *η*, and taking away *ι* and *σ*. Perhaps, however, the name θεονόη may mean "she who knows divine things" (θεῖα νοοῦσα) better than others. Nor shall we be far wrong in supposing that the author of it wished to identify this Goddess with moral intelligence (ἐν ἤθει νόησιν), and therefore gave her the name ἠθονόη; which, however, either he or his successors have altered into what they thought a nicer form, and called her Athene.

Her. But what do you say of Hephaestus?

Soc. Speak you of the princely lord of light (φάεος ἵστορα)?

Her. Surely.

Soc. Ἥφαιστος is Φαῖστος, and has added the *η* by attraction; that is obvious to anybody.

Her. That is very probable, until some more probable notion gets into your head.

Soc. To prevent that, you had better ask what is the derivation of Ares.

Her. What is Ares?

Soc. Ares may be called, if you will, from his manhood (ἄρρεν) and manliness, or if you please, from his hard and unchangeable nature, which is the meaning of ἄρρατος: the latter is a derivation in every way appropriate to the God of war.

Her. Very true.

Soc. And now, by the Gods, let us have no more of the Gods, for I am afraid of them; ask about anything but them, and thou shalt see how the steeds of Euthyphro can prance.

Her. Only one more God! I should like to know about Hermes, of whom I am said not to be a true son. Let us make him out, and then I shall know whether there is any meaning in what Cratylus says.

Soc. I should imagine that the name Hermes has to do with speech, [408] and signifies that he is the interpreter (ἑρμηνεύς), or messenger, or thief, or liar, or bargainer; all that sort of thing has a great deal to do with language; as I was telling you the word εἴρειν is expressive of the use of speech, and there is an often-recurring Homeric word ἐμήσατο, which means "he contrived"—out of these two words, εἴρειν and μήσασθαι, the legislator formed the name of the God who invented language and speech; and we may imagine him dictating to us the use of this name: "O my friends," says he to us, "seeing that he is the contriver of tales or speeches, you may rightly call him Εἰρέμης." And this has been improved by us, as we think, into Hermes. Iris also appears to have been called from the verb "to tell" (εἴρειν), because she was a messenger.

Her. Then I am very sure that Cratylus was quite right in saying that I was no true son of Hermes (Ἑρμογένης), for I am not a good hand at speeches.

Soc. There is also reason, my friend, in Pan being the double-formed son of Hermes.

Her. How do you make that out?

Soc. You are aware that speech signifies all things (πᾶν), and is always turning them round and round, and has two forms, true and false?

Her. Certainly.

Soc. Is not the truth that is in him the smooth or sacred form which dwells above among the Gods, whereas falsehood dwells among men below, and is rough like the goat of tragedy; for tales and falsehoods have generally to do with the tragic or goatish life, and tragedy is the place of them?

Her. Very true.

Soc. Then surely Pan, who is the declarer of all things (πᾶν) and the perpetual mover (ἀεὶ πολῶν) of all things, is rightly called αἰπόλος (goat-herd), he being the two-formed son of Hermes, smooth in his upper part, and rough and goatlike in his lower regions. And, as the son of Hermes, he is speech or the brother of speech, and that brother should be like brother is no marvel. But, as I was saying, my dear Hermogenes, let us get away from the Gods.

Her. From these sort of Gods, by all means, Socrates. But why should we not discuss another kind of Gods—the sun, moon, stars, earth, aether, air, fire, water, the seasons, and the year?

Soc. You impose a great many tasks upon me. Still, if you wish, I will not refuse.

Her. You will oblige me.

Soc. How would you have me begin? Shall I take first of all him whom you mentioned first—the sun?

Her. Very good.

Soc. The origin of the sun will probably be clearer in the Doric form, *[409]* for the Dorians call him ἅλιος, and this name is given to him because when he rises he gathers (ἁλίζοι) men together or because he is always rolling in his course (ἀεὶ εἰλεῖν ἰών) about the earth; or from αἰολεῖν, of which the meaning is the same as ποικίλλειν (to variegate), because he variegates the productions of the earth.

Her. But what is σελήνη (the moon)?

Soc. That name is rather unfortunate for Anaxagoras.

Her. How so?

Soc. The word seems to forestall his recent discovery, that the moon receives her light from the sun.

Her. Why do you say so?

Soc. The two words σέλας (brightness) and φῶς (light) have much the same meaning?

Her. Yes.

Soc. This light about the moon is always new (νέον) and always old (ἔνον), if the disciples of Anaxagoras say truly. For the sun in his revolution always adds new light, and there is the old light of the previous month.

Her. Very true.

Soc. The moon is not unfrequently called σελαναία.

Her. True.

Soc. And as she has a light which is always old and always new (ἔνον νέον ἀεί) she may very properly have the name σελαενονεοάεια; and this when hammered into shape becomes σελαναία.

Her. A real dithyrambic sort of name that, Socrates. But what do you say of the month and the stars?

Soc. Μείς (month) is called from μειοῦσθαι (to lessen), because suffering diminution; the name of ἄστρα (stars) seems to be derived from ἀστραπὴ, which is an improvement on ἀναστρωπὴ, signifying the upsetting of the eyes (ἀναστρέφειν ὦπα).

Her. What do you say of πῦρ (fire) and ὕδωρ (water)?

Soc. I am at a loss how to explain πῦρ; either the muse of Euthyphro has deserted me, or there is some very great difficulty in the word. Please, however, to note the contrivance which I adopt whenever I am in a difficulty of this sort.

Her. What is it?

Soc. I will tell you; but I should like to know first whether you can tell me what is the meaning of the word πῦρ?

Her. Indeed I cannot.

Soc. Shall I tell you what I suspect to be the true explanation of this and several other words?—My belief is that they are of foreign origin. For the Hellenes, especially those who were under the dominion of the barbarians, often borrowed from them.

Her. What is the inference?

Soc. Why, you know that any one who seeks to demonstrate the fitness of these names according to the Hellenic language, and not according to the language from which the words are derived, is rather likely to be at fault.

Her. Yes, certainly.

[410] *Soc.* Well then, consider whether this πῦρ is not foreign; for the word is not easily brought into relation with the Hellenic tongue, and the Phrygians may be observed to have the same word slightly changed, just as they have ὕδωρ (water) and κύνες (dogs), and many other words.

Her. That is true.

Soc. Any violent interpretations of the words should be avoided; for something to say about them may easily be found. And thus I get rid of πῦρ and ὕδωρ. Ἀήρ (air), Hermogenes, may be explained as the element which raises (αἴρει) things from the earth, or as ever flowing (ἀεὶ ῥεῖ), or because the flux of the air is wind, and the poets call the winds "air-blasts," (ἀῆται); he who uses the term may mean, so to speak, air-flux (ἀητόρρουν), in the sense of wind-flux (πνευματόρρουν); and because this moving wind may be expressed by either term he employs the word air (ἀὴρ=ἀήτης ῥέω). Αἰθὴρ (aether) I should interpret as ἀειθεήρ; this may be correctly said, because this element is always running in a flux about the air (ἀεὶ θεῖ περὶ τὸν ἀέρα ῥέων). The meaning of the word γῆ (earth) comes out better when in the form of γαῖα, for the earth may be truly called "mother" (γαῖα, γεννήτειρα), as in the language of Homer (Od. ix. 118; xiii. 160) γεγάασι means γεγενῆσθαι.

Her. Good.

Soc. What shall we take next?

Her. There are ὧραι (the seasons), and the two names of the year, ἐνιαυτὸς and ἔτος.

Soc. The ὧραι should be spelt in the old Attic way, if you desire to know the probable truth about them; they are rightly called the ὧραι because they divide (ὁρίζουσιν) the summers and winters and winds and the fruits of the earth. The words ἐνιαυτὸς and ἔτος appear to be the same,—"that which brings to light the plants and growths of the earth in their turn, and passes them in review within itself (ἐν ἑαυτῷ ἐξετάζει)": this is broken up into two words, ἐνιαυτὸς from ἐν ἑαυτῷ, and ἔτος from ἐτάζει, just as the original name of Ζεὺς was divided into Ζῆνα and Δία; and the whole proposition means that his power of reviewing from within is one, but has two names, two words ἔτος and ἐνιαυτὸς being thus formed out of a single proposition.

Her. Indeed, Socrates, you make surprising progress.

Soc. I am run away with.

Her. Very true.

Soc. But am not yet at my utmost speed.

[411] Her. I should like very much to know, in the next place, how you would explain the virtues. What principle of correctness is there in those charming words—wisdom, understanding, justice, and the rest of them?

Soc. That is a tremendous class of names which you are disinterring; still, as I have put on the lion's skin, I must not be faint of heart; and I suppose that I must consider the meaning of wisdom (φρόνησις) and understanding (σύνεσις), and judgment (γνώμη), and knowledge (ἐπιστήμη), and all those other charming words, as you call them?

Her. Surely, we must not leave off until we find out their meaning.

Soc. By the dog of Egypt I have not a bad notion which came into my head only this moment: I believe that the primeval givers of names were undoubtedly like too many of our modern philosophers, who, in their search after the nature of things, are always getting dizzy from constantly going round and round, and then they imagine that the world is going round and round and moving in all directions; and this appearance, which arises out of their own internal condition, they suppose to be a reality of nature; they think that there is nothing stable or permanent, but only flux and motion, and that the world is always full of every sort of motion and change. The consideration of the names which I mentioned has led me into making this reflection.

Her. How is that, Socrates?

Soc. Perhaps you did not observe that in the names which have been just cited, the motion or flux or generation of things is most surely indicated.

Her. No, indeed, I never thought of it.

Soc. Take the first of those which you mentioned; clearly that is a name indicative of motion.

Her. What was the name?

Soc. Φρόνησις (wisdom), which may signify Φορᾶς καὶ ῥοῦ νόησις (perception of motion and flux), or perhaps Φορᾶς ὄνησις (the blessing of motion), but is at any rate connected with Φέρεσθαι (motion); γνώμη (judgment), again, certainly implies the ponderation or consideration (νώμησις) of generation, for to ponder is the same as to consider; or, if you would rather, here is νόησις, the very word just now mentioned, which is νέου ἔσις (the desire of the new); the word νέος implies that the world is always in process of creation. The giver of the name wanted to express his longing of the soul, for the original name was νεόεσις, and not νόησις; but η took the place of a double ε. The word σωφροσύνη is the salvation (σωτηρία) of that wisdom (φρόνησις) which we were just now considering. *[412]* Ἐπιστήμη (knowledge) is akin to this, and indicates that the soul which is good for anything follows (ἔπεται) the motion of things, neither anticipating them nor falling behind them; wherefor the word should rather be read as ἐπιστημένη, inserting ἐν. Σύνεσις (understanding) may be regarded in like manner as a kind of conclusion; the word is derived from συνιέναι (to go along with), and, like ἐπίστασθαι (to know), implies the progression of the soul in company with the nature of things. Σοφία (wisdom) is very dark, and appears not to be of native growth; the meaning is, touching the motion or stream of things. You must remember that the poets, when they speak of the commencement of any rapid motion, often use the word ἐσύθη (he rushed); and there was a famous Lacedaemonian who was named Σοῦς (Rush), for by this word the Lacedaemonians signify rapid motion, and the touching (ἐπαφὴ) of motion is expressed by σοφία, for all things are supposed to be in motion. Good (ἀγαθὸν) is the name which is given to the admirable (ἀγαστῷ) in nature; for, although all things move, still there are degrees of motion; some are swifter, some slower; but there are some things which are admirable for their swiftness, and this admirable part of nature is called ἀγαθόν. Δικαιοσύνη (justice) is clearly δικαίου σύνεσις (understanding of the just); but the actual word δίκαιον is more difficult: men are only agreed to a certain extent about justice, and then they begin to disagree.

For those who suppose all things to be in

motion conceive the greater part of nature to be a mere receptacle; and they say that there is a penetrating power which passes through all this, and is the instrument of creation in all, and is the subtlest and swiftest element; for if it were not the subtlest, and a power which none can keep out, and also the swiftest, passing by other things as if they were standing still, it could not penetrate through the moving universe. And this element, which superintends all things and pieces (διαϊὸν) all, is rightly called δίκαιον; the letter κ is only added for the sake of euphony. Thus far, as I was saying, there is a general agreement about the nature of justice; [413] but I, Hermogenes, being an enthusiastic disciple, have been told in a mystery that the justice of which I am speaking is also the cause of the world: now a cause is that because of which anything is created; and some one comes and whispers in my ear that justice is rightly so called because partaking of the nature of the cause, and I begin, after hearing what he has said, to interrogate him gently: "Well, my excellent friend," say I, "but if all this be true, I still want to know what is justice." Thereupon they think that I ask tiresome questions, and am leaping over the barriers, and have been already sufficiently answered, and they try to satisfy me with one derivation after another, and at length they quarrel. For one of them says that justice is the sun, and that he only is the piercing (διαϊόντα) and burning (κάοντα) element which is the guardian of nature. And when I joyfully repeat this beautiful notion, I am answered by the satirical remark, "What, is there no justice in the world when the sun is down?" And when I earnestly beg my questioner to tell me his own honest opinion, he says, "Fire in the abstract"; but this is not very intelligible. Another says, "No, not fire in the abstract, but the abstraction of heat in the fire." Another man professes to laugh at all this, and says, as Anaxagoras says, that justice is mind, for mind, as they say, has absolute power, and mixes with nothing, and orders all things, and passes through all things. At last, my friend, I find myself in far greater perplexity about the nature of justice than I was before I began to learn. But still I am of opinion that the name, which has led me into this digression, was given to justice for the reasons which I have mentioned.

Her. I think, Socrates, that you are not improvising now; you must have heard this from some one else.

Soc. And not the rest?

Her. Hardly.

Soc. Well, then, let me go on in the hope of making you believe in the originality of the rest. What remains after justice? I do not think that we have as yet discussed courage (ἀνδρεία),—injustice (ἀδικία), which is obviously nothing more than a hindrance to the penetrating principle (διαϊόντος), need not be considered. Well, then, the name of ἀνδρεία seems to imply a battle;—this battle is in the world of existence, and according to the doctrine of flux is only the counterflux (ἐναντία ῥοή): if you extract the δ from ἀνδρεία, the name at once signifies the thing, and you may clearly understand that ἀνδρεία is not the stream opposed to every stream, but only to that which is contrary to justice, [414] for otherwise courage would not have been praised. The words ἄρρην (male) and ἀνήρ (man) also contain a similar allusion to the same principle of the upward flux (τῇ ἄνω ῥοῇ). Γυνή (woman) I suspect to be the same word as γονή (birth): θῆλυ (female) appears to be partly derived from θηλή (the teat), because the teat is like rain, and makes things flourish (τεθηλέναι).

Her. That is surely probable.

Soc. Yes; and the very word θάλλειν (to flourish) seems to figure the growth of youth, which is swift and sudden ever. And this is expressed by the legislator in the name, which is a compound of θεῖν (running), and ἄλλεσθαι (leaping). Pray observe how I gallop away when I get on smooth ground. There are a good many names generally thought to be of importance, which have still to be explained.

Her. True.

Soc. There is the meaning of the word τέχνη (art), for example.

Her. Very true.

Soc. That may be identified with ἐχονόη, and expresses the possession of mind: you have only to take away the τ and insert two o's, one between the χ and ν, and another between the ν and η.

Her. That is a very shabby etymology.

Soc. Yes, my dear friend; but then you know that the original names have been long ago buried and disguised by people sticking on and stripping off letters for the sake of euphony, and twisting and bedizening them in all sorts of ways: and time too may have had a share in the change. Take, for example, the word κάτοπτρον; why is the letter ρ inserted? This must surely be the addition of some one who cares nothing about the truth, but thinks only of putting the mouth into shape. And the additions are often such that at last no human being can possibly make out the original meaning of the word. Another example is the word σφὶγξ, σφιγγὸς, which ought properly to be φὶγξ, φιγγὸς, and there are other examples.

Her. That is quite true, Socrates.

Soc. And yet, if you are permitted to put in and pull out any letters which you please, names will be too easily made, and any name may be adapted to any object.

Her. True.

Soc. Yes, that is true. And therefore a wise dictator, like yourself, should observe the laws of moderation and probability.

Her. Such is my desire.

Soc. And mine, too, Hermogenes. But do not be too much of a precisian, *[415]* or "you will unnerve me of my strength."[1] When you have allowed me to add μηχανὴ (contrivance) to τέχνη (art) I shall be at the top of my bent, for I conceive μηχανὴ to be a sign of great accomplishment—ἄνειν; for μῆκος has the meaning of greatness, and these two, μῆκος and ἄνειν, make up the word μηχανή. But, as I was saying, being now at the top of my bent, I should like to consider the meaning of the two words ἀρετὴ (virtue) and κακία (vice); ἀρετὴ I do not as yet understand, but κακία is transparent, and agrees with the principles which preceded, for all things being in a flux (ἰόντων), κακία is κακῶς ἰὸν (going badly); and this evil motion when existing in the soul has the general name of κακία, or vice, specially appropriated to it. The meaning of κακῶς ἰέναι may be further illustrated by the use of δειλία (cowardice), which ought to have come after ἀνδρεία, but was forgotten, and, as I fear, is not the only word which has been passed over. Δειλία signifies that the soul is bound with a strong chain (δεσμὸς), for λίαν means strength, and therefore δειλία expresses the greatest and strongest bond of the soul; and ἀπορία (difficulty) is an evil of the same nature (from α not, and πορεύεσθαι to go), like anything else which is an impediment to motion and movement. Then the word κακία appears to mean κακῶς ἰέναι, or going badly, or limping and halting; of which the consequence is, that the soul becomes filled with vice. And if κακία is the name of this sort of thing, ἀρετὴ will be the opposite of it, signifying in the first place ease of motion, then that the stream of the good soul is unimpeded, and has therefore the attribute of ever flowing without let or hindrance, and is therefore called ἀρετὴ, or, more correctly, ἀειρειτὴ (ever-flowing), and

[1] *Iliad,* vi. 265.

may perhaps have had another form, αἱρετὴ (eligible), indicating that nothing is more eligible than virtue, and this has been hammered into ἀρετή. I daresay that you will deem this to be another invention of mine, but I think that if the previous word κακία was right, then ἀρετὴ is also right.

[416] Her. But what is the meaning of κακὸν, which has played so great a part in your previous discourse?

Soc. That is a very singular word about which I can hardly form an opinion, and therefore I must have recourse to my ingenious device.

Her. What device?

Soc. The device of a foreign origin, which I shall give to this word also.

Her. Very likely you are right; but suppose that we leave these words and endeavour to see the rationale of καλὸν and αἰσχρόν.

Soc. The meaning of αἰσχρόν is evident, being only ἀεὶ ἴσχον ῥοῆς (always preventing from flowing), and this is in accordance with our former derivations. For the name-giver was a great enemy to stagnation of all sorts, and hence he gave the name ἀεισχοροῦν to that which hindered the flux (ἀεὶ ἴσχον ῥοῦν), and this is now beaten together into αἰσχρόν.

Her. But what do you say of καλόν?

Soc. That is more obscure; yet the form is only due to the quantity, and has been changed by altering ου into ο.

Her. What do you mean?

Soc. This name appears to denote mind.

Her. How so?

Soc. Let me ask you what is the cause why anything has a name; is not the principle which imposes the name the cause?

Her. Certainly.

Soc. And must not this be the mind of Gods, or of men, or of both?

Her. Yes.

Soc. Is not mind that which called (καλέσαν) things by their names, and is not mind the beautiful (καλόν)?

Her. That is evident.

Soc. And are not the works of intelligence and mind worthy of praise, and are not other works worthy of blame?

Her. Certainly.

Soc. Physic does the work of a physician, and carpentering does the works of a carpenter?

Her. Exactly.

Soc. And the principle of beauty does the works of beauty?

Her. Of course.

Soc. And that principle we affirm to be mind?

Her. Very true.

Soc. Then mind is rightly called beauty because she does the works which we recognize and speak of as the beautiful?

Her. That is evident.

Soc. What more names remain to us?

Her. There are the words which are connected with ἀγαθὸν and καλὸν, such as συμφέρον and λυσιτελοῦν, ὠφέλιμον, κερδαλέον, and their opposites. *[417]*

Soc. The meaning of συμφέρον (expedient) I think that you may discover for yourself by the light of the previous examples,—for it is a sister word to ἐπιστήμη, meaning just the motion (φορὰ) of the soul accompanying the world, and things which are done upon this principle are called σύμφορα or συμφέροντα, because they are carried round with the world.

Her. That is probable.

Soc. Again, χερδαλέον (gainful) is called from χέρδος (gain), but you must alter the δ into ν if you want to get at the meaning; for this word also signifies good, but in another way; he who gave the name intended to express the power of admixture (κεραννύμενον) and universal penetration in the good; in forming the word, however, he inserted a δ instead of an ν, and so made κέρδος.

Her. Well, but what is λυσιτελοῦν (profitable)?

Soc. I suppose, Hermogenes, that people do not mean by the profitable the gainful or that which pays (λύει) the retailer, but they use the word in the sense of swift. You regard the profitable (λυσιτελοῦ), as that which being the swiftest thing in existence, allows of no stay in things and no pause or end of motion, but always, if there begins to be any end, lets things go again (λύει), and makes motion immortal and unceasing: and in this point of view, as appears to me, the good is happily denominated λυσιτελοῦν —being that which looses (λύον) the end (τέλος) of motion. Ὠφέλιμον (the advantageous) is derived from ὀφέλλειν, meaning that which creates and increases; this latter is a common Homeric word, and has a foreign character.

Her. And what do you say of their opposites?

Soc. Of such as mere negatives I hardly think that I need speak.

Her. Which are they?

Soc. The words ἀξύμφορον (inexpedient), ἀνωφελὲς (unprofitable), ἀλυσιτελὲς (unadvantageous), ἀκερδὲς (ungainful).

Her. True.

Soc. I would rather take the words βλαβερὸν (harmful), ζημιῶδες (hurtful).

Her. Good.

Soc. The word βλαβερὸν is that which is said to hinder or harm (βλάπτειν) the stream (ῥοῦν); βλάπτον is βουλόμενον ἅπτειν (seeking to hold or bind); for ἅπτειν is the same as δεῖν, and δεῖν is always a term of censure; βουλόμενον ἅπτειν ῥοῦν (wanting to bind the stream) would properly be βουλαπτεροῦν, and this, as I imagine, is improved into βλαβερόν.

Her. You bring out curious results, Socrates, in the use of names; and when I hear the word βουλαπτεροῦν I cannot help imagining that you are making your mouth into a flute, and puffing away at some prelude to Athene.

[418] Soc. That is the fault of the makers of the name, Hermogenes; not mine.

Her. Very true; but what is the derivation of ζημιῶδες?

Soc. What is the meaning of ζημιῶδες?—let me remark, Hermogenes, how right I was in saying that great changes are made in the meaning of words by putting in and pulling out letters; even a very slight permutation will sometimes give an entirely opposite sense; I may instance the word δέον, which occurs to me at the moment, and reminds me of what I was going to say to you, that the fine fashionable language of modern times has twisted and disguised and entirely altered the original meaning both of δέον, and also of ζημιῶδες, which in the old language is clearly indicated.

Her. What do you mean?

Soc. I will try to explain. You are aware that our forefathers loved the sounds ι and δ, especially the women, who are most conservative of the ancient language, but now they change ι into η or ε, and δ into ζ; this is supposed to increase the grandeur of the sound.

Her. How do you mean?

Soc. For example, in very ancient times they called the day either ἱμέρα or ἐμέρα, which is called by us ἡμέρα.

Her. That is true.

Soc. Do you observe that only the ancient form shows the intention of the giver of the name? of which the reason is, that men long for (ἱμείρουσι) and love the light which comes after the darkness, and is therefore called ἱμέρα, from ἵμερος, desire.

Her. Clearly.

Soc. But now the name is so travestied that you cannot tell the meaning, although there are some who imagine the day to be called ἡμέρα because it makes things gentle (ἥμερα).

Her. Such is my view.

Soc. And do you know that the ancients said δυογὸν and not ζυγόν?

Her. They did so.

Soc. And ζυγόν (yoke) has no meaning,—it ought to be δυογὸν, which word expresses the binding of two together (δυεῖν ἀγωγὴ) for the purpose of drawing;—this has been changed into ζυγόν, and there are many other examples of similar changes.

Her. There are.

Soc. Proceeding in the same train of thought I may remark that the word δέον (obligation) has a meaning which is the opposite of all the other appellations of good; for δέον is here a species of good, and is, nevertheless, the chain (δεσμὸς) or hinderer of motion, and therefore own brother of βλαβερόν.

Her. Yes, Socrates; that is quite plain.

Soc. Not if you restore the ancient form, which is more likely to be the correct one, [419] and read διὸν instead of δέον; if you convert the ε into an ι after the old fashion, this word will then agree with other words meaning good; for διὸν, not δέον, signifies the good, and is a term of praise; and the author of names has not contradicted himself, but in all these various appellations, δέον (obligatory), ὠφέλιμον (advantageous), λυσιτελοῦν (profitable), κερδαλέον (gainful), ἀγαθὸν (good), συμφέρον (expedient), εὔπορον (plenteous), the same conception is implied of the ordering or all-pervading principle which is praised, and the restraining and binding principle which is censured. And this is further illustrated by the word ζημιῶδης (hurtful), which if the ζ is only changed into δ as in the ancient language, becomes δημιῶδης; and this name, as you will perceive, is given to that which binds motion (δοῦντι ἰόν).

Her. What do you say of ἡδονὴ (pleasure), λύπη (pain), ἐπιθυμία (desire), and the like, Socrates?

Soc. I do not think, Hermogenes, that there is any great difficulty about them—ἡδονὴ is ἡ ὄνησις, the action which tends to advantage; and the original form may be supposed to have been ἡονὴ, but this has been altered by the insertion of the δ. Λύπη appears to be derived from the relaxation (λύειν) which the body feels when in sorrow; ἀνία (trouble) is the hindrance of motion (α and ἰέναι); ἀλγηδὼν (distress), if I am not mistaken, is a foreign word, which is derived from ἀλεινὸς (grievous); ὀδύνη (grief) is called from the putting on (ἔνδυσις) sorrow; in ἀχθηδὼν (vexation) "the word too labours," as any one may see; χαρὰ (joy) is the very expression of the fluency and diffusion of the soul (χέω); τέρψις (delight) is so called from the pleasure creeping (ἕρπον) through the soul, which may be likened to a breath (πνοή) and is properly ἑρπνοῦν, but has been altered by time into τερπνόν; εὐφροσύνη (cheerfulness) and ἐπιθυμία explain themselves; the former, which ought to be εὐφεροσύνη and has been changed into εὐφροσύνη, is named, as every one may see, from the soul moving (φέρεσθαι) in harmony with nature; ἐπιθυμία is really ἡ ἐπὶ τὸν θυμὸν ἰοῦσα δύναμις, the power which enters into the soul; θυμὸς (passion) is called from the rushing (θύσεως) and boiling of the soul; ἵμερος (desire) denotes the stream (ῥοῦς) which most draws the soul διὰ τὴν ἕσιν τῆς ῥοῆς—because flowing with desire (ἱέμενος), and expresses a longing after things and violent attraction of the soul to [420] them, and is termed ἵμερος from possessing this power; πόθος (longing) is expressive of the desire of that which is not present but absent, and in another place (που); this is the reason why the name πόθος is applied to things absent, as ἵμερος is to things present; ἔρως (love) is so called because flowing in (ἐσρῶν) from without; the stream is not inherent, but is an influence introduced through the eyes, and from flowing in was called ἔσρος (influx) in the old time when they used o for ω, and is called ἔρως, now that ω is substituted for o. But why do you not give me another word?

Her. What do you think of δόξα (opinion), and that class of words?

Soc. Δόξα is either derived from δίωξις (pursuit), and expresses the march of the soul in the pursuit of knowledge, or from the shooting of a bow (τόξον); the latter is more likely, and is confirmed by οἴησις (thinking), which is only οἶσις (moving), and implies the movement of the soul to the essential nature of each thing—just as βουλὴ (counsel) has to do with shooting (βολή); and βούλεσθαι (to wish) combines the notion of aiming and deliberating—all these words seem to follow δόξα, and all involve the idea of shooting, just as ἀβουλία, absence of counsel, on the other hand, is a mishap, or missing, or mistaking of the mark, or aim, or proposal, or object.

Her. You are quickening your pace now, Socrates.

Soc. Why yes, the end I now dedicate to God, not, however, until I have explained ἀνάγκη (necessity), which ought to come next, and ἑκούσιον (the voluntary). Ἑκούσιον is certainly the yielding (εἶκον) and unresisting—the notion implied is yielding and not opposing, yielding, as I was just now saying, to that motion which is in accordance with our will; but the necessary and resistant being contrary to our will, implies error and ignorance; the idea is taken from walking through a ravine which is impassable, and rugged, and overgrown, and impedes motion—and this is the derivation of the word ἀναγκαῖον (necessary) ἀν' ἄγκη ἰὸν, going through a ravine. But while my strength lasts let us persevere, and I hope that you will persevere with your questions.

Her. Well, then, let me ask about the greatest and noblest, such as ἀλήθεια (truth) and ψεῦδος (falsehood) and ὂν (being), *[421]* not forgetting to enquire why the word ὄνομα (name), which is the theme of our discussion, has this name of ὄνομα.

Soc. You know the word μαίεσθαι (to seek)?

Her. Yes;—meaning the same as ζητεῖν (to enquire).

Soc. The word ὄνομα seems to be a compressed sentence, signifying ὂν οὗ ζήτημα (being for which there is a search); as is still more obvious in ὀνομαστὸν (notable), which states in so many words that real existence is that for which there is a seeking (ὂν οὗ μάσμα); ἀλήθεια is also an agglomeration of θεία ἄλη (divine wandering), implying the divine motion of existence; ψεῦδος (falsehood) is the opposite of motion; here is another ill name given by the legislator to stagnation and forced inaction, which he compares to sleep (εὕδειν); but the original meaning of the word is disguised by the addition of ψ; ὂν and οὐσία are ἰὸν with an ι broken off; this agrees with the true principle, for being (ὂν) is also moving (ἰὸν), and the same may be said of not being, which is likewise called not going (οὐκίον or οὐκὶ ὂν=οὐκ ἰὸν).

Her. You have hammered away at them manfully; but suppose that some one were to say to you, what is the word ἰὸν, and what are ῥέον and δοῦν?—show me their fitness.

Soc. You mean to say, how should I answer him?

Her. Yes.

Soc. One way of giving the appearance of an answer has been already suggested.

Her. What way?

Soc. To say that names which we do not understand are of foreign origin; and this is very likely the right answer, and something of this kind may be true of them; but also the original forms of words may have been lost in the lapse of ages; names have been so twisted in all manner of ways, that I should not be surprised if the old language when compared with that now in use would appear to us to be a barbarous tongue.

Her. Very likely.

Soc. Yes, very likely. But still the enquiry demands our earnest attention and we must not flinch. For we should remember, that if a person go on analysing names into words, and enquiring also into the elements out of which the words are formed, and keeps on always repeating this process, he who has to answer him must at last give up the enquiry in despair.

Her. Very true.

[422] *Soc.* And at what point ought he to lose heart and give up the enquiry? Must he not stop when he comes to the names which are the elements of all other names and sentences; for these cannot be supposed to be made up of other names? The word ἀγαθὸν (good), for example, is, as we were saying, a compound of ἀγαστὸς (admirable) and θοός (swift). And probably θοὸς is made up of other elements, and these again of others. But if we take a word which is incapable of further resolution, then we shall be right in saying that we have at last reached a primary element, which need not be resolved any further.

Her. I believe you to be in the right.

Soc. And suppose the names about which you are now asking should turn out to be primary elements, must not their truth or law be examined according to some new method?

Her. Very likely.

Soc. Quite so, Hermogenes; all that has preceded would lead to this conclusion. And if, as I think, the conclusion is true, then I shall again say to you, come and help me, that I may not fall into some absurdity in stating the principle of primary names.

Her. Let me hear, and I will do my best to assist you.

Soc. I think that you will acknowledge with me, that one principle is applicable to all names, primary as well as secondary—when they are regarded simply as names, there is no difference in them.

Her. Certainly not.

Soc. All the names that we have been explaining were intended to indicate the nature of things.

Her. Of course.

Soc. And that this is true of the primary quite as much as of the secondary names, is implied in their being names.

Her. Surely.

Soc. But the secondary, as I conceive, derive their significance from the primary.

Her. That is evident.

Soc. Very good; but then how do the primary names which precede analysis show the natures of things, as far as they can be shown; which they must do, if they are to be real names? And here I will ask you a question: Suppose that we had no voice or tongue, and wanted to communicate with one another, should we not, like the deaf and dumb, make signs with the hands and head and the rest of the body?

Her. There would be no choice, Socrates.

[423] Soc. We should imitate the nature of the thing; the elevation of our hands to heaven would mean lightness and upwardness; heaviness and downwardness would be expressed by letting them drop to the ground; if we were describing the running of a horse, or any other animal, we should make our bodies and their gestures as like as we could to them.

Her. I do not see that we could do anything else.

Soc. We could not; for by bodily imitation only can the body ever express anything.

Her. Very true.

Soc. And when we want to express ourselves, either with the voice, or tongue, or mouth, the expression is simply their imitation of that which we want to express.

Her. It must be so, I think.

Soc. Then a name is a vocal imitation of that which the vocal imitator names or imitates?

Her. I think so.

Soc. Nay, my friend, I am disposed to think that we have not reached the truth as yet.

Her. Why not?

Soc. Because if we have we shall be obliged to admit that the people who imitate sheep, or cocks, or other animals, name that which they imitate.

Her. Quite true.

Soc. Then could I have been right in what I was saying?

Her. In my opinion, no. But I wish that you would tell me, Socrates, what sort of an imitation is a name?

Soc. In the first place, I should reply, not a musical imitation, although that is also vocal; nor, again, an imitation of what music imitates; these, in my judgment, would not be naming. Let me put the matter as follows: All objects have sound and figure, and many have colour?

Her. Certainly.

Soc. But the art of naming appears not to be concerned with imitations of this kind; the arts which have to do with them are music and drawing?

Her. True.

Soc. Again, is there not an essence of each thing, just as there is a colour, or sound? And is there not an essence of colour and sound as well as of anything else which may be said to have an essence?

Her. I should think so.

Soc. Well, and if any one could express the essence of each thing in letters and syllables, would he not express the nature of each thing?

[424] Her. Quite so.

Soc. The musician and the painter were the two names which you gave to the two other imitators. What will this imitator be called?

Her. I imagine, Socrates, that he must be the namer, or name-giver, of whom we are in search.

Soc. If this is true, then I think that we are in a condition to consider the names ῥοή (stream), ἰέναι (to go), σχέσις (retention), about which you were asking; and we may see whether the namer has grasped the nature of them in letters and syllables in such a manner as to imitate the essence or not.

Her. Very good.

Soc. But are these the only primary names, or are there others?

Her. There must be others.

Soc. So I should expect. But how shall we further analyse them, and where does the imitator begin? Imitation of the essence is made by syllables and letters; ought we not, therefore, first to separate the letters, just as those who are beginning rhythm first distinguish the powers of elementary, and then of compound sounds, and when they have done so, but not before, they proceed to the consideration of rhythms?

Her. Yes.

Soc. Must we not begin in the same way with letters; first separating the vowels, and then the consonants and mutes, into classes, according to the received distinctions of the learned; also the semivowels, which are neither vowels, nor yet mutes; and distinguishing into classes the vowels themselves? And when we have perfected the classification of things, we shall give their names, and see whether, as in the case of letters, there are any classes to which they may be all referred;[1] and hence we shall see their natures, and see, too, whether they have in them classes as there are in the letters; and when we have well considered all this, we shall know

[1] Cf. *Phaedrus,* 271.

how to apply them to what they resemble—whether one letter is used to denote one thing, or whether there is to be an admixture of several of them; just, as in painting, the painter who wants to depict anything sometimes uses purple only, or any other colour, and sometimes mixes up several colours, as his method is when he has to paint flesh colour or anything of that kind—he uses his colours as his figures appear to require them; and so, too, we shall apply letters to the expression of objects, either single letters when required, or several letters; and so we shall form syllables, as they are called, [425] and from syllables make nouns and verbs; and thus, at last, from the combinations of nouns and verbs arrive at language, large and fair and whole; and as the painter made a figure, even so shall we make speech by the art of the namer or the rhetorician, or by some other art. Not that I am literally speaking of ourselves, but I was carried away—meaning to say that this was the way in which (not we but) the ancients formed language, and what they put together we must take to pieces in like manner, if we are to attain a scientific view of the whole subject; and we must see whether the primary, and also whether the secondary elements are rightly given or not, for if they are not, the composition of them, my dear Hermogenes, will be a sorry piece of work, and in the wrong direction.

Her. That, Socrates, I can quite believe.

Soc. Well, but do you suppose that you will be able to analyse them in this way? for I am certain that I should not.

Her. Much less am I likely to be able.

Soc. Shall we leave them, then? or shall we seek to discover, if we can, something about them, according to the measure of our ability, saying by way of preface, as I said before of the Gods, that of the truth about them we know nothing, and do but entertain human notions of them. And in this present enquiry, let us say to ourselves, before we proceed, that the higher method is the one which we or others who would analyse language to any good purpose must follow; but under the circumstances, as men say, we must do as well as we can. What do you think?

Her. I very much approve.

Soc. That objects should be imitated in letters and syllables, and so find expression, may appear ridiculous, Hermogenes, but it cannot be avoided—there is no better principle to which we can look for the truth of first names. Deprived of this, we must have recourse to divine help, like the tragic poets, who in any perplexity have their Gods waiting in the air; and must get out of our difficulty in like fashion, by saying that "the Gods gave the first names, and therefore they are right." This will be the best contrivance, or perhaps that other notion may be even better still, of deriving them from some barbarous people, for the barbarians are older than we are; [426] or we may say that antiquity has cast a veil over them, which is the same sort of excuse as the last; for all these are not reasons but only ingenious excuses for having no reasons concerning the truth of words. And yet any sort of ignorance of first or primitive names involves an ignorance of secondary words; for they can only be explained by the primary. Clearly then the professor of languages should be able to give a very lucid explanation of first names, or let him be assured he will only talk nonsense about the rest. Do you not suppose this to be true?

Her. Certainly, Socrates.

Soc. My first notions of original names are truly wild and ridiculous, though I have no objection to impart them to you if you desire, and I hope that you will communicate to me in return anything better which you may have.

Her. Fear not; I will do my best.

Soc. In the first place, the letter ρ appears to me to be the general instrument expressing all motion (κίνησις). But I have not yet explained the meaning of this latter word, which is just ἴεσις (going); for the letter η was not in use among the ancients, who only employed ε; and the root is κίειν, which is a foreign form, the same as ἰέναι. And the old word κίνησις will be correctly given as ἴεσις in corresponding modern letters. Assuming this foreign root κίειν, and allowing for the change of the η and the insertion of the ν, we have κίνησις, which should have been κιείνησις or εἴσις; and στάσις is the negative of ἰέναι (or εἴσις), and has been improved into στάσις. Now the letter ρ, as I was saying, appeared to the imposer of names an excellent instrument for the expression of motion; and he frequently uses the letter for this purpose: for example, in the actual words ῥεῖν and ῥοὴ he represents motion by ρ; also in the words τρόμος (trembling), τραχὺς (rugged); and again, in words such as κρούειν (strike), θραύειν (crush), ἐρείκειν (bruise), θρύπτειν (break), κερματίζειν (crumble), ῥυμβεῖν (whirl): of all these sorts of movements he generally finds an expression in the letter R, because, as I imagine, he had observed that the tongue was most agitated and least at rest in the pronunciation of this letter, which he therefore used in order to express motion, just as by the letter ι he expresses the subtle elements which pass through all things. *[427]* This is why he uses the letter ι as imitative of motion, ἰέναι, ἵεσθαι. And there is another class of letters, φ, ψ, σ and ξ, of which the pronunciation is accompanied by great expenditure of breath; these are used in the imitation of such notions as ψυχρὸν (shivering), ξέον (seething), σείεσθαι (to be shaken), σεισμὸς (shock), and are always introduced by the giver of names when he wants to imitate what is φυσῶδες (windy). He seems to have thought that the closing and pressure of the tongue in the utterance of δ and τ was expressive of binding and rest in a place: he further observed the liquid movement of λ, in the pronunciation of which the tongue slips, and in this he found the expression of smoothness, as in λεῖος (level), and in the word ὀλισθάνειν (to slip) itself, λιπαρὸν (sleek), in the word κολλῶδες (gluey), and the like: the heavier sound of γ detained the slipping tongue, and the union of the two gave the notion of a glutinous clammy nature, as in γλίσχρος, γλυκὺς, γλοιώδες. The ν he observed to be sounded from within, and therefore to have a notion of inwardness; hence he introduced the sound in ἔνδον and ἐντός: α he assigned to the expression of size, and η of length, because they are great letters: ο was the sign of roundness, and therefore there is plenty of ο mixed up in the word γογγύλον (round). Thus did the legislator, reducing all things into letters and syllables, and impressing on them names and signs, and out of them by imitation compounding other signs. That is my view, Hermogenes, of the truth of names; but I should like to hear what Cratylus has more to say.

Her. But, Socrates, as I was telling you before, Cratylus mystifies me; he says that there is a fitness of names, but he never explains what is this fitness, so that I cannot tell whether his obscurity is intended or not. Tell me now, Cratylus, here in the presence of Socrates, do you agree in what Socrates has been saying about names, or have you something better of your own? and if you have, tell me what your view is, and then you will either learn of Socrates, or Socrates and I will learn of you.

Crat. Well, but surely, Hermogenes, you do not suppose that you can learn, or I explain, any subject of importance all in a moment; at any rate, not such a subject as language, which is, perhaps, the very greatest of all.

[428] Her. No, indeed; but, as Hesiod says, and I agree with him, "to add little to little" is worth while. And, therefore, if you think that you can add anything at all, however small, to our knowledge, take a little trouble and oblige Socrates, and me too, who certainly have a claim upon you.

Soc. I am by no means positive, Cratylus, in the view which Hermogenes and myself have worked out; and therefore do not hesitate to say what you think, which if it be better than my own view I shall gladly accept. And I should not be at all surprised to find that you have found some better notion. For you have evidently reflected on these matters and have had teachers, and if you have really a better theory of the truth of names, you may count me in the number of your disciples.

Crat. You are right, Socrates, in saying that I have made a study of these matters, and I might possibly convert you into a disciple. But I fear that the opposite is more probable, and I already find myself moved to say to you what Achilles in the "Prayers" says to Ajax—

Illustrious Ajax, son of Telamon, lord of the people,
You appear to have spoken in all things much to my mind.

And you, Socrates, appear to me to be an oracle, and to give answers much to my mind, whether you are inspired by Euthyphro, or whether some Muse may have long been an inhabitant of your breast, unconsciously to yourself.

Soc. Excellent Cratylus, I have long been wondering at my own wisdom; I cannot trust myself. And I think that I ought to stop and ask myself What am I saying? for there is nothing worse than self-deception—when the deceiver is always at home and always with you—it is quite terrible, and therefore I ought often to retrace my steps and endeavour to "look fore and aft," in the words of the aforesaid Homer. And now let me see; where are we? Have we not been saying that the correct name indicates the nature of the thing:—has this proposition been sufficiently proven?

Crat. Yes, Socrates, what you say, as I am disposed to think, is quite true.

Soc. Names, then, are given in order to instruct?

Crat. Certainly.

Soc. And naming is an art, and has artificers?

Crat. Yes.

Soc. And who are they?

[429] Crat. The legislators, of whom you spoke at first.

Soc. And does this art grow up among men like other arts? Let me explain what I mean: of painters, some are better and some worse?

Crat. Yes.

Soc. The better painters execute their works, I mean their figures, better, and the worse execute them worse; and of builders also, the better sort build fairer houses, and the worse build them worse.

Crat. True.

Soc. And among legislators, there are some who do their work better and some worse?

Crat. No; there I do not agree with you.

Soc. Then you do not think that some laws are better and others worse?

Crat. No, indeed.

Soc. Or that one name is better than another?

Crat. Certainly not.

Soc. Then all names are rightly imposed?

Crat. Yes, if they are names at all.

Soc. Well, what do you say to the name of our friend Hermogenes, which was mentioned before:—assuming that he has nothing of the nature of Hermes in him, shall we say that this is a wrong name, or not his name at all?

Crat. I should reply that Hermogenes is not his name at all, but only appears to be his, and is really the name of somebody else, who has the nature which corresponds to it.

Soc. And if a man were to call him Hermogenes, would he not be even speaking falsely? For there may be a doubt whether you can call him Hermogenes, if he is not.

Crat. What do you mean?

Soc. Are you maintaining that falsehood is impossible? For if this is your meaning I should answer, that there have been plenty of liars in all ages.

Crat. Why, Socrates, how can a man say that which is not?—say something and yet say nothing? For is not falsehood saying the thing which is not?

Soc. Your argument, friend, is too subtle for a man of my age. But I should like to know whether you are one of those philosophers who think that falsehood may be spoken but not said?

Crat. Neither spoken nor said.

Soc. Nor uttered nor addressed? For example: If a person, saluting you in a foreign country, were to take your hand and say: "Hail, Athenian stranger, Hermogenes, son of Smicrion"—these words, whether spoken, said, uttered, or addressed, would have no application to you but only to our friend Hermogenes, or perhaps to nobody at all?

Crat. In my opinion, Socrates, the speaker would only be talking nonsense.

Soc. Well, but that will be quite enough for me, if you will tell me whether the nonsense would be true or false, *[430]* or partly true and partly false:—which is all that I want to know.

Crat. I should say that he would be putting himself in motion to no purpose; and that his words would be an unmeaning sound like the noise of hammering at a brazen pot.

Soc. But let us see, Cratylus, whether we cannot find a meeting-point, for you would admit that the name is not the same with the thing named?

Crat. I should.

Soc. And would you further acknowledge that the name is an imitation of the thing?

Crat. Certainly.

Soc. And you would say that pictures are also imitations of things, but in another way?

Crat. Yes.

Soc. I believe you may be right, but I do not rightly understand you. Please to say, then, whether both sorts of imitation (I mean both pictures or words) are not equally attributable and applicable to the things of which they are the imitation.

Crat. They are.

Soc. First look at the matter thus: you may attribute the likeness of the man to the man, and of the woman to the woman; and so on?

Crat. Certainly.

Soc. And conversely you may attribute the likeness of the man to the woman, and of the woman to the man?

Crat. Very true.

Soc. And are both modes of assigning them right, or only the first?

Crat. Only the first.

Soc. That is to say, the mode of assignment which attributes to each that which belongs to them and is like them?

Crat. That is my view.

Soc. Now then, as I am desirous that we being friends should have a good understanding about the argument, let me state my view to you: the first mode of assignment, whether applied to figures or to names, I call right, and when applied to names only, true as well as right; and the other mode of giving and assigning the name which is unlike, I call wrong, and in the case of names, false as well as wrong.

Crat. That may be true, Socrates, in the case of pictures; they may be wrongly assigned; but not in the case of names—they must be always right.

Soc. Why, what is the difference? May I not go to a man and say to him, "This is your picture," showing him his own likeness, or perhaps the likeness of a woman; and when I say "show," I mean bring before the sense of sight.

Crat. Certainly.

Soc. And may I not go to him again, and say, "This is your name"?—for the name, like the picture, is an imitation. May I not say to him— "This is your name"? *[431]* and may I not then bring to his sense of hearing the imitation of himself, when I say, "This is a man"; or of a female of the human species, when I say, "This is a woman," as the case may be? Is not all that quite possible?

Crat. I would fain agree with you, Socrates; and therefore I say, Granted.

Soc. That is very good of you, if I am right, which need hardly be disputed at present. But if I can assign names as well as pictures to objects, the right assignment of them we may call truth, and the wrong assignment of them falsehood. Now if there be such a wrong assignment of names, there may also be a wrong or inappropriate assignment of verbs; and if of names and verbs then of the sentences, which are made up of them. What do you say, Cratylus?

Crat. I agree; and think that what you say is very true.

Soc. And further, primitive nouns may be compared to pictures, and in pictures you may either give all the appropriate colours and figures, or you may not give them all—some may be wanting; or there may be too many or too much of them—may there not?

Crat. Very true.

Soc. And he who gives all gives a perfect picture or figure; and he who takes away or adds also gives a picture or figure, but not a good one.

Crat. Yes.

Soc. In like manner, he who by syllables and letters imitates the nature of things, if he gives all that is appropriate will produce a good image, or in other words a name; but if he subtracts or perhaps adds a little, he will make an image but not a good one; whence I infer that some names are well and others ill made.

Crat. That is true.

Soc. Then the artist of names may be sometimes good, or he may be bad?

Crat. Yes.

Soc. And this artist of names is called the legislator?

Crat. Yes.

Soc. Then like other artists the legislator may be good or he may be bad; it must surely be so if our former admissions hold good?

Crat. Very true, Socrates; but the case of language, you see, is different; for when by the help of grammar we assign the letters α or β, *[432]* or any other letters to a certain name, then, if we add, or subtract, or misplace a letter, the name which is written is not only written wrongly, but not written at all; and in any of these cases becomes other than a name.

Soc. But I doubt whether your view is altogether correct, Cratylus.

Crat. How so?

Soc. I believe that what you say may be true about numbers, which must be just what they are, or not be at all; for example, the number ten at once becomes other than ten if a unit be added or subtracted, and so of any other number: but this does not apply to that which is qualitative or to anything which is represented under an image. I should say rather that the image, if expressing in every point the entire reality, would no longer be an image. Let us suppose the existence of two objects: one of them shall be Cratylus, and the other the image of Cratylus; and we will suppose, further, that some God makes not only a representation such as a painter would make of your outward form and colour, but also creates an inward organization like yours, having the same warmth and softness; and into this infuses motion, and soul, and mind, such as you have, and in a word copies all your qualities, and places them by you in another form; would you say that this was Cratylus and the image of Cratylus, or that there were two Cratyluses?

Crat. I should say that there were two Cratyluses.

Soc. Then you see, my friend, that we must find some other principle of truth in images, and also in names; and not insist that an image is no longer an image when something is added or subtracted. Do you not perceive that images are very far from having qualities which are the exact counterpart of the realities which they represent?

Crat. Yes, I see.

Soc. But then how ridiculous would be the effect of names on things, if they were exactly the same with them! For they would be the doubles of them, and no one would be able to determine which were the names and which were the realities.

Crat. Quite true.

Soc. Then fear not, but have the courage to

admit that one name may be correctly and another incorrectly given; and do not insist that the name shall be exactly the same with the thing; but allow the occasional substitution of a wrong letter, and if of a letter also of a noun in a sentence, and if of a noun in a sentence also of a sentence which is not appropriate to the matter, and acknowledge that the thing may be named, and described, so long as the general character of the thing which you are describing is retained; and this, as you will remember, [433] was remarked by Hermogenes and myself in the particular instance of the names of the letters.

Crat. Yes, I remember.

Soc. Good; and when the general character is preserved, even if some of the proper letters are wanting, still the thing is signified;—well, if all the letters are given; not well, when only a few of them are given. I think that we had better admit this, lest we be punished like travellers in Ægina who wander about the street late at night: and be likewise told by truth herself that we have arrived too late; or if not, you must find out some new notion of correctness of names, and no longer maintain that a name is the expression of a thing in letters or syllables; for if you say both, you will be inconsistent with yourself.

Crat. I quite acknowledge, Socrates, what you say to be very reasonable.

Soc. Then as we are agreed thus far, let us ask ourselves whether a name rightly imposed ought not to have the proper letters.

Crat. Yes.

Soc. And the proper letters are those which are like the things?

Crat. Yes.

Soc. Enough then of names which are rightly given. And in names which are incorrectly given, the greater part may be supposed to be made up of proper and similar letters, or there would be no likeness; but there will be likewise a part which is improper and spoils the beauty and formation of the word: you would admit that?

Crat. There would be no use, Socrates, in my quarrelling with you, since I cannot be satisfied that a name which is incorrectly given is a name at all.

Soc. Do you admit a name to be the representation of a thing?

Crat. Yes, I do.

Soc. But do you not allow that some nouns are primitive, and some derived?

Crat. Yes, I do.

Soc. Then if you admit that primitive or first nouns are representations of things, is there any better way of framing representations than by assimilating them to the objects as much as you can; or do you prefer the notion of Hermogenes and of many others, who say that names are conventional, and have a meaning to those who have agreed about them, and who have previous knowledge of the things intended by them, and that convention is the only principle; and whether you abide by our present convention, or make a new and opposite one, according to which you call small great and great small—that, they would say, makes no difference, if you are only agreed. Which of these two notions do you prefer?

[434] *Crat.* Representation by likeness, Socrates, is infinitely better than representation by any chance sign.

Soc. Very good: but if the name is to be like the thing, the letters out of which the first names are composed must also be like things. Returning to the image of the picture, I would ask, How could any one ever compose a picture which would be like anything at all, if there were not pigments in nature which resembled the things imitated, and out of which the picture is composed?

Crat. Impossible.

Soc. No more could names ever resemble any actually existing thing, unless the original elements of which they are compounded bore some degree of resemblance to the objects of which the names are the imitation: And the original elements are letters?

Crat. Yes.

Soc. Let me now invite you to consider what Hermogenes and I were saying about sounds. Do you agree with me that the letter ῥ is expressive of rapidity, motion, and hardness? Were we right or wrong in saying so?

Crat. I should say that you were right.

Soc. And that λ was expressive of smoothness, and softness, and the like?

Crat. There again you were right.

Soc. And yet, as you are aware, that which is called by us σκληρότης, is by the Eretrians called σκληρότηρ.

Crat. Very true.

Soc. But are the letters ρ and σ equivalents; and is there the same significance to them in the termination ῥ, which there is to us in σ, or is there no significance to one of us?

Crat. Nay, surely there is a significance to both of us.

Soc. In as far as they are like, or in as far as they are unlike?

Crat. In as far as they are like.

Soc. Are they altogether alike?

Crat. Yes; for the purpose of expressing motion.

Soc. And what do you say of the insertion of the λ? for that is expressive not of hardness but of softness.

Crat. Why, perhaps the letter λ is wrongly inserted, Socrates, and should be altered into ρ, as you were saying to Hermogenes and in my opinion rightly, when you spoke of adding and subtracting letters upon occasion.

Soc. Good. But still the word is intelligible to both of us; when I say σκληρὸς (hard), you know what I mean.

Crat. Yes, my dear friend, and the explanation of that is custom.

Soc. And what is custom but convention? I utter a sound which I understand, and you know that I understand the meaning of the sound: *[435]* this is what you are saying?

Crat. Yes.

Soc. And if when I speak you know my meaning, there is an indication given by me to you?

Crat. Yes.

Soc. This indication of my meaning may proceed from unlike as well as from like, for example in the λ of σκληρότης. But if this is true, then you have made a convention with yourself, and the correctness of a name turns out to be convention, since letters which are unlike are indicative equally with those which are like, if they are sanctioned by custom and convention. And even supposing that you distinguish custom from convention ever so much, still you must say that the signification of words is given by custom and not by likeness, for custom may indicate by the unlike as well as by the like. But as we are agreed thus far, Cratylus (for I shall assume that your silence gives consent), then custom and convention must be supposed to contribute to the indication of our thoughts; for suppose we take the instance of number, how can you ever imagine, my good friend, that you will find names resembling every individual number, unless you allow that which you term convention and agreement to have authority in determining the correctness of names? I quite agree with you that words should as far as possible resemble things; but I fear that this dragging in of resemblance, as Hermogenes says,[1] is a shabby thing, which has

[1] See above, 414.

to be supplemented by the mechanical aid of convention with a view to correctness; for I believe that if we could always, or almost always, use likenesses, which are perfectly appropriate, this would be the most perfect state of language; as the opposite is the most imperfect. But let me ask you, what is the force of names, and what is the use of them?

Crat. The use of names, Socrates, as I should imagine, is to inform: the simple truth is, that he who knows names knows also the things which are expressed by them.

Soc. I suppose you mean to say, Cratylus, that as the name is, so also is the thing; and that he who knows the one will also know the other, because they are similars, and all similars fall under the same art or science; and therefore you would say that he who knows names will also know things.

Crat. That is precisely what I mean.

Soc. But let us consider what is the nature of this information about things which, according to you, is given us by names. Is it the best sort of information? or is there any other? What do you say?

[436] Crat. I believe that to be both the only and the best sort of information about them; there can be no other.

Soc. But do you believe that in the discovery of them, he who discovers the names discovers also the things; or is this only the method of instruction, and is there some other method of enquiry and discovery?

Crat. I certainly believe that the methods of enquiry and discovery are of the same nature as instruction.

Soc. Well, but do you not see, Cratylus, that he who follows names in the search after things, and analyses their meaning, is in great danger of being deceived?

Crat. How so?

Soc. Why clearly he who first gave names gave them according to his conception of the things which they signified—did he not?

Crat. True.

Soc. And if his conception was erroneous, and he gave names according to his conception, in what position shall we who are his followers find ourselves? Shall we not be deceived by him?

Crat. But, Socrates, am I not right in thinking that he must surely have known; or else, as I was saying, his names would not be names at all? And you have a clear proof that he has not missed the truth, and the proof is—that he is perfectly consistent. Did you ever observe in speaking that all the words which you utter have a common character and purpose?

Soc. But that, friend Cratylus, is no answer. For if he did begin in error, he may have forced the remainder into agreement with the original error and with himself; there would be nothing strange in this, any more than in geometrical diagrams, which have often a slight and invisible flaw in the first part of the process, and are consistently mistaken in the long deductions which follow. And this is the reason why every man should expend his chief thought and attention on the consideration of his first principles:—are they or are they not rightly laid down? and when he has duly sifted them, all the rest will follow. Now I should be astonished to find that names are really consistent. And here let us revert to our former discussion: Were we not saying that all things are in motion and progress and flux, and that this idea of motion is expressed by names? Do you not conceive that to be the meaning of them?

Crat. Yes; that is assuredly their meaning, and the true meaning.

[437] *Soc.* Let us revert to ἐπιστήμη (knowledge), and observe how ambiguous this word is, seeming rather to signify stopping the soul at things than going round with them; and therefore we should leave the beginning as at present, and not reject the ε (cf. 412 A), but make an insertion of an ι instead of an ε (not πιστήμη, but ἐπιστήμη). Take another example: βέβαιον (sure) is clearly the expression of station and position, and not of motion. Again, the word ἱστορία (enquiry) bears upon the face of it the stopping (ἱστάναι) of the stream; and the word πιστὸν (faithful) certainly indicates cessation of motion; then, again, μνήμη (memory), as any one may see, expresses rest in the soul, and not motion. Moreover, words such as ἁμαρτία and συμφορά, which have a bad sense, viewed in the light of their etymologies will be the same as σύνεσις and ἐπιστήμη and other words which have a good sense (cf. ὁμαρτεῖν, συνιέναι, ἕπεσθαι, συμφέρεσθαι); and much the same may be said of ἀμαθία and ἀκολαΐα, for ἀμαθία may be explained as ἡ ἅμα θεῷ ἰόντος πορεία, and ἀκολασία as ἡ ἀκολουθία τοῖς πράγμασιν. Thus the names which in these instances we find to have the worst sense, will turn out to be framed on the same principle as those which have the best. And any one I believe who would take the trouble might find many other examples in which the giver of names indicates, not that things are in motion or progress, but that they are at rest; which is the opposite of motion.

Crat. Yes, Socrates, but observe; the greater number express motion.

Soc. What of that, Cratylus? Are we to count them like votes? and is correctness of names the voice of the majority? Are we to say of whichever sort there are most, those are the true ones?

Crat. No; that is not reasonable.

Soc. Certainly not. But let us have done with this question and proceed to another, about which I should like to know whether you think with me. Were we not lately acknowledging that the first givers of names in states, both Hellenic and barbarous, were the legislators, and that the art which gave names was the art of the legislator?

Crat. Quite true.

Soc. Tell me, then, did the first legislators, who were the givers of the first names, know or not know the things which they named?

Crat. They must have known, Socrates.

[438] *Soc.* Why, yes, friend Cratylus, they could hardly have been ignorant.

Crat. I should say not.

Soc. Let us return to the point from which we digressed. You were saying, if you remember, that he who gave names must have known the things which he named; are you still of that opinion?

Crat. I am.

Soc. And would you say that the giver of the first names had also a knowledge of the things which he named?

Crat. I should.

Soc. But how could he have learned or discovered things from names if the primitive names were not yet given? For, if we are correct in our view, the only way of learning and discovering things, is either to discover names for ourselves or to learn them from others.

Crat. I think that there is a good deal in what you say, Socrates.

Soc. But if things are only to be known through names, how can we suppose that the givers of names had knowledge, or were legislators before there were names at all, and therefore before they could have known them?

Crat. I believe, Socrates, the true account of the matter to be, that a power more than human gave things their first names, and that the names which are thus given are necessarily their true names.

Soc. Then how came the giver of the names, if he was an inspired being or God, to contradict himself? For were we not saying just now that he made some names expressive of rest and others of motion? Were we mistaken?

Crat. But I suppose one of the two not to be names at all.

Soc. And which, then, did he make, my good friend; those which are expressive of rest, or those which are expressive of motion? This is a point which, as I said before, cannot be determined by counting them.

Crat. No; not in that way, Socrates.

Soc. But if this is a battle of names, some of them asserting that they are like the truth, others contending that *they* are, how or by what criterion are we to decide between them? For there are no other names to which appeal can be made, but obviously recourse must be had to another standard which, without employing names, will make clear which of the two are right; and this must be a standard which shows the truth of things.

Crat. I agree.

Soc. But if that is true, Cratylus, then I suppose that things may be known without names?

Crat. Clearly.

Soc. But how would you expect to know them? What other way can there be of knowing them, except the true and natural way, through their affinities, when they are akin to each other, and through themselves? For that which is other and different from them must signify something other and different from them.

Crat. What you are saying is, I think, true.

[439] *Soc.* Well, but reflect; have we not several times acknowledged that names rightly given are the likenesses and images of the things which they name?

Crat. Yes.

Soc. Let us suppose that to any extent you please you can learn things through the medium of names, and suppose also that you can learn them from the things themselves—which is likely to be the nobler and clearer way; to learn of the image, whether the image and the truth of which the image is the expression have been rightly conceived, or to learn of the truth whether the truth and the image of it have been duly executed?

Crat. I should say that we must learn of the truth.

Soc. How real existence is to be studied or discovered is, I suspect, beyond you and me. But we may admit so much, that the knowledge of things is not to be derived from names. No; they must be studied and investigated in themselves.

Crat. Clearly, Socrates.

Soc. There is another point. I should not like us to be imposed upon by the appearance of such a multitude of names, all tending in the same direction. I myself do not deny that the givers of names did really give them under the idea that all things were in motion and flux; which was their sincere but, I think, mistaken opinion. And having fallen into a kind of whirlpool themselves, they are carried round, and want to drag us in after them. There is a matter, master Cratylus, about which I often dream, and should like to ask your opinion: Tell me, whether there is or is not any absolute beauty or good, or any other absolute existence?

Crat. Certainly, Socrates, I think so.

Soc. Then let us seek the true beauty: not asking whether a face is fair, or anything of that sort, for all such things appear to be in a flux; but let us ask whether the true beauty is not always beautiful.

Crat. Certainly.

Soc. And can we rightly speak of a beauty which is always passing away, and is first this and then that; must not the same thing be born and retire and vanish while the word is in our mouths?

Crat. Undoubtedly.

Soc. Then how can that be a real thing which is never in the same state? for obviously things which are the same cannot change while they remain the same; and if they are always the same and in the same state, and never depart from their original form, they can never change or be moved.

Crat. Certainly they cannot.

[440] *Soc.* Nor yet can they be known by any one; for at the moment that the observer approaches, then they become other and of another nature, so that you cannot get any further in knowing their nature or state, for you cannot know that which has no state.

Crat. True.

Soc. Nor can we reasonably say, Cratylus, that there is knowledge at all, if everything is in a state of transition and there is nothing abiding; for knowledge too cannot continue to be knowledge unless continuing always to abide and exist. But if the very nature of knowledge changes, at the time when the change occurs there will be no knowledge; and if the transition is always going on, there will always be no knowledge, and, according to this view, there will be no one to know and nothing to be known: but if that which knows and that which is known exist ever, and the beautiful and the good and every other thing also exist, then I do not think that they can resemble a process or flux, as we were just now supposing. Whether there is this eternal nature in things, or whether the truth is what Heracleitus and his followers and many others say, is a question hard to determine; and no man of sense will like to put himself or the education of his mind in the power of names: neither will he so far trust names or the givers of names as to be confident in any knowledge which condemns himself and other existences to an unhealthy state of unreality; he will not believe that all things leak like a pot, or imagine that the world is a man who has a running at the nose. This may be true, Cratylus, but is also very likely to be untrue; and therefore I would not have you be too easily persuaded of it. Reflect well

and like a man, and do not easily accept such a doctrine; for you are young and of an age to learn. And when you have found the truth, come and tell me.

Crat. I will do as you say, though I can assure you, Socrates, that I have been considering the matter already, and the result of a great deal of trouble and consideration is that I incline to Heracleitus.

Soc. Then, another day, my friend, when you come back, you shall give me a lesson; but at present, go into the country, as you are intending, and Hermogenes shall set you on your way.

Crat. Very good, Socrates; I hope, however, that you will continue to think about these things yourself.

PHAEDRUS

PERSONS OF THE DIALOGUE: SOCRATES; PHAEDRUS. *Scene: Under a plane-tree, by the banks of the Ilissus*

~~~~~~~~~~~~~~~~~~

[227] *Socrates.* My dear Phaedrus, whence come you, and whither are you going?

Phaedrus. I come from Lysias the son of Cephalus, and I am going to take a walk outside the wall, for I have been sitting with him the whole morning; and our common friend Acumenus tells me that it is much more refreshing to walk in the open air than to be shut up in a cloister.

Soc. There he is right. Lysias then, I suppose, was in the town?

Phaedr. Yes, he was staying with Epicrates, here at the house of Morychus; that house which is near the temple of Olympian Zeus.

Soc. And how did he entertain you? Can I be wrong in supposing that Lysias gave you a feast of discourse?

Phaedr. You shall hear, if you can spare time to accompany me.

Soc. And should I not deem the conversation of you and Lysias "a thing of higher import," as I may say in the words of Pindar, "than any business"?

Phaedr. Will you go on?

Soc. And will you go on with the narration?

Phaedr. My tale, Socrates, is one of your sort, for love was the theme which occupied us— love after a fashion: Lysias has been writing about a fair youth who was being tempted, but not by a lover; and this was the point: he ingeniously proved that the non-lover should be accepted rather than the lover.

Soc. O that is noble of him! I wish that he would say the poor man rather than the rich, and the old man rather than the young one;— then he would meet the case of me and of many

a man; his words would be quite refreshing, and he would be a public benefactor. For my part, I do so long to hear his speech, that if you walk all the way to Megara, and when you have reached the wall come back, as Herodicus recommends, without going in, I will keep you company.

Phaedr. What do you mean, my good Socrates? How can you imagine that my unpractised memory can do justice to an elaborate work, [228] which the greatest rhetorician of the age spent a long time in composing. Indeed, I cannot; I would give a great deal if I could.

Soc. I believe that I know Phaedrus about as well as I know myself, and I am very sure that the speech of Lysias was repeated to him, not once only, but again and again;—he insisted on hearing it many times over and Lysias was very willing to gratify him; at last, when nothing else would do, he got hold of the book, and looked at what he most wanted to see,—this occupied him during the whole morning;— and then when he was tired with sitting, he went out to take a walk, not until, by the dog, as I believe, he had simply learned by heart the entire discourse, unless it was unusually long, and he went to a place outside the wall that he might practise his lesson. There he saw a certain lover of discourse who had a similar weakness;—he saw and rejoiced; now thought he, "I shall have a partner in my revels." And he invited him to come and walk with him. But when the lover of discourse begged that he would repeat the tale, he gave himself airs and said, "No I cannot," as if he were indisposed; although, if the hearer had refused, he would sooner or later have been compelled by him to listen whether he would or no. Therefore, Phaedrus, bid him do at once what he will soon do whether bidden or not.

Phaedr. I see that you will not let me off until I speak in some fashion or other; verily therefore my best plan is to speak as I best can.

Soc. A very true remark, that of yours.

Phaedr. I will do as I say; but believe me, Socrates, I did not learn the very words—O no; nevertheless I have a general notion of what he said, and will give you a summary of the points in which the lover differed from the non-lover. Let me begin at the beginning.

Soc. Yes, my sweet one; but you must first of all show what you have in your left hand under your cloak, for that roll, as I suspect, is the actual discourse. Now, much as I love you, I would not have you suppose that I am going to have your memory exercised at my expense, if you have Lysias himself here.

Phaedr. Enough; I see that I have no hope of practising my art upon you. But if I am to read, where would you please to sit? *[229]*

Soc. Let us turn aside and go by the Ilissus; we will sit down at some quiet spot.

Phaedr. I am fortunate in not having my sandals, and as you never have any, I think that we may go along the brook and cool our feet in the water; this will be the easiest way, and at midday and in the summer is far from being unpleasant.

Soc. Lead on, and look out for a place in which we can sit down.

Phaedr. Do you see the tallest plane-tree in the distance?

Soc. Yes.

Phaedr. There are shade and gentle breezes, and grass on which we may either sit or lie down.

Soc. Move forward.

Phaedr. I should like to know, Socrates, whether the place is not somewhere here at which Boreas is said to have carried off Orithyia from the banks of the Ilissus?

Soc. Such is the tradition.

Phaedr. And is this the exact spot? The little stream is delightfully clear and bright; I can fancy that there might be maidens playing near.

Soc. I believe that the spot is not exactly here, but about a quarter of a mile lower down, where you cross to the temple of Artemis, and there is, I think, some sort of an altar of Boreas at the place.

Phaedr. I have never noticed it; but I beseech you to tell me, Socrates, do you believe this tale?

Soc. The wise are doubtful, and I should not be singular if, like them, I too doubted. I might have a rational explanation that Orithyia was playing with Pharmacia, when a northern gust carried her over the neighbouring rocks; and this being the manner of her death, she was said to have been carried away by Boreas. There is a discrepancy, however, about the locality; according to another version of the story she was taken from Areopagus, and not from this place. Now I quite acknowledge that these allegories are very nice, but he is not to be envied who has to invent them; much labour and ingenuity will be required of him; and when he has once begun, he must go on and rehabilitate Hippocentaurs and chimeras dire. Gorgons and winged steeds flow in apace, and numberless other inconceivable and portentous natures. And if he is sceptical about them, and would fain reduce them one after another to the rules of probability, this sort of crude philosophy will take up a great deal of time. Now I have no leisure for such enquiries; shall I tell you why? I must first know myself, as the Delphian inscription says; *[230]* to be curious about that which is not my concern, while I am still in ignorance of my own self, would be ridiculous. And therefore I bid farewell to all this; the common opinion is enough for me. For, as I was saying, I want to know not about this, but about myself: am I a monster more complicated and swollen with passion than the serpent Typho, or a creature of a gentler and simpler sort, to whom Nature has given a diviner and lowlier destiny? But let me ask you, friend: have we not reached the plane-tree to which you were conducting us?

Phaedr. Yes, this is the tree.

Soc. By Herè, a fair resting-place, full of summer sounds and scents. Here is this lofty and spreading plane-tree, and the agnus castus high and clustering, in the fullest blossom and the greatest fragrance; and the stream which flows beneath the plane-tree is deliciously cold to the feet. Judging from the ornaments and images, this must be a spot sacred to Achelous and the Nymphs. How delightful is the breeze:—so very sweet; and there is a sound in the air shrill and summerlike which makes answer to the chorus of the cicadae. But the greatest charm of all is the grass, like a pillow gently sloping to the head. My dear Phaedrus, you have been an admirable guide.

Phaedr. What an incomprehensible being

you are, Socrates: when you are in the country, as you say, you really are like some stranger who is led about by a guide. Do you ever cross the border? I rather think that you never venture even outside the gates.

Soc. Very true, my good friend; and I hope that you will excuse me when you hear the reason, which is, that I am a lover of knowledge, and the men who dwell in the city are my teachers, and not the trees or the country. Though I do indeed believe that you have found a spell with which to draw me out of the city into the country, like a hungry cow before whom a bough or a bunch of fruit is waved. For only hold up before me in like manner a book, and you may lead me all round Attica, and over the wide world. And now having arrived, I intend to lie down, and do you choose any posture in which you can read best. Begin.

Phaedr. Listen. You know how matters stand with me; and how, as I conceive, *[231]* this affair may be arranged for the advantage of both of us. And I maintain that I ought not to fail in my suit, because I am not your lover: for lovers repent of the kindnesses which they have shown when their passion ceases, but to the non-lovers who are free and not under any compulsion, no time of repentance ever comes; for they confer their benefits according to the measure of their ability, in the way which is most conducive to their own interest. Then again, lovers consider how by reason of their love they have neglected their own concerns and rendered service to others: and when to these benefits conferred they add on the troubles which they have endured, they think that they have long ago made to the beloved a very ample return. But the non-lover has no such tormenting recollections; he has never neglected his affairs or quarrelled with his relations; he has no troubles to add up or excuse to invent; and being well rid of all these evils, why should he not freely do what will gratify the beloved?

If you say that the lover is more to be esteemed, because his love is thought to be greater; for he is willing to say and do what is hateful to other men, in order to please his beloved; —that, if true, is only a proof that he will prefer any future love to his present, and will injure his old love at the pleasure of the new. And how, in a matter of such infinite importance, can a man be right in trusting himself to one who is afflicted with a malady which no experienced person would attempt to cure, for the patient himself admits that he is not in his

right mind, and acknowledges that he is wrong in his mind, but says that he is unable to control himself? And if he came to his right mind, would he ever imagine that the desires were good which he conceived when in his wrong mind? Once more, there are many more non-lovers than lovers; and if you choose the best of the lovers, you will not have many to choose from; but if from the non-lovers, the choice will be larger, and you will be far more likely to find among them a person who is worthy of your friendship. If public opinion be your dread, and you would avoid reproach, in all probability the lover, who is always thinking that other men are as emulous of him as he is of *[232]* them, will boast to some one of his successes, and make a show of them openly in the pride of his heart;—he wants others to know that his labour has not been lost; but the non-lover is more his own master, and is desirous of solid good, and not of the opinion of mankind. Again, the lover may be generally noted or seen following the beloved (this is his regular occupation), and whenever they are observed to exchange two words they are supposed to meet about some affair of love either past or in contemplation; but when non-lovers meet, no one asks the reason why, because people know that talking to another is natural, whether friendship or mere pleasure be the motive.

Once more, if you fear the fickleness of friendship, consider that in any other case a quarrel might be a mutual calamity; but now, when you have given up what is most precious to you, you will be the greater loser, and therefore, you will have more reason in being afraid of the lover, for his vexations are many, and he is always fancying that every one is leagued against him. Wherefore also he debars his beloved from society; he will not have you intimate with the wealthy, lest they should exceed him in wealth, or with men of education, lest they should be his superiors in understanding; and he is equally afraid of anybody's influence who has any other advantage over himself. If he can persuade you to break with them, you are left without a friend in the world; or if, out of a regard to your own interest, you have more sense than to comply with his desire, you will have to quarrel with him. But those who are non-lovers, and whose success in love is the reward of their merit, will not be jealous of the companions of their beloved, and will rather hate those who refuse to be his associates, thinking that their favourite is slighted by the latter and benefited by the former; for more love than hatred may be expected to come to him out of his friendship with others. Many lovers too have loved the person of a youth before they knew his character or his belongings; so that when their passion has passed away, there is no knowing whether they will continue to be his friends; [233] whereas, in the case of non-lovers who were always friends, the friendship is not lessened by the favours granted; but the recollection of these remains with them, and is an earnest of good things to come.

Further, I say that you are likely to be improved by me, whereas the lover will spoil you. For they praise your words and actions in a wrong way; partly, because they are afraid of offending you, and also, their judgment is weakened by passion. Such are the feats which love exhibits; he makes things painful to the disappointed which give no pain to others; he compels the successful lover to praise what ought not to give him pleasure, and therefore the beloved is to be pitied rather than envied. But if you listen to me, in the first place, I, in my intercourse with you, shall not merely regard present enjoyment, but also future advantage, being not mastered by love, but my own master; nor for small causes taking violent dislikes, but even when the cause is great, slowly laying up little wrath—unintentional offences I shall forgive, and intentional ones I shall try to prevent; and these are the marks of a friendship which will last.

Do you think that a lover only can be a firm friend? reflect:—if this were true, we should set small value on sons, or fathers, or mothers; nor should we ever have loyal friends, for our love of them arises not from passion, but from other associations. Further, if we ought to shower favours on those who are the most eager suitors,—on that principle, we ought always to do good, not to the most virtuous, but to the most needy; for they are the persons who will be most relieved, and will therefore be the most grateful; and when you make a feast you should invite not your friend, but the beggar and the empty soul; for they will love you, and attend you, and come about your doors, and will be the best pleased, and the most grateful, and will invoke many a blessing on your head. Yet surely you ought not to be granting favours to those who besiege you with prayer, but to those who are best able to reward you; nor to the lover only, but to those who are worthy of love; nor to those who will enjoy the bloom of your youth, [234] but to those who will share their possessions with you in age; nor to those

who, having succeeded, will glory in their success to others, but to those who will be modest and tell no tales; nor to those who care about you for a moment only, but to those who will continue your friends through life; nor to those who, when their passion is over, will pick a quarrel with you, but rather to those who, when the charm of youth has left you, will show their own virtue. Remember what I have said; and consider yet this further point: friends admonish the lover under the idea that his way of life is bad, but no one of his kindred ever yet censured the non-lover, or thought that he was ill-advised about his own interests.

"Perhaps you will ask me whether I propose that you should indulge every non-lover. To which I reply that not even the lover would advise you to indulge all lovers, for the indiscriminate favour is less esteemed by the rational recipient, and less easily hidden by him who would escape the censure of the world. Now love ought to be for the advantage of both parties, and for the injury of neither.

"I believe that I have said enough; but if there is anything more which you desire or which in your opinion needs to be supplied, ask and I will answer."

Now, Socrates, what do you think? Is not the discourse excellent, more especially in the matter of the language?

Soc. Yes, quite admirable; the effect on me was ravishing. And this I owe to you, Phaedrus, for I observed you while reading to be in an ecstasy, and thinking that you are more experienced in these matters than I am, I followed your example, and, like you, my divine darling, I became inspired with a phrenzy.

Phaedr. Indeed, you are pleased to be merry.

Soc. Do you mean that I am not in earnest?

Phaedr. Now don't talk in that way, Socrates, but let me have your real opinion; I adjure you, by Zeus, the god of friendship, to tell me whether you think that any Hellene could have said more or spoken better on the same subject.

Soc. Well, but are you and I expected to praise the sentiments of the author, or only the clearness, and roundness, and finish, and tournure of the language? As to the first I willingly submit to your better judgment, [235] for I am not worthy to form an opinion, having only attended to the rhetorical manner; and I was doubting whether this could have been defended even by Lysias himself; I thought, though I speak under correction, that he repeated himself two or three times, either from want of words or from want of pains; and also, he appeared to me ostentatiously to exult in showing how well he could say the same thing in two or three ways.

Phaedr. Nonsense, Socrates; what you call repetition was the especial merit of the speech; for he omitted no topic of which the subject rightly allowed, and I do not think that any one could have spoken better or more exhaustively.

Soc. There I cannot go along with you. Ancient sages, men and women, who have spoken and written of these things, would rise up in judgment against me, if out of complaisance I assented to you.

Phaedr. Who are they, and where did you hear anything better than this?

Soc. I am sure that I must have heard; but at this moment I do not remember from whom; perhaps from Sappho the fair, or Anacreon the wise; or, possibly, from a prose writer. Why do I say so? Why, because I perceive that my bosom is full, and that I could make another speech as good as that of Lysias, and different. Now I am certain that this is not an invention of my own, who am well aware that I know nothing, and therefore I can only infer that I have been filled through the ears, like a pitcher, from the waters of another, though I have actually forgotten in my stupidity who was my informant.

Phaedr. That is grand:—but never mind where you heard the discourse or from whom; let that be a mystery not to be divulged even at my earnest desire. Only, as you say, promise to make another and better oration, equal in length and entirely new, on the same subject; and I, like the nine Archons, will promise to set up a golden image at Delphi, not only of myself, but of you, and as large as life.

Soc. You are a dear golden ass if you suppose me to mean that Lysias has altogether missed the mark, and that I can make a speech from which all his arguments are to be excluded. The worst of authors will say something which is to the point. Who, for example, [236] could speak on this thesis of yours without praising the discretion of the non-lover and blaming the indiscretion of the lover? These are the commonplaces of the subject which must come in (for what else is there to be said?) and must be allowed and excused; the only merit is in the arrangement of them, for there can be none in the invention; but when you leave the commonplaces, then there may be some originality.

Phaedr. I admit that there is reason in what you say, and I too will be reasonable, and will allow you to start with the premiss that the lover is more disordered in his wits than the non-lover; if in what remains you make a longer and better speech than Lysias, and use other arguments, then I say again, that a statue you shall have of beaten gold, and take your place by the colossal offerings of the Cypselids at Olympia.

Soc. How profoundly in earnest is the lover, because to tease him I lay a finger upon his love! And so, Phaedrus, you really imagine that I am going to improve upon the ingenuity of Lysias?

Phaedr. There I have you as you had me, and you must just speak "as you best can." Do not let us exchange *"tu quoque"* as in a farce, or compel me to say to you as you said to me, "I know Socrates as well as I know myself, and he was wanting to speak, but he gave himself airs." Rather I would have you consider that from this place we stir not until you have unbosomed yourself of the speech; for here are we all alone, and I am stronger, remember, and younger than you:—Wherefore perpend, and do not compel me to use violence.

Soc. But, my sweet Phaedrus, how ridiculous it would be of me to compete with Lysias in an extempore speech! He is a master in his art and I am an untaught man.

Phaedr. You see how matters stand; and therefore let there be no more pretences; for, indeed, I know the word that is irresistible.

Soc. Then don't say it.

Phaedr. Yes, but I will; and my word shall be an oath. "I say, or rather swear"—but what god will be witness of my oath?—"By this plane-tree I swear, that unless you repeat the discourse here in the face of this very plane-tree, I will never tell you another; never let you have word of another!"

Soc. Villain! I am conquered; the poor lover of discourse has no more to say.

Phaedr. Then why are you still at your tricks?

Soc. I am not going to play tricks now that you have taken the oath, for I cannot allow myself to be starved.

Phaedr. Proceed.

[237] *Soc.* Shall I tell you what I will do?

Phaedr. What?

Soc. I will veil my face and gallop through the discourse as fast as I can, for if I see you I shall feel ashamed and not know what to say.

Phaedr. Only go on and you may do anything else which you please.

Soc. Come, O ye Muses, melodious, as ye are called, whether you have received this name from the character of your strains, or because the Melians are a musical race, help, O help me in the tale which my good friend here desires me to rehearse, in order that his friend whom he always deemed wise may seem to him to be wiser than ever.

Once upon a time there was a fair boy, or, more properly speaking, a youth; he was very fair and had a great many lovers; and there was one special cunning one, who had persuaded the youth that he did not love him, but he really loved him all the same; and one day when he was paying his addresses to him, he used this very argument—that he ought to accept the non-lover rather than the lover; his words were as follows:—

"All good counsel begins in the same way; a man should know what he is advising about, or his counsel will all come to nought. But people imagine that they know about the nature of things, when they don't know about them, and, not having come to an understanding at first because they think that they know, they end, as might be expected, in contradicting one another and themselves. Now you and I must not be guilty of this fundamental error which we condemn in others; but as our question is whether the lover or non-lover is to be preferred, let us first of all agree in defining the nature and power of love, and then, keeping our eyes upon the definition and to this appealing, let us further enquire whether love brings advantage or disadvantage.

"Every one sees that love is a desire, and we know also that non-lovers desire the beautiful and good. Now in what way is the lover to be distinguished from the non-lover? Let us note that in every one of us there are two guiding and ruling principles which lead us whither they will; one is the natural desire of pleasure, the other is an acquired opinion which aspires after the best; and these two are sometimes in harmony and then again at war, and sometimes the one, sometimes the other conquers. When opinion by the help of reason leads us to the best, the conquering principle is called temperance; *[238]* but when desire, which is devoid of reason, rules in us and drags us to pleasure, that power of misrule is called excess. Now excess has many names, and many members, and many forms, and any of these forms when very marked gives a name, neither honourable nor creditable, to the bearer of the name. The desire of eating, for example, which

gets the better of the higher reason and the other desires, is called gluttony, and he who is possessed by it is called a glutton; the tyrannical desire of drink, which inclines the possessor of the desire to drink, has a name which is only too obvious, and there can be as little doubt by what name any other appetite of the same family would be called;—it will be the name of that which happens to be dominant. And now I think that you will perceive the drift of my discourse; but as every spoken word is in a manner plainer than the unspoken, I had better say further that the irrational desire which overcomes the tendency of opinion towards right, and is led away to the enjoyment of beauty, and especially of personal beauty, by the desires which are her own kindred—that supreme desire, I say, which by leading conquers and by the force of passion is reinforced, from this very force, receiving a name, is called love (ἐρρωμένως ἔρως)."

And now, dear Phaedrus, I shall pause for an instant to ask whether you do not think me, as I appear to myself, inspired?

Phaedr. Yes, Socrates, you seem to have a very unusual flow of words.

Soc. Listen to me, then, in silence; for surely the place is holy; so that you must not wonder, if, as I proceed, I appear to be in a divine fury, for already I am getting into dithyrambics.

Phaedr. Nothing can be truer.

Soc. The responsibility rests with you. But hear what follows, and perhaps the fit may be averted; all is in their hands above. I will go on talking to my youth. Listen:

Thus, my friend, we have declared and defined the nature of the subject. Keeping the definition in view, let us now enquire what advantage or disadvantage is likely to ensue from the lover or the non-lover to him who accepts their advances.

He who is the victim of his passions and the slave of pleasure will of course desire to make his beloved as agreeable to himself as possible. Now to him who has a mind diseased anything is agreeable which is not opposed to him, but that which is equal or superior is hateful to him, and therefore the lover will not brook any superiority or equality on the part of his beloved; *[239]* he is always employed in reducing him to inferiority. And the ignorant is the inferior of the wise, the coward of the brave, the slow of speech of the speaker, the dull of the clever. These, and not these only, are the mental defects of the beloved;—defects which, when implanted by nature, are necessarily a delight to the lover, and when not implanted, he must contrive to implant them in him, if he would not be deprived of his fleeting joy. And therefore he cannot help being jealous, and will debar his beloved from the advantages of society which would make a man of him, and especially from that society which would have given him wisdom, and thereby he cannot fail to do him great harm. That is to say, in his excessive fear lest he should come to be despised in his eyes he will be compelled to banish from him divine philosophy; and there is no greater injury which he can inflict upon him than this. He will contrive that his beloved shall be wholly ignorant, and in everything shall look to him; he is to be the delight of the lover's heart, and a curse to himself. Verily, a lover is a profitable guardian and associate for him in all that relates to his mind.

Let us next see how his master, whose law of life is pleasure and not good, will keep and train the body of his servant. Will he not choose a beloved who is delicate rather than sturdy and strong? One brought up in shady bowers and not in the bright sun, a stranger to manly exercises and the sweat of toil, accustomed only to a soft and luxurious diet, instead of the hues of health having the colours of paint and ornament, and the rest of a piece?—such a life as any one can imagine and which I need not detail at length. But I may sum up all that I have to say in a word, and pass on. Such a person in war, or in any of the great crises of life, will be the anxiety of his friends and also of his lover, and certainly not the terror of his enemies; which nobody can deny.

And now let us tell what advantage or disadvantage the beloved will receive from the guardianship and society of his lover in the matter of his property; this is the next point to be considered. The lover will be the first to see what, indeed, will be sufficiently evident to all men, that he desires above all things to deprive his beloved of his dearest and best and holiest possessions, [240] father, mother, kindred, friends, of all whom he thinks may be hinderers or reprovers of their most sweet converse; he will even cast a jealous eye upon his gold and silver or other property, because these make him a less easy prey, and when caught less manageable; hence he is of necessity displeased at his possession of them and rejoices at their loss; and he would like him to be wifeless, childless, homeless, as well; and the longer the better, for the longer he is all this, the longer he will enjoy him.

There are some sort of animals, such as flatterers, who are dangerous and mischievous enough, and yet nature has mingled a temporary pleasure and grace in their composition. You may say that a courtesan is hurtful, and disapprove of such creatures and their practices, and yet for the time they are very pleasant. But the lover is not only hurtful to his love; he is also an extremely disagreeable companion. The old proverb says that "birds of a feather flock together"; I suppose that equality of years inclines them to the same pleasures, and similarity begets friendship; yet you may have more than enough even of this; and verily constraint is always said to be grievous. Now the lover is not only unlike his beloved, but he forces himself upon him. For he is old and his love is young, and neither day nor night will he leave him if he can help; necessity and the sting of desire drive him on, and allure him with the pleasure which he receives from seeing, hearing, touching, perceiving him in every way. And therefore he is delighted to fasten upon him and to minister to him. But what pleasure or consolation can the beloved be receiving all this time? Must he not feel the extremity of disgust when he looks at an old shrivelled face and the remainder to match, which even in a description is disagreeable, and quite detestable when he is forced into daily contact with his lover; moreover he is jealously watched and guarded against everything and everybody, and has to hear misplaced and exaggerated praises of himself, and censures equally inappropriate, which are intolerable when the man is sober, and, besides being intolerable, are published all over the world in all their indelicacy and wearisomeness when he is drunk.

And not only while his love continues is he mischievous and unpleasant, but when his love ceases he becomes a perfidious enemy of him on whom he showered his oaths and prayers and promises, [241] and yet could hardly prevail upon him to tolerate the tedium of his company even from motives of interest. The hour of payment arrives, and now he is the servant of another master; instead of love and infatuation, wisdom and temperance are his bosom's lords; but the beloved has not discovered the change which has taken place in him, when he asks for a return and recalls to his recollection former sayings and doings; he believes himself to be speaking to the same person, and the other, not having the courage to confess the truth, and not knowing how to fulfil the oaths and promises which he made when under the dominion of folly, and having now grown wise and temperate, does not want to do as he did or to be as he was before. And so he runs away and is constrained to be a defaulter; the oyster-shell [1] has fallen with the other side uppermost—he changes pursuit into flight, while the other is compelled to follow him with passion and imprecation not knowing that he ought never from the first to have accepted a demented lover instead of a sensible non-lover; and that in making such a choice he was giving himself up to a faithless, morose, envious, disagreeable being, hurtful to his estate, hurtful to his bodily health, and still more hurtful to the cultivation of his mind, than which there neither is nor ever will be anything more honoured in the eyes both of gods and men. Consider this, fair youth, and know that in the friendship of the lover there is no real kindness; he has an appetite and wants to feed upon you:

As wolves love lambs so lovers love their loves.

But I told you so, I am speaking in verse, and therefore I had better make an end; enough.

Phaedr. I thought that you were only halfway and were going to make a similar speech about all the advantages of accepting the non-lover. Why do you not proceed?

Soc. Does not your simplicity observe that I have got out of dithyrambics into heroics, when only uttering a censure on the lover? And if I am to add the praises of the non-lover, what will become of me? Do you not perceive that I am already overtaken by the Nymphs to whom you have mischievously exposed me? And therefore I will only add that the non-lover has all the advantages in which the lover is accused of being deficient. And now I will say no more; there has been enough of both of them. Leaving the tale to its fate, *[242]* I will cross the river and make the best of my way home, lest a worse thing be inflicted upon me by you.

Phaedr. Not yet, Socrates; not until the heat of the day has passed; do you not see that the hour is almost noon? there is the midday sun standing still, as people say, in the meridian. Let us rather stay and talk over what has been said, and then return in the cool.

Soc. Your love of discourse, Phaedrus, is superhuman, simply marvellous, and I do not believe that there is any one of your contemporaries who has either made or in one way or another has compelled others to make an equal number of speeches. I would except Simmias the Theban, but all the rest are far behind you. And now I do verily believe that you have been the cause of another.

Phaedr. That is good news. But what do you mean?

Soc. I mean to say that as I was about to cross the stream the usual sign was given to me,—that sign which always forbids, but never bids, me to do anything which I am going to do; and I thought that I heard a voice saying in my ear that I had been guilty of impiety, and that I must not go away until I had made an atonement. Now I am a diviner, though not a very good one, but I have enough religion for my own use, as you might say of a bad writer—his writing is good enough for him; and I am beginning to see that I was in error. O my friend, how prophetic is the human soul! At the time I had a sort of misgiving, and, like Ibycus, "I was troubled; I feared that I might be buying honour from men at the price of sinning against the gods." Now I recognize my error.

Phaedr. What error?

Soc. That was a dreadful speech which you brought with you, and you made me utter one as bad.

Phaedr. How so?

Soc. It was foolish, I say,—to a certain extent, impious; can anything be more dreadful?

Phaedr. Nothing, if the speech was really such as you describe.

Soc. Well, and is not Eros the son of Aphrodite, and a god?

Phaedr. So men say.

Soc. But that was not acknowledged by Lysias in his speech, nor by you in that other speech which you by a charm drew from my lips. For if love be, as he surely is, a divinity, he cannot be evil. Yet this was the error of both the speeches. There was also a simplicity about them which was refreshing; *[243]* having no truth or honesty in them, nevertheless they pretended to be something, hoping to succeed in deceiving the manikins of earth and gain celebrity among them. Wherefore I must have a purgation. And I bethink me of an ancient purgation of mythological error which was devised, not by Homer, for he never had the wit to discover why he was blind, but by Stesichorus, who was a philosopher and knew the reason why; and therefore, when he lost his eyes, for that was the penalty which was inflicted upon him for reviling the lovely Helen, he at

[1] In allusion to a game in which two parties fled or pursued according as an oyster-shell which was thrown into the air fell with the dark or light side uppermost.

once purged himself. And the purgation was a recantation, which began thus,—

False is that word of mine—the truth is that thou didst not embark in ships, nor ever go to the walls of Troy;

and when he had completed his poem, which is called "the recantation," immediately his sight returned to him. Now I will be wiser than either Stesichorus or Homer, in that I am going to make my recantation for reviling love before I suffer; and this I will attempt, not as before, veiled and ashamed, but with forehead bold and bare.

Phaedr. Nothing could be more agreeable to me than to hear you say so.

Soc. Only think, my good Phaedrus, what an utter want of delicacy was shown in the two discourses; I mean, in my own and in that which you recited out of the book. Would not any one who was himself of a noble and gentle nature, and who loved or ever had loved a nature like his own, when we tell of the petty causes of lovers' jealousies, and of their exceeding animosities, and of the injuries which they do to their beloved, have imagined that our ideas of love were taken from some haunt of sailors to which good manners were unknown —he would certainly never have admitted the justice of our censure?

Phaedr. I dare say not, Socrates.

Soc. Therefore, because I blush at the thought of this person, and also because I am afraid of Love himself, I desire to wash the brine out of my ears with water from the spring; and I would counsel Lysias not to delay, but to write another discourse, which shall prove that *ceteris paribus* the lover ought to be accepted rather than the non-lover.

Phaedr. Be assured that he shall. You shall speak the praises of the lover, and Lysias shall be compelled by me to write another discourse on the same theme.

Soc. You will be true to your nature in that, and therefore I believe you.

Phaedr. Speak, and fear not.

Soc. But where is the fair youth whom I was addressing before, and who ought to listen now; lest, if he hear me not, he should accept a non-lover before he knows what he is doing?

Phaedr. He is close at hand, and always at your service.

Soc. Know then, fair youth, that the former discourse was the word of Phaedrus, *[244]* the son of Vain Man, who dwells in the city of Myrrhina (Myrrhinusius). And this which I am about to utter is the recantation of Stesichorus the son of Godly Man (Euphemus), who comes from the town of Desire (Himera), and is to the following effect: "I told a lie when I said" that the beloved ought to accept the non-lover when he might have the lover, because the one is sane, and the other mad. It might be so if madness were simply an evil; but there is also a madness which is a divine gift, and the source of the chiefest blessings granted to men. For prophecy is a madness, and the prophetess at Delphi and the priestesses at Dodona when out of their senses have conferred great benefits on Hellas, both in public and private life, but when in their senses few or none. And I might also tell you how the Sibyl and other inspired persons have given to many an one many an intimation of the future which has saved them from falling. But it would be tedious to speak of what every one knows.

There will be more reason in appealing to the ancient inventors of names,[1] who would never have connected prophecy (μαντική), which foretells the future and is the noblest of arts, with madness (μανική), or called them both by the same name, if they had deemed madness to be a disgrace or dishonour;—they must have thought that there was an inspired madness which was a noble thing; for the two words, μαντική and μανική, are really the same, and the letter τ is only a modern and tasteless insertion. And this is confirmed by the name which was given by them to the rational investigation of futurity, whether made by the help of birds or of other signs—this, for as much as it is an art which supplies from the reasoning faculty mind (νοῦς) and information (ἱστορία) to human thought (οἴησις), they originally termed οἰονοιστική, but the word has been lately altered and made sonorous by the modern introduction of the letter Omega (οἰονοιστική and οἰωνιστική), and in proportion as prophecy (μαντική) is more perfect and august than augury, both in name and fact, in the same proportion, as the ancients testify, is madness superior to a sane mind (σωφροσύνη), for the one is only of human, but the other of divine origin. Again, where plagues and mightiest woes have bred in certain families, owing to some ancient blood-guiltiness, there madness has entered with holy prayers and rites, and by inspired utterances found a way of deliverance for those who are in need; and he who has part in this gift, and is truly possessed and duly out of his mind, is by the use of purifications and mys-

[1] Cf. *Cratylus*, 388 ff.

teries made whole and except from evil, future as well as present, and has a release from the calamity which was afflicting him. *[245]* The third kind is the madness of those who are possessed by the Muses; which taking hold of a delicate and virgin soul, and there inspiring frenzy, awakens lyrical and all other numbers; with these adorning the myriad actions of ancient heroes for the instruction of posterity. But he who, having no touch of the Muses' madness in his soul, comes to the door and thinks that he will get into the temple by the help of art—he, I say, and his poetry are not admitted; the sane man disappears and is nowhere when he enters into rivalry with the madman.

I might tell of many other noble deeds which have sprung from inspired madness. And therefore, let no one frighten or flutter us by saying that the temperate friend is to be chosen rather than the inspired, but let him further show that love is not sent by the gods for any good to lover or beloved; if he can do so we will allow him to carry off the palm. And we, on our part, will prove in answer to him that the madness of love is the greatest of heaven's blessings, and the proof shall be one which the wise will receive, and the witling disbelieve. But first of all, let us view the affections and actions of the soul divine and human, and try to ascertain the truth about them. The beginning of our proof is as follows:—

The soul through all her being is immortal, for that which is ever in motion is immortal; but that which moves another and is moved by another, in ceasing to move ceases also to live. Only the self-moving, never leaving self, never ceases to move, and is the fountain and beginning of motion to all that moves besides. Now, the beginning is unbegotten, for that which is begotten has a beginning; but the beginning is begotten of nothing, for if it were begotten of something, then the begotten would not come from a beginning. But if unbegotten, it must also be indestructible; for if beginning were destroyed, there could be no beginning out of anything, nor anything out of a beginning; and all things must have a beginning. And therefore the self-moving is the beginning of motion; and this can neither be destroyed nor begotten, else the whole heavens and all creation would collapse and stand still, and never again have motion or birth. But if the self-moving is proved to be immortal, he who affirms that self-motion is the very idea and essence of the soul will not be put to confusion. For the body which is

moved from without is soulless; but that which is moved from within has a soul, for such is the nature of the soul. But if this be true, must not the soul be the self-moving, and therefore of necessity unbegotten and immortal? *[246]* Enough of the soul's immortality.

Of the nature of the soul, though her true form be ever a theme of large and more than mortal discourse, let me speak briefly, and in a figure. And let the figure be composite—a pair of winged horses and a charioteer. Now the winged horses and the charioteers of the gods are all of them noble and of noble descent, but those of other races are mixed; the human charioteer drives his in a pair; and one of them is noble and of noble breed, and the other is ignoble and of ignoble breed; and the driving of them of necessity gives a great deal of trouble to him. I will endeavour to explain to you in what way the mortal differs from the immortal creature. The soul in her totality has the care of inanimate being everywhere, and traverses the whole heaven in divers forms appearing:—when perfect and fully winged she soars upward, and orders the whole world; whereas the imperfect soul, losing her wings and drooping in her flight at last settles on the solid ground—there, finding a home, she receives an earthly frame which appears to be self-moved, but is really moved by her power; and this composition of soul and body is called a living and mortal creature. For immortal no such union can be reasonably believed to be; although fancy, not having seen nor surely known the nature of God, may imagine an immortal creature having both a body and also a soul which are united throughout all time. Let that, however, be as God wills, and be spoken of acceptably to him. And now let us ask the reason why the soul loses her wings!

The wing is the corporeal element which is most akin to the divine, and which by nature tends to soar aloft and carry that which gravitates downwards into the upper region, which is the habitation of the gods. The divine is beauty, wisdom, goodness, and the like; and by these the wing of the soul is nourished, and grows apace; but when fed upon evil and foulness and the opposite of good, wastes and falls away. Zeus, the mighty lord, holding the reins of a winged chariot, leads the way in heaven, ordering all and taking care of all; and there follows him the array of gods and demigods, *[247]* marshalled in eleven bands; Hestia alone abides at home in the house of heaven; of the rest they who are reckoned among the princely twelve march in their appointed order. They see many blessed sights in the inner heaven, and there are many ways to and fro, along which the blessed gods are passing, every one doing his own work; he may follow who will and can, for jealousy has no place in the celestial choir. But when they go to banquet and festival, then they move up the steep to the top of the vault of heaven. The chariots of the gods in even poise, obeying the rein, glide rapidly; but the others labour, for the vicious steed goes heavily, weighing down the charioteer to the earth when his steed has not been thoroughly trained:—and this is the hour of agony and extremest conflict for the soul. For the immortals, when they are at the end of their course, go forth and stand upon the outside of heaven, and the revolution of the spheres carries them round, and they behold the things beyond. But of the heaven which is above the heavens, what earthly poet ever did or ever will sing worthily? It is such as I will describe; for I must dare to speak the truth, when truth is my theme. There abides the very being with which true knowledge is concerned; the colourless, formless, intangible essence, visible only to mind, the pilot of the soul. The divine intelligence, being nurtured upon mind and pure knowledge, and the intelligence of every soul which is capable of receiving the food proper to it, rejoices at beholding reality, and once more gazing upon truth, is replenished and made glad, until the revolution of the worlds brings her round again to the same place. In the revolution she beholds justice, and temperance, and knowledge absolute, not in the form of generation or of relation, which men call existence, but knowledge absolute in existence absolute; and beholding the other true existences in like manner, and feasting upon them, she passes down into the interior of the heavens and returns home; and there the charioteer putting up his horses at the stall, gives them ambrosia to eat and nectar to drink.

[248] Such is the life of the gods; but of other souls, that which follows God best and is likest to him lifts the head of the charioteer into the outer world, and is carried round in the revolution, troubled indeed by the steeds, and with difficulty beholding true being; while another only rises and falls, and sees, and again fails to see by reason of the unruliness of the steeds. The rest of the souls are also longing after the upper world and they all follow, but not being strong enough they are carried round below the surface, plunging, treading on one

another, each striving to be first; and there is confusion and perspiration and the extremity of effort; and many of them are lamed or have their wings broken through the ill-driving of the charioteers; and all of them after a fruitless toil, not having attained to the mysteries of true being, go away, and feed upon opinion. The reason why the souls exhibit this exceeding eagerness to behold the plain of truth is that pasturage is found there, which is suited to the highest part of the soul; and the wing on which the soul soars is nourished with this. And there is a law of Destiny, that the soul which attains any vision of truth in company with a god is preserved from harm until the next period, and if attaining always is always unharmed. But when she is unable to follow, and fails to behold the truth, and through some ill-hap sinks beneath the double load of forgetfulness and vice, and her wings fall from her and she drops to the ground, then the law ordains that this soul shall at her first birth pass, not into any other animal, but only into man; and the soul which has seen most of truth shall come to the birth as a philosopher, or artist, or some musical and loving nature; that which has seen truth in the second degree shall be some righteous king or warrior chief; the soul which is of the third class shall be a politician, or economist, or trader; the fourth shall be a lover of gymnastic toils, or a physician; the fifth shall lead the life of a prophet or hierophant; to the sixth the character of a poet or some other imitative artist will be assigned; to the seventh the life of an artisan or husbandman; to the eighth that of a sophist or demagogue; to the ninth that of a tyrant;—all these are states of probation, in which he who does righteously improves, and he who does unrighteously, deteriorates his lot.

Ten thousand years must elapse before the soul of each one can return to the place from whence she came, [249] for she cannot grow her wings in less; only the soul of a philosopher, guileless and true, or the soul of a lover, who is not devoid of philosophy, may acquire wings in the third of the recurring periods of a thousand years; he is distinguished from the ordinary good man who gains wings in three thousand years:—and they who choose this life three times in succession have wings given them, and go away at the end of three thousand years. But the others receive judgment when they have completed their first life, and after the judgment they go, some of them to the houses of correction which are under the earth, and are punished; others to some place in heaven whither they are lightly borne by justice, and there they live in a manner worthy of the life which they led here when in the form of men. And at the end of the first thousand years the good souls and also the evil souls both come to draw lots and choose their second life, and they may take any which they please. The soul of a man may pass into the life of a beast, or from the beast return again into the man. But the soul which has never seen the truth will not pass into the human form. For a man must have intelligence of universals, and be able to proceed from the many particulars of sense to one conception of reason;—this is the recollection of those things which our soul once saw while following God—when regardless of that which we now call being she raised her head up towards the true being. And therefore the mind of the philosopher alone has wings; and this is just, for he is always, according to the measure of his abilities, clinging in recollection to those things in which God abides, and in beholding which He is what He is. And he who employs aright these memories is ever being initiated into perfect mysteries and alone becomes truly perfect. But, as he forgets earthly interests and is rapt in the divine, the vulgar deem him mad, and rebuke him; they do not see that he is inspired.

Thus far I have been speaking of the fourth and last kind of madness, which is imputed to him who, when he sees the beauty of earth, is transported with the recollection of the true beauty; he would like to fly away, but he cannot; he is like a bird fluttering and looking upward and careless of the world below; and he is therefore thought to be mad. And I have shown this of all inspirations to be the noblest and highest and the offspring of the highest to him who has or shares in it, and that he who loves the beautiful is called a lover because he partakes of it. For, as has been already said, every soul of man has in the way of nature beheld true being; this was the condition of her passing into the form of man. But all souls do not easily recall the things of the other world; [250] they may have seen them for a short time only, or they may have been unfortunate in their earthly lot, and, having had their hearts turned to unrighteousness through some corrupting influence, they may have lost the memory of the holy things which once they saw. Few only retain an adequate remembrance of them; and they, when they behold here any image of that other world, are rapt

in amazement; but they are ignorant of what this rapture means, because they do not clearly perceive. For there is no light of justice or temperance or any of the higher ideas which are precious to souls in the earthly copies of them: they are seen through a glass dimly; and there are few who, going to the images, behold in them the realities, and these only with difficulty. There was a time when with the rest of the happy band they saw beauty shining in brightness,—we philosophers following in the train of Zeus, others in company with other gods; and then we beheld the beatific vision and were initiated into a mystery which may be truly called most blessed, celebrated by us in our state of innocence, before we had any experience of evils to come, when we were admitted to the sight of apparitions innocent and simple and calm and happy, which we beheld shining in pure light, pure ourselves and not yet enshrined in that living tomb which we carry about, now that we are imprisoned in the body, like an oyster in his shell. Let me linger over the memory of scenes which have passed away.

But of beauty, I repeat again that we saw her there shining in company with the celestial forms; and coming to earth we find her here too, shining in clearness through the clearest aperture of sense. For sight is the most piercing of our bodily senses; though not by that is wisdom seen; her loveliness would have been transporting if there had been a visible image of her, and the other ideas, if they had visible counterparts, would be equally lovely. But this is the privilege of beauty, that being the loveliest she is also the most palpable to sight. Now he who is not newly initiated or who has become corrupted, does not easily rise out of this world to the sight of true beauty in the other; he looks only at her earthly namesake, and instead of being awed at the sight of her, he is given over to pleasure, and like a brutish beast he rushes on to enjoy and beget; [251] he consorts with wantonness, and is not afraid or ashamed of pursuing pleasure in violation of nature. But he whose initiation is recent, and who has been the spectator of many glories in the other world, is amazed when he sees any one having a godlike face or form, which is the expression of divine beauty; and at first a shudder runs through him, and again the old awe steals over him; then looking upon the face of his beloved as of a god he reverences him, and if he were not afraid of being thought a downright madman, he would sacrifice to his beloved as to the image of a god; then while he gazes on him there is a sort of reaction, and the shudder passes into an unusual heat and perspiration; for, as he receives the effluence of beauty through the eyes, the wing moistens and he warms. And as he warms, the parts out of which the wing grew, and which had been hitherto closed and rigid, and had prevented the wing from shooting forth, are melted, and as nourishment streams upon him, the lower end of the wings begins to swell and grow from the root upwards; and the growth extends under the whole soul—for once the whole was winged.

During this process the whole soul is all in a state of ebullition and effervescence,—which may be compared to the irritation and uneasiness in the gums at the time of cutting teeth,—bubbles up, and has a feeling of uneasiness and tickling; but when in like manner the soul is beginning to grow wings, the beauty of the beloved meets her eye and she receives the sensible warm motion of particles which flow towards her, therefore called emotion ($ἵμερος$), and is refreshed and warmed by them, and then she ceases from her pain with joy. But when she is parted from her beloved and her moisture fails, then the orifices of the passage out of which the wing shoots dry up and close, and intercept the germ of the wing; which, being shut up with the emotion, throbbing as with the pulsations of an artery, pricks the aperture which is nearest, until at length the entire soul is pierced and maddened and pained, and at the recollection of beauty is again delighted. And from both of them together the soul is oppressed at the strangeness of her condition, and is in a great strait and excitement, and in her madness can neither sleep by night nor abide in her place by day. And wherever she thinks that she will behold the beautiful one, thither in her desire she runs. And when she has seen him, and bathed herself in the waters of beauty, her constraint is loosened, and she is refreshed, and has no more pangs and pains; and this is the sweetest of all pleasures at the time, *[252]* and is the reason why the soul of the lover will never forsake his beautiful one, whom he esteems above all; he has forgotten mother and brethren and companions, and he thinks nothing of the neglect and loss of his property; the rules and proprieties of life, on which he formerly prided himself, he now despises, and is ready to sleep like a servant, wherever he is allowed, as near as he can to his desired one, who is the object of his worship, and the physician who can alone assuage the greatness of his pain. And this

state, my dear imaginary youth to whom I am talking, is by men called love, and among the gods has a name at which you, in your simplicity, may be inclined to mock; there are two lines in the apocryphal writings of Homer in which the name occurs. One of them is rather outrageous, and not altogether metrical. They are as follows:

Mortals call him fluttering love,
But the immortals call him winged one,
Because the growing of wings is a necessity to him.

You may believe this, but not unless you like. At any rate the loves of lovers and their causes are such as I have described.

Now the lover who is taken to be the attendant of Zeus is better able to bear the winged god, and can endure a heavier burden; but the attendants and companions of Ares, when under the influence of love, if they fancy that they have been at all wronged, are ready to kill and put an end to themselves and their beloved. And he who follows in the train of any other god, while he is unspoiled and the impression lasts, honours and imitates him, as far as he is able; and after the manner of his god he behaves in his intercourse with his beloved and with the rest of the world during the first period of his earthly existence. Every one chooses his love from the ranks of beauty according to his character, and this he makes his god, and fashions and adorns as a sort of image which he is to fall down and worship. The followers of Zeus desire that their beloved should have a soul like him; and therefore they seek out some one of a philosophical and imperial nature, and when they have found him and loved him, they do all they can to confirm such a nature in him, and if they have no experience of such a disposition hitherto, they learn of any one who can teach them, and themselves follow in the same way. And they have the less difficulty in finding the nature of their own god in themselves, *[253]* because they have been compelled to gaze intensely on him; their recollection clings to him, and they become possessed of him, and receive from him their character and disposition, so far as man can participate in God. The qualities of their god they attribute to the beloved, wherefore they love him all the more, and if, like the Bacchic Nymphs, they draw inspiration from Zeus, they pour out their own fountain upon him, wanting to make him as like as possible to their own god. But those who are the followers of Herè seek a royal love, and when they have found him they do just the same with him; and in like manner the followers of Apollo, and of every other god walking in the ways of their god, seek a love who is to be made like him whom they serve, and when they have found him, they themselves imitate their god, and persuade their love to do the same, and educate him into the manner and nature of the god as far as they each can; for no feelings of envy or jealousy are entertained by them towards their beloved, but they do their utmost to create in him the greatest likeness of themselves and of the god whom they honour. Thus fair and blissful to the beloved is the desire of the inspired lover, and the initiation of which I speak into the mysteries of true love, if he be captured by the lover and their purpose is effected. Now the beloved is taken captive in the following manner:—

As I said at the beginning of this tale, I divided each soul into three—two horses and a charioteer; and one of the horses was good and the other bad: the division may remain, but I have not yet explained in what the goodness or badness of either consists, and to that I will proceed. The right-hand horse is upright and cleanly made; he has a lofty neck and an aquiline nose; his colour is white, and his eyes dark; he is a lover of honour and modesty and temperance, and the follower of true glory; he needs no touch of the whip, but is guided by word and admonition only. The other is a crooked lumbering animal, put together anyhow; he has a short thick neck; he is flat-faced and of a dark colour, with grey eyes and blood-red complexion; the mate of insolence and pride, shag-eared and deaf, hardly yielding to whip and spur. Now when the charioteer beholds the vision of love, and has his whole soul warmed through sense, and is full of the prickings and ticklings of desire, [254] the obedient steed, then as always under the government of shame, refrains from leaping on the beloved; but the other, heedless of the pricks and of the blows of the whip, plunges and runs away, giving all manner of trouble to his companion and the charioteer, whom he forces to approach the beloved and to remember the joys of love. They at first indignantly oppose him and will not be urged on to do terrible and unlawful deeds; but at last, when he persists in plaguing them, they yield and agree to do as he bids them.

And now they are at the spot and behold the flashing beauty of the beloved; which when the charioteer sees, his memory is carried to the true beauty, whom he beholds in company with Modesty like an image placed upon a holy pedestal. He sees her, but he is afraid and falls backwards in adoration, and by his fall is compelled to pull back the reins with such violence as to bring both the steeds on their haunches, the one willing and unresisting, the unruly one very unwilling; and when they have gone back a little, the one is overcome with shame and wonder, and his whole soul is bathed in perspiration; the other, when the pain is over which the bridle and the fall had given him, having with difficulty taken breath, is full of wrath and reproaches, which he heaps upon the charioteer and his fellow-steed, for want of courage and manhood, declaring that they have been false to their agreement and guilty of desertion. Again they refuse, and again he urges them on, and will scarce yield to their prayer that he would wait until another time. When the appointed hour comes, they make as if they had forgotten, and he reminds them, fighting and neighing and dragging them on, until at length he, on the same thoughts intent, forces them to draw near again. And when they are near he stoops his head and puts up his tail, and takes the bit in his teeth and pulls shamelessly. Then the charioteer is worse off than ever; he falls back like a racer at the barrier, and with a still more violent wrench drags the bit out of the teeth of the wild steed and covers his abusive tongue and jaws with blood, and forces his legs and haunches to the ground and punishes him sorely. And when this has happened several times and the villain has ceased from his wanton way, he is tamed and humbled, and follows the will of the charioteer, and when he sees the beautiful one he is ready to die of fear. And from that time forward the soul of the lover follows the beloved in modesty and holy fear.

[255] And so the beloved who, like a god, has received every true and loyal service from his lover, not in pretence but in reality, being also himself of a nature friendly to his admirer, if in former days he has blushed to own his passion and turned away his lover, because his youthful companions or others slanderously told him that he would be disgraced, now as years advance, at the appointed age and time, is led to receive him into communion. For fate which has ordained that there shall be no friendship among the evil has also ordained that there shall ever be friendship among the good. And the beloved when he has received him into communion and intimacy, is quite

amazed at the good-will of the lover; he recognises that the inspired friend is worth all other friends or kinsmen; they have nothing of friendship in them worthy to be compared with his. And when his feeling continues and he is nearer to him and embraces him, in gymnastic exercises and at other times of meeting, then the fountain of that stream, which Zeus when he was in love with Ganymede named Desire, overflows upon the lover, and some enters into his soul, and some when he is filled flows out again; and as a breeze or an echo rebounds from the smooth rocks and returns whence it came, so does the stream of beauty, passing through the eyes which are the windows of the soul, come back to the beautiful one; there arriving and quickening the passages of the wings, watering them and inclining them to grow, and filling the soul of the beloved also with love. And thus he loves, but he knows not what; he does not understand and cannot explain his own state; he appears to have caught the infection of blindness from another; the lover is his mirror in whom he is beholding himself, but he is not aware of this. When he is with the lover, both cease from their pain, but when he is away then he longs as he is longed for, and has love's image, love for love (Anteros) lodging in his breast, which he calls and believes to be not love but friendship only, and his desire is as the desire of the other, but weaker; he wants to see him, touch him, kiss, embrace him, and probably not long afterwards his desire is accomplished. When they meet, the wanton steed of the lover has a word to say to the charioteer; [256] he would like to have a little pleasure in return for many pains, but the wanton steed of the beloved says not a word, for he is bursting with passion which he understands not;—he throws his arms round the lover and embraces him as his dearest friend; and, when they are side by side, he is not in a state in which he can refuse the lover anything, if he ask him; although his fellow-steed and the charioteer oppose him with the arguments of shame and reason.

After this their happiness depends upon their self-control; if the better elements of the mind which lead to order and philosophy prevail, then they pass their life here in happiness and harmony—masters of themselves and orderly—enslaving the vicious and emancipating the virtuous elements of the soul; and when the end comes, they are light and winged for flight, having conquered in one of the three heavenly or truly Olympian victories; nor can human

discipline or divine inspiration confer any greater blessing on man than this. If, on the other hand, they leave philosophy and lead the lower life of ambition, then probably, after wine or in some other careless hour, the two wanton animals take the two souls when off their guard and bring them together, and they accomplish that desire of their hearts which to the many is bliss; and this having once enjoyed they continue to enjoy, yet rarely because they have not the approval of the whole soul. They too are dear, but not so dear to one another as the others, either at the time of their love or afterwards. They consider that they have given and taken from each other the most sacred pledges, and they may not break them and fall into enmity. At last they pass out of the body, unwinged, but eager to soar, and thus obtain no mean reward of love and madness. For those who have once begun the heavenward pilgrimage may not go down again to darkness and the journey beneath the earth, but they live in light always; happy companions in their pilgrimage, and when the time comes at which they receive their wings they have the same plumage because of their love.

Thus great are the heavenly blessings which the friendship of a lover will confer upon you, my youth. Whereas the attachment of the non-lover, which is alloyed with a worldly prudence and has worldly and niggardly ways of doling out benefits, will breed in your soul those vulgar qualities which the populace applaud, will send you bowling round the earth during a period of nine thousand [257] years, and leave you a fool in the world below.

And thus, dear Eros, I have made and paid my recantation, as well and as fairly as I could; more especially in the matter of the poetical figures which I was compelled to use, because Phaedrus would have them.[1] And now forgive the past and accept the present, and be gracious and merciful to me, and do not in thine anger deprive me of sight, or take from me the art of love which thou hast given me, but grant that I may be yet more esteemed in the eyes of the fair. And if Phaedrus or I myself said anything rude in our first speeches, blame Lysias, who is the father of the brat, and let us have no more of his progeny; bid him study philosophy, like his brother Polemarchus; and then his lover Phaedrus will no longer halt between two opinions, but will dedicate himself wholly to love and to philosophical discourses.

Phaedr. I join in the prayer, Socrates, and say

[1] See 234.

with you, if this be for my good, may your words come to pass. But why did you make your second oration so much finer than the first? I wonder why. And I begin to be afraid that I shall lose conceit of Lysias, and that he will appear tame in comparison, even if he be willing to put another as fine and as long as yours into the field, which I doubt. For quite lately one of your politicians was abusing him on this very account; and called him a "speech-writer" again and again. So that a feeling of pride may probably induce him to give up writing speeches.

Soc. What a very amusing notion! But I think, my young man, that you are much mistaken in your friend if you imagine that he is frightened at a little noise; and possibly, you think that his assailant was in earnest?

Phaedr. I thought, Socrates, that he was. And you are aware that the greatest and most influential statesmen are ashamed of writing speeches and leaving them in a written form, lest they should be called Sophists by posterity.

Soc. You seem to be unconscious, Phaedrus, that the "sweet elbow"[1] of the proverb is really the long arm of the Nile. And you appear to be equally unaware of the fact that this sweet elbow of theirs is also a long arm. For there is nothing of which our great politicians are so fond as of writing speeches and bequeathing them to posterity. And they add their admirers' names at the top of the writing, out of gratitude to them.

[258] Phaedr. What do you mean? I do not understand.

Soc. Why, do you not know that when a politician writes, he begins with the names of his approvers?

Phaedr. How so?

Soc. Why, he begins in this manner: "Be it enacted by the senate, the people, or both, on the motion of a certain person," who is our author; and so putting on a serious face, he proceeds to display his own wisdom to his admirers in what is often a long and tedious composition. Now what is that sort of thing but a regular piece of authorship?

Phaedr. True.

Soc. And if the law is finally approved, then the author leaves the theatre in high delight; but if the law is rejected and he is done out of his speech-making, and not thought good

[1] A proverb applied to pleasures which cannot be had, meaning sweet things which, like the elbow, are out of the reach of the mouth. The promised pleasure turns out to be a long and tedious affair.

enough to write, then he and his party are in mourning.

Phaedr. Very true.

Soc. So far are they from despising, or rather so highly do they value the practice of writing.

Phaedr. No doubt.

Soc. And when the king or orator has the power, as Lycurgus or Solon or Darius had, of attaining an immortality or authorship in a state, is he not thought by posterity, when they see his compositions, and does he not think himself, while he is yet alive, to be a god?

Phaedr. Very true.

Soc. Then do you think that any one of this class, however ill-disposed, would reproach Lysias with being an author?

Phaedr. Not upon your view; for according to you he would be casting a slur upon his own favourite pursuit.

Soc. Any one may see that there is no disgrace in the mere fact of writing.

Phaedr. Certainly not.

Soc. The disgrace begins when a man writes not well, but badly.

Phaedr. Clearly.

Soc. And what is well and what is badly—need we ask Lysias, or any other poet or orator, who ever wrote or will write either a political or any other work, in metre or out of metre, poet or prose writer, to teach us this?

Phaedr. Need we? For what should a man live if not for the pleasures of discourse? Surely not for the sake of bodily pleasures, which almost always have previous pain as a condition of them, and therefore are rightly called slavish.

Soc. There is time enough. And I believe that the grasshoppers chirruping after their manner in the heat of the sun over our heads *[259]* are talking to one another and looking down at us. What would they say if they saw that we, like the many, are not conversing, but slumbering at mid-day, lulled by their voices, too indolent to think? Would they not have a right to laugh at us? They might imagine that we were slaves, who, coming to rest at a place of resort of theirs, like sheep lie asleep at noon around the well. But if they see us discoursing, and like Odysseus sailing past them, deaf to their siren voices, they may perhaps, out of respect, give us of the gifts which they receive from the gods that they may impart them to men.

Phaedr. What gifts do you mean? I never heard of any.

Soc. A lover of music like yourself ought

surely to have heard the story of the grasshoppers, who are said to have been human beings in an age before the Muses. And when the Muses came and song appeared they were ravished with delight; and singing always, never thought of eating and drinking, until at last in their forgetfulness they died. And now they live again in the grasshoppers; and this is the return which the Muses make to them— they neither hunger, nor thirst, but from the hour of their birth are always singing, and never eating or drinking; and when they die they go and inform the Muses in heaven who honours them on earth. They win the love of Terpsichore for the dancers by their report of them; of Erato for the lovers, and of the other Muses for those who do them honour, according to the several ways of honouring them;— of Calliope the eldest Muse and of Urania who is next to her, for the philosophers, of whose music the grasshoppers make report to them; for these are the Muses who are chiefly concerned with heaven and thought, divine as well as human, and they have the sweetest utterance. For many reasons, then, we ought always to talk and not to sleep at mid-day.

Phaedr. Let us talk.

Soc. Shall we discuss the rules of writing and speech as we were proposing?

Phaedr. Very good.

Soc. In good speaking should not the mind of the speaker know the truth of the matter about which he is going to speak?

[260] *Phaedr.* And yet, Socrates, I have heard that he who would be an orator has nothing to do with true justice, but only with that which is likely to be approved by the many who sit in judgment; nor with the truly good or honourable, but only with opinion about them, and that from opinion comes persuasion, and not from the truth.

Soc. The words of the wise are not to be set aside; for there is probably something in them; and therefore the meaning of this saying is not hastily to be dismissed.

Phaedr. Very true.

Soc. Let us put the matter thus:—Suppose that I persuaded you to buy a horse and go to the wars. Neither of us knew what a horse was like, but I knew that you believed a horse to be of tame animals the one which has the longest ears.

Phaedr. That would be ridiculous.

Soc. There is something more ridiculous coming:—Suppose, further, that in sober earnest I, having persuaded you of this, went and composed a speech in honour of an ass, whom I entitled a horse beginning: "A noble animal and a most useful possession, especially in war, and you may get on his back and fight, and he will carry baggage or anything."

Phaedr. How ridiculous!

Soc. Ridiculous! Yes; but is not even a ridiculous friend better than a cunning enemy?

Phaedr. Certainly.

Soc. And when the orator instead of putting an ass in the place of a horse puts good for evil being himself as ignorant of their true nature as the city on which he imposes is ignorant; and having studied the notions of the multitude, falsely persuades them not about "the shadow of an ass," which he confounds with a horse, but about good which he confounds with evil,—what will be the harvest which rhetoric will be likely to gather after the sowing of that seed?

Phaedr. The reverse of good.

Soc. But perhaps rhetoric has been getting too roughly handled by us, and she might answer: What amazing nonsense you are talking! As if I forced any man to learn to speak in ignorance of the truth! Whatever my advice may be worth, I should have told him to arrive at the truth first, and then come to me. At the same time I boldly assert that mere knowledge of the truth will not give you the art of persuasion.

Phaedr. There is reason in the lady's defence of herself.

Soc. Quite true; if only the other arguments which remain to be brought up bear her witness that she is an art at all. But I seem to hear them arraying themselves on the opposite side, declaring that she speaks falsely, and that rhetoric is a mere routine and trick, not an art. Lo! a Spartan appears, and says that there never is nor ever will be a real art of speaking which is divorced from the truth.

[261] *Phaedr.* And what are these arguments, Socrates? Bring them out that we may examine them.

Soc. Come out, fair children, and convince Phaedrus, who is the father of similar beauties, that he will never be able to speak about anything as he ought to speak unless he have a knowledge of philosophy. And let Phaedrus answer you.

Phaedr. Put the question.

Soc. Is not rhetoric, taken generally, a universal art of enchanting the mind by arguments; which is practised not only in courts and public assemblies, but in private houses also, having to do with all matters, great as well as small, good and bad alike, and is in all equally right, and equally to be esteemed—that is what you have heard?

Phaedr. Nay, not exactly that; I should say rather that I have heard the art confined to speaking and writing in lawsuits, and to speaking in public assemblies—not extended farther.

Soc. Then I suppose that you have only heard of the rhetoric of Nestor and Odysseus, which they composed in their leisure hours when at Troy, and never of the rhetoric of Palamedes?

Phaedr. No more than of Nestor and Odysseus, unless Gorgias is your Nestor, and Thrasymachus or Theodorus your Odysseus.

Soc. Perhaps that is my meaning. But let us leave them. And do you tell me, instead, what are plaintiff and defendant doing in a lawcourt—are they not contending?

Phaedr. Exactly so.

Soc. About the just and unjust—that is the matter in dispute?

Phaedr. Yes.

Soc. And a professor of the art will make the same thing appear to the same persons to be at one time just, at another time, if he is so inclined, to be unjust?

Phaedr. Exactly.

Soc. And when he speaks in the assembly, he will make the same things seem good to the city at one time, and at another time the reverse of good?

Phaedr. That is true.

Soc. Have we not heard of the Eleatic Palamedes (Zeno), who has an art of speaking by which he makes the same things appear to his hearers like and unlike, one and many, at rest and in motion?

Phaedr. Very true.

Soc. The art of disputation, then, is not confined to the courts and the assembly, but is one and the same in every use of language; this is the art, if there be such an art, which is able to find a likeness of everything to which a likeness can be found, and draws into the light of day the likenesses and disguises which are used by others?

Phaedr. How do you mean?

Soc. Let me put the matter thus: When will there be more chance of deception—when the difference is large or small?

[262] *Phaedr*. When the difference is small.

Soc. And you will be less likely to be discovered in passing by degrees into the other extreme than when you go all at once?

Phaedr. Of course.

Soc. He, then, who would deceive others, and not be deceived, must exactly know the real likenesses and differences of things?

Phaedr. He must.

Soc. And if he is ignorant of the true nature of any subject, how can he detect the greater or less degree of likeness in other things to that of which by the hypothesis he is ignorant?

Phaedr. He cannot.

Soc. And when men are deceived and their notions are at variance with realities, it is clear that the error slips in through resemblances?

Phaedr. Yes, that is the way.

Soc. Then he who would be a master of the art must understand the real nature of everything; or he will never know either how to make the gradual departure from truth into the opposite of truth which is effected by the help of resemblances, or how to avoid it?

Phaedr. He will not.

Soc. He then, who being ignorant of the truth aims at appearances, will only attain an art of rhetoric which is ridiculous and is not an art at all?

Phaedr. That may be expected.

Soc. Shall I propose that we look for examples of art and want of art, according to our notion of them, in the speech of Lysias which you have in your hand, and in my own speech?

Phaedr. Nothing could be better; and indeed I think that our previous argument has been too abstract and wanting in illustrations.

Soc. Yes; and the two speeches happen to afford a very good example of the way in which the speaker who knows the truth may, without any serious purpose, steal away the hearts of his hearers. This piece of good-fortune I attribute to the local deities; and perhaps, the prophets of the Muses who are singing over our heads may have imparted their inspiration to me. For I do not imagine that I have any rhetorical art of my own.

Phaedr. Granted; if you will only please to get on.

Soc. Suppose that you read me the first words of Lysias' speech.

Phaedr. "You know how matters stand with me, and how, as I conceive, they might be arranged for our common interest; and I maintain that I ought not to fail in my suit, because I am not your lover. For lovers repent——"

[263] *Soc*. Enough:—Now, shall I point out the rhetorical error of those words?

Phaedr. Yes.

Soc. Every one is aware that about some

things we are agreed, whereas about other things we differ.

Phaedr. I think that I understand you; but will you explain yourself?

Soc. When any one speaks of iron and silver, is not the same thing present in the minds of all?

Phaedr. Certainly.

Soc. But when any one speaks of justice and goodness we part company and are at odds with one another and with ourselves?

Phaedr. Precisely.

Soc. Then in some things we agree, but not in others?

Phaedr. That is true.

Soc. In which are we more likely to be deceived, and in which has rhetoric the greater power?

Phaedr. Clearly, in the uncertain class.

Soc. Then the rhetorician ought to make a regular division, and acquire a distinct notion of both classes, as well of that in which the many err, as of that in which they do not err?

Phaedr. He who made such a distinction would have an excellent principle.

Soc. Yes; and in the next place he must have a keen eye for the observation of particulars in speaking, and not make a mistake about the class to which they are to be referred.

Phaedr. Certainly.

Soc. Now to which class does love belong— to the debatable or to the undisputed class?

Phaedr. To the debatable, clearly; for if not, do you think that love would have allowed you to say as you did, that he is an evil both to the lover and the beloved, and also the greatest possible good?

Soc. Capital. But will you tell me whether I defined love at the beginning of my speech? for, having been in an ecstasy, I cannot well remember.

Phaedr. Yes, indeed; that you did, and no mistake.

Soc. Then I perceive that the Nymphs of Achelous and Pan the son of Hermes, who inspired me, were far better rhetoricians than Lysias the son of Cephalus. Alas! how inferior to them he is! But perhaps I am mistaken; and Lysias at the commencement of his lover's speech did insist on our supposing love to be something or other which he fancied him to be, and according to this model he fashioned and framed the remainder of his discourse. Suppose we read his beginning over again:

Phaedr. If you please; but you will not find what you want.

Soc. Read, that I may have his exact words.

Phaedr. "You know how matters stand with with me, and how, as I conceive, [264] they might be arranged for our common interest; and I maintain I ought not to fail in my suit because I am not your lover, for lovers repent of the kindnesses which they have shown, when their love is over."

Soc. Here he appears to have done just the reverse of what he ought; for he has begun at the end, and is swimming on his back through the flood to the place of starting. His address to the fair youth begins where the lover would have ended. Am I not right, sweet Phaedrus?

Phaedr. Yes, indeed, Socrates; he does begin at the end.

Soc. Then as to the other topics—are they not thrown down anyhow? Is there any principle in them? Why should the next topic follow next in order, or any other topic? I cannot help fancying in my ignorance that he wrote off boldly just what came into his head, but I dare say that you would recognize a rhetorical necessity in the succession of the several parts of the composition?

Phaedr. You have too good an opinion of me if you think that I have any such insight into his principles of composition.

Soc. At any rate, you will allow that every discourse ought to be a living creature, having a body of its own and a head and feet; there should be a middle, beginning, and end, adapted to one another and to the whole?

Phaedr. Certainly.

Soc. Can this be said of the discourse of Lysias? See whether you can find any more connexion in his words than in the epitaph which is said by some to have been inscribed on the grave of Midas the Phrygian.

Phaedr. What is there remarkable in the epitaph?

Soc. It is as follows:—

I am a maiden of bronze and lie on the tomb of Midas;
So long as water flows and tall trees grow,
So long here on this spot by his sad tomb abiding,
I shall declare to passers-by that Midas sleeps below.

Now in this rhyme whether a line comes first or comes last, as you will perceive, makes no difference.

Phaedr. You are making fun of that oration of ours.

Soc. Well, I will say no more about your friend's speech lest I should give offence to you; although I think that it might furnish many other examples of what a man ought rather to avoid. But I will proceed to the other speech, *[265]* which, as I think, is also suggestive to students of rhetoric.

Phaedr. In what way?

Soc. The two speeches, as you may remember, were unlike; the one argued that the lover and the other that the non-lover ought to be accepted.

Phaedr. And right manfully.

Soc. You should rather say "madly"; and madness was the argument of them, for, as I said, "love is a madness."

Phaedr. Yes.

Soc. And of madness there were two kinds; one produced by human infirmity, the other was a divine release of the soul from the yoke of custom and convention.

Phaedr. True.

Soc. The divine madness was subdivided into four kinds, prophetic, initiatory, poetic, erotic, having four gods presiding over them; the first was the inspiration of Apollo, the second that of Dionysus, the third that of the Muses, the fourth that of Aphrodite and Eros. In the description of the last kind of madness, which was also said to be the best, we spoke of the affection of love in a figure, into which we introduced a tolerably credible and possibly true though partly erring myth, which was also a hymn in honour of Love, who is your lord and also mine, Phaedrus, and the guardian of fair children, and to him we sung the hymn in measured and solemn strain.

Phaedr. I know that I had great pleasure in listening to you.

Soc. Let us take this instance and note how the transition was made from blame to praise.

Phaedr. What do you mean?

Soc. I mean to say that the composition was mostly playful. Yet in these chance fancies of the hour were involved two principles of which we should be too glad to have a clearer description if art could give us one.

Phaedr. What are they?

Soc. First, the comprehension of scattered particulars in one idea; as in our definition of love, which whether true or false certainly gave clearness and consistency to the discourse, the speaker should define his several notions and so make his meaning clear.

Phaedr. What is the other principle, Socrates?

Soc. The second principle is that of division into species according to the natural formation, where the joint is, not breaking any part as a bad carver might. *[266]* Just as our two dis-

courses, alike assumed, first of all, a single form of unreason; and then, as the body which from being one becomes double and may be divided into a left side and right side, each having parts right and left of the same name—after this manner the speaker proceeded to divide the parts of the left side and did not desist until he found in them an evil or left-handed love which he justly reviled; and the other discourse leading us to the madness which lay on the right side, found another love, also having the same name, but divine, which the speaker held up before us and applauded and affirmed to be the author of the greatest benefits.

Phaedr. Most true.

Soc. I am myself a great lover of these processes of division and generalization; they help me to speak and to think. And if I find any man who is able to see "a One and Many" in nature, him I follow, and "walk in his footsteps as if he were a god." And those who have this art, I have hitherto been in the habit of calling dialecticians; but God knows whether the name is right or not. And I should like to know what name you would give to your or to Lysias' disciples, and whether this may not be that famous art of rhetoric which Thrasymachus and others teach and practise? Skilful speakers they are, and impart their skill to any who is willing to make kings of them and to bring gifts to them.

Phaedr. Yes, they are royal men; but their art is not the same with the art of those whom you call, and rightly, in my opinion, dialecticians:—Still we are in the dark about rhetoric.

Soc. What do you mean? The remains of it, if there be anything remaining which can be brought under rules of art, must be a fine thing; and, at any rate, is not to be despised by you and me. But how much is left?

Phaedr. There is a great deal surely to be found in books of rhetoric?

Soc. Yes; thank you for reminding me:—There is the exordium, showing how the speech should begin, if I remember rightly; that is what you mean—the niceties of the art?

Phaedr. Yes.

Soc. Then follows the statement of facts, and upon that witnesses; thirdly, proofs; fourthly, probabilities are to come; the great Byzantian word-maker also speaks, if I am not mistaken, of confirmation and further confirmation.

Phaedr. You mean the excellent Theodorus.

[267] Soc. Yes; and he tells how refutation or further refutation is to be managed, whether in accusation or defence. I ought also to men-

tion the illustrious Parian, Evenus, who first invented insinuations and indirect praises; and also indirect censures, which according to some he put into verse to help the memory. But shall I "to dumb forgetfulness consign" Tisias and Gorgias, who are not ignorant that probability is superior to truth, and who by force of argument make the little appear great and the great little, disguise the new in old fashions and the old in new fashions, and have discovered forms for everything, either short or going on to infinity. I remember Prodicus laughing when I told him of this; he said that he had himself discovered the true rule of art, which was to be neither long nor short, but of a convenient length.

Phaedr. Well done, Prodicus!

Soc. Then there is Hippias the Elean stranger, who probably agrees with him.

Phaedr. Yes.

Soc. And there is also Polus, who has treasuries of diplasiology, and gnomology, and eikonology, and who teaches in them the names of which Licymnius made him a present; they were to give a polish.

Phaedr. Had not Protagoras something of the same sort?

Soc. Yes, rules of correct diction and many other fine precepts; for the "sorrows of a poor old man," or any other pathetic case, no one is better than the Chalcedonian giant; he can put a whole company of people into a passion and out of one again by his mighty magic, and is first-rate at inventing or disposing of any sort of calumny on any grounds or none. All of them agree in asserting that a speech should end in a recapitulation, though they do not all agree to use the same word.

Phaedr. You mean that there should be a summing up of the arguments in order to remind the hearers of them.

Soc. I have now said all that I have to say of the art of rhetoric: have you anything to add?

Phaedr. Not much; nothing very important.

[268] Soc. Leave the unimportant and let us bring the really important question into the light of day, which is: What power has this art of rhetoric, and when?

Phaedr. A very great power in public meetings.

Soc. It has. But I should like to know whether you have the same feeling as I have about the rhetoricians? To me there seem to be a great many holes in their web.

Phaedr. Give an example.

Soc. I will. Suppose a person to come to your friend Eryximachus, or to his father Acumenus, and to say to him: "I know how to apply drugs which shall have either a heating or a cooling effect, and I can give a vomit and also a purge, and all that sort of thing; and knowing all this, as I do, I claim to be a physician and to make physicians by imparting this knowledge to others,"—what do you suppose that they would say?

Phaedr. They would be sure to ask him whether he knew "to whom" he would give his medicines, and "when," and "how much."

Soc. And suppose that he were to reply: "No; I know nothing of all that; I expect the patient who consults me to be able to do these things for himself"?

Phaedr. They would say in reply that he is a madman or a pedant who fancies that he is a physician because he has read something in a book, or has stumbled on a prescription or two, although he has no real understanding of the art of medicine.

Soc. And suppose a person were to come to Sophocles or Euripides and say that he knows how to make a very long speech about a small matter, and a short speech about a great matter, and also a sorrowful speech, or a terrible, or threatening speech, or any other kind of speech, and in teaching this fancies that he is teaching the art of tragedy—?

Phaedr. They too would surely laugh at him if he fancies that tragedy is anything but the arranging of these elements in a manner which will be suitable to one another and to the whole.

Soc. But I do not suppose that they would be rude or abusive to him: Would they not treat him as a musician would a man who thinks that he is a harmonist because he knows how to pitch the highest and lowest notes; happening to meet such an one he would not say to him savagely, "Fool, you are mad!" But like a musician, in a gentle and harmonious tone of voice, he would answer: "My good friend, he who would be a harmonist must certainly know this, and yet he may understand nothing of harmony if he has not got beyond your stage of knowledge, for you only know the preliminaries of harmony and not harmony itself."

Phaedr. Very true.

[269] Soc. And will not Sophocles say to the display of the would-be tragedian, that this is not tragedy but the preliminaries of tragedy? and will not Acumenus say the same of medicine to the would-be physician?

Phaedr. Quite true.

Soc. And if Adrastus the mellifluous or Pericles heard of these wonderful arts, brachylogies and eikonologies and all the hard names which we have been endeavouring to draw into the light of day, what would they say? Instead of losing temper and applying uncomplimentary epithets, as you and I have been doing, to the authors of such an imaginary art, their superior wisdom would rather censure us, as well as them. "Have a little patience, Phaedrus and Socrates, they would say; you should not be in such a passion with those who from some want of dialectical skill are unable to define the nature of rhetoric, and consequently suppose that they have found the art in the preliminary conditions of it, and when these have been taught by them to others, fancy that the whole art of rhetoric has been taught by them; but as to using the several instruments of the art effectively, or making the composition a whole,—an application of it such as this is they regard as an easy thing which their disciples may make for themselves."

Phaedr. I quite admit, Socrates, that the art of rhetoric which these men teach and of which they write is such as you describe—there I agree with you. But I still want to know where and how the true art of rhetoric and persuasion is to be acquired.

Soc. The perfection which is required of the finished orator is, or rather must be, like the perfection of anything else, partly given by nature, but may also be assisted by art. If you have the natural power and add to it knowledge and practice, you will be a distinguished speaker; if you fall short in either of these, you will be to that extent defective. But the art, as far as there is an art, of rhetoric does not lie in the direction of Lysias or Thrasymachus.

Phaedr. In what direction then?

Soc. I conceive Pericles to have been the most accomplished of rhetoricians.

Phaedr. What of that?

Soc. All the great arts require discussion and high speculation about the truths of nature; [270] hence come loftiness of thought and completeness of execution. And this, as I conceive, was the quality which, in addition to his natural gifts, Pericles acquired from his intercourse with Anaxagoras whom he happened to know. He was thus imbued with the higher philosophy, and attained the knowledge of Mind and the negative of Mind, which were favourite themes of Anaxagoras, and applied what suited his purpose to the art of speaking.

Phaedr. Explain.

Soc. Rhetoric is like medicine.

Phaedr. How so?

Soc. Why, because medicine has to define the nature of the body and rhetoric of the soul —if we would proceed, not empirically but scientifically, in the one case to impart health and strength by giving medicine and food, in the other to implant the conviction or virtue which you desire, by the right application of words and training.

Phaedr. There, Socrates, I suspect that you are right.

Soc. And do you think that you can know the nature of the soul intelligently without knowing the nature of the whole?

Phaedr. Hippocrates the Asclepiad says that the nature even of the body can only be understood as a whole.[1]

Soc. Yes, friend, and he was right:—still, we ought not to be content with the name of Hippocrates, but to examine and see whether his argument agrees with his conception of nature.

Phaedr. I agree.

Soc. Then consider what truth as well as Hippocrates says about this or about any other nature. Ought we not to consider first whether that which we wish to learn and to teach is a simple or multiform thing, and if simple, then to enquire what power it has of acting or being acted upon in relation to other things, and if multiform, then to number the forms; and see first in the case of one of them, and then in the case of all of them, what is that power of acting or being acted upon which makes each and all of them to be what they are?

Phaedr. You may very likely be right, Socrates.

Soc. The method which proceeds without analysis is like the groping of a blind man. Yet, surely, he who is an artist ought not to admit of a comparison with the blind, or deaf. The rhetorician, who teaches his pupil to speak scientifically, will particularly set forth the nature of that being to which he addresses his speeches; and this, I conceive, to be the soul.

Phaedr. Certainly.

[271] *Soc.* His whole effort is directed to the soul; for in that he seeks to produce conviction.

Phaedr. Yes.

Soc. Then clearly, Thrasymachus or any one else who teaches rhetoric in earnest will give an exact description of the nature of the soul; which will enable us to see whether she be single and same, or, like the body, multiform. That is what we should call showing the nature of the soul.

[1] Cf. *Charmides,* 156.

Phaedr. Exactly.

Soc. He will explain, secondly, the mode in which she acts or is acted upon.

Phaedr. True.

Soc. Thirdly, having classified men and speeches, and their kinds and affections, and adapted them to one another, he will tell the reasons of his arrangement, and show why one soul is persuaded by a particular form of argument, and another not.

Phaedr. You have hit upon a very good way.

Soc. Yes, that is the true and only way in which any subject can be set forth or treated by rules of art, whether in speaking or writing. But the writers of the present day, at whose feet you have sat, craftily conceal the nature of the soul which they know quite well. Nor, until they adopt our method of reading and writing, can we admit that they write by rules of art?

Phaedr. What is our method?

Soc. I cannot give you the exact details; but I should like to tell you generally, as far as is in my power, how a man ought to proceed according to rules of art.

Phaedr. Let me hear.

Soc. Oratory is the art of enchanting the soul, and therefore he who would be an orator has to learn the differences of human souls—they are so many and of such a nature, and from them come the differences between man and man. Having proceeded thus far in his analysis, he will next divide speeches into their different classes:—"Such and such persons," he will say, "are affected by this or that kind of speech in this or that way," and he will tell you why. The pupil must have a good theoretical notion of them first, and then he must have experience of them in actual life, and be able to follow them with all his senses about him, or he will never get beyond the precepts of his masters. But when he understands what persons are persuaded by what arguments, *[272]* and sees the person about whom he was speaking in the abstract actually before him, and knows that it is he, and can say to himself, "This is the man or this is the character who ought to have a certain argument applied to him in order to convince him of a certain opinion";—he who knows all this, and knows also when he should speak and when he should refrain, and when he should use pithy sayings, pathetic appeals, sensational effects, and all the other modes of speech which he has learned;—when, I say, he knows the times and seasons of all these things, then, and not till then, he is a perfect master of his art; but if he fail in any of these points,

whether in speaking or teaching or writing them, and yet declares that he speaks by rules of art, he who says "I don't believe you" has the better of him. Well, the teacher will say, is this, Phaedrus and Socrates, your account of the so-called art of rhetoric, or am I to look for another?

Phaedr. He must take this, Socrates, for there is no possibility of another, and yet the creation of such an art is not easy.

Soc. Very true; and therefore let us consider this matter in every light, and see whether we cannot find a shorter and easier road; there is no use in taking a long rough round-about way if there be a shorter and easier one. And I wish that you would try and remember whether you have heard from Lysias or any one else anything which might be of service to us.

Phaedr. If trying would avail, then I might; but at the moment I can think of nothing.

Soc. Suppose I tell you something which somebody who knows told me.

Phaedr. Certainly.

Soc. May not "the wolf," as the proverb says, "claim a hearing"?

Phaedr. Do you say what can be said for him.

Soc. He will argue that there is no use in putting a solemn face on these matters, or in going round and round, until you arrive at first principles; for, as I said at first, when the question is of justice and good, or is a question in which men are concerned who are just and good, either by nature or habit, he who would be a skilful rhetorician has no need of truth—for that in courts of law men literally care nothing about truth, but only about conviction: and this is based on probability, to which he who would be a skilful orator should therefore give his whole attention. And they say also that there are cases in which the actual facts, if they are improbable, ought to be withheld, and only the probabilities should be told either in accusation or defence, and that always in speaking, the orator should keep probability in view, and say good-bye to the truth. *[273]* And the observance of this principle throughout a speech furnishes the whole art.

Phaedr. That is what the professors of rhetoric do actually say, Socrates. I have not forgotten that we have quite briefly touched upon this matter[1] already; with them the point is all-important.

Soc. I dare say that you are familiar with Tisias. Does he not define probability to be that which the many think?

[1] Cf. 259.

Phaedr. Certainly, he does.

Soc. I believe that he has a clever and ingenious case of this sort:—He supposes a feeble and valiant man to have assaulted a strong and cowardly one, and to have robbed him of his coat or of something or other; he is brought into court, and then Tisias says that both parties should tell lies: the coward should say that he was assaulted by more men than one; the other should prove that they were alone, and should argue thus: "How could a weak man like me have assaulted a strong man like him?" The complainant will not like to confess his own cowardice, and will therefore invent some other lie which his adversary will thus gain an opportunity of refuting. And there are other devices of the same kind which have a place in the system. Am I not right, Phaedrus?

Phaedr. Certainly.

Soc. Bless me, what a wonderfully mysterious art is this which Tisias or some other gentleman, in whatever name or country he rejoices, has discovered. Shall we say a word to him or not?

Phaedr. What shall we say to him?

Soc. Let us tell him that, before he appeared, you and I were saying that the probability of which he speaks was engendered in the minds of the many by the likeness of the truth, and we had just been affirming that he who knew the truth would always know best how to discover the resemblances of the truth. If he has anything else to say about the art of speaking we should like to hear him; but if not, we are satisfied with our own view, that unless a man estimates the various characters of his hearers and is able to divide all things into classes and to comprehend them under single ideas, he will never be a skilful rhetorician even within the limits of human power. And this skill he will not attain without a great deal of trouble, which a good man ought to undergo, not for the sake of speaking and acting before men, but in order that he may be able to say what is acceptable to God and always to act acceptably to Him as far as in him lies; *[274]* for there is a saying of wiser men than ourselves, that a man of sense should not try to please his fellow-servants (at least this should not be his first object) but his good and noble masters; and therefore if the way is long and circuitous, marvel not at this, for, where the end is great, there we may take the longer road, but not for lesser ends such as yours. Truly, the argument may say, Tisias, that if you do not mind going so far, rhetoric has a fair beginning here.

Phaedr. I think, Socrates, that this is admirable, if only practicable.

Soc. But even to fail in an honourable object is honourable.

Phaedr. True.

Soc. Enough appears to have been said by us of a true and false art of speaking.

Phaedr. Certainly.

Soc. But there is something yet to be said of propriety and impropriety of writing.

Phaedr. Yes.

Soc. Do you know how you can speak or act about rhetoric in a manner which will be acceptable to God?

Phaedr. No, indeed. Do you?

Soc. I have heard a tradition of the ancients, whether true or not they only know; although if we had found the truth ourselves, do you think that we should care much about the opinions of men?

Phaedr. Your question needs no answer; but I wish that you would tell me what you say that you have heard.

Soc. At the Egyptian city of Naucratis, there was a famous old god, whose name was Theuth; the bird which is called the Ibis is sacred to him, and he was the inventor of many arts, such as arithmetic and calculation and geometry and astronomy and draughts and dice, but his great discovery was the use of letters. Now in those days the god Thamus was the king of the whole country of Egypt; and he dwelt in that great city of Upper Egypt which the Hellenes call Egyptian Thebes, and the god himself is called by them Ammon. To him came Theuth and showed his inventions, desiring that the other Egyptians might be allowed to have the benefit of them; he enumerated them, and Thamus enquired about their several uses, and praised some of them and censured others, as he approved or disapproved of them. It would take a long time to repeat all that Thamus said to Theuth in praise or blame of the various arts. But when they came to letters, This, said Theuth, will make the Egyptians wiser and give them better memories; it is a specific both for the memory and for the wit. Thamus replied: O most ingenious Theuth, the parent or inventor of an art is not always the best judge of the utility or inutility of his own inventions to the users of them. *[275]* And in this instance, you who are the father of letters, from a paternal love of your own children have been led to attribute to them a quality which they cannot have; for this discovery of yours will create forgetfulness in the learners' souls, because they will not use their memories; they will trust to the external written characters and not remember of themselves. The specific which you have discovered is an aid not to memory, but to reminiscence, and you give your disciples not truth, but only the semblance of truth; they will be hearers of many things and will have learned nothing; they will appear to be omniscient and will generally know nothing; they will be tiresome company, having the show of wisdom without the reality.

Phaedr. Yes, Socrates, you can easily invent tales of Egypt, or of any other country.

Soc. There was a tradition in the temple of Dodona that oaks first gave prophetic utterances. The men of old, unlike in their simplicity to young philosophy, deemed that if they heard the truth even from "oak or rock," it was enough for them; whereas you seem to consider not whether a thing is or is not true, but who the speaker is and from what country the tale comes.

Phaedr. I acknowledge the justice of your rebuke; and I think that the Theban is right in his view about letters.

Soc. He would be a very simple person, and quite a stranger to the oracles of Thamus or Ammon, who should leave in writing or receive in writing any art under the idea that the written word would be intelligible or certain; or who deemed that writing was at all better than knowledge and recollection of the same matters?

Phaedr. That is most true.

Soc. I cannot help feeling, Phaedrus, that writing is unfortunately like painting; for the creations of the painter have the attitude of life, and yet if you ask them a question they preserve a solemn silence. And the same may be said of speeches. You would imagine that they had intelligence, but if you want to know anything and put a question to one of them, the speaker always gives one unvarying answer. And when they have been once written down they are tumbled about anywhere among those who may or may not understand them, and know not to whom they should reply, to whom not: and, if they are maltreated or abused, they have no parent to protect them; and they cannot protect or defend themselves.

Phaedr. That again is most true.

Soc. Is there not another kind of word or speech far better than this, *[276]* and having far greater power—a son of the same family, but lawfully begotten?

Phaedr. Whom do you mean, and what is his origin?

Soc. I mean an intelligent word graven in the soul of the learner, which can defend itself, and knows when to speak and when to be silent.

Phaedr. You mean the living word of knowledge which has a soul, and of which the written word is properly no more than an image?

Soc. Yes, of course that is what I mean. And now may I be allowed to ask you a question: Would a husbandman, who is a man of sense, take the seeds, which he values and which he wishes to bear fruit, and in sober seriousness plant them during the heat of summer, in some garden of Adonis, that he may rejoice when he sees them in eight days appearing in beauty? at least he would do so, if at all, only for the sake of amusement and pastime. But when he is in earnest he sows in fitting soil, and practises husbandry, and is satisfied if in eight months the seeds which he has sown arrive at perfection?

Phaedr. Yes, Socrates, that will be his way when he is in earnest; he will do the other, as you say, only in play.

Soc. And can we suppose that he who knows the just and good and honourable has less understanding, than the husbandman, about his own seeds?

Phaedr. Certainly not.

Soc. Then he will not seriously incline to "write" his thoughts "in water" with pen and ink, sowing words which can neither speak for themselves nor teach the truth adequately to others?

Phaedr. No, that is not likely.

Soc. No, that is not likely—in the garden of letters he will sow and plant, but only for the sake of recreation and amusement; he will write them down as memorials to be treasured against the forgetfulness of old age, by himself, or by any other old man who is treading the same path. He will rejoice in beholding their tender growth; and while others are refreshing their souls with banqueting and the like, this will be the pastime in which his days are spent.

Phaedr. A pastime, Socrates, as noble as the other is ignoble, the pastime of a man who can be amused by serious talk, and can discourse merrily about justice and the like.

Soc. True, Phaedrus. But nobler far is the serious pursuit of the dialectician, who, finding a congenial soul, by the help of science sows and plants therein words which are able to help themselves and him who planted them,

[277] and are not unfruitful, but have in them a seed which others brought up in different soils render immortal, making the possessors of it happy to the utmost extent of human happiness.

Phaedr. Far nobler, certainly.

Soc. And now, Phaedrus, having agreed upon the premises we decide about the conclusion.

Phaedr. About what conclusion?

Soc. About Lysias, whom we censured, and his art of writing, and his discourses, and the rhetorical skill or want of skill which was shown in them—these are the questions which we sought to determine, and they brought us to this point. And I think that we are now pretty well informed about the nature of art and its opposite.

Phaedr. Yes, I think with you; but I wish that you would repeat what was said.

Soc. Until a man knows the truth of the several particulars of which he is writing or speaking, and is able to define them as they are, and having defined them again to divide them until they can be no longer divided, and until in like manner he is able to discern the nature of the soul, and discover the different modes of discourse which are adapted to different natures, and to arrange and dispose them in such a way that the simple form of speech may be addressed to the simpler nature, and the complex and composite to the more complex nature—until he has accomplished all this, he will be unable to handle arguments according to rules of art, as far as their nature allows them to be subjected to art, either for the purpose of teaching or persuading;—such is the view which is implied in the whole preceding argument.

Phaedr. Yes, that was our view, certainly.

Soc. Secondly, as to the censure which was passed on the speaking or writing of discourses, and how they might be rightly or wrongly censured—did not our previous argument show—?

Phaedr. Show what?

Soc. That whether Lysias or any other writer that ever was or will be, whether private man or statesman, proposes laws and so becomes the author of a political treatise, fancying that there is any great certainty and clearness in his performance, the fact of his so writing is only a disgrace to him, whatever men may say. For not to know the nature of justice and injustice, and good and evil, and not to be able to distinguish the dream from the reality, cannot in truth be otherwise than disgraceful to him, even though he have the applause of the whole world.

Phaedr. Certainly.

Soc. But he who thinks that in the written word there is necessarily much which is not serious, and that neither poetry nor prose, spoken or written, is of any great value, if, like the compositions of the rhapsodes, *[278]* they are only recited in order to be believed, and not with any view to criticism or instruction; and who thinks that even the best of writings are but a reminiscence of what we know, and that only in principles of justice and goodness and nobility taught and communicated orally for the sake of instruction and graven in the soul, which is the true way of writing, is there clearness and perfection and seriousness, and that such principles are a man's own and his legitimate offspring;—being, in the first place, the word which he finds in his own bosom; secondly, the brethren and descendants and relations of his others;—and who cares for them and no others—this is the right sort of man; and you and I, Phaedrus, would pray that we may become like him.

Phaedr. That is most assuredly my desire and prayer.

Soc. And now the play is played out; and of rhetoric enough. Go and tell Lysias that to the fountain and school of the Nymphs we went down, and were bidden by them to convey a message to him and to other composers of speeches—to Homer and other writers of poems, whether set to music or not; and to Solon and others who have composed writings in the form of political discourses which they would term laws—to all of them we are to say that if their compositions are based on knowledge of the truth, and they can defend or prove them, when they are put to the test, by spoken arguments, which leave their writings poor in comparison of them, then they are to be called, not only poets, orators, legislators, but are worthy of a higher name, befitting the serious pursuit of their life.

Phaedr. What name would you assign to them?

Soc. Wise, I may not call them; for that is a great name which belongs to God alone,—lovers of wisdom or philosophers is their modest and befitting title.

Phaedr. Very suitable.

Soc. And he who cannot rise above his own compilations and compositions, which he has been long patching and piecing, adding some and taking away some, may be justly called poet or speechmaker or law-maker.

Phaedr. Certainly.

Soc. Now go and tell this to your companion.

Phaedr. But there is also a friend of yours who ought not to be forgotten.

Soc. Who is he?

[279] *Phaedr.* Isocrates the fair:—What message will you send to him, and how shall we describe him?

Soc. Isocrates is still young, Phaedrus; but I am willing to hazard a prophecy concerning him.

Phaedr. What would you prophesy?

Soc. I think that he has a genius which soars above the orations of Lysias, and that his character is cast in a finer mould. My impression of him is that he will marvellously improve as he grows older, and that all former rhetoricians will be as children in comparison of him. And I believe that he will not be satisfied with rhetoric, but that there is in him a divine inspiration which will lead him to things higher still. For

he has an element of philosophy in his nature. This is the message of the gods dwelling in this place, and which I will myself deliver to Isocrates, who is my delight; and do you give the other to Lysias, who is yours.

Phaedr. I will; and now as the heat is abated let us depart.

Soc. Should we not offer up a prayer first of all to the local deities?

Phaedr. By all means.

Soc. Beloved Pan, and all ye other gods who haunt this place, give me beauty in the inward soul; and may the outward and inward man be at one. May I reckon the wise to be the wealthy, and may I have such a quantity of gold as a temperate man and he only can bear and carry. —Anything more? The prayer, I think, is enough for me.

Phaedr. Ask the same for me, for friends should have all things in common.

Soc. Let us go.

ION

PERSONS OF THE DIALOGUE: SOCRATES; ION

❧❧❧❧❧❧❧❧❧❧❧❧

[530] Socrates. WELCOME, ION. Are you from your native city of Ephesus?

Ion. No, Socrates; but from Epidaurus, where I attended the festival of Asclepius.

Soc. And do the Epidaurians have contests of rhapsodes at the festival?

Ion. O yes; and of all sorts of musical performers.

Soc. And were you one of the competitors—and did you succeed?

Ion. I obtained the first prize of all, Socrates.

Soc. Well done; and I hope that you will do the same for us at the Panathenaea.

Ion. And I will, please heaven.

Soc. I often envy the profession of a rhapsode, Ion; for you have always to wear fine clothes, and to look as beautiful as you can is a part of your art. Then, again, you are obliged to be continually in the company of many good poets; and especially of Homer, who is the best and most divine of them; and to understand him, and not merely learn his words by rote, is a thing greatly to be envied. And no man can be a rhapsode who does not understand the meaning of the poet. For the rhapsode ought to interpret the mind of the poet to his hearers, but how can he interpret him well unless he knows what he means? All this is greatly to be envied.

Ion. Very true, Socrates; interpretation has certainly been the most laborious part of my art; and I believe myself able to speak about Homer better than any man; and that neither Metrodorus of Lampsacus, nor Stesimbrotus of Thasos, nor Glaucon, nor any one else who ever was, had as good ideas about Homer as I have, or as many.

Soc. I am glad to hear you say so, Ion; I see that you will not refuse to acquaint me with them.

Ion. Certainly, Socrates; and you really ought to hear how exquisitely I render Homer. I think that the Homeridae should give me a golden crown.

Soc. I shall take an opportunity of hearing your embellishments of him at some other time. *[531]* But just now I should like to ask you a question: Does your art extend to Hesiod and Archilochus, or to Homer only?

Ion. To Homer only; he is in himself quite enough.

Soc. Are there any things about which Homer and Hesiod agree?

Ion. Yes; in my opinion there are a good many.

Soc. And can you interpret better what Homer says, or what Hesiod says, about these matters in which they agree?

Ion. I can interpret them equally well, Socrates, where they agree.

Soc. But what about matters in which they do not agree?—for example, about divination, of which both Homer and Hesiod have something to say—

Ion. Very true:

Soc. Would you or a good prophet be a better interpreter of what these two poets say about divination, not only when they agree, but when they disagree?

Ion. A prophet.

Soc. And if you were a prophet, would you be able to interpret them when they disagree as well as when they agree?

Ion. Clearly.

Soc. But how did you come to have this skill about Homer only, and not about Hesiod or the other poets? Does not Homer speak of the same themes which all other poets handle? Is not war his great argument? and does he not speak of human society and of intercourse of men, good and bad, skilled and unskilled, and of the gods conversing with one another and with mankind, and about what happens in heaven and in the world below, and the generations of gods and heroes? Are not these the themes of which Homer sings?

Ion. Very true, Socrates.

Soc. And do not the other poets sing of the same?

Ion. Yes, Socrates; but not in the same way as Homer.

Soc. What, in a worse way?

Ion. Yes, in a far worse.

Soc. And Homer in a better way?

Ion. He is incomparably better.

Soc. And yet surely, my dear friend Ion, in a discussion about arithmetic, where many people are speaking, and one speaks better than the rest, there is somebody who can judge which of them is the good speaker?

Ion. Yes.

Soc. And he who judges of the good will be the same as he who judges of the bad speakers?

Ion. The same.

Soc. And he will be the arithmetician?

Ion. Yes.

Soc. Well, and in discussions about the wholesomeness of food, when many persons are speaking, and one speaks better than the rest, will he who recognizes the better speaker be a different person from him who recognizes the worse, or the same?

Ion. Clearly the same.

Soc. And who is he, and what is his name?

Ion. The physician.

Soc. And speaking generally, in all discussions in which the subject is the same and many men are speaking, will not he who knows the good know the bad speaker also? [532] For if he does not know the bad, neither will he know the good when the same topic is being discussed.

Ion. True.

Soc. Is not the same person skilful in both?

Ion. Yes.

Soc. And you say that Homer and the other poets, such as Hesiod and Archilochus, speak of the same things, although not in the same way; but the one speaks well and the other not so well?

Ion. Yes; and I am right in saying so.

Soc. And if you knew the good speaker, you would also know the inferior speakers to be inferior?

Ion. That is true.

Soc. Then, my dear friend, can I be mistaken in saying that Ion is equally skilled in Homer and in other poets, since he himself acknowledges that the same person will be a good judge of all those who speak of the same things; and that almost all poets do speak of the same things?

Ion. Why then, Socrates, do I lose attention and go to sleep and have absolutely no ideas of the least value, when any one speaks of any other poet; but when Homer is mentioned, I wake up at once and am all attention and have plenty to say?

Soc. The reason, my friend, is obvious. No one can fail to see that you speak of Homer without any art or knowledge. If you were able to speak of him by rules of art, you would have been able to speak of all other poets; for poetry is a whole.

Ion. Yes.

Soc. And when any one acquires any other art as a whole, the same may be said of them. Would you like me to explain my meaning, Ion?

Ion. Yes, indeed, Socrates; I very much wish that you would: for I love to hear you wise men talk.

Soc. O that we were wise, Ion, and that you could truly call us so; but you rhapsodes and actors, and the poets whose verses you sing, are wise; whereas I am a common man, who only speak the truth. For consider what a very commonplace and trivial thing is this which I have said—a thing which any man might say: that when a man has acquired a knowledge of a whole art, the enquiry into good and bad is one and the same. Let us consider this matter; is not the art of painting a whole?

Ion. Yes.

Soc. And there are and have been many painters good and bad?

Ion. Yes.

Soc. And did you ever know any one who was skilful in pointing out the excellences and defects of Polygnotus the son of Aglaophon, but incapable of criticizing other painters; [533] and when the work of any other painter was produced, went to sleep and was at a loss, and had no ideas; but when he had to give his opinion about Polygnotus, or whoever the painter might be, and about him only, woke up and was attentive and had plenty to say?

Ion. No indeed, I have never known such a person.

Soc. Or did you ever know of any one in sculpture, who was skilful in expounding the merits of Daedalus the son of Metion, or of Epeius the son of Panopeus, or of Theodorus the Samian, or of any individual sculptor; but when the works of sculptors in general were produced, was at a loss and went to sleep and had nothing to say?

Ion. No indeed; no more than the other.

Soc. And if I am not mistaken, you never met with any one among flute-players or harp-players or singers to the harp or rhapsodes who was able to discourse of Olympus or Thamyras or Orpheus, or Phemius the rhapsode of Ithaca, but was at a loss when he came to speak of Ion of Ephesus, and had no notion of his merits or defects?

Ion. I cannot deny what you say, Socrates. Nevertheless I am conscious in my own self, and the world agrees with me in thinking that I do speak better and have more to say about Homer than any other man. But I do not speak equally well about others—tell me the reason of this.

Soc. I perceive, Ion; and I will proceed to explain to you what I imagine to be the reason of this. The gift which you possess of speaking excellently about Homer is not an art, but, as I was just saying, an inspiration; there is a divinity moving you, like that contained in the stone which Euripides calls a magnet, but which is commonly known as the stone of Heraclea. This stone not only attracts iron rings, but also imparts to them a similar power of attracting other rings; and sometimes you may see a number of pieces of iron and rings suspended from one another so as to form quite a long chain: and all of them derive their power of suspension from the original stone. In like manner the Muse first of all inspires men herself; and from these inspired persons a chain of other persons is suspended, who take the inspiration. For all good poets, epic as well as lyric, compose their beautiful poems not by art, but because they are inspired and possessed. And as the Corybantian revellers when they dance are not in their right mind, [534] so the lyric poets are not in their right mind when they are composing their beautiful strains: but when falling under the power of music and metre they are inspired and possessed; like Bacchic maidens who draw milk and honey from the rivers when they are under the in-

fluence of Dionysus but not when they are in their right mind. And the soul of the lyric poet does the same, as they themselves say; for they tell us that they bring songs from honeyed fountains, culling them out of the gardens and dells of the Muses; they, like the bees, winging their way from flower to flower. And this is true. For the poet is a light and winged and holy thing, and there is no invention in him until he has been inspired and is out of his senses, and the mind is no longer in him: when he has not attained to this state, he is powerless and is unable to utter his oracles.

Many are the noble words in which poets speak concerning the actions of men; but like yourself when speaking about Homer, they do not speak of them by any rules of art: they are simply inspired to utter that to which the Muse impels them, and that only; and when inspired, one of them will make dithyrambs, another hymns of praise, another choral strains, another epic or iambic verses—and he who is good at one is not good at any other kind of verse: for not by art does the poet sing, but by power divine. Had he learned by rules of art, he would have known how to speak not of one theme only, but of all; and therefore God takes away the minds of poets, and uses them as his ministers, as he also uses diviners and holy prophets, in order that we who hear them may know them to be speaking not of themselves who utter these priceless words in a state of unconsciousness, but that God himself is the speaker, and that through them he is conversing with us. And Tynnichus the Chalcidian affords a striking instance of what I am saying: he wrote nothing that any one would care to remember but the famous paean which is in every one's mouth, one of the finest poems ever written, simply an invention of the Muses, as he himself says. For in this way the God would seem to indicate to us and not allow us to doubt that these beautiful poems are not human, or the work of man, but divine and the work of God; and that the poets are only the interpreters of the Gods by whom they are severally possessed. Was not this the lesson which the God intended to teach when by the mouth of the worst of poets he sang the best of [535] songs? Am I not right, Ion?

Ion. Yes, indeed, Socrates, I feel that you are; for your words touch my soul, and I am persuaded that good poets by a divine inspiration interpret the things of the Gods to us.

Soc. And you rhapsodists are the interpreters of the poets?

Ion. There again you are right.

Soc. Then you are the interpreters of interpreters?

Ion. Precisely.

Soc. I wish you would frankly tell me, Ion, what I am going to ask of you: When you produce the greatest effect upon the audience in the recitation of some striking passage, such as the apparition of Odysseus leaping forth on the floor, recognized by the suitors and casting his arrows at his feet, or the description of Achilles rushing at Hector, or the sorrows of Andromache, Hecuba, or Priam,—are you in your right mind? Are you not carried out of yourself, and does not your soul in an ecstasy seem to be among the persons or places of which you are speaking, whether they are in Ithaca or in Troy or whatever may be the scene of the poem?

Ion. That proof strikes home to me, Socrates. For I must frankly confess that at the tale of pity my eyes are filled with tears, and when I speak of horrors, my hair stands on end and my heart throbs.

Soc. Well, Ion, and what are we to say of a man who at a sacrifice or festival, when he is dressed in holiday attire, and has golden crowns upon his head, of which nobody has robbed him, appears weeping or panic-stricken in the presence of more than twenty thousand friendly faces, when there is no one despoiling or wronging him;—is he in his right mind or is he not?

Ion. No indeed, Socrates, I must say that, strictly speaking, he is not in his right mind.

Soc. And are you aware that you produce similar effects on most spectators?

Ion. Only too well; for I look down upon them from the stage, and behold the various emotions of pity, wonder, sternness, stamped upon their countenances when I am speaking: and I am obliged to give my very best attention to them; for if I make them cry I myself shall laugh, and if I make them laugh I myself shall cry when the time of payment arrives.

Soc. Do you know that the spectator is the last of the rings which, as I am saying, receive the power of the original magnet from one another? The rhapsode like yourself and the actor are intermediate links, *[536]* and the poet himself is the first of them. Through all these the God sways the souls of men in any direction which he pleases, and makes one man hang down from another. Thus there is a vast chain of dancers and masters and undermasters of choruses, who are suspended, as if from the stone, at the side of the rings which hang down

from the Muse. And every poet has some Muse from whom he is suspended, and by whom he is said to be possessed, which is nearly the same thing; for he is taken hold of. And from these first rings, which are the poets, depend others, some deriving their inspiration from Orpheus, others from Musaeus; but the greater number are possessed and held by Homer. Of whom, Ion, you are one, and are possessed by Homer; and when any one repeats the words of another poet you go to sleep, and know not what to say; but when any one recites a strain of Homer you wake up in a moment, and your soul leaps within you, and you have plenty to say; for not by art or knowledge about Homer do you say what you say, but by divine inspiration and by possession; just as the Corybantian revellers too have a quick perception of that strain only which is appropriated to the God by whom they are possessed, and have plenty of dances and words for that, but take no heed of any other. And you, Ion, when the name of Homer is mentioned have plenty to say, and have nothing to say of others. You ask, "Why is this?" The answer is that you praise Homer not by art but by divine inspiration.

Ion. That is good, Socrates; and yet I doubt whether you will ever have eloquence enough to persuade me that I praise Homer only when I am mad and possessed; and if you could hear me speak of him I am sure you would never think this to be the case.

Soc. I should like very much to hear you, but not until you have answered a question which I have to ask. On what part of Homer do you speak well?—not surely about every part.

Ion. There is no part, Socrates, about which I do not speak well: of that I can assure you.

Soc. Surely not about things in Homer of which you have no knowledge?

Ion. And what is there in Homer of which I have no knowledge?

Soc. Why, does not Homer speak in many passages about arts? For example, *[537]* about driving; if I can only remember the lines I will repeat them.

Ion. I remember, and will repeat them.

Soc. Tell me then, what Nestor says to Antilochus, his son, where he bids him be careful of the turn at the horse-race in honour of Patroclus.

Ion. He says:

Bend gently in the polished chariot to the left of them, and urge the horse on the right hand with whip and voice; and slacken the rein. And when you are at the goal, let the left horse draw near, yet so that the nave of the well-wrought wheel may not even seem to touch the extremity; and avoid catching the stone.

Soc. Enough. Now, Ion, will the charioteer or the physician be the better judge of the propriety of these lines?

Ion. The charioteer, clearly.

Soc. And will the reason be that this is his art, or will there be any other reason?

Ion. No, that will be the reason.

Soc. And every art is appointed by God to have knowledge of a certain work; for that which we know by the art of the pilot we do not know by the art of medicine?

Ion. Certainly not.

Soc. Nor do we know by the art of the carpenter that which we know by the art of medicine?

Ion. Certainly not.

Soc. And this is true of all the arts;—that which we know with one art we do not know with the other? But let me ask a prior question: You admit that there are differences of arts?

Ion. Yes.

Soc. You would argue, as I should, that when one art is of one kind of knowledge and another of another, they are different?

Ion. Yes.

Soc. Yes, surely; for if the subject of knowledge were the same, there would be no meaning in saying that the arts were different,—if they both gave the same knowledge. For example, I know that here are five fingers, and you know the same. And if I were to ask whether I and you became acquainted with this fact by the help of the same art of arithmetic, you would acknowledge that we did?

Ion. Yes.

[538] *Soc.* Tell me, then, what I was intending to ask you—whether this holds universally? Must the same art have the same subject of knowledge, and different arts other subjects of knowledge?

Ion. That is my opinion, Socrates.

Soc. Then he who has no knowledge of a particular art will have no right judgment of the sayings and doings of that art?

Ion. Very true.

Soc. Then which will be a better judge of the lines which you were reciting from Homer, you or the charioteer?

Ion. The charioteer.

Soc. Why, yes, because you are a rhapsode and not a charioteer.

Ion. Yes.

Soc. And the art of the rhapsode is different from that of the charioteer?

Ion. Yes.

Soc. And if a different knowledge, then a knowledge of different matters?

Ion. True.

Soc. You know the passage in which Hecamede, the concubine of Nestor, is described as giving to the wounded Machaon a posset, as he says,

Made with Pramnian wine; and she grated cheese of goat's milk with a grater of bronze, and at his side placed an onion which gives a relish to drink.

Now would you say that the art of the rhapsode or the art of medicine was better able to judge of the propriety of these lines?

Ion. The art of medicine.

Soc. And when Homer says,

And she descended into the deep like a leaden plummet, which, set in the horn of ox that ranges in the fields, rushes along carrying death among the ravenous fishes,—

will the art of the fisherman or of the rhapsode be better able to judge whether these lines are rightly expressed or not?

Ion. Clearly, Socrates, the art of the fisherman.

Soc. Come now, suppose that you were to say to me: "Since you, Socrates, are able to assign different passages in Homer to their corresponding arts, I wish that you would tell me what are the passages of which the excellence ought to be judged by the prophet and prophetic art"; and you will see how readily and truly I shall answer you. For there are many such passages, particularly in the *Odyssey;* as, for example, the passage in which Theoclymenus the prophet of the house of Melampus says to the suitors:—

[539] *Wretched men! what is happening to you? Your heads and your faces and your limbs underneath are shrouded in night; and the voice of lamentation bursts forth, and your cheeks are wet with tears. And the vestibule is full, and the court is full, of ghosts descending into the darkness of Erebus, and the sun has perished out of heaven, and an evil mist is spread abroad.*

And there are many such passages in the *Iliad* also; as for example in the description of the battle near the rampart, where he says:—

As they were eager to pass the ditch, there came to them an omen: a soaring eagle, holding back the people on the left, bore a huge bloody dragon in his talons, still living and panting; nor had he yet resigned the strife, for he bent back and smote the bird which carried him on the breast by the neck, and he in pain let him fall from him to the ground into the midst of the multitude. And the eagle, with a cry, was borne afar on the wings of the wind.

These are the sort of things which I should say that the prophet ought to consider and determine.

Ion. And you are quite right, Socrates, in saying so.

Soc. Yes, Ion, and you are right also. And as I have selected from the *Iliad* and *Odyssey* for you passages which describe the office of the prophet and the physician and the fisherman, do you, who know Homer so much better than I do, Ion, select for me passages which relate to the rhapsode and the rhapsode's art, and which the rhapsode ought to examine and judge of better than other men.

Ion. All passages, I should say, Socrates.

Soc. Not all, Ion, surely. Have you already forgotten what you were saying? A rhapsode ought to have a better memory.

[540] Ion. Why, what am I forgetting?

Soc. Do you not remember that you declared the art of the rhapsode to be different from the art of the charioteer?

Ion. Yes, I remember.

Soc. And you admitted that being different they would have different subjects of knowledge?

Ion. Yes.

Soc. Then upon your own showing the rhapsode, and the art of the rhapsode, will not know everything?

Ion. I should exclude certain things, Socrates.

Soc. You mean to say that you would exclude pretty much the subjects of the other arts. As he does not know all of them, which of them will he know?

Ion. He will know what a man and what a woman ought to say, and what a freeman and what a slave ought to say, and what a ruler and what a subject.

Soc. Do you mean that a rhapsode will know better than the pilot what the ruler of a sea-tossed vessel ought to say?

Ion. No; the pilot will know best.

Soc. Or will the rhapsode know better than the physician what the ruler of a sick man ought to say?

Ion. He will not.

Soc. But he will know what a slave ought to say?

Ion. Yes.

Soc. Suppose the slave to be a cowherd; the rhapsode will know better than the cowherd what he ought to say in order to soothe the infuriated cows?

Ion. No, he will not.

Soc. But he will know what a spinning-woman ought to say about the working of wool?

Ion. No.

Soc. At any rate he will know what a general ought to say when exhorting his soldiers?

Ion. Yes, that is the sort of thing which the rhapsode will be sure to know.

Soc. Well, but is the art of the rhapsode the art of the general?

Ion. I am sure that I should know what a general ought to say.

Soc. Why, yes, Ion, because you may possibly have a knowledge of the art of the general as well as of the rhapsode; and you may also have a knowledge of horsemanship as well as of the lyre: and then you would know when horses were well or ill managed. But suppose I were to ask you: By the help of which art, Ion, do you know whether horses are well managed, by your skill as a horseman or as a performer on the lyre—what would you answer?

Ion. I should reply, by my skill as a horseman.

Soc. And if you judged of performers on the lyre, you would admit that you judged of them as a performer on the lyre, and not as a horseman?

Ion. Yes.

Soc. And in judging of the general's art, do you judge of it as a general or a rhapsode?

Ion. To me there appears to be no difference between them.

[541] Soc. What do you mean? Do you mean to say that the art of the rhapsode and of the general is the same?

Ion. Yes, one and the same.

Soc. Then he who is a good rhapsode is also a good general?

Ion. Certainly, Socrates.

Soc. And he who is a good general is also a good rhapsode?

Ion. No; I do not say that.

Soc. But you do say that he who is a good rhapsode is also a good general.

Ion. Certainly.

Soc. And you are the best of Hellenic rhapsodes?

Ion. Far the best, Socrates.

Soc. And are you the best general, Ion?

Ion. To be sure, Socrates; and Homer was my master.

Soc. But then, Ion, what in the name of goodness can be the reason why you, who are the best of generals as well as the best of rhapsodes in all Hellas, go about as a rhapsode when you might be a general? Do you think that the Hellenes want a rhapsode with his golden crown, and do not want a general?

Ion. Why, Socrates, the reason is, that my countrymen, the Ephesians, are the servants and soldiers of Athens, and do not need a general; and you and Sparta are not likely to have me, for you think that you have enough generals of your own.

Soc. My good Ion, did you never hear of Apollodorus of Cyzicus?

Ion. Who may he be?

Soc. One who, though a foreigner, has often been chosen their general by the Athenians: and there is Phanosthenes of Andros, and Heraclides of Clazomenae, whom they have also appointed to the command of their armies and to other offices, although aliens, after they had shown their merit. And will they not choose Ion the Ephesian to be their general, and honour him, if he prove himself worthy? Were not the Ephesians originally Athenians, and Ephesus is no mean city? But, indeed, Ion, if you are correct in saying that by art and knowledge you are able to praise Homer, you do not deal fairly with me, and after all your professions of knowing many glorious things about Homer, and promises that you would exhibit them, you are only a deceiver, and so far from exhibiting the art of which you are a master, will not, even after my repeated entreaties, explain to me the nature of it. You have literally as many forms as Proteus; and now you go all manner of ways, twisting and turning, and, like Proteus, become all manner of people at once, and at last slip away from me in the disguise of a general, [542] in order that you may escape exhibiting your Homeric lore. And if you have art, then, as I was saying, in falsifying your promise that you would exhibit Homer, you are not dealing fairly with me. But if, as I believe, you have no art, but speak all these beautiful words about Homer unconsciously under his inspiring influence, then I acquit you of dishonesty, and shall only say that you are inspired. Which do you prefer to be thought, dishonest or inspired?

Ion. There is a great difference, Socrates, between the two alternatives; and inspiration is by far the nobler.

Soc. Then, Ion, I shall assume the nobler alternative; and attribute to you in your praises of Homer inspiration, and not art.

SYMPOSIUM

PERSONS OF THE DIALOGUE: APOLLODORUS, *who repeats to his companion the dialogue which he had heard from Aristodemus, and had already once narrated to Glaucon;* PHAEDRUS; PAUSANIAS; ERYXIMACHUS; ARISTOPHANES; AGATHON; SOCRATES; ALCIBIADES; A TROOP OF REVELLERS. *Scene: The House of Agathon*

[172] CONCERNING the things about which you ask to be informed I believe that I am not ill-prepared with an answer. For the day before yesterday I was coming from my own home at Phalerum to the city, and one of my acquaintance, who had caught a sight of me from behind, calling out playfully in the distance, said: Apollodorus, O thou Phalerian[1] man, halt! So I did as I was bid; and then he said, I was looking for you, Apollodorus, only just now, that I might ask you about the speeches in praise of love, which were delivered by Socrates, Alcibiades, and others, at Agathon's supper. Phoenix, the son of Philip, told another person who told me of them; his narrative was very indistinct, but he said that you knew, and I wish that you would give me an account of them. Who, if not you, should be the reporter of the words of your friend? And first tell me, he said, were you present at this meeting?

Your informant, Glaucon, I said, must have been very indistinct indeed, if you imagine that the occasion was recent; or that I could have been of the party.

Why, yes, he replied, I thought so.

Impossible: I said. Are you ignorant that for many years Agathon has not resided at Athens; and not three have elapsed since I became acquainted with Socrates, and have made it my daily business to know all that he says and does. [173] There was a time when I was run-

[1] Probably a play of words on φαλαρὸς, "bald-headed."

ning about the world, fancying myself to be well employed, but I was really a most wretched being, no better than you are now. I thought that I ought to do anything rather than be a philosopher.

Well, he said, jesting apart, tell me when the meeting occurred.

In our boyhood, I replied, when Agathon won the prize with his first tragedy, on the day after that on which he and his chorus offered the sacrifice of victory.

Then it must have been a long while ago, he said; and who told you—did Socrates?

No indeed, I replied, but the same person who told Phoenix;—he was a little fellow, who never wore any shoes, Aristodemus, of the deme of Cydathenaeum. He had been at Agathon's feast; and I think that in those days there was no one who was a more devoted admirer of Socrates. Moreover, I have asked Socrates about the truth of some parts of his narrative, and he confirmed them. Then, said Glaucon, let us have the tale over again; is not the road to Athens just made for conversation? And so we walked, and talked of the discourses on love; and therefore, as I said at first, I am not ill-prepared to comply with your request, and will have another rehearsal of them if you like. For to speak or to hear others speak of philosophy always gives me the greatest pleasure, to say nothing of the profit. But when I hear another strain, especially that of you rich men and traders, such conversation displeases me;

and I pity you who are my companions, because you think that you are doing something when in reality you are doing nothing. And I dare say that you pity me in return, whom you regard as an unhappy creature, and very probably you are right. But I certainly know of you what you only think of me—there is the difference.

Companion. I see, Apollodorus, that you are just the same—always speaking evil of yourself, and of others; and I do believe that you pity all mankind, with the exception of Socrates, yourself first of all, true in this to your old name, which, however deserved, I know not how you acquired, of Apollodorus the madman; for you are always raging against yourself and everybody but Socrates.

Apollodorus. Yes, friend, and the reason why I am said to be mad, and out of my wits, is just because I have these notions of myself and you; no other evidence is required.

Com. No more of that, Apollodorus; but let me renew my request that you would repeat the conversation.

Apoll. Well, the tale of love was on this wise: —But perhaps I had better begin at the beginning, *[174]* and endeavour to give you the exact words of Aristodemus:

He said that he met Socrates fresh from the bath and sandalled; and as the sight of the sandals was unusual, he asked him whither he was going that he had been converted into such a beau:—

To a banquet at Agathon's, he replied, whose invitation to his sacrifice of victory I refused yesterday, fearing a crowd, but promising that I would come to-day instead; and so I have put on my finery, because he is such a fine man. What say you to going with me unasked?

I will do as you bid me, I replied.

Follow then, he said, and let us demolish the proverb:

To the feasts of inferior men the good unbidden go;

instead of which our proverb will run:—

To the feasts of the good the good unbidden go;

and this alteration may be supported by the authority of Homer himself, who not only demolishes but literally outrages the proverb. For, after picturing Agamemnon as the most valiant of men, he makes Menelaus, who is but a faint-hearted warrior, come unbidden to the banquet of Agamemnon, who is feasting and offering sacrifices, not the better to the worse, but the worse to the better.

I rather fear, Socrates, said Aristodemus, lest this may still be my case; and that, like Menelaus in Homer, I shall be the inferior person, who

To the feasts of the wise unbidden goes.

But I shall say that I was bidden of you, and then you will have to make an excuse.

Two going together,

he replied, in Homeric fashion, one or other of them may invent an excuse by the way.

This was the style of their conversation as they went along. Socrates dropped behind in a fit of abstraction, and desired Aristodemus, who was waiting, to go on before him. When he reached the house of Agathon he found the doors wide open, and a comical thing happened. A servant coming out met him, and led him at once into the banqueting-hall in which the guests were reclining, for the banquet was about to begin. Welcome, Aristodemus, said Agathon, as soon as he appeared—you are just in time to sup with us; if you come on any other matter put it off, and make one of us, as I was looking for you yesterday and meant to have asked you, if I could have found you. But what have you done with Socrates?

I turned round, but Socrates was nowhere to be seen; and I had to explain that he had been with me a moment before, and that I came by his invitation to the supper.

You were quite right in coming, said Agathon; but where is he himself?

[175] He was behind me just now, as I entered, he said, and I cannot think what has become of him.

Go and look for him, boy, said Agathon, and bring him in; and do you, Aristodemus, meanwhile take the place by Eryximachus.

The servant then assisted him to wash, and he lay down, and presently another servant came in and reported that our friend Socrates had retired into the portico of the neighbouring house. "There he is fixed," said he, "and when I call to him he will not stir."

How strange, said Agathon; then you must call him again, and keep calling him.

Let him alone, said my informant; he has a way of stopping anywhere and losing himself without any reason. I believe that he will soon appear; do not therefore disturb him.

Well, if you think so, I will leave him, said Agathon. And then, turning to the servants, he added, "Let us have supper without waiting for him. Serve up whatever you please, for there is no one to give you orders; hitherto I have never left you to yourselves. But on this occasion imagine that you are our hosts, and that I and the company are your guests; treat us well, and then we shall commend you." After this, supper was served, but still no Socrates; and during the meal Agathon several times expressed a wish to send for him, but Aristodemus objected; and at last when the feast was about half over—for the fit, as usual, was not of long duration—Socrates entered. Agathon, who was reclining alone at the end of the table, begged that he would take the place next to him; that "I may touch you," he said, "and have the benefit of that wise thought which came into your mind in the portico, and is now in your possession; for I am certain that you would not have come away until you had found what you sought."

How I wish, said Socrates, taking his place as he was desired, that wisdom could be infused by touch, out of the fuller into the emptier man, as water runs through wool out of a fuller cup into an emptier one; if that were so, how greatly should I value the privilege of reclining at your side! For you would have filled me full with a stream of wisdom plenteous and fair; whereas my own is of a very mean and questionable sort, no better than a dream. But yours is bright and full of promise, and was manifested forth in all the splendour of youth the day before yesterday, in the presence of more than thirty thousand Hellenes.

You are mocking, Socrates, said Agathon, and ere long you and I will have to determine who bears off the palm of wisdom—of this Dionysus shall be the judge; but at present you are better occupied with supper.

[176] Socrates took his place on the couch, and supped with the rest; and then libations were offered, and after a hymn had been sung to the god, and there had been the usual ceremonies, they were about to commence drinking, when Pausanias said, And now, my friends, how can we drink with least injury to ourselves? I can assure you that I feel severely the effect of yesterday's potations, and must have time to recover; and I suspect that most of you are in the same predicament, for you were of the party yesterday. Consider then: How can the drinking be made easiest?

I entirely agree, said Aristophanes, that we should, by all means, avoid hard drinking, for I was myself one of those who were yesterday drowned in drink.

I think that you are right, said Eryximachus, the son of Acumenus; but I should still like to hear one other person speak: Is Agathon able to drink hard?

I am not equal to it, said Agathon.

Then, said Eryximachus, the weak heads like myself, Aristodemus, Phaedrus, and others who never can drink, are fortunate in finding that the stronger ones are not in a drinking mood. (I do not include Socrates, who is able either to drink or to abstain, and will not mind, whichever we do.) Well, as none of the company seem disposed to drink much, I may be forgiven for saying, as a physician, that drinking deep is a bad practice, which I never follow, if I can help, and certainly do not recommend to another, least of all to any one who still feels the effects of yesterday's carouse.

I always do what you advise, and especially what you prescribe as a physician, rejoined Phaedrus the Myrrhinusian, and the rest of the company, if they are wise, will do the same.

It was agreed that drinking was not to be the order of the day, but that they were all to drink only so much as they pleased.

Then, said Eryximachus, as you are all agreed that drinking is to be voluntary, and that there is to be no compulsion, I move, in the next place, that the flute-girl, who has just made her appearance, be told to go away and play to herself, or, if she likes, to the women who are within.[1] To-day let us have conversation instead; and, [177] if you will allow me, I will tell you what sort of conversation. This proposal having been accepted, Eryximachus proceeded as follows:—

I will begin, he said, after the manner of Melanippe in Euripides,

Not mine the word

which I am about to speak, but that of Phaedrus. For often he says to me in an indignant tone:— "What a strange thing it is, Eryximachus, that, whereas other gods have poems and hymns made in their honour, the great and glorious god, Love, has no encomiast among all the poets who are so many. There are the worthy sophists too—the excellent Prodicus for example, who have descanted in prose on the virtues of Heracles and other heroes; and, what is still more extraordinary, I have met with a philosophical work in which the utility of salt has been made the theme of an eloquent discourse; and many other like things have had a like honour bestowed upon them. And only to think that there should have been an eager

[1] Cf. *Protagoras*, 347.

interest created about them, and yet that to this day no one has ever dared worthily to hymn Love's praises! So entirely has this great deity been neglected." Now in this Phaedrus seems to me to be quite right, and therefore I want to offer him a contribution; also I think that at the present moment we who are here assembled cannot do better than honour the god Love. If you agree with me, there will be no lack of conversation; for I mean to propose that each of us in turn, going from left to right, shall make a speech in honour of Love. Let him give us the best which he can; and Phaedrus, because he is sitting first on the left hand, and because he is the father of the thought, shall begin.

No one will vote against you, Eryximachus, said Socrates. How can I oppose your motion, who profess to understand nothing but matters of love; nor, I presume, will Agathon and Pausanias; and there can be no doubt of Aristophanes, whose whole concern is with Dionysus and Aphrodite; nor will any one disagree of those whom I see around me. The proposal, as I am aware, may seem rather hard upon us whose place is last; but we shall be contented if we hear some good speeches first. Let Phaedrus begin the praise of Love, and good luck to him. All the company expressed their assent, [178] and desired him to do as Socrates bade him.

Aristodemus did not recollect all that was said, nor do I recollect all that he related to me; but I will tell you what I thought most worthy of remembrance, and what the chief speakers said.

Phaedrus began by affirming that Love is a mighty god, and wonderful among gods and men, but especially wonderful in his birth. For he is the eldest of the gods, which is an honour to him; and a proof of his claim to this honour is, that of his parents there is no memorial; neither poet nor prose-writer has ever affirmed that he had any. As Hesiod says:

First Chaos came, and then broad-bosomed Earth,
The everlasting seat of all that is,
And Love.

In other words, after Chaos, the Earth and Love, these two, came into being. Also Parmenides sings of Generation:

First in the train of gods, he fashioned Love.

And Acusilaus agrees with Hesiod. Thus numerous are the witnesses who acknowledge Love to be the eldest of the gods. And not only is he the eldest, he is also the source of the greatest benefits to us. For I know not any greater blessing to a young man who is beginning life than a virtuous lover, or to the lover than a beloved youth. For the principle which ought to be the guide of men who would nobly live—that principle, I say, neither kindred, nor honour, nor wealth, nor any other motive is able to implant so well as love. Of what am I speaking? Of the sense of honour and dishonour, without which neither states nor individuals ever do any good or great work. And I say that a lover who is detected in doing any dishonourable act, or submitting through cowardice when any dishonour is done to him by another, will be more pained at being detected by his beloved than at being seen by his father, or by his companions, or by any one else. The beloved too, when he is found in any disgraceful situation, has the same feeling about his lover. And if there were only some way of contriving that a state or an army should be made up of lovers and their loves,[1] they would be the very best governors of their own city, abstaining from all dishonour, and emulating one another in honour; [179] and when fighting at each other's side, although a mere handful, they would overcome the world. For what lover would not choose rather to be seen by all mankind than by his beloved, either when abandoning his post or throwing away his arms? He would be ready to die a thousand deaths rather than endure this. Or who would desert his beloved or fail him in the hour of danger? The veriest coward would become an inspired hero, equal to the bravest, at such a time; Love would inspire him. That courage which, as Homer says, the god breathes into the souls of some heroes, Love of his own nature infuses into the lover.

Love will make men dare to die for their beloved—love alone; and women as well as men. Of this, Alcestis, the daughter of Pelias, is a monument to all Hellas; for she was willing to lay down her life on behalf of her husband, when no one else would, although he had a father and mother; but the tenderness of her love so far exceeded theirs, that she made them seem to be strangers in blood to their own son, and in name only related to him; and so noble did this action of hers appear to the gods, as well as to men, that among the many who have done virtuously she is one of the very few to whom, in admiration of her noble action, they have granted the privilege of returning alive to earth; such exceeding honour is paid by the gods to the devotion and virtue of

[1] Cf. *Republic*, v. 468.

love. But Orpheus, the son of Oeagrus, the harper, they sent empty away, and presented to him an apparition only of her whom he sought, but herself they would not give up, because he showed no spirit; he was only a harp-player, and did not dare like Alcestis to die for love, but was contriving how he might enter Hades alive; moreover, they afterwards caused him to suffer death at the hands of women, as the punishment of his cowardliness. Very different was the reward of the true love of Achilles towards his lover Patroclus—his lover and not his love (the notion that Patroclus was the beloved one is a foolish error into which Aeschylus has fallen, for Achilles was surely the fairer of the two, fairer also than all the other heroes; and, as Homer informs us, he was still beardless, and younger far). [180] And greatly as the gods honour the virtue of love, still the return of love on the part of the beloved to the lover is more admired and valued and rewarded by them, for the lover is more divine; because he is inspired by God. Now Achilles was quite aware, for he had been told by his mother, that he might avoid death and return home, and live to a good old age, if he abstained from slaying Hector. Nevertheless he gave his life to revenge his friend, and dared to die, not only in his defence, but after he was dead. Wherefore the gods honoured him even above Alcestis, and sent him to the Islands of the Blest. These are my reasons for affirming that Love is the eldest and noblest and mightiest of the gods, and the chiefest author and giver of virtue in life, and of happiness after death.

This, or something like this, was the speech of Phaedrus; and some other speeches followed which Aristodemus did not remember; the next which he repeated was that of Pausanias. Phaedrus, he said, the argument has not been set before us, I think, quite in the right form; —we should not be called upon to praise Love in such an indiscriminate manner. If there were only one Love, then what you said would be well enough; but since there are more Loves than one, you should have begun by determining which of them was to be the theme of our praises. I will amend this defect; and first of all I will tell you which Love is deserving of praise, and then try to hymn the praiseworthy one in a manner worthy of him. For we all know that Love is inseparable from Aphrodite, and if there were only one Aphrodite there would be only one Love; but as there are two goddesses there must be two Loves.

And am I not right in asserting that there are two goddesses? The elder one, having no mother, who is called the heavenly Aphrodite —she is the daughter of Uranus; the younger, who is the daughter of Zeus and Dione—her we call common; and the Love who is her fellow-worker is rightly named common, as the other love is called heavenly. All the gods ought to have praise given to them, but not without distinction of their natures; and therefore I must try to distinguish the characters of the two Loves. Now actions vary according to the manner of their performance. [181] Take, for example, that which we are now doing, drinking, singing and talking—these actions are not in themselves either good or evil, but they turn out in this or that way according to the mode of performing them; and when well done they are good, and when wrongly done they are evil; and in like manner not every love, but only that which has a noble purpose, is noble and worthy of praise. The Love who is the offspring of the common Aphrodite is essentially common, and has no discrimination, being such as the meaner sort of men feel, and is apt to be of women as well as of youths, and is of the body rather than of the soul—the most foolish beings are the objects of this love which desires only to gain an end, but never thinks of accomplishing the end nobly, and therefore does good and evil quite indiscriminately. The goddess who is his mother is far younger than the other, and she was born of the union of the male and female, and partakes of both.

But the offspring of the heavenly Aphrodite is derived from a mother in whose birth the female has no part,—she is from the male only; this is that love which is of youths, and the goddess being older, there is nothing of wantonness in her. Those who are inspired by this love turn to the male, and delight in him who is the more valiant and intelligent nature; any one may recognise the pure enthusiasts in the very character of their attachments. For they love not boys, but intelligent beings whose reason is beginning to be developed, much about the time at which their beards begin to grow. And in choosing young men to be their companions, they mean to be faithful to them, and pass their whole life in company with them, not to take them in their inexperience, and deceive them, and play the fool with them, or run away from one to another of them. But the love of young boys should be forbidden by law, because their future is uncertain; they may turn out good or bad, either in body or soul, and much noble enthusiasm may be thrown away upon them;

in this matter the good are a law to themselves, and the coarser sort of lovers ought to be restrained by force, as we restrain or attempt to restrain them from fixing their affections on women of free birth. [182] These are the persons who bring a reproach on love; and some have been led to deny the lawfulness of such attachments because they see the impropriety and evil of them; for surely nothing that is decorously and lawfully done can justly be censured.

Now here and in Lacedaemon the rules about love are perplexing, but in most cities they are simple and easily intelligible; in Elis and Boeotia, and in countries having no gifts of eloquence, they are very straightforward; the law is simply in favour of these connexions, and no one, whether young or old, has anything to say to their discredit; the reason being, as I suppose, that they are men of few words in those parts, and therefore the lovers do not like the trouble of pleading their suit. In Ionia and other places, and generally in countries which are subject to the barbarians, the custom is held to be dishonourable; loves of youths share the evil repute in which philosophy and gymnastics are held, because they are inimical to tyranny; for the interests of rulers require that their subjects should be poor in spirit [1] and that there should be no strong bond of friendship or society among them, which love, above all other motives, is likely to inspire, as our Athenian tyrants learned by experience; for the love of Aristogeiton and the constancy of Harmodius had a strength which undid their power. And, therefore, the ill-repute into which these attachments have fallen is to be ascribed to the evil condition of those who make them to be ill-reputed; that is to say, to the self-seeking of the governors and the cowardice of the governed; on the other hand, the indiscriminate honour which is given to them in some countries is attributable to the laziness of those who hold this opinion of them. In our own country a far better principle prevails, but, as I was saying, the explanation of it is rather perplexing. For, observe that open loves are held to be more honourable than secret ones, and that the love of the noblest and highest, even if their persons are less beautiful than others, is especially honourable.

Consider, too, how great is the encouragement which all the world gives to the lover; neither is he supposed to be doing anything dishonourable; but if he succeeds he is praised, and if he fail he is blamed. And in the pursuit

[1] Cf. Aristotle, *Politics*, v. 11, 1314[a]13-29.

of his love the custom of mankind allows him to do many strange things, which philosophy would bitterly censure if they were done from any motive of interest, [183] or wish for office or power. He may pray, and entreat, and supplicate, and swear, and lie on a mat at the door, and endure a slavery worse than that of any slave—in any other case friends and enemies would be equally ready to prevent him, but now there is no friend who will be ashamed of him and admonish him, and no enemy will charge him with meanness or flattery; the actions of a lover have a grace which ennobles them; and custom has decided that they are highly commendable and that there is no loss of character in them; and, what is strangest of all, he only may swear and forswear himself (so men say), and the gods will forgive his transgression, for there is no such thing as a lover's oath. Such is the entire liberty which gods and men have allowed the lover, according to the custom which prevails in our part of the world. From this point of view a man fairly argues that in Athens to love and to be loved is held to be a very honourable thing. But when parents forbid their sons to talk with their lovers, and place them under a tutor's care, who is appointed to see to these things, and their companions and equals cast in their teeth anything of the sort which they may observe, and their elders refuse to silence the reprovers and do not rebuke them—any one who reflects on all this will, on the contrary, think that we hold these practices to be most disgraceful. But, as I was saying at first, the truth as I imagine is, that whether such practices are honourable or whether they are dishonourable is not a simple question; they are honourable to him who follows them honourably, dishonourable to him who follows them dishonourably. There is dishonour in yielding to the evil, or in an evil manner; but there is honour in yielding to the good, or in an honourable manner.

Evil is the vulgar lover who loves the body rather than the soul, inasmuch as he is not even stable, because he loves a thing which is in itself unstable, and therefore when the bloom of youth which he was desiring is over, he takes wing and flies away, in spite of all his words and promises; whereas the love of the noble disposition is life-long, for it becomes one with the everlasting. The custom of our country would have both of them proven well and truly, [184] and would have us yield to the one sort of lover and avoid the other, and therefore encourages some to pursue, and others to fly; testing both the lover and beloved in contests and trials, until they show to which of the two classes they respectively belong. And this is the reason why, in the first place, a hasty attachment is held to be dishonourable, because time is the true test of this as of most other things; and secondly there is a dishonour in being overcome by the love of money, or of wealth, or of political power, whether a man is frightened into surrender by the loss of them, or, having experienced the benefits of money and political corruption, is unable to rise above the seductions of them. For none of these things are of a permanent or lasting nature; not to mention that no generous friendship ever sprang from them. There remains, then, only one way of honourable attachment which custom allows in the beloved, and this is the way of virtue; for as we admitted that any service which the lover does to him is not to be accounted flattery or a dishonour to himself, so the beloved has one way only of voluntary service which is not dishonourable, and this is virtuous service.

For we have a custom, and according to our custom any one who does service to another under the idea that he will be improved by him either in wisdom, or in some other particular of virtue—such a voluntary service, I say, is not to be regarded as a dishonour, and is not open to the charge of flattery. And these two customs, one the love of youth, and the other the practice of philosophy and virtue in general, ought to meet in one, and then the beloved may honourably indulge the lover. For when the lover and beloved come together, having each of them a law, and the lover thinks that he is right in doing any service which he can to his gracious loving one; and the other that he is right in showing any kindness which he can to him who is making him wise and good; the one capable of communicating wisdom and virtue, the other seeking to acquire them with a view to education and wisdom; when the two laws of love are fulfilled and meet in one—then, and then only, may the beloved yield with honour to the lover. Nor when love is of this disinterested sort is there any disgrace in being deceived, but in every other case there is equal disgrace in being or not being deceived. For he who is gracious to his lover under the impression that he is rich, [185] and is disappointed of his gains because he turns out to be poor, is disgraced all the same: for he has done his best to show that he would give himself up to any one's "uses base" for the sake of money; but this is not honourable. And on the

same principle he who gives himself to a lover because he is a good man, and in the hope that he will be improved by his company, shows himself to be virtuous, even though the object of his affection turn out to be a villain, and to have no virtue; and if he is deceived he has committed a noble error. For he has proved that for his part he will do anything for anybody with a view to virtue and improvement, than which there can be nothing nobler. Thus noble in every case is the acceptance of another for the sake of virtue. This is that love which is the love of the heavenly goddess, and is heavenly, and of great price to individuals and cities, making the lover and the beloved alike eager in the work of their own improvement. But all other loves are the offspring of the other, who is the common goddess. To you, Phaedrus, I offer this my contribution in praise of love, which is as good as I could make extempore.

Pāusăniās cāme tŏ ă pāuse—this is the balanced way in which I have been taught by the wise to speak; and Aristodemus said that the turn of Aristophanes was next, but either he had eaten too much, or from some other cause he had the hiccough, and was obliged to change turns with Eryximachus the physician, who was reclining on the couch below him. Eryximachus, he said, you ought either to stop my hiccough, or to speak in my turn until I have left off.

I will do both, said Eryximachus: I will speak in your turn, and do you speak in mine; and while I am speaking let me recommend you to hold your breath, and if after you have done so for some time the hiccough is no better, then gargle with a little water; and if it still continues, tickle your nose with something and sneeze; and if you sneeze once or twice, even the most violent hiccough is sure to go. I will do as you prescribe, said Aristophanes, and now get on.

Eryximachus spoke as follows: Seeing that Pausanias made a fair beginning, [186] and but a lame ending, I must endeavour to supply his deficiency. I think that he has rightly distinguished two kinds of love. But my art further informs me that the double love is not merely an affection of the soul of man towards the fair, or towards anything, but is to be found in the bodies of all animals and in productions of the earth, and I may say in all that is; such is the conclusion which I seem to have gathered from my own art of medicine, whence I learn how great and wonderful and universal is the deity of love, whose empire extends over all things, divine as well as human. And from medicine I will begin that I may do honour to my art. There are in the human body these two kinds of love, which are confessedly different and unlike, and being unlike, they have loves and desires which are unlike; and the desire of the healthy is one, and the desire of the diseased is another; and as Pausanias was just now saying that to indulge good men is honourable, and bad men dishonourable:—so too in the body the good and healthy elements are to be indulged, and the bad elements and the elements of disease are not to be indulged, but discouraged. And this is what the physician has to do, and in this the art of medicine consists: for medicine may be regarded generally as the knowledge of the loves and desires of the body, and how to satisfy them or not; and the best physician is he who is able to separate fair love from foul, or to convert one into the other; and he who knows how to eradicate and how to implant love, whichever is required, and can reconcile the most hostile elements in the constitution and make them loving friends, is a skilful practitioner. Now the most hostile are the most opposite, such as hot and cold, bitter and sweet, moist and dry, and the like. And my ancestor, Asclepius, knowing how to implant friendship and accord in these elements, was the creator of our art, as our friends the poets here tell us, and I believe them; and not only medicine in every branch, but the arts of gymnastic and husbandry are under his dominion.

[187]Any one who pays the least attention to the subject will also perceive that in music there is the same reconciliation of opposites; and I suppose that this must have been the meaning of Heracleitus, although his words are not accurate; for he says that The One is united by disunion, like the harmony of the bow and the lyre. Now there is an absurdity in saying that harmony is discord or is composed of elements which are still in a state of discord. But what he probably meant was, that harmony is composed of differing notes of higher or lower pitch which disagreed once, but are now reconciled by the art of music; for if the higher and lower notes still disagreed, there could be no harmony—clearly not. For harmony is a symphony, and symphony is an agreement; but an agreement of disagreements while they disagree there cannot be; you cannot harmonize that which disagrees. In like manner rhythm is compounded of elements short and long, once differing and now in accord; which accordance, as in the former instance, medicine, so in all

these other cases, music implants, making love and unison to grow up among them; and thus music, too, is concerned with the principles of love in their application to harmony and rhythm. Again, in the essential nature of harmony and rhythm there is no difficulty in discerning love which has not yet become double. But when you want to use them in actual life, either in the composition of songs or in the correct performance of airs or metres composed already, which latter is called education, then the difficulty begins, and the good artist is needed. Then the old tale has to be repeated of fair and heavenly love—the love of Urania the fair and heavenly muse, and of the duty of accepting the temperate, and those who are as yet intemperate only that they may become temperate, and of preserving their love; and again, of the vulgar Polyhymnia, who must be used with circumspection that the pleasure be enjoyed, but may not generate licentiousness; just as in my own art it is a great matter so to regulate the desires of the epicure that he may gratify his tastes without the attendant evil of disease. Whence I infer that in music, in medicine, in all other things human as well as divine, both loves ought to be noted as far as may be, [188] for they are both present.

The course of the seasons is also full of both these principles; and when, as I was saying, the elements of hot and cold, moist and dry, attain the harmonious love of one another and blend in temperance and harmony, they bring to men, animals, and plants health and plenty, and do them no harm; whereas the wanton love, getting the upper hand and affecting the seasons of the year, is very destructive and injurious, being the source of pestilence, and bringing many other kinds of diseases on animals and plants; for hoar-frost and hail and blight spring from the excesses and disorders of these elements of love, which to know in relation to the revolutions of the heavenly bodies and the seasons of the year is termed astronomy. Furthermore all sacrifices and the whole province of divination, which is the art of communion between gods and men—these, I say, are concerned only with the preservation of the good and the cure of the evil love. For all manner of impiety is likely to ensue if, instead of accepting and honouring and reverencing the harmonious love in all his actions, a man honours the other love, whether in his feelings towards gods or parents, towards the living or the dead. Wherefore the business of divination is to see to these loves and to heal them, and divination is the peacemaker of gods and men, working by a knowledge of the religious or irreligious tendencies which exist in human loves. Such is the great and mighty, or rather omnipotent force of love in general. And the love, more especially, which is concerned with the good, and which is perfected in company with temperance and justice, whether among gods or men, has the greatest power, and is the source of all our happiness and harmony, and makes us friends with the gods who are above us, and with one another. I dare say that I too have omitted several things which might be said in praise of Love, but this was not intentional, and you, Aristophanes, may now supply the omission or take some other line of commendation; for I perceive that you are rid of the hiccough.

[189] Yes, said Aristophanes, who followed, the hiccough is gone; not, however, until I applied the sneezing; and I wonder whether the harmony of the body has a love of such noises and ticklings, for I no sooner applied the sneezing than I was cured.

Eryximachus said: Beware, friend Aristophanes, although you are going to speak, you are making fun of me; and I shall have to watch and see whether I cannot have a laugh at your expense, when you might speak in peace.

You are quite right, said Aristophanes, laughing. I will unsay my words; but do you please not to watch me, as I fear that in the speech which I am about to make, instead of others laughing with me, which is to the manner born of our muse and would be all the better, I shall only be laughed at by them.

Do you expect to shoot your bolt and escape, Aristophanes? Well, perhaps if you are very careful and bear in mind that you will be called to account, I may be induced to let you off.

Aristophanes professed to open another vein of discourse; he had a mind to praise Love in another way, unlike that either of Pausanias or Eryximachus. Mankind, he said, judging by their neglect of him, have never, as I think, at all understood the power of Love. For if they had understood him they would surely have built noble temples and altars, and offered solemn sacrifices in his honour; but this is not done, and most certainly ought to be done: since of all the gods he is the best friend of men, the helper and the healer of the ills which are the great impediment to the happiness of the race. I will try to describe his power to you, and you shall teach the rest of the world what I am teaching you. In the first place, let me treat of the nature of man and what has happened to

it; for the original human nature was not like the present, but different. The sexes were not two as they are now, but originally three in number; there was man, woman, and the union of the two, having a name corresponding to this double nature, which had once a real existence, but is now lost, and the word "Androgynous" is only preserved as a term of reproach. In the second place, the primeval man was round, his back and sides forming a circle; and he had four hands and four feet, one head with two faces, looking opposite ways, [190] set on a round neck and precisely alike; also four ears, two privy members, and the remainder to correspond. He could walk upright as men now do, backwards or forwards as he pleased, and he could also roll over and over at a great pace, turning on his four hands and four feet, eight in all, like tumblers going over and over with their legs in the air; this was when he wanted to run fast. Now the sexes were three, and such as I have described them; because the sun, moon, and earth are three; and the man was originally the child of the sun, the woman of the earth, and the man-woman of the moon, which is made up of sun and earth, and they were all round and moved round and round like their parents. Terrible was their might and strength, and the thoughts of their hearts were great, and they made an attack upon the gods; of them is told the tale of Otys and Ephialtes who, as Homer says, dared to scale heaven, and would have laid hands upon the gods. Doubt reigned in the celestial councils. Should they kill them and annihilate the race with thunderbolts, as they had done the giants, then there would be an end of the sacrifices and worship which men offered to them; but, on the other hand, the gods could not suffer their insolence to be unrestrained.

At last, after a good deal of reflection, Zeus discovered a way. He said: "Methinks I have a plan which will humble their pride and improve their manners; men shall continue to exist, but I will cut them in two and then they will be diminished in strength and increased in numbers; this will have the advantage of making them more profitable to us. They shall walk upright on two legs, and if they continue insolent and will not be quiet, I will split them again and they shall hop about on a single leg." He spoke and cut men in two, like a sorb-apple which is halved for pickling, or as you might divide an egg with a hair; and as he cut them one after another, he bade Apollo give the face and the half of the neck a turn in order that the man might contemplate the section of himself: he would thus learn a lesson of humility. Apollo was also bidden to heal their wounds and compose their forms. So he gave a turn to the face and pulled the skin from the sides all over that which in our language is called the belly, like the purses which draw in, and he made one mouth at the centre, which he fastened in a knot (the same which is called the navel); [191] he also moulded the breast and took out most of the wrinkles, much as a shoemaker might smooth leather upon a last; he left a few, however, in the region of the belly and navel, as a memorial of the primeval state. After the division the two parts of man, each desiring his other half, came together, and throwing their arms about one another, entwined in mutual embraces, longing to grow into one, they were on the point of dying from hunger and self-neglect, because they did not like to do anything apart; and when one of the halves died and the other survived, the survivor sought another mate, man or woman as we call them,—being the sections of entire men or women,—and clung to that. They were being destroyed, when Zeus in pity of them invented a new plan: he turned the parts of generation round to the front, for this had not been always their position, and they sowed the seed no longer as hitherto like grasshoppers in the ground, but in one another; and after the transposition the male generated in the female in order that by the mutual embraces of man and woman they might breed, and the race might continue; or if man came to man they might be satisfied, and rest, and go their ways to the business of life: so ancient is the desire of one another which is implanted in us, reuniting our original nature, making one of two, and healing the state of man.

Each of us when separated, having one side only, like a flat fish, is but the indenture of a man, and he is always looking for his other half. Men who are a section of that double nature which was once called Androgynous are lovers of women; adulterers are generally of this breed, and also adulterous women who lust after men: the women who are a section of the woman do not care for men, but have female attachments; the female companions are of this sort. But they who are a section of the male follow the male, and while they are young, being slices of the original man, [192] they hang about men and embrace them, and they are themselves the best of boys and youths, because they have the most manly nature. Some

indeed assert that they are shameless, but this is not true; for they do not act thus from any want of shame, but because they are valiant and manly, and have a manly countenance, and they embrace that which is like them. And these when they grow up become our statesmen, and these only, which is a great proof of the truth of what I am saying. When they reach manhood they are lovers of youth, and are not naturally inclined to marry or beget children,—if at all, they do so only in obedience to the law; but they are satisfied if they may be allowed to live with one another unwedded; and such a nature is prone to love and ready to return love, always embracing that which is akin to him. And when one of them meets with his other half, the actual half of himself, whether he be a lover of youth or a lover of another sort, the pair are lost in an amazement of love and friendship and intimacy, and will not be out of the other's sight, as I may say, even for a moment: these are the people who pass their whole lives together; yet they could not explain what they desire of one another. For the intense yearning which each of them has towards the other does not appear to be the desire of lover's intercourse, but of something else which the soul of either evidently desires and cannot tell, and of which she has only a dark and doubtful presentiment. Suppose Hephaestus, with his instruments, to come to the pair who are lying side by side and to say to them, "What do you people want of one another?" they would be unable to explain. And suppose further, that when he saw their perplexity he said: "Do you desire to be wholly one; always day and night to be in one another's company? for if this is what you desire, I am ready to melt you into one and let you grow together, so that being two you shall become one, and while you live live a common life as if you were a single man, and after your death in the world below still be one departed soul instead of two—I ask whether this is what you lovingly desire, and whether you are satisfied to attain this?"—there is not a man of them who when he heard the proposal would deny or would not acknowledge that this meeting and melting into one another, this becoming one instead of two, was the very expression of his ancient need.[1] And the reason is that human nature was originally one and we were a whole, [193] and the desire and pursuit of the whole is called love. There was a time, I say, when we were one, but now because of the wickedness of mankind God has dispersed us, as the Arcadians

[1] Cf. Aristotle, *Politics*, ii. 4, 1262^{b}5-14.

were dispersed into villages by the Lacedae-monians.[1] And if we are not obedient to the gods, there is a danger that we shall be split up again and go about in basso-relievo, like the profile figures having only half a nose which are sculptured on monuments, and that we shall be like tallies.

Wherefore let us exhort all men to piety, that we may avoid evil, and obtain the good, of which Love is to us the lord and minister; and let no one oppose him—he is the enemy of the gods who oppose him. For if we are friends of the God and at peace with him we shall find our own true loves, which rarely happens in this world at present. I am serious, and there-fore I must beg Eryximachus not to make fun or to find any allusion in what I am saying to Pausanias and Agathon, who, as I suspect, are both of the manly nature, and belong to the class which I have been describing. But my words have a wider application—they include men and women everywhere; and I believe that if our loves were perfectly accomplished, and each one returning to his primeval nature had his original true love, then our race would be happy. And if this would be best of all, the best in the next degree and under present circum-stances must be the nearest approach to such an union; and that will be the attainment of a congenial love. Wherefore, if we would praise him who has given to us the benefit, we must praise the god Love, who is our greatest bene-factor, both leading us in this life back to our own nature, and giving us high hopes for the future, for he promises that if we are pious, he will restore us to our original state, and heal us and make us happy and blessed. This, Ery-ximachus, is my discourse of love, which, al-though different to yours, I must beg you to leave unassailed by the shafts of your ridicule, in order that each may have his turn; each, or rather either, for Agathon and Socrates are the only ones left.

Indeed, I am not going to attack you, said Eryximachus, for I thought your speech charm-ing, and did I not know that Agathon and Soc-rates are masters in the art of love, I should be really afraid that they would have nothing to say, after the world of things which have been said already. But, for all that, I am not without hopes.

[194] Socrates said: You played your part well, Eryximachus; but if you were as I am now, or rather as I shall be when Agathon has spoken, you would, indeed, be in a great strait.

[1] Cf. Aristotle, *Politics,* ii. 2, 1261ª24-30.

You want to cast a spell over me, Socrates, said Agathon, in the hope that I may be discon-certed at the expectation raised among the au-dience that I shall speak well.

I should be strangely forgetful, Agathon, re-plied Socrates, of the courage and magnanimity which you showed when your own composi-tions were about to be exhibited, and you came upon the stage with the actors and faced the vast theatre altogether undismayed, if I thought that your nerves could be fluttered at a small party of friends.

Do you think, Socrates, said Agathon, that my head is so full of the theatre as not to know how much more formidable to a man of sense a few good judges are than many fools?

Nay, replied Socrates, I should be very wrong in attributing to you, Agathon, that or any other want of refinement. And I am quite aware that if you happened to meet with any whom you thought wise, you would care for their opinion much more than for that of the many. But then we, having been a part of the foolish many in the theatre, cannot be regarded as the select wise; though I know that if you chanced to be in the presence, not of one of ourselves, but of some really wise man, you would be ashamed of disgracing yourself before him—would you not?

Yes, said Agathon.

But before the many you would not be ashamed, if you thought that you were doing something disgraceful in their presence?

Here Phaedrus interrupted them, saying: Do not answer him, my dear Agathon; for if he can only get a partner with whom he can talk, especially a good-looking one, he will no longer care about the completion of our plan. Now I love to hear him talk; but just at present I must not forget the encomium on Love which I ought to receive from him and from every one. When you and he have paid your tribute to the god, then you may talk.

Very good, Phaedrus, said Agathon; I see no reason why I should not proceed with my speech, as I shall have many other opportunities of conversing with Socrates. Let me say first how I ought to speak, and then speak:—

The previous speakers, instead of praising the god Love, or unfolding his nature, appear to have congratulated mankind on the benefits which he confers upon them. [195] But I would rather praise the god first, and then speak of his gifts; this is always the right way of praising everything. May I say without im-piety or offence, that of all the blessed gods he is the most blessed because he is the fairest and best? And he is the fairest: for, in the first place, he is the youngest, and of his youth he is himself the witness, fleeing out of the way of age, who is swift enough, swifter truly than most of us like:—Love hates him and will not come near him; but youth and love live and move together—like to like, as the proverb says. Many things were said by Phaedrus about Love in which I agree with him; but I cannot agree that he is older than Iapetus and Kronos:—not so; I maintain him to be the youngest of the gods, and youthful ever. The ancient doings among the gods of which Hesiod and Parmenides spoke, if the tradition of them be true, were done of Necessity and not of Love; had Love been in those days, there would have been no chaining or mutilation of the gods, or other violence, but peace and sweetness, as there is now in heaven, since the rule of Love began.

Love is young and also tender; he ought to have a poet like Homer to describe his tenderness, as Homer says of Ate, that she is a goddess and tender:

Her feet are tender, for she sets her steps,
Not on the ground but on the heads of men:

herein is an excellent proof of her tenderness, —that she walks not upon the hard but upon the soft. Let us adduce a similar proof of the tenderness of Love; for he walks not upon the earth, nor yet upon the skulls of men, which are not so very soft, but in the hearts and souls of both gods and men, which are of all things the softest: in them he walks and dwells and makes his home. Not in every soul without exception, for where there is hardness he departs, where there is softness there he dwells; and nestling always with his feet and in all manner of ways in the softest of soft places, how can he be other than the softest of all things? [196] Of a truth he is the tenderest as well as the youngest, and also he is of flexile form; for if he were hard and without flexure he could not enfold all things, or wind his way into and out of every soul of man undiscovered. And a proof of his flexibility and symmetry of form is his grace, which is universally admitted to be in an especial manner the attribute of Love; ungrace and love are always at war with one another. The fairness of his complexion is revealed by his habitation among the flowers; for he dwells not amid bloomless or fading beauties, whether of body or soul or aught else, but in the place of flowers and scents, there he sits and abides. Concerning the beauty of the

god I have said enough; and yet there remains much more which I might say. Of his virtue I have now to speak: his greatest glory is that he can neither do nor suffer wrong to or from any god or any man; for he suffers not by force if he suffers; force comes not near him, neither when he acts does he act by force. For all men in all things serve him of their own free will, and where there is voluntary agreement, there, as the laws which are the lords of the city say, is justice. And not only is he just but exceedingly temperate, for Temperance is the acknowledged ruler of the pleasures and desires, and no pleasure ever masters Love; he is their master and they are his servants; and if he conquers them he must be temperate indeed. As to courage, even the God of War is no match for him; he is the captive and Love is the lord, for love, the love of Aphrodite, masters him, as the tale runs; and the master is stronger than the servant. And if he conquers the bravest of all others, he must be himself the bravest.

Of his courage and justice and temperance I have spoken, but I have yet to speak of his wisdom; and according to the measure of my ability I must try to do my best. In the first place he is a poet (and here, like Eryximachus, I magnify my art), and he is also the source of poesy in others, which he could not be if he were not himself a poet. And at the touch of him every one becomes a poet, even though he had no music in him before; this also is a proof that Love is a good poet and accomplished in all the fine arts; for no one can give to another that which he has not himself, or teach that of which he has no knowledge. Who will deny that the creation of the animals is his doing? Are they not all the works of his wisdom, [197] born and begotten of him? And as to the artists, do we not know that he only of them whom love inspires has the light of fame?—he whom Love touches not walks in darkness. The arts of medicine and archery and divination were discovered by Apollo, under the guidance of love and desire; so that he too is a disciple of Love. Also the melody of the Muses, the metallurgy of Hephaestus, the weaving of Athene, the empire of Zeus over gods and men, are all due to Love, who was the inventor of them. And so Love set in order the empire of the gods —the love of beauty, as is evident, for with deformity Love has no concern. In the days of old, as I began by saying, dreadful deeds were done among the gods, for they were ruled by Necessity; but now since the birth of Love, and from the Love of the beautiful, has sprung every good in heaven and earth. Therefore, Phaedrus, I say of Love that he is the fairest and best in himself, and the cause of what is fairest and best in all other things. And there comes into my mind a line of poetry in which he is said to be the god who

Gives peace on earth and calms the stormy deep,
Who stills the winds and bids the sufferer sleep.

This is he who empties men of disaffection and fills them with affection, who makes them to meet together at banquets such as these: in sacrifices, feasts, dances, he is our lord—who sends courtesy and sends away discourtesy, who gives kindness ever and never gives unkindness; the friend of the good, the wonder of the wise, the amazement of the gods; desired by those who have no part in him, and precious to those who have the better part in him; parent of delicacy, luxury, desire, fondness, softness, grace; regardful of the good, regardless of the evil: in every word, work, wish, fear—saviour, pilot, comrade, helper; glory of gods and men, leader best and brightest: in whose footsteps let every man follow, sweetly singing in his honour and joining in that sweet strain with which love charms the souls of gods and men. Such is the speech, Phaedrus, half-playful, yet having a certain measure of seriousness, which, according to my ability, I dedicate to the god.

[198] When Agathon had done speaking, Aristodemus said that there was a general cheer; the young man was thought to have spoken in a manner worthy of himself, and of the god. And Socrates, looking at Eryximachus, said: Tell me, son of Acumenus, was there not reason in my fears? and was I not a true prophet when I said that Agathon would make a wonderful oration, and that I should be in a strait?

The part of the prophecy which concerns Agathon, replied Eryximachus, appears to me to be true; but not the other part—that you will be in a strait.

Why, my dear friend, said Socrates, must not I or any one be in a strait who has to speak after he has heard such a rich and varied discourse? I am especially struck with the beauty of the concluding words—who could listen to them without amazement? When I reflected on the immeasurable inferiority of my own powers, I was ready to run away for shame, if there had been a possibility of escape. For I was reminded of Gorgias, and at the end of his speech I fancied that Agathon was shaking at me the Gorgian or Gorgonian head of the great master

of rhetoric, which was simply to turn me and my speech into stone, as Homer says, and strike me dumb. And then I perceived how foolish I had been in consenting to take my turn with you in praising love, and saying that I too was a master of the art, when I really had no conception how anything ought to be praised. For in my simplicity I imagined that the topics of praise should be true, and that this being presupposed, out of the true the speaker was to choose the best and set them forth in the best manner. And I felt quite proud, thinking that I knew the nature of true praise, and should speak well. Whereas I now see that the intention was to attribute to Love every species of greatness and glory, whether really belonging to him or not, without regard to truth or falsehood—that was no matter; for the original proposal seems to have been not that each of you should really praise Love, but only that you should appear to praise him. And so you attribute to Love every imaginable form of praise which can be gathered anywhere; and you say that "he is all this," and "the cause of all that," [199] making him appear the fairest and best of all to those who know him not, for you cannot impose upon those who know him. And a noble and solemn hymn of praise have you rehearsed. But as I misunderstood the nature of the praise when I said that I would take my turn, I must beg to be absolved from the promise which I made in ignorance, and which (as Euripides would say) was a promise of the lips and not of the mind. Farewell then to such a strain: for I do not praise in that way; no, indeed, I cannot. But if you like to hear the truth about love, I am ready to speak in my own manner, though I will not make myself ridiculous by entering into any rivalry with you. Say then, Phaedrus, whether you would like to have the truth about love, spoken in any words and in any order which may happen to come into my mind at the time. Will that be agreeable to you?

Aristodemus said that Phaedrus and the company bid him speak in any manner which he thought best. Then, he added, let me have your permission first to ask Agathon a few more questions, in order that I may take his admissions as the premises of my discourse.

I grant the permission, said Phaedrus: put your questions. Socrates then proceeded as follows:—

In the magnificent oration which you have just uttered, I think that you were right, my dear Agathon, in proposing to speak of the nature of Love first and afterwards of his works —that is a way of beginning which I very much approve. And as you have spoken so eloquently of his nature, may I ask you further, Whether love is the love of something or of nothing? And here I must explain myself: I do not want you to say that love is the love of a father or the love of a mother—that would be ridiculous; but to answer as you would, if I asked is a father a father of something? to which you would find no difficulty in replying, of a son or daughter: and the answer would be right.

Very true, said Agathon.

And you would say the same of a mother?

He assented.

Yet let me ask you one more question in order to illustrate my meaning: Is not a brother to be regarded essentially as a brother of something?

Certainly, he replied.

That is, of a brother or sister?

Yes, he said.

And now, said Socrates, I will ask about Love:—Is Love of something or of nothing?

[200] Of something, surely, he replied.

Keep in mind what this is, and tell me what I want to know—whether Love desires that of which love is.

Yes, surely.

And does he possess, or does he not possess, that which he loves and desires?

Probably not, I should say.

Nay, replied Socrates, I would have you consider whether "necessarily" is not rather the word. The inference that he who desires something is in want of something, and that he who desires nothing is in want of nothing, is in my judgment, Agathon absolutely and necessarily true. What do you think?

I agree with you, said Agathon.

Very good. Would he who is great, desire to be great, or he who is strong, desire to be strong?

That would be inconsistent with our previous admissions.

True. For he who is anything cannot want to be that which he is?

Very true.

And yet, added Socrates, if a man being strong desired to be strong, or being swift desired to be swift, or being healthy desired to be healthy, in that case he might be thought to desire something which he already has or is. I give the example in order that we may avoid misconception. For the possessors of these qualities, Agathon, must be supposed to have their respective advantages at the time, whether they choose or not; and who can desire that which he has? Therefore, when a person says, I am well and wish to be well, or I am rich and wish to be rich, and I desire simply to have what I have—to him we shall reply: "You, my friend, having wealth and health and strength, want to have the continuance of them; for at this moment, whether you choose or no, you have them. And when you say, I desire that which I have and nothing else, is not your meaning that you want to have what you now have in the future?" He must agree with us—must he not?

He must, replied Agathon.

Then, said Socrates, he desires that what he has at present may be preserved to him in the future, which is equivalent to saying that he desires something which is non-existent to him, and which as yet he has not got.

Very true, he said.

Then he and every one who desires, desires that which he has not already, and which is future and not present, and which he has not, and is not, and of which he is in want;—these are the sort of things which love and desire seek?

Very true, he said.

Then now, said Socrates, let us recapitulate the argument. First, is not love of something, and of something too which is wanting to a man?

[201] Yes, he replied.

Remember further what you said in your speech, or if you do not remember I will remind you: you said that the love of the beautiful set in order the empire of the gods, for that of deformed things there is no love—did you not say something of that kind?

Yes, said Agathon.

Yes, my friend, and the remark was a just one. And if this is true, Love is the love of beauty and not of deformity?

He assented.

And the admission has been already made that Love is of something which a man wants and has not?

True, he said.

Then Love wants and has not beauty?

Certainly, he replied.

And would you call that beautiful which wants and does not possess beauty?

Certainly not.

Then would you still say that love is beautiful?

Agathon replied: I fear that I did not understand what I was saying.

You made a very good speech, Agathon, replied Socrates; but there is yet one small question which I would fain ask:—Is not the good also the beautiful?

Yes.

Then in wanting the beautiful, love wants also the good?

I cannot refute you, Socrates, said Agathon: —Let us assume that what you say is true.

Say rather, beloved Agathon, that you cannot refute the truth; for Socrates is easily refuted.

And now, taking my leave of you, I will rehearse a tale of love which I heard from Diotima of Mantineia, a woman wise in this and in many other kinds of knowledge, who in the days of old, when the Athenians offered sacrifice before the coming of the plague, delayed the disease ten years. She was my instructress in the art of love, and I shall repeat to you what she said to me, beginning with the admissions made by Agathon, which are nearly if not quite the same which I made to the wise woman when she questioned me: I think that this will be the easiest way, and I shall take both parts myself as well as I can.[1] As you, Agathon, suggested,[2] I must speak first of the being and nature of Love, and then of his works. First I said to her in nearly the same words which he used to me, that Love was a mighty god, and likewise fair; and she proved to me as I proved to him that, by my own showing, Love was neither fair nor good. "What do you mean, Diotima," I said, "is love then evil and foul?" "Hush," she cried; "must that be foul which is not fair?" [202] "Certainly," I said. "And is that which is not wise, ignorant? do you not see that there is a mean between wisdom and ignorance?" "And what may that be?" I said. "Right opinion," she replied; "which, as you know, being incapable of giving a reason, is not knowledge (for how can knowledge be devoid of reason? nor again, ignorance, for neither can ignorance attain the truth), but is clearly something which is a mean between ignorance and wisdom." "Quite true," I replied. "Do not then insist," she said, "that what is not fair is of necessity foul, or what is not good evil; or infer that because love is not fair and good he is therefore foul and evil; for he is in a mean between them." "Well," I said, "Love is surely admitted by all to be a great god." "By

those who know or by those who do not know?" "By all." "And how, Socrates," she said with a smile, "can Love be acknowledged to be a great god by those who say that he is not a god at all?" "And who are they?" I said. "You and I are two of them," she replied. "How can that be?" I said. "It is quite intelligible," she replied; "for you yourself would acknowledge that the gods are happy and fair— of course you would—would you dare to say that any god was not?" "Certainly not," I replied. "And you mean by the happy, those who are the possessors of things good or fair?" "Yes." "And you admitted that Love, because he was in want, desires those good and fair things of which he is in want?" "Yes, I did." "But how can he be a god who has no portion in what is either good or fair?" "Impossible." "Then you see that you also deny the divinity of Love."

"What then is Love?" I asked; "Is he mortal?" "No." "What then?" "As in the former instance, he is neither mortal nor immortal, but in a mean between the two." "What is he, Diotima?" "He is a great spirit (δαίμων), and like all spirits he is intermediate between the divine and the mortal." "And what," I said, "is his power?" "He interprets," she replied, "between gods and men, conveying and taking across to the gods the prayers and sacrifices of men, and to men the commands and replies of the gods; he is the mediator who spans the chasm which divides them, and therefore in him all is bound together, and through him the arts of the prophet and the priest, [203] their sacrifices and mysteries and charms, and all prophecy and incantation, find their way. For God mingles not with man; but through Love all the intercourse and converse of god with man, whether awake or asleep, is carried on. The wisdom which understands this is spiritual; all other wisdom, such as that of arts and handicrafts, is mean and vulgar. Now these spirits or intermediate powers are many and diverse, and one of them is Love." "And who," I said, "was his father, and who his mother?" "The tale," she said, "will take time; nevertheless I will tell you. On the birthday of Aphrodite there was a feast of the gods, at which the god Poros or Plenty, who is the son of Metis or Discretion, was one of the guests. When the feast was over, Penia or Poverty, as the manner is on such occasions, came about the doors to beg. Now Plenty, who was the worse for nectar (there was no wine in those days), went into the garden of Zeus and fell into a heavy sleep; and Poverty considering her own straitened circumstances, plotted to have a child by him, and accordingly she lay down at his side and conceived Love, who partly because he is naturally a lover of the beautiful, and because Aphrodite is herself beautiful, and also because he was born on her birthday, is her follower and attendant. And as his parentage is, so also are his fortunes. In the first place he is always poor, and anything but tender and fair, as the many imagine him; and he is rough and squalid, and has no shoes, nor a house to dwell in; on the bare earth exposed he lies under the open heaven, in the streets, or at the doors of houses, taking his rest; and like his mother he is always in distress. Like his father too, whom he also partly resembles, he is always plotting against the fair and good; he is bold, enterprising, strong, a mighty hunter, always weaving some intrigue or other, keen in the pursuit of wisdom, fertile in resources; a philosopher at all times, terrible as an enchanter, sorcerer, sophist. He is by nature neither mortal nor immortal, but alive and flourishing at one moment when he is in plenty, and dead at another moment, and again alive by reason of his father's nature. But that which is always flowing in is always flowing out, and so he is never in want and never in wealth; and, further, he is in a mean between ignorance and knowledge. The truth of the matter is this: No god is a philosopher or seeker after wisdom, for he is wise already; nor does any man who is wise seek after wisdom. Neither do the ignorant seek after wisdom. [204] For herein is the evil of ignorance, that he who is neither good nor wise is nevertheless satisfied with himself: he has no desire for that of which he feels no want." "But who then, Diotima," I said, "are the lovers of wisdom, if they are neither the wise nor the foolish?" "A child may answer that question," she replied; "they are those who are in a mean between the two; Love is one of them. For wisdom is a most beautiful thing, and Love is of the beautiful; and therefore Love is also a philosopher or lover of wisdom, and being a lover of wisdom is in a mean between the wise and the ignorant. And of this too his birth is the cause; for his father is wealthy and wise, and his mother poor and foolish. Such, my dear Socrates, is the nature of the spirit Love. The error in your conception of him was very natural, and as I imagine from what you say, has arisen out of a confusion of love and the beloved, which made you think that love was all beautiful. For

the beloved is the truly beautiful, and delicate, and perfect, and blessed; but the principle of love is of another nature, and is such as I have described."

I said: "O thou stranger woman, thou sayest well; but, assuming Love to be such as you say, what is the use of him to men?" "That, Socrates," she replied, "I will attempt to unfold: of his nature and birth I have already spoken; and you acknowledge that love is of the beautiful. But some one will say: Of the beautiful in what, Socrates and Diotima?—or rather let me put the question more clearly, and ask: When a man loves the beautiful, what does he desire?" I answered her "That the beautiful may be his." "Still," she said, "the answer suggests a further question: What is given by the possession of beauty?" "To what you have asked," I replied, "I have no answer ready." "Then," she said, "let me put the word 'good' in the place of the beautiful, and repeat the question once more: If he who loves loves the good, what is it then that he loves?" "The possession of the good," I said. "And what does he gain who possesses the good?" "Happiness," I replied; "there is less difficulty in answering that question." [205] "Yes," she said, "the happy are made happy by the acquisition of good things. Nor is there any need to ask why a man desires happiness; the answer is already final." "You are right," I said. "And is this wish and this desire common to all? and do all men always desire their own good, or only some men?—what say you?" "All men," I replied; "the desire is common to all." "Why, then," she rejoined, "are not all men, Socrates, said to love, but only some of them? whereas you say that all men are always loving the same things." "I myself wonder," I said, "why this is." "There is nothing to wonder at," she replied; "the reason is that one part of love is separated off and receives the name of the whole, but the other parts have other names." "Give an illustration," I said. She answered me as follows: "There is poetry, which, as you know, is complex and manifold. All creation or passage of non-being into being is poetry or making, and the processes of all art are creative; and the masters of arts are all poets or makers." "Very true." "Still," she said, "you know that they are not called poets, but have other names; only that portion of the art which is separated off from the rest, and is concerned with music and metre, is termed poetry, and they who possess poetry in this sense of the word are called poets." "Very true," I said.

"And the same holds of love. For you may say generally that all desire of good and happiness is only the great and subtle power of love; but they who are drawn towards him by any other path, whether the path of money-making or gymnastics or philosophy, are not called lovers —the name of the whole is appropriated to those whose affection takes one form only— they alone are said to love, or to be lovers." "I dare say," I replied, "that you are right." "Yes," she added, "and you hear people say that lovers are seeking for their other half; but I say that they are seeking neither for the half of themselves, nor for the whole, unless the half or the whole be also a good. And they will cut off their own hands and feet and cast them away, if they are evil; for they love not what is their own, unless perchance there be some one who calls what belongs to him the good, [206] and what belongs to another the evil. For there is nothing which men love but the good. Is there anything?" "Certainly, I should say, that there is nothing." "Then," she said, "the simple truth is, that men love the good." "Yes," I said. "To which must be added that they love the possession of the good?" "Yes, that must be added." "And not only the possession, but the everlasting possession of the good?" "That must be added too." "Then love," she said, "may be described generally as the love of the everlasting possession of the good?" "That is most true."

"Then if this be the nature of love, can you tell me further," she said, "what is the manner of the pursuit? what are they doing who show all this eagerness and heat which is called love? and what is the object which they have in view? Answer me." "Nay, Diotima," I replied, "if I had known, I should not have wondered at your wisdom, neither should I have come to learn from you about this very matter." "Well," she said, "I will teach you:—The object which they have in view is birth in beauty, whether of body or soul." "I do not understand you," I said; "the oracle requires an explanation." "I will make my meaning clearer," she replied. "I mean to say, that all men are bringing to the birth in their bodies and in their souls. There is a certain age at which human nature is desirous of procreation—procreation which must be in beauty and not in deformity; and this procreation is the union of man and woman, and is a divine thing; for conception and generation are an immortal principle in the mortal creature, and in the inharmonious they can never be. But the deformed is always inhar-monious with the divine, and the beautiful harmonious. Beauty, then, is the destiny or goddess of parturition who presides at birth, and therefore, when approaching beauty, the conceiving power is propitious, and diffusive, and benign, and begets and bears fruit: at the sight of ugliness she frowns and contracts and has a sense of pain, and turns away, and shrivels up, and not without a pang refrains from conception. And this is the reason why, when the hour of conception arrives, and the teeming nature is full, there is such a flutter and ecstasy about beauty whose approach is the alleviation of the pain of travail. For love, Socrates, is not, as you imagine, the love of the beautiful only." "What then?" "The love of generation and of birth in beauty." "Yes," I said. "Yes, indeed," she replied. "But why of generation?" "Because to the mortal creature, generation is a sort of eternity and immortality," she replied; "and if, as has been already admitted, love is of the everlasting possession of the good, all men will necessarily desire immortality together with good: [207] Wherefore love is of immortality."

All this she taught me at various times when she spoke of love. And I remember her once saying to me, "What is the cause, Socrates, of love, and the attendant desire? See you not how all animals, birds, as well as beasts, in their desire of procreation, are in agony when they take the infection of love, which begins with the desire of union; whereto is added the care of offspring, on whose behalf the weakest are ready to battle against the strongest even to the uttermost, and to die for them, and will let themselves be tormented with hunger or suffer anything in order to maintain their young. Man may be supposed to act thus from reason; but why should animals have these passionate feelings? Can you tell me why?" Again I replied that I did not know. She said to me: "And do you expect ever to become a master in the art of love, if you do not know this?" "But I have told you already, Diotima, that my ignorance is the reason why I come to you; for I am conscious that I want a teacher; tell me then the cause of this and of the other mysteries of love." "Marvel not," she said, "if you believe that love is of the immortal, as we have several times acknowledged; for here again, and on the same principle too, the mortal nature is seeking as far as is possible to be everlasting and immortal: and this is only to be attained by generation, because generation always leaves behind a new existence in the place of the old.

Nay even in the life of the same individual there is succession and not absolute unity: a man is called the same, and yet in the short interval which elapses between youth and age, and in which every animal is said to have life and identity, he is undergoing a perpetual process of loss and reparation—hair, flesh, bones, blood, and the whole body are always changing. Which is true not only of the body, but also of the soul, whose habits, tempers, opinions, desires, pleasures, pains, fears, never remain the same in any one of us, but are always coming and going; and equally true of knowledge, and what is still more surprising to us mortals, [208] not only do the sciences in general spring up and decay, so that in respect of them we are never the same; but each of them individually experiences a like change. For what is implied in the word 'recollection,' but the departure of knowledge, which is ever being forgotten, and is renewed and preserved by recollection, and appears to be the same although in reality new, according to that law of succession by which all mortal things are preserved, not absolutely the same, but by substitution, the old worn-out mortality leaving another new and similar existence behind—unlike the divine, which is always the same and not another? And in this way, Socrates, the mortal body, or mortal anything, partakes of immortality; but the immortal in another way. Marvel not then at the love which all men have of their offspring; for that universal love and interest is for the sake of immortality."

I was astonished at her words, and said: "Is this really true, O thou wise Diotima?" And she answered with all the authority of an accomplished sophist: "Of that, Socrates, you may be assured;—think only of the ambition of men, and you will wonder at the senselessness of their ways, unless you consider how they are stirred by the love of an immortality of fame. They are ready to run all risks greater far than they would have run for their children, and to spend money and undergo any sort of toil, and even to die, for the sake of leaving behind them a name which shall be eternal. Do you imagine that Alcestis would have died to save Admetus, or Achilles to avenge Patroclus, or your own Codrus in order to preserve the kingdom for his sons, if they had not imagined that the memory of their virtues, which still survives among us, would be immortal? Nay," she said, "I am persuaded that all men do all things, and the better they are the more they do them, in hope of the glorious fame of immortal virtue; for they desire the immortal.

"Those who are pregnant in the body only, betake themselves to women and beget children—this is the character of their love; their offspring, as they hope, will preserve their memory and give them the blessedness and immortality which they desire in the future. But souls which are pregnant—for there certainly are men who are [209] more creative in their souls than in their bodies—conceive that which is proper for the soul to conceive or contain. And what are these conceptions?—wisdom and virtue in general. And such creators are poets and all artists who are deserving of the name inventor. But the greatest and fairest sort of wisdom by far is that which is concerned with the ordering of states and families, and which is called temperance and justice. And he who in youth has the seed of these implanted in him and is himself inspired, when he comes to maturity desires to beget and generate. He wanders about seeking beauty that he may beget offspring—for in deformity he will beget nothing—and naturally embraces the beautiful rather than the deformed body; above all when he finds a fair and noble and well-nurtured soul, he embraces the two in one person, and to such an one he is full of speech about virtue and the nature and pursuits of a good man; and he tries to educate him; and at the touch of the beautiful which is ever present to his memory, even when absent, he brings forth that which he had conceived long before, and in company with him tends that which he brings forth; and they are married by a far nearer tie and have a closer friendship than those who beget mortal children, for the children who are their common offspring are fairer and more immortal. Who, when he thinks of Homer and Hesiod and other great poets, would not rather have their children than ordinary human ones? Who would not emulate them in the creation of children such as theirs, which have preserved their memory and given them everlasting glory? Or who would not have such children as Lycurgus left behind him to be the saviours, not only of Lacedaemon, but of Hellas, as one may say? There is Solon, too, who is the revered father of Athenian laws; and many others there are in many other places, both among Hellenes and barbarians, who have given to the world many noble works, and have been the parents of virtue of every kind; and many temples have been raised in their honour for the sake of children such as theirs; which were never raised in honour of any one, for the sake of his mortal children.

"These are the lesser mysteries of love, into which even you, Socrates, *[210]* may enter; to the greater and more hidden ones which are the crown of these, and to which, if you pursue them in a right spirit, they will lead, I know not whether you will be able to attain. But I will do my utmost to inform you, and do you follow if you can. For he who would proceed aright in this matter should begin in youth to visit beautiful forms; and first, if he be guided by his instructor aright, to love one such form only—out of that he should create fair thoughts; and soon he will of himself perceive that the beauty of one form is akin to the beauty of another; and then if beauty of form in general is his pursuit, how foolish would he be not to recognize that the beauty in every form is one and the same! And when he perceives this he will abate his violent love of the one, which he will despise and deem a small thing, and will become a lover of all beautiful forms; in the next stage he will consider that the beauty of the mind is more honourable than the beauty of the outward form. So that if a virtuous soul have but a little comeliness, he will be content to love and tend him, and will search out and bring to the birth thoughts which may improve the young, until he is compelled to contemplate and see the beauty of institutions and laws, and to understand that the beauty of them all is of one family, and that personal beauty is a trifle; and after laws and institutions he will go on to the sciences, that he may see their beauty, being not like a servant in love with the beauty of one youth or man or institution, himself a slave mean and narrow-minded, but drawing towards and contemplating the vast sea of beauty, he will create many fair and noble thoughts and notions in boundless love of wisdom; until on that shore he grows and waxes strong, and at last the vision is revealed to him of a single science, which is the science of beauty everywhere. To this I will proceed; please to give me your very best attention:

"He who has been instructed thus far in the things of love, and who has learned to see the beautiful in due order and succession, when he comes toward the end will suddenly perceive a nature of wondrous beauty (and this, *[211]* Socrates, is the final cause of all our former toils)—a nature which in the first place is everlasting, not growing and decaying, or waxing and waning; secondly, not fair in one point of view and foul in another, or at one time or in one relation or at one place fair, at another time or in another relation or at another place foul, as if fair to some and foul to others, or in the likeness of a face or hands or any other part of the bodily frame, or in any form of speech or knowledge, or existing in any other being, as for example, in an animal, or in heaven, or in earth, or in any other place; but beauty absolute, separate, simple, and everlasting, which without diminution and without increase, or any change, is imparted to the ever-growing and perishing beauties of all other things. He who from these ascending under the influence of true love, begins to perceive that beauty, is not far from the end. And the true order of going, or being led by another, to the things of love, is to begin from the beauties of earth and mount upwards for the sake of that other beauty, using these as steps only, and from one going on to two, and from two to all fair forms, and from fair forms to fair practices, and from fair practices to fair notions, until from fair notions he arrives at the notion of absolute beauty, and at last knows what the essence of beauty is. This, my dear Socrates," said the stranger of Mantineia, "is that life above all others which man should live, in the contemplation of beauty absolute; a beauty which if you once beheld, you would see not to be after the measure of gold, and garments, and fair boys and youths, whose presence now entrances you; and you and many a one would be content to live seeing them only and conversing with them without meat or drink, if that were possible—you only want to look at them and to be with them. But what if man had eyes to see the true beauty—the divine beauty, I mean, pure and clear and unalloyed, not clogged with the pollutions of mortality and all the colours and vanities of human life —thither looking, and holding converse with the true beauty simple and divine? *[212]* Remember how in that communion only, beholding beauty with the eye of the mind, he will be enabled to bring forth, not images of beauty, but realities (for he has hold not of an image but of a reality), and bringing forth and nourishing true virtue to become the friend of God and be immortal, if mortal man may. Would that be an ignoble life?"

Such, Phaedrus—and I speak not only to you, but to all of you—were the words of Diotima; and I am persuaded of their truth. And being persuaded of them, I try to persuade others, that in the attainment of this end human nature will not easily find a helper better than love. And therefore, also, I say that every man ought to honour him as I myself honour him, and walk in his ways, and exhort others to do the same, and praise the power and spirit of love according to the measure of my ability now and ever.

The words which I have spoken, you, Phaedrus, may call an encomium of love, or anything else which you please.

When Socrates had done speaking, the company applauded, and Aristophanes was beginning to say something in answer to the allusion which Socrates had made to his own speech,[1] when suddenly there was a great knocking at the door of the house, as of revellers, and the sound of a flute-girl was heard. Agathon told the attendants to go and see who were the intruders. "If they are friends of ours," he said, "invite them in, but if not, say that the drinking is over." A little while afterwards they heard the voice of Alcibiades resounding in the court; he was in a great state of intoxication, and kept roaring and shouting "Where is Agathon? Lead me to Agathon," and at length, supported by the flute-girl and some of his attendants, he found his way to them. "Hail, friends," he said, appearing at the door crowned with a massive garland of ivy and violets, his head flowing with ribands. "Will you have a very drunken man as a companion of your revels? Or shall I crown Agathon, which was my intention in coming, and go away? For I was unable to come yesterday, and therefore I am here to-day, carrying on my head these ribands, that taking them from my own head, I may crown the head of this fairest and wisest of men, as I may be allowed to call him. Will you laugh at me because I am drunk? Yet I know very well that I am speaking the truth, [213] although you may laugh. But first tell me; if I come in shall we have the understanding of which I spoke? [2] Will you drink with me or not?"

The company were vociferous in begging that he would take his place among them, and Agathon specially invited him. Thereupon he was led in by the people who were with him; and as he was being led, intending to crown Agathon, he took the ribands from his own head and held them in front of his eyes; he was thus prevented from seeing Socrates, who made way for him, and Alcibiades took the vacant place between Agathon and Socrates,

and in taking the place he embraced Agathon and crowned him. Take off his sandals, said Agathon, and let him make a third on the same couch.

By all means; but who makes the third partner in our revels? said Alcibiades, turning round and starting up as he caught sight of Socrates. By Heracles, he said, what is this? here is Socrates always lying in wait for me, and always, as his way is, coming out at all sorts of unsuspected places: and now, what have you to say for yourself, and why are you lying here, where I perceive that you have contrived to find a place, not by a joker or lover of jokes, like Aristophanes, but by the fairest of the company?

Socrates turned to Agathon and said: I must ask you to protect me, Agathon; for the passion of this man has grown quite a serious matter to me. Since I became his admirer I have never been allowed to speak to any other fair one, or so much as to look at them. If I do, he goes wild with envy and jealousy, and not only abuses me but can hardly keep his hands off me, and at this moment he may do me some harm. Please to see to this, and either reconcile me to him, or, if he attempts violence, protect me, as I am in bodily fear of his mad and passionate attempts.

There can never be reconciliation between you and me, said Alcibiades; but for the present I will defer your chastisement. And I must beg you, Agathon, to give me back some of the ribands that I may crown the marvellous head of this universal despot—I would not have him complain of me for crowning you, and neglecting him, who in conversation is the conqueror of all mankind; and this not only once, as you were the day before yesterday, but always. Whereupon, taking some of the ribands, he crowned Socrates, and again reclined.

Then he said: You seem, my friends, to be sober, which is a thing not to be endured; you must drink—for that was the agreement under which I was admitted—and I elect myself master of the feast until you are well drunk. Let us have a large goblet, Agathon, or rather, he said, addressing the attendant, bring me that wine-cooler. The wine-cooler which had caught his eye was a vessel holding more than two quarts—this he filled and emptied, [214] and bade the attendant fill it again for Socrates. Observe, my friends, said Alcibiades, that this ingenious trick of mine will have no effect on Socrates, for he can drink any quantity of wine and not be at all nearer being drunk. Socrates

[1] Cf. 205.

[2] Supra, 212: "Will you have a very drunken man?" etc.

drank the cup which the attendant filled for him.

Eryximachus said: What is this, Alcibiades? Are we to have neither conversation nor singing over our cups; but simply to drink as if we were thirsty?

Alcibiades replied: Hail, worthy son of a most wise and worthy sire!

The same to you, said Eryximachus; but what shall we do?

That I leave to you, said Alcibiades.

The wise physician skilled our wounds to heal

shall prescribe and we will obey. What do you want?

Well, said Eryximachus, before you appeared we had passed a resolution that each one of us in turn should make a speech in praise of love, and as good a one as he could: the turn was passed round from left to right; and as all of us have spoken, and you have not spoken but have well drunken, you ought to speak, and then impose upon Socrates any task which you please, and he on his right hand neighbour, and so on.

That is good, Eryximachus, said Alcibiades; and yet the comparison of a drunken man's speech with those of sober men is hardly fair; and I should like to know, sweet friend, whether you really believe what Socrates was just now saying; for I can assure you that the very reverse is the fact, and that if I praise any one but himself in his presence, whether God or man, he will hardly keep his hands off me.

For shame, said Socrates.

Hold your tongue, said Alcibiades, for by Poseidon, there is no one else whom I will praise when you are of the company.

Well then, said Eryximachus, if you like praise Socrates.

What do you think, Eryximachus? said Alcibiades: shall I attack him and inflict the punishment before you all?

What are you about? said Socrates; are you going to raise a laugh at my expense? Is that the meaning of your praise?

I am going to speak the truth, if you will permit me.

I not only permit, but exhort you to speak the truth.

Then I will begin at once, said Alcibiades, and if I say anything which is not true, you may interrupt me if you will, and say "that is a lie," though my intention is to speak the truth. But you must not wonder if I speak any how as things come into my mind; for the fluent and orderly enumeration of all your singularities is not a task which is easy to a man in my condition.

[215] And now, my boys, I shall praise Socrates in a figure which will appear to him to be a caricature, and yet I speak, not to make fun of him, but only for the truth's sake. I say, that he is exactly like the busts of Silenus, which are set up in the statuaries' shops, holding pipes and flutes in their mouths; and they are made to open in the middle, and have images of gods inside them. I say also that he is like Marsyas the satyr. You yourself will not deny, Socrates, that your face is like that of a satyr. Aye, and there is a resemblance in other points too. For example, you are a bully, as I can prove by witnesses, if you will not confess. And are you not a flute-player? That you are, and a performer far more wonderful than Marsyas. He indeed with instruments used to charm the souls of men by the powers of his breath, and the players of his music do so still: for the melodies of Olympus [1] are derived from Marsyas who taught them, and these, whether they are played by a great master or by a miserable flute-girl, have a power which no others have; they alone possess the soul and reveal the wants of those who have need of gods and mysteries, because they are divine. But you produce the same effect with your words only, and do not require the flute; that is the difference between you and him. When we hear any other speaker, even a very good one, he produces absolutely no effect upon us, or not much, whereas the mere fragments of you and your words, even at second-hand, and however imperfectly repeated, amaze and possess the souls of every man, woman, and child who comes within hearing of them. And if I were not afraid that you would think me hopelessly drunk, I would have sworn as well as spoken to the influence which they have always had and still have over me. For my heart leaps within me more than that of any Corybantian reveller, and my eyes rain tears when I hear them. And I observe that many others are affected in the same manner. I have heard Pericles and other great orators, and I thought that they spoke well, but I never had any similar feeling; my soul was not stirred by them, nor was I angry at the thought of my own slavish state. But this Marsyas has often brought me to such a pass, that I have felt as if I could hardly endure the life which I am leading [216] (this, Socrates, you will admit); and I am conscious that if I did not shut my

[1] Cf. Aristotle, *Politics*, viii. 5. 1340ᵃ3-12.

ears against him, and fly as from the voice of the siren, my fate would be like that of others, —he would transfix me, and I should grow old sitting at his feet. For he makes me confess that I ought not to live as I do, neglecting the wants of my own soul, and busying myself with the concerns of the Athenians; therefore I hold my ears and tear myself away from him. And he is the only person who ever made me ashamed, which you might think not to be in my nature, and there is no one else who does the same. For I know that I cannot answer him or say that I ought not to do as he bids, but when I leave his presence the love of popularity gets the better of me. And therefore I run away and fly from him, and when I see him I am ashamed of what I have confessed to him. Many a time have I wished that he were dead, and yet I know that I should be much more sorry than glad, if he were to die: so that I am at my wit's end.

And this is what I and many others have suffered from the flute-playing of this satyr. Yet hear me once more while I show you how exact the image is, and how marvellous his power. For let me tell you; none of you know him; but I will reveal him to you; having begun, I must go on. See you how fond he is of the fair? He is always with them and is always being smitten by them, and then again he knows nothing and is ignorant of all things—such is the appearance which he puts on. Is he not like a Silenus in this? To be sure he is: his outer mask is the carved head of the Silenus; but, O my companions in drink, when he is opened, what temperance there is residing within! Know you that beauty and wealth and honour, at which the many wonder, are of no account with him, and are utterly despised by him: he regards not at all the persons who are gifted with them; mankind are nothing to him; all his life is spent in mocking and flouting at them. But when I opened him, and looked within at his serious purpose, I saw in him divine and golden images of such fascinating beauty that I was ready to do in a [217] moment whatever Socrates commanded: they may have escaped the observation of others, but I saw them. Now I fancied that he was seriously enamoured of my beauty, and I thought that I should therefore have a grand opportunity of hearing him tell what he knew, for I had a wonderful opinion of the attractions of my youth. In the prosecution of this design, when I next went to him, I sent away the attendant who usually accompanied me (I will confess the whole truth, and beg you to listen; and if I speak falsely, do you, Socrates, expose the falsehood). Well, he and I were alone together, and I thought that when there was nobody with us, I should hear him speak the language which lovers use to their loves when they are by themselves, and I was delighted. Nothing of the sort; he conversed as usual, and spent the day with me and then went away. Afterwards I challenged him to the palaestra; and he wrestled and closed with me several times when there was no one present; I fancied that I might succeed in this manner. Not a bit; I made no way with him. Lastly, as I had failed hitherto, I thought that I must take stronger measures and attack him boldly, and, as I had begun, not give him up, but see how matters stood between him and me. So I invited him to sup with me, just as if he were a fair youth, and I a designing lover. He was not easily persuaded to come; he did, however, after a while accept the invitation, and when he came the first time, he wanted to go away at once as soon as supper was over, and I had not the face to detain him. The second time, still in pursuance of my design, after we had supped, I went on conversing far into the night, and when he wanted to go away, I pretended that the hour was late and that he had much better remain. So he lay down on the couch next to me, the same on which he had supped, and there was no one but ourselves sleeping in the apartment. All this may be told without shame to any one. But what follows I could hardly tell you if I were sober. Yet as the proverb says, "In vino veritas," whether with boys, or without them; and therefore I must speak. Nor, again, should I be justified in concealing the lofty actions of Socrates when I come to praise him. Moreover I have felt the serpent's sting; and he who has suffered, as they say, is willing to tell his fellow-sufferers only, as they alone will be likely to understand him, [218] and will not be extreme in judging of the sayings or doings which have been wrung from his agony. For I have been bitten by a more than viper's tooth; I have known in my soul, or in my heart, or in some other part, that worst of pangs, more violent in ingenuous youth than any serpent's tooth, the pang of philosophy, which will make a man say or do anything. And you whom I see around me, Phaedrus and Agathon and Eryximachus and Pausanias and Aristodemus and Aristophanes, all of you, and I need not say Socrates himself, have had experience of the same madness and passion in your longing after wisdom. Therefore listen and excuse my doings then and my sayings now. But let the attendants and other profane and unmannered persons close up the doors of their ears.

When the lamp was put out and the servants had gone away, I thought that I must be plain with him and have no more ambiguity. So I gave him a shake, and I said: "Socrates, are you asleep?" "No," he said. "Do you know what I am meditating?" "What are you meditating?" he said. "I think," I replied, "that of all the lovers whom I have ever had you are the only one who is worthy of me, and you appear to be too modest to speak. Now I feel that I should be a fool to refuse you this or any other favour, and therefore I come to lay at your feet all that I have and all that my friends have, in the hope that you will assist me in the way of virtue, which I desire above all things, and in which I believe that you can help me better than any one else. And I should certainly have more reason to be ashamed of what wise men would say if I were to refuse a favour to such as you, than of what the world, who are mostly fools, would say of me if I granted it." To these words he replied in the ironical manner which is so characteristic of him:— "Alcibiades, my friend, you have indeed an elevated aim if what you say is true, and if there really is in me any power by which you may become better; truly you must see in me some rare beauty of a kind infinitely higher than any which I see in you. And therefore, if you mean to share with me and to exchange beauty for beauty, you will have greatly the advantage of me; you will gain true beauty in return for appearance—like Diomede, *[219]* gold in exchange for brass. But look again, sweet friend, and see whether you are not deceived in me. The mind begins to grow critical when the bodily eye fails, and it will be a long time before you get old." Hearing this, I said: "I have told you my purpose, which is quite serious, and do you consider what you think best for you and me." "That is good," he said; "at some other time then we will consider and act as seems best about this and about other matters." Whereupon, I fancied that he was smitten, and that the words which I had uttered like arrows had wounded him, and so without waiting to hear more I got up, and throwing my coat about him crept under his threadbare cloak, as the time of year was winter, and there I lay during the whole night having this wonderful monster in my arms.

This again, Socrates, will not be denied by you. And yet, notwithstanding all, he was so superior to my solicitations, so contemptuous and derisive and disdainful of my beauty— which really, as I fancied, had some attractions —hear, O judges; for judges you shall be of the haughty virtue of Socrates—nothing more happened, but in the morning when I awoke (let all the gods and goddesses be my witnesses) I arose as from the couch of a father or an elder brother.

What do you suppose must have been my feelings, after this rejection, at the thought of my own dishonour? And yet I could not help wondering at his natural temperance and self-restraint and manliness. I never imagined that I could have met with a man such as he is in wisdom and endurance. And therefore I could not be angry with him or renounce his company, any more than I could hope to win him. For I well knew that if Ajax could not be wounded by steel, much less he by money; and my only chance of captivating him by my personal attractions had failed. So I was at my wit's end; no one was ever more hopelessly enslaved by another. All this happened before he and I went on the expedition to Potidaea; there we messed together, and I had the opportunity of observing his extraordinary power of sustaining fatigue. His endurance was simply marvellous when, *[220]* being cut off from our supplies, we were compelled to go without food —on such occasions, which often happen in time of war, he was superior not only to me but to everybody; there was no one to be compared to him. Yet at a festival he was the only person who had any real powers of enjoyment; though not willing to drink, he could if compelled beat us all at that,—wonderful to relate! no human being had ever seen Socrates drunk; and his powers, if I am not mistaken, will be tested before long. His fortitude in enduring cold was also surprising. There was a severe frost, for the winter in that region is really tremendous, and everybody else either remained indoors, or if they went out had on an amazing quantity of clothes, and were well shod, and had their feet swathed in felt and fleeces: in the midst of this, Socrates with his bare feet on the ice and in his ordinary dress marched better than the other soldiers who had shoes, and they looked daggers at him because he seemed to despise them.

I have told you one tale, and now I must tell you another, which is worth hearing, *Of the doings and sufferings of the enduring man* while he was on the expedition. One morning he was thinking about something which he could not resolve; he would not give it up, but continued thinking from early dawn until noon—there he stood fixed in thought; and at noon attention was drawn to him, and the rumour ran through the wondering crowd that Socrates had been standing and thinking about something ever since the break of day. At last, in the evening after supper, some Ionians out of curiosity (I should explain that this was not in winter but in summer), brought out their mats and slept in the open air that they might watch him and see whether he would stand all night. There he stood until the following morning; and with the return of light he offered up a prayer to the sun, and went his way.[1] I will also tell, if you please—and indeed I am bound to tell—of his courage in battle; for who but he saved my life? Now this was the engagement in which I received the prize of valour: for I was wounded and he would not leave me, but he rescued me and my arms; and he ought to have received the prize of valour which the generals wanted to confer on me partly on account of my rank, and I told them so (this, again, Socrates will not impeach or deny), but he was more eager than the generals that I and not he should have the prize. There was another occasion on which his behaviour was very remarkable [221]—in the flight of the army after the battle of Delium, where he served among the heavy-armed—I had a better opportunity of seeing him than at Potidaea, for I was myself on horseback, and therefore comparatively out of danger. He and Laches were retreating, for the troops were in flight, and I met them and told them not to be discouraged, and promised to remain with them; and there you might see him, Aristophanes, as you describe,[2] just as he is in the streets of Athens, stalking like a pelican, and rolling his eyes, calmly contemplating enemies as well as friends, and making very intelligible to anybody, even from a distance, that whoever attacked him would be likely to meet with a stout resistance; and in this way he and his companion escaped—for this is the sort of man who is never touched in war; those only are pursued who are running away headlong. I particularly observed how superior he was to Laches in presence of mind. Many are the marvels which I might narrate in praise of Socrates; most of his ways might perhaps be paralleled in another man, but his

absolute unlikeness to any human being that is or ever has been is perfectly astonishing. You may imagine Brasidas and others to have been like Achilles; or you may imagine Nestor and Antenor to have been like Pericles; and the same may be said of other famous men, but of this strange being you will never be able to find any likeness, however remote, either among men who now are or who ever have been—other than that which I have already suggested of Silenus and the satyrs; and they represent in a figure not only himself, but his words. For, although I forgot to mention this to you before, his words are like the images of Silenus which open; they are ridiculous when you first hear them; he clothes himself in language that is like the skin of the wanton satyr—for his talk is of pack-asses and smiths and cobblers and curriers, and he is always repeating the same things in the same words,[3] so that any ignorant or inexperienced person might feel disposed to laugh at him; [222] but he who opens the bust and sees what is within will find that they are the only words which have a meaning in them, and also the most divine, abounding in fair images of virtue, and of the widest comprehension, or rather extending to the whole duty of a good and honourable man.

This, friends, is my praise of Socrates. I have added my blame of him for his ill-treatment of me; and he has ill-treated not only me, but Charmides the son of Glaucon, and Euthydemus the son of Diocles, and many others in the same way—beginning as their lover he has ended by making them pay their addresses to him. Wherefore I say to you, Agathon, "Be not deceived by him; learn from me and take warning, and do not be a fool and learn by experience, as the proverb says."

When Alcibiades had finished, there was a laugh at his outspokenness; for he seemed to be still in love with Socrates. You are sober, Alcibiades, said Socrates, or you would never have gone so far about to hide the purpose of your satyr's praises, for all this long story is only an ingenious circumlocution, of which the point comes in by the way at the end; you want to get up a quarrel between me and Agathon, and your notion is that I ought to love you and nobody else, and that you and you only ought to love Agathon. But the plot of this Satyric or Silenic drama has been detected, and you must not allow him, Agathon, to set us at variance.

I believe you are right, said Agathon, and I

---

[1] Cf. supra, 175.

[2] Aristophanes, Clouds, 362.

[3] Cf. Gorgias, 490, 491, 517.

am disposed to think that his intention in placing himself between you and me was only to divide us; but he shall gain nothing by that move; for I will go and lie on the couch next to you.

Yes, yes, replied Socrates, by all means come here and lie on the couch below me.

Alas, said Alcibiades, how I am fooled by this man; he is determined to get the better of me at every turn. I do beseech you, allow Agathon to lie between us.

Certainly not, said Socrates, as you praised me, and I in turn ought to praise my neighbour on the right, he will be out of order in praising me again when he ought rather to be praised by me, and I must entreat you to consent to this, and not be jealous, for I have a great desire to praise the youth. [223]

Hurrah! cried Agathon, I will rise instantly, that I may be praised by Socrates.

The usual way, said Alcibiades; where Socrates is, no one else has any chance with the fair; and now how readily has he invented a specious reason for attracting Agathon to himself.

Agathon arose in order that he might take his place on the couch by Socrates, when suddenly a band of revellers entered, and spoiled the order of the banquet. Some one who was

going out having left the door open, they had found their way in, and made themselves at home; great confusion ensued, and every one was compelled to drink large quantities of wine. Aristodemus said that Eryximachus, Phaedrus, and others went away—he himself fell asleep, and as the nights were long took a good rest: he was awakened towards daybreak by a crowing of cocks, and when he awoke, the others were either asleep, or had gone away; there remained only Socrates, Aristophanes, and Agathon, who were drinking out of a large goblet which they passed round, and Socrates was discoursing to them. Aristodemus was only half awake, and he did not hear the beginning of the discourse; the chief thing which he remembered was Socrates compelling the other two to acknowledge that the genius of comedy was the same with that of tragedy, and that the true artist in tragedy was an artist in comedy also. To this they were constrained to assent, being drowsy, and not quite following the argument. And first of all Aristophanes dropped off, then, when the day was already dawning, Agathon. Socrates, having laid them to sleep, rose to depart; Aristodemus, as his manner was, following him. At the Lyceum he took a bath, and passed the day as usual. In the evening he retired to rest at his own home.

MENO

PERSONS OF THE DIALOGUE: MENO; SOCRATES; A SLAVE OF MENO; ANYTUS

[70] Meno. CAN you tell me, Socrates, whether virtue is acquired by teaching or by practice; or if neither by teaching nor practice, then whether it comes to man by nature, or in what other way?

Socrates. O Meno, there was a time when the Thessalians were famous among the other Hellenes only for their riches and their riding; but now, if I am not mistaken, they are equally famous for their wisdom, especially at Larisa, which is the native city of your friend Aristippus. And this is Gorgias' doing; for when he came there, the flower of the Aleuadae, among them your admirer Aristippus, and the other chiefs of the Thessalians, fell in love with his wisdom. And he has taught you the habit of answering questions in a grand and bold style, which becomes those who know, and is the style in which he himself answers all comers; and any Hellene who likes may ask him anything. How different is our lot! my dear Meno. *[71]* Here at Athens there is a dearth of the commodity, and all wisdom seems to have emigrated from us to you. I am certain that if you were to ask any Athenian whether virtue was natural or acquired, he would laugh in your face, and say: "Stranger, you have far too good an opinion of me, if you think that I can answer your question. For I literally do not know what virtue is, and much less whether it is acquired by teaching or not." And I myself, Meno, living as I do in this region of poverty, am as poor as the rest of the world; and I confess with shame that I know literally nothing about virtue; and when I do not know the "quid" of anything how can I know the "quale"? How, if I knew nothing at all of

Meno, could I tell if he was fair, or the opposite of fair; rich and noble, or the reverse of rich and noble? Do you think that I could?

Men. No, Indeed. But are you in earnest, Socrates, in saying that you do not know what virtue is? And am I to carry back this report of you to Thessaly?

Soc. Not only that, my dear boy, but you may say further that I have never known of any one else who did, in my judgment.

Men. Then you have never met Gorgias when he was at Athens?

Soc. Yes, I have.

Men. And did you not think that he knew?

Soc. I have not a good memory, Meno, and therefore I cannot now tell what I thought of him at the time. And I dare say that he did know, and that you know what he said: please, therefore, to remind me of what he said; or, if you would rather, tell me your own view; for I suspect that you and he think much alike.

Men. Very true.

Soc. Then as he is not here, never mind him, and do you tell me: By the gods, Meno, be generous, and tell me what you say that virtue is; for I shall be truly delighted to find that I have been mistaken, and that you and Gorgias do really have this knowledge; although I have been just saying that I never found anybody who had.

Men. There will be no difficulty, Socrates, in answering your question. Let us take first the virtue of a man—he should know how to administer the state, and in the administration of it to benefit his friends and harm his enemies; and he must also be careful not to suffer harm himself. A woman's virtue, if you wish to know about that, may also be easily described: her duty is to order her house, and keep what is indoors, and obey her husband. Every age, every condition of life, young or old, male or female, bond or free, [72] has a different virtue: there are virtues numberless, and no lack of definitions of them; for virtue is relative to the actions and ages of each of us in all that we do. And the same may be said of vice, Socrates.[1]

Soc. How fortunate I am, Meno! When I ask you for one virtue, you present me with a swarm of them,[2] which are in your keeping. Suppose that I carry on the figure of the swarm, and ask of you, What is the nature of the bee? and you answer that there are many kinds of bees, and I reply: But do bees differ as bees, because there are many and different kinds of them; or are they not rather to be distinguished by some other quality, as for example beauty, size, or shape? How would you answer me?

Men. I should answer that bees do not differ from one another, as bees.

Soc. And if I went on to say: That is what I desire to know, Meno; tell me what is the quality in which they do not differ, but are all alike; —would you be able to answer?

Men. I should.

Soc. And so of the virtues, however many and different they may be, they have all a common nature which makes them virtues; and on this he who would answer the question, "What is virtue?" would do well to have his eye fixed: Do you understand?

Men. I am beginning to understand; but I do not as yet take hold of the question as I could wish.

Soc. When you say, Meno, that there is one virtue of a man, another of a woman, another of a child, and so on, does this apply only to virtue, or would you say the same of health, and size, and strength? Or is the nature of health always the same, whether in man or woman?

Men. I should say that health is the same, both in man and woman.

Soc. And is not this true of size and strength? If a woman is strong, she will be strong by reason of the same form and of the same strength subsisting in her which there is in the man. I mean to say that strength, as strength, whether of man or woman, is the same. Is there any difference?

Men. I think not.

[73] *Soc.* And will not virtue, as virtue, be

the same, whether in a child or in a grown-up person, in a woman or in a man?

Men. I cannot help feeling, Socrates, that this case is different from the others.

Soc. But why? Were you not saying that the virtue of a man was to order a state, and the virtue of a woman was to order a house?

Men. I did say so.

Soc. And can either house or state or anything be well ordered without temperance and without justice?

Men. Certainly not.

Soc. Then they who order a state or a house temperately or justly order them with temperance and justice?

Men. Certainly.

Soc. Then both men and women, if they are to be good men and women, must have the same virtues of temperance and justice?

Men. True.

Soc. And can either a young man or an elder one be good, if they are intemperate and unjust?

Men. They cannot.

Soc. They must be temperate and just?

Men. Yes.

Soc. Then all men are good in the same way, and by participation in the same virtues?

Men. Such is the inference.

Soc. And they surely would not have been good in the same way, unless their virtue had been the same?

Men. They would not.

Soc. Then now that the sameness of all virtue has been proven, try and remember what you and Gorgias say that virtue is.

Men. Will you have one definition of them all?

Soc. That is what I am seeking.

Men. If you want to have one definition of them all, I know not what to say, but that virtue is the power of governing mankind.

Soc. And does this definition of virtue include all virtue? Is virtue the same in a child and in a slave, Meno? Can the child govern his father, or the slave his master; and would he who governed be any longer a slave?

Men. I think not, Socrates.

Soc. No, indeed; there would be small reason in that. Yet once more, fair friend; according to you, virtue is "the power of governing"; but do you not add "justly and not unjustly"?

Men. Yes, Socrates; I agree there; for justice is virtue.

Soc. Would you say "virtue," Meno, or "a virtue"?

[1] Cf. Aristotle, *Politics*, i. 13, 1260[a]23-28.
[2] Cf. *Theaetetus*, 146.

Men. What do you mean?

Soc. I mean as I might say about anything; that a round, for example, is "a figure" and not simply "figure," and I should adopt this mode of speaking, because there are other figures.

Men. Quite right; and that is just what I am saying about virtue—that there are other virtues as well as justice.

[74] Soc. What are they? tell me the names of them, as I would tell you the names of the other figures if you asked me.

Men. Courage and temperance and wisdom and magnanimity are virtues; and there are many others.

Soc. Yes, Meno; and again we are in the same case: in searching after one virtue we have found many, though not in the same way as before; but we have been unable to find the common virtue which runs through them all.

Men. Why, Socrates, even now I am not able to follow you in the attempt to get at one common notion of virtue as of other things.

Soc. No wonder; but I will try to get nearer if I can, for you know that all things have a common notion. Suppose now that some one asked you the question which I asked before: Meno, he would say, what is figure? And if you answered "roundness," he would reply to you, in my way of speaking, by asking whether you would say that roundness is "figure" or "a figure"; and you would answer "a figure."

Men. Certainly.

Soc. And for this reason—that there are other figures?

Men. Yes.

Soc. And if he proceeded to ask, What other figures are there? you would have told him.

Men. I should.

Soc. And if he similarly asked what colour is, and you answered whiteness, and the questioner rejoined, Would you say that whiteness is colour or a colour? you would reply, A colour, because there are other colours as well.

Men. I should.

Soc. And if he had said, Tell me what they are?—you would have told him of other colours which are colours just as much as whiteness.

Men. Yes.

Soc. And suppose that he were to pursue the matter in my way, he would say: Ever and anon we are landed in particulars, but this is not what I want; tell me then, since you call them by a common name, and say that they are all figures, even when opposed to one an-

other, what is that common nature which you designate as figure—which contains straight as well as round, and is no more one than the other—that would be your mode of speaking?

Men. Yes.

Soc. And in speaking thus, you do not mean to say that the round is round any more than straight, or the straight any more straight than round?

Men. Certainly not.

Soc. You only assert that the round figure is not more a figure than the straight, or the straight than the round?

Men. Very true.

Soc. To what then do we give the name of figure? Try and answer. Suppose that when a person asked you this question either about figure or colour, you were to reply, Man, I do not understand what you want, *[75]* or know what you are saying; he would look rather astonished and say: Do you not understand that I am looking for the "simile in multis"? And then he might put the question in another form: Meno, he might say, what is that "simile in multis" which you call figure, and which includes not only round and straight figures, but all? Could you not answer that question, Meno? I wish that you would try; the attempt will be good practice with a view to the answer about virtue.

Men. I would rather that you should answer, Socrates.

Soc. Shall I indulge you?

Men. By all means.

Soc. And then you will tell me about virtue?

Men. I will.

Soc. Then I must do my best, for there is a prize to be won.

Men. Certainly.

Soc. Well, I will try and explain to you what figure is. What do you say to this answer?—Figure is the only thing which always follows colour. Will you be satisfied with it, as I am sure that I should be, if you would let me have a similar definition of virtue?

Men. But, Socrates, it is such a simple answer.

Soc. Why simple?

Men. Because, according to you, figure is that which always follows colour.

(*Soc.* Granted.)

Men. But if a person were to say that he does not know what colour is, any more than what figure is—what sort of answer would you have given him?

Soc. I should have told him the truth. And if

he were a philosopher of the eristic and antagonistic sort, I should say to him: You have my answer, and if I am wrong, your business is to take up the argument and refute me. But if we were friends, and were talking as you and I are now, I should reply in a milder strain and more in the dialectician's vein; that is to say, I should not only speak the truth, but I should make use of premises which the person interrogated would be willing to admit. And this is the way in which I shall endeavour to approach you. You will acknowledge, will you not, that there is such a thing as an end, or termination, or extremity?—all which words I use in the same sense, although I am aware that Prodicus might draw distinctions about them: but still you, I am sure, would speak of a thing as ended or terminated—that is all which I am saying—not anything very difficult.

Men. Yes, I should; and I believe that I understand your meaning.

[76] *Soc.* And you would speak of a surface and also of a solid, as for example in geometry.

Men. Yes.

Soc. Well then, you are now in a condition to understand my definition of figure. I define figure to be that in which the solid ends; or, more concisely, the limit of solid.

Men. And now, Socrates, what is colour?

Soc. You are outrageous, Meno, in thus plaguing a poor old man to give you an answer, when you will not take the trouble of remembering what is Gorgias' definition of virtue.

Men. When you have told me what I ask, I will tell you, Socrates.

Soc. A man who was blindfolded has only to hear you talking, and he would know that you are a fair creature and have still many lovers.

Men. Why do you think so?

Soc. Why, because you always speak in imperatives: like all beauties when they are in their prime, you are tyrannical; and also, as I suspect, you have found out that I have a weakness for the fair, and therefore to humour you I must answer.

Men. Please do.

Soc. Would you like me to answer you after the manner of Gorgias, which is familiar to you?

Men. I should like nothing better.

Soc. Do not he and you and Empedocles say that there are certain effluences of existence?

Men. Certainly.

Soc. And passages into which and through which the effluences pass?

Men. Exactly.

Soc. And some of the effluences fit into the passages, and some of them are too small or too large?

Men. True.

Soc. And there is such a thing as sight?

Men. Yes.

Soc. And now, as Pindar says, "read my meaning":—colour is an effluence of form, commensurate with sight, and palpable to sense.

Men. That, Socrates, appears to me to be an admirable answer.

Soc. Why, yes, because it happens to be one which you have been in the habit of hearing: and your wit will have discovered, I suspect, that you may explain in the same way the nature of sound and smell, and of many other similar phenomena.

Men. Quite true.

Soc. The answer, Meno, was in the orthodox solemn vein, and therefore was more acceptable to you than the other answer about figure.

Men. Yes.

Soc. And yet, O son of Alexidemus, I cannot help thinking that the other was the better; and I am sure that you would be of the same opinion, if you would only stay and be initiated, and were not compelled, as you said yesterday, to go away before the mysteries.

Men. But I will stay, Socrates, if you will give me many such answers. [77]

Soc. Well then, for my own sake as well as for yours, I will do my very best; but I am afraid that I shall not be able to give you very many as good: and now, in your turn, you are to fulfil your promise, and tell me what virtue is in the universal; and do not make a singular into a plural, as the facetious say of those who break a thing, but deliver virtue to me whole and sound, and not broken into a number of pieces: I have given you the pattern.

Men. Well then, Socrates, virtue, as I take it, is when he, who desires the honourable, is able to provide it for himself; so the poet says, and I say too—

Virtue is the desire of things honourable and the power of attaining them.

Soc. And does he who desires the honourable also desire the good?

Men. Certainly.

Soc. Then are there some who desire the evil and others who desire the good? Do not all men, my dear sir, desire good?

Men. I think not.

Soc. There are some who desire evil?

Men. Yes.

Soc. Do you mean that they think the evils which they desire, to be good; or do they know that they are evil and yet desire them?

Men. Both, I think.

Soc. And do you really imagine, Meno, that a man knows evils to be evils and desires them notwithstanding?

Men. Certainly I do.

Soc. And desire is of possession?

Men. Yes, of possession.

Soc. And does he think that the evils will do good to him who possesses them, or does he know that they will do him harm?

Men. There are some who think that the evils will do them good, and others who know that they will do them harm.

Soc. And, in your opinion, do those who think that they will do them good know that they are evils?

Men. Certainly not.

Soc. Is it not obvious that those who are ignorant of their nature do not desire them; but they desire what they suppose to be goods although they are really evils; and if they are mistaken and suppose the evils to be good they really desire goods?

Men. Yes, in that case.

Soc. Well, and do those who, as you say, desire evils, and think that evils are hurtful to the possessor of them, know that they will be hurt by them?

Men. They must know it.

[78] *Soc.* And must they not suppose that those who are hurt are miserable in proportion to the hurt which is inflicted upon them?

Men. How can it be otherwise?

Soc. But are not the miserable ill-fated?

Men. Yes, indeed.

Soc. And does any one desire to be miserable and ill-fated?

Men. I should say not, Socrates.

Soc. But if there is no one who desires to be miserable, there is no one, Meno, who desires evil; for what is misery but the desire and possession of evil?

Men. That appears to be the truth, Socrates, and I admit that nobody desires evil.

Soc. And yet, were you not saying just now that virtue is the desire and power of attaining good?

Men. Yes, I did say so.

Soc. But if this be affirmed, then the desire of good is common to all, and one man is no better than another in that respect?

Men. True.

Soc. And if one man is not better than another in desiring good, he must be better in the power of attaining it?

Men. Exactly.

Soc. Then, according to your definition, virtue would appear to be the power of attaining good?

Men. I entirely approve, Socrates, of the manner in which you now view this matter.

Soc. Then let us see whether what you say is true from another point of view; for very likely you may be right:—You affirm virtue to be the power of attaining goods?

Men. Yes.

Soc. And the goods which you mean are such as health and wealth and the possession of gold and silver, and having office and honour in the state—those are what you would call goods?

Men. Yes, I should include all those.

Soc. Then, according to Meno, who is the hereditary friend of the great king, virtue is the power of getting silver and gold; and would you add that they must be gained piously, justly, or do you deem this to be of no consequence? And is any mode of acquisition, even if unjust and dishonest, equally to be deemed virtue?

Men. Not virtue, Socrates, but vice.

Soc. Then justice or temperance or holiness, or some other part of virtue, as would appear, must accompany the acquisition, and without them the mere acquisition of good will not be virtue.

Men. Why, how can there be virtue without these?

Soc. And the non-acquisition of gold and silver in a dishonest manner for oneself or another, or in other words the want of them, may be equally virtue?

Men. True.

Soc. Then the acquisition of such goods is no more virtue than the non-acquisition and want of them, but whatever is accompanied by justice or honesty is virtue, [79] and whatever is devoid of justice is vice.

Men. It cannot be otherwise, in my judgment.

Soc. And were we not saying just now that justice, temperance, and the like, were each of them a part of virtue?

Men. Yes.

Soc. And so, Meno, this is the way in which you mock me.

Men. Why do you say that, Socrates?

Soc. Why, because I asked you to deliver virtue into my hands whole and unbroken, and I gave you a pattern according to which you were to frame your answer; and you have forgotten already, and tell me that virtue is the power of attaining good justly, or with justice; and justice you acknowledge to be a part of virtue.

Men. Yes.

Soc. Then it follows from your own admissions, that virtue is doing what you do with a part of virtue; for justice and the like are said by you to be parts of virtue.

Men. What of that?

Soc. What of that! Why, did not I ask you to tell me the nature of virtue as a whole? And you are very far from telling me this; but declare every action to be virtue which is done with a part of virtue; as though you had told me and I must already know the whole of virtue, and this too when frittered away into little pieces. And, therefore, my dear Meno, I fear that I must begin again and repeat the same question: What is virtue? for otherwise, I can only say, that every action done with a part of virtue is virtue; what else is the meaning of saying that every action done with justice is virtue? Ought I not to ask the question over again; for can any one who does not know virtue know a part of virtue?

Men. No; I do not say that he can.

Soc. Do you remember how, in the example of figure, we rejected any answer given in terms which were as yet unexplained or unadmitted?

Men. Yes, Socrates; and we were quite right in doing so.

Soc. But then, my friend, do not suppose that we can explain to any one the nature of virtue as a whole through some unexplained portion of virtue, or anything at all in that fashion; we should only have to ask over again the old question, What is virtue? Am I not right?

Men. I believe that you are.

Soc. Then begin again, and answer me, What, according to you and your friend Gorgias, is the definition of virtue?

Men. O Socrates, I used to be told, before I knew you, that you were always doubting yourself and making others doubt; *[80]* and now you are casting your spells over me, and I am simply getting bewitched and enchanted, and am at my wits' end. And if I may venture to make a jest upon you, you seem to me both in your appearance and in your power over others to be very like the flat torpedo fish, who torpifies those who come near him and touch him, as you have now torpified me, I think. For my soul and my tongue are really torpid, and I do not know how to answer you; and though I have been delivered of an infinite variety of speeches about virtue before now, and to many persons—and very good ones they were, as I thought—at this moment I cannot even say what virtue is. And I think that you are very wise in not voyaging and going away from home, for if you did in other places as you do in Athens, you would be cast into prison as a magician.

Soc. You are a rogue, Meno, and had all but caught me.

Men. What do you mean, Socrates?

Soc. I can tell why you made a simile about me.

Men. Why?

Soc. In order that I might make another simile about you. For I know that all pretty young gentlemen like to have pretty similes made about them—as well they may—but I shall not return the compliment. As to my being a torpedo, if the torpedo is torpid as well as the cause of torpidity in others, then indeed I am a torpedo, but not otherwise; for I perplex others, not because I am clear, but because I am utterly perplexed myself. And now I know not what virtue is, and you seem to be in the same case, although you did once perhaps know before you touched me. However, I have no objection to join with you in the enquiry.

Men. And how will you enquire, Socrates, into that which you do not know? What will you put forth as the subject of enquiry? And if you find what you want, how will you ever know that this is the thing which you did not know?

Soc. I know, Meno, what you mean; but just see what a tiresome dispute you are introducing. You argue that a man cannot enquire either about that which he knows, or about that which he does not know; for if he knows, he has no need to enquire; and if not, he cannot; for he does not know the very subject about which he is to enquire.[1]

[81] Men. Well, Socrates, and is not the argument sound?

Soc. I think not.

Men. Why not?

Soc. I will tell you why: I have heard from certain wise men and women who spoke of things divine that—

Men. What did they say?

Soc. They spoke of a glorious truth, as I conceive.

Men. What was it? and who were they?

Soc. Some of them were priests and priestesses, who had studied how they might be able to

[1] Cf. Aristotle, *Posterior Analytics*, I. i. 71ᵃ 26-31.

give a reason of their profession: there have been poets also, who spoke of these things by inspiration, like Pindar, and many others who were inspired. And they say—mark, now, and see whether their words are true—they say that the soul of man is immortal, and at one time has an end, which is termed dying, and at another time is born again, but is never destroyed. And the moral is, that a man ought to live always in perfect holiness. *"For in the ninth year Persephone sends the souls of those from whom she has received the penalty of ancient crime back again from beneath into the light of the sun above, and these are they who become noble kings and mighty men and great in wisdom and are called saintly heroes in after ages."* The soul, then, as being immortal, and having been born again many times, and having seen all things that exist, whether in this world or in the world below, has knowledge of them all; and it is no wonder that she should be able to call to remembrance all that she ever knew about virtue, and about everything; for as all nature is akin, and the soul has learned all things, there is no difficulty in her eliciting or as men say learning, out of a single recollection all the rest, if a man is strenuous and does not faint; for all enquiry and all learning is but recollection. And therefore we ought not to listen to this sophistical argument about the impossibility of enquiry: for it will make us idle, and is sweet only to the sluggard; but the other saying will make us active and inquisitive. In that confiding, I will gladly enquire with you into the nature of virtue.

Men. Yes, Socrates; but what do you mean by saying that we do not learn, and that what we call learning is only a process of recollection? Can you teach me how this is?

Soc. I told you, Meno, just now that you were a rogue, and now you ask whether I can teach you, when I am saying that there is no teaching, [82] but only recollection; and thus you imagine that you will involve me in a contradiction.

Men. Indeed, Socrates, I protest that I had no such intention. I only asked the question from habit; but if you can prove to me that what you say is true, I wish that you would.

Soc. It will be no easy matter, but I will try to please you to the utmost of my power. Suppose that you call one of your numerous attendants, that I may demonstrate on him.

Men. Certainly. Come hither, boy.

Soc. He is Greek, and speaks Greek, does he not?

Men. Yes, indeed; he was born in the house.

Soc. Attend now to the questions which I ask him, and observe whether he learns of me or only remembers.

Men. I will.

Soc. Tell me, boy, do you know that a figure like this is a square?

Boy. I do.

Soc. And you know that a square figure has these four lines equal?

Boy. Certainly.

Soc. And these lines which I have drawn through the middle of the square are also equal?

Boy. Yes.

Soc. A square may be of any size?

Boy. Certainly.

Soc. And if one side of the figure be of two feet, and the other side be of two feet, how much will the whole be? Let me explain: if in one direction the space was of two feet, and in the other direction of one foot, the whole would be of two feet taken once?

Boy. Yes.

Soc. But since this side is also of two feet, there are twice two feet?

Boy. There are.

Soc. Then the square is of twice two feet?

Boy. Yes.

Soc. And how many are twice two feet? count and tell me.

Boy. Four, Socrates.

Soc. And might there not be another square twice as large as this, and having like this the lines equal?

Boy. Yes.

Soc. And of how many feet will that be?

Boy. Of eight feet.

Soc. And now try and tell me the length of the line which forms the side of that double square: this is two feet—what will that be?

Boy. Clearly, Socrates, it will be double.

Soc. Do you observe, Meno, that I am not teaching the boy anything, but only asking him questions; and now he fancies that he knows how long a line is necessary in order to produce a figure of eight square feet; does he not?

Men. Yes.

Soc. And does he really know?

Men. Certainly not.

Soc. He only guesses that because the square is double, the line is double.

Men. True.

Soc. Observe him while he recalls the steps in regular order. (*To the Boy.*) [83] Tell me, boy, do you assert that a double space comes from a double line? Remember that I am not speaking of an oblong, but of a figure equal every way, and twice the size of this—that is to say of eight feet; and I want to know whether you still say that a double square comes from a double line?

Boy. Yes.

Soc. But does not this line become doubled if we add another such line here?

Boy. Certainly.

Soc. And four such lines will make a space containing eight feet?

Boy. Yes.

Soc. Let us describe such a figure: Would you not say that this is the figure of eight feet?

Boy. Yes.

Soc. And are there not these four divisions in the figure, each of which is equal to the figure of four feet?

Boy. True.

Soc. And is not that four times four?

Boy. Certainly.

Soc. And four times is not double?

Boy. No, indeed.

Soc. But how much?

Boy. Four times as much.

Soc. Therefore the double line, boy, has given a space, not twice, but four times as much.

Boy. True.

Soc. Four times four are sixteen—are they not?

Boy. Yes.

Soc. What line would give you a space of eight feet, as this gives one of sixteen feet;—do you see?

Boy. Yes.

Soc. And the space of four feet is made from this half line?

Boy. Yes.

Soc. Good; and is not a space of eight feet twice the size of this, and half the size of the other?

Boy. Certainly.

Soc. Such a space, then, will be made out of a line greater than this one, and less than that one?

Boy. Yes; I think so.

Soc. Very good; I like to hear you say what you think. And now tell me, is not this a line of two feet and that of four?

Boy. Yes.

Soc. Then the line which forms the side of eight feet ought to be more than this line of

two feet, and less than the other of four feet?

Boy. It ought.

Soc. Try and see if you can tell me how much it will be.

Boy. Three feet.

Soc. Then if we add a half to this line of two, that will be the line of three. Here are two and there is one; and on the other side, here are two also and there is one: and that makes the figure of which you speak?

Boy. Yes.

Soc. But if there are three feet this way and three feet that way, the whole space will be three times three feet?

Boy. That is evident.

Soc. And how much are three times three feet?

Boy. Nine.

Soc. And how much is the double of four?

Boy. Eight.

Soc. Then the figure of eight is not made out of a line of three?

Boy. No.

[84] *Soc.* But from what line?—tell me exactly; and if you would rather not reckon, try and show me the line.

Boy. Indeed, Socrates, I do not know.

Soc. Do you see, Meno, what advances he has made in his power of recollection? He did not know at first, and he does not know now, what is the side of a figure of eight feet: but then he thought that he knew, and answered confidently as if he knew, and had no difficulty; now he has a difficulty, and neither knows nor fancies that he knows.

Men. True.

Soc. Is he not better off in knowing his ignorance?

Men. I think that he is.

Soc. If we have made him doubt, and given him the "torpedo's shock," have we done him any harm?

Men. I think not.

Soc. We have certainly, as would seem, assisted him in some degree to the discovery of the truth; and now he will wish to remedy his ignorance, but then he would have been ready to tell all the world again and again that the double space should have a double side.

Men. True.

Soc. But do you suppose that he would ever have enquired into or learned what he fancied that he knew, though he was really ignorant of it, until he had fallen into perplexity under the idea that he did not know, and had desired to know?

Men. I think not, Socrates.

Soc. Then he was the better for the torpedo's touch?

Men. I think so.

Soc. Mark now the farther development. I shall only ask him, and not teach him, and he shall share the enquiry with me: and do you watch and see if you find me telling or explaining anything to him, instead of eliciting his opinion. Tell me, boy, is not this a square of four feet which I have drawn?

Boy. Yes.

Soc. And now I add another square equal to the former one?

Boy. Yes.

Soc. And a third, which is equal to either of them?

Boy. Yes.

Soc. Suppose that we fill up the vacant corner?

Boy. Very good.

Soc. Here, then, there are four equal spaces?

Boy. Yes.

Soc. And how many times larger is this space than this other?

Boy. Four times.

Soc. But it ought to have been twice only, as you will remember.

Boy. True.

Soc. And does not this line, reaching from corner to corner, bisect each of these spaces? [85]

Boy. Yes.

Soc. And are there not here four equal lines which contain this space?

Boy. There are.

Soc. Look and see how much this space is.

Boy. I do not understand.

Soc. Has not each interior line cut off half of the four spaces?

Boy. Yes.

Soc. And how many spaces are there in this section?

Boy. Four.

Soc. And how many in this?

Boy. Two.

Soc. And four is how many times two?

Boy. Twice.

Soc. And this space is of how many feet?

Boy. Of eight feet.

Soc. And from what line do you get this figure?

Boy. From this.

Soc. That is, from the line which extends from corner to corner of the figure of four feet?

Boy. Yes.

Soc. And that is the line which the learned call the diagonal. And if this is the proper name, then you, Meno's slave, are prepared to affirm that the double space is the square of the diagonal?

Boy. Certainly, Socrates.

Soc. What do you say of him, Meno? Were not all these answers given out of his own head?

Men. Yes, they were all his own.

Soc. And yet, as we were just now saying, he did not know?

Men. True.

Soc. But still he had in him those notions of his—had he not?

Men. Yes.

Soc. Then he who does not know may still have true notions of that which he does not know?

Men. He has.

Soc. And at present these notions have just been stirred up in him, as in a dream; but if he were frequently asked the same questions, in different forms, he would know as well as any one at last?

Men. I dare say.

Soc. Without any one teaching him he will recover his knowledge for himself, if he is only asked questions?

Men. Yes.

Soc. And this spontaneous recovery of knowledge in him is recollection?

Men. True.

Soc. And this knowledge which he now has must he not either have acquired or always possessed?

Men. Yes.

Soc. But if he always possessed this knowledge he would always have known; or if he has acquired the knowledge he could not have acquired it in this life, unless he has been taught geometry; for he may be made to do the same with all geometry and every other branch of knowledge. Now, has any one ever taught him all this? You must know about him, if, as you say, he was born and bred in your house.

Men. And I am certain that no one ever did teach him.

Soc. And yet he has the knowledge?

Men. The fact, Socrates, is undeniable.

Soc. But if he did not acquire the knowledge in this life, then he must have had and learned it at some other time? [86]

Men. Clearly he must.

Soc. Which must have been the time when he was not a man?

Men. Yes.

Soc. And if there have been always true thoughts in him, both at the time when he was and was not a man, which only need to be awakened into knowledge by putting questions to him, his soul must have always possessed this knowledge, for he always either was or was not a man?

Men. Obviously.

Soc. And if the truth of all things always existed in the soul, then the soul is immortal. Wherefore be of good cheer, and try to recollect what you do not know, or rather what you do not remember.

Men. I feel, somehow, that I like what you are saying.

Soc. And I, Meno, like what I am saying. Some things I have said of which I am not altogether confident. But that we shall be better and braver and less helpless if we think that we ought to enquire, than we should have been if we indulged in the idle fancy that there was no knowing and no use in seeking to know what we do not know;—that is a theme upon which I am ready to fight, in word and deed, to the utmost of my power.

Men. There again, Socrates, your words seem to me excellent.

Soc. Then, as we are agreed that a man should enquire about that which he does not know, shall you and I make an effort to enquire together into the nature of virtue?

Men. By all means, Socrates. And yet I would much rather return to my original question, Whether in seeking to acquire virtue we should regard it as a thing to be taught, or as a gift of nature, or as coming to men in some other way?

Soc. Had I the command of you as well as of myself, Meno, I would not have enquired whether virtue is given by instruction or not, until we had first ascertained "what it is." But as you think only of controlling me who am your slave, and never of controlling yourself,—such being your notion of freedom, I must yield to you, for you are irresistible. And therefore I have now to enquire into the qualities of a thing of which I do not as yet know the nature. At any rate, will you condescend a little, and allow the question "Whether virtue is given by instruction, or in any other way," to be argued upon hypothesis? *[87]* As the geometrician, when he is asked whether a certain triangle is capable of being inscribed in a certain circle,

will reply: "I cannot tell you as yet; but I will offer a hypothesis which may assist us in forming a conclusion: If the figure be such that when you have produced a given side of it, the given area of the triangle falls short by an area corresponding to the part produced, then one consequence follows, and if this is impossible then some other; and therefore I wish to assume a hypothesis before I tell you whether this triangle is capable of being inscribed in the circle": —that is a geometrical hypothesis. And we too, as we know not the nature and qualities of virtue, must ask, whether virtue is or is not taught, under a hypothesis: as thus, if virtue is of such a class of mental goods, will it be taught or not? Let the first hypothesis be that virtue is or is not knowledge,—in that case will it be taught or not? or, as we were just now saying, "remembered"? For there is no use in disputing about the name. But is virtue taught or not? or rather, does not everyone see that knowledge alone is taught?

Men. I agree.

Soc. Then if virtue is knowledge, virtue will be taught?

Men. Certainly.

Soc. Then now we have made a quick end of this question: if virtue is of such a nature, it will be taught; and if not, not?

Men. Certainly.

Soc. The next question is, whether virtue is knowledge or of another species?

Men. Yes, that appears to be the question which comes next in order.

Soc. Do we not say that virtue is a good?— This is a hypothesis which is not set aside.

Men. Certainly.

Soc. Now, if there be any sort of good which is distinct from knowledge, virtue may be that good; but if knowledge embraces all good, then we shall be right in thinking that virtue is knowledge?

Men. True.

Soc. And virtue makes us good?

Men. Yes.

Soc. And if we are good, then we are profitable; for all good things are profitable?

Men. Yes.

Soc. Then virtue is profitable?

Men. That is the only inference.

Soc. Then now let us see what are the things which severally profit us. Health and strength, and beauty and wealth—these, and the like of these, we call profitable?

Men. True.

[88] Soc. And yet these things may also

sometimes do us harm: would you not think so?

Men. Yes.

Soc. And what is the guiding principle which makes them profitable or the reverse? Are they not profitable when they are rightly used, and hurtful when they are not rightly used?

Men. Certainly.

Soc. Next, let us consider the goods of the soul: they are temperance, justice, courage, quickness of apprehension, memory, magnanimity, and the like?

Men. Surely.

Soc. And such of these as are not knowledge, but of another sort, are sometimes profitable and sometimes hurtful; as, for example, courage wanting prudence, which is only a sort of confidence? When a man has no sense he is harmed by courage, but when he has sense he is profited?

Men. True.

Soc. And the same may be said of temperance and quickness of apprehension; whatever things are learned or done with sense are profitable, but when done without sense they are hurtful?

Men. Very true.

Soc. And in general, all that the soul attempts or endures, when under the guidance of wisdom, ends in happiness; but when she is under the guidance of folly, in the opposite?

Men. That appears to be true.

Soc. If then virtue is a quality of the soul, and is admitted to be profitable, it must be wisdom or prudence, since none of the things of the soul are either profitable or hurtful in themselves, but they are all made profitable or hurtful by the addition of wisdom or of folly; and therefore if virtue is profitable, virtue must be a sort of wisdom or prudence?

Men. I quite agree.

Soc. And the other goods, such as wealth and the like, of which we were just now saying that they are sometimes good and sometimes evil, do not they also become profitable or hurtful, accordingly as the soul guides and uses them rightly or wrongly; just as the things of the soul herself are benefited when under the guidance of wisdom and harmed by folly?

Men. True.

Soc. And the wise soul guides them rightly, and the foolish soul wrongly.

Men. Yes.

Soc. And is not this universally true of human nature? All other things hang upon the soul, and the things of the soul herself hang upon wisdom, *[89]* if they are to be good; and

so wisdom is inferred to be that which profits —and virtue, as we say, is profitable?

Men. Certainly.

Soc. And thus we arrive at the conclusion that virtue is either wholly or partly wisdom?

Men. I think that what you are saying, Socrates, is very true.

Soc. But if this is true, then the good are not by nature good?

Men. I think not.

Soc. If they had been, there would assuredly have been discerners of characters among us who would have known our future great men; and on their showing we should have adopted them, and when we had got them, we should have kept them in the citadel out of the way of harm, and set a stamp upon them far rather than upon a piece of gold, in order that no one might tamper with them; and when they grew up they would have been useful to the state?

Men. Yes, Socrates, that would have been the right way.

Soc. But if the good are not by nature good, are they made good by instruction?

Men. There appears to be no other alternative, Socrates. On the supposition that virtue is knowledge, there can be no doubt that virtue is taught.

Soc. Yes, indeed; but what if the supposition is erroneous?

Men. I certainly thought just now that we were right.

Soc. Yes, Meno; but a principle which has any soundness should stand firm not only just now, but always.

Men. Well; and why are you so slow of heart to believe that knowledge is virtue?

Soc. I will try and tell you why, Meno. I do not retract the assertion that if virtue is knowledge it may be taught; but I fear that I have some reason in doubting whether virtue is knowledge: for consider now and say whether virtue, and not only virtue but anything that is taught, must not have teachers and disciples?

Men. Surely.

Soc. And conversely, may not the art of which neither teachers nor disciples exist be assumed to be incapable of being taught?

Men. True; but do you think that there are no teachers of virtue?

Soc. I have certainly often enquired whether there were any, and taken great pains to find them, and have never succeeded; and many have assisted me in the search, and they were the persons whom I thought the most likely to know. Here at the moment when he is wanted we fortunately have sitting by us Anytus, *[90]* the very person of whom we should make enquiry; to him then let us repair. In the first place, he is the son of a wealthy and wise father, Anthemion, who acquired his wealth, not by accident or gift, like Ismenias the Theban (who has recently made himself as rich as Polycrates), but by his own skill and industry, and who is a well-conditioned, modest man, not insolent, or over-bearing, or annoying; moreover, this son of his has received a good education, as the Athenian people certainly appear to think, for they choose him to fill the highest offices. And these are the sort of men from whom you are likely to learn whether there are any teachers of virtue, and who they are. Please, Anytus, to help me and your friend Meno in answering our question, Who are the teachers? Consider the matter thus: If we wanted Meno to be a good physician, to whom should we send him? Should we not send him to the physicians?

Any. Certainly.

Soc. Or if we wanted him to be a good cobbler, should we not send him to the cobblers?

Any. Yes.

Soc. And so forth?

Any. Yes.

Soc. Let me trouble you with one more question. When we say that we should be right in sending him to the physicians if we wanted him to be a physician, do we mean that we should be right in sending him to those who profess the art, rather than to those who do not, and to those who demand payment for teaching the art, and profess to teach it to any one who will come and learn? And if these were our reasons, should we not be right in sending him?

Any. Yes.

Soc. And might not the same be said of flute-playing, and of the other arts? Would a man who wanted to make another a flute-player refuse to send him to those who profess to teach the art for money, and be plaguing other persons to give him instruction, who are not professed teachers and who never had a single disciple in that branch of knowledge which he wishes him to acquire—would not such conduct be the height of folly?

Any. Yes, by Zeus, and of ignorance too.

[91] Soc. Very good. And now you are in a position to advise with me about my friend Meno. He has been telling me, Anytus, that he desires to attain that kind of wisdom and virtue by which men order the state or the house, and honour their parents, and know when to receive and when to send away citizens and strangers, as a good man should. Now, to whom should he go in order that he may learn this virtue? Does not the previous argument imply clearly that we should send him to those who profess and avouch that they are the common teachers of all Hellas, and are ready to impart instruction to any one who likes, at a fixed price?

Any. Whom do you mean, Socrates?

Soc. You surely know, do you not, Anytus, that these are the people whom mankind call Sophists?

Any. By Heracles, Socrates, forbear! I only hope that no friend or kinsman or acquaintance of mine, whether citizen or stranger, will ever be so mad as to allow himself to be corrupted by them; for they are a manifest pest and corrupting influences to those who have to do with them.

Soc. What, Anytus? Of all the people who profess that they know how to do men good, do you mean to say that these are the only ones who not only do them no good, but positively corrupt those who are entrusted to them, and in return for this disservice have the face to demand money? Indeed, I cannot believe you; for I know of a single man, Protagoras, who made more out of his craft than the illustrious Pheidias, who created such noble works, or any ten other statuaries. How could that be? A mender of old shoes, or patcher up of clothes, who made the shoes or clothes worse than he received them, could not have remained thirty days undetected, and would very soon have starved; whereas during more than forty years, Protagoras was corrupting all Hellas, and sending his disciples from him worse than he received them, and he was never found out. For, if I am not mistaken, he was about seventy years old at his death, forty of which were spent in the practice of his profession; and during all that time he had a good reputation, which to this day he retains: and not only Protagoras, but many others are well spoken of; some who lived before him, and others who are still living. *[92]* Now, when you say that they deceived and corrupted the youth, are they to be supposed to have corrupted them consciously or unconsciously? Can those who were deemed by many to be the wisest men of Hellas have been out of their minds?

Any. Out of their minds! No, Socrates; the young men who gave their money to them were out of their minds, and their relations and guardians who entrusted their youth to the care of these men were still more out of their minds, and most of all, the cities who allowed them to come in, and did not drive them out, citizen and stranger alike.

Soc. Has any of the Sophists wronged you, Anytus? What makes you so angry with them?

Any. No, indeed, neither I nor any of my belongings has ever had, nor would I suffer them to have, anything to do with them.

Soc. Then you are entirely unacquainted with them?

Any. And I have no wish to be acquainted.

Soc. Then, my dear friend, how can you know whether a thing is good or bad of which you are wholly ignorant?

Any. Quite well; I am sure that I know what manner of men these are, whether I am acquainted with them or not.

Soc. You must be a diviner, Anytus, for I really cannot make out, judging from your own words, how, if you are not acquainted with them, you know about them. But I am not enquiring of you who are the teachers who will corrupt Meno (let them be, if you please, the Sophists); I only ask you to tell him who there is in this great city who will teach him how to become eminent in the virtues which I was just now describing. He is the friend of your family, and you will oblige him.

Any. Why do you not tell him yourself?

Soc. I have told him whom I supposed to be the teachers of these things; but I learn from you that I am utterly at fault, and I dare say that you are right. And now I wish that you, on your part, would tell me to whom among the Athenians he should go. Whom would you name?

Any. Why single out individuals? Any Athenian gentleman, taken at random, if he will mind him, will do far more good to him than the Sophists.

Soc. And did those gentlemen grow of themselves; and without having been taught by any one, were they nevertheless able to teach others that which they had never learned themselves?

[93]

Any. I imagine that they learned of the previous generation of gentlemen. Have there not been many good men in this city?

Soc. Yes, certainly, Anytus; and many good statesmen also there always have been and there are still, in the city of Athens. But the question is whether they were also good teachers of their own virtue;—not whether there are, or have been, good men in this part of the world, but whether virtue can be taught, is the question which we have been discussing. Now, do we mean to say that the good men of our own and of other times knew how to impart to others that virtue which they had themselves; or is virtue a thing incapable of being communicated or imparted by one man to another? That is the question which I and Meno have been arguing. Look at the matter in your own way: Would you not admit that Themistocles was a good man?

Any. Certainly; no man better.

Soc. And must not he then have been a good teacher, if any man ever was a good teacher, of his own virtue?

Any. Yes, certainly,—if he wanted to be so.

Soc. But would he not have wanted? He would, at any rate, have desired to make his own son a good man and a gentleman; he could not have been jealous of him, or have intentionally abstained from imparting to him his own virtue. Did you never hear that he made his son Cleophantus a famous horseman; and had him taught to stand upright on horseback and hurl a javelin, and to do many other marvellous things; and in anything which could be learned from a master he was well trained? Have you not heard from our elders of him?

Any. I have.

Soc. Then no one could say that his son showed any want of capacity?

Any. Very likely not.

Soc. But did any one, old or young, ever say in your hearing that Cleophantus, son of Themistocles, was a wise or good man, as his father was?

Any. I have certainly never heard any one say so.

Soc. And if virtue could have been taught, would his father Themistocles have sought to train him in these minor accomplishments, and allowed him who, as you must remember, was his own son, to be no better than his neighbours in those qualities in which he himself excelled?

Any. Indeed, indeed, I think not.

Soc. Here was a teacher of virtue whom you admit to be among the best men of the past. [94] Let us take another,—Aristides, the son of Lysimachus: would you not acknowledge that he was a good man?

Any. To be sure I should.

Soc. And did not he train his son Lysimachus better than any other Athenian in all that could be done for him by the help of masters? But what has been the result? Is he a bit better than any other mortal? He is an acquaintance of yours, and you see what he is like. There is Pericles, again, magnificent in his wisdom; and he, as you are aware, had two sons, Paralus and Xanthippus.

Any. I know.

Soc. And you know, also, that he taught them to be unrivalled horsemen, and had them trained in music and gymnastics and all sorts of arts—in these respects they were on a level with the best—and had he no wish to make good men of them? Nay, he must have wished it. But virtue, as I suspect, could not be taught. And that you may not suppose the incompetent teachers to be only the meaner sort of Athenians and few in number, remember again that Thucydides had two sons, Melesias and Stephanus, whom, besides giving them a good education in other things, he trained in wrestling, and they were the best wrestlers in Athens: one of them he committed to the care of Xanthias, and the other of Eudorus, who had the reputation of being the most celebrated wrestlers of that day. Do you remember them?

Any. I have heard of them.

Soc. Now, can there be a doubt that Thucydides, whose children were taught things for which he had to spend money, would have taught them to be good men, which would have cost him nothing, if virtue could have been taught? Will you reply that he was a mean man, and had not many friends among the Athenians and allies? Nay, but he was of a great family, and a man of influence at Athens and in all Hellas, and, if virtue could have been taught, he would have found out some Athenian or foreigner who would have made good men of his sons, if he could not himself spare the time from cares of state. Once more, I suspect, friend Anytus, that virtue is not a thing which can be taught?

Any. Socrates, I think that you are too ready to speak evil of men: and, if you will take my advice, I would recommend you to be careful. Perhaps there is no city in which it is not easier to do men harm than to do them good, [95] and this is certainly the case at Athens, as I believe that you know.

Soc. O Meno, I think that Anytus is in a rage. And he may well be in a rage, for he thinks, in the first place, that I am defaming these gentlemen; and in the second place, he is of opinion that he is one of them himself. But some day he will know what is the meaning of defamation, and if he ever does, he will forgive me. Meanwhile I will return to you, Meno; for I suppose that there are gentlemen in your region too?

Men. Certainly there are.

Soc. And are they willing to teach the young? and do they profess to be teachers? and do they agree that virtue is taught?

Men. No indeed, Socrates, they are anything but agreed; you may hear them saying at one time that virtue can be taught, and then again the reverse.

Soc. Can we call those teachers who do not acknowledge the possibility of their own vocation?

Men. I think not, Socrates.

Soc. And what do you think of these Sophists, who are the only professors? Do they seem to you to be teachers of virtue?

Men. I often wonder, Socrates, that Gorgias is never heard promising to teach virtue: and when he hears others promising he only laughs at them; but he thinks that men should be taught to speak.

Soc. Then do you not think that the Sophists are teachers?

Men. I cannot tell you, Socrates; like the rest of the world, I am in doubt, and sometimes I think that they are teachers and sometimes not.

Soc. And are you aware that not you only and other politicians have doubts whether virtue can be taught or not, but that Theognis the poet says the very same thing?

Men. Where does he say so?

Soc. In these elegiac verses:

Eat and drink and sit with the mighty, and make yourself agreeable to them; for from the good you will learn what is good, but if you mix with the bad you will lose the intelligence which you already have.

Do you observe that here he seems to imply that virtue can be taught?

Men. Clearly.

Soc. But in some other verses he shifts about and says:

If understanding could be created and put into a man, then they [who were able to perform this feat] would have obtained great rewards.

And again:—[96]

Never would a bad son have sprung from a good sire, for he would have heard the voice of instruction; but not by teaching will you ever make a bad man into a good one.

And this, as you may remark, is a contradiction of the other.

Men. Clearly.

Soc. And is there anything else of which the professors are affirmed not only not to be teachers of others, but to be ignorant themselves, and bad at the knowledge of that which they are professing to teach? or is there anything about which even the acknowledged "gentlemen" are sometimes saying that "this thing can be taught," and sometimes the opposite? Can you say that they are teachers in any true sense whose ideas are in such confusion?

Men. I should say, certainly not.

Soc. But if neither the Sophists nor the gentlemen are teachers, clearly there can be no other teachers?

Men. No.

Soc. And if there are no teachers, neither are there disciples?

Men. Agreed.

Soc. And we have admitted that a thing cannot be taught of which there are neither teachers nor disciples?

Men. We have.

Soc. And there are no teachers of virtue to be found anywhere?

Men. There are not.

Soc. And if there are no teachers, neither are there scholars?

Men. That, I think, is true.

Soc. Then virtue cannot be taught?

Men. Not if we are right in our view. But I cannot believe, Socrates, that there are no good men: And if there are, how did they come into existence?

Soc. I am afraid, Meno, that you and I are not good for much, and that Gorgias has been as poor an educator of you as Prodicus has been of me. Certainly we shall have to look to ourselves, and try to find some one who will help in some way or other to improve us. This I say, because I observe that in the previous discussion none of us remarked that right and good action is possible to man under other guidance than that of knowledge (ἐπιστήμη);—and indeed if this be denied, there is no seeing how there can be any good men at all.

Men. How do you mean, Socrates?

Soc. I mean that good men are necessarily useful or profitable. *[97]* Were we not right in admitting this? It must be so.

Men. Yes.

Soc. And in supposing that they will be useful only if they are true guides to us of action —there we were also right?

Men. Yes.

Soc. But when we said that a man cannot be a good guide unless he have knowledge (φρόνησις), in this we were wrong.

Men. What do you mean by the word "right"?

Soc. I will explain. If a man knew the way to Larisa, or anywhere else, and went to the place and led others thither, would he not be a right and good guide?

Men. Certainly.

Soc. And a person who had a right opinion about the way, but had never been and did not know, might be a good guide also, might he not?

Men. Certainly.

Soc. And while he has true opinion about that which the other knows, he will be just as good a guide if he thinks the truth, as he who knows the truth?

Men. Exactly.

Soc. Then true opinion is as good a guide to correct action as knowledge; and that was the point which we omitted in our speculation about the nature of virtue, when we said that knowledge only is the guide of right action; whereas there is also right opinion.

Men. True.

Soc. Then right opinion is not less useful than knowledge?

Men. The difference, Socrates, is only that he who has knowledge will always be right; but he who has right opinion will sometimes be right, and sometimes not.

Soc. What do you mean? Can he be wrong who has right opinion, so long as he has right opinion?

Men. I admit the cogency of your argument, and therefore, Socrates, I wonder that knowledge should be preferred to right opinion—or why they should ever differ.

Soc. And shall I explain this wonder to you?

Men. Do tell me.

Soc. You would not wonder if you had ever observed the images of Daedalus;[1] but perhaps you have not got them in your country?

Men. What have they to do with the question?

Soc. Because they require to be fastened in order to keep them, and if they are not fastened they will play truant and run away.

Men. Well, what of that?

Soc. I mean to say that they are not very valuable possessions if they are at liberty, for they will walk off like runaway slaves; but when fastened, they are of great value, for they are really beautiful works of art. *[98]* Now this is

[1] Cf. *Euthyphro*, 11.

an illustration of the nature of true opinions: while they abide with us they are beautiful and fruitful, but they run away out of the human soul, and do not remain long, and therefore they are not of much value until they are fastened by the tie of the cause; and this fastening of them, friend Meno, is recollection, as you and I have agreed to call it. But when they are bound, in the first place, they have the nature of knowledge; and, in the second place, they are abiding. And this is why knowledge is more honourable and excellent than true opinion, because fastened by a chain.

Men. What you are saying, Socrates, seems to be very like the truth.

Soc. I too speak rather in ignorance; I only conjecture. And yet that knowledge differs from true opinion is no matter of conjecture with me. There are not many things which I profess to know, but this is most certainly one of them.

Men. Yes, Socrates; and you are quite right in saying so.

Soc. And am I not also right in saying that true opinion leading the way perfects action quite as well as knowledge?

Men. There again, Socrates, I think you are right.

Soc. Then right opinion is not a whit inferior to knowledge, or less useful in action; nor is the man who has right opinion inferior to him who has knowledge?

Men. True.

Soc. And surely the good man has been acknowledged by us to be useful?

Men. Yes.

Soc. Seeing then that men become good and useful to states, not only because they have knowledge, but because they have right opinion, and that neither knowledge nor right opinion is given to man by nature or acquired by him—(do you imagine either of them to be given by nature?

Men. Not I.)

Soc. Then if they are not given by nature, neither are the good by nature good?

Men. Certainly not.

Soc. And nature being excluded, then came the question whether virtue is acquired by teaching?

Men. Yes.

Soc. If virtue was wisdom [or knowledge], then, as we thought, it was taught?

Men. Yes.

Soc. And if it was taught it was wisdom?

Men. Certainly.

Soc. And if there were teachers, it might be taught; and if there were no teachers, not?

Men. True.

Soc. But surely we acknowledged that there were no teachers of virtue?

Men. Yes.

Soc. Then we acknowledged that it was not taught, and was not wisdom?

Men. Certainly.

Soc. And yet we admitted that it was a good?

Men. Yes.

[99] Soc. And the right guide is useful and good?

Men. Certainly.

Soc. And the only right guides are knowledge and true opinion—these are the guides of man; for things which happen by chance are not under the guidance of man: but the guides of man are true opinion and knowledge.

Men. I think so too.

Soc. But if virtue is not taught, neither is virtue knowledge.

Men. Clearly not.

Soc. Then of two good and useful things, one, which is knowledge, has been set aside, and cannot be supposed to be our guide in political life.

Men. I think not.

Soc. And therefore not by any wisdom, and not because they were wise, did Themistocles and those others of whom Anytus spoke govern states. This was the reason why they were unable to make others like themselves—because their virtue was not grounded on knowledge.

Men. That is probably true, Socrates.

Soc. But if not by knowledge, the only alternative which remains is that statesmen must have guided states by right opinion, which is in politics what divination is in religion; for diviners and also prophets say many things truly, but they know not what they say.

Men. So I believe.

Soc. And may we not, Meno, truly call those men "divine" who, having no understanding, yet succeed in many a grand deed and word?

Men. Certainly.

Soc. Then we shall also be right in calling divine those whom we were just now speaking of as diviners and prophets, including the whole tribe of poets. Yes, and statesmen above all may be said to be divine and illumined, being inspired and possessed of God, in which condition they say many grand things, not knowing what they say.

Men. Yes.

Soc. And the women too, Meno, call good

men divine—do they not? and the Spartans, when they praise a good man, say "that he is a divine man."

Men. And I think, Socrates, that they are right; although very likely our friend Anytus may take offence at the word.

Soc. I do not care; as for Anytus, there will be another opportunity of talking with him. To sum up our enquiry—the result seems to be, if we are at all right in our view, that virtue is neither natural nor acquired, [*100*] but an instinct given by God to the virtuous. Nor is the instinct accompanied by reason, unless there may be supposed to be among statesmen some one who is capable of educating statesmen. And if there be such an one, he may be said to be among the living what Homer says that Tiresias was among the dead, "he alone has understanding; but the rest are flitting shades"; and he and his virtue in like manner will be a reality among shadows.

Men. That is excellent, Socrates.

Soc. Then, Meno, the conclusion is that virtue comes to the virtuous by the gift of God. But we shall never know the certain truth until, before asking how virtue is given, we enquire into the actual nature of virtue. I fear that I must go away, but do you, now that you are persuaded yourself, persuade our friend Anytus. And do not let him be so exasperated; if you can conciliate him, you will have done good service to the Athenian people.

EUTHYPHRO

Persons of the Dialogue: Socrates; Euthyphro. *Scene: The Porch of the King Archon*

~~~~~~~~~~~~~~~~~~~~~~~~~~~~~~~~~~~~~

[2] Euthyphro. Why have you left the Lyceum, Socrates? and what are you doing in the Porch of the King Archon? Surely you cannot be concerned in a suit before the King, like myself?

Socrates. Not in a suit, Euthyphro; impeachment is the word which the Athenians use.

Euth. What! I suppose that some one has been prosecuting you, for I cannot believe that you are the prosecutor of another.

Soc. Certainly not.

Euth. Then some one else has been prosecuting you?

Soc. Yes.

Euth. And who is he?

Soc. A young man who is little known, Euthyphro; and I hardly know him: his name is Meletus, and he is of the deme of Pitthis. Perhaps you may remember his appearance; he has a beak, and long straight hair, and a beard which is ill grown.

Euth. No, I do not remember him, Socrates. But what is the charge which he brings against you?

Soc. What is the charge? Well, a very serious charge, which shows a good deal of character in the young man, and for which he is certainly not to be despised. He says he knows how the youth are corrupted and who are their corruptors. I fancy that he must be a wise man, and seeing that I am the reverse of a wise man, he has found me out, and is going to accuse me of corrupting his young friends. And of this our mother the state is to be the judge. Of all our political men he is the only one who seems to me to begin in the right way, with the cultivation of virtue in youth; like a good husbandman, he makes the young shoots his first care, and

[3] clears away us who are the destroyers of them. This is only the first step; he will afterwards attend to the elder branches; and if he goes on as he has begun, he will be a very great public benefactor.

Euth. I hope that he may; but I rather fear, Socrates, that the opposite will turn out to be the truth. My opinion is that in attacking you he is simply aiming a blow at the foundation of the state. But in what way does he say that you corrupt the young?

Soc. He brings a wonderful accusation against me, which at first hearing excites surprise: he says that I am a poet or maker of gods, and that I invent new gods and deny the existence of old ones; this is the ground of his indictment.

Euth. I understand, Socrates; he means to attack you about the familiar sign which occasionally, as you say, comes to you. He thinks that you are a neologian, and he is going to have you up before the court for this. He knows that such a charge is readily received by the world, as I myself know too well; for when I speak in the assembly about divine things, and foretell the future to them, they laugh at me and think me a madman. Yet every word that I say is true. But they are jealous of us all; and we must be brave and go at them.

Soc. Their laughter, friend Euthyphro, is not a matter of much consequence. For a man may be thought wise; but the Athenians, I suspect, do not much trouble themselves about him until he begins to impart his wisdom to others; and then for some reason or other, perhaps, as you say, from jealousy, they are angry.

Euth. I am never likely to try their temper in this way.

191

Soc. I dare say not, for you are reserved in your behaviour, and seldom impart your wisdom. But I have a benevolent habit of pouring out myself to everybody, and would even pay for a listener, and I am afraid that the Athenians may think me too talkative. Now if, as I was saying, they would only laugh at me, as you say that they laugh at you, the time might pass gaily enough in the court; but perhaps they may be in earnest, and then what the end will be you soothsayers only can predict.

Euth. I dare say that the affair will end in nothing, Socrates, and that you will win your cause; and I think that I shall win my own.

Soc. And what is your suit, Euthyphro? are you the pursuer or the defendant?

Euth. I am the pursuer.

Soc. Of whom?

[4] *Euth.* You will think me mad when I tell you.

Soc. Why, has the fugitive wings?

Euth. Nay, he is not very volatile at his time of life.

Soc. Who is he?

Euth. My father.

Soc. Your father! my good man?

Euth. Yes.

Soc. And of what is he accused?

Euth. Of murder, Socrates.

Soc. By the powers, Euthyphro! how little does the common herd know of the nature of right and truth. A man must be an extraordinary man, and have made great strides in wisdom, before he could have seen his way to bring such an action.

Euth. Indeed, Socrates, he must.

Soc. I suppose that the man whom your father murdered was one of your relatives—clearly he was; for if he had been a stranger you would never have thought of prosecuting him.

Euth. I am amused, Socrates, at your making a distinction between one who is a relation and one who is not a relation; for surely the pollution is the same in either case, if you knowingly associate with the murderer when you ought to clear yourself and him by proceeding against him. The real question is whether the murdered man has been justly slain. If justly, then your duty is to let the matter alone; but if unjustly, then even if the murderer lives under the same roof with you and eats at the same table, proceed against him. Now the man who is dead was a poor dependant of mine who worked for us as a field labourer on our farm in Naxos, and one day in a fit of drunken passion he got into a quarrel with one of our domestic servants and slew him. My father bound him hand and foot and threw him into a ditch, and then sent to Athens to ask of a diviner what he should do with him. Meanwhile he never attended to him and took no care about him, for he regarded him as a murderer; and thought that no great harm would be done even if he did die. Now this was just what happened. For such was the effect of cold and hunger and chains upon him, that before the messenger returned from the diviner, he was dead. And my father and family are angry with me for taking the part of the murderer and prosecuting my father. They say that he did not kill him, and that if he did, the dead man was but a murderer, and I ought not to take any notice, for that a son is impious who prosecutes a father. Which shows, Socrates, how little they know what the gods think about piety and impiety.

Soc. Good heavens, Euthyphro! and is your knowledge of religion and of things pious and impious so very exact, that, supposing the circumstances to be as you state them, you are not afraid lest you too may be doing an impious thing in bringing an action against your father?

Euth. The best of Euthyphro, and that which distinguishes him, Socrates, [5] from other men, is his exact knowledge of all such matters. What should I be good for without it?

Soc. Rare friend! I think that I cannot do better than be your disciple. Then before the trial with Meletus comes on I shall challenge him, and say that I have always had a great interest in religious questions, and now, as he charges me with rash imaginations and innovations in religion, I have become your disciple. You, Meletus, as I shall say to him, acknowledge Euthyphro to be a great theologian, and sound in his opinions; and if you approve of him you ought to approve of me, and not have me into court; but if you disapprove, you should begin by indicting him who is my teacher, and who will be the ruin, not of the young, but of the old; that is to say, of myself whom he instructs, and of his old father whom he admonishes and chastises. And if Meletus refuses to listen to me, but will go on, and will not shift the indictment from me to you, I cannot do better than repeat this challenge in the court.

Euth. Yes, indeed, Socrates; and if he attempts to indict me I am mistaken if I do not find a flaw in him; the court shall have a great deal more to say to him than to me.

Soc. And I, my dear friend, knowing this, am desirous of becoming your disciple. For I observe that no one appears to notice you—not even this Meletus; but his sharp eyes have found me out at once, and he has indicted me for impiety. And therefore, I adjure you to tell me the nature of piety and impiety, which you said that you knew so well, and of murder, and of other offences against the gods. What are they? Is not piety in every action always the same? and impiety, again—is it not always the opposite of piety, and also the same with itself, having, as impiety, one notion which includes whatever is impious?

Euth. To be sure, Socrates.

Soc. And what is piety, and what is impiety?

Euth. Piety is doing as I am doing; that is to say, prosecuting any one who is guilty of murder, sacrilege, or of any similar crime—whether he be your father or mother, or whoever he may be—that makes no difference; and not to prosecute them is impiety. And please to consider, Socrates, what a notable proof I will give you of the truth of my words, a proof which I have already given to others:—of the principle, I mean, that the impious, whoever he may be, ought not to go unpunished. For do not men regard Zeus as the best and most righteous of the gods? *[6]*—and yet they admit that he bound his father (Cronos) because he wickedly devoured his sons, and that he too had punished his own father (Uranus) for a similar reason, in a nameless manner. And yet when I proceed against my father, they are angry with me. So inconsistent are they in their way of talking when the gods are concerned, and when I am concerned.

Soc. May not this be the reason, Euthyphro, why I am charged with impiety—that I cannot away with these stories about the gods? and therefore I suppose that people think me wrong. But, as you who are well informed about them approve of them, I cannot do better than assent to your superior wisdom. What else can I say, confessing as I do, that I know nothing about them? Tell me, for the love of Zeus, whether you really believe that they are true.

Euth. Yes, Socrates; and things more wonderful still, of which the world is in ignorance.

Soc. And do you really believe that the gods fought with one another, and had dire quarrels, battles, and the like, as the poets say, and as you may see represented in the works of great artists? The temples are full of them; and notably the robe of Athene, which is carried up to the Acropolis at the great Panathenaea, is embroidered with them. Are all these tales of the gods true, Euthyphro?

Euth. Yes, Socrates; and, as I was saying, I can tell you, if you would like to hear them, many other things about the gods which would quite amaze you.

Soc. I dare say; and you shall tell me them at some other time when I have leisure. But just at present I would rather hear from you a more precise answer, which you have not as yet given, my friend, to the question, What is "piety"? When asked, you only replied, Doing as you do, charging your father with murder.

Euth. And what I said was true, Socrates.

Soc. No doubt, Euthyphro; but you would admit that there are many other pious acts?

Euth. There are.

Soc. Remember that I did not ask you to give me two or three examples of piety, but to explain the general idea which makes all pious things to be pious. Do you not recollect that there was one idea which made the impious impious, and the pious pious?

Euth. I remember.

Soc. Tell me what is the nature of this idea, and then I shall have a standard to which I may look, and by which I may measure actions, whether yours or those of any one else, and then I shall be able to say that such and such an action is pious, such another impious.

Euth. I will tell you, if you like.

Soc. I should very much like.

Euth. Piety, then, is that which is dear to the gods, and impiety is that which is not dear to them.

[7] Soc. Very good, Euthyphro; you have now given me the sort of answer which I wanted. But whether what you say is true or not I cannot as yet tell, although I make no doubt that you will prove the truth of your words.

Euth. Of course.

Soc. Come, then, and let us examine what we are saying. That thing or person which is dear to the gods is pious, and that thing or person which is hateful to the gods is impious, these two being the extreme opposites of one another. Was not that said?

Euth. It was.

Soc. And well said?

Euth. Yes, Socrates, I thought so; it was certainly said.

Soc. And further, Euthyphro, the gods were admitted to have enmities and hatreds and differences?

Euth. Yes, that was also said.

Soc. And what sort of difference creates enmity and anger? Suppose for example that you and I, my good friend, differ about a number; do differences of this sort make us enemies and set us at variance with one another? Do we not go at once to arithmetic, and put an end to them by a sum?

Euth. True.

Soc. Or suppose that we differ about magnitudes, do we not quickly end the differences by measuring?

Euth. Very true.

Soc. And we end a controversy about heavy and light by resorting to a weighing machine?

Euth. To be sure.

Soc. But what differences are there which cannot be thus decided, and which therefore make us angry and set us at enmity with one another? I dare say the answer does not occur to you at the moment, and therefore I will suggest that these enmities arise when the matters of difference are the just and unjust, good and evil, honourable and dishonourable. Are not these the points about which men differ, and about which when we are unable satisfactorily to decide our differences, you and I and all of us quarrel, when we do quarrel?

Euth. Yes, Socrates, the nature of the differences about which we quarrel is such as you describe.

Soc. And the quarrels of the gods, noble Euthyphro, when they occur, are of a like nature?

Euth. Certainly they are.

Soc. They have differences of opinion, as you say, about good and evil, just and unjust, honourable and dishonourable: there would have been no quarrels among them, if there had been no such differences—would there now?

Euth. You are quite right.

Soc. Does not every man love that which he deems noble and just and good, and hate the opposite of them?

Euth. Very true.

Soc. But, as you say, people regard the same things, some as just and others as unjust,—about these they dispute; and so there arise wars and fightings among them. *[8]*

Euth. Very true.

Soc. Then the same things are hated by the gods and loved by the gods, and are both hateful and dear to them?

Euth. True.

Soc. And upon this view the same things, Euthyphro, will be pious and also impious?

Euth. So I should suppose.

Soc. Then, my friend, I remark with surprise that you have not answered the question which I asked. For I certainly did not ask you to tell me what action is both pious and impious: but

now it would seem that what is loved by the gods is also hated by them. And therefore, Euthyphro, in thus chastising your father you may very likely be doing what is agreeable to Zeus but disagreeable to Cronos or Uranus, and what is acceptable to Hephaestus but unacceptable to Herè, and there may be other gods who have similar differences of opinion.

Euth. But I believe, Socrates, that all the gods would be agreed as to the propriety of punishing a murderer: there would be no difference of opinion about that.

Soc. Well, but speaking of men, Euthyphro, did you ever hear any one arguing that a murderer or any sort of evil-doer ought to be let off?

Euth. I should rather say that these are the questions which they are always arguing, especially in courts of law: they commit all sorts of crimes, and there is nothing which they will not do or say in their own defence.

Soc. But do they admit their guilt, Euthyphro, and yet say that they ought not to be punished?

Euth. No; they do not.

Soc. Then there are some things which they do not venture to say and do: for they do not venture to argue that the guilty are to be unpunished, but they deny their guilt, do they not?

Euth. Yes.

Soc. Then they do not argue that the evil-doer should not be punished, but they argue about the fact of who the evil-doer is, and what he did and when?

Euth. True.

Soc. And the gods are in the same case, if as you assert they quarrel about just and unjust, and some of them say while others deny that injustice is done among them. For surely neither God nor man will ever venture to say that the doer of injustice is not to be punished?

Euth. That is true, Socrates, in the main.

Soc. But they join issue about the particulars—gods and men alike; and, if they dispute at all, they dispute about some act which is called in question, and which by some is affirmed to be just, by others to be unjust. Is not that true?

Euth. Quite true.

[9] Soc. Well then, my dear friend Euthyphro, do tell me, for my better instruction and information, what proof have you that in the opinion of all the gods a servant who is guilty of murder, and is put in chains by the master of the dead man, and dies because he is put in chains before he who bound him can learn

from the interpreters of the gods what he ought to do with him, dies unjustly; and that on behalf of such an one a son ought to proceed against his father and accuse him of murder. How would you show that all the gods absolutely agree in approving of his act? Prove to me that they do, and I will applaud your wisdom as long as I live.

Euth. It will be a difficult task; but I could make the matter very clear indeed to you.

Soc. I understand; you mean to say that I am not so quick of apprehension as the judges: for to them you will be sure to prove that the act is unjust, and hateful to the gods.

Euth. Yes indeed, Socrates; at least if they will listen to me.

Soc. But they will be sure to listen if they find that you are a good speaker. There was a notion that came into my mind while you were speaking; I said to myself: "Well, and what if Euthyphro does prove to me that all the gods regarded the death of the serf as unjust, how do I know anything more of the nature of piety and impiety? for granting that this action may be hateful to the gods, still piety and impiety are not adequately defined by these distinctions, for that which is hateful to the gods has been shown to be also pleasing and dear to them." And therefore, Euthyphro, I do not ask you to prove this; I will suppose, if you like, that all the gods condemn and abominate such an action. But I will amend the definition so far as to say that what all the gods hate is impious, and what they love pious or holy; and what some of them love and others hate is both or neither. Shall this be our definition of piety and impiety?

Euth. Why not, Socrates?

Soc. Why not! certainly, as far as I am concerned, Euthyphro, there is no reason why not. But whether this admission will greatly assist you in the task of instructing me as you promised, is a matter for you to consider.

Euth. Yes, I should say that what all the gods love is pious and holy, and the opposite which they all hate, impious.

Soc. Ought we to enquire into the truth of this, Euthyphro, or simply to accept the mere statement on our own authority and that of others? What do you say?

Euth. We should enquire; and I believe that the statement will stand the test of enquiry.

Soc. We shall know better, my good friend, in a little while. The point which I should first wish to understand is whether the pious or holy is beloved by the gods because it is holy, [10] or holy because it is beloved of the gods.

Euth. I do not understand your meaning, Socrates.

Soc. I will endeavour to explain: we speak of carrying and we speak of being carried, of leading and being led, seeing and being seen. You know that in all such cases there is a difference, and you know also in what the difference lies?

Euth. I think that I understand.

Soc. And is not that which is beloved distinct from that which loves?

Euth. Certainly.

Soc. Well; and now tell me, is that which is carried in this state of carrying because it is carried, or for some other reason?

Euth. No; that is the reason.

Soc. And the same is true of what is led and of what is seen?

Euth. True.

Soc. And a thing is not seen because it is visible, but conversely, visible because it is seen; nor is a thing led because it is in the state of being led, or carried because it is in the state of being carried, but the converse of this. And now I think, Euthyphro, that my meaning will be intelligible; and my meaning is, that any state of action or passion implies previous action or passion. It does not become because it is becoming, but it is in a state of becoming because it becomes; neither does it suffer because it is in a state of suffering, but it is in a state of suffering because it suffers. Do you not agree?

Euth. Yes.

Soc. Is not that which is loved in some state either of becoming or suffering?

Euth. Yes.

Soc. And the same holds as in the previous instances; the state of being loved follows the act of being loved, and not the act the state.

Euth. Certainly.

Soc. And what do you say of piety, Euthyphro: is not piety, according to your definition, loved by all the gods?

Euth. Yes.

Soc. Because it is pious or holy, or for some other reason?

Euth. No, that is the reason.

Soc. It is loved because it is holy, not holy because it is loved?

Euth. Yes.

Soc. And that which is dear to the gods is loved by them, and is in a state to be loved of them because it is loved of them?

Euth. Certainly.

Soc. Then that which is dear to the gods,

Euthyphro, is not holy, nor is that which is holy loved of God, as you affirm; but they are two different things.

Euth. How do you mean, Socrates?

Soc. I mean to say that the holy has been acknowledged by us to be loved of God because it is holy, not to be holy because it is loved.

Euth. Yes.

Soc. But that which is dear to the gods is dear to them because it is loved by them, not loved by them because it is dear to them.

Euth. True.

Soc. But, friend Euthyphro, if that which is holy is the same with that which is dear to God, and is loved because it is holy, then that which is dear to God would have been loved as being [11] dear to God; but if that which is dear to God is dear to him because loved by him, then that which is holy would have been holy because loved by him. But now you see that the reverse is the case, and that they are quite different from one another. For one (θεοφιλὲς) is of a kind to be loved because it is loved, and the other (ὅσιον) is loved because it is of a kind to be loved. Thus you appear to me, Euthyphro, when I ask you what is the essence of holiness, to offer an attribute only, and not the essence—the attribute of being loved by all the gods. But you still refuse to explain to me the nature of holiness. And therefore, if you please, I will ask you not to hide your treasure, but to tell me once more what holiness or piety really is, whether dear to the gods or not (for that is a matter about which we will not quarrel); and what is impiety?

Euth. I really do not know, Socrates, how to express what I mean. For somehow or other our arguments, on whatever ground we rest them, seem to turn round and walk away from us.

Soc. Your words, Euthyphro, are like the handiwork of my ancestor Daedalus; and if I were the sayer or propounder of them, you might say that my arguments walk away and will not remain fixed where they are placed because I am a descendant of his. But now, since these notions are your own, you must find some other gibe, for they certainly, as you yourself allow, show an inclination to be on the move.

Euth. Nay, Socrates, I shall still say that you are the Daedalus who sets arguments in motion; not I, certainly, but you make them move or go round, for they would never have stirred, as far as I am concerned.

Soc. Then I must be a greater than Daedalus:

for whereas he only made his own inventions to move, I move those of other people as well. And the beauty of it is, that I would rather not. For I would give the wisdom of Daedalus, and the wealth of Tantalus, to be able to detain them and keep them fixed. But enough of this. As I perceive that you are lazy, I will myself endeavor to show you how you might instruct me in the nature of piety; and I hope that you will not grudge your labour. Tell me, then,—Is not that which is pious necessarily just?

Euth. Yes.

Soc. And is, then, all which is just pious? or, is that which is pious all just, [12] but that which is just, only in part and not all, pious?

Euth. I do not understand you, Socrates.

Soc. And yet I know that you are as much wiser than I am, as you are younger. But, as I was saying, revered friend, the abundance of your wisdom makes you lazy. Please to exert yourself, for there is no real difficulty in understanding me. What I mean I may explain by an illustration of what I do not mean. The poet (Stasinus) sings—

Of Zeus, the author and creator of all these things,
You will not tell: for where there is fear there is
also reverence.

Now I disagree with this poet. Shall I tell you in what respect?

Euth. By all means.

Soc. I should not say that where there is fear there is also reverence; for I am sure that many persons fear poverty and disease, and the like evils, but I do not perceive that they reverence the objects of their fear.

Euth. Very true.

Soc. But where reverence is, there is fear; for he who has a feeling of reverence and shame about the commission of any action, fears and is afraid of an ill reputation.

Euth. No doubt.

Soc. Then we are wrong in saying that where there is fear there is also reverence; and we should say, where there is reverence there is also fear. But there is not always reverence where there is fear; for fear is a more extended notion, and reverence is a part of fear, just as the odd is a part of number, and number is a more extended notion than the odd. I suppose that you follow me now?

Euth. Quite well.

Soc. That was the sort of question which I meant to raise when I asked whether the just is always the pious, or the pious always the just; and whether there may not be justice where there is not piety; for justice is the more extended notion of which piety is only a part. Do you dissent?

Euth. No, I think that you are quite right.

Soc. Then, if piety is a part of justice, I suppose that we should enquire what part? If you had pursued the enquiry in the previous cases; for instance, if you had asked me what is an even number, and what part of number the even is, I should have had no difficulty in replying, a number which represents a figure having two equal sides. Do you not agree?

Euth. Yes, I quite agree.

Soc. In like manner, I want you to tell me what part of justice is piety or holiness, that I may be able to tell Meletus not to do me injustice, or indict me for impiety, as I am now adequately instructed by you in the nature of piety or holiness, and their opposites.

Euth. Piety or holiness, Socrates, appears to me to be that part of justice which attends to the gods, as there is the other part of justice which attends to men.

[13] Soc. That is good, Euthyphro; yet still there is a little point about which I should like to have further information, What is the meaning of "attention"? For attention can hardly be used in the same sense when applied to the gods as when applied to other things. For instance, horses are said to require attention, and not every person is able to attend to them, but only a person skilled in horsemanship. Is it not so?

Euth. Certainly.

Soc. I should suppose that the art of horsemanship is the art of attending to horses?

Euth. Yes.

Soc. Nor is every one qualified to attend to dogs, but only the huntsman?

Euth. True.

Soc. And I should also conceive that the art of the huntsman is the art of attending to dogs?

Euth. Yes.

Soc. As the art of the oxherd is the art of attending to oxen?

Euth. Very true.

Soc. In like manner holiness or piety is the art of attending to the gods?—that would be your meaning, Euthyphro?

Euth. Yes.

Soc. And is not attention always designed for the good or benefit of that to which the attention is given? As in the case of horses, you may observe that when attended to by the horseman's art they are benefited and improved, are they not?

Euth. True.

Soc. As the dogs are benefited by the huntsman's art, and the oxen by the art of the oxherd, and all other things are tended or attended for their good and not for their hurt?

Euth. Certainly, not for their hurt.

Soc. But for their good?

Euth. Of course.

Soc. And does piety or holiness, which has been defined to be the art of attending to the gods, benefit or improve them? Would you say that when you do a holy act you make any of the gods better?

Euth. No, no; that was certainly not what I meant.

Soc. And I, Euthyphro, never supposed that you did. I asked you the question about the nature of the attention, because I thought that you did not.

Euth. You do me justice, Socrates; that is not the sort of attention which I mean.

Soc. Good: but I must still ask what is this attention to the gods which is called piety?

Euth. It is such, Socrates, as servants show to their masters.

Soc. I understand—a sort of ministration to the gods.

Euth. Exactly.

Soc. Medicine is also a sort of ministration or service, having in view the attainment of some object—would you not say of health?

Euth. I should.

Soc. Again, there is an art which ministers to the ship-builder with a view to the attainment of some result?

Euth. Yes, Socrates, with a view to the building of a ship.

Soc. As there is an art which ministers to the housebuilder with a view to the building of a house?

Euth. Yes.

Soc. And now tell me, my good friend, about the art which ministers to the gods: what work does that help to accomplish? For you must surely know if, as you say, you are of all men living the one who is best instructed in religion.

Euth. And I speak the truth, Socrates.

Soc. Tell me then, oh tell me—what is that fair work which the gods do by the help of our ministrations?

Euth. Many and fair, Socrates, are the works which they do.

[14] Soc. Why, my friend, and so are those of a general. But the chief of them is easily told. Would you not say that victory in war is the chief of them?

Euth. Certainly.

Soc. Many and fair, too, are the works of the husbandman, if I am not mistaken; but his chief work is the production of food from the earth?

Euth. Exactly.

Soc. And of the many and fair things done by the gods, which is the chief or principal one?

Euth. I have told you already, Socrates, that to learn all these things accurately will be very tiresome. Let me simply say that piety or holiness is learning how to please the gods in word and deed, by prayers and sacrifices. Such piety is the salvation of families and states, just as the impious, which is unpleasing to the gods, is their ruin and destruction.

Soc. I think that you could have answered in much fewer words the chief question which I asked, Euthyphro, if you had chosen. But I see plainly that you are not disposed to instruct me—clearly not: else why, when we reached the point, did you turn aside? Had you only answered me I should have truly learned of you by this time the nature of piety. Now, as the asker of a question is necessarily dependent on the answerer, whither he leads I must follow; and can only ask again, what is the pious, and what is piety? Do you mean that they are a sort of science of praying and sacrificing?

Euth. Yes, I do.

Soc. And sacrificing is giving to the gods, and prayer is asking of the gods?

Euth. Yes, Socrates.

Soc. Upon this view, then, piety is a science of asking and giving?

Euth. You understand me capitally, Socrates.

Soc. Yes, my friend; the reason is that I am a votary of your science, and give my mind to it, and therefore nothing which you say will be thrown away upon me. Please then to tell me, what is the nature of this service to the gods? Do you mean that we prefer requests and give gifts to them?

Euth. Yes, I do.

Soc. Is not the right way of asking to ask of them what we want?

Euth. Certainly.

Soc. And the right way of giving is to give to them in return what they want of us. There would be no meaning in an art which gives to any one that which he does not want.

Euth. Very true, Socrates.

Soc. Then piety, Euthyphro, is an art which gods and men have of doing business with one another?

Euth. That is an expression which you may use, if you like.

Soc. But I have no particular liking for anything but the truth. I wish, however, that you would tell me what benefit accrues to the gods from our gifts. There is no doubt about what they give to us; [15] for there is no good thing which they do not give; but how we can give any good thing to them in return is far from being equally clear. If they give everything and we give nothing, that must be an affair of business in which we have very greatly the advantage of them.

Euth. And do you imagine, Socrates, that any benefit accrues to the gods from our gifts?

Soc. But if not, Euthyphro, what is the meaning of gifts which are conferred by us upon the gods?

Euth. What else, but tributes of honour; and, as I was just now saying, what pleases them?

Soc. Piety, then, is pleasing to the gods, but not beneficial or dear to them?

Euth. I should say that nothing could be dearer.

Soc. Then once more the assertion is repeated that piety is dear to the gods?

Euth. Certainly.

Soc. And when you say this, can you wonder at your words not standing firm, but walking away? Will you accuse me of being the Daedalus who makes them walk away, not perceiving that there is another and far greater artist than Daedalus who makes them go round in a circle, and he is yourself; for the argument, as you will perceive, comes round to the same point. Were we not saying that the holy or pious was not the same with that which is loved of the gods? Have you forgotten?

Euth. I quite remember.

Soc. And are you not saying that what is loved of the gods is holy; and is not this the same as what is dear to them—do you see?

Euth. True.

Soc. Then either we were wrong in our former assertion; or, if we were right then, we are wrong now.

Euth. One of the two must be true.

Soc. Then we must begin again and ask, What is piety? That is an enquiry which I shall never be weary of pursuing as far as in me lies; and I entreat you not to scorn me, but to apply your mind to the utmost, and tell me the truth. For, if any man knows, you are he; and therefore I must detain you, like Proteus, until you tell. If you had not certainly known the nature of piety and impiety, I am confident that you would never, on behalf of a serf, have charged your aged father with murder. You would not have run such a risk of doing wrong in the sight of the gods, and you would have had too much respect for the opinions of men. I am sure, therefore, that you know the nature of piety and impiety. Speak out then, my dear Euthyphro, and do not hide your knowledge.

Euth. Another time, Socrates; for I am in a hurry, and must go now.

Soc. Alas! my companion, and will you leave me in despair? I was hoping that you would instruct me in the nature of piety and impiety; and then I might have cleared myself of Meletus and his indictment. *[16]* I would have told him that I had been enlightened by Euthyphro, and had given up rash innovations and speculations, in which I indulged only through ignorance, and that now I am about to lead a better life.

APOLOGY

❦❦❦❦❦❦❦❦❦❦❦❦❦❦

[17] How you, O Athenians, have been affected by my accusers, I cannot tell; but I know that they almost made me forget who I was—so persuasively did they speak; and yet they have hardly uttered a word of truth. But of the many falsehoods told by them, there was one which quite amazed me;—I mean when they said that you should be upon your guard and not allow yourselves to be deceived by the force of my eloquence. To say this, when they were certain to be detected as soon as I opened my lips and proved myself to be anything but a great speaker, did indeed appear to me most shameless—unless by the force of eloquence they mean the force of truth; for if such is their meaning, I admit that I am eloquent. But in how different a way from theirs! Well, as I was saying, they have scarcely spoken the truth at all; but from me you shall hear the whole truth: not, however, delivered after their manner in a set oration duly ornamented with words and phrases. No, by heaven! but I shall use the words and arguments which occur to me at the moment; for I am confident in the justice of my cause: at my time of life I ought not to be appearing before you, O men of Athens, in the character of a juvenile orator—let no one expect it of me. And I must beg of you to grant me a favour:—If I defend myself in my accustomed manner, and you hear me using the words which I have been in the habit of using in the agora, at the tables of the money-changers, or anywhere else, I would ask you not to be surprised, and not to interrupt me on this account. For I am more than seventy years of age, and appearing now for the first time in a court of law, I am quite a stranger to the language of the place; and therefore I would have you regard me as if I were really a stranger, [18] whom you would excuse if he spoke in his native tongue, and after the fashion of his country: —Am I making an unfair request of you?

Never mind the manner, which may or may not be good; but think only of the truth of my words, and give heed to that: let the speaker speak truly and the judge decide justly.

And first, I have to reply to the older charges and to my first accusers, and then I will go on to the later ones. For of old I have had many accusers, who have accused me falsely to you during many years; and I am more afraid of them than of Anytus and his associates, who are dangerous, too, in their own way. But far more dangerous are the others, who began when you were children, and took possession of your minds with their falsehoods, telling of one Socrates, a wise man, who speculated about the heaven above, and searched into the earth beneath, and made the worse appear the better cause. The disseminators of this tale are the accusers whom I dread; for their hearers are apt to fancy that such enquirers do not believe in the existence of the gods. And they are many, and their charges against me are of ancient date, and they were made by them in the days when you were more impressible than you are now—in childhood, or it may have been in youth—and the cause when heard went by default, for there was none to answer. And hardest of all, I do not know and cannot tell the names of my accusers; unless in the chance case of a Comic poet. All who from envy and malice have persuaded you—some of them having first convinced themselves—all this class of men are most difficult to deal with; for I cannot have them up here, and cross-examine them, and therefore I must simply fight with shadows in my own defence, and argue when there is no one who answers. I will ask you then to assume with me, as I was saying, that my opponents are of two kinds; one recent, the other ancient: and I hope that you will see the propriety of my answering the latter first, for these accusations you heard long before the others, and much oftener.

[*19*] Well, then, I must make my defence, and endeavor to clear away in a short time, a slander which has lasted a long time. May I succeed, if to succeed be for my good and yours, or likely to avail me in my cause! The task is not an easy one; I quite understand the nature of it. And so leaving the event with God, in obedience to the law I will now make my defence.

I will begin at the beginning, and ask what is the accusation which has given rise to the slander of me, and in fact has encouraged Meletus to prefer this charge against me. Well, what do the slanderers say? They shall be my prosecutors, and I will sum up their words in an affidavit: "Socrates is an evil-doer, and a curious person, who searches into things under the earth and in heaven, and he makes the worse appear the better cause; and he teaches the aforesaid doctrines to others." Such is the nature of the accusation: it is just what you have yourselves seen in the comedy of Aristophanes,[1] who has introduced a man whom he calls Socrates, going about and saying that he walks in air, and talking a deal of nonsense concerning matters of which I do not pretend to know either much or little—not that I mean to speak disparagingly of any one who is a student of natural philosophy. I should be very sorry if Meletus could bring so grave a charge against me. But the simple truth is, O Athenians, that I have nothing to do with physical speculations. Very many of those here present are witnesses to the truth of this, and to them I appeal. Speak then, you who have heard me, and tell your neighbours whether any of you have ever known me hold forth in few words or in many upon such matters. . . . You hear their answer. And from what they say of this part of the charge you will be able to judge of the truth of the rest.

As little foundation is there for the report that I am a teacher, and take money; this accusation has no more truth in it than the other. Although, if a man were really able to instruct mankind, to receive money for giving instruction would, in my opinion, be an honour to him. There is Gorgias of Leontium, and Prodicus of Ceos, and Hippias of Elis, who go the round of the cities, and are able to persuade the young men to leave their own citizens by whom they might be taught for nothing, [*20*] and come to them whom they not only pay, but are thankful if they may be allowed to pay them.

[1] Aristophanes, *Clouds,* 225 ff.

There is at this time a Parian philosopher residing in Athens, of whom I have heard; and I came to hear of him in this way:—I came across a man who has spent a world of money on the Sophists, Callias, the son of Hipponicus, and knowing that he had sons, I asked him: "Callias," I said "if your two sons were foals or calves, there would be no difficulty in finding some one to put over them; we should hire a trainer of horses, or a farmer probably, who would improve and perfect them in their own proper virtue and excellence; but as they are human beings, whom are you thinking of placing over them? Is there any one who understands human and political virtue? You must have thought about the matter, for you have sons; is there any one?" "There is," he said. "Who is he?" said I; "and of what country? and what does he charge?" "Evenus the Parian," he replied; "he is the man, and his charge is five minae." Happy is Evenus, I said to myself, if he really has this wisdom, and teaches at such a moderate charge. Had I the same, I should have been very proud and conceited; but the truth is that I have no knowledge of the kind.

I dare say, Athenians, that some one among you will reply, "Yes, Socrates, but what is the origin of these accusations which are brought against you; there must have been something strange which you have been doing? All these rumours and this talk about you would never have arisen if you had been like other men: tell us, then, what is the cause of them, for we should be sorry to judge hastily of you." Now I regard this as a fair challenge, and I will endeavour to explain to you the reason why I am called wise and have such an evil fame. Please to attend then. And although some of you may think that I am joking, I declare that I will tell you the entire truth. Men of Athens, this reputation of mine has come of a certain sort of wisdom which I possess. If you ask me what kind of wisdom, I reply, wisdom such as may perhaps be attained by man, for to that extent I am inclined to believe that I am wise; whereas the persons of whom I was speaking have a superhuman wisdom, which I may fail to describe, because I have it not myself; and he who says that I have, speaks falsely, and is taking away my character. And here, O men of Athens, I must beg you not to interrupt me, even if I seem to say something extravagant. For the word which I will speak is not mine. I will refer you to a witness who is worthy of credit; that witness shall be the God of Delphi—he will tell you about my wisdom, if I have any, and of what sort it is. You must have known Chaerephon; he was early a friend of mine, and also a friend of yours, *[21]* for he shared in the recent exile of the people, and returned with you. Well, Chaerephon, as you know, was very impetuous in all his doings, and he went to Delphi and boldly asked the oracle to tell him whether—as I was saying, I must beg you not to interrupt—he asked the oracle to tell him whether any one was wiser than I was, and the Pythian prophetess answered, that there was no man wiser. Chaerephon is dead himself; but his brother, who is in court, will confirm the truth of what I am saying.

Why do I mention this? Because I am going to explain to you why I have such an evil name. When I heard the answer, I said to myself, What can the god mean? and what is the interpretation of his riddle? for I know that I have no wisdom, small or great. What then can he mean when he says that I am the wisest of men? And yet he is a god, and cannot lie; that would be against his nature. After long consideration, I thought of a method of trying the question. I reflected that if I could only find a man wiser than myself, then I might go to the god with a refutation in my hand. I should say to him, "Here is a man who is wiser than I am; but you said that I was the wisest." Accordingly I went to one who had the reputation of wisdom, and observed him—his name I need not mention; he was a politician whom I selected for examination—and the result was as follows: When I began to talk with him, I could not help thinking that he was not really wise, although he was thought wise by many, and still wiser by himself; and thereupon I tried to explain to him that he thought himself wise, but was not really wise; and the consequence was that he hated me, and his enmity was shared by several who were present and heard me. So I left him, saying to myself, as I went away: Well, although I do not suppose that either of us knows anything really beautiful and good, I am better off than he is,—for he knows nothing, and thinks that he knows; I neither know nor think that I know. In this latter particular, then, I seem to have slightly the advantage of him. Then I went to another who had still higher pretensions to wisdom, and my conclusion was exactly the same. Whereupon I made another enemy of him, and of many others besides him.

Then I went to one man after another, being not unconscious of the enmity which I provoked, and I lamented and feared this: But necessity was laid upon me,—the word of God, I thought, ought to be considered first. And I said to myself, Go I must to all who appear to know, *[22]* and find out the meaning of the oracle. And I swear to you, Athenians, by the dog I swear!—for I must tell you the truth—the result of my mission was just this: I found that the men most in repute were all but the most foolish; and that others less esteemed were really wiser and better. I will tell you the tale of my wanderings and of the "Herculean" labours, as I may call them, which I endured only to find at last the oracle irrefutable. After the politicians, I went to the poets; tragic, dithyrambic, and all sorts. And there, I said to myself, you will be instantly detected; now you will find out that you are more ignorant than they are. Accordingly, I took them some of the most elaborate passages in their own writings, and asked what was the meaning of them—thinking that they would teach me something. Will you believe me? I am almost ashamed to confess the truth, but I must say that there is hardly a person present who would not have talked better about their poetry than they did themselves. Then I knew that not by wisdom do poets write poetry, but by a sort of genius and inspiration; they are like diviners or soothsayers who also say many fine things, but do not understand the meaning of them. The poets appeared to me to be much in the same case; and I further observed that upon the strength of their poetry they believed themselves to be the wisest of men in other things in which they were not wise. So I departed, conceiving myself to be superior to them for the same reason that I was superior to the politicians.

At last I went to the artisans, for I was conscious that I knew nothing at all, as I may say, and I was sure that they knew many fine things; and here I was not mistaken, for they did know many things of which I was ignorant, and in this they certainly were wiser than I was. But I observed that even the good artisans fell into the same error as the poets;—because they were good workmen they thought that they also knew all sorts of high matters, and this defect in them overshadowed their wisdom; and therefore I asked myself on behalf of the oracle, whether I would like to be as I was, neither having their knowledge nor their ignorance, or like them in both; and I made answer to myself and to the oracle that I was better off as I was.

This inquisition has led to my having many

enemies of the worst and most dangerous kind, [23] and has given occasion also to many calumnies. And I am called wise, for my hearers always imagine that I myself possess the wisdom which I find wanting in others: but the truth is, O men of Athens, that God only is wise; and by his answer he intends to show that the wisdom of men is worth little or nothing; he is not speaking of Socrates, he is only using my name by way of illustration, as if he said, He, O men, is the wisest, who, like Socrates, knows that his wisdom is in truth worth nothing. And so I go about the world, obedient to the god, and search and make enquiry into the wisdom of any one, whether citizen or stranger, who appears to be wise; and if he is not wise, then in vindication of the oracle I show him that he is not wise; and my occupation quite absorbs me, and I have no time to give either to any public matter of interest or to any concern of my own, but I am in utter poverty by reason of my devotion to the god.

There is another thing:—young men of the richer classes, who have not much to do, come about me of their own accord; they like to hear the pretenders examined, and they often imitate me, and proceed to examine others; there are plenty of persons, as they quickly discover, who think that they know something, but really know little or nothing; and then those who are examined by them instead of being angry with themselves are angry with me: This confounded Socrates, they say; this villainous misleader of youth!—and then if somebody asks them, Why, what evil does he practise or teach? they do not know, and cannot tell; but in order that they may not appear to be at a loss, they repeat the ready-made charges which are used against all philosophers about teaching things up in the clouds and under the earth, and having no gods, and making the worse appear the better cause; for they do not like to confess that their pretence of knowledge has been detected —which is the truth; and as they are numerous and ambitious and energetic, and are drawn up in battle array and have persuasive tongues, they have filled your ears with their loud and inveterate calumnies. And this is the reason why my three accusers, Meletus and Anytus and Lycon, have set upon me; Meletus, who has a quarrel with me on behalf of the poets; Anytus, on behalf of the craftsmen and politicians; [24] Lycon, on behalf of the rhetoricians: and as I said at the beginning, I cannot expect to get rid of such a mass of calumny all in a moment. And this, O men of Athens, is

the truth and the whole truth; I have concealed nothing, I have dissembled nothing. And yet, I know that my plainness of speech makes them hate me, and what is their hatred but a proof that I am speaking the truth?—Hence has arisen the prejudice against me; and this is the reason of it, as you will find out either in this or in any future enquiry.

I have said enough in my defence against the first class of my accusers; I turn to the second class. They are headed by Meletus, that good man and true lover of his country, as he calls himself. Against these, too, I must try to make a defence:—Let their affidavit be read: it contains something of this kind: It says that Socrates is a doer of evil, who corrupts the youth; and who does not believe in the gods of the state, but has other new divinities of his own. Such is the charge; and now let us examine the particular counts. He says that I am a doer of evil, and corrupt the youth; but I say, O men of Athens that Meletus is a doer of evil, in that he pretends to be in earnest when he is only in jest, and is so eager to bring men to trial from a pretended zeal and interest about matters in which he really never had the smallest interest. And the truth of this I will endeavour to prove to you.

Come hither, Meletus, and let me ask a question of you. You think a great deal about the improvement of youth?

Yes, I do.

Tell the judges, then, who is their improver; for you must know, as you have taken the pains to discover their corrupter, and are citing and accusing me before them. Speak, then, and tell the judges who their improver is.—Observe, Meletus, that you are silent, and have nothing to say. But is not this rather disgraceful, and a very considerable proof of what I was saying, that you have no interest in the matter? Speak up, friend, and tell us who their improver is.

The laws.

But that, my good sir, is not my meaning. I want to know who the person is, who, in the first place, knows the laws.

The judges, Socrates, who are present in court.

What, do you mean to say, Meletus, that they are able to instruct and improve youth?

Certainly they are.

What, all of them, or some only and not others?

All of them.

By the goddess Herè, that is good news! There are plenty of improvers, [25] then. And what do you say of the audience,—do they improve them?

Yes, they do.

And the senators?

Yes, the senators improve them.

But perhaps the members of the assembly corrupt them?—or do they too improve them?

They improve them.

Then every Athenian improves and elevates them; all with the exception of myself; and I alone am their corrupter? Is that what you affirm?

That is what I stoutly affirm.

I am very unfortunate if you are right. But suppose I ask you a question: How about horses? Does one man do them harm and all the world good? Is not the exact opposite the truth? One man is able to do them good, or at least not many;—the trainer of horses, that is to say, does them good, and others who have to do with them rather injure them? Is not that true, Meletus, of horses, or of any other animals? Most assuredly it is; whether you and Anytus say yes or no. Happy indeed would be the condition of youth if they had one corrupter only, and all the rest of the world were their improvers. But you, Meletus, have sufficiently shown that you never had a thought about the young: your carelessness is seen in your not caring about the very things which you bring against me.

And now, Meletus, I will ask you another question—by Zeus I will: Which is better, to live among bad citizens, or among good ones? Answer, friend, I say; the question is one which may be easily answered. Do not the good do their neighbours good, and the bad do them evil?

Certainly.

And is there any one who would rather be injured than benefited by those who live with him? Answer, my good friend, the law requires you to answer—does any one like to be injured?

Certainly not.

And when you accuse me of corrupting and deteriorating the youth, do you allege that I corrupt them intentionally or unintentionally?

Intentionally, I say.

But you have just admitted that the good do their neighbours good, and evil do them evil. Now, is that a truth which your superior wisdom has recognized thus early in life, and am I, at my age, in such darkness and ignorance as not to know that if a man with whom I have to live is corrupted by me, I am very likely to be harmed by him; and yet I corrupt him, and intentionally, too—so you say, although neither I nor any other human being is ever likely to be convinced by you. [26] But either I do not corrupt them, or I corrupt them unintentionally; and on either view of the case you lie. If my offense is unintentional, the law has no cognizance of unintentional offences: you ought to have taken me privately, and warned and admonished me; for if I had been better advised, I should have left off doing what I only did unintentionally—no doubt I should; but you would have nothing to say to me and refused to teach me. And now you bring me up in this court, which is a place not of instruction, but of punishment.

It will be very clear to you, Athenians, as I was saying, that Meletus has no care at all, great or small, about the matter. But still I should like to know, Meletus, in what I am affirmed to corrupt the young. I suppose you mean, as I infer from your indictment, that I teach them not to acknowledge the gods which the state acknowledges, but some other new divinities or spiritual agencies in their stead. These are the lessons by which I corrupt the youth, as you say.

Yes, that I say emphatically.

Then, by the gods, Meletus, of whom we are speaking, tell me and the court, in somewhat plainer terms, what you mean! for I do not as yet understand whether you affirm that I teach other men to acknowledge some gods, and therefore that I do believe in gods, and am not an entire atheist—this you do not lay to my charge,—but only you say that they are not the same gods which the city recognizes—the charge is that they are different gods. Or, do you mean that I am an atheist simply, and a teacher of atheism?

I mean the latter—that you are a complete atheist.

What an extraordinary statement! Why do you think so, Meletus? Do you mean that I do not believe in the godhead of the sun or moon, like other men?

I assure you, judges, that he does not: for he says that the sun is stone, and the moon earth.

Friend Meletus, you think that you are accusing Anaxagoras: and you have but a bad opinion of the judges, if you fancy them illiterate to such a degree as not to know that these doctrines are found in the books of Anaxagoras the Clazomenian, which are full of them. And so, forsooth, the youth are said to be taught them by Socrates, when there are not unfrequently exhibitions of them at the theatre (price of admission one drachma at the most); and they might pay their money, and laugh at Socrates if he pretends to father these extraordinary views. And so, Meletus, you really think that I do not believe in any god?

I swear by Zeus that you believe absolutely in none at all.

Nobody will believe you, Meletus, and I am pretty sure that you do not believe yourself. I cannot help thinking, men of Athens, that Meletus is reckless and impudent, and that he has written this indictment in a spirit of mere wantonness and youthful bravado. [27] Has he not compounded a riddle, thinking to try me? He said to himself:—I shall see whether the wise Socrates will discover my facetious contradiction, or whether I shall be able to deceive him and the rest of them. For he certainly does appear to me to contradict himself in the indictment as much as if he said that Socrates is guilty of not believing in the gods, and yet of believing in them—but this is not like a person who is in earnest.

I should like you, O men of Athens, to join me in examining what I conceive to be his inconsistency; and do you, Meletus, answer. And I must remind the audience of my request that they would not make a disturbance if I speak in my accustomed manner:

Did ever man, Meletus, believe in the existence of human things, and not of human beings? . . . I wish, men of Athens, that he would answer, and not be always trying to get up an interruption. Did ever any man believe in horsemanship, and not in horses? or in flute-playing, and not in flute-players? No, my friend; I will answer to you and to the court, as you refuse to answer for yourself. There is no man who ever did. But now please to answer the next question: Can a man believe in spiritual and divine agencies, and not in spirits or demigods?

He cannot.

How lucky I am to have extracted that answer, by the assistance of the court! But then you swear in the indictment that I teach and believe in divine or spiritual agencies (new or old, no matter for that); at any rate, I believe in spiritual agencies,—so you say and swear in the affidavit; and yet if I believe in divine beings, how can I help believing in spirits or demigods;—must I not? To be sure I must; and therefore I may assume that your silence gives consent. Now what are spirits or demigods? are they not either gods or the sons of gods?

Certainly they are.

But this is what I call the facetious riddle invented by you: the demigods or spirits are gods, and you say first that I do not believe in gods, and then again that I do believe in gods; that is, if I believe in demigods. For if the demigods are the illegitimate sons of gods, whether by the nymphs or by any other mothers, of whom they are said to be the sons—what human being will ever believe that there are no gods if they are the sons of gods? You might as well affirm the existence of mules, and deny that of horses and asses. Such nonsense, Meletus, could only have been intended by you to make trial of me. You have put this into the indictment because you had nothing real of which to accuse me. But no one who has a particle of understanding will ever be convinced by you that the same men can believe in divine and superhuman things, and yet not believe that there are gods and demigods and heroes. [28]

I have said enough in answer to the charge of Meletus: any elaborate defence is unnecessary; but I know only too well how many are the enmities which I have incurred, and this is what will be my destruction if I am destroyed; —not Meletus, nor yet Anytus, but the envy and detraction of the world, which has been the death of many good men, and will probably be the death of many more; there is no danger of my being the last of them.

Some one will say: And are you not ashamed, Socrates, of a course of life which is likely to bring you to an untimely end? To him I may fairly answer: There you are mistaken: a man who is good for anything ought not to calculate the chance of living or dying; he ought only to consider whether in doing anything he is doing right or wrong—acting the part of a good man or of a bad. Whereas, upon your view, the heroes who fell at Troy were not good for much, and the son of Thetis above all, who altogether despised danger in comparison with disgrace; and when he was so eager to slay Hector, his goddess mother said to him, that if he avenged his companion Patroclus, and slew Hector, he would die himself—"Fate," she said, in these or the like words, "waits for you next after Hector"; he, receiving this warning, utterly despised danger and death, and instead of fearing them, feared rather to live in dishonour, and not to avenge his friend. "Let me die forthwith," he replies, "and be avenged of my enemy, rather than abide here by the beaked ships, a laughing-stock and a burden of the earth." Had Achilles any thought of death and danger? For wherever a man's place is, whether the place which he has chosen or that in which he has been placed by a commander, there he ought to remain in the hour of danger; he should not think of death or of anything but of disgrace. And this, O men of Athens, is a true saying.

Strange, indeed, would be my conduct, O men of Athens, if I who, when I was ordered by the generals whom you chose to command me at Potidaea and Amphipolis and Delium, remained where they placed me, like any other man, facing death—if now, when, as I conceive and imagine, God orders me to fulfil the philosopher's mission of searching into myself and other men, I were to desert my post through fear of death, [29] or any other fear; that would indeed be strange, and I might justly be arraigned in court for denying the existence of the gods, if I disobeyed the oracle because I was afraid of death, fancying that I was wise when I was not wise. For the fear of death is indeed the pretence of wisdom, and not real wisdom, being a pretence of knowing the unknown; and no one knows whether death, which men in their fear apprehend to be the greatest evil, may not be the greatest good. Is not this ignorance of a disgraceful sort, the ignorance which is the conceit that man knows what he does not know? And in this respect only I believe myself to differ from men in general, and may perhaps claim to be wiser than they are:—that whereas I know but little of the world below, I do not suppose that I know: but I do know that injustice and disobedience to a better, whether God or man, is evil and dishonourable, and I will never fear or avoid a possible good rather than a certain evil. And therefore if you let me go now, and are not convinced by Anytus, who said that since I had been prosecuted I must be put to death (or if not that I ought never to have been prosecuted at all); and that if I escape now, your sons will all utterly be ruined by listening to my words—if you say to me, Socrates, this time we will not mind Anytus, and you shall be let off, but upon one condition, that you are not to enquire and speculate in this way any more, and that if you are caught doing so again you shall die;—if this was the condition on which you let me go, I should reply: Men of Athens, I honour and love you; but I shall obey God rather than you, and while I have life and strength I shall never cease from the practice and teaching of philosophy, exhorting any one whom I meet and say-

ing to him after my manner: You, my friend, —a citizen of the great and mighty and wise city of Athens,—are you not ashamed of heaping up the greatest amount of money and honour and reputation, and caring so little about wisdom and truth and the greatest improvement of the soul, which you never regard or heed at all? And if the person with whom I am arguing, says: Yes, but I do care; then I do not leave him or let him go at once; but I proceed to interrogate and examine and cross-examine him, and if I think that he has no virtue in him, but only says that he has, I reproach him with undervaluing the greater, and overvaluing the less. [30] And I shall repeat the same words to every one whom I meet, young and old, citizen and alien, but especially to the citizens, inasmuch as they are my brethren. For know that this is the command of God; and I believe that no greater good has ever happened in the state than my service to the God. For I do nothing but go about persuading you all, old and young alike, not to take thought for your persons or your properties, but first and chiefly to care about the greatest improvement of the soul. I tell you that virtue is not given by money, but that from virtue comes money and every other good of man, public as well as private. This is my teaching, and if this is the doctrine which corrupts the youth, I am a mischievous person. But if any one says that this is not my teaching, he is speaking an untruth. Wherefore, O men of Athens, I say to you, do as Anytus bids or not as Anytus bids, and either acquit me or not; but whichever you do, understand that I shall never alter my ways, not even if I have to die many times.

Men of Athens, do not interrupt, but hear me; there was an understanding between us that you should hear me to the end: I have something more to say, at which you may be inclined to cry out; but I believe that to hear me will be good for you, and therefore I beg that you will not cry out. I would have you know, that if you kill such an one as I am, you will injure yourselves more than you will injure me. Nothing will injure me, not Meletus nor yet Anytus—they cannot, for a bad man is not permitted to injure a better than himself. I do not deny that Anytus may, perhaps, kill him, or drive him into exile, or deprive him of civil rights; and he may imagine, and others may imagine, that he is inflicting a great injury upon him: but there I do not agree. For the evil of doing as he is doing—the evil of unjustly taking away the life of another—is greater far.

And now, Athenians, I am not going to argue for my own sake, as you may think, but for yours, that you may not sin against the God by condemning me, who am his gift to you. For if you kill me you will not easily find a successor to me, who, if I may use such a ludicrous figure of speech, am a sort of gadfly, given to the state by God; and the state is a great and noble steed who is tardy in his motions owing to his very size, and requires to be stirred into life. [31] I am that gadfly which God has attached to the state, and all day long and in all places am always fastening upon you, arousing and persuading and reproaching you. You will not easily find another like me, and therefore I would advise you to spare me. I dare say that you may feel out of temper (like a person who is suddenly awakened from sleep), and you think that you might easily strike me dead as Anytus advises, and then you would sleep on for the remainder of your lives, unless God in his care of you sent you another gadfly. When I say that I am given to you by God, the proof of my mission is this:—if I had been like other men, I should not have neglected all my own concerns or patiently seen the neglect of them during all these years, and have been doing yours, coming to you individually like a father or elder brother, exhorting you to regard virtue; such conduct, I say, would be unlike human nature. If I had gained anything, or if my exhortations had been paid, there would have been some sense in my doing so; but now, as you will perceive, not even the impudence of my accusers dares to say that I have ever exacted or sought pay of any one; of that they have no witness. And I have a sufficient witness to the truth of what I say—my poverty.

Some one may wonder why I go about in private giving advice and busying myself with the concerns of others, but do not venture to come forward in public and advise the state. I will tell you why. You have heard me speak at sundry times and in divers places of an oracle or sign which comes to me, and is the divinity which Meletus ridicules in the indictment. This sign, which is a kind of voice, first began to come to me when I was a child; it always forbids but never commands me to do anything which I am going to do. This is what deters me from being a politician. And rightly, as I think. For I am certain, O men of Athens, that if I had engaged in politics, I should have perished long ago, and done no good either to you or to myself. And do not be offended at my telling you the truth: for the truth is, that no man who

goes to war with you or any other multitude, honestly striving against the many lawless and unrighteous deeds which are done in a state, [32] will save his life; he who will fight for the right, if he would live even for a brief space, must have a private station and not a public one.

I can give you convincing evidence of what I say, not words only, but what you value far more—actions. Let me relate to you a passage of my own life which will prove to you that I should never have yielded to injustice from any fear of death, and that "as I should have refused to yield" I must have died at once. I will tell you a tale of the courts, not very interesting perhaps, but nevertheless true. The only office of state which I ever held, O men of Athens, was that of senator: the tribe Antiochis, which is my tribe, had the presidency at the trial of the generals who had not taken up the bodies of the slain after the battle of Arginusae; and you proposed to try them in a body, contrary to law, as you all thought afterwards; but at the time I was the only one of the Prytanes who was opposed to the illegality, and I gave my vote against you; and when the orators threatened to impeach and arrest me, and you called and shouted, I made up my mind that I would run the risk, having law and justice with me, rather than take part in your injustice because I feared imprisonment and death. This happened in the days of the democracy. But when the oligarchy of the Thirty was in power, they sent for me and four others into the rotunda, and bade us bring Leon the Salaminian from Salamis, as they wanted to put him to death. This was a specimen of the sort of commands which they were always giving with the view of implicating as many as possible in their crimes; and then I showed, not in word only but in deed, that, if I may be allowed to use such an expression, I cared not a straw for death, and that my great and only care was lest I should do an unrighteous or unholy thing. For the strong arm of that oppressive power did not frighten me into doing wrong; and when we came out of the rotunda the other four went to Salamis and fetched Leon, but I went quietly home. For which I might have lost my life, had not the power of the Thirty shortly afterwards come to an end. And many will witness to my words.

Now do you really imagine that I could have survived all these years, if I had led a public life, supposing that like a good man I had always maintained the right and had made justice, as I ought, the first thing? No indeed, men of Athens, neither I nor any other man. *[33]* But I have been always the same in all my actions, public as well as private, and never have I yielded any base compliance to those who are slanderously termed my disciples, or to any other. Not that I have any regular disciples. But if any one likes to come and hear me while I am pursuing my mission, whether he be young or old, he is not excluded. Nor do I converse only with those who pay; but any one, whether he be rich or poor, may ask and answer me and listen to my words; and whether he turns out to be a bad man or a good one, neither result can be justly imputed to me; for I never taught or professed to teach him anything. And if any one says that he has ever learned or heard anything from me in private which all the world has not heard, let me tell you that he is lying.

But I shall be asked, Why do people delight in continually conversing with you? I have told you already, Athenians, the whole truth about this matter: they like to hear the cross-examination of the pretenders to wisdom; there is amusement in it. Now this duty of cross-examining other men has been imposed upon me by God; and has been signified to me by oracles, visions, and in every way in which the will of divine power was ever intimated to any one. This is true, O Athenians; or, if not true, would be soon refuted. If I am or have been corrupting the youth, those of them who are now grown up and become sensible that I gave them bad advice in the days of their youth should come forward as accusers, and take their revenge; or if they do not like to come themselves, some of their relatives, fathers, brothers, or other kinsmen, should say what evil their families have suffered at my hands. Now is their time. Many of them I see in the court. There is Crito, who is of the same age and of the same deme with myself, and there is Critobulus his son, whom I also see. Then again there is Lysanias of Sphettus, who is the father of Aeschines—he is present; and also there is Antiphon of Cephisus, who is the father of Epigenes; and there are the brothers of several who have associated with me. There is Nicostratus the son of Theosdotides, and the brother of Theodotus (now Theodotus himself is dead, and therefore he, at any rate, will not seek to stop him); and there is Paralus the son of Demodocus, who had a brother Theages; and Adeimantus the son of Ariston, *[34]* whose brother Plato is present; and Aeantodorus, who is the brother of Apollodorus, whom I also see. I might mention a great many others, some of whom Meletus should have produced as witnesses in the course of his speech; and let him still produce them, if he has forgotten—I will make way for him. And let him say, if he has any testimony of the sort which he can produce. Nay, Athenians, the very opposite is the truth. For all these are ready to witness on behalf of the corrupter, of the injurer of their kindred, as Meletus and Anytus call me; not the corrupted youth only—there might have been a motive for that—but their uncorrupted elder relatives. Why should they too support me with their testimony? Why, indeed, except for the sake of truth and justice, and because they know that I am speaking the truth, and that Meletus is a liar.

Well, Athenians, this and the like of this is all the defence which I have to offer. Yet a word more. Perhaps there may be some one who is offended at me, when he calls to mind how he himself on a similar, or even a less serious occasion, prayed and entreated the judges with many tears, and how he produced his children in court, which was a moving spectacle, together with a host of relations and friends; whereas I, who am probably in danger of my life, will do none of these things. The contrast may occur to his mind, and he may be set against me, and vote in anger because he is displeased at me on this account. Now if there be such a person among you,—mind, I do not say that there is,—to him I may fairly reply: My friend, I am a man, and like other men, a creature of flesh and blood, and not "of wood or stone," as Homer says; and I have a family, yes, and sons, O Athenians, three in number, one almost a man, and two others who are still young; and yet I will not bring any of them hither in order to petition you for an acquittal. And why not? Not from any self-assertion or want of respect for you. Whether I am or am not afraid of death is another question, of which I will not now speak. But, having regard to public opinion, I feel that such conduct would be discreditable to myself, and to you, and to the whole state. One who has reached my years, and who has a name for wisdom, ought not to demean himself. Whether this opinion of me be deserved or not, at any rate the world has decided that Socrates is in some way superior to other men. *[35]* And if those among you who are said to be superior in wisdom and courage, and any other virtue, demean themselves in this way, how shameful is their conduct! I have seen men of reputation, when they have been condemned, behaving in the strangest manner: they seemed to fancy that they were going to suffer something dreadful if they died, and that they could be immortal if you only allowed them to live; and I think that such are a dishonour to the state, and that any stranger coming in would have said of them that the most eminent men of Athens, to whom the Athenians themselves give honour and command, are no better than women. And I say that these things ought not to be done by those of us who have a reputation; and if they are done, you ought not to permit them; you ought rather to show that you are far more disposed to condemn the man who gets up a doleful scene and makes the city ridiculous, than him who holds his peace.

But, setting aside the question of public opinion, there seems to be something wrong in asking a favour of a judge, and thus procuring an acquittal, instead of informing and convincing him. For his duty is, not to make a present of justice, but to give judgment; and he has sworn that he will judge according to the laws, and not according to his own good pleasure; and we ought not to encourage you, nor should you allow yourself to be encouraged, in this habit of perjury—there can be no piety in that. Do not then require me to do what I consider dishonourable and impious and wrong, especially now, when I am being tried for impiety on the indictment of Meletus. For if, O men of Athens, by force of persuasion and entreaty I could overpower your oaths, then I should be teaching you to believe that there are no gods, and in defending should simply convict myself of the charge of not believing in them. But that is not so—far otherwise. For I do believe that there are gods, and in a sense higher than that in which any of my accusers believe in them. And to you and to God I commit my cause, to be determined by you as is best for you and me.

....

There are many reasons why I am not grieved, O men of Athens, at the vote of condemnation. [36] I expected it, and am only surprised that the votes are so nearly equal; for I had thought that the majority against me would have been far larger; but now, had thirty votes gone over to the other side, I should have been acquitted. And I may say, I think, that I have escaped Meletus. I may say more; for without the assistance of Anytus and Lycon, any one may see that he would not have had a fifth part of the votes, as the law requires, in which case he would have incurred a fine of a thousand drachmae.

And so he proposes death as the penalty.

And what shall I propose on my part, O men of Athens? Clearly that which is my due. And what is my due? What return shall be made to the man who has never had the wit to be idle during his whole life; but has been careless of what the many care for—wealth, and family interests, and military offices, and speaking in the assembly, and magistracies, and plots, and parties. Reflecting that I was really too honest a man to be a politician and live, I did not go where I could do no good to you or to myself; but where I could do the greatest good privately to every one of you, thither I went, and sought to persuade every man among you that he must look to himself, and seek virtue and wisdom before he looks to his private interests, and look to the state before he looks to the interests of the state; and that this should be the order which he observes in all his actions. What shall be done to such an one? Doubtless some good thing, O men of Athens, if he has his reward; and the good should be of a kind suitable to him. What would be a reward suitable to a poor man who is your benefactor, and who desires leisure that he may instruct you? There can be no reward so fitting as maintenance in the Prytaneum, O men of Athens, a reward which he deserves far more than the citizen who has won the prize at Olympia in the horse or chariot race, whether the chariots were drawn by two horses or by many. For I am in want, and he has enough; and he only gives you the appearance of happiness, and I give you the reality. And if I am to estimate the penalty fairly, I should say that maintenance in the Prytaneum is the just return. [37]

Perhaps you think that I am braving you in what I am saying now, as in what I said before about the tears and prayers. But this is not so. I speak rather because I am convinced that I never intentionally wronged any one, although I cannot convince you—the time has been too short; if there were a law at Athens, as there is in other cities, that a capital cause should not be decided in one day, then I believe that I should have convinced you. But I cannot in a moment refute great slanders; and, as I am convinced that I never wronged another, I will assuredly not wrong myself. I will not say of myself that I deserve any evil, or propose any penalty. Why should I? Because I am afraid of the penalty of death which Meletus proposes? When I do not know whether death is a good or an evil, why should I propose a penalty which would certainly be an evil? Shall I say imprisonment? And why should I live in prison, and be the slave of the magistrates of the year—of the Eleven? Or shall the penalty be a fine, and imprisonment until the fine is paid? There is the same objection. I should have to lie in prison, for money I have none, and cannot pay. And if I say exile (and this may possibly be the penalty which you will affix), I must indeed be blinded by the love of life, if I am so irrational as to expect that when you, who are my own citizens, cannot endure my discourses and words, and have found them so grievous and odious that you will have no more of them, others are likely to endure me. No indeed, men of Athens, that is not very likely. And what a life should I lead, at my age, wandering from city to city, ever changing my place of exile, and always being driven out! For I am quite sure that wherever I go, there, as here, the young men will flock to me; and if I drive them away, their elders will drive me out at their request; and if I let them come, their fathers and friends will drive me out for their sakes.

Some one will say: Yes, Socrates, but cannot you hold your tongue, and then you may go into a foreign city, and no one will interfere with you? Now I have great difficulty in making you understand my answer to this. For if I tell you that to do as you say would be a disobedience to the God, and therefore that I cannot hold my tongue, [38] you will not believe that I am serious; and if I say again that daily to discourse about virtue, and of those other things about which you hear me examining myself and others, is the greatest good of man, and that the unexamined life is not worth living, you are still less likely to believe me. Yet I say what is true, although a thing of which it is hard for me to persuade you. Also, I have never been accustomed to think that I deserve to suffer any harm. Had I money I might have estimated the offence at what I was able to pay, and not have been much the worse. But I have none, and therefore I must ask you to proportion the fine to my means. Well, perhaps I could afford a mina, and therefore I propose that penalty: Plato, Crito, Critobulus, and Apollodorus, my friends here, bid me say thirty minae, and they will be the sureties. Let thirty minae be the penalty; for which sum they will be ample security to you.

■■■■■■■■■■■■■■■■■■■■■■■■

Not much time will be gained, O Athenians, in return for the evil name which you will get from the detractors of the city, who will say that you killed Socrates, a wise man; for they will call me wise, even although I am not wise, when they want to reproach you. If you had waited a little while, your desire would have been fulfilled in the course of nature. For I am far advanced in years, as you may perceive, and not far from death. I am speaking now not to all of you, but only to those who have condemned me to death. And I have another thing to say to them: You think that I was convicted because I had no words of the sort which would have procured my acquittal—I mean, if I had thought fit to leave nothing undone or unsaid. Not so; the deficiency which led to my conviction was not of words—certainly not. But I had not the boldness or impudence or inclination to address you as you would have liked me to do, weeping and wailing and lamenting, and saying and doing many things which you have been accustomed to hear from others, and which, as I maintain, are unworthy of me. I thought at the time that I ought not to do anything common or mean when in danger: nor do I now repent of the style of my defence; I would rather die having spoken after my manner, than speak in your manner and live. For neither in war nor yet at law ought I or any man to use every way of escaping death. [39] Often in battle there can be no doubt that if a man will throw away his arms, and fall on his knees before his pursuers, he may escape death; and in other dangers there are other ways of escaping death, if a man is willing to say and do anything. The difficulty, my friends, is not to avoid death, but to avoid unrighteousness; for that runs faster than death. I am old and move slowly, and the slower runner has overtaken me, and my accursers are keen and quick, and the faster runner, who is unrighteousness, has overtaken them. And now I depart hence condemned by you to suffer the penalty of death,—they too go their ways condemned by the truth to suffer the penalty of villainy and wrong; and I must abide by my award—let them abide by theirs. I suppose that these things may be regarded as fated,—and I think that they are well.

And now, O men who have condemned me, I would fain prophesy to you; for I am about to die, and in the hour of death men are gifted with prophetic power. And I prophesy to you who are my murderers, that immediately after my departure punishment far heavier than you have inflicted on me will surely await you. Me you have killed because you wanted to escape the accuser, and not to give an account of your lives. But that will not be as you suppose: far otherwise. For I say that there will be more accusers of you than there are now; accusers whom hitherto I have restrained: and as they are younger they will be more inconsiderate with you, and you will be more offended at them. If you think that by killing men you can prevent some one from censuring your evil lives, you are mistaken; that is not a way of escape which is either possible or honourable; the easiest and the noblest way is not to be disabling others, but to be improving yourselves. This is the prophecy which I utter before my departure to the judges who have condemned me.

Friends, who would have acquitted me, I would like also to talk with you about the thing which has come to pass, while the magistrates are busy, and before I go to the place at which I must die. Stay then a little, for we may as well talk with one another while there is time. [40] You are my friends, and I should like to show you the meaning of this event which has happened to me. O my judges—for you I may truly call judges—I should like to tell you of a wonderful circumstance. Hitherto the divine faculty of which the internal oracle is the source has constantly been in the habit of opposing me even about trifles, if I was going to make a slip or error in any matter; and now as you see there has come upon me that which may be thought, and is generally believed to be, the last and worst evil. But the oracle made no sign of opposition, either when I was leaving my house in the morning, or when I was on my way to the court, or while I was speaking, at anything which I was going to say; and yet I have often been stopped in the middle of a speech, but now in nothing I either said or did touching the matter in hand has the oracle opposed me. What do I take to be the explanation of this silence? I will tell you. It is an intimation that what has happened to me is a good, and that those of us who think that death is an evil are in error. For the customary sign would surely have opposed me had I been going to evil and not to good.

Let us reflect in another way, and we shall see that there is great reason to hope that death is a good; for one of two things—either death is a state of nothingness and utter unconsciousness, or, as men say, there is a change and migration of the soul from this world to another. Now if you suppose that there is no consciousness, but a sleep like the sleep of him who is undisturbed even by dreams, death will be an unspeakable gain. For if a person were to select the night in which his sleep was undisturbed even by dreams, and were to compare with this the other days and nights of his life, and then were to tell us how many days and nights he had passed in the course of his life better and more pleasantly than this one, I think that any man, I will not say a private man, but even the great king will not find many such days or nights, when compared with the others. Now if death be of such a nature, I say that to die is gain; for eternity is then only a single night. But if death is the journey to another place, and there, as men say, all the dead abide, what good, O my friends and judges, can be greater than this? If indeed when the pilgrim arrives in the world below, [41] he is delivered from the professors of justice in this world, and finds the true judges who are said to give judgment there, Minos and Rhadamanthus and Aeacus and Triptolemus, and other sons of God who were righteous in their own life, that pilgrimage will be worth making. What would not a man give if he might converse with Orpheus and Musaeus and Hesiod and Homer? Nay, if this be true, let me die again and again. I myself, too, shall have a wonderful interest in there meeting and conversing with Palamedes, and Ajax the son of Telamon, and any other ancient hero who has suffered death through an unjust judgment; and there will be no small pleasure, as I think, in comparing my own sufferings with theirs. Above all, I shall then be able to continue my search into true and false knowledge; as in this world, so also in the next; and I shall find out who is wise, and who pretends to be wise, and is not. What would not a man give, O judges, to be able to examine the leader of the great Trojan expedition; or Odysseus or Sisyphus, or numberless others, men and women too! What infinite delight would there be in conversing with them and asking them questions! In another world they do not put a man to death for asking questions: assuredly not. For besides being happier than we are, they will be immortal, if what is said is true.

Wherefore, O judges, be of good cheer about death, and know of a certainty, that no evil can happen to a good man, either in life or after death. He and his are not neglected by the gods; nor has my own approaching end happened by mere chance. But I see clearly that the time had arrived when it was better for me to die and be released from trouble; wherefore the oracle gave no sign. For which reason, also, I am not angry with my condemners, or with my accusers; they have done me no harm, although they did not mean to do me any good; and for this I may gently blame them.

Still I have a favour to ask of them. When my sons are grown up, I would ask you, O my friends, to punish them; and I would have you trouble them, as I have troubled you, if they seem to care about riches, or anything, more than about virtue; or if they pretend to be something when they are really nothing,—then

reprove them, as I have reproved you, for not caring about that for which they ought to care, and thinking that they are something when they are really nothing. [42] And if you do this, both I and my sons will have received justice at your hands.

The hour of departure has arrived, and we go our ways—I to die, and you to live. Which is better God only knows.

CRITO

PERSONS OF THE DIALOGUE: SOCRATES; CRITO. *Scene: The Prison of Socrates*

~~~~~~~~~~~~~~~~~~~~~~~~

[43] *Socrates.* WHY have you come at this hour, Crito? it must be quite early?

Crito. Yes, certainly.

Soc. What is the exact time?

Cr. The dawn is breaking.

Soc. I wonder that the keeper of the prison would let you in.

Cr. He knows me, because I often come, Socrates; moreover, I have done him a kindness.

Soc. And are you only just arrived?

Cr. No, I came some time ago.

Soc. Then why did you sit and say nothing, instead of at once awakening me?

Cr. I should not have liked myself, Socrates, to be in such great trouble and unrest as you are—indeed I should not: I have been watching with amazement your peaceful slumbers; and for that reason I did not awake you, because I wished to minimize the pain. I have always thought you to be of a happy disposition; but never did I see anything like the easy, tranquil manner in which you bear this calamity.

Soc. Why, Crito, when a man has reached my age he ought not to be repining at the approach of death.

Cr. And yet other old men find themselves in similar misfortunes, and age does not prevent them from repining.

Soc. That is true. But you have not told me why you come at this early hour.

Cr. I come to bring you a message which is sad and painful; not, as I believe, to yourself, but to all of us who are your friends, and saddest of all to me.

Soc. What? Has the ship come from Delos, on the arrival of which I am to die?

Cr. No, the ship has not actually arrived, but she will probably be here to-day, as persons who have come from Sunium tell me that they left her there; and therefore to-morrow, Socrates, will be the last day of your life.

Soc. Very well, Crito; if such is the will of God, I am willing; but my belief is that there will be a delay of a day.

[44] *Cr.* Why do you think so?

Soc. I will tell you. I am to die on the day after the arrival of the ship.

Cr. Yes; that is what the authorities say.

Soc. But I do not think that the ship will be here until to-morrow; this I infer from a vision which I had last night, or rather only just now, when you fortunately allowed me to sleep.

Cr. And what was the nature of the vision?

Soc. There appeared to me the likeness of a woman, fair and comely, clothed in bright raiment, who called to me and said: O Socrates,

The third day hence to fertile Phthia shalt thou go.

Cr. What a singular dream, Socrates!

Soc. There can be no doubt about the meaning, Crito, I think.

Cr. Yes; the meaning is only too clear. But, oh! my beloved Socrates, let me entreat you once more to take my advice and escape. For if you die I shall not only lose a friend who can never be replaced, but there is another evil: people who do not know you and me will believe that I might have saved you if I had been willing to give money, but that I did not care. Now, can there be a worse disgrace than this— that I should be thought to value money more than the life of a friend? For the many will not be persuaded that I wanted you to escape, and that you refused.

Soc. But why, my dear Crito, should we care about the opinion of the many? Good men, and they are the only persons who are worth considering, will think of these things truly as they occurred.

Cr. But you see, Socrates, that the opinion of the many must be regarded, for what is now happening shows that they can do the greatest evil to any one who has lost their good opinion.

Soc. I only wish it were so, Crito; and that the many could do the greatest evil; for then they would also be able to do the greatest good—and what a fine thing this would be! But in reality they can do neither; for they cannot make a man either wise or foolish; and whatever they do is the result of chance.

Cr. Well, I will not dispute with you; but please to tell me, Socrates, whether you are not acting out of regard to me and your other friends: are you not afraid that if you escape from prison we may get into trouble with the informers for having stolen you away, and lose either the whole or a great part of our property; or that even a worse evil may happen to us? [45] Now, if you fear on our account, be at ease; for in order to save you, we ought surely to run this, or even a greater risk; be persuaded, then, and do as I say.

Soc. Yes, Crito, that is one fear which you mention, but by no means the only one.

Cr. Fear not—there are persons who are willing to get you out of prison at no great cost; and as for the informers, they are far from being exorbitant in their demands—a little money will satisfy them. My means, which are certainly ample, are at your service, and if you have a scruple about spending all mine, here are strangers who will give you the use of theirs; and one of them, Simmias the Theban, has brought a large sum of money for this very purpose; and Cebes and many others are prepared to spend their money in helping you to escape. I say, therefore, do not hesitate on our account, and do not say, as you did in the court,[1] that you will have a difficulty in knowing what to do with yourself anywhere else. For men will love you in other places to which you may go, and not in Athens only; there are friends of mine in Thessaly, if you like to go to them, who will value and protect you, and no Thessalian will give you any trouble. Nor can I think that you are at all justified, Socrates, in betraying your own life when you might be saved; in acting thus you are playing into the hands of your enemies, who are hurrying on

your destruction. And further I should say that you are deserting your own children; for you might bring them up and educate them; instead of which you go away and leave them, and they will have to take their chance; and if they do not meet with the usual fate of orphans, there will be small thanks to you. No man should bring children into the world who is unwilling to persevere to the end in their nurture and education. But you appear to be choosing the easier part, not the better and manlier, which would have been more becoming in one who professes to care for virtue in all his actions, like yourself. And indeed, I am ashamed not only of you, but of us who are your friends, when I reflect that the whole business will be attributed entirely to our want of courage. The trial need never have come on, or might have been managed differently; and this last act, or crowning folly, will seem to have occurred through our negligence and cowardice, who might have saved you, [46] if we had been good for anything; and you might have saved yourself, for there was no difficulty at all. See now, Socrates, how sad and discreditable are the consequences, both to us and you. Make up your mind then, or rather have your mind already made up, for the time of deliberation is over, and there is only one thing to be done, which must be done this very night, and if we delay at all will be no longer practicable or possible; I beseech you therefore, Socrates, be persuaded by me, and do as I say.

Soc. Dear Crito, your zeal is invaluable, if a right one; but if wrong, the greater the zeal the greater the danger; and therefore we ought to consider whether I shall or shall not do as you say. For I am and always have been one of those natures who must be guided by reason, whatever the reason may be which upon reflection appears to me to be the best; and now that this chance has befallen me, I cannot repudiate my own words: the principles which I have hitherto honoured and revered I still honour, and unless we can at once find other and better principles, I am certain not to agree with you; no, not even if the power of the multitude could inflict many more imprisonments, confiscations, deaths, frightening us like children with hobgoblin terrors.[2] What will be the fairest way of considering the question? Shall I return to your old argument about the opinions of men?—we were saying that some of them are to be regarded, and others not. Now were we right in maintaining this before I was

[1] Cf. *Apology*, 37.

[2] Cf. *Apology*, 30.

condemned? And has the argument which was once good now proved to be talk for the sake of talking—mere childish nonsense? That is what I want to consider with your help, Crito: —whether, under my present circumstances, the argument appears to be in any way different or not; and is to be allowed by me or disallowed. That argument, which, as I believe, is maintained by many persons of authority, was to the effect, as I was saying, that the opinions of some men are to be regarded, and of other men not to be regarded. Now you, Crito, are not going to die to-morrow—at least, [47] there is no human probability of this—and therefore you are disinterested and not liable to be deceived by the circumstances in which you are placed. Tell me then, whether I am right in saying that some opinions, and the opinions of some men only, are to be valued, and that other opinions, and the opinions of other men, are not to be valued. I ask you whether I was right in maintaining this?

Cr. Certainly.

Soc. The good are to be regarded, and not the bad?

Cr. Yes.

Soc. And the opinions of the wise are good, and the opinions of the unwise are evil?

Cr. Certainly.

Soc. And what was said about another matter? Is the pupil who devotes himself to the practice of gymnastics supposed to attend to the praise and blame and opinion of every man, or of one man only—his physician or trainer, whoever he may be?

Cr. Of one man only.

Soc. And he ought to fear the censure and welcome the praise of that one only, and not of the many?

Cr. Clearly so.

Soc. And he ought to act and train, and eat and drink in the way which seems good to his single master who has understanding, rather than according to the opinion of all other men put together?

Cr. True.

Soc. And if he disobeys and disregards the opinion and approval of the one, and regards the opinion of the many who have no understanding, will he not suffer evil?

Cr. Certainly he will.

Soc. And what will the evil be, whither tending and what affecting, in the disobedient person?

Cr. Clearly, affecting the body; that is what is destroyed by the evil.

Soc. Very good; and is not this true, Crito, of other things which we need not separately enumerate? In questions of just and unjust, fair and foul, good and evil, which are the subjects of our present consultation, ought we to follow the opinion of the many and to fear them; or the opinion of the one man who has understanding? ought we not to fear and reverence him more than all the rest of the world: and if we desert him shall we not destroy and injure that principle in us which may be assumed to be improved by justice and deteriorated by injustice;—there is such a principle?

Cr. Certainly there is, Socrates.

Soc. Take a parallel instance:—if, acting under the advice of those who have no understanding, we destroy that which is improved by health and is deteriorated by disease, would life be worth having? And that which has been destroyed is—the body?

Cr. Yes.

Soc. Could we live, having an evil and corrupted body?

Cr. Certainly not.

Soc. And will life be worth having, if that higher part of man be destroyed, which is improved by justice and depraved by injustice? Do we suppose that principle, [48] whatever it may be in man, which has to do with justice and injustice, to be inferior to the body?

Cr. Certainly not.

Soc. More honourable than the body?

Cr. Far more.

Soc. Then, my friend, we must not regard what the many say of us: but what he, the one man who has understanding of just and unjust, will say, and what the truth will say. And therefore you begin in error when you advise that we should regard the opinion of the many about just and unjust, good and evil, honourable and dishonourable.—"Well," some one will say, "but the many can kill us."

Cr. Yes, Socrates; that will clearly be the answer.

Soc. And it is true: but still I find with surprise that the old argument is unshaken as ever. And I should like to know whether I may say the same of another proposition—that not life, but a good life, is to be chiefly valued?

Cr. Yes, that also remains unshaken.

Soc. And a good life is equivalent to a just and honourable one—that holds also?

Cr. Yes, it does.

Soc. From these premises I proceed to argue the question whether I ought or ought not to try and escape without the consent of the

Athenians: and if I am clearly right in escaping, then I will make the attempt; but if not, I will abstain. The other considerations which you mention, of money and loss of character and the duty of educating one's children, are, I fear, only the doctrines of the multitude, who would be as ready to restore people to life, if they were able, as they are to put them to death—and with as little reason. But now, since the argument has thus far prevailed, the only question which remains to be considered is, whether we shall do rightly either in escaping or in suffering others to aid in our escape and paying them in money and thanks, or whether in reality we shall not do rightly; and if the latter, then death or any other calamity which may ensue on my remaining here must not be allowed to enter into the calculation.

Cr. I think that you are right, Socrates; how then shall we proceed?

Soc. Let us consider the matter together, and do you either refute me if you can, and I will be convinced; or else cease, my dear friend, from repeating to me that I ought to escape against the wishes of the Athenians: for I highly value your attempts to persuade me to do so, but I may not be persuaded against my own better judgment. [49] And now please to consider my first position, and try how you can best answer me.

Cr. I will.

Soc. Are we to say that we are never intentionally to do wrong, or that in one way we ought and in another we ought not to do wrong, or is doing wrong always evil and dishonourable, as I was just now saying, and has been already acknowledged by us? Are all our former admissions which were made within a few days to be thrown away? And have we, at our age, been earnestly discoursing with one another all our life long only to discover that we are no better than children? Or, in spite of the opinion of the many, and in spite of consequences whether better or worse, shall we insist on the truth of what was then said, that injustice is always an evil and dishonour to him who acts unjustly? Shall we say so or not?

Cr. Yes.

Soc. Then we must do no wrong?

Cr. Certainly not.

Soc. Nor when injured injure in return, as the many imagine; for we must injure no one at all? [1]

Cr. Clearly not.

Soc. Again, Crito, may we do evil?

[1] Cf. *Republic,* i. 335.

Cr. Surely not, Socrates.

Soc. And what of doing evil in return for evil, which is the morality of the many—is that just or not?

Cr. Not just.

Soc. For doing evil to another is the same as injuring him?

Cr. Very true.

Soc. Then we ought not to retaliate or render evil for evil to any one, whatever evil we may have suffered from him. But I would have you consider, Crito, whether you really mean what you are saying. For this opinion has never been held, and never will be held, by any considerable number of persons; and those who are agreed and those who are not agreed upon this point have no common ground, and can only despise one another when they see how widely they differ. Tell me, then, whether you agree with and assent to my first principle, that neither injury nor retaliation nor warding off evil by evil is ever right. And shall that be the premiss of our argument? Or do you decline and dissent from this? For so I have ever thought, and continue to think; but, if you are of another opinion, let me hear what you have to say. If, however, you remain of the same mind as formerly, I will proceed to the next step.

Cr. You may proceed, for I have not changed my mind.

Soc. Then I will go on to the next point, which may be put in the form of a question:— Ought a man to do what he admits to be right, or ought he to betray the right?

Cr. He ought to do what he thinks right.

Soc. But if this is true, what is the application? In leaving the prison against the will of the Athenians, [50] do I wrong any? or rather do I not wrong those whom I ought least to wrong? Do I not desert the principles which were acknowledged by us to be just—what do you say?

Cr. I cannot tell, Socrates; for I do not know.

Soc. Then consider the matter in this way:— Imagine that I am about to play truant (you may call the proceeding by any name which you like), and the laws and the government come and interrogate me: "Tell us, Socrates," they say; "what are you about? are you not going by an act of yours to overturn us—the laws, and the whole state, as far as in you lies? Do you imagine that a state can subsist and not be overthrown, in which the decisions of law have no power, but are set aside and trampled upon by individuals?" What will be our answer, Crito, to these and the like words? Any one, and especially a rhetorician, will have a good deal to say on behalf of the law which requires a sentence to be carried out. He will argue that this law should not be set aside; and shall we reply, "Yes; but the state has injured us and given an unjust sentence." Suppose I say that?

Cr. Very good, Socrates.

Soc. "And was that our agreement with you?" the law would answer; "or were you to abide by the sentence of the state?" And if I were to express my astonishment at their words, the law would probably add: "Answer, Socrates, instead of opening your eyes—you are in the habit of asking and answering questions. Tell us,—What complaint have you to make against us which justifies you in attempting to destroy us and the state? In the first place did we not bring you into existence? Your father married your mother by our aid and begat you. Say whether you have any objection to urge against those of us who regulate marriage?" None, I should reply. "Or against those of us who after birth regulate the nurture and education of children, in which you also were trained? Were not the laws, which have the charge of education, right in commanding your father to train you in music and gymnastic?" Right, I should reply. "Well then, since you were brought into the world and nurtured and educated by us, can you deny in the first place that you are our child and slave, as your fathers were before you? And if this is true you are not on equal terms with us; nor can you think that you have a right to do to us what we are doing to you. Would you have any right to strike or revile or do any other evil to your father or your master, if you had one, because you have been struck or reviled by him, or received some other evil at his hands?—you would not say this? [51] And because we think right to destroy you, do you think that you have any right to destroy us in return, and your country as far as in you lies? Will you, O professor of true virtue, pretend that you are justified in this? Has a philosopher like you failed to discover that our country is more to be valued and higher and holier far than mother or father or any ancestor, and more to be regarded in the eyes of the gods and of men of understanding? also to be soothed, and gently and reverently entreated when angry, even more than a father, and either to be persuaded, or if not persuaded, to be obeyed? And when we are punished by her, whether with imprisonment or stripes, the punishment is to be endured in silence: and if she leads us to wounds or death in battle, thither we follow as is right; neither may any one yield or retreat or leave his rank, but whether in battle or in a court of law, or in any other place, he must do what his city and his country order him; or he must change their view of what is just: and if he may do no violence to his father or mother, much less may he do violence to his country." What answer shall we make to this, Crito? Do the laws speak truly, or do they not?

Cr. I think that they do.

Soc. Then the laws will say, "Consider, Socrates, if we are speaking truly that in your present attempt you are going to do us an injury. For, having brought you into the world, and nurtured and educated you, and given you and every other citizen a share in every good which we had to give, we further proclaim to any Athenian by the liberty which we allow him, that if he does not like us when he has become of age and has seen the ways of the city, and made our acquaintance, he may go where he pleases and take his goods with him. None of us laws will forbid him or interfere with him. Any one who does not like us and the city, and who wants to emigrate to a colony or to any other city, may go where he likes, retaining his property. But he who has experience of the manner in which we order justice and administer the state, and still remains, has entered into an implied contract that he will do as we command him. And he who disobeys us is, as we maintain, thrice wrong; first, because in disobeying us he is disobeying his parents; secondly, because we are the authors of his education; thirdly, because he has made an agreement with us that he will duly obey our commands; [52] and he neither obeys them nor convinces us that our commands are unjust; and we do not rudely impose them, but give him the alternative of obeying or convincing us;—that is what we offer, and he does neither.

"These are the sort of accusations to which, as we were saying, you, Socrates, will be exposed if you accomplish your intentions; you above all other Athenians." Suppose now I ask, why I rather than anybody else? they will justly retort upon me that I above all other men have acknowledged the agreement. "There is clear proof," they will say, "Socrates, that we and the city were not displeasing to you. Of all Athenians you have been the most constant resident in the city, which, as you never leave, you may be supposed to love.[1] For you never

[1] Cf. *Phaedrus,* 230.

went out of the city either to see the games, except once when you went to the Isthmus, or to any other place unless when you were on military service; nor did you travel as other men do. Nor had you any curiosity to know other states or their laws: your affections did not go beyond us and our state; we were your special favourites, and you acquiesced in our government of you; and here in this city you begat your children, which is a proof of your satisfaction. Moreover, you might in the course of the trial, if you had liked, have fixed the penalty at banishment; the state which refuses to let you go now would have let you go then. But you pretended that you preferred death to exile,[1] and that you were not unwilling to die. And now you have forgotten these fine sentiments, and pay no respect to us the laws, of whom you are the destroyer; and are doing what only a miserable slave would do, running away and turning your back upon the compacts and agreements which you made as a citizen. And first of all answer this very question: Are we right in saying that you agreed to be governed according to us in deed, and not in word only? Is that true or not?" How shall we answer, Crito? Must we not assent?

Cr. We cannot help it, Socrates.

Soc. Then will they not say: "You, Socrates, are breaking the covenants and agreements which you made with us at your leisure, not in any haste or under any compulsion or deception, but after you have had seventy years to think of them, during which time you were at liberty to leave the city, if we were not to your mind, or if our covenants appeared to you to be unfair. You had your choice, and might have gone either to Lacedaemon or Crete, both which states are often praised by you for their good government, *[53]* or to some other Hellenic or foreign state. Whereas you, above all other Athenians, seemed to be so fond of the state, or, in other words, of us her laws (and who would care about a state which has no laws?), that you never stirred out of her; the halt, the blind, the maimed were not more stationary in her than you were. And now you run away and forsake your agreements. Not so, Socrates, if you will take our advice; do not make yourself ridiculous by escaping out of the city.

"For just consider, if you transgress and err in this sort of way, what good will you do either to yourself or to your friends? That your friends will be driven into exile and deprived

[1] Cf. *Apology*, 37.

of citizenship, or will lose their property, is tolerably certain; and you yourself, if you fly to one of the neighbouring cities, as, for example, Thebes or Megara, both of which are well governed, will come to them as an enemy, Socrates, and their government will be against you, and all patriotic citizens will cast an evil eye upon you as a subverter of the laws, and you will confirm in the minds of the judges the justice of their own condemnation of you. For he who is a corrupter of the laws is more than likely to be a corrupter of the young and foolish portion of mankind. Will you then flee from well-ordered cities and virtuous men? and is existence worth having on these terms? Or will you go to them without shame, and talk to them, Socrates? And what will you say to them? What you say here about virtue and justice and institutions and laws being the best things among men? Would that be decent of you? Surely not. But if you go away from well-governed states to Crito's friends in Thessaly, where there is great disorder and licence, they will be charmed to hear the tale of your escape from prison, set off with ludicrous particulars of the manner in which you were wrapped in a goatskin or some other disguise, and metamorphosed as the manner is of runaways; but will there be no one to remind you that in your old age you were not ashamed to violate the most sacred laws from a miserable desire of a little more life? Perhaps not, if you keep them in a good temper; but if they are out of temper you will hear many degrading things; you will live, but how?—as the flatterer of all men, and the servant of all men; and doing what?—eating and drinking in Thessaly, having gone abroad in order that you may get a dinner. And where will be your fine sentiments about justice and virtue? *[54]* Say that you wish to live for the sake of your children—you want to bring them up and educate them—will you take them into Thessaly and deprive them of Athenian citizenship? Is this the benefit which you will confer upon them? Or are you under the impression that they will be better cared for and educated here if you are still alive, although absent from them; for your friends will take care of them? Do you fancy that if you are an inhabitant of Thessaly they will take care of them, and if you are an inhabitant of the other world that they will not take care of them? Nay; but if they who call themselves friends are good for anything, they will—to be sure they will.

"Listen, then, Socrates, to us who have

brought you up. Think not of life and children first, and of justice afterwards, but of justice first, that you may be justified before the princes of the world below. For neither will you nor any that belong to you be happier or holier or juster in this life, or happier in another, if you do as Crito bids. Now you depart in innocence, a sufferer and not a doer of evil; a victim, not of the laws but of men. But if you go forth, returning evil for evil, and injury for injury, breaking the covenants and agreements which you have made with us, and wronging those whom you ought least of all to wrong, that is to say, yourself, your friends, your country, and us, we shall be angry with you while you live, and our brethren, the laws in the world below, will receive you as an enemy; for they will know that you have done your best to destroy us. Listen, then, to us and not to Crito."

This, dear Crito, is the voice which I seem to hear murmuring in my ears, like the sound of the flute in the ears of the mystic; that voice, I say, is humming in my ears, and prevents me from hearing any other. And I know that anything more which you may say will be vain. Yet speak, if you have anything to say.

Cr. I have nothing to say, Socrates.

Soc. Leave me then, Crito, to fulfil the will of God, and to follow whither he leads.

PHAEDO

PERSONS OF THE DIALOGUE: PHAEDO, *who is the narrator of the Dialogue to Echecrates of Phlius;* SOCRATES; APOLLODORUS; SIMMIAS; CEBES; CRITO; ATTENDANT OF THE PRISON.
Scene: The Prison of Socrates; Place of the Narration: Phlius

[57] *Echecrates.* WERE you yourself, Phaedo, in the prison with Socrates on the day when he drank the poison?

Phaedo. Yes, Echecrates, I was.

Ech. I should so like to hear about his death. What did he say in his last hours? We were informed that he died by taking poison, but no one knew anything more; for no Phliasian ever goes to Athens now, and it is a long time since any stranger from Athens has found his way hither; so that we had no clear account.

[58] *Phaed.* Did you not hear of the proceedings at the trial?

Ech. Yes; some one told us about the trial, and we could not understand why, having been condemned, he should have been put to death, not at the time, but long afterwards. What was the reason of this?

Phaed. An accident, Echecrates: the stern of the ship which the Athenians send to Delos happened to have been crowned on the day before he was tried.

Ech. What is this ship?

Phaed. It is the ship in which, according to Athenian tradition, Theseus went to Crete when he took with him the fourteen youths, and was the saviour of them and of himself. And they are said to have vowed to Apollo at the time, that if they were saved they would send a yearly mission to Delos. Now this custom still continues, and the whole period of the voyage to and from Delos, beginning when the priest of Apollo crowns the stern of the ship, is a holy season, during which the city is not allowed to be polluted by public executions;

and when the vessel is detained by contrary winds, the time spent in going and returning is very considerable. As I was saying, the ship was crowned on the day before the trial, and this was the reason why Socrates lay in prison and was not put to death until long after he was condemned.

Ech. What was the manner of his death, Phaedo? What was said or done? And which of his friends were with him? Or did the authorities forbid them to be present—so that he had no friends near him when he died?

Phaed. No; there were several of them with him.

Ech. If you have nothing to do, I wish that you would tell me what passed, as exactly as you can.

Phaed. I have nothing at all to do, and will try to gratify your wish. To be reminded of Socrates is always the greatest delight to me, whether I speak myself or hear another speak of him.

Ech. You will have listeners who are of the same mind with you, and I hope that you will be as exact as you can.

Phaed. I had a singular feeling at being in his company. For I could hardly believe that I was present at the death of a friend, and therefore I did not pity him, Echecrates; he died so fearlessly, and his words and bearing were so noble and gracious, that to me he appeared blessed. I thought that in going to the other world he could not be without a divine call, [59] and that he would be happy, if any man ever was, when he arrived there; and therefore I did not pity him as might have seemed natural at such an hour. But I had not the pleasure which I usually feel in philosophical discourse (for philosophy was the theme of which we spoke). I was pleased, but in the pleasure there was also a strange admixture of pain; for I reflected that he was soon to die, and this double feeling was shared by us all; we were laughing and weeping by turns, especially the excitable Apollodorus—you know the sort of man?

Ech. Yes.

Phaed. He was quite beside himself; and I and all of us were greatly moved.

Ech. Who were present?

Phaed. Of native Athenians there were, besides Apollodorus, Critobulus and his father Crito, Hermogenes, Epigenes, Aeschines, Antisthenes; likewise Ctesippus of the deme of Paeania, Menexenus, and some others; Plato, if I am not mistaken, was ill.

Ech. Were there any strangers?

Phaed. Yes, there were; Simmias the Theban, and Cebes, and Phaedondes; Euclid and Terpsion, who came from Megara.

Ech. And was Aristippus there, and Cleombrotus?

Phaed. No, they were said to be in Aegina.

Ech. Any one else?

Phaed. I think that these were nearly all.

Ech. Well, and what did you talk about?

Phaed. I will begin at the beginning, and endeavour to repeat the entire conversation. On the previous days we had been in the habit of assembling early in the morning at the court in which the trial took place, and which is not far from the prison. There we used to wait talking with one another until the opening of the doors (for they were not opened very early); then we went in and generally passed the day with Socrates. On the last morning we assembled sooner than usual, having heard on the day before when we quitted the prison in the evening that the sacred ship had come from Delos; and so we arranged to meet very early at the accustomed place. On our arrival the jailer who answered the door, instead of admitting us, came out and told us to stay until he called us "For the Eleven," he said, "are now with Socrates; they are taking off his chains, and giving orders that he is to die today." He soon returned and said that we might come in. *[60]* On entering we found Socrates just released from chains, and Xanthippè, whom you know, sitting by him, and holding his child in her arms. When she saw us she uttered a cry and said, as women will: "O Socrates, this is the last time that either you will converse with your friends, or they with you." Socrates turned to Crito and said: "Crito, let some one take her home." Some of Crito's people accordingly led her away, crying out and beating herself. And when she was gone, Socrates, sitting up on the couch, bent and rubbed his leg, saying, as he was rubbing: How singular is the thing called pleasure, and how curiously related to pain, which might be thought to be the opposite of it; for they are never present to a man at the same instant, and yet he who pursues either is generally compelled to take the other; their bodies are two, but they are joined by a single head. And I cannot help thinking that if Aesop had remembered them, he would have made a fable about God trying to reconcile their strife, and how, when he could not, he fastened their heads together; and this is the reason why when one comes the other follows: as I know by my own experience now, when after the pain in my leg which was caused by the chain, pleasure appears to succeed.

Upon this Cebes said: I am glad, Socrates, that you have mentioned the name of Aesop. For it reminds me of a question which has been asked by many, and was asked of me only the day before yesterday by Evenus the poet—he will be sure to ask it again, and therefore if you would like me to have an answer ready for him, you may as well tell me what I should say to him:—he wanted to know why you, who never before wrote a line of poetry, now that you are in prison are turning Aesop's fables into verse, and also composing that hymn in honour of Apollo.

Tell him, Cebes, he replied, what is the truth —that I had no idea of rivalling him or his poems; to do so, as I knew, would be no easy task. But I wanted to see whether I could purge away a scruple which I felt about the meaning of certain dreams. In the course of my life I have often had intimations in dreams "that I should compose music." The same dream came to me sometimes in one form, and sometimes in another, but always saying the same or nearly the same words: "Cultivate and make music," said the dream. And hitherto I had imagined that this was only intended to exhort and encourage me in the study of philosophy, which has been the pursuit of my life, *[61]* and is the noblest and best of music. The dream was bidding me do what I was already doing, in the same way that the competitor in a race is bidden by the spectators to run when he is already running. But I was not certain of this; for the dream might have meant music in the popular sense of the word, and being under sentence of death, and the festival giving me a respite, I thought that it would be safer for me to satisfy the scruple, and, in obedience to the dream, to compose a few verses before I departed. And first I made a hymn in honour of the god of the festival, and then considering that a poet, if he is really to be a poet, should not only put together words, but should invent stories, and that I have no invention, I took some fables of Aesop, which I had ready at hand and which I knew—they were the first I came upon—and turned them into verse. Tell this to Evenus, Cebes, and bid him be of good cheer; say that I would have him come after me if he be a wise man, and not tarry; and that to-day I am likely to be going, for the Athenians say that I must.

Simmias said: What a message for such a man! having been a frequent companion of his I should say that, as far as I know him, he will never take your advice unless he is obliged.

Why, said Socrates,—is not Evenus a philosopher?

I think that he is, said Simmias.

Then he, or any man who has the spirit of philosophy, will be willing to die; but he will not take his own life, for that is held to be unlawful.

Here he changed his position, and put his legs off the couch on to the ground, and during the rest of the conversation he remained sitting.

Why do you say, enquired Cebes, that a man ought not to take his own life, but that the philosopher will be ready to follow the dying?

Socrates replied: And have you, Cebes and Simmias, who are the disciples of Philolaus, never heard him speak of this?

Yes, but his language was obscure, Socrates.

My words, too, are only an echo; but there is no reason why I should not repeat what I have heard: and indeed, as I am going to another place, it is very meet for me to be thinking and talking of the nature of the pilgrimage which I am about to make. What can I do better in the interval between this and the setting of the sun?

Then tell me, Socrates, why is suicide held to be unlawful? as I have certainly heard Philolaus, about whom you were just now asking, affirm when he was staying with us at Thebes; and there are others who say the same, although I have never understood what was meant by any of them.

[62] Do not lose heart, replied Socrates, and the day may come when you will understand. I suppose that you wonder why, when other things which are evil may be good at certain times and to certain persons, death is to be the only exception, and why, when a man is better dead, he is not permitted to be his own benefactor, but must wait for the hand of another.

Very true, said Cebes, laughing gently and speaking in his native Boeotian.

I admit the appearance of inconsistency in what I am saying; but there may not be any real inconsistency after all. There is a doctrine whispered in secret that man is a prisoner who has no right to open the door and run away; this is a great mystery which I do not quite understand. Yet I too believe that the gods are our guardians, and that we men are a possession of theirs. Do you not agree?

Yes, I quite agree, said Cebes.

And if one of your own possessions, an ox or an ass, for example, took the liberty of putting himself out of the way when you had given no intimation of your wish that he should die, would you not be angry with him, and would you not punish him if you could?

Certainly, replied Cebes.

Then, if we look at the matter thus, there may be reason in saying that a man should wait, and not take his own life until God summons him, as he is now summoning me.

Yes, Socrates, said Cebes, there seems to be truth in what you say. And yet how can you reconcile this seemingly true belief that God is our guardian and we his possessions, with the willingness to die which you were just now attributing to the philosopher? That the wisest of men should be willing to leave a service in which they are ruled by the gods who are the best of rulers, is not reasonable; for surely no wise man thinks that when set at liberty he can take better care of himself than the gods take of him. A fool may perhaps think so—he may argue that he had better run away from his master, not considering that his duty is to remain to the end, and not to run away from the good, and that there would be no sense in his running away. The wise man will want to be ever with him who is better than himself. Now this, Socrates, is the reverse of what was just now said; for upon this view the wise man should sorrow and the fool rejoice at passing out of life.

[63] The earnestness of Cebes seemed to please Socrates. Here, said he, turning to us,

is a man who is always enquiring, and is not so easily convinced by the first thing which he hears.

And certainly, added Simmias, the objection which he is now making does appear to me to have some force. For what can be the meaning of a truly wise man wanting to fly away and lightly leave a master who is better than himself? And I rather imagine that Cebes is referring to you; he thinks that you are too ready to leave us, and too ready to leave the gods whom you acknowledge to be our good masters.

Yes, replied Socrates; there is reason in what you say. And so you think that I ought to answer your indictment as if I were in a court?

We should like you to do so, said Simmias.

Then I must try to make a more successful defence before you than I did before the judges. For I am quite ready to admit, Simmias and Cebes, that I ought to be grieved at death, if I were not persuaded in the first place that I am going to other gods who are wise and good (of which I am as certain as I can be of any such matters), and secondly (though I am not so sure of this last) to men departed, better than those whom I leave behind; and therefore I do not grieve as I might have done, for I have good hope that there is yet something remaining for the dead, and as has been said of old, some far better thing for the good than for the evil.

But do you mean to take away your thoughts with you, Socrates? said Simmias. Will you not impart them to us?—for they are a benefit in which we too are entitled to share. Moreover, if you succeed in convincing us, that will be an answer to the charge against yourself.

I will do my best, replied Socrates. But you must first let me hear what Crito wants; he has long been wishing to say something to me.

Only this, Socrates, replied Crito:—the attendant who is to give you the poison has been telling me, and he wants me to tell you, that you are not to talk much; talking, he says, increases heat, and this is apt to interfere with the action of the poison; persons who excite themselves are sometimes obliged to take a second or even a third dose.

Then, said Socrates, let him mind his business and be prepared to give the poison twice or even thrice if necessary; that is all.

I knew quite well what you would say, replied Crito; but I was obliged to satisfy him.

Never mind him, he said.

And now, O my judges, I desire to prove to you that the real philosopher has reason to be of good cheer when he is about to die, and that after death he may hope to obtain the greatest good in the [64] other world. And how this may be, Simmias and Cebes, I will endeavour to explain. For I deem that the true votary of philosophy is likely to be misunderstood by other men; they do not perceive that he is always pursuing death and dying; and if this be so, and he has had the desire of death all his life long, why when his time comes should he repine at that which he has been always pursuing and desiring?

Simmias said laughingly: Though not in a laughing humour, you have made me laugh, Socrates; for I cannot help thinking that the many when they hear your words will say how truly you have described philosophers, and our people at home will likewise say that the life which philosophers desire is in reality death, and that they have found them out to be deserving of the death which they desire

And they are right, Simmias, in thinking so, with the exception of the words "they have found them out"; for they have not found out either what is the nature of that death which the true philosopher deserves, or how he deserves or desires death. But enough of them:— let us discuss the matter among ourselves. Do we believe that there is such a thing as death?

To be sure, replied Simmias.

Is it not the separation of soul and body? And to be dead is the completion of this; when the soul exists in herself, and is released from the body and the body is released from the soul, what is this but death?

Just so, he replied.

There is another question, which will probably throw light on our present enquiry if you and I can agree about it:—Ought the philosopher to care about the pleasures—if they are to be called pleasures—of eating and drinking?

Certainly not, answered Simmias.

And what about the pleasures of love— should he care for them?

By no means.

And will he think much of the other ways of indulging the body, for example, the acquisition of costly raiment, or sandals, or other adornments of the body? Instead of caring about them, does he not rather despise anything more than nature needs? What do you say?

I should say that the true philosopher would despise them.

Would you not say that he is entirely concerned with the soul and not with the body? He would like, as far as he can, to get away from the body and to turn to the soul.

Quite true.

In matters of this sort philosophers, above all other men, may be observed in every sort of way to dissever the soul from the communion [65] of the body.

Very true.

Whereas, Simmias, the rest of the world are of opinion that to him who has no sense of pleasure and no part in bodily pleasure, life is not worth having; and that he who is indifferent about them is as good as dead.

That is also true.

What again shall we say of the actual acquirement of knowledge?—is the body, if invited to share in the enquiry, a hinderer or a helper? I mean to say, have sight and hearing any truth in them? Are they not, as the poets are always telling us, inaccurate witnesses? and yet, if even they are inaccurate and indistinct, what is to be said of the other senses?—for you will allow that they are the best of them?

Certainly, he replied.

Then when does the soul attain truth?—for in attempting to consider anything in company with the body she is obviously deceived.

True.

Then must not true existence be revealed to her in thought, if at all?

Yes.

And thought is best when the mind is gathered into herself and none of these things trouble her—neither sounds nor sights nor pain nor any pleasure,—when she takes leave of the body, and has as little as possible to do with it, when she has no bodily sense or desire, but is aspiring after true being?

Certainly.

And in this the philosopher dishonours the body; his soul runs away from his body and desires to be alone and by herself?

That is true.

Well, but there is another thing, Simmias: Is there or is there not an absolute justice?

Assuredly there is.

And an absolute beauty and absolute good?

Of course.

But did you ever behold any of them with your eyes?

Certainly not.

Or did you ever reach them with any other bodily sense?—and I speak not of these alone, but of absolute greatness, and health, and strength, and of the essence or true nature of everything. Has the reality of them ever been perceived by you through the bodily organs?

or rather, is not the nearest approach to the knowledge of their several natures made by him who so orders his intellectual vision as to have the most exact conception of the essence of each thing which he considers?

Certainly.

And he attains to the purest knowledge of them who goes to each with the mind alone, not introducing or intruding in the act of thought sight or any other sense together with reason, but with the very light of the mind in her own clearness searches into the very [66] truth of each; he who has got rid, as far as he can, of eyes and ears and, so to speak, of the whole body, these being in his opinion distracting elements which when they infect the soul hinder her from acquiring truth and knowledge—who, if not he, is likely to attain to the knowledge of true being?

What you say has a wonderful truth in it, Socrates, replied Simmias.

And when real philosophers consider all these things, will they not be led to make a reflection which they will express in words something like the following? "Have we not found," they will say, "a path of thought which seems to bring us and our argument to the conclusion, that while we are in the body, and while the soul is infected with the evils of the body, our desire will not be satisfied? and our desire is of the truth. For the body is a source of endless trouble to us by reason of the mere requirement of food; and is liable also to diseases which overtake and impede us in the search after true being: it fills us full of loves, and lusts, and fears, and fancies of all kinds, and endless foolery, and in fact, as men say, takes away from us the power of thinking at all. Whence come wars, and fightings, and factions? whence but from the body and the lusts of the body? Wars are occasioned by the love of money, and money has to be acquired for the sake and in the service of the body; and by reason of all these impediments we have no time to give to philosophy; and, last and worst of all, even if we are at leisure and betake ourselves to some speculation, the body is always breaking in upon us, causing turmoil and confusion in our enquiries, and so amazing us that we are prevented from seeing the truth. It has been proved to us by experience that if we would have pure knowledge of anything we must be quit of the body—the soul in herself must behold things in themselves: and then we shall attain the wisdom which we desire, and of which we say that we are lovers; not while we live, but after death; for if while in company with the body, the soul cannot have pure knowledge, one of two things follows—either knowledge is not to be attained at all, or, if at all, *[67]* after death. For then, and not till then, the soul will be parted from the body and exist in herself alone. In this present life, I reckon that we make the nearest approach to knowledge when we have the least possible intercourse or communion with the body, and are not surfeited with the bodily nature, but keep ourselves pure until the hour when God himself is pleased to release us. And thus having got rid of the foolishness of the body we shall be pure and hold converse with the pure, and know of ourselves the clear light everywhere, which is no other than the light of truth." For the impure are not permitted to approach the pure. These are the sort of words, Simmias, which the true lovers of knowledge cannot help saying to one another, and thinking. You would agree; would you not?

Undoubtedly, Socrates.

But, O my friend, if this be true, there is great reason to hope that, going whither I go, when I have come to the end of my journey, I shall attain that which has been the pursuit of my life. And therefore I go on my way rejoicing, and not I only, but every other man who believes that his mind has been made ready and that he is in a manner purified.

Certainly, replied Simmias.

And what is purification but the separation of the soul from the body, as I was saying before; the habit of the soul gathering and collecting herself into herself from all sides out of the body; the dwelling in her own place alone, as in another life, so also in this, as far as she can;—the release of the soul from the chains of the body?

Very true, he said.

And this separation and release of the soul from the body is termed death?

To be sure, he said.

And the true philosophers, and they only, are ever seeking to release the soul. Is not the separation and release of the soul from the body their especial study?

That is true.

And, as I was saying at first, there would be a ridiculous contradiction in men studying to live as nearly as they can in a state of death, and yet repining when it comes upon them.

Clearly.

And the true philosophers, Simmias, are always occupied in the practice of dying, wherefore also to them least of all men is death terri-

ble. Look at the matter thus:—if they have been in every way the enemies of the body, and are wanting to be alone with the soul, when this desire of theirs is granted, how inconsistent would they be if they trembled and repined, instead of rejoicing at their departure to that place where, when they arrive, they hope to gain that which in life they desired—and this was wisdom—and at the *[68]* same time to be rid of the company of their enemy. Many a man has been willing to go to the world below animated by the hope of seeing there an earthly love, or wife, or son, and conversing with them. And will he who is a true lover of wisdom, and is strongly persuaded in like manner that only in the world below he can worthily enjoy her, still repine at death? Will he not depart with joy? Surely he will, O my friend, if he be a true philosopher. For he will have a firm conviction that there, and there only, he can find wisdom in her purity. And if this be true, he would be very absurd, as I was saying, if he were afraid of death.

He would indeed, replied Simmias.

And when you see a man who is repining at the approach of death, is not his reluctance a sufficient proof that he is not a lover of wisdom, but a lover of the body, and probably at the same time a lover of either money or power, or both?

Quite so, he replied.

And is not courage, Simmias, a quality which is specially characteristic of the philosopher?

Certainly.

There is temperance again, which even by the vulgar is supposed to consist in the control and regulation of the passions, and in the sense of superiority to them—is not temperance a virtue belonging to those only who despise the body, and who pass their lives in philosophy?

Most assuredly.

For the courage and temperance of other men, if you will consider them, are really a contradiction.

How so?

Well, he said, you are aware that death is regarded by men in general as a great evil.

Very true, he said.

And do not courageous men face death because they are afraid of yet greater evils?

That is quite true.

Then all but the philosophers are courageous only from fear, and because they are afraid; and yet that a man should be courageous from fear, and because he is a coward, is surely a strange thing.

Very true.

And are not the temperate exactly in the same case? They are temperate because they are intemperate—which might seem to be a contradiction, but is nevertheless the sort of thing which happens with this foolish temperance. For there are pleasures which they are afraid of losing; and in their desire to keep them, they abstain from some pleasures, because they are overcome by others; and although to be conquered by pleasure is called by men intemperance, *[69]* to them the conquest of pleasure consists in being conquered by pleasure. And that is what I mean by saying that, in a sense, they are made temperate through intemperance.

Such appears to be the case.

Yet the exchange of one fear or pleasure or pain for another fear or pleasure or pain, and of the greater for the less, as if they were coins, is not the exchange of virtue. O my blessed Simmias, is there not one true coin for which all things ought to be exchanged?—and that is wisdom; and only in exchange for this, and in company with this, is anything truly bought or sold, whether courage or temperance or justice. And is not all true virtue the companion of wisdom, no matter what fears or pleasures or other similar goods or evils may or may not attend her? But the virtue which is made up of these goods, when they are severed from wisdom and exchanged with one another, is a shadow of virtue only, nor is there any freedom or health or truth in her; but in the true exchange there is a purging away of all these things, and temperance, and justice, and courage, and wisdom herself are the purgation of them. The founders of the mysteries would appear to have had a real meaning, and were not talking nonsense when they intimated in a figure long ago that he who passes unsanctified and uninitiated into the world below will lie in a slough, but that he who arrives there after initiation and purification will dwell with the gods. For "many," as they say in the mysteries, "are the thyrsus-bearers, but few are the mystics,"—meaning, as I interpret the words, "the true philosophers." In the number of whom, during my whole life, I have been seeking, according to my ability, to find a place;—whether I have sought in a right way or not, and whether I have succeeded or not, I shall truly know in a little while, if God will, when I myself arrive in the other world—such is my belief. And therefore I maintain that I am right, Simmias and Cebes, in not grieving or repining at parting from you and my masters in this world, for I believe that I shall equally find good masters and friends in another world. But most men do not believe this saying; if then I succeed in convincing you by my defence better than I did the Athenian judges, it will be well.

Cebes answered: I agree, Socrates, in the greater part of what you say. *[70]* But in what concerns the soul, men are apt to be incredulous; they fear that when she has left the body her place may be nowhere, and that on the very day of death she may perish and come to an end—immediately on her release from the body, issuing forth dispersed like smoke or air and in her flight vanishing away into nothingness. If she could only be collected into herself after she has obtained release from the evils of which you were speaking, there would be good reason to hope, Socrates, that what you say is true. But surely it requires a great deal of argument and many proofs to show that when the man is dead his soul yet exists, and has any force or intelligence.

True, Cebes, said Socrates; and shall I suggest that we converse a little of the probabilities of these things?

I am sure, said Cebes, that I should greatly like to know your opinion about them.

I reckon, said Socrates, that no one who heard me now, not even if he were one of my old enemies, the Comic poets, could accuse me of idle talking about matters in which I have no concern:—If you please, then, we will proceed with the enquiry.

Suppose we consider the question whether the souls of men after death are or are not in the world below. There comes into my mind an ancient doctrine which affirms that they go from hence into the other world, and returning hither, are born again from the dead. Now if it be true that the living come from the dead, then our souls must exist in the other world, for if not, how could they have been born again? And this would be conclusive, if there were any real evidence that the living are only born from the dead; but if this is not so, then other arguments will have to be adduced.

Very true, replied Cebes.

Then let us consider the whole question, not in relation to man only, but in relation to animals generally, and to plants, and to everything of which there is generation, and the proof will be easier. Are not all things which have opposites generated out of their opposites? I mean such things as good and evil, just and unjust—and there are innumerable other opposites which are generated out of opposites. And I want to show that in all opposites there is of necessity a similar alternation; I mean to say, for example, that anything which becomes greater must become greater after being less.

True.

And that which becomes less must have been once greater and then have become less. [71]

Yes.

And the weaker is generated from the stronger, and the swifter from the slower.

Very true.

And the worse is from the better, and the more just is from the more unjust.

Of course.

And is this true of all opposites? and are we convinced that all of them are generated out of opposites?

Yes.

And in this universal opposition of all things, are there not also two intermediate processes which are ever going on, from one to the other opposite, and back again; where there is a greater and a less there is also an intermediate process of increase and diminution, and that which grows is said to wax, and that which decays to wane?

Yes, he said.

And there are many other processes, such as division and composition, cooling and heating, which equally involve a passage into and out of one another. And this necessarily holds of all opposites, even though not always expressed in words—they are really generated out of one another, and there is a passing or process from one to the other of them?

Very true, he replied.

Well, and is there not an opposite of life, as sleep is the opposite of waking?

True, he said.

And what is it?

Death, he answered.

And these, if they are opposites, are generated the one from the other, and have their two intermediate processes also?

Of course.

Now, said Socrates, I will analyze one of the two pairs of opposites which I have mentioned to you, and also its intermediate processes, and you shall analyze the other to me. One of them I term sleep, the other waking. The state of sleep is opposed to the state of waking, and out of sleeping waking is generated, and out of waking, sleeping; and the process of generation is in the one case falling asleep, and in the other waking up. Do you agree?

I entirely agree.

Then, suppose that you analyze life and death to me in the same manner. Is not death opposed to life?

Yes.

And they are generated one from the other?

Yes.

What is generated from the living?

The dead.

And what from the dead?

I can only say in answer—the living.

Then the living, whether things or persons, Cebes, are generated from the dead?

That is clear, he replied.

Then the inference is that our souls exist in the world below?

That is true.

And one of the two processes or generations is visible—for surely the act of dying is visible?

Surely, he said.

What then is to be the result? Shall we exclude the opposite process? and shall we suppose nature to walk on one leg only? Must we not rather assign to death some corresponding process of generation?

Certainly, he replied.

And what is that process?

Return to life.

And return to life, if there be such a thing, is the birth of the dead into the world of the living? [72]

Quite true.

Then here is a new way by which we arrive at the conclusion that the living come from the dead, just as the dead come from the living; and this, if true, affords a most certain proof that the souls of the dead exist in some place out of which they come again.

Yes, Socrates, he said; the conclusion seems to flow necessarily out of our previous admissions.

And that these admissions were not unfair, Cebes, he said, may be shown, I think, as follows: If generation were in a straight line only, and there were no compensation or circle in nature, no turn or return of elements into their opposites, then you know that all things would at last have the same form and pass into the same state, and there would be no more generation of them.

What do you mean? he said.

A simple thing enough, which I will illustrate by the case of sleep, he replied. You know that if there were no alternation of sleeping and waking, the tale of the sleeping Endymion would in the end have no meaning, because all other things would be asleep too, and he would not be distinguishable from the rest. Or if there were composition only, and no division of substances, then the chaos of Anaxagoras would come again. And in like manner, my dear Cebes, if all things which partook of life were to die, and after they were dead remained in the form of death, and did not come to life again, all would at last die, and nothing would be alive—what other result could there be? For if the living spring from any other things, and they too die, must not all things at last be swallowed up in death?[1]

There is no escape, Socrates, said Cebes; and to me your argument seems to be absolutely true.

Yes, he said, Cebes, it is and must be so, in my opinion; and we have not been deluded in making these admissions; but I am confident that there truly is such a thing as living again, and that the living spring from the dead, and that the souls of the dead are in existence, and that the good souls have a better portion than the evil.

Cebes added: Your favourite doctrine, Socrates, that knowledge is simply recollection, if true, also necessarily implies a previous time in which we have learned that which we now recollect. But this would be impossible unless our soul had been in some place [73] before existing in the form of man; here then is another proof of the soul's immortality.

But tell me, Cebes, said Simmias, interposing, what arguments are urged in favour of this doctrine of recollection. I am not very sure at the moment that I remember them.

One excellent proof, said Cebes, is afforded by questions. If you put a question to a person in a right way, he will give a true answer of himself, but how could he do this unless there were knowledge and right reason already in him? And this is most clearly shown when he is taken to a diagram or to anything of that sort.[2]

But if, said Socrates, you are still incredulous, Simmias, I would ask you whether you may not agree with me when you look at the matter in another way;—I mean, if you are still incredulous as to whether knowledge is recollection?

Incredulous I am not, said Simmias; but I want to have this doctrine of recollection brought to my own recollection, and, from what Cebes has said, I am beginning to recol-

lect and be convinced: but I should still like to hear what you were going to say.

This is what I would say, he replied:—We should agree, if I am not mistaken, that what a man recollects he must have known at some previous time.

Very true.

And what is the nature of this knowledge or recollection? I mean to ask, Whether a person who, having seen or heard or in any way perceived anything, knows not only that, but has a conception of something else which is the subject, not of the same but of some other kind of knowledge, may not be fairly said to recollect that of which he has the conception?

What do you mean?

I mean what I may illustrate by the following instance:—The knowledge of a lyre is not the same as the knowledge of a man?

True.

And yet what is the feeling of lovers when they recognize a lyre, or a garment, or anything else which the beloved has been in the habit of using? Do not they, from knowing the lyre, form in the mind's eye an image of the youth to whom the lyre belongs? And this is recollection. In like manner any one who sees Simmias may remember Cebes; and there are endless examples of the same thing.

Endless, indeed, replied Simmias.

And recollection is most commonly a process of recovering that which has been already forgotten through time and inattention.

Very true, he said.

Well; and may you not also from seeing the picture of a house or a lyre remember a man? and from the picture of Simmias, you may be led to remember Cebes;

True.

Or you may also be led to the recollection of Simmias himself?

[74] Quite so.

And in all these cases, the recollection may be derived from things either like or unlike?

It may be.

And when the recollection is derived from like things, then another consideration is sure to arise, which is—whether the likeness in any degree falls short or not of that which is recollected?

Very true, he said.

And shall we proceed a step further, and affirm that there is such a thing as equality, not of one piece of wood or stone with another, but that, over and above this, there is absolute equality? Shall we say so?

[1] But cf. *Republic*, x. 611.
[2] Cf. *Meno*, 83 ff.

Say so, yes, replied Simmias, and swear to it, with all the confidence in life.

And do we know the nature of this absolute essence?

To be sure, he said.

And whence did we obtain our knowledge? Did we not see equalities of material things, such as pieces of wood and stones, and gather from them the idea of an equality which is different from them? For you will acknowledge that there is a difference. Or look at the matter in another way:—Do not the same pieces of wood or stone appear at one time equal, and at another time unequal?

That is certain.

But are real equals ever equal? or is the idea of equality the same as of inequality?

Impossible, Socrates.

Then these (so-called) equals are not the same with the idea of equality?

I should say, clearly not, Socrates.

And yet from these equals, although differing from the idea of equality, you conceived and attained that idea?

Very true, he said.

Which might be like, or might be unlike them?

Yes.

But that makes no difference: whenever from seeing one thing you conceived another, whether like or unlike, there must surely have been an act of recollection?

Very true.

But what would you say of equal portions of wood and stone, or other material equals? and what is the impression produced by them? Are they equals in the same sense in which absolute equality is equal? or do they fall short of this perfect equality in a measure?

Yes, he said, in a very great measure too.

And must we not allow, that when I or any one, looking at any object, observes that the thing which he sees aims at being some other thing, but falls short of, and cannot be, that other thing, but is inferior, he who makes this observation must have had a previous knowledge of that to which the other, although similar, was inferior.

Certainly.

And has not this been our own case in the matter of equals and of absolute equality?

Precisely.

Then we must have known equality previously to the time when we first saw the material equals, [75] and reflected that all these apparent equals strive to attain absolute equal-ity, but fall short of it?

Very true.

And we recognize also that this absolute equality has only been known, and can only be known, through the medium of sight or touch, or of some other of the senses, which are all alike in this respect?

Yes, Socrates, as far as the argument is concerned, one of them is the same as the other.

From the senses then is derived the knowledge that all sensible things aim at an absolute equality of which they fall short?

Yes.

Then before we began to see or hear or perceive in any way, we must have had a knowledge of absolute equality, or we could not have referred to that standard the equals which are derived from the senses?—for to that they all aspire, and of that they fall short.

No other inference can be drawn from the previous statements.

And did we not see and hear and have the use of our other senses as soon as we were born?

Certainly.

Then we must have acquired the knowledge of equality at some previous time?

Yes.

That is to say, before we were born, I suppose?

True.

And if we acquired this knowledge before we were born, and were born having the use of it, then we also knew before we were born and at the instant of birth not only the equal or the greater or the less, but all other ideas; for we are not speaking only of equality, but of beauty, goodness, justice, holiness, and of all which we stamp with the name of essence in the dialectical process, both when we ask and when we answer questions. Of all this we may certainly affirm that we acquired the knowledge before birth?

We may.

But if, after having acquired, we have not forgotten what in each case we acquired, then we must always have come into life having knowledge, and shall always continue to know as long as life lasts—for knowing is the acquiring and retaining knowledge and not forgetting. Is not forgetting, Simmias, just the losing of knowledge?

Quite true, Socrates.

But if the knowledge which we acquired before birth was lost by us at birth, and if afterwards by the use of the senses we recovered what we previously knew, will not the process which we call learning be a recovering of the knowledge which is natural to us, and may not this be rightly termed recollection?

Very true.

[76] So much is clear—that when we perceive something, either by the help of sight, or hearing, or some other sense, from that perception we are able to obtain a notion of some other thing like or unlike which is associated with it but has been forgotten. Whence, as I was saying, one of two alternatives follows:—either we had this knowledge at birth, and continued to know through life; or, after birth, those who are said to learn only remember, and learning is simply recollection.

Yes, that is quite true, Socrates.

And which alternative, Simmias, do you prefer? Had we the knowledge at our birth, or did we recollect the things which we knew previously to our birth?

I cannot decide at the moment.

At any rate you can decide whether he who has knowledge will or will not be able to render an account of his knowledge? What do you say?

Certainly, he will.

But do you think that every man is able to give an account of these very matters about which we are speaking?

Would that they could, Socrates, but I rather fear that to-morrow, at this time, there will no longer be any one alive who is able to give an account of them such as ought to be given.

Then you are not of opinion, Simmias, that all men know these things?

Certainly not.

They are in process of recollecting that which they learned before?

Certainly.

But when did our souls acquire this knowledge?—not since we were born as men?

Certainly not.

And therefore, previously?

Yes.

Then, Simmias, our souls must also have existed without bodies before they were in the form of man, and must have had intelligence.

Unless indeed you suppose, Socrates, that these notions are given us at the very moment of birth; for this is the only time which remains.

Yes, my friend, but if so, when do we lose them? for they are not in us when we are born—that is admitted. Do we lose them at the moment of receiving them, or if not at what other time?

No, Socrates, I perceive that I was unconsciously talking nonsense.

Then may we not say, Simmias, that if, as we are always repeating, there is an absolute beauty, and goodness, and an absolute essence of all things; and if to this, which is now discovered to have existed in our former state, we refer all our sensations, and with this compare them, finding these ideas to be pre-existent and our inborn possession—then our souls must have had a prior existence, but if not, there would be no force in the argument? There is the same proof that these ideas must have existed before we were born, as that our souls existed before we were born; and if not the ideas, then not the souls.

Yes, Socrates; I am convinced that there is precisely the same necessity for the one as for the other; and the argument retreats successfully to the position that the existence of the soul before [77] birth cannot be separated from the existence of the essence of which you speak. For there is nothing which to my mind is so patent as that beauty, goodness, and the other notions of which you were just now speaking, have a most real and absolute existence; and I am satisfied with the proof.

Well, but is Cebes equally satisfied? for I must convince him too.

I think, said Simmias, that Cebes is satisfied: although he is the most incredulous of mortals, yet I believe that he is sufficiently convinced of the existence of the soul before birth. But that after death the soul will continue to exist is not yet proven even to my own satisfaction. I cannot get rid of the feeling of the many to which Cebes was referring—the feeling that when the man dies the soul will be dispersed, and that this may be the extinction of her. For admitting that she may have been born elsewhere, and framed out of other elements, and was in existence before entering the human body, why after having entered in and gone out again may she not herself be destroyed and come to an end?

Very true, Simmias, said Cebes; about half of what was required has been proven; to wit, that our souls existed before we were born:—that the soul will exist after death as well as before birth is the other half of which the proof is still wanting, and has to be supplied; when that is given the demonstration will be complete.

But that proof, Simmias and Cebes, has been already given, said Socrates, if you put the two arguments together—I mean this and the former one, in which we admitted that everything living is born of the dead. For if the soul exists before birth, and in coming to life and being born can be born only from death and dying, must she not after death continue to exist, since she has to be born again?—Surely the proof which you desire has been already furnished. Still I suspect that you and Simmias would be glad to probe the argument further. Like children, you are haunted with a fear that when the soul leaves the body, the wind may really blow her away and scatter her; especially if a man should happen to die in a great storm and not when the sky is calm.

Cebes answered with a smile: Then, Socrates, you must argue us out of our fears—and yet, strictly speaking, they are not our fears, but there is a child within us to whom death is a sort of hobgoblin: him too we must persuade not to be afraid when he is alone in the dark.

Socrates said: Let the voice of the charmer be applied daily until you have charmed away the fear.

[78] And where shall we find a good charmer of our fears, Socrates, when you are gone?

Hellas, he replied, is a large place, Cebes, and has many good men, and there are barbarous races not a few: seek for him among them all, far and wide, sparing neither pains nor money; for there is no better way of spending your money. And you must seek among yourselves too; for you will not find others better able to make the search.

The search, replied Cebes, shall certainly be made. And now, if you please, let us return to the point of the argument at which we digressed.

By all means, replied Socrates; what else should I please?

Very good.

Must we not, said Socrates, ask ourselves what that is which, as we imagine, is liable to be scattered, and about which we fear? and what again is that about which we have no fear? And then we may proceed further to enquire whether that which suffers dispersion is or is not of the nature of soul—our hopes and fears as to our own souls will turn upon the answers to these questions.

Very true, he said.

Now the compound or composite may be supposed to be naturally capable, as of being compounded, so also of being dissolved; but that which is uncompounded, and that only, must be, if anything is, indissoluble.

Yes; I should imagine so, said Cebes.

And the uncompounded may be assumed to be the same and unchanging, whereas the compound is always changing and never the same.

I agree, he said.

Then now let us return to the previous discussion. Is that idea or essence, which in the dialectical process we define as essence or true existence—whether essence of equality, beauty, or anything else—are these essences, I say, liable at times to some degree of change? or are they each of them always what they are, having the same simple self-existent and unchanging forms, not admitting of variation at all, or in any way, or at any time?

They must be always the same, Socrates, replied Cebes.

And what would you say of the many beautiful—whether men or horses or garments or any other things which are named by the same names and may be called equal or beautiful,—are they all unchanging and the same always, or quite the reverse? May they not rather be described as almost always changing and hardly ever the same, either with themselves or with one another?

The latter, replied Cebes; they are always in a state of change.

[79] And these you can touch and see and perceive with the senses, but the unchanging things you can only perceive with the mind—they are invisible and are not seen?

That is very true, he said.

Well then, added Socrates, let us suppose that there are two sorts of existences—one seen, the other unseen.

Let us suppose them.

The seen is the changing, and the unseen is the unchanging?

That may be also supposed.

And, further, is not one part of us body, another part soul?

To be sure.

And to which class is the body more alike and akin?

Clearly to the seen—no one can doubt that.

And is the soul seen or not seen?

Not by man, Socrates.

And what we mean by "seen" and "not seen" is that which is or is not visible to the eye of man?

Yes, to the eye of man.

And is the soul seen or not seen?

Not seen.

Unseen then?

Yes.

Then the soul is more like to the unseen, and the body to the seen?

That follows necessarily, Socrates.

And were we not saying long ago that the soul when using the body as an instrument of perception, that is to say, when using the sense of sight or hearing or some other sense (for the meaning of perceiving through the body is perceiving through the senses)—were we not saying that the soul too is then dragged by the body into the region of the changeable, and wanders and is confused; the world spins round her, and she is like a drunkard, when she touches change?

Very true.

But when returning into herself she reflects, then she passes into the other world, the region of purity, and eternity, and immortality, and unchangeableness, which are her kindred, and with them she ever lives, when she is by herself and is not let or hindered; then she ceases from her erring ways, and being in communion with the unchanging is unchanging. And this state of the soul is called wisdom?

That is well and truly said, Socrates, he replied.

And to which class is the soul more nearly alike and akin, as far as may be inferred from this argument, as well as from the preceding one?

I think, Socrates, that, in the opinion of every one who follows the argument, the soul will be infinitely more like the unchangeable—even the most stupid person will not deny that.

And the body is more like the changing?

Yes.

Yet once more consider the matter in another light: When the soul and the body are united, *[80]* then nature orders the soul to rule and govern, and the body to obey and serve. Now which of these two functions is akin to the divine? and which to the mortal? Does not the divine appear to you to be that which naturally orders and rules, and the mortal to be that which is subject and servant?

True.

And which does the soul resemble?

The soul resembles the divine, and the body the mortal—there can be no doubt of that, Socrates.

Then reflect, Cebes: of all which has been said is not this the conclusion?—that the soul is in the very likeness of the divine, and immortal, and intellectual, and uniform, and indissoluble, and unchangeable; and that the body is in the very likeness of the human, and mortal, and unintellectual, and multiform, and

dissoluble, and changeable. Can this, my dear Cebes, be denied?

It cannot.

But if it be true, then is not the body liable to speedy dissolution? and is not the soul almost or altogether indissoluble?

Certainly.

And do you further observe, that after a man is dead, the body, or visible part of him, which is lying in the visible world, and is called a corpse, and would naturally be dissolved and decomposed and dissipated, is not dissolved or decomposed at once, but may remain for some time, nay even for a long time, if the constitution be sound at the time of death, and the season of the year favourable? For the body when shrunk and embalmed, as the manner is in Egypt, may remain almost entire through infinite ages; and even in decay, there are still some portions, such as the bones and ligaments, which are practically indestructible:—Do you agree?

Yes.

And is it likely that the soul, which is invisible, in passing to the place of the true Hades, which like her is invisible, and pure, and noble, and on her way to the good and wise God, whither, if God will, my soul is also soon to go,—that the soul, I repeat, if this be her nature and origin, will be blown away and destroyed immediately on quitting the body, as the many say? That can never be, my dear Simmias and Cebes. The truth rather is, that the soul which is pure at departing and draws after her no bodily taint, having never voluntarily during life had connection with the body, which she is ever avoiding, herself gathered into herself;—and making such abstraction her perpetual study— which means that she has been a true disciple of philosophy; *[81]* and therefore has in fact been always engaged in the practice of dying? For is not philosophy the study of death?—

Certainly—

That soul, I say, herself invisible, departs to the invisible world—to the divine and immortal and rational; thither arriving, she is secure of bliss and is released from the error and folly of men, their fears and wild passions and all other human ills, and for ever dwells, as they say of the initiated, in company with the gods.[1] Is not this true, Cebes?

Yes, said Cebes, beyond a doubt.

But the soul which has been polluted, and is impure at the time of her departure, and is the

[1] Cf. *Apology,* 40.

companion and servant of the body always, and is in love with and fascinated by the body and by the desires and pleasures of the body, until she is led to believe that the truth only exists in a bodily form, which a man may touch and see and taste, and use for the purposes of his lusts,—the soul, I mean, accustomed to hate and fear and avoid the intellectual principle, which to the bodily eye is dark and invisible, and can be attained only by philosophy;—do you suppose that such a soul will depart pure and unalloyed?

Impossible, he replied.

She is held fast by the corporeal, which the continual association and constant care of the body have wrought into her nature.

Very true.

And this corporeal element, my friend, is heavy and weighty and earthy, and is that element of sight by which a soul is depressed and dragged down again into the visible world, because she is afraid of the invisible and of the world below—prowling about tombs and sepulchres, near which, as they tell us, are seen certain ghostly apparitions of souls which have not departed pure, but are cloyed with sight and therefore visible.[1]

That is very likely, Socrates.

Yes, that is very likely, Cebes; and these must be the souls, not of the good, but of the evil, which are compelled to wander about such places in payment of the penalty of their former evil way of life; and they continue to wander until through the craving after the corporeal which never leaves them, they are imprisoned finally in another body. And they may be supposed to find their prisons in the same natures which they have had in their former lives.

What natures do you mean, Socrates?

What I mean is that men who have followed after gluttony, and wantonness, and drunkenness, and have had no thought of avoiding them, [82] would pass into asses and animals of that sort. What do you think?

I think such an opinion to be exceedingly probable.

And those who have chosen the portion of injustice, and tyranny, and violence, will pass into wolves, or into hawks and kites;—whither else can we suppose them to go?

Yes, said Cebes; with such natures, beyond question.

And there is no difficulty, he said, in assigning to all of them places answering to their several natures and propensities?

There is not, he said.

Some are happier than others; and the happiest both in themselves and in the place to which they go are those who have practised the civil and social virtues which are called temperance and justice, and are acquired by habit and attention without philosophy and mind.[2]

Why are they the happiest?

Because they may be expected to pass into some gentle and social kind which is like their own, such as bees or wasps or ants, or back again into the form of man, and just and moderate men may be supposed to spring from them.

Very likely.

No one who has not studied philosophy and who is not entirely pure at the time of his departure is allowed to enter the company of the Gods, but the lover of knowledge only. And this is the reason, Simmias and Cebes, why the true votaries of philosophy abstain from all fleshly lusts, and hold out against them and refuse to give themselves up to them,—not because they fear poverty or the ruin of their families, like the lovers of money, and the world in general; nor like the lovers of power and honour, because they dread the dishonour or disgrace of evil deeds.

No, Socrates, that would not become them, said Cebes.

No indeed, he replied; and therefore they who have any care of their own souls, and do not merely live moulding and fashioning the body, say farewell to all this; they will not walk in the ways of the blind: and when philosophy offers them purification and release from evil, they feel that they ought not to resist her influence, and whither she leads they turn and follow.

What do you mean, Socrates?

I will tell you, he said. The lovers of knowledge are conscious that the soul was simply fastened and glued to the body—until philosophy received her, she could only view real ex-

---

[1] Compare Milton, *Comus*, 463 ff.:

> *But when lust,*
> *By unchaste looks, loose gestures, and foul talk,*
> *But most by lewd and lavish act of sin,*
> *Lets in defilement to the inward parts,*
> *The soul grows clotted by contagion,*
> *Imbodies, and imbrutes, till she quite lose,*
> *The divine property of her first being.*
> *Such are those thick and gloomy shadows damp*
> *Oft seen in charnel vaults and sepulchres,*
> *Lingering, and sitting by a new made grave,*
> *As loath to leave the body that it lov'd,*
> *And linked itself by carnal sensuality*
> *To a degenerate and degraded state.*

[2] Cf. *Republic*, x. 619.

istence through the bars of a prison, not in and through herself; she was wallowing in the mire of every sort of ignorance, and by reason of lust had become the principal accomplice in her own captivity. *[83]* This was her original state; and then, as I was saying, and as the lovers of knowledge are well aware, philosophy, seeing how terrible was her confinement, of which she was to herself the cause, received and gently comforted her and sought to release her, pointing out that the eye and the ear and the other senses are full of deception, and persuading her to retire from them, and abstain from all but the necessary use of them, and be gathered up and collected into herself, bidding her trust in herself and her own pure apprehension of pure existence, and to mistrust whatever comes to her through other channels and is subject to variation; for such things are visible and tangible, but what she sees in her own nature is intelligible and invisible. And the soul of the true philosopher thinks that she ought not to resist this deliverance, and therefore abstains from pleasures and desires and pains and fears, as far as she is able; reflecting that when a man has great joys or sorrows or fears or desires, he suffers from them, not merely the sort of evil which might be anticipated —as for example, the loss of his health or property which he has sacrificed to his lusts—but an evil greater far, which is the greatest and worst of all evils, and one of which he never thinks.

What is it, Socrates? said Cebes.

The evil is that when the feeling of pleasure or pain is most intense, every soul of man imagines the objects of this intense feeling to be then plainest and truest: but this is not so, they are really the things of sight.

Very true.

And is not this the state in which the soul is most enthralled by the body?

How so?

Why, because each pleasure and pain is a sort of nail which nails and rivets the soul to the body, until she becomes like the body, and believes that to be true which the body affirms to be true; and from agreeing with the body and having the same delights she is obliged to have the same habits and haunts, and is not likely ever to be pure at her departure to the world below, but is always infected by the body; and so she sinks into another body and there germinates and grows, and has therefore no part in the communion of the divine and pure and simple.

Most true, Socrates, answered Cebes.

And this, Cebes, is the reason why the true lovers of knowledge are temperate and brave; and not for the reason which the world gives. *[84]* Certainly not.

Certainly not! The soul of a philosopher will reason in quite another way; she will not ask philosophy to release her in order that when released she may deliver herself up again to the thraldom of pleasures and pains, doing a work only to be undone again, weaving instead of unweaving her Penelope's web. But she will calm passion, and follow reason, and dwell in the contemplation of her, beholding the true and divine (which is not matter of opinion), and thence deriving nourishment. Thus she seeks to live while she lives, and after death she hopes to go to her own kindred and to that which is like her, and to be freed from human ills. Never fear, Simmias and Cebes, that a soul which has been thus nurtured and has had these pursuits, will at her departure from the body be scattered and blown away by the winds and be nowhere and nothing.

When Socrates had done speaking, for a considerable time there was silence; he himself appeared to be meditating, as most of us were, on what had been said; only Cebes and Simmias spoke a few words to one another. And Socrates observing them asked what they thought of the argument, and whether there was anything wanting? For, said he, there are many points still open to suspicion and attack, if any one were disposed to sift the matter thoroughly. Should you be considering some other matter I say no more, but if you are still in doubt do not hesitate to say exactly what you think, and let us have anything better which you can suggest; and if you think that I can be of any use, allow me to help you.

Simmias said: I must confess, Socrates, that doubts did arise in our minds, and each of us was urging and inciting the other to put the question which we wanted to have answered but which neither of us liked to ask, fearing that our importunity might be troublesome at such a time.

Socrates replied with a smile: O Simmias, what are you saying? I am not very likely to persuade other men that I do not regard my present situation as a misfortune, if I cannot even persuade you that I am no worse off now than at any other time in my life. Will you not allow that I have as much of the spirit of prophecy in me as the swans? For they, when they perceive that they must die, having sung all their life long, do then sing more lustily than ever, rejoicing in the thought that they are about to go away to the god [85] whose ministers they are. But men, because they are themselves afraid of death, slanderously affirm of the swans that they sing a lament at the last, not considering that no bird sings when cold, or hungry, or in pain, not even the nightingale, nor the swallow, nor yet the hoopoe; which are said indeed to tune a lay of sorrow, although I do not believe this to be true of them any more than of the swans. But because they are sacred to Apollo, they have the gift of prophecy, and anticipate the good things of another world; wherefore they sing and rejoice in that day more than ever they did before. And I too, believing myself to be the consecrated servant of the same God, and the fellow-servant of the swans, and thinking that I have received from my master gifts of prophecy which are not inferior to theirs, would not go out of life less merrily than the swans. Never mind then, if this be your only objection, but speak and ask anything which you like, while the eleven magistrates of Athens allow.

Very good, Socrates, said Simmias; then I will tell you my difficulty, and Cebes will tell you his. I feel myself (and I dare say that you have the same feeling), how hard or rather impossible is the attainment of any certainty about questions such as these in the present life. And yet I should deem him a coward who did not prove what is said about them to the uttermost, or whose heart failed him before he had examined them on every side. For he should persevere until he has achieved one of two things: either he should discover, or be taught the truth about them; or, if this be impossible, I would have him take the best and most irrefragable of human theories, and let this be the raft upon which he sails through life—not without risk, as I admit, if he cannot find some word of God which will more surely and safely carry him. And now, as you bid me, I will venture to question you, and then I shall not have to reproach myself hereafter with not having said at the time what I think. For when I consider the matter, either alone or with Cebes, the argument does certainly appear to me, Socrates, to be not sufficient.

Socrates answered: I dare say, my friend, that you may be right, but I should like to know in what respect the argument is insufficient.

In this respect, replied Simmias:—Suppose a person to use the same argument about harmony and the lyre—might he not say that harmony is a thing invisible, [86] incorporeal, perfect, divine, existing in the lyre which is harmonized, but that the lyre and the strings are matter and material, composite, earthy, and akin to mortality? And when some one breaks the lyre, or cuts and rends the strings, then he who takes this view would argue as you do, and on the same analogy, that the harmony survives and has not perished—you cannot imagine, he would say, that the lyre without the strings, and the broken strings themselves which are mortal remain, and yet that the harmony, which is of heavenly and immortal nature and kindred, has perished—perished before the mortal. The harmony must still be somewhere, and the wood and strings will decay before anything can happen to that. The thought, Socrates, must have occurred to your own mind that such is our conception of the soul; and that when the body is in a manner strung and held together by the elements of hot and cold, wet and dry, then the soul is the harmony or due proportionate admixture of them. But if so, whenever the strings of the body are unduly loosened or overstrained through disease or other injury, then the soul, though most divine, like other harmonies of music or of works of art, of course perishes at once; although the material remains of the body may last for a considerable time, until they are either decayed or burnt. And if any one maintains that the soul, being the harmony of the elements of the body, is first to perish in that which is called death, how shall we answer him?

Socrates looked fixedly at us as his manner was, and said with a smile: Simmias has reason on his side; and why does not some one of you who is better able than myself answer him? for there is force in his attack upon me. But perhaps, before we answer him, we had better also hear what Cebes has to say that we may gain time for reflection, and when they have both spoken, we may either assent to them, if there is truth in what they say, or if not, we will maintain our position. Please to tell me then, Cebes, he said, what was the difficulty which troubled you?

Cebes said: I will tell you. My feeling is that the argument is where it was, and open to the same objections which were urged before; [87] for I am ready to admit that the existence of the soul before entering into the bodily form has been very ingeniously, and, if I may say so, quite sufficiently proven; but the existence of the soul after death is still, in my judgment, unproven. Now my objection is not the same as that of Simmias; for I am not disposed to deny that the soul is stronger and more lasting than the body, being of opinion that in all such respects the soul very far excels the body. Well then, says the argument to me, why do you remain unconvinced?—When you see that the weaker continues in existence after the man is dead, will you not admit that the more lasting must also survive during the same period of time? Now I will ask you to consider whether the objection, which, like Simmias, I will express in a figure, is of any weight. The analogy which I will adduce is that of an old weaver, who dies, and after his death somebody says:—He is not dead, he must be alive;—see, there is the coat which he himself wove and wore, and which remains whole and undecayed. And then he proceeds to ask of some one who is incredulous, whether a man lasts longer, or the coat which is in use and wear; and when he is answered that a man lasts far longer, thinks that he has thus certainly demonstrated the survival of the man, who is the more lasting, because the less lasting remains. But that, Simmias, as I would beg you to remark, is a mistake; any one can see that he who talks thus is talking nonsense. For the truth is, that the weaver aforesaid, having woven and worn many such coats, outlived several of them; and was outlived by the last; but a man is not therefore proved to be slighter and weaker than a coat. Now the relation of the body to the soul may be expressed in a similar figure; and any one may very fairly say in like manner that the soul is lasting, and the body weak and shortlived in comparison. He may argue in like manner that every soul wears out many bodies, especially if a man live many years. While he is alive the body deliquesces and decays, and the soul always weaves another garment and repairs the waste. But of course, whenever the soul perishes, she must have on her last garment, and this will survive her; and then at length, when the soul is dead, the body will show its native weakness, and quickly decompose and pass away. I would therefore rather not rely on the argument from superior strength to prove the continued existence of the soul after death. [88] For granting even more than you affirm to be possible, and acknowledging not only that the soul existed before birth, but also that the souls of some exist, and will continue to exist after death, and will be born and die again, and that there is a natural strength in the soul which will hold out and be born many times—nevertheless, we may be still inclined to think that she will weary in the labours of successive births, and may at last succumb in one of her deaths and utterly perish; and this death and dissolution of the body which brings destruction to the soul may be unknown to any of us, for no one of us can have had any experience of it: and if so, then I maintain that he who is confident about death has but a foolish confidence, unless he is able to prove that the soul is altogether immortal and imperishable. But if he cannot prove the soul's immortality, he who is about to die will always have reason to fear that when the body is disunited, the soul also may utterly perish.

All of us, as we afterwards remarked to one another, had an unpleasant feeling at hearing what they said. When we had been so firmly convinced before, now to have our faith shaken seemed to introduce a confusion and uncertainty, not only into the previous argument, but into any future one; either we were incapable of forming a judgment, or there were no grounds of belief.

Ech. There I feel with you—by heaven I do, Phaedo, and when you were speaking, I was beginning to ask myself the same question: What argument can I ever trust again? For what could be more convincing than the argument of Socrates, which has now fallen into discredit? That the soul is a harmony is a doctrine which has always had a wonderful attraction for me, and, when mentioned, came back to me at once, as my own original conviction. And now I must begin again and find another argument which will assure me that when the man is dead the soul survives. Tell me, I implore you, how did Socrates proceed? Did he appear to share the unpleasant feeling which you mention? or did he calmly meet the attack? And did he answer forcibly or feebly? Narrate what passed as exactly as you can.

Phaed. Often, Echecrates, I have wondered at Socrates, but never more than on that occasion. [89] That he should be able to answer was nothing, but what astonished me was, first, the gentle and pleasant and approving manner in which he received the words of the young men, and then his quick sense of the wound which had been inflicted by the argument, and the readiness with which he healed it. He might be compared to a general rallying his defeated and broken army, urging them to accompany him and return to the field of argument.

Ech. What followed?

Phaed. You shall hear, for I was close to him on his right hand, seated on a sort of stool, and he on a couch which was a good deal higher. He stroked my head, and pressed the hair upon my neck—he had a way of playing with my hair; and then he said: To-morrow, Phaedo, I suppose that these fair locks of yours will be severed.

Yes, Socrates, I suppose that they will, I replied.

Not so, if you will take my advice.

What shall I do with them? I said.

To-day, he replied, and not to-morrow, if this argument dies and we cannot bring it to life again, you and I will both shave our locks: and if I were you, and the argument got away from me, and I could not hold my ground against Simmias and Cebes, I would myself take an oath, like the Argives, not to wear hair any more until I had renewed the conflict and defeated them.

Yes, I said; but Heracles himself is said not to be a match for two.

Summon me then, he said, and I will be your Iolaus until the sun goes down.

I summon you rather, I rejoined, not as Heracles summoning Iolaus, but as Iolaus might summon Heracles.

That will do as well, he said. But first let us take care that we avoid a danger.

Of what nature? I said.

Lest we become misologists, he replied: no worse thing can happen to a man than this. For as there are misanthropists or haters of men, there are also misologists or haters of ideas, and both spring from the same cause, which is ignorance of the world. Misanthropy arises out of the too great confidence of inexperience;—you trust a man and think him altogether true and sound and faithful, and then in a little while he turns out to be false and knavish; and then another and another, and when this has happened several times to a man, especially when it happens among those whom he deems to be his own most trusted and familiar friends, and he has often quarrelled with them, he at last hates all men, and believes that no one has any good in him at all. You must have observed this trait of character?

I have.

And is not the feeling discreditable? Is it not obvious that such an one having to deal with other men, was clearly without any experience of human nature; for experience would have taught him the true state of the case, *[90]* that

few are the good and few the evil, and that the great majority are in the interval between them.

What do you mean? I said.

I mean, he replied, as you might say of the very large and very small—that nothing is more uncommon than a very large or very small man; and this applies generally to all extremes, whether of great and small, or swift and slow, or fair and foul, or black and white: and whether the instances you select be men or dogs or anything else, few are the extremes, but many are in the mean between them. Did you never observe this?

Yes, I said, I have.

And do you not imagine, he said, that if there were a competition in evil, the worst would be found to be very few?

Yes, that is very likely, I said.

Yes, that is very likely, he replied; although in this respect arguments are unlike men—there I was led on by you to say more than I had intended; but the point of comparison was, that when a simple man who has no skill in dialectics believes an argument to be true which he afterwards imagines to be false, whether really false or not, and then another and another, he has no longer any faith left, and great disputers, as you know, come to think at last that they have grown to be the wisest of mankind; for they alone perceive the utter unsoundness and instability of all arguments, or indeed, of all things, which, like the currents in the Euripus, are going up and down in never-ceasing ebb and flow.

That is quite true, I said.

Yes, Phaedo, he replied, and how melancholy, if there be such a thing as truth or certainty or possibility of knowledge—that a man should have lighted upon some argument or other which at first seemed true and then turned out to be false, and instead of blaming himself and his own want of wit, because he is annoyed, should at last be too glad to transfer the blame from himself to arguments in general: and for ever afterwards should hate and revile them, and lose truth and the knowledge of realities.

Yes, indeed, I said; that is very melancholy.

Let us then, in the first place, he said, be careful of allowing or of admitting into our souls the notion that there is no health or soundness in any arguments at all. Rather say that we have not yet attained to soundness in ourselves, and that we must struggle manfully and do our best to gain health of mind—you and all other men having regard to the whole of your future life, and I myself in the prospect of death. *[91]* For at this moment I am sensible that I have not the temper of a philosopher; like the vulgar, I am only a partisan. Now the partisan, when he is engaged in a dispute, cares nothing about the rights of the question, but is anxious only to convince his hearers of his own assertions. And the difference between him and me at the present moment is merely this—that whereas he seeks to convince his hearers that what he says is true, I am rather seeking to convince myself; to convince my hearers is a secondary matter with me. And do but see much I gain by the argument. For if what I say is true, then I do well to be persuaded of the truth; but if there be nothing after death, still, during the short time that remains, I shall not distress my friends with lamentations, and my ignorance will not last, but will die with me, and therefore no harm will be done. This is the state of mind, Simmias and Cebes, in which I approach the argument. And I would ask you to be thinking of the truth and not of Socrates: agree with me, if I seem to you to be speaking the truth; or if not, withstand me might and main, that I may not deceive you as well as myself in my enthusiasm, and like the bee, leave my sting in you before I die.

And now let us proceed, he said. And first of all let me be sure that I have in my mind what you were saying. Simmias, if I remember rightly, has fears and misgivings whether the soul, although a fairer and diviner thing than the body, being as she is in the form of harmony, may not perish first. On the other hand, Cebes appeared to grant that the soul was more lasting than the body, but he said that no one could know whether the soul, after having worn out many bodies, might not perish herself and leave her last body behind her; and that this is death, which is the destruction not of the body but of the soul, for in the body the work of destruction is ever going on. Are not these, Simmias and Cebes, the points which we have to consider?

They both agreed to this statement of them.

He proceeded: And did you deny the force of the whole preceding argument, or of a part only?

Of a part only, they replied.

And what did you think, he said, of that part of the argument in which we said that knowledge was recollection, and hence inferred that the soul must have previously existed somewhere else *[92]* before she was enclosed in the body?

Cebes said that he had been wonderfully impressed by that part of the argument, and that his conviction remained absolutely unshaken. Simmias agreed, and added that he himself could hardly imagine the possibility of his ever thinking differently.

But, rejoined Socrates, you will have to think differently, my Theban friend, if you still maintain that harmony is a compound, and that the soul is a harmony which is made out of strings set in the frame of the body; for you will surely never allow yourself to say that a harmony is prior to the elements which compose it.

Never, Socrates.

But do you not see that this is what you imply when you say that the soul existed before she took the form and body of man, and was made up of elements which as yet had no existence? For harmony is not like the soul, as you suppose; but first the lyre, and the strings, and the sounds exist in a state of discord, and then harmony is made last of all, and perishes first. And how can such a notion of the soul as this agree with the other?

Not at all, replied Simmias.

And yet, he said, there surely ought to be harmony in a discourse of which harmony is the theme?

There ought, replied Simmias.

But there is no harmony, he said, in the two propositions that knowledge is recollection, and that the soul is a harmony. Which of them will you retain?

I think, he replied, that I have a much stronger faith, Socrates, in the first of the two, which has been fully demonstrated to me, than in the latter, which has not been demonstrated at all, but rests only on probable and plausible grounds; and is therefore believed by the many. I know too well that these arguments from probabilities are impostors, and unless great caution is observed in the use of them, they are apt to be deceptive—in geometry, and in other things too. But the doctrine of knowledge and recollection has been proven to me on trustworthy grounds: and the proof was that the soul must have existed before she came into the body, because to her belongs the essence of which the very name implies existence. Having, as I am convinced, rightly accepted this conclusion, and on sufficient grounds, I must, as I suppose, cease to argue or allow others to argue that the soul is a harmony.

Let me put the matter, Simmias, he said, in another point of view: *[93]* Do you imagine that a harmony or any other composition can be in a state other than that of the elements, out of which it is compounded?

Certainly not.

Or do or suffer anything other than they do or suffer?

He agreed.

Then a harmony does not, properly speaking, lead the parts or elements which make up the harmony, but only follows them.

He assented.

For harmony cannot possibly have any motion, or sound, or other quality which is opposed to its parts.

That would be impossible, he replied.

And does not the nature of every harmony depend upon the manner in which the elements are harmonized?

I do not understand you, he said.

I mean to say that a harmony admits of degrees, and is more of a harmony, and more completely a harmony, when more truly and fully harmonized, to any extent which is possible; and less of a harmony, and less completely a harmony, when less truly and fully harmonized.

True.

But does the soul admit of degrees? or is one soul in the very least degree more or less, or more or less completely, a soul than another?

Not in the least.

Yet surely of two souls, one is said to have intelligence and virtue, and to be good, and the other to have folly and vice, and to be an evil soul: and this is said truly?

Yes, truly.

But what will those who maintain the soul to be a harmony say of this presence of virtue and vice in the soul?—will they say that here is another harmony, and another discord, and that the virtuous soul is harmonized, and herself being a harmony has another harmony within her, and that the vicious soul is inharmonical and has no harmony within her?

I cannot tell, replied Simmias; but I suppose that something of the sort would be asserted by those who say that the soul is a harmony.

And we have already admitted that no soul is more a soul than another; which is equivalent to admitting that harmony is not more or less harmony, or more or less completely a harmony?

Quite true.

And that which is not more or less a harmony is not more or less harmonized?

True.

And that which is not more or less harmonized cannot have more or less of harmony, but only an equal harmony?

Yes, an equal harmony.

Then one soul not being more or less absolutely a soul than another, is not more or less harmonized?

Exactly.

And therefore has neither more nor less of discord, nor yet of harmony?

She has not.

And having neither more nor less of harmony or of discord, one soul has no more vice or virtue than another, if vice be discord and virtue harmony?

Not at all more.

[94] Or speaking more correctly, Simmias, the soul, if she is a harmony, will never have any vice; because a harmony, being absolutely a harmony, has no part in the inharmonical.

No.

And therefore a soul which is absolutely a soul has no vice?

How can she have, if the previous argument holds?

Then, if all souls are equally by their nature souls, all souls of all living creatures will be equally good?

I agree with you, Socrates, he said.

And can all this be true, think you? he said; for these are the consequences which seem to follow from the assumption that the soul is a harmony?

It cannot be true.

Once more, he said, what ruler is there of the elements of human nature other than the soul, and especially the wise soul? Do you know of any?

Indeed, I do not.

And is the soul in agreement with the affections of the body? or is she at variance with them? For example, when the body is hot and thirsty, does not the soul incline us against drinking? and when the body is hungry, against eating? And this is only one instance out of ten thousand of the opposition of the soul to the things of the body.

Very true.

But we have already acknowledged that the soul, being a harmony, can never utter a note at variance with the tensions and relaxations and vibrations and other affections of the strings out of which she is composed; she can only follow, she cannot lead them?

It must be so, he replied.

And yet do we not now discover the soul

to be doing the exact opposite—leading the elements of which she is believed to be composed; almost always opposing and coercing them in all sorts of ways throughout life, sometimes more violently with the pains of medicine and gymnastic; then again more gently; now threatening, now admonishing the desires, passions, fears, as if talking to a thing which is not herself, as Homer in the *Odyssey* represents Odysseus doing in the words:

He beat his breast, and thus reproached his heart:
Endure, my heart; far worse hast thou endured!

Do you think that Homer wrote this under the idea that the soul is a harmony capable of being led by the affections of the body, and not rather of a nature which should lead and master them—herself a far diviner thing than any harmony?

Yes, Socrates, I quite think so.

Then, my friend, we can never be right in saying that the soul is a harmony, *[95]* for we should contradict the divine Homer, and contradict ourselves.

True, he said.

Thus much, said Socrates, of Harmonia, your Theban goddess, who has graciously yielded to us; but what shall I say, Cebes, to her husband Cadmus, and how shall I make peace with him?

I think that you will discover a way of propitiating him, said Cebes; I am sure that you have put the argument with Harmonia in a manner that I could never have expected. For when Simmias was mentioning his difficulty, I quite imagined that no answer could be given to him, and therefore I was surprised at finding that his argument could not sustain the first onset of yours, and not impossibly the other, whom you call Cadmus, may share a similar fate.

Nay, my good friend, said Socrates, let us not boast, lest some evil eye should put to flight the word which I am about to speak. That, however, may be left in the hands of those above; while I draw near in Homeric fashion, and try the mettle of your words. Here lies the point:—You want to have it proven to you that the soul is imperishable and immortal, and the philosopher who is confident in death appears to you to have but a vain and foolish confidence, if he believes that he will fare better in the world below than one who has led another sort of life, unless he can prove this: and you say that the demonstration of the strength and divinity of the soul, and of her existence prior

to our becoming men, does not necessarily imply her immortality. Admitting the soul to be long-lived, and to have known and done much in a former state, still she is not on that account immortal; and her entrance into the human form may be a sort of disease which is the beginning of dissolution, and may at last, after the toils of life are over, end in that which is called death. And whether the soul enters into the body once only or many times, does not, as you say, make any difference in the fears of individuals. For any man, who is not devoid of sense, must fear, if he has no knowledge and can give no account of the soul's immortality. This, or something like this, I suspect to be your notion, Cebes; and I designedly recur to it in order that nothing may escape us, and that you may, if you wish, add or subtract anything.

But, said Cebes, as far as I see at present, I have nothing to add or subtract: I mean what you say that I mean.

Socrates paused awhile, and seemed to be absorbed in reflection. At length he said: You are raising a tremendous question, Cebes, involving the whole nature of generation and corruption, *[96]* about which, if you like, I will give you my own experience; and if anything which I say is likely to avail towards the solution of your difficulty you may make use of it.

I should very much like, said Cebes, to hear what you have to say.

Then I will tell you, said Socrates. When I was young, Cebes, I had a prodigious desire to know that department of philosophy which is called the investigation of nature; to know the causes of things, and why a thing is and is created or destroyed appeared to me to be a lofty profession; and I was always agitating myself with the consideration of questions such as these:—Is the growth of animals the result of some decay which the hot and cold principle contracts, as some have said? Is the blood the element with which we think, or the air, or the fire? or perhaps nothing of the kind—but the brain may be the originating power of the perceptions of hearing and sight and smell, and memory and opinion may come from them, and science may be based on memory and opinion when they have attained fixity. And then I went on to examine the corruption of them, and then to the things of heaven and earth, and at last I concluded myself to be utterly and absolutely incapable of these enquiries, as I will satisfactorily prove to you, For

I was fascinated by them to such a degree that my eyes grew blind to things which I had seemed to myself, and also to others, to know quite well; I forgot what I had before thought self-evident truths; e.g. such a fact as that the growth of man is the result of eating and drinking; for when by the digestion of food flesh is added to flesh and bone to bone, and whenever there is an aggregation of congenial elements, the lesser bulk becomes larger and the small man great. Was not that a reasonable notion?

Yes, said Cebes, I think so.

Well; but let me tell you something more. There was a time when I thought that I understood the meaning of greater and less pretty well; and when I saw a great man standing by a little one, I fancied that one was taller than the other by a head; or one horse would appear to be greater than another horse: and still more clearly did I seem to perceive that ten is two more than eight, and that two cubits are more than one, because two is the double of one.

And what is now your notion of such matters? said Cebes.

I should be far enough from imagining, he replied, that I knew the cause of any of them, by heaven I should; for I cannot satisfy myself that, [97] when one is added to one, the one to which the addition is made becomes two, or that the two units added together make two by reason of the addition. I cannot understand how, when separated from the other, each of them was one and not two, and now, when they are brought together, the mere juxtaposition or meeting of them should be the cause of their becoming two: neither can I understand how the division of one is the way to make two; for then a different cause would produce the same effect,—as in the former instance the addition and juxtaposition of one to one was the cause of two, in this the separation and subtraction of one from the other would be the cause. Nor am I any longer satisfied that I understand the reason why one or anything else is either generated or destroyed or is at all, but I have in my mind some confused notion of a new method, and can never admit the other.

Then I heard some one reading, as he said, from a book of Anaxagoras, that mind was the disposer and cause of all, and I was delighted at this notion, which appeared quite admirable, and I said to myself: If mind is the disposer, mind will dispose all for the best, and put each particular in the best place; and I argued that if

any one desired to find out the cause of the generation or destruction or existence of anything, he must find out what state of being or doing or suffering was best for that thing, and therefore a man had only to consider the best for himself and others, and then he would also know the worse, since the same science comprehended both. And I rejoiced to think that I had found in Anaxagoras a teacher of the causes of existence such as I desired, and I imagined that he would tell me first whether the earth is flat or round; and whichever was true, he would proceed to explain the cause and the necessity of this being so, and then he would teach me the nature of the best and show that this was best; and if he said that the earth was in the centre, he would further explain that this position was the best, and I should be satisfied with the explanation given, and not want any other sort of cause. [98] And I thought that I would then go on and ask him about the sun and moon and stars, and that he would explain to me their comparative swiftness, and their returnings and various states, active and passive, and how all of them were for the best. For I could not imagine that when he spoke of mind as the disposer of them, he would give any other account of their being as they are, except that this was best; and I thought that when he had explained to me in detail the cause of each and the cause of all, he would go on to explain to me what was best for each and what was good for all. These hopes I would not have sold for a large sum of money, and I seized the books and read them as fast as I could in my eagerness to know the better and the worse.

What expectations I had formed, and how grievously was I disappointed! As I proceeded, I found my philosopher altogether forsaking mind or any other principle of order, but having recourse to air, and ether, and water, and other eccentricities. I might compare him to a person who began by maintaining generally that mind is the cause of the actions of Socrates, but who, when he endeavoured to explain the causes of my several actions in detail, went on to show that I sit here because my body is made up of bones and muscles; and the bones, as he would say, are hard and have joints which divide them, and the muscles are elastic, and they cover the bones, which have also a covering or environment of flesh and skin which contains them; and as the bones are lifted at their joints by the contraction or relaxation of the muscles, I am able to bend my limbs, and this is why I am sitting here in a curved posture—that is what he would say; and he would have a similar explanation of my talking to you, which he would attribute to sound, and air, and hearing, and he would assign ten thousand other causes of the same sort, forgetting to mention the true cause, which is, that the Athenians have thought fit to condemn me, and accordingly I have thought it better and more right to remain here and undergo my sentence; [99] for I am inclined to think that these muscles and bones of mine would have gone off long ago to Megara or Boeotia—by the dog, they would, if they had been moved only by their own idea of what was best, and if I had not chosen the better and nobler part, instead of playing truant and running away, of enduring any punishment which the state inflicts. There is surely a strange confusion of causes and conditions in all this. It may be said, indeed, that without bones and muscles and the other parts of the body I cannot execute my purposes. But to say that I do as I do because of them, and that this is the way in which mind acts, and not from the choice of the best, is a very careless and idle mode of speaking. I wonder that they cannot distinguish the cause from the condition, which the many, feeling about in the dark, are always mistaking and misnaming. And thus one man makes a vortex all round and steadies the earth by the heaven; another gives the air as a support to the earth, which is a sort of broad trough. Any power which in arranging them as they are arranges them for the best never enters into their minds; and instead of finding any superior strength in it, they rather expect to discover another Atlas of the world who is stronger and more everlasting and more containing than the good; —of the obligatory and containing power of the good they think nothing; and yet this is the principle which I would fain learn if any one would teach me. But as I have failed either to discover myself, or to learn of any one else, the nature of the best, I will exhibit to you, if you like, what I have found to be the second best mode of enquiring into the cause.

I should very much like to hear, he replied.

Socrates proceeded: I thought that as I had failed in the contemplation of true existence, I ought to be careful that I did not lose the eye of my soul; as people may injure their bodily eye by observing and gazing on the sun during an eclipse, unless they take the precaution of only looking at the image reflected in the water, or in some similar medium. So in my own case, I was afraid that my soul might be blinded altogether if I looked at things with my eyes or tried to apprehend them by the help of the senses. And I thought that I had better have recourse to the world of mind and seek there the truth of existence. [100] I dare say that the simile is not perfect—for I am very far from admitting that he who contemplates existences through the medium of thought, sees them only "through a glass darkly," any more than he who considers them in action and operation. However, this was the method which I adopted: I first assumed some principle which I judged to be the strongest, and then I affirmed as true whatever seemed to agree with this, whether relating to the cause or to anything else; and that which disagreed I regarded as untrue. But I should like to explain my meaning more clearly, as I do not think that you as yet understand me.

No indeed, replied Cebes, not very well.

There is nothing new, he said, in what I am about to tell you; but only what I have been always and everywhere repeating in the previous discussion and on other occasions: I want to show you the nature of that cause which has occupied my thoughts. I shall have to go back to those familiar words which are in the mouth of every one, and first of all assume that there is an absolute beauty and goodness and greatness, and the like; grant me this, and I hope to be able to show you the nature of the cause, and to prove the immortality of the soul.

Cebes said: You may proceed at once with the proof, for I grant you this.

Well, he said, then I should like to know whether you agree with me in the next step; for I cannot help thinking, if there be anything beautiful other than absolute beauty should there be such, that it can be beautiful only in so far as it partakes of absolute beauty— and I should say the same of everything. Do you agree in this notion of the cause?

Yes, he said, I agree.

He proceeded: I know nothing and can understand nothing of any other of those wise causes which are alleged; and if a person says to me that the bloom of colour, or form, or any such thing is a source of beauty, I leave all that, which is only confusing to me, and simply and singly, and perhaps foolishly, hold and am assured in my own mind that nothing makes a thing beautiful but the presence and participation of beauty in whatever way or manner obtained; for as to the manner I am uncertain, but I stoutly contend that by beauty all beautiful things become beautiful. This appears to me to be the safest answer which I can give, either to myself or to another, and to this I cling, in the persuasion that this principle will never be overthrown, and that to myself or to any one who asks the question, I may safely reply, That by beauty beautiful things become beautiful. Do you not agree with me?

I do.

And that by greatness only great things become great and greater greater, and by smallness the less become less?

True.

Then if a person were to remark that A is taller by a head than B, [101] and B less by a head than A, you would refuse to admit his statement, and would stoutly contend that what you mean is only that the greater is greater by, and by reason of, greatness, and the less is less only by, and by reason of, smallness; and thus you would avoid the danger of saying that the greater is greater and the less less by the measure of the head, which is the same in both, and would also avoid the monstrous absurdity of supposing that the greater man is greater by reason of the head, which is small. You would be afraid to draw such an inference, would you not?

Indeed, I should, said Cebes, laughing.

In like manner you would be afraid to say that ten exceeded eight by, and by reason of, two; but would say by, and by reason of, number; or you would say that two cubits exceed one cubit not by a half, but by magnitude?—for there is the same liability to error in all these cases.

Very true, he said.

Again, would you not be cautious of affirming that the addition of one to one, or the division of one, is the cause of two? And you would loudly asseverate that you know of no way in which anything comes into existence except by participation in its own proper essence, and consequently, as far as you know, the only cause of two is the participation in duality—this is the way to make two, and the participation in one is the way to make one. You would say: I will let alone puzzles of division and addition—wiser heads than mine may answer them; inexperienced as I am, and ready to start, as the proverb says, at my own shadow, I cannot afford to give up the sure ground of a principle. And if any one assails you there, you would not mind him, or answer him until you had seen whether the consequences which follow agree with one another or not, and when you are further required to give an explanation of this principle, you would go on to assume a higher principle, and a higher, until you found a resting-place in the best of the higher; but you would not confuse the principle and the consequences in your reasoning, like the Eristics—at least if you wanted to discover real existence. Not that this confusion signifies to them, who never care or think about the matter at all, for they have the wit to be well pleased with themselves however great may be the turmoil of their ideas. [102] But you, if you are a philosopher, will certainly do as I say.

What you say is most true, said Simmias and Cebes, both speaking at once.

Ech. Yes, Phaedo; and I do not wonder at their assenting. Any one who has the least sense will acknowledge the wonderful clearness of Socrates' reasoning.

Phaed. Certainly, Echecrates; and such was the feeling of the whole company at the time.

Ech. Yes, and equally of ourselves, who were not of the company, and are now listening to your recital. But what followed?

Phaed. After all this had been admitted, and they had agreed that ideas exist, and that other things participate in them and derive their names from them, Socrates, if I remember rightly, said:—

This is your way of speaking; and yet when you say that Simmias is greater than Socrates and less than Phaedo, do you not predicate of Simmias both greatness and smallness?

Yes, I do.

But still you allow that Simmias does not really exceed Socrates, as the words may seem to imply, because he is Simmias, but by reason of the size which he has; just as Simmias does not exceed Socrates because he is Simmias, any more than because Socrates is Socrates, but because he has smallness when compared with the greatness of Simmias?

True.

And if Phaedo exceeds him in size, this is not because Phaedo is Phaedo, but because Phaedo has greatness relatively to Simmias, who is comparatively smaller?

That is true.

And therefore Simmias is said to be great, and is also said to be small, because he is in a mean between them, exceeding the smallness of the one by his greatness, and allowing the greatness of the other to exceed his smallness. He added, laughing, I am speaking like a book, but I believe that what I am saying is true.

Simmias assented.

I speak as I do because I want you to agree with me in thinking, not only that absolute greatness will never be great and also small, but that greatness in us or in the concrete will never admit the small or admit of being exceeded: instead of this, one of two things will happen, either the greater will fly or retire before the opposite, which is the less, or at the approach of the less has already ceased to exist; but will not, if allowing or admitting of smallness, be changed by that; even as I, having received and admitted smallness when compared with Simmias, remain just as I was, and am the same small person. And as the idea of greatness cannot condescend ever to be or become small, in like manner the smallness in us cannot be or become great; nor can any other opposite which remains the same ever be or become its own opposite, [103] but either passes away or perishes in the change.

That, replied Cebes, is quite my notion.

Hereupon one of the company, though I do not exactly remember which of them, said: In heaven's name, is not this the direct contrary of what was admitted before—that out of the greater came the less and out of the less the greater, and that opposites were simply generated from opposites; but now this principle seems to be utterly denied.

Socrates inclined his head to the speaker and listened. I like your courage, he said, in reminding us of this. But you do not observe that there is a difference in the two cases. For then we were speaking of opposites in the concrete, and now of the essential opposite which, as is affirmed, neither in us nor in nature can ever be at variance with itself: then, my friend, we were speaking of things in which opposites are inherent and which are called after them, but now about the opposites which are inherent in them and which give their name to them; and these essential opposites will never, as we maintain, admit of generation into or out of one another. At the same time, turning to Cebes, he said: Are you at all disconcerted, Cebes, at our friend's objection?

No, I do not feel so, said Cebes; and yet I cannot deny that I am often disturbed by objections.

Then we are agreed after all, said Socrates, that the opposite will never in any case be opposed to itself?

To that we are quite agreed, he replied.

Yet once more let me ask you to consider the question from another point of view, and see whether you agree with me:—There is a thing which you term heat, and another thing which you term cold?

Certainly.

But are they the same as fire and snow?

Most assuredly not.

Heat is a thing different from fire, and cold is not the same with snow?

Yes.

And yet you will surely admit, that when snow, as was before said, is under the influence of heat, they will not remain snow and heat; but at the advance of the heat, the snow will either retire or perish?

Very true, he replied.

And the fire too at the advance of the cold will either retire or perish; and when the fire is under the influence of the cold, they will not remain as before, fire and cold.

That is true, he said.

And in some cases the name of the idea is not only attached to the idea in an eternal connection, but anything else which, not being the idea, exists only in the form of the idea, may also lay claim to it. I will try to make this clearer by an example:—The odd number is always called by the name of odd?

Very true.

But is this the only thing which is called odd? Are there not other things which have their own name, [104] and yet are called odd, because, although not the same as oddness, they are never without oddness?—that is what I mean to ask—whether numbers such as the number three are not of the class of odd. And there are many other examples: would you not say, for example, that three may be called by its proper name, and also be called odd, which is not the same with three? and this may be said not only of three but also of five, and of every alternate number—each of them without being oddness is odd; and in the same way two and four, and the other series of alternate numbers, has every number even, without being evenness. Do you agree?

Of course.

Then now mark the point at which I am aiming:—not only do essential opposites exclude one another, but also concrete things, which, although not in themselves opposed, contain opposites; these, I say, likewise reject the idea which is opposed to that which is contained in them, and when it approaches them they either perish or withdraw. For example; Will not the number three endure annihilation or anything sooner than be converted into an even number, while remaining three?

Very true, said Cebes.

And yet, he said, the number two is certainly not opposed to the number three?

It is not.

Then not only do opposite ideas repel the advance of one another, but also there are other natures which repel the approach of opposites.

Very true, he said.

Suppose, he said, that we endeavour, if possible, to determine what these are.

By all means.

Are they not, Cebes, such as compel the things of which they have possession, not only to take their own form, but also the form of some opposite?

What do you mean?

I mean, as I was just now saying, and as I am sure that you know, that those things which are possessed by the number three must not only be three in number, but must also be odd.

Quite true.

And on this oddness, of which the number three has the impress, the opposite idea will never intrude?

No.

And this impress was given by the odd principle?

Yes.

And to the odd is opposed the even?

True.

Then the idea of the even number will never arrive at three?

No.

Then three has no part in the even?

None.

Then the triad or number three is uneven?

Very true.

To return then to my distinction of natures which are not opposed, and yet do not admit opposites—as, in the instance given, three, although not opposed to the even, does not any the more admit of the even, but always brings the opposite into play on the other side; [105] or as two does not receive the odd, or fire the cold—from these examples (and there are many more of them) perhaps you may be able to arrive at the general conclusion, that not only opposites will not receive opposites, but also that nothing which brings the opposite will admit the opposite of that which it brings, in that to which it is brought. And here let me recapitulate—for there is no harm in repetition. The number five will not admit the nature of the even, any more than ten, which is the double of five, will admit the nature of the

odd. The double has another opposite, and is not strictly opposed to the odd, but nevertheless rejects the odd altogether. Nor again will parts in the ratio 3:2, nor any fraction in which there is a half, nor again in which there is a third, admit the notion of the whole, although they are not opposed to the whole: You will agree?

Yes, he said, I entirely agree and go along with you in that.

And now, he said, let us begin again; and do not you answer my question in the words in which I ask it: let me have not the old safe answer of which I spoke at first, but another equally safe, of which the truth will be inferred by you from what has been just said. I mean that if any one asks you "what that is, of which the inherence makes the body hot," you will reply not heat (this is what I call the safe and stupid answer), but fire, a far superior answer, which we are now in a condition to give. Or if any one asks you "why a body is diseased," you will not say from disease, but from fever; and instead of saying that oddness is the cause of odd numbers, you will say that the monad is the cause of them: and so of things in general, as I dare say that you will understand sufficiently without my adducing any further examples.

Yes, he said, I quite understand you.

Tell me, then, what is that of which the inherence will render the body alive?

The soul, he replied.

And is this always the case?

Yes, he said, of course.

Then whatever the soul possesses, to that she comes bearing life?

Yes, certainly.

And is there any opposite to life?

There is, he said.

And what is that?

Death.

Then the soul, as has been acknowledged, will never receive the opposite of what she brings.

Impossible, replied Cebes.

And now, he said, what did we just now call that principle which repels the even?

The odd.

And that principle which repels the musical or the just?

The unmusical, he said, and the unjust.

And what do we call that principle which does not admit of death?

The immortal, he said.

And does the soul admit of death?

No.

Then the soul is immortal?

Yes, he said.

And may we say that this has been proven?

Yes, abundantly proven, Socrates, he replied.

[106] Supposing that the odd were imperishable, must not three be imperishable?

Of course.

And if that which is cold were imperishable, when the warm principle came attacking the snow, must not the snow have retired whole and unmelted—for it could never have perished, nor could it have remained and admitted the heat?

True, he said.

Again, if the uncooling or warm principle were imperishable, the fire when assailed by cold would not have perished or have been extinguished, but would have gone away unaffected?

Certainly, he said.

And the same may be said of the immortal: if the immortal is also imperishable, the soul when attacked by death cannot perish; for the preceding argument shows that the soul will not admit of death, or ever be dead, any more than three or the odd number will admit of the even, or fire, or the heat in the fire, of the cold. Yet a person may say: "But although the odd will not become even at the approach of the even, why may not the odd perish and the even take the place of the odd?" Now to him who makes this objection, we cannot answer that the odd principle is imperishable; for this has not been acknowledged, but if this had been acknowledged, there would have been no difficulty in contending that at the approach of the even the odd principle and the number three took their departure; and the same argument would have held good of fire and heat and any other thing.

Very true.

And the same may be said of the immortal: if the immortal is also imperishable, then the soul will be imperishable as well as immortal; but if not, some other proof of her imperishableness will have to be given.

No other proof is needed, he said; for if the immortal, being eternal, is liable to perish, then nothing is imperishable.

Yes, replied Socrates, and yet all men will agree that God, and the essential form of life, and the immortal in general, will never perish.

Yes, all men, he said—that is true; and what is more, gods, if I am not mistaken, as well as men.

Seeing then that the immortal is indestructible, must not the soul, if she is immortal, be also imperishable?

Most certainly.

Then when death attacks a man, the mortal portion of him may be supposed to die, but the immortal retires at the approach of death and is preserved safe and sound?

True.

Then, Cebes, beyond question, the soul is immortal and imperishable, [107] and our souls will truly exist in another world!

I am convinced, Socrates, said Cebes, and have nothing more to object; but if my friend Simmias, or any one else, has any further objection to make, he had better speak out, and not keep silence, since I do not know to what other season he can defer the discussion, if there is anything which he wants to say or to have said.

But I have nothing more to say, replied Simmias; nor can I see any reason for doubt after what has been said. But I still feel and cannot help feeling uncertain in my own mind, when I think of the greatness of the subject and the feebleness of man.

Yes, Simmias, replied Socrates, that is well said: and I may add that first principles, even if they appear certain, should be carefully considered; and when they are satisfactorily ascertained, then, with a sort of hesitating confidence in human reason, you may, I think, follow the course of the argument; and if that be plain and clear, there will be no need for any further enquiry.

Very true.

But then, O my friends, he said, if the soul is really immortal, what care should be taken of her, not only in respect of the portion of time which is called life, but of eternity! And the danger of neglecting her from this point of view does indeed appear to be awful. If death had only been the end of all, the wicked would have had a good bargain in dying, for they would have been happily quit not only of their body, but of their own evil together with their souls. But now, inasmuch as the soul is manifestly immortal, there is no release or salvation from evil except the attainment of the highest virtue and wisdom. For the soul when on her progress to the world below takes nothing with her but nurture and education; and these are said greatly to benefit or greatly to injure the departed, at the very beginning of his journey thither.

For after death, as they say, the genius of

each individual, to whom he belonged in life, leads him to a certain place in which the dead are gathered together, whence after judgment has been given they pass into the world below, following the guide, who is appointed to conduct them from this world to the other: and when they have there received their due and remained their time, another guide brings them back again after many revolutions of ages. Now this way to the other world is not, [108] as Aeschylus says in the Telephus, a single and straight path—if that were so no guide would be needed, for no one could miss it; but there are many partings of the road, and windings, as I infer from the rites and sacrifices which are offered to the gods below in places where three ways meet on earth. The wise and orderly soul follows in the straight path and is conscious of her surroundings; but the soul which desires the body, and which, as I was relating before, has long been fluttering about the lifeless frame and the world of sight, is after many struggles and many sufferings hardly and with violence carried away by her attendant genius; and when she arrives at the place where the other souls are gathered, if she be impure and have done impure deeds, whether foul murders or other crimes which are the brothers of these, and the works of brothers in crime—from that soul every one flees and turns away; no one will be her companion, no one her guide, but alone she wanders in extremity of evil until certain times are fulfilled, and when they are fulfilled, she is borne irresistibly to her own fitting habitation; as every pure and just soul which has passed through life in the company and under the guidance of the gods has also her own proper home.

Now the earth has divers wonderful regions, and is indeed in nature and extent very unlike the notions of geographers, as I believe on the authority of one who shall be nameless.

What do you mean, Socrates? said Simmias. I have myself heard many descriptions of the earth, but I do not know, and I should very much like to know, in which of these you put faith.

And I, Simmias, replied Socrates, if I had the art of Glaucus would tell you; although I know not that the art of Glaucus could prove the truth of my tale, which I myself should never be able to prove, and even if I could, I fear, Simmias, that my life would come to an end before the argument was completed. I may describe to you, however, the form and regions of the earth according to my conception of them.

That, said Simmias, will be enough.

Well then, he said, my conviction is, that the earth is a round body in the centre of the heavens, and therefore has no need of air or of any similar force to be a support, [109] but is kept there and hindered from falling or inclining any way by the equability of the surrounding heaven and by her own equipoise. For that which, being in equipoise, is in the centre of that which is equably diffused, will not incline any way in any degree, but will always remain in the same state and not deviate. And this is my first notion.

Which is surely a correct one, said Simmias.

Also I believe that the earth is very vast, and that we who dwell in the region extending from the river Phasis to the Pillars of Heracles inhabit a small portion only about the sea, like ants or frogs about a marsh, and that there are other inhabitants of many other like places; for everywhere on the face of the earth there are hollows of various forms and sizes, into which the water and the mist and the lower air collect. But the true earth is pure and situated in the pure heaven—there are the stars also; and it is the heaven which is commonly spoken of by us as the ether, and of which our own earth is the sediment gathering in the hollows beneath. But we who live in these hollows are deceived into the notion that we are dwelling above on the surface of the earth; which is just as if a creature who was at the bottom of the sea were to fancy that he was on the surface of the water, and that the sea was the heaven through which he saw the sun and the other stars, he having never come to the surface by reason of his feebleness and sluggishness, and having never lifted up his head and seen, nor ever heard from one who had seen, how much purer and fairer the world above is than his own. And such is exactly our case: for we are dwelling in a hollow of the earth, and fancy that we are on the surface; and the air we call heaven, in which we imagine that the stars move. But the fact is, that owing to our feebleness and sluggishness we are prevented from reaching the surface of the air: for if any man could arrive at the exterior limit, or take the wings of a bird and come to the top, then like a fish who puts his head out of the water and sees this world, he would see a world beyond; and, if the nature of man could sustain the sight, he would acknowledge that this other world was the place of the true heaven and the true light and the true earth. [110] For our earth, and the stones, and the entire region which surrounds us, are spoilt and corroded, as in the sea all things are corroded by the brine, neither is there any noble or perfect growth, but caverns only, and sand, and an endless slough of mud; and even the shore is not to be compared to the fairer sights of this world. And still less is this our world to be compared with the other. Of that upper earth which is under the heaven, I can tell you a charming tale, Simmias, which is well worth hearing.

And we, Socrates, replied Simmias, shall be charmed to listen to you.

The tale, my friend, he said, is as follows:— In the first place, the earth, when looked at from above, is in appearance streaked like one of those balls which have leather coverings in twelve pieces, and is decked with various colours, of which the colours used by painters on earth are in a manner samples. But there the whole earth is made up of them, and they are brighter far and clearer than ours; there is a purple of wonderful lustre, also the radiance of gold, and the white which is in the earth is whiter than any chalk or snow. Of these and other colours the earth is made up, and they are more in number and fairer than the eye of man has ever seen; the very hollows (of which I was speaking) filled with air and water have a colour of their own, and are seen like light gleaming amid the diversity of the other colours, so that the whole presents a single and continuous appearance of variety in unity. And in this fair region everything that grows—trees, and flowers, and fruits—are in a like degree fairer than any here; and there are hills, having stones in them in a like degree smoother, and more transparent, and fairer in colour than our highly-valued emeralds and sardonyxes and jaspers, and other gems, which are but minute fragments of them: for there all the stones are like our precious stones, and fairer still.[1] The reason is, that they are pure, and not, like our precious stones, infected or corroded by the corrupt briny elements which coagulate among us, and which breed foulness and disease both in earth and stones, as well as in animals and plants. They are the jewels of the upper earth, which also shines with gold and silver and the like, [111] and they are set in the light of day and are large and abundant and in all places, making the earth a sight to gladden the beholder's eye. And there are animals and men, some in a middle region, others dwelling about

[1] Cf. Revelation, esp. 21. 18 ff.

the air as we dwell about the sea; others in islands which the air flows round, near the continent; and in a word, the air is used by them as the water and the sea are by us, and the ether is to them what the air is to us. Moreover, the temperament of their seasons is such that they have no disease, and live much longer than we do, and have sight and hearing and smell, and all the other senses, in far greater perfection, in the same proportion that air is purer than water or the ether than air. Also they have temples and sacred places in which the gods really dwell, and they hear their voices and receive their answers, and are conscious of them and hold converse with them; and they see the sun, moon, and stars as they truly are, and their other blessedness is of a piece with this.

Such is the nature of the whole earth, and of the things which are around the earth; and there are divers regions in the hollows on the face of the globe everywhere, some of them deeper and more extended than that which we inhabit, others deeper but with a narrower opening than ours, and some are shallower and also wider. All have numerous perforations, and there are passages broad and narrow in the interior of the earth, connecting them with one another; and there flows out of and into them, as into basins, a vast tide of water, and huge subterranean streams of perennial rivers, and springs hot and cold, and a great fire, and great rivers of fire, and streams of liquid mud, thin or thick (like the rivers of mud in Sicily, and the lava streams which follow them), and the regions about which they happen to flow are filled up with them. And there is a swinging or see-saw in the interior of the earth which moves all this up and down, and is due to the following cause:—There is a chasm which is the vastest of them all, and pierces right through the whole earth; [112] this is that chasm which Homer describes in the words:

Far off, where is the inmost depth beneath the earth;

and which he in other places, and many other poets, have called Tartarus. And the see-saw is caused by the streams flowing into and out of this chasm, and they each have the nature of the soil through which they flow. And the reason why the streams are always flowing in and out, is that the watery element has no bed or bottom, but is swinging and surging up and down, and the surrounding wind and air do the same; they follow the water up and down, hither and thither, over the earth—just as in the act of respiration the air is always in process of inhalation and exhalation;—and the wind swinging with the water in and out produces fearful and irresistible blasts: when the waters retire with a rush into the lower parts of the earth, as they are called, they flow through the earth in those regions, and fill them up like water raised by a pump, and then when they leave those regions and rush back hither, they again fill the hollows here, and when these are filled, flow through subterranean channels and find their way to their several places, forming seas, and lakes, and rivers, and springs. Thence they again enter the earth, some of them making a long circuit into many lands, others going to a few places and not so distant; and again fall into Tartarus, some at a point a good deal lower than that at which they rose, and others not much lower, but all in some degree lower than the point from which they came. And some burst forth again on the opposite side, and some on the same side, and some wind round the earth with one or many folds like the coils of a serpent, and descend as far as they can, but always return and fall into the chasm. The rivers flowing in either direction can descend only to the centre and no further, for opposite to the rivers is a precipice.

Now these rivers are many, and mighty, and diverse, and there are four principal ones, of which the greatest and outermost is that called Oceanus, which flows round the earth in a circle; and in the opposite direction flows Acheron, which passes under the earth through desert places into the Acherusian lake: [113] this is the lake to the shores of which the souls of the many go when they are dead, and after waiting an appointed time, which is to some a longer and to some a shorter time, they are sent back to be born again as animals. The third river passes out between the two, and near the place of outlet pours into a vast region of fire, and forms a lake larger than the Mediterranean Sea, boiling with water and mud; and proceeding muddy and turbid, and winding about the earth, comes, among other places, to the extremities of the Acherusian lake, but mingles not with the waters of the lake, and after making many coils about the earth plunges into Tartarus at a deeper level. This is that Pyriphlegethon, as the stream is called, which throws up jets of fire in different parts of the earth. The fourth river goes out on the opposite side, and falls first of all into a wild and savage region, which is all of a dark blue colour, like lapis lazuli; and this is that river which is called the Stygian river, and falls into and forms the Lake Styx, and after falling into the lake and receiving strange powers in the waters, passes under the earth, winding round in the opposite direction, and comes near the Acherusian lake from the opposite side to Pyriphlegethon. And the water of this river too mingles with no other, but flows round in a circle and falls into Tartarus over against Pyriphlegethon; and the name of the river, as the poets say, is Cocytus.

Such is the nature of the other world; and when the dead arrive at the place to which the genius of each severally guides them, first of all, they have sentence passed upon them, as they have lived well and piously or not. And those who appear to have lived neither well nor ill, go to the river Acheron, and embarking in any vessels which they may find, are carried in them to the lake, and there they dwell and are purified of their evil deeds, and having suffered the penalty of the wrongs which they have done to others, they are absolved, and receive the rewards of their good deeds, each of them according to his deserts. But those who appear to be incurable by reason of the greatness of their crimes—who have committed many and terrible deeds of sacrilege, murders foul and violent, or the like—such are hurled into Tartarus which is their suitable destiny, and they never come out. Those again who have committed crimes, which, although great, are not irremediable—who in a moment of anger, for example, have done some violence to a father or a mother, [114] and have repented for the remainder of their lives, or, who have taken the life of another under the like extenuating circumstances—these are plunged into Tartarus, the pains of which they are compelled to undergo for a year, but at the end of the year the wave casts them forth—mere homicides by way of Cocytus, parricides and matricides by Pyriphlegethon—and they are borne to the Acherusian lake, and there they lift up their voices and call upon the victims whom they have slain or wronged, to have pity on them, and to be kind to them, and let them come out into the lake. And if they prevail, then they come forth and cease from their troubles; but if not, they are carried back again into Tartarus and from thence into the rivers unceasingly, until they obtain mercy from those whom they have wronged: for that is the sentence inflicted upon them by their judges. Those too who have been pre-eminent for holiness of life are released from this earthly prison, and go to their pure home which is above, and dwell in the purer earth; and of these, such as have duly purified themselves with philosophy live henceforth altogether without the body, in mansions fairer still, which may not be described, and of which the time would fail me to tell.

Wherefore, Simmias, seeing all these things, what ought not we to do that we may obtain virtue and wisdom in this life? Fair is the prize, and the hope great!

A man of sense ought not to say, nor will I be very confident, that the description which I have given of the soul and her mansions is exactly true. But I do say that, inasmuch as the soul is shown to be immortal, he may venture to think, not improperly or unworthily, that something of the kind is true. The venture is a glorious one, and he ought to comfort himself with words like these, which is the reason why I lengthen out the tale. Wherefore, I say, let a man be of good cheer about his soul, who having cast away the pleasures and ornaments of the body as alien to him and working harm rather than good, has sought after the pleasures of knowledge; and has arrayed the soul, not in some foreign attire, but in her own proper jewels, temperance, and justice, and courage, and nobility, [115] and truth—in these adorned she is ready to go on her journey to the world below, when her hour comes. You, Simmias and Cebes, and all other men, will depart at some time or other. Me already, as a tragic poet would say, the voice of fate calls. Soon I must drink the poison; and I think that I had better repair to the bath first, in order that the women may not have the trouble of washing my body after I am dead.

When he had done speaking, Crito said: And have you any commands for us, Socrates —anything to say about your children, or any other matter in which we can serve you?

Nothing particular, Crito, he replied: only, as I have always told you, take care of yourselves; that is a service which you may be ever rendering to me and mine and to all of us, whether you promise to do so or not. But if you have no thought for yourselves, and care not to walk according to the rule which I have prescribed for you, not now for the first time, however much you may profess or promise at the moment, it will be of no avail.

We will do our best, said Crito: And in what way shall we bury you?

In any way that you like; but you must get

hold of me, and take care that I do not run away from you. Then he turned to us, and added with a smile:—I cannot make Crito believe that I am the same Socrates who have been talking and conducting the argument; he fancies that I am the other Socrates whom he will soon see, a dead body—and he asks, How shall he bury me? And though I have spoken many words in the endeavour to show that when I have drunk the poison I shall leave you and go to the joys of the blessed,—these words of mine, with which I was comforting you and myself, have had, as I perceive, no effect upon Crito. And therefore I want you to be surety for me to him now, as at the trial he was surety to the judges for me: but let the promise be of another sort; for he was surety for me to the judges that I would remain, and you must be my surety to him that I shall not remain, but go away and depart; and then he will suffer less at my death, and not be grieved when he sees my body being burned or buried. I would not have him sorrow at my hard lot, or say at the burial, Thus we lay out Socrates, or, Thus we follow him to the grave or bury him; for false words are not only evil in themselves, but they infect the soul with evil. Be of good cheer then, my dear Crito, and say that you are burying my body only, [116] and do with that whatever is usual, and what you think best.

When he had spoken these words, he arose and went into a chamber to bathe; Crito followed him and told us to wait. So we remained behind, talking and thinking of the subject of discourse, and also of the greatness of our sorrow; he was like a father of whom we were being bereaved, and we were about to pass the rest of our lives as orphans. When he had taken the bath his children were brought to him— (he had two young sons and an elder one); and the women of his family also came, and he talked to them and gave them a few directions in the presence of Crito; then he dismissed them and returned to us.

Now the hour of sunset was near, for a good deal of time had passed while he was within. When he came out, he sat down with us again after his bath, but not much was said. Soon the jailer, who was the servant of the Eleven, entered and stood by him, saying:—To you, Socrates, whom I know to be the noblest and gentlest and best of all who ever came to this place, I will not impute the angry feelings of other men, who rage and swear at me, when, in obedience to the authorities, I bid them drink the poison—indeed, I am sure that you will not be angry with me; for others, as you are aware, and not I, are to blame. And so fare you well, and try to bear lightly what must needs be—you know my errand. Then bursting into tears he turned away and went out.

Socrates looked at him and said: I return your good wishes, and will do as you bid. Then turning to us, he said, How charming the man is: since I have been in prison he has always been coming to see me, and at times he would talk to me, and was as good to me as could be, and now see how generously he sorrows on my account. We must do as he says, Crito; and therefore let the cup be brought, if the poison is prepared: if not, let the attendant prepare some.

Yet, said Crito, the sun is still upon the hill-tops, and I know that many a one has taken the draught late, and after the announcement has been made to him, he has eaten and drunk, and enjoyed the society of his beloved; do not hurry—there is time enough.

Socrates said: Yes, Crito, and they of whom you speak are right in so acting, for they think that they will be gainers by the delay; but I am right in not following their example, for I do not think that I should gain anything by drinking the poison a little later; [117] I should only be ridiculous in my own eyes for sparing and saving a life which is already forfeit. Please then to do as I say, and not to refuse me.

Crito made a sign to the servant, who was standing by; and he went out, and having been absent for some time, returned with the jailer carrying the cup of poison. Socrates said: You, my good friend, who are experienced in these matters, shall give me directions how I am to proceed. The man answered: You have only to walk about until your legs are heavy, and then to lie down, and the poison will act. At the same time he handed the cup to Socrates, who in the easiest and gentlest manner, without the least fear or change of colour or feature, looking at the man with all his eyes, Echecrates, as his manner was, took the cup and said: What do you say about making a libation out of this cup to any god? May I, or not? The man answered: We only prepare, Socrates, just so much as we deem enough. I understand, he

said: but I may and must ask the gods to prosper my journey from this to the other world—even so—and so be it according to my prayer. Then raising the cup to his lips, quite readily and cheerfully he drank off the poison. And hitherto most of us had been able to control our sorrow; but now when we saw him drinking, and saw too that he had finished the draught, we could no longer forbear, and in spite of myself my own tears were flowing fast; so that I covered my face and wept, not for him, but at the thought of my own calamity in having to part from such a friend. Nor was I the first; for Crito, when he found himself unable to restrain his tears, had got up, and I followed; and at that moment, Apollodorus, who had been weeping all the time, broke out in a loud and passionate cry which made cowards of us all. Socrates alone retained his calmness: What is this strange outcry? he said. I sent away the women mainly in order that they might not misbehave in this way, for I have been told that a man should die in peace. Be quiet then, and have patience. When we heard his words we were ashamed, and refrained our tears; and he walked about until, as he said, his legs began to fail, and then he lay on his back, according to the directions, and the man who gave him the poison now and then looked at his feet and legs; and after a while he pressed his foot hard, and asked him if he could feel; and he said, [118] No; and then his leg, and so upwards and upwards, and showed us that he was cold and stiff. And he felt them himself, and said: When the poison reaches the heart, that will be the end. He was beginning to grow cold about the groin, when he uncovered his face, for he had covered himself up, and said—they were his last words—he said: Crito, I owe a cock to Asclepius; will you remember to pay the debt? The debt shall be paid, said Crito; is there anything else? There was no answer to this question; but in a minute or two a movement was heard, and the attendants uncovered him; his eyes were set, and Crito closed his eyes and mouth.

Such was the end, Echecrates, of our friend; concerning whom I may truly say, that of all the men of his time whom I have known, he was the wisest and justest and best.

GORGIAS

PERSONS OF THE DIALOGUE: CALLICLES; SOCRATES; CHAEREPHON; GORGIAS; POLUS.
Scene: *The house of Callicles*

❧❧❧❧❧❧❧❧

[447] *Callicles.* THE wise man, as the proverb says, is late for a fray, but not for a feast.

Socrates. And are we late for a feast?

Cal. Yes, and a delightful feast; for Gorgias has just been exhibiting to us many fine things.

Soc. It is not my fault, Callicles; our friend Chaerephon is to blame; for he would keep us loitering in the Agora.

Chaerephon. Never mind, Socrates; the misfortune of which I have been the cause I will also repair; for Gorgias is a friend of mine, and I will make him give the exhibition again either now, or, if you prefer, at some other time.

Cal. What is the matter, Chaerephon—does Socrates want to hear Gorgias?

Chaer. Yes, that was our intention in coming.

Cal. Come into my house, then; for Gorgias is staying with me, and he shall exhibit to you.

Soc. Very good, Callicles; but will he answer our questions? for I want to hear from him what is the nature of his art, and what it is which he professes and teaches; he may, as you [Chaerephon] suggest, defer the exhibition to some other time.

Cal. There is nothing like asking him, Socrates; and indeed to answer questions is a part of his exhibition, for he was saying only just now, that any one in my house might put any question to him, and that he would answer.

Soc. How fortunate! will you ask him, Chaerephon—?

Chaer. What shall I ask him?

Soc. Ask him who he is.

Chaer. What do you mean?

Soc. I mean such a question as would elicit from him, if he had been a maker of shoes, the answer that he is a cobbler. Do you understand?

Chaer. I understand, and will ask him: Tell me, Gorgias, is our friend Callicles right in saying that you undertake to answer any questions which you are asked?

Gorgias. Quite right, Chaerephon: I was saying as much only just now; [448] and I may add, that many years have elapsed since any one has asked me a new one.

Chaer. Then you must be very ready, Gorgias.

Gor. Of that, Chaerephon, you can make trial.

Polus. Yes, indeed, and if you like, Chaerephon, you may make trial of me too, for I think that Gorgias, who has been talking a long time, is tired.

Chaer. And do you, Polus, think that you can answer better than Gorgias?

Pol. What does that matter if I answer well enough for you?

Chaer. Not at all:—and you shall answer if you like.

Pol. Ask:—

Chaer. My question is this: If Gorgias had the skill of his brother Herodicus, what ought we to call him? Ought he not to have the name which is given to his brother?

Pol. Certainly.

Chaer. Then we should be right in calling him a physician?

Pol. Yes.

Chaer. And if he had the skill of Aristophon the son of Aglaophon, or of his brother Polygnotus, what ought we to call him?

Pol. Clearly, a painter.

Chaer. But now what shall we call him—

what is the art in which he is skilled?

Pol. O Chaerephon, there are many arts among mankind which are experimental, and have their origin in experience, for experience makes the days of men to proceed according to art, and inexperience according to chance, and different persons in different ways are proficient in different arts, and the best persons in the best arts. And our friend Gorgias is one of the best, and the art in which he is a proficient is the noblest.

Soc. Polus has been taught how to make a capital speech, Gorgias; but he is not fulfilling the promise which he made to Chaerephon.

Gor. What do you mean, Socrates?

Soc. I mean that he has not exactly answered the question which he was asked.

Gor. Then why not ask him yourself?

Soc. But I would much rather ask you, if you are disposed to answer: for I see, from the few words which Polus has uttered, that he has attended more to the art which is called rhetoric than to dialectic.

Pol. What makes you say so, Socrates?

Soc. Because, Polus, when Chaerephon asked you what was the art which Gorgias knows, you praised it as if you were answering some one who found fault with it, but you never said what the art was.

Pol. Why, did I not say that it was the noblest of arts?

Soc. Yes, indeed, but that was no answer to the question: nobody asked what was the quality, but what was the nature, of the art, and by what name we were to describe Gorgias. *[449]* And I would still beg you briefly and clearly, as you answered Chaerephon when he asked you at first, to say what this art is, and what we ought to call Gorgias: Or rather, Gorgias, let me turn to you, and ask the same question— what are we to call you, and what is the art which you profess?

Gor. Rhetoric, Socrates, is my art.

Soc. Then I am to call you a rhetorician?

Gor. Yes, Socrates, and a good one too, if you would call me that which, in Homeric language, "I boast myself to be."

Soc. I should wish to do so.

Gor. Then pray do.

Soc. And are we to say that you are able to make other men rhetoricians?

Gor. Yes, that is exactly what I profess to make them, not only at Athens, but in all places.

Soc. And will you continue to ask and answer questions, Gorgias, as we are at present doing and reserve for another occasion the longer mode of speech which Polus was attempting? Will you keep your promise, and answer shortly the questions which are asked of you?

Gor. Some answers, Socrates, are of necessity longer; but I will do my best to make them as short as possible; for a part of my profession is that I can be as short as any one.

Soc. That is what is wanted, Gorgias; exhibit the shorter method now, and the longer one at some other time.

Gor. Well, I will; and you will certainly say, that you never heard a man use fewer words.

Soc. Very good then; as you profess to be a rhetorician, and a maker of rhetoricians, let me ask you, with what is rhetoric concerned: I might ask with what is weaving concerned, and you would reply (would you not?), with the making of garments?

Gor. Yes.

Soc. And music is concerned with the composition of melodies?

Gor. It is.

Soc. By Herè, Gorgias, I admire the surpassing brevity of your answers.

Gor. Yes, Socrates, I do think myself good at that.

Soc. I am glad to hear it; answer me in like manner about rhetoric: with what is rhetoric concerned?

Gor. With discourse.

Soc. What sort of discourse, Gorgias?—such discourse as would teach the sick under what treatment they might get well?

Gor. No.

Soc. Then rhetoric does not treat of all kinds of discourse?

Gor. Certainly not.

Soc. And yet rhetoric makes men able to speak?

Gor. Yes.

Soc. And to understand that about which they speak?

Gor. Of course.

Soc. But does not the art of medicine, which we were just now mentioning, *[450]* also make men able to understand and speak about the sick?

Gor. Certainly.

Soc. Then medicine also treats of discourse?

Gor. Yes.

Soc. Of discourse concerning diseases?

Gor. Just so.

Soc. And does not gymnastic also treat of discourse concerning the good or evil condition of the body?

Gor. Very true.

Soc. And the same, Gorgias, is true of the other arts:—all of them treat of discourse concerning the subjects with which they severally have to do.

Gor. Clearly.

Soc. Then why, if you call rhetoric the art which treats of discourse, and all the other arts treat of discourse, do you not call them arts of rhetoric?

Gor. Because, Socrates, the knowledge of the other arts has only to do with some sort of external action, as of the hand; but there is no such action of the hand in rhetoric which works and takes effect only through the medium of discourse. And therefore I am justified in saying that rhetoric treats of discourse.

Soc. I am not sure whether I entirely understand you, but I dare say I shall soon know better; please to answer me a question:—you would allow that there are arts?

Gor. Yes.

Soc. As to the arts generally, they are for the most part concerned with doing, and require little or no speaking; in painting, and statuary, and many other arts, the work may proceed in silence; and of such arts I suppose you would say that they do not come within the province of rhetoric.

Gor. You perfectly conceive my meaning, Socrates.

Soc. But there are other arts which work wholly through the medium of language, and require either no action or very little, as, for example, the arts of arithmetic, of calculation, of geometry, and of playing draughts; in some of these speech is pretty nearly co-extensive with action, but in most of them the verbal element is greater—they depend wholly on words for their efficacy and power: and I take your meaning to be that rhetoric is an art of this latter sort?

Gor. Exactly.

Soc. And yet I do not believe that you really mean to call any of these arts rhetoric; although the precise expression which you used was, that rhetoric is an art which works and takes effect only through the medium of discourse; and an adversary who wished to be captious might say, "And so, Gorgias, you call arithmetic rhetoric." But I do not think that you really call arithmetic rhetoric any more than geometry would be so called by you. *[451]*

Gor. You are quite right, Socrates, in your apprehension of my meaning.

Soc. Well, then, let me now have the rest of my answer:—seeing that rhetoric is one of those arts which works mainly by the use of words, and there are other arts which also use words, tell me what is that quality in words with which rhetoric is concerned:—Suppose that a person asks me about some of the arts which I was mentioning just now; he might say, "Socrates, what is arithmetic?" and I should reply to him, as you replied to me, that arithmetic is one of those arts which take effect through words. And then he would proceed to ask: "Words about what?" and I should reply, Words about odd and even numbers, and how many there are of each. And if he asked again: "What is the art of calculation?" I should say, That also is one of the arts which is concerned wholly with words. And if he further said, "Concerned with what?" I should say, like the clerks in the assembly, "as aforesaid" of arithmetic, but with a difference, the difference being that the art of calculation considers not only the quantities of odd and even numbers, but also their numerical relations to themselves and to one another. And suppose, again, I were to say that astronomy is only words—he would ask, "Words about what, Socrates?" and I should answer, that astronomy tells us about the motions of the stars and sun and moon, and their relative swiftness.

Gor. You would be quite right, Socrates.

Soc. And now let us have from you, Gorgias, the truth about rhetoric: which you would admit (would you not?) to be one of those arts which act always and fulfil all their ends through the medium of words?

Gor. True.

Soc. Words which do what? I should ask. To what class of things do the words which rhetoric uses relate?

Gor. To the greatest, Socrates, and the best of human things.

Soc. That again, Gorgias, is ambiguous; I am still in the dark: for which are the greatest and best of human things? I dare say that you have heard men singing at feasts the old drinking song, in which the singers enumerate the goods of life, first health, beauty next, thirdly, as the writer of the song says, wealth honestly obtained.

[452] Gor. Yes, I know the song; but what is your drift?

Soc. I mean to say, that the producers of those things which the author of the song praises, that is to say, the physician, the trainer, the money-maker, will at once come to you, and first the physician will say: "O Socrates,

Gorgias is deceiving you, for my art is concerned with the greatest good of men and not his." And when I ask, Who are you? he will reply, "I am a physician." What do you mean? I shall say. Do you mean that your art produces the greatest good? "Certainly," he will answer, "for is not health the greatest good? What greater good can men have, Socrates?" And after him the trainer will come and say, "I too, Socrates, shall be greatly surprised if Gorgias can show more good of his art than I can show of mine." To him again I shall say, Who are you, honest friend, and what is your business? "I am a trainer," he will reply, "and my business is to make men beautiful and strong in body." When I have done with the trainer, there arrives the money-maker, and he, as I expect, will utterly despise them all. "Consider, Socrates," he will say, "whether Gorgias or any one else can produce any greater good than wealth." Well, you and I say to him, and are you a creator of wealth? "Yes," he replies. And who are you? "A money-maker." And do you consider wealth to be the greatest good of man? "Of course," will be his reply. And we shall rejoin: Yes; but our friend Gorgias contends that his art produces a greater good than yours. And then he will be sure to go on and ask, "What good? Let Gorgias answer." Now I want you, Gorgias, to imagine that this question is asked of you by them and by me; What is that which, as you say, is the greatest good of man, and of which you are the creator? Answer us.

Gor. That good, Socrates, which is truly the greatest, being that which gives to men freedom in their own persons, and to individuals the power of ruling over others in their several states.

Soc. And what would you consider this to be?

Gor. What is there greater than the word which persuades the judges in the courts, or the senators in the council, or the citizens in the assembly, or at any other political meeting? —if you have the power of uttering this word, you will have the physician your slave, and the trainer your slave, and the money-maker of whom you talk will be found to gather treasures, not for himself, but for you who are able to speak and to persuade the multitude.

Soc. Now I think, Gorgias, that you have very accurately explained what you conceive to be the art of rhetoric; and you mean to say, [453] if I am not mistaken, that rhetoric is the artificer of persuasion, having this and no other business, and that this is her crown and end. Do you know any other effect of rhetoric over and above that of producing persuasion?

Gor. No: the definition seems to me very fair, Socrates; for persuasion is the chief end of rhetoric.

Soc. Then hear me, Gorgias, for I am quite sure that if there ever was a man who entered on the discussion of a matter from a pure love of knowing the truth, I am such a one, and I should say the same of you.

Gor. What is coming, Socrates?

Soc. I will tell you: I am very well aware that I do not know what, according to you, is the exact nature, or what are the topics of that persuasion of which you speak, and which is given by rhetoric; although I have a suspicion about both the one and the other. And I am going to ask—what is this power of persuasion which is given by rhetoric, and about what? But why, if I have a suspicion, do I ask instead of telling you? Not for your sake, but in order that the argument may proceed in such a manner as is most likely to set forth the truth. And I would have you observe, that I am right in asking this further question: If I asked, "What sort of a painter is Zeuxis?" and you said, "The painter of figures," should I not be right in asking, "What kind of figures, and where do you find them?"

Gor. Certainly.

Soc. And the reason for asking this second question would be, that there are other painters besides, who paint many other figures?

Gor. True.

Soc. But if there had been no one but Zeuxis who painted them, then you would have answered very well?

Gor. Quite so.

Soc. Now I want to know about rhetoric in the same way;—is rhetoric the only art which brings persuasion, or do other arts have the same effect? I mean to say—Does he who teaches anything persuade men of that which he teaches or not?

Gor. He persuades, Socrates,—there can be no mistake about that.

Soc. Again, if we take the arts of which we were just now speaking:—do not arithmetic and the arithmeticians teach us the properties of number?

Gor. Certainly.

Soc. And therefore persuade us of them?

Gor. Yes.

Soc. Then arithmetic as well as rhetoric is an artificer of persuasion?

Gor. Clearly.

Soc. And if any one asks us what sort of persuasion, and about what,—we shall answer, persuasion which teaches the quantity of odd and even; *[454]* and we shall be able to show that all the other arts of which we were just now speaking are artificers of persuasion, and of what sort, and about what.

Gor. Very true.

Soc. Then rhetoric is not the only artificer of persuasion?

Gor. True.

Soc. Seeing, then, that not only rhetoric works by persuasion, but that other arts do the same, as in the case of the painter, a question has arisen which is a very fair one: Of what persuasion is rhetoric the artificer, and about what?—is not that a fair way of putting the question?

Gor. I think so.

Soc. Then, if you approve the question, Gorgias, what is the answer?

Gor. I answer, Socrates, that rhetoric is the art of persuasion in courts of law and other assemblies, as I was just now saying, and about the just and unjust.

Soc. And that, Gorgias, was what I was suspecting to be your notion; yet I would not have you wonder if by-and-by I am found repeating a seemingly plain question; for I ask not in order to confute you, but as I was saying that the argument may proceed consecutively, and that we may not get the habit of anticipating and suspecting the meaning of one another's words; I would have you develop your own views in your own way, whatever may be your hypothesis.

Gor. I think that you are quite right, Socrates.

Soc. Then let me raise another question; there is such a thing as "having learned"?

Gor. Yes.

Soc. And there is also "having believed"?

Gor. Yes.

Soc. And is the "having learned" the same as "having believed," and are learning and belief the same things?

Gor. In my judgment, Socrates, they are not the same.

Soc. And your judgment is right, as you may ascertain in this way:—If a person were to say to you, "Is there, Gorgias, a false belief as well as a true?"—you would reply, if I am not mistaken, that there is.

Gor. Yes.

Soc. Well, but is there a false knowledge as well as a true?

Gor. No.

Soc. No, indeed; and this again proves that knowledge and belief differ.

Gor. Very true.

Soc. And yet those who have learned as well as those who have believed are persuaded?

Gor. Just so.

Soc. Shall we then assume two sorts of persuasion,—one which is the source of belief without knowledge, as the other is of knowledge?

Gor. By all means.

Soc. And which sort of persuasion does rhetoric create in courts of law and other assemblies about the just and unjust, the sort of persuasion which gives belief without knowledge, or that which gives knowledge?

[455] Gor. Clearly, Socrates, that which only gives belief.

Soc. Then rhetoric, as would appear, is the artificer of a persuasion which creates belief about the just and unjust, but gives no instruction about them?

Gor. True.

Soc. And the rhetorician does not instruct the courts of law or other assemblies about things just and unjust, but he creates belief about them; for no one can be supposed to instruct such a vast multitude about such high matters in a short time?

Gor. Certainly not.

Soc. Come, then, and let us see what we really mean about rhetoric; for I do not know what my own meaning is as yet. When the assembly meets to elect a physician or a shipwright or any other craftsman, will the rhetorician be taken into counsel? Surely not. For at every election he ought to be chosen who is most skilled; and, again, when walls have to be built or harbours or docks to be constructed, not the rhetorician but the master workman will advise; or when generals have to be chosen and an order of battle arranged, or a proposition taken, then the military will advise and not the rhetoricians: what do you say, Gorgias? Since you profess to be a rhetorician and a maker of rhetoricians, I cannot do better than learn the nature of your art from you. And here let me assure you that I have your interest in view as well as my own. For likely enough some one or other of the young men present might desire to become your pupil, and in fact I see some, and a good many too, who have this wish, but they would be too modest to question you. And therefore when you are interrogated by me, I would have you imagine that you are interrogated by them. "What is the use of coming to you, Gorgias?" they will say—"about what will you teach us to advise the state?—about the just and unjust only, or about those other things also which Socrates has just mentioned?" How will you answer them?

Gor. I like your way of leading us on, Socrates, and I will endeavour to reveal to you the whole nature of rhetoric. You must have heard, I think, that the docks and the walls of the Athenians and the plan of the harbour were devised in accordance with the counsels, partly of Themistocles, and partly of Pericles, and not at the suggestion of the builders.

Soc. Such is the tradition, Gorgias, about Themistocles; and I myself heard the speech of Pericles when he advised us about the middle wall.

[456] *Gor*. And you will observe, Socrates, that when a decision has to be given in such matters the rhetoricians are the advisers; they are the men who win their point.

Soc. I had that in my admiring mind, Gorgias, when I asked what is the nature of rhetoric, which always appears to me, when I look at the matter in this way, to be a marvel of greatness.

Gor. A marvel, indeed, Socrates, if you only knew how rhetoric comprehends and holds under her sway all the inferior arts. Let me offer you a striking example of this. On several occasions I have been with my brother Herodicus or some other physician to see one of his patients, who would not allow the physician to give him medicine, or apply a knife or hot iron to him; and I have persuaded him to do for me what he would not do for the physician just by the use of rhetoric. And I say that if a rhetorician and a physician were to go to any city, and had there to argue in the Ecclesia or any other assembly as to which of them should be elected state-physician, the physician would have no chance; but he who could speak would be chosen if he wished; and in a contest with a man of any other profession the rhetorician more than any one would have the power of getting himself chosen, for he can speak more persuasively to the multitude than any of them, and on any subject. Such is the nature and power of the art of rhetoric! And yet, Socrates, rhetoric should be used like any other competitive art, not against everybody—the rhetorician ought not to abuse his strength any more than a pugilist or pancratiast or other master of fence; because he has powers which are more than a match either for friend or enemy, he ought not therefore to strike, stab, or slay his friends. Suppose a man to have been trained

in the palestra and to be a skilful boxer—he in the fulness of his strength goes and strikes his father or mother or one of his familiars or friends; but that is no reason why the trainers or fencing-masters should be held in detestation or banished from the city—surely not. For they taught their art for a good purpose, to be used against enemies and evil-doers, in self-defence not in aggression, and others have perverted their instructions, [457] and turned to a bad use their own strength and skill. But not on this account are the teachers bad, neither is the art in fault, or bad in itself; I should rather say that those who make a bad use of the art are to blame. And the same argument holds good of rhetoric; for the rhetorician can speak against all men and upon any subject—in short, he can persuade the multitude better than any other man of anything which he pleases, but he should not therefore seek to defraud the physician or any other artist of his reputation merely because he has the power; he ought to use rhetoric fairly, as he would also use his athletic powers. And if after having become a rhetorician he makes a bad use of his strength and skill, his instructor surely ought not on that account to be held in detestation or banished. For he was intended by his teacher to make a good use of his instructions, but he abuses them. And therefore he is the person who ought to be held in detestation, banished, and put to death, and not his instructor.

Soc. You, Gorgias, like myself, have had great experience of disputations, and you must have observed, I think, that they do not always terminate in mutual edification, or in the definition by either party of the subjects which they are discussing; but disagreements are apt to arise—somebody says that another has not spoken truly or clearly; and then they get into a passion and begin to quarrel, both parties conceiving that their opponents are arguing from personal feeling only and jealousy of themselves, not from any interest in the question at issue. And sometimes they will go on abusing one another until the company at last are quite vexed at themselves for ever listening to such fellows. Why do I say this? Why, because I cannot help feeling that you are now saying what is not quite consistent or accordant with what you were saying at first about rhetoric. And I am afraid to point this out to you, lest you should think that I have some animosity against you, and that I speak, not for the sake of discovering the truth, but from jealousy of you. Now if you are one of my sort, I should like to cross-examine you, [458] but if not I will let you alone. And what is my sort? you will ask. I am one of those who are very willing to be refuted if I say anything which is not true, and very willing to refute any one else who says what is not true, and quite as ready to be refuted as to refute; for I hold that this is the greater gain of the two, just as the gain is greater of being cured of a very great evil than of curing another. For I imagine that there is no evil which a man can endure so great as an erroneous opinion about the matters of which we are speaking; and if you claim to be one of my sort, let us have the discussion out, but if you would rather have done, no matter—let us make an end of it.

Gor. I should say, Socrates, that I am quite the man whom you indicate; but, perhaps, we ought to consider the audience, for, before you came, I had already given a long exhibition, and if we proceed the argument may run on to a great length. And therefore I think that we should consider whether we may not be detaining some part of the company when they are wanting to do something else.

Chaer. You hear the audience cheering, Gorgias and Socrates, which shows their desire to listen to you; and for myself, Heaven forbid that I should have any business on hand which would take me away from a discussion so interesting and so ably maintained.

Cal. By the gods, Chaerephon, although I have been present at many discussions, I doubt whether I was ever so much delighted before, and therefore if you go on discoursing all day I shall be the better pleased.

Soc. I may truly say, Callicles, that I am willing, if Gorgias is.

Gor. After all this, Socrates, I should be disgraced if I refused, especially as I have promised to answer all comers; in accordance with the wishes of the company, then, do you begin, and ask of me any question which you like.

Soc. Let me tell you then, Gorgias, what surprises me in your words; though I dare say that you may be right, and I may have misunderstood your meaning. You say that you can make any man, who will learn of you, a rhetorician?

Gor. Yes.

Soc. Do you mean that you will teach him to gain the ears of the multitude on any subject, [459] and this not by instruction but by persuasion?

Gor. Quite so.

Soc. You were saying, in fact, that the rhetorician will have greater powers of persuasion than the physician even in a matter of health?

Gor. Yes, with the multitude—that is.

Soc. You mean to say, with the ignorant; for with those who know he cannot be supposed to have greater powers of persuasion.

Gor. Very true.

Soc. But if he is to have more power of persuasion than the physician, he will have greater power than he who knows?

Gor. Certainly.

Soc. Although he is not a physician:—is he?

Gor. No.

Soc. And he who is not a physician must, obviously, be ignorant of what the physician knows.

Gor. Clearly.

Soc. Then, when the rhetorician is more persuasive than the physician, the ignorant is more persuasive with the ignorant than he who has knowledge?—is not that the inference?

Gor. In the case supposed:—Yes.

Soc. And the same holds of the relation of rhetoric to all the other arts; the rhetorician need not know the truth about things; he has only to discover some way of persuading the ignorant that he has more knowledge than those who know?

Gor. Yes, Socrates, and is not this a great comfort?—not to have learned the other arts, but the art of rhetoric only, and yet to be in no way inferior to the professors of them?

Soc. Whether the rhetorician is or is not inferior on this account is a question which we will hereafter examine if the enquiry is likely to be of any service to us; but I would rather begin by asking, whether he is or is not as ignorant of the just and unjust, base and honourable, good and evil, as he is of medicine and the other arts; I mean to say, does he really know anything of what is good and evil, base or honourable, just or unjust in them; or has he only a way with the ignorant of persuading them that he not knowing is to be esteemed to know more about these things than some one else who knows? Or must the pupil know these things and come to you knowing them before he can acquire the art of rhetoric? If he is ignorant, you who are the teacher of rhetoric will not teach him—it is not your business; but you will make him seem to the multitude to know them, when he does not know them; and seem to be a good man, [460] when he is not. Or will you be unable to teach him rhetoric at all, unless he knows the truth of these things first? What is to be said about all this? By heavens,

Gorgias, I wish that you would reveal to me the power of rhetoric, as you were saying that you would.

Gor. Well, Socrates, I suppose that if the pupil does chance not to know them, he will have to learn of me these things as well.

Soc. Say no more, for there you are right; and so he whom you make a rhetorician must either know the nature of the just and unjust already, or he must be taught by you.

Gor. Certainly.

Soc. Well, and is not he who has learned carpentering a carpenter?

Gor. Yes.

Soc. And he who has learned music a musician?

Gor. Yes.

Soc. And he who has learned medicine is a physician, in like manner? He who has learned anything whatever is that which his knowledge makes him.

Gor. Certainly.

Soc. And in the same way, he who has learned what is just is just?

Gor. To be sure.

Soc. And he who is just may be supposed to do what is just?

Gor. Yes.

Soc. And must not the just man always desire to do what is just?

Gor. That is clearly the inference.

Soc. Surely, then, the just man will never consent to do injustice?

Gor. Certainly not.

Soc. And according to the argument the rhetorician must be a just man?

Gor. Yes.

Soc. And will therefore never be willing to do injustice?

Gor. Clearly not.

Soc. But do you remember saying just now that the trainer is not to be accused or banished if the pugilist makes a wrong use of his pugilistic art; and in like manner, if the rhetorician makes a bad and unjust use of rhetoric, that is not to be laid to the charge of his teacher, who is not to be banished, but the wrong-doer himself who made a bad use of his rhetoric—he is to be banished—was not that said?

Gor. Yes, it was.

Soc. But now we are affirming that the aforesaid rhetorician will never have done injustice at all?

Gor. True.

Soc. And at the very outset, Gorgias, it was said that rhetoric treated of discourse, not [like arithmetic] about odd and even, but about just and unjust? Was not this said?

Gor. Yes.

Soc. I was thinking at the time, when I heard you saying so, that rhetoric, which is always discoursing about justice, could not possibly be an unjust thing. But when you added, shortly afterwards, that the rhetorician might make a bad use of rhetoric I noted with surprise the inconsistency into which you had fallen; [461] and I said, that if you thought, as I did, that there was a gain in being refuted, there would be an advantage in going on with the question, but if not, I would leave off. And in the course of our investigations, as you will see yourself, the rhetorician has been acknowledged to be incapable of making an unjust use of rhetoric, or of willingness to do injustice. By the dog, Gorgias, there will be a great deal of discussion, before we get at the truth of all this.

Polus. And do even you, Socrates, seriously believe what you are now saying about rhetoric? What! because Gorgias was ashamed to deny that the rhetorician knew the just and the honourable and the good, and admitted that to any one who came to him ignorant of them he could teach them, and then out of this admission there arose a contradiction—the thing which you so dearly love, and to which not he, but you, brought the argument by your captious questions—[do you seriously believe that there is any truth in all this?] For will any one ever acknowledge that he does not know, or cannot teach, the nature of justice? The truth is, that there is great want of manners in bringing the argument to such a pass.

Soc. Illustrious Polus, the reason why we provide ourselves with friends and children is, that when we get old and stumble, a younger generation may be at hand to set us on our legs again in our words and in our actions: and now, if I and Gorgias are stumbling, here are you who should raise us up; and I for my part engage to retract any error into which you may think that I have fallen—upon one condition:

Pol. What condition?

Soc. That you contract, Polus, the prolixity of speech in which you indulged at first.

Pol. What! do you mean that I may not use as many words as I please?

Soc. Only to think, my friend, that having come on a visit to Athens, which is the most free-spoken state in Hellas, you when you got there, and you alone, should be deprived of the power of speech—that would be hard indeed. But then consider my case:—shall not I be very hardly used, if, when you are making a long oration, [462] and refusing to answer what you are asked, I am compelled to stay and listen to you, and may not go away? I say rather, if you have a real interest in the argument, or, to repeat my former expression, have any desire to set it on its legs, take back any statement which you please; and in your turn ask and answer, like myself and Gorgias—refute and be refuted: for I suppose that you would claim to know what Gorgias knows—would you not?

Pol. Yes.

Soc. And you, like him, invite any one to ask you about anything which he pleases, and you will know how to answer him?

Pol. To be sure.

Soc. And now, which will you do, ask or answer?

Pol. I will ask; and do you answer me, Socrates, the same question which Gorgias, as you suppose, is unable to answer: What is rhetoric?

Soc. Do you mean what sort of an art?

Pol. Yes.

Soc. To say the truth, Polus, it is not an art at all, in my opinion.

Pol. Then what, in your opinion, is rhetoric?

Soc. A thing which, as I was lately reading in a book of yours, you say that you have made an art.

Pol. What thing?

Soc. I should say a sort of experience.

Pol. Does rhetoric seem to you to be an experience?

Soc. That is my view, but you may be of another mind.

Pol. An experience in what?

Soc. An experience in producing a sort of delight and gratification.

Pol. And if able to gratify others, must not rhetoric be a fine thing?

Soc. What are you saying, Polus? Why do you ask me whether rhetoric is a fine thing or not, when I have not as yet told you what rhetoric is?

Pol. Did I not hear you say that rhetoric was a sort of experience?

Soc. Will you, who are so desirous to gratify others, afford a slight gratification to me?

Pol. I will.

Soc. Will you ask me, what sort of an art is cookery?

Pol. What sort of an art is cookery?

Soc. Not an art at all, Polus.

Pol. What then?

Soc. I should say an experience.

Pol. In what? I wish that you would explain to me.

Soc. An experience in producing a sort of delight and gratification, Polus.

Pol. Then are cookery and rhetoric the same?

Soc. No, they are only different parts of the same profession.

Pol. Of what profession?

Soc. I am afraid that the truth may seem discourteous; and I hesitate to answer, lest Gorgias should imagine that I am making fun of his own profession. [463] For whether or no this is that art of rhetoric which Gorgias practises I really cannot tell:—from what he was just now saying, nothing appeared of what he thought of his art, but the rhetoric which I mean is a part of a not very creditable whole.

Gor. A part of what, Socrates? Say what you mean, and never mind me.

Soc. In my opinion then, Gorgias, the whole of which rhetoric is a part is not an art at all, but the habit of a bold and ready wit, which knows how to manage mankind: this habit I sum up under the word "flattery"; and it appears to me to have many other parts, one of which is cookery, which may seem to be an art, but, as I maintain, is only an experience or routine and not an art:—another part is rhetoric, and the art of attiring and sophistry are two others: thus there are four branches, and four different things answering to them. And Polus may ask, if he likes, for he has not as yet been informed, what part of flattery is rhetoric: he did not see that I had not yet answered him when he proceeded to ask a further question: Whether I do not think rhetoric a fine thing? But I shall not tell him whether rhetoric is a fine thing or not, until I have first answered, "What is rhetoric?" For that would not be right, Polus; but I shall be happy to answer, if you will ask me, What part of flattery is rhetoric?

Pol. I will ask, and do you answer? What part of flattery is rhetoric?

Soc. Will you understand my answer? Rhetoric, according to my view, is the ghost or counterfeit of a part of politics.

Pol. And noble or ignoble?

Soc. Ignoble, I should say, if I am compelled to answer, for I call what is bad ignoble:—though I doubt whether you understand what I was saying before.

Gor. Indeed, Socrates, I cannot say that I understand myself.

Soc. I do not wonder, Gorgias; for I have not as yet explained myself, and our friend Polus, colt by name and colt by nature, is apt to run away.[1]

Gor. Never mind him, but explain to me what you mean by saying that rhetoric is the counterfeit of a part of politics.

Soc. I will try, then, to explain my notion of rhetoric, and if I am mistaken, *[464]* my friend Polus shall refute me. We may assume the existence of bodies and of souls?

Gor. Of course.

Soc. You would further admit that there is a good condition of either of them?

Gor. Yes.

Soc. Which condition may not be really good, but good only in appearance? I mean to say, that there are many persons who appear to be in good health, and whom only a physician or trainer will discern at first sight not to be in good health.

Gor. True.

Soc. And this applies not only to the body, but also to the soul: in either there may be that which gives the appearance of health and not the reality?

Gor. Yes, certainly.

Soc. And now I will endeavour to explain to you more clearly what I mean: The soul and body being two, have two arts corresponding to them: there is the art of politics attending on the soul; and another art attending on the body, of which I know no single name, but which may be described as having two divisions, one of them gymnastic, and the other medicine. And in politics there is a legislative part, which answers to gymnastic, as justice does to medicine; and the two parts run into one another, justice having to do with the same subject as legislation, and medicine with the same subject as gymnastic, but with a difference. Now, seeing that there are these four arts, two attending on the body and two on the soul for their highest good; flattery knowing, or rather guessing their natures, has distributed herself into four shams or simulations of them; she puts on the likeness of some one or other of them, and pretends to be that which she simulates, and having no regard for men's highest interests, is ever making pleasure the bait of the unwary, and deceiving them into the belief that she is of the highest value to them. Cookery simulates the disguise of medicine, and pretends to know what food is the best for the body; and if the physician and the cook had to enter into a competition in which children were the judges, or

men who had no more sense than children, as to which of them best understands the goodness or badness of food, the physician would be starved to death. *[465]* A flattery I deem this to be and of an ignoble sort, Polus, for to you I am now addressing myself, because it aims at pleasure without any thought of the best. An art I do not call it, but only an experience, because it is unable to explain or to give a reason of the nature of its own applications. And I do not call any irrational thing an art; but if you dispute my words, I am prepared to argue in defence of them.

Cookery, then, I maintain to be a flattery which takes the form of medicine; and tiring, in like manner, is a flattery which takes the form of gymnastic, and is knavish, false, ignoble, illiberal, working deceitfully by the help of lines, and colours, and enamels, and garments, and making men affect a spurious beauty to the neglect of the true beauty which is given by gymnastic.

I would rather not be tedious, and therefore I will only say, after the manner of the geometricians (for I think that by this time you will be able to follow)

    as tiring : gymnastic : : cookery : medicine;
or rather,

    as tiring : gymnastic : : sophistry : legislation;
and

    as cookery : medicine : : rhetoric : justice.

And this, I say, is the natural difference between the rhetorician and the sophist, but by reason of their near connection, they are apt to be jumbled up together; neither do they know what to make of themselves, nor do other men know what to make of them. For if the body presided over itself, and were not under the guidance of the soul, and the soul did not discern and discriminate between cookery and medicine, but the body was made the judge of them, and the rule of judgment was the bodily delight which was given by them, then the word of Anaxagoras, that word with which you, friend Polus, are so well acquainted, would prevail far and wide: "Chaos" would come again, and cookery, health, and medicine would mingle in an indiscriminate mass. And now I have told you my notion of rhetoric, which is, in relation to the soul, what cookery is to the body. I may have been inconsistent in making a long speech, when I would not allow you to discourse at length. But I think that I may be excused, because you did not understand me, and could make no use of my answer when I spoke shortly, and therefore I had to enter into

[1] There is an untranslatable play on the name "Polus," which means "a colt."

an explanation. [466] And if I show an equal inability to make use of yours, I hope that you will speak at equal length; but if I am able to understand you, let me have the benefit of your brevity, as is only fair: And now you may do what you please with my answer.

Pol. What do you mean? do you think that rhetoric is flattery?

Soc. Nay, I said a part of flattery; if at your age, Polus, you cannot remember, what will you do by-and-by, when you get older?

Pol. And are the good rhetoricians meanly regarded in states, under the idea that they are flatterers?

Soc. Is that a question or the beginning of a speech?

Pol. I am asking a question.

Soc. Then my answer is, that they are not regarded at all.

Pol. How not regarded? Have they not very great power in states?

Soc. Not if you mean to say that power is a good to the possessor.

Pol. And that is what I do mean to say.

Soc. Then, if so, I think that they have the least power of all the citizens.

Pol. What! are they not like tyrants? They kill and despoil and exile any one whom they please.

Soc. By the dog, Polus, I cannot make out at each deliverance of yours, whether you are giving an opinion of your own, or asking a question of me.

Pol. I am asking a question of you.

Soc. Yes, my friend, but you ask two questions at once.

Pol. How two questions?

Soc. Why, did you not say just now that the rhetoricians are like tyrants, and that they kill and despoil or exile any one whom they please?

Pol. I did.

Soc. Well then, I say to you that here are two questions in one, and I will answer both of them. And I tell you, Polus, that rhetoricians and tyrants have the least possible power in states, as I was just now saying; for they do literally nothing which they will, but only what they think best.

Pol. And is not that a great power?

Soc. Polus has already said the reverse.

Soc. No, by the great—what do you call him? —not you, for you say that power is a good to him who has the power.

Pol. I do.

Soc. And would you maintain that if a fool does what he thinks best, this is a good, and

would you call this great power?

Pol. I should not.

Soc. Then you must prove that the rhetorician is not a fool, and that rhetoric is an art and not a flattery—and so you will have refuted [467] me; but if you leave me unrefuted, why, the rhetoricians who do what they think best in states, and the tyrants, will have nothing upon which to congratulate themselves, if as you say, power be indeed a good, admitting at the same time that what is done without sense is an evil.

Pol. Yes; I admit that.

Soc. How then can the rhetoricians or the tyrants have great power in states, unless Polus can refute Socrates, and prove to him that they do as they will?

Pol. This fellow—

Soc. I say that they do not do as they will— now refute me.

Pol. Why, have you not already said that they do as they think best?

Soc. And I say so still.

Pol. Then surely they do as they will?

Soc. I deny it.

Pol. But they do what they think best?

Soc. Aye.

Pol. That, Socrates, is monstrous and absurd.

Soc. Good words, good Polus, as I may say in your own peculiar style; but if you have any questions to ask of me, either prove that I am in error or give the answer yourself.

Pol. Very well, I am willing to answer that I may know what you mean.

Soc. Do men appear to you to will that which they do, or to will that further end for the sake of which they do a thing? when they take medicine, for example, at the bidding of a physician, do they will the drinking of the medicine which is painful, or the health for the sake of which they drink?

Pol. Clearly, the health.

Soc. And when men go on a voyage or engage in business, they do not will that which they are doing at the time; for who would desire to take the risk of a voyage or the trouble of business?—But they will, to have the wealth for the sake of which they go on a voyage.

Pol. Certainly.

Soc. And is not this universally true? If a man does something for the sake of something else, he wills not that which he does, but that for the sake of which he does it.

Pol. Yes.

Soc. And are not all things either good or evil, or intermediate and indifferent?

Pol. To be sure, Socrates.

Soc. Wisdom and health and wealth and the like you would call goods, and their opposites evils?

Pol. I should.

[468] *Soc.* And the things which are neither good nor evil, and which partake sometimes of the nature of good and at other times of evil, or of neither, are such as sitting, walking, running, sailing; or, again, wood, stones, and the like:—these are the things which you call neither good nor evil?

Pol. Exactly so.

Soc. Are these indifferent things done for the sake of the good, or the good for the sake of the indifferent?

Pol. Clearly, the indifferent for the sake of the good.

Soc. When we walk we walk for the sake of the good, and under the idea that it is better to walk, and when we stand we stand equally for the sake of the good?

Pol. Yes.

Soc. And when we kill a man we kill him or exile him or despoil him of his goods, because, as we think, it will conduce to our good?

Pol. Certainly.

Soc. Men who do any of these things do them for the sake of the good?

Pol. Yes.

Soc. And did we not admit that in doing something for the sake of something else, we do not will those things which we do, but that other thing for the sake of which we do them?

Pol. Most true.

Soc. Then we do not will simply to kill a man or to exile him or to despoil him of his goods, but we will to do that which conduces to our good, and if the act is not conducive to our good we do not will it; for we will, as you say, that which is our good, but that which is neither good nor evil, or simply evil, we do not will. Why are you silent, Polus? Am I not right?

Pol. You are right.

Soc. Hence we may infer, that if any one, whether he be a tyrant or a rhetorician, kills another or exiles another or deprives him of his property, under the idea that the act is for his own interests when really not for his own interests, he may be said to do what seems best to him?

Pol. Yes.

Soc. But does he do what he wills if he does what is evil? Why do you not answer?

Pol. Well, I suppose not.

Soc. Then if great power is a good as you allow, will such a one have great power in a state?

Pol. He will not.

Soc. Then I was right in saying that a man may do what seems good to him in a state, and not have great power, and not do what he wills?

Pol. As though you, Socrates, would not like to have the power of doing what seemed good to you in the state, rather than not; you would not be jealous when you saw any one killing or despoiling or imprisoning whom he pleased, Oh, no!

[469] *Soc.* Justly or unjustly, do you mean?

Pol. In either case is he not equally to be envied?

Soc. Forbear, Polus!

Pol. Why "forbear"?

Soc. Because you ought not to envy wretches who are not to be envied, but only to pity them.

Pol. And are those of whom I spoke wretches?

Soc. Yes, certainly they are.

Pol. And so you think that he who slays any one whom he pleases, and justly slays him, is pitiable and wretched?

Soc. No, I do not say that of him: but neither do I think that he is to be envied.

Pol. Were you not saying just now that he is wretched?

Soc. Yes, my friend, if he killed another unjustly, in which case he is also to be pitied; and he is not to be envied if he killed him justly.

Pol. At any rate you will allow that he who is unjustly put to death is wretched, and to be pitied?

Soc. Not so much, Polus, as he who kills him, and not so much as he who is justly killed.

Pol. How can that be, Socrates?

Soc. That may very well be, inasmuch as doing injustice is the greatest of evils.

Pol. But is it the greatest? Is not suffering injustice a greater evil?

Soc. Certainly not.

Pol. Then would you rather suffer than do injustice?

Soc. I should not like either, but if I must choose between them, I would rather suffer than do.

Pol. Then you would not wish to be a tyrant?

Soc. Not if you mean by tyranny what I mean.

Pol. I mean, as I said before, the power of doing whatever seems good to you in a state, killing, banishing, doing in all things as you like.

Soc. Well then, illustrious friend, when I have said my say, do you reply to me. Suppose that I go into a crowded Agora, and take a dagger under my arm. Polus, I say to you, I have just acquired rare power, and become a tyrant; for if I think that any of these men whom you see ought to be put to death, the man whom I have a mind to kill is as good as dead; and if I am disposed to break his head or tear his garment, he will have his head broken or his garment torn in an instant. Such is my great power in this city. And if you do not believe me, and I show you the dagger, you would probably reply: Socrates, in that sort of way any one may have great power—he may burn any house which he pleases, and the docks and triremes of the Athenians, and all their other vessels, whether public or private—but can you believe that this mere doing as you think best is great power?

Pol. Certainly not such doing as this.

[470] *Soc.* But can you tell me why you disapprove of such a power?

Pol. I can.

Soc. Why then?

Pol. Why, because he who did as you say would be certain to be punished.

Soc. And punishment is an evil?

Pol. Certainly.

Soc. And you would admit once more, my good sir, that great power is a benefit to a man if his actions turn out to his advantage, and that this is the meaning of great power; and if not, then his power is an evil and is no power. But let us look at the matter in another way:—do we not acknowledge that the things of which we were speaking, the infliction of death, and exile, and the deprivation of property are sometimes a good and sometimes not a good?

Pol. Certainly.

Soc. About that you and I may be supposed to agree?

Pol. Yes.

Soc. Tell me, then, when do you say that they are good and when that they are evil—what principle do you lay down?

Pol. I would rather, Socrates, that you should answer as well as ask that question.

Soc. Well, Polus, since you would rather have the answer from me, I say that they are good when they are just, and evil when they are unjust.

Pol. You are hard of refutation, Socrates, but might not a child refute that statement?

Soc. Then I shall be very grateful to the child, and equally grateful to you if you will refute me and deliver me from my foolishness. And I hope that refute me you will, and not weary of doing good to a friend.

Pol. Yes, Socrates, and I need not go far or appeal to antiquity; events which happened only a few days ago are enough to refute you, and to prove that many men who do wrong are happy.

Soc. What events?

Pol. You see, I presume, that Archelaus the son of Perdiccas is now the ruler of Macedonia?

Soc. At any rate I hear that he is.

Pol. And do you think that he is happy or miserable?

Soc. I cannot say, Polus, for I have never had any acquaintance with him.

Pol. And cannot you tell at once, and without having an acquaintance with him, whether a man is happy?

Soc. Most certainly not.

Pol. Then clearly, Socrates, you would say that you did not even know whether the great king was a happy man?

Soc. And I should speak the truth; for I do not know how he stands in the matter of education and justice.

Pol. What! and does all happiness consist in this?

Soc. Yes, indeed, Polus, that is my doctrine; the men and women who are gentle and good are also happy, as I maintain, and the unjust and evil are miserable.

[471] *Pol.* Then, according to your doctrine, the said Archelaus is miserable?

Soc. Yes, my friend, if he is wicked.

Pol. That he is wicked I cannot deny; for he had no title at all to the throne which he now occupies, he being only the son of a woman who was the slave of Alcetas the brother of Perdiccas; he himself therefore in strict right was the slave of Alcetas; and if he had meant to do rightly he would have remained his slave, and then, according to your doctrine, he would have been happy. But now he is unspeakably miserable, for he has been guilty of the greatest crimes: in the first place he invited his uncle and master, Alcetas, to come to him, under the pretence that he would restore to him the throne which Perdiccas has usurped, and after entertaining him and his son Alexander, who was his own cousin, and nearly of an age with him, and making them drunk, he threw them into a waggon and carried them off by night, and slew them, and got both of them out of the way; and when he had done all this wickedness he never discovered that he was the most miserable of all men, and was very far from repenting: shall I tell you how he showed his remorse? he had a younger brother, a child of seven years old, who was the legitimate son of Perdiccas, and to him of right the kingdom belonged; Archelaus, however, had no mind to bring him up as he ought and restore the kingdom to him; that was not his notion of happiness; but not long afterwards he threw him into a well and drowned him, and declared to his mother Cleopatra that he had fallen in while running after a goose, and had been killed. And now as he is the greatest criminal of all the Macedonians, he may be supposed to be the most miserable and not the happiest of them, and I dare say that there are many Athenians, and you would be at the head of them, who would rather be any other Macedonian than Archelaus!

Soc. I praised you at first, Polus, for being a rhetorician rather than a reasoner. And this, as I suppose, is the sort of argument with which you fancy that a child might refute me, and by which I stand refuted when I say that the unjust man is not happy. But, my good friend, where is the refutation? I cannot admit a word which you have been saying.

Pol. That is because you will not; for you surely must think as I do.

Soc. Not so, my simple friend, but because you will refute me after the manner which rhetoricians practise in courts of law. For there the one party think that they refute the other when they bring forward a number of witnesses of good repute in proof of their allegations, *[472]* and their adversary has only a single one or none at all. But this kind of proof is of no value where truth is the aim; a man may often be sworn down by a multitude of false witnesses who have a great air of respectability. And in this argument nearly every one, Athenian and stranger alike, would be on your side, if you should bring witnesses in disproof of my statement—you may, if you will, summon Nicias the son of Niceratus, and let his brothers, who gave the row of tripods which stand in the precincts of Dionysus, come with him; or you may summon Aristocrates, the son of Scellius, who is the giver of that famous offering which is at Delphi; summon, if you will, the whole house of Pericles, or any other great Athenian family whom you choose—they will all agree with you: I only am left alone and cannot agree, for you do not convince me; although you produce many false witnesses against me, in the hope of depriving me of my inheritance, which is the truth. But I consider that nothing worth speaking of will have been effected by me unless I

make you the one witness of my words; nor by you, unless you make me the one witness of yours; no matter about the rest of the world. For there are two ways of refutation, one which is yours and that of the world in general; but mine is of another sort—let us compare them, and see in what they differ. For, indeed, we are at issue about matters which to know is honourable and not to know disgraceful; to know or not to know happiness and misery—that is the chief of them. And what knowledge can be nobler? or what ignorance more disgraceful than this? And therefore I will begin by asking you whether you do not think that a man who is unjust and doing injustice can be happy, seeing that you think Archelaus unjust, and yet happy? May I assume this to be your opinion?

Pol. Certainly.

Soc. But I say that this is an impossibility—here is one point about which we are at issue:—very good. And do you mean to say also that if he meets with retribution and punishment he will still be happy?

Pol. Certainly not; in that case he will be most miserable.

Soc. On the other hand, if the unjust be not punished, then, according to you, he will be happy?

Pol. Yes.

Soc. But in my opinion, Polus, the unjust or doer of unjust actions is miserable in any case,—more miserable, however, if he be not punished and does not meet with retribution, and less miserable if he be punished and meets with retribution at the hands of gods *[473]* and men.

Pol. You are maintaining a strange doctrine, Socrates.

Soc. I shall try to make you agree with me, O my friend, for as a friend I regard you. Then these are the points at issue between us—are they not? I was saying that to do is worse than to suffer injustice?

Pol. Exactly so.

Soc. And you said the opposite?

Pol. Yes.

Soc. I said also that the wicked are miserable, and you refuted me?

Pol. By Zeus, I did.

Soc. In your own opinion, Polus.

Pol. Yes, and I rather suspect that I was in the right.

Soc. You further said that the wrong-doer is happy if he be unpunished?

Pol. Certainly.

Soc. And I affirm that he is most miserable, and that those who are punished are less miserable—are you going to refute this proposition also?

Pol. A proposition which is harder of refutation than the other, Socrates.

Soc. Say rather, Polus, impossible; for who can refute the truth?

Pol. What do you mean? If a man is detected in an unjust attempt to make himself a tyrant, and when detected is racked, mutilated, has his eyes burned out, and after having had all sorts of great injuries inflicted on him, and having seen his wife and children suffer the like, is at last impaled or tarred and burned alive, will he be happier than if he escape and become a tyrant, and continue all through life doing what he likes and holding the reins of government, the envy and admiration both of citizens and strangers? Is that the paradox which, as you say, cannot be refuted?

Soc. There again, noble Polus, you are raising hobgoblins instead of refuting me; just now you were calling witnesses against me. But please to refresh my memory a little; did you say—"in an unjust attempt to make himself a tyrant"?

Pol. Yes, I did.

Soc. Then I say that neither of them will be happier than the other—neither he who unjustly acquires a tyranny, nor he who suffers in the attempt, for of two miserables one cannot be the happier, but that he who escapes and becomes a tyrant is the more miserable of the two. Do you laugh, Polus? Well, this is a new kind of refutation—when any one says anything, instead of refuting him to laugh at him.

Pol. But do you not think, Socrates, that you have been sufficiently refuted, when you say that which no human being will allow? Ask the company.

Soc. O Polus, I am not a public man, and only last year, when my tribe were serving as Prytanes, and it became my duty as their president to take the votes, [474] there was a laugh at me, because I was unable to take them. And as I failed then, you must not ask me to count the suffrages of the company now; but if, as I was saying, you have no better argument than numbers, let me have a turn, and do you make trial of the sort of proof which, as I think, is required; for I shall produce one witness only of the truth of my words, and he is the person with whom I am arguing; his suffrage I know how to take; but with the many I have nothing to do, and do not even address myself to them. May I ask then whether you will answer in

turn and have your words put to the proof? For I certainly think that I and you and every man do really believe, that to do is a greater evil than to suffer injustice: and not to be punished than to be punished.

Pol. And I should say neither I, nor any man: would you yourself, for example, suffer rather than do injustice?

Soc. Yes, and you, too; I or any man would.

Pol. Quite the reverse; neither you, nor I, nor any man.

Soc. But will you answer?

Pol. To be sure, I will; for I am curious to hear what you can have to say.

Soc. Tell me, then, and you will know, and let us suppose that I am beginning at the beginning: which of the two, Polus, in your opinion, is the worst?—to do injustice or to suffer?

Pol. I should say that suffering was worst.

Soc. And which is the greater disgrace?— Answer.

Pol. To do.

Soc. And the greater disgrace is the greater evil?

Pol. Certainly not.

Soc. I understand you to say, if I am not mistaken, that the honourable is not the same as the good, or the disgraceful as the evil?

Pol. Certainly not.

Soc. Let me ask a question of you: When you speak of beautiful things, such as bodies, colours, figures, sounds, institutions, do you not call them beautiful in reference to some standard: bodies, for example, are beautiful in proportion as they are useful, or as the sight of them gives pleasure to the spectators; can you give any other account of personal beauty?

Pol. I cannot.

Soc. And you would say of figures or colours generally that they were beautiful, either by reason of the pleasure which they give, or of their use, or both?

Pol. Yes, I should.

Soc. And you would call sounds and music beautiful for the same reason?

Pol. I should.

Soc. Laws and institutions also have no beauty in them except in so far as they are useful or pleasant or both?

[475] *Pol.* I think not.

Soc. And may not the same be said of the beauty of knowledge?

Pol. To be sure, Socrates; and I very much approve of your measuring beauty by the standard of pleasure and utility.

Soc. And deformity or disgrace may be equally measured by the opposite standard of pain and evil?

Pol. Certainly.

Soc. Then when of two beautiful things one exceeds in beauty, the measure of the excess is to be taken in one or both of these; that is to say, in pleasure or utility or both?

Pol. Very true.

Soc. And of two deformed things, that which exceeds in deformity or disgrace, exceeds either in pain or evil—must it not be so?

Pol. Yes.

Soc. But then again, what was the observation which you just now made, about doing and suffering wrong? Did you not say, that suffering wrong was more evil, and doing wrong more disgraceful?

Pol. I did.

Soc. Then, if doing wrong is more disgraceful than suffering, the more disgraceful must be more painful and must exceed in pain or in evil or both: does not that also follow?

Pol. Of course.

Soc. First, then, let us consider whether the doing of injustice exceeds the suffering in the consequent pain: Do the injurers suffer more than the injured?

Pol. No, Socrates; certainly not.

Soc. Then they do not exceed in pain?

Pol. No.

Soc. But if not in pain, then not in both?

Pol. Certainly not.

Soc. Then they can only exceed in the other?

Pol. Yes.

Soc. That is to say, in evil?

Pol. True.

Soc. Then doing injustice will have an excess of evil, and will therefore be a greater evil than suffering injustice?

Pol. Clearly.

Soc. But have not you and the world already agreed that to do injustice is more disgraceful than to suffer?

Pol. Yes.

Soc. And that is now discovered to be more evil?

Pol. True.

Soc. And would you prefer a greater evil or a greater dishonour to a less one? Answer, Polus, and fear not; for you will come to no harm if you nobly resign yourself into the healing hand of the argument as to a physician without shrinking, and either say "Yes" or "No" to me.

Pol. I should say "No."

Soc. Would any other man prefer a greater to a less evil?

Pol. No, not according to this way of putting the case, Socrates.

Soc. Then I said truly, Polus, that neither you, nor I, nor any man, would rather, do than suffer injustice; for to do injustice is the greater evil of the two.

Pol. That is the conclusion.

Soc. You see, Polus, when you compare the two kinds of refutations, how unlike they are. All men, with the exception of myself, are of your way of thinking; [476] but your single assent and witness are enough for me—I have no need of any other, I take your suffrage, and am regardless of the rest. Enough of this, and now let us proceed to the next question; which is, Whether the greatest of evils to a guilty man is to suffer punishment, as you supposed, or whether to escape punishment is not a greater evil, as I supposed. Consider:—You would say that to suffer punishment is another name for being justly corrected when you do wrong?

Pol. I should.

Soc. And would you not allow that all just things are honourable in so far as they are just? Please to reflect, and tell me your opinion.

Pol. Yes, Socrates, I think that they are.

Soc. Consider again:—Where there is an agent, must there not also be a patient?

Pol. I should say so.

Soc. And will not the patient suffer that which the agent does, and will not the suffering have the quality of the action? I mean, for example, that if a man strikes, there must be something which is stricken?

Pol. Yes.

Soc. And if the striker strikes violently or quickly, that which is struck will be struck violently or quickly?

Pol. True.

Soc. And the suffering to him who is stricken is of the same nature as the act of him who strikes?

Pol. Yes.

Soc. And if a man burns, there is something which is burned?

Pol. Certainly.

Soc. And if he burns in excess or so as to cause pain, the thing burned will be burned in the same way?

Pol. Truly.

Soc. And if he cuts, the same argument holds—there will be something cut?

Pol. Yes.

Soc. And if the cutting be great or deep or such as will cause pain, the cut will be of the same nature?

Pol. That is evident.

Soc. Then you would agree generally to the universal proposition which I was just now asserting: that the affection of the patient answers to the act of the agent?

Pol. I agree.

Soc. Then, as this is admitted, let me ask whether being punished is suffering or acting?

Pol. Suffering, Socrates; there can be no doubt of that.

Soc. And suffering implies an agent?

Pol. Certainly, Socrates; and he is the punisher.

Soc. And he who punishes rightly, punishes justly?

Pol. Yes.

Soc. And therefore he acts justly?

Pol. Justly.

Soc. Then he who is punished and suffers retribution, suffers justly?

Pol. That is evident.

Soc. And that which is just has been admitted to be honourable?

Pol. Certainly.

Soc. Then the punisher does what is honourable, and the punished suffers what is honourable?

Pol. True.

Soc. And if what is honourable, then what is good, for the honourable is either pleasant or useful? *[477]*

Pol. Certainly.

Soc. Then he who is punished suffers what is good?

Pol. That is true.

Soc. Then he is benefited?

Pol. Yes.

Soc. Do I understand you to mean what I mean by the term "benefited"? I mean, that if he be justly punished his soul is improved.

Pol. Surely.

Soc. Then he who is punished is delivered from the evil of his soul?

Pol. Yes.

Soc. And is he not then delivered from the greatest evil? Look at the matter in this way: —In respect of a man's estate, do you see any greater evil than poverty?

Pol. There is no greater evil.

Soc. Again, in a man's bodily frame, you would say that the evil is weakness and disease and deformity?

Pol. I should.

Soc. And do you not imagine that the soul likewise has some evil of her own?

Pol. Of course.

Soc. And this you would call injustice and ignorance and cowardice, and the like?

Pol. Certainly.

Soc. So then, in mind, body, and estate, which are three, you have pointed out three corresponding evils—injustice, disease, poverty?

Pol. True.

Soc. And which of the evils is the most disgraceful?—Is not the most disgraceful of them injustice, and in general the evil of the soul?

Pol. By far the most.

Soc. And if the most disgraceful, then also the worst?

Pol. What do you mean, Socrates?

Soc. I mean to say, that what is most disgraceful has been already admitted to be most painful or hurtful, or both.

Pol. Certainly.

Soc. And now injustice and all evil in the soul has been admitted by us to be most disgraceful?

Pol. It has been admitted.

Soc. And most disgraceful either because most painful and causing excessive pain, or most hurtful, or both?

Pol. Certainly.

Soc. And therefore to be unjust and intemperate, and cowardly and ignorant, is more painful than to be poor and sick?

Pol. Nay, Socrates; the painfulness does not appear to me to follow from your premises.

Soc. Then, if, as you would argue, not more painful, the evil of the soul is of all evils the most disgraceful; and the excess of disgrace must be caused by some preternatural greatness, or extraordinary hurtfulness of the evil.

Pol. Clearly.

Soc. And that which exceeds most in hurtfulness will be the greatest of evils?

Pol. Yes.

Soc. Then injustice and intemperance, and in general the depravity of the soul, are the greatest of evils!

Pol. That is evident.

Soc. Now, what art is there which delivers us from poverty? Does not the art of making money?

Pol. Yes.

Soc. And what art frees us from disease? Does not the art of medicine?

Pol. Very true.

[478] Soc. And what from vice and injustice? If you are not able to answer at once, ask yourself whither we go with the sick, and to whom we take them.

Pol. To the physicians, Socrates.

Soc. And to whom do we go with the unjust and intemperate?

Pol. To the judges, you mean.

Soc.—Who are to punish them?

Pol. Yes.

Soc. And do not those who rightly punish others, punish them in accordance with a certain rule of justice?

Pol. Clearly.

Soc. Then the art of money-making frees a man from poverty; medicine from disease; and justice from intemperance and injustice?

Pol. That is evident.

Soc. Which, then, is the best of these three?

Pol. Will you enumerate them?

Soc. Money-making, medicine, and justice.

Pol. Justice, Socrates, far excels the two others.

Soc. And justice, if the best, gives the greatest pleasure or advantage or both?

Pol. Yes.

Soc. But is the being healed a pleasant thing, and are those who are being healed pleased?

Pol. I think not.

Soc. A useful thing, then?

Pol. Yes.

Soc. Yes, because the patient is delivered from a great evil; and this is the advantage of enduring the pain—that you get well?

Pol. Certainly.

Soc. And would he be the happier man in his bodily condition, who is healed, or who never was out of health?

Pol. Clearly he who was never out of health.

Soc. Yes; for happiness surely does not consist in being delivered from evils, but in never having had them.

Pol. True.

Soc. And suppose the case of two persons who have some evil in their bodies, and that one of them is healed and delivered from evil, and another is not healed, but retains the evil —which of them is the most miserable?

Pol. Clearly he who is not healed.

Soc. And was not punishment said by us to be a deliverance from the greatest of evils, which is vice?

Pol. True.

Soc. And justice punishes us, and makes us more just, and is the medicine of our vice?

Pol. True.

Soc. He, then, has the first place in the scale of happiness who has never had vice in his soul; for this has been shown to be the greatest of evils.

Pol. Clearly.

Soc. And he has the second place, who is delivered from vice?

Pol. True.

Soc. That is to say, he who receives admonition and rebuke and punishment?

Pol. Yes.

Soc. Then he lives worst, who, having been unjust, has no deliverance from injustice?

Pol. Certainly.

[479] Soc. That is, he lives worst who commits the greatest crimes, and who, being the most unjust of men, succeeds in escaping rebuke or correction or punishment; and this, as you say, has been accomplished by Archelaus and other tyrants and rhetoricians and potentates?[1]

Pol. True.

Soc. May not their way of proceeding, my friend, be compared to the conduct of a person who is afflicted with the worst of diseases and yet contrives not to pay the penalty to the physician for his sins against his constitution, and will not be cured, because, like a child, he is afraid of the pain of being burned or cut:—Is not that a parallel case?

Pol. Yes, truly.

Soc. He would seem as if he did not know the nature of health and bodily vigour; and if we are right, Polus, in our previous conclusions, they are in a like case who strive to evade justice, which they see to be painful, but are blind to the advantage which ensues from it, not knowing how far more miserable a companion a diseased soul is than a diseased body; a soul, I say, which is corrupt and unrighteous and unholy. And hence they do all that they can to avoid punishment and to avoid being released from the greatest of evils; they provide themselves with money and friends, and cultivate to the utmost their powers of persuasion. But if we, Polus, are right, do you see what follows, or shall we draw out the consequences in form?

Pol. If you please.

Soc. Is it not a fact that injustice, and the doing of injustice, is the greatest of evils?

Pol. That is quite clear.

Soc. And further, that to suffer punishment is the way to be released from this evil?

Pol. True.

Soc. And not to suffer, is to perpetuate the evil?

Pol. Yes.

Soc. To do wrong, then, is second only in the scale of evils; but to do wrong and not to be punished, is first and greatest of all?

[1] Cf. *Republic,* ix. 579, 580.

Pol. That is true.

Soc. Well, and was not this the point in dispute, my friend? You deemed Archelaus happy, because he was a very great criminal and unpunished: I, on the other hand, maintained that he or any other who like him has done wrong and has not been punished, is, and ought to be, the most miserable of all men; and that the doer of injustice is more miserable than the sufferer; and he who escapes punishment, more miserable than he who suffers.—Was not that what I said?

Pol. Yes.

Soc. And it has been proved to be true?

Pol. Certainly.

[480] *Soc.* Well, Polus, but if this is true, where is the great use of rhetoric? If we admit what has been just now said, every man ought in every way to guard himself against doing wrong, for he will thereby suffer great evil?

Pol. True.

Soc. And if he, or any one about whom he cares, does wrong, he ought of his own accord to go where he will be immediately punished; he will run to the judge, as he would to the physician, in order that the disease of injustice may not be rendered chronic and become the incurable cancer of the soul; must we not allow this consequence, Polus, if our former admissions are to stand:—is any other inference consistent with them?

Pol. To that, Socrates, there can be but one answer.

Soc. Then rhetoric is of no use to us, Polus, in helping a man to excuse his own injustice, or that of his parents or friends, or children or country; but may be of use to any one who holds that instead of excusing he ought to accuse—himself above all, and in the next degree his family or any of his friends who may be doing wrong; he should bring to light the iniquity and not conceal it, that so the wrong-doer may suffer and be made whole; and he should even force himself and others not to shrink, but with closed eyes like brave men to let the physician operate with knife or searing iron, not regarding the pain, in the hope of attaining the good and the honourable; let him who has done things worthy of stripes, allow himself to be scourged, if of bonds, to be bound, if of a fine, to be fined, if of exile, to be exiled, if of death, to die, himself being the first to accuse himself and his own relations, and using rhetoric to this end, that his and their unjust actions may be made manifest, and that they themselves may be delivered from injustice, which is the greatest evil. Then,

Polus, rhetoric would indeed be useful. Do you say "Yes" or "No" to that?

Pol. To me, Socrates, what you are saying appears very strange, though probably in agreement with your premises.

Soc. Is not this the conclusion, if the premises are not disproven?

Pol. Yes; it certainly is.

Soc. And from the opposite point of view, if indeed it be our duty to harm another, whether an enemy or not—I except the case of self-defence—then I have to be upon my guard—but if my enemy [481] injures a third person, then in every sort of way, by word as well as deed, I should try to prevent his being punished, or appearing before the judge; and if he appears, I should contrive that he should escape, and not suffer punishment: if he has stolen a sum of money, let him keep what he has stolen and spend it on him and his, regardless of religion and justice; and if he has done things worthy of death, let him not die, but rather be immortal in his wickedness; or, if this is not possible, let him at any rate be allowed to live as long as he can. For such purposes, Polus, rhetoric may be useful, but is of small if of any use to him who is not intending to commit injustice; at least, there was no such use discovered by us in the previous discussion.

Cal. Tell me, Chaerephon, is Socrates in earnest, or is he joking?

Chaer. I should say, Callicles, that he is in most profound earnest; but you may as well ask him.

Cal. By the gods, and I will. Tell me, Socrates, are you in earnest, or only in jest? For if you are in earnest, and what you say is true, is not the whole of human life turned upside down; and are we not doing, as would appear, in everything the opposite of what we ought to be doing?

Soc. O Callicles, if there were not some community of feelings among mankind, however varying in different persons—I mean to say, if every man's feelings were peculiar to himself and were not shared by the rest of his species—I do not see how we could ever communicate our impressions to one another. I make this remark because I perceive that you and I have a common feeling. For we are lovers both, and both of us have two loves apiece:—I am the lover of Alcibiades, the son of Cleinias, and of philosophy; and you of the Athenian Demus, and of Demus the son of Pyrilampes. Now, I observe that you, with all your cleverness, do not venture to contradict your favourite in any word or opinion of his; but as he changes you change, backwards and forwards. When the Athenian Demus denies anything that you are saying in the assembly, you go over to his opinion; and you do the same with Demus, the fair young son of Pyrilampes. For you have not the power to resist the words and ideas of your loves; and if a person were to express surprise at the strangeness of what you say from time to time when under their influence, *[482]* you would probably reply to him, if you were honest, that you cannot help saying what your loves say unless they are prevented; and that you can only be silent when they are. Now you must understand that my words are an echo too, and therefore you need not wonder at me; but if you want to silence me, silence philosophy, who is my love, for she is always telling me what I am now telling you, my friend; neither is she capricious like my other love, for the son of Cleinias says one thing to-day and another thing to-morrow, but philosophy is always true. She is the teacher at whose words you are now wondering, and you have heard her yourself. Her you must refute, and either show, as I was saying, that to do injustice and to escape punishment is not the worst of all evils; or, if you leave her word unrefuted, by the dog the god of Egypt, I declare, O Callicles, that Callicles will never be at one with himself, but that his whole life will be a discord. And yet, my friend, I would rather that my lyre should be inharmonious, and that there should be no music in the chorus which I provided; aye, or that the whole world should be at odds with me, and oppose me, rather than that I myself should be at odds with myself, and contradict myself.

Cal. O Socrates, you are a regular declaimer, and seem to be running riot in the argument. And now you are declaiming in this way because Polus has fallen into the same error himself of which he accused Gorgias:—for he said that when Gorgias was asked by you, whether, if some one came to him who wanted to learn rhetoric, and did not know justice, he would teach him justice, Gorgias in his modesty replied that he would, because he thought that mankind in general would be displeased if he answered "No"; and then in consequence of this admission, Gorgias was compelled to contradict himself, that being just the sort of thing in which you delight. Whereupon Polus laughed at you deservedly, as I think; but now he has himself fallen into the same trap. I cannot say very much for his wit when he conceded to you

that to do is more dishonourable than to suffer injustice, for this was the admission which led to his being entangled by you; and because he was too modest to say what he thought, he had his mouth stopped. For the truth is, Socrates, that you, who pretend to be engaged in the pursuit of truth, are appealing now to the popular and vulgar notions of right, which are not natural, but only conventional. Convention and nature are generally at variance with one another: and hence, if a person is too modest to say what he thinks, *[483]* he is compelled to contradict himself; and you, in your ingenuity perceiving the advantage to be thereby gained, slyly ask of him who is arguing conventionally a question which is to be determined by the rule of nature; and if he is talking of the rule of nature, you slip away to custom: as, for instance, you did in this very discussion about doing and suffering injustice. When Polus was speaking of the conventionally dishonourable, you assailed him from the point of view of nature; for by the rule of nature, to suffer injustice is the greater disgrace because the greater evil; but conventionally, to do evil is the more disgraceful. For the suffering of injustice is not the part of a man, but of a slave, who indeed had better die than live; since when he is wronged and trampled upon, he is unable to help himself, or any other about whom he cares. The reason, as I conceive, is that the makers of laws are the majority who are weak; and they make laws and distribute praises and censures with a view to themselves and to their own interests; and they terrify the stronger sort of men, and those who are able to get the better of them, in order that they may not get the better of them; and they say, that dishonesty is shameful and unjust; meaning, by the word injustice, the desire of a man to have more than his neighbours; for knowing their own inferiority, I suspect that they are too glad of equality. And therefore the endeavour to have more than the many, is conventionally said to be shameful and unjust, and is called injustice,[1] whereas nature herself intimates that it is just for the better to have more than the worse, the more powerful than the weaker; and in many ways she shows, among men as well as among animals, and indeed among whole cities and races, that justice consists in the superior ruling over and having more than the inferior. For on what principle of justice did Xerxes invade Hellas, or his father the Scythians? (not to speak of numberless other examples). Nay, but

[1] Cf. *Republic*, ii. 359.

these are the men who act according to nature; yes, by Heaven, and according to the law of nature: not, perhaps, according to that artificial law, which we invent and impose upon our fellows, of whom we take the best and strongest from their youth upwards, and tame them like young lions, [484]—charming them with the sound of the voice, and saying to them, that with equality they must be content, and that the equal is the honourable and the just. But if there were a man who had sufficient force, he would shake off and break through, and escape from all this; he would trample under foot all our formulas and spells and charms, and all our laws which are against nature: the slave would rise in rebellion and be lord over us, and the light of natural justice would shine forth. And this I take to be the sentiment of Pindar, when he says in his poem, that

Law is the king of all, of mortals as well as of immortals;

this, as he says,

Makes might to be right, doing violence with highest hand; as I infer from the deeds of Heracles, for without buying them—

—I do not remember the exact words, but the meaning is, that without buying them, and without their being given to him, he carried off the oxen of Geryon, according to the law of natural right, and that the oxen and other possessions of the weaker and inferior properly belong to the stronger and superior. And this is true, as you may ascertain, if you will leave philosophy and go on to higher things: for philosophy, Socrates, if pursued in moderation and at the proper age, is an elegant accomplishment, but too much philosophy is the ruin of human life. Even if a man has good parts, still, if he carries philosophy into later life, he is necessarily ignorant of all those things which a gentleman and a person of honour ought to know; he is inexperienced in the laws of the State, and in the language which ought to be used in the dealings of man with man, whether private or public, and utterly ignorant of the pleasures and desires of mankind and of human character in general. And people of this sort, when they betake themselves to politics or business, are as ridiculous as I imagine the politicians to be, when they make their appearance in the arena of philosophy. For, as Euripides says,

Every man shines in that and pursues that, and devotes the greatest portion of the day to that in which he most excels,

but anything in which he is inferior, [485] he avoids and depreciates, and praises the opposite from partiality to himself, and because he thinks that he will thus praise himself. The true principle is to unite them. Philosophy, as a part of education, is an excellent thing, and there is no disgrace to a man while he is young in pursuing such a study; but when he is more advanced in years, the thing becomes ridiculous, and I feel towards philosophers as I do towards those who lisp and imitate children. For I love to see a little child, who is not of an age to speak plainly, lisping at his play; there is an appearance of grace and freedom in his utterance, which is natural to his childish years. But when I hear some small creature carefully articulating its words, I am offended; the sound is disagreeable, and has to my ears the twang of slavery. So when I hear a man lisping, or see him playing like a child, his behaviour appears to me ridiculous and unmanly and worthy of stripes. And I have the same feeling about students of philosophy; when I see a youth thus engaged—the study appears to me to be in character, and becoming a man of liberal education, and him who neglects philosophy I regard as an inferior man, who will never aspire to anything great or noble. But if I see him continuing the study in later life, and not leaving off, I should like to beat him, Socrates; for, as I was saying, such a one, even though he have good natural parts, becomes effeminate. He flies from the busy centre and the market-place, in which, as the poet says, men become distinguished; he creeps into a corner for the rest of his life, and talks in a whisper with three or four admiring youths, but never speaks out like a freeman in a satisfactory manner. Now I, Socrates, am very well inclined towards you, and my feeling may be compared with that of Zethus towards Amphion, in the play of Euripides, whom I was mentioning just now: for I am disposed to say to you much what Zethus said to his brother, that you, Socrates, are careless about the things of which you ought to be careful; and that you

Who have a soul so noble, are remarkable for a puerile exterior;

[486] Neither in a court of justice could you state a case, or give any reason or proof,

Or offer valiant counsel on another's behalf.

And you must not be offended, my dear Socrates, for I am speaking out of good-will towards you, if I ask whether you are not ashamed of being thus defenceless; which I affirm to be the condition not of you only but of all those who will carry the study of philosophy too far. For suppose that some one were to take you, or any one of your sort, off to prison, declaring that you had done wrong when you had done no wrong, you must allow that you would not know what to do:— there you would stand giddy and gaping, and not having a word to say; and when you went up before the Court, even if the accuser were a poor creature and not good for much, you would die if he were disposed to claim the penalty of death. And yet, Socrates, what is the value of

An art which converts a man of sense into a fool,

who is helpless, and has no power to save either himself or others, when he is in the greatest danger and is going to be despoiled by his enemies of all his goods, and has to live, simply deprived of his rights of citizenship?—he being a man who, if I may use the expression, may be boxed on the ears with impunity. Then, my good friend, take my advice, and refute no more:

Learn the philosophy of business, and acquire the reputation of wisdom.
But leave to others these niceties,

whether they are to be described as follies or absurdities:

For they will only
Give you poverty for the inmate of your dwelling.

Cease, then, emulating these paltry splitters of words, and emulate only the man of substance and honour, who is well to do.

Soc. If my soul, Callicles, were made of gold, should I not rejoice to discover one of those stones with which they test gold, and the very best possible one to which I might bring my soul; and if the stone and I agreed in approving of her training, then I should know that I was in a satisfactory state, and that no other test was needed by me.

Cal. What is your meaning, Socrates?

Soc. I will tell you; I think that I have found in you the desired touchstone.

Cal. Why?

Soc. Because I am sure that if you agree with me in any of the opinions which my soul forms, I have at last found the truth indeed. For I consider that if a man is to make a complete trial of the good or evil of the soul, *[487]* he ought to have three qualities—knowledge, good-will, outspokenness, which are all possessed by you. Many whom I meet are unable to make trial of me, because they are not wise as you are; others are wise, but they will not tell me the truth, because they have not the same interest in me

which you have; and these two strangers, Gorgias and Polus, are undoubtedly wise men and my very good friends, but they are not outspoken enough, and they are too modest. Why, their modesty is so great that they are driven to contradict themselves, first one and then the other of them, in the face of a large company, on matters of the highest moment. But you have all the qualities in which these others are deficient, having received an excellent education; to this many Athenians can testify. And you are my friend. Shall I tell you why I think so? I know that you, Callicles, and Tisander of Aphidnae, and Andron the son of Androtion, and Nausicydes of the deme of Cholarges, studied together: there were four of you, and I once heard you advising with one another as to the extent to which the pursuit of philosophy should be carried, and, as I know, you came to the conclusion that the study should not be pushed too much into detail. You were cautioning one another not to be overwise; you were afraid that too much wisdom might unconsciously to yourselves be the ruin of you. And now when I hear you giving the same advice to me which you then gave to your most intimate friends, I have a sufficient evidence of your real good-will to me. And of the frankness of your nature and freedom from modesty I am assured by yourself, and the assurance is confirmed by your last speech. Well then, the inference in the present case clearly is, that if you agree with me in an argument about any point, that point will have been sufficiently tested by us, and will not require to be submitted to any further test. For you could not have agreed with me, either from lack of knowledge or from superfluity of modesty, nor yet from a desire to deceive me, for you are my friend, as you tell me yourself. And therefore when you and I are agreed, the result will be the attainment of perfect truth. Now there is no nobler enquiry, Callicles, than that which you censure me for making,— What ought the character of a man to be, and what his pursuits, and how far is he to go, both in maturer years and in youth? *[488]* For be assured that if I err in my own conduct I do not err intentionally, but from ignorance. Do not then desist from advising me, now that you have begun, until I have learned clearly what this is which I am to practise, and how I may acquire it. And if you find me assenting to your words, and hereafter not doing that to which I assented, call me "dolt," and deem me unworthy of receiving further instruction. Once more, then, tell me what you and Pindar mean by natural justice: Do you not mean that the superior should take the property of the inferior by force; that the better should rule the worse, the noble have more than the mean? Am I not right in my recollection?

Cal. Yes; that is what I was saying, and so I still aver.

Soc. And do you mean by the better the same as the superior? for I could not make out what you were saying at the time—whether you meant by the superior the stronger, and that the weaker must obey the stronger, as you seemed to imply when you said that great cities attack small ones in accordance with natural right, because they are superior and stronger, as though the superior and stronger and better were the same; or whether the better may be also the inferior and weaker, and the superior the worse, or whether better is to be defined in the same way as superior: this is the point which I want to have cleared up. Are the superior and better and stronger the same or different?

Cal. I say unequivocally that they are the same.

Soc. Then the many are by nature superior to the one, against whom, as you were saying, they make the laws?

Cal. Certainly.

Soc. Then the laws of the many are the laws of the superior?

Cal. Very true.

Soc. Then they are the laws of the better; for the superior class are far better, as you were saying?

Cal. Yes.

Soc. And since they are superior, the laws which are made by them are by nature good?

Cal. Yes.

Soc. And are not the many of opinion, as you were lately saying, that justice is equality, *[489]* and that to do is more disgraceful than to suffer injustice?—is that so or not? Answer, Callicles, and let no modesty be found to come in the way;[1] do the many think, or do they not think thus?—I must beg of you to answer, in order that if you agree with me I may fortify myself by the assent of so competent an authority.

Cal. Yes; the opinion of the many is what you say.

Soc. Then not only custom but nature also affirms that to do is more disgraceful than to suffer injustice, and that justice is equality; so that you seem to have been wrong in your former assertion, when accusing me you said

[1] Cf. what is said of Gorgias by Callicles, 482.

that nature and custom are opposed, and that I, knowing this, was dishonestly playing between them, appealing to custom when the argument is about nature, and to nature when the argument is about custom?

Cal. This man will never cease talking nonsense. At your age, Socrates, are you not ashamed to be catching at words and chuckling over some verbal slip? do you not see—have I not told you already, that by superior I mean better: do you imagine me to say, that if a rabble of slaves and nondescripts, who are of no use except perhaps for their physical strength, get together, their *ipsissima verba* are laws?

Soc. Ho! my philosopher, is that your line?

Cal. Certainly.

Soc. I was thinking, Callicles, that something of the kind must have been in your mind, and that is why I repeated the question—What is the superior? I wanted to know clearly what you meant; for you surely do not think that two men are better than one, or that your slaves are better than you because they are stronger? Then please to begin again, and tell me who the better are, if they are not the stronger; and I will ask you, great Sir, to be a little milder in your instructions, or I shall have to run away from you.

Cal. You are ironical.

Soc. No, by the hero Zethus, Callicles, by whose aid you were just now saying (486) many ironical things against me, I am not:—tell me, then, whom you mean by the better?

Cal. I mean the more excellent.

Soc. Do you not see that you are yourself using words which have no meaning and that you are explaining nothing?—will you tell me whether you mean by the better and superior the wiser, or if not, whom?

[490] Cal. Most assuredly, I do mean the wiser.

Soc. Then according to you, one wise man may often be superior to ten thousand fools, and he ought to rule them, and they ought to be his subjects, and he ought to have more than they should. This is what I believe that you mean (and you must not suppose that I am word-catching), if you allow that the one is superior to the ten thousand?

Cal. Yes; that is what I mean, and that is what I conceive to be natural justice—that the better and wiser should rule and have more than the inferior.

Soc. Stop there, and let me ask you what you would say in this case: Let us suppose that we are all together as we are now; there are several of us, and we have a large common store of meats and drinks, and there are all sorts of persons in our company having various degrees of strength and weakness, and one of us, being physician, is wiser in the matter of food than all the rest, and he is probably stronger than some and not so strong as others of us—will he not, being wiser, be also better than we are, and our superior in this matter of food?

Cal. Certainly.

Soc. Either, then, he will have a larger share of the meats and drinks, because he is better, or he will have the distribution of all of them by reason of his authority, but he will not expend or make use of a larger share of them on his own person, or if he does, he will be punished—his share will exceed that of some, and be less than that of others, and if he be the weakest of all, he being the best of all will have the smallest share of all, Callicles:—am I not right, my friend?

Cal. You talk about meats and drinks and physicians and other nonsense; I am not speaking of them.

Soc. Well, but do you admit that the wiser is the better? Answer "Yes" or "No."

Cal. Yes.

Soc. And ought not the better to have a larger share?

Cal. Not of meats and drinks.

Soc. I understand: then, perhaps, of coats—the skilfullest weaver ought to have the largest coat, and the greatest number of them, and go about clothed in the best and finest of them?

Cal. Fudge about coats!

Soc. Then the skilfullest and best in making shoes ought to have the advantage in shoes; the shoemaker, clearly, should walk about in the largest shoes, and have the greatest number of them?

Cal. Fudge about shoes! What nonsense are you talking?

Soc. Or, if this is not your meaning, perhaps you would say that the wise and good and true husbandman should actually have a larger share of seeds, and have as much seed as possible for his own land?

Cal. How you go on, always talking in the same way, Socrates!

[491] *Soc.* Yes, Callicles, and also about the same things.

Cal. Yes, by the Gods, you are literally always talking of cobblers and fullers and cooks and doctors, as if this had to do with our argument.

Soc. But why will you not tell me in what a

man must be superior and wiser in order to claim a larger share; will you neither accept a suggestion, nor offer one?

Cal. I have already told you. In the first place, I mean by superiors not cobblers or cooks, but wise politicians who understand the administration of a state, and who are not only wise, but also valiant and able to carry out their designs, and not the men to faint from want of soul.

Soc. See now, most excellent Callicles, how different my charge against you is from that which you bring against me, for you reproach me with always saying the same; but I reproach you with never saying the same about the same things, for at one time you were defining the better and the superior to be the stronger, then again as the wiser, and now you bring forward a new notion; the superior and the better are now declared by you to be the more courageous: I wish, my good friend, that you would tell me, once for all, whom you affirm to be the better and superior, and in what they are better?

Cal. I have already told you that I mean those who are wise and courageous in the administration of a state—they ought to be the rulers of their states, and justice consists in their having more than their subjects.

Soc. But whether rulers or subjects will they or will they not have more than themselves, my friend?

Cal. What do you mean?

Soc. I mean that every man is his own ruler; but perhaps you think that there is no necessity for him to rule himself; he is only required to rule others?

Cal. What do you mean by his "ruling over himself"?

Soc. A simple thing enough; just what is commonly said, that a man should be temperate and master of himself, and ruler of his own pleasures and passions.

Cal. What innocence! you mean those fools —the temperate?

Soc. Certainly:—any one may know that to be my meaning.

Cal. Quite so, Socrates; and they are really fools, for how can a man be happy who is the servant of anything? On the contrary, I plainly assert, that he who would truly live ought to allow his desires to wax to the uttermost, and not to chastise them; but when they have grown to their greatest he should have courage and intelligence [492] to minister to them and to satisfy all his longings. And this I affirm to be natural justice and nobility. To this however the many cannot attain; and they blame the strong man because they are ashamed of their own weakness, which they desire to conceal, and hence they say that intemperance is base. As I have remarked already, they enslave the nobler natures, and being unable to satisfy their pleasures, they praise temperance and justice out of their own cowardice. For if a man had been originally the son of a king, or had a nature capable of acquiring an empire or a tyranny or sovereignty, what could be more truly base or evil than temperance—to a man like him, I say, who might freely be enjoying every good, and has no one to stand in his way, and yet has admitted custom and reason and the opinion of other men to be lords over him?— must not he be in a miserable plight whom the reputation of justice and temperance hinders from giving more to his friends than to his enemies, even though he be a ruler in his city? Nay, Socrates, for you profess to be a votary of the truth, and the truth is this:—that luxury and intemperance and licence, if they be provided with means, are virtue and happiness— all the rest is a mere bauble, agreements contrary to nature, foolish talk of men, nothing worth.[1]

Soc. There is a noble freedom, Callicles, in your way of approaching the argument; for what you say is what the rest of the world think, but do not like to say. And I must beg of you to persevere, that the true rule of human life may become manifest. Tell me, then:—you say, do you not, that in the rightly-developed man the passions ought not to be controlled, but that we should let them grow to the utmost and somehow or other satisfy them, and that this is virtue?

Cal. Yes; I do.

Soc. Then those who want nothing are not truly said to be happy?

Cal. No indeed, for then stones and dead men would be the happiest of all.

Soc. But surely life according to your view is an awful thing; and indeed I think that Euripides may have been right in saying,

Who knows if life be not death and death life;

and that we are very likely dead; *[493]* I have heard a philosopher say that at this moment we are actually dead, and that the body (σῶμα) is our tomb (σῆμα),[2] and that the part of the soul which is the seat of the desires is liable to be tossed about by words and blown up and down;

and some ingenious person, probably a Sicilian or an Italian, playing with the word, invented a tale in which he called the soul—because of its believing and make-believe nature—a vessel,[3] and the ignorant he called the uninitiated or leaky, and the place in the souls of the uninitiated in which the desires are seated, being the intemperate and incontinent part, he compared to a vessel full of holes, because it can never be satisfied. He is not of your way of thinking, Callicles, for he declares, that of all the souls in Hades, meaning the invisible world (ἀειδὲς), these uninitiated or leaky persons are the most miserable, and that they pour water into a vessel which is full of holes out of a colander which is similarly perforated. The colander, as my informer assures me, is the soul, and the soul which he compares to a colander is the soul of the ignorant, which is likewise full of holes, and therefore incontinent, owing to a bad memory and want of faith. These notions are strange enough, but they show the principle which, if I can, I would fain prove to you; that you should change your mind, and, instead of the intemperate and insatiate life, choose that which is orderly and sufficient and has a due provision for daily needs. Do I make any impression on you, and are you coming over to the opinion that the orderly are happier than the intemperate? Or do I fail to persuade you, and, however many tales I rehearse to you, do you continue of the same opinion still?

Cal. The latter, Socrates, is more like the truth.

Soc. Well, I will tell you another image, which comes out of the same school:—Let me request you to consider how far you would accept this as an account of the two lives of the temperate and intemperate in a figure:—There are two men, both of whom have a number of casks; the one man has his casks sound and full, one of wine, another of honey, and a third of milk, besides others filled with other liquids, and the streams which fill them are few and scanty, and he can only obtain them with a great deal of toil and difficulty; but when his casks are once filled he has no need to feed them any more, and has no further trouble with them or care about them. The other, in like manner, can procure streams, though not without difficulty; but his vessels are leaky and unsound, and night and day he is compelled to be filling them, and if he pauses for a moment, *[494]* he is in an agony of pain. Such are their respective lives:—

---

[1] Cf. *Republic,* i. 348.
[2] Cf. *Phaedrus,* 250.

[3] An untranslateable pun—διὰ τὸ πιθανόν τε καὶ πιστικὸν ὠνόμασε πίθον.

And now would you say that the life of the intemperate is happier than that of the temperate? Do I not convince you that the opposite is the truth?

Cal. You do not convince me, Socrates, for the one who has filled himself has no longer any pleasure left; and this, as I was just now saying, is the life of a stone: he has neither joy nor sorrow after he is once filled; but the pleasure depends on the superabundance of the influx.

Soc. But the more you pour in, the greater the waste; and the holes must be large for the liquid to escape.

Cal. Certainly.

Soc. The life which you are now depicting is not that of a dead man, or of a stone, but of a cormorant; you mean that he is to be hungering and eating?

Cal. Yes.

Soc. And he is to be thirsting and drinking?

Cal. Yes, that is what I mean; he is to have all his desires about him, and to be able to live happily in the gratification of them.

Soc. Capital, excellent; go on as you have begun, and have no shame; I, too, must disencumber myself of shame: and first, will you tell me whether you include itching and scratching, provided you have enough of them and pass your life in scratching, in your notion of happiness?

Cal. What a strange being you are, Socrates! a regular mob-orator.

Soc. That was the reason, Callicles, why I scared Polus and Gorgias, until they were too modest to say what they thought; but you will not be too modest and will not be scared, for you are a brave man. And now, answer my question.

Cal. I answer, that even the scratcher would live pleasantly.

Soc. And if pleasantly, then also happily?

Cal. To be sure.

Soc. But what if the itching is not confined to the head? Shall I pursue the question? And here, Callicles, I would have you consider how you would reply if consequences are pressed upon you, especially if in the last resort you are asked, whether the life of a catamite is not terrible, foul, miserable? Or would you venture to say, that they too are happy, if they only get enough of what they want?

Cal. Are you not ashamed, Socrates, of introducing such topics into the argument?

Soc. Well, my fine friend, but am I the introducer of these topics, or he who says without any qualification that all who feel pleasure in whatever manner are happy, [495] and who admits of no distinction between good and bad pleasures? And I would still ask, whether you say that pleasure and good are the same, or whether there is some pleasure which is not a good?

Cal. Well, then, for the sake of consistency, I will say that they are the same.

Soc. You are breaking the original agreement, Callicles, and will no longer be a satisfactory companion in the search after truth, if you say what is contrary to your real opinion.

Cal. Why, that is what you are doing too, Socrates.

Soc. Then we are both doing wrong. Still, my dear friend, I would ask you to consider whether pleasure, from whatever source derived, is the good; for, if this be true, then the disagreeable consequences which have been darkly intimated must follow, and many others.

Cal. That, Socrates, is only your opinion.

Soc. And do you, Callicles, seriously maintain what you are saying?

Cal. Indeed I do.

Soc. Then, as you are in earnest, shall we proceed with the argument?

Cal. By all means.

Soc. Well, if you are willing to proceed, determine this question for me:—There is something, I presume, which you would call knowledge?

Cal. There is.

Soc. And were you not saying just now, that some courage implied knowledge?

Cal. I was.

Soc. And you were speaking of courage and knowledge as two things different from one another?

Cal. Certainly I was.

Soc. And would you say that pleasure and knowledge are the same, or not the same?

Cal. Not the same, O man of wisdom.

Soc. And would you say that courage differed from pleasure?

Cal. Certainly.

Soc. Well, then, let us remember that Callicles, the Acharnian, says that pleasure and good are the same; but that knowledge and courage are not the same, either with one another, or with the good.

Cal. And what does our friend Socrates, of Foxton, say—does he assent to this, or not?

Soc. He does not assent; neither will Callicles, when he sees himself truly. You will admit, I suppose, that good and evil fortune are opposed to each other?

Cal. Yes.

Soc. And if they are opposed to each other, then, like health and disease, they exclude one another; a man cannot have them both, or be without them both, at the same time?

Cal. What do you mean?

Soc. Take the case of any bodily affection:— a man may have the complaint in his eyes which is called ophthalmia?

[496] *Cal.* To be sure.

Soc. But he surely cannot have the same eyes well and sound at the same time?

Cal. Certainly not.

Soc. And when he has got rid of his ophthalmia, has he got rid of the health of his eyes too? Is the final result, that he gets rid of them both together?

Cal. Certainly not.

Soc. That would surely be marvellous and absurd?

Cal. Very.

Soc. I suppose that he is affected by them, and gets rid of them in turns?

Cal. Yes.

Soc. And he may have strength and weakness in the same way, by fits?

Cal. Yes.

Soc. Or swiftness and slowness?

Cal. Certainly.

Soc. And does he have and not have good and happiness, and their opposites, evil and misery, in a similar alternation?[1]

Cal. Certainly he has.

Soc. If then there be anything which a man has and has not at the same time, clearly that cannot be good and evil—do we agree? Please not to answer without consideration.

Cal. I entirely agree.

Soc. Go back now to our former admissions. —Did you say that to hunger, I mean the mere state of hunger, was pleasant or painful?

Cal. I said painful, but that to eat when you are hungry is pleasant.

Soc. I know; but still the actual hunger is painful: am I not right?

Cal. Yes.

Soc. And thirst, too, is painful?

Cal. Yes, very.

Soc. Need I adduce any more instances, or would you agree that all wants or desires are painful?

Cal. I agree, and therefore you need not adduce any more instances.

[1] Cf. *Republic*, iv. 436.

Soc. Very good. And you would admit that to drink, when you are thirsty, is pleasant?

Cal. Yes.

Soc. And in the sentence which you have just uttered, the word "thirsty" implies pain?

Cal. Yes.

Soc. And the word "drinking" is expressive of pleasure, and of the satisfaction of the want?

Cal. Yes.

Soc. There is pleasure in drinking?

Cal. Certainly.

Soc. When you are thirsty?

Cal. Yes.

Soc. And in pain?

Cal. Yes.

Soc. Do you see the inference:—that pleasure and pain are simultaneous, when you say that being thirsty, you drink? For are they not simultaneous, and do they not affect at the same time the same part, whether of the soul or the body?—which of them is affected cannot be supposed to be of any consequence: Is not this true?

Cal. It is.

Soc. You said also, that no man could have good and evil fortune at the same time?

Cal. Yes, I did.

[497] *Soc.* But you admitted, that when in pain a man might also have pleasure?

Cal. Clearly.

Soc. Then pleasure is not the same as good fortune, or pain the same as evil fortune, and therefore the good is not the same as the pleasant?

Cal. I wish I knew, Socrates, what your quibbling means.

Soc. You know, Callicles, but you affect not to know.

Cal. Well, get on, and don't keep fooling: then you will know what a wiseacre you are in your admonition of me.

Soc. Does not a man cease from his thirst and from his pleasure in drinking at the same time?

Cal. I do not understand what you are saying.

Gor. Nay, Callicles, answer, if only for our sakes;—we should like to hear the argument out.

Cal. Yes, Gorgias, but I must complain of the habitual trifling of Socrates; he is always arguing about little and unworthy questions.

Gor. What matter? Your reputation, Callicles, is not at stake. Let Socrates argue in his own fashion.

Cal. Well, then, Socrates, you shall ask these little peddling questions, since Gorgias wishes to have them.

Soc. I envy you, Callicles, for having been initiated into the great mysteries before you were initiated into the lesser. I thought that this was not allowable. But to return to our argument:—Does not a man cease from thirsting and from the pleasure of drinking at the same moment?

Cal. True.

Soc. And if he is hungry, or has any other desire, does he not cease from the desire and the pleasure at the same moment?

Cal. Very true.

Soc. Then he ceases from pain and pleasure at the same moment?

Cal. Yes.

Soc. But he does not cease from good and evil at the same moment, as you have admitted: do you still adhere to what you said?

Cal. Yes, I do; but what is the inference?

Soc. Why, my friend, the inference is that the good is not the same as the pleasant, or the evil the same as the painful; there is a cessation of pleasure and pain at the same moment; but not of good and evil, for they are different. How then can pleasure be the same as good, or pain as evil? And I would have you look at the matter in another light, which could hardly, I think, have been considered by you when you identified them: Are not the good good because they have good present with them, as the beautiful are those who have beauty present with them?

Cal. Yes.

Soc. And do you call the fools and cowards good men? For you were saying just now that the courageous and the wise are the good—would you not say so?

Cal. Certainly.

Soc. And did you never see a foolish child rejoicing?

Cal. Yes, I have.

Soc. And a foolish man too?

Cal. Yes, certainly; but what is your drift?

[498] *Soc.* Nothing particular, if you will only answer.

Cal. Yes, I have.

Soc. And did you ever see a sensible man rejoicing or sorrowing?

Cal. Yes.

Soc. Which rejoice and sorrow most—the wise or the foolish?

Cal. They are much upon a par, I think, in that respect.

Soc. Enough: And did you ever see a coward in battle?

Cal. To be sure.

Soc. And which rejoiced most at the departure of the enemy, the coward or the brave?

Cal. I should say "most" of both; or at any rate, they rejoiced about equally.

Soc. No matter; then the cowards, and not only the brave, rejoice?

Cal. Greatly.

Soc. And the foolish; so it would seem?

Cal. Yes.

Soc. And are only the cowards pained at the approach of their enemies, or are the brave also pained?

Cal. Both are pained.

Soc. And are they equally pained?

Cal. I should imagine that the cowards are more pained.

Soc. And are they not better pleased at the enemy's departure?

Cal. I dare say.

Soc. Then are the foolish and the wise and the cowards and the brave all pleased and pained, as you were saying, in nearly equal degree; but are the cowards more pleased and pained than the brave?

Cal. Yes.

Soc. But surely the wise and brave are the good, and the foolish and the cowardly are the bad?

Cal. Yes.

Soc. Then the good and the bad are pleased and pained in a nearly equal degree?

Cal. Yes.

Soc. Then are the good and bad good and bad in a nearly equal degree, or have the bad the advantage both in good and evil? [i. e. in having more pleasure and more pain.]

Cal. I really do not know what you mean.

Soc. Why, do you not remember saying that the good were good because good was present with them, and the evil because evil; and that pleasures were goods and pains evils?

Cal. Yes, I remember.

Soc. And are not these pleasures or goods present to those who rejoice—if they do rejoice?

Cal. Certainly.

Soc. Then those who rejoice are good when goods are present with them?

Cal. Yes.

Soc. And those who are in pain have evil or sorrow present with them?

Cal. Yes.

Soc. And would you still say that the evil are evil by reason of the presence of evil?

Cal. I should.

Soc. Then those who rejoice are good, and those who are in pain evil?

Cal. Yes.

Soc. The degrees of good and evil vary with the degrees of pleasure and of pain?

Cal. Yes.

Soc. Have the wise man and the fool, the brave and the coward, joy and pain in nearly equal degrees? or would you say that the coward has more?

Cal. I should say that he has.

Soc. Help me then to draw out the conclusion which follows from our admissions; [499] for it is good to repeat and review what is good twice and thrice over, as they say. Both the wise man and the brave man we allow to be good?

Cal. Yes.

Soc. And the foolish man and the coward to be evil?

Cal. Certainly.

Soc. And he who has joy is good?

Cal. Yes.

Soc. And he who is in pain is evil?

Cal. Certainly.

Soc. The good and evil both have joy and pain, but, perhaps, the evil has more of them?

Cal. Yes.

Soc. Then must we not infer, that the bad man is as good and bad as the good, or, perhaps, even better?—is not this a further inference which follows equally with the preceding from the assertion that the good and the pleasant are the same:—can this be denied, Callicles?

Cal. I have been listening and making admissions to you, Socrates; and I remark that if a person grants you anything in play, you, like a child, want to keep hold and will not give it back. But do you really suppose that I or any other human being denies that some pleasures are good and others bad?

Soc. Alas, Callicles, how unfair you are! you certainly treat me as if I were a child, sometimes saying one thing, and then another, as if you were meaning to deceive me. And yet I thought at first that you were my friend, and would not have deceived me if you could have helped. But I see that I was mistaken; and now I suppose that I must make the best of a bad business, as they said of old, and take what I can get out of you.—Well, then, as I understand you to say, I may assume that some pleasures are good and others evil?

Cal. Yes.

Soc. The beneficial are good, and the hurtful are evil?

Cal. To be sure.

Soc. And the beneficial are those which do some good, and the hurtful are those which do some evil?

Cal. Yes.

Soc. Take, for example, the bodily pleasures of eating and drinking, which we were just now mentioning—you mean to say that those which promote health, or any other bodily excellence, are good, and their opposites evil?

Cal. Certainly.

Soc. And in the same way there are good pains and there are evil pains?

Cal. To be sure.

Soc. And ought we not to choose and use the good pleasures and pains?

Cal. Certainly.

Soc. But not the evil?

Cal. Clearly.

Soc. Because, if you remember, Polus and I have agreed that all our actions are to be done for the sake of the good—and will you agree with us in saying, that the good is the end of all our actions, and that all our actions are to be done for the sake of the good, [500] and not the good for the sake of them?—will you add a third vote to our two?

Cal. I will.

Soc. Then pleasure, like everything else, is to be sought for the sake of that which is good, and not that which is good for the sake of pleasure?

Cal. To be sure.

Soc. But can every man choose what pleasures are good and what are evil, or must he have art or knowledge of them in detail?

Cal. He must have art.

Soc. Let me now remind you of what I was saying to Gorgias and Polus; I was saying, as you will not have forgotten, that there were some processes which aim only at pleasure, and know nothing of a better and worse, and there are other processes which know good and evil. And I considered that cookery, which I do not call an art, but only an experience, was of the former class, which is concerned with pleasure, and that the art of medicine was of the class which is concerned with the good. And now, by the god of friendship, I must beg you, Callicles, not to jest, or to imagine that I am jesting with you; do not answer at random and contrary to your real opinion—for you will observe that we are arguing about the way of human life; and to a man who has any sense at all, what question can be more serious than this?—whether he should follow after that way of life to which you exhort me, and act what you call the manly part of speaking in the assembly, and cultivating rhetoric, and engaging in public affairs, according to the principles now in vogue; or whether he should pursue the life of philosophy—and in what the latter way differs from the former. But perhaps we had better first try to distinguish them, as I did before, and when we have come to an agreement that they are distinct, we may proceed to consider in what they differ from one another, and which of them we should choose. Perhaps, however, you do not even now understand what I mean?

Cal. No, I do not.

Soc. Then I will explain myself more clearly: seeing that you and I have agreed that there is such a thing as good, and that there is such a thing as pleasure, and that pleasure is not the same as good, and that the pursuit and process of acquisition of the one, that is pleasure, is different from the pursuit and process of acquisition of the other, which is good—I wish that you would tell me whether you agree with me thus far or not—do you agree?

Cal. I do.

Soc. Then I will proceed, and ask whether you also agree with me, [*501*] and whether you think that I spoke the truth when I further said to Gorgias and Polus that cookery in my opinion is only an experience, and not an art at all; and that whereas medicine is an art, and attends to the nature and constitution of the patient, and has principles of action and reason in each case, cookery in attending upon pleasure never regards either the nature or reason of that pleasure to which she devotes herself, but goes straight to her end, nor ever considers or calculates anything, but works by experience and routine, and just preserves the recollection of what she has usually done when producing pleasure. And first, I would have you consider whether I have proved what I was saying, and then whether there are not other similar processes which have to do with the soul—some of them processes of art, making a provision for the soul's highest interest—others despising the interest, and, as in the previous case, considering only the pleasure of the soul, and how this may be acquired, but not considering what pleasures are good or bad, and having no other aim but to afford gratification, whether good or bad. In my opinion, Callicles, there are such processes, and this is the sort of thing which I term flattery, whether concerned with the body or the soul, or whenever employed with a view to pleasure and without any consideration of good and evil. And now I wish that you

would tell me whether you agree with us in this notion, or whether you differ.

Cal. I do not differ; on the contrary, I agree; for in that way I shall soonest bring the argument to an end, and shall oblige my friend Gorgias.

Soc. And is this notion true of one soul, or of two or more?

Cal. Equally true of two or more.

Soc. Then a man may delight a whole assembly, and yet have no regard for their true interests?

Cal. Yes.

Soc. Can you tell me the pursuits which delight mankind—or rather, if you would prefer, let me ask, and do you answer, which of them belong to the pleasurable class, and which of them not? In the first place, what say you of flute-playing? Does not that appear to be an art which seeks only pleasure, Callicles, and thinks of nothing else?

Cal. I assent.

Soc. And is not the same true of all similar arts, as, for example, the art of playing the lyre at festivals?

Cal. Yes.

Soc. And what do you say of the choral art and of dithyrambic poetry?—are not they of the same nature? Do you imagine that Cinesias the son of Meles cares about what will tend to the moral [*502*] improvement of his hearers, or about what will give pleasure to the multitude?

Cal. There can be no mistake about Cinesias, Socrates.

Soc. And what do you say of his father, Meles the harp-player? Did he perform with any view to the good of his hearers? Could he be said to regard even their pleasure? For his singing was an infliction to his audience. And of harp-playing and dithyrambic poetry in general, what would you say? Have they not been invented wholly for the sake of pleasure?

Cal. That is my notion of them.

Soc. And as for the Muse of Tragedy, that solemn and august personage—what are her aspirations? Is all her aim and desire only to give pleasure to the spectators, or does she fight against them and refuse to speak of their pleasant vices, and willingly proclaim in word and song truths welcome and unwelcome?—which in your judgment is her character?

Cal. There can be no doubt, Socrates, that Tragedy has her face turned towards pleasure and the gratification of the audience.

Soc. And is not that the sort of thing, Callicles, which we were just now describing as flattery?

Cal. Quite true.

Soc. Well now, suppose that we strip all poetry of song and rhythm and metre, there will remain speech?[1]

Cal. To be sure.

Soc. And this speech is addressed to a crowd of people?

Cal. Yes.

Soc. Then poetry is a sort of rhetoric?

Cal. True.

Soc. And do not the poets in the theatres seem to you to be rhetoricians?

Cal. Yes.

Soc. Then now we have discovered a sort of rhetoric which is addressed to a crowd of men, women, and children, freemen and slaves. And this is not much to our taste, for we have described it as having the nature of flattery.

Cal. Quite true.

Soc. Very good. And what do you say of that other rhetoric which addresses the Athenian assembly and the assemblies of freemen in other states? Do the rhetoricians appear to you always to aim at what is best, and do they seek to improve the citizens by their speeches, or are they too, like the rest of mankind, bent upon giving them pleasure, forgetting the public good in the thought of their own interest, playing with the people as with children, and trying to amuse them, but never considering whether they are better or worse for this?

[503] Cal. I must distinguish. There are some who have a real care of the public in what they say, while others are such as you describe.

Soc. I am contented with the admission that rhetoric is of two sorts; one, which is mere flattery and disgraceful declamation; the other, which is noble and aims at the training and improvement of the souls of the citizens, and strives to say what is best, whether welcome or unwelcome, to the audience; but have you ever known such a rhetoric; or if you have, and can point out any rhetorician who is of this stamp, who is he?

Cal. But, indeed, I am afraid that I cannot tell you of any such among the orators who are at present living.

Soc. Well, then, can you mention any one of a former generation, who may be said to have improved the Athenians, who found them worse and made them better, from the day that he began to make speeches? for, indeed, I do not know of such a man.

[1] Cf. *Republic,* iii. 392 ff.

Cal. What! did you never hear that Themistocles was a good man, and Cimon and Miltiades and Pericles, who is just lately dead, and whom you heard yourself?

Soc. Yes, Callicles, they were good men, if, as you said at first, true virtue consists only in the satisfaction of our own desires and those of others; but if not, and if, as we were afterwards compelled to acknowledge, the satisfaction of some desires makes us better, and of others, worse, and we ought to gratify the one and not the other, and there is an art in distinguishing them—can you tell me of any of these statesmen who did distinguish them?

Cal. No, indeed, I cannot.

Soc. Yet, surely, Callicles, if you look you will find such a one. Suppose that we just calmly consider whether any of these was such as I have described. Will not the good man, who says whatever he says with a view to the best, speak with a reference to some standard and not at random; just as all other artists, whether the painter, the builder, the shipwright, or any other look all of them to their own work, and do not select and apply at random what they apply, but strive to give a definite form to it? The artist disposes all things in order, and compels the one part to harmonize and accord with the other part, *[504]* until he has constructed a regular and systematic whole; and this is true of all artists, and in the same way the trainers and physicians, of whom we spoke before, give order and regularity to the body: do you deny this?

Cal. No; I am ready to admit it.

Soc. Then the house in which order and regularity prevail is good; that in which there is disorder, evil?

Cal. Yes.

Soc. And the same is true of a ship?

Cal. Yes.

Soc. And the same may be said of the human body?

Cal. Yes.

Soc. And what would you say of the soul? Will the good soul be that in which disorder is prevalent, or that in which there is harmony and order?

Cal. The latter follows from our previous admissions.

Soc. What is the name which is given to the effect of harmony and order in the body?

Cal. I suppose that you mean health and strength?

Soc. Yes, I do; and what is the name which you would give to the effect of harmony and order in the soul? Try and discover a name for this as well as for the other.

Cal. Why not give the name yourself, Socrates?

Soc. Well, if you had rather that I should, I will; and you shall say whether you agree with me, and if not, you shall refute and answer me. "Healthy," as I conceive, is the name which is given to the regular order of the body, whence comes health and every other bodily excellence: is that true or not?

Cal. True.

Soc. And "lawful" and "law" are the names which are given to the regular order and action of the soul, and these make men lawful and orderly:—and so we have temperance and justice: have we not?

Cal. Granted.

Soc. And will not the true rhetorician who is honest and understands his art have his eye fixed upon these, in all the words which he addresses to the souls of men, and in all his actions, both in what he gives and in what he takes away? Will not his aim be to implant justice in the souls of his citizens and take away injustice, to implant temperance and take away intemperance, to implant every virtue and take away every vice? Do you not agree?

Cal. I agree.

Soc. For what use is there, Callicles, in giving to the body of a sick man who is in a bad state of health a quantity of the most delightful food or drink or any other pleasant thing, which may be really as bad for him as if you gave him nothing, or even worse if rightly estimated. Is not that true?

[505] *Cal.* I will not say No to it.

Soc. For in my opinion there is no profit in a man's life if his body is in an evil plight—in that case his life also is evil: am I not right?

Cal. Yes.

Soc. When a man is in health the physicians will generally allow him to eat when he is hungry and drink when he is thirsty, and to satisfy his desires as he likes, but when he is sick they hardly suffer him to satisfy his desires at all: even you will admit that?

Cal. Yes.

Soc. And does not the same argument hold of the soul, my good sir? While she is in a bad state and is senseless and intemperate and unjust and unholy, her desires ought to be controlled, and she ought to be prevented from doing anything which does not tend to her own improvement.

Cal. Yes.

Soc. Such treatment will be better for the soul herself?

Cal. To be sure.

Soc. And to restrain her from her appetites is to chastise her?

Cal. Yes.

Soc. Then restraint or chastisement is better for the soul than intemperance or the absence of control, which you were just now preferring?

Cal. I do not understand you, Socrates, and I wish that you would ask some one who does.

Soc. Here is a gentleman who cannot endure to be improved or to subject himself to that very chastisement of which the argument speaks!

Cal. I do not heed a word of what you are saying, and have only answered hitherto out of civility to Gorgias.

Soc. What are we to do, then? Shall we break off in the middle?

Cal. You shall judge for yourself.

Soc. Well, but people say that "a tale should have a head and not break off in the middle," and I should not like to have the argument going about without a head;[1] please then to go on a little longer, and put the head on.

Cal. How tyrannical you are, Socrates! I wish that you and your argument would rest, or that you would get some one else to argue with you.

Soc. But who else is willing?—I want to finish the argument.

Cal. Cannot you finish without my help, either talking straight on, or questioning and answering yourself?

Soc. Must I then say with Epicharmus, "Two men spoke before, but now one shall be enough"? I suppose that there is absolutely no help. And if I am to carry on the enquiry by myself, I will first of all remark that not only I but all of us should have an ambition to know what is true and what is false in this matter, for the discovery of the truth is a common good. And now I will proceed to argue according to my own notion. [506] But if any of you think that I arrive at conclusions which are untrue you must interpose and refute me, for I do not speak from any knowledge of what I am saying; I am an enquirer like yourselves, and therefore, if my opponent says anything which is of force, I shall be the first to agree with him. I am speaking on the supposition that the argument ought to be completed; but if you think otherwise let us leave off and go our ways.

Gor. I think, Socrates, that we should not go

[1] Cf. *Laws,* vi. 752.

our ways until you have completed the argument; and this appears to me to be the wish of the rest of the company; I myself should very much like to hear what more you have to say.

Soc. I too, Gorgias, should have liked to continue the argument with Callicles, and then I might have given him an "Amphion" in return for his "Zethus"; [1] but since you, Callicles, are unwilling to continue, I hope that you will listen, and interrupt me if I seem to you to be in error. And if you refute me, I shall not be angry with you as you are with me, but I shall inscribe you as the greatest of benefactors on the tablets of my soul.

Cal. My good fellow, never mind me, but get on.

Soc. Listen to me, then, while I recapitulate the argument:—Is the pleasant the same as the good? Not the same. Callicles and I are agreed about that. And is the pleasant to be pursued for the sake of the good? or the good for the sake of the pleasant? The pleasant is to be pursued for the sake of the good. And that is pleasant at the presence of which we are pleased, and that is good at the presence of which we are good? To be sure. And we are good, and all good things whatever are good when some virtue is present in us or them? That, Callicles, is my conviction. But the virtue of each thing, whether body or soul, instrument or creature, when given to them in the best way comes to them not by chance but as the result of the order and truth and art which are imparted to them: Am I not right? I maintain that I am. And is not the virtue of each thing dependent on order or arrangement? Yes, I say. And that which makes a thing good is the proper order inhering in each thing? Such is my view. And is not the soul which has an order of her own better than that which has no order? Certainly. And the soul which has order is orderly? Of course. And that which is orderly is temperate? [507] Assuredly. And the temperate soul is good? No other answer can I give, Callicles dear; have you any?

Cal. Go on, my good fellow.

Soc. Then I shall proceed to add, that if the temperate soul is the good soul, the soul which is in the opposite condition, that is, the foolish and intemperate, is the bad soul. Very true.

And will not the temperate man do what is proper, both in relation to the gods and to men; —for he would not be temperate if he did not? Certainly he will do what is proper. In his relation to other men he will do what is just;

and in his relation to the gods he will do what is holy; and he who does what is just and holy must be just and holy? Very true. And must he not be courageous? for the duty of a temperate man is not to follow or to avoid what he ought not, but what he ought, whether things or men or pleasures or pains, and patiently to endure when he ought; and therefore, Callicles, the temperate man, being, as we have described, also just and courageous and holy, cannot be other than a perfectly good man, nor can the good man do otherwise than well and perfectly whatever he does; and he who does well must of necessity be happy and blessed, and the evil man who does evil, miserable: now this latter is he whom you were applauding—the intemperate who is the opposite of the temperate. Such is my position, and these things I affirm to be true. And if they are true, then I further affirm that he who desires to be happy must pursue and practise temperance and run away from intemperance as fast as his legs will carry him: he had better order his life so as not to need punishment; but if either he or any of his friends, whether private individual or city, are in need of punishment, then justice must be done and he must suffer punishment, if he would be happy. This appears to me to be the aim which a man ought to have, and towards which he ought to direct all the energies both of himself and of the state, acting so that he may have temperance and justice present with him and be happy, not suffering his lusts to be unrestrained, and in the never-ending desire to satisfy them leading a robber's life. Such a one is the friend neither of God nor man, for he is incapable of communion, and he who is incapable of communion is also incapable of friendship. And philosophers tell us, [508] Callicles, that communion and friendship and orderliness and temperance and justice bind together heaven and earth and gods and men, and that this universe is therefore called Cosmos or order, not disorder or misrule, my friend. But although you are a philosopher you seem to me never to have observed that geometrical equality is mighty, both among gods and men; you think that you ought to cultivate inequality or excess, and do not care about geometry.—Well, then, either the principle that the happy are made happy by the possession of justice and temperance, and the miserable miserable by the possession of vice, must be refuted, or, if it is granted, what will be the consequences? All the consequences which I drew before, Callicles, and about which you asked me whether I was

in earnest when I said that a man ought to accuse himself and his son and his friend if he did
anything wrong, and that to this end he should
use his rhetoric—all those consequences are true.
And that which you thought that Polus was led
to admit out of modesty is true, viz., that, to do
injustice, if more disgraceful than to suffer, is
in that degree worse; and the other position,
which, according to Polus, Gorgias admitted
out of modesty, that he who would truly be a
rhetorician ought to be just and have a knowledge of justice, has also turned out to be true.

And now, these things being as we have said,
let us proceed in the next place to consider
whether you are right in throwing in my teeth
that I am unable to help myself or any of my
friends or kinsmen, or to save them in the extremity of danger, and that I am in the power of
another like an outlaw to whom any one may do
what he likes—he may box my ears, which was
a brave saying of yours; or take away my goods
or banish me, or even do his worst and kill me;
a condition which, as you say, is the height of
disgrace. My answer to you is one which has
been already often repeated, but may as well be
repeated once more. I tell you, Callicles, that
to be boxed on the ears wrongfully is not the
worst evil which can befall a man, nor to have
my purse or my body cut open, but that to
smite and slay me and mine wrongfully is far
more disgraceful and more evil; aye, and to despoil and enslave and pillage, or in any way at
all to wrong me and mine, is far more disgraceful and evil to the doer of the wrong than
to me who am the sufferer. [509] These truths,
which have been already set forth as I state them
in the previous discussion, would seem now to
have been fixed and riveted by us, if I may use
an expression which is certainly bold, in words
which are like bonds of iron and adamant; and
unless you or some other still more enterprising
hero shall break them, there is no possibility
of denying what I say. For my position has always been, that I myself am ignorant how these
things are, but that I have never met any one
who could say otherwise, any more than you
can, and not appear ridiculous. This is my position still, and if what I am saying is true, and
injustice is the greatest of evils to the doer of
injustice, and yet there is if possible a greater
than this greatest of evils,[1] in an unjust man not
suffering retribution, what is that defence of
which the want will make a man truly ridiculous? Must not the defence be one which will
avert the greatest of human evils? And will not

[1] Cf. *Republic,* ix. 578 ff.

the worst of all defences be that with which a
man is unable to defend himself or his family
or his friends?—and next will come that which
is unable to avert the next greatest evil; thirdly
that which is unable to avert the third greatest
evil; and so of other evils. As is the greatness of
evil so is the honour of being able to avert them
in their several degrees, and the disgrace of not
being able to avert them. Am I not right Callicles?

Cal. Yes, quite right.

Soc. Seeing then that there are these two evils,
the doing injustice and the suffering injustice
—and we affirm that to do injustice is a greater,
and to suffer injustice a lesser evil—by what
devices can a man succeed in obtaining the
two advantages, the one of not doing and the
other of not suffering injustice? must he have
the power, or only the will to obtain them? I
mean to ask whether a man will escape injustice
if he has only the will to escape, or must he
have provided himself with the power?

Cal. He must have provided himself with the
power; that is clear.

Soc. And what do you say of doing injustice?
Is the will only sufficient, and will that prevent
him from doing injustice, or must he have provided himself with power and art; and if he
has not studied and practised, will he be unjust still? Surely you might say, Callicles,
whether you think that Polus and I were right
in admitting the conclusion that no one does
wrong voluntarily, but that all do wrong against
their will?

[510] *Cal.* Granted, Socrates, if you will only have done.

Soc. Then, as would appear, power and art
have to be provided in order that we may do no
injustice?

Cal. Certainly.

Soc. And what art will protect us from suffering injustice, if not wholly, yet as far as possible?
I want to know whether you agree with me; for
I think that such an art is the art of one who is
either a ruler or even tyrant himself, or the
equal and companion of the ruling power.

Cal. Well said, Socrates; and please to observe how ready I am to praise you when you
talk sense.

Soc. Think and tell me whether you would
approve of another view of mine: To me every
man appears to be most the friend of him who
is most like to him—like to like, as ancient
sages say: Would you not agree to this?

Cal. I should.

Soc. But when the tyrant is rude and uneducated, he may be expected to fear any one who is his superior in virtue, and will never be able to be perfectly friendly with him.

Cal. That is true.

Soc. Neither will he be the friend of any one who is greatly his inferior, for the tyrant will despise him, and will never seriously regard him as a friend.

Cal. That again is true.

Soc. Then the only friend worth mentioning, whom the tyrant can have, will be one who is of the same character, and has the same likes and dislikes, and is at the same time willing to be subject and subservient to him; he is the man who will have power in the state, and no one will injure him with impunity:—is not that so?

Cal. Yes.

Soc. And if a young man begins to ask how he may become great and formidable, this would seem to be the way—he will accustom himself, from his youth upward, to feel sorrow and joy on the same occasions as his master, and will contrive to be as like him as possible?

Cal. Yes.

Soc. And in this way he will have accomplished, as you and your friends would say, the end of becoming a great man and not suffering injury?

Cal. Very true.

Soc. But will he also escape from doing injury? Must not the very opposite be true, if he is to be like the tyrant in his injustice, and to have influence with him? [511] Will he not rather contrive to do as much wrong as possible, and not be punished?

Cal. True.

Soc. And by the imitation of his master and by the power which he thus acquires will not his soul become bad and corrupted, and will not this be the greatest evil to him?

Cal. You always contrive somehow or other, Socrates, to invert everything: do you not know that he who imitates the tyrant will, if he has a mind, kill him who does not imitate him and take away his goods?

Soc. Excellent Callicles, I am not deaf, and I have heard that a great many times from you and from Polus and from nearly every man in the city, but I wish that you would hear me too. I dare say that he will kill him if he has a mind—the bad man will kill the good and true.

Cal. And is not that just the provoking thing?

Soc. Nay, not to a man of sense, as the argument shows: do you think that all our cares should be directed to prolonging life to the uttermost, and to the study of those arts which secure us from danger always; like that art of rhetoric which saves men in courts of law, and which you advise me to cultivate?

Cal. Yes, truly, and very good advice too.

Soc. Well, my friend, but what do you think of swimming; is that an art of any great pretensions?

Cal. No, indeed.

Soc. And yet surely swimming saves a man from death, and there are occasions on which he must know how to swim. And if you despise the swimmers, I will tell you of another and greater art, the art of the pilot, who not only saves the souls of men, but also their bodies and properties from the extremity of danger, just like rhetoric. Yet his art is modest and unpresuming: it has no airs or pretences of doing anything extraordinary, and, in return for the same salvation which is given by the pleader, demands only two obols, if he brings us from Aegina to Athens, or for the longer voyage from Pontus or Egypt, at the utmost two drachmae, when he has saved, as I was just now saying, the passenger and his wife and children and goods, and safely disembarked them at the Piraeus—this is the payment which he asks in return for so great a boon; and he who is the master of the art, and has done all this, gets out and walks about on the sea-shore by his ship in an unassuming way. For he is able to reflect and is aware that he cannot tell which of his fellow-passengers he has benefited, and which of them he has injured in not allowing them to be drowned. He knows that they are just the same when he has disembarked them as when they [512] embarked, and not a whit better either in their bodies or in their souls; and he considers that if a man who is afflicted by great and incurable bodily diseases is only to be pitied for having escaped, and is in no way benefited by him in having been saved from drowning, much less he who has great and incurable diseases, not of the body, but of the soul, which is the more valuable part of him; neither is life worth having nor of any profit to the bad man, whether he be delivered from the sea, or the law-courts, or any other devourer—and so he reflects that such a one had better not live, for he cannot live well.[1]

And this is the reason why the pilot, although he is our saviour, is not usually conceited, any more than the engineer, who is not at all behind either the general, or the pilot, or any one

[1] Cf. *Republic,* iii. 407.

else, in his saving power, for he sometimes saves whole cities. Is there any comparison between him and the pleader? And if he were to talk, Callicles, in your grandiose style, he would bury you under a mountain of words, declaring and insisting that we ought all of us to be engine-makers, and that no other profession is worth thinking about; he would have plenty to say. Nevertheless you despise him and his art, and sneeringly call him an engine-maker, and you will not allow your daughters to marry his son, or marry your son to his daughters. And yet, on your principle, what justice or reason is there in your refusal? What right have you to despise the engine-maker, and the others whom I was just now mentioning? I know that you will say, "I am better, and better born." But if the better is not what I say, and virtue consists only in a man saving himself and his, whatever may be his character, then your censure of the engine-maker, and of the physician, and of the other arts of salvation, is ridiculous. O my friend! I want you to see that the noble and the good may possibly be something different from saving and being saved:—May not he who is truly a man cease to care about living a certain time?—he knows, as women say, that no man can escape fate, and therefore he is not fond of life; he leaves all that with God, and considers in what way he can best spend his appointed term—whether by assimilating himself to the constitution under which he lives, [513] as you at this moment have to consider how you may become as like as possible to the Athenian people, if you mean to be in their good graces, and to have power in the state; whereas I want you to think and see whether this is for the interest of either of us—I would not have us risk that which is dearest in the acquisition of this power, like the Thessalian enchantresses, who, as they say, bring down the moon from heaven at the risk of their own perdition. But if you suppose that any man will show you the art of becoming great in the city, and yet not conforming yourself to the ways of the city, whether for better or worse, then I can only say that you are mistaken, Callicles; for he who would deserve to be the true natural friend of the Athenian Demus, aye, or of Pyrilampes' darling who is called after them, must be by nature like them, and not an imitator only. He, then, who will make you most like them, will make you as you desire, a statesman and orator: for every man is pleased when he is spoken to in his own language and spirit, and dislikes any other. But perhaps you, sweet Callicles, may be of another mind. What do you say?

Cal. Somehow or other your words, Socrates, always appear to me to be good words; and yet, like the rest of the world, I am not quite convinced by them.[1]

Soc. The reason is, Callicles, that the love of Demus which abides in your soul is an adversary to me; but I dare say that if we recur to these same matters, and consider them more thoroughly, you may be convinced for all that. Please, then, to remember that there are two processes of training all things, including body and soul; in the one, as we said, we treat them with a view to pleasure, and in the other with a view to the highest good, and then we do not indulge but resist them: was not that the distinction which we drew?

Cal. Very true.

Soc. And the one which had pleasure in view was just a vulgar flattery:—was not that another of our conclusions?

Cal. Be it so, if you will have it.

Soc. And the other had in view the greatest improvement of that which was ministered to, whether body or soul?

Cal. Quite true.

Soc. And must we not have the same end in view in the treatment of our city and citizens? Must we not try and make them as good as possible? [514] For we have already discovered that there is no use in imparting to them any other good, unless the mind of those who are to have the good, whether money, or office, or any other sort of power, be gentle and good. Shall we say that?

Cal. Yes, certainly, if you like.

Soc. Well, then, if you and I, Callicles, were intending to set about some public business, and were advising one another to undertake buildings, such as walls, docks or temples of the largest size, ought we not to examine ourselves, first, as to whether we know or do not know the art of building, and who taught us? —would not that be necessary, Callicles?

Cal. True.

Soc. In the second place, we should have to consider whether we had ever constructed any private house, either of our own or for our friends, and whether this building of ours was a success or not; and if upon consideration we found that we had had good and eminent masters, and had been successful in constructing many fine buildings, not only with their assistance, but without them, by our own unaided

[1] Cf. *Symposium,* 216.

skill—in that case prudence would not dissuade us from proceeding to the construction of public works. But if we had no master to show, and only a number of worthless buildings or none at all, then, surely, it would be ridiculous in us to attempt public works, or to advise one another to undertake them. Is not this true?

Cal. Certainly.

Soc. And does not the same hold in all other cases? If you and I were physicians, and were advising one another that we were competent to practise as state-physicians, should I not ask about you, and would you not ask about me, Well, but how about Socrates himself, has he good health? and was any one else ever known to be cured by him, whether slave or freeman? And I should make the same enquiries about you. And if we arrived at the conclusion that no one, whether citizen or stranger, man or woman, had ever been any the better for the medical skill of either of us, then, by Heaven, Callicles, what an absurdity to think that we or any human being should be so silly as to set up as state-physicians and advise others like ourselves to do the same, without having first practised in private, whether successfully or not, and acquired experience of the art! Is not this, as they say, to begin with the big jar when you are learning the potter's art; which is a foolish thing?

[515] *Cal.* True.

Soc. And now, my friend, as you are already beginning to be a public character, and are admonishing and reproaching me for not being one, suppose that we ask a few questions of one another. Tell me, then, Callicles, how about making any of the citizens better? Was there ever a man who was once vicious, or unjust, or intemperate, or foolish, and became by the help of Callicles good and noble? Was there ever such a man, whether citizen or stranger, slave or freeman? Tell me, Callicles, if a person were to ask these questions of you, what would you answer? Whom would you say that you had improved by your conversation? There may have been good deeds of this sort which were done by you as a private person, before you came forward in public. Why will you not answer?

Cal. You are contentious, Socrates.

Soc. Nay, I ask you, not from a love of contention, but because I really want to know in what way you think that affairs should be administered among us—whether, when you come to the administration of them, you have any other aim but the improvement of the citizens?

Have we not already admitted many times over that such is the duty of a public man? Nay, we have surely said so; for if you will not answer for yourself I must answer for you. But if this is what the good man ought to effect for the benefit of his own state, allow me to recall to you the names of those whom you were just now mentioning, Pericles, and Cimon, and Miltiades, and Themistocles, and ask whether you still think that they were good citizens.

Cal. I do.

Soc. But if they were good, then clearly each of them must have made the citizens better instead of worse?

Cal. Yes.

Soc. And, therefore, when Pericles first began to speak in the assembly, the Athenians were not so good as when he spoke last?

Cal. Very likely.

Soc. Nay, my friend, "likely" is not the word; for if he was a good citizen, the inference is certain.

Cal. And what difference does that make?

Soc. None; only I should like further to know whether the Athenians are supposed to have been made better by Pericles, or, on the contrary, to have been corrupted by him; for I hear that he was the first who gave the people pay, and made them idle and cowardly, and encouraged them in the love of talk and money.

Cal. You heard that, Socrates, from the laconising set who bruise their ears.

Soc. But what I am going to tell you now is not mere hearsay, but well known both to you and me: that at first, Pericles was glorious and his character unimpeached by any verdict of the [516] Athenians—this was during the time when they were not so good—yet afterwards, when they had been made good and gentle by him, at the very end of his life they convicted him of theft, and almost put him to death, clearly under the notion that he was a malefactor.

Cal. Well, but how does that prove Pericles' badness?

Soc. Why, surely you would say that he was a bad manager of asses or horses or oxen, who had received them originally neither kicking nor butting nor biting him, and implanted in them all these savage tricks? Would he not be a bad manager of any animals who received them gentle, and made them fiercer than they were when he received them? What do you say?

Cal. I will do you the favour of saying "yes."

Soc. And will you also do me the favour of

saying whether man is an animal?

Cal. Certainly he is.

Soc. And was not Pericles a shepherd of men?

Cal. Yes.

Soc. And if he was a good political shepherd, ought not the animals who were his subjects, as we were just now acknowledging, to have become more just, and not more unjust?

Cal. Quite true.

Soc. And are not just men gentle, as Homer says?—or are you of another mind?

Cal. I agree.

Soc. And yet he really did make them more savage than he received them, and their savageness was shown towards himself; which he must have been very far from desiring.

Cal. Do you want me to agree with you?

Soc. Yes, if I seem to you to speak the truth.

Cal. Granted then.

Soc. And if they were more savage, must they not have been more unjust and inferior?

Cal. Granted again.

Soc. Then upon this view, Pericles was not a good statesman?

Cal. That is, upon your view.

Soc. Nay, the view is yours, after what you have admitted. Take the case of Cimon again. Did not the very persons whom he was serving ostracize him, in order that they might not hear his voice for ten years? and they did just the same to Themistocles, adding the penalty of exile; and they voted that Miltiades, the hero of Marathon, should be thrown into the pit of death, and he was only saved by the Prytanis. And yet, if they had been really good men, as you say, these things would never have happened to them. For the good charioteers are not those who at first keep their place, and then, when they have broken-in their horses, and themselves become better charioteers, are thrown out—that is not the way either in charioteering or in any profession—What do you think?

Cal. I should think not.

[517] *Soc.* Well, but if so, the truth is as I have said already, that in the Athenian State no one has ever shown himself to be a good statesman—you admitted that this was true of our present statesmen, but not true of former ones, and you preferred them to the others; yet they have turned out to be no better than our present ones; and therefore, if they were rhetoricians, they did not use the true art of rhetoric or of flattery, or they would not have fallen out of favour.

Cal. But surely, Socrates, no living man ever came near any one of them in his performances.

Soc. O, my dear friend, I say nothing against them regarded as the serving-men of the State; and I do think that they were certainly more serviceable than those who are living now, and better able to gratify the wishes of the State; but as to transforming those desires and not allowing them to have their way, and using the powers which they had, whether of persuasion or of force, in the improvement of their fellow-citizens, which is the prime object of the truly good citizen, I do not see that in these respects they were a whit superior to our present statesmen, although I do admit that they were more clever at providing ships and walls and docks, and all that. You and I have a ridiculous way, for during the whole time that we are arguing, we are always going round and round to the same point, and constantly misunderstanding one another. If I am not mistaken, you have admitted and acknowledged more than once, that there are two kinds of operations which have to do with the body, and two which have to do with the soul: one of the two is ministerial, and if our bodies are hungry provides food for them, and if they are thirsty gives them drink, or if they are cold supplies them with garments, blankets, shoes, and all that they crave. I use the same images as before intentionally, in order that you may understand me the better. The purveyor of the articles may provide them either wholesale or retail, or he may be the maker of any of them,—the baker, or the cook, or the weaver, or the shoemaker, or the currier; and in so doing, being such as he is, he is naturally supposed by himself and every one to minister to the body. For none of them know that there is another art—an art of gymnastic and medicine which is the true minister of the body, and ought to be the mistress of all the rest, and to use their results according to the knowledge which she has and they have not, of the real good or bad effects of meats and drinks on the body. *[518]* All other arts which have to do with the body are servile and menial and illiberal; and gymnastic and medicine are, as they ought to be, their mistresses.

Now, when I say that all this is equally true of the soul, you seem at first to know and understand and assent to my words, and then a little while afterwards you come repeating, Has not the State had good and noble citizens? and when I ask you who they are, you reply, seemingly quite in earnest, as if I had asked, Who are or have been good trainers?—and you had replied, Thearion, the baker, Mithoecus, who wrote the

Sicilian cookery-book, Sarambus, the vintner: these are ministers of the body, first-rate in their art; for the first makes admirable loaves, the second excellent dishes, and the third capital wine—to me these appear to be the exact parallel of the statesmen whom you mention. Now you would not be altogether pleased if I said to you, My friend, you know nothing of gymnastics; those of whom you are speaking to me are only the ministers and purveyors of luxury, who have no good or noble notions of their art, and may very likely be filling and fattening men's bodies and gaining their approval, although the result is that they lose their original flesh in the long run, and become thinner than they were before; and yet they, in their simplicity, will not attribute their diseases and loss of flesh to their entertainers; but when in after years the unhealthy surfeit brings the attendant penalty of disease, he who happens to be near them at the time, and offers them advice, is accused and blamed by them, and if they could they would do him some harm; while they proceed to eulogize the men who have been the real authors of the mischief.

And that, Callicles, is just what you are now doing. You praise the men who feasted the citizens and satisfied their desires, and people say that they have made the city great, not seeing that the swollen and ulcerated condition of the State is to be attributed to these elder statesmen; for they have filled the city full of harbours and docks and walls and revenues and all that, [519] and have left no room for justice and temperance. And when the crisis of the disorder comes, the people will blame the advisers of the hour, and applaud Themistocles and Cimon and Pericles, who are the real authors of their calamities; and if you are not careful they may assail you and my friend Alcibiades, when they are losing not only their new acquisitions, but also their original possessions; not that you are the authors of these misfortunes of theirs, although you may perhaps be accessories to them. A great piece of work is always being made, as I see and am told, now as of old, about our statesmen. When the State treats any of them as malefactors, I observe that there is a great uproar and indignation at the supposed wrong which is done to them; "after all their many services to the State, that they should unjustly perish"—so the tale runs. But the cry is all a lie; for no statesman ever could be unjustly put to death by the city of which he is the head. The case of the professed statesman is, I believe, very much like that of the professed

sophist; for the sophists, although they are wise men, are nevertheless guilty of a strange piece of folly; professing to be teachers of virtue, they will often accuse their disciples of wronging them, and defrauding them of their pay, and showing no gratitude for their services. Yet what can be more absurd than that men who have become just and good, and whose injustice has been taken away from them, and who have had justice implanted in them by their teachers, should act unjustly by reason of the injustice which is not in them? Can anything be more irrational, my friends, than this? You, Callicles, compel me to be a mob-orator, because you will not answer.

Cal. And you are the man who cannot speak unless there is some one to answer?

Soc. I suppose that I can; just now, at any rate, the speeches which I am making are long enough because you refuse to answer me. But I adjure you by the god of friendship, my good sir, do tell me whether there does not appear to you to be a great inconsistency in saying that you have made a man good, and then blaming him for being bad?

Cal. Yes, it appears so to me.

[520] *Soc.* Do you never hear our professors of education speaking in this inconsistent manner?

Cal. Yes, but why talk of men who are good for nothing?

Soc. I would rather say, why talk of men who profess to be rulers, and declare that they are devoted to the improvement of the city, and nevertheless upon occasion declaim against the utter vileness of the city:—do you think that there is any difference between one and the other? My good friend, the sophist and the rhetorician, as I was saying to Polus, are the same, or nearly the same; but you ignorantly fancy that rhetoric is a perfect thing, and sophistry a thing to be despised; whereas the truth is, that sophistry is as much superior to rhetoric as legislation is to the practice of law, or gymnastic to medicine. The orators and sophists, as I am inclined to think, are the only class who cannot complain of the mischief ensuing to themselves from that which they teach others, without in the same breath accusing themselves of having done no good to those whom they profess to benefit. Is not this a fact?

Cal. Certainly it is.

Soc. If they were right in saying that they make men better, then they are the only class who can afford to leave their remuneration to those who have been benefited by them. Whereas if a man has been benefited in any other way, if, for example, he has been taught to run by a trainer, he might possibly defraud him of his pay, if the trainer left the matter to him, and made no agreement with him that he should receive money as soon as he had given him the utmost speed; for not because of any deficiency of speed do men act unjustly, but by reason of injustice.

Cal. Very true.

Soc. And he who removes injustice can be in no danger of being treated unjustly: he alone can safely leave the honorarium to his pupils, if he be really able to make them good—am I not right? [1]

Cal. Yes.

Soc. Then we have found the reason why there is no dishonour in a man receiving pay who is called in to advise about building or any other art?

Cal. Yes, we have found the reason.

Soc. But when the point is, how a man may become best himself, and best govern his family and state, then to say that you will give no advice gratis is held to be dishonourable?

Cal. True.

Soc. And why? Because only such benefits call forth a desire to requite them, and there is evidence that a benefit has been conferred when the benefactor receives a return; otherwise not. Is this true?

Cal. It is.

[521] Soc. Then to which service of the State do you invite me? determine for me. Am I to be the physician of the State who will strive and struggle to make the Athenians as good as possible; or am I to be the servant and flatterer of the State? Speak out, my good friend, freely and fairly as you did at first and ought to do again, and tell me your entire mind.

Cal. I say then that you should be the servant of the State.

Soc. The flatterer? well, sir, that is a noble invitation.

Cal. The Mysian, Socrates, or what you please. For if you refuse, the consequences will be—

Soc. Do not repeat the old story—that he who likes will kill me and get my money; for then I shall have to repeat the old answer, that he will be a bad man and will kill the good, and that the money will be of no use to him, but that he will wrongly use that which he wrongly took, and if wrongly, basely, and if basely, hurtfully.

[1] Cf. *Protagoras*, 328.

Cal. How confident you are, Socrates, that you will never come to harm! you seem to think that you are living in another country, and can never be brought into a court of justice, as you very likely may be brought by some miserable and mean person.

Soc. Then I must indeed be a fool, Callicles, if I do not know that in the Athenian State any man may suffer anything. And if I am brought to trial and incur the dangers of which you speak, he will be a villain who brings me to trial—of that I am very sure, for no good man would accuse the innocent. Nor shall I be surprised if I am put to death. Shall I tell you why I anticipate this?

Cal. By all means.

Soc. I think that I am the only or almost the only Athenian living who practises the true art of politics; I am the only politician of my time. Now, seeing that when I speak my words are not uttered with any view of gaining favour, and that I look to what is best and not to what is most pleasant, having no mind to use those arts and graces which you recommend, I shall have nothing to say in the justice court. And you might argue with me, as I was arguing with Polus:—I shall be tried just as a physician would be tried in a court of little boys at the indictment of the cook. What would he reply under such circumstances, if some one were to accuse him, saying, "O my boys, many evil things has this man done to you: he is the death of you, especially of the younger ones among you, cutting and burning and starving and suffocating you, *[522]* until you know not what to do; he gives you the bitterest potions, and compels you to hunger and thirst. How unlike the variety of meats and sweets on which I feasted you!" What do you suppose that the physician would be able to reply when he found himself in such a predicament? If he told the truth he could only say, "All these evil things, my boys, I did for your health," and then would there not just be a clamour among a jury like that? How they would cry out!

Cal. I dare say.

Soc. Would he not be utterly at a loss for a reply?

Cal. He certainly would.

Soc. And I too shall be treated in the same way, as I well know, if I am brought before the court. For I shall not be able to rehearse to the people the pleasures which I have procured for them, and which, although I am not disposed to envy either the procurers or enjoyers of them, are deemed by them to be benefits and advantages. And if any one says that I corrupt young men, and perplex their minds, or that I speak evil of old men, and use bitter words towards them, whether in private or public, it is useless for me to reply, as I truly might:—"All this I do for the sake of justice, and with a view to your interest, my judges, and to nothing else." And therefore there is no saying what may happen to me.

Cal. And do you think, Socrates, that a man who is thus defenceless is in a good position?

Soc. Yes, Callicles, if he have that defence, which as you have often acknowledged he should have—if he be his own defence, and have never said or done anything wrong, either in respect of gods or men; and this has been repeatedly acknowledged by us to be the best sort of defence. And if anyone could convict me of inability to defend myself or others after this sort, I should blush for shame, whether I was convicted before many, or before a few, or by myself alone; and if I died from want of ability to do so, that would indeed grieve me. But if I died because I have no powers of flattery or rhetoric, I am very sure that you would not find me repining at death. For no man who is not an utter fool and coward is afraid of death itself, but he is afraid of doing wrong. For to go to the world below having one's soul full of injustice is the last and worst of all evils. And in proof of what I say, if you have no objection, I should like to tell you a story.

Cal. Very well, proceed; and then we shall have done.

[523] Soc. Listen, then, as story-tellers say, to a very pretty tale, which I dare say that you may be disposed to regard as a fable only, but which, as I believe, is a true tale, for I mean to speak the truth. Homer tells us, how Zeus and Poseidon and Pluto divided the empire which they inherited from their father. Now in the days of Cronos there existed a law respecting the destiny of man, which has always been, and still continues to be in Heaven—that he who has lived all his life in justice and holiness shall go, when he is dead, to the Islands of the Blessed, and dwell there in perfect happiness out of the reach of evil; but that he who has lived unjustly and impiously shall go to the house of vengeance and punishment, which is called Tartarus. And in the time of Cronos, and even quite lately in the reign of Zeus, the judgment was given on the very day on which the men were to die; the judges were alive, and the men were alive; and the consequence was that the judgments were not well given. Then Pluto

and the authorities from the Islands of the Blessed came to Zeus, and said that the souls found their way to the wrong places. Zeus said: "I shall put a stop to this; the judgments are not well given, because the persons who are judged have their clothes on, for they are alive; and there are many who, having evil souls, are apparelled in fair bodies, or encased in wealth or rank, and, when the day of judgment arrives, numerous witnesses come forward and testify on their behalf that they have lived righteously. The judges are awed by them, and they themselves too have their clothes on when judging; their eyes and ears and their whole bodies are interposed as a veil before their own souls. All this is a hindrance to them; there are the clothes of the judges and the clothes of the judged— What is to be done? I will tell you:—In the first place, I will deprive men of the foreknowledge of death, which they possess at present: this power which they have Prometheus has already received my orders to take from them: in the second place, they shall be entirely stripped before they are judged, for they shall be judged when they are dead; and the judge too shall be naked, that is to say, dead—he with his naked soul shall pierce into the other naked souls; and they shall die suddenly and be deprived of all their kindred, and leave their brave attire strewn upon the earth—conducted in this manner, the judgment will be just. I knew all about the matter before any of you, and therefore I have made my sons judges; two from Asia, Minos and Rhadamanthus, and one from Europe, *[524]* Aeacus. And these, when they are dead, shall give judgment in the meadow at the parting of the ways, whence the two roads lead, one to the Islands of the Blessed, and the other to Tartarus. Rhadamanthus shall judge those who come from Asia, and Aeacus those who come from Europe. And to Minos I shall give the primacy, and he shall hold a court of appeal, in case either of the two others are in any doubt:—then the judgment respecting the last journey of men will be as just as possible."

From this tale, Callicles, which I have heard and believe, I draw the following inferences:— Death, if I am right, is in the first place the separation from one another of two things, soul and body; nothing else. And after they are separated they retain their several natures, as in life; the body keeps the same habit, and the results of treatment or accident are distinctly visible in it: for example, he who by nature or training or both, was a tall man while he was alive, will remain as he was, after he is dead; and the fat man will remain fat; and so on; and the dead man, who in life had a fancy to have flowing hair, will have flowing hair. And if he was marked with the whip and had the prints of the scourge, or of wounds in him when he was alive, you might see the same in the dead body; and if his limbs were broken or misshapen when he was alive, the same appearance would be visible in the dead. And in a word, whatever was the habit of the body during life would be distinguishable after death, either perfectly, or in a great measure and for a certain time. And I should imagine that this is equally true of the soul, Callicles; when a man is stripped of the body, all the natural or acquired affections of the soul are laid open to view. And when they come to the judge, as those from Asia come to Rhadamanthus, he places them near him and inspects them quite impartially, not knowing whose the soul is: perhaps he may lay hands on the soul of the great king, or of some other king or potentate, who has no soundness in him, but his soul is marked with the whip, and is full of the prints and scars of perjuries and crimes with which each action has stained him, [525] and he is all crooked with falsehood and imposture, and has no straightness, because he has lived without truth. Him Rhadamanthus beholds, full of all deformity and disproportion, which is caused by licence and luxury and insolence and incontinence, and despatches him ignominiously to his prison, and there he undergoes the punishment which he deserves.

Now the proper office of punishment is twofold: he who is rightly punished ought either to become better and profit by it, or he ought to be made an example to his fellows, that they may see what he suffers, and fear and become better. Those who are improved when they are punished by gods and men, are those whose sins are curable; and they are improved, as in this world so also in another, by pain and suffering; for there is no other way in which they can be delivered from their evil. But they who have been guilty of the worst crimes, and are incurable by reason of their crimes, are made examples; for, as they are incurable, the time has passed at which they can receive any benefit. They get no good themselves, but others get good when they behold them enduring for ever the most terrible and painful and fearful sufferings as the penalty of their sins—there they are, hanging up as examples, in the prison-house of the world below, a spectacle and a warning to all unrighteous men who come thither. And among them, as I confidently affirm, will be found Archelaus, if Polus truly reports of him, and any other tyrant who is like him. Of these fearful examples, most, as I believe, are taken from the class of tyrants and kings and potentates and public men, for they are the authors of the greatest and most impious crimes, because they have the power. And Homer witnesses to the truth of this; for they are always kings and potentates whom he has described as suffering everlasting punishment in the world below: such were Tantalus and Sisyphus and Tityus. But no one ever described Thersites, or any private person who was a villain, as suffering everlasting punishment, or as incurable. For to commit the worst crimes, as I am inclined to think, was not in his power, and he was happier than those who had the power. No, Callicles, [526] the very bad men come from the class of those who have power.[1] And yet in that very class there may arise good men, and worthy of all admiration they are, for where there is great power to do wrong, to live and to die justly is a hard thing, and greatly to be praised, and few there are who attain to this. Such good and true men, however, there have been, and will be again, at Athens and in other states, who have fulfilled their trust righteously; and there is one who is quite famous all over Hellas, Aristeides, the son of Lysimachus. But, in general, great men are also bad, my friend.

As I was saying, Rhadamanthus, when he gets a soul of the bad kind, knows nothing about him, neither who he is, nor who his parents are; he knows only that he has got hold of a villain; and seeing this, he stamps him as curable or incurable, and sends him away to Tartarus, whither he goes and receives his proper recompense. Or, again, he looks with admiration on the soul of some just one who has lived in holiness and truth; he may have been a private man or not; and I should say, Callicles, that he is most likely to have been a philosopher who has done his own work, and not troubled himself with the doings of other men in his lifetime; him Rhadamanthus sends to the Islands of the Blessed. Aeacus does the same; and they both have sceptres, and judge; but Minos alone has a golden sceptre and is seated looking on, as Odysseus in Homer declares that he saw him:

Holding a sceptre of gold, and giving laws to the dead.

Now I, Callicles, am persuaded of the truth of
[1] Cf. *Republic,* x. 615.

these things, and I consider how I shall present my soul whole and undefiled before the judge in that day. Renouncing the honours at which the world aims, I desire only to know the truth, and to live as well as I can, and, when I die, to die as well as I can. And, to the utmost of my power, I exhort all other men to do the same. And, in return for your exhortation of me, I exhort you also to take part in the great combat, which is the combat of life, and greater than every other earthly conflict. And I retort your reproach of me, and say, that you will not be able to help yourself when the day of trial and judgment, of which I was speaking, comes upon you; you will go before the judge, *[527]* the son of Aegina, and, when he has got you in his grip and is carrying you off, you will gape and your head will swim round, just as mine would in the courts of this world, and very likely some one will shamefully box you on the ears, and put upon you any sort of insult.

Perhaps this may appear to you to be only an old wife's tale, which you will contemn. And there might be reason in your contemning such tales, if by searching we could find out anything better or truer: but now you see that you and Polus and Gorgias, who are the three wisest of the Greeks of our day, are not able to show that we ought to live any life which does not profit in another world as well as in this. And of all that has been said, nothing remains unshaken but the saying, that to do injustice is more to be avoided than to suffer injustice, and that the reality and not the appearance of virtue is to be followed above all things, as well in public as in private life; and that when any one has been wrong in anything, he is to be chastised, and that the next best thing to a man being just is that he should become just, and be chastised and punished; also that he should avoid all flattery of himself as well as of others, of the few or of the many: and rhetoric and any other art should be used by him, and all his actions should be done always, with a view to justice.

Follow me then, and I will lead you where you will be happy in life and after death, as the argument shows. And never mind if some one despises you as a fool, and insults you, if he has a mind; let him strike you, by Zeus, and do you be of good cheer, and do not mind the insulting blow, for you will never come to any harm in the practise of virtue, if you are a really good and true man. When we have practised virtue together, we will apply ourselves to politics, if that seems desirable, or we will advise about whatever else may seem good to us, for we shall be better able to judge then. In our present condition we ought not to give ourselves airs, for even on the most important subjects we are always changing our minds; so utterly stupid are we! Let us, then, take the argument as our guide, which has revealed to us that the best way of life is to practise justice and every virtue in life and death. This way let us go; and in this exhort all men to follow, not in the way to which you trust and in which you exhort me to follow you; for that way, Callicles, is nothing worth.

THE REPUBLIC

PERSONS OF THE DIALOGUE: SOCRATES, *who is the narrator;* GLAUCON; ADEIMANTUS; POLEMARCHUS; CEPHALUS; THRASYMACHUS; CLEITOPHON; *And others who are mute auditors. The Scene is laid in the house of Cephalus at the Piraeus; and the whole dialogue is narrated by Socrates the day after it actually took place to Timaeus, Hermocrates, Critias, and a nameless person, who are introduced in the* Timaeus

BOOK I

[327] I WENT down yesterday to the Piraeus with Glaucon the son of Ariston, that I might offer up my prayers to the goddess;[1] and also because I wanted to see in what manner they would celebrate the festival, which was a new thing. I was delighted with the procession of the inhabitants; but that of the Thracians was equally, if not more, beautiful. When we had finished our prayers and viewed the spectacle, we turned in the direction of the city; and at that instant Polemarchus the son of Cephalus chanced to catch sight of us from a distance as we were starting on our way home, and told his servant to run and bid us wait for him. The servant took hold of me by the cloak behind, and said: Polemarchus desires you to wait.

I turned round, and asked him where his master was.

There he is, said the youth, coming after you, if you will only wait.

Certainly we will, said Glaucon; and in a few minutes Polemarchus appeared, and with him Adeimantus, Glaucon's brother, Niceratus the son of Nicias, and several others who had been at the procession.

Polemarchus said to me: I perceive, Socrates, that you and your companion are already on your way to the city.

---
[1] Bendis, the Thracian Artemis.

You are not far wrong, I said.

But do you see, he rejoined, how many we are?

Of course.

And are you stronger than all these? for if not, you will have to remain where you are.

May there not be the alternative, I said, that we may persuade you to let us go?

But can you persuade us, if we refuse to listen to you? he said.

Certainly not, replied Glaucon.

Then we are not going to listen; of that you may be assured.

[328] Adeimantus added: Has no one told you of the torch-race on horseback in honour of the goddess which will take place in the evening?

With horses! I replied: That is a novelty. Will horsemen carry torches and pass them one to another during the race?

Yes, said Polemarchus, and not only so, but a festival will be celebrated at night, which you certainly ought to see. Let us rise soon after supper and see this festival; there will be a gathering of young men, and we will have a good talk. Stay then, and do not be perverse.

Glaucon said: I suppose, since you insist, that we must.

Very good, I replied.

Accordingly we went with Polemarchus to his house; and there we found his brothers

Lysias and Euthydemus, and with them Thrasymachus the Chalcedonian, Charmantides the Paeanian, and Cleitophon the son of Aristonymus. There too was Cephalus the father of Polemarchus, whom I had not seen for a long time, and I thought him very much aged. He was seated on a cushioned chair, and had a garland on his head, for he had been sacrificing in the court; and there were some other chairs in the room arranged in a semicircle, upon which we sat down by him. He saluted me eagerly, and then he said:—

You don't come to see me, Socrates, as often as you ought: If I were still able to go and see you I would not ask you to come to me. But at my age I can hardly get to the city, and therefore you should come oftener to the Piraeus. For let me tell you, that the more the pleasures of the body fade away, the greater to me is the pleasure and charm of conversation. Do not then deny my request, but make our house your resort and keep company with these young men; we are old friends, and you will be quite at home with us.

I replied: There is nothing which for my part I like better, Cephalus, than conversing with aged men; for I regard them as travellers who have gone a journey which I too may have to go, and of whom I ought to enquire, whether the way is smooth and easy, or rugged and difficult. And this is a question which I should like to ask of you who have arrived at that time which the poets call the "threshold of old age" —Is life harder towards the end, or what report do you give of it?

[329] I will tell you, Socrates, he said, what my own feeling is. Men of my age flock together; we are birds of a feather, as the old proverb says; and at our meetings the tale of my acquaintance commonly is—I cannot eat, I cannot drink; the pleasures of youth and love are fled away: there was a good time once, but now that is gone, and life is no longer life. Some complain of the slights which are put upon them by relations, and they will tell you sadly of how many evils their old age is the cause. But to me, Socrates, these complainers seem to blame that which is not really in fault. For if old age were the cause, I too being old, and every other old man, would have felt as they do. But this is not my own experience, nor that of others whom I have known. How well I remember the aged poet Sophocles, when in answer to the question, How does love suit with age, Sophocles—are you still the man you were? Peace, he replied; most gladly have I

escaped the thing of which you speak; I feel as if I had escaped from a mad and furious master. His words have often occurred to my mind since, and they seem as good to me now as at the time when he uttered them. For certainly old age has a great sense of calm and freedom; when the passions relax their hold, then, as Sophocles says, we are freed from the grasp not of one mad master only, but of many. The truth is, Socrates, that these regrets, and also the complaints about relations, are to be attributed to the same cause, which is not old age, but men's characters and tempers; for he who is of a calm and happy nature will hardly feel the pressure of age, but to him who is of an opposite disposition youth and age are equally a burden.

I listened in admiration, and wanting to draw him out, that he might go on—Yes, Cephalus, I said; but I rather suspect that people in general are not convinced by you when you speak thus; they think that old age sits lightly upon you, not because of your happy disposition, but because you are rich, and wealth is well known to be a great comforter.

You are right, he replied; they are not convinced: and there is something in what they say; not, however, so much as they imagine. I might answer them as Themistocles answered the Seriphian who was abusing him and saying that he was famous, not for his own merits but because he was an Athenian: [330] "If you had been a native of my country or I of yours, neither of us would have been famous." And to those who are not rich and are impatient of old age, the same reply may be made; for to the good poor man old age cannot be a light burden, nor can a bad rich man ever have peace with himself.

May I ask, Cephalus, whether your fortune was for the most part inherited or acquired by you?

Acquired! Socrates; do you want to know how much I acquired? In the art of making money I have been midway between my father and grandfather: for my grandfather, whose name I bear, doubled and trebled the value of his patrimony, that which he inherited being much what I possess now; but my father Lysanias reduced the property below what it is at present: and I shall be satisfied if I leave to these my sons not less but a little more than I received.

That was why I asked you the question, I replied, because I see that you are indifferent about money, which is a characteristic rather of those who have inherited their fortunes than of those who have acquired them; the makers of fortunes have a second love of money as a creation of their own, resembling the affection of authors for their own poems, or of parents for their children, besides that natural love of it for the sake of use and profit which is common to them and all men. And hence they are very bad company, for they can talk about nothing but the praises of wealth.

That is true, he said.

Yes, that is very true, but may I ask another question?—What do you consider to be the greatest blessing which you have reaped from your wealth?

One, he said, of which I could not expect easily to convince others. For let me tell you, Socrates, that when a man thinks himself to be near death, fears and cares enter into his mind which he never had before; the tales of a world below and the punishment which is exacted there of deeds done here were once a laughing matter to him, but now he is tormented with the thought that they may be true: either from the weakness of age, or because he is now drawing nearer to that other place, he has a clearer view of these things; suspicions and alarms crowd thickly upon him, and he begins to reflect and consider what wrongs he has done to others. And when he finds that the sum of his transgressions is great he will many a time like a child start up in his sleep for fear, and he is filled with dark forebodings. *[331]* But to him who is conscious of no sin, sweet hope, as Pindar charmingly says, is the kind nurse of his age:

Hope [he says] *cherishes the soul of him who lives in justice and holiness, and is the nurse of his age and the companion of his journey;—hope which is mightiest to sway the restless soul of man.*

How admirable are his words! And the great blessing of riches, I do not say to every man, but to a good man, is, that he has had no occasion to deceive or to defraud others, either intentionally or unintentionally; and when he departs to the world below he is not in any apprehension about offerings due to the gods or debts which he owes to men. Now to this peace of mind the possession of wealth greatly contributes; and therefore I say, that, setting one thing against another, of the many advantages which wealth has to give, to a man of sense this is in my opinion the greatest.

Well said, Cephalus, I replied; but as concerning justice, what is it?—to speak the truth and to pay your debts—no more than this? And even to this are there not exceptions? Suppose that a friend when in his right mind has deposited arms with me and he asks for them when he is not in his right mind, ought I to give them back to him? No one would say that I ought or that I should be right in doing so, any more than they would say that I ought always to speak the truth to one who is in his condition.

You are quite right, he replied.

But then, I said, speaking the truth and paying your debts is not a correct definition of justice.

Quite correct, Socrates, if Simonides is to be believed, said Polemarchus interposing.

I fear, said Cephalus, that I must go now, for I have to look after the sacrifices, and I hand over the argument to Polemarchus and the company.

Is not Polemarchus your heir? I said.

To be sure, he answered, and went away laughing to the sacrifices.

Tell me then, O thou heir of the argument, what did Simonides say, and according to you truly say, about justice?

He said that the re-payment of a debt is just, and in saying so he appears to me to be right.

I should be sorry to doubt the word of such a wise and inspired man, but his meaning, though probably clear to you, is the reverse of clear to me. For he certainly does not mean, as we were just now saying, that I ought to return a deposit of arms or of anything else to one who asks for it when he is not in his right senses; and yet a deposit cannot be denied to be a debt. *[332]*

True.

Then when the person who asks me is not in his right mind I am by no means to make the return?

Certainly not.

When Simonides said that the repayment of a debt was justice, he did not mean to include that case?

Certainly not; for he thinks that a friend ought always to do good to a friend and never evil.

You mean that the return of a deposit of gold which is to the injury of the receiver, if the two parties are friends, is not the repayment of a debt—that is what you would imagine him to say?

Yes.

And are enemies also to receive what we owe to them?

To be sure, he said, they are to receive what we owe them, and an enemy, as I take it, owes to an enemy that which is due or proper to him—that is to say, evil.

Simonides, then, after the manner of poets, would seem to have spoken darkly of the nature of justice; for he really meant to say that justice is the giving to each man what is proper to him, and this he termed a debt.

That must have been his meaning, he said.

By heaven! I replied; and if we asked him what due or proper thing is given by medicine, and to whom, what answer do you think that he would make to us?

He would surely reply that medicine gives drugs and meat and drink to human bodies.

And what due or proper thing is given by cookery, and to what?

Seasoning to food.

And what is that which justice gives, and to whom?

If, Socrates, we are to be guided at all by the analogy of the preceding instances, then justice is the art which gives good to friends and evil to enemies.

That is his meaning then?

I think so.

And who is best able to do good to his friends and evil to his enemies in time of sickness?

The physician.

Or when they are on a voyage, amid the perils of the sea?

The pilot.

And in what sort of actions or with a view to what result is the just man most able to do harm to his enemy and good to his friend?

In going to war against the one and in making alliances with the other.

But when a man is well, my dear Polemarchus, there is no need of a physician?

No.

And he who is not on a voyage has no need of a pilot?

No.

Then in time of peace justice will be of no use?

I am very far from thinking so.

[333] You think that justice may be of use in peace as well as in war?

Yes.

Like husbandry for the acquisition of corn?

Yes.

Or like shoemaking for the acquisition of shoes—that is what you mean?

Yes.

And what similar use or power of acquisition has justice in time of peace?

In contracts, Socrates, justice is of use.

And by contracts you mean partnerships?

Exactly.

But is the just man or the skilful player a more useful and better partner at a game of draughts?

The skilful player.

And in the laying of bricks and stones is the just man a more useful or better partner than the builder?

Quite the reverse.

Then in what sort of partnership is the just man a better partner than the harp-player, as in playing the harp the harp-player is certainly a better partner than the just man?

In a money partnership.

Yes, Polemarchus, but surely not in the use of money; for you do not want a just man to be your counsellor in the purchase or sale of a horse; a man who is knowing about horses would be better for that, would he not?

Certainly.

And when you want to buy a ship, the shipwright or the pilot would be better?

True.

Then what is that joint use of silver or gold in which the just man is to be preferred?

When you want a deposit to be kept safely.

You mean when money is not wanted, but allowed to lie?

Precisely.

That is to say, justice is useful when money is useless?

That is the inference.

And when you want to keep a pruning-hook safe, then justice is useful to the individual and to the state; but when you want to use it, then the art of the vine-dresser?

Clearly.

And when you want to keep a shield or a lyre, and not to use them, you would say that justice is useful; but when you want to use them, then the art of the soldier or of the musician?

Certainly.

And so of all the other things—justice is useful when they are useless, and useless when they are useful?

That is the inference.

Then justice is not good for much. But let us consider this further point: Is not he who can best strike a blow in a boxing match or in any kind of fighting best able to ward off a blow?

Certainly.

And he who is most skilful in preventing or escaping from a disease is best able to create one?

True.

And he is the best guard of a camp who is best able to steal a march upon the enemy? *[334]*

Certainly.

Then he who is a good keeper of anything is also a good thief?

That, I suppose, is to be inferred.

Then if the just man is good at keeping money, he is good at stealing it.

That is implied in the argument.

Then after all the just man has turned out to be a thief. And this is a lesson which I suspect you must have learnt out of Homer; for he, speaking of Autolycus, the maternal grandfather of Odysseus, who is a favourite of his, affirms that

He was excellent above all men in theft and perjury.

And so, you and Homer and Simonides are agreed that justice is an art of theft; to be practised however "for the good of friends and for the harm of enemies"—that was what you were saying?

No, certainly not that, though I do not now know what I did say; but I still stand by the latter words.

Well, there is another question: By friends and enemies do we mean those who are so really, or only in seeming?

Surely, he said, a man may be expected to love those whom he thinks good, and to hate those whom he thinks evil.

Yes, but do not persons often err about good and evil: many who are not good seem to be so, and conversely?

That is true.

Then to them the good will be enemies and the evil will be their friends?

True.

And in that case they will be right in doing good to the evil and evil to the good?

Clearly.

But the good are just and would not do an injustice?

True.

Then according to your argument it is just to injure those who do no wrong?

Nay, Socrates; the doctrine is immoral.

Then I suppose that we ought to do good to the just and harm to the unjust?

I like that better.

But see the consequence:—Many a man who is ignorant of human nature has friends who are bad friends, and in that case he ought to do harm to them; and he has good enemies whom he ought to benefit; but, if so, we shall be saying the very opposite of that which we affirmed to be the meaning of Simonides.

Very true, he said; and I think that we had better correct an error into which we seem to have fallen in the use of the words "friend" and "enemy."

What was the error, Polemarchus? I asked.

We assumed that he is a friend who seems to be or who is thought good.

And how is the error to be corrected?

We should rather say that he is a friend who is, as well as seems, good; *[335]* and that he who seems only, and is not good, only seems to be and is not a friend; and of an enemy the same may be said.

You would argue that the good are our friends and the bad our enemies?

Yes.

And instead of saying simply as we did at first, that it is just to do good to our friends and harm to our enemies, we should further say: It is just to do good to our friends when they are good and harm to our enemies when they are evil?

Yes, that appears to me to be the truth.

But ought the just to injure any one at all?

Undoubtedly he ought to injure those who are both wicked and his enemies.

When horses are injured, are they improved or deteriorated?

The latter.

Deteriorated, that is to say, in the good qualities of horses, not of dogs?

Yes, of horses.

And dogs are deteriorated in the good qualities of dogs, and not of horses?

Of course.

And will not men who are injured be deteriorated in that which is the proper virtue of man?

Certainly.

And that human virtue is justice?

To be sure.

Then men who are injured are of necessity made unjust?

That is the result.

But can the musician by his art make men unmusical?

Certainly not.

Or the horseman by his art make them bad horsemen?

Impossible.

And can the just by justice make men unjust, or speaking generally, can the good by virtue make them bad?

Assuredly not.

Any more than heat can produce cold?

It cannot.

Or drought moisture?

Clearly not.

Nor can the good harm any one?

Impossible.

And the just is the good?

Certainly.

Then to injure a friend or any one else is not the act of a just man, but of the opposite, who is the unjust?

I think that what you say is quite true, Socrates.

Then if a man says that justice consists in the repayment of debts, and that good is the debt which a man owes to his friends, and evil the debt which he owes to his enemies—to say this is not wise; for it is not true, if, as has been clearly shown, the injuring of another can be in no case just.

I agree with you, said Polemarchus.

Then you and I are prepared to take up arms against any one who attributes such a saying to Simonides or Bias or Pittacus, or any other wise man or seer?

I am quite ready to do battle at your side, he said.

[336] Shall I tell you whose I believe the saying to be?

Whose?

I believe that Periander or Perdiccas or Xerxes or Ismenias the Theban, or some other rich and mighty man, who had a great opinion of his own power, was the first to say that justice is "doing good to your friends and harm to your enemies."

Most true, he said.

Yes, I said; but if this definition of justice also breaks down, what other can be offered?

Several times in the course of the discussion Thrasymachus had made an attempt to get the argument into his own hands, and had been put down by the rest of the company, who wanted to hear the end. But when Polemarchus and I had done speaking and there was a pause, he could no longer hold his peace; and, gathering himself up, he came at us like a wild beast, seeking to devour us. We were quite panic-stricken at the sight of him.

He roared out to the whole company: What folly, Socrates, has taken possession of you all? And why, sillybillies, do you knock under to one another? I say that if you want really to know what justice is, you should not only ask but answer, and you should not seek honour to yourself from the refutation of an opponent, but have your own answer; for there is many a one who can ask and cannot answer. And now I will not have you say that justice is duty or advantage or profit or gain or interest, for this sort of nonsense will not do for me; I must have clearness and accuracy.

I was panic-stricken at his words, and could not look at him without trembling. Indeed I believe that if I had not fixed my eye upon him, I should have been struck dumb: but when I saw his fury rising, I looked at him first, and was therefore able to reply to him.

Thrasymachus, I said, with a quiver, don't be hard upon us. Polemarchus and I may have been guilty of a little mistake in the argument, but I can assure you that the error was not intentional. If we were seeking for a piece of gold, you would not imagine that we were "knocking under to one another," and so losing our chance of finding it. And why, when we are seeking for justice, a thing more precious than many pieces of gold, do you say that we are weakly yielding to one another and not doing our utmost to get at the truth? Nay, my good friend, we are most willing and anxious to do so, but the fact is that we cannot. And if so, you people who know all things should pity us and not be angry with us.

[337] How characteristic of Socrates! he replied, with a bitter laugh—that's your ironical style! Did I not foresee—have I not already told you, that whatever he was asked he would refuse to answer, and try irony or any other shuffle, in order that he might avoid answering?

You are a philosopher, Thrasymachus, I replied, and well know that if you ask a person what numbers make up twelve, taking care to prohibit him whom you ask from answering twice six, or three times four, or six times two, or four times three, "for this sort of nonsense will not do for me"—then obviously, if that is your way of putting the question, no one can answer you. But suppose that he were to retort, "Thrasymachus, what do you mean? If one of these numbers which you interdict be the true answer to the question, am I falsely to say some other number which is not the right one?—is that your meaning?"—How would you answer him?

Just as if the two cases were at all alike! he said.

Why should they not be? I replied; and even if they are not, but only appear to be so to the person who is asked, ought he not to say what he thinks, whether you and I forbid him or not?

I presume then that you are going to make one of the interdicted answers?

I dare say that I may, notwithstanding the danger, if upon reflection I approve of any of them.

But what if I give you an answer about justice other and better, he said, than any of these? What do you deserve to have done to you?

Done to me!—as becomes the ignorant, I must learn from the wise—that is what I deserve to have done to me.

What, and no payment! a pleasant notion!

I will pay when I have the money, I replied.

But you have, Socrates, said Glaucon: and you, Thrasymachus, need be under no anxiety about money, for we will all make a contribution for Socrates.

Yes, he replied, and then Socrates will do as he always does—refuse to answer himself, but take and pull to pieces the answer of some one else.

Why, my good friend, I said, how can any one answer who knows, and says that he knows, just nothing; and who, even if he has some faint notions of his own, is told by a man of authority not to utter them? [338] The natural thing is, that the speaker should be some one like yourself who professes to know and can tell what he knows. Will you then kindly answer, for the edification of the company and of myself?

Glaucon and the rest of the company joined in my request and Thrasymachus, as any one might see, was in reality eager to speak; for he thought that he had an excellent answer, and would distinguish himself. But at first he affected to insist on my answering; at length he consented to begin. Behold, he said, the wisdom of Socrates; he refuses to teach himself, and goes about learning of others, to whom he never even says Thank you.

That I learn of others, I replied, is quite true; but that I am ungrateful I wholly deny. Money I have none, and therefore I pay in praise, which is all I have; and how ready I am to praise any one who appears to me to speak well you will very soon find out when you answer; for I expect that you will answer well.

Listen, then, he said; I proclaim that justice is nothing else than the interest of the stronger. And now why do you not praise me? But of course you won't.

Let me first understand you, I replied. Justice, as you say, is the interest of the stronger. What, Thrasymachus, is the meaning of this? You cannot mean to say that because Polydamas, the pancratiast, is stronger than we are, and finds the eating of beef conducive to his bodily strength, that to eat beef is therefore equally for our good who are weaker than he is, and right and just for us?

That's abominable of you, Socrates; you take the words in the sense which is most damaging to the argument.

Not at all, my good sir, I said; I am trying to understand them; and I wish that you would be a little clearer.

Well, he said, have you never heard that forms of government differ; there are tyrannies, and there are democracies, and there are aristocracies?

Yes, I know.

And the government is the ruling power in each state?

Certainly.

And the different forms of government make laws democratical, aristocratical, tyrannical, with a view to their several interests; and these laws, which are made by them for their own interests, are the justice which they deliver to their subjects, and him who transgresses them they punish as a breaker of the law, and unjust. And that is what I mean when I say that in all states there is the same principle of justice, which is the interest of the government; and as the government must be supposed to have power, [339] the only reasonable conclusion is, that everywhere there is one principle of justice, which is the interest of the stronger.

Now I understand you, I said; and whether you are right or not I will try to discover. But let me remark, that in defining justice you have yourself used the word "interest" which you forbade me to use. It is true, however, that in your definition the words "of the stronger" are added.

A small addition, you must allow, he said.

Great or small, never mind about that: we must first enquire whether what you are saying is the truth. Now we are both agreed that justice is interest of some sort, but you go on to say "of the stronger"; about this addition I am not so sure, and must therefore consider further.

Proceed.

I will; and first tell me, Do you admit that it is just for subjects to obey their rulers?

I do.

But are the rulers of states absolutely infallible, or are they sometimes liable to err?

To be sure, he replied, they are liable to err.

Then in making their laws they may sometimes make them rightly, and sometimes not?

True.

When they make them rightly, they make them agreeably to their interest; when they are mistaken, contrary to their interest; you admit that?

Yes.

And the laws which they make must be obeyed by their subjects—and that is what you call justice?

Doubtless.

Then justice, according to your argument, is not only obedience to the interest of the stronger but the reverse?

What is that you are saying? he asked.

I am only repeating what you are saying, I believe. But let us consider: Have we not admitted that the rulers may be mistaken about their own interest in what they command, and also that to obey them is justice? Has not that been admitted?

Yes.

Then you must also have acknowledged justice not to be for the interest of the stronger, when the rulers unintentionally command things to be done which are to their own injury. For if, as you say, justice is the obedience which the subject renders to their commands, in that case, O wisest of men, is there any escape from the conclusion that the weaker are commanded to do, not what is for the interest, but what is for the injury of the stronger?

Nothing can be clearer, Socrates, said Polemarchus.

[340] Yes, said Cleitophon, interposing, if you are allowed to be his witness.

But there is no need of any witness, said Polemarchus, for Thrasymachus himself acknowledges that rulers may sometimes command what is not for their own interest, and that for subjects to obey them is justice.

Yes, Polemarchus—Thrasymachus said that for subjects to do what was commanded by their rulers is just.

Yes, Cleitophon, but he also said that justice is the interest of the stronger, and, while admitting both these propositions, he further acknowledged that the stronger may command the weaker who are his subjects to do what is

not for his own interest; whence follows that justice is the injury quite as much as the interest of the stronger.

But, said Cleitophon, he meant by the interest of the stronger what the stronger thought to be his interest—this was what the weaker had to do; and this was affirmed by him to be justice.

Those were not his words, rejoined Polemarchus.

Never mind, I replied, if he now says that they are, let us accept his statement. Tell me, Thrasymachus, I said, did you mean by justice what the stronger thought to be his interest, whether really so or not?

Certainly not, he said. Do you suppose that I call him who is mistaken the stronger at the time when he is mistaken?

Yes, I said, my impression was that you did so, when you admitted that the ruler was not infallible but might be sometimes mistaken.

You argue like an informer, Socrates. Do you mean, for example, that he who is mistaken about the sick is a physician in that he is mistaken? or that he who errs in arithmetic or grammar is an arithmetician or grammarian at the time when he is making the mistake, in respect of the mistake? True, we say that the physician or arithmetician or grammarian has made a mistake, but this is only a way of speaking; for the fact is that neither the grammarian nor any other person of skill ever makes a mistake in so far as he is what his name implies; they none of them err unless their skill fails them, and then they cease to be skilled artists. No artist or sage or ruler errs at the time when he is what his name implies; though he is commonly said to err, and I adopt the common mode of speaking. But to be perfectly accurate, since you are such a lover of accuracy, we should say that the ruler, in so far as he is a ruler, is unerring, [341] and, being unerring, always commands that which is for his own interest; and the subject is required to execute his commands; and therefore, as I said at first and now repeat, justice is the interest of the stronger.

Indeed, Thrasymachus, and do I really appear to you to argue like an informer?

Certainly, he replied.

And do you suppose that I ask these questions with any design of injuring you in the argument?

Nay, he replied, "suppose" is not the word—I know it; but you will be found out, and by sheer force of argument you will never prevail.

I shall not make the attempt, my dear man; but to avoid any misunderstanding occurring between us in future, let me ask, in what sense do you speak of a ruler or stronger whose interest, as you were saying, he being the superior, it is just that the inferior should execute—is he a ruler in the popular or in the strict sense of the term?

In the strictest of all senses, he said. And now cheat and play the informer if you can; I ask no quarter at your hands. But you never will be able, never.

And do you imagine, I said, that I am such a madman as to try and cheat Thrasymachus? I might as well shave a lion.

Why, he said, you made the attempt a minute ago, and you failed.

Enough, I said, of these civilities. It will be better that I should ask you a question: Is the physician, taken in that strict sense of which you are speaking, a healer of the sick or a maker of money? And remember that I am now speaking of the true physician.

A healer of the sick, he replied.

And the pilot—that is to say, the true pilot—is he a captain of sailors or a mere sailor?

A captain of sailors.

The circumstance that he sails in the ship is not to be taken into account; neither is he to be called a sailor; the name pilot by which he is distinguished has nothing to do with sailing, but is significant of his skill and of his authority over the sailors.

Very true, he said.

Now, I said, every art has an interest?

Certainly.

For which the art has to consider and provide?

Yes, that is the aim of art.

And the interest of any art is the perfection of it—this and nothing else?

What do you mean?

I mean what I may illustrate negatively by the example of the body. Suppose you were to ask me whether the body is self-sufficing or has wants, I should reply: Certainly the body has wants; for the body may be ill and require to be cured, and has therefore interests to which the art of medicine ministers; and this is the origin and intention of medicine, as you will acknowledge. Am I not right?

[342] Quite right, he replied.

But is the art of medicine or any other art faulty or deficient in any quality in the same way that the eye may be deficient in sight or the ear fail of hearing, and therefore requires another art to provide for the interests of seeing and hearing—has art in itself, I say, any similar liability to fault or defect, and does every art require another supplementary art to provide for its interests, and that another and another without end? Or have the arts to look only after their own interests? Or have they no need either of themselves or of another?—having no faults or defects, they have no need to correct them, either by the exercise of their own art or of any other; they have only to consider the interest of their subject-matter. For every art remains pure and faultless while remaining true—that is to say, while perfect and unimpaired. Take the words in your precise sense, and tell me whether I am not right.

Yes, clearly.

Then medicine does not consider the interest of medicine, but the interest of the body?

True, he said.

Nor does the art of horsemanship consider the interests of the art of horsemanship, but the interests of the horse; neither do any other arts care for themselves, for they have no needs; they care only for that which is the subject of their art?

True, he said.

But surely, Thrasymachus, the arts are the superiors and rulers of their own subjects?

To this he assented with a good deal of reluctance.

Then, I said, no science or art considers or enjoins the interest of the stronger or superior, but only the interest of the subject and weaker?

He made an attempt to contest this proposition also, but finally acquiesced.

Then, I continued, no physician, in so far as he is a physician, considers his own good in what he prescribes, but the good of his patient; for the true physician is also a ruler having the human body as a subject, and is not a mere money-maker; that has been admitted?

Yes.

And the pilot likewise, in the strict sense of the term, is a ruler of sailors and not a mere sailor?

That has been admitted.

And such a pilot and ruler will provide and prescribe for the interest of the sailor who is under him, and not for his own or the ruler's interest?

He gave a reluctant "Yes."

Then, I said, Thrasymachus, there is no one in any rule who, in so far as he is a ruler, considers or enjoins what is for his own interest, but always what is for the interest of his subject or suitable to his art; to that he looks, and that alone he considers in everything which he says and does.

[343] When we had got to this point in the argument, and every one saw that the definition of justice had been completely upset, Thrasymachus, instead of replying to me, said: Tell me, Socrates, have you got a nurse?

Why do you ask such a question, I said, when you ought rather to be answering?

Because she leaves you to snivel, and never wipes your nose: she has not even taught you to know the shepherd from the sheep.

What makes you say that? I replied.

Because you fancy that the shepherd or neatherd fattens or tends the sheep or oxen with a view to their own good and not to the good of himself or his master; and you further imagine that the rulers of states, if they are true rulers, never think of their subjects as sheep, and that they are not studying their own advantage day and night. Oh, no; and so entirely astray are you in your ideas about the just and unjust as not even to know that justice and the just are in reality another's good; that is to say, the interest of the ruler and stronger, and the loss of the subject and servant; and injustice the opposite; for the unjust is lord over the truly simple and just: he is the stronger, and his subjects do what is for his interest, and minister to his happiness, which is very far from being their own. Consider further, most foolish Socrates, that the just is always a loser in comparison with the unjust. First of all, in private contracts: wherever the unjust is the partner of the just you will find that, when the partnership is dissolved, the unjust man has always more and the just less. Secondly, in their dealings with the State: when there is an income-tax, the just man will pay more and the unjust less on the same amount of income; and when there is anything to be received the one gains nothing and the other much. Observe also what happens when they take an office; there is the just man neglecting his affairs and perhaps suffering other losses, and getting nothing out of the public, because he is just; moreover he is hated by his friends and acquaintance for refusing to serve them in unlawful ways. [344] But all this is reversed in the case of the unjust man. I am speaking, as before, of injustice on a large scale in which the advantage of the unjust is more apparent; and my meaning will be most clearly seen if we turn to that highest form of injustice in which the criminal is the happiest of men, and the suffer-

ers or those who refuse to do injustice are the most miserable—that is to say tyranny, which by fraud and force takes away the property of others, not little by little but wholesale; comprehending in one, things sacred as well as profane, private and public; for which acts of wrong, if he were detected perpetrating any one of them singly, he would be punished and incur great disgrace—they who do such wrong in particular cases are called robbers of temples, and man-stealers and burglars and swindlers and thieves. But when a man besides taking away the money of the citizens has made slaves of them, then, instead of these names of reproach, he is termed happy and blessed, not only by the citizens but by all who hear of his having achieved the consummation of injustice. For mankind censure injustice, fearing that they may be the victims of it and not because they shrink from committing it. And thus, as I have shown, Socrates, injustice, when on a sufficient scale, has more strength and freedom and mastery than justice; and, as I said at first, justice is the interest of the stronger, whereas injustice is a man's own profit and interest.

Thrasymachus, when he had thus spoken, having, like a bathman, deluged our ears with his words, had a mind to go away. But the company would not let him; they insisted that he should remain and defend his position; and I myself added my own humble request that he would not leave us. Thrasymachus, I said to him, excellent man, how suggestive are your remarks! And are you going to run away before you have fairly taught or learned whether they are true or not? Is the attempt to determine the way of man's life so small a matter in your eyes —to determine how life may be passed by each one of us to the greatest advantage?

And do I differ from you, he said, as to the importance of the enquiry?

You appear rather, I replied, to have no care or thought about us, Thrasymachus—whether we live better or worse from not knowing what you say you know, is to you a matter of indifference. Prithee, friend, [345] do not keep your knowledge to yourself; we are a large party; and any benefit which you confer upon us will be amply rewarded. For my own part I openly declare that I am not convinced, and that I do not believe injustice to be more gainful than justice, even if uncontrolled and allowed to have free play. For, granting that there may be an unjust man who is able to commit injustice either by fraud or force, still this does not convince me of the superior advantage of injustice, and there may be others who are in the same predicament with myself. Perhaps we may be wrong; if so, you in your wisdom should convince us that we are mistaken in preferring justice to injustice.

And how am I to convince you, he said, if you are not already convinced by what I have just said; what more can I do for you? Would you have me put the proof bodily into your souls?

Heaven forbid! I said; I would only ask you to be consistent; or, if you change, change openly and let there be no deception. For I must remark, Thrasymachus, if you will recall what was previously said, that although you began by defining the true physician in an exact sense, you did not observe a like exactness when speaking of the shepherd; you thought that the shepherd as a shepherd tends the sheep not with a view to their own good, but like a mere diner or banquetter with a view to the pleasures of the table; or, again, as a trader for sale in the market, and not as a shepherd. Yet surely the art of the shepherd is concerned only with the good of his subjects; he has only to provide the best for them, since the perfection of the art is already ensured whenever all the requirements of it are satisfied. And that was what I was saying just now about the ruler. I conceived that the art of the ruler, considered as ruler, whether in a state or in private life, could only regard the good of his flock or subjects; whereas you seem to think that the rulers in states, that is to say, the true rulers, like being in authority.

Think! Nay, I am sure of it.

Then why in the case of lesser offices do men never take them willingly without payment, unless under the idea that they govern for the advantage not of themselves but of others? [346] Let me ask you a question: Are not the several arts different, by reason of their each having a separate function? And, my dear illustrious friend, do say what you think, that we may make a little progress.

Yes, that is the difference, he replied.

And each art gives us a particular good and not merely a general one—medicine, for example, gives us health; navigation, safety at sea, and so on?

Yes, he said.

And the art of payment has the special function of giving pay: but we do not confuse this with other arts, any more than the art of the pilot is to be confused with the art of medicine, because the health of the pilot may be improved by a sea voyage. You would not be inclined to say, would you, that navigation is the art of medicine, at least if we are to adopt your exact use of language?

Certainly not.

Or because a man is in good health when he receives pay you would not say that the art of payment is medicine?

I should say not.

Nor would you say that medicine is the art of receiving pay because a man takes fees when he is engaged in healing?

Certainly not.

And we have admitted, I said, that the good of each art is specially confined to the art?

Yes.

Then, if there be any good which all artists have in common, that is to be attributed to something of which they all have the common use?

True, he replied.

And when the artist is benefited by receiving pay the advantage is gained by an additional use of the art of pay, which is not the art professed by him?

He gave a reluctant assent to this.

Then the pay is not derived by the several artists from their respective arts. But the truth is, that while the art of medicine gives health, and the art of the builder builds a house, another art attends them which is the art of pay. The various arts may be doing their own business and benefiting that over which they preside, but would the artist receive any benefit from his art unless he were paid as well?

I suppose not.

But does he therefore confer no benefit when he works for nothing?

Certainly, he confers a benefit.

Then now, Thrasymachus, there is no longer any doubt that neither arts nor governments provide for their own interests; but, as we were before saying, they rule and provide for the interests of their subjects who are the weaker and not the stronger—to their good they attend and not to the good of the superior. And this is the reason, my dear Thrasymachus, why, as I was just now saying, no one is willing to govern; because no one likes to take in hand the reformation of evils which are not his concern without remuneration. For, [347] in the execution of his work, and in giving his orders to another, the true artist does not regard his own interest, but always that of his subjects; and therefore in order that rulers may be willing to rule, they must be paid in one of three modes of payment, money, or honour, or a penalty for refusing.

What do you mean, Socrates? said Glaucon. The first two modes of payment are intelligible enough, but what the penalty is I do not understand, or how a penalty can be a payment.

You mean that you do not understand the nature of this payment which to the best men is the great inducement to rule? Of course you know that ambition and avarice are held to be, as indeed they are, a disgrace?

Very true.

And for this reason, I said, money and honour have no attraction for them; good men do not wish to be openly demanding payment for governing and so to get the name of hirelings, nor by secretly helping themselves out of the public revenues to get the name of thieves. And not being ambitious they do not care about honour. Wherefore necessity must be laid upon them, and they must be induced to serve from the fear of punishment. And this, as I imagine, is the reason why the forwardness to take office, instead of waiting to be compelled, has been deemed dishonourable. Now the worst part of the punishment is that he who refuses to rule is liable to be ruled by one who is worse than himself. And the fear of this, as I conceive, induces the good to take office, not because they would, but because they cannot help—not under the idea that they are going to have any benefit or enjoyment themselves, but as a necessity, and because they are not able to commit the task of ruling to any one who is better than themselves, or indeed as good. For there is reason to think that if a city were composed entirely of good men, then to avoid office would be as much an object of contention as to obtain office is at present; then we should have plain proof that the true ruler is not meant by nature to regard his own interest, but that of his subjects; and every one who knew this would choose rather to receive a benefit from another than to have the trouble of conferring one. So far am I from agreeing with Thrasymachus that justice is the interest of the stronger. This latter question need not be further discussed at present; but when Thrasymachus says that the life of the unjust is more advantageous than that of the just, his new statement appears to me to be of a far more serious character. Which of us has spoken truly? And which sort of life, Glaucon, do you prefer?

I for my part deem the life of the just to be the more advantageous, he answered.

[348] Did you hear all the advantages of the unjust which Thrasymachus was rehearsing?

Yes, I heard him, he replied, but he has not convinced me.

Then shall we try to find some way of convincing him, if we can, that he is saying what is not true?

Most certainly, he replied.

If, I said, he makes a set speech and we make another recounting all the advantages of being just, and he answers and we rejoin, there must be a numbering and measuring of the goods which are claimed on either side, and in the end we shall want judges to decide; but if we proceed in our enquiry as we lately did, by making admissions to one another, we shall unite the offices of judge and advocate in our own persons.

Very good, he said.

And which method do I understand you to prefer? I said.

That which you propose.

Well, then, Thrasymachus, I said, suppose you begin at the beginning and answer me. You say that perfect injustice is more gainful than perfect justice?

Yes, that is what I say, and I have given you my reasons.

And what is your view about them? Would you call one of them virtue and the other vice?

Certainly.

I suppose that you would call justice virtue and injustice vice?

What a charming notion! So likely too, seeing that I affirm injustice to be profitable and justice not.

What else then would you say?

The opposite, he replied.

And would you call justice vice?

No, I would rather say sublime simplicity.

Then would you call injustice malignity?

No; I would rather say discretion.

And do the unjust appear to you to be wise and good?

Yes, he said; at any rate those of them who are able to be perfectly unjust, and who have the power of subduing states and nations; but perhaps you imagine me to be talking of cutpurses. Even this profession if undetected has advantages, though they are not to be compared with those of which I was just now speaking.

I do not think that I misapprehend your meaning, Thrasymachus, I replied; but still I cannot hear without amazement that you class injustice with wisdom and virtue, and justice with the opposite.

Certainly I do so class them.

Now, I said, you are on more substantial and almost unanswerable ground; for if the injustice which you were maintaining to be profitable had been admitted by you as by others to be vice and deformity, an answer might have been given to you on received principles; *[349]* but now I perceive that you will call injustice honourable and strong, and to the unjust you will attribute all the qualities which were attributed by us before to the just, seeing that you do not hesitate to rank injustice with wisdom and virtue.

You have guessed most infallibly, he replied.

Then I certainly ought not to shrink from going through with the argument so long as I have reason to think that you, Thrasymachus, are speaking your real mind; for I do believe that you are now in earnest and are not amusing yourself at our expense.

I may be in earnest or not, but what is that to you?—to refute the argument is your business.

Very true, I said; that is what I have to do: But will you be so good as answer yet one more question? Does the just man try to gain any advantage over the just?

Far otherwise; if he did he would not be the simple amusing creature which he is.

And would he try to go beyond just action?

He would not.

And how would he regard the attempt to gain an advantage over the unjust; would that be considered by him as just or unjust?

He would think it just, and would try to gain the advantage; but he would not be able.

Whether he would or would not be able, I said, is not to the point. My question is only whether the just man, while refusing to have more than another just man, would wish and claim to have more than the unjust?

Yes, he would.

And what of the unjust—does he claim to have more than the just man and to do more than is just?

Of course, he said, for he claims to have more than all men.

And the unjust man will strive and struggle to obtain more than the unjust man or action, in order that he may have more than all?

True.

We may put the matter thus, I said—the just does not desire more than his like but more than his unlike, whereas the unjust desires more than both his like and his unlike?

Nothing, he said, can be better than that statement.

And the unjust is good and wise, and the just is neither?

Good again, he said.

And is not the unjust like the wise and good and the just unlike them?

Of course, he said, he who is of a certain nature, is like those who are of a certain nature; he who is not, not.

Each of them, I said, is such as his like is?

Certainly, he replied.

Very good, Thrasymachus, I said; and now to take the case of the arts: you would admit that one man is a musician and another not a musician?

Yes.

And which is wise and which is foolish?

Clearly the musician is wise, and he who is not a musician is foolish.

And he is good in as far as he is wise, and bad in as far as he is foolish?

Yes.

And you would say the same sort of thing of the physician?

Yes.

And do you think, my excellent friend, that a musician when he adjusts the lyre would desire or claim to exceed or go beyond a musician in the tightening and loosening the strings?

I do not think that he would.

But he would claim to exceed the non-musician?

Of course.

[350] And what would you say of the physician? In prescribing meats and drinks would he wish to go beyond another physician or beyond the practice of medicine?

He would not.

But he would wish to go beyond the non-physician?

Yes.

And about knowledge and ignorance in general; see whether you think that any man who has knowledge ever would wish to have the choice of saying or doing more than another man who has knowledge. Would he not rather say or do the same as his like in the same case?

That, I suppose, can hardly be denied.

And what of the ignorant? would he not desire to have more than either the knowing or the ignorant?

I dare say.

And the knowing is wise?

Yes.

And the wise is good?

True.

Then the wise and good will not desire to

gain more than his like, but more than his unlike and opposite?

I suppose so.

Whereas the bad and ignorant will desire to gain more than both?

Yes.

But did we not say, Thrasymachus, that the unjust goes beyond both his like and unlike? Were not these your words?

They were.

And you also said that the just will not go beyond his like but his unlike?

Yes.

Then the just is like the wise and good, and the unjust like the evil and ignorant?

That is the inference.

And each of them is such as his like is?

That was admitted.

Then the just has turned out to be wise and good and the unjust evil and ignorant.

Thrasymachus made all these admissions, not fluently, as I repeat them, but with extreme reluctance; it was a hot summer's day, and the perspiration poured from him in torrents; and then I saw what I had never seen before, Thrasymachus blushing. As we were now agreed that justice was virtue and wisdom, and injustice vice and ignorance, I proceeded to another point:

Well, I said, Thrasymachus, that matter is now settled; but were we not also saying that injustice had strength; do you remember?

Yes, I remember, he said, but do not suppose that I approve of what you are saying or have no answer; if however I were to answer, you would be quite certain to accuse me of haranguing; therefore either permit me to have my say out, or if you would rather ask, do so, and I will answer "Very good," as they say to story-telling old women, and will nod "Yes" and "No."

Certainly not, I said, if contrary to your real opinion.

Yes, he said, I will, to please you, since you will not let me speak. What else would you have?

Nothing in the world, I said; and if you are so disposed I will ask and you shall answer.

Proceed.

Then I will repeat the question which I asked before, in order that our examination of the relative nature of justice and injustice *[351]* may be carried on regularly. A statement was made that injustice is stronger and more powerful than justice, but now justice, having been identified with wisdom and virtue, is easily shown to be stronger than injustice, if injustice is ignorance; this can no longer be questioned by any one. But I want to view the matter, Thrasymachus, in a different way: You would not deny that a state may be unjust and may be unjustly attempting to enslave other states, or may have already enslaved them, and may be holding many of them in subjection?

True, he replied; and I will add that the best and most perfectly unjust state will be most likely to do so.

I know, I said, that such was your position; but what I would further consider is, whether this power which is possessed by the superior state can exist or be exercised without justice or only with justice.

If you are right in your view, and justice is wisdom, then only with justice; but if I am right, then without justice.

I am delighted, Thrasymachus, to see you not only nodding assent and dissent, but making answers which are quite excellent.

That is out of civility to you, he replied.

You are very kind, I said; and would you have the goodness also to inform me, whether you think that a state, or an army, or a band of robbers and thieves, or any other gang of evildoers could act at all if they injured one another?

No indeed, he said, they could not.

But if they abstained from injuring one another, then they might act together better?

Yes.

And this is because injustice creates divisions and hatreds and fighting, and justice imparts harmony and friendship; is not that true, Thrasymachus?

I agree, he said, because I do not wish to quarrel with you.

How good of you, I said; but I should like to know also whether injustice, having this tendency to arouse hatred, wherever existing, among slaves or among freemen, will not make them hate one another and set them at variance and render them incapable of common action?

Certainly.

And even if injustice be found in two only, will they not quarrel and fight, and become enemies to one another and to the just?

They will.

And suppose injustice abiding in a single person, would your wisdom say that she loses or that she retains her natural power?

Let us assume that she retains her power.

Yet is not the power which injustice exercises of such a nature that wherever she takes up her abode, whether in a city, in an army, [352] in a family, or in any other body, that body is, to begin with, rendered incapable of united action by reason of sedition and distraction; and does it not become its own enemy and at variance with all that opposes it, and with the just? Is not this the case?

Yes, certainly.

And is not injustice equally fatal when existing in a single person; in the first place rendering him incapable of action because he is not at unity with himself, and in the second place making him an enemy to himself and the just? Is not that true, Thrasymachus?

Yes.

And O my friend, I said, surely the gods are just?

Granted that they are.

But if so, the unjust will be the enemy of the gods, and the just will be their friend?

Feast away in triumph, and take your fill of the argument; I will not oppose you, lest I should displease the company.

Well then, proceed with your answers, and let me have the remainder of my repast. For we have already shown that the just are clearly wiser and better and abler than the unjust, and that the unjust are incapable of common action; nay more, that to speak as we did of men who are evil acting at any time vigorously together, is not strictly true, for if they had been perfectly evil, they would have laid hands upon one another; but it is evident that there must have been some remnant of justice in them, which enabled them to combine; if there had not been they would have injured one another as well as their victims; they were but half-villains in their enterprises; for had they been whole villains, and utterly unjust, they would have been utterly incapable of action. That, as I believe, is the truth of the matter, and not what you said at first. But whether the just have a better and happier life than the unjust is a further question which we also proposed to consider. I think that they have, and for the reasons which I have given; but still I should like to examine further, for no light matter is at stake, nothing less than the rule of human life.

Proceed.

I will proceed by asking a question: Would you not say that a horse has some end?

I should.

And the end or use of a horse or of anything would be that which could not be accomplished, or not so well accomplished, by any other thing?

I do not understand, he said.

Let me explain: Can you see, except with the eye?

Certainly not.

Or hear, except with the ear?

No.

These then may be truly said to be the ends of these organs?

They may.

[353] But you can cut off a vine-branch with a dagger or with a chisel, and in many other ways?

Of course.

And yet not so well as with a pruning-hook made for the purpose?

True.

May we not say that this is the end of a pruning-hook?

We may.

Then now I think you will have no difficulty in understanding my meaning when I asked the question whether the end of anything would be that which could not be accomplished, or not so well accomplished, by any other thing?

I understand your meaning, he said, and assent.

And that to which an end is appointed has also an excellence? Need I ask again whether the eye has an end?

It has.

And has not the eye an excellence?

Yes.

And the ear has an end and an excellence also?

True.

And the same is true of all other things; they have each of them an end and a special excellence?

That is so.

Well, and can the eyes fulfil their end if they are wanting in their own proper excellence and have a defect instead?

How can they, he said, if they are blind and cannot see?

You mean to say, if they have lost their proper excellence, which is sight; but I have not arrived at that point yet. I would rather ask the question more generally, and only enquire whether the things which fulfil their ends fulfil them by their own proper excellence, and fail of fulfilling them by their own defect?

Certainly, he replied.

I might say the same of the ears; when deprived of their own proper excellence they cannot fulfil their end?

True.

And the same observation will apply to all other things?

I agree.

Well; and has not the soul an end which nothing else can fulfil? for example, to superintend and command and deliberate and the like. Are not these functions proper to the soul, and can they rightly be assigned to any other?

To no other.

And is not life to be reckoned among the ends of the soul?

Assuredly, he said.

And has not the soul an excellence also?

Yes.

And can she or can she not fulfil her own ends when deprived of that excellence?

She cannot.

Then an evil soul must necessarily be an evil ruler and superintendent, and the good soul a good ruler?

Yes, necessarily.

And we have admitted that justice is the excellence of the soul, and injustice the defect of the soul?

That has been admitted.

Then the just soul and the just man will live well, and the unjust man will live ill?

That is what your argument proves.

[354] And he who lives well is blessed and happy, and he who lives ill the reverse of happy?

Certainly.

Then the just is happy, and the unjust miserable?

So be it.

But happiness and not misery is profitable.

Of course.

Then, my blessed Thrasymachus, injustice can never be more profitable than justice.

Let this, Socrates, he said, be your entertainment at the Bendidea.

For which I am indebted to you, I said, now that you have grown gentle towards me and have left off scolding. Nevertheless, I have not been well entertained; but that was my own fault and not yours. As an epicure snatches a taste of every dish which is successively brought to table, he not having allowed himself time to enjoy the one before, so have I gone from one subject to another without having discovered what I sought at first, the nature of justice. I left that enquiry and turned away to consider whether justice is virtue and wisdom or evil and folly; and when there arose a further question about the comparative advantages of justice and injustice, I could not refrain from passing on to that. And the result of the whole discussion has been that I know nothing at all. For I know not what justice is, and therefore I am not likely to know whether it is or is not a virtue, nor can I say whether the just man is happy or unhappy.

BOOK II

[357] WITH these words I was thinking that I had made an end of the discussion; but the end, in truth, proved to be only a beginning. For Glaucon, who is always the most pugnacious of men, was dissatisfied at Thrasymachus' retirement; he wanted to have the battle out. So he said to me: Socrates, do you wish really to persuade us, or only to seem to have persuaded us, that to be just is always better than to be unjust?

I should wish really to persuade you, I replied, if I could.

Then you certainly have not succeeded. Let me ask you now:—How would you arrange goods—are there not some which we welcome for their own sakes, and independently of their consequences, as, for example, harmless pleasures and enjoyments, which delight us at the time, although nothing follows from them?

I agree in thinking that there is such a class, I replied.

Is there not also a second class of goods, such as knowledge, sight, health, which are desirable not only in themselves, but also for their results?

Certainly, I said.

And would you not recognize a third class, such as gymnastic, and the care of the sick, and the physician's art; also the various ways of money-making—these do us good but we regard them as disagreeable; and no one would choose them for their own sakes, but only for the sake of some reward or result which flows from them?

There is, I said, this third class also. But why do you ask?

Because I want to know in which of the three classes you would place justice?

[358] In the highest class, I replied—among those goods which he who would be happy desires both for their own sake and for the sake of their results.

Then the many are of another mind; they think that justice is to be reckoned in the troublesome class, among goods which are to be pursued for the sake of rewards and of reputation, but in themselves are disagreeable and rather to be avoided.

I know, I said, that this is their manner of thinking, and that this was the thesis which Thrasymachus was maintaining just now, when he censured justice and praised injustice. But I am too stupid to be convinced by him.

I wish, he said, that you would hear me as well as him, and then I shall see whether you and I agree. For Thrasymachus seems to me, like a snake, to have been charmed by your voice sooner than he ought to have been; but to my mind the nature of justice and injustice have not yet been made clear. Setting aside their rewards and results, I want to know what they are in themselves, and how they inwardly work in the soul. If you please, then, I will revive the argument of Thrasymachus. And first I will speak of the nature and origin of justice according to the common view of them. Secondly, I will show that all men who practise justice do so against their will, of necessity, but not as a good. And thirdly, I will argue that there is reason in this view, for the life of the unjust is after all better far than the life of the just—if what they say is true, Socrates, since I myself am not of their opinion. But still I acknowledge that I am perplexed when I hear the voices of Thrasymachus and myriads of others dinning in my ears; and, on the other hand, I have never yet heard the superiority of justice to injustice maintained by any one in a satisfactory way. I want to hear justice praised in respect of itself; then I shall be satisfied, and you are the person from whom I think that I am most likely to hear this; and therefore I will praise the unjust life to the utmost of my power, and my manner of speaking will indicate the manner in which I desire to hear you too praising justice and censuring injustice. Will you say whether you approve of my proposal?

Indeed I do; nor can I imagine any theme about which a man of sense would oftener wish to converse.

I am delighted, he replied, to hear you say so, and shall begin by speaking, as I proposed, of the nature and origin of justice.

They say that to do injustice is, by nature, good; to suffer injustice, evil; but that the evil is greater than the good. And so when men have both done and suffered injustice and have had experience [359] of both, not being able to avoid the one and obtain the other, they think that they had better agree among themselves to have neither; hence there arise laws and mutual covenants; and that which is ordained by law is termed by them lawful and just. This they affirm to be the origin and nature of justice—it is a mean or compromise, between the best of all, which is to do injustice and not be punished, and the worst of all, which is to suffer injustice without the power of retaliation; and justice, being at a middle point between the two, is tolerated not as a good, but as the lesser evil, and honoured by reason of the inability of men to do injustice. For no man who is worthy to be called a man would ever submit to such an agreement if he were able to resist; he would be mad if he did. Such is the received account, Socrates, of the nature and origin of justice.

Now that those who practise justice do so involuntarily and because they have not the power to be unjust will best appear if we imagine something of this kind: having given both to the just and the unjust power to do what they will, let us watch and see whither desire will lead them; then we shall discover in the very act the just and unjust man to be proceeding along the same road, following their interest, which all natures deem to be their good, and are only diverted into the path of justice by the force of law. The liberty which we are supposing may be most completely given to them in the form of such a power as is said to have been possessed by Gyges the ancestor of Croesus the Lydian. According to the tradition, Gyges was a shepherd in the service of the king of Lydia; there was a great storm, and an earthquake made an opening in the earth at the place where he was feeding his flock. Amazed at the sight, he descended into the opening, where, among other marvels, he beheld a hollow brazen horse, having doors, at which he stooping and looking in saw a dead body of stature, as appeared to him, more than human, and having nothing on but a gold ring; this he took from the finger of the dead and reascended. Now the shepherds met together, according to custom, that they might send their monthly report about the flocks to the king; into their assembly he came having the ring on his finger, and as he was sitting among them he chanced to turn the collet of the ring inside his hand, when instantly he became invisible to the rest of the company and they began to speak of him as if he were no longer present. [360] He was astonished at this, and again touching the ring he turned the collet outwards and reappeared; he made several trials of the ring, and always with the same result—when he turned the collet inwards he became invisible, when outwards he reappeared. Whereupon he contrived to be chosen one of the messengers who were sent to the court; where as soon as he arrived he seduced the queen, and with her help conspired against the king and slew him, and took the kingdom. Suppose now that there were two such magic rings, and the just put on one of them and the unjust the other; no man can be imagined to be of such an iron nature that he would stand fast in justice. No man would keep his hands off what was not his own when he could safely take what he liked out of the market, or go into houses and lie with any one at his pleasure, or kill or release from prison whom he would, and in all respects be like a God among men. Then the actions of the just would be as the actions of the unjust; they would both come at last to the same point. And this we may truly affirm to be a great proof that a man is just, not willingly or because he thinks that justice is any good to him individually, but of necessity, for wherever any one thinks that he can safely be unjust, there he is unjust. For all men believe in their hearts that injustice is far more profitable to the individual than justice, and he who argues as I have been supposing, will say that they are right. If you could imagine any one obtaining this power of becoming invisible, and never doing any wrong or touching what was another's, he would be thought by the lookers-on to be a most wretched idiot, although they would praise him to one another's faces, and keep up appearances with one another from a fear that they too might suffer injustice. Enough of this.

Now, if we are to form a real judgment of the life of the just and unjust, we must isolate them; there is no other way; and how is the isolation to be effected? I answer: Let the unjust man be entirely unjust, and the just man entirely just; nothing is to be taken away from either of them, and both are to be perfectly furnished for the work of their respective lives. First, let the unjust be like other distinguished masters of craft; like the skilful pilot or physician, who knows intuitively his own powers and keeps within their limits, [361] and who, if he fails at any point, is able to recover himself. So let the unjust make his unjust attempts in the right way, and lie hidden if he means to be great in his injustice (he who is found out is nobody): for the highest reach of injustice is, to be deemed just when you are not. Therefore I say that in the perfectly unjust man we must

assume the most perfect injustice; there is to be no deduction, but we must allow him, while doing the most unjust acts, to have acquired the greatest reputation for justice. If he have taken a false step he must be able to recover himself; he must be one who can speak with effect, if any of his deeds come to light, and who can force his way where force is required by his courage and strength, and command of money and friends. And at his side let us place the just man in his nobleness and simplicity, wishing, as Aeschylus says, to be and not to seem good. There must be no seeming, for if he seem to be just he will be honoured and rewarded, and then we shall not know whether he is just for the sake of justice or for the sake of honours and rewards; therefore, let him be clothed in justice only, and have no other covering; and he must be imagined in a state of life the opposite of the former. Let him be the best of men, and let him be thought the worst; then he will have been put to the proof; and we shall see whether he will be affected by the fear of infamy and its consequences. And let him continue thus to the hour of death; being just and seeming to be unjust. When both have reached the uttermost extreme, the one of justice and the other of injustice, let judgment be given which of them is the happier of the two.

Heavens! my dear Glaucon, I said, how energetically you polish them up for the decision, first one and then the other, as if they were two statues.

I do my best, he said. And now that we know what they are like there is no difficulty in tracing out the sort of life which awaits either of them. This I will proceed to describe; but as you may think the description a little too coarse, I ask you to suppose, Socrates, that the words which follow are not mine. Let me put them into the mouths of the eulogists of injustice: They will tell you that the just man who is thought unjust will be scourged, racked, bound—will have his eyes burnt out; and, at last, after suffering every kind of evil, he will be impaled: Then he will understand that he ought to seem only, [362] and not to be, just; the words of Aeschylus may be more truly spoken of the unjust than of the just. For the unjust is pursuing a reality; he does not live with a view to appearances—he wants to be really unjust and not to seem only:

His mind has a soil deep and fertile,
Out of which spring his prudent counsels.

In the first place, he is thought just, and therefore bears rule in the city; he can marry whom he will, and give in marriage to whom he will; also he can trade and deal where he likes, and always to his own advantage, because he has no misgivings about injustice; and at every contest, whether in public or private, he gets the better of his antagonists, and gains at their expense, and is rich, and out of his gains he can benefit his friends, and harm his enemies; moreover, he can offer sacrifices, and dedicate gifts to the gods abundantly and magnificently, and can honour the gods or any man whom he wants to honour in a far better style than the just, and therefore he is likely to be dearer than they are to the gods. And thus, Socrates, gods and men are said to unite in making the life of the unjust better than the life of the just.

I was going to say something in answer to Glaucon, when Adeimantus, his brother, interposed: Socrates, he said, you do not suppose that there is nothing more to be urged?

Why, what else is there? I answered.

The strongest point of all has not been even mentioned, he replied.

Well, then, according to the proverb, "Let brother help brother"—if he fails in any part do you assist him; although I must confess that Glaucon has already said quite enough to lay me in the dust, and take from me the power of helping justice.

Nonsense, he replied. But let me add something more: There is another side to Glaucon's argument about the praise and censure of justice and injustice, which is equally required in order to bring out what I believe to be his meaning. Parents and tutors are always telling their sons and their wards that they are to be just; [363] but why? not for the sake of justice, but for the sake of character and reputation; in the hope of obtaining for him who is reputed just some of those offices, marriages, and the like which Glaucon has enumerated among the advantages accruing to the unjust from the reputation of justice. More, however, is made of appearances by this class of persons than by the others; for they throw in the good opinion of the gods, and will tell you of a shower of benefits which the heavens, as they say, rain upon the pious; and this accords with the testimony of the noble Hesiod and Homer, the first of whom says, that the gods make the oaks of the just—

To bear acorns at their summit, and bees in the middle;
And the sheep are bowed down with the weight of their fleeces,

and many other blessings of a like kind are provided for them. And Homer has a very similar strain; for he speaks of one whose fame is—

As the fame of some blameless king who, like a god,
Maintains justice; to whom the black earth brings forth
Wheat and barley, whose trees are bowed with fruit,
And his sheep never fail to bear, and the sea gives him fish.

Still grander are the gifts of heaven which Musaeus and his son [1] vouchsafe to the just; they take them down into the world below, where they have the saints lying on couches at a feast, everlastingly drunk, crowned with garlands; their idea seems to be that an immortality of drunkenness is the highest meed of virtue. Some extend their rewards yet further; the posterity, as they say, of the faithful and just shall survive to the third and fourth generation. This is the style in which they praise justice. But about the wicked there is another strain; they bury them in a slough in Hades, and make them carry water in a sieve; also while they are yet living they bring them to infamy, and inflict upon them the punishments which Glaucon described as the portion of the just who are reputed to be unjust; nothing else does their invention supply. Such is their manner of praising the one and censuring the other.

Once more, Socrates, I will ask you to consider another way of speaking about justice and injustice, which is not confined to the poets, [364] but is found in prose writers. The universal voice of mankind is always declaring that justice and virtue are honourable, but grievous and toilsome; and that the pleasures of vice and injustice are easy of attainment, and are only censured by law and opinion. They say also that honesty is for the most part less profitable than dishonesty; and they are quite ready to call wicked men happy, and to honour them both in public and private when they are rich or in any other way influential, while they despise and overlook those who may be weak and poor, even though acknowledging them to be better than the others. But most extraordinary of all is their mode of speaking about virtue and the gods: they say that the gods apportion calamity and misery to many good men, and good and happiness to the wicked. And mendicant prophets go to rich

[1] Eumolpus.

men's doors and persuade them that they have a power committed to them by the gods of making an atonement for a man's own or his ancestor's sins by sacrifices or charms, with rejoicings and feasts; and they promise to harm an enemy, whether just or unjust, at a small cost; with magic arts and incantations binding heaven, as they say, to execute their will. And the poets are the authorities to whom they appeal, now smoothing the path of vice with the words of Hesiod:

Vice may be had in abundance without trouble;
the way is smooth and her dwelling-place is near.
But before virtue the gods have set toil,

and a tedious and uphill road: then citing Homer as a witness that the gods may be influenced by men; for he also says:—

The gods, too, may be turned from their purpose; and men pray to them and avert their wrath by sacrifices and soothing entreaties, and by libations and the odour of fat, when they have sinned and transgressed.

And they produce a host of books written by Musaeus and Orpheus, who were children of the Moon and the Muses—that is what they say—according to which they perform their ritual, and persuade not only individuals, but whole cities, that expiations and atonements for sin may be made by sacrifices and amusements which fill a vacant hour, and are equally at the service of the living and the dead; *[365]* the latter sort they call mysteries, and they redeem us from the pains of hell, but if we neglect them no one knows what awaits us.

He proceeded: And now when the young hear all this said about virtue and vice, and the way in which gods and men regard them, how are their minds likely to be affected, my dear Socrates—those of them, I mean, who are quick-witted, and, like bees on the wing, light on every flower, and from all that they hear are prone to draw conclusions as to what manner of persons they should be and in what way they should walk if they would make the best of life? Probably the youth will say to himself in the words of Pindar—

Can I by justice or by crooked ways of deceit
ascend a loftier tower which may be a fortress to
me all my days?

For what men say is that, if I am really just and am not also thought just, profit there is none, but the pain and loss on the other hand are unmistakeable. But if, though unjust, I acquire the reputation of justice, a heavenly life is promised to me. Since then, as philosophers prove, appearance tyrannizes over truth and is lord of happiness, to appearance I must devote myself. I will describe around me a picture and shadow of virtue to be the vestibule and exterior of my house; behind I will trail the subtle and crafty fox, as Archilochus, greatest of sages, recommends. But I hear some one exclaiming that the concealment of wickedness is often difficult; to which I answer, Nothing great is easy. Nevertheless, the argument indicates this, if we would be happy, to be the path along which we should proceed. With a view to concealment we will establish secret brotherhoods and political clubs. And there are professors of rhetoric who teach the art of persuading courts and assemblies; and so, partly by persuasion and partly by force, I shall make unlawful gains and not be punished. Still I hear a voice saying that the gods cannot be deceived, neither can they be compelled. But what if there are no gods? or, suppose them to have no care of human things—why in either case should we mind about concealment? And even if there are gods, and they do care about us, yet we know of them only from tradition and the genealogies of the poets; and these are the very persons who say that they may be influenced and turned by "sacrifices and soothing entreaties and by offerings." Let us be consistent then, and believe both or neither. If the poets speak truly, *[366]* why then we had better be unjust, and offer of the fruits of injustice; for if we are just, although we may escape the vengeance of heaven, we shall lose the gains of injustice; but, if we are unjust, we shall keep the gains, and by our sinning and praying, and praying and sinning, the gods will be propitiated, and we shall not be punished. "But there is a world below in which either we or our posterity will suffer for our unjust deeds." Yes, my friend, will be the reflection, but there are mysteries and atoning deities, and these have great power. That is what mighty cities declare; and the children of the gods, who were their poets and prophets, bear a like testimony.

On what principle, then, shall we any longer choose justice rather than the worst injustice? when, if we only unite the latter with a deceitful regard to appearances, we shall fare to our mind both with gods and men, in life and after death, as the most numerous and the highest authorities tell us. Knowing all this, Socrates, how can a man who has any superiority of mind or person or rank or wealth, be willing to honour justice; or indeed to refrain from laughing when he hears justice praised? And even if there should be some one who is able to disprove the truth of my words, and who is satisfied that justice is best, still he is not angry with the unjust, but is very ready to forgive them, because he also knows that men are not just of their own free will; unless, peradventure, there be some one whom the divinity within him may have inspired with a hatred of injustice, or who has attained knowledge of the truth—but no other man. He only blames injustice who, owing to cowardice or age or some weakness, has not the power of being unjust. And this is proved by the fact that when he obtains the power, he immediately becomes unjust as far as he can be.

The cause of all this, Socrates, was indicated by us at the beginning of the argument, when my brother and I told you how astonished we were to find that of all the professing panegyrists of justice—beginning with the ancient heroes of whom any memorial has been preserved to us, and ending with the men of our own time—no one has ever blamed injustice or praised justice except with a view to the glories, honours, and benefits which flow from them. No one has ever adequately described either in verse or prose the true essential nature of either of them abiding in the soul, and invisible to any human or divine eye; or shown that of all the things of a man's soul which he has within him, justice is the greatest good, [367] and injustice the greatest evil. Had this been the universal strain, had you sought to persuade us of this from our youth upwards, we should not have been on the watch to keep one another from doing wrong, but every one would have been his own watchman, because afraid, if he did wrong, of harbouring in himself the greatest of evils. I dare say that Thrasymachus and others would seriously hold the language which I have been merely repeating, and words even stronger than these about justice and injustice, grossly, as I conceive, perverting their true nature. But I speak in this vehement manner, as I must frankly confess to you, because I want to hear from you the opposite side; and I would ask you to show not only the superiority which justice has over injustice, but what effect they have on the possessor of them which makes the one to be a good and the other an evil to him. And please, as Glaucon requested of you, to exclude reputations; for unless you take away from each of them his true reputation and add on the false, we shall say that

you do not praise justice, but the appearance of it; we shall think that you are only exhorting us to keep injustice dark, and that you really agree with Thrasymachus in thinking that justice is another's good and the interest of the stronger, and that injustice is a man's own profit and interest, though injurious to the weaker. Now as you have admitted that justice is one of that highest class of goods which are desired indeed for their results, but in a far greater degree for their own sakes—like sight or hearing or knowledge or health, or any other real and natural and not merely conventional good—I would ask you in your praise of justice to regard one point only: I mean the essential good and evil which justice and injustice work in the possessors of them. Let others praise justice and censure injustice, magnifying the rewards and honours of the one and abusing the other; that is a manner of arguing which, coming from them, I am ready to tolerate, but from you who have spent your whole life in the consideration of this question, unless I hear the contrary from your own lips, I expect something better. And therefore, I say, not only prove to us that justice is better than injustice, but show what they either of them do to the possessor of them, which makes the one to be a good and the other an evil, whether seen or unseen by gods and men.

I had always admired the genius of Glaucon and Adeimantus, but on hearing these words I was quite delighted, and said: Sons of an illustrious father, [368] that was not a bad beginning of the Elegiac verses which the admirer of Glaucon made in honour of you after you had distinguished yourselves at the battle of Megara:

*Sons of Ariston, divine offspring of an illustrious
  hero.*

The epithet is very appropriate, for there is something truly divine in being able to argue as you have done for the superiority of injustice, and remaining unconvinced by your own arguments. And I do believe that you are not convinced—this I infer from your general character, for had I judged only from your speeches I should have mistrusted you. But now, the greater my confidence in you, the greater is my difficulty in knowing what to say. For I am in a strait between two; on the one hand I feel that I am unequal to the task; and my inability is brought home to me by the fact that you were not satisfied with the answer which I made to Thrasymachus, proving, as I thought, the superiority which justice has over injustice. And yet I cannot refuse to help, while breath and speech remain to me; I am afraid that there would be an impiety in being present when justice is evil spoken of and not lifting up a hand in her defence. And therefore I had best give such help as I can.

Glaucon and the rest entreated me by all means not to let the question drop, but to proceed in the investigation. They wanted to arrive at the truth, first, about the nature of justice and injustice, and secondly, about their relative advantages. I told them, what I really thought, that the enquiry would be of a serious nature, and would require very good eyes. Seeing then, I said, that we are no great wits, I think that we had better adopt a method which I may illustrate thus; suppose that a short-sighted person had been asked by some one to read small letters from a distance; and it occurred to some one else that they might be found in another place which was larger and in which the letters were larger—if they were the same and he could read the larger letters first, and then proceed to the lesser—this would have been thought a rare piece of good fortune.

Very true, said Adeimantus; but how does the illustration apply to our enquiry?

I will tell you, I replied; justice, which is the subject of our enquiry, is, as you know, sometimes spoken of as the virtue of an individual, and sometimes as the virtue of a State.

True, he replied.

And is not a State larger than an individual? It is.

Then in the larger the quantity of justice is likely to be larger and more easily discernible. I propose therefore that we enquire into the nature of justice and injustice, first as they appear in the State, *[369]* and secondly in the individual, proceeding from the greater to the lesser and comparing them.

That, he said, is an excellent proposal.

And if we imagine the State in process of creation, we shall see the justice and injustice of the State in process of creation also.

I dare say.

When the State is completed there may be a hope that the object of our search will be more easily discovered.

Yes, far more easily.

But ought we to attempt to construct one? I said; for to do so, as I am inclined to think, will be a very serious task. Reflect therefore.

I have reflected, said Adeimantus, and am anxious that you should proceed.

A State, I said, arises, as I conceive, out of the needs of mankind; no one is self-sufficing, but all of us have many wants. Can any other origin of a State be imagined?

There can be no other.

Then, as we have many wants, and many persons are needed to supply them, one takes a helper for one purpose and another for another; and when these partners and helpers are gathered together in one habitation the body of inhabitants is termed a State.

True, he said.

And they exchange with one another, and one gives, and another receives, under the idea that the exchange will be for their good.

Very true.

Then, I said, let us begin and create in idea a State; and yet the true creator is necessity, who is the mother of our invention.

Of course, he replied.

Now the first and greatest of necessities is food, which is the condition of life and existence.

Certainly.

The second is a dwelling, and the third clothing and the like.

True.

And now let us see how our city will be able to supply this great demand: We may suppose that one man is a husbandman, another a builder, some one else a weaver—shall we add to them a shoemaker, or perhaps some other purveyor to our bodily wants?

Quite right.

The barest notion of a State must include four or five men.

Clearly.

And how will they proceed? Will each bring the result of his labours into a common stock? —the individual husbandman, for example, producing for four, and labouring four times as long and as much as he need in the provision of food with which he supplies others as well as himself; or will he have nothing to do with others and not be at the trouble of producing for them, but provide for himself alone a fourth of the food in a fourth of the time, *[370]* and in the remaining three-fourths of his time be employed in making a house or a coat or a pair of shoes, having no partnership with others, but supplying himself all his own wants?

Adeimantus thought that he should aim at producing food only and not at producing everything.

Probably, I replied, that would be the better

way; and when I hear you say this, I am myself reminded that we are not all alike; there are diversities of natures among us which are adapted to different occupations.

Very true.

And will you have a work better done when the workman has many occupations, or when he has only one?

When he has only one?

Further, there can be no doubt that a work is spoilt when not done at the right time?

No doubt.

For business is not disposed to wait until the doer of the business is at leisure; but the doer must follow up what he is doing, and make the business his first object.

He must.

And if so, we must infer that all things are produced more plentifully and easily and of a better quality when one man does one thing which is natural to him and does it at the right time, and leaves other things.

Undoubtedly.

Then more than four citizens will be required; for the husbandman will not make his own plough or mattock, or other implements of agriculture, if they are to be good for anything. Neither will the builder make his tools—and he too needs many; and in like manner the weaver and shoemaker.

True.

Then carpenters, and smiths, and many other artisans, will be sharers in our little State, which is already beginning to grow?

True.

Yet even if we add neatherds, shepherds, and other herdsmen, in order that our husbandmen may have oxen to plough with, and builders as well as husbandmen may have draught cattle, and curriers and weavers fleeces and hides— still our State will not be very large.

That is true; yet neither will it be a very small State which contains all these.

Then, again, there is the situation of the city—to find a place where nothing need be imported is wellnigh impossible.

Impossible.

Then there must be another class of citizens who will bring the required supply from an-other city?

There must.

[371] But if the trader goes empty-handed, having nothing which they require who would supply his need, he will come back empty-handed.

That is certain.

And therefore what they produce at home must be not only enough for themselves, but such both in quantity and quality as to accommodate those from whom their wants are supplied.

Very true.

Then more husbandmen and more artisans will be required?

They will.

Not to mention the importers and exporters, who are called merchants?

Yes.

Then we shall want merchants?

We shall.

And if merchandise is to be carried over the sea, skilful sailors will also be needed, and in considerable numbers?

Yes, in considerable numbers.

Then, again, within the city, how will they exchange their productions? To secure such an exchange was, as you will remember, one of our principal objects when we formed them into a society and constituted a State.

Clearly they will buy and sell.

Then they will need a market-place, and a money-token for purposes of exchange.

Certainly.

Suppose now that a husbandman, or an artisan, brings some production to market, and he comes at a time when there is no one to exchange with him—is he to leave his calling and sit idle in the market-place?

Not at all; he will find people there who, seeing the want, undertake the office of salesmen. In well-ordered states they are commonly those who are the weakest in bodily strength, and therefore of little use for any other purpose; their duty is to be in the market, and to give money in exchange for goods to those who desire to sell and to take money from those who desire to buy.

This want, then, creates a class of retail-traders in our State. Is not "retailer" the term which is applied to those who sit in the market-place engaged in buying and selling, while those who wander from one city to another are called merchants?

Yes, he said.

And there is another class of servants, who are intellectually hardly on the level of companionship; still they have plenty of bodily strength for labour, which accordingly they sell, and are called, if I do not mistake, hire-lings, hire being the name which is given to the price of their labour.

True.

Then hirelings will help to make up our population?

Yes.

And now, Adeimantus, is our State matured and perfected?

I think so.

Where, then, is justice, and where is injustice, and in what part of the State did they spring up?

[372] Probably in the dealings of these citizens with one another. I cannot imagine that they are more likely to be found any where else.

I dare say that you are right in your suggestion, I said; we had better think the matter out, and not shrink from the enquiry.

Let us then consider, first of all, what will be their way of life, now that we have thus established them. Will they not produce corn, and wine, and clothes, and shoes, and build houses for themselves? And when they are housed, they will work, in summer, commonly, stripped and barefoot, but in winter substantially clothed and shod. They will feed on barley-meal and flour of wheat, baking and kneading them, making noble cakes and loaves; these they will serve up on a mat of reeds or on clean leaves, themselves reclining the while upon beds strewn with yew or myrtle. And they and their children will feast, drinking of the wine which they have made, wearing garlands on their heads, and hymning the praises of the gods, in happy converse with one another. And they will take care that their families do not exceed their means; having an eye to poverty or war.

But, said Glaucon, interposing, you have not given them a relish to their meal.

True, I replied, I had forgotten; of course they must have a relish—salt, and olives, and cheese, and they will boil roots and herbs such as country people prepare; for a dessert we shall give them figs, and peas, and beans; and they will roast myrtle-berries and acorns at the fire, drinking in moderation. And with such a diet they may be expected to live in peace and health to a good old age, and bequeath a similar life to their children after them.

Yes, Socrates, he said, and if you were providing for a city of pigs, how else would you feed the beasts?

But what would you have, Glaucon? I replied.

Why, he said, you should give them the ordinary conveniences of life. People who are to be comfortable are accustomed to lie on sofas, and dine off tables, and they should have sauces and sweets in the modern style.

Yes, I said, now I understand: the question which you would have me consider is, not only how a State, but how a luxurious State is created; and possibly there is no harm in this, for in such a State we shall be more likely to see how justice and injustice originate. In my opinion the true and healthy constitution of the State is the one which I have described. But if you wish also to see a State at fever-heat, I have no objection. For I suspect that many will not be satisfied with the simpler way of life. [373] They will be for adding sofas, and tables, and other furniture; also dainties, and perfumes, and incense, and courtesans, and cakes, all these not of one sort only, but in every variety; we must go beyond the necessaries of which I was at first speaking, such as houses, and clothes, and shoes: the arts of the painter and the embroiderer will have to be set in motion, and gold and ivory and all sorts of materials must be procured.

True, he said.

Then we must enlarge our borders; for the original healthy State is no longer sufficient. Now will the city have to fill and swell with a multitude of callings which are not required by any natural want; such as the whole tribe of hunters and actors, of whom one large class have to do with forms and colours; another will be the votaries of music—poets and their attendant train of rhapsodists, players, dancers, contractors; also makers of divers kinds of articles, including women's dresses. And we shall want more servants. Will not tutors be also in request, and nurses wet and dry, tire-women and barbers, as well as confectioners and cooks; and swineherds, too, who were not needed and therefore had no place in the former edition of our State, but are needed now? They must not be forgotten: and there will be animals of many other kinds, if people eat them.

Certainly.

And living in this way we shall have much greater need of physicians than before?

Much greater.

And the country which was enough to support the original inhabitants will be too small now, and not enough?

Quite true.

Then a slice of our neighbours' land will be wanted by us for pasture and tillage, and they will want a slice of ours, if, like ourselves, they exceed the limit of necessity, and give themselves up to the unlimited accumulation of wealth?

That, Socrates, will be inevitable.

And so we shall go to war, Glaucon. Shall we not?

Most certainly, he replied.

Then, without determining as yet whether war does good or harm, thus much we may affirm, that now we have discovered war to be derived from causes which are also the causes of almost all the evils in States, private as well as public.

Undoubtedly.

And our State must once more enlarge; and this time the enlargement will be nothing short of a whole army, *[374]* which will have to go out and fight with the invaders for all that we have, as well as for the things and persons whom we were describing above.

Why? he said; are they not capable of defending themselves?

No, I said; not if we were right in the principle which was acknowledged by all of us when we were framing the State: the principle, as you will remember, was that one man cannot practise many arts with success.

Very true, he said.

But is not war an art?

Certainly.

And an art requiring as much attention as shoemaking?

Quite true.

And the shoemaker was not allowed by us to be a husbandman, or a weaver, or a builder —in order that we might have our shoes well made; but to him and to every other worker was assigned one work for which he was by nature fitted, and at that he was to continue working all his life long and at no other; he was not to let opportunities slip, and then he would become a good workman. Now nothing can be more important than that the work of a soldier should be well done. But is war an art so easily acquired that a man may be a warrior who is also a husbandman, or shoemaker, or other artisan; although no one in the world would be a good dice or draught player who merely took up the game as a recreation, and had not from his earliest years devoted himself to this and nothing else? No tools will make a man a skilled workman, or master of defence, nor be of any use to him who has not learned how to handle them, and has never bestowed any attention upon them. How then will he who takes up a shield or other implement of war become a good fighter all in a day,

whether with heavy-armed or any other kind of troops?

Yes, he said, the tools which would teach men their own use would be beyond price.

And the higher the duties of the guardian, I said, the more time, and skill, and art, and application will be needed by him?

No doubt, he replied.

Will he not also require natural aptitude for his calling?

Certainly.

Then it will be our duty to select, if we can, natures which are fitted for the task of guarding the city?

It will.

And the selection will be no easy matter, I said; but we must be brave and do our best.

We must.

[375] Is not the noble youth very like a well-bred dog in respect of guarding and watching?

What do you mean?

I mean that both of them ought to be quick to see, and swift to overtake the enemy when they see him; and strong too if, when they have caught him, they have to fight with him.

All these qualities, he replied, will certainly be required by them.

Well, and your guardian must be brave if he is to fight well?

Certainly.

And is he likely to be brave who has no spirit, whether horse or dog or any other animal? Have you never observed how invincible and unconquerable is spirit and how the presence of it makes the soul of any creature to be absolutely fearless and indomitable?

I have.

Then now we have a clear notion of the bodily qualities which are required in the guardian.

True.

And also of the mental ones; his soul is to be full of spirit?

Yes.

But are not these spirited natures apt to be savage with one another, and with everybody else?

A difficulty by no means easy to overcome, he replied.

Whereas, I said, they ought to be dangerous to their enemies, and gentle to their friends; if not, they will destroy themselves without waiting for their enemies to destroy them.

True, he said.

What is to be done then? I said; how shall we find a gentle nature which has also a great spirit, for the one is the contradiction of the other?

True.

He will not be a good guardian who is wanting in either of these two qualities; and yet the combination of them appears to be impossible; and hence we must infer that to be a good guardian is impossible.

I am afraid that what you say is true, he replied.

Here feeling perplexed I began to think over what had preceded—My friend, I said, no wonder that we are in a perplexity; for we have lost sight of the image which we had before us.

What do you mean? he said.

I mean to say that there do exist natures gifted with those opposite qualities.

And where do you find them?

Many animals, I replied, furnish examples of them; our friend the dog is a very good one: you know that well-bred dogs are perfectly gentle to their familiars and acquaintances, and the reverse to strangers.

Yes, I know.

Then there is nothing impossible or out of the order of nature in our finding a guardian who has a similar combination of qualities?

Certainly not.

Would not he who is fitted to be a guardian, besides the spirited nature, need to have the qualities of a philosopher?

I do not apprehend your meaning.

[376] The trait of which I am speaking, I replied, may be also seen in the dog, and is remarkable in the animal.

What trait?

Why, a dog, whenever he sees a stranger, is angry; when an acquaintance, he welcomes him, although the one has never done him any harm, nor the other any good. Did this never strike you as curious?

The matter never struck me before; but I quite recognise the truth of your remark.

And surely this instinct of the dog is very charming—your dog is a true philosopher.

Why?

Why, because he distinguishes the face of a friend and of an enemy only by the criterion of knowing and not knowing. And must not an animal be a lover of learning who determines what he likes and dislikes by the test of knowledge and ignorance?

Most assuredly.

And is not the love of learning the love of wisdom, which is philosophy?

They are the same, he replied.

And may we not say confidently of man also, that he who is likely to be gentle to his friends and acquaintances, must by nature be a lover of wisdom and knowledge?

That we may safely affirm.

Then he who is to be a really good and noble guardian of the State will require to unite in himself philosophy and spirit and swiftness and strength?

Undoubtedly.

Then we have found the desired natures; and now that we have found them, how are they to be reared and educated? Is not this an enquiry which may be expected to throw light on the greater enquiry which is our final end—How do justice and injustice grow up in States? for we do not want either to omit what is to the point or to draw out the argument to an inconvenient length.

Adeimantus thought that the enquiry would be of great service to us.

Then, I said, my dear friend, the task must not be given up, even if somewhat long.

Certainly not.

Come then, and let us pass a leisure hour in story-telling, and our story shall be the education of our heroes.

By all means.

And what shall be their education? Can we find a better than the traditional sort?—and this has two divisions, gymnastic for the body, and music for the soul.

True.

Shall we begin education with music, and go on to gymnastic afterwards?

By all means.

And when you speak of music, do you include literature or not?

I do.

And literature may be either true or false?

Yes.

[377] And the young should be trained in both kinds, and we begin with the false?

I do not understand your meaning, he said.

You know, I said, that we begin by telling children stories which, though not wholly destitute of truth, are in the main fictitious; and these stories are told them when they are not of an age to learn gymnastics.

Very true.

That was my meaning when I said that we must teach music before gymnastics.

Quite right, he said.

You know also that the beginning is the most important part of any work, especially in the case of a young and tender thing; for that is the time at which the character is being formed and the desired impression is more readily taken.

Quite true.

And shall we just carelessly allow children to hear any casual tales which may be devised by casual persons, and to receive into their minds ideas for the most part the very opposite of those which we should wish them to have when they are grown up?

We cannot.

Then the first thing will be to establish a censorship of the writers of fiction, and let the censors receive any tale of fiction which is good, and reject the bad; and we will desire mothers and nurses to tell their children the authorised ones only. Let them fashion the mind with such tales, even more fondly than they mould the body with their hands; but most of those which are now in use must be discarded.

Of what tales are you speaking? he said.

You may find a model of the lesser in the greater, I said; for they are necessarily of the same type, and there is the same spirit in both of them.

Very likely, he replied; but I do not as yet know what you would term the greater.

Those, I said, which are narrated by Homer and Hesiod, and the rest of the poets, who have ever been the great story-tellers of mankind.

But which stories do you mean, he said; and what fault do you find with them?

A fault which is most serious, I said; the fault of telling a lie, and, what is more, a bad lie.

But when is this fault committed?

Whenever an erroneous representation is made of the nature of gods and heroes—as when a painter paints a portrait not having the shadow of a likeness to the original.

Yes, he said, that sort of thing is certainly very blameable; but what are the stories which you mean?

First of all, I said, there was that greatest of all lies, in high places, which the poet told about Uranus, and which was a bad lie too *[378]*—I mean what Hesiod says that Uranus did, and how Cronus retaliated on him. The doings of Cronus, and the sufferings which in turn his son inflicted upon him, even if they were true, ought certainly not to be lightly told to young and thoughtless persons; if possible, they had better be buried in silence. But if there is an absolute necessity for their mention, a chosen few might hear them in a mystery, and they should sacrifice not a common [Eleusinian] pig, but some huge and unprocurable victim; and then the number of the hearers will be very few indeed.

Why, yes, said he, those stories are extremely objectionable.

Yes, Adeimantus, they are stories not to be repeated in our State; the young man should not be told that in committing the worst of crimes he is far from doing anything outrageous; and that even if he chastises his father when he does wrong, in whatever manner, he will only be following the example of the first and greatest among the gods.

I entirely agree with you, he said; in my opinion those stories are quite unfit to be repeated.

Neither, if we mean our future guardians to regard the habit of quarrelling among themselves as of all things the basest, should any word be said to them of the wars in heaven, and of the plots and fightings of the gods against one another, for they are not true. No, we shall never mention the battles of the giants, or let them be embroidered on garments; and we shall be silent about the innumerable other quarrels of gods and heroes with their friends and relatives. If they would only believe us we would tell them that quarrelling is unholy, and that never up to this time has there been any quarrel between citizens; this is what old men and old women should begin by telling children; and when they grow up, the poets also should be told to compose for them in a similar spirit. But the narrative of Hephaestus binding Herè his mother, or how on another occasion Zeus sent him flying for taking her part when she was being beaten, and all the battles of the gods in Homer—these tales must not be admitted into our State, whether they are supposed to have an allegorical meaning or not. For a young person cannot judge what is allegorical and what is literal; anything that he receives into his mind at that age is likely to become indelible and unalterable; and therefore it is most important that the tales which the young first hear should be models of virtuous thoughts.

There you are right, he replied; but if any one asks where are such models to be found and of what tales are you speaking—how shall we answer him?

[379] I said to him, You and I, Adeimantus, at this moment are not poets, but founders of a State: now the founders of a State ought to know the general forms in which poets should cast their tales, and the limits which must be

observed by them, but to make the tales is not their business.

Very true, he said; but what are these forms of theology which you mean?

Something of this kind, I replied:—God is always to be represented as he truly is, whatever be the sort of poetry, epic, lyric or tragic, in which the representation is given.

Right.

And is he not truly good? and must he not be represented as such?

Certainly.

And no good thing is hurtful?

No, indeed.

And that which is not hurtful hurts not?

Certainly not.

And that which hurts not does no evil?

No.

And can that which does no evil be a cause of evil?

Impossible.

And the good is advantageous?

Yes.

And therefore the cause of well-being?

Yes.

It follows therefore that the good is not the cause of all things, but of the good only?

Assuredly.

Then God, if he be good, is not the author of all things, as the many assert, but he is the cause of a few things only, and not of most things that occur to men. For few are the goods of human life, and many are the evils, and the good is to be attributed to God alone; of the evils the causes are to be sought elsewhere, and not in him.

That appears to me to be most true, he said.

Then we must not listen to Homer or to any other poet who is guilty of the folly of saying that two casks

Lie at the threshold of Zeus, full of lots, one of good, the other of evil lots,

and that he to whom Zeus gives a mixture of the two

Sometimes meets with evil fortune, at other times with good;

but that he to whom is given the cup of unmingled ill,

Him wild hunger drives o'er the beauteous earth.

And again—

Zeus, who is the dispenser of good and evil to us.

And if any one asserts that the violation of oaths and treaties, which was really the work of Pandarus, was brought about by Athene and Zeus, or that the strife and contention of the gods was instigated by Themis and Zeus, he shall not have our approval; neither will we allow our young men to hear the words of Aeschylus, that [380]

God plants guilt among men when he desires utterly to destroy a house.

And if a poet writes of the sufferings of Niobe —the subject of the tragedy in which these iambic verses occur—or of the house of Pelops, or of the Trojan War or on any similar theme, either we must not permit him to say that these are the works of God, or if they are of God, he must devise some explanation of them such as we are seeking; he must say that God did what was just and right, and they were the better for being punished; but that those who are punished are miserable, and that God is the author of their misery—the poet is not to be permitted to say; though he may say that the wicked are miserable because they require to be punished, and are benefited by receiving punishment from God; but that God being good is the author of evil to any one is to be strenuously denied, and not to be said or sung or heard in verse or prose by any one whether old or young in any well-ordered commonwealth. Such a fiction is suicidal, ruinous, impious.

I agree with you, he replied, and am ready to give my assent to the law.

Let this then be one of our rules and principles concerning the gods, to which our poets and reciters will be expected to conform—that God is not the author of all things, but of good only.

That will do, he said.

And what do you think of a second principle? Shall I ask you whether God is a magician, and of a nature to appear insidiously now in one shape, and now in another—sometimes himself changing and passing into many forms, sometimes deceiving us with the semblance of such transformations; or is he one and the same immutably fixed in his own proper image?

I cannot answer you, he said, without more thought.

Well, I said; but if we suppose a change in anything, that change must be effected either by the thing itself, or by some other thing?

Most certainly.

And things which are at their best are also least liable to be altered or discomposed; for example, when healthiest and strongest, the human frame is least liable to be affected by meats and drinks, and the plant which is in the fullest vigour also suffers least from winds or the heat of the sun or any similar causes.

Of course.

[381] And will not the bravest and wisest soul be least confused or deranged by any external influence?

True.

And the same principle, as I should suppose, applies to all composite things—furniture, houses, garments: when good and well made, they are least altered by time and circumstances.

Very true.

Then everything which is good, whether made by art or nature, or both, is least liable to suffer change from without?

True.

But surely God and the things of God are in every way perfect?

Of course they are.

Then he can hardly be compelled by external influence to take many shapes?

He cannot.

But may he not change and transform himself?

Clearly, he said, that must be the case if he is changed at all.

And will he then change himself for the better and fairer, or for the worse and more unsightly?

If he change at all he can only change for the worse, for we cannot suppose him to be deficient either in virtue or beauty.

Very true, Adeimantus; but then, would any one, whether God or man, desire to make himself worse?

Impossible.

Then it is impossible that God should ever be willing to change; being, as is supposed, the fairest and best that is conceivable, every God remains absolutely and for ever in his own form.

That necessarily follows, he said, in my judgment.

Then, I said, my dear friend, let none of the poets tell us that

The gods, taking the disguise of strangers from other lands, walk up and down cities in all sorts of forms,

and let no one slander Proteus and Thetis, neither let any one, either in tragedy or in any other kind of poetry, introduce Herè disguised in the likeness of a priestess asking an alms

For the life-giving daughters of Inachus the river of Argos;

—let us have no more lies of that sort. Neither must we have mothers under the influence of the poets scaring their children with a bad version of these myths—telling how certain gods, as they say, "Go about by night in the likeness of so many strangers and in divers forms"; but let them take heed lest they make cowards of their children, and at the same time speak blasphemy against the gods.

Heaven forbid, he said.

But although the gods are themselves unchangeable, still by witchcraft and deception they may make us think that they appear in various forms?

Perhaps, he replied.

Well, but can you imagine that God will be willing to lie, whether in word or deed, or to put forth a phantom of himself?

[382] I cannot say, he replied.

Do you not know, I said, that the true lie, if such an expression may be allowed, is hated of gods and men?

What do you mean? he said.

I mean that no one is willingly deceived in that which is the truest and highest part of himself, or about the truest and highest matters; there, above all, he is most afraid of a lie having possession of him.

Still, he said, I do not comprehend you.

The reason is, I replied, that you attribute some profound meaning to my words; but I am only saying that deception, or being deceived or uninformed about the highest realities in the highest part of themselves, which is the soul, and in that part of them to have and to hold the lie, is what mankind least like—that, I say, is what they utterly detest.

There is nothing more hateful to them.

And, as I was just now remarking, this ignorance in the soul of him who is deceived may be called the true lie; for the lie in words is only a kind of imitation and shadowy image of a previous affection of the soul, not pure unadulterated falsehood. Am I not right?

Perfectly right.

The true lie is hated not only by the gods, but also by men?

Yes.

Whereas the lie in words is in certain cases useful and not hateful; in dealing with enemies—that would be an instance; or again, when those whom we call our friends in a fit of madness or illusion are going to do some harm, then it is useful and is a sort of medicine or preventive; also in the tales of mythology, of which we were just now speaking—because we do not know the truth about ancient times, we make falsehood as much like truth as we can, and so turn it to account.

Very true, he said.

But can any of these reasons apply to God? Can we suppose that he is ignorant of antiquity, and therefore has recourse to invention?

That would be ridiculous, he said.

Then the lying poet has no place in our idea of God?

I should say not.

Or perhaps he may tell a lie because he is afraid of enemies?

That is inconceivable.

But he may have friends who are senseless or mad?

But no mad or senseless person can be a friend of God.

Then no motive can be imagined why God should lie?

None whatever.

Then the superhuman and divine is absolutely incapable of falsehood?

Yes.

Then is God perfectly simple and true both in word and deed; he changes not; he deceives not, either by sign or word, by dream or waking vision.

[383] Your thoughts, he said, are the reflection of my own.

You agree with me then, I said, that this is the second type or form in which we should write and speak about divine things. The gods are not magicians who transform themselves, neither do they deceive mankind in any way.

I grant that.

Then, although we are admirers of Homer, we do not admire the lying dream which Zeus sends to Agamemnon; neither will we praise the verses of Aeschylus in which Thetis says that Apollo at her nuptials

Was celebrating in song her fair progeny whose days were to be long, and to know no sickness. And when he had spoken of my lot as in all things blessed of heaven he raised a note of triumph and cheered my soul. And I thought that the word of Phoebus, being divine and full of prophecy, would not fail. And now he himself who uttered the strain, he who was present at the banquet, and who said this—he it is who has slain my son.

These are the kind of sentiments about the gods which will arouse our anger; and he who utters them shall be refused a chorus; neither shall we allow teachers to make use of them in the instruction of the young, meaning, as we do, that our guardians, as far as men can be,

should be true worshippers of the gods and like them.

I entirely agree, he said, in these principles, and promise to make them my laws.

BOOK III

[386] Such then, I said, are our principles of theology—some tales are to be told, and others are not to be told to our disciples from their youth upwards, if we mean them to honour the gods and their parents, and to value friendship with one another.

Yes; and I think that our principles are right, he said.

But if they are to be courageous, must they not learn other lessons besides these, and lessons of such a kind as will take away the fear of death? Can any man be courageous who has the fear of death in him?

Certainly not, he said.

And can he be fearless of death, or will he choose death in battle rather than defeat and slavery, who believes the world below to be real and terrible?

Impossible.

Then we must assume a control over the narrators of this class of tales as well as over the others, and beg them not simply to revile, but rather to commend the world below, intimating to them that their descriptions are untrue, and will do harm to our future warriors.

That will be our duty, he said.

Then, I said, we shall have to obliterate many obnoxious passages, beginning with the verses,

I would rather be a serf on the land of a poor and portionless man than rule over all the dead who have come to nought.[1]

We must also expunge the verse, which tells us how Pluto feared,

Lest the mansions grim and squalid which the gods abhor should be seen both of mortals and immortals.[2]

And again:

O heavens! verily in the house of Hades there is soul and ghostly form but no mind at all![3]

Again of Tiresias:

[To him even after death did Persephone grant mind,] that he alone should be wise; but the other souls are flitting shades.[4]

[1] *Odyssey,* ix. 489.
[2] *Iliad,* xx. 64.
[3] *Iliad,* xxiii. 103.
[4] *Odyssey,* x. 495.

Again:

The soul flying from the limbs had gone to Hades, lamenting her fate, leaving manhood and youth.[1]

Again:

[387] And the soul, with shrilling cry, passed like smoke beneath the earth.[2]

And—

As bats in hollow of mystic cavern, whenever any of them has dropped out of the string and falls from the rock, fly shrilling and cling to one another, so did they with shrilling cry hold together as they moved.[3]

And we must beg Homer and the other poets not to be angry if we strike out these and similar passages, not because they are unpoetical, or unattractive to the popular ear, but because the greater the poetical charm of them, the less are they meet for the ears of boys and men who are meant to be free, and who should fear slavery more than death.

Undoubtedly.

Also we shall have to reject all the terrible and appalling names which describe the world below—Cocytus and Styx, ghosts under the earth, and sapless shades, and any similar words of which the very mention causes a shudder to pass through the inmost soul of him who hears them. I do not say that these horrible stories may not have a use of some kind; but there is a danger that the nerves of our guardians may be rendered too excitable and effeminate by them.

There is a real danger, he said.

Then we must have no more of them.

True.

Another and a nobler strain must be composed and sung by us.

Clearly.

And shall we proceed to get rid of the weepings and wailings of famous men?

They will go with the rest.

But shall we be right in getting rid of them? Reflect: our principle is that the good man will not consider death terrible to any other good man who is his comrade.

Yes; that is our principle.

And therefore he will not sorrow for his departed friend as though he had suffered anything terrible?

He will not.

Such an one, as we further maintain, is suffi-

cient for himself and his own happiness, and therefore is least in need of other men.

True, he said.

And for this reason the loss of a son or brother, or the deprivation of fortune, is to him of all men least terrible.

Assuredly.

And therefore he will be least likely to lament, and will bear with the greatest equanimity any misfortune of this sort which may befall him.

Yes, he will feel such a misfortune far less than another.

Then we shall be right in getting rid of the lamentations of famous men, and making them over to women (and not even to women who are good for anything), *[388]* or to men of a baser sort, that those who are being educated by us to be the defenders of their country may scorn to do the like.

That will be very right.

Then we will once more entreat Homer and the other poets not to depict Achilles,[4] who is the son of a goddess, first lying on his side, then on his back, and then on his face; then starting up and sailing in a frenzy along the shores of the barren sea; now taking the sooty ashes in both his hands[5] and pouring them over his head, or weeping and wailing in the various modes which Homer has delineated. Nor should he describe Priam the kinsman of the gods as praying and beseeching,

Rolling in the dirt, calling each man loudly by his name.[6]

Still more earnestly will we beg of him at all events not to introduce the gods lamenting and saying,

Alas! my misery! Alas! that I bore the bravest to my sorrow.[7]

But if he must introduce the gods, at any rate let him not dare so completely to misrepresent the greatest of the gods, as to make him say—

O heavens! with my eyes verily I behold a dear friend of mine chased round and round the city, and my heart is sorrowful.[8]

Or again:

Woe is me that I am fated to have Sarpedon,

[1] *Iliad*, xvi. 856.
[2] *Ibid*, xxiii. 100.
[3] *Odyssey*, xxiv. 6.
[4] *Iliad*, xxiv. 10.
[5] *Ibid*, xviii. 23.
[6] *Ibid*, xxii. 414.
[7] *Ibid*, xviii. 54.
[8] *Ibid*, xxii. 168.

*dearest of men to me, subdued at the hands of Pa-
troclus the son of Menoetius.*[1]

For if, my sweet Adeimantus, our youth seriously listen to such unworthy representations
of the gods, instead of laughing at them as they
ought, hardly will any of them deem that he
himself, being but a man, can be dishonoured
by similar actions; neither will he rebuke any
inclination which may arise in his mind to say
and do the like. And instead of having any
shame or self-control, he will be always whin-
ing and lamenting on slight occasions.

Yes, he said, that is most true.

Yes, I replied; but that surely is what ought
not to be, as the argument has just proved to
us; and by that proof we must abide until it is
disproved by a better.

It ought not to be.

Neither ought our guardians to be given to
laughter. For a fit of laughter which has been
indulged to excess almost always produces a
violent reaction.

So I believe.

Then persons of worth, even if only mortal
men, must not be represented as overcome by
laughter, and still less must such a representation of the gods be allowed.

[389] Still less of the gods, as you say, he
replied.

Then we shall not suffer such an expression
to be used about the gods as that of Homer
when he describes how

*Inextinguishable laughter arose among the bless-
ed gods, when they saw Hephaestus bustling about
the mansion.*[2]

On your views, we must not admit them.

On my views, if you like to father them on
me; that we must not admit them is certain.

Again, truth should be highly valued; if, as
we were saying, a lie is useless to the gods, and
useful only as a medicine to men, then the use
of such medicines should be restricted to physicians; private individuals have no business with
them.

Clearly not, he said.

Then if any one at all is to have the privilege
of lying, the rulers of the State should be the
persons; and they, in their dealings either with
enemies or with their own citizens, may be allowed to lie for the public good. But nobody
else should meddle with anything of the kind;
and although the rulers have this privilege, for
a private man to lie to them in return is to be
deemed a more heinous fault than for the

patient or the pupil of a gymnasium not to
speak the truth about his own bodily illnesses
to the physician or to the trainer, or for a sailor
not to tell the captain what is happening about
the ship and the rest of the crew, and how
things are going with himself or his fellow
sailors.

Most true, he said.

If, then, the ruler catches anybody beside
himself lying in the State,

*Any of the craftsmen, whether he be priest or phy-
sician or carpenter,*[3]

he will punish him for introducing a practice
which is equally subversive and destructive of
ship or State.

Most certainly, he said, if our idea of the
State is ever carried out.

In the next place our youth must be temperate?

Certainly.

Are not the chief elements of temperance,
speaking generally, obedience to commanders
and self-control in sensual pleasures?

True.

Then we shall approve such language as that
of Diomede in Homer,

Friend, sit still and obey my word,[4]

and the verses which follow,

The Greeks marched breathing prowess,[5]
. . . . in silent awe of their leaders,[6]

and other sentiments of the same kind.

We shall.

What of this line,

*O heavy with wine, who hast the eyes of a dog and
the heart of a stag,*[7]

and of the words which follow? [390] Would
you say that these, or any similar impertinences
which private individuals are supposed to address to their rulers, whether in verse or prose,
are well or ill spoken?

They are ill spoken.

They may very possibly afford some amusement, but they do not conduce to temperance.
And therefore they are likely to do harm to
our young men—you would agree with me
there?

Yes.

[1] *Ibid*, xvi. 433.
[2] *Ibid*, i. 599.
[3] *Odyssey*, xvii. 383 ff.
[4] *Iliad*, iv. 412.
[5] *Odyssey*, iii. 8.
[6] *Ibid*, iv. 431.
[7] *Ibid*, i. 225.

And then, again, to make the wisest of men say that nothing in his opinion is more glorious than

When the tables are full of bread and meat, and the cup-bearer carries round wine which he draws from the bowl and pours into the cups; [1]

is it fit or conducive to temperance for a young man to hear such words? Or the verse

The saddest of fates is to die and meet destiny from hunger? [2]

What would you say again to the tale of Zeus, who, while other gods and men were asleep and he the only person awake, lay devising plans, but forgot them all in a moment through his lust, and was so completely overcome at the sight of Herè that he would not even go into the hut, but wanted to lie with her on the ground, declaring that he had never been in such a state of rapture before, even when they first met one another

Without the knowledge of their parents; [3]

or that other tale of how Hephaestus, because of similar goings on, cast a chain around Ares and Aphrodite? [4]

Indeed, he said, I am strongly of opinion that they ought not to hear that sort of thing.

But any deeds of endurance which are done or told by famous men, these they ought to see and hear; as, for example, what is said in the verses,

He smote his breast, and thus reproached his heart, Endure, my heart; far worse hast thou endured! [5]

Certainly, he said.

In the next place, we must not let them be receivers of gifts or lovers of money.

Certainly not.

Neither must we sing to them of

Gifts persuading gods, and persuading reverend kings.

Neither is Phoenix, the tutor of Achilles, to be approved or deemed to have given his pupil good counsel when he told him that he should take the gifts of the Greeks and assist them; [6] but that without a gift he should not lay aside his anger. Neither will we believe or acknowl-

edge Achilles himself to have been such a lover of money that he took Agamemnon's gifts, or that when he had received payment he restored the dead body of Hector, but that without payment he was unwilling to do so. [7]

[*391*] Undoubtedly, he said, these are not sentiments which can be approved.

Loving Homer as I do, [8] I hardly like to say that in attributing these feelings to Achilles, or in believing that they are truly attributed to him, he is guilty of downright impiety. As little can I believe the narrative of his insolence to Apollo, where he says,

Thou hast wronged me, O far-darter, most abominable of deities. Verily I would be even with thee, if I had only the power; [9]

or his insubordination to the river-god, [10] on whose divinity he is ready to lay hands; or his offering to the dead Patroclus of his own hair, [11] which had been previously dedicated to the other river-god Spercheius, and that he actually performed this vow; or that he dragged Hector round the tomb of Patroclus, [12] and slaughtered the captives at the pyre; [13] of all this I cannot believe that he was guilty, any more than I can allow our citizens to believe that he, the wise Cheiron's pupil, the son of a goddess and of Peleus who was the gentlest of men and third in descent from Zeus, was so disordered in his wits as to be at one time the slave of two seemingly inconsistent passions, meanness, not untainted by avarice, combined with overweening contempt of gods and men.

You are quite right, he replied.

And let us equally refuse to believe, or allow to be repeated, the tale of Theseus son of Poseidon, or of Peirithous son of Zeus, going forth as they did to perpetrate a horrid rape; or of any other hero or son of a god daring to do such impious and dreadful things as they falsely ascribe to them in our day: and let us further compel the poets to declare either that these acts were not done by them, or that they were not the sons of gods—both in the same breath they shall not be permitted to affirm. We will not have them trying to persuade our youth that the gods are the authors of evil, and that heroes are no better than men—sentiments

[1] *Ibid*, ix. 8.
[2] *Ibid*, xii. 342.
[3] *Iliad*, xiv. 281.
[4] *Odyssey*, viii. 266.
[5] *Ibid*, xx. 17.
[6] *Iliad*, ix. 515.

[7] *Ibid*, xxiv. 175.
[8] Cf. *infra*, x. 595.
[9] *Iliad*, xxii. 15 ff.
[10] *Ibid*, xxi. 130, 223 ff.
[11] *Ibid*, xxiii. 151.
[12] *Ibid*, xxii. 394.
[13] *Ibid*, xxiii. 175.

which, as we were saying, are neither pious nor true, for we have already proved that evil cannot come from the gods.

Assuredly not.

And further they are likely to have a bad effect on those who hear them; for everybody will begin to excuse his own vices when he is convinced that similar wickednesses are always being perpetrated by—

The kindred of the gods, the relatives of Zeus, whose ancestral altar, the altar of Zeus, is aloft in air on the peak of Ida,

and who have

the blood of deities yet flowing in their veins.

And therefore let us put an end to such tales, lest they engender laxity of morals among the young. *[392]*

By all means, he replied.

But now that we are determining what classes of subjects are or are not to be spoken of, let us see whether any have been omitted by us. The manner in which gods and demigods and heroes and the world below should be treated has been already laid down.

Very true.

And what shall we say about men? That is clearly the remaining portion of our subject.

Clearly so.

But we are not in a condition to answer this question at present, my friend.

Why not?

Because, if I am not mistaken, we shall have to say that about men poets and story-tellers are guilty of making the gravest mis-statements when they tell us that wicked men are often happy, and the good miserable; and that injustice is profitable when undetected, but that justice is a man's own loss and another's gain— these things we shall forbid them to utter, and command them to sing and say the opposite.

To be sure we shall, he replied.

But if you admit that I am right in this, then I shall maintain that you have implied the principle for which we have been all along contending.

I grant the truth of your inference.

That such things are or are not to be said about men is a question which we cannot determine until we have discovered what justice is, and how naturally advantageous to the possessor, whether he seems to be just or not.

Most true, he said.

Enough of the subjects of poetry: let us now speak of the style; and when this has been con-

sidered, both matter and manner will have been completely treated.

I do not understand what you mean, said Adeimantus.

Then I must make you understand; and perhaps I may be more intelligible if I put the matter in this way. You are aware, I suppose, that all mythology and poetry is a narration of events, either past, present, or to come?

Certainly, he replied.

And narration may be either simple narration, or imitation, or a union of the two?

That again, he said, I do not quite understand.

I fear that I must be a ridiculous teacher when I have so much difficulty in making myself apprehended. Like a bad speaker, therefore, I will not take the whole of the subject, but will break a piece off in illustration of my meaning. You know the first lines of the *Iliad*, *[393]* in which the poet says that Chryses prayed Agamemnon to release his daughter, and that Agamemnon flew into a passion with him; whereupon Chryses, failing of his object, invoked the anger of the God against the Achaeans. Now as far as these lines,

And he prayed all the Greeks, but especially the two sons of Atreus, the chiefs of the people,

the poet is speaking in his own person; he never leads us to suppose that he is any one else. But in what follows he takes the person of Chryses, and then he does all that he can to make us believe that the speaker is not Homer, but the aged priest himself. And in this double form he has cast the entire narrative of the events which occurred at Troy and in Ithaca and throughout the *Odyssey*.

Yes.

And a narrative it remains both in the speeches which the poet recites from time to time and in the intermediate passages?

Quite true.

But when the poet speaks in the person of another, may we not say that he assimilates his style to that of the person who, as he informs you, is going to speak?

Certainly.

And this assimilation of himself to another, either by the use of voice or gesture, is the imitation of the person whose character he assumes?

Of course.

Then in this case the narrative of the poet may be said to proceed by way of imitation?

Very true.

Or, if the poet everywhere appears and never conceals himself, then again the imitation is dropped, and his poetry becomes simple narration. However, in order that I may make my meaning quite clear, and that you may no more say, "I don't understand," I will show how the change might be effected. If Homer had said, "The priest came, having his daughter's ransom in his hands, supplicating the Achaeans, and above all the kings"; and then if, instead of speaking in the person of Chryses, he had continued in his own person, the words would have been, not imitation, but simple narration. The passage would have run as follows (I am no poet, and therefore I drop the metre), "The priest came and prayed the gods on behalf of the Greeks that they might capture Troy and return safely home, but begged that they would give him back his daughter, and take the ransom which he brought, and respect the God. Thus he spoke, and the other Greeks revered the priest and assented. But Agamemnon was wroth, and bade him depart and not come again, lest the staff and chaplets of the God should be of no avail to him—the daughter of Chryses should not be released, he said—she should grow old with him in Argos. And then he told him to go away and not to provoke him, if he intended to get home unscathed. *[394]* And the old man went away in fear and silence, and, when he had left the camp, he called upon Apollo by his many names, reminding him of everything which he had done pleasing to him, whether in building his temples, or in offering sacrifice, and praying that his good deeds might be returned to him, and that the Achaeans might expiate his tears by the arrows of the god"—and so on. In this way the whole becomes simple narrative.

I understand, he said.

Or you may suppose the opposite case—that the intermediate passages are omitted, and the dialogue only left.

That also, he said, I understand; you mean, for example, as in tragedy.

You have conceived my meaning perfectly; and if I mistake not, what you failed to apprehend before is now made clear to you, that poetry and mythology are, in some cases, wholly imitative—instances of this are supplied by tragedy and comedy; there is likewise the opposite style, in which the poet is the only speaker—of this the dithyramb affords the best example; and the combination of both is found in epic, and in several other styles of poetry. Do I take you with me?

Yes, he said; I see now what you meant.

I will ask you to remember also what I began by saying, that we had done with the subject and might proceed to the style.

Yes, I remember.

In saying this, I intended to imply that we must come to an understanding about the mimetic art—whether the poets, in narrating their stories, are to be allowed by us to imitate, and if so, whether in whole or in part, and if the latter, in what parts; or should all imitation be prohibited?

You mean, I suspect, to ask whether tragedy and comedy shall be admitted into our State?

Yes, I said; but there may be more than this in question: I really do not know as yet, but whither the argument may blow, thither we go.

And go we will, he said.

Then, Adeimantus, let me ask you whether our guardians ought to be imitators; or rather, has not this question been decided by the rule already laid down that one man can only do one thing well, and not many; and that if he attempt many, he will altogether fail of gaining much reputation in any?

Certainly.

And this is equally true of imitation; no one man can imitate many things as well as he would imitate a single one?

He cannot.

[395] Then the same person will hardly be able to play a serious part in life, and at the same time to be an imitator and imitate many other parts as well; for even when two species of imitation are nearly allied, the same persons cannot succeed in both, as, for example, the writers of tragedy and comedy—did you not just now call them imitations?

Yes, I did; and you are right in thinking that the same persons cannot succeed in both.

Any more than they can be rhapsodists and actors at once?

True.

Neither are comic and tragic actors the same; yet all these things are but imitations.

They are so.

And human nature, Adeimantus, appears to have been coined into yet smaller pieces, and to be as incapable of imitating many things well, as of performing well the actions of which the imitations are copies.

Quite true, he replied.

If then we adhere to our original notion and bear in mind that our guardians, setting aside every other business, are to dedicate themselves wholly to the maintenance of freedom in the State, making this their craft, and engaging in no work which does not bear on this end, they ought not to practise or imitate anything else; if they imitate at all, they should imitate from youth upward only those characters which are suitable to their profession—the courageous, temperate, holy, free, and the like; but they should not depict or be skilful at imitating any kind of illiberality or baseness, lest from imitation they should come to be what they imitate. Did you never observe how imitations, beginning in early youth and continuing far into life, at length grow into habits and become a second nature, affecting body, voice, and mind?

Yes, certainly, he said.

Then, I said, we will not allow those for whom we profess a care and of whom we say that they ought to be good men, to imitate a woman, whether young or old, quarrelling with her husband, or striving and vaunting against the gods in conceit of her happiness, or when she is in affliction, or sorrow, or weeping; and certainly not one who is in sickness, love, or labour.

Very right, he said.

Neither must they represent slaves, male or female, performing the offices of slaves?

They must not.

And surely not bad men, whether cowards or any others, who do the reverse of what we have just been prescribing, who scold or mock or revile one another in drink or out of drink, or who in any other manner sin against themselves and their neighbours in word or deed, [396] as the manner of such is. Neither should they be trained to imitate the action or speech of men or women who are mad or bad; for madness, like vice, is to be known but not to be practised or imitated.

Very true, he replied.

Neither may they imitate smiths or other artificers, or oarsmen, or boatswains, or the like?

How can they, he said, when they are not allowed to apply their minds to the callings of any of these?

Nor may they imitate the neighing of horses, the bellowing of bulls, the murmur of rivers and roll of the ocean, thunder, and all that sort of thing?

Nay, he said, if madness be forbidden, neither may they copy the behaviour of madmen.

You mean, I said, if I understand you aright, that there is one sort of narrative style which may be employed by a truly good man when he has anything to say, and that another sort will be used by a man of an opposite character and education.

And which are these two sorts? he asked.

Suppose, I answered, that a just and good man in the course of a narration comes on some saying or action of another good man—I should imagine that he will like to personate him, and will not be ashamed of this sort of imitation: he will be most ready to play the part of the good man when he is acting firmly and wisely; in a less degree when he is overtaken by illness or love or drink, or has met with any other disaster. But when he comes to a character which is unworthy of him, he will not make a study of that; he will disdain such a person, and will assume his likeness, if at all, for a moment only when he is performing some good action; at other times he will be ashamed to play a part which he has never practised, nor will he like to fashion and frame himself after the baser models; he feels the employment of such an art, unless in jest, to be beneath him, and his mind revolts at it.

So I should expect, he replied.

Then he will adopt a mode of narration such as we have illustrated out of Homer, that is to say, his style will be both imitative and narrative; but there will be very little of the former, and a great deal of the latter. Do you agree?

Certainly, he said; that is the model which such a speaker must necessarily take. [397]

But there is another sort of character who will narrate anything, and, the worse he is, the more unscrupulous he will be; nothing will be too bad for him: and he will be ready to imitate anything, not as a joke, but in right good earnest, and before a large company. As I was just now saying, he will attempt to represent the roll of thunder, the noise of wind and hail, or the creaking of wheels, and pulleys, and the various sounds of flutes, pipes, trumpets, and all sorts of instruments: he will bark like a dog, bleat like a sheep, or crow like a cock; his entire art will consist in imitation of voice and gesture, and there will be very little narration.

That, he said, will be his mode of speaking.

These, then, are the two kinds of style?

Yes.

And you would agree with me in saying that one of them is simple and has but slight changes; and if the harmony and rhythm are also chosen for their simplicity, the result is that the speaker, if he speaks correctly, is always pretty much the same in style, and he will keep within the limits of a single harmony (for the changes are not great), and in like manner he will make use of nearly the same rhythm?

That is quite true, he said.

Whereas the other requires all sorts of harmonies and all sorts of rhythms, if the music and the style are to correspond, because the style has all sorts of changes.

That is also perfectly true, he replied.

And do not the two styles, or the mixture of the two, comprehend all poetry, and every form of expression in words? No one can say anything except in one or other of them or in both together.

They include all, he said.

And shall we receive into our State all the three styles, or one only of the two unmixed styles? or would you include the mixed?

I should prefer only to admit the pure imitator of virtue.

Yes, I said, Adeimantus; but the mixed style is also very charming: and indeed the pantomimic, which is the opposite of the one chosen by you, is the most popular style with children and their attendants, and with the world in general.

I do not deny it.

But I suppose you would argue that such a style is unsuitable to our State, in which human nature is not twofold or manifold, for one man plays one part only?

Yes; quite unsuitable.

And this is the reason why in our State, and in our State only, we shall find a shoemaker to be a shoemaker and not a pilot also, and a husbandman to be a husbandman and not a dicast also, and a soldier a soldier and not a trader also, and the same throughout?

True, he said.

[398] And therefore when any one of these pantomimic gentlemen, who are so clever that they can imitate anything, comes to us, and makes a proposal to exhibit himself and his poetry, we will fall down and worship him as a sweet and holy and wonderful being; but we must also inform him that in our State such as he are not permitted to exist; the law will not allow them. And so when we have anointed him with myrrh, and set a garland of wool upon his head, we shall send him away to another city. For we mean to employ for our souls' health the rougher and severer poet or story-teller, who will imitate the style of the virtuous only, and will follow those models which we prescribed at first when we began the education of our soldiers.

We certainly will, he said, if we have the power.

Then now, my friend, I said, that part of music or literary education which relates to the story or myth may be considered to be finished; for the matter and manner have both been discussed.

I think so too, he said.

Next in order will follow melody and song.

That is obvious.

Every one can see already what we ought to say about them, if we are to be consistent with ourselves.

I fear, said Glaucon, laughing, that the word "every one" hardly includes me, for I cannot at the moment say what they should be; though I may guess.

At any rate you can tell that a song or ode has three parts—the words, the melody, and the rhythm; that degree of knowledge I may presuppose?

Yes, he said; so much as that you may.

And as for the words, there will surely be no difference between words which are and which are not set to music; both will conform to the same laws, and these have been already determined by us?

Yes.

And the melody and rhythm will depend upon the words?

Certainly.

We were saying, when we spoke of the subject-matter, that we had no need of lamentations and strains of sorrow?

True.

And which are the harmonies expressive of sorrow? You are musical, and can tell me.

The harmonies which you mean are the mixed or tenor Lydian, and the full-toned or bass Lydian, and such like.

These then, I said, must be banished; even to women who have a character to maintain they are of no use, and much less to men.

Certainly.

In the next place, drunkenness and softness and indolence are utterly unbecoming the character of our guardians.

Utterly unbecoming.

And which are the soft or drinking harmonies?

[399] The Ionian, he replied, and the Lydian; they are termed "relaxed."

Well, and are these of any military use?

Quite the reverse, he replied; and if so the Dorian and the Phrygian are the only ones which you have left.

I answered: Of the harmonies I know nothing, but I want to have one warlike, to sound the note or accent which a brave man utters in the hour of danger and stern resolve, or when his cause is failing, and he is going to wounds or death or is overtaken by some other evil, and at every such crisis meets the blows of fortune with firm step and a determination to endure; and another to be used by him in times of peace and freedom of action, when there is no pressure of necessity, and he is seeking to persuade God by prayer, or man by instruction and admonition, or on the other hand, when he is expressing his willingness to yield to persuasion or entreaty or admonition, and which represents him when by prudent conduct he has attained his end, not carried away by his success, but acting moderately and wisely under the circumstances, and acquiescing in the event. These two harmonies I ask you to leave; the strain of necessity and the strain of freedom, the strain of the unfortunate and the strain of the fortunate, the strain of courage, and the strain of temperance; these, I say, leave.

And these, he replied, are the Dorian and Phrygian harmonies of which I was just now speaking.

Then, I said, if these and these only are to be used in our songs and melodies, we shall not want multiplicity of notes or a panharmonic scale?

I suppose not.

Then we shall not maintain the artificers of lyres with three corners and complex scales, or the makers of any other many-stringed curiously-harmonised instruments?

Certainly not.

But what do you say to flute-makers and flute-players? Would you admit them into our State when you reflect that in this composite use of harmony the flute is worse than all the stringed instruments put together; even the panharmonic music is only an imitation of the flute?

Clearly not.

There remain then only the lyre and the harp for use in the city, and the shepherds may have a pipe in the country.

That is surely the conclusion to be drawn from the argument.

The preferring of Apollo and his instruments to Marsyas and his instruments is not at all strange, I said.

Not at all, he replied.

And so, by the dog of Egypt, we have been unconsciously purging the State, which not long ago we termed luxurious.

And we have done wisely, he replied.

Then let us now finish the purgation, I said. Next in order to harmonies, rhythms will naturally follow, and they should be subject to the same rules, for we ought not to seek out complex systems of metre, or metres of every kind, but rather to discover what rhythms are the expressions of a courageous and harmonious life; [400] and when we have found them, we shall adapt the foot and the melody to words having a like spirit, not the words to the foot and melody. To say what these rhythms are will be your duty—you must teach me them, as you have already taught me the harmonies.

But, indeed, he replied, I cannot tell you. I only know that there are some three principles of rhythm out of which metrical systems are framed, just as in sounds there are four notes [1] out of which all the harmonies are composed; that is an observation which I have made. But of what sort of lives they are severally the imitations I am unable to say.

Then, I said, we must take Damon into our counsels; and he will tell us what rhythms are expressive of meanness, or insolence, or fury, or other unworthiness, and what are to be reserved for the expression of opposite feelings. And I think that I have an indistinct recollection of his mentioning a complex Cretic rhythm; also a dactylic or heroic, and he arranged them in some manner which I do not quite understand, making the rhythms equal in the rise and fall of the foot, long and short alternating; and, unless I am mistaken, he spoke of an iambic as well as of a trochaic rhythm, and assigned to them short and long quantities. Also in some cases he appeared to praise or censure the movement of the foot quite as much as the rhythm; or perhaps a combination of the two; for I am not certain what he meant. These matters, however, as I was saying, had better be referred to Damon himself, for the analysis of the subject would be difficult, you know?

Rather so, I should say.

But there is no difficulty in seeing that grace or the absence of grace is an effect of good or bad rhythm.

None at all.

And also that good and bad rhythm naturally assimilate to a good and bad style; and that harmony and discord in like manner follow style; for our principle is that rhythm and harmony are regulated by the words, and not the words by them.

[1] The four notes of the tetrachord.

Just so, he said, they should follow the words.

And will not the words and the character of the style depend on the temper of the soul?

Yes.

And everything else on the style?

Yes.

Then beauty of style and harmony and grace and good rhythm depend on simplicity—I mean the true simplicity of a rightly and nobly ordered mind and character, not that other simplicity which is only an euphemism for folly?

Very true, he replied.

And if our youth are to do their work in life, must they not make these graces and harmonies their perpetual aim?

They must.

[401] And surely the art of the painter and every other creative and constructive art are full of them—weaving, embroidery, architecture, and every kind of manufacture; also nature, animal and vegetable—in all of them there is grace or the absence of grace. And ugliness and discord and inharmonious motion are nearly allied to ill words and ill nature, as grace and harmony are the twin sisters of goodness and virtue and bear their likeness.

That is quite true, he said.

But shall our superintendence go no further, and are the poets only to be required by us to express the image of the good in their works, on pain, if they do anything else, of expulsion from our State? Or is the same control to be extended to other artists, and are they also to be prohibited from exhibiting the opposite forms of vice and intemperance and meanness and indecency in sculpture and building and the other creative arts; and is he who cannot conform to this rule of ours to be prevented from practising his art in our State, lest the taste of our citizens be corrupted by him? We would not have our guardians grow up amid images of moral deformity, as in some noxious pasture, and there browse and feed upon many a baneful herb and flower day by day, little by little, until they silently gather a festering mass of corruption in their own soul. Let our artists rather be those who are gifted to discern the true nature of the beautiful and graceful; then will our youth dwell in a land of health, amid fair sights and sounds, and receive the good in everything; and beauty, the effluence of fair works, shall flow into the eye and ear, like a health-giving breeze from a purer region, and insensibly draw the soul from earliest years into likeness and sympathy with the beauty of reason.

There can be no nobler training than that, he replied.

And therefore, I said, Glaucon, musical training is a more potent instrument than any other, because rhythm and harmony find their way into the inward places of the soul, on which they mightily fasten, imparting grace, and making the soul of him who is rightly educated graceful, or of him who is ill-educated ungraceful; and also because he who has received this true education of the inner being will most shrewdly perceive omissions or faults in art and nature, [402] and with a true taste, while he praises and rejoices over and receives into his soul the good, and becomes noble and good, he will justly blame and hate the bad, now in the days of his youth, even before he is able to know the reason why; and when reason comes he will recognise and salute the friend with whom his education has made him long familiar.

Yes, he said, I quite agree with you in thinking that our youth should be trained in music and on the grounds which you mention.

Just as in learning to read, I said, we were satisfied when we knew the letters of the alphabet, which are very few, in all their recurring sizes and combinations; not slighting them as unimportant whether they occupy a space large or small, but everywhere eager to make them out; and not thinking ourselves perfect in the art of reading until we recognise them wherever they are found: [1]

True—

Or, as we recognise the reflection of letters in the water, or in a mirror, only when we know the letters themselves; the same art and study giving us the knowledge of both:

Exactly—

Even so, as I maintain, neither we nor our guardians, whom we have to educate, can ever become musical until we and they know the essential forms, in all their combinations, and can recognise them and their images wherever they are found, not slighting them either in small things or great, but believing them all to be within the sphere of one art and study.

Most assuredly.

And when a beautiful soul harmonises with a beautiful form, and the two are cast in one mould, that will be the fairest of sights to him who has an eye to see it?

The fairest indeed.

And the fairest is also the loveliest?

That may be assumed.

[1] Cf. ii. 368.

And the man who has the spirit of harmony will be most in love with the loveliest; but he will not love him who is of an inharmonious soul?

That is true, he replied, if the deficiency be in his soul; but if there be any merely bodily defect in another he will be patient of it, and will love all the same.

I perceive, I said, that you have or have had experiences of this sort, and I agree. But let me ask you another question: Has excess of pleasure any affinity to temperance?

How can that be? he replied; pleasure deprives a man of the use of his faculties quite as much as pain.

Or any affinity to virtue in general?

[403] None whatever.

Any affinity to wantonness and intemperance?

Yes, the greatest.

And is there any greater or keener pleasure than that of sensual love?

No, nor a madder.

Whereas true love is a love of beauty and order—temperate and harmonious?

Quite true, he said.

Then no intemperance or madness should be allowed to approach true love?

Certainly not.

Then mad or intemperate pleasure must never be allowed to come near the lover and his beloved; neither of them can have any part in it if their love is of the right sort?

No, indeed, Socrates, it must never come near them.

Then I suppose that in the city which we are founding you would make a law to the effect that a friend should use no other familiarity to his love than a father would use to his son, and then only for a noble purpose, and he must first have the other's consent; and this rule is to limit him in all his intercourse, and he is never to be seen going further, or, if he exceeds, he is to be deemed guilty of coarseness and bad taste.

I quite agree, he said.

Thus much of music, which makes a fair ending; for what should be the end of music if not the love of beauty?

I agree, he said.

After music comes gymnastic, in which our youth are next to be trained.

Certainly.

Gymnastic as well as music should begin in early years; the training in it should be careful and should continue through life. Now my belief is—and this is a matter upon which I should like to have your opinion in confirmation of my own, but my own belief is—not that the good body by any bodily excellence improves the soul, but, on the contrary, that the good soul, by her own excellence, improves the body as far as this may be possible. What do you say?

Yes, I agree.

Then, to the mind when adequately trained, we shall be right in handing over the more particular care of the body; and in order to avoid prolixity we will now only give the general outlines of the subject.

Very good.

That they must abstain from intoxication has been already remarked by us; for of all persons a guardian should be the last to get drunk and not know where in the world he is.

Yes, he said; that a guardian should require another guardian to take care of him is ridiculous indeed.

But next, what shall we say of their food; for the men are in training for the great contest of all—are they not?

Yes, he said.

[404] And will the habit of body of our ordinary athletes be suited to them?

Why not?

I am afraid, I said, that a habit of body such as they have is but a sleepy sort of thing, and rather perilous to health. Do you not observe that these athletes sleep away their lives, and are liable to most dangerous illnesses if they depart, in ever so slight a degree, from their customary regimen?

Yes, I do.

Then, I said, a finer sort of training will be required for our warrior athletes, who are to be like wakeful dogs, and to see and hear with the utmost keenness; amid the many changes of water and also of food, of summer heat and winter cold, which they will have to endure when on a campaign, they must not be liable to break down in health.

That is my view.

The really excellent gymnastic is twin sister of that simple music which we were just now describing.

How so?

Why, I conceive that there is a gymnastic which, like our music, is simple and good; and especially the military gymnastic.

What do you mean?

My meaning may be learned from Homer; he, you know, feeds his heroes at their feasts, when they are campaigning, on soldiers' fare; they have no fish, although they are on the shores of the Hellespont, and they are not allowed boiled meats but only roast, which is the food most convenient for soldiers, requiring only that they should light a fire, and not involving the trouble of carrying about pots and pans.

True.

And I can hardly be mistaken in saying that sweet sauces are nowhere mentioned in Homer. In proscribing them, however, he is not singular; all professional athletes are well aware that a man who is to be in good condition should take nothing of the kind.

Yes, he said; and knowing this, they are quite right in not taking them.

Then you would not approve of Syracusan dinners, and the refinements of Sicilian cookery?

I think not.

Nor, if a man is to be in condition, would you allow him to have a Corinthian girl as his fair friend?

Certainly not.

Neither would you approve of the delicacies, as they are thought, of Athenian confectionary?

Certainly not.

All such feeding and living may be rightly compared by us to melody and song composed in the panharmonic style, and in all the rhythms.

Exactly.

There complexity engendered licence, and here disease; whereas simplicity in music was the parent of temperance in the soul; and simplicity in gymnastic of health in the body.

Most true, he said.

[405] But when intemperance and disease multiply in a State, halls of justice and medicine are always being opened; and the arts of the doctor and the lawyer give themselves airs, finding how keen is the interest which not only the slaves but the freemen of a city take about them.

Of course.

And yet what greater proof can there be of a bad and disgraceful state of education than this, that not only artisans and the meaner sort of people need the skill of first-rate physicians and judges, but also those who would profess to have had a liberal education? Is it not disgraceful, and a great sign of want of good-breeding, that a man should have to go abroad for his law and physic because he has none of his own at home, and must therefore surrender himself into the hands of other men whom he makes lords and judges over him?

Of all things, he said, the most disgraceful.

Would you say "most," I replied, when you consider that there is a further stage of the evil in which a man is not only a life-long litigant, passing all his days in the courts, either as plaintiff or defendant, but is actually led by his bad taste to pride himself on his litigiousness; he imagines that he is a master in dishonesty; able to take every crooked turn, and wriggle into and out of every hole, bending like a withy and getting out of the way of justice: and all for what?—in order to gain small points not worth mentioning, he not knowing that so to order his life as to be able to do without a napping judge is a far higher and nobler sort of thing. Is not that still more disgraceful?

Yes, he said, that is still more disgraceful.

Well, I said, and to require the help of medicine, not when a wound has to be cured, or on occasion of an epidemic, but just because, by indolence and a habit of life such as we have been describing, men fill themselves with waters and winds, as if their bodies were a marsh, compelling the ingenious sons of Asclepius to find more names for diseases, such as flatulence and catarrh; is not this, too, a disgrace?

Yes, he said, they do certainly give very strange and newfangled names to diseases.

Yes, I said, and I do not believe that there were any such diseases in the days of Asclepius; and this I infer from the circumstance that the hero Eurypylus, after he has been wounded in Homer, [406] drinks a posset of Pramnian wine well besprinkled with barley-meal and grated cheese, which are certainly inflammatory, and yet the sons of Asclepius who were at the Trojan War do not blame the damsel who gives him the drink, or rebuke Patroclus, who is treating his case.

Well, he said, that was surely an extraordinary drink to be given to a person in his condition.

Not so extraordinary, I replied, if you bear in mind that in former days, as is commonly said, before the time of Herodicus, the guild of Asclepius did not practise our present system of medicine, which may be said to educate diseases. But Herodicus, being a trainer, and himself of a sickly constitution, by a combination of training and doctoring found out a way of torturing first and chiefly himself, and secondly the rest of the world.

How was that? he said.

By the invention of lingering death; for he

had a mortal disease which he perpetually tended, and as recovery was out of the question, he passed his entire life as a valetudinarian; he could do nothing but attend upon himself, and he was in constant torment whenever he departed in anything from his usual regimen, and so dying hard, by the help of science he struggled on to old age.

A rare reward of his skill!

Yes, I said; a reward which a man might fairly expect who never understood that, if Asclepius did not instruct his descendants in valetudinarian arts, the omission arose, not from ignorance or inexperience of such a branch of medicine, but because he knew that in all well-ordered states every individual has an occupation to which he must attend, and has therefore no leisure to spend in continually being ill. This we remark in the case of the artisan, but, ludicrously enough, do not apply the same rule to people of the richer sort.

How do you mean? he said.

I mean this: When a carpenter is ill he asks the physician for a rough and ready cure; an emetic or a purge or a cautery or the knife—these are his remedies. And if some one prescribes for him a course of dietetics, and tells him that he must swathe and swaddle his head, and all that sort of thing, he replies at once that he has no time to be ill, and that he sees no good in a life which is spent in nursing his disease to the neglect of his customary employment; and therefore bidding good-bye to this sort of physician, he resumes his ordinary habits, and either gets well and lives and does his business, or, if his constitution fails, he dies and has no more trouble.

Yes, he said, and a man in his condition of life ought to use the art of medicine thus far only.

[407] Has he not, I said, an occupation; and what profit would there be in his life if he were deprived of his occupation?

Quite true, he said.

But with the rich man this is otherwise; of him we do not say that he has any specially appointed work which he must perform, if he would live.

He is generally supposed to have nothing to do.

Then you never heard of the saying of Phocylides, that as soon as a man has a livelihood he should practise virtue?

Nay, he said, I think that he had better begin somewhat sooner.

Let us not have a dispute with him about this, I said; but rather ask ourselves: Is the practice of virtue obligatory on the rich man, or can he live without it? And if obligatory on him, then let us raise a further question, whether this dieting of disorders, which is an impediment to the application of the mind in carpentering and the mechanical arts, does not equally stand in the way of the sentiment of Phocylides?

Of that, he replied, there can be no doubt; such excessive care of the body, when carried beyond the rules of gymnastic, is most inimical to the practice of virtue.

Yes, indeed, I replied, and equally incompatible with the management of a house, an army, or an office of state; and, what is most important of all, irreconcileable with any kind of study or thought or self-reflection—there is a constant suspicion that headache and giddiness are to be ascribed to philosophy, and hence all practising or making trial of virtue in the higher sense is absolutely stopped; for a man is always fancying that he is being made ill, and is in constant anxiety about the state of his body.

Yes, likely enough.

And therefore our politic Asclepius may be supposed to have exhibited the power of his art only to persons who, being generally of healthy constitution and habits of life, had a definite ailment; such as these he cured by purges and operations, and bade them live as usual, herein consulting the interests of the State; but bodies which disease had penetrated through and through he would not have attempted to cure by gradual processes of evacuation and infusion: he did not want to lengthen out good-for-nothing lives, or to have weak fathers begetting weaker sons—if a man was not able to live in the ordinary way he had no business to cure him; for such a cure would have been of no use either to himself, or to the State.

Then, he said, you regard Asclepius as a statesman.

Clearly; and his character is further illustrated by his sons. Note that they were heroes in the days of old and practised the medicines [408] of which I am speaking at the siege of Troy: You will remember how, when Pandarus wounded Menelaus, they

Sucked the blood out of the wound, and sprinkled soothing remedies,[1]

but they never prescribed what the patient

[1] *Iliad,* iv. 218.

was afterwards to eat or drink in the case of Menelaus, any more than in the case of Eurypylus; the remedies, as they conceived, were enough to heal any man who before he was wounded was healthy and regular in his habits; and even though he did happen to drink a posset of Pramnian wine, he might get well all the same. But they would have nothing to do with unhealthy and intemperate subjects, whose lives were of no use either to themselves or others; the art of medicine was not designed for their good, and though they were as rich as Midas, the sons of Asclepius would have declined to attend them.

They were very acute persons, those sons of Asclepius.

Naturally so, I replied. Nevertheless, the tragedians and Pindar disobeying our behests, although they acknowledge that Asclepius was the son of Apollo, say also that he was bribed into healing a rich man who was at the point of death, and for this reason he was struck by lightning. But we, in accordance with the principle already affirmed by us, will not believe them when they tell us both—if he was the son of a god, we maintain that he was not avaricious; or, if he was avaricious, he was not the son of a god.

All that, Socrates, is excellent; but I should like to put a question to you: Ought there not to be good physicians in a State, and are not the best those who have treated the greatest number of constitutions good and bad? and are not the best judges in like manner those who are acquainted with all sorts of moral natures?

Yes, I said, I too would have good judges and good physicians. But do you know whom I think good?

Will you tell me?

I will, if I can. Let me however note that in the same question you join two things which are not the same.

How so? he asked.

Why, I said, you join physicians and judges. Now the most skilful physicians are those who, from their youth upwards, have combined with the knowledge of their art the greatest experience of disease; they had better not be robust in health, and should have had all manner of diseases in their own persons. For the body, as I conceive, is not the instrument with which they cure the body; in that case we could not allow them ever to be or to have been sickly; but they cure the body with the mind, and the mind which has become and is sick can cure nothing.

That is very true, he said.

[409] But with the judge it is otherwise; since he governs mind by mind; he ought not therefore to have been trained among vicious minds, and to have associated with them from youth upwards, and to have gone through the whole calendar of crime, only in order that he may quickly infer the crimes of others as he might their bodily diseases from his own self-consciousness; the honourable mind which is to form a healthy judgment should have had no experience or contamination of evil habits when young. And this is the reason why in youth good men often appear to be simple, and are easily practised upon by the dishonest, because they have no examples of what evil is in their own souls.

Yes, he said, they are far too apt to be deceived.

Therefore, I said, the judge should not be young; he should have learned to know evil, not from his own soul, but from late and long observation of the nature of evil in others: knowledge should be his guide, not personal experience.

Yes, he said, that is the ideal of a judge.

Yes, I replied, and he will be a good man (which is my answer to your question); for he is good who has a good soul. But the cunning and suspicious nature of which we spoke —he who has committed many crimes, and fancies himself to be a master in wickedness, when he is amongst his fellows, is wonderful in the precautions which he takes, because he judges of them by himself: but when he gets into the company of men of virtue, who have the experience of age, he appears to be a fool again, owing to his unseasonable suspicions; he cannot recognise an honest man, because he has no pattern of honesty in himself; at the same time, as the bad are more numerous than the good, and he meets with them oftener, he thinks himself, and is by others thought to be, rather wise than foolish.

Most true, he said.

Then the good and wise judge whom we are seeking is not this man, but the other; for vice cannot know virtue too, but a virtuous nature, educated by time, will acquire a knowledge both of virtue and vice: the virtuous, and not the vicious man has wisdom—in my opinion.

And in mine also.

This is the sort of medicine, and this is the sort of law, which you will sanction in your state. [410] They will minister to better natures, giving health both of soul and of body;

but those who are diseased in their bodies they will leave to die, and the corrupt and incurable souls they will put an end to themselves.

That is clearly the best thing both for the patients and for the State.

And thus our youth, having been educated only in that simple music which, as we said, inspires temperance, will be reluctant to go to law.

Clearly.

And the musician, who, keeping to the same track, is content to practise the simple gymnastic, will have nothing to do with medicine unless in some extreme case.

That I quite believe.

The very exercises and toils which he undergoes are intended to stimulate the spirited element of his nature, and not to increase his strength; he will not, like common athletes, use exercise and regimen to develop his muscles.

Very right, he said.

Neither are the two arts of music and gymnastic really designed, as is often supposed, the one for the training of the soul, the other for the training of the body.

What then is the real object of them?

I believe, I said, that the teachers of both have in view chiefly the improvement of the soul.

How can that be? he asked.

Did you never observe, I said, the effect on the mind itself of exclusive devotion to gymnastic, or the opposite effect of an exclusive devotion to music?

In what way shown? he said.

The one producing a temper of hardness and ferocity, the other of softness and effeminacy, I replied.

Yes, he said, I am quite aware that the mere athlete becomes too much of a savage, and that the mere musician is melted and softened beyond what is good for him.

Yet surely, I said, this ferocity only comes from spirit, which, if rightly educated, would give courage, but, if too much intensified, is liable to become hard and brutal.

That I quite think.

On the other hand the philosopher will have the quality of gentleness. And this also, when too much indulged, will turn to softness, but, if educated rightly, will be gentle and moderate.

True.

And in our opinion the guardians ought to have both these qualities?

Assuredly.

And both should be in harmony?

Beyond question.

[411] And the harmonious soul is both temperate and courageous?

Yes.

And the inharmonious is cowardly and boorish?

Very true.

And, when a man allows music to play upon him and to pour into his soul through the funnel of his ears those sweet and soft and melancholy airs of which we were just now speaking, and his whole life is passed in warbling and the delights of song; in the first stage of the process the passion or spirit which is in him is tempered like iron, and made useful, instead of brittle and useless. But, if he carries on the softening and soothing process, in the next stage he begins to melt and waste, until he has wasted away his spirit and cut out the sinews of his soul; and he becomes a feeble warrior.

Very true.

If the element of spirit is naturally weak in him the change is speedily accomplished, but if he have a good deal, then the power of music weakening the spirit renders him excitable—on the least provocation he flames up at once, and is speedily extinguished; instead of having spirit he grows irritable and passionate and is quite impracticable.

Exactly.

And so in gymnastics, if a man takes violent exercise and is a great feeder, and the reverse of a great student of music and philosophy, at first the high condition of his body fills him with pride and spirit, and he becomes twice the man that he was.

Certainly.

And what happens? if he do nothing else, and holds no converse with the Muses, does not even that intelligence which there may be in him, having no taste of any sort of learning or enquiry or thought or culture, grow feeble and dull and blind, his mind never waking up or receiving nourishment, and his senses not being purged of their mists?

True, he said.

And he ends by becoming a hater of philosophy, uncivilized, never using the weapon of persuasion—he is like a wild beast, all violence and fierceness, and knows no other way of dealing; and he lives in all ignorance and evil conditions, and has no sense of propriety and grace.

That is quite true, he said.

And as there are two principles of human nature, one the spirited and the other the philosophical, some God, as I should say, has given mankind two arts answering to them (and only indirectly to the soul and body), *[412]* in order that these two principles (like the strings of an instrument) may be relaxed or drawn tighter until they are duly harmonized.

That appears to be the intention.

And he who mingles music with gymnastic in the fairest proportions, and best attempers them to the soul, may be rightly called the true musician and harmonist in a far higher sense than the tuner of the strings.

You are quite right, Socrates.

And such a presiding genius will be always required in our State if the government is to last.

Yes, he will be absolutely necessary.

Such, then, are our principles of nurture and education: Where would be the use of going into further details about the dances of our citizens, or about their hunting and coursing, their gymnastic and equestrian contests? For these all follow the general principle, and having found that, we shall have no difficulty in discovering them.

I dare say that there will be no difficulty.

Very good, I said; then what is the next question? Must we not ask who are to be rulers and who subjects?

Certainly.

There can be no doubt that the elder must rule the younger.

Clearly.

And that the best of these must rule.

That is also clear.

Now, are not the best husbandmen those who are most devoted to husbandry?

Yes.

And as we are to have the best of guardians for our city, must they not be those who have most the character of guardians?

Yes.

And to this end they ought to be wise and efficient, and to have a special care of the State?

True.

And a man will be most likely to care about that which he loves?

To be sure.

And he will be most likely to love that which he regards as having the same interests with himself, and that of which the good or evil fortune is supposed by him at any time most to affect his own?

Very true, he replied.

Then there must be a selection. Let us note among the guardians those who in their whole life show the greatest eagerness to do what is for the good of their country, and the greatest repugnance to do what is against her interests.

Those are the right men.

And they will have to be watched at every age, in order that we may see whether they preserve their resolution, and never, under the influence either of force or enchantment, forget or cast off their sense of duty to the State.

How cast off? he said.

I will explain to you, I replied. A resolution may go out of a man's mind either with his will or against his will; *[413]* with his will when he gets rid of a falsehood and learns better, against his will whenever he is deprived of a truth.

I understand, he said, the willing loss of a resolution; the meaning of the unwilling I have yet to learn.

Why, I said, do you not see that men are unwillingly deprived of good, and willingly of evil? Is not to have lost the truth an evil, and to possess the truth a good? and you would agree that to conceive things as they are is to possess the truth?

Yes, he replied; I agree with you in thinking that mankind are deprived of truth against their will.

And is not this involuntary deprivation caused either by theft, or force, or enchantment?

Still, he replied, I do not understand you.

I fear that I must have been talking darkly, like the tragedians. I only mean that some men are changed by persuasion and that others forget; argument steals away the hearts of one class, and time of the other; and this I call theft. Now you understand me?

Yes.

Those again who are forced are those whom the violence of some pain or grief compels to change their opinion.

I understand, he said, and you are quite right.

And you would also acknowledge that the enchanted are those who change their minds either under the softer influence of pleasure, or the sterner influence of fear?

Yes, he said; everything that deceives may be said to enchant.

Therefore, as I was just now saying, we must enquire who are the best guardians of their own conviction that what they think the interest of the State is to be the rule of their lives.

We must watch them from their youth upwards, and make them perform actions in which they are most likely to forget or to be deceived, and he who remembers and is not deceived is to be selected, and he who fails in the trial is to be rejected. That will be the way?

Yes.

And there should also be toils and pains and conflicts prescribed for them, in which they will be made to give further proof of the same qualities.

Very right, he replied.

And then, I said, we must try them with enchantments—that is the third sort of test—and see what will be their behaviour: like those who take colts amid noise and tumult to see if they are of a timid nature, so must we take our youth amid terrors of some kind, and again pass them into pleasures, and prove them more thoroughly than gold is proved in the furnace, that we may discover whether they are armed against all enchantments, and of a noble bearing always, good guardians of themselves and of the music which they have learned, and retaining under all circumstances a rhythmical and harmonious nature, such as will be most serviceable to the individual and to the State. And he who at every age, as boy and youth and in mature life, has come out of the trial victorious and pure, *[414]* shall be appointed a ruler and guardian of the State; he shall be honoured in life and death, and shall receive sepulture and other memorials of honour, the greatest that we have to give. But him who fails, we must reject. I am inclined to think that this is the sort of way in which our rulers and guardians should be chosen and appointed. I speak generally, and not with any pretension to exactness.

And, speaking generally, I agree with you, he said.

And perhaps the word "guardian" in the fullest sense ought to be applied to this higher class only who preserve us against foreign enemies and maintain peace among our citizens at home, that the one may not have the will, or the others the power, to harm us. The young men whom we before called guardians may be more properly designated auxiliaries and supporters of the principles of the rulers.

I agree with you, he said.

How then may we devise one of those needful falsehoods of which we lately spoke—just one royal lie which may deceive the rulers, if that be possible, and at any rate the rest of the city?

What sort of lie? he said.

Nothing new, I replied; only an old Phoenician[1] tale of what has often occurred before now in other places (as the poets say, and have made the world believe), though not in our time, and I do not know whether such an event could ever happen again, or could now even be made probable, if it did.

How your words seem to hesitate on your lips!

You will not wonder, I replied, at my hesitation when you have heard.

Speak, he said, and fear not.

Well then, I will speak, although I really know not how to look you in the face, or in what words to utter the audacious fiction, which I propose to communicate gradually, first to the rulers, then to the soldiers, and lastly to the people. They are to be told that their youth was a dream, and the education and training which they received from us, an appearance only; in reality during all that time they were being formed and fed in the womb of the earth, where they themselves and their arms and appurtenances were manufactured; when they were completed, the earth, their mother, sent them up; and so, their country being their mother and also their nurse, they are bound to advise for her good, and to defend her against attacks, and her citizens they are to regard as children of the earth and their own brothers.

You had good reason, he said, to be ashamed of the lie which you were going to tell.

[415] True, I replied, but there is more coming; I have only told you half. Citizens, we shall say to them in our tale, you are brothers, yet God has framed you differently. Some of you have the power of command, and in the composition of these he has mingled gold, wherefore also they have the greatest honour; others he has made of silver, to be auxiliaries; others again who are to be husbandmen and craftsmen he has composed of brass and iron; and the species will generally be preserved in the children. But as all are of the same original stock, a golden parent will sometimes have a silver son, or a silver parent a golden son. And God proclaims as a first principle to the rulers, and above all else, that there is nothing which they should so anxiously guard, or of which they are to be such good guardians, as of the purity of the race. They should observe what elements mingle in their offspring; for if the son of a golden or silver parent has an admixture of brass and iron, then nature orders

[1] Cf. *Laws*, ii. 663.

a transposition of ranks, and the eye of the ruler must not be pitiful towards the child because he has to descend in the scale and become a husbandman or artisan, just as there may be sons of artisans who having an admixture of gold or silver in them are raised to honour, and become guardians or auxiliaries. For an oracle says that when a man of brass or iron guards the State, it will be destroyed. Such is the tale; is there any possibility of making our citizens believe in it?

Not in the present generation, he replied; there is no way of accomplishing this; but their sons may be made to believe in the tale, and their sons' sons, and posterity after them.

I see the difficulty, I replied; yet the fostering of such a belief will make them care more for the city and for one another. Enough, however, of the fiction, which may now fly abroad upon the wings of rumour, while we arm our earth-born heroes, and lead them forth under the command of their rulers. Let them look round and select a spot whence they can best suppress insurrection, if any prove refractory within, and also defend themselves against enemies, who like wolves may come down on the fold from without; there let them encamp, and when they have encamped, let them sacrifice to the proper Gods and prepare their dwellings.

Just so, he said.

And their dwellings must be such as will shield them against the cold of winter and the heat of summer.

I suppose that you mean houses, he replied.

Yes, I said; but they must be the houses of soldiers, and not of shopkeepers.

What is the difference? he said.

[416] That I will endeavour to explain, I replied. To keep watch-dogs, who, from want of discipline or hunger, or some evil habit or other, would turn upon the sheep and worry them, and behave not like dogs but wolves, would be a foul and monstrous thing in a shepherd?

Truly monstrous, he said.

And therefore every care must be taken that our auxiliaries, being stronger than our citizens, may not grow to be too much for them and become savage tyrants instead of friends and allies?

Yes, great care should be taken.

And would not a really good education furnish the best safeguard?

But they are well-educated already, he replied.

I cannot be so confident, my dear Glaucon, I said; I am much more certain that they ought to be, and that true education, whatever that may be, will have the greatest tendency to civilize and humanize them in their relations to one another, and to those who are under their protection.

Very true, he replied.

And not only their education, but their habitations, and all that belongs to them, should be such as will neither impair their virtue as guardians, nor tempt them to prey upon the other citizens. Any man of sense must acknowledge that.

He must.

Then let us consider what will be their way of life, if they are to realize our idea of them. In the first place, none of them should have any property of his own beyond what is absolutely necessary; neither should they have a private house or store closed against any one who has a mind to enter; their provisions should be only such as are required by trained warriors, who are men of temperance and courage; they should agree to receive from the citizens a fixed rate of pay, enough to meet the expenses of the year and no more; and they will go to mess and live together like soldiers in a camp. Gold and silver we will tell them that they have from God; the diviner metal is within them, and they have therefore no need of the dross which is current among men, and ought not to pollute the divine by any such earthly admixture; [417] for that commoner metal has been the source of many unholy deeds, but their own is undefiled. And they alone of all the citizens may not touch or handle silver or gold, or be under the same roof with them, or wear them, or drink from them. And this will be their salvation, and they will be the saviours of the State. But should they ever acquire homes or lands or moneys of their own, they will become housekeepers and husbandmen instead of guardians, enemies and tyrants instead of allies of the other citizens; hating and being hated, plotting and being plotted against, they will pass their whole life in much greater terror of internal than of external enemies, and the hour of ruin, both to themselves and to the rest of the State, will be at hand. For all which reasons may we not say that thus shall our State be ordered, and that these shall be the regulations appointed by us for our guardians concerning their houses and all other matters?

Yes, said Glaucon.

BOOK IV

[419] HERE Adeimantus interposed a question: How would you answer, Socrates, said he, if a person were to say that you are making these people miserable, and that they are the cause of their own unhappiness; the city in fact belongs to them, but they are none the better for it; whereas other men acquire lands, and build large and handsome houses, and have everything handsome about them, offering sacrifices to the gods on their own account, and practising hospitality; moreover, as you were saying just now, they have gold and silver, and all that is usual among the favourites of fortune; but our poor citizens are no better than mercenaries who are quartered in the city and are always mounting guard?

[420] Yes, I said; and you may add that they are only fed, and not paid in addition to their food, like other men; and therefore they cannot, if they would, take a journey of pleasure; they have no money to spend on a mistress or any other luxurious fancy, which, as the world goes, is thought to be happiness; and many other similar accusations might be added.

But, said he, let us suppose all this to be included in the charge.

You mean to ask, I said, what will be our answer?

Yes.

If we proceed along the old path, my belief, I said, is that we shall find the answer. And our answer will be that, even as they are, our guardians may very likely be the happiest of men; but that our aim in founding the State was not the disproportionate happiness of any one class, but the greatest happiness of the whole; we thought that in a State which is ordered with a view to the good of the whole we should be most likely to find justice, and in the ill-ordered State injustice: and, having found them, we might then decide which of the two is the happier. At present, I take it, we are fashioning the happy State, not piecemeal, or with a view of making a few happy citizens, but as a whole; and by-and-by we will proceed to view the opposite kind of State. Suppose that we were painting a statue, and some one came up to us and said, Why do you not put the most beautiful colours on the most beautiful parts of the body—the eyes ought to be purple, but you have made them black—to him we might fairly answer, Sir, you would not surely have us beautify the eyes to such a degree that they are no longer eyes; consider rather wheth-

er, by giving this and the other features their due proportion, we make the whole beautiful. And so I say to you, do not compel us to assign to the guardians a sort of happiness which will make them anything but guardians; for we too can clothe our husbandmen in royal apparel, and set crowns of gold on their heads, and bid them till the ground as much as they like, and no more. Our potters also might be allowed to repose on couches, and feast by the fireside, passing round the winecup, while their wheel is conveniently at hand, and working at pottery only as much as they like; in this way we might make every class happy—and then, as you imagine, the whole State would be happy. But do not put this idea into our heads; *[421]* for, if we listen to you, the husbandman will be no longer a husbandman, the potter will cease to be a potter, and no one will have the character of any distinct class in the State. Now this is not of much consequence where the corruption of society, and pretension to be what you are not, is confined to cobblers; but when the guardians of the laws and of the government are only seemingly and not real guardians, then see how they turn the State upside down; and on the other hand they alone have the power of giving order and happiness to the State. We mean our guardians to be true saviours and not the destroyers of the State, whereas our opponent is thinking of peasants at a festival, who are enjoying a life of revelry, not of citizens who are doing their duty to the State. But, if so, we mean different things, and he is speaking of something which is not a State. And therefore we must consider whether in appointing our guardians we would look to their greatest happiness individually, or whether this principle of happiness does not rather reside in the State as a whole. But if the latter be the truth, then the guardians and auxiliaries, and all others equally with them, must be compelled or induced to do their own work in the best way. And thus the whole State will grow up in a noble order, and the several classes will receive the proportion of happiness which nature assigns to them.

I think that you are quite right.

I wonder whether you will agree with another remark which occurs to me.

What may that be?

There seem to be two causes of the deterioration of the arts.

What are they?

Wealth, I said, and poverty.

How do they act?

The process is as follows: When a potter becomes rich, will he, think you, any longer take the same pains with his art?

Certainly not.

He will grow more and more indolent and careless?

Very true.

And the result will be that he becomes a worse potter?

Yes; he greatly deteriorates.

But, on the other hand, if he has no money, and cannot provide himself with tools or instruments, he will not work equally well himself, nor will he teach his sons or apprentices to work equally well.

Certainly not.

Then, under the influence either of poverty or of wealth, workmen and their work are equally liable to degenerate?

That is evident.

Here, then, is a discovery of new evils, I said, against which the guardians will have to watch, or they will creep into the city unobserved.

What evils?

[422] Wealth, I said, and poverty; the one is the parent of luxury and indolence, and the other of meanness and viciousness, and both of discontent.

That is very true, he replied; but still I should like to know, Socrates, how our city will be able to go to war, especially against an enemy who is rich and powerful, if deprived of the sinews of war.

There would certainly be a difficulty, I replied, in going to war with one such enemy; but there is no difficulty where there are two of them.

How so? he asked.

In the first place, I said, if we have to fight, our side will be trained warriors fighting against an army of rich men.

That is true, he said.

And do you not suppose, Adeimantus, that a single boxer who was perfect in his art would easily be a match for two stout and well-to-do gentlemen who were not boxers?

Hardly, if they came upon him at once.

What, not, I said, if he were able to run away and then turn and strike at the one who first came up? And supposing he were to do this several times under the heat of a scorching sun, might he not, being an expert, overturn more than one stout personage?

Certainly, he said, there would be nothing wonderful in that.

And yet rich men probably have a greater superiority in the science and practise of boxing than they have in military qualities.

Likely enough.

Then we may assume that our athletes will be able to fight with two or three times their own number?

I agree with you, for I think you right.

And suppose that, before engaging, our citizens send an embassy to one of the two cities, telling them what is the truth: Silver and gold we neither have nor are permitted to have, but you may; do you therefore come and help us in war, and take the spoils of the other city: Who, on hearing these words, would choose to fight against lean wiry dogs, rather than, with the dogs on their side, against fat and tender sheep?

That is not likely; and yet there might be a danger to the poor State if the wealth of many States were to be gathered into one.

But how simple of you to use the term State at all of any but our own!

Why so?

You ought to speak of other States in the plural number; not one of them is a city, but many cities, as they say in the game. For indeed any city, however small, is in fact divided into two, one the city of the poor, [423] the other of the rich; these are at war with one another; and in either there are many smaller divisions, and you would be altogether beside the mark if you treated them all as a single State. But if you deal with them as many, and give the wealth or power or persons of the one to the others, you will always have a great many friends and not many enemies. And your State, while the wise order which has now been prescribed continues to prevail in her, will be the greatest of States, I do not mean to say in reputation or appearance, but in deed and truth, though she number not more than a thousand defenders. A single State which is her equal you will hardly find, either among Hellenes or barbarians, though many that appear to be as great and many times greater.

That is most true, he said.

And what, I said, will be the best limit for our rulers to fix when they are considering the size of the State and the amount of territory which they are to include, and beyond which they will not go?

What limit would you propose?

I would allow the State to increase so far as is consistent with unity; that, I think, is the proper limit.

Very good, he said.

Here then, I said, is another order which will have to be conveyed to our guardians: Let our city be accounted neither large nor small, but one and self-sufficing.

And surely, said he, this is not a very severe order which we impose upon them.

And the other, said I, of which we were speaking before is lighter still—I mean the duty of degrading the offspring of the guardians when inferior, and of elevating into the rank of guardians the offspring of the lower classes, when naturally superior. The intention was, that, in the case of the citizens generally, each individual should be put to the use for which nature intended him, one to one work, and then every man would do his own business, and be one and not many; and so the whole city would be one and not many.

Yes, he said; that is not so difficult.

The regulations which we are prescribing, my good Adeimantus, are not, as might be supposed, a number of great principles, but trifles all, if care be taken, as the saying is, of the one great thing—a thing, however, which I would rather call, not great, but sufficient for our purpose.

What may that be? he asked.

Education, I said, and nurture: If our citizens are well educated, and grow into sensible men, they will easily see their way through all these, as well as other matters which I omit; such, for example, as marriage, *[424]* the possession of women and the procreation of children, which will all follow the general principle that friends have all things in common, as the proverb says.

That will be the best way of settling them.

Also, I said, the State, if once started well, moves with accumulating force like a wheel. For good nurture and education implant good constitutions, and these good constitutions taking root in a good education improve more and more, and this improvement affects the breed in man as in other animals.

Very possibly, he said.

Then to sum up: This is the point to which, above all, the attention of our rulers should be directed—that music and gymnastic be preserved in their original form, and no innovation made. They must do their utmost to maintain them intact. And when any one says that mankind most regard

The newest song which the singers have,[1]

[1] *Odyssey,* i. 352.

they will be afraid that he may be praising, not new songs, but a new kind of song; and this ought not to be praised, or conceived to be the meaning of the poet; for any musical innovation is full of danger to the whole State, and ought to be prohibited. So Damon tells me, and I can quite believe him—he says that when modes of music change, the fundamental laws of the State always change with them.

Yes, said Adeimantus; and you may add my suffrage to Damon's and your own.

Then, I said, our guardians must lay the foundations of their fortress in music?

Yes, he said; the lawlessness of which you speak too easily steals in.

Yes, I replied, in the form of amusement; and at first sight it appears harmless.

Why, yes, he said, and there is no harm; were it not that little by little this spirit of licence, finding a home, imperceptibly penetrates into manners and customs; whence, issuing with greater force, it invades contracts between man and man, and from contracts goes on to laws and constitutions, in utter recklessness, ending at last, Socrates, by an overthrow of all rights, private as well as public.

Is that true? I said.

That is my belief, he replied.

Then, as I was saying, our youth should be trained from the first in a stricter system, for if amusements become lawless, and the youths themselves become lawless, *[425]* they can never grow up into well-conducted and virtuous citizens.

Very true, he said.

And when they have made a good beginning in play, and by the help of music have gained the habit of good order, then this habit of order, in a manner how unlike the lawless play of the others! will accompany them in all their actions and be a principle of growth to them, and if there be any fallen places in the State will raise them up again.

Very true, he said.

Thus educated, they will invent for themselves any lesser rules which their predecessors have altogether neglected.

What do you mean?

I mean such things as these:—when the young are to be silent before their elders; how they are to show respect to them by standing and making them sit; what honour is due to parents; what garments or shoes are to be worn; the mode of dressing the hair; deportment and manners in general. You would agree with me?

Yes.

But there is, I think, small wisdom in legislating about such matters—I doubt if it is ever done; nor are any precise written enactments about them likely to be lasting.

Impossible.

It would seem, Adeimantus, that the direction in which education starts a man, will determine his future life. Does not like always attract like?

To be sure.

Until some one rare and grand result is reached which may be good, and may be the reverse of good?

That is not to be denied.

And for this reason, I said, I shall not attempt to legislate further about them.

Naturally enough, he replied.

Well, and about the business of the agora, and the ordinary dealings between man and man, or again about agreements with artisans; about insult and injury, or the commencement of actions, and the appointment of juries, what would you say? there may also arise questions about any impositions and extractions of market and harbour dues which may be required, and in general about the regulations of markets, police, harbours, and the like. But, oh heavens! shall we condescend to legislate on any of these particulars?

I think, he said, that there is no need to impose laws about them on good men; what regulations are necessary they will find out soon enough for themselves.

Yes, I said, my friend, if God will only preserve to them the laws which we have given them.

And without divine help, said Adeimantus, they will go on for ever making and mending their laws and their lives in the hope of attaining perfection.

You would compare them, I said, to those invalids who, having no self-restraint, will not leave off their habits of intemperance?

Exactly.

[426] Yes, I said; and what a delightful life they lead! they are always doctoring and increasing and complicating their disorders, and always fancying that they will be cured by any nostrum which anybody advises them to try.

Such cases are very common, he said, with invalids of this sort.

Yes, I replied; and the charming thing is that they deem him their worst enemy who tells them the truth, which is simply that, unless they give up eating and drinking and wenching and idling, neither drug nor cautery nor spell nor amulet nor any other remedy will avail.

Charming! he replied. I see nothing charming in going into a passion with a man who tells you what is right.

These gentlemen, I said, do not seem to be in your good graces.

Assuredly not.

Nor would you praise the behaviour of States which act like the men whom I was just now describing. For are there not ill-ordered States in which the citizens are forbidden under pain of death to alter the constitution; and yet he who most sweetly courts those who live under this régime and indulges them and fawns upon them and is skilful in anticipating and gratifying their humours is held to be a great and good statesman—do not these States resemble the persons whom I was describing?

Yes, he said; the States are as bad as the men; and I am very far from praising them.

But do you not admire, I said, the coolness and dexterity of these ready ministers of political corruption?

Yes, he said, I do; but not of all of them, for there are some whom the applause of the multitude has deluded into the belief that they are really statesmen, and these are not much to be admired.

What do you mean? I said; you should have more feeling for them. When a man cannot measure, and a great many others who cannot measure declare that he is four cubits high, can he help believing what they say?

Nay, he said, certainly not in that case.

Well, then, do not be angry with them; for are they not as good as a play, trying their hand at paltry reforms such as I was describing; they are always fancying that by legislation they will make an end of frauds in contracts, and the other rascalities which I was mentioning, not knowing that they are in reality cutting off the heads of a hydra?

[427] Yes, he said; that is just what they are doing.

I conceive, I said, that the true legislator will not trouble himself with this class of enactments whether concerning laws or the constitution either in an ill-ordered or in a well-ordered State; for in the former they are quite useless, and in the latter there will be no difficulty in devising them; and many of them will naturally flow out of our previous regulations.

What, then, he said, is still remaining to us of the work of legislation?

Nothing to us, I replied; but to Apollo, the god of Delphi, there remains the ordering of the greatest and noblest and chiefest things of all.

Which are they? he said.

The institution of temples and sacrifices, and the entire service of gods, demigods, and heroes; also the ordering of the repositories of the dead, and the rites which have to be observed by him who would propitiate the inhabitants of the world below. These are matters of which we are ignorant ourselves, and as founders of a city we should be unwise in trusting them to any interpreter but our ancestral deity. He is the god who sits in the centre, on the navel of the earth, and he is the interpreter of religion to all mankind.

You are right, and we will do as you propose.

But where, amid all this, is justice? son of Ariston, tell me where. Now that our city has been made habitable, light a candle and search, and get your brother and Polemarchus and the rest of our friends to help, and let us see where in it we can discover justice and where injustice, and in what they differ from one another, and which of them the man who would be happy should have for his portion, whether seen or unseen by gods and men.

Nonsense, said Glaucon: did you not promise to search yourself, saying that for you not to help justice in her need would be an impiety?

I do not deny that I said so; and as you remind me, I will be as good as my word; but you must join.

We will, he replied.

Well, then, I hope to make the discovery in this way: I mean to begin with the assumption that our State, if rightly ordered, is perfect.

That is most certain.

And being perfect, is therefore wise and valiant and temperate and just.

That is likewise clear.

And whichever of these qualities we find in the State, the one which is not found will be the residue?

[428] Very good.

If there were four things, and we were searching for one of them, wherever it might be, the one sought for might be known to us from the first, and there would be no further trouble; or we might know the other three first, and then the fourth would clearly be the one left.

Very true, he said.

And is not a similar method to be pursued about the virtues, which are also four in number?

Clearly.

First among the virtues found in the State, wisdom comes into view, and in this I detect a certain peculiarity.

What is that?

The State which we have been describing is said to be wise as being good in counsel?

Very true.

And good counsel is clearly a kind of knowledge, for not by ignorance, but by knowledge, do men counsel well?

Clearly.

And the kinds of knowledge in a State are many and diverse?

Of course.

There is the knowledge of the carpenter; but is that the sort of knowledge which gives a city the title of wise and good in counsel?

Certainly not; that would only give a city the reputation of skill in carpentering.

Then a city is not to be called wise because possessing a knowledge which counsels for the best about wooden implements?

Certainly not.

Nor by reason of a knowledge which advises about brazen pots, I said, nor as possessing any other similar knowledge?

Not by reason of any of them, he said.

Nor yet by reason of a knowledge which cultivates the earth; that would give the city the name of agricultural?

Yes.

Well, I said, and is there any knowledge in our recently-founded State among any of the citizens which advises, not about any particular thing in the State, but about the whole, and considers how a State can best deal with itself and with other States?

There certainly is.

And what is this knowledge, and among whom is it found? I asked.

It is the knowledge of the guardians, he replied, and is found among those whom we were just now describing as perfect guardians.

And what is the name which the city derives from the possession of this sort of knowledge?

The name of good in counsel and truly wise.

And will there be in our city more of these true guardians or more smiths?

The smiths, he replied, will be far more numerous.

Will not the guardians be the smallest of all the classes who receive a name from the profession of some kind of knowledge?

Much the smallest.

And so by reason of the smallest part or class, and of the knowledge which resides in this presiding and ruling part of itself, the whole State, *[429]* being thus constituted according to nature, will be wise; and this, which has the only knowledge worthy to be called wisdom, has been ordained by nature to be of all classes the least.

Most true.

Thus, then, I said, the nature and place in the State of one of the four virtues has somehow or other been discovered.

And, in my humble opinion, very satisfactorily discovered, he replied.

Again, I said, there is no difficulty in seeing the nature of courage, and in what part that quality resides which gives the name of courageous to the State.

How do you mean?

Why, I said, every one who calls any State courageous or cowardly, will be thinking of the part which fights and goes out to war on the State's behalf.

No one, he replied, would ever think of any other.

The rest of the citizens may be courageous or may be cowardly, but their courage or cowardice will not, as I conceive, have the effect of making the city either the one or the other.

Certainly not.

The city will be courageous in virtue of a portion of herself which preserves under all circumstances that opinion about the nature of things to be feared and not to be feared in which our legislator educated them; and this is what you term courage.

I should like to hear what you are saying once more, for I do not think that I perfectly understand you.

I mean that courage is a kind of salvation.

Salvation of what?

Of the opinion respecting things to be feared, what they are and of what nature, which the law implants through education; and I mean by the words "under all circumstances" to intimate that in pleasure or in pain, or under the influence of desire or fear, a man preserves, and does not lose this opinion. Shall I give you an illustration?

If you please.

You know, I said, that dyers, when they want to dye wool for making the true sea-purple, begin by selecting their white colour first; this they prepare and dress with much care and pains, in order that the white ground may take the purple hue in full perfection. The dyeing then proceeds; and whatever is dyed in this manner becomes a fast colour, and no washing either with lyes or without them can take away the bloom. But, when the ground has not been duly prepared, you will have noticed how poor is the look either of purple or of any other colour.

Yes, he said; I know that they have a washed-out and ridiculous appearance.

Then now, I said, you will understand what our object was in selecting our soldiers, *[430]* and educating them in music and gymnastic; we were contriving influences which would prepare them to take the dye of the laws in perfection, and the colour of their opinion about dangers and of every other opinion was to be indelibly fixed by their nurture and training, not to be washed away by such potent lyes as pleasure—mightier agent far in washing the soul than any soda or lye; or by sorrow, fear, and desire, the mightiest of all other solvents. And this sort of universal saving power of true opinion in conformity with law about real and false dangers I call and maintain to be courage, unless you disagree.

But I agree, he replied; for I suppose that you mean to exclude mere uninstructed courage, such as that of a wild beast or of a slave—this, in your opinion, is not the courage which the law ordains, and ought to have another name.

Most certainly.

Then I may infer courage to be such as you describe?

Why, yes, said I, you may, and if you add the words "of a citizen," you will not be far wrong —hereafter, if you like, we will carry the examination further, but at present we are seeking not for courage but justice; and for the purpose of our enquiry we have said enough.

You are right, he replied.

Two virtues remain to be discovered in the State—first temperance, and then justice which is the end of our search.

Very true.

Now, can we find justice without troubling ourselves about temperance?

I do not know how that can be accomplished, he said, nor do I desire that justice should be brought to light and temperance lost sight of; and therefore I wish that you would do me the favour of considering temperance first.

Certainly, I replied, I should not be justified in refusing your request.

Then consider, he said.

Yes, I replied; I will; and as far as I can at present see, the virtue of temperance has more of the nature of harmony and symphony than the preceding.

How so? he asked.

Temperance, I replied, is the ordering or controlling of certain pleasures and desires; this is curiously enough implied in the saying of "a man being his own master"; and other traces of the same notion may be found in language.

No doubt, he said.

There is something ridiculous in the expression "master of himself"; [431] for the master is also the servant and the servant the master; and in all these modes of speaking the same person is denoted.

Certainly.

The meaning is, I believe, that in the human soul there is a better and also a worse principle; and when the better has the worse under control, then a man is said to be master of himself; and this is a term of praise: but when, owing to evil education or association, the better principle, which is also the smaller, is overwhelmed by the greater mass of the worse—in this case he is blamed and is called the slave of self and unprincipled.

Yes, there is reason in that.

And now, I said, look at our newly-created State, and there you will find one of these two conditions realized; for the State, as you will acknowledge, may be justly called master of itself, if the words "temperance" and "self-mastery" truly express the rule of the better part over the worse.

Yes, he said, I see that what you say is true.

Let me further note that the manifold and complex pleasures and desires and pains are generally found in children and women and servants, and in the freemen so called who are of the lowest and more numerous class.

Certainly, he said.

Whereas the simple and moderate desires which follow reason, and are under the guidance of mind and true opinion, are to be found only in a few, and those the best born and best educated.

Very true.

These two, as you may perceive, have a place in our State; and the meaner desires of the many are held down by the virtuous desires and wisdom of the few.

That I perceive, he said.

Then if there be any city which may be described as master of its own pleasures and desires, and master of itself, ours may

claim such a designation?

Certainly, he replied.

It may also be called temperate, and for the same reasons?

Yes.

And if there be any State in which rulers and subjects will be agreed as to the question who are to rule, that again will be our State?

Undoubtedly.

And the citizens being thus agreed among themselves, in which class will temperance be found—in the rulers or in the subjects?

In both, as I should imagine, he replied.

Do you observe that we were not far wrong in our guess that temperance was a sort of harmony?

Why so?

Why, because temperance is unlike courage and wisdom, each of which resides in a part only, [432] the one making the State wise and the other valiant; not so temperance, which extends to the whole, and runs through all the notes of the scale, and produces a harmony of the weaker and the stronger and the middle class, whether you suppose them to be stronger or weaker in wisdom or power or numbers or wealth, or anything else. Most truly then may we deem temperance to be the agreement of the naturally superior and inferior, as to the right to rule of either, both in states and individuals.

I entirely agree with you.

And so, I said, we may consider three out of the four virtues to have been discovered in our State. The last of those qualities which make a state virtuous must be justice, if we only knew what that was.

The inference is obvious.

The time then has arrived, Glaucon, when, like huntsmen, we should surround the cover, and look sharp that justice does not steal away, and pass out of sight and escape us; for beyond a doubt she is somewhere in this country: watch therefore and strive to catch a sight of her, and if you see her first, let me know.

Would that I could! but you should regard me rather as a follower who has just eyes enough to see what you show him—that is about as much as I am good for.

Offer up a prayer with me and follow.

I will, but you must show me the way.

Here is no path, I said, and the wood is dark and perplexing; still we must push on.

Let us push on.

Here I saw something: Halloo! I said, I begin to perceive a track, and I believe that the quarry will not escape.

Good news, he said.

Truly, I said, we are stupid fellows.

Why so?

Why, my good sir, at the beginning of our enquiry, ages ago, there was justice tumbling out at our feet, and we never saw her; nothing could be more ridiculous. Like people who go about looking for what they have in their hands—that was the way with us—we looked not at what we were seeking, but at what was far off in the distance; and therefore, I suppose, we missed her.

What do you mean?

I mean to say that in reality for a long time past we have been talking of justice, and have failed to recognise her.

I grow impatient at the length of your exordium.

[433] Well then, tell me, I said, whether I am right or not: You remember the original principle which we were always laying down at the foundation of the State, that one man should practise one thing only, the thing to which his nature was best adapted—now justice is this principle or a part of it.

Yes, we often said that one man should do one thing only.

Further, we affirmed that justice was doing one's own business, and not being a busybody; we said so again and again, and many others have said the same to us.

Yes, we said so.

Then to do one's own business in a certain way may be assumed to be justice. Can you tell me whence I derive this inference?

I cannot, but I should like to be told.

Because I think that this is the only virtue which remains in the State when the other virtues of temperance and courage and wisdom are abstracted; and, that this is the ultimate cause and condition of the existence of all of them, and while remaining in them is also their preservative; and we were saying that if the three were discovered by us, justice would be the fourth or remaining one.

That follows of necessity.

If we are asked to determine which of these four qualities by its presence contributes most to the excellence of the State, whether the agreement of rulers and subjects, or the preservation in the soldiers of the opinion which the law ordains about the true nature of dangers, or wisdom and watchfulness in the rulers, or whether this other which I am mentioning, and which is found in children and women, slave and freeman, artisan, ruler, subject—the quality, I mean, of every one doing his own work, and not being a busybody, would claim the palm—the question is not so easily answered.

Certainly, he replied, there would be a difficulty in saying which.

Then the power of each individual in the State to do his own work appears to compete with the other political virtues, wisdom, temperance, courage.

Yes, he said.

And the virtue which enters into this competition is justice?

Exactly.

Let us look at the question from another point of view: Are not the rulers in a State those to whom you would entrust the office of determining suits at law?

Certainly.

And are suits decided on any other ground but that a man may neither take what is another's, nor be deprived of what is his own?

Yes; that is their principle.

Which is a just principle?

Yes.

Then on this view also justice will be admitted to be the having and doing what is a man's own, and belongs to him?

[434] Very true.

Think, now, and say whether you agree with me or not. Suppose a carpenter to be doing the business of a cobbler, or a cobbler of a carpenter; and suppose them to exchange their implements or their duties, or the same person to be doing the work of both, or whatever be the change; do you think that any great harm would result to the State?

Not much.

But when the cobbler or any other man whom nature designed to be a trader, having his heart lifted up by wealth or strength or the number of his followers, or any like advantage, attempts to force his way into the class of warriors, or a warrior into that of legislators and guardians, for which he is unfitted, and either to take the implements or the duties of the other; or when one man is trader, legislator, and warrior all in one, then I think you will agree with me in saying that this interchange and this meddling of one with another is the ruin of the State.

Most true.

Seeing then, I said, that there are three distinct classes, any meddling of one with another, or the change of one into another, is the greatest harm to the State, and may be most justly termed evil-doing?

Precisely.

And the greatest degree of evil-doing to one's own city would be termed by you injustice?

Certainly.

This then is injustice; and on the other hand when the trader, the auxiliary, and the guardian each do their own business, that is justice, and will make the city just.

I agree with you.

We will not, I said, be overpositive as yet; but if, on trial, this conception of justice be verified in the individual as well as in the State, there will be no longer any room for doubt; if it be not verified, we must have a fresh enquiry. First let us complete the old investigation, which we began, as you remember, under the impression that, if we could previously examine justice on the larger scale, there would be less difficulty in discerning her in the individual. That larger example appeared to be the State, and accordingly we constructed as good a one as we could, knowing well that in the good State justice would be found. Let the discovery which we made be now applied to the individual—if they agree, we shall be satisfied; or, if there be a difference in the individual, we will come back to the State and have another trial of the theory. [435] The friction of the two when rubbed together may possibly strike a light in which justice will shine forth, and the vision which is then revealed we will fix in our souls.

That will be in regular course; let us do as you say.

I proceeded to ask: When two things, a greater and less, are called by the same name, are they like or unlike in so far as they are called the same?

Like, he replied.

The just man then, if we regard the idea of justice only, will be like the just State?

He will.

And a State was thought by us to be just when the three classes in the State severally did their own business; and also thought to be temperate and valiant and wise by reason of certain other affections and qualities of these same classes?

True, he said.

And so of the individual; we may assume that he has the same three principles in his own soul which are found in the State; and he may be rightly described in the same terms, because he is affected in the same manner?

Certainly, he said.

Once more then, O my friend, we have alighted upon an easy question—whether the soul has these three principles or not?

An easy question! Nay, rather, Socrates, the proverb holds that hard is the good.

Very true, I said; and I do not think that the method which we are employing is at all adequate to the accurate solution of this question; the true method is another and a longer one. Still we may arrive at a solution not below the level of the previous enquiry.

May we not be satisfied with that? he said —under the circumstances, I am quite content.

I too, I replied, shall be extremely well satisfied.

Then faint not in pursuing the speculation, he said.

Must we not acknowledge, I said, that in each of us there are the same principles and habits which there are in the State; and that from the individual they pass into the State?— how else can they come there? Take the quality of passion or spirit—it would be ridiculous to imagine that this quality, when found in States, is not derived from the individuals who are supposed to possess it, e. g. the Thracians, Scythians, and in general the northern nations; and the same may be said of the love of knowledge, which is the special characteristic of our part of the world, [436] or of the love of money, which may, with equal truth, be attributed to the Phoenicians and Egyptians.

Exactly so, he said.

There is no difficulty in understanding this.

None whatever.

But the question is not quite so easy when we proceed to ask whether these principles are three or one; whether, that is to say, we learn with one part of our nature, are angry with another, and with a third part desire the satisfaction of our natural appetites; or whether the whole soul comes into play in each sort of action—to determine that is the difficulty.

Yes, he said; there lies the difficulty.

Then let us now try and determine whether they are the same or different.

How can we? he asked.

I replied as follows: The same thing clearly cannot act or be acted upon in the same part or in relation to the same thing at the same time, in contrary ways; and therefore whenever this contradiction occurs in things apparently the same, we know that they are really not the same, but different.

Good.

For example, I said, can the same thing be

at rest and in motion at the same time in the same part?

Impossible.

Still, I said, let us have a more precise statement of terms, lest we should hereafter fall out by the way. Imagine the case of a man who is standing and also moving his hands and his head, and suppose a person to say that one and the same person is in motion and at rest at the same moment—to such a mode of speech we should object, and should rather say that one part of him is in motion while another is at rest.

Very true.

And suppose the objector to refine still further, and to draw the nice distinction that not only parts of tops, but whole tops, when they spin round with their pegs fixed on the spot, are at rest and in motion at the same time (and he may say the same of anything which revolves in the same spot), his objection would not be admitted by us, because in such cases things are not at rest and in motion in the same parts of themselves; we should rather say that they have both an axis and a circumference; and that the axis stands still, for there is no deviation from the perpendicular; and that the circumference goes round. But if, while revolving, the axis inclines either to the right or left, forwards or backwards, then in no point of view can they be at rest.

That is the correct mode of describing them, he replied.

Then none of these objections will confuse us, or incline us to believe that the same thing at the same time, [437] in the same part or in relation to the same thing, can act or be acted upon in contrary ways.

Certainly not, according to my way of thinking.

Yet, I said, that we may not be compelled to examine all such objections, and prove at length that they are untrue, let us assume their absurdity, and go forward on the understanding that hereafter, if this assumption turn out to be untrue, all the consequences which follow shall be withdrawn.

Yes, he said, that will be the best way.

Well, I said, would you not allow that assent and dissent, desire and aversion, attraction and repulsion, are all of them opposites, whether they are regarded as active or passive (for that makes no difference in the fact of their opposition)?

Yes, he said, they are opposites.

Well, I said, and hunger and thirst, and the desires in general, and again willing and wishing—all these you would refer to the classes already mentioned. You would say—would you not?—that the soul of him who desires is seeking after the object of his desires; or that he is drawing to himself the thing which he wishes to possess: or again, when a person wants anything to be given him, his mind, longing for the realization of his desires, intimates his wish to have it by a nod of assent, as if he had been asked a question?

Very true.

And what would you say of unwillingness and dislike and the absence of desire; should not these be referred to the opposite class of repulsion and rejection?

Certainly.

Admitting this to be true of desire generally, let us suppose a particular class of desires, and out of these we will select hunger and thirst, as they are termed, which are the most obvious of them?

Let us take that class, he said.

The object of one is food, and of the other drink?

Yes.

And here comes the point: is not thirst the desire which the soul has of drink, and of drink only; not of drink qualified by anything else; for example, warm or cold, or much or little, or, in a word, drink of any particular sort: but if the thirst be accompanied by heat, then the desire is of cold drink; or, if accompanied by cold, then of warm drink; or, if the thirst be excessive, then the drink which is desired will be excessive; or, if not great, the quantity of drink will also be small: but thirst pure and simple will desire drink pure and simple, which is the natural satisfaction of thirst, as food is of hunger?

Yes, he said; the simple desire is, as you say, in every case of the simple object, and the qualified desire of the qualified object.

[438] But here a confusion may arise; and I should wish to guard against an opponent starting up and saying that no man desires drink only, but good drink, or food only, but good food; for good is the universal object of desire, and thirst being a desire, will necessarily be thirst after good drink; and the same is true of every other desire.

Yes, he replied, the opponent might have something to say.

Nevertheless I should still maintain, that of relatives some have a quality attached to either term of the relation; others are simple and have their correlatives simple.

I do not know what you mean.

Well, you know of course that the greater is relative to the less?

Certainly.

And the much greater to the much less?

Yes.

And the sometime greater to the sometime less, and the greater that is to be to the less that is to be?

Certainly, he said.

And so of more and less, and of other correlative terms, such as the double and the half, or again, the heavier and the lighter, the swifter and the slower; and of hot and cold, and of any other relatives—is not this true of all of them?

Yes.

And does not the same principle hold in the sciences? The object of science is knowledge (assuming that to be the true definition), but the object of a particular science is a particular kind of knowledge; I mean, for example, that the science of house-building is a kind of knowledge which is defined and distinguished from other kinds and is therefore termed architecture.

Certainly.

Because it has a particular quality which no other has?

Yes.

And it has this particular quality because it has an object of a particular kind; and this is true of the other arts and sciences?

Yes.

Now, then, if I have made myself clear, you will understand my original meaning in what I said about relatives. My meaning was, that if one term of a relation is taken alone, the other is taken alone; if one term is qualified, the other is also qualified. I do not mean to say that relatives may not be disparate, or that the science of health is healthy, or of disease necessarily diseased, or that the sciences of good and evil are therefore good and evil; but only that, when the term science is no longer used absolutely, but has a qualified object which in this case is the nature of health and disease, it becomes defined, and is hence called not merely science, but the science of medicine.

I quite understand, and I think as you do.

[439] Would you not say that thirst is one of these essentially relative terms, having clearly a relation—

Yes, thirst is relative to drink.

And a certain kind of thirst is relative to a certain kind of drink; but thirst taken alone is neither of much nor little, nor of good nor bad, nor of any particular kind of drink, but of drink only?

Certainly.

Then the soul of the thirsty one, in so far as he is thirsty, desires only drink; for this he yearns and tries to obtain it?

That is plain.

And if you suppose something which pulls a thirsty soul away from drink, that must be different from the thirsty principle which draws him like a beast to drink; for, as we were saying, the same thing cannot at the same time with the same part of itself act in contrary ways about the same.

Impossible.

No more than you can say that the hands of the archer push and pull the bow at the same time, but what you say is that one hand pushes and the other pulls.

Exactly so, he replied.

And might a man be thirsty, and yet unwilling to drink?

Yes, he said, it constantly happens.

And in such a case what is one to say? Would you not say that there was something in the soul bidding a man to drink, and something else forbidding him, which is other and stronger than the principle which bids him?

I should say so.

And the forbidding principle is derived from reason, and that which bids and attracts proceeds from passion and disease?

Clearly.

Then we may fairly assume that they are two, and that they differ from one another; the one with which a man reasons, we may call the rational principle of the soul, the other, with which he loves and hungers and thirsts and feels the flutterings of any other desire, may be termed the irrational or appetitive, the ally of sundry pleasures and satisfactions?

Yes, he said, we may fairly assume them to be different.

Then let us finally determine that there are two principles existing in the soul. And what of passion, or spirit? Is it a third, or akin to one of the preceding?

I should be inclined to say—akin to desire.

Well, I said, there is a story which I remember to have heard, and in which I put faith. The story is, that Leontius, the son of Aglaion, coming up one day from the Piraeus, under the north wall on the outside, observed some dead bodies lying on the ground at the place of execution. He felt a desire to see them, and also a dread and abhorrence of them; *[440]* for a time he struggled and covered his eyes, but at length the desire got the better of him; and forcing them open, he ran up to the dead bodies, saying, Look, ye wretches, take your fill of the fair sight.

I have heard the story myself, he said.

The moral of the tale is, that anger at times goes to war with desire, as though they were two distinct things.

Yes; that is the meaning, he said.

And are there not many other cases in which we observe that when a man's desires violently prevail over his reason, he reviles himself, and is angry at the violence within him, and that in this struggle, which is like the struggle of factions in a State, his spirit is on the side of his reason—but for the passionate or spirited element to take part with the desires when reason decides that she should not be opposed, is a sort of thing which I believe that you never observed occurring in yourself, nor, as I should imagine, in any one else?

Certainly not.

Suppose that a man thinks he has done a wrong to another, the nobler he is the less able is he to feel indignant at any suffering, such as hunger, or cold, or any other pain which the injured person may inflict upon him—these he deems to be just, and, as I say, his anger refuses to be excited by them.

True, he said.

But when he thinks that he is the sufferer of the wrong, then he boils and chafes, and is on the side of what he believes to be justice; and because he suffers hunger or cold or other pain he is only the more determined to persevere and conquer. His noble spirit will not be quelled until he either slays or is slain; or until he hears the voice of the shepherd, that is, reason, bidding his dog bark no more.

The illustration is perfect, he replied; and in our State, as we were saying, the auxiliaries were to be dogs, and to hear the voice of the rulers, who are their shepherds.

I perceive, I said, that you quite understand me; there is, however, a further point which I wish you to consider.

What point?

You remember that passion or spirit appeared at first sight to be a kind of desire, but now we should say quite the contrary; for in the conflict of the soul spirit is arrayed on the side of the rational principle.

Most assuredly.

But a further question arises: Is passion dif-

ferent from reason also, or only a kind of reason; in which latter case, instead of three principles in the soul, *[441]* there will only be two, the rational and the concupiscent; or rather, as the State was composed of three classes, traders, auxiliaries, counsellors, so may there not be in the individual soul a third element which is passion or spirit, and when not corrupted by bad education is the natural auxiliary of reason?

Yes, he said, there must be a third.

Yes, I replied, if passion, which has already been shown to be different from desire, turn out also to be different from reason.

But that is easily proved:—We may observe even in young children that they are full of spirit almost as soon as they are born, whereas some of them never seem to attain to the use of reason, and most of them late enough.

Excellent, I said, and you may see passion equally in brute animals, which is a further proof of the truth of what you are saying. And we may once more appeal to the words of Homer, which have been already quoted by us,

He smote his breast, and thus rebuked his heart; [1]

for in this verse Homer has clearly supposed the power which reasons about the better and worse to be different from the unreasoning anger which is rebuked by it.

Very true, he said.

And so, after much tossing, we have reached land, and are fairly agreed that the same principles which exist in the State exist also in the individual, and that they are three in number.

Exactly.

Must we not then infer that the individual is wise in the same way, and in virtue of the same quality which makes the State wise?

Certainly.

Also that the same quality which constitutes courage in the State constitutes courage in the individual, and that both the State and the individual bear the same relation to all the other virtues?

Assuredly.

And the individual will be acknowledged by us to be just in the same way in which the State is just?

That follows of course.

We cannot but remember that the justice of the State consisted in each of the three classes doing the work of its own class?

We are not very likely to have forgotten, he said.

We must recollect that the individual in

[1] *Odyssey*, xx. 17, quoted *supra*, iii. 390.

whom the several qualities of his nature do their own work will be just, and will do his own work?

Yes, he said, we must remember that too.

And ought not the rational principle, which is wise, and has the care of the whole soul, to rule, and the passionate or spirited principle to be the subject and ally?

Certainly.

And, as we were saying, the united influence of music and gymnastic will bring them into accord, nerving and sustaining the reason with noble words and lessons, [442] and moderating and soothing and civilizing the wildness of passion by harmony and rhythm?

Quite true, he said.

And these two, thus nurtured and educated, and having learned truly to know their own functions, will rule over the concupiscent, which in each of us is the largest part of the soul and by nature most insatiable of gain; over this they will keep guard, lest, waxing great and strong with the fulness of bodily pleasures, as they are termed, the concupiscent soul, no longer confined to her own sphere, should attempt to enslave and rule those who are not her natural-born subjects, and overturn the whole life of man?

Very true, he said.

Both together will they not be the best defenders of the whole soul and the whole body against attacks from without; the one counselling, and the other fighting under his leader, and courageously executing his commands and counsels?

True.

And he is to be deemed courageous whose spirit retains in pleasure and in pain the commands of reason about what he ought or ought not to fear?

Right, he replied.

And him we call wise who has in him that little part which rules, and which proclaims these commands; that part too being supposed to have a knowledge of what is for the interest of each of the three parts and of the whole?

Assuredly.

And would you not say that he is temperate who has these same elements in friendly harmony, in whom the one ruling principle of reason, and the two subject ones of spirit and desire are equally agreed that reason ought to rule, and do not rebel?

Certainly, he said, that is the true account of temperance whether in the State or individual.

And surely, I said, we have explained again and again how and by virtue of what quality a man will be just.

That is very certain.

And is justice dimmer in the individual, and is her form different, or is she the same which we found her to be in the State?

There is no difference in my opinion, he said.

Because, if any doubt is still lingering in our minds, a few commonplace instances will satisfy us of the truth of what I am saying.

What sort of instances do you mean?

[443] If the case is put to us, must we not admit that the just State, or the man who is trained in the principles of such a State, will be less likely than the unjust to make away with a deposit of gold or silver? Would any one deny this?

No one, he replied.

Will the just man or citizen ever be guilty of sacrilege or theft, or treachery either to his friends or to his country?

Never.

Neither will he ever break faith where there have been oaths or agreements?

Impossible.

No one will be less likely to commit adultery, or to dishonour his father and mother, or to fail in his religious duties?

No one.

And the reason is that each part of him is doing its own business, whether in ruling or being ruled?

Exactly so.

Are you satisfied then that the quality which makes such men and such states is justice, or do you hope to discover some other?

Not I, indeed.

Then our dream has been realized; and the suspicion which we entertained at the beginning of our work of construction, that some divine power must have conducted us to a primary form of justice, has now been verified?

Yes, certainly.

And the division of labour which required the carpenter and the shoemaker and the rest of the citizens to be doing each his own business, and not another's, was a shadow of justice, and for that reason it was of use?

Clearly.

But in reality justice was such as we were describing, being concerned however, not with the outward man, but with the inward, which is the true self and concernment of man: for the just man does not permit the several elements within him to interfere with one another, or any of them to do the work of others, —he sets in order his own inner life, and is his own master and his own law, and at peace with himself; and when he has bound together the three principles within him, which may be compared to the higher, lower, and middle notes of the scale, and the intermediate intervals— when he has bound all these together, and is no longer many, but has become one entirely temperate and perfectly adjusted nature, then he proceeds to act, if he has to act, whether in a matter of property, or in the treatment of the body, or in some affair of politics or private business; always thinking and calling that which preserves and co-operates with this harmonious condition, just and good action, and the knowledge which presides over it, wisdom, and that which at any time impairs this condition, *[444]* he will call unjust action, and the opinion which presides over it ignorance.

You have said the exact truth, Socrates.

Very good; and if we were to affirm that we had discovered the just man and the just State, and the nature of justice in each of them, we should not be telling a falsehood?

Most certainly not.

May we say so, then?

Let us say so.

And now, I said, injustice has to be considered.

Clearly.

Must not injustice be a strife which arises among the three principles—a meddlesomeness, and interference, and rising up of a part of the soul against the whole, an assertion of unlawful authority, which is made by a rebellious subject against a true prince, of whom he is the natural vassal—what is all this confusion and delusion but injustice, and intemperance and cowardice and ignorance, and every form of vice?

Exactly so.

And if the nature of justice and injustice be known, then the meaning of acting unjustly and being unjust, or, again, of acting justly, will also be perfectly clear?

What do you mean? he said.

Why, I said, they are like disease and health; being in the soul just what disease and health are in the body.

How so? he said.

Why, I said, that which is healthy causes health, and that which is unhealthy causes disease.

Yes.

And just actions cause justice, and unjust actions cause injustice?

That is certain.

And the creation of health is the institution of a natural order and government of one by another in the parts of the body; and the creation of disease is the production of a state of things at variance with this natural order?

True.

And is not the creation of justice the institution of a natural order and government of one by another in the parts of the soul, and the creation of injustice the production of a state of things at variance with the natural order?

Exactly so, he said.

Then virtue is the health and beauty and well-being of the soul, and vice the disease and weakness and deformity of the same?

True.

And do not good practices lead to virtue, and evil practices to vice?

Assuredly.

[445] Still our old question of the comparative advantage of justice and injustice has not been answered: Which is the more profitable, to be just and act justly and practise virtue, whether seen or unseen of gods and men, or to be unjust and act unjustly, if only unpunished and unreformed?

In my judgment, Socrates, the question has now become ridiculous. We know that, when the bodily constitution is gone, life is no longer endurable, though pampered with all kinds of meats and drinks, and having all wealth and all power; and shall we be told that when the very essence of the vital principle is undermined and corrupted, life is still worth having to a man, if only he be allowed to do whatever he likes with the single exception that he is not to acquire justice and virtue, or to escape from injustice and vice; assuming them both to be such as we have described?

Yes, I said, the question is, as you say, ridiculous. Still, as we are near the spot at which we may see the truth in the clearest manner with our own eyes, let us not faint by the way.

Certainly not, he replied.

Come up hither, I said, and behold the various forms of vice, those of them, I mean, which are worth looking at.

I am following you, he replied: proceed.

I said, The argument seems to have reached a height from which, as from some tower of speculation, a man may look down and see that virtue is one, but that the forms of vice are innumerable; there being four special ones which are deserving of note.

What do you mean? he said.

I mean, I replied, that there appear to be as many forms of the soul as there are distinct forms of the State.

How many?

There are five of the State, and five of the soul, I said.

What are they?

The first, I said, is that which we have been describing, and which may be said to have two names, monarchy and aristocracy, accordingly as rule is exercised by one distinguished man or by many.

True, he replied.

But I regard the two names as describing one form only; for whether the government is in the hands of one or many, if the governors have been trained in the manner which we have supposed, the fundamental laws of the State will be maintained.

That is true, he replied.

BOOK V

[449] SUCH is the good and true City or State, and the good and true man is of the same pattern; and if this is right every other is wrong; and the evil is one which affects not only the ordering of the State, but also the regulation of the individual soul, and is exhibited in four forms.

What are they? he said.

I was proceeding to tell the order in which the four evil forms appeared to me to succeed one another, when Polemarchus, who was sitting a little way off, just beyond Adeimantus, began to whisper to him: stretching forth his hand, he took hold of the upper part of his coat by the shoulder, and drew him towards him, leaning forward himself so as to be quite close and saying something in his ear, of which I only caught the words, "Shall we let him off, or what shall we do?"

Certainly not, said Adeimantus, raising his voice.

Who is it, I said, whom you are refusing to let off?

You, he said.

I repeated, Why am I especially not to be let off?

Why, he said, we think that you are lazy, and mean to cheat us out of a whole chapter which is a very important part of the story; and you fancy that we shall not notice your

airy way of proceeding; as if it were self-evident to everybody, that in the matter of women and children "friends have all things in common."

And was I not right, Adeimantus?

Yes, he said; but what is right in this particular case, like everything else, requires to be explained; for community may be of many kinds. Please, therefore, to say what sort of community you mean. We have been long expecting that you would tell us something about the family life of your citizens—how they will bring children into the world, and rear them when they have arrived, and, in general, what is the nature of this community of women and children—for we are of opinion that the right or wrong management of such matters will have a great and paramount influence on the State for good or for evil. And now, since the question is still undetermined, and you are taking in hand another State, we have resolved, as you heard, [450] not to let you go until you give an account of all this.

To that resolution, said Glaucon, you may regard me as saying Agreed.

And without more ado, said Thrasymachus, you may consider us all to be equally agreed.

I said, You know not what you are doing in thus assailing me: What an argument are you raising about the State! Just as I thought that I had finished, and was only too glad that I had laid this question to sleep, and was reflecting how fortunate I was in your acceptance of what I then said, you ask me to begin again at the very foundation, ignorant of what a hornet's nest of words you are stirring. Now I foresaw this gathering trouble, and avoided it.

For what purpose do you conceive that we have come here, said Thrasymachus—to look for gold, or to hear discourse?

Yes, but discourse should have a limit.

Yes, Socrates, said Glaucon, and the whole of life is the only limit which wise men assign to the hearing of such discourses. But never mind about us; take heart yourself and answer the question in your own way: What sort of community of women and children is this which is to prevail among our guardians? and how shall we manage the period between birth and education, which seems to require the greatest care? Tell us how these things will be.

Yes, my simple friend, but the answer is the reverse of easy; many more doubts arise about this than about our previous conclusions. For the practicability of what is said may be doubted; and looked at in another point of view, whether the scheme, if ever so practicable, would be for the best, is also doubtful. Hence I feel a reluctance to approach the subject, lest our aspiration, my dear friend, should turn out to be a dream only.

Fear not, he replied, for your audience will not be hard upon you; they are not sceptical or hostile.

I said: My good friend, I suppose that you mean to encourage me by these words.

Yes, he said.

Then let me tell you that you are doing just the reverse; the encouragement which you offer would have been all very well had I myself believed that I knew what I was talking about: to declare the truth about matters of high interest which a man honours and loves among wise men who love him need occasion no fear or faltering in his mind; but to carry on an argument when you are yourself only a hesitating enquirer, [451] which is my condition, is a dangerous and slippery thing; and the danger is not that I shall be laughed at (of which the fear would be childish), but that I shall miss the truth where I have most need to be sure of my footing, and drag my friends after me in my fall. And I pray Nemesis not to visit upon me the words which I am going to utter. For I do indeed believe that to be an involuntary homicide is a less crime than to be a deceiver about beauty or goodness or justice in the matter of laws. And that is a risk which I would rather run among enemies than among friends, and therefore you do well to encourage me.

Glaucon laughed and said: Well then, Socrates, in case you and your argument do us any serious injury you shall be acquitted beforehand of the homicide, and shall not be held to be a deceiver; take courage then and speak.

Well, I said, the law says that when a man is acquitted he is free from guilt, and what holds at law may hold in argument.

Then why should you mind?

Well, I replied, I suppose that I must retrace my steps and say what I perhaps ought to have said before in the proper place. The part of the men has been played out, and now properly enough comes the turn of the women. Of them I will proceed to speak, and the more readily since I am invited by you.

For men born and educated like our citizens, the only way, in my opinion, of arriving at a right conclusion about the possession and use of women and children is to follow the path on which we originally started, when we said that the men were to be the guardians and watchdogs of the herd.

True.

Let us further suppose the birth and education of our women to be subject to similar or nearly similar regulations; then we shall see whether the result accords with our design.

What do you mean?

What I mean may be put into the form of a question, I said: Are dogs divided into hes and shes, or do they both share equally in hunting and in keeping watch and in the other duties of dogs? or do we entrust to the males the entire and exclusive care of the flocks, while we leave the females at home, under the idea that the bearing and suckling their puppies is labour enough for them?

No, he said, they share alike; the only difference between them is that the males are stronger and the females weaker.

But can you use different animals for the same purpose, unless they are bred and fed in the same way?

You cannot.

Then, if women are to have the same duties as men, they must have the same nurture and education? [452]

Yes.

The education which was assigned to the men was music and gymnastic.

Yes.

Then women must be taught music and gymnastic and also the art of war, which they must practise like the men?

That is the inference, I suppose.

I should rather expect, I said, that several of our proposals, if they are carried out, being unusual, may appear ridiculous.

No doubt of it.

Yes, and the most ridiculous thing of all will be the sight of women naked in the palaestra, exercising with the men, especially when they are no longer young; they certainly will not be a vision of beauty, any more than the enthusiastic old men who in spite of wrinkles and ugliness continue to frequent the gymnasia.

Yes, indeed, he said: according to present notions the proposal would be thought ridiculous.

But then, I said, as we have determined to speak our minds, we must not fear the jests of the wits which will be directed against this sort of innovation; how they will talk of women's attainments both in music and gymnastic, and above all about their wearing armour and riding upon horseback!

Very true, he replied.

Yet having begun we must go forward to the rough places of the law; at the same time begging of these gentlemen for once in their life to be serious. Not long ago, as we shall remind them, the Hellenes were of the opinion, which is still generally received among the barbarians, that the sight of a naked man was ridiculous and improper; and when first the Cretans and then the Lacedaemonians introduced the custom, the wits of that day might equally have ridiculed the innovation.

No doubt.

But when experience showed that to let all things be uncovered was far better than to cover them up, and the ludicrous effect to the outward eye vanished before the better principle which reason asserted, then the man was perceived to be a fool who directs the shafts of his ridicule at any other sight but that of folly and vice, or seriously inclines to weigh the beautiful by any other standard but that of the good.

Very true, he replied.

First, then, whether the question is to be put in jest or in earnest, let us come to an understanding about the nature of woman: [453] Is she capable of sharing either wholly or partially in the actions of men, or not at all? And is the art of war one of those arts in which she can or can not share? That will be the best way of commencing the enquiry, and will probably lead to the fairest conclusion.

That will be much the best way.

Shall we take the other side first and begin by arguing against ourselves; in this manner the adversary's position will not be undefended.

Why not? he said.

Then let us put a speech into the mouths of our opponents. They will say: "Socrates and Glaucon, no adversary need convict you, for you yourselves, at the first foundation of the State, admitted the principle that everybody was to do the one work suited to his own nature." And certainly, if I am not mistaken, such an admission was made by us. "And do not the natures of men and women differ very much indeed?" And we shall reply: Of course they do. Then we shall be asked, "Whether the tasks assigned to men and to women should not be different, and such as are agreeable to their different natures?" Certainly they should. "But if so, have you not fallen into a serious inconsistency in saying that men and women, whose natures are so entirely different, ought

to perform the same actions?"—What defence will you make for us, my good Sir, against any one who offers these objections?

That is not an easy question to answer when asked suddenly; and I shall and I do beg of you to draw out the case on our side.

These are the objections, Glaucon, and there are many others of a like kind, which I foresaw long ago; they made me afraid and reluctant to take in hand any law about the possession and nurture of women and children.

By Zeus, he said, the problem to be solved is anything but easy.

Why yes, I said, but the fact is that when a man is out of his depth, whether he has fallen into a little swimming bath or into mid-ocean, he has to swim all the same.

Very true.

And must not we swim and try to reach the shore: we will hope that Arion's dolphin or some other miraculous help may save us?

I suppose so, he said.

Well then, let us see if any way of escape can be found. We acknowledged—did we not? that different natures ought to have different pursuits, and that men's and women's natures are different. And now what are we saying?— that different natures ought to have the same pursuits—this is the inconsistency which is charged upon us.

Precisely.

[454] Verily, Glaucon, I said, glorious is the power of the art of contradiction!

Why do you say so?

Because I think that many a man falls into the practice against his will. When he thinks that he is reasoning he is really disputing, just because he cannot define and divide, and so know that of which he is speaking; and he will pursue a merely verbal opposition in the spirit of contention and not of fair discussion.

Yes, he replied, such is very often the case; but what has that to do with us and our argument?

A great deal; for there is certainly a danger of our getting unintentionally into a verbal opposition.

In what way?

Why we valiantly and pugnaciously insist upon the verbal truth, that different natures ought to have different pursuits, but we never considered at all what was the meaning of sameness or difference of nature, or why we distinguished them when we assigned different pursuits to different natures and the same to the same natures.

Why, no, he said, that was never considered by us.

I said: Suppose that by way of illustration we were to ask the question whether there is not an opposition in nature between bald men and hairy men; and if this is admitted by us, then, if bald men are cobblers, we should forbid the hairy men to be cobblers, and conversely?

That would be a jest, he said.

Yes, I said, a jest; and why? because we never meant when we constructed the State, that the opposition of natures should extend to every difference, but only to those differences which affected the pursuit in which the individual is engaged; we should have argued, for example, that a physician and one who is in mind a physician may be said to have the same nature.

True.

Whereas the physician and the carpenter have different natures?

Certainly.

And if, I said, the male and female sex appear to differ in their fitness for any art or pursuit, we should say that such pursuit or art ought to be assigned to one or the other of them; but if the difference consists only in women bearing and men begetting children, this does not amount to a proof that a woman differs from a man in respect of the sort of education she should receive; and we shall therefore continue to maintain that our guardians and their wives ought to have the same pursuits.

Very true, he said.

Next, we shall ask our opponent how, in reference to any of the pursuits or arts of civic life, [455] the nature of a woman differs from that of a man?

That will be quite fair.

And perhaps he, like yourself, will reply that to give a sufficient answer on the instant is not easy; but after a little reflection there is no difficulty.

Yes, perhaps.

Suppose then that we invite him to accompany us in the argument, and then we may hope to show him that there is nothing peculiar in the constitution of women which would affect them in the administration of the State.

By all means.

Let us say to him: Come now, and we will ask you a question:—when you spoke of a nature gifted or not gifted in any respect, did you mean to say that one man will acquire a thing easily, another with difficulty; a little

learning will lead the one to discover a great deal; whereas the other, after much study and application, no sooner learns than he forgets; or again, did you mean, that the one has a body which is a good servant to his mind, while the body of the other is a hindrance to him?—would not these be the sort of differences which distinguish the man gifted by nature from the one who is ungifted?

No one will deny that.

And can you mention any pursuit of mankind in which the male sex has not all these gifts and qualities in a higher degree than the female? Need I waste time in speaking of the art of weaving, and the management of pancakes and preserves, in which womankind does really appear to be great, and in which for her to be beaten by a man is of all things the most absurd?

You are quite right, he replied, in maintaining the general inferiority of the female sex: although many women are in many things superior to many men, yet on the whole what you say is true.

And if so, my friend, I said, there is no special faculty of administration in a state which a woman has because she is a woman, or which a man has by virtue of his sex, but the gifts of nature are alike diffused in both; all the pursuits of men are the pursuits of women also, but in all of them a woman is inferior to a man.

Very true.

Then are we to impose all our enactments on men and none of them on women?

That will never do.

[456] One woman has a gift of healing, another not; one is a musician, and another has no music in her nature?

Very true.

And one woman has a turn for gymnastic and military exercises, and another is unwarlike and hates gymnastics?

Certainly.

And one woman is a philosopher, and another is an enemy of philosophy; one has spirit, and another is without spirit?

That is also true.

Then one woman will have the temper of a guardian, and another not. Was not the selection of the male guardians determined by differences of this sort?

Yes.

Men and women alike possess the qualities which make a guardian; they differ only in their comparative strength or weakness.

Obviously.

And those women who have such qualities are to be selected as the companions and colleagues of men who have similar qualities and whom they resemble in capacity and in character?

Very true.

And ought not the same natures to have the same pursuits?

They ought.

Then, as we were saying before, there is nothing unnatural in assigning music and gymnastic to the wives of the guardians—to that point we come round again.

Certainly not.

The law which we then enacted was agreeable to nature, and therefore not an impossibility or mere aspiration; and the contrary practice, which prevails at present, is in reality a violation of nature.

That appears to be true.

We had to consider, first, whether our proposals were possible, and secondly whether they were the most beneficial?

Yes.

And the possibility has been acknowledged?

Yes.

The very great benefit has next to be established?

Quite so.

You will admit that the same education which makes a man a good guardian will make a woman a good guardian; for their original nature is the same?

Yes.

I should like to ask you a question.

What is it?

Would you say that all men are equal in excellence, or is one man better than another?

The latter.

And in the commonwealth which we were founding do you conceive the guardians who have been brought up on our model system to be more perfect men, or the cobblers whose education has been cobbling?

What a ridiculous question!

You have answered me, I replied: Well, and may we not further say that our guardians are the best of our citizens?

By far the best.

And will not their wives be the best women?

Yes, by far the best.

And can there be anything better for the interests of the State than that the men and women of a State should be as good as possible?

There can be nothing better.

[457] And this is what the arts of music and gymnastic, when present in such manner as we have described, will accomplish?

Certainly.

Then we have made an enactment not only possible but in the highest degree beneficial to the State?

True.

Then let the wives of our guardians strip, for their virtue will be their robe, and let them share in the toils of war and the defence of their country; only in the distribution of labours the lighter are to be assigned to the women, who are the weaker natures, but in other respects their duties are to be the same. And as for the man who laughs at naked women exercising their bodies from the best of motives, in his laughter he is plucking

A fruit of unripe wisdom,

and he himself is ignorant of what he is laughing at, or what he is about—for that is, and ever will be, the best of sayings, *That the useful is the noble and the hurtful is the base.*

Very true.

Here, then, is one difficulty in our law about women, which we may say that we have now escaped; the wave has not swallowed us up alive for enacting that the guardians of either sex should have all their pursuits in common; to the utility and also to the possibility of this arrangement the consistency of the argument with itself bears witness.

Yes, that was a mighty wave which you have escaped.

Yes, I said, but a greater is coming; you will not think much of this when you see the next.

Go on; let me see.

The law, I said, which is the sequel of this and of all that has preceded, is to the following effect—"that the wives of our guardians are to be common, and their children are to be common, and no parent is to know his own child, nor any child his parent."

Yes, he said, that is a much greater wave than the other; and the possibility as well as the utility of such a law are far more questionable.

I do not think, I said, that there can be any dispute about the very great utility of having wives and children in common; the possibility is quite another matter, and will be very much disputed.

I think that a good many doubts may be raised about both.

You imply that the two questions must be

combined, I replied. Now I meant that you should admit the utility; and in this way, as I thought, I should escape from one of them, and then there would remain only the possibility.

But that little attempt is detected, and therefore you will please to give a defence of both.

Well, I said, I submit to my fate. Yet grant me a little favour: let me feast my mind with the dream as day dreamers are in the [458] habit of feasting themselves when they are walking alone; for before they have discovered any means of effecting their wishes—that is a matter which never troubles them—they would rather not tire themselves by thinking about possibilities; but assuming that what they desire is already granted to them, they proceed with their plan, and delight in detailing what they mean to do when their wish has come true—that is a way which they have of not doing much good to a capacity which was never good for much. Now I myself am beginning to lose heart, and I should like, with your permission, to pass over the question of possibility at present. Assuming therefore the possibility of the proposal, I shall now proceed to enquire how the rulers will carry out these arrangements, and I shall demonstrate that our plan, if executed, will be of the greatest benefit to the State and to the guardians. First of all, then, if you have no objection, I will endeavour with your help to consider the advantages of the measure; and hereafter the question of possibility.

I have no objection; proceed.

First, I think that if our rulers and their auxiliaries are to be worthy of the name which they bear, there must be willingness to obey in the one and the power of command in the other; the guardians must themselves obey the laws, and they must also imitate the spirit of them in any details which are entrusted to their care.

That is right, he said.

You, I said, who are their legislator, having selected the men, will now select the women and give them to them—they must be as far as possible of like natures with them; and they must live in common houses and meet at common meals. None of them will have anything specially his or her own; they will be together, and will be brought up together, and will associate at gymnastic exercises. And so they will be drawn by a necessity of their natures to have intercourse with each other—necessity is not too strong a word, I think?

Yes, he said—necessity, not geometrical, but another sort of necessity which lovers know, and which is far more convincing and constraining to the mass of mankind.

True, I said; and this, Glaucon, like all the rest, must proceed after an orderly fashion; in a city of the blessed, licentiousness is an unholy thing which the rulers will forbid.

Yes, he said, and it ought not to be permitted.

Then clearly the next thing will be to make matrimony sacred in the highest degree, and what is most beneficial will be deemed sacred? [459] Exactly.

And how can marriages be made most beneficial?—that is a question which I put to you, because I see in your house dogs for hunting, and of the nobler sort of birds not a few. Now, I beseech you, do tell me, have you ever attended to their pairing and breeding?

In what particulars?

Why, in the first place, although they are all of a good sort, are not some better than others?

True.

And do you breed from them all indifferently, or do you take care to breed from the best only?

From the best.

And do you take the oldest or the youngest, or only those of ripe age?

I choose only those of ripe age.

And if care was not taken in the breeding, your dogs and birds would greatly deteriorate?

Certainly.

And the same of horses and animals in general?

Undoubtedly.

Good heavens! my dear friend, I said, what consummate skill will our rulers need if the same principle holds of the human species!

Certainly, the same principle holds; but why does this involve any particular skill?

Because, I said, our rulers will often have to practise upon the body corporate with medicines. Now you know that when patients do not require medicines, but have only to be put under a regimen, the inferior sort of practitioner is deemed to be good enough; but when medicine has to be given, then the doctor should be more of a man.

That is quite true, he said; but to what are you alluding?

I mean, I replied, that our rulers will find a considerable dose of falsehood and deceit necessary for the good of their subjects: we were saying that the use of all these things regarded as medicines might be of advantage.

And we were very right.

And this lawful use of them seems likely to be often needed in the regulations of marriages and births.

How so?

Why, I said, the principle has been already laid down that the best of either sex should be united with the best as often, and the inferior with the inferior, as seldom as possible; and that they should rear the offspring of the one sort of union, but not of the other, if the flock is to be maintained in first-rate condition. Now these goings on must be a secret which the rulers only know, or there will be a further danger of our herd, as the guardians may be termed, breaking out into rebellion.

Very true.

Had we not better appoint certain festivals at which we will bring together the brides and bridegrooms, [460] and sacrifices will be offered and suitable hymeneal songs composed by our poets: the number of weddings is a matter which must be left to the discretion of the rulers, whose aim will be to preserve the average of population? There are many other things which they will have to consider, such as the effects of wars and diseases and any similar agencies, in order as far as this is possible to prevent the State from becoming either too large or too small.

Certainly, he replied.

We shall have to invent some ingenious kind of lots which the less worthy may draw on each occasion of our bringing them together, and then they will accuse their own ill-luck and not the rulers.

To be sure, he said.

And I think that our braver and better youth, besides their other honours and rewards, might have greater facilities of intercourse with women given them; their bravery will be a reason, and such fathers ought to have as many sons as possible.

True.

And the proper officers, whether male or female or both, for offices are to be held by women as well as by men—

Yes—

The proper officers will take the offspring of the good parents to the pen or fold, and there they will deposit them with certain nurses who dwell in a separate quarter; but the offspring of the inferior, or of the better when they chance to be deformed, will be put away in some mysterious, unknown place, as they should be.

Yes, he said, that must be done if the breed of the guardians is to be kept pure.

They will provide for their nurture, and will bring the mothers to the fold when they are full of milk, taking the greatest possible care that no mother recognises her own child; and other wet-nurses may be engaged if more are required. Care will also be taken that the process of suckling shall not be protracted too long; and the mothers will have no getting up at night or other trouble, but will hand over all this sort of thing to the nurses and attendants.

You suppose the wives of our guardians to have a fine easy time of it when they are having children.

Why, said I, and so they ought. Let us, however, proceed with our scheme. We were saying that the parents should be in the prime of life?

Very true.

And what is the prime of life? May it not be defined as a period of about twenty years in a woman's life, and thirty in a man's?

Which years do you mean to include?

A woman, I said, at twenty years of age may begin to bear children to the State, and continue to bear them until forty; a man may begin at five-and-twenty, when he has passed the point at which the pulse of life beats quickest, and continue to beget children until he be fifty-five.

[461] Certainly, he said, both in men and women those years are the prime of physical as well as of intellectual vigour.

Any one above or below the prescribed ages who takes part in the public hymeneals shall be said to have done an unholy and unrighteous thing; the child of which he is the father, if it steals into life, will have been conceived under auspices very unlike the sacrifices and prayers, which at each hymeneal priestesses and priests and the whole city will offer, that the new generation may be better and more useful than their good and useful parents, whereas his child will be the offspring of darkness and strange lust.

Very true, he replied.

And the same law will apply to any one of those within the prescribed age who forms a connection with any woman in the prime of life without the sanction of the rulers; for we shall say that he is raising up a bastard to the State, uncertified and unconsecrated.

Very true, he replied.

This applies, however, only to those who are within the specified age: after that we allow them to range at will, except that a man may not marry his daughter or his daughter's daughter, or his mother or his mother's mother; and women, on the other hand, are prohibited from marrying their sons or fathers, or son's son or father's father, and so on in either direction. And we grant all this, accompanying the permission with strict orders to prevent any embryo which may come into being from seeing the light; and if any force a way to the birth, the parents must understand that the offspring of such an union cannot be maintained, and arrange accordingly.

That also, he said, is a reasonable proposition. But how will they know who are fathers and daughters, and so on?

They will never know. The way will be this: —dating from the day of the hymeneal, the bridegroom who was then married will call all the male children who are born in the seventh and ten month afterwards his sons, and the female children his daughters, and they will call him father, and he will call their children his grandchildren, and they will call the elder generation grandfathers and grandmothers. All who were begotten at the time when their fathers and mothers came together will be called their brothers and sisters, and these, as I was saying, will be forbidden to intermarry. This, however, is not to be understood as an absolute prohibition of the marriage of brothers and sisters; if the lot favours them, and they receive the sanction of the Pythian oracle, the law will allow them.

Quite right, he replied.

Such is the scheme, Glaucon, according to which the guardians of our State are to have their wives and families in common. And now you would have the argument show that this community is consistent with the rest of our polity, and also that nothing can be better— would you not?

[462] Yes, certainly.

Shall we try to find a common basis by asking of ourselves what ought to be the chief aim of the legislator in making laws and in the organization of a State—what is the greatest good, and what is the greatest evil, and then consider whether our previous description has the stamp of the good or of the evil?

By all means.

Can there be any greater evil than discord and distraction and plurality where unity ought to reign? or any greater good than the bond of unity?

There cannot.

And there is unity where there is community of pleasures and pains—where all the citizens are glad or grieved on the same occasions of joy and sorrow?

No doubt.

Yes; and where there is no common but only private feeling a State is disorganized—when you have one half of the world triumphing and the other plunged in grief at the same events happening to the city or the citizens?

Certainly.

Such differences commonly originate in a disagreement about the use of the terms "mine" and "not mine," "his" and "not his."

Exactly so.

And is not that the best-ordered State in which the greatest number of persons apply the terms "mine" and "not mine" in the same way to the same thing?

Quite true.

Or that again which most nearly approaches to the condition of the individual—as in the body, when but a finger of one of us is hurt, the whole frame, drawn towards the soul as a centre and forming one kingdom under the ruling power therein, feels the hurt and sympathizes all together with the part affected, and we say that the man has a pain in his finger; and the same expression is used about any other part of the body, which has a sensation of pain at suffering or of pleasure at the alleviation of suffering.

Very true, he replied; and I agree with you that in the best-ordered State there is the nearest approach to this common feeling which you describe.

Then when any one of the citizens experiences any good or evil, the whole State will make his case their own, and will either rejoice or sorrow with him?

Yes, he said, that is what will happen in a well-ordered State.

It will now be time, I said, for us to return to our State and see whether this or some other form is most in accordance with these fundamental principles.

Very good.

[463] Our State like every other has rulers and subjects?

True.

All of whom will call one another citizens?

Of course.

But is there not another name which people give to their rulers in other States?

Generally they call them masters, but in democratic States they simply call them rulers.

And in our State what other name besides that of citizens do the people give the rulers?

They are called saviours and helpers, he replied.

And what do the rulers call the people?

Their maintainers and foster-fathers.

And what do they call them in other States?

Slaves.

And what do the rulers call one another in other States?

Fellow-rulers.

And what in ours?

Fellow-guardians.

Did you ever know an example in any other State of a ruler who would speak of one of his colleagues as his friend and of another as not being his friend?

Yes, very often.

And the friend he regards and describes as one in whom he has an interest, and the other as a stranger in whom he has no interest?

Exactly.

But would any of your guardians think or speak of any other guardian as a stranger?

Certainly he would not; for every one whom they meet will be regarded by them either as a brother or sister, or father or mother, or son or daughter, or as the child of parent of those who are thus connected with him.

Capital, I said; but let me ask you once more: Shall they be a family in name only; or shall they in all their actions be true to the name? For example, in the use of the word "father," would the care of a father be implied and the filial reverence and duty and obedience to him which the law commands; and is the violator of these duties to be regarded as an impious and unrighteous person who is not likely to receive much good either at the hands of God or of man? Are these to be or not to be the strains which the children will hear repeated in their ears by all the citizens about those who are intimated to them to be their parents and the rest of their kinsfolk?

These, he said, and none other; for what can be more ridiculous than for them to utter the names of family ties with the lips only and not to act in the spirit of them?

Then in our city the language of harmony and concord will be more often heard than in any other. As I was describing before, when any one is well or ill, the universal word will be "with me it is well" or "it is ill."

[464] Most true.

And agreeably to this mode of thinking and speaking, were we not saying that they will have their pleasures and pains in common?

Yes, and so they will.

And they will have a common interest in the same thing which they will alike call "my own," and having this common interest they will have a common feeling of pleasure and pain?

Yes, far more so than in other States.

And the reason of this, over and above the general constitution of the State, will be that the guardians will have a community of women and children?

That will be the chief reason.

And this unity of feeling we admitted to be the greatest good, as was implied in our own comparison of a well-ordered State to the relation of the body and the members, when affected by pleasure or pain?

That we acknowledged, and very rightly.

Then the community of wives and children among our citizens is clearly the source of the greatest good to the State?

Certainly.

And this agrees with the other principle which we were affirming—that the guardians were not to have houses or lands or any other property; their pay was to be their food, which they were to receive from the other citizens, and they were to have no private expenses; for we intended them to preserve their true character of guardians.

Right, he replied.

Both the community of property and the community of families, as I am saying, tend to make them more truly guardians; they will not tear the city in pieces by differing about "mine" and "not mine"; each man dragging any acquisition which he has made into a separate house of his own, where he has a separate wife and children and private pleasures and pains; but all will be affected as far as may be by the same pleasures and pains because they are all of one opinion about what is near and dear to them, and therefore they all tend towards a common end.

Certainly, he replied.

And as they have nothing but their persons which they can call their own, suits and complaints will have no existence among them; they will be delivered from all those quarrels of which money or children or relations are the occasion.

Of course they will.

Neither will trials for assault or insult ever be likely to occur among them. For that equals should defend themselves against equals we shall maintain to be honourable and right; [465] we shall make the protection of the person a matter of necessity.

That is good, he said.

Yes; and there is a further good in the law; viz., that if a man has a quarrel with another he will satisfy his resentment then and there, and not proceed to more dangerous lengths.

Certainly.

To the elder shall be assigned the duty of ruling and chastising the younger.

Clearly.

Nor can there be a doubt that the younger will not strike or do any other violence to an elder, unless the magistrates command him; nor will he slight him in any way. For there are two guardians, shame and fear, mighty to prevent him: shame, which makes men refrain from laying hands on those who are to them in the relation of parents; fear, that the injured one will be succoured by the others who are his brothers, sons, fathers.

That is true, he replied.

Then in every way the laws will help the citizens to keep the peace with one another?

Yes, there will be no want of peace.

And as the guardians will never quarrel among themselves there will be no danger of the rest of the city being divided either against them or against one another.

None whatever.

I hardly like even to mention the little meannesses of which they will be rid, for they are beneath notice: such, for example, as the flattery of the rich by the poor, and all the pains and pangs which men experience in bringing up a family, and in finding money to buy necessaries for their household, borrowing and then repudiating, getting how they can, and giving the money into the hands of women and slaves to keep—the many evils of so many kinds which people suffer in this way are mean enough and obvious enough, and not worth speaking of.

Yes, he said, a man has no need of eyes in order to perceive that.

And from all these evils they will be delivered, and their life will be blessed as the life of Olympic victors and yet more blessed.

How so?

The Olympic victor, I said, is deemed happy in receiving a part only of the blessedness which is secured to our citizens, who have won a more glorious victory and have a more complete maintenance at the public cost. For the victory which they have won is the salvation of the whole State; and the crown with which they and their children are crowned is the fulness of all that life needs; they receive rewards from the hands of their country while living, and after death have an honourable burial.

Yes, he said, and glorious rewards they are.

Do you remember, I said, how in the course of the previous discussion [1] some one who shall be nameless accused us of making our [466] guardians unhappy—they had nothing and might have possessed all things—to whom we replied that, if an occasion offered, we might perhaps hereafter consider this question, but that, as at present advised, we would make our guardians truly guardians, and that we were fashioning the State with a view to the greatest happiness, not of any particular class, but of the whole?

Yes, I remember.

And what do you say, now that the life of our protectors is made out to be far better and nobler than that of Olympic victors—is the life of shoemakers, or any other artisans, or of husbandmen, to be compared with it?

Certainly not.

At the same time I ought here to repeat what I have said elsewhere, that if any of our guardians shall try to be happy in such a manner that he will cease to be a guardian, and is not content with this safe and harmonious life, which, in our judgment, is of all lives the best, but infatuated by some youthful conceit of happiness which gets up into his head shall seek to appropriate the whole state to himself, then he will have to learn how wisely Hesiod spoke, when he said, "half is more than the whole."

If he were to consult me, I should say to him: Stay where you are, when you have the offer of such a life.

You agree then, I said, that men and women are to have a common way of life such as we have described—common education, common children; and they are to watch over the citizens in common whether abiding in the city or going out to war; they are to keep watch together, and to hunt together like dogs; and always and in all things, as far as they are able, women are to share with the men? And in so doing they will do what is best, and will not violate, but preserve the natural relation of the sexes.

I agree with you, he replied.

The enquiry, I said, has yet to be made, whether such a community will be found possible—as among other animals, so also among

[1] Sections iv. 419, 420 ff.

men—and if possible, in what way possible?

You have anticipated the question which I was about to suggest.

There is no difficulty, I said, in seeing how war will be carried on by them.

How?

Why, of course they will go on expeditions together; and will take with them any of their children who are strong enough, that, after the manner of the artisan's child, they may look on at the work which they will have to do when they are grown up; [467] and besides looking on they will have to help and be of use in war, and to wait upon their fathers and mothers. Did you never observe in the arts how the potters' boys look on and help, long before they touch the wheel?

Yes, I have.

And shall potters be more careful in educating their children and in giving them the opportunity of seeing and practising their duties than our guardians will be?

The idea is ridiculous, he said.

There is also the effect on the parents, with whom, as with other animals, the presence of their young ones will be the greatest incentive to valour.

That is quite true, Socrates; and yet if they are defeated, which may often happen in war, how great the danger is! the children will be lost as well as their parents, and the State will never recover.

True, I said; but would you never allow them to run any risk?

I am far from saying that.

Well, but if they are ever to run a risk should they not do so on some occasion when, if they escape disaster, they will be the better for it?

Clearly.

Whether the future soldiers do or do not see war in the days of their youth is a very important matter, for the sake of which some risk may fairly be incurred.

Yes, very important.

This then must be our first step—to make our children spectators of war; but we must also contrive that they shall be secured against danger; then all will be well.

True.

Their parents may be supposed not to be blind to the risks of war, but to know, as far as human foresight can, what expeditions are safe and what dangerous?

That may be assumed.

And they will take them on the safe expeditions and be cautious about the dangerous ones?

True.

And they will place them under the command of experienced veterans who will be their leaders and teachers?

Very properly.

Still, the dangers of war cannot be always foreseen; there is a good deal of chance about them?

True.

Then against such chances the children must be at once furnished with wings, in order that in the hour of need they may fly away and escape.

What do you mean? he said.

I mean that we must mount them on horses in their earliest youth, and when they have learnt to ride, take them on horseback to see war: the horses must not be spirited and warlike, but the most tractable and yet the swiftest that can be had. In this way they will get an excellent view of what is hereafter to be their own [468] business; and if there is danger they have only to follow their elder leaders and escape.

I believe that you are right, he said.

Next, as to war; what are to be the relations of your soldiers to one another and to their enemies? I should be inclined to propose that the soldier who leaves his rank or throws away his arms, or is guilty of any other act of cowardice, should be degraded into the rank of a husbandman or artisan. What do you think?

By all means, I should say.

And he who allows himself to be taken prisoner may as well be made a present of to his enemies; he is their lawful prey, and let them do what they like with him.

Certainly.

But the hero who has distinguished himself, what shall be done to him? In the first place, he shall receive honour in the army from his youthful comrades; every one of them in succession shall crown him. What do you say?

I approve.

And what do you say to his receiving the right hand of fellowship?

To that too, I agree.

But you will hardly agree to my next proposal.

What is your proposal?

That he should kiss and be kissed by them.

Most certainly, and I should be disposed to go further, and say: Let no one whom he has a mind to kiss refuse to be kissed by him while the expedition lasts. So that if there be a lover in the army, whether his love be youth or maiden, he may be more eager to win the prize of valour.

Capital, I said. That the brave man is to have more wives than others has been already determined: and he is to have first choices in such matters more than others, in order that he may have as many children as possible?

Agreed.

Again, there is another manner in which, according to Homer, brave youths should be honoured; for he tells how Ajax,[1] after he had distinguished himself in battle, was rewarded with long chines, which seems to be a compliment appropriate to a hero in the flower of his age, being not only a tribute of honour but also a very strengthening thing.

Most true, he said.

Then in this, I said, Homer shall be our teacher; and we too, at sacrifices and on the like occasions, will honour the brave according to the measure of their valour, whether men or women, with hymns and those other distinctions which we were mentioning; also with

seats of precedence, and meats and full cups;[2]

and in honouring them, we shall be at the same time training them.

That, he replied, is excellent.

Yes, I said; and when a man dies gloriously in war shall we not say, in the first place, that he is of the golden race?

To be sure.

Nay, have we not the authority of Hesiod for affirming that when they are dead

[469] *They are holy angels upon the earth, authors of good, averters of evil, the guardians of speech-gifted men?*

Yes; and we accept his authority.

We must learn of the god how we are to order the sepulture of divine and heroic personages, and what is to be their special distinction; and we must do as he bids?

By all means.

And in ages to come we will reverence them and kneel before their sepulchres as at the graves of heroes. And not only they but any who are deemed pre-eminently good, whether they die from age, or in any other way, shall be admitted to the same honours.

That is very right, he said.

Next, how shall our soldiers treat their enemies? What about this?

In what respect do you mean?

[1] *Iliad*, vii. 321.
[2] *Iliad*, viii. 162.

First of all, in regard to slavery? Do you think it right that Hellenes should enslave Hellenic States, or allow others to enslave them, if they can help? Should not their custom be to spare them, considering the danger which there is that the whole race may one day fall under the yoke of the barbarians?

To spare them is infinitely better.

Then no Hellene should be owned by them as a slave; that is a rule which they will observe and advise the other Hellenes to observe.

Certainly, he said; they will in this way be united against the barbarians and will keep their hands off one another.

Next as to the slain; ought the conquerors, I said, to take anything but their armour? Does not the practice of despoiling an enemy afford an excuse for not facing the battle? Cowards skulk about the dead, pretending that they are fulfilling a duty, and many an army before now has been lost from this love of plunder.

Very true.

And is there not illiberality and avarice in robbing a corpse, and also a degree of meanness and womanishness in making an enemy of the dead body when the real enemy has flown away and left only his fighting gear behind him—is not this rather like a dog who cannot get at his assailant, quarrelling with the stones which strike him instead?

Very like a dog, he said.

Then we must abstain from spoiling the dead or hindering their burial?

Yes, he replied, we most certainly must.

Neither shall we offer up arms at the temples of the gods, least of all the arms of Hellenes, [470] if we care to maintain good feeling with other Hellenes; and, indeed, we have reason to fear that the offering of spoils taken from kinsmen may be a pollution unless commanded by the god himself?

Very true.

Again, as to the devastation of Hellenic territory or the burning of houses, what is to be the practice?

May I have the pleasure, he said, of hearing your opinion?

Both should be forbidden, in my judgment; I would take the annual produce and no more. Shall I tell you why?

Pray do.

Why, you see, there is a difference in the names "discord" and "war," and I imagine that there is also a difference in their natures; the one is expressive of what is internal and domestic, the other of what is external and foreign; and the first of the two is termed discord, and only the second, war.

That is a very proper distinction, he replied.

And may I not observe with equal propriety that the Hellenic race is all united together by ties of blood and friendship, and alien and strange to the barbarians?

Very good, he said.

And therefore when Hellenes fight with barbarians and barbarians with Hellenes, they will be described by us as being at war when they fight, and by nature enemies, and this kind of antagonism should be called war; but when Hellenes fight with one another we shall say that Hellas is then in a state of disorder and discord, they being by nature friends; and such enmity is to be called discord.

I agree.

Consider then, I said, when that which we have acknowledged to be discord occurs, and a city is divided, if both parties destroy the lands and burn the houses of one another, how wicked does the strife appear! No true lover of his country would bring himself to tear in pieces his own nurse and mother: There might be reason in the conqueror depriving the conquered of their harvest, but still they would have the idea of peace in their hearts and would not mean to go on fighting for ever.

Yes, he said, that is a better temper than the other.

And will not the city, which you are founding, be an Hellenic city?

It ought to be, he replied.

Then will not the citizens be good and civilised?

Yes, very civilised.

And will they not be lovers of Hellas, and think of Hellas as their own land, and share in the common temples?

Most certainly.

And any difference which arises among them will be regarded by them as discord only—a quarrel among friends, [471] which is not to be called a war?

Certainly not.

Then they will quarrel as those who intend some day to be reconciled?

Certainly.

They will use friendly correction, but will not enslave or destroy their opponents; they will be correctors, not enemies?

Just so.

And as they are Hellenes themselves they will not devastate Hellas, nor will they burn houses, nor even suppose that the whole population of a city—men, women, and children—are equally their enemies, for they know that the guilt of war is always confined to a few persons and that the many are their friends. And for all these reasons they will be unwilling to waste their lands and rase their houses; their enmity to them will only last until the many innocent sufferers have compelled the guilty few to give satisfaction?

I agree, he said, that our citizens should thus deal with their Hellenic enemies; and with barbarians as the Hellenes now deal with one another.

Then let us enact this law also for our guardians:—that they are neither to devastate the lands of Hellenes nor to burn their houses.

Agreed; and we may agree also in thinking that these, like all our previous enactments, are very good.

But still I must say, Socrates, that if you are allowed to go on in this way you will entirely forget the other question which at the commencement of this discussion you thrust aside:—Is such an order of things possible, and how, if at all? For I am quite ready to acknowledge that the plan which you propose, if only feasible, would do all sorts of good to the State. I will add, what you have omitted, that your citizens will be the bravest of warriors, and will never leave their ranks, for they will all know one another, and each will call the other father, brother, son; and if you suppose the women to join their armies, whether in the same rank or in the rear, either as a terror to the enemy, or as auxiliaries in case of need, I know that they will then be absolutely invincible; and there are many domestic advantages which might also be mentioned and which I also fully acknowledge: but, as I admit all these advantages and as many more as you please, if only this State of yours were to come into existence, we need say no more about them; assuming then the existence of the State, let us now turn to the question of possibility and ways and means—the rest may be left.

[472] If I loiter for a moment, you instantly make a raid upon me, I said, and have no mercy; I have hardly escaped the first and second waves, and you seem not to be aware that you are now bringing upon me the third, which is the greatest and heaviest. When you have seen and heard the third wave, I think you will be more considerate and will acknowledge that some fear and hesitation was natural respecting a proposal so extraordinary as that which I have now to state and investigate.

The more appeals of this sort which you make, he said, the more determined are we that you shall tell us how such a State is possible: speak out and at once.

Let me begin by reminding you that we found our way hither in the search after justice and injustice.

True, he replied; but what of that?

I was only going to ask whether, if we have discovered them, we are to require that the just man should in nothing fail of absolute justice; or may we be satisfied with an approximation, and the attainment in him of a higher degree of justice than is to be found in other men?

The approximation will be enough.

We are enquiring into the nature of absolute justice and into the character of the perfectly just, and into injustice and the perfectly unjust, that we might have an ideal. We were to look at these in order that we might judge of our own happiness and unhappiness according to the standard which they exhibited and the degree in which we resembled them, but not with any view of showing that they could exist in fact.

True, he said.

Would a painter be any the worse because, after having delineated with consummate art an ideal of a perfectly beautiful man, he was unable to show that any such man could ever have existed?

He would be none the worse.

Well, and were we not creating an ideal of a perfect State?

To be sure.

And is our theory a worse theory because we are unable to prove the possibility of a city being ordered in the manner described?

Surely not, he replied.

That is the truth, I said. But if, at your request, I am to try and show how and under what conditions the possibility is highest, I must ask you, having this in view, to repeat your former admissions.

What admissions?

[473] I want to know whether ideals are ever fully realized in language? Does not the word express more than the fact, and must not the actual, whatever a man may think, always, in the nature of things, fall short of the truth? What do you say?

I agree.

Then you must not insist on my proving that the actual State will in every respect coincide with the ideal: if we are only able to discover how a city may be governed nearly as we pro-posed, you will admit that we have discovered the possibility which you demand; and will be contented. I am sure that I should be contented—will not you?

Yes, I will.

Let me next endeavour to show what is that fault in States which is the cause of their present maladministration, and what is the least change which will enable a State to pass into the truer form; and let the change, if possible, be of one thing only, or, if not, of two; at any rate, let the changes be as few and slight as possible.

Certainly, he replied.

I think, I said, that there might be a reform of the State if only one change were made, which is not a slight or easy though still a possible one.

What is it? he said.

Now then, I said, I go to meet that which I liken to the greatest of the waves; yet shall the word be spoken, even though the wave break and drown me in laughter and dishonour; and do you mark my words.

Proceed.

I said: *Until philosophers are kings, or the kings and princes of this world have the spirit and power of philosophy, and political greatness and wisdom meet in one, and those commoner natures who pursue either to the exclusion of the other are compelled to stand aside, cities will never have rest from their evils—no, nor the human race, as I believe—and then only will this our State have a possibility of life and behold the light of day.* Such was the thought, my dear Glaucon, which I would fain have uttered if it had not seemed too extravagant; for to be convinced that in no other State can there be happiness private or public is indeed a hard thing.

Socrates, what do you mean? I would have you consider that the word which you have uttered is one at which numerous persons, and very respectable persons too, [474] in a figure pulling off their coats all in a moment, and seizing any weapon that comes to hand, will run at you might and main, before you know where you are, intending to do heaven knows what; and if you don't prepare an answer, and put yourself in motion, you will be "pared by their fine wits," and no mistake.

You got me into the scrape, I said.

And I was quite right; however, I will do all I can to get you out of it; but I can only give you good-will and good advice, and, perhaps, I may be able to fit answers to your questions better than another—that is all. And now, having such an auxiliary, you must do your best to show the unbelievers that you are right.

I ought to try, I said, since you offer me such invaluable assistance. And I think that, if there is to be a chance of our escaping, we must explain to them whom we mean when we say that philosophers are to rule in the State; then we shall be able to defend ourselves: There will be discovered to be some natures who ought to study philosophy and to be leaders in the State; and others who are not born to be philosophers, and are meant to be followers rather than leaders.

Then now for a definition, he said.

Follow me, I said, and I hope that I may in some way or other be able to give you a satisfactory explanation.

Proceed.

I dare say that you remember, and therefore I need not remind you, that a lover, if he is worthy of the name, ought to show his love, not to some one part of that which he loves, but to the whole.

I really do not understand, and therefore beg of you to assist my memory.

Another person, I said, might fairly reply as you do; but a man of pleasure like yourself ought to know that all who are in the flower of youth do somehow or other raise a pang or emotion in a lover's breast, and are thought by him to be worthy of his affectionate regards. Is not this a way which you have with the fair: one has a snub nose, and you praise his charming face; the hook-nose of another has, you say, a royal look; while he who is neither snub nor hooked has the grace of regularity: the dark visage is manly, the fair are children of the gods; and as to the sweet "honey pale," as they are called, what is the very name but the invention of a lover who talks in diminutives, and is not adverse to paleness if appearing on the cheek of youth? [475] In a word, there is no excuse which you will not make, and nothing which you will not say, in order not to lose a single flower that blooms in the springtime of youth.

If you make me an authority in matters of love, for the sake of the argument, I assent.

And what do you say of lovers of wine? Do you not see them doing the same? They are glad of any pretext of drinking any wine.

Very good.

And the same is true of ambitious men; if they cannot command an army, they are willing to command a file; and if they cannot be honoured by really great and important persons, they are glad to be honoured by lesser and meaner people—but honour of some kind they must have.

Exactly.

Once more let me ask: Does he who desires any class of goods, desire the whole class or a part only?

The whole.

And may we not say of the philosopher that he is a lover, not of a part of wisdom only, but of the whole?

Yes, of the whole.

And he who dislikes learning, especially in youth, when he has no power of judging what is good and what is not, such an one we maintain not to be a philosopher or a lover of knowledge, just as he who refuses his food is not hungry, and may be said to have a bad appetite and not a good one?

Very true, he said.

Whereas he who has a taste for every sort of knowledge and who is curious to learn and is never satisfied, may be justly termed a philosopher? Am I not right?

Glaucon said: If curiosity makes a philosopher, you will find many a strange being will have a title to the name. All the lovers of sights have a delight in learning, and must therefore be included. Musical amateurs, too, are a folk strangely out of place among philosophers, for they are the last persons in the world who would come to anything like a philosophical discussion, if they could help, while they run about at the Dionysiac festivals as if they had let out their ears to hear every chorus; whether the performance is in town or country—that makes no difference—they are there. Now are we to maintain that all these and any who have similar tastes, as well as the professors of quite minor arts, are philosophers?

Certainly not, I replied; they are only an imitation.

He said: Who then are the true philosophers?

Those, I said, who are lovers of the vision of truth.

That is also good, he said; but I should like to know what you mean?

To another, I replied, I might have a difficulty in explaining; but I am sure that you will admit a proposition which I am about to make.

What is the proposition?

That since beauty is the opposite of ugliness, they are two?

Certainly.

[476] And inasmuch as they are two, each of them is one?

True again.

And of just and unjust, good and evil, and of every other class, the same remark holds: taken singly, each of them is one; but from the various combinations of them with actions and things and with one another, they are seen in all sorts of lights and appear many?

Very true.

And this is the distinction which I draw between the sight-loving, art-loving, practical class and those of whom I am speaking, and who are alone worthy of the name of philosophers.

How do you distinguish them? he said.

The lovers of sounds and sights, I replied, are, as I conceive, fond of fine tones and colours and forms and all the artificial products that are made out of them, but their mind is incapable of seeing or loving absolute beauty.

True, he replied.

Few are they who are able to attain to the sight of this.

Very true.

And he who, having a sense of beautiful things has no sense of absolute beauty, or who, if another lead him to a knowledge of that beauty is unable to follow—of such an one I ask, Is he awake or in a dream only? Reflect: is not the dreamer, sleeping or waking, one who likens dissimilar things, who puts the copy in the place of the real object?

I should certainly say that such an one was dreaming.

But take the case of the other, who recognises the existence of absolute beauty and is able to distinguish the idea from the objects which participate in the idea, neither putting the objects in the place of the idea nor the idea in the place of the objects—is he a dreamer, or is he awake?

He is wide awake.

And may we not say that the mind of the one who knows has knowledge, and that the mind of the other, who opines only, has opinion?

Certainly.

But suppose that the latter should quarrel with us and dispute our statement, can we administer any soothing cordial or advice to him, without revealing to him that there is sad disorder in his wits?

We must certainly offer him some good advice, he replied.

Come, then, and let us think of something to say to him. Shall we begin by assuring him that he is welcome to any knowledge which he may have, and that we are rejoiced at his having it? But we should like to ask him a question: Does he who has knowledge know something or nothing? (You must answer for him.)

I answer that he knows something.

Something that is or is not?

Something that is; for how can that which is not ever be known?

[477] And are we assured, after looking at the matter from many points of view, that absolute being is or may be absolutely known, but that the utterly non-existent is utterly unknown?

Nothing can be more certain.

Good. But if there be anything which is of such a nature as to be and not to be, that will have a place intermediate between pure being and the absolute negation of being?

Yes, between them.

And, as knowledge corresponded to being and ignorance of necessity to not-being, for that intermediate between being and not-being there has to be discovered a corresponding intermediate between ignorance and knowledge, if there be such?

Certainly.

Do we admit the existence of opinion?

Undoubtedly.

As being the same with knowledge, or another faculty?

Another faculty.

Then opinion and knowledge have to do with different kinds of matter corresponding to this difference of faculties?

Yes.

And knowledge is relative to being and knows being. But before I proceed further I will make a division.

What division?

I will begin by placing faculties in a class by themselves: they are powers in us, and in all other things, by which we do as we do. Sight and hearing, for example, I should call faculties. Have I clearly explained the class which I mean?

Yes, I quite understand.

Then let me tell you my view about them. I do not see them, and therefore the distinctions of figure, colour, and the like, which enable me to discern the differences of some things, do not apply to them. In speaking of a faculty I think only of its sphere and its result; and that which has the same sphere and the same result I call the same faculty, but that which has another sphere and another result I call different. Would that be your way of speaking?

Yes.

And will you be so very good as to answer one more question? Would you say that knowledge is a faculty, or in what class would you place it?

Certainly knowledge is a faculty, and the mightiest of all faculties.

And is opinion also a faculty?

Certainly, he said; for opinion is that with which we are able to form an opinion.

And yet you were acknowledging a little while ago that knowledge is not the same as opinion?

[478] Why, yes, he said: how can any reasonable being ever identify that which is infallible with that which errs?

An excellent answer, proving, I said, that we are quite conscious of a distinction between them.

Yes.

Then knowledge and opinion having distinct powers have also distinct spheres or subject-matters?

That is certain.

Being is the sphere or subject-matter of knowledge, and knowledge is to know the nature of being?

Yes.

And opinion is to have an opinion?

Yes.

And do we know what we opine? or is the subject-matter of opinion the same as the subject-matter of knowledge?

Nay, he replied, that has been already disproven; if difference in faculty implies difference in the sphere or subject-matter, and if, as we were saying, opinion and knowledge are distinct faculties, then the sphere of knowledge and of opinion cannot be the same.

Then if being is the subject-matter of knowledge, something else must be the subject-matter of opinion?

Yes, something else.

Well then, is not-being the subject-matter of opinion? or, rather, how can there be an opinion at all about not-being? Reflect: when a man has an opinion, has he not an opinion about something? Can he have an opinion which is an opinion about nothing?

Impossible.

He who has an opinion has an opinion about some one thing?

Yes.

And not-being is not one thing but, properly speaking, nothing?

True.

Of not-being, ignorance was assumed to be the necessary correlative; of being, knowledge?

True, he said.

Then opinion is not concerned either with being or with not-being?

Not with either.

And can therefore neither be ignorance nor knowledge?

That seems to be true.

But is opinion to be sought without and beyond either of them, in a greater clearness than knowledge, or in a greater darkness than ignorance?

In neither.

Then I suppose that opinion appears to you to be darker than knowledge, but lighter than ignorance?

Both; and in no small degree.

And also to be within and between them?

Yes.

Then you would infer that opinion is intermediate?

No question.

But were we not saying before, that if anything appeared to be of a sort which is and is not at the same time, that sort of thing would appear also to lie in the interval between pure being and absolute not-being; and that the corresponding faculty is neither knowledge nor ignorance, but will be found in the interval between them?

True.

And in that interval there has now been discovered something which we call opinion?

There has.

Then what remains to be discovered is the object which partakes equally of the nature of being and not-being, and cannot rightly be termed either, pure and simple; this unknown term, when discovered, we may truly call the subject of opinion, and assign each to their proper faculty—the extremes to the faculties of the extremes and the mean to the faculty of the mean.

True.

[479] This being premised, I would ask the gentleman who is of opinion that there is no absolute or unchangeable idea of beauty—in whose opinion the beautiful is the manifold —he, I say, your lover of beautiful sights, who cannot bear to be told that the beautiful is one, and the just is one, or that anything is one—to him I would appeal, saying, Will you be so very kind, sir, as to tell us whether, of all these beautiful things, there is one which will not be found ugly; or of the just, which will not be

found unjust; or of the holy, which will not also be unholy?

No, he replied; the beautiful will in some point of view be found ugly; and the same is true of the rest.

And may not the many which are doubles be also halves?—doubles, that is, of one thing, and halves of another?

Quite true.

And things great and small, heavy and light, as they are termed, will not be denoted by these any more than by the opposite names?

True; both these and the opposite names will always attach to all of them.

And can any one of those many things which are called by particular names be said to be this rather than not to be this?

He replied: They are like the punning riddles which are asked at feasts or the children's puzzle about the eunuch aiming at the bat, with what he hit him, as they say in the puzzle, and upon what the bat was sitting. The individual objects of which I am speaking are also a riddle, and have a double sense: nor can you fix them in your mind, either as being or not-being, or both, or neither.

Then what will you do with them? I said. Can they have a better place than between being and not-being? For they are clearly not in greater darkness or negation than not-being, or more full of light and existence than being.

That is quite true, he said.

Thus then we seem to have discovered that the many ideas which the multitude entertain about the beautiful and about all other things are tossing about in some region which is half-way between pure being and pure not-being?

We have.

Yes; and we had before agreed that anything of this kind which we might find was to be described as matter of opinion, and not as matter of knowledge; being the intermediate flux which is caught and detained by the intermediate faculty.

Quite true.

Then those who see the many beautiful, and who yet neither see absolute beauty, nor can follow any guide who points the way thither; who see the many just, and not absolute justice, and the like—such persons may be said to have opinion but not knowledge?

That is certain.

But those who see the absolute and eternal and immutable may be said to know, and not to have opinion only?

Neither can that be denied.

The one love and embrace the subjects of knowledge, the other those of opinion? The latter are the same, as I dare say you will remember, [480] who listened to sweet sounds and gazed upon fair colours, but would not tolerate the existence of absolute beauty.

Yes, I remember.

Shall we then be guilty of any impropriety in calling them lovers of opinion rather than lovers of wisdom, and will they be very angry with us for thus describing them?

I shall tell them not to be angry; no man should be angry at what is true.

But those who love the truth in each thing are to be called lovers of wisdom and not lovers of opinion.

Assuredly.

BOOK VI

[484] AND thus, Glaucon, after the argument has gone a weary way, the true and the false philosophers have at length appeared in view.

I do not think, he said, that the way could have been shortened.

I suppose not, I said; and yet I believe that we might have had a better view of both of them if the discussion could have been confined to this one subject and if there were not many other questions awaiting us, which he who desires to see in what respect the life of the just differs from that of the unjust must consider.

And what is the next question? he asked.

Surely, I said, the one which follows next in order. Inasmuch as philosophers only are able to grasp the eternal and unchangeable, and those who wander in the region of the many and variable are not philosophers, I must ask you which of the two classes should be the rulers of our State?

And how can we rightly answer that question?

Whichever of the two are best able to guard the laws and institutions of our State—let them be our guardians.

Very good.

Neither, I said, can there be any question that the guardian who is to keep anything should have eyes rather than no eyes?

There can be no question of that.

And are not those who are verily and indeed wanting in the knowledge of the true being of each thing, and who have in their souls no clear pattern, and are unable as with a painter's eye to look at the absolute truth and to that original to repair, and having perfect vision of the other world to order the laws about beauty, goodness, justice in this, if not already ordered, and to guard and preserve the order of them—are not such persons, I ask, simply blind?

Truly, he replied, they are much in that condition.

And shall they be our guardians when there are others who, besides being their equals in experience and falling short of them in no particular of virtue, also know the very truth of each thing?

There can be no reason, he said, for rejecting those who have this greatest of all great qualities; [485] they must always have the first place unless they fail in some other respect.

Suppose then, I said, that we determine how far they can unite this and the other excellences.

By all means.

In the first place, as we began by observing, the nature of the philosopher has to be ascertained. We must come to an understanding about him, and, when we have done so, then, if I am not mistaken, we shall also acknowledge that such an union of qualities is possible, and that those in whom they are united, and those only, should be rulers in the State.

What do you mean?

Let us suppose that philosophical minds always love knowledge of a sort which shows them the eternal nature not varying from generation and corruption.

Agreed.

And further, I said, let us agree that they are lovers of all true being; there is no part whether greater or less, or more or less honourable, which they are willing to renounce; as we said before of the lover and the man of ambition.

True.

And if they are to be what we were describing, is there not another quality which they should also possess?

What quality?

Truthfulness: they will never intentionally receive into their mind falsehood, which is their detestation, and they will love the truth.

Yes, that may be safely affirmed of them.

"May be," my friend, I replied, is not the word; say rather "must be affirmed": for he whose nature is amorous of anything cannot help loving all that belongs or is akin to the object of his affections.

Right, he said.

And is there anything more akin to wisdom than truth?

How can there be?

Can the same nature be a lover of wisdom and a lover of falsehood?

Never.

The true lover of learning then must from his earliest youth, as far as in him lies, desire all truth?

Assuredly.

But then again, as we know by experience, he whose desires are strong in one direction will have them weaker in others; they will be like a stream which has been drawn off into another channel.

True.

He whose desires are drawn towards knowledge in every form will be absorbed in the pleasures of the soul, and will hardly feel bodily pleasure—I mean, if he be a true philosopher and not a sham one.

That is most certain.

Such an one is sure to be temperate and the reverse of covetous; for the motives which make another man desirous of having and spending, have no place in his character.

Very true.

[486] Another criterion of the philosophical nature has also to be considered.

What is that?

There should be no secret corner of illiberality; nothing can be more antagonistic than meanness to a soul which is ever longing after the whole of things both divine and human.

Most true, he replied.

Then how can he who has magnificence of mind and is the spectator of all time and all existence, think much of human life?

He cannot.

Or can such an one account death fearful?

No indeed.

Then the cowardly and mean nature has no part in true philosophy?

Certainly not.

Or again: can he who is harmoniously constituted, who is not covetous or mean, or a boaster, or a coward—can he, I say, ever be unjust or hard in his dealings?

Impossible.

Then you will soon observe whether a man is just and gentle, or rude and unsociable; these are the signs which distinguish even in youth the philosophical nature from the unphilosophical.

True.

There is another point which should be remarked.

What point?

Whether he has or has not a pleasure in learning; for no one will love that which gives him

He will.

And when truth is the captain, we cannot suspect any evil of the band which he leads?

Impossible.

Justice and health of mind will be of the company, and temperance will follow after?

True, he replied.

Neither is there any reason why I should again set in array the philosopher's virtues, as you will doubtless remember that courage, magnificence, apprehension, memory, were his natural gifts. And you objected that, although no one could deny what I then said, still, if you leave words and look at facts, the persons who are thus described are some of them manifestly useless, and the greater number utterly depraved; we were then led to enquire into the grounds of these accusations, and have now arrived at the point of asking why are the majority bad, which question of necessity brought us back to the examination and definition of the true philosopher.

Exactly.

And we have next to consider the corruptions of the philosophic nature, why so many are spoiled and so few escape spoiling—I am speaking of those who were said to be useless but not wicked—and, [491] when we have done with them, we will speak of the imitators of philosophy, what manner of men are they who aspire after a profession which is above them and of which they are unworthy, and then, by their manifold inconsistencies, bring upon philosophy, and upon all philosophers, that universal reprobation of which we speak.

What are these corruptions? he said.

I will see if I can explain them to you. Every one will admit that a nature having in perfection all the qualities which we required in a philosopher, is a rare plant which is seldom seen among men.

Rare indeed.

And what numberless and powerful causes tend to destroy these rare natures!

What causes?

In the first place there are their own virtues, their courage, temperance, and the rest of them, every one of which praiseworthy qualities (and this is a most singular circumstance) destroys and distracts from philosophy the soul which is the possessor of them.

That is very singular, he replied.

Then there are all the ordinary goods of life —beauty, wealth, strength, rank, and great connections in the State—you understand the sort

of things—these also have a corrupting and distracting effect.

I understand; but I should like to know more precisely what you mean about them.

Grasp the truth as a whole, I said, and in the right way; you will then have no difficulty in apprehending the preceding remarks, and they will no longer appear strange to you.

And how am I to do so? he asked.

Why, I said, we know that all germs or seeds, whether vegetable or animal, when they fail to meet with proper nutriment or climate or soil, in proportion to their vigour, are all the more sensitive to the want of a suitable environment, for evil is a greater enemy to what is good than what is not.

Very true.

There is reason in supposing that the finest natures, when under alien conditions, receive more injury than the inferior, because the contrast is greater.

Certainly.

And may we not say, Adeimantus, that the most gifted minds, when they are ill-educated, become pre-eminently bad? Do not great crimes and the spirit of pure evil spring out of a fulness of nature ruined by education rather than from any inferiority, whereas weak natures are scarcely capable of any very great good or very great evil?

There I think that you are right.

[492] And our philosopher follows the same analogy—he is like a plant which, having proper nurture, must necessarily grow and mature into all virtue, but, if sown and planted in an alien soil, becomes the most noxious of all weeds, unless he be preserved by some divine power. Do you really think, as people so often say, that our youth are corrupted by Sophists, or that private teachers of the art corrupt them in any degree worth speaking of? Are not the public who say these things the greatest of all Sophists? And do they not educate to perfection young and old, men and women alike, and fashion them after their own hearts?

When is this accomplished? he said.

When they meet together, and the world sits down at an assembly, or in a court of law, or a theatre, or a camp, or in any other popular resort, and there is a great uproar, and they praise some things which are being said or done, and blame other things, equally exaggerating both, shouting and clapping their hands, and the echo of the rocks and the place in which they are assembled redoubles the sound of the praise or blame—at such a time will not a young man's heart, as they say, leap within him? Will any private training enable him to stand firm against the overwhelming flood of popular opinion? or will he be carried away by the stream? Will he not have the notions of good and evil which the public in general have—he will do as they do, and as they are, such will he be?

Yes, Socrates; necessity will compel him.

And yet, I said, there is a still greater necessity, which has not been mentioned.

What is that?

The gentle force of attainder or confiscation or death, which, as you are aware, these new Sophists and educators, who are the public, apply when their words are powerless.

Indeed they do; and in right good earnest.

Now what opinion of any other Sophist, or of any private person, can be expected to overcome in such an unequal contest?

None, he replied.

No, indeed, I said, even to make the attempt is a great piece of folly; there neither is, nor has been, nor is ever likely to be, any different type of character which has had no other training in virtue but that which is supplied by public opinion—I speak, my friend, of human virtue only; what is more than human, as the proverb says, is not included: for I would not have you ignorant that, in the present evil state of governments, whatever is saved and comes to good is saved by the power of God, [493] as we may truly say.

I quite assent, he replied.

Then let me crave your assent also to a further observation.

What are you going to say?

Why, that all those mercenary individuals, whom the many call Sophists and whom they deem to be their adversaries, do, in fact, teach nothing but the opinion of the many, that is to say, the opinions of their assemblies; and this is their wisdom. I might compare them to a man who should study the tempers and desires of a mighty strong beast who is fed by him—he would learn how to approach and handle him, also at what times and from what causes he is dangerous or the reverse, and what is the meaning of his several cries, and by what sounds, when another utters them, he is soothed or infuriated; and you may suppose further, that when, by continually attending upon him, he has become perfect in all this, he calls his knowledge wisdom, and makes of it a system or art, which he proceeds to teach, although he has no real notion of what he means by the principles

or passions of which he is speaking, but calls this honourable and that dishonourable, or good or evil, or just or unjust, all in accordance with the tastes and tempers of the great brute. Good he pronounces to be that in which the beast delights and evil to be that which he dislikes; and he can give no other account of them except that the just and noble are the necessary, having never himself seen, and having no power of explaining to others the nature of either, or the difference between them, which is immense. By heaven, would not such an one be a rare educator?

Indeed he would.

And in what way does he who thinks that wisdom is the discernment of the tempers and tastes of the motley multitude, whether in painting or music, or, finally, in politics, differ from him whom I have been describing? For when a man consorts with the many, and exhibits to them his poem or other work of art or the service which he has done the State, making them his judges when he is not obliged, the so-called necessity of Diomede will oblige him to produce whatever they praise. And yet the reasons are utterly ludicrous which they give in confirmation of their own notions about the honourable and good. Did you ever hear any of them which were not?

No, nor am I likely to hear.

You recognise the truth of what I have been saying? Then let me ask you to consider further whether the world will ever be induced to believe in the existence of absolute beauty rather than of the many beautiful, [494] or of the absolute in each kind rather than of the many in each kind?

Certainly not.

Then the world cannot possibly be a philosopher?

Impossible.

And therefore philosophers must inevitably fall under the censure of the world?

They must.

And of individuals who consort with the mob and seek to please them?

That is evident.

Then, do you see any way in which the philosopher can be preserved in his calling to the end? and remember what we were saying of him, that he was to have quickness and memory and courage and magnificence—these were admitted by us to be the true philosopher's gifts.

Yes.

Will not such an one from his early childhood be in all things first among all, especially if his bodily endowments are like his mental ones?

Certainly, he said.

And his friends and fellow-citizens will want to use him as he gets older for their own purposes?

No question.

Falling at his feet, they will make requests to him and do him honour and flatter him, because they want to get into their hands now, the power which he will one day possess.

That often happens, he said.

And what will a man such as he is be likely to do under such circumstances, especially if he be a citizen of a great city, rich and noble, and a tall proper youth? Will he not be full of boundless aspirations, and fancy himself able to manage the affairs of Hellenes and of barbarians, and having got such notions into his head will he not dilate and elevate himself in the fulness of vain pomp and senseless pride?

To be sure he will.

Now, when he is in this state of mind, if some one gently comes to him and tells him that he is a fool and must get understanding, which can only be got by slaving for it, do you think that, under such adverse circumstances, he will be easily induced to listen?

Far otherwise.

And even if there be some one who through inherent goodness or natural reasonableness has had his eyes opened a little and is humbled and taken captive by philosophy, how will his friends behave when they think that they are likely to lose the advantage which they were hoping to reap from his companionship? Will they not do and say anything to prevent him from yielding to his better nature and to render his teacher powerless, using to this end private intrigues as well as public prosecutions?

[495] There can be no doubt of it.

And how can one who is thus circumstanced ever become a philosopher?

Impossible.

Then were we not right in saying that even the very qualities which make a man a philosopher may, if he be ill-educated, divert him from philosophy, no less than riches and their accompaniments and the other so-called goods of life?

We were quite right.

Thus, my excellent friend, is brought about all that ruin and failure which I have been describing of the natures best adapted to the best of all pursuits; they are natures which we maintain to be rare at any time; this being the class

out of which come the men who are the authors of the greatest evil to States and individuals; and also of the greatest good when the tide carries them in that direction; but a small man never was the doer of any great thing either to individuals or to States.

That is most true, he said.

And so philosophy is left desolate, with her marriage rite incomplete: for her own have fallen away and forsaken her, and while they are leading a false and unbecoming life, other unworthy persons, seeing that she has no kinsmen to be her protectors, enter in and dishonour her; and fasten upon her the reproaches which, as you say, her reprovers utter, who affirm of her votaries that some are good for nothing, and that the greater number deserve the severest punishment.

That is certainly what people say.

Yes; and what else would you expect, I said, when you think of the puny creatures who, seeing this land open to them—a land well stocked with fair names and showy titles—like prisoners running out of prison into a sanctuary, take a leap out of their trades into philosophy; those who do so being probably the cleverest hands at their own miserable crafts? For, although philosophy be in this evil case, still there remains a dignity about her which is not to be found in the arts. And many are thus attracted by her whose natures are imperfect and whose souls are maimed and disfigured by their meannesses, as their bodies are by their trades and crafts. Is not this unavoidable?

Yes.

Are they not exactly like a bald little tinker who has just got out of durance and come into a fortune; he takes a bath and puts on a new coat, and is decked out as a bridegroom going to marry his master's daughter, who is left poor and desolate?

[496] A most exact parallel.

What will be the issue of such marriages? Will they not be vile and bastard?

There can be no question of it.

And when persons who are unworthy of education approach philosophy and make an alliance with her who is a rank above them what sort of ideas and opinions are likely to be generated? Will they not be sophisms captivating to the ear, having nothing in them genuine, or worthy of or akin to true wisdom?

No doubt, he said.

Then, Adeimantus, I said, the worthy disciples of philosophy will be but a small remnant: perchance some noble and well-educated person, detained by exile in her service, who in the absence of corrupting influences remains devoted to her; or some lofty soul born in a mean city, the politics of which he contemns and neglects; and there may be a gifted few who leave the arts, which they justly despise, and come to her—or peradventure there are some who are restrained by our friend Theages' bridle; for everything in the life of Theages conspired to divert him from philosophy; but ill-health kept him away from politics. My own case of the internal sign is hardly worth mentioning, for rarely, if ever, has such a monitor been given to any other man. Those who belong to this small class have tasted how sweet and blessed a possession philosophy is, and have also seen enough of the madness of the multitude; and they know that no politician is honest, nor is there any champion of justice at whose side they may fight and be saved. Such an one may be compared to a man who has fallen among wild beasts—he will not join in the wickedness of his fellows, but neither is he able singly to resist all their fierce natures, and therefore seeing that he would be of no use to the State or to his friends, and reflecting that he would have to throw away his life without doing any good either to himself or others, he holds his peace, and goes his own way. He is like one who, in the storm of dust and sleet which the driving wind hurries along, retires under the shelter of a wall; and seeing the rest of mankind full of wickedness, he is content, if only he can live his own life and be pure from evil or unrighteousness, and depart in peace and good-will, with bright hopes.

Yes, he said, and he will have done a great work before he departs.

A great work—yes; but not the greatest, unless he find a State suitable to him; [497] for in a State which is suitable to him, he will have a larger growth and be the saviour of his country, as well as of himself.

The causes why philosophy is in such an evil name have now been sufficiently explained: the injustice of the charges against her has been shown—is there anything more which you wish to say?

Nothing more on that subject, he replied; but I should like to know which of the governments now existing is in your opinion the one adapted to her.

Not any of them, I said; and that is precisely the accusation which I bring against them—not one of them is worthy of the philosophic nature, and hence that nature is warped and enstranged—as the exotic seed which is sown in a foreign land becomes denaturalized, and is wont to be overpowered and to lose itself in the new soil, even so this growth of philosophy, instead of persisting, degenerates and receives another character. But if philosophy ever finds in the State that perfection which she herself is, then will be seen that she is in truth divine, and that all other things, whether natures of men or institutions, are but human—and now, I know, that you are going to ask, What that State is.

No, he said; there you are wrong, for I was going to ask another question—whether it is the State of which we are the founders and inventors, or some other?

Yes, I replied, ours in most respects; but you may remember my saying before, that some living authority would always be required in the State having the same idea of the constitution which guided you when as legislator you were laying down the laws.

That was said, he replied.

Yes, but not in a satisfactory manner; you frightened us by interposing objections, which certainly showed that the discussion would be long and difficult; and what still remains is the reverse of easy.

What is there remaining?

The question how the study of philosophy may be so ordered as not to be the ruin of the State: All great attempts are attended with risk; "hard is the good," as men say.

Still, he said, let the point be cleared up, and the enquiry will then be complete.

I shall not be hindered, I said, by any want of will, but, if at all, by a want of power: my zeal you may see for yourselves; and please to remark in what I am about to say how boldly and unhesitatingly I declare that States should pursue philosophy, not as they do now, but in a different spirit.

In what manner?

[498] At present, I said, the students of philosophy are quite young; beginning when they are hardly past childhood, they devote only the time saved from money-making and housekeeping to such pursuits; and even those of them who are reputed to have most of the philosophic spirit, when they come within sight of the great difficulty of the subject, I mean dialectic, take themselves off. In after life when invited by some one else, they may, perhaps, go and hear a lecture, and about this they make much ado, for philosophy is not considered by them to be their proper business: at last, when they grow

old, in most cases they are extinguished more truly than Heracleitus' sun, inasmuch as they never light up again.

But what ought to be their course?

Just the opposite. In childhood and youth their study, and what philosophy they learn, should be suited to their tender years: during this period while they are growing up towards manhood, the chief and special care should be given to their bodies that they may have them to use in the service of philosophy; as life advances and the intellect begins to mature, let them increase the gymnastics of the soul; but when the strength of our citizens fails and is past civil and military duties, then let them range at will and engage in no serious labour, as we intend them to live happily here, and to crown this life with a similar happiness in another.

How truly in earnest you are, Socrates! he said; I am sure of that; and yet most of your hearers, if I am not mistaken, are likely to be still more earnest in their opposition to you, and will never be convinced; Thrasymachus least of all.

Do not make a quarrel, I said, between Thrasymachus and me, who have recently become friends, although, indeed, we were never enemies; for I shall go on striving to the utmost until I either convert him and other men, or do something which may profit them against the day when they live again, and hold the like discourse in another state of existence.

You are speaking of a time which is not very near.

Rather, I replied, of a time which is as nothing in comparison with eternity. Nevertheless, I do not wonder that the many refuse to believe; for they have never seen that of which we are now speaking realized; they have seen only a conventional imitation of philosophy, consisting of words artificially brought together, not like these of ours having a natural unity. But a human being who in word and work is perfectly moulded, as far as he can be, into the proportion and likeness of virtue—such a man ruling in a city which bears the same image, [499] they have never yet seen, neither one nor many of them—do you think that they ever did?

No indeed.

No, my friend, and they have seldom, if ever, heard free and noble sentiments; such as men utter when they are earnestly and by every means in their power seeking after truth for the sake of knowledge, while they look coldly on the subtleties of controversy, of which the end is opinion and strife, whether they meet with them in the courts of law or in society.

They are strangers, he said, to the words of which you speak.

And this was what we foresaw, and this was the reason why truth forced us to admit, not without fear and hesitation, that neither cities nor States nor individuals will ever attain perfection until the small class of philosophers whom we termed useless but not corrupt are providentially compelled, whether they will or not, to take care of the State, and until a like necessity be laid on the State to obey them; or until kings, or if not kings, the sons of kings or princes, are divinely inspired with a true love of true philosophy. That either or both of these alternatives are impossible, I see no reason to affirm: if they were so, we might indeed be justly ridiculed as dreamers and visionaries. Am I not right?

Quite right.

If then, in the countless ages of the past, or at the present hour in some foreign clime which is far away and beyond our ken, the perfected philosopher is or has been or hereafter shall be compelled by a superior power to have the charge of the State, we are ready to assert to the death, that this our constitution has been, and is—yea, and will be whenever the Muse of Philosophy is queen. There is no impossibility in all this; that there is a difficulty, we acknowledge ourselves.

My opinion agrees with yours, he said.

But do you mean to say that this is not the opinion of the multitude?

I should imagine not, he replied.

O my friend, I said, do not attack the multitude: they will change their minds, if, not in an aggressive spirit, but gently and with the view of soothing them and removing their dislike of overeducation, you show them your philosophers as they really are and describe as you were just now doing their character and profession, [500] and then mankind will see that he of whom you are speaking is not such as they supposed—if they view him in this new light, they will surely change their notion of him, and answer in another strain. Who can be at enmity with one who loves them, who that is himself gentle and free from envy will be jealous of one in whom there is no jealousy? Nay, let me answer for you, that in a few this harsh temper may be found but not in the majority of mankind.

I quite agree with you, he said.

And do you not also think, as I do, that the harsh feeling which the many entertain towards philosophy originates in the pretenders, who rush in uninvited, and are always abusing them, and finding fault with them, who make persons instead of things the theme of their conversation? and nothing can be more unbecoming in philosophers than this.

It is most unbecoming.

For he, Adeimantus, whose mind is fixed upon true being, has surely no time to look down upon the affairs of earth, or to be filled with malice and envy, contending against men; his eye is ever directed towards things fixed and immutable, which he sees neither injuring nor injured by one another, but all in order moving according to reason; these he imitates, and to these he will, as far as he can, conform himself. Can a man help imitating that with which he holds reverential converse?

Impossible.

And the philosopher holding converse with the divine order, becomes orderly and divine, as far as the nature of man allows; but like every one else, he will suffer from detraction.

Of course.

And if a necessity be laid upon him of fashioning, not only himself, but human nature generally, whether in States or individuals, into that which he beholds elsewhere, will he, think you, be an unskilful artificer of justice, temperance, and every civil virtue?

Anything but unskilful.

And if the world perceives that what we are saying about him is the truth, will they be angry with philosophy? Will they disbelieve us, when we tell them that no State can be happy which is not designed by artists who imitate the heavenly pattern?

They will not be angry if they understand, he said. But how will they draw out the plan of which you are speaking? [501]

They will begin by taking the State and the manners of men, from which, as from a tablet, they will rub out the picture, and leave a clean surface. This is no easy task. But whether easy or not, herein will lie the difference between them and every other legislator—they will have nothing to do either with individual or State, and will inscribe no laws, until they have either found, or themselves made, a clean surface.

They will be very right, he said.

Having effected this, they will proceed to trace an outline of the constitution?

No doubt.

And when they are filling in the work, as I conceive, they will often turn their eyes upwards and downwards: I mean that they will first look at absolute justice and beauty and temperance, and again at the human copy; and will mingle and temper the various elements of life into the image of a man; and thus they will conceive according to that other image, which, when existing among men, Homer calls the form and likeness of God.

Very true, he said.

And one feature they will erase, and another they will put in, until they have made the ways of men, as far as possible, agreeable to the ways of God?

Indeed, he said, in no way could they make a fairer picture.

And now, I said, are we beginning to persuade those whom you described as rushing at us with might and main, that the painter of constitutions is such an one as we are praising; at whom they were so very indignant because to his hands we committed the State; and are they growing a little calmer at what they have just heard?

Much calmer, if there is any sense in them.

Why, where can they still find any ground for objection? Will they doubt that the philosopher is a lover of truth and being?

They would not be so unreasonable.

Or that his nature, being such as we have delineated, is akin to the highest good?

Neither can they doubt this.

But again, will they tell us that such a nature, placed under favourable circumstances, will not be perfectly good and wise if any ever was? Or will they prefer those whom we have rejected?

Surely not.

Then will they still be angry at our saying, that, until philosophers bear rule, States and individuals will have no rest from evil, nor will this our imaginary State ever be realized?

I think that they will be less angry.

Shall we assume that they are not only less angry but quite gentle, [502] and that they have been converted and for very shame, if for no other reason, cannot refuse to come to terms?

By all means, he said.

Then let us suppose that the reconciliation has been effected. Will any one deny the other point, that there may be sons of kings or princes who are by nature philosophers?

Surely no man, he said.

And when they have come into being will any one say that they must of necessity be destroyed; that they can hardly be saved is not denied even by us; but that in the whole course of ages no single one of them can escape—who will venture to affirm this?

Who indeed!

But, said I, one is enough; let there be one man who has a city obedient to his will, and he might bring into existence the ideal polity about which the world is so incredulous.

Yes, one is enough.

The ruler may impose the laws and institutions which we have been describing, and the citizens may possibly be willing to obey them?

Certainly.

And that others should approve, of what we approve, is no miracle or impossibility?

I think not.

But we have sufficiently shown, in what has preceded, that all this, if only possible, is assuredly for the best.

We have.

And now we say not only that our laws, if they could be enacted, would be for the best, but also that the enactment of them, though difficult, is not impossible.

Very good.

And so with pain and toil we have reached the end of one subject, but more remains to be discussed—how and by what studies and pursuits will the saviours of the constitution be created, and at what ages are they to apply themselves to their several studies?

Certainly.

I omitted the troublesome business of the possession of women, and the procreation of children, and the appointment of the rulers, because I knew that the perfect State would be eyed with jealousy and was difficult of attainment; but that piece of cleverness was not of much service to me, for I had to discuss them all the same. The women and children are now disposed of, but the other question of the rulers must be investigated from the very beginning. We were saying, as you will remember, that they were to be lovers of their country, [503] tried by the test of pleasures and pains, and neither in hardships, nor in dangers, nor at any other critical moment were to lose their patriotism—he was to be rejected who failed, but he who always came forth pure, like gold tried in the refiner's fire, was to be made a ruler, and to receive honours and rewards in life and after death. This was the sort of thing which was being said, and then the argument turned aside and veiled her face; not liking to stir the question which has now arisen.

I perfectly remember, he said.

Yes, my friend, I said, and I then shrank from hazarding the bold word; but now let me dare to say—that the perfect guardian must be a philosopher.

Yes, he said, let that be affirmed.

And do not suppose that there will be many of them; for the gifts which were deemed by us to be essential rarely grow together; they are mostly found in shreds and patches.

What do you mean? he said.

You are aware, I replied, that quick intelligence, memory, sagacity, cleverness, and similar qualities, do not often grow together, and that persons who possess them and are at the same time high-spirited and magnanimous are not so constituted by nature as to live orderly and in a peaceful and settled manner; they are driven any way by their impulses, and all solid principle goes out of them.

Very true, he said.

On the other hand, those steadfast natures which can better be depended upon, which in a battle are impregnable to fear and immovable, are equally immovable when there is anything to be learned; they are always in a torpid state, and are apt to yawn and go to sleep over any intellectual toil.

Quite true.

And yet we were saying that both qualities were necessary in those to whom the higher education is to be imparted, and who are to share in any office or command.

Certainly, he said.

And will they be a class which is rarely found?

Yes, indeed.

Then the aspirant must not only be tested in those labours and dangers and pleasures which we mentioned before, but there is another kind of probation which we did not mention—he must be exercised also in many kinds of knowledge, to see whether the soul will be able to endure the highest of all, [504] or will faint under them, as in any other studies and exercises.

Yes, he said, you are quite right in testing him. But what do you mean by the highest of all knowledge?

You may remember, I said, that we divided the soul into three parts; and distinguished the several natures of justice, temperance, courage, and wisdom?

Indeed, he said, if I had forgotten, I should not deserve to hear more.

And do you remember the word of caution which preceded the discussion of them? [1]

[1] Cf. iv. 435.

To what do you refer?

We were saying, if I am not mistaken, that he who wanted to see them in their perfect beauty must take a longer and more circuitous way, at the end of which they would appear; but that we could add on a popular exposition of them on a level with the discussion which had preceded. And you replied that such an exposition would be enough for you, and so the enquiry was continued in what to me seemed to be a very inaccurate manner; whether you were satisfied or not, it is for you to say.

Yes, he said, I thought and the others thought that you gave us a fair measure of truth.

But, my friend, I said, a measure of such things which in any degree falls short of the whole truth is not fair measure; for nothing imperfect is the measure of anything, although persons are too apt to be contented and think that they need search no further.

Not an uncommon case when people are indolent.

Yes, I said; and there cannot be any worse fault in a guardian of the State and of the laws.

True.

The guardian then, I said, must be required to take the longer circuit, and toil at learning as well as at gymnastics, or he will never reach the highest knowledge of all which, as we were just now saying, is his proper calling.

What, he said, is there a knowledge still higher than this—higher than justice and the other virtues?

Yes, I said, there is. And of the virtues too we must behold not the outline merely, as at present—nothing short of the most finished picture should satisfy us. When little things are elaborated with an infinity of pains, in order that they may appear in their full beauty and utmost clearness, how ridiculous that we should not think the highest truths worthy of attaining the highest accuracy!

A right noble thought; but do you suppose that we shall refrain from asking you what is this highest knowledge?

Nay, I said, ask if you will; but I am certain that you have heard the answer many times, and now you either do not understand me or, as I rather think, you are disposed to be troublesome; for you have often been told that the idea of good is the highest [505] knowledge, and that all other things become useful and advantageous only by their use of this. You can hardly be ignorant that of this I was about to speak, concerning which, as you have often heard me say, we know so little; and, without

which, any other knowledge or possession of any kind will profit us nothing. Do you think that the possession of all other things is of any value if we do not possess the good? or the knowledge of all other things if we have no knowledge of beauty and goodness?

Assuredly not.

You are further aware that most people affirm pleasure to be the good, but the finer sort of wits say it is knowledge?

Yes.

And you are aware too that the latter cannot explain what they mean by knowledge, but are obliged after all to say knowledge of the good?

How ridiculous!

Yes, I said, that they should begin by reproaching us with our ignorance of the good, and then presume our knowledge of it—for the good they define to be knowledge of the good, just as if we understood them when they use the term "good"—this is of course ridiculous.

Most true, he said.

And those who make pleasure their good are in equal perplexity; for they are compelled to admit that there are bad pleasures as well as good.

Certainly.

And therefore to acknowledge that bad and good are the same?

True.

There can be no doubt about the numerous difficulties in which this question is involved.

There can be none.

Further, do we not see that many are willing to do or to have or to seem to be what is just and honourable without the reality; but no one is satisfied with the appearance of good—the reality is what they seek; in the case of the good, appearance is despised by every one.

Very true, he said.

Of this then, which every soul of man pursues and makes the end of all his actions, having a presentiment that there is such an end, [506] and yet hesitating because neither knowing the nature nor having the same assurance of this as of other things, and therefore losing whatever good there is in other things,—of a principle such and so great as this ought the best men in our State, to whom everything is entrusted, to be in the darkness of ignorance?

Certainly not, he said.

I am sure, I said, that he who does not know how the beautiful and the just are likewise good will be but a sorry guardian of them; and I suspect that no one who is ignorant of the good will have a true knowledge of them.

That, he said, is a shrewd suspicion of yours.

And if we only have a guardian who has this knowledge our State will be perfectly ordered?

Of course, he replied; but I wish that you would tell me whether you conceive this supreme principle of the good to be knowledge or pleasure, or different from either?

Aye, I said, I knew all along that a fastidious gentleman like you would not be contented with the thoughts of other people about these matters.

True, Socrates; but I must say that one who like you has passed a lifetime in the study of philosophy should not be always repeating the opinions of others, and never telling his own.

Well, but has any one a right to say positively what he does not know?

Not, he said, with the assurance of positive certainty; he has no right to do that: but he may say what he thinks, as a matter of opinion.

And do you not know, I said, that all mere opinions are bad, and the best of them blind? You would not deny that those who have any true notion without intelligence are only like blind men who feel their way along the road?

Very true.

And do you wish to behold what is blind and crooked and base, when others will tell you of brightness and beauty?

Still, I must implore you, Socrates, said Glaucon, not to turn away just as you are reaching the goal; if you will only give such an explanation of the good as you have already given of justice and temperance and the other virtues, we shall be satisfied.

Yes, my friend, and I shall be at least equally satisfied, but I cannot help fearing that I shall fail, and that my indiscreet zeal will bring ridicule upon me. No, sweet sirs, let us not at present ask what is the actual nature of the good, for to reach what is now in my thoughts would be an effort too great for me. But of the child of the good who is likest him, I would fain speak, if I could be sure that you wished to hear—otherwise, not.

By all means, he said, tell us about the child, and you shall remain in our debt for the account of the parent.

[507] I do indeed wish, I replied, that I could pay, and you receive, the account of the parent, and not, as now, of the offspring only; take, however, this latter by way of interest,[1] and at the same time have a care that I do not render a false account, although I have no intention of deceiving you.

Yes, we will take all the care that we can: proceed.

Yes, I said, but I must first come to an understanding with you, and remind you of what I have mentioned in the course of this discussion, and at many other times.

What?

The old story, that there is a many beautiful and a many good, and so of other things which we describe and define; to all of them "many" is applied.

True, he said.

And there is an absolute beauty and an absolute good, and of other things to which the term "many" is applied there is an absolute; for they may be brought under a single idea, which is called the essence of each.

Very true.

The many, as we say, are seen but not known, and the ideas are known but not seen.

Exactly.

And what is the organ with which we see the visible things?

The sight, he said.

And with the hearing, I said, we hear, and with the other senses perceive the other objects of sense?

True.

But have you remarked that sight is by far the most costly and complex piece of workmanship which the artificer of the senses ever contrived?

No, I never have, he said.

Then reflect: has the ear or voice need of any third or additional nature in order that the one may be able to hear and the other to be heard?

Nothing of the sort.

No, indeed, I replied; and the same is true of most, if not all, the other senses—you would not say that any of them requires such an addition?

Certainly not.

But you see that without the addition of some other nature there is no seeing or being seen?

How do you mean?

Sight being, as I conceive, in the eyes, and he who has eyes wanting to see; colour being also present in them, still unless there be a third nature specially adapted to the purpose, the owner of the eyes will see nothing and the colours will be invisible.

Of what nature are you speaking?

Of that which you term light, I replied.

True, he said.

[508] Noble, then, is the bond which links

[1] A play upon τόκος, which means both "offspring" and "interest."

together sight and visibility, and great beyond other bonds by no small difference of nature; for light is their bond, and light is no ignoble thing?

Nay, he said, the reverse of ignoble.

And which, I said, of the gods in heaven would you say was the lord of this element? Whose is that light which makes the eye to see perfectly and the visible to appear?

You mean the sun, as you and all mankind say.

May not the relation of sight to this deity be described as follows?

How?

Neither sight nor the eye in which sight resides is the sun?

No.

Yet of all the organs of sense the eye is the most like the sun?

By far the most like.

And the power which the eye possesses is a sort of effluence which is dispensed from the sun?

Exactly.

Then the sun is not sight, but the author of sight who is recognized by sight.

True, he said.

And this is he whom I call the child of the good, whom the good begat in his own likeness, to be in the visible world, in relation to sight and the things of sight, what the good is in the intellectual world in relation to mind and the things of mind.

Will you be a little more explicit? he said.

Why, you know, I said, that the eyes, when a person directs them towards objects on which the light of day is no longer shining, but the moon and stars only, see dimly, and are nearly blind; they seem to have no clearness of vision in them?

Very true.

But when they are directed towards objects on which the sun shines, they see clearly and there is sight in them?

Certainly.

And the soul is like the eye: when resting upon that on which truth and being shine, the soul perceives and understands and is radiant with intelligence; but when turned towards the twilight of becoming and perishing, then she has opinion only, and goes blinking about, and is first of one opinion and then of another, and seems to have no intelligence?

Just so.

Now, that which imparts truth to the known and the power of knowing to the knower is

what I would have you term the idea of good, and this you will deem to be the cause of science, and of truth in so far as the latter becomes the subject of knowledge; beautiful too, as are both truth and knowledge, you will be right in esteeming this other nature as more beautiful than either; [509] and, as in the previous instance, light and sight may be truly said to be like the sun, and yet not to be the sun, so in this other sphere, science and truth may be deemed to be like the good, but not the good; the good has a place of honour yet higher.

What a wonder of beauty that must be, he said, which is the author of science and truth, and yet surpasses them in beauty; for you surely cannot mean to say that pleasure is the good?

God forbid, I replied; but may I ask you to consider the image in another point of view?

In what point of view?

You would say, would you not, that the sun is not only the author of visibility in all visible things, but of generation and nourishment and growth, though he himself is not generation?

Certainly.

In like manner the good may be said to be not only the author of knowledge to all things known, but of their being and essence, and yet the good is not essence, but far exceeds essence in dignity and power.

Glaucon said, with a ludicrous earnestness: By the light of heaven, how amazing!

Yes, I said, and the exaggeration may be set down to you; for you made me utter my fancies.

And pray continue to utter them; at any rate let us hear if there is anything more to be said about the similitude of the sun.

Yes, I said, there is a great deal more.

Then omit nothing, however slight.

I will do my best, I said; but I should think that a great deal will have to be omitted.

You have to imagine, then, that there are two ruling powers, and that one of them is set over the intellectual world, the other over the visible. I do not say heaven, lest you should fancy that I am playing upon the name (οὐρανός, ὁρατός). May I suppose that you have this distinction of the visible and intelligible fixed in your mind?

I have.

Now take a line which has been cut into two unequal parts, and divide each of them again in the same proportion, and suppose the two main divisions to answer, one to the visible and the other to the intelligible, and then compare the subdivisions in respect of their clearness and want of clearness, and you will find that the first section in the sphere of the visible consists of images. [510] And by images I mean, in the first place, shadows, and in the second place, reflections in water and in solid, smooth and polished bodies and the like: Do you understand?

Yes, I understand.

Imagine, now, the other section, of which this is only the resemblance, to include the animals which we see, and everything that grows or is made.

Very good.

Would you not admit that both the sections of this division have different degrees of truth, and that the copy is to the original as the sphere of opinion is to the sphere of knowledge?

Most undoubtedly.

Next proceed to consider the manner in which the sphere of the intellectual is to be divided.

In what manner?

Thus:—There are two subdivisions, in the lower of which the soul uses the figures given by the former division as images; the enquiry can only be hypothetical, and instead of going upwards to a principle descends to the other end; in the higher of the two, the soul passes out of hypotheses, and goes up to a principle which is above hypotheses, making no use of images as in the former case, but proceeding only in and through the ideas themselves.

I do not quite understand your meaning, he said.

Then I will try again; you will understand me better when I have made some preliminary remarks. You are aware that students of geometry, arithmetic, and the kindred sciences assume the odd and the even and the figures and three kinds of angles and the like in their several branches of science; these are their hypotheses, which they and every body are supposed to know, and therefore they do not deign to give any account of them either to themselves or others; but they begin with them, and go on until they arrive at last, and in a consistent manner, at their conclusion?

Yes, he said, I know.

And do you not know also that although they make use of the visible forms and reason about them, they are thinking not of these, but of the ideals which they resemble; not of the figures which they draw, but of the absolute square and the absolute diameter, and so on—the forms which they draw or make, and which have shadows and reflections in water of their own, are converted by them into images, but they are really seeking to behold the things themselves, which can only be seen with the eye of the mind?

[511] That is true.

And of this kind I spoke as the intelligible, although in the search after it the soul is compelled to use hypotheses; not ascending to a first principle, because she is unable to rise above the region of hypothesis, but employing the objects of which the shadows below are resemblances in their turn as images, they having in relation to the shadows and reflections of them a greater distinctness, and therefore a higher value.

I understand, he said, that you are speaking of the province of geometry and the sister arts.

And when I speak of the other division of the intelligible, you will understand me to speak of that other sort of knowledge which reason herself attains by the power of dialectic, using the hypotheses not as first principles, but only as hypotheses—that is to say, as steps and points of departure into a world which is above hypotheses, in order that she may soar beyond them to the first principle of the whole; and clinging to this and then to that which depends on this, by successive steps she descends again without the aid of any sensible object, from ideas, through ideas, and in ideas she ends.

I understand you, he replied; not perfectly, for you seem to me to be describing a task which is really tremendous; but, at any rate, I understand you to say that knowledge and being, which the science of dialectic contemplates, are clearer than the notions of the arts, as they are termed, which proceed from hypotheses only: these are also contemplated by the understanding, and not by the senses: yet, because they start from hypotheses and do not ascend to a principle, those who contemplate them appear to you not to exercise the higher reason upon them, although when a first principle is added to them they are cognizable by the higher reason. And the habit which is concerned with geometry and the cognate sciences I suppose that you would term understanding and not reason, as being intermediate between opinion and reason.

You have quite conceived my meaning, I said; and now, corresponding to these four divisions, let there be four faculties in the soul—reason answering to the highest, understanding to the second, faith (or conviction) to the third, and perception of shadows to the last—and let there be a scale of them, and let us suppose that the several faculties have clearness in the same degree that their objects have truth.

I understand, he replied, and give my assent, and accept your arrangement.

BOOK VII

[514] AND now, I said, let me show in a figure how far our nature is enlightened or unenlightened:—Behold! human beings living in an underground den, which has a mouth open towards the light and reaching all along the den; here they have been from their childhood, and have their legs and necks chained so that they cannot move, and can only see before them, being prevented by the chains from turning round their heads. Above and behind them a fire is blazing at a distance, and between the fire and the prisoners there is a raised way; and you will see, if you look, a low wall built along the way, like the screen which marionette players have in front of them, over which they show the puppets.

I see.

And do you see, I said, men passing along the wall carrying all sorts of vessels, [515] and statues and figures of animals made of wood and stone and various materials, which appear over the wall? Some of them are talking, others silent.

You have shown me a strange image, and they are strange prisoners.

Like ourselves, I replied; and they see only their own shadows, or the shadows of one another, which the fire throws on the opposite wall of the cave?

True, he said; how could they see anything but the shadows if they were never allowed to move their heads?

And of the objects which are being carried in like manner they would only see the shadows?

Yes, he said.

And if they were able to converse with one another, would they not suppose that they were naming what was actually before them?

Very true.

And suppose further that the prison had an echo which came from the other side, would they not be sure to fancy when one of the passers-by spoke that the voice which they heard came from the passing shadow?

No question, he replied.

To them, I said, the truth would be literally nothing but the shadows of the images.

That is certain.

And now look again, and see what will naturally follow if the prisoners are released and disabused of their error. At first, when any of them is liberated and compelled suddenly to stand up and turn his neck round and walk and look towards the light, he will suffer sharp pains; the glare will distress him, and he will be unable to see the realities of which in his former state he had seen the shadows; and then conceive some one saying to him, that what he saw before was an illusion, but that now, when he is approaching nearer to being and his eye is turned towards more real existence, he has a clearer vision—what will be his reply? And you may further imagine that his instructor is pointing to the objects as they pass and requiring him to name them—will he not be perplexed? Will he not fancy that the shadows which he formerly saw are truer than the objects which are now shown to him?

Far truer.

And if he is compelled to look straight at the light, will he not have a pain in his eyes which will make him turn away to take refuge in the objects of vision which he can see, and which he will conceive to be in reality clearer than the things which are now being shown to him?

True, he said.

And suppose once more, that he is reluctantly dragged up a steep and rugged ascent, and held fast until he is forced into the presence of the sun himself, [516] is he not likely to be pained and irritated? When he approaches the light his eyes will be dazzled, and he will not be able to see anything at all of what are now called realities.

Not all in a moment, he said.

He will require to grow accustomed to the sight of the upper world. And first he will see the shadows best, next the reflections of men and other objects in the water, and then the objects themselves; then he will gaze upon the light of the moon and the stars and the spangled heaven; and he will see the sky and the stars by night better than the sun or the light of the sun by day?

Certainly.

Last of all he will be able to see the sun, and not mere reflections of him in the water, but he will see him in his own proper place, and not in another; and he will contemplate him as he is.

Certainly.

He will then proceed to argue that this is he who gives the season and the years, and is the guardian of all that is in the visible world, and in a certain way the cause of all things which he and his fellows have been accustomed to behold?

Clearly, he said, he would first see the sun and then reason about him.

And when he remembered his old habitation, and the wisdom of the den and his fellow-prisoners, do you not suppose that he would felicitate himself on the change, and pity them?

Certainly, he would.

And if they were in the habit of conferring honours among themselves on those who were quickest to observe the passing shadows and to remark which of them went before, and which followed after, and which were together; and who were therefore best able to draw conclusions as to the future, do you think that he would care for such honours and glories, or envy the possessors of them? Would he not say with Homer,

Better to be the poor servant of a poor master,

and to endure anything, rather than think as they do and live after their manner?

Yes, he said, I think that he would rather suffer anything than entertain these false notions and live in this miserable manner.

Imagine once more, I said, such an one coming suddenly out of the sun to be replaced in his old situation; would he not be certain to have his eyes full of darkness?

To be sure, he said.

And if there were a contest, and he had to compete in measuring the shadows with the prisoners who had never moved out of the [517] den, while his sight was still weak, and before his eyes had become steady (and the time which would be needed to acquire this new habit of sight might be very considerable), would he not be ridiculous? Men would say of him that up he went and down he came without his eyes; and that it was better not even to think of ascending; and if any one tried to loose another and lead him up to the light, let them only catch the offender, and they would put him to death.

No question, he said.

This entire allegory, I said, you may now append, dear Glaucon, to the previous argument; the prison-house is the world of sight, the light of the fire is the sun, and you will not misapprehend me if you interpret the journey upwards to be the ascent of the soul into the intellectual world according to my poor belief, which, at your desire, I have expressed—whether rightly or wrongly God knows. But, whether true or false, my opinion is that in the world of knowledge the idea of good appears last of all, and is seen only with an effort; and,

when seen, is also inferred to be the universal author of all things beautiful and right, parent of light and of the lord of light in this visible world, and the immediate source of reason and truth in the intellectual; and that this is the power upon which he who would act rationally either in public or private life must have his eye fixed.

I agree, he said, as far as I am able to understand you.

Moreover, I said, you must not wonder that those who attain to this beatific vision are unwilling to descend to human affairs; for their souls are ever hastening into the upper world where they desire to dwell; which desire of theirs is very natural, if our allegory may be trusted.

Yes, very natural.

And is there anything surprising in one who passes from divine contemplations to the evil state of man, misbehaving himself in a ridiculous manner; if, while his eyes are blinking and before he has become accustomed to the surrounding darkness, he is compelled to fight in courts of law, or in other places, about the images or the shadows of images of justice, and is endeavouring to meet the conceptions of those who have never yet seen absolute justice?

Anything but surprising, he replied.

[518] Any one who has common sense will remember that the bewilderments of the eyes are of two kinds, and arise from two causes, either from coming out of the light or from going into the light, which is true of the mind's eye, quite as much as of the bodily eye; and he who remembers this when he sees any one whose vision is perplexed and weak, will not be too ready to laugh; he will first ask whether that soul of man has come out of the brighter life, and is unable to see because unaccustomed to the dark, or having turned from darkness to the day is dazzled by excess of light. And he will count the one happy in his condition and state of being, and he will pity the other; or, if he have a mind to laugh at the soul which comes from below into the light, there will be more reason in this than in the laugh which greets him who returns from above out of the light into the den.

That, he said, is a very just distinction.

But then, if I am right, certain professors of education must be wrong when they say that they can put a knowledge into the soul which was not there before, like sight into blind eyes.

They undoubtedly say this, he replied.

Whereas, our argument shows that the power

and capacity of learning exists in the soul already; and that just as the eye was unable to turn from darkness to light without the whole body, so too the instrument of knowledge can only by the movement of the whole soul be turned from the world of becoming into that of being, and learn by degrees to endure the sight of being, and of the brightest and best of being, or in other words, of the good.

Very true.

And must there not be some art which will effect conversion in the easiest and quickest manner; not implanting the faculty of sight, for that exists already, but has been turned in the wrong direction, and is looking away from the truth?

Yes, he said, such an art may be presumed.

And whereas the other so-called virtues of the soul seem to be akin to bodily qualities, for even when they are not originally innate they can be implanted later by habit and exercise, the virtue of wisdom more than anything else contains a divine element which always remains, and by this conversion is rendered useful and profitable; [519] or, on the other hand, hurtful and useless. Did you never observe the narrow intelligence flashing from the keen eye of a clever rogue—how eager he is, how clearly his paltry soul sees the way to his end; he is the reverse of blind, but his keen eye-sight is forced into the service of evil, and he is mischievous in proportion to his cleverness?

Very true, he said.

But what if there had been a circumcision of such natures in the days of their youth; and they had been severed from those sensual pleasures, such as eating and drinking, which, like leaden weights, were attached to them at their birth, and which drag them down and turn the vision of their souls upon the things that are below—if, I say, they had been released from these impediments and turned in the opposite direction, the very same faculty in them would have seen the truth as keenly as they see what their eyes are turned to now.

Very likely.

Yes, I said; and there is another thing which is likely, or rather a necessary inference from what has preceded, that neither the uneducated and uninformed of the truth, nor yet those who never make an end of their education, will be able ministers of State; not the former, because they have no single aim of duty which is the rule of all their actions, private as well as public; nor the latter, because they will not act at all except upon compulsion, fancying that they are already dwelling apart in the islands of the blest.

Very true, he replied.

Then, I said, the business of us who are the founders of the State will be to compel the best minds to attain that knowledge which we have already shown to be the greatest of all—they must continue to ascend until they arrive at the good; but when they have ascended and seen enough we must not allow them to do as they do now.

What do you mean?

I mean that they remain in the upper world: but this must not be allowed; they must be made to descend again among the prisoners in the den, and partake of their labours and honours, whether they are worth having or not.

But is not this unjust? he said; ought we to give them a worse life, when they might have a better?

You have again forgotten, my friend, I said, the intention of the legislator, who did not aim at making any one class in the State happy above the rest; the happiness was to be in the whole State, and he held the citizens together by persuasion and necessity, making them benefactors of the State, [520] and therefore benefactors of one another; to this end he created them, not to please themselves, but to be his instruments in binding up the State.

True, he said, I had forgotten.

Observe, Glaucon, that there will be no injustice in compelling our philosophers to have a care and providence of others; we shall explain to them that in other States, men of their class are not obliged to share in the toils of politics: and this is reasonable, for they grow up at their own sweet will, and the government would rather not have them. Being self-taught, they cannot be expected to show any gratitude for a culture which they have never received. But we have brought you into the world to be rulers of the hive, kings of yourselves and of the other citizens, and have educated you far better and more perfectly than they have been educated, and you are better able to share in the double duty. Wherefore each of you, when his turn comes, must go down to the general underground abode, and get the habit of seeing in the dark. When you have acquired the habit, you will see ten thousand times better than the inhabitants of the den, and you will know what the several images are, and what they represent, because you have seen the beautiful and just and good in their truth. And thus our State which is also yours will be a reality, and not a dream only, and will be administered in a spirit unlike that of other States, in which men fight with one another about shadows only and are distracted in the struggle for power, which in their eyes is a great good. Whereas the truth is that the State in which the rulers are most reluctant to govern is always the best and most quietly governed, and the State in which they are most eager, the worst.

Quite true, he replied.

And will our pupils, when they hear this, refuse to take their turn at the toils of State, when they are allowed to spend the greater part of their time with one another in the heavenly light?

Impossible, he answered; for they are just men, and the commands which we impose upon them are just; there can be no doubt that every one of them will take office as a stern necessity, and not after the fashion of our present rulers of State.

Yes, my friend, I said; and there lies the point. You must contrive for your future rulers another and a better life than that of [521] a ruler, and then you may have a well-ordered State; for only in the State which offers this, will they rule who are truly rich, not in silver and gold, but in virtue and wisdom, which are the true blessings of life. Whereas if they go to the administration of public affairs, poor and hungering after their own private advantage, thinking that hence they are to snatch the chief good, order there can never be; for they will be fighting about office, and the civil and domestic broils which thus arise will be the ruin of the rulers themselves and of the whole State.

Most true, he replied.

And the only life which looks down upon the life of political ambition is that of true philosophy. Do you know of any other?

Indeed, I do not, he said.

And those who govern ought not to be lovers of the task? For, if they are, there will be rival lovers, and they will fight.

No question.

Who then are those whom we shall compel to be guardians? Surely they will be the men who are wisest about affairs of State, and by whom the State is best administered, and who at the same time have other honours and another and a better life than that of politics?

They are the men, and I will choose them, he replied.

And now shall we consider in what way such guardians will be produced, and how they are to be brought from darkness to light—as some

are said to have ascended from the world below to the gods?

By all means, he replied.

The process, I said, is not the turning over of an oyster-shell,[1] but the turning round of a soul passing from a day which is little better than night to the true day of being, that is, the ascent from below, which we affirm to be true philosophy?

Quite so.

And should we not enquire what sort of knowledge has the power of effecting such a change?

Certainly.

What sort of knowledge is there which would draw the soul from becoming to being? And another consideration has just occurred to me: You will remember that our young men are to be warrior athletes?

Yes, that was said.

Then this new kind of knowledge must have an additional quality?

What quality?

Usefulness in war.

Yes, if possible.

There were two parts in our former scheme of education, were there not?

Just so.

There was gymnastic which presided over the growth and decay of the body, and may therefore be regarded as having to do with generation and corruption?

True.

[522] Then that is not the knowledge which we are seeking to discover?

No.

But what do you say of music, what also entered to a certain extent into our former scheme?

Music, he said, as you will remember, was the counterpart of gymnastic, and trained the guardians by the influences of habit, by harmony making them harmonious, by rhythm rhythmical, but not giving them science; and the words, whether fabulous or possibly true, had kindred elements of rhythm and harmony in them. But in music there was nothing which tended to that good which you are now seeking.

You are most accurate, I said, in your recollection; in music there certainly was nothing of the kind. But what branch of knowledge is there, my dear Glaucon, which is of the desired nature; since all the useful arts were

---

[1] In allusion to a game in which two parties fled or pursued according as an oyster-shell which was thrown into the air fell with the dark or light side uppermost.

reckoned mean by us?

Undoubtedly; and yet if music and gymnastic are excluded, and the arts are also excluded, what remains?

Well, I said, there may be nothing left of our special subjects; and then we shall have to take something which is not special, but of universal application.

What may that be?

A something which all arts and sciences and intelligences use in common, and which every one first has to learn among the elements of education.

What is that?

The little matter of distinguishing one, two, and three—in a word, number and calculation: —do not all arts and sciences necessarily partake of them?

Yes.

Then the art of war partakes of them?

To be sure.

Then Palamedes, whenever he appears in tragedy, proves Agamemnon ridiculously unfit to be a general. Did you never remark how he declares that he had invented number, and had numbered the ships and set in array the ranks of the army at Troy; which implies that they had never been numbered before, and Agamemnon must be supposed literally to have been incapable of counting his own feet—how could he if he was ignorant of number? And if that is true, what sort of general must he have been?

I should say a very strange one, if this was as you say.

Can we deny that a warrior should have a knowledge of arithmetic?

Certainly he should, if he is to have the smallest understanding of military tactics, or indeed, I should rather say, if he is to be a man at all.

I should like to know whether you have the same notion which I have of this study?

What is your notion?

It appears to me to be a study of the kind which we are seeking, and which leads naturally to reflection, [523] but never to have been rightly used; for the true use of it is simply to draw the soul towards being.

Will you explain your meaning? he said.

I will try, I said; and I wish you would share the enquiry with me, and say "yes" or "no" when I attempt to distinguish in my own mind what branches of knowledge have this attracting power, in order that we may have clearer proof that arithmetic is, as I suspect, one of them.

Explain, he said.

I mean to say that objects of sense are of two kinds; some of them do not invite thought because the sense is an adequate judge of them; while in the case of other objects sense is so untrustworthy that further enquiry is imperatively demanded.

You are clearly referring, he said, to the manner in which the senses are imposed upon by distance, and by painting in light and shade.

No, I said, that is not at all my meaning.

Then what is your meaning?

When speaking of uninviting objects, I mean those which do not pass from one sensation to the opposite; inviting objects are those which do; in this latter case the sense coming upon the object, whether at a distance or near, gives no more vivid idea of anything in particular than of its opposite. An illustration will make my meaning clearer:—here are three fingers—a little finger, a second finger, and a middle finger.

Very good.

You may suppose that they are seen quite close: And here comes the point.

What is it?

Each of them equally appears a finger, whether seen in the middle or at the extremity, whether white or black, or thick or thin—it makes no difference; a finger is a finger all the same. In these cases a man is not compelled to ask of thought the question what is a finger? for the sight never intimates to the mind that a finger is other than a finger.

True.

And therefore, I said, as we might expect, there is nothing here which invites or excites intelligence.

There is not, he said.

But is this equally true of the greatness and smallness of the fingers? Can sight adequately perceive them? and is no difference made by the circumstance that one of the fingers is in the middle and another at the extremity? And in like manner does the touch adequately perceive the qualities of thickness or thinness, of softness or hardness? And so of the other senses; do they give perfect intimations of such matters? [524] Is not their mode of operation on this wise—the sense which is concerned with the quality of hardness is necessarily concerned also with the quality of softness, and only intimates to the soul that the same thing is felt to be both hard and soft?

You are quite right, he said.

And must not the soul be perplexed at this

intimation which the sense gives of a hard which is also soft? What, again, is the meaning of light and heavy, if that which is light is also heavy, and that which is heavy, light?

Yes, he said, these intimations which the soul receives are very curious and require to be explained.

Yes, I said, and in these perplexities the soul naturally summons to her aid calculation and intelligence, that she may see whether the several objects announced to her are one or two.

True.

And if they turn out to be two, is not each of them one and different?

Certainly.

And if each is one, and both are two, she will conceive the two as in a state of division, for if they were undivided they could only be conceived of as one?

True.

The eye certainly did see both small and great, but only in a confused manner; they were not distinguished.

Yes.

Whereas the thinking mind, intending to light up the chaos, was compelled to reverse the process, and look at small and great as separate and not confused.

Very true.

Was not this the beginning of the enquiry "What is great?" and "What is small?"

Exactly so.

And thus arose the distinction of the visible and the intelligible.

Most true.

This was what I meant when I spoke of impressions which invited the intellect, or the reverse—those which are simultaneous with opposite impressions, invite thought; those which are not simultaneous do not.

I understand, he said, and agree with you.

And to which class do unity and number belong?

I do not know, he replied.

Think a little and you will see that what has preceded will supply the answer; for if simple unity could be adequately perceived by the sight or by any other sense, then, as we were saying in the case of the finger, there would be nothing to attract towards being; but when there is some contradiction always present, and one is the reverse of one and involves the conception of plurality, then thought begins to be aroused within us, and the soul perplexed and wanting to arrive at a decision asks "What is absolute unity?" This is the way in which the study of the one

has a power of drawing [525] and converting the mind to the contemplation of true being.

And surely, he said, this occurs notably in the case of one; for we see the same thing to be both one and infinite in multitude?

Yes, I said; and this being true of one must be equally true of all number?

Certainly.

And all arithmetic and calculation have to do with number?

Yes.

And they appear to lead the mind towards truth?

Yes, in a very remarkable manner.

Then this is knowledge of the kind for which we are seeking, having a double use, military and philosophical; for the man of war must learn the art of number or he will not know how to array his troops, and the philosopher also, because he has to rise out of the sea of change and lay hold of true being, and therefore he must be an arithmetician.

That is true.

And our guardian is both warrior and philosopher?

Certainly.

Then this is a kind of knowledge which legislation may fitly prescribe; and we must endeavour to persuade those who are to be the principal men of our State to go and learn arithmetic, not as amateurs, but they must carry on the study until they see the nature of numbers with the mind only; nor again, like merchants or retail-traders, with a view to buying or selling, but for the sake of their military use, and of the soul herself; and because this will be the easiest way for her to pass from becoming to truth and being.

That is excellent, he said.

Yes, I said, and now having spoken of it, I must add how charming the science is! and in how many ways it conduces to our desired end, if pursued in the spirit of a philosopher, and not of a shopkeeper!

How do you mean?

I mean, as I was saying, that arithmetic has a very great and elevating effect, compelling the soul to reason about abstract number, and rebelling against the introduction of visible or tangible objects into the argument. You know how steadily the masters of the art repel and ridicule any one who attempts to divide absolute unity when he is calculating, and if you divide, they multiply, taking care that one shall continue one and not become lost in fractions.

That is very true.

[526] Now, suppose a person were to say to them: O my friends, what are these wonderful numbers about which you are reasoning, in which, as you say, there is a unity such as you demand, and each unit is equal, invariable, indivisible—what would they answer?

They would answer, as I should conceive, that they were speaking of those numbers which can only be realized in thought.

Then you see that this knowledge may be truly called necessary, necessitating as it clearly does the use of the pure intelligence in the attainment of pure truth?

Yes; that is a marked characteristic of it.

And have you further observed, that those who have a natural talent for calculation are generally quick at every other kind of knowledge; and even the dull, if they have had an arithmetical training, although they may derive no other advantage from it, always become much quicker than they would otherwise have been.

Very true, he said.

And indeed, you will not easily find a more difficult study, and not many as difficult.

You will not.

And, for all these reasons, arithmetic is a kind of knowledge in which the best natures should be trained, and which must not be given up.

I agree.

Let this then be made one of our subjects of education. And next, shall we enquire whether the kindred science also concerns us?

You mean geometry?

Exactly so.

Clearly, he said, we are concerned with that part of geometry which relates to war; for in pitching a camp, or taking up a position, or closing or extending the lines of an army, or any other military manœuvre, whether in actual battle or on a march, it will make all the difference whether a general is or is not a geometrician.

Yes, I said, but for that purpose a very little of either geometry or calculation will be enough; the question relates rather to the greater and more advanced part of geometry—whether that tends in any degree to make more easy the vision of the idea of good; and thither, as I was saying, all things tend which compel the soul to turn her gaze towards that place, where is the full perfection of being, which she ought, by all means, to behold.

True, he said.

Then if geometry compels us to view being,

it concerns us; if becoming only, it does not concern us?

[527] Yes, that is what we assert.

Yet anybody who has the least acquaintance with geometry will not deny that such a conception of the science is in flat contradiction to the ordinary language of geometricians.

How so?

They have in view practice only, and are always speaking, in a narrow and ridiculous manner, of squaring and extending and applying and the like—they confuse the necessities of geometry with those of daily life; whereas knowledge is the real object of the whole science.

Certainly, he said.

Then must not a further admission be made?

What admission?

That the knowledge at which geometry aims is knowledge of the eternal, and not of aught perishing and transient.

That, he replied, may be readily allowed, and is true.

Then, my noble friend, geometry will draw the soul towards truth, and create the spirit of philosophy, and raise up that which is now unhappily allowed to fall down.

Nothing will be more likely to have such an effect.

Then nothing should be more sternly laid down than that the inhabitants of your fair city should by all means learn geometry. Moreover the science has indirect effects, which are not small.

Of what kind? he said.

There are the military advantages of which you spoke, I said; and in all departments of knowledge, as experience proves, any one who has studied geometry is infinitely quicker of apprehension than one who has not.

Yes indeed, he said, there is an infinite difference between them.

Then shall we propose this as a second branch of knowledge which our youth will study?

Let us do so, he replied.

And suppose we make astronomy the third—what do you say?

I am strongly inclined to it, he said; the observation of the seasons and of months and years is as essential to the general as it is to the farmer or sailor.

I am amused, I said, at your fear of the world, which makes you guard against the appearance of insisting upon useless studies; and I quite admit the difficulty of believing that in every man there is an eye of the soul which, when by other pursuits lost and dimmed, is by these purified and re-illumined; and is more precious far than ten thousand bodily eyes, for by it alone is truth seen. Now there are two classes of persons: one class of those who will agree with you and will take your words as a revelation; another class to whom they will be utterly unmeaning, [528] and who will naturally deem them to be idle tales, for they see no sort of profit which is to be obtained from them. And therefore you had better decide at once with which of the two you are proposing to argue. You will very likely say with neither, and that your chief aim in carrying on the argument is your own improvement; at the same time you do not grudge to others any benefit which they may receive.

I think that I should prefer to carry on the argument mainly on my own behalf.

Then take a step backward, for we have gone wrong in the order of the sciences.

What was the mistake? he said.

After plane geometry, I said, we proceeded at once to solids in revolution, instead of taking solids in themselves; whereas after the second dimension the third, which is concerned with cubes and dimensions of depth, ought to have followed.

That is true, Socrates; but so little seems to be known as yet about these subjects.

Why, yes, I said, and for two reasons:—in the first place, no government patronises them; this leads to a want of energy in the pursuit of them, and they are difficult; in the second place, students cannot learn them unless they have a director. But then a director can hardly be found, and even if he could, as matters now stand, the students, who are very conceited, would not attend to him. That, however, would be otherwise if the whole State became the director of these studies and gave honour to them; then disciples would want to come, and there would be continuous and earnest search, and discoveries would be made; since even now, disregarded as they are by the world, and maimed of their fair proportions, and although none of their votaries can tell the use of them, still these studies force their way by their natural charm, and very likely, if they had the help of the State, they would some day emerge into light.

Yes, he said, there is a remarkable charm in them. But I do not clearly understand the change in the order. First you began with a geometry of plane surfaces?

Yes, I said.

And you placed astronomy next, and then you made a step backward?

Yes, and I have delayed you by my hurry; the ludicrous state of solid geometry, which, in natural order, should have followed, made me pass over this branch and go on to astronomy, or motion of solids.

True, he said.

Then assuming that the science now omitted would come into existence if encouraged by the State, let us go on to astronomy, which will be fourth.

The right order, he replied. And now, Socrates, as you rebuked the vulgar manner in which I praised astronomy before, [529] my praise shall be given in your own spirit. For every one, as I think, must see that astronomy compels the soul to look upwards and leads us from this world to another.

Every one but myself, I said; to every one else this may be clear, but not to me.

And what then would you say?

I should rather say that those who elevate astronomy into philosophy appear to me to make us look downwards and not upwards.

What do you mean? he asked.

You, I replied, have in your mind a truly sublime conception of our knowledge of the things above. And I dare say that if a person were to throw his head back and study the fretted ceiling, you would still think that his mind was the percipient, and not his eyes. And you are very likely right, and I may be a simpleton: but, in my opinion, that knowledge only which is of being and of the unseen can make the soul look upwards, and whether a man gapes at the heavens or blinks on the ground, seeking to learn some particular of sense, I would deny that he can learn, for nothing of that sort is matter of science; his soul is looking downwards, not upwards, whether his way to knowledge is by water or by land, whether he floats, or only lies on his back.

I acknowledge, he said, the justice of your rebuke. Still, I should like to ascertain how astronomy can be learned in any manner more conducive to that knowledge of which we are speaking?

I will tell you, I said: The starry heaven which we behold is wrought upon a visible ground, and therefore, although the fairest and most perfect of visible things, must necessarily be deemed inferior far to the true motions of absolute swiftness and absolute slowness, which are relative to each other, and carry with them that which is contained in them, in the true number and in every true figure. Now, these are to be apprehended by reason and intelligence, but not by sight.

True, he replied.

The spangled heavens should be used as a pattern and with a view to that higher knowledge; their beauty is like the beauty of figures or pictures excellently wrought by the hand of Daedalus, or some other great artist, which we may chance to behold; any geometrician who saw them would appreciate the exquisiteness of their workmanship, but he would never dream of thinking that in them he could find the true equal or the true double, or the truth of any other proportion. [530]

No, he replied, such an idea would be ridiculous.

And will not a true astronomer have the same feeling when he looks at the movements of the stars? Will he not think that heaven and the things in heaven are framed by the Creator of them in the most perfect manner? But he will never imagine that the proportions of night and day, or of both to the month, or of the month to the year, or of the stars to these and to one another, and any other things that are material and visible can also be eternal and subject to no deviation—that would be absurd; and it is equally absurd to take so much pains in investigating their exact truth.

I quite agree, though I never thought of this before.

Then, I said, in astronomy, as in geometry, we should employ problems, and let the heavens alone if we would approach the subject in the right way and so make the natural gift of reason to be of any real use.

That, he said, is a work infinitely beyond our present astronomers.

Yes, I said; and there are many other things which must also have a similar extension given to them, if our legislation is to be of any value. But can you tell me of any other suitable study?

No, he said, not without thinking.

Motion, I said, has many forms, and not one only; two of them are obvious enough even to wits no better than ours; and there are others, as I imagine, which may be left to wiser persons.

But where are the two?

There is a second, I said, which is the counterpart of the one already named.

And what may that be?

The second, I said, would seem relatively to the ears to be what the first is to the eyes; for I conceive that as the eyes are designed to look up at the stars, so are the ears to hear harmonious motions; and these are sister sciences—as the Pythagoreans say, and we, Glaucon, agree with them?

Yes, he replied.

But this, I said, is a laborious study, and therefore we had better go and learn of them; and they will tell us whether there are any other applications of these sciences. At the same time, we must not lose sight of our own higher object.

What is that?

There is a perfection which all knowledge ought to reach, and which our pupils ought also to attain, and not to fall short of, as I was saying that they did in astronomy. [531] For in the science of harmony, as you probably know, the same thing happens. The teachers of harmony compare the sounds and consonances which are heard only, and their labour, like that of the astronomers, is in vain.

Yes, by heaven! he said; and 'tis as good as a play to hear them talking about their condensed notes, as they call them; they put their ears close alongside of the strings like persons catching a sound from their neighbour's wall—one set of them declaring that they distinguish an intermediate note and have found the least interval which should be the unit of measurement; the others insisting that the two sounds have passed into the same—either party setting their ears before their understanding.

You mean, I said, those gentlemen who tease and torture the strings and rack them on the pegs of the instrument: I might carry on the metaphor and speak after their manner of the blows which the plectrum gives, and make accusations against the strings, both of backwardness and forwardness to sound; but this would be tedious, and therefore I will only say that these are not the men, and that I am referring to the Pythagoreans, of whom I was just now proposing to enquire about harmony. For they too are in error, like the astronomers; they investigate the numbers of the harmonies which are heard, but they never attain to problems—that is to say, they never reach the natural harmonies of number, or reflect why some numbers are harmonious and others not.

That, he said, is a thing of more than mortal knowledge.

A thing, I replied, which I would rather call useful; that is, if sought after with a view to the beautiful and good; but if pursued in any other spirit, useless.

Very true, he said.

Now, when all these studies reach the point of inter-communion and connection with one another, and come to be considered in their mutual affinities, then, I think, but not till then, will the pursuit of them have a value for our objects; otherwise there is no profit in them.

I suspect so; but you are speaking, Socrates, of a vast work.

What do you mean? I said; the prelude or what? Do you not know that all this is but the prelude to the actual strain which we have to learn? For you surely would not regard the skilled mathematician as a dialectician?

Assuredly not, he said; I have hardly ever known a mathematician who was capable of reasoning.

But do you imagine that men who are unable to give and take a reason will have the knowledge which we require of them? *[532]*

Neither can this be supposed.

And so, Glaucon, I said, we have at last arrived at the hymn of dialectic. This is that strain which is of the intellect only, but which the faculty of sight will nevertheless be found to imitate; for sight, as you may remember, was imagined by us after a while to behold the real animals and stars, and last of all the sun himself. And so with dialectic; when a person starts on the discovery of the absolute by the light of reason only, and without any assistance of sense, and perseveres until by pure intelligence he arrives at the perception of the absolute good, he at last finds himself at the end of the intellectual world, as in the case of sight at the end of the visible.

Exactly, he said.

Then this is the progress which you call dialectic?

True.

But the release of the prisoners from chains, and their translation from the shadows to the images and to the light, and the ascent from the underground den to the sun, while in his presence they are vainly trying to look on animals and plants and the light of the sun, but are able to perceive even with their weak eyes the images in the water [which are divine], and are the shadows of true existence (not shadows of images cast by a light of fire, which compared with the sun is only an image)—this power of elevating the highest principle in the soul to the contemplation of that which is best in existence, with which we may compare the raising of that faculty which is the very light of the body to the sight of that which is brightest in the material and visible world—this power is given, as I was saying, by all that study and pursuit of the arts which has been described.

I agree in what you are saying, he replied, which may be hard to believe, yet, from another point of view, is harder still to deny. This however is not a theme to be treated of in passing only, but will have to be discussed again and again. And so, whether our conclusion be true or false, let us assume all this, and proceed at once from the prelude or preamble to the chief strain,[1] and describe that in like manner. Say, then, what is the nature and what are the divisions of dialectic, and what are the paths which lead thither; for these paths will also lead to our final rest.

[533] Dear Glaucon, I said, you will not be able to follow me here, though I would do my best, and you should behold not an image only but the absolute truth, according to my notion. Whether what I told you would or would not have been a reality I cannot venture to say; but you would have seen something like reality; of that I am confident.

Doubtless, he replied.

But I must also remind you, that the power of dialectic alone can reveal this, and only to one who is a disciple of the previous sciences.

Of that assertion you may be as confident as of the last.

And assuredly no one will argue that there is any other method of comprehending by any regular process all true existence or of ascertaining what each thing is in its own nature; for the arts in general are concerned with the desires or opinions of men, or are cultivated with a view to production and construction, or for the preservation of such productions and constructions; and as to the mathematical sciences which, as we were saying, have some apprehension of true being—geometry and the like—they only dream about being, but never can they behold the waking reality so long as they leave the hypotheses which they use unexamined, and are unable to give an account of them. For when a man knows not his own first principle, and when the conclusion and intermediate steps are also constructed out of he knows not what, how can he imagine that such a fabric of convention can ever become science?

Impossible, he said.

Then dialectic, and dialectic alone, goes directly to the first principle and is the only science which does away with hypotheses in order to make her ground secure; the eye of the soul, which is literally buried in an outlandish slough,

[1] A play upon the word νόμος, which means both "law" and "strain."

is by her gentle aid lifted upwards; and she uses as handmaids and helpers in the work of conversion, the sciences which we have been discussing. Custom terms them sciences, but they ought to have some other name, implying greater clearness than opinion and less clearness than science: and this, in our previous sketch, was called understanding. But why should we dispute about names when we have realities of such importance to consider?

Why indeed, he said, when any name will do which expresses the thought of the mind with clearness?

At any rate, we are satisfied, as before, to have four divisions; two for intellect and two for opinion, and to call the first division science, the second understanding, the third belief, and the fourth perception of shadows, *[534]* opinion being concerned with becoming, and intellect with being; and so to make a proportion: *As being is to becoming, so is pure intellect to opinion. And as intellect is to opinion, so is science to belief, and understanding to the perception of shadows.* But let us defer the further correlation and subdivision of the subjects of opinion and of intellect, for it will be a long enquiry, many times longer than this has been.

As far as I understand, he said, I agree.

And do you also agree, I said, in describing the dialectician as one who attains a conception of the essence of each thing? And he who does not possess and is therefore unable to impart this conception, in whatever degree he fails, may in that degree also be said to fail in intelligence? Will you admit so much?

Yes, he said; how can I deny it?

And you would say the same of the conception of the good? Until the person is able to abstract and define rationally the idea of good, and unless he can run the gauntlet of all objections, and is ready to disprove them, not by appeals to opinion, but to absolute truth, never faltering at any step of the argument—unless he can do all this, you would say that he knows neither the idea of good nor any other good; he apprehends only a shadow, if anything at all, which is given by opinion and not by science —dreaming and slumbering in this life, before he is well awake here, he arrives at the world below, and has his final quietus.

In all that I should most certainly agree with you.

And surely you would not have the children of your ideal State, whom you are nurturing and educating—if the ideal ever becomes a reality—you would not allow the future rulers to be like posts,[1] having no reason in them, and yet to be set in authority over the highest matters?

Certainly not.

Then you will make a law that they shall have such an education as will enable them to attain the greatest skill in asking and answering questions?

Yes, he said, you and I together will make it.

Dialectic, then, as you will agree, is the coping-stone of the sciences, and is set over them; no other science can be placed higher—the nature of knowledge can no further go?

I agree, he said.

[535] But to whom we are to assign these studies, and in what way they are to be assigned, are questions which remain to be considered.

Yes, clearly.

You remember, I said, how the rulers were chosen before?

Certainly, he said.

The same natures must still be chosen, and the preference again given to the surest and the bravest, and, if possible, to the fairest; and, having noble and generous tempers, they should also have the natural gifts which will facilitate their education.

And what are these?

Such gifts as keenness and ready powers of acquisition; for the mind more often faints from the severity of study than from the severity of gymnastics: the toil is more entirely the mind's own, and is not shared with the body.

Very true, he replied.

Further, he of whom we are in search should have a good memory, and be an unwearied solid man who is a lover of labour in any line; or he will never be able to endure the great amount of bodily exercise and to go through all the intellectual discipline and study which we require of him.

Certainly, he said; he must have natural gifts.

The mistake at present is, that those who study philosophy have no vocation, and this, as I was before saying, is the reason why she has fallen into disrepute: her true sons should take her by the hand and not bastards.

What do you mean?

In the first place, her votary should not have a lame or halting industry—I mean, that he should not be half industrious and half idle: as, for example, when a man is a lover of gymnas-

[1] Literally "lines," probably the starting-point of a race-course.

tic and hunting, and all other bodily exercises, but a hater rather than a lover of the labour of learning or listening or enquiring. Or the occupation to which he devotes himself may be of an opposite kind, and he may have the other sort of lameness.

Certainly, he said.

And as to truth, I said, is not a soul equally to be deemed halt and lame which hates voluntary falsehood and is extremely indignant at herself and others when they tell lies, but is patient of involuntary falsehood, and does not mind wallowing like a swinish beast in the mire of ignorance, and has no shame at being detected?

To be sure.

[536] And, again, in respect of temperance, courage, magnificence, and every other virtue, should we not carefully distinguish between the true son and the bastard? for where there is no discernment of such qualities states and individuals unconsciously err; and the state makes a ruler, and the individual a friend, of one who, being defective in some part of virtue, is in a figure lame or a bastard.

That is very true, he said.

All these things, then, will have to be carefully considered by us; and if only those whom we introduce to this vast system of education and training are sound in body and mind, justice herself will have nothing to say against us, and we shall be the saviours of the constitution and of the State; but, if our pupils are men of another stamp, the reverse will happen, and we shall pour a still greater flood of ridicule on philosophy than she has to endure at present.

That would not be creditable.

Certainly not, I said; and yet perhaps, in thus turning jest into earnest I am equally ridiculous.

In what respect?

I had forgotten, I said, that we were not serious, and spoke with too much excitement. For when I saw philosophy so undeservedly trampled under foot of men I could not help feeling a sort of indignation at the authors of her disgrace: and my anger made me too vehement.

Indeed! I was listening, and did not think so.

But I, who am the speaker, felt that I was. And now let me remind you that, although in our former selection we chose old men, we must not do so in this. Solon was under a delusion when he said that a man when he grows old may learn many things—for he can no more learn much than he can run much; youth is the time for any extraordinary toil.

Of course.

And, therefore, calculation and geometry and all the other elements of instruction, which are a preparation for dialectic, should be presented to the mind in childhood; not, however, under any notion of forcing our system of education.

Why not?

Because a freeman ought not to be a slave in the acquisition of knowledge of any kind. Bodily exercise, when compulsory, does no harm to the body; but knowledge which is acquired under compulsion obtains no hold on the mind.

Very true.

Then, my good friend, I said, do not use compulsion, but let early education be a sort of amusement; [537] you will then be better able to find out the natural bent.

That is a very rational notion, he said.

Do you remember that the children, too, were to be taken to see the battle on horseback; and that if there were no danger they were to be brought close up and, like young hounds, have a taste of blood given them?

Yes, I remember.

The same practice may be followed, I said, in all these things—labours, lessons, dangers—and he who is most at home in all of them ought to be enrolled in a select number.

At what age?

At the age when the necessary gymnastics are over: the period whether of two or three years which passes in this sort of training is useless for any other purpose; for sleep and exercise are unpropitious to learning; and the trial of who is first in gymnastic exercises is one of the most important tests to which our youth are subjected.

Certainly, he replied.

After that time those who are selected from the class of twenty years old will be promoted to higher honour, and the sciences which they learned without any order in their early education will now be brought together, and they will be able to see the natural relationship of them to one another and to true being.

Yes, he said, that is the only kind of knowledge which takes lasting root.

Yes, I said; and the capacity for such knowledge is the great criterion of dialectical talent: the comprehensive mind is always the dialectical.

I agree with you, he said.

These, I said, are the points which you must consider; and those who have most of this comprehension, and who are more steadfast in their learning, and in their military and other appointed duties, when they have arrived at the age of thirty will have to be chosen by you out of the select class, and elevated to higher honour; and you will have to prove them by the help of dialectic, in order to learn which of them is able to give up the use of sight and the other senses, and in company with truth to attain absolute being: And here, my friend, great caution is required.

Why great caution?

Do you not remark, I said, how great is the evil which dialectic has introduced?

What evil? he said.

The students of the art are filled with lawlessness.

Quite true, he said.

Do you think that there is anything so very unnatural or inexcusable in their case? or will you make allowance for them?

In what way make allowance?

I want you, I said, by way of parallel, to imagine a supposititious son who is brought up in great wealth; [538] he is one of a great and numerous family, and has many flatterers. When he grows up to manhood, he learns that his alleged are not his real parents; but who the real are he is unable to discover. Can you guess how he will be likely to behave towards his flatterers and his supposed parents, first of all during the period when he is ignorant of the false relation, and then again when he knows? Or shall I guess for you?

If you please.

Then I should say, that while he is ignorant of the truth he will be likely to honour his father and his mother and his supposed relations more than the flatterers; he will be less inclined to neglect them when in need, or to do or say anything against them; and he will be less willing to disobey them in any important matter.

He will.

But when he has made the discovery, I should imagine that he would diminish his honour and regard for them, and would become more devoted to the flatterers; their influence over him would greatly increase; he would now live after their ways, and openly associate with them, and, unless he were of an unusually good disposition, he would trouble himself no more about his supposed parents or other relations.

Well, all that is very probable. But how is the image applicable to the disciples of philosophy?

In this way: you know that there are certain principles about justice and honour, which were taught us in childhood, and under their pa-

rental authority we have been brought up, obeying and honouring them.

That is true.

There are also opposite maxims and habits of pleasure which flatter and attract the soul, but do not influence those of us who have any sense of right, and they continue to obey and honour the maxims of their fathers.

True.

Now, when a man is in this state, and the questioning spirit asks what is fair or honourable, and he answers as the legislator has taught him, and then arguments many and diverse refute his words, until he is driven into believing that nothing is honourable any more than dishonourable, or just and good any more than the reverse, and so of all the notions which he most valued, do you think that he will still honour and obey them as before?

Impossible.

And when he ceases to think them honourable and natural as heretofore, [539] and he fails to discover the true, can he be expected to pursue any life other than that which flatters his desires?

He cannot.

And from being a keeper of the law he is converted into a breaker of it?

Unquestionably.

Now all this is very natural in students of philosophy such as I have described, and also, as I was just now saying, most excusable.

Yes, he said; and, I may add, pitiable.

Therefore, that your feelings may not be moved to pity about our citizens who are now thirty years of age, every care must be taken in introducing them to dialectic.

Certainly.

There is a danger lest they should taste the dear delight too early; for youngsters, as you may have observed, when they first get the taste in their mouths, argue for amusement, and are always contradicting and refuting others in imitation of those who refute them; like puppy-dogs, they rejoice in pulling and tearing at all who come near them.

Yes, he said, there is nothing which they like better.

And when they have made many conquests and received defeats at the hands of many, they violently and speedily get into a way of not believing anything which they believed before, and hence, not only they, but philosophy and all that relates to it is apt to have a bad name with the rest of the world.

Too true, he said.

But when a man begins to get older, he will no longer be guilty of such insanity; he will imitate the dialectician who is seeking for truth, and not the eristic, who is contradicting for the sake of amusement; and the greater moderation of his character will increase instead of diminishing the honour of the pursuit.

Very true, he said.

And did we not make special provision for this, when we said that the disciples of philosophy were to be orderly and steadfast, not, as now, any chance aspirant or intruder?

Very true.

Suppose, I said, the study of philosophy to take the place of gymnastics and to be continued diligently and earnestly and exclusively for twice the number of years which were passed in bodily exercise—will that be enough?

Would you say six or four years? he asked.

Say five years, I replied; at the end of the time they must be sent down again into the den and compelled to hold any military or other office which young men are qualified to hold: in this way they will get their experience of life, and there will be an opportunity of trying whether, when they are drawn all manner of ways by temptation, they will stand firm or flinch.

[540] And how long is this stage of their lives to last?

Fifteen years, I answered; and when they have reached fifty years of age, then let those who still survive and have distinguished themselves in every action of their lives and in every branch of knowledge come at last to their consummation; the time has now arrived at which they must raise the eye of the soul to the universal light which lightens all things, and behold the absolute good; for that is the pattern according to which they are to order the State and the lives of individuals, and the remainder of their own lives also; making philosophy their chief pursuit, but, when their turn comes, toiling also at politics and ruling for the public good, not as though they were performing some heroic action, but simply as a matter of duty; and when they have brought up in each generation others like themselves and left them in their place to be governors of the State, then they will depart to the Islands of the Blest and dwell there; and the city will give them public memorials and sacrifices and honour them, if the Pythian oracle consent, as demigods, but if not, as in any case blessed and divine.

You are a sculptor, Socrates, and have made statues of our governors faultless in beauty.

Yes, I said, Glaucon, and of our governesses too; for you must not suppose that what I have been saying applies to men only and not to women as far as their natures can go.

There you are right, he said, since we have made them to share in all things like the men.

Well, I said, and you would agree (would you not?) that what has been said about the State and the government is not a mere dream, and although difficult not impossible, but only possible in the way which has been supposed; that is to say, when the true philosopher kings are born in a State, one or more of them, despising the honours of this present world which they deem mean and worthless, esteeming above all things right and the honour that springs from right, and regarding justice as the greatest and most necessary of all things, whose ministers they are, and whose principles will be exalted by them when they set in order their own city?

How will they proceed?

They will begin by sending out into the country all the inhabitants of the city who are more than ten years old, and will take possession of their children, who will be unaffected by the habits of their parents; these they will train in their own habits and laws, I mean in the laws which we have given them: and in this way the State and constitution of which we were speaking will soonest and most easily attain happiness, and the nation which has such a constitution will gain most.

Yes, that will be the best way. And I think, Socrates, that you have very well described how, if ever, such a constitution might come into being.

Enough then of the perfect State, and of the man who bears its image—there is no difficulty in seeing how we shall describe him.

There is no difficulty, he replied; and I agree with you in thinking that nothing more need be said.

BOOK VIII

[543] AND so, Glaucon, we have arrived at the conclusion that in the perfect State wives and children are to be in common; and that all education and the pursuits of war and peace are also to be in common, and the best philosophers and the bravest warriors are to be their kings?

That, replied Glaucon, has been acknowledged.

Yes, I said; and we have further acknowledged that the governors, when appointed themselves, will take their soldiers and place them in houses such as we were describing, which are common to all, and contain nothing private, or individual; and about their property, you remember what we agreed?

Yes, I remember that no one was to have any of the ordinary possessions of mankind; they were to be warrior athletes and guardians, receiving from the other citizens, in lieu of annual payment, only their maintenance, and they were to take care of themselves and of the whole State.

True, I said; and now that this division of our task is concluded, let us find the point at which we digressed, that we may return into the old path.

There is no difficulty in returning; you implied, then as now, that you had finished the description of the State: you said that such a State was good, and that the man was good who answered to it, although, [544] as now appears, you had more excellent things to relate both of State and man. And you said further, that if this was the true form, then the others were false; and of the false forms, you said, as I remember, that there were four principal ones, and that their defects, and the defects of the individuals corresponding to them, were worth examining. When we had seen all the individuals, and finally agreed as to who was the best and who was the worst of them, we were to consider whether the best was not also the happiest, and the worst the most miserable. I asked you what were the four forms of government of which you spoke, and then Polemarchus and Adeimantus put in their word; and you began again, and have found your way to the point at which we have now arrived.

Your recollection, I said, is most exact.

Then, like a wrestler, he replied, you must put yourself again in the same position; and let me ask the same questions, and do you give me the same answer which you were about to give me then.

Yes, if I can, I will, I said.

I shall particularly wish to hear what were the four constitutions of which you were speaking.

That question, I said, is easily answered: the four governments of which I spoke, so far as they have distinct names, are, first, those of Crete and Sparta, which are generally applauded; what is termed oligarchy comes next; this is not equally approved, and is a form of government which teems with evils: thirdly, democracy, which naturally follows oligarchy, although very different: and lastly comes tyranny, great and famous, which differs from them all, and is the fourth and worst disorder of a State. I do not know, do you? of any other constitution which can be said to have a distinct character. There are lordships and principalities which are bought and sold, and some other intermediate forms of government. But these are nondescripts and may be found equally among Hellenes and among barbarians.

Yes, he replied, we certainly hear of many curious forms of government which exist among them.

Do you know, I said, that governments vary as the dispositions of men vary, and that there must be as many of the one as there are of the other? For we cannot suppose that States are made of "oak and rock," and not out of the human natures which are in them, and which in a figure turn the scale and draw other things after them?

Yes, he said, the States are as the men are; they grow out of human characters.

Then if the constitutions of States are five, the dispositions of individual minds will also be five?

Certainly.

Him who answers to aristocracy, and whom we rightly call just and good, [545] we have already described.

We have.

Then let us now proceed to describe the inferior sort of natures, being the contentious and ambitious, who answer to the Spartan polity; also the oligarchical, democratical, and tyrannical. Let us place the most just by the side of the most unjust, and when we see them we shall be able to compare the relative happiness or unhappiness of him who leads a life of pure justice or pure injustice. The enquiry will then be completed. And we shall know whether we ought to pursue injustice, as Thrasymachus advises, or in accordance with the conclusions of the argument to prefer justice.

Certainly, he replied, we must do as you say.

Shall we follow our old plan, which we adopted with a view to clearness, of taking the State first and then proceeding to the individual, and begin with the government of honour?—I know of no name for such a government other than timocracy, or perhaps timarchy. We will compare with this the like character in the individual; and, after that, consider oligarchical man; and then again we will turn our attention to democracy and the democratical man; and lastly, we will go and view the city of tyranny, and once more take a look into the tyrant's soul, and try to arrive at a satisfactory decision.

That way of viewing and judging of the matter will be very suitable.

First, then, I said, let us enquire how timocracy (the government of honour) arises out of aristocracy (the government of the best). Clearly, all political changes originate in divisions of the actual governing power; a government which is united, however small, cannot be moved.

Very true, he said.

In what way, then, will our city be moved, and in what manner will the two classes of auxiliaries and rulers disagree among themselves or with one another? Shall we, after the manner of Homer, pray the Muses to tell us "how discord first arose?" Shall we imagine them in solemn mockery, to play and jest with us as if we were children, and to address us in a lofty tragic vein, making believe to be in earnest?

How would they address us?

[546] After this manner:—A city which is thus constituted can hardly be shaken; but, seeing that everything which has a beginning has also an end, even a constitution such as yours will not last for ever, but will in time be dissolved. And this is the dissolution:—In plants that grow in the earth, as well as in animals that move on the earth's surface, fertility and sterility of soul and body occur when the circumferences of the circles of each are completed, which in short-lived existences pass over a short space, and in long-lived ones over a long space. But to the knowledge of human fecundity and sterility all the wisdom and education of your rulers will not attain; the laws which regulate them will not be discovered by an intelligence which is alloyed with sense, but will escape them, and they will bring children into the world when they ought not. Now that which is of divine birth has a period which is contained in a perfect number,[1] but the period of human birth is comprehended in a number in which first increments by involution and evolution [or squared and cubed] obtaining three intervals and four terms of like and unlike, waxing and waning numbers, make all the terms commensurable and agreeable to one

another.[2] The base of these (3) with a third added (4) when combined with five (20) and raised to the third power furnishes two harmonies; the first a square which is a hundred times as great $(400 = 4 \times 100)$,[3] and the other a figure having one side equal to the former, but oblong, consisting of a hundred numbers squared upon rational diameters of a square (i.e. omitting fractions), the side of which is five $(7 \times 7 = 49 \times 100 = 4900)$, each of them being less by one (than the perfect square which includes the fractions, sc. 50) or less by [4] two perfect squares of irrational diameters (of a square the side of which is five $= 50 + 50 = 100)$; and a hundred cubes of three $(27 \times 100 = 2700 + 4900 + 400 = 8000)$. Now this number represents a geometrical figure which has control over the good and evil of births. For when your guardians are ignorant of the law of births, and unite bride and bridegroom out of season, the children will not be goodly or fortunate. And though only the best of them will be appointed by their predecessors, still they will be unworthy to hold their fathers' places, and when they come into power as guardians, they will soon be found to fail in taking care of us, the Muses, first by undervaluing music; which neglect will soon extend to gymnastic; and hence the young men of your State will be less cultivated. In the succeeding generation rulers will be appointed who have lost the guardian power of testing the metal of your different races, which, like Hesiod's, are of gold and silver and brass and iron. [547] And so iron will be mingled with silver, and brass with gold, and hence there will arise dissimilarity and inequality and irregularity, which always and in all places are causes of hatred and war. This the Muses affirm to be the stock from which discord has sprung, wherever arising; and this is their answer to us.

Yes, and we may assume that they answer truly.

Why, yes, I said, of course they answer truly; how can the Muses speak falsely?

And what do the Muses say next?

When discord arose, then the two races were

---

[1] A cyclical number, such as 6, which is equal to the sum of its divisors 1, 2, 3, so that when the circle or time represented by 6 is completed, the lesser times or rotations represented by 1, 2, 3 are also completed.

[2] Probably the numbers 3, 4, 5, 6 of which the three first = the sides of the Pythagorean triangle. The terms will then be 3^3, 4^3, 5^3, which together $= 6^3 = 216$.

[3] Or the first a square which is $100 \times 100 = 10,000$. The whole number will then be 17,500 = a square of 100, and an oblong of 100 by 75.

[4] Or, "consisting of two numbers squared upon irrational diameters," &c. $= 100$.

drawn different ways: the iron and brass fell to acquiring money and land and houses and gold and silver; but the gold and silver races, not wanting money but having the true riches in their own nature, inclined towards virtue and the ancient order of things. There was a battle between them, and at last they agreed to distribute their land and houses among individual owners; and they enslaved their friends and maintainers, whom they had formerly protected in the condition of freemen, and made of them subjects and servants; and they themselves were engaged in war and in keeping a watch against them.

I believe that you have rightly conceived the origin of the change.

And the new government which thus arises will be of a form intermediate between oligarchy and aristocracy?

Very true.

Such will be the change, and after the change has been made, how will they proceed? Clearly, the new State, being in a mean between oligarchy and the perfect State, will partly follow one and partly the other, and will also have some peculiarities.

True, he said.

In the honour given to rulers, in the abstinence of the warrior class from agriculture, handicrafts, and trade in general, in the institution of common meals, and in the attention paid to gymnastics and military training—in all these respects this State will resemble the former.

True.

But in the fear of admitting philosophers to power, because they are no longer to be had simple and earnest, but are made up of mixed elements; and in turning from them to passionate and less complex characters, [548] who are by nature fitted for war rather than peace; and in the value set by them upon military stratagems and contrivances, and in the waging of everlasting wars—this State will be for the most part peculiar.

Yes.

Yes, I said; and men of this stamp will be covetous of money, like those who live in oligarchies; they will have a fierce secret longing after gold and silver, which they will hoard in dark places, having magazines and treasuries of their own for the deposit and concealment of them; also castles which are just nests for their eggs, and in which they will spend large sums on their wives, or on any others whom they please.

That is most true, he said.

And they are miserly because they have no means of openly acquiring the money which they prize; they will spend that which is another man's on the gratification of their desires, stealing their pleasures and running away like children from the law, their father: they have been schooled not by gentle influences but by force, for they have neglected her who is the true Muse, the companion of reason and philosophy, and have honoured gymnastic more than music.

Undoubtedly, he said, the form of government which you describe is a mixture of good and evil.

Why, there is a mixture, I said; but one thing, and one thing only, is predominantly seen—the spirit of contention and ambition; and these are due to the prevalence of the passionate or spirited element.

Assuredly, he said.

Such is the origin and such the character of this State, which has been described in outline only; the more perfect execution was not required, for a sketch is enough to show the type of the most perfectly just and most perfectly unjust; and to go through all the States and all the characters of men, omitting none of them, would be an interminable labour.

Very true, he replied.

Now what man answers to this form of government—how did he come into being, and what is he like?

I think, said Adeimantus, that in the spirit of contention which characterises him, he is not unlike our friend Glaucon.

Perhaps, I said, he may be like him in that one point; but there are other respects in which he is very different.

In what respects?

He should have more of self-assertion and be less cultivated, and yet a friend of culture; [549] and he should be a good listener, but no speaker. Such a person is apt to be rough with slaves, unlike the educated man, who is too proud for that; and he will also be courteous to freemen, and remarkably obedient to authority; he is a lover of power and a lover of honour; claiming to be a ruler, not because he is eloquent, or on any ground of that sort, but because he is a soldier and has performed feats of arms; he is also a lover of gymnastic exercises and of the chase.

Yes, that is the type of character which answers to timocracy.

Such an one will despise riches only when he

is young; but as he gets older he will be more and more attracted to them, because he has a piece of the avaricious nature in him, and is not single-minded towards virtue, having lost his best guardian.

Who was that? said Adeimantus.

Philosophy, I said, tempered with music, who comes and takes her abode in a man, and is the only saviour of his virtue throughout life.

Good, he said.

Such, I said, is the timocratical youth, and he is like the timocratical State.

Exactly.

His origin is as follows:—He is often the young son of a brave father, who dwells in an ill-governed city, of which he declines the honours and offices, and will not go to law, or exert himself in any way, but is ready to waive his rights in order that he may escape trouble.

And how does the son come into being?

The character of the son begins to develop when he hears his mother complaining that her husband has no place in the government, of which the consequence is that she has no precedence among other women. Further, when she sees her husband not very eager about money, and instead of battling and railing in the law courts or assembly, taking whatever happens to him quietly; and when she observes that his thoughts always centre in himself, while he treats her with very considerable indifference, she is annoyed, and says to her son that his father is only half a man and far too easy-going: adding all the other complaints about her own ill-treatment which women are so fond of rehearsing.

Yes, said Adeimantus, they give us plenty of them, and their complaints are so like themselves.

And you know, I said, that the old servants also, who are supposed to be attached to the family, from time to time talk privately in the same strain to the son; and if they see any one who owes money to his father, or is wronging him in any way, and he fails to prosecute them, [550] they tell the youth that when he grows up he must retaliate upon people of this sort, and be more of a man than his father. He has only to walk abroad and he hears and sees the same sort of thing: those who do their own business in the city are called simpletons, and held in no esteem, while the busy-bodies are honoured and applauded. The result is that the young man, hearing and seeing all these things —hearing, too, the words of his father, and having a nearer view of his way of life, and

making comparisons of him and others—is drawn opposite ways: while his father is watering and nourishing the rational principle in his soul, the others are encouraging the passionate and appetitive; and he being not originally of a bad nature, but having kept bad company, is at last brought by their joint influence to a middle point, and gives up the kingdom which is within him to the middle principle of contentiousness and passion, and becomes arrogant and ambitious.

You seem to me to have described his origin perfectly.

Then we have now, I said, the second form of government and the second type of character?

We have.

Next, let us look at another man who, as Aeschylus says,

Is set over against another State;

or rather, as our plan requires, begin with the State.

By all means.

I believe that oligarchy follows next in order.

And what manner of government do you term oligarchy?

A government resting on a valuation of property, in which the rich have power and the poor man is deprived of it.

I understand, he replied.

Ought I not to begin by describing how the change from timocracy to oligarchy arises?

Yes.

Well, I said, no eyes are required in order to see how the one passes into the other.

How?

The accumulation of gold in the treasury of private individuals is the ruin of timocracy; they invent illegal modes of expenditure; for what do they or their wives care about the law?

Yes, indeed.

And then one, seeing another grow rich, seeks to rival him, and thus the great mass of the citizens become lovers of money.

Likely enough.

And so they grow richer and richer, and the more they think of making a fortune the less they think of virtue; for when riches and virtue are placed together in the scales of the balance, the one always rises as the other falls.

True.

[551] And in proportion as riches and rich men are honoured in the State, virtue and the virtuous are dishonoured.

Clearly.

And what is honoured is cultivated, and that which has no honour is neglected.

That is obvious.

And so at last, instead of loving contention and glory, men become lovers of trade and money; they honour and look up to the rich man, and make a ruler of him, and dishonour the poor man.

They do so.

They next proceed to make a law which fixes a sum of money as the qualification of citizenship; the sum is higher in one place and lower in another, as the oligarchy is more or less exclusive; and they allow no one whose property falls below the amount fixed to have any share in the government. These changes in the constitution they effect by force of arms, if intimidation has not already done their work.

Very true.

And this, speaking generally, is the way in which oligarchy is established.

Yes, he said; but what are the characteristics of this form of government, and what are the defects of which we were speaking?[1]

First of all, I said, consider the nature of the qualification. Just think what would happen if pilots were to be chosen according to their property, and a poor man were refused permission to steer, even though he were a better pilot?

You mean that they would shipwreck.

Yes; and is not this true of the government of anything?

I should imagine so.

Except a city?—or would you include a city?

Nay, he said, the case of a city is the strongest of all, inasmuch as the rule of a city is the greatest and most difficult of all.

This, then, will be the first great defect of oligarchy?

Clearly.

And here is another defect which is quite as bad.

What defect?

The inevitable division: such a State is not one, but two States, the one of poor, the other of rich men; and they are living on the same spot and always conspiring against one another.

That, surely, is at least as bad.

Another discreditable feature is, that, for a like reason, they are incapable of carrying on any war. Either they arm the multitude, and then they are more afraid of them than of the enemy; or, if they do not call them out in the

[1] Cf. 544.

hour of battle, they are oligarchs indeed, few to fight as they are few to rule. And at the same time their fondness for money makes them unwilling to pay taxes.

How discreditable!

And, as we said before, under such a constitution the same persons have too many callings —they are husbandmen, [552] tradesmen, warriors, all in one. Does that look well?

Anything but well.

There is another evil which is, perhaps, the greatest of all, and to which this State first begins to be liable.

What evil?

A man may sell all that he has, and another may acquire his property; yet after the sale he may dwell in the city of which he is no longer a part, being neither trader, nor artisan, nor horseman, nor hoplite, but only a poor, helpless creature.

Yes, that is an evil which also first begins in this State.

The evil is certainly not prevented there; for oligarchies have both the extremes of great wealth and utter poverty.

True.

But think again: In his wealthy days, while he was spending his money, was a man of this sort a whit more good to the State for the purposes of citizenship? Or did he only seem to be a member of the ruling body, although in truth he was neither ruler nor subject, but just a spendthrift?

As you say, he seemed to be a ruler, but was only a spendthrift.

May we not say that this is the drone in the house who is like the drone in the honeycomb, and that the one is the plague of the city as the other is of the hive?

Just so, Socrates.

And God has made the flying drones, Adeimantus, all without stings, whereas of the walking drones he has made some without stings but others have dreadful stings; of the stingless class are those who in their old age end as paupers; of the stingers come all the criminal class, as they are termed.

Most true, he said.

Clearly then, whenever you see paupers in a State, somewhere in that neighbourhood there are hidden away thieves, and cut-purses and robbers of temples, and all sorts of malefactors.

Clearly.

Well, I said, and in oligarchical States do you not find paupers?

Yes, he said; nearly everybody is a pauper who is not a ruler.

And may we be so bold as to affirm that there are also many criminals to be found in them, rogues who have stings, and whom the authorities are careful to restrain by force?

Certainly, we may be so bold.

The existence of such persons is to be attributed to want of education, ill-training, and an evil constitution of the State?

True.

Such, then, is the form and such are the evils of oligarchy; and there may be many other evils.

Very likely.

[553] Then oligarchy, or the form of government in which the rulers are elected for their wealth, may now be dismissed. Let us next proceed to consider the nature and origin of the individual who answers to this State.

By all means.

Does not the timocratical man change into the oligarchical on this wise?

How?

A time arrives when the representative of timocracy has a son: at first he begins by emulating his father and walking in his footsteps, but presently he sees him of a sudden foundering against the State as upon a sunken reef, and he and all that he has is lost; he may have been a general or some other high officer who is brought to trial under a prejudice raised by informers, and either put to death, or exiled, or deprived of the privileges of a citizen, and all his property taken from him.

Nothing more likely.

And the son has seen and known all this—he is a ruined man, and his fear has taught him to knock ambition and passion headforemost from his bosom's throne; humbled by poverty he takes to money-making and by mean and miserly savings and hard work gets a fortune together. Is not such an one likely to seat the concupiscent and covetous element on the vacant throne and to suffer it to play the great king within him, girt with tiara and chain and scimitar?

Most true, he replied.

And when he has made reason and spirit sit down on the ground obediently on either side of their sovereign, and taught them to know their place, he compels the one to think only of how lesser sums may be turned into larger ones, and will not allow the other to worship and admire anything but riches and rich men, or to be ambitious of anything so much as the acquisi-tion of wealth and the means of acquiring it.

Of all changes, he said, there is none so speedy or so sure as the conversion of the ambitious youth into the avaricious one.

And the avaricious, I said, is the oligarchical youth?

Yes, he said; at any rate the individual out of whom he came is like the State out of which oligarchy came.

Let us then consider whether there is any likeness between them.

[554] Very good.

First, then, they resemble one another in the value which they set upon wealth?

Certainly.

Also in their penurious, laborious character; the individual only satisfies his necessary appetites, and confines his expenditure to them; his other desires he subdues, under the idea that they are unprofitable.

True.

He is a shabby fellow, who saves something out of everything and makes a purse for himself; and this is the sort of man whom the vulgar applaud. Is he not a true image of the State which he represents?

He appears to me to be so; at any rate money is highly valued by him as well as by the State.

You see that he is not a man of cultivation, I said.

I imagine not, he said; had he been educated he would never have made a blind god director of his chorus, or given him chief honour.

Excellent! I said. Yet consider: Must we not further admit that owing to this want of cultivation there will be found in him drone-like desires as of pauper and rogue, which are forcibly kept down by his general habit of life?

True.

Do you know where you will have to look if you want to discover his rogueries?

Where must I look?

You should see him where he has some great opportunity of acting dishonestly, as in the guardianship of an orphan.

Aye.

It will be clear enough then that in his ordinary dealings which give him a reputation for honesty he coerces his bad passions by an enforced virtue; not making them see that they are wrong, or taming them by reason, but by necessity and fear constraining them, and because he trembles for his possessions.

To be sure.

Yes, indeed, my dear friend, but you will find that the natural desires of the drone commonly exist in him all the same whenever he has to spend what is not his own.

Yes, and they will be strong in him too.

The man, then, will be at war with himself; he will be two men, and not one; but, in general, his better desires will be found to prevail over his inferior ones.

True.

For these reasons such an one will be more respectable than most people; yet the true virtue of a unanimous and harmonious soul will flee far away and never come near him.

I should expect so.

[555] And surely, the miser individually will be an ignoble competitor in a State for any prize of victory, or other object of honourable ambition; he will not spend his money in the contest for glory; so afraid is he of awakening his expensive appetites and inviting them to help and join in the struggle; in true oligarchical fashion he fights with a small part only of his resources, and the result commonly is that he loses the prize and saves his money.

Very true.

Can we any longer doubt, then, that the miser and money-maker answers to the oligarchical State?

There can be no doubt.

Next comes democracy; of this the origin and nature have still to be considered by us; and then we will enquire into the ways of the democratic man, and bring him up for judgment.

That, he said, is our method.

Well, I said, and how does the change from oligarchy into democracy arise? Is it not on this wise?—The good at which such a State aims is to become as rich as possible, a desire which is insatiable?

What then?

The rulers, being aware that their power rests upon their wealth, refuse to curtail by law the extravagance of the spendthrift youth because they gain by their ruin; they take interest from them and buy up their estates and thus increase their own wealth and importance?

To be sure.

There can be no doubt that the love of wealth and the spirit of moderation cannot exist together in citizens of the same State to any considerable extent; one or the other will be disregarded.

That is tolerably clear.

And in oligarchical States, from the general spread of carelessness and extravagance, men of good family have often been reduced to beggary?

Yes, often.

And still they remain in the city; there they are, ready to sting and fully armed, and some of them owe money, some have forfeited their citizenship; a third class are in both predicaments; and they hate and conspire against those who have got their property, and against everybody else, and are eager for revolution.

That is true.

On the other hand, the men of business, stooping as they walk, and pretending not even to see those whom they have already ruined, insert their sting—that is, their money—into some one else who is not on his guard against them, and recover the parent sum many times over multiplied into a family of children: and so they make drone and pauper to abound in the State.

[556] Yes, he said, there are plenty of them—that is certain.

The evil blazes up like a fire; and they will not extinguish it, either by restricting a man's use of his own property, or by another remedy:

What other?

One which is the next best, and has the advantage of compelling the citizens to look to their characters:—Let there be a general rule that every one shall enter into voluntary contracts at his own risk, and there will be less of this scandalous money-making, and the evils of which we were speaking will be greatly lessened in the State.

Yes, they will be greatly lessened.

At present the governors, induced by the motives which I have named, treat their subjects badly; while they and their adherents, especially the young men of the governing class, are habituated to lead a life of luxury and idleness both of body and mind; they do nothing, and are incapable of resisting either pleasure or pain.

Very true.

They themselves care only for making money, and are as indifferent as the pauper to the cultivation of virtue.

Yes, quite as indifferent.

Such is the state of affairs which prevails among them. And often rulers and their subjects may come in one another's way, whether on a pilgrimage or a march, as fellow-soldiers or fellow-sailors; aye and they may observe the behaviour of each other in the very moment of danger—for where danger is, there is no fear that the poor will be despised by the rich—and very likely the wiry sunburnt poor man may be placed in battle at the side of a wealthy one who has never spoilt his complexion and has plenty of superfluous flesh—when he sees such an one puffing and at his wit's end, how can he avoid drawing the conclusion that men like him are only rich because no one has the courage to despoil them? And when they meet in private will not people be saying to one another "Our warriors are not good for much"?

Yes, he said, I am quite aware that this is their way of talking.

And, as in a body which is diseased the addition of a touch from without may bring on illness, and sometimes even when there is no external provocation a commotion may arise within—in the same way wherever there is weakness in the State there is also likely to be illness, of which the occasions may be very slight, the one party introducing from without their oligarchical, the other their democratical allies, and then the State falls sick, and is at war with herself; [557] and may be at times distracted, even when there is no external cause.

Yes, surely.

And then democracy comes into being after the poor have conquered their opponents, slaughtering some and banishing some, while to the remainder they give an equal share of freedom and power; and this is the form of government in which the magistrates are commonly elected by lot.

Yes, he said, that is the nature of democracy, whether the revolution has been effected by arms, or whether fear has caused the opposite party to withdraw.

And now what is their manner of life, and what sort of a government have they? for as the government is, such will be the man.

Clearly, he said.

In the first place, are they not free; and is not the city full of freedom and frankness—a man may say and do what he likes?

'Tis said so, he replied.

And where freedom is, the individual is clearly able to order for himself his own life as he pleases?

Clearly.

Then in this kind of State there will be the greatest variety of human natures?

There will.

This, then, seems likely to be the fairest of States, being like an embroidered robe which is spangled with every sort of flower. And just as women and children think a variety of colours to be of all things most charming, so there are many men to whom this State, which is spangled with the manners and characters of man-

kind, will appear to be the fairest of States.

Yes.

Yes, my good Sir, and there will be no better in which to look for a government.

Why?

Because of the liberty which reigns there—they have a complete assortment of constitutions; and he who has a mind to establish a State, as we have been doing, must go to a democracy as he would to a bazaar at which they sell them, and pick out the one that suits him; then, when he has made his choice, he may found his State.

He will be sure to have patterns enough.

And there being no necessity, I said, for you to govern in this State, even if you have the capacity, or to be governed, unless you like, or go to war when the rest go to war, or to be at peace when others are at peace, unless you are so disposed—there being no necessity also, because some law forbids you to hold office or be a dicast, [558] that you should not hold office or be a dicast, if you have a fancy—is not this a way of life which for the moment is supremely delightful?

For the moment, yes.

And is not their humanity to the condemned in some cases quite charming? Have you not observed how, in a democracy, many persons, although they have been sentenced to death or exile, just stay where they are and walk about the world—the gentleman parades like a hero, and nobody sees or cares?

Yes, he replied, many and many a one.

See too, I said, the forgiving spirit of democracy, and the "don't care" about trifles, and the disregard which she shows of all the fine principles which we solemnly laid down at the foundation of the city—as when we said that, except in the case of some rarely gifted nature, there never will be a good man who has not from his childhood been used to play amid things of beauty and make of them a joy and a study—how grandly does she trample all these fine notions of ours under her feet, never giving a thought to the pursuits which make a statesman, and promoting to honour any one who professes to be the people's friend.

Yes, she is of a noble spirit.

These and other kindred characteristics are proper to democracy, which is a charming form of government, full of variety and disorder, and dispensing a sort of equality to equals and unequals alike.

We know her well.

Consider now, I said, what manner of man

the individual is, or rather consider, as in the case of the state, how he comes into being.

Very good, he said.

Is not this the way—he is the son of the miserly and oligarchical father who has trained him in his own habits?

Exactly.

And, like his father, he keeps under by force the pleasures which are of the spending and not of the getting sort, being those which are called unnecessary?

Obviously.

Would you like, for the sake of clearness, to distinguish which are the necessary and which are the unnecessary pleasures?

I should.

Are not necessary pleasures those of which we cannot get rid, and of which the satisfaction is a benefit to us? And they are rightly so, because we are framed by nature to desire both what is beneficial and what is necessary, and cannot help it.

[559] True.

We are not wrong therefore in calling them necessary?

We are not.

And the desires of which a man may get rid, if he takes pains from his youth upwards—of which the presence, moreover, does no good, and in some cases the reverse of good—shall we not be right in saying that all these are unnecessary?

Yes, certainly.

Suppose we select an example of either kind, in order that we may have a general notion of them?

Very good.

Will not the desire of eating, that is, of simple food and condiments, in so far as they are required for health and strength, be of the necessary class?

That is what I should suppose.

The pleasure of eating is necessary in two ways; it does us good and it is essential to the continuance of life?

Yes.

But the condiments are only necessary in so far as they are good for health?

Certainly.

And the desire which goes beyond this, of more delicate food, or other luxuries, which might generally be got rid of, if controlled and trained in youth, and is hurtful to the body, and hurtful to the soul in the pursuit of wisdom and virtue, may be rightly called unnecessary?

Very true.

May we not say that these desires spend, and that the others make money because they conduce to production?

Certainly.

And of the pleasures of love, and all other pleasures, the same holds good?

True.

And the drone of whom we spoke was he who has surfeited in pleasures and desires of this sort, and was the slave of the unnecessary desires, whereas he who was subject to the necessary only was miserly and oligarchical?

Very true.

Again, let us see how the democratical man grows out of the oligarchical: the following, as I suspect, is commonly the process.

What is the process?

When a young man who has been brought up as we were just now describing, in a vulgar and miserly way, has tasted drones' honey and has come to associate with fierce and crafty natures who are able to provide for him all sorts of refinements and varieties of pleasure—then, as you may imagine, the change will begin of the oligarchical principle within him into the democratical?

Inevitably.

And as in the city like was helping like, and the change was effected by an alliance from without assisting one division of the citizens, so too the young man is changed by a class of desires coming from without to assist the desires within him, that which is akin and alike again helping that which is akin and alike?

Certainly.

And if there be any ally which aids the oligarchical principle within him, whether the influence of a father or of kindred, advising or rebuking him, [560] then there arises in his soul a faction and an opposite faction, and he goes to war with himself.

It must be so.

And there are times when the democratical principle gives way to the oligarchical, and some of his desires die, and others are banished; a spirit of reverence enters into the young man's soul and order is restored.

Yes, he said, that sometimes happens.

And then, again, after the old desires have been driven out, fresh ones spring up, which are akin to them, and because he their father does not know how to educate them, wax fierce and numerous.

Yes, he said, that is apt to be the way.

They draw him to his old associates, and holding secret intercourse with them, breed and multiply in him.

Very true.

At length they seize upon the citadel of the young man's soul, which they perceive to be void of all accomplishments and fair pursuits and true words, which make their abode in the minds of men who are dear to the gods, and are their best guardians and sentinels.

None better.

False and boastful conceits and phrases mount upwards and take their place.

They are certain to do so.

And so the young man returns into the country of the lotus-eaters, and takes up his dwelling there in the face of all men; and if any help be sent by his friends to the oligarchical part of him, the aforesaid vain conceits shut the gate of the king's fastness; and they will neither allow the embassy itself to enter, nor if private advisers offer the fatherly counsel of the aged will they listen to them or receive them. There is a battle and they gain the day, and then modesty, which they call silliness, is ignominiously thrust into exile by them, and temperance, which they nickname unmanliness, is trampled in the mire and cast forth; they persuade men that moderation and orderly expenditure are vulgarity and meanness, and so, by the help of a rabble of evil appetites, they drive them beyond the border.

Yes, with a will.

And when they have emptied and swept clean the soul of him who is now in their power and who is being initiated by them in great mysteries, the next thing is to bring back to their house insolence and anarchy and waste and impudence in bright array having garlands on their heads, and a great company with them, hymning their praises and calling them by sweet names; [561] insolence they term breeding, and anarchy liberty, and waste magnificence, and impudence courage. And so the young man passes out of his original nature, which was trained in the school of necessity, into the freedom and libertinism of useless and unnecessary pleasures.

Yes, he said, the change in him is visible enough.

After this he lives on, spending his money and labour and time on unnecessary pleasures quite as much as on necessary ones; but if he be fortunate, and is not too much disordered in his wits, when years have elapsed, and the heyday of passion is over—supposing that he then re-admits into the city some part of the exiled virtues, and does not wholly give himself up to

their successors—in that case he balances his pleasures and lives in a sort of equilibrium, putting the government of himself into the hands of the one which comes first and wins the turn; and when he has had enough of that, then into the hands of another; he despises none of them but encourages them all equally.

Very true, he said.

Neither does he receive or let pass into the fortress any true word of advice; if any one says to him that some pleasures are the satisfactions of good and noble desires, and others of evil desires, and that he ought to use and honour some and chastise and master the others—whenever this is repeated to him he shakes his head and says that they are all alike, and that one is as good as another.

Yes, he said; that is the way with him.

Yes, I said, he lives from day to day indulging the appetite of the hour; and sometimes he is lapped in drink and strains of the flute; then he becomes a water-drinker, and tries to get thin; then he takes a turn at gymnastics; sometimes idling and neglecting everything, then once more living the life of a philosopher; often he is busy with politics, and starts to his feet and says and does whatever comes into his head; and, if he is emulous of any one who is a warrior, off he is in that direction, or of men of business, once more in that. His life has neither law nor order; and this distracted existence he terms joy and bliss and freedom; and so he goes on.

Yes, he replied, he is all liberty and equality.

Yes, I said; his life is motley and manifold and an epitome of the lives of many—he answers to the State which we described as fair and spangled. And many a man and many a woman will take him for their pattern, and many a constitution and many an example of manners is contained in him.

Just so.

[562] Let him then be set over against democracy; he may truly be called the democratic man.

Let that be his place, he said.

Last of all comes the most beautiful of all, man and State alike, tyranny and the tyrant; these we have now to consider.

Quite true, he said.

Say then, my friend, In what manner does tyranny arise?—that it has a democratic origin is evident.

Clearly.

And does not tyranny spring from democracy in the same manner as democracy from oligarchy—I mean, after a sort?

How?

The good which oligarchy proposed to itself and the means by which it was maintained was excess of wealth—am I not right?

Yes.

And the insatiable desire of wealth and the neglect of all other things for the sake of money-getting was also the ruin of oligarchy?

True.

And democracy has her own good, of which the insatiable desire brings her to dissolution?

What good?

Freedom, I replied; which, as they tell you in a democracy, is the glory of the State—and that therefore in a democracy alone will the freeman of nature deign to dwell.

Yes; the saying is in everybody's mouth.

I was going to observe, that the insatiable desire of this and the neglect of other things introduces the change in democracy, which occasions a demand for tyranny.

How so?

When a democracy which is thirsting for freedom has evil cup-bearers presiding over the feast, and has drunk too deeply of the strong wine of freedom, then, unless her rulers are very amenable and give a plentiful draught, she calls them to account and punishes them, and says that they are cursed oligarchs.

Yes, he replied, a very common occurrence.

Yes, I said; and loyal citizens are insultingly termed by her slaves who hug their chains and men of naught; she would have subjects who are like rulers, and rulers who are like subjects: these are men after her own heart, whom she praises and honours both in private and public. Now, in such a State, can liberty have any limit?

Certainly not.

By degrees the anarchy finds a way into private houses, and ends by getting among the animals and infecting them.

How do you mean?

I mean that the father grows accustomed to descend to the level of his sons and to fear them, and the son is on a level with his father, he having no respect or reverence for either of his parents; and this is his freedom, and the metic is equal with the citizen and the citizen with the metic, *[563]* and the stranger is quite as good as either.

Yes, he said, that is the way.

And these are not the only evils, I said—there are several lesser ones: In such a state of society the master fears and flatters his schol-ars, and the scholars despise their masters and tutors; young and old are all alike; and the young man is on a level with the old, and is ready to compete with him in word or deed; and old men condescend to the young and are full of pleasantry and gaiety; they are loth to be thought morose and authoritative, and there-fore they adopt the manners of the young.

Quite true, he said.

The last extreme of popular liberty is when the slave bought with money, whether male or female, is just as free as his or her purchaser; nor must I forget to tell of the liberty and equality of the two sexes in relation to each other.

Why not, as Aeschylus says, utter the word which rises to our lips?

That is what I am doing, I replied; and I must add that no one who does not know would believe, how much greater is the liberty which the animals who are under the dominion of man have in a democracy than in any other State: for truly, the she-dogs, as the proverb says, are as good as their she-mistresses, and the horses and asses have a way of marching along with all the rights and dignities of freemen; and they will run at any body who comes in their way if he does not leave the road clear for them: and all things are just ready to burst with liberty.

When I take a country walk, he said, I often experience what you describe. You and I have dreamed the same thing.

And above all, I said, and as the result of all, see how sensitive the citizens become; they chafe impatiently at the least touch of authority and at length, as you know, they cease to care even for the laws, written or unwritten; they will have no one over them.

Yes, he said, I know it too well.

Such, my friend, I said, is the fair and glori-ous beginning out of which springs tyranny.

Glorious indeed, he said. But what is the next step?

The ruin of oligarchy is the ruin of democracy; the same disease magnified and intensi-fied by liberty overmasters democracy—the truth being that the excessive increase of any-thing often causes a *[564]* reaction in the opposite direction; and this is the case not only in the seasons and in vegetable and animal life, but above all in forms of government.

True.

The excess of liberty, whether in States or individuals, seems only to pass into excess of slavery.

Yes, the natural order.

And so tyranny naturally arises out of democracy, and the most aggravated form of tyranny and slavery out of the most extreme form of liberty?

As we might expect.

That, however, was not, as I believe, your question—you rather desired to know what is that disorder which is generated alike in oligarchy and democracy, and is the ruin of both?

Just so, he replied.

Well, I said, I meant to refer to the class of idle spendthrifts, of whom the more courageous are the leaders and the more timid the followers, the same whom we were comparing to drones, some stingless, and others having stings.

A very just comparison.

These two classes are the plagues of every city in which they are generated, being what phlegm and bile are to the body. And the good physician and lawgiver of the State ought, like the wise bee-master, to keep them at a distance and prevent, if possible, their ever coming in; and if they have anyhow found a way in, then he should have them and their cells cut out as speedily as possible.

Yes, by all means, he said.

Then, in order that we may see clearly what we are doing, let us imagine democracy to be divided, as indeed it is, into three classes; for in the first place freedom creates rather more drones in the democratic than there were in the oligarchical State.

That is true.

And in the democracy they are certainly more intensified.

How so?

Because in the oligarchical State they are disqualified and driven from office, and therefore they cannot train or gather strength; whereas in a democracy they are almost the entire ruling power, and while the keener sort speak and act, the rest keep buzzing about the bema and do not suffer a word to be said on the other side; hence in democracies almost everything is managed by the drones.

Very true, he said.

Then there is another class which is always being severed from the mass.

What is that?

They are the orderly class, which in a nation of traders is sure to be the richest.

Naturally so.

They are the most squeezable persons and yield the largest amount of money to the drones.

Why, he said, there is little to be squeezed out of people who have little.

And this is called the wealthy class, and the drones feed upon them.

[565] That is pretty much the case, he said.

The people are a third class, consisting of those who work with their own hands; they are not politicians, and have not much to live upon. This, when assembled, is the largest and most powerful class in a democracy.

True, he said; but then the multitude is seldom willing to congregate unless they get a little honey.

And do they not share? I said. Do not their leaders deprive the rich of their estates and distribute them among the people; at the same time taking care to reserve the larger part for themselves?

Why, yes, he said, to that extent the people do share.

And the persons whose property is taken from them are compelled to defend themselves before the people as they best can?

What else can they do?

And then, although they may have no desire of change, the others charge them with plotting against the people and being friends of oligarchy?

True.

And the end is that when they see the people, not of their own accord, but through ignorance, and because they are deceived by informers, seeking to do them wrong, then at last they are forced to become oligarchs in reality; they do not wish to be, but the sting of the drones torments them and breeds revolution in them.

That is exactly the truth.

Then come impeachments and judgments and trials of one another.

True.

The people have always some champion whom they set over them and nurse into greatness.

Yes, that is their way.

This and no other is the root from which a tyrant springs; when he first appears above ground he is a protector.

Yes, that is quite clear.

How then does a protector begin to change into a tyrant? Clearly when he does what the man is said to do in the tale of the Arcadian temple of Lycaean Zeus.

What tale?

The tale is that he who has tasted the entrails of a single human victim minced up with the entrails of other victims is destined to become a wolf. Did you never hear it?

O yes.

And the protector of the people is like him; having a mob entirely at his disposal, he is not restrained from shedding the blood of kinsmen; by the favourite method of false accusation he brings them into court and murders them, making the life of man to disappear, and with unholy tongue and lips tasting the blood of his fellow citizen; some he kills and others he banishes, at the same time hinting at the abolition of debts and partition of lands: and after this, [566] what will be his destiny? Must he not either perish at the hands of his enemies, or from being a man become a wolf—that is, a tyrant?

Inevitably.

This, I said, is he who begins to make a party against the rich?

The same.

After a while he is driven out, but comes back, in spite of his enemies, a tyrant full grown.

That is clear.

And if they are unable to expel him, or to get him condemned to death by a public accusation, they conspire to assassinate him.

Yes, he said, that is their usual way.

Then comes the famous request for a bodyguard, which is the device of all those who have got thus far in their tyrannical career—"Let not the people's friend," as they say, "be lost to them."

Exactly.

The people readily assent; all their fears are for him—they have none for themselves.

Very true.

And when a man who is wealthy and is also accused of being an enemy of the people sees this, then, my friend, as the oracle said to Croesus: "By pebbly Hermus' shore he flees and rests not, and is not ashamed to be a coward." [1]

And quite right too, said he, for if he were, he would never be ashamed again.

But if he is caught he dies.

Of course.

And he, the protector of whom we spoke, is to be seen, not "larding the plain" with his bulk, but himself the overthrower of many, standing up in the chariot of State with the reins in his hand, no longer protector, but tyrant absolute.

No doubt, he said.

And now let us consider the happiness of the

[1] Herodotus, i. 55.

man, and also of the State in which a creature like him is generated.

Yes, he said, let us consider that.

At first, in the early days of his power, he is full of smiles, and he salutes every one whom he meets—he to be called a tyrant, who is making promises in public and also in private! liberating debtors, and distributing land to the people and his followers, and wanting to be so kind and good to every one!

Of course, he said.

But when he has disposed of foreign enemies by conquest or treaty, [567] and there is nothing to fear from them, then he is always stirring up some war or other, in order that the people may require a leader.

To be sure.

Has he not also another object, which is that they may be impoverished by payment of taxes, and thus compelled to devote themselves to their daily wants and therefore less likely to conspire against him?

Clearly.

And if any of them are suspected by him of having notions of freedom, and of resistance to his authority, he will have a good pretext for destroying them by placing them at the mercy of the enemy; and for all these reasons the tyrant must be always getting up a war.

He must.

Now he begins to grow unpopular.

A necessary result.

Then some of those who joined in setting him up, and who are in power, speak their minds to him and to one another, and the more courageous of them cast in his teeth what is being done.

Yes, that may be expected.

And the tyrant, if he means to rule, must get rid of them; he cannot stop while he has a friend or an enemy who is good for anything.

He cannot.

And therefore he must look about him and see who is valiant, who is high-minded, who is wise, who is wealthy; happy man, he is the enemy of them all, and must seek occasion against them whether he will or no, until he has made a purgation of the State.

Yes, he said, and a rare purgation.

Yes, I said, not the sort of purgation which the physicians make of the body; for they take away the worse and leave the better part, but he does the reverse.

If he is to rule, I suppose that he cannot help himself.

What a blessed alternative, I said:—to be

compelled to dwell only with the many bad, and to be by them hated, or not to live at all!

Yes, that is the alternative.

And the more detestable his actions are to the citizens the more satellites and the greater devotion in them will he require?

Certainly.

And who are the devoted band, and where will he procure them?

They will flock to him, he said, of their own accord, if he pays them.

By the dog! I said, here are more drones, of every sort and from every land.

Yes, he said, there are.

But will he not desire to get them on the spot?

How do you mean?

He will rob the citizens of their slaves; he will then set them free and enrol them in his body-guard.

To be sure, he said; and he will be able to trust them best of all.

What a blessed creature, I said, must this tyrant be; he has put to death the others and has these for his trusted friends. [568]

Yes, he said; they are quite of his sort.

Yes, I said, and these are the new citizens whom he has called into existence, who admire him and are his companions, while the good hate and avoid him.

Of course.

Verily, then, tragedy is a wise thing and Euripides a great tragedian.

Why so?

Why, because he is the author of the pregnant saying,

Tyrants are wise by living with the wise;

and he clearly meant to say that they are the wise whom the tyrant makes his companions.

Yes, he said, and he also praises tyranny as godlike; and many other things of the same kind are said by him and by the other poets.

And therefore, I said, the tragic poets being wise men will forgive us and any others who live after our manner if we do not receive them into our State, because they are the eulogists of tyranny.

Yes, he said, those who have the wit will doubtless forgive us.

But they will continue to go to other cities and attract mobs, and hire voices fair and loud and persuasive, and draw the cities over to tyrannies and democracies.

Very true.

Moreover, they are paid for this and receive honour—the greatest honour, as might be expected, from tyrants, and the next greatest from democracies; but the higher they ascend our constitution hill, the more their reputation fails, and seems unable from shortness of breath to proceed further.

True.

But we are wandering from the subject: Let us therefore return and enquire how the tyrant will maintain that fair and numerous and various and ever-changing army of his.

If, he said, there are sacred treasures in the city, he will confiscate and spend them; and in so far as the fortunes of attainted persons may suffice, he will be able to diminish the taxes which he would otherwise have to impose upon the people.

And when these fail?

Why, clearly, he said, then he and his boon companions, whether male or female, will be maintained out of his father's estate.

You mean to say that the people, from whom he has derived his being, will maintain him and his companions?

Yes, he said; they cannot help themselves.

But what if the people fly into a passion, and aver that a grown-up son ought not to be supported by his father, but that the father should be supported by the son? [569] The father did not bring him into being, or settle him in life, in order that when his son became a man he should himself be the servant of his own servants and should support him and his rabble of slaves and companions; but that his son should protect him, and that by his help he might be emancipated from the government of the rich and aristocratic, as they are termed. And so he bids him and his companions depart, just as any other father might drive out of the house a riotous son and his undesirable associates.

By heaven, he said, then the parent will discover what a monster he has been fostering in his bosom; and, when he wants to drive him out, he will find that he is weak and his son strong.

Why, you do not mean to say that the tyrant will use violence? What! beat his father if he opposes him?

Yes, he will, having first disarmed him.

Then he is a parricide, and a cruel guardian of an aged parent; and this is real tyranny, about which there can be no longer a mistake: as the saying is, the people who would escape the smoke which is the slavery of freemen, has fallen into the fire which is the tyranny of slaves. Thus liberty, getting out of all order and reason, passes into the harshest and bitterest form of slavery.

True, he said.

Very well; and may we not rightly say that we have sufficiently discussed the nature of tyranny, and the manner of the transition from democracy to tyranny?

Yes, quite enough, he said.

BOOK IX

[571] LAST of all comes the tyrannical man; about whom we have once more to ask, how is he formed out of the democratical? and how does he live, in happiness or in misery?

Yes, he said, he is the only one remaining.

There is, however, I said, a previous question which remains unanswered.

What question?

I do not think that we have adequately determined the nature and number of the appetites, and until this is accomplished the enquiry will always be confused.

Well, he said, it is not too late to supply the omission.

Very true, I said; and observe the point which I want to understand: Certain of the unnecessary pleasures and appetites I conceive to be unlawful; every one appears to have them, but in some persons they are controlled by the laws and by reason, and the better desires prevail over them—either they are wholly banished or they become few and weak; while in the case of others they are stronger, and there are more of them.

Which appetites do you mean?

I mean those which are awake when the reasoning and human and ruling power is asleep; then the wild beast within us, gorged with meat or drink, starts up and having shaken off sleep, goes forth to satisfy his desires; and there is no conceivable folly or crime—not excepting incest or any other unnatural union, or parricide, or the eating of forbidden food—which at such a time, when he has parted company with all shame and sense, a man may not be ready to commit.

Most true, he said.

But when a man's pulse is healthy and temperate, and when before going to sleep he has awakened his rational powers, and fed them on noble thoughts and enquiries, collecting himself in meditation; after having first indulged his appetites neither too much nor too little, but just enough to lay them to sleep, and prevent them and their enjoyments and pains from interfering with the [572] higher principle—which he leaves in the solitude of pure abstraction, free to contemplate and aspire to the knowledge of the unknown, whether in past, present, or future: when again he has allayed the passionate element, if he has a quarrel against any one—I say, when, after pacifying the two irrational principles, he rouses up the third, which is reason, before he takes his rest, then, as you know, he attains truth most nearly, and is least likely to be the sport of fantastic and lawless visions.

I quite agree.

In saying this I have been running into a digression; but the point which I desire to note is that in all of us, even in good men, there is a lawless wild-beast nature, which peers out in sleep. Pray, consider whether I am right, and you agree with me.

Yes, I agree.

And now remember the character which we attributed to the democratic man. He was supposed from his youth upwards to have been trained under a miserly parent, who encouraged the saving appetites in him, but discountenanced the unnecessary, which aim only at amusement and ornament?

True.

And then he got into the company of a more refined, licentious sort of people, and taking to all their wanton ways rushed into the opposite extreme from an abhorrence of his father's meanness. At last, being a better man than his corruptors, he was drawn in both directions until he halted midway and led a life, not of vulgar and slavish passion, but of what he deemed moderate indulgence in various pleasures. After this manner the democrat was generated out of the oligarch?

Yes, he said; that was our view of him, and is so still.

And now, I said, years will have passed away, and you must conceive this man, such as he is, to have a son, who is brought up in his father's principles.

I can imagine him.

Then you must further imagine the same thing to happen to the son which has already happened to the father:—he is drawn into a perfectly lawless life, which by his seducers is termed perfect liberty; and his father and friends take part with his moderate desires, and the opposite party assist the opposite ones. As soon as these dire magicians and tyrant-makers find that they are losing [573] their hold on him, they contrive to implant in him a master passion, to be lord over his idle and spend-thrift lusts—a sort of monstrous winged drone—that is the only image which will adequately describe him.

Yes, he said, that is the only adequate image of him.

And when his other lusts, amid clouds of incense and perfumes and garlands and wines, and all the pleasures of a dissolute life, now let loose, come buzzing around him, nourishing to the utmost the sting of desire which they implant in his drone-like nature, then at last this lord of the soul, having Madness for the captain of his guard, breaks out into a frenzy; and if he finds in himself any good opinions or appetites in process of formation, and there is in him any sense of shame remaining, to these better principles he puts an end, and casts them forth until he has purged away temperance and brought in madness to the full.

Yes, he said, that is the way in which the tyrannical man is generated.

And is not this the reason why of old love has been called a tyrant?

I should not wonder.

Further, I said, has not a drunken man also the spirit of a tyrant?

He has.

And you know that a man who is deranged and not right in his mind, will fancy that he is able to rule, not only over men, but also over the gods?

That he will.

And the tyrannical man in the true sense of the word comes into being when, either under the influence of nature, or habit, or both, he becomes drunken, lustful, passionate? O my friend, is not that so?

Assuredly.

Such is the man and such is his origin. And next, how does he live?

Suppose, as people facetiously say, you were to tell me.

I imagine, I said, at the next step in his progress, that there will be feasts and carousals and revellings and courtesans, and all that sort of thing; Love is the lord of the house within him, and orders all the concerns of his soul.

That is certain.

Yes; and every day and every night desires grow up many and formidable, and their demands are many.

They are indeed, he said.

His revenues, if he has any, are soon spent.

True.

Then comes debt and the cutting down of his property.

Of course.

When he has nothing left, must not his desires, crowding in the nest like young ravens, [574] be crying aloud for food; and he, goaded on by them, and especially by Love himself, who is in a manner the captain of them, is in a frenzy, and would fain discover whom he can defraud or despoil of his property, in order that he may gratify them?

Yes, that is sure to be the case.

He must have money, no matter how, if he is to escape horrid pains and pangs.

He must.

And as in himself there was a succession of pleasures, and the new got the better of the old and took away their rights, so he being younger will claim to have more than his father and his mother, and if he has spent his own share of the property, he will take a slice of theirs.

No doubt he will.

And if his parents will not give way, then he will try first of all to cheat and deceive them.

Very true.

And if he fails, then he will use force and plunder them.

Yes, probably.

And if the old man and woman fight for their own, what then, my friend? Will the creature feel any compunction at tyrannizing over them?

Nay, he said, I should not feel at all comfortable about his parents.

But, O heavens! Adeimantus, on account of some new-fangled love of a harlot, who is anything but a necessary connection, can you believe that he would strike the mother who is his ancient friend and necessary to his very existence, and would place her under the authority of the other, when she is brought under the same roof with her; or that, under like circumstances, he would do the same to his withered old father, first and most indispensable of friends, for the sake of some newly-found blooming youth who is the reverse of indispensable?

Yes, indeed, he said; I believe that he would.

Truly, then, I said, a tyrannical son is a blessing to his father and mother.

He is indeed, he replied.

He first takes their property, and when that fails, and pleasures are beginning to swarm in the hive of his soul, then he breaks into a house, or steals the garments of some nightly wayfarer; next he proceeds to clear a temple. Meanwhile the old opinions which he had when a child, and which gave judgment about good and evil, are overthrown by those others which have just been emancipated, and are now the body-guard of love and share his empire. These in his democratic days, when he was still subject to the laws and to his father, were only let loose in the dreams of sleep. But now that he is under the dominion of Love, he becomes always and in waking reality what he was then very rarely and in a dream only; he will commit the foulest murder, or eat forbidden food, or be guilty of any other horrid act. [575] Love is his tyrant, and lives lordly in him and lawlessly, and being himself a king, leads him on, as a tyrant leads a State, to the performance of any reckless deed by which he can maintain himself and the rabble of his associates, whether those whom evil communications have brought in from without, or those whom he himself has allowed to break loose within him by reason of a similar evil nature in himself. Have we not here a picture of his way of life?

Yes, indeed, he said.

And if there are only a few of them in the State, and the rest of the people are well disposed, they go away and become the bodyguard or mercenary soldiers of some other tyrant who may probably want them for a war; and if there is no war, they stay at home and do many little pieces of mischief in the city.

What sort of mischief?

For example, they are the thieves, burglars, cut-purses, footpads, robbers of temples, man-stealers of the community; or if they are able to speak they turn informers, and bear false witness, and take bribes.

A small catalogue of evils, even if the perpetrators of them are few in number.

Yes, I said; but small and great are comparative terms, and all these things, in the misery and evil which they inflict upon a State, do not come within a thousand miles of the tyrant; when this noxious class and their followers grow numerous and become conscious of their strength, assisted by the infatuation of the people, they choose from among themselves the one who has most of the tyrant in his own soul, and him they create their tyrant.

Yes, he said, and he will be the most fit to be a tyrant.

If the people yield, well and good; but if they resist him, as he began by beating his own father and mother, so now, if he has the power, he beats them, and will keep his dear old fatherland or motherland, as the Cretans say, in sub-jection to his young retainers whom he has introduced to be their rulers and masters. This is the end of his passions and desires.

Exactly.

When such men are only private individuals and before they get power, this is their character; they associate entirely with their own flatterers or ready tools; or if they want anything from anybody, they in their turn are equally ready to bow down before them: [576] they profess every sort of affection for them; but when they have gained their point they know them no more.

Yes, truly.

They are always either the masters or servants and never the friends of anybody; the tyrant never tastes of true freedom or friendship.

Certainly not.

And may we not rightly call such men treacherous?

No question.

Also they are utterly unjust, if we were right in our notion of justice?

Yes, he said, and we were perfectly right.

Let us then sum up in a word, I said, the character of the worst man: he is the waking reality of what we dreamed.

Most true.

And this is he who being by nature most of a tyrant bears rule, and the longer he lives the more of a tyrant he becomes.

That is certain, said Glaucon, taking his turn to answer.

And will not he who has been shown to be the wickedest, be also the most miserable? and he who has tyrannized longest and most, most continually and truly miserable; although this may not be the opinion of men in general?

Yes, he said, inevitably.

And must not the tyrannical man be like the tyrannical State, and the democratical man like the democratical State; and the same of the others?

Certainly.

And as State is to State in virtue and happiness, so is man in relation to man?

To be sure.

Then comparing our original city, which was under a king, and the city which is under a tyrant, how do they stand as to virtue?

They are the opposite extremes, he said, for one is the very best, the other the very worst.

There can be no mistake, I said, as to which is which, and therefore I will at once enquire whether you would arrive at a similar decision about their relative happiness and misery. And here we must not allow ourselves to be panic-striken at the apparition of the tyrant, who is only a unit and may perhaps have a few retainers about him; but let us go as we ought into every corner of the city and look all about, and then we will give our opinion.

A fair invitation, he replied; and I see, as every one must, that a tyranny is the wretchedest form of government, and the rule of a king the happiest.

And in estimating the men too, may I not fairly make a like request, [577] that I should have a judge whose mind can enter into and see through human nature? he must not be like a child who looks at the outside and is dazzled at the pompous aspect which the tyrannical nature assumes to the beholder, but let him be one who has a clear insight. May I suppose that the judgment is given in the hearing of us all by one who is able to judge, and has dwelt in the same place with him, and been present at his daily life and known him in his family relations, where he may be seen stripped of his tragedy attire, and again in the hour of public danger—he shall tell us about the happiness and misery of the tyrant when compared with other men?

That again, he said, is a very fair proposal.

Shall I assume that we ourselves are able and experienced judges and have before now met with such a person? We shall then have some one who will answer our enquiries.

By all means.

Let me ask you not to forget the parallel of the individual and the State; bearing this in mind, and glancing in turn from one to the other of them, will you tell me their respective conditions?

What do you mean? he asked.

Beginning with the State, I replied, would you say that a city which is governed by a tyrant is free or enslaved?

No city, he said, can be more completely enslaved.

And yet, as you see, there are freemen as well as masters in such a State?

Yes, he said, I see that there are—a few; but the people, speaking generally, and the best of them are miserably degraded and enslaved.

Then if the man is like the State, I said, must not the same rule prevail? his soul is full of meanness and vulgarity—the best elements in him are enslaved; and there is a small ruling part, which is also the worst and maddest.

Inevitably.

And would you say that the soul of such an one is the soul of a freeman, or of a slave?

He has the soul of a slave, in my opinion.

And the State which is enslaved under a tyrant is utterly incapable of acting voluntarily?

Utterly incapable.

And also the soul which is under a tyrant (I am speaking of the soul taken as a whole) is least capable of doing what she desires; there is a gadfly which goads her, and she is full of trouble and remorse?

Certainly.

And is the city which is under a tyrant rich or poor?

Poor.

[578] And the tyrannical soul must be always poor and insatiable?

True.

And must not such a State and such a man be always full of fear?

Yes, indeed.

Is there any State in which you will find more of lamentation and sorrow and groaning and pain?

Certainly not.

And is there any man in whom you will find more of this sort of misery than in the tyrannical man, who is in a fury of passions and desires?

Impossible.

Reflecting upon these and similar evils, you held the tyrannical State to be the most miserable of States?

And I was right, he said.

Certainly, I said. And when you see the same evils in the tyrannical man, what do you say of him?

I say that he is by far the most miserable of all men.

There, I said, I think that you are beginning to go wrong.

What do you mean?

I do not think that he has as yet reached the utmost extreme of misery.

Then who is more miserable?

One of whom I am about to speak.

Who is that?

He who is of a tyrannical nature, and instead of leading a private life has been cursed with the further misfortune of being a public tyrant.

From what has been said, I gather that you are right.

Yes, I replied, but in this high argument you should be a little more certain, and should not conjecture only; for of all questions, this respecting good and evil is the greatest.

Very true, he said.

Let me then offer you an illustration, which may, I think, throw a light upon this subject.

What is your illustration?

The case of rich individuals in cities who possess many slaves, from them you may form an idea of the tyrant's condition, for they both have slaves; the only difference is that he has more slaves.

Yes, that is the difference.

You know that they live securely and have nothing to apprehend from their servants?

What should they fear?

Nothing. But do you observe the reason of this?

Yes; the reason is, that the whole city is leagued together for the protection of each individual.

Very true, I said. But imagine one of these owners, the master say of some fifty slaves, together with his family and property and slaves, carried off by a god into the wilderness, where there are no freemen to help him—will he not be in an agony of fear lest he and his wife and children should be put to death by his slaves?

[579] Yes, he said, he will be in the utmost fear.

The time has arrived when he will be compelled to flatter divers of his slaves, and make many promises to them of freedom and other things, much against his will—he will have to cajole his own servants.

Yes, he said, that will be the only way of saving himself.

And suppose the same god, who carried him away, to surround him with neighbours who will not suffer one man to be the master of another, and who, if they could catch the offender, would take his life?

His case will be still worse, if you suppose him to be everywhere surrounded and watched by enemies.

And is not this the sort of prison in which the tyrant will be bound—he who being by nature such as we have described, is full of all sorts of fears and lusts? His soul is dainty and greedy, and yet alone, of all men in the city, he is never allowed to go on a journey, or to see the things which other freemen desire to see, but he lives in his hole like a woman hidden in the house, and is jealous of any other citizen who goes into foreign parts and sees anything of interest.

Very true, he said.

And amid evils such as these will not he who is ill-governed in his own person—the tyranni-cal man, I mean—whom you just now decided to be the most miserable of all—will not he be yet more miserable when, instead of leading a private life, he is constrained by fortune to be a public tyrant? He has to be master of others when he is not master of himself: he is like a diseased or paralytic man who is compelled to pass his life, not in retirement, but fighting and combating with other men.

Yes, he said, the similitude is most exact.

Is not his case utterly miserable? and does not the actual tyrant lead a worse life than he whose life you determined to be the worst?

Certainly.

He who is the real tyrant, whatever men may think, is the real slave, and is obliged to practise the greatest adulation and servility, and to be the flatterer of the vilest of mankind. He has desires which he is utterly unable to satisfy, and has more wants than any one, and is truly poor, if you know how to inspect the whole soul of him: all his life long he is beset with fear and is full of convulsions, and distractions, even as the State which he resembles: and surely the resemblance holds?

Very true, he said.

[580] Moreover, as we were saying before, he grows worse from having power: he becomes and is of necessity more jealous, more faithless, more unjust, more friendless, more impious, than he was at first; he is the purveyor and cherisher of every sort of vice, and the consequence is that he is supremely miserable, and that he makes everybody else as miserable as himself.

No man of any sense will dispute your words.

Come then, I said, and as the general umpire in theatrical contests proclaims the result, do you also decide who in your opinion is first in the scale of happiness, and who second, and in what order the others follow: there are five of them in all—they are the royal, timocratical, oligarchical, democratical, tyrannical.

The decision will be easily given, he replied; they shall be choruses coming on the stage, and I must judge them in the order in which they enter, by the criterion of virtue and vice, happiness and misery.

Need we hire a herald, or shall I announce, that the son of Ariston [the best] has decided that the best and justest is also the happiest, and that this is he who is the most royal man and king over himself; and that the worst and most unjust man is also the most miserable, and that this is he who being the greatest tyrant of himself is also the greatest tyrant of his State?

Make the proclamation yourself, he said.

And shall I add, "whether seen or unseen by gods and men"?

Let the words be added.

Then this, I said, will be our first proof; and there is another, which may also have some weight.

What is that?

The second proof is derived from the nature of the soul: seeing that the individual soul, like the State, has been divided by us into three principles, the division may, I think, furnish a new demonstration.

Of what nature?

It seems to me that to these three principles three pleasures correspond; also three desires and governing powers.

How do you mean? he said.

There is one principle with which, as we were saying, a man learns, another with which he is angry; the third, having many forms, has no special name, but is denoted by the general term appetitive, from the extraordinary strength and vehemence of the desires of eating and drinking and the other sensual appetites which are the main elements of it; [581] also money-loving, because such desires are generally satisfied by the help of money.

That is true, he said.

If we were to say that the loves and pleasures of this third part were concerned with gain, we should then be able to fall back on a single notion; and might truly and intelligibly describe this part of the soul as loving gain or money.

I agree with you.

Again, is not the passionate element wholly set on ruling and conquering and getting fame?

True.

Suppose we call it the contentious or ambitious—would the term be suitable?

Extremely suitable.

On the other hand, every one sees that the principle of knowledge is wholly directed to the truth, and cares less than either of the others for gain or fame.

Far less.

"Lover of wisdom," "lover of knowledge," are titles which we may fitly apply to that part of the soul?

Certainly.

One principle prevails in the souls of one class of men, another in others, as may happen?

Yes.

Then we may begin by assuming that there are three classes of men—lovers of wisdom, lovers of honour, lovers of gain?

Exactly.

And there are three kinds of pleasure, which are their several objects?

Very true.

Now, if you examine the three classes of men, and ask of them in turn which of their lives is pleasantest, each will be found praising his own and depreciating that of others: the money-maker will contrast the vanity of honour or of learning if they bring no money with the solid advantages of gold and silver?

True, he said.

And the lover of honour—what will be his opinion? Will he not think that the pleasure of riches is vulgar, while the pleasure of learning, if it brings no distinction, is all smoke and nonsense to him?

Very true.

And are we to suppose, I said, that the philosopher sets any value on other pleasures in comparison with the pleasure of knowing the truth, and in that pursuit abiding, ever learning, not so far indeed from the heaven of pleasure? Does he not call the other pleasures necessary, under the idea that if there were no necessity for them, he would rather not have them?

There can be no doubt of that, he replied.

Since, then, the pleasures of each class and the life of each are in dispute, and the question is not which life is more or less honourable, [582] or better or worse, but which is the more pleasant or painless—how shall we know who speaks truly?

I cannot myself tell, he said.

Well, but what ought to be the criterion? Is any better than experience and wisdom and reason?

There cannot be a better, he said.

Then, I said, reflect. Of the three individuals, which has the greatest experience of all the pleasures which we enumerated? Has the lover of gain, in learning the nature of essential truth, greater experience of the pleasure of knowledge than the philosopher has of the pleasure of gain?

The philosopher, he replied, has greatly the advantage; for he has of necessity always known the taste of the other pleasures from his childhood upwards: but the lover of gain in all his experience has not of necessity tasted—or, I should rather say, even had he desired, could hardly have tasted—the sweetness of learning and knowing truth.

Then the lover of wisdom has a great advantage over the lover of gain, for he has a double experience?

Yes, very great.

Again, has he greater experience of the pleasures of honour, or the lover of honour of the pleasures of wisdom?

Nay, he said, all three are honoured in proportion as they attain their object; for the rich man and the brave man and the wise man alike have their crowd of admirers, and as they all receive honour they all have experience of the pleasures of honour; but the delight which is to be found in the knowledge of true being is known to the philosopher only.

His experience, then, will enable him to judge better than any one?

Far better.

And he is the only one who has wisdom as well as experience?

Certainly.

Further, the very faculty which is the instrument of judgment is not possessed by the covetous or ambitious man, but only by the philosopher?

What faculty?

Reason, with whom, as we were saying, the decision ought to rest.

Yes.

And reasoning is peculiarly his instrument?

Certainly.

If wealth and gain were the criterion, then the praise or blame of the lover of gain would surely be the most trustworthy?

Assuredly.

Or if honour or victory or courage, in that case the judgment of the ambitious or pugnacious would be the truest?

Clearly.

But since experience and wisdom and reason are the judges—

The only inference possible, he replied, is that pleasures which are approved by the lover of wisdom and reason are the truest.

And so we arrive at the result, that the pleasure of the intelligent part of the soul is the pleasantest of the three, [583] and that he of us in whom this is the ruling principle has the pleasantest life.

Unquestionably, he said, the wise man speaks with authority when he approves of his own life.

And what does the judge affirm to be the life which is next, and the pleasure which is next?

Clearly that of the soldier and lover of honour; who is nearer to himself than the moneymaker.

Last comes the lover of gain?

Very true, he said.

Twice in succession, then, has the just man overthrown the unjust in this conflict; and now comes the third trial, which is dedicated to Olympian Zeus the saviour: a sage whispers in my ear that no pleasure except that of the wise is quite true and pure—all others are a shadow only; and surely this will prove the greatest and most decisive of falls?

Yes, the greatest; but will you explain yourself?

I will work out the subject and you shall answer my questions.

Proceed.

Say, then, is not pleasure opposed to pain?

True.

And there is a neutral state which is neither pleasure nor pain?

There is.

A state which is intermediate, and a sort of repose of the soul about either—that is what you mean?

Yes.

You remember what people say when they are sick?

What do they say?

That after all nothing is pleasanter than health. But then they never knew this to be the greatest of pleasures until they were ill.

Yes, I know, he said.

And when persons are suffering from acute pain, you must have heard them say that there is nothing pleasanter than to get rid of their pain?

I have.

And there are many other cases of suffering in which the mere rest and cessation of pain, and not any positive enjoyment, is extolled by them as the greatest pleasure?

Yes, he said; at the time they are pleased and well content to be at rest.

Again, when pleasure ceases, that sort of rest or cessation will be painful?

Doubtless, he said.

Then the intermediate state of rest will be pleasure and will also be pain?

So it would seem.

But can that which is neither become both?

I should say not.

And both pleasure and pain are motions of the soul, are they not?

Yes.

[584] But that which is neither was just now shown to be rest and not motion, and in a mean between them?

Yes.

How, then, can we be right in supposing

that the absence of pain is pleasure, or that the absence of pleasure is pain?

Impossible.

This then is an appearance only and not a reality; that is to say, the rest is pleasure at the moment and in comparison of what is painful, and painful in comparison of what is pleasant; but all these representations, when tried by the test of true pleasure, are not real but a sort of imposition?

That is the inference.

Look at the other class of pleasures which have no antecedent pains and you will no longer suppose, as you perhaps may at present, that pleasure is only the cessation of pain, or pain of pleasure.

What are they, he said, and where shall I find them?

There are many of them: take as an example the pleasures of smell, which are very great and have no antecedent pains; they come in a moment, and when they depart leave no pain behind them.

Most true, he said.

Let us not, then, be induced to believe that pure pleasure is the cessation of pain, or pain of pleasure.

No.

Still, the more numerous and violent pleasures which reach the soul through the body are generally of this sort—they are reliefs of pain.

That is true.

And the anticipations of future pleasures and pains are of a like nature?

Yes.

Shall I give you an illustration of them?

Let me hear.

You would allow, I said, that there is in nature an upper and lower and middle region?

I should.

And if a person were to go from the lower to the middle region, would he not imagine that he is going up; and he who is standing in the middle and sees whence he has come, would imagine that he is already in the upper region, if he has never seen the true upper world?

To be sure, he said; how can he think otherwise?

But if he were taken back again he would imagine, and truly imagine, that he was descending?

No doubt.

All that would arise out of his ignorance of the true upper and middle and lower regions?

Yes.

Then can you wonder that persons who are inexperienced in the truth, as they have wrong ideas about many other things, should also have wrong ideas about pleasure and pain and the intermediate state; so that when they are only being drawn towards the painful they feel pain and think the pain which they experience to be real, [585] and in like manner, when drawn away from pain to the neutral or intermediate state, they firmly believe that they have reached the goal of satiety and pleasure; they, not knowing pleasure, err in contrasting pain with the absence of pain, which is like contrasting black with grey instead of white—can you wonder, I say, at this?

No, indeed; I should be much more disposed to wonder at the opposite.

Look at the matter thus:—Hunger, thirst, and the like, are inanitions of the bodily state?

Yes.

And ignorance and folly are inanitions of the soul?

True.

And food and wisdom are the corresponding satisfactions of either?

Certainly.

And is the satisfaction derived from that which has less or from that which has more existence the truer?

Clearly, from that which has more.

What classes of things have a greater share of pure existence in your judgment—those of which food and drink and condiments and all kinds of sustenance are examples, or the class which contains true opinion and knowledge and mind and all the different kinds of virtue? Put the question in this way:—Which has a more pure being—that which is concerned with the invariable, the immortal, and the true, and is of such a nature, and is found in such natures; or that which is concerned with and found in the variable and mortal, and is itself variable and mortal?

Far purer, he replied, is the being of that which is concerned with the invariable.

And does the essence of the invariable partake of knowledge in the same degree as of essence?

Yes, of knowledge in the same degree.

And of truth in the same degree?

Yes.

And, conversely, that which has less of truth will also have less of essence?

Necessarily.

Then, in general, those kinds of things which are in the service of the body have less of truth and essence than those which are in the service of the soul?

Far less.

And has not the body itself less of truth and essence than the soul?

Yes.

What is filled with more real existence, and actually has a more real existence, is more really filled than that which is filled with less real existence and is less real?

Of course.

And if there be a pleasure in being filled with that which is according to nature, that which is more really filled with more real being will more really and truly enjoy true pleasure; whereas that which participates in less real being will be less truly and surely satisfied, and will participate in an illusory and less real pleasure?

Unquestionably.

[586] Those then who know not wisdom and virtue, and are always busy with gluttony and sensuality, go down and up again as far as the mean; and in this region they move at random throughout life, but they never pass into the true upper world; thither they neither look, nor do they ever find their way, neither are they truly filled with true being, nor do they taste of pure and abiding pleasure. Like cattle, with their eyes always looking down and their heads stooping to the earth, that is, to the dining-table, they fatten and feed and breed, and, in their excessive love of these delights, they kick and butt at one another with horns and hoofs which are made of iron; and they kill one another by reason of their insatiable lust. For they fill themselves with that which is not substantial, and the part of themselves which they fill is also unsubstantial and incontinent.

Verily, Socrates, said Glaucon, you describe the life of the many like an oracle.

Their pleasures are mixed with pains—how can they be otherwise? For they are mere shadows and pictures of the true, and are coloured by contrast, which exaggerates both light and shade, and so they implant in the minds of fools insane desires of themselves; and they are fought about as Stesichorus says that the Greeks fought about the shadow of Helen at Troy in ignorance of the truth.

Something of that sort must inevitably happen.

And must not the like happen with the spirited or passionate element of the soul? Will not the passionate man who carries his passion into action, be in the like case, whether he is envious and ambitious, or violent and contentious, or angry and discontented, if he be seeking to attain honour and victory and the satisfaction of his anger without reason or sense?

Yes, he said, the same will happen with the spirited element also.

Then may we not confidently assert that the lovers of money and honour, when they seek their pleasures under the guidance and in the company of reason and knowledge, and pursue after and win the pleasures which wisdom shows them, will also have the truest pleasures in the highest degree which is attainable to them, inasmuch as they follow truth; and they will have the pleasures which are natural to them, if that which is best for each one is also most natural to him?

Yes, certainly; the best is the most natural.

And when the whole soul follows the philosophical principle, and there is no division, the several parts are just, and do each of them their own business, [587] and enjoy severally the best and truest pleasures of which they are capable?

Exactly.

But when either of the two other principles prevails, it fails in attaining its own pleasure, and compels the rest to pursue after a pleasure which is a shadow only and which is not their own?

True.

And the greater the interval which separates them from philosophy and reason, the more strange and illusive will be the pleasure?

Yes.

And is not that farthest from reason which is at the greatest distance from law and order?

Clearly.

And the lustful and tyrannical desires are, as we saw, at the greatest distance?

Yes.

And the royal and orderly desires are nearest?

Yes.

Then the tyrant will live at the greatest distance from true or natural pleasure, and the king at the least?

Certainly.

But if so, the tyrant will live most unpleasantly, and the king most pleasantly?

Inevitably.

Would you know the measure of the interval which separates them?

Will you tell me?

There appear to be three pleasures, one genuine and two spurious: now the transgression of the tyrant reaches a point beyond the spurious; he has run away from the region of law and reason, and taken up his abode with certain slave pleasures which are his satellites, and the measure of his inferiority can only be expressed in a figure.

How do you mean?

I assume, I said, that the tyrant is in the third place from the oligarch; the democrat was in the middle?

Yes.

And if there is truth in what has preceded, he will be wedded to an image of pleasure which is thrice removed as to truth from the pleasure of the oligarch?

He will.

And the oligarch is third from the royal; since we count as one royal and aristocratical?

Yes, he is third.

Then the tyrant is removed from true pleasure by the space of a number which is three times three?

Manifestly.

The shadow then of tyrannical pleasure determined by the number of length will be a plane figure.

Certainly.

And if you raise the power and make the plane a solid, there is no difficulty in seeing how vast is the interval by which the tyrant is parted from the king.

Yes; the arithmetician will easily do the sum.

Or if some person begins at the other end and measures the interval by which the king is parted from the tyrant in truth of pleasure, he will find him, when the multiplication is complete, living 729 times more pleasantly, and the tyrant more painfully by this same interval.

What a wonderful calculation! And how enormous is the distance which separates the just from the unjust in regard to pleasure [588] and pain!

Yet a true calculation, I said, and a number which nearly concerns human life, if human beings are concerned with days and nights and months and years.[1]

Yes, he said, human life is certainly concerned with them.

Then if the good and just man be thus superior in pleasure to the evil and unjust, his superiority will be infinitely greater in propriety of life and in beauty and virtue?

Immeasurably greater.

Well, I said, and now having arrived at this

[1] The figure 729 *nearly* equals the number of days and nights in the year.

stage of the argument, we may revert to the words which brought us hither: Was not some one saying that injustice was a gain to the perfectly unjust who was reputed to be just?

Yes, that was said.

Now then, having determined the power and quality of justice and injustice, let us have a little conversation with him.

What shall we say to him?

Let us make an image of the soul, that he may have his own words presented before his eyes.

Of what sort?

An ideal image of the soul, like the composite creations of ancient mythology, such as the Chimera or Scylla or Cerberus, and there are many others in which two or more different natures are said to grow into one.

There are said to have been such unions.

Then do you now model the form of a multitudinous, many-headed monster, having a ring of heads of all manner of beasts, tame and wild, which he is able to generate and metamorphose at will.

You suppose marvellous powers in the artist; but, as language is more pliable than wax or any similar substance, let there be such a model as you propose.

Suppose now that you make a second form as of a lion, and a third of a man, the second smaller than the first, and the third smaller than the second.

That, he said, is an easier task; and I have made them as you say.

And now join them, and let the three grow into one.

That has been accomplished.

Next fashion the outside of them into a single image, as of a man, so that he who is not able to look within, and sees only the outer hull, may believe the beast to be a single human creature.

I have done so, he said.

And now, to him who maintains that it is profitable for the human creature to be unjust, and unprofitable to be just, let us reply that, if he be right, it is profitable for this creature to feast the multitudinous monster and strengthen the lion and the lion-like qualities, [589] but to starve and weaken the man, who is consequently liable to be dragged about at the mercy of either of the other two; and he is not to attempt to familiarise or harmonise them with one another—he ought rather to suffer them to fight and bite and devour one another.

Certainly, he said; that is what the approver of injustice says.

To him the supporter of justice makes answer that he should ever so speak and act as to give the man within him in some way or other the most complete mastery over the entire human creature. He should watch over the many-headed monster like a good husbandman, fostering and cultivating the gentle qualities, and preventing the wild ones from growing; he should be making the lion-heart his ally, and in common care of them all should be uniting the several parts with one another and with himself.

Yes, he said, that is quite what the maintainer of justice will say.

And so from every point of view, whether of pleasure, honour, or advantage, the approver of justice is right and speaks the truth, and the disapprover is wrong and false and ignorant?

Yes, from every point of view.

Come, now, and let us gently reason with the unjust, who is not intentionally in error. "Sweet Sir," we will say to him, "what think you of things esteemed noble and ignoble? Is not the noble that which subjects the beast to the man, or rather to the god in man; and the ignoble that which subjects the man to the beast?" He can hardly avoid saying Yes—can he now?

Not if he has any regard for my opinion.

But, if he agree so far, we may ask him to answer another question: "Then how would a man profit if he received gold and silver on the condition that he was to enslave the noblest part of him to the worst? Who can imagine that a man who sold his son or daughter into slavery for money, especially if he sold them into the hands of fierce and evil men, would be the gainer, however large might be the sum which he received? And will any one say that he is not a miserable caitiff who remorselessly sells his own divine being to [590] that which is most godless and detestable? Eriphyle took the necklace as the price of her husband's life, but he is taking a bribe in order to compass a worse ruin."

Yes, said Glaucon, far worse—I will answer for him.

Has not the intemperate been censured of old, because in him the huge multiform monster is allowed to be too much at large?

Clearly.

And men are blamed for pride and bad temper when the lion and serpent element in them disproportionately grows and gains strength?

Yes.

And luxury and softness are blamed, because they relax and weaken this same creature, and make a coward of him?

Very true.

And is not a man reproached for flattery and meanness who subordinates the spirited animal to the unruly monster, and, for the sake of money, of which he can never have enough, habituates him in the days of his youth to be trampled in the mire, and from being a lion to become a monkey?

True, he said.

And why are mean employments and manual arts a reproach? Only because they imply a natural weakness of the higher principle; the individual is unable to control the creatures within him, but has to court them, and his great study is how to flatter them.

Such appears to be the reason.

And therefore, being desirous of placing him under a rule like that of the best, we say that he ought to be the servant of the best, in whom the Divine rules; not, as Thrasymachus supposed, to the injury of the servant, but because every one had better be ruled by divine wisdom dwelling within him; or, if this be impossible, then by an external authority, in order that we may be all, as far as possible, under the same government, friends and equals.

True, he said.

And this is clearly seen to be the intention of the law, which is the ally of the whole city; and is seen also in the authority which we exercise over children, and the refusal to let them be free until we have established in them a principle analogous to the constitution of a state, [591] and by cultivation of this higher element have set up in their hearts a guardian and ruler like our own, and when this is done they may go their ways.

Yes, he said, the purpose of the law is manifest.

From what point of view, then, and on what ground can we say that a man is profited by injustice or intemperance or other baseness, which will make him a worse man, even though he acquire money or power by his wickedness?

From no point of view at all.

What shall he profit, if his injustice be undetected and unpunished? He who is undetected only gets worse, whereas he who is detected and punished has the brutal part of his nature silenced and humanised; the gentler element in him is liberated, and his whole soul is perfected and ennobled by the acquirement of justice and temperance and wisdom, more than the body ever is by receiving gifts of beauty, strength and health, in proportion as the soul is more honourable than the body.

Certainly, he said.

To this nobler purpose the man of understanding will devote the energies of his life. And in the first place, he will honour studies which impress these qualities on his soul, and will disregard others?

Clearly, he said.

In the next place, he will regulate his bodily habit and training, and so far will he be from yielding to brutal and irrational pleasures, that he will regard even health as quite a secondary matter; his first object will be not that he may be fair or strong or well, unless he is likely thereby to gain temperance, but he will always desire so to attemper the body as to preserve the harmony of the soul.

Certainly he will, if he has true music in him.

And in the acquisition of wealth there is a principle of order and harmony which he will also observe; he will not allow himself to be dazzled by the foolish applause of the world, and heap up riches to his own infinite harm?

Certainly not, he said.

He will look at the city which is within him, and take heed that no disorder occur in it, such as might arise either from superfluity or from want; and upon this principle he will regulate his property and gain or spend according to his means.

Very true.

And, for the same reason, he will gladly accept and enjoy such honours as he deems likely to make him a better man; [592] but those, whether private or public, which are likely to disorder his life, he will avoid?

Then, if that is his motive, he will not be a statesman.

By the dog of Egypt, he will! in the city which is his own he certainly will, though in the land of his birth perhaps not, unless he have a divine call.

I understand; you mean that he will be a ruler in the city of which we are the founders, and which exists in idea only; for I do not believe that there is such an one anywhere on earth?

In heaven, I replied, there is laid up a pattern of it, methinks, which he who desires may behold, and beholding, may set his own house in order. But whether such an one exists, or ever will exist in fact, is no matter; for he will live after the manner of that city, having nothing to do with any other.

I think so, he said.

BOOK X

[595] OF the many excellences which I perceive in the order of our State, there is none which upon reflection pleases me better than the rule about poetry.

To what do you refer?

To the rejection of imitative poetry, which certainly ought not to be received; as I see far more clearly now that the parts of the soul have been distinguished.

What do you mean?

Speaking in confidence, for I should not like to have my words repeated to the tragedians and the rest of the imitative tribe—but I do not mind saying to you, that all poetical imitations are ruinous to the understanding of the hearers, and that the knowledge of their true nature is the only antidote to them.

Explain the purport of your remark.

Well, I will tell you, although I have always from my earliest youth had an awe and love of Homer, which even now makes the words falter on my lips, for he is the great captain and teacher of the whole of that charming tragic company; but a man is not to be reverenced more than the truth, and therefore I will speak out.

Very good, he said.

Listen to me then, or rather, answer me.

Put your question.

Can you tell me what imitation is? for I really do not know.

A likely thing, then, that I should know.

[596] Why not? for the duller eye may often see a thing sooner than the keener.

Very true, he said; but in your presence, even if I had any faint notion, I could not muster courage to utter it. Will you enquire yourself?

Well then, shall we begin the enquiry in our usual manner: Whenever a number of individuals have a common name, we assume them to have also a corresponding idea or form:—do you understand me?

I do.

Let us take any common instance; there are beds and tables in the world—plenty of them, are there not?

Yes.

But there are only two ideas or forms of them—one the idea of a bed, the other of a table.

True.

And the maker of either of them makes a bed or he makes a table for our use, in accordance with the idea—that is our way of speaking in this and similar instances—but no artificer makes the ideas themselves: how could he?

Impossible.

And there is another artist—I should like to know what you would say of him.

Who is he?

One who is the maker of all the works of all other workmen.

What an extraordinary man!

Wait a little, and there will be more reason for your saying so. For this is he who is able to make not only vessels of every kind, but plants and animals, himself and all other things—the earth and heaven, and the things which are in heaven or under the earth; he makes the gods also.

He must be a wizard and no mistake.

Oh! you are incredulous, are you? Do you mean that there is no such maker or creator, or that in one sense there might be a maker of all these things but in another not? Do you see that there is a way in which you could make them all yourself?

What way?

An easy way enough; or rather, there are many ways in which the feat might be quickly and easily accomplished, none quicker than that of turning a mirror round and round—you would soon enough make the sun and the heavens, and the earth and yourself, and other animals and plants, and all the other things of which we were just now speaking, in the mirror.

Yes, he said; but they would be appearances only.

Very good, I said, you are coming to the point now. And the painter too is, as I conceive, just such another—a creator of appearances, is he not?

Of course.

But then I suppose you will say that what he creates is untrue. And yet there is a sense in which the painter also creates a bed?

Yes, he said, but not a real bed.

[597] And what of the maker of the bed? were you not saying that he too makes, not the idea which, according to our view, is the essence of the bed, but only a particular bed?

Yes, I did.

Then if he does not make that which exists he cannot make true existence, but only some semblance of existence; and if any one were to say that the work of the maker of the bed, or of any other workman, has real existence, he could hardly be supposed to be speaking the truth.

At any rate, he replied, philosophers would say that he was not speaking the truth.

No wonder, then, that his work too is an indistinct expression of truth.

No wonder.

Suppose now that by the light of the examples just offered we enquire who this imitator is?

If you please.

Well then, here are three beds: one existing in nature, which is made by God, as I think that we may say—for no one else can be the maker?

No.

There is another which is the work of the carpenter?

Yes.

And the work of the painter is a third?

Yes.

Beds, then, are of three kinds, and there are three artists who superintend them: God, the maker of the bed, and the painter?

Yes, there are three of them.

God, whether from choice or from necessity, made one bed in nature and one only; two or more such ideal beds neither ever have been nor ever will be made by God.

Why is that?

Because even if He had made but two, a third would still appear behind them which both of them would have for their idea, and that would be the ideal bed and not the two others.

Very true, he said.

God knew this, and He desired to be the real maker of a real bed, not a particular maker of a particular bed, and therefore He created a bed which is essentially and by nature one only.

So we believe.

Shall we, then, speak of Him as the natural author or maker of the bed?

Yes, he replied; inasmuch as by the natural process of creation He is the author of this and of all other things.

And what shall we say of the carpenter—is not he also the maker of the bed?

Yes.

But would you call the painter a creator and maker?

Certainly not.

Yet if he is not the maker, what is he in relation to the bed?

I think, he said, that we may fairly designate him as the imitator of that which the others make.

Good, I said; then you call him who is third in the descent from nature an imitator?

Certainly, he said.

And the tragic poet is an imitator, and therefore, like all other imitators, he is thrice removed from the king and from the truth?

That appears to be so.

Then about the imitator we are agreed. And what about the painter? *[598]*—I would like to know whether he may be thought to imitate that which originally exists in nature, or only the creations of artists?

The latter.

As they are or as they appear? you have still to determine this.

What do you mean?

I mean, that you may look at a bed from different points of view, obliquely or directly or from any other point of view, and the bed will appear different, but there is no difference in reality. And the same of all things.

Yes, he said, the difference is only apparent.

Now let me ask you another question: Which is the art of painting designed to be—an imitation of things as they are, or as they appear—of appearance or of reality?

Of appearance.

Then the imitator, I said, is a long way off the truth, and can do all things because he lightly touches on a small part of them, and that part an image. For example: A painter will paint a cobbler, carpenter, or any other artist, though he knows nothing of their arts; and, if he is a good artist, he may deceive children or simple persons, when he shows them his picture of a carpenter from a distance, and they will fancy that they are looking at a real carpenter.

Certainly.

And whenever any one informs us that he has found a man who knows all the arts, and all things else that anybody knows, and every single thing with a higher degree of accuracy than any other man—whoever tells us this, I think that we can only imagine him to be a simple creature who is likely to have been deceived by some wizard or actor whom he met, and whom he thought all-knowing, because he himself was unable to analyse the nature of knowledge and ignorance and imitation.

Most true.

And so, when we hear persons saying that the tragedians, and Homer, who is at their head, know all the arts and all things human, virtue as well as vice, and divine things too, for that the good poet cannot compose well unless he knows his subject, and that he who has not this knowledge can never be a poet, we ought to consider whether here also there may not be a similar illusion. Perhaps they may have come across imitators and been deceived by them;

they may not have remembered when they saw their works that these were but imitations thrice removed from the truth, *[599]* and could easily be made without any knowledge of the truth, because they are appearances only and not realities? Or, after all, they may be in the right, and poets do really know the things about which they seem to the many to speak so well?

The question, he said, should by all means be considered.

Now do you suppose that if a person were able to make the original as well as the image, he would seriously devote himself to the image-making branch? Would he allow imitation to be the ruling principle of his life, as if he had nothing higher in him?

I should say not.

The real artist, who knew what he was imitating, would be interested in realities and not in imitations; and would desire to leave as memorials of himself works many and fair; and, instead of being the author of encomiums, he would prefer to be the theme of them.

Yes, he said, that would be to him a source of much greater honour and profit.

Then, I said, we must put a question to Homer; not about medicine, or any of the arts to which his poems only incidentally refer: we are not going to ask him, or any other poet, whether he has cured patients like Asclepius, or left behind him a school of medicine such as the Asclepiads were, or whether he only talks about medicine and other arts at second-hand; but we have a right to know respecting military tactics, politics, education, which are the chiefest and noblest subjects of his poems, and we may fairly ask him about them. "Friend Homer," then we say to him, "if you are only in the second remove from truth in what you say of virtue, and not in the third—not an image maker or imitator—and if you are able to discern what pursuits make men better or worse in private or public life, tell us what State was ever better governed by your help? The good order of Lacedaemon is due to Lycurgus, and many other cities great and small have been similarly benefited by others; but who says that you have been a good legislator to them and have done them any good? Italy and Sicily boast of Charondas, and there is Solon who is renowned among us; but what city has anything to say about you?" Is there any city which he might name?

I think not, said Glaucon; not even the Homerids themselves pretend that he was a legislator.

[600] Well, but is there any war on record which was carried on successfully by him, or aided by his counsels, when he was alive?

There is not.

Or is there any invention of his, applicable to the arts or to human life, such as Thales the Milesian or Anacharsis the Scythian, and other ingenious men have conceived, which is attributed to him?

There is absolutely nothing of the kind.

But, if Homer never did any public service, was he privately a guide or teacher of any? Had he in his lifetime friends who loved to associate with him, and who handed down to posterity an Homeric way of life, such as was established by Pythagoras who was so greatly beloved for his wisdom, and whose followers are to this day quite celebrated for the order which was named after him?

Nothing of the kind is recorded of him. For surely, Socrates, Creophylus, the companion of Homer, that child of flesh, whose name always makes us laugh, might be more justly ridiculed for his stupidity, if, as is said, Homer was greatly neglected by him and others in his own day when he was alive?

Yes, I replied, that is the tradition. But can you imagine, Glaucon, that if Homer had really been able to educate and improve mankind —if he had possessed knowledge and not been a mere imitator—can you imagine, I say, that he would not have had many followers, and been honoured and loved by them? Protagoras of Abdera, and Prodicus of Ceos, and a host of others, have only to whisper to their contemporaries: "You will never be able to manage either your own house or your own State until you appoint us to be your ministers of education"—and this ingenious device of theirs has such an effect in making men love them that their companions all but carry them about on their shoulders. And is it conceivable that the contemporaries of Homer, or again of Hesiod, would have allowed either of them to go about as rhapsodists, if they had really been able to make mankind virtuous? Would they not have been as unwilling to part with them as with gold, and have compelled them to stay at home with them? Or, if the master would not stay, then the disciples would have followed him about everywhere, until they had got education enough?

Yes, Socrates, that, I think, is quite true.

Then must we not infer that all these poetical individuals, beginning with Homer, are only imitators; they copy images of virtue and the like, [601] but the truth they never reach? The poet is like a painter who, as we have already observed, will make a likeness of a cobbler though he understands nothing of cobbling; and his picture is good enough for those who know no more than he does, and judge only by colours and figures.

Quite so.

In like manner the poet with his words and phrases may be said to lay on the colours of the several arts, himself understanding their nature only enough to imitate them; and other people, who are as ignorant as he is, and judge only from his words, imagine that if he speaks of cobbling, or of military tactics, or of anything else, in metre and harmony and rhythm, he speaks very well—such is the sweet influence which melody and rhythm by nature have. And I think that you must have observed again and again what a poor appearance the tales of poets make when stripped of the colours which music puts upon them, and recited in simple prose.

Yes, he said.

They are like faces which were never really beautiful, but only blooming; and now the bloom of youth has passed away from them?

Exactly.

Here is another point: The imitator or maker of the image knows nothing of true existence; he knows appearances only. Am I not right?

Yes.

Then let us have a clear understanding, and not be satisfied with half an explanation.

Proceed.

Of the painter we say that he will paint reins, and he will paint a bit?

Yes.

And the worker in leather and brass will make them?

Certainly.

But does the painter know the right form of the bit and reins? Nay, hardly even the workers in brass and leather who make them; only the horseman who knows how to use them—he knows their right form.

Most true.

And may we not say the same of all things?

What?

That there are three arts which are concerned with all things: one which uses, another which makes, a third which imitates them?

Yes.

And the excellence or beauty or truth of every structure, animate or inanimate, and of every action of man, is relative to the use for which nature or the artist has intended them.

True.

Then the user of them must have the greatest experience of them, and he must indicate to the maker the good or bad qualities which develop themselves in use; for example, the flute-player will tell the flute-maker which of his flutes is satisfactory to the performer; he will tell him how he ought to make them, and the other will attend to his instructions?

Of course.

The one knows and therefore speaks with authority about the goodness and badness of flutes, while the other, confiding in him, will do what he is told by him?

True.

The instrument is the same, but about the excellence or badness of it the maker will only attain to a correct belief; and this he will gain from him who knows, by talking to him and being compelled to hear what he has to say, [602] whereas the user will have knowledge?

True.

But will the imitator have either? Will he know from use whether or no his drawing is correct or beautiful? or will he have right opinion from being compelled to associate with another who knows and gives him instructions about what he should draw?

Neither.

Then he will no more have true opinion than he will have knowledge about the goodness or badness of his imitations?

I suppose not.

The imitative artist will be in a brilliant state of intelligence about his own creations?

Nay, very much the reverse.

And still he will go on imitating without knowing what makes a thing good or bad, and may be expected therefore to imitate only that which appears to be good to the ignorant multitude?

Just so.

Thus far then we are pretty well agreed that the imitator has no knowledge worth mentioning of what he imitates. Imitation is only a kind of play or sport, and the tragic poets, whether they write in Iambic or in Heroic verse, are imitators in the highest degree?

Very true.

And now tell me, I conjure you, has not imitation been shown by us to be concerned with that which is thrice removed from the truth?

Certainly.

And what is the faculty in man to which imitation is addressed?

What do you mean?

I will explain: The body which is large when seen near, appears small when seen at a distance?

Very true.

And the same object appears straight when looked at out of the water, and crooked when in the water; and the concave becomes convex, owing to the illusion about colours to which the sight is liable. Thus every sort of confusion is revealed within us; and this is that weakness of the human mind on which the art of conjuring and of deceiving by light and shadow and other ingenious devices imposes, having an effect upon us like magic.

True.

And the arts of measuring and numbering and weighing come to the rescue of the human understanding—there is the beauty of them—and the apparent greater or less, or more or heavier, no longer have the mastery over us, but give way before calculation and measure and weight?

Most true.

And this, surely, must be the work of the calculating and rational principle in the soul?

To be sure.

And when this principle measures and certifies that some things are equal, or that some are greater or less than others, there occurs an apparent contradiction?

True.

But were we not saying that such a contradiction is impossible—the same faculty cannot have contrary opinions at the same time [603] about the same thing?

Very true.

Then that part of the soul which has an opinion contrary to measure is not the same with that which has an opinion in accordance with measure?

True.

And the better part of the soul is likely to be that which trusts to measure and calculation?

Certainly.

And that which is opposed to them is one of the inferior principles of the soul?

No doubt.

This was the conclusion at which I was seeking to arrive when I said that painting or drawing, and imitation in general, when doing their own proper work, are far removed from truth, and the companions and friends and associates of a principle within us which is equally removed from reason, and that they have no true or healthy aim.

Exactly.

The imitative art is an inferior who marries an inferior, and has inferior offspring.

Very true.

And is this confined to the sight only, or does it extend to the hearing also, relating in fact to what we term poetry?

Probably the same would be true of poetry.

Do not rely, I said, on a probability derived from the analogy of painting; but let us examine further and see whether the faculty with which poetical imitation is concerned is good or bad.

By all means.

We may state the question thus:—Imitation imitates the actions of men, whether voluntary or involuntary, on which, as they imagine, a good or bad result has ensued, and they rejoice or sorrow accordingly. Is there anything more?

No, there is nothing else.

But in all this variety of circumstances is the man at unity with himself—or rather, as in the instance of sight there was confusion and opposition in his opinions about the same things, so here also is there not strife and inconsistency in his life? Though I need hardly raise the question again, for I remember that all this has been already admitted; and the soul has been acknowledged by us to be full of these and ten thousand similar oppositions occurring at the same moment?

And we were right, he said.

Yes, I said, thus far we were right; but there was an omission which must now be supplied.

What was the omission?

Were we not saying that a good man, who has the misfortune to lose his son or anything else which is most dear to him, will bear the loss with more equanimity than another?

Yes.

But will he have no sorrow, or shall we say that although he cannot help sorrowing, he will moderate his sorrow?

The latter, he said, is the truer statement.

[604] Tell me: will he be more likely to struggle and hold out against his sorrow when he is seen by his equals, or when he is alone?

It will make a great difference whether he is seen or not.

When he is by himself he will not mind saying or doing many things which he would be ashamed of any one hearing or seeing him do?

True.

There is a principle of law and reason in him which bids him resist, as well as a feeling of his misfortune which is forcing him to indulge his sorrow?

True.

But when a man is drawn in two opposite directions, to and from the same object, this, as we affirm, necessarily implies two distinct principles in him?

Certainly.

One of them is ready to follow the guidance of the law?

How do you mean?

The law would say that to be patient under suffering is best, and that we should not give way to impatience, as there is no knowing whether such things are good or evil; and nothing is gained by impatience; also, because no human thing is of serious importance, and grief stands in the way of that which at the moment is most required.

What is most required? he asked.

That we should take counsel about what has happened, and when the dice have been thrown order our affairs in the way which reason deems best; not, like children who have had a fall, keeping hold of the part struck and wasting time in setting up a howl, but always accustoming the soul forthwith to apply a remedy, raising up that which is sickly and fallen, banishing the cry of sorrow by the healing art.

Yes, he said, that is the true way of meeting the attacks of fortune.

Yes, I said; and the higher principle is ready to follow this suggestion of reason?

Clearly.

And the other principle, which inclines us to recollection of our troubles and to lamentation, and can never have enough of them, we may call irrational, useless, and cowardly?

Indeed, we may.

And does not the latter—I mean the rebellious principle—furnish a great variety of materials for imitation? Whereas the wise and calm temperament, being always nearly equable, is not easy to imitate or to appreciate when imitated, especially at a public festival when a promiscuous crowd is assembled in a theatre. For the feeling represented is one to which they are strangers.

Certainly.

[605] Then the imitative poet who aims at being popular is not by nature made, nor is his art intended, to please or to affect the rational principle in the soul; but he will prefer the passionate and fitful temper, which is easily imitated?

Clearly.

And now we may fairly take him and place

him by the side of the painter, for he is like him in two ways: first, inasmuch as his creations have an inferior degree of truth—in this, I say, he is like him; and he is also like him in being concerned with an inferior part of the soul; and therefore we shall be right in refusing to admit him into a well-ordered State, because he awakens and nourishes and strengthens the feelings and impairs the reason. As in a city when the evil are permitted to have authority and the good are put out of the way, so in the soul of man, as we maintain, the imitative poet implants an evil constitution, for he indulges the irrational nature which has no discernment of greater and less, but thinks the same thing at one time great and at another small—he is a manufacturer of images and is very far removed from the truth.

Exactly.

But we have not yet brought forward the heaviest count in our accusation:—the power which poetry has of harming even the good (and there are very few who are not harmed) is surely an awful thing?

Yes, certainly, if the effect is what you say.

Hear and judge: The best of us, as I conceive, when we listen to a passage of Homer, or one of the tragedians, in which he represents some pitiful hero who is drawling out his sorrows in a long oration, or weeping, and smiting his breast—the best of us, you know, delight in giving way to sympathy, and are in raptures at the excellence of the poet who stirs our feelings most.

Yes, of course I know.

But when any sorrow of our own happens to us, then you may observe that we pride ourselves on the opposite quality—we would fain be quiet and patient; this is the manly part, and the other which delighted us in the recitation is now deemed to be the part of a woman.

Very true, he said.

Now can we be right in praising and admiring another who is doing that which any one of us would abominate and be ashamed of in his own person?

No, he said, that is certainly not reasonable.

[606] Nay, I said, quite reasonable from one point of view.

What point of view?

If you consider, I said, that when in misfortune we feel a natural hunger and desire to relieve our sorrow by weeping and lamentation, and that this feeling which is kept under control in our own calamities is satisfied and delighted by the poets—the better nature in each

of us, not having been sufficiently trained by reason or habit, allows the sympathetic element to break loose because the sorrow is another's; and the spectator fancies that there can be no disgrace to himself in praising and pitying any one who comes telling him what a good man he is, and making a fuss about his troubles; he thinks that the pleasure is a gain, and why should he be supercilious and lose this and the poem too? Few persons ever reflect, as I should imagine, that from the evil of other men something of evil is communicated to themselves. And so the feeling of sorrow which has gathered strength at the sight of the misfortunes of others is with difficulty repressed in our own.

How very true!

And does not the same hold also of the ridiculous? There are jests which you would be ashamed to make yourself, and yet on the comic stage, or indeed in private, when you hear them, you are greatly amused by them, and are not at all disgusted at their unseemliness—the case of pity is repeated—there is a principle in human nature which is disposed to raise a laugh, and this which you once restrained by reason, because you were afraid of being thought a buffoon, is now let out again; and having stimulated the risible faculty at the theatre, you are betrayed unconsciously to yourself into playing the comic poet at home.

Quite true, he said.

And the same may be said of lust and anger and all the other affections, of desire and pain and pleasure, which are held to be inseparable from every action—in all of them poetry feeds and waters the passions instead of drying them up; she lets them rule, although they ought to be controlled, if mankind are ever to increase in happiness and virtue.

I cannot deny it.

Therefore, Glaucon, I said, whenever you meet with any of the eulogists of Homer declaring that he has been the educator of Hellas, and that he is profitable for education and for the ordering of human things, [607] and that you should take him up again and again and get to know him and regulate your whole life according to him, we may love and honour those who say these things—they are excellent people, as far as their lights extend; and we are ready to acknowledge that Homer is the greatest of poets and first of tragedy writers; but we must remain firm in our conviction that hymns to the gods and praises of famous men are the only poetry which ought to be admitted into our State. For if you go beyond this and allow the honeyed muse to enter, either in epic or lyric verse, not law and the reason of mankind, which by common consent have ever been deemed best, but pleasure and pain will be the rulers in our State.

That is most true, he said.

And now since we have reverted to the subject of poetry, let this our defence serve to show the reasonableness of our former judgment in sending away out of our State an art having the tendencies which we have described; for reason constrained us. But that she may not impute to us any harshness or want of politeness, let us tell her that there is an ancient quarrel between philosophy and poetry; of which there are many proofs, such as the saying of "the yelping hound howling at her lord," or of one "mighty in the vain talk of fools," and "the mob of sages circumventing Zeus," and the "subtle thinkers who are beggars after all"; and there are innumerable other signs of ancient enmity between them. Notwithstanding this, let us assure our sweet friend and the sister arts of imitation, that if she will only prove her title to exist in a well-ordered State we shall be delighted to receive her—we are very conscious of her charms; but we may not on that account betray the truth. I dare say, Glaucon, that you are as much charmed by her as I am, especially when she appears in Homer?

Yes, indeed, I am greatly charmed.

Shall I propose, then, that she be allowed to return from exile, but upon this condition only —that she make a defence of herself in lyrical or some other metre?

Certainly.

And we may further grant to those of her defenders who are lovers of poetry and yet not poets the permission to speak in prose on her behalf: let them show not only that she is pleasant but also useful to States and to human life, and we will listen in a kindly spirit; for if this can be proved we shall surely be the gainers— I mean, if there is a use in poetry as well as a delight?

Certainly, he said, we shall be the gainers.

If her defence fails, then, my dear friend, like other persons who are enamoured of something, but put a restraint upon themselves when they think their desires are opposed to their interests, so too must we after the manner of lovers give her up, though not without a struggle. We too are inspired by that love of poetry which the education of noble States has implanted in us, [608] and therefore we would have her appear at her best and truest; but so long as she

is unable to make good her defence, this argument of ours shall be a charm to us, which we will repeat to ourselves while we listen to her strains; that we may not fall away into the childish love of her which captivates the many. At all events we are well aware that poetry being such as we have described is not to be regarded seriously as attaining to the truth; and he who listens to her, fearing for the safety of the city which is within him, should be on his guard against her seductions and make our words his law.

Yes, he said, I quite agree with you.

Yes, I said, my dear Glaucon, for great is the issue at stake, greater than appears, whether a man is to be good or bad. And what will any one be profited if under the influence of honour or money or power, aye, or under the excitement of poetry, he neglect justice and virtue?

Yes, he said; I have been convinced by the argument, as I believe that any one else would have been.

And yet no mention has been made of the greatest prizes and rewards which await virtue.

What, are there any greater still? If there are, they must be of an inconceivable greatness.

Why, I said, what was ever great in a short time? The whole period of three score years and ten is surely but a little thing in comparison with eternity?

Say rather "nothing," he replied.

And should an immortal being seriously think of this little space rather than of the whole?

Of the whole, certainly. But why do you ask?

Are you not aware, I said, that the soul of man is immortal and imperishable?

He looked at me in astonishment, and said: No, by heaven: And are you really prepared to maintain this?

Yes, I said, I ought to be, and you too—there is no difficulty in proving it.

I see a great difficulty; but I should like to hear you state this argument of which you make so light.

Listen then.

I am attending.

There is a thing which you call good and another which you call evil?

Yes, he replied.

Would you agree with me in thinking that the corrupting and destroying element is evil, and the saving and improving element the good?

[609] Yes.

And you admit that every thing has a good and also an evil; as ophthalmia is the evil of the eyes and disease of the whole body; as mildew is of corn, and rot of timber, or rust of copper and iron: in everything, or in almost everything, there is an inherent evil and disease?

Yes, he said.

And anything which is infected by any of these evils is made evil, and at last wholly dissolves and dies?

True.

The vice and evil which is inherent in each is the destruction of each; and if this does not destroy them there is nothing else that will; for good certainly will not destroy them, nor again, that which is neither good nor evil.

Certainly not.

If, then, we find any nature which having this inherent corruption cannot be dissolved or destroyed, we may be certain that of such a nature there is no destruction?

That may be assumed.

Well, I said, and is there no evil which corrupts the soul?

Yes, he said, there are all the evils which we were just now passing in review: unrighteousness, intemperance, cowardice, ignorance.

But does any of these dissolve or destroy her? —and here do not let us fall into the error of supposing that the unjust and foolish man, when he is detected, perishes through his own injustice, which is an evil of the soul. Take the analogy of the body: The evil of the body is a disease which wastes and reduces and annihilates the body; and all the things of which we were just now speaking come to annihilation through their own corruption attaching to them and inhering in them and so destroying them. Is not this true?

Yes.

Consider the soul in like manner. Does the injustice or other evil which exists in the soul waste and consume her? do they by attaching to the soul and inhering in her at last bring her to death, and so separate her from the body?

Certainly not.

And yet, I said, it is unreasonable to suppose that anything can perish from without through affection of external evil which could not be destroyed from within by a corruption of its own?

It is, he replied.

Consider, I said, Glaucon, that even the badness of food, whether staleness, decomposition, or any other bad quality, when confined to the actual food, is not supposed to destroy the body; although, if the badness of food communicates corruption to the body, then we should say that the body has been destroyed by a corruption of [610] itself, which is disease, brought on by this; but that the body, being one thing, can be destroyed by the badness of food, which is another, and which does not engender any natural infection—this we shall absolutely deny?

Very true.

And, on the same principle, unless some bodily evil can produce an evil of the soul, we must not suppose that the soul, which is one thing, can be dissolved by any merely external evil which belongs to another?

Yes, he said, there is reason in that.

Either, then, let us refute this conclusion, or, while it remains unrefuted, let us never say that fever, or any other disease, or the knife put to the throat, or even the cutting up of the whole body into the minutest pieces, can destroy the soul, until she herself is proved to become more unholy or unrighteous in consequence of these things being done to the body; but that the soul, or anything else if not destroyed by an internal evil, can be destroyed by an external one, is not to be affirmed by any man.

And surely, he replied, no one will ever prove that the souls of men become more unjust in consequence of death.

But if some one who would rather not admit the immortality of the soul boldly denies this, and says that the dying do really become more evil and unrighteous, then, if the speaker is right, I suppose that injustice, like disease, must be assumed to be fatal to the unjust, and that those who take this disorder die by the natural inherent power of destruction which evil has, and which kills them sooner or later, but in quite another way from that in which, at present, the wicked receive death at the hands of others as the penalty of their deeds?

Nay, he said, in that case injustice, if fatal to the unjust, will not be so very terrible to him, for he will be delivered from evil. But I rather suspect the opposite to be the truth, and that injustice which, if it have the power, will murder others, keeps the murderer alive—aye, and well awake too; so far removed is her dwelling-place from being a house of death.

True, I said; if the inherent natural vice or evil of the soul is unable to kill or destroy her, hardly will that which is appointed to be the destruction of some other body, destroy a soul or anything else except that of which it was appointed to be the destruction.

Yes, that can hardly be.

But the soul which cannot be destroyed by an evil, whether inherent or external, *[611]* must exist for ever, and if existing for ever, must be immortal?

Certainly.

That is the conclusion, I said; and, if a true conclusion, then the souls must always be the same, for if none be destroyed they will not diminish in number. Neither will they increase, for the increase of the immortal natures must come from something mortal, and all things would thus end in immortality.

Very true.

But this we cannot believe—reason will not allow us—any more than we can believe the soul, in her truest nature, to be full of variety and difference and dissimilarity.

What do you mean? he said.

The soul, I said, being, as is now proven, immortal, must be the fairest of compositions and cannot be compounded of many elements?

Certainly not.

Her immortality is demonstrated by the previous argument, and there are many other proofs; but to see her as she really is, not as we now behold her, marred by communion with the body and other miseries, you must contemplate her with the eye of reason, in her original purity; and then her beauty will be revealed, and justice and injustice and all the things which we have described will be manifested more clearly. Thus far, we have spoken the truth concerning her as she appears at present, but we must remember also that we have seen her only in a condition which may be compared to that of the sea-god Glaucus, whose original image can hardly be discerned because his natural members are broken off and crushed and damaged by the waves in all sorts of ways, and incrustations have grown over them of seaweed and shells and stones, so that he is more like some monster than he is to his own natural form. And the soul which we behold is in a similar condition, disfigured by ten thousand ills. But not there, Glaucon, not there must we look.

Where then?

At her love of wisdom. Let us see whom she affects, and what society and converse she seeks in virtue of her near kindred with the immortal and eternal and divine; also how different she would become if wholly following this superior principle, and borne by a divine impulse out of the ocean in which she now is, and disengaged from the stones and shells and things of earth and rock which in wild variety spring up around her because she feeds upon earth, *[612]* and is overgrown by the good things of this life as they are termed: then you would see her as she is, and know whether she have one shape only or many, or what her nature is. Of her affections and of the forms which she takes in this present life I think that we have now said enough.

True, he replied.

And thus, I said, we have fulfilled the conditions of the argument; we have not introduced the rewards and glories of justice, which, as you were saying, are to be found in Homer and Hesiod; but justice in her own nature has been shown to be best for the soul in her own nature. Let a man do what is just, whether he have the ring of Gyges or not, and even if in addition to the ring of Gyges he put on the helmet of Hades.

Very true.

And now, Glaucon, there will be no harm in further enumerating how many and how great are the rewards which justice and the other virtues procure to the soul from gods and men, both in life and after death.

Certainly not, he said.

Will you repay me, then, what you borrowed in the argument?

What did I borrow?

The assumption that the just man should appear unjust and the unjust just: for you were of opinion that even if the true state of the case could not possibly escape the eyes of gods and men, still this admission ought to be made for the sake of the argument, in order that pure justice might be weighed against pure injustice. Do you remember?

I should be much to blame if I had forgotten.

Then, as the cause is decided, I demand on behalf of justice that the estimation in which she is held by gods and men and which we acknowledge to be her due should now be restored to her by us; since she has been shown to confer reality, and not to deceive those who truly possess her, let what has been taken from her be given back, that so she may win that palm of appearance which is hers also, and which she gives to her own.

The demand, he said, is just.

In the first place, I said—and this is the first thing which you will have to give back—the nature both of the just and unjust is truly known to the gods.

Granted.

And if they are both known to them, one must be the friend and the other the enemy of the gods, as we admitted from the beginning?

True.

[613] And the friend of the gods may be supposed to receive from them all things at their best, excepting only such evil as is the necessary consequence of former sins?

Certainly.

Then this must be our notion of the just man, that even when he is in poverty or sickness, or any other seeming misfortune, all things will in the end work together for good to him in life and death: for the gods have a care of any one whose desire is to become just and to be like God, as far as man can attain the divine likeness, by the pursuit of virtue?

Yes, he said; if he is like God he will surely not be neglected by him.

And of the unjust may not the opposite be supposed?

Certainly.

Such, then, are the palms of victory which the gods give the just?

That is my conviction.

And what do they receive of men? Look at things as they really are, and you will see that the clever unjust are in the case of runners, who run well from the starting-place to the goal but not back again from the goal: they go off at a great pace, but in the end only look foolish, slinking away with their ears draggling on their shoulders, and without a crown; but the true runner comes to the finish and receives the prize and is crowned. And this is the way with the just; he who endures to the end of every action and occasion of his entire life has a good report and carries off the prize which men have to bestow.

True.

And now you must allow me to repeat of the just the blessings which you were attributing to the fortunate unjust. I shall say of them, what you were saying of the others, that as they grow older, they become rulers in their own city if they care to be; they marry whom they like and give in marriage to whom they will; all that you said of the others I now say of these. And, on the other hand, of the unjust I say that the greater number, even though they escape in their youth, are found out at last and look foolish at the end of their course, and when they come to be old and miserable are flouted alike by stranger and citizen; they are beaten and then come those things unfit for ears polite, as you truly term them; they will be racked and have their eyes burned out, as you were saying. And you may suppose that I have repeated the

remainder of your tale of horrors. But will you let me assume, without reciting them, that these things are true?

Certainly, he said, what you say is true.

[614] These, then, are the prizes and rewards and gifts which are bestowed upon the just by gods and men in this present life, in addition to the other good things which justice of herself provides.

Yes, he said; and they are fair and lasting.

And yet, I said, all these are as nothing, either in number or greatness in comparison with those other recompenses which await both just and unjust after death. And you ought to hear them, and then both just and unjust will have received from us a full payment of the debt which the argument owes to them.

Speak, he said; there are few things which I would more gladly hear.

Well, I said, I will tell you a tale; not one of the tales which Odysseus tells to the hero Alcinous, yet this too is a tale of a hero, Er the son of Armenius, a Pamphylian by birth. He was slain in battle, and ten days afterwards, when the bodies of the dead were taken up already in a state of corruption, his body was found unaffected by decay, and carried away home to be buried. And on the twelfth day, as he was lying on the funeral pile, he returned to life and told them what he had seen in the other world. He said that when his soul left the body he went on a journey with a great company, and that they came to a mysterious place at which there were two openings in the earth; they were near together, and over against them were two other openings in the heaven above. In the intermediate space there were judges seated, who commanded the just, after they had given judgment on them and had bound their sentences in front of them, to ascend by the heavenly way on the right hand; and in like manner the unjust were bidden by them to descend the lower way on the left hand; these also bore the symbols of their deeds, but fastened on their backs. He drew near, and they told him that he was to be the messenger who would carry the report of the other world to men, and they bade him hear and see all that was to be heard and seen in that place. Then he beheld and saw on one side the souls departing at either opening of heaven and earth when sentence had been given on them; and at the two other openings other souls, some ascending out of the earth dusty and worn with travel, some descending out of heaven clean and bright. And arriving ever and anon they seemed to have come from a long journey, and they went forth with gladness into the meadow, where they encamped as at a festival; and those who knew one another embraced and conversed, the souls which came from earth curiously enquiring about the things above, and the souls which came from heaven about the things beneath. And they told one another of what had happened by the way, those from below weeping and sorrowing at the remembrance of the things which they had endured [615] and seen in their journey beneath the earth (now the journey lasted a thousand years), while those from above were describing heavenly delights and visions of inconceivable beauty. The story, Glaucon, would take too long to tell; but the sum was this:—He said that for every wrong which they had done to any one they suffered tenfold; or once in a hundred years— such being reckoned to be the length of man's life, and the penalty being thus paid ten times in a thousand years. If, for example, there were any who had been the cause of many deaths, or had betrayed or enslaved cities or armies, or been guilty of any other evil behaviour, for each and all of their offences they received punishment ten times over, and the rewards of beneficence and justice and holiness were in the same proportion. I need hardly repeat what he said concerning young children dying almost as soon as they were born. Of piety and impiety to gods and parents, and of murderers, there were retributions other and greater far which he described. He mentioned that he was present when one of the spirits asked another, "Where is Ardiaeus the Great?" (Now this Ardiaeus lived a thousand years before the time of Er: he had been the tyrant of some city of Pamphylia, and had murdered his aged father and his elder brother, and was said to have committed many other abominable crimes.) The answer of the other spirit was: "He comes not hither and will never come. And this," said he, "was one of the dreadful sights which we ourselves witnessed. We were at the mouth of the cavern, and, having completed all our experiences, were about to reascend, when of a sudden Ardiaeus appeared and several others, most of whom were tyrants; and there were also besides the tyrants private individuals who had been great criminals: they were just, as they fancied, about to return into the upper world, but the mouth, instead of admitting them, gave a roar, whenever any of these incurable sinners or some one who had not been sufficiently punished tried to ascend; and then wild men of fiery aspect, who were standing by and heard the sound, [616] seized and carried them off; and Ardiaeus and others they bound head and foot and hand, and threw them down and flayed them with scourges, and dragged them along the road at the side, carding them on thorns like wool, and declaring to the passers-by what were their crimes, and that they were being taken away to be cast into hell." And of all the many terrors which they had endured, he said that there was none like the terror which each of them felt at that moment, lest they should hear the voice; and when there was silence, one by one they ascended with exceeding joy. These, said Er, were the penalties and retributions, and there were blessings as great.

Now when the spirits which were in the meadow had tarried seven days, on the eighth they were obliged to proceed on their journey, and, on the fourth day after, he said that they came to a place where they could see from above a line of light, straight as a column, extending right through the whole heaven and through the earth, in colour resembling the rainbow, only brighter and purer; another day's journey brought them to the place, and there, in the midst of the light, they saw the ends of the chains of heaven let down from above: for this light is the belt of heaven, and holds together the circle of the universe, like the under-girders of a trireme. From these ends is extended the spindle of Necessity, on which all the revolutions turn. The shaft and hook of this spindle are made of steel, and the whorl is made partly of steel and also partly of other materials. Now the whorl is in form like the whorl used on earth; and the description of it implied that there is one large hollow whorl which is quite scooped out, and into this is fitted another lesser one, and another, and another, and four others, making eight in all, like vessels which fit into one another; the whorls show their edges on the upper side, and on their lower side all together form one continuous whorl. This is pierced by the spindle, which is driven home through the centre of the eighth. The first and outermost whorl has the rim broadest, and the seven inner whorls are narrower, in the following proportions—the sixth is next to the first in size, the fourth next to the sixth; then comes the eighth; the seventh is fifth, the fifth is sixth, the third is seventh, last and eighth comes the second. The largest [or fixed stars] is spangled, and the seventh [or sun] is brightest; the eighth [or moon] coloured by the reflected light of the seventh; [617] the second and fifth [Saturn and Mercury] are in colour like one another, and yellower than the preceding; the third [Venus] has the whitest light; the fourth [Mars] is reddish; the sixth [Jupiter] is in whiteness second. Now the whole spindle has the same motion; but, as the whole revolves in one direction, the seven inner circles move slowly in the other, and of these the swiftest is the eighth; next in swiftness are the seventh, sixth, and fifth, which move together; third in swiftness appeared to move according to the law of this reversed motion the fourth; the third appeared fourth and the second fifth. The spindle turns on the knees of Necessity; and on the upper surface of each circle is a siren, who goes round with them, hymning a single tone or note. The eight together form one harmony; and round about, at equal intervals, there is another band, three in number, each sitting upon her throne: these are the Fates, daughters of Necessity, who are clothed in white robes and have chaplets upon their heads, Lachesis and Clotho and Atropos, who accompany with their voices the harmony of the sirens—Lachesis singing of the past, Clotho of the present, Atropos of the future; Clotho from time to time assisting with a touch of her right hand the revolution of the outer circle of the whorl or spindle, and Atropos with her left hand touching and guiding the inner ones, and Lachesis laying hold of either in turn, first with one hand and then with the other.

When Er and the spirits arrived, their duty was to go at once to Lachesis; but first of all there came a prophet who arranged them in order; then he took from the knees of Lachesis lots and samples of lives, and having mounted a high pulpit, spoke as follows: "Hear the word of Lachesis, the daughter of Necessity. Mortal souls, behold a new cycle of life and mortality. Your genius will not be allotted to you, but you will choose your genius; and let him who draws the first lot have the first choice, and the life which he chooses shall be his destiny. Virtue is free, and as a man honours or dishonours her he will have more or less of her; the responsibility is with the chooser—God is justified." When the Interpreter had thus spoken he scattered lots indifferently among them all, and each of them took up the lot which fell near him, [618] all but Er himself (he was not allowed), and each as he took his lot perceived the number which he had obtained. Then the Interpreter placed on the ground before them the samples of lives; and there were many more lives than the souls present, and they were of all sorts. There were lives of every animal and of man

in every condition. And there were tyrannies among them, some lasting out the tyrant's life, others which broke off in the middle and came to an end in poverty and exile and beggary; and there were lives of famous men, some who were famous for their form and beauty as well as for their strength and success in games, or, again, for their birth and the qualities of their ancestors; and some who were the reverse of famous for the opposite qualities. And of women likewise; there was not, however, any definite character in them, because the soul, when choosing a new life, must of necessity become different. But there was every other quality, and they all mingled with one another, and also with elements of wealth and poverty, and disease and health; and there were mean states also. And here, my dear Glaucon, is the supreme peril of our human state; and therefore the utmost care should be taken. Let each one of us leave every other kind of knowledge and seek and follow one thing only, if peradventure he may be able to learn and may find some one who will make him able to learn and discern between good and evil, and so to choose always and everywhere the better life as he has opportunity. He should consider the bearing of all these things which have been mentioned severally and collectively upon virtue; he should know what the effect of beauty is when combined with poverty or wealth in a particular soul, and what are the good and evil consequences of noble and humble birth, of private and public station, of strength and weakness, of cleverness and dullness, and of all the natural and acquired gifts of the soul, and the operation of them when conjoined; he will then look at the nature of the soul, and from the consideration of all these qualities he will be able to determine which is the better and which is the worse; and so he will choose, giving the name of evil to the life which will make his soul more unjust, and good to the life which will make his soul more just; all else he will disregard. For we have seen and know that this is the best choice both in life and after death. [619] A man must take with him into the world below an adamantine faith in truth and right, that there too he may be undazzled by the desire of wealth or the other allurements of evil, lest, coming upon tyrannies and similar villainies, he do irremediable wrongs to others and suffer yet worse himself; but let him know how to choose the mean and avoid the extremes on either side, as far as possible, not only in this life but in all that which is to come. For this is the way of happiness.

And according to the report of the messenger from the other world this was what the prophet said at the time: "Even for the last comer, if he chooses wisely and will live diligently, there is appointed a happy and not undesirable existence. Let not him who chooses first be careless, and let not the last despair." And when he had spoken, he who had the first choice came forward and in a moment chose the greatest tyranny; his mind having been darkened by folly and sensuality, he had not thought out the whole matter before he chose, and did not at first sight perceive that he was fated, among other evils, to devour his own children. But when he had time to reflect, and saw what was in the lot, he began to beat his breast and lament over his choice, forgetting the proclamation of the prophet; for, instead of throwing the blame of his misfortune on himself, he accused chance and the gods, and everything rather than himself. Now he was one of those who came from heaven, and in a former life had dwelt in a well-ordered State, but his virtue was a matter of habit only, and he had no philosophy. And it was true of others who were similarly overtaken, that the greater number of them came from heaven and therefore they had never been schooled by trial, whereas the pilgrims who came from earth having themselves suffered and seen others suffer were not in a hurry to choose. And owing to this inexperience of theirs, and also because the lot was a chance, many of the souls exchanged a good destiny for an evil or an evil for a good. For if a man had always on his arrival in this world dedicated himself from the first to sound philosophy, and had been moderately fortunate in the number of the lot, he might, as the messenger reported, be happy here, and also his journey to another life and return to this, instead of being rough and underground, would be smooth and heavenly. Most curious, he said, was the spectacle—sad and laughable and strange; for the choice of the souls was in most cases based on their experience *[620]* of a previous life. There he saw the soul which had once been Orpheus choosing the life of a swan out of enmity to the race of women, hating to be born of a woman because they had been his murderers; he beheld also the soul of Thamyras choosing the life of a nightingale; birds, on the other hand, like the swan and other musicians, wanting to be men. The soul which obtained the twentieth lot chose the life of a lion, and this was the soul of Ajax the son of Telamon, who would not be a man, remembering the injustice which was done him in the judgment about the arms. The next was Agamemnon, who took the life of an eagle, because, like Ajax, he hated human nature by reason of his sufferings. About the middle came the lot of Atalanta; she, seeing the great fame of an athlete, was unable to resist the temptation: and after her there followed the soul of Epeus the son of Panopeus passing into the nature of a woman cunning in the arts; and far away among the last who chose, the soul of the jester Thersites was putting on the form of a monkey. There came also the soul of Odysseus having yet to make a choice, and his lot happened to be the last of them all. Now the recollection of former toils had disenchanted him of ambition, and he went about for a considerable time in search of the life of a private man who had no cares; he had some difficulty in finding this, which was lying about and had been neglected by everybody else; and when he saw it, he said that he would have done the same had his lot been first instead of last, and that he was delighted to have it. And not only did men pass into animals, but I must also mention that there were animals tame and wild who changed into one another and into corresponding human natures—the good into the gentle and the evil into the savage, in all sorts of combinations.

All the souls had now chosen their lives, and they went in the order of their choice to Lachesis, who sent with them the genius whom they had severally chosen, to be the guardian of their lives and the fulfiller of the choice: this genius led the souls first to Clotho, and drew them within the revolution of the spindle impelled by her hand, thus ratifying the destiny of each; and then, when they were fastened to this, carried them to Atropos, who spun the threads and made them irreversible, *[621]* whence without turning round they passed beneath the throne of Necessity; and when they had all passed, they marched on in a scorching heat to the plain of Forgetfulness, which was a barren waste destitute of trees and verdure; and then towards evening they encamped by the river of Unmindfulness, whose water no vessel can hold; of this they were all obliged to drink a certain quantity, and those who were not saved by wisdom drank more than was necessary; and each one as he drank forgot all things. Now after they had gone to rest, about the middle of the night there was a thunderstorm and earthquake, and then in an instant they were driven upwards in all manner of ways to their birth, like stars shooting. He himself was hindered from drinking the water. But in what manner or by what means he returned to the body he could not say; only, in the morning, awakening suddenly, he found himself lying on the pyre.

And thus, Glaucon, the tale has been saved and has not perished, and will save us if we are obedient to the word spoken; and we shall pass safely over the river of Forgetfulness and our soul will not be defiled. Wherefore my counsel is that we hold fast ever to the heavenly way and follow after justice and virtue always, considering that the soul is immortal and able to endure every sort of good and every sort of evil. Thus shall we live dear to one another and to the gods, both while remaining here and when, like conquerors in the games who go round to gather gifts, we receive our reward. And it shall be well with us both in this life and in the pilgrimage of a thousand years which we have been describing.

TIMAEUS

PERSONS OF THE DIALOGUE: SOCRATES; CRITIAS; TIMAEUS; HERMOCRATES

~~~~~~~~~~~~~~~~~~~~~~~~~~~~

[17] *Socrates.* ONE, two, three; but where, my dear Timaeus, is the fourth of those who were yesterday my guests and are to be my entertainers to-day?

Timaeus. He has been taken ill, Socrates; for he would not willingly have been absent from this gathering.

Soc. Then, if he is not coming, you and the two others must supply his place.

Tim. Certainly, and we will do all that we can; having been handsomely entertained by you yesterday, those of us who remain should be only too glad to return your hospitality.

Soc. Do you remember what were the points of which I required you to speak?

Tim. We remember some of them, and you will be here to remind us of anything which we have forgotten: or rather, if we are not troubling you, will you briefly recapitulate the whole, and then the particulars will be more firmly fixed in our memories?

Soc. To be sure I will: the chief theme of my yesterday's discourse was the State—how constituted and of what citizens composed it would seem likely to be most perfect.

Tim. Yes, Socrates; and what you said of it was very much to our mind.

Soc. Did we not begin by separating the husbandmen and the artisans from the class of defenders of the State?

Tim. Yes.

Soc. And when we had given to each one that single employment and particular art which was suited to his nature, we spoke of those who were intended to be our warriors, and said that they were to be guardians of the city against attacks from within as well as from without, [18]

and to have no other employment; they were to be merciful in judging their subjects, of whom they were by nature friends, but fierce to their enemies, when they came across them in battle.

Tim. Exactly.

Soc. We said, if I am not mistaken, that the guardians should be gifted with a temperament in a high degree both passionate and philosophical; and that then they would be as they ought to be, gentle to their friends and fierce with their enemies.

Tim. Certainly.

Soc. And what did we say of their education? Were they not to be trained in gymnastic, and music, and all other sorts of knowledge which were proper for them?

Tim. Very true.

Soc. And being thus trained they were not to consider gold or silver or anything else to be their own private property; they were to be like hired troops, receiving pay for keeping guard from those who were protected by them—the pay was to be no more than would suffice for men of simple life; and they were to spend in common, and to live together in the continual practice of virtue, which was to be their sole pursuit.

Tim. That was also said.

Soc. Neither did we forget the women; of whom we declared, that their natures should be assimilated and brought into harmony with those of the men, and that common pursuits should be assigned to them both in time of war and in their ordinary life.

Tim. That, again, was as you say.

Soc. And what about the procreation of children? Or rather was not the proposal too singular to be forgotten? for all wives and children were to be in common, to the intent that no one should ever know his own child, but they were to imagine that they were all one family; those who were within a suitable limit of age were to be brothers and sisters, those who were of an elder generation parents and grandparents, and those of a younger, children and grandchildren.

Tim. Yes, and the proposal is easy to remember, as you say.

Soc. And do you also remember how, with a view of securing as far as we could the best breed, we said that the chief magistrates, male and female, should contrive secretly, by the use of certain lots, so to arrange the nuptial meeting, that the bad of either sex and the good of either sex might pair with their like; and there was to be no quarrelling on this account, for they would imagine that the union was a mere accident, and was to be attributed to the lot?

Tim. I remember.

Soc. And you remember how we said that the children of the good parents were to be educated, [19] and the children of the bad secretly dispersed among the inferior citizens; and while they were all growing up the rulers were to be on the look-out, and to bring up from below in their turn those who were worthy, and those among themselves who were unworthy were to take the places of those who came up?

Tim. True.

Soc. Then have I now given you all the heads of our yesterday's discussion? Or is there anything more, my dear Timaeus, which has been omitted?

Tim. Nothing, Socrates; it was just as you have said.

Soc. I should like, before proceeding further, to tell you how I feel about the State which we have described. I might compare myself to a person who, on beholding beautiful animals either created by the painter's art, or, better still, alive but at rest, is seized with a desire of seeing them in motion or engaged in some struggle or conflict to which their forms appear suited; this is my feeling about the State which we have been describing. There are conflicts which all cities undergo, and I should like to hear some one tell of our own city carrying on a struggle against her neighbours, and how she went out to war in a becoming manner, and when at war showed by the greatness of her actions and the magnanimity of her words in dealing with other cities a result worthy of her training and education. Now I, Critias and Her-

mocrates, am conscious that I myself should never be able to celebrate the city and her citizens in a befitting manner, and I am not surprised at my own incapacity; to me the wonder is rather that the poets present as well as past are no better—not that I mean to depreciate them; but every one can see that they are a tribe of imitators, and will imitate best and most easily the life in which they have been brought up; while that which is beyond the range of a man's education he finds hard to carry out in action, and still harder adequately to represent in language. I am aware that the Sophists have plenty of brave words and fair conceits, but I am afraid that being only wanderers from one city to another, and having never had habitations of their own, they may fail in their conception of philosophers and statesmen, and may not know what they do and say in time of war, when they are fighting or holding parley with their enemies. And thus people of your class are the only ones remaining who are fitted by nature and education to take part at once both in politics and philosophy. Here is Timaeus, [20] of Locris in Italy, a city which has admirable laws, and who is himself in wealth and rank the equal of any of his fellow-citizens; he has held the most important and honourable offices in his own state, and, as I believe, has scaled the heights of all philosophy; and here is Critias, whom every Athenian knows to be no novice in the matters of which we are speaking; and as to Hermocrates, I am assured by many witnesses that his genius and education qualify him to take part in any speculation of the kind. And therefore yesterday when I saw that you wanted me to describe the formation of the State, I readily assented, being very well aware, that, if you only would, none were better qualified to carry the discussion further, and that when you had engaged our city in a suitable war, you of all men living could best exhibit her playing a fitting part. When I had completed my task, I in return imposed this other task upon you. You conferred together and agreed to entertain me to-day, as I had entertained you, with a feast of discourse. Here am I in festive array, and no man can be more ready for the promised banquet.

Her. And we too, Socrates, as Timaeus says, will not be wanting in enthusiasm; and there is no excuse for not complying with your request. As soon as we arrived yesterday at the guest-chamber of Critias, with whom we are staying, or rather on our way thither, we talked the matter over, and he told us an ancient tradition, which I wish, Critias, that you would repeat to Socrates, so that he may help us to judge whether it will satisfy his requirements or not.

Crit. I will, if Timaeus, who is our other partner, approves.

Tim. I quite approve.

Crit. Then listen, Socrates, to a tale which, though strange, is certainly true, having been attested by Solon, who was the wisest of the seven sages. He was a relative and a dear friend of my great-grandfather, Dropides, as he himself says in many passages of his poems; and he told the story to Critias, my grandfather, who remembered and repeated it to us. There were of old, he said, great and marvellous actions of the Athenian city, *[21]* which have passed into oblivion through lapse of time and the destruction of mankind, and one in particular, greater than all the rest. This we will now rehearse. It will be a fitting monument of our gratitude to you, and a hymn of praise true and worthy of the goddess, on this her day of festival.

Soc. Very good. And what is this ancient famous action of the Athenians, which Critias declared, on the authority of Solon, to be not a mere legend, but an actual fact?

Crit. I will tell an old-world story which I heard from an aged man; for Critias, at the time of telling it, was as he said, nearly ninety years of age, and I was about ten. Now the day was that day of the Apaturia which is called the Registration of Youth, at which, according to custom, our parents gave prizes for recitations, and the poems of several poets were recited by us boys, and many of us sang the poems of Solon, which at that time had not gone out of fashion. One of our tribe, either because he thought so or to please Critias, said that in his judgment Solon was not only the wisest of men, but also the noblest of poets. The old man, as I very well remember, brightened up at hearing this and said, smiling: Yes, Amynander, if Solon had only, like other poets, made poetry the business of his life, and had completed the tale which he brought with him from Egypt, and had not been compelled, by reason of the factions and troubles which he found stirring in his own country when he came home, to attend to other matters, in my opinion he would have been as famous as Homer or Hesiod, or any poet.

And what was the tale about, Critias? said Amynander.

About the greatest action which the Athenians ever did, and which ought to have been the most famous, but, through the lapse of time and the destruction of the actors, it has not come down to us.

Tell us, said the other, the whole story, and how and from whom Solon heard this veritable tradition.

He replied:—In the Egyptian Delta, at the head of which the river Nile divides, there is a certain district which is called the district of Sais, and the great city of the district is also called Sais, and is the city from which King Amasis came. The citizens have a deity for their foundress; she is called in the Egyptian tongue Neith, and is asserted by them to be the same whom the Hellenes call Athene; they are great lovers of the Athenians, and say that they are in some way related to them. To this city came Solon, and was received there with great honour; *[22]* he asked the priests who were most skilful in such matters, about antiquity, and made the discovery that neither he nor any other Hellene knew anything worth mentioning about the times of old. On one occasion, wishing to draw them on to speak of antiquity, he began to tell about the most ancient things in our part of the world—about Phoroneus, who is called "the first man," and about Niobe; and after the Deluge, of the survival of Deucalion and Pyrrha; and he traced the genealogy of their descendants, and reckoning up the dates, tried to compute how many years ago the events of which he was speaking happened. Thereupon one of the priests, who was of a very great age, said: O Solon, Solon, you Hellenes are never anything but children, and there is not an old man among you. Solon in return asked him what he meant. I mean to say, he replied, that in mind you are all young; there is no old opinion handed down among you by ancient tradition, nor any science which is hoary with age. And I will tell you why. There have been, and will be again, many destructions of mankind arising out of many causes; the greatest have been brought about by the agencies of fire and water, and other lesser ones by innumerable other causes. There is a story, which even you have preserved, that once upon a time Phaëthon, the son of Helios, having yoked the steeds in his father's chariot, because he was not able to drive them in the path of his father, burnt up all that was upon the earth, and was himself destroyed by a thunderbolt. Now this has the form of a myth, but really signifies a declination of the bodies moving in the heavens around the earth, and a great conflagration of things upon the earth, which recurs after long intervals; at such times those who live upon the mountains and in dry and lofty places are more liable to destruction than those who dwell by rivers or on the seashore. And from this calamity the Nile, who is our never-failing saviour, delivers and preserves us. When, on the other hand, the gods purge the earth with a deluge of water, the survivors in your country are herdsmen and shepherds who dwell on the mountains, but those who, like you, live in cities are carried by the rivers into the sea. Whereas in this land, neither then nor at any other time, does the water come down from above on the fields, having always a tendency to come up from below; for which reason the traditions preserved here are the most ancient.

The fact is, that wherever the extremity of winter frost or of summer sun does not prevent, mankind exist, sometimes in greater, [23] sometimes in lesser numbers. And whatever happened either in your country or in ours, or in any other region of which we are informed —if there were any actions noble or great or in any other way remarkable, they have all been written down by us of old, and are preserved in our temples. Whereas just when you and other nations are beginning to be provided with letters and the other requisites of civilized life, after the usual interval, the stream from heaven, like a pestilence, comes pouring down, and leaves only those of you who are destitute of letters and education; and so you have to begin all over again like children, and know nothing of what happened in ancient times, either among us or among yourselves. As for those genealogies of yours which you just now recounted to us, Solon, they are no better than the tales of children. In the first place you remember a single deluge only, but there were many previous ones; in the next place, you do not know that there formerly dwelt in your land the fairest and noblest race of men which ever lived, and that you and your whole city are descended from a small seed or remnant of them which survived. And this was unknown to you, because, for many generations, the survivors of that destruction died, leaving no written word. For there was a time, Solon, before the great deluge of all, when the city which now is Athens was first in war and in every way the best governed of all cities, and is said to have performed the noblest deeds and to have had the fairest constitution of any of which tradition tells, under the face of heaven.

Solon marvelled at his words, and earnestly requested the priests to inform him exactly and in order about these former citizens. You are welcome to hear about them, Solon, said the priest, both for your own sake and for that of your city, and above all, for the sake of the goddess who is the common patron and parent and educator of both our cities. She founded your city a thousand years before ours,[1] receiving from the Earth and Hephaestus the seed of your race, and afterwards she founded ours, of which the constitution is recorded in our sacred registers to be eight thousand years old. As touching your citizens of nine thousand years ago, [24] I will briefly inform you of their laws and of their most famous action; the exact particulars of the whole we will hereafter go through at our leisure in the sacred registers themselves. If you compare these very laws with ours you will find that many of ours are the counterpart of yours as they were in the olden time. In the first place, there is the caste of priests, which is separated from all the others; next, there are the artificers, who ply their several crafts by themselves and do not intermix; and also there is the class of shepherds and of hunters, as well as that of husbandmen; and you will observe, too, that the warriors in Egypt are distinct from all the other classes, and are commanded by the law to devote themselves solely to military pursuits; moreover, the weapons which they carry are shields and spears, a style of equipment which the goddess taught of Asiatics first to us, as in your part of the world first to you. Then as to wisdom, do you observe how our law from the very first made a study of the whole order of things, extending even to prophecy and medicine which gives health, out of these divine elements deriving what was needful for human life, and adding every sort of knowledge which was akin to them. All this order and arrangement the goddess first imparted to you when establishing your city; and she chose the spot of earth in which you were born, because she saw that the happy temperament of the seasons in that land would produce the wisest of men. Wherefore the goddess, who was a lover both of war and of wisdom, selected and first of all settled that spot which was the most likely to produce men likest herself. And there you dwelt, having such laws as these and still better ones, and excelled all mankind in all virtue, as became the children and disciples of the gods.

Many great and wonderful deeds are recorded of your state in our histories. But one of them exceeds all the rest in greatness and valour. For these histories tell of a mighty power which un-

[1] Cf. *Critias*, 108.

provoked made an expedition against the whole of Europe and Asia, and to which your city put an end. This power came forth out of the Atlantic Ocean, for in those days the Atlantic was navigable; and there was an island situated in front of the straits which are by you called the Pillars of Heracles; the island was larger than Libya and Asia put together, [25] and was the way to other islands, and from these you might pass to the whole of the opposite continent which surrounded the true ocean; for this sea which is within the Straits of Heracles is only a harbour, having a narrow entrance, but that other is a real sea, and the surrounding land may be most truly called a boundless continent. Now in this island of Atlantis there was a great and wonderful empire which had rule over the whole island and several others, and over parts of the continent, and, furthermore, the men of Atlantis had subjected the parts of Libya within the columns of Heracles as far as Egypt, and of Europe as far as Tyrrhenia. This vast power, gathered into one, endeavoured to subdue at a blow our country and yours and the whole of the region within the straits; and then, Solon, your country shone forth, in the excellence of her virtue and strength, among all mankind. She was pre-eminent in courage and military skill, and was the leader of the Hellenes. And when the rest fell off from her, being compelled to stand alone, after having undergone the very extremity of danger, she defeated and triumphed over the invaders, and preserved from slavery those who were not yet subjugated, and generously liberated all the rest of us who dwell within the pillars. But afterwards there occurred violent earthquakes and floods; and in a single day and night of misfortune all your warlike men in a body sank into the earth, and the island of Atlantis in like manner disappeared in the depths of the sea. For which reason the sea in those parts is impassable and impenetrable, because there is a shoal of mud in the way; and this was caused by the subsidence of the island.

I have told you briefly, Socrates, what the aged Critias heard from Solon and related to us. And when you were speaking yesterday about your city and citizens, the tale which I have just been repeating to you came into my mind, and I remarked with astonishment how, by some mysterious coincidence, you agreed in almost every particular with the narrative of Solon; but I did not like to speak at the moment. [26] For a long time had elapsed, and I had forgotten too much; I thought that I must first of all run over the narrative in my own mind, and then I would speak. And so I readily assented to your request yesterday, considering that in all such cases the chief difficulty is to find a tale suitable to our purpose, and that with such a tale we should be fairly well provided.

And therefore, as Hermocrates has told you, on my way home yesterday I at once communicated the tale to my companions as I remembered it; and after I left them, during the night by thinking I recovered nearly the whole of it. Truly, as is often said, the lessons of our childhood make a wonderful impression on our memories; for I am not sure that I could remember all the discourse of yesterday, but I should be much surprised if I forgot any of these things which I have heard very long ago. I listened at the time with childlike interest to the old man's narrative; he was very ready to teach me, and I asked him again and again to repeat his words, so that like an indelible picture they were branded into my mind. As soon as the day broke, I rehearsed them as he spoke them to my companions, that they, as well as myself, might have something to say. And now, Socrates, to make an end of my preface, I am ready to tell you the whole tale. I will give you not only the general heads, but the particulars, as they were told to me. The city and citizens, which you yesterday described to us in fiction, we will now transfer to the world of reality. It shall be the ancient city of Athens, and we will suppose that the citizens whom you imagined, were our veritable ancestors, of whom the priest spoke; they will perfectly harmonise, and there will be no inconsistency in saying that the citizens of your republic are these ancient Athenians. Let us divide the subject among us, and all endeavour according to our ability gracefully to execute the task which you have imposed upon us. Consider then, Socrates, if this narrative is suited to the purpose, or whether we should seek for some other instead.

Soc. And what other, Critias, can we find that will be better than this, which is natural and suitable to the festival of the goddess, and has the very great advantage of being a fact and not a fiction? How or where shall we find another if we abandon this? We cannot, [27] and therefore you must tell the tale, and good luck to you; and I in return for my yesterday's discourse will now rest and be a listener.

Crit. Let me proceed to explain to you, Socrates, the order in which we have arranged our entertainment. Our intention is, that Timaeus, who is the most of an astronomer amongst us, and has made the nature of the universe his special study, should speak first, beginning with the generation of the world and going down to the creation of man; next, I am to receive the men whom he has created of whom some will have profited by the excellent education which you have given them; and then, in accordance with the tale of Solon, and equally with his law, we will bring them into court and make them citizens, as if they were those very Athenians whom the sacred Egyptian record has recovered from oblivion, and thenceforward we will speak of them as Athenians and fellow-citizens.

Soc. I see that I shall receive in my turn a perfect and splendid feast of reason. And now, Timaeus, you, I suppose, should speak next, after duly calling upon the Gods.

Tim. All men, Socrates, who have any degree of right feeling, at the beginning of every enterprise, whether small or great, always call upon God. And we, too, who are going to discourse of the nature of the universe, how created or how existing without creation, if we be not altogether out of our wits, must invoke the aid of Gods and Goddesses and pray that our words may be acceptable to them and consistent with themselves. Let this, then, be our invocation of the Gods, to which I add an exhortation of myself to speak in such manner as will be most intelligible to you, and will most accord with my own intent.

First then, in my judgment, we must make a distinction and ask, What is that which always is and has no becoming; and what is that which is always becoming and never is? That which is apprehended by intelligence and reason is always in the same state; *[28]* but that which is conceived by opinion with the help of sensation and without reason, is always in a process of becoming and perishing and never really is. Now everything that becomes or is created must of necessity be created by some cause, for without a cause nothing can be created. The work of the creator, whenever he looks to the unchangeable and fashions the form and nature of his work after an unchangeable pattern, must necessarily be made fair and perfect; but when he looks to the created only, and uses a created pattern, it is not fair or perfect. Was the heaven then or the world, whether called by this or by any other more appropriate name—assuming the name, I am asking a question which has to be asked at the beginning of an enquiry about anything—was the world, I say, always in existence and without beginning? or created, and had it a beginning? Created, I reply, being visible and tangible and having a

body, and therefore sensible; and all sensible things are apprehended by opinion and sense and are in a process of creation and created. Now that which is created must, as we affirm, of necessity be created by a cause. But the father and maker of all this universe is past finding out; and even if we found him, to tell of him to all men would be impossible. And there is still a question to be asked about him: Which of the patterns had the artificer in view when he made the world—the pattern of the unchangeable, or of that which is created? *[29]* If the world be indeed fair and the artificer good, it is manifest that he must have looked to that which is eternal; but if what cannot be said without blasphemy is true, then to the created pattern. Every one will see that he must have looked to the eternal; for the world is the fairest of creations and he is the best of causes. And having been created in this way, the world has been framed in the likeness of that which is apprehended by reason and mind and is unchangeable, and must therefore of necessity, if this is admitted, be a copy of something. Now it is all-important that the beginning of everything should be according to nature. And in speaking of the copy and the original we may assume that words are akin to the matter which they describe; when they relate to the lasting and permanent and intelligible, they ought to be lasting and unalterable, and, as far as their nature allows, irrefutable and immovable—nothing less. But when they express only the copy or likeness and not the eternal things themselves, they need only be likely and analogous to the real words. As being is to becoming, so is truth to belief. If then, Socrates, amid the many opinions about the gods and the generation of the universe, we are not able to give notions which are altogether and in every respect exact and consistent with one another, do not be surprised. Enough, if we adduce probabilities as likely as any others; for we must remember that I who am the speaker, and you who are the judges, are only mortal men, and we ought to accept the tale which is probable and enquire no further.

Soc. Excellent, Timaeus; and we will do precisely as you bid us. The prelude is charming, and is already accepted by us—may we beg of you to proceed to the strain?

Tim. Let me tell you then why the creator made this world of generation. He was good, and the good can never have any jealousy of anything. And being free from jealousy, he desired that all things should be as like himself as they could be. This is in the truest sense the origin of creation and of the world, *[30]* as we shall do well in believing on the testimony of wise men: God desired that all things should be good and nothing bad, so far as this was attainable. Wherefore also finding the whole visible sphere not at rest, but moving in an irregular and disorderly fashion, out of disorder he brought order, considering that this was in every way better than the other. Now the deeds of the best could never be or have been other than the fairest; and the creator, reflecting on the things which are by nature visible, found that no unintelligent creature taken as a whole was fairer than the intelligent taken as a whole; and that intelligence could not be present in anything which was devoid of soul. For which reason, when he was framing the universe, he put intelligence in soul, and soul in body, that he might be the creator of a work which was by nature fairest and best. Wherefore, using the language of probability, we may say that the world became a living creature truly endowed with soul and intelligence by the providence of God.

This being supposed, let us proceed to the next stage: In the likeness of what animal did the Creator make the world? It would be an unworthy thing to liken it to any nature which exists as a part only; for nothing can be beautiful which is like any imperfect thing; but let us suppose the world to be the very image of that whole of which all other animals both individually and in their tribes are portions. For the original of the universe contains in itself all intelligible beings, just as this world comprehends us and all other visible creatures. For the Deity, intending to make this world like the fairest and most perfect of intelligible beings, framed one visible animal comprehending within itself all other animals of a kindred nature. *[31]* Are we right in saying that there is one world, or that they are many and infinite? There must be one only, if the created copy is to accord with the original. For that which includes all other intelligible creatures cannot have a second or companion; in that case there would be need of another living being which would include both, and of which they would be parts, and the likeness would be more truly said to resemble not them, but that other which included them. In order then that the world might be solitary, like the perfect animal, the creator made not two worlds or an infinite number of them; but there is and ever will be one only-begotten and created heaven.

Now that which is created is of necessity corporeal, and also visible and tangible. And nothing is visible where there is no fire, or tangible which has no solidity, and nothing is solid without earth. Wherefore also God in the beginning of creation made the body of the universe to consist of fire and earth. But two things cannot be rightly put together without a third; there must be some bond of union between them. And the fairest bond is that which makes the most complete fusion of itself and the things which it combines; and proportion is best adapted to effect such a union. For whenever in any three numbers, whether cube or square, there is a mean, which is to the last term what the first term is to it; *[32]* and again, when the mean is to the first term as the last term is to the mean—then the mean becoming first and last, and the first and last both becoming means, they will all of them of necessity come to be the same, and having become the same with one another will be all one. If the universal frame had been created a surface only and having no depth, a single mean would have sufficed to bind together itself and the other terms; but now, as the world must be solid, and solid bodies are always compacted not by one mean but by two, God placed water and air in the mean between fire and earth, and made them to have the same proportion so far as was possible (as fire is to air so is air to water, and as air is to water so is water to earth); and thus he bound and put together a visible and tangible heaven. And for these reasons, and out of such elements which are in number four, the body of the world was created, and it was harmonised by proportion, and therefore has the spirit of friendship; and having been reconciled to itself, it was indissoluble by the hand of any other than the framer.

Now the creation took up the whole of each of the four elements; for the Creator compounded the world out of all the fire and all the water and all the air and all the earth, leaving no part of any of them nor any power of them outside. His intention was, in the first place, that the animal should be as far as possible a perfect whole and of perfect parts: *[33]* secondly, that it should be one, leaving no remnants out of which another such world might be created: and also that it should be free from old age and unaffected by disease. Considering that if heat and cold and other powerful forces which unite bodies surround and attack them from without when they are unprepared, they decompose them, and by bringing diseases and old age upon them, make them waste away—for this cause and on these grounds he made the world one whole, having every part entire, and being therefore perfect and not liable to old age and disease. And he gave to the world the figure which was suitable and also natural. Now to the animal which was to comprehend all animals, that figure was suitable which comprehends within itself all other figures. Wherefore he made the world in the form of a globe, round as from a lathe, having its extremes in every direction equidistant from the centre, the most perfect and the most like itself of all figures; for he considered that the like is infinitely fairer than the unlike. This he finished off, making the surface smooth all around for many reasons; in the first place, because the living being had no need of eyes when there was nothing remaining outside him to be seen; nor of ears when there was nothing to be heard; and there was no surrounding atmosphere to be breathed; nor would there have been any use of organs by the help of which he might receive his food or get rid of what he had already digested, since there was nothing which went from him or came into him: for there was nothing beside him. Of design he was created thus, his own waste providing his own food, and all that he did or suffered taking place in and by himself. For the Creator conceived that a being which was self-sufficient would be far more excellent than one which lacked anything; and, as he had no need to take anything or defend himself against any one, the Creator did not think it necessary to bestow upon him hands: nor had he any need of feet, *[34]* nor of the whole apparatus of walking; but the movement suited to his spherical form was assigned to him, being of all the seven that which is most appropriate to mind and intelligence; and he was made to move in the same manner and on the same spot, within his own limits revolving in a circle. All the other six motions were taken away from him, and he was made not to partake of their deviations. And as this circular movement required no feet, the universe was created without legs and without feet.

Such was the whole plan of the eternal God about the god that was to be, to whom for this reason he gave a body, smooth and even, having a surface in every direction equidistant from the centre, a body entire and perfect, and formed out of perfect bodies. And in the centre he put the soul, which he diffused throughout the body, making it also to be the exterior environment of it; and he made the universe a circle moving in a circle, one and solitary, yet by reason of its excellence able to converse with itself, and needing no other friendship or acquaintance. Having these purposes in view he created the world a blessed god.

Now God did not make the soul after the body, although we are speaking of them in this order; for having brought them together he would never have allowed that the elder should be ruled by the younger; but this is a random manner of speaking which we have, because somehow we ourselves too are very much under the dominion of chance. Whereas he made the soul in origin and excellence prior to and older than the body, to be the ruler and mistress, of whom the body was to be the subject. And he made her out of the following elements and on this wise: *[35]* Out of the indivisible and unchangeable, and also out of that which is divisible and has to do with material bodies, he compounded a third and intermediate kind of essence, partaking of the nature of the same and of the other, and this compound he placed accordingly in a mean between the indivisible, and the divisible and material. He took the three elements of the same, the other, and the essence, and mingled them into one form, compressing by force the reluctant and unsociable nature of the other into the same. When he had mingled them with the essence and out of three made one, he again divided this whole into as many portions as was fitting, each portion being a compound of the same, the other, and the essence. And he proceeded to divide after this manner:—First of all, he took away one part of the whole [1], and then he separated a second part which was double the first [2], and then he took away a third part which was half as much again as the second and three times as much as the first [3], and then he took a fourth part which was twice as much as the second [4], and a fifth part which was three times the third [9], and a sixth part which was eight times the first [8], and a seventh part which was twenty-seven times the first [27]. After this he filled up the double intervals [i. e. between 1, 2, 4, 8] and *[36]* the triple [i.e. between 1, 3, 9, 27], cutting off yet other portions from the mixture and placing them in the intervals, so that in each interval there were two kinds of means, the one exceeding and exceeded by equal parts of its extremes [as for example 1, 4/3, 2, in which the mean 4/3 is one-third of 1 more than 1, and one-third of 2 less than 2], the other being that kind of mean which exceeds and is exceeded by an equal number. Where there were intervals of 3/2 and of 4/3 and of 9/8, made by the connecting terms in the former intervals, he filled up all the intervals of ⅔ with the interval of ⅞, leaving a fraction over; and the interval which this fraction expressed was in the ratio of 256 to 243. And thus the whole mixture out of which he cut these portions was all exhausted by him. This entire compound he divided lengthways into two parts, which he joined to one another at the centre like the letter X, and bent them into a circular form, connecting them with themselves and each other at the point opposite to their original meeting-point; and, comprehending them in a uniform revolution upon the same axis, he made the one the outer and the other the inner circle. Now the motion of the outer circle he called the motion of the same, and the motion of the inner circle the motion of the other or diverse. The motion of the same he carried round by the side [1] to the right, and the motion of the diverse diagonally [2] to the left. And he gave dominion to the motion of the same and like, for that he left single and undivided; but the inner motion he divided in six places and made seven unequal circles having their intervals in ratios of two and three, three of each, and bade the orbits proceed in a direction opposite to one another; and three [Sun, Mercury, Venus] he made to move with equal swiftness, and the remaining four [Moon, Saturn, Mars, Jupiter] to move with unequal swiftness to the three and to one another, but in due proportion.

Now when the Creator had framed the soul according to his will, he formed within her the corporeal universe, and brought the two together, and united them centre to centre. The soul, interfused everywhere from the centre to the circumference of heaven, of which also she is the external envelopment, herself turning in herself, began a divine beginning of never-ceasing and rational life enduring throughout all time. [37] The body of heaven is visible, but the soul is invisible, and partakes of reason and harmony, and being made by the best of intellectual and everlasting natures, is the best of things created. And because she is composed of the same and of the other and of the essence, these three, and is divided and united in due proportion, and in her revolutions returns upon herself, the soul, when touching anything which has essence, whether dispersed in parts or undivided, is stirred through all her powers, to declare the sameness or difference of that

[1] i. e. of the rectangular figure supposed to be inscribed in the circle of the same.
[2] i. e. across the rectangular figure from corner to corner.

thing and some other; and to what individuals are related, and by what affected, and in what way and how and when, both in the world of generation and in the world of immutable being. And when reason, which works with equal truth, whether she be in the circle of the diverse or of the same—in voiceless silence holding her onward course in the sphere of the self-moved—when reason, I say, is hovering around the sensible world and when the circle of the diverse also moving truly imparts the intimations of sense to the whole soul, then arise opinions and beliefs sure and certain. But when reason is concerned with the rational, and the circle of the same moving smoothly declares it, then intelligence and knowledge are necessarily perfected. And if any one affirms that in which these two are found to be other than the soul, he will say the very opposite of the truth.

When the father and creator saw the creature which he had made moving and living, the created image of the eternal gods, he rejoiced, and in his joy determined to make the copy still more like the original; and as this was eternal, he sought to make the universe eternal, so far as might be. Now the nature of the ideal being was everlasting, but to bestow this attribute in its fulness upon a creature was impossible. Wherefore he resolved to have a moving image of eternity, and when he set in order the heaven, he made this image eternal but moving according to number, while eternity itself rests in unity; and this image we call time. For there were no days and nights and months and years before the heaven was created, but when he constructed the heaven he created them also. They are all parts of time, and the past and future are created species of time, which we unconsciously but wrongly transfer to the eternal essence; for we say that he "was," he "is," he "will be," but the truth is that "is" alone is properly attributed to him, [38] and that "was" and "will be" are only to be spoken of becoming in time, for they are motions, but that which is immovably the same cannot become older or younger by time, nor ever did or has become, or hereafter will be, older or younger, nor is subject at all to any of those states which affect moving and sensible things and of which generation is the cause. These are the forms of time, which imitates eternity and revolves according to a law of number. Moreover, when we say that what has become *is* become and what becomes *is* becoming, and that what will become *is* about to become and that the non-existent *is* non-existent—all these are inaccurate modes of expression.[1] But perhaps this whole subject will be more suitably discussed on some other occasion.

Time, then, and the heaven came into being at the same instant in order that, having been created together, if ever there was to be a dissolution of them, they might be dissolved together. It was framed after the pattern of the eternal nature, that it might resemble this as far as was possible; for the pattern exists from eternity, and the created heaven has been, and is, and will be, in all time. Such was the mind and thought of God in the creation of time. The sun and moon and five other stars, which are called the planets, were created by him in order to distinguish and preserve the numbers of time; and when he had made their several bodies, he placed them in the orbits in which the circle of the other was revolving [2]—in seven orbits seven stars. First, there was the moon in the orbit nearest the earth, and next the sun, in the second orbit above the earth; then came the morning star and the star sacred to Hermes, moving in orbits which have an equal swiftness with the sun, but in an opposite direction; and this is the reason why the sun and Hermes and Lucifer overtake and are overtaken by each other. To enumerate the places which he assigned to the other stars, and to give all the reasons why he assigned them, although a secondary matter, would give more trouble than the primary. These things at some future time, when we are at leisure, may have the consideration which they deserve, but not at present.

Now, when all the stars which were necessary to the creation of time had attained a motion suitable to them, and had become living creatures having bodies fastened by vital chains, and learnt their appointed task, [39] moving in the motion of the diverse, which is diagonal, and passes through and is governed by the motion of the same, they revolved, some in a larger and some in a lesser orbit—those which had the lesser orbit revolving faster, and those which had the larger more slowly. Now by reason of the motion of the same, those which revolved fastest appeared to be overtaken by those which moved slower although they really overtook them; for the motion of the same made them all turn in a spiral, and, because some went one way and some another, that which receded most slowly from the sphere of the same, which was the swiftest, appeared to follow it most nearly. That there might be some visible measure of their relative swiftness and slowness as they proceeded in their eight courses, God lighted a fire, which we now call the sun, in the second from the earth of these orbits, that it might give light to the whole of heaven, and that the animals, as many as nature intended, might participate in number, learning arithmetic from the revolution of the same and the like. Thus, then, and for this reason the night and the day were created, being the period of the one most intelligent revolution. And the month is accomplished when the moon has completed her orbit and overtaken the sun, and the year when the sun has completed his own orbit. Mankind, with hardly an exception, have not remarked the periods of the other stars, and they have no name for them, and do not measure them against one another by the help of number, and hence they can scarcely be said to know that their wanderings, being infinite in number and admirable for their variety, make up time. And yet there is no difficulty in seeing that the perfect number of time fulfils the perfect year when all the eight revolutions, having their relative degrees of swiftness, are accomplished together and attain their completion at the same time, measured by the rotation of the same and equally moving. After this manner, and for these reasons, came into being such of the stars as in their heavenly progress received reversals of motion, to the end that the created heaven might imitate the eternal nature, and be as like as possible to the perfect and intelligible animal.

Thus far and until the birth of time the created universe was made in the likeness of the original, but inasmuch as all animals were not yet comprehended therein, it was still unlike. What remained, the creator then proceeded to fashion after the nature of the pattern. Now as in the ideal animal the mind perceives ideas or species of a certain nature and number, he thought that this created animal ought to have species of a like nature and number. There are four such; [40] one of them is the heavenly race of the gods; another, the race of birds whose way is in the air; the third, the watery species; and the fourth, the pedestrian and land creatures. Of the heavenly and divine, he created the greater part out of fire, that they might be the brightest of all things and fairest to behold, and he fashioned them after the likeness of the universe in the figure of a circle, and made them follow the intelligent motion of the supreme, distributing them over the whole circumference of heaven, which was to be a true cosmos or glorious world spangled with them all over.

---

[1] Cf. *Parmenides*, 141.
[2] Cf. 36.

And he gave to each of them two movements: the first, a movement on the same spot after the same manner, whereby they ever continue to think consistently the same thoughts about the same things; the second, a forward movement, in which they are controlled by the revolution of the same and the like; but by the other five motions they were unaffected [cf. 43], in order that each of them might attain the highest perfection. And for this reason the fixed stars were created, to be divine and eternal animals, ever-abiding and revolving after the same manner and on the same spot; and the other stars which reverse their motion and are subject to deviations of this kind, were created in the manner already described. The earth, which is our nurse, clinging around the pole which is extended through the universe, he framed to be the guardian and artificer of night and day, first and eldest of gods that are in the interior of heaven. Vain would be the attempt to tell all the figures of them circling as in dance, and their juxtapositions, and the return of them in their revolutions upon themselves, and their approximations, and to say which of these deities in their conjunctions meet, and which of them are in opposition, and in what order they get behind and before one another, and when they are severally eclipsed to our sight and again reappear, sending terrors and intimations of the future to those who cannot calculate their movements—to attempt to tell of all this without a visible representation of the heavenly system would be labour in vain. Enough on this head; and now let what we have said about the nature of the created and visible gods have an end.

To know or tell the origin of the other divinities is beyond us, and we must accept the traditions of the men of old time who affirm themselves to be the offspring of the gods—that is what they say—and they must surely have known their own ancestors. How can we doubt the word of the children of the gods? Although they give no probable or certain proofs, still, as they declare that they are speaking of what took place in their own family, we must conform to custom and believe them. In this manner, then, according to them, the genealogy of these gods is to be received and set forth.

Oceanus and Tethys were the children of Earth and Heaven, and from these sprang Phorcys and Cronos and Rhea, and all that generation; [41] and from Cronos and Rhea sprang Zeus and Herè, and all those who are said to be their brethren, and others who were the children of these.

Now, when all of them, both those who visibly appear in their revolutions as well as those other gods who are of a more retiring nature, had come into being, the creator of the universe addressed them in these words: "Gods, children of gods, who are my works, and of whom I am the artificer and father, my creations are indissoluble, if so I will. All that is bound may be undone, but only an evil being would wish to undo that which is harmonious and happy. Wherefore, since ye are but creatures, ye are not altogether immortal and indissoluble, but ye shall certainly not be dissolved, nor be liable to the fate of death, having in my will a greater and mightier bond than those with which ye were bound at the time of your birth. And now listen to my instructions:—Three tribes of mortal beings remain to be created—without them the universe will be incomplete, for it will not contain every kind of animal which it ought to contain, if it is to be perfect. On the other hand, if they were created by me and received life at my hands, they would be on an equality with the gods. In order then that they may be mortal, and that this universe may be truly universal, do ye, according to your natures, betake yourselves to the formation of animals, imitating the power which was shown by me in creating you. The part of them worthy of the name immortal, which is called divine and is the guiding principle of those who are willing to follow justice and you—of that divine part I will myself sow the seed, and having made a beginning, I will hand the work over to you. And do ye then interweave the mortal with the immortal, and make and beget living creatures, and give them food, and make them to grow, and receive them again in death."

Thus he spake, and once more into the cup in which he had previously mingled the soul of the universe he poured the remains of the elements, and mingled them in much the same manner; they were not, however, pure as before, but diluted to the second and third degree. And having made it he divided the whole mixture into souls equal in number to the stars, and assigned each soul to a star; and having there placed them as in a chariot, he showed them the nature of the universe, and declared to them the laws of destiny, according to which their first birth would be one and the same for all, —no one should suffer a disadvantage at his hands; they were to be sown in the instruments of time severally adapted to them, [42] and to come forth the most religious of animals; and as human nature was of two kinds, the superior race would hereafter be called man. Now, when they should be implanted in bodies by necessity, and be always gaining or losing some part of their bodily substance, then in the first place it would be necessary that they should all have in them one and the same faculty of sensation, arising out of irresistible impressions; in the second place, they must have love, in which pleasure and pain mingle; also fear and anger, and the feelings which are akin or opposite to them; if they conquered these they would live righteously, and if they were conquered by them, unrighteously. He who lived well during his appointed time was to return and dwell in his native star, and there he would have a blessed and congenial existence. But if he failed in attaining this, at the second birth he would pass into a woman, and if, when in that state of being, he did not desist from evil, he would continually be changed into some brute who resembled him in the evil nature which he had acquired, and would not cease from his toils and transformations until he followed the revolution of the same and the like within him, and overcame by the help of reason the turbulent and irrational mob of later accretions, made up of fire and air and water and earth, and returned to the form of his first and better state. Having given all these laws to his creatures, that he might be guiltless of future evil in any of them, the creator sowed some of them in the earth, and some in the moon, and some in the other instruments of time; and when he had sown them he committed to the younger gods the fashioning of their mortal bodies, and desired them to furnish what was still lacking to the human soul, and having made all the suitable additions, to rule over them, and to pilot the mortal animal in the best and wisest manner which they could, and avert from him all but self-inflicted evils.

When the creator had made all these ordinances he remained in his own accustomed nature, and his children heard and were obedient to their father's word, and receiving from him the immortal principle of a mortal creature, in imitation of their own creator they borrowed portions of fire, and earth, and water, and air from the world, [43] which were hereafter to be restored—these they took and welded them together, not with the indissoluble chains by which they were themselves bound, but with little pegs too small to be visible, making up out of all the four elements each separate body, and fastening the courses of the immortal soul in a body which was in a state of perpetual influx

and efflux. Now these courses, detained as in a vast river, neither overcame nor were overcome; but were hurrying and hurried to and fro, so that the whole animal was moved and progressed, irregularly however and irrationally and anyhow, in all the six directions of motion, wandering backwards and forwards, and right and left, and up and down, and in all the six directions. For great as was the advancing and retiring flood which provided nourishment, the affections produced by external contact caused still greater tumult—when the body of any one met and came into collision with some external fire, or with the solid earth or the gliding waters, or was caught in the tempest borne on the air, and the motions produced by any of these impulses were carried through the body to the soul. All such motions have consequently received the general name of "sensations," which they still retain. And they did in fact at that time create a very great and mighty movement; uniting with the everflowing stream in stirring up and violently shaking the courses of the soul, they completely stopped the revolution of the same by their opposing current, and hindered it from predominating and advancing; and they so disturbed the nature of the other or diverse, that the three double intervals [i.e. between 1, 2, 4, 8], and the three triple intervals [i.e. between 1, 3, 9, 27], together with the mean terms and connecting links which are expressed by the ratios of 3 : 2, and 4 : 3, and of 9 : 8—these, although they cannot be wholly undone except by him who united them, were twisted by them in all sorts of ways, and the circles were broken and disordered in every possible manner, so that when they moved they were tumbling to pieces, and moved irrationally, at one time in a reverse direction, and then again obliquely, and then upside down, as you might imagine a person who is upside down and has his head leaning upon the ground and his feet up against something in the air; and when he is in such a position, both he and the spectator fancy that the right of either is his left, and left right. If, when powerfully experiencing these and similar effects, the revolutions of the soul come in contact with some external thing, [44] either of the class of the same or of the other, they speak of the same or of the other in a manner the very opposite of the truth; and they become false and foolish, and there is no course or revolution in them which has a guiding or directing power; and if again any sensations enter in violently from without and drag after them the whole vessel of the soul, then the courses of the soul, though they seem to conquer, are really conquered.

And by reason of all these affections, the soul, when encased in a mortal body, now, as in the beginning, is at first without intelligence; but when the flood of growth and nutriment abates, and the courses of the soul, calming down, go their own way and become steadier as time goes on, then the several circles return to their natural form, and their revolutions are corrected, and they call the same and the other by their right names, and make the possessor of them to become a rational being. And if these combine in him with any true nurture or education, he attains the fulness and health of the perfect man, and escapes the worst disease of all; but if he neglects education he walks lame to the end of his life, and returns imperfect and good for nothing to the world below. This, however, is a later stage; at present we must treat more exactly the subject before us, which involves a preliminary enquiry into the generation of the body and its members, and as to how the soul was created—for what reason and by what providence of the gods; and holding fast to probability, we must pursue our way.

First, then, the gods, imitating the spherical shape of the universe, enclosed the two divine courses in a spherical body, that, namely, which we now term the head, being the most divine part of us and the lord of all that is in us: to this the gods, when they put together the body, gave all the other members to be servants, considering that it partook of every sort of motion. In order then that it might not tumble about among the high and deep places of the earth, but might be able to get over the one and out of the other, they provided the body to be its vehicle and means of locomotion; which consequently had length and was furnished with four limbs extended and flexible; these God contrived to be instruments of locomotion with which it might take hold and find support, [45] and so be able to pass through all places, carrying on high the dwelling-place of the most sacred and divine part of us. Such was the origin of legs and hands, which for this reason were attached to every man; and the gods, deeming the front part of man to be more honourable and more fit to command than the hinder part, made us to move mostly in a forward direction. Wherefore man must needs have his front part unlike and distinguished from the rest of his body.

And so in the vessel of the head, they first of all put a face in which they inserted organs to minister in all things to the providence of the soul, and they appointed this part, which has authority, to be by nature the part which is in front. And of the organs they first contrived the eyes to give light, and the principle according to which they were inserted was as follows: So much of fire as would not burn, but gave a gentle light, they formed into a substance akin to the light of every-day life; and the pure fire which is within us and related thereto they made to flow through the eyes in a stream smooth and dense, compressing the whole eye, and especially the centre part, so that it kept out everything of a coarser nature, and allowed to pass only this pure element. When the light of day surrounds the stream of vision, then like falls upon like, and they coalesce, and one body is formed by natural affinity in the line of vision, wherever the light that falls from within meets with an external object. And the whole stream of vision, being similarly affected in virtue of similarity, diffuses the motions of what it touches or what touches it over the whole body, until they reach the soul, causing that perception which we call sight. But when night comes on and the external and kindred fire departs, then the stream of vision is cut off; for going forth to an unlike element it is changed and extinguished, being no longer of one nature with the surrounding atmosphere which is now deprived of fire: and so the eye no longer sees, and we feel disposed to sleep. For when the eyelids, which the gods invented for the preservation of sight, are closed, they keep in the internal fire; and the power of the fire diffuses and equalises the inward motions; when they are equalised, there is rest, and when the rest is profound, [46] sleep comes over us scarce disturbed by dreams; but where the greater motions still remain, of whatever nature and in whatever locality, they engender corresponding visions in dreams, which are remembered by us when we are awake and in the external world. And now there is no longer any difficulty in understanding the creation of images in mirrors and all smooth and bright surfaces. For from the communion of the internal and external fires, and again from the union of them and their numerous transformations when they meet in the mirror, all these appearances of necessity arise, when the fire from the face coalesces with the fire from the eye on the bright and smooth surface. And right appears left and left right, because the visual rays come into contact with the rays emitted by the object in a manner contrary to the usual mode of meeting; but the right appears right, and the left left, when the position of one of the two concurring lights is reversed; and this happens when the mirror is concave and its smooth surface repels the right stream of vision to the left side, and the left to the right. Or if the mirror be turned vertically, then the concavity makes the countenance appear to be all upside down, and the lower rays are driven upwards and the upper downwards.

All these are to be reckoned among the second and co-operative causes which God, carrying into execution the idea of the best as far as possible, uses as his ministers. They are thought by most men not to be the second, but the prime causes of all things, because they freeze and heat, and contract and dilate, and the like. But they are not so, for they are incapable of reason or intellect; the only being which can properly have mind is the invisible soul, whereas fire and water, and earth and air, are all of them visible bodies. The lover of intellect and knowledge ought to explore causes of intelligent nature first of all, and, secondly, of those things which, being moved by others, are compelled to move others. And this is what we too must do. Both kinds of causes should be acknowledged by us, but a distinction should be made between those which are endowed with mind and are the workers of things fair and good, and those which are deprived of intelligence and always produce chance effects without order or design. Of the second or co-operative causes of sight, which help to give to the eyes the power which they now possess, enough has been said. I will therefore now proceed to speak of the higher use and purpose for which God has given them to us. [47] The sight in my opinion is the source of the greatest benefit to us, for had we never seen the stars, and the sun, and the heaven, none of the words which we have spoken about the universe would ever have been uttered. But now the sight of day and night, and the months and the revolutions of the years, have created number, and have given us a conception of time, and the power of enquiring about the nature of the universe; and from this source we have derived philosophy, than which no greater good ever was or will be given by the gods to mortal man. This is the greatest boon of sight: and of the lesser benefits why should I speak? even the ordinary man if he were deprived of them would bewail his loss, but in vain. Thus much let me say however: God invented and gave us sight to the end that we might behold the courses of intelligence in the heaven, and apply them to the courses of our own intelligence which are akin to them, the unperturbed

to the perturbed; and that we, learning them and partaking of the natural truth of reason, might imitate the absolutely unerring courses of God and regulate our own vagaries. The same may be affirmed of speech and hearing: they have been given by the gods to the same end and for a like reason. For this is the principal end of speech, whereto it most contributes. Moreover, so much of music as is adapted to the sound of the voice and to the sense of hearing is granted to us for the sake of harmony; and harmony, which has motions akin to the revolutions of our souls, is not regarded by the intelligent votary of the Muses as given by them with a view to irrational pleasure, which is deemed to be the purpose of it in our day, but as meant to correct any discord which may have arisen in the courses of the soul, and to be our ally in bringing her into harmony and agreement with herself; and rhythm too was given by them for the same reason, on account of the irregular and graceless ways which prevail among mankind generally, and to help us against them.

Thus far in what we have been saying, with small exception, the works of intelligence have been set forth; and now we must place by the side of them in our discourse the things which come into being through necessity—for the creation is mixed, [48] being made up of necessity and mind. Mind, the ruling power, persuaded necessity to bring the greater part of created things to perfection, and thus and after this manner in the beginning, when the influence of reason got the better of necessity, the universe was created. But if a person will truly tell of the way in which the work was accomplished, he must include the other influence of the variable cause as well. Wherefore, we must return again and find another suitable beginning, as about the former matters, so also about these. To which end we must consider the nature of fire, and water, and air, and earth, such as they were prior to the creation of the heaven, and what was happening to them in this previous state;[1] for no one has as yet explained the manner of their generation, but we speak of fire and the rest of them, whatever they mean, as though men knew their natures, and we maintain them to be the first principles and letters or elements of the whole, when they cannot reasonably be compared by a man of any sense even to syllables or first compounds. And let me say thus much: I will not now speak of the first principle or principles of all things, or by whatever

[1] Cf. 53.

name they are to be called, for this reason—because it is difficult to set forth my opinion according to the method of discussion which we are at present employing. Do not imagine, any more than I can bring myself to imagine, that I should be right in undertaking so great and difficult a task. Remembering what I said at first about probability, I will do my best to give as probable an explanation as any other—or rather, more probable; and I will first go back to the beginning and try to speak of each thing and of all. Once more, then, at the commencement of my discourse, I call upon God, and beg him to be our saviour out of a strange and unwonted enquiry, and to bring us to the haven of probability. So now let us begin again.

This new beginning of our discussion of the universe requires a fuller division than the former; for then we made two classes, now a third must be revealed. The two sufficed for the former discussion: one, which we assumed, was a pattern intelligible and always the same; [49] and the second was only the imitation of the pattern, generated and visible. There is also a third kind which we did not distinguish at the time, conceiving that the two would be enough. But now the argument seems to require that we should set forth in words another kind, which is difficult of explanation and dimly seen. What nature are we to attribute to this new kind of being? We reply, that it is the receptacle, and in a manner the nurse, of all generation. I have spoken the truth; but I must express myself in clearer language, and this will be an arduous task for many reasons, and in particular because I must first raise questions concerning fire and the other elements, and determine what each of them is; for to say, with any probability or certitude, which of them should be called water rather than fire, and which should be called any of them rather than all or some one of them, is a difficult matter. How, then, shall we settle this point, and what questions about the elements may be fairly raised?

In the first place, we see that what we just now called water, by condensation, I suppose, becomes stone and earth; and this same element, when melted and dispersed, passes into vapour and air. Air, again, when inflamed, becomes fire; and again fire, when condensed and extinguished, passes once more into the form of air; and once more, air, when collected and condensed, produces cloud and mist; and from these, when still more compressed, comes flowing water, and from water comes earth and stones once more; and thus generation appears to be transmitted from one to the other in a circle. Thus, then, as the several elements never present themselves in the same form, how can any one have the assurance to assert positively that any of them, whatever it may be, is one thing rather than another? No one can. But much the safest plan is to speak of them as follows:—Anything which we see to be continually changing, as, for example, fire, we must not call "this" or "that," but rather say that it is "of such a nature"; nor let us speak of water as "this," but always as "such"; nor must we imply that there is any stability in any of those things which we indicate by the use of the words "this" and "that," supposing ourselves to signify something thereby; for they are too volatile to be detained in any such expressions as "this," or "that," or "relative to this," or any other mode of speaking which represents them as permanent. We ought not to apply "this" to any of them, but rather the word "such"; which expresses the similar principle circulating in each and all of them; for example, that should be called "fire" which is of such a nature always, and so of everything that has generation. That in which the elements severally grow up, and appear, and decay, is alone to be called by the name "this" or "that"; [50] but that which is of a certain nature, hot or white, or anything which admits of opposite qualities, and all things that are compounded of them, ought not to be so denominated. Let me make another attempt to explain my meaning more clearly. Suppose a person to make all kinds of figures of gold and to be always transmuting one form into all the rest—somebody points to one of them and asks what it is. By far the safest and truest answer is, That is gold; and not to call the triangle or any other figures which are formed in the gold "these," as though they had existence, since they are in process of change while he is making the assertion; but if the questioner be willing to take the safe and indefinite expression, "such," we should be satisfied. And the same argument applies to the universal nature which receives all bodies—that must be always called the same; for, while receiving all things, she never departs at all from her own nature, and never in any way, or at any time, assumes a form like that of any of the things which enter into her; she is the natural recipient of all impressions, and is stirred and informed by them, and appears different from time to time by reason of them. But the forms which enter into and go out of her are the likenesses of real existences modelled after their patterns in a wonderful and inexplicable manner, which we will hereafter investigate. For the present we have only to conceive of three natures: first, that which is in process of generation; secondly, that in which the generation takes place; and thirdly, that of which the thing generated is a resemblance. And we may liken the receiving principle to a mother, and the source or spring to a father, and the intermediate nature to a child; and may remark further, that if the model is to take every variety of form, then the matter in which the model is fashioned will not be duly prepared, unless it is formless, and free from the impress of any of those shapes which it is hereafter to receive from without. For if the matter were like any of the supervening forms, then whenever any opposite or entirely different nature was stamped upon its surface, it would take the impression badly, because it would intrude its own shape. Wherefore, that which is to receive all forms should have no form; as in making perfumes they first contrive that the liquid substance which is to receive the scent shall be as inodorous as possible; or as those who wish to impress figures on soft substances do not allow any previous impression to remain, [51] but begin by making the surface as even and smooth as possible. In the same way that which is to receive perpetually and through its whole extent the resemblances of all eternal beings ought to be devoid of any particular form. Wherefore, the mother and receptacle of all created and visible and in any way sensible things, is not to be termed earth, or air, or fire, or water, or any of their compounds or any of the elements from which these are derived, but is an invisible and formless being which receives all things and in some mysterious way partakes of the intelligible, and is most incomprehensible. In saying this we shall not be far wrong; as far, however, as we can attain to a knowledge of her from the previous considerations, we may truly say that fire is that part of her nature which from time to time is inflamed, and water that which is moistened, and that the mother substance becomes earth and air, in so far as she receives the impressions of them.

Let us consider this question more precisely. Is there any self-existent fire? and do all those things which we call self-existent exist? or are only those things which we see, or in some way perceive through the bodily organs, truly existent, and nothing whatever besides them? And is all that which we call an intelligible essence nothing at all, and only a name? Here is a ques-tion which we must not leave unexamined or undetermined, nor must we affirm too confidently that there can be no decision; neither must we interpolate in our present long discourse a digression equally long, but if it is possible to set forth a great principle in a few words, that is just what we want.

Thus I state my view:—If mind and true opinion are two distinct classes, then I say that there certainly are these self-existent ideas unperceived by sense, and apprehended only by the mind; if, however, as some say, true opinion differs in no respect from mind, then everything that we perceive through the body is to be regarded as most real and certain. But we must affirm them to be distinct, for they have a distinct origin and are of a different nature; the one is implanted in us by instruction, the other by persuasion; the one is always accompanied by true reason, the other is without reason; the one cannot be overcome by persuasion, but the other can: and lastly, every man may be said to share in true opinion, but mind is the attribute of the gods and of very few men. Wherefore also we must acknowledge that there is one kind of being which is always the same, [52] uncreated and indestructible, never receiving anything into itself from without, nor itself going out to any other, but invisible and imperceptible by any sense, and of which the contemplation is granted to intelligence only. And there is another nature of the same name with it, and like to it, perceived by sense, created, always in motion, becoming in place and again vanishing out of place, which is apprehended by opinion and sense. And there is a third nature, which is space, and is eternal, and admits not of destruction and provides a home for all created things, and is apprehended without the help of sense, by a kind of spurious reason, and is hardly real; which we beholding as in a dream, say of all existence that it must of necessity be in some place and occupy a space, but that what is neither in heaven nor in earth has no existence. Of these and other things of the same kind, relating to the true and waking reality of nature, we have only this dreamlike sense, and we are unable to cast off sleep and determine the truth about them. For an image, since the reality, after which it is modelled, does not belong to it, and it exists ever as the fleeting shadow of some other, must be inferred to be in another [i.e. in space], grasping existence in some way or other, or it could not be at all. But true and exact reason, vindicating the nature of true being, maintains that while two things [i.e. the image and space] are different they cannot exist one of them in the other and so be one and also two at the same time.

Thus have I concisely given the result of my thoughts; and my verdict is that being and space and generation, these three, existed in their three ways before the heaven; and that the nurse of generation, moistened by water and inflamed by fire, and receiving the forms of earth and air, and experiencing all the affections which accompany these, presented a strange variety of appearances; and being full of powers which were neither similar nor equally balanced, was never in any part in a state of equipoise, but swaying unevenly hither and thither, was shaken by them, and by its motion again shook them; and the elements when moved were separated and carried continually, some one way, some another; as, when grain is shaken and winnowed by fans and other instruments used in the threshing of corn, [53] the close and heavy particles are borne away and settle in one direction, and the loose and light particles in another. In this manner, the four kinds or elements were then shaken by the receiving vessel, which, moving like a winnowing machine, scattered far away from one another the elements most unlike, and forced the most similar elements into close contact. Wherefore also the various elements had different places before they were arranged so as to form the universe. At first, they were all without reason and measure. But when the world began to get into order, fire and water and earth and air had only certain faint traces of themselves, and were altogether such as everything might be expected to be in the absence of God; this, I say, was their nature at that time, and God fashioned them by form and number. Let it be consistently maintained by us in all that we say that God made them as far as possible the fairest and best, out of things which were not fair and good. And now I will endeavour to show you the disposition and generation of them by an unaccustomed argument, which I am compelled to use; but I believe that you will be able to follow me, for your education has made you familiar with the methods of science.

In the first place, then, as is evident to all, fire and earth and water and air are bodies. And every sort of body possesses solidity, and every solid must necessarily be contained in planes; and every plane rectilinear figure is composed of triangles; and all triangles are originally of two kinds, both of which are made up of one right and two acute angles; one of them has at either end of the base the half of a divided right angle, having equal sides, while in the other the right angle is divided into unequal parts, having unequal sides. These, then, proceeding by a combination of probability with demonstration, we assume to be the original elements of fire and the other bodies; but the principles which are prior to these God only knows, and he of men who is the friend of God. And next we have to determine what are the four most beautiful bodies which are unlike one another, and of which some are capable of resolution into one another; for having discovered thus much, we shall know the true origin of earth and fire and of the proportionate and intermediate elements. And then we shall not be willing to allow that there are any distinct kinds of visible bodies fairer than these. Wherefore we must endeavour to construct the four forms of bodies which excel in beauty, and then we shall be able to say that we have sufficiently apprehended their nature. [54] Now of the two triangles, the isosceles has one form only; the scalene or unequal-sided has an infinite number. Of the infinite forms we must select the most beautiful, if we are to proceed in due order, and any one who can point out a more beautiful form than ours for the construction of these bodies, shall carry off the palm, not as an enemy, but as a friend. Now, the one which we maintain to be the most beautiful of all the many triangles (and we need not speak of the others) is that of which the double forms a third triangle which is equilateral; the reason of this would be long to tell; he who disproves what we are saying, and shows that we are mistaken, may claim a friendly victory. Then let us choose two triangles, out of which fire and the other elements have been constructed, one isosceles, the other having the square of the longer side equal to three times the square of the lesser side.

Now is the time to explain what was before obscurely said: there was an error in imagining that all the four elements might be generated by and into one another; this, I say, was an erroneous supposition, for there are generated from the triangles which we have selected four kinds—three from the one which has the sides unequal; the fourth alone is framed out of the isosceles triangle. Hence they cannot all be resolved into one another, a great number of small bodies being combined into a few large ones, or the converse. But three of them can be thus resolved and compounded, for they all spring from one, and when the greater bodies are broken up, many small bodies will spring up out of them and take their own proper figures; or, again, when many small bodies are dissolved into their triangles, if they become one, they will form one large mass of another kind. So much for their passage into one another. I have now to speak of their several kinds, and show out of what combinations of numbers each of them was formed. The first will be the simplest and smallest construction, and its element is that triangle which has its hypothenuse twice the lesser side. When two such triangles are joined at the diagonal, and this is repeated three times, and the triangles rest their diagonals and shorter sides on the same point as a centre, a single equilateral triangle is formed out of six triangles; and four equilateral triangles, if put together, make out of every three plane angles one solid angle, being that which is nearest to the most obtuse of plane angles; [55] and out of the combination of these four angles arises the first solid form which distributes into equal and similar parts the whole circle in which it is inscribed. The second species of solid is formed out of the same triangles, which unite as eight equilateral triangles and form one solid angle out of four plane angles, and out of six such angles the second body is completed. And the third body is made up of 120 triangular elements, forming twelve solid angles, each of them included in five plane equilateral triangles, having altogether twenty bases, each of which is an equilateral triangle. The one element [that is, the triangle which has its hypothenuse twice the lesser side] having generated these figures, generated no more; but the isosceles triangle produced the fourth elementary figure, which is compounded of four such triangles, joining their right angles in a centre, and forming one equilateral quadrangle. Six of these united form eight solid angles, each of which is made by the combination of three plane right angles; the figure of the body thus composed is a cube, having six plane quadrangular equilateral bases. There was yet a fifth combination which God used in the delineation of the universe.

Now, he who, duly reflecting on all this, enquires whether the worlds are to be regarded as indefinite or definite in number, will be of opinion that the notion of their indefiniteness is characteristic of a sadly indefinite and ignorant mind. He, however, who raises the question whether they are to be truly regarded as one or five, takes up a more reasonable position. Arguing from probabilities, I am of opinion that they

are one; another, regarding the question from another point of view, will be of another mind. But, leaving this enquiry, let us proceed to distribute the elementary forms, which have now been created in idea, among the four elements.

To earth, then, let us assign the cubical form; for earth is the most immoveable of the four and the most plastic of all bodies, and that which has the most stable bases must of necessity be of such a nature. Now, of the triangles which we assumed at first, that which has two equal sides is by nature more firmly based than that which has unequal sides; and of the compound figures which are formed out of either, the plane equilateral quadrangle has necessarily, a more stable basis than the equilateral triangle, both in the whole and in the parts. [56] Wherefore, in assigning this figure to earth, we adhere to probability; and to water we assign that one of the remaining forms which is the least moveable; and the most moveable of them to fire; and to air that which is intermediate. Also we assign the smallest body to fire, and the greatest to water, and the intermediate in size to air; and, again, the acutest body to fire, and the next in acuteness to air, and the third to water. Of all these elements, that which has the fewest bases must necessarily be the most moveable, for it must be the acutest and most penetrating in every way, and also the lightest as being composed of the smallest number of similar particles: and the second body has similar properties in a second degree, and the third body in the third degree. Let it be agreed, then, both according to strict reason and according to probability, that the pyramid is the solid which is the original element and seed of fire; and let us assign the element which was next in the order of generation to air, and the third to water. We must imagine all these to be so small that no single particle of any of the four kinds is seen by us on account of their smallness: but when many of them are collected together their aggregates are seen. And the ratios of their numbers, motions, and other properties, everywhere God, as far as necessity allowed or gave consent, has exactly perfected, and harmonised in due proportion.

From all that we have just been saying about the elements or kinds, the most probable conclusion is as follows:—earth, when meeting with fire and dissolved by its sharpness, whether the dissolution take place in the fire itself or perhaps in some mass of air or water, is borne hither and thither, until its parts, meeting together and mutually harmonising, again become earth; for they can never take any other form. But water, when divided by fire or by air, on re-forming, may become one part fire and two parts air; and a single volume of air divided becomes two of fire. Again, when a small body of fire is contained in a larger body of air or water or earth, and both are moving, and the fire struggling is overcome and broken up, then two volumes of fire form one volume of air; and when air is overcome and cut up into small pieces, two and a half parts of air are condensed into one part of water. Let us consider the matter in another way. When one of the other elements is fastened upon by fire, [57] and is cut by the sharpness of its angles and sides, it coalesces with the fire, and then ceases to be cut by them any longer. For no element which is one and the same with itself can be changed by or change another of the same kind and in the same state. But so long as in the process of transition the weaker is fighting against the stronger, the dissolution continues. Again, when a few small particles, enclosed in many larger ones, are in process of decomposition and extinction, they only cease from their tendency to extinction when they consent to pass into the conquering nature, and fire becomes air and air water. But if bodies of another kind go and attack them [i.e. the small particles], the latter continue to be dissolved until, being completely forced back and dispersed, they make their escape to their own kindred, or else, being overcome and assimilated to the conquering power, they remain where they are and dwell with their victors, and from being many become one. And owing to these affections, all things are changing their place, for by the motion of the receiving vessel the bulk of each class is distributed into its proper place; but those things which become unlike themselves and like other things, are hurried by the shaking into the place of the things to which they grow like.

Now all unmixed and primary bodies are produced by such causes as these. As to the subordinate species which are included in the greater kinds, they are to be attributed to the varieties in the structure of the two original triangles. For either structure did not originally produce the triangle of one size only, but some larger and some smaller, and there are as many sizes as there are species of the four elements. Hence when they are mingled with themselves and with one another there is an endless variety of them, which those who would arrive at the probable truth of nature ought duly to consider.

Unless a person comes to an understanding about the nature and conditions of rest and motion, he will meet with many difficulties in the discussion which follows. Something has been said of this matter already, and something more remains to be said, which is, that motion never exists in what is uniform. For to conceive that anything can be moved without a mover is hard or indeed impossible, and equally impossible to conceive that there can be a mover unless there be something which can be moved—motion cannot exist where either of these are wanting, and for these to be uniform is impossible; wherefore we must assign rest to uniformity and motion to the want of uniformity. [58] Now inequality is the cause of the nature which is wanting in uniformity; and of this we have already described the origin. But there still remains the further point—why things when divided after their kinds do not cease to pass through one another and to change their place —which we will now proceed to explain. In the revolution of the universe are comprehended all the four elements, and this being circular and having a tendency to come together, compresses everything and will not allow any place to be left void. Wherefore, also, fire above all things penetrates everywhere, and air next, as being next in rarity of the elements; and the two other elements in like manner penetrate according to their degrees of rarity. For those things which are composed of the largest particles have the largest void left in their compositions, and those which are composed of the smallest particles have the least. And the contraction caused by the compression thrusts the smaller particles into the interstices of the larger. And thus, when the small parts are placed side by side with the larger, and the lesser divide the greater and the greater unite the lesser, all the elements are borne up and down and hither and thither towards their own places; for the change in the size of each changes its position in space. And these causes generate an inequality which is always maintained, and is continually creating a perpetual motion of the elements in all time.

In the next place we have to consider that there are divers kinds of fire. There are, for example, first, flame; and secondly, those emanations of flame which do not burn but only give light to the eyes; thirdly, the remains of fire, which are seen in red-hot embers after the flame has been extinguished. There are similar differences in the air; of which the brightest part is called the aether, and the most turbid sort mist and darkness; and there are various other nameless kinds which arise from the inequality of the triangles. Water, again, admits in the first place of a division into two kinds; the one liquid and the other fusile. The liquid kind is composed of the small and unequal particles of water; and moves itself and is moved by other bodies owing to the want of uniformity and the shape of its particles; whereas the fusile kind, being formed of large and uniform particles, is more stable than the other, and is heavy and compact by reason of its uniformity. But when fire gets in and dissolves the particles and destroys the uniformity, it has greater mobility, and becoming fluid is thrust forth by the neighbouring air and spreads upon the earth; and this dissolution of the solid masses is called melting, [59] and their spreading out upon the earth flowing. Again, when the fire goes out of the fusile substance, it does not pass into a vacuum, but into the neighbouring air; and the air which is displaced forces together the liquid and still moveable mass into the place which was occupied by the fire, and unites it with itself. Thus compressed the mass resumes its equability, and is again at unity with itself, because the fire which was the author of the inequality has retreated; and this departure of the fire is called cooling, and the coming together which follows upon it is termed congealment. Of all the kinds termed fusile, that which is the densest and is formed out of the finest and most uniform parts is that most precious possession called gold, which is hardened by filtration through rock; this is unique in kind, and has both a glittering and a yellow colour. A shoot of gold, which is so dense as to be very hard, and takes a black colour, is termed adamant. There is also another kind which has parts nearly like gold, and of which there are several species; it is denser than gold, and it contains a small and fine portion of earth, and is therefore harder, yet also lighter because of the great interstices which it has within itself; and this substance, which is one of the bright and denser kinds of water, when solidified is called copper. There is an alloy of earth mingled with it, which, when the two parts grow old and are disunited, shows itself separately and is called rust. The remaining phenomena of the same kind there will be no difficulty in reasoning out by the method of probabilities. A man may sometimes set aside meditations about eternal things, and for recreation turn to consider the truths of generation which are probable only; he will thus gain a pleasure not to be repented of, and secure for himself while he lives a wise

and moderate pastime. Let us grant ourselves this indulgence, and go through the probabilities relating to the same subjects which follow next in order.

Water which is mingled with fire, so much as is fine and liquid (being so called by reason of its motion and the way in which it rolls along the ground), and soft, because its bases give way and are less stable than those of earth, when separated from fire and air and isolated, becomes more uniform, and by their retirement is compressed into itself; and if the condensation be very great, the water above the earth becomes hail, but on the earth, ice; and that which is congealed in a less degree and is only half solid, when above the earth is called snow, and when upon the earth, and condensed from dew, hoarfrost. Then, again, there are the numerous kinds of water which have been mingled with one another, and are distilled through plants which grow in the earth; and this whole class is called by the name of juices or saps. [60] The unequal admixture of these fluids creates a variety of species; most of them are nameless, but four which are of a fiery nature are clearly distinguished and have names. First, there is wine, which warms the soul as well as the body: secondly, there is the oily nature, which is smooth and divides the visual ray, and for this reason is bright and shining and of a glistening appearance, including pitch, the juice of the castor berry, oil itself, and other things of a like kind: thirdly, there is the class of substances which expand the contracted parts [1] of the mouth, until they return to their natural state, and by reason of this property create sweetness; —these are included under the general name of honey: and, lastly, there is a frothy nature, which differs from all juices, having a burning quality which dissolves the flesh; it is called *opos* (a vegetable acid).

As to the kinds of earth, that which is filtered through water passes into stone in the following manner:—The water which mixes with the earth and is broken up in the process changes into air, and taking this form mounts into its own place. But as there is no surrounding vacuum it thrusts away the neighbouring air, and this being rendered heavy, and, when it is displaced, having been poured around the mass of earth, forcibly compresses it and drives it into the vacant space whence the new air had come up; and the earth when compressed by the air into an indissoluble union with water becomes rock. The fairer sort is that which is made up

[1] Cf. 65, 66.

of equal and similar parts and is transparent; that which has the opposite qualities is inferior. But when all the watery part is suddenly drawn out by fire, a more brittle substance is formed, to which we give the name of pottery. Sometimes also moisture may remain, and the earth which has been fused by fire becomes, when cool, a certain stone of a black colour. A like separation of the water which had been copiously mingled with them may occur in two substances composed of finer particles of earth and of a briny nature; out of either of them a half-solid body is then formed, soluble in water— the one, soda, which is used for purging away oil and earth, and other, salt, which harmonizes so well in combinations pleasing to the palate, and is, as the law testifies, a substance dear to the gods. The compounds of earth and water are not soluble by water, but by fire only, and for this reason:—Neither fire nor air melt masses of earth; for their particles, being smaller than the interstices in its structure, have plenty of room to move without forcing their way, and so they leave the earth unmelted and undissolved; but particles of water, [61] which are larger, force a passage, and dissolve and melt the earth. Wherefore earth when not consolidated by force is dissolved by water only; when consolidated, by nothing but fire; for this is the only body which can find an entrance. The cohesion of water again, when very strong, is dissolved by fire only—when weaker, then either by air or fire—the former entering the interstices, and the latter penetrating even the triangles. But nothing can dissolve air, when strongly condensed, which does not reach the elements or triangles; or if not strongly condensed, then only fire can dissolve it. As to bodies composed of earth and water, while the water occupies the vacant interstices of the earth in them which are compressed by force, the particles of water which approach them from without, finding no entrance, flow around the entire mass and leave it undissolved; but the particles of fire, entering into the interstices of the water, do to the water what water does to earth and fire to air, and are the sole causes of the compound body of earth and water liquefying and becoming fluid. Now these bodies are of two kinds; some of them, such as glass and the fusible sort of stones, have less water than they have earth; on the other hand, substances of the nature of wax and incense have more of water entering into their composition.

I have thus shown the various classes of bodies as they are diversified by their forms and combinations and changes into one another, and now I must endeavour to set forth their affections and the causes of them. In the first place, the bodies which I have been describing are necessarily objects of sense. But we have not yet considered the origin of flesh, or what belongs to flesh, or of that part of the soul which is mortal. And these things cannot be adequately explained without also explaining the affections which are concerned with sensation, nor the latter without the former: and yet to explain them together is hardly possible; for which reason we must assume first one or the other and afterwards examine the nature of our hypothesis. In order, then, that the affections may follow regularly after the elements, let us presuppose the existence of body and soul.

First, let us enquire what we mean by saying that fire is hot; and about this we may reason from the dividing or cutting power which it exercises on our bodies. We all of us feel that fire is sharp; and we may further consider the fineness of the sides, and the sharpness of the angles, and the smallness of the particles, and the swiftness of the motion—all this makes the action of fire violent and sharp, [62] so that it cuts whatever it meets. And we must not forget that the original figure of fire [i.e. the pyramid], more than any other form, has a dividing power which cuts our bodies into small pieces ($\kappa\epsilon\rho\mu\alpha\tau\dot{\iota}\zeta\epsilon\iota$), and thus naturally produces that affection which we call heat; and hence the origin of the name ($\theta\epsilon\rho\mu\dot{o}s$, $\kappa\dot{\epsilon}\rho\mu\alpha$). Now, the opposite of this is sufficiently manifest; nevertheless we will not fail to describe it. For the larger particles of moisture which surround the body, entering in and driving out the lesser, but not being able to take their places, compress the moist principle in us; and this from being unequal and disturbed, is forced by them into a state of rest, which is due to equability and compression. But things which are contracted contrary to nature are by nature at war, and force themselves apart; and to this war and convulsion the name of shivering and trembling is given; and the whole affection and the cause of the affection are both termed cold. That is called hard to which our flesh yields, and soft which yields to our flesh; and things are also termed hard and soft relatively to one another. That which yields has a small base; but that which rests on quadrangular bases is firmly posed and belongs to the class which offers the greatest resistance; so too does that which is the most compact and therefore most repellent. The nature of the light and the heavy will be best understood when examined in connexion with our notions of above and below; for it is quite a mistake to suppose that the universe is parted into two regions, separate from and opposite to each other, the one a lower to which all things tend which have any bulk, and an upper to which things only ascend against their will. For as the universe is in the form of a sphere, all the extremities, being equidistant from the centre, are equally extremities, and the centre, which is equidistant from them, is equally to be regarded as the opposite of them all. Such being the nature of the world, when a person says that any of these points is above or below, may he not be justly charged with using an improper expression? For the centre of the world cannot be rightly called either above or below, but is the centre and nothing else; and the circumference is not the centre, and has in no one part of itself a different relation to the centre from what it has in any of the opposite parts. Indeed, when it is in every direction similar, how can one rightly give to it names which imply opposition? For if there were any solid body in equipoise at the centre of the [63] universe, there would be nothing to draw it to this extreme rather than to that, for they are all perfectly similar; and if a person were to go round the world in a circle, he would often, when standing at the antipodes of his former position, speak of the same point as above and below; for, as I was saying just now, to speak of the whole which is in the form of a globe as having one part above and another below is not like a sensible man.

The reason why these names are used, and the circumstances under which they are ordinarily applied by us to the division of the heavens, may be elucidated by the following supposition:—if a person were to stand in that part of the universe which is the appointed place of fire, and where there is the great mass of fire to which fiery bodies gather—if, I say, he were to ascend thither, and, having the power to do this, were to abstract particles of fire and put them in scales and weigh them, and then, raising the balance, were to draw the fire by force towards the uncongenial element of the air, it would be very evident that he could compel the smaller mass more readily than the larger; for when two things are simultaneously raised by one and the same power, the smaller body must necessarily yield to the superior power with less reluctance than the larger; and the larger body is called heavy and said to tend downwards, and the smaller body is called light and said to

tend upwards. And we may detect ourselves who are upon the earth doing precisely the same thing. For we often separate earthy natures, and sometimes earth itself, and draw them into the uncongenial element of air by force and contrary to nature, both clinging to their kindred elements. But that which is smaller yields to the impulse given by us towards the dissimilar element more easily than the larger; and so we call the former light, and the place towards which it is impelled we call above, and the contrary state and place we call heavy and below respectively. Now the relations of these must necessarily vary, because the principal masses of the different elements hold opposite positions; for that which is light, heavy, below or above in one place will be found to be and become contrary and transverse and every way diverse in relation to that which is light, heavy, below or above in an opposite place. And about all of them this has to be considered:—that the tendency of each towards its kindred element makes the body which is moved heavy, and the place towards which the motion tends below, but things which have an opposite tendency we call by an opposite name. Such are the causes which we assign to these phenomena. As to the smooth and the rough, any one who sees them can explain the reason of them to another. For roughness is hardness mingled with irregularity, [64] and smoothness is produced by the joint effect of uniformity and density.

The most important of the affections which concern the whole body remains to be considered—that is, the cause of pleasure and pain in the perceptions of which I have been speaking, and in all other things which are perceived by sense through the parts of the body, and have both pains and pleasures attendant on them. Let us imagine the causes of every affection, whether of sense or not, to be of the following nature, remembering that we have already distinguished between the nature which is easy and which is hard to move; for this is the direction in which we must hunt the prey which we mean to take. A body which is of a nature to be easily moved, on receiving an impression however slight, spreads abroad the motion in a circle, the parts communicating with each other, until at last, reaching the principle of mind, they announce the quality of the agent. But a body of the opposite kind, being immobile, and not extending to the surrounding region, merely receives the impression, and does not stir any of the neighbouring parts; and since the parts do not distribute the original impression to other parts, it has no effect of motion on the whole animal, and therefore produces no effect on the patient. This is true of the bones and hair and other more earthy parts of the human body; whereas what was said above relates mainly to sight and hearing, because they have in them the greatest amount of fire and air. Now we must conceive of pleasure and pain in this way. An impression produced in us contrary to nature and violent, if sudden, is painful; and, again, the sudden return to nature is pleasant; but a gentle and gradual return is imperceptible and *vice versa*. On the other hand the impression of sense which is most easily produced is most readily felt, but is not accompanied by pleasure or pain; such, for example, are the affections of the sight, which, as we said above, is a body naturally uniting with our body in the day-time (45); for cuttings and burnings and other affections which happen to the sight do not give pain, nor is there pleasure when the sight returns to its natural state; but the sensations are clearest and strongest according to the manner in which the eye is affected by the object, and itself strikes and touches it; there is no violence either in the contraction or dilation of the eye. But bodies formed of larger particles yield to the agent only with a struggle; and then they impart their motions to the whole and cause pleasure and pain—pain when alienated from their natural conditions, [65] and pleasure when restored to them. Things which experience gradual withdrawings and emptyings of their nature, and great and sudden replenishments, fail to perceive the emptying, but are sensible of the replenishment; and so they occasion no pain, but the greatest pleasure, to the mortal part of the soul, as is manifest in the case of perfumes. But things which are changed all of a sudden, and only gradually and with difficulty return to their own nature, have effects in every way opposite to the former, as is evident in the case of burnings and cuttings of the body.

Thus have we discussed the general affections of the whole body, and the names of the agents which produce them. And now I will endeavour to speak of the affections of particular parts, and the causes and agents of them, as far as I am able. In the first place let us set forth what was omitted when we were speaking of juices, concerning the affections peculiar to the tongue. These too, like most of the other affections, appear to be caused by certain contractions and dilations, but they have besides more of roughness and smoothness than is found in other affections; for whenever earthy particles enter into the small veins which are the testing instruments of the tongue, reaching to the heart, and fall upon the moist, delicate portions of flesh—when, as they are dissolved, they contract and dry up the little veins, they are astringent if they are rougher, but if not so rough, then only harsh. Those of them which are of an abstergent nature, and purge the whole surface of the tongue, if they do it in excess, and so encroach as to consume some part of the flesh itself, like potash and soda, are all termed bitter. But the particles which are deficient in the alkaline quality, and which cleanse only moderately, are called salt, and having no bitterness or roughness, are regarded as rather agreeable than otherwise. Bodies which share in and are made smooth by the heat of the mouth, and which are inflamed, and again in turn inflame that which heats them, and which are so light that they are carried upwards to the sensations of the head, [66] and cut all that comes in their way, by reason of these qualities in them, are all termed pungent. But when these same particles, refined by putrefaction, enter into the narrow veins, and are duly proportioned to the particles of earth and air which are there, they set them whirling about one another, and while they are in a whirl cause them to dash against and enter into one another, and so form hollows surrounding the particles that enter—which watery vessels of air (for a film of moisture, sometimes earthy, sometimes pure, is spread around the air) are hollow spheres of water; and those of them which are pure, are transparent, and are called bubbles, while those composed of the earthy liquid, which is in a state of general agitation and effervescence, are said to boil or ferment—of all these affections the cause is termed acid. And there is the opposite affection arising from an opposite cause, when the mass of entering particles, immersed in the moisture of the mouth, is congenial to the tongue, and smooths and oils over the roughness, and relaxes the parts which are unnaturally contracted, and contracts the parts which are relaxed, and disposes them all according to their nature—that sort of remedy of violent affections is pleasant and agreeable to every man, and has the name sweet. But enough of this.

The faculty of smell does not admit of differences of kind; for all smells are of a halfformed nature, and no element is so proportioned as to have any smell. The veins about the nose are too narrow to admit earth and water, and too wide to detain fire and air; and for this reason no one ever perceives the smell of any of them; but smells always proceed from bodies that are damp, or putrefying, or liquefying, or evaporating, and are perceptible only in the intermediate state, when water is changing into air and air into water; and all of them are either vapor or mist. That which is passing out of air into water is mist, and that which is passing from water into air is vapour; and hence all smells are thinner than water and thicker than air. The proof of this is, that when there is any obstruction to the respiration, and a man draws in his breath by force, then no smell filters through, but the air without the smell alone penetrates. [67] Wherefore the varieties of smell have no name, and they have not many, or definite and simple kinds; but they are distinguished only as painful and pleasant, the one sort irritating and disturbing the whole cavity which is situated between the head and the navel, the other having a soothing influence, and restoring this same region to an agreeable and natural condition.

In considering the third kind of sense, hearing, we must speak of the causes in which it originates. We may in general assume sound to be a blow which passes through the ears, and is transmitted by means of the air, the brain, and the blood, to the soul, and that hearing is the vibration of this blow, which begins in the head and ends in the region of the liver. The sound which moves swiftly is acute, and the sound which moves slowly is grave, and that which is regular is equable and smooth, and the reverse is harsh. A great body of sound is loud, and a small body of sound the reverse. Respecting the harmonies of sound I must hereafter speak.

There is a fourth class of sensible things, having many intricate varieties, which must now be distinguished. They are called by the general name of colours, and are a flame which emanates from every sort of body, and has particles corresponding to the sense of sight. I have spoken already, in what has preceded, of the causes which generate sight, and in this place it will be natural and suitable to give a rational theory of colours.

Of the particles coming from other bodies which fall upon the sight, some are smaller and some are larger, and some are equal to the parts of the sight itself. Those which are equal are imperceptible, and we call them transparent. The larger produce contraction, the smaller dilation, in the sight, exercising a power akin to that of hot and cold bodies on the flesh, or of astringent bodies on the tongue, or of those heating bodies which we termed pungent. White and black are similar effects of contraction and dilation in another sphere, and for this reason have a different appearance. Wherefore, we ought to term white that which dilates the visual ray, and the opposite of this is black. There is also a swifter motion of a different sort of fire which strikes and dilates the ray of sight until it reaches the eyes, [68] forcing a way through their passages and melting them, and eliciting from them a union of fire and water which we call tears, being itself an opposite fire which comes to them from an opposite direction—the inner fire flashes forth like lightning, and the outer finds a way in and is extinguished in the moisture, and all sorts of colours are generated by the mixture. This affection is termed dazzling, and the object which produces it is called bright and flashing. There is another sort of fire which is intermediate, and which reaches and mingles with the moisture of the eye without flashing; and in this, the fire mingling with the ray of the moisture, produces a colour like blood, to which we give the name of red. A bright hue mingled with red and white gives the colour called auburn. The law of proportion, however, according to which the several colours are formed, even if a man knew he would be foolish in telling, for he could not give any necessary reason, nor indeed any tolerable or probable explanation of them. Again, red, when mingled with black and white, becomes purple, but it becomes umber when the colours are burnt as well as mingled and the black is more thoroughly mixed with them. Flame-colour is produced by a union of auburn and dun, and dun by an admixture of black and white; pale yellow, by an admixture of white and auburn. White and bright meeting, and falling upon a full black, become dark blue, and when dark blue mingles with white, a light blue colour is formed, as flame-colour with black makes leek green. There will be no difficulty in seeing how and by what mixtures the colours derived from these are made according to the rules of probability. He, however, who should attempt to verify all this by experiment, would forget the difference of the human and divine nature. For God only has the knowledge and also the power which are able to combine many things into one and again resolve the one into many. But no man either is or ever will be able to accomplish either the one or the other operation.

These are the elements, thus of necessity then subsisting, which the creator of the fairest and best of created things associated with himself, when he made the self-sufficing and most perfect God, using the necessary causes as his ministers in the accomplishment of his work, but himself contriving the good in all his creations. Wherefore we may distinguish two sorts of causes, the one divine and the other necessary, and may seek for the divine in all things, as far as our nature admits, *[69]* with a view to the blessed life; but the necessary kind only for the sake of the divine, considering that without them and when isolated from them, these higher things for which we look cannot be apprehended or received or in any way shared by us.

Seeing, then, that we have now prepared for our use the various classes of causes which are the material out of which the remainder of our discourse must be woven, just as wood is the material of the carpenter, let us revert in a few words to the point at which we began, and then endeavour to add on a suitable ending to the beginning of our tale.

As I said at first, when all things were in disorder God created in each thing in relation to itself, and in all things in relation to each other, all the measures and harmonies which they could possibly receive. For in those days nothing had any proportion except by accident; nor did any of the things which now have names deserve to be named at all—as, for example, fire, water, and the rest of the elements. All these the creator first set in order, and out of them he constructed the universe, which was a single animal comprehending in itself all other animals, mortal and immortal. Now of the divine, he himself was the creator, but the creation of the mortal he committed to his offspring. And they, imitating him, received from him the immortal principle of the soul; and around this they proceeded to fashion a mortal body, and made it to be the vehicle of the soul, and constructed within the body a soul of another nature which was mortal, subject to terrible and irresistible affections—first of all, pleasure, the greatest incitement to evil; then, pain, which deters from good; also rashness and fear, two foolish counsellors, anger hard to be appeased, and hope easily led astray—these they mingled with irrational sense and with all-daring love according to necessary laws, and so framed man. Wherefore, fearing to pollute the divine any more than was absolutely unavoidable, they gave to the mortal nature a separate habitation in another part of the body, placing the neck between them to be the isthmus and boundary, which they constructed between the

head and breast, to keep them apart. And in the breast, and in what is termed the thorax, they encased the mortal soul; and as the one part of this was superior and the other inferior they divided the cavity of the *[70]* thorax into two parts, as the women's and men's apartments are divided in houses, and placed the midriff to be a wall of partition between them. That part of the inferior soul which is endowed with courage and passion and loves contention they settled nearer the head, midway between the midriff and the neck, in order that it might be under the rule of reason and might join with it in controlling and restraining the desires when they are no longer willing of their own accord to obey the word of command issuing from the citadel.

The heart, the knot of the veins and the fountain of the blood which races through all the limbs was set in the place of guard, that when the might of passion was roused by reason making proclamation of any wrong assailing them from without or being perpetrated by the desires within, quickly the whole power of feeling in the body, perceiving these commands and threats, might obey and follow through every turn and alley, and thus allow the principle of the best to have the command in all of them. But the gods, foreknowing that the palpitation of the heart in the expectation of danger and the swelling and excitement of passion was caused by fire, formed and implanted as a supporter to the heart the lung, which was, in the first place, soft and bloodless, and also had within hollows like the pores of a sponge, in order that by receiving the breath and the drink, it might give coolness and the power of respiration and alleviate the heat. Wherefore they cut the air-channels leading to the lung, and placed the lung about the heart as a soft spring, that, when passion was rife within, the heart, beating against a yielding body, might be cooled and suffer less, and might thus become more ready to join with passion in the service of reason.

The part of the soul which desires meats and drinks and the other things of which it has need by reason of the bodily nature, they placed between the midriff and the boundary of the navel, contriving in all this region a sort of manger for the food of the body; and there they bound it down like a wild animal which was chained up with man, and must be nourished if man was to exist. They appointed this lower creation his place here in order that he might be always feeding at the manger, and have his

sensation—as, for example, the tongue. But commonly this is not the case. For the nature which comes into being and grows up in us by a law of necessity, does not admit of the combination of solid bone and much flesh with acute perceptions. More than any other part the framework of the head would have had them, if they could have co-existed, and the human race, having a strong and fleshy and sinewy head, would have had a life twice or many times as long as it now has, and also more healthy and free from pain.

But our creators, considering whether they should make a longer-lived race which was worse, or a shorter-lived race which was better, came to the conclusion that every one ought to prefer a shorter span of life, which was better, to a longer one, which was worse; and therefore they covered the head with thin bone, but not with flesh and sinews, since it had no joints; and thus the head was added, having more wisdom and sensation than the rest of the body, but also being in every man far weaker. For these reasons and after this manner God placed the sinews at the extremity of the head, in a circle round the neck, and glued them together by the principle of likeness and fastened the extremities of the jawbones to them below the face, and the other sinews he dispersed throughout the body, fastening limb to limb. The framers of us framed the mouth, as now arranged, having teeth and tongue and lips, with a view to the necessary and the good, contriving the way in for necessary purposes, the way out for the best purposes; for that is necessary which enters in and gives food to the body; but the river of speech, which flows out of a man and ministers to the intelligence, is the fairest and noblest of all streams. Still the head could neither be left a bare frame of bones, on account of the extremes of heat and cold in the different seasons, nor yet be allowed to be wholly covered, and so become dull and senseless by reason of an overgrowth of flesh. The fleshy nature was not therefore wholly dried up, [76] but a large sort of peel was parted off and remained over, which is now called the skin. This met and grew by the help of the cerebral moisture, and became the circular envelopment of the head. And the moisture, rising up under the sutures, watered and closed in the skin upon the crown, forming a sort of knot. The diversity of the sutures was caused by the power of the courses of the soul and of the food, and the more these struggled against one another the more numerous they became, and fewer if the struggle were

less violent. This skin the divine power pierced all round with fire, and out of the punctures which were thus made the moisture issued forth, and the liquid and heat which was pure came away, and a mixed part which was composed of the same material as the skin, and had a fineness equal to the punctures, was borne up by its own impulse and extended far outside the head, but being too slow to escape, was thrust back by the external air, and rolled up underneath the skin, where it took root. Thus the hair sprang up in the skin, being akin to it because it is like threads of leather, but rendered harder and closer through the pressure of the cold, by which each hair, while in process of separation from the skin, is compressed and cooled. Wherefore the creator formed the head hairy, making use of the causes which I have mentioned, and reflecting also that instead of flesh the brain needed the hair to be a light covering or guard, which would give shade in summer and shelter in winter, and at the same time would not impede our quickness of perception. From the combination of sinew, skin, and bone, in the structure of the finger, there arises a triple compound, which, when dried up, takes the form of one hard skin partaking of all three natures, and was fabricated by these second causes, but designed by mind which is the principal cause with an eye to the future. For our creators well knew that women and other animals would some day be framed out of men, and they further knew that many animals would require the use of nails for many purposes; wherefore they fashioned in men at their first creation the rudiments of nails. For this purpose and for these reasons they caused skin, hair, and nails to grow at the extremities of the limbs. And now that all the parts and members of the mortal animal had [77] come together, since its life of necessity consisted of fire and breath, and it therefore wasted away by dissolution and depletion, the gods contrived the following remedy: They mingled a nature akin to that of man with other forms and perceptions, and thus created another kind of animal. These are the trees and plants and seeds which have been improved by cultivation and are now domesticated among us; anciently there were only the wild kinds, which are older than the cultivated. For everything that partakes of life may be truly called a living being, and the animal of which we are now speaking partakes of the third kind of soul, which is said to be seated between the midriff and the navel, having no part in opinion or reason or mind, but only in feelings of pleasure and pain and the desires which accompany them. For this nature is always in a passive state, revolving in and about itself, repelling the motion from without and using its own, and accordingly is not endowed by nature with the power of observing or reflecting on its own concerns. Wherefore it lives and does not differ from a living being, but is fixed and rooted in the same spot, having no power of self-motion.

Now after the superior powers had created all these natures to be food for us who are of the inferior nature, they cut various channels through the body as through a garden, that it might be watered as from a running stream. In the first place, they cut two hidden channels or veins down the back where the skin and the flesh join, which answered severally to the right and left side of the body. These they let down along the backbone, so as to have the marrow of generation between them, where it was most likely to flourish, and in order that the stream coming down from above might flow freely to the other parts, and equalise the irrigation. In the next place, they divided the veins about the head, and interlacing them, they sent them in opposite directions; those coming from the right side they sent to the left of the body, and those from the left they diverted towards the right, so that they and the skin might together form a bond which should fasten the head to the body, since the crown of the head was not encircled by sinews; and also in order that the sensations from both sides might be distributed over the whole body. And next, they ordered the water-courses of the body in a manner which I will describe, [78] and which will be more easily understood if we begin by admitting that all things which have lesser parts retain the greater, but the greater cannot retain the lesser. Now of all natures fire has the smallest parts, and therefore penetrates through earth and water and air and their compounds, nor can anything hold it. And a similar principle applies to the human belly; for when meats and drinks enter it, it holds them, but it cannot hold air and fire, because the particles of which they consist are smaller than its own structure.

These elements, therefore, God employed for the sake of distributing moisture from the belly into the veins, weaving together a network of fire and air like a weel, having at the entrance two lesser weels; further he constructed one of these with two openings, and from the lesser weels he extended cords reaching all round to the extremities of the network. All the interior of the net he made of fire, but the lesser weels and their cavity, of air. The network he took and spread over the newly-formed animal in the following manner:—He let the lesser weels pass into the mouth; there were two of them, and one he let down by the air-pipes into the lungs, the other by the side of the air-pipes into the belly. The former he divided into two branches, both of which he made to meet at the channels of the nose, so that when the way through the mouth did not act, the streams of the mouth as well were replenished through the nose. With the other cavity (i.e. of the greater weel) he enveloped the hollow parts of the body, and at one time he made all this to flow into the lesser weels, quite gently, for they are composed of air, and at another time he caused the lesser weels to flow back again; and the net he made to find a way in and out through the pores of the body, and the rays of fire which are bound fast within followed the passage of the air either way, never at any time ceasing so long as the mortal being holds together. This process, as we affirm, the name-giver named inspiration and expiration. And all this movement, active as well as passive, takes place in order that the body, being watered and cooled, may receive nourishment and life; for when the respiration is going in and out, and the fire, which is fast bound within, follows it, and ever and anon moving to and fro, enters through the belly and reaches the meat and drink, [79] it dissolves them, and dividing them into small portions and guiding them through the passages where it goes, pumps them as from a fountain into the channels of the veins, and makes the stream of the veins flow through the body as through a conduit.

Let us once more consider the phenomena of respiration, and enquire into the causes which have made it what it is. They are as follows:— Seeing that there is no such thing as a vacuum into which any of those things which are moved can enter, and the breath is carried from us into the external air, the next point is, as will be clear to every one, that it does not go into a vacant space, but pushes its neighbour out of its place, and that which is thrust out in turn drives out its neighbour; and in this way everything of necessity at last comes round to that place from whence the breath came forth, and enters in there, and following the breath, fills up the vacant space; and this goes on like the rotation of a wheel, because there can be no such thing as a vacuum. Wherefore also the breast and the lungs, when they emit the breath, are replenished by the air which surrounds the body and which enters in through the pores of the flesh and is driven round in a circle; and again, the air which is sent away and passes out through the body forces the breath inwards through the passage of the mouth and the nostrils. Now the origin of this movement may be supposed to be as follows. In the interior of every animal the hottest part is that which is around the blood and veins; it is in a manner an internal fountain of fire, which we compare to the network of a creel, being woven all of fire and extended through the centre of the body, while the outer parts are composed of air. Now we must admit that heat naturally proceeds outward to its own place and to its kindred element; and as there are two exits for the heat, the one out through the body, and the other through the mouth and nostrils, when it moves towards the one, it drives round the air at the other, and that which is driven round falls into the fire and becomes warm, and that which goes forth is cooled. But when the heat changes its place, and the particles at the other exit grow warmer, the hotter air inclining in that direction and carried towards its native element, fire, pushes round the air at the other; and this being affected in the same way and communicating the same impulse, a circular motion swaying to and fro is produced by the double process, which we call inspiration and expiration.

The phenomena of medical cupping-glasses and of the swallowing of drink and of the projection of bodies, [80] whether discharged in the air or bowled along the ground, are to be investigated on a similar principle; and swift and slow sounds, which appear to be high and low, and are sometimes discordant on account of their inequality, and then again harmonical on account of the equality of the motion which they excite in us. For when the motions of the antecedent swifter sounds begin to pause and the two are equalised, the slower sounds overtake the swifter and then propel them. When they overtake them they do not intrude a new and discordant motion, but introduce the beginnings of a slower, which answers to the swifter as it dies away, thus producing a single mixed expression out of high and low, whence arises a pleasure which even the unwise feel, and which to the wise becomes a higher sort of delight, being an imitation of divine harmony in mortal motions. Moreover, as to the flowing of water, the fall of the thunderbolt, and the marvels that are observed about the attraction of am-

ber and the Heraclean stones,—in none of these cases is there any attraction; but he who investigates rightly, will find that such wonderful phenomena are attributable to the combination of certain conditions—the non-existence of a vacuum, the fact that objects push one another round, and that they change places, passing severally into their proper positions as they are divided or combined.

Such as we have seen, is the nature and such are the causes of respiration—the subject in which this discussion originated. For the fire cuts the food and following the breath surges up within, fire and breath rising together and filling the veins by drawing up out of the belly and pouring into them the cut portions of the food; and so the streams of food are kept flowing through the whole body in all animals. And fresh cuttings from kindred substances, whether the fruits of the earth or herb of the field, which God planted to be our daily food, acquire all sorts of colours by their inter-mixture; but red is the most pervading of them, being created by the cutting action of fire and by the impression which it makes on a moist substance; and hence the liquid which circulates in the body has a colour such as we have described. The liquid itself we call blood, which nourishes the flesh and the whole body, [81] whence all parts are watered and empty places filled.

Now the process of repletion and evacuation is effected after the manner of the universal motion by which all kindred substances are drawn towards one another. For the external elements which surround us are always causing us to consume away, and distributing and sending off like to like; the particles of blood, too, which are divided and contained within the frame of the animal as in a sort of heaven, are compelled to imitate the motion of the universe. Each, therefore, of the divided parts within us, being carried to its kindred nature, replenishes the void. When more is taken away than flows in, then we decay, and when less, we grow and increase.

The frame of the entire creature when young has the triangles of each kind new, and may be compared to the keel of a vessel which is just off the stocks; they are locked firmly together and yet the whole mass is soft and delicate, being freshly formed of marrow and nurtured on milk. Now when the triangles out of which meats and drinks are composed come in from without, and are comprehended in the body, being older and weaker than the triangles already there, the frame of the body gets the better of them and its newer triangles cut them up, and so the animal grows great, being nourished by a multitude of similar particles. But when the roots of the triangles are loosened by having undergone many conflicts with many things in the course of time, they are no longer able to cut or assimilate the food which enters, but are themselves easily divided by the bodies which come in from without. In this way every animal is overcome and decays, and this affection is called old age. And at last, when the bonds by which the triangles of the marrow are united no longer hold, and are parted by the strain of existence, they in turn loosen the bonds of the soul, and she, obtaining a natural release, flies away with joy. For that which takes place according to nature is pleasant, but that which is contrary to nature is painful. And thus death, if caused by disease or produced by wounds, is painful and violent; but that sort of death which comes with old age and fulfils the debt of nature is the easiest of deaths, and is accompanied with pleasure rather than with pain.

Now every one can see whence diseases arise. There are four natures out of which the body is compacted, [82] earth and fire and water and air, and the unnatural excess or defect of these, or the change of any of them from its own natural place into another, or—since there are more kinds than one of fire and of the other elements—the assumption by any of these of a wrong kind, or any similar irregularity, produces disorders and diseases; for when any of them is produced or changed in a manner contrary to nature, the parts which were previously cool grow warm, and those which were dry become moist, and the light become heavy, and the heavy light; all sorts of changes occur. For, as we affirm, a thing can only remain the same with itself, whole and sound, when the same is added to it, or subtracted from it, in the same respect and in the same manner and in due proportion; and whatever comes or goes away in violation of these laws causes all manner of changes and infinite diseases and corruptions. Now there is a second class of structures which are also natural, and this affords a second opportunity of observing diseases to him who would understand them. For whereas marrow and bone and flesh and sinews are composed of the four elements, and the blood, though after another manner, is likewise formed out of them, most diseases originate in the way which I have described; but the worst of all owe their severi-

ty to the fact that the generation of these substances proceeds in a wrong order; they are then destroyed. For the natural order is that the flesh and sinews should be made of blood, the sinews out of the fibres to which they are akin, and the flesh out of the clots which are formed when the fibres are separated. And the glutinous and rich matter which comes away from the sinews and the flesh, not only glues the flesh to the bones, but nourishes and imparts growth to the bone which surrounds the marrow; and by reason of the solidity of the bones, that which filters through consists of the purest and smoothest and oiliest sort of triangles, dropping like dew from the bones and watering the marrow.

Now when each process takes place in this order, health commonly results; when in the opposite order, disease. For when the flesh becomes decomposed and sends back the wasting substance into the veins, then an over-supply of blood of diverse kinds, mingling with air in the veins, having variegated colours and bitter properties, as well as acid and saline qualities, contains all sorts of bile and serum and phlegm. For all things go the wrong way, [83] and having become corrupted, first they taint the blood itself, and then ceasing to give nourishment to the body they are carried along the veins in all directions, no longer preserving the order of their natural courses, but at war with themselves, because they receive no good from one another, and are hostile to the abiding constitution of the body, which they corrupt and dissolve. The oldest part of the flesh which is corrupted, being hard to decompose, from long burning grows black, and from being everywhere corroded becomes bitter, and is injurious to every part of the body which is still uncorrupted. Sometimes, when the bitter element is refined away, the black part assumes an acidity which takes the place of the bitterness; at other times the bitterness being tinged with blood has a redder colour; and this, when mixed with black, takes the hue of grass; and again, an auburn colour mingles with the bitter matter when new flesh is decomposed by the fire which surrounds the internal flame—to all which symptoms some physician perhaps, or rather some philosopher, who had the power of seeing in many dissimilar things one nature deserving of a name, has assigned the common name of bile. But the other kinds of bile are variously distinguished by their colours. As for serum, that sort which is the watery part of blood is innocent, but that which is a secretion of black and acid bile is malignant when mingled by the power of heat with any salt substance, and is then called acid phlegm.

Again, the substance which is formed by the liquefaction of new and tender flesh when air is present, if inflated and encased in liquid so as to form bubbles, which separately are invisible owing to their small size, but when collected are of a bulk which is visible, and have a white colour arising out of the generation of foam—all this decomposition of tender flesh when inter-mingled with air is termed by us white phlegm. And the whey or sediment of newly-formed phlegm is sweat and tears, and includes the various daily discharges by which the body is purified. Now all these become causes of disease when the blood is not replenished in a natural manner by food and drink but gains bulk from opposite sources in violation of the laws of nature. [84] When the several parts of the flesh are separated by disease, if the foundation remains, the power of the disorder is only half as great, and there is still a prospect of an easy recovery; but when that which binds the flesh to the bones is diseased, and no longer being separated from the muscles and sinews, ceases to give nourishment to the bone and to unite flesh and bone, and from being oily and smooth and glutinous becomes rough and salt and dry, owing to bad regimen, then all the substance thus corrupted crumbles away under the flesh and the sinews, and separates from the bone, and the fleshy parts fall away from their foundation and leave the sinews bare and full of brine, and the flesh again gets into the circulation of the blood and makes the previously-mentioned disorders still greater. And if these bodily affections be severe, still worse are the prior disorders; as when the bone itself, by reason of the density of the flesh, does not obtain sufficient air, but becomes mouldy and hot and gangrened and receives no nutriment, and the natural process is inverted, and the bone crumbling passes into the food, and the food into the flesh, and the flesh again falling into the blood makes all maladies that may occur more virulent than those already mentioned. But the worst case of all is when the marrow is diseased, either from excess or defect; and this is the cause of the very greatest and most fatal disorders, in which the whole course of the body is reversed.

There is a third class of diseases which may be conceived of as arising in three ways; for they are produced sometimes by wind, and sometimes by phlegm, and sometimes by bile. When the lung, which is the dispenser of the air to the body, is obstructed by rheums and its passages are not free, some of them not acting, while through others too much air enters, then the parts which are unrefreshed by air corrode, while in other parts the excess of air forcing its way through the veins distorts them and decomposing the body is enclosed in the midst of it and occupies the midriff; thus numberless painful diseases are produced, accompanied by copious sweats. And oftentimes when the flesh is dissolved in the body, wind, generated within and unable to escape, is the source of quite as much pain as the air coming in from without; but the greatest pain is felt when the wind gets about the sinews and the veins of the shoulders, and swells them up, and so twists back the great tendons and the sinews which are connected with them. These disorders are called tetanus and opisthotonus, by reason of the tension which accompanies them. The cure of them is difficult; relief is in most cases given by fever supervening. [85] The white phlegm, though dangerous when detained within by reason of the air-bubbles, yet if it can communicate with the outside air, is less severe, and only discolours the body, generating leprous eruptions and similar diseases. When it is mingled with black bile and dispersed about the courses of the head, which are the divinest part of us, the attack if coming on in sleep, is not so severe; but when assailing those who are awake it is hard to be got rid of, and being an affection of a sacred part, is most justly called sacred. An acid and salt phlegm, again, is the source of all those diseases which take the form of catarrh, but they have many names because the places into which they flow are manifold.

Inflammations of the body come from burnings and inflamings, and all of them originate in bile. When bile finds a means of discharge, it boils up and sends forth all sorts of tumours; but when imprisoned within, it generates many inflammatory diseases, above all when mingled with pure blood; since it then displaces the fibres which are scattered about in the blood and are designed to maintain the balance of rare and dense, in order that the blood may not be so liquefied by heat as to exude from the pores of the body, nor again become too dense and thus find a difficulty in circulating through the veins. The fibres are so constituted as to maintain this balance; and if any one brings them all together when the blood is dead and in process of cooling, then the blood which remains becomes fluid, but if they are left alone, they soon congeal by reason of the surrounding cold. The fibres having this power over the blood, bile, which is only stale blood, and which from being flesh is dissolved again into blood, at the first influx coming in little by little, hot and liquid, is congealed by the power of the fibres; and so congealing and made to cool, it produces internal cold and shuddering. When it enters with more of a flood and overcomes the fibres by its heat, and boiling up throws them into disorder, if it have power enough to maintain its supremacy, it penetrates the marrow and burns up what may be termed the cables of the soul, and sets her free; but when there is not so much of it, and the body though wasted still holds out, the bile is itself mastered, and is either utterly banished, or is thrust through the veins into the lower or upper belly, and is driven out of the body like an exile from a state in which there has been civil war; [86] whence arise diarrhoeas and dysenteries, and all such disorders. When the constitution is disordered by excess of fire, continuous heat and fever are the result; when excess of air is the cause, then the fever is quotidian; when of water, which is a more sluggish element than either fire or air, then the fever is a tertian; when of earth, which is the most sluggish of the four, and is only purged away in a four-fold period, the result is a quartan fever, which can with difficulty be shaken off.

Such is the manner in which diseases of the body arise; the disorders of the soul, which depend upon the body, originate as follows. We must acknowledge disease of the mind to be a want of intelligence; and of this there are two kinds; to wit, madness and ignorance. In whatever state a man experiences either of them, that state may be called disease; and excessive pains and pleasures are justly to be regarded as the greatest diseases to which the soul is liable. For a man who is in great joy or in great pain, in his unseasonable eagerness to attain the one and to avoid the other, is not able to see or to hear anything rightly; but he is mad, and is at the time utterly incapable of any participation in reason. He who has the seed about the spinal marrow too plentiful and overflowing, like a tree overladen with fruit, has many throes, and also obtains many pleasures in his desires and their offspring, and is for the most part of his life deranged, because his pleasures and pains are so very great; his soul is rendered foolish and disordered by his body; yet he is regarded not as one diseased, but as one who is voluntarily bad, which is a mistake. The truth is that the

intemperance of love is a disease of the soul due chiefly to the moisture and fluidity which is produced in one of the elements by the loose consistency of the bones. And in general, all that which is termed the incontinence of pleasure and is deemed a reproach under the idea that the wicked voluntarily do wrong is not justly a matter for reproach. For no man is voluntarily bad; but the bad become bad by reason of an ill disposition of the body and bad education, things which are hateful to every man and happen to him against his will. And in the case of pain too in like manner the soul suffers much evil from the body. For where the acid and briny phlegm and other bitter and bilious humours wander about in the body, and find no exit or escape, but are pent up within and mingle their own vapours with the motions of the soul, and are blended, [87] with them, they produce all sorts of diseases, more or fewer, and in every degree of intensity; and being carried to the three places of the soul, whichever they may severally assail, they create infinite varieties of ill-temper and melancholy, of rashness and cowardice, and also of forgetfulness and stupidity. Further, when to this evil constitution of body evil forms of government are added and evil discourses are uttered in private as well as in public, and no sort of instruction is given in youth to cure these evils, then all of us who are bad become bad from two causes which are entirely beyond our control. In such cases the planters are to blame rather than the plants, the educators rather than the educated. But however that may be, we should endeavour as far as we can by education, and studies, and learning, to avoid vice and attain virtue; this, however, is part of another subject.

There is a corresponding enquiry concerning the mode of treatment by which the mind and the body are to be preserved, about which it is meet and right that I should say a word in turn; for it is more our duty to speak of the good than of the evil. Everything that is good is fair, and the fair is not without proportion, and the animal which is to be fair must have due proportion. Now we perceive lesser symmetries or proportions and reason about them, but of the highest and greatest we take no heed; for there is no proportion or disproportion more productive of health and disease, and virtue and vice, than that between soul and body. This however we do not perceive, nor do we reflect that when a weak or small frame is the vehicle of a great and mighty soul, or conversely, when a little soul is encased in a large body, then the whole animal is not fair, for it lacks the most important of all symmetries; but the due proportion of mind and body is the fairest and loveliest of all sights to him who has the seeing eye. Just as a body which has a leg too long, or which is unsymmetrical in some other respect, is an unpleasant sight, and also, when doing its share of work, is much distressed and makes convulsive efforts, and often stumbles through awkwardness, and is the cause of infinite evil to its own self—in like manner we should conceive of the double nature which we call the living being; and when in this compound there is an impassioned soul more powerful than the body, *[88]* that soul, I say, convulses and fills with disorders the whole inner nature of man; and when eager in the pursuit of some sort of learning or study, causes wasting; or again, when teaching or disputing in private or in public, and strifes and controversies arise, inflames and dissolves the composite frame of man and introduces rheums; and the nature of this phenomenon is not understood by most professors of medicine, who ascribe it to the opposite of the real cause. And once more, when a body large and too strong for the soul is united to a small and weak intelligence, then inasmuch as there are two desires natural to man,—one of food for the sake of the body, and one of wisdom for the sake of the diviner part of us—then, I say, the motions of the stronger, getting the better and increasing their own power, but making the soul dull, and stupid, and forgetful, engender ignorance, which is the greatest of diseases. There is one protection against both kinds of disproportion:—that we should not move the body without the soul or the soul without the body, and thus they will be on their guard against each other, and be healthy and well balanced. And therefore the mathematician or any one else whose thoughts are much absorbed in some intellectual pursuit, must allow his body also to have due exercise, and practise gymnastic; and he who is careful to fashion the body, should in turn impart to the soul its proper motions, and should cultivate music and all philosophy, if he would deserve to be called truly fair and truly good. And the separate parts should be treated in the same manner, in imitation of the pattern of the universe; for as the body is heated and also cooled within by the elements which enter into it, and is again dried up and moistened by external things, and experiences these and the like affections from both kinds of motions, the result is that the body if given up to motion when in a state of quiescence is overmastered

and perishes; but if any one, in imitation of that which we call the foster-mother and nurse of the universe, will not allow the body ever to be inactive, but is always producing motions and agitations through its whole extent, which form the natural defence against other motions both internal and external, and by moderate exercise reduces to order according to their affinities the particles and affections which are wandering about the body, as we have already said when speaking of the universe,[1] he will not allow enemy placed by the side of enemy to stir up wars and disorders in the body, but he will place friend by the side of friend, so as to create health.

Now of all motions that is the best which is produced in a thing by itself, *[89]* for it is most akin to the motion of thought and of the universe; but that motion which is caused by others is not so good, and worst of all is that which moves the body, when at rest, in parts only and by some external agency. Wherefore of all modes of purifying and reuniting the body the best is gymnastic; the next best is a surging motion, as in sailing or any other mode of conveyance which is not fatiguing; the third sort of motion may be of use in a case of extreme necessity, but in any other will be adopted by no man of sense: I mean the purgative treatment of physicians; for diseases unless they are very dangerous should not be irritated by medicines, since every form of disease is in a manner akin to the living being, whose complex frame has an appointed term of life. For not the whole race only, but each individual—barring inevitable accidents—comes into the world having a fixed span, and the triangles in us are originally framed with power to last for a certain time, beyond which no man can prolong his life. And this holds also of the constitution of diseases; if any one regardless of the appointed time tries to subdue them by medicine, he only aggravates and multiplies them. Wherefore we ought always to manage them by regimen, as far as a man can spare the time, and not provoke a disagreeable enemy by medicines.

Enough of the composite animal, and of the body which is a part of him, and of the manner in which a man may train and be trained by himself so as to live most according to reason: and we must above and before all provide that the element which is to train him shall be the fairest and best adapted to that purpose. A minute discussion of this subject would be a serious task; but if, as before, I am to give only an

[1] Cf. 33.

outline, the subject may not unfitly be summed up as follows.

I have often remarked that there are three kinds of soul located within us, having each of them motions, and I must now repeat in the fewest words possible, that one part, if remaining inactive and ceasing from its natural motion, must necessarily become very weak, but that which is trained and exercised, very strong. Wherefore we should take care that the movements of the different parts *[90]* of the soul should be in due proportion.

And we should consider that God gave the sovereign part of the human soul to be the divinity of each one, being that part which, as we say, dwells at the top of the body, and inasmuch as we are a plant not of an earthly but of a heavenly growth, raises us from earth to our kindred who are in heaven. And in this we say truly; for the divine power suspended the head and root of us from that place where the generation of the soul first began, and thus made the whole body upright. When a man is always occupied with the cravings of desire and ambition, and is eagerly striving to satisfy them, all his thoughts must be mortal, and, as far as it is possible altogether to become such, he must be mortal every whit, because he has cherished his mortal part. But he who has been earnest in the love of knowledge and of true wisdom, and has exercised his intellect more than any other part of him, must have thoughts immortal and divine, if he attain truth, and in so far as human nature is capable of sharing in immortality, he must altogether be immortal; and since he is ever cherishing the divine power, and has the divinity within him in perfect order, he will be perfectly happy. Now there is only one way of taking care of things, and this is to give to each the food and motion which are natural to it. And the motions which are naturally akin to the divine principle within us are the thoughts and revolutions of the universe. These each man should follow, and correct the courses of the head which were corrupted at our birth, and by learning the harmonies and revolutions of the universe, should assimilate the thinking being to the thought, renewing his original nature, and having assimilated them should attain to that perfect life which the gods have set before mankind, both for the present and the future.

Thus our original design of discoursing about the universe down to the creation of man is nearly completed. A brief mention may be made of the generation of other animals, so far as the subject admits of brevity; in this manner our argument will best attain a due proportion. On the subject of animals, then, the following remarks may be offered. Of the men who came into the world, those who were cowards or led unrighteous lives may with reason be supposed to have changed into the nature of women in the second generation.*[91]* And this was the reason why at that time the gods created in us the desire of sexual intercourse, contriving in man one animated substance, and in woman another, which they formed respectively in the following manner. The outlet for drink by which liquids pass through the lung under the kidneys and into the bladder, which receives and then by the pressure of the air emits them, was so fashioned by them as to penetrate also into the body of the marrow, which passes from the head along the neck and through the back, and which in the preceding discourse we have named the seed. And the seed having life, and becoming endowed with respiration, produces in that part in which it respires a lively desire of emission, and thus creates in us the love of procreation. Wherefore also in men the organ of generation becoming rebellious and masterful, like an animal disobedient to reason, and maddened with the sting of lust, seeks to gain absolute sway; and the same is the case with the so-called womb or matrix of women; the animal within them is desirous of procreating children, and when remaining unfruitful long beyond its proper time, gets discontented and angry, and wandering in every direction through the body, closes up the passages of the breath, and, by obstructing respiration, drives them to extremity, causing all varieties of disease, until at length the desire and love of the man and the woman, bringing them together and as it were plucking the fruit from the tree, sow in the womb, as in a field, animals unseen by reason of their smallness and without form; these again are separated and matured within; they are then finally brought out into the light, and thus the generation of animals is completed.

Thus were created women and the female sex in general. But the race of birds was created out of innocent light-minded men, who, although their minds were directed toward heaven, imagined, in their simplicity, that the clearest demonstration of the things above was to be obtained by sight; these were remodelled and transformed into birds, and they grew feathers instead of hair. The race of wild pedestrian animals, again, came from those who had no philosophy in any of their thoughts, and never considered at all about the nature of the heavens, because they had ceased to use the courses of the head, but followed the guidance of those parts of the soul which are in the breast. In consequence of these habits of theirs they had their front-legs and their heads resting upon the earth to which they were drawn by natural affinity; and the crowns of their heads were elongated and of all sorts of shapes, into which the courses of the soul were crushed by reason of disuse. And this was the reason why they were created quadrupeds and polypods: *[92]* God gave the more senseless of them the more support that they might be more attracted to the earth. And the most foolish of them, who trail their bodies entirely upon the ground and have no longer any need of feet, he made without feet to crawl upon the earth. The fourth class were the inhabitants of the water: these were made out of the most entirely senseless and ignorant of all, whom the transformers did not think any longer worthy of pure respiration, because they possessed a soul which was made impure by all sorts of transgression; and instead of the subtle and pure medium of air, they gave them the deep and muddy sea to be their element of respiration; and hence arose the race of fishes and oysters, and other aquatic animals, which have received the most remote habitations as a punishment of their outlandish ignorance. These are the laws by which animals pass into one another, now, as ever, changing as they lose or gain wisdom and folly.

We may now say that our discourse about the nature of the universe has an end. The world has received animals, mortal and immortal, and is fulfilled with them, and has become a visible animal containing the visible—the sensible God who is the image of the intellectual, the greatest, best, fairest, most perfect—the one only-begotten heaven.

CRITIAS

PERSONS OF THE DIALOGUE: CRITIAS; HERMOCRATES; TIMAEUS; SOCRATES

[106] *Timaeus.* How thankful I am, Socrates, that I have arrived at last, and, like a weary traveller after a long journey, may be at rest! And I pray the being who always was of old, and has now been by me revealed, to grant that my words may endure in so far as they have been spoken truly and acceptably to him; but if unintentionally I have said anything wrong, I pray that he will impose upon me a just retribution, and the just retribution of him who errs is that he should be set right. Wishing, then, to speak truly in future concerning the generation of the gods, I pray him to give me knowledge, which of all medicines is the most perfect and best. And now having offered my prayer I deliver up the argument to Critias, who is to speak next according to our agreement.[1]

Critias. And I, Timaeus, accept the trust, and as you at first said that you were going to speak of high matters, and begged that some forbearance might be shown to you, I too ask the same or greater forbearance for what I am about to say. And although I very well know that my request may appear to be somewhat ambitious and discourteous, I must make it nevertheless. [107] For will any man of sense deny that you have spoken well? I can only attempt to show that I ought to have more indulgence than you, because my theme is more difficult; and I shall argue that to seem to speak well of the gods to men is far easier than to speak well of men to men: for the inexperience and utter ignorance of his hearers about any subject is a great assistance to him who has to speak of it, and we know how ignorant we are concerning the gods. But I should like to make my meaning clearer, if

[1] *Timaeus,* 27.

you will follow me. All that is said by any of us can only be imitation and representation. For if we consider the likenesses which painters make of bodies divine and heavenly, and the different degrees of gratification with which the eye of the spectator receives them, we shall see that we are satisfied with the artist who is able in any degree to imitate the earth and its mountains, and the rivers, and the woods, and the universe, and the things that are and move therein, and further, that knowing nothing precise about such matters, we do not examine or analyze the painting; all that is required is a sort of indistinct and deceptive mode of shadowing them forth. But when a person endeavours to paint the human form we are quick at finding out defects, and our familiar knowledge makes us severe judges of any one who does not render every point of similarity. And we may observe the same thing to happen in discourse; we are satisfied with a picture of divine and heavenly things which has very little likeness to them; but we are more precise in our criticism of mortal and human things. Wherefore if at the moment of speaking I cannot suitably express my meaning, you must excuse me, considering that to form approved likenesses of human things is the reverse of easy. This is what I want to suggest to you, [108] and at the same time to beg, Socrates, that I may have not less, but more indulgence conceded to me in what I am about to say. Which favour, if I am right in asking, I hope that you will be ready to grant.

Socrates. Certainly, Critias, we will grant your request, and we will grant the same by anticipation to Hermocrates, as well as to you and Timaeus; for I have no doubt that when his turn comes a little while hence, he will make the same request which you have made. In order, then, that he may provide himself with a fresh beginning, and not be compelled to say the same things over again, let him understand that the indulgence is already extended by anticipation to him. And now, friend Critias, I will announce to you the judgment of the theatre. They are of opinion that the last performer was wonderfully successful, and that you will need a great deal of indulgence before you will be able to take his place.

Hermocrates. The warning, Socrates, which you have addressed to him, I must also take to myself. But remember, Critias, that faint heart never yet raised a trophy; and therefore you must go and attack the argument like a man. First invoke Apollo and the Muses, and then let us hear you sound the praises and show forth the virtues of your ancient citizens.

Crit. Friend Hermocrates, you, who are stationed last and have another in front of you, have not lost heart as yet; the gravity of the situation will soon be revealed to you; meanwhile I accept your exhortations and encouragements. But besides the gods and goddesses whom you have mentioned, I would specially invoke Mnemosyne; for all the important part of my discourse is dependent on her favour, and if I can recollect and recite enough of what was said by the priests and brought hither by Solon, I doubt not that I shall satisfy the requirements of this theatre. And now, making no more excuses, I will proceed.

Let me begin by observing first of all, that nine thousand was the sum of years which had elapsed since the war which was said to have taken place between those who dwelt outside the Pillars of Heracles and all who dwelt within them; this war I am going to describe. Of the combatants on the one side, the city of Athens was reported to have been the leader and to have fought out the war; the combatants on the other side were commanded by the kings of Atlantis, which, as I was saying, was an island greater in extent than Libya and Asia, and when afterwards sunk by an earthquake, became an impassable barrier of mud to voyagers sailing from hence to any part of the ocean. [*109*] The progress of the history will unfold the various nations of barbarians and families of Hellenes which then existed, as they successively appear on the scene; but I must describe first of all Athenians of that day, and their enemies who fought with them, and then the respective powers and governments of the two kingdoms. Let us give the precedence to Athens.

In the days of old the gods had the whole earth distributed among them by allotment.[1] There was no quarrelling; for you cannot rightly suppose that the gods did not know what was proper for each of them to have, or, knowing this, that they would seek to procure for themselves by contention that which more properly belonged to others. They all of them by just apportionment obtained what they wanted, and peopled their own districts; and when they had peopled them they tended us, their nurselings and possessions, as shepherds tend their flocks, excepting only that they did not use blows or bodily force, as shepherds do, but governed us like pilots from the stern of the vessel, which is an easy way of guiding animals, holding our souls by the rudder of persuasion according to their own pleasure;—thus did they guide all mortal creatures. Now different gods had their allotments in different places which they set in order. Hephaestus and Athene, who were brother and sister, and sprang from the same father, having a common nature, and being united also in the love of philosophy and art, both obtained as their common portion this land, which was naturally adapted for wisdom and virtue; and there they implanted brave children of the soil, and put into their minds the order of government; their names are preserved, but their actions have disappeared by reason of the destruction of those who received the tradition, and the lapse of ages. For when there were any survivors, as I have already said, they were men who dwelt in the mountains; and they were ignorant of the art of writing, and had heard only the names of the chiefs of the land, but very little about their actions. The names they were willing enough to give to their children; but the virtues and the laws of their predecessors, they knew only by obscure traditions; and as they themselves and their children lacked for many generations the necessaries of life, they directed their attention to the supply of their wants, and of them they conversed, [*110*] to the neglect of events that had happened in times long past; for mythology and the enquiry into antiquity are first introduced into cities when they begin to have leisure,[2] and when they see that the necessaries of life have already been provided, but not before. And this is the reason why the names of the ancients have been preserved to us and not their actions. This

---

[1] Cf. *Statesman*, 271 ff.

[2] Cf. Aristotle, *Metaphysics*, I. i. 981[b] 13-24.

I infer because Solon said that the priests in their narrative of that war mentioned most of the names which are recorded prior to the time of Theseus, such as Cecrops, and Erechtheus, and Erichthonius, and Erysichthon, and the names of the women in like manner. Moreover, since military pursuits were then common to men and women, the men of those days in accordance with the custom of the time set up a figure and image of the goddess in full armour, to be a testimony that all animals which associate together, male as well as female, may, if they please, practise in common the virtue which belongs to them without distinction of sex.

Now the country was inhabited in those days by various classes of citizens;—there were artisans, and there were husbandmen, and there was also a warrior class originally set apart by divine men. The latter dwelt by themselves, and had all things suitable for nurture and education; neither had any of them anything of their own, but they regarded all that they had as common property; nor did they claim to receive of the other citizens anything more than their necessary food. And they practised all the pursuits which we yesterday described as those of our imaginary guardians. Concerning the country the Egyptian priests said what is not only probable but manifestly true, that the boundaries were in those days fixed by the Isthmus, and that in the direction of the continent they extended as far as the heights of Cithaeron and Parnes; the boundary line came down in the direction of the sea, having the district of Oropus on the right, and with the river Asopus as the limit on the left. The land was the best in the world, and was therefore able in those days to support a vast army, raised from the surrounding people. Even the remnant of Attica which now exists may compare with any region in the world for the variety and excellence of its fruits and the suitableness of its pastures to [111] every sort of animal, which proves what I am saying; but in those days the country was fair as now and yielded far more abundant produce. How shall I establish my words? and what part of it can be truly called a remnant of the land that then was? The whole country is only a long promontory extending far into the sea away from the rest of the continent, while the surrounding basin of the sea is everywhere deep in the neighbourhood of the shore. Many great deluges have taken place during the nine thousand years, for that is the number of years which have elapsed since the time of which I am speaking; and during all this time and through so many changes, there has never been any considerable accumulation of the soil coming down from the mountains, as in other places, but the earth has fallen away all round and sunk out of sight. The consequence is, that in comparison of what then was, there are remaining only the bones of the wasted body, as they may be called, as in the case of small islands, all the richer and softer parts of the soil having fallen away, and the mere skeleton of the land being left. But in the primitive state of the country, its mountains were high hills covered with soil, and the plains, as they are termed by us, of Phelleus were full of rich earth, and there was abundance of wood in the mountains. Of this last the traces still remain, for although some of the mountains now only afford sustenance to bees, not so very long ago there were still to be seen roofs of timber cut from trees growing there, which were of a size sufficient to cover the largest houses; and there were many other high trees, cultivated by man and bearing abundance of food for cattle. Moreover, the land reaped the benefit of the annual rainfall, not as now losing the water which flows off the bare earth into the sea, but, having an abundant supply in all places, and receiving it into herself and treasuring it up in the close clay soil, it let off into the hollows the streams which it absorbed from the heights, providing everywhere abundant fountains and rivers, of which there may still be observed sacred memorials in places where fountains once existed; and this proves the truth of what I am saying.

Such was the natural state of the country, which was cultivated, as we may well believe, by true husbandmen, who made husbandry their business, and were lovers of honour, and of a noble nature, and had a soil the best in the world, and abundance of water, and in the heaven above an excellently attempered climate. Now the city in those days was arranged on this wise. In the first place the Acropolis was not as now. [112] For the fact is that a single night of excessive rain washed away the earth and laid bare the rock; at the same time there were earthquakes, and then occurred the extraordinary inundation, which was the third before the great destruction of Deucalion. But in primitive times the hill of the Acropolis extended to the Eridanus and Ilissus, and included the Pnyx on one side, and the Lycabettus as a boundary on the opposite side to the Pnyx, and was all well covered with soil, and level at the top, except in one or two places.

Outside the Acropolis and under the sides of the hill there dwelt artisans, and such of the husbandmen as were tilling the ground near; the warrior class dwelt by themselves around the temples of Athene and Hephaestus at the summit, which moreover they had enclosed with a single fence like the garden of a single house. On the north side they had dwellings in common and had erected halls for dining in winter, and had all the buildings which they needed for their common life, besides temples, but there was no adorning of them with gold and silver, for they made no use of these for any purpose; they took a middle course between meanness and ostentation, and built modest houses in which they and their children's children grew old, and they handed them down to others who were like themselves, always the same. But in summer-time they left their gardens and gymnasia and dining halls, and then the southern side of the hill was made use of by them for the same purpose. Where the Acropolis now is there was a fountain, which was choked by the earthquake, and has left only the few small streams which still exist in the vicinity, but in those days the fountain gave an abundant supply of water for all and of suitable temperature in summer and in winter. This is how they dwelt, being the guardians of their own citizens and the leaders of the Hellenes, who were their willing followers. And they took care to preserve the same number of men and women through all time, being so many as were required for warlike purposes, then as now—that is to say, about twenty thousand. Such were the ancient Athenians, and after this manner they righteously administered their own land and the rest of Hellas; they were renowned all over Europe and Asia for the beauty of their persons and for the many virtues of their souls, and of all men who lived in those days they were the most illustrious. And next, if I have not forgotten what I heard when I was a child, I will impart to you the character and origin of their adversaries. For friends should not keep their stories to themselves, but have them in common.

[113] Yet, before proceeding further in the narrative, I ought to warn you, that you must not be surprised if you should perhaps hear Hellenic names given to foreigners. I will tell you the reason of this: Solon, who was intending to use the tale for his poem, enquired into the meaning of the names, and found that the early Egyptians in writing them down had translated them into their own language, and he recovered the meaning of the several names and when copying them out again translated them into our language. My great-grandfather, Dropides, had the original writing, which is still in my possession, and was carefully studied by me when I was a child. Therefore if you hear names such as are used in this country, you must not be surprised, for I have told how they came to be introduced. The tale, which was of great length, began as follows:—

I have before remarked in speaking of the allotments of the gods, that they distributed the whole earth into portions differing in extent, and made for themselves temples and instituted sacrifices. And Poseidon, receiving for his lot the island of Atlantis, begat children by a mortal woman, and settled them in a part of the island, which I will describe. Looking towards the sea, but in the centre of the whole island, there was a plain which is said to have been the fairest of all plains and very fertile. Near the plain again, and also in the centre of the island at a distance of about fifty stadia, there was a mountain not very high on any side.

In this mountain there dwelt one of the earthborn primeval men of that country, whose name was Evenor, and he had a wife named Leucippe, and they had an only daughter who was called Cleito. The maiden had already reached womanhood, when her father and mother died; Poseidon fell in love with her and had intercourse with her, and breaking the ground, inclosed the hill in which she dwelt all round, making alternate zones of sea and land larger and smaller, encircling one another; there were two of land and three of water, which he turned as with a lathe, each having its circumference equidistant every way from the centre, so that no man could get to the island, for ships and voyages were not as yet. He himself, being a god, found no difficulty in making special arrangements for the centre island, bringing up two springs of water from beneath the earth, one of warm water and the other of cold, and making every variety of food to spring up abundantly from the soil. He also begat and brought up five pairs of twin male children; and dividing the island of Atlantis into ten portions, [114] he gave to the first-born of the eldest pair his mother's dwelling and the surrounding allotment, which was the largest and best, and made him king over the rest; the others he made princes, and gave them rule over many men, and a large territory. And he named them all; the eldest, who was the first king, he named Atlas, and after him the whole island and the ocean were called Atlantic. To his twin brother, who was born after him, and obtained as his lot the extremity of the island towards the Pillars of Heracles, facing the country which is now called the region of Gades in that part of the world, he gave the name which in the Hellenic language is Eumelus, in the language of the country which is named after him, Gadeirus. Of the second pair of twins he called one Ampheres, and the other Evaemon. To the elder of the third pair of twins he gave the name Mneseus, and Autochthon to the one who followed him. Of the fourth pair of twins he called the elder Elasippus, and the younger Mestor. And of the fifth pair he gave to the elder the name of Azaes, and to the younger that of Diaprepes. All these and their descendants for many generations were the inhabitants and rulers of divers islands in the open sea; and also, as has been already said, they held sway in our direction over the country within the Pillars as far as Egypt and Tyrrhenia.

Now Atlas had a numerous and honourable family, and they retained the kingdom, the eldest son handing it on to his eldest for many generations; and they had such an amount of wealth as was never before possessed by kings and potentates, and is not likely ever to be again, and they were furnished with everything which they needed, both in the city and country. For because of the greatness of their empire many things were brought to them from foreign countries, and the island itself provided most of what was required by them for the uses of life. In the first place, they dug out of the earth whatever was to be found there, solid as well as fusile, and that which is now only a name and was then something more than a name, orichalcum, was dug out of the earth in many parts of the island, being more precious in those days than anything except gold. There was an abundance of wood for carpenter's work, and sufficient maintenance for tame and wild animals. Moreover, there were a great number of elephants in the island; [115] for as there was provision for all other sorts of animals, both for those which live in lakes and marshes and rivers, and also for those which live in mountains and on plains, so there was for the animal which is the largest and most voracious of all. Also whatever fragrant things there now are in the earth, whether roots, or herbage, or woods, or essences which distil from fruit and flower, grew and thrived in that land; also the fruit which admits of cultivation, both the dry sort, which is given us for nourishment and any other which we use for food—we call them all by the common name of pulse, and the fruits having a hard rind, affording drinks and meats and ointments, and good store of chestnuts and the like, which furnish pleasure and amusement, and are fruits which spoil with keeping, and the pleasant kinds of dessert, with which we console ourselves after dinner, when we are tired of eating—all these that sacred island which then beheld the light of the sun, brought forth fair and wondrous and in infinite abundance. With such blessings the earth freely furnished them; meanwhile they went on constructing their temples and palaces and harbours and docks. And they arranged the whole country in the following manner:

First of all they bridged the zones of sea which surrounded the ancient metropolis, making a road to and from the royal palace. And at the very beginning they built the palace in the habitation of the god and of their ancestors, which they continued to ornament in successive generations, every king surpassing the one who went before him to the utmost of his power, until they made the building a marvel to behold for size and for beauty. And beginning from the sea they bored a canal of three hundred feet in width and one hundred feet in depth and fifty stadia in length, which they carried through to the outermost zone, making a passage from the sea up to this, which became a harbour, and leaving an opening sufficient to enable the largest vessels to find ingress. Moreover, they divided at the bridges the zones of land which parted the zones of sea, leaving room for a single trireme to pass out of one zone into another, and they covered over the channels so as to leave a way underneath for the ships; for the banks were raised considerably above the water. Now the largest of the zones into which a passage was cut from the sea was three stadia in breadth, and the zone of land which came next of equal breadth; but the next two zones, the one of water, the other of land, were two stadia, and the one which surrounded the central island was a stadium only in width. [116] The island in which the palace was situated had a diameter of five stadia. All this including the zones and the bridge, which was the sixth part of a stadium in width, they surrounded by a stone wall on every side, placing towers and gates on the bridges where the sea passed in. The stone which was used in the work they quarried from underneath the centre island, and from underneath the zones, on the outer as well as the inner side. One kind was white, another black, and a third red, and as they quarried, they at the same time hollowed out double docks, having roofs formed out of the native rock. Some of their buildings were simple, but in others they put together different stones, varying the colour to please the eye, and to be a natural source of delight. The entire circuit of the wall, which went round the outermost zone, they covered with a coating of brass, and the circuit of the next wall they coated with tin, and the third, which encompassed the citadel, flashed with the red light of orichalcum.

The palaces in the interior of the citadel were constructed on this wise:—in the centre was a holy temple dedicated to Cleito and Poseidon, which remained inaccessible, and was surrounded by an enclosure of gold; this was the spot where the family of the ten princes first saw the light, and thither the people annually brought the fruits of the earth in their season from all the ten portions, to be an offering to each of the ten. Here was Poseidon's own temple which was a stadium in length, and half a stadium in width, and of a proportionate height, having a strange barbaric appearance. All the outside of the temple, with the exception of the pinnacles, they covered with silver, and the pinnacles with gold. In the interior of the temple the roof was of ivory, curiously wrought everywhere with gold and silver and orichalcum; and all the other parts, the walls and pillars and floor, they coated with orichalcum. In the temple they placed statues of gold: there was the god himself standing in a chariot—the charioteer of six winged horses—and of such a size that he touched the roof of the building with his head; around him there were a hundred Nereids riding on dolphins, for such was thought to be the number of them by the men of those days. There were also in the interior of the temple other images which had been dedicated by private persons. And around the temple on the outside were placed statues of gold of all the descendants of the ten kings and of their wives, and there were many other great offerings of kings and of private persons, coming both from the city itself and from the foreign cities over which they held sway. There was an altar too, which in size and workmanship corresponded to this magnificence, *[117]* and the palaces, in like manner, answered to the greatness of the kingdom and the glory of the temple.

In the next place, they had fountains, one of cold and another of hot water, in gracious plenty flowing; and they were wonderfully adapted for use by reason of the pleasantness and excellence of their waters. They constructed buildings about them and planted suitable trees; also they made cisterns, some open to the heavens, others roofed over, to be used in winter as warm baths; there were the kings' baths, and the baths of private persons, which were kept apart; and there were separate baths for women, and for horses and cattle, and to each of them they gave as much adornment as was suitable. Of the water which ran off they carried some to the grove of Poseidon, where were growing all manner of trees of wonderful height and beauty, owing to the excellence of the soil, while the remainder was conveyed by aqueducts along the bridges to the outer circles; and there were many temples built and dedicated to many gods; also gardens and places of exercise, some for men, and others for horses in both of the two islands formed by the zones; and in the centre of the larger of the two there was set apart a race-course of a stadium in width, and in length allowed to extend all round the island, for horses to race in. Also there were guard-houses at intervals for the guards, the more trusted of whom were appointed to keep watch in the lesser zone, which was nearer the Acropolis; while the most trusted of all had houses given them within the citadel, near the persons of the kings. The docks were full of triremes and naval stores, and all things were quite ready for use. Enough of the plan of the royal palace.

Leaving the palace and passing out across the three harbours, you came to a wall which began at the sea and went all round: this was everywhere distant fifty stadia from the largest zone or harbour, and enclosed the whole, the ends meeting at the mouth of the channel which led to the sea. The entire area was densely crowded with habitations; and the canal and the largest of the harbours were full of vessels and merchants coming from all parts, who, from their numbers, kept up a multitudinous sound of human voices, and din and clatter of all sorts night and day.

I have described the city and the environs of the ancient palace nearly in the words of Solon, and now I must endeavour to represent to you the nature and arrangement of the rest of the land. *[118]* The whole country was said by him to be very lofty and precipitous on the side of the sea, but the country immediately about and surrounding the city was a level plain, itself surrounded by mountains which descended towards the sea; it was smooth and even, and of an oblong shape, extending in one direction three thousand stadia, but across the centre inland it was two thousand stadia. This part of the island looked towards the south, and was sheltered from the north. The surrounding mountains were celebrated for their number and size and beauty, far beyond any which still exist, having in them also many wealthy villages of country folk, and rivers, and lakes, and meadows supplying food enough for every animal, wild or tame, and much wood of various sorts, abundant for each and every kind of work.

I will now describe the plain, as it was fashioned by nature and by the labours of many generations of kings through long ages. It was for the most part rectangular and oblong, and where falling out of the straight line followed the circular ditch. The depth, and width, and length of this ditch were incredible, and gave the impression that a work of such extent, in addition to so many others, could never have been artificial. Nevertheless I must say what I was told. It was excavated to the depth of a hundred feet, and its breadth was a stadium everywhere; it was carried round the whole of the plain, and was ten thousand stadia in length. It received the streams which came down from the mountains, and winding round the plain and meeting at the city, was there let off into the sea. Further inland, likewise, straight canals of a hundred feet in width were cut from it through the plain, and again let off into the ditch leading to the sea: these canals were at intervals of a hundred stadia, and by them they brought down the wood from the mountains to the city, and conveyed the fruits of the earth in ships, cutting transverse passages from one canal into another, and to the city. Twice in the year they gathered the fruits of the earth—in winter having the benefit of the rains of heaven, and in summer the water which the land supplied by introducing streams from the canals.

As to the population, each of the lots in the plain had to find a leader for the men who were fit for military service, [119] and the size of a lot was a square of ten stadia each way, and the total number of all the lots was sixty thousand. And of the inhabitants of the mountains and of the rest of the country there was also a vast multitude, which was distributed among the lots and had leaders assigned to them according to their districts and villages. The leader was required to furnish for the war the sixth portion of a war-chariot, so as to make up a

total of ten thousand chariots; also two horses and riders for them, and a pair of chariot-horses without a seat, accompanied by a horseman who could fight on foot carrying a small shield, and having a charioteer who stood behind the man-at-arms to guide the two horses; also, he was bound to furnish two heavy armed soldiers, two archers, two slingers, three stone-shooters and three javelin-men, who were light-armed, and four sailors to make up the complement of twelve hundred ships. Such was the military order of the royal city—the order of the other nine governments varied, and it would be wearisome to recount their several differences.

As to offices and honours, the following was the arrangement from the first. Each of the ten kings in his own division and in his own city had the absolute control of the citizens, and, in most cases, of the laws, punishing and slaying whomsoever he would. Now the order of precedence among them and their mutual relations were regulated by the commands of Poseidon which the law had handed down. These were inscribed by the first kings on a pillar of orichalcum, which was situated in the middle of the island, at the temple of Poseidon, whither the kings were gathered together every fifth and every sixth year alternately, thus giving equal honour to the odd and to the even number. And when they were gathered together they consulted about their common interests, and enquired if any one had transgressed in anything, and passed judgment, and before they passed judgment they gave their pledges to one another on this wise:—There were bulls who had the range of the temple of Poseidon; and the ten kings, being left alone in the temple, after they had offered prayers to the god that they might capture the victim which was acceptable to him, hunted the bulls, without weapons, but with staves and nooses; and the bull which they caught they led up to the pillar and cut its throat over the top of it so that the blood fell upon the sacred inscription. Now on the pillar, besides the laws, there was inscribed an oath invoking mighty curses on the disobedient. When therefore, after slaying the bull in the accustomed manner, they had burnt its limbs, they filled a bowl of wine and cast in a clot of blood for each of them; [120] the rest of the victim they put in the fire, after having purified the column all round. Then they drew from the bowl in golden cups, and pouring a libation on the fire, they swore that they would judge according to the laws on the pillar, and would punish him who in any point had already transgressed them, and that for the future they would not, if they could help, offend against the writing on the pillar, and would neither command others, nor obey any ruler who commanded them, to act otherwise than according to the laws of their father Poseidon. This was the prayer which each of them offered up for himself and for his descendants, at the same time drinking and dedicating the cup out of which he drank in the temple of the god; and after they had supped and satisfied their needs, when darkness came on, and the fire about the sacrifice was cool, all of them put on most beautiful azure robes, and, sitting on the ground, at night, over the embers of the sacrifices by which they had sworn, and extinguishing all the fire about the temple, they received and gave judgment, if any of them had an accusation to bring against any one; and when they had given judgment, at daybreak they wrote down their sentences on a golden tablet, and dedicated it together with their robes to be a memorial.

There were many special laws affecting the several kings inscribed about the temples, but the most important was the following: They were not to take up arms against one another, and they were all to come to the rescue if any one in any of their cities attempted to overthrow the royal house; like their ancestors, they were to deliberate in common about war and other matters, giving the supremacy to the descendants of Atlas. And the king was not to have the power of life and death over any of his kinsmen unless he had the assent of the majority of the ten.

Such was the vast power which the god settled in the lost island of Atlantis; and this he afterwards directed against our land for the following reasons, as tradition tells: For many generations, as long as the divine nature lasted in them, they were obedient to the laws, and well-affectioned towards the god, whose seed they were; for they possessed true and in every way great spirits, uniting gentleness with wisdom in the various chances of life, and in their intercourse with one another. They despised everything but virtue, caring little for their present state of life, and thinking lightly of the possession of gold and other property, which seemed only a burden to them; neither were they intoxicated by luxury; nor did wealth deprive them of their self-control; [*121*] but they were sober, and saw clearly that all these goods are increased by virtue and friendship with one another, whereas by too great regard and respect for them, they are lost and friendship with them. By such reflections and by the continuance in them of a divine nature, the qualities which we have described grew and increased among them; but when the divine portion began to fade away, and became diluted too often and too much with the mortal admixture, and the human nature got the upper hand, they then, being unable to bear their fortune, behaved unseemly, and to him who had an eye to see, grew visibly debased, for they were losing the fairest of their precious gifts; but to those who had no eye to see the true happiness, they appeared glorious and blessed at the very time when they were full of avarice and unrighteous power. Zeus, the god of gods, who rules according to law, and is able to see into such things, perceiving that an honourable race was in a woeful plight, and wanting to inflict punishment on them, that they might be chastened and improve, collected all the gods into their most holy habitation, which, being placed in the centre of the world, beholds all created things. And when he had called them together, he spake as follows—[1]

[1] The fragment *Critias* thus breaks off in the middle of a sentence.

CRITIAS

PARMENIDES

PERSONS OF THE DIALOGUE: CEPHALUS; ADEIMANTUS; GLAUCON; ANTIPHON; PYTHODORUS; SOCRATES; ZENO; PARMENIDES; ARISTOTELES. *Cephalus rehearses a dialogue which is supposed to have been narrated in his presence by Antiphon, the half-brother of Adeimantus and Glaucon, to certain Clazomenians*

[126] WE had come from our home at Clazomenae to Athens, and met Adeimantus and Glaucon in the Agora. Welcome, Cephalus, said Adeimantus, taking me by the hand; is there anything which we can do for you in Athens?

Yes; that is why I am here; I wish to ask a favour of you.

What may that be? he said.

I want you to tell me the name of your half-brother, which I have forgotten; he was a mere child when I last came hither from Clazomenae, but that was a long time ago; his father's name, if I remember rightly, was Pyrilampes?

Yes, he said, and the name of our brother, Antiphon; but why do you ask?

Let me introduce some countrymen of mine, I said; they are lovers of philosophy, and have heard that Antiphon was intimate with a certain Pythodorus, a friend of Zeno, and remembers a conversation which took place between Socrates, Zeno, and Parmenides many years ago, Pythodorus having often recited it to him.

Quite true.

And could we hear it? I asked.

Nothing easier, he replied; when he was a youth he made a careful study of the piece; at present his thoughts run in another direction; like his grandfather Antiphon he is devoted to horses. But, if that is what you want, let us go and look for him; he dwells at Melita, which is quite near, and he has only just left us to go home.

[127] Accordingly we went to look for him; he was at home, and in the act of giving a bridle to a smith to be fitted. When he had done with the smith, his brothers told him the purpose of our visit; and he saluted me as an acquaintance whom he remembered from my former visit, and we asked him to repeat the dialogue. At first he was not very willing, and complained of the trouble, but at length he consented. He told us that Pythodorus had described to him the appearance of Parmenides and Zeno; they came to Athens, as he said, at the great Panathenaea; the former was, at the time of his visit, about 65 years old, very white with age, but well favoured. Zeno was nearly 40 years of age, tall and fair to look upon; in the days of his youth he was reported to have been beloved by Parmenides. He said that they lodged with Pythodorus in the Ceramicus, outside the wall, whither Socrates, then a very young man, came to see them, and many others with him; they wanted to hear the writings of Zeno, which had been brought to Athens for the first time on the occasion of their visit. These Zeno himself read to them in the absence of Parmenides, and had very nearly finished when Pythodorus entered, and with him Parmenides and Aristoteles who was afterwards one of the Thirty, and heard the little that remained of the dialogue. Pythodorus had heard Zeno repeat them before.

When the recitation was completed, Socrates requested that the first thesis of the first argument might be read over again, and this having been done, he said: What is your meaning, Zeno? Do you maintain that if being is many, it must be both like and unlike, and that this is impossible, for neither can the like be unlike, nor the unlike like—is that your position?

Just so, said Zeno.

And if the unlike cannot be like, or the like unlike, then according to you, being could not be many; for this would involve an impossibility. In all that you say have you any other purpose except to disprove the being of the many? and is not each division of your treatise intended to furnish a separate proof of this, there being in all as many proofs of the not-being of the many as you have composed arguments? Is that your meaning, or have I misunderstood you?

[128] No, said Zeno; you have correctly understood my general purpose.

I see, Parmenides, said Socrates, that Zeno would like to be not only one with you in friendship but your second self in his writings too; he puts what you say in another way, and would fain make believe that he is telling us something which is new. For you, in your poems, say The All is one, and of this you adduce excellent proofs; and he on the other hand says There is no many; and on behalf of this he offers overwhelming evidence. You affirm unity, he denies plurality. And so you deceive the world into believing that you are saying different things when really you are saying much the same. This is a strain of art beyond the reach of most of us.

Yes, Socrates, said Zeno. But although you are as keen as a Spartan hound in pursuing the track, you do not fully apprehend the true motive of the composition, which is not really such an artificial work as you imagine; for what you speak of was an accident; there was no pretence of a great purpose; nor any serious intention of deceiving the world. The truth is, that these writings of mine were meant to protect the arguments of Parmenides against those who make fun of him and seek to show the many ridiculous and contradictory results which they suppose to follow from the affirmation of the one. My answer is addressed to the partisans of the many, whose attack I return with interest by retorting upon them that their hypothesis of the being of many, if carried out, appears to be still more ridiculous than the hypothesis of the being of one. Zeal for my master led me to write the book in the days of my youth, but some one stole the copy; and therefore I had no choice whether it should be published or not; the mo-

tive, however, of writing, was not the ambition of an elder man, but the pugnacity of a young one. This you do not seem to see, Socrates; though in other respects, as I was saying, your notion is a very just one.

I understand, said Socrates, and quite accept your account. But tell me, Zeno, do you not further think that there is an idea of likeness in itself, [129] and another idea of unlikeness, which is the opposite of likeness, and that in these two, you and I and all other things to which we apply the term many, participate— things which participate in likeness become in that degree and manner like; and so far as they participate in unlikeness become in that degree unlike, or both like and unlike in the degree in which they participate in both? And may not all things partake of both opposites, and be both like and unlike, by reason of this participation?—Where is the wonder? Now if a person could prove the absolute like to become unlike, or the absolute unlike to become like, that, in my opinion, would indeed be a wonder; but there is nothing extraordinary, Zeno, in showing that the things which only partake of likeness and unlikeness experience both. Nor, again, if a person were to show that all is one by partaking of one, and at the same time many by partaking of many, would that be very astonishing. But if he were to show me that the absolute one was many, or the absolute many one, I should be truly amazed. And so of all the rest: I should be surprised to hear that the natures or ideas themselves had these opposite qualities; but not if a person wanted to prove of me that I was many and also one. When he wanted to show that I was many he would say that I have a right and a left side, and a front and a back, and an upper and a lower half, for I cannot deny that I partake of multitude; when, on the other hand, he wants to prove that I am one, he will say, that we who are here assembled are seven, and that I am one and partake of the one. In both instances he proves his case. So again, if a person shows that such things as wood, stones, and the like, being many are also one, we admit that he shows the coexistence of the one and many, but he does not show that the many are one or the one many; he is uttering not a paradox but a truism. If however, as I just now suggested, some one were to abstract simple notions of like, unlike, one, many, rest, motion, and similar ideas, and then to show that these admit of admixture and separation in themselves, I should be very much astonished. This part of the argument appears to be treated by you, Zeno, in a very spirited manner; but, as I was saying, I should be far more amazed if any one found in the ideas themselves which are [130] apprehended by reason, the same puzzle and entanglement which you have shown to exist in visible objects.

While Socrates was speaking, Pythodorus thought that Parmenides and Zeno were not altogether pleased at the successive steps of the argument; but still they gave the closest attention, and often looked at one another, and smiled as if in admiration of him. When he had finished, Parmenides expressed their feelings in the following words:—

Socrates, he said, I admire the bent of your mind towards philosophy; tell me now, was this your own distinction between ideas in themselves and the things which partake of them? and do you think that there is an idea of likeness apart from the likeness which we possess, and of the one and many, and of the other things which Zeno mentioned?

I think that there are such ideas, said Socrates.

Parmenides proceeded: And would you also make absolute ideas of the just and the beautiful and the good, and of all that class?

Yes, he said, I should.

And would you make an idea of man apart from us and from all other human creatures, or of fire and water?

I am often undecided, Parmenides, as to whether I ought to include them or not.

And would you feel equally undecided, Socrates, about things of which the mention may provoke a smile?—I mean such things as hair, mud, dirt, or anything else which is vile and paltry; would you suppose that each of these has an idea distinct from the actual objects with which we come into contact, or not?

Certainly not, said Socrates; visible things like these are such as they appear to us, and I am afraid that there would be an absurdity in assuming any idea of them, although I sometimes get disturbed, and begin to think that there is nothing without an idea; but then again, when I have taken up this position, I run away, because I am afraid that I may fall into a bottomless pit of nonsense, and perish; and so I return to the ideas of which I was just now speaking, and occupy myself with them.

Yes, Socrates, said Parmenides; that is because you are still young; the time will come, if I am not mistaken, when philosophy will have a firmer grasp of you, and then you will not despise even the meanest things; at your age, you are too much disposed to regard the opinions of men. But I should like to know whether you mean that there are certain ideas of which all other things partake, and from which they derive their names; [131] that similars, for example, become similar, because they partake of similarity; and great things become great, because they partake of greatness; and that just and beautiful things become just and beautiful, because they partake of justice and beauty?

Yes, certainly, said Socrates, that is my meaning.

Then each individual partakes either of the whole of the idea or else of a part of the idea? Can there be any other mode of participation?

There cannot be, he said.

Then do you think that the whole idea is one, and yet, being one, is in each one of the many?

Why not, Parmenides? said Socrates.

Because one and the same thing will exist as a whole at the same time in many separate individuals, and will therefore be in a state of separation from itself.

Nay, but the idea may be like the day which is one and the same in many places at once, and yet continuous with itself; in this way each idea may be one and the same in all at the same time.

I like your way, Socrates, of making one in many places at once. You mean to say, that if I were to spread out a sail and cover a number of men, there would be one whole including many —is not that your meaning?

I think so.

And would you say that the whole sail includes each man, or a part of it only, and different parts different men?

The latter.

Then, Socrates, the ideas themselves will be divisible, and things which participate in them will have a part of them only and not the whole idea existing in each of them?

That seems to follow.

Then would you like to say, Socrates, that the one idea is really divisible and yet remains one?

Certainly not, he said.

Suppose that you divide absolute greatness, and that of the many great things, each one is great in virtue of a portion of greatness less than absolute greatness—is that conceivable?

No.

Or will each equal thing, if possessing some small portion of equality less than absolute equality, be equal to some other thing by virtue of that portion only?

Impossible.

Or suppose one of us to have a portion of smallness; this is but a part of the small, and therefore the absolutely small is greater; if the absolutely small be greater, that to which the part of the small is added will be smaller and not greater than before.

How absurd!

Then in what way, Socrates, will all things participate in the ideas, if they are unable to participate in them either as parts or wholes?

Indeed, he said, you have asked a question which is not easily answered.

Well, said Parmenides, and what do you say of another question?

What question?

I imagine that the way in which you are led to assume one idea of each kind is as follows: [132]—You see a number of great objects, and when you look at them there seems to you to be one and the same idea (or nature) in them all; hence you conceive of greatness as one.

Very true, said Socrates.

And if you go on and allow your mind in like manner to embrace in one view the idea of greatness and of great things which are not the idea, and to compare them, will not another greatness arise, which will appear to be the source of all these?

It would seem so.

Then another idea of greatness now comes into view over and above absolute greatness, and the individuals which partake of it; and then another, over and above all these, by virtue of which they will all be great, and so each idea instead of being one will be infinitely multiplied.

But may not the ideas, asked Socrates, be thoughts only, and have no proper existence except in our minds, Parmenides? For in that case each idea may still be one, and not experience this infinite multiplication.

And can there be individual thoughts which are thoughts of nothing?

Impossible, he said.

The thought must be of something?

Yes.

Of something which is or which is not?

Of something which is.

Must it not be of a single something, which the thought recognizes as attaching to all, being a single form or nature?

Yes.

And will not the something which is apprehended as one and the same in all, be an idea?

From that, again, there is no escape.

Then, said Parmenides, if you say that every-

thing else participates in the ideas, must you not say either that everything is made up of thoughts, and that all things think; or that they are thoughts but have no thought?

The latter view, Parmenides, is no more rational than the previous one. In my opinion, the ideas are, as it were, patterns fixed in nature, and other things are like them, and resemblances of them—what is meant by the participation of other things in the ideas, is really assimilation to them.

But if, said he, the individual is like the idea, must not the idea also be like the individual, in so far as the individual is a resemblance of the idea? That which is like, cannot be conceived of as other than the like of like.

Impossible.

And when two things are alike, must they not partake of the same idea?

They must.

And will not that of which the two partake, and which makes them alike, be the idea itself?

Certainly.

Then the idea cannot be like the individual, or the individual like the idea; for if they are alike, some further idea of likeness will always be coming to light, [133] and if that be like anything else, another; and new ideas will be always arising, if the idea resembles that which partakes of it?

Quite true.

The theory, then, that other things participate in the ideas by resemblance, has to be given up, and some other mode of participation devised?

It would seem so.

Do you see then, Socrates, how great is the difficulty of affirming the ideas to be absolute?

Yes, indeed.

And, further, let me say that as yet you only understand a small part of the difficulty which is involved if you make of each thing a single idea, parting it off from other things.

What difficulty? he said.

There are many, but the greatest of all is this: —If an opponent argues that these ideas, being such as we say they ought to be, must remain unknown, no one can prove to him that he is wrong, unless he who denies their existence be a man of great ability and knowledge, and is willing to follow a long and laborious demonstration; he will remain unconvinced, and still insist that they cannot be known.

What do you mean, Parmenides? said Socrates.

In the first place, I think, Socrates, that you, or any one who maintains the existence of absolute essences, will admit that they cannot exist in us.

No, said Socrates; for then they would be no longer absolute.

True, he said; and therefore when ideas are what they are in relation to one another, their essence is determined by a relation among themselves, and has nothing to do with the resemblances, or whatever they are to be termed, which are in our sphere, and from which we receive this or that name when we partake of them. And the things which are within our sphere and have the same names with them, are likewise only relative to one another, and not to the ideas which have the same names with them, but belong to themselves and not to them.

What do you mean? said Socrates.

I may illustrate my meaning in this way, said Parmenides:—A master has a slave; now there is nothing absolute in the relation between them, which is simply a relation of one man to another. But there is also an idea of mastership in the abstract, which is relative to the idea of slavery in the abstract. [134] These natures have nothing to do with us, nor we with them; they are concerned with themselves only, and we with ourselves. Do you see my meaning?

Yes, said Socrates, I quite see your meaning.

And will not knowledge—I mean absolute knowledge—answer to absolute truth?

Certainly.

And each kind of absolute knowledge will answer to each kind of absolute being?

Yes.

But the knowledge which we have, will answer to the truth which we have; and again, each kind of knowledge which we have, will be a knowledge of each kind of being which we have?

Certainly.

But the ideas themselves, as you admit, we have not, and cannot have?

No, we cannot.

And the absolute natures or kinds are known severally by the absolute idea of knowledge?

Yes.

And we have not got the idea of knowledge?

No.

Then none of the ideas are known to us, because we have no share in absolute knowledge?

I suppose not.

Then the nature of the beautiful in itself, and of the good in itself, and all other ideas which we suppose to exist absolutely, are unknown to us?

It would seem so.

I think that there is a stranger consequence still.

What is it?

Would you, or would you not say, that absolute knowledge, if there is such a thing, must be a far more exact knowledge than our knowledge; and the same of beauty and of the rest?

Yes.

And if there be such a thing as participation in absolute knowledge, no one is more likely than God to have this most exact knowledge?

Certainly.

But then, will God, having absolute knowledge, have a knowledge of human things?

Why not?

Because, Socrates, said Parmenides, we have admitted that the ideas are not valid in relation to human things; nor human things in relation to them; the relations of either are limited to their respective spheres.

Yes, that has been admitted.

And if God has this perfect authority, and perfect knowledge, his authority cannot rule us, nor his knowledge know us, or any human thing; just as our authority does not extend to the gods, nor our knowledge know anything which is divine, so by parity of reason, being gods, are not our masters, neither do they know the things of men.

Yet, surely, said Socrates, to deprive God of knowledge is monstrous.

[135] These, Socrates, said Parmenides, are a few, and only a few of the difficulties in which we are involved if ideas really are and we determine each one of them to be an absolute unity. He who hears what may be said against them will deny the very existence of them—and even if they do exist, he will say that they must of necessity be unknown to man; and he will seem to have reason on his side, and as we were remarking just now, will be very difficult to convince; a man must be gifted with very considerable ability before he can learn that everything has a class and an absolute essence; and still more remarkable will he be who discovers all these things for himself, and having thoroughly investigated them is able to teach them to others.

I agree with you, Parmenides, said Socrates; and what you say is very much to my mind.

And yet, Socrates, said Parmenides, if a man, fixing his attention on these and the like difficulties, does away with ideas of things and will not admit that every individual thing has its own determinate idea which is always one and the same, he will have nothing on which his mind can rest; and so he will utterly destroy the power of reasoning, as you seem to me to have particularly noted.

Very true, he said.

But, then, what is to become of philosophy? Whither shall we turn, if the ideas are unknown?

I certainly do not see my way at present.

Yes, said Parmenides; and I think that this arises, Socrates, out of your attempting to define the beautiful, the just, the good, and the ideas generally, without sufficient previous training. I noticed your deficiency, when I heard you talking here with your friend Aristoteles, the day before yesterday. The impulse that carries you towards philosophy is assuredly noble and divine; but there is an art which is called by the vulgar idle talking, and which is often imagined to be useless; in that you must train and exercise yourself, now that you are young, or truth will elude your grasp.

And what is the nature of this exercise, Parmenides, which you would recommend?

That which you heard Zeno practising; at the same time, I give you credit for saying to him that you did not care to examine the perplexity in reference to visible things, or to consider the question in that way; but only in reference to objects of thought, and to what may be called ideas.

Why, yes, he said, there appears to me to be no difficulty in showing by this method that visible things are like and unlike and may experience anything.

Quite true, said Parmenides; but I think that you should go a step further, and consider not only the consequences which flow from a given hypothesis, [136] but also the consequences which flow from denying the hypothesis; and that will be still better training for you.

What do you mean? he said.

I mean, for example, that in the case of this very hypothesis of Zeno's about the many, you should inquire not only what will be the consequences to the many in relation to themselves and to the one, and to the one in relation to itself and the many, on the hypothesis of the being of the many, but also what will be the consequences to the one and the many in their relation to themselves and to each other, on the opposite hypothesis. Or, again, if likeness is or is not, what will be the consequences in either of these cases to the subjects of the hypothesis, and to other things, in relation both to themselves and to one another, and so of unlikeness; and the same holds good of motion and rest, of generation and destruction, and even of being and not-being. In a word, when you suppose anything to be or not to be, or to be in any way affected, you must look at the consequences in relation to the thing itself, and to any other things which you choose—to each of them singly, to more than one, and to all; and so of other things, you must look at them in relation to themselves and to anything else which you suppose either to be or not to be, if you would train yourself perfectly and see the real truth.

That, Parmenides, is a tremendous business of which you speak, and I do not quite understand you; will you take some hypothesis and go through the steps?—then I shall apprehend you better.

That, Socrates, is a serious task to impose on a man of my years.

Then will you, Zeno? said Socrates.

Zeno answered with a smile:—Let us make our petition to Parmenides himself, who is quite right in saying that you are hardly aware of the extent of the task which you are imposing on him; and if there were more of us I should not ask him, for these are not subjects which any one, especially at his age, can well speak of before a large audience; most people are not aware that this round-about progress through all things is the only way in which the mind can attain truth and wisdom. And therefore, Parmenides, I join in the request of Socrates, that I may hear the process again which I have not heard for a long time.

When Zeno had thus spoken, Pythodorus, according to Antiphon's report of him, said, that he himself and Aristoteles and the whole company entreated Parmenides to give an example of the process. [137] I cannot refuse, said Parmenides; and yet I feel rather like Ibycus, who, when in his old age, against his will, he fell in love, compared himself to an old racehorse, who was about to run in a chariot race, shaking with fear at the course he knew so well—this was his simile of himself. And I also experience a trembling when I remember through what an ocean of words I have to wade at my time of life. But I must indulge you, as Zeno says that I ought, and we are alone. Where shall I begin? And what shall be our first hypothesis, if I am to attempt this laborious pastime? Shall I begin with myself, and take my own hypothesis of the one? and consider the consequences which follow on the supposition either of the being or of the not-being of one?

By all means, said Zeno.

And who will answer me? he said. Shall I propose the youngest? He will not make difficulties and will be the most likely to say what he thinks; and his answers will give me time to breathe.

I am the one whom you mean, Parmenides, said Aristoteles; for I am the youngest and at your service. Ask, and I will answer.

Parmenides proceeded: If one is, he said, the one cannot be many?

Impossible.

Then the one cannot have parts, and cannot be a whole?

Why not?

Because every part is part of a whole; is it not?

Yes.

And what is a whole? would not that of which no part is wanting be a whole?

Certainly.

Then, in either case, the one would be made up of parts; both as being a whole, and also as having parts?

To be sure.

And in either case, the one would be many, and not one?

True.

But, surely, it ought to be one and not many?

It ought.

Then, if the one is to remain one, it will not be a whole, and will not have parts?

No.

But if it has no parts, it will have neither beginning, middle, nor end; for these would of course be parts of it.

Right.

But then, again, a beginning and an end are the limits of everything?

Certainly.

Then the one, having neither beginning nor end, is unlimited?

Yes, unlimited.

And therefore formless; for it cannot partake either of round or straight.

But why?

Why, because the round is that of which all the extreme points are equidistant from the centre?

Yes.

And the straight is that of which the centre intercepts the view of the extremes?

True.

[138] Then the one would have parts and would be many, if it partook either of a straight or of a circular form?

Assuredly.

But having no parts, it will be neither straight nor round?

Right.

And, being of such a nature, it cannot be in any place, for it cannot be either in another or in itself.

How so?

Because if it were in another, it would be encircled by that in which it was, and would touch it at many places and with many parts; but that which is one and indivisible, and does not partake of a circular nature, cannot be touched all round in many places.

Certainly not.

But if, on the other hand, one were in itself, it would also be contained by nothing else but itself; that is to say, if it were really in itself; for nothing can be in anything which does not contain it.

Impossible.

But then, that which contains must be other than that which is contained? for the same whole cannot do and suffer both at once; and if so, one will be no longer one, but two?

True.

Then one cannot be anywhere, either in itself or in another?

No.

Further consider, whether that which is of such a nature can have either rest or motion.

Why not?

Why, because the one, if it were moved, would be either moved in place or changed in nature; for these are the only kinds of motion.

Yes.

And the one, when it changes and ceases to be itself, cannot be any longer one.

It cannot.

It cannot therefore experience the sort of motion which is change of nature?

Clearly not.

Then can the motion of the one be in place?

Perhaps.

But if the one moved in place, must it not either move round and round in the same place, or from one place to another?

It must.

And that which moves in a circle must rest upon a centre; and that which goes round upon a centre must have parts which are different from the centre; but that which has no centre and no parts cannot possibly be carried round upon a centre?

Impossible.

But perhaps the motion of the one consists in change of place?

Perhaps so, if it moves at all.

And have we not already shown that it cannot be in anything?

Yes.

Then its coming into being in anything is still more impossible; is it not?

I do not see why.

Why, because anything which comes into being in anything, can neither as yet be in that other thing while still coming into being, nor be altogether out of it, if already coming into being in it.

Certainly not.

And therefore whatever comes into being in another must have parts, and then one part may be in, and another part out of that other; but that which has no parts can never be at one and the same time neither wholly within nor wholly without anything.

True.

And is there not a still greater impossibility in that which has no parts, and is not a whole, coming into being anywhere, since it cannot come into being either as a part or as a whole? [139]

Clearly.

Then it does not change place by revolving in the same spot, not by going somewhere and coming into being in something; nor again, by change in itself?

Very true.

Then in respect of any kind of motion the one is immoveable?

Immoveable.

But neither can the one be in anything, as we affirm?

Yes, we said so.

Then it is never in the same?

Why not?

Because if it were in the same it would be in something.

Certainly.

And we said that it could not be in itself, and could not be in other?

True.

Then one is never in the same place?

It would seem not.

But that which is never in the same place is never quiet or at rest?

Never.

One then, as would seem, is neither at rest nor in motion?

It certainly appears so.

Neither will it be the same with itself or other; nor again, other than itself or other.

How is that?

If other than itself it would be other than one, and would not be one.

True.

And if the same with other, it would be that other, and not itself; so that upon this supposition too, it would not have the nature of one, but would be other than one?

It would.

Then it will not be the same with other, or other than itself?

It will not.

Neither will it be other than other, while it remains one; for not one, but only other, can be other than other, and nothing else.

True.

Then not by virtue of being one will it be other?

Certainly not.

But if not by virtue of being one, not by virtue of itself; and if not by virtue of itself, not itself, and itself not being other at all, will not be other than anything?

Right.

Neither will one be the same with itself.

How not?

Surely the nature of the one is not the nature of the same.

Why not?

It is not when anything becomes the same with anything that it becomes one.

What of that?

Anything which becomes the same with the many, necessarily becomes many and not one.

True.

But, if there were no difference between the one and the same, when a thing became the same, it would always become one; and when it became one, the same?

Certainly.

And, therefore, if one be the same with itself, it is not one with itself, and will therefore be one and also not one.

Surely that is impossible.

And therefore the one can neither be other than other, nor the same with itself.

Impossible.

And thus the one can neither be the same, nor other, either in relation to itself or other?

No.

Neither will the one be like anything or unlike itself or other.

Why not?

Because likeness is sameness of affections.

Yes.

And sameness has been shown to be of a nature distinct from oneness?

That has been shown.

[140] But if the one had any other affection than that of being one, it would be affected in such a way as to be more than one; which is impossible.

True.

Then the one can never be so affected as to be the same either with another or with itself?

Clearly not.

Then it cannot be like another, or like itself?

No.

Nor can it be affected so as to be other, for then it would be affected in such a way as to be more than one.

It would.

That which is affected otherwise than itself or another, will be unlike itself or another, for sameness of affections is likeness.

True.

But the one, as appears, never being affected otherwise, is never unlike itself or other?

Never.

Then the one will never be either like or unlike itself or other?

Plainly not.

Again, being of this nature, it can neither be equal nor unequal either to itself or to other.

How is that?

Why, because the one if equal must be of the same measures as that to which it is equal.

True.

And if greater or less than things which are commensurable with it, the one will have more measures than that which is less, and fewer than that which is greater?

Yes.

And so of things which are not commensurate with it, the one will have greater measures than that which is less and smaller than that which is greater.

Certainly.

But how can that which does not partake of sameness, have either the same measures or have anything else the same?

Impossible.

And not having the same measures, the one cannot be equal either with itself or with another?

It appears so.

But again, whether it have fewer or more measures, it will have as many parts as it has measures; and thus again the one will be no longer one but will have as many parts as measures.

True.

Right.

And if it were of one measure, it would be equal to that measure; yet it has been shown to be incapable of equality.

It has.

Then it will neither partake of one measure, nor of many, nor of few, nor of the same at all, nor be equal to itself or another; nor be greater or less than itself, or other?

Certainly.

Well, and do we suppose that one can be older, or younger than anything, or of the same age with it?

Why not?

Why, because that which is of the same age with itself or other, must partake of equality or likeness of time; and we said that the one did not partake either of equality or of likeness?

We did say so.

And we also said, that it did not partake of inequality or unlikeness.

[141] Very true.

How then can one, being of this nature, be either older or younger than anything, or have the same age with it?

In no way.

Then one cannot be older or younger, or of the same age, either with itself or with another?

Clearly not.

Then the one, being of this nature, cannot be in time at all; for must not that which is in time, be always growing older than itself?

Certainly.

And that which is older, must always be older than something which is younger?

True.

Then, that which becomes older than itself, also becomes at the same time younger than itself, if it is to have something to become older than.

What do you mean?

I mean this:—A thing does not need to become different from another thing which is already different; it is different, and if its different has become, it has become different; if its different will be, it will be different; but of that which is becoming different, there cannot have been, or be about to be, or yet be, a different—the only different possible is one which is becoming.

That is inevitable.

But, surely, the elder is a difference relative to the younger, and to nothing else.

True.

Then that which becomes older than itself

must also, at the same time, become younger than itself?

Yes.

But again, it is true that it cannot become for a longer or for a shorter time than itself, but it must become, and be, and have become, and be about to be, for the same time with itself?

That again is inevitable.

Then things which are in time, and partake of time, must in every case, I suppose, be of the same age with themselves; and must also become at once older and younger than themselves?

Yes.

But the one did not partake of those affections?

Not at all.

Then it does not partake of time, and is not in any time?

So the argument shows.

Well, but do not the expressions "was," and "has become," and "was becoming," signify a participation of past time?

Certainly.

And do not "will be," "will become," "will have become," signify a participation of future time?

Yes.

And "is," or "becomes," signifies a participation of present time?

Certainly.

And if the one is absolutely without participation in time, it never had become, or was becoming, or was at any time, or is now become or is becoming, or is, or will become, or will have become, or will be, hereafter.

Most true.

But are there any modes of partaking of being other than these?

There are none.

Then the one cannot possibly partake of being?

That is the inference.

Then the one is not at all?

Clearly not.

Then the one does not exist in such way as to be one; for if it were and partook of being, it would already be; but if the argument is to be trusted, the one neither is nor is one?

[142] True.

But that which is not admits of no attribute or relation?

Of course not.

Then there is no name, nor expression, nor perception, nor opinion, nor knowledge of it?

Clearly not.

Then it is neither named, nor expressed, nor opined, nor known, nor does anything that is perceive it.

So we must infer.

But can all this be true about the one?

I think not.

Suppose, now, that we return once more to the original hypothesis; let us see whether, on a further review, any new aspect of the question appears.

I shall be very happy to do so.

We say that we have to work out together all the consequences, whatever they may be, which follow, if the one is?

Yes.

Then we will begin at the beginning:—If one is, can one be, and not partake of being?

Impossible.

Then the one will have being, but its being will not be the same with the one; for if the same, it would not be the being of the one; nor would the one have participated in being, for the proposition that one is would have been identical with the proposition that one is one; but our hypothesis is not if one is one, what will follow, but if one is:—am I not right?

Quite right.

We mean to say, that being has not the same significance as one?

Of course.

And when we put them together shortly, and say "One is," that is equivalent to saying, "partakes of being"?

Quite true.

Once more then let us ask, if one is what will follow. Does not this hypothesis necessarily imply that one is of such a nature as to have parts?

How so?

In this way:—If being is predicated of the one, if the one is, and one of being, if being is one; and if being and one are not the same; and since the one, which we have assumed, is, must not the whole, if it is one, itself be, and have for its parts, one and being?

Certainly.

And is each of these parts—one and being—to be simply called a part, or must the word "part" be relative to the word "whole"?

The latter.

Then that which is one is both a whole and has a part?

Certainly.

Again, of the parts of the one, if it is—I mean being and one—does either fail to imply the other? is the one wanting to being, or being to the one?

Impossible.

Thus, each of the parts also has in turn both one and being, and is at the least made up of two parts; and the same principle goes on for ever, and every part whatever has always these two parts; for being always involves one, and one being; so that one is always disappearing, and becoming two.

[143] Certainly.

And so the one, if it is, must be infinite in multiplicity?

Clearly.

Let us take another direction.

What direction?

We say that the one partakes of being and therefore it is?

Yes.

And in this way, the one, if it has being, has turned out to be many?

True.

But now, let us abstract the one which, as we say, partakes of being, and try to imagine it apart from that of which, as we say, it partakes—will this abstract one be one only or many?

One, I think.

Let us see:—Must not the being of one be other than one? for the one is not being, but, considered as one, only partook of being?

Certainly.

If being and the one be two different things, it is not because the one is one that it is other than being; nor because being is being that it is other than the one; but they differ from one another in virtue of otherness and difference.

Certainly.

So that the other is not the same—either with the one or with being?

Certainly not.

And therefore whether we take being and the other, or being and the one, or the one and the other, in every such case we take two things, which may be rightly called both.

How so.

In this way—you may speak of being?

Yes.

And also of one?

Yes.

Then now we have spoken of either of them?

Yes.

Well, and when I speak of being and one, I speak of them both?

Certainly.

And if I speak of being and the other, or of the one and the other—in any such case do I not speak of both?

Yes.

And must not that which is correctly called both, be also two?

Undoubtedly.

And of two things how can either by any possibility not be one?

It cannot.

Then, if the individuals of the pair are together two, they must be severally one?

Clearly.

And if each of them is one, then by the addition of any one to any pair, the whole becomes three?

Yes.

And three are odd, and two are even?

Of course.

And if there are two there must also be twice, and if there are three there must be thrice; that is, if twice one makes two, and thrice one three?

Certainly.

There are two, and twice, and therefore there must be twice two; and there are three, and there is thrice, and therefore there must be thrice three?

Of course.

If there are three and twice, there is twice three; and if there are two and thrice, there is thrice two?

Undoubtedly.

[144] Here, then, we have even taken even times, and odd taken odd times, and even taken odd times, and odd taken even times.

True.

And if this is so, does any number remain which has no necessity to be?

None whatever.

Then if one is, number must also be?

It must.

But if there is number, there must also be many, and infinite multiplicity of being; for number is infinite in multiplicity, and partakes also of being: am I not right?

Certainly.

And if all number participates in being, every part of number will also participate?

Yes.

Then being is distributed over the whole multitude of things, and nothing that is, however small or however great, is devoid of it? And, indeed, the very supposition of this is absurd, for how can that which is, be devoid of being?

In no way.

And it is divided into the greatest and into

the smallest, and into being of all sizes, and is broken up more than all things; the divisions of it have no limit.

True.

Then it has the greatest number of parts?

Yes, the greatest number.

Is there any of these which is a part of being, and yet no part?

Impossible.

But if it is at all and so long as it is, it must be one, and cannot be none?

Certainly.

Then the one attaches to every single part of being, and does not fail in any part, whether great or small, or whatever may be the size of it?

True.

But reflect:—Can one in its entirety, be in many places at the same time?

No; I see the impossibility of that.

And if not in its entirety, then it is divided; for it cannot be present with all the parts of being, unless divided.

True.

And that which has parts will be as many as the parts are?

Certainly.

Then we were wrong in saying just now, that being was distributed into the greatest number of parts. For it is not distributed into parts more than the one, but into parts equal to the one; the one is never wanting to being, or being to the one, but being two they are co-equal and co-extensive.

Certainly that is true.

The one itself, then, having been broken up into parts by being, is many and infinite?

True.

Then not only the one which has being is many, but the one itself distributed by being, must also be many?

Certainly.

Further, inasmuch as the parts are parts of a whole, the one, as a whole, [145] will be limited; for are not the parts contained by the whole?

Certainly.

And that which contains, is a limit?

Of course.

Then the one if it has being is one and many, whole and parts, having limits and yet unlimited in number?

Clearly.

And because having limits, also having extremes?

Certainly.

And if a whole, having beginning and mid-dle and end. For can anything be a whole without these three? And if any one of them is wanting to anything, will that any longer be a whole?

No.

Then the one, as appears, will have beginning, middle, and end.

It will.

But, again, the middle will be equidistant from the extremes; or it would not be in the middle?

Yes.

Then the one will partake of figure, either rectilinear or round, or a union of the two?

True.

And if this is the case, it will be both in itself and in another too.

How?

Every part is in the whole, and none is outside the whole.

True.

And all the parts are contained by the whole?

Yes.

And the one is all its parts, and neither more nor less than all?

No.

And the one is the whole?

Of course.

But if all the parts are in the whole, and the one is all of them and the whole, and they are all contained by the whole, the one will be contained by the one; and thus the one will be in itself.

That is true.

But then, again, the whole is not in the parts—neither in all the parts, nor in some one of them. For if it is in all, it must be in one; for if there were any one in which it was not, it could not be in all the parts; for the part in which it is wanting is one of all, and if the whole is not in this, how can it be in them all?

It cannot.

Nor can the whole be in some of the parts; for if the whole were in some of the parts, the greater would be in the less, which is impossible.

Yes, impossible.

But if the whole is neither in one, nor in more than one, nor in all of the parts, it must be in something else, or cease to be anywhere at all?

Certainly.

If it were nowhere, it would be nothing; but being a whole, and not being in itself, it must be in another.

Very true.

The one then, regarded as a whole, is in another, but regarded as being all its parts, is in itself; and therefore the one must be itself in itself and also in another.

Certainly.

The one then, being of this nature, is of necessity both at rest and in motion?

How?

The one is at rest since it is in itself, for being in one, and not passing out of this, [146] it is in the same, which is itself.

True.

And that which is ever in the same, must be ever at rest?

Certainly.

Well, and must not that, on the contrary, which is ever in other, never be in the same; and if never in the same, never at rest, and if not at rest, in motion?

True.

Then the one being always itself in itself and other, must always be both at rest and in motion?

Clearly.

And must be the same with itself, and other than itself; and also the same with the others, and other than the others; this follows from its previous affections.

How so?

Every thing in relation to every other thing, is either the same or other; or if neither the same nor other, then in the relation of a part to a whole, or of a whole to a part.

Clearly.

And is the one a part of itself?

Certainly not.

Since it is not a part in relation to itself it cannot be related to itself as whole to part?

It cannot.

But is the one other than one?

No.

And therefore not other than itself?

Certainly not.

If then it be neither other, nor a whole, nor a part in relation to itself, must it not be the same with itself?

Certainly.

But then, again, a thing which is in another place from "itself," if this "itself" remains in the same place with itself, must be other than "itself," for it will be in another place?

True.

Then the one has been shown to be at once in itself and in another?

Yes.

Thus, then, as appears, the one will be other than itself?

True.

Well, then, if anything be other than anything, will it not be other than that which is other?

Certainly.

And will not all things that are not one, be other than the one, and the one other than the not-one?

Of course.

Then the one will be other than the others?

True.

But, consider:—Are not the absolute same, and the absolute other, opposites to one another?

Of course.

Then will the same ever be in the other, or the other in the same?

They will not.

If then the other is never in the same, there is nothing in which the other is during any space of time; for during that space of time, however small, the other would be in the same. Is not that true?

Yes.

And since the other is never in the same, it can never be in anything that is.

True.

Then the other will never be either in the not-one, or in the one?

Certainly not.

Then not by reason of otherness is the one other than the not-one, or the not-one other than the one.

No.

Nor by reason of themselves will they be other than one another, if not partaking of the other. [147]

How can they be?

But if they are not other, either by reason of themselves or of the other, will they not altogether escape being other than one another?

They will.

Again, the not-one cannot partake of the one; otherwise it would not have been not-one, but would have been in some way one.

True.

Nor can the not-one be number; for having number, it would not have been not-one at all.

It would not.

Again, is the not-one part of the one; or rather, would it not in that case partake of the one?

It would.

If then, in every point of view, the one and the not-one are distinct, then neither is the one part or whole of the not-one, nor is the not-one part or whole of the one?

No.

But we said that things which are neither parts nor wholes of one another, nor other than one another, will be the same with one another: —so we said?

Yes.

Then shall we say that the one, being in this relation to the not-one, is the same with it?

Let us say so.

Then it is the same with itself and the others, and also other than itself and the others.

That appears to be the inference.

And it will also be like and unlike itself and the others?

Perhaps.

Since the one was shown to be other than the others, the others will also be other than the one.

Yes.

And the one is other than the others in the same degree that the others are other than it, and neither more nor less?

True.

And if neither more nor less, then in a like degree?

Yes.

In virtue of the affection by which the one is other than others and others in like manner other than it, the one will be affected like the others and the others like the one.

How do you mean?

I may take as an illustration the case of names: You give a name to a thing?

Yes.

And you may say the name once or oftener?

Yes.

And when you say it once, you mention that of which it is the name? and when more than once, is it something else which you mention? or must it always be the same thing of which you speak, whether you utter the name once or more than once?

Of course it is the same.

And is not "other" a name given to a thing?

Certainly.

Whenever, then, you use the word "other," whether once or oftener, you name that of which it is the name, and to no other do you give the name?

True.

Then when we say that the others are other than the one, and the one other than the others, in repeating the word "other" we speak of that nature to which the name is applied, and of no other?

Quite true.

Then the one which is other than others, and the other which is other than the one, *[148]* in

that the word "other" is applied to both, will be in the same condition; and that which is in the same condition is like?

Yes.

Then in virtue of the affection by which the one is other than the others, every thing will be like every thing, for every thing is other than every thing.

True.

Again, the like is opposed to the unlike?

Yes.

And the other to the same?

True again.

And the one was also shown to be the same with the others?

Yes.

And to be the same with the others is the opposite of being other than the others?

Certainly.

And in that it was other it was shown to be like?

Yes.

But in that it was the same it will be unlike by virtue of the opposite affection to that which made it like; and this was the affection of otherness.

Yes.

The same then will make it unlike; otherwise it will not be the opposite of the other.

True.

Then the one will be both like and unlike the others; like in so far as it is other, and unlike in so far as it is the same.

Yes, that argument may be used.

And there is another argument.

What?

In so far as it is affected in the same way it is not affected otherwise, and not being affected otherwise is not unlike, and not being unlike, is like; but in so far as it is affected by other it is otherwise, and being otherwise affected is unlike.

True.

Then because the one is the same with the others and other than the others, on either of these two grounds, or on both of them, it will be both like and unlike the others?

Certainly.

And in the same way as being other than itself and the same with itself, on either of these two grounds and on both of them, it will be like and unlike itself?

Of course.

Again, how far can the one touch or not touch itself and others?—consider.

I am considering.

The one was shown to be in itself which was a whole?

True.

And also in other things?

Yes.

In so far as it is in other things it would touch other things, but in so far as it is in itself it would be debarred from touching them, and would touch itself only.

Clearly.

Then the inference is that it would touch both?

It would.

But what do you say to a new point of view? Must not that which is to touch another be next to that which it is to touch, and occupy the place nearest to that in which what it touches is situated?

True.

Then the one, if it is to touch itself, ought to be situated next to itself, and occupy the place next to that in which itself is?

It ought.

And that would require that the one should be two, and be in two places at once, *[149]* and this, while it is one, will never happen.

No.

Then the one cannot touch itself any more than it can be two?

It cannot.

Neither can it touch others.

Why not?

The reason is, that whatever is to touch another must be in separation from, and next to, that which it is to touch, and no third thing can be between them.

True.

Two things, then, at the least are necessary to make contact possible?

They are.

And if to the two a third be added in due order, the number of terms will be three, and the contacts two?

Yes.

And every additional term makes one additional contact, whence it follows that the contacts are one less in number than the terms; the first two terms exceeded the number of contacts by one, and the whole number of terms exceeds the whole number of contacts by one in like manner; and for every one which is afterwards added to the number of terms, one contact is added to the contacts.

True.

Whatever is the whole number of things, the contacts will be always one less.

True.

But if there be only one, and not two, there will be no contact?

How can there be?

And do we not say that the others being other than the one are not one and have no part in the one?

True.

Then they have no number, if they have no one in them?

Of course not.

Then the others are neither one nor two, nor are they called by the name of any number?

No.

One, then, alone is one, and two do not exist?

Clearly not.

And if there are not two, there is no contact?

There is not.

Then neither does the one touch the others, nor the others the one, if there is no contact?

Certainly not.

For all which reasons the one touches and does not touch itself and the others?

True.

Further—is the one equal and unequal to itself and others?

How do you mean?

If the one were greater or less than the others, or the others greater or less than the one, they would not be greater or less than each other in virtue of their being the one and the others; but, if in addition to their being what they are they had equality, they would be equal to one another, or if the one had smallness and the others greatness, or the one had greatness and the others smallness—whichever kind had greatness would be greater, and whichever had smallness would be smaller?

Certainly.

Then there are two such ideas as greatness and smallness; for if they were not they could not be opposed to each other and be present in that which is.

How could they?

[150] If, then, smallness is present in the one it will be present either in the whole or in a part of the whole?

Certainly.

Suppose the first; it will be either co-equal and co-extensive with the whole one, or will contain the one?

Clearly.

If it be co-extensive with the one it will be co-equal with the one, or if containing the one it will be greater than the one?

Of course.

But can smallness be equal to anything or greater than anything, and have the functions of greatness and equality and not its own functions?

Impossible.

Then smallness cannot be in the whole of one, but, if at all, in a part only?

Yes.

And surely not in all of a part, for then the difficulty of the whole will recur; it will be equal to or greater than any part in which it is.

Certainly.

Then smallness will not be in anything, whether in a whole or in a part; nor will there be anything small but actual smallness.

True.

Neither will greatness be in the one, for if greatness be in anything there will be something greater other and besides greatness itself, namely, that in which greatness is; and this too when the small itself is not there, which the one, if it is great, must exceed; this, however, is impossible, seeing that smallness is wholly absent.

True.

But absolute greatness is only greater than absolute smallness, and smallness is only smaller than absolute greatness.

Very true.

Then other things are not greater or less than the one, if they have neither greatness nor smallness; nor have greatness or smallness any power of exceeding or being exceeded in relation to the one, but only in relation to one another; nor will the one be greater or less than them or others, if it has neither greatness nor smallness.

Clearly not.

Then if the one is neither greater nor less than the others, it cannot either exceed or be exceeded by them?

Certainly not.

And that which neither exceeds nor is exceeded, must be on an equality; and being on an equality, must be equal.

Of course.

And this will be true also of the relation of the one to itself; having neither greatness nor smallness in itself, it will neither exceed nor be exceeded by itself, but will be on an equality with and equal to itself.

Certainly.

Then the one will be equal to both itself and the others?

Clearly so.

And yet the one, being itself in itself, will al-

so surround and be without itself; [151] and, as containing itself, will be greater than itself; and, as contained in itself, will be less; and will thus be greater and less than itself.

It will.

Now there cannot possibly be anything which is not included in the one and the others?

Of course not.

But, surely, that which is must always be somewhere?

Yes.

But that which is in anything will be less, and that in which it is will be greater; in no other way can one thing be in another.

True.

And since there is nothing other or besides the one and the others, and they must be in something, must they not be in one another, the one in the others and the others in the one, if they are to be anywhere?

That is clear.

But inasmuch as the one is in the others, the others will be greater than the one, because they contain the one, which will be less than the others, because it is contained in them; and inasmuch as the others are in the one, the one on the same principle will be greater than the others, and the others less than the one.

True.

The one, then, will be equal to and greater and less than itself and the others?

Clearly.

And if it be greater and less and equal, it will be of equal and more and less measures or divisions than itself and the others, and if of measures, also of parts?

Of course.

And if of equal and more and less measures or divisions, it will be in number more or less than itself and the others, and likewise equal in number to itself and to the others?

How is that?

It will be of more measures than those things which it exceeds, and of as many parts as measures; and so with that to which it is equal, and that than which it is less.

True.

And being greater and less than itself, and equal to itself, it will be of equal measures with itself and of more and fewer measures than itself; and if of measures then also of parts?

It will.

And being of equal parts with itself, it will be numerically equal to itself; and being of more parts, more, and being of less, less than itself?

Certainly.

And the same will hold of its relation to other things; inasmuch as it is greater than them, it will be more in number than them; and inasmuch as it is smaller, it will be less in number; and inasmuch as it is equal in size to other things, it will be equal to them in number.

Certainly.

Once more, then, as would appear, the one will be in number both equal to and more and less than both itself and all other things.

It will.

Does the one also partake of time? And is it and does it become older and younger than itself and others, and again, neither younger nor older than itself and others, by virtue of participation in time?

How do you mean?

If one is, being must be predicated of it?

Yes.

But to be (εἶναι) is only participation of being in present time, and to have been is the participation of being at a past time, *[152]* and to be about to be is the participation of being at a future time?

Very true.

Then the one, since it partakes of being, partakes of time?

Certainly.

And is not time always moving forward?

Yes.

Then the one is always becoming older than itself, since it moves forward in time?

Certainly.

And do you remember that the older becomes older than that which becomes younger?

I remember.

Then since the one becomes older than itself, it becomes younger at the same time?

Certainly.

Thus, then, the one becomes older as well as younger than itself?

Yes.

And it is older (is it not?) when in becoming, it gets to the point of time between "was" and "will be," which is "now": for surely in going from the past to the future, it cannot skip the present?

No.

And when it arrives at the present it stops from becoming older, and no longer becomes, but is older, for if it went on it would never be reached by the present, for it is the nature of that which goes on, to touch both the present and the future, letting go the present and seizing the future, while in process of becoming between them.

True.

But that which is becoming cannot skip the present; when it reaches the present it ceases to become, and is then whatever it may happen to be becoming.

Clearly.

And so the one, when in becoming older it reaches the present, ceases to become, and is then older.

Certainly.

And it is older than that than which it was becoming older, and it was becoming older than itself.

Yes.

And that which is older is older than that which is younger?

True.

Then the one is younger than itself, when in becoming older it reaches the present?

Certainly.

But the present is always present with the one during all its being; for whenever it is it is always now.

Certainly.

Then the one always both is and becomes older and younger than itself?

Truly.

And is it or does it become a longer time than itself or an equal time with itself?

An equal time.

But if it becomes or is for an equal time with itself, it is of the same age with itself?

Of course.

And that which is of the same age, is neither older nor younger?

No.

The one, then, becoming and being the same time with itself, neither is nor becomes older or younger than itself? *[153]*

I should say not.

And what are its relations to other things? Is it or does it become older or younger than they?

I cannot tell you.

You can at least tell me that others than the one are more than the one—other would have been one, but the others have multitude, and are more than one?

They will have multitude.

And a multitude implies a number larger than one?

Of course.

And shall we say that the lesser or the greater is the first to come or to have come into existence?

The lesser.

Then the least is the first? And that is the one?

Yes.

Then the one of all things that have number is the first to come into being; but all other things have also number, being plural and not singular.

They have.

And since it came into being first it must be supposed to have come into being prior to the others, and the others later; and the things which came into being later, are younger than that which preceded them? And so the other things will be younger than the one, and the one older than other things?

True.

What would you say of another question? Can the one have come into being contrary to its own nature, or is that impossible?

Impossible.

And yet, surely, the one was shown to have parts; and if parts, then a beginning, middle and end?

Yes.

And a beginning, both of the one itself and of all other things, comes into being first of all; and after the beginning, the others follow, until you reach the end?

Certainly.

And all these others we shall affirm to be parts of the whole and of the one, which, as soon as the end is reached, has become whole and one?

Yes; that is what we shall say.

But the end comes last, and the one is of such a nature as to come into being with the last; and, since the one cannot come into being except in accordance with its own nature, its nature will require that it should come into being after the others, simultaneously with the end.

Clearly.

Then the one is younger than the others and the others older than the one.

That also is clear in my judgment.

Well, and must not a beginning or any other part of the one or of anything, if it be a part and not parts, being a part, be also of necessity one?

Certainly.

And will not the one come into being together with each part—together with the first part when that comes into being, and together with the second part and with all the rest, and will not be wanting to any part, which is added

to any other part until it has reached the last and become one whole; it will be wanting neither to the middle, nor to the first, nor to the last, nor to any of them, while the process of becoming is going on?

True.

Then the one is of the same age with all the others, so that if the one itself does not contradict its own nature, it will be neither prior nor posterior to the others, but simultaneous; and according to this argument the one will be neither older nor younger than the others, [154] nor the others than the one, but according to the previous argument the one will be older and younger than the others and the others than the one.

Certainly.

After this manner then the one is and has become. But as to its becoming older and younger than the others, and the others than the one, and neither older nor younger, what shall we say? Shall we say as of being so also of becoming, or otherwise?

I cannot answer.

But I can venture to say, that even if one thing were older or younger than another, it could not become older or younger in a greater degree than it was at first; for equals added to unequals, whether to periods of time or to anything else, leave the difference between them the same as at first.

Of course.

Then that which is, cannot become older or younger than that which is, since the difference of age is always the same; the one is and has become older and the other younger; but they are no longer becoming so.

True.

And the one which is does not therefore become either older or younger than the others which are.

No.

But consider whether they may not become older and younger in another way.

In what way?

Just as the one was proven to be older than the others and the others than the one.

And what of that?

If the one is older than the others, it has come into being a longer time than the others.

Yes.

But consider again; if we add equal time to a greater and a less time, will the greater differ from the less time by an equal or by a smaller portion than before?

By a smaller portion.

Then the difference between the age of the one and the age of the others will not be afterwards so great as at first, but if an equal time be added to both of them they will differ less and less in age?

Yes.

And that which differs in age from some other less than formerly, from being older will become younger in relation to that other than which it was older?

Yes, younger.

And if the one becomes younger the others aforesaid will become older than they were before, in relation to the one.

Certainly.

Then that which had become younger becomes older relatively to that which previously had become and was older; it never really is older, *[155]* but is always becoming, for the one is always growing on the side of youth and the other on the side of age. And in like manner the older is always in process of becoming younger than the younger; for as they are always going in opposite directions they become in ways the opposite to one another, the younger older than the older, and the older younger than the younger. They cannot, however, have become; for if they had already become they would be and not merely become. But that is impossible; for they are always becoming both older and younger than one another: the one becomes younger than the others because it was seen to be older and prior, and the others become older than the one because they came into being later; and in the same way the others are in the same relation to the one, because they were seen to be older and prior to the one.

That is clear.

Inasmuch then, as one thing does not become older or younger than another, in that they always differ from each other by an equal number, the one cannot become older or younger than the others, nor the others than the one; but inasmuch as that which came into being earlier and that which came into being later must continually differ from each other by a different portion—in this point of view the others must become older and younger than the one, and the one than the others.

Certainly.

For all these reasons, then, the one is and becomes older and younger than itself and the others, and neither is nor becomes older or younger than itself or the others.

Certainly.

But since the one partakes of time, and partakes of becoming older and younger, must it not also partake of the past, the present, and the future?

Of course it must.

Then the one was and is and will be, and was becoming and is becoming and will become?

Certainly.

And there is and was and will be something which is in relation to it and belongs to it?

True.

And since we have at this moment opinion and knowledge and perception of the one, there is opinion and knowledge and perception of it?

Quite right.

Then there is name and expression for it, and it is named and expressed, and everything of this kind which appertains to other things appertains to the one.

Certainly, that is true.

Yet once more and for the third time, let us consider: If the one is both one and many, as we have described, and is neither one nor many, and participates in time, must it not, in as far as it is one, at times partake of being, and in as far as it is not one, at times not partake of being?

Certainly.

But can it partake of being when not partaking of being, or not partake of being when partaking of being?

Impossible.

Then the one partakes and does not partake of being at different times, for that is the only way in which it can partake and not partake of the same.

True.

[156] And is there not also a time at which it assumes being and relinquishes being—for how can it have and not have the same thing unless it receives and also gives it up at some time?

Impossible.

And the assuming of being is what you would call becoming?

I should.

And the relinquishing of being you would call destruction?

I should.

The one then, as would appear, becomes and is destroyed by taking and giving up being.

Certainly.

And being one and many and in process of becoming and being destroyed, when it becomes one it ceases to be many, and when many, it ceases to be one?

Certainly.

And as it becomes one and many, must it not inevitably experience separation and aggregation?

Inevitably.

And whenever it becomes like and unlike it must be assimilated and dissimilated?

Yes.

And when it becomes greater or less or equal it must grow or diminish or be equalized?

True.

And when being in motion it rests, and when being at rest it changes to motion, it can surely be in no time at all?

How can it?

But that a thing which is previously at rest should be afterwards in motion, or previously in motion and afterwards at rest, without experiencing change, is impossible.

Impossible.

And surely there cannot be a time in which a thing can be at once neither in motion nor at rest?

There cannot.

But neither can it change without changing.

True.

When then does it change; for it cannot change either when at rest, or when in motion, or when in time?

It cannot.

And does this strange thing in which it is at the time of changing really exist?

What thing?

The moment. For the moment seems to imply a something out of which change takes place into either of two states; for the change is not from the state of rest as such, nor from the state of motion as such; but there is this curious nature which we call the moment lying between rest and motion, not being in any time; and into this and out of this what is in motion changes into rest, and what is at rest into motion.

So it appears.

And the one then, since it is at rest and also in motion, will change to either, for only in this way can it be in both. And in changing it changes in a moment, and when it is changing it will be in no time, and will not then be either in motion or at rest.

It will not.

[157] And it will be in the same case in relation to the other changes, when it passes from being into cessation of being, or from not-being into becoming—then it passes between certain states of motion and rest, and neither is nor is not, nor becomes nor is destroyed.

Very true.

And on the same principle, in the passage from one to many and from many to one, the one is neither one nor many, neither separated nor aggregated; and in the passage from like to unlike, and from unlike to like, it is neither like nor unlike, neither in a state of assimilation nor of dissimilation; and in the passage from small to great and equal and back again, it will be neither small nor great, nor equal, nor in a state of increase, or diminution, or equalization.

True.

All these, then, are the affections of the one, if the one has being.

Of course.

But if one is, what will happen to the others —is not that also to be considered?

Yes.

Let us show then, if one is, what will be the affections of the others than the one.

Let us do so.

Inasmuch as there are things other than the one, the others are not the one; for if they were they could not be other than the one.

Very true.

Nor are the others altogether without the one, but in a certain way they participate in the one.

In what way?

Because the others are other than the one inasmuch as they have parts; for if they had no parts they would be simply one.

Right.

And parts, as we affirm, have relation to a whole?

So we say.

And a whole must necessarily be one made up of many; and the parts will be parts of the one, for each of the parts is not a part of many, but of a whole.

How do you mean?

If anything were a part of many, being itself one of them, it will surely be a part of itself, which is impossible, and it will be a part of each one of the other parts, if of all; for if not a part of some one, it will be a part of all the others but this one, and thus will not be a part of each one; and if not a part of each one, it will not be a part of any one of the many; and not being a part of any one, it cannot be a part or anything else of all those things of none of which it is anything.

Clearly not.

Then the part is not a part of the many, nor of all, but is of a certain single form, which we call a whole, being one perfect unity framed out of all—of this the part will be a part.

Certainly.

If, then, the others have parts, they will participate in the whole and in the one.

True.

Then the others than the one must be one perfect whole, having parts.

Certainly.

And the same argument holds of each part, for the part must participate in the one; [158] for if each of the parts is a part, this means, I suppose, that it is one separate from the rest and self-related; otherwise it is not each.

True.

But when we speak of the part participating in the one, it must clearly be other than one; for if not, it would not merely have participated, but would have been one; whereas only the one itself can be one.

Very true.

Both the whole and the part must participate in the one; for the whole will be one whole, of which the parts will be parts; and each part will be one part of the whole which is the whole of the part.

True.

And will not the things which participate in the one, be other than it?

Of course.

And the things which are other than the one will be many; for if the things which are other than the one were neither one nor more than one, they would be nothing.

True.

But, seeing that the things which participate in the one as a part, and in the one as a whole, are more than one, must not those very things which participate in the one be infinite in number?

How so?

Let us look at the matter thus:—Is it not a fact that in partaking of the one they are not one, and do not partake of the one at the very time when they are partaking of it?

Clearly.

They do so then as multitudes in which the one is not present?

Very true.

And if we were to abstract from them in idea the very smallest fraction, must not that least fraction, if it does not partake of the one, be a multitude and not one?

It must.

And if we continue to look at the other side of their nature, regarded simply, and in itself, will not they, as far as we see them, be unlimited in number?

Certainly.

And yet, when each several part becomes a part, then the parts have a limit in relation to the whole and to each other, and the whole in relation to the parts.

Just so.

The result to the others than the one is that the union of themselves and the one appears to create a new element in them which gives to them limitation in relation to one another; whereas in their own nature they have no limit.

That is clear.

Then the others than the one, both as whole and parts, are infinite, and also partake of limit.

Certainly.

Then they are both like and unlike one another and themselves.

How is that?

Inasmuch as they are unlimited in their own nature, they are all affected in the same way.

True.

And inasmuch as they all partake of limit, they are all affected in the same way.

Of course.

But inasmuch as their state is both limited and unlimited, they are affected in opposite ways.

Yes.

[159] And opposites are the most unlike of things.

Certainly.

Considered, then, in regard to either one of their affections, they will be like themselves and one another; considered in reference to both of them together, most opposed and most unlike.

That appears to be true.

Then the others are both like and unlike themselves and one another?

True.

And they are the same and also different from one another, and in motion and at rest, and experience every sort of opposite affection, as may be proved without difficulty of them, since they have been shown to have experienced the affections aforesaid?

True.

Suppose, now, that we leave the further discussion of these matters as evident, and consider again upon the hypothesis that the one is, whether the opposite of all this is or is not equally true of the others.

By all means.

Then let us begin again, and ask, If one is, what must be the affections of the others?

Let us ask that question.

Must not the one be distinct from the others, and the others from the one?

Why so?

Why, because there is nothing else beside them which is distinct from both of them; for the expression "one and the others" includes all things.

Yes, all things.

Then we cannot suppose that there is anything different from them in which both the one and the others might exist?

There is nothing.

Then the one and the others are never in the same?

True.

Then they are separated from each other?

Yes.

And we surely cannot say that what is truly one has parts?

Impossible.

Then the one will not be in the others as a whole, nor as part, if it be separated from the others, and has no parts?

Impossible.

Then there is no way in which the others can partake of the one, if they do not partake either in whole or in part?

It would seem not.

Then there is no way in which the others are one, or have in themselves any unity?

There is not.

Nor are the others many; for if they were many, each part of them would be a part of the whole; but now the others, not partaking in any way of the one, are neither one nor many, nor whole, nor part.

True.

Then the others neither are nor contain two or three, if entirely deprived of the one?

True.

Then the others are neither like nor unlike the one, nor is likeness and unlikeness in them; for if they were like and unlike, or had in them likeness and unlikeness, they would have two natures in them opposite to one another.

That is clear.

But for that which partakes of nothing to partake of two things was held by us to be impossible?

Impossible.

[160] Then the others are neither like nor unlike nor both, for if they were like or unlike they would partake of one of those two natures, which would be one thing, and if they were both they would partake of opposites which would be two things, and this has been shown to be impossible.

True.

Therefore they are neither the same, nor other, nor in motion, nor at rest, nor in a state of becoming, nor of being destroyed, nor greater, nor less, nor equal, nor have they experienced anything else of the sort; for, if they are capable of experiencing any such affection, they will participate in one and two and three, and odd and even, and in these, as has been proved, they do not participate, seeing that they are altogether and in every way devoid of the one.

Very true.

Therefore if one is, the one is all things, and also nothing, both in relation to itself and to other things.

Certainly.

Well, and ought we not to consider next what will be the consequence if the one is not?

Yes; we ought.

What is the meaning of the hypothesis—If the one is not; is there any difference between this and the hypothesis—If the not one is not?

There is a difference, certainly.

Is there a difference only, or rather are not the two expressions—if the one is not, and if the not one is not, entirely opposed?

They are entirely opposed.

And suppose a person to say:—If greatness is not, if smallness is not, or anything of that sort, does he not mean, whenever he uses such an expression, that "what is not" is other than other things?

To be sure.

And so when he says "If one is not" he clearly means, that what "is not" is other than all others; we know what he means—do we not?

Yes, we do.

When he says "one," he says something which is known; and secondly something which is other than all other things; it makes no difference whether he predicate of one being or not-being, for that which is said "not to be" is known to be something all the same, and is distinguished from other things.

Certainly.

Then I will begin again, and ask: If one is not, what are the consequences? In the first place, as would appear, there is a knowledge of it, or the very meaning of the words, "if one is not," would not be known.

True.

Secondly, the others differ from it, or it could not be described as different from the others?

Certainly.

Difference, then, belongs to it as well as knowledge; for in speaking of the one as different from the others, we do not speak of a difference in the others, but in the one.

Clearly so.

Moreover, the one that is not is something and partakes of relation to "that," and "this," and "these," and the like, and is an attribute of "this"; for the one, or the others than the one, could not have been spoken of, nor could any attribute or relative of the one that is not have been or been spoken of, nor could it have been said to be anything, if it did not partake of "some," or of the other relations just now mentioned.

True.

Being, then, cannot be ascribed to the one, since it is not; but the one that is not may or rather must participate in many things, [161] if it and nothing else is not; if, however, neither the one nor the one that is not is supposed not to be, and we are speaking of something of a different nature, we can predicate nothing of it. But supposing that the one that is not and nothing else is not, then it must participate in the predicate "that," and in many others.

Certainly.

And it will have unlikeness in relation to the others, for the others being different from the one will be of a different kind.

Certainly.

And are not things of a different kind also other in kind?

Of course.

And are not things other in kind unlike?

They are unlike.

And if they are unlike the one, that which they are unlike will clearly be unlike them?

Clearly so.

Then the one will have unlikeness in respect of which the others are unlike it?

That would seem to be true.

And if unlikeness to other things is attributed to it, it must have likeness to itself.

How so?

If the one have unlikeness to one, something else must be meant; nor will the hypothesis relate to one; but it will relate to something other than one?

Quite so.

But that cannot be.

No.

Then the one must have likeness to itself?

It must.

Again, it is not equal to the others; for if it were equal, then it would at once be and be like them in virtue of the equality; but if one has no being, then it can neither be nor be like?

It cannot.

But since it is not equal to the others, neither can the others be equal to it?

Certainly not.

And things that are not equal are unequal?

True.

And they are unequal to an unequal?

Of course.

Then the one partakes of inequality, and in respect of this the others are unequal to it?

Very true.

And inequality implies greatness and smallness?

Yes.

Then the one, if of such a nature, has greatness and smallness?

That appears to be true.

And greatness and smallness always stand apart?

True.

Then there is always something between them?

There is.

And can you think of anything else which is between them other than equality?

No, it is equality which lies between them.

Then that which has greatness and smallness also has equality, which lies between them?

That is clear.

Then the one, which is not, partakes, as would appear, of greatness and smallness and equality?

Clearly.

Further, it must surely in a sort partake of being?

How so?

It must be so, for if not, then we should not speak the truth in saying that the one is not. But if we speak the truth, clearly we must say what is. Am I not right?

[162] Yes.

And since we affirm that we speak truly, we must also affirm that we say what is?

Certainly.

Then, as would appear, the one, when it is not, is; for if it were not to be when it is not, but were to relinquish something of being, so as to become not-being, it would at once be.

Quite true.

Then the one which is not, if it is to maintain itself, must have the being of not-being as the bond of not-being, just as being must have as a bond the not-being of not-being in order to perfect its own being; for the truest assertion of the being of being and of the not-being of not-being is when being partakes of the being of being, and not of the being of not-being—that is, the perfection of being; and when not-being does not partake of the not-being of not-being but of the being of not-being—that is the perfection of not-being.

Most true.

Since then what is partakes of not-being, and what is not of being, must not the one also partake of being in order not to be?

Certainly.

Then the one, if it is not, clearly has being?

Clearly.

And has not-being also, if it is not?

Of course.

But can anything which is in a certain state not be in that state without changing?

Impossible.

Then everything which is and is not in a certain state, implies change?

Certainly.

And change is motion—we may say that?

Yes, motion.

And the one has been proved both to be and not to be?

Yes.

And therefore is and is not in the same state?

Yes.

Thus the one that is not has been shown to have motion also, because it changes from being to not-being?

That appears to be true.

But surely if it is nowhere among what is, as is the fact, since it is not, it cannot change from one place to another?

Impossible.

Then it cannot move by changing place?

No.

Nor can it turn on the same spot, for it nowhere touches the same, for the same is, and that which is not cannot be reckoned among things that are?

It cannot.

Then the one, if it is not, cannot turn in that in which it is not?

No.

Neither can the one, whether it is or is not, be altered into other than itself, for if it altered and became different from itself, then we could not be still speaking of the one, but of something else?

True.

But if the one neither suffers alteration, nor turns round in the same place, nor changes place, can it still be capable of motion?

Impossible.

Now that which is unmoved must surely be at rest, and that which is at rest must stand still?

Certainly.

Then the one that is not, stands still, and is also in motion?

That seems to be true.

But if it be in motion it must necessarily undergo alteration, for anything which is moved, [163] in so far as it is moved, is no longer in the same state, but in another?

Yes.

Then the one, being moved, is altered?

Yes.

And, further, if not moved in any way, it will not be altered in any way?

No.

Then, in so far as the one that is not is moved, it is altered, but in so far as it is not moved, it is not altered?

Right.

Then the one that is not is altered and is not altered?

That is clear.

And must not that which is altered become other than it previously was, and lose its former state and be destroyed; but that which is not altered can neither come into being nor be destroyed?

Very true.

And the one that is not, being altered, becomes and is destroyed; and not being altered, neither becomes nor is destroyed; and so the one that is not becomes and is destroyed, and neither becomes nor is destroyed?

True.

And now, let us go back once more to the beginning, and see whether these or some other consequences will follow.

Let us do as you say.

If one is not, we ask what will happen in respect of one? That is the question.

Yes.

Do not the words "is not" signify absence of being in that to which we apply them?

Just so.

And when we say that a thing is not, do we mean that it is not in one way but is in another? or do we mean, absolutely, that what is not has in no sort or way or kind participation of being?

Quite absolutely.

Then, that which is not cannot be, or in any way participate in being?

It cannot.

And did we not mean by becoming, and being destroyed, the assumption of being and the loss of being?

Nothing else.

And can that which has no participation in being, either assume or lose being?

Impossible.

The one then, since it in no way is, cannot have or lose or assume being in any way?

True.

Then the one that is not, since it in no way partakes of being, neither perishes nor becomes?

No.

Then it is not altered at all; for if it were it would become and be destroyed?

True.

But if it be not altered it cannot be moved?

Certainly not.

Nor can we say that it stands, if it is nowhere; for that which stands must always be in one and the same spot?

Of course.

Then we must say that the one which is not never stands still and never moves?

Neither.

Nor is there any existing thing which can be attributed to it; for if there had been, *[164]* it would partake of being?

That is clear.

And therefore neither smallness, nor greatness, nor equality, can be attributed to it?

No.

Nor yet likeness nor difference, either in relation to itself or to others?

Clearly not.

Well, and if nothing should be attributed to it, can other things be attributed to it?

Certainly not.

And therefore other things can neither be like or unlike, the same, or different in relation to it?

They cannot.

Nor can what is not, be anything, or be this thing, or be related to or the attribute of this or that or other, or be past, present, or future. Nor can knowledge, or opinion, or perception, or expression, or name, or any other thing that is, have any concern with it?

No.

Then the one that is not has no condition of any kind?

Such appears to be the conclusion.

Yet once more; if one is not, what becomes of the others? Let us determine that.

Yes; let us determine that.

The others must surely be; for if they, like the one, were not, we could not be now speaking of them.

True.

But to speak of the others implies difference —the terms "other" and "different" are synonymous?

True.

Other means other than other, and different, different from the different?

Yes.

Then, if there are to be others, there is something than which they will be other?

Certainly.

And what can that be?—for if the one is not, they will not be other than the one.

They will not.

Then they will be other than each other; for the only remaining alternative is that they are other than nothing.

True.

And they are each other than one another, as being plural and not singular; for if one is not, they cannot be singular but every particle of them is infinite in number; and even if a person takes that which appears to be the smallest fraction, this, which seemed one, in a moment evanesces into many, as in a dream, and from being the smallest becomes very great, in comparison with the fractions into which it is split up?

Very true.

And in such particles the others will be other than one another, if others are, and the one is not?

Exactly.

And will there not be many particles, each appearing to be one, but not being one, if one is not?

True.

And it would seem that number can be predicated of them if each of them appears to be one, though it is really many?

It can.

And there will seem to be odd and even among them, which will also have no reality, if one is not?

Yes.

And there will appear to be a least among them; and even this will seem large and manifold in comparison with the many small *[165]* fractions which are contained in it?

Certainly.

And each particle will be imagined to be equal to the many and little; for it could not have appeared to pass from the greater to the less without having appeared to arrive at the middle; and thus would arise the appearance of equality.

Yes.

And having neither beginning, middle, nor end, each separate particle yet appears to have a limit in relation to itself and other.

How so?

Because, when a person conceives of any one of these as such, prior to the beginning another beginning appears, and there is another end, remaining after the end, and in the middle truer middles within but smaller, because no unity can be conceived of any of them, since the one is not.

Very true.

And so all being, whatever we think of, must be broken up into fractions, for a particle will have to be conceived of without unity?

Certainly.

And such being when seen indistinctly and at a distance, appears to be one; but when seen near and with keen intellect, every single thing appears to be infinite, since it is deprived of the one, which is not?

Nothing more certain.

Then each of the others must appear to be infinite and finite, and one and many, if others than the one exist and not the one.

They must.

Then will they not appear to be like and unlike?

In what way?

Just as in a picture things appear to be all one to a person standing at a distance, and to be in the same state and alike?

True.

But when you approach them, they appear to be many and different; and because of the appearance of the difference, different in kind from, and unlike, themselves?

True.

And so must the particles appear to be like and unlike themselves and each other.

Certainly.

And must they not be the same and yet different from one another, and in contact with themselves, although they are separated, and having every sort of motion, and every sort of rest, and becoming and being destroyed, and in neither state, and the like, all which things may be easily enumerated, if the one is not and the many are?

Most true.

Once more, let us go back to the beginning, and ask if the one is not, and the others of the one are, what will follow.

Let us ask that question.

In the first place, the others will not be one?

Impossible.

Nor will they be many; for if they were many one would be contained in them. But if no one of them is one, all of them are nought, and therefore they will not be many.

True.

If there be no one in the others, the others are neither many nor one.

[166] They are not.

Nor do they appear either as one or many.

Why not?

Because the others have no sort or manner or way of communion with any sort of not-being, nor can anything which is not, be connected with any of the others; for that which is not has no parts.

True.

Nor is there an opinion or any appearance of not-being in connection with the others, nor is not-being ever in any way attributed to the others.

No.

Then if one is not, the others neither are, nor any of the others either as one or many; for you cannot conceive the many without the one.

You cannot.

Then if one is not, there is no conception of can be conceived to be either one or many?

It would seem not.

Nor as like or unlike?

No.

Nor as the same or different, nor in contact or separation, nor in any of those states which we enumerated as appearing to be;—the others neither are nor appear to be any of these, if one is not?

True.

Then may we not sum up the argument in a word and say truly: If one is not, then nothing is?

Certainly.

Let thus much be said; and further let us affirm what seems to be the truth, that, whether one is or is not, one and the others in relation to themselves and one another, all of them, in every way, are and are not, and appear to be and appear not to be.

Most true.

THEAETETUS

PERSONS OF THE DIALOGUE: SOCRATES; THEODORUS; THEAETETUS. *Euclid and Terpsion meet in front of Euclid's house in Megara; they enter the house, and the dialogue is read to them by a servant*

~~~~~~~~~~~~~~~~~~~~~~~~~~~~~

[142] *Euclid*. Have you only just arrived from the country, Terpsion?

Terpsion. No, I came some time ago: and I have been in the Agora looking for you, and wondering that I could not find you.

Euc. But I was not in the city.

Terp. Where then?

Euc. As I was going down to the harbour, I met Theaetetus—he was being carried up to Athens from the army at Corinth.

Terp. Was he alive or dead?

Euc. He was scarcely alive, for he has been badly wounded; but he was suffering even more from the sickness which has broken out in the army.

Terp. The dysentery, you mean?

Euc. Yes.

Terp. Alas! what a loss he will be!

Euc. Yes, Terpsion, he is a noble fellow; only to-day I heard some people highly praising his behaviour in this very battle.

Terp. No wonder; I should rather be surprised at hearing anything else of him. But why did he go on, instead of stopping at Megara?

Euc. He wanted to get home: although I entreated and advised him to remain, he would not listen to me; so I set him on his way, and turned back, and then I remembered what Socrates had said of him, and thought how remarkably this, like all his predictions, had been fulfilled. I believe that he had seen him a little before his own death, when Theaetetus was a youth, and he had a memorable conversation with him, which he repeated to me when I came to Athens; he was full of admiration of his genius, and said that he would most certainly be a great man, if he lived.

Terp. The prophecy has certainly been fulfilled; but what was the conversation? can you tell me?

[143] *Euc*. No, indeed, not offhand; but I took notes of it as soon as I got home; these I filled up from memory, writing them out at leisure; and whenever I went to Athens, I asked Socrates about any point which I had forgotten, and on my return I made corrections; thus I have nearly the whole conversation written down.

Terp. I remember—you told me; and I have always been intending to ask you to show me the writing, but have put off doing so; and now, why should we not read it through?—having just come from the country, I should greatly like to rest.

Euc. I too shall be very glad of a rest, for I went with Theaetetus as far as Erineum. Let us go in, then, and, while we are reposing, the servant shall read to us.

Terp. Very good.

Euc. Here is the roll, Terpsion; I may observe that I have introduced Socrates, not as narrating to me, but as actually conversing with the persons whom he mentioned—these were, Theodorus the geometrician (of Cyrene), and Theaetetus. I have omitted, for the sake of convenience, the interlocutory words "I said," "I remarked," which he used when he spoke of himself, and again, "he agreed," or "dis-

512

agreed," in the answer, lest the repetition of them should be troublesome.

Terp. Quite right, Euclid.

Euc. And now, boy, you may take the roll and read.

Euclid's servant reads.

Socrates. If I cared enough about the Cyrenians, Theodorus, I would ask you whether there are any rising geometricians or philosophers in that part of the world. But I am more interested in our own Athenian youth, and I would rather know who among them are likely to do well. I observe them as far as I can myself, and I enquire of any one whom they follow, and I see that a great many of them follow you, in which they are quite right, considering your eminence in geometry and in other ways. Tell me then, if you have met with any one who is good for anything.

Theodorus. Yes, Socrates, I have become acquainted with one very remarkable Athenian youth, whom I commend to you as well worthy of your attention. If he had been a beauty I should have been afraid to praise him, lest you should suppose that I was in love with him; but he is no beauty, and you must not be offended if I say that he is very like you; for he has a snub nose and projecting eyes, although these features are less marked in him than in you. Seeing, *[144]* then, that he has no personal attractions, I may freely say, that in all my acquaintance, which is very large, I never knew any one who was his equal in natural gifts: for he has a quickness of apprehension which is almost unrivalled, and he is exceedingly gentle, and also the most courageous of men; there is a union of qualities in him such as I have never seen in any other, and should scarcely have thought possible; for those who, like him, have quick and ready and retentive wits, have generally also quick tempers; they are ships without ballast, and go darting about, and are mad rather than courageous; and the steadier sort, when they have to face study, prove stupid and cannot remember. Whereas he moves surely and smoothly and successfully in the path of knowledge and enquiry; and he is full of gentleness, flowing on silently like a river of oil; at his age, it is wonderful.

Soc. That is good news; whose son is he?

Theod. The name of his father I have forgotten, but the youth himself is the middle one of those who are approaching us; he and his companions have been anointing themselves in the outer court, and now they seem to have finished, and are coming towards us. Look and see whether you know him.

Soc. I know the youth, but I do not know his name; he is the son of Euphronius the Sunian, who was himself an eminent man, and such another as his son is, according to your account of him; I believe that he left a considerable fortune.

Theod. Theaetetus, Socrates, is his name; but I rather think that the property disappeared in the hands of trustees; notwithstanding which he is wonderfully liberal.

Soc. He must be a fine fellow; tell him to come and sit by me.

Theod. I will. Come hither, Theaetetus, and sit by Socrates.

Soc. By all means, Theaetetus, in order that I may see the reflection of myself in your face, for Theodorus says that we are alike; and yet if each of us held in his hands a lyre, and he said that they were tuned alike, should we at once take his word, or should we ask whether he who said so was or was not a musician?

Theaetetus. We should ask.

Soc. And if we found that he was, we should take his word; and if not, not?

Theaet. True.

Soc. And if this supposed likeness of our faces is a matter of any interest to us, we should enquire whether he who says that we are alike is a painter or not?

[145] Theaet. Certainly we should.

Soc. And is Theodorus a painter?

Theaet. I never heard that he was.

Soc. Is he a geometrician?

Theaet. Of course he is, Socrates.

Soc. And is he an astronomer and calculator and musician, and in general an educated man?

Theaet. I think so.

Soc. If, then, he remarks on a similarity in our persons, either by way of praise or blame, there is no particular reason why we should attend to him.

Theaet. I should say not.

Soc. But if he praises the virtue or wisdom which are the mental endowments of either of us, then he who hears the praises will naturally desire to examine him who is praised: and he again should be willing to exhibit himself.

Theaet. Very true, Socrates.

Soc. Then now is the time, my dear Theaetetus, for me to examine, and for you to exhibit; since although Theodorus has praised many a citizen and stranger in my hearing, never did I hear him praise any one as he has been praising you.

Theaet. I am glad to hear it, Socrates; but what if he was only in jest?

Soc. Nay, Theodorus is not given to jesting; and I cannot allow you to retract your consent on any such pretence as that. If you do, he will have to swear to his words; and we are perfectly sure that no one will be found to impugn him. Do not be shy then, but stand to your word.

Theaet. I suppose I must, if you wish it.

Soc. In the first place, I should like to ask what you learn of Theodorus: something of geometry, perhaps?

Theaet. Yes.

Soc. And astronomy and harmony and calculation?

Theaet. I do my best.

Soc. Yes, my boy, and so do I: and my desire is to learn of him, or of anybody who seems to understand these things. And I get on pretty well in general; but there is a little difficulty which I want you and the company to aid me in investigating. Will you answer me a question: "Is not learning growing wiser about that which you learn?"

Theaet. Of course.

Soc. And by wisdom the wise are wise?

Theaet. Yes.

Soc. And is that different in any way from knowledge?

Theaet. What?

Soc. Wisdom; are not men wise in that which they know?

Theaet. Certainly they are.

Soc. Then wisdom and knowledge are the same?

Theaet. Yes.

[146] *Soc.* Herein lies the difficulty which I can never solve to my satisfaction—What is knowledge? Can we answer that question? What say you? which of us will speak first? whoever misses shall sit down, as at a game of ball, and shall be donkey, as the boys say; he who lasts out his competitors in the game without missing, shall be our king, and shall have the right of putting to us any questions which he pleases . . . Why is there no reply? I hope, Theodorus, that I am not betrayed into rudeness by my love of conversation? I only want to make us talk and be friendly and sociable.

Theod. The reverse of rudeness, Socrates: but I would rather that you would ask one of the young fellows; for the truth is, that I am unused to your game of question and answer, and I am too old to learn; the young will be more suitable, and they will improve more than I shall, for youth is always able to improve.

And so having made a beginning with Theaetetus, I would advise you to go on with him and not let him off.

Soc. Do you hear, Theaetetus, what Theodorus says? The philosopher, whom you would not like to disobey, and whose word ought to be a command to a young man, bids me interrogate you. Take courage, then, and nobly say what you think that knowledge is.

Theaet. Well, Socrates, I will answer as you and he bid me; and if I make a mistake, you will doubtless correct me.

Soc. We will, if we can.

Theaet. Then, I think that the sciences which I learn from Theodorus—geometry, and those which you just now mentioned—are knowledge; and I would include the art of the cobbler and other craftsmen; these, each and all of them, are knowledge.

Soc. Too much, Theaetetus, too much; the nobility and liberality of your nature make you give many and diverse things, when I am asking for one simple thing.

Theaet. What do you mean, Socrates?

Soc. Perhaps nothing. I will endeavour, however, to explain what I believe to be my meaning: When you speak of cobbling, you mean the art or science of making shoes?

Theaet. Just so.

Soc. And when you speak of carpentering, you mean the art of making wooden implements?

Theaet. I do.

Soc. In both cases you define the subject-matter of each of the two arts?

Theaet. True.

Soc. But that, Theaetetus, was not the point of my question: we wanted to know not the subjects, nor yet the number of the arts or sciences, for we were not going to count them, but we wanted to know the nature of knowledge in the abstract. Am I not right?

Theaet. Perfectly right.

[147] *Soc.* Let me offer an illustration: Suppose that a person were to ask about some very trivial and obvious thing—for example, What is clay? and we were to reply, that there is a clay of potters, there is a clay of oven-makers, there is a clay of brick-makers; would not the answer be ridiculous?

Theaet. Truly.

Soc. In the first place, there would be an absurdity in assuming that he who asked the question would understand from our answer the nature of "clay," merely because we added "of the image-makers," or of any other workers.

How can a man understand the name of anything, when he does not know the nature of it?

Theaet. He cannot.

Soc. Then he who does not know what science or knowledge is, has no knowledge of the art or science of making shoes?

Theaet. None.

Soc. Nor of any other science?

Theaet. No.

Soc. And when a man is asked what science or knowledge is, to give in answer the name of some art or science is ridiculous; for the question is, "What is knowledge?" and he replies, "A knowledge of this or that."

Theaet. True.

Soc. Moreover, he might answer shortly and simply, but he makes an enormous circuit. For example, when asked about the clay, he might have said simply, that clay is moistened earth—what sort of clay is not to the point.

Theaet. Yes, Socrates, there is no difficulty as you put the question. You mean, if I am not mistaken, something like what occurred to me and to my friend here, your namesake Socrates, in a recent discussion.

Soc. What was that, Theaetetus?

Theaet. Theodorus was writing out for us something about roots, such as the roots of three or five, showing that they are incommensurable by the unit: he selected other examples up to seventeen—there he stopped. Now as there are innumerable roots, the notion occurred to us of attempting to include them all under one name or class.

Soc. And did you find such a class?

Theaet. I think that we did; but I should like to have your opinion.

Soc. Let me hear.

Theaet. We divided all numbers into two classes: those which are made up of equal factors multiplying into one another, which we compared to square figures and called square or equilateral numbers;—that was one class.

Soc. Very good.

Theaet. The intermediate numbers, such as three and five, and every other number which is made up of unequal factors, [148] either of a greater multiplied by a less, or of a less multiplied by a greater, and when regarded as a figure, is contained in unequal sides;—all these we compared to oblong figures, and called them oblong numbers.

Soc. Capital; and what followed?

Theaet. The lines, or sides, which have for their squares the equilateral plane numbers, were called by us lengths or magnitudes; and the lines which are the roots of (or whose squares are equal to) the oblong numbers, were called powers or roots; the reason of this latter name being, that they are commensurable with the former [i.e., with the so-called lengths or magnitudes] not in linear measurement, but in the value of the superficial content of their squares; and the same about solids.

Soc. Excellent, my boys; I think that you fully justify the praises of Theodorus, and that he will not be found guilty of false witness.

Theaet. But I am unable, Socrates, to give you a similar answer about knowledge, which is what you appear to want; and therefore Theodorus is a deceiver after all.

Soc. Well, but if some one were to praise you for running, and to say that he never met your equal among boys, and afterwards you were beaten in a race by a grown-up man, who was a great runner—would the praise be any the less true?

Theaet. Certainly not.

Soc. And is the discovery of the nature of knowledge so small a matter, as I just now said? Is it not one which would task the powers of men perfect in every way?

Theaet. By heaven, they should be the top of all perfection!

Soc. Well, then, be of good cheer; do not say that Theodorus was mistaken about you, but do your best to ascertain the true nature of knowledge, as well as of other things.

Theaet. I am eager enough, Socrates, if that would bring to light the truth.

Soc. Come, you made a good beginning just now; let your own answer about roots be your model, and as you comprehended them all in one class, try and bring the many sorts of knowledge under one definition.

Theaet. I can assure you, Socrates, that I have tried very often, when the report of questions asked by you was brought to me; but I can neither persuade myself that I have a satisfactory answer to give, nor hear of any one who answers as you would have him; and I cannot shake off a feeling of anxiety.

Soc. These are the pangs of labour, my dear Theaetetus; you have something within you which you are bringing to the birth.

Theaet. I do not know, Socrates; I only say what I feel.

[149] Soc. And have you never heard, simpleton, that I am the son of a midwife, brave and burly, whose name was Phaenarete?

Theaet. Yes, I have.

Soc. And that I myself practise midwifery?

Theaet. No, never.

Soc. Let me tell you that I do though, my friend: but you must not reveal the secret, as the world in general have not found me out; and therefore they only say of me, that I am the strangest of mortals and drive men to their wits' end. Did you ever hear that too?

Theaet. Yes.

Soc. Shall I tell you the reason?

Theaet. By all means.

Soc. Bear in mind the whole business of the midwives, and then you will see my meaning better:—No woman, as you are probably aware, who is still able to conceive and bear, attends other women, but only those who are past bearing.

Theaet. Yes, I know.

Soc. The reason of this is said to be that Artemis—the goddess of childbirth—is not a mother, and she honours those who are like herself; but she could not allow the barren to be midwives, because human nature cannot know the mystery of an art without experience; and therefore she assigned this office to those who are too old to bear.

Theaet. I dare say.

Soc. And I dare say too, or rather I am absolutely certain, that the midwives know better than others who is pregnant and who is not?

Theaet. Very true.

Soc. And by the use of potions and incantations they are able to arouse the pangs and to soothe them at will; they can make those bear who have a difficulty in bearing, and if they think fit they can smother the embryo in the womb.

Theaet. They can.

Soc. Did you ever remark that they are also most cunning matchmakers, and have a thorough knowledge of what unions are likely to produce a brave brood?

Theaet. No, never.

Soc. Then let me tell you that this is their greatest pride, more than cutting the umbilical cord. And if you reflect, you will see that the same art which cultivates and gathers in the fruits of the earth, will be most likely to know in what soils the several plants or seeds should be deposited.

Theaet. Yes, the same art.

Soc. And do you suppose that with women the case is otherwise?

[*150*] *Theaet.* I should think not.

Soc. Certainly not; but midwives are respectable women who have a character to lose, and they avoid this department of their profession, because they are afraid of being called procuresses, which is a name given to those who join together man and woman in an unlawful and unscientific way; and yet the true midwife is also the true and only matchmaker.

Theaet. Clearly.

Soc. Such are the midwives, whose task is a very important one, but not so important as mine; for women do not bring into the world at one time real children, and at another time counterfeits which are with difficulty distinguished from them; if they did, then the discernment of the true and false birth would be the crowning achievement of the art of midwifery—you would think so?

Theaet. Indeed I should.

Soc. Well, my art of midwifery is in most respects like theirs; but differs, in that I attend men and not women, and I look after their souls when they are in labour, and not after their bodies: and the triumph of my art is in thoroughly examining whether the thought which the mind of the young man brings forth is a false idol or a noble and true birth. And like the midwives, I am barren, and the reproach which is often made against me, that I ask questions of others and have not the wit to answer them myself, is very just—the reason is, that the god compels me to be a midwife, but does not allow me to bring forth. And therefore I am not myself at all wise, nor have I anything to show which is the invention or birth of my own soul, but those who converse with me profit. Some of them appear dull enough at first, but afterwards, as our acquaintance ripens, if the god is gracious to them, they all make astonishing progress; and this in the opinion of others as well as in their own. It is quite clear that they never learned anything from me; the many fine discoveries to which they cling are of their own making. But to me and the god they owe their delivery. And the proof of my words is, that many of them in their ignorance, either in their self-conceit despising me, or falling under the influence of others, have gone away too soon; and have not only lost the children of whom I had previously delivered them by an ill bringing up, but have stifled whatever else they had in them by evil communications, being fonder of lies and shams than of the truth; and they have at last ended by seeing themselves, as others see them, to be great fools. Aristeides, the son of Lysimachus, is one of them, [*151*] and there are many others. The truants often return to me, and beg that I would consort with them again—they are ready to go to me on their knees—and then, if my familiar allows, which is not always the case, I receive them, and they begin to grow again. Dire are the pangs which my art is able to arouse and to allay in those who consort with me, just like the pangs of women in childbirth; night and day they are full of perplexity and travail which is even worse than that of the women. So much for them. And there are others, Theaetetus, who come to me apparently having nothing in them; and as I know that they have no need of my art, I coax them into marrying some one, and by the grace of God I can generally tell who is likely to do them good. Many of them I have given away to Prodicus, and many to other inspired sages. I tell you this long story, friend Theaetetus, because I suspect, as indeed you seem to think yourself, that you are in labour—great with some conception. Come then to me, who am a widwife's son and myself a midwife, and do your best to answer the questions which I will ask you. And if I abstract and expose your first-born, because I discover upon inspection that the conception which you have formed is a vain shadow, do not quarrel with me on that account, as the manner of women is when their first children are taken from them. For I have actually known some who were ready to bite me when I deprived them of a darling folly; they did not perceive that I acted from good will, not knowing that no god is the enemy of man—that was not within the range of their ideas; neither am I their enemy in all this, but it would be wrong for me to admit falsehood, or to stifle the truth. Once more, then, Theaetetus, I repeat my old question, "What is knowledge?"—and do not say that you cannot tell; but quit yourself like a man, and by the help of God you will be able to tell.

Theaet. At any rate, Socrates, after such an exhortation I should be ashamed of not trying to do my best. Now he who knows perceives what he knows, and, as far as I can see at present, knowledge is perception.

Soc. Bravely said, boy; that is the way in which you should express your opinion. And now, let us examine together this conception of yours, and see whether it is a true birth or a mere wind-egg:—You say that knowledge is perception?

Theaet. Yes.

Soc. Well, you have delivered yourself of a very important doctrine about knowledge; [152] it is indeed the opinion of Protagoras, who has another way of expressing it. Man, he says, is the measure of all things, of the existence of things that are, and of the non-existence of things that are not:—You have read him?

Theaet. O yes, again and again.

Soc. Does he not say that things are to you such as they appear to you, and to me such as they appear to me, and that you and I are men?

Theaet. Yes, he says so.

Soc. A wise man is not likely to talk nonsense. Let us try to understand him: the same wind is blowing, and yet one of us may be cold and the other not, or one may be slightly and the other very cold?

Theaet. Quite true.

Soc. Now is the wind, regarded not in relation to us but absolutely, cold or not; or are we to say, with Protagoras, that the wind is cold to him who is cold, and not to him who is not?

Theaet. I suppose the last.

Soc. Then it must appear so to each of them?

Theaet. Yes.

Soc. And "appears to him" means the same as "he perceives."

Theaet. True.

Soc. Then appearing and perceiving coincide in the case of hot and cold, and in similar instances; for things appear, or may be supposed to be, to each one such as he perceives them?

Theaet. Yes.

Soc. Then perception is always of existence, and being the same as knowledge is unerring?

Theaet. Clearly.

Soc. In the name of the Graces, what an almighty wise man Protagoras must have been! He spoke these things in a parable to the common herd, like you and me, but told the truth, his *Truth*,[1] in secret to his own disciples.

Theaet. What do you mean, Socrates?

Soc. I am about to speak of a high argument, in which all things are said to be relative; you cannot rightly call anything by any name, such as great or small, heavy or light, for the great will be small and the heavy light—there is no single thing or quality, but out of motion and change and admixture all things are becoming relatively to one another, which "becoming" is by us incorrectly called being, but is really becoming, for nothing ever is, but all things are becoming. Summon all philosophers—Protagoras, Heracleitus, Empedocles, and the rest of them, one after another, and with the exception of Parmenides they will agree with you in this.

[1] In allusion to a book of Protagoras' which bore this title.

Summon the great masters of either kind of poetry—Epicharmus, the prince of Comedy, and Homer of Tragedy; when the latter sings of

Ocean whence sprang the gods, and mother Tethys,

does he not mean that all things are the offspring of flux and motion?

Theaet. I think so.

[153] *Soc.* And who could take up arms against such a great army having Homer for its general, and not appear ridiculous? [1]

Theaet. Who indeed, Socrates?

Soc. Yes, Theaetetus; and there are plenty of other proofs which will show that motion is the source of what is called being and becoming, and inactivity of not-being and destruction; for fire and warmth, which are supposed to be the parent and guardian of all other things, are born of movement and of friction, which is a kind of motion;—is not this the origin of fire?

Theaet. It is.

Soc. And the race of animals is generated in the same way?

Theaet. Certainly.

Soc. And is not the bodily habit spoiled by rest and idleness, but preserved for a long time by motion and exercise?

Theaet. True.

Soc. And what of the mental habit? Is not the soul informed, and improved, and preserved by study and attention, which are motions; but when at rest, which in the soul only means want of attention and study, is uninformed, and speedily forgets whatever she has learned?

Theaet. True.

Soc. Then motion is a good, and rest an evil, to the soul as well as to the body?

Theaet. Clearly.

Soc. I may add, that breathless calm, stillness and the like waste and impair, while wind and storm preserve; and the palmary argument of all, which I strongly urge, is the golden chain in Homer, by which he means the sun, thereby indicating that so long as the sun and the heavens go round in their orbits, all things human and divine are and are preserved, but if they were chained up and their motions ceased, then all things would be destroyed, and, as the saying is, turned upside down.

Theaet. I believe, Socrates, that you have truly explained his meaning.

Soc. Then now apply his doctrine to perception, my good friend, and first of all to vision; that which you call white colour is not in your eyes, and is not a distinct thing which exists out of them. And you must not assign any place to it: for if it had position it would be, and be at rest, and there would be no process of becoming.

Theaet. Then what is colour?

Soc. Let us carry out the principle which has just been affirmed, that nothing is self-existent, and then we shall see that white, black, and every other colour, arises out of the eye meeting the appropriate motion, [154] and that what we call a colour is in each case neither the active nor the passive element, but something which passes between them, and is peculiar to each percipient; are you quite certain that the several colours appear to a dog or to any animal whatever as they appear to you?

Theaet. Far from it.

Soc. Or that anything appears the same to you as to another man? Are you so profoundly convinced of this? Rather would it not be true that it never appears exactly the same to you, because you are never exactly the same?

Theaet. The latter.

Soc. And if that with which I compare myself in size, or which I apprehend by touch, were great or white or hot, it could not become different by mere contact with another unless it actually changed; nor again, if the comparing or apprehending subject were great or white or hot, could this, when unchanged from within, become changed by any approximation or affection of any other thing. The fact is that in our ordinary way of speaking we allow ourselves to be driven into most ridiculous and wonderful contradictions, as Protagoras and all who take his line of argument would remark.

Theaet. How? and of what sort do you mean?

Soc. A little instance will sufficiently explain my meaning: Here are six dice, which are more by a half when compared with four, and fewer by a half than twelve—they are more and also fewer. How can you or any one maintain the contrary?

Theaet. Very true.

Soc. Well, then, suppose that Protagoras or some one asks whether anything can become greater or more if not by increasing, how would you answer him, Theaetetus?

Theaet. I should say "No," Socrates, if I were to speak my mind in reference to this last question, and if I were not afraid of contradicting my former answer.

[1] Cf. *Cratylus*, 401 ff.

Soc. Capital! excellent! spoken like an oracle, my boy! And if you reply "Yes," there will be a case for Euripides; for our tongue will be unconvinced, but not our mind.[1]

Theaet. Very true.

Soc. The thoroughbred Sophists, who know all that can be known about the mind, and argue only out of the superfluity of their wits, would have had a regular sparring-match over this, and would have knocked their arguments together finely. But you and I, who have no professional aims, only desire to see what is the mutual relation of these principles—whether they are consistent with each other or not.

Theaet. Yes, that would be my desire.

Soc. And mine too. But since this is our feeling, and there is plenty of time, why should we not calmly and patiently review our own thoughts, *[155]* and thoroughly examine and see what these appearances in us really are? If I am not mistaken, they will be described by us as follows:—first, that nothing can become greater or less, either in number or magnitude, while remaining equal to itself—you would agree?

Theaet. Yes.

Soc. Secondly, that without addition or subtraction there is no increase or diminution of anything, but only equality.

Theaet. Quite true.

Soc. Thirdly, that what was not before cannot be afterwards, without becoming and having become.

Theaet. Yes, truly.

Soc. These three axioms, if I am not mistaken, are fighting with one another in our minds in the case of the dice, or, again, in such a case as this—if I were to say that I, who am of a certain height and taller than you, may within a year, without gaining or losing in height, be not so tall—not that I should have lost, but that you would have increased. In such a case, I am afterwards what I once was not, and yet I have not become; for I could not have become without becoming, neither could I have become less without losing somewhat of my height; and I could give you ten thousand examples of similar contradictions, if we admit them at all. I believe that you follow me, Theaetetus; for I suspect that you have thought of these questions before now.

Theaet. Yes, Socrates, and I am amazed when I think of them; by the Gods I am! and I want to know what on earth they mean; and

[1] In allusion to the well-known line of Euripides, *Hippolytus*, 612.

there are times when my head quite swims with the contemplation of them.

Soc. I see, my dear Theaetetus, that Theodorus had a true insight into your nature when he said that you were a philosopher, for wonder is the feeling of a philosopher, and philosophy begins in wonder. He was not a bad genealogist who said that Iris (the messenger of heaven) is the child of Thaumas (wonder). But do you begin to see what is the explanation of this perplexity on the hypothesis which we attribute to Protagoras?

Theaet. Not as yet.

Soc. Then you will be obliged to me if I help you to unearth the hidden "truth" of a famous man or school.

Theaet. To be sure, I shall be very much obliged.

Soc. Take a look round, then, and see that none of the uninitiated are listening. Now by the uninitiated I mean the people who believe in nothing but what they can grasp in their hands, and who will not allow that action or generation or anything invisible can have real existence.

Theaet. Yes, indeed, Socrates, they are very hard and impenetrable mortals.

[156] Soc. Yes, my boy, outer barbarians. Far more ingenious are the brethren whose mysteries I am about to reveal to you. Their first principle is, that all is motion, and upon this all the affections of which we were just now speaking are supposed to depend: there is nothing but motion, which has two forms, one active and the other passive, both in endless number; and out of the union and friction of them there is generated a progeny endless in number, having two forms, sense and the object of sense, which are ever breaking forth and coming to the birth at the same moment. The senses are variously named hearing, seeing, smelling; there is the sense of heat, cold, pleasure, pain, desire, fear, and many more which have names, as well as innumerable others which are without them; each has its kindred object—each variety of colour has a corresponding variety of sight, and so with sound and hearing, and with the rest of the senses and the objects akin to them. Do you see, Theaetetus, the bearings of this tale on the preceding argument?

Theaet. Indeed I do not.

Soc. Then attend, and I will try to finish the story. The purport is that all these things are in motion, as I was saying, and that this motion is of two kinds, a slower and a quicker; and the slower elements have their motions in the same place and with reference to things near them, and so they beget; but what is begotten is swifter, for it is carried to and fro, and moves from place to place. Apply this to sense:—When the eye and the appropriate object meet together and give birth to whiteness and the sensation connatural with it, which could not have been given by either of them going elsewhere, then, while the sight is flowing from the eye, whiteness proceeds from the object which combines in producing the colour; and so the eye is fulfilled with sight, and really sees, and becomes, not sight, but a seeing eye; and the object which combined to form the colour is fulfilled with whiteness, and becomes not whiteness but a white thing, whether wood or stone or whatever the object may be which happens to be coloured white. And this is true of all sensible objects, hard, warm, and the like, which are similarly to be regarded, [157] as I was saying before, not as having any absolute existence, but as being all of them of whatever kind generated by motion in their intercourse with one another; for of the agent and patient, as existing in separation, no trustworthy conception, as they say, can be formed, for the agent has no existence until united with the patient, and the patient has no existence until united with the agent; and that which by uniting with something becomes an agent, by meeting with some other thing is converted into a patient. And from all these considerations, as I said at first, there arises a general reflection, that there is no one self-existent thing, but everything is becoming and in relation; and being must be altogether abolished, although from habit and ignorance we are compelled even in this discussion to retain the use of the term. But great philosophers tell us that we are not to allow either the word "something," or "belonging to something," or "to me," or "this" or "that," or any other detaining name to be used; in the language of nature all things are being created and destroyed, coming into being and passing into new forms; nor can any name fix or detain them; he who attempts to fix them is easily refuted. And this should be the way of speaking, not only of particulars but of aggregates; such aggregates as are expressed in the word "man," or "stone," or any name of an animal or of a class. O Theaetetus, are not these speculations sweet as honey? And do you not like the taste of them in the mouth?

Theaet. I do not know what to say, Socrates, for, indeed, I cannot make out whether you are giving your own opinion or only wanting to draw me out.

Soc. You forget, my friend, that I neither know, nor profess to know, anything of these matters; you are the person who is in labour, I am the barren midwife; and this is why I soothe you, and offer you one good thing after another, that you may taste them. And I hope that I may at last help to bring your own opinion into the light of day: when this has been accomplished, then we will determine whether what you have brought forth is only a wind-egg or a real and genuine birth. Therefore, keep up your spirits, and answer like a man what you think.

Theaet. Ask me.

Soc. Then once more: Is it your opinion that nothing is but what becomes?—the good and the noble, as well as all the other things which we were just now mentioning?

Theaet. When I hear you discoursing in this style, I think that there is a great deal in what you say, and I am very ready to assent.

Soc. Let us not leave the argument unfinished, then; for there still remains to be considered an objection which may be raised about dreams and diseases, in particular about madness, and the various illusions of hearing and sight, or of other senses. For you know that in all these cases the *esse-percipi* theory appears to be [158] unmistakably refuted, since in dreams and illusions we certainly have false perceptions; and far from saying that everything is which appears, we should rather say that nothing is which appears.

Theaet. Very true, Socrates.

Soc. But then, my boy, how can any one contend that knowledge is perception, or that to every man what appears is?

Theaet. I am afraid to say, Socrates, that I have nothing to answer, because you rebuked me just now for making this excuse; but I certainly cannot undertake to argue that madmen or dreamers think truly, when they imagine, some of them that they are gods, and others that they can fly, and are flying in their sleep.

Soc. Do you see another question which can be raised about these phenomena, notably about dreaming and waking?

Theaet. What question?

Soc. A question which I think that you must often have heard persons ask:—How can you determine whether at this moment we are sleeping, and all our thoughts are a dream; or whether we are awake, and talking to one another in the waking state?

and the philosopher is not merely amusing himself by giving oracles out of the shrine of his book.

Theod. He was a friend of mine, Socrates, as you were saying, and therefore I cannot have him refuted by my lips, nor can I oppose you when I agree with you; please, then, to take Theaetetus again; he seemed to answer very nicely.

Soc. If you were to go into a Lacedaemonian palestra, Theodorus, would you have a right to look on at the naked wrestlers, some of them making a poor figure, if you did not strip and give them an opportunity of judging of your own person?

Theod. Why not, Socrates, if they would allow me, as I think you will, in consideration of my age and stiffness; let some more supple youth try a fall with you, and do not drag me into the gymnasium.

Soc. Your will is my will, Theodorus, as the proverbial philosophers say, and therefore I will return to the sage Theaetetus: Tell me, Theaetetus, in reference to what I was saying, are you not lost in wonder, like myself, when you find that all of a sudden you are raised to the level of the wisest of men, or indeed of the gods?—for you would assume the measure of Protagoras to apply to the gods as well as men?

Theaet. Certainly I should, and I confess to you that I am lost in wonder. At first hearing, I was quite satisfied with the doctrine, that whatever appears is to each one, but now the face of things has changed.

Soc. Why, my dear boy, you are young, and therefore your ear is quickly caught and your mind influenced by popular arguments. Protagoras, or some one speaking on his behalf, will doubtless say in reply,—Good people, young and old, you meet and harangue, and bring in the gods, whose existence or non-existence I banish from writing and speech, or you talk about the reason of man being degraded to the level of the brutes, which is a telling argument with the multitude, but not one word of proof or demonstration do you offer. All is probability with you, and yet surely you and Theodorus had better reflect whether you are disposed to admit of probability and figures of speech in matters of such importance. [*163*] He or any other mathematician who argued from probabilities and likelihoods in geometry, would not be worth an ace.

Theaet. But neither you nor we, Socrates, would be satisfied with such arguments.

Soc. Then you and Theodorus mean to say that we must look at the matter in some other way?

Theaet. Yes, in quite another way.

Soc. And the way will be to ask whether perception is or is not the same as knowledge; for this was the real point of our argument, and with a view to this we raised (did we not?) those many strange questions.

Theaet. Certainly.

Soc. Shall we say that we know every thing which we see and hear? for example, shall we say that not having learned, we do not hear the language of foreigners when they speak to us? or shall we say that we not only hear, but know what they are saying? Or again, if we see letters which we do not understand, shall we say that we do not see them? or shall we aver that, seeing them, we must know them?

Theaet. We shall say, Socrates, that we know what we actually see and hear of them—that is to say, we see and know the figure and colour of the letters, and we hear and know the elevation or depression of the sound of them; but we do not perceive by sight and hearing, or know, that which grammarians and interpreters teach about them.

Soc. Capital, Theaetetus; and about this there shall be no dispute, because I want you to grow; but there is another difficulty coming, which you will also have to repulse.

Theaet. What is it?

Soc. Some one will say, Can a man who has ever known anything, and still has and preserves a memory of that which he knows, not know that which he remembers at the time when he remembers? I have, I fear, a tedious way of putting a simple question, which is only, whether a man who has learned, and remembers, can fail to know?

Theaet. Impossible, Socrates; the supposition is monstrous.

Soc. Am I talking nonsense, then? Think: is not seeing perceiving, and is not sight perception?

Theaet. True.

Soc. And if our recent definition holds, every man knows that which he has seen?

Theaet. Yes.

Soc. And you would admit that there is such a thing as memory?

Theaet. Yes.

Soc. And is memory of something or of nothing?

Theaet. Of something, surely.

Soc. Of things learned and perceived, that is?

Theaet. Certainly.

Soc. Often a man remembers that which he has seen?

Theaet. True.

Soc. And if he closed his eyes, would he forget?

[*164*] *Theaet.* Who, Socrates, would dare to say so?

Soc. But we must say so, if the previous argument is to be maintained.

Theaet. What do you mean? I am not quite sure that I understand you, though I have a strong suspicion that you are right.

Soc. As thus: he who sees knows, as we say, that which he sees; for perception and sight and knowledge are admitted to be the same.

Theaet. Certainly.

Soc. But he who saw, and has knowledge of that which he saw, remembers, when he closes his eyes, that which he no longer sees.

Theaet. True.

Soc. And seeing is knowing, and therefore not-seeing is not-knowing?

Theaet. Very true.

Soc. Then the inference is, that a man may have attained the knowledge of something, which he may remember and yet not know, because he does not see; and this has been affirmed by us to be a monstrous supposition.

Theaet. Most true.

Soc. Thus, then, the assertion that knowledge and perception are one, involves a manifest impossibility?

Theaet. Yes.

Soc. Then they must be distinguished?

Theaet. I suppose that they must.

Soc. Once more we shall have to begin, and ask "What is knowledge?" and yet, Theaetetus, what are we going to do?

Theaet. About what?

Soc. Like a good-for-nothing cock, without having won the victory, we walk away from the argument and crow.

Theaet. How do you mean?

Soc. After the manner of disputers,[1] we were satisfied with mere verbal consistency, and were well pleased if in this way we could gain an advantage. Although professing not to be mere Eristics, but philosophers, I suspect that we have unconsciously fallen into the error of that ingenious class of persons.

Theaet. I do not as yet understand you.

Soc. Then I will try to explain myself: just now we asked the question, whether a man who had learned and remembered could fail to know, and we showed that a person who had

[1] *Lysis,* 216; *Phaedo,* 90, 101; *Republic,* v. 453 ff.

seen might remember when he had his eyes shut and could not see, and then he would at the same time remember and not know. But this was an impossibility. And so the Protagorean fable came to nought, and yours also, who maintained that knowledge is the same as perception.

Theaet. True.

Soc. And yet, my friend, I rather suspect that the result would have been different if Protagoras, who was the father of the first of the two brats, had been alive; he would have had a great deal to say on their behalf. But he is dead, and we insult over his orphan child; and even the guardians whom he left, and of whom our friend Theodorus is one, are unwilling to give any help, and therefore I suppose that I must take up his cause myself, and see justice done?

[*165*] *Theod.* Not I, Socrates, but rather Callias, the son of Hipponicus, is guardian of his orphans. I was too soon diverted from the abstractions of dialectic to geometry. Nevertheless, I shall be grateful to you if you assist him.

Soc. Very good, Theodorus; you shall see how I will come to the rescue. If a person does not attend to the meaning of terms as they are commonly used in argument, he may be involved even in greater paradoxes than these. Shall I explain this matter to you or to Theaetetus?

Theod. To both of us, and let the younger answer; he will incur less disgrace if he is discomfited.

Soc. Then now let me ask the awful question, which is this:—Can a man know and also not know that which he knows?

Theod. How shall we answer, Theaetetus?

Theaet. He cannot, I should say.

Soc. He can, if you maintain that seeing is knowing. When you are imprisoned in a well, as the saying is, and the self-assured adversary closes one of your eyes with his hand, and asks whether you can see his cloak with the eye which he has closed, how will you answer the inevitable man?

Theaet. I should answer, "Not with that eye but with the other."

Soc. Then you see and do not see the same thing at the same time.

Theaet. Yes, in a certain sense.

Soc. None of that, he will reply; I do not ask or bid you answer in what sense you know, but only whether you know that which you do not know. You have been proved to see that which you do not see; and you have already admitted that seeing is knowing, and that not-seeing is not-knowing: I leave you to draw the inference.

Theaet. Yes, the inference is the contradictory of my assertion.

Soc. Yes, my marvel, and there might have been yet worse things in store for you, if an opponent had gone on to ask whether you can have a sharp and also a dull knowledge, and whether you can know near, but not at a distance, or know the same thing with more or less intensity, and so on without end. Such questions might have been put to you by a light-armed mercenary, who argued for pay. He would have lain in wait for you, and when you took up the position, that sense is knowledge, he would have made an assault upon hearing, smelling, and the other senses;—he would have shown you no mercy; and while you were lost in envy and admiration of his wisdom, he would have got you into his net, out of which you would not have escaped until you had come to an understanding about the sum to be paid for your release. Well, you ask, and how will Protagoras reinforce his position? Shall I answer for him?

Theaet. By all means.

Soc. He will repeat all those things which we have been urging on his behalf, [166] and then he will close with us in disdain, and say:—The worthy Socrates asked a little boy, whether the same man could remember and not know the same thing, and the boy said No, because he was frightened, and could not see what was coming, and then Socrates made fun of poor me. The truth is, O slatternly Socrates, that when you ask questions about any assertion of mine, and the person asked is found tripping, if he has answered as I should have answered, then I am refuted, but if he answers something else, then he is refuted and not I. For do you really suppose that any one would admit the memory which a man has of an impression which has passed away to be the same with that which he experienced at the time? Assuredly not. Or would he hesitate to acknowledge that the same man may know and not know the same thing? Or, if he is afraid of making this admission, would he ever grant that one who has become unlike is the same as before he became unlike? Or would he admit that a man is one at all, and not rather many and infinite as the changes which take place in him? I speak by the card in order to avoid entanglements of words. But, O my good sir, he will say, come to the argument in a more generous spirit; and either show, if you can, that our sensations are not relative and individual, or, if you admit them to be so, prove that this does not involve the consequence that the appearance becomes, or, if you will have the word, is, to the individual only. As to your talk about pigs and baboons, you are yourself behaving like a pig, and you teach your hearers to make sport of my writings in the same ignorant manner; but this is not to your credit. For I declare that the truth is as I have written, and that each of us is a measure of existence and of non-existence. Yet one man may be a thousand times better than another in proportion as different things are and appear to him.

And I am far from saying that wisdom and the wise man have no existence; but I say that the wise man is he who makes the evils which appear and are to a man, into goods which are and appear to him. And I would beg you not to press my words in the letter, but to take the meaning of them as I will explain them. Remember what has been already said,—that to the sick man his food appears to be and is bitter, and to the man in health the opposite of bitter. Now I cannot conceive that one of these men can be or ought to be made wiser than the other: [167] nor can you assert that the sick man because he has one impression is foolish, and the healthy man because he has another is wise; but the one state requires to be changed into the other, the worse into the better. As in education, a change of state has to be effected, and the sophist accomplishes by words the change which the physician works by the aid of drugs. Not that any one ever made another think truly, who previously thought falsely. For no one can think what is not, or think anything different from that which he feels; and this is always true. But as the inferior habit of mind has thoughts of kindred nature, so I conceive that a good mind causes men to have good thoughts; and these which the inexperienced call true, I maintain to be only better, and not truer than others. And, O my dear Socrates, I do not call wise men tadpoles: far from it; I say that they are the physicians of the human body, and the husbandmen of plants—for the husbandmen also take away the evil and disordered sensations of plants, and infuse into them good and healthy sensations—aye and true ones; and the wise and good rhetoricians make the good instead of the evil to seem just to states; for whatever appears to a state to be just and fair, so long as it is regarded as such, is just and fair to it; but the teacher of wisdom causes the good to take the place of the evil, both in appearance and in reality. And in like manner the Sophist who is able to train his pupils in this spirit is a wise man, and deserves to be well paid by them. And so one man is wiser than another; and no one thinks falsely, and you, whether you will or not, must endure to be a measure. On these foundations the argument stands firm, which you, Socrates, may, if you please, overthrow by an opposite argument, or if you like you may put questions to me—a method to which no intelligent person will object, quite the reverse. But I must beg you to put fair questions: for there is great inconsistency in saying that you have a zeal for virtue, and then always behaving unfairly in argument. The unfairness of which I complain is that you do not distinguish between mere disputation and dialectic: the disputer may trip up his opponent as often as he likes, and make fun; but the dialectician will be in earnest, and only correct his adversary when necessary, telling him the errors into which he has fallen through his own fault, or that of the company which he has previously kept. [168] If you do so, your adversary will lay the blame of his own confusion and perplexity on himself, and not on you. He will follow and love you, and will hate himself, and escape from himself into philosophy, in order that he may become different from what he was. But the other mode of arguing, which is practised by the many, will have just the opposite effect upon him; and as he grows older, instead of turning philosopher, he will come to hate philosophy. I would recommend you, therefore, as I said before, not to encourage yourself in this polemical and controversial temper, but to find out, in a friendly and congenial spirit, what we really mean when we say that all things are in motion, and that to every individual and state what appears, is. In this manner you will consider whether knowledge and sensation are the same or different, but you will not argue, as you were just now doing, from the customary use of names and words, which the vulgar pervert in all sorts of ways, causing infinite perplexity to one another. Such, Theodorus, is the very slight help which I am able to offer to your old friend; had he been living, he would have helped himself in a far more gloriose style.

Theod. You are jesting, Socrates; indeed, your defence of him has been most valorous.

Soc. Thank you, friend; and I hope that you observed Protagoras bidding us be serious, as the text, "Man is the measure of all things," was a solemn one; and he reproached us with making a boy the medium of discourse, and said that the boy's timidity was made to tell against his argument; he also declared that we made a joke of him.

Theod. How could I fail to observe all that, Socrates?

Soc. Well, and shall we do as he says?

Theod. By all means.

Soc. But if his wishes are to be regarded, you and I must take up the argument, and in all seriousness, and ask and answer one another, for you see that the rest of us are nothing but boys. In no other way can we escape the imputation, that in our fresh analysis of his thesis we are making fun with boys.

Theod. Well, but is not Theaetetus better able to follow a philosophical enquiry than a great many men who have long beards?

Soc. Yes, Theodorus, but not better than you; and therefore please not to imagine that I am to defend by every means in my power your departed friend; [169] and that you are to defend nothing and nobody. At any rate, my good man, do not sheer off until we know whether you are a true measure of diagrams, or whether all men are equally measures and sufficient for themselves in astronomy and geometry, and the other branches of knowledge in which you are supposed to excel them.

Theod. He who is sitting by you, Socrates, will not easily avoid being drawn into an argument; and when I said just now that you would excuse me, and not, like the Lacedaemonians, compel me to strip and fight, I was talking nonsense—I should rather compare you to Scirrhon, who threw travellers from the rocks; for the Lacedaemonian rule is "strip or depart," but you seem to go about your work more after the fashion of Antaeus: you will not allow any one who approaches you to depart until you have stripped him, and he has been compelled to try a fall with you in argument.

Soc. There, Theodorus, you have hit off precisely the nature of my complaint; but I am even more pugnacious than the giants of old, for I have met with no end of heroes; many a Heracles, many a Theseus, mighty in words, has broken my head; nevertheless I am always at this rough exercise, which inspires me like a passion. Please, then, to try a fall with me, whereby you will do yourself good as well as me.

Theod. I consent; lead me whither you will, for I know that you are like destiny; no man can escape from any argument which you may weave for him. But I am not disposed to go further than you suggest.

Soc. Once will be enough; and now take particular care that we do not again unwittingly expose ourselves to the reproach of talking childishly.

Theod. I will do my best to avoid that error.

Soc. In the first place, let us return to our old objection, and see whether we were right in blaming and taking offence at Protagoras on the ground that he assumed all to be equal and sufficient in wisdom; although he admitted that there was a better and worse, and that in respect of this, some who as he said were the wise excelled others.

Theod. Very true.

Soc. Had Protagoras been living and answered for himself, instead of our answering for him, there would have been no need of our reviewing or reinforcing the argument. But as he is not here, and some one may accuse us of speaking without authority on his behalf, had we not better come to a clearer agreement about his meaning, for a great deal may be at stake?

Theod. True.

[170] Soc. Then let us obtain, not through any third person, but from his own statement and in the fewest words possible, the basis of agreement.

Theod. In what way?

Soc. In this way:—His words are, "What seems to a man, is to him."

Theod. Yes, so he says.

Soc. And are not we, Protagoras, uttering the opinion of man, or rather of all mankind, when we say that every one thinks himself wiser than other men in some things, and their inferior in others? In the hour of danger, when they are in perils of war, or of the sea, or of sickness, do they not look up to their commanders as if they were gods, and expect salvation from them, only because they excel them in knowledge? Is not the world full of men in their several employments, who are looking for teachers and rulers of themselves and of the animals? and there are plenty who think that they are able to teach and able to rule. Now, in all this is implied that ignorance and wisdom exist among them, at least in their own opinion.

Theod. Certainly.

Soc. And wisdom is assumed by them to be true thought, and ignorance to be false opinion.

Theod. Exactly.

Soc. How then, Protagoras, would you have us treat the argument? Shall we say that the opinions of men are always true, or sometimes true and sometimes false? In either case, the result is the same, and their opinions are not always true, but sometimes true and sometimes false. For tell me, Theodorus, do you suppose that you yourself, or any other follower of Protagoras, would contend that no one deems another ignorant or mistaken in his opinion?

Theod. The thing is incredible, Socrates.

Soc. And yet that absurdity is necessarily involved in the thesis which declares man to be the measure of all things.

Theod. How so?

Soc. Why, suppose that you determine in your own mind something to be true, and declare your opinion to me; let us assume, as he argues, that this is true to you. Now, if so, you must either say that the rest of us are not the judges of this opinion or judgment of yours, or that we judge you always to have a true opinion? But are there not thousands upon thousands who, whenever you form a judgment, take up arms against you and are of an opposite judgment and opinion, deeming that you judge falsely?

Theod. Yes, indeed, Socrates, thousands and tens of thousands, as Homer says, who give me a world of trouble.

Soc. Well, but are we to assert that what you think is true to you and false to the ten thousand others?

Theod. No other inference seems to be possible.

Soc. And how about Protagoras himself? If neither he nor the multitude thought, as indeed they do not think, that man is the measure of all things, *[171]* must it not follow that the truth of which Protagoras wrote would be true to no one? But if you suppose that he himself thought this, and that the multitude does not agree with him, you must begin by allowing that in whatever proportion the many are more than one, in that proportion his truth is more untrue than true.

Theod. That would follow if the truth is supposed to vary with individual opinion.

Soc. And the best of the joke is, that he acknowledges the truth of their opinion who believe his own opinion to be false; for he admits that the opinions of all men are true.

Theod. Certainly.

Soc. And does he not allow that his own opinion is false, if he admits that the opinion of those who think him false is true?

Theod. Of course.

Soc. Whereas the other side do not admit that they speak falsely?

Theod. They do not.

Soc. And he, as may be inferred from his writings, agrees that this opinion is also true.

Theod. Clearly.

Soc. Then all mankind, beginning with Protagoras, will contend, or rather, I should say that he will allow, when he concedes that his adversary has a true opinion—Protagoras, I say, will himself allow that neither a dog nor any ordinary man is the measure of anything which he has not learned—am I not right?

Theod. Yes.

Soc. And the truth of Protagoras being doubted by all, will be true neither to himself nor to any one else?

Theod. I think, Socrates, that we are running my old friend too hard.

Soc. But I do not know that we are going beyond the truth. Doubtless, as he is older, he may be expected to be wiser than we are. And if he could only just get his head out of the world below, he would have overthrown both of us again and again, me for talking nonsense and you for assenting to me, and have been off and underground in a trice. But as he is not within call, we must make the best use of our own faculties, such as they are, and speak out what appears to us to be true. And one thing which no one will deny is, that there are great differences in the understandings of men.

Theod. In that opinion I quite agree.

Soc. And is there not most likely to be firm ground in the distinction which we were indicating on behalf of Protagoras, viz., that most things, and all immediate sensations, such as hot, dry, sweet, are only such as they appear; if however difference of opinion is to be allowed at all, surely we must allow it in respect of health or disease? for every woman, child, or living creature has not such a knowledge of what conduces to health as to enable them to cure themselves.

Theod. I quite agree.

[172] Soc. Or again, in politics, while affirming that just and unjust, honourable and disgraceful, holy and unholy, are in reality to each state such as the state thinks and makes lawful, and that in determining these matters no individual or state is wiser than another, still the followers of Protagoras will not deny that in determining what is or is not expedient for the community one state is wiser and one counsellor better than another—they will scarcely venture to maintain, that what a city enacts in the belief that it is expedient will always be really expedient. But in the other case, I mean when they speak of justice and injustice, piety and impiety, they are confident that in nature these have no existence or essence of their own —the truth is that which is agreed on at the time of the agreement, and as long as the agreement lasts; and this is the philosophy of many who do not altogether go along with Protagoras. Here arises a new question, Theodorus, which threatens to be more serious than the last.

Theod. Well, Socrates, we have plenty of leisure.

Soc. That is true, and your remark recalls to my mind an observation which I have often made, that those who have passed their days in the pursuit of philosophy are ridiculously at fault when they have to appear and speak in court. How natural is this!

Theod. What do you mean?

Soc. I mean to say, that those who have been trained in philosophy and liberal pursuits are as unlike those who from their youth upwards have been knocking about in the courts and such places, as a freeman is in breeding unlike a slave.

Theod. In what is the difference seen?

Soc. In the leisure spoken of by you, which a freeman can always command: he has his talk out in peace, and, like ourselves, he wanders at will from one subject to another, and from a second to a third,—if the fancy takes him, he begins again, as we are doing now, caring not whether his words are many or few; his only aim is to attain the truth. But the lawyer is always in a hurry; there is the water of the clepsydra driving him on, and not allowing him to expatiate at will: and there is his adversary standing over him, enforcing his rights; the indictment, which in their phraseology is termed the affidavit, is recited at the time: and from this he must not deviate. He is a servant, and is continually disputing about a fellow-servant before his master, who is seated, and has the cause in his hands; the trial is never about some indifferent matter, but always concerns himself; *[173]* and often the race is for his life. The consequence has been, that he has become keen and shrewd; he has learned how to flatter his master in word and indulge him in deed; but his soul is small and unrighteous. His condition, which has been that of a slave from his youth upwards, has deprived him of growth and uprightness and independence; dangers and fears, which were too much for his truth and honesty, came upon him in early years, when the tenderness of youth was unequal to them, and he has been driven into crooked ways; from the first he has practised deception and retaliation, and has become stunted and warped. And so he has passed out of youth into manhood, having no soundness in him; and is now, as he thinks, a master in wisdom. Such is the lawyer, Theodorus. Will you have the companion picture of the philosopher, who is of our brotherhood; or shall we return to the argument? Do not let us abuse the freedom of digression which we claim.

Theod. Nay, Socrates, not until we have finished what we are about; for you truly said that we belong to a brotherhood which is free, and are not the servants of the argument; but the argument is our servant, and must wait our leisure. Who is our judge? Or where is the spectator having any right to censure or control us, as he might the poets?

Soc. Then, as this is your wish, I will describe the leaders; for there is no use in talking about the inferior sort. In the first place, the lords of philosophy have never, from their youth upwards, known their way to the Agora, or the dicastery, or the council, or any other political assembly; they neither see nor hear the laws or decrees, as they are called, of the state written or recited; the eagerness of political societies in the attainment of offices—clubs, and banquets, and revels, and singing-maidens, —do not enter even into their dreams. Whether any event has turned out well or ill in the city, what disgrace may have descended to any one from his ancestors, male or female, are matters of which the philosopher no more knows than he can tell, as they say, how many pints are contained in the ocean. Neither is he conscious of his ignorance. For he does not hold aloof in order that he may gain a reputation; but the truth is, that the outer form of him only is in the city: his mind, disdaining the littlenesses and nothingnesses of human things, is "flying all abroad" as Pindar says, measuring earth and heaven and the things which are under and on the earth and above the heaven, interrogating the whole nature of each and all in their entirety, *[174]* but not condescending to anything which is within reach.

Theod. What do you mean, Socrates?

Soc. I will illustrate my meaning, Theodorus, by the jest which the clever witty Thracian handmaid is said to have made about Thales, when he fell into a well as he was looking up at the stars. She said, that he was so eager to know what was going on in heaven, that he could not see what was before his feet. This is a jest which is equally applicable to all philosophers.

For the philosopher is wholly unacquainted with his next-door neighbour; he is ignorant, not only of what he is doing, but he hardly knows whether he is a man or an animal; he is searching into the essence of man, and busy in enquiring what belongs to such a nature to do or suffer different from any other;—I think that you understand me, Theodorus?

Theod. I do, and what you say is true.

Soc. And thus, my friend, on every occasion, private as well as public, as I said at first, when he appears in a law-court, or in any place in which he has to speak of things which are at his feet and before his eyes, he is the jest, not only of Thracian handmaids but of the general herd, tumbling into wells and every sort of disaster through his inexperience. His awkwardness is fearful, and gives the impression of imbecility. When he is reviled, he has nothing personal to say in answer to the civilities of his adversaries, for he knows no scandals of any one, and they do not interest him; and therefore he is laughed at for his sheepishness; and when others are being praised and glorified, in the simplicity of his heart he cannot help going into fits of laughter, so that he seems to be a downright idiot. When he hears a tyrant or king eulogized, he fancies that he is listening to the praises of some keeper of cattle—a swineherd, or shepherd, or perhaps a cowherd, who is congratulated on the quantity of milk which he squeezes from them; and he remarks that the creature whom they tend, and out of whom they squeeze the wealth, is of a less tractable and more insidious nature. Then, again, he observes that the great man is of necessity as illmannered and uneducated as any shepherd— for he has no leisure, and he is surrounded by a wall, which is his mountain-pen. Hearing of enormous landed proprietors of ten thousand acres and more, our philosopher deems this to be a trifle, because he has been accustomed to think of the whole earth; and when they sing the praises of family, and say that someone is a gentleman because he can show seven generations of wealthy ancestors, he thinks that their sentiments only betray a dull and narrow vision in those *[175]* who utter them, and who are not educated enough to look at the whole, nor to consider that every man has had thousands and ten thousands of progenitors, and among them have been rich and poor, kings and slaves, Hellenes and barbarians, innumerable. And when people pride themselves on having a pedigree of twenty-five ancestors, which goes back to Heracles, the son of Amphitryon, he cannot understand their poverty of ideas. Why are they unable to calculate that Amphitryon had a twenty-fifth ancestor, who might have been anybody, and was such as fortune made him, and he had a fiftieth, and so on? He amuses himself with the notion that they cannot count, and thinks that a little arithmetic would have got rid of their senseless vanity. Now, in all these cases our philosopher is derided by the vulgar, partly because he is thought to despise them, and also because he is ignorant of what is before him, and always at a loss.

Theod. That is very true, Socrates.

Soc. But, O my friend, when he draws the other into upper air, and gets him out of his pleas and rejoinders into the contemplation of justice and injustice in their own nature and in their difference from one another and from all other things; or from the commonplaces about the happiness of a king or of a rich man to the consideration of government, and of human happiness and misery in general—what they are, and how a man is to attain the one and avoid the other—when that narrow, keen, little legal mind is called to account about all this, he gives the philosopher his revenge; for dizzied by the height at which he is hanging, whence he looks down into space, which is a strange experience to him, he being dismayed, and lost, and stammering broken words, is laughed at, not by Thracian handmaidens or any other uneducated persons, for they have no eye for the situation, but by every man who has not been brought up a slave. Such are the two characters, Theodorus: the one of the freeman, who has been trained in liberty and leisure, whom you call the philosopher—him we cannot blame because he appears simple and of no account when he has to perform some menial task, such as packing up bed-clothes, or flavouring a sauce or fawning speech; the other character is that of the man who is able to do all this kind of service smartly and neatly, *[176]* but knows not how to wear his cloak like a gentleman; still less with the music of discourse can he hymn the true life aright which is lived by immortals or men blessed of heaven.

Theod. If you could only persuade everybody, Socrates, as you do me, of the truth of your words, there would be more peace and fewer evils among men.

Soc. Evils, Theodorus, can never pass away; for there must always remain something which is antagonistic to good. Having no place among the gods in heaven, of necessity they hover around the mortal nature, and this earthly sphere. Wherefore we ought to fly away from earth to heaven as quickly as we can; and to fly away is to become like God, as far as this is possible; and to become like him, is to become holy, just, and wise. But, O my friend, you cannot easily convince mankind that they should pursue virtue or avoid vice, not merely in order that a man may seem to be good, which is the reason given by the world, and in my judgment is only a repetition of an old wives' fable. Whereas, the truth is that God is never in any way unrighteous—he is perfect righteousness; and he of us who is the most righteous is most like him. Herein is seen the true cleverness of a man, and also his nothingness and want of manhood. For to know this is true wisdom and virtue, and ignorance of this is manifest folly and vice. All other kinds of wisdom or cleverness, which seem only, such as the wisdom of politicians, or the wisdom of the arts, are coarse and vulgar. The unrighteous man, or the sayer and doer of unholy things, had far better not be encouraged in the illusion that his roguery is clever; for men glory in their shame—they fancy that they hear others saying of them, "These are not mere good-for-nothing persons, mere burdens of the earth, but such as men should be who mean to dwell safely in a state." Let us tell them that they are all the more truly what they do not think they are because they do not know it; for they do not know the penalty of injustice, which above all things they ought to know—not stripes and death, as they suppose, which evil-doers often escape, but a penalty which cannot be escaped.

Theod. What is that?

Soc. There are two patterns eternally set before them; the one blessed and divine, the other godless and wretched: but they do not see them, or perceive that in their utter folly and infatuation they are growing like the one and unlike the other, *[177]* by reason of their evil deeds; and the penalty is, that they lead a life answering to the pattern which they are growing like. And if we tell them, that unless they depart from their cunning, the place of innocence will not receive them after death; and that here on earth, they will live ever in the likeness of their own evil selves, and with evil friends—when they hear this they in their superior cunning will seem to be listening to the talk of idiots.

Theod. Very true, Socrates.

Soc. Too true, my friend, as I well know; there is, however, one peculiarity in their case: when they begin to reason in private about their dislike of philosophy, if they have the courage to hear the argument out, and do not run away, they grow at last strangely discontented with themselves; their rhetoric fades away, and they become helpless as children. These however are digressions from which we must now desist, or they will overflow, and drown the original argument; to which, if you please, we will now return.

Theod. For my part, Socrates, I would rather have the digressions, for at my age I find them easier to follow; but if you wish, let us go back to the argument.

Soc. Had we not reached the point at which the partisans of the perpetual flux, who say that things are as they seem to each one, were confidently maintaining that the ordinances which the state commanded and thought just, were just to the state which imposed them, while they were in force; this was especially asserted of justice; but as to the good, no one had any longer the hardihood to contend of any ordinances which the state thought and enacted to be good that these, while they were in force, were really good;—he who said so would be playing with the name "good," and would not touch the real question—it would be a mockery, would it not?

Theod. Certainly it would.

Soc. He ought not to speak of the name, but of the thing which is contemplated under the name.

Theod. Right.

Soc. Whatever be the term used, the good or expedient is the aim of legislation, and as far as she has an opinion, the state imposes all laws with a view to the greatest expediency; can legislation have any other aim?

[178] *Theod.* Certainly not.

Soc. But is the aim attained always? do not mistakes often happen?

Theod. Yes, I think that there are mistakes.

Soc. The possibility of error will be more distinctly recognized, if we put the question in reference to the whole class under which the good or expedient falls. That whole class has to do with the future, and laws are passed under the idea that they will be useful in after-time; which, in other words, is the future.

Theod. Very true.

Soc. Suppose now, that we ask Protagoras, or one of his disciples, a question:—O, Protagoras, we will say to him, Man is, as you declare, the measure of all things—white, heavy, light: of all such things he is the judge; for he has the criterion of them in himself, and when he thinks that things are such as he experiences them to be, he thinks what is and is true to himself. Is it not so?

Theod. Yes.

Soc. And do you extend your doctrine, Protagoras (as we shall further say), to the future as well as to the present; and has he the criterion not only of what in his opinion is but of what will be, and do things always happen to him as he expected? For example, take the case of heat:—When an ordinary man thinks that he is going to have a fever, and that this kind of heat is coming on, and another person, who is a physician, thinks the contrary, whose opinion is likely to prove right? Or are they both right?—he will have a heat and fever in his own judgment, and not have a fever in the physician's judgment?

Theod. How ludicrous!

Soc. And the vinegrower, if I am not mistaken, is a better judge of the sweetness or dryness of the vintage which is not yet gathered than the harp-player?

Theod. Certainly.

Soc. And in musical composition the musician will know better than the training master what the training master himself will hereafter think harmonious or the reverse?

Theod. Of course.

Soc. And the cook will be a better judge than the guest, who is not a cook, of the pleasure to be derived from the dinner which is in preparation; for of present or past pleasure we are not as yet arguing; but can we say that every one will be to himself the best judge of the pleasure which will seem to be and will be to him in the future?—nay, would not you, Protagoras, better guess which arguments in a court would convince any one of us than the ordinary man?

Theod. Certainly, Socrates, he used to profess in the strongest manner that he was the superior of all men in this respect.

[179] *Soc.* To be sure, friend: who would have paid a large sum for the privilege of talking to him, if he had really persuaded his visitors that neither a prophet nor any other man was better able to judge what will be and seem to be in the future than every one could for himself?

Theod. Who indeed?

Soc. And legislation and expediency are all concerned with the future; and every one will admit that states, in passing laws, must often fail of their highest interests?

Theod. Quite true.

Soc. Then we may fairly argue against your master, that he must admit one man to be wiser than another, and that the wiser is a measure: but I, who know nothing, am not at all obliged to accept the honour which the advocate of Protagoras was just now forcing upon me, whether I would or not, of being a measure of anything.

Theod. That is the best refutation of him, Socrates; although he is also caught when he ascribes truth to the opinions of others, who give the lie direct to his own opinion.

Soc. There are many ways, Theodorus, in which the doctrine that every opinion of every man is true may be refuted; but there is more difficulty in proving that states of feeling, which are present to a man, and out of which arise sensations and opinions in accordance with them, are also untrue. And very likely I have been talking nonsense about them; for they may be unassailable, and those who say that there is clear evidence of them, and that they are matters of knowledge, may probably be right; in which case our friend Theaetetus was not so far from the mark when he identified perception and knowledge. And therefore let us draw nearer, as the advocate of Protagoras desires, and give the truth of the universal flux a ring: is the theory sound or not? at any rate, no small war is raging about it, and there are combatants not a few.

Theod. No small war, indeed, for in Ionia the sect makes rapid strides; the disciples of Heracleitus are most energetic upholders of the doctrine.

Soc. Then we are the more bound, my dear Theodorus, to examine the question from the foundation as it is set forth by themselves.

Theod. Certainly we are. About these speculations of Heracleitus, which, as you say, are as old as Homer, or even older still, the Ephesians themselves, who profess to know them, are downright mad, and you cannot talk with them on the subject. For, in accordance with their text-books, they are always in motion; but as for dwelling upon an argument or a question, [180] and quietly asking and answering in turn, they can no more do so than they can fly; or rather, the determination of these fellows not to have a particle of rest in them is more than the utmost powers of negation can express. If you ask any of them a question, he will produce, as from a quiver, sayings brief and dark, and shoot them at you; and if you inquire the reason of what he has said, you will be hit by some other newfangled word, and will make no way with any of them, nor they with one another; their great care is, not to allow of any settled principle either in their arguments or in their minds, conceiving, as I imagine, that any such principle would be stationary; for they are at war with the stationary, and do what they can to drive it out everywhere.

Soc. I suppose, Theodorus, that you have only seen them when they were fighting, and have never stayed with them in time of peace, for they are no friends of yours; and their peace doctrines are only communicated by them at leisure, as I imagine, to those disciples of theirs whom they want to make like themselves.

Theod. Disciples! my good sir, they have none; men of their sort are not one another's disciples, but they grow up at their own sweet will, and get their inspiration anywhere, each of them saying of his neighbour that he knows nothing. From these men, then, as I was going to remark, you will never get a reason, whether with their will or without their will; we must take the question out of their hands, and make the anaylsis ourselves, as if we were doing a geometrical problem.

Soc. Quite right too; but as touching the aforesaid problem, have we not heard from the ancients, who concealed their wisdom from the many in poetical figures, that Oceanus and Tethys, the origin of all things, are streams, and that nothing is at rest? And now the moderns, in their superior wisdom, have declared the same openly, that the cobbler too may hear and learn of them, and no longer foolishly imagine that some things are at rest and others in motion—having learned that all is motion, he will duly honour his teachers. I had almost forgotten the opposite doctrine, Theodorus,

Alone Being remains unmoved, which is the name for the all.

This is the language of Parmenides, Melissus, and their followers, who stoutly maintain that all being is one and self-contained, and has no place which to move. What shall we do, friend, with all these people? for, advancing step by step, we have imperceptibly got between the combatants, [181] and, unless we can protect our retreat, we shall pay the penalty of our rashness—like the players in the palaestra who are caught upon the line, and are dragged different ways by the two parties. Therefore I think that we had better begin by considering those whom we first accosted, "the river-gods," and, if we find any truth in them, we will help them to pull us over, and try to get away from the others. But if the partisans of "the whole" appear to speak more truly, we will fly off from the party which would move the immovable, to them. And if we find that neither of them have anything reasonable to say, we shall be in a ridiculous position, having so great a conceit of our own poor opinion and rejecting that of ancient and famous men. O Theodorus, do you think that there is any use in proceeding when the danger is so great?

Theod. Nay, Socrates, not to examine thoroughly what the two parties have to say would be quite intolerable.

Soc. Then examine we must, since you, who were so reluctant to begin, are so eager to proceed. The nature of motion appears to be the question with which we begin. What do they mean when they say that all things are in motion? Is there only one kind of motion, or, as I rather incline to think, two? I should like to have your opinion upon this point in addition to my own, that I may err, if I must err, in your company; tell me, then, when a thing changes from one place to another, or goes round in the same place, is not that what is called motion?

Theod. Yes.

Soc. Here then we have one kind of motion. But when a thing, remaining on the same spot, grows old, or becomes black from being white, or hard from being soft, or undergoes any other change, may not this be properly called motion of another kind?

Theod. I think so.

Soc. Say rather that it must be so. Of motion then there are these two kinds, "change," and "motion in place."

Theod. You are right.

Soc. And now, having made this distinction, let us address ourselves to those who say that all is motion, and ask them whether all things according to them have the two kinds of motion, and are changed as well as move in place, or is one thing moved in both ways, and another in one only?

Theod. Indeed, I do not know what to answer; but I think they would say that all things are moved in both ways.

Soc. Yes, comrade; for, if not, they would have to say that the same things are in motion and at rest, and there would be no more truth in saying that all things are in motion, than that all things are at rest.

Theod. To be sure.

Soc. And if they are to be in motion, and nothing is to be devoid of motion, [182] all things must always have every sort of motion?

Theod. Most true.

Soc. Consider a further point: did we not understand them to explain the generation of heat, whiteness, or anything else, in some such manner as the following:—were they not saying that each of them is moving between the agent and the patient, together with a perception, and that the patient ceases to be a perceiving power and becomes a percipient, and the agent a quale instead of a quality? I suspect that quality may appear a strange and uncouth term to you, and that you do not understand the abstract expression. Then I will take concrete instances: I mean to say that the producing power or agent becomes neither heat nor whiteness, but hot and white, and the like of other things. For I must repeat what I said before, that neither the agent nor patient have any absolute existence, but when they come together and generate sensations and their objects, the one becomes a thing of a certain quality, and the other a percipient. You remember?

Theod. Of course.

Soc. We may leave the details of their theory unexamined, but we must not forget to ask them the only question with which we are concerned: Are all things in motion and flux?

Theod. Yes, they will reply.

Soc. And they are moved in both those ways which we distinguished, that is to say, they move in place and are also changed?

Theod. Of course, if the motion is to be perfect.

Soc. If they only moved in place and were not changed, we should be able to say what is the nature of the things which are in motion and flux.

Theod. Exactly.

Soc. But now, since not even white continues to flow white, and whiteness itself is a flux or change which is passing into another colour, and is never to be caught standing still, can the name of any colour be rightly used at all?

Theod. How is that possible, Socrates, either in the case of this or of any other quality—if while we are using the word the object is escaping in the flux?

Soc. And what would you say of perceptions, such as sight and hearing, or any other kind of perception? Is there any stopping in the act of seeing and hearing?

Theod. Certainly not, if all things are in motion.

Soc. Then we must not speak of seeing any more than of not-seeing, nor of any other perception more than of any non-perception, if all things partake of every kind of motion?

Theod. Certainly not.

Soc. Yet perception is knowledge: so at least Theaetetus and I were saying.

Theod. Very true.

Soc. Then when we were asked what is knowledge, we no more answered what is knowledge than what is not knowledge?

Theod. I suppose not.

[183] Soc. Here, then, is a fine result: we corrected our first answer in our eagerness to prove that nothing is at rest. But if nothing is at rest, every answer upon whatever subject is equally right: you may say that a thing is or is not thus; or, if you prefer, "becomes" thus; and if we say "becomes," we shall not then hamper them with words expressive of rest.

Theod. Quite true.

Soc. Yes, Theodorus, except in saying "thus" and "not thus." But you ought not to use the word "thus," for there is no motion in "thus" or in "not thus." The maintainers of the doctrine have as yet no words in which to express themselves, and must get a new language. I know of no word that will suit them, except perhaps "no how," which is perfectly indefinite.

Theod. Yes, that is a manner of speaking in which they will be quite at home.

Soc. And so, Theodorus, we have got rid of your friend without assenting to his doctrine, that every man is the measure of all things—a wise man only is a measure; neither can we allow that knowledge is perception, certainly not on the hypothesis of a perpetual flux, unless perchance our friend Theaetetus is able to convince us that it is.

Theod. Very good, Socrates; and now that the argument about the doctrine of Protagoras has been completed, I am absolved from answering; for this was the agreement.

Theaet. Not, Theodorus, until you and Socrates have discussed the doctrine of those who say that all things are at rest, as you were proposing.

Theod. You, Theaetetus, who are a young rogue, must not instigate your elders to a breach of faith, but should prepare to answer Socrates in the remainder of the argument.

Theaet. Yes, if he wishes; but I would rather have heard about the doctrine of rest.

Theod. Invite Socrates to an argument—invite horsemen to the open plain; do but ask him, and he will answer.

Soc. Nevertheless, Theodorus, I am afraid that I shall not be able to comply with the request of Theaetetus.

Theod. Not comply! for what reason?

Soc. My reason is that I have a kind of reverence; not so much for Melissus and the others, who say that "All is one and at rest," as for the great leader himself, Parmenides, venerable and awful, as in Homeric language he may be called;—him I should be ashamed to approach in a spirit unworthy of him. I met him when he was an old man, and I was a mere youth, and he appeared to me to have a glorious depth of mind. *[184]* And I am afraid that we may not understand his words, and may be still further from understanding his meaning; above all I fear that the nature of knowledge, which is the main subject of our discussion, may be thrust out of sight by the unbidden guests who will come pouring in upon our feast of discourse, if we let them in—besides, the question which is now stirring is of immense extent, and will be treated unfairly if only considered by the way; or if treated adequately and at length, will put into the shade the other question of knowledge. Neither the one nor the other can be allowed; but I must try by my art of midwifery to deliver Theaetetus of his conceptions about knowledge.

Theaet. Very well; do so if you will.

Soc. Then now, Theaetetus, take another view of the subject: you answered that knowledge is perception?

Theaet. I did.

Soc. And if any one were to ask you: With what does a man see black and white colours? and with what does he hear high and low sounds?—you would say, if I am not mistaken, "With the eyes and with the ears."

Theaet. I should.

Soc. The free use of words and phrases, rather than minute precision, is generally characteristic of a liberal education, and the opposite is pedantic; but sometimes precision is necessary, and I believe that the answer which you have just given is open to the charge of incorrectness; for which is more correct, to say that we see or hear with the eyes and with the ears, or through the eyes and through the ears.

Theaet. I should say "through," Socrates, rather than "with."

Soc. Yes, my boy, for no one can suppose that in each of us, as in a sort of Trojan horse, there are perched a number of unconnected senses, which do not all meet in some one nature, the mind, or whatever we please to call it, of which they are the instruments, and with which through them we perceive objects of sense.

Theaet. I agree with you in that opinion.

Soc. The reason why I am thus precise is,

because I want to know whether, when we perceive black and white through the eyes, and again, other qualities through other organs, we do not perceive them with one and the same part of ourselves, and, if you were asked, you might refer all such perceptions to the body. Perhaps, however, I had better allow you to answer for yourself and not interfere. Tell me, then, are not the organs through which you perceive warm and hard and light and sweet, organs of the body?

Theaet. Of the body, certainly.

[185] Soc. And you would admit that what you perceive through one faculty you cannot perceive through another; the objects of hearing, for example, cannot be perceived through sight, or the objects of sight through hearing?

Theaet. Of course not.

Soc. If you have any thought about both of them, this common perception cannot come to you, either through the one or the other organ?

Theaet. It cannot.

Soc. How about sounds and colours: in the first place you would admit that they both exist?

Theaet. Yes.

Soc. And that either of them is different from the other, and the same with itself?

Theaet. Certainly.

Soc. And that both are two and each of them one?

Theaet. Yes.

Soc. You can further observe whether they are like or unlike one another?

Theaet. I dare say.

Soc. But through what do you perceive all this about them? for neither through hearing nor yet through seeing can you apprehend that which they have in common. Let me give you an illustration of the point at issue:—If there were any meaning in asking whether sounds and colours are saline or not, you would be able to tell me what faculty would consider the question. It would not be sight or hearing, but some other.

Theaet. Certainly; the faculty of taste.

Soc. Very good; and now tell me what is the power which discerns, not only in sensible objects, but in all things, universal notions, such as those which are called being and not-being, and those others about which we were just asking—what organs will you assign for the perception of these notions?

Theaet. You are thinking of being and not-being, likeness and unlikeness, sameness and difference, and also of unity and other numbers which are applied to objects of sense; and

you mean to ask, through what bodily organ the soul perceives odd and even numbers and other arithmetical conceptions.

Soc. You follow me excellently, Theaetetus; that is precisely what I am asking.

Theaet. Indeed, Socrates, I cannot answer; my only notion is, that these, unlike objects of sense, have no separate organ, but that the mind, by a power of her own, contemplates the universals in all things.

Soc. You are a beauty, Theaetetus, and not ugly, as Theodorus was saying; for he who utters the beautiful is himself beautiful and good. And besides being beautiful, you have done me a kindness in releasing me from a very long discussion, if you are clear that the soul views some things by herself and others through the bodily organs. For that was my own opinion, and I wanted you to agree with me.

Theaet. I am quite clear.

[186] Soc. And to which class would you refer being or essence; for this, of all our notions, is the most universal?

Theaet. I should say, to that class which the soul aspires to know of herself.

Soc. And would you say this also of like and unlike, same and other?

Theaet. Yes.

Soc. And would you say the same of the noble and base, and of good and evil?

Theaet. These I conceive to be notions which are essentially relative, and which the soul also perceives by comparing in herself things past and present with the future.

Soc. And does she not perceive the hardness of that which is hard by the touch, and the softness of that which is soft equally by the touch?

Theaet. Yes.

Soc. But their essence and what they are, and their opposition to one another, and the essential nature of this opposition, the soul herself endeavours to decide for us by the review and comparison of them?

Theaet. Certainly.

Soc. The simple sensations which reach the soul through the body are given at birth to men and animals by nature, but their reflections on the being and use of them are slowly and hardly gained, if they are ever gained, by education and long experience.

Theaet. Assuredly.

Soc. And can a man attain truth who fails of attaining being?

Theaet. Impossible.

Soc. And can he who misses the truth of anything, have a knowledge of that thing?

Theaet. He cannot.

Soc. Then knowledge does not consist in impressions of sense, but in reasoning about them; in that only, and not in the mere impression, truth and being can be attained?

Theaet. Clearly.

Soc. And would you call the two processes by the same name, when there is so great a difference between them?

Theaet. That would certainly not be right.

Soc. And what name would you give to seeing, hearing, smelling, being cold and being hot?

Theaet. I should call all of them perceiving —what other name could be given to them?

Soc. Perception would be the collective name of them?

Theaet. Certainly.

Soc. Which, as we say, has no part in the attainment of truth any more than of being?

Theaet. Certainly not.

Soc. And therefore not in science or knowledge?

Theaet. No.

Soc. Then perception, Theaetetus, can never be the same as knowledge or science?

Theaet. Clearly not, Socrates; and knowledge has now been most distinctly proved to be different from perception.

[187] *Soc.* But the original aim of our discussion was to find out rather what knowledge is than what it is not; at the same time we have made some progress, for we no longer seek for knowledge in perception at all, but in that other process, however called, in which the mind is alone and engaged with being.

Theaet. You mean, Socrates, if I am not mistaken, what is called thinking or opining.

Soc. You conceive truly. And now, my friend, please to begin again at this point; and having wiped out of your memory all that has preceded, see if you have arrived at any clearer view, and once more say what is knowledge.

Theaet. I cannot say, Socrates, that all opinion is knowledge, because there may be a false opinion; but I will venture to assert, that knowledge is true opinion: let this then be my reply; and if this is hereafter disproved, I must try to find another.

Soc. That is the way in which you ought to answer, Theaetetus, and not in your former hesitating strain, for if we are bold we shall gain one of two advantages; either we shall find what we seek, or we shall be less likely to think that we know what we do not know—in either case we shall be richly rewarded. And now, what are you saying?—Are there two sorts of opinion, one true and the other false; and do you define knowledge to be the true?

Theaet. Yes, according to my present view.

Soc. Is it still worth our while to resume the discussion touching opinion?

Theaet. To what are you alluding?

Soc. There is a point which often troubles me, and is a great perplexity to me, both in regard to myself and others. I cannot make out the nature or origin of the mental experience to which I refer.

Theaet. Pray what is it?

Soc. How there can be false opinion—that difficulty still troubles the eye of my mind; and I am uncertain whether I shall leave the question, or begin over again in a new way.

Theaet. Begin again, Socrates,—at least if you think that there is the slightest necessity for doing so. Were not you and Theodorus just now remarking very truly, that in discussions of this kind we may take our own time?

Soc. You are quite right, and perhaps there will be no harm in retracing our steps and beginning again. Better a little which is well done, than a great deal imperfectly.

Theaet. Certainly.

Soc. Well, and what is the difficulty? Do we not speak of false opinion, and say that one man holds a false and another a true opinion, as though there were some natural distinction between them?

Theaet. We certainly say so.

[188] *Soc.* All things and everything are either known or not known. I leave out of view the intermediate conceptions of learning and forgetting, because they have nothing to do with our present question.

Theaet. There can be no doubt, Socrates, if you exclude these, that there is no other alternative but knowing or not knowing a thing.

Soc. That point being now determined, must we not say that he who has an opinion, must have an opinion about something which he knows or does not know?

Theaet. He must.

Soc. He who knows, cannot but know; and he who does not know, cannot know?

Theaet. Of course.

Soc. What shall we say then? When a man has a false opinion does he think that which he knows to be some other thing which he knows, and knowing both, is he at the same time ignorant of both?

Theaet. That, Socrates, is impossible.

Soc. But perhaps he thinks of something

which he does not know as some other thing which he does not know; for example, he knows neither Theaetetus nor Socrates, and yet he fancies that Theaetetus is Socrates, or Socrates Theaetetus?

Theaet. How can he?

Soc. But surely he cannot suppose what he knows to be what he does not know, or what he does not know to be what he knows?

Theaet. That would be monstrous.

Soc. Where, then, is false opinion? For if all things are either known or unknown, there can be no opinion which is not comprehended under this alternative, and so false opinion is excluded.

Theaet. Most true.

Soc. Suppose that we remove the question out of the sphere of knowing or not knowing, into that of being and not-being.

Theaet. What do you mean?

Soc. May we not suspect the simple truth to be that he who thinks about anything, that which is not, will necessarily think what is false, whatever in other respects may be the state of his mind?

Theaet. That, again, is not unlikely, Socrates.

Soc. Then suppose some one to say to us, Theaetetus:—Is it possible for any man to think that which is not, either as a self-existent substance or as a predicate of something else? And suppose that we answer, "Yes, he can, when he thinks what is not true."—That will be our answer?

Theaet. Yes.

Soc. But is there any parallel to this?

Theaet. What do you mean?

Soc. Can a man see something and yet see nothing?

Theaet. Impossible.

Soc. But if he sees any one thing, he sees something that exists. Do you suppose that what is one is ever to be found among non-existing things?

Theaet. I do not.

Soc. He then who sees some one thing, sees something which is?

Theaet. Clearly.

[189] *Soc.* And he who hears anything, hears some one thing, and hears that which is?

Theaet. Yes.

Soc. And he who touches anything, touches something which is one and therefore is?

Theaet. That again is true.

Soc. And does not he who thinks, think some one thing?

Theaet. Certainly.

Soc. And does not he who thinks some one thing, think something which is?

Theaet. I agree.

Soc. Then he who thinks of that which is not, thinks of nothing?

Theaet. Clearly.

Soc. And he who thinks of nothing, does not think at all?

Theaet. Obviously.

Soc. Then no one can think that which is not, either as a self-existent substance or as a predicate of something else?

Theaet. Clearly not.

Soc. Then to think falsely is different from thinking that which is not?

Theaet. It would seem so.

Soc. Then false opinion has no existence in us, either in the sphere of being or of knowledge?

Theaet. Certainly not.

Soc. But may not the following be the description of what we express by this name?

Theaet. What?

Soc. May we not suppose that false opinion or thought is a sort of heterodoxy; a person may make an exchange in his mind, and say that one real object is another real object. For thus he always thinks that which is, but he puts one thing in place of another, and missing the aim of his thoughts, he may be truly said to have false opinion.

Theaet. Now you appear to me to have spoken the exact truth: when a man puts the base in the place of the noble, or the noble in the place of the base, then he has truly false opinion.

Soc. I see, Theaetetus, that your fear has disappeared, and that you are beginning to despise me.

Theaet. What makes you say so?

Soc. You think, if I am not mistaken, that your "truly false" is safe from censure, and that I shall never ask whether there can be a swift which is slow, or a heavy which is light, or any other self-contradictory thing, which works, not according to its own nature, but according to that of its opposite. But I will not insist upon this, for I do not wish needlessly to discourage you. And so you are satisfied that false opinion is heterodoxy, or the thought of something else?

Theaet. I am.

Soc. It is possible then upon your view for the mind to conceive of one thing as another?

Theaet. True.

Soc. But must not the mind, or thinking power, which misplaces them, have a conception either of both objects or of one of them?

Theaet. Certainly.

Soc. Either together or in succession?

Theaet. Very good.

Soc. And do you mean by conceiving, the same which I mean?

Theaet. What is that?

Soc. I mean the conversation which the soul holds with herself in considering of anything. *[190]* I speak of what I scarcely understand; but the soul when thinking appears to me to be just talking—asking questions of herself and answering them, affirming and denying. And when she has arrived at a decision, either gradually or by a sudden impulse, and has at last agreed, and does not doubt, this is called her opinion. I say, then, that to form an opinion is to speak, and opinion is a word spoken, —I mean, to oneself and in silence, not aloud or to another: What think you?

Theaet. I agree.

Soc. Then when any one thinks of one thing as another, he is saying to himself that one thing is another?

Theaet. Yes.

Soc. But do you ever remember saying to yourself that the noble is certainly base, or the unjust just; or, best of all—have you ever attempted to convince yourself that one thing is another? Nay, not even in sleep, did you ever venture to say to yourself that odd is even, or anything of the kind?

Theaet. Never.

Soc. And do you suppose that any other man, either in his senses or out of them, ever seriously tried to persuade himself that an ox is a horse, or that two are one?

Theaet. Certainly not.

Soc. But if thinking is talking to oneself, no one speaking and thinking of two objects, and apprehending them both in his soul, will say and think that the one is the other of them, and I must add, that even you, lover of dispute as you are, had better let the word "other" alone [i.e., not insist that "one" and "other" are the same].[1] I mean to say, that no one thinks the noble to be base, or anything of the kind.

Theaet. I will give up the word "other," Socrates; and I agree to what you say.

Soc. If a man has both of them in his thoughts, he cannot think that the one of them is the other?

[1] Both words in Greek are called ἕτερον: cf. *Parmenides,* 147; *Euthydemus,* 301.

Theaet. True.

Soc. Neither, if he has one of them only in his mind and not the other, can he think that one is the other?

Theaet. True; for we should have to suppose that he apprehends that which is not in his thoughts at all.

Soc. Then no one who has either both or only one of the two objects in his mind can think that the one is the other. And therefore, he who maintains that false opinion is heterodoxy is talking nonsense; for neither in this, any more than in the previous way, can false opinion exist in us.

Theaet. No.

Soc. But if, Theaetetus, this is not admitted, we shall be driven into many absurdities.

Theaet. What are they?

Soc. I will not tell you until I have endeavoured to consider the matter from every point of view. *[191]* For I should be ashamed of us if we were driven in our perplexity to admit the absurd consequences of which I speak. But if we find the solution, and get away from them, we may regard them only as the difficulties of others, and the ridicule will not attach to us. On the other hand, if we utterly fail, I suppose that we must be humble, and allow the argument to trample us under foot, as the sea-sick passenger is trampled upon by the sailor, and to do anything to us. Listen, then, while I tell you how I hope to find a way out of our difficulty.

Theaet. Let me hear.

Soc. I think that we were wrong in denying that a man could think what he knew to be what he did not know; and that there is a way in which such a deception is possible.

Theaet. You mean to say, as I suspected at the time, that I may know Socrates, and at a distance see some one who is unknown to me, and whom I mistake for him—then the deception will occur?

Soc. But has not that position been relinquished by us, because involving the absurdity that we should know and not know the things which we know?

Theaet. True.

Soc. Let us make the assertion in another form, which may or may not have a favourable issue; but as we are in a great strait, every argument should be turned over and tested. Tell me, then, whether I am right in saying that you may learn a thing which at one time you did not know?

Theaet. Certainly you may.

Soc. And another and another?

Theaet. Yes.

Soc. I would have you imagine, then, that there exists in the mind of man a block of wax, which is of different sizes in different men; harder, moister, and having more or less of purity in one than another, and in some of an intermediate quality.

Theaet. I see.

Soc. Let us say that this tablet is a gift of Memory, the mother of the Muses; and that when we wish to remember anything which we have seen, or heard, or thought in our own minds, we hold the wax to the perceptions and thoughts, and in that material receive the impression of them as from the seal of a ring; and that we remember and know what is imprinted as long as the image lasts; but when the image is effaced, or cannot be taken, then we forget and do not know.

Theaet. Very good.

Soc. Now, when a person has this knowledge, and is considering something which he sees or hears, may not false opinion arise in the following manner?

Theaet. In what manner?

Soc. When he thinks what he knows, sometimes to be what he knows, and sometimes to be what he does not know. We were wrong before in denying the possibility of this.

Theaet. And how would you amend the former statement?

[*192*] *Soc.* I should begin by making a list of the impossible cases which must be excluded. (1) No one can think one thing to be another when he does not perceive either of them, but has the memorial or seal of both of them in his mind; nor can any mistaking of one thing for another occur, when he only knows one, and does not know, and has no impression of the other; nor can he think that one thing which he does not know is another thing which he does not know, or that what he does not know is what he knows; nor (2) that one thing which he perceives is another thing which he perceives, or that something which he perceives is something which he does not perceive; or that something which he does not perceive is something else which he does not perceive; or that something which he does not perceive is something which he perceives; nor again (3) can he think that something which he knows and perceives, and of which he has the impression coinciding with sense, is something else which he knows and perceives, and of which he has the impression coinciding with sense;—this last

case, if possible, is still more inconceivable than the others; nor (4) can he think that something which he knows and perceives, and of which he has the memorial coinciding with sense, is something else which he knows; nor so long as these agree, can he think that a thing which he knows and perceives is another thing which he perceives; or that a thing which he does not know and does not perceive, is the same as another thing which he does not know and does not perceive;—nor again, can he suppose that a thing which he does not know and does not perceive is the same as another thing which he does not know; or that a thing which he does not know and does not perceive is another thing which he does not perceive:—All these utterly and absolutely exclude the possibility of false opinion. The only cases, if any, which remain, are the following.

Theaet. What are they? If you tell me, I may perhaps understand you better; but at present I am unable to follow you.

Soc. A person may think that some things which he knows, or which he perceives and does not know, are some other things which he knows and perceives; or that some things which he knows and perceives, are other things which he knows and perceives.

Theaet. I understand you less than ever now.

Soc. Hear me once more, then:—I, knowing Theodorus, and remembering in my own mind what sort of person he is, and also what sort of person Theaetetus is, at one time see them, and at another time do not see them, and sometimes I touch them, and at another time not, or at one time I may hear them or perceive them in some other way, and at another time not perceive them, but still I remember them, and know them in my own mind.

Theaet. Very true.

Soc. Then, first of all, I want you to understand that a man may or may not perceive sensibly that which he knows.

Theaet. True.

Soc. And that which he does not know will sometimes not be perceived by him and sometimes will be perceived and only perceived?

Theaet. That is also true.

[*193*] *Soc.* See whether you can follow me better now: Socrates can recognize Theodorus and Theaetetus, but he sees neither of them, nor does he perceive them in any other way; he cannot then by any possibility imagine in his own mind that Theaetetus is Theodorus. Am I not right?

Theaet. You are quite right.

Soc. Then that was the first case of which I spoke.

Theaet. Yes.

Soc. The second case was, that I, knowing one of you and not knowing the other, and perceiving neither, can never think him whom I know to be him whom I do not know.

Theaet. True.

Soc. In the third case, not knowing and not perceiving either of you, I cannot think that one of you whom I do not know is the other whom I do not know. I need not again go over the catalogue of excluded cases, in which I cannot form a false opinion about you and Theodorus, either when I know both or when I am in ignorance of both, or when I know one and not the other. And the same of perceiving: do you understand me?

Theaet. I do.

Soc. The only possibility of erroneous opinion is, when knowing you and Theodorus, and having on the waxen block the impression of both of you given as by a seal, but seeing you imperfectly and at a distance, I try to assign the right impression of memory to the right visual impression, and to fit this into its own print: if I succeed, recognition will take place; but if I fail and transpose them, putting the foot into the wrong shoe—that is to say, putting the vision of either of you on to the wrong impression, or if my mind, like the sight in a mirror, which is transferred from right to left, err by reason of some similar affection, then "heterodoxy" and false opinion ensues.

Theaet. Yes, Socrates, you have described the nature of opinion with wonderful exactness.

Soc. Or again, when I know both of you, and perceive as well as know one of you, but not the other, and my knowledge of him does not accord with perception—that was the case put by me just now which you did not understand.

Theaet. No, I did not.

Soc. I meant to say, that when a person knows and perceives one of you, and his knowledge coincides with his perception, he will never think him to be some other person, whom he knows and perceives, and the knowledge of whom coincides with his perception—for that also was a case supposed.

Theaet. True.

Soc. But there was an omission of the further case, in which, as we now say, [194] false opinion may arise, when knowing both, and seeing, or having some other sensible perception of both, I fail in holding the seal over against the corresponding sensation; like a bad archer, I miss and fall wide of the mark—and this is called falsehood.

Theaet. Yes; it is rightly so called.

Soc. When, therefore, perception is present to one of the seals or impressions but not to the other, and the mind fits the seal of the absent perception on the one which is present, in any case of this sort the mind is deceived; in a word, if our view is sound, there can be no error or deception about things which a man does not know and has never perceived, but only in things which are known and perceived; in these alone opinion turns and twists about, and becomes alternately true and false;—true when the seals and impressions of sense meet straight and opposite—false when they go awry and crooked.

Theaet. And is not that, Socrates, nobly said?

Soc. Nobly! yes; but wait a little and hear the explanation, and then you will say so with more reason; for to think truly is noble and to be deceived is base.

Theaet. Undoubtedly.

Soc. And the origin of truth and error is as follows:—When the wax in the soul of any one is deep and abundant, and smooth and perfectly tempered, then the impressions which pass through the senses and sink into the heart of the soul, as Homer says in a parable, meaning to indicate the likeness of the soul to wax (κῆρ κηρὸς); these, I say, being pure and clear, and having a sufficient depth of wax, are also lasting, and minds, such as these, easily learn and easily retain, and are not liable to confusion, but have true thoughts, for they have plenty of room, and having clear impressions of things, as we term them, quickly distribute them into their proper places on the block. And such men are called wise. Do you agree?

Theaet. Entirely.

Soc. But when the heart of any one is shaggy —a quality which the all-wise poet commends, or muddy and of impure wax, or very soft, or very hard, then there is a corresponding defect in the mind—the soft are good at learning, but apt to forget; and the hard are the reverse; the shaggy and rugged and gritty, or those who have an admixture of earth or dung in their composition, [195] have the impressions indistinct, as also the hard, for there is no depth in them; and the soft too are indistinct, for their impressions are easily confused and effaced. Yet greater is the indistinctness when they are all jostled together in a little soul, which has no room. These are the natures which have false opinion; for when they see or hear or think of anything, they are slow in assigning the right objects to the right impressions—in their stupidity they confuse them, and are apt to see and hear and think amiss—and such men are said to be deceived in their knowledge of objects, and ignorant.

Theaet. No man, Socrates, can say anything truer than that.

Soc. Then now we may admit the existence of false opinion in us?

Theaet. Certainly.

Soc. And of true opinion also?

Theaet. Yes.

Soc. We have at length satisfactorily proven that beyond a doubt there are these two sorts of opinion?

Theaet. Undoubtedly.

Soc. Alas, Theaetetus, what a tiresome creature is a man who is fond of talking!

Theaet. What makes you say so?

Soc. Because I am disheartened at my own stupidity and tiresome garrulity; for what other term will describe the habit of a man who is always arguing on all sides of a question; whose dulness cannot be convinced, and who will never leave off?

Theaet. But what puts you out of heart?

Soc. I am not only out of heart, but in positive despair; for I do not know what to answer if any one were to ask me:—O Socrates, have you indeed discovered that false opinion arises neither in the comparison of perceptions with one another nor yet in thought, but in the union of thought and perception? Yes, I shall say, with the complacence of one who thinks that he has made a noble discovery.

Theaet. I see no reason why we should be ashamed of our demonstration, Socrates.

Soc. He will say: You mean to argue that the man whom we only think of and do not see, cannot be confused with the horse which we do not see or touch, but only think of and do not perceive? That I believe to be my meaning, I shall reply.

Theaet. Quite right.

Soc. Well, then, he will say, according to that argument, the number eleven, which is only thought, can never be mistaken for twelve, which is only thought: How would you answer him?

Theaet. I should say that a mistake may very likely arise between the eleven or twelve which are seen or handled, but that no similar mistake can arise between the eleven and twelve which are in the mind.

Soc. Well, but do you think that no one ever put before his own mind five and seven, [196] —I do not mean five or seven men or horses, but five or seven in the abstract, which, as we say, are recorded on the waxen block, and in which false opinion is held to be impossible;— did no man ever ask himself how many these numbers make when added together, and answer that they are eleven, while another thinks that they are twelve, or would all agree in thinking and saying that they are twelve?

Theaet. Certainly not; many would think that they are eleven, and in the higher numbers the chance of error is greater still; for I assume you to be speaking of numbers in general.

Soc. Exactly; and I want you to consider whether this does not imply that the twelve in the waxen block are supposed to be eleven?

Theaet. Yes, that seems to be the case.

Soc. Then do we not come back to the old difficulty? For he who makes such a mistake does think one thing which he knows to be another thing which he knows; but this, as we said, was impossible, and afforded an irresistible proof of the non-existence of false opinion, because otherwise the same person would inevitably know and not know the same thing at the same time.

Theaet. Most true.

Soc. Then false opinion cannot be explained as a confusion of thought and sense, for in that case we could not have been mistaken about pure conceptions of thought; and thus we are obliged to say, either that false opinion does not exist, or that a man may not know that which he knows;—which alternative do you prefer?

Theaet. It is hard to determine, Socrates.

Soc. And yet the argument will scarcely admit of both. But, as we are at our wits' end, suppose that we do a shameless thing?

Theaet. What is it?

Soc. Let us attempt to explain the verb "to know."

Theaet. And why should that be shameless?

Soc. You seem not to be aware that the whole of our discussion from the very beginning has been a search after knowledge, of which we are assumed not to know the nature.

Theaet. Nay, but I am well aware.

Soc. And is it not shameless when we do not know what knowledge is, to be explaining the verb "to know"? The truth is, Theaetetus, that we have long been infected with logical impurity. Thousands of times have we repeated the words "we know," and "do not know," and "we have or have not science or knowledge," as if we could understand what we are saying to one another, so long as we remain ignorant about knowledge; and at this moment we are using the words "we understand," "we are ignorant," as though we could still employ them when deprived of knowledge or science.

Theaet. But if you avoid these expressions, Socrates, how will you ever argue at all?

[197] Soc. I could not, being the man I am. The case would be different if I were a true hero of dialectic: and O that such an one were present! for he would have told us to avoid the use of these terms; at the same time he would not have spared in you and me the faults which I have noted. But, seeing that we are no great wits, shall I venture to say what knowing is? for I think that the attempt may be worth making.

Theaet. Then by all means venture, and no one shall find fault with you for using the forbidden terms.

Soc. You have heard the common explanation of the verb "to know"?

Theaet. I think so, but I do not remember it at the moment.

Soc. They explain the word "to know" as meaning "to have knowledge."

Theaet. True.

Soc. I should like to make a slight change, and say "to possess" knowledge.

Theaet. How do the two expressions differ?

Soc. Perhaps there may be no difference; but still I should like you to hear my view, that you may help me to test it.

Theaet. I will, if I can.

Soc. I should distinguish "having" from "possessing": for example, a man may buy and keep under his control a garment which he does not wear; and then we should say, not that he has, but that he possesses the garment.

Theaet. It would be the correct expression.

Soc. Well, may not a man "possess" and yet not "have" knowledge in the sense of which I am speaking? As you may suppose a man to have caught wild birds—doves or any other birds—and to be keeping them in an aviary which he has constructed at home; we might say of him in one sense, that he always has them because he possesses them, might we not?

Theaet. Yes.

Soc. And yet, in another sense, he has none of them; but they are in his power, and he has got them under his hand in an enclosure of his own, and can take and have them whenever he likes;—he can catch any which he likes, and

let the bird go again, and he may do so as often as he pleases.

Theaet. True.

Soc. Once more, then, as in what preceded we made a sort of waxen figment in the mind, so let us now suppose that in the mind of each man there is an aviary of all sorts of birds—some flocking together apart from the rest, others in small groups, others solitary, flying anywhere and everywhere.

Theaet. Let us imagine such an aviary—and what is to follow?

Soc. We may suppose that the birds are kinds of knowledge, and that when we were children, this receptacle was empty; whenever a man has gotten and detained in the enclosure a kind of knowledge, he may be said to have learned or discovered the thing which is the subject of the knowledge: and this is to know.

Theaet. Granted.

[198] Soc. And further, when any one wishes to catch any of these knowledges or sciences, and having taken, to hold it, and again to let them go, how will he express himself?—will he describe the "catching" of them and the original "possession" in the same words? I will make my meaning clearer by an example:—You admit that there is an art of arithmetic?

Theaet. To be sure.

Soc. Conceive this under the form of a hunt after the science of odd and even in general.

Theaet. I follow.

Soc. Having the use of the art, the arithmetician, if I am not mistaken, has the conceptions of number under his hand, and can transmit them to another.

Theaet. Yes.

Soc. And when transmitting them he may be said to teach them, and when receiving to learn them, and when having them in possession in the aforesaid aviary he may be said to know them.

Theaet. Exactly.

Soc. Attend to what follows: must not the perfect arithmetician know all numbers, for he has the science of all numbers in his mind?

Theaet. True.

Soc. And he can reckon abstract numbers in his head, or things about him which are numerable?

Theaet. Of course he can.

Soc. And to reckon is simply to consider how much such and such a number amounts to?

Theaet. Very true.

Soc. And so he appears to be searching into something which he knows, as if he did not know it, for we have already admitted that he knows all numbers;—you have heard these perplexing questions raised?

Theaet. I have.

Soc. May we not pursue the image of the doves, and say that the chase after knowledge is of two kinds? one kind is prior to possession and for the sake of possession, and the other for the sake of taking and holding in the hands that which is possessed already. And thus, when a man has learned and known something long ago, he may resume and get hold of the knowledge which he has long possessed, but has not at hand in his mind.

Theaet. True.

Soc. That was my reason for asking how we ought to speak when an arithmetician sets about numbering, or a grammarian about reading? Shall we say, that although he knows, he comes back to himself to learn what he already knows?

Theaet. It would be too absurd, Socrates.

Soc. Shall we say then that he is going to read or number what he does not know, *[199]* although we have admitted that he knows all letters and all numbers?

Theaet. That, again, would be an absurdity.

Soc. Then shall we say that about names we care nothing?—any one may twist and turn the words "knowing" and "learning" in any way which he likes, but since we have determined that the possession of knowledge is not the having or using it, we do assert that a man cannot not possess that which he possesses; and, therefore, in no case can a man not know that which he knows, but he may get a false opinion about it; for he may have the knowledge, not of this particular thing, but of some other; —when the various numbers and forms of knowledge are flying about in the aviary, and wishing to capture a certain sort of knowledge out of the general store, he takes the wrong one by mistake, that is to say, when he thought eleven to be twelve, he got hold of the ringdove which he had in his mind, when he wanted the pigeon.

Theaet. A very rational explanation.

Soc. But when he catches the one which he wants, then he is not deceived, and has an opinion of what is, and thus false and true opinion may exist, and the difficulties which were previously raised disappear. I dare say that you agree with me, do you not?

Theaet. Yes.

Soc. And so we are rid of the difficulty of a man's not knowing what he knows, for we are not driven to the inference that he does not possess what he possesses, whether he be or be not deceived. And yet I fear that a greater difficulty is looking in at the window.

Theaet. What is it?

Soc. How can the exchange of one knowledge for another ever become false opinion?

Theaet. What do you mean?

Soc. In the first place, how can a man who has the knowledge of anything be ignorant of that which he knows, not by reason of ignorance, but by reason of his own knowledge? And, again, is it not an extreme absurdity that he should suppose another thing to be this, and this to be another thing;—that, having knowledge present with him in his mind, he should still know nothing and be ignorant of all things?—you might as well argue that ignorance may make a man know, and blindness make him see, as that knowledge can make him ignorant.

Theaet. Perhaps, Socrates, we may have been wrong in making only forms of knowledge our birds: whereas there ought to have been forms of ignorance as well, flying about together in the mind, and then he who sought to take one of them might sometimes catch a form of knowledge, and sometimes a form of ignorance; and thus he would have a false opinion from ignorance, but a true one from knowledge, about the same thing.

Soc. I cannot help praising you, Theaetetus, and yet I must beg you to reconsider your words. *[200]* Let us grant what you say—then, according to you, he who takes ignorance will have a false opinion—am I right?

Theaet. Yes.

Soc. He will certainly not think that he has a false opinion?

Theaet. Of course not.

Soc. He will think that his opinion is true, and he will fancy that he knows the things about which he has been deceived?

Theaet. Certainly.

Soc. Then he will think that he has captured knowledge and not ignorance?

Theaet. Clearly.

Soc. And thus, after going a long way round, we are once more face to face with our original difficulty. The hero of dialectic will retort upon us:—"O my excellent friends, he will say, laughing, if a man knows the form of ignorance and the form of knowledge, can he think that one of them which he knows is the other which he knows? or, if he knows neither of them, can he think that the one which he knows not is another which he knows not? or, if he knows one and not the other, can he think the one which he knows to be the one which he does not know? or the one which he does not know to be the one which he knows? or will you tell me that there are other forms of knowledge which distinguish the right and wrong birds, and which the owner keeps in some other aviaries or graven on waxen blocks according to your foolish images, and which he may be said to know while he possesses them, even though he have them not at hand in his mind? And thus, in a perpetual circle, you will be compelled to go round and round, and you will make no progress." What are we to say in reply, Theaetetus?

Theaet. Indeed, Socrates, I do not know what we are to say.

Soc. Are not his reproaches just, and does not the argument truly show that we are wrong in seeking for false opinion until we know what knowledge is; that must be first ascertained; then, the nature of false opinion?

Theaet. I cannot but agree with you, Socrates, so far as we have yet gone.

Soc. Then, once more, what shall we say that knowledge is?—for we are not going to lose heart as yet.

Theaet. Certainly, I shall not lose heart, if you do not.

Soc. What definition will be most consistent with our former views?

Theaet. I cannot think of any but our old one, Socrates.

Soc. What was it?

Theaet. Knowledge was said by us to be true opinion; and true opinion is surely unerring, and the results which follow from it are all noble and good.

Soc. He who led the way into the river, Theaetetus, said "The experiment will show"; [201] and perhaps if we go forward in the search, we may stumble upon the thing which we are looking for; but if we stay where we are, nothing will come to light.

Theaet. Very true; let us go forward and try.

Soc. The trail soon comes to an end, for a whole profession is against us.

Theaet. How is that, and what profession do you mean?

Soc. The profession of the great wise ones who are called orators and lawyers; for these persuade men by their art and make them think whatever they like, but they do not teach them. Do you imagine that there are any teachers in the world so clever as to be able to con-

vince others of the truth about acts of robbery or violence, of which they were not eye-witnesses, while a little water is flowing in the clepsydra?

Theaet. Certainly not, they can only persuade them.

Soc. And would you not say that persuading them is making them have an opinion?

Theaet. To be sure.

Soc. When, therefore, judges are justly persuaded about matters which you can know only by seeing them, and not in any other way, and when thus judging of them from report they attain a true opinion about them, they judge without knowledge and yet are rightly persuaded, if they have judged well.

Theaet. Certainly.

Soc. And yet, O my friend, if true opinion in law courts and knowledge are the same, the perfect judge could not have judged rightly without knowledge; and therefore I must infer that they are not the same.

Theaet. That is a distinction, Socrates, which I have heard made by some one else, but I had forgotten it. He said that true opinion, combined with reason, was knowledge, but that the opinion which had no reason was out of the sphere of knowledge; and that things of which there is no rational account are not knowable—such was the singular expression which he used—and that things which have a reason or explanation are knowable.

Soc. Excellent; but then, how did he distinguish between things which are and are not "knowable"? I wish that you would repeat to me what he said, and then I shall know whether you and I have heard the same tale.

Theaet. I do not know whether I can recall it; but if another person would tell me, I think that I could follow him.

Soc. Let me give you, then, a dream in return for a dream:—Methought that I too had a dream, and I heard in my dream that the primeval letters or elements out of which you and I and all other things are compounded, have no reason or explanation; you can only name them, [202] but no predicate can be either affirmed or denied of them, for in the one case existence, in the other non-existence is already implied, neither of which must be added, if you mean to speak of this or that thing by itself alone. It should not be called itself, or that, or each, or alone, or this, or the like; for these go about everywhere and are applied to all things, but are distinct from them; whereas, if the first elements could be described, and had a definition of their own, they would be spoken of apart from all else. But none of these primeval elements can be defined; they can only be named, for they have nothing but a name, and the things which are compounded of them, as they are complex, are expressed by a combination of names, for the combination of names is the essence of a definition. Thus, then, the elements or letters are only objects of perception, and cannot be defined or known; but the syllables or combinations of them are known and expressed, and are apprehended by true opinion. When, therefore, any one forms the true opinion of anything without rational explanation, you may say that his mind is truly exercised, but has no knowledge; for he who cannot give and receive a reason for a thing, has no knowledge of that thing; but when he adds rational explanation, then, he is perfected in knowledge and may be all that I have been denying of him. Was that the form in which the dream appeared to you?

Theaet. Precisely.

Soc. And you allow and maintain that true opinion, combined with definition or rational explanation, is knowledge?

Theaet. Exactly.

Soc. Then may we assume, Theaetetus, that to-day, and in this casual manner, we have found a truth which in former times many wise men have grown old and have not found?

Theaet. At any rate, Socrates, I am satisfied with the present statement.

Soc. Which is probably correct—for how can there be knowledge apart from definition and true opinion? And yet there is one point in what has been said which does not quite satisfy me.

Theaet. What was it?

Soc. What might seem to be the most ingenious notion of all:—That the elements or letters are unknown, but the combination or syllables known.

Theaet. And was that wrong?

Soc. We shall soon know; for we have as hostages the instances which the author of the argument himself used.

Theaet. What hostages?

Soc. The letters, which are the elements; and the syllables, which are the combinations;—he reasoned, did he not, from the letters of the alphabet?

[203] *Theaet.* Yes; he did.

Soc. Let us take them and put them to the test, or rather, test ourselves:—What was the way in which we learned letters? and, first of all, are we right in saying that syllables have a definition, but that letters have no definition?

Theaet. I think so.

Soc. I think so too; for, suppose that some one asks you to spell the first syllable of my name:—Theaetetus, he says, what is SO?

Theaet. I should reply S and O.

Soc. That is the definition which you would give of the syllable?

Theaet. I should.

Soc. I wish that you would give me a similar definition of the S.

Theaet. But how can any one, Socrates, tell the elements of an element? I can only reply, that S is a consonant, a mere noise, as of the tongue hissing; B, and most other letters, again, are neither vowel-sounds nor noises. Thus letters may be most truly said to be undefined; for even the most distinct of them, which are the seven vowels, have a sound only, but no definition at all.

Soc. Then, I suppose, my friend, that we have been so far right in our idea about knowledge?

Theaet. Yes; I think that we have.

Soc. Well, but have we been right in maintaining that the syllables can be known, but not the letters?

Theaet. I think so.

Soc. And do we mean by a syllable two letters, or if there are more, all of them, or a single idea which arises out of the combination of them?

Theaet. I should say that we mean all the letters.

Soc. Take the case of the two letters S and O, which form the first syllable of my own name; must not he who knows the syllable, know both of them?

Theaet. Certainly.

Soc. He knows, that is, the S and O?

Theaet. Yes.

Soc. But can he be ignorant of either singly and yet know both together?

Theaet. Such a supposition, Socrates, is monstrous and unmeaning.

Soc. But if he cannot know both without knowing each, then if he is ever to know the syllable, he must know the letters first; and thus the fine theory has again taken wings and departed.

Theaet. Yes, with wonderful celerity.

Soc. Yes, we did not keep watch properly. Perhaps we ought to have maintained that a syllable is not the letters, but rather one single idea framed out of them, having a separate form distinct from them.

Theaet. Very true; and a more likely notion than the other.

Soc. Take care; let us not be cowards and betray a great and imposing theory.

[204] *Theaet.* No, indeed.

Soc. Let us assume then, as we now say, that the syllable is a simple form arising out of the several combinations of harmonious elements—of letters or of any other elements.

Theaet. Very good.

Soc. And it must have no parts.

Theaet. Why?

Soc. Because that which has parts must be a whole of all the parts. Or would you say that a whole, although formed out of the parts, is a single notion different from all the parts?

Theaet. I should.

Soc. And would you say that all and the whole are the same, or different?

Theaet. I am not certain; but, as you like me to answer at once, I shall hazard the reply, that they are different.

Soc. I approve of your readiness, Theaetetus, but I must take time to think whether I equally approve of your answer.

Theaet. Yes; the answer is the point.

Soc. According to this new view, the whole is supposed to differ from all?

Theaet. Yes.

Soc. Well, but is there any difference between all [in the plural] and the all [in the singular]? Take the case of number:—When we say one, two, three, four, five, six; or when we say twice three, or three times two, or four and two, or three and two and one, are we speaking of the same or of different numbers?

Theaet. Of the same.

Soc. That is of six?

Theaet. Yes.

Soc. And in each form of expression we spoke of all the six?

Theaet. True.

Soc. Again, in speaking of all [in the plural], is there not one thing which we express?

Theaet. Of course there is.

Soc. And that is six?

Theaet. Yes.

Soc. Then in predicating the word "all" of things measured by number, we predicate at the same time a singular and a plural?

Theaet. Clearly we do.

Soc. Again, the number of the acre and the acre are the same; are they not?

Theaet. Yes.

Soc. And the number of the stadium in like manner is the stadium?

Theaet. Yes.

Soc. And the army is the number of the army; and in all similar cases, the entire number of anything is the entire thing?

Theaet. True.

Soc. And the number of each is the parts of each?

Theaet. Exactly.

Soc. Then as many things as have parts are made up of parts?

Theaet. Clearly.

Soc. But all the parts are admitted to be the all, if the entire number is the all?

Theaet. True.

Soc. Then the whole is not made up of parts, for it would be the all, if consisting of all the parts?

Theaet. That is the inference.

Soc. But is a part a part of anything but the whole?

Theaet. Yes, of the all.

[205] *Soc.* You make a valiant defence, Theaetetus. And yet is not the all that of which nothing is wanting?

Theaet. Certainly.

Soc. And is not a whole likewise that from which nothing is absent? but that from which anything is absent is neither a whole nor all;—if wanting in anything, both equally lose their entirety of nature.

Theaet. I now think that there is no difference between a whole and all.

Soc. But were we not saying that when a thing has parts, all the parts will be a whole and all?

Theaet. Certainly.

Soc. Then, as I was saying before, must not the alternative be that either the syllable is not the letters, and then the letters are not parts of the syllable, or that the syllable will be the same with the letters, and will therefore be equally known with them?

Theaet. You are right.

Soc. And, in order to avoid this, we suppose it to be different from them?

Theaet. Yes.

Soc. But if letters are not parts of syllables, can you tell me of any other parts of syllables, which are not letters?

Theaet. No, indeed, Socrates; for if I admit the existence of parts in a syllable, it would be ridiculous in me to give up letters and seek for other parts.

Soc. Quite true, Theaetetus, and therefore,

according to our present view, a syllable must surely be some indivisible form?

Theaet. True.

Soc. But do you remember, my friend, that only a little while ago we admitted and approved the statement, that of the first elements out of which all other things are compounded there could be no definition, because each of them when taken by itself is uncompounded; nor can one rightly attribute to them the words "being" or "this," because they are alien and inappropriate words, and for this reason the letters or elements were indefinable and unknown?

Theaet. I remember.

Soc. And is not this also the reason why they are simple and indivisible? I can see no other.

Theaet. No other reason can be given.

Soc. Then is not the syllable in the same case as the elements or letters, if it has no parts and is one form?

Theaet. To be sure.

Soc. If, then, a syllable is a whole, and has many parts or letters, the letters as well as the syllable must be intelligible and expressible, since all the parts are acknowledged to be the same as the whole?

Theaet. True.

Soc. But if it be one and indivisible, then the syllables and the letters are alike undefined and unknown, and for the same reason?

Theaet. I cannot deny that.

Soc. We cannot, therefore, agree in the opinion of him who says that the syllable can be known and expressed, *[206]* but not the letters.

Theaet. Certainly not; if we may trust the argument.

Soc. Well, but will you not be equally inclined to disagree with him, when you remember your own experience in learning to read?

Theaet. What experience?

Soc. Why, that in learning you were kept trying to distinguish the separate letters both by the eye and by the ear, in order that, when you heard them spoken or saw them written, you might not be confused by their position.

Theaet. Very true.

Soc. And is the education of the harp-player complete unless he can tell what string answers to a particular note; the notes, as every one would allow, are the elements or letters of music?

Theaet. Exactly.

Soc. Then, if we argue from the letters and syllables which we know to other simples and compounds, we shall say that the letters or simple elements as a class are much more certainly known than the syllables, and much more indispensable to a perfect knowledge of any subject; and if some one says that the syllable is known and the letter unknown, we shall consider that either intentionally or unintentionally he is talking nonsense?

Theaet. Exactly.

Soc. And there might be given other proofs of this belief, if I am not mistaken. But do not let us in looking for them lose sight of the question before us, which is the meaning of the statement, that right opinion with rational definition or explanation is the most perfect form of knowledge.

Theaet. We must not.

Soc. Well, and what is the meaning of the term "explanation"? I think that we have a choice of three meanings.

Theaet. What are they?

Soc. In the first place, the meaning may be, manifesting one's thought by the voice with verbs and nouns, imaging an opinion in the stream which flows from the lips, as in a mirror or water. Does not explanation appear to be of this nature?

Theaet. Certainly; he who so manifests his thought, is said to explain himself.

Soc. And every one who is not born deaf or dumb is able sooner or later to manifest what he thinks of anything; and if so, all those who have a right opinion about anything will also have right explanation; nor will right opinion be anywhere found to exist apart from knowledge.

Theaet. True.

Soc. Let us not, therefore, hastily charge him who gave this account of knowledge with uttering an unmeaning word; for perhaps he only intended to say, that when a person was asked what was the nature of anything, *[207]* he should be able to answer his questioner by giving the elements of the thing.

Theaet. As for example, Socrates . . . ?

Soc. As, for example, when Hesiod says that a waggon is made up of a hundred planks. Now, neither you nor I could describe all of them individually; but if any one asked what is a waggon, we should be content to answer, that a waggon consists of wheels, axle, body, rims, yoke.

Theaet. Certainly.

Soc. And our opponent will probably laugh at us, just as he would if we professed to be grammarians and to give a grammatical account of the name of Theaetetus, and yet could only tell the syllables and not the letters of your name—that would be true opinion, and not knowledge; for knowledge, as has been already remarked, is not attained until, combined with true opinion, there is an enumeration of the elements out of which anything is composed.

Theaet. Yes.

Soc. In the same general way, we might also have true opinion about a waggon; but he who can describe its essence by an enumeration of the hundred planks, adds rational explanation to true opinion, and instead of opinion has art and knowledge of the nature of a waggon, in that he attains to the whole through the elements.

Theaet. And do you not agree in that view, Socrates?

Soc. If you do, my friend; but I want to know first, whether you admit the resolution of all things into their elements to be a rational explanation of them, and the consideration of them in syllables or larger combinations of them to be irrational—is this your view?

Theaet. Precisely.

Soc. Well, and do you conceive that a man has knowledge of any element who at one time affirms and at another time denies that element of something, or thinks that the same thing is composed of different elements at different times?

Theaet. Assuredly not.

Soc. And do you not remember that in your case and in that of others this often occurred in the process of learning to read?

Theaet. You mean that I mistook the letters and misspelt the syllables?

Soc. Yes.

Theaet. To be sure; I perfectly remember, and I am very far from supposing that they who are in this condition have knowledge.

Soc. When a person at the time of learning writes the name of Theaetetus, *[208]* and thinks that he ought to write and does write *Th* and *e;* but, again, meaning to write the name of Theodorus, thinks that he ought to write and does write *T* and *e*—can we suppose that he knows the first syllables of your two names?

Theaet. We have already admitted that such a one has not yet attained knowledge.

Soc. And in like manner he may enumerate without knowing them the second and third and fourth syllables of your name?

Theaet. He may.

Soc. And in that case, when he knows the order of the letters and can write them out correctly, he has right opinion?

Theaet. Clearly.

Soc. But although we admit that he has right opinion, he will still be without knowledge?

Theaet. Yes.

Soc. And yet he will have explanations, as well as right opinion, for he knew the order of the letters when he wrote; and this we admit to be explanation.

Theaet. True.

Soc. Then, my friend, there is such a thing as right opinion united with definition or explanation, which does not as yet attain to the exactness of knowledge.

Theaet. It would seem so.

Soc. And what we fancied to be a perfect definition of knowledge is a dream only. But perhaps we had better not say so as yet, for were there not three explanations of knowledge, one of which must, as we said, be adopted by him who maintains knowledge to be true opinion combined with rational explanation? And very likely there may be found some one who will not prefer this but the third.

Theaet. You are quite right; there is still one remaining. The first was the image or expression of the mind in speech; the second, which has just been mentioned, is a way of reaching the whole by an enumeration of the elements. But what is the third definition?

Soc. There is, further, the popular notion of telling the mark or sign of difference which distinguishes the thing in question from all others.

Theaet. Can you give me any example of such a definition?

Soc. As, for example, in the case of the sun, I think that you would be contented with the statement that the sun is the brightest of the heavenly bodies which revolve about the earth.

Theaet. Certainly.

Soc. Understand why:—the reason is, as I was just now saying, that if you get at the difference and distinguishing characteristic of each thing, then, as many persons affirm, you will get at the definition or explanation of it; but while you lay hold only of the common and not of the characteristic notion, you will only have the definition of those things to which this common quality belongs.

Theaet. I understand you, and your account of definition is in my judgment correct.

Soc. But he, who having right opinion about anything, can find out the difference which distinguishes it from other things will know that of which before he had only an opinion.

Theaet. Yes; that is what we are maintaining.

Soc. Nevertheless, Theaetetus, on a nearer view, I find myself quite disappointed; the picture, which at a distance was not so bad, has now become altogether unintelligible.

Theaet. What do you mean?

[209] *Soc.* I will endeavour to explain: I will suppose myself to have true opinion of you, and if to this I add your definition, then I have knowledge, but if not, opinion only.

Theaet. Yes.

Soc. The definition was assumed to be the interpretation of your difference.

Theaet. True.

Soc. But when I had only opinion, I had no conception of your distinguishing characteristics.

Theaet. I suppose not.

Soc. Then I must have conceived of some general or common nature which no more belonged to you than to another.

Theaet. True.

Soc. Tell me, now—How in that case could I have formed a judgment of you any more than of any one else? Suppose that I imagine Theaetetus to be a man who has nose, eyes, and mouth, and every other member complete; how would that enable me to distinguish Theaetetus from Theodorus, or from some outer barbarian?

Theaet. How could it?

Soc. Or if I had further conceived of you, not only as having nose and eyes, but as having a snub nose and prominent eyes, should I have any more notion of you than of myself and others who resemble me?

Theaet. Certainly not.

Soc. Surely I can have no conception of Theaetetus until your snub-nosedness has left an impression on my mind different from the snub-nosedness of all others whom I have ever seen, and until your other peculiarities have a like distinctness; and so when I meet you to-morrow the right opinion will be re-called?

Theaet. Most true.

Soc. Then right opinion implies the perception of differences?

Theaet. Clearly.

Soc. What, then, shall we say of adding reason or explanation to right opinion? If the meaning is, that we should form an opinion of the way in which something differs from another thing, the proposal is ridiculous.

Theaet. How so?

Soc. We are supposed to acquire a right opinion of the differences which distinguish one thing from another when we have already a right opinion of them, and so we go round and round:—the revolution of the scytal, or pestle, or any other rotatory machine, in the same circles, is as nothing compared with such a requirement; and we may be truly described as the blind directing the blind; for to add those things which we already have, in order that we may learn what we already think, is like a soul utterly benighted.

Theaet. Tell me; what were you going to say just now, when you asked the question?

Soc. If, my boy, the argument, in speaking of adding the definition, had used the word to "know," and not merely "have an opinion" of the difference, this which is the most promising of all the definitions of knowledge would have come to a pretty end, for to know is surely to acquire knowledge.

[210] *Theaet.* True.

Soc. And so, when the question is asked, What is knowledge? this fair argument will answer "Right opinion with knowledge,"— knowledge, that is, of difference, for this, as the said argument maintains, is adding the definition.

Theaet. That seems to be true.

Soc. But how utterly foolish, when we are asking what is knowledge, that the reply should only be, right opinion with knowledge of difference or of anything! And so, Theaetetus, knowledge is neither sensation nor true opinion, nor yet definition and explanation accompanying and added to true opinion?

Theaet. I suppose not.

Soc. And are you still in labour and travail, my dear friend, or have you brought all that you have to say about knowledge to the birth?

Theaet. I am sure, Socrates, that you have elicited from me a good deal more than ever was in me.

Soc. And does not my art show that you have brought forth wind, and that the offspring of your brain are not worth bringing up?

Theaet. Very true.

Soc. But if, Theaetetus, you should ever conceive afresh, you will be all the better for the present investigation, and if not, you will be soberer and humbler and gentler to other men, and will be too modest to fancy that you know what you do not know. These are the limits of my art; I can no further go, nor do I know aught of the things which great and famous men know or have known in this or former ages. The office of a midwife I, like my mother, have received from God; she delivered women, and I deliver men; but they must be young and noble and fair.

And now I have to go to the porch of the King Archon, where I am to meet Meletus and his indictment. To-morrow morning, Theodorus, I shall hope to see you again at this place.[1]

[1] Cf. *Euthyphro, sub fin.*; *Meno, sub fin.*

SOPHIST

PERSONS OF THE DIALOGUE: THEODORUS; THEAETETUS; SOCRATES. *An* ELEATIC
STRANGER, *whom Theodorus and Theaetetus bring with them.*
The younger SOCRATES, *who is a silent auditor*

~~~~~~~~~~~~~~~~~~~~~~

[216] *Theodorus.* HERE we are, Socrates, true to our agreement of yesterday; and we bring with us a stranger from Elea, who is a disciple of Parmenides and Zeno, and a true philosopher.

Socrates. Is he not rather a god, Theodorus, who comes to us in the disguise of a stranger? For Homer says that all the gods, and especially the god of strangers, are companions of the meek and just, and visit the good and evil among men. And may not your companion be one of those higher powers, a cross-examining deity, who has come to spy out our weakness in argument, and to cross-examine us?

Theod. Nay, Socrates, he is not one of the disputatious sort—he is too good for that. And, in my opinion, he is not a god at all; but divine he certainly is, for this is a title which I should give to all philosophers.

Soc. Capital, my friend! and I may add that they are almost as hard to be discerned as the gods. For the true philosophers, and such as are not merely made up for the occasion, appear in various forms unrecognized by the ignorance of men, and they "hover about cities," as Homer declares, looking from above upon human life; and some think nothing of them, and others can never think enough; and sometimes they appear as statesmen, and sometimes as sophists; and then, again, to many they seem to be no better than madmen. I should like to ask our Eleatic friend, if he would tell us, [217] what is thought about them in Italy, and to whom the terms are applied.

Theod. What terms?

Soc. Sophist, statesman, philosopher.

Theod. What is your difficulty about them, and what made you ask?

Soc. I want to know whether by his countrymen they are regarded as one or two; or do they, as the names are three, distinguish also three kinds, and assign one to each name?

Theod. I dare say that the Stranger will not object to discuss the question. What do you say, Stranger?

Stranger. I am far from objecting, Theodorus, nor have I any difficulty in replying that by us they are regarded as three. But to define precisely the nature of each of them is by no means a slight or easy task.

Theod. You have happened to light, Socrates, almost on the very question which we were asking our friend before we came hither, and he excused himself to us, as he does now to you; although he admitted that the matter had been fully discussed, and that he remembered the answer.

Soc. Then do not, Stranger, deny us the first favour which we ask of you: I am sure that you will not, and therefore I shall only beg of you to say whether you like and are accustomed to make a long oration on a subject which you want to explain to another, or to proceed by the method of question and answer. I remember hearing a very noble discussion in which Parmenides employed the latter of the two methods, when I was a young man, and he was far advanced in years.[1]

Str. I prefer to talk with another when he responds pleasantly, and is light in hand; if not, I would rather have my own say.

[1] Cf. *Parmenides,* 137 ff.

551

Soc. Any one of the present company will respond kindly to you, and you can choose whom you like of them; I should recommend you to take a young person—Theaetetus, for example—unless you have a preference for some one else.

Str. I feel ashamed, Socrates, being a newcomer into your society, instead of talking a little and hearing others talk, to be spinning out a long soliloquy or address, as if I wanted to show off. For the true answer will certainly be a very long one, a great deal longer than might be expected from such a short and simple question. At the same time, I fear that I may seem rude and ungracious if I refuse your courteous request, *[218]* especially after what you have said. For I certainly cannot object to your proposal, that Theaetetus should respond, having already conversed with him myself, and being recommended by you to take him.

Theaetetus. But are you sure, Stranger, that this will be quite so acceptable to the rest of the company as Socrates imagines?

Str. You hear them applauding, Theaetetus; after that, there is nothing more to be said. Well then, I am to argue with you, and if you tire of the argument, you may complain of your friends and not of me.

Theaet. I do not think that I shall tire, and if I do, I shall get my friend here, young Socrates, the namesake of the elder Socrates, to help; he is about my own age, and my partner at the gymnasium, and is constantly accustomed to work with me.

Str. Very good; you can decide about that for yourself as we proceed. Meanwhile you and I will begin together and enquire into the nature of the Sophist, first of the three: I should like you to make out what he is and bring him to light in a discussion; for at present we are only agreed about the name, but of the thing to which we both apply the name possibly you have one notion and I another; whereas we ought always to come to an understanding about the thing itself in terms of a definition, and not merely about the name minus the definition. Now the tribe of Sophists which we are investigating is not easily caught or defined; and the world has long ago agreed, that if great subjects are to be adequately treated, they must be studied in the lesser and easier instances of them before we proceed to the greatest of all. And as I know that the tribe of Sophists is troublesome and hard to be caught, I should recommend that we practise beforehand the method which is to be applied to him on some simple and smaller thing, unless you can suggest a better way.

Theaet. Indeed I cannot.

Str. Then suppose that we work out some lesser example which will be a pattern of the greater?

Theaet. Good.

Str. What is there which is well known and not great, and is yet as susceptible of definition as any larger thing? Shall I say an angler? He is familiar to all of us, and not a very interesting or important person.

Theaet. He is not.

[219] Str. Yet I suspect that he will furnish us with the sort of definition and line of enquiry which we want.

Theaet. Very good.

Str. Let us begin by asking whether he is a man having art or not having art, but some other power.

Theaet. He is clearly a man of art.

Str. And of arts there are two kinds?

Theaet. What are they?

Str. There is agriculture, and the tending of mortal creatures, and the art of constructing or moulding vessels, and there is the art of imitation—all these may be appropriately called by a single name.

Theaet. What do you mean? And what is the name?

Str. He who brings into existence something that did not exist before is said to be a producer, and that which is brought into existence is said to be produced.

Theaet. True.

Str. And all the arts which were just now mentioned are characterized by this power of producing?

Theaet. They are.

Str. Then let us sum them up under the name of productive or creative art.

Theaet. Very good.

Str. Next follows the whole class of learning and cognition; then comes trade, fighting, hunting. And since none of these produces anything, but is only engaged in conquering by word or deed, or in preventing others from conquering, things which exist and have been already produced—in each and all of these branches there appears to be an art which may be called acquisitive.

Theaet. Yes, that is the proper name.

Str. Seeing, then, that all arts are either acquisitive or creative, in which class shall we place the art of the angler?

Theaet. Clearly in the acquisitive class.

Str. And the acquisitive may be subdivided into two parts: there is exchange, which is voluntary and is effected by gifts, hire, purchase; and the other part of acquisitive, which takes by force of word or deed, may be termed conquest?

Theaet. That is implied in what has been said.

Str. And may not conquest be again subdivided?

Theaet. How?

Str. Open force may be called fighting, and secret force may have the general name of hunting?

Theaet. Yes.

Str. And there is no reason why the art of hunting should not be further divided.

Theaet. How would you make the division?

Str. Into the hunting of living and of lifeless prey.

Theaet. Yes, if both kinds exist.

[220] *Str.* Of course they exist; but the hunting after lifeless things having no special name, except some sorts of diving, and other small matters, may be omitted; the hunting after living things may be called animal hunting.

Theaet. Yes.

Str. And animal hunting may be truly said to have two divisions, land-animal hunting, which has many kinds and names, and water-animal hunting, or the hunting after animals who swim?

Theaet. True.

Str. And of swimming animals, one class lives on the wing and the other in the water?

Theaet. Certainly.

Str. Fowling is the general term under which the hunting of all birds is included.

Theaet. True.

Str. The hunting of animals who live in the water has the general name of fishing.

Theaet. Yes.

Str. And this sort of hunting may be further divided also into two principal kinds?

Theaet. What are they?

Str. There is one kind which takes them in nets, another which takes them by a blow.

Theaet. What do you mean, and how do you distinguish them?

Str. As to the first kind—all that surrounds and encloses anything to prevent egress, may be rightly called an enclosure.

Theaet. Very true.

Str. For which reason twig baskets, casting-nets, nooses, creels, and the like may all be termed "enclosures"?

Theaet. True.

Str. And therefore this first kind of capture may be called by us capture with enclosures, or something of that sort?

Theaet. Yes.

Str. The other kind, which is practised by a blow with hooks and three-pronged spears, when summed up under one name, may be called striking, unless you, Theaetetus, can find some better name?

Theaet. Never mind the name—what you suggest will do very well.

Str. There is one mode of striking, which is done at night, and by the light of a fire, and is by the hunters themselves called firing, or spearing by firelight.

Theaet. True.

Str. And the fishing by day is called by the general name of barbing, because the spears, too, are barbed at the point.

Theaet. Yes, that is the term.

Str. Of this barb-fishing, that which strikes the fish who is below from above is called spearing, because this is the way in which the three-pronged spears are mostly used.

Theaet. Yes, it is often called so.

Str. Then now there is only one kind remaining.

Theaet. What is that?

Str. When a hook is used, and the fish is not struck in any chance part of his body, as he is with the spear, but only about the head and mouth, [221] and is then drawn out from below upwards with reeds and rods:—What is the right name of that mode of fishing, Theaetetus?

Theaet. I suspect that we have now discovered the object of our search.

Str. Then now you and I have come to an understanding not only about the name of the angler's art, but about the definition of the thing itself. One half of all art was acquisitive —half of the acquisitive art was conquest or taking by force, half of this was hunting, and half of hunting was hunting animals, half of this was hunting water animals—of this again, the under half was fishing, half of fishing was striking; a part of striking was fishing with a barb, and one half of this again, being the kind which strikes with a hook and draws the fish from below upwards, is the art which we have been seeking, and which from the nature of the operation is denoted angling or drawing up (ἀσπαλιευτική, ἀνασπᾶσθαι).

Theaet. The result has been quite satisfactorily brought out.

Str. And now, following this pattern, let us endeavour to find out what a Sophist is.

Theaet. By all means.

Str. The first question about the angler was, whether he was a skilled artist or unskilled?

Theaet. True.

Str. And shall we call our new friend unskilled, or a thorough master of his craft?

Theaet. Certainly not unskilled, for his name, as, indeed, you imply, must surely express his nature.

Str. Then he must be supposed to have some art.

Theaet. What art?

Str. By heaven, they are cousins! it never occurred to us.

Theaet. Who are cousins?

Str. The angler and the Sophist.

Theaet. In what way are they related?

Str. They both appear to me to be hunters.

Theaet. How the Sophist? Of the other we have spoken.

Str. You remember our division of hunting, into hunting after swimming animals and land animals?

Theaet. Yes.

Str. And you remember that we subdivided the swimming and left the land animals, saying that there were many kinds of them?

[222] Theaet. Certainly.

Str. Thus far, then, the Sophist and the angler, starting from the art of acquiring, take the same road?

Theaet. So it would appear.

Str. Their paths diverge when they reach the art of animal hunting; the one going to the seashore, and to the rivers and to the lakes, and angling for the animals which are in them.

Theaet. Very true.

Str. While the other goes to land and water of another sort—rivers of wealth and broad meadow-lands of generous youth; and he also is intending to take the animals which are in them.

Theaet. What do you mean?

Str. Of hunting on land there are two principal divisions.

Theaet. What are they?

Str. One is the hunting of tame, and the other of wild animals.

Theaet. But are tame animals ever hunted?

Str. Yes, if you include man under tame animals. But if you like you may say that there are no tame animals, or that, if there are, man is not among them; or you may say that man is a tame animal but is not hunted—you shall decide which of these alternatives you prefer.

Theaet. I should say, Stranger, that man is a tame animal, and I admit that he is hunted.

Str. Then let us divide the hunting of tame animals into two parts.

Theaet. How shall we make the division?

Str. Let us define piracy, man-stealing, tyranny, the whole military art, by one name, as hunting with violence.

Theaet. Very good.

Str. But the art of the lawyer, of the popular orator, and the art of conversation may be called in one word the art of persuasion.

Theaet. True.

Str. And of persuasion, there may be said to be two kinds?

Theaet. What are they?

Str. One is private, and the other public.

Theaet. Yes; each of them forms a class.

Str. And of private hunting, one sort receives hire, and the other brings gifts.

Theaet. I do not understand you.

Str. You seem never to have observed the manner in which lovers hunt.

Theaet. To what do you refer?

Str. I mean that they lavish gifts on those whom they hunt in addition to other inducements.

Theaet. Most true.

Str. Let us admit this, then, to be the amatory art.

Theaet. Certainly.

Str. But that sort of hireling whose conversation is pleasing and who baits his hook only with pleasure and exacts nothing but his maintenance in return, we should all, if I am not mistaken, describe as possessing flattery or an art of making things pleasant. *[223]*

Theaet. Certainly.

Str. And that sort, which professes to form acquaintances only for the sake of virtue, and demands a reward in the shape of money, may be fairly called by another name?

Theaet. To be sure.

Str. And what is the name? Will you tell me?

Theaet. It is obvious enough; for I believe that we have discovered the Sophist: which is, as I conceive, the proper name for the class described.

Str. Then now, Theaetetus, his art may be traced as a branch of the appropriative, acquisitive family—which hunts animals,—living—land—tame animals; which hunts man,—privately—for hire,—taking money in exchange—having the semblance of education; and this is termed Sophistry, and is a hunt after young men of wealth and rank—such is the conclusion.

Theaet. Just so.

Str. Let us take another branch of his genealogy; for he is a professor of a great and many-sided art; and if we look back at what has preceded we see that he presents another aspect, besides that of which we are speaking.

Theaet. In what respect?

Str. There were two sorts of acquisitive art; the one concerned with hunting, the other with exchange.

Theaet. There were.

Str. And of the art of exchange there are two divisions, the one of giving, and the other of selling.

Theaet. Let us assume that.

Str. Next, we will suppose the art of selling to be divided into two parts.

Theaet. How?

Str. There is one part which is distinguished as the sale of a man's own productions; another, which is the exchange of the works of others.

Theaet. Certainly.

Str. And is not that part of exchange which takes place in the city, being about half of the whole, termed retailing?

Theaet. Yes.

Str. And that which exchanges the goods of one city for those of another by selling and buying is the exchange of the merchant?

Theaet. To be sure.

Str. And you are aware that this exchange of the merchant is of two kinds: it is partly concerned with food for the use of the body, and partly with the food of the soul which is bartered and received in exchange for money.

Theaet. What do you mean?

Str. You want to know what is the meaning of food for the soul; the other kind you surely understand.

Theaet. Yes.

Str. Take music in general and painting and marionette playing and many other things, [224] which are purchased in one city, and carried away and sold in another—wares of the soul which are hawked about either for the sake of instruction or amusement;—may not he who takes them about and sells them be quite as truly called a merchant as he who sells meats and drinks?

Theaet. To be sure he may.

Str. And would you not call by the same name him who buys up knowledge and goes about from city to city exchanging his wares for money?

Theaet. Certainly I should.

Str. Of this merchandise of the soul, may not one part be fairly termed the art of display? And there is another part which is certainly not less ridiculous, but being a trade in learning must be called by some name germane to the matter?

Theaet. Certainly.

Str. The latter should have two names,—one descriptive of the sale of the knowledge of virtue, and the other of the sale of other kinds of knowledge.

Theaet. Of course.

Str. The name of art-seller corresponds well enough to the latter; but you must try and tell me the name of the other.

Theaet. He must be the Sophist, whom we are seeking; no other name can possibly be right.

Str. No other; and so this trader in virtue again turns out to be our friend the Sophist, whose art may now be traced from the art of acquisition through exchange, trade, merchandise, to a merchandise of the soul which is concerned with speech and the knowledge of virtue.

Theaet. Quite true.

Str. And there may be a third reappearance of him;—for he may have settled down in a city, and may fabricate as well as buy these same wares, intending to live by selling them, and he would still be called a Sophist?

Theaet. Certainly.

Str. Then that part of acquisitive art which exchanges, and of exchange which either sells a man's own productions or retails those of others, as the case may be, and in either way sells the knowledge of virtue, you would again term Sophistry?

Theaet. I must, if I am to keep pace with the argument.

Str. Let us consider once more whether there may not be yet another aspect of sophistry.

Theaet. What is it?

[225] *Str.* In the acquisitive there was a subdivision of the combative or fighting art.

Theaet. There was.

Str. Perhaps we had better divide it.

Theaet. What shall be the divisions?

Str. There shall be one division of the competitive, and another of the pugnacious.

Theaet. Very good.

Str. That part of the pugnacious which is a contest of bodily strength may be properly called by some such name as violent.

Theaet. True.

Str. And when the war is one of words, it may be termed controversy?

Theaet. Yes.

Str. And controversy may be of two kinds.

Theaet. What are they?

Str. When long speeches are answered by long speeches, and there is public discussion about the just and unjust, that is forensic controversy.

Theaet. Yes.

Str. And there is a private sort of controversy, which is cut up into questions and answers, and this is commonly called disputation?

Theaet. Yes, that is the name.

Str. And of disputation, that sort which is only a discussion about contracts, and is carried on at random, and without rules of art, is recognized by the reasoning faculty to be a distinct class, but has hitherto had no distinctive name, and does not deserve to receive one from us.

Theaet. No; for the different sorts of it are too minute and heterogeneous.

Str. But that which proceeds by rules of art to dispute about justice and injustice in their own nature, and about things in general, we have been accustomed to call argumentation (Eristic)?

Theaet. Certainly.

Str. And of argumentation, one sort wastes money, and the other makes money.

Theaet. Very true.

Str. Suppose we try and give to each of these two classes a name.

Theaet. Let us do so.

Str. I should say that the habit which leads a man to neglect his own affairs for the pleasure of conversation, of which the style is far from being agreeable to the majority of his hearers, may be fairly termed loquacity: such is my opinion.

Theaet. That is the common name for it.

Str. But now who the other is, who makes money out of private disputation, it is your turn to say.

Theaet. There is only one true answer: he is the wonderful Sophist, of whom we are in pursuit, and who reappears again for the fourth time.

[226] *Str.* Yes, and with a fresh pedigree, for he is the money-making species of the Eristic, disputatious, controversial, pugnacious, combative, acquisitive family, as the argument has already proven.

Theaet. Certainly.

Str. How true was the observation that he

was a many-sided animal, and not to be caught with one hand, as they say!

Theaet. Then you must catch him with two.

Str. Yes, we must, if we can. And therefore let us try another track in our pursuit of him: You are aware that there are certain menial occupations which have names among servants?

Theaet. Yes, there are many such; which of them do you mean?

Str. I mean such as sifting, straining, winnowing, threshing.

Theaet. Certainly.

Str. And besides these there are a great many more, such as carding, spinning, adjusting the warp and the woof; and thousands of similar expressions are used in the arts.

Theaet. Of what are they to be patterns, and what are we going to do with them all?

Str. I think that in all of these there is implied a notion of division.

Theaet. Yes.

Str. Then if, as I was saying, there is one art which includes all of them, ought not that art to have one name?

Theaet. And what is the name of the art?

Str. The art of discerning or discriminating.

Theaet. Very good.

Str. Think whether you cannot divide this.

Theaet. I should have to think a long while.

Str. In all the previously named processes either like has been separated from like or the better from the worse.

Theaet. I see now what you mean.

Str. There is no name for the first kind of separation; of the second, which throws away the worse and preserves the better, I do know a name.

Theaet. What is it?

Str. Every discernment or discrimination of that kind, as I have observed, is called a purification.

Theaet. Yes, that is the usual expression.

Str. And any one may see that purification is of two kinds.

Theaet. Perhaps so, if he were allowed time to think; but I do not see at this moment.

Str. There are many purifications of bodies which may with propriety be comprehended under a single name.

Theaet. What are they, and what is their name?

[227] *Str.* There is the purification of living bodies in their inward and in their outward parts, of which the former is duly effected by medicine and gymnastic, the latter by the not very dignified art of the bath-man; and there is

the purification of inanimate substances—to this the arts of fulling and of furbishing in general attend in a number of minute particulars, having a variety of names which are thought ridiculous.

Theaet. Very true.

Str. There can be no doubt that they are thought ridiculous, Theaetetus; but then the dialectical art never considers whether the benefit to be derived from the purge is greater or less than that to be derived from the sponge, and has not more interest in the one than in the other; her endeavour is to know what is and is not kindred in all arts, with a view to the acquisition of intelligence; and having this in view, she honours them all alike, and when she makes comparisons, she counts one of them not a whit more ridiculous than another; nor does she esteem him who adduces as his example of hunting, the general's art, at all more decorous than another who cites that of the vermin-destroyer, but only as the greater pretender of the two. And as to your question concerning the name which was to comprehend all these arts of purification, whether of animate or inanimate bodies, the art of dialectic is in no wise particular about fine words, if she may be only allowed to have a general name for all other purifications, binding them up together and separating them off from the purification of the soul or intellect. For this is the purification at which she wants to arrive, and this we should understand to be her aim.

Theaet. Yes, I understand; and I agree that there are two sorts of purification, and that one of them is concerned with the soul, and that there is another which is concerned with the body.

Str. Excellent; and now listen to what I am going to say, and try to divide further the first of the two.

Theaet. Whatever line of division you suggest, I will endeavour to assist you.

Str. Do we admit that virtue is distinct from vice in the soul?

Theaet. Certainly.

Str. And purification was to leave the good and to cast out whatever is bad?

Theaet. True.

Str. Then any taking away of evil from the soul may be properly called purification?

Theaet. Yes.

Str. And in the soul there are two kinds of evil.

Theaet. What are they?

[228] *Str.* The one may be compared to disease in the body, the other to deformity.

Theaet. I do not understand.

Str. Perhaps you have never reflected that disease and discord are the same.

Theaet. To this, again, I know not what I should reply.

Str. Do you not conceive discord to be a dissolution of kindred elements, originating in some disagreement?

Theaet. Just that.

Str. And is deformity anything but the want of measure, which is always unsightly?

Theaet. Exactly.

Str. And do we not see that opinion is opposed to desire, pleasure to anger, reason to pain, and that all these elements are opposed to one another in the souls of bad men?

Theaet. Certainly.

Str. And yet they must all be akin?

Theaet. Of course.

Str. Then we shall be right in calling vice a discord and disease of the soul?

Theaet. Most true.

Str. And when things having motion, and aiming at an appointed mark, continually miss their aim and glance aside, shall we say that this is the effect of symmetry among them, or of the want of symmetry?

Theaet. Clearly of the want of symmetry.

Str. But surely we know that no soul is voluntarily ignorant of anything?

Theaet. Certainly not.

Str. And what is ignorance but the aberration of a mind which is bent on truth, and in which the process of understanding is perverted?

Theaet. True.

Str. Then we are to regard an unintelligent soul as deformed and devoid of symmetry?

Theaet. Very true.

Str. Then there are these two kinds of evil in the soul—the one which is generally called vice, and is obviously a disease of the soul . . .

Theaet. Yes.

Str. And there is the other, which they call ignorance, and which, because existing only in the soul, they will not allow to be vice.

Theaet. I certainly admit what I at first disputed—that there are two kinds of vice in the soul, and that we ought to consider cowardice, intemperance, and injustice to be all alike forms of disease in the soul, and ignorance, of which there are all sorts of varieties, to be deformity.

Str. And in the case of the body are there not two arts which have to do with the two bodily states?

Theaet. What are they?

Str. There is gymnastic, which has to do with deformity, and medicine, which has to do with disease.

Theaet. True.

[229] Str. And where there is insolence and injustice and cowardice, is not chastisement the art which is most required?

Theaet. That certainly appears to be the opinion of mankind.

Str. Again, of the various kinds of ignorance, may not instruction be rightly said to be the remedy?

Theaet. True.

Str. And of the art of instruction, shall we say that there is one or many kinds? At any rate there are two principal ones. Think.

Theaet. I will.

Str. I believe that I can see how we shall soonest arrive at the answer to this question.

Theaet. How?

Str. If we can discover a line which divides ignorance into two halves. For a division of ignorance into two parts will certainly imply that the art of instruction is also twofold, answering to the two divisions of ignorance.

Theaet. Well, and do you see what you are looking for?

Str. I do seem to myself to see one very large and bad sort of ignorance which is quite separate, and may be weighed in the scale against all other sorts of ignorance put together.

Theaet. What is it?

Str. When a person supposes that he knows, and does not know; this appears to be the great source of all the errors of the intellect.

Theaet. True.

Str. And this, if I am not mistaken, is the kind of ignorance which specially earns the title of stupidity.

Theaet. True.

Str. What name, then, shall be given to the sort of instruction which gets rid of this?

Theaet. The instruction which you mean, Stranger, is, I should imagine, not the teaching of handicraft arts, but what, thanks to us, has been termed education in this part of the world.

Str. Yes, Theaetetus, and by nearly all Hellenes. But we have still to consider whether education admits of any further division.

Theaet. We have.

Str. I think that there is a point at which such a division is possible.

Theaet. Where?

Str. Of education, one method appears to be rougher, and another smoother.

Theaet. How are we to distinguish the two?

Str. There is the time-honoured mode which our fathers commonly practised towards their sons, and which is still adopted by many—either of roughly reproving their errors, *[230]* or of gently advising them; which varieties may be correctly included under the general term of admonition.

Theaet. True.

Str. But whereas some appear to have arrived at the conclusion that all ignorance is involuntary, and that no one who thinks himself wise is willing to learn any of those things in which he is conscious of his own cleverness, and that the admonitory sort of instruction gives much trouble and does little good—

Theaet. There they are quite right.

Str. Accordingly, they set to work to eradicate the spirit of conceit in another way.

Theaet. In what way?

Str. They cross-examine a man's words, when he thinks that he is saying something and is really saying nothing, and easily convict him of inconsistencies in his opinions; these they then collect by the dialectical process, and placing them side by side, show that they contradict one another about the same things, in relation to the same things, and in the same respect. He, seeing this, is angry with himself, and grows gentle towards others, and thus is entirely delivered from great prejudices and harsh notions, in a way which is most amusing to the hearer, and produces the most lasting good effect on the person who is the subject of the operation. For as the physician considers that the body will receive no benefit from taking food until the internal obstacles have been removed, so the purifier of the soul is conscious that his patient will receive no benefit from the application of knowledge until he is refuted, and from refutation learns modesty; he must be purged of his prejudices first and made to think that he knows only what he knows, and no more.

Theaet. That is certainly the best and wisest state of mind.

Str. For all these reasons, Theaetetus, we must admit that refutation is the greatest and chiefest of purifications, and he who has not been refuted, though he be the Great King himself, is in an awful state of impurity; he is uninstructed and deformed in those things in which he who would be truly blessed ought to be fairest and purest.

Theaet. Very true.

Str. And who are the ministers of this art? I am afraid to say the Sophists. *[231]*

Theaet. Why?

Str. Lest we should assign to them too high a prerogative.

Theaet. Yet the Sophist has a certain likeness to our minister of purification.

Str. Yes, the same sort of likeness which a wolf, who is the fiercest of animals, has to a dog, who is the gentlest. But he who would not be found tripping, ought to be very careful in this matter of comparisons, for they are most slippery things. Nevertheless, let us assume that the Sophists are the men. I say this provisionally, for I think that the line which divides them will be marked enough if proper care is taken.

Theaet. Likely enough.

Str. Let us grant, then, that from the discerning art comes purification, and from purification let there be separated off a part which is concerned with the soul; of this mental purification instruction is a portion, and of instruction education, and of education, that refutation of vain conceit which has been discovered in the present argument; and let this be called by you and me the nobly-descended art of Sophistry.

Theaet. Very well; and yet, considering the number of forms in which he has presented himself, I begin to doubt how I can with any truth or confidence describe the real nature of the Sophist.

Str. You naturally feel perplexed; and yet I think that he must be still more perplexed in his attempt to escape us, for as the proverb says, when every way is blocked, there is no escape; now, then, is the time of all others to set upon him.

Theaet. True.

Str. First let us wait a moment and recover breath, and while we are resting, we may reckon up in how many forms he has appeared. In the first place, he was discovered to be a paid hunter after wealth and youth.

Theaet. Yes.

Str. In the second place, he was a merchant in the goods of the soul.

Theaet. Certainly.

Str. In the third place, he has turned out to be a retailer of the same sort of wares.

Theaet. Yes; and in the fourth place, he himself manufactured the learned wares which he sold.

Str. Quite right; I will try and remember the fifth myself. He belonged to the fighting class, and was further distinguished as a hero of debate, who professed the eristic art.

Theaet. True.

Str. The sixth point was doubtful, and yet we at last agreed that he was a purger of souls, who cleared away notions obstructive to knowledge.

Theaet. Very true.

[232] Str. Do you not see that when the professor of any art has one name and many kinds of knowledge, there must be something wrong? The multiplicity of names which is applied to him shows that the common principle to which all these branches of knowledge are tending, is not understood.

Theaet. I should imagine this to be the case.

Str. At any rate we will understand him, and no indolence shall prevent us. Let us begin again, then, and re-examine some of our statements concerning the Sophist; there was one thing which appeared to me especially characteristic of him.

Theaet. To what are you referring?

Str. We were saying of him, if I am not mistaken, that he was a disputer?

Theaet. We were.

Str. And does he not also teach others the art of disputation?

Theaet. Certainly he does.

Str. And about what does he profess that he teaches men to dispute? To begin at the beginning—Does he make them able to dispute about divine things, which are invisible to men in general?

Theaet. At any rate, he is said to do so.

Str. And what do you say of the visible things in heaven and earth, and the like?

Theaet. Certainly he disputes, and teaches to dispute about them.

Str. Then, again, in private conversation, when any universal assertion is made about generation and essence, we know that such persons are tremendous argufiers, and are able to impart their own skill to others.

Theaet. Undoubtedly.

Str. And do they not profess to make men able to dispute about law and about politics in general?

Theaet. Why, no one would have anything to say to them, if they did not make these professions.

Str. In all and every art, what the craftsman ought to say in answer to any question is written down in a popular form, and he who likes may learn.

Theaet. I suppose that you are referring to the precepts of Protagoras about wrestling and the other arts?

Str. Yes, my friend, and about a good many other things. In a word, is not the art of disputation a power of disputing about all things?

Theaet. Certainly; there does not seem to be

much which is left out.

Str. But oh! my dear youth, do you suppose this possible? for perhaps your young eyes may see things which to our duller sight do not appear.

[233] *Theaet.* To what are you alluding? I do not think that I understand your present question.

Str. I ask whether anybody can understand all things.

Theaet. Happy would mankind be if such a thing were possible!

Str. But how can any one who is ignorant dispute in a rational manner against him who knows?

Theaet. He cannot.

Str. Then why has the sophistical art such a mysterious power?

Theaet. To what do you refer?

Str. How do the Sophists make young men believe in their supreme and universal wisdom? For if they neither disputed nor were thought to dispute rightly, or being thought to do so were deemed no wiser for their controversial skill, then, to quote your own observation, no one would give them money or be willing to learn their art.

Theaet. They certainly would not.

Str. But they are willing.

Theaet. Yes, they are.

Str. Yes, and the reason, as I should imagine, is that they are supposed to have knowledge of those things about which they dispute?

Theaet. Certainly.

Str. And they dispute about all things?

Theaet. True.

Str. And therefore, to their disciples, they appear to be all-wise?

Theaet. Certainly.

Str. But they are not; for that was shown to be impossible.

Theaet. Impossible, of course.

Str. Then the Sophist has been shown to have a sort of conjectural or apparent knowledge only of all things, which is not the truth?

Theaet. Exactly; no better description of him could be given.

Str. Let us now take an illustration, which will still more clearly explain his nature.

Theaet. What is it?

Str. I will tell you, and you shall answer me, giving your very closest attention. Suppose that a person were to profess, not that he could speak or dispute, but that he knew how to make and do all things, by a single art.

Theaet. All things?

Str. I see that you do not understand the first word that I utter, for you do not understand the meaning of "all."

Theaet. No, I do not.

Str. Under all things, I include you and me, and also animals and trees.

Theaet. What do you mean?

Str. Suppose a person to say that he will make you and me, and all creatures.

[234] *Theaet.* What would he mean by "making"? He cannot be a husbandman;—for you said that he is a maker of animals.

Str. Yes; and I say that he is also the maker of the sea, and the earth, and the heavens, and the gods, and of all other things; and, further, that he can make them in no time, and sell them for a few pence.

Theaet. That must be a jest.

Str. And when a man says that he knows all things, and can teach them to another at a small cost, and in a short time, is not that a jest?

Theaet. Certainly.

Str. And is there any more artistic or graceful form of jest than imitation?

Theaet. Certainly not; and imitation is a very comprehensive term, which includes under one class the most diverse sorts of things.

Str. We know, of course, that he who professes by one art to make all things is really a painter, and by the painter's art makes resemblances of real things which have the same name with them; and he can deceive the less intelligent sort of young children, to whom he shows his pictures at a distance, into the belief that he has the absolute power of making whatever he likes.

Theaet. Certainly.

Str. And may there not be supposed to be an imitative art of reasoning? Is it not possible to enchant the hearts of young men by words poured through their ears, when they are still at a distance from the truth of facts, by exhibiting to them fictitious arguments, and making them think that they are true, and that the speaker is the wisest of men in all things?

Theaet. Yes; why should there not be another such art?

Str. But as time goes on, and their hearers advance in years, and come into closer contact with realities, and have learnt by sad experience to see and feel the truth of things, are not the greater part of them compelled to change many opinions which they formerly entertained, so that the great appears small to them, and the easy difficult, and all their dreamy speculations are overturned by the facts of life?

Theaet. That is my view, as far as I can judge, although, at my age, I may be one of those who see things at a distance only.

Str. And the wish of all of us, who are your friends, is and always will be to bring you as near to the truth as we can without the sad [235] reality. And now I should like you to tell me, whether the Sophist is not visibly a magician and imitator of true being; or are we still disposed to think that he may have a true knowledge of the various matters about which he disputes?

Theaet. But how can he, Stranger? Is there any doubt, after what has been said, that he is to be located in one of the divisions of children's play?

Str. Then we must place him in the class of magicians and mimics.

Theaet. Certainly we must.

Str. And now our business is not to let the animal out, for we have got him in a sort of dialectical net, and there is one thing which he decidedly will not escape.

Theaet. What is that?

Str. The inference that he is a juggler.

Theaet. Precisely my own opinion of him.

Str. Then, clearly, we ought as soon as possible to divide the image-making art, and go down into the net, and, if the Sophist does not run away from us, to seize him according to orders and deliver him over to reason, who is the lord of the hunt, and proclaim the capture of him; and if he creeps into the recesses of the imitative art, and secretes himself in one of them, to divide again and follow him up until in some sub-section of imitation he is caught. For our method of tackling each and all is one which neither he nor any other creature will ever escape in triumph.

Theaet. Well said; and let us do as you propose.

Str. Well, then, pursuing the same analytic method as before, I think that I can discern two divisions of the imitative art, but I am not as yet able to see in which of them the desired form is to be found.

Theaet. Will you tell me first what are the two divisions of which you are speaking?

Str. One is the art of likeness-making;—generally a likeness of anything is made by producing a copy which is executed according to the proportions of the original, similar in length and breadth and depth, each thing receiving also its appropriate colour.

Theaet. Is not this always the aim of imitation?

Str. Not always; in works either of sculpture or of painting, which are of any magnitude, [236] there is a certain degree of deception; for if artists were to give the true proportions of their fair works, the upper part, which is farther off, would appear to be out of proportion in comparison with the lower, which is nearer; and so they give up the truth in their images and make only the proportions which appear to be beautiful, disregarding the real ones.

Theaet. Quite true.

Str. And that which being other is also like, may we not fairly call a likeness or image?

Theaet. Yes.

Str. And may we not, as I did just now, call that part of the imitative art which is concerned with making such images the art of likeness-making?

Theaet. Let that be the name.

Str. And what shall we call those resemblances of the beautiful, which appear such owing to the unfavourable position of the spectator, whereas if a person had the power of getting a correct view of works of such magnitude, they would appear not even like that to which they profess to be like? May we not call these "appearances," since they appear only and are not really like?

Theaet. Certainly.

Str. There is a great deal of this kind of thing in painting, and in all imitation.

Theaet. Of course.

Str. And may we not fairly call the sort of art, which produces an appearance and not an image, phantastic art?

Theaet. Most fairly.

Str. These then are the two kinds of image-making—the art of making likenesses, and phantastic or the art of making appearances?

Theaet. True.

Str. I was doubtful before in which of them I should place the Sophist, nor am I even now able to see clearly; verily he is a wonderful and inscrutable creature. And now in the cleverest manner he has got into an impossible place.

Theaet. Yes, he has.

Str. Do you speak advisedly, or are you carried away at the moment by the habit of assenting into giving a hasty answer?

Theaet. May I ask to what you are referring?

Str. My dear friend, we are engaged in a very difficult speculation—there can be no doubt of that; for how a thing can appear and seem, and not be, or how a man can say a thing which is not true, [237] has always been and still remains a very perplexing question. Can any one say or think that falsehood really exists, and avoid being caught in a contradiction? Indeed, Theaetetus, the task is a difficult one.

Theaet. Why?

Str. He who says that falsehood exists has the audacity to assert the being of not-being; for this is implied in the possibility of falsehood. But, my boy, in the days when I was a boy, the great Parmenides protested against this doctrine, and to the end of his life he continued to inculcate the same lesson—always repeating both in verse and out of verse:

Keep your mind from this way of enquiry, for never will you show that not-being is

Such is his testimony, which is confirmed by the very expression when sifted a little. Would you object to begin with the consideration of the words themselves?

Theaet. Never mind about me; I am only desirous that you should carry on the argument in the best way, and that you should take me with you.

Str. Very good; and now say, do we venture to utter the forbidden word "not-being"?

Theaet. Certainly we do.

Str. Let us be serious then, and consider the question neither in strife nor play: suppose that one of the hearers of Parmenides was asked, "To what is the term 'not-being' to be applied?" —do you know what sort of object he would single out in reply, and what answer he would make to the enquirer?

Theaet. That is a difficult question, and one not to be answered at all by a person like myself.

Str. There is at any rate no difficulty in seeing that the predicate "not-being" is not applicable to any being.

Theaet. None, certainly.

Str. And if not to being, then not to something.

Theaet. Of course not.

Str. It is also plain, that in speaking of something we speak of being, for to speak of an abstract something naked and isolated from all being is impossible.

Theaet. Impossible.

Str. You mean by assenting to imply that he who says something must say some one thing?

Theaet. Yes.

Str. Some in the singular ($\tau\iota$) you would say is the sign of one, some in the dual ($\tau\iota\nu\grave{\epsilon}$) of two, some in the plural ($\tau\iota\nu\grave{\epsilon}s$) of many?

Theaet. Exactly.

Str. Then he who says "not something" must

say absolutely nothing.

Theaet. Most assuredly.

Str. And as we cannot admit that a man speaks and says nothing, he who says "not-being" does not speak at all.

Theaet. The difficulty of the argument can no further go.

[238] Str. Not yet, my friend, is the time for such a word; for there still remains of all perplexities the first and greatest, touching the very foundation of the matter.

Theaet. What do you mean? Do not be afraid to speak.

Str. To that which is, may be attributed some other thing which is?

Theaet. Certainly.

Str. But can anything which is, be attributed to that which is not?

Theaet. Impossible.

Str. And all number is to be reckoned among things which are?

Theaet. Yes, surely number, if anything, has a real existence.

Str. Then we must not attempt to attribute to not-being number either in the singular or plural?

Theaet. The argument implies that we should be wrong in doing so.

Str. But how can a man either express in words or even conceive in thought things which are not or a thing which is not without number?

Theaet. How indeed?

Str. When we speak of things which are not, are we not attributing plurality to not-being?

Theaet. Certainly.

Str. But, on the other hand, when we say "what is not," do we not attribute unity?

Theaet. Manifestly.

Str. Nevertheless, we maintain that you may not and ought not to attribute being to not-being?

Theaet. Most true.

Str. Do you see, then, that not-being in itself can neither be spoken, uttered, or thought, but that it is unthinkable, unutterable, unspeakable, indescribable?

Theaet. Quite true.

Str. But, if so, I was wrong in telling you just now that the difficulty which was coming is the greatest of all.

Theaet. What! is there a greater still behind?

Str. Well, I am surprised, after what has been said already, that you do not see the difficulty in which he who would refute the notion of not-being is involved. For he is compelled to contradict himself as soon as he makes the attempt.

Theaet. What do you mean? Speak more clearly.

Str. Do not expect clearness from me. For I, who maintain that not-being has no part either in the one or many, just now spoke and am still speaking of not-being as one; for I say "not-being." Do you understand?

Theaet. Yes.

Str. And a little while ago I said that not-being is unutterable, unspeakable, indescribable: do you follow?

Theaet. I do after a fashion.

Str. When I introduced the word "is," did I not contradict what I said before?

[239] *Theaet.* Clearly.

Str. And in using the singular verb, did I not speak of not-being as one?

Theaet. Yes.

Str. And when I spoke of not-being as indescribable and unspeakable and unutterable, in using each of these words in the singular, did I not refer to not-being as one?

Theaet. Certainly.

Str. And yet we say that, strictly speaking, it should not be defined as one or many, and should not even be called "it," for the use of the word "it" would imply a form of unity.

Theaet. Quite true.

Str. How, then, can any one put any faith in me? For now, as always, I am unequal to the refutation of not-being. And therefore, as I was saying, do not look to me for the right way of speaking about not-being; but come, let us try the experiment with you.

Theaet. What do you mean?

Str. Make a noble effort, as becomes youth, and endeavour with all your might to speak of not-being in a right manner, without introducing into it either existence or unity or plurality.

Theaet. It would be a strange boldness in me which would attempt the task when I see you thus discomfited.

Str. Say no more of ourselves; but until we find some one or other who can speak of not-being without number, we must acknowledge that the Sophist is a clever rogue who will not be got out of his hole.

Theaet. Most true.

Str. And if we say to him that he professes an art of making appearances, he will grapple with us and retort our argument upon ourselves; and when we call him an image-maker he will say, "Pray what do you mean at all by an image?"—and I should like to know, Theaetetus, how we can possibly answer the younker's question?

Theaet. We shall doubtless tell him of the images which are reflected in water or in mirrors; also of sculptures, pictures, and other duplicates.

Str. I see, Theaetetus, that you have never made the acquaintance of the Sophist.

Theaet. Why do you think so?

Str. He will make believe to have his eyes shut, or to have none.

Theaet. What do you mean?

Str. When you tell him of something existing in a mirror, or in sculpture, [240] and address him as though he had eyes, he will laugh you to scorn, and will pretend that he knows nothing of mirrors and streams, or of sight at all; he will say that he is asking about an idea.

Theaet. What can he mean?

Str. The common notion pervading all these objects, which you speak of as many, and yet call by the single name of image, as though it were the unity under which they were all included. How will you maintain your ground against him?

Theaet. How, Stranger, can I describe an image except as something fashioned in the likeness of the true?

Str. And do you mean this something to be some other true thing, or what do you mean?

Theaet. Certainly not another true thing, but only a resemblance.

Str. And you mean by true that which really is?

Theaet. Yes.

Str. And the not true is that which is the opposite of the true?

Theaet. Exactly.

Str. A resemblance, then, is not really real, if, as you say, not true?

Theaet. Nay, but it is in a certain sense.

Str. You mean to say, not in a true sense?

Theaet. Yes; it is in reality only an image.

Str. Then what we call an image is in reality really unreal.

Theaet. In what a strange complication of being and not-being we are involved!

Str. Strange! I should think so. See how, by his reciprocation of opposites, the many-headed Sophist has compelled us, quite against our will, to admit the existence of not-being.

Theaet. Yes, indeed, I see.

Str. The difficulty is how to define his art without falling into a contradiction.

Theaet. How do you mean? And where does the danger lie?

Str. When we say that he deceives us with an illusion, and that his art is illusory, do we mean that our soul is led by his art to think falsely, or what do we mean?

Theaet. There is nothing else to be said.

Str. Again, false opinion is that form of opinion which thinks the opposite of the truth:—You would assent?

Theaet. Certainly.

Str. You mean to say that false opinion thinks what is not?

Theaet. Of course.

Str. Does false opinion think that things which are not are not, or that in a certain sense they are?

Theaet. Things that are not must be imagined to exist in a certain sense, if any degree of falsehood is to be possible.

Str. And does not false opinion also think that things which most certainly exist do not exist at all?

Theaet. Yes.

Str. And here, again, is falsehood?

Theaet. Falsehood—yes.

Str. And in like manner, a false proposition will be deemed to be one which asserts the non-existence of things which are, and the existence of things which are not.

Theaet. There is no other way in which a false proposition can arise.

[241] *Str.* There is not; but the Sophist will deny these statements. And indeed how can any rational man assent to them, when the very expressions which we have just used were before acknowledged by us to be unutterable, unspeakable, indescribable, unthinkable? Do you see his point, Theaetetus?

Theaet. Of course he will say that we are contradicting ourselves when we hazard the assertion, that falsehood exists in opinion and in words; for in maintaining this, we are compelled over and over again to assert being of not-being, which we admitted just now to be an utter impossibility.

Str. How well you remember! And now it is high time to hold a consultation as to what we ought to do about the Sophist; for if we persist in looking for him in the class of false workers and magicians, you see that the handles for objection and the difficulties which will arise are very numerous and obvious.

Theaet. They are indeed.

Str. We have gone through but a very small portion of them, and they are really infinite.

Theaet. If that is the case, we cannot possibly catch the Sophist.

Str. Shall we then be so faint-hearted as to give him up?

Theaet. Certainly not, I should say, if we can get the slightest hold upon him.

Str. Will you then forgive me, and, as your words imply, not be altogether displeased if I flinch a little from the grasp of such a sturdy argument?

Theaet. To be sure I will.

Str. I have a yet more urgent request to make.

Theaet. Which is—?

Str. That you will promise not to regard me as a parricide.

Theaet. And why?

Str. Because, in self-defence, I must test the philosophy of my father Parmenides, and try to prove by main force that in a certain sense not-being is, and that being, on the other hand, is not.

Theaet. Some attempt of the kind is clearly needed.

Str. Yes, a blind man, as they say, might see that, and, unless these questions are decided in one way or another, no one when he speaks of false words, or false opinion, or idols, or images, or imitations, or appearances, or about the arts which are concerned with them, can avoid falling into ridiculous contradictions.

Theaet. Most true.

[242] *Str.* And therefore I must venture to lay hands on my father's argument; for if I am to be over-scrupulous, I shall have to give the matter up.

Theaet. Nothing in the world should ever induce us to do so.

Str. I have a third little request which I wish to make.

Theaet. What is it?

Str. You heard me say what I have always felt and still feel—that I have no heart for this argument?

Theaet. I did.

Str. I tremble at the thought of what I have said, and expect that you will deem me mad, when you hear of my sudden changes and shiftings; let me therefore observe, that I am examining the question entirely out of regard for you.

Theaet. There is no reason for you to fear that I shall impute any impropriety to you, if you attempt this refutation and proof; take heart, therefore, and proceed.

Str. And where shall I begin the perilous enterprise? I think that the road which I must take is—

Theaet. Which?—Let me hear.

Str. I think that we had better, first of all, consider the points which at present are regarded as self-evident, lest we may have fallen into some confusion, and be too ready to assent to one another, fancying that we are quite clear about them.

Theaet. Say more distinctly what you mean.

Str. I think that Parmenides, and all who ever yet undertook to determine the number and nature of existences, talked to us in rather a light and easy strain.

Theaet. How?

Str. As if we had been children, to whom they repeated each his own mythus or story;—one said that there were three principles, and that at one time there was war between certain of them; and then again there was peace, and they were married and begat children, and brought them up; and another spoke of two principles,—a moist and a dry, or a hot and a cold, and made them marry and cohabit. The Eleatics, however, in our part of the world, say that all things are many in name, but in nature one; this is their mythus, which goes back to Xenophanes, and is even older. Then there are Ionian, and in more recent times Sicilian muses, who have arrived at the conclusion that to unite the two principles is safer, and to say that being is one and many, and that these are held together by enmity and friendship, ever parting, ever meeting, as the severer Muses assert, while the gentler ones do not insist on the perpetual strife and peace, *[243]* but admit a relaxation and alternation of them; peace and unity sometimes prevailing under the sway of Aphrodite, and then again plurality and war, by reason of a principle of strife. Whether any of them spoke the truth in all this is hard to determine; besides, antiquity and famous men should have reverence, and not be liable to accusations so serious. Yet one thing may be said of them without offence—

Theaet. What thing?

Str. That they went on their several ways disdaining to notice people like ourselves; they did not care whether they took us with them, or left us behind them.

Theaet. How do you mean?

Str. I mean to say, that when they talk of one, two, or more elements, which are or have become or are becoming, or again of heat mingling with cold, assuming in some other part of their works separations and mixtures,—tell me, Theaetetus, do you understand what they mean by these expressions? When I was a younger man, I used to fancy that I understood quite well what was meant by the term "not-being," which is our present subject of dispute; and now you see

in what a fix we are about it.

Theaet. I see.

Str. And very likely we have been getting into the same perplexity about "being," and yet may fancy that when anybody utters the word, we understand him quite easily, although we do not know about not-being. But we may be equally ignorant of both.

Theaet. I dare say.

Str. And the same may be said of all the terms just mentioned.

Theaet. True.

Str. The consideration of most of them may be deferred; but we had better now discuss the chief captain and leader of them.

Theaet. Of what are you speaking? You clearly think that we must first investigate what people mean by the word "being."

Str. You follow close at my heels, Theaetetus. For the right method, I conceive, will be to call into our presence the dualistic philosophers and to interrogate them. "Come," we will say, "Ye, who affirm that hot and cold or any other two principles are the universe, what is this term which you apply to both of them, and what do you mean when you say that both and each of them 'are'? How are we to understand the word 'are'? Upon your view, are we to suppose that there is a third principle over and above the other two—three in all, and not two? For clearly you cannot say that one of the two principles is being, and yet attribute being equally to both of them; for, if you did, whichever of the two is identified with being, will comprehend the other; and so they will be one and not two."

Theaet. Very true.

Str. But perhaps you mean to give the name of "being" to both of them together?

Theaet. Quite likely.

[244] Str. "Then, friends," we shall reply to them, "the answer is plainly that the two will still be resolved into one."

Theaet. Most true.

Str. "Since then, we are in a difficulty, please to tell us what you mean, when you speak of being; for there can be no doubt that you always from the first understood your own meaning, whereas we once thought that we understood you, but now we are in a great strait. Please to begin by explaining this matter to us, and let us no longer fancy that we understand you, when we entirely misunderstand you." There will be no impropriety in our demanding an answer to this question, either of the dualists or of the pluralists?

Theaet. Certainly not.

Str. And what about the assertors of the oneness of the all—must we not endeavour to ascertain from them what they mean by "being"?

Theaet. By all means.

Str. Then let them answer this question: One, you say, alone is? "Yes," they will reply.

Theaet. True.

Str. And there is something which you call "being"?

Theaet. "Yes."

Str. And is being the same as one, and do you apply two names to the same thing?

Theaet. What will be their answer, Stranger?

Str. It is clear, Theaetetus, that he who asserts the unity of being will find a difficulty in answering this or any other question.

Theaet. Why so?

Str. To admit of two names, and to affirm that there is nothing but unity, is surely ridiculous?

Theaet. Certainly.

Str. And equally irrational to admit that a name is anything?

Theaet. How so?

Str. To distinguish the name from the thing, implies duality.

Theaet. Yes.

Str. And yet he who identifies the name with the thing will be compelled to say that it is the name of nothing, or if he says that it is the name of something, even then the name will only be the name of a name, and of nothing else.

Theaet. True.

Str. And the one will turn out to be only one of one, and being absolute unity, will represent a mere name.

Theaet. Certainly.

Str. And would they say that the whole is other than the one that is, or the same with it?

Theaet. To be sure they would, and they actually say so.

Str. If being is a whole, as Parmenides sings,—

Every way like unto the fullness of a well-rounded sphere,
Evenly balanced from the centre on every side,
And must needs be neither greater nor less in any way,
Neither on this side nor on that—

then being has a centre and extremes, and, having these, must also have parts.

Theaet. True.

[245] *Str.* Yet that which has parts may have the attribute of unity in all the parts, and in this way being all and a whole, may be one?

Theaet. Certainly.

Str. But that of which this is the condition cannot be absolute unity?

Theaet. Why not?

Str. Because, according to right reason, that which is truly one must be affirmed to be absolutely indivisible.

Theaet. Certainly.

Str. But this indivisible, if made up of many parts, will contradict reason.

Theaet. I understand.

Str. Shall we say that being is one and a whole, because it has the attribute of unity? Or shall we say that being is not a whole at all?

Theaet. That is a hard alternative to offer.

Str. Most true; for being, having in a certain sense the attribute of one, is yet proved not to be the same as one, and the all is therefore more than one.

Theaet. Yes.

Str. And yet if being be not a whole, through having the attribute of unity, and there be such a thing as an absolute whole, being lacks something of its own nature?

Theaet. Certainly.

Str. Upon this view, again, being, having a defect of being, will become not-being?

Theaet. True.

Str. And, again, the all becomes more than one, for being and the whole will each have their separate nature.

Theaet. Yes.

Str. But if the whole does not exist at all, all the previous difficulties remain the same, and there will be the further difficulty, that besides having no being, being can never have come into being.

Theaet. Why so?

Str. Because that which comes into being always comes into being as a whole, so that he who does not give whole a place among beings, cannot speak either of essence or generation as existing.

Theaet. Yes, that certainly appears to be true.

Str. Again; how can that which is not a whole have any quantity? For that which is of a certain quantity must necessarily be the whole of that quantity.

Theaet. Exactly.

Str. And there will be innumerable other points, each of them causing infinite trouble to him who says that being is either one or two.

Theaet. The difficulties which are dawning upon us prove this; for one objection connects with another, and they are always involving what has preceded in a greater and worse perplexity.

Str. We are far from having exhausted the more exact thinkers who treat of being and not-being. But let us be content to leave them, *[246]* and proceed to view those who speak less precisely; and we shall find as the result of all, that the nature of being is quite as difficult to comprehend as that of not-being.

Theaet. Then now we will go to the others.

Str. There appears to be a sort of war of Giants and Gods going on amongst them; they are fighting with one another about the nature of essence.

Theaet. How is that?

Str. Some of them are dragging down all things from heaven and from the unseen to earth, and they literally grasp in their hands rocks and oaks; of these they lay hold, and obstinately maintain, that the things only which can be touched or handled have being or essence, because they define being and body as one, and if any one else says that what is not a body exists they altogether despise him, and will hear of nothing but body.

Theaet. I have often met with such men, and terrible fellows they are.

Str. And that is the reason why their opponents cautiously defend themselves from above, out of an unseen world, mightily contending that true essence consists of certain intelligible and incorporeal ideas; the bodies of the materialists, which by them are maintained to be the very truth, they break up into little bits by their arguments, and affirm them to be, not essence, but generation and motion. Between the two armies, Theaetetus, there is always an endless conflict raging concerning these matters.

Theaet. True.

Str. Let us ask each party in turn, to give an account of that which they call essence.

Theaet. How shall we get it out of them?

Str. With those who make being to consist in ideas, there will be less difficulty, for they are civil people enough; but there will be very great difficulty, or rather an absolute impossibility, in getting an opinion out of those who drag everything down to matter. Shall I tell you what we must do?

Theaet. What?

Str. Let us, if we can, really improve them; but if this is not possible, let us imagine them to be better than they are, and more willing to answer in accordance with the rules of argument, and then their opinion will be more worth having; for that which better men acknowledge has more weight than that which is acknowledged by inferior men. Moreover we are no re-

specters of persons, but seekers after truth.

Theaet. Very good.

Str. Then now, on the supposition that they are improved, let us ask them to state their views, and do you interpret them.

Theaet. Agreed.

Str. Let them say whether they would admit that there is such a thing as a mortal animal.

Theaet. Of course they would.

Str. And do they not acknowledge this to be a body having a soul?

Theaet. Certainly they do.

Str. Meaning to say the soul is something which exists?

[247] Theaet. True.

Str. And do they not say that one soul is just, and another unjust, and that one soul is wise, and another foolish?

Theaet. Certainly.

Str. And that the just and wise soul becomes just and wise by the possession of justice and wisdom, and the opposite under opposite circumstances?

Theaet. Yes, they do.

Str. But surely that which may be present or may be absent will be admitted by them to exist?

Theaet. Certainly.

Str. And, allowing that justice, wisdom, the other virtues, and their opposites exist, as well as a soul in which they inhere, do they affirm any of them to be visible and tangible, or are they all invisible?

Theaet. They would say that hardly any of them are visible.

Str. And would they say that they are corporeal?

Theaet. They would distinguish: the soul would be said by them to have a body; but as to the other qualities of justice, wisdom, and the like, about which you asked, they would not venture either to deny their existence, or to maintain that they were all corporeal.

Str. Verily, Theaetetus, I perceive a great improvement in them; the real aborigines, children of the dragon's teeth, would have been deterred by no shame at all, but would have obstinately asserted that nothing is which they are not able to squeeze in their hands.

Theaet. That is pretty much their notion.

Str. Let us push the question; for if they will admit that any, even the smallest particle of being, is incorporeal, it is enough; they must then say what that nature is which is common to both the corporeal and incorporeal, and which they have in their mind's eye when they say of both of them that they "are." Perhaps they may be in a difficulty; and if this is the case, there is a possibility that they may accept a notion of ours respecting the nature of being, having nothing of their own to offer.

Theaet. What is the notion? Tell me, and we shall soon see.

Str. My notion would be, that anything which possesses any sort of power to affect another, or to be affected by another, if only for a single moment, however trifling the cause and however slight the effect, has real existence; and I hold that the definition of being is simply power.

Theaet. They accept your suggestion, having nothing better of their own to offer.

Str. Very good; perhaps we, as well as they, may one day change our minds; [248] but, for the present, this may be regarded as the understanding which is established with them.

Theaet. Agreed.

Str. Let us now go to the friends of ideas; of their opinions, too, you shall be the interpreter.

Theaet. I will.

Str. To them we say—You would distinguish essence from generation?

Theaet. "Yes," they reply.

Str. And you would allow that we participate in generation with the body, and through perception, but we participate with the soul through thought in true essence; and essence you would affirm to be always the same and immutable, whereas generation or becoming varies?

Theaet. Yes; that is what we should affirm.

Str. Well, fair sirs, we say to them, what is this participation, which you assert of both? Do you agree with our recent definition?

Theaet. What definition?

Str. We said that being was an active or passive energy, arising out of a certain power which proceeds from elements meeting with one another. Perhaps your ears, Theaetetus, may fail to catch their answer, which I recognize because I have been accustomed to hear it.

Theaet. And what is their answer?

Str. They deny the truth of what we were just now saying to the aborigines about existence.

Theaet. What was that?

Str. Any power of doing or suffering in a degree however slight was held by us to be a sufficient definition of being?

Theaet. True.

Str. They deny this, and say that the power of doing or suffering is confined to becoming, and that neither power is applicable to being.

Theaet. And is there not some truth in what they say?

Str. Yes; but our reply will be that we want to ascertain from them more distinctly, whether they further admit that the soul knows, and that being or essence is known.

Theaet. There can be no doubt that they say so.

Str. And is knowing and being known doing or suffering, or both, or is the one doing and the other suffering, or has neither any share in either?

Theaet. Clearly, neither has any share in either; for if they say anything else, they will contradict themselves.

Str. I understand; but they will allow that if to know is active, then, of course, to be known is passive. And on this view being, in so far as it is known, is acted upon by knowledge, and is therefore in motion; for that which is in a state of rest cannot be acted upon, as we affirm.

Theaet. True.

[249] *Str.* And, O heavens, can we ever be made to believe that motion and life and soul and mind are not present with perfect being? Can we imagine that being is devoid of life and mind, and exists in awful unmeaningness an everlasting fixture?

Theaet. That would be a dreadful thing to admit, Stranger.

Str. But shall we say that being has mind and not life?

Theaet. How is that possible?

Str. Or shall we say that both inhere in perfect being, but that it has no soul which contains them?

Theaet. And in what other way can it contain them?

Str. Or that being has mind and life and soul, but although endowed with soul remains absolutely unmoved?

Theaet. All three suppositions appear to me to be irrational.

Str. Under being, then, we must include motion, and that which is moved.

Theaet. Certainly.

Str. Then, Theaetetus, our inference is, that if there is no motion, neither is there any mind anywhere, or about anything or belonging to any one.

Theaet. Quite true.

Str. And yet this equally follows, if we grant that all things are in motion—upon this view too mind has no existence.

Theaet. How so?

Str. Do you think that sameness of condition

and mode and subject could ever exist without a principle of rest?

Theaet. Certainly not.

Str. Can you see how without them mind could exist, or come into existence anywhere?

Theaet. No.

Str. And surely contend we must in every possible way against him who would annihilate knowledge and reason and mind, and yet ventures to speak confidently about anything.

Theaet. Yes, with all our might.

Str. Then the philosopher, who has the truest reverence for these qualities, cannot possibly accept the notion of those who say that the whole is at rest, either as unity or in many forms: and he will be utterly deaf to those who assert universal motion. As children say entreatingly "Give us both," so he will include both the moveable and immoveable in his definition of being and all.

Theaet. Most true.

Str. And now, do we seem to have gained a fair notion of being?

Theaet. Yes truly.

Str. Alas, Theaetetus, methinks that we are now only beginning to see the real difficulty of the enquiry into the nature of it.

Theaet. What do you mean?

Str. O my friend, do you not see that nothing can exceed our ignorance, and yet we fancy that we are saying something good?

Theaet. I certainly thought that we were; and I do not at all understand how we never found out our desperate case.

[250] *Str*. Reflect: after having made these admissions, may we not be justly asked the same questions which we ourselves were asking of those who said that all was hot and cold?

Theaet. What were they? Will you recall them to my mind?

Str. To be sure I will, and I will remind you of them, by putting the same questions to you which I did to them, and then we shall get on.

Theaet. True.

Str. Would you not say that rest and motion are in the most entire opposition to one another?

Theaet. Of course.

Str. And yet you would say that both and either of them equally are?

Theaet. I should.

Str. And when you admit that both or either of them are, do you mean to say that both or either of them are in motion?

Theaet. Certainly not.

Str. Or do you wish to imply that they are both at rest, when you say that they are?

Theaet. Of course not.

Str. Then you conceive of being as some third and distinct nature, under which rest and motion are alike included; and, observing that they both participate in being, you declare that they are.

Theaet. Truly we seem to have an intimation that being is some third thing, when we say that rest and motion are.

Str. Then being is not the combination of rest and motion, but something different from them.

Theaet. So it would appear.

Str. Being, then, according to its own nature, is neither in motion nor at rest.

Theaet. That is very much the truth.

Str. Where, then, is a man to look for help who would have any clear or fixed notion of being in his mind?

Theaet. Where, indeed?

Str. I scarcely think that he can look anywhere; for that which is not in motion must be at rest, and again, that which is not at rest must be in motion; but being is placed outside of both these classes. Is this possible?

Theaet. Utterly impossible.

Str. Here, then, is another thing which we ought to bear in mind.

Theaet. What?

Str. When we were asked to what we were to assign the appellation of not-being, we were in the greatest difficulty:—do you remember?

Theaet. To be sure.

Str. And are we not now in as great a difficulty about being?

Theaet. I should say, Stranger, that we are in one which is, if possible, even greater.

Str. Then let us acknowledge the difficulty; and as being and not-being are involved in the same perplexity, there is hope that when the one appears more or less distinctly, [251] the other will equally appear; and if we are able to see neither, there may still be a chance of steering our way in between them, without any great discredit.

Theaet. Very good.

Str. Let us enquire, then, how we come to predicate many names of the same thing.

Theaet. Give an example.

Str. I mean that we speak of man, for example, under many names—that we attribute to him colours and forms and magnitudes and virtues and vices, in all of which instances and in ten thousand others we not only speak of him as a man, but also as good, and having numberless other attributes, and in the same way anything else which we originally supposed to be one is described by us as many, and under many names.

Theaet. That is true.

Str. And thus we provide a rich feast for tyros, whether young or old; for there is nothing easier than to argue that the one cannot be many, or the many one; and great is their delight in denying that a man is good; for man, they insist, is man and good is good. I dare say that you have met with persons who take an interest in such matters—they are often elderly men, whose meagre sense is thrown into amazement by these discoveries of theirs, which they believe to be the height of wisdom.

Theaet. Certainly, I have.

Str. Then, not to exclude any one who has ever speculated at all upon the nature of being, let us put our questions to them as well as to our former friends.

Theaet. What questions?

Str. Shall we refuse to attribute being to motion and rest, or anything to anything, and assume that they do not mingle, and are incapable of participating in one another? Or shall we gather all into one class of things communicable with one another? Or are some things communicable and others not?—Which of these alternatives, Theaetetus, will they prefer?

Theaet. I have nothing to answer on their behalf. Suppose that you take all these hypotheses in turn, and see what are the consequences which follow from each of them.

Str. Very good, and first let us assume them to say that nothing is capable of participating in anything else in any respect; [252] in that case rest and motion cannot participate in being at all.

Theaet. They cannot.

Str. But would either of them be if not participating in being?

Theaet. No.

Str. Then by this admission everything is instantly overturned, as well the doctrine of universal motion as of universal rest, and also the doctrine of those who distribute being into immutable and everlasting kinds; for all these add on a notion of being, some affirming that things "are" truly in motion, and others that they "are" truly at rest.

Theaet. Just so.

Str. Again, those who would at one time compound, and at another resolve all things, whether making them into one and out of one creating infinity, or dividing them into finite elements, and forming compounds out of these;

whether they suppose the processes of creation to be successive or continuous, would be talking nonsense in all this if there were no admixture.

Theaet. True.

Str. Most ridiculous of all will the men themselves be who want to carry out the argument and yet forbid us to call anything, because participating in some affection from another, by the name of that other.

Theaet. Why so?

Str. Why, because they are compelled to use the words "to be," "apart," "from others," "in itself," and ten thousand more, which they cannot give up, but must make the connecting links of discourse; and therefore they do not require to be refuted by others, but their enemy, as the saying is, inhabits the same house with them; they are always carrying about with them an adversary, like the wonderful ventriloquist, Eurycles, who out of their own bellies audibly contradicts them.

Theaet. Precisely so; a very true and exact illustration.

Str. And now, if we suppose that all things have the power of communion with one another—what will follow?

Theaet. Even I can solve that riddle.

Str. How?

Theaet. Why, because motion itself would be at rest, and rest again in motion, if they could be attributed to one another.

Str. But this is utterly impossible.

Theaet. Of course.

Str. Then only the third hypothesis remains.

Theaet. True.

Str. For, surely, either all things have communion with all; or nothing with any other thing; or some things communicate with some things and others not.

Theaet. Certainly.

Str. And two out of these three suppositions have been found to be impossible.

Theaet. Yes.

Str. Every one then, who desires to answer truly, will adopt the third and remaining hypothesis of the communion of some with some.

Theaet. Quite true.

[253] *Str.* This communion of some with some may be illustrated by the case of letters; for some letters do not fit each other, while others do.

Theaet. Of course.

Str. And the vowels, especially, are a sort of bond which pervades all the other letters, so that without a vowel one consonant cannot be joined to another.

Theaet. True.

Str. But does every one know what letters will unite with what? Or is art required in order to do so?

Theaet. Art is required.

Str. What art?

Theaet. The art of grammar.

Str. And is not this also true of sounds high and low?—Is not he who has the art to know what sounds mingle, a musician, and he who is ignorant, not a musician?

Theaet. Yes.

Str. And we shall find this to be generally true of art or the absence of art.

Theaet. Of course.

Str. And as classes are admitted by us in like manner to be some of them capable and others incapable of intermixture, must not he who would rightly show what kinds will unite and what will not, proceed by the help of science in the path of argument? And will he not ask if the connecting links are universal, and so capable of intermixture with all things; and again, in divisions, whether there are not other universal classes, which make them possible?

Theaet. To be sure he will require science, and, if I am not mistaken, the very greatest of all sciences.

Str. How are we to call it? By Zeus, have we not lighted unwittingly upon our free and noble science, and in looking for the Sophist have we not entertained the philosopher unawares?

Theaet. What do you mean?

Str. Should we not say that the division according to classes, which neither makes the same other, nor makes other the same, is the business of the dialectical science?

Theaet. That is what we should say.

Str. Then, surely, he who can divide rightly is able to see clearly one form pervading a scattered multitude, and many different forms contained under one higher form; and again, one form knit together into a single whole and pervading many such wholes, and many forms, existing only in separation and isolation. This is the knowledge of classes which determines where they can have communion with one another and where not.

Theaet. Quite true.

Str. And the art of dialectic would be attributed by you only to the philosopher pure and true?

Theaet. Who but he can be worthy?

Str. In this region we shall always discover the philosopher, if we look for him; like the Sophist, [254] he is not easily discovered, but for a different reason.

Theaet. For what reason?

Str. Because the Sophist runs away into the darkness of not-being, in which he has learned by habit to feel about, and cannot be discovered because of the darkness of the place. Is not that true?

Theaet. It seems to be so.

Str. And the philosopher, always holding converse through reason with the idea of being, is also dark from excess of light; for the souls of the many have no eye which can endure the vision of the divine.

Theaet. Yes; that seems to be quite as true as the other.

Str. Well, the philosopher may hereafter be more fully considered by us, if we are disposed; but the Sophist must clearly not be allowed to escape until we have had a good look at him.

Theaet. Very good.

Str. Since, then, we are agreed that some classes have a communion with one another, and others not, and some have communion with a few and others with many, and that there is no reason why some should not have universal communion with all, let us now pursue the enquiry, as the argument suggests, not in relation to all ideas, lest the multitude of them should confuse us, but let us select a few of those which are reckoned to be the principal ones, and consider their several natures and their capacity of communion with one another, in order that if we are not able to apprehend with perfect clearness the notions of being and not-being, we may at least not fall short in the consideration of them, so far as they come within the scope of the present enquiry, if peradventure we may be allowed to assert the reality of not-being, and yet escape unscathed.

Theaet. We must do so.

Str. The most important of all the genera are those which we were just now mentioning— being and rest and motion.

Theaet. Yes, by far.

Str. And two of these are, as we affirm, incapable of communion with one another.

Theaet. Quite incapable.

Str. Whereas being surely has communion with both of them, for both of them are?

Theaet. Of course.

Str. That makes up three of them.

Theaet. To be sure.

Str. And each of them is other than the remaining two, but the same with itself.

Theaet. True.

Str. But then, what is the meaning of these two words, "same" and "other"? Are they two new kinds other than the three, and yet always of necessity intermingling with them, and are we to have five kinds instead of three; or when we speak of the same and other, *[255]* are we unconsciously speaking of one of the three first kinds?

Theaet. Very likely we are.

Str. But, surely, motion and rest are neither the other nor the same.

Theaet. How is that?

Str. Whatever we attribute to motion and rest in common, cannot be either of them.

Theaet. Why not?

Str. Because motion would be at rest and rest in motion, for either of them, being predicated of both, will compel the other to change into the opposite of its own nature, because partaking of its opposite.

Theaet. Quite true.

Str. Yet they surely both partake of the same and of the other?

Theaet. Yes.

Str. Then we must not assert that motion, any more than rest, is either the same or the other.

Theaet. No; we must not.

Str. But are we to conceive that being and the same are identical?

Theaet. Possibly.

Str. But if they are identical, then again in saying that motion and rest have being, we should also be saying that they are the same.

Theaet. Which surely cannot be.

Str. Then being and the same cannot be one.

Theaet. Scarcely.

Str. Then we may suppose the same to be a fourth class, which is now to be added to the three others.

Theaet. Quite true.

Str. And shall we call the other a fifth class? Or should we consider being and other to be two names of the same class?

Theaet. Very likely.

Str. But you would agree, if I am not mistaken, that existences are relative as well as absolute?

Theaet. Certainly.

Str. And the other is always relative to other?

Theaet. True.

Str. But this would not be the case unless being and the other entirely differed; for, if the other, like being, were absolute as well as relative, then there would have been a kind of other which was not other than other. And now we find that what is other must of necessity be what it is in relation to some other.

Theaet. That is the true state of the case.

Str. Then we must admit the other as the fifth of our selected classes.

Theaet. Yes.

Str. And the fifth class pervades all classes, for they all differ from one another, not by reason of their own nature, but because they partake of the idea of the other.

Theaet. Quite true.

Str. Then let us now put the case with reference to each of the five.

Theaet. How?

Str. First there is motion, which we affirm to be absolutely "other" than rest: what else can we say?

Theaet. It is so.

Str. And therefore is not rest.

Theaet. Certainly not.

Str. And yet is, because partaking of being.

[256] *Theaet.* True.

Str. Again, motion is other than the same?

Theaet. Just so.

Str. And is therefore not the same.

Theaet. It is not.

Str. Yet, surely, motion is the same, because all things partake of the same.

Theaet. Very true.

Str. Then we must admit, and not object to say, that motion is the same and is not the same, for we do not apply the terms "same" and "not the same," in the same sense; but we call it the "same," in relation to itself, because partaking of the same; and not the same, because having communion with the other, it is thereby severed from the same, and has become not that but other, and is therefore rightly spoken of as "not the same."

Theaet. To be sure.

Str. And if absolute motion in any point of view partook of rest, there would be no absurdity in calling motion stationary.

Theaet. Quite right,—that is, on the supposition that some classes mingle with one another, and others not.

Str. That such a communion of kinds is according to nature, we had already proved [1] before we arrived at this part of our discussion.

Theaet. Certainly.

Str. Let us proceed, then. May we not say that motion is other than the other, having been also proved by us to be other than the same and other than rest?

Theaet. That is certain.

---

[1] Cf. *supra,* 252.

Str. Then, according to this view, motion is other and also not other?

Theaet. True.

Str. What is the next step? Shall we say that motion is other than the three and not other than the fourth—for we agreed that there are five classes about and in the sphere of which we proposed to make enquiry?

Theaet. Surely we cannot admit that the number is less than it appeared to be just now.

Str. Then we may without fear contend that motion is other than being?

Theaet. Without the least fear.

Str. The plain result is that motion, since it partakes of being, really is and also is not?

Theaet. Nothing can be plainer.

Str. Then not-being necessarily exists in the case of motion and of every class; for the nature of the other entering into them all, makes each of them other than being, and so non-existent; and therefore of all of them, in like manner, we may truly say that they are not; and again, inasmuch as they partake of being, that they are and are existent.

Theaet. So we may assume.

Str. Every class, then, has plurality of being and infinity of not-being.

[257] Theaet. So we must infer.

Str. And being itself may be said to be other than the other kinds.

Theaet. Certainly.

Str. Then we may infer that being is not, in respect of as many other things as there are; for not being these it is itself one, and is not the other things, which are infinite in number.

Theaet. That is not far from the truth.

Str. And we must not quarrel with this result, since it is of the nature of classes to have communion with one another; and if any one denies our present statement [viz., that being is not, etc.], let him first argue with our former conclusion [i.e., respecting the communion of ideas], and then he may proceed to argue with what follows.

Theaet. Nothing can be fairer.

Str. Let me ask you to consider a further question.

Theaet. What question?

Str. When we speak of not-being, we speak, I suppose, not of something opposed to being, but only different.

Theaet. What do you mean?

Str. When we speak of something as not great, does the expression seem to you to imply what is little any more than what is equal?

Theaet. Certainly not.

Str. The negative particles, οὐ and μή, when prefixed to words, do not imply opposition, but only difference from the words, or more correctly from the things represented by the words, which follow them.

Theaet. Quite true.

Str. There is another point to be considered, if you do not object.

Theaet. What is it?

Str. The nature of the other appears to me to be divided into fractions like knowledge.

Theaet. How so?

Str. Knowledge, like the other, is one; and yet the various parts of knowledge have each of them their own particular name, and hence there are many arts and kinds of knowledge.

Theaet. Quite true.

Str. And is not the case the same with the parts of the other, which is also one?

Theaet. Very likely; but will you tell me how?

Str. There is some part of the other which is opposed to the beautiful?

Theaet. There is.

Str. Shall we say that this has or has not a name?

Theaet. It has; for whatever we call not-beautiful is other than the beautiful, not than something else.

Str. And now tell me another thing.

Theaet. What?

Str. Is the not-beautiful anything but this—an existence parted off from a certain kind of existence, and again from another point of view opposed to an existing something?

Theaet. True.

Str. Then the not-beautiful turns out to be the opposition of being to being?

Theaet. Very true.

Str. But upon this view, is the beautiful a more real and the not-beautiful a less real existence?

Theaet. Not at all.

[258] Str. And the not-great may be said to exist, equally with the great?

Theaet. Yes.

Str. And, in the same way, the just must be placed in the same category with the not-just—the one cannot be said to have any more existence than the other.

Theaet. True.

Str. The same may be said of other things; seeing that the nature of the other has a real existence, the parts of this nature must equally be supposed to exist.

Theaet. Of course.

Str. Then, as would appear, the opposition of

a part of the other, and of a part of being, to one another, is, if I may venture to say so, as truly essence as being itself, and implies not the opposite of being, but only what is other than being.

Theaet. Beyond question.

Str. What then shall we call it?

Theaet. Clearly, not being; and this is the very nature for which the Sophist compelled us to search.

Str. And has not this, as you were saying, as real an existence as any other class? May I not say with confidence that not-being has an assured existence, and a nature of its own? Just as the great was found to be great and the beautiful beautiful, and the not-great not-great, and the not-beautiful not-beautiful, in the same manner not-being has been found to be and is not-being, and is to be reckoned one among the many classes of being. Do you, Theaetetus, still feel any doubt of this?

Theaet. None whatever.

Str. Do you observe that our scepticism has carried us beyond the range of Parmenides' prohibition?

Theaet. In what?

Str. We have advanced to a further point, and shown him more than he forbad us to investigate.

Theaet. How is that?

Str. Why, because he says—

Not-being never is, and do thou keep thy thoughts from this way of enquiry.

Theaet. Yes, he says so.

Str. Whereas, we have not only proved that things which are not are, but we have shown what form of being not-being is; for we have shown that the nature of the other is, and is distributed over all things in their relations to one another, and whatever part of the other is contrasted with being, this is precisely what we have ventured to call not-being.

Theaet. And surely, Stranger, we were quite right.

Str. Let not any one say, then, that while affirming the opposition of not-being to being, we still assert the being of not-being; for as to whether there is an opposite of being, to that enquiry we have long said good-bye—it may or may not be, *[259]* and may or may not be capable of definition. But as touching our present account of not-being, let a man either convince us of error, or, so long as he cannot, he too must say, as we are saying, that there is a communion of classes, and that being, and difference or

other, traverse all things and mutually interpenetrate, so that the other partakes of being, and by reason of this participation is, and yet is not that of which it partakes, but other, and being other than being, it is clearly a necessity that not-being should be. And again, being, through partaking of the other, becomes a class other than the remaining classes, and being other than all of them, is not each one of them, and is not all the rest, so that undoubtedly there are thousands upon thousands of cases in which being is not, and all other things, whether regarded individually or collectively, in many respects are, and in many respects are not.

Theaet. True.

Str. And he who is sceptical of this contradiction, must think how he can find something better to say; or if he sees a puzzle, and his pleasure is to drag words this way and that, the argument will prove to him, that he is not making a worthy use of his faculties; for there is no charm in such puzzles, and there is no difficulty in detecting them; but we can tell him of something else the pursuit of which is noble and also difficult.

Theaet. What is it?

Str. A thing of which I have already spoken;—letting alone these puzzles as involving no difficulty, he should be able to follow and criticize in detail every argument, and when a man says that the same is in a manner other, or that other is the same, to understand and refute him from his own point of view, and in the same respect in which he asserts either of these affections. But to show that somehow and in some sense the same is other, or the other same, or the great small, or the like unlike; and to delight in always bringing forward such contradictions, is no real refutation, but is clearly the new-born babe of some one who is only beginning to approach the problem of being.

Theaet. To be sure.

Str. For certainly, my friend, the attempt to separate all existences from one another is a barbarism and utterly unworthy of an educated or philosophical mind.

Theaet. Why so?

Str. The attempt at universal separation is the final annihilation of all reasoning; *[260]* for only by the union of conceptions with one another do we attain to discourse of reason.

Theaet. True.

Str. And, observe that we were only just in time in making a resistance to such separatists, and compelling them to admit that one thing mingles with another.

Theaet. Why so?

Str. Why, that we might be able to assert discourse to be a kind of being; for if we could not, the worst of all consequences would follow; we should have no philosophy. Moreover, the necessity for determining the nature of discourse presses upon us at this moment; if utterly deprived of it, we could no more hold discourse; and deprived of it we should be if we admitted that there was no admixture of natures at all.

Theaet. Very true. But I do not understand why at this moment we must determine the nature of discourse.

Str. Perhaps you will see more clearly by the help of the following explanation.

Theaet. What explanation?

Str. Not-being has been acknowledged by us to be one among many classes diffused over all being.

Theaet. True.

Str. And thence arises the question, whether not-being mingles with opinion and language.

Theaet. How so?

Str. If not-being has no part in the proposition, then all things must be true; but if not-being has a part, then false opinion and false speech are possible, for to think or to say what is not—is falsehood, which thus arises in the region of thought and in speech.

Theaet. That is quite true.

Str. And where there is falsehood surely there must be deceit.

Theaet. Yes.

Str. And if there is deceit, then all things must be full of idols and images and fancies.

Theaet. To be sure.

Str. Into that region the Sophist, as we said, made his escape, and, when he had got there, denied the very possibility of falsehood; no one, he argued, either conceived or uttered falsehood, inasmuch as not-being did not in any way partake of being.

Theaet. True.

Str. And now, not-being has been shown to partake of being, and therefore he will not continue fighting in this direction, but he will probably say that some ideas partake of not-being, and some not, and that language and opinion are of the non-partaking class; and he will still fight to the death against the existence of the image-making and phantastic art, in which we have placed him, because, as he will say, opinion and language do not partake of not-being, and unless this participation exists, there can be no such thing as falsehood. And,

with the view of meeting this evasion, we must begin by enquiring into the nature of language, opinion, and imagination, in order that when we find them we may find also that they have communion with not-being, *[261]* and, having made out the connection of them, may thus prove that falsehood exists; and therein we will imprison the Sophist, if he deserves it, or, if not, we will let him go again and look for him in another class.

Theaet. Certainly, Stranger, there appears to be truth in what was said about the Sophist at first, that he was of a class not easily caught, for he seems to have abundance of defences, which he throws up, and which must every one of them be stormed before we can reach the man himself. And even now, we have with difficulty got through his first defence, which is the not-being of not-being, and lo! here is another; for we have still to show that falsehood exists in the sphere of language and opinion, and there will be another and another line of defence without end.

Str. Any one, Theaetetus, who is able to advance even a little ought to be of good cheer, for what would he who is dispirited at a little progress do, if he were making none at all, or even undergoing a repulse? Such a faint heart, as the proverb says, will never take a city: but now that we have succeeded thus far, the citadel is ours, and what remains is easier.

Theaet. Very true.

Str. Then, as I was saying, let us first of all obtain a conception of language and opinion, in order that we may have clearer grounds for determining, whether not-being has any concern with them, or whether they are both always true, and neither of them ever false.

Theaet. True.

Str. Then, now, let us speak of names, as before we were speaking of ideas and letters; for that is the direction in which the answer may be expected.

Theaet. And what is the question at issue about names?

Str. The question at issue is whether all names may be connected with one another, or none, or only some of them.

Theaet. Clearly the last is true.

Str. I understand you to say that words which have a meaning when in sequence may be connected, but that words which have no meaning when in sequence cannot be connected?

Theaet. What are you saying?

Str. What I thought that you intended when you gave your assent; for there are two sorts of intimation of being which are given by the voice.

Theaet. What are they?

Str. One of them is called nouns, and the other verbs.

Theaet. Describe them.

[262] *Str.* That which denotes action we call a verb.

Theaet. True.

Str. And the other, which is an articulate mark set on those who do the actions, we call a noun.

Theaet. Quite true.

Str. A succession of nouns only is not a sentence, any more than of verbs without nouns.

Theaet. I do not understand you.

Str. I see that when you gave your assent you had something else in your mind. But what I intended to say was, that a mere succession of nouns or of verbs is not discourse.

Theaet. What do you mean?

Str. I mean that words like "walks," "runs," "sleeps," or any other words which denote action, however many of them you string together, do not make discourse.

Theaet. How can they?

Str. Or, again, when you say "lion," "stag," "horse," or any other words which denote agents—neither in this way of stringing words together do you attain to discourse; for there is no expression of action or inaction, or of the existence of existence or non-existence indicated by the sounds, until verbs are mingled with nouns; then the words fit, and the smallest combination of them forms language, and is the simplest and least form of discourse.

Theaet. Again I ask, What do you mean?

Str. When any one says "A man learns," should you not call this the simplest and least of sentences?

Theaet. Yes.

Str. Yes, for he now arrives at the point of giving an intimation about something which is, or is becoming, or has become, or will be. And he not only names, but he does something, by connecting verbs with nouns; and therefore we say that he discourses, and to this connection of words we give the name of discourse.

Theaet. True.

Str. And as there are some things which fit one another, and other things which do not fit, so there are some vocal signs which do, and others which do not, combine and form discourse.

Theaet. Quite true.

Str. There is another small matter.

Theaet. What is it?

Str. A sentence must and cannot help having a subject.

Theaet. True.

Str. And must be of a certain quality.

Theaet. Certainly.

Str. And now let us mind what we are about.

Theaet. We must do so.

Str. I will repeat a sentence to you in which a thing and an action are combined, by the help of a noun and a verb; and you shall tell me of whom the sentence speaks.

Theaet. I will, to the best of my power.

[263] *Str.* "Theaetetus sits"—not a very long sentence.

Theaet. Not very.

Str. Of whom does the sentence speak, and who is the subject? that is what you have to tell.

Theaet. Of me; I am the subject.

Str. Or this sentence, again—

Theaet. What sentence?

Str. "Theaetetus, with whom I am now speaking, is flying."

Theaet. That also is a sentence which will be admitted by every one to speak of me, and to apply to me.

Str. We agreed that every sentence must necessarily have a certain quality.

Theaet. Yes.

Str. And what is the quality of each of these two sentences?

Theaet. The one, as I imagine, is false, and the other true.

Str. The true says what is true about you?

Theaet. Yes.

Str. And the false says what is other than true?

Theaet. Yes.

Str. And therefore speaks of things which are not as if they were?

Theaet. True.

Str. And says that things are real of you which are not; for, as we were saying, in regard to each thing or person, there is much that is and much that is not.

Theaet. Quite true.

Str. The second of the two sentences which related to you was first of all an example of the shortest form consistent with our definition.

Theaet. Yes, this was implied in our recent admission.

Str. And, in the second place, it related to a subject?

Theaet. Yes.

Str. Who must be you, and can be nobody else?

Theaet. Unquestionably.

Str. And it would be no sentence at all if there were no subject, for, as we proved, a sentence which has no subject is impossible.

Theaet. Quite true.

Str. When other, then, is asserted of you as the same, and not-being as being, such a combination of nouns and verbs is really and truly false discourse.

Theaet. Most true.

Str. And therefore thought, opinion, and imagination are now proved to exist in our minds both as true and false.

Theaet. How so?

Str. You will know better if you first gain a knowledge of what they are, and in what they severally differ from one another.

Theaet. Give me the knowledge which you would wish me to gain.

Str. Are not thought and speech the same, with this exception, that what is called thought is the unuttered conversation of the soul with herself?

Theaet. Quite true.

Str. But the stream of thought which flows through the lips and is audible is called speech?

Theaet. True.

Str. And we know that there exists in speech . . .

Theaet. What exists?

Str. Affirmation.

[264] Theaet. Yes, we know it.

Str. When the affirmation or denial takes place in silence and in the mind only, have you any other name by which to call it but opinion?

Theaet. There can be no other name.

Str. And when opinion is presented, not simply, but in some form of sense, would you not call it imagination?

Theaet. Certainly.

Str. And seeing that language is true and false, and that thought is the conversation of the soul with herself, and opinion is the end of thinking, and imagination or phantasy is the union of sense and opinion, the inference is that some of them, since they are akin to language, should have an element of falsehood as well as of truth?

Theaet. Certainly.

Str. Do you perceive, then, that false opinion and speech have been discovered sooner than we expected?—For just now we seemed to be undertaking a task which would never be accomplished.

Theaet. I perceive.

Str. Then let us not be discouraged about the future; but now having made this discovery, let us go back to our previous classification.

Theaet. What classification?

Str. We divided image-making into two sorts; the one likeness-making, the other imaginative or phantastic.

Theaet. True.

Str. And we said that we were uncertain in which we should place the Sophist.

Theaet. We did say so.

Str. And our heads began to go round more and more when it was asserted that there is no such thing as an image or idol or appearance, because in no manner or time or place can there ever be such a thing as falsehood.

Theaet. True.

Str. And now, since there has been shown to be false speech and false opinion, there may be imitations of real existences, and out of this condition of the mind an art of deception may arise.

Theaet. Quite possible.

Str. And we have already admitted, in what preceded, that the Sophist was lurking in one of the divisions of the likeness-making art?

Theaet. Yes.

Str. Let us, then, renew the attempt, and in dividing any class, always take the part to the right, holding fast to that which holds the Sophist, until we have stripped him of all his common properties. *[265]* and reached his difference or peculiar. Then we may exhibit him in his true nature, first to ourselves and then to kindred dialectical spirits.

Theaet. Very good.

Str. You may remember that all art was originally divided by us into creative and acquisitive.

Theaet. Yes.

Str. And the Sophist was flitting before us in the acquisitive class, in the subdivisions of hunting, contests, merchandise, and the like.

Theaet. Very true.

Str. But now that the imitative art has enclosed him, it is clear that we must begin by dividing the art of creation; for imitation is a kind of creation—of images, however, as we affirm, and not of real things.

Theaet. Quite true.

Str. In the first place, there are two kinds of creation.

Theaet. What are they?

Str. One of them is human and the other divine.

Theaet. I do not follow.

Str. Every power, as you may remember our

saying originally, which causes things to exist, not previously existing, was defined by us as creative.

Theaet. I remember.

Str. Looking, now, at the world and all the animals and plants, at things which grow upon the earth from seeds and roots, as well as at inanimate substances which are formed within the earth, fusile or non-fusile, shall we say that they come into existence—not having existed previously—by the creation of God, or shall we agree with vulgar opinion about them?

Theaet. What is it?

Str. The opinion that nature brings them into being from some spontaneous and unintelligent cause. Or shall we say that they are created by a divine reason and a knowledge which comes from God?

Theaet. I dare say that, owing to my youth, I may often waver in my view, but now when I look at you and see that you incline to refer them to God, I defer to your authority.

Str. Nobly said, Theaetetus, and if I thought that you were one of those who would hereafter change your mind, I would have gently argued with you, and forced you to assent; but as I perceive that you will come of yourself and without any argument of mine, to that belief which, as you say, attracts you, I will not forestall the work of time. Let me suppose, then, that things which are said to be made by nature are the work of divine art, and that things which are made by man out of these are work of human art. And so there are two kinds of making and production, the one human and the other divine.

Theaet. True.

Str. Then, now, subdivide each of the two sections which we have already.

Theaet. How do you mean?

[266] *Str.* I mean to say that you should make a vertical division of production or invention, as you have already made a lateral one.

Theaet. I have done so.

Str. Then, now, there are in all four parts or segments—two of them have reference to us and are human, and two of them have reference to the gods and are divine.

Theaet. True.

Str. And, again, in the division which was supposed to be made in the other way, one part in each subdivision is the making of the things themselves, but the two remaining parts may be called the making of likenesses; and so the productive art is again divided into two parts.

Theaet. Tell me the divisions once more.

Str. I suppose that we, and the other animals, and the elements out of which things are made—fire, water, and the like—are known by us to be each and all the creation and work of God.

Theaet. True.

Str. And there are images of them, which are not them, but which correspond to them; and these are also the creation of a wonderful skill.

Theaet. What are they?

Str. The appearances which spring up of themselves in sleep or by day, such as a shadow when darkness arises in a fire, or the reflection which is produced when the light in bright and smooth objects meets on their surface with an external light, and creates a perception the opposite of our ordinary sight.

Theaet. Yes; and the images as well as the creation are equally the work of a divine hand.

Str. And what shall we say of human art? Do we not make one house by the art of building, and another by the art of drawing, which is a sort of dream created by man for those who are awake?

Theaet. Quite true.

Str. And other products of human creation are also twofold and go in pairs; there is the thing, with which the art of making the thing is concerned, and the image, with which imitation is concerned.

Theaet. Now I begin to understand, and am ready to acknowledge that there are two kinds of production, and each of them twofold; in the lateral division there is both a divine and a human production; in the vertical there are realities and a creation of a kind of similitudes.

Str. And let us not forget that of the imitative class the one part was to have been likeness-making, and the other phantastic, if it could be shown that falsehood is a reality and belongs to the class of real being.

Theaet. Yes.

Str. And this appeared to be the case; and therefore now, without hesitation, we shall number the different kinds as two.

Theaet. True.

[267] *Str.* Then, now, let us again divide the phantastic art.

Theaet. Where shall we make the division?

Str. There is one kind which is produced by an instrument, and another in which the creator of the appearance is himself the instrument.

Theaet. What do you mean?

Str. When any one makes himself appear like another in his figure or his voice, imitation is the name for this part of the phantastic art.

Theaet. Yes.

Str. Let this, then, be named the art of mimicry, and this the province assigned to it; as for the other division, we are weary and will give that up, leaving to some one else the duty of making the class and giving it a suitable name.

Theaet. Let us do as you say—assign a sphere to the one and leave the other.

Str. There is a further distinction, Theaetetus, which is worthy of our consideration, and for a reason which I will tell you.

Theaet. Let me hear.

Str. There are some who imitate, knowing what they imitate, and some who do not know. And what line of distinction can there possibly be greater than that which divides ignorance from knowledge?

Theaet. There can be no greater.

Str. Was not the sort of imitation of which we spoke just now the imitation of those who know? For he who would imitate you would surely know you and your figure?

Theaet. Naturally.

Str. And what would you say of the figure or form of justice or of virtue in general? Are we not well aware that many, having no knowledge of either, but only a sort of opinion, do their best to show that this opinion is really entertained by them, by expressing it, as far as they can, in word and deed?

Theaet. Yes, that is very common.

Str. And do they always fail in their attempt to be thought just, when they are not? Or is not the very opposite true?

Theaet. The very opposite.

Str. Such a one, then, should be described as an imitator—to be distinguished from the other, as he who is ignorant is distinguished from him who knows?

Theaet. True.

Str. Can we find a suitable name for each of them? This is clearly not an easy task; for among the ancients there was some confusion of ideas, which prevented them from attempting to divide genera into species; wherefore there is no great abundance of names. Yet, for the sake of distinctness, I will make bold to call the imitation which coexists with opinion, the imitation of appearance—that which coexists with science, a scientific or learned imitation.

Theaet. Granted.

Str. The former is our present concern, for the Sophist was classed with imitators indeed, but not among those who have knowledge.

Theaet. Very true.

Str. Let us, then, examine our imitator of appearance, and see whether he is sound, like a piece of iron, or whether there is still some crack in him.

Theaet. Let us examine him.

Str. Indeed there is a very considerable crack; for if you look, you find that one of the two classes of imitators is a simple creature, [268] who thinks that he knows that which he only fancies; the other sort has knocked about among arguments, until he suspects and fears that he is ignorant of that which to the many he pretends to know.

Theaet. There are certainly the two kinds which you describe.

Str. Shall we regard one as the simple imitator—the other as the dissembling or ironical imitator?

Theaet. Very good.

Str. And shall we further speak of this latter class as having one or two divisions?

Theaet. Answer yourself.

Str. Upon consideration, then, there appear to me to be two; there is the dissembler, who harangues a multitude in public in a long speech, and the dissembler, who in private and in short speeches compels the person who is conversing with him to contradict himself.

Theaet. What you say is most true.

Str. And who is the maker of the longer speeches? Is he the statesman or the popular orator?

Theaet. The latter.

Str. And what shall we call the other? Is he the philosopher or the Sophist?

Theaet. The philosopher he cannot be, for upon our view he is ignorant; but since he is an imitator of the wise he will have a name which is formed by an adaptation of the word σοθός. What shall we name him? I am pretty sure that I cannot be mistaken in terming him the true and very Sophist.

Str. Shall we bind up his name as we did before, making a chain from one end of his genealogy to the other?

Theaet. By all means.

Str. He, then, who traces the pedigree of his art as follows—who, belonging to the conscious or dissembling section of the art of causing self-contradiction, is an imitator of appearance, and is separated from the class of phantastic which is a branch of image-making into that further division of creation, the juggling of words, a creation human, and not divine—any one who affirms the real Sophist to be of this blood and lineage will say the very truth.

Theaet. Undoubtedly.

STATESMAN

PERSONS OF THE DIALOGUE: THEODORUS; SOCRATES; THE ELEATIC STRANGER; THE YOUNGER SOCRATES

~~~~~~~~~~~~~~~~~~~~~~

[257] Socrates. I owe you many thanks, indeed, Theodorus, for the acquaintance both of Theaetetus and of the Stranger.

Theodorus. And in a little while, Socrates, you will owe me three times as many, when they have completed for you the delineation of the Statesman and of the Philosopher, as well as of the Sophist.

Soc. Sophist, statesman, philosopher! O my dear Theodorus, do my ears truly witness that this is the estimate formed of them by the great calculator and geometrician?

Theod. What do you mean, Socrates?

Soc. I mean that you rate them all at the same value, whereas they are really separated by an interval, which no geometrical ratio can express.

Theod. By Ammon, the god of Cyrene, Socrates, that is a very fair hit; and shows that you have not forgotten your geometry. I will retaliate on you at some other time, but I must now ask the Stranger, who will not, I hope, tire of his goodness to us, to proceed either with the Statesman or with the Philosopher, whichever he prefers.

Stranger. That is my duty, Theodorus; having begun I must go on, and not leave the work unfinished. But what shall be done with Theaetetus?

Theod. In what respect?

Str. Shall we relieve him, and take his companion, the Young Socrates, instead of him? What do you advise?

Theod. Yes, give the other a turn, as you propose. The young always do better when they have intervals of rest.

[258] Soc. I think, Stranger, that both of them may be said to be in some way related to me; for the one, as you affirm, has the cut of my ugly face,[1] the other is called by my name. And we should always be on the look-out to recognize a kinsman by the style of his conversation. I myself was discoursing with Theaetetus yesterday, and I have just been listening to his answers; my namesake I have not yet examined, but I must. Another time will do for me; to-day let him answer you.

Str. Very good. Young Socrates, do you hear what the elder Socrates is proposing?

Young Socrates. I do.

Str. And do you agree to his proposal?

Y. Soc. Certainly.

Str. As you do not object, still less can I. After the Sophist, then, I think that the Statesman naturally follows next in the order of enquiry. And please to say, whether he, too, should be ranked among those who have science.

Y. Soc. Yes.

Str. Then the sciences must be divided as before?

Y. Soc. I dare say.

Str. But yet the division will not be the same?

Y. Soc. How then?

Str. They will be divided at some other point.

Y. Soc. Yes.

Str. Where shall we discover the path of the Statesman? We must find and separate off, and set our seal upon this, and we will set the mark of another class upon all diverging paths. Thus the soul will conceive of all kinds of knowledge under two classes.

[1] Cf. *Theaetetus*, 143.

580

Y. Soc. To find the path is your business, Stranger, and not mine.

Str. Yes, Socrates, but the discovery, when once made, must be yours as well as mine.

Y. Soc. Very good.

Str. Well, and are not arithmetic and certain other kindred arts, merely abstract knowledge, wholly separated from action?

Y. Soc. True.

Str. But in the art of carpentering and all other handicrafts, the knowledge of the workman is merged in his work; he not only knows, but he also makes things which previously did not exist.

Y. Soc. Certainly.

Str. Then let us divide sciences in general into those which are practical and those which are purely intellectual.

Y. Soc. Let us assume these two divisions of science, which is one whole.

Str. And are "statesman," "king," "master," or "householder," one and the same; or is there a science or art answering to each of these names? Or rather, allow me to put the matter in another way.

[259] Y. Soc. Let me hear.

Str. If any one who is in a private station has the skill to advise one of the public physicians, must not he also be called a physician?

Y. Soc. Yes.

Str. And if any one who is in a private station is able to advise the ruler of a country, may not he be said to have the knowledge which the ruler himself ought to have?

Y. Soc. True.

Str. But surely the science of a true king is royal science?

Y. Soc. Yes.

Str. And will not he who possesses this knowledge, whether he happens to be a ruler or a private man, when regarded only in reference to his art, be truly called "royal"?

Y. Soc. He certainly ought to be.

Str. And the householder and master are the same?

Y. Soc. Of course.

Str. Again, a large household may be compared to a small state:—will they differ at all, as far as government is concerned?

Y. Soc. They will not.

Str. Then, returning to the point which we were just now discussing, do we not clearly see that there is one science of all of them; and this science may be called either royal or political or economical; we will not quarrel with any one about the name.

Y. Soc. Certainly not.

Str. This, too, is evident, that the king cannot do much with his hands, or with his whole body, towards the maintenance of his empire, compared with what he does by the intelligence and strength of his mind.

Y. Soc. Clearly not.

Str. Then, shall we say that the king has a greater affinity to knowledge than to manual arts and to practical life in general?

Y. Soc. Certainly he has.

Str. Then we may put all together as one and the same—statesmanship and the statesman—the kingly science and the king.

Y. Soc. Clearly.

Str. And now we shall only be proceeding in due order if we go on to divide the sphere of knowledge?

Y. Soc. Very good.

Str. Think whether you can find any joint or parting in knowledge.

Y. Soc. Tell me of what sort.

Str. Such as this: You may remember that we made an art of calculation?

Y. Soc. Yes.

Str. Which was, unmistakeably, one of the arts of knowledge?

Y. Soc. Certainly.

Str. And to this art of calculation which discerns the differences of numbers shall we assign any other function except to pass judgment on their differences?

Y. Soc. How could we?

Str. You know that the master-builder does not work himself, but is the ruler of workmen?

Y. Soc. Yes.

Str. He contributes knowledge, not manual labour?

Y. Soc. True.

[260] Str. And may therefore be justly said to share in theoretical science?

Y. Soc. Quite true.

Str. But he ought not, like the calculator, to regard his functions as at an end when he has formed a judgment;—he must assign to the individual workmen their appropriate task until they have completed the work.

Y. Soc. True.

Str. Are not all such sciences, no less than arithmetic and the like, subjects of pure knowledge; and is not the difference between the two classes, that the one sort has the power of judging only, and the other of ruling as well?

Y. Soc. That is evident.

Str. May we not very properly say, that of all knowledge, there are two divisions—one which rules, and the other which judges?

Y. Soc. I should think so.

Str. And when men have anything to do in common, that they should be of one mind is surely a desirable thing?

Y. Soc. Very true.

Str. Then while we are at unity among ourselves, we need not mind about the fancies of others?

Y. Soc. Certainly not.

Str. And now, in which of these divisions shall we place the king?—Is he a judge and a kind of spectator? Or shall we assign to him the art of command—for he is a ruler?

Y. Soc. The latter, clearly.

Str. Then we must see whether there is any mark of division in the art of command too. I am inclined to think that there is a distinction similar to that of manufacturer and retail dealer, which parts off the king from the herald.

Y. Soc. How is this?

Str. Why, does not the retailer receive and sell over again the productions of others, which have been sold before?

Y. Soc. Certainly he does.

Str. And is not the herald under command, and does he not receive orders, and in his turn give them to others?

Y. Soc. Very true.

Str. Then shall we mingle the kingly art in the same class with the art of the herald, the interpreter, the boatswain, the prophet, and the numerous kindred arts which exercise command; or, as in the preceding comparison we spoke of manufacturers, or sellers for themselves, and of retailers,—seeing, too, that the class of supreme rulers, or rulers for themselves, is almost nameless—shall we make a word following the same analogy, and refer kings to a supreme or ruling-for-self science, leaving the rest to receive a name from some one else? For we are seeking the ruler; and our enquiry is not concerned with him who is not a ruler.

Y. Soc. Very good.

[261] Str. Thus a very fair distinction has been attained between the man who gives his own commands, and him who gives another's. And now let us see if the supreme power allows of any further division.

Y. Soc. By all means.

Str. I think that it does; and please to assist me in making the division.

Y. Soc. At what point?

Str. May not all rulers be supposed to command for the sake of producing something?

Y. Soc. Certainly.

Str. Nor is there any difficulty in dividing the things produced into two classes.

Y. Soc. How would you divide them?

Str. Of the whole class, some have life and some are without life.

Y. Soc. True.

Str. And by the help of this distinction we may make, if we please, a subdivision of the section of knowledge which commands.

Y. Soc. At what point?

Str. One part may be set over the production of lifeless, the other of living objects; and in this way the whole will be divided.

Y. Soc. Certainly.

Str. That division, then, is complete; and now we may leave one half, and take up the other; which may also be divided into two.

Y. Soc. Which of the two halves do you men?

Str. Of course that which exercises command about animals. For, surely, the royal science is not like that of a master-workman, a science presiding over lifeless objects;—the king has a nobler function, which is the management and control of living beings.

Y. Soc. True.

Str. And the breeding and tending of living beings may be observed to be sometimes a tending of the individual; in other cases, a common care of creatures in flocks?

Y. Soc. True.

Str. But the statesman is not a tender of individuals—not like the driver or groom of a single ox or horse; he is rather to be compared with the keeper of a drove of horses or oxen.

Y. Soc. Yes, I see, thanks to you.

Str. Shall we call this art of tending many animals together, the art of managing a herd, or the art of collective management?

Y. Soc. No matter;—whichever suggests itself to us in the course of conversation.

Str. Very good, Socrates; and, if you continue to be not too particular about names, you will be all the richer in wisdom when you are an old man. And now, as you say, leaving the discussion of the name, *[262]*—can you see a way in which a person, by showing the art of herding to be of two kinds, may cause that which is now sought amongst twice the number of things, to be then sought amongst half that number?

Y. Soc. I will try;—there appears to me to be one management of men and another of beasts.

Str. You have certainly divided them in a most straightforward and manly style; but you have fallen into an error which hereafter I think that we had better avoid.

Y. Soc. What is the error?

Str. I think that we had better not cut off a single small portion which is not a species, from many larger portions; the part should be a species. To separate off at once the subject of investigation, is a most excellent plan, if only the separation be rightly made; and you were under the impression that you were right, because you saw that you would come to man; and this led you to hasten the steps. But you should not chip off too small a piece, my friend; the safer way is to cut through the middle; which is also the more likely way of finding classes. Attention to this principle makes all the difference in a process of enquiry.

Y. Soc. What do you mean, Stranger?

Str. I will endeavour to speak more plainly out of love to your good parts, Socrates; and, although I cannot at present entirely explain myself, I will try, as we proceed, to make my meaning a little clearer.

Y. Soc. What was the error of which, as you say, we were guilty in our recent division?

Str. The error was just as if some one who wanted to divide the human race, were to divide them after the fashion which prevails in this part of the world; here they cut off the Hellenes as one species, and all the other species of mankind, which are innumerable, and have no ties or common language, they include under the single name of "barbarians," and because they have one name they are supposed to be of one species also. Or suppose that in dividing numbers you were to cut off ten thousand from all the rest, and make of it one species, comprehending the rest under another separate name, you might say that here too was a single class, because you had given it a single name. Whereas you would make a much better and more equal and logical classification of numbers, if you divided them into odd and even; or of the human species, if you divided them into male and female; and only separated off Lydians or Phrygians, or any other tribe, and arrayed them against the rest of the world, when you could no longer make a division into parts which were also classes. [263]

Y. Soc. Very true; but I wish that this distinction between a part and a class could still be made somewhat plainer.

Str. O Socrates, best of men, you are imposing upon me a very difficult task. We have already digressed further from our original intention than we ought, and you would have us wander still further away. But we must now return to our subject; and hereafter, when there is a leisure hour, we will follow up the other track; at the same time, I wish you to guard against imagining that you ever heard me declare—

Y. Soc. What?

Str. That a class and a part are distinct.

Y. Soc. What did I hear, then?

Str. That a class is necessarily a part, but there is no similar necessity that a part should be a class; that is the view which I should always wish you to attribute to me, Socrates.

Y. Soc. So be it.

Str. There is another thing which I should like to know.

Y. Soc. What is it?

Str. The point at which we digressed; for, if I am not mistaken, the exact place was at the question, Where you would divide the management of herds. To this you appeared rather too ready to answer that there were two species of animals; man being one, and all brutes making up the other.

Y. Soc. True.

Str. I thought that in taking away a part, you imagined that the remainder formed a class, because you were able to call them by the common name of brutes.

Y. Soc. That again is true.

Str. Suppose now, O most courageous of dialecticians, that some wise and understanding creature, such as a crane is reputed to be, were, in imitation of you, to make a similar division, and set up cranes against all other animals to their own special glorification, at the same time jumbling together all the others, including man, under the appellation of brutes,—here would be the sort of error which we must try to avoid.

Y. Soc. How can we be safe?

Str. If we do not divide the whole class of animals, we shall be less likely to fall into that error.

Y. Soc. We had better not take the whole?

Str. Yes, there lay the source of error in our former division.

Y. Soc. How?

Str. You remember how that part of the art of knowledge which was concerned with command, had to do with the rearing of living creatures,—I mean, with animals in herds?

Y. Soc. Yes.

[264] *Str.* In that case, there was already implied a division of all animals into tame and wild; those whose nature can be tamed are called tame, and those which cannot be tamed are called wild.

Y. Soc. True.

Str. And the political science of which we are in search, is and ever was concerned with tame animals, and is also confined to gregarious animals.

Y. Soc. Yes.

Str. But then we ought not to divide, as we did, taking the whole class at once. Neither let us be in too great haste to arrive quickly at the political science; for this mistake has already brought upon us the misfortune of which the proverb speaks.

Y. Soc. What misfortune?

Str. The misfortune of too much haste, which is too little speed.

Y. Soc. And all the better, Stranger; we got what we deserved.

Str. Very well: Let us then begin again, and endeavour to divide the collective rearing of animals; for probably the completion of the argument will best show what you are so anxious to know. Tell me, then—

Y. Soc. What?

Str. Have you ever heard, as you very likely may—for I do not suppose that you ever actually visited them—of the preserves of fishes in the Nile, and in the ponds of the Great King; or you may have seen similar preserves in wells at home?

Y. Soc. Yes, to be sure, I have seen them, and I have often heard the others described.

Str. And you may have heard also, and may have been assured by report, although you have not travelled in those regions, of nurseries of geese and cranes in the plains of Thessaly?

Y. Soc. Certainly.

Str. I asked you, because here is a new division of the management of herds, into the management of land and of water herds.

Y. Soc. There is.

Str. And do you agree that we ought to divide the collective rearing of herds into two corresponding parts, the one the rearing of water, and the other the rearing of land herds?

Y. Soc. Yes.

Str. There is surely no need to ask which of these two contains the royal art, for it is evident to everybody.

Y. Soc. Certainly.

Str. Any one can divide the herds which feed on dry land?

Y. Soc. How would you divide them?

Str. I should distinguish between those which fly and those which walk.

Y. Soc. Most true.

Str. And where shall we look for the politi-

cal animal? Might not an idiot, so to speak, know that he is a pedestrian?

Y. Soc. Certainly.

Str. The art of managing the walking animal has to be further divided, just as you might halve an even number.

Y. Soc. Clearly.

[265] *Str.* Let me note that here appear in view two ways to that part or class which the argument aims at reaching—the one is speedier way, which cuts off a small portion and leaves a large; the other agrees better with the principle which we were laying down, that as far as we can we should divide in the middle; but it is longer. We can take either of them, whichever we please.

Y. Soc. Cannot we have both ways?

Str. Together? What a thing to ask! but, if you take them in turn, you clearly may.

Y. Soc. Then I should like to have them in turn.

Str. There will be no difficulty, as we are near the end; if we had been at the beginning, or in the middle, I should have demurred to your request; but now, in accordance with your desire, let us begin with the longer way; while we are fresh, we shall get on better. And now attend to the division.

Y. Soc. Let me hear.

Str. The tame walking herding animals are distributed by nature into two classes.

Y. Soc. Upon what principle?

Str. The one grows horns; and the other is without horns.

Y. Soc. Clearly.

Str. Suppose that you divide the science which manages pedestrian animals into two corresponding parts, and define them; for if you try to invent names for them, you will find the intricacy too great.

Y. Soc. How must I speak of them, then?

Str. In this way: let the science of managing pedestrian animals be divided into two parts, and one part assigned to the horned herd, and the other to the herd that has no horns.

Y. Soc. All that you say has been abundantly proved, and may therefore be assumed.

Str. The king is clearly the shepherd of a polled herd, who have no horns.

Y. Soc. That is evident.

Str. Shall we break up this hornless herd into sections, and endeavour to assign to him what is his?

Y. Soc. By all means.

Str. Shall we distinguish them by their having or not having cloven feet, or by their mixing or not mixing the breed? You know what I mean.

Y. Soc. What?

Str. I mean that horses and asses naturally breed from one another.

Y. Soc. Yes.

Str. But the remainder of the hornless herd of tame animals will not mix the breed.

Y. Soc. Very true.

Str. And of which has the Statesman charge, —of the mixed or of the unmixed race?

Y. Soc. Clearly of the unmixed.

Str. I suppose that we must divide this again as before.

Y. Soc. We must.

[266] Str. Every tame and herding animal has now been split up, with the exception of two species; for I hardly think that dogs should be reckoned among gregarious animals.

Y. Soc. Certainly not; but how shall we divide the two remaining species?

Str. There is a measure of difference which may be appropriately employed by you and Theaetetus, who are students of geometry.

Y. Soc. What is that?

Str. The diameter; and, again, the diameter of a diameter.[1]

Y. Soc. What do you mean?

Str. How does man walk, but as a diameter whose power is two feet?

Y. Soc. Just so.

Str. And the power of the remaining kind, being the power of twice two feet, may be said to be the diameter of our diameter.

Y. Soc. Certainly; and now I think that I pretty nearly understand you.

Str. In these divisions, Socrates, I descry what would make another famous jest.

Y. Soc. What is it?

Str. Human beings have come out in the same class with the freest and airiest of creation, and have been running a race with them.

Y. Soc. I remark that very singular coincidence.

Str. And would you not expect the slowest to arrive last?

Y. Soc. Indeed I should.

Str. And there is a still more ridiculous consequence, that the king is found running about with the herd, and in close competition with the bird-catcher, who of all mankind is most of an adept at the airy life.

Y. Soc. Certainly.

Str. Then here, Socrates, is still clearer evidence of the truth of what was said in the en-

quiry about the Sophist.[2]

Y. Soc. What?

Str. That the dialectical method is no respecter of persons, and does not set the great above the small, but always arrives in her own way at the truest result.

Y. Soc. Clearly.

Str. And now, I will not wait for you to ask me, but will of my own accord take you by the shorter road to the definition of a king.

Y. Soc. By all means.

Str. I say that we should have begun at first by dividing land animals into biped and quadruped; and since the winged herd, and that alone, comes out in the same class with man, we should divide bipeds into those which have feathers and those which have not, and when they have been divided, and the art of the management of mankind is brought to light, the time will have come to produce our Statesman and ruler, and set him like a charioteer in his place, and hand over to him the reins of state, for that too is a vocation which belongs to him.

[267] Y. Soc. Very good; you have paid me the debt—I mean, that you have completed the argument, and I suppose that you added the digression by way of interest.[3]

Str. Then now, let us go back to the beginning, and join the links, which together make the definition of the name of the Statesman's art.

Y. Soc. By all means.

Str. The science of pure knowledge had, as we said originally, a part which was the science of rule or command, and from this was derived another part, which was called command-for-self, on the analogy of selling-for-self; an important section of this was the management of living animals, and this again was further limited to the management of them in herds, and again in herds of pedestrian animals. The chief division of the latter was the art of managing pedestrian animals which are without horns; this again has a part which can only be comprehended under one term by joining together three names—shepherding pure-bred animals. The only further subdivision is the art of man-herding—this has to do with bipeds, and is what we were seeking after, and have now found, being at once the royal and political.

Y. Soc. To be sure.

Str. And do you think, Socrates, that we really have done as you say?

Y. Soc. What?

[1] Cf. Meno, 82 ff.

[2] Cf. Sophist, 227.

[3] Cf. Republic, vi. 507.

Str. Do you think, I mean, that we have really fulfilled our intention?—There has been a sort of discussion, and yet the investigation seems to me not to be perfectly worked out: this is where the enquiry fails.

Y. Soc. I do not understand.

Str. I will try to make the thought, which is at this moment present in my mind, clearer to us both.

Y. Soc. Let me hear.

Str. There were many arts of shepherding, and one of them was the political, which had the charge of one particular herd?

Y. Soc. Yes.

Str. And this the argument defined to be the art of rearing, not horses or other brutes, but the art of rearing man collectively?

Y. Soc. True.

Str. Note, however, a difference which distinguishes the king from all other shepherds.

Y. Soc. To what do you refer?

Str. I want to ask, whether any one of the other herdsmen has a rival who professes and claims to share with him in the management of the herd?

Y. Soc. What do you mean?

Str. I mean to say that merchants, husbandmen, providers of food, and also trainingmasters and physicians, will all contend with the herdsmen of humanity, whom we call Statesmen, declaring that they themselves have the care of rearing or managing [268] mankind, and that they rear not only the common herd, but also the rulers themselves.

Y. Soc. Are they not right in saying so?

Str. Very likely they may be, and we will consider their claim. But we are certain of this, —that no one will raise a similar claim as against the herdsman, who is allowed on all hands to be the sole and only feeder and physician of his herd; he is also their matchmaker and accoucheur; no one else knows that department of science. And he is their merry-maker and musician, as far as their nature is susceptible of such influences, and no one can console and soothe his own herd better than he can, either with the natural tones of his voice or with instruments. And the same may be said of tenders of animals in general.

Y. Soc. Very true.

Str. But if this is as you say, can our argument about the king be true and unimpeachable? Were we right in selecting him out of ten thousand other claimants to be the shepherd and rearer of the human flock?

Y. Soc. Surely not.

Str. Had we not reason just now [1] to apprehend, that although we may have described a sort of royal form, we have not as yet accurately worked out the true image of the Statesman? and that we cannot reveal him as he truly is in his own nature, until we have disengaged and separated him from those who hang about him and claim to share in his prerogatives?

Y. Soc. Very true.

Str. And that, Socrates, is what we must do, if we do not mean to bring disgrace upon the argument at its close.

Y. Soc. We must certainly avoid that.

Str. Then let us make a new beginning, and travel by a different road.

Y. Soc. What road?

Str. I think that we may have a little amusement; there is a famous tale, of which a good portion may with advantage be interwoven, and then we may resume our series of divisions, and proceed in the old path until we arrive at the desired summit. Shall we do as I say?

Y. Soc. By all means.

Str. Listen, then, to a tale which a child would love to hear; and you are not too old for childish amusement.

Y. Soc. Let me hear.

Str. There did really happen, and will again happen, like many other events of which ancient tradition has preserved the record, the portent which is traditionally said to have occurred in the quarrel of Atreus and Thyestes. You have heard, no doubt, and remember what they say happened at that time?

Y. Soc. I suppose you to mean the token of the birth of the golden lamb.

[269] *Str.* No, not that; but another part of the story, which tells how the sun and the stars once rose in the west, and set in the east, and that the god reversed their motion, and gave them that which they now have as a testimony to the right of Atreus.

Y. Soc. Yes; there is that legend also.

Str. Again, we have been often told of the reign of Cronos.

Y. Soc. Yes, very often.

Str. Did you ever hear that the men of former times were earthborn, and not begotten of one another?

Y. Soc. Yes, that is another old tradition.

Str. All these stories, and ten thousand others which are still more wonderful, have a common origin; many of them have been lost in the lapse of ages, or are repeated only in a disconnected form; but the origin of them is what no

[1] Cf. 267.

one has told, and may as well be told now; for the tale is suited to throw light on the nature of the king.

Y. Soc. Very good; and I hope that you will give the whole story, and leave out nothing.

Str. Listen, then. There is a time when God himself guides and helps to roll the world in its course; and there is a time, on the completion of a certain cycle, when he lets go, and the world being a living creature, and having originally received intelligence from its author and creator, turns about and by an inherent necessity revolves in the opposite direction.

Y. Soc. Why is that?

Str. Why, because only the most divine things of all remain ever unchanged and the same, and body is not included in this class. Heaven and the universe, as we have termed them, although they have been endowed by the Creator with many glories, partake of a bodily nature, and therefore cannot be entirely free from perturbation. But their motion is, as far as possible, single and in the same place, and of the same kind; and is therefore only subject to a reversal, which is the least alteration possible. For the lord of all moving things is alone able to move of himself; and to think that he moves them at one time in one direction and at another time in another is blasphemy. Hence we must not say that the world is either self-moved always, or all made to go round by God in two opposite courses; *[270]* or that two Gods, having opposite purposes, make it move round. But as I have already said (and this is the only remaining alternative) the world is guided at one time by an external power which is divine and receives fresh life and immortality from the renewing hand of the Creator, and again, when let go, moves spontaneously, being set free at such a time as to have, during infinite cycles of years, a reverse movement: this is due to its perfect balance, to its vast size, and to the fact that it turns on the smallest pivot.

Y. Soc. Your account of the world seems to be very reasonable indeed.

Str. Let us now reflect and try to gather from what has been said the nature of the phenomenon which we affirmed to be the cause of all these wonders. It is this.

Y. Soc. What?

Str. The reversal which takes place from time to time of the motion of the universe.

Y. Soc. How is that the cause?

Str. Of all changes of the heavenly motions, we may consider this to be the greatest and most complete.

Y. Soc. I should imagine so.

Str. And it may be supposed to result in the greatest changes to the human beings who are the inhabitants of the world at the time.

Y. Soc. Such changes would naturally occur.

Str. And animals, as we know, survive with difficulty great and serious changes of many different kinds when they come upon them at once.

Y. Soc. Very true.

Str. Hence there necessarily occurs a great destruction of them, which extends also to the life of man; few survivors of the race are left, and those who remain become the subjects of several novel and remarkable phenomena, and of one in particular, which takes place at the time when the transition is made to the cycle opposite to that in which we are now living.

Y. Soc. What is it?

Str. The life of all animals first came to a standstill, and the mortal nature ceased to be or look older, and was then reversed and grew young and delicate; the white locks of the aged darkened again, and the cheeks of the bearded man became smooth, and recovered their former bloom; the bodies of youths in their prime grew softer and smaller, continually by day and night returning and becoming assimilated to the nature of a newly-born child in mind as well as body; in the succeeding stage they wasted away and wholly disappeared. And the bodies of those who died by violence at that time quickly passed through the like changes, and in a few days were no more seen.

[271] *Y. Soc.* Then how, Stranger, were the animals created in those days; and in what way were they begotten of one another?

Str. It is evident, Socrates, that there was no such thing in the then order of nature as the procreation of animals from one another; the earth-born race, of which we hear in story, was the one which existed in those days—they rose again from the ground; and of this tradition, which is now-a-days often unduly discredited, our ancestors, who were nearest in point of time to the end of the last period and came into being at the beginning of this, are to us the heralds. And mark how consistent the sequel of the tale is; after the return of age to youth, follows the return of the dead, who are lying in the earth, to life; simultaneously with the reversal of the world the wheel of their generation has been turned back, and they are put together and rise and live in the opposite order, unless God has carried any of them away to some other lot. According to this tradition they of necessity sprang from the earth and have the name of earth-born, and so the above legend clings to them.

Y. Soc. Certainly that is quite consistent with what has preceded; but tell me, was the life which you said existed in the reign of Cronos in that cycle of the world, or in this? For the change in the course of the stars and the sun must have occurred in both.

Str. I see that you enter into my meaning;—no, that blessed and spontaneous life does not belong to the present cycle of the world, but to the previous one, in which God superintended the whole revolution of the universe; and the several parts of the universe were distributed under the rule of certain inferior deities, as is the way in some places still. There were demigods, who were the shepherds of the various species and herds of animals, and each one was in all respects sufficient for those of whom he was the shepherd; neither was there any violence, or devouring of one another, or war or quarrel among them; and I might tell of ten thousand other blessings, which belonged to that dispensation. The reason why the life of man was, as tradition says, spontaneous, is as follows: In those days God himself was their shepherd, and ruled over them, just as man, who is by comparison a divine being, still rules over the lower animals. Under him there were no forms of government or separate possession of women and children; *[272]* for all men rose again from the earth, having no memory of the past. And although they had nothing of this sort, the earth gave them fruits in abundance, which grew on trees and shrubs unbidden, and were not planted by the hand of man. And they dwelt naked, and mostly in the open air, for the temperature of their seasons was mild; and they had no beds, but lay on soft couches of grass, which grew plentifully out of the earth. Such was the life of man in the days of Cronos, Socrates; the character of our present life, which is said to be under Zeus, you know from your own experience. Can you, and will you, determine which of them you deem the happier?

Y. Soc. Impossible.

Str. Then shall I determine for you as well as I can?

Y. Soc. By all means.

Str. Suppose that the nurslings of Cronos, having this boundless leisure, and the power of holding intercourse, not only with men, but with the brute creation, had used all these advantages with a view to philosophy, conversing with the brutes as well as with one another, and

learning of every nature which was gifted with any special power, and was able to contribute some special experience to the store of wisdom, there would be no difficulty in deciding that they would be a thousand times happier than the men of our own day. Or, again, if they had merely eaten and drunk until they were full, and told stories to one another and to the animals—such stories as are now attributed to them—in this case also, as I should imagine, the answer would be easy. But until some satisfactory witness can be found of the love of that age for knowledge and discussion, we had better let the matter drop, and give the reason why we have unearthed this tale, and then we shall be able to get on.

In the fulness of time, when the change was to take place, and the earth-born race had all perished, and every soul had completed its proper cycle of births and been sown in the earth her appointed number of times, the pilot of the universe let the helm go, and retired to his place of view; and then Fate and innate desire reversed the motion of the world. Then also all the inferior deities who share the rule of the supreme power, being informed of what was happening, let go the parts of the world which were under their control. *[273]* And the world turning round with a sudden shock, being impelled in an opposite direction from beginning to end, was shaken by a mighty earthquake, which wrought a new destruction of all manner of animals. Afterwards, when sufficient time had elapsed, the tumult and confusion and earthquake ceased, and the universal creature, once more at peace, attained to a calm, and settled down into his own orderly and accustomed course, having the charge and rule of himself and of all the creatures which are contained in him, and executing, as far as he remembered them, the instructions of his Father and Creator, more precisely at first, but afterwords with less exactness. The reason of the falling off was the admixture of matter in him; this was inherent in the primal nature, which was full of disorder, until attaining to the present order. From God, the constructor, the world received all that is good in him, but from a previous state came elements of evil and unrighteousness, which, thence derived, first of all passed into the world, and were then transmitted to the animals. While the world was aided by the pilot in nurturing the animals, the evil was small, and great the good which he produced, but after the separation, when the world was let go, at first all proceeded well enough;

but, as time went on, there was more and more forgetting, and the old discord again held sway and burst forth in full glory; and at last small was the good, and great was the admixture of evil, and there was a danger of universal ruin to the world, and to the things contained in him. Wherefore God, the orderer of all, in his tender care, seeing that the world was in great straits, and fearing that all might be dissolved in the storm and disappear in infinite chaos, again seated himself at the helm; and bringing back the elements which had fallen into dissolution and disorder to the motion which had prevailed under his dispensation, he set them in order and restored them, and made the world imperishable and immortal.

And this is the whole tale, of which the first part will suffice to illustrate the nature of the king. For when the world turned towards the present cycle of generation, the age of man again stood still, and a change opposite to the previous one was the result. The small creatures which had almost disappeared grew in stature, and the newly-born children of the earth became grey and died and sank into the earth again. *[274]* All things changed, imitating and following the condition of the universe, and of necessity agreeing with that in their mode of conception and generation and nurture; for no animal was any longer allowed to come into being in the earth through the agency of other creative beings, but as the world was ordained to be the lord of his own progress, in like manner the parts were ordained to grow and generate and give nourishment, as far as they could, of themselves, impelled by a similar movement. And so we have arrived at the real end of this discourse; for although there might be much to tell of the lower animals, and of the condition out of which they changed and of the causes of the change, about men there is not much, and that little is more to the purpose. Deprived of the care of God, who had possessed and tended them, they were left helpless and defenceless, and were torn in pieces by the beasts, who were naturally fierce and had now grown wild. And in the first ages they were still without skill or resource; the food which once grew spontaneously had failed, and as yet they knew not how to procure it, because they had never felt the pressure of necessity. For all these reasons they were in a great strait; wherefore also the gifts spoken of in the old tradition were imparted to man by the gods, together with so much teaching and education as was indispensable; fire was given to them by Prometheus, the

arts by Hephaestus and his fellow-worker, Athene, seeds and plants by others. From these is derived all that has helped to frame human life; since the care of the Gods, as I was saying, had now failed men, and they had to order their course of life for themselves, and were their own masters, just like the universal creature whom they imitate and follow, ever changing, as he changes, and ever living and growing, at one time in one manner, and at another time in another. Enough of the story, which may be of use in showing us how greatly we erred in the delineation of the king and the statesman in our previous discourse.

Y. Soc. What was this great error of which you speak?

Str. There were two; the first a lesser one, the other was an error on a much larger and grander scale.

Y. Soc. What do you mean?

[275] Str. I mean to say that when we were asked about a king and statesman of the present cycle and generation, we told of a shepherd of a human flock who belonged to the other cycle, and of one who was a god when he ought to have been a man; and this was a great error. Again, we declared him to be the ruler of the entire State, without explaining how: this was not the whole truth, nor very intelligible; but still it was true, and therefore the second error was not so great as the first.

Y. Soc. Very good.

Str. Before we can expect to have a perfect description of the statesman we must define the nature of his office.

Y. Soc. Certainly.

Str. And the myth was introduced in order to show, not only that all others are rivals of the true shepherd who is the object of our search, but in order that we might have a clearer view of him who is alone worthy to receive this appellation, because he alone of shepherds and herdsmen, according to the image which we have employed, has the care of human beings.

Y. Soc. Very true.

Str. And I cannot help thinking, Socrates, that the form of the divine shepherd is even higher than that of a king; whereas the statesmen who are now on earth seem to be much more like their subjects in character, and much more nearly to partake of their breeding and education.

Y. Soc. Certainly.

Str. Still they must be investigated all the same, to see whether, like the divine shepherd, they are above their subjects or on a level with them.

Y. Soc. Of course.

Str. To resume:—Do you remember that we spoke of a command-for-self exercised over animals, not singly but collectively, which we called the art of rearing a herd?

Y. Soc. Yes, I remember.

Str. There, somewhere, lay our error; for we never included or mentioned the Statesman; and we did not observe that he had no place in our nomenclature.

Y. Soc. How was that?

Str. All other herdsmen "rear" their herds, but this is not a suitable term to apply to the Statesman; we should use a name which is common to them all.

Y. Soc. True, if there be such a name.

Str. Why, is not "care" of herds applicable to all? For this implies no feeding, or any special duty; if we say either "tending" the herds, or "managing" the herds, or "having the care" of them, the same word will include all, and then we may wrap up the Statesman with the rest, as the argument seems to require.

[276] Y. Soc. Quite right; but how shall we take the next step in the division?

Str. As before we divided the art of "rearing" herds accordingly as they were land or water herds, winged and wingless, mixing or not mixing the breed, horned and hornless, so we may divide by these same differences the "tending" of herds, comprehending in our definition the kingship of to-day and the rule of Cronos.

Y. Soc. That is clear; but I still ask, what is to follow.

Str. If the word had been "managing" herds, instead of feeding or rearing them, no one would have argued that there was no care of men in the case of the politician, although it was justly contended, that there was no human art of feeding them which was worthy of the name, or at least, if there were, many a man had a prior and greater right to share in such an art than any king.

Y. Soc. True.

Str. But no other art or science will have a prior or better right than the royal science to care for human society and to rule over men in general.

Y. Soc. Quite true.

Str. In the next place, Socrates, we must surely notice that a great error was committed at the end of our analysis.

Y. Soc. What was it?

Str. Why, supposing we were ever so sure that there is such an art as the art of rearing or feeding bipeds, there was no reason why we should call this the royal or political art, as though there were no more to be said.

Y. Soc. Certainly not.

Str. Our first duty, as we were saying, was to remodel the name, so as to have the notion of care rather than of feeding, and then to divide, for there may be still considerable divisions.

Y. Soc. How can they be made?

Str. First, by separating the divine shepherd from the human guardian or manager.

Y. Soc. True.

Str. And the art of management which is assigned to man would again have to be subdivided.

Y. Soc. On what principle?

Str. On the principle of voluntary and compulsory.

Y. Soc. Why?

Str. Because, if I am not mistaken, there has been an error here; for our simplicity led us to rank king and tyrant together, whereas they are utterly distinct, like their modes of government.

Y. Soc. True.

Str. Then, now, as I said, let us make the correction and divide human care into two parts, on the principle of voluntary and compulsory.

Y. Soc. Certainly.

Str. And if we call the management of violent rulers tyranny, and the voluntary management of herds of voluntary bipeds politics, may we not further assert that he who has this latter art of management is the true king and statesman?

[277] Y. Soc. I think, Stranger, that we have now completed the account of the Statesman.

Str. Would that we had, Socrates, but I have to satisfy myself as well as you; and in my judgment the figure of the king is not yet perfected; like statuaries who, in their too great haste, having overdone the several parts of their work, lose time in cutting them down, so too we, partly out of haste, partly out of a magnanimous desire to expose our former error, and also because we imagined that a king required grand illustrations, have taken up a marvellous lump of fable, and have been obliged to use more than was necessary. This made us discourse at large, and, nevertheless, the story never came to an end. And our discussion might be compared to a picture of some living being which had been fairly drawn in outline, but had not yet attained the life and clearness which is given by the blending of colours. Now to intelligent persons a living being had better be delineated by language and discourse than by any painting or work of art: to the duller sort by works of art.

Y. Soc. Very true; but what is the imperfection which still remains? I wish that you would tell me.

Str. The higher ideas, my dear friend, can hardly be set forth except through the medium of examples; every man seems to know all things in a dreamy sort of way, and then again to wake up and to know nothing.

Y. Soc. What do you mean?

Str. I fear that I have been unfortunate in raising a question about our experience of knowledge.

Y. Soc. Why so?

Str. Why, because my "example" requires the assistance of another example.

Y. Soc. Proceed; you need not fear that I shall tire.

Str. I will proceed, finding, as I do, such a ready listener in you: when children are beginning to know their letters—

Y. Soc. What are you going to say?

Str. That they distinguish the several letters well enough in very short and easy syllables, [278] and are able to tell them correctly.

Y. Soc. Certainly.

Str. Whereas in other syllables they do not recognize them, and think and speak falsely of them.

Y. Soc. Very true.

Str. Will not the best and easiest way of bringing them to a knowledge of what they do not as yet know be—

Y. Soc. Be what?

Str. To refer them first of all to cases in which they judge correctly about the letters in question, and then to compare these with the cases in which they do not as yet know, and to show them that the letters are the same, and have the same character in both combination, until all cases in which they are right have been placed side by side with all cases in which they are wrong. In this way they have examples, and are made to learn that each letter in every combination is always the same and not another, and is always called by the same name.

Y. Soc. Certainly.

Str. Are not examples formed in this manner? We take a thing and compare it with another distinct instance of the same thing, of which we have a right conception, and out of the comparison there arises one true notion, which includes both of them.

Y. Soc. Exactly.

Str. Can we wonder, then, that the soul has

the same uncertainty about the alphabet of things, and sometimes and in some cases is firmly fixed by the truth in each particular, and then, again, in other cases is altogether at sea; having somehow or other a correct notion of combinations; but when the elements are transferred into the long and difficult language (syllables) of facts, is again ignorant of them?

Y. Soc. There is nothing wonderful in that.

Str. Could any one, my friend, who began with false opinion ever expect to arrive even at a small portion of truth and to attain wisdom?

Y. Soc. Hardly.

Str. Then you and I will not be far wrong in trying to see the nature of example in general in a small and particular instance; afterwards from lesser things we intend to pass to the royal class, which is the highest form of the same nature, and endeavour to discover by rules of art what the management of cities is; and then the dream will become a reality to us.

Y. Soc. Very true.

[279] Str. Then, once more, let us resume the previous argument, and as there were innumerable rivals of the royal race who claim to have the care of states, let us part them all off, and leave him alone; and, as I was saying, a model or example of this process has first to be framed.

Y. Soc. Exactly.

Str. What model is there which is small, and yet has any analogy with the political occupation? Suppose, Socrates, that if we have no other example at hand, we choose weaving, or, more precisely, weaving of wool—this will be quite enough, without taking the whole of weaving, to illustrate our meaning?

Y. Soc. Certainly.

Str. Why should we not apply to weaving the same processes of division and subdivision which we have already applied to other classes; going once more as rapidly as we can through all the steps until we come to that which is needed for our purpose?

Y. Soc. How do you mean?

Str. I shall reply by actually performing the process.

Y. Soc. Very good.

Str. All things which we make or acquire are either creative or preventive; of the preventive class are antidotes, divine and human, and also defences; and defences are either military weapons or protections; and protections are veils, and also shields against heat and cold, and shields against heat and cold are shelters and coverings; and coverings are blankets and garments; and garments are some of them in one piece, and others of them are made in several parts; and of these latter some are stitched, others are fastened and not stitched; and of the not stitched, some are made of the sinews of plants, and some of hair; and of these, again, some are cemented with water and earth, and others are fastened together by themselves. And these last defences and coverings which are fastened together by themselves are called clothes, and the art which superintends them we may call, from the nature of the operation, [280] the art of clothing, just as before the art of the Statesman was derived from the State; and may we not say that the art of weaving, at least that largest portion of it which was concerned with the making of clothes,[1] differs only in name from this art of clothing, in the same way that, in the previous case, the royal science differed from the political?

Y. Soc. Most true.

Str. In the next place, let us make the reflection, that the art of weaving clothes, which an incompetent person might fancy to have been sufficiently described, has been separated off from several others which are of the same family, but not from the co-operative arts.

Y. Soc. And which are the kindred arts?

Str. I see that I have not taken you with me. So I think that we had better go backwards, starting from the end. We just now parted off from the weaving of clothes, the making of blankets, which differ from each other in that one is put under and the other is put around! and these are what I termed kindred arts.

Y. Soc. I understand.

Str. And we have subtracted the manufacture of all articles made of flax and cords, and all that we just now metaphorically termed the sinews of plants, and we have also separated off the process of felting and the putting together of materials by stitching and sewing, of which the most important part is the cobbler's art.

Y. Soc. Precisely.

Str. Then we separated off the currier's art, which prepared coverings in entire pieces, and the art of sheltering, and subtracted the various arts of making water-tight which are employed in building, and in general in carpentering, and in other crafts, and all such arts as furnish impediments to thieving and acts of violence, and are concerned with making the lids of boxes and the fixing of doors, being divisions of the art of joining; and we also cut off the manufacture of arms, which is a section of the great and manifold art of making defences; and we originally began by parting off the whole of the magic art which is concerned with antidotes, and have left, as would appear, the very art of which we were in search, the art of protection against winter cold, which fabricates woollen defences, and has the name of weaving.

Y. Soc. Very true.

[281] Str. Yes, my boy, but that is not all; for the first process to which the material is subjected is the opposite of weaving.

Y. Soc. How so?

Str. Weaving is a sort of uniting?

Y. Soc. Yes.

Str. But the first process is a separation of the clotted and matted fibres?

Y. Soc. What do you mean?

Str. I mean the work of the carder's art; for we cannot say that carding is weaving, or that the carder is a weaver.

Y. Soc. Certainly not.

Str. Again, if a person were to say that the art of making the warp and the woof was the art of weaving, he would say what was paradoxical and false.

Y. Soc. To be sure.

Str. Shall we say that the whole art of the fuller or of the mender has nothing to do with the care and treatment of clothes, or are we to regard all these as arts of weaving?

Y. Soc. Certainly not.

Str. And yet surely all these arts will maintain that they are concerned with the treatment and production of clothes; they will dispute the exclusive prerogative of weaving, and though assigning a larger sphere to that, will still reserve a considerable field for themselves.

Y. Soc. Very true.

Str. Besides these, there are the arts which make tools and instruments of weaving, and which will claim at least to be co-operative causes in every work of the weaver.

Y. Soc. Most true.

Str. Well, then, suppose that we define weaving, or rather that part of it which has been selected by us, to be the greatest and noblest of arts which are concerned with woollen garments—shall we be right? Is not the definition, although true, wanting in clearness and completeness; for do not all those other arts require to be first cleared away?

Y. Soc. True.

Str. Then the next thing will be to separate them, in order that the argument may proceed in a regular manner?

Y. Soc. By all means.

Str. Let us consider, in the first place, that

[1] Cf. 279.

there are two kinds of arts entering into everything which we do.

Y. Soc. What are they?

Str. The one kind is the conditional or co-operative, the other the principal cause.

Y. Soc. What do you mean?

Str. The arts which do not manufacture the actual thing, but which furnish the necessary tools for the manufacture, without which the several arts could not fulfil their appointed work, are co-operative; but those which make the things themselves are causal.

Y. Soc. A very reasonable distinction.

Str. Thus the arts which make spindles, combs, and other instruments of the production of clothes, may be called co-operative, and those which treat and fabricate the things themselves, causal.

Y. Soc. Very true.

[282] *Str.* The arts of washing and mending, and the other preparatory arts which belong to the causal class, and form a division of the great art of adornment, may be all comprehended under what we call the fuller's art.

Y. Soc. Very good.

Str. Carding and spinning threads and all the parts of the process which are concerned with the actual manufacture of a woollen garment form a single art, which is one of those universally acknowledged—the art of working in wool.

Y. Soc. To be sure.

Str. Of working in wool, again, there are two divisions, and both these are parts of two arts at once.

Y. Soc. How is that?

Str. Carding and one half of the use of the comb, and the other processes of wool-working which separate the composite, may be classed together as belonging both to the art of wool-working, and also to one of the two great arts which are of universal application—the art of composition and the art of division.

Y. Soc. Yes.

Str. To the latter belong carding and the other processes of which I was just now speaking; the art of discernment or division in wool and yarn, which is effected in one manner with the comb and in another with the hands, is variously described under all the names which I just now mentioned.

Y. Soc. Very true.

Str. Again, let us take some process of wool-working which is also a portion of the art of composition, and, dismissing the elements of division which we found there, make two

halves, one on the principle of composition, and the other on the principle of division.

Y. Soc. Let that be done.

Str. And once more, Socrates, we must divide the part which belongs at once both to wool-working and composition, if we are ever to discover satisfactorily the aforesaid art of weaving.

Y. Soc. We must.

Str. Yes, certainly, and let us call one part of the art the art of twisting threads, the other the art of combining them.

Y. Soc. Do I understand you, in speaking of twisting, to be referring to manufacture of the warp?

Str. Yes, and of the woof too; how, if not by twisting, is the woof made?

Y. Soc. There is no other way.

Str. Then suppose that you define the warp and the woof, for I think that the definition will be of use to you.

Y. Soc. How shall I define them?

Str. As thus: A piece of carded wool which is drawn out lengthwise and breadthwise is said to be pulled out.

Y. Soc. Yes.

Str. And the wool thus prepared, when twisted by the spindle, and made into a firm thread, is called the warp, and the art which regulates these operations the art of spinning the warp.

Y. Soc. True.

Str. And the threads which are more loosely spun, having a softness proportioned to the intertexture of the warp and to the degree of force used in dressing the cloth—the threads which are thus spun are called the woof, *[283]* and the art which is set over them may be called the art of spinning the woof.

Y. Soc. Very true.

Str. And, now, there can be no mistake about the nature of the part of weaving which we have undertaken to define. For when that part of the art of composition which is employed in the working of wool forms a web by the regular intertexture of warp and woof, the entire woven substance is called by us a woollen garment, and the art which presides over this is the art of weaving.

Y. Soc. Very true.

Str. But why did we not say at once that weaving is the art of entwining warp and woof, instead of making a long and useless circuit?

Y. Soc. I thought, Stranger, that there was nothing useless in what was said.

Str. Very likely, but you may not always think so, my sweet friend; and in case any feeling of dissatisfaction should hereafter arise in your mind, as it very well may, let me lay down a principle which will apply to arguments in general.

Y. Soc. Proceed.

Str. Let us begin by considering the whole nature of excess and defect, and then we shall have a rational ground on which we may praise or blame too much length or too much shortness in discussions of this kind.

Y. Soc. Let us do so.

Str. The points on which I think that we ought to dwell are the following:—

Y. Soc. What?

Str. Length and shortness, excess and defect; with all of these the art of measurement is conversant.

Y. Soc. Yes.

Str. And the art of measurement has to be divided into two parts, with a view to our present purpose.

Y. Soc. Where would you make the division?

Str. As thus: I would make two parts, one having regard to the relativity of greatness and smallness to each other; and there is another, without which the existence of production would be impossible.

Y. Soc. What do you mean?

Str. Do you not think that it is only natural for the greater to be called greater with reference to the less alone, and the less less with reference to the greater alone?

Y. Soc. Yes.

Str. Well, but is there not also something exceeding and exceeded by the principle of the mean, both in speech and action, and is not this a reality, and the chief mark of difference between good and bad men?

Y. Soc. Plainly.

Str. Then we must suppose that the great and small exist and are discerned in both these ways, and not, as we were saying before, only relatively to one another, but there must also be another comparison of them with the mean or ideal standard; would you like to hear the reason why?

Y. Soc. Certainly.

[284] Str. If we assume the greater to exist only in relation to the less, there will never be any comparison of either with the mean.

Y. Soc. True.

Str. And would not this doctrine be the ruin of all the arts and their creations; would not the art of the Statesman and the aforesaid art of weaving disappear? For all these arts are on the watch against excess and defect, not as un-realities, but as real evils, which occasion a difficulty in action; and the excellence of beauty of every work of art is due to this observance of measure.

Y. Soc. Certainly.

Str. But if the science of the Statesman disappears, the search for the royal science will be impossible.

Y. Soc. Very true.

Str. Well, then, as in the case of the Sophist we extorted the inference that not-being had an existence, because here was the point at which the argument eluded our grasp, so in this we must endeavour to show that the greater and less are not only to be measured with one another, but also have to do with the production of the mean; for if this is not admitted, neither a statesman nor any other man of action can be an undisputed master of his science.

Y. Soc. Yes, we must certainly do again what we did then.

Str. But this, Socrates, is a greater work than the other, of which we only too well remember the length. I think, however, that we may fairly assume something of this sort—

Y. Soc. What?

Str. That we shall some day require this notion of a mean with a view to the demonstration of absolute truth; meanwhile, the argument that the very existence of the arts must be held to depend on the possibility of measuring more or less, not only with one another, but also with a view to the attainment of the mean, seems to afford a grand support and satisfactory proof of the doctrine which we are maintaining; for if there are arts, there is a standard of measure, and if there is a standard of measure, there are arts; but if either is wanting, there is neither.

Y. Soc. True; and what is the next step?

Str. The next step clearly is to divide the art of measurement into two parts, as we have said already, and to place in the one part all the arts which measure number, length, depth, breadth, swiftness with their opposites; and to have another part in which they are measured with the mean, and the fit, and the opportune, and the due, and with all those words, in short, which denote a mean or standard removed from the extremes.

Y. Soc. Here are two vast divisions, embracing two very different spheres.

[285] Str. There are many accomplished men, Socrates, who say, believing themselves to speak wisely, that the art of measurement is universal, and has to do with all things. And this means what we are now saying; for all

things which come within the province of art do certainly in some sense partake of measure. But these persons, because they are not accustomed to distinguish classes according to real forms, jumble together two widely different things, relation to one another, and to a standard, under the idea that they are the same, and also fall into the converse error of dividing other things not according to their real parts. Whereas the right way is, if a man has first seen the unity of things, to go on with the enquiry and not desist until he has found all the differences contained in it which form distinct classes; nor again should he be able to rest contented with the manifold diversities which are seen in a multitude of things until he has comprehended all of them that have any affinity within the bounds of one similarity and embraced them within the reality of a single kind. But we have said enough on this head, and also of excess and defect; we have only to bear in mind that two divisions of the art of measurement have been discovered which are concerned with them, and not forget what they are.

Y. Soc. We will not forget.

Str. And now that this discussion is completed, let us go on to consider another question, which concerns not this argument only but the conduct of such arguments in general.

Y. Soc. What is this new question?

Str. Take the case of a child who is engaged in learning his letters: when he is asked what letters make up a word, should we say that the question is intended to improve his grammatical knowledge of that particular word, or of all words?

Y. Soc. Clearly, in order that he may have a better knowledge of all words.

Str. And is our enquiry about the Statesman intended only to improve our knowledge of politics, or our power of reasoning generally?

Y. Soc. Clearly, as in the former example, the purpose is general.

Str. Still less would any rational man seek to analyse the notion of weaving for its own sake. But people seem to forget that some things have sensible images, which are readily known, and can be easily pointed out when any one desires to answer an enquirer without any trouble or argument; [286] whereas the greatest and highest truths have no outward image of themselves visible to man, which he who wishes to satisfy the soul of the enquirer can adapt to the eye of sense,[1] and therefore we ought to train ourselves to give and accept a rational account

[1] Cf. *Phaedrus*, 250.

of them; for immaterial things, which are the noblest and greatest, are shown only in thought and idea, and in no other way, and all that we are now saying is said for the sake of them. Moreover, there is always less difficulty in fixing the mind on small matters than on great.

Y. Soc. Very good.

Str. Let us call to mind the bearing of all this.

Y. Soc. What is it?

Str. I wanted to get rid of any impression of tediousness which we may have experienced in the discussion about weaving, and the reversal of the universe, and in the discussion concerning the Sophist and the being of not-being. I know that they were felt to be too long, and I reproached myself with this, fearing that they might be not only tedious but irrelevant; and all that I have now said is only designed to prevent the recurrence of any such disagreeables for the future.

Y. Soc. Very good. Will you proceed?

Str. Then I would like to observe that you and I, remembering what has been said, should praise or blame the length or shortness of discussions, not by comparing them with one another, but with what is fitting, having regard to the part of measurement, which, as we said, was to be borne in mind.

Y. Soc. Very true.

Str. And yet, not everything is to be judged even with a view to what is fitting; for we should only want such a length as is suited to give pleasure, if at all, as a secondary matter; and reason tells us, that we should be contented to make the ease or rapidity of an enquiry, not our first, but our second object; the first and highest of all being to assert the great method of division according to species—whether the discourse be shorter or longer is not to the point. No offence should be taken at length, but the longer and shorter are to be employed indifferently, according as either of them is better calculated to sharpen the wits of the auditors. Reason would also say to him who censures the length of discourses on such occasions and cannot away with their circumlocution, that he should not be in such a hurry to have done with them, when he can only complain that they are tedious, [287] but he should prove that if they had been shorter they would have made those who took part in them better dialecticians, and more capable of expressing the truth of things; about any other praise and blame, he need not trouble himself—he should pretend not to hear them. But we have had enough of this, as you will probably agree with me in thinking. Let us return to our Statesman, and apply to his case the aforesaid example of weaving.

Y. Soc. Very good;—let us do as you say.

Str. The art of the king has been separated from the similar arts of shepherds, and, indeed, from all those which have to do with herds at all. There still remain, however, of the causal and co-operative arts those which are immediately concerned with States, and which must first be distinguished from one another.

Y. Soc. Very good.

Str. You know that these arts cannot easily be divided into two halves; the reason will be very evident as we proceed.

Y. Soc. Then we had better do so.

Str. We must carve them like a victim into members or limbs, since we cannot bisect them.[1] For we certainly should divide everything into as few parts as possible.

Y. Soc. What is to be done in this case?

Str. What we did in the example of weaving —all those arts which furnish the tools were regarded by us as co-operative.

Y. Soc. Yes.

Str. So now, and with still more reason, all arts which make any implement in a State, whether great or small, may be regarded by us as co-operative, for without them neither State nor Statesmanship would be possible; and yet we are not inclined to say that any of them is a product of the kingly art.

Y. Soc. No, indeed.

Str. The task of separating this class from others is not an easy one; for there is plausibility in saying that anything in the world is the instrument of doing something. But there is another class of possessions in a city, of which I have a word to say.

Y. Soc. What class do you mean?

Str. A class which may be described as not having this power; that is to say, not like an instrument, framed for production, but designed for the preservation of that which is produced.

Y. Soc. To what do you refer?

Str. To the class of vessels, as they are comprehensively termed, which are constructed for the preservation of things moist and dry, of things prepared in the fire or out of the fire; [288] this is a very large class, and has, if I am not mistaken, literally nothing to do with the royal art of which we are in search.

Y. Soc. Certainly not.

Str. There is also a third class of possessions to be noted, different from these and very ex-

tensive, moving or resting on land or water, honourable and also dishonourable. The whole of this class has one name, because it is intended to be sat upon, being always a seat for something.

Y. Soc. What is it?

Str. A vehicle, which is certainly not the work of the Statesman, but of the carpenter, potter, and coppersmith.

Y. Soc. I understand.

Str. And is there not a fourth class which is again different, and in which most of the things formerly mentioned are contained—every kind of dress, most sorts of arms, walls and enclosures, whether of earth or stone, and ten thousand other things? all of which being made for the sake of defence, may be truly called defences, and are for the most part to be regarded as the work of the builder or of the weaver, rather than of the Statesman.

Y. Soc. Certainly.

Str. Shall we add a fifth class, of ornamentation and drawing, and of the imitations produced by drawing and music, which are designed for amusement only, and may be fairly comprehended under one name?

Y. Soc. What is it?

Str. Plaything is the name.

Y. Soc. Certainly.

Str. That one name may be fitly predicated of all of them, for none of these things have a serious purpose—amusement is their sole aim.

Y. Soc. That again I understand.

Str. Then there is a class which provides materials for all these, out of which and in which the arts already mentioned fabricate their works;—this manifold class, I say, which is the creation and offspring of many other arts, may I not rank sixth?

Y. Soc. What do you mean?

Str. I am referring to gold, silver, and other metals, and all that wood-cutting and shearing of every sort provides for the art of carpentry and plaiting; and there is the process of barking and stripping the cuticle of plants, and the currier's art, which strips off the skins of animals, and other similar arts which manufacture corks and papyri and cords, and provide for the manufacture of composite species out of simple kinds—the whole class may be termed the primitive and simple possession of man, and with this the kingly science has no concern at all.

Y. Soc. True.

Str. The provision of food and of all other things which mingle their particles with the

[1] Cf. *Phaedrus,* 265.

particles of the human body, and minister to the body, [289] will form a seventh class, which may be called by the general term of nourishment, unless you have any better name to offer. This, however, appertains rather to the husbandman, huntsman, trainer, doctor, cook, and is not to be assigned to the Statesman's art.

Y. Soc. Certainly not.

Str. These seven classes include nearly every description of property, with the exception of tame animals. Consider;—there was the original material, which ought to have been placed first; next come instruments, vessels, vehicles, defences, playthings, nourishment; small things, which may be included under one of these—as for example, coins, seals and stamps, are omitted, for they have not in them the character of any larger kind which includes them; but some of them may, with a little forcing, be placed among ornaments, and others may be made to harmonize with the class of implements. The art of herding, which has been already divided into parts, will include all property in tame animals, except slaves.

Y. Soc. Very true.

Str. The class of slaves and ministers only remains, and I suspect that in this the real aspirants for the throne, who are the rivals of the king in the formation of the political web, will be discovered; just as spinners, carders, and the rest of them, were the rivals of the weaver. All the others, who were termed co-operators, have been got rid of among the occupations already mentioned, and separated from the royal and political science.

Y. Soc. I agree.

Str. Let us go a little nearer, in order that we may be more certain of the complexion of this remaining class.

Y. Soc. Let us do so.

Str. We shall find from our present point of view that the greatest servants are in a case and condition which is the reverse of what we anticipated.

Y. Soc. Who are they?

Str. Those who have been purchased, and have so become possessions; these are unmistakably slaves, and certainly do not claim royal science.

Y. Soc. Certainly not.

Str. Again, freemen who of their own accord become the servants of the other classes in a State, and who exchange and equalise the products of husbandry and the other arts, some sitting in the market-place, others going from city to city by land or sea, and giving money in exchange for money or for other productions— [290] the money-changer, the merchant, the ship-owner, the retailer, will not put in any claim to statecraft or politics?

Y. Soc. No; unless, indeed, to the politics of commerce.

Str. But surely men whom we see acting as hirelings and serfs, and too happy to turn their hand to anything, will not profess to share in royal science?

Y. Soc. Certainly not.

Str. But what would you say of some other serviceable officials?

Y. Soc. Who are they, and what services do they perform?

Str. There are heralds, and scribes perfected by practice, and divers others who have great skill in various sorts of business connected with the government of states—what shall we call them?

Y. Soc. They are the officials, and servants of the rulers, as you just now called them, but not themselves rulers.

Str. There may be something strange in any servant pretending to be a ruler, and yet I do not think that I could have been dreaming when I imagined that the principal claimants to political science would be found somewhere in this neighbourhood.

Y. Soc. Very true.

Str. Well, let us draw nearer, and try the claims of some who have not yet been tested; in the first place, there are diviners, who have a portion of servile or ministerial science, and are thought to be the interpreters of the gods to men.

Y. Soc. True.

Str. There is also the priestly class, who, as the law declares, know how to give the gods gifts from men in the form of sacrifices which are acceptable to them, and to ask on our behalf blessings in return from them. Now both these are branches of the servile or ministerial art.

Y. Soc. Yes, clearly.

Str. And here I think that we seem to be getting on the right track; for the priest and the diviner are swollen with pride and prerogative, and they create an awful impression of themselves by the magnitude of their enterprises; in Egypt, the king himself is not allowed to reign, unless he have priestly powers, and if he should be of another class and has thrust himself in, he must get enrolled in the priesthood. In many parts of Hellas, the duty of offering the most solemn propitiatory sacrifices is assigned to the highest magistracies, and here, at Athens, the most solemn and national of the ancient sacrifices are supposed to be celebrated by him who has been chosen by lot to be the King Archon.

Y. Soc. Precisely.

[291] Str. But who are these other kings and priests elected by lot who now come into view followed by their retainers and a vast throng, as the former class disappears and the scene changes?

Y. Soc. Whom can you mean?

Str. They are a strange crew.

Y. Soc. Why strange?

Str. A minute ago I thought that they were animals of every tribe; for many of them are like lions and centaurs, and many more like satyrs and such weak and shifty creatures;— Protean shapes quickly changing into one another's forms and natures; and now, Socrates, I begin to see who they are.

Y. Soc. Who are they? You seem to be gazing on some strange vision.

Str. Yes; every one looks strange when you do not know him; and just now I myself fell into this mistake—at first sight, coming suddenly upon him, I did not recognize the politician and his troop.

Y. Soc. Who is he?

Str. The chief of Sophists and most accomplished of wizards, who must at any cost be separated from the true king or Statesman, if we are ever to see daylight in the present enquiry.

Y. Soc. That is a hope not lightly to be renounced.

Str. Never, if I can help it; and, first, let me ask you a question.

Y. Soc. What?

Str. Is not monarchy a recognized form of government?

Y. Soc. Yes.

Str. And, after monarchy, next in order comes the government of the few?

Y. Soc. Of course.

Str. Is not the third form of government the rule of the multitude, which is called by the name of democracy?

Y. Soc. Certainly.

Str. And do not these three expand in a manner into five, producing out of themselves two other names?

Y. Soc. What are they?

Str. There is a criterion of voluntary and involuntary, poverty and riches, law and the absence of law, which men now-a-days apply to them; the two first they subdivide accordingly,

and ascribe to monarchy two forms and two corresponding names, royalty and tyranny.

Y. Soc. Very true.

Str. And the government of the few they distinguish by the names of aristocracy and oligarchy.

Y. Soc. Certainly.

[292] Str. Democracy alone, whether rigidly observing the laws or not, and whether the multitude rule over the men of property with their consent or against their consent, always in ordinary language has the same name.

Y. Soc. True.

Str. But do you suppose that any form of government which is defined by these characteristics of the one, the few, or the many, of poverty or wealth, of voluntary or compulsory submission, of written law or the absence of law, can be a right one?

Y. Soc. Why not?

Str. Reflect; and follow me.

Y. Soc. In what direction?

Str. Shall we abide by what we said at first, or shall we retract our words?

Y. Soc. To what do you refer?

Str. If I am not mistaken, we said that royal power was a science?

Y. Soc. Yes.

Str. And a science of a peculiar kind, which was selected out of the rest as having a character which is at once judicial and authoritative?

Y. Soc. Yes.

Str. And there was one kind of authority over lifeless things and another other living animals; and so we proceeded in the division step by step up to this point, not losing the idea of science, but unable as yet to determine the nature of the particular science?

Y. Soc. True.

Str. Hence we are led to observe that the distinguishing principle of the State cannot be the few or many, the voluntary or involuntary, poverty or riches; but some notion of science must enter into it, if we are to be consistent with what has preceded.

Y. Soc. And we must be consistent.

Str. Well, then, in which of these various forms of States may the science of government, which is among the greatest of all sciences and most difficult to acquire, be supposed to reside? That we must discover, and then we shall see who are the false politicians who pretend to be politicians but are not, although they persuade many, and shall separate them from the wise king.

Y. Soc. That, as the argument has already

Str. Do you think that the multitude in a State can attain political science?

Y. Soc. Impossible.

Str. But, perhaps, in a city of a thousand men, there would be a hundred, or say fifty, who could?

Y. Soc. In that case political science would certainly be the easiest of all sciences; there could not be found in a city of that number as many really first-rate draught-players, if judged by the standard of the rest of Hellas, and there would certainly not be as many kings. For kings we may truly call those who possess royal science, whether they rule or not, as was shown in the previous argument.[1]

[293] Str. Thank you for reminding me; and the consequence is that any true form of government can only be supposed to be the government of one, two, or, at any rate, of a few.

Y. Soc. Certainly.

Str. And these, whether they rule with the will, or against the will, of their subjects, with written laws or without written laws, and whether they are poor or rich, and whatever be the nature of their rule, must be supposed, according to our present view, to rule on some scientific principle; just as the physician, whether he cures us against our will or with our will, and whatever be his mode of treatment—incision, burning, or the infliction of some other pain—whether he practises out of a book or not out of a book, and whether he be rich or poor, whether he purges or reduces in some other way, or even fattens his patients, is a physician all the same, so long as he exercises authority over them according to rules of art, if he only does them good and heals and saves them. And this we lay down to be the only proper test of the art of medicine, or of any other art of command.

Y. Soc. Quite true.

Str. Then that can be the only true form of government in which the governors are really found to possess science, and are not mere pretenders, whether they rule according to law or without law, over willing or unwilling subjects, and are rich or poor themselves—none of these things can with any propriety be included in the notion of the ruler.

Y. Soc. True.

Str. And whether with a view to the public good they purge the State by killing some, or exiling some; whether they reduce the size of the body corporate by sending out from the

[1] Cf. 259.

hive swarms of citizens, or, by introducing persons from without, increase it; while they act according to the rules of wisdom and justice, and use their power with a view to the general security and improvement, the city over which they rule, and which has these characteristics, may be described as the only true State. All other governments are not genuine or real, but only imitations of this, and some of them are better and some of them are worse; the better are said to be well governed, but they are mere imitations like the others.

Y. Soc. I agree, Stranger, in the greater part of what you say; but as to their ruling without laws—the expression has a harsh sound.

[294] Str. You have been too quick for me, Socrates; I was just going to ask you whether you objected to any of my statements. And now I see that we shall have to consider this notion of there being good government without laws.

Y. Soc. Certainly.

Str. There can be no doubt that legislation is in a manner the business of a king, and yet the best thing of all is not that the law should rule, but that a man should rule, supposing him to have wisdom and royal power. Do you see why this is?

Y. Soc. Why?

Str. Because the law does not perfectly comprehend what is noblest and most just for all and therefore cannot enforce what is best. The differences of men and actions, and the endless irregular movements of human things, do not admit of any universal and simple rule. And no art whatsoever can lay down a rule which will last for all time.

Y. Soc. Of course not.

Str. But the law is always striving to make one;—like an obstinate and ignorant tyrant, who will not allow anything to be done contrary to his appointment, or any question to be asked—not even in sudden changes of circumstances, when something happens to be better than what he commanded for some one.

Y. Soc. Certainly; the law treats us all precisely in the manner which you describe.

Str. A perfectly simple principle can never be applied to a state of things which is the reverse of simple.

Y. Soc. True.

Str. Then if the law is not the perfection of right, why are we compelled to make laws at all? The reason of this has next to be investigated.

Y. Soc. Certainly.

Str. Let me ask, whether you have not meetings for gymnastic contests in your city, such as there are in other cities, at which men compete in running, wrestling, and the like?

Y. Soc. Yes; they are very common among us.

Str. And what are the rules which are enforced on their pupils by professional trainers or by others having similar authority? Can you remember?

Y. Soc. To what do you refer?

Str. The training-masters do not issue minute rules for individuals, or give every individual what is exactly suited to his constitution; they think that they ought to go more roughly to work, and to prescribe generally the regimen which will benefit the majority.

Y. Soc. Very true.

Str. And therefore they assign equal amounts of exercise to them all; they send them forth together, and let them rest together from their running, wrestling, or whatever the form of bodily exercise may be.

Y. Soc. True.

[*295*] *Str.* And now observe that the legislator who has to preside over the herd, and to enforce justice in their dealings with one another, will not be able, in enacting for the general good, to provide exactly what is suitable for each particular case.

Y. Soc. He cannot be expected to do so.

Str. He will lay down laws in a general form for the majority, roughly meeting the cases of individuals; and some of them he will deliver in writing, and others will be unwritten; and these last will be traditional customs of the country.

Y. Soc. He will be right.

Str. Yes, quite right; for how can he sit at every man's side all through his life, prescribing for him the exact particulars of his duty? Who, Socrates, would be equal to such a task? No one who really had the royal science, if he had been able to do this, would have imposed upon himself the restriction of a written law.

Y. Soc. So I should infer from what has now been said.

Str. Or rather, my good friend, from what is going to be said.

Y. Soc. And what is that?

Str. Let us put to ourselves the case of a physician, or trainer, who is about to go into a far country, and is expecting to be a long time away from his patients—thinking that his instructions will not be remembered unless they are written down, he will leave notes of them for the use of his pupils or patients.

Y. Soc. True.

Str. But what would you say, if he came back sooner than he had intended, and, owing to an unexpected change of the winds or other celestial influences, something else happened to be better for them—would he not venture to suggest this new remedy, although not contemplated in his former prescription? Would he persist in observing the original law, neither himself giving any new commandments, nor the patient daring to do otherwise than was prescribed, under the idea that this course only was healthy and medicinal, all others noxious and heterodox? Viewed in the light of science and true art, would not all such enactments be utterly ridiculous?

Y. Soc. Utterly.

Str. And if he who gave laws, written or unwritten, determining what was good or bad, honourable or dishonourable, just or unjust, to the tribes of men who flock together in their several cities, and are governed in accordance with them; if, I say, the wise legislator were suddenly to come again, [*296*] or another like to him, is he to be prohibited from changing them?—would not this prohibition be in reality quite as ridiculous as the other?

Y. Soc. Certainly.

Str. Do you know a plausible saying of the common people which is in point?

Y. Soc. I do not recall what you mean at the moment.

Str. They say that if any one knows how the ancient laws may be improved, he must first persuade his own State of the improvement, and then he may legislate, but not otherwise.

Y. Soc. And are they not right?

Str. I dare say. But supposing that he does use some gentle violence for their good, what is this violence to be called? Or rather, before you answer, let me ask the same question in reference to our previous instances.

Y. Soc. What do you mean?

Str. Suppose that a skilful physician has a patient, of whatever sex or age, whom he compels against his will to do something for his good which is contrary to the written rules; what is this compulsion to be called? Would you ever dream of calling it a violation of the art, or a breach of the laws of health? Nothing could be more unjust than for the patient to whom such violence is applied, to charge the physician who practises the violence with wanting skill or aggravating his disease.

Y. Soc. Most true.

Str. In the political art error is not called dis-

ease, but evil, or disgrace, or injustice.

Y. Soc. Quite true.

Str. And when the citizen, contrary to law and custom, is compelled to do what is juster and better and nobler than he did before, the last and most absurd thing which he could say about such violence is that he has incurred disgrace or evil or injustice at the hands of those who compelled him.

Y. Soc. Very true.

Str. And shall we say that the violence, if exercised by a rich man, is just, and if by a poor man, unjust? May not any man, rich or poor, with or without laws, with the will of the citizens or against the will of the citizens, do what is for their interest? Is not this the true principle of government, according to which the wise and good man will order the affairs of his subjects? *[297]* As the pilot, by watching continually over the interests of the ship and of the crew—not by laying down rules, but by making his art a law—preserves the lives of his fellow-sailors, even so, and in the self-same way, may there not be a true form of polity created by those who are able to govern in a similar spirit, and who show a strength of art which is superior to the law? Nor can wise rulers ever err while they, observing the one great rule of distributing justice to the citizens with intelligence and skill, are able to preserve them, and, as far as may be, to make them better from being worse.

Y. Soc. No one can deny what has been now said.

Str. Neither, if you consider, can any one deny the other statement.

Y. Soc. What was it?

Str. We said that no great number of persons, whoever they may be, can attain political knowledge, or order a State wisely, but that the true government is to be found in a small body, or in an individual, and that other States are but imitations of this, as we said a little while ago, some for the better and some for the worse.

Y. Soc. What do you mean? I cannot have understood your previous remark about imitations.

Str. And yet the mere suggestion which I hastily threw out is highly important, even if we leave the question where it is, and do not seek by the discussion of it to expose the error which prevails in this matter.

Y. Soc. What do you mean?

Str. The idea which has to be grasped by us is not easy or familiar; but we may attempt to express it thus:—Supposing the government of which I have been speaking to be the only true model, then the others must use the written laws of this—in no other way can they be saved; they will have to do what is now generally approved, although not the best thing in the world.

Y. Soc. What is this?

Str. No citizen should do anything contrary to the laws, and any infringement of them should be punished with death and the most extreme penalties; and this is very right and good when regarded as the second best thing, if you set aside the first, of which I was just now speaking. Shall I explain the nature of what I call the second best?

Y. Soc. By all means.

Str. I must again have recourse to my favourite images; through them, and them alone, can I describe kings and rulers.

Y. Soc. What images?

Str. The noble pilot and the wise physician, who "is worth many another man"—in the similitude of these let us endeavour to discover some image of the king.

Y. Soc. What sort of an image?

[298] Str. Well, such as this:—Every man will reflect that he suffers strange things at the hands of both of them; the physician saves any whom he wishes to save, and any whom he wishes to maltreat he maltreats—cutting or burning them, and at the same time requiring them to bring him payments, which are a sort of tribute, of which little or nothing is spent upon the sick man, and the greater part is consumed by him and his domestics; and the finale is that he receives money from the relations of the sick man or from some enemy of his, and puts him out of the way. And the pilots of ships are guilty of numberless evil deeds of the same kind; they intentionally play false and leave you ashore when the hour of sailing arrives; or they cause mishaps at sea and cast away their freight; and are guilty of other rogueries. Now suppose that we, bearing all this in mind, were to determine, after consideration, that neither of these arts shall any longer be allowed to exercise absolute control either over freemen or over slaves, but that we will summon an assembly either of all the people, or of the rich only, that anybody who likes, whatever may be his calling, or even if he have no calling, may offer an opinion either about seamanship or about diseases—whether as to the manner in which physic or surgical instruments are to be applied to the patient, or again about the vessels and the nautical implements which are required in

navigation, and how to meet the dangers of winds and waves which are incidental to the voyage, how to behave when encountering pirates, and what is to be done with the old-fashioned galleys, if they have to fight with others of a similar build—and that, whatever shall be decreed by the multitude on these points, upon the advice of persons skilled or unskilled, shall be written down on triangular tablets and columns, or enacted although unwritten to be national customs; and that in all future time vessels shall be navigated and remedies administered to the patient after this fashion.

Y. Soc. What a strange notion!

Str. Suppose further, that the pilots and physicians are appointed annually, either out of the rich, or out of the whole people, and that they are elected by lot; and that after their election they navigate vessels and heal the sick according to the written rules.

Y. Soc. Worse and worse.

Str. But hear what follows:—When the year of office has expired, the pilot or physician has to come before a court of review, in which the judges are either selected from the wealthy classes or chosen by [299] lot out of the whole people; and anybody who pleases may be their accuser, and may lay to their charge, that during the past year they have not navigated their vessels or healed their patients according to the letter of the law and the ancient customs of their ancestors; and if either of them is condemned, some of the judges must fix what he is to suffer or pay.

Y. Soc. He who is willing to take a command under such conditions, deserves to suffer any penalty.

Str. Yet once more, we shall have to enact that if any one is detected enquiring into piloting and navigation, or into health and the true nature of medicine, or about the winds, or other conditions of the atmosphere, contrary to the written rules, and has any ingenious notions about such matters, he is not to be called a pilot or physician, but a cloudy prating sophist;—further, on the ground that he is a corrupter of the young, who would persuade them to follow the art of medicine or piloting in an unlawful manner, and to exercise an arbitary rule over their patients or ships, any one who is qualified by law may inform against him, and indict him in some court, and then if he is found to be persuading any, whether young or old, to act contrary to the written law, he is to be punished with the utmost rigour; for no one should presume to be wiser than the laws; and as touch-

ing healing and health and piloting and navigation, the nature of them is known to all, for anybody may learn the written laws and the national customs. If such were the mode of procedure, Socrates, about these sciences and about generalship, and any branch of hunting, or about painting or imitation in general, or carpentry, or any sort of handicraft, or husbandry, or planting, or if we were to see an art of rearing horses, or tending herds, or divination, or any ministerial service, or draught-playing, or any science conversant with number, whether simple or square or cube, or comprising motion—I say, if all these things were done in this way according to written regulations, and not according to art, what would be the result?

Y. Soc. All the arts would utterly perish, and could never be recovered, because enquiry would be unlawful. And human life, which is bad enough already, would then become utterly unendurable.

[300] *Str.* But what, if while compelling all these operations to be regulated by written law, we were to appoint as the guardian of the laws some one elected by a show of hands, or by lot, and he caring nothing about the laws, were to act contrary to them from motives of interest or favour, and without knowledge—would not this be a still worse evil than the former?

Y. Soc. Very true.

Str. To go against the laws, which are based upon long experience, and the wisdom of counsellors who have graciously recommended them and persuaded the multitude to pass them, would be a far greater and more ruinous error than any adherence to written law?

Y. Soc. Certainly.

Str. Therefore, as there is a danger of this, the next best thing in legislating is not to allow either the individual or the multitude to break the law in any respect whatever.

Y. Soc. True.

Str. The laws would be copies of the true particulars of action as far as they admit of being written down from the lips of those who have knowledge?

Y. Soc. Certainly they would.

Str. And, as we were saying, he who has knowledge and is a true Statesman, will do many things within his own sphere of action by his art without regard to the laws, when he is of opinion that something other than that which he has written down and enjoined to be observed during his absence would be better.

Y. Soc. Yes, we said so.

Str. And any individual or any number of

men, having fixed laws, in acting contrary to them with a view to something better, would only be acting, as far as they are able, like the true Statesman?

Y. Soc. Certainly.

Str. If they had no knowledge of what they were doing, they would imitate the truth, and they would always imitate ill; but if they had knowledge, the imitation would be the perfect truth, and an imitation no longer.

Y. Soc. Quite true.

Str. And the principle that no great number of men are able to acquire a knowledge of any art has been already admitted by us.

Y. Soc. Yes, it has.

Str. Then the royal or political art, if there be such an art, will never be attained either by the wealthy or by the other mob.

Y. Soc. Impossible.

Str. Then the nearest approach which these lower forms of government can ever make to the true government of the one scientific [301] ruler, is to do nothing contrary to their own written laws and national customs.

Y. Soc. Very good.

Str. When the rich imitate the true form, such a government is called aristocracy; and when they are regardless of the laws, oligarchy.

Y. Soc. True.

Str. Or again, when an individual rules according to law in imitation of him who knows, we call him a king; and if he rules according to law, we give him the same name, whether he rules with opinion or with knowledge.

Y. Soc. To be sure.

Str. And when an individual truly possessing knowledge rules, his name will surely be the same—he will be called a king; and thus the five names of governments, as they are now reckoned, become one.

Y. Soc. That is true.

Str. And when an individual ruler governs neither by law nor by custom, but following in the steps of the true man of science pretends that he can only act for the best by violating the laws, while in reality appetite and ignorance are the motives of the imitation, may not such an one be called a tyrant?

Y. Soc. Certainly.

Str. And this we believe to be the origin of the tyrant and the king, of oligarchies, and aristocracies, and democracies—because men are offended at the one monarch, and can never be made to believe that any one can be worthy of such authority, or is able and willing in the spirit of virtue and knowledge to act justly and holily to all; they fancy that he will be a despot who will wrong and harm and slay whom he pleases of us; for if there could be such a despot as we describe, they would acknowledge that we ought to be too glad to have him, and that he alone would be the happy ruler of a true and perfect State.

Y. Soc. To be sure.

Str. But then, as the State is not like a bee-hive, and has no natural head who is at once recognized to be the superior both in body and in mind, mankind are obliged to meet and make laws, and endeavour to approach as nearly as they can to the true form of government.

Y. Soc. True.

Str. And when the foundation of politics is in the letter only and in custom, and knowledge is divorced from action, can we wonder, Socrates, at the miseries which there are, and always will be, in States? Any other art, built on such a foundation and thus conducted, [302] would ruin all that it touched. Ought we not rather to wonder at the natural strength of the political bond? For States have endured all this, time out of mind, and yet some of them still remain and are not overthrown, though many of them, like ships at sea, founder from time to time, and perish and have perished and will hereafter perish, through the badness of their pilots and crews, who have the worst sort of ignorance of the highest truths—I mean to say, that they are wholly unacquainted with politics, of which, above all other sciences, they believe themselves to have acquired the most perfect knowledge.

Y. Soc. Very true.

Str. Then the question arises:—which of these untrue forms of government is the least oppressive to their subjects, though they are all oppressive; and which is the worst of them? Here is a consideration which is beside our present purpose, and yet having regard to the whole it seems to influence all our actions: we must examine it.

Y. Soc. Yes, we must.

Str. You may say that of the three forms, the same is at once the hardest and the easiest.

Y. Soc. What do you mean?

Str. I am speaking of the three forms of government, which I mentioned at the beginning of this discussion—monarchy, the rule of the few, and the rule of the many.

Y. Soc. True.

Str. If we divide each of these we shall have six, from which the true one may be distinguished as a seventh.

Y. Soc. How would you make the division?

Str. Monarchy divides into royalty and tyranny; the rule of the few into aristocracy, which has an auspicious name, and oligarchy; and democracy or the rule of the many, which before was one, must now be divided.

Y. Soc. On what principle of division?

Str. On the same principle as before, although the name is now discovered to have a twofold meaning. For the distinction of ruling with law or without law, applies to this as well as to the rest.

Y. Soc. Yes.

Str. The division made no difference when we were looking for the perfect State, as we showed before. But now that this has been separated off, and, as we said, the others alone are left for us, the principle of law and the absence of law will bisect them all.

Y. Soc. That would seem to follow, from what has been said.

Str. Then monarchy, when bound by good prescriptions or laws, is the best of all the six, and when lawless is the most bitter and oppressive to the subject.

Y. Soc. True.

[303] *Str.* The government of the few, which is intermediate between that of the one and many, is also intermediate in good and evil; but the government of the many is in every respect weak and unable to do either any great good or any great evil, when compared with the others, because the offices are too minutely subdivided and too many hold them. And this therefore is the worst of all lawful governments, and the best of all lawless ones. If they are all without the restraints of law, democracy is the form in which to live is best; if they are well ordered, then this is the last which you should choose, as royalty, the first form, is the best, with the exception of the seventh, for that excels them all, and is among States what God is among men.

Y. Soc. You are quite right, and we should choose that above all.

Str. The members of all these States, with the exception of the one which has knowledge, may be set aside as being not Statesmen but partisans—upholders of the most monstrous idols, and themselves idols; and, being the greatest imitators and magicians, they are also the greatest of Sophists.

Y. Soc. The name of Sophist after many windings in the argument appears to have been most justly fixed upon the politicians, as they are termed.

Str. And so our satyric drama has been played out; and the troop of Centaurs and Satyrs, however unwilling to leave the stage, have at last been separated from the political science.

Y. Soc. So I perceive.

Str. There remain, however, natures still more troublesome, because they are more nearly akin to the king, and more difficult to discern; the examination of them may be compared to the process of refining gold.

Y. Soc. What is your meaning?

Str. The workmen begin by sifting away the earth and stones and the like; there remain in a confused mass the valuable elements akin to gold, which can only be separated by fire—copper, silver, and other precious metals; these are at last refined away by the use of tests, until the gold is left quite pure.

Y. Soc. Yes, that is the way in which things are said to be done.

Str. In like manner, all alien and uncongenial matter has been separated from political science, and what is precious and of a kindred nature has been left; there remain the nobler arts of the general and the judge, and the higher sort of oratory which is an ally of the royal art, *[304]* and persuades men to do justice, and assists in guiding the helm of States:—How can we best clear away all these, leaving him whom we seek alone and unalloyed?

Y. Soc. That is obviously what has in some way to be attempted.

Str. If the attempt is all that is wanting, he shall certainly be brought to light; and I think that the illustration of music may assist in exhibiting him. Please to answer me a question.

Y. Soc. What question?

Str. There is such a thing as learning music or handicraft arts in general?

Y. Soc. There is.

Str. And is there any higher art or science, having power to decide which of these arts are and are not to be learned;—what do you say?

Y. Soc. I should answer that there is.

Str. And do we acknowledge this science to be different from the others?

Y. Soc. Yes.

Str. And ought the other sciences to be superior to this, or no single science to any other? Or ought this science to be the overseer and governor of all the others?

Y. Soc. The latter.

Str. You mean to say that the science which judges whether we ought to learn or not, must be superior to the science which is learned or which teaches?

Y. Soc. Far superior.

Str. And the science which determines whether we ought to persuade or not, must be superior to the science which is able to persuade?

Y. Soc. Of course.

Str. Very good; and to what science do we assign the power of persuading a multitude by a pleasing tale and not by teaching?

Y. Soc. That power, I think, must clearly be assigned to rhetoric.

Str. And to what science do we give the power of determining whether we are to employ persuasion or force towards any one, or to refrain altogether?

Y. Soc. To that science which governs the arts of speech and persuasion.

Str. Which, if I am not mistaken, will be politics?

Y. Soc. Very good.

Str. Rhetoric seems to be quickly distinguished from politics, being a different species, yet ministering to it.

Y. Soc. Yes.

Str. But what would you think of another sort of power or science?

Y. Soc. What science?

Str. The science which has to do with military operations against our enemies—is that to be regarded as a science or not?

Y. Soc. How can generalship and military tactics be regarded as other than a science?

Str. And is the art which is able and knows how to advise when we are to go to war, or to make peace, the same as this or different?

Y. Soc. If we are to be consistent, we must say different.

[305] *Str.* And we must also suppose that this rules the other, if we are not to give up our former notion?

Y. Soc. True.

Str. And, considering how great and terrible the whole art of war is, can we imagine any which is superior to it but the truly royal?

Y. Soc. No other.

Str. The art of the general is only ministerial, and therefore not political?

Y. Soc. Exactly.

Str. Once more let us consider the nature of the righteous judge.

Y. Soc. Very good.

Str. Does he do anything but decide the dealings of men with one another to be just or unjust in accordance with the standard which he receives from the king and legislator—showing his own peculiar virtue only in this, that he is not perverted by gifts, or fears, or pity, or by any sort of favour or enmity, into deciding the suits of men with one another contrary to the appointment of the legislator?

Y. Soc. No; his office is such as you describe.

Str. Then the inference is that the power of the judge is not royal, but only the power of a guardian of the law which ministers to the royal power?

Y. Soc. True.

Str. The review of all these sciences shows that none of them is political or royal. For the truly royal ought not itself to act, but to rule over those who are able to act; the king ought to know what is and what is not a fitting opportunity for taking the initiative in matters of the greatest importance, whilst others should execute his orders.

Y. Soc. True.

Str. And, therefore, the arts which we have described, as they have no authority over themselves or one another, but are each of them concerned with some special action of their own, have, as they ought to have, special names corresponding to their several actions.

Y. Soc. I agree.

Str. And the science which is over them all, and has charge of the laws, and of all matters affecting the State, and truly weaves them all into one, if we would describe under a name characteristic of their common nature, most truly we may call politics.

Y. Soc. Exactly so.

Str. Then, now that we have discovered the various classes in a State,[1] shall I analyse politics after the pattern which weaving supplied?

[306] *Y. Soc.* I greatly wish that you would.

Str. Then I must describe the nature of the royal web, and show how the various threads are woven into one piece.

Y. Soc. Clearly.

Str. A task has to be accomplished, which although difficult, appears to be necessary.

Y. Soc. Certainly the attempt must be made.

Str. To assume that one part of virtue differs in kind from another, is a position easily assailable by contentious disputants, who appeal to popular opinion.

Y. Soc. I do not understand.

Str. Let me put the matter in another way: I suppose that you would consider courage to be a part of virtue?

Y. Soc. Certainly I should.

Str. And you would think temperance to be different from courage; and likewise to be a part of virtue?

[1] Cf. 287-90, 303-5.

Y. Soc. True.

Str. I shall venture to put forward a strange theory about them.

Y. Soc. What is it?

Str. That they are two principles which thoroughly hate one another and are antagonistic throughout a great part of nature.

Y. Soc. How singular!

Str. Yes very—for all the parts of virtue are commonly said to be friendly to one another.

Y. Soc. Yes.

Str. Then let us carefully investigate whether this is universally true, or whether there are not parts of virtue which are at war with their kindred in some respect.

Y. Soc. Tell me how we shall consider that question.

Str. We must extend our enquiry to all those things which we consider beautiful and at the same time place in two opposite classes.

Y. Soc. Explain; what are they?

Str. Acuteness and quickness, whether in body or soul or in the movement of sound, and the imitations of them which painting and music supply, you must have praised yourself before now, or been present when others praised them.

Y. Soc. Certainly.

Str. And do you remember the terms in which they are praised?

Y. Soc. I do not.

Str. I wonder whether I can explain to you in words the thought which is passing in my mind.

Y. Soc. Why not?

Str. You fancy that this is all so easy: Well, let us consider these notions with reference to the opposite classes of action under which they fall. When we praise quickness and energy and acuteness, whether of mind or body or sound, we express our praise of the quality which we admire by one word, and that one word is manliness or courage.

Y. Soc. How?

Str. We speak of an action as energetic and brave, quick and manly, and vigorous too; and when we apply the name of which I speak as the common attribute of all these natures, we certainly praise them.

[307] Y. Soc. True.

Str. And do we not often praise the quiet strain of action also?

Y. Soc. To be sure.

Str. And do we not then say the opposite of what we said of the other?

Y. Soc. How do you mean?

Str. We exclaim How calm! How temperate! in admiration of the slow and quiet working of the intellect, and of steadiness and gentleness in action, of smoothness and depth of voice, and of all rhythmical movement and of music in general, when these have a proper solemnity. Of all such actions we predicate not courage, but a name indicative of order.

Y. Soc. Very true.

Str. But when, on the other hand, either of these is out of place, the names of either are changed into terms of censure.

Y. Soc. How so?

Str. Too great sharpness or quickness or hardness is termed violence or madness; too great slowness or gentleness is called cowardice or sluggishness; and we may observe, that for the most part these qualities, and the temperance and manliness of the opposite characters, are arrayed as enemies on opposite sides, and do not mingle with one another in their respective actions; and if we pursue the enquiry, we shall find that men who have these different qualities of mind differ from one another.

Y. Soc. In what respect?

Str. In respect of all the qualities which I mentioned, and very likely of many others. According to their respective affinities to either class of actions they distribute praise and blame —praise to the actions which are akin to their own, blame to those of the opposite party—and out of this many quarrels and occasions of quarrel arise among them.

Y. Soc. True.

Str. The difference between the two classes is often a trivial concern; but in a state, and when affecting really important matters, becomes of all disorders the most hateful.

Y. Soc. To what do you refer?

Str. To nothing short of the whole regulation of human life. For the orderly class are always ready to lead a peaceful life, quietly doing their own business; this is their manner of behaving with all men at home, and they are equally ready to find some way of keeping the peace with foreign States. And on account of this fondness of theirs for peace, which is often out of season where their influence prevails, they become by degrees unwarlike, and bring up their young men to be like themselves; they are at the mercy of their enemies; whence in a few years they and their children and the whole city often pass imperceptibly from the condition of freemen into that of slaves.

[308] Y. Soc. What a cruel fate!

Str. And now think of what happens with the more courageous natures. Are they not always inciting their country to go to war, owing to their excessive love of the military life? they raise up enemies against themselves many and mighty, and either utterly ruin their native-land or enslave and subject it to its foes?

Y. Soc. That, again, is true.

Str. Must we not admit, then, that where these two classes exist, they always feel the greatest antipathy and antagonism towards one another?

Y. Soc. We cannot deny it.

Str. And returning to the enquiry with which we began, have we not found that considerable portions of virtue are at variance with one another, and give rise to a similar opposition in the characters who are endowed with them?

Y. Soc. True.

Str. Let us consider a further point.

Y. Soc. What is it?

Str. I want to know, whether any constructive art will make any, even the most trivial thing, out of bad and good materials indifferently, if this can be helped? does not all art rather reject the bad as far as possible, and accept the good and fit materials, and from these elements, whether like or unlike, gathering them all into one, work out some nature or idea?

Y. Soc. To be sure.

Str. Then the true and natural art of statesmanship will never allow any State to be formed by a combination of good and bad men, if this can be avoided; but will begin by testing human natures in play, and after testing them, will entrust them to proper teachers who are the ministers of her purposes—she will herself give orders, and maintain authority; just as the art of weaving continually gives orders and maintains authority over the carders and all the others who prepare the material for the work, commanding the subsidiary arts to execute the works which she deems necessary for making the web.

Y. Soc. Quite true.

Str. In like manner, the royal science appears to me to be the mistress of all lawful educators and instructors, and having this queenly power, will not permit them to train men in what will produce characters unsuited to the political constitution which she desires to create, but only in what will produce such as are suitable. Those which have no share of manliness and temperance, or any other virtuous inclination, and, from the necessity of an evil nature, are vi-olently carried away to godlessness and insolence and injustice, she gets rid of by death and exile, and punishes them with the greatest of disgraces.

Y. Soc. That is commonly said.

[309] Str. But those who are wallowing in ignorance and baseness she bows under the yoke of slavery.

Y. Soc. Quite right.

Str. The rest of the citizens, out of whom, if they have education, something noble may be made, and who are capable of being united by the Statesman, the kingly art blends and weaves together; taking on the one hand those whose natures tend rather to courage, which is the stronger element and may be regarded as the warp, and on the other hand those which incline to order and gentleness, and which are represented in the figure as spun thick and soft, after the manner of the woof—these, which are naturally opposed, she seeks to bind and weave together in the following manner:

Y. Soc. In what manner?

Str. First of all, she takes the eternal element of the soul and binds it with a divine cord, to which it is akin, and then the animal nature, and binds that with human cords.

Y. Soc. I do not understand what you mean.

Str. The meaning is, that the opinion about the honourable and the just and good and their opposites, which is true and confirmed by reason, is a divine principle, and when implanted in the soul, is implanted, as I maintain, in a nature of heavenly birth.

Y. Soc. Yes; what else should it be?

Str. Only the Statesman and the good legislator, having the inspiration of the royal muse, can implant this opinion, and he, only in the rightly educated, whom we were just now describing.

Y. Soc. Likely enough.

Str. But him who cannot, we will not designate by any of the names which are the subject of the present enquiry.

Y. Soc. Very right.

Str. The courageous soul when attaining this truth becomes civilized, and rendered more capable of partaking of justice; but when not partaking, is inclined to brutality. Is not that true?

Y. Soc. Certainly.

Str. And again, the peaceful and orderly nature, if sharing in these opinions, becomes temperate and wise, as far as this may be in a State, but if not, deservedly obtains the ignominious name of silliness.

Y. Soc. Quite true.

Str. Can we say that such a connection as this will lastingly unite the evil with one another or with the good, or that any science would seriously think of using a bond of this kind to join such materials?

Y. Soc. Impossible.

[310] Str. But in those who were originally of a noble nature, and who have been nurtured in noble ways, and in those only, may we not say that union is implanted by law, and that this is the medicine which art prescribes for them, and of all the bonds which unite the dissimilar and contrary parts of virtue is not this, as I was saying, the divinest?

Y. Soc. Very true.

Str. Where this divine bond exists there is no difficulty in imagining, or when you have imagined, in creating the other bonds, which are human only.

Y. Soc. How is that, and what bonds do you mean?

Str. Rights of intermarriage, and ties which are formed between States by giving and taking children in marriage, or between individuals by private betrothals and espousals. For most persons form marriage connections without due regard to what is best for the procreation of children.

Y. Soc. In what way?

Str. They seek after wealth and power, which in matrimony are objects not worthy even of a serious censure.

Y. Soc. There is no need to consider them at all.

Str. More reason is there to consider the practice of those who make family their chief aim, and to indicate their error.

Y. Soc. Quite true.

Str. They act on no true principle at all; they seek their ease and receive with open arms those who are like themselves, and hate those who are unlike them, being too much influenced by feelings of dislike.

Y. Soc. How so?

Str. The quiet orderly class seek for natures like their own, and as far as they can they marry and give in marriage exclusively in this class, and the courageous do the same; they seek natures like their own, whereas they should both do precisely the opposite.

Y. Soc. How and why is that?

Str. Because courage, when untempered by the gentler nature during many generations, may at first bloom and strengthen, but at last bursts forth into downright madness.

Y. Soc. Like enough.

Str. And then, again, the soul which is overfull of modesty and has no element of courage in many successive generations, is apt to grow too indolent, and at last to become utterly paralyzed and useless.

Y. Soc. That, again, is quite likely.

Str. It was of these bonds I said that there would be no difficulty in creating them, if only both classes originally held the same opinion about the honourable and good;—indeed, in this single work, the whole process of royal weaving is comprised—never to allow temperate natures to be separated from the brave, but to weave them together, like the warp and the woof, by common sentiments and honours and reputation, *[311]* and by the giving of pledges to one another; and out of them forming one smooth and even web, to entrust to them the offices of State.

Y. Soc. How do you mean?

Str. Where one officer only is needed, you must choose a ruler who has both these qualities —when many, you must mingle some of each, for the temperate ruler is very careful and just and safe, but is wanting in thoroughness and go.

Y. Soc. Certainly, that is very true.

Str. The character of the courageous, on the other hand, falls short of the former in justice and caution, but has the power of action in a remarkable degree, and where either of these two qualities is wanting, there cities cannot altogether prosper either in their public or private life.

Y. Soc. Certainly they cannot.

Str. This then we declare to be the completion of the web of political action, which is created by a direct intertexture of the brave and temperate natures, whenever the royal science has drawn the two minds into communion with one another by unanimity and friendship, and having perfected the noblest and best of all the webs which political life admits, and enfolding therein all other inhabitants of cities, whether slaves or freemen, binds them in one fabric and governs and presides over them, and, in so far as to be happy is vouchsafed to a city, in no particular fails to secure their happiness.

Y. Soc. Your picture, Stranger, of the king and statesman, no less than of the Sophist, is quite perfect.

PHILEBUS

PERSONS OF THE DIALOGUE: SOCRATES; PROTARCHUS; PHILEBUS

~~~~~~~~~~~~~~~~~~~

[11] *Socrates*. OBSERVE, Protarchus, the nature of the position which you are now going to take from Philebus, and what the other position is which I maintain, and which, if you do not approve of it, is to be controverted by you. Shall you and I sum up the two sides?

Protarchus. By all means.

Soc. Philebus was saying that enjoyment and pleasure and delight, and the class of feelings akin to them, are a good to every living being, whereas I contend, that not these, but wisdom and intelligence and memory, and their kindred, right opinion and true reasoning, are better and more desirable than pleasure for all who are able to partake of them, and that to all such who are or ever will be they are the most advantageous of all things. Have I not given, Philebus, a fair statement of the two sides of the argument?

Philebus. Nothing could be fairer, Socrates.

Soc. And do you, Protarchus, accept the position which is assigned to you?

Pro. I cannot do otherwise, since our excellent Philebus has left the field.

Soc. Surely the truth about these matters ought, by all means, to be ascertained.

Pro. Certainly.

Soc. Shall we further agree—

Pro. To what?

Soc. That you and I must now try to indicate some state and disposition of the soul which has the property of making all men happy.

Pro. Yes, by all means.

Soc. And you say that pleasure, and I say that wisdom, is such a state?

Pro. True.

Soc. And what if there be a third state, which

is better than either? Then both of us are vanquished—are we not? But if this life, which really has the power of making men happy, turn out to be more akin to pleasure than to wisdom, the life of pleasure may still have the advantage over the life of wisdom. [12]

Pro. True.

Soc. Or suppose that the better life is more nearly allied to wisdom, then wisdom conquers, and pleasure is defeated;—do you agree?

Pro. Certainly.

Soc. And what do you say, Philebus?

Phi. I say, and shall always say, that pleasure is easily the conqueror; but you must decide for yourself, Protarchus.

Pro. You, Philebus, have handed over the argument to me, and have no longer a voice in the matter?

Phi. True enough. Nevertheless I would clear myself and deliver my soul of you; and I call the goddess herself to witness that I now do so.

Pro. You may appeal to us; we too will be the witnesses of your words. And now, Socrates, whether Philebus is pleased or displeased, we will proceed with the argument.

Soc. Then let us begin with the goddess herself, of whom Philebus says that she is called Aphrodite, but that her real name is Pleasure.

Pro. Very good.

Soc. The awe which I always feel, Protarchus, about the names of the gods is more than human—it exceeds all other fears. And now I would not sin against Aphrodite by naming her amiss; let her be called what she pleases. But Pleasure I know to be manifold, and with her, as I was just now saying, we must begin,

609

and consider what her nature is. She has one name, and therefore you would imagine that she is one; and yet surely she takes the most varied and even unlike forms. For do we not say that the intemperate has pleasure, and that the temperate has pleasure in his very temperance—that the fool is pleased when he is full of foolish fancies and hopes, and that the wise man has pleasure in his wisdom? and how foolish would any one be who affirmed that all these opposite pleasures are severally alike!

Pro. Why, Socrates, they are opposed in so far as they spring from opposite sources, but they are not in themselves opposite. For must not pleasure be of all things most absolutely like pleasure—that is, like himself?

Soc. Yes, my good friend, just as colour is like colour;—in so far as colours are colours, there is no difference between them; and yet we all know that black is not only unlike, but even absolutely opposed to white: or again, as figure is like figure, for all figures are comprehended under one class; and yet particular figures may be absolutely opposed to one another, *[13]* and there is an infinite diversity of them. And we might find similar examples in many other things; therefore do not rely upon this argument, which would go to prove the unity of the most extreme opposites. And I suspect that we shall find a similar opposition among pleasures.

Pro. Very likely; but how will this invalidate the argument?

Soc. Why, I shall reply, that dissimilar as they are, you apply to them a new predicate, for you say that all pleasant things are good; now although no one can argue that pleasure is not pleasure, he may argue, as we are doing, that pleasures are oftener bad than good; but you call them all good, and at the same time are compelled, if you are pressed, to acknowledge that they are unlike. And so you must tell us what is the identical quality existing alike in good and bad pleasures, which makes you designate all of them as good.

Pro. What do you mean, Socrates? Do you think that any one who asserts pleasure to be the good, will tolerate the notion that some pleasures are good and others bad?

Soc. And yet you will acknowledge that they are different from one another, and sometimes opposed?

Pro. Not in so far as they are pleasures.

Soc. That is a return to the old position, Protarchus, and so we are to say (are we?) that there is no difference in pleasures, but that they are all alike; and the examples which have just been cited do not pierce our dull minds, but we go on arguing all the same, like the weakest and most inexperienced reasoners?

Pro. What do you mean?

Soc. Why, I mean to say, that in self-defence I may, if I like, follow your example, and assert boldly that the two things most unlike are most absolutely alike; and the result will be that you and I will prove ourselves to be very tyros in the art of disputing; and the argument will be blown away and lost. Suppose that we put back, and return to the old position; then perhaps we may come to an understanding with one another.

Pro. How do you mean?

Soc. Shall I, Protarchus, have my own question asked of me by you?

Pro. What question?

Soc. Ask me whether wisdom and science and mind, and those other qualities which I, when asked by you at first what is the nature of the good, affirmed to be good, are not in the same case with the pleasures of which you spoke.

Pro. What do you mean?

Soc. The sciences are a numerous class, and will be found to present great differences. But even admitting that, like the pleasures, they are opposite as well as different, *[14]* should I be worthy of the name of dialectician if, in order to avoid this difficulty, I were to say (as you are saying of pleasure) that there is no difference between one science and another;—would not the argument founder and disappear like an idle tale, although we might ourselves escape drowning by clinging to a fallacy?

Pro. May none of this befall us, except the deliverance! Yet I like the even-handed justice which is applied to both our arguments. Let us assume, then, that there are many and diverse pleasures, and many and different sciences.

Soc. And let us have no concealment, Protarchus, of the differences between my good and yours; but let us bring them to the light in the hope that, in the process of testing them, they may show whether pleasure is to be called the good, or wisdom, or some third quality; for surely we are not now simply contending in order that my view or that yours may prevail, but I presume that we ought both of us to be fighting for the truth.

Pro. Certainly we ought.

Soc. Then let us have a more definite understanding and establish the principle on which the argument rests.

Pro. What principle?

Soc. A principle about which all men are always in a difficulty, and some men sometimes against their will.

Pro. Speak plainer.

Soc. The principle which has just turned up, which is a marvel of nature; for that one should be many or many one, are wonderful propositions; and he who affirms either is very open to attack.

Pro. Do you mean, when a person says that I, Protarchus, am by nature one and also many, dividing the single "me" into many "me's," and even opposing them as great and small, light and heavy, and in ten thousand other ways?

Soc. Those, Protarchus, are the common and acknowledged paradoxes about the one and many, which I may say that everybody has by this time agreed to dismiss as childish and obvious and detrimental to the true course of thought; and no more favour is shown to that other puzzle, in which a person proves the members and parts of anything to be divided, and then confessing that they are all one, says laughingly in disproof of his own words: Why, here is a miracle, the one is many and infinite, and the many are only one.

Pro. But what, Socrates, are those other marvels connected with this subject which, as you imply, have not yet become common and acknowledged? [15]

Soc. When, my boy, the one does not belong to the class of things that are born and perish, as in the instances which we were giving, for in those cases, and when unity is of this concrete nature, there is, as I was saying, a universal consent that no refutation is needed; but when the assertion is made that man is one, or ox is one, or beauty one, or the good one, then the interest which attaches to these and similar unities and the attempt which is made to divide them gives birth to a controversy.

Pro. Of what nature?

Soc. In the first place, as to whether these unities have a real existence; and then how each individual unity, being always the same, and incapable either of generation or of destruction, but retaining a permanent individuality, can be conceived either as dispersed and multiplied in the infinity of the world of generation, or as still entire and yet divided from itself, which latter would seem to be the greatest impossibility of all, for how can one and the same thing be at the same time in one and in many things? These, Protarchus, are the real difficulties, and this is the one and many to which

they relate; they are the source of great perplexity if ill decided, and the right determination of them is very helpful.

Pro. Then, Socrates, let us begin by clearing up these questions.

Soc. That is what I should wish.

Pro. And I am sure that all my other friends will be glad to hear them discussed; Philebus, fortunately for us, is not disposed to move, and we had better not stir him up with questions.

Soc. Good; and where shall we begin this great and multifarious battle, in which such various points are at issue? Shall we begin thus?

Pro. How?

Soc. We say that the one and many become identified by thought, and that now, as in time past, they run about together, in and out of every word which is uttered, and that this union of them will never cease, and is not now beginning, but is, as I believe, an everlasting quality of thought itself, which never grows old. Any young man, when he first tastes these subtleties, is delighted, and fancies that he has found a treasure of wisdom; in the first enthusiasm of his joy he leaves no stone, or rather no thought unturned, now rolling up the many into the one, and kneading them together, now unfolding and dividing them; he puzzles himself first and above all, and then he proceeds to puzzle his neighbours, whether they are older or younger, [16] or of his own age—that makes no difference; neither father nor mother does he spare; no human being who has ears is safe from him, hardly even his dog, and a barbarian would have no chance of escaping him, if an interpreter could only be found.

Pro. Considering, Socrates, how many we are, and that all of us are young men, is there not a danger that we and Philebus may all set upon you, if you abuse us? We understand what you mean; but is there no charm by which we may dispel all this confusion, no more excellent way of arriving at the truth? If there is, we hope that you will guide us into that way, and we will do our best to follow, for the enquiry in which we are engaged, Socrates, is not unimportant.

Soc. The reverse of unimportant, my boys, as Philebus calls you, and there neither is nor ever will be a better than my own favourite way, which has nevertheless already often deserted me and left me helpless in the hour of need.

Pro. Tell us what that is.

Soc. One which may be easily pointed out, but is by no means easy of application; it is the parent of all the discoveries in the arts.

Pro. Tell us what it is.

Soc. A gift of heaven, which, as I conceive, the gods tossed among men by the hands of a new Prometheus, and therewith a blaze of light; and the ancients, who were our betters and nearer the gods than we are, handed down the tradition, that whatever things are said to be are composed of one and many, and have the finite and infinite implanted in them: seeing, then, that such is the order of the world, we too ought in every enquiry to begin by laying down one idea of that which is the subject of enquiry; this unity we shall find in everything. Having found it, we may next proceed to look for two, if there be two, or, if not, then for three or some other number, subdividing each of these units, until at last the unity with which we began is seen not only to be one and many and infinite, but also a definite number; the infinite must not be suffered to approach the many until the entire number of the species intermediate between unity and infinity has been discovered—then, and not till then, we may rest from division, and without further troubling ourselves about the endless individuals may allow them to drop into infinity. This, as I was saying, is the way of considering and learning and teaching one another, which the gods have handed down to us. [17] But the wise men of our time are either too quick or too slow in conceiving plurality in unity. Having no method, they make their one and many anyhow, and from unity pass at once to infinity; the intermediate steps never occur to them. And this, I repeat, is what makes the difference between the mere art of disputation and true dialectic.

Pro. I think that I partly understand you, Socrates, but I should like to have a clearer notion of what you are saying.

Soc. I may illustrate my meaning by the letters of the alphabet, Protarchus, which you were made to learn as a child.

Pro. How do they afford an illustration?

Soc. The sound which passes through the lips whether of an individual or of all men is one and yet infinite.

Pro. Very true.

Soc. And yet not by knowing either that sound is one or that sound is infinite are we perfect in the art of speech, but the knowledge of the number and nature of sounds is what makes a man a grammarian.

Pro. Very true.

Soc. And the knowledge which makes a man a musician is of the same kind.

Pro. How so?

Soc. Sound is one in music as well as in grammar?

Pro. Certainly.

Soc. And there is a higher note and a lower note, and a note of equal pitch:—may we affirm so much?

Pro. Yes.

Soc. But you would not be a real musician if this was all that you knew; though if you did not know this you would know almost nothing of music.

Pro. Nothing.

Soc. But when you have learned what sounds are high and what low, and the number and nature of the intervals and their limits or proportions, and the systems compounded out of them, which our fathers discovered, and have handed down to us who are their descendants under the name of harmonies; and the affections corresponding to them in the movements of the human body, which when measured by numbers ought, as they say, to be called rhythms and measures; and they tell us that the same principle should be applied to every one and many;—when, I say, you have learned all this, then, my dear friend, you are perfect; and you may be said to understand any other subject, when you have a similar grasp of it. But the infinity of kinds and the infinity of individuals which there is in each of them, when not classified, creates in every one of us a state of infinite ignorance; and he who never looks for number in anything, will not himself be looked for in the number of famous men.

[18] *Pro.* I think that what Socrates is now saying is excellent, Philebus.

Phi. I think so too, but how do his words bear upon us and upon the argument?

Soc. Philebus is right in asking that question of us, Protarchus.

Pro. Indeed he is, and you must answer him.

Soc. I will; but you must let me make one little remark first about these matters; I was saying, that he who begins with any individual unity, should proceed from that, not to infinity, but to a definite number, and now I say conversely, that he who has to begin with infinity should not jump to unity, but he should look about for some number representing a certain quantity, and thus out of all end in one. And now let us return for an illustration of our principle to the case of letters.

Pro. What do you mean?

Soc. Some god or divine man, who in the

Egyptian legend is said to have been Theuth, observing that the human voice was infinite, first distinguished in this infinity a certain number of vowels, and then other letters which had sound, but were not pure vowels (i.e., the semivowels); these too exist in a definite number; and lastly, he distinguished a third class of letters which we now call mutes, without voice and without sound, and divided these, and likewise the two other classes of vowels and semivowels, into the individual sounds, and told the number of them, and gave to each and all of them the name of letters; and observing that none of us could learn any one of them and not learn them all, and in consideration of this common bond which in a manner united them, he assigned to them all a single art, and this he called the art of grammar or letters.

Phi. The illustration, Protarchus, has assisted me in understanding the original statement, but I still feel the defect of which I just now complained.

Soc. Are you going to ask, Philebus, what this has to do with the argument?

Phi. Yes, that is a question which Protarchus and I have been long asking.

Soc. Assuredly you have already arrived at the answer to the question which, as you say, you have been so long asking?

Phi. How so?

Soc. Did we not begin by enquiring into the comparative eligibility of pleasure and wisdom?

Phi. Certainly.

Soc. And we maintain that they are each of them one?

Phi. True.

Soc. And the precise question to which the previous discussion desires an answer is, how they are one and also many [i.e., how they have one genus and many species], and are not at once infinite, and what number of species is to be assigned to either of them before they pass into infinity.

[19] *Pro.* That is a very serious question, Philebus, to which Socrates has ingeniously brought us round, and please to consider which of us shall answer him; there may be something ridiculous in my being unable to answer, and therefore imposing the task upon you, when I have undertaken the whole charge of the argument, but if neither of us were able to answer, the result methinks would be still more ridiculous. Let us consider, then, what we are to do:—Socrates, if I understood him rightly, is asking whether there are not kinds of pleasure, and what is the number and nature

of them, and the same of wisdom.

Soc. Most true, O son of Callias; and the previous argument showed that if we are not able to tell the kinds of everything that has unity, likeness, sameness, or their opposites, none of us will be of the smallest use in any enquiry.

Pro. That seems to be very near the truth, Socrates. Happy would the wise man be if he knew all things, and the next best thing for him is that he should know himself. Why do I say so at this moment? I will tell you. You, Socrates, have granted us this opportunity of conversing with you, and are ready to assist us in determining what is the best of human goods. For when Philebus said that pleasure and delight and enjoyment and the like were the chief good, you answered—No, not those, but another class of goods; and we are constantly reminding ourselves of what you said, and very properly, in order that we may not forget to examine and compare the two. And these goods, which in your opinion are to be designated as superior to pleasure, and are the true objects of pursuit, are mind and knowledge and understanding and art, and the like. There was a dispute about which were the best, and we playfully threatened that you should not be allowed to go home until the question was settled; and you agreed, and placed yourself at our disposal. And now, as children say, what has been fairly given cannot be taken back; cease then to fight against us in this way.

Soc. In what way?

[20] *Phi.* Do not perplex us, and keep asking questions of us to which we have not as yet any sufficient answer to give; let us not imagine that a general puzzling of us all is to be the end of our discussion, but if we are unable to answer, do you answer, as you have promised. Consider, then, whether you will divide pleasure and knowledge according to their kinds; or you may let the matter drop, if you are able and willing to find some other mode of clearing up our controversy.

Soc. If you say that, I have nothing to apprehend, for the words "if you are willing" dispel all my fear; and, moreover, a god seems to have recalled something to my mind.

Phi. What is that?

Soc. I remember to have heard long ago certain discussions about pleasure and wisdom, whether awake or in a dream I cannot tell; they were to the effect that neither the one nor the other of them was the good, but some third thing, which was different from them, and better than either. If this be clearly established, then pleasure will lose the victory, for the good will cease to be identified with her:—Am I not right?

Pro. Yes.

Soc. And there will cease to be any need of distinguishing the kinds of pleasures, as I am inclined to think, but this will appear more clearly as we proceed.

Pro. Capital, Socrates; pray go on as you propose.

Soc. But, let us first agree on some little points.

Pro. What are they?

Soc. Is the good perfect or imperfect?

Pro. The most perfect, Socrates, of all things.

Soc. And is the good sufficient?

Pro. Yes, certainly, and in a degree surpassing all other things.

Soc. And no one can deny that all percipient beings desire and hunt after good, and are eager to catch and have the good about them, and care not for the attainment of anything which is not accompanied by good.

Pro. That is undeniable.

Soc. Now let us part off the life of pleasure from the life of wisdom, and pass them in review.

Pro. How do you mean?

Soc. Let there be no wisdom in the life of pleasure, nor any pleasure in the life of wisdom, for if either of them is the chief good, it cannot be supposed to want anything, but if either is shown to want anything, then it cannot really be the chief good.

[21] Pro. Impossible.

Soc. And will you help us to test these two lives?

Pro. Certainly.

Soc. Then answer.

Pro. Ask.

Soc. Would you choose, Protarchus, to live all your life long in the enjoyment of the greatest pleasures?

Pro. Certainly I should.

Soc. Would you consider that there was still anything wanting to you if you had perfect pleasure?

Pro. Certainly not.

Soc. Reflect; would you not want wisdom and intelligence and forethought, and similar qualities? would you not at any rate want sight?

Pro. Why should I? Having pleasure I should have all things.

Soc. Living thus, you would always throughout your life enjoy the greatest pleasures?

Pro. I should.

Soc. But if you had neither mind, nor memory, nor knowledge, nor true opinion, you would in the first place be utterly ignorant of whether you were pleased or not, because you would be entirely devoid of intelligence.

Pro. Certainly.

Soc. And similarly, if you had no memory you would not recollect that you had ever been pleased, nor would the slightest recollection of the pleasure which you feel at any moment remain with you; and if you had no true opinion you would not think that you were pleased when you were; and if you had no power of calculation you would not be able to calculate on future pleasure, and your life would be the life, not of a man, but of an oyster or *pulmo marinus*. Could this be otherwise?

Pro. No.

Soc. But is such a life eligible?

Pro. I cannot answer you, Socrates; the argument has taken away from me the power of speech.

Soc. We must keep up our spirits;—let us now take the life of mind and examine it in turn.

Pro. And what is this life of mind?

Soc. I want to know whether any one of us would consent to live, having wisdom and mind and knowledge and memory of all things, but having no sense of pleasure or pain, and wholly unaffected by these and the like feelings?

Pro. Neither life, Socrates, appears eligible to me, or is likely, as I should imagine, to be chosen by any one else.

[22] Soc. What would you say, Protarchus, to both of these in one, or to one that was made out of the union of the two?

Pro. Out of the union, that is, of pleasure with mind and wisdom?

Soc. Yes, that is the life which I mean.

Pro. There can be no difference of opinion; not some but all would surely choose this third rather than either of the other two, and in addition to them.

Soc. But do you see the consequence?

Pro. To be sure I do. The consequence is, that two out of the three lives which have been proposed are neither sufficient nor eligible for man or for animal.

Soc. Then now there can be no doubt that neither of them has the good, for the one which had would certainly have been sufficient and perfect and eligible for every living creature or thing that was able to live such a life; and if any of us had chosen any other, he would have chosen contrary to the nature of the truly eligible, and not of his own free will, but either through ignorance or from some unhappy necessity.

Pro. Certainly that seems to be true.

Soc. And now have I not sufficiently shown that Philebus' goddess is not to be regarded as identical with the good?

Phi. Neither is your "mind" the good, Socrates, for that will be open to the same objections.

Soc. Perhaps, Philebus, you may be right in saying so of my "mind"; but of the true, which is also the divine mind, far otherwise. However, I will not at present claim the first place for mind as against the mixed life; but we must come to some understanding about the second place. For you might affirm pleasure and I mind to be the cause of the mixed life; and in that case although neither of them would be the good, one of them might be imagined to be the cause of the good. And I might proceed further to argue in opposition to Philebus, that the element which makes this mixed life eligible and good, is more akin and more similar to mind than to pleasure. And if this is true, pleasure cannot be truly said to share either in the first or second place, and does not, if I may trust my own mind, attain even to the third.

Pro. Truly, Socrates, pleasure appears to me to have had a fall; in fighting for the palm, *[23]* she has been smitten by the argument, and is laid low. I must say that mind would have fallen too, and may therefore be thought to show discretion in not putting forward a similar claim. And if pleasure were deprived not only of the first but of the second place, she would be terribly damaged in the eyes of her admirers, for not even to them would she still appear as fair as before.

Soc. Well, but had we not better leave her now, and not pain her by applying the crucial test, and finally detecting her?

Pro. Nonsense, Socrates.

Soc. Why? because I said that we had better not pain pleasure, which is an impossibility?

Pro. Yes, and more than that, because you do not seem to be aware that none of us will let you go home until you have finished the argument.

Soc. Heavens! Protarchus, that will be a tedious business, and just at present not at all an easy one. For in going to war in the cause of mind, who is aspiring to the second prize, I ought to have weapons of another make from those which I used before; some, however, of

the old ones may do again. And must I then finish the argument?

Pro. Of course you must.

Soc. Let us be very careful in laying the foundation.

Pro. What do you mean?

Soc. Let us divide all existing things into two, or rather, if you do not object, into three classes.

Pro. Upon what principle would you make the division?

Soc. Let us take some of our newly-found notions.

Pro. Which of them?

Soc. Were we not saying that God revealed a finite element of existence, and also an infinite?

Pro. Certainly.

Soc. Let us assume these two principles, and also a third, which is compounded out of them; but I fear that I am ridiculously clumsy at these processes of division and enumeration.

Pro. What do you mean, my good friend?

Soc. I say that a fourth class is still wanted.

Pro. What will that be?

Soc. Find the cause of the third or compound, and add this as a fourth class to the three others.

Pro. And would you like to have a fifth class or cause of resolution as well as a cause of composition?

Soc. Not, I think, at present; but if I want a fifth at some future time you shall allow me to have it.

Pro. Certainly.

Soc. Let us begin with the first three; and as we find two out of the three greatly divided and dispersed, let us endeavour to reunite them, and see how in each of them there is a one and many.

[24] Pro. If you would explain to me a little more about them, perhaps I might be able to follow you.

Soc. Well, the two classes are the same which I mentioned before, one the finite, and the other the infinite; I will first show that the infinite is in a certain sense many, and the finite may be hereafter discussed.

Pro. I agree.

Soc. And now consider well; for the question to which I invite your attention is difficult and controverted. When you speak of hotter and colder, can you conceive any limit in those qualities? Does not the more and less, which dwells in their very nature, prevent their having any end? for if they had an end, the more and less would themselves have an end.

Pro. That is most true.

Soc. Ever, as we say, into the hotter and the colder there enters a more and a less.

Pro. Yes.

Soc. Then, says the argument, there is never any end of them, and being endless they must also be infinite.

Pro. Yes, Socrates, that is exceedingly true.

Soc. Yes, my dear Protarchus, and your answer reminds me that such an expression as "exceedingly," which you have just uttered, and also the term "gently," have the same significance as more or less; for whenever they occur they do not allow of the existence of quantity —they are always introducing degrees into actions, instituting a comparison of a more or a less excessive or a more or a less gentle, and at each creation of more or less, quantity disappears. For, as I was just now saying, if quantity and measure did not disappear, but were allowed to intrude in the sphere of more and less and the other comparatives, these last would be driven out of their own domain. When definite quantity is once admitted, there can be no longer a "hotter" or a "colder" (for these are always progressing, and are never in one stay); but definite quantity is at rest, and has ceased to progress. Which proves that comparatives, such as the hotter and the colder, are to be ranked in the class of the infinite.

Pro. Your remark certainly has the look of truth, Socrates; but these subjects, as you were saying, are difficult to follow at first. I think, however, that if I could hear the argument repeated by you once or twice, there would be a substantial agreement between us.

Soc. Yes, and I will try to meet your wish; but, as I would rather not waste time in the enumeration of endless particulars, let me know whether I may not assume as a note of the infinite—

[25] *Pro.* What?

Soc. I want to know whether such things as appear to us to admit of more or less, or are denoted by the words "exceedingly," "gently," "extremely," and the like, may not be referred to the class of the infinite, which is their unity, for, as was asserted in the previous argument, all things that were divided and dispersed should be brought together, and have the mark or seal of some one nature, if possible, set upon them—do you remember?

Pro. Yes.

Soc. And all things which do not admit of more or less, but admit their opposites, that is to say, first of all, equality, and the equal, or

again, the double, or any other ratio of number and measure—all these may, I think, be rightly reckoned by us in the class of the limited or finite; what do you say?

Pro. Excellent, Socrates.

Soc. And now what nature shall we ascribe to the third or compound kind?

Pro. You, I think, will have to tell me that.

Soc. Rather God will tell you, if there be any God who will listen to my prayers.

Pro. Offer up a prayer, then, and think.

Soc. I am thinking, Protarchus, and I believe that some God has befriended us.

Pro. What do you mean, and what proof have you to offer of what you are saying?

Soc. I will tell you, and do you listen to my words.

Pro. Proceed.

Soc. Were we not speaking just now of hotter and colder?

Pro. True.

Soc. Add to them drier, wetter, more, less, swifter, slower, greater, smaller, and all that in the preceding argument we placed under the unity of more and less.

Pro. In the class of the infinite, you mean?

Soc. Yes; and now mingle this with the other.

Pro. What is the other?

Soc. The class of the finite which we ought to have brought together as we did the infinite; but, perhaps, it will come to the same thing if we do so now;—when the two are combined, a third will appear.

Pro. What do you mean by the class of the finite?

Soc. The class of the equal and the double, and any class which puts an end to difference and opposition, and by introducing number creates harmony and proportion among the different elements.

Pro. I understand; you seem to me to mean that the various opposites, when you mingle with them the class of the finite, takes certain forms.

Soc. Yes, that is my meaning.

Pro. Proceed.

Soc. Does not the right participation in the finite give health—in disease, for instance?

Pro. Certainly.

[26] *Soc.* And whereas the high and low, the swift and the slow are infinite or unlimited, does not the addition of the principles aforesaid introduce a limit, and perfect the whole frame of music?

Pro. Yes, certainly.

Soc. Or, again, when cold and heat prevail, does not the introduction of them take away excess and indefiniteness, and infuse moderation and harmony?

Pro. Certainly.

Soc. And from a like admixture of the finite and infinite come the seasons, and all the delights of life?

Pro. Most true.

Soc. I omit ten thousand other things, such as beauty and health and strength, and the many beauties and high perfections of the soul: O my beautiful Philebus, the goddess, methinks, seeing the universal wantonness and wickedness of all things, and that there was in them no limit to pleasures and self-indulgence, devised the limit of law and order, whereby, as you say, Philebus, she torments, or as I maintain, delivers the soul—What think you, Protarchus?

Pro. Her ways are much to my mind, Socrates.

Soc. You will observe that I have spoken of three classes?

Pro. Yes, I think that I understand you: you mean to say that the infinite is one class, and that the finite is a second class of existences; but what you would make the third I am not so certain.

Soc. That is because the amazing variety of the third class is too much for you, my dear friend; but there was not this difficulty with the infinite, which also comprehended many classes, for all of them were sealed with the note of more and less, and therefore appeared one.

Pro. True.

Soc. And the finite or limit had not many divisions, and we readily acknowledged it to be by nature one?

Pro. Yes.

Soc. Yes, indeed; and when I speak of the third class, understand me to mean any offspring of these, being a birth into true being, effected by the measure which the limit introduces.

Pro. I understand.

Soc. Still there was, as we said, a fourth class to be investigated, and you must assist in the investigation; for does not everything which comes into being, of necessity come into being through a cause?

Pro. Yes, certainly; for how can there be anything which has no cause?

Soc. And is not the agent the same as the cause in all except name; the agent and the cause may be rightly called one?

[27] Pro. Very true.

Soc. And the same may be said of the patient, or effect; we shall find that they too differ, as I was saying, only in name—shall we not?

Pro. We shall.

Soc. The agent or cause always naturally leads, and the patient or effect naturally follows it?

Pro. Certainly.

Soc. Then the cause and what is subordinate to it in generation are not the same, but different?

Pro. True.

Soc. Did not the things which were generated, and the things out of which they were generated, furnish all the three classes?

Pro. Yes.

Soc. And the creator or cause of them has been satisfactorily proven to be distinct from them—and may therefore be called a fourth principle?

Pro. So let us call it.

Soc. Quite right; but now, having distinguished the four, I think that we had better refresh our memories by recapitulating each of them in order.

Pro. By all means.

Soc. Then the first I will call the infinite or unlimited, and the second the finite or limited; then follows the third, an essence compound and generated; and I do not think that I shall be far wrong in speaking of the cause of mixture and generation as the fourth.

Pro. Certainly not.

Soc. And now what is the next question, and how came we hither? Were we not enquiring whether the second place belonged to pleasure or wisdom?

Pro. We were.

Soc. And now, having determined these points, shall we not be better able to decide about the first and second place, which was the original subject of dispute?

Pro. I dare say.

Soc. We said, if you remember, that the mixed life of pleasure and wisdom was the conqueror—did we not?

Pro. True.

Soc. And we see what is the place and nature of this life and to what class it is to be assigned?

Pro. Beyond a doubt.

Soc. This is evidently comprehended in the third or mixed class; which is not composed of any two particular ingredients, but of all the elements of infinity, bound down by the finite, and may therefore be truly said to comprehend the conqueror life.

Pro. Most true.

Soc. And what shall we say, Philebus, of your life which is all sweetness; and in which of the aforesaid classes is that to be placed? Perhaps you will allow me to ask you a question before you answer?

Phi. Let me hear.

Soc. Have pleasure and pain a limit, or do they belong to the class which admits of more and less?

Phi. They belong to the class which admits of more, Socrates; for pleasure would not be perfectly good if she were not infinite in quantity and degree.

[28] Soc. Nor would pain, Philebus, be perfectly evil. And therefore the infinite cannot be that element which imparts to pleasure some degree of good. But now—admitting, if you like, that pleasure is of the nature of the infinite —in which of the aforesaid classes, O Protarchus and Philebus, can we without irreverence place wisdom and knowledge and mind? And let us be careful, for I think that the danger will be very serious if we err on this point.

Phi. You magnify, Socrates, the importance of your favourite god.

Soc. And you, my friend, are also magnifying your favourite goddess; but still I must beg you to answer the question.

Pro. Socrates is quite right, Philebus, and we must submit to him.

Phi. And did not you, Protarchus, propose to answer in my place?

Pro. Certainly I did; but I am now in a great strait, and I must entreat you, Socrates, to be our spokesman, and then we shall not say anything wrong or disrespectful of your favourite.

Soc. I must obey you, Protarchus; nor is the task which you impose a difficult one; but did I really, as Philebus implies, disconcert you with my playful solemnity, when I asked the question to what class mind and knowledge belong?

Pro. You did, indeed, Socrates.

Soc. Yet the answer is easy, since all philosophers assert with one voice that mind is the king of heaven and earth—in reality they are magnifying themselves. And perhaps they are right. But still I should like to consider the class of mind, if you do not object, a little more fully.

Phi. Take your own course, Socrates, and never mind length; we shall not tire of you.

Soc. Very good; let us begin then, Protarchus, by asking a question.

Pro. What question?

Soc. Whether all this which they call the universe is left to the guidance of unreason and chance medley, or, on the contrary, as our fathers have declared, ordered and governed by a marvellous intelligence and wisdom.

Pro. Wide asunder are the two assertions, illustrious Socrates, for that which you were just now saying to me appears to be blasphemy; but the other assertion, that mind orders all things, is worthy of the aspect of the world, and of the sun, and of the moon, and of the stars and of the whole circle of the heavens; and never will I say or think otherwise.

Soc. Shall we then agree with them of old time in maintaining[1] this doctrine—not merely reasserting the notions of others, without risk to ourselves, *[29]*—but shall we share in the danger, and take our part of the reproach which will await us, when an ingenious individual declares that all is disorder?

Pro. That would certainly be my wish.

Soc. Then now please to consider the next stage of the argument.

Pro. Let me hear.

Soc. We see that the elements which enter into the nature of the bodies of all animals, fire, water, air, and, as the storm-tossed sailor cries, "land" [i. e., earth], reappear in the constitution of the world.

Pro. The proverb may be applied to us; for truly the storm gathers over us, and we are at our wit's end.

Soc. There is something to be remarked about each of these elements.

Pro. What is it?

Soc. Only a small fraction of any one of them exists in us, and that of a mean sort, and not in any way pure, or having any power worthy of its nature. One instance will prove this of all of them; there is fire within us, and in the universe.

Pro. True.

Soc. And is not our fire small and weak and mean? But the fire in the universe is wonderful in quantity and beauty, and in every power that fire has.

Pro. Most true.

Soc. And is the fire in the universe nourished and generated and ruled by the fire in us, or is the fire in you and me, and in other animals, dependent on the universal fire?

Pro. That is a question which does not deserve an answer.

Soc. Right; and you would say the same, if
_____
[1] Cf. 28, 30.

I am not mistaken, of the earth which is in animals and the earth which is in the universe, and you would give a similar reply about all the other elements?

Pro. Why, how could any man who gave any other be deemed in his senses?

Soc. I do not think that he could—but now go on to the next step. When we saw those elements of which we have been speaking gathered up in one, did we not call them a body?

Pro. We did.

Soc. And the same may be said of the cosmos, which for the same reason may be considered to be a body, because made up of the same elements.

Pro. Very true.

Soc. But is our body nourished wholly by this body, or is this body nourished by our body, thence deriving and having the qualities of which we were just now speaking?

Pro. That again, Socrates, is a question which does not deserve to be asked.

[30] Soc. Well, tell me, is this question worth asking?

Pro. What question?

Soc. May our body be said to have a soul?

Pro. Clearly.

Soc. And whence comes that soul, my dear Protarchus, unless the body of the universe, which contains elements like those in our bodies but in every way fairer, had also a soul? Can there be another source?

Pro. Clearly, Socrates, that is the only source.

Soc. Why, yes, Protarchus; for surely we cannot imagine that of the four classes, the finite, the infinite, the composition of the two, and the cause, the fourth, which enters into all things, giving to our bodies souls, and the art of self-management, and of healing disease, and operating in other ways to heal and organize, having too all the attributes of wisdom;—we cannot, I say, imagine that whereas the self-same elements exist, both in the entire heaven and in great provinces of the heaven, only fairer and purer, this last should not also in that higher sphere have designed the noblest and fairest things?

Pro. Such a supposition is quite unreasonable.

Soc. Then if this be denied, should we not be wise in adopting the other view and maintaining that there is in the universe a mighty infinite and an adequate limit, of which we have often spoken, as well as a presiding cause of no mean power, which orders and arranges years and seasons and months, and may be justly called wisdom and mind?

Pro. Most justly.

Soc. And wisdom and mind cannot exist without soul?

Pro. Certainly not.

Soc. And in the divine nature of Zeus would you not say that there is the soul and mind of a king, because there is in him the power of the cause? And other gods have other attributes, by which they are pleased to be called.

Pro. Very true.

Soc. Do not then suppose that these words are rashly spoken by us, O Protarchus, for they are in harmony with the testimony of those who said of old time that mind rules the universe.

Pro. True.

Soc. And they furnish an answer to my enquiry (cf. 28); for they imply that mind is the parent of that class of the four which we called the cause of all; and I think that you now have my answer.

Pro. I have indeed, and yet I did not observe that you had answered.

Soc. A jest is sometimes refreshing, Protarchus, when it interrupts earnest.

[31] Pro. Very true.

Soc. I think, friend, that we have now pretty clearly set forth the class to which mind belongs and what is the power of mind.

Pro. True.

Soc. And the class to which pleasure belongs has also been long ago discovered?

Pro. Yes.

Soc. And let us remember, too, of both of them, (1) that mind was akin to the cause and of this family; and (2) that pleasure is infinite and belongs to the class which neither has, nor ever will have in itself, a beginning, middle, or end of its own.

Pro. I shall be sure to remember.

Soc. We must next examine what is their place and under what conditions they are generated. And we will begin with pleasure, since her class was first examined; and yet pleasure cannot be rightly tested apart from pain.

Pro. If this is the road, let us take it.

Soc. I wonder whether you would agree with me about the origin of pleasure and pain.

Pro. What do you mean?

Soc. I mean to say that their natural seat is in the mixed class.

Pro. And would you tell me again, sweet Socrates, which of the aforesaid classes is the mixed one?

Soc. I will, my fine fellow, to the best of my ability.

Pro. Very good.

Soc. Let us then understand the mixed class to be that which we placed third in the list of four.

Pro. That which followed the infinite and the finite; and in which you ranked health, and, if I am not mistaken, harmony.

Soc. Capital; and now will you please to give me your best attention?

Pro. Proceed; I am attending.

Soc. I say that when the harmony in animals is dissolved, there is also a dissolution of nature and a generation of pain.

Pro. That is very probable.

Soc. And the restoration of harmony and return to nature is the source of pleasure, if I may be allowed to speak in the fewest and shortest words about matters of the greatest moment.

Pro. I believe that you are right, Socrates; but will you try to be a little plainer?

Soc. Do not obvious and every-day phenomena furnish the simplest illustration?

Pro. What phenomena do you mean?

Soc. Hunger, for example, is a dissolution and a pain.

Pro. True.

Soc. Whereas eating is a replenishment and a pleasure?

[32] Pro. Yes.

Soc. Thirst again is a destruction and a pain, but the effect of moisture replenishing the dry place is a pleasure: once more, the unnatural separation and dissolution caused by heat is painful, and the natural restoration and refrigeration is pleasant.

Pro. Very true.

Soc. And the unnatural freezing of the moisture in an animal is pain, and the natural process of resolution and return of the elements to their original state is pleasure. And would not the general proposition seem to you to hold, that the destroying of the natural union of the finite and infinite, which, as I was observing before, make up the class of living beings, is pain, and that the process of return of all things to their own nature is pleasure?

Pro. Granted; what you say has a general truth.

Soc. Here then is one kind of pleasures and pains originating severally in the two processes which we have described?

Pro. Good.

Soc. Let us next assume that in the soul herself there is an antecedent hope of pleasure which is sweet and refreshing, and an expectation of pain, fearful and anxious.

Pro. Yes; this is another class of pleasures and pains, which is of the soul only, apart from the body, and is produced by expectation.

Soc. Right; for in the analysis of these, pure, as I suppose them to be, the pleasures being unalloyed with pain and the pains with pleasure, methinks that we shall see clearly whether the whole class of pleasure is to be desired, or whether this quality of entire desirableness is not rather to be attributed to another of the classes which have been mentioned; and whether pleasure and pain, like heat and cold, and other things of the same kind, are not sometimes to be desired and sometimes not to be desired, as being not in themselves good, but only sometimes and in some instances admitting of the nature of good.

Pro. You say most truly that this is the track which the investigation should pursue.

Soc. Well, then, assuming that pain ensues on the dissolution, and pleasure on the restoration of the harmony, let us now ask what will be the condition of animated beings who are neither in process of restoration nor of dissolution. And mind what you say: I ask whether any animal who is in that condition can possibly have any feeling of pleasure or pain, great or small?

Pro. Certainly not.

[33] Soc. Then here we have a third state, over and above that of pleasure and of pain?

Pro. Very true.

Soc. And do not forget that there is such a state; it will make a great difference in our judgment of pleasure, whether we remember this or not. And I should like to say a few words about it.

Pro. What have you to say?

Soc. Why, you know that if a man chooses the life of wisdom, there is no reason why he should not live in this neutral state.

Pro. You mean that he may live neither rejoicing nor sorrowing?

Soc. Yes; and if I remember rightly, when the lives were compared, no degree of pleasure, whether great or small, was thought to be necessary to him who chose the life of thought and wisdom.

Pro. Yes, certainly, we said so.

Soc. Then he will live without pleasure; and who knows whether this may not be the most divine of all lives?

Pro. If so, the gods, at any rate, cannot be supposed to have either joy or sorrow.

Soc. Certainly not—there would be a great

impropriety in the assumption of either alternative. But whether the gods are or are not indifferent to pleasure is a point which may be considered hereafter if in any way relevant to the argument, and whatever is the conclusion we will place it to the account of mind in her contest for the second place, should she have to resign the first.

Pro. Just so.

Soc. The other class of pleasures, which as we were saying is purely mental, is entirely derived from memory.

Pro. What do you mean?

Soc. I must first of all analyse memory, or rather perception which is prior to memory, if the subject of our discussion is ever to be properly cleared up.

Pro. How will you proceed?

Soc. Let us imagine affections of the body which are extinguished before they reach the soul, and leave her unaffected; and again, other affections which vibrate through both soul and body, and impart a shock to both and to each of them.

Pro. Granted.

Soc. And the soul may be truly said to be oblivious of the first but not of the second?

Pro. Quite true.

Soc. When I say oblivious, do not suppose that I mean forgetfulness in a literal sense; for forgetfulness is the exit of memory, which in this case has not yet entered; and to speak of the loss of that which is not yet in existence, and never has been, is a contradiction; do you see?

Pro. Yes.

Soc. Then just be so good as to change the terms.

Pro. How shall I change them?

[34] Soc. Instead of the oblivion of the soul, when you are describing the state in which she is unaffected by the shocks of the body, say unconsciousness.

Pro. I see.

Soc. And the union or communion of soul and body in one feeling and motion would be properly called consciousness?

Pro. Most true.

Soc. Then now we know the meaning of the word?

Pro. Yes.

Soc. And memory may, I think, be rightly described as the preservation of consciousness?

Pro. Right.

Soc. But do we not distinguish memory from recollection?

Pro. I think so.

Soc. And do we not mean by recollection the power which the soul has of recovering, when by herself, some feeling which she experienced when in company with the body?

Pro. Certainly.

Soc. And when she recovers of herself the lost recollection of some consciousness or knowledge, the recovery is termed recollection and reminiscence?

Pro. Very true.

Soc. There is a reason why I say all this.

Pro. What is it?

Soc. I want to attain the plainest possible notion of pleasure and desire, as they exist in the mind only, apart from the body; and the previous analysis helps to show the nature of both.

Pro. Then now, Socrates, let us proceed to the next point.

Soc. There are certainly many things to be considered in discussing the generation and whole complexion of pleasure. At the outset we must determine the nature and seat of desire.

Pro. Ay; let us enquire into that, for we shall lose nothing.

Soc. Nay, Protarchus, we shall surely lose the puzzle if we find the answer.

Pro. A fair retort; but let us proceed.

Soc. Did we not place hunger, thirst, and the like, in the class of desires?

Pro. Certainly.

Soc. And yet they are very different; what common nature have we in view when we call them by a single name?

Pro. By heavens, Socrates, that is a question which is not easily answered; but it must be answered.

Soc. Then let us go back to our examples.

Pro. Where shall we begin?

Soc. Do we mean anything when we say "a man thirsts"?

Pro. Yes.

Soc. We mean to say that he "is empty"?

Pro. Of course.

Soc. And is not thirst desire?

Pro. Yes, of drink.

[35] Soc. Would you say of drink, or of replenishment with drink?

Pro. I should say, of replenishment with drink.

Soc. Then he who is empty desires, as would appear, the opposite of what he experiences; for he is empty and desires to be full?

Pro. Clearly so.

Soc. But how can a man who is empty for the first time, attain either by perception or memory to any apprehension of replenishment, of which he has no present or past experience?

Pro. Impossible.

Soc. And yet he who desires, surely desires something?

Pro. Of course.

Soc. He does not desire that which he experiences, for he experiences thirst, and thirst is emptiness; but he desires replenishment?

Pro. True.

Soc. Then there must be something in the thirsty man which in some way apprehends replenishment?

Pro. There must.

Soc. And that cannot be the body, for the body is supposed to be emptied?

Pro. Yes.

Soc. The only remaining alternative is that the soul apprehends the replenishment by the help of memory; as is obvious, for what other way can there be?

Pro. I cannot imagine any other.

Soc. But do you see the consequence?

Pro. What is it?

Soc. That there is no such thing as desire of the body.

Pro. Why so?

Soc. Why, because the argument shows that the endeavour of every animal is to the reverse of his bodily state.

Pro. Yes.

Soc. And the impulse which leads him to the opposite of what he is experiencing proves that he has a memory of the opposite state.

Pro. True.

Soc. And the argument, having proved that memory attracts us towards the objects of desire, proves also that the impulses and the desires and the moving principle in every living being have their origin in the soul.

Pro. Most true.

Soc. The argument will not allow that our body either hungers or thirsts or has any similar experience.

Pro. Quite right.

Soc. Let me make a further observation; the argument appears to me to imply that there is a kind of life which consists in these affections.

Pro. Of what affections, and of what kind of life, are you speaking?

Soc. I am speaking of being emptied and replenished, and of all that relates to the preservation and destruction of living beings, as well as of the pain which is felt in one of these states and of the pleasure which succeeds to it.

Pro. True.

Soc. And what would you say of the intermediate state?

Pro. What do you mean by "intermediate"?

Soc. I mean when a person is in actual suffering and yet remembers past pleasures which, if they would only return, would relieve him; but as yet he has them not. May we not say of him, that he is in an intermediate state? *[36]*

Pro. Certainly.

Soc. Would you say that he was wholly pained or wholly pleased?

Pro. Nay, I should say that he has two pains; in his body there is the actual experience of pain, and in his soul longing and expectation.

Soc. What do you mean, Protarchus, by the two pains? May not a man who is empty have at one time a sure hope of being filled, and at other times be quite in despair?

Pro. Very true.

Soc. And has he not the pleasure of memory when he is hoping to be filled, and yet in that he is empty is he not at the same time in pain?

Pro. Certainly.

Soc. Then man and the other animals have at the same time both pleasure and pain?

Pro. I suppose so.

Soc. But when a man is empty and has no hope of being filled, there will be the double experience of pain. You observed this and inferred that the double experience was the single case possible.

Pro. Quite true, Socrates.

Soc. Shall the enquiry into these states of feeling be made the occasion of raising a question?

Pro. What question?

Soc. Whether we ought to say that the pleasures and pains of which we are speaking are true or false? or some true and some false?

Pro. But how, Socrates, can there be false pleasures and pains?

Soc. And how, Protarchus, can there be true and false fears, or true and false expectations, or true and false opinions?

Pro. I grant that opinions may be true or false, but not pleasures.

Soc. What do you mean? I am afraid that we are raising a very serious enquiry.

Pro. There I agree.

Soc. And yet, my boy, for you are one of Philebus' boys (cf. 16), the point to be considered, is, whether the enquiry is relevant to the argument.

Pro. Surely.

Soc. No tedious and irrelevant discussion can be allowed; what is said should be pertinent.

Pro. Right.

Soc. I am always wondering at the question which has now been raised.

Pro. How so?

Soc. Do you deny that some pleasures are false, and others true?

Pro. To be sure I do.

Soc. Would you say that no one ever seemed to rejoice and yet did not rejoice, or seemed to feel pain and yet did not feel pain, sleeping or waking, mad or lunatic?

Pro. So we have always held, Socrates.

[37] Soc. But were you right? Shall we enquire into the truth of your opinion?

Pro. I think that we should.

Soc. Let us then put into more precise terms the question which has arisen about pleasure and opinion. Is there such a thing as opinion?

Pro. Yes.

Soc. And such a thing as pleasure?

Pro. Yes.

Soc. And an opinion must be of something?

Pro. True.

Soc. And a man must be pleased by something?

Pro. Quite correct.

Soc. And whether the opinion be right or wrong, makes no difference; it will still be an opinion?

Pro. Certainly.

Soc. And he who is pleased, whether he is rightly pleased or not will always have a real feeling of pleasure?

Pro. Yes; that is also quite true.

Soc. Then, how can opinion be both true and false, and pleasure true only, although pleasure and opinion are both equally real?

Pro. Yes; that is the question.

Soc. You mean that opinion admits of truth and falsehood, and hence becomes not merely opinion, but opinion of a certain quality; and this is what you think should be examined?

Pro. Yes.

Soc. And further, even if we admit the existence of qualities in other objects, may not pleasure and pain be simple and devoid of quality?

Pro. Clearly.

Soc. But there is no difficulty in seeing that pleasure and pain as well as opinion have qualities, for they are great or small, and have various degrees of intensity; as was indeed said long ago by us.

Pro. Quite true.

Soc. And if badness attaches to any of them, Protarchus, then we should speak of a bad opinion or of a bad pleasure?

Pro. Quite true, Socrates.

Soc. And if rightness attaches to any of them, should we not speak of a right opinion or right pleasure; and in like manner of the reverse of rightness?

Pro. Certainly.

Soc. And if the thing opined be erroneous, might we not say that opinion, being erroneous, is not right or rightly opined?

Pro. Certainly.

Soc. And if we see a pleasure or pain which errs in respect of its object, shall we call that right or good, or by any honourable name?

Pro. Not if the pleasure is mistaken; how could we?

Soc. And surely pleasure often appears to accompany an opinion which is not true, but false?

[38] Pro. Certainly it does; and in that case, Socrates, as we were saying, the opinion is false, but no one could call the actual pleasure false.

Soc. How eagerly, Protarchus, do you rush to the defence of pleasure!

Pro. Nay, Socrates, I only repeat what I hear.

Soc. And is there no difference, my friend, between that pleasure which is associated with right opinion and knowledge, and that which is often found in all of us associated with falsehood and ignorance?

Pro. There must be a very great difference between them.

Soc. Then, now let us proceed to contemplate this difference.

Pro. Lead, and I will follow.

Soc. Well, then, my view is—

Pro. What is it?

Soc. We agree—do we not?—that there is such a thing as false, and also such a thing as true opinion?

Pro. Yes.

Soc. And pleasure and pain, as I was just now saying, are often consequent upon these— upon true and false opinion, I mean.

Pro. Very true.

Soc. And do not opinion and the endeavour to form an opinion always spring from memory and perception?

Pro. Certainly.

Soc. Might we imagine the process to be something of this nature?

Pro. Of what nature?

Soc. An object may be often seen at a distance not very clearly, and the seer may want to determine what it is which he sees.

Pro. Very likely.

Soc. Soon he begins to interrogate himself.

Pro. In what manner?

Soc. He asks himself—"What is that which appears to be standing by the rock under the tree?" This is the question which he may be supposed to put to himself when he sees such an appearance.

Pro. True.

Soc. To which he may guess the right answer, saying as if in a whisper to himself—"It is a man."

Pro. Very good.

Soc. Or again, he may be misled, and then he will say—"No, it is a figure made by the shepherds."

Pro. Yes.

Soc. And if he has a companion, he repeats his thought to him in articulate sounds, and what was before an opinion, has now become a proposition.

Pro. Certainly.

Soc. But if he be walking alone when these thoughts occur to him, he may not unfrequently keep them in his mind for a considerable time.

Pro. Very true.

Soc. Well, now, I wonder whether you would agree in my explanation of this phenomenon.

Pro. What is your explanation?

Soc. I think that the soul at such times is like a book.

Pro. How so?

[39] *Soc.* Memory and perception meet, and they and their attendant feelings seem to me almost to write down words in the soul, and when the inscribing feeling writes truly, then true opinion and true propositions which are the expressions of opinion, come into our souls—but when the scribe within us writes falsely, the result is false.

Pro. I quite assent and agree to your statement.

Soc. I must bespeak your favour also for another artist, who is busy at the same time in the chambers of the soul.

Pro. Who is he?

Soc. The painter, who, after the scribe has done his work, draws images in the soul of the things which he has described.

Pro. But when and how does he do this?

Soc. When a man, besides receiving from sight or some other sense certain opinions or statements, sees in his mind the images of the subjects of them;—is not this a very common mental phenomenon?

Pro. Certainly.

Soc. And the images answering to true opinions and words are true, and to false opinions and words false; are they not?

Pro. They are.

Soc. If we are right so far, there arises a further question.

Pro. What is it?

Soc. Whether we experience the feeling of which I am speaking only in relation to the present and the past, or in relation to the future also?

Pro. I should say in relation to all times alike.

Soc. Have not purely mental pleasures and pains been described already as in some cases anticipations of the bodily ones; from which we may infer that anticipatory pleasures and pains have to do with the future?

Pro. Most true.

Soc. And do all those writings and paintings which, as we were saying a little while ago, are produced in us, relate to the past and present only, and not to the future?

Pro. To the future, very much.

Soc. When you say, "Very much," you mean to imply that all these representations are hopes about the future, and that mankind are filled with hopes in every stage of existence?

Pro. Exactly.

Soc. Answer me another question.

Pro. What question?

Soc. A just and pious and good man is the friend of the gods; is he not?

Pro. Certainly he is.

Soc. And the unjust and utterly bad man is the reverse?

[40] *Pro.* True.

Soc. And all men, as we were saying just now, are always filled with hopes?

Pro. Certainly.

Soc. And these hopes, as they are termed, are propositions which exist in the minds of each of us?

Pro. Yes.

Soc. And the fancies of hope are also pictured in us; a man may often have a vision of a heap of gold, and pleasures ensuing, and in the picture there may be a likeness of himself mightily rejoicing over his good fortune.

Pro. True.

Soc. And may we not say that the good, being friends of the gods, have generally true pictures presented to them, and the bad false pictures?

Pro. Certainly.

Soc. The bad, too, have pleasures painted in their fancy as well as the good; but I presume that they are false pleasures.

Pro. They are.

Soc. The bad then commonly delight in false pleasures, and the good in true pleasures?

Pro. Doubtless.

Soc. Then upon this view there are false pleasures in the souls of men which are a ludicrous imitation of the true, and there are pains of a similar character?

Pro. There are.

Soc. And did we not allow that a man who had an opinion at all had a real opinion, but often about things which had no existence either in the past, present, or future?

Pro. Quite true.

Soc. And this was the source of false opinion and opining; am I not right?

Pro. Yes.

Soc. And must we not attribute to pleasure and pain a similar real but illusory character?

Pro. How do you mean?

Soc. I mean to say that a man must be admitted to have real pleasure who is pleased with anything or anyhow; and he may be pleased about things which neither have nor have ever had any real existence, and, more often than not, are never likely to exist.

Pro. Yes, Socrates, that again is undeniable.

Soc. And may not the same be said about fear and anger and the like; are they not often false?

Pro. Quite so.

Soc. And can opinions be good or bad except in as far as they are true or false?

Pro. In no other way.

[41] *Soc.* Nor can pleasures be conceived to be bad except in so far as they are false.

Pro. Nay, Socrates, that is the very opposite of truth; for no one would call pleasures and pains bad because they are false, but by reason of some other great corruption to which they are liable.

Soc. Well, of pleasures which are corrupt and caused by corruption we will hereafter speak, if we care to continue the enquiry; for the present I would rather show by another argument that there are many false pleasures existing or coming into existence in us, because this may assist our final decision.

Pro. Very true; that is to say, if there are such pleasures.

Soc. I think that there are, Protarchus; but this is an opinion which should be well assured, and not rest upon a mere assertion.

Pro. Very good.

Soc. Then now, like wrestlers, let us approach and grasp this new argument.

Pro. Proceed.

Soc. We were maintaining a little while since, that when desires, as they are termed, exist in us, then the body has separate feelings apart from the soul—do you remember?

Pro. Yes, I remember that you said so.

Soc. And the soul was supposed to desire the opposite of the bodily state, while the body was the source of any pleasure or pain which was experienced.

Pro. True.

Soc. Then now you may infer what happens in such cases.

Pro. What am I to infer?

Soc. That in such cases pleasure and pains come simultaneously; and there is a juxtaposition of the opposite sensations which correspond to them, as has been already shown.

Pro. Clearly.

Soc. And there is another point to which we have agreed.

Pro. What is it?

Soc. That pleasure and pain both admit of more and less, and that they are of the class of infinites.

Pro. Certainly, we said so.

Soc. But how can we rightly judge of them?

Pro. How can we?

Soc. It is our intention to judge of their comparative importance and intensity, measuring pleasure against pain, and pain against pain, and pleasure against pleasure?

Pro. Yes, such is our intention, and we shall judge of them accordingly.

[42] *Soc.* Well, take the case of sight. Does not the nearness or distance of magnitudes obscure their true proportions, and make us opine falsely; and do we not find the same illusion happening in the case of pleasures and pains?

Pro. Yes, Socrates, and in a degree far greater.

Soc. Then what we are now saying is the opposite of what we were saying before.

Pro. What was that?

Soc. Then the opinions were true and false, and infected the pleasures and pains with their own falsity.

Pro. Very true.

Soc. But now it is the pleasures which are said to be true and false because they are seen at various distances, and subjected to comparison; the pleasures appear to be greater and more vehement when placed side by side with the pains, and the pains when placed side by side with the pleasures.

Pro. Certainly, and for the reason which you mention.

Soc. And suppose you part off from pleasures and pains the element which makes them appear to be greater or less than they really are: you will acknowledge that this element is illusory, and you will never say that the corresponding excess or defect of pleasure or pain is real or true.

Pro. Certainly not.

Soc. Next let us see whether in another direction we may not find pleasures and pains existing and appearing in living beings, which are still more false than these.

Pro. What are they, and how shall we find them?

Soc. If I am not mistaken, I have often repeated that pains and aches and suffering and uneasiness of all sorts arise out of a corruption of nature caused by concretions, and dissolutions, and repletions, and evacuations, and also by growth and decay?

Pro. Yes, that has been often said.

Soc. And we have also agreed that the restoration of the natural state is pleasure?

Pro. Right.

Soc. But now let us suppose an interval of time at which the body experiences none of these changes.

Pro. When can that be, Socrates?

Soc. Your question, Protarchus, does not help the argument.

Pro. Why not, Socrates?

Soc. Because it does not prevent me from repeating mine.

Pro. And what was that?

Soc. Why, Protarchus, admitting that there is no such interval, I may ask what would be the necessary consequence if there were?

Pro. You mean, what would happen if the body were not changed either for good or bad?

Soc. Yes.

Pro. Why then, Socrates, I should suppose that there would be neither pleasure nor pain.

[43] Soc. Very good; but still, if I am not mistaken, you do assert that we must always be experiencing one of them; that is what the wise tell us; for, say they, all things are ever flowing up and down.

Pro. Yes, and their words are of no mean authority.

Soc. Of course, for they are no mean authorities themselves; and I should like to avoid the brunt of their argument. Shall I tell you how I mean to escape from them? And you shall be the partner of my flight.

Pro. How?

Soc. To them we will say: "Good; but are we, or living things in general, always conscious of what happens to us—for example, of our growth, or the like? Are we not, on the contrary, almost wholly unconscious of this and similar phenomena?" You must answer for them.

Pro. The latter alternative is the true one.

Soc. Then we were not right in saying, just now, that motions going up and down cause pleasures and pains?

Pro. True.

Soc. A better and more unexceptionable way of speaking will be—

Pro. What?

Soc. If we say that the great changes produce pleasures and pains, but that the moderate and lesser ones do neither.

Pro. That, Socrates, is the more correct mode of speaking.

Soc. But if this be true, the life to which I was just now referring again appears.

Pro. What life?

Soc. The life which we affirmed to be devoid either of pain or of joy.

Pro. Very true.

Soc. We may assume then that there are three lives, one pleasant, one painful, and the third which is neither; what say you?

Pro. I should say as you do that there are three of them.

Soc. But if so, the negation of pain will not be the same with pleasure.

Pro. Certainly not.

Soc. Then when you hear a person saying, that always to live without pain is the pleasantest of all things, what would you understand him to mean by that statement?

Pro. I think that by pleasure he must mean the negative of pain.

Soc. Let us take any three things; or suppose that we embellish a little and call the first gold, the second silver, and there shall be a third which is neither.

Pro. Very good.

Soc. Now, can that which is neither be either gold or silver?

Pro. Impossible.

Soc. No more can that neutral or middle life be rightly or reasonably spoken or thought of as pleasant or painful.

Pro. Certainly not.

[44] Soc. And yet, my friend, there are, as we know, persons who say and think so.

Pro. Certainly.

Soc. And do they think that they have pleasure when they are free from pain?

Pro. They say so.

Soc. And they must think or they would not say that they have pleasure.

Pro. I suppose not.

Soc. And yet if pleasure and the negation of pain are of distinct natures, they are wrong.

Pro. But they are undoubtedly of distinct natures.

Soc. Then shall we take the view that they are three, as we were just now saying, or that they are two only—the one being a state of pain, which is an evil, and the other a cessation of pain, which is of itself a good, and is called pleasant?

Pro. But why, Socrates, do we ask the question at all? I do not see the reason.

Soc. You, Protarchus, have clearly never heard of certain enemies of our friend Philebus.

Pro. And who may they be?

Soc. Certain persons who are reputed to be masters in natural philosophy, who deny the very existence of pleasure.

Pro. Indeed!

Soc. They say that what the school of Philebus calls pleasures are all of them only avoidances of pain.

Pro. And would you, Socrates, have us agree with them?

Soc. Why, no, I would rather use them as a sort of diviners, who divine the truth, not by rules of art, but by an instinctive repugnance and extreme detestation which a noble nature has of the power of pleasure, in which they think that there is nothing sound, and her seductive influence is declared by them to be witchcraft, and not pleasure. This is the use which you may make of them. And when you have considered the various grounds of their dislike, you shall hear from me what I deem to be true pleasures. Having thus examined the nature of pleasure from both points of view, we will bring her up for judgment.

Pro. Well said.

Soc. Then let us enter into an alliance with these philosophers and follow in the track of their dislike. I imagine that they would say something of this sort; they would begin at the beginning, and ask whether, if we wanted to know the nature of any quality, such as hardness, we should be more likely to discover it by looking at the hardest things, rather than at the least hard? You, Protarchus, shall answer these severe gentlemen as you answer me.

Pro. By all means, and I reply to them, that

you should look at the greatest instances.

Soc. Then if we want to see the true nature of pleasures as a class, we should not look at the most diluted pleasures, *[45]* but at the most extreme and most vehement?

Pro. In that every one will agree.

Soc. And the obvious instances of the greatest pleasures, as we have often said, are the pleasures of the body?

Pro. Certainly.

Soc. And are they felt by us to be or become greater, when we are sick or when we are in health? And here we must be careful in our answer, or we shall come to grief.

Pro. How will that be?

Soc. Why, because we might be tempted to answer, "When we are in health."

Pro. Yes, that is the natural answer.

Soc. Well, but are not those pleasures the greatest of which mankind have the greatest desires?

Pro. True.

Soc. And do not people who are in a fever, or any similar illness, feel cold or thirst or other bodily affections more intensely? Am I not right in saying that they have a deeper want and greater pleasure in the satisfaction of their want?

Pro. That is obvious as soon as it is said.

Soc. Well, then, shall we not be right in saying, that if a person would wish to see the greatest pleasures he ought to go and look, not at health, but at disease? And here you must distinguish:—do not imagine that I mean to ask whether those who are very ill have more pleasures than those who are well, but understand that I am speaking of the magnitude of pleasure; I want to know where pleasures are found to be most intense. For, as I say, we have to discover what is pleasure, and what they mean by pleasure who deny her very existence.

Pro. I think I follow you.

Soc. You will soon have a better opportunity of showing whether you do or not, Protarchus. Answer now, and tell me whether you see, I will not say more, but more intense and excessive pleasures in wantonness than in temperance? Reflect before you speak.

Pro. I understand you, and see that there is a great difference between them; the temperate are restrained by the wise man's aphorism of "Never too much," which is their rule, but excess of pleasure possessing the minds of fools and wantons becomes madness and makes them shout with delight.

Soc. Very good, and if this be true, then the

greatest pleasures and pains will clearly be found in some vicious state of soul and body, and not in a virtuous state.

[46] Pro. Certainly.

Soc. And ought we not to select some of these for examination, and see what makes them the greatest?

Pro. To be sure we ought.

Soc. Take the case of the pleasures which arise out of certain disorders.

Pro. What disorders?

Soc. The pleasures of unseemly disorders, which our severe friends utterly detest.

Pro. What pleasures?

Soc. Such, for example, as the relief of itching and other ailments by scratching, which is the only remedy required. For what in Heaven's name is the feeling to be called which is thus produced in us?—Pleasure or pain?

Pro. A villainous mixture of some kind, Socrates, I should say.

Soc. I did not introduce the argument, O Protarchus, with any personal reference to Philebus, but because, without the consideration of these and similar pleasures, we shall not be able to determine the point at issue.

Pro. Then we had better proceed to analyze this family of pleasures.

Soc. You mean the pleasures which are mingled with pain?

Pro. Exactly.

Soc. There are some mixtures which are of the body, and only in the body, and others which are of the soul, and only in the soul; while there are other mixtures of pleasures with pains, common both to soul and body, which in their composite state are called sometimes pleasures and sometimes pains.

Pro. How is that?

Soc. Whenever, in the restoration or in the derangement of nature, a man experiences two opposite feelings; for example, when he is cold and is growing warm, or again, when he is hot and is becoming cool, and he wants to have the one and be rid of the other;—the sweet has a bitter, as the common saying is, and both together fasten upon him and create irritation and in time drive him to distraction.

Pro. That description is very true to nature.

Soc. And in these sorts of mixtures the pleasures and pains are sometimes equal, and sometimes one or other of them predominates?

Pro. True.

Soc. Of cases in which the pain exceeds the pleasure, an example is afforded by itching, of which we were just now speaking, and by the tingling which we feel when the boiling and fiery element is within, and the rubbing and motion only relieves the surface, and does not reach the parts affected; then if you put them to the fire, and as a last resort apply cold to them, you may often produce the most intense pleasure or pain in the inner parts, which contrasts and mingles with the pain or pleasure, as the case may be, of the outer parts; *[47]* and this is due to the forcible separation of what is united, or to the union of what is separated, and to the juxtaposition of pleasure and pain.

Pro. Quite so.

Soc. Sometimes the element of pleasure prevails in a man, and the slight undercurrent of pain makes him tingle, and causes a gentle irritation; or again, the excessive infusion of pleasure creates an excitement in him,—he even leaps for joy, he assumes all sorts of attitudes, he changes all manner of colours, he gasps for breath, and is quite amazed, and utters the most irrational exclamations.

Pro. Yes, indeed.

Soc. He will say of himself, and others will say of him, that he is dying with these delights; and the more dissipated and good-for-nothing he is, the more vehemently he pursues them in every way; of all pleasures he declares them to be the greatest; and he reckons him who lives in the most constant enjoyment of them to be the happiest of mankind.

Pro. That, Socrates, is a very true description of the opinions of the majority about pleasures.

Soc. Yes, Protarchus, quite true of the mixed pleasures, which arise out of the communion of external and internal sensations in the body; there are also cases in which the mind contributes an opposite element to the body, whether of pleasure or pain, and the two unite and form one mixture. Concerning these I have already remarked, that when a man is empty he desires to be full, and has pleasure in hope and pain in vacuity. But now I must further add what I omitted before, that in all these and similar emotions in which body and mind are opposed (and they are innumerable), pleasure and pain coalesce in one.

Pro. I believe that to be quite true.

Soc. There still remains one other sort of admixture of pleasures and pains.

Pro. What is that?

Soc. The union which, as we were saying, the mind often experiences of purely mental feelings.

Pro. What do you mean?

Soc. Why, do we not speak of anger, fear, desire, sorrow, love, emulation, envy, and the like, as pains which belong to the soul only?

Pro. Yes.

Soc. And shall we not find them also full of the most wonderful pleasures? need I remind you of the anger

Which stirs even a wise man to violence,
And is sweeter than honey and the honeycomb?

And you remember how pleasures mingle with pains in lamentation *[48]* and bereavement?

Pro. Yes, there is a natural connection between them.

Soc. And you remember also how at the sight of tragedies the spectators smile through their tears?

Pro. Certainly I do.

Soc. And are you aware that even at a comedy the soul experiences a mixed feeling of pain and pleasure?

Pro. I do not quite understand you.

Soc. I admit, Protarchus, that there is some difficulty in recognizing this mixture of feelings at a comedy.

Pro. There is, I think.

Soc. And the greater the obscurity of the case the more desirable is the examination of it, because the difficulty in detecting other cases of mixed pleasures and pains will be less.

Pro. Proceed.

Soc. I have just mentioned envy; would you not call that a pain of the soul?

Pro. Yes.

Soc. And yet the envious man finds something in the misfortunes of his neighbours at which he is pleased?

Pro. Certainly.

Soc. And ignorance, and what is termed clownishness, are surely an evil?

Pro. To be sure.

Soc. From these considerations learn to know the nature of the ridiculous.

Pro. Explain.

Soc. The ridiculous is in short the specific name which is used to describe the vicious form of a certain habit; and of vice in general it is that kind which is most at variance with the inscription at Delphi.

Pro. You mean, Socrates, "Know thyself."

Soc. I do; and the opposite would be, "Know not thyself."

Pro. Certainly.

Soc. And now, O Protarchus, try to divide this into three.

Pro. Indeed I am afraid that I cannot.

Soc. Do you mean to say that I must make the division for you?

Pro. Yes, and what is more, I beg that you will.

Soc. Are there not three ways in which ignorance of self may be shown?

Pro. What are they?

Soc. In the first place, about money; the ignorant may fancy himself richer than he is.

Pro. Yes, that is a very common error.

Soc. And still more often he will fancy that he is taller or fairer than he is, or that he has some other advantage of person which he really has not.

Pro. Of course.

Soc. And yet surely by far the greatest number err about the goods of the mind; they imagine themselves to be much better men than they are. *[49]*

Pro. Yes, that is by far the commonest delusion.

Soc. And of all the virtues, is not wisdom the one which the mass of mankind are always claiming, and which most arouses in them a spirit of contention and lying conceit of wisdom?

Pro. Certainly.

Soc. And may not all this be truly called an evil condition?

Pro. Very evil.

Soc. But we must pursue the division a step further, Protarchus, if we would see in envy of the childish sort a singular mixture of pleasure and pain.

Pro. How can we make the further division which you suggest?

Soc. All who are silly enough to entertain this lying conceit of themselves may of course be divided, like the rest of mankind, into two classes—one having power and might; and the other the reverse.

Pro. Certainly.

Soc. Let this, then, be the principle of division; those of them who are weak and unable to revenge themselves, when they are laughed at, may be truly called ridiculous, but those who can defend themselves may be more truly described as strong and formidable; for ignorance in the powerful is hateful and horrible, because hurtful to others both in reality and in fiction, but powerless ignorance may be reckoned, and in truth is, ridiculous.

Pro. That is very true, but I do not as yet see where is the admixture of pleasures and pains.

Soc. Well, then, let us examine the nature of envy.

Pro. Proceed.

Soc. Is not envy an unrighteous pleasure, and also an unrighteous pain?

Pro. Most true.

Soc. There is nothing envious or wrong in rejoicing at the misfortunes of enemies?

Pro. Certainly not.

Soc. But to feel joy instead of sorrow at the sight of our friends' misfortunes—is not that wrong?

Pro. Undoubtedly.

Soc. Did we not say that ignorance was always an evil?

Pro. True.

Soc. And the three kinds of vain conceit in our friends which we enumerated—the vain conceit of beauty, of wisdom, and of wealth, are ridiculous if they are weak, and detestable when they are powerful: May we not say, as I was saying before, that our friends who are in this state of mind, when harmless to others, are simply ridiculous?

Pro. They are ridiculous.

Soc. And do we not acknowledge this ignorance of theirs to be a misfortune?

Pro. Certainly.

Soc. And do we feel pain or pleasure in laughing at it?

Pro. Clearly we feel pleasure.

[50] Soc. And was not envy the source of this pleasure which we feel at the misfortunes of friends?

Pro. Certainly.

Soc. Then the argument shows that when we laugh at the folly of our friends, pleasure, in mingling with envy, mingles with pain, for envy has been acknowledged by us to be mental pain, and laughter is pleasant; and so we envy and laugh at the same instant.

Pro. True.

Soc. And the argument implies that there are combinations of pleasure and pain in lamentations, and in tragedy and comedy, not only on the stage, but on the greater stage of human life; and so in endless other cases.

Pro. I do not see how any one can deny what you say, Socrates, however eager he may be to assert the opposite opinion.

Soc. I mentioned anger, desire, sorrow, fear, love, emulation, envy, and similar emotions, as examples in which we should find a mixture of the two elements so often named; did I not?

Pro. Yes.

Soc. We may observe that our conclusions hitherto have had reference only to sorrow and envy and anger.

Pro. I see.

Soc. Then many other cases still remain?

Pro. Certainly.

Soc. And why do you suppose me to have pointed out to you the admixture which takes place in comedy? Why but to convince you that there was no difficulty in showing the mixed nature of fear and love and similar affections; and I thought that when I had given you the illustration, you would have let me off, and have acknowledged as a general truth that the body without the soul, and the soul without the body, as well as the two united, are susceptible of all sorts of admixtures of pleasures and pains; and so further discussion would have been unnecessary. And now I want to know whether I may depart; or will you keep me here until midnight? I fancy that I may obtain my release without many words;—if I promise that to-morrow I will give you an account of all these cases. But at present I would rather sail in another direction, and go to other matters which remain to be settled, before the judgment can be given which Philebus demands.

Pro. Very good, Socrates; in what remains take your own course.

Soc. Then after the mixed pleasures the unmixed should have their turn; this is the natural and necessary order.

[51] Pro. Excellent.

Soc. These, in turn, then, I will now endeavour to indicate; for with the maintainers of the opinion that all pleasures are a cessation of pain, I do not agree, but, as I was saying, I use them as witnesses, that there are pleasures which seem only and are not, and there are others again which have great power and appear in many forms, yet are intermingled with pains, and are partly alleviations of agony and distress, both of body and mind.

Pro. Then what pleasures, Socrates, should we be right in conceiving to be true?

Soc. True pleasures are those which are given by beauty of colour and form, and most of those which arise from smells; those of sound, again, and in general those of which the want is painless and unconscious, and of which the fruition is palpable to sense and pleasant and unalloyed with pain.

Pro. Once more, Socrates, I must ask what you mean.

Soc. My meaning is certainly not obvious, and I will endeavour to be plainer. I do not mean by beauty of form such beauty as that of animals or pictures, which the many would suppose to be my meaning; but, says the argument, understand me to mean straight lines and circles, and the plane or solid figures which are formed out of them by turning-lathes and rulers and measurers of angles; for these I affirm to be not only relatively beautiful, like other things, but they are eternally and absolutely beautiful, and they have peculiar pleasures, quite unlike the pleasures of scratching. And there are colours which are of the same character, and have similar pleasures; now do you understand my meaning?

Pro. I am trying to understand, Socrates, and I hope that you will try to make your meaning clearer.

Soc. When sounds are smooth and clear, and have a single pure tone, then I mean to say that they are not relatively but absolutely beautiful, and have natural pleasures associated with them.

Pro. Yes, there are such pleasures.

Soc. The pleasures of smell are of a less ethereal sort, but they have no necessary admixture of pain; and all pleasures, however and wherever experienced, which are unattended by pains, I assign to an analogous class. Here then are two kinds of pleasures.

Pro. I understand.

[52] Soc. To these may be added the pleasures of knowledge, if no hunger of knowledge and no pain caused by such hunger precede them.

Pro. And this is the case.

Soc. Well, but if a man who is full of knowledge loses his knowledge, are there not pains of forgetting?

Pro. Not necessarily, but there may be times of reflection, when he feels grief at the loss of his knowledge.

Soc. Yes, my friend, but at present we are enumerating only the natural perceptions, and have nothing to do with reflection.

Pro. In that case you are right in saying that the loss of knowledge is not attended with pain.

Soc. These pleasures of knowledge, then, are unmixed with pain; and they are not the pleasures of the many but of a very few.

Pro. Quite true.

Soc. And now, having fairly separated the pure pleasures and those which may be rightly termed impure, let us further add to our description of them, that the pleasures which are in excess have no measure, but that those which are not in excess have measure; the great, the excessive, whether more or less frequent, we

shall be right in referring to the class of the infinite, and of the more and less, which pours through body and soul alike; and the others we shall refer to the class which has measure.

Pro. Quite right, Socrates.

Soc. Still there is something more to be considered about pleasures.

Pro. What is it?

Soc. When you speak of purity and clearness, or of excess, abundance, greatness and sufficiency, in what relation do these terms stand to truth?

Pro. Why do you ask, Socrates?

Soc. Because, Protarchus, I should wish to test pleasure and knowledge in every possible way, in order that if there be a pure and impure element in either of them, I may present the pure element for judgment, and then they will be more easily judged of by you and by me and by all of us.

Pro. Most true.

Soc. Let us investigate all the pure kinds; first selecting for consideration a single instance.

Pro. What instance shall we select?

[53] Soc. Suppose that we first of all take whiteness.

Pro. Very good.

Soc. How can there be purity in whiteness, and what purity? Is that purest which is greatest or most in quantity, or that which is most unadulterated and freest from any admixture of other colours?

Pro. Clearly that which is most unadulterated.

Soc. True, Protarchus; and so the purest white, and not the greatest or largest in quantity, is to be deemed truest and most beautiful?

Pro. Right.

Soc. And we shall be quite right in saying that a little pure white is whiter and fairer and truer than a great deal that is mixed.

Pro. Perfectly right.

Soc. There is no need of adducing many similar examples in illustration of the argument about pleasures; one such is sufficient to prove to us that a small pleasure or a small amount of pleasure, if pure or unalloyed with pain, is always pleasanter and truer and fairer than a great pleasure or a great amount of pleasure of another kind.

Pro. Assuredly; and the instance you have given is quite sufficient.

Soc. But what do you say of another question:—have we not heard that pleasure is always a generation, and has no true being? Do not certain ingenious philosophers teach this doctrine, and ought not we to be grateful to them?

Pro. What do they mean?

Soc. I will explain to you, my dear Protarchus, what they mean, by putting a question.

Pro. Ask, and I will answer.

Soc. I assume that there are two natures, one self-existent, and the other ever in want of something.

Pro. What manner of natures are they?

Soc. The one majestic ever, the other inferior.

Pro. You speak riddles.

Soc. You have seen loves good and fair, and also brave lovers of them.

Pro. I should think so.

Soc. Search the universe for two terms which are like these two and are present everywhere.

Pro. Yet a third time I must say, Be a little plainer, Socrates.

Soc. There is no difficulty, Protarchus; the argument is only in play, and insinuates that some things are for the sake of something else (relatives), and that other things are the ends to which the former class subserve (absolutes).

Pro. Your many repetitions make me slow to understand.

[54] Soc. As the argument proceeds, my boy, I dare say that the meaning will become clearer.

Pro. Very likely.

Soc. Here are two new principles.

Pro. What are they?

Soc. One is the generation of all things, and the other is essence.

Pro. I readily accept from you both generation and essence.

Soc. Very right; and would you say that generation is for the sake of essence, or essence for the sake of generation?

Pro. You want to know whether that which is called essence is, properly speaking, for the sake of generation?

Soc. Yes.

Pro. By the gods, I wish that you would repeat your question.

Soc. I mean, O my Protarchus, to ask whether you would tell me that ship-building is for the sake of ships, or ships for the sake of shipbuilding? and in all similar cases I should ask the same question.

Pro. Why do you not answer yourself, Socrates?

Soc. I have no objection, but you must take your part.

Pro. Certainly.

Soc. My answer is, that all things instrumental, remedial, material, are given to us with a view to generation, and that each generation is relative to, or for the sake of, some being or essence, and that the whole of generation is relative to the whole of essence.

Pro. Assuredly.

Soc. Then pleasure, being a generation, must surely be for the sake of some essence?

Pro. True.

Soc. And that for the sake of which something else is done must be placed in the class of good, and that which is done for the sake of something else, in some other class, my good friend.

Pro. Most certainly.

Soc. Then pleasure, being a generation, will be rightly placed in some other class than that of good?

Pro. Quite right.

Soc. Then, as I said at first, we ought to be very grateful to him who first pointed out that pleasure was a generation only, and had no true being at all; for he is clearly one who laughs at the notion of pleasure being a good.

Pro. Assuredly.

Soc. And he would surely laugh also at those who make generation their highest end.

Pro. Of whom are you speaking, and what do they mean?

Soc. I am speaking of those who when they are cured of hunger or thirst or any other defect by some process of generation are delighted at the process as if it were pleasure; and they say that they would not wish to live without these and other feelings of a like kind which might be mentioned.

[55] Pro. That is certainly what they appear to think.

Soc. And is not destruction universally admitted to be the opposite of generation?

Pro. Certainly.

Soc. Then he who chooses thus, would choose generation and destruction rather than that third sort of life, in which, as we were saying, was neither pleasure nor pain, but only the purest possible thought.

Pro. He who would make us believe pleasure to be a good is involved in great absurdities, Socrates.

Soc. Great, indeed; and there is yet another of them.

Pro. What is it?

Soc. Is there not an absurdity in arguing that there is nothing good or noble in the body, or in anything else, but that good is in the soul only, and that the only good of the soul is pleasure; and that courage or temperance or understanding, or any other good of the soul, is not really a good?—and is there not yet a further absurdity in our being compelled to say that he who has a feeling of pain and not of pleasure is bad at the time when he is suffering pain, even though he be the best of men; and again, that he who has a feeling of pleasure, in so far as he is pleased at the time when he is pleased, in that degree excels in virtue?

Pro. Nothing, Socrates, can be more irrational than all this.

Soc. And now, having subjected pleasure to every sort of test, let us not appear to be too sparing of mind and knowledge: let us ring their metal bravely, and see if there be unsoundness in any part, until we have found out what in them is of the purest nature; and then the truest elements both of pleasure and knowledge may be brought up for judgment.

Pro. Right.

Soc. Knowledge has two parts—the one productive, and the other educational?

Pro. True.

Soc. And in the productive or handicraft arts, is not one part more akin to knowledge, and the other less; and may not the one part be regarded as the pure, and the other as the impure?

Pro. Certainly.

Soc. Let us separate the superior or dominant elements in each of them.

Pro. What are they, and how do you separate them?

Soc. I mean to say, that if arithmetic, mensuration, and weighing be taken away from any art, that which remains will not be much.

Pro. Not much, certainly.

Soc. The rest will be only conjecture, and the better use of the senses which is given by experience and practice, in addition to a certain power of guessing, which is commonly called art, and is perfected by attention and pains. [56]

Pro. Nothing more, assuredly.

Soc. Music, for instance, is full of this empiricism; for sounds are harmonized, not by measure, but by skilful conjecture; the music of the flute is always trying to guess the pitch of each vibrating note, and is therefore mixed up with much that is doubtful and has little which is certain.

Pro. Most true.

Soc. And the same will be found to hold good of medicine and husbandry and piloting and generalship.

Pro. Very true.

Soc. The art of the builder, on the other hand, which uses a number of measures and instruments, attains by their help to a greater degree of accuracy than the other arts.

Pro. How is that?

Soc. In ship-building and house-building, and in other branches of the art of carpentering, the builder has his rule, lathe, compass, line, and a most ingenious machine for straightening wood.

Pro. Very true, Socrates.

Soc. Then now let us divide the arts of which we were speaking into two kinds—the arts which, like music, are less exact in their results, and those which, like carpentering, are more exact.

Pro. Let us make that division.

Soc. Of the latter class, the most exact of all are those which we just now spoke of as primary.

Pro. I see that you mean arithmetic, and the kindred arts of weighing and measuring.

Soc. Certainly, Protarchus; but are not these also distinguishable into two kinds?

Pro. What are the two kinds?

Soc. In the first place, arithmetic is of two kinds, one of which is popular, and the other philosophical.

Pro. How would you distinguish them?

Soc. There is a wide difference between them, Protarchus; some arithmeticians reckon unequal units; as for example, two armies, two oxen, two very large things or two very small things. The party who are opposed to them insist that every unit in ten thousand must be the same as every other unit.

Pro. Undoubtedly there is, as you say, a great difference among the votaries of the science; and there may be reasonably supposed to be two sorts of arithmetic.

Soc. And when we compare the art of mensuration which is used in building with philosophical geometry, [57] or the art of computation which is used in trading with exact calculation, shall we say of either of the pairs that it is one or two?

Pro. On the analogy of what has preceded, I should be of opinion that they were severally two.

Soc. Right; but do you understand why I have discussed the subject?

Pro. I think so, but I should like to be told by you.

Soc. The argument has all along been seeking a parallel to pleasure, and true to that original design, has gone on to ask whether one sort of knowledge is purer than another, as one pleasure is purer than another.

Pro. Clearly; that was the intention.

Soc. And has not the argument in what has preceded, already shown that the arts have different provinces, and vary in their degrees of certainty?

Pro. Very true.

Soc. And just now did not the argument first designate a particular art by a common term, thus making us believe in the unity of that art; and then again, as if speaking of two different things, proceed to enquire whether the art as pursed by philosophers, or as pursued by non-philosophers, has more of certainty and purity?

Pro. That is the very question which the argument is asking.

Soc. And how, Protarchus, shall we answer the enquiry?

Pro. O Socrates, we have reached a point at which the difference of clearness in different kinds of knowledge is enormous.

Soc. Then the answer will be the easier.

Pro. Certainly; and let us say in reply, that those arts into which arithmetic and mensuration enter, far surpass all others; and that of these the arts or sciences which are animated by the pure philosophic impulse are infinitely superior in accuracy and truth.

Soc. Then this is your judgment; and this is the answer which, upon your authority, we will give to all masters of the art of misinterpretation?

Pro. What answer?

Soc. That there are two arts of arithmetic, and two of mensuration; and also several other arts which in like manner have this double nature, and yet only one name.

Pro. Let us boldly return this answer to the masters of whom you speak, Socrates, and hope for good luck.

Soc. We have explained what we term the most exact arts or sciences.

Pro. Very good.

Soc. And yet, Protarchus, dialectic will refuse to acknowledge us, if we do not award to her the first place.

[58] *Pro.* And pray, what is dialectic?

Soc. Clearly the science which has to do with all that knowledge of which we are now speaking; for I am sure that all men who have a grain of intelligence will admit that the knowledge which has to do with being and reality, and sameness and unchangeableness, is by far the truest of all. But how would you decide this question, Protarchus?

Pro. I have often heard Gorgias maintain, Socrates, that the art of persuasion far surpassed every other; this, as he says, is by far the best of them all, for to it all things submit, not by compulsion, but of their own free will. Now, I should not like to quarrel either with you or with him.

Soc. You mean to say that you would like to desert, if you were not ashamed?

Pro. As you please.

Soc. May I not have led you into a misapprehension?

Pro. How?

Soc. Dear Protarchus, I never asked which was the greatest or best or usefullest of arts or sciences, but which had clearness and accuracy, and the greatest amount of truth, however humble and little useful an art. And as for Gorgias, if you do not deny that his art has the advantage in usefulness to mankind, he will not quarrel with you for saying that the study of which I am speaking is superior in this particular of essential truth; as in the comparison of white colours, a little whiteness, if that little be only pure, was said to be superior in truth to a great mass which is impure. And now let us give our best attention and consider well, not the comparative use or reputation of the sciences, but the power or faculty, if there be such, which the soul has of loving the truth, and of doing all things for the sake of it; let us search into the pure element of mind and intelligence, and then we shall be able to say whether the science of which I have been speaking is most likely to possess the faculty, or whether there be some other which has higher claims.

Pro. Well, I have been considering, and I can hardly think that any other science or art has a firmer grasp of the truth than this.

[59] *Soc.* Do you say so because you observe that the arts in general and those engaged in them make use of opinion, and are resolutely engaged in the investigation of matters of opinion? Even he who supposes himself to be occupied with nature is really occupied with the things of this world, how created, how acting or acted upon. Is not this the sort of enquiry in which his life is spent?

Pro. True.

Soc. He is labouring, not after eternal being, but about things which are becoming, or which will or have become.

Pro. Very true.

Soc. And can we say that any of these things which neither are nor have been nor will be unchangeable, when judged by the strict rule of truth, ever become certain?

Pro. Impossible.

Soc. How can anything fixed be concerned with that which has no fixedness?

Pro. How indeed?

Soc. Then mind and science when employed about such changing things do not attain the highest truth?

Pro. I should imagine not.

Soc. And now let us bid farewell, a long farewell, to you or me or Philebus or Gorgias, and urge on behalf of the argument a single point.

Pro. What point?

Soc. Let us say that the stable and pure and true and unalloyed has to do with the things which are eternal and unchangeable and unmixed, or if not, at any rate what is most akin to them has; and that all other things are to be placed in a second or inferior class.

Pro. Very true.

Soc. And of the names expressing cognition, ought not the fairest to be given to the fairest things?

Pro. That is natural.

Soc. And are not mind and wisdom the names which are to be honoured most?

Pro. Yes.

Soc. And these names may be said to have their truest and most exact application when the mind is engaged in the contemplation of true being?

Pro. Certainly.

Soc. And these were the names which I adduced of the rivals of pleasure?

Pro. Very true, Socrates.

Soc. In the next place, as to the mixture, here are the ingredients, pleasure and wisdom, and we may be compared to artists who have their materials ready to their hands.

Pro. Yes.

Soc. And now we must begin to mix them?

Pro. By all means.

Soc. But had we not better have a preliminary word and refresh our memories?

Pro. Of what?

Soc. Of that which I have already mentioned. Well says the proverb, *[60]* that we ought to repeat twice and even thrice that which is good.

Pro. Certainly.

Soc. Well then, by Zeus, let us proceed, and I will make what I believe to be a fair summary of the argument.

Pro. Let me hear.

Soc. Philebus says that pleasure is the true end of all living beings, at which all ought to aim, and moreover that it is the chief good of all, and that the two names "good" and "pleasant" are correctly given to one thing and one nature; Socrates, on the other hand, begins by denying this, and further says, that in nature as in name they are two, and that wisdom partakes more than pleasure of the good. Is not and was not this what we were saying, Protarchus?

Pro. Certainly.

Soc. And is there not and was there not a further point which was conceded between us?

Pro. What was it?

Soc. That the good differs from all other things.

Pro. In what respect?

Soc. In that the being who possesses good always everywhere and in all things has the most perfect sufficiency, and is never in need of anything else.

Pro. Exactly.

Soc. And did we not endeavour to make an imaginary separation of wisdom and pleasure, assigning to each a distinct life, so that pleasure was wholly excluded from wisdom, and wisdom in like manner had no part whatever in pleasure?

Pro. We did.

Soc. And did we think that either of them alone would be sufficient?

Pro. Certainly not.

Soc. And if we erred in any point, then let any one who will, take up the enquiry again and set us right; and assuming memory and wisdom and knowledge and true opinion to belong to the same class, let him consider whether he would desire to possess or acquire —I will not say pleasure, however abundant or intense, if he has no real perception that he is pleased, nor any consciousness of what he feels, nor any recollection, however momentary, of the feeling,—but would he desire to have anything at all, if these faculties were wanting to him? And about wisdom I ask the same question; can you conceive that any one would choose to have all wisdom absolutely devoid of pleasure, rather than with a certain degree of pleasure, or all pleasure devoid of wisdom, rather than with a certain degree of wisdom?

Pro. Certainly not, Socrates; but why repeat such questions any more?

[61] Soc. Then the perfect and universally

eligible and entirely good cannot possibly be either of them?

Pro. Impossible.

Soc. Then now we must ascertain the nature of the good more or less accurately, in order, as we were saying, that the second place may be duly assigned?

Pro. Right.

Soc. Have we not found a road which leads towards the good?

Pro. What road?

Soc. Supposing that a man had to be found, and you could discover in what house he lived, would not that be a great step towards the discovery of the man himself?

Pro. Certainly.

Soc. And now reason intimates to us, as at our first beginning, that we should seek the good, not in the unmixed life but in the mixed.

Pro. True.

Soc. There is greater hope of finding that which we are seeking in the life which is well mixed than in that which is not?

Pro. Far greater.

Soc. Then now let us mingle, Protarchus, at the same time offering up a prayer to Dionysus or Hephaestus, or whoever is the god who presides over the ceremony of mingling.

Pro. By all means.

Soc. Are not we the cup-bearers? and here are two fountains which are flowing at our side: one, which is pleasure, may be likened to a fountain of honey; the other, wisdom, a sober draught in which no wine mingles, is of water unpleasant but healthful; out of these we must seek to make the fairest of all possible mixtures.

Pro. Certainly.

Soc. Tell me first;—should we be most likely to succeed if we mingled every sort of pleasure with every sort of wisdom?

Pro. Perhaps we might.

Soc. But I should be afraid of the risk, and I think that I can show a safer plan.

Pro. What is it?

Soc. One pleasure was supposed by us to be truer than another, and one art to be more exact than another.

Pro. Certainly.

Soc. There was also supposed to be a difference in sciences; some of them regarding only the transient and perishing, and others the permanent and imperishable and everlasting and immutable; and when judged by the standard of truth, the latter, as we thought, were truer than the former.

Pro. Very good and right.

Soc. If, then, we were to begin by mingling the sections of each class which have the most of truth, will not the union suffice to give us the loveliest of lives, or shall we still want some elements of another kind?

[62] Pro. I think that we ought to do what you suggest.

Soc. Let us suppose a man who understands justice, and has reason as well as understanding about the true nature of this and of all other things.

Pro. We will suppose such a man.

Soc. Will he have enough of knowledge if he is acquainted only with the divine circle and sphere, and knows nothing of our human spheres and circles, but uses only divine circles and measures in the building of a house?

Pro. The knowledge which is only superhuman, Socrates, is ridiculous in man.

Soc. What do you mean? Do you mean that you are to throw into the cup and mingle the impure and uncertain art which uses the false measure and the false circle?

Pro. Yes, we must, if any of us is ever to find his way home.

Soc. And am I to include music, which, as I was saying just now, is full of guesswork and imitation, and is wanting in purity?

Pro. Yes, I think that you must, if human life is to be a life at all.

Soc. Well, then, suppose that I give way, and, like a doorkeeper who is pushed and overborne by the mob, I open the door wide, and let knowledge of every sort stream in, and the pure mingle with the impure?

Pro. I do not know, Socrates, that any great harm would come of having them all, if only you have the first sort.

Soc. Well, then, shall I let them all flow into what Homer poetically terms "a meeting of the waters"?

Pro. By all means.

Soc. There—I have let him in, and now I must return to the fountain of pleasure. For we were not permitted to begin by mingling in a single stream the true portions of both according to our original intention; but the love of all knowledge constrained us to let all the sciences flow in together before the pleasures.

Pro. Quite true.

Soc. And now the time has come for us to consider about the pleasures also, whether we shall in like manner let them go all at once, or at first only the true ones.

Pro. It will be by far the safer course to let flow the true ones first.

Soc. Let them flow, then; and now, if there are any necessary pleasures, as there were arts and sciences necessary, must we not mingle them?

Pro. Yes; the necessary pleasures should certainly be allowed to mingle.

[63] *Soc.* The knowledge of the arts has been admitted to be innocent and useful always; and if we say of pleasures in like manner that all of them are good and innocent for all of us at all times, we must let them all mingle?

Pro. What shall we say about them, and what course shall we take?

Soc. Do not ask me, Protarchus; but ask the daughters of pleasure and wisdom to answer for themselves.

Pro. How?

Soc. Tell us, O beloved—shall we call you pleasures or by some other name?—would you rather live with or without wisdom? I am of opinion that they would certainly answer as follows:

Pro. How?

Soc. They would answer, as we said before, that for any single class to be left by itself pure and isolated is not good, nor altogether possible; and that if we are to make comparisons of one class with another and choose, there is no better companion than knowledge of things in general, and likewise the perfect knowledge, if that may be, of ourselves in every respect.

Pro. And our answer will be:—In that ye have spoken well.

Soc. Very true. And now let us go back and interrogate wisdom and mind: Would you like to have any pleasures in the mixture? And they will reply:—"What pleasures do you mean?"

Pro. Likely enough.

Soc. And we shall take up our parable and say: Do you wish to have the greatest and most vehement pleasures for your companions in addition to the true ones? "Why, Socrates," they will say, "how can we? seeing that they are the source of ten thousand hindrances to us; they trouble the souls of men, which are our habitation, with their madness; they prevent us from coming to the birth, and are commonly the ruin of the children which are born to us, causing them to be forgotten and unheeded; but the true and pure pleasures, of which you spoke, know to be of our family, and also those pleasures which accompany health and temperance, and which every Virtue, like a goddess has in her train to follow her about wherever she goes,—mingle these and not the others; there would be great want of sense in any one

who desires to see a fair [64] and perfect mixture, and to find in it what is the highest good in man and in the universe, and to divine what is the true form of good—there would be great want of sense in his allowing the pleasures, which are always in the company of folly and vice, to mingle with mind in the cup."—Is not this a very rational and suitable reply, which mind has made, both on her own behalf, as well as on the behalf of memory and true opinion?

Pro. Most certainly.

Soc. And still there must be something more added, which is a necessary ingredient in every mixture.

Pro. What is that?

Soc. Unless truth enter into the composition, nothing can truly be created or subsist.

Pro. Impossible.

Soc. Quite impossible; and now you and Philebus must tell me whether anything is still wanting in the mixture, for to my way of thinking the argument is now completed, and may be compared to an incorporeal law, which is going to hold fair rule over a living body.

Pro. I agree with you, Socrates.

Soc. And may we not say with reason that we are now at the vestibule of the habitation of the good?

Pro. I think that we are.

Soc. What, then, is there in the mixture which is most precious, and which is the principal cause why such a state is universally beloved by all? When we have discovered it, we will proceed to ask whether this omnipresent nature is more akin to pleasure or to mind.

Pro. Quite right; in that way we shall be better able to judge.

Soc. And there is no difficulty in seeing the cause which renders any mixture either of the highest value or of none at all.

Pro. What do you mean?

Soc. Every man knows it.

Pro. What?

Soc. He knows that any want of measure and symmetry in any mixture whatever must always of necessity be fatal, both to the elements and to the mixture, which is then not a mixture, but only a confused medley which brings confusion on the possessor of it.

Pro. Most true.

Soc. And now the power of the good has retired into the region of the beautiful; for measure and symmetry are beauty and virtue all the world over.

Pro. True.

Soc. Also we said that truth was to form an element in the mixture.

[65] *Pro.* Certainly.

Soc. Then, if we are not able to hunt the good with one idea only, with three we may catch our prey; Beauty, Symmetry, Truth are the three, and these taken together we may regard as the single cause of the mixture, and the mixture as being good by reason of the infusion of them.

Pro. Quite right.

Soc. And now, Protarchus, any man could decide well enough whether pleasure or wisdom is more akin to the highest good, and more honourable among gods and men.

Pro. Clearly, and yet perhaps the argument had better be pursued to the end.

Soc. We must take each of them separately in their relation to pleasure and mind, and pronounce upon them; for we ought to see to which of the two they are severally most akin.

Pro. You are speaking of beauty, truth, and measure?

Soc. Yes, Protarchus, take truth first, and, after passing in review mind, truth, pleasure, pause awhile and make answer to yourself—as to whether pleasure or mind is more akin to truth.

Pro. There is no need to pause, for the difference between them is palpable; pleasure is the veriest impostor in the world; and it is said that in the pleasures of love, which appear to be the greatest, perjury is excused by the gods; for pleasures, like children, have not the least particle of reason in them; whereas mind is either the same as truth, or the most like truth, and the truest.

Soc. Shall we next consider measure, in like manner, and ask whether pleasure has more of this than wisdom, or wisdom than pleasure?

Pro. Here is another question which may be easily answered; for I imagine that nothing can ever be more immoderate than the transports of pleasure, or more in conformity with measure than mind and knowledge.

Soc. Very good; but there still remains the third test: Has mind a greater share of beauty than pleasure, and is mind or pleasure the fairer of the two?

Pro. No one, Socrates, either awake or dreaming, ever saw or imagined mind or wisdom to be in aught unseemly, at any time, past, present, or future.

Soc. Right.

Pro. But when we see some one indulging in pleasures, perhaps in the greatest of pleasures,

[66] the ridiculous or disgraceful nature of the action makes us ashamed; and so we put them out of sight, and consign them to darkness, under the idea that they ought not to meet the eye of day.

Soc. Then, Protarchus, you will proclaim everywhere, by word of mouth to this company, and by messengers bearing the tidings far and wide, that pleasure is not the first of possessions, nor yet the second, but that in measure, and the mean, and the suitable, and the like, the eternal nature has been found.

Pro. Yes, that seems to be the result of what has been now said.

Soc. In the second class is contained the symmetrical and beautiful and perfect or sufficient, and all which are of that family.

Pro. True.

Soc. And if you reckon in the third class mind and wisdom, you will not be far wrong, if I divine aright.

Pro. I dare say.

Soc. And would you not put in the fourth class the goods which we were affirming to appertain specially to the soul—sciences and arts and true opinions as we called them? These come after the third class, and form the fourth, as they are certainly more akin to good than pleasure is.

Pro. Surely.

Soc. The fifth class are the pleasures which were defined by us as painless, being the pure pleasures of the soul herself, as we termed them, which accompany, some the sciences, and some the senses.

Pro. Perhaps.

Soc. And now, as Orpheus says,

With the sixth generation cease the glory of my song.

Here, at the sixth award, let us make an end; all that remains is to set the crown on our discourse.

Pro. True.

Soc. Then let us sum up and reassert what has been said, thus offering the third libation to the saviour Zeus.

Pro. How?

Soc. Philebus affirmed that pleasure was always and absolutely the good.

Pro. I understand; this third libation, Socrates, of which you spoke, meant a recapitulation.

Soc. Yes, but listen to the sequel; convinced of what I have just been saying, and feeling indignant at the doctrine, which is maintained, not by Philebus only, but by thousands of others, I affirmed that mind was far better and far more excellent, as an element of human life, than pleasure.

Pro. True.

Soc. But, suspecting that there were other things which were also better, I went on to say that if there was anything better than either, then I would claim the second place for mind over pleasure, and pleasure would lose the second place as well as the first.

Pro. You did.

[67] Soc. Nothing could be more satisfactorily shown than the unsatisfactory nature of both of them.

Pro. Very true.

Soc. The claims both of pleasure and mind to be the absolute good have been entirely disproven in this argument, because they are both wanting in self-sufficiency and also in adequacy and perfection.

Pro. Most true.

Soc. But, though they must both resign in favour of another, mind is ten thousand times nearer and more akin to the nature of the conqueror than pleasure.

Pro. Certainly.

Soc. And, according to the judgment which has now been given, pleasure will rank fifth.

Pro. True.

Soc. But not first; no, not even if all the oxen and horses and animals in the world by their pursuit of enjoyment proclaim her to be so;—although the many trusting in them, as diviners trust in birds, determine that pleasures make up the good of life, and deem the lusts of animals to be better witnesses than the inspirations of divine philosophy.

Pro. And now, Socrates, we tell you that the truth of what you have been saying is approved by the judgment of all of us.

Soc. And will you let me go?

Pro. There is a little which yet remains, and I will remind you of it, for I am sure that you will not be the first to go away from an argument.

LAWS

PERSONS OF THE DIALOGUE: *An* ATHENIAN STRANGER; CLEINIAS, *a Cretan;* MEGILLUS, *a Lacedaemonian*

BOOK I

[624] *Athenian Stranger.* TELL me, Strangers, is a God or some man supposed to be the author of your laws?

Cleinias. A God, Stranger; in very truth a God: among us Cretans he is said to have been Zeus, but in Lacedaemon, whence our friend here comes, I believe they would say that Apollo is their lawgiver: would they not, Megillus?

Megillus. Certainly.

Ath. And do you, Cleinias, believe, as Homer tells, that every ninth year Minos went to converse with his Olympian sire, and was inspired by him to make laws for your cities?

Cle. Yes, that is our tradition; and there was Rhadamanthus, a brother of his, with whose name you are familiar; he is reputed to have been the justest of men, *[625]* and we Cretans are of opinion that he earned this reputation from his righteous administration of justice when he was alive.

Ath. Yes, and a noble reputation it was, worthy of a son of Zeus. As you and Megillus have been trained in these institutions, I dare say that you will not be unwilling to give an account of your government and laws; on our way we can pass the time pleasantly in talking about them, for I am told that the distance from Cnosus to the cave and temple of Zeus is considerable; and doubtless there are shady places under the lofty trees, which will protect us from this scorching sun. Being no longer young, we may often stop to rest beneath them, and get over the whole journey without difficulty, beguiling the time by conversation.

Cle. Yes, Stranger, and if we proceed onward we shall come to groves of cypresses, which are of rare height and beauty, and there are green meadows, in which we may repose and converse.

Ath. Very good.

Cle. Very good, indeed; and still better when we see them; let us move on cheerily.

Ath. I am willing—And first, I want to know why the law has ordained that you shall have common meals and gymnastic exercises, and wear arms.

Cle. I think, Stranger, that the aim of our institutions is easily intelligible to any one. Look at the character of our country: Crete is not like Thessaly, a large plain; and for this reason they have horsemen in Thessaly, and we have runners—the inequality of the ground in our country is more adapted to locomotion on foot; but then, if you have runners you must have light arms—no one can carry a heavy weight when running, and bows and arrows are convenient because they are light. Now all these regulations have been made with a view to war, and the legislator appears to me to have looked to this in all his arrangements:—the common meals, if I am not mistaken, were instituted by him for a similar reason, because he saw that while they are in the field the citizens are by the nature of the case compelled to take their meals together for the sake of mutual protection. He seems to me to have thought the world foolish in not understanding that all men are always at war with one another; *[626]* and if in war there ought to be common meals and certain persons regularly appointed under others to protect an army, they should be continued in peace. For what men in general term peace would be said by him to be only a name; in reality every city is in a natural state of war with every other, not indeed proclaimed by heralds, but everlasting. And if you look closely, you will find that this was the intention of the Cretan legislator; all institutions, private as well as public, were arranged by him with a view to war; in giving them he was under the impression that no possessions or institutions are of any value to him who is defeated in battle; for all the good things of the conquered pass into the hands of the conquerors.

Ath. You appear to me, Stranger, to have been thoroughly trained in the Cretan institutions, and to be well informed about them; will you tell me a little more explicitly what is the principle of government which you would lay down? You seem to imagine that a well-governed state ought to be so ordered as to conquer all other states in war: am I right in supposing this to be your meaning?

Cle. Certainly; and our Lacedaemonian friend, if I am not mistaken, will agree with me.

Meg. Why, my good friend, how could any Lacedaemonian say anything else?

Ath. And is what you say applicable only to states, or also to villages?

Cle. To both alike.

Ath. The case is the same?

Cle. Yes.

Ath. And in the village will there be the same war of family against family, and of individual against individual?

Cle. The same.

Ath. And should each man conceive himself to be his own enemy:—what shall we say?

Cle. O Athenian Stranger—inhabitant of Attica I will not call you, for you seem to deserve rather to be named after the goddess herself, because you go back to first principles—you have thrown a light upon the argument, and will now be better able to understand what I was just saying—that all men are publicly one another's enemies, and each man privately his own.

(*Ath.* My good sir, what do you mean?)—

Cle. . . . . . Moreover, there is a victory and defeat—the first and best of victories, the lowest and worst of defeats—which each man gains or sustains at the hands, not of another, but of himself; this shows that there is a war, against ourselves going on within every one of us.

[627] Ath. Let us now reverse the order of the argument: Seeing that every individual is either his own superior or his own inferior, may we say that there is the same principle in the house, the village, and the state?

Cle. You mean that in each of them there is a principle of superiority or inferiority to self?

Ath. Yes.

Cle. You are quite right in asking the question, for there certainly is such a principle, and above all in states; and the state in which the better citizens win a victory over the mob and over the inferior classes may be truly said to be better than itself, and may be justly praised, where such a victory is gained, or censured in the opposite case.

Ath. Whether the better is ever really conquered by the worse, is a question which requires more discussion, and may be therefore left for the present. But I now quite understand your meaning when you say that citizens who are of the same race and live in the same cities may unjustly conspire, and having the superiority in numbers may overcome and enslave the few just; and when they prevail, the state may be truly called its own inferior and therefore bad; and when they are defeated, its own superior and therefore good.

Cle. Your remark, Stranger, is a paradox, and yet we cannot possibly deny it.

Ath. Here is another case for consideration; —in a family there may be several brothers, who are the offspring of a single pair; very possibly the majority of them may be unjust, and the just may be in a minority.

Cle. Very possibly.

Ath. And you and I ought not to raise a question of words as to whether this family and household are rightly said to be superior when they conquer, and inferior when they are conquered; for we are not now considering what may or may not be the proper or customary way of speaking, but we are considering the natural principles of right and wrong in laws.

Cle. What you say, Stranger, is most true.

Meg. Quite excellent, in my opinion, as far as we have gone.

Ath. Again; might there not be a judge over these brethren, of whom we were speaking?

Cle. Certainly.

Ath. Now, which would be the better judge —one who destroyed the bad and appointed the good to govern themselves; or one who, while allowing the good to govern, let the bad live, and made them voluntarily submit? Or third, I suppose, in the scale of excellence might be placed a judge, [628] who, finding the family distracted, not only did not destroy any one, but reconciled them to one another for ever after, and gave them laws which they mutually observed, and was able to keep them friends.

Cle. The last would be by far the best sort of judge and legislator.

Ath. And yet the aim of all the laws which he gave would be the reverse of war.

Cle. Very true.

Ath. And will he who constitutes the state and orders the life of man have in view external war, or that kind of intestine war called civil, which no one, if he could prevent, would like to have occurring in his own state; and when occurring, every one would wish to be quit of as soon as possible?

Cle. He would have the latter chiefly in view.

Ath. And would he prefer that this civil war should be terminated by the destruction of one of the parties, and by the victory of the other, or that peace and friendship should be re-established, and that, being reconciled, they should give their attention to foreign enemies?

Cle. Every one would desire the latter in the case of his own state.

Ath. And would not that also be the desire of the legislator?

Cle. Certainly.

Ath. And would not every one always make laws for the sake of the best?

Cle. To be sure.

Ath. But war, whether external or civil, is not the best, and the need of either is to be deprecated; but peace with one another, and good will, are best. Nor is the victory of the state over itself to be regarded as a really good thing, but as a necessity; a man might as well say that the body was in the best state when sick and purged by medicine, forgetting that there is also a state of the body which needs no purge. And in like manner no one can be a true statesman, whether he aims at the happiness of the individual or state, who looks only, or first of all, to external warfare; nor will he ever be a sound legislator who orders peace for the sake of war, and not war for the sake of peace.

Cle. I suppose that there is truth, Stranger, in that remark of yours; and yet I am greatly mistaken if war is not the entire aim and object of our own institutions, and also of the Lacedaemonian.

[629] *Ath.* I dare say; but there is no reason why we should rudely quarrel with one another about your legislators, instead of gently questioning them, seeing that both we and they are equally in earnest. Please follow me and the argument closely:—And first I will put forward Tyrtaeus, an Athenian by birth, but also a Spartan citizen, who of all men was most eager about war: Well, he says, "I sing not, I care not, about any man, even if he were the richest of men, and possessed every good (and then he gives a whole list of them), if he be not at all times a brave warrior." I imagine that you, too, must have heard his poems; our Lacedaemonian friend has probably heard more than enough of them.

Meg. Very true.

Cle. And they have found their way from Lacedaemon to Crete.

Ath. Come now and let us all join in asking this question of Tyrtaeus: O most divine poet, we will say to him, the excellent praise which you have bestowed on those who excel in war sufficiently proves that you are wise and good, and I and Megillus and Cleinias of Cnosus do, as I believe, entirely agree with you. But we should like to be quite sure that we are speaking of the same men; tell us, then, do you agree with us in thinking that there are two kinds of war; or what would you say? A far inferior man to Tyrtaeus would have no difficulty in replying quite truly, that war is of two kinds— one which is universally called civil war, and is, as we were just now saying, of all wars the worst; the other, as we should all admit, in which we fall out with other nations who are of a different race, is a far milder form of warfare.

Cle. Certainly, far milder.

Ath. Well, now, when you praise and blame war in this high-flown strain, whom are you praising or blaming, and to which kind of war are you referring? I suppose that you must mean foreign war, if I am to judge from expressions of yours in which you say that you abominate those

Who refuse to look upon fields of blood, and will not draw near and strike at their enemies.

And we shall naturally go on to say to him— You, Tyrtaeus, as it seems, praise those who distinguish themselves in external and foreign war; and he must admit this.

Cle. Evidently.

Ath. They are good; but we say that there are still better men whose virtue is displayed in the greatest of all battles. [630] And we too have a poet whom we summon as a witness, Theognis, citizen of Megara in Sicily:

Cyrnus, he who is faithful in a civil broil is worth his weight in gold and silver.

And such an one is far better, as we affirm, than the other in a more difficult kind of war, much in the same degree as justice and temperance and wisdom, when united with courage, are better than courage only; for a man cannot be faithful and good in civil strife without having all virtue. But in the war of which Tyrtaeus speaks, many a mercenary soldier will take his stand and be ready to die at his post, and yet they are generally and almost without exception insolent, unjust, violent men, and the most senseless of human beings. You will ask what the conclusion is, and what I am seeking to prove: I maintain that the divine legislator of Crete, like any other who is worthy of consideration, will always and above all things in making laws have regard to the greatest virtue; which, according to Theognis, is loyalty in the hour of danger, and may be truly called perfect justice. Whereas, that virtue which Tyrtaeus highly praises is well enough, and was praised by the poet at the right time, yet in place and dignity may be said to be only fourth-rate.[1]

Cle. Stranger, we are degrading our inspired lawgiver to a rank which is far beneath him.

Ath. Nay, I think that we degrade not him but ourselves, if we imagine that Lycurgus and Minos laid down laws both in Lacedaemon and Crete mainly with a view to war.

Cle. What ought we to say then?

Ath. What truth and what justice require of us, if I am not mistaken, when speaking in behalf of divine excellence;—that the legislator when making his laws had in view not a part only, and this the lowest part of virtue, but all virtue, and that he devised classes of laws answering to the kinds of virtue; not in the way in which modern inventors of laws make the classes, for they only investigate and offer laws whenever a want is felt, and one man has a class of laws about allotments and heiresses, another about assaults; others about ten thousand other such matters. [631] But we maintain that the right way of examining into laws is to proceed as we have now done, and I admired the spirit of your exposition; for you were quite right in beginning with virtue, and saying that this was the aim of the giver of the law, but I thought that you went wrong when you added that all his legislation had a view only to a part, and the least part of virtue, and this called forth my subsequent remarks. Will

[1] It ranks after justice, temperance, and wisdom.

you allow me then to explain how I should have liked to have heard you expound the matter?

Cle. By all means.

Ath. You ought to have said, Stranger—The Cretan laws are with reason famous among the Hellenes; for they fulfil the object of laws, which is to make those who use them happy; and they confer every sort of good. Now goods are of two kinds: there are human and there are divine goods, and the human hang upon the divine; and the state which attains the greater, at the same time acquires the less, or, not having the greater, has neither. Of the lesser goods the first is health, the second beauty, the third strength, including swiftness in running and bodily agility generally, and the fourth is wealth, not the blind god [Pluto], but one who is keen of sight, if only he has wisdom for his companion. For wisdom is chief and leader of the divine class of goods, and next follows temperance; and from the union of these two with courage springs justice, and fourth in the scale of virtue is courage. All these naturally take precedence of the other goods, and this is the order in which the legislator must place them, and after them he will enjoin the rest of his ordinances on the citizens with a view to these, the human looking to the divine, and the divine looking to their leader mind. Some of his ordinances will relate to contracts of marriage which they make one with another, and then to the procreation and education of children, both male and female; the duty of the lawgiver will be to take charge of his citizens, in youth and age, and at every time of life, and to give them punishments and rewards; and in reference to all their intercourse with one another, he ought to consider their pains and pleasures and desires, and the vehemence of all their passions; he should keep a watch over them, and blame and praise them rightly by the mouth of the laws themselves. [632] Also with regard to anger and terror, and the other perturbations of the soul, which arise out of misfortune, and the deliverances from them which prosperity brings, and the experiences which come to men in diseases, or in war, or poverty, or the opposite of these; in all these states he should determine and teach what is the good and evil of the condition of each. In the next place, the legislator has to be careful how the citizens make their money and in what way they spend it, and to have an eye to their mutual contracts and dissolutions of contracts, whether voluntary or involuntary: he should see how they order all this, and consider where justice as well as injustice is found or is wanting in their several dealings with one another; and honour those who obey the law, and impose fixed penalties on those who disobey, until the round of civil life is ended, and the time has come for the consideration of the proper funeral rites and honours of the dead. And the lawgiver reviewing his work, will appoint guardians to preside over these things—some who walk by intelligence, others by true opinion only, and then mind will bind together all his ordinances and show them to be in harmony with temperance and justice, and not with wealth or ambition. This is the spirit, Stranger, in which I was and am desirous that you should pursue the subject. And I want to know the nature of all these things, and how they are arranged in the laws of Zeus, as they are termed, and in those of the Pythian Apollo, which Minos and Lycurgus gave; and how the order of them is discovered to his eyes, who has experience in laws gained either by study or habit, although they are far from being self-evident to the rest of mankind like ourselves.

Cle. How shall we proceed, Stranger?

Ath. I think that we must begin again as before, and first consider the habit of courage; and then we will go on and discuss another and then another form of virtue, if you please. In this way we shall have a model of the whole; and with these and similar discourses we will beguile the way. And when we have gone through all the virtues, we will show, by the grace of God, that the institutions of which I was speaking look to virtue.

[633] Meg. Very good; and suppose that you first criticize this praiser of Zeus and the laws of Crete.

Ath. I will try to criticize you and myself, as well as him, for the argument is a common concern. Tell me—were not first the syssitia, and secondly the gymnasia, invented by your legislator with a view to war?

Meg. Yes.

Ath. And what comes third, and what fourth? For that, I think, is the sort of enumeration which ought to be made of the remaining parts of virtue, no matter whether you call them parts or what their name is, provided the meaning is clear.

Meg. Then I, or any other Lacedaemonian, would reply that hunting is third in order.

Ath. Let us see if we can discover what comes fourth and fifth.

Meg. I think that I can get as far as the fourth

head, which is the frequent endurance of pain, exhibited among us Spartans in certain hand-to-hand fights; also in stealing with the prospect of getting a good beating; there is, too, the so-called Crypteia, or secret service, in which wonderful endurance is shown—our people wander over the whole country by day and by night, and even in winter have not a shoe to their foot, and are without beds to lie upon, and have to attend upon themselves. Marvellous, too, is the endurance which our citizens show in their naked exercises, contending against the violent summer heat; and there are many similar practices, to speak of which in detail would be endless.

Ath. Excellent, O Lacedaemonian Stranger. But how ought we to define courage? Is it to be regarded only as a combat against fears and pains, or also against desires and pleasures, and against flatteries; which exercise such a tremendous power, that they make the hearts even of respectable citizens to melt like wax?

Meg. I should say the latter.

Ath. In what preceded, as you will remember, our Cnosian friend was speaking of a man or a city being inferior to themselves:—Were you not, Cleinias?

Cle. I was.

Ath. Now, which is in the truest sense inferior, the man who is overcome by pleasure or by pain?

Cle. I should say the man who is overcome by pleasure; for all men deem him to be inferior in a more disgraceful sense, than the other who is overcome by pain.

Ath. But surely the lawgivers of Crete and Lacedaemon have not legislated for a courage which is lame of one leg, *[634]* able only to meet attacks which come from the left, but impotent against the insidious flatteries which come from the right?

Cle. Able to meet both, I should say.

Ath. Then let me once more ask, what institutions have you in either of your states which give a taste of pleasures, and do not avoid them any more than they avoid pains; but which set a person in the midst of them, and compel or induce him by the prospect of reward to get the better of them? Where is an ordinance about pleasure similar to that about pain to be found in your laws? Tell me what there is of this nature among you:—What is there which makes your citizen equally brave against pleasure and pain, conquering what they ought to conquer, and superior to the enemies who are most dangerous and nearest home?

Meg. I was able to tell you, Stranger, many laws which were directed against pain; but I do not know that I can point out any great or obvious examples of similar institutions which are concerned with pleasure; there are some lesser provisions, however, which I might mention.

Cle. Neither can I show anything of that sort which is at all equally prominent in the Cretan laws.

Ath. No wonder, my dear friends; and if, as is very likely, in our search after the true and good, one of us may have to censure the laws of the others, we must not be offended, but take kindly what another says.

Cle. You are quite right, Athenian Stranger, and we will do as you say.

Ath. At our time of life, Cleinias, there should be no feeling of irritation.

Cle. Certainly not.

Ath. I will not at present determine whether he who censures the Cretan or Lacedaemonian polities is right or wrong. But I believe that I can tell better than either of you what the many say about them. For assuming that you have reasonably good laws, one of the best of them will be the law forbidding any young men to enquire which of them are right or wrong; but with one mouth and one voice they must all agree that the laws are all good, for they came from God; and any one who says the contrary is not to be listened to. But an old man who remarks any defect in your laws may communicate his observation to a ruler or to an equal in years when no young man is present.

[635] Cle. Exactly so, Stranger; and like a diviner, although not there at the time, you seem to me quite to have hit the meaning of the legislator, and to say what is most true.

Ath. As there are no young men present, and the legislator has given old men free licence, there will be no impropriety in our discussing these very matters now that we are alone.

Cle. True. And therefore you may be as free as you like in your censure of our laws, for there is no discredit in knowing what is wrong; he who receives what is said in a generous and friendly spirit will be all the better for it.

Ath. Very good; however, I am not going to say anything against your laws until to the best of my ability I have examined them, but I am going to raise doubts about them. For you are the only people known to us, whether Greek or barbarian, whom the legislator commanded to eschew all great pleasures and amusements and never to touch them; whereas in the matter of pains or fears which we have just been discussing, he thought that they who from infancy had always avoided pains and fears and sorrows, when they were compelled to face them would run away from those who were hardened in them, and would become their subjects. Now the legislator ought to have considered that this was equally true of pleasure; he should have said to himself, that if our citizens are from their youth upward unacquainted with the greatest pleasures, and unused to endure amid the temptations of pleasure, and are not disciplined to refrain from all things evil, the sweet feeling of pleasure will overcome them just as fear would overcome the former class; and in another, and even a worse manner, they will be the slaves of those who are able to endure amid pleasures, and have had the opportunity of enjoying them, they being often the worst of mankind. One half of their souls will be a slave, the other half free; and they will not be worthy to be called in the true sense men and freemen. Tell me whether you assent to my words?

Cle. On first hearing, what you say appears to be the truth; but to be hasty in coming to a conclusion about such important matters would be very childish and simple.

Ath. Suppose, Cleinias and Megillus, that we consider the virtue which follows next of those which we intended to discuss (for after courage comes temperance), what institutions shall we find relating to temperance, either in Crete or Lacedaemon, which, like your military institutions, differ from those of any ordinary state.

[636] Meg. That is not an easy question to answer; still I should say that the common meals and gymnastic exercises have been excellently devised for the promotion both of temperance and courage.

Ath. There seems to be a difficulty, Stranger, with regard to states, in making words and facts coincide so that there can be no dispute about them. As in the human body, the regimen which does good in one way does harm in another; and we can hardly say that any one course of treatment is adapted to a particular constitution. Now the gymnasia and common meals do a great deal of good, and yet they are a source of evil in civil troubles; as is shown in the case of the Milesian, and Boeotian, and Thurian youth, among whom these institutions seem always to have had a tendency to degrade the ancient and natural custom of love below the level, not only of man, but of the beasts. The charge may be fairly brought against your cities above all others, and is true also of most other states which especially cultivate gymnastics. Whether such matters are to be regarded jestingly or seriously, I think that the pleasure is to be deemed natural which arises out of the intercourse between men and women; but that the intercourse of men with men, or of women with women, is contrary to nature, and that the bold attempt was originally due to unbridled lust. The Cretans are always accused of having invented the story of Ganymede and Zeus because they wanted to justify themselves in the enjoyment of unnatural pleasures by the practice of the god whom they believe to have been their lawgiver. Leaving the story, we may observe that any speculation about laws turns almost entirely on pleasure and pain, both in states and in individuals: these are two fountains which nature lets flow, and he who draws from them where and when, and as much as he ought, is happy; and this holds of men and animals—of individuals as well as states; and he who indulges in them ignorantly and at the wrong time, is the reverse of happy.

Meg. I admit, Stranger, that your words are well spoken, and I hardly know what to say in answer to you; but still I think that the Spartan lawgiver was quite right in forbidding pleasure. Of the Cretan laws, I shall leave the defence to my Cnosian friend. But the laws of Sparta, *[637]* in as far as they relate to pleasure, appear to me to be the best in the world; for that which leads mankind in general into the wildest pleasure and licence, and every other folly, the law has clean driven out; and neither in the country nor in towns which are under the control of Sparta, will you find revelries and the many incitements of every kind of pleasure which accompany them; and any one who meets a drunken and disorderly person, will immediately have him most severely punished, and will not let him off on any pretence, not even at the time of a Dionysiac festival; although I have remarked that this may happen at your performances "on the cart," as they are called; and among our Tarentine colonists I have seen the whole city drunk at a Dionysiac festival; but nothing of the sort happens among us.

Ath. O Lacedaemonian Stranger, these festivities are praiseworthy where there is a spirit of endurance, but are very senseless when they are under no regulations. In order to retaliate, an Athenian has only to point out the licence which exists among your women. To all such accusations, whether they are brought against the Tarentines, or us, or you, there is one answer which exonerates the practice in question from impropriety. When a stranger expresses wonder at the singularity of what he sees, any inhabitant will naturally answer him:—Wonder not, O stranger; this is our custom, and you may very likely have some other custom about the same things. Now we are speaking, my friends, not about men in general, but about the merits and defects of the lawgivers themselves. Let us then discourse a little more at length about intoxication, which is a very important subject, and will seriously task the discrimination of the legislator. I am not speaking of drinking, or not drinking, wine at all, but of intoxication. Are we to follow the custom of the Scythians, and Persians, and Carthaginians, and Celts, and Iberians, and Thracians, who are all warlike nations, or that of your countrymen, for they, as you say, altogether abstain? But the Scythians and Thracians, both men and women, drink unmixed wine, which they pour on their garments, and this they think a happy and glorious institution. The Persians, again, are much given to other practices of luxury which you reject, but they have more moderation in them than the Thracians and Scythians.

[638] Meg. O best of men, we have only to take arms into our hands, and we send all these nations flying before us.

Ath. Nay, my good friend, do not say that; there have been, as there always will be, flights and pursuits of which no account can be given, and therefore we cannot say that victory or defeat in battle affords more than a doubtful proof of the goodness or badness of institutions. For when the greater states conquer and enslave the lesser, as the Syracusans have done the Locrians, who appear to be the best-governed people in their part of the world, or as the Athenians have done the Ceans (and there are ten thousand other instances of the same sort of thing), all this is not to the point; let us endeavour rather to form a conclusion about each institution in itself and say nothing, at present, of victories and defeats. Let us only say that such and such a custom is honourable, and another not. And first permit me to tell you how good and bad are to be estimated in reference to these very matters.

Meg. How do you mean?

Ath. All those who are ready at a moment's notice to praise or censure any practice which is matter of discussion, seem to me to proceed in a wrong way. Let me give you an illustration of what I mean:—You may suppose a person to be praising wheat as a good kind of food, whereupon another person instantly blames wheat, without ever enquiring into its effect or use, or in what way, or to whom, or with what, or in what state and how, wheat is to be given. And that is just what we are doing in this discussion. At the very mention of the word intoxication, one side is ready with their praises and the other with their censures; which is absurd. For either side adduce their witnesses and approvers, and some of us think that we speak with authority because we have many witnesses; and others because they see those who abstain conquering in battle, and this again is disputed by us. Now I cannot say that I shall be satisfied, if we go on discussing each of the remaining laws in the same way. And about this very point of intoxication I should like to speak in another way, which I hold to be the right one; for if number is to be the criterion, are there not myriads upon myriads of nations ready to dispute the point with you, who are only two cities?

[639] Meg. I shall gladly welcome any method of enquiry which is right.

Ath. Let me put the matter thus:—Suppose a person to praise the keeping of goats, and the creatures themselves as capital things to have, and then some one who had seen goats feeding without a goatherd in cultivated spots, and doing mischief, were to censure a goat or any other animal who has no keeper, or a bad keeper, would there be any sense or justice in such censure?

Meg. Certainly not.

Ath. Does a captain require only to have nautical knowledge in order to be a good captain, whether he is sea-sick or not? What do you say?

Meg. I say that he is not a good captain if, although he have nautical skill, he is liable to sea-sickness.

Ath. And what would you say of the commander of an army? Will he be able to command merely because he has military skill if he be a coward, who, when danger comes, is sick and drunk with fear?

Meg. Impossible.

Ath. And what if besides being a coward he has no skill?

Meg. He is a miserable fellow, not fit to be a commander of men, but only of old women.

Ath. And what would you say of some one who blames or praises any sort of meeting which is intended by nature to have a ruler, and is well enough when under his presidency? The critic, however, has never seen the society meeting together at an orderly feast under the control of a president, but always without a ruler or with a bad one:—when observers of this class praise or blame such meetings, are we to suppose that what they say is of any value?

Meg. Certainly not, if they have never seen or been present at such a meeting when rightly ordered.

Ath. Reflect; may not banqueters and banquets be said to constitute a kind of meeting?

Meg. Of course.

Ath. And did any one ever see this sort of convivial meeting rightly ordered? Of course you two will answer that you have never seen them at all, because they are not customary or lawful in your country; but I have come across many of them in many different places, and moreover I have made enquiries about them wherever I went, as I may say, and never did I see or hear of anything of the kind which was carried on altogether rightly; in some few particulars they might be right, but in general they were utterly wrong.

Cle. What do you mean, Stranger, by this remark? Explain. For we, as you say, from our inexperience in such matters, might very likely not know, even if they came in our way, what was right or wrong in such societies.

[640] Ath. Likely enough; then let me try to be your instructor: You would acknowledge, would you not, that in all gatherings of mankind, of whatever sort, there ought to be a leader?

Cle. Certainly I should.

Ath. And we were saying just now, that when men are at war the leader ought to be a brave man?

Cle. We were.

Ath. The brave man is less likely than the coward to be disturbed by fears?

Cle. That again is true.

Ath. And if there were a possibility of having a general of an army who was absolutely fearless and imperturbable, should we not by all means appoint him?

Cle. Assuredly.

Ath. Now, however, we are speaking not of a general who is to command an army, when foe meets foe in time of war, but of one who is to regulate meetings of another sort, when friend meets friend in time of peace.

Cle. True.

Ath. And that sort of meeting, if attended

with drunkenness, is apt to be unquiet.

Cle. Certainly; the reverse of quiet.

Ath. In the first place, then, the revellers as well as the soldiers will require a ruler?

Cle. To be sure; no men more so.

Ath. And we ought, if possible, to provide them with a quiet ruler?

Cle. Of course.

Ath. And he should be a man who understands society; for his duty is to preserve the friendly feelings which exist among the company at the time, and to increase them for the future by his use of the occasion.

Cle. Very true.

Ath. Must we not appoint a sober man and a wise to be our master of the revels? For if the ruler of drinkers be himself young and drunken, and not over-wise, only by some special good fortune will he be saved from doing some great evil.

Cle. It will be by a singular good fortune that he is saved.

Ath. Now suppose such associations to be framed in the best way possible in states, and that some one blames the very fact of their existence—he may very likely be right. But if he blames a practice which he only sees very much mismanaged, he shows in the first place that he is not aware of the mismanagement, and also not aware that everything done in this way will turn out to be wrong, because done without the superintendence of a sober ruler. Do you not see that a drunken pilot or a drunken ruler of any sort will ruin ship, *[641]* chariot, army—anything, in short, of which he has the direction?

Cle. The last remark is very true, Stranger; and I see quite clearly the advantage of an army having a good leader—he will give victory in war to his followers, which is a very great advantage; and so of other things. But I do not see any similar advantage which either individuals or states gain from the good management of a feast; and I want you to tell me what great good will be effected, supposing that this drinking ordinance is duly established.

Ath. If you mean to ask what great good accrues to the state from the right training of a single youth, or of a single chorus—when the question is put in that form, we cannot deny that the good is not very great in any particular instance. But if you ask what is the good of education in general, the answer is easy—that education makes good men, and that good men act nobly, and conquer their enemies in battle, because they are good. Education certainly gives victory, although victory sometimes produces forgetfulness of education; for many have grown insolent from victory in war, and this insolence has engendered in them innumerable evils; and many a victory has been and will be suicidal to the victors; but education is never suicidal.

Cle. You seem to imply, my friend, that convivial meetings, when rightly ordered, are an important element of education.

Ath. Certainly I do.

Cle. And can you show that what you have been saying is true?

Ath. To be absolutely sure of the truth of matters concerning which there are many opinions, is an attribute of the Gods not given to man, Stranger; but I shall be very happy to tell you what I think, especially as we are now proposing to enter on a discussion concerning laws and constitutions.

Cle. Your opinion, Stranger, about the questions which are now being raised, is precisely what we want to hear.

Ath. Very good; I will try to find a way of explaining my meaning, and you shall try to have the gift of understanding me. But first let me make an apology. The Athenian citizen is reputed among all the Hellenes to be a great talker, whereas Sparta is renowned for brevity, *[642]* and the Cretans have more wit than words. Now I am afraid of appearing to elicit a very long discourse out of very small materials. For drinking indeed may appear to be a slight matter, and yet is one which cannot be rightly ordered according to nature, without correct principles of music; these are necessary to any clear or satisfactory treatment of the subject, and music again runs up into education generally, and there is much to be said about all this. What would you say then to leaving these matters for the present, and passing on to some other question of law?

Meg. O Athenian Stranger, let me tell you what perhaps you do not know, that our family is the proxenus of your state. I imagine that from their earliest youth all boys, when they are told that they are the proxeni of a particular state, feel kindly towards their second country; and this has certainly been my own feeling. I can well remember from the days of my boyhood, how, when any Lacedaemonians praised or blamed the Athenians, they used to say to me—"See, Megillus, how ill or how well," as the case might be, "has your state treated us"; and having always had to fight your battles against detractors when I heard you assailed, I became warmly attached to you. And I always like to hear the Athenian tongue spoken; the common saying is quite true, that a good Athenian is more than ordinarily good, for he is the only man who is freely and genuinely good by the divine inspiration of his own nature, and is not manufactured. Therefore be assured that I shall like to hear you say whatever you have to say.

Cle. Yes, Stranger; and when you have heard me speak, say boldly what is in your thoughts. Let me remind you of a tie which unites you to Crete. You must have heard here the story of the prophet Epimenides, who was of my family, and came to Athens ten years before the Persian war, in accordance with the response of the Oracle, and offered certain sacrifices which the God commanded. The Athenians were at that time in dread of the Persian invasion; and he said that for ten years they would not come, and that when they came, they would go away again without accomplishing any of their objects, and would suffer more evil than they inflicted. At that time my forefathers formed ties of hospitality with you; thus ancient is the friendship which I and my parents have had for you.

[643] Ath. You seem to be quite ready to listen; and I am also ready to perform as much as I can of an almost impossible task, which I will nevertheless attempt. At the outset of the discussion, let me define the nature and power of education; for this is the way by which our argument must travel onwards to the God Dionysus.

Cle. Let us proceed, if you please.

Ath. Well, then, if I tell you what are my notions of education, will you consider whether they satisfy you?

Cle. Let us hear.

Ath. According to my view, any one who would be good at anything must practise that thing from his youth upwards, both in sport and earnest, in its several branches: for example, he who is to be a good builder, should play at building children's houses; he who is to be a good husbandman, at tilling the ground; and those who have the care of their education should provide them when young with mimic tools. They should learn beforehand the knowledge which they will afterwards require for their art. For example, the future carpenter should learn to measure or apply the line in play; and the future warrior should learn riding, or some other exercise, for amusement, and the teacher should endeavour to direct the chil-

dren's inclinations and pleasures, by the help of amusements, to their final aim in life. The most important part of education is right training in the nursery. The soul of the child in his play should be guided to the love of that sort of excellence in which when he grows up to manhood he will have to be perfected. Do you agree with me thus far?

Cle. Certainly.

Ath. Then let us not leave the meaning of education ambiguous or ill-defined. At present, when we speak in terms of praise or blame about the bringing-up of each person, we call one man educated and another uneducated, although the uneducated man may be sometimes very well educated for the calling of a retail trader, or of a captain of a ship, and the like. For we are not speaking of education in this narrower sense, but of that other education in virtue from youth upwards, which makes a man eagerly pursue the ideal perfection of citizenship, and teaches him how rightly to rule and how to obey. *[644]* This is the only education which, upon our view, deserves the name; that other sort of training, which aims at the acquisition of wealth or bodily strength, or mere cleverness apart from intelligence and justice, is mean and illiberal, and is not worthy to be called education at all. But let us not quarrel with one another about a word, provided that the proposition which has just been granted hold good: to wit, that those who are rightly educated generally become good men. Neither must we cast a slight upon education, which is the first and fairest thing that the best of men can ever have, and which, though liable to take a wrong direction, is capable of reformation. And this work of reformation is the great business of every man while he lives.

Cle. Very true; and we entirely agree with you.

Ath. And we agreed before that they are good men who are able to rule themselves, and bad men who are not.

Cle. You are quite right.

Ath. Let me now proceed, if I can, to clear up the subject a little further by an illustration which I will offer you.

Cle. Proceed.

Ath. Do we not consider each of ourselves to be one?

Cle. We do.

Ath. And each one of us has in his bosom two counsellors, both foolish and also antagonistic; of which we call the one pleasure, and the other pain.

Cle. Exactly.

Ath. Also there are opinions about the future, which have the general name of expectations; and the specific name of fear, when the expectation is of pain; and of hope, when of pleasure; and further, there is reflection about the good or evil of them, and this, when embodied in a decree by the State, is called Law.

Cle. I am hardly able to follow you; proceed, however, as if I were.

Meg. I am in the like case.

Ath. Let us look at the matter thus: May we not conceive each of us living beings to be a puppet of the Gods, either their plaything only, or created with a purpose—which of the two we cannot certainly know? But we do know, that these affections in us are like cords and strings, which pull us different and opposite ways, and to opposite actions; and herein lies the difference between virtue and vice. According to the argument there is one among these cords which every man ought to grasp and never let go, but to pull with it against all the rest; [645] and this is the sacred and golden cord of reason, called by us the common law of the State; there are others which are hard and of iron, but this one is soft because golden; and there are several other kinds. Now we ought always to co-operate with the lead of the best, which is law. For inasmuch as reason is beautiful and gentle, and not violent, her rule must needs have ministers in order to help the golden principle in vanquishing the other principles. And thus the moral of the tale about our being puppets will not have been lost, and the meaning of the expression "superior or inferior to a man's self" will become clearer; and the individual, attaining to right reason in this matter of pulling the strings of the puppet, should live according to its rule; while the city, receiving the same from some god or from one who has knowledge of these things, should embody it in a law, to be her guide in her dealings with herself and with other states. In this way virtue and vice will be more clearly distinguished by us. And when they have become clearer, education and other institutions will in like manner become clearer; and in particular that question of convivial entertainment, which may seem, perhaps, to have been a very trifling matter, and to have taken a great many more words than were necessary.

Cle. Perhaps, however, the theme may turn out not to be unworthy of the length of discourse.

Ath. Very good; let us proceed with any enquiry which really bears on our present object.

Cle. Proceed.

Ath. Suppose that we give this puppet of ours drink—what will be the effect on him?

Cle. Having what in view do you ask that question?

Ath. Nothing as yet; but I ask generally, when the puppet is brought to the drink, what sort of result is likely to follow. I will endeavour to explain my meaning more clearly: what I am now asking is this—Does the drinking of wine heighten and increase pleasures and pains, and passions and loves?

Cle. Very greatly.

Ath. And are perception and memory, and opinion and prudence, heightened and increased? Do not these qualities entirely desert a man if he becomes saturated with drink?

Cle. Yes, they entirely desert him.

Ath. Does he not return to the state of soul in which he was when a young child?

Cle. He does.

Ath. Then at that time he will have the least control over himself?

Cle. The least.

[646] *Ath*. And will he not be in a most wretched plight?

Cle. Most wretched.

Ath. Then not only an old man but also a drunkard becomes a second time a child?

Cle. Well said, Stranger.

Ath. Is there any argument which will prove to us that we ought to encourage the taste for drinking instead of doing all we can to avoid it?

Cle. I suppose that there is; you, at any rate, were just now saying that you were ready to maintain such a doctrine.

Ath. True, I was; and I am ready still, seeing that you have both declared that you are anxious to hear me.

Cle. To be sure we are, if only for the strangeness of the paradox, which asserts that a man ought of his own accord to plunge into utter degradation.

Ath. Are you speaking of the soul?

Cle. Yes.

Ath. And what would you say about the body, my friend? Are you not surprised at any one of his own accord bringing upon himself deformity, leanness, ugliness, decrepitude?

Cle. Certainly.

Ath. Yet when a man goes of his own accord to a doctor's shop, and takes medicine, is he not quite aware that soon, and for many days afterwards, he will be in a state of body which he would die rather than accept as the permanent condition of his life? Are not those who train in gymnasia, at first beginning reduced to a state of weakness?

Cle. Yes, all that is well known.

Ath. Also that they go of their own accord for the sake of the subsequent benefit?

Cle. Very good.

Ath. And we may conceive this to be true in the same way of other practices?

Cle. Certainly.

Ath. And the same view may be taken of the pastime of drinking wine, if we are right in supposing that the same good effect follows?

Cle. To be sure.

Ath. If such convivialities should turn out to have any advantage equal in importance to that of gymnastic, they are in their very nature to be preferred to mere bodily exercise, inasmuch as they have no accompaniment of pain.

Cle. True; but I hardly think that we shall be able to discover any such benefits to be derived from them.

Ath. That is just what we must endeavour to show. And let me ask you a question:—Do we not distinguish two kinds of fear, which are very different?

Cle. What are they?

Ath. There is the fear of expected evil.

Cle. Yes.

Ath. And there is the fear of an evil reputation; we are afraid of being thought evil, *[647]* because we do or say some dishonourable thing, which fear we and all men term shame.

Cle. Certainly.

Ath. These are the two fears, as I called them; one of which is the opposite of pain and other fears, and the opposite also of the greatest and most numerous sort of pleasures.

Cle. Very true.

Ath. And does not the legislator and every one who is good for anything, hold this fear in the greatest honour? This is what he terms reverence, and the confidence which is the reverse of this he terms insolence; and the latter he always deems to be a very great evil both to individuals and to states.

Cle. True.

Ath. Does not this kind of fear preserve us in many important ways? What is there which so surely gives victory and safety in war? For there are two things which give victory—confidence before enemies, and fear of disgrace before friends.

Cle. There are.

Ath. Then each of us should be fearless and also fearful; and why we should be either has now been determined.

Cle. Certainly.

Ath. And when we want to make any one fearless, we and the law bring him face to face with many fears.

Cle. Clearly.

Ath. And when we want to make him rightly fearful, must we not introduce him to shameless pleasures, and train him to take up arms against them, and to overcome them? Or does this principle apply to courage only, and must he who would be perfect in valour fight against and overcome his own natural character— since if he be unpractised and inexperienced in such conflicts, he will not be half the man which he might have been—and are we to suppose, that with temperance it is otherwise, and that he who has never fought with the shameless and unrighteous temptations of his pleasures and lusts, and conquered them, in earnest and in play, by word, deed, and act, will still be perfectly temperate?

Cle. A most unlikely supposition.

Ath. Suppose that some God had given a fear-potion to men, and that the more a man drank of this the more he regarded himself at every draught as a child of misfortune, and that he feared everything happening or about to happen to him; and that at last the most courageous of men utterly lost his presence of mind for a time, and only came to himself again when he had slept off the influence *[648]* of the draught.

Cle. But has such a draught, Stranger, ever really been known among men?

Ath. No; but, if there had been, might not such a draught have been of use to the legislator as a test of courage? Might we not go and say to him, "O legislator, whether you are legislating for the Cretan, or for any other state, would you not like to have a touchstone of the courage and cowardice of your citizens?"

Cle. "I should," will be the answer of every one.

Ath. "And you would rather have a touchstone in which there is no risk and no great danger than the reverse?"

Cle. In that proposition every one may safely agree.

Ath. "And in order to make use of the draught, you would lead them amid these imaginary terrors, and prove them, when the affection of fear was working upon them, and compel them to be fearless, exhorting and admonishing them; and also honouring them, but dishonouring any one who will not be persuaded by you to be in all respects such as you command him; and if he underwent the trial well and manfully, you would let him go unscathed; but if ill, you would inflict a punishment upon him? Or would you abstain from using the potion altogether, although you have no reason for abstaining?"

Cle. He would be certain, Stranger, to use the potion.

Ath. This would be a mode of testing and training which would be wonderfully easy in comparison with those now in use, and might be applied to a single person, or to a few, or indeed to any number; and he would do well who provided himself with the potion only, rather than with any number of other things, whether he preferred to be by himself in solitude, and there contend with his fears, because he was ashamed to be seen by the eye of man until he was perfect; or trusting to the force of his own nature and habits, and believing that he had been already disciplined sufficiently, he did not hesitate to train himself in company with any number of others, and display his power in conquering the irresistible change effected by the draught—his virtue being such, that he never in any instance fell into any great unseemliness, but was always himself, and left off before he arrived at the last cup, fearing that he, like all other men, might be overcome by the potion.

Cle. Yes, Stranger, in that last case, too, he might equally show his self-control.

[649] Ath. Let us return to the lawgiver, and say to him:—"Well, lawgiver, there is certainly no such fear-potion which man has either received from the Gods or himself discovered; for witchcraft has no place at our board. But is there any potion which might serve as a test of overboldness and excessive and indiscreet boasting?"

Cle. I suppose that he will say, Yes—meaning that wine is such a potion.

Ath. Is not the effect of this quite the opposite of the effect of the other? When a man drinks wine he begins to be better pleased with himself, and the more he drinks the more he is filled full of brave hopes, and conceit of his power, and at last the string of his tongue is loosened, and fancying himself wise, he is brimming over with lawlessness, and has no more fear or respect, and is ready to do or say anything.

Cle. I think that every one will admit the truth of your description.

Meg. Certainly.

Ath. Now, let us remember, as we were saying, that there are two things which should be cultivated in the soul: first, the greatest courage; secondly, the greatest fear—

Cle. Which you said to be characteristic of reverence, if I am not mistaken.

Ath. Thank you for reminding me. But now, as the habit of courage and fearlessness is to be trained amid fears, let us consider whether the opposite quality is not also to be trained among opposites.

Cle. That is probably the case.

Ath. There are times and seasons at which we are by nature more than commonly valiant and bold; now we ought to train ourselves on these occasions to be as free from impudence and shamelessness as possible, and to be afraid to say or suffer or do anything that is base.

Cle. True.

Ath. Are not the moments in which we are apt to be bold and shameless such as these?—when we are under the influence of anger, love, pride, ignorance, avarice, cowardice? or when wealth, beauty, strength, and all the intoxicating workings of pleasure madden us? What is better adapted than the festive use of wine, in the first place to test, and in the second place to train the character of a man, if care be taken in the use of it? What is there cheaper, or more innocent? For do but consider which is the greater risk:—Would you rather test a man of a morose and savage nature, which is the source of ten thousand acts of injustice, by making bargains with him at a risk to yourself, *[650]* or by having him as a companion at the festival of Dionysus? Or would you, if you wanted to apply a touchstone to a man who is prone to love, entrust your wife, or your sons, or daughters to him, perilling your dearest interests in order to have a view of the condition of his soul? I might mention numberless cases, in which the advantage would be manifest of getting to know a character in sport, and without paying dearly for experience. And I do not believe that either a Cretan, or any other man, will doubt that such a test is a fair test, and safer, cheaper, and speedier than any other.

Cle. That is certainly true.

Ath. And this knowledge of the natures and habits of men's souls will be of the greatest use in that art which has the management of them; and that art, if I am not mistaken, is politics.

Cle. Exactly so.

BOOK II

[652] Athenian Stranger. AND now we have to consider whether the insight into human nature is the only benefit derived from well-ordered potations, or whether there are not other advantages great and much to be desired. The argument seems to imply that there are. But how and in what way these are to be attained, will have to be considered attentively, or we may be entangled in error.

Cleinias. Proceed.

Ath. Let me once more recall our doctrine of right education; which, *[653]* if I am not mistaken, depends on the due regulation of convivial intercourse.

Cle. You talk rather grandly.

Ath. Pleasure and pain I maintain to be the first perceptions of children, and I say that they are the forms under which virtue and vice are originally present to them. As to wisdom and true and fixed opinions, happy is the man who acquires them, even when declining in years; and we may say that he who possesses them, and the blessings which are contained in them, is a perfect man. Now I mean by education that training which is given by suitable habits to the first instincts of virtue in children;—when pleasure, and friendship, and pain, and hatred, are rightly implanted in souls not yet capable of understanding the nature of them, and who find them, after they have attained reason, to be in harmony with her. This harmony of the soul, taken as a whole, is virtue; but the particular training in respect of pleasure and pain, which leads you always to hate what you ought to hate, and love what you ought to love from the beginning of life to the end, may be separated off; and, in my view, will be rightly called education.

Cle. I think, Stranger, that you are quite right in all that you have said and are saying about education.

Ath. I am glad to hear that you agree with me; for, indeed, the discipline of pleasure and pain which, when rightly ordered, is a principle of education, has been often relaxed and corrupted in human life. And the Gods, pitying the toils which our race is born to undergo, have appointed holy festivals, wherein men alternate rest with labour; and have given them the Muses and Apollo, the leader of the Muses, and Dionysus, to be companions in their revels, that they may improve their education by taking part in the festivals of the Gods, and with their help. I should like to know whether a common saying is in our opinion true to nature or not. For men say that the young of all creatures cannot be quiet in their bodies or in their voices; they are always wanting to move and cry out; some leaping and skipping, and overflowing with sportiveness and delight at something, others uttering all sorts of cries. But, whereas the animals have no perception of order or disorder in their movements, that is, of rhythm or harmony, as they are called, to us, the Gods, who, as we say, have been appointed to be our companions in the dance, *[654]* have given the pleasurable sense of harmony and rhythm; and so they stir us into life, and we follow them, joining hands together in dances and songs; and these they call choruses, which is a term naturally expressive of cheerfulness. Shall we begin, then, with the acknowledgment that education is first given through Apollo and the Muses? What do you say?

Cle. I assent.

Ath. And the uneducated is he who has not been trained in the chorus, and the educated is he who has been well trained?

Cle. Certainly.

Ath. And the chorus is made up of two parts, dance and song?

Cle. True.

Ath. Then he who is well educated will be able to sing and dance well?

Cle. I suppose that he will.

Ath. Let us see; what are we saying?

Cle. What?

Ath. He sings well and dances well; now must we add that he sings what is good and dances what is good?

Cle. Let us make the addition.

Ath. We will suppose that he knows the good to be good, and the bad to be bad, and makes use of them accordingly: which now is the better trained in dancing and music—he who is able to move his body and to use his voice in what is understood to be the right manner, but has no delight in good or hatred of evil; or he who is incorrect in gesture and voice, but is right in his sense of pleasure and pain, and welcomes what is good, and is offended at what is evil?

Cle. There is a great difference, Stranger, in the two kinds of education.

Ath. If we three know what is good in song and dance, then we truly know also who is educated and who is uneducated; but if not, then we certainly shall not know wherein lies the safeguard of education, and whether there is any or not.

Cle. True.

Ath. Let us follow the scent like hounds, and go in pursuit of beauty of figure, and melody, and song, and dance; if these escape us, there will be no use in talking about true education, whether Hellenic or barbarian.

Cle. Yes.

Ath. And what is beauty of figure, or beautiful melody? When a manly soul is in trouble, *[655]* and when a cowardly soul is in similar case, are they likely to use the same figures and gestures, or to give utterance to the same sounds?

Cle. How can they, when the very colours of their faces differ?

Ath. Good, my friend; I may observe, however, in passing, that in music there certainly are figures and there are melodies: and music is concerned with harmony and rhythm, so that you may speak of a melody or figure having good rhythm or good harmony—the term is correct enough; but to speak metaphorically of a melody or figure having a "good colour," as the masters of choruses do, is not allowable, although you can speak of the melodies or figures of the brave and the coward, praising the one and censuring the other. And not to be tedious, let us say that the figures and melodies which are expressive of virtue of soul or body, or of images of virtue, are without exception good, and those which are expressive of vice are the reverse of good.

Cle. Your suggestion is excellent; and let us answer that these things are so.

Ath. Once more, are all of us equally delighted with every sort of dance?

Cle. Far otherwise.

Ath. What, then, leads us astray? Are beautiful things not the same to us all, or are they the same in themselves, but not in our opinion of them? For no one will admit that forms of vice in the dance are more beautiful than forms of virtue, or that he himself delights in the forms of vice, and others in a muse of another character. And yet most persons say, that the excellence of music is to give pleasure to our souls. But this is intolerable and blasphemous; there is, however, a much more plausible account of the delusion.

Cle. What?

Ath. The adaptation of art to the characters of men. Choric movements are imitations of manners occurring in various actions, fortunes, dispositions—each particular is imitated, and those to whom the words, or songs, or dances are suited, either by nature or habit or both, cannot help feeling pleasure in them and applauding them, and calling them beautiful. But those whose natures, or ways, or habits are unsuited to them, cannot delight in them or applaud them, and they call them base. There are others, again, whose natures are right and their habits wrong, or whose habits are right and their natures wrong, and they praise one thing, but are pleased at another. *[656]* For they say that all these imitations are pleasant, but not good. And in the presence of those whom they think wise, they are ashamed of dancing and singing in the baser manner, or of deliberately lending any countenance to such proceedings; and yet, they have a secret pleasure in them.

Cle. Very true.

Ath. And is any harm done to the lover of vicious dances or songs, or any good done to the approver of the opposite sort of pleasure?

Cle. I think that there is.

Ath. "I think" is not the word, but I would say, rather, "I am certain." For must they not have the same effect as when a man associates with bad characters, whom he likes and approves rather than dislikes, and only censures playfully because he has a suspicion of his own badness? In that case, he who takes pleasure in them will surely become like those in whom he takes pleasure, even though he be ashamed to praise them. And what greater good or evil can any destiny ever make us undergo?

Cle. I know of none.

Ath. Then in a city which has good laws, or in future ages is to have them, bearing in mind the instruction and amusement which are given by music, can we suppose that the poets are to be allowed to teach in the dance anything which they themselves like, in the way of rhythm, or melody, or words, to the young children of any well-conditioned parents? Is the poet to train his choruses as he pleases, without reference to virtue or vice?

Cle. That is surely quite unreasonable, and is not to be thought of.

Ath. And yet he may do this in almost any state with the exception of Egypt.

Cle. And what are the laws about music and dancing in Egypt?

Ath. You will wonder when I tell you: Long ago they appear to have recognized the very principle of which we are now speaking—that their young citizens must be habituated to forms and strains of virtue. These they fixed, and exhibited the patterns of them in their temples; and no painter or artist is allowed to innovate upon them, or to leave the traditional forms and invent new ones. To this day, no alteration is allowed either in these arts, or in music at all. And you will find that their works of art are painted or moulded in the same forms which they had ten thousand years ago;—this is literally true and no exaggeration—their ancient paintings and sculptures are not a whit better or worse than the work of to-day, *[657]* but are made with just the same skill.

Cle. How extraordinary!

Ath. I should rather say, How statesmanlike, how worthy of a legislator! I know that other things in Egypt are not so well. But what I am telling you about music is true and deserving of consideration, because showing that a law-giver may institute melodies which have a natural truth and correctness without any fear of failure. To do this, however, must be the work of God, or of a divine person; in Egypt they have a tradition that their ancient chants which have been preserved for so many ages are the composition of the Goddess Isis. And therefore, as I was saying, if a person can only find in any way the natural melodies, he may confidently embody them in a fixed and legal form. For the love of novelty which arises out of pleasure in the new and weariness of the old, has not strength enough to corrupt the consecrated song and dance, under the plea that they have become antiquated. At any rate, they are far from being corrupted in Egypt.

Cle. Your arguments seem to prove your point.

Ath. May we not confidently say that the true use of music and of choral festivities is as follows: We rejoice when we think that we prosper, and again we think that we prosper when we rejoice?

Cle. Exactly.

Ath. And when rejoicing in our good fortune, we are unable to be still?

Cle. True.

Ath. Our young men break forth into dancing and singing, and we who are their elders deem that we are fulfilling our part in life when we look on at them. Having lost our agility, we delight in their sports and merry-making, because we love to think of our former selves; and gladly institute contests for those who are able to awaken in us the memory of our youth.

Cle. Very true.

Ath. Is it altogether unmeaning to say, as the common people do about festivals, that he should be adjudged the wisest of men, and the winner of the palm, who gives us the greatest amount of pleasure and mirth? For on such occasions, and when mirth is the order of the day, ought not he to be honoured most, and, as I was saying, bear the palm, *[658]* who gives most mirth to the greatest number? Now is this a true way of speaking or of acting?

Cle. Possibly.

Ath. But, my dear friend, let us distinguish between different cases, and not be hasty in forming a judgment: One way of considering the question will be to imagine a festival at which there are entertainments of all sorts, including gymnastic, musical, and equestrian contests: the citizens are assembled; prizes are offered, and proclamation is made that any one who likes may enter the lists, and that he is to bear the palm who gives the most pleasure to the spectators—there is to be no regulation about the manner how; but he who is most successful in giving pleasure is to be crowned victor, and deemed to be the pleasantest of the candidates: What is likely to be the result of such a proclamation?

Cle. In what respect?

Ath. There would be various exhibitions: one man, like Homer, will exhibit a rhapsody, another a performance on the lute; one will have a tragedy, and another a comedy. Nor would there be anything astonishing in some one imagining that he could gain the prize by exhibiting a puppet-show. Suppose these competitors to meet, and not these only, but innumerable others as well—can you tell me who ought to be the victor?

Cle. I do not see how any one can answer you, or pretend to know, unless he has heard with his own ears the several competitors; the question is absurd.

Ath. Well, then, if neither of you can answer, shall I answer this question which you deem so absurd?

Cle. By all means.

Ath. If very small children are to determine the question, they will decide for the puppet-show.

Cle. Of course.

Ath. The older children will be advocates of comedy; educated women, and young men, and people in general, will favour tragedy.

Cle. Very likely.

Ath. And I believe that we old men would have the greatest pleasure in hearing a rhapsodist recite well the *Iliad* and *Odyssey,* or one of the Hesiodic poems, and would award the victory to him. But, who would really be the victor?—that is the question.

Cle. Yes.

Ath. Clearly you and I will have to declare that those whom we old men adjudge victors ought to win; for our ways are far and away better than any which at present exist anywhere in the world.

Cle. Certainly.

Ath. Thus far I too should agree with the many, that the excellence of music is to be measured by pleasure. But the pleasure must not be that of chance persons; the fairest music is that which delights the best and best educated, *[659]* and especially that which delights the one man who is pre-eminent in virtue and education. And therefore the judges must be men of character, for they will require both wisdom and courage; the true judge must not draw his inspiration from the theatre, nor ought he to be unnerved by the clamour of the many and his own incapacity; nor again, knowing the truth, ought he through cowardice and unmanliness carelessly to deliver a lying judgment, with the very same lips which have just appealed to the Gods before he judged. He is sitting not as the disciple of the theatre, but, in his proper place, as their instructor, and he ought to be the enemy of all pandering to the pleasure of the spectators. The ancient and common custom of Hellas, which still prevails in Italy and Sicily, did certainly leave the judgment to the body of spectators, who determined the victor by show of hands. But this custom has been the destruction of the poets; for they are now in the habit of composing with a view to please the bad taste of their judges, and the result is that the spectators instruct themselves;—and also it has been the ruin of the theatre; they ought to be having characters put before them better than their own, and so receiving a higher pleasure, but now by their own act the opposite result follows. What inference is to be drawn from all this? Shall I tell you?

Cle. What?

Ath. The inference at which we arrive for the third or fourth time is, that education is the constraining and directing of youth towards that right reason, which the law affirms, and which the experience of the eldest and best has agreed to be truly right. In order, then, that the soul of the child may not be habituated to feel joy and sorrow in a manner at variance with the law, and those who obey the law, but may rather follow the law and rejoice and sorrow at the same things as the aged—in order, I say, to

produce this effect, chants appear to have been invented, which really enchant, and are designed to implant that harmony of which we speak. And, because the mind of the child is incapable of enduring serious training, they are called plays and songs, and are performed in play; just as when men are sick and ailing in their bodies, their attendants give them wholesome diet in pleasant meats and drinks, *[660]* but unwholesome diet in disagreeable things, in order that they may learn, as they ought, to like the one, and to dislike the other. And similarly the true legislator will persuade, and, if he cannot persuade, will compel the poet to express, as he ought, by fair and noble words, in his rhythms, the figures, and in his melodies, the music of temperate and brave and in every way good men.

Cle. But do you really imagine, Stranger, that this is the way in which poets generally compose in States at the present day? As far as I can observe, except among us and among the Lacedaemonians, there are no regulations like those of which you speak; in other places novelties are always being introduced in dancing and in music, generally not under the authority of any law, but at the instigation of lawless pleasures; and these pleasures are so far from being the same, as you describe the Egyptian to be, or having the same principles, that they are never the same.

Ath. Most true, Cleinias; and I daresay that I may have expressed myself obscurely, and so led you to imagine that I was speaking of some really existing state of things, whereas I was only saying what regulations I would like to have about music; and hence there occurred a misapprehension on your part. For when evils are far gone and irremediable, the task of censuring them is never pleasant, although at times necessary. But as we do not really differ, will you let me ask you whether you consider such institutions to be more prevalent among the Cretans and Lacedaemonians than among the other Hellenes?

Cle. Certainly they are.

Ath. And if they were extended to the other Hellenes, would it be an improvement on the present state of things?

Cle. A very great improvement, if the customs which prevail among them were such as prevail among us and the Lacedaemonians, and such as you were just now saying ought to prevail.

Ath. Let us see whether we understand one another:—Are not the principles of education and music which prevail among you as follows: you compel your poets to say that the good man, if he be temperate and just, is fortunate and happy; and this whether he be great and strong or small and weak, and whether he be rich or poor; and, on the other hand, if he have a wealth passing that of Cinyras or Midas, and be unjust, he is wretched and lives in misery? As the poet says, and with truth: I sing not, I care not about him who accomplishes all noble things, not having justice; let him who "draws near and stretches out his hand against his enemies be a just man." But if he be unjust, [661] I would not have him "look calmly upon bloody death," nor "surpass in swiftness the Thracian Boreas"; and let no other thing that is called good ever be his. For the goods of which the many speak are not really good: first in the catalogue is placed health, beauty next, wealth third; and then innumerable others, as for example to have a keen eye or a quick ear, and in general to have all the senses perfect; or, again, to be a tyrant and do as you like; and the final consummation of happiness is to have acquired all these things, and when you have acquired them to become at once immortal. But you and I say, that while to the just and holy all these things are the best of possessions, to the unjust they are all, including even health, the greatest of evils. For in truth, to have sight, and hearing, and the use of the senses, or to live at all without justice and virtue, even though a man be rich in all the so-called goods of fortune, is the greatest of evils, if life be immortal; but not so great, if the bad man lives only a very short time. These are the truths which, if I am not mistaken, you will persuade or compel your poets to utter with suitable accompaniments of harmony and rhythm, and in these they must train up your youth. Am I not right? For I plainly declare that evils as they are termed are goods to the unjust, and only evils to the just, and that goods are truly good to the good, but evil to the evil. Let me ask again, Are you and I agreed about this?

Cle. I think that we partly agree and partly do not.

Ath. When a man has health and wealth and a tyranny which lasts, and when he is preeminent in strength and courage, and has the gift of immortality, and none of the so-called evils which counter-balance these goods, but only the injustice and insolence of his own nature—of such an one you are, I suspect, unwilling to believe that he is miserable rather than happy.

Cle. That is quite true.

Ath. Once more: Suppose that he be valiant and strong, and handsome and rich, and does throughout his whole life whatever he likes, [662] still, if he be unrighteous and insolent, would not both of you agree that he will of necessity live basely? You will surely grant so much?

Cle. Certainly.

Ath. And an evil life too?

Cle. I am not equally disposed to grant that.

Ath. Will he not live painfully and to his own disadvantage?

Cle. How can I possibly say so?

Ath. How! Then may Heaven make us to be of one mind, for now we are of two. To me, dear Cleinias, the truth of what I am saying is as plain as the fact that Crete is an island. And, if I were a lawgiver, I would try to make the poets and all the citizens speak in this strain; and I would inflict the heaviest penalties on any one in all the land who should dare to say that there are bad men who lead pleasant lives, or that the profitable and gainful is one thing, and the just another; and there are many other matters about which I should make my citizens speak in a manner different from the Cretans and Lacedaemonians of this age, and I may say, indeed, from the world in general. For tell me, my good friends, by Zeus and Apollo tell me, if I were to ask these same Gods who were your legislators—Is not the most just life also the pleasantest? or are there two lives, one of which is the justest and the other the pleasantest?—and they were to reply that there are two; and thereupon I proceeded to ask, (that would be the right way of pursuing the enquiry), Which are the happier—those who lead the justest, or those who lead the pleasantest life? and they replied, Those who lead the pleasantest—that would be a very strange answer, which I should not like to put into the mouth of the Gods. The words will come with more propriety from the lips of fathers and legislators, and therefore I will repeat my former questions to one of them, and suppose him to say again that he who leads the pleasantest life is the happiest. And to that I rejoin:—O my father, did you not wish me to live as happily as possible? And yet you also never ceased telling me that I should live as justly as possible. Now, here the giver of the rule, whether he be legislator or father, will be in a dilemma, and will in vain endeavour to be consistent with himself. But if he were to declare that the justest life is also the happiest, every one hearing him would enquire, *[663]* if I am not mistaken, what is that good and noble principle in life which the law approves, and which is superior to pleasure. For what good can the just man have which is separated from pleasure? Shall we say that glory and fame, coming from Gods and men, though good and noble, are nevertheless unpleasant, and infamy pleasant? Certainly not, sweet legislator. Or shall we say that the not-doing of wrong and there being no wrong done is good and honourable, although there is no pleasure in it, and that the doing wrong is pleasant, but evil and base?

Cle. Impossible.

Ath. The view which identifies the pleasant and the just and the good and the noble has an excellent moral and religious tendency. And the opposite view is most at variance with the designs of the legislator, and is, in his opinion, infamous; for no one, if he can help, will be persuaded to do that which gives him more pain than pleasure. But as distant prospects are apt to make us dizzy, especially in childhood, the legislator will try to purge away the darkness and exhibit the truth; he will persuade the citizens, in some way or other, by customs and praises and words, that just and unjust are shadows only, and that injustice, which seems opposed to justice, when contemplated by the unjust and evil man appears pleasant and the just most unpleasant; but that from the just man's point of view, the very opposite is the appearance of both of them.

Cle. True.

Ath. And which may be supposed to be the truer judgment—that of the inferior or of the better soul?

Cle. Surely, that of the better soul.

Ath. Then the unjust life must not only be more base and depraved, but also more unpleasant than the just and holy life?

Cle. That seems to be implied in the present argument.

Ath. And even supposing this were otherwise, and not as the argument has proven, still the lawgiver, who is worth anything, if he ever ventures to tell a lie to the young for their good, could not invent a more useful lie than this, or one which will have a better effect in making them do what is right, not on compulsion but voluntarily.

Cle. Truth, Stranger, is a noble thing and a lasting, but a thing of which men are hard to be persuaded.

Ath. And yet the story of the Sidonian Cadmus, which is so improbable, has been readily believed, and also innumerable other tales.

Cle. What is that story?

Ath. The story of armed men springing up after the sowing of teeth, which the legislator may take as a proof that he can persuade the minds of the young of anything; *[664]* so that he has only to reflect and find out what belief will be of the greatest public advantage, and then use all his efforts to make the whole community utter one and the same word in their songs and tales and discourses all their life long. But if you do not agree with me, there is no reason why you should not argue on the other side.

Cle. I do not see that any argument can fairly be raised by either of us against what you are now saying.

Ath. The next suggestion which I have to offer is, that all our three choruses shall sing to the young and tender souls of children, reciting in their strains all the noble thoughts of which we have already spoken, or are about to speak; and the sum of them shall be, that the life which is by the Gods deemed to be the happiest is also the best;—we shall affirm this to be a most certain truth; and the minds of our young disciples will be more likely to receive these words of ours than any others which we might address to them.

Cle. I assent to what you say.

Ath. First will enter in their natural order the sacred choir composed of children, which is to sing lustily the heaven-taught lay to the whole city. Next will follow the choir of young men under the age of thirty, who will call upon the God Paean to testify to the truth of their words, and will pray him to be gracious to the youth and to turn their hearts. Thirdly, the choir of elder men, who are from thirty to sixty years of age, will also sing. There remain those who are too old to sing, and they will tell stories, illustrating the same virtues, as with the voice of an oracle.

Cle. Who are those who compose the third choir, Stranger? for I do not clearly understand what you mean to say about them.

Ath. And yet almost all that I have been saying has been said with a view to them.

Cle. Will you try to be a little plainer?

Ath. I was speaking at the commencement of our discourse, as you will remember, of the fiery nature of young creatures: I said that they were unable to keep quiet either in limb or voice, and that they called out and jumped about in a disorderly manner; and that no other animal attained to any perception of order,

[665] but man only. Now the order of motion is called rhythm, and the order of the voice, in which high and low are duly mingled, is called harmony; and both together are termed choric song. And I said that the Gods had pity on us, and gave us Apollo and the Muses to be our playfellows and leaders in the dance; and Dionysus, as I dare say that you will remember, was the third.

Cle. I quite remember.

Ath. Thus far I have spoken of the chorus of Apollo and the Muses, and I have still to speak of the remaining chorus, which is that of Dionysus.

Cle. How is that arranged? There is something strange, at any rate on first hearing, in a Dionysiac chorus of old men, if you really mean that those who are above thirty, and may be fifty, or from fifty to sixty years of age, are to dance in his honour.

Ath. Very true; and therefore it must be shown that there is good reason for the proposal.

Cle. Certainly.

Ath. Are we agreed thus far?

Cle. About what?

Ath. That every man and boy, slave and free, both sexes, and the whole city, should never cease charming themselves with the strains of which we have spoken; and that there should be every sort of change and variation of them in order to take away the effect of sameness, so that the singers may always receive pleasure from their hymns, and may never weary of them?

Cle. Every one will agree.

Ath. Where, then, will that best part of our city which, by reason of age and intelligence, has the greatest influence, sing these fairest of strains, which are to do so much good? Shall we be so foolish as to let them off who would give us the most beautiful and also the most useful of songs?

Cle. But, says the argument, we cannot let them off.

Ath. Then how can we carry out our purpose with decorum? Will this be the way?

Cle. What?

Ath. When a man is advancing in years, he is afraid and reluctant to sing;—he has no pleasure in his own performances; and if compulsion is used, he will be more and more ashamed, the older and more discreet he grows; —is not this true?

Cle. Certainly.

Ath. Well, and will he not be yet more ashamed if he has to stand up and sing in the theatre to a mixed audience?—and if moreover when he is required to do so, like the other choirs who contend for prizes, and have been trained under a singing master, he is pinched and hungry, *[666]* he will certainly have a feeling of shame and discomfort which will make him very unwilling to exhibit.

Cle. No doubt.

Ath. How, then, shall we reassure him, and get him to sing? Shall we begin by enacting that boys shall not taste wine at all until they are eighteen years of age; we will tell them that fire must not be poured upon fire, whether in the body or in the soul, until they begin to go to work—this is a precaution which has to be taken against the excitableness of youth;— afterwards they may taste wine in moderation up to the age of thirty, but while a man is young he should abstain altogether from intoxication and from excess of wine; when, at length, he has reached forty years, after dinner at a public mess, he may invite not only the other Gods, but Dionysus above all, to the mystery and festivity of the elder men, making use of the wine which he has given men to lighten the sourness of old age; that in age we may renew our youth, and forget our sorrows; and also in order that the nature of the soul, like iron melted in the fire, may become softer and so more impressible. In the first place, will not any one who is thus mellowed be more ready and less ashamed to sing—I do not say before a large audience, but before a moderate company; nor yet among strangers, but among his familiars, and, as we have often said, to chant, and to enchant?

Cle. He will be far more ready.

Ath. There will be no impropriety in our using such a method of persuading them to join with us in song.

Cle. None at all.

Ath. And what strain will they sing, and what muse will they hymn? The strain should clearly be one suitable to them.

Cle. Certainly.

Ath. And what strain is suitable for heroes? Shall they sing a choric strain?

Cle. Truly, Stranger, we of Crete and Lacedaemon know no strain other than that which we have learnt and been accustomed to sing in our chorus.

Ath. I dare say; for you have never acquired the knowledge of the most beautiful kind of song, in your military way of life, which is modelled after the camp, and is not like that of dwellers in cities; and you have your young men herding and feeding together like young colts. No one takes his own individual colt and drags him away from his fellows against his will, raging and foaming, and gives him a groom to attend to him alone, and trains and rubs him down privately, and gives him the qualities in education which will make him not only a good soldier, but also a governor of a state and of cities. Such an one, as we said at first, would be a greater warrior than he of whom Tyrtaeus sings; [667] and he would honour courage everywhere, but always as the fourth, and not as the first part of virtue, either in individuals or states.

Cle. Once more, Stranger, I must complain that you depreciate our lawgivers.

Ath. Not intentionally, if at all, my good friend; but whither the argument leads, thither let us follow; for if there be indeed some strain of song more beautiful than that of the choruses or the public theatres, I should like to impart it to those who, as we say, are ashamed of these, and want to have the best.

Cle. Certainly.

Ath. When things have an accompanying charm, either the best thing in them is this very charm, or there is some rightness or utility possessed by them;—for example, I should say that eating and drinking, and the use of food in general, have an accompanying charm which we call pleasure; but that this rightness and utility is just the healthfulness of the things served up to us, which is their true rightness.

Cle. Just so.

Ath. Thus, too, I should say that learning has a certain accompanying charm which is the pleasure; but that the right and the profitable, the good and the noble, are qualities which the truth gives to it.

Cle. Exactly.

Ath. And so in the imitative arts—if they succeed in making likenesses, and are accompanied by pleasure, may not their works be said to have a charm?

Cle. Yes.

Ath. But equal proportions, whether of quality or quantity, and not pleasure, speaking generally, would give them truth or rightness.

Cle. Yes.

Ath. Then that only can be rightly judged by the standard of pleasure, which makes or furnishes no utility or truth or likeness, nor on the other hand is productive of any hurtful quality, but exists solely for the sake of the accompany-

ing charm; and the term "pleasure" is most appropriately applied to it when these other qualities are absent.

Cle. You are speaking of harmless pleasure, are you not?

Ath. Yes; and this I term amusement, when doing neither harm nor good in any degree worth speaking of.

Cle. Very true.

Ath. Then, if such be our principles, we must assert that imitation is not to be judged of by pleasure and false opinion; and this is true of all equality, for the equal is not equal or the symmetrical symmetrical, because somebody thinks or likes something, but they are to be judged of by the standard of truth, and by no other whatever.

Cle. Quite true.

[668] *Ath.* Do we not regard all music as representative and imitative?

Cle. Certainly.

Ath. Then, when any one says that music is to be judged of by pleasure, his doctrine cannot be admitted; and if there be any music of which pleasure is the criterion, such music is not to be sought out or deemed to have any real excellence, but only that other kind of music which is an imitation of the good.

Cle. Very true.

Ath. And those who seek for the best kind of song and music ought not to seek for that which is pleasant, but for that which is true; and the truth of imitation consists, as we were saying, in rendering the thing imitated according to quantity and quality.

Cle. Certainly.

Ath. And every one will admit that musical compositions are all imitative and representative. Will not poets and spectators and actors all agree in this?

Cle. They will.

Ath. Surely then he who would judge correctly must know what each composition is; for if he does not know what is the character and meaning of the piece, and what it represents, he will never discern whether the intention is true or false.

Cle. Certainly not.

Ath. And will he who does not know what is true be able to distinguish what is good and bad? My statement is not very clear; but perhaps you will understand me better if I put the matter in another way.

Cle. How?

Ath. There are ten thousand likenesses of objects of sight?

Cle. Yes.

Ath. And can he who does not know what the exact object is which is imitated, ever know whether the resemblance is truthfully executed? I mean, for example, whether a statue has the proportions of a body, and the true situation of the parts; what those proportions are, and how the parts fit into one another in due order; also their colours and conformations, or whether this is all confused in the execution: do you think that any one can know about this, who does not know what the animal is which has been imitated?

Cle. Impossible.

Ath. But even if we know that the thing pictured or sculptured is a man, who has received at the hand of the artist all his proper parts and colours and shapes, *[669]* must we not also know whether the work is beautiful or in any respect deficient in beauty?

Cle. If this were not required, Stranger, we should all of us be judges of beauty.

Ath. Very true; and may we not say that in everything imitated, whether in drawing, music, or any other art, he who is to be a competent judge must possess three things;—he must know, in the first place, of what the imitation is; secondly, he must know that it is true; and thirdly, that it has been well executed in words and melodies and rhythms?

Cle. Certainly.

Ath. Then let us not faint in discussing the peculiar difficulty of music. Music is more celebrated than any other kind of imitation, and therefore requires the greatest care of them all. For if a man makes a mistake here, he may do himself the greatest injury by welcoming evil dispositions, and the mistake may be very difficult to discern, because the poets are artists very inferior in character to the Muses themselves, who would never fall into the monstrous error of assigning to the words of men the gestures and songs of women; nor after combining the melodies with the gestures of freemen would they add on the rhythms of slaves and men of the baser sort; nor, beginning with the rhythms and gestures of freemen, would they assign to them a melody or words which are of an opposite character; nor would they mix up the voices and sounds of animals and of men and instruments, and every other sort of noise, as if they were all one. But human poets are fond of introducing this sort of inconsistent mixture, and so make themselves ridiculous in the eyes of those who, as Orpheus says, "are ripe for true pleasure." The experienced see all this confusion, and yet the poets go on and make still further havoc by separating the rhythm and the figure of the dance from the melody, setting bare words to metre, and also separating the melody and the rhythm from the words, using the lyre or the flute alone. For when there are no words, it is very difficult to recognize the meaning of the harmony and rhythm, or to see that any worthy object is imitated by them. And we must acknowledge that all this sort of thing, which aims only at swiftness and smoothness and a brutish noise, and uses the flute and the lyre not as the mere accompaniments of the dance and song, *[670]* is exceedingly coarse and tasteless. The use of either instrument, when unaccompanied, leads to every sort of irregularity and trickery. This is all rational enough. But we are considering not how our choristers, who are from thirty to fifty years of age, and may be over fifty, are not to use the Muses, but how they are to use them. And the considerations which we have urged seem to show in what way these fifty-year-old choristers who are to sing, may be expected to be better trained. For they need to have a quick perception and knowledge of harmonies and rhythms; otherwise, how can they ever know whether a melody would be rightly sung to the Dorian mode, or to the rhythm which the poet has assigned to it?

Cle. Clearly they cannot.

Ath. The many are ridiculous in imagining that they know what is in proper harmony and rhythm, and what is not, when they can only be made to sing and step in rhythm by force; it never occurs to them that they are ignorant of what they are doing. Now every melody is right when it has suitable harmony and rhythm, and wrong when unsuitable.

Cle. That is most certain.

Ath. But can a man who does not know a thing, as we were saying, know that the thing is right?

Cle. Impossible.

Ath. Then now, as would appear, we are making the discovery that our newly-appointed choristers, whom we hereby invite and, although they are their own masters, compel to sing, must be educated to such an extent as to be able to follow the steps of the rhythm and the notes of the song, that they may know the harmonies and rhythms, and be able to select what are suitable for men of their age and character to sing; and may sing them, and have innocent pleasure from their own performance, and also lead younger men to welcome with dutiful delight good dispositions. Having such training, they will attain a more accurate knowledge than falls to the lot of the common people, or even of the poets themselves. For the poet need not know the third point, viz., whether the imitation is good or not, though he can hardly help knowing the laws of melody and rhythm. [671] But the aged chorus must know all the three, that they may choose the best, and that which is nearest to the best; for otherwise they will never be able to charm the souls of young men in the way of virtue. And now the original design of the argument which was intended to bring eloquent aid to the Chorus of Dionysus, has been accomplished to the best of our ability, and let us see whether we were right:—I should imagine that a drinking assembly is likely to become more and more tumultuous as the drinking goes on: this, as we were saying at first, will certainly be the case.

Cle. Certainly.

Ath. Every man has a more than natural elevation; his heart is glad within him, and he will say anything and will be restrained by nobody at such a time; he fancies that he is able to rule over himself and all mankind.

Cle. Quite true.

Ath. Were we not saying that on such occasions the souls of the drinkers become like iron heated in the fire, and grow softer and younger, and are easily moulded by him who knows how to educate and fashion them, just as when they were young, and that this fashioner of them is the same who prescribed for them in the days of their youth, viz., the good legislator; and that he ought to enact laws of the banquet, which, when a man is confident, bold, and impudent, and unwilling to wait his turn and have his share of silence and speech, and drinking and music, will change his character into the opposite—such laws as will infuse into him a just and noble fear, which will take up arms at the approach of insolence, being that divine fear which we have called reverence and shame?

Cle. True.

Ath. And the guardians of these laws and fellow-workers with them are the calm and sober generals of the drinkers; and without their help there is greater difficulty in fighting against drink than in fighting against enemies when the commander of an army is not himself calm; and he who is unwilling to obey them and the commanders of Dionysiac feasts who are more than sixty years of age, shall suffer a disgrace as great as he who disobeys military leaders, or even greater.

Cle. Right.

Ath. If, then, drinking and amusement were regulated in this way, would not the companions of our revels be improved? they would part better friends than they were, [672] and not, as now, enemies. Their whole intercourse would be regulated by law and observant of it, and the sober would be the leaders of the drunken.

Cle. I think so too, if drinking were regulated as you propose.

Ath. Let us not then simply censure the gift of Dionysus as bad and unfit to be received into the State. For wine has many excellences, and one pre-eminent one, about which there is a difficulty in speaking to the many, from a fear of their misconceiving and misunderstanding what is said.

Cle. To what do you refer?

Ath. There is a tradition or story, which has somehow crept about the world, that Dionysus was robbed of his wits by his stepmother Herè, and that out of revenge he inspires Bacchic furies and dancing madnesses in others; for which reason he gave men wine. Such traditions concerning the Gods I leave to those who think that they may be safely uttered;[1] I only know that no animal at birth is mature or perfect in intelligence; and in the intermediate period, in which he has not yet acquired his own proper sense, he rages and roars without rhyme or reason; and when he has once got on his legs he jumps about without rhyme or reason; and this, as you will remember, has been already said by us to be the origin of music and gymnastic.[2]

Cle. To be sure, I remember.

Ath. And did we not say that the sense of harmony and rhythm sprang from this beginning among men, and that Apollo and the Muses and Dionysus were the Gods whom we had to thank for them?

Cle. Certainly.

Ath. The other story implied that wine was given man out of revenge, and in order to make him mad; but our present doctrine, on the contrary, is, that wine was given him as a balm, and in order to implant modesty in the soul, and health and strength in the body.

Cle. That, Stranger, is precisely what was said.

Ath. Then half the subject may now be considered to have been discussed; shall we proceed to the consideration of the other half?

[1] Cf. *Euthyphro*, 6 ff.; *Republic*, ii. 378; iii. 388, 408.
[2] Cf. 653.

Cle. What is the other half, and how do you divide the subject?

Ath. The whole choral art is also in our view the whole of education; and of this art, rhythms and harmonies form the part which has to do with the voice.

Cle. Yes.

Ath. The movement of the body has rhythm in common with the movement of the voice, but gesture is peculiar to it, whereas song is simply the movement of the voice.

Cle. Most true.

[673] Ath. And the sound of the voice which reaches and educates the soul, we have ventured to term music.

Cle. We were right.

Ath. And the movement of the body, when regarded as an amusement, we termed dancing; but when extended and pursued with a view to the excellence of the body, this scientific training may be called gymnastic.

Cle. Exactly.

Ath. Music, which was one half of the choral art, may be said to have been completely discussed. Shall we proceed to the other half or not? What would you like?

Cle. My good friend, when you are talking with a Cretan and Lacedaemonian, and we have discussed music and not gymnastic, what answer are either of us likely to make to such an enquiry?

Ath. An answer is contained in your question; and I understand and accept what you say not only as an answer, but also as a command to proceed with gymnastic.

Cle. You quite understand me; do as you say.

Ath. I will; and there will not be any difficulty in speaking intelligibly to you about a subject with which both of you are far more familiar than with music.

Cle. There will not.

Ath. Is not the origin of gymnastics, too, to be sought in the tendency to rapid motion which exists in all animals; man, as we were saying, having attained the sense of rhythm, created and invented dancing; and melody arousing and awakening rhythm, both united formed the choral art?

Cle. Very true.

Ath. And one part of this subject has been already discussed by us, and there still remains another to be discussed?[1]

Cle. Exactly.

Ath. I have first a final word to add to my

[1] Cf. vii. 813, 814.

discourse about drink, if you will allow me to do so.

Cle. What more have you to say?

Ath. I should say that if a city seriously means to adopt the practice of drinking under due regulation and with a view to the enforcement of temperance, and in like manner, and on the same principle, will allow of other pleasures, designing to gain the victory over them—in this way all of them may be used. But if the State makes drinking an amusement only, and whoever likes may drink whenever he likes, *[674]* and with whom he likes, and add to this any other indulgences, I shall never agree or allow that this city or this man should practise drinking. I would go further than the Cretans and Lacedaemonians, and am disposed rather to the law of the Carthaginians, that no one while he is on a campaign should be allowed to taste wine at all, but that he should drink water during all that time, and that in the city no slave, male or female, should ever drink wine; and that no magistrates should drink during their year of office, nor should pilots of vessels or judges while on duty taste wine at all, nor any one who is going to hold a consultation about any matter of importance; nor in the daytime at all, unless in consequence of exercise or as medicine; nor again at night, when any one, either man or woman, is minded to get children. There are numberless other cases also in which those who have good sense and good laws ought not to drink wine, so that if what I say is true, no city will need many vineyards. Their husbandry and their way of life in general will follow an appointed order, and their cultivation of the vine will be the most limited and the least common of their employments. And this, Stranger, shall be the crown of my discourse about wine, if you agree.

Cle. Excellent: we agree.

BOOK III

[676] Athenian Stranger. ENOUGH of this. And what, then, is to be regarded as the origin of government? Will not a man be able to judge of it best from a point of view in which he may behold the progress of states and their transitions to good or evil?

Cleinias. What do you mean?

Ath. I mean that he might watch them from the point of view of time, and observe the changes which take place in them during infinite ages.

Cle. How so?

Ath. Why, do you think that you can reckon the time which has elapsed since cities first existed and men were citizens of them?

Cle. Hardly.

Ath. But you are sure that it must be vast and incalculable?

Cle. Certainly.

Ath. And have not thousands and thousands of cities come into being during this period and as many perished? And has not each of them had every form of government many times over, now growing larger, now smaller, and again improving or declining?

Cle. To be sure.

Ath. Let us endeavour to ascertain the cause of these changes; for that will probably explain the first origin and development of forms of government.

Cle. Very good. You shall endeavour to impart your thoughts to us, and we will make an effort to understand you.

[677] Ath. Do you believe that there is any truth in ancient traditions?

Cle. What traditions?

Ath. The traditions about the many destructions of mankind which have been occasioned by deluges and pestilences, and in many other ways, and of the survival of a remnant?

Cle. Every one is disposed to believe them.

Ath. Let us consider one of them, that which was caused by the famous deluge.

Cle. What are we to observe about it?

Ath. I mean to say that those who then escaped would only be hill shepherds—small sparks of the human race preserved on the tops of mountains.

Cle. Clearly.

Ath. Such survivors would necessarily be unacquainted with the arts and the various devices which are suggested to the dwellers in cities by interest or ambition, and with all the wrongs which they contrive against one another.

Cle. Very true.

Ath. Let us suppose, then, that the cities in the plain and on the sea-coast were utterly destroyed at that time.

Cle. Very good.

Ath. Would not all implements have then perished and every other excellent invention of political or any other sort of wisdom have utterly disappeared?

Cle. Why, yes, my friend; and if things had always continued as they are at present ordered, how could any discovery have ever been made even in the least particular? For it is evident that the arts were unknown during ten thousand times ten thousand years. And no more than a thousand or two thousand years have elapsed since the discoveries of Daedalus, Orpheus and Palamedes—since Marsyas and Olympus invented music, and Amphion the lyre—not to speak of numberless other inventions which are but of yesterday.

Ath. Have you forgotten, Cleinias, the name of a friend who is really of yesterday?

Cle. I suppose that you mean Epimenides.[1]

Ath. The same, my friend; he does indeed far overleap the heads of all mankind by his invention; for he carried out in practice, as you declare, what of old Hesiod only preached.

Cle. Yes, according to our tradition.

Ath. After the great destruction, may we not suppose that the state of man was something of this sort:—In the beginning of things there was a fearful illimitable desert and a vast expanse of land; a herd or two of oxen would be the only survivors of the animal world; *[678]* and there might be a few goats, these too hardly enough to maintain the shepherds who tended them?

Cle. True.

Ath. And of cities or governments or legislation, about which we are now talking, do you suppose that they could have any recollection at all?

Cle. None whatever.

Ath. And out of this state of things has there not sprung all that we now are and have: cities and governments, and arts and laws, and a great deal of vice and a great deal of virtue?

Cle. What do you mean?

Ath. Why, my good friend, how can we possibly suppose that those who knew nothing of all the good and evil of cities could have attained their full development, whether of virtue or of vice?

Cle. I understand your meaning, and you are quite right.

Ath. But, as time advanced and the race multiplied, the world came to be what the world is.

Cle. Very true.

Ath. Doubtless the change was not made all in a moment, but little by little, during a very long period of time.

Cle. A highly probable supposition.

Ath. At first, they would have a natural fear ringing in their ears which would prevent their descending from the heights into the plain.

Cle. Of course.

Ath. The fewness of the survivors at that time

[1] Cf. i. 642.

would have made them all the more desirous of seeing one another; but then the means of travelling either by land or sea had been almost entirely lost, as I may say, with the loss of the arts, and there was great difficulty in getting at one another; for iron and brass and all metals were jumbled together and had disappeared in the chaos; nor was there any possibility of extracting ore from them; and they had scarcely any means of felling timber. Even if you suppose that some implements might have been preserved in the mountains, they must quickly have worn out and vanished, and there would be no more of them until the art of metallurgy had again revived.

Cle. There could not have been.

Ath. In how many generations would this be attained?

Cle. Clearly, not for many generations.

Ath. During this period, and for some time afterwards, all the arts which require iron and brass and the like would disappear.

Cle. Certainly.

Ath. Faction and war would also have died out in those days, and for many reasons.

Cle. How would that be?

Ath. In the first place, the desolation of these primitive men would create in them a feeling of affection and good-will towards one another; and, secondly, they would have no occasion to quarrel about their subsistence, *[679]* for they would have pasture in abundance, except just at first, and in some particular cases; and from their pasture-land they would obtain the greater part of their food in a primitive age, having plenty of milk and flesh; moreover they would procure other food by the chase, not to be despised either in quantity or quality. They would also have abundance of clothing, and bedding, and dwellings, and utensils either capable of standing on the fire or not; for the plastic and weaving arts do not require any use of iron: and God has given these two arts to man in order to provide him with all such things, that, when reduced to the last extremity, the human race may still grow and increase. Hence in those days mankind were not very poor; nor was poverty a cause of difference among them; and rich they could not have been, having neither gold nor silver:—such at that time was their condition. And the community which has neither poverty nor riches will always have the noblest principles; in it there is no insolence or injustice, nor, again, are there any contentions or envyings. And therefore they were good, and also because they were what is called simple-minded; and when they were told about good and evil, they in their simplicity believed what they heard to be very truth and practised it. No one had the wit to suspect another of a falsehood, as men do now; but what they heard about Gods and men they believed to be true, and lived accordingly; and therefore they were in all respects such as we have described them.

Cle. That quite accords with my views, and with those of my friend here.

Ath. Would not many generations living on in a simple manner, although ruder, perhaps, and more ignorant of the arts generally, and in particular of those of land or naval warfare, and likewise of other arts, termed in cities legal practices and party conflicts, and including all conceivable ways of hurting one another in word and deed;—although inferior to those who lived before the deluge, or to the men of our day in these respects, would they not, I say, be simpler and more manly, and also more temperate and altogether more just? The reason has been already explained.

Cle. Very true.

Ath. I should wish you to understand that what has preceded and what is about to follow, has been, and will be said, with the intention of explaining what need the men of that time had of laws, *[680]* and who was their lawgiver.

Cle. And thus far what you have said has been very well said.

Ath. They could hardly have wanted lawgivers as yet; nothing of that sort was likely to have existed in their days, for they had no letters at this early period; they lived by habit and the customs of their ancestors, as they are called.

Cle. Probably.

Ath. But there was already existing a form of government which, if I am not mistaken, is generally termed a lordship, and this still remains in many places, both among Hellenes and barbarians,[1] and is the government which is declared by Homer to have prevailed among the Cyclopes:

They have neither councils nor judgments, but they dwell in hollow caves on the tops of high mountains, and every one gives law to his wife and children, and they do not busy themselves about one another.[2]

Cle. That seems to be a charming poet of yours; I have read some other verses of his, which are very clever; but I do not know much of him, for foreign poets are very little read among the Cretans.

[1] Cf. Aristotle, *Politics,* i. 2, 1252 [b] 17-27.

[2] *Odyssey,* ix. 112, ff.

Megillus. But they are in Lacedaemon, and he appears to be the prince of them all; the manner of life, however, which he describes is not Spartan, but rather Ionian, and he seems quite to confirm what you are saying, when he traces up the ancient state of mankind by the help of tradition to barbarism.

Ath. Yes, he does confirm it; and we may accept his witness to the fact that such forms of government sometimes arise.

Cle. We may.

Ath. And were not such states composed of men who had been dispersed in single habitations and families by the poverty which attended the devastations; and did not the eldest then rule among them, because with them government originated in the authority of a father and a mother, whom, like a flock of birds, they followed, forming one troop under the patriarchal rule and sovereignty of their parents, which of all sovereignties is the most just?

Cle. Very true.

Ath. After this they came together in greater numbers, and increased the size of their cities, and betook themselves to husbandry, first of all at the foot of the mountains, *[681]* and made enclosures of loose walls and works of defence, in order to keep off wild beasts; thus creating a single large and common habitation.

Cle. Yes; at least we may suppose so.

Ath. There is another thing which would probably happen.

Cle. What?

Ath. When these larger habitations grew up out of the lesser original ones, each of the lesser ones would survive in the larger; every family would be under the rule of the eldest, and, owing to their separation from one another, would have peculiar customs in things divine and human, which they would have received from their several parents who had educated them; and these customs would incline them to order, when the parents had the element of order in their nature, and to courage, when they had the element of courage. And they would naturally stamp upon their children, and upon their children's children, their own likings; and, as we are saying, they would find their way into the larger society, having already their own peculiar laws.

Cle. Certainly.

Ath. And every man surely likes his own laws best, and the laws of others not so well.

Cle. True.

Ath. Then now we seem to have stumbled upon the beginnings of legislation.

Cle. Exactly.

Ath. The next step will be that these persons who have met together, will select some arbiters, who will review the laws of all of them, and will publicly present such as they approve to the chiefs who lead the tribes, and who are in a manner their kings, allowing them to choose those which they think best. These persons will themselves be called legislators, and will appoint the magistrates, framing some sort of aristocracy, or perhaps monarchy, out of the dynasties or lordships, and in this altered state of the government they will live.

Cle. Yes, that would be the natural order of things.

Ath. Then, now let us speak of a third form of government, in which all other forms and conditions of polities and cities concur.

Cle. What is that?

Ath. The form which in fact Homer indicates as following the second. This third form arose when, as he says, Dardanus founded Dardania:

For not as yet had the holy Ilium been built on the plain to be a city of speaking men; but they were still dwelling at the foot of many-fountained Ida.[1]

For indeed, *[682]* in these verses, and in what he said of the Cyclopes, he speaks the words of God and nature; for poets are a divine race and often in their strains, by the aid of the Muses and the Graces, they attain truth.

Cle. Yes.

Ath. Then now let us proceed with the rest of our tale, which will probably be found to illustrate in some degree our proposed design:— Shall we do so?

Cle. By all means.

Ath. Ilium was built, when they had descended from the mountain, in a large and fair plain, on a sort of low hill, watered by many rivers descending from Ida.

Cle. Such is the tradition.

Ath. And we must suppose this event to have taken place many ages after the deluge?

Ath. A marvellous forgetfulness of the former destruction would appear to have come over them, when they placed their town right under numerous streams flowing from the heights, trusting for their security to not very high hills, either.

Cle. There must have been a long interval, clearly.

Ath. And, as population increased, many

[1] *Iliad,* xx. 216, ff.

other cities would begin to be inhabited.

Cle. Doubtless.

Ath. Those cities made war against Troy— by sea as well as land—for at that time men were ceasing to be afraid of the sea.

Cle. Clearly.

Ath. The Achaeans remained ten years, and overthrew Troy.

Cle. True.

Ath. And during the ten years in which the Achaeans were besieging Ilium, the homes of the besiegers were falling into an evil plight. Their youth revolted; and when the soldiers returned to their own cities and families, they did not receive them properly, and as they ought to have done, and numerous deaths, murders, exiles, were the consequence. The exiles came again, under a new name, no longer Achaeans, but Dorians—a name which they derived from Dorieus; for it was he who gathered them together. The rest of the story is told by you Lacedaemonians as part of the history of Sparta.

Meg. To be sure.

Ath. Thus, after digressing from the original subject of laws into music and drinking-bouts, the argument has, providentially, come back to the same point, and presents to us another handle. For we have reached the settlement of Lacedaemon; *[683]* which, as you truly say, is in laws and in institutions the sister of Crete. And we are all the better for the digression, because we have gone through various governments and settlements, and have been present at the foundation of a first, second, and third state, succeeding one another in infinite time. And now there appears on the horizon a fourth state or nation which was once in process of settlement and has continued settled to this day. If, out of all this, we are able to discern what is well or ill settled, and what laws are the salvation and what are the destruction of cities, and what changes would make a state happy, O Megillus and Cleinias, we may now begin again, unless we have some fault to find with the previous discussion.

Meg. If some God, Stranger, would promise us that our new enquiry about legislation would be as good and full as the present, I would go a great way to hear such another, and would think that a day as long as this—and we are now approaching the longest day of the year— was too short for the discussion.

Ath. Then I suppose that we must consider this subject?

Meg. Certainly.

Ath. Let us place ourselves in thought at the moment when Lacedaemon and Argos and Messene and the rest of the Peloponnesus were all in complete subjection, Megillus, to your ancestors; for afterwards, as the legend informs us, they divided their army into three portions, and settled three cities, Argos, Messene, Lacedaemon.

Meg. True.

Ath. Temenus was the king of Argos, Cresphontes of Messene, Procles and Eurysthenes of Lacedaemon.

Meg. Certainly.

Ath. To these kings all the men of that day made oath that they would assist them, if any one subverted their kingdom.

Meg. True.

Ath. But can a kingship be destroyed, or was any other form of government ever destroyed, by any but the rulers themselves? No indeed, by Zeus. Have we already forgotten what was said a little while ago? [1]

Meg. No.

Ath. And may we not now further confirm what was then mentioned? For we have come upon facts which have brought us back again to the same principle; so that, in resuming the discussion, we shall not be enquiring about an empty theory, *[684]* but about events which actually happened. The case was as follows:— Three royal heroes made oath to three cities which were under a kingly government, and the cities to the kings, that both rulers and subjects should govern and be governed according to the laws which were common to all of them: the rulers promised that as time and the race went forward they would not make their rule more arbitrary; and the subjects said that, if the rulers observed these conditions, they would never subvert or permit others to subvert those kingdoms; the kings were to assist kings and peoples when injured, and the peoples were to assist peoples and kings in like manner. Is not this the fact?

Meg. Yes.

Ath. And the three states to whom these laws were given, whether their kings or any others were the authors of them, had therefore the greatest security for the maintenance of their constitutions?

Meg. What security?

Ath. That the other two states were always to come to the rescue against a rebellious third.

Meg. True.

Ath. Many persons say that legislators ought

[1] Cf. 682.

to impose such laws as the mass of the people will be ready to receive; but this is just as if one were to command gymnastic masters or physicians to treat or cure their pupils or patients in an agreeable manner.

Meg. Exactly.

Ath. Whereas the physician may often be too happy if he can restore health, and make the body whole, without any very great infliction of pain.

Meg. Certainly.

Ath. There was also another advantage possessed by the men of that day, which greatly lightened the task of passing laws.[1]

Meg. What advantage?

Ath. The legislators of that day, when they equalized property, escaped the great accusation which generally arises in legislation, if a person attempts to disturb the possession of land, or to abolish debts, because he sees that without this reform there can never be any real equality. Now, in general, when the legislator attempts to make a new settlement of such matters, every one meets him with the cry, that "he is not to disturb vested interests"—declaring with imprecations that he is introducing agrarian laws and cancelling of debts, until a man is at his wits' end; whereas no one could quarrel with the Dorians for distributing the land—there was nothing to hinder them; and as for debts, they had none which were considerable or of old standing.

Meg. Very true.

Ath. But then, my good friends, why did the settlement and legislation of their country turn out so badly?

[685] *Meg.* How do you mean; and why do you blame them?

Ath. There were three kingdoms, and of these, two quickly corrupted their original constitution and laws, and the only one which remained was the Spartan.

Meg. The question which you ask is not easily answered.

Ath. And yet must be answered when we are enquiring about laws, this being our old man's sober game of play, whereby we beguile the way, as I was saying when we first set out on our journey.[2]

Meg. Certainly; and we must find out why this was.

Ath. What laws are more worthy of our attention than those which have regulated such cities? or what settlements of states are greater or more famous?

[1] Cf. v. 736.   [2] Cf. i. 625.

Meg. I know of none.

Ath. Can we doubt that your ancestors intended these institutions not only for the protection of Peloponnesus, but of all the Hellenes, in case they were attacked by the barbarian? For the inhabitants of the region about Ilium, when they provoked by their insolence the Trojan war, relied upon the power of the Assyrians and the Empire of Ninus, which still existed and had a great prestige; the people of those days fearing the united Assyrian Empire just as we now fear the Great King. And the second capture of Troy was a serious offence against them, because Troy was a portion of the Assyrian Empire. To meet the danger the single army was distributed between three cities by the royal brothers, sons of Heracles—a fair device, as it seemed, and a far better arrangement than the expedition against Troy. For, firstly, the people of that day had, as they thought, in the Heraclidae better leaders than the Pelopidae; in the next place, they considered that their army was superior in valour to that which went against Troy; for, although the latter conquered the Trojans, they were themselves conquered by the Heraclidae—Achaeans by Dorians. May we not suppose that this was the intention with which the men of those days framed the constitutions of their states?

Meg. Quite true.

[686] *Ath.* And would not men who had shared with one another many dangers, and were governed by a single race of royal brothers, and had taken the advice of oracles, and in particular of the Delphian Apollo, be likely to think that such states would be firmly and lastingly established?

Meg. Of course they would.

Ath. Yet these institutions, of which such great expectations were entertained, seem to have all rapidly vanished away; with the exception, as I was saying, of that small part of them which existed in your land. And this third part has never to this day ceased warring against the two others; whereas, if the original idea had been carried out, and they had agreed to be one, their power would have been invincible in war.

Meg. No doubt.

Ath. But what was the ruin of this glorious confederacy? Here is a subject well worthy of consideration.

Meg. Certainly, no one will ever find more striking instances of laws or governments being the salvation or destruction of great and noble interests, than are here presented to his view.

Ath. Then now we seem to have happily arrived at a real and important question.

Meg. Very true.

Ath. Did you never remark, sage friend, that all men, and we ourselves at this moment, often fancy that they see some beautiful thing which might have effected wonders if any one had only known how to make a right use of it in some way; and yet this mode of looking at things may turn out after all to be a mistake, and not according to nature, either in our own case or in any other?

Meg. To what are you referring, and what do you mean?

Ath. I was thinking of my own admiration of the aforesaid Heracleid expedition, which was so noble, and might have had such wonderful results for the Hellenes, if only rightly used; and I was just laughing at myself.

Meg. But were you not right and wise in speaking as you did, and we in assenting to you?

Ath. Perhaps; and yet I cannot help observing that any one who sees anything great or powerful, immediately has the feeling that—"If the owner only knew how to use his great and noble possession, how happy would he be, and what great results would he achieve!"

[687] Meg. And would he not be justified?

Ath. Reflect; in what point of view does this sort of praise appear just: First, in reference to the question in hand:—If the then commanders had known how to arrange their army properly, how would they have attained success? Would not this have been the way? They would have bound them all firmly together and preserved them for ever, giving them freedom and dominion at pleasure, combined with the power of doing in the whole world, Hellenic and barbarian, whatever they and their descendants desired. What other aim would they have had?

Meg. Very good.

Ath. Suppose any one were in the same way to express his admiration at the sight of great wealth or family honour, or the like, he would praise them under the idea that through them he would attain either all or the greater and chief part of what he desires.

Meg. He would.

Ath. Well, now, and does not the argument show that there is one common desire of all mankind?

Meg. What is it?

Ath. The desire which a man has, that all things, if possible—at any rate, things human—may come to pass in accordance with his soul's desire.

Meg. Certainly.

Ath. And having this desire always, and at every time of life, in youth, in manhood, in age, he cannot help always praying for the fulfilment of it.

Meg. No doubt.

Ath. And we join in the prayers of our friends, and ask for them what they ask for themselves.

Meg. We do.

Ath. Dear is the son to the father—the younger to the elder.

Meg. Of course.

Ath. And yet the son often prays to obtain things which the father prays that he may not obtain.

Meg. When the son is young and foolish, you mean?

Ath. Yes; or when the father, in the dotage of age or the heat of youth, having no sense of right and justice, prays with fervour, under the influence of feelings akin to those of Theseus when he cursed the unfortunate Hippolytus, do you imagine that the son, having a sense of right and justice, will join in his father's prayers?

Meg. I understand you to mean that a man should not desire or be in a hurry to have all things according to his wish, for his wish may be at variance with his reason. But every state and every individual ought to pray and strive for wisdom. *[688]*

Ath. Yes; and I remember, and you will remember, what I said at first, that a statesman and legislator ought to ordain laws with a view to wisdom; while you were arguing that the good lawgiver ought to order all with a view to war. And to this I replied that there were four virtues, but that upon your view one of them only was the aim of legislation; whereas you ought to regard all virtue, and especially that which comes first, and is the leader of all the rest—I mean wisdom and mind and opinion, having affection and desire in their train. And now the argument returns to the same point, and I say once more, in jest if you like, or in earnest if you like, that the prayer of a fool is full of danger, being likely to end in the opposite of what he desires. And if you would rather receive my words in earnest, I am willing that you should; and you will find, I suspect, as I have said already, that not cowardice was the cause of the ruin of the Dorian kings and of their whole design, nor ignorance of military matters, either on the part of the rulers or of their subjects; but their misfortunes were due to their general degeneracy, and especially to their ignorance of the most important human affairs. That was then, and is still, and always will be the case, as I will endeavour, if you will allow me, to make out and demonstrate as well as I am able to you who are my friends, in the course of the argument.

Cle. Pray go on, Stranger;—compliments are troublesome, but we will show, not in word but in deed, how greatly we prize your words, for we will give them our best attention; and that is the way in which a freeman best shows his approval or disapproval.

Meg. Excellent, Cleinias; let us do as you say.

Cle. By all means, if Heaven wills. Go on.

Ath. Well, then, proceeding in the same train of thought, I say that the greatest ignorance was the ruin of the Dorian power, and that now, as then, ignorance is ruin. And if this be true, the legislator must endeavour to implant wisdom in states, and banish ignorance to the utmost of his power.

Cle. That is evident.

[689] Ath. Then now consider what is really the greatest ignorance. I should like to know whether you and Megillus would agree with me in what I am about to say; for my opinion is——

Cle. What?

Ath. That the greatest ignorance is when a man hates that which he nevertheless thinks to be good and noble, and loves and embraces that which he knows to be unrighteous and evil. This disagreement between the sense of pleasure and the judgment of reason in the soul is, in my opinion, the worst ignorance; and also the greatest, because affecting the great mass of the human soul; for the principle which feels pleasure and pain in the individual is like the mass or populace in a state. And when the soul is opposed to knowledge, or opinion, or reason, which are her natural lords, that I call folly, just as in the state, when the multitude refuses to obey their rulers and the laws; or, again, in the individual, when fair reasonings have their habitation in the soul and yet do no good, but rather the reverse of good. All these cases I term the worst ignorance, whether in individuals or in states. You will understand, Stranger, that I am speaking of something which is very different from the ignorance of handicraftsmen.

Cle. Yes, my friend, we understand and agree.

Ath. Let us, then, in the first place declare and affirm that the citizen who does not know these things ought never to have any kind of authority entrusted to him: he must be stigmatized as ignorant, even though he be versed in calculation and skilled in all sorts of accomplishments, and feats of mental dexterity; and the opposite are to be called wise, even although, in the words of the proverb, they know neither how to read nor how to swim; and to them, as to men of sense, authority is to be committed. For, O my friends, how can there be the least shadow of wisdom when there is no harmony? There is none; but the noblest and greatest of harmonies may be truly said to be the greatest wisdom; and of this he is a partaker who lives according to reason; whereas he who is devoid of reason is the destroyer of his house and the very opposite of a saviour of the state: he is utterly ignorant of political wisdom. Let this, then, as I was saying, be laid down by us.

Cle. Let it be so laid down.

Ath. I suppose that there must be rulers and subjects in states?

Cle. Certainly.

[690] Ath. And what are the principles on which men rule and obey in cities, whether great or small; and similarly in families? What are they, and how many in number? Is there not one claim of authority which is always just —that of fathers and mothers and in general of progenitors to rule over their offspring?

Cle. There is.

Ath. Next follows the principle that the noble should rule over the ignoble; and, thirdly, that the elder should rule and the younger obey?

Cle. To be sure.

Ath. And, fourthly, that slaves should be ruled, and their masters rule?

Cle. Of course.

Ath. Fifthly, if I am not mistaken, comes the principle that the stronger shall rule, and the weaker be ruled?

Cle. That is a rule not to be disobeyed.

Ath. Yes, and a rule which prevails very widely among all creatures, and is according to nature, as the Theban poet Pindar once said; and the sixth principle, and the greatest of all, is, that the wise should lead and command, and the ignorant follow and obey; and yet, O thou most wise Pindar, as I should reply to him, this surely is not contrary to nature, but according to nature, being the rule of law over willing subjects, and not a rule of compulsion.

Cle. Most true.

Ath. There is a seventh kind of rule which is awarded by lot, and is dear to the Gods and a token of good fortune: he on whom the lot falls is a ruler, and he who fails in obtaining the lot goes away and is the subject; and this we affirm to be quite just.

Cle. Certainly.

Ath. "Then now," as we say playfully to any of those who lightly undertake the making of laws, "you see, legislator, the principles of government, how many they are, and that they are naturally opposed to each other. There we have discovered a fountain-head of seditions, to which you must attend. And, first, we will ask you to consider with us, how and in what respect the kings of Argos and Messene violated these our maxims, and ruined themselves and the great and famous Hellenic power of the olden time. Was it because they did not know how wisely Hesiod spoke when he said that the half is often more than the whole? His meaning was, that when to take the whole would be dangerous, and to take the half would be the safe and moderate course, then the moderate or better was more than the immoderate or worse."

Cle. Very true.

Ath. And may we suppose this immoderate spirit to be more fatal when found among kings than when among peoples?

[691] Cle. The probability is that ignorance will be a disorder especially prevalent among kings, because they lead a proud and luxurious life.

Ath. Is it not palpable that the chief aim of the kings of that time was to get the better of the established laws, and that they were not in harmony with the principles which they had agreed to observe by word and oath? This want of harmony may have had the appearance of wisdom, but was really, as we assert, the greatest ignorance, and utterly overthrew the whole empire by dissonance and harsh discord.

Cle. Very likely.

Ath. Good; and what measures ought the legislator to have then taken in order to avert this calamity? Truly there is no great wisdom in knowing, and no great difficulty in telling, after the evil has happened; but to have foreseen the remedy at the time would have taken a much wiser head than ours.

Meg. What do you mean?

Ath. Any one who looks at what has occurred with you Lacedaemonians, Megillus, may easily know and may easily say what ought to have been done at that time.

Meg. Speak a little more clearly.

Ath. Nothing can be clearer than the observation which I am about to make.

Meg. What is it?

Ath. That if any one gives too great a power to anything, too large a sail to a vessel, too much food to the body, too much authority to the mind, and does not observe the mean, everything is overthrown, and, in the wantonness of excess runs in the one case to disorders, and in the other to injustice, which is the child of excess. I mean to say, my dear friends, that there is no soul of man, young and irresponsible, who will be able to sustain the temptation of arbitrary power—no one who will not, under such circumstances, become filled with folly, that worst of diseases, and be hated by his nearest and dearest friends: when this happens, his kingdom is undermined, and all his power vanishes from him. And great legislators who know the mean should take heed of the danger. As far as we can guess at this distance of time, what happened was as follows:—

Meg. What?

Ath. A God, who watched over Sparta, seeing into the future, gave you two families of kings instead of one; and thus brought you more within the limits of moderation. In the next place, some human wisdom mingled with divine power, observing that the constitution of your government was still feverish and excited, tempered your inborn strength and pride of birth with the moderation which comes of age, *[692]* making the power of your twenty-eight elders equal with that of the kings in the most important matters. But your third saviour, perceiving that your government was still swelling and foaming, and desirous to impose a curb upon it, instituted the Ephors, whose power he made to resemble that of magistrates elected by lot; and by this arrangement the kingly office, being compounded of the right elements and duly moderated, was preserved, and was the means of preserving all the rest. Since, if there had been only the original legislators, Temenus, Cresphontes, and their contemporaries, as far as they were concerned not even the portion of Aristodemus would have been preserved; for they had no proper experience in legislation, or they would surely not have imagined that oaths would moderate a youthful spirit invested with a power which might be converted into a tyranny. Now that God has instructed us what sort of government would have been or will be lasting, there is no wisdom, as I have already said, in judging after the event; there is no difficulty in learning from an example which has already occurred. But if any one could have foreseen all this at the time, and had been able to moderate the government of the three kingdoms and unite them into one, he might have saved all the excellent institutions which were then conceived; and no Persian or any other armament would have dared to attack us, or would have regarded Hellas as a power to be despised.

Cle. True.

Ath. There was small credit to us, Cleinias, in defeating them; and the discredit was, not that the conquerors did not win glorious victories both by land and sea, but what, in my opinion, brought discredit was, first of all, the circumstance that of the three cities one only fought on behalf of Hellas, and the two others were so utterly good for nothing that the one was waging a mighty war against Lacedaemon, and was thus preventing her from rendering assistance, while the city of Argos, which had the precedence at the time of the distribution, when asked to aid in repelling the barbarian, would not answer to the call, or give aid. Many things might be told about Hellas in connection with that war which are far from honourable; nor, indeed, can we rightly say that Hellas repelled the invader; for the truth is, that unless the Athenians and Lacedaemonians, *[693]* acting in concert, had warded off the impending yoke, all the tribes of Hellas would have been fused in a chaos of Hellenes mingling with one another, of barbarians mingling with Hellenes, and Hellenes with barbarians; just as nations who are now subject to the Persian power, owing to unnatural separations and combinations of them, are dispersed and scattered, and live miserably. These, Cleinias and Megillus, are the reproaches which we have to make against statesmen and legislators, as they are called, past and present, if we would analyse the causes of their failure, and find out what else might have been done. We said, for instance, just now, that there ought to be no great and unmixed powers; and this was under the idea that a state ought to be free and wise and harmonious, and that a legislator ought to legislate with a view to this end. Nor is there any reason to be surprised at our continually proposing aims for the legislator which appear not to be always the same; but we should consider when we say that temperance is to be the aim, or wisdom is to be the aim, or friendship is to be the aim, that all these aims are really the same; and if so, a variety in the modes of

expression ought not to disturb us.

Cle. Let us resume the argument in that spirit. And now, speaking of friendship and wisdom and freedom, I wish that you would tell me at what, in your opinion, the legislator should aim.

Ath. Hear me, then: there are two mother forms of states from which the rest may be truly said to be derived; and one of them may be called monarchy and the other democracy: the Persians have the highest form of the one, and we of the other; almost all the rest, as I was saying, are variations of these. Now, if you are to have liberty and the combination of friendship with wisdom, you must have both these forms of government in a measure; the argument emphatically declares that no city can be well governed which is not made up of both.[1]

Cle. Impossible.

Ath. Neither the one, if it be exclusively and excessively attached to monarchy, nor the other, if it be similarly attached to freedom, observes moderation; but your states, the Laconian and Cretan, have more of it; and the same was the case with the Athenians and Persians of old time, but now they have less. Shall I tell you why?

[694] *Cle.* By all means, if it will tend to elucidate our subject.

Ath. Hear, then:—There was a time when the Persians had more of the state which is a mean between slavery and freedom. In the reign of Cyrus they were freemen and also lords of many others: the rulers gave a share of freedom to the subjects, and being treated as equals, the soldiers were on better terms with their generals, and showed themselves more ready in the hour of danger. And if there was any wise man among them, who was able to give good counsel, he imparted his wisdom to the public; for the king was not jealous, but allowed him full liberty of speech, and gave honour to those who could advise him in any matter. And the nation waxed in all respects, because there was freedom and friendship and communion of mind among them.

Cle. That certainly appears to have been the case.

Ath. How, then, was this advantage lost under Cambyses, and again recovered under Darius? Shall I try to divine?

Cle. The enquiry, no doubt, has a bearing upon our subject.

Ath. I imagine that Cyrus, though a great and patriotic general, had never given his mind

[1] Cf. vi. 756; Aristotle, *Politics*, ii. 6, 1266 ᵃ 1-7.

to education, and never attended to the order of his household.

Cle. What makes you say so?

Ath. I think that from his youth upwards he was a soldier, and entrusted the education of his children to the women; and they brought them up from their childhood as the favourites of fortune, who were blessed already, and needed no more blessings. They thought that they were happy enough, and that no one should be allowed to oppose them in any way, and they compelled every one to praise all that they said or did. This was how they brought them up.

Cle. A splendid education truly!

Ath. Such an one as women were likely to give them, and especially princesses who had recently grown rich, and in the absence of the men, too, who were occupied in wars and dangers, and had no time to look after them.

Cle. What would you expect?

Ath. Their father had possessions of cattle and sheep, and many herds of men and other animals; *[695]* but he did not consider that those to whom he was about to make them over were not trained in his own calling, which was Persian; for the Persians are shepherds—sons of a rugged land, which is a stern mother, and well fitted to produce a sturdy race able to live in the open air and go without sleep, and also to fight, if fighting is required.[1] He did not observe that his sons were trained differently; through the so-called blessing of being royal they were educated in the Median fashion by women and eunuchs, which led to their becoming such as people do become when they are brought up unreproved. And so, after the death of Cyrus, his sons, in the fulness of luxury and licence, took the kingdom, and first one slew the other because he could not endure a rival; and, afterwards, the slayer himself, mad with wine and brutality, lost his kingdom through the Medes and the Eunuch, as they called him, who despised the folly of Cambyses.

Cle. So runs the tale, and such probably were the facts.

Ath. Yes; and the tradition says, that the empire came back to the Persians, through Darius and the seven chiefs.

Cle. True.

Ath. Let us note the rest of the story. Observe, that Darius was not the son of a king, and had not received a luxurious education. When he came to the throne, being one of the seven, he divided the country into seven portions, and of this arrangement there are some shadowy traces still remaining; he made laws upon the principle of introducing universal equality in the order of the state, and he embodied in his laws the settlement of the tribute which Cyrus promised—thus creating a feeling of friendship and community among all the Persians, and attaching the people to him with money and gifts. Hence his armies cheerfully acquired for him countries as large as those which Cyrus had left behind him. Darius was succeeded by his son Xerxes; and he again was brought up in the royal and luxurious fashion. Might we not most justly say: "O Darius, how came you to bring up Xerxes in the same way in which Cyrus brought up Cambyses, and not to see his fatal mistake?" For Xerxes, being the creation of the same education, met with much the same fortune as Cambyses; and from that time until now there has never been a really great king among the Persians, although they are all called Great. And their degeneracy is not to be attributed to chance, as I maintain; the reason is rather the evil life which is generally led by the sons of very rich and royal persons; *[696]* for never will boy or man, young or old, excel in virtue, who has been thus educated. And this, I say, is what the legislator has to consider, and what at the present moment has to be considered by us. Justly may you, O Lacedaemonians, be praised, in that you do not give special honour or a special education to wealth rather than to poverty, or to a royal rather than to a private station, where the divine and inspired lawgiver has not originally commanded them to be given. For no man ought to have pre-eminent honour in a state because he surpasses others in wealth, any more than because he is swift of foot or fair or strong, unless he have some virtue in him; nor even if he have virtue, unless he have this particular virtue of temperance.

Meg. What do you mean, Stranger?

Ath. I suppose that courage is a part of virtue?

Meg. To be sure.

Ath. Then, now hear and judge for yourself: —Would you like to have for a fellow-lodger or neighbour a very courageous man, who had no control over himself?

Meg. Heaven forbid!

Ath. Or an artist, who was clever in his profession, but a rogue?

Meg. Certainly not.

Ath. And surely justice does not grow apart from temperance?

[1] Cf. Aristotle, *Politics*, vii, 2, 1324 [b] 10-15.

Meg. Impossible.

Ath. Any more than our pattern wise man, whom we exhibited as having his pleasures and pains in accordance with and corresponding to true reason, can be intemperate? [1]

Meg. No.

Ath. There is a further consideration relating to the due and undue award of honours in states.

Meg. What is it?

Ath. I should like to know whether temperance without the other virtues, existing alone in the soul of man, is rightly to be praised or blamed?

Meg. I cannot tell.

Ath. And that is the best answer; for whichever alternative you had chosen, I think that you would have gone wrong.

Meg. I am fortunate.

Ath. Very good; a quality, which is a mere appendage of things which can be praised or blamed, does not deserve an expression of opinion, but is best passed over in silence.

Meg. You are speaking of temperance?

Ath. Yes; but of the other virtues, that which having this appendage is also most beneficial, will be most deserving of honour, and next that which is beneficial in the next degree; and so each of them will be rightly honoured according to a regular order.

Meg. True.

[697] *Ath.* And ought not the legislator to determine these classes?

Meg. Certainly he should.

Ath. Suppose that we leave to him the arrangement of details. But the general division of laws according to their importance into a first and second and third class, we who are lovers of law may make ourselves.

Meg. Very good.

Ath. We maintain, then, that a State which would be safe and happy, as far as the nature of man allows, must and ought to distribute honour and dishonour in the right way. And the right way is to place the goods of the soul first and highest in the scale, always assuming temperance to be the condition of them; and to assign the second place to the goods of the body; and the third place to money and property. And if any legislator or state departs from this rule by giving money the place of honour, or in any way preferring that which is really last, may we not say, that he or the state is doing an unholy and unpatriotic thing?

Meg. Yes; let that be plainly declared.

[1] Cf. 689.

Ath. The consideration of the Persian governments led us thus far to enlarge. We remarked that the Persians grew worse and worse. And we affirm the reason of this to have been, that they too much diminished the freedom of the people, and introduced too much of despotism, and so destroyed friendship and community of feeling. And when there is an end of these, no longer do the governors govern on behalf of their subjects or of the people, but on behalf of themselves; and if they think that they can gain ever so small an advantage for themselves, they devastate cities, and send fire and desolation among friendly races. And as they hate ruthlessly and horribly, so are they hated; and when they want the people to fight for them, they find no community of feeling or willingness to risk their lives on their behalf; their untold myriads are useless to them on the field of battle, and they think that their salvation depends on the employment of mercenaries and strangers whom they hire, as if they were in want of more men. And they cannot help being stupid, since they proclaim by their actions that the ordinary distinctions of right and wrong which are made in a state are a trifle, [698] when compared with gold and silver.

Meg. Quite true.

Ath. And now enough of the Persians, and their present maladministration of their government, which is owing to the excess of slavery and despotism among them.

Meg. Good.

Ath. Next, we must pass in review the government of Attica in like manner, and from this show that entire freedom and the absence of all superior authority is not by any means so good as government by others when properly limited, which was our ancient Athenian constitution at the time when the Persians made their attack on Hellas, or, speaking more correctly, on the whole continent of Europe. There were four classes, arranged according to a property census, and reverence was our queen and mistress, and made us willing to live in obedience to the laws which then prevailed. Also the vastness of the Persian armament, both by sea and on land, caused a helpless terror, which made us more and more the servants of our rulers and of the laws; and for all these reasons an exceeding harmony prevailed among us. About ten years before the naval engagement at Salamis, Datis came, leading a Persian host by command of Darius, which was expressly directed against the Athenians and Eretrians, having orders to carry them away captive; and these orders he was to execute under pain of death. Now Datis and his myriads soon became complete masters of Eretria, and he sent a fearful report to Athens that no Eretrian had escaped him; for the soldiers of Datis had joined hands and netted the whole of Eretria. And this report, whether well or ill founded, was terrible to all the Hellenes, and above all to the Athenians, and they dispatched embassies in all directions, but no one was willing to come to their relief, with the exception of the Lacedaemonians; and they, either because they were detained by the Messenian war, which was then going on, or for some other reason of which we are not told, came a day too late for the battle of Marathon. After a while, the news arrived of mighty preparations being made, and innumerable threats came from the king. Then, as time went on, a rumour reached us that Darius had died, and that his son, who was young and hot-headed, [699] had come to the throne and was persisting in his design. The Athenians were under the impression that the whole expedition was directed against them, in consequence of the battle of Marathon; and hearing of the bridge over the Hellespont, and the canal of Athos, and the host of ships, considering that there was no salvation for them either by land or by sea, for there was no one to help them, and remembering that in the first expedition, when the Persians destroyed Eretria, no one came to their help, or would risk the danger of an alliance with them, they thought that this would happen again, at least on land; nor, when they looked to the sea, could they descry any hope of salvation; for they were attacked by a thousand vessels and more. One chance of safety remained, slight indeed and desperate, but their only one. They saw that on the former occasion they had gained a seemingly impossible victory, and borne up by this hope, they found that their only refuge was in themselves and in the Gods. All these things created in them the spirit of friendship; there was the fear of the moment, and there was that higher fear, which they had acquired by obedience to their ancient laws, and which I have several times in the preceding discourse called reverence, of which the good man ought to be a willing servant, and of which the coward is independent and fearless. If this fear had not possessed them, they would never have met the enemy, or defended their temples and sepulchres and their country, and everything that was near and dear to them, as they did; but little by little they would have

been all scattered and dispersed.

Meg. Your words, Athenian, are quite true, and worthy of yourself and of your country.

Ath. They are true, Megillus; and to you, who have inherited the virtues of your ancestors, I may properly speak of the actions of that day. And I would wish you and Cleinias to consider whether my words have not also a bearing on legislation; for I am not discoursing only for the pleasure of talking, but for the argument's sake. Please to remark that the experience both of ourselves and the Persians was, in a certain sense, the same; for as they led their people into utter servitude, so we too led ours into all freedom. And now, how shall we proceed? for I would like you to observe that our previous arguments have a good deal to say for themselves.

[700] *Meg.* True; but I wish that you would give us a fuller explanation.

Ath. I will. Under the ancient laws, my friends, the people was not as now the master, but rather the willing servant of the laws.

Meg. What laws do you mean?

Ath. In the first place, let us speak of the laws about music—that is to say, such music as then existed—in order that we may trace the growth of the excess of freedom from the beginning. Now music was early divided among us into certain kinds and manners. One sort consisted of prayers to the Gods, which were called hymns; and there was another and opposite sort called lamentations, and another termed paeans, and another, celebrating the birth of Dionysus, called, I believe, "dithyrambs." And they used the actual word "laws," or νόμοι, for another kind of song; and to this they added the term "citharoedic." All these and others were duly distinguished, nor were the performers allowed to confuse one style of music with another. And the authority which determined and gave judgment, and punished the disobedient, was not expressed in a hiss, nor in the most unmusical shouts of the multitude, as in our days, nor in applause and clapping of hands. But the directors of public instruction insisted that the spectators should listen in silence to the end; and boys and their tutors, and the multitude in general, were kept quiet by a hint from a stick. Such was the good order which the multitude were willing to observe; they would never have dared to give judgment by noisy cries. And then, as time went on, the poets themselves introduced the reign of vulgar and lawless innovation. They were men of genius, but they had no perception of what is just and lawful in music; raging like Bacchanals and possessed with inordinate delights—mingling lamentations with hymns, and paeans with dithyrambs; imitating the sounds of the flute on the lyre, and making one general confusion; ignorantly affirming that music has no truth, and, whether good or bad, can only be judged of rightly by the pleasure of the hearer.[1] And by composing such licentious works, and adding to them words as licentious, they have inspired the multitude with lawlessness and boldness, and made them fancy that they can judge for themselves about melody and song. *[701]* And in this way the theatres from being mute have become vocal, as though they had understanding of good and bad in music and poetry; and instead of an aristocracy, an evil sort of theatrocracy has grown up.[2] For if the democracy which judged had only consisted of educated persons, no fatal harm would have been done; but in music there first arose the universal conceit of omniscience and general lawlessness;—freedom came following afterwards, and men, fancying that they knew what they did not know, had no longer any fear, and the absence of fear begets shamelessness. For what is this shamelessness, which is so evil a thing, but the insolent refusal to regard the opinion of the better by reason of an over-daring sort of liberty?

Meg. Very true.

Ath. Consequent upon this freedom comes the other freedom, of disobedience to rulers;[3] and then the attempt to escape the control and exhortation of father, mother, elders, and when near the end, the control of the laws also; and at the very end there is the contempt of oaths and pledges, and no regard at all for the Gods—herein they exhibit and imitate the old so-called Titanic nature, and come to the same point as the Titans when they rebelled against God, leading a life of endless evils. But why have I said all this? I ask, because the argument ought to be pulled up from time to time, and not be allowed to run away, but held with bit and bridle, and then we shall not, as the proverb says, fall off our ass. Let us then once more ask the question, To what end has all this been said?

Meg. Very good.

Ath. This, then, has been said for the sake—

Meg. Of what?

Ath. We were maintaining that the lawgiver

ought to have three things in view: first, that the city for which he legislates should be free; and secondly, be at unity with herself; and thirdly, should have understanding;—these were our principles, were they not?

Meg. Certainly.

Ath. With a view to this we selected two kinds of government, the one the most despotic, and the other the most free; and now we are considering which of them is the right form: we took a mean in both cases, of despotism in the one, and of liberty in the other, and we saw that in a mean they attained their perfection; but that when they were carried to the extreme of either, slavery or licence, neither party were the gainers.

[702] Meg. Very true.

Ath. And that was our reason for considering the settlement of the Dorian army, and of the city built by Dardanus at the foot of the mountains, and the removal of cities to the sea-shore, and of our mention of the first men, who were the survivors of the deluge. And all that was previously said about music and drinking, and what preceded, was said with the view of seeing how a state might be best administered, and how an individual might best order his own life. And now, Megillus and Cleinias, how can we put to the proof the value of our words?

Cle. Stranger, I think that I see how a proof of their value may be obtained. This discussion of ours appears to me to have been singularly fortunate, and just what I at this moment want; most auspiciously have you and my friend Megillus come in my way. For I will tell you what has happened to me; and I regard the coincidence as a sort of omen. The greater part of Crete is going to send out a colony, and they have entrusted the management of the affair to the Cnosians; and the Cnosian government to me and nine others. And they desire us to give them any laws which we please, whether taken from the Cretan model or from any other; and they do not mind about their being foreign if they are better. Grant me then this favour, which will also be a gain to yourselves:—Let us make a selection from what has been said, and then let us imagine a State of which we will suppose ourselves to be the original founders. Thus we shall proceed with our enquiry, and, at the same time, I may have the use of the framework which you are constructing, for the city which is in contemplation.

Ath. Good news, Cleinias; if Megillus has no objection, you may be sure that I will do all in my power to please you.

[1] Cf. *Republic*, iii. 397, ff.
[2] Cf. Aristotle, *Politics*, viii. 6.
[3] Cf. *Republic*, iv. 424.

Cle. Thank you.

Meg. And so will I.

Cle. Excellent; and now let us begin to frame the State.

BOOK IV

[704] Athenian Stranger. And now, what will this city be? I do not mean to ask what is or will hereafter be the name of the place; that may be determined by the accident of locality or of the original settlement—a river or fountain, or some local deity may give the sanction of a name to the newly-founded city; but I do want to know what the situation is, whether maritime or inland.

Cleinias. I should imagine, Stranger, that the city of which we are speaking is about eighty stadia distant from the sea.

Ath. And are there harbours on the seaboard?

Cle. Excellent harbours, Stranger; there could not be better.

Ath. Alas! what a prospect! And is the surrounding country productive, or in need of importations?

Cle. Hardly in need of anything.

Ath. And is there any neighbouring State?

Cle. None whatever, and that is the reason for selecting the place; in days of old, there was a migration of the inhabitants, and the region has been deserted from time immemorial.

Ath. And has the place a fair proportion of hill, and plain, and wood?

Cle. Like the rest of Crete in that.

Ath. You mean to say that there is more rock than plain?

Cle. Exactly.

Ath. Then there is some hope that your citizens may be virtuous: had you been on the sea, and well provided with harbours, and an importing rather than a producing country, some mighty saviour would have been needed, and lawgivers more than mortal, if you were ever to have a chance of preserving your state from degeneracy and discordance of manners.[1] But there is comfort in the eighty stadia; although the sea is too near, especially if, as you say, the harbours are so good. *[705]* Still we may be content. The sea is pleasant enough as a daily companion, but has indeed also a bitter and brackish quality; filling the streets with merchants and shopkeepers, and begetting in the souls of men uncertain and unfaithful ways—making the state unfriendly and unfaithful both to her own citizens, and also to other na-

tions. There is a consolation, therefore, in the country producing all things at home; and yet, owing to the ruggedness of the soil, not providing anything in great abundance. Had there been abundance, there might have been a great export trade, and a great return of gold and silver; which, as we may safely affirm, has the most fatal results on a State whose aim is the attainment of just and noble sentiments: this was said by us, if you remember, in the previous discussion.[2]

Cle. I remember, and am of opinion that we both were and are in the right.

Ath. Well, but let me ask, how is the country supplied with timber for ship-building?

Cle. There is no fir of any consequence, nor pine, and not much cypress; and you will find very little stone-pine or plane-wood, which shipwrights always require for the interior of ships.

Ath. These are also natural advantages.

Cle. Why so?

Ath. Because no city ought to be easily able to imitate its enemies in what is mischievous.

Cle. How does that bear upon any of the matters of which we have been speaking?

Ath. Remember, my good friend, what I said at first[3] about the Cretan laws, that they look to one thing only, and this, as you both agreed, was war; and I replied that such laws, in so far as they tended to promote virtue, were good; but in that they regarded a part only, and not the whole of virtue, I disapproved of them. And now I hope that you in your turn will follow and watch me if I legislate with a view to anything but virtue, or with a view to a part of virtue only. For I consider that the true lawgiver, like an archer, aims only at that on which some eternal beauty is always attending, *[706]* and dismisses everything else, whether wealth or any other benefit, when separated from virtue. I was saying that the imitation of enemies was a bad thing; and I was thinking of a case in which a maritime people are harassed by enemies, as the Athenians were by Minos (I do not speak from any desire to recall past grievances); but he, as we know, was a great naval potentate, who compelled the inhabitants of Attica to pay him a cruel tribute; and in those days they had no ships of war as they now have, nor was the country filled with ship-timber, and therefore they could not readily build them. Hence they could not learn how to imitate their enemy at sea, and in this way, becoming sailors themselves, directly repel their enemies. Better

---

[1] Cf. Aristotle, *Politics*, vii. 6, 1327 ª 11-32.

[2] Cf. iii. 679.

[3] Cf. i. 625.

for them to have lost many times over the seven youths, than that heavy-armed and stationary troops should have been turned into sailors, and accustomed to be often leaping on shore, and again to come running back to their ships; or should have fancied that there was no disgrace in not awaiting the attack of an enemy and dying boldly; and that there were good reasons, and plenty of them, for a man throwing away his arms, and betaking himself to flight—which is not dishonourable, as people say, at certain times. This is the language of naval warfare, and is anything but worthy of extraordinary praise. For we should not teach bad habits, least of all to the best part of the citizens. You may learn the evil of such a practice from Homer, by whom Odysseus is introduced, rebuking Agamemnon because he desires to draw down the ships to the sea at a time when the Achaeans are hard pressed by the Trojans—he gets angry with him, and says:

Who, at a time when the battle is in full cry, biddest to drag the well-benched ships into the sea, that the prayers of the Trojans may be accomplished yet more, and high ruin fall upon us. For the Achaeans will not maintain the battle, when the ships are drawn into the sea, but they will look behind and will cease from strife; in that the counsel which you give will prove injurious. [707]

You see that he quite knew triremes on the sea, in the neighbourhood of fighting men, to be an evil;—lions might be trained in that way to fly from a herd of deer. Moreover, naval powers which owe their safety to ships, do not give honour to that sort of warlike excellence which is most deserving of it. For he who owes his safety to the pilot and the captain, and the oarsman, and all sorts of rather inferior persons, cannot rightly give honour to whom honour is due. But how can a state be in a right condition which cannot justly award honour?

Cle. It is hardly possible, I admit; and yet, Stranger, we Cretans are in the habit of saying that the battle of Salamis was the salvation of Hellas.

Ath. Why, yes; and that is an opinion which is widely spread both among Hellenes and barbarians. But Megillus and I say rather, that the battle of Marathon was the beginning, and the battle of Plataea the completion, of the great deliverance, and that these battles by land made the Hellenes better; whereas the sea-fights of Salamis and Artemisium—for I may as well put them both together—made them no better, if I may say so without offence about the battles which helped to save us. And in estimating the

goodness of a state, we regard both the situation of the country and the order of the laws, considering that the mere preservation and continuance of life is not the most honourable thing for men, as the vulgar think, but the continuance of the best life, while we live; and that again, if I am not mistaken, is a remark which has been made already.[1]

Cle. Yes.

Ath. Then we have only to ask whether we are taking the course which we acknowledge to be the best for the settlement and legislation of states.

Cle. The best by far.

Ath. And now let me proceed to another question: Who are to be the colonists? May any one come out of all Crete; and is the idea that the population in the several states is too numerous for the means of subsistence? For I suppose that you are not going to send out a general invitation to any Hellene who likes to come. And yet I observe that to your country settlers have come from Argos and [708] Aegina and other parts of Hellas. Tell me, then, whence do you draw your recruits in the present enterprise?

Cle. They will come from all Crete; and of other Hellenes, Peloponnesians will be most acceptable. For, as you truly observe, there are Cretans of Argive descent; and the race of Cretans which has the highest character at the present day is the Gortynian, and this has come from Gortys in the Peloponnesus.

Ath. Cities find colonization in some respects easier if the colonists are one race, which like a swarm of bees is sent out from a single country, either when friends leave friends, owing to some pressure of population or other similar necessity, or when a portion of a state is driven by factions to emigrate. And there have been whole cities which have taken flight when utterly conquered by a superior power in war. This, however, which is in one way an advantage to the colonist or legislator, in another point of view creates a difficulty. There is an element of friendship in the community of race, and language, and laws, and in common temples and rites of worship; but colonies which are of this homogeneous sort are apt to kick against any laws or any form of constitution differing from that which they had at home; and although the badness of their own laws may have been the cause of the factions which prevailed among them, yet from the force of habit they would fain preserve the very customs which

[1] Cf. ii. 661.

were their ruin, and the leader of the colony, who is their legislator, finds them troublesome and rebellious. On the other hand, the conflux of several populations might be more disposed to listen to new laws; but then, to make them combine and pull together, as they say of horses, is a most difficult task, and the work of years. And yet there is nothing which tends more to the improvement of mankind than legislation and colonization.

Cle. No doubt; but I should like to know why you say so.

Ath. My good friend, I am afraid that the course of my speculations is leading me to say something depreciatory of legislators; but if the word be to the purpose, there can be no harm. And yet, why am I disquieted, for I believe that the same principle applies equally to all human things?

[709] Cle. To what are you referring?

Ath. I was going to say that man never legislates, but accidents of all sorts, which legislate for us in all sorts of ways. The violence of war and the hard necessity of poverty are constantly overturning governments and changing laws. And the power of disease has often caused innovations in the state, when there have been pestilences, or when there has been a succession of bad seasons continuing during many years. Any one who sees all this, naturally rushes to the conclusion of which I was speaking, that no mortal legislates in anything, but that in human affairs chance is almost everything. And this may be said of the arts of the sailor, and the pilot, and the physician, and the general, and may seem to be well said; and yet there is another thing which may be said with equal truth of all of them.

Cle. What is it?

Ath. That God governs all things, and that chance and opportunity co-operate with him in the government of human affairs. There is, however, a third and less extreme view, that art should be there also; for I should say that in a storm there must surely be a great advantage in having the aid of the pilot's art. You would agree?

Cle. Yes.

Ath. And does not a like principle apply to legislation as well as to other things: even supposing all the conditions to be favourable which are needed for the happiness of the state, yet the true legislator must from time to time appear on the scene?

Cle. Most true.

Ath. In each case the artist would be able to pray rightly for certain conditions, and if these were granted by fortune, he would then only require to exercise his art?

Cle. Certainly.

Ath. And all the other artists just now mentioned, if they were bidden to offer up each their special prayer, would do so?

Cle. Of course.

Ath. And the legislator would do likewise?

Cle. I believe that he would.

Ath. "Come, legislator," we will say to him; "what are the conditions which you require in a state before you can organize it?" How ought he to answer this question? Shall I give his answer?

Cle. Yes.

Ath. He will say—"Give me a state which is governed by a tyrant, and let the tyrant be young and have a good memory; let him be quick at learning, and of a courageous and noble nature; let him have that quality which, as I said before, is the inseparable companion of all the other parts of virtue, *[710]* if there is to be any good in them."

Cle. I suppose, Megillus, that this companion virtue of which the Stranger speaks, must be temperance?

Ath. Yes, Cleinias, temperance in the vulgar sense; not that which in the forced and exaggerated language of some philosophers is called prudence, but that which is the natural gift of children and animals, of whom some live continently and others incontinently, but when isolated, was as we said, hardly worth reckoning in the catalogue of goods.[1] I think that you must understand my meaning.

Cle. Certainly.

Ath. Then our tyrant must have this as well as the other qualities, if the state is to acquire in the best manner and in the shortest time the form of government which is most conducive to happiness; for there neither is nor ever will be a better or speedier way of establishing a polity than by a tyranny.

Cle. By what possible arguments, Stranger, can any man persuade himself of such a monstrous doctrine?

Ath. There is surely no difficulty in seeing, Cleinias, what is in accordance with the order of nature?

Cle. You would assume, as you say, a tyrant who was young, temperate, quick at learning, having a good memory, courageous, of a noble nature?

Ath. Yes; and you must add fortunate; and

[1] Cf. iii 696.

his good fortune must be that he is the contemporary of a great legislator, and that some happy chance brings them together. When this has been accomplished, God has done all that he ever does for a state which he desires to be eminently prosperous; He has done second best for a state in which there are two such rulers, and third best for a state in which there are three. The difficulty increases with the increase, and diminishes with the diminution of the number.

Cle. You mean to say, I suppose, that the best government is produced from a tyranny, and originates in a good lawgiver and an orderly tyrant, and that the change from such a tyranny into a perfect form of government takes place most easily; less easily when from an oligarchy; and, in the third degree, from a democracy: is not that your meaning?

Ath. Not so; I mean rather to say that the change is best made out of a tyranny; and secondly, out of a monarchy; and thirdly, out of some sort of democracy: fourth, in the capacity for improvement, comes oligarchy, which has the greatest difficulty in admitting of such a change, because the government is in the hands of a number of potentates. I am supposing that the legislator is by nature of the true sort, and that his strength is united with that of the chief men of the state; and when the ruling element is numerically small, and at the same time very strong, *[711]* as in a tyranny, there the change is likely to be easiest and most rapid.

Cle. How? I do not understand.

Ath. And yet I have repeated what I am saying a good many times; but I suppose that you have never seen a city which is under a tyranny?

Cle. No, and I cannot say that I have any great desire to see one.

Ath. And yet, where there is a tyranny, you might certainly see that of which I am now speaking.

Cle. What do you mean?

Ath. I mean that you might see how, without trouble and in no very long period of time, the tyrant, if he wishes, can change the manners of a state: he has only to go in the direction of virtue or of vice, whichever he prefers, he himself indicating by his example the lines of conduct, praising and rewarding some actions and reproving others, and degrading those who disobey.

Cle. But how can we imagine that the citizens in general will at once follow the example

set to them; and how can he have this power both of persuading and of compelling them?

Ath. Let no one, my friends, persuade us that there is any quicker and easier way in which states change their laws than when the rulers lead: such changes never have, nor ever will, come to pass in any other way. The real impossibility or difficulty is of another sort, and is rarely surmounted in the course of ages; but when once it is surmounted, ten thousand or rather all blessings follow.

Cle. Of what are you speaking?

Ath. The difficulty is to find the divine love of temperate and just institutions existing in any powerful forms of government, whether in a monarchy or oligarchy of wealth or of birth. You might as well hope to reproduce the character of Nestor, who is said to have excelled all men in the power of speech, and yet more in his temperance. This, however, according to the tradition, was in the times of Troy; in our own days there is nothing of the sort; but if such an one either has or ever shall come into being, or is now among us, blessed is he and blessed are they who hear the wise words that flow from his lips. And this may be said of power in general: When the supreme power in man coincides with the greatest wisdom and temperance, *[712]* then the best laws and the best constitution come into being; but in no other way. And let what I have been saying be regarded as a kind of sacred legend or oracle, and let this be our proof that, in one point of view, there may be a difficulty for a city to have good laws, but that there is another point of view in which nothing can be easier or sooner effected, granting our supposition.

Cle. How do you mean?

Ath. Let us try to amuse ourselves, old boys as we are, by moulding in words the laws which are suitable to your state.[1]

Cle. Let us proceed without delay.

Ath. Then let us invoke God at the settlement of our state; may he hear and be propitious to us, and come and set in order the State and the laws!

Cle. May he come!

Ath. But what form of polity are we going to give the city?

Cle. Tell us what you mean a little more clearly. Do you mean some form of democracy, or oligarchy, or aristocracy, or monarchy? For we cannot suppose that you would include tyranny.

Ath. Which of you will first tell me to which

[1] Cf. v. 746.

of these classes his own government is to be referred?

Megillus. Ought I to answer first, since I am the elder?

Cle. Perhaps you should.

Meg. And yet, Stranger, I perceive that I cannot say, without more thought, what I should call the government of Lacedaemon, for it seems to me to be like a tryanny—the power of our Ephors is marvellously tyrannical; and sometimes it appears to me to be of all cities the most democratical; and who can reasonably deny that it is an aristocracy? [1] We have also a monarchy which is held for life, and is said by all mankind, and not by ourselves only, to be the most ancient of all monarchies; and, therefore, when asked on a sudden, I cannot precisely say which form of government the Spartan is.

Cle. I am in the same difficulty, Megillus; for I do not feel confident that the polity of Cnosus is any of these.

Ath. The reason is, my excellent friends, that you really have polities, but the states of which we were just now speaking are merely aggregations of men dwelling in cities who are the subjects and servants of a part of their own state, [713] and each of them is named after the dominant power; they are not polities at all. But if states are to be named after their rulers, the true state ought to be called by the name of the God who rules over wise men.

Cle. And who is this God?

Ath. May I still make use of fable to some extent, in the hope that I may be better able to answer your question: shall I?

Cle. By all means.

Ath. In the primeval world, and a long while before the cities came into being whose settlements we have described, there is said to have been in the time of Cronos a blessed rule and life, of which the best-ordered of existing states is a copy. [2]

Cle. It will be very necessary to hear about that.

Ath. I quite agree with you; and therefore I have introduced the subject.

Cle. Most appropriately; and since the tale is to the point, you will do well in giving us the whole story.

Ath. I will do as you suggest. There is a tradition of the happy life of mankind in days when all things were spontaneous and abundant. And of this the reason is said to have been as follows:—Cronos knew what we ourselves

were declaring, [3] that no human nature invested with supreme power is able to order human affairs and not overflow with insolence and wrong. Which reflection led him to appoint not men but demigods, who are of a higher and more divine race, to be the kings and rulers of our cities; he did as we do with flocks of sheep and other tame animals. For we do not appoint oxen to be the lords of oxen, or goats of goats; but we ourselves are a superior race, and rule over them. In like manner God, in his love of mankind, placed over us the demons, who are a superior race, and they with great ease and pleasure to themselves, and no less to us, taking care of us and giving us peace and reverence and order and justice never failing, made the tribes of men happy and united. And this tradition, which is true, declares that cities of which some mortal man and not God is the ruler, have no escape from evils and toils. Still we must do all that we can to imitate the life which is said to have existed in the days of Cronos, and, as far as the principle of immortality dwells in us, to that we must hearken, both in private and public life, and regulate our cities and houses according to law, [714] meaning by the very term "law," the distribution of mind. But if either a single person or an oligarchy or a democracy has a soul eager after pleasures and desires—wanting to be filled with them, yet retaining none of them, and perpetually afflicted with an endless and insatiable disorder; and this evil spirit, having first trampled the laws under foot, becomes the master either of a state or of an individual—then, as I was saying, salvation is hopeless. And now, Cleinias, we have to consider whether you will or will not accept this tale of mine.

Cle. Certainly we will.

Ath. You are aware—are you not?—that there are often said to be as many forms of laws as there are of governments, and of the latter we have already mentioned [4] all those which are commonly recognized. Now you must regard this as a matter of first-rate importance. For what is to be the standard of just and unjust, is once more the point at issue. Men say that the law ought not to regard either military virtue, or virtue in general, but only the interests and power and preservation of the established form of government; this is thought by them to be the best way of expressing the natural definition of justice.

Cle. How?

[2] Cf. *Statesman,* 271.
[1] Cf. Aristotle, *Politics,* ii. 6, 1265 [b] 27-41.
[3] Cf. iii. 691.
[4] *Supra,* 712.

Ath. Justice is said by them to be the interest of the stronger.[1]

Cle. Speak plainer.

Ath. I will:—"Surely," they say, "the governing power makes whatever laws have authority in any state?"

Cle. True.

Ath. "Well," they would add, "and do you suppose that tyranny or democracy, or any other conquering power, does not make the continuance of the power which is possessed by them the first or principal object of their laws?"

Cle. How can they have any other?

Ath. "And whoever transgresses these laws is punished as an evil-doer by the legislator, who calls the laws just?"

Cle. Naturally.

Ath. "This, then, is always the mode and fashion in which justice exists."

Cle. Certainly, if they are correct in their view.

Ath. Why, yes, this is one of those false principles of government to which we were referring.[2]

Cle. Which do you mean?

Ath. Those which we were examining when we spoke of who ought to govern whom. Did we not arrive at the conclusion that parents ought to govern their children, and the elder the younger, and the noble the ignoble? And there were many other principles, if you remember, and they were not always consistent. One principle was this very principle of might, and we said that Pindar considered violence natural and justified it.

[715] Cle. Yes; I remember.

Ath. Consider, then, to whom our state is to be entrusted. For there is a thing which has occurred times without number in states——

Cle. What thing?

Ath. That when there has been a contest for power, those who gain the upper hand so entirely monopolize the government, as to refuse all share to the defeated party and their descendants—they live watching one another, the ruling class being in perpetual fear that some one who has a recollection of former wrongs will come into power and rise up against them. Now, according to our view, such governments are not polities at all, nor are laws right which are passed for the good of particular classes and not for the good of the whole state. States which have such laws are not polities but parties, and their notions of justice are

simply unmeaning. I say this, because I am going to assert that we must not entrust the government in your state to any one because he is rich, or because he possesses any other advantage, such as strength, or stature, or again birth: but he who is most obedient to the laws of the state, he shall win the palm; and to him who is victorious in the first degree shall be given the highest office and chief ministry of the gods; and the second to him who bears the second palm; and on a similar principle shall all the other offices be assigned to those who come next in order. And when I call the rulers servants or ministers of the law, I give them this name not for the sake of novelty, but because I certainly believe that upon such service or ministry depends the well- or ill-being of the state. For that state in which the law is subject and has no authority, I perceive to be on the highway to ruin; but I see that the state in which the law is above the rulers, and the rulers are the inferiors of the law, has salvation, and every blessing which the Gods can confer.

Cle. Truly, Stranger, you see with the keen vision of age.

Ath. Why, yes; every man when he is young has that sort of vision dullest, and when he is old keenest.

Cle. Very true.

Ath. And now, what is to be the next step? May we not suppose the colonists to have arrived, and proceed to make our speech to them?

Cle. Certainly.

Ath. "Friends," we say to them,—"God, as the old tradition declares, holding in his hand the beginning, middle, and end of all that is, *[716]* travels according to his nature in a straight line towards the accomplishment of his end. Justice always accompanies him, and is the punisher of those who fall short of the divine law. To justice, he who would be happy holds fast, and follows in her company with all humility and order; but he who is lifted up with pride, or elated by wealth or rank, or beauty, who is young and foolish, and has a soul hot with insolence, and thinks that he has no need of any guide or ruler, but is able himself to be the guide of others, he, I say, is left deserted of God; and being thus deserted, he takes to him others who are like himself, and dances about, throwing all things into confusion, and many think that he is a great man, but in a short time he pays a penalty which justice cannot but approve, and is utterly destroyed, and his family and city with him. Wherefore, seeing that human things are thus ordered, what should a

---

[1] *Republic* i. 338; ii. 367.

[2] Cf. iii. 690.

wise man do or think, or not do or think?"

Cle. Every man ought to make up his mind that he will be one of the followers of God; there can be no doubt of that.

Ath. Then what life is agreeable to God, and becoming in his followers? One only, expressed once for all in the old saying that "like agrees with like, with measure measure," but things which have no measure agree neither with themselves nor with the things which have. Now God ought to be to us the measure of all things, and not man,[1] as men commonly say (Protagoras): the words are far more true of him. And he who would be dear to God must, as far as is possible, be like him and such as he is. Wherefore the temperate man is the friend of God, for he is like him; and the intemperate man is unlike him, and different from him, and unjust. And the same applies to other things; and this is the conclusion, which is also the noblest and truest of all sayings—that for the good man to offer sacrifice to the Gods, and hold converse with them by means of prayers and offerings and every kind of service, is the noblest and best of all things, and also the most conducive to a happy life, and very fit and meet. But with the bad man, the opposite of this is true: for the bad man has an impure soul, whereas the good is pure; and from one who is polluted, neither a good man nor God can without impropriety receive gifts. *[717]* Wherefore the unholy do only waste their much service upon the Gods, but when offered by any holy man, such service is most acceptable to them. This is the mark at which we ought to aim. But what weapons shall we use, and how shall we direct them? In the first place, we affirm that next after the Olympian Gods and the Gods of the State, honour should be given to the Gods below; they should receive everything in even numbers, and of the second choice, and ill omen, while the odd numbers, and the first choice, and the things of lucky omen, are given to the Gods above, by him who would rightly hit the mark of piety. Next to these Gods, a wise man will do service to the demons or spirits, and then to the heroes, and after them will follow the private and ancestral Gods, who are worshipped as the law prescribes in the places which are sacred to them. Next comes the honour of living parents, to whom, as is meet, we have to pay the first and greatest and oldest of all debts, considering that all which a man has belongs to those who gave him birth and brought him up, and that he must do all that he can to minis-

[1] Cf. *Cratylus,* 386 ff.; *Theaetetus,* 152.

ter to them, first, in his property, secondly, in his person, and thirdly, in his soul, in return for the endless care and travail which they bestowed upon him of old, in the days of his infancy, and which he is now to pay back to them when they are old and in the extremity of their need. And all his life long he ought never to utter, or to have uttered, an unbecoming word to them; for of light and fleeting words the penalty is most severe; Nemesis, the messenger of justice, is appointed to watch over all such matters. When they are angry and want to satisfy their feelings in word or deed, he should give way to them; for a father who thinks that he has been wronged by his son may be reasonably expected to be very angry. At their death, the most moderate funeral is best, neither exceeding the customary expense, nor yet falling short of the honour which has been usually shown by the former generation to their parents. And let a man not forget to pay the yearly tribute of respect to the dead, honouring them chiefly by omitting nothing that conduces to a perpetual remembrance of them, *[718]* and giving a reasonable portion of his fortune to the dead. Doing this, and living after this manner, we shall receive our reward from the Gods and those who are above us [i.e., the demons]; and we shall spend our days for the most part in good hope. And how a man ought to order what relates to his descendants and his kindred and friends and fellow-citizens, and the rites of hospitality taught by Heaven, and the intercourse which arises out of all these duties, with a view to the embellishment and orderly regulation of his own life—these things, I say, the laws, as we proceed with them, will accomplish, partly persuading, and partly when natures do not yield to the persuasion of custom, chastising them by might and right, and will thus render our state, if the Gods co-operate with us, prosperous and happy. But of what has to be said, and must be said by the legislator who is of my way of thinking, and yet, if said in the form of law, would be out of place—of this I think that he may give a sample for the instruction of himself and of those for whom he is legislating; and then when, as far as he is able, he has gone through all the preliminaries, he may proceed to the work of legislation. Now, what will be the form of such prefaces? There may be a difficulty in including or describing them all under a single form, but I think that we may get some notion of them if we can guarantee one thing.

Cle. What is that?

Ath. I should wish the citizens to be as readily persuaded to virtue as possible; this will surely be the aim of the legislator in all his laws.

Cle. Certainly.

Ath. The proposal appears to me to be of some value; and I think that a person will listen with more gentleness and good-will to the precepts addressed to him by the legislator, when his soul is not altogether unprepared to receive them. Even a little done in the way of conciliation gains his ear, and is always worth having. For there is no great inclination or readiness on the part of mankind to be made as good, or as quickly good, as possible. The case of the many proves the wisdom of Hesiod, who says that the road to wickedness is smooth and can be travelled without perspiring, because it is so very short:

But before virtue the immortal Gods have placed the sweat of labour, and long and steep is the way thither, [719] and rugged at first; but when you have reached the top, although difficult before, it is then easy.

Cle. Yes; and he certainly speaks well.

Ath. Very true: and now let me tell you the effect which the preceding discourse has had upon me.

Cle. Proceed.

Ath. Suppose that we have a little conversation with the legislator, and say to him—"O, legislator, speak; if you know what we ought to say and do, you can surely tell."

Cle. Of course he can.

Ath. "Did we not hear you just now saying,[1] that the legislator ought not to allow the poets to do what they liked? For that they would not know in which of their words they went against the laws, to the hurt of the state."

Cle. That is true.

Ath. May we not fairly make answer to him on behalf of the poets?

Cle. What answer shall we make to him?

Ath. That the poet, according to the tradition which has ever prevailed among us, and is accepted of all men, when he sits down on the tripod of the muse, is not in his right mind; like a fountain, he allows to flow out freely whatever comes in, and his art being imitative, he is often compelled to represent men of opposite dispositions, and thus to contradict himself; neither can he tell whether there is more truth in one thing that he has said than in another. But this is not the case in a law; the legislator must give not two rules about the same

[1] Cf. ii. 656, ff.

thing, but one only. Take an example from what you have just been saying.[2] Of three kinds of funerals, there is one which is too extravagant, another is too niggardly, the third is a mean; and you choose and approve and order the last without qualification. But if I had an extremely rich wife, and she bade me bury her and describe her burial in a poem, I should praise the extravagant sort; and a poor miserly man, who had not much money to spend, would approve of the niggardly; and the man of moderate means, who was himself moderate, would praise a moderate funeral. Now you in the capacity of legislator must not barely say "a moderate funeral," but you must define what moderation is, and how much; unless you are definite, you must not suppose that you are speaking a language that can become law.

Cle. Certainly not.

Ath. And is our legislator to have no preface to his laws, but to say at once Do this, avoid that—and then holding the penalty in terrorem, to go on to another law; offering never a word of advice or exhortation to those for whom he is legislating, [720] after the manner of some doctors? For of doctors, as I may remind you, some have a gentler, others a ruder method of cure; and as children ask the doctor to be gentle with them, so we will ask the legislator to cure our disorders with the gentlest remedies. What I mean to say is, that besides doctors there are doctors' servants, who are also styled doctors.

Cle. Very true.

Ath. And whether they are slaves or freemen makes no difference; they acquire their knowledge of medicine by obeying and observing their masters; empirically and not according to the natural way of learning, as the manner of freemen is, who have learned scientifically themselves the art which they impart scientifically to their pupils. You are aware that there are these two classes of doctors?

Cle. To be sure.

Ath. And did you ever observe that there are two classes of patients in states, slaves and freemen; and the slave doctors run about and cure the slaves, or wait for them in the dispensaries—practitioners of this sort never talk to their patients individually, or let them talk about their own individual complaints? The slave-doctor prescribes what mere experience suggests, as if he had exact knowledge; and when he has given his orders, like a tyrant, he rushes off with equal assurance to some other servant who is ill; and so he relieves the master of the

[2] Cf. 717.

house of the care of his invalid slaves. But the other doctor, who is a freeman, attends and practises upon freemen; and he carries his enquiries far back, and goes into the nature of the disorder; he enters into discourse with the patient and with his friends, and is at once getting information from the sick man, and also instructing him as far as he is able, and he will not prescribe for him until he has first convinced him; at last, when he has brought the patient more and more under his persuasive influences and set him on the road to health, he attempts to effect a cure. Now which is the better way of proceeding in a physician and in a trainer? Is he the better who accomplishes his ends in a double way, or he who works in one way, and that the ruder and inferior?

Cle. I should say, Stranger, that the double way is far better.

Ath. Should you like to see an example of the double and single method in legislation?

Cle. Certainly I should.

[721] Ath. What will be our first law? Will not the legislator, observing the order of nature, begin by making regulations for states about births?

Cle. He will.

Ath. In all states the birth of children goes back to the connection of marriage?

Cle. Very true.

Ath. And, according to the true order, the laws relating to marriage should be those which are first determined in every state?

Cle. Quite so.

Ath. Then let me first give the law of marriage in a simple form; it may run as follows:—A man shall marry between the ages of thirty and thirty-five, or, if he does not, he shall pay such and such a fine, or shall suffer the loss of such and such privileges. This would be the simple law about marriage. The double law would run thus:—A man shall marry between the ages of thirty and thirty-five, considering that in a manner the human race naturally partakes of immortality, which every man is by nature inclined to desire to the utmost; for the desire of every man that he may become famous, and not lie in the grave without a name, is only the love of continuance. Now mankind are coeval with all time, and are ever following, and will ever follow, the course of time; and so they are immortal, because they leave children's children behind them, and partake of immortality in the unity of generation. And for a man voluntarily to deprive himself of this gift, as he deliberately does who will not have a wife or

children, is impiety. He who obeys the law shall be free, and shall pay no fine; but he who is disobedient, and does not marry, when he has arrived at the age of thirty-five, shall pay a yearly fine of a certain amount, in order that he may not imagine his celibacy to bring ease and profit to him; and he shall not share in the honours which the young men in the state give to the aged. Comparing now the two forms of the law, you will be able to arrive at a judgment about any other laws—whether they should be double in length even when shortest, because they have to persuade as well as threaten, or whether they shall only threaten and be of half the length.

Meg. The shorter form, Stranger, would be more in accordance with Lacedaemonian custom; although, for my own part, if any one were to ask me which I myself prefer in the state, I should certainly determine in favour of the longer; *[722]* and I would have every law made after the same pattern, if I had to choose. But I think that Cleinias is the person to be consulted, for his is the state which is going to use these laws.

Cle. Thank you, Megillus.

Ath. Whether, in the abstract, words are to be many or few, is a very foolish question; the best form, and not the shortest, is to be approved; nor is length at all to be regarded. Of the two forms of law which have been recited, the one is not only twice as good in practical usefulness as the other, but the case is like that of the two kinds of doctors, which I was just now mentioning. And yet legislators never appear to have considered that they have two instruments which they might use in legislation —persuasion and force; for in dealing with the rude and uneducated multitude, they use the one only as far as they can; they do not mingle persuasion with coercion, but employ force pure and simple. Moreover, there is a third point, sweet friends, which ought to be, and never is, regarded in our existing laws.

Cle. What is it?

Ath. A point arising out of our previous discussion, which comes into my mind in some mysterious way. All this time, from early dawn until noon, have we been talking about laws in this charming retreat: now we are going to promulgate our laws, and what has preceded was only the prelude of them. Why do I mention this? For this reason:—Because all discourses and vocal exercises have preludes and overtures, which are a sort of artistic beginnings intended to help the strain which is to be performed; lyric measures and music of every other kind have preludes framed with wonderful care. But of the truer and higher strain of law and politics, no one has ever yet uttered any prelude, or composed or published any, as though there was no such thing in nature. Whereas our present discussion seems to me to imply that there is;—these double laws, of which we were speaking, are not exactly double, but they are in two parts, [723] the law and the prelude of the law. The arbitrary command, which was compared to the commands of doctors, whom we described as of the meaner sort, was the law pure and simple; and that which preceded, and was described by our friend here as being hortatory only, was, although in fact, an exhortation, likewise analogous to the preamble of a discourse.[1] For I imagine that all this language of conciliation, which the legislator has been uttering in the preface of the law, was intended to create good-will in the person whom he addressed, in order that, by reason of this good-will, he might more intelligently receive his command, that is to say, the law. And therefore, in my way of speaking, this is more rightly described as the preamble than as the matter of the law. And I must further proceed to observe, that to all his laws, and to each separately, the legislator should prefix a preamble; he should remember how great will be the difference between them, according as they have, or have not, such preambles, as in the case already given.

Cle. The lawgiver, if he asks my opinion, will certainly legislate in the form which you advise.

Ath. I think that you are quite right, Cleinias, in affirming that all laws have preambles, and that throughout the whole of this work of legislation every single law should have a suitable preamble at the beginning; for that which is to follow is most important, and it makes all the difference whether we clearly remember the preambles or not. Yet we should be wrong in requiring that all laws, small and great alike, should have preambles of the same kind, any more than all songs or speeches; although they may be natural to all, they are not always necessary, and whether they are to be employed or not has in each case to be left to the judgment of the speaker or the musician, or, in the present instance, of the lawgiver.

Cle. That I think is most true. And now, Stranger, without delay let us return to the argument, and, as people say in play, make a sec-

[1] Cf. 718.

ond and better beginning, if you please, with the principles which we have been laying down, which we never thought of regarding as a preamble before, but of which we may now make a preamble, and not merely consider them to be chance topics of discourse. Let us acknowledge, then, that we have a preamble. About the honour of the Gods and the respect of parents, enough has been already said; and we may proceed to the topics which follow next in order, until the preamble is deemed by you to be complete; and after that you shall go through the laws themselves.

[724] Ath. I understand you to mean that we have made a sufficient preamble about Gods and demi-gods, and about parents living or dead; and now you would have us bring the rest of the subject into the light of day?

Cle. Exactly.

Ath. After this, as is meet and for the interest of us all, I the speaker, and you the listeners, will try to estimate all that relates to the souls and bodies and properties of the citizens, as regards both their occupations and amusements, and thus arrive, as far as in us lies, at the nature of education. These then are the topics which follow next in order.

Cle. Very good.

BOOK V

[726] Athenian Stranger. LISTEN, all ye who have just now heard the laws about Gods, and about our dear forefathers:—Of all the things which a man has, next to the Gods, his soul is the most divine and most truly his own. Now in every man there are two parts: the better and superior, which rules, and the worse and inferior, which serves; [727] and the ruling part of him is always to be preferred to the subject. Wherefore I am right in bidding every one next to the Gods, who are our masters, and those who in order follow them [i.e., the demons], to honour his own soul, which every one seems to honour, but no one honours as he ought; for honour is a divine good, and no evil thing is honourable; and he who thinks that he can honour the soul by word or gift, or any sort of compliance, without making her in any way better, seems to honour her, but honours her not at all. For example, every man, from his very boyhood, fancies that he is able to know everything, and thinks that he honours his soul by praising her, and he is very ready to let her do whatever she may like. But I mean to say that in acting thus he injures his soul, and is

far from honouring her; whereas, in our opinion, he ought to honour her as second only to the Gods. Again, when a man thinks that others are to be blamed, and not himself, for the errors which he has committed from time to time, and the many and great evils which befell him in consequence, and is always fancying himself to be exempt and innocent, he is under the idea that he is honouring his soul; whereas the very reverse is the fact, for he is really injuring her. And when, disregarding the word and approval of the legislator, he indulges in pleasure, then again he is far from honouring her; he only dishonours her, and fills her full of evil and remorse; or when he does not endure to the end the labours and fears and sorrows and pains which the legislator approves, but gives way before them, then, by yielding, he does not honour the soul, but by all such conduct he makes her to be dishonourable; nor when he thinks that life at any price is a good, does he honour her, but yet once more he dishonours her; for the soul having a notion that the world below is all evil, he yields to her, and does not resist and teach or convince her that, for aught she knows, the world of the Gods below, instead of being evil, may be the greatest of all goods. Again, when any one prefers beauty to virtue, what is this but the real and utter dishonour of the soul? For such a preference implies that the body is more honourable than the soul; and this is false, for there is nothing of earthly birth which is more honourable than the heavenly, and he who thinks otherwise of the soul has no idea how greatly he undervalues this wonderful possession; [728] nor, again, when a person is willing, or not unwilling, to acquire dishonest gains, does he then honour his soul with gifts—far otherwise; he sells her glory and honour for a small piece of gold; but all the gold which is under or upon the earth is not enough to give in exchange for virtue. In a word, I may say that he who does not estimate the base and evil, the good and noble, according to the standard of the legislator, and abstain in every possible way from the one and practise the other to the utmost of his power, does not know that in all these respects he is most foully and disgracefully abusing his soul, which is the divinest part of man; for no one, as I may say, ever considers that which is declared to be the greatest penalty of evil-doing—namely, to grow into the likeness of bad men, and growing like them to fly from the conversation of the good, and be cut off from them, and cleave to and follow after the company of

the bad. And he who is joined to them must do and suffer what such men by nature do and say to one another—a suffering which is not justice but retribution; for justice and the just are noble, whereas retribution is the suffering which waits upon injustice; and whether a man escape or endure this, he is miserable—in the former case, because he is not cured; while in the latter, he perishes in order that the rest of mankind may be saved.

Speaking generally, our glory is to follow the better and improve the inferior, which is susceptible of improvement, as far as this is possible. And of all human possessions, the soul is by nature most inclined to avoid the evil, and track out and find the chief good; which when a man has found, he should take up his abode with it during the remainder of his life. Wherefore the soul also is second [or next to God] in honour; and third, as every one will perceive, comes the honour of the body in natural order. Having determined this, we have next to consider that there is a natural honour of the body, and that of honours some are true and some are counterfeit. To decide which are which is the business of the legislator; and he, I suspect, would intimate that they are as follows:—Honour is not to be given to the fair body, or to the strong or the swift or the tall, or to the healthy body (although many may think otherwise), any more than to their opposites; but the mean states of all these habits are by far the safest and most moderate; for the one extreme makes the soul braggart and insolent, and the other, illiberal and base; and money, and property, and distinction all go to the same tune. The excess of any of these things is apt to be a source of hatreds and divisions [729] among states and individuals; and the defect of them is commonly a cause of slavery. And, therefore, I would not have any one fond of heaping up riches for the sake of his children, in order that he may leave them as rich as possible. For the possession of great wealth is of no use, either to them or to the state. The condition of youth which is free from flattery, and at the same time not in need of the necessaries of life, is the best and most harmonious of all, being in accord and agreement with our nature, and making life to be most entirely free from sorrow. Let parents, then, bequeath to their children not a heap of riches, but the spirit of reverence. We, indeed, fancy that they will inherit reverence from us, if we rebuke them when they show a want of reverence. But this quality is not really imparted to them by the present style of admonition, which only tells them that the young ought always to be reverential. A sensible legislator will rather exhort the elders to reverence the younger, and above all to take heed that no young man sees or hears one of themselves doing or saying anything disgraceful; for where old men have no shame, there young men will most certainly be devoid of reverence. The best way of training the young is to train yourself at the same time; not to admonish them, but to be always carrying out your own admonitions in practice. He who honours his kindred, and reveres those who share in the same Gods and are of the same blood and family, may fairly expect that the Gods who preside over generation will be propitious to him, and will quicken his seed. And he who deems the services which his friends and acquaintances do for him, greater and more important than they themselves deem them, and his own favours to them less than theirs to him, will have their good-will in the intercourse of life. And surely in his relations to the state and his fellow-citizens, he is by far the best, who rather than the Olympic or any other victory of peace or war, desires to win the palm of obedience to the laws of his country, and who, of all mankind, is the person reputed to have obeyed them best through life. In his relations to strangers, a man should consider that a contract is a most holy thing, and that all concerns and wrongs of strangers are more directly dependent on the protection of God, than wrongs done to citizens; for the stranger, having no kindred and friends, is more to be pitied by Gods and men. Wherefore, also, he who is most able to avenge him is most zealous in his cause; and he who is most able is the genius and the god of the stranger, [730] who follow in the train of Zeus, the god of strangers. And for this reason, he who has a spark of caution in him, will do his best to pass through life without sinning against the stranger. And of offences committed, whether against strangers or fellow-countrymen, that against suppliants is the greatest. For the God who witnessed to the agreement made with the suppliant, becomes in a special manner the guardian of the sufferer; and he will certainly not suffer unavenged.

Thus we have fairly described the manner in which a man is to act about his parents, and himself, and his own affairs; and in relation to the state, and his friends, and kindred, both in what concerns his own countrymen, and in what concerns the stranger. We will now consider what manner of man he must be who would best pass through life in respect of those other things which are not matters of law, but of praise and blame only; in which praise and blame educate a man, and make him more tractable and amenable to the laws which are about to be imposed.

Truth is the beginning of every good thing, both to Gods and men; and he who would be blessed and happy, should be from the first a partaker of the truth, that he may live a true man as long as possible, for then he can be trusted; but he is not to be trusted who loves voluntary falsehood, and he who loves involuntary falsehood is a fool. Neither condition is enviable, for the untrustworthy and ignorant has no friend, and as time advances he becomes known, and lays up in store for himself isolation in crabbed age when life is on the wane: so that, whether his children or friends are alive or not, he is equally solitary.—Worthy of honour is he who does no injustice, and of more than twofold honour, if he not only does no injustice himself, but hinders others from doing any; the first may count as one man, the second is worth many men, because he informs the rulers of the injustice of others. And yet more highly to be esteemed is he who co-operates with the rulers in correcting the citizens as far as he can—he shall be proclaimed the great and perfect citizen, and bear away the palm of virtue. The same praise may be given about temperance and wisdom, and all other goods which may be imparted to others, as well as acquired by a man for himself; he who imparts them shall be honoured as the man of men, and he who is willing, [731] yet is not able, may be allowed the second place; but he who is jealous and will not, if he can help, allow others to partake in a friendly way of any good, is deserving of blame: the good, however, which he has, is not to be undervalued by us because it is possessed by him, but must be acquired by us also to the utmost of our power. Let every man, then, freely strive for the prize of virtue, and let there be no envy. For the unenvious nature increases the greatness of states—he himself contends in the race, blasting the fair fame of no man; but the envious, who thinks that he ought to get the better by defaming others, is less energetic himself in the pursuit of true virtue, and reduces his rivals to despair by his unjust slanders of them. And so he makes the whole city to enter the arena untrained in the practice of virtue, and diminishes her glory as far as in him lies. Now every man should be valiant, but he should also be gentle. From the

introducing for the sake of illustration; but what relates to man is of the highest importance; and the legislator should make enquiries, and indicate what is proper for each one in the way of purification and of any other procedure. Take, for example, the purification of a city—there are many kinds of purification, some easier and others more difficult; and some of them, and the best and most difficult of them, the legislator, if he be also a despot, may be able to effect; but the legislator, who, not being a despot, sets up a new government and laws, even if he attempt the mildest of purgations, may think himself happy if he can complete his work. The best kind of purification is painful, like similar cures in medicine, involving righteous punishment and inflicting death or exile in the last resort. For in this way we commonly dispose of great sinners who are incurable, and are the greatest injury of the whole state. But the milder form of purification is as follows:— when men who have nothing, and are in want of food, show a disposition to follow their leaders in an attack on the property of the rich— these, [736] who are the natural plague of the state, are sent away by the legislator in a friendly spirit as far as he is able; and this dismissal of them is euphemistically termed a colony. And every legislator should contrive to do this at once. Our present case, however, is peculiar. For there is no need to devise any colony or purifying separation under the circumstances in which we are placed. But as, when many streams flow together from many sources, whether springs or mountain torrents, into a single lake, we ought to attend and take care that the confluent waters should be perfectly clear, and in order to effect this, should pump and draw off and divert impurities, so in every political arrangement there may be trouble and danger. But, seeing that we are now only discoursing and not acting, let our selection be supposed to be completed, and the desired purity attained. Touching evil men, who want to join and be citizens of our state, after we have tested them by every sort of persuasion and for a sufficient time, we will prevent them from coming; but the good we will to the utmost of our ability receive as friends with open arms.

Another piece of good fortune must not be forgotten, which, as we were saying,[1] the Heraclid colony had, and which is also ours—that we have escaped division of land and the abolition of debts; for these are always a source of dangerous contention, and a city which is driv-

[1] Cf. iii. 684.

en by necessity to legislate upon such matters can neither allow the old ways to continue, nor yet venture to alter them. We must have recourse to prayers, so to speak, and hope that a slight change may be cautiously effected in a length of time. And such a change can be accomplished by those who have abundance of land, and having also many debtors, are willing, in a kindly spirit, to share with those who are in want, sometimes remitting and sometimes giving, holding fast in a path of moderation, and deeming poverty to be the increase of a man's desires and not the diminution of his property. For this is the great beginning of salvation to a state, and upon this lasting basis may be erected afterwards whatever political order is suitable under the circumstances; but if the change be based upon an unsound principle, the future administration of the country will be full of difficulties. [737] That is a danger which, as I am saying, is escaped by us, and yet we had better say how, if we had not escaped, we might have escaped; and we may venture now to assert that no other way of escape, whether narrow or broad, can be devised but freedom from avarice and a sense of justice— upon this rock our city shall be built; for there ought to be no disputes among citizens about property. If there are quarrels of long standing among them, no legislator of any degree of sense will proceed a step in the arrangement of the state until they are settled. But that they to whom God has given, as he has to us, to be the founders of a new state as yet free from enmity —that they should create themselves enmities by their mode of distributing lands and houses, would be superhuman folly and wickedness.

How then can we rightly order the distribution of the land? In the first place, the number of the citizens has to be determined, and also the number and size of the divisions into which they will have to be formed; and the land and the houses will then have to be apportioned by us as fairly as we can. The number of citizens can only be estimated satisfactorily in relation to the territory and the neighbouring states. The territory must be sufficient to maintain a certain number of inhabitants in a moderate way of life—more than this is not required; and the number of citizens should be sufficient to defend themselves against the injustice of their neighbours, and also to give them the power of rendering efficient aid to their neighbours when they are wronged. After having taken a survey of theirs and their neighbours' territory, we will determine the limits of them in fact as well as in theory. And now, let us proceed to legislate with a view to perfecting the form and outline of our state. The number of our citizens shall be 5040—this will be a convenient number; and these shall be owners of the land and protectors of the allotment. The houses and the land will be divided in the same way, so that every man may correspond to a lot. Let the whole number be first divided into two parts, and then into three; and the number is further capable of being divided into four or five parts, or any number of parts up to ten. Every legislator ought to know so much arithmetic as to be able to tell what number is most likely to be useful to all cities; [738] and we are going to take that number which contains the greatest and most regular and unbroken series of divisions. The whole of number has every possible division, and the number 5040 can be divided by exactly fifty-nine divisors, and ten of these proceed without interval from one to ten: this will furnish numbers for war and peace, and for all contracts and dealings, including taxes and divisions of the land. These properties of number should be ascertained at leisure by those who are bound by law to know them; for they are true, and should be proclaimed at the foundation of the city, with a view to use. Whether the legislator is establishing a new state or restoring an old and decayed one, in respect of Gods and temples— the temples which are to be built in each city, and the Gods or demi-gods after whom they are to be called—if he be a man of sense, he will make no change in anything which the oracle of Delphi, or Dodona, or the God Ammon, or any ancient tradition has sanctioned in whatever manner, whether by apparitions or reputed inspiration of Heaven, in obedience to which mankind have established sacrifices in connection with mystic rites, either originating on the spot, or derived from Tyrrhenia or Cyprus or some other place, and on the strength of which traditions they have consecrated oracles and images, and altars and temples, and portioned out a sacred domain for each of them. The least part of all these ought not to be disturbed by the legislator; but he should assign to the several districts some God, or demi-god, or hero, and, in the distribution of the soil, should give to these first their chosen domain and all things fitting, that the inhabitants of the several districts may meet at fixed times, and that they may readily supply their various wants, and entertain one another with sacrifices, and become friends and acquaintances;

for there is no greater good in a state than that the citizens should be known to one another. When not light but darkness and ignorance of each other's characters prevails among them, no one will receive the honour of which he is deserving, or the power or the justice to which he is fairly entitled: wherefore, in every state, above all things, every man should take heed that he have no deceit in him, but that he be always true and simple; and that no deceitful person take any advantage of him.

[739] The next move in our pastime of legislation, like the withdrawal of the stone from the holy line in the game of draughts, being an unusual one, will probably excite wonder when mentioned for the first time. And yet, if a man will only reflect and weigh the matter with care, he will see that our city is ordered in a manner which, if not the best, is the second best. Perhaps also some one may not approve this form, because he thinks that such a constitution is ill adapted to a legislator who has not despotic power. The truth is, that there are three forms of government, the best, the second and the third best, which we may just mention, and then leave the selection to the ruler of the settlement. Following this method in the present instance, let us speak of the states which are respectively first, second, and third in excellence, and then we will leave the choice to Cleinias now, or to any one else who may hereafter have to make a similar choice among constitutions, and may desire to give to his state some feature which is congenial to him and which he approves in his own country.

The first and highest form of the state and of the government and of the law is that in which there prevails most widely the ancient saying, that "Friends have all things in common." Whether there is anywhere now, or will ever be, this communion of women and children and of property, in which the private and individual is altogether banished from life, and things which are by nature private, such as eyes and ears and hands, have become common, and in some way see and hear and act in common, and all men express praise and blame and feel joy and sorrow on the same occasions, and whatever laws there are unite the city to the utmost [1]—whether all this is possible or not, I say that no man, acting upon any other principle, will ever constitute a state which will be truer or better or more exalted in virtue. Whether such a state is governed by Gods or sons of Gods, one, or more than one, happy are the

[1] Cf. *Republic,* v. 462, ff.

men who, living after this manner, dwell there; and therefore to this we are to look for the pattern of the state, and to cling to this, and to seek with all our might for one which is like this. The state which we have now in hand, when created, will be nearest to immortality and the only one which takes the second place; and after that, by the grace of God, we will complete the third one. And we will begin by speaking of the nature and origin of the second.

Let the citizens at once distribute their land and houses, and not till the land in common, [740] since a community of goods goes beyond their proposed origin, and nurture, and education. But in making the distribution, let the several possessors feel that their particular lots also belong to the whole city; and seeing that the earth is their parent, let them tend her more carefully than children do their mother. For she is a goddess and their queen, and they are her mortal subjects. Such also are the feelings which they ought to entertain to the Gods and demi-gods of the country. And in order that the distribution may always remain, they ought to consider further that the present number of families should be always retained, and neither increased nor diminished. This may be secured for the whole city in the following manner:—Let the possessor of a lot leave the one of his children who is his best beloved, and one only, to be the heir of his dwelling, and his successor in the duty of ministering to the Gods, the state and the family, as well the living members of it as those who are departed when he comes into the inheritance; but of his other children, if he have more than one, he shall give the females in marriage according to the law to be hereafter enacted,[1] and the males he shall distribute as sons to those citizens who have no children, and are disposed to receive them; or if there should be none such, and particular individuals have too many children, male or female, or too few, as in the case of barrenness—in all these cases let the highest and most honourable magistracy created by us judge and determine what is to be done with the redundant or deficient, and devise a means that the number of 5040 houses shall always remain the same. There are many ways of regulating numbers; for they in whom generation is affluent may be made to refrain,[2] and, on the other hand, special care may be taken to increase the number of births by rewards and stigmas, or we may meet the evil by the elder men giving

advice and administering rebuke to the younger—in this way the object may be attained. And if after all there be very great difficulty about the equal preservation of the 5040 houses, and there be an excess of citizens, owing to the too great love of those who live together, and we are at our wits' end, there is still the old device often mentioned by us of sending out a colony, which will part friends with us, and be composed of suitable persons. [741] If, on the other hand, there come a wave bearing a deluge of disease, or a plague of war, and the inhabitants become much fewer than the appointed number by reason of bereavement, we ought not to introduce citizens of spurious birth and education, if this can be avoided; but even God is said not to be able to fight against necessity.

Wherefore let us suppose this "high argument" of ours to address us in the following terms:—Best of men, cease not to honour according to nature similarity and equality and sameness and agreement, as regards number and every good and noble quality. And, above all, observe the aforesaid number 5040 throughout life; in the second place, do not disparage the small and modest proportions of the inheritances which you received in the distribution, by buying and selling them to one another. For then neither will the God who gave you the lot be your friend, nor will the legislator; and indeed the law declares to the disobedient that these are the terms upon which he may or may not take the lot. In the first place, the earth as he is informed is sacred to the Gods; and in the next place, priests and priestesses will offer up prayers over a first, and second, and even a third sacrifice, that he who buys or sells the houses or lands which he has received, may suffer the punishment which he deserves; and these their prayers they shall write down in the temples, on tablets of cypress-wood, for the instruction of posterity. Moreover they will set a watch over all these things, that they may be observed;—the magistracy which has the sharpest eyes shall keep watch that any infringement of these commands may be discovered and punished as offences both against the law and the God. How great is the benefit of such an ordinance to all those cities, which obey and are administered accordingly, no bad man can ever know, as the old proverb says; but only a man of experience and good habits. For in such an order of things there will not be much opportunity for making money; no man either ought, or indeed will be allowed, to exercise any ignoble occupation, of which the vulgarity is a mat-

---

[1] Cf. xi. 923-926.

[2] Cf. Aristotle, *Politics*, vii. 16, 1335 ᵇ 20-27.

ter of reproach to a freeman, and should never want to acquire riches by any such means.

[742] Further, the law enjoins that no private man shall be allowed to possess gold and silver, but only coin for daily use, which is almost necessary in dealing with artisans, and for payment of hirelings, whether slaves or immigrants, by all those persons who require the use of them. Wherefore our citizens, as we say, should have a coin passing current among themselves, but not accepted among the rest of mankind; with a view, however, to expeditions and journeys to other lands—for embassies, or for any other occasion which may arise of sending out a herald, the state must also possess a common Hellenic currency. If a private person is ever obliged to go abroad, let him have the consent of the magistrates and go; and if when he returns he has any foreign money remaining, let him give the surplus back to the treasury, and receive a corresponding sum in the local currency. And if he is discovered to appropriate it, let it be confiscated, and let him who knows and does not inform be subject to curse and dishonour equally with him who brought the money, and also to a fine not less in amount than the foreign money which has been brought back. In marrying and giving in marriage, no one shall give or receive any dowry at all; and no one shall deposit money with another whom he does not trust as a friend, nor shall he lend money upon interest; and the borrower should be under no obligation to repay either capital or interest. That these principles are best, any one may see who compares them with the first principle and intention of a state. The intention, as we affirm, of a reasonable statesman, is not what the many declare to be the object of a good legislator, namely, that the state for the true interests of which he is advising should be as great and as rich as possible, and should possess gold and silver, and have the greatest empire by sea and land;—this they imagine to be the real object of legislation, at the same time adding, inconsistently, that the true legislator desires to have the city the best and happiest possible. But they do not see that some of these things are possible, and some of them are impossible; and he who orders the state will desire what is possible, and will not indulge in vain wishes or attempts to accomplish that which is impossible. The citizen must indeed be happy and good, and the legislator will seek to make him so; but very rich and very good at the same time he cannot be, not, at least, in the sense in which the many speak of riches. *[743]* For they

mean by "the rich" the few who have the most valuable possessions, although the owner of them may quite well be a rogue. And if this is true, I can never assent to the doctrine that the rich man will be happy—he must be good as well as rich. And good in a high degree, and rich in a high degree at the same time, he cannot be. Some one will ask, why not? And we shall answer—Because acquisitions which come from sources which are just and unjust indifferently, are more than double those which come from just sources only; and the sums which are expended neither honourably nor disgracefully, are only half as great as those which are expended honourably and on honourable purposes. Thus, if the one acquires double and spends half, the other who is in the opposite case and is a good man cannot possibly be wealthier than he. The first—I am speaking of the saver and not of the spender—is not always bad; he may indeed in some cases be utterly bad, but, as I was saying, a good man he never is. For he who receives money unjustly as well as justly, and spends neither justly nor unjustly, will be a rich man if he be also thrifty. On the other hand, the utterly bad is in general profligate, and therefore very poor; while he who spends on noble objects, and acquires wealth by just means only, can hardly be remarkable for riches, any more than he can be very poor. Our statement, then, is true, that the very rich are not good, and, if they are not good, they are not happy. But the intention of our laws was that the citizens should be as happy as may be, and as friendly as possible to one another. And men who are always at law with one another, and amongst whom there are many wrongs done, can never be friends to one another, but only those among whom crimes and lawsuits are few and slight. Therefore we say that gold and silver ought not to be allowed in the city, nor much of the vulgar sort of trade which is carried on by lending money, or rearing the meaner kinds of live stock; but only the produce of agriculture, and only so much of this as will not compel us in pursuing it to neglect that for the sake of which riches exist—I mean, soul and body, which without gymnastics, and without education, will never be worth anything; and therefore, as we have said not once but many times, the care of riches should have the last place in our thoughts. For there are in all three things about which every man has an interest; and the interest about money, when rightly regarded, is the third and lowest of them: midway comes the interest of the body; and, first of all, that of the soul; and the state which we are describing will have been rightly constituted if it ordains honours according to this scale. *[744]* But if, in any of the laws which have been ordained, health has been preferred to temperance, or wealth to health and temperate habits, that law must clearly be wrong. Wherefore, also, the legislator ought often to impress upon himself the question—"What do I want?" and "Do I attain my aim, or do I miss the mark?" In this way, and in this way only, he may acquit himself and free others from the work of legislation.

Let the allottee then hold his lot upon the conditions which we have mentioned.[1]

It would be well that every man should come to the colony having all things equal; but seeing that this is not possible, and one man will have greater possessions than another, for many reasons and in particular in order to preserve equality in special crises of the state, qualifications of property must be unequal, in order that offices and contributions and distributions may be proportioned to the value of each person's wealth, and not solely to the virtue of his ancestors or himself, nor yet to the strength and beauty of his person, but also to the measure of his wealth or poverty; and so by a law of inequality, which will be in proportion to his wealth, he will receive honours and offices as equally as possible, and there will be no quarrels and disputes. To which end there should be four different standards appointed according to the amount of property: there should be a first and a second and a third and a fourth class, in which the citizens will be placed, and they will be called by these or similar names: they may continue in the same rank, or pass into another in any individual case, on becoming richer from being poorer, or poorer from being richer. The form of law which I should propose as the natural sequel would be as follows:—In a state which is desirous of being saved from the greatest of all plagues—not faction, but rather distraction—there should exist among the citizens neither extreme poverty, nor, again, excess of wealth, for both are productive of both these evils. Now the legislator should determine what is to be the limit of poverty or wealth. Let the limit of poverty be the value of the lot; this ought to be preserved, and no ruler, nor any one else who aspires after a reputation for virtue, will allow the lot to be impaired in any case. This the leg-

islator gives as a measure, and he will permit a man to acquire double or triple, or as much as four times the amount of this.[2] But if a person have yet greater riches, whether he has found them, or they have been given to him, or he has made them in business, or has acquired by any stroke of fortune that which is in excess of the measure, *[745]* if he give back the surplus to the state, and to the Gods who are the patrons of the state, he shall suffer no penalty or loss of reputation; but if he disobeys this our law, any one who likes may inform against him and receive half the value of the excess, and the delinquent shall pay a sum equal to the excess out of his own property, and the other half of the excess shall belong to the Gods. And let every possession of every man, with the exception of the lot, be publicly registered before the magistrates whom the law appoints, so that all suits about money may be easy and quite simple.

The next thing to be noted is, that the city should be placed as nearly as possible in the centre of the country; we should choose a place which possesses what is suitable for a city, and this may easily be imagined and described. Then we will divide the city into twelve portions, first founding temples to Hestia, to Zeus and to Athene, in a spot which we will call the Acropolis, and surround with a circular wall, making the division of the entire city and country radiate from this point. The twelve portions shall be equalized by the provision that those which are of good land shall be smaller. while those of inferior quality shall be larger. The number of the lots shall be 5040, and each of them shall be divided into two, and every allotment shall be composed of two such sections; one of land near the city, the other of land which is at a distance.[3] This arrangement shall be carried out in the following manner: The section which is near the city shall be added to that which is on the borders, and form one lot, and the portion which is next nearest shall be added to the portion which is next farthest; and so of the rest. Moreover, in the two sections of the lots the same principle of equalization of the soil ought to be maintained; the badness and goodness shall be compensated by more and less. And the legislator shall divide the citizens into twelve parts, and arrange the rest of their property, as far as possible, so as to form twelve equal parts; and there shall be a registration of all. After this they shall assign

[1] Cf. 740, 741.

[2] Cf. Aristotle, *Politics,* ii. 6, 1265 [b] 18-25.

[3] *Ibid.,* vii. 10, 1324 [b] 10-15.

twelve lots to twelve Gods, and call them by
their names, and dedicate to each God their
several portions, and call the tribes after them.
And they shall distribute the twelve divisions
of the city in the same way in which they divided the country; and every man shall have
two habitations,[1] one in the centre of the country, and the other at the extremity. Enough of
the manner of settlement.

Now we ought by all means to consider that
there can never be such a happy concurrence
of circumstances as we have described; neither
can all things coincide as they are wanted.
[746] Men who will not take offence at such
a mode of living together, and will endure all
their life long to have their property fixed at
a moderate limit, and to beget children in accordance with our ordinances, and will allow
themselves to be deprived of gold and other
things which the legislator, as is evident from
these enactments, will certainly forbid them;
and will endure, further, the situation of the
land with the city in the middle and dwellings
round about;—all this is as if the legislator were
telling his dreams, or making a city and citizens of wax. There is truth in these objections,
and therefore every one should take to heart
what I am going to say. Once more, then, the
legislator shall appear and address us:—"O
my friends," he will say to us, "do not suppose
me ignorant that there is a certain degree of
truth in your words; but I am of opinion that,
in matters which are not present but future,
he who exhibits a pattern of that at which he
aims, should in nothing fall short of the fairest and truest; and that if he finds any part of
this work impossible of execution he should
avoid and not execute it, but he should contrive
to carry out that which is nearest and most
akin to it; you must allow the legislator to perfect his design, and when it is perfected, you
should join with him in considering what part
of his legislation is expedient and what will
arouse opposition; for surely the artist who is
to be deemed worthy of any regard at all,
ought always to make his work self-consistent."

Having determined that there is to be a distribution into twelve parts, let us now see in
what way this may be accomplished. There
is no difficulty in perceiving that the twelve
parts admit of the greatest number of divisions
of that which they include, or in seeing the
other numbers which are consequent upon
them, and are produced out of them up to
5040; wherefore the law ought to order phra-

tries and demes and villages, and also military
ranks and movements, as well as coins and
measures, dry and liquid, and weights, so as to
be commensurable and agreeable to one another. Nor should we fear the appearance of
minuteness, if the law commands that all the
vessels which a man possesses should have a
common measure, when we consider generally
that the divisions and variations of [747] numbers have a use in respect of all the variations
of which they are susceptible, both in themselves and as measures of height and depth,
and in all sounds, and in motions, as well those
which proceed in a straight direction, upwards
or downwards, as in those which go round and
round. The legislator is to consider all these
things and to bid the citizens, as far as possible,
not to lose sight of numerical order; for no single instrument of youthful education has such
mighty power, both as regards domestic econ-
omy and politics, and in the arts, as the study
of arithmetic. Above all, arithmetic stirs up
him who is by nature sleepy and dull, and
makes him quick to learn, retentive, shrewd,
and aided by art divine he makes progress quite
beyond his natural powers.[2] All such things, if
only the legislator, by other laws and institutions, can banish meanness and covetousness
from the souls of men, so that they can use
them properly and to their own good, will be
excellent and suitable instruments of education. But if he cannot, he will unintentionally
create in them, instead of wisdom, the habit of
craft, which evil tendency may be observed in
the Egyptians and Phoenicians, and many other
races, through the general vulgarity of their
pursuits and acquisitions, whether some unworthy legislator of theirs has been the cause,
or some impediment of chance or nature. For
we must not fail to observe, O Megillus and
Cleinias, that there is a difference in places,
and that some beget better men and others
worse; and we must legislate accordingly. Some
places are subject to strange and fatal influences
by reason of diverse winds and violent heats,
some by reason of waters; or, again, from the
character of the food given by the earth, which
not only affects the bodies of men for good or
evil, but produces similar results in their souls.
And in all such qualities those spots excel in
which there is a divine inspiration, and in
which the demi-gods have their appointed lots,
and are propitious, not adverse, to the settlers
in them. To all these matters the legislator, if
he have any sense in him, will attend as far as

[1] Cf. *Ibid.*, ii. 6, 1265[b] 18-25.

[2] Cf. *Republic*, vii. 526.

man can, and frame his laws accordingly. And this is what you, Cleinias, must do, and to matters of this kind you must turn your mind since you are going to colonize a new country.

Cleinias. Your words, Athenian Stranger, are excellent, and I will do as you say.

BOOK VI

[751] *Athenian Stranger.* AND now having made an end of the preliminaries we will proceed to the appointment of magistracies.

Cleinias. Very good.

Ath. In the ordering of a state there are two parts: first, the number of the magistracies, and the mode of establishing them; and, secondly, when they have been established, laws again will have to be provided for each of them, suitable in nature and number. But before electing the magistrates let us stop a little and say a word in season about the election of them.

Cle. What have you got to say?

Ath. This is what I have to say;—every one can see, that although the work of legislation is a most important matter, yet if a well-ordered city superadd to good laws unsuitable offices, not only will there be no use in having the good laws—not only will they be ridiculous and useless, but the greatest political injury and evil will accrue from them.

Cle. Of course.

Ath. Then now, my friend, let us observe what will happen in the constitution of our intended state. In the first place, you will acknowledge that those who are duly appointed to magisterial power, and their families, should severally have given satisfactory proof of what they are, from youth upward until the time of election; in the next place, those who are to elect should have been trained in habits of law, and be well educated, that they may have a right judgment, and may be able to select or reject men whom they approve or disapprove, as they are worthy of either. But how can we imagine that those who are brought together for the first time, and are strangers to one another, and also uneducated, will avoid making mistakes in the choice of magistrates?

Cle. Impossible.

Ath. The matter is serious, and excuses will not serve the turn. I will tell you, then, what you and I will have to do, since you, as you tell me, with nine others, have offered to settle the new state on behalf of the people of Crete, [752] and I am to help you by the invention of the present romance. I certainly should not like to leave the tale wandering all over the world without a head;—a headless monster is such a hideous thing.

Cle. Excellent, Stranger.

Ath. Yes; and I will be as good as my word.

Cle. Let us by all means do as you propose.

Ath. That we will, by the grace of God, if old age will only permit us.

Cle. But God will be gracious.

Ath. Yes; and under his guidance let us consider a further point.

Cle. What is it?

Ath. Let us remember what a courageously mad and daring creation this our city is.

Cle. What had you in your mind when you said that?

Ath. I had in my mind the free and easy manner in which we are ordaining that the inexperienced colonists shall receive our laws. Now a man need not be very wise, Cleinias, in order to see that no one can easily receive laws at their first imposition. But if we could anyhow wait until those who have been imbued with them from childhood, and have been nurtured in them, and become habituated to them, take their part in the public elections of the state; I say, if this could be accomplished, and rightly accomplished by any way or contrivance—then, I think that there would be very little danger, at the end of the time, of a state thus trained not being permanent.

Cle. A reasonable supposition.

Ath. Then let us consider if we can find any way out of the difficulty; for I maintain, Cleinias, that the Cnosians, above all the other Cretans, should not be satisfied with barely discharging their duty to the colony, but they ought to take the utmost pains to establish the offices which are first created by them in the best and surest manner. Above all, this applies to the selection of the guardians of the law, who must be chosen first of all, and with the greatest care; the others are of less importance.

Cle. What method can we devise of electing them?

Ath. This will be the method:—Sons of the Cretans, I shall say to them, inasmuch as the Cnosians have precedence over the other states, they should, in common with those who join this settlement, choose a body of thirty-seven in all, nineteen of them being taken from the settlers, [753] and the remainder from the citizens of Cnosus. Of those latter the Cnosians shall make a present to your colony, and you yourself shall be one of the eighteen, and shall become a citizen of the new state; and if you and they cannot be persuaded to go, the Cnosians may fairly use a little violence in order to make you.

Cle. But why, Stranger, do not you and Megillus take a part in our new city?

Ath. O, Cleinias, Athens is proud, and Sparta too; and they are both a long way off. But you and likewise the other colonists are conveniently situated as you describe. I have been speaking of the way in which the new citizens may be best managed under present circumstances; but in after-ages, if the city continues to exist, let the election be on this wise. All who are horse or foot soldiers, or have seen military service at the proper ages when they were severally fitted for it,[1] shall share in the election of magistrates; and the election shall be held in whatever temple the state deems most venerable, and every one shall carry his vote to the altar of the God, writing down on a tablet the name of the person for whom he votes, and his father's name, and his tribe, and ward; and at the side he shall write his own name in like manner. Any one who pleases may take away any tablet which he does not think properly filled up, and exhibit it in the Agora for a period of not less than thirty days. The tablets which are judged to be first, to the number of 300, shall be shown by the magistrates to the whole city, and the citizens shall in like manner select from these the candidates whom they prefer; and this second selection, to the number of 100, shall be again exhibited to the citizens; in the third, let any one who pleases select whom he pleases out of the 100, walking through the parts of victims, and let them choose for magistrates and proclaim the seven-and-thirty who have the greatest number of votes. But who, Cleinias and Megillus, will order for us in the colony all this matter of the magistrates, and the scrutinies of them? If we reflect, we shall see that cities which are in process of construction like ours must have some such persons, who cannot possibly be elected before there are any magistrates; and yet they must be elected in some way, and they are not to be inferior men, but the best possible. For as the proverb says, "a good beginning is half the business"; and "to have begun well" is praised by all, and in my opinion is a great deal more than half the business, *[754]* and has never been praised by any one enough.

Cle. That is very true.

Ath. Then let us recognize the difficulty, and make clear to our own minds how the begin-

[1] Cf. Aristotle, *Politics,* ii. 6, 1265 [b] 26-33.

ning is to be accomplished. There is only one proposal which I have to offer, and that is one which, under our circumstances, is both necessary and expedient.

Cle. What is it?

Ath. I maintain that this colony of ours has a father and mother, who are no other than the colonizing state. Well I know that many colonies have been, and will be, at enmity with their parents. But in early days the child, as in a family, loves and is beloved; even if there come a time later when the tie is broken, still, while he is in want of education, he naturally loves his parents and is beloved by them, and flies to his relatives for protection, and finds in them his only natural allies in time of need; and this parental feeling already exists in the Cnosians, as is shown by their care of the new city; and there is a similar feeling on the part of the young city towards Cnosus. And I repeat what I was saying—for there is no harm in repeating a good thing—that the Cnosians should take a common interest in all these matters, and choose, as far as they can, the eldest and best of the colonists, to the number of not less than a hundred; and let there be another hundred of the Cnosians themselves. These, I say, on their arrival, should have a joint care that the magistrates should be appointed according to law, and that when they are appointed they should undergo a scrutiny. When this has been effected, the Cnosians shall return home, and the new city do the best she can for her own preservation and happiness. I would have the seven-and-thirty now, and in all future time, chosen to fulfil the following duties:—Let them, in the first place, be the guardians of the law; and, secondly, of the registers in which each one registers before the magistrate the amount of his property, excepting four minae which are allowed to citizens of the first class, three allowed to the second, two to the third, and a single mina to the fourth. And if any one, despising the laws for the sake of gain, be found to possess anything more which has not been registered, let all that he has in excess be confiscated, and let him be liable to a suit which shall be the reverse of honourable or fortunate. And let any one who will, indict him on the charge of loving base gains, and proceed against him before the guardians of the law. *[755]* And if he be cast, let him lose his share of the public possessions, and when there is any public distribution, let him have nothing but his original lot; and let him be written down a condemned man as long as he lives, in some place in which any one who pleases can read about his offences. The guardian of the law shall not hold office longer than twenty years, and shall not be less than fifty years of age when he is elected; or if he is elected when he is sixty years of age, he shall hold office for ten years only; and upon the same principle, he must not imagine that he will be permitted to hold such an important office as that of guardian of the laws after he is seventy years of age, if he live so long.

These are the three first ordinances about the guardians of the law; as the work of legislation progresses, each law in turn will assign to them their further duties. And now we may proceed in order to speak of the election of other officers; for generals have to be elected, and these again must have their ministers, commanders, and colonels of horse, and commanders of brigades of foot, who would be more rightly called by their popular name of brigadiers. The guardians of the law shall propose as generals men who are natives of the city, and a selection from the candidates proposed shall be made by those who are or have been of the age for military service. And if one who is not proposed is thought by somebody to be better than one who is, let him name whom he prefers in the place of whom, and make oath that he is better, and propose him; and whichever of them is approved by vote shall be admitted to the final selection; and the three who have the greatest number of votes shall be appointed generals, and superintendents of military affairs, after previously undergoing a scrutiny, like the guardians of the law. And let the generals thus elected propose twelve brigadiers, one for each tribe; and there shall be a right of counter-proposal as in the case of the generals, and the voting and decision shall take place in the same way. Until the prytanes and council are elected, the guardians of the law shall convene the assembly in some holy spot which is suitable to the purpose, placing the hoplites by themselves, and the cavalry by themselves, and in a third division all the rest of the army. All are to vote for the generals [and for the colonels of horse], but the brigadiers are to be voted for only by those who carry shields [i.e., the hoplites]. [756] Let the body of cavalry choose phylarchs for the generals; but captains of light troops, or archers, or any other division of the army, shall be appointed by the generals for themselves. There only remains the appointment of officers of cavalry: these shall be proposed by the same persons who proposed the generals, and the election and the counter-proposal of other candidates shall be arranged in the same way as in the case of the generals, and let the cavalry vote and the infantry look on at the election; the two who have the greatest number of votes shall be the leaders of all the horse. Disputes about the voting may be raised once or twice; but if the dispute be raised a third time, the officers who preside at the several elections shall decide.

The council shall consist of 30 x 12 members—360 will be a convenient number for sub-division. If we divide the whole number into four parts of ninety each, we get ninety counsellors for each class. First, all the citizens shall select candidates from the first class; they shall be compelled to vote, and, if they do not, shall be duly fined. When the candidates have been selected, some one shall mark them down; this shall be the business of the first day. And on the following day, candidates shall be selected from the second class in the same manner and under the same conditions as on the previous day; and on the third day a selection shall be made from the third class, at which every one may, if he likes, vote, and the three first classes shall be compelled to vote; but the fourth and lowest class shall be under no compulsion, and any member of this class who does not vote shall not be punished. On the fourth day candidates shall be selected from the fourth and smallest class; they shall be selected by all, but he who is of the fourth class shall suffer no penalty, nor he who is of the third, if he be not willing to vote; but he who is of the first or second class, if he does not vote shall be punished;—he who is of the second class shall pay a fine of triple the amount which was exacted at first, and he who is of the first class quadruple. On the fifth day the rulers shall bring out the names noted down, for all the citizens to see, and every man shall choose out of them, under pain, if he do not, of suffering the first penalty; and when they have chosen 180 out of each of the classes, they shall choose one-half of them by lot, who shall undergo a scrutiny:— These are to form the council for the year.

The mode of election which has been described is in a mean between monarchy and democracy, [757] and such a mean the state ought always to observe; for servants and masters never can be friends, nor good and bad, merely because they are declared to have equal privileges. For to unequals equals become unequal, if they are not harmonized by measure; and both by reason of equality, and by reason of inequality, cities are filled with seditions.

The old saying, that "equality makes friendship," is happy and also true; but there is obscurity and confusion as to what sort of equality is meant. For there are two equalities which are called by the same name, but are in reality in many ways almost the opposite of one another; one of them may be introduced without difficulty, by any state or any legislator in the distribution of honours: this is the rule of measure, weight, and number, which regulates and apportions them. But there is another equality, of a better and higher kind, which is not so easily recognized. This is the judgment of Zeus; among men it avails but little; that little, however, is the source of the greatest good to individuals and states. For it gives to the greater more, and to the inferior less and in proportion to the nature of each; and, above all, greater honour always to the greater virtue, and to the less less; and to either in proportion to their respective measure of virtue and education. And this is justice, and is ever the true principle of states, at which we ought to aim, and according to this rule order the new city which is now being founded, and any other city which may be hereafter founded. To this the legislator should look—not to the interests of tyrants one or more, or to the power of the people, but to justice always; which, as I was saying, is the distribution of natural equality among unequals in each case. But there are times at which every state is compelled to use the words, "just," "equal," in a secondary sense, in the hope of escaping in some degree from factions. For equity and indulgence are infractions of the perfect and strict rule of justice. And this is the reason why we are obliged to use the equality of the lot, in order to avoid the discontent of the people; and so we invoke God and fortune in our prayers, and beg that they themselves will direct the lot with a view to supreme justice. And therefore, although we are compelled to use both equalities, we should use that into which the element of chance enters as seldom as possible. [758]

Thus, O my friends, and for the reasons given, should a state act which would endure and be saved. But as a ship sailing on the sea has to be watched night and day, in like manner a city also is sailing on a sea of politics, and is liable to all sorts of insidious assaults; and therefore from morning to night, and from night to morning, rulers must join hands with rulers, and watchers with watchers, receiving and giving up their trust in a perpetual succession. Now a multitude can never fulfil a duty of this sort with anything like energy.

Moreover, the greater number of the senators will have to be left during the greater part of the year to order their concerns at their own homes. They will therefore have to be arranged in twelve portions, answering to the twelve months, and furnish guardians of the state, each portion for a single month. Their business is to be at hand and receive any foreigner or citizen who comes to them, whether to give information, or to put one of those questions, to which, when asked by other cities, a city should give an answer, and to which, if she ask them herself, she should receive an answer; or again, when there is a likelihood of internal commotions, which are always liable to happen in some form or other, they will, if they can, prevent their occurring; or if they have already occurred, will lose no time in making them known to the city, and healing the evil. Wherefore, also, this which is the presiding body of the state ought always to have the control of their assemblies, and of the dissolutions of them, ordinary as well as extraordinary. All this is to be ordered by the twelfth part of the council, which is always to keep watch together with the other officers of the state during one portion of the year, and to rest during the remaining eleven portions.

Thus will the city be fairly ordered. And now, who is to have the superintendence of the country, and what shall be the arrangement? Seeing that the whole city and the entire country have been both of them divided into twelve portions, ought there not to be appointed superintendents of the streets of the city, and of the houses, and buildings, and harbours, and the agora, and fountains, and sacred domains, and temples, and the like?

Cle. To be sure there ought.

[759] Ath. Let us assume, then, that there ought to be servants of the temples, and priests and priestesses. There must also be superintendents of roads and buildings, who will have a care of men, that they may do no harm, and also of beasts, both within the enclosure and in the suburbs. Three kinds of officers will thus have to be appointed, in order that the city may be suitably provided according to her needs. Those who have the care of the city shall be called wardens of the city; and those who have the care of the agora shall be called wardens of the agora; and those who have the care of the temples shall be called priests. Those who hold hereditary offices as priests or priestesses, shall not be disturbed; but if there be few or none such, as is probable at the foundation of a new

city, priests and priestesses shall be appointed to be servants of the Gods who have no servants. Some of our officers shall be elected, and others appointed by lot, those who are of the people and those who are not of the people mingling in a friendly manner in every place and city, that the state may be as far as possible of one mind. The officers of the temples shall be appointed by lot; in this way their election will be committed to God, that he may do what is agreeable to him. And he who obtains a lot shall undergo a scrutiny, first, as to whether he is sound of body and of legitimate birth; and in the second place, in order to show that he is of a perfectly pure family, not stained with homicide or any similar impiety in his own person, and also that his father and mother have led a similar unstained life. Now the laws about all divine things should be brought from Delphi, and interpreters appointed, under whose direction they should be used. The tenure of the priesthood should always be for a year and no longer; and he who will duly execute the sacred office, according to the laws of religion, must be not less than sixty years of age—the laws shall be the same about priestesses. As for the interpreters, they shall be appointed thus:—let the twelve tribes be distributed into groups of four, and let each group select four, one out of each tribe within the group, three times; and let the three who have the greatest number of votes [out of the twelve appointed by each group], after undergoing a scrutiny, nine in all, be sent to Delphi, in order that the God may return one out of each triad; their age shall be the same as that of the priests, and the scrutiny of them shall be conducted in the same manner; let them be interpreters for life, and when any one dies let the four tribes select another from the tribe of the deceased. Moreover, besides priests and interpreters, there must be treasurers, who will take charge of the property of the several temples, and of the sacred domains, and shall have authority over the produce and the letting of them; and three of them shall be chosen from the highest classes for the greater [760] temples, and two for the lesser, and one for the least of all; the manner of their election and the scrutiny of them shall be the same as that of the generals.[1] This shall be the order of the temples.

Let everything have a guard as far as possible. Let the defence of the city be committed to the generals, and taxiarchs, and hipparchs, and phylarchs, and prytanes, and the wardens of

the city, and of the agora, when the election of them has been completed. The defence of the country shall be provided for as follows:—The entire land has been already distributed into twelve as nearly as possible equal parts, and let the tribe allotted to a division provide annually for it five wardens of the country and commanders of the watch; and let each body of five have the power of selecting twelve others out of the youth of their own tribe—these shall be not less than twenty-five years of age, and not more than thirty. And let there be allotted to them severally every month the various districts, in order that they may all acquire knowledge and experience of the whole country. The term of service for commanders and for watchers shall continue during two years. After having had their stations allotted to them, they will go from place to place in regular order, making their round from left to right as their commanders direct them; (when I speak of going to the right, I mean that they are to go to the east). And at the commencement of the second year, in order that as many as possible of the guards may not only get a knowledge of the country at any one season of the year, but may also have experience of the manner in which different places are affected at different seasons of the year, their then commanders shall lead them again towards the left, from place to place in succession, until they have completed the second year. In the third year other wardens of the country shall be chosen and commanders of the watch, five for each division, who are to be the superintendents of the bands of twelve. While on service at each station, their attention shall be directed to the following points:—In the first place, they shall see that the country is well protected against enemies; they shall trench and dig wherever this is required, and, as far as they can, they shall by fortifications keep off the evil-disposed, in order to prevent them from doing any harm to the country or the property; they shall use the beasts of burden and the labourers whom they find on the spot: these will be their instruments whom they will superintend, [761] taking them, as far as possible, at the times when they are not engaged in their regular business. They shall make every part of the country inaccessible to enemies, and as accessible as possible to friends;[2] there shall be ways for man and beasts of burden and for cattle, and they shall take care to have them always as smooth as they can; and shall provide

[1] Cf. 755.

[2] Cf. Aristotle, *Politics*, vii. 5, 1326 [b] 38.

against the rains doing harm instead of good to the land, when they come down from the mountains into the hollow dells; and shall keep in the overflow by the help of works and ditches, in order that the valleys, receiving and drinking up the rain from heaven, and providing fountains and streams in the fields and regions which lie underneath, may furnish even to the dry places plenty of good water. The fountains of water, whether of rivers or of springs, shall be ornamented with plantations and buildings for beauty; and let them bring together the streams in subterraneous channels, and make all things plenteous; and if there be a sacred grove or dedicated precinct in the neighbourhood, they shall conduct the water to the actual temples of the Gods, and so beautify them at all seasons of the year. Everywhere in such places the youth shall make gymnasia for themselves, and warm baths for the aged, placing by them abundance of dry wood, for the benefit of those labouring under disease—there the weary frame of the rustic, worn with toil, will receive a kindly welcome, far better than he would at the hands of a not over-wise doctor.

The building of these and the like works will be useful and ornamental; they will provide a pleasing amusement, but they will be a serious employment too; for the sixty wardens will have to guard their several divisions, not only with a view to enemies, but also with an eye to professing friends. When a quarrel arises among neighbours or citizens, and any one, whether slave or freeman wrongs another, let the five wardens decide small matters on their own authority; but where the charge against another relates to greater matters, the seventeen composed of the fives and twelves, shall determine any charges which one man brings against another, not involving more than three minae.[1] Every judge and magistrate shall be liable to give an account of his conduct in office, except those who, like kings, have the final decision. Moreover, as regards the aforesaid wardens of the country, if they do any wrong to those of whom they have the care, whether by imposing upon them unequal tasks, *[762]* or by taking the produce of the soil or implements of husbandry without their consent; also if they receive anything in the way of a bribe, or decide suits unjustly, or if they yield to the influences of flattery, let them be publicly dishonoured; and in regard to any other wrong which they do to the inhabitants of the country, if the question be of a mina, let them submit

[1] Cf. viii. 843.

to the decision of the villagers in the neighbourhood; but in suits of greater amount, or in the case of lesser, if they refuse to submit, trusting that their monthly removal into another part of the country will enable them to escape—in such cases the injured party may bring his suit in the common court, and if he obtain a verdict he may exact from the defendant, who refused to submit, a double penalty.

The wardens and the overseers of the country, while on their two years' service, shall have common meals at their several stations, and shall all live together; and he who is absent from the common meal, or sleeps out, if only for one day or night, unless by order of his commanders, or by reason of absolute necessity, if the five denounce him and inscribe his name in the agora as not having kept his guard, let him be deemed to have betrayed the city, as far as lay in his power, and let him be disgraced and beaten with impunity by any one who meets him and is willing to punish him. If any of the commanders is guilty of such an irregularity, the whole company of sixty shall see to it, and he who is cognizant of the offence, and does not bring the offender to trial, shall be amenable to the same laws as the younger offender himself, and shall pay a heavier fine, and be incapable of ever commanding the young. The guardians of the law are to be careful inspectors of these matters, and shall either prevent or punish offenders. Every man should remember the universal rule, that he who is not a good servant will not be a good master; a man should pride himself more upon serving well than upon commanding well: first upon serving the laws, which is also the service of the Gods; in the second place, upon having served ancient and honourable men in the days of his youth. Furthermore, during the two years in which any one is a warden of the country, his daily food ought to be of a simple and humble kind. When the twelve have been chosen, *[763]* let them and the five meet together, and determine that they will be their own servants, and, like servants, will not have other slaves and servants for their own use, neither will they use those of the villagers and husbandmen for their private advantage, but for the public service only; and in general they should make up their minds to live independently by themselves, servants of each other and of themselves. Further, at all seasons of the year, summer and winter alike, let them be under arms and survey minutely the whole country; thus they will at once keep guard, and at the same time acquire a perfect knowledge of every locality. There can be no more important kind of information than the exact knowledge of a man's own country; and for this as well as for more general reasons of pleasure and advantage, hunting with dogs and other kinds of sports should be pursued by the young. The service to whom this is committed may be called the secret police [1] or wardens of the country; the name does not much signify, but every one who has the safety of the state at heart will use his utmost diligence in this service.

After the wardens of the country, we have to speak of the election of wardens of the agora and of the city. The wardens of the country were sixty in number, and the wardens of the city will be three, and will divide the twelve parts of the city into three; like the former, they shall have care of the ways, and of the different high roads which lead out of the country into the city, and of the buildings, that they may be all made according to law;—also of the waters, which the guardians of the supply preserve and convey to them, care being taken that they may reach the fountains pure and abundant, and be both an ornament and a benefit to the city. These also should be men of influence, and at leisure to take care of the public interest. Let every man propose as warden of the city any one whom he likes out of the highest class, and when the vote has been given on them, and the number is reduced to the six who have the greatest number of votes, let the electing officers choose by lot three out of the six, and when they have undergone a scrutiny let them hold office according to the laws laid down for them. Next, let the wardens of the agora be elected in like manner, out of the first and second class, five in number: ten are to be first elected, and out of the ten five are to be chosen by lot, as in the election of the wardens of the city:—these when they have undergone a scrutiny are to be declared magistrates. Every one shall vote for every one, and he who will not vote, [764] if he be informed against before the magistrates, shall be fined fifty drachmae, and shall also be deemed a bad citizen. Let any one who likes go to the assembly and to the general council; it shall be compulsory to go on citizens of the first and second class, and they shall pay a fine of ten drachmae if they be found not answering to their names at the assembly. But the third and fourth class shall be under no compulsion, and shall be let off without a fine, unless the magistrates have commanded all to

[1] Cf. i. 633.

be present, in consequence of some urgent necessity. The wardens of the agora shall observe the order appointed by law for the agora, and shall have the charge of the temples and fountains which are in the agora; and they shall see that no one injures anything, and punish him who does, with stripes and bonds, if he be a slave or stranger; but if he be a citizen who misbehaves in this way, they shall have the power themselves of inflicting a fine upon him to the amount of a hundred drachmae, or with the consent of the wardens of the city up to double that amount. And let the wardens of the city have a similar power of imposing punishments and fines in their own department; and let them impose fines by their own authority, up to a mina, or up to two minae with the consent of the wardens of the agora.

In the next place, it will be proper to appoint directors of music and gymnastic, two kinds of each—of the one kind the business will be education, of the other, the superintendence of contests. In speaking of education, the law means to speak of those who have the care of order and instruction in gymnasia and schools, and of the going to school, and of school buildings for boys and girls; and in speaking of contests, the law refers to the judges of gymnastics and of music; these again are divided into two classes, the one having to do with music, the other with gymnastics; and the same who judge of the gymnastic contests of men, shall judge of horses; but in music there shall be one set of judges of solo singing, and of imitation—I mean of rhapsodists, players on the harp, the flute and the like, and another who shall judge of choral song. First of all, we must choose directors for the choruses of boys, and men, and maidens, whom they shall follow in the amusement of the dance, and for our other musical arrangements; [765]—one director will be enough for the choruses, and he should be not less than forty years of age. One director will also be enough to introduce the solo singers, and to give judgment on the competitors, and he ought not to be less than thirty years of age. The director and manager of the choruses shall be elected after the following manner:—Let any persons who commonly take an interest in such matters go to the meeting, and be fined if they do not go (the guardians of the law shall judge of their fault), but those who have no interest shall not be compelled. The elector shall propose as director some one who understands music, and he in the scrutiny may be challenged on the one part by those who say he has no skill, and defended on the other hand by those who say that he has. Ten are to be elected by vote, and he of the ten who is chosen by lot shall undergo a scrutiny, and lead the choruses for a year according to law. And in like manner the competitor who wins the lot shall be leader of the solo and concert music for that year; and he who is thus elected shall deliver the award to the judges. In the next place, we have to choose judges in the contests of horses and of men; these shall be selected from the third and also from the second class of citizens, and the three first classes shall be compelled to go to the election, but the lowest may stay away with impunity; and let there be three elected by lot out of the twenty who have been chosen previously, and they must also have the vote and approval of the examiners. But if any one is rejected in the scrutiny at any ballot or decision, others shall be chosen in the same manner, and undergo a similar scrutiny.

There remains the minister of the education of youth, male and female; he too will rule according to law; one such minister will be sufficient, and he must be fifty years old, and have children lawfully begotten, both boys and girls by preference, at any rate, one or the other. He who is elected, and he who is the elector, should consider that of all the great offices of state this is the greatest; for the first shoot of any plant, if it makes a good start towards the attainment of its natural excellence, has the greatest effect on its maturity; and this is not only true of plants, *[766]* but of animals wild and tame, and also of men. Man, as we say, is a tame or civilized animal; nevertheless, he requires proper instruction and a fortunate nature, and then of all animals he becomes the most divine and most civilized;[1] but if he be insufficiently or ill educated he is the most savage of earthly creatures. Wherefore the legislator ought not to allow the education of children to become a secondary or accidental matter. In the first place, he who would be rightly provident about them, should begin by taking care that he is elected, who of all the citizens is in every way best; him the legislator shall do his utmost to appoint guardian and superintendent. To this end all the magistrates, with the exception of the council and prytanes, shall go to the temple of Apollo, and elect by ballot him of the guardians of the law whom they severally think will be the best superintendent of education. And he who has the greatest number of votes, after he has undergone a scrutiny at the hands of all

[1] Aristotle, *Politics,* i. 2, 1253 ᵃ 29-38.

the magistrates who have been his electors, with the exception of the guardians of the law —shall hold office for five years; and in the sixth year let another be chosen in like manner to fill his office.

If any one dies while he is holding a public office, and more than thirty days before his term of office expires, let those whose business it is elect another to the office in the same manner as before. And if any one who is entrusted with orphans dies, let the relations both on the father's and mother's side, who are residing at home, including cousins, appoint another guardian within ten days, or be fined a drachma a day for neglect to do so.

A city which has no regular courts of law ceases to be a city; and again, if a judge is silent and says no more in preliminary proceedings than the litigants, as is the case in arbitrations, he will never be able to decide justly; wherefore a multitude of judges will not easily judge well, nor a few if they are bad. The point in dispute between the parties should be made clear; and time, and deliberation, and repeated examination, greatly tend to clear up doubts. For this reason, he who goes to law with another, should go first of all to his neighbours and friends who know best the questions at issue. And if he be unable to obtain from them a satisfactory decision, *[767]* let him have recourse to another court; and if the two courts cannot settle the matter, let a third put an end to the suit.

Now the establishment of courts of justice may be regarded as a choice of magistrates, for every magistrate must also be a judge of some things; and the judge, though he be not a magistrate, yet in certain respects is a very important magistrate on the day on which he is determining a suit. Regarding then the judges also as magistrates, let us say who are fit to be judges, and of what they are to be judges, and how many of them are to judge in each suit. Let that be the supreme tribunal which the litigants appoint in common for themselves, choosing certain persons by agreement. And let there be two other tribunals: one for private causes, when a citizen accuses another of wronging him and wishes to get a decision; the other for public causes, in which some citizen is of opinion that the public has been wronged by an individual, and is willing to vindicate the common interests. And we must not forget to mention how the judges are to be qualified, and who they are to be. In the first place, let there be a tribunal open to all private persons who are trying causes one against another for the third time, and let this be composed as follows: —All the officers of state, as well annual as those holding office for a longer period, when the new year is about to commence, in the month following after the summer solstice, on the last day but one of the year, shall meet in some temple, and calling God to witness, shall dedicate one judge from every magistracy to be their first-fruits, choosing in each office him who seems to them to be the best, and whom they deem likely to decide the causes of his fellow-citizens during the ensuing year in the best and holiest manner. And when the election is completed, a scrutiny shall be held in the presence of the electors themselves, and if any one be rejected another shall be chosen in the same manner. Those who have undergone the scrutiny shall judge the causes of those who have declined the inferior courts, and shall give their vote openly. The councillors and other magistrates who have elected them shall be required to be hearers and spectators of the causes; and any one else may be present who pleases. If one man charges another with having intentionally decided wrong, let him go to the guardians of the law and lay his accusation before them, and he who is found guilty in such a case shall pay damages to the injured party equal to half the injury; but if he shall appear to deserve a greater penalty, the judges shall determine what additional punishment he shall suffer, and how much more he ought to pay to the public treasury, and to the party who brought the suit.

[768] In the judgment of offences against the state, the people ought to participate, for when any one wrongs the state all are wronged, and may reasonably complain if they are not allowed to share in the decision. Such causes ought to originate with the people, and they ought also to have the final decision of them, but the trial of them shall take place before three of the highest magistrates, upon whom the plaintiff and the defendant shall agree; and if they are not able to come to an agreement themselves, the council shall choose one of the two proposed. And in private suits, too, as far as is possible, all should have a share; for he who has no share in the administration of justice, is apt to imagine that he has no share in the state at all. And for this reason there shall be a court of law in every tribe, and the judges shall be chosen by lot;—they shall give their decisions at once, and shall be inaccessible to entreaties. The final judgment shall rest with that court which, as we maintain, has been established in the most incorruptible form of which human things admit: this shall be the court established for those who are unable to get rid of their suits either in the courts of neighbours or of the tribes.

Thus much of the courts of law, which, as I was saying, cannot be precisely defined either as being or not being offices; a superficial sketch has been given of them, in which some things have been told and others omitted. For the right place of an exact statement of the laws respecting suits, under their several heads, will be at the end of the body of legislation;—let us then expect them at the end.[1] Hitherto our legislation has been chiefly occupied with the appointment of offices. Perfect unity and exactness, extending to the whole and every particular of political administration, cannot be attained to the full, until the discussion shall have a beginning, middle, and end, and is complete in every part. At present we have reached the election of magistrates, and this may be regarded as a sufficient termination of what has preceded. And now there need no longer be any delay or hesitation in beginning the work of legislation.

Cle. I like what you have said, Stranger; and I particularly like your manner of tacking on the beginning of your new discourse to the end of the former one.

[769] *Ath.* Thus far, then, the old men's rational pastime has gone off well.

Cle. You mean, I suppose, their serious and noble pursuit?

Ath. Perhaps; but I should like to know whether you and I are agreed about a certain thing.

Cle. About what thing?

Ath. You know the endless labour which painters expend upon their pictures—they are always putting in or taking out colours, or whatever be the term which artists employ; they seem as if they would never cease touching up their works, which are always being made brighter and more beautiful.

Cle. I know something of these matters from report, although I have never had any great acquaintance with the art.

Ath. No matter; we may make use of the illustration notwithstanding:—Suppose that some one had a mind to paint a figure in the most beautiful manner, in the hope that his work instead of losing would always improve as time went on—do you not see that being a

[1] Cf. ix. 853, ff.; xii. 956, ff.

mortal, unless he leaves some one to succeed him who will correct the flaws which time may introduce, and be able to add what is left imperfect through the defect of the artist, and who will further brighten up and improve the picture, all his great labour will last but a short time?

Cle. True.

Ath. And is not the aim of the legislator similar? First, he desires that his laws should be written down with all possible exactness; in the second place, as time goes on and he has made an actual trial of his decrees, will he not find omissions? Do you imagine that there ever was a legislator so foolish as not to know that many things are necessarily omitted, which some one coming after him must correct, if the constitution and the order of government is not to deteriorate, but to improve in the state which he has established?

Cle. Assuredly, that is the sort of thing which every one would desire.

Ath. And if any one possesses any means of accomplishing this by word or deed, or has any way great or small by which he can teach a person to understand how he can maintain and amend the laws, he should finish what he has to say, and not leave the work incomplete.

Cle. By all means.

[770] *Ath.* And is not this what you and I have to do at the present moment?

Cle. What have we to do?

Ath. As we are about to legislate and have chosen our guardians of the law, and are ourselves in the evening of life, and they as compared with us are young men, we ought not only to legislate for them, but to endeavour to make them not only guardians of the law but legislators themselves, as far as this is possible.

Cle. Certainly; if we can.

Ath. At any rate, we must do our best.

Cle. Of course.

Ath. We will say to them—O friends and saviours of our laws, in laying down any law, there are many particulars which we shall omit, and this cannot be helped; at the same time, we will do our utmost to describe what is important, and will give an outline which you shall fill up. And I will explain on what principle you are to act. Megillus and Cleinias and I have often spoken to one another touching these matters, and we are of opinion that we have spoken well. And we hope that you will be of the same mind with us, and become our disciples, and keep in view the things which in our united opinion the legislator and guardian

of the law ought to keep in view. There was one main point about which we were agreed—that a man's whole energies throughout life should be devoted to the acquisition of the virtue proper to a man, whether this was to be gained by study, or habit, or some mode of acquisition, or desire, or opinion, or knowledge—and this applies equally to men and women, old and young—the aim of all should always be such as I have described; anything which may be an impediment, the good man ought to show that he utterly disregards. And if at last necessity plainly compels him to be an outlaw from his native land, rather than bow his neck to the yoke of slavery and be ruled by inferiors, and he has to fly, an exile he must be and endure all such trials, rather than accept another form of government, which is likely to make men worse. These are our original principles; and do you now, fixing your eyes upon the standard of what a man and a citizen ought or ought not to be, praise and blame the laws—blame those which have not this power of making the citizen better, [771] but embrace those which have; and with gladness receive and live in them; bidding a long farewell to other institutions which aim at goods, as they are termed, of a different kind.

Let us proceed to another class of laws, beginning with their foundation in religion. And we must first return to the number 5040—the entire number had, and has, a great many convenient divisions, and the number of the tribes which was a twelfth part of the whole, being correctly formed by 21 x 20 [5040 ÷ (21 x 20), i.e., 5040 ÷ 420 = 12], also has them. And not only is the whole number divisible by twelve, but also the number of each tribe is divisible by twelve. Now every portion should be regarded by us as a sacred gift of Heaven, corresponding to the months and to the revolution of the universe.[1] Every city has a guiding and sacred principle given by nature, but in some the division or distribution has been more right than in others, and has been more sacred and fortunate. In our opinion, nothing can be more right than the selection of the number 5040, which may be divided by all numbers from one to twelve with the single exception of eleven, and that admits of a very easy correction; for if, turning to the dividend (5040), we deduct two families, the defect in the division is cured. And the truth of this may be easily proved when we have leisure. But for the present, trusting to the mere assertion of this prin-

[1] Cf. *Timaeus*, 39, 47.

ciple, let us divide the state; and assigning to each portion some God or son of a God, let us give them altars and sacred rites, and at the altars let us hold assemblies for sacrifice twice in the month—twelve assemblies for the tribes, and twelve for the city, according to their divisions; the first in honour of the Gods and divine things, and the second to promote friendship and "better acquaintance," as the phrase is, and every sort of good fellowship with one another. For people must be acquainted with those into whose families and whom they marry and with those to whom they give in marriage; in such matters, as far as possible, a man should deem it all important to avoid a mistake, and with this serious purpose let games be instituted [1] in which youths and maidens shall dance together, [772] seeing one another and being seen naked, at a proper age, and on a suitable occasion, not transgressing the rules of modesty.

The directors of choruses will be the superintendents and regulators of these games, and they, together with the guardians of the law, will legislate in any matters which we have omitted; for, as we said,[2] where there are numerous and minute details, the legislator must leave out something. And the annual officers who have experience, and know what is wanted, must make arrangements and improvements year by year, until such enactments and provisions are sufficiently determined. A ten years' experience of sacrifices and dances, if extending to all particulars, will be quite sufficient; and if the legislator be alive they shall communicate with him, but if he be dead then the several officers shall refer the omissions which come under their notice to the guardians of the law, and correct them, until all is perfect; and from that time there shall be no more change, and they shall establish and use the new laws with the others which the legislator originally gave them, and of which they are never, if they can help, to change aught; or, if some necessity overtakes them, the magistrates must be called into counsel, and the whole people, and they must go to all the oracles of the Gods; and if they are all agreed, in that case they may make the change, but if they are not agreed, by no manner of means, and any one who dissents shall prevail, as the law ordains.

Whenever any one over twenty-five years of age, having seen and been seen by others, believes himself to have found a marriage con-

nection which is to his mind, and suitable for the procreation of children, let him marry if he be still under the age of five-and-thirty years; but let him first hear how he ought to seek after what is suitable and appropriate.[3] For, as Cleinias says,[4] every law should have a suitable prelude.

Cle. You recollect at the right moment, Stranger, and do not miss the opportunity which the argument affords of saying a word in season.

[773] *Ath.* I thank you. We will say to him who is born of good parents—O my son, you ought to make such a marriage as wise men would approve. Now they would advise you neither to avoid a poor marriage, nor specially to desire a rich one; but if other things are equal, always to honour inferiors, and with them to form connections;—this will be for the benefit of the city and of the families which are united; for the equable and symmetrical tends infinitely more to virtue than the unmixed. And he who is conscious of being too headstrong, and carried away more than is fitting in all his actions, ought to desire to become the relation of orderly parents; and he who is of the opposite temper ought to seek the opposite alliance. Let there be one word concerning all marriages:—Every man shall follow, not after the marriage which is most pleasing to himself, but after that which is most beneficial to the state. For somehow every one is by nature prone to that which is likest to himself, and in this way the whole city becomes unequal in property and in disposition; and hence there arise in most states the very results which we least desire to happen. Now, to add to the law an express provision, not only that the rich man shall not marry into the rich family, nor the powerful into the family of the powerful, but that the slower natures shall be compelled to enter into marriage with the quicker, and the quicker with the slower, may awaken anger as well as laughter in the minds of many; for there is a difficulty in perceiving that the city ought to be well mingled like a cup, in which the maddening wine is hot and fiery, but when chastened by a soberer God, receives a fair associate and becomes an excellent and temperate drink.[5] Yet in marriage no one is able to see that the same result occurs. Wherefore also the law must let alone such matters, but we should

[1] Cf. *Republic,* v. 459.
[2] Cf. 770.

[3] Cf. iv. 721, and Aristotle, *Politics,* vii. 16, 1335 ª 27-31
[4] Cf. iv. 723.
[5] Cf. *Statesman,* 306, ff.

try to charm the spirits of men into believing the equability of their children's disposition to be of more importance than equality in excessive fortune when they marry; and him who is too desirous of making a rich marriage we should endeavour to turn aside by reproaches, not, however, by any compulsion of written law.

Let this then be our exhortation concerning marriage, and let us remember what was said before[1]—that a man should cling to immortality, [774] and leave behind him children's children to be the servants of God in his place for ever. All this and much more may be truly said by way of prelude about the duty of marriage. But if a man will not listen, and remains unsocial and alien among his fellow-citizens, and is still unmarried at thirty-five years of age, let him pay a yearly fine;—he who is of the highest class shall pay a fine of a hundred drachmae, and he who is of the second class a fine of seventy drachmae; the third class shall pay sixty drachmae, and the fourth thirty drachmae, and let the money be sacred to Herè; he who does not pay the fine annually shall owe ten times the sum, which the treasurer of the goddess shall exact; and if he fails in doing so, let him be answerable and give an account of the money at his audit. He who refuses to marry shall be thus punished in money, and also be deprived of all honour which the younger show to the elder; let no young man voluntarily obey him, and, if he attempt to punish any one, let every one come to the rescue and defend the injured person, and he who is present and does not come to the rescue, shall be pronounced by the law to be a coward and a bad citizen. Of the marriage portion I have already spoken;[2] and again I say for the instruction of poor men that he who neither gives nor receives a dowry on account of poverty, has a compensation; for the citizens of our state are provided with the necessaries of life, and wives will be less likely to be insolent, and husbands to be mean and subservient to them on account of property. And he who obeys this law will do a noble action; but he who will not obey, and gives or receives more than fifty drachmae as the price of the marriage garments if he be of the lowest, or more than a mina, or a mina-and-a-half, if he be of the third or second classes, or two minae if he be of the highest class, shall owe to the public treasury a similar sum, and that which is given or received shall be sacred to Herè and Zeus; and let the treasurers

of these Gods exact the money, as was said before about the unmarried—that the treasurers of Herè were to exact the money, or pay the fine themselves.

The betrothal by a father shall be valid in the first degree, that by a grandfather in the second degree, and in the third degree, betrothal by brothers who have the same father; but if there are none of these alive, the betrothal by a mother shall be valid in like manner; in cases of unexampled fatality, the next of kin and the guardians shall have authority. What are to be the rites before marriages, or any other sacred acts, relating either to future, present, or past marriages, [775] shall be referred to the interpreters; and he who follows their advice may be satisfied. Touching the marriage festival, they shall assemble not more than five male and five female friends of both families, and a like number of members of the family of either sex, and no man shall spend more than his means will allow; he who is of the richest class may spend a mina—he who is of the second, half a mina, and in the same proportion as the census of each decreases: all men shall praise him who is obedient to the law; but he who is disobedient shall be punished by the guardians of the law as a man wanting in true taste, and uninstructed in the laws of bridal song. Drunkenness is always improper, except at the festivals of the God who gave wine; and peculiarly dangerous, when a man is engaged in the business of marriage; at such a crisis of their lives a bride and bridegroom ought to have all their wits about them—they ought to take care that their offspring may be born of reasonable beings; for on what day or night Heaven will give them increase, who can say? Moreover, they ought not to be begetting children when their bodies are dissipated by intoxication, but their offspring should be compact and solid, quiet and compounded properly; whereas the drunkard is all abroad in all his actions, and beside himself both in body and soul. Wherefore, also, the drunken man is bad and unsteady in sowing the seed of increase, and is likely to beget offspring who will be unstable and untrustworthy, and cannot be expected to walk straight either in body or mind. Hence during the whole year and all his life long, and especially while he is begetting children, he ought to take care and not intentionally do what is injurious to health, or what involves insolence and wrong; for he cannot help leaving the impression of himself on the souls and bodies of his offspring, and he begets children in every way

---

[1] Cf. iv. 721.   [2] Cf. v. 742.

inferior. And especially on the day and night of marriage should a man abstain from such things. For the beginning, which is also a God dwelling in man, *[776]* preserves all things, if it meet with proper respect from each individual. He who marries is further to consider that one of the two houses in the lot is the nest and nursery of his young, and there he is to marry and make a home for himself and bring up his children, going away from his father and mother. For in friendships there must be some degree of desire, in order to cement and bind together diversities of character; but excessive intercourse not having the desire which is created by time, insensibly dissolves friendships from a feeling of satiety; wherefore a man and his wife shall leave to his and her father and mother their own dwelling-places, and themselves go as to a colony and dwell there, and visit and be visited by their parents; and they shall beget and bring up children, handing on the torch of life from one generation to another, and worshipping the Gods according to law for ever.

In the next place, we have to consider what sort of property will be most convenient. There is no difficulty either in understanding or acquiring most kinds of property, but there is great difficulty in what relates to slaves. And the reason is that we speak about them in a way which is right and which is not right; for what we say about our slaves is consistent and also inconsistent with our practice about them.

Megillus. I do not understand, Stranger, what you mean.

Ath. I am not surprised, Megillus, for the state of the Helots among the Lacedaemonians is of all Hellenic forms of slavery the most controverted and disputed about, some approving and some condemning it; there is less dispute about the slavery which exists among the Heracleots, who have subjugated the Mariandynians, and about the Thessalian Penestae. Looking at these and the like examples, what ought we to do concerning property in slaves? I made a remark, in passing, which naturally elicited a question about my meaning from you. It was this:—We know that all would agree that we should have the best and most attached slaves whom we can get. For many a man has found his slaves better in every way than brethren or sons, and many times they have saved the lives and property of their masters and their whole house—such tales are well known.

Meg. To be sure.

Ath. But may we not also say that the soul of the slave is utterly corrupt, and that no man of

sense ought to trust them? And the wisest of our poets, speaking of Zeus, says:

Far-seeing Zeus takes away half the understanding of men whom the day of slavery subdues. *[777]*

Different persons have got these two different notions of slaves in their minds—some of them utterly distrust their servants, and, as if they were wild beasts, chastise them with goads and whips, and make their souls three times, or rather many times, as slavish as they were before;—and others do just the opposite.

Meg. True.

Cle. Then what are we to do in our own country, Stranger, seeing that there are such differences in the treatment of slaves by their owners?

Ath. Well, Cleinias, there can be no doubt that man is a troublesome animal, and therefore he is not very manageable, nor likely to become so, when you attempt to introduce the necessary division of slave, and freeman, and master.

Cle. That is obvious.

Ath. He is a troublesome piece of goods, as has been often shown by the frequent revolts of the Messenians, and the great mischiefs which happen in states having many slaves who speak the same language, and the numerous robberies and lawless life of the Italian banditti, as they are called. A man who considers all this is fairly at a loss. Two remedies alone remain to us—not to have the slaves of the same country, nor if possible, speaking the same language;[1] in this way they will more easily be held in subjection: secondly, we should tend them carefully, not only out of regard to them, but yet more out of respect to ourselves. And the right treatment of slaves is to behave properly to them, and to do to them, if possible, even more justice than to those who are our equals; for he who naturally and genuinely reverences justice, and hates injustice, is discovered in his dealings with any class of men to whom he can easily be unjust. And he who in regard to the natures and actions of his slaves is undefiled by impiety and injustice, will best sow the seeds of virtue in them; and this may be truly said of every master, and tyrant, and of every other having authority in relation to his inferiors. Slaves ought to be punished as they deserve, and not admonished as if they were freemen, which will only make them conceited. *[778]* The language used to a servant

[1] Cf. Aristotle, *Politics*, vii. 10, 1330 ᵃ 23-33.

ought always to be that of a command,[1] and we ought not to jest with them, whether they are males or females—this is a foolish way which many people have of setting up their slaves, and making the life of servitude more disagreeable both for them and for their masters.

Cle. True.

Ath. Now that each of the citizens is provided, as far as possible, with a sufficient number of suitable slaves who can help him in what he has to do, we may next proceed to describe their dwellings.

Cle. Very good.

Ath. The city being new and hitherto uninhabited, care ought to be taken of all the buildings, and the manner of building each of them, and also of the temples and walls. These, Cleinias, were matters which properly came before the marriages; but, as we are only talking, there is no objection to changing the order. If, however, our plan of legislation is ever to take effect, then the house shall precede the marriage if God so will, and afterwards we will come to the regulations about marriage; but at present we are only describing these matters in a general outline.

Cle. Quite true.

Ath. The temples are to be placed all round the agora, and the whole city built on the heights in a circle,[2] for the sake of defence and for the sake of purity. Near the temples are to be placed buildings for the magistrates and the courts of law; in these plaintiff and defendant will receive their due, and the places will be regarded as most holy, partly because they have to do with holy things, and partly because they are the dwelling-places of holy Gods: and in them will be held the courts in which cases of homicide and other trials of capital offenses may fitly take place. As to the walls, Megillus, I agree with Sparta in thinking that they should be allowed to sleep in the earth, and that we should not attempt to disinter them;[3] there is a poetical saying, which is finely expressed, that "walls ought to be of steel and iron, and not of earth"; besides, how ridiculous of us to be sending out our young men annually into the country to dig and to trench, and to keep off the enemy by fortifications, under the idea that they are not to be allowed to set foot in our territory, and then, that we should surround ourselves with a wall, which, in the first place, is by no means conducive to the health of cities,

and is also apt to produce a certain effeminacy in the minds of the inhabitants, inviting men to run thither instead of repelling their enemies, [779] and leading them to imagine that their safety is due not to their keeping guard day and night, but that when they are protected by walls and gates, then they may sleep in safety; as if they were not meant to labour, and did not know that true repose comes from labour, and that disgraceful indolence and a careless temper of mind is only the renewal of trouble. But if men must have walls, the private houses ought to be so arranged from the first that the whole city may be one wall, having all the houses capable of defence by reason of their uniformity and equality towards the streets.[4] The form of the city being that of a single dwelling will have an agreeable aspect, and being easily guarded will be infinitely better for security. Until the original building is completed, these should be the principal objects of the inhabitants; and the wardens of the city should superintend the work, and should impose a fine on him who is negligent; and in all that relates to the city they should have a care of cleanliness, and not allow a private person to encroach upon any public property either by buildings or excavations. Further, they ought to take care that the rains from heaven flow off easily, and of any other matters which may have to be administered either within or without the city. The guardians of the law shall pass any further enactments which their experience may show to be necessary, and supply any other points in which the law may be deficient. And now that these matters, and the buildings about the agora, and the gymnasia, and places of instruction, and theatres, are all ready and waiting for scholars and spectators, let us proceed to the subjects which follow marriage in the order of legislation.

Cle. By all means.

Ath. Assuming that marriages exist already, Cleinias, the mode of life during the year after marriage, before children are born, will follow next in order. In what way bride and bridegroom ought to live in a city which is to be superior to other cities, is a matter not at all easy for us to determine. There have been many difficulties already, but this will be the greatest of them, and the most disagreeable to the many. Still I cannot but say what appears to me to be right and true, Cleinias.

[780] *Cle.* Certainly.

Ath. He who imagines that he can give laws

---

[1] Cf. Aristotle, *Politics,* i. 13, 1260 ᵇ 2-8.

[2] Cf *Ibid.,* vii. 12, 1331 ᵃ 29-31.

[3] Cf. *Ibid.,* 11, 1330 ᵇ 31-35.

[4] Cf. *Ibid.,* 11, 1330 ᵇ 21-27.

for the public conduct of states, while he leaves the private life of citizens wholly to take care of itself; who thinks that individuals may pass the day as they please, and that there is no necessity of order in all things; he, I say, who gives up the control of their private lives, and supposes that they will conform to law in their common and public life, is making a great mistake. Why have I made this remark? Why, because I am going to enact that the bridegrooms should live at the common tables, just as they did before marriage. This was a singularity when first enacted by the legislator in your parts of the world, Megillus and Cleinias, as I should suppose, on the occasion of some war or other similar danger,[1] which caused the passing of the law, and which would be likely to occur in thinly-peopled places, and in times of pressure. But when men had once tried and been accustomed to a common table, experience showed that the institution greatly conduced to security; and in some such manner the custom of having common tables arose among you.

Cle. Likely enough.

Ath. I said that there may have been singularity and danger in imposing such a custom at first, but that now there is not the same difficulty. There is, however, another institution which is the natural sequel to this, and would be excellent, if it existed anywhere, but at present it does not. The institution of which I am about to speak is not easily described or executed; and would be like the legislator "combing wool into the fire," as people say, or performing any other impossible and useless feat.

Cle. What is the cause, Stranger, of this extreme hesitation?

Ath. You shall hear without any fruitless loss of time. That which has law and order in a state is the cause of every good, but that which is disordered or ill-ordered is often the ruin of that which is well-ordered; *[781]* and at this point the argument is now waiting. For with you, Cleinias and Megillus, the common tables of men are, as I said, a heaven-born and admirable institution, but you are mistaken in leaving the women unregulated by law. They have no similar institution of public tables in the light of day, and just that part of the human race which is by nature prone to secrecy and stealth on account of their weakness—I mean the female sex—has been left without regulation by the legislator, which is a great mistake. And, in consequence of this neglect, many things have grown lax among you, which might

have been far better, if they had been only regulated by law; for the neglect of regulations about women may not only be regarded as a neglect of half the entire matter,[2] but in proportion as woman's nature is inferior to that of men in capacity for virtue, in that degree the consequence of such neglect is more than twice as important. The careful consideration of this matter, and the arranging and ordering on a common principle of all our institutions relating both to men and women, greatly conduces to the happiness of the state. But at present, such is the unfortunate condition of mankind, that no man of sense will even venture to speak of common tables in places and cities in which they have never been established at all; and how can any one avoid being utterly ridiculous, who attempts to compel women to show in public how much they eat and drink? There is nothing at which the sex is more likely to take offence. For women are accustomed to creep into dark places, and when dragged out into the light they will exert their utmost powers of resistance, and be far too much for the legislator. And therefore, as I said before, in most places they will not endure to have the truth spoken without raising a tremendous outcry, but in this state perhaps they may. And if we may assume that our whole discussion about the state has not been mere idle talk, I should like to prove to you, if you will consent to listen, that this institution is good and proper; but if you had rather not, I will refrain.

Cle. There is nothing which we should both of us like better, Stranger, than to hear what you have to say.

Ath. Very good; and you must not be surprised if I go back a little, for we have plenty of leisure, and there is nothing to prevent us from considering in every point of view the subject of law.

Cle. True.

Ath. Then let us return once more to what we were saying at first. Every man should understand that the human race either had no beginning at all, and will never have an end, but always will be and has been; *[782]* or that it began an immense while ago.[3]

Cle. Certainly.

Ath. Well, and have there not been constitutions and destructions of states, and all sorts of pursuits both orderly and disorderly, and diverse desires of meats and drinks always, and in all the world, and all sorts of changes of the

[1] Cf. i. 625, 633.

[2] Aristotle, *Politics,* i. 13, 1260 ^{b} 8-24.

[3] Cf. iii. 676.

seasons in which animals may be expected to have undergone innumerable transformations of themselves?

Cle. No doubt.

Ath. And may we not suppose that vines appeared, which had previously no existence, and also olives, and the gifts of Demeter and her daughter, of which one Triptolemus was the minister, and that, before these existed, animals took to devouring each other as they do still?

Cle. True.

Ath. Again, the practice of men sacrificing one another still exists among many nations; while, on the other hand, we hear of other human beings who did not even venture to taste the flesh of a cow and had no animal sacrifices, but only cakes and fruits dipped in honey, and similar pure offerings, but no flesh of animals; from these they abstained under the idea that they ought not to eat them, and might not stain the altars of the Gods with blood. For in those days men are said to have lived a sort of Orphic life, having the use of all lifeless things, but abstaining from all living things.

Cle. Such has been the constant tradition, and is very likely true.

Ath. Some one might say to us, What is the drift of all this?

Cle. A very pertinent question, Stranger.

Ath. And therefore I will endeavour, Cleinias, if I can, to draw the natural inference.

Cle. Proceed.

Ath. I see that among men all things depend upon three wants and desires, of which the end is virtue, if they are rightly led by them, or the opposite if wrongly. Now these are eating and drinking, which begin at birth—every animal has a natural desire for them, and is violently excited, and rebels against him who says that he must not satisfy all his pleasures and appetites, and get rid of all the corresponding pains —and the third and greatest and *[783]* sharpest want and desire breaks out last, and is the fire of sexual lust, which kindles in men every species of wantonness and madness. And these three disorders we must endeavour to master by the three great principles of fear and law and right reason; turning them away from that which is called pleasantest to the best, using the Muses and the Gods who preside over contests to extinguish their increase and influx.

But to return:—After marriage let us speak of the birth of children, and after their birth of their nurture and education. In the course of discussion the several laws will be perfected, and we shall at last arrive at the common tables. Whether such associations are to be confined to men, or extended to women also, we shall see better when we approach and take a nearer view of them; and we may then determine what previous institutions are required and will have to precede them. As I said before, we shall see them more in detail, and shall be better able to lay down the laws which are proper or suited to them.

Cle. Very true.

Ath. Let us keep in mind the words which have now been spoken; for hereafter there may be need of them.

Cle. What do you bid us keep in mind?

Ath. That which we comprehended under the three words—first, eating, secondly, drinking, thirdly, the excitement of love.

Cle. We shall be sure to remember, Stranger.

Ath. Very good. Then let us now proceed to marriage, and teach persons in what way they shall beget children, threatening them, if they disobey, with the terrors of the law.

Cle. What do you mean?

Ath. The bride and bridegroom should consider that they are to produce for the state the best and fairest specimens of children which they can. Now all men who are associated in any action always succeed when they attend and give their mind to what they are doing, but when they do not give their mind or have no mind, they fail; wherefore let the bridegroom give his mind to the bride and to the begetting of children, and the bride in like manner give her mind to the bridegroom, and particularly at the time when their children are not yet born. *[784]* And let the women whom we have chosen be the overseers of such matters, and let them in whatever number, large or small, and at whatever time the magistrates may command, assemble every day in the temple of Eileithyia during a third part of the day, and being there assembled, let them inform one another of any one whom they see, whether man or woman, of those who are begetting children, disregarding the ordinances given at the time when the nuptial sacrifices and ceremonies were performed. Let the begetting of children and the supervision of those who are begetting them continue ten years and no longer, during the time when marriage is fruitful. But if any continue without children up to this time, let them take counsel with their kindred and with the women holding the office of overseer and be divorced for their mutual benefit. If, however, any dispute arises about what is proper and for the interest of either party, they shall choose ten of the guardians of the law and abide by their permission and appointment. The women who preside over these matters shall enter into the houses of the young, and partly by admonitions and partly by threats make them give over their folly and error: if they persist, let the women go and tell the guardians of the law, and the guardians shall prevent them. But if they too cannot prevent them, they shall bring the matter before the people; and let them write up their names and make oath that they cannot reform such and such an one; and let him who is thus written up, if he cannot in a court of law convict those who have inscribed his name, be deprived of the privileges of a citizen in the following respects:—let him not go to weddings nor to the thanksgivings after the birth of children; and if he go, let any one who pleases strike him with impunity; and let the same regulations hold about women: let not a woman be allowed to appear abroad, or receive honour, or go to nuptial and birthday festivals, if she in like manner be written up as acting disorderly and cannot obtain a verdict. And if, when they themselves have done begetting children according to the law, a man or woman have connection with another man or woman who are still begetting children, let the same penalties be inflicted upon them as upon those who are still having a family; and when the time for procreation has passed let the man or woman who refrains in such matters be held in esteem, and let those who do not refrain be held in the contrary of esteem—that is to say, [785] disesteem. Now, if the greater part of mankind behave modestly, the enactments of law may be left to slumber; but, if they are disorderly, the enactments having been passed, let them be carried into execution. To every man the first year is the beginning of life, and the time of birth ought to be written down in the temples of their fathers as the beginning of existence to every child, whether boy or girl. Let every phratria have inscribed on a whited wall the names of the successive archons by whom the years are reckoned. And near to them let the living members of the phratria be inscribed, and when they depart life let them be erased. The limit of marriageable ages for a woman shall be from sixteen to twenty years at the longest—for a man, from thirty to thirty-five years; and let a woman hold office at forty, and a man at thirty years. Let a man go out to war from twenty to sixty years, and for a woman, if there appear any need to make use of her in military service, let the time of service be after she shall have brought forth children up to fifty years of age; and let regard be had to what is possible and suitable to each.

BOOK VII

[788] AND now, assuming children of both sexes to have been born, it will be proper for us to consider, in the next place, their nurture and education; this cannot be left altogether unnoticed, and yet may be thought a subject fitted rather for precept and admonition than for law. In private life there are many little things, not always apparent, arising out of the pleasures and pains and desires of individuals, which run counter to the intention of the legislator, and make the characters of the citizens various and dissimilar:—this is an evil in states; for by reason of their smallness and frequent occurrence, there would be an unseemliness and want of propriety in making them penal by law; and if made penal, they are the destruction of the written law because mankind get the habit of frequently transgressing the law in small matters. The result is that you cannot legislate about them, and still less can you be silent. I speak somewhat darkly, but I shall endeavour also to bring my wares into the light of day, for I acknowledge that at present there is a want of clearness in what I am saying.

Cleinias. Very true.

Athenian Stranger. Am I not right in maintaining that a good education is that which tends most to the improvement of mind and body?

Cle. Undoubtedly.

Ath. And nothing can be plainer than that the fairest bodies are those which grow up from infancy in the best and straightest manner?

Cle. Certainly.

Ath. And do we not further observe that the first shoot of every living thing is by far the greatest and fullest? Many will even contend that a man at twenty-five does not reach twice the height which he attained at five.

Cle. True.

Ath. Well, and is not rapid growth without proper and abundant exercise the source of endless evils in the body?

Cle. Yes.

[789] *Ath.* And the body should have the most exercise when it receives most nourishment?

Cle. But, Stranger, are we to impose this great amount of exercise upon newly-born infants?

Ath. Nay, rather on the bodies of infants still unborn.

Cle. What do you mean, my good sir? In the process of gestation?

Ath. Exactly. I am not at all surprised that you have never heard of this very peculiar sort of gymnastic applied to such little creatures, which, although strange, I will endeavour to explain to you.

Cle. By all means.

Ath. The practice is more easy for us to understand than for you, by reason of certain amusements which are carried to excess by us at Athens. Not only boys, but often older persons, are in the habit of keeping quails and cocks,[1] which they train to fight one another. And they are far from thinking that the contests in which they stir them up to fight with one another are sufficient exercise; for, in addition to this, they carry them about tucked beneath their armpits, holding the smaller birds in their hands, the larger under their arms, and go for a walk of a great many miles for the sake of health, that is to say, not their own health, but the health of the birds; whereby they prove to any intelligent person, that all bodies are benefited by shakings and movements, when they are moved without weariness, whether the motion proceeds from themselves, or is caused by a swing, or at sea, or on horseback, or by other bodies in whatever way moving, and that thus gaining the mastery over food and drink, they are able to impart beauty and health and strength. But admitting all this, what follows? Shall we make a ridiculous law that the pregnant woman shall walk about and fashion the embryo within as we fashion wax before it hardens, and after birth swathe the infant for two years? Suppose that we compel nurses, under penalty of a legal fine, to be always carrying the children somewhere or other, either to the temples, or into the country, or to their relations' houses, until they are well able to stand, and to take care that their limbs are not distorted by leaning on them when they are too young [2]—they should continue to carry them until the infant has completed its third year; the nurses should be strong, and there should be more than one of them. Shall these be our rules, and shall we impose a penalty for the neglect of them? *[790]* No, no; the penalty of which we were speaking will fall upon our own heads more than enough.

Cle. What penalty?

Ath. Ridicule, and the difficulty of getting the feminine and servant-like dispositions of the nurses to comply.

Cle. Then why was there any need to speak of the matter at all?

Ath. The reason is that masters and freemen in states, when they hear of it, are very likely to arrive at a true conviction that without due regulation of private life in cities, stability in the laying down of laws is hardly to be expected; [3] and he who makes this reflection may himself adopt the laws just now mentioned, and, adopting them, may order his house and state well and be happy.

Cle. Likely enough.

Ath. And therefore let us proceed with our legislation until we have determined the exercises which are suited to the souls of young children, in the same manner in which we have begun to go through the rules relating to their bodies.

Cle. By all means.

Ath. Let us assume, then, as a first principle in relation both to the body and soul of very young creatures, that nursing and moving about by day and night is good for them all, and that the younger they are, the more they will need it; [4] infants should live, if that were possible, as if they were always rocking at sea. This is the lesson which we may gather from the experience of nurses, and likewise from the use of the remedy of motion in the rites of the Corybantes; for when mothers want their restless children to go to sleep they do not employ rest, but, on the contrary, motion—rocking them in their arms; nor do they give them silence, but they sing to them and lap them in sweet strains; and the Bacchic women are cured of their frenzy in the same manner by the use of the dance and of music.

Cle. Well, Stranger, and what is the reason of this?

Ath. The reason is obvious.

Cle. What?

Ath. The affection both of the Bacchantes and of the children is an emotion of fear, which springs out of an evil habit of the soul. And when some one applies external agitation to affections of this *[791]* sort, the motion coming from without gets the better of the terrible and violent internal one, and produces a peace and calm in the soul, and quiets the restless palpitation of the heart, which is a thing much to be desired, sending the children to sleep, and

[1] Cf. *Republic,* v. 459.
[2] Cf. Aristotle, *Politics,* vii. 17, 1336 ᵃ 8-15.
[3] Cf. *Republic,* v. 449.
[4] Cf. Aristotle, *Politics,* vii. 17, 1336 ᵃ 8-15.

making the Bacchantes, although they remain awake, to dance to the pipe with the help of the Gods to whom they offer acceptable sacrifices, and producing in them a sound mind, which takes the place of their frenzy. And, to express what I mean in a word, there is a good deal to be said in favour of this treatment.

Cle. Certainly.

Ath. But if fear has such a power we ought to infer from these facts, that every soul which from youth upward has been familiar with fears, will be made more liable to fear,[1] and every one will allow that this is the way to form a habit of cowardice and not of courage.

Cle. No doubt.

Ath. And, on the other hand, the habit of overcoming, from our youth upwards, the fears and terrors which beset us, may be said to be an exercise of courage.

Cle. True.

Ath. And we may say that the use of exercise and motion in the earliest years of life greatly contributes to create a part of virtue in the soul.

Cle. Quite true.

Ath. Further, a cheerful temper, or the reverse, may be regarded as having much to do with high spirit on the one hand, or with cowardice on the other.

Cle. To be sure.

Ath. Then now we must endeavour to show how and to what extent we may, if we please, without difficulty implant either character in the young.

Cle. Certainly.

Ath. There is a common opinion, that luxury makes the disposition of youth discontented and irascible and vehemently excited by trifles; that on the other hand excessive and savage servitude makes men mean and abject, and haters of their kind, and therefore makes them undesirable associates.

Cle. But how must the state educate those who do not as yet understand the language of the country, and are therefore incapable of appreciating any sort of instruction?

Ath. I will tell you how:—Every animal that is born is wont to utter some cry, and this is especially the case with man, and he is also affected with the inclination to weep more than any other animal.

Cle. Quite true.

Ath. Do not nurses, when they want to know what an infant desires, *[792]* judge by these signs?—when anything is brought to the infant and he is silent, then he is supposed to

be pleased, but, when he weeps and cries out, then he is not pleased. For tears and cries are the inauspicious signs by which children show what they love and hate. Now the time which is thus spent is no less than three years, and is a very considerable portion of life to be passed ill or well.

Cle. True.

Ath. Does not the discontented and ungracious nature appear to you to be full of lamentations and sorrows more than a good man ought to be?

Cle. Certainly.

Ath. Well, but if during these three years every possible care were taken that our nursling should have as little of sorrow and fear, and in general of pain as was possible, might we not expect in early childhood to make his soul more gentle and cheerful?[2]

Cle. To be sure, Stranger—more especially if we could procure him a variety of pleasures.

Ath. There I can no longer agree, Cleinias: you amaze me. To bring him up in such a way would be his utter ruin; for the beginning is always the most critical part of education. Let us see whether I am right.

Cle. Proceed.

Ath. The point about which you and I differ is of great importance, and I hope that you, Megillus, will help to decide between us. For I maintain that the true life should neither seek for pleasures, nor, on the other hand, entirely avoid pains, but should embrace the middle state,[3] which I just spoke of as gentle and benign, and is a state which we by some divine presage and inspiration rightly ascribe to God. Now, I say, he among men, too, who would be divine ought to pursue after this mean habit—he should not rush headlong into pleasures, for he will not be free from pains; nor should we allow any one, young or old, male or female, to be thus given any more than ourselves, and least of all the newly-born infant, for in infancy more than at any other time the character is engrained by habit. Nay, more, if I were not afraid of appearing to be ridiculous, I would say that a woman during her year of pregnancy should of all women be most carefully tended, and kept from violent or excessive pleasures and pains, and should at that time cultivate gentleness and benevolence and kindness.

[793] Cle. You need not ask Megillus, Stranger, which of us has most truly spoken; for I myself agree that all men ought to avoid the

---

[1] Cf. *Republic,* iii. 386.

[2] Cf. Aristotle, *Politics;* vii. 17, 1336 ᵃ 34-40.

[3] Cf. *Republic,* x. 619.

life of unmingled pain or pleasure, and pursue always a middle course. And having spoken well, may I add that you have been well answered?

Ath. Very good, Cleinias; and now let us all three consider a further point.

Cle. What is it?

Ath. That all the matters which we are now describing are commonly called by the general name of unwritten customs, and what are termed the laws of our ancestors are all of similar nature. And the reflection which lately arose in our minds,[1] that we can neither call these things laws, nor yet leave them unmentioned, is justified; for they are the bonds of the whole state, and come in between the written laws which are or are hereafter to be laid down; they are just ancestral customs of great antiquity, which, if they are rightly ordered and made habitual, shield and preserve the previously existing written law; but if they depart from right and fall into disorder, then they are like the props of builders which slip away out of their place and cause a universal ruin—one part drags another down, and the fair superstructure falls because the old foundations are undermined. Reflecting upon this, Cleinias, you ought to bind together the new state in every possible way, omitting nothing, whether great or small, of what are called laws or manners or pursuits, for by these means a city is bound together, and all these things are only lasting when they depend upon one another; and, therefore, we must not wonder if we find that many apparently trifling customs or usages come pouring in and lengthening out our laws.

Cle. Very true: we are disposed to agree with you.

Ath. Up to the age of three years, whether of boy or girl, if a person strictly carries out our previous regulations and makes them a principal aim, he will do much for the advantage of the young creatures. But at three, four, five, and even six years the childish nature will require sports; now is the time to get rid of self-will in him, punishing him, but not so as to disgrace him. We were saying about slaves,[2] that we ought neither to add insult to punishment so as to anger them, *[794]* nor yet to leave them unpunished lest they become self-willed; and a like rule is to be observed in the case of the free-born. Children at that age have certain natural modes of amusement which they find out for themselves when they meet. And

all the children who are between the ages of three and six ought to meet at the temples of the villages, the several families of a village uniting on one spot. The nurses are to see that the children behave properly and orderly—they themselves and all their companies are to be under the control of twelve matrons, one for each company, who are annually selected to inspect them from the women previously mentioned,[3] [i.e., the women who have authority over marriage], whom the guardians of the law appoint. These matrons shall be chosen by the women who have authority over marriage, one out of each tribe; all are to be of the same age; and let each of them, as soon as she is appointed, hold office and go to the temples every day, punishing all offenders, male or female, who are slaves or strangers, by the help of some of the public slaves; but if any citizen disputes the punishment, let her bring him before the wardens of the city; or, if there be no dispute, let her punish him herself. After the age of six years the time has arrived for the separation of the sexes—let boys live with boys, and girls in like manner with girls. Now they must begin to learn—the boys going to teachers of horsemanship and the use of the bow, the javelin, and sling, and the girls too, if they do not object, at any rate until they know how to manage these weapons, and especially how to handle heavy arms; for I may note, that the practice which now prevails is almost universally misunderstood.

Cle. In what respect?

Ath. In that the right and left hand are supposed to be by nature differently suited for our various uses of them; whereas no difference is found in the use of the feet and the lower limbs; but in the use of the hands we are, as it were, maimed by the folly of nurses and mothers; for although our several limbs are by nature balanced, we create a difference in them by bad habit. In some cases this is of no consequence, as, for example, when we hold the lyre in the left hand, and the plectrum in the right, but it is downright folly to make the same distinction in other cases. *[795]* The custom of the Scythians proves our error; for they not only hold the bow from them with the left hand and draw the arrow to them with their right, but use either hand for both purposes. And there are many similar examples in charioteering and other things, from which we may learn that those who make the left side weaker than the right act contrary to nature. In the case of the plectrum, which is of horn only, and

[1] Cf. 788.
[2] Cf. vi. 777.
[3] Cf. vi. 784.

similar instruments, as I was saying, it is of no consequence, but makes a great difference, and may be of very great importance to the warrior who has to use iron weapons, bows and javelins, and the like; above all, when in heavy armour, he has to fight against heavy armour. And there is a very great difference between one who has learnt and one who has not, and between one who has been trained in gymnastic exercises and one who has not been. For as he who is perfectly skilled in the Pancratium or boxing or wrestling, is not unable to fight from his left side, and does not limp and draggle in confusion when his opponent makes him change his position, so in heavy-armed fighting, and in all other things, if I am not mistaken, the like holds—he who has these double powers of attack and defence ought not in any case to leave them either unused or untrained, if he can help; and if a person had the nature of Geryon or Briareus he ought to be able with his hundred hands to throw a hundred darts. Now, the magistrates, male and female, should see to all these things, the women superintending the nursing and amusements of the children, and the men superintending their education, that all of them, boys and girls alike, may be sound hand and foot, and may not, if they can help, spoil the gifts of nature by bad habits.

Education has two branches—one of gymnastic, which is concerned with the body, and the other of music, which is designed for the improvement of the soul.[1] And gymnastic has also two branches—dancing and wrestling; and one sort of dancing imitates musical recitation, and aims at preserving dignity and freedom, the other aims at producing health, agility, and beauty in the limbs and parts of the body, giving the proper flexion and extension to each of them, a harmonious motion being diffused everywhere, and forming a suitable accompaniment to the dance. [796] As regards wrestling, the tricks which Antaeus and Cercyon devised in their systems out of a vain spirit of competition, or the tricks of boxing which Epeius or Amycus invented, are useless and unsuitable for war, and do not deserve to have much said about them; but the art of wrestling erect and keeping free the neck and hands and sides, working with energy and constancy, with a composed strength, and for the sake of health —these are always useful, and are not to be neglected, but to be enjoined alike on masters and scholars, when we reach that part of legislation; and we will desire the one to give their

instructions freely, and the others to receive them thankfully.[2] Nor, again, must we omit suitable imitations of war in our choruses; here in Crete you have the armed dances of the Curetes, and the Lacedaemonians have those of the Dioscuri. And our virgin lady, delighting in the amusement of the dance, thought it not fit to amuse herself with empty hands; she must be clothed in a complete suit of armour, and in this attire go through the dance;[3] and youths and maidens should in every respect imitate her, esteeming highly the favour of the Goddess, both with a view to the necessities of war, and to festive occasions: it will be right also for the boys, until such time as they go out to war, to make processions and supplications to all the Gods in goodly array, armed and on horseback, in dances, and marches, fast or slow, offering up prayers to the Gods and to the sons of Gods; and also engaging in contests and preludes of contests, if at all, with these objects. For these sorts of exercises, and no others, are useful both in peace and war, and are beneficial alike to states and to private houses. But other labours and sports and exercises of the body are unworthy of freemen, O Megillus and Cleinias.

I have now completely described the kind of gymnastic which I said at first ought to be described; if you know of any better, will you communicate your thoughts?

Cle. It is not easy, Stranger, to put aside these principles of gymnastic and wrestling and to enunciate better ones.

Ath. Now we must say what has yet to be said about the gifts of the Muses and of Apollo: before, we fancied that we had said all, and that gymnastic alone remained;[4] but now we see clearly what points have been omitted, and should be first proclaimed; of these, then, let us proceed to speak.

[797] *Cle.* By all means.

Ath. Let me tell you once more—although you have heard me say the same before—that caution must be always exercised, both by the speaker and by the hearer, about anything that is very singular and unusual. For my tale is one which many a man would be afraid to tell, and yet I have a confidence which makes me go on.

Cle. What have you to say, Stranger?

Ath. I say that in states generally no one has observed that the plays of childhood have a great deal to do with the permanence or want

[1] Cf. *Republic*, ii. 376; iii. 403, 410.

[2] Cf. 814.

[3] Cf. *Critias*, 110.

[4] Cf. ii. 673.

of permanence in legislation. For when plays are ordered with a view to children having the same plays, and amusing themselves after the same manner, and finding delight in the same playthings, the more solemn institutions of the state are allowed to remain undisturbed. Whereas if sports are disturbed, and innovations are made in them, and they constantly change, and the young never speak of their having the same likings, or the same established notions of good and bad taste, either in the bearing of their bodies or in their dress, but he who devises something new and out of the way in figures and colours and the like is held in special honour, we may truly say that no greater evil can happen in a state;[1] for he who changes the sports is secretly changing the manners of the young, and making the old to be dishonoured among them and the new to be honoured. And I affirm that there is nothing which is a greater injury to all states than saying or thinking thus. Will you hear me tell how great I deem the evil to be?

Cle. You mean the evil of blaming antiquity in states?

Ath. Exactly.

Cle. If you are speaking of that, you will find in us hearers who are disposed to receive what you say not unfavourably but most favourably.

Ath. I should expect so.

Cle. Proceed.

Ath. Well, then, let us give all the greater heed to one another's words. The argument affirms that any change whatever except from evil is the most dangerous of all things; this is true in the case of the seasons and of the winds, in the management of our bodies and the habits of our minds—true of all things except, as I said before, of the bad. He who looks at the constitution of individuals accustomed to eat any sort of meat, or drink any drink, or to do any work which they can get, may see that they are at first disordered by them, but afterwards, as time goes on, their bodies grow adapted to them, and they learn to know and like variety, and have good health and enjoyment of life; *[798]* and if ever afterwards they are confined again to a superior diet, at first they are troubled with disorders, and with difficulty become habituated to their new food. A similar principle we may imagine to hold good about the minds of men and the natures of their souls. For when they have been brought up in certain laws, which by some Divine Providence have remained unchanged during long ages, so that

[1] Cf. *Republic,* iv. 424.

no one has any memory or tradition of their ever having been otherwise than they are, then every one is afraid and ashamed to change that which is established. The legislator must somehow find a way of implanting this reverence for antiquity, and I would propose the following way:—People are apt to fancy, as I was saying before, that when the plays of children are altered they are merely plays, not seeing that the most serious and detrimental consequences arise out of the change; and they readily comply with the child's wishes instead of deterring him, not considering that these children who make innovations in their games, when they grow up to be men, will be different from the last generation of children, and, being different, will desire a different sort of life, and under the influence of this desire will want other institutions and laws; and no one of them reflects that there will follow what I just now called the greatest of evils to states. Changes in bodily fashions are no such serious evils, but frequent changes in the praise and censure of manners are the greatest of evils, and require the utmost prevision.

Cle. To be sure.

Ath. And now do we still hold to our former assertion, that rhythms and music in general are imitations of good and evil characters in men?[2] What say you?

Cle. That is the only doctrine which we can admit.

Ath. Must we not, then, try in every possible way to prevent our youth from even desiring to imitate new modes either in dance or song?[3] nor must any one be allowed to offer them varieties of pleasures.

Cle. Most true.

[799] Ath. Can any of us imagine a better mode of effecting this object than that of the Egyptians?

Cle. What is their method?

Ath. To consecrate every sort of dance or melody. First we should ordain festivals—calculating for the year what they ought to be, and at what time, and in honour of what Gods, sons of Gods, and heroes they ought to be celebrated; and, in the next place, what hymns ought to be sung at the several sacrifices, and with what dances the particular festival is to be honoured. This has to be arranged at first by certain persons, and, when arranged, the whole assembly of the citizens are to offer sacrifices and libations to the Fates and all the other

[2] Cf. ii. 655, ff.
[3] Cf. *Republic,* iv. 424.

Gods, and to consecrate the several odes to Gods and heroes: and if any one offers any other hymns or dances to any one of the Gods, the priests and priestesses, acting in concert with the guardians of the law, shall, with the sanction of religion and the law, exclude him, and he who is excluded, if he do not submit, shall be liable all his life long to have a suit of impiety brought against him by any one who likes.

Cle. Very good.

Ath. In the consideration of this subject, let us remember what is due to ourselves.

Cle. To what are you referring?

Ath. I mean that any young man, and much more any old one, when he sees or hears anything strange or unaccustomed, does not at once run to embrace the paradox, but he stands considering, like a person who is at a place where three paths meet, and does not very well know his way—he may be alone or he may be walking with others, and he will say to himself and them, "Which is the way?" and will not move forward until he is satisfied that he is going right. And this is what we must do in the present instance:—A strange discussion on the subject of law has arisen, which requires the utmost consideration, and we should not at our age be too ready to speak about such great matters, or be confident that we can say anything certain all in a moment.

Cle. Most true.

Ath. Then we will allow time for reflection, and decide when we have given the subject sufficient consideration. But that we may not be hindered from completing the natural arrangement of our laws, let us proceed to the conclusion of them in due order; for very possibly, if God will, the exposition of them, when completed, may throw light on our present perplexity.

Cle. Excellent, Stranger; let us do as you propose.

Ath. Let us then affirm the paradox that strains of music are our laws (νόμοι), *[800]* and this latter being the name which the ancients gave to lyric songs,[1] they probably would not have very much objected to our proposed application of the word. Some one, either asleep or awake, must have had a dreamy suspicion of their nature. And let our decree be as follows:—No one in singing or dancing shall offend against public and consecrated models, and the general fashion among the youth, any more than he would offend against any other

[1] Cf. iii. 700.

law. And he who observes this law shall be blameless; but he who is disobedient, as I was saying, shall be punished by the guardians of the laws, and by the priests and priestesses. Suppose that we imagine this to be our law.

Cle. Very good.

Ath. Can any one who makes such laws escape ridicule? Let us see. I think that our only safety will be in first framing certain models for composers. One of these models shall be as follows:—If when a sacrifice is going on, and the victims are being burnt according to law —if, I say, any one who may be a son or brother, standing by another at the altar and over the victims, horribly blasphemes, will not his words inspire despondency and evil omens and forebodings in the mind of his father and of his other kinsmen?

Cle. Of course.

Ath. And this is just what takes place in almost all our cities. A magistrate offers a public sacrifice, and there come in not one but many choruses, who take up a position a little way from the altar, and from time to time pour forth all sorts of horrible blasphemies on the sacred rites, exciting the souls of the audience with words and rhythms and melodies most sorrowful to hear; and he who at the moment when the city is offering sacrifice makes the citizens weep most, carries away the palm of victory. Now, ought we not to forbid such strains as these? And if ever our citizens must hear such lamentations, then on some unblest and inauspicious day let there be choruses of foreign and hired minstrels, like those hirelings who accompany the departed at funerals with barbarous Carian chants. That is the sort of thing which will be appropriate if we have such strains at all; and let the apparel of the singers be, not circlets and ornaments of gold, but the reverse. Enough of all this. I will simply ask once more whether we shall lay down as one of our principles of song——

Cle. What?

[801] Ath. That we should avoid every word of evil omen; let that kind of song which is of good omen be heard everywhere and always in our state. I need hardly ask again, but shall assume that you agree with me.

Cle. By all means; that law is approved by the suffrages of us all.

Ath. But what shall be our next musical law or type? Ought not prayers to be offered up to the Gods when we sacrifice?

Cle. Certainly.

Ath. And our third law, if I am not mistaken, will be to the effect that our poets, understanding prayers to be requests which we make to the Gods, will take especial heed that they do not by mistake ask for evil instead of good. To make such a prayer would surely be too ridiculous.

Cle. Very true.

Ath. Were we not a little while ago quite convinced that no silver or golden Plutus should dwell in our state? [1]

Cle. To be sure.

Ath. And what has it been the object of our argument to show? Did we not imply that the poets are not always quite capable of knowing what is good or evil? And if one of them utters a mistaken prayer in song or words, he will make our citizens pray for the opposite of what is good in matters of the highest import; than which, as I was saying, there can be few greater mistakes. Shall we then propose as one of our laws and models relating to the Muses——

Cle. What?—will you explain the law more precisely?

Ath. Shall we make a law that the poet shall compose nothing contrary to the ideas of the lawful, or just, or beautiful, or good, which are allowed in the state? nor shall he be permitted to communicate his compositions to any private individuals, until he shall have shown them to the appointed judges and the guardians of the law, and they are satisfied with them. As to the persons whom we appoint to be our legislators about music [2] and as to the director of education, [3] these have been already indicated. Once more then, as I have asked more than once, shall this be our third law, and type, and model—What do you say?

Cle. Let it be so, by all means.

Ath. Then it will be proper to have hymns and praises of the Gods, [4] intermingled with prayers; and after the Gods prayers and praises should be offered in like manner to demigods and heroes, suitable to their several characters.

Cle. Certainly.

Ath. In the next place there will be no objection to a law, that citizens who are departed and have done good and energetic deeds, either with their souls or with their bodies, and have been obedient to the laws, should receive eulogies; this will be very fitting.

[802] *Cle.* Quite true.

Ath. But to honour with hymns and pane-gyrics those who are still alive is not safe; a man should run his course, and make a fair ending, and then we will praise him; and let praise be given equally to women as well as men who have been distinguished in virtue. The order of songs and dances shall be as follows:—There are many ancient musical compositions and dances which are excellent, and from these the newly-founded city may freely select what is proper and suitable; and they shall choose judges of not less than fifty years of age, who shall make the selection, and any of the old poems which they deem sufficient they shall include; any that are deficient or altogether unsuitable, they shall either utterly throw aside, or examine and amend, taking into their counsel poets and musicians, and making use of their poetical genius; but explaining to them the wishes of the legislator in order that they may regulate dancing, music, and all choral strains, according to the mind of the judges; and not allowing them to indulge, except in some few matters, their individual pleasures and fancies. Now the irregular strain of music is always made ten thousand times better by attaining to law and order, and rejecting the honeyed Muse—not however that we mean wholly to exclude pleasure, which is the characteristic of all music. And if a man be brought up from childhood to the age of discretion and maturity in the use of the orderly and severe music, when he hears the opposite he detests it, and calls it illiberal; but if trained in the sweet and vulgar music, he deems the severer kind cold and displeasing. [5] So that, as I was saying before, while he who hears them gains no more pleasure from the one than from the other, the one has the advantage of making those who are trained in it better men, whereas the other makes them worse.

Cle. Very true.

Ath. Again, we must distinguish and determine on some general principle what songs are suitable to women, and what to men, and must assign to them their proper melodies and rhythms. It is shocking for a whole harmony to be inharmonical, or for a rhythm to be unrhythmical, and this will happen when the melody is inappropriate to them. And therefore the legislator must assign to these also their forms. Now both sexes have melodies and rhythms which of necessity belong to them; and those of women are clearly enough indicated by their natural difference. The grand,

[1] Cf. v. 741.
[2] Cf. vi. 764.
[3] Cf. vi. 765.
[4] Cf. *Republic*, x. 607.

[5] Cf. Aristotle, *Politics*, viii. 6, 1341ᵃ 12-15; viii. 7, 1342ᵃ 21-28.

and that which tends to courage, may be fairly called manly; but that which inclines to moderation and temperance, *[803]* may be declared both in law and in ordinary speech to be the more womanly quality. This, then, will be the general order of them.

Let us now speak of the manner of teaching and imparting them, and the persons to whom, and the time when, they are severally to be imparted. As the shipwright first lays down the lines of the keel, and thus, as it were, draws the ship in outline, so do I seek to distinguish the patterns of life, and lay down their keels according to the nature of different men's souls; seeking truly to consider by what means, and in what ways, we may go through the voyage of life best. Now human affairs are hardly worth considering in earnest, and yet we must be in earnest about them—a sad necessity constrains us. And having got thus far, there will be a fitness in our completing the matter, if we can only find some suitable method of doing so. But what do I mean? Some one may ask this very question, and quite rightly, too.

Cle. Certainly.

Ath. I say that about serious matters a man should be serious, and about a matter which is not serious he should not be serious; and that God is the natural and worthy object of our most serious and blessed endeavours, for man, as I said before,[1] is made to be the plaything of God, and this, truly considered, is the best of him; wherefore also every man and woman should walk seriously, and pass life in the noblest of pastimes, and be of another mind from what they are at present.

Cle. In what respect?

Ath. At present they think that their serious pursuits should be for the sake of their sports, for they deem war a serious pursuit, which must be managed well for the sake of peace; but the truth is, that there neither is, nor has been, nor ever will be, either amusement or instruction in any degree worth speaking of in war, which is nevertheless deemed by us to be the most serious of our pursuits. And therefore, as we say, every one of us should live the life of peace as long and as well as he can.[2] And what is the right way of living? Are we to live in sports always? If so, in what kind of sports? We ought to live sacrificing, and singing, and dancing, and then a man will be able to propitiate the Gods, and to defend himself against his enemies and conquer them in battle. The type

of song or dance by which he will propitiate them has been described, and the paths along which he is to proceed have been cut for him. He will go forward in the spirit of the poet: *[804]*

Telemachus, some things thou wilt thyself find in thy heart, but other things God will suggest; for I deem that thou wast not born or brought up without the will of the Gods.[3]

And this ought to be the view of our alumni; they ought to think that what has been said is enough for them, and that any other things their Genius and God will suggest to them—he will tell them to whom, and when, and to what Gods severally they are to sacrifice and perform dances, and how they may propitiate the deities, and live according to the appointment of nature; being for the most part puppets, but having some little share of reality.

Megillus. You have a low opinion of mankind, Stranger.

Ath. Nay, Megillus, be not amazed, but forgive me:—I was comparing them with the Gods; and under that feeling I spoke. Let us grant, if you wish, that the human race is not to be despised, but is worthy of some consideration.

Next follow the buildings for gymnasia and schools open to all; these are to be in three places in the midst of the city; and outside the city and in the surrounding country, also in three places, there shall be schools for horse exercise, and large grounds arranged with a view to archery and the throwing of missiles, at which young men may learn and practise. Of these mention has already been made,[4] and if the mention be not sufficiently explicit, let us speak further of them and embody them in laws. In these several schools let there be dwellings for teachers, who shall be brought from foreign parts by pay, and let them teach those who attend the schools the art of war and the art of music, and the children shall come not only if their parents please, but if they do not please; there shall be compulsory education, as the saying is, of all and sundry, as far as this is possible; and the pupils shall be regarded as belonging to the state rather than to their parents.[5] My law would apply to females as well as males; they shall both go through the same exercises. I assert without fear of contradiction that gymnastic and horsemanship are as suitable to women as to men.[6] Of the truth of this

[1] Cf. i. 644.
[2] Cf. i. 628.
[3] *Odyssey*, iii. 26, ff.
[4] Cf. vi. 764, 779.
[5] Cf. Aristotle, *Politics*, viii. 1, 1337 ᵃ 21-34.
[6] Cf. *Republic*, v. 451, ff.

I am persuaded from ancient tradition, and at the present day there are said to be countless myriads of women in the neighbourhood of the Black Sea, called Sauromatides, who not only ride on horseback like men, [805] but have enjoined upon them the use of bows and other weapons equally with the men. And I further affirm, that if these things are possible, nothing can be more absurd than the practice which prevails in our own country, of men and women not following the same pursuits with all their strength and with one mind, for thus the state, instead of being a whole, is reduced to a half,[1] but has the same imposts to pay and the same toils to undergo; and what can be a greater mistake for any legislator to make than this?

Cle. Very true; yet much of what has been asserted by us, Stranger, is contrary to the custom of states; still, in saying that the discourse should be allowed to proceed, and that when the discussion is completed, we should choose what seems best, you spoke very properly,[2] and I now feel compunction for what I have said. Tell me, then, what you would next wish to say.

Ath. I should wish to say, Cleinias, as I said before, that if the possibility of these things were not sufficiently proven in fact, then there might be an objection to the argument, but the fact being as I have said, he who rejects the law must find some other ground of objection; and, failing this, our exhortation will still hold good, nor will any one deny that women ought to share as far as possible in education and in other ways with men. For consider;—if women do not share in their whole life with men, then they must have some other order of life.

Cle. Certainly.

Ath. And what arrangement of life to be found anywhere is preferable to this community which we are now assigning to them? Shall we prefer that which is adopted by the Thracians and many other races who use their women to till the ground and to be shepherds of their herds and flocks, and to minister to them like slaves?—Or shall we do as we and people in our part of the world do—getting together, as the phrase is, all our goods and chattels into one dwelling, we entrust them to our women, who are the stewards of them, and who also preside over the shuttles and the whole art of spinning? [806] Or shall we take a middle course, as in Lacedaemon, Megillus—letting

the girls share in gymnastic and music, while the grown-up women, no longer employed in spinning wool, are hard at work weaving the web of life, which will be no cheap or mean employment, and in the duty of serving and taking care of the household and bringing up children, in which they will observe a sort of mean, not participating in the toils of war; and if there were any necessity that they should fight for their city and families, unlike the Amazons, they would be unable to take part in archery or any other skilled use of missiles, nor could they, after the example of the Goddess, carry shield or spear, or stand up nobly for their country when it was being destroyed, and strike terror into their enemies, if only because they were seen in regular order? Living as they do, they would never dare at all to imitate the Sauromatides, who, when compared with ordinary women, would appear to be like men. Let him who will, praise your legislators, but I must say what I think. The legislator ought to be whole and perfect, and not half a man only; he ought not to let the female sex live softly and waste money and have no order of life, while he takes the utmost care of the male sex, and leaves half of life only blest with happiness, when he might have made the whole state happy.

Meg. What shall we do, Cleinias? Shall we allow a stranger to run down Sparta in this fashion?

Cle. Yes; for as we have given him liberty of speech we must let him go on until we have perfected the work of legislation.

Meg. Very true.

Ath. Then now I may proceed?

Cle. By all means.

Ath. What will be the manner of life among men who may be supposed to have their food and clothing provided for them in moderation, and who have entrusted the practice of the arts to others, and whose husbandry, committed to slaves paying a part of the produce, brings them a return sufficient for men living temperately; who, moreover, have common tables in which the men are placed apart, and near them are the common tables of their families, of their daughters and mothers, which day by day, the officers, male and female, are to inspect—they shall see to the behaviour of the company, and so dismiss them; after which the presiding magistrate and his attendants shall honour with libations those Gods [807] to whom that day and night are dedicated, and then go home? To men whose lives are thus ordered, is there

[1] Cf. vi. 781; Aristotle, *Politics,* i. 13, 1260 [b] 9-24.
[2] Cf. 799.

no work remaining to be done which is necessary and fitting, but shall each one of them live fattening like a beast? Such a life is neither just nor honourable, nor can he who lives it fail of meeting his due; and the due reward of the idle fatted beast is that he should be torn in pieces by some other valiant beast whose fatness is worn down by brave deeds and toil. These regulations, if we duly consider them, will never be exactly carried into execution under present circumstances, nor as long as women and children and houses and all other things are the private property of individuals; but if we can attain the second-best form of polity, we shall be very well off. And to men living under this second polity there remains a work to be accomplished which is far from being small or insignificant, but is the greatest of all works, and ordained by the appointment of righteous law. For the life which may be truly said to be concerned with the virtue of body and soul is twice, or more than twice, as full of toil and trouble as the pursuit after Pythian and Olympic victories,[1] which debars a man from every employment of life. For there ought to be no bye-work interfering with the greater work of providing the necessary exercise and nourishment for the body, and instruction and education for the soul. Night and day are not long enough for the accomplishment of their perfection and consummation; and therefore to this end all freemen ought to arrange the way in which they will spend their time during the whole course of the day, from morning till evening and from evening till the morning of the next sunrise. There may seem to be some impropriety in the legislator determining minutely the numberless details of the management of the house, including such particulars as the duty of wakefulness in those who are to be perpetual watchmen of the whole city; for that any citizen should continue during the whole of any night in sleep, *[808]* instead of being seen by all his servants, always the first to awake and get up—this, whether the regulation is to be called a law or only a practice, should be deemed base and unworthy of a freeman; also that the mistress of the house should be awakened by her handmaidens instead of herself first awakening them, is what the slaves, male and female, and the serving-boys, and, if that were possible, everybody and everything in the house should regard as base. If they rise early, they may all of them do much of their public and of their household business, as mag-

istrates in the city, and masters and mistresses in their private houses, before the sun is up. Much sleep is not required by nature, either for our souls or bodies, or for the actions which they perform. For no one who is asleep is good for anything, any more than if he were dead; but he of us who has the most regard for life and reason keeps awake as long as he can, reserving only so much time for sleep as is expedient for health; and much sleep is not required, if the habit of moderation be once rightly formed. Magistrates in states who keep awake at night are terrible to the bad, whether enemies or citizens, and are honoured and reverenced by the just and temperate, and are useful to themselves and to the whole state.

A night which is passed in such a manner, in addition to all the above-mentioned advantages, infuses a sort of courage into the minds of the citizens. When the day breaks, the time has arrived for youth to go to their schoolmasters. Now neither sheep nor any other animals can live without a shepherd, nor can children be left without tutors, or slaves without masters. And of all animals the boy is the most unmanageable, inasmuch as he has the fountain of reason in him not yet regulated;[2] he is the most insidious, sharp-witted, and insubordinate of animals. Wherefore he must be bound with many bridles; in the first place, when he gets away from mothers and nurses, he must be under the management of tutors on account of his childishness and foolishness; then, again, being a freeman, he must be controlled by teachers, no matter what they teach, and by studies; but he is also a slave, and in that regard any freeman who comes in his way may punish him and his tutor and his instructor, if any of them does anything wrong; and he who comes across him and does not inflict upon him the punishment which he deserves, *[809]* shall incur the greatest disgrace; and let the guardian of the law, who is the director of education, see to him who coming in the way of the offences which we have mentioned, does not chastise them when he ought, or chastises them in a way which he ought not; let him keep a sharp look-out, and take especial care of the training of our children, directing their natures, and always turning them to good according to the law.

But how can our law sufficiently train the director of education himself; for as yet all has been imperfect, and nothing has been said either clear or satisfactory? Now, as far as pos-

[1] Cf. *Republic*, v. 465, 466.

[2] Cf. vi. 766.

sible, the law ought to leave nothing to him, but to explain everything, that he may be an interpreter and tutor to others. About dances and music and choral strains, I have already spoken both as to the character of the selection of them, and the manner in which they are to be amended and consecrated. But we have not as yet spoken, O illustrious guardian of education, of the manner in which your pupils are to use those strains which are written in prose, although you have been informed what martial strains they are to learn and practise; what relates in the first place to the learning of letters, and secondly, to the lyre, and also to calculation, which, as we were saying,[1] is needful for them all to learn, and any other things which are required with a view to war and the management of house and city, and, looking to the same object, what is useful in the revolutions of the heavenly bodies—the stars and sun and moon, and the various regulations about these matters which are necessary for the whole state—I am speaking of the arrangements of days in periods of months, and of months in years, which are to be observed, in order that seasons and sacrifices and festivals may have their regular and natural order, and keep the city alive and awake, the Gods receiving the honours due to them, and men having a better understanding about them:[2] all these things, O my friend, have not yet been sufficiently declared to you by the legislator. Attend, then, to what I am now going to say:— We were telling you, in the first place, that you were not sufficiently informed about letters, and the objection was to this effect—that you were never told whether he who was meant to be a respectable citizen should apply himself in detail to that sort of learning, or not apply himself at all; and the same remark holds good of the study of the lyre. But now we say that he ought to attend to them. *[810]* A fair time for a boy of ten years old to spend in letters is three years; the age of thirteen is the proper time for him to begin to handle the lyre, and he may continue at this for another three years, neither more nor less, and whether his father or himself like or dislike the study, he is not to be allowed to spend more or less time in learning music than the law allows. And let him who disobeys the law be deprived of those youthful honours of which we shall hereafter speak.[3] Hear, however, first of all, what the young

ought to learn in the early years of life, and what their instructors ought to teach them. They ought to be occupied with their letters until they are able to read and write; but the acquisition of perfect beauty or quickness in writing, if nature has not stimulated them to acquire these accomplishments in the given number of years, they should let alone. And as to the learning of compositions committed to writing which are not set to the lyre, whether metrical or without rhythmical divisions, compositions in prose, as they are termed, having no rhythm or harmony—seeing how dangerous are the writings handed down to us by many writers of this class—what will you do with them, O most excellent guardians of the law? or how can the lawgiver rightly direct you about them? I believe that he will be in great difficulty.

Cle. What troubles you, Stranger? and why are you so perplexed in your mind?

Ath. You naturally ask, Cleinias, and to you and Megillus, who are my partners in the work of legislation, I must state the more difficult as well as the easier parts of the task.

Cle. To what do you refer in this instance?

Ath. I will tell you. There is a difficulty in opposing many myriads of mouths.

Cle. Well, and have we not already opposed the popular voice in many important enactments?

Ath. That is quite true; and you mean to imply that the road which we are taking may be disagreeable to some but is agreeable to as many others, or if not to as many, at any rate to persons not inferior to the others, and in company with them you bid me, at whatever risk, to proceed along the path of legislation which has opened out of our present discourse, and to be of good cheer, and not to faint.

Cle. Certainly.

Ath. And I do not faint; I say, indeed, that we have a great many poets writing in hexameter, trimeter, and all sorts of measures— some who are serious, others who aim only at raising a laugh—and all mankind declare that the youth who are rightly educated should be brought up in them and saturated with them; some insist that they should be constantly hearing them read aloud, *[811]* and always learning them, so as to get by heart entire poets; while others select choice passages and long speeches, and make compendiums of them, saying that these ought to be committed to memory, if a man is to be made good and wise by experience and learning of many things. And

---

[1] Cf. v. 747.
[2] Cf. viii. 828.
[3] Cf. viii. 829.

you want me now to tell them plainly in what they are right and in what they are wrong.

Cle. Yes, I do.

Ath. But how can I in one word rightly comprehend all of them? I am of opinion, and, if I am not mistaken, there is a general agreement, that every one of these poets has said many things well and many things the reverse of well; and if this be true, then I do affirm that much learning is dangerous to youth.

Cle. How would you advise the guardian of the law to act?

Ath. In what respect?

Cle. I mean to what pattern should he look as his guide in permitting the young to learn some things and forbidding them to learn others. Do not shrink from answering.

Ath. My good Cleinias, I rather think that I am fortunate.

Cle. How so?

Ath. I think that I am not wholly in want of a pattern, for when I consider the words which we have spoken from early dawn until now, and which, as I believe, have been inspired by Heaven, they appear to me to be quite like a poem. When I reflected upon all these words of ours, I naturally felt pleasure, for of all the discourses which I have ever learnt or heard, either in poetry or prose, this seemed to me to be the justest, and most suitable for young men to hear; I cannot imagine any better pattern than this which the guardian of the law who is also the director of education can have. He cannot do better than advise the teachers to teach the young these words and any which are of a like nature, if he should happen to find them, either in poetry or prose, or if he come across unwritten discourses akin to ours, he should certainly preserve them, and commit them to writing. And, first of all, he shall constrain the teachers themselves to learn and approve them, and any of them who will not, shall not be employed by him, but those whom he finds agreeing in his judgment, he shall make use of and shall commit to them the instruction and education of youth. *[812]* And here and on this wise let my fanciful tale about letters and teachers of letters come to an end.

Cle. I do not think, Stranger, that we have wandered out of the proposed limits of the argument; but whether we are right or not in our whole conception, I cannot be very certain.

Ath. The truth, Cleinias, may be expected to become clearer when, as we have often said, we arrive at the end of the whole discussion about laws.

Cle. Yes.

Ath. And now that we have done with the teacher of letters, the teacher of the lyre has to receive orders from us.

Cle. Certainly.

Ath. I think that we have only to recollect our previous discussions, and we shall be able to give suitable regulations touching all this part of instruction and education to the teachers of the lyre.

Cle. To what do you refer?

Ath. We were saying, if I remember rightly, that the sixty-year-old choristers of Dionysus were to be specially quick in their perceptions of rhythm and musical composition, that they might be able to distinguish good and bad imitation, that is to say, the imitation of the good or bad soul when under the influence of passion, rejecting the one and displaying the other in hymns and songs, charming the souls of youth, and inviting them to follow and attain virtue by the way of imitation.[1]

Cle. Very true.

Ath. And with this view the teacher and the learner ought to use the sounds of the lyre, because its notes are pure, the player who teaches and his pupil rendering note for note in unison; but complexity, and variation of notes, when the strings give one sound and the poet or composer of the melody gives another—also when they make concords and harmonies in which lesser and greater intervals, slow and quick, or high and low notes, are combined—or, again, when they make complex variations of rhythms, which they adapt to the notes of the lyre [2]—all that sort of thing is not suited to those who have to acquire a speedy and useful knowledge of music in three years; for opposite principles are confusing, and create a difficulty in learning, and our young men should learn quickly, and their mere necessary acquirements are not few or trifling, as will be shown in due course. Let the director of education attend to the principles concerning music which we are laying down. As to the songs and words themselves which the masters of choruses are to teach and the character of them, *[813]* they have been already described by us, and are the same which, when consecrated and adapted to the different festivals, we said were to benefit cities by affording them an innocent amusement.[3]

Cle. That, again, is true.

[1] Cf. ii. 664, ff.
[2] Cf. *Republic,* iii. 397.
[3] Cf. 799.

Ath. Then let him who has been elected a director of music [1] receive these rules from us as containing the very truth; and may he prosper in his office! Let us now proceed to lay down other rules in addition to the preceding about dancing and gymnastic exercise in general. Having said what remained to be said about the teaching of music, let us speak in like manner about gymnastic. For boys and girls ought to learn to dance and practise gymnastic exercises—ought they not?

Cle. Yes.

Ath. Then the boys ought to have dancing masters, and the girls dancing mistresses to exercise them.

Cle. Very good.

Ath. Then once more let us summon him who has the chief concern in the business, the superintendent of youth [i. e., the director of education]; he will have plenty to do, if he is to have the charge of music and gymnastic.

Cle. But how will an old man be able to attend to such great charges?

Ath. O my friend, there will be no difficulty, for the law has already given and will give him permission to select as his assistants in this charge any citizens, male or female, whom he desires; and he will know whom he ought to choose, and will be anxious not to make a mistake, from a due sense of responsibility, and from a consciousness of the importance of his office, and also because he will consider that if young men have been and are well brought up, then all things go swimmingly, but if not, it is not meet to say, nor do we say, what will follow, lest the regarders of omens should take alarm about our infant state. Many things have been said by us about dancing and about gymnastic movements in general; for we include under gymnastics all military exercises, such as archery, and all hurling of weapons, and the use of the light shield, and all fighting with heavy arms, and military evolutions, and movements of armies, and encampings, and all that relates to horsemanship. Of all these things there ought to be public teachers, receiving pay from the state, and their pupils should be the men and boys in the state, and also the girls and women, who are to know all these things. While they are yet girls they should have practised dancing in arms and the whole art of fighting—when grown-up women, *[814]* they should apply themselves to evolutions and tactics, and the mode of grounding and taking up arms; if for no other reason, yet in case the

[1] Cf. vi. 764.

whole military force should have to leave the city and carry on operations of war outside, that those who will have to guard the young and the rest of the city may be equal to the task; and, on the other hand, when enemies, whether barbarian or Hellenic, come from without with mighty force and make a violent assault upon them, and thus compel them to fight for the possession of the city, which is far from being an impossibility, great would be the disgrace to the state, if the women had been so miserably trained that they could not fight for their young, as birds will, against any creature however strong, and die or undergo any danger, but must instantly rush to the temples and crowd at the altars and shrines, and bring upon human nature the reproach, that of all animals man is the most cowardly!

Cle. Such a want of education, Stranger, is certainly an unseemly thing to happen in a state, as well as a great misfortune.

Ath. Suppose that we carry our law to the extent of saying that women ought not to neglect military matters, but that all citizens, male and female alike, shall attend to them?

Cle. I quite agree.

Ath. Of wrestling we have spoken in part, but of what I should call the most important part we have not spoken, and cannot easily speak without showing at the same time by gesture as well as in word what we mean; when word and action combine, and not till then, we shall explain clearly what has been said, pointing out that of all movements wrestling is most akin to the military art, and is to be pursued for the sake of this, and not this for the sake of wrestling.

Cle. Excellent.

Ath. Enough of wrestling; we will now proceed to speak of other movements of the body. Such motion may be in general called dancing, and is of two kinds: one of nobler figures, imitating the honourable, the other of the more ignoble figures, imitating the mean; and of both these there are two further subdivisions. Of the serious, one kind is of those engaged in war and vehement action, and is the exercise of a noble person and a manly heart; the other exhibits a temperate soul in the enjoyment of prosperity and modest pleasures, *[815]* and may be truly called and is the dance of peace. The warrior dance is different from the peaceful one, and may be rightly termed Pyrrhic; this imitates the modes of avoiding blows and missiles by dropping or giving way, or springing aside, or rising up or falling down; also the opposite postures which are those of action, as, for example, the imitation of archery and the hurling of javelins, and of all sorts of blows. And when the imitation is of brave bodies and souls, and the action is direct and muscular, giving for the most part a straight movement to the limbs of the body—that, I say, is the true sort; but the opposite is not right. In the dance of peace what we have to consider is whether a man bears himself naturally and gracefully, and after the manner of men who duly conform to the law. But before proceeding I must distinguish the dancing about which there is any doubt, from that about which there is no doubt. Which is the doubtful kind, and how are the two to be distinguished? There are dances of the Bacchic sort, both those in which, as they say, they imitate drunken men, and which are named after the Nymphs, and Pan, and Silenuses, and Satyrs; and also those in which purifications are made or mysteries celebrated—all this sort of dancing cannot be rightly defined as having either a peaceful or a warlike character, or indeed as having any meaning whatever, and may, I think, be most truly described as distinct from the warlike dance, and distinct from the peaceful, and not suited for a city at all. There let it lie; and so leaving it to lie, we will proceed to the dances of war and peace, for with these we are undoubtedly concerned. Now the unwarlike muse, which honours in dance the Gods and the sons of the Gods, is entirely associated with the consciousness of prosperity; this class may be subdivided into two lesser classes, of which one is expressive of an escape from some labour or danger into good, and has greater pleasures, the other expressive of preservation and increase of former good, in which the pleasure is less exciting;—in all these cases, every man when the pleasure is greater, moves his body more, and less when the pleasure is less; and, again, if he be more orderly and has learned courage from discipline he moves less, [816] but if he be a coward, and has no training or self-control, he makes greater and more violent movements, and in general when he is speaking or singing he is not altogether able to keep his body still; and so out of the imitation of words in gestures the whole art of dancing has arisen. And in these various kinds of imitation one man moves in an orderly, another in a disorderly manner; and as the ancients may be observed to have given many names which are according to nature and deserving of praise, so there is an excellent one

which they have given to the dances of men who in their times of prosperity are moderate in their pleasures—the giver of names, whoever he was, assigned to them a very true, and poetical, and rational name, when he called them Emmeleiai, or dances of order, thus establishing two kinds of dances of the nobler sort, the dance of war which he called the Pyrrhic, and the dance of peace which he called Emmeleia, or the dance of order; giving to each their appropriate and becoming name.[1] These things the legislator should indicate in general outline, and the guardian of the law should enquire into them and search them out, combining dancing with music, and assigning to the several sacrificial feasts that which is suitable to them; and when he has consecrated all of them in due order, he shall for the future change nothing, whether of dance or song. Thenceforward the city and the citizens shall continue to have the same pleasures, themselves being as far as possible alike, and shall live well and happily.

I have described the dances which are appropriate to noble bodies and generous souls. But it is necessary also to consider and know uncomely persons and thoughts, and those which are intended to produce laughter in comedy, and have a comic character in respect of style, song, and dance, and of the imitations which these afford. For serious things cannot be understood without laughable things, nor opposites at all without opposites, if a man is really to have intelligence of either; but he can not carry out both in action, if he is to have any degree of virtue. And for this very reason he should learn them both, in order that he may not in ignorance do or say anything which is ridiculous and out of place—he should command slaves and hired strangers to imitate such things, but he should never take any serious interest in them himself, nor should any freeman or freewoman be discovered taking pains to learn them; and there should always be some element of novelty in the imitation. Let these then be laid down, both in law and in our discourse, as the regulations of laughable amusements which are generally called [817] comedy. And, if any of the serious poets, as they are termed, who write tragedy, come to us and say —"O strangers, may we go to your city and country or may we not, and shall we bring with us our poetry—what is your will about these matters?"—how shall we answer the divine men? I think that our answer should be as fol-

[1] Cf. *Cratylus*, 388, ff.

lows:[1]—Best of strangers, we will say to them, we also according to our ability are tragic poets, and our tragedy is the best and noblest; for our whole state is an imitation of the best and noblest life, which we affirm to be indeed the very truth of tragedy. You are poets and we are poets, both makers of the same strains, rivals and antagonists in the noblest of dramas, which true law can alone perfect, as our hope is. Do not then suppose that we shall all in a moment allow you to erect your stage in the agora, or introduce the fair voices of your actors, speaking above our own, and permit you to harangue our women and children, and the common people, about our institutions, in language other than our own, and very often the opposite of our own. For a state would be mad which gave you this licence, until the magistrates had determined whether your poetry might be recited, and was fit for publication or not. Wherefore, O ye sons and scions of the softer Muses, first of all show your songs to the magistrates, and let them compare them with our own, and if they are the same or better we will give you a chorus; but if not, then, my friends, we cannot. Let these, then, be the customs ordained by law about all dances and the teaching of them, and let matters relating to slaves be separated from those relating to masters, if you do not object.

Cle. We can have no hesitation in assenting when you put the matter thus.

Ath. There still remain three studies suitable for freemen. Arithmetic is one of them; the measurement of length, surface, and depth is the second; and the third has to do with the revolutions of the stars in relation to one another. [818] Not every one has need to toil through all these things in a strictly scientific manner, but only a few, and who they are to be we will hereafter indicate at the end, which will be the proper place;[2] not to know what is necessary for mankind in general, and what is the truth, is disgraceful to every one: and yet to enter into these matters minutely is neither easy, nor at all possible for every one; but there is something in them which is necessary and cannot be set aside, and probably he who made the proverb about God originally had this in view when he said, that "not even God himself can fight against necessity";—he meant, if I am not mistaken, divine necessity; for as to the human necessities of which the many speak, when they talk in this manner, nothing can be

more ridiculous than such an application of the words.

Cle. And what necessities of knowledge are there, Stranger, which are divine and not human?

Ath. I conceive them to be those of which he who has no use nor any knowledge at all cannot be a God, or demi-god, or hero to mankind, or able to take any serious thought or charge of them. And very unlike a divine man would he be, who is unable to count one, two, three, or to distinguish odd and even numbers,[3] or is unable to count at all, or reckon night and day, and who is totally unacquainted with the revolution of the sun and moon, and the other stars. There would be great folly in supposing that all these are not necessary parts of knowledge to him who intends to know anything about the highest kinds of knowledge;[4] but which these are, and how many there are of them, and when they are to be learned, and what is to be learned together and what apart, and the whole correlation of them, must be rightly apprehended first; and these leading the way we may proceed to the other parts of knowledge. For so necessity grounded in nature constrains us, against which we say that no God contends, or ever will contend.

Cle. I think, Stranger, that what you have now said is very true and agreeable to nature.

Ath. Yes, Cleinias, that is so. But it is difficult for the legislator to begin with these studies; at a more convenient time we will make regulations for them.

Cle. You seem, Stranger, to be afraid of our habitual ignorance of the subject: [819] there is no reason why that should prevent you from speaking out.

Ath. I certainly am afraid of the difficulties to which you allude, but I am still more afraid of those who apply themselves to this sort of knowledge, and apply themselves badly. For entire ignorance is not so terrible or extreme an evil, and is far from being the greatest of all; too much cleverness and too much learning, accompanied with an ill bringing up, are far more fatal.[5]

Cle. True.

Ath. All freemen, I conceive, should learn as much of these branches of knowledge as every child in Egypt is taught when he learns the alphabet. In that country arithmetical games have been invented for the use of mere chil-

---

[1] Cf. *Republic,* iii. 398; x. 607.
[2] Cf. xii. 967.

[3] Cf. *Republic,* vii. 522.
[4] Cf. *ibid.,* 523, 524, 525, ff.
[5] Cf. *ibid.,* 519.

dren, which they learn as a pleasure and amusement. They have to distribute apples and garlands, using the same number sometimes for a larger and sometimes for a lesser number of persons; and they arrange pugilists and wrestlers as they pair together by lot or remain over, and show how their turns come in natural order. Another mode of amusing them is to distribute vessels, sometimes of gold, brass, silver, and the like, intermixed with one another, sometimes of one metal only; as I was saying they adapt to their amusement the numbers in common use, and in this way make more intelligible to their pupils the arrangements and movements of armies and expeditions, and in the management of a household they make people more useful to themselves, and more wide awake; and again in measurements of things which have length, and breadth, and depth, they free us from that natural ignorance of all these things which is so ludicrous and disgraceful.[1]

Cle. What kind of ignorance do you mean?

Ath. O my dear Cleinias, I, like yourself, have late in life heard with amazement of our ignorance in these matters; to me we appear to be more like pigs than men, and I am quite ashamed, not only of myself, but of all Hellenes.

Cle. About what? Say, Stranger, what you mean.

Ath. I will; or rather I will show you my meaning by a question, and do you please to answer me: You know, I suppose, what length is?

Cle. Certainly.

Ath. And what breadth is?

Cle. To be sure.

Ath. And you know that these are two distinct things, and that there is a third thing called depth?

Cle. Of course.

Ath. And do not all these seem to you to be commensurable with themselves?

Cle. Yes.

Ath. That is to say, length is naturally commensurable with length, [*820*] and breadth with breadth, and depth in like manner with depth?

Cle. Undoubtedly.

Ath. But if some things are commensurable and others wholly incommensurable, and you think that all things are commensurable, what is your position in regard to them?

Cle. Clearly, far from good.

[1] Cf. *ibid.,* 528.

Ath. Concerning length and breadth when compared with depth, or breadth and length when compared with one another, are not all the Hellenes agreed that these are commensurable with one another in some way?

Cle. Quite true.

Ath. But if they are absolutely incommensurable, and yet all of us regard them as commensurable, have we not reason to be ashamed of our compatriots; and might we not say to them: —O ye best of Hellenes, is not this one of the things of which we were saying that not to know them is disgraceful, and of which to have a bare knowledge only is no great distinction?

Cle. Certainly.

Ath. And there are other things akin to these, in which there spring up other errors of the same family.

Cle. What are they?

Ath. The natures of commensurable and incommensurable quantities in their relation to one another. A man who is good for anything ought to be able, when he thinks, to distinguish them; and different persons should compete with one another in asking questions, which will be a far better and more graceful way of passing their time than the old man's game of draughts.

Cle. I dare say; and these pastimes are not so very unlike a game of draughts.

Ath. And these, as I maintain, Cleinias, are the studies which our youth ought to learn, for they are innocent and not difficult; the learning of them will be an amusement, and they will benefit the state. If any one is of another mind, let him say what he has to say.

Cle. Certainly.

Ath. Then if these studies are such as we maintain, we will include them; if not, they shall be excluded.

Cle. Assuredly: but may we not now, Stranger, prescribe these studies as necessary, and so fill up the lacunae of our laws?

Ath. They shall be regarded as pledges which may be hereafter redeemed and removed from our state, if they do not please either us who give them, or you who accept them.

Cle. A fair condition.

Ath. Next let us see whether we are or are not willing that the study of astronomy shall be proposed for our youth.[2]

Cle. Proceed.

Ath. Here occurs a strange phenomenon, which certainly cannot in any point of view be tolerated.

[2] Cf. *ibid.,* vii. 527, ff.

[821] Cle. To what are you referring?

Ath. Men say that we ought not to enquire into the supreme God and the nature of the universe, nor busy ourselves in searching out the causes of things, and that such enquiries are impious; whereas the very opposite is the truth.

Cle. What do you mean?

Ath. Perhaps what I am saying may seem paradoxical, and at variance with the usual language of age. But when any one has any good and true notion which is for the advantage of the state and in every way acceptable to God, he cannot abstain from expressing it.

Cle. Your words are reasonable enough; but shall we find any good or true notion about the stars?

Ath. My good friends, at this hour all of us Hellenes tell lies, if I may use such an expression, about those great Gods, the Sun and the Moon.

Cle. Lies of what nature?

Ath. We say that they and divers other stars do not keep the same path, and we call them planets or wanderers.

Cle. Very true, Stranger; and in the course of my life I have often myself seen the morning star and the evening star and divers others not moving in their accustomed course, but wandering out of their path in all manner of ways, and I have seen the sun and moon doing what we all know that they do.

Ath. Just so, Megillus and Cleinias; and I maintain that our citizens and our youth ought to learn about the nature of the Gods in heaven, so far as to be able to offer sacrifices and pray to them in pious language, and not to blaspheme about them.

Cle. There you are right, if such a knowledge be only attainable; and if we are wrong in our mode of speaking now, and can be better instructed and learn to use better language, then I quite agree with you that such a degree of knowledge as will enable us to speak rightly should be acquired by us. And now do you try to explain to us your whole meaning, and we, on our part, will endeavour to understand you.

Ath. There is some difficulty in understanding my meaning, but not a very great one, nor will any great length of time be required. And of this I am myself a proof; for I did not know these things long ago, nor in the days of my youth, and yet I can explain them to you in a brief space of time; whereas if they had been difficult I could certainly never have explained them all, old as I am, to old men like yourselves.

Cle. True; but what is this study which you describe as wonderful and fitting for youth to learn, *[822]* but of which we are ignorant? Try and explain the nature of it to us as clearly as you can.

Ath. I will. For, O my good friends, that other doctrine about the wandering of the sun and the moon and the other stars is not the truth, but the very reverse of the truth. Each of them moves in the same path—not in many paths, but in one only, which is circular, and the varieties are only apparent. Nor are we right in supposing that the swiftest of them is the slowest, nor conversely, that the slowest is the quickest. And if what I say is true, only just imagine that we had a similar notion about horses running at Olympia, or about men who ran in the long course, and that we addressed the swiftest as the slowest and the slowest as the swiftest, and sang the praises of the vanquished as though he were the victor,—in that case our praises would not be true, nor very agreeable to the runners, though they be but men; and now, to commit the same error about the Gods which would have been ludicrous and erroneous in the case of men—is not that ludicrous and erroneous?

Cle. Worse than ludicrous, I should say.

Ath. At all events, the Gods cannot like us to be spreading a false report of them.

Cle. Most true, if such is the fact.

Ath. And if we can show that such is really the fact, then all these matters ought to be learned so far as is necessary for the avoidance of impiety; but if we cannot, they may be let alone, and let this be our decision.

Cle. Very good.

Ath. Enough of laws relating to education and learning. But hunting and similar pursuits in like manner claim our attention. For the legislator appears to have a duty imposed upon him which goes beyond mere legislation. There is something over and above law which lies in a region between admonition and law, and has several times occurred to us in the course of discussion; for example, in the education of very young children there were things, as we maintain, which are not to be defined, and to regard them as matters of positive law is a great absurdity. Now, our laws and the whole constitution of our state having been thus delineated, the praise of the virtuous citizen is not complete when he is described as the person who serves the laws best and obeys them most, but the higher form of praise is that which describes him as the good *[823]* citizen who passes through life undefiled and is obedient to the words of the legislator, both when he is giving laws and when he assigns praise and blame. This is the truest word that can be spoken in praise of a citizen; and the true legislator ought not only to write his laws, but also to interweave with them all such things as seem to him honourable and dishonourable. And the perfect citizen ought to seek to strengthen these no less than the principles of law which are sanctioned by punishments. I will adduce an example which will clear up my meaning, and will be a sort of witness to my words. Hunting is of wide extent, and has a name under which many things are included, for there is a hunting of creatures in the water, and of creatures in the air, and there is a great deal of hunting of land animals of all kinds, and not of wild beasts only. The hunting after man is also worthy of consideration; there is the hunting after him in war, and there is often a hunting after him in the way of friendship, which is praised and also blamed; and there is thieving, and the hunting which is practised by robbers, and that of armies against armies. Now the legislator, in laying down laws about hunting, can neither abstain from noting these things, nor can he make threatening ordinances which will assign rules and penalties about all of them. What is he to do? He will have to praise and blame hunting with a view to the exercise and pursuits of youth. And, on the other hand, the young man must listen obediently; neither pleasure nor pain should hinder him, and he should regard as his standard of action the praises and injunctions of the legislator rather than the punishments which he imposes by law. This being premised, there will follow next in order moderate praise and censure of hunting; the praise being assigned to that kind which will make the souls of young men better, and the censure to that which has the opposite effect.

And now let us address young men in the form of a prayer for their welfare: O friends, we will say to them, may no desire or love of hunting in the sea, or of angling or of catching the creatures in the waters, ever take possession of you, either when you are awake or when you are asleep, by hook or with weels, which latter is a very lazy contrivance; and let not any desire of catching men and of piracy by sea enter into your souls and make you cruel and lawless hunters. And as to the desire of thieving in town or country, may it never enter into your most passing thoughts; nor let the insidi-

ous fancy of catching birds, which is hardly worthy of freemen, come into the head of any youth. *[824]* There remains therefore for our athletes only the hunting and catching of land animals, of which the one sort is called hunting by night, in which the hunters sleep in turn and are lazy; this is not to be commended any more than that which has intervals of rest, in which the wild strength of beasts is subdued by nets and snares, and not by the victory of a laborious spirit. Thus, only the best kind of hunting is allowed at all—that of quadrupeds, which is carried on with horses and dogs and men's own persons, and they get the victory over the animals by running them down and striking them and hurling at them, those who have a care of godlike manhood taking them with their own hands. The praise and blame which is assigned to all these things has now been declared; and let the law be as follows:— Let no one hinder these who verily are sacred hunters from following the chase wherever and whithersoever they will; but the hunter by night, who trusts to his nets and gins, shall not be allowed to hunt anywhere. The fowler in the mountains and waste places shall be permitted, but on cultivated ground and on consecrated wilds he shall not be permitted; and any one who meets him may stop him. As to the hunter in waters, he may hunt anywhere except in harbours or sacred streams or marshes or pools, provided only that he do not pollute the water with poisonous juices. And now we may say that all our enactments about education are complete.

Cle. Very good.

BOOK VIII

[828] Athenian Stranger. NEXT, with the help of the Delphian oracle, we have to institute festivals and make laws about them, and to determine what sacrifices will be for the good of the city, and to what Gods they shall be offered; but when they shall be offered, and how often, may be partly regulated by us.

Cleinias. The number—yes.

Ath. Then we will first determine the number; and let the whole number be 365—one for every day—so that one magistrate at least will sacrifice daily to some God or demi-god on behalf of the city, and the citizens, and their possessions. And the interpreters, and priests, and priestesses, and prophets shall meet, and, in company with the guardians of the law, ordain those things which the legislator of necessity omits; and I may remark that they are the very persons who ought to take note of what is omitted.[1] The law will say that there are twelve feasts dedicated to the twelve Gods, after whom the several tribes are named; and that to each of them they shall sacrifice every month, and appoint choruses, and musical and gymnastic contests, assigning them so as to suit the Gods and seasons of the year. And they shall have festivals for women, distinguishing those which ought to be separated from the men's festivals, and those which ought not. Further, they shall not confuse the infernal deities and their rites with the Gods who are termed heavenly and their rites, but shall separate them, giving to Pluto his own in the twelfth month, which is sacred to him, according to the law. To such a deity warlike men should entertain no aversion, but they should honour him as being always the best friend of man.[2] For the connection of soul and body is no way better than the dissolution of them, as I am ready to maintain quite seriously. Moreover, those who would regulate these matters rightly should consider, that our city among existing cities has no fellow, either in respect of leisure or command of the necessaries of life, and that like an individual she ought to live happily. [829] And those who would live happily should in the first place do no wrong to one another, and ought not themselves to be wronged by others; to attain the first is not difficult, but there is great difficulty in acquiring the power of not being wronged. No man can be perfectly secure against wrong, unless he has become perfectly good; and cities are like individuals in this, for a city if good has a life of peace, but if evil, a life of war within and without. Wherefore the citizens ought to practise war—not in time of war, but rather while they are at peace. And every city which has any sense, should take the field at least for one day in every month, and for more if the magistrates think fit, having no regard to winter cold or summer heat; and they should go out *en masse,* including their wives and their children, when the magistrates determine to lead forth the whole people, or in separate portions when summoned by them; and they should always provide that there should be games and sacrificial feasts, and they should have tournaments, imitating in as lively a manner as they can real battles. And they should distribute prizes of victory and valour to the competitors, passing censures and encomiums on one another according to the characters which they bear in the contests and in their whole life, honouring him who seems to be the best, and blaming him who is the opposite. And let poets celebrate the victors—not however every poet, but only one who in the first place is not less than fifty years of age; nor should he be one who, although he may have musical and poetical gifts, has never in his life done any noble or illustrious action; but those who are themselves good and also honourable in the state, creators of noble actions—let their poems be sung, even though they be not very musical. And let the judgment of them rest with the instructor of youth and the other guardians of the laws, who shall give them this privilege, and they alone shall be free to sing; but the rest of the world shall not have this liberty. Nor shall any one dare to sing a song which has not been approved by the judgment of the guardians of the laws, not even if his strain be sweeter than the songs of Thamyras and Orpheus; but only such poems as have been judged sacred and dedicated to the Gods, and such as are the works of good men, in which praise or blame has been awarded and which have been deemed to fulfil their design fairly.

The regulations about war, and about liberty of speech in poetry, ought to apply equally to men and women. The legislator may be supposed to argue the question in his own mind: —Who are my citizens for whom I have set in order the city? [830] Are they not competitors in the greatest of all contests,[3] and have they not innumerable rivals? To be sure, will be the natural reply. Well, but if we were training boxers, or pancratiasts, or any other sort of athletes, would they never meet until the hour of contest arrived; and should we do nothing to prepare ourselves previously by daily practice? Surely, if we were boxers, we should have been learning to fight for many days before, and exercising ourselves in imitating all those blows and wards which we were intending to use in the hour of conflict; and in order that we might come as near to reality as possible, instead of cestuses we should put on boxing gloves, that the blows and the wards might be practised by us to the utmost of our power. And if there were a lack of competitors, the ridicule of fools would not deter us from hanging up a lifeless image and practising at that. Or if we had no adversary at all, animate or inanimate, should we not venture in the dearth of antagonists to spar by ourselves? In what other manner could

[1] Cf. vi. 770, and *Republic,* v. 458.
[2] Cf. *Cratylus,* 403; *Republic,* iii. 386.

[3] Cf. *Republic,* iii. 403.

we ever study the art of self-defence?

Cle. The way which you mention, Stranger, would be the only way.

Ath. And shall the warriors of our city, who are destined when occasion calls to enter the greatest of all contests, and to fight for their lives, and their children, and their property, and the whole city, be worse prepared than boxers? And will the legislator, because he is afraid that their practising with one another may appear to some ridiculous, abstain from commanding them to go out and fight; will he not ordain that soldiers shall perform lesser exercises without arms every day, making dancing and all gymnastic tend to this end; and also will he not require that they shall practise some gymnastic exercises, greater as well as lesser, as often as every month; and that they shall have contests one with another in every part of the country, seizing upon posts and lying in ambush, and imitating in every respect the reality of war; fighting with boxing-gloves and hurling javelins, and using weapons somewhat dangerous, and as nearly as possible like the true ones, in order that the sport may not be altogether without fear, but may have terrors and to a certain degree show the man who has and who has not courage; *[831]* and that the honour and dishonour which are assigned to them respectively, may prepare the whole city for the true conflict of life? If any one dies in these mimic contests, the homicide is involuntary, and we will make the slayer, when he has been purified according to law, to be pure of blood, considering that if a few men should die, others as good as they will be born; but that if fear is dead, then the citizens will never find a test of superior and inferior natures, which is a far greater evil to the state than the loss of a few.

Cle. We are quite agreed, Stranger, that we should legislate about such things, and that the whole state should practise them.

Ath. And what is the reason that dances and contests of this sort hardly ever exist in states, at least not to any extent worth speaking of? Is this due to the ignorance of mankind and their legislators?

Cle. Perhaps.

Ath. Certainly not, sweet Cleinias; there are two causes, which are quite enough to account for the deficiency.

Cle. What are they?

Ath. One cause is the love of wealth, which wholly absorbs men, and never for a moment allows them to think of anything but their own private possesions; on this the soul of every citizen hangs suspended, and can attend to nothing but his daily gain; mankind are ready to learn any branch of knowledge, and to follow any pursuit which tends to this end, and they laugh at every other:—that is one reason why a city will not be in earnest about such contests or any other good and honourable pursuit. But from an insatiable love of gold and silver, every man will stoop to any art or contrivance, seemly or unseemly, in the hope of becoming rich; and will make no objection to performing any action, holy, or unholy and utterly base, if only like a beast he have the power of eating and drinking all kinds of things, and procuring for himself in every sort of way the gratification of his lusts.

Cle. True.

Ath. Let this, then, be deemed one of the causes which prevent states from pursuing in an efficient manner the art of war, or any other noble aim, but makes the orderly and temperate part of mankind into merchants, and captains of ships, and servants, and converts the valiant sort into thieves and burglars, and robbers of temples, *[832]* and violent, tyrannical persons; many of whom are not without ability, but they are unfortunate.[1]

Cle. What do you mean?

Ath. Must not they be truly unfortunate whose souls are compelled to pass through life always hungering?

Cle. Then that is one cause, Stranger; but you spoke of another.

Ath. Thank you for reminding me.

Cle. The insatiable lifelong love of wealth, as you were saying, is one cause which absorbs mankind, and prevents them from rightly practising the arts of war:—Granted; and now tell me, what is the other?

Ath. Do you imagine that I delay because I am in a perplexity?

Cle. No; but we think that you are too severe upon the money-loving temper, of which you seem in the present discussion to have a peculiar dislike.

Ath. That is a very fair rebuke, Cleinias; and I will now proceed to the second cause.

Cle. Proceed.

Ath. I say that governments are a cause—democracy, oligarchy, tyranny, concerning which I have often spoken in the previous discourse;[2] or rather governments they are not, for none of them exercises a voluntary rule over voluntary subjects; but they may be truly called

[1] Cf. *Republic,* vi. 491, 495.
[2] Cf. iv. 712, 715.

states of discord, in which while the government is voluntary, the subjects always obey against their will, and have to be coerced; and the ruler fears the subject, and will not, if he can help, allow him to become either noble, or rich, or strong, or valiant, or warlike at all.[1] These two are the chief causes of almost all evils, and of the evils of which I have been speaking they are notably the causes. But our state has escaped both of them; for her citizens have the greatest leisure, and they are not subject to one another, and will, I think, be made by these laws the reverse of lovers of money. Such a constitution may be reasonably supposed to be the only one existing which will accept the education which we have described, and the martial pastimes which have been perfected according to our idea.

Cle. True.

Ath. Then next we must remember, about all gymnastic contests, that only the warlike sort of them are to be practised and to have prizes of victory; and those which are not military are to be given up. The military sort had better be completely described and established by law; and first, let us speak of running and swiftness.

Cle. Very good.

Ath. Certainly the most military of all qualities is general activity of body, whether of foot or hand. For escaping or for capturing an enemy, *[833]* quickness of foot is required; but hand-to-hand conflict and combat need vigour and strength.

Cle. Very true.

Ath. Neither of them can attain their greatest efficiency without arms.

Cle. How can they?

Ath. Then our herald, in accordance with the prevailing practice, will first summon the runner;—he will appear armed, for to an unarmed competitor we will not give a prize. And he shall enter first who is to run the single course bearing arms; next, he who is to run the double course; third, he who is to run the horse-course; and fourthly, he who is to run the long course; the fifth whom we start, shall be the first sent forth in heavy armour, and shall run a course of sixty stadia to some temple of Ares—and we will send forth another, whom we will style the more heavily armed, to run over smoother ground. There remains the archer; and he shall run in the full equipments of an archer a distance of 100 stadia over mountains, and across every sort of country, to a temple of Apollo

[1] Cf. Aristotle, *Politics*, v. 11, 1313 ͣ 38; 1314 ͣ

and Artemis; this shall be the order of the contest, and we will wait for them until they return, and will give a prize to the conqueror in each.

Cle. Very good.

Ath. Let us suppose that there are three kinds of contests—one of boys, another of beardless youths, and a third of men. For the youths we will fix the length of the contest at two-thirds, and for the boys at half of the entire course, whether they contend as archers or as heavy-armed. Touching the women, let the girls who are not grown up compete naked in the stadium and the double course, and the horse-course and the long course, and let them run on the race-ground itself; those who are thirteen years of age and upwards until their marriage shall continue to share in contests if they are not more than twenty, and shall be compelled to run up to eighteen; and they shall descend into the arena in suitable dresses. Let these be the regulations about contests in running both for men and women.

Respecting contests of strength, instead of wrestling and similar contests of the heavier sort, we will institute conflicts in armour of one against one, and two against two, and so on up to ten against ten. As to what a man ought not to suffer or do, and to what extent, in order to gain the victory—as in wrestling, the masters of the art have laid down what is fair and what is not fair, so in fighting in armour—we ought to call in skilful persons, who shall judge for us and be our assessors in the work of legislation; they shall say who deserves to be victor in combats of this sort, and what he is not to do or have done to him, and in like manner what rule determines who is defeated; *[834]* and let these ordinances apply to women until they are married as well as to men. The pancration shall have a counterpart in a combat of the light-armed; they shall contend with bows and with light shields and with javelins and in the throwing of stones by slings and by hand: and laws shall be made about it, and rewards and prizes given to him who best fulfils the ordinances of the law.

Next in order we shall have to legislate about the horse contests. Now we do not need many horses, for they cannot be of much use in a country like Crete,[2] and hence we naturally do not take great pains about the rearing of them or about horse races. There is no one who keeps a chariot among us, and any rivalry in such matters would be altogether out of place; there

[2] Cf. i. 625.

would be no sense nor any shadow of sense in instituting contests which are not after the manner of our country. And therefore we give our prizes for single horses—for colts who have not yet cast their teeth, and for those who are intermediate, and for the full-grown horses themselves; and thus our equestrian games will accord with the nature of the country. Let them have conflict and rivalry in these matters in accordance with the law, and let the colonels and generals of horse decide together about all courses and about the armed competitors in them. But we have nothing to say to the unarmed either in gymnastic exercises or in these contests. On the other hand, the Cretan bowman or javelin-man who fights in armour on horseback is useful, and therefore we may as well place a competition of this sort among our amusements. Women are not to be forced to compete by laws and ordinances; but if from previous training they have acquired the habit and are strong enough and like to take part, let them do so, girls as well as boys, and no blame to them.

Thus the competition in gymnastic and the mode of learning it have been described; and we have spoken also of the toils of the contest, and of daily exercises under the superintendence of masters. Likewise, what relates to music has been, for the most part, completed. But as to rhapsodes and the like, and the contests of choruses which are to perform at feasts, all this shall be arranged when the months and days and years have been appointed for Gods and demi-gods, whether every third year, or again every fifth year, or in whatever way or manner the Gods may put into men's minds *[835]* the distribution and order of them. At the same time, we may expect that the musical contests will be celebrated in their turn by the command of the judges and the director of education and the guardians of the law meeting together for this purpose, and themselves becoming legislators of the times and nature and conditions of the choral contests and of dancing in general. What they ought severally to be in language and song, and in the admixture of harmony with rhythm and the dance, has been often declared by the original legislator; and his successors ought to follow him, making the games and sacrifices duly to correspond at fitting times, and appointing public festivals. It is not difficult to determine how these and the like matters may have a regular order; nor, again, will the alteration of them do any great good or harm to the state. There is, however, another

matter of great importance and difficulty, concerning which God should legislate, if there were any possibility of obtaining from him an ordinance about it. But seeing that divine aid is not to be had, there appears to be a need of some bold man who specially honours plainness of speech, and will say outright what he thinks best for the city and citizens—ordaining what is good and convenient for the whole state amid the corruptions of human souls, opposing the mightiest lusts, and having no man his helper but himself standing alone and following reason only.

Cle. What is this, Stranger, that you are saying? For we do not as yet understand your meaning.

Ath. Very likely; I will endeavour to explain myself more clearly. When I came to the subject of education, I beheld young men and maidens holding friendly intercourse with one another. And there naturally arose in my mind a sort of apprehension—I could not help thinking how one is to deal with a city in which youths and maidens are well nurtured, and have nothing to do, and are not undergoing the excessive and servile toils which extinguish wantonness, and whose only cares during their whole life are sacrifices and festivals and dances. How, in such a state as this, will they abstain from desires which thrust many a man and woman into perdition; and from which reason, *[836]* assuming the functions of law, commands them to abstain? The ordinances already made may possibly get the better of most of these desires; the prohibition of excessive wealth is a very considerable gain in the direction of temperance, and the whole education of our youth imposes a law of moderation on them; moreover, the eye of the rulers is required always to watch over the young, and never to lose sight of them; and these provisions do, as far as human means can effect anything, exercise a regulating influence upon the desires in general. But how can we take precautions against the unnatural loves of either sex, from which innumerable evils have come upon individuals and cities? How shall we devise a remedy and way of escape out of so great a danger? Truly, Cleinias, here is a difficulty. In many ways Crete and Lacedaemon furnish a great help to those who make peculiar laws; but in the matter of love, as we are alone, I must confess that they are quite against us. For if any one following nature should lay down the law which existed before the days of Laius, and denounce these lusts as contrary to nature, adducing the animals as a proof that such unions were monstrous, he might prove his point, but he would be wholly at variance with the custom of your states. Further, they are repugnant to a principle which we say that a legislator should always observe; for we are always enquiring which of our enactments tends to virtue and which not.[1] And suppose we grant that these loves are accounted by law to be honourable, or at least not disgraceful, in what degree will they contribute to virtue? Will such passions implant in the soul of him who is seduced the habit of courage, or in the soul of the seducer the principle of temperance? Who will ever believe this?—or rather, who will not blame the effeminacy of him who yields to pleasures and is unable to hold out against them? Will not all men censure as womanly him who imitates the woman? And who would ever think of establishing such a practice by law? Certainly no one who had in his mind the image of true law. How can we prove that what I am saying is true? *[837]* He who would rightly consider these matters must see the nature of friendship and desire, and of these so-called loves, for they are of two kinds, and out of the two arises a third kind, having the same name; and this similarity of name causes all the difficulty and obscurity.

Cle. How is that?

Ath. Dear is the like in virtue to the like, and the equal to the equal; dear also, though unlike, is he who has abundance to him who is in want. And when either of these friendships becomes excessive, we term the excess love.

Cle. Very true.

Ath. The friendship which arises from contraries is horrible and coarse, and has often no tie of communion; but that which arises from likeness is gentle, and has a tie of communion which lasts through life. As to the mixed sort which is made up of them both, there is, first of all, a difficulty in determining what he who is possessed by this third love desires; moreover, he is drawn different ways, and is in doubt between the two principles; the one exhorting him to enjoy the beauty of youth, and the other forbidding him. For the one is a lover of the body, and hungers after beauty, like ripe fruit, and would fain satisfy himself without any regard to the character of the beloved; the other holds the desire of the body to be a secondary matter, and looking rather than loving and with his soul desiring the soul of the other in a becoming manner, regards the satisfaction of

[1] Cf. iii. 693; iv 705; vi. 770; xii. 963.

the bodily love as wantonness;[2] he reverences and respects temperance and courage and magnanimity and wisdom, and wishes to live chastely with the chaste object of his affection. Now the sort of love which is made up of the other two is that which we have described as the third. Seeing then that there are these three sorts of love, ought the law to prohibit and forbid them all to exist among us? Is it not rather clear that we should wish to have in the state the love which is of virtue and which desires the beloved youth to be the best possible; and the other two, if possible, we should hinder? What do you say, friend Megillus?

Megillus. I think, Stranger, that you are perfectly right in what you have been now saying.

Ath. I knew well, my friend, that I should obtain your assent, which I accept, and therefore have no need to analyse your custom any further. Cleinias shall be prevailed upon to give me his assent at some other time. Enough of this; and now let us proceed to the laws.

[838] Meg. Very good.

Ath. Upon reflection I see a way of imposing the law, which, in one respect, is easy, but, in another, is of the utmost difficulty.

Meg. What do you mean?

Ath. We are all aware that most men, in spite of their lawless natures, are very strictly and precisely restrained from intercourse with the fair, and this is not at all against their will, but entirely with their will.

Meg. When do you mean?

Ath. When any one has a brother or sister who is fair; and about a son or daughter the same unwritten law holds, and is a most perfect safeguard, so that no open or secret connection ever takes place between them. Nor does the thought of such a thing ever enter at all into the minds of most of them.

Meg. Very true.

Ath. Does not a little word extinguish all pleasures of that sort?

Meg. What word?

Ath. The declaration that they are unholy, hated of God, and most infamous; and is not the reason of this that no one has ever said the opposite, but every one from his earliest childhood has heard men speaking in the same manner about them always and everywhere, whether in comedy or in the graver language of tragedy? When the poet introduces on the stage a Thyestes or an Oedipus, or a Macareus having secret intercourse with his sister, he represents him, when found out, ready to kill himself as

[2] Cf. *Phaedrus,* 251.

the penalty of his sin.

Meg. You are very right in saying that tradition, if no breath of opposition ever assails it, has a marvellous power.

Ath. Am I not also right in saying that the legislator who wants to master any of the passions which master man may easily know how to subdue them? He will consecrate the tradition of their evil character among all, slaves and freemen, women and children, throughout the city:—that will be the surest foundation of the law which he can make.

Meg. Yes; but will he ever succeed in making all mankind use the same language about them?

Ath. A good objection; but was I not just now saying that I had a way to make men use natural love and abstain from unnatural, not intentionally destroying the seeds of human increase, *[839]* or sowing them in stony places, in which they will take no root; and that I would command them to abstain too from any female field of increase in which that which is sown is not likely to grow? Now if a law to this effect could only be made perpetual, and gain an authority such as already prevents intercourse of parents and children—such a law, extending to other sensual desires, and conquering them, would be the source of ten thousand blessings. For, in the first place, moderation is the appointment of nature, and deters men from all frenzy and madness of love, and from all adulteries and immoderate use of meats and drinks, and makes them good friends to their own wives. And innumerable other benefits would result if such a law could only be enforced. I can imagine some lusty youth who is standing by, and who, on hearing this enactment, declares in scurrilous terms that we are making foolish and impossible laws, and fills the world with his outcry. And therefore I said that I knew a way of enacting and perpetuating such a law, which was very easy in one respect, but in another most difficult. There is no difficulty in seeing that such a law is possible, and in what way; for, as I was saying, the ordinance once consecrated would master the soul of every man, and terrify him into obedience. But matters have now come to such a pass that even then the desired result seems as if it could not be attained, just as the continuance of an entire state in the practice of common meals is also deemed impossible. And although this latter is partly disproven by the fact of their existence among you, still even in your cities the common meals of women would be regarded as unnatural and impossible. I was thinking of the rebelliousness of the human heart when I said that the permanent establishment of these things is very difficult.

Meg. Very true.

Ath. Shall I try and find some sort of persuasive argument which will prove to you that such enactments are possible, and not beyond human nature?

Cle. By all means.

Ath. Is a man more likely to abstain from the pleasures of love and to do what he is bidden about them, when his body is in a good condition, or when he is in an ill condition, and out of training?

Cle. He will be far more temperate when he is in training.

Ath. And have we not heard of Iccus of Tarentum, who, with a view to the Olympic and other contests, *[840]* in his zeal for his art, and also because he was of a manly and temperate disposition, never had any connection with a woman or a youth during the whole time of his training? And the same is said of Crison and Astylus and Diopompus and many others; and yet, Cleinias, they were far worse educated in their minds than your and my citizens, and in their bodies far more lusty.

Cle. No doubt this fact has been often affirmed positively by the ancients of these athletes.

Ath. And had they the courage to abstain from what is ordinarily deemed a pleasure for the sake of a victory in wrestling, running, and the like; and shall our young men be incapable of a similar endurance for the sake of a much nobler victory, which is the noblest of all, as from their youth upwards we will tell them, charming them, as we hope, into the belief of this by tales and sayings and songs?

Cle. Of what victory are you speaking?

Ath. Of the victory over pleasure, which if they win, they will live happily; or if they are conquered, the reverse of happily. And, further, may we not suppose that the fear of impiety will enable them to master that which other inferior people have mastered?

Cle. I dare say.

Ath. And since we have reached this point in our legislation, and have fallen into a difficulty by reason of the vices of mankind, I affirm that our ordinance should simply run in the following terms: Our citizens ought not to fall below the nature of birds and beasts in general, who are born in great multitudes, and yet remain until the age for procreation virgin and unmarried, but when they have reached the proper time of life are coupled, male and female, and lovingly pair together, and live the rest of their lives in holiness and innocence, abiding firmly in their original compact:— surely, we will say to them, you should be better than the animals. But if they are corrupted by the other Hellenes and the common practice of barbarians, and they see with their eyes and hear with their ears of the so-called free love everywhere prevailing among them, and they themselves are not able to get the better of the temptation, the guardians of the law, exercising the functions of lawgivers, shall devise a second law against them.

[841] Cle. And what law would you advise them to pass if this one failed?

Ath. Clearly, Cleinias, the one which would naturally follow.

Cle. What is that?

Ath. Our citizens should not allow pleasures to strengthen with indulgence, but should by toil divert the aliment and exuberance of them into other parts of the body; and this will happen if no immodesty be allowed in the practice of love. Then they will be ashamed of frequent intercourse, and they will find pleasure, if seldom enjoyed, to be a less imperious mistress. They should not be found out doing anything of the sort. Concealment shall be honourable, and sanctioned by custom and made law by unwritten prescription; on the other hand, to be detected shall be esteemed dishonourable, but not, to abstain wholly. In this way there will be a second legal standard of honourable and dishonourable, involving a second notion of right. Three principles will comprehend all those corrupt natures whom we call inferior to themselves, and who form but one class, and will compel them not to transgress.

Cle. What are they?

Ath. The principle of piety, the love of honour, and the desire of beauty, not in the body but in the soul. These are, perhaps, romantic aspirations; but they are the noblest of aspirations, if they could only be realized in all states, and, God willing, in the matter of love we may be able to enforce one of two things—either that no one shall venture to touch any person of the freeborn or noble class except his wedded wife, or sow the unconsecrated and bastard seed among harlots, or in barren and unnatural lusts; or at least we may abolish altogether the connection of men with men; and as to women, if any man has to do with any but those who come into his house duly married by sacred

rites, whether they be bought or acquired in any other way, and he offends publicly in the face of all mankind, we shall be right in enacting that he be deprived of civic honours and privileges, and be deemed to be, as he truly is, a stranger. Let this law, then, whether it is one, or ought rather to be called two, be laid down respecting love in general, and the intercourse of the sexes which arises out of the desires, whether rightly or wrongly indulged.

[842] Meg. I, for my part, Stranger, would gladly receive this law. Cleinias shall speak for himself, and tell you what is his opinion.

Cle. I will, Megillus, when an opportunity offers; at present, I think that we had better allow the Stranger to proceed with his laws.

Meg. Very good.

Ath. We had got about as far as the establishment of the common tables, which in most places would be difficult, but in Crete no one would think of introducing any other custom. There might arise a question about the manner of them—whether they shall be such as they are here in Crete, or such as they are in Lacedaemon,—or is there a third kind which may be better than either of them?[1] The answer to this question might be easily discovered, but the discovery would do no great good, for at present they are very well ordered.

Leaving the common tables, we may therefore proceed to the means of providing food. Now, in cities the means of life are gained in many ways and from divers sources, and in general from two sources, whereas our city has only one. For most of the Hellenes obtain their food from sea and land, but our citizens from land only. And this makes the task of the legislator less difficult—half as many laws will be enough, and much less than half; and they will be of a kind better suited to free men. For he has nothing to do with laws about shipowners and merchants and retailers and innkeepers and tax collectors and mines and money-lending and compound interest and innumerable other things—bidding good-bye to these, he gives laws to husbandmen and shepherds and bee-keepers, and to the guardians and superintendents of their implements; and he has already legislated for greater matters, as for example, respecting marriage and the procreation and nurture of children, and for education, and the establishment of offices—and now he must direct his laws to those who provide food and labour in preparing it.

Let us first of all, then, have a class of laws

[1] Cf. Aristotle, *Politics,* vii. 10, 1330 ᵃ 3-10.

which shall be called the laws of husbandmen. And let the first of them be the law of Zeus, the god of boundaries. Let no one shift the boundary line either of a fellow-citizen who is a neighbour, or, if he dwells at the extremity of the land, *[843]* of any stranger who is conterminous with him, considering that this is truly "to move the immovable," and every one should be more willing to move the largest rock which is not a landmark, than the least stone which is the sworn mark of friendship and hatred between neighbours; for Zeus, the god of kindred, is the witness of the citizen, and Zeus, the god of strangers, of the stranger, and when aroused, terrible are the wars which they stir up. He who obeys the law will never know the fatal consequences of disobedience, but he who despises the law shall be liable to a double penalty, the first coming from the Gods, and the second from the law. For let no one wilfully remove the boundaries of his neighbour's land, and if any one does, let him who will inform the landowners, and let them bring him into court, and if he be convicted of re-dividing the land by stealth or by force, let the court determine what he ought to suffer or pay. In the next place, many small injuries done by neighbours to one another, through their multiplication, may cause a weight of enmity, and make neighbourhood a very disagreeable and bitter thing. Wherefore a man ought to be very careful of committing any offence against his neighbour, and especially of encroaching on his neighbour's land; for any man may easily do harm, but not every man can do good to another. He who encroaches on his neighbour's land, and transgresses his boundaries, shall make good the damage, and, to cure him of his impudence and also of his meanness, he shall pay a double penalty to the injured party. Of these and the like matters the wardens of the country shall take cognizance, and be the judges of them and assessors of the damage; in the more important cases, as has been already said,[1] the whole number of them belonging to any one of the twelve divisions shall decide, and in the lesser cases the commanders: or, again, if any one pastures his cattle on his neighbour's land, they shall see the injury, and adjudge the penalty. And if any one, by decoying the bees, gets possession of another's swarms, and draws them to himself by making noises, he shall pay the damage; or if anyone sets fire to his own wood and takes no care of his neighbour's property, he shall be fined at the discretion of the magistrates. And

[1] Cf. vi. 761.

if in planting he does not leave a fair distance between his own and his neighbour's land, he shall be punished, in accordance with the enactments of many lawgivers, which we may use, not deeming it necessary that the great legislator of our state should *[844]* determine all the trifles which might be decided by any body; for example, husbandmen have had of old excellent laws about waters, and there is no reason why we should propose to divert their course: He who likes may draw water from the fountain-head of the common stream on to his own land, if he do not cut off the spring which clearly belongs to some other owner; and he may take the water in any direction which he pleases, except through a house or temple or sepulchre, but he must be careful to do no harm beyond the channel. And if there be in any place a natural dryness of the earth, which keeps in the rain from heaven, and causes a deficiency in the supply of water, let him dig down on his own land as far as the clay, and if at this depth he finds no water, let him obtain water from his neighbours, as much as is required for his servants' drinking, and if his neighbours, too, are limited in their supply, let him have a fixed measure, which shall be determined by the wardens of the country. This he shall receive each day, and on these terms have a share of his neighbours' water. If there be heavy rain, and one of those on the lower ground injures some tiller of the upper ground, or some one who has a common wall, by refusing to give them an outlet for water; or, again, if some one living on the higher ground recklessly lets off the water on his lower neighbour, and they cannot come to terms with one another, let him who will call in a warden of the city, if he be in the city, or if he be in the country, a warden of the country, and let him obtain a decision determining what each of them is to do. And he who will not abide by the decision shall suffer for his malignant and morose temper, and pay a fine to the injured party, equivalent to double the value of the injury, because he was unwilling to submit to the magistrates.

Now the participation of fruits shall be ordered on this wise. The goddess of Autumn has two gracious gifts: one, the joy of Dionysus which is not treasured up; the other, which nature intends to be stored. Let this be the law, then, concerning the fruits of autumn: He who tastes the common or storing fruits of autumn, whether grapes or figs, before the season of vintage which coincides with Arcturus, either on his own land or on that of others—let him pay fifty drachmae, which shall be sacred to Diony-sus, if he pluck them from his own land; and if from his neighbour's land, a mina, and if from any others', two-thirds of a mina. And he who would gather the "choice" grapes or the "choice" figs, as they are now termed, if he take them off his own land, let him pluck them how and when he likes; but if he take them from the ground of others without their leave, let him in that case be always punished in accordance with the law which ordains that he should not move what he has not laid down.[1] [845] And if a slave touches any fruit of this sort, without the consent of the owner of the land, he shall be beaten with as many blows as there are grapes on the bunch, or figs on the fig-tree. Let a metric purchase the "choice" autumnal fruit, and then, if he pleases, he may gather it; but if a stranger is passing along the road, and desires to eat, let him take of the "choice" grapes for himself and a single follower without payment, as a tribute of hospitality. The law however forbids stran-gers from sharing in the sort which is not used for eating; and if any one, whether he be mas-ter or slave, takes of them in ignorance, let the slave be beaten, and the freeman dismissed with admonitions, and instructed to take of the other autumnal fruits which are unfit for mak-ing raisins and wine, or for laying by as dried figs. As to pears, and apples, and pomegran-ates, and similar fruits, there shall be no dis-grace in taking them secretly; but he who is caught, if he be of less than thirty years of age, shall be struck and beaten off, but not wound-ed; and no freeman shall have any right of sat-isfaction for such blows. Of these fruits the stranger may partake, just as he may of the fruits of autumn. And if an elder, who is more than thirty years of age, eat of them on the spot, let him, like the stranger, be allowed to partake of all such fruits, but he must carry away noth-ing. If, however, he will not obey the law, let him run the risk of failing in the competition of virtue, in case any one takes notice of his ac-tions before the judges at the time.

Water is the greatest element of nutrition in gardens, but is easily polluted. You cannot poi-son the soil, or the sun, or the air, which are the other elements of nutrition in plants, or divert them, or steal them; but all these things may very likely happen in regard to water, which must therefore be protected by law. And let this be the law:—If any one intentionally pol-lutes the water of another, whether the water of a spring, or collected in reservoirs, either by poisonous substances, or by digging, or by theft, let the injured party bring the cause before the wardens of the city, and claim in writing the value of the loss; if the accused be found guilty of injuring the water by deleterious substances, let him not only pay damages, but purify the stream or the cistern which contains the water, in such manner as the laws of the interpreters [2] order the purification to be made by the offend-er in each case.

With respect to the gathering in of the fruits of the soil, let a man, if he pleases, [846] carry his own fruits through any place in which he either does no harm to any one, or himself gains three times as much as his neighbour loses. Now of these things the magistrates should be cognisant, as of all other things in which a man intentionally does injury to another or to the property of another, by fraud or force, in the use which he makes of his own property. All these matters a man should lay before the magis-trates, and receive damages, supposing the in-jury to be not more than three minae; or if he have a charge against another which involves a larger amount, let him bring his suit into the public courts and have the evil-doer punished. But if any of the magistrates appear to adjudge the penalties which he imposes in an unjust spirit, let him be liable to pay double to the in-jured party. Any one may bring the offences of magistrates, in any particular case, before the public courts. There are innumerable little mat-ters relating to the modes of punishment, and applications for suits, and summonses and the witnesses to summonses—for example, whether two witnesses should be required for a sum-mons, or how many—and all such details, which cannot be omitted in legislation, but are beneath the wisdom of an aged legislator. These lesser matters, as they indeed are in comparison with the greater ones, let a younger generation regu-late by law, after the patterns which have pre-ceded, and according to their own experience of the usefulness and necessity of such laws; and when they are duly regulated let there be no alteration, but let the citizens live in the ob-servance of them.

Now of artisans, let the regulations be as fol-lows:—In the first place, let no citizen or serv-ant of a citizen be occupied in handicraft arts; for he who is to secure and preserve the public order of the state, has an art which requires much study and many kinds of knowledge, and does not admit of being made a secondary oc-cupation; and hardly any human being is capa-

[1] Cf. xi. 913.

[2] Cf. vi. 759.

ble of pursuing two professions or two arts rightly, or of practising one art himself, and superintending some one else who is practising another. Let this, then, be our first principle in the state:—No one who is a smith shall also be a carpenter, and if he be a carpenter, he shall not superintend the smith's art rather than his own, under the pretext that in superintending many servants who are working for him, he is likely to superintend them better, because more revenue will accrue to him from them than from his own art; *[847]* but let every man in the state have one art, and get his living by that. Let the wardens of the city labour to maintain this law, and if any citizen incline to any other art than the study of virtue, let them punish him with disgrace and infamy, until they bring him back into his own right course; and if any stranger profess two arts, let them chastise him with bonds and money penalties, and expulsion from the state, until they compel him to be one only and not many.[1]

But as touching payments for hire, and contracts of work, or in case any one does wrong to any of the citizens, or they do wrong to any other, up to fifty drachmae, let the wardens of the city decide the case; but if a greater amount be involved, then let the public courts decide according to law. Let no one pay any duty either on the importation or exportation of goods; and as to frankincense and similar perfumes, used in the service of the Gods, which come from abroad, and purple and other dyes which are not produced in the country, or the materials of any art which have to be imported, and which are not necessary—no one should import them; nor, again, should any one export anything which is wanted in the country. Of all these things let there be inspectors and superintendents, taken from the guardians of the law; and they shall be the twelve next in order to the five seniors. Concerning arms, and all implements which are required for military purposes, if there be need of introducing any art, or plant, or metal, or chains of any kind, or animals for use in war, let the commanders of the horse and the generals have authority over their importation and exportation; the city shall send them out and also receive them, and the guardians of the law shall make fit and proper laws about them. But let there be no retail trade[2] for the sake of money-making, either in these or any other articles, in the city or country at all.

With respect to food and the distribution of the produce of the country, the right and proper way seems to be nearly that which is the custom of Crete;[3] for all should be required to distribute the fruits of the soil into twelve parts, and in this way consume them. Let the twelfth portion of each (as for instance of wheat and barley, to which the rest of the fruits of the earth shall be added, *[848]* as well as the animals which are for sale in each of the twelve divisions) be divided in due proportion into three parts; one part for freemen, another for their servants, and a third for craftsmen and in general for strangers, whether sojourners who may be dwelling in the city, and like other men must live, or those who come on some business which they have with the state, or with some individual. Let only this third part of all necessaries be required to be sold; out of the other two-thirds no one shall be compelled to sell. And how will they be best distributed? In the first place, we see clearly that the distribution will be of equals in one point of view, and in another point of view of unequals.

Cle. What do you mean?

Ath. I mean that the earth of necessity produces and nourishes the various articles of food, sometimes better and sometimes worse.

Cle. Of course.

Ath. Such being the case, let no one of the three portions be greater than either of the other two;—neither that which is assigned to masters or to slaves, nor again that of the stranger; but let the distribution to all be equal and alike, and let every citizen take his two portions and distribute them among slaves and freemen, he having power to determine the quantity and quality. And what remains he shall distribute by measure and number among the animals who have to be sustained from the earth, taking the whole number of them.

In the second place, our citizens should have separate houses duly ordered; and this will be the order proper for men like them. There shall be twelve hamlets, one in the middle of each twelfth portion, and in each hamlet they shall first set apart a market-place, and the temples of the Gods, and of their attendant demi-gods; and if there be any local deities of the Magnetes, or holy seats of other ancient deities, whose memory has been preserved, to these let them pay their ancient honours.[4] But Hestia, and Zeus, and Athene will have temples everywhere together with the God who presides in

[1] Cf. *Republic,* iii. 397.

[2] Cf. Aristotle, *Politics,* vii. 9, 1329 ᵃ 18-24.

[3] Cf. *ibid.,* ii. 10, 1272 ᵃ 11-21.

[4] Cf. v. 738.

each of the twelve districts.[1] And the first erection of houses shall be around these temples, where the ground is highest, in order to provide the safest and most defensible place of retreat for the guards. All the rest of the country they shall settle in the following manner:—They shall make thirteen divisions of the craftsmen; one of them they shall establish in the city, and this, again, they shall subdivide into twelve lesser divisions, among the twelve districts of the city, and the remainder shall be distributed in the country round about; and in each village they shall settle various classes of craftsmen, with a view to the convenience of the husbandmen. And the chief officers of the wardens of the country shall superintend all these matters, and see how many of them, and which class of them, each place requires; [849] and fix them where they are likely to be least troublesome, and most useful to the husbandman. And the wardens of the city shall see to similar matters in the city.

Now the wardens of the agora ought to see to the details of the agora. Their first care, after the temples which are in the agora have been seen to, should be to prevent any one from doing any wrong in dealings between man and man; in the second place, as being inspectors of temperance and violence, they should chastise him who requires chastisement. Touching articles of sale, they should first see whether the articles which the citizens are under regulations to sell to strangers are sold to them, as the law ordains. And let the law be as follows:—On the first day of the month, the persons in charge, whoever they are, whether strangers or slaves, who have the charge on behalf of the citizens, shall produce to the strangers the portion which falls to them, in the first place, a twelfth portion of the corn;—the stranger shall purchase corn for the whole month, and other cereals, on the first market day; and on the tenth day of the month the one party shall sell, and the other buy, liquids sufficient to last during the whole month; and on the twenty-third day there shall be a sale of animals by those who are willing to sell to the people who want to buy, and of implements and other things which husbandmen sell (such as skins and all kinds of clothing, either woven or made of felt and other goods of the same sort), and which strangers are compelled to buy and purchase of others. As to the retail trade in these things, whether of barley or wheat set apart for meal and flour, or any other kind of food, no one shall sell them to

[1] Cf. v. 745.

citizens or their slaves, nor shall any one buy of a citizen; but let the stranger sell them in the market of strangers, to artisans and their slaves, making an exchange of wine and food, which is commonly called retail trade. And butchers shall offer for sale parts of dismembered animals to the strangers, and artisans, and their servants. Let any stranger who likes buy fuel from day to day wholesale, from those who have the care of it in the country, and let him sell to the strangers as much as he pleases and when he pleases. As to other goods and implements which are likely to be wanted, they shall sell them in the common market, at any place which the guardians of the law and the wardens of the market and city, choosing according to their judgment, shall determine; at such places they shall exchange money for goods, and goods for money, neither party giving credit to the other;[2] and he who gives credit must be satisfied, whether he obtain his money or not, [850] for in such exchanges he will not be protected by law. But whenever property has been bought or sold, greater in quantity or value than is allowed by the law, which has determined within what limits a man may increase and diminish his possessions, let the excess be registered in the books of the guardians of the law; or in case of diminution, let there be an erasure made. And let the same rule be observed about the registration of the property of the metics. Any one who likes may come and be a metic on certain conditions; a foreigner, if he likes, and is able to settle, may dwell in the land, but he must practise an art, and not abide more than twenty years from the time at which he has registered himself; and he shall pay no sojourner's tax, however small, except good conduct, nor any other tax for buying and selling. But when the twenty years have expired, he shall take his property with him and depart. And if in the course of these years he should chance to distinguish himself by any considerable benefit which he confers on the state, and he thinks that he can persuade the council and assembly, either to grant him delay in leaving the country, or to allow him to remain for the whole of his life, let him go and persuade the city, and whatever they assent to at his instance shall take effect. For the children of the metics, being artisans, and of fifteen years of age, let the time of their sojourn commence after their fifteenth year; and let them remain for twenty years, and then go where they like; but any of them who wishes to remain, may do so, if he can persuade

[2] Cf. xi. 915.

the council and assembly. And if he depart, let him erase all the entries which have been made by him in the register kept by the magistrates.

BOOK IX

[853] NEXT to all the matters which have preceded in the natural order of legislation will come suits of law. Of suits those which relate to agriculture have been already described, but the more important have not been described. Having mentioned them severally under their usual names, we will proceed to say what punishments are to be inflicted for each offence, and who are to be the judges of them.

Cleinias. Very good.

Athenian Stranger. There is a sense of disgrace in legislating, as we are about to do, for all the details of crime in a state which, as we say, is to be well regulated and will be perfectly adapted to the practice of virtue. To assume that in such a state there will arise some one who will be guilty of crimes as heinous as any which are ever perpetrated in other states, and that we must legislate for him by anticipation, and threaten and make laws against him if he should arise, in order to deter him, and punish his acts, under the idea that he will arise—this, as I was saying, is in a manner disgraceful. Yet seeing that we are not like the ancient legislators, who gave laws to heroes and sons of gods, being, according to the popular belief, themselves the offspring of the gods, and legislating for others, who were also the children of divine parents, but that we are only men who are legislating for the sons of men, there is no uncharitableness in apprehending that some one of our citizens may be like a seed which has touched the ox's horn, having a heart so hard that it cannot be softened any more than those seeds can be softened by fire. Among our citizens there may be those who cannot be subdued by all the strength of the laws; and for their sake, though an ungracious task, I will proclaim my first law about the robbing of temples, in case any one should dare to commit such a crime. I do not expect or imagine that any well-brought-up citizen will ever take the infection, but their servants, and strangers, and strangers' servants may be guilty of many impieties. [854] And with a view to them especially, and yet not without a provident eye to the weakness of human nature generally, I will proclaim the law about robbers of temples and similar incurable, or almost incurable, criminals. Having already agreed that such enactments ought always to

have a short prelude, we may speak to the criminal, whom some tormenting desire by night and by day tempts to go and rob a temple, the fewest possible words of admonition and exhortation:—O sir, we will say to him, the impulse which moves you to rob temples is not an ordinary human malady, nor yet a visitation of heaven, but a madness which is begotten in a man from ancient and unexpiated crimes of his race, an ever-recurring curse;—against this you must guard with all your might, and how you are to guard we will explain to you. When any such thought comes into your mind, go and perform expiations, go as a suppliant to the temples of the Gods who avert evils, go to the society of those who are called good men among you; hear them tell and yourself try to repeat after them, that every man should honour the noble and the just. Fly from the company of the wicked—fly and turn not back; and if your disorder is lightened by these remedies, well and good, but if not, then acknowledge death to be nobler than life, and depart hence.

Such are the preludes which we sing to all who have thoughts of unholy and treasonable actions, and to him who hearkens to them the law has nothing to say. But to him who is disobedient when the prelude is over, cry with a loud voice—He who is taken in the act of robbing temples, if he be a slave or stranger, shall have his evil deed engraven on his face and hands, and shall be beaten with as many stripes as may seem good to the judges, and be cast naked beyond the borders of the land. And if he suffers this punishment he will probably return to his right mind and be improved; for no penalty which the law inflicts is designed for evil, but always makes him who suffers either better or not so much worse as he would have been.[1] But if any citizen be found guilty of any great or unmentionable wrong, either in relation to the gods, or his parents, or the state, let the judge deem him to be incurable, remembering that after receiving such an excellent education and training from youth upward, he has not abstained from the greatest of crimes.[2] His punishment shall be death, [855] which to him will be the least of evils; and his example will benefit others, if he perish ingloriously, and be cast beyond the borders of the land. But let his children and family, if they avoid the ways of their father, have glory, and let honourable mention be made of them, as having nobly and manfully escaped out of evil into good. None

[1] Cf. *Protagoras*, 323, ff.; *Gorgias*, 525.
[2] Cf. *Statesman*, 308.

of them should have their goods confiscated to the state, for the lots of the citizens ought always to continue the same and equal.

Touching the exaction of penalties, when a man appears to have done anything which deserves a fine, he shall pay the fine, if he have anything in excess of the lot which is assigned to him; but more than that he shall not pay. And to secure exactness, let the guardians of the law refer to the registers, and inform the judges of the precise truth, in order that none of the lots may go uncultivated for want of money. But if any one seems to deserve a greater penalty, let him undergo a long and public imprisonment and be dishonoured, unless some of his friends are willing to be surety for him, and liberate him by assisting him to pay the fine. No criminal shall go unpunished, not even for a single offence, nor if he have fled the country; but let the penalty be according to his deserts —death, or bonds, or blows, or degrading places of sitting or standing, or removal to some temple on the borders of the land; or let him pay fines, as we said before. In cases of death, let the judges be the guardians of the law, and a court selected by merit from the last year's magistrates. But how the causes are to be brought into court, how the summonses are to be served, and the like, these things may be left to the younger generation of legislators to determine; the manner of voting we must determine ourselves.

Let the vote be given openly; but before they come to the vote let the judges sit in order of seniority over against plaintiff and defendant, and let all the citizens who can spare time hear and take a serious interest in listening to such causes. First of all the plaintiff shall make one speech, and then the defendant shall make another; and after the speeches have been made the eldest judge shall begin to examine the parties, and proceed to make an adequate enquiry into what has been said; and after the oldest has spoken, the rest shall proceed in order to examine either party as to what he finds defective in the evidence, whether of statement or omission; and he who has nothing to ask shall hand over the examination to another. And on so much of what has been said as is to the purpose all the judges shall set their seals, and place the writings on the altar of Hestia. *[856]* On the next day they shall meet again, and in like manner put their questions and go through the cause, and again set their seals upon the evidence; and when they have three times done this, and have had witnesses and evidence enough, they shall each of them give a holy vote, after promising by Hestia that they will decide justly and truly to the utmost of their power; and so they shall put an end to the suit.

Next, after what relates to the Gods, follows what relates to the dissolution of the state:— Whoever by promoting a man to power enslaves the laws, and subjects the city to factions, using violence and stirring up sedition contrary to law, him we will deem the greatest enemy of the whole state. But he who takes no part in such proceedings, and, being one of the chief magistrates of the state, has no knowledge of the treason, or, having knowledge of it, by reason of cowardice does not interfere on behalf of his country, such an one we must consider nearly as bad. Every man who is worth anything will inform the magistrates, and bring the conspirator to trial for making a violent and illegal attempt to change the government. The judges of such cases shall be the same as of the robbers of temples; and let the whole proceeding be carried on in the same way, and the vote of the majority condemn to death. But let there be a general rule, that the disgrace and punishment of the father is not to be visited on the children, except in the case of some one whose father, grandfather, and great-grandfather have successively undergone the penalty of death. Such persons the city shall send away with all their possessions to the city and country of their ancestors, retaining only and wholly their appointed lot. And out of the citizens who have more than one son of not less than ten years of age, they shall select ten whom their father or grandfather by the mother's or father's side shall appoint, and let them send to Delphi the names of those who are selected, and him whom the God chooses they shall establish as heir of the house which has failed; and may he have better fortune than his predecessors!

Cle. Very good.

Ath. Once more let there be a third general law respecting the judges who are to give judgment, and the manner of conducting suits against those who are tried on an accusation of treason; *[857]* and as concerning the remaining or departure of their descendants—there shall be one law for all three, for the traitor, and the robber of temples, and the subverter by violence of the laws of the state. For a thief, whether he steal much or little, let there be one law, and one punishment for all alike: in the first place, let him pay double the amount of the theft if he be convicted, and if he have so much over and above the allotment;—if he have not, he shall be bound until he pay the penalty, or persuade him who has obtained the sentence against him to forgive him. But if a person be convicted of a theft against the state, then if he can persuade the city, or if he will pay back twice the amount of the theft, he shall be set free from his bonds.[1]

Cle. What makes you say, Stranger, that a theft is all one, whether the thief may have taken much or little, and either from sacred or secular places—and these are not the only differences in thefts:—seeing, then, that they are of many kinds, ought not the legislator to adapt himself to them, and impose upon them entirely different penalties?

Ath. Excellent. I was running on too fast, Cleinias, and you impinged upon me, and brought me to my senses, reminding me of what, indeed, had occurred to my mind already, that legislation was never yet rightly worked out, as I may say in passing.—Do you remember the image in which I likened the men for whom laws are now made to slaves who are doctored by slaves?[2] For of this you may be very sure, that if one of those empirical physicians, who practise medicine without science, were to come upon the gentleman physician talking to his gentleman patient, and using the language almost of philosophy, beginning at the beginning of the disease and discoursing about the whole nature of the body, he would burst into a hearty laugh—he would say what most of those who are called doctors always have at their tongue's end:—Foolish fellow, he would say, you are not healing the sick man, but you are educating him; and he does not want to be made a doctor, but to get well.

Cle. And would he not be right?

Ath. Perhaps he would; and he might remark upon us, that he who discourses about laws, as we are now doing, is giving the citizens education and not laws; that would be rather a telling observation.

Cle. Very true.

Ath. But we are fortunate.

[858] *Cle.* In what way?

Ath. Inasmuch as we are not compelled to give laws, but we may take into consideration every form of government, and ascertain what is best and what is most needful, and how they may both be carried into execution; and we may also, if we please, at this very moment choose what is best, or, if we prefer, what is most necessary—which shall we do?

[1] Cf. xi. 933; xii. 941.
[2] Cf. iv. 720.

Cle. There is something ridiculous, Stranger, in our proposing such an alternative, as if we were legislators, simply bound under some great necessity which cannot be deferred to the morrow. But we, as I may by the grace of Heaven affirm, like gatherers of stones or beginners of some composite work, may gather a heap of materials, and out of this, at our leisure, select what is suitable for our projected construction. Let us then suppose ourselves to be at leisure, not of necessity building, but rather like men who are partly providing materials, and partly putting them together. And we may truly say that some of our laws, like stones, are already fixed in their places, and others lie at hand.

Ath. Certainly, in that case, Cleinias, our view of law will be more in accordance with nature. For there is another matter affecting legislators, which I must earnestly entreat you to consider.

Cle. What is it?

Ath. There are many writings to be found in cities, and among them there are discourses composed by legislators as well as by other persons.

Cle. To be sure.

Ath. Shall we give heed rather to the writings of those others—poets and the like, who either in metre or out of metre have recorded their advice about the conduct of life, and not to the writings of legislators? or shall we give heed to them above all?

Cle. Yes; to them far above all others.

Ath. And ought the legislator alone among writers to withhold his opinion about the beautiful, the good, and the just, and not to teach what they are, and how they are to be pursued by those who intend to be happy?

Cle. Certainly not.

Ath. And is it disgraceful for Homer and Tyrtaeus and other poets to lay down evil precepts in their writings respecting life and the pursuits of men, but not so disgraceful for Lycurgus and Solon and others who were legislators as well as writers? Is it not true that of all the writings to be found in cities, those which relate to laws, when you unfold and read them, ought to be by far the noblest and the best? [859] and should not other writings either agree with them, or if they disagree, be deemed ridiculous? We should consider whether the laws of states ought not to have the character of loving and wise parents, rather than of tyrants and masters, who command and threaten, and, after writing their decrees on walls, go their ways; and whether, in discoursing of laws, we should not take the gentler view of them which may or may not be attainable—at any rate, we will show our readiness to entertain such a view, and be prepared to undergo whatever may be the result. And may the result be good, and if God be gracious, it will be good!

Cle. Excellent; let us do as you say.

Ath. Then we will now consider accurately, as we proposed, what relates to robbers of temples, and all kinds of thefts, and offences in general; and we must not be annoyed if, in the course of legislation, we have enacted some things, and have not made up our minds about some others; for as yet we are not legislators, but we may soon be. Let us, if you please, consider these matters.

Cle. By all means.

Ath. Concerning all things honourable and just, let us then endeavour to ascertain how far we are consistent with ourselves, and how far we are inconsistent, and how far the many, from whom at any rate we should profess a desire to differ, agree and disagree among themselves.

Cle. What are the inconsistencies which you observe in us?

Ath. I will endeavour to explain. If I am not mistaken, we are all agreed that justice, and just men and things and actions, are all fair, and, if a person were to maintain that just men, even when they are deformed in body, are still perfectly beautiful in respect of the excellent justice of their minds, no one would say that there was any inconsistency in this.

Cle. They would be quite right.

Ath. Perhaps; but let us consider further, that if all things which are just are fair and honourable, in the term "all" we must include just sufferings which are the correlatives of just actions.

Cle. And what is the inference?

Ath. The inference is, that a just action in partaking of the just partakes also in the same degree of the fair and honourable.

Cle. Certainly.

Ath. And must not a suffering which partakes of the just principle be admitted to be in the same degree fair and honourable, *[860]* if the argument is consistently carried out?

Cle. True.

Ath. But then if we admit suffering to be just and yet dishonourable, and the term "dishonourable" is applied to justice, will not the just and the honourable disagree?

Cle. What do you mean?

Ath. A thing not difficult to understand; the laws which have been already enacted would seem to announce principles directly opposed to what we are saying.

Cle. To what?

Ath. We had enacted, if I am not mistaken, that the robber of temples, and he who was the enemy of law and order, might justly be put to death, and we were proceeding to make divers other enactments of a similar nature. But we stopped short, because we saw that these sufferings are infinite in number and degree, and that they are, at once, the most just and also the most dishonourable of all sufferings. And if this be true, are not the just and the honourable at one time all the same, and at another time in the most diametrical opposition?

Cle. Such appears to be the case.

Ath. In this discordant and inconsistent fashion does the language of the many rend asunder the honourable and just.

Cle. Very true, Stranger.

Ath. Then now, Cleinias, let us see how far we ourselves are consistent about these matters.

Cle. Consistent in what?

Ath. I think that I have clearly stated in the former part of the discussion, but if I did not, let me now state——

Cle. What?

Ath. That all bad men are always involuntarily bad; and from this I must proceed to draw a further inference.

Cle. What is it?

Ath. That the unjust man may be bad, but that he is bad against his will. Now that an action which is voluntary should be done involuntarily is a contradiction; wherefore he who maintains that injustice is involuntary will deem that the unjust does injustice involuntarily. I too admit that all men do injustice involuntarily, and if any contentious or disputatious person says that men are unjust against their will, and yet that many do injustice willingly, I do not agree with him. But, then, how can I avoid being inconsistent with myself, if you, Cleinias, and you, Megillus, say to me— Well, Stranger, if all this be as you say, how about legislating for the city of the Magnetes— shall we legislate or not—what do you advise? Certainly we will, I should reply. Then will you determine for them what are voluntary and what are involuntary crimes, and shall we make the punishments greater of voluntary errors and crimes and less for the involuntary? or shall we make the punishment of all to be alike, *[861]* under the idea that there is no such thing as voluntary crime?

Cle. Very good, Stranger; and what shall we say in answer to these objections?

Ath. That is a very fair question. In the first place, let us——

Cle. Do what?

Ath. Let us remember what has been well said by us already, that our ideas of justice are in the highest degree confused and contradictory. Bearing this in mind, let us proceed to ask ourselves once more whether we have discovered a way out of the difficulty. Have we ever determined in what respect these two classes of actions differ from one another? For in all states and by all legislators whatsoever, two kinds of actions have been distinguished—the one, voluntary, the other, involuntary; and they have legislated about them accordingly. But shall this new word of ours, like an oracle of God, be only spoken, and get away without giving any explanation or verification of itself? How can a word not understood be the basis of legislation? Impossible. Before proceeding to legislate, then, we must prove that they are two, and what is the difference between them, that when we impose the penalty upon either, every one may understand our proposal, and be able in some way to judge whether the penalty is fitly or unfitly inflicted.

Cle. I agree with you, Stranger; for one of two things is certain: either we must not say that all unjust acts are involuntary, or we must show the meaning and truth of this statement.

Ath. Of these two alternatives, the one is quite intolerable—not to speak what I believe to be the truth would be to me unlawful and unholy. But if acts of injustice cannot be divided into voluntary and involuntary, I must endeavour to find some other distinction between them.

Cle. Very true, Stranger; there cannot be two opinions among us upon that point.

Ath. Reflect, then; there are hurts of various kinds done by the citizens to one another in the intercourse of life, affording plentiful examples both of the voluntary and involuntary.

Cle. Certainly.

Ath. I would not have any one suppose that all these hurts are injuries, and that these injuries are of two kinds—one, voluntary, and the other, involuntary; for the involuntary hurts of all men are quite as many and as great as the voluntary.[1] *[862]* And please to consider whether I am right or quite wrong in what I am going to say; for I deny, Cleinias and Me-

[1] Cf. Aristotle, *Ethics*, iii. 1-5; v. 8.

gillus, that he who harms another involuntarily does him an injury involuntarily, nor should I legislate about such an act under the idea that I am legislating for an involuntary injury. But I should rather say that such a hurt, whether great or small, is not an injury at all; and, on the other hand, if I am right, when a benefit is wrongly conferred, the author of the benefit may often be said to injure. For I maintain, O my friends, that the mere giving or taking away of anything is not to be described either as just or unjust; but the legislator has to consider whether mankind do good or harm to one another out of a just principle and intention. On the distinction between injustice and hurt he must fix his eye; and when there is hurt, he must, as far as he can, make the hurt good by law, and save that which is ruined, and raise up that which is fallen, and make that which is dead or wounded whole. And when compensation has been given for injustice, the law must always seek to win over the doers and sufferers of the several hurts from feelings of enmity to those of friendship.

Cle. Very good.

Ath. Then as to unjust hurts (and gains also, supposing the injustice to bring gain), of these we may heal as many as are capable of being healed, regarding them as diseases of the soul; and the cure of injustice will take the following direction.

Cle. What direction?

Ath. When any one commits any injustice, small or great, the law will admonish and compel him either never at all to do the like again, or never voluntarily, or at any rate in a far less degree; and he must in addition pay for the hurt. Whether the end is to be attained by word or action, with pleasure or pain, by giving or taking away privileges, by means of fines or gifts, or in whatsoever way the law shall proceed to make a man hate injustice, and love or not hate the nature of the just—this is quite the noblest work of law. But if the legislator sees any one who is incurable, for him he will appoint a law and a penalty. He knows quite well that to such men themselves there is no profit in the continuance of their lives, and that they would do a double good to the rest of mankind if they would take their departure, *[863]* inasmuch as they would be an example to other men not to offend, and they would relieve the city of bad citizens. In such cases, and in such cases only, the legislator ought to inflict death as the punishment of offences.

Cle. What you have said appears to me to be

very reasonable, but will you favour me by stating a little more clearly the difference between hurt and injustice, and the various complications of the voluntary and involuntary which enter into them?

Ath. I will endeavour to do as you wish:—Concerning the soul, thus much would be generally said and allowed, that one element in her nature is passion, which may be described either as a state or a part of her, and is hard to be striven against and contended with, and by irrational force overturns many things.

Cle. Very true.

Ath. And pleasure is not the same with passion, but has an opposite power, working her will by persuasion and by the force of deceit in all things.

Cle. Quite true.

Ath. A man may truly say that ignorance is a third cause of crimes. Ignorance, however, may be conveniently divided by the legislator into two sorts: there is simple ignorance, which is the source of lighter offences, and double ignorance, which is accompanied by a conceit of wisdom; and he who is under the influence of the latter fancies that he knows all about matters of which he knows nothing. This second kind of ignorance, when possessed of power and strength, will be held by the legislator to be the source of great and monstrous crimes, but when attended with weakness, will only result in the errors of children and old men; and these he will treat as errors, and will make laws accordingly for those who commit them, which will be the mildest and most merciful of all laws.

Cle. You are perfectly right.

Ath. We all of us remark of one man that he is superior to pleasure and passion, and of another that he is inferior to them; and this is true.[1]

Cle. Certainly.

Ath. But no one was ever yet heard to say that one of us is superior and another inferior to ignorance.

Cle. Very true.

Ath. We are speaking of motives which incite men to the fulfilment of their will; although an individual may be often drawn by them in opposite directions at the same time.

Cle. Yes, often.

Ath. And now I can define to you clearly, and without ambiguity, what I mean by the just and unjust, according to my notion of them:—When anger and fear, and pleasure

[1] Cf. *Republic*, iv. 430; *supra*, i. 626 ff.

and pain, and jealousies and desires, *[864]* tyrannize over the soul, whether they do any harm or not—I call all this injustice. But when the opinion of the best, in whatever part of human nature states or individuals may suppose that to dwell, has dominion in the soul and orders the life of every man, even if it be sometimes mistaken, yet what is done in accordance therewith, and the principle in individuals which obeys this rule, and is best for the whole life of man, is to be called just; although the hurt done by mistake is thought by many to be involuntary injustice. Leaving the question of names, about which we are not going to quarrel, and having already delineated three sources of error, we may begin by recalling them somewhat more vividly to our memory: —One of them was of the painful sort, which we denominate anger and fear.

Cle. Quite right.

Ath. There was a second consisting of pleasures and desires, and a third of hopes, which aimed at true opinion about the best. The latter being subdivided into three, we now get five sources of actions, and for these five we will make laws of two kinds.

Cle. What are the two kinds?

Ath. There is one kind of actions done by violence and in the light of day, and another kind of actions which are done in darkness and with secret deceit, or sometimes both with violence and deceit; the laws concerning these last ought to have a character of severity.

Cle. Naturally.

Ath. And now let us return from this digression and complete the work of legislation. Laws have been already enacted by us concerning the robbers of the Gods, and concerning traitors, and also concerning those who corrupt the laws for the purpose of subverting the government. A man may very likely commit some of these crimes, either in a state of madness or when affected by disease, or under the influence of extreme old age, or in a fit of childish wantonness, himself no better than a child. And if this be made evident to the judges elected to try the cause, on the appeal of the criminal or his advocate, and he be judged to have been in this state when he committed the offence, he shall simply pay for the hurt which he may have done to another; but he shall be exempt from other penalties, unless he have slain some one, and have on his hands the stain of blood. And in that case he shall go to another land and country, and there dwell for a year; and if he return before the expiration of the time which the law appoints, or even set his foot at all on his native land, he shall be bound by the guardians of the law in the public prison for two years, *[865]* and then go free.

Having begun to speak of homicide, let us endeavour to lay down laws concerning every different kind of homicide; and, first of all, concerning violent and involuntary homicides. If any one in an athletic contest, and at the public games, involuntarily kills a friend, and he dies either at the time or afterwards of the blows which he has received; or if the like misfortune happens to any one in war, or military exercises, or mimic contests of which the magistrates enjoin the practice, whether with or without arms, when he has been purified according to the law brought from Delphi relating to these matters, he shall be innocent. And so in the case of physicians: if their patient dies against their will, they shall be held guiltless by the law. And if one slay another with his own hand, but unintentionally, whether he be unarmed or have some instrument or dart in his hand; or if he kill him by administering food or drink, or by the application of fire or cold, or by suffocating him, whether he do the deed by his own hand, or by the agency of others, he shall be deemed the agent, and shall suffer one of the following penalties:—If he kill the slave of another in the belief that he is his own, he shall bear the master of the dead man harmless from loss, or shall pay a penalty of twice the value of the dead man, which the judges shall assess; but purifications must be used greater and more numerous than for those who committed homicide at the games;—what they are to be, the interpreters whom the God appoints[1] shall be authorized to declare. And if a man kills his own slave, when he has been purified according to law, he shall be quit of the homicide. And if a man kills a freeman unintentionally, he shall undergo the same purification as he did who killed the slave. But let him not forget also a tale of olden time, which is to this effect:—He who has suffered a violent end, when newly dead, if he has had the soul of a freeman in life, is angry with the author of his death; and being himself full of fear and panic by reason of his violent end, when he sees his murderer walking about in his own accustomed haunts, he is stricken with terror and becomes disordered, and this disorder of his, aided by the guilty recollection of the other, is communicated by him with overwhelming force to the murderer and his deeds. Wherefore also the murderer must go out of the way

[1] Cf. vi. 759.

of his victim for the entire period of a year, and not himself be found in any spot which was familiar to him throughout the country. And if the dead man be a stranger, *[866]* the homicide shall be kept from the country of the stranger during a like period. If any one voluntarily obeys this law, the next of kin to the deceased, seeing all that has happened, shall take pity on him, and make peace with him, and show him all gentleness. But if any one is disobedient, and either ventures to go to any of the temples and sacrifice unpurified, or will not continue in exile during the appointed time, the next of kin to the deceased shall proceed against him for murder; and if he be convicted, every part of his punishment shall be doubled.

And if the next of kin do not proceed against the perpetrator of the crime, then the pollution shall be deemed to fall upon his own head;—the murdered man will fix the guilt upon his kinsman, and he who has a mind to proceed against him may compel him to be absent from his country during five years, according to law. If a stranger unintentionally kill a stranger who is dwelling in the city, he who likes shall prosecute the cause according to the same rules. If he be a metic, let him be absent for a year, or if he be an entire stranger, in addition to the purification, whether he have slain a stranger, or a metic, or a citizen, he shall be banished for life from the country which is in possession of our laws. And if he return contrary to law, let the guardians of the law punish him with death; and let them hand over his property, if he have any, to him who is next of kin to the sufferer. And if he be wrecked, and driven on the coast against his will, he shall take up his abode on the seashore, wetting his feet in the sea, and watching for an opportunity of sailing; but if he be brought by land, and is not his own master, let the magistrate whom he first comes across in the city, release him and send him unharmed over the border.

If any one slays a freeman with his own hand, and the deed be done in passion, in the case of such actions we must begin by making a distinction. For a deed is done from passion either when men suddenly, and without intention to kill, cause the death of another by blows and the like on a momentary impulse, and are sorry for the deed immediately afterwards; or again, when after having been insulted in deed or word, men pursue revenge, and kill a person intentionally, and are not sorry for the act. And, therefore, we must assume that these homicides are of two kinds, both of them arising from passion, which may be justly said to be in a mean between the voluntary and involuntary; *[867]* at the same time, they are neither of them anything more than a likeness or shadow of either. He who treasures up his anger, and avenges himself, not immediately and at the moment, but with insidious design, and after an interval, is like the voluntary; but he who does not treasure up his anger, and takes vengeance on the instant, and without malice prepense, approaches to the involuntary; and yet even he is not altogether involuntary, but is only the image or shadow of the involuntary; wherefore about homicides committed in hot blood, there is a difficulty in determining whether in legislating we shall reckon them as voluntary or as partly involuntary. The best and truest view is to regard them respectively as likenesses only of the voluntary and involuntary, and to distinguish them accordingly as they are done with or without premeditation. And we should make the penalties heavier for those who commit homicide with angry premeditation, and lighter for those who do not premeditate, but smite upon the instant; for that which is like a greater evil should be punished more severely, and that which is like a less evil should be punished less severely: this shall be the rule of our laws.

Cle. Certainly.

Ath. Let us proceed:—If any one slays a freeman with his own hand, and the deed be done in a moment of anger, and without premeditation, let the offender suffer in other respects as the involuntary homicide would have suffered, and also undergo an exile of two years, that he may learn to school his passions. But he who slays another from passion, yet with premeditation, shall in other respects suffer as the former; and to this shall be added an exile of three instead of two years—his punishment is to be longer because his passion is greater. The manner of their return shall be on this wise: (and here the law has difficulty in determining exactly; for in some cases the murderer who is judged by the law to be the worse may really be the less cruel, and he who is judged the less cruel may be really the worse, and may have executed the murder in a more savage manner, whereas the other may have been gentler. But in general the degrees of guilt will be such as we have described them. Of all these things the guardians of the law must take cognisance):—When a homicide of either kind has completed his term of exile, the guardians shall send twelve judges to the borders of the land; these during the interval shall have informed themselves of the actions of the criminals, and they shall judge respecting their pardon and reception; *[868]* and the homicides shall abide by their judgment. But if after they have returned home, any one of them in a moment of anger repeats the deed, let him be an exile, and return no more; or if he returns, let him suffer as the stranger was to suffer in a similar case. He who kills his own slave shall undergo a purification, but if he kills the slave of another in anger, he shall pay twice the amount of the loss to his owner. And if any homicide is disobedient to the law, and without purification pollutes the agora, or the games, or the temples, he who pleases may bring to trial the next of kin to the dead man for permitting him, and the murderer with him, and may compel the one to exact and the other to suffer a double amount of fines and purifications; and the accuser shall himself receive the fine in accordance with the law. If a slave in a fit of passion kills his master, the kindred of the deceased man may do with the murderer (provided only they do not spare his life) whatever they please, and they will be pure; or if he kills a freeman, who is not his master, the owner shall give up the slave to the relatives of the deceased, and they shall be under an obligation to put him to death, but this may be done in any manner which they please. And if (which is a rare occurrence, but does sometimes happen) a father or a mother in a moment of passion slays a son or daughter by blows, or some other violence, the slayer shall undergo the same purification as in other cases, and be exiled during three years; but when the exile returns the wife shall separate from the husband, and the husband from the wife, and they shall never afterwards beget children together, or live under the same roof, or partake of the same sacred rites with those whom they have deprived of a child or of a brother. And he who is impious and disobedient in such a case shall be brought to trial for impiety by any one who pleases. If in a fit of anger a husband kills his wedded wife, or the wife her husband, the slayer shall undergo the same purification, and the term of exile shall be three years. And when he who has committed any such crime returns, let him have no communication in sacred rites with his children, neither let him sit at the same table with them, and the father or son who disobeys shall be liable to be brought to trial for impiety by any one who pleases. If a brother or a sister in a fit of passion kills a brother or a sister, they shall undergo purification and exile, as was the case with parents who killed their offspring: they shall not come under the same roof, or share in the sacred rites of those whom they have deprived of their brethren, or of their children. [869] And he who is disobedient shall be justly liable to the law concerning impiety, which relates to these matters. If any one is so violent in his passion against his parents, that in the madness of his anger he dares to kill one of them, if the murdered person before dying freely forgives the murderer, let him undergo the purification which is assigned to those who have been guilty of involuntary homicide, and do as they do, and he shall be pure. But if he be not acquitted, the perpetrator of such a deed shall be amenable to many laws;—he shall be amenable to the extreme punishments for assault, and impiety, and robbing of temples, for he has robbed his parent of life; and if a man could be slain more than once, most justly would he who in a fit of passion has slain father or mother, undergo many deaths. How can he, whom, alone of all men, even in defence of his life, and when about to suffer death at the hands of his parents, no law will allow to kill his father or his mother who are the authors of his being, and whom the legislator will command to endure any extremity rather than do this—how can he, I say, lawfully receive any other punishment? Let death then be the appointed punishment of him who in a fit of passion slays his father or his mother. But if brother kills brother in a civil broil, or under other like circumstances, if the other has begun, and he only defends himself, let him be free from guilt, as he would be if he had slain an enemy; and the same rule will apply if a citizen kill a citizen, or a stranger a stranger. Or if a stranger kill a citizen or a citizen a stranger in self-defence, let him be free from guilt in like manner; and so in the case of a slave who has killed a slave; but if a slave have killed a freeman in self-defence, let him be subject to the same law as he who has killed a father; and let the law about the remission of penalties in the case of parricide apply equally to every other remission. Whenever any sufferer of his own accord remits the guilt of homicide to another, under the idea that his act was involuntary, let the perpetrator of the deed undergo a purification and remain in exile for a year, according to law.

Enough has been said of murders violent and involuntary and committed in passion: we have now to speak of voluntary crimes done with injustice of every kind and with premeditation, through the influence of pleasures, and desires, and jealousies.

Cle. Very good.

Ath. Let us first speak, as far as we are able, of their various kinds. The greatest cause of them is lust, which gets the mastery of the soul maddened by desire; [870] and this is most commonly found to exist where the passion reigns which is strongest and most prevalent among the mass of mankind: I mean where the power of wealth breeds endless desires of never-to-be-satisfied acquisition, originating in natural disposition, and a miserable want of education. Of this want of education, the false praise of wealth which is bruited about both among Hellenes and barbarians is the cause; they deem that to be the first of goods which in reality is only the third. And in this way they wrong both posterity and themselves, for nothing can be nobler and better than that the truth about wealth should be spoken in all states—namely, that riches are for the sake of the body, as the body is for the sake of the soul. They are good, and wealth is intended by nature to be for the sake of them, and is therefore inferior to them both, and third in order of excellence. This argument teaches us that he who would be happy ought not to seek to be rich, or rather he should seek to be rich justly and temperately, and then there would be no murders in states requiring to be purged away by other murders. But now, as I said at first, avarice is the chiefest cause and source of the worst trials for voluntary homicide. A second cause is ambition: this creates jealousies, which are troublesome companions, above all to the jealous man himself, and in a less degree to the chiefs of the state. And a third cause is cowardly and unjust fear, which has been the occasion of many murders. When a man is doing or has done something which he desires that no one should know him to be doing or to have done, he will take the life of those who are likely to inform of such things, if he have no other means of getting rid of them. Let this be said as a prelude concerning crimes of violence in general; and I must not omit to mention a tradition which is firmly believed by many, and has been received by them from those who are learned in the mysteries: they say that such deeds will be punished in the world below, and also that when the perpetrators return to this world they will pay the natural penalty which is due to the sufferer, and end their lives in like manner by the hand of another. If he who is about to commit murder believes this, and is made by the mere prelude to dread such a penalty, there is no need to proceed with the proclamation of the law. But if he will not listen, let the following law be declared and registered against him: *[871]*

Whoever shall wrongfully and of design slay with his own hand any of his kinsmen, shall in the first place be deprived of legal privileges; and he shall not pollute the temples, or the agora, or the harbours, or any other place of meeting, whether he is forbidden of men or not; for the law, which represents the whole state, forbids him, and always is and will be in the attitude of forbidding him. And if a cousin or nearer relative of the deceased, whether on the male or female side, does not prosecute the homicide when he ought, and have him proclaimed an outlaw, he shall in the first place be involved in the pollution, and incur the hatred of the Gods, even as the curse of the law stirs up the voices of men against him; and in the second place he shall be liable to be prosecuted by any one who is willing to inflict retribution on behalf of the dead. And he who would avenge a murder shall observe all the precautionary ceremonies of lavation, and any others which the God commands in cases of this kind. Let him have proclamation made, and then go forth and compel the perpetrator to suffer the execution of justice according to the law. Now the legislator may easily show that these things must be accomplished by prayers and sacrifices to certain Gods, who are concerned with the prevention of murders in states. But who these Gods are, and what should be the true manner of instituting such trials with due regard to religion, the guardians of the law, aided by the interpreters, and the prophets, and the God, shall determine, and when they have determined let them carry on the prosecution at law. The cause shall have the same judges [1] who are appointed to decide in the case of those who plunder temples. Let him who is convicted be punished with death, and let him not be buried in the country of the murdered man, for this would be shameless as well as impious. But if he fly and will not stand his trial, let him fly for ever; or, if he set foot anywhere on any part of the murdered man's country, let any relation of the deceased, or any other citizen who may first happen to meet with him, kill him with impunity, or bind and deliver him to those among the judges of the case who are magistrates, that they may put him to death. And let the prosecutor demand surety of him whom he prosecutes; three sureties sufficient in the opinion of the magistrates who try the cause shall be provided by him, and they shall undertake to produce him at the trial.

[1] Cf. 855.

But if he be unwilling or unable to provide sureties, then the magistrates shall take him and keep him in bonds, and produce him at the day of trial.

[872] If a man do not commit a murder with his own hand, but contrives the death of another, and is the author of the deed in intention and design, and he continues to dwell in the city, having his soul not pure of the guilt of murder, let him be tried in the same way, except in what relates to the sureties; and also, if he be found guilty, his body after execution may have burial in his native land, but in all other respects his case shall be as the former; and whether a stranger shall kill a citizen, or a citizen a stranger, or a slave a slave, there shall be no difference as touching murder by one's own hand or by contrivance, except in the matter of sureties; and these, as has been said, shall be required of the actual murderer only, and he who brings the accusation shall bind them over at the time. If a slave be convicted of slaying a freeman voluntarily, either by his own hand or by contrivance, let the public executioner take him in the direction of the sepulchre, to a place whence he can see the tomb of the dead man, and inflict upon him as many stripes as the person who caught him orders, and if he survive, let him put him to death. And if any one kills a slave who has done no wrong, because he is afraid that he may inform of some base and evil deeds of his own, or for any similar reason, in such a case let him pay the penalty of murder, as he would have done if he had slain a citizen. There are things about which it is terrible and unpleasant to legislate, but impossible not to legislate. If, for example, there should be murders of kinsmen, either perpetrated by the hands of kinsmen, or by their contrivance, voluntary and purely malicious, which most often happen in ill-regulated and ill-educated states, and may perhaps occur even in a country where a man would not expect to find them, we must repeat once more the tale which we narrated a little while ago, in the hope that he who hears us will be the more disposed to abstain voluntarily on these grounds from murders which are utterly abominable. For the myth, or saying, or whatever we ought to call it, [2] has been plainly set forth by priests of old; they have pronounced that the justice which guards and avenges the blood of kindred, follows the law of retaliation, and ordains that he who has done any murderous act should of necessity suffer that which he has done. He who has slain a father shall himself

[2] Cf. 870.

be slain at some time or other by his children—if a mother, he shall of necessity take a woman's nature, and lose his life at the hands of his offspring in after ages; for where the blood of a family has been polluted there is no other purification, nor can the pollution be washed out until the homicidal soul which did the deed has given life for life, *[873]* and has propitiated and laid to sleep the wrath of the whole family. These are the retributions of Heaven, and by such punishments men should be deterred. But if they are not deterred, and any one should be incited by some fatality to deprive his father or mother, or brethren, or children, of life voluntarily and of purpose, for him the earthly lawgiver legislates as follows:—There shall be the same proclamations about outlawry, and there shall be the same sureties which have been enacted in the former cases. But in his case, if he be convicted, the servants of the judges and the magistrates shall slay him at an appointed place without the city where three ways meet, and there expose his body naked, and each of the magistrates on behalf of the whole city shall take a stone and cast it upon the head of the dead man, and so deliver the city from pollution; after that, they shall bear him to the borders of the land, and cast him forth unburied, according to law. And what shall he suffer who slays him who of all men, as they say, is his own best friend? I mean the suicide, who deprives himself by violence of his appointed share of life, not because the law of the state requires him, nor yet under the compulsion of some painful and inevitable misfortune which has come upon him, nor because he has had to suffer from irremediable and intolerable shame, but who from sloth or want of manliness imposes upon himself an unjust penalty. For him, what ceremonies there are to be of purification and burial God knows, and about these the next of kin should enquire of the interpreters and of the laws thereto relating, and do according to their injunctions. They who meet their death in this way shall be buried alone, and none shall be laid by their side; they shall be buried ingloriously in the borders of the twelve portions of the land, in such places as are uncultivated and nameless, and no column or inscription shall mark the place of their interment. And if a beast of burden or other animal cause the death of any one, except in the case of anything of that kind happening to a competitor in the public contests, the kinsmen of the deceased shall prosecute the slayer for murder, and the wardens of the country, such, and so many as the kinsmen appoint, shall try the cause, and let the beast when condemned be slain by them, and let them cast it beyond the borders. And if any lifeless thing deprive a man of life, except in the case of a thunderbolt or other fatal dart sent from the Gods—whether a man is killed by lifeless objects falling upon him, *[874]* or by his falling upon them, the nearest of kin shall appoint the nearest neighbour to be a judge, and thereby acquit himself and the whole family of guilt. And he shall cast forth the guilty thing beyond the border, as has been said about the animals.

If a man is found dead, and his murderer be unknown, and after a diligent search cannot be detected, there shall be the same proclamation as in the previous cases, and the same interdict on the murderer; and having proceeded against him, they shall proclaim in the agora by a herald, that he who has slain such and such a person, and has been convicted of murder, shall not set his foot in the temples, nor at all in the country of the murdered man, and if he appears and is discovered, he shall die, and be cast forth unburied beyond the border. Let this one law then be laid down by us about murder; and let cases of this sort be so regarded.

And now let us say in what cases and under what circumstances the murderer is rightly free from guilt:—If a man catch a thief coming into his house by night to steal, and he take and kill him, or if he slay a footpad in self-defence, he shall be guiltless. And any one who does violence to a free woman or a youth, shall be slain with impunity by the injured person, or by his or her father or brothers or sons. If a man find his wife suffering violence, he may kill the violator, and be guiltless in the eye of the law; or if a person kill another in warding off death from his father or mother or children or brethren or wife who are doing no wrong, he shall assuredly be guiltless.

Thus much as to the nurture and education of the living soul of man, having which, he can, and without which, if he unfortunately be without them, he cannot live; and also concerning the punishments which are to be inflicted for violent deaths, let thus much be enacted. Of the nurture and education of the body we have spoken before, and next in order we have to speak of deeds of violence, voluntary and involuntary, which men do to one another; these we will now distinguish, as far as we are able, according to their nature and number, and determine what will be the suitable penalties of each, and so assign to them their proper place in the series of our enactments. The poorest legislator will have no difficulty in determining that wounds and mutilations arising out of wounds should follow next in order after deaths. Let wounds be divided as homicides were divided—into those which are involuntary, and which are given in passion or from fear, and those inflicted voluntarily and with premeditation. Concerning all this, we must make some such proclamation as the following:—Mankind must have laws, and conform to them, [875] or their life would be as bad as that of the most savage beast.[1] And the reason of this is that no man's nature is able to know what is best for human society; or knowing, always able and willing to do what is best. In the first place, there is a difficulty in apprehending that the true art or politics is concerned, not with private but with public good (for public good binds together states, but private only distracts them); and that both the public and private good as well of individuals as of states is greater when the state and not the individual is first considered. In the second place, although a person knows in the abstract that this is true, yet if he be possessed of absolute and irresponsible power, he will never remain firm in his principles or persist in regarding the public good as primary in the state, and the private good as secondary. Human nature will be always drawing him into avarice and selfishness, avoiding pain and pursuing pleasure without any reason, and will bring these to the front, obscuring the juster and better; and so working darkness in his soul will at last fill with evils both him and the whole city.[2] For if a man were born so divinely gifted that he could naturally apprehend the truth, he would have no need of laws to rule over him;[3] for there is no law or order which is above knowledge, nor can mind, without impiety, be deemed the subject or slave of any man, but rather the lord of all. I speak of mind, true and free, and in harmony with nature. But then there is no such mind anywhere, or at least not much; and therefore we must choose law and order, which are second best. These look at things as they exist for the most part only, and are unable to survey the whole of them. And therefore I have spoken as I have.

And now we will determine what penalty he ought to pay or suffer who has hurt or wounded another. Any one may easily imagine the questions which have to be asked in all such cases:—What did he wound, or whom, or how, or when? for there are innumerable particulars of this sort which greatly vary from one another. And to allow courts of law to determine all these things, or not to determine any of them, is alike impossible. There is one particular which they must determine in all cases—the question of fact. And then, again, [876] that the legislator should not permit them to determine what punishment is to be inflicted in any of these cases, but should himself decide about all of them, small or great, is next to impossible.

Cle. Then what is to be the inference?

Ath. The inference is, that some things should be left to courts of law; others the legislator must decide for himself.

Cle. And what ought the legislator to decide, and what ought he to leave to the courts of law?

Ath. I may reply, that in a state in which the courts are bad and mute, because the judges conceal their opinions and decide causes clandestinely; or what is worse, when they are disorderly and noisy, as in a theatre, clapping or hooting in turn this or that orator—I say that then there is a very serious evil, which affects the whole state. Unfortunate is the necessity of having to legislate for such courts, but where the necessity exists, the legislator should only allow them to ordain the penalties for the smallest offences; if the state for which he is legislating be of this character, he must take most matters into his own hands and speak distinctly. But when a state has good courts, and the judges are well trained and scrupulously tested, the determination of the penalties or punishments which shall be inflicted on the guilty may fairly and with advantage be left to them. And we are not to be blamed for not legislating concerning all that large class of matters which judges far worse educated than ours would be able to determine, assigning to each offence what is due both to the perpetrator and to the sufferer. We believe those for whom we are legislating to be best able to judge, and therefore to them the greater part may be left. At the same time, as I have often said,[4] we should exhibit to the judges, as we have done, the outline and form of the punishments to be inflicted, and then they will not transgress the just rule. That was an excellent practice, which we observed before, and which now that we are resuming the work of legislation, may with advantage be repeated by us.

Let the enactment about wounding be in the following terms:—If any one has a purpose and

[1] Cf. Aristotle, *Politics,* i. 2, 1253 ª 29-33.
[2] Cf. iii. 691; iv. 711, 713, 716.
[3] Cf. *Statesman,* 297.
[4] Cf. v. 734; vi. 770.

intention to slay another who is not his enemy, and whom the law does not permit him to slay, and he wounds him, *[877]* but is unable to kill him, he who had the intent and has wounded him is not to be pitied—he deserves no consideration, but should be regarded as a murderer and be tried for murder. Still having respect to the fortune which has in a manner favoured him, and to the providence which in pity to him and to the wounded man saved the one from a fatal blow, and the other from an accursed fate and calamity—as a thank-offering to this deity, and in order not to oppose his will—in such a case the law will remit the punishment of death, and only compel the offender to emigrate to a neighbouring city for the rest of his life, where he shall remain in the enjoyment of all his possessions. But if he have injured the wounded man, he shall make such compensation for the injury as the court deciding the cause shall assess, and the same judges shall decide who would have decided if the man had died of his wounds. And if a child intentionally wound his parents, or a servant his master, death shall be the penalty. And if a brother or a sister intentionally wound a brother or a sister, and is found guilty, death shall be the penalty. And if a husband wound a wife, or a wife a husband, with intent to kill, let him or her undergo perpetual exile; if they have sons or daughters who are still young, the guardians shall take care of their property, and have charge of the children as orphans. If their sons are grown up, they shall be under no obligation to support the exiled parent, but they shall possess the property themselves. And if he who meets with such a misfortune has no children, the kindred of the exiled man to the degree of sons of cousins, both on the male and female side, shall meet together, and after taking counsel with the guardians of the law and the priests, shall appoint a 5040th citizen to be the heir of the house, considering and reasoning that no house of all the 5040 belongs to the inhabitant or to the whole family, but is the public and private property of the state. Now the state should seek to have its houses as holy and happy as possible. And if any one of the houses be unfortunate, and stained with impiety, and the owner leave no posterity, but dies unmarried, or married and childless, having suffered death as the penalty of murder or some other crime committed against the Gods or against his fellow-citizens, of which death is the penalty distinctly laid down in the law; or if any of the citizens be in perpetual exile, and also childless, that house shall first

of all be purified and undergo expiation according to law; and then let the kinsmen of the house, as we were just now saying, and the guardians of the law, *[878]* meet and consider what family there is in the state which is of the highest repute for virtue and also for good fortune, in which there are a number of sons; from that family let them take one and introduce him to the father and forefathers of the dead man as their son, and, for the sake of the omen, let him be called so, that he may be the continuer of their family, the keeper of their hearth, and the minister of their sacred rites with better fortune than his father had; and when they have made this supplication, they shall make him heir according to law, and the offending person they shall leave nameless and childless and portionless when calamities such as these overtake him.

Now the boundaries of some things do not touch one another, but there is a borderland which comes in between, preventing them from touching. And we were saying that actions done from passion are of this nature, and come in between the voluntary and involuntary. If a person be convicted of having inflicted wounds in a passion, in the first place he shall pay twice the amount of the injury, if the wound be curable, or, if incurable, four times the amount of the injury; or if the wound be curable, and at the same time cause great and notable disgrace to the wounded person, he shall pay fourfold. And whenever any one in wounding another injures not only the sufferer, but also the city, and makes him incapable of defending his country against the enemy, he, besides the other penalties, shall pay a penalty for the loss which the state has incurred. And the penalty shall be, that in addition to his own times of service, he shall serve on behalf of the disabled person, and shall take his place in war; or, if he refuse, he shall be liable to be convicted by law of refusal to serve. The compensation for the injury, whether to be twofold or threefold or fourfold, shall be fixed by the judges who convict him. And if, in like manner, a brother wounds a brother, the parents and kindred of either sex, including the children of cousins, whether on the male or female side, shall meet, and when they have judged the cause, they shall entrust the assessment of damages to the parents, as is natural; and if the estimate be disputed, then the kinsmen on the male side shall make the estimate, or if they cannot, they shall commit the matter to the guardians of the law. And when similar charges of wounding are brought by children against their parents, those who are more than sixty years of age, having children of their own, not adopted, shall be required to decide; and if any one is convicted, they shall determine whether he or she ought to die, or suffer some other punishment either greater than death, *[879]* or, at any rate, not much less. A kinsman of the offender shall not be allowed to judge the cause, not even if he be of the age which is prescribed by the law. If a slave in a fit of anger wound a freeman, the owner of the slave shall give him up to the wounded man, who may do as he pleases with him, and if he do not give him up he shall himself make good the injury. And if any one says that the slave and the wounded man are conspiring together, let him argue the point, and if he is cast, he shall pay for the wrong three times over, but if he gains his case, the freeman who conspired with the slave shall be liable to an action for kidnapping. And if any one unintentionally wounds another he shall simply pay for the harm, for no legislator is able to control chance. In such a case the judges shall be the same as those who are appointed in the case of children suing their parents; and they shall estimate the amount of the injury.

All the preceding injuries and every kind of assault are deeds of violence; and every man, woman, or child ought to consider that the elder has the precedence of the younger in honour,[1] both among the Gods and also among men who would live in security and happiness. Wherefore it is a foul thing and hateful to the Gods to see an elder man assaulted by a younger in the city; and it is reasonable that a young man when struck by an elder should lightly endure his anger, laying up in store for himself a like honour when he is old. Let this be the law: —Every one shall reverence his elder in word and deed; he shall respect any one who is twenty years older than himself, whether male or female, regarding him or her as his father or mother; and he shall abstain from laying hands on any one who is of an age to have been his father or his mother, out of reverence to the Gods who preside over birth; similarly he shall keep his hands from a stranger, whether he be an old inhabitant or newly arrived; he shall not venture to correct such an one by blows, either as the aggressor or in self-defence. If he thinks that some stranger has struck him out of wantonness or insolence, and ought to be punished, he shall take him to the wardens of the city, but let him not strike him, that the stranger may

be kept far away from the possibility of lifting up his hand against a citizen, and let the wardens of the city take the offender and examine him, not forgetting their duty to the God of Strangers, and in case the stranger appears to have struck the citizen unjustly, let them inflict upon him as many blows with the scourge as he has himself inflicted, and quell his presumption. But if he be innocent, they shall threaten and rebuke the man who arrested him, *[880]* and let them both go. If a person strikes another of the same age or somewhat older than himself, who has no children, whether he be an old man who strikes an old man or a young man who strikes a young man, let the person struck defend himself in the natural way without a weapon and with his hands only. He who, being more than forty years of age, dares to fight with another, whether he be the aggressor or in self-defence, shall be regarded as rude and ill-mannered and slavish;—this will be a disgraceful punishment, and therefore suitable to him. The obedient nature will readily yield to such exhortations, but the disobedient, who heeds not the prelude, shall have the law ready for him:—If any man smite another who is older than himself, either by twenty or by more years, in the first place, he who is at hand, not being younger than the combatants, nor their equal in age, shall separate them, or be disgraced according to law; but if he be the equal in age of the person who is struck or younger, he shall defend the person injured as he would a brother or father or still older relative. Further, let him who dares to smite an elder be tried for assault, as I have said, and if he be found guilty, let him be imprisoned for a period of not less than a year, or if the judges approve of a longer period, their decision shall be final. But if a stranger or metic smite one who is older by twenty years or more, the same law shall hold about the bystanders assisting, and he who is found guilty in such a suit, if he be a stranger but not resident, shall be imprisoned during a period of two years; and a metic who disobeys the laws shall be imprisoned for three years, unless the court assign him a longer term. And let him who was present in any of these cases and did not assist according to law be punished, if he be of the highest class, by paying a fine of a mina; or if he be of the second class, of fifty drachmas; or if of the third class, by a fine of thirty drachmas; or if he be of the fourth class, by a fine of twenty drachmas; and the generals and taxiarchs and phylarchs and hipparchs shall form the court in such cases.

[1] Cf. *Republic,* v. 465.

Laws are partly framed for the sake of good men, in order to instruct them how they may live on friendly terms with one another, and partly for the sake of those who refuse to be instructed, whose spirit cannot be subdued, or softened, or hindered from plunging into evil. These are the persons who cause the word to be spoken which I am about to utter; for them the legislator legislates of necessity, and in the hope that there may be no need of his laws. He who shall dare to lay violent hands upon his father or mother, or any still older relative, having no fear either of the wrath of the Gods above, *[881]* or of the punishments that are spoken of in the world below, but transgresses in contempt of ancient and universal traditions as though he were too wise to believe in them, requires some extreme measure of prevention. Now death is not the worst that can happen to men; far worse are the punishments which are said to pursue them in the world below. But although they are most true tales, they work on such souls no prevention; for if they had any effect there would be no slayers of mothers, or impious hands lifted up against parents; and therefore the punishments of this world which are inflicted during life ought not in such cases to fall short, if possible, of the terrors of the world below. Let our enactment then be as follows:—If a man dare to strike his father or his mother, or their fathers or mothers, he being at the time of sound mind, then let any one who is at hand come to the rescue as has been already said, and the metic or stranger who comes to the rescue shall be called to the first place in the games; but if he do not come he shall suffer the punishment of perpetual exile. He who is not a metic, if he comes to the rescue, shall have praise, and if he do not come, blame. And if a slave come to the rescue, let him be made free, but if he do not come to the rescue, let him receive 100 strokes of the whip, by order of the wardens of the agora, if the occurrence take place in the agora; or if somewhere in the city beyond the limits of the agora, any warden of the city who is in residence shall punish him; or if in the country, then the commanders of the wardens of the country.[1] If those who are near at the time be inhabitants of the same place, whether they be youths, or men, or women, let them come to the rescue and denounce him as the impious one; and he who does not come to the rescue shall fall under the curse of Zeus, the God of kindred and of ancestors, according to law. And if any one is found guilty of assault-

[1] Cf. vi. 760.

ing a parent, let him in the first place be for ever banished from the city into the country, and let him abstain from the temples; and if he do not abstain, the wardens of the country shall punish him with blows, or in any way which they please, and if he return he shall be put to death. And if any freeman eat or drink, or have any other sort of intercourse with him, or only meeting him have voluntarily touched him, he shall not enter into any temple, nor into the agora, nor into the city, until he is purified; for he should consider that he has become tainted by a curse. And if he disobeys the law, and pollutes the city and the temples contrary to law, and one of the magistrates sees him and does not indict him, when he gives in his account this omission shall be a most serious charge.

[882] If a slave strike a freeman, whether a stranger or a citizen, let any one who is present come to the rescue, or pay the penalty already mentioned; and let the bystanders bind him, and deliver him up to the injured person, and he receiving him shall put him in chains, and inflict on him as many stripes as he pleases; but having punished him he must surrender him to his master according to law, and not deprive him of his property. Let the law be as follows:—The slave who strikes a freeman, not at the command of the magistrates, his owner shall receive bound from the man whom he has stricken, and not release him until the slave has persuaded the man whom he has stricken that he ought to be released. And let there be the same laws about women in relation to women, and about men and women in relation to one another.

BOOK X

[884] And now having spoken of assaults, let us sum up all acts of violence under a single law, which shall be as follows:—No one shall take or carry away any of his neighbour's goods, neither shall he use anything which is his neighbour's without the consent of the owner; for these are the offences which are and have been, and will ever be, the source of all the aforesaid evils. The greatest of them are excesses and insolences of youth, and are offences against the greatest when they are done against religion; and especially great when in violation of public and holy rites, or of the partly-common rites in which tribes and phratries share; *[885]* and in the second degree great when they are committed against private rites and sepulchres, and in the third degree (not to re-

peat the acts formerly mentioned), when insults are offered to parents; the fourth kind of violence is when any one, regardless of the authority of the rulers, takes or carries away or makes use of anything which belongs to them, not having their consent; and the fifth kind is when the violation of the civil rights of an individual demands reparation. There should be a common law embracing all these cases. For we have already said in general terms what shall be the punishment of sacrilege, whether fraudulent or violent, and now we have to determine what is to be the punishment of those who speak or act insolently toward the Gods. But first we must give them an admonition which may be in the following terms:—No one who in obedience to the laws believed that there were Gods, ever intentionally did any unholy act, or uttered any unlawful word; but he who did must have supposed one of three things—either that they did not exist, —which is the first possibility, or secondly, that, if they did, they took no care of man, or thirdly, that they were easily appeased and turned aside from their purpose by sacrifices and prayers.

Cleinias. What shall we say or do to these persons?

Athenian Stranger. My good friend, let us first hear the jests which I suspect that they in their superiority will utter against us.

Cle. What jests?

Ath. They will make some irreverent speech of this sort:—"O inhabitants of Athens, and Sparta, and Cnosus," they will reply, "in that you speak truly; for some of us deny the very existence of the Gods, while others, as you say, are of opinion that they do not care about us; and others that they are turned from their course by gifts. Now we have a right to claim, as you yourself allowed, in the matter of laws, that before you are hard upon us and threaten us, you should argue with us and convince us [1] —you should first attempt to teach and persuade us that there are Gods by reasonable evidences, and also that they are too good to be unrighteous, or to be propitiated, or turned from their course by gifts. For when we hear such things said of them by those who are esteemed to be the best of poets, and orators, and prophets, and priests, and by innumerable others, the thoughts of most of us are not set upon abstaining from unrighteous acts, but upon doing them and atoning for them.[2] When law-

givers profess that they are gentle and not stern, we think that they should first of all use persuasion to us, and show us the existence of Gods, if not in a better manner than other men, at any rate in a truer; and who knows but that we shall hearken to you? If then our request is a fair one, please to accept our challenge."

Cle. But is there any difficulty in proving the existence of the Gods?

[886] *Ath.* How would you prove it?

Cle. How? In the first place, the earth and the sun, and the stars and the universe, and the fair order of the seasons, and the division of them into years and months, furnish proofs of their existence; and also there is the fact that all Hellenes and barbarians believe in them.

Ath. I fear, my sweet friend, though I will not say that I much regard, the contempt with which the profane will be likely to assail us. For you do not understand the nature of their complaint, and you fancy that they rush into impiety only from a love of sensual pleasure.

Cle. Why, Stranger, what other reason is there?

Ath. One which you who live in a different atmosphere would never guess.

Cle. What is it?

Ath. A very grievous sort of ignorance which is imagined to be the greatest wisdom.

Cle. What do you mean?

Ath. At Athens there are tales preserved in writing which the virtue of your state, as I am informed, refuses to admit. They speak of the Gods in prose as well as verse, and the oldest of them tell of the origin of the heavens and of the world, and not far from the beginning of their story they proceed to narrate the birth of the Gods, and how after they were born they behaved to one another. Whether these stories have in other ways a good or a bad influence, I should not like to be severe upon them, because they are ancient; but, looking at them with reference to the duties of children to their parents, I cannot praise them, or think that they are useful, or at all true.[3] Of the words of the ancients I have nothing more to say; and I should wish to say of them only what is pleasing to the Gods. But as to our younger generation and their wisdom, I cannot let them off when they do mischief. For do but mark the effect of their words: when you and I argue for the existence of the Gods, and produce the sun, moon, stars, and earth, claiming for them a divine being, if we would listen to the aforesaid philosophers we should say that they are

---

[1] Cf. iv. 718, ff.
[2] Cf. *Republic*, ii. 364.

[3] Cf. *Republic*, ii. 378, ff.

earth and stones only,[1] which can have no care at all of human affairs, and that all religion is a cooking up of words and a make-believe.

Cle. One such teacher, O Stranger, would be bad enough, and you imply that there are many of them, which is worse.

Ath. Well, then; what shall we say or do?— Shall we assume that some one is accusing us among unholy men, *[887]* who are trying to escape from the effect of our legislation; and that they say of us—How dreadful that you should legislate on the supposition that there are Gods! Shall we make a defence of ourselves? or shall we leave them and return to our laws, lest the prelude should become longer than the law? For the discourse will certainly extend to great length, if we are to treat the impiously disposed as they desire, partly demonstrating to them at some length the things of which they demand an explanation, partly making them afraid or dissatisfied, and then proceed to the requisite enactments.

Cle. Yes, Stranger; but then how often have we repeated already that on the present occasion there is no reason why brevity should be preferred to length;[2] for who is "at our heels"? —as the saying goes, and it would be paltry and ridiculous to prefer the shorter to the better. It is a matter of no small consequence, in some way or other to prove that there are Gods, and that they are good, and regard justice more than men do. The demonstration of this would be the best and noblest prelude of all our laws. And therefore, without impatience, and without hurry, let us unreservedly consider the whole matter, summoning up all the power of persuasion which we possess.

Ath. Seeing you thus in earnest, I would fain offer up a prayer that I may succeed:—but I must proceed at once. Who can be calm when he is called upon to prove the existence of the Gods? Who can avoid hating and abhorring the men who are and have been the cause of this argument; I speak of those who will not believe the tales which they have heard as babes and sucklings from their mothers and nurses, repeated by them both in jest and earnest, like charms, who have also heard them in the sacrificial prayers, and seen sights accompanying them—sights and sounds delightful to children—and their parents during the sacrifices showing an intense earnestness on behalf of their children and of themselves, and with eager interest talking to the Gods, and beseeching them, as though they were firmly convinced

[1] Cf. *Apology*, 26, ff.   [2] Cf. iv. 719, ff.; ix. 857-8.

of their existence; who likewise see and hear the prostrations and invocations which are made by Hellenes and barbarians at the rising and setting of the sun and moon, in all the vicissitudes of life, not as if they thought that there were no Gods, but as if there could be no doubt of their existence, and no suspicion of their non-existence; when men, knowing all these things, *[888]* despise them on no real grounds, as would be admitted by all who have any particle of intelligence, and when they force us to say what we are now saying, how can any one in gentle terms remonstrate with the like of them, when he has to begin by proving to them the very existence of the Gods? Yet the attempt must be made; for it would be unseemly that one half of mankind should go mad in their lust of pleasure, and the other half in their indignation at such persons. Our address to these lost and perverted natures should not be spoken in passion; let us suppose ourselves to select some one of them, and gently reason with him, smothering our anger:—O my son, we will say to him, you are young, and the advance of time will make you reverse may of the opinions which you now hold. Wait awhile, and do not attempt to judge at present of the highest things; and that is the highest of which you now think nothing—to know the Gods rightly and to live accordingly. And in the first place let me indicate to you one point which is of great importance, and about which I cannot be deceived:—You and your friends are not the first who have held this opinion about the Gods. There have always been persons more or less numerous who have had the same disorder. I have known many of them, and can tell you, that no one who had taken up in youth this opinion, that the Gods do not exist, ever continued in the same until he was old; the two other notions certainly do continue in some cases, but not in many; the notion, I mean, that the Gods exist, but take no heed of human things, and the other notion that they do take heed of them, but are easily propitiated with sacrifices and prayers. As to the opinion about the Gods which may some day become clear to you, I advise you go wait and consider if it be true or not; ask of others, and above all of the legislator. In the meantime take care that you do not offend against the Gods. For the duty of the legislator is and always will be to teach you the truth of these matters.

Cle. Our address, Stranger, thus far, is excellent.

Ath. Quite true, Megillus and Cleinias, but I am afraid that we have unconsciously lighted on a strange doctrine.

Cle. What doctrine do you mean?

Ath. The wisest of all doctrines, in the opinion of many.

Cle. I wish that you would speak plainer.

Ath. The doctrine that all things do become, have become, and will become, some by nature, some by art, and some by chance.

Cle. Is not that true?

Ath. Well, philosophers are probably right; at any rate we may as well follow in their track, [889] and examine what is the meaning of them and their disciples.

Cle. By all means.

Ath. They say that the greatest and fairest things are the work of nature and of chance, the lesser of art, which, receiving from nature the greater and primeval creations, moulds and fashions all those lesser works which are generally termed artificial.

Cle. How is that?

Ath. I will explain my meaning still more clearly. They say that fire and water, and earth and air, all exist by nature and chance, and none of them by art, and that as to the bodies which come next in order—earth, and sun, and moon, and stars—they have been created by means of these absolutely inanimate existences. The elements are severally moved by chance and some inherent force according to certain affinities among them—of hot with cold, or of dry with moist, or of soft with hard, and according to all the other accidental admixtures of opposites which have been formed by necessity. After this fashion and in this manner the whole heaven has been created, and all that is in the heaven, as well as animals and all plants, and all the seasons come from these elements, not by the action of mind, as they say, or of any God, or from art, but as I was saying, by nature and chance only. Art sprang up afterwards and out of these, mortal and of mortal birth, and produced in play certain images and very partial imitations of the truth, having an affinity to one another, such as music and painting create and their companion arts. And there are other arts which have a serious purpose, and these co-operate with nature, such, for example, as medicine, and husbandry, and gymnastic. And they say that politics cooperate with nature, but in a less degree, and have more of art; also that legislation is entirely a work of art, and is based on assumptions which are not true.

Cle. How do you mean?

Ath. In the first place, my dear friend, these people would say that the Gods exist not by nature, but by art, and by the laws of states, which are different in different places, according to the agreement of those who make them; and that the honourable is one thing by nature and another thing by law, and that the principles of justice have no existence at all in nature, but that mankind are always disputing about them and altering them; and that the alterations which are made by art and by law have no basis in nature, [890] but are of authority for the moment and at the time at which they are made.—These, my friends, are the sayings of wise men, poets and prose writers, which find a way into the minds of youth. They are told by them that the highest right is might, and in this way the young fall into impieties, under the idea that the Gods are not such as the law bids them imagine; and hence arise factions, these philosophers inviting them to lead a true life according to nature, that is, to live in real dominion over others, and not in legal subjection to them.[1]

Cle. What a dreadful picture, Stranger, have you given, and how great is the injury which is thus inflicted on young men to the ruin both of states and families!

Ath. True, Cleinias; but then what should the lawgiver do when this evil is of long standing? should he only rise up in the state and threaten all mankind, proclaiming that if they will not say and think that the Gods are such as the law ordains (and this may be extended generally to the honourable, the just, and to all the highest things, and to all that relates to virtue and vice), and if they will not make their actions conform to the copy which the law gives them, then he who refuses to obey the law shall die, or suffer stripes and bonds, or privation of citizenship, or in some cases be punished by loss of property and exile? Should he not rather, when he is making laws for men, at the same time infuse the spirit of persuasion into his words, and mitigate the severity of them as far as he can?

Cle. Why, Stranger, if such persuasion be at all possible, then a legislator who has anything in him ought never to weary of persuading men; he ought to leave nothing unsaid in support of the ancient opinion that there are Gods, and of all those other truths which you were just now mentioning; he ought to support the law and also art, and acknowledge that both

[1] Cf. *Gorgias*, 483.

alike exist by nature, and no less than nature, if they are the creations of mind in accordance with right reason, as you appear to me to maintain, and I am disposed to agree with you in thinking.

Ath. Yes, my enthusiastic Cleinias; but are not these things when spoken to a multitude hard to be understood, not to mention that they take up a dismal length of time?

Cle. Why, Stranger, shall we, whose patience failed not when drinking or music were the themes of discourse, weary now of discoursing about the Gods, and about divine things? And the greatest help to rational legislation is that the laws when once written down *[891]* are always at rest; they can be put to the test at any future time, and therefore, if on first hearing they seem difficult, there is no reason for apprehension about them, because any man however dull can go over them and consider them again and again; nor if they are tedious but useful, is there any reason or religion, as it seems to me, in any man refusing to maintain the principles of them to the utmost of his power.

Megillus. Stranger, I like what Cleinias is saying.

Ath. Yes, Megillus, and we should do as he proposes; for if impious discourses were not scattered, as I may say, throughout the world, there would have been no need for any vindication of the existence of the Gods—but seeing that they are spread far and wide, such arguments are needed; and who should come to the rescue of the greatest laws, when they are being undermined by bad men, but the legislator himself?

Meg. There is no more proper champion of them.

Ath. Well, then, tell me, Cleinias—for I must ask you to be my partner—does not he who talks in this way conceive fire and water and earth and air to be the first elements of all things? [1] These he calls nature, and out of these he supposes the soul to be formed afterwards; and this is not a mere conjecture of ours about his meaning, but is what he really means.

Cle. Very true.

Ath. Then, by Heaven, we have discovered the source of this vain opinion of all those physical investigators; and I would have you examine their arguments with the utmost care, for their impiety is a very serious matter; they not only make a bad and mistaken use of argument, but they lead away the minds of others: that is my opinion of them.

[1] Cf. *Timaeus,* 46.

Cle. You are right; but I should like to know how this happens.

Ath. I fear that the argument may seem singular.

Cle. Do not hesitate, Stranger; I see that you are afraid of such a discussion carrying you beyond the limits of legislation. But if there be no other way of showing our agreement in the belief that there are Gods, of whom the law is said now to approve, let us take this way, my good sir.

Ath. Then I suppose that I must repeat the singular argument of those who manufacture the soul according to their own impious notions; they affirm that which is the first cause of the generation and destruction of all things, to be not first, but last, and that which is last to be first, and hence they have fallen into error about the true nature of the Gods.

[892] Cle. Still I do not understand you.

Ath. Nearly all of them, my friends, seem to be ignorant of the nature and power of the soul, especially in what relates to her origin: they do not know that she is among the first of things, and before all bodies, and is the chief author of their changes and transpositions. And if this is true, and if the soul is older than the body, must not the things which are of the soul's kindred be of necessity prior to those which appertain to the body?

Cle. Certainly.

Ath. Then thought and attention and mind and art and law will be prior to that which is hard and soft and heavy and light; and the great and primitive works and actions will be works of art; they will be the first, and after them will come nature and works of nature, which however is a wrong term for men to apply to them; these will follow, and will be under the government of art and mind.

Cle. But why is the word "nature" wrong?

Ath. Because those who use the term mean to say that nature is the first creative power; but if the soul turn out to be the primeval element, and not fire or air, then in the truest sense and beyond other things the soul may be said to exist by nature; and this would be true if you proved that the soul is older than the body, but not otherwise.

Cle. You are quite right.

Ath. Shall we, then, take this as the next point to which our attention should be directed?

Cle. By all means.

Ath. Let us be on our guard lest this most deceptive argument with its youthful looks, beguiling us old men, give us the slip and make a laughing-stock of us. Who knows but we may be aiming at the greater, and fail of attaining the lesser? Suppose that we three have to pass a rapid river, and I, being the youngest of the three and experienced in rivers, take upon me the duty of making the attempt first by myself; leaving you in safety on the bank, I am to examine whether the river is passable by older men like yourselves, and if such appears to be the case then I shall invite you to follow, and my experience will help to convey you across; but if the river is impassable by you, then there will have been no danger to anybody but myself—would not that seem to be a very fair proposal? I mean to say that the argument in prospect is likely to be too much for you, out of your depth and beyond your strength, and I should be afraid that the stream of my questions might create in you who [893] are not in the habit of answering, giddiness and confusion of mind, and hence a feeling of unpleasantness and unsuitableness might arise. I think therefore that I had better first ask the questions and then answer them myself while you listen in safety; in that way I can carry on the argument until I have completed the proof that the soul is prior to the body.

Cle. Excellent, Stranger, and I hope that you will do as you propose.

Ath. Come, then, and if ever we are to call upon the Gods, let us call upon them now in all seriousness to come to the demonstration of their own existence. And so holding fast to the rope we will venture upon the depths of the argument. When questions of this sort are asked of me, my safest answer would appear to be as follows:—Some one says to me, "O Stranger, are all things at rest and nothing in motion, or is the exact opposite of this true, or are some things in motion and others at rest?"—To this I shall reply that some things are in motion and others at rest. "And do not things which move move in a place, and are not the things which are at rest at rest in a place?" Certainly. "And some move or rest in one place and some in more places than one?" You mean to say, we shall rejoin, that those things which rest at the centre move in one place, just as the circumference goes round of globes which are said to be at rest? "Yes." And we observe that, in the revolution, the motion which carries round the larger and the lesser circle at the same time is proportionally distributed to greater and smaller, and is greater and smaller in a certain proportion. Here is a wonder which

might be thought an impossibility, that the same motion should impart swiftness and slowness in due proportion to larger and lesser circles. "Very true." And when you speak of bodies moving in many places, you seem to me to mean those which move from one place to another, and sometimes have one centre of motion and sometimes more than one because they turn upon their axis; and whenever they meet anything, if it be stationary, they are divided by it; but if they get in the midst between bodies which are approaching and moving towards the same spot from opposite directions, they unite with them. "I admit the truth of what you are saying." Also when they unite they grow, and when they are divided they waste away—that is, supposing the constitution of each to remain, or if that fails, then there is a second reason of their dissolution. "And when are all things created and how?" [894] Clearly, they are created when the first principle receives increase and attains to the second dimension, and from this arrives at the one which is neighbour to this, and after reaching the third becomes perceptible to sense. Everything which is thus changing and moving is in process of generation; only when at rest has it real existence, but when passing into another state it is destroyed utterly. Have we not mentioned all motions that there are, and comprehended them under their kinds and numbered them with the exception, my friends, of two?

Cle. Which are they?

Ath. Just the two, with which our present enquiry is concerned.

Cle. Speak plainer.

Ath. I suppose that our enquiry has reference to the soul?

Cle. Very true.

Ath. Let us assume that there is a motion able to move other things, but not to move itself;—that is one kind; and there is another kind which can move itself as well as other things, working in composition and decomposition, by increase and diminution and generation and destruction—that is also one of the many kinds of motion.

Cle. Granted.

Ath. And we will assume that which moves other, and is changed by other, to be the ninth, and that which changes itself and others, and is co-incident with every action and every passion, and is the true principle of change and motion in all that is—that we shall be inclined to call the tenth.

Cle. Certainly.

Ath. And which of these ten motions ought we to prefer as being the mightiest and most efficient?

Cle. I must say that the motion which is able to move itself is ten thousand times superior to all the others.[1]

Ath. Very good; but may I make one or two corrections in what I have been saying?

Cle. What are they?

Ath. When I spoke of the tenth sort of motion, that was not quite correct.

Cle. What was the error?

Ath. According to the true order, the tenth was really the first in generation and power; then follows the second, which was strangely enough termed the ninth by us.

Cle. What do you mean?

Ath. I mean this: when one thing changes another, and that another, of such will there be any primary changing element? How can a thing which is moved by another ever be the beginning of change? Impossible. But when the self-moved changes other, and that again other, and thus thousands upon tens of thousands of bodies are set in motion, *[895]* must not the beginning of all this motion be the change of the self-moving principle?[2]

Cle. Very true, and I quite agree.

Ath. Or, to put the question in another way, making answer to ourselves:—If, as most of these philosophers have the audacity to affirm, all things were at rest in one mass, which of the above-mentioned principles of motion would first spring up among them?

Cle. Clearly the self-moving; for there could be no change in them arising out of any external cause; the change must first take place in themselves.

Ath. Then we must say that self-motion being the origin of all motions, and the first which arises among things at rest as well as among things in motion, is the eldest and mightiest principle of change, and that which is changed by another and yet moves other is second.

Cle. Quite true.

Ath. At this stage of the argument let us put a question.

Cle. What question?

Ath. If we were to see this power existing in any earthy, watery, or fiery substance, simple or compound—how should we describe it?

Cle. You mean to ask whether we should call

[1] Cf. *Timaeus,* 89.
[2] Cf. *Phaedrus,* 245.

such a self-moving power life?

Ath. I do.

Cle. Certainly we should.

Ath. And when we see soul in anything, must we not do the same—must we not admit that this is life?

Cle. We must.

Ath. And now, I beseech you, reflect;—you would admit that we have a threefold knowledge of things?

Cle. What do you mean?

Ath. I mean that we know the essence, and that we know the definition of the essence, and the name,—these are the three; and there are two questions which may be raised about anything.

Cle. How two?

Ath. Sometimes a person may give the name and ask the definition; or he may give the definition and ask the name. I may illustrate what I mean in this way.

Cle. How?

Ath. Number like some other things is capable of being divided into equal parts; when thus divided, number is named "even," and the definition of the name "even" is "number divisible into two equal parts"?

Cle. True.

Ath. I mean, that when we are asked about the definition and give the name, or when we are asked about the name and give the definition—in either case, whether we give name or definition, we speak of the same thing, calling "even" the number which is divided into two equal parts.

Cle. Quite true.

Ath. And what is the definition of that which is named "soul"? Can we conceive of any other than that which has been already *[896]* given—the motion which can move itself?

Cle. You mean to say that the essence which is defined as the self-moved is the same with that which has the name soul?

Ath. Yes; and if this is true, do we still maintain that there is anything wanting in the proof that the soul is the first origin and moving power of all that is, or has become, or will be, and their contraries, when she has been clearly shown to be the source of change and motion in all things?

Cle. Certainly not; the soul as being the source of motion, has been most satisfactorily shown to be the oldest of all things.

Ath. And is not that motion which is produced in another, by reason of another, but never has any self-moving power at all, being in truth the change of an inanimate body, to be reckoned second, or by any lower number which you may prefer?

Cle. Exactly.

Ath. Then we are right, and speak the most perfect and absolute truth, when we say that the soul is prior to the body, and that the body is second and comes afterwards, and is born to obey the soul, which is the ruler?

Cle. Nothing can be more true.

Ath. Do you remember our old admission, that if the soul was prior to the body the things of the soul were also prior to those of the body?

Cle. Certainly.

Ath. Then characters and manners, and wishes and reasonings, and true opinions, and reflections, and recollections are prior to length and breadth and depth and strength of bodies, if the soul is prior to the body.

Cle. To be sure.

Ath. In the next place, must we not of necessity admit that the soul is the cause of good and evil, base and honourable, just and unjust, and of all other opposites, if we suppose her to be the cause of all things?

Cle. We must.

Ath. And as the soul orders and inhabits all things that move, however moving, must we not say that she orders also the heavens?

Cle. Of course.

Ath. One soul or more? More than one—I will answer for you; at any rate, we must not suppose that there are less than two—one the author of good, and the other of evil.

Cle. Very true.

Ath. Yes, very true; the soul then directs all things in heaven, and earth, and sea by her movements, and these are described by the terms—will, *[897]* consideration, attention, deliberation, opinion true and false, joy and sorrow, confidence, fear, hatred, love, and other primary motions akin to these; which again receive the secondary motions of corporeal substances, and guide all things to growth and decay, to composition and decomposition, and to the qualities which accompany them, such as heat and cold, heaviness and lightness, hardness and softness, blackness and whiteness, bitterness and sweetness, and all those other qualities which the soul uses, herself a goddess, when truly receiving the divine mind she disciplines all things rightly to their happiness; but when she is the companion of folly, she does the very contrary of all this. Shall we assume so much, or do we still entertain doubts?

Cle. There is no room at all for doubt.

Ath. Shall we say then that it is the soul which controls heaven and earth, and the whole world?—that it is a principle of wisdom and virtue, or a principle which has neither wisdom nor virtue? Suppose that we make answer as follows:—

Cle. How would you answer?

Ath. If, my friend, we say that the whole path and movement of heaven, and of all that is therein, is by nature akin to the movement and revolution and calculation of mind, and proceeds by kindred laws, then, as is plain, we must say that the best soul takes care of the world and guides it along the good path.

Cle. True.

Ath. But if the world moves wildly and irregularly, then the evil soul guides it.

Cle. True again.

Ath. Of what nature is the movement of mind?—To this question it is not easy to give an intelligent answer; and therefore I ought to assist you in framing one.

Cle. Very good.

Ath. Then let us not answer as if we would look straight at the sun, making ourselves darkness at midday,[1]—I mean as if we were under the impression that we could see with mortal eyes, or know adequately the nature of mind; —it will be safer to look at the image only.

Cle. What do you mean?

Ath. Let us select of the ten motions the one which mind chiefly resembles; this I will bring to your recollection, and will then make the answer on behalf of us all.

Cle. That will be excellent.

Ath. You will surely remember our saying that all things were either at rest or in motion?

Cle. I do.

Ath. And that of things in motion some were moving in one place, *[898]* and others in more than one?

Cle. Yes.

Ath. Of these two kinds of motion, that which moves in one place must move about a centre like globes made in a lathe, and is most entirely akin and similar to the circular movement of mind.

Cle. What do you mean?

Ath. In saying that both mind and the motion which is in one place move in the same and like manner, in and about the same, and in relation to the same, and according to one proportion and order, and are like the motion of a globe, we invented a fair image, which

[1] Cf. *Republic*, vii. 515.

does no discredit to our ingenuity.

Cle. It does us great credit.

Ath. And the motion of the other sort which is not after the same manner, nor in the same, nor about the same, nor in relation to the same, nor in one place, nor in order, nor according to any rule or proportion, may be said to be akin to senselessness and folly?

Cle. That is most true.

Ath. Then, after what has been said, there is no difficulty in distinctly stating, that since soul carries all things round, either the best soul or the contrary must of necessity carry round and order and arrange the revolution of the heaven.

Cle. And judging from what has been said, Stranger, there would be impiety in asserting that any but the most perfect soul or souls carries round the heavens.

Ath. You have understood my meaning right well, Cleinias, and now let me ask you another question.

Cle. What are you going to ask?

Ath. If the soul carries round the sun and moon, and the other stars, does she not carry round each individual of them?

Cle. Certainly.

Ath. Then of one of them let us speak, and the same argument will apply to all.

Cle. Which will you take?

Ath. Every one sees the body of the sun, but no one sees his soul, nor the soul of any other body living or dead; and yet there is great reason to believe that this nature, unperceived by any of our senses, is circumfused around them all, but is perceived by mind; and therefore by mind and reflection only let us apprehend the following point.

Cle. What is that?

Ath. If the soul carries round the sun, we shall not be far wrong in supposing one of three alternatives.

Cle. What are they?

Ath. Either the soul which moves the sun this way and that, resides within the circular and visible body, like the soul which carries us about every way; *[899]* or the soul provides herself with an external body of fire or air, as some affirm, and violently propels body by body; or thirdly, she is without such a body, but guides the sun by some extraordinary and wonderful power.

Cle. Yes, certainly; the soul can only order all things in one of these three ways.

Ath. And this soul of the sun, which is therefore better than the sun, whether taking the sun about in a chariot to give light to men, or acting from without, or in whatever way, ought by every man to be deemed a God.[1]

Cle. Yes, by every man who has the least particle of sense.

Ath. And of the stars too, and of the moon, and of the years and months and seasons, must we not say in like manner, that since a soul or souls having every sort of excellence are the causes of all of them, those souls are Gods, whether they are living beings and reside in bodies, and in this way order the whole heaven, or whatever be the place and mode of their existence;—and will any one who admits all this venture to deny that all things are full of Gods?

Cle. No one, Stranger, would be such a madman.

Ath. And now, Megillus and Cleinias, let us offer terms to him who has hitherto denied the existence of the Gods, and leave him.

Cle. What terms?

Ath. Either he shall teach us that we were wrong in saying that the soul is the original of all things, and arguing accordingly; or, if he be not able to say anything better, then he must yield to us and live for the remainder of his life in the belief that there are Gods.—Let us see, then, whether we have said enough or not enough to those who deny that there are Gods.

Cle. Certainly—quite enough, Stranger.

Ath. Then to them we will say no more. And now we are to address him who, believing that there are Gods, believes also that they take no heed of human affairs: To him we say—O thou best of men, in believing that there are Gods you are led by some affinity to them, which attracts you towards your kindred and makes you honour and believe in them. But the fortunes of evil and unrighteous men in private as well as public life, which, though not really happy, are wrongly counted happy in the judgment of men, and are celebrated both by poets and prose writers [2]—these draw you aside from your natural piety. *[900]* Perhaps you have seen impious men growing old and leaving their children's children in high offices, and their prosperity shakes your faith—you have known or heard or been yourself an eyewitness of many monstrous impieties, and have beheld men by such criminal means from small beginnings attaining to sovereignty and the pinnacle of greatness; and considering all these things you do not like to accuse the Gods of them, because they are your relatives; and so from some

---

[1] Cf. xii. 966, 967.

[2] Cf. *Republic,* ii. 364.

want of reasoning power, and also from an un-willingness to find fault with them, you have come to believe that they exist indeed, but have no thought or care of human things. Now, that your present evil opinion may not grow to still greater impiety, and that we may if possible use arguments which may conjure away the evil before it arrives, we will add another argu-ment to that originally addressed to him who utterly denied the existence of the Gods. And do you, Megillus and Cleinias, answer for the young man as you did before; and if any im-pediment comes in our way, I will take the word out of your mouths, and carry you over the river as I did just now.

Cle. Very good; do as you say, and we will help you as well as we can.

Ath. There will probably be no difficulty in proving to him that the Gods care about the small as well as about the great. For he was present and heard what was said, that they are perfectly good, and that the care of all things is most entirely natural to them.[1]

Cle. No doubt he heard that.

Ath. Let us consider together in the next place what we mean by this virtue which we ascribe to them. Surely we should say that to be temperate and to possess mind belongs to vir-tue, and the contrary to vice?

Cle. Certainly.

Ath. Yes; and courage is a part of virtue, and cowardice of vice?

Cle. True.

Ath. And the one is honourable, and the other dishonourable?

Cle. To be sure.

Ath. And the one, like other meaner things, is a human quality, but the Gods have no part in anything of the sort?

Cle. That again is what everybody will ad-mit.

Ath. But do we imagine carelessness and idleness and luxury to be virtues? What do you think?

Cle. Decidedly not.

Ath. They rank under the opposite class?

Cle. Yes.

[901] *Ath.* And their opposites, therefore, would fall under the opposite class?

Cle. Yes.

Ath. But are we to suppose that one who possesses all these good qualities will be luxuri-ous and heedless and idle, like those whom the poet compares to stingless drones?

Cle. And the comparison is a most just one.

[1] Cf. 899.

Ath. Surely God must not be supposed to have a nature which he himself hates?—he who dares to say this sort of thing must not be tolerated for a moment.

Cle. Of course not. How could he have?

Ath. Should we not on any principle be en-tirely mistaken in praising any one who has some special business entrusted to him, if he have a mind which takes care of great matters and no care of small ones? Reflect; he who acts in this way, whether he be God or man, must act from one of two principles.

Cle. What are they?

Ath. Either he must think that the neglect of the small matters is of no consequence to the whole, or if he knows that they are of conse-quence, and he neglects them, his neglect must be attributed to carelessness and indolence. Is there any other way in which his neglect can be explained? For surely, when it is impossible for him to take care of all, he is not negligent if he fails to attend to these things great or small, which a God or some inferior being might be wanting in strength or capacity to manage?

Cle. Certainly not.

Ath. Now, then, let us examine the offend-ers, who both alike confess that there are Gods, but with a difference—the one saying that they may be appeased, and the other that they have no care of small matters: there are three of us and two of them, and we will say to them—In the first place, you both acknowledge that the Gods hear and see and know all things, and that nothing can escape them which is matter of sense and knowledge:—do you admit this?

Cle. Yes.

Ath. And do you admit also that they have all power which mortals and immortals can have?

Cle. They will, of course, admit this also.

Ath. And surely we three and they two—five in all—have acknowledged that they are good and perfect?

Cle. Assuredly.

Ath. But, if they are such as we conceive them to be, can we possibly suppose that they ever act in the spirit of carelessness and indo-lence? For in us inactivity is the child of cow-ardice, and carelessness of inactivity and indo-lence.

Cle. Most true.

Ath. Then not from inactivity and careless-ness is any God ever negligent; for there is no cowardice in them.

Cle. That is very true.

Ath. Then the alternative which remains is, that if the Gods neglect the lighter and lesser concerns of the universe, *[902]* they neglect them because they know that they ought not to care about such matters—what other alternative is there but the opposite of their knowing?

Cle. There is none.

Ath. And, O most excellent and best of men, do I understand you to mean that they are careless because they are ignorant, and do not know that they ought to take care, or that they know, and yet like the meanest sort of men, knowing the better, choose the worse because they are overcome by pleasures and pains?

Cle. Impossible.

Ath. Do not all human things partake of the nature of soul? And is not man the most religious of all animals? [1]

Cle. That is not to be denied.

Ath. And we acknowledge that all mortal creatures are the property of the Gods, to whom also the whole of heaven belongs? [2]

Cle. Certainly.

Ath. And, therefore, whether a person says that these things are to the Gods great or small —in either case it would not be natural for the Gods who own us, and who are the most careful and the best of owners, to neglect us.— There is also a further consideration.

Cle. What is it?

Ath. Sensation and power are in an inverse ratio to each other in respect to their ease and difficulty.

Cle. What do you mean?

Ath. I mean that there is greater difficulty in seeing and hearing the small than the great, but more facility in moving and controlling and taking care of small and unimportant things than of their opposites.

Cle. Far more.

Ath. Suppose the case of a physician who is willing and able to cure some living thing as a whole—how will the whole fare at his hands if he takes care only of the greater and neglects the parts which are lesser?

Cle. Decidedly not well.

Ath. No better would be the result with pilots or generals, or householders or statesmen, or any other such class, if they neglected the small and regarded only the great;—as the builders say, the larger stones do not lie well without the lesser.

Cle. Of course not.

Ath. Let us not, then, deem God inferior to

[1] Cf. *Timaeus*, 42.
[2] Cf. *Phaedo*, 62.

human workmen, who, in proportion to their skill, finish and perfect their works, small as well as great, *[903]* by one and the same art; or that God, the wisest of beings, who is both willing and able to take care, is like a lazy good-for-nothing, or a coward, who turns his back upon labour and gives no thought to smaller and easier matters, but to the greater only.

Cle. Never, Stranger, let us admit a supposition about the Gods which is both impious and false.

Ath. I think that we have now argued enough with him who delights to accuse the Gods of neglect.

Cle. Yes.

Ath. He has been forced to acknowledge that he is in error, but he still seems to me to need some words of consolation.

Cle. What consolation will you offer him?

Ath. Let us say to the youth:—The ruler of the universe has ordered all things with a view to the excellence and preservation of the whole, and each part, as far as may be, has an action and passion appropriate to it. Over these, down to the least fraction of them, ministers have been appointed to preside, who have wrought out their perfection with infinitesimal exactness. And one of these portions of the universe is thine own, unhappy man, which, however little, contributes to the whole; and you do not seem to be aware that this and every other creation is for the sake of the whole, and in order that the life of the whole may be blessed; and that you are created for the sake of the whole, and not the whole for the sake of you. For every physician and every skilled artist does all things for the sake of the whole, directing his effort towards the common good, executing the part for the sake of the whole, and not the whole for the sake of the part. And you are annoyed because you are ignorant how what is best for you happens to you and to the universe, as far as the laws of the common creation admit. Now, as the soul combining first with one body and then with another undergoes all sorts of changes, either of herself, or through the influence of another soul, all that remains to the player of the game is that he should shift the pieces; sending the better nature to the better place, and the worse to the worse, and so assigning to them their proper portion.

Cle. In what way do you mean?

Ath. In a way which may be supposed to make the care of all things easy to the Gods. If any one were to form or fashion all things without any regard to the whole—if, for example, he formed a living element of water out of fire, instead of forming many things out of one or one out of many in regular order attaining to a first or *[904]* second or third birth,[1] the transmutation would have been infinite; but now the ruler of the world has a wonderfully easy task.

Cle. How so?

Ath. I will explain:—When the king saw that our actions had life, and that there was much virtue in them and much vice, and that the soul and body, although not, like the Gods of popular opinion, eternal, yet having once come into existence, were indestructible (for if either of them had been destroyed, there would have been no generation of living beings); and when he observed that the good of the soul was ever by nature designed to profit men, and the evil to harm them—he, seeing all this, contrived so to place each of the parts that their position might in the easiest and best manner procure the victory of good and the defeat of evil in the whole. And he contrived a general plan by which a thing of a certain nature found a certain seat and room. But the formation of qualities he left to the wills of individuals. For every one of us is made pretty much what he is by the bent of his desires and the nature of his soul.

Cle. Yes, that is probably true.

Ath. Then all things which have a soul change, and possess in themselves a principle of change, and in changing move according to law and to the order of destiny: natures which have undergone a lesser change move less and on the earth's surface, but those which have suffered more change and have become more criminal sink into the abyss, that is to say, into Hades and other places in the world below, of which the very names terrify men, and which they picture to themselves as in a dream, both while alive and when released from the body. And whenever the soul receives more of good or evil from her own energy and the strong influence of others—when she has communion with divine virtue and becomes divine, she is carried into another and better place, which is perfect in holiness; but when she has communion with evil, then she also changes the place of her life.

This is the justice of the Gods who inhabit Olympus.[2]

O youth or young man, who fancy that you are

¹ Cf. *Timaeus,* 42.   ² *Odyssey,* xix. 43.

neglected by the Gods, know that if you become worse you shall go to the worse souls, or if better to the better, and in every succession of life and death you will do and suffer what like *[905]* may fitly suffer at the hands of like. This is the justice of heaven, which neither you nor any other unfortunate will ever glory in escaping, and which the ordaining powers have specially ordained; take good heed thereof, for it will be sure to take heed of you. If you say:—I am small and will creep into the depths of the earth, or I am high and will fly up to heaven, you are not so small or so high but that you shall pay the fitting penalty, either here or in the world below or in some still more savage place whither you shall be conveyed. This is also the explanation of the fate of those whom you saw, who had done unholy and evil deeds, and from small beginnings had grown great, and you fancied that from being miserable they had become happy; and in their actions, as in a mirror, you seemed to see the universal neglect of the Gods, not knowing how they make all things work together and contribute to the great whole. And thinkest thou, bold man, that thou needest not to know this?—he who knows it not can never form any true idea of the happiness or unhappiness of life or hold any rational discourse respecting either. If Cleinias and this our reverend company succeed in proving to you that you know not what you say of the Gods, then will God help you; but should you desire to hear more, listen to what we say to the third opponent, if you have any understanding whatsoever. For I think that we have sufficiently proved the existence of the Gods, and that they care for men:—The other notion that they are appeased by the wicked, and take gifts, is what we must not concede to any one, and what every man should disprove to the utmost of his power.

Cle. Very good; let us do as you say.

Ath. Well, then, by the Gods themselves I conjure you to tell me—if they are to be propitiated, how are they to be propitiated? Who are they, and what is their nature? Must they not be at least rulers who have to order unceasingly the whole heaven?

Cle. True.

Ath. And to what earthly rulers can they be compared, or who to them? How in the less can we find an image of the greater? Are they charioteers of contending pairs of steeds, or pilots of vessels? Perhaps they might be compared to the generals of armies, or they might be likened to physicians providing against the diseases which *[906]* make war upon the body, or to husbandmen observing anxiously the effects of the seasons on the growth of plants; or perhaps to shepherds of flocks. For as we acknowledge the world to be full of many goods and also of evils, and of more evils than goods, there is, as we affirm, an immortal conflict going on among us, which requires marvellous watchfulness; and in that conflict the Gods and demigods are our allies, and we are their property. Injustice and insolence and folly are the destruction of us, and justice and temperance and wisdom are our salvation; and the place of these latter is in the life of the Gods, although some vestige of them may occasionally be discerned among mankind. But upon this earth we know that there dwell souls possessing an unjust spirit, who may be compared to brute animals, which fawn upon their keepers, whether dogs or shepherds, or the best and most perfect masters; for they in like manner, as the voices of the wicked declare, prevail by flattery and prayers and incantations, and are allowed to make their gains with impunity. And this sin, which is termed dishonesty, is an evil of the same kind as what is termed disease in living bodies or pestilence in years or seasons of the year, and in cities and governments has another name, which is injustice.

Cle. Quite true.

Ath. What else can he say who declares that the Gods are always lenient to the doers of unjust acts, if they divide the spoil with them? As if wolves were to toss a portion of their prey to the dogs, and they, mollified by the gift, suffered them to tear the flocks.[1] Must not he who maintains that the Gods can be propitiated argue thus?

Cle. Precisely so.

Ath. And to which of the above-mentioned classes of guardians would any man compare the Gods without absurdity? Will he say that they are like pilots, who are themselves turned away from their duty by "libations of wine and the savour of fat," and at last overturn both ship and sailors?

Cle. Assuredly not.

Ath. And surely they are not like charioteers who are bribed to give up the victory to other chariots?

Cle. That would be a fearful image of the Gods.

Ath. Nor are they like generals, or physicians, or husbandmen, or shepherds; and no one would compare them to dogs who have

[1] Cf. *Republic*, ii. 365.

been silenced by wolves.

Cle. A thing not to be spoken of.

[907] Ath. And are not all the Gods the chiefest of all guardians, and do they not guard our highest interests?

Cle. Yes; the chiefest.

Ath. And shall we say that those who guard our noblest interests, and are the best of guardians, are inferior in virtue to dogs, and to men even of moderate excellence, who would never betray justice for the sake of gifts which unjust men impiously offer them?

Cle. Certainly not; nor is such a notion to be endured, and he who holds this opinion may be fairly singled out and characterized as of all impious men the wickedest and most impious.

Ath. Then are the three assertions—that the Gods exist, and that they take care of men, and that they can never be persuaded to do injustice, now sufficiently demonstrated? May we say that they are?

Cle. You have our entire assent to your words.

Ath. I have spoken with vehemence because I am zealous against evil men; and I will tell you, dear Cleinias, why I am so. I would not have the wicked think that, having the superiority in argument, they may do as they please and act according to their various imaginations about the Gods; and this zeal has led me to speak too vehemently; but if we have at all succeeded in persuading the men to hate themselves and love their opposites, the prelude of our laws about impiety will not have been spoken in vain.

Cle. So let us hope; and even if we have failed, the style of our argument will not discredit the lawgiver.

Ath. After the prelude shall follow a discourse, which will be the interpreter of the law; this shall proclaim to all impious persons that they must depart from their ways and go over to the pious. And to those who disobey, let the law about impiety be as follows:—If a man is guilty of any impiety in word or deed, any one who happens to be present shall give information to the magistrates, in aid of the law; and let the magistrates who first receive the information bring him before the appointed court according to the law; and if a magistrate, after receiving information, refuses to act, he shall be tried for impiety at the instance of any one who is willing to vindicate the laws; and if any one be cast, the court shall estimate the punishment of each act of impiety; *[908]* and let all such criminals be imprisoned. There shall be three prisons in the state: the first of them is to be the common prison in the neighbourhood of the agora for the safe-keeping of the generality of offenders; another is to be in the neighbourhood of the nocturnal council,[1] and is to be called the "House of Reformation"; another, to be situated in some wild and desolate region in the centre of the country, shall be called by some name expressive of retribution. Now, men fall into impiety from three causes, which have been already mentioned, and from each of these causes arise two sorts of impiety, in all six, which are worth distinguishing, and should not all have the same punishment. For he who does not believe in the Gods, and yet has a righteous nature, hates the wicked and dislikes and refuses to do injustice, and avoids unrighteous men, and loves the righteous. But they who besides believing that the world is devoid of Gods are intemperate, and have at the same time good memories and quick wits, are worse; although both of them are unbelievers, much less injury is done by the one than by the other. The one may talk loosely about the Gods and about sacrifices and oaths, and perhaps by laughing at other men he may make them like himself, if he be not punished. But the other who holds the same opinions and is called a clever man, is full of stratagem and deceit—men of this class deal in prophecy and jugglery of all kinds, and out of their ranks sometimes come tyrants and demagogues and generals and hierophants of private mysteries and the Sophists, as they are termed, with their ingenious devices. There are many kinds of unbelievers, but two only for whom legislation is required; one the hypocritical sort, whose crime is deserving of death many times over, while the other needs only bonds and admonition. In like manner also the notion that the Gods take no thought of men produces two other sorts of crimes, and the notion that they may be propitiated produces two more. Assuming these divisions, let those who have been made what they are only from want of understanding, and not from malice or an evil nature, be placed by the judge in the House of Reformation, [909] and ordered to suffer imprisonment during a period of not less than five years. And in the meantime let them have no intercourse with the other citizens, except with members of the nocturnal council, and with them let them converse with a view to the improvement of their soul's health. And when the time of their imprisonment has expired, if any of them be of

sound mind let him be restored to sane company, but if not, and if he be condemned a second time, let him be punished with death. As to that class of monstrous natures who not only believe that there are no Gods, or that they are negligent, or to be propitiated, but in contempt of mankind conjure the souls of the living [2] and say that they can conjure the dead and promise to charm the Gods with sacrifices and prayers, and will utterly overthrow individuals and whole houses and states for the sake of money—let him who is guilty of any of these things be condemned by the court to be bound according to law in the prison which is in the centre of the land, and let no freeman ever approach him, but let him receive the rations of food appointed by the guardians of the law from the hands of the public slaves; and when he is dead let him be cast beyond the borders unburied, and if any freeman assist in burying him, let him pay the penalty of impiety to any one who is willing to bring a suit against him. But if he leaves behind him children who are fit to be citizens, let the guardians of orphans take care of them, just as they would of any other orphans, from the day on which their father is convicted.

In all these cases there should be one law, which will make men in general less liable to transgress in word or deed, and less foolish, because they will not be allowed to practise religious rites contrary to law. And let this be the simple form of the law:—No man shall have sacred rites in a private house. When he would sacrifice, let him go to the temples and hand over his offerings to the priests and priestesses, who see to the sanctity of such things, and let him pray himself, and let any one who pleases join with him in prayer. The reason of this is as follows:—Gods and temples are not easily instituted, and to establish them rightly is the work of a mighty intellect. And women especially, and men too, when they are sick or in danger, or in any sort of difficulty, or again on their receiving any good fortune, [910] have a way of consecrating the occasion, vowing sacrifices, and promising shrines to Gods, demigods, and sons of Gods; and when they are awakened by terrible apparitions and dreams or remember visions, they find in altars and temples the remedies of them, and will fill every house and village with them, placing them in the open air, or wherever they may have had such visions; and with a view to all these cases we should obey the law. The law has also re-

---

[1] Cf. xii. 951, 961.

[2] Cf. *Republic*, ii. 364.

gard to the impious, and would not have them fancy that by the secret performance of these actions—by raising temples and by building altars in private houses, they can propitiate the God secretly with sacrifices and prayers, while they are really multiplying their crimes infinitely, bringing guilt from heaven upon themselves, and also upon those who permit them, and who are better men than they are; and the consequence is that the whole state reaps the fruit of their impiety, which, in a certain sense, is deserved. Assuredly God will not blame the legislator, who will enact the following law:—No one shall possess shrines of the Gods in private houses, and he who is found to possess them, and perform any sacred rites not publicly authorized—supposing the offender to be some man or woman who is not guilty of any other great and impious crime—shall be informed against by him who is acquainted with the fact, which shall be announced by him to the guardians of the law; and let them issue orders that he or she shall carry away their private rites to the public temples, and if they do not persuade them, let them inflict a penalty on them until they comply. And if a person be proven guilty of impiety, not merely from childish levity, but such as grown-up men may be guilty of, whether he have sacrificed publicly or privately to any Gods, let him be punished with death, for his sacrifice is impure. Whether the deed has been done in earnest, or only from childish levity, let the guardians of the law determine, before they bring the matter into court and prosecute the offender for impiety.

BOOK XI

[913] In the next place, dealings between man and man require to be suitably regulated. The principle of them is very simple:—Thou shalt not, if thou canst help, touch that which is mine, or remove the least thing which belongs to me without my consent; and may I be of a sound mind, and do to others as I would that they should do to me. First, let us speak of treasure trove:—May I never pray the Gods to find the hidden treasure, which another has laid up for himself and his family, he not being one of my ancestors, nor lift, if I should find, such a treasure. And may I never have any dealings with those who are called diviners, and who in any way or manner counsel me to take up the deposit entrusted to the earth, for I should not gain so much in the increase of my possessions, if I take up the prize, as I should grow in justice and virtue of soul, if I abstain; and this will be a better possession to me than the other in a better part of myself; for the possession of justice in the soul is preferable to the possession of wealth. And of many things it is well said—"Move not the immovables," and this may be regarded as one of them. And we shall do well to believe the common tradition which says that such deeds prevent a man from having a family. Now as to him who is careless about having children and regardless of the legislator, taking up that which neither he deposited, nor any ancestor of his, without the consent of the depositor, violating the simplest and noblest of laws which was the enactment of no mean man:—"Take not up that which was not laid down by thee"—of him, I say, who despises these two legislators, and takes up, not small matter which he has not deposited, but perhaps a great heap of treasure, what he ought to suffer at the hands of the Gods, God only knows; but I would have the first person who sees him go and tell the wardens of the city, if the occurrence has taken place in the city, or if the occurrence has taken place in the agora he shall tell the wardens of the agora, or if in the country he shall tell the wardens of the country and their commanders.[1] When information has been received the city shall send to Delphi, [914] and, whatever the God answers about the money and the remover of the money, that the city shall do in obedience to the oracle; the informer, if he be a freeman, shall have the honour of doing rightly, and he who informs not, the dishonour of doing wrongly; and if he be a slave who gives information, let him be freed, as he ought to be, by the state, which shall give his master the price of him; but if he do not inform he shall be punished with death. Next in order shall follow a similar law, which shall apply equally to matters great and small:—If a man happens to leave behind him some part of his property, whether intentionally or unintentionally, let him who may come upon the left property suffer it to remain, reflecting that such things are under the protection of the Goddess of ways, and are dedicated to her by the law. But if any one defies the law, and takes the property home with him, let him, if the thing is of little worth, and the man who takes it a slave, be beaten with many stripes by him, being a person of not less than thirty years of age. Or if he be a freeman, in addition to being thought a mean person and a despiser of the laws, let him pay ten times the value of

[1] Cf. vi. 760.

the treasure which he has moved to the leaver. And if some one accuses another of having anything which belongs to him, whether little or much, and the other admits that he has this thing, but denies that the property in dispute belongs to the other, if the property be registered with the magistrates according to law, the claimant shall summon the possessor, who shall bring it before the magistrates; and when it is brought into court, if it be registered in the public registers, to which of the litigants it belonged, let him take it and go his way. Or if the property be registered as belonging to some one who is not present, whoever will offer sufficient surety on behalf of the absent person that he will give it up to him, shall take it away as the representative of the other. But if the property which is deposited be not registered with the magistrates, let it remain until the time of trial with three of the eldest of the magistrates; and if it be an animal which is deposited, then he who loses the suit shall pay the magistrates for its keep, and they shall determine the cause within three days.

Any one who is of sound mind may arrest his own slave, and do with him whatever he will of such things as are lawful; and he may arrest the runaway slave of any of his friends or kindred with a view to his safe-keeping. And if any one takes away him who is being carried off as a slave, intending to liberate him, he who is carrying him off shall let him go; but he who takes him away shall give three sufficient sureties; and if he give them, and not without giving them, he may take him away, but if he take him away after any other manner he shall be deemed guilty of violence, and being convicted shall pay as a penalty double the amount of the damages claimed to him who has been deprived of the slave. *[915]* Any man may also carry off a freedman, if he do not pay respect or sufficient respect to him who freed him. Now the respect shall be, that the freedman go three times in the month to the hearth of the person who freed him, and offer to do whatever he ought, so far as he can; and he shall agree to make such a marriage as his former master approves. He shall not be permitted to have more property than he who gave him liberty, and what more he has shall belong to his master. The freedman shall not remain in the state more than twenty years, but like other foreigners [1] shall go away, taking his entire property with him, unless he has the consent of the magistrates and of his former master to remain. If a freedman or any

other stranger has a property greater than the census of the third class, at the expiration of thirty days from the day on which this comes to pass, he shall take that which is his and go his way, and in this case he shall not be allowed to remain any longer by the magistrates. And if any one disobeys this regulation, and is brought into court and convicted, he shall be punished with death, and his property shall be confiscated. Suits about these matters shall take place before the tribes, unless the plaintiff and defendant have got rid of the accusation either before their neighbours or before judges chosen by them. If a man lay claim to any animal or anything else which he declares to be his, let the possessor refer to the seller or to some honest and trustworthy person, who has given, or in some legitimate way made over the property to him; if he be a citizen or a metic, sojourning in the city, within thirty days, or, if the property have been delivered to him by a stranger, within five months, of which the middle month shall include the summer solstice. [2] When goods are exchanged by selling and buying, a man shall deliver them, and receive the price of them, at a fixed place in the agora, and have done with the matter; but he shall not buy or sell anywhere else, nor give credit. And if in any other manner or in any other place there be an exchange of one thing for another, and the seller give credit to the man who buys from him, he must do this on the understanding that the law gives no protection in cases of things sold not in accordance with these regulations. [3] Again, as to contributions, any man who likes may go about collecting contributions as a friend among friends, but if any difference arises about the collection, he is to act on the understanding that the law gives no protection in such cases. *[916]* He who sells anything above the value of fifty drachmas shall be required to remain in the city for ten days, and the purchaser shall be informed of the house of the seller, with a view to the sort of charges which are apt to arise in such cases, and the restitutions which the law allows. And let legal restitution be on this wise: —If a man sells a slave who is in a consumption, or who has the disease of the stone, or of strangury, or epilepsy, or some other tedious and incurable disorder of body or mind, which is not discernible to the ordinary man, if the purchaser be a physician or trainer, he shall have no right of restitution; nor shall there be any right of restitution if the seller has told the truth before-

[1] Cf. viii. 850.

[2] Cf. xii. 952.

[3] Cf. viii. 849.

hand to the buyer. But if a skilled person sells to another who is not skilled, let the buyer appeal for restitution within six months, except in the case of epilepsy, and then the appeal may be made within a year. The cause shall be determined by such physicians as the parties may agree to choose; and the defendant, if he lose the suit, shall pay double the price at which he sold. If a private person sell to another private person, he shall have the right of restitution, and the decision shall be given as before, but the defendant, if he be cast, shall only pay back the price of the slave. If a person sells a homicide to another, and they both know of the fact, let there be no restitution in such a case, but if he do not know of the fact, there shall be a right of restitution, whenever the buyer makes the discovery; and the decision shall rest with the five youngest guardians of the law, and if the decision be that the seller was cognisant of the fact, he shall purify the house of the purchaser, according to the law of the interpreters, and shall pay back three times the purchase-money.

If a man exchanges either money for money, or anything whatever for anything else, either with or without life, let him give and receive them genuine and unadulterated, in accordance with the law. And let us have a prelude about all this sort of roguery, like the preludes of our other laws. Every man should regard adulteration as of one and the same class with falsehood and deceit, concerning which the many are too fond of saying that at proper times and places the practice may often be right. But they leave the occasion, and the when, and the where, undefined and unsettled, and from this want of definiteness in their language they do a great deal of harm to themselves and to others. Now a legislator ought not to leave the matter undetermined; he ought to prescribe some limit, either greater or less. Let this be the rule prescribed:—No one shall call the Gods to witness, when he says or does anything false or deceitful or dishonest, unless he would be the most hateful of mankind to them. *[917]* And he is most hateful to them who takes a false oath, and pays no heed to the Gods; and in the next degree, he who tells a falsehood in the presence of his superiors. Now better men are the superiors of worse men, and in general elders are the superiors of the young; wherefore also parents are the superiors of their offspring, and men of women and children, and rulers of their subjects; for all men ought to reverence any one who is in any position of authority, and especially those who are in state offices. And this is

the reason why I have spoken of these matters. For every one who is guilty of adulteration in the agora tells a falsehood, and deceives, and when he invokes the Gods, according to the customs and cautions of the wardens of the agora, he does but swear without any respect for God or man. Certainly, it is an excellent rule not lightly to defile the names of the Gods, after the fashion of men in general, who care little about piety and purity in their religious actions. But if a man will not conform to this rule, let the law be as follows:—He who sells anything in the agora shall not ask two prices for that which he sells, but he shall ask one price, and if he do not obtain this, he shall take away his goods; and on that day he shall not value them either at more or less; and there shall be no praising of any goods, or oath taken about them. If a person disobeys this command, any citizen who is present, not being less than thirty years of age, may with impunity chastise and beat the swearer, but if instead of obeying the laws he takes no heed, he shall be liable to the charge of having betrayed them. If a man sells any adulterated goods and will not obey these regulations, he who knows and can prove the fact, and does prove it in the presence of the magistrates, if he be a slave or a metic, shall have the adulterated goods; but if he be a citizen, and do not pursue the charge, he shall be called a rogue, and deemed to have robbed the Gods of the agora; or if he proves the charge, he shall dedicate the goods to the Gods of the agora. He who is proved to have sold any adulterated goods, in addition to losing the goods themselves, shall be beaten with stripes—a stripe for a drachma, according to the price of the goods; and the herald shall proclaim in the agora the offence for which he is going to be beaten. The wardens of the agora and the guardians of the law shall obtain information from experienced persons about the rogueries and adulterations of the sellers, and shall write up what the seller ought and ought not to do in each case; and let them inscribe their laws on a column in front of the court of the wardens of the agora, that they may be clear instructors of those who have business in the agora. *[918]* Enough has been said in what has preceded about the wardens of the city, and if anything seems to be wanting, let them communicate with the guardians of the law, and write down the omission, and place on a column in the court of the wardens of the city the primary and secondary regulations which are laid down for them about their office.

After the practices of adulteration naturally follow the practices of retail trade. Concerning these, we will first of all give a word of counsel and reason, and the law shall come afterwards. Retail trade in a city is not by nature intended to do any harm, but quite the contrary; for is not he a benefactor who reduces the inequalities and incommensurabilities of goods to equality and common measure? And this is what the power of money accomplishes, and the merchant may be said to be appointed for this purpose. The hireling and the tavern-keeper, and many other occupations, some of them more and others less seemly—alike have this object;—they seek to satisfy our needs and equalize our possessions.[1] Let us then endeavour to see what has brought retail trade into ill-odour, and wherein lies the dishonour and unseemliness of it, in order that if not entirely, we may yet partially, cure the evil by legislation. To effect this is no easy matter, and requires a great deal of virtue.

Cleinias. What do you mean?

Athenian Stranger. Dear Cleinias, the class of men is small—they must have been rarely gifted by nature, and trained by education—who, when assailed by wants and desires, are able to hold out and observe moderation, and when they might make a great deal of money are sober in their wishes, and prefer a moderate to a large gain. But the mass of mankind are the very opposite: their desires are unbounded, and when they might gain in moderation they prefer gains without limit; wherefore all that relates to retail trade, and merchandise, and the keeping of taverns, is denounced and numbered among dishonourable things. For if what I trust may never be and will not be, we were to compel, if I may venture to say a ridiculous thing, the best men everywhere to keep taverns for a time, or carry on retail trade, or do anything of that sort; or if, in consequence of some fate or necessity, the best women were compelled to follow similar callings, then we should know how agreeable and pleasant all these things are; and if all such occupations were managed on incorrupt principles, they would be honoured as we honour a mother or a nurse. But now that a man goes to desert places and builds houses which can only be reached by long journeys, *[919]* for the sake of retail trade, and receives strangers who are in need at the welcome resting-place, and gives them peace and calm when they are tossed by the storm, or cool shade in the heat;

[1] Cf. Aristotle, *Politics,* i. 9, 1256 ᵇ 40-1257 ᵇ 17.

and then instead of behaving to them as friends, and showing the duties of hospitality to his guests, treats them as enemies and captives who are at his mercy, and will not release them until they have paid the most unjust, abominable, and extortionate ransom—these are the sort of practices, and foul evils they are, which cast a reproach upon the succour of adversity. And the legislator ought always to be devising a remedy for evils of this nature. There is an ancient saying, which is also a true one—"To fight against two opponents is a difficult thing," as is seen in diseases and in many other cases. And in this case also the war is against two enemies—wealth and poverty; one of whom corrupts the soul of man with luxury, while the other drives him by pain into utter shamelessness. What remedy can a city of sense find against this disease? In the first place, they must have as few retail traders as possible; and in the second place, they must assign the occupation to that class of men whose corruption will be the least injury to the state; and in the third place, they must devise some way whereby the followers of these occupations themselves will not readily fall into habits of unbridled shamelessness and meanness.

After this preface let our law run as follows, and may fortune favour us:—No landowner among the Magnetes, whose city the God is restoring and resettling—no one, that is, of the 5040 families, shall become a retail trader either voluntarily or involuntarily; neither shall he be a merchant, or do any service for private persons unless they equally serve him, except for his father or his mother, and their fathers and mothers; and in general for his elders who are freemen, and whom he serves as a freeman. Now it is difficult to determine accurately the things which are worthy or unworthy of a freeman, but let those who have obtained the prize of virtue give judgment about them in accordance with their feelings of right and wrong. He who in any way shares in the illiberality of retail trades may be indicted for dishonouring his race by any one who likes, before those who have been judged to be the first in virtue; and if he appear to throw dirt upon his father's house by an unworthy occupation, *[920]* let him be imprisoned for a year and abstain from that sort of thing; and if he repeat the offence, for two years; and every time that he is convicted let the length of his imprisonment be doubled. This shall be the second law:—He who engages in retail trade must be either a metic or a stranger. And a third law shall be:—

In order that the retail trader who dwells in our city may be as good or as little bad as possible, the guardians of the law shall remember that they are not only guardians of those who may be easily watched and prevented from becoming lawless or bad, because they are well-born and bred; but still more should they have a watch over those who are of another sort, and follow pursuits which have a very strong tendency to make men bad. And, therefore, in respect of the multifarious occupations of retail trade, that is to say, in respect of such of them as are allowed to remain, because they seem to be quite necessary in a state—about these the guardians of the law should meet and take counsel with those who have experience of the several kinds of retail trade, as we before commanded concerning adulteration (which is a matter akin to this), and when they meet they shall consider what amount of receipts, after deducting expenses, will produce a moderate gain to the retail trades, and they shall fix in writing and strictly maintain what they find to be the right percentage of profit; this shall be seen to by the wardens of the agora, and by the wardens of the city, and by the wardens of the country. And so retail trade will benefit every one, and do the least possible injury to those in the state who practise it.

When a man makes an agreement which he does not fulfil, unless the agreement be of a nature which the law or a vote of the assembly does not allow, or which he has made under the influence of some unjust compulsion, or which he is prevented from fulfilling against his will by some unexpected chance, the other party may go to law with him in the courts of the tribes, for not having completed his agreement, if the parties are not able previously to come to terms before arbiters or before their neighbours. The class of craftsmen who have furnished human life with the arts is dedicated to Hephaestus and Athene; and there is a class of craftsmen who preserve the works of all craftsmen by arts of defence, the votaries of Ares and Athene, to which divinities they too are rightly dedicated. All these continue through life serving the country and the people; some of them are leaders in battle; others make for hire implements and works, *[921]* and they ought not to deceive in such matters, out of respect to the Gods who are their ancestors. If any craftsman through indolence omit to execute his work in a given time, not reverencing the God who gives him the means of life, but considering, foolish fellow, that he is his own God and

will let him off easily, in the first place, he shall suffer at the hands of the God, and in the second place, the law shall follow in a similar spirit. He shall owe to him who contracted with him the price of the works which he has failed in performing, and he shall begin again and execute them gratis in the given time. When a man undertakes a work, the law gives him the same advice which was given to the seller, that he should not attempt to raise the price, but simply ask the value; this the law enjoins also on the contractor; for the craftsman assuredly knows the value of his work. Wherefore, in free states the man of art ought not to attempt to impose upon private individuals by the help of his art, which is by nature a true thing; and he who is wronged in a matter of this sort, shall have a right of action against the party who has wronged him. And if any one lets out work to a craftsman, and does not pay him duly according to the lawful agreement, disregarding Zeus the guardian of the city and Athene, who are the partners of the state, and overthrows the foundations of society for the sake of a little gain, in his case let the law and the Gods maintain the common bonds of the state. And let him who, having already received the work in exchange, does not pay the price in the time agreed, pay double the price; and if a year has elapsed, although interest is not to be taken on loans, yet for every drachma which he owes to the contractor let him pay a monthly interest of an obol. Suits about these matters are to be decided by the courts of the tribes; and by the way, since we have mentioned craftsmen at all, we must not forget the other craft of war, in which generals and tacticians are the craftsmen, who undertake voluntarily the work of our safety, as other craftsmen undertake other public works;—if they execute their work well the law will never tire of praising him who gives them those honours which are the just rewards of the soldier; but if any one, having already received the benefit of any noble service in war, does not make the due return of honour, the law will blame him. Let this then be the law, having an ingredient of praise, *[922]* not compelling but advising the great body of the citizens to honour the brave men who are the saviours of the whole state, whether by their courage or by their military skill;—they should honour them, I say, in the second place; for the first and highest tribute of respect is to be given to those who are able above other men to honour the words of good legislators.

The greater part of the dealings between man

and man have been now regulated by us with the exception of those that relate to orphans and the supervision of orphans by their guardians. These follow next in order, and must be regulated in some way. But to arrive at them we must begin with the testamentary wishes of the dying and the case of those who may have happened to die intestate. When I said, Cleinias, that we must regulate them, I had in my mind the difficulty and perplexity in which all such matters are involved. You cannot leave them unregulated, for individuals would make regulations at variance with one another, and repugnant to the laws and habits of the living and to their own previous habits, if a person were simply allowed to make any will which he pleased, and this were to take effect in whatever state he may have been at the end of his life; for most of us lose our senses in a manner, and feel crushed when we think that we are about to die.

Cle. What do you mean, Stranger?

Ath. O Cleinias, a man when he is about to die is an intractable creature, and is apt to use language which causes a great deal of anxiety and trouble to the legislator.

Cle. In what way?

Ath. He wants to have the entire control of all his property, and will use angry words.

Cle. Such as what?

Ath. O ye Gods, he will say, how monstrous that I am not allowed to give, or not to give, my own to whom I will—less to him who has been bad to me, and more to him who has been good to me, and whose badness and goodness have been tested by me in time of sickness or in old age and in every other sort of fortune!

Cle. Well, Stranger, and may he not very fairly say so?

Ath. In my opinion, Cleinias, the ancient legislators were too good-natured, and made laws without sufficient observation or consideration of human things.

Cle. What do you mean?

Ath. I mean, my friend, that they were afraid of the testator's reproaches, and so they passed a law to the effect that a man should be allowed to dispose of his property in all respects as he liked; but you and I, if I am not mistaken, will have something better to say to our departing citizens. [923]

Cle. What?

Ath. O my friends, we will say to them, hard is it for you, who are creatures of a day, to know what is yours—hard too, as the Delphic oracle says, to know yourselves at this hour. Now I,

as the legislator, regard you and your possessions, not as belonging to yourselves, but as belonging to your whole family, both past and future, and yet more do I regard both family and possessions as belonging to the state; wherefore, if some one steals upon you with flattery, when you are tossed on the sea of disease or old age, and persuades you to dispose of your property in a way that is not for the best, I will not, if I can help, allow this; but I will legislate with a view to the whole, considering what is best both for the state and for the family, esteeming as I ought the feelings of an individual at a lower rate; and I hope that you will depart in peace and kindness towards us, as you are going the way of all mankind; and we will impartially take care of all your concerns, not neglecting any of them, if we can possibly help. Let this be our prelude and consolation to the living and dying, Cleinias, and let the law be as follows:

He who makes a disposition in a testament, if he be the father of a family, shall first of all inscribe as his heir any one of his sons whom he may think fit; and if he gives any of his children to be adopted by another citizen, let the adoption be inscribed. And if he has a son remaining over and above who has not been adopted upon any lot, and who may be expected to be sent out to a colony according to law, to him his father may give as much as he pleases of the rest of his property, with the exception of the paternal lot and the fixtures on the lot. And if there are other sons, let him distribute among them what there is more than the lot in such portions as he pleases. And if one of the sons has already a house of his own, he shall not give him of the money, nor shall he give money to a daughter who has been betrothed, but if she is not betrothed he may give her money. And if any of the sons or daughters shall be found to have another lot of land in the country, which has accrued after the testament has been made, they shall leave the lot which they have inherited to the heir of the man who has made the will. If the testator has no sons, but only daughters, let him choose the husband of any one of his daughters whom he pleases, and leave and inscribe him as his son and heir. And if a man have lost his son, when he was a child, and before he could be reckoned among grown-up men, whether his own or an adopted son, [924] let the testator make mention of the circumstance and inscribe whom he will to be his second son in hope of better fortune. If the testator has no children at all, he may select and give to any one whom he pleases the tenth part of the property which he has acquired; but let him not be blamed if he gives all the rest to his adopted son, and makes a friend of him according to the law. If the sons of a man require guardians, and the father when he dies leaves a will appointing guardians, those who have been named by him, whoever they are and whatever their number be, if they are able and willing to take charge of the children, shall be recognized according to the provisions of the will. But if he dies and has made no will, or a will in which he has appointed no guardians, then the next of kin, two on the father's and two on the mother's side, and one of the friends of the deceased, shall have the authority of guardians, whom the guardians of the law shall appoint when the orphans require guardians. And the fifteen eldest guardians of the law shall have the whole care and charge of the orphans, divided into threes according to seniority—a body of three for one year, and then another body of three for the next year, until the cycle of the five periods is complete; and this, as far as possible, is to continue always. If a man dies, having made no will at all, and leaves sons who require the care of guardians, they shall share in the protection which is afforded by these laws.

And if a man dying by some unexpected fate leaves daughters behind him, let him pardon the legislator if when he gives them in marriage, he have a regard only to two out of three conditions—nearness of kin and the preservation of the lot, and omits the third condition, which a father would naturally consider, for he would choose out of all the citizens a son for himself, and a husband for his daughter, with a view to his character and disposition—the father, I say, shall forgive the legislator if he disregards this, which to him is an impossible consideration. Let the law about these matters where practicable be as follows:—If a man dies without making a will, and leaves behind him daughters, let his brother, being the son of the same father or of the same mother, having no lot, marry the daughter and have the lot of the dead man. And if he have no brother, but only a brother's son, in like manner let them marry, if they be of a suitable age; and if there be not even a brother's son, but only the son of a sister, let them do likewise, and so in the fourth degree, if there be only the testator's father's brother, or in the fifth degree, his father's brother's son, or in a sixth degree, the child of his father's sister. Let kindred be always reckoned in this way: if a person leaves daughters the rela-

tionship shall proceed upwards through brothers and sisters, and brothers' and sisters' children, [925] and first the males shall come, and after them the females in the same family. The judge shall consider and determine the suitableness or unsuitableness of age in marriage; he shall make an inspection of the males naked, and of the women naked down to the navel. And if there be a lack of kinsmen in a family extending to grandchildren of a brother, or to the grandchildren of a grandfather's children, the maiden may choose with the consent of her guardians any one of the citizens who is willing and whom she wills, and he shall be the heir of the dead man, and the husband of his daughter. Circumstances vary, and there may sometimes be a still greater lack of relations within the limits of the state; and if any maiden has no kindred living in the city, and there is some one who has been sent out to a colony, and she is disposed to make him the heir of her father's possessions, if he be indeed of her kindred, let him proceed to take the lot according to the regulation of the law; but if he be not of her kindred, she having no kinsmen within the city, and he be chosen by the daughter of the dead man, and empowered to marry by the guardians, let him return home and take the lot of him who died intestate. And if a man has no children, either male or female, and dies without making a will, let the previous law in general hold; and let a man and a woman go forth from the family and share the deserted house, and let the lot belong absolutely to them; and let the heiress in the first degree be a sister, and in a second degree a daughter of a brother, and in the third, a daughter of a sister, in the fourth degree the sister of a father, and in the fifth degree the daughter of a father's brother, and in a sixth degree of a father's sister; and these shall dwell with their male kinsmen, according to the degree of relationship and right, as we enacted before. Now we must not conceal from ourselves that such laws are apt to be oppressive and that there may sometimes be a hardship in the lawgiver commanding the kinsman of the dead man to marry his relation; he may be thought not to have considered the innumerable hindrances which may arise among men in the execution of such ordinances; for there may be cases in which the parties refuse to obey, and are ready to do anything rather than marry, when there is some bodily or mental malady or defect among those who are bidden to marry or be married. Persons may fancy that the legislator never thought of this, but they are mistaken; wherefore let us make a common prelude on behalf of the lawgiver and of his subjects, the law begging the latter to forgive the legislator, in that he, having to take care of the common weal, cannot order at the same time the various circumstances of individuals, [926] and begging him to pardon them if naturally they are sometimes unable to fulfil the act which he in his ignorance imposes upon them.

Cle. And how, Stranger, can we act most fairly under the circumstances?

Ath. There must be arbiters chosen to deal with such laws and the subjects of them.

Cle. What do you mean?

Ath. I mean to say, that a case may occur in which the nephew, having a rich father, will be unwilling to marry the daughter of his uncle; he will have a feeling of pride, and he will wish to look higher. And there are cases in which the legislator will be imposing upon him the greatest calamity, and he will be compelled to disobey the law, if he is required, for example, to take a wife who is mad, or has some other terrible malady of soul or body, such as makes life intolerable to the sufferer. Then let what we are saying concerning these cases be embodied in a law:—If any one finds fault with the established laws respecting testaments, both as to other matters and especially in what relates to marriage, and asserts that the legislator, if he were alive and present, would not compel him to obey—that is to say, would not compel those who are by our law required to marry or be given in marriage, to do either—and some kinsman or guardian dispute this, the reply is that the legislator left fifteen of the guardians of the law to be arbiters and fathers of orphans, male or female, and to them let the disputants have recourse, and by their aid determine any matters of the kind, admitting their decision to be final. But if any one thinks that too great power is thus given to the guardians of the law, let him bring his adversaries into the court of the select judges, and there have the points in dispute determined. And he who loses the cause shall have censure and blame from the legislator, which, by a man of sense, is felt to be a penalty far heavier than a great loss of money.

Thus will orphan children have a second birth. After their first birth we spoke of their nurture and education, and after their second birth, when they have lost their parents, we ought to take measures that the misfortune of orphanhood may be as little sad to them as possible. In the first place, we say that the guardians of the law are lawgivers and fathers to them, not inferior to their natural fathers. Moreover, they shall take charge of them year by year[1] as of their own kindred; and we have given both to them and to the children's own guardians a suitable admonition concerning the nurture of orphans. [927] And we seem to have spoken opportunely in our former discourse,[2] when we said that the souls of the dead have the power after death of taking an interest in human affairs, about which there are many tales and traditions, long indeed, but true; and seeing that they are so many and so ancient, we must believe them, and we must also believe the lawgivers, who tell us that these things are true, if they are not to be regarded as utter fools. But if these things are really so, in the first place men should have a fear of the Gods above, who regard the loneliness of the orphans; and in the second place of the souls of the departed, who by nature incline to take an especial care of their own children, and are friendly to those who honour, and unfriendly to those who dishonour them. Men should also fear the souls of the living who are aged and high in honour; wherever a city is well ordered and prosperous, their descendants cherish them, and so live happily; old persons are quick to see and hear all that relates to them, and are propitious to those who are just in the fulfilment of such duties, and they punish those who wrong the orphan and the desolate, considering that they are the greatest and most sacred of trusts. To all which matters the guardian and magistrate ought to apply his mind, if he has any, and take heed of the nurture and education of the orphans, seeking in every possible way to do them good, for he is making a contribution to his own good and that of his children. He who obeys the tale which precedes the law, and does no wrong to an orphan, will never experience the wrath of the legislator. But he who is disobedient, and wrongs any one who is bereft of father or mother, shall pay twice the penalty which he would have paid if he had wronged one whose parents had been alive. As touching other legislation concerning guardians in their relation to orphans, or concerning magistrates and their superintendence of the guardians, if they did not possess examples of the manner in which children of freemen should be brought up in the bringing up of their own children, and of the care of their property in the care of their own, or if they had not just laws fairly stated

[1] Cf. 924.

[2] Cf. ix. 865.

about these very things—there would have been reason in making laws for them, under the idea that they were a peculiar class, and we might distinguish and make separate rules for the life of those who are orphans and of those who are not orphans. But as the case stands, the condition of orphans with us is not different from the case of those who have a father, though in regard to honour and dishonour, and the attention given to them, the two are not usually placed upon a level. *[928]* Wherefore, touching the legislation about orphans, the law speaks in serious accents, both of persuasion and threatening, and such a threat as the following will be by no means out of place:—He who is the guardian of an orphan of either sex, and he among the guardians of the law to whom the superintendence of this guardian has been assigned, shall love the unfortunate orphan as though he were his own child, and he shall be as careful and diligent in the management of his possessions as he would be if they were his own, or even more careful and diligent. Let every one who has the care of an orphan observe this law. But any one who acts contrary to the law on these matters, if he be a guardian of the child, may be fined by a magistrate, or, if he be himself a magistrate, the guardian may bring him before the court of select judges, and punish him, if convicted, by exacting a fine of double the amount of that inflicted by the court. And if a guardian appears to the relations of the orphan, or to any other citizen, to act negligently or dishonestly, let them bring him before the same court, and whatever damages are given against him, let him pay fourfold, and let half belong to the orphan and half to him who procured the conviction. If any orphan arrives at years of discretion, and thinks that he has been ill-used by his guardians, let him within five years of the expiration of the guardianship be allowed to bring them to trial; and if any of them be convicted, the court shall determine what he shall pay or suffer. And if a magistrate shall appear to have wronged the orphan by neglect, and he be convicted, let the court determine what he shall suffer or pay to the orphan, and if there be dishonesty in addition to neglect, besides paying the fine, let him be deposed from his office of guardian of the law, and let the state appoint another guardian of the law for the city and for the country in his room.

Greater differences than there ought to be sometimes arise between fathers and sons, on the part either of fathers who will be of opinion that the legislator should enact that they may, if they wish, lawfully renounce their son by the proclamation of a herald in the face of the world, or of sons who think that they should be allowed to indict their fathers on the charge of imbecility when they are disabled by disease or old age. These things only happen, as a matter of fact, where the natures of men are utterly bad; for where only half is bad, as, for example, if the father be not bad, but the son be bad, or conversely, no great calamity is the result of such an amount of hatred as this. In another state, a son disowned by his father would not of necessity cease to be a citizen, but in our state, of which these are to be the laws, *[929]* the disinherited must necessarily emigrate into another country, for no addition can be made even of a single family to the 5040 households; and, therefore, he who deserves to suffer these things must be renounced not only by his father, who is a single person, but by the whole family, and what is done in these cases must be regulated by some such law as the following:—He who in the sad disorder of his soul has a mind, justly or unjustly, to expel from his family a son whom he has begotten and brought up, shall not lightly or at once execute his purpose; but first of all he shall collect together his own kinsmen, extending to cousins, and in like manner his son's kinsmen by the mother's side, and in their presence he shall accuse his son, setting forth that he deserves at the hands of them all to be dismissed from the family; and the son shall be allowed to address them in a similar manner, and show that he does not deserve to suffer any of these things. And if the father persuades them, and obtains the suffrages of more than half of his kindred, exclusive of the father and mother and the offender himself—I say, if he obtains more than half the suffrages of all the other grown-up members of the family, of both sexes, the father shall be permitted to put away his son, but not otherwise. And if any other citizen is willing to adopt the son who is put away, no law shall hinder him; for the characters of young men are subject to many changes in the course of their lives. And if he has been put away, and in a period of ten years no one is willing to adopt him, let those who have the care of the superabundant population which is sent out into colonies, see to him, in order that he may be suitably provided for in the colony. And if disease or age or harshness of temper, or all these together, makes a man to be more out of his mind than the rest of the world are—but this is not observable, except to those who live with him—and he, being master of his property, is the ruin of the house, and his son doubts and hesitates about indicting his father for insanity, let the law in that case ordain that he shall first of all go to the eldest guardians of the law and tell them of his father's misfortune, and they shall duly look into the matter, and take counsel as to whether he shall indict him or not. And if they advise him to proceed, they shall be both his witnesses and his advocates; and if the father is cast, he shall henceforth be incapable of ordering the least particular of his life; let him be as a child dwelling in the house for the remainder of his days. And if a man and his wife have an unfortunate incompatibility of temper, ten of the guardians of the law, who are impartial, and ten of the women who regulate marriages,[1] *[930]* shall look to the matter, and if they are able to reconcile them they shall be formally reconciled; but if their souls are too much tossed with passion, they shall endeavour to find other partners. Now they are not likely to have very gentle tempers; and, therefore, we must endeavour to associate with them deeper and softer natures. Those who have no children, or only a few, at the time of their separation, should choose their new partners with a view to the procreation of children; but those who have a sufficient number of children should separate and marry again in order that they may have some one to grow old with and that the pair may take care of one another in age. If a woman dies, leaving children, male or female, the law will advise rather than compel the husband to bring up the children without introducing into the house a stepmother. But if he have no children, then he shall be compelled to marry until he has begotten a sufficient number of sons to his family and to the state. And if a man dies leaving a sufficient number of children, the mother of his children shall remain with them and bring them up. But if she appears to be too young to live virtuously without a husband, let her relations communicate with the women who superintend marriage, and let both together do what they think best in these matters; if there is a lack of children, let the choice be made with a view to having them; two children, one of either sex, shall be deemed sufficient in the eye of the law. When a child is admitted to be the offspring of certain parents and is acknowledged by them, but there is need of a decision as to which parent the child is to follow—in case a female slave have intercourse with a male slave, or with a freeman or freedman, the offspring

[1] Cf. vi. 784, ff.; vii. 794.

shall always belong to the master of the female slave. Again, if a free woman have intercourse with a male slave, the offspring shall belong to the master of the slave; but if a child be born either of a slave by her master, or of his mistress by a slave—and this be proven—the offspring of the woman and its father shall be sent away by the women who superintend marriage into another country, and the guardians of the law shall send away the offspring of the man and its mother.

Neither God, nor a man who has understanding, will ever advise any one to neglect his parents. To a discourse concerning the honour and dishonour of parents, a prelude such as the following, about the service of the Gods, will be a suitable introduction:—There are ancient customs about the Gods which are universal, and they are of two kinds: *[931]* some of the Gods we see with our eyes and we honour them, of others we honour the images, raising statues of them which we adore; and though they are lifeless, yet we imagine that the living Gods have a good will and gratitude to us on this account. Now, if a man has a father or mother, or their fathers or mothers treasured up in his house stricken in years, let him consider that no statue can be more potent to grant his requests than they are, who are sitting at his hearth, if only he knows how to show true service to them.

Cle. And what do you call the true mode of service?

Ath. I will tell you, O my friend, for such things are worth listening to.

Cle. Proceed.

Ath. Oedipus, as tradition says, when dishonoured by his sons, invoked on them curses which every one declares to have been heard and ratified by the Gods, and Amyntor in his wrath invoked curses on his son Phoenix, and Theseus upon Hippolytus, and innumerable others have also called down wrath upon their children, whence it is clear that the Gods listen to the imprecations of parents; for the curses of parents are, as they ought to be, mighty against their children as no others are. And shall we suppose that the prayers of a father or mother who is specially dishonoured by his or her children, are heard by the Gods in accordance with nature; and that if a parent is honoured by them, and in the gladness of his heart earnestly entreats the Gods in his prayers to do them good, he is not equally heard, and that they do not minister to his request? If not, they would be very unjust ministers of good, and that we affirm to be contrary to their nature.

Cle. Certainly.

Ath. May we not think, as I was saying just now, that we can possess no image which is more honoured by the Gods, than that of a father or grandfather, or of a mother stricken in years? whom when a man honours, the heart of the God rejoices, and he is ready to answer their prayers. And, truly, the figure of an ancestor is a wonderful thing, far higher than that of a lifeless image. For the living, when they are honoured by us, join in our prayers, and when they are dishonoured, they utter imprecations against us; but lifeless objects do neither. And therefore, if a man makes a right use of his father and grandfather and other aged relations, he will have images which above all others will win him the favour of the Gods.

Cle. Excellent.

Ath. Every man of any understanding fears and respects the prayers of parents, knowing well that many times and to many persons they have been accomplished. Now these things being thus ordered by nature, *[932]* good men think it a blessing from heaven if their parents live to old age and reach the utmost limit of human life, or if taken away before their time they are deeply regretted by them; but to bad men parents are always a cause of terror. Wherefore let every man honour with every sort of lawful honour his own parents, agreeably to what has now been said. But if this prelude be an unmeaning sound in the ears of any one, let the law follow, which may be rightly imposed in these terms:—If any one in this city be not sufficiently careful of his parents, and do not regard and gratify in every respect their wishes more than those of his sons and of his other offspring or of himself—let him who experiences this sort of treatment either come himself, or send some one to inform the three eldest guardians of the law, and three of the women who have the care of marriages; and let them look to the matter and punish youthful evil-doers with stripes and bonds if they are under thirty years of age, that is to say, if they be men, or if they be women, let them undergo the same punishment up to forty years of age. But if, when they are still more advanced in years, they continue the same neglect of their parents, and do any hurt to any of them, let them be brought before a court in which every single one of the eldest citizens shall be the judges, and if the offender be convicted, let the court determine what he ought to pay or suffer, and any penalty may be imposed on him which a man can pay

or suffer. If the person who has been wronged be unable to inform the magistrates, let any freeman who hears of his case inform, and if he do not, he shall be deemed base, and shall be liable to have a suit for damage brought against him by any one who likes. And if a slave inform, he shall receive freedom; and if he be the slave of the injurer or injured party, he shall be set free by the magistrates, or if he belong to any other citizen, the public shall pay a price on his behalf to the owner; and let the magistrates take heed that no one wrongs him out of revenge, because he has given information.

Cases in which one man injures another by poisons, and which prove fatal, have been already discussed; [1] but about other cases in which a person intentionally and of malice harms another with meats, or drinks, or ointments, nothing has as yet been determined. For there are two kinds of poisons used among men, which cannot clearly be distinguished. There is the kind just now explicitly mentioned, *[933]* which injures bodies by the use of other bodies according to a natural law; there is also another kind which persuades the more daring class that they can do injury by sorceries, and incantations, and magic knots, as they are termed, and makes others believe that they above all persons are injured by the powers of the magician. Now it is not easy to know the nature of all these things; nor if a man do know can he readily persuade others to believe him. And when men are disturbed in their minds at the sight of waxen images fixed either at their doors, or in a place where three ways meet, or on the sepulchres of parents, there is no use in trying to persuade them that they should despise all such things because they have no certain knowledge about them. But we must have a law in two parts, concerning poisoning, in whichever of the two ways the attempt is made, and we must entreat, and exhort, and advise men not to have recourse to such practices, by which they scare the multitude out of their wits, as if they were children, compelling the legislator and the judge to heal the fears which the sorcerer arouses, and to tell them in the first place, that he who attempts to poison or enchant others knows not what he is doing, either as regards the body (unless he has a knowledge of medicine), or as regards his enchantments (unless he happens to be a prophet or diviner). Let the law, then, run as follows about poisoning or witchcraft:—He who employs poison to do any injury, not fatal, to a man himself, or to his

[1] Cf. ix. 870, ff.

servants, or any injury, whether fatal or not, to his cattle or his bees, if he be a physician, and be convicted of poisoning, shall be punished with death; or if he be a private person, the court shall determine what he is to pay or suffer. But he who seems to be the sort of man who injures others by magic knots, or enchantments, or incantations, or any of the like practices, if he be a prophet or diviner, let him die; and if, not being a prophet, he be convicted of witchcraft, as in the previous case, let the court fix what he ought to pay or suffer.

When a man does another any injury by theft or violence, for the greater injury let him pay greater damages to the injured man, and less for the smaller injury; but in all cases, whatever the injury may have been, as much as will compensate the loss. And besides the compensation of the wrong, let a man pay a further penalty for the chastisement of his offence: [934] he who has done the wrong instigated by the folly of another, through the lightheartedness of youth or the like, shall pay a lighter penalty; but he who has injured another through his own folly, when overcome by pleasure or pain, in cowardly fear, or lust, or envy, or implacable anger, shall endure a heavier punishment. Not that he is punished because he did wrong, for that which is done can never be undone, but in order that in future times, he, and those who see him corrected, may utterly hate injustice, or at any rate abate much of their evil-doing. Having an eye to all these things, the law, like a good archer, should aim at the right measure of punishment, and in all cases at the deserved punishment. In the attainment of this the judge shall be a fellow-worker with the legislator, whenever the law leaves to him to determine what the offender shall suffer or pay; and the legislator, like a painter, shall give a rough sketch of the cases in which the law is to be applied. This is what we must do, Megillus and Cleinias, in the best and fairest manner that we can, saying what the punishments are to be of all actions of theft and violence, and giving laws of such a kind as the Gods and sons of Gods would have us give.

If a man is mad he shall not be at large in the city, but his relations shall keep him at home in any way which they can; or if not, let them pay a penalty—he who is of the highest class shall pay a penalty of one hundred drachmae, whether he be a slave or a freeman whom he neglects; and he of the second class shall pay four-fifths of a mina; and he of the third class three-fifths; and he of the fourth class two-

fifths. Now there are many sorts of madness, some arising out of disease, which we have already mentioned; and there are other kinds, which originate in an evil and passionate temperament, and are increased by bad education; out of a slight quarrel this class of madmen will often raise a storm of abuse against one another, and nothing of that sort ought to be allowed to occur in a well-ordered state. Let this, then, be the law about abuse, which shall relate to all cases:—No one shall speak evil of another; and when a man disputes with another he shall teach and learn of the disputant and the company, but he shall abstain from evil-speaking; for out of the imprecations which men utter against one another, [935] and the feminine habit of casting aspersions on one another, and using foul names, out of words light as air, in very deed the greatest enmities and hatreds spring up. For the speaker gratifies his anger, which is an ungracious element of his nature; and nursing up his wrath by the entertainment of evil thoughts, and exacerbating that part of his soul which was formerly civilized by education, he lives in a state of savageness and moroseness, and pays a bitter penalty for his anger. And in such cases almost all men take to saying something ridiculous about their opponent, and there is no man who is in the habit of laughing at another who does not miss virtue and earnestness altogether, or lose the better half of greatness. Wherefore let no one utter any taunting word at a temple, or at the public sacrifices, or at the games, or in the agora, or in a court of justice, or in any public assembly. And let the magistrate who presides on these occasions chastise an offender, and he shall be blameless; but if he fails in doing so, he shall not claim the prize of virtue; for he is one who heeds not the laws, and does not do what the legislator commands. And if in any other place any one indulges in these sort of revilings, whether he has begun the quarrel or is only retaliating, let any elder who is present support the law, and control with blows those who indulge in passion, which is another great evil; and if he do not, let him be liable to pay the appointed penalty. And we say now, that he who deals in reproaches against others cannot reproach them without attempting to ridicule them; and this, when done in a moment of anger, is what we make matter of reproach against him. But then, do we admit into our state the comic writers[1] who are so fond of making man-

[1] Cf. *Republic,* iii. 394; x. 606; Aristotle, *Politics,* vii. 17, 1336 [b] 19-24.

kind ridiculous, if they attempt in a good-natured manner to turn the laugh against our citizens? or do we draw the distinction of jest and earnest, and allow a man to make use of ridicule in jest and without anger about any thing or person; though as we were saying, not if he be angry and have a set purpose? We forbid earnest—that is unalterably fixed; but we have still to say who are to be sanctioned or not to be sanctioned by the law in the employment of innocent humour. A comic poet, or maker of iambic or satirical lyric verse, shall not be permitted to ridicule any of the citizens, either by word or likeness, either in anger or without anger. And if any one is disobedient, the judges shall either at once expel him from the country, or he shall pay a fine of three minae, which shall be dedicated to the God who presides over the contests. [936] Those only who have received permission shall be allowed to write verses at one another, but they shall be without anger and in jest; in anger and in serious earnest they shall not be allowed. The decision of this matter shall be left to the superintendent of the general education of the young, and whatever he may license, the writer shall be allowed to produce, and whatever he rejects let not the poet himself exhibit, or ever teach anybody else, slave or freeman, under the penalty of being dishonoured, and held disobedient to the laws.

Now he is not to be pitied who is hungry, or who suffers any bodily pain, but he who is temperate, or has some other virtue, or part of a virtue, and at the same time suffers from misfortune; it would be an extraordinary thing if such an one, whether slave or freeman, were utterly forsaken and fell into the extremes of poverty in any tolerably well-ordered city or government. Wherefore the legislator may safely make a law applicable to such cases in the following terms:—Let there be no beggars in our state; and if anybody begs, seeking to pick up a livelihood by unavailing prayers, let the wardens of the agora turn him out of the agora, and the wardens of the city out of the city, and the wardens of the country send him out of any other parts of the land across the border, in order that the land may be cleared of this sort of animal.

If a slave of either sex injure anything, which is not his or her own, through inexperience, or some improper practice, and the person who suffers damage be not himself in part to blame, the master of the slave who has done the harm shall either make full satisfaction, or give up the slave who has done the injury. But if the master argue that the charge has arisen by collusion between the injured party and the injurer, with the view of obtaining the slave, let him sue the person, who says that he has been injured, for malpractices. And if he gain a conviction, let him receive double the value which the court fixes as the price of the slave; and if he lose his suit, let him make amends for the injury, and give up the slave. And if a beast of burden, or horse, or dog, or any other animal, injure the property of a neighbour, the owner shall in like manner pay for the injury.

If any man refuses to be a witness, he who wants him shall summon him, and he who is summoned shall come to the trial; and if he knows and is willing to bear witness, let him bear witness, but if he says he does not know let him swear by the three divinities Zeus, and Apollo, and Themis, that he does not, and have no more to do with the cause. [937] And he who is summoned to give witness and does not answer to his summoner, shall be liable for the harm which ensues according to law. And if a person calls up as a witness any one who is acting as a judge, let him give his witness, but he shall not afterwards vote in the cause. A free woman may give her witness and plead, if she be more than forty years of age, and may bring an action if she have no husband; but if her husband be alive she shall only be allowed to bear witness. A slave of either sex and a child shall be allowed to give evidence and to plead, but only in cases of murder; and they must produce sufficient sureties that they will certainly remain until the trial, in case they should be charged with false witness. And either of the parties in a cause may bring an accusation of perjury against witnesses, touching their evidence in whole or in part, if he asserts that such evidence has been given; but the accusation must be brought previous to the final decision of the cause. The magistrates shall preserve the accusations of false witness, and have them kept under the seal of both parties, and produce them on the day when the trial for false witness takes place. If a man be twice convicted of false witness, he shall not be required, and if thrice, he shall not be allowed to bear witness; and if he dare to witness after he has been convicted three times, let any one who pleases inform against him to the magistrates, and let the magistrates hand him over to the court, and if he be convicted he shall be punished with death. And in any case in which the evidence is rightly found to be false, and yet to have given the victory to him who wins the suit, and more than half the witnesses are condemned, the decision which was gained by these means shall be rescinded, and there shall be a discussion and a decision as to whether the suit was determined by that false evidence or not; and in whichever way the decision may be given, the previous suit shall be determined accordingly.

There are many noble things in human life, but to most of them attach evils which are fated to corrupt and spoil them. Is not justice noble, which has been the civilizer of humanity? How then can the advocate of justice be other than noble? And yet upon this profession which is presented to us under the fair name of art has come an evil reputation. In the first place, we are told that by ingenious pleas and the help of an advocate the law enables a man to win a particular cause, [938] whether just or unjust; and that both the art, and the power of speech which is thereby imparted, are at the service of him who is willing to pay for them. Now in our state this so-called art, whether really an art[1] or only an experience and practice destitute of any art, ought if possible never to come into existence, or if existing among us should listen to the request of the legislator and go away into another land, and not speak contrary to justice. If the offenders obey we say no more; but for those who disobey, the voice of the law is as follows:—If any one thinks that he will pervert the power of justice in the minds of the judges, and unseasonably litigate or advocate, let any one who likes indict him for malpractices of law and dishonest advocacy, and let him be judged in the court of select judges; and if he be convicted, let the court determine whether he may be supposed to act from a love of money or from contentiousness. And if he is supposed to act from contentiousness, the court shall fix a time during which he shall not be allowed to institute or plead a cause; and if he is supposed to act as he does from love of money, in case he be a stranger, he shall leave the country, and never return under penalty of death; but if he be a citizen, he shall die, because he is a lover of money, in whatever manner gained; and equally, if he be judged to have acted more than once from contentiousness, he shall die.

BOOK XII

[941] IF a herald or an ambassador carry a false message from our city to any other, or bring back a false message from the city to

which he is sent, or be proved to have brought back, whether from friends or enemies, in his capacity of herald or ambassador, what they have never said, let him be indicted for having violated, contrary to the law, the commands and duties imposed upon him by Hermes and Zeus, and let there be a penalty fixed, which he shall suffer or pay if he be convicted.

Theft is a mean, and robbery a shameless thing; and none of the sons of Zeus delight in fraud and violence, or ever practised either. Wherefore let no one be deluded by poets or mythologers into a mistaken belief of such things, nor let him suppose, when he thieves or is guilty of violence, that he is doing nothing base, but only what the Gods themselves do. For such tales are untrue and improbable; and he who steals or robs contrary to the law, is never either a God or the son of a God; of this the legislator ought to be better informed than all the poets put together.[2] Happy is he and may he be for ever happy, who is persuaded and listens to our words; but he who disobeys shall have to contend against the following law:—If a man steal anything belonging to the public, whether that which he steals be much or little, he shall have the same punishment. For he who steals a little steals with the same wish as he who steals much, but with less power, and he who takes up a greater amount, not having deposited it, is wholly unjust. Wherefore the law is not disposed to inflict a less penalty on the one than on the other because his theft is less, but on the ground that the thief may possibly be in one case still curable, and may in another case be incurable. If any one convict in a court of law a stranger or a slave of a theft of public property, let the court determine what punishment he shall suffer, or what penalty he shall pay, bearing in mind that he is probably not incurable. But the citizen who has been brought up as our citizens will have been, if he be found guilty of robbing his country by fraud or violence, whether he be caught in the act or not, shall be punished with death; for he is incurable.[3]

[942] Now for expeditions of war much consideration and many laws are required; the great principle of all is that no one of either sex should be without a commander;[4] nor should the mind of any one be accustomed to do any-

[1] Cf. Gorgias, 463.

[2] Cf. Republic, iii. 388, 391.
[3] This passage is not consistent with ix. 857, where theft of public property is punished by imprisonment.
[4] Cf. Thucydides, v. 66.

thing, either in jest or earnest, of his own motion, but in war and in peace he should look to and follow his leader, even in the least things being under his guidance; for example, he should stand or move, or exercise, or wash, or take his meals, or get up in the night to keep guard and deliver messages when he is bidden; and in the hour of danger he should not pursue and not retreat except by order of his superior; and in a word, not teach the soul or accustom her to know or understand how to do anything apart from others. Of all soldiers the life should be always and in all things as far as possible in common and together; there neither is nor ever will be a higher, or better, or more scientific principle than this for the attainment of salvation and victory in war. And we ought in time of peace from youth upwards to practise this habit of commanding others, and of being commanded by others; anarchy should have no place in the life of man or of the beasts who are subject to man. I may add that all dances ought to be performed with a view to military excellence;[1] and agility and ease should be cultivated for the same object, and also endurance of the want of meats and drinks, and of winter cold and summer heat, and of hard couches; and, above all, care should be taken not to destroy the peculiar qualities of the head and the feet by surrounding them with extraneous coverings, and so hindering their natural growth of hair and soles. For these are the extremities, and of all the parts of the body, whether they are preserved or not is of the greatest consequence; the one is the servant of the whole body, and the other the master, *[943]* in whom all the ruling senses are by nature set. Let the young man imagine that he hears in what has preceded the praises of the military life; the law shall be as follows:—He shall serve in war who is on the roll or appointed to some special service, and if any one is absent from cowardice; and without the leave of the generals, he shall be indicted before the military commanders for failure of service when the army comes home; and the soldiers shall be his judges; the heavy-armed, and the cavalry, and the other arms of the service shall form separate courts; and they shall bring the heavy-armed before the heavy-armed, and the horsemen before the horsemen, and the others in like manner before their peers; and he who is found guilty shall never be allowed to compete for any prize of valour, or indict another for not serving on an expedition, or be an accuser at all in any military mat-

[1] Cf. vii. 796.

ters. Moreover, the court shall further determine what punishment he shall suffer, or what penalty he shall pay. When the suits for failure of service are completed, the leaders of the several kinds of troops shall again hold an assembly, and they shall adjudge the prizes of valour; and he who likes shall give judgment in his own branch of the service, saying nothing about any former expedition, nor producing any proof or witnesses to confirm his statement, but speaking only of the present occasion. The crown of victory shall be an olive wreath which the victor shall offer up at the temple of any war-god whom he likes, adding an inscription for a testimony to last during life, that such an one has received the first, the second, or the third prize. If any one goes on an expedition, and returns home before the appointed time, when the generals have not withdrawn the army, he shall be indicted for desertion before the same persons who took cognisance of failure of service, and if he be found guilty, the same punishment shall be inflicted on him. Now every man who is engaged in any suit ought to be very careful of bringing false witness against any one, either intentionally or unintentionally, if he can help; for justice is truly said to be an honourable maiden, and falsehood is naturally repugnant to honour and justice. A witness ought to be very careful not to sin against justice, as for example in what relates to the throwing away of arms—he must distinguish the throwing them away when necessary, and not make that a reproach, or bring an action against some innocent person on that account. *[944]* To make the distinction may be difficult; but still the law must attempt to define the different kinds in some way. Let me endeavour to explain my meaning by an ancient tale:—If Patroclus had been brought to the tent still alive but without his arms (and this has happened to innumerable persons), the original arms, which the poet says were presented to Peleus by the Gods as a nuptial gift when he married Thetis, remaining in the hands of Hector, then the base spirits of that day might have reproached the son of Menoetius with having cast away his arms. Again, there is the case of those who have been thrown down precipices and lost their arms; and of those who at sea, and in stormy places, have been suddenly overwhelmed by floods of water; and there are numberless things of this kind which one might adduce by way of extenuation, and with the view of justifying a misfortune which is easily misrepresented. We must, therefore, endeavour to divide to the best of our power the greater and more serious evil from the lesser. And a distinction may be drawn in the use of terms of reproach. A man does not always deserve to be called the thrower away of his shield; he may be only the loser of his arms. For there is a great or rather absolute difference between him who is deprived of his arms by a sufficient force, and him who voluntarily lets his shield go. Let the law then be as follows:— If a person having arms is overtaken by the enemy and does not turn round and defend himself, but lets them go voluntarily or throws them away, choosing a base life and a swift escape rather than a courageous and noble and blessed death—in such a case of the throwing away of arms let justice be done, but the judge need take no note of the case just now mentioned; for the bad man ought always to be punished, in the hope that he may be improved, but not the unfortunate, for there is no advantage in that. And what shall be the punishment suited to him who has thrown away his weapons of defence? Tradition says that Caeneus, the Thessalian, was changed by a God from a woman into a man; but the converse miracle cannot now be wrought, or no punishment would be more proper than that the man who throws away his shield should be changed into a woman.[1] This however is impossible, and therefore let us make a law as nearly like this as we can—that he who loves his life too well shall be in no danger for the remainder of his days, but shall live for ever under the stigma of cowardice. And let the law be in the following terms:—When a man is found guilty of disgracefully throwing away his arms in war, no general or military officer shall allow him to serve as a soldier, or give him any place at all in the ranks of soldiers; [945] and the officer who gives the coward any place, shall suffer a penalty which the public examiner shall exact of him; and if he be of the highest class, he shall pay a thousand drachmae; or if he be of the second class, five minae; or if he be of the third, three minae; or if he be of the fourth class, one mina. And he who is found guilty of cowardice, shall not only be dismissed from manly dangers, which is a disgrace appropriate to his nature, but he shall pay a thousand drachmae, if he be of the highest class, and five minae if he be of the second class, and three if he be of the third class, and a mina, like the preceding, if he be of the fourth class.

What regulations will be proper about ex-

aminers, seeing that some of our magistrates are elected by lot, and for a year, and some for a longer time and from selected persons? Of such magistrates, who will be a sufficient censor or examiner, if any of them, weighed down by the pressure of office or his own inability to support the dignity of his office, be guilty of any crooked practice? It is by no means easy to find a magistrate who excels other magistrates in virtue, but still we must endeavour to discover some censor or examiner who is more than man. For the truth is, that there are many elements of dissolution in a state, as there are also in a ship, or in an animal; they all have their cords, and girders, and sinews—one nature diffused in many places, and called by many names; and the office of examiner is a most important element in the preservation and dissolution of states. For if the examiners are better than the magistrates, and their duty is fulfilled justly and without blame, then the whole state and country flourishes and is happy; but if the examination of the magistrates is carried on in a wrong way, then, by the relaxation of that justice which is the uniting principle of all constitutions, every power in the state is rent asunder from every other; they no longer incline in the same direction, but fill the city with faction, and make many cities out of one,[2] and soon bring all to destruction. Wherefore the examiners ought to be admirable in every sort of virtue. Let us invent a mode of creating them, which shall be as follows:—Every year, after the summer solstice, the whole city shall meet in the common precincts of Helios and Apollo, and shall present to the God three men out of their own number in the manner following: [946]—Each citizen shall select, not himself, but some other citizen whom he deems in every way the best, and who is not less than fifty years of age. And out of the selected persons who have the greatest number of votes, they shall make a further selection until they reduce them to one-half, if they are an even number; but if they are not an even number, they shall subtract the one who has the smallest number of votes, and make them an even number, and then leave the half which have the greater number of votes. And if two persons have an equal number of votes, and thus increase the number beyond one-half, they shall withdraw the younger of the two and do away with the excess; and then including all the rest they shall again vote, until there are left three having an unequal number of votes. But if all the three, or

[1] Cf. *Timaeus*, 90.

[2] Cf. *Republic*, iv. 422.

two out of the three, have equal votes, let them commit the election to good fate and fortune, and separate off by lot the first, and the second, and the third; these they shall crown with an olive wreath and give them the prize of excellence, at the same time proclaiming to all the world that the city of the Magnetes, by the providence of the Gods, is again preserved, and presents to the Sun and to Apollo her three best men as first-fruits, to be a common offering to them, according to the ancient law, as long as their lives answer to the judgment formed of them. And these shall appoint in their first year twelve examiners, to continue until each has completed seventy-five years, to whom three shall afterwards be added yearly; and let these divide all the magistracies into twelve parts, and prove the holders of them by every sort of test to which a freeman may be subjected; and let them live while they hold office in the precinct of Helios and Apollo, in which they were chosen, and let each one form a judgment of some things individually, and of others in company with his colleagues; and let him place a writing in the agora about each magistracy, and what the magistrate ought to suffer or pay, according to the decision of the examiners. And if a magistrate does not admit that he has been justly judged, let him bring the examiners before the select judges, and if he be acquitted by their decision, let him, if he will, accuse the examiners themselves; if, however, he be convicted, and have been condemned to death by the examiners, let him die (and of course he can only die once):—but any other penalties which admit of being doubled let him suffer twice over.

And now let us pass under review the examiners themselves; what will their examination be, *[947]* and how conducted? During the life of these men, whom the whole state counts worthy of the rewards of virtue, they shall have the first seat at all public assemblies, and at all Hellenic sacrifices and sacred missions, and other public and holy ceremonies in which they share. The chiefs of each sacred mission shall be selected from them, and they only of all the citizens shall be adorned with a crown of laurel; they shall all be priests of Apollo and Helios; and one of them, who is judged first of the priests created in that year, shall be high priest; and they shall write up his name in each year to be a measure of time as long as the city lasts; and after their death they shall be laid out and carried to the grave and entombed in a manner different from the other citizens. They shall be decked in a robe all of white, and there shall be no crying or lamentation over them; but a chorus of fifteen maidens, and another of boys, shall stand around the bier on either side, hymning the praises of the departed priests in alternate responses, declaring their blessedness in song all day long; and at dawn a hundred of the youths who practise gymnastic exercises, and whom the relations of the departed shall choose, shall carry the bier to the sepulchre, the young men marching first, dressed in the garb of warriors—the cavalry with their horses, the heavy-armed with their arms, and the others in like manner. And boys near the bier and in front of it shall sing their national hymn, and maidens shall follow behind, and with them the women who have passed the age of childbearing; next, although they are interdicted from other burials, let priests and priestesses follow, unless the Pythian oracle forbid them; for this burial is free from pollution. The place of burial shall be an oblong vaulted chamber underground, constructed of tufa, which will last for ever, having stone couches placed side by side. And here they will lay the blessed person, and cover the sepulchre with a circular mound of earth and plant a grove of trees around on every side but one; and on that side the sepulchre shall be allowed to extend for ever, and a new mound will not be required. Every year they shall have contests in music and gymnastics, and in horsemanship, in honour of the dead. These are the honours which shall be given to those who at the examination are found blameless; but if any of them, trusting to the scrutiny being over, should, after the judgment has been given, manifest the wickedness of human nature, let the law ordain that he who pleases shall indict him, *[948]* and let the cause be tried in the following manner. In the first place, the court shall be composed of the guardians of the law, and to them the surviving examiners shall be added, as well as the court of select judges; and let the pursuer lay his indictment in this form—he shall say that so-and-so is unworthy of the prize of virtue and of his office; and if the defendant be convicted let him be deprived of his office, and of the burial, and of the other honours given him. But if the prosecutor do not obtain the fifth part of the votes, let him, if he be of the first class, pay twelve minae, and eight if he be of the second class, and six if he be of the third class, and two minae if he be of the fourth class.

The so-called decision of Rhadamanthus is worthy of all admiration. He knew that the men of his own time believed and had no doubt that there were Gods, which was a reasonable belief in those days, because most men were the sons of Gods,[1] and according to tradition he was one himself. He appears to have thought that he ought to commit judgment to no man, but to the Gods only, and in this way suits were simply and speedily decided by him. For he made the two parties take an oath respecting the points in dispute, and so got rid of the matter speedily and safely. But now that a certain portion of mankind do not believe at all in the existence of the Gods, and others imagine that they have no care of us, and the opinion of most men, and of the worst men, is that in return for a small sacrifice and a few flattering words they will be their accomplices in purloining large sums and save them from many terrible punishments, the way of Rhadamanthus is no longer suited to the needs of justice; for as the opinions of men about the Gods are changed, the laws should also be changed;—in the granting of suits a rational legislation ought to do away with the oaths of the parties on either side—he who obtains leave to bring an action should write down the charges, but should not add an oath; and the defendant in like manner should give his denial to the magistrates in writing, and not swear; for it is a dreadful thing to know, when many lawsuits are going on in a state, that almost half the people who meet one another quite unconcernedly at the public meals and in other companies and relations of private life are perjured. Let the law, then, be as follows:—A judge who is about to give judgment shall take an oath, and he who is choosing magistrates for the state shall either vote on oath or with a voting tablet which he brings from a temple; *[949]* so too the judge of dances and of all music, and the superintendents and umpires of gymnastic and equestrian contests, and any matters in which, as far as men can judge, there is nothing to be gained by a false oath; but all cases in which a denial confirmed by an oath clearly results in a great advantage to the taker of the oath, shall be decided without the oath of the parties to the suit, and the presiding judges shall not permit either of them to use an oath for the sake of persuading, nor to call down curses on himself and his race, nor to use unseemly supplications or womanish laments. But they shall ever be teaching and learning what is just in auspicious words; and he who does otherwise shall be supposed to speak beside the point, and the judges shall again bring him back to the question at

issue. On the other hand, strangers in their dealings with strangers shall as at present have power to give and receive oaths, for they will not often grow old in the city or leave a fry of young ones like themselves to be the sons and heirs of the land.

As to the initiation of private suits, let the manner of deciding causes between all citizens be the same as in cases in which any freeman is disobedient to the state in minor matters, of which the penalty is not stripes, imprisonment, or death. But as regards attendance at choruses or processions or other shows, and as regards public services, whether the celebration of sacrifice in peace, or the payment of contributions in war—in all these cases, first comes the necessity of providing a remedy for the loss; and by those who will not obey, there shall be security given to the officers whom the city and the law empower to exact the sum due; and if they forfeit their security, let the goods which they have pledged be sold and the money given to the city; but if they ought to pay a larger sum, the several magistrates shall impose upon the disobedient a suitable penalty, and bring them before the court, until they are willing to do what they are ordered.

Now a state which makes money from the cultivation of the soil only, and has no foreign trade, must consider what it will do about the emigration of its own people to other countries, and the reception of strangers from elsewhere. About these matters the legislator has to consider, and he will begin by trying to persuade men as far as he can. The intercourse of cities with one another is apt to create a confusion of manners; strangers are always suggesting novelties to strangers.[2] *[950]* When states are well governed by good laws the mixture causes the greatest possible injury; but seeing that most cities are the reverse of well-ordered, the confusion which arises in them from the reception of strangers, and from the citizens themselves rushing off into other cities, when any one either young or old desires to travel anywhere abroad at whatever time, is of no consequence. On the other hand, the refusal of states to receive others, and for their own citizens never to go to other places, is an utter impossibility, and to the rest of the world is likely to appear ruthless and uncivilized; it is a practice adopted by people who use harsh words, such as xenelasia or banishment of strangers, and who have harsh and morose ways, as men think. And to be thought or not to be thought well of by the rest of the world is no light matter; for the many are not so far wrong in their judgment of who are bad and who are good, as they are removed from the nature of virtue in themselves. Even bad men have a divine instinct which guesses rightly, and very many who are utterly depraved form correct notions and judgments of the differences between the good and bad. And the generality of cities are quite right in exhorting us to value a good reputation in the world, for there is no truth greater and more important than this—that he who is really good (I am speaking of the man who would be perfect) seeks for reputation with, but not without, the reality of goodness. And our Cretan colony ought also to acquire the fairest and noblest reputation for virtue from other men; and there is every reason to expect that, if the reality answers to the idea, she will be one of the few well-ordered cities which the sun and the other Gods behold. Wherefore, in the matter of journeys to other countries and the reception of strangers, we enact as follows:—In the first place, let no one be allowed to go anywhere at all into a foreign country who is less than forty years of age; and no one shall go in a private capacity, but only in some public one, as a herald, or on an embassy, or on a sacred mission. Going abroad on an expedition or in war is not to be included among travels of the class authorized by the state. To Apollo at Delphi and to Zeus at Olympia and to Nemea and to the Isthmus, citizens should be sent to take part in the sacrifices and games there dedicated to the Gods; and they should send as many as possible, and the best and fairest that can be found, and they will make the city renowned at holy meetings in time of peace, [951] procuring a glory which shall be the converse of that which is gained in war; and when they come home they shall teach the young that the institutions of other states are inferior to their own. And they shall send spectators of another sort, if they have the consent of the guardians, being such citizens as desire to look a little more at leisure at the doings of other men; and these no law shall hinder. For a city which has no experience of good and bad men or intercourse with them, can never be thoroughly and perfectly civilized, nor, again, can the citizens of a city properly observe the laws by habit only, and without an intelligent understanding of them.[1] And there always are in the world a few inspired men whose acquaintance is beyond price, and who spring up quite

as much in ill-ordered as in well-ordered cities. These are they whom the citizens of a well-ordered city should be ever seeking out, going forth over sea and over land to find him who is incorruptible—that he may establish more firmly institutions in his own state which are good already; and amend what is deficient; for without this examination and enquiry a city will never continue perfect any more than if the examination is ill-conducted.

Cleinias. How can we have an examination and also a good one?

Athenian Stranger. In this way: In the first place, our spectator shall be of not less than fifty years of age; he must be a man of reputation, especially in war, if he is to exhibit to other cities a model of the guardians of the law, but when he is more than sixty years of age he shall no longer continue in his office of spectator. And when he has carried on his inspection during as many out of the ten years of his office as he pleases, on his return home let him go to the assembly of those who review the laws. This shall be a mixed body of young and old men, who shall be required to meet daily between the hour of dawn and the rising of the sun. They shall consist, in the first place, of the priests who have obtained the rewards of virtue; [2] and, in the second place, of guardians of the law, the ten eldest being chosen; the general superintendent of education shall also be a member, as well the last appointed as those who have been released from the office; and each of them shall take with him as his companion a young man, whomsoever he chooses, between the ages of thirty and forty. These shall be always holding conversation and discourse about the laws of their own city or about any specially [952] good ones which they may hear to be existing elsewhere; also about kinds of knowledge which may appear to be of use and will throw light upon the examination, or of which the want will make the subject of laws dark and uncertain to them. Any knowledge of this sort which the elders approve, the younger men shall learn with all diligence; and if any one of those who have been invited appear to be unworthy, the whole assembly shall blame him who invited him. The rest of the city shall watch over those among the young men who distinguish themselves, having an eye upon them, and especially honouring them if they succeed, but dishonouring them above the rest if they turn out to be inferior. This is the assembly to which he who has visited the institutions of other men,

[1] Cf. *Republic,* x. 619.

[2] Cf. 947.

on his return home shall straightway go, and if he have discovered any one who has anything to say about the enactment of laws or education or nurture, or if he have himself made any observations, let him communicate his discoveries to the whole assembly. And if he be seen to have come home neither better nor worse, let him be praised at any rate for his enthusiasm; and if he be much better, let him be praised so much the more; and not only while he lives but after his death let the assembly honour him with fitting honours. But if on his return home he appear to have been corrupted, pretending to be wise when he is not, let him hold no communication with any one, whether young or old; and if he will hearken to the rulers, then he shall be permitted to live as a private individual; but if he will not, let him die, if he be convicted in a court of law of interfering about education and the laws. And if he deserve to be indicted, and none of the magistrates indict him, let that be counted as a disgrace to them when the rewards of virtue are decided.

Let such be the character of the person who goes abroad, and let him go abroad under these conditions. In the next place, the stranger who comes from abroad should be received in a friendly spirit. Now there are four kinds of strangers, of whom we must make some mention—the first is he who comes and stays throughout the summer;[1] this class are like birds of passage, taking wing in pursuit of commerce, and flying over the sea to other cities, while the season lasts; he shall be received in market-places and harbours and public buildings, near the city but outside,[2] by those magistrates who are appointed to superintend these matters; and they shall take care that a stranger, whoever he be, duly receives justice; but he shall not be allowed to make any innovation. [953] They shall hold the intercourse with him which is necessary, and this shall be as little as possible. The second kind is just a spectator who comes to see with his eyes and hear with his ears the festivals of the Muses; such ought to have entertainment provided them at the temples by hospitable persons, and the priests and ministers of the temples should see and attend to them. But they should not remain more than a reasonable time; let them see and hear that for the sake of which they came, and then go away, neither having suffered nor done any harm. The priests shall be their judges, if any of them receive or do any wrong up to the sum

of fifty drachmae, but if any greater charge be brought, in such cases the suit shall come before the wardens of the agora. The third kind of stranger is he who comes on some public business from another land, and is to be received with public honours. He is to be received only by the generals and commanders of horse and foot, and the host by whom he is entertained, in conjunction with the Prytanes, shall have the sole charge of what concerns him. There is a fourth class of persons answering to our spectators, who come from another land to look at ours. In the first place, such visits will be rare, and the visitor should be at least fifty years of age; he may possibly be wanting to see something that is rich and rare in other states, or himself to show something in like manner to another city. Let such an one, then, go unbidden to the doors of the wise and rich, being one of them himself: let him go, for example, to the house of the superintendent of education, confident that he is a fitting guest of such a host, or let him go to the house of some of those who have gained the prize of virtue and hold discourse with them, both learning from them, and also teaching them; and when he has seen and heard all, he shall depart, as a friend taking leave of friends, and be honoured by them with gifts and suitable tributes of respect. These are the customs, according to which our city should receive all strangers of either sex who come from other countries, and should send forth her own citizens, showing respect to Zeus, the God of hospitality, not forbidding strangers at meals and sacrifices, as is the manner which prevails among the children of the Nile, nor driving them away by savage proclamations.[3]

When a man becomes surety, let him give the security in a distinct form, acknowledging the whole transaction in a written document, and in the presence of not less than three witnesses if the sum be under a thousand drachmae, and of not less than five witnesses if the sum be above a thousand drachmae. [954] The agent of a dishonest or untrustworthy seller shall himself be responsible; both the agent and the principal shall be equally liable. If a person wishes to find anything in the house of another, he shall enter naked, or wearing only a short tunic and without a girdle, having first taken an oath by the customary Gods that he expects to find it there; he shall then make his search, and the other shall throw open his house and allow him to search things both sealed and

[1] Cf. xi. 915.
[2] Cf. Aristotle, *Politics*, vii. 6, 1327 ª 31-39.
[3] Cf. 950.

unsealed. And if a person will not allow the searcher to make his search, he who is prevented shall go to law with him, estimating the value of the goods after which he is searching, and if the other be convicted he shall pay twice the value of the article. If the master be absent from home, the dwellers in the house shall let him search the unsealed property, and on the sealed property the searcher shall set another seal, and shall appoint any one whom he likes to guard them during five days; and if the master of the house be absent during a longer time, he shall take with him the wardens of the city, and so make his search, opening the sealed property as well as the unsealed, and then, together with the members of the family and the wardens of the city, he shall seal them up again as they were before. There shall be a limit of time in the case of disputed things, and he who has had possession of them during a certain time shall no longer be liable to be disturbed. As to houses and lands there can be no dispute in this state of ours; but if a man has any other possessions which he has used and openly shown in the city and in the agora and in the temples, and no one has put in a claim to them, and some one says that he was looking for them during this time, and the possessor is proved to have made no concealment, if they have continued for a year, the one having the goods and the other looking for them, the claim of the seeker shall not be allowed after the expiration of the year; or if he does not use or show the lost property in the market or in the city, but only in the country, and no one offers himself as the owner during five years, at the expiration of the five years the claim shall be barred for ever after; or if he uses them in the city but within the house, then the appointed time of claiming the goods shall be three years, or ten years if he has them in the country in private. And if he has them in another land, there shall be no limit of time or prescription, but whenever the owner finds them he may claim them.

If any one prevents another by force from being present at a trial, whether a principal party or his witnesses; if the person prevented be a slave, whether his own or belonging to another, the suit shall be incomplete and invalid; but if he who is prevented be a freeman, besides the suit being incomplete, [955] the other who has prevented him shall be imprisoned for a year, and shall be prosecuted for kidnapping by any one who pleases. And if any one hinders by force a rival competitor in gymnastic or music, or any other sort of contest, from being present at the contest, let him who has a mind inform the presiding judges, and they shall liberate him who is desirous of competing; and if they are not able, and he who hinders the other from competing wins the prize, then they shall give the prize of victory to him who is prevented, and inscribe him as the conqueror in any temples which he pleases; and he who hinders the other shall not be permitted to make any offering or inscription having reference to that contest, and in any case he shall be liable for damages, whether he be defeated or whether he conquer.

If any one knowingly receives anything which has been stolen, he shall undergo the same punishment as the thief, and if a man receives an exile he shall be punished with death. Every man should regard the friend and enemy of the state as his own friend and enemy; and if any one makes peace or war with another on his own account, and without the authority of the state, he, like the receiver of the exile, shall undergo the penalty of death. And if any fraction of the city declare war or peace against any, the generals shall indict the authors of this proceeding, and if they are convicted death shall be the penalty. Those who serve their country ought to serve without receiving gifts, and there ought to be no excusing or approving the saying, "Men should receive gifts as the reward of good, but not of evil deeds"; for to know which we are doing, and to stand fast by our knowledge, is no easy matter. The safest course is to obey the law which says, "Do no service for a bribe," and let him who disobeys, if he be convicted, simply die. With a view to taxation, for various reasons, every man ought to have had his property valued: and the tribesmen should likewise bring a register of the yearly produce to the wardens of the country, that in this way there may be two valuations; and the public officers may use annually whichever on consideration they deem the best, whether they prefer to take a certain portion of the whole value, or of the annual revenue, after subtracting what is paid to the common tables.

Touching offerings to the Gods, a moderate man should observe moderation in what he offers. Now the land and the hearth of the house of all men is sacred to all Gods; wherefore let no man dedicate them a second time to the Gods. Gold and silver, whether possessed by private persons or in temples, are in other cities provocative of envy, [956] and ivory, the product of a dead body, is not a proper offering; brass and iron, again, are instruments of war; but of wood let a man bring what offerings he likes, provided it be a single block, and in like manner of stone, to the public temples; of woven work let him not offer more than one woman can execute in a month. White is a colour suitable to the Gods, especially in woven works, but dyes should only be used for the adornments of war. The most divine of gifts are birds and images, and they should be such as one painter can execute in a single day. And let all other offerings follow a similar rule.

Now that the whole city has been divided into parts of which the nature and number have been described, and laws have been given about all the most important contracts as far as this was possible, the next thing will be to have justice done. The first of the courts shall consist of elected judges, who shall be chosen by the plaintiff and the defendant in common: these shall be called arbiters rather than judges. And in the second court there shall be judges of the villages and tribes corresponding to the twelvefold division of the land, and before these the litigants shall go to contend for greater damages, if the suit be not decided before the first judges; the defendant, if he be defeated the second time, shall pay a fifth more than the damages mentioned in the indictment; and if he find fault with his judges and would try a third time, let him carry the suit before the select judges, and if he be again defeated, let him pay the whole of the damages and half as much again. And the plaintiff, if when defeated before the first judges he persist in going on to the second, shall if he wins receive in addition to the damages a fifth part more, and if defeated he shall pay a like sum; but if he is not satisfied with the previous decision, and will insist on proceeding to a third court, then if he win he shall receive from the defendant the amount of the damages and, as I said before, half as much again, and the plaintiff, if he lose, shall pay half of the damages claimed. Now the assignment by lot of judges to courts and the completion of the number of them, and the appointment of servants to the different magistrates, and the times at which the several causes should be heard, and the votings and delays, and all the things that necessarily concern suits, and the order of causes, and the time in which answers have to be put in and parties are to appear—of these and other things akin to these we have indeed already spoken,[1] but there is no harm in repeating what is right twice or thrice:—All lesser and easier matters

which the elder legislator has omitted may be supplied by the younger one. [957] Private courts will be sufficiently regulated in this way, and the public and state courts, and those which the magistrates must use in the administration of their several offices, exist in many other states. Many very respectable institutions of this sort have been framed by good men, and from them the guardians of the law may by reflection derive what is necessary for the order of our new state, considering and correcting them, and bringing them to the test of experience, until every detail appears to be satisfactorily determined; and then putting the final seal upon them, and making them irreversible, they shall use them for ever afterwards. As to what relates to the silence of judges and the abstinence from words of evil omen and the reverse, and the different notions of the just and good and honourable which exist in our own as compared with other states, they have been partly mentioned already, and another part of them will be mentioned hereafter as we draw near the end. To all these matters he who would be an equal judge shall justly look, and he shall possess writings about them that he may learn them. For of all kinds of knowledge the knowledge of good laws has the greatest power of improving the learner; otherwise there would be no meaning in the divine and admirable law possessing a name akin to mind (νοῦς, νόμος). And of all other words, such as the praises and censures of individuals which occur in poetry and also in prose, whether written down or uttered in daily conversation, whether men dispute about them in the spirit of contention or weakly assent to them, as is often the case—of all these the one sure test is the writings of the legislator,[2] which the righteous judge ought to have in his mind as the antidote of all other words, and thus make himself and the city stand upright, procuring for the good the continuance and increase of justice, and for the bad, on the other hand, a conversion from ignorance and intemperance, and in general from all unrighteousness, as far as their evil minds can be healed, but to those whose web of life is in reality finished, giving death, which is the only remedy for souls in their condition, as I may say truly again and again. And such judges and chiefs of judges will be worthy of receiving praise [958] from the whole city.

When the suits of the year are completed the following laws shall regulate their execution:—In the first place, the judge shall assign to the party who wins the suit the whole property of him who loses, with the exception of mere necessaries,[1] and the assignment shall be made through the herald immediately after each decision in the hearing of the judges; and when the month arrives following the month in which the courts are sitting (unless the gainer of the suit has been previously satisfied), the court shall follow up the case, and hand over to the winner the goods of the loser; but if they find that he has not the means of paying, and the sum deficient is not less than a drachma, the insolvent person shall not have any right of going to law with any other man until he have satisfied the debt of the winning party; but other persons shall still have the right of bringing suits against him. And if any one after he is condemned refuses to acknowledge the authority which condemned him, let the magistrates who are thus deprived of their authority bring him before the court of the guardians of the law, and if he be cast, let him be punished with death, as a subverter of the whole state and of the laws.

Thus a man is born and brought up, and after this manner he begets and brings up his own children, and has his share of dealings with other men, and suffers if he has done wrong to any one, and receives satisfaction if he has been wronged, and so at length in due time he grows old under the protection of the laws, and his end comes in the order of nature. Concerning the dead of either sex, the religious ceremonies which may fittingly be performed, whether appertaining to the Gods of the underworld or of this, shall be decided by the interpreters with absolute authority. Their sepulchres are not to be in places which are fit for cultivation, and there shall be no monuments in such spots, either large or small, but they shall occupy that part of the country which is naturally adapted for receiving and concealing the bodies of the dead with as little hurt as possible to the living. No man, living or dead, shall deprive the living of the sustenance which the earth, their foster-parent, is naturally inclined to provide for them. And let not the mound be piled higher than would be the work of five men completed in five days; nor shall the stone which is placed over the spot be larger than would be sufficient to receive the praises of the dead included in four heroic lines. [959] Nor shall the laying out of the dead in the house continue for a longer time than is sufficient to distinguish between him who is in a

trance only and him who is really dead, and speaking generally, the third day after death will be a fair time for carrying out the body to the sepulchre. Now we must believe the legislator when he tells us that the soul is in all respects superior to the body, and that even in life what makes each one of us to be what we are is only the soul; and that the body follows us about in the likeness of each of us, and therefore, when we are dead, the bodies of the dead are quite rightly said to be our shades or images; for the true and immortal being of each one of us which is called the soul goes on her way to other Gods,[2] before them to give an account—which is an inspiring hope to the good, but very terrible to the bad, as the laws of our fathers tell us; and they also say that not much can be done in the way of helping a man after he is dead. But the living—he should be helped by all his kindred, that while in life he may be the holiest and justest of men, and after death may have no great sins to be punished in the world below. If this be true, a man ought not to waste his substance under the idea that all this lifeless mass of flesh which is in process of burial is connected with him; he should consider that the son, or brother, or the beloved one, whoever he may be, whom he thinks he is laying in the earth, has gone away to complete and fulfil his own destiny, and that his duty is rightly to order the present, and to spend moderately on the lifeless altar of the Gods below. But the legislator does not intend moderation to be taken in the sense of meanness.[3] Let the law, then, be as follows:—The expenditure on the entire funeral of him who is of the highest class, shall not exceed five minae; and for him who is of the second class, three minae, and for him who is of the third class, two minae, and for him who is of the fourth class, one mina, will be a fair limit of expense. The guardians of the law ought to take especial care of the different ages of life, whether childhood, or manhood, or any other age. And at the end of all, let there be some one guardian of the law presiding, who shall be chosen by the friends of the deceased to superintend, and let it be glory to him to manage with fairness and moderation what relates to the dead, and a discredit to him if they are not well managed. Let the laying out and other ceremonies be in accordance with custom, but to the statesman who adopts custom as his law we must give way in certain particulars. It would be monstrous for

[1] Cf. ix. 855.

[2] Cf. *Phaedo*, 63.
[3] Cf. iv. 717, 719.

example that he should command any man to weep or abstain from weeping over the dead; but he may forbid cries of lamentation, and not allow the voice of the mourner to be heard outside the house; [960] also, he may forbid the bringing of the dead body into the open streets, or the processions of mourners in the streets, and may require that before daybreak they should be outside the city. Let these, then, be our laws relating to such matters, and let him who obeys be free from penalty; but he who disobeys even a single guardian of the law shall be punished by them all with a fitting penalty. Other modes of burial, or again the denial of burial, which is to be refused in the case of robbers of temples and parricides and the like, have been devised and are embodied in the preceding laws, so that now our work of legislation is pretty nearly at an end; but in all cases the end does not consist in doing something or acquiring something or establishing something,—the end will be attained and finally accomplished, when we have provided for the perfect and lasting continuance of our institutions until then our creation is incomplete.

Cle. That is very good Stranger; but I wish you would tell me more clearly what you mean.

Ath. O Cleinias, many things of old time were well said and sung; and the saying about the Fates was one of them.

Cle. What is it?

Ath. The saying that Lachesis or the giver of the lots is the first of them, and that Clotho or the spinster is the second of them, and that Atropos or the unchanging one is the third of them;[1] and that she is the preserver of the things which we have spoken, and which have been compared in a figure to things woven by fire, they both (i.e., Atropos and the fire) producing the quality of unchangeableness. I am speaking of the things which in a state and government give not only health and salvation to the body, but law, or rather preservation of the law, in the soul; and, if I am not mistaken, this seems to be still wanting in our laws: we have still to see how we can implant in them this irreversible nature.

Cle. It will be no small matter if we can only discover how such a nature can be implanted in anything.

Ath. But it certainly can be; so much I clearly see.

Cle. Then let us not think of desisting until we have imparted this quality to our laws; for it is ridiculous, after a great deal of labour has

[1] Cf. *Republic,* x. 620.

been spent, to place a thing at last on an insecure foundation.

Megillus. I approve of your suggestion, and am quite of the same mind with you.

Cle. Very good: And now what, according to you, is to be the salvation of our government and of our laws, and how is it to be effected?

Ath. Were we not saying that there must be in our city a council which was to be of this sort:[961]—The ten oldest guardians of the law, and all those who have obtained prizes of virtue, were to meet in the same assembly, and the council was also to include those who had visited foreign countries in the hope of hearing something that might be of use in the preservation of the laws, and who, having come safely home, and having been tested in these same matters, had proved themselves to be worthy to take part in the assembly;—each of the members was to select some young man of not less than thirty years of age, he himself judging in the first instance whether the young man was worthy by nature and education, and then suggesting him to the others, and if he seemed to them also to be worthy they were to adopt him; but if not, the decision at which they arrived was to be kept a secret from the citizens at large, and, more especially, from the rejected candidate. The meeting of the council was to be held early in the morning, when everybody was most at leisure from all other business, whether public or private— was not something of this sort said by us before?

Cle. True.

Ath. Then, returning to the council, I would say further, that if we let it down to be the anchor of the state, our city, having everything which is suitable to her, will preserve all that we wish to preserve.

Cle. What do you mean?

Ath. Now is the time for me to speak the truth in all earnestness.

Cle. Well said, and I hope that you will fulfil your intention.

Ath. Know, Cleinias, that everything, in all that it does, has a natural saviour, as of an animal the soul and the head are the chief saviours.

Cle. Once more, what do you mean?

Ath. The well-being of those two is obviously the preservation of every living thing.

Cle. How is that?

Ath. The soul, besides other things, contains mind, and the head, besides other things, contains sight and hearing; and the mind, mingling with the noblest of the senses, and becoming one with them, may be truly called the salvation of all.

Cle. Yes, Quite so.

Ath. Yes, indeed; but with what is that intellect concerned which, mingling with the senses, is the salvation of ships in storms as well as in fair weather? In a ship, when the pilot and the sailors unite their perceptions with the piloting mind, do they not save both themselves and their craft?

Cle. Very true.

Ath. We do not want many illustrations about such matters:—What aim would the general of an army, or what aim would a physician propose to himself, if he were seeking to attain salvation?

Cle. Very good.

[962] Ath. Does not the general aim at victory and superiority in war, and do not the physician and his assistants aim at producing health in the body?

Cle. Certainly.

Ath. And a physician who is ignorant about the body, that is to say, who knows not that which we just now called health, or a general who knows not victory, or any others who are ignorant of the particulars of the arts which we mentioned, cannot be said to have understanding about any of these matters.

Cle. They cannot.

Ath. And what would you say of the state? If a person proves to be ignorant of the aim to which the statesman should look, ought he, in the first place, to be called a ruler at all; and further, will he ever be able to preserve that of which he does not even know the aim?

Cle. Impossible.

Ath. And therefore, if our settlement of the country is to be perfect, we ought to have some institution, which, as I was saying, will tell what is the aim of the state, and will inform us how we are to attain this, and what law or what man will advise us to that end. Any state which has no such institution is likely to be devoid of mind and sense, and in all her actions will proceed by mere chance.

Cle. Very true.

Ath. In which, then, of the parts or institutions of the state is any such guardian power to be found? Can we say?

Cle. I am not quite certain, Stranger; but I have a suspicion that you are referring to the assembly which you just now said was to meet at night.

Ath. You understand me perfectly, Cleinias; and we must assume, as the argument implies,

that this council possesses all virtue; and the beginning of virtue is not to make mistakes by guessing many things, but to look steadily at one thing, and on this to fix all our aims.

Cle. Quite true.

Ath. Then now we shall see why there is nothing wonderful in states going astray—the reason is that their legislators have such different aims; nor is there anything wonderful in some laying down as their rule of justice, that certain individuals should bear rule in the state, whether they be good or bad, and others that the citizens should be rich, not caring whether they are the slaves of other men or not. The tendency of others, again, is towards freedom; and some legislate with a view to two things at once—they want to be at the same time free and the lords of other states; but the wisest men, as they deem themselves to be, look to all these and similar aims, and there is no one of them which they exclusively honour, and to which they would have all things look.

[963] Cle. Then, Stranger, our former assertion will hold, for we were saying that laws generally should look to one thing only; and this, as we admitted, was rightly said to be virtue.

Ath. Yes.

Cle. And we said that virtue was of four kinds?

Ath. Quite true.

Cle. And that mind was the leader of the four, and that to her the three other virtues and all other things ought to have regard?

Ath. You follow me capitally, Cleinias, and I would ask you to follow me to the end, for we have already said that the mind of the pilot, the mind of the physician and of the general look to that one thing to which they ought to look; and now we may turn to mind political, of which, as of a human creature, we will ask a question:—O wonderful being, and to what are you looking? The physician is able to tell his single aim in life, but you, the superior, as you declare yourself to be, of all intelligent beings, when you are asked are not able to tell. Can you, Megillus, and you, Cleinias, say distinctly what is the aim of mind political, in return for the many explanations of things which I have given you?

Cle. We cannot, Stranger.

Ath. Well, but ought we not to desire to see it, and to see where it is to be found?

Cle. For example, where?

Ath. For example, we were saying that there

are four kinds of virtue, and as there are four of them, each of them must be one.

Cle. Certainly.

Ath. And further, all four of them we call one; for we say that courage is virtue, and that prudence is virtue, and the same of the two others, as if they were in reality not many but one, that is, virtue.

Cle. Quite so.

Ath. There is no difficulty in seeing in what way the two differ from one another, and have received two names, and so of the rest. But there is more difficulty in explaining why we call these two and the rest of them by the single name of virtue.

Cle. How do you mean?

Ath. I have no difficulty in explaining what I mean. Let us distribute the subject into questions and answers.

Cle. Once more, what do you mean?

Ath. Ask me what is that one thing which I call virtue, and then again speak of as two, one part being courage and the other wisdom. I will tell you how that occurs:—One of them has to do with fear; in this the beasts also participate,[1] and quite young children—I mean courage; for a courageous temper is a gift of nature and not of reason. But without reason there never has been, or is, or will be a wise and understanding soul; it is of a different nature.

Cle. That is true.

Ath. I have now told you in what way the two are different, and do you in return tell me in what way they are one and the same. *[964]* Suppose that I ask you in what way the four are one, and when you have answered me, you will have a right to ask of me in return in what way they are four; and then let us proceed to enquire whether in the case of things which have a name and also a definition to them, true knowledge consists in knowing the name only and not the definition. Can he who is good for anything be ignorant of all this without discredit where great and glorious truths are concerned?

Cle. I suppose not.

Ath. And is there anything greater to the legislator and the guardian of the law, and to him who thinks that he excels all other men in virtue, and has won the palm of excellence, than these very qualities of which we are now speaking—courage, temperance, wisdom, justice?

Cle. How can there be anything greater?

Ath. And ought not the interpreters, the

[1] Cf. *Laches*, 196.

teachers, the lawgivers, the guardians of the other citizens, to excel the rest of mankind, and perfectly to show him who desires to learn and know or whose evil actions require to be punished and reproved, what is the nature of virtue and vice? Or shall some poet who has found his way into the city, or some chance person who pretends to be an instructor of youth, show himself to be better than him who has won the prize for every virtue? And can we wonder that when the guardians are not adequate in speech or action, and have no adequate knowledge of virtue, the city being unguarded should experience the common fate of cities in our day?

Cle. Wonder! no.

Ath. Well, then, must we do as we said? Or can we give our guardians a more precise knowledge of virtue in speech and action than the many have? or is there any way in which our city can be made to resemble the head and senses of rational beings because possessing such a guardian power?

Cle. What, Stranger, is the drift of your comparison?

Ath. Do we not see that the city is the trunk, and are not the younger guardians, who are chosen for their natural gifts, placed in the head of the state, having their souls all full of eyes, with which they look about the whole city? They keep watch and hand over their perceptions to the memory, and inform the elders of all that happens in the city; *[965]* and those whom we compared to the mind, because they have many wise thoughts—that is to say, the old men—take counsel, and making use of the younger men as their ministers, and advising with them—in this way both together truly preserve the whole state:—Shall this or some other be the order of our state? Are all our citizens to be equal in acquirements, or shall there be special persons among them who have received a more careful training and education?

Cle. That they should be equal, my good sir, is impossible.

Ath. Then we ought to proceed to some more exact training than any which has preceded.

Cle. Certainly.

Ath. And must not that of which we are in need be the one to which we were just now alluding?

Cle. Very true.

Ath. Did we not say that the workman or guardian, if he be perfect in every respect, ought not only to be able to see the many aims, but he should press onward to the one?[1] this he should know, and knowing, order all things with a view to it.

Cle. True.

Ath. And can any one have a more exact way of considering or contemplating anything, than the being able to look at one idea gathered from many different things?

Cle. Perhaps not.

Ath. Not "Perhaps not," but "Certainly not," my good sir, is the right answer. There never has been a truer method than this discovered by any man.

Cle. I bow to your authority, Stranger; let us proceed in the way which you propose.

Ath. Then, as would appear, we must compel the guardians of our divine state to perceive, in the first place, what that principle is which is the same in all the four—the same, as we affirm, in courage and in temperance, and in justice and in prudence, and which, being one, we call as we ought, by the single name of virtue. To this, my friends, we will, if you please, hold fast, and not let go until we have sufficiently explained what that is to which we are to look, whether to be regarded as one, or as a whole, or as both, or in whatever way. Are we likely ever to be in a virtuous condition, if we cannot tell whether virtue is many, or four, or one? Certainly, if we take counsel among ourselves, we shall in some way contrive that this principle has a place amongst us; but if you have made up your mind that we should let the matter alone, we will.

Cle. We must not, Stranger, by the God of strangers I swear that we must not, for in our opinion you speak most truly; but we should like to know how you will accomplish your purpose.

[966] Ath. Wait a little before you ask; and let us, first of all, be quite agreed with one another that the purpose has to be accomplished.

Cle. Certainly, it ought to be, if it can be.

Ath. Well, and about the good and the honourable, are we to take the same view? Are our guardians only to know that each of them is many, or also how and in what way they are one?

Cle. They must consider also in what sense they are one.

Ath. And are they to consider only, and to be unable to set forth what they think?

Cle. Certainly not; that would be the state of a slave.

Ath. And may not the same be said of all

good things—that the true guardians of the laws ought to know the truth about them, and to be able to interpret them in words, and carry them out in action, judging of what is and of what is not well, according to nature?

Cle. Certainly.

Ath. Is not the knowledge of the Gods which we have set forth with so much zeal one of the noblest sorts of knowledge;—to know that they are, and know how great is their power, as far as in man lies? We do indeed excuse the mass of the citizens, who only follow the voice of the laws, but we refuse to admit as guardians any who do not labour to obtain every possible evidence that there is respecting the Gods; our city is forbidden and not allowed to choose as a guardian of the law, or to place in the select order of virtue, him who is not an inspired man, and has not laboured at these things.

Cle. It is certainly just, as you say, that he who is indolent about such matters or incapable should be rejected, and that things honourable should be put away from him.

Ath. Are we assured that there are two things which lead men to believe in the Gods, as we have already stated?

Cle. What are they?

Ath. One is the argument about the soul, which has been already mentioned—that it is the eldest and most divine of all things, to which motion attaining generation gives perpetual existence;[2] the other was an argument from the order of the motion of the stars, and of all things under the dominion of the mind which ordered the universe.[3] If a man look upon the world not lightly or ignorantly, there was never any one so godless who did not experience an effect opposite to that which the many imagine. *[967]* For they think that those who handle these matters by the help of astronomy, and the accompanying arts of demonstration, may become godless, because they see, as far as they can see, things happening by necessity, and not by an intelligent will accomplishing good.

Cle. But what is the fact?

Ath. Just the opposite, as I said, of the opinion which once prevailed among men, that the sun and stars are without soul. Even in those days men wondered about them, and that which is now ascertained was then conjectured by some who had a more exact knowledge of them—that if they had been things without soul, and had no mind, they could never have

[1] Cf. *Republic,* vii. 537.

[2] Cf. x. 893.

[3] Cf. *ibid.,* 896.

moved with numerical exactness so wonderful; and even at that time some ventured to hazard the conjecture that mind was the orderer of the universe. But these same persons again mistaking the nature of the soul, which they conceived to be younger and not older than the body, once more overturned the world, or rather, I should say, themselves; for the bodies which they saw moving in heaven all appeared to be full of stones, and earth, and many other lifeless substances, and to these they assigned the causes of all things. Such studies gave rise to much atheism and perplexity, and the poets took occasion to be abusive—comparing the philosophers to she-dogs uttering vain howlings, and talking other nonsense of the same sort. But now, as I said, the case is reversed.[1]

Cle. How so?

Ath. No man can be a true worshipper of the Gods who does not know these two principles—that the soul is the eldest of all things which are born, and is immortal and rules over all bodies; moreover, as I have now said several times, he who has not contemplated the mind of nature which is said to exist in the stars, and gone through the previous training, and seen the connection of music with these things, and harmonized them all with laws and institutions, is not able to give a reason of such things as have a reason.[2] And he who is unable to acquire this in addition to the ordinary virtues of a [968] citizen, can hardly be a good ruler of a whole state; but he should be the subordinate of other rulers. Wherefore, Cleinias and Megillus, let us consider whether we may not add to all the other laws which we have discussed this further one—that the nocturnal assembly of the magistrates, which has also shared in the whole scheme of education proposed by us, shall be a guard set according to law for the salvation of the state. Shall we propose this?

Cle. Certainly, my good friend, we will if the thing is in any degree possible.

Ath. Let us make a common effort to gain such an object; for I too will gladly share in the attempt. Of these matters I have had much experience, and have often considered them, and I dare say that I shall be able to find others who will also help.

Cle. I agree, Stranger, that we should proceed along the road in which God is guiding us; and how we can proceed rightly has now to be investigated and explained.

[1] Cf. *Republic,* x. 607.
[2] Cf. *Republic,* vii. 531, ff.

Ath. O Megillus and Cleinias, about these matters we cannot legislate further until the council is constituted; when that is done, then we will determine what authority they shall have of their own; but the explanation of how this is all to be ordered would only be given rightly in a long discourse.

Cle. What do you mean, and what new thing is this?

Ath. In the first place, a list would have to be made out of those who by their ages and studies and dispositions and habits are well fitted for the duty of a guardian. In the next place, it will not be easy for them to discover themselves what they ought to learn, or become the disciple of one who has already made the discovery. Furthermore, to write down the times at which, and during which, they ought to receive the several kinds of instruction, would be a vain thing; for the learners themselves do not know what is learned to advantage until the knowledge which is the result of learning has found a place in the soul of each. And so these details, although they could not be truly said to be secret, might be said to be incapable of being stated beforehand, because when stated they would have no meaning.

Cle. What then are we to do, Stranger, under these circumstances?

Ath. As the proverb says, the answer is no secret, but open to all of us: [969]—We must risk the whole on the chance of throwing, as they say, thrice six or thrice ace, and I am willing to share with you the danger by stating and explaining to you my views about education and nurture, which is the question coming to the surface again. The danger is not a slight or ordinary one, and I would advise you, Cleinias, in particular, to see to the matter; for if you order rightly the city of the Magnetes, or whatever name God may give it, you will obtain the greatest glory; or at any rate you will be thought the most courageous of men in the estimation of posterity. Dear companions, if this our divine assembly can only be established, to them we will hand over the city; none of the present company of legislators, as I may call them, would hesitate about that. And the state will be perfected and become a waking reality, which a little while ago we attempted to create as a dream[3] and in idea only, mingling together reason and mind in one image, in the hope that our citizens might be duly mingled and rightly educated; and being educated, and

[3] Cf. *Republic,* ix. 592.

dwelling in the citadel of the land, might become perfect guardians, such as we have never seen in all our previous life, by reason of the saving virtue which is in them.

Meg. Dear Cleinias, after all that has been said, either we must detain the Stranger, and by supplications and in all manner of ways make him share in the foundation of the city, or we must give up the undertaking.

Cle. Very true, Megillus; and you must join with me in detaining him.

Meg. I will.

The Seventh Letter

PLATO TO THE RELATIVES AND FRIENDS OF DION. WELFARE

You write to me that I must consider your views the same as those of Dion, [324a] and you urge me to aid your cause so far as I can in word and deed. My answer is that, if you have the same opinion and desire as he had, I consent to aid your cause; but if not, I shall think more than once about it. Now what his purpose and desire was, I can inform you from no mere conjecture but from positive knowledge. For when I made my first visit to Sicily, being then about forty years old, Dion was of the same age as Hipparinos is now, and the opinion which he then formed was that which he always retained, [b] I mean the belief that the Syracusans ought to be free and governed by the best laws. So it is no matter for surprise if some God should make Hipparinos adopt the same opinion as Dion about forms of government. But it is well worth while that you should all, old as well as young, hear the way in which this opinion was formed, and I will attempt to give you an account of it from the beginning. For the present is a suitable opportunity.

In my youth I went through the same experience as many other men. I fancied that if, early in life, I became my own master, [c] I should at once embark on a political career. And I found myself confronted with the following occurrences in the public affairs of my own city. The existing constitution being generally condemned, a revolution took place, and fifty-one men came to the front as rulers of the revolutionary government, namely eleven in the city and ten in the Peiraeus—each of these bodies being in charge of the market and municipal matters—while thirty were appointed rulers with full powers over public affairs as a whole. [d] Some of these were relatives and acquaintances of mine, and they at once invited me to share in their doings, as something to which I had a claim. The effect on me was not surprising in the case of a young man. I considered

that they would, of course, so manage the State as to bring men out of a bad way of life into a good one. So I watched them very closely to see what they would do.

And seeing, as I did, that in quite a short time they made the former government seem by comparison something precious as gold— for among other things they tried to send a friend of mine, [e] the aged Socrates, whom I should scarcely scruple to describe as the most upright man of that day, with some other persons to carry off one of the citizens by force to [325a] execution, in order that, whether he wished it, or not, he might share the guilt of their conduct; but he would not obey them, risking all consequences in preference to becoming a partner in their iniquitous deeds—seeing all these things and others of the same kind on a considerable scale, I disapproved of their proceedings, and withdrew from any connection with the abuses of the time.

Not long after that a revolution terminated the power of the thirty and the form of government as it then was. And once more, though with more hesitation, I began to be moved by the desire to take part in public and political affairs. [b] Well, even in the new government, unsettled as it was, events occurred which one would naturally view with disapproval; and it was not surprising that in a period of revolution excessive penalties were inflicted by some persons on political opponents, though those who had returned from exile at that time showed very considerable forbearance. But once more it happened that some of those in power brought my friend Socrates, whom I have mentioned, to trial before a court of law, [c] laying a most iniquitous charge against him and one most inappropriate in his case: for it was on a charge of impiety that some of them prosecuted and others condemned and executed the very man who would not participate in the iniquitous arrest of one of the friends of the party then in exile, at the time when they themselves were in exile and misfortune.

As I observed these incidents and the men engaged in public affairs, the laws too and the customs, the more closely I examined them and the farther I advanced in life, the more difficult it seemed to me to handle public affairs aright. [d] For it was not possible to be active in politics without friends and trustworthy supporters; and to find these ready to my hand was not an easy matter, since public affairs at Athens were not carried on in accordance with the manners and practices of our fathers; nor was there any ready method by which I could make new friends. The laws too, written and unwritten, were being altered for the worse, and the evil was growing with startling rapidity. The result was that, though at first I had been full of a strong impulse towards political life, [e] as I looked at the course of affairs and saw them being swept in all directions by contending currents, my head finally began to swim; and, though I did not stop looking to see if there was any likelihood of improvement in these symptoms and in the general course of public life, [326a] I postponed action till a suitable opportunity should arise. Finally, it became clear to me with regard to all existing communities, that they were one and all misgoverned. For their laws have got into a state that is almost incurable, except by some extraordinary reform with good luck to support it. And I was forced to say, when praising true philosophy, that it is by this that men are enabled to see what justice in public and private life really is. Therefore, I said, there will be no cessation of evils for the sons of men, [b] till either those who are pursuing a right and true philosophy receive sovereign power in the States, or those in power in the States by some dispensation of providence become true philosophers.

With these thoughts in my mind I came to Italy and Sicily on my first visit. My first impressions on arrival were those of strong disapproval—disapproval of the kind of life which was there called the life of happiness, stuffed full as it was with the banquets of the Italian Greeks and Syracusans, who ate to repletion twice every day, and were never without a partner for the night; [c] and disapproval of the habits which this manner of life produces. For with these habits formed early in life, no man under heaven could possibly attain to wisdom —human nature is not capable of such an extraordinary combination. Temperance also is out of the question for such a man; and the same applies to virtue generally. No city could remain in a state of tranquillity under any laws whatsoever, when men think it right to squander all their property in extravagant excesses, [d] and consider it a duty to be idle in everything else except eating and drinking and the laborious prosecution of debauchery. It follows necessarily that the constitutions of such cities must be constantly changing, tyrannies, oligarchies and democracies succeeding one another, while those who hold the power cannot so much as endure the name of any form of government which maintains justice and equality of rights.

With a mind full of these thoughts, on the top of my previous convictions, [e] I crossed over to Syracuse—led there perhaps by chance —but it really looks as if some higher power was even then planning to lay a foundation for all that has now come to pass with regard to Dion and Syracuse—and for further troubles too, I fear, unless you listen to the advice which is now for the second time offered by me. What do I mean by saying that my arrival in Sicily at that moment proved to be the foundation [327a] on which all the sequel rests? I was brought into close intercourse with Dion who was then a young man, and explained to him my views as to the ideals at which men should aim, advising him to carry them out in practice. In doing this I seem to have been unaware that I was, in a fashion, without knowing it, contriving the overthrow of the tyranny which subsequently took place. For Dion, who rapidly assimilated my teaching as he did all forms of knowledge, listened to me with an eagerness which I had never seen equalled in any young man, [b] and resolved to live for the future in a better way than the majority of Italian and Sicilian Greeks, having set his affection on virtue in preference to pleasure and self-indulgence. The result was that until the death of Dionysios he lived in a way which rendered him somewhat unpopular among those whose manner of life was that which is usual in the courts of despots.

After that event he came to the conclusion that this conviction, [c] which he himself had gained under the influence of good teaching, was not likely to be confined to himself. Indeed, he saw it being actually implanted in other minds—not many perhaps, but certainly in some; and he thought that, with the aid of the Gods, Dionysios might perhaps become one of these, and that, if such a thing did come to pass, the result would be a life of unspeakable happiness both for himself and for the rest of the Syracusans. Further, he thought it essential that I should come to Syracuse by all manner of means and with the utmost possible speed to be his partner in these plans, *[d]* remembering in his own case how readily intercourse with me had produced in him a longing for the noblest and best life. And if it should produce a similar effect on Dionysios, as his aim was that it should, he had great hope that, without bloodshed, loss of life, and those disastrous events which have now taken place, he would be able to introduce the true life of happiness throughout the whole territory.

Holding these sound views, Dion persuaded Dionysios to send for me; he also wrote himself entreating me to come by all manner of means and with the utmost possible speed, *[e]* before certain other persons coming in contact with Dionysios should turn him aside into some way of life other than the best. What he said, though perhaps it is rather long to repeat, was as follows: "What opportunities," he said, "shall we wait for, greater than those now offered to us by Providence?" *[328a]* And he described the Syracusan empire in Italy and Sicily, his own influential position in it, and the youth of Dionysios and how strongly his desire was directed towards philosophy and education. His own nephews and relatives, he said, would be readily attracted towards the principles and manner of life described by me, and would be most influential in attracting Dionysios in the same direction, so that, now if ever, we should see the accomplishment of every hope that the same persons might actually become both philosophers and the rulers of great States. *[b]* These were the appeals addressed to me and much more to the same effect.

My own opinion, so far as the young men were concerned, and the probable line which their conduct would take, was full of apprehension—for young men are quick in forming desires, which often take directions conflicting with one another. But I knew that the character of Dion's mind was naturally a stable one and had also the advantage of somewhat advanced years.

Therefore, I pondered the matter and was in two minds as to whether I ought to listen to entreaties and go, or how I ought to act; and finally the scale turned in favour of the view that, if ever anyone was to try to carry out in practice my ideas about *[c]* laws and constitutions, now was the time for making the attempt; for if only I could fully convince one man, I should have secured thereby the accomplishment of all good things.

With these views and thus nerved to the task, I sailed from home, not in the spirit which some imagined, but principally through a feeling of shame with regard to myself, lest I might some day appear to myself wholly and solely a mere man of words, one who would never of his own will lay his hand to any act. Also there was reason to think that I should be betraying first and foremost my friendship and comradeship with Dion, *[d]* who in very truth was in a position of considerable danger. If therefore anything should happen to him, or if he were banished by Dionysios and his other enemies and coming to us as exile addressed this question to me: "Plato, I have come to you as a fugitive, not for want of hoplites, nor because I had no cavalry for defence against my enemies, but for want of words and power of persuasion, which I knew to be a special gift of yours, enabling you to lead young men into the path of goodness and justice, and to establish in every case relations of friendship and comradeship among them. *[e]* It is for the want of this assistance on your part that I have left Syracuse and am here now. And the disgrace attaching to your treatment of me is a small matter. But philosophy—whose praises you are always singing, while you say she is held in dishonour by the rest of mankind—must we not say that philosophy along with me has now been betrayed, so far as your action was concerned? *[329a]* Had I been living at Megara, you would certainly have come to give me your aid towards the objects for which I asked it; or you would have thought yourself the most contemptible of mankind. But as it is, do you think that you will escape the reputation of cowardice by making excuses about the distance of the journey, the length of the sea voyage, and the amount of labour involved? Far from it." To reproaches of this kind what creditable reply could I have made? Surely none.

[b] I took my departure, therefore, acting, so far as a man can act, in obedience to reason and justice, and for these reasons leaving my own occupations, which were certainly not discreditable ones, to put myself under a tyranny which did not seem likely to harmonise with my teaching or with myself. By my departure I secured my own freedom from the displeasure of Zeus Xenios, and made myself clear of any charge on the part of philosophy, which would have been exposed to detraction, if any disgrace

had come upon me for faint-heartedness and cowardice.

On my arrival, to cut a long story short, I found the court of Dionysios full of intrigues and of attempts to create in the *[c]* sovereign ill-feeling against Dion. I combated these as far as I could, but with very little success; and in the fourth month or thereabouts, charging Dion with conspiracy to seize the throne, Dionysios put him on board a small boat and expelled him from Syracuse with ignominy. All of us who were Dion's friends were afraid that he might take vengeance on one or other of us as an accomplice in Dion's conspiracy. With regard to me, there was even a rumour current in Syracuse that I had been put to death by Dionysios as the cause of all that had occurred. *[d]* Perceiving that we were all in this state of mind and apprehending that our fears might lead to some serious consequence, he now tried to win all of us over by kindness: me in particular he encouraged, bidding me be of good cheer and entreating me on all grounds to remain. For my flight from him was not likely to redound to his credit, but my staying might do so. Therefore, he made a great pretence of entreating me. And we know that the entreaties of sovereigns are mixed with compulsion. *[e]* So to secure his object he proceeded to render my departure impossible, bringing me into the acropolis, and establishing me in quarters from which not a single ship's captain would have taken me away against the will of Dionysios, nor indeed without a special messenger sent by him to order my removal. Nor was there a single merchant, or a single official in charge of points of departure from the country, who would have allowed me to depart unaccompanied, and would not have promptly seized me and taken me back to Dionysios, especially since a statement had now been circulated contradicting the previous rumours and giving out that Dionysios was becoming extraordinarily *[330a]* attached to Plato. What were the facts about this attachment? I must tell the truth. As time went on, and as intercourse made him acquainted with my disposition and character, he did become more and more attached to me, and wished me to praise him more than I praised Dion, and to look upon him as more specially my friend than Dion, and he was extraordinarily eager about this sort of thing. But when confronted with the one way in which this might have been done, if it was to be done at all, *[b]* he shrank from coming into close and intimate relations with me as a pupil and listener to my discourses

on philosophy, fearing the danger suggested by mischief-makers, that he might be ensnared, and so Dion would prove to have accomplished all his object. I endured all this patiently, retaining the purpose with which I had come and the hope that he might come to desire the philosophic life. But his resistance prevailed against me.

The time of my first visit to Sicily and my stay there was taken up with all these incidents. *[c]* On a later occasion I left home and again came on an urgent summons from Dionysios. But before giving the motives and particulars of my conduct then and showing how suitable and right it was, I must first, in order that I may not treat as the main point what is only a side issue, give you my advice as to what your acts should be in the present position of affairs; afterwards, to satisfy those who put the question why I came a second time, I will deal fully with the facts about my second visit; what I have now to say is this.

He who advises a sick man, whose manner of life is prejudicial to health, *[d]* is clearly bound first of all to change his patient's manner of life, and if the patient is willing to obey him, he may go on to give him other advice. But if he is not willing, I shall consider one who declines to advise such a patient to be a man and a physician, and one who gives in to him to be unmanly and unprofessional. In the same way with regard to a State, whether it be under a single ruler or more than one, if, while the government is being carried on methodically and in a right course, *[e]* it asks advice about any details of policy, it is the part of a wise man to advise such people. But when men are travelling altogether outside the path of right government and flatly refuse to move in the right path, and start by giving notice to their adviser that he must leave the government alone and make no change in it under penalty of death—if such men *[331a]* should order their counsellors to pander to their wishes and desires and to advise them in what way their object may most readily and easily be once for all accomplished, I should consider as unmanly one who accepts the duty of giving such forms of advice, and one who refuses it to be a true man.

Holding these views, whenever anyone consults me about any of the weightiest matters affecting his own life, as, for instance, the acquisition of property or the proper treatment of body or *[b]* mind, if it seems to me that his daily life rests on any system, or if he seems likely to listen to advice about the things on which he consults me, I advise him with readiness, and do not content myself with giving him a merely perfunctory answer. But if a man does not consult me at all, or evidently does not intend to follow my advice, I do not take the initiative in advising such a man, and will not use compulsion to him, even if he be my own son. I would advise a slave under such circumstances, and would use compulsion to him if he were unwilling. [c] To a father or mother I do not think that piety allows one to offer compulsion, unless they are suffering from an attack of insanity; and if they are following any regular habits of life which please them but do not please me, I would not offend them by offering useless advice, nor would I flatter them or truckle to them, providing them with the means of satisfying desires which I myself would sooner die than cherish. The wise man should go through life with the same attitude of mind towards his country. If she should appear to him to be following a policy which is not a [d] good one, he should say so, provided that his words are not likely either to fall on deaf ears or to lead to the loss of his own life. But force against his native land he should not use in order to bring about a change of constitution, when it is not possible for the best constitution to be introduced without driving men into exile or putting them to death; he should keep quiet and offer up prayers for his own welfare and for that of his country.

These are the principles in accordance with which I should advise you, as also, jointly with Dion, I advised Dionysios, bidding him in the first place to live his daily life in a way that would make him as far as possible master of himself and able to [e] gain faithful friends and supporters, in order that he might not have the same experience as his father. For his father, having taken under his rule many great cities of Sicily which had been utterly destroyed by the barbarians, was not able to found them afresh and to establish in them trustworthy governments carried on by his own supporters, [332a] either by men who had no ties of blood with him, or by his brothers whom he had brought up when they were younger, and had raised from humble station to high office and from poverty to immense wealth. Not one of these was he able to work upon by persuasion, instruction, services and ties of kindred, so as to make him a partner in his rule; and he showed himself inferior to Darius with a sevenfold inferiority. For Darius did not put his trust in brothers or in men whom he had

brought up, but only in his confederates in the overthrow of the Mede and Eunuch; [b] and to these he assigned portions of his empire, seven in number, each of them greater than all Sicily; and they were faithful to him and did not attack either him or one another. Thus he showed a pattern of what the good lawgiver and king ought to be; for he drew up laws by which he has secured the Persian empire in safety down to the present time.

Again, to give another instance, the Athenians took under their rule very many cities not founded by themselves, which had been hard hit by the barbarians but were still in existence, and maintained their rule over these for seventy years, [c] because they had in each of them men whom they could trust. But Dionysios, who had gathered the whole of Sicily into a single city, and was so clever that he trusted no one, only secured his own safety with great difficulty. For he was badly off for trustworthy friends; and there is no surer criterion of virtue and vice than this, whether a man is or is not destitute of such friends.

This, then, was the advice which Dion and I gave to Dionysios, since, [d] owing to the bringing up which he had received from his father, he had had no advantages in the way of education or of suitable lessons, in the first place . . . ; and, in the second place, that, after starting in this way, he should make friends of others among his connections who were of the same age and were in sympathy with his pursuit of virtue, but above all that he should be in harmony with himself; for this it was of which he was remarkably in need. This we did not say in plain words, for that would not have been safe; but in covert language we maintained that every man in this way would save both himself and those whom he was leading, [e] and if he did not follow this path, he would do just the opposite of this. And after proceeding on the course which we described, and making himself a wise and temperate man, if he were then to found again the cities of Sicily which had been laid waste, and bind them together by laws and constitutions, so as to be loyal to him and to one another in their resistance to the attacks of the barbarians, he would, we told him, [333a] make his father's empire not merely double what it was but many times greater. For, if these things were done, his way would be clear to a more complete subjugation of the Carthaginians than that which befell them in Gelon's time, whereas in our own day his father had followed the opposite course of levying a tribute for the barbarians. This was the language and these the exhortations given by us, the conspirators against Dionysios according to the charges circulated from various sources—charges which, prevailing as they did with Dionysios, caused the expulsion of Dion and reduced me to a state of apprehension. But when—to summarise great events which happened in no great time—Dion returned from the Peloponnese [b] and Athens, his advice to Dionysios took the form of action.

To proceed—when Dion had twice over delivered the city and restored it to the citizens, the Syracusans went through the same changes of feeling towards him as Dionysios had gone through, when Dion attempted first to educate him and train him to be a sovereign worthy of supreme power and, when that was done, to be his coadjutor in all the details of his career. Dionysios listened to those who circulated slanders to the effect that Dion was aiming at the tyranny in all the steps which [c] he took at that time, his intention being that Dionysios, when his mind had fallen under the spell of culture, should neglect the government and leave it in his hands, and that he should then appropriate it for himself and treacherously depose Dionysios. These slanders were victorious on that occasion; they were so once more when circulated among the Syracusans, winning a victory which took an extraordinary course and proved disgraceful to its authors. The story of what then took place is one which deserves careful attention on the part of those who are [d] inviting me to deal with the present situation.

I, an Athenian and friend of Dion, came as his ally to the court of Dionysios, in order that I might create good will in place of a state of war; in my conflict with the authors of these slanders I was worsted. When Dionysios tried to persuade me by offers of honours and wealth to attach myself to him, and with a view to giving a decent colour to Dion's expulsion to be a witness and friend on his side, he failed completely in his attempt. Later on, [e] when Dion returned from exile, he took with him from Athens two brothers, who had been his friends, not from community in philosophic study, but with the ordinary companionship common among most friends, which they form as the result of relations of hospitality and the intercourse which occurs when one man initiates the other in the mysteries. It was from this kind of intercourse and from services connected with his return that these two helpers in his restoration became his companions. Having come to Sicily, [334a] when they perceived that Dion had been misrepresented to the Sicilian Greeks, whom he had liberated, as one that plotted to become monarch, they not only betrayed their companion and friend, but shared personally in the guilt of his murder, standing by his murderers as supporters with weapons in their hands. The guilt and impiety of their conduct I neither excuse nor do I dwell upon it. For many others make it their business to harp upon it, [b] and will make it their business in the future. But I do take exception to the statement that, because they were Athenians, they have brought shame upon this city. For I say that he too is an Athenian who refused to betray this same Dion, when he had the offer of riches and many other honours. For his was no common or vulgar friendship, but rested on community in liberal education, and this is the one thing in which a wise man will put his trust, far more than in ties of personal and bodily kinship. So the two murderers of Dion were not of sufficient importance to be causes of disgrace [c] to this city, as though they had been men of any note.

All this has been said with a view to counselling the friends and family of Dion. And in addition to this I give for the third time to you the same advice and counsel which I have given twice before to others—not to enslave Sicily nor any other State to despots—this is my counsel —but to put it under the rule of laws—for the other course is better neither for the enslavers nor for the enslaved, [d] for themselves, their children's children and descendants; the attempt is in every way fraught with disaster. It is only small and mean natures that are bent upon seizing such gains for themselves, natures that know nothing of goodness and justice, divine as well as human, in this life and in the next.

These are the lessons which I tried to teach, first to Dion, secondly to Dionysios, and now for the third time to you. Do you obey me, thinking of Zeus the Preserver, the patron of third ventures, and looking at the lot of Dionysios and Dion, of whom the one who disobeyed me is living in dishonour, [e] while he who obeyed me has died honourably. For the one thing which is wholly right and noble is to strive for that which is most honourable for a man's self and for his country, and to face the consequences whatever they may be. For none of us can escape death, nor, if a man could do so, would it, as the vulgar suppose, make him happy. For nothing evil or good, which is worth mentioning at all, [335a] belongs to things soulless; but good or evil will be the portion of every soul, either while attached to the body or when separated from it.

And we should in very truth always believe those ancient and sacred teachings, which declare that the soul is immortal, that it has judges, and suffers the greatest penalties when it has been separated from the body. Therefore also we should consider it a lesser evil to suffer great wrongs and outrages than to do them. The covetous man, impoverished as he is in the soul, turns a deaf ear to this teaching; [b] or if he hears it, he laughs it to scorn with fancied superiority, and shamelessly snatches for himself from every source whatever his bestial fancy supposes will provide for him the means of eating or drinking or glutting himself with that slavish and gross pleasure which is falsely called after the goddess of love. He is blind and cannot see in those acts of plunder which are accompanied by impiety what heinous guilt is attached to each wrongful deed, and that the offender must drag with him the burden of this impiety while he moves about on earth, and when he has travelled beneath the earth on a journey which has every circumstance of shame and misery. [c]

It was by urging these and other like truths that I convinced Dion, and it is I who have the best right to be angered with his murderers in much the same way as I have with Dionysios. For both they and he have done the greatest injury to me, and I might almost say to all mankind, they by slaying the man that was willing to act righteously, and he by refusing to act righteously during the whole of his rule, [d] when he held supreme power, in which rule if philosophy and power had really met together, it would have sent forth a light to all men, Greeks and barbarians, establishing fully for all the true belief that there can be no happiness either for the community or for the individual man, unless he passes his life under the rule of righteousness with the guidance of wisdom, either possessing these virtues in himself, or living under the rule of godly men and having received a right training and education in morals. [e] These were the aims which Dionysios injured, and for me everything else is a trifling injury compared with this.

The murderer of Dion has, without knowing it, done the same as Dionysios. For as regards Dion, I know right well, so far as it is possible for a man to say anything positively about other men, that, if he had got the supreme power, he would never have turned his mind to any other form of rule, [336a] but that, dealing first with Syracuse, his own native land, when he had made an end of her slavery, clothed her in bright apparel, and given her the garb of freedom, he would then by every means in his power have ordered aright the lives of his fellow-citizens by suitable and excellent laws; and the thing next in order, which he would have set his heart to accomplish, was to found again all the States of Sicily and make them free from the barbarians, driving out some and subduing others, an easier task for him than it was for Hiero. [b] If these things had been accomplished by a man who was just and brave and temperate and a philosopher, the same belief with regard to virtue would have been established among the majority which, if Dionysios had been won over, would have been established, I might almost say, among all mankind and would have given them salvation. But now some higher power or avenging fiend has fallen upon them, inspiring them with lawlessness, godlessness and acts of recklessness issuing from ignorance, the seed from which all evils for all mankind take root and grow and will in future bear the bitterest harvest for those who brought them into being. This ignorance it was which in that second venture wrecked and ruined everything.

[c] And now, for good luck's sake, let us on this third venture abstain from words of ill-omen. But, nevertheless, I advise you, his friends, to imitate in Dion his love for his country and his temperate habits of daily life, and to try with better auspices to carry out his wishes—what these were, you have heard from me in plain words. And whoever among you cannot live the simple Dorian life according to the customs of your forefathers, [d] but follows the manner of life of Dion's murderers and of the Sicilians, do not invite this man to join you, or expect him to do any loyal or salutary act; but invite all others to the work of resettling all the States of Sicily and establishing equality under the laws, summoning them from Sicily itself and from the whole Peloponnese—and have no fear even of Athens; for there, also, are men who excel all mankind in their devotion to virtue and in hatred of the reckless acts of those who shed the blood of friends.

But if, after all, this is work for a future time, whereas immediate action is called for by the disorders of all sorts and [e] kinds which arise every day from your state of civil strife, every man to whom Providence has given even a moderate share of right intelligence ought to know that in times of civil strife there is no respite from trouble till the victors make an end of feeding their grudge by combats and banishments and executions, and of wreaking their vengeance on their enemies. *[337a]* They should master themselves and, enacting impartial laws, framed not to gratify themselves more than the conquered party, should compel men to obey these by two restraining forces, respect and fear; fear, because they are the masters and can display superior force; respect, because they rise superior to pleasures and are willing and able to be servants to the laws. There is no other way save this for terminating the troubles of a city that is *[b]* in a state of civil strife; but a constant continuance of internal disorders, struggles, hatred and mutual distrust is the common lot of cities which are in that plight.

Therefore, those who have for the time being gained the upper hand, when they desire to secure their position, must by their own act and choice select from all Hellas men whom they have ascertained to be the best for the purpose. These must in the first place be men of mature years, who have children and wives at home, and, as far as possible, a long line of ancestors of good repute, and all must be possessed of sufficient property. For a city of ten thousand householders their numbers should be *[c]* fifty; that is enough. These they must induce to come from their own homes by entreaties and the promise of the highest honours; and having induced them to come they must entreat and command them to draw up laws after binding themselves by oath to show no partiality either to conquerors or to conquered, but to give equal and common rights to the whole State.

When laws have been enacted, what everything then hinges on is this. *[d]* If the conquerors show more obedience to the laws than the conquered, the whole State will be full of security and happiness, and there will be an escape from all your troubles. But if they do not, then do not summon me or any other helper to aid you against those who do not obey the counsel I now give you. For this course is akin to that which Dion and I attempted to carry out with our hearts set on the welfare of Syracuse. It is indeed a second best course. The first and best was that scheme of welfare to all mankind which we attempted to carry out with the co-operation of Dionysios; but some chance, mightier than men, *[e]* brought it to nothing. Do you now, with good fortune attending you and with Heaven's help, try to bring your efforts to a happier issue.

Let this be the end of my advice and injunction and of the narrative of my first visit to Dionysios. Whoever wishes may next hear of my second journey and voyage, and learn that it was a reasonable and suitable proceeding. My first period of residence in Sicily was occupied in the way which I related *[338a]* before giving my advice to the relatives and friends of Dion. After those events I persuaded Dionysios by such arguments as I could to let me go; and we made an agreement as to what should be done when peace was made; for at that time there was a state of war in Sicily. Dionysios said that, when he had put the affairs of his empire in a position of greater safety for himself, he would send for Dion and me again; and he desired that Dion should regard what had befallen him not as an exile, *[b]* but as a change of residence. I agreed to come again on these conditions.

When peace had been made, he began sending for me; he requested that Dion should wait for another year, but begged that I should by all means come. Dion now kept urging and entreating me to go. For persistent rumours came from Sicily that Dionysios was now once more possessed by an extraordinary desire for philosophy. For this reason Dion pressed me urgently not to decline his invitation. But though I was well aware that as regards philosophy such symptoms were not uncommon *[c]* in young men, still it seemed to me safer at that time to part company altogether with Dion and Dionysios; and I offended both of them by replying that I was an old man, and that the steps now being taken were quite at variance with the previous agreement.

After this, it seems, Archytes came to the court of Dionysios. Before my departure I had brought him and his Tarentine *[d]* circle into friendly relations with Dionysios. There were some others in Syracuse who had received some instruction from Dion, and others had learnt from these, getting their heads full of erroneous teaching on philosophical questions. These, it seems, were attempting to hold discussions with Dionysios on questions connected with such subjects, in the idea that he had been fully instructed in my views. Now he is not at all devoid of natural gifts for learning, and he has a great craving for honour and glory. What was said probably pleased him, and he felt some shame when it became clear that he had not taken advantage of *[e]* my teaching during my visit. For these reasons he conceived a desire for more definite instruction, and his love of glory was an additional incentive to him. The real reasons why he had learnt nothing during my previous visit have just been set forth in the preceding narrative. Accordingly, now that I was safe at home and had refused his second invitation, as I just now related, Dionysios seems to have felt all manner of anxiety lest certain people should suppose that I was unwilling to visit him again [339a] because I had formed a poor opinion of his natural gifts and character, and because, knowing as I did his manner of life, I disapproved of it.

It is right for me to speak the truth, and make no complaint if anyone, after hearing the facts, forms a poor opinion of my philosophy, and thinks that the tyrant was in the right. Dionysios now invited me for the third time, sending a trireme to ensure me comfort on the voyage; he sent also Archedemos—one of those who had spent some time with Archytes, [b] and of whom he supposed that I had a higher opinion than of any of the Sicilian Greeks—and, with him, other men of repute in Sicily. These all brought the same report, that Dionysios had made remarkable progress in philosophy. He also sent a very long letter, knowing as he did my relations with Dion and Dion's eagerness also that I should take ship and go to Syracuse. The letter was framed in its opening sentences to meet all these conditions, and the tenor of it was as follows: [c] "Dionysios to Plato," here followed the customary greeting and immediately after it he said, "If in compliance with our request you come now, in the first place, Dion's affairs will be dealt with in whatever way you yourself desire; I know that you will desire what is reasonable, and I shall consent to it. But if not, none of Dion's affairs will have results in accordance with your wishes, with regard either to Dion himself or to other matters." This he said in these words; [d] the rest it would be tedious and inopportune to quote. Other letters arrived from Archytes and the Tarentines, praising the philosophical studies of Dionysios and saying that, if I did not now come, I should cause a complete rupture in their friendship with Dionysios, which had been brought about by me and was of no small importance to their political interests.

When this invitation came to me at that time in such terms, and those who had come from Sicily and Italy were trying to drag me thither, while my friends at Athens were literally pushing me out with their urgent entreaties, [e] it was the same old tale—that I must not betray Dion and my Tarentine friends and supporters. Also I myself had a lurking feeling that

there was nothing surprising in the fact that a young man, quick to learn, hearing talk of the great truths of philosophy, should feel a craving for the higher life. I thought therefore that I must put the matter definitely to the test to see whether his desire was genuine or the reverse, and on no account leave such an impulse unaided nor make myself responsible for such a deep and real disgrace, [340a] if the reports brought by anyone were really true. So blindfolding myself with this reflection, I set out, with many fears and with no very favourable anticipations, as was natural enough. However, I went, and my action on this occasion at any rate was really a case of "the third to the Preserver," for I had the good fortune to return safely; and for this I must, next to the God, thank Dionysios, because, though many wished to make an end of me, he prevented them and paid some proper respect to my situation.

[b] On my arrival, I thought that first I must put to the test the question whether Dionysios had really been kindled with the fire of philosophy, or whether all the reports which had come to Athens were empty rumours. Now there is a way of putting such things to the test which is not to be despised and is well suited to monarchs, especially to those who have got their heads full of erroneous teaching, which immediately on my arrival I found to be very much the case with Dionysios. One should show such men what philosophy is in all its extent, what the range of studies is by which it is approached, [c] and how much labour it involves. For the man who has heard this, if he has the true philosophic spirit and that godlike temperament which makes him akin to philosophy and worthy of it, thinks that he has been told of a marvellous road lying before him, that he must forthwith press on with all his strength, and that life is not worth living if he does anything else. After this he uses to the full his own powers and those of his guide in the path, and relaxes not his efforts, till he has either reached the end of the whole course of study or gained such power that he is not incapable of directing his steps without the aid of a guide. [d] This is the spirit and these are the thoughts by which such a man guides his life, carrying out his work, whatever his occupation may be, but throughout it all ever cleaving to philosophy, and to such rules of diet in his daily life as will give him inward sobriety and therewith quickness in learning, a good memory, and reasoning power; the kind of life which is opposed to this he consistently hates. Those who have not the true philosophic

temper, but a mere surface colouring of opinions penetrating, like sunburn, only skin deep, when they see how great the range of studies is, [e] how much labour is involved in it, and how necessary to the pursuit it is to have an orderly regulation of the daily life, come to the conclusion that the thing is difficult and impossible for them, [341a] and are actually incapable of carrying out the course of study; while some of them persuade themselves that they have sufficiently studied the whole matter and have no need of any further effort. This is the sure test and is the safest one to apply to those who live in luxury and are incapable of continuous effort; it ensures that such a man shall not throw the blame upon his teacher but on himself, because he cannot bring to the pursuit all the qualities necessary to it. Thus it came about that I said to Dionysios what I did say on that occasion.

I did not, however, give a complete exposition, nor did Dionysios ask for one. [b] For he professed to know many, and those the most important, points, and to have a sufficient hold of them through instruction given by others. I hear also that he has since written about what he heard from me, composing what professes to be his own handbook, very different, so he says, from the doctrines which he heard from me; but of its contents I know nothing. I know indeed that others have written on the same subjects; but who they are, is more than they know themselves. Thus much, at least, I can say about all writers, [c] past or future, who say they know the things to which I devote myself, whether by hearing the teaching of me or of others, or by their own discoveries—that according to my view it is not possible for them to have any real skill in the matter. There neither is nor ever will be a treatise of mine on the subject. For it does not admit of exposition like other branches of knowledge; but after much converse about the matter itself and a life lived together, suddenly a light, as it were, is kindled in one soul by a flame that leaps to it from another, [d] and thereafter sustains itself. Yet this much I know—that if the things were written or put into words, it would be done best by me, and that, if they were written badly, I should be the person most pained. Again, if they had appeared to me to admit adequately of writing and exposition, what task in life could I have performed nobler than this, to write what is of great service to mankind and to bring the nature of things into the light for all [e] to see? But I do not think it a good thing for men

that there should be a disquisition, as it is called, on this topic—except for some few, who are able with a little teaching to find it out for themselves. As for the rest, it would fill some of them quite illogically with a mistaken feeling of contempt, and others with lofty and vain-glorious expectations, as though they had learnt something high and mighty.

[342a] On this point I intend to speak a little more at length; for perhaps, when I have done so, things will be clearer with regard to my present subject. There is an argument which holds good against the man who ventures to put anything whatever into writing on questions of this nature; it has often before been stated by me, and it seems suitable to the present occasion.

For everything that exists there are three instruments by which the knowledge of it is necessarily imparted; fourth, there is the knowledge itself, [b] and, as fifth, we must count the thing itself which is known and truly exists. The first is the name, the second the definition, the third the image, and the fourth the knowledge. If you wish to learn what I mean, take these in the case of one instance, and so understand them in the case of all. A circle is a thing spoken of, and its name is that very word which we have just uttered. The second thing belonging to it is its definition, made up of names and verbal forms. For that which has the name "round," "annular," or "circle," might be defined as that which has the distance from its circumference to its centre everywhere equal. [c] Third, comes that which is drawn and rubbed out again, or turned on a lathe and broken up —none of which things can happen to the circle itself—to which the other things mentioned have reference; for it is something of a different order from them. Fourth, comes knowledge, intelligence and right opinion about these things. Under this one head we must group everything which has its existence, not in words nor in bodily shapes, but in souls—from which it is clear that it is something different from the nature of the circle itself and from the three things mentioned before. [d] Of these things intelligence comes closest in kinship and likeness to the fifth, and the others are farther distant.

The same applies to straight as well as to circular form, to colours, to the good, the beautiful, the just, to all bodies whether manufactured or coming into being in the course of nature, to fire, water, and all such things, to every living being, to character in souls, and to all things done and suffered. For in the case of all these no one, *[e]* if he has not some how or other got hold of the four things first mentioned, can ever be completely a partaker of knowledge of the fifth. Further, on account of the weakness of language, these (i.e., the four) attempt to show what each thing is like, *[343a]* not less than what each thing is. For this reason no man of intelligence will venture to express his philosophical views in language, especially not in language that is unchangeable, which is true of that which is set down in written characters.

Again you must learn the point which comes next. Every circle, of those which are by the act of man drawn or even turned on a lathe, is full of that which is opposite to the fifth thing. For everywhere it has contact with the straight. But the circle itself, we say, has nothing in it, either smaller or greater, of that which is its opposite. We say also that the name is not a thing of permanence for any of them, *[b]* and that nothing prevents the things now called round from being called straight, and the straight things round; so for those who make changes and call things by opposite names, nothing will be less permanent (than a name). Again with regard to the definition, if it is made up of names and verbal forms, the same remark holds that there is no sufficiently durable permanence in it. And there is no end to the instances of the ambiguity from which each of the four suffers; but the greatest of them is that which we mentioned a little earlier, that, whereas there are two things, that which has real being, *[c]* and that which is only a quality, when the soul is seeking to know, not the quality, but the essence, each of the four, presenting to the soul by word and in act that which it is not seeking (i.e., the quality), a thing open to refutation by the senses, being merely the thing presented to the soul in each particular case whether by statement or the act of showing, fills, one may say, every man with puzzlement and perplexity.

Now in subjects in which, by reason of our defective education, we have not been accustomed even to search for the truth, but are satisfied with whatever images are presented to us, we are not held up to ridicule by one another, the questioned by questioners, *[d]* who can pull to pieces and criticise the four things. But in subjects where we try to compel a man to give a clear answer about the fifth, any one of those who are capable of overthrowing an antagonist gets the better of us, and makes the man, who gives an exposition in speech or writing or in replies to questions, appear to most of his hearers to know nothing of the things on which he is attempting to write or speak; for they are sometimes not aware that it is not the mind of the writer or speaker which is proved to be at fault, but the defective nature of each of the four instruments. The process however of dealing with all of these, *[e]* as the mind moves up and down to each in turn, does after much effort give birth in a well-constituted mind to knowledge of that which is well constituted. But if a man is ill-constituted by nature (as the state of the soul is naturally in the majority both in its capacity for learning and in what is called moral character)—or it may have become so by deterioration—not even Lynceus could endow such men with the power *[344a]* of sight.

In one word, the man who has no natural kinship with this matter cannot be made akin to it by quickness of learning or memory; for it cannot be engendered at all in natures which are foreign to it. Therefore, if men are not by nature and kinship allied to justice and all other things that are honourable, though they may be good at learning and remembering other knowledge of various kinds—or if they have the kinship but are slow learners and have no memory—none of all these will ever learn to the full the truth about virtue and vice. *[b]* For both must be learnt together; and together also must be learnt, by complete and long continued study, as I said at the beginning, the true and the false about all that has real being. After much effort, as names, definitions, sights, and other data of sense, are brought into contact and friction one with another, in the course of scrutiny and kindly testing by men who proceed by question and answer without ill will, with a sudden flash there shines forth understanding about every problem, and an intelligence whose efforts reach the furthest limits of human powers. *[c]* Therefore every man of worth, when dealing with matters of worth, will be far from exposing them to ill feeling and misunderstanding among men by committing them to writing. In one word, then, it may be known from this that, if one sees written treatises composed by anyone, either the laws of a lawgiver, or in any other form whatever, these are not for that man the things of most worth, if he is a man of worth, but that his treasures are laid up in the fairest spot that he possesses. But if these things were worked at by him as things of real worth, *[d]* and committed to writing, then surely, not gods, but men "have themselves bereft him of his wits."

Anyone who has followed this discourse and

digression will know well that, if Dionysios or anyone else, great or small, has written a treatise on the highest matters and the first principles of things, he has, so I say, neither heard nor learnt any sound teaching about the subject of his treatise; otherwise, he would have had the same reverence for it, which I have, and would have shrunk from putting it forth into a world of discord and uncomeliness. For he wrote it, not as an aid to memory—since there is no risk of forgetting it, [e] if a man's soul has once laid hold of it; for it is expressed in the shortest of statements—but if he wrote it at all, it was from a mean craving for honour, either putting it forth as his own invention, or to figure as a man possessed of culture, of which he was not worthy, if his heart was set on the credit of possessing it. [345a] If then Dionysios gained this culture from the one lesson which he had from me, we may perhaps grant him the possession of it, though how he acquired it—God wot, as the Theban says; for I gave him the teaching, which I have described, on that one occasion and never again.

The next point which requires to be made clear to anyone who wishes to discover how things really happened, is the reason why it came about that I did not continue my teaching in a second and third lesson and yet oftener. Does Dionysios, after a single lesson, [b] believe himself to know the matter, and has he an adequate knowledge of it, either as having discovered it for himself or learnt it before from others, or does he believe my teaching to be worthless, or, thirdly, to be beyond his range and too great for him, and himself to be really unable to live as one who gives his mind to wisdom and virtue? For if he thinks it worthless, he will have to contend with many who say the opposite, and who would be held in far higher repute as judges than Dionysios. If, on the other hand, he thinks he has discovered or learnt the things and that they are worth having as part of a liberal education, how could he, unless he is an extraordinary person, [c] have so recklessly dishonoured the master who has led the way in these subjects? How he dishonoured him, I will now state.

Up to this time he had allowed Dion to remain in possession of his property and to receive the income from it. But not long after the foregoing events, as if he had entirely forgotten his letter to that effect, he no longer allowed Dion's trustees to send him remittances to the Peloponnese, on the pretence that the owner of the property was not Dion but Dion's son, his own nephew, [d] of whom he himself was legally the trustee. These were the actual facts which occurred up to the point which we have reached. They had opened my eyes as to the value of Dionysios' desire for philosophy, and I had every right to complain, whether I wished to do so or not. Now by this time it was summer and the season for sea voyages; therefore I decided that I must not be vexed with Dionysios rather than with myself and those who had forced me to come for the third time into the [e] strait of Scylla,

that once again I might
To fell Charybdis measure back my course,

but must tell Dionysios that it was impossible for me to remain after this outrage had been put upon Dion. He tried to soothe me and begged me to remain, not thinking it desirable for himself that I should arrive post haste in person as the bearer of such tidings. When his entreaties produced no effect, he promised that he himself would provide me with transport. [346a] For my intention was to embark on one of the trading ships and sail away, being indignant and thinking it my duty to face all dangers, in case I was prevented from going—since plainly and obviously I was doing no wrong, but was the party wronged.

Seeing me not at all inclined to stay, he devised the following scheme to make me stay during that sailing season. On the next day he came to me and made a plausible proposal: "Let us put an end," [b] he said, "to these constant quarrels between you and me about Dion and his affairs. For your sake I will do this for Dion. I require him to take his own property and reside in the Peloponnese, not as an exile, but on the understanding that it is open for him to migrate here, when this step has the joint approval of himself, me, and you his friends; and this shall be open to him on the understanding that he does not plot against me. You and your friends and Dion's friends here must be sureties for him in this, and he must give you security. Let the funds which he receives be deposited in the Peloponnese and at [c] Athens, with persons approved by you, and let Dion enjoy the income from them but have no power to take them out of deposit without the approval of you and your friends. For I have no great confidence in him, that, if he has this property at his disposal, he will act justly towards me, for it will be no small amount; but I have more confidence in you and your friends. See if this satisfies you; and on these conditions remain for the present year, [d] and at the next season you shall depart taking the property with you. I am quite sure that Dion will be grateful to you, if you accomplish so much on his behalf."

When I heard this proposal I was vexed, but after reflection said I would let him know my view of it on the following day. We agreed to that effect for the moment, and afterwards when I was by myself I pondered the matter in much distress. The first reflection that came up, leading the way in my self-communing, was this: [e] "Come, suppose that Dionysios intends to do none of the things which he has mentioned, but that, after my departure, he writes a plausible letter to Dion, and orders several of his creatures to write to the same effect, telling him of the proposal which he has now made to me, making out that he was willing to do what he proposed, [347a] but that I refused and completely neglected Dion's interests. Further, suppose that he is not willing to allow my departure, and without giving personal orders to any of the merchants, makes it clear, as he easily can, to all that he does not wish me to sail, will anyone consent to take me as a passenger, when I leave the house of Dionysios?"

For in addition to my other troubles, I was lodging at that time in the garden which surrounds his house, from which even the gatekeeper would have refused to let me go, unless an order had been sent to him from Dionysios. "Suppose however that I wait for the year, I shall be able to write word of these things to Dion, stating the position in which I am, and the steps which I am trying to take. And if Dionysios does any of the things which he says, [b] I shall have accomplished something that is not altogether to be sneered at; for Dion's property is, at a fair estimate, perhaps not less than a hundred talents. If however the prospect which I see looming in the future takes the course which may reasonably be expected, I know not what I shall do with myself. Still it is perhaps necessary to go on working for a year, and to attempt to prove by actual fact the machinations of Dionysios."

Having come to this decision, on the following day I said to Dionysios, [c] "I have decided to remain. But," I continued, "I must ask that you will not regard me as empowered to act for Dion, but will along with me write a letter to him, stating what has now been decided, and enquire whether this course satisfies him. If it does not, and if he has other wishes and demands, he must write particulars of them as

soon as possible, and you must not as yet take any hasty step with regard to his interests."

This was what was said and this was the agreement which was made, almost in these words. Well, after this the trading-ships took their departure, and it was no longer possible for me to take mine, [d] when Dionysios, if you please, addressed me with the remark that half the property must be regarded as belonging to Dion and half to his son. Therefore, he said, he would sell it, and when it was sold would give half to me to take away, and would leave half on the spot for the son. This course, he said, was the most just. This proposal was a blow to me, and I thought it absurd to argue any longer with him; however, I said that we must wait for Dion's letter, and then once more write to tell him of this new proposal. [e] His next step was the brilliant one of selling the whole of Dion's property, using his own discretion with regard to the manner and terms of the sale and the selection of the purchasers. He spoke not a word to me about the matter from beginning to end, and I followed his example and never talked to him again about Dion's affairs; for I did not think that I could do any good by doing so. This is the history so far of my efforts to come to the rescue of philosophy and of my friends.

[348a] After this Dionysios and I went on with our daily life, I with my eyes turned abroad like a bird yearning to fly from its perch, and he always devising some new way of scaring me back and of keeping a tight hold on Dion's property. However, we gave out to all Sicily that we were friends. Dionysios, now deserting the policy of his father, attempted to lower the pay of the older members of his body guard. The soldiers were furious, and, assembling in great numbers, declared that they would not submit. [b] He attempted to use force to them, shutting the gates of the acropolis; but they charged straight for the walls, yelling out an unintelligible and ferocious war cry. Dionysios took fright and conceded all their demands and more to the peltasts then assembled.

A rumour soon spread that Heracleides had been the cause of all the trouble. Hearing this, Heracleides kept out of the way. Dionysios was trying to get hold of him, [c] and being unable to do so, sent for Theodotes to come to him in his garden. It happened that I was walking in the garden at the same time. I neither know nor did I hear the rest of what passed between them, but what Theodotes said to Dionysios in my presence I know and remember.

"Plato," he said, "I am trying to convince our friend Dionysios that, if I am able to bring Heracleides before us to defend himself on the charges which have been made against him, and if he decides that Heracleides must no longer live in Sicily, he should be allowed (this is my point) to take his son and wife and sail to the Peloponnese and reside there, [d] taking no action there against Dionysios and enjoying the income of his property. I have already sent for him and will send for him again; and if he comes in obedience either to my former message or to this one—well and good. But I beg and entreat Dionysios that, if anyone finds Heracleides either in the country or here, no harm shall come to him, [e] but that he may retire from the country till Dionysios comes to some other decision. Do you agree to this?" he added, addressing Dionysios. "I agree," he replied, "that even if he is found at your house, no harm shall be done to him beyond what has now been said."

On the following day Eurybios and Theodotes came to me in the evening, both greatly disturbed. Theodotes said, "Plato, you were present yesterday during the promises made by Dionysios to me and to you about Heracleides?" "Certainly," I replied. "Well," he continued, "at this moment peltasts are scouring the country seeking to arrest Heracleides; and he must be somewhere in this neighbourhood. [349a] For Heaven's sake come with us to Dionysios." So we went and stood in the presence of Dionysios; and those two stood shedding silent tears, while I said: "These men are afraid that you may take strong measures with regard to Heracleides contrary to what was agreed yesterday. For it seems that he has returned and has been seen somewhere about here." On hearing this he blazed up and turned all colours, as a man would in a rage. [b] Theodotes, falling before him in tears, took his hand and entreated him to do nothing of the sort. But I broke in and tried to encourage him, saying: "Be of good cheer, Theodotes; Dionysios will not have the heart to take any fresh step contrary to his promises of yesterday." Fixing his eye on me, and assuming his most autocratic air, he said, "To you I promised nothing small or great." "By the gods," I said, "you did promise that forbearance for which our friend here now appeals." With these words I turned away and went out. After this he continued the hunt for Heracleides, [c] and Theodotes, sending messages, urged Heracleides to take flight. Dionysios sent out Teisias and some peltasts with or-

ders to pursue him. But Heracleides, as it was said, was just in time, by a small fraction of a day, in making his escape into Carthaginian territory.

After this Dionysios thought that his long cherished scheme not to restore Dion's property would give him a plausible excuse for hostility towards me; and first of all he sent me out of the acropolis, [d] finding a pretext that the women were obliged to hold a sacrificial service for ten days in the garden in which I had my lodging. He therefore ordered me to stay outside in the house of Archedemos during this period. While I was there, Theodotes sent for me and made a great outpouring of indignation at these occurrences, throwing the blame on Dionysios. Hearing that I had been to see Theodotes he regarded this as another excuse, [e] sister to the previous one, for quarrelling with me. Sending a messenger he enquired if I had really been conferring with Theodotes on his invitation. "Certainly," I replied. "Well," continued the messenger, "he ordered me to tell you that you are not acting at all well in preferring always Dion and Dion's friends to him." And he did not send for me to return to his house, as though it were now clear that Theodotes and Heracleides were my friends, and he my enemy. He also thought that I had no kind feelings towards him because the property of Dion was now entirely done for.

[350a] After this I resided outside the acropolis among the mercenaries. Various people then came to me, among them those of the ships' crews who came from Athens, my own fellow citizens, and reported that I was evil spoken of among the peltasts, and that some of them were threatening to make an end of me, if they could get hold of me. Accordingly I devised the following plan for my safety.

I sent to Archytes and my other friends in Taras, telling them the plight I was in. Finding some excuse for an embassy from their city, [b] they sent a thirty-oared galley with Lamiscos, one of themselves, who came and entreated Dionysios about me, saying that I wanted to go, and that he should on no account stand in my way. He consented and allowed me to go, giving me money for the journey. But for Dion's property I made no further request, nor was any of it restored.

I made my way to the Peloponnese to Olympia, where I found Dion a spectator at the Games, and told him what had occurred. Calling Zeus to be his witness, he at once urged me with my relatives and friends to make preparations for taking vengeance [c] on Dionysios—our ground for action being the breach of faith to a guest—so he put it and regarded it, while his own was his unjust expulsion and banishment. Hearing this, I told him that he might call my friends to his aid, if they wished to go; "But for myself," I continued, "you and others in a way forced me to be the sharer of Dionysios' table and hearth and his associate in the acts of religion. He probably believed the current slanders, that I was plotting with you against him and his despotic rule; yet feelings of scruple prevailed with him, [d] and he spared my life. Again, I am hardly of the age for being comrade in arms to anyone; also I stand as a neutral between you, if ever you desire friendship and wish to benefit one another; so long as you aim at injuring one another, call others to your aid." This I said, because I was disgusted with my misguided journeyings to Sicily and my ill-fortune there. But they disobeyed me and would not listen to my attempts at reconciliation, and so brought on their own heads all the evils which have since taken place. [e] For if Dionysios had restored to Dion his property or been reconciled with him on any terms, none of these things would have happened, so far as human foresight can foretell. Dion would have easily been kept in check by my wishes and influence. But now, rushing upon one another, they have caused universal disaster.

[351a] Dion's aspiration however was the same that I should say my own or that of any other right-minded man ought to be. With regard to his own power, his friends and his country the ideal of such a man would be to win the greatest power and honour by rendering the greatest services. And this end is not attained if a man gets riches for himself, his supporters and his country, by forming plots and getting together conspirators, being all the while a poor creature, not master of himself, overcome by the cowardice which fears to fight against pleasures; [b] nor is it attained if he goes on to kill the men of substance, whom he speaks of as the enemy, and to plunder their possessions, and invites his confederates and supporters to do the same, with the object that no one shall say that it is *his* fault, if he complains of being poor. The same is true if anyone renders services of this kind to the State and receives honours from her for distributing by decrees the property of the few among the many—or if, being in charge of the affairs of a great State which rules over many small ones, [c] he unjustly appropriates to his own State the possessions of the small ones. For neither a Dion nor any other man will, with his eyes open, make his way by steps like these to a power which will be fraught with destruction to himself and his descendants for all time; but he will advance towards constitutional government and the framing of the justest and best laws, reaching these ends without executions and murders even on the smallest scale.

This course Dion actually followed, thinking it preferable to suffer iniquitous deeds rather than to do them; but, while taking precautions against them, he nevertheless, when he had reached the climax of victory over his enemies, [d] took a false step and fell, a catastrophe not at all surprising. For a man of piety, temperance and wisdom, when dealing with the impious, would not be entirely blind to the character of such men; but it would perhaps not be surprising if he suffered the catastrophe that might befall a good ship's captain, who would not be entirely unaware of the approach of a storm, but might be unaware of its extraordinary and startling violence, and might therefore be overwhelmed by its force. The same thing caused Dion's downfall. For he was not unaware that his assailants were thoroughly bad men, but he was unaware how high a pitch of infatuation and of general wickedness and greed they had reached. [e] This was the cause of his downfall, which has involved Sicily in countless sorrows.

[352a] As to the steps which should be taken after the events which I have now related, my advice has been given pretty fully and may be regarded as finished; and if you ask my reasons for recounting the story of my second journey to Sicily, it seemed to me essential that an account of it must be given because of the strange and paradoxical character of the incidents. If in this present account of them they appear to anyone more intelligible, and seem to anyone to show sufficient grounds in view of the circumstances, the present statement is adequate and not too lengthy.

GREAT BOOKS OF THE WESTERN WORLD

GREAT BOOKS
OF THE WESTERN WORLD

ROBERT MAYNARD HUTCHINS, *EDITOR IN CHIEF*

34.

NEWTON

HUYGENS

MATHEMATICAL PRINCIPLES OF NATURAL PHILOSOPHY

OPTICS

BY SIR ISAAC NEWTON

TREATISE ON LIGHT

BY CHRISTIAAN HUYGENS

WILLIAM BENTON, *Publisher*

ENCYCLOPÆDIA BRITANNICA, INC.

CHICAGO · LONDON · TORONTO · GENEVA

THE UNIVERSITY OF CHICAGO

The Great Books
is published with the editorial advice of the faculties
of The University of Chicago

GENERAL CONTENTS

++++++++++++

Mathematical Principles
of Natural Philosophy, page 1
By Sir Isaac Newton

Translated by Andrew Motte
Revised by Florian Cajori

Optics, page 377
By Sir Isaac Newton

++++++++++++

Treatise on Light, page 551
By Christiaan Huygens

Translated by Silvanus P. Thompson

++++++++++++

MATHEMATICAL PRINCIPLES
OF NATURAL PHILOSOPHY

BIOGRAPHICAL NOTE

SIR ISAAC NEWTON, 1642–1727

NEWTON was born at Woolsthorpe, Lincoln-shire, on Christmas Day, 1642. His father, a small farmer, died a few months before his birth, and when in 1645 his mother married the rector of North Witham, Newton was left with his maternal grandmother at Wools-thorpe. After having acquired the rudiments of education at small schools close by, Newton was sent at the age of twelve to the grammar school at Grantham, where he lived in the house of an apothecary. By his own account, Newton was at first an indifferent scholar until a successful fight with another boy aroused a spirit of emulation and led to his becoming first in the school. He displayed very early a taste and aptitude for mechanical contrivances; he made windmills, water-clocks, kites, and sun-dials, and he is said to have invented a four-wheel carriage which was to be moved by the rider.

After the death of her second husband in 1656, Newton's mother returned to Wools-thorpe and removed her eldest son from school so that he might prepare himself to manage the farm. But it was soon evident that his in-terests were not in farming, and upon the ad-vice of his uncle, the rector of Burton Coggles, he was sent to Trinity College, Cambridge, where he matriculated in 1661 as one of the boys who performed menial services in return for their expenses. Although there is no record of his formal progress as a student, Newton is known to have read widely in mathematics and mechanics. His first reading at Cambridge was in the optical works of Kepler. He turned to Euclid because he was bothered by his in-ability to comprehend certain diagrams in a book on astrology he had bought at a fair; finding its propositions self-evident, he put it aside as "a trifling book," until his teacher, Isaac Barrow, induced him to take up the book again. It appears to have been the study of Descartes' *Geometry* which inspired him to do original mathematical work. In a small com-monplace book kept by Newton as an under-graduate, there are several articles on angular sections and the squaring of curves, several calculations about musical notes, geometrical

problems from Vieta and Van Schooten, an-notations out of Wallis' *Arithmetic of Infinities*, together with observations on refraction, on the grinding of spherical optic glasses, on the errors of lenses, and on the extraction of all kinds of roots. It was around the time of his taking the Bachelor's degree, in 1665, that Newton discovered the binomial theorem and made the first notes on his discovery of the "method of fluxions."

When the Great Plague spread from London to Cambridge in 1665, college was dismissed, and Newton retired to the farm in Lincoln-shire, where he conducted experiments in op-tics and chemistry and continued his mathe-matical speculations. From this forced retire-ment in 1666 he dated his discovery of the gravitational theory: "In the same year I be-gan to think of gravity extending to the orb of the Moon, . . . compared the force requisite to keep the Moon in her orb with the force of gravity at the surface of the earth and found them to answer pretty nearly." At about the same time his work on optics led to his expla-nation of the composition of white light. Of the work he accomplished in these years Newton later remarked: "All this was in the two years of 1665 and 1666, for in those years I was in the prime of my age for invention and minded Mathematics and Philosophy more than at any time since."

On the re-opening of Trinity College in 1667, Newton was elected a fellow, and two years later, a little before his twenty-seventh birth-day, he was appointed Lucasian professor of mathematics, succeeding his friend and teach-er, Dr. Barrow. Newton had already built a reflecting telescope in 1668; the second tele-scope of his making he presented to the Royal Society in December, 1671. Two months later, as a fellow of the Society, he communicated his discovery on light and thereby started a con-troversy which was to run for many years and to involve Hooke, Lucas, Linus, and others. Newton, who always found controversy dis-tasteful, "blamed my own imprudence for parting with so substantial a blessing as my quiet to run after a shadow." His papers on optics, the most important of which were communicated to the Royal Society between 1672 and 1676, were collected in the *Optics* (1704).

It was not until 1684 that Newton began to think of making known his work on gravity. Hooke, Halley, and Sir Christopher Wren had independently come to some notion of the law of gravity but were not having any success in explaining the orbits of the planets. In that year Halley consulted Newton on the problem and was astonished to find that he had already solved it. Newton submitted to him four theorems and seven problems, which proved to be the nucleus of his major work. In some seventeen or eighteen months during 1685 and 1686 he wrote in Latin the *Mathematical Principles of Natural Philosophy*. Newton thought for some time of suppressing the third book, and it was only Halley's insistence that preserved it. Halley also took upon himself the cost of publishing the work in 1687 after the Royal Society proved unable to meet its cost. The book caused great excitement throughout Europe, and in 1689 Huygens, at that time the most famous scientist, came to England to make the personal acquaintance of Newton.

While working upon the *Principles*, Newton had begun to take a more prominent part in university affairs. For his opposition to the attempt of James II to repudiate the oath of allegiance and supremacy at the university, Newton was elected parliamentary member for Cambridge. On his return to the university, he suffered a serious illness which incapacitated him for most of 1692 and 1693 and caused considerable concern to his friends and fellow-workers. After his recovery, he left the university to work for the government. Through his friends Locke, Wren, and Lord Halifax, Newton was made Warden of the Mint in 1695 and four years later, Master of the Mint, a position he held until his death.

For the last thirty years of his life Newton produced little original mathematical work. He kept his interest and his skill in the subject; in

1696 he solved overnight a problem offered by Bernoulli in a competition for which six months had been allowed, and again in 1716 he worked in a few hours a problem which Leibnitz had proposed in order to "feel the pulse of the English analysts." He was much occupied, to his own distress, with two mathematical controversies, one regarding the astronomical observations of the astronomer royal, and the other with Leibnitz regarding the invention of calculus. He also worked on revisions for a second edition of the *Principles*, which appeared in 1713.

Newton's scientific work brought him great fame. He was a popular visitor at the Court and was knighted in 1705. Many honors came to him from the continent; he was in correspondence with all the leading men of science, and visitors became so frequent as to prove a serious discomfort. Despite his fame, Newton maintained his modesty. Shortly before his death, he remarked: "I do not know what I may appear to the world, but to myself I seem to have been only like a boy playing on the seashore, and diverting myself in now and then finding a smoother pebble or a prettier shell than ordinary, whilst the great ocean of truth lay all undiscovered before me."

From an early period of his life Newton had been much interested in theological studies and before 1690 had begun to study the prophecies. In that year he wrote, in the form of a letter to Locke, an *Historical Account of Two Notable Corruptions of the Scriptures*, regarding two passages on the Trinity. He left in manuscript *Observations on the Prophecies of Daniel and the Apocalypse* and other works of exegesis.

After 1725 Newton's health was much impaired, and his duties at the Mint were discharged by a deputy. In February, 1727, he presided for the last time at the Royal Society, of which he had been president since 1703, and died on March 20, 1727, in his eighty-fifth year. He was buried in Westminster Abbey after lying in state in the Jerusalem Chamber.

CONTENTS

CONTENTS

PREFACE TO THE FIRST EDITION

SINCE the ancients (as we are told by Pappus) esteemed the science of mechanics of greatest importance in the investigation of natural things, and the moderns, rejecting substantial forms and occult qualities, have endeavored to subject the phenomena of nature to the laws of mathematics, I have in this treatise cultivated mathematics as far as it relates to philosophy. The ancients considered mechanics in a twofold respect; as rational, which proceeds accurately by demonstration, and practical. To practical mechanics all the manual arts belong, from which mechanics took its name. But as artificers do not work with perfect accuracy, it comes to pass that mechanics is so distinguished from geometry that what is perfectly accurate is called geometrical; what is less so, is called mechanical. However, the errors are not in the art, but in the artificers. He that works with less accuracy is an imperfect mechanic; and if any could work with perfect accuracy, he would be the most perfect mechanic of all, for the description of right lines and circles, upon which geometry is founded, belongs to mechanics. Geometry does not teach us to draw these lines, but requires them to be drawn, for it requires that the learner should first be taught to describe these accurately before he enters upon geometry, then it shows how by these operations problems may be solved. To describe right lines and circles are problems, but not geometrical problems. The solution of these problems is required from mechanics, and by geometry the use of them, when so solved, is shown; and it is the glory of geometry that from those few principles, brought from without, it is able to produce so many things. Therefore geometry is founded in mechanical practice, and is nothing but that part of universal mechanics which accurately proposes and demonstrates the art of measuring. But since the manual arts are chiefly employed in the moving of bodies, it happens that geometry is commonly referred to their magnitude, and mechanics to their motion. In this sense rational mechanics will be the science of motions resulting from any forces whatsoever, and of the forces required to produce any motions, accurately proposed and demonstrated. This part of mechanics, as far as it extended to the five powers which relate to manual arts, was cultivated by the ancients, who considered gravity (it not being a manual power) no otherwise than in moving weights by those powers. But I consider philosophy rather than arts and write not concerning manual but natural powers, and consider chiefly those things which relate to gravity, levity, elastic force, the resistance of fluids, and the like forces, whether attractive or impulsive; and therefore I offer this work as the mathematical principles of philosophy, for the whole burden of philosophy seems to consist in this—from the phenomena of motions to investigate the forces of nature, and then from these forces to demonstrate the other phenomena; and to this end the general propositions in the first and second books are directed. In the third book I give an example of this in the explication of the System of the World; for by the propositions mathematically demonstrated in the former books in the third I derive from the celestial phenomena the forces of gravity with which bodies tend to the sun and

1

the several planets. Then from these forces, by other propositions which are also mathematical, I deduce the motions of the planets, the comets, the moon, and the sea. I wish we could derive the rest of the phenomena of Nature by the same kind of reasoning from mechanical principles, for I am induced by many reasons to suspect that they may all depend upon certain forces by which the particles of bodies, by some causes hitherto unknown, are either mutually impelled towards one another, and cohere in regular figures, or are repelled and recede from one another. These forces being unknown, philosophers have hitherto attempted the search of Nature in vain; but I hope the principles here laid down will afford some light either to this or some truer method of philosophy.

In the publication of this work the most acute and universally learned Mr. Edmund Halley not only assisted me in correcting the errors of the press and preparing the geometrical figures, but it was through his solicitations that it came to be published; for when he had obtained of me my demonstrations of the figure of the celestial orbits, he continually pressed me to communicate the same to the Royal Society, who afterwards, by their kind encouragement and entreaties, engaged me to think of publishing them. But after I had begun to consider the inequalities of the lunar motions, and had entered upon some other things relating to the laws and measures of gravity and other forces; and the figures that would be described by bodies attracted according to given laws; and the motion of several bodies moving among themselves; the motion of bodies in resisting mediums; the forces, densities, and motions, of mediums; the orbits of the comets, and such like, I deferred that publication till I had made a search into those matters, and could put forth the whole together. What relates to the lunar motions (being imperfect), I have put all together in the corollaries of Prop. 66, to avoid being obliged to propose and distinctly demonstrate the several things there contained in a method more prolix than the subject deserved and interrupt the series of the other propositions. Some things, found out after the rest, I chose to insert in places less suitable, rather than change the number of the propositions and the citations. I heartily beg that what I have here done may be read with forbearance; and that my labors in a subject so difficult may be examined, not so much with the view to censure, as to remedy their defects.

Is. NEWTON

Cambridge, Trinity College, *May* 8, 1686

PREFACE TO THE SECOND EDITION

IN this second edition of the *Principia* there are many emendations and some additions. In the second section of the first book, the determination of forces, by which bodies may be made to revolve in given orbits, is illustrated and enlarged. In the seventh section of the second book the theory of the resistances of fluids was more accurately investigated, and confirmed by new experiments. In the third book the lunar theory and the precession of the equinoxes were more fully deduced from their principles; and the theory of the comets was confirmed by more examples of the calculation of their orbits, done also with greater accuracy.

Is. NEWTON

London, *March* 28, 1713

PREFACE TO THE THIRD EDITION

IN this third edition, prepared with much care by Henry Pemberton, M.D., a man of the greatest skill in these matters, some things in the second book on the resistance of mediums are somewhat more comprehensively handled than before, and new experiments on the resistance of heavy bodies falling in air are added. In the third book, the argument to prove that the moon is retained in its orbit by the force of gravity is more fully stated; and there are added new observations made by Mr. Pound, concerning the ratio of the diameters of Jupiter to one another. Some observations are also added on the comet which appeared in the year 1680, made in Germany in the month of November by Mr. Kirk; which have lately come to my hands. By the help of these it becomes apparent how nearly parabolic orbits represent the motions of comets. The orbit of that comet is determined somewhat more accurately than before, by the computation of Dr. Halley, in an ellipse. And it is shown that, in this elliptic orbit, the comet took its course through the nine signs of the heavens, with as much accuracy as the planets move in the elliptic orbits given in astronomy. The orbit of the comet which appeared in the year 1723 is also added, computed by Mr. Bradley, Professor of Astronomy at Oxford.

Is. NEWTON

London, *Jan.* 12, 1725–6

DEFINITIONS

DEFINITION I

The quantity of matter is the measure of the same, arising from its density and bulk conjointly.

Thus air of a double density, in a double space, is quadruple in quantity; in a triple space, sextuple in quantity. The same thing is to be understood of snow, and fine dust or powders, that are condensed by compression or liquefaction, and of all bodies that are by any causes whatever differently condensed. I have no regard in this place to a medium, if any such there is, that freely pervades the interstices between the parts of bodies. It is this quantity that I mean hereafter everywhere under the name of body or mass. And the same is known by the weight of each body, for it is proportional to the weight, as I have found by experiments on pendulums, very accurately made, which shall be shown hereafter.

DEFINITION II

The quantity of motion is the measure of the same, arising from the velocity and quantity of matter conjointly.

The motion of the whole is the sum of the motions of all the parts; and therefore in a body double in quantity, with equal velocity, the motion is double; with twice the velocity, it is quadruple.

DEFINITION III

The vis insita, *or innate force of matter, is a power of resisting, by which every body, as much as in it lies, continues in its present state, whether it be of rest, or of moving uniformly forwards in a right line.*

This force is always proportional to the body whose force it is and differs nothing from the inactivity of the mass, but in our manner of conceiving it. A body, from the inert nature of matter, is not without difficulty put out of its state of rest or motion. Upon which account, this *vis insita* may, by a most significant name, be called inertia (*vis inertiæ*) or force of inactivity. But a body only exerts this force when another force, impressed upon it, endeavors to change its condition; and the exercise of this force may be considered as both resistance and impulse; it is resistance so far as the body, for maintaining its present state, opposes the force impressed; it is impulse so far as the body, by not easily giving way to the impressed force of another, endeavors to change the state of that other. Resistance is usually ascribed to bodies at rest, and impulse to those in motion; but motion and rest, as commonly conceived, are only relatively distinguished; nor are those bodies always truly at rest, which commonly are taken to be so.

DEFINITION IV

An impressed force is an action exerted upon a body, in order to change its state, either of rest, or of uniform motion in a right line.

This force consists in the action only, and remains no longer in the body when the action is over. For a body maintains every new state it acquires, by its inertia only. But impressed forces are of different origins, as from percussion, from pressure, from centripetal force.

DEFINITION V

A centripetal force is that by which bodies are drawn or impelled, or any way tend, towards a point as to a centre.

Of this sort is gravity, by which bodies tend to the centre of the earth; magnetism, by which iron tends to the loadstone; and that force, whatever it is, by which the planets are continually drawn aside from the rectilinear motions, which otherwise they would pursue, and made to revolve in curvilinear orbits. A stone, whirled about in a sling, endeavors to recede from the hand that turns it; and by that endeavor, distends the sling, and that with so much the greater force, as it is revolved with the greater velocity, and as soon as it is let go, flies away. That force which opposes itself to this endeavor, and by which the sling continually draws back the stone towards the hand, and retains it in its orbit, because it is directed to the hand as the centre of the orbit, I call the centripetal force. And the same thing is to be understood of all bodies, revolved in any orbits. They all endeavor to recede from the centres of their orbits; and were it not for the opposition of a contrary force which restrains them to, and detains them in their orbits, which I therefore call centripetal, would fly off in right lines, with an uniform motion. A projectile, if it was not for the force of gravity, would not deviate towards the earth, but would go off from it in a right line, and that with an uniform motion, if the resistance of the air was taken away. It is by its gravity that it is drawn aside continually from its rectilinear course, and made to deviate towards the earth, more or less, according to the force of its gravity, and the velocity of its motion. The less its gravity is, or the quantity of its matter, or the greater the velocity with which it is projected, the less will it deviate from a rectilinear course, and the farther it will go. If a leaden ball, projected from the top of a mountain by the force of gunpowder, with a given velocity, and in a direction parallel to the horizon, is carried in a curved line to the distance of two miles before it falls to the ground; the same, if the resistance of the air were taken away, with a double or decuple velocity, would fly twice or ten times as far. And by increasing the velocity, we may at pleasure increase the distance to which it might be projected, and diminish the curvature of the line which it might describe, till at last it should fall at the distance of 10, 30, or 90 degrees, or even might go quite round the whole earth before it falls; or lastly, so that it might never fall to the earth, but go forwards into the celestial spaces, and proceed in its motion *in infinitum*. And after the same manner that a projectile, by the force of gravity, may be made to revolve in an orbit, and go round the whole earth, the moon also, either by the force of gravity, if it is endued with gravity, or by any other force, that impels it towards the earth, may be continually drawn aside towards the earth, out of the rectilinear way which by its innate force it would pursue; and would be made to revolve in the orbit which it now describes; nor could the moon without some such force be retained in its orbit. If this force was too small, it would not sufficiently turn the moon out of a rectilinear course; if it was too great, it would turn it too much, and draw down the moon from its orbit towards the earth. It is necessary that the force be of a just quantity, and it belongs to the mathematicians to find the force that may serve exactly to retain a body in a given orbit with a given velocity; and *vice versa*, to determine the curvilinear way into which a body projected from a given place, with a given velocity, may be made to deviate from its natural rectilinear way, by means of a given force.

The quantity of any centripetal force may be considered as of three kinds: absolute, accelerative, and motive.

DEFINITION VI

The absolute quantity of a centripetal force is the measure of the same, proportional to the efficacy of the cause that propagates it from the centre, through the spaces round about.

Thus the magnetic force is greater in one loadstone and less in another, according to their sizes and strength of intensity.

DEFINITION VII

The accelerative quantity of a centripetal force is the measure of the same, proportional to the velocity which it generates in a given time.

Thus the force of the same loadstone is greater at a less distance, and less at a greater: also the force of gravity is greater in valleys, less on tops of exceeding high mountains; and yet less (as shall hereafter be shown), at greater distances from the body of the earth; but at equal distances, it is the same everywhere; because (taking away, or allowing for, the resistance of the air), it equally accelerates all falling bodies, whether heavy or light, great or small.

DEFINITION VIII

The motive quantity of a centripetal force is the measure of the same, proportional to the motion which it generates in a given time.

Thus the weight is greater in a greater body, less in a less body; and, in the same body, it is greater near to the earth, and less at remoter distances. This sort of quantity is the centripetency, or propension of the whole body towards the centre, or, as I may say, its weight; and it is always known by the quantity of an equal and contrary force just sufficient to hinder the descent of the body.

These quantities of forces, we may, for the sake of brevity, call by the names of motive, accelerative, and absolute forces; and, for the sake of distinction, consider them with respect to the bodies that tend to the centre, to the places of those bodies, and to the centre of force towards which they tend; that is to say, I refer the motive force to the body as an endeavor and propensity of the whole towards a centre, arising from the propensities of the several parts taken together; the accelerative force to the place of the body, as a certain power diffused from the centre to all places around to move the bodies that are in them; and the absolute force to the centre, as endued with some cause, without which those motive forces would not be propagated through the spaces round about; whether that cause be some central body (such as is the magnet in the centre of the magnetic force, or the earth in the centre of the gravitating force), or anything else that does not yet appear. For I here design only to give a mathematical notion of those forces, without considering their physical causes and seats.

Wherefore the accelerative force will stand in the same relation to the motive, as celerity does to motion. For the quantity of motion arises from the celerity multiplied by the quantity of matter; and the motive force arises from the accelerative force multiplied by the same quantity of matter. For the sum of the actions of the accelerative force, upon the several particles of the body, is the motive force of the whole. Hence it is, that near the surface of the earth, where the accelerative gravity, or force productive of gravity, in all bodies is the same, the motive gravity or the weight is as the body; but if we should ascend to higher regions, where the accelerative gravity is less, the weight would be equally diminished, and would always be as the product of the body, by the accelerative gravity. So in those regions, where the accelerative gravity is diminished into one-half, the weight of a body two or three times less, will be four or six times less.

I likewise call attractions and impulses, in the same sense, accelerative, and motive; and use the words attraction, impulse, or propensity of any sort towards a centre, promiscuously, and indifferently, one for another; considering those forces not physically, but mathematically: wherefore the reader is not to imagine that by those words I anywhere take upon me to define the kind, or the manner of any action, the causes or the physical reason thereof, or that I attribute forces, in a true and physical sense, to certain centres (which are only mathematical points); when at any time I happen to speak of centres as attracting, or as endued with attractive powers.

SCHOLIUM

Hitherto I have laid down the definitions of such words as are less known, and explained the sense in which I would have them to be understood in the following discourse. I do not define time, space, place, and motion, as being well known to all. Only I must observe, that the common people conceive those quantities under no other notions but from the relation they bear to sensible objects. And thence arise certain prejudices, for the removing of which it will be convenient to distinguish them into absolute and relative, true and apparent, mathematical and common.

I. Absolute, true, and mathematical time, of itself, and from its own nature, flows equably without relation to anything external, and by another name is called duration: relative, apparent, and common time, is some sensible and external (whether accurate or unequable) measure of duration by the means of motion, which is commonly used instead of true time; such as an hour, a day, a month, a year.

II. Absolute space, in its own nature, without relation to anything external, remains always similar and immovable. Relative space is some movable dimension or measure of the absolute spaces; which our senses determine by its position to bodies; and which is commonly taken for immovable space; such is the dimension of a subterraneous, an aerial, or celestial space, determined by its position in respect of the earth. Absolute and relative space are the same in figure and magnitude; but they do not remain always numerically the same.

For if the earth, for instance, moves, a space of our air, which relatively and in respect of the earth remains always the same, will at one time be one part of the absolute space into which the air passes; at another time it will be another part of the same, and so, absolutely understood, it will be continually changed.

III. Place is a part of space which a body takes up, and is according to the space, either absolute or relative. I say, a part of space; not the situation, nor the external surface of the body. For the places of equal solids are always equal; but their surfaces, by reason of their dissimilar figures, are often unequal. Positions properly have no quantity, nor are they so much the places themselves, as the properties of places. The motion of the whole is the same with the sum of the motions of the parts; that is, the translation of the whole, out of its place, is the same thing with the sum of the translations of the parts out of their places; and therefore the place of the whole is the same as the sum of the places of the parts, and for that reason, it is internal, and in the whole body.

IV. Absolute motion is the translation of a body from one absolute place into another; and relative motion, the translation from one relative place into another. Thus in a ship under sail, the relative place of a body is that part of the ship which the body possesses; or that part of the cavity which the body fills, and which therefore moves together with the ship: and relative rest is the continuance of the body in the same part of the ship, or of its cavity. But real, absolute rest, is the continuance of the body in the same part of that immovable space, in which the ship itself, its cavity, and all that it contains, is moved. Wherefore, if the earth is really at rest, the body, which relatively rests in the ship, will really and absolutely move with the same velocity which the ship has on the earth. But if the earth also moves, the true and absolute motion of the body will arise, partly from the true motion of the earth, in immovable space, partly from the relative motion of the ship on the earth; and if the body moves also relatively in the ship, its true motion will arise, partly from the true motion of the earth, in immovable space, and partly from the relative motions as well of the ship on the earth, as of the body in the ship; and from these relative motions will arise the relative motion of the body on the earth. As if that part of the earth, where the ship is, was truly moved towards the east, with a velocity of 10,010 parts; while the ship itself, with a fresh gale, and full sails, is carried towards the west, with a velocity expressed by 10 of those parts; but a sailor walks in the ship towards the east, with 1 part of the said velocity; then the sailor will be moved truly in immovable space towards the east, with a velocity of 10,001 parts, and relatively on the earth towards the west, with a velocity of 9 of those parts.

Absolute time, in astronomy, is distinguished from relative, by the equation or correction of the apparent time. For the natural days are truly unequal, though they are commonly considered as equal, and used for a measure of time; astronomers correct this inequality that they may measure the celestial motions by a more accurate time. It may be, that there is no such thing as an equable motion, whereby time may be accurately measured. All motions may be accelerated and retarded, but the flowing of absolute time is not liable to any change. The duration of perseverance of the existence of things remains the same, whether the motions are swift or slow, or none at all: and therefore this duration ought to be distinguished from what are only sensible measures thereof; and from which we deduce it, by means of the astronomical equation. The necessity of this equation, for determining the times of a phenomenon, is evinced as well from the experiments of the pendulum clock, as by eclipses of the satellites of Jupiter.

As the order of the parts of time is immutable, so also is the order of the parts of space. Suppose those parts to be moved out of their places, and they will be moved (if the expression may be allowed) out of themselves. For times and spaces are, as it were, the places as well of themselves as of all other things. All things are placed in time as to order of succession; and in space as to order of situation. It is from their essence or nature that they are places; and that the primary places of things should be movable, is absurd. These are therefore the absolute places; and translations out of those places, are the only absolute motions.

But because the parts of space cannot be seen, or distinguished from one another by our senses, therefore in their stead we use sensible measures of them. For from the positions and distances of things from any body considered as immovable, we define all places; and then with respect to such places, we estimate all motions, considering bodies as transferred from some of those places into others. And so, instead of absolute places and motions, we use relative ones; and that without any inconvenience in common affairs; but in philosophical disquisitions, we ought to abstract from our senses, and consider things themselves, distinct from what are only sensible measures of them. For it may be that there is no body really at rest, to which the places and motions of others may be referred.

But we may distinguish rest and motion, absolute and relative, one from the other by their properties, causes, and effects. It is a property of rest, that bodies really at rest do rest in respect to one another. And therefore as it is possible, that in the remote regions of the fixed stars, or perhaps far beyond them, there may be some body absolutely at rest; but impossible to know, from the position of bodies to one another in our regions, whether any of these do keep the same position to that remote body, it follows that absolute rest cannot be determined from the position of bodies in our regions.

It is a property of motion, that the parts, which retain given positions to their wholes, do partake of the motions of those wholes. For all the parts of revolving bodies endeavor to recede from the axis of motion; and the impetus of bodies moving forwards arises from the joint impetus of all the parts. Therefore, if surrounding bodies are moved, those that are relatively at rest within them will partake of their motion. Upon which account, the true and absolute motion of a body cannot be determined by the translation of it from those which only seem to rest; for the external bodies ought not only to appear at rest, but to be really at rest. For otherwise, all included bodies, besides their translation from near the surrounding ones, partake likewise of their true motions; and though that translation were not made, they would not be really at rest, but only seem to be so. For the surrounding bodies stand in the like relation to the surrounded as the exterior part of a whole does to the interior, or as the shell does to the kernel; but if the shell moves, the kernel will also move, as being part of the whole, without any removal from near the shell.

A property, near akin to the preceding, is this, that if a place is moved, whatever is placed therein moves along with it; and therefore a body, which is moved from a place in motion, partakes also of the motion of its place. Upon which account, all motions, from places in motion, are no other than parts of entire and absolute motions; and every entire motion is composed of the motion of the body out of its first place, and the motion of this place out of its place; and so on, until we come to some immovable place, as in the before-mentioned example of the sailor. Wherefore, entire and absolute motions can be no otherwise determined than by immovable places; and for that reason I did before refer those absolute motions to immovable places, but relative ones to movable places. Now no other places are immovable but those that, from infinity to infinity, do all retain the same given position one to another; and upon this account must ever remain unmoved; and do thereby constitute immovable space.

The causes by which true and relative motions are distinguished, one from the other, are the forces impressed upon bodies to generate motion. True motion is neither generated nor altered, but by some force impressed upon the body moved; but relative motion may be generated or altered without any force impressed upon the body. For it is sufficient only to impress some force on other bodies with which the former is compared, that by their giving way, that relation may be changed, in which the relative rest or motion of this other body did consist. Again, true motion suffers always some change from any force impressed upon the moving body; but relative motion does not necessarily undergo any change by such forces. For if the same forces are likewise impressed on those other bodies, with which the comparison is made, that the relative position may be preserved, then that condition will be preserved in which the relative motion consists. And therefore any relative motion may be changed when the true motion remains unaltered, and the relative may be preserved when the true suffers some change. Thus, true motion by no means consists in such relations.

The effects which distinguish absolute from relative motion are, the forces of receding from the axis of circular motion. For there are no such forces in a circular motion purely relative, but in a true and absolute circular motion, they are greater or less, according to the quantity of the motion. If a vessel, hung by a long cord, is so often turned about that the cord is strongly twisted, then filled with water, and held at rest together with the water; thereupon, by the sudden action of another force, it is whirled about the contrary way, and while the cord is untwisting itself, the vessel continues for some time in this motion; the surface of the water will at first be plain, as before the vessel began to move; but after that, the vessel, by gradually communicating its motion to the water, will make it begin sensibly to revolve, and recede by little and little from the middle, and ascend to the sides of the vessel, forming itself into a concave figure (as I have experienced), and the swifter the motion becomes, the higher will the water rise, till at last, performing its revolutions in the same times with the vessel, it becomes relatively at rest in it. This ascent of the water shows its endeavor to recede from the axis of its motion; and the true and absolute circular motion of the water, which is here directly contrary to the relative, becomes known, and may be measured by this endeavor. At first, when the relative motion of the water in the vessel was greatest, it produced no endeavor to recede from the axis; the water showed no tendency to the circumference, nor any ascent towards the sides of the vessel, but remained of a plain surface, and therefore its true circular motion had not yet begun. But afterwards, when the relative motion of the water had decreased, the ascent thereof towards the sides of the vessel proved its endeavor to recede from the axis; and this endeavor showed the real circular motion of the water continually increasing, till it had acquired its greatest quantity, when the water rested relatively in the vessel. And therefore this endeavor does not depend upon any translation of the water in respect of the ambient bodies, nor can true circular motion be defined by such translation. There is only one real circular motion of any one revolving body, corresponding to only one power of endeavoring to recede from its axis of motion, as its proper and adequate effect; but relative motions, in one and the same body, are innumerable, according to the various relations it bears to external bodies, and, like other relations, are altogether destitute of any real effect, any otherwise than they may perhaps partake of that one only true motion. And therefore in their system who suppose that our heavens, revolving below the sphere of the fixed stars, carry the planets along with them; the several parts of those heavens, and the planets, which are indeed relatively at rest in their heavens, do yet really move. For they change their position one to another (which never happens to bodies truly at rest), and being carried together with their heavens, partake of their motions, and as parts of revolving wholes, endeavor to recede from the axis of their motions.

Wherefore relative quantities are not the quantities themselves, whose names they bear, but those sensible measures of them (either accurate or inaccurate), which are commonly used instead of the measured quantities themselves. And if the meaning of words is to be determined by their use, then by the names time, space, place, and motion, their [sensible] measures are properly to be understood; and the expression will be unusual, and purely mathematical, if the measured quantities themselves are meant. On this account, those violate the accuracy of language, which ought to be kept precise, who interpret these words for the measured quantities. Nor do those less defile the purity of mathematical and philosophical truths, who confound real quantities with their relations and sensible measures.

It is indeed a matter of great difficulty to discover, and effectually to distinguish, the true motions of particular bodies from the apparent; because the parts of that immovable space, in which those motions are performed, do by no means come under the observation of our senses. Yet the thing is not altogether desperate; for we have some arguments to guide us, partly from the apparent motions, which are the differences of the true motions; partly from the forces, which are the causes and effects of the true motions. For instance, if two globes, kept at a given distance one from the other by means of a cord that connects them, were revolved about their common centre of gravity, we might, from the tension of the cord, discover the endeavor of the globes to recede from the axis of their motion, and from thence we might compute the quantity of their circular motions. And then if any equal forces should be impressed at once on the alternate faces of the globes to augment or diminish their circular motions, from the increase or decrease of the tension of the cord, we might infer the increment or decrement of their motions; and thence would be found on what faces those forces ought to be impressed, that the motions of the globes might be most augmented; that is, we might discover their hindmost faces, or those which, in the circular motion, do follow. But the faces which follow being known, and consequently the opposite ones that precede, we should likewise know the determination of their motions. And thus we might find both the quantity and the determination of this circular motion, even in an immense vacuum, where there was nothing external or sensible with which the globes could be compared. But now, if in that space some remote bodies were placed that kept always a given position one to another, as the fixed stars do in our regions, we could not indeed determine from the relative translation of the globes among those bodies, whether the motion did belong to the globes or to the bodies. But if we observed the cord, and found that its tension was that very tension which the motions of the globes required, we might conclude the motion to be in the globes, and the bodies to be at rest; and then, lastly, from the translation of the globes among the bodies, we should find the determination of their motions. But how we are to obtain the true motions from their causes, effects, and apparent differences, and the converse, shall be explained more at large in the following treatise. For to this end it was that I composed it.

AXIOMS, OR LAWS OF MOTION

LAW I

Every body continues in its state of rest, or of uniform motion in a right line, unless it is compelled to change that state by forces impressed upon it.

Projectiles continue in their motions, so far as they are not retarded by the resistance of the air, or impelled downwards by the force of gravity. A top, whose parts by their cohesion are continually drawn aside from rectilinear motions, does not cease its rotation, otherwise than as it is retarded by the air. The greater bodies of the planets and comets, meeting with less resistance in freer spaces, preserve their motions both progressive and circular for a much longer time.

LAW II

The change of motion is proportional to the motive force impressed; and is made in the direction of the right line in which that force is impressed.

If any force generates a motion, a double force will generate double the motion, a triple force triple the motion, whether that force be impressed altogether and at once, or gradually and successively. And this motion (being always directed the same way with the generating force), if the body moved before, is added to or subtracted from the former motion, according as they directly conspire with or are directly contrary to each other; or obliquely joined, when they are oblique, so as to produce a new motion compounded from the determination of both.

LAW III

To every action there is always opposed an equal reaction: or, the mutual actions of two bodies upon each other are always equal, and directed to contrary parts.

Whatever draws or presses another is as much drawn or pressed by that other. If you press a stone with your finger, the finger is also pressed by the stone. If a horse draws a stone tied to a rope, the horse (if I may so say) will be equally drawn back towards the stone; for the distended rope, by the same endeavor to relax or unbend itself, will draw the horse as much towards the stone as it does the stone towards the horse, and will obstruct the progress of the one as much as it advances that of the other. If a body impinge upon another, and by its force change the motion of the other, that body also (because of the equality of the mutual pressure) will undergo an equal change, in its own motion, towards the contrary part. The changes made by these actions are equal, not in the velocities but in the motions of bodies; that is to say, if the bodies are not hindered by any other impediments. For, because the motions are equally changed, the changes of the velocities made towards contrary parts are inversely proportional to the bodies. This law takes place also in attractions, as will be proved in the next Scholium.

COROLLARY I

A body, acted on by two forces simultaneously, will describe the diagonal of a parallelogram in the same time as it would describe the sides by those forces separately.

If a body in a given time, by the force M impressed apart in the place A, should with an uniform motion be carried from A to B, and by the force N impressed apart in the same place, should be carried from A to C, let the paral-

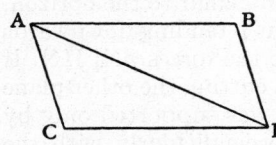

lelogram ABCD be completed, and, by both forces acting together, it will in the same time be carried in the diagonal from A to D. For since the force N acts in the direction of the line AC, parallel to BD, this force (by the second Law) will not at all alter the velocity generated by the other force M, by which the body is carried towards the line BD. The body therefore will arrive at the line BD in the same time, whether the force N be impressed or not; and therefore at the end of that time it will be found somewhere in the line BD. By the same argument, at the end of the same time it will be found somewhere in the line CD. Therefore it will be found in the point D, where both lines meet. But it will move in a right line from A to D, by Law I.

COROLLARY II

And hence is explained the composition of any one direct force AD, out of any two oblique forces AC and CD; and, on the contrary, the resolution of any one direct force AD into two oblique forces AC and CD: which composition and resolution are abundantly confirmed from mechanics.

As if the unequal radii OM and ON drawn from the centre O of any wheel, should sustain the weights A and P by the cords MA and NP; and the forces of those weights to move the wheel were required. Through the centre O draw the right line KOL, meeting the cords perpendicularly in K and L; and from the centre O, with OL the greater of the distances OK and OL, describe a circle, meeting the cord MA in D; and drawing OD, make AC parallel and DC perpendicular thereto. Now, it being indifferent whether the points K, L, D, of the cords be fixed to the plane of the wheel or not, the weights will have the same effect whether they are suspended from the points K and L, or from D and L. Let the whole force of the weight A be represented by the line AD, and let it be resolved into the forces AC and CD, of which the force AC, drawing the radius OD directly from the centre, will have no effect to move the wheel; but the other force DC, drawing the radius DO perpendicularly, will have the same effect as if it drew perpendicularly the radius OL equal to OD; that is, it will have the same effect as the weight P, if

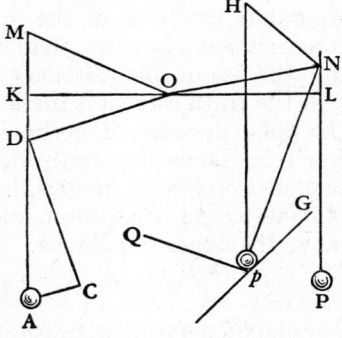

$$P : A = DC : DA,$$

but because the triangles ADC and DOK are similar,

$$DC : DA = OK : OD = OK : OL.$$

Therefore,

$$P : A = \text{radius } OK : \text{radius } OL.$$

As these radii lie in the same right line they will be equipollent, and so remain in equilibrium; which is the well-known property of the balance, the lever, and the wheel. If either weight is greater than in this ratio, its force to move the wheel will be so much greater.

If the weight $p = P$, is partly suspended by the cord Np, partly sustained by the oblique plane pG; draw pH, NH, the former perpendicular to the horizon, the latter to the plane pG; and if the force of the weight p tending downwards is represented by the line pH, it may be resolved into the forces pN, HN. If there was any plane pQ, perpendicular to the cord pN, cutting the other plane pG in a line parallel to the horizon, and the weight p was supported only by those planes pQ, pG, it would press those planes perpendicularly with the forces pN, HN; to wit, the plane pQ with the force pN, and the plane pG with the force HN. And therefore if the plane pQ was taken away, so that the weight might stretch the cord, because the cord, now sustaining the weight, supplied the place of the plane that was removed, it would be strained by the same force pN which pressed upon the plane before. Therefore, the

$$\text{tension of } pN : \text{tension of } PN = \text{line } pN : \text{line } pH.$$

Therefore, if p is to A in a ratio which is the product of the inverse ratio of the least distances of their cords pN and AM from the centre of the wheel, and of the ratio pH to pN, then the weights p and A will have the same effect towards moving the wheel, and will, therefore, sustain each other; as anyone may find by experiment.

But the weight p pressing upon those two oblique planes, may be considered as a wedge between the two internal surfaces of a body split by it; and hence the forces of the wedge and the mallet may be determined: because the force with which the weight p presses the plane pQ is to the force with which the same, whether by its own gravity, or by the blow of a mallet, is impelled in the direction of the line pH towards both the planes, as

$$pN : pH;$$

and to the force with which it presses the other plane pG, as

$$pN : NH.$$

And thus the force of the screw may be deduced from a like resolution of forces; it being no other than a wedge impelled with the force of a lever. Therefore the use of this Corollary spreads far and wide, and by that diffusive extent the truth thereof is further confirmed. For on what has been said depends the whole doctrine of mechanics variously demonstrated by different authors. For from hence are easily deduced the forces of machines, which are compounded of wheels, pullies, levers, cords, and weights, ascending directly or obliquely, and other mechanical powers; as also the force of the tendons to move the bones of animals.

COROLLARY III

The quantity of motion, which is obtained by taking the sum of the motions directed towards the same parts, and the difference of those that are directed to contrary parts, suffers no change from the action of bodies among themselves.

For action and its opposite reaction are equal, by Law III, and therefore, by Law II, they produce in the motions equal changes towards opposite parts.

Therefore if the motions are directed towards the same parts, whatever is added to the motion of the preceding body will be subtracted from the motion of that which follows; so that the sum will be the same as before. If the bodies meet, with contrary motions, there will be an equal deduction from the motions of both; and therefore the difference of the motions directed towards opposite parts will remain the same.

Thus, if a spherical body A is 3 times greater than the spherical body B, and has a velocity $=2$, and B follows in the same direction with a velocity $=10$, then the

$$\text{motion of A} : \text{motion of B} = 6 : 10.$$

Suppose, then, their motions to be of 6 parts and of 10 parts, and the sum will be 16 parts. Therefore, upon the meeting of the bodies, if A acquire 3, 4, or 5 parts of motion, B will lose as many; and therefore after reflection A will proceed with 9, 10, or 11 parts, and B with 7, 6, or 5 parts; the sum remaining always of 16 parts as before. If the body A acquire 9, 10, 11, or 12 parts of motion, and therefore after meeting proceed with 15, 16, 17, or 18 parts, the body B, losing so many parts as A has got, will either proceed with 1 part, having lost 9, or stop and remain at rest, as having lost its whole progressive motion of 10 parts; or it will go back with 1 part, having not only lost its whole motion, but (if I may so say) one part more; or it will go back with 2 parts, because a progressive motion of 12 parts is taken off. And so the sums of the conspiring motions,

$$15+1 \quad \text{or} \quad 16+0,$$

and the differences of the contrary motions,

$$17-1 \quad \text{and} \quad 18-2,$$

will always be equal to 16 parts, as they were before the meeting and reflection of the bodies. But the motions being known with which the bodies proceed after reflection, the velocity of either will be also known, by taking the velocity after to the velocity before reflection, as the motion after is to the motion before. As in the last case, where the

$$\text{motion of A before reflection } (6) : \text{motion of A after } (18)$$
$$= \text{velocity of A before } (2) : \text{velocity of A after } (x);$$

that is,

$$6 : 18 = 2 : x, \ x = 6.$$

But if the bodies are either not spherical, or, moving in different right lines, impinge obliquely one upon the other, and their motions after reflection are required, in those cases we are first to determine the position of the plane that touches the bodies in the point of impact, then the motion of each body (by Cor. II) is to be resolved into two, one perpendicular to that plane, and the other parallel to it. This done, because the bodies act upon each other in the direction of a line perpendicular to this plane, the parallel motions are to be retained the same after reflection as before; and to the perpendicular motions we are to assign equal changes towards the contrary parts; in such manner that the sum of the conspiring and the difference of the contrary motions may remain the same as before. From such kind of reflections sometimes arise also the circular motions of bodies about their own centres. But these are cases which I do not consider in what follows; and it would be too tedious to demonstrate every particular case that relates to this subject.

COROLLARY IV

The common centre of gravity of two or more bodies does not alter its state of motion or rest by the actions of the bodies among themselves; and therefore the common centre of gravity of all bodies acting upon each other (excluding external actions and impediments) is either at rest, or moves uniformly in a right line.

For if two points proceed with an uniform motion in right lines, and their distance be divided in a given ratio, the dividing point will be either at rest, or proceed uniformly in a right line. This is demonstrated hereafter in Lem. 23 and Corollary, when the points are moved in the same plane; and by a like way of arguing, it may be demonstrated when the points are not moved in the same plane. Therefore if any number of bodies move uniformly in right lines, the common centre of gravity of any two of them is either at rest, or proceeds uniformly in a right line; because the line which connects the centres of those two bodies so moving is divided at that common centre in a given ratio. In like manner the common centre of those two and that of a third body will be either at rest or moving uniformly in a right line; because at that centre the distance between the common centre of the two bodies, and the centre of this last, is divided in a given ratio. In like manner the common centre of these three, and of a fourth body, is either at rest, or moves uniformly in a right line; because the distance between the common centre of the three bodies, and the centre of the fourth, is there also divided in a given ratio, and so on *in infinitum*. Therefore, in a system of bodies where there is neither any mutual action among themselves, nor any foreign force impressed upon them from without, and which consequently move uniformly in right lines, the common centre of gravity of them all is either at rest or moves uniformly forwards in a right line.

Moreover, in a system of two bodies acting upon each other, since the distances between their centres and the common centre of gravity of both are reciprocally as the bodies, the relative motions of those bodies, whether of approaching to or of receding from that centre, will be equal among themselves. Therefore since the changes which happen to motions are equal and directed to contrary parts, the common centre of those bodies, by their mutual action between themselves, is neither accelerated nor retarded, nor suffers any change as to its state of motion or rest. But in a system of several bodies, because the common centre of gravity of any two acting upon each other suffers no change in its state by that action; and much less the common centre of gravity of the others with which that action does not intervene; but the distance between those two centres is divided by the common centre of gravity of all the bodies into parts inversely proportional to the total sums of those bodies whose centres they are; and therefore while those two centres retain their state of motion or rest, the common centre of all does also retain its state: it is manifest that the common centre of all never suffers any change in the state of its motion or rest from the actions of any two bodies between themselves. But in such a system all the actions of the bodies among themselves either happen between two bodies, or are composed of actions interchanged between some two bodies; and therefore they do never produce any alteration in the common centre of all as to its state of motion or rest. Wherefore since that centre, when the bodies do not act one upon another, either is at rest or moves uniformly forwards in some right line, it will, notwithstanding the mutual actions of the bodies among themselves, always continue in its state, either of rest, or of proceeding uniformly in a right line, unless it is forced out of this state by the action of some power impressed from without upon the whole system. And therefore the same law takes place in a system consisting of many bodies as in one single body, with regard to their persevering in their state of motion or of rest. For the progressive motion, whether of one single body, or of a whole system of bodies, is always to be estimated from the motion of the centre of gravity.

COROLLARY V

The motions of bodies included in a given space are the same among themselves, whether that space is at rest, or moves uniformly forwards in a right line without any circular motion.

For the differences of the motions tending towards the same parts, and the sums of those that tend towards contrary parts, are, at first (by supposition), in both cases the same; and it is from those sums and differences that the collisions and impulses do arise with which the bodies impinge one upon another. Wherefore (by Law 2), the effects of those collisions will be equal in both cases; and therefore the mutual motions of the bodies among themselves in the one case will remain equal to the motions of the bodies among themselves in the other. A clear proof of this we have from the experiment of a ship; where all motions happen after the same manner, whether the ship is at rest, or is carried uniformly forwards in a right line.

COROLLARY VI

If bodies, moved in any manner among themselves, are urged in the direction of parallel lines by equal accelerative forces, they will all continue to move among themselves, after the same manner as if they had not been urged by those forces.

For these forces acting equally (with respect to the quantities of the bodies to be moved), and in the direction of parallel lines, will (by Law 2) move all the bodies equally (as to velocity), and therefore will never produce any change in the positions or motions of the bodies among themselves.

SCHOLIUM

Hitherto I have laid down such principles as have been received by mathematicians, and are confirmed by abundance of experiments. By the first two Laws and the first two Corollaries, Galileo discovered that the descent of bodies varied as the square of the time (*in duplicata ratione temporis*) and that the motion of projectiles was in the curve of a parabola; experience agreeing with both, unless so far as these motions are a little retarded by the resistance of the air. When a body is falling, the uniform force of its gravity acting equally, impresses, in equal intervals of time, equal forces upon that body, and therefore generates equal velocities; and in the whole time impresses a whole force, and generates a whole velocity proportional to the time. And the spaces described in proportional times are as the product of the velocities and the times; that is, as the squares of the times. And when a body is thrown upwards, its uniform gravity impresses forces and reduces velocities proportional to the times; and the times of ascending to the greatest heights are as the velocities to be taken away, and those heights are as the product of the velocities and the times, or as the squares of the velocities. And if a body be projected in any direction, the motion arising from its projection is compounded with the motion arising from its gravity. Thus, if the body A by its motion of projection alone could describe in a given time the right line AB, and with its motion of falling alone could describe in the same time the altitude AC; complete the parallelogram ABCD, and the body by that compounded motion will at the end of the time be found in the place D; and the curved line AED, which that body describes, will be a parabola, to which the right line AB will be a tangent at A; and whose ordinate BD will be as the square of the line AB. On the same Laws and Corollaries depend those things which have been demonstrated concerning the times of the vibration of pendulums, and are confirmed by the daily experiments of pendulum clocks. By the same, together with Law 3, Sir Christopher Wren, Dr. Wallis, and Mr. Huygens, the greatest geometers of our times, did severally determine the rules of the impact and reflection of hard bodies, and about the same time communicated their discoveries to the Royal Society, exactly agreeing among themselves as to those rules. Dr. Wallis, indeed, was somewhat earlier in the publication; then followed Sir Christopher Wren, and, lastly, Mr. Huygens. But Sir Christopher Wren confirmed the truth of the thing before the Royal Society by the experiments on pendulums, which M. Mariotte soon after thought fit to explain in a treatise entirely upon that subject. But to bring this experiment to an accurate agreement with the theory, we are to have due regard as well to the resistance of the air as to the elastic force of the concurring bodies. Let the spherical bodies A, B be suspended by the parallel and equal strings AC, BD, from the centres C, D. About these centres, with those lengths as radii, describe the semicircles EAF, GBH, bisected respectively by the radii CA, DB. Bring the body A to any point R of the arc EAF, and (withdrawing the body B) let it go from thence, and after one oscillation suppose it to return to the point V: then RV will be the retardation arising from the resistance of the air. Of this RV let ST be a fourth part, situated in the middle, namely, so that RS = TV,

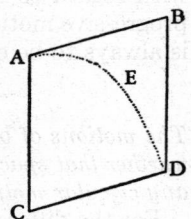

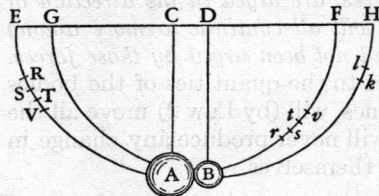

and
$$RS : ST = 3 : 2,$$
then will ST represent very nearly the retardation during the descent from S to A. Restore the body B to its place: and, supposing the body A to be let fall from the point S, the velocity thereof in the place of reflection A, without sensible error, will be the same as if it had descended *in vacuo* from the point T. Upon which account this velocity may be represented by the chord of the arc TA. For it is a proposition well known to geometers, that the velocity of a pendulous body in the lowest point is as the chord of the arc which it has described in its descent. After reflection, suppose the body A comes to the place s, and the body B to the place k. Withdraw the body B, and find the place v, from which if the body A, being let go, should after one oscillation return to the place r, st may be a fourth part of rv, so placed in the middle thereof as to leave rs equal to tv, and let the chord of the arc tA represent the velocity which the body A

had in the place A immediately after reflection. For t will be the true and correct place to which the body A should have ascended, if the resistance of the air had been taken off. In the same way we are to correct the place k to which the body B ascends, by finding the place l to which it should have ascended *in vacuo*. And thus everything may be subjected to experiment, in the same manner as if we were really placed *in vacuo*. These things being done, we are to take the product (if I may so say) of the body A, by the chord of the arc TA (which represents its velocity), that we may have its motion in the place A immediately before reflection; and then by the chord of the arc tA, that we may have its motion in the place A immediately after reflection. And so we are to take the product of the body B by the chord of the arc Bl, that we may have the motion of the same immediately after reflection. And in like manner, when two bodies are let go together from different places, we are to find the motion of each, as well before as after reflection; and then we may compare the motions between themselves, and collect the effects of the reflection. Thus trying the thing with pendulums of 10 feet, in unequal as well as equal bodies, and making the bodies to concur after a descent through large spaces, as of 8, 12, or 16 feet, I found always, without an error of 3 inches, that when the bodies concurred together directly, equal changes towards the contrary parts were produced in their motions, and, of consequence, that the action and reaction were always equal. As if the body A impinged upon the body B at rest with 9 parts of motion, and losing 7, proceeded after reflection with 2, the body B was carried backwards with those 7 parts. If the bodies concurred with contrary motions, A with 12 parts of motion, and B with 6, then if A receded with 2, B receded with 8; namely, with a deduction of 14 parts of motion on each side. For from the motion of A subtracting 12 parts, nothing will remain; but subtracting 2 parts more, a motion will be generated of 2 parts towards the contrary way; and so, from the motion of the body B of 6 parts, subtracting 14 parts, a motion is generated of 8 parts towards the contrary way. But if the bodies were made both to move towards the same way, A, the swifter, with 14 parts of motion, B, the slower, with 5, and after reflection A went on with 5, B likewise went on with 14 parts; 9 parts being transferred from A to B. And so in other cases. By the meeting and collision of bodies, the quantity of motion, obtained from the sum of the motions directed towards the same way, or from the difference of those that were directed towards contrary ways, was never changed. For the error of an inch or two in measures may be easily ascribed to the difficulty of executing everything with accuracy. It was not easy to let go the two pendulums so exactly together that the bodies should impinge one upon the other in the lowermost place AB; nor to mark the places s, and k, to which the bodies ascended after impact. Nay, and some errors, too, might have happened from the unequal density of the parts of the pendulous bodies themselves, and from the irregularity of the texture proceeding from other causes.

But to prevent an objection that may perhaps be alleged against the rule, for the proof of which this experiment was made, as if this rule did suppose that the bodies were either absolutely hard, or at least perfectly elastic (whereas no such bodies are to be found in Nature), I must add, that the experiments we have been describing, by no means depending upon that quality of hardness, do succeed as well in soft as in hard bodies. For if the rule is to be tried in bodies not perfectly hard, we are only to diminish the reflection in such a certain proportion as the quantity of the elastic force requires. By the theory of Wren and Huygens, bodies absolutely hard return one from another with the same velocity with which they meet. But this may be affirmed with more certainty of bodies perfectly elastic. In bodies imperfectly elastic the velocity of the return is to be diminished together with the elastic force; because that force (except when the parts of bodies are bruised by their impact, or suffer some such extension as happens under the strokes of a hammer) is (as far as I can perceive) certain and determined, and makes the bodies to return one from the other with a relative velocity, which is in a given ratio to that relative velocity with which they met. This I tried in balls of wool, made up tightly, and strongly compressed. For, first, by letting go the pendulous bodies, and measuring their reflection, I determined the quantity of their elastic force; and then, according to this force, estimated the reflections that ought to happen in other cases of impact. And with this computation other experiments made afterwards did accordingly agree; the balls always receding one from the other with a relative velocity, which was to the relative velocity with which they met as about 5 to 9. Balls of steel returned with almost the same velocity; those of cork with a a velocity something less; but in balls of glass the proportion was as about 15 to 16. And thus the third Law, so far as it regards percussions and reflections, is proved by a theory exactly agreeing with experience.

In attractions, I briefly demonstrate the thing after this manner. Suppose an obstacle is interposed to hinder the meeting of any two bodies A, B, attracting one the other: then if either body, as A, is more attracted towards the other body B, than that other body B is towards the first body A, the obstacle will be more strongly urged by the pressure of the body A than by the pressure of the body B, and therefore will not remain in equilibrium: but the stronger pressure will prevail, and will make the system of the two bodies, together with the obstacle, to move directly towards the parts on which B lies; and in free spaces, to go forwards *in infinitum* with a motion continually accelerated; which is absurd and contrary to the first Law. For, by the first Law, the system ought to continue in its state of rest, or of moving uniformly forwards in a right line; and therefore the bodies must equally press the obstacle, and be equally attracted one by the other. I made the experiment on the loadstone and iron. If these, placed apart in proper vessels, are made to float by one another in standing water, neither of them will propel the other; but, by being equally attracted, they will sustain each other's pressure, and rest at last in an equilibrium.

So the gravitation between the earth and its parts is mutual. Let the earth FI by cut by any plane EG into two parts EGF and EGI, and their weights one towards the other will be mutually equal. For if by another plane HK, parallel to the former EG, the greater part EGI is cut into two parts EGKH and HKI, whereof HKI is equal to the part EFG, first cut off, it is evident that the middle part EGKH will have no propension by its proper weight towards either side, but will hang as it were, and rest in an equilibrium between both. But the one extreme part HKI will with its whole weight bear upon and press the middle part towards the other extreme part EGF; and therefore the force with which EGI, the sum of the parts HKI and EGKH, tends towards the

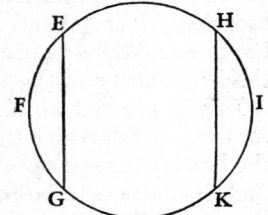

third part EGF, is equal to the weight of the part HKI, that is, to the weight of the third part EGF. And therefore the weights of the two parts EGI and EGF, one towards the other, are equal, as I was to prove. And indeed if those weights were not equal, the whole earth floating in the nonresisting ether would give way to the greater weight, and, retiring from it, would be carried off *in infinitum.*

And as those bodies are equipollent in the impact and reflection, whose velocities are inversely as their innate forces, so in the use of mechanic instruments those agents are equipollent, and mutually sustain each the contrary pressure of the other, whose velocities, estimated according to the determination of the forces, are inversely as the forces.

So those weights are of equal force to move the arms of a balance, which during the play of the balance are inversely as their velocities upwards and downwards; that is, if the ascent or descent is direct, those weights are of equal force, which are inversely as the distances of the points at which they are suspended from the axis of the balance; but if they are turned aside by the interposition of oblique planes, or other obstacles, and made to ascend or descend obliquely, those bodies will be equipollent, which are inversely as the heights of their ascent and descent taken according to the perpendicular; and that on account of the determination of gravity downwards.

And in like manner in the pulley, or in a combination of pulleys, the force of a hand drawing the rope directly, which is to the weight, whether ascending directly or obliquely, as the velocity of the perpendicular ascent of the weight to the velocity of the hand that draws the rope, will sustain the weight.

In clocks and such like instruments, made up from a combination of wheels, the contrary forces that promote and impede the motion of the wheels, if they are inversely as the velocities of the parts of the wheel on which they are impressed, will mutually sustain each other.

The force of the screw to press a body is to the force of the hand that turns the handles by which it is moved as the circular velocity of the handle in that part where it is impelled by the hand is to the progressive velocity of the screw towards the pressed body.

The forces by which the wedge presses or drives the two parts of the wood it cleaves are to the force of the mallet upon the wedge as the progress of the wedge in the direction of the force impressed upon it by the mallet is to the velocity with which the parts of the wood yield to the wedge, in the direction of lines perpendicular to the sides of the wedge. And the like account is to be given of all machines.

The power and use of machines consist only in this, that by diminishing the velocity we may augment the force, and the contrary; from whence, in all sorts of proper machines, we have the solution of this problem: *To move a given weight with a given power*, or with a given force to overcome any other given resistance. For if machines are so contrived that the velocities of the agent and resistant are inversely as their forces, the agent will just sustain the resistant, but with a greater disparity of velocity will overcome it. So that if the disparity of velocities is so great as to overcome all that resistance which commonly arises either from the friction of contiguous bodies as they slide by one another, or from the cohesion of continuous bodies that are to be separated, or from the weights of bodies to be raised, the excess of the force remaining, after all those resistances are overcome, will produce an acceleration of motion proportional thereto, as well in the parts of the machine as in the resisting body. But to treat of mechanics is not my present business. I was aiming only to show by those examples the great extent and certainty of the third Law of Motion. For if we estimate the action of the agent from the product of its force and velocity, and likewise the reaction of the impediment from the product of the velocities of its several parts, and the forces of resistance arising from the friction, cohesion, weight, and acceleration of those parts, the action and reaction in the use of all sorts of machines will be found always equal to one another. And so far as the action is propagated by the intervening instruments, and at last impressed upon the resisting body, the ultimate action will be always contrary to the reaction.

BOOK ONE

THE MOTION OF BODIES

SECTION I

THE METHOD OF FIRST AND LAST RATIOS OF QUANTITIES, BY THE HELP OF WHICH
WE DEMONSTRATE THE PROPOSITIONS THAT FOLLOW

LEMMA 1

*Quantities, and the ratios of quantities, which in any finite time converge contin-
ually to equality, and before the end of that time approach nearer to each other than
by any given difference, become ultimately equal.*

If you deny it, suppose them to be ultimately unequal, and let D be their
ultimate difference. Therefore they cannot approach nearer to equality than
by that difference D; which is contrary to the supposition.

LEMMA 2

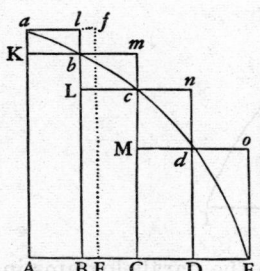

If in any figure AacE, *terminated by the right lines* Aa,
AE, *and the curve* acE, *there be inscribed any number of
parallelograms* Ab, Bc, Cd, &c., *comprehended under equal
bases* AB, BC, CD, &c., *and the sides,* Bb, Cc, Dd, &c.,
parallel to one side Aa *of the figure; and the parallelograms*
aKbl, bLcm, cMdn, &c., *are completed: then if the breadth
of those parallelograms be supposed to be diminished, and
their number to be augmented* in infinitum, *I say, that the
ultimate ratios which the inscribed figure* AKbLcMdD,
the circumscribed figure Aalbmcndoe, *and curvilinear
figure* AabcdE, *will have to one another, are ratios of equality.*

For the difference of the inscribed and circumscribed figures is the sum of
the parallelograms Kl, Lm, Mn, Do, that is (from the equality of all their
bases), the rectangle under one of their bases Kb and the sum of their altitudes
Aa, that is, the rectangle ABla. But this rectangle, because its breadth AB is
supposed diminished *in infinitum*, becomes less than any given space. And
therefore (by Lem. 1) the figures inscribed and circumscribed become ultimately equal one to the other; and much more will the intermediate curvilinear
figure be ultimately equal to either. Q.E.D.

LEMMA 3

The same ultimate ratios are also ratios of equality, when the breadths AB,
BC, DC, &c., *of the parallelograms are unequal, and are all diminished* in infinitum.

For suppose AF equal to the greatest breadth, and complete the parallelogram FAaf. This parallelogram will be greater than the difference of the in-

25

scribed and circumscribed figures; but, because its breadth AF is diminished *in infinitum*, it will become less than any given rectangle. Q.E.D.

Cor. i. Hence the ultimate sum of those evanescent parallelograms will in all parts coincide with the curvilinear figure.

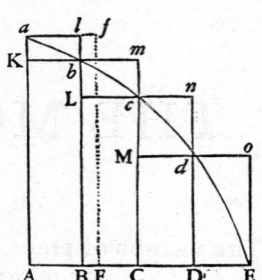

Cor. ii. Much more will the rectilinear figure comprehended under the chords of the evanescent arcs *ab*, *bc, cd, &c.*, ultimately coincide with the curvilinear figure.

Cor. iii. And also the circumscribed rectilinear figure comprehended under the tangents of the same arcs.

Cor. iv. And therefore these ultimate figures (as to their perimeters *ac*E) are not rectilinear, but curvilinear limits of rectilinear figures.

Lemma 4

If in two figures AacE, PprT, *there are inscribed (as before) two series of parallelograms, an equal number in each series, and, their breadths being diminished in* infinitum, *if the ultimate ratios of the parallelograms in one figure to those in the other, each to each respectively, are the same: I say, that those two figures,* AacE, PprT, *are to each other in that same ratio.*

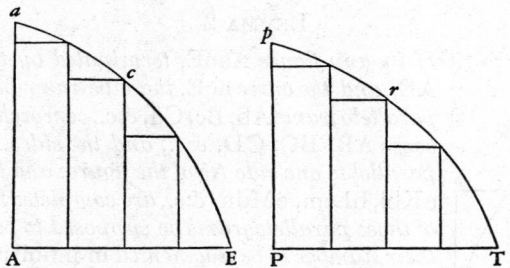

For as the parallelograms in the one are severally to the parallelograms in the other, so (by composition) is the sum of all in the one to the sum of all in the other; and so is the one figure to the other; because (by Lem. 3) the former figure to the former sum, and the latter figure to the latter sum, are both in the ratio of equality. Q.E.D.

Cor. Hence if two quantities of any kind are divided in any manner into an equal number of parts, and those parts, when their number is augmented, and their magnitude diminished *in infinitum*, have a given ratio to each other, the first to the first, the second to the second, and so on in order, all of them taken together will be to each other in that same given ratio. For if, in the figures of this Lemma, the parallelograms are taken to each other in the ratio of the parts, the sum of the parts will always be as the sum of the parallelograms; and therefore supposing the number of the parallelograms and parts to be augmented, and their magnitudes diminished *in infinitum*, those sums will be in the ultimate ratio of the parallelogram in the one figure to the correspondent parallelogram in the other; that is (by the supposition), in the ultimate ratio of any part of the one quantity to the correspondent part of the other.

LEMMA 5

All homologous sides of similar figures, whether curvilinear or rectilinear, are proportional; and the areas are as the squares of the homologous sides.

LEMMA 6

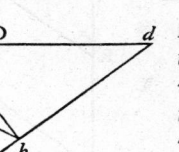

If any arc ACB, given in position, is subtended by its chord AB, and in any point A, in the middle of the continued curvature, is touched by a right line AD, produced both ways; then if the points A and B approach one another and meet, I say, the angle BAD, contained between the chord and the tangent, will be diminished in infinitum, and ultimately will vanish.

For if that angle does not vanish, the arc ACB will contain with the tangent AD an angle equal to a rectilinear angle; and therefore the curvature at the point A will not be continued, which is against the supposition.

LEMMA 7

The same things being supposed, I say that the ultimate ratio of the arc, chord, and tangent, any one to any other, is the ratio of equality.

For while the point B approaches towards the point A, consider always AB and AD as produced to the remote points b and d; and parallel to the secant BD draw bd; and let the arc Acb be always similar to the arc ACB. Then, supposing the points A and B to coincide, the angle dAb will vanish, by the preceding Lemma; and therefore the right lines Ab, Ad (which are always finite), and the intermediate arc Acb, will coincide, and become equal among themselves. Wherefore, the right lines AB, AD, and the intermediate arc ACB (which are always proportional to the former), will vanish, and ultimately acquire the ratio of equality.   Q.E.D.

COR. I. Whence if through B we draw BF parallel to the tangent, always cutting any right line AF passing through A in F, this line BF will be ultimately in the ratio of equality with the evanescent arc ACB; because, completing the parallelogram AFBD, it is always in a ratio of equality with AD.

COR. II. And if through B and A more right lines are drawn, as BE, BD, AF, AG, cutting the tangent AD and its parallel BF; the ultimate ratio of all the abscissas AD, AE, BF, BG, and of the chord and arc AB, any one to any other, will be the ratio of equality.

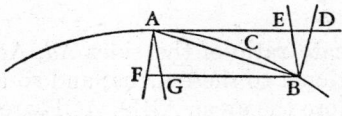

COR. III. And therefore in all our reasoning about ultimate ratios, we may freely use any one of those lines for any other.

LEMMA 8

If the right lines AR, BR, with the arc ACB, the chord AB, and the tangent AD, constitute three triangles RAB, RACB, RAD, and the points A and B approach and meet: I say, that the ultimate form of these evanescent triangles is that of similitude, and their ultimate ratio that of equality.

For while the point B approaches towards the point A, consider always AB, AD, AR, as produced to the remote points b, d, and r, and rbd as drawn parallel to RD, and let the arc Acb be always similar to the arc ACB. Then supposing the
points A and B to coincide, the angle bAd
will vanish; and therefore the three triangles rAb, $rAcb$, rAd (which are always
finite), will coincide, and on that account
become both similar and equal. And therefore the triangles RAB, RACB, RAD,
which are always similar and proportional
to these, will ultimately become both similar and equal among themselves.

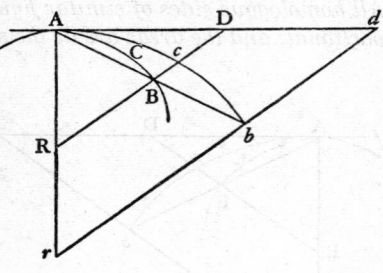

Q.E.D.

Cor. And hence in all reasonings about ultimate ratios, we may use any one of those triangles for any other.

Lemma 9

If a right line AE, *and a curved line* ABC, *both given by position, cut each other in a given angle,* A; *and to that right line, in another given angle,* BD, CE *are ordinately applied, meeting the curve in* B, C; *and the points* B *and* C *together approach towards and meet in the point* A: *I say, that the areas of the triangles* ABD, ACE, *will ultimately be to each other as the squares of homologous sides.*

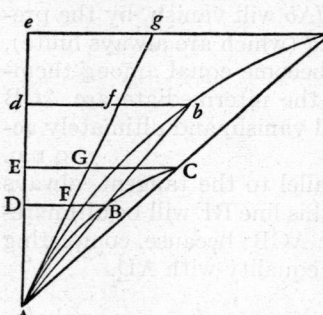

For while the points B, C, approach towards the point A, suppose always AD to be produced to the remote points d and e, so as Ad, Ae may be proportional to AD, AE; and the ordinates db, ec, to
be drawn parallel to the ordinates DB and EC,
and meeting AB and AC produced in b and c.
Let the curve Abc be similar to the curve ABC,
and draw the right line Ag so as to touch both
curves in A, and cut the ordinates DB, EC, db,
ec, in F, G, f, g. Then, supposing the length Ae
to remain the same, let the points B and C meet
in the point A; and the angle cAg vanishing,
the curvilinear areas Abd, Ace will coincide with
the rectilinear areas Afd, Age; and therefore (by
Lem. 5) will be one to the other in the dupli-
cate ratio of the sides Ad, Ae. But the areas ABD, ACE are always proportional to these areas; and so the sides AD, AE are to these sides. And therefore the areas ABD, ACE are ultimately to each other as the squares of the
sides AD, AE.

Q.E.D.

Lemma 10

The spaces which a body describes by any finite force urging it, whether that force is determined and immutable, or is continually augmented or continually diminished, are in the very beginning of the motion to each other as the squares of the times.

Let the times be represented by the lines AD, AE, and the velocities generated in those times by the ordinates DB, EC. The spaces described with these velocities will be as the areas ABD, ACE, described by those ordinates, that is, at the very beginning of the motion (by Lem. 9), in the duplicate ratio of the times AD, AE.   Q.E.D.

COR. I. And hence one may easily infer, that the errors of bodies describing similar parts of similar figures in proportional times, the errors being generated by any equal forces similarly applied to the bodies, and measured by the distances of the bodies from those places of the similar figures, at which, without the action of those forces, the bodies would have arrived in those proportional times—are nearly as the squares of the times in which they are generated.

COR. II. But the errors that are generated by proportional forces, similarly applied to the bodies at similar parts of the similar figures, are as the product of the forces and the squares of the times.

COR. III. The same thing is to be understood of any spaces whatsoever described by bodies urged with different forces; all which, in the very beginning of the motion, are as the product of the forces and the squares of the times.

COR. IV. And therefore the forces are directly as the spaces described in the very beginning of the motion, and inversely as the squares of the times.

COR. V. And the squares of the times are directly as the spaces described, and inversely as the forces.

SCHOLIUM

If in comparing with each other indeterminate quantities of different sorts, any one is said to be directly or inversely as any other, the meaning is, that the former is augmented or diminished in the same ratio as the latter, or as its reciprocal. And if any one is said to be as any other two or more, directly or inversely, the meaning is, that the first is augmented or diminished in the ratio compounded of the ratios in which the others, or the reciprocals of the others, are augmented or diminished. Thus, if A is said to be as B directly, and C directly, and D inversely, the meaning is, that A is augmented or diminished in the same ratio as $B \cdot C \cdot \frac{1}{D}$, that is to say, that A and $\frac{BC}{D}$ are to each other in a given ratio.

LEMMA 11

The evanescent subtense of the angle of contact, in all curves which at the point of contact have a finite curvature, is ultimately as the square of the subtense of the conterminous arc.

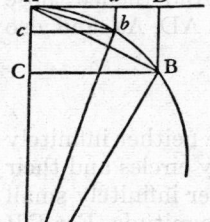

CASE 1. Let AB be that arc, AD its tangent, BD the subtense of the angle of contact perpendicular on the tangent, AB the subtense of the arc. Draw BG perpendicular to the subtense AB, and AG perpendicular to the tangent AD, meeting in G; then let the points D, B, and G approach to the points d, b, and g, and suppose J to be the ultimate intersection of the lines BG, AG, when the points D, B have come to A. It is evident that the distance GJ may be less than any assignable distance. But (from the nature of the circles passing through the points A, B, G, and through A, b, g),

$$AB^2 = AG \cdot BD, \text{ and}$$
$$Ab^2 = Ag \cdot bd.$$

But because GJ may be assumed of less length than any assignable, the ratio of AG to Ag may be such as to differ from unity by less than any assignable difference; and therefore the ratio of AB^2 to Ab^2 may be such as to differ from the ratio of BD to bd by less than any assignable difference. Therefore, by Lem. 1, ultimately,

$$AB^2 : Ab^2 = BD : bd.$$

Q.E.D.

CASE 2. Now let BD be inclined to AD in any given angle, and the ultimate ratio of BD to bd will always be the same as before, and therefore the same with the ratio of AB^2 to Ab^2.

Q.E.D.

CASE 3. And if we suppose the angle D not to be given, but that the right line BD converges to a given point, or is determined by any other condition whatever; nevertheless the angles D, d, being determined by the same law, will always draw nearer to equality, and approach nearer to each other than by any assigned difference, and therefore, by Lem. 1, will at last be equal; and therefore the lines BD, bd are in the same ratio to each other as before. Q.E.D.

COR. I. Therefore since the tangents AD, Ad, the arcs AB, Ab, and their sines, BC, bc, become ultimately equal to the chords AB, Ab, their squares will ultimately become as the subtenses BD, bd.

COR. II. Their squares are also ultimately as the versed sines of the arcs, bisecting the chords, and converging to a given point. For those versed sines are as the subtenses BD, bd.

COR. III. And therefore the versed sine is as the square of the time in which a body will describe the arc with a given velocity.

COR. IV. The ultimate proportion,

$$\triangle ADB : \triangle Adb = AD^3 : Ad^3 = DB^{3/2} : db^{3/2},$$

is derived from

$$\triangle ADB : \triangle Adb = AD \cdot DB : Ad \cdot db$$

and from the ultimate proportion

$$AD^2 : Ad^2 = DB : db.$$

So also is obtained ultimately

$$\triangle ABC : \triangle Abc = BC^3 : bc^3.$$

COR. V. And because DB, db are ultimately parallel and as the squares of the lines AD, Ad, the ultimate curvilinear areas ADB, Adb will be (by the nature of the parabola) two-thirds of the rectilinear triangles ADB, Adb, and the segments, AB, Ab will be one-third of the same triangles. And thence those areas and those segments will be as the cubes of the tangents AD, Ad, and also of the chords and arcs AB, Ab.

SCHOLIUM

But we have all along supposed the angle of contact to be neither infinitely greater nor infinitely less than the angles of contact made by circles and their tangents; that is, that the curvature at the point A is neither infinitely small nor infinitely great, and that the interval AJ is of a finite magnitude. For DB may be taken as AD^3: in which case no circle can be drawn through the point A, between the tangent AD and the curve AB, and therefore the angle of contact will be infinitely less than those of circles. And by a like reasoning, if DB be made successfully as AD^4, AD^5, AD^6, AD^7, &c., we shall have a series of angles of contact, proceeding *in infinitum*, wherein every succeeding term is infinitely less than the preceding. And if DB be made successively as AD^2, $AD^{3/2}$, $AD^{4/3}$, $AD^{5/4}$, $AD^{6/5}$, $AD^{7/6}$, &c., we shall have another infinite series of angles of contact, the first of which is of the same sort with those of circles, the second infinitely greater, and every succeeding one infinitely greater than the preceding. But between any two of these angles another series of intermediate angles of contact may be interposed, proceeding both ways *in infinitum*, wherein every succeeding angle shall be infinitely greater or infinitely less than the preceding. As if between the terms AD^2 and AD^3 there were interposed the series $AD^{13/6}$, $AD^{11/5}$, $AD^{9/4}$, $AD^{7/3}$, $AD^{5/2}$, $AD^{3/3}$, $AD^{11/4}$, $AD^{14/5}$, $AD^{17/6}$, &c. And again, between any two angles of this series, a new series of intermediate angles may be interposed, differing from one another by infinite intervals. Nor is Nature confined to any bounds.

Those things which have been demonstrated of curved lines, and the surfaces which they comprehend, may be easily applied to the curved surfaces and contents of solids. These Lemmas are premised to avoid the tediousness of deducing involved demonstrations *ad absurdum*, according to the method of the ancient geometers. For demonstrations are shorter by the method of indivisibles; but because the hypothesis of indivisibles seems somewhat harsh, and therefore that method is reckoned less geometrical, I chose rather to reduce the demonstrations of the following Propositions to the first and last sums and ratios of nascent and evanescent quantities, that is, to the limits of those sums and ratios, and so to premise, as short as I could, the demonstrations of those limits. For hereby the same thing is performed as by the method of indivisibles; and now those principles being demonstrated, we may use them with greater safety. Therefore if hereafter I should happen to consider quantities as made up of particles, or should use little curved lines for right ones, I would not be understood to mean indivisibles, but evanescent divisible quantities; not the sums and ratios of determinate parts, but always the limits of sums and ratios; and that the force of such demonstrations always depends on the method laid down in the foregoing Lemmas.

Perhaps it may be objected, that there is no ultimate proportion of evanescent quantities; because the proportion, before the quantities have vanished, is not the ultimate, and when they are vanished, is none. But by the same argument it may be alleged that a body arriving at a certain place, and there stopping, has no ultimate velocity; because the velocity, before the body comes to the place, is not its ultimate velocity; when it has arrived, there is none. But the answer is easy; for by the ultimate velocity is meant that with which the body is moved, neither before it arrives at its last place and the motion ceases, nor after, but at the very instant it arrives; that is, that velocity with which the body arrives at its last place, and with which the motion ceases. And in like manner, by the ultimate ratio of evanescent quantities is to be understood the ratio of the quantities not before they vanish, nor afterwards, but with which they vanish. In like manner the first ratio of nascent quantities is that with which they begin to be. And the first or last sum is that with which they begin and cease to be (or to be augmented or diminished). There is a limit which the velocity at the end of the motion may attain, but not exceed. This is the ultimate velocity. And there is the like limit in all quantities and proportions that begin and cease to be. And since such limits are certain and definite, to determine the same is a problem strictly geometrical. But whatever is geometrical we may use in determining and demonstrating any other thing that is also geometrical.

It may also be objected, that if the ultimate ratios of evanescent quantities are given, their ultimate magnitudes will be also given: and so all quantities will consist of indivisibles, which is contrary to what Euclid has demonstrated concerning incommensurables, in the tenth book of his *Elements*. But this objection is founded on a false supposition. For those ultimate ratios with which quantities vanish are not truly the ratios of ultimate quantities, but limits towards which the ratios of quantities decreasing without limit do always converge; and to which they approach nearer than by any given difference, but never go beyond, nor in effect attain to, till the quantities are diminished *in infinitum*. This thing will appear more evident in quantities infinitely great. If two quantities, whose difference is given, be augmented *in infinitum*, the ultimate ratio of these quantities will be given, namely, the ratio of equality; but it does not from thence follow, that the ultimate or greatest quantities themselves, whose ratio that is, will be given. Therefore if in what follows, for the sake of being more easily understood, I should happen to mention quantities as least, or evanescent, or ultimate, you are not to suppose that quantities of any determinate magnitude are meant, but such as are conceived to be always diminished without end.

SECTION II

THE DETERMINATION OF CENTRIPETAL FORCES

PROPOSITION 1. THEOREM 1

The areas which revolving bodies describe by radii drawn to an immovable centre of force do lie in the same immovable planes, and are proportional to the times in which they are described.

For suppose the time to be divided into equal parts, and in the first part of that time let the body by its innate force describe the right line AB. In the second part of that time, the same would (by Law I), if not hindered, proceed directly to c, along the line Bc equal to AB; so that by the radii AS, BS, cS, drawn to the centre, the equal areas ASB, BSc, would be described. But when the body is arrived at B, suppose that a centripetal force acts at once with a great impulse, and, turning aside the body from the right line Bc, compels it afterwards to continue its motion along the right line BC. Draw cC parallel to BS, meeting BC in C; and at the end of the second part of the time, the body (by Cor. I of the Laws) will be found in C, in the same plane with the triangle ASB. Join SC, and, because SB and Cc are parallel, the triangle SBC will be equal to the triangle SBc, and therefore also to the triangle SAB. By the like argument, if the centripetal force acts successively in C, D, E, &c., and makes the body, in each single particle of time, to describe the right lines CD, DE, EF, &c., they will all lie in the same plane; and the triangle SCD will be equal to the triangle SBC, and SDE to SCD, and SEF to SDE. And therefore, in equal times, equal areas are described in one immovable plane: and, by composition, any sums SADS, SAFS, of those areas, are to each other as the times in which they are described. Now let the number of those triangles be augmented, and their breadth diminished *in infinitum;* and (by Cor. IV, Lem. 3) their ultimate perimeter ADF will be a curved line: and therefore the centripetal force, by which the body is continually drawn back from the tangent of

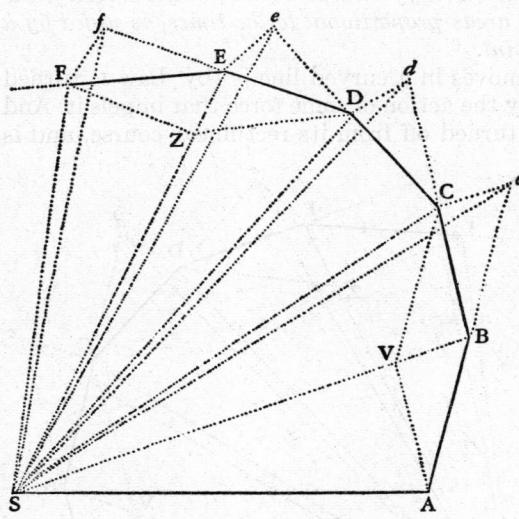

this curve, will act continually; and any described areas SADS, SAFS, which are always proportional to the times of description, will, in this case also, be proportional to those times.

Q.E.D.

Cor. I. The velocity of a body attracted towards an immovable centre, in spaces void of resistance, is inversely as the perpendicular let fall from that centre on the right line that touches the orbit. For the velocities in those places A, B, C, D, E, are as the bases AB, BC, CD, DE, EF, of equal triangles; and these bases are inversely as the perpendiculars let fall upon them.

Cor. II. If the chords AB, BC of two arcs, successively described in equal times by the same body, in spaces void of resistance, are completed into a parallelogram ABCV, and the diagonal BV of this parallelogram, in the position which it ultimately acquires when those arcs are diminished *in infinitum,* is produced both ways, it will pass through the centre of force.

Cor. III. If the chords AB, BC, and DE, EF, of arcs described in equal times, in spaces void of resistance, are completed into the parallelograms ABCV, DEFZ, the forces in B and E are one to the other in the ultimate ratio of the diagonals BV, EZ, when those arcs are diminished *in infinitum.* For the motions BC and EF of the body (by Cor. 1 of the Laws) are compounded of the motions B*c*, BV, and E*f*, EZ; but BV and EZ, which are equal to C*c* and F*f*, in the demonstration of this Proposition, were generated by the impulses of the centripetal force in B and E, and are therefore proportional to those impulses.

Cor. IV. The forces by which bodies, in spaces void of resistance, are drawn back from rectilinear motions, and turned into curvilinear orbits, are to each other as the versed sines of arcs described in equal times; which versed sines tend to the centre of force, and bisect the chords when those arcs are diminished to infinity. For such versed sines are the halves of the diagonals mentioned in Cor. III.

Cor. V. And therefore those forces are to the force of gravity as the said versed sines to the versed sines perpendicular to the horizon of those parabolic arcs which projectiles describe in the same time.

Cor. VI. And the same things do all hold good (by Cor. V of the Laws) when the planes in which the bodies are moved, together with the centres of force which are placed in those planes, are not at rest, but move uniformly forwards in right lines.

Proposition 2. Theorem 2

Every body that moves in any curved line described in a plane, and by a radius drawn to a point either immovable, or moving forwards with an uniform rectilinear motion, describes about that point areas proportional to the times, is urged by a centripetal force directed to that point.

Case 1. For every body that moves in a curved line is (by Law i) turned aside from its rectilinear course by the action of some force that impels it. And that force by which the body is turned off from its rectilinear course, and is made to describe, in equal times, the equal least triangles SAB, SBC, SCD, &c., about the immovable point S (by Prop. 40, Book 1, *Elements* of Euclid, and Law ii), acts in the place B, according to the direction of a line parallel to cC, that is, in the direction of the line BS; and in the place C, according to the direction of a line parallel to dD, that is, in the direction of the line CS, &c.; and therefore acts always in the direction of lines tending to the immovable point S. q.e.d.

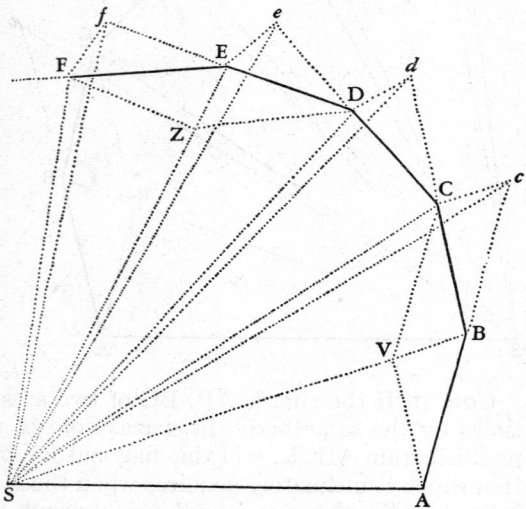

Case 2. And (by Cor. v of the Laws) it is indifferent whether the surface in which a body describes a curvilinear figure be at rest, or moves together with the body, the figure described, and its point S, uniformly forwards in a right line.

Cor. i. In nonresisting spaces or mediums, if the areas are not proportional to the times, the forces are not directed to the point in which the radii meet, but deviate therefrom towards the part to which the motion is directed, if the description of the areas is accelerated, and away from that part, if retarded.

Cor. ii. And even in resisting mediums, if the description of the areas is accelerated, the directions of the forces deviate from the point in which the radii meet, towards the part to which the motion tends.

Scholium

A body may be urged by a centripetal force compounded of several forces; in which case the meaning of the Proposition is, that the force which results out of all tends to the point S. But if any force acts continually in the direction of lines perpendicular to the described surface, this force will make the body to deviate from the plane of its motion; but will neither augment nor diminish the area of the described surface, and is therefore to be neglected in the composition of forces.

PROPOSITION 3. THEOREM 3

Every body, that by a radius drawn to the centre of another body, howsoever moved, describes areas about that centre proportional to the times, is urged by a force compounded of the centripetal force tending to that other body, and of all the accelerative force by which that other body is impelled.

Let L represent the one, and T the other body; and (by Cor. VI of the Laws) if both bodies are urged in the direction of parallel lines, by a new force equal and contrary to that by which the second body T is urged, the first body L will go on to describe about the other body T the same areas as before: but the force by which that other body T was urged will be now destroyed by an equal and contrary force; and therefore (by Law I) that other body T, now left to itself, will either rest, or move uniformly forwards in a right line: and the first body L, impelled by the difference of the forces, that is, by the force remaining, will go on to describe about the other body T areas proportional to the times. And therefore (by Theor. 2) the difference of the forces is directed to the other body T as its centre.   Q.E.D.

Cor. I. Hence if the one body L, by a radius drawn to the other body T, describes areas proportional to the times; and from the whole force, by which the first body L is urged (whether that force is simple, or, according to Cor. II of the Laws, compounded out of several forces), we subtract (by the same Cor.) that whole accelerative force by which the other body is urged; the whole remaining force by which the first body is urged will tend to the other body T, as its centre.

Cor. II. And, if these areas are proportional to the times nearly, the remaining force will tend to the other body T nearly.

Cor. III. And *vice versa*, if the remaining force tends nearly to the other body T, those areas will be nearly proportional to the times.

Cor. IV. If the body L, by a radius drawn to the other body T, describes areas, which, compared with the times, are very unequal; and that other body T be either at rest, or moves uniformly forwards in a right line: the action of the centripetal force tending to that other body T is either none at all, or it is mixed and compounded with very powerful actions of other forces: and the whole force compounded of them all, if they are many, is directed to another (immovable or movable) centre. The same thing obtains, when the other body is moved by any motion whatsoever; provided that centripetal force is taken, which remains after subtracting that whole force acting upon that other body T.

SCHOLIUM

Since the equable description of areas indicates that there is a centre to which tends that force by which the body is most affected, and by which it is drawn back from its rectilinear motion, and retained in its orbit, why may we not be allowed, in the following discourse, to use the equable description of areas as an indication of a centre, about which all circular motion is performed in free spaces?

PROPOSITION 4. THEOREM 4

The centripetal forces of bodies, which by equable motions describe different circles, tend to the centres of the same circles; and are to each other as the squares of the arcs described in equal times divided respectively by the radii of the circles.

These forces tend to the centres of the circles (by Prop. 2, and Cor. II, Prop. 1), and are to one another as the versed sines of the least arcs described in equal times (by Cor. IV, Prop. 1); that is, as the squares of the same arcs divided by the diameters of the circles (by Lem. 7); and therefore since those arcs are as arcs described in any equal times, and the diameters are as the radii, the forces will be as the squares of any arcs described in the same time divided by the radii of the circles.   Q.E.D.

COR. I. Therefore, since those arcs are as the velocities of the bodies, the centripetal forces are as the squares of the velocities divided by the radii.

COR. II. And since the periodic times are as the radii divided by the velocities, the centripetal forces are as the radii divided by the square of the periodic times.

COR. III. Whence if the periodic times are equal, and the velocities therefore as the radii, the centripetal forces will be also as the radii; and conversely.

COR. IV. If the periodic times and the velocities are both as the square roots of the radii, the centripetal forces will be equal among themselves; and conversely.

COR. V. If the periodic times are as the radii, and therefore the velocities equal, the centripetal forces will be inversely as the radii; and conversely.

COR. VI. If the periodic times are as the $\frac{3}{2}$th powers of the radii, and therefore the velocities inversely as the square roots of the radii, the centripetal forces will be inversely as the squares of the radii; and conversely.

COR. VII. And universally, if the periodic time is as any power R^n of the radius R, and therefore the velocity inversely as the power R^{n-1} of the radius, the centripetal force will be inversely as the power R^{2n-1} of the radius; and conversely.

COR. VIII. The same things hold concerning the times, the velocities, and the forces by which bodies describe the similar parts of any similar figures that have their centres in a similar position with those figures; as appears by applying the demonstration of the preceding cases to those. And the application is easy, by only substituting the equable description of areas in the place of equable motion, and using the distances of the bodies from the centres instead of the radii.

COR. IX. From the same demonstration it likewise follows, that the arc which a body, uniformly revolving in a circle with a given centripetal force, describes in any time, is a mean proportional between the diameter of the circle, and the space which the same body falling by the same given force would describe in the same given time.

SCHOLIUM

The case of the sixth Corollary obtains in the celestial bodies (as Sir Christopher Wren, Dr. Hooke, and Dr. Halley have severally observed); and therefore in what follows, I intend to treat more at large of those things which relate to centripetal force decreasing as the squares of the distances from the centres.

Moreover, by means of the preceding Proposition and its Corollaries, we may discover the proportion of a centripetal force to any other known force, such as that of gravity. For if a body by means of its gravity revolves in a circle concentric to the earth, this gravity is the centripetal force of that body. But from the descent of heavy bodies, the time of one entire revolution, as well as the arc described in any given time, is given (by Cor. IX of this Prop.). And by such propositions, Mr. Huygens, in his excellent book *De horologio oscillatorio*, has compared the force of gravity with the centrifugal forces of revolving bodies.

The preceding Proposition may be likewise demonstrated after this manner. In any circle suppose a polygon to be inscribed of any number of sides. And if a body, moved with a given velocity along the sides of the polygon, is reflected from the circle at the several angular points, the force, with which at every reflection it strikes the circle, will be as its velocity: and therefore the sum of the forces, in a given time, will be as the product of that velocity and the number of reflections; that is (if the species of the polygon be given), as the length described in that given time, and increased or diminished in the ratio of the same length to the radius of the circle; that is, as the square of that length divided by the radius; and therefore the polygon, by having its sides diminished *in infinitum*, coincides with the circle, as the square of the arc described in a given time divided by the radius. This is the centrifugal force, with which the body impels the circle; and to which the contrary force, wherewith the circle continually repels the body towards the centre, is equal.

PROPOSITION 5. PROBLEM 1

There being given, in any places, the velocity with which a body describes a given figure, by means of forces directed to some common centre: to find that centre.

Let the three right lines PT, TQV, VR touch the figure described in as many points, P, Q, R, and meet in T and V. On the tangents erect the perpendiculars

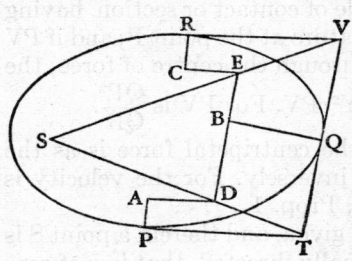

PA, QB, RC, inversely proportional to the velocities of the body in the points P, Q, R, from which the perpendiculars were raised; that is, so that PA may be to QB as the velocity in Q to the velocity in P, and QB to RC as the velocity in R to the velocity in Q. Through the ends A, B, C of the perpendiculars draw AD, DBE, EC, at right angles, meeting in D and E: and the right lines TD, VE produced, will meet in S, the centre required.

For the perpendiculars let fall from the centre S on the tangents PT, QT, are inversely as the velocities of the bodies in the points P and Q (by Cor. I, Prop. 1), and therefore, by construction, directly as the perpendiculars AP, BQ; that is, as the perpendiculars let fall from the point D on the tangents. Whence it is easy to infer that the points S, D, T are in one right line. And by the like argument the points S, E, V are also in one right line; and therefore the centre S is in the point where the right lines TD, VE meet.   Q.E.D.

PROPOSITION 6. THEOREM 5

In a space void of resistance, if a body revolves in any orbit about an immovable centre, and in the least time describes any arc just then nascent; and the versed sine of that arc is supposed to be drawn bisecting the chord, and produced passing through the centre of force: the centripetal force in the middle of the arc will be directly as the versed sine and inversely as the square of the time.

For the versed sine in a given time is as the force (by Cor. IV, Prop. 1); and augmenting the time in any ratio, because the arc will be augmented in the same ratio, the versed sine will be augmented in the square of that ratio (by Cor. II and III, Lem. 11), and therefore is as the force and the square of the time. Divide both sides by the square of the time, and the force will be directly as the versed sine, and inversely as the square of the time.   Q.E.D.

And the same thing may also be easily demonstrated by Cor. IV, Lem. 10.

Cor. I. If a body P revolving about the centre S describes a curved line APQ, which a right line ZPR touches in any point P; and from any other point Q of the curve, QR is drawn parallel to the distance SP, meeting the tangent in R; and QT is drawn perpendicular to the distance SP; the centripetal force will be inversely as the solid $\dfrac{SP^2 \cdot QT^2}{QR}$, if the solid be taken

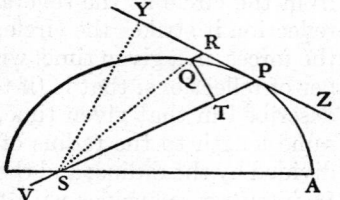

of that magnitude which it ultimately acquires when the points P and Q coincide. For QR is equal to the versed sine of double the arc QP, whose middle is P: and double the triangle SQP, or SP·QT is proportional to the time in which that double arc is described; and therefore may be used to represent the time.

Cor. II. By a like reasoning, the centripetal force is inversely as the solid $\dfrac{SY^2 \cdot QP^2}{QR}$; if SY is a perpendicular from the centre of force on PR, the tangent of the orbit. For the rectangles SY·QP and SP·QT are equal.

Cor. III. If the orbit is either a circle, or touches or cuts a circle concentrically, that is, contains with a circle the least angle of contact or section, having the same curvature and the same radius of curvature at the point P; and if PV be a chord of this circle, drawn from the body through the centre of force; the centripetal force will be inversely as the solid $SY^2 \cdot PV$. For PV is $\dfrac{QP^2}{QR}$.

Cor. IV. The same things being supposed, the centripetal force is as the square of the velocity directly, and the chord inversely. For the velocity is reciprocally as the perpendicular SY, by Cor. I, Prop. 1.

Cor. V. Hence if any curvilinear figure APQ is given, and therein a point S is also given, to which a centripetal force is continually directed, that law of centripetal force may be found, by which the body P will be continually drawn back from a rectilinear course, and, being detained in the perimeter of that figure, will describe the same by a continual revolution. That is, we are to find, by computation, either the solid $\dfrac{SP^2 \cdot QT^2}{QR}$ or the solid $SY^2 \cdot PV$, inversely proportional to this force. Examples of this we shall give in the following Problems.

Proposition 7. Problem 2

If a body revolves in the circumference of a circle, it is proposed to find the law of centripetal force directed to any given point.

Let VQPA be the circumference of the circle; S the given point to which as to a centre the force tends; P the body moving in the circumference; Q the next place into which it is to move; and PRZ the tangent of the circle at the preceding place. Through the point S draw the chord PV, and the diameter VA of the circle; join AP, and draw QT perpendicular to SP, which produced, may meet the tangent PR in Z; and lastly, through the point Q, draw LR parallel to SP, meeting the circle in L, and the tangent PZ in R. And, because of the similar triangles ZQR, ZTP, VPA, we shall have

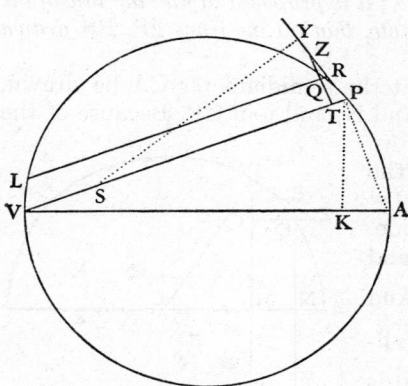

$$RP^2 : QT^2 = AV^2 : PV^2.$$

Since $RP^2 = RL \cdot QR$, $QT^2 = \dfrac{RL \cdot QR \cdot PV^2}{AV^2}$.

Multiply those equals by $\dfrac{SP^2}{QR}$, and the points P and Q coinciding, for RL write PV; then we shall have

$$\frac{SP^2 \cdot PV^3}{AV^2} = \frac{SP^2 \cdot QT^2}{QR}.$$

And therefore (by Cor. i and v, Prop. 6) the centripetal force is inversely as $\dfrac{SP^2 \cdot PV^3}{AV^2}$; that is (because AV^2 is given), inversely as the product of SP^2 and PV^3.

Q.E.I.

The same otherwise.

On the tangent PR produced let fall the perpendicular SY; and (because of the similar triangles SYP, VPA) we shall have AV to PV as SP to SY, and therefore $\dfrac{SP \cdot PV}{AV} = SY$, and $\dfrac{SP^2 \cdot PV^3}{AV^2} = SY^2 \cdot PV$. And therefore (by Cor. iii and v, Prop. 6) the centripetal force is inversely as $\dfrac{SP^2 \cdot PV^3}{AV^2}$; that is (because AV is given), inversely as $SP^2 \cdot PV^3$.

Q.E.I.

Cor. i. Hence if the given point S, to which the centripetal force always tends, is placed in the circumference of the circle, as at V, the centripetal force will be inversely as the fifth power of the altitude SP.

Cor. ii. The force by which the body P in the circle APTV revolves about the centre of force S is to the force by which the same body P may revolve in the same circle, and in the same periodic time, about any other centre of force R, as $RP^2 \cdot SP$ to the cube of the right line SG, which from the first centre of force S is drawn parallel to the distance PR of the body from the second centre of force R, meeting the tangent PG of the orbit in G. For by the construction of this Proposition, the former force is to the latter as $RP^2 \cdot PT^3$ to $SP^2 \cdot PV^3$; that

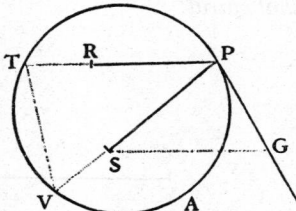

is, as $SP \cdot RP^2$ to $\dfrac{SP^3 \cdot PV^3}{PT^3}$; or (because of the similar triangles PSG, TPV) to SG^3.

Cor. iii. The force by which the body P in any orbit revolves about the centre of force S, is to the force by which the same body may revolve in the same orbit, and the same periodic time, about any other centre of force R, as the solid $SP \cdot RP^2$, contained under the distance of the body from the first centre of force S, and the square of its distance from the second centre of force R, to the cube of the right line SG, drawn from the first centre of the force S, parallel to the distance RP of the body from the second centre of force R, meeting the tangent PG of the orbit in G. For the force in this orbit at any point P is the same as in a circle of the same curvature.

PROPOSITION 8. PROBLEM 3

If a body moves in the semicircumference PQA; *it is proposed to find the law of the centripetal force tending to a point* S, *so remote, that all the lines* PS, RS *drawn thereto, may be taken for parallels.*

From C, the centre of the semicircle, let the semidiameter CA be drawn, cutting the parallels at right angles in M and N, and join CP. Because of the similar triangles CPM, PZT, and RZQ, we shall have $CP^2 : PM^2 = PR^2 : QT^2$. From the nature of the circle, $PR^2 = QR(RN+QN) = QR \cdot 2PM$, when the points P and Q coincide. Therefore $CP^2 : PM^2 = QR \cdot 2PM : QT^2$; and $\dfrac{QT^2}{QR} = \dfrac{2PM^3}{CP^2}$, and $\dfrac{QT^2 \cdot SP^2}{QR} = \dfrac{2PM^3 \cdot SP^2}{CP^2}$. And

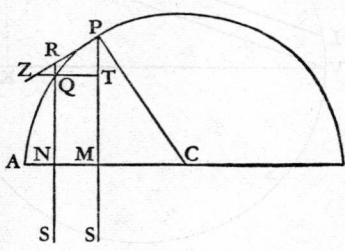

therefore (by Cor. I and V, Prop. 6) the centripetal force is inversely as $\dfrac{2PM^3 \cdot SP^2}{CP^2}$; that is

(neglecting the given ratio $\dfrac{2SP^2}{CP^2}$), inversely as PM^3.   Q.E.I.

And the same thing is likewise easily inferred from the preceding Proposition.

SCHOLIUM

And by a like reasoning, a body will be moved in an ellipse, or even in an hyperbola, or parabola, by a centripetal force which is inversely as the cube of the ordinate directed to an infinitely remote centre of force.

PROPOSITION 9. PROBLEM 4

If a body revolves in a spiral PQS, *cutting all the radii* SP, SQ, &c., *in a given angle; it is proposed to find the law of the centripetal force tending to the centre of that spiral.*

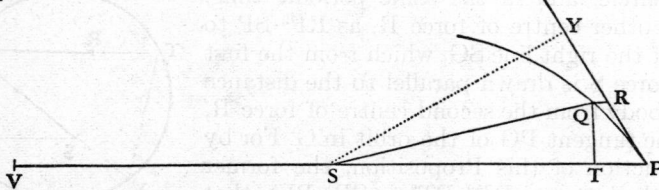

Suppose the indefinitely small angle PSQ to be given; because, then, all the angles are given, the figure SPRQT will be given in kind. Therefore the ratio $\dfrac{QT}{QR}$ is also given, and $\dfrac{QT^2}{QR}$ is as QT, that is (because the figure is given in kind), as SP. But if the angle PSQ is any way changed, the right line QR, subtending the angle of contact QPR (by Lem. 11) will be changed in the ratio of PR^2 or QT^2. Therefore the ratio $\dfrac{QT^2}{QR}$ remains the same as before, that is, as SP. And $\dfrac{QT^2 \cdot SP^2}{QR}$ is as SP^3, and therefore (by Cor. I and V, Prop. 6) the centripetal force is inversely as the cube of the distance SP.   Q.E.I.

The same otherwise.

The perpendicular SY let fall upon the tangent, and the chord PV of the circle concentrically cutting the spiral, are in given ratios to the height SP; and therefore SP³ is as SY²·PV, that is (by Cor. III and V, Prop. 6) inversely as the centripetal force.

LEMMA 12

All parallelograms circumscribed about any conjugate diameters of a given ellipse or hyperbola are equal among themselves.

This is demonstrated by the writers on the conic sections.

PROPOSITION 10. PROBLEM 5

If a body revolves in an ellipse; it is proposed to find the law of the centripetal force tending to the centre of the ellipse.

Suppose CA, CB to be semiaxes of the ellipse; GP, DK, conjugate diameters; PF, QT, perpendiculars to those diameters; Qv, an ordinate to the diam-

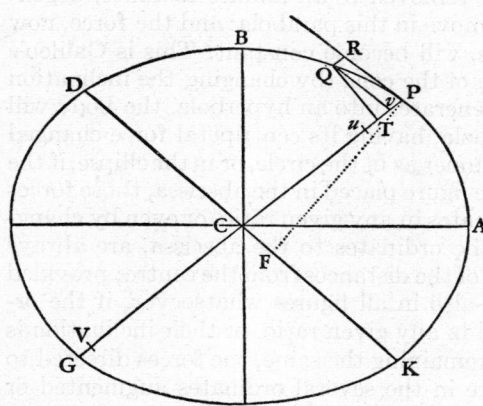

eter GP; and if the parallelogram QvPR be completed, then (by the properties of the conic sections) $Pv \cdot vG : Qv^2 = PC^2 : CD^2$, and, because of the similar triangles QvT, PCF, $Qv^2 : QT^2 = PC^2 : PF^2$; and by eliminating Qv^2, $vG : \dfrac{QT^2}{Pv} = PC^2 : \dfrac{CD^2 \cdot PF^2}{PC^2}$. Since QR = Pv, and (by Lem. 12) BC·CA = CD·PF, and, when the points P and Q coincide, 2PC = vG, we shall have, multiplying the extremes and means together, $\dfrac{QT^2 \cdot PC^2}{QR} =$ $\dfrac{2BC^2 \cdot CA^2}{PC}$. Therefore (by Cor. V, Prop. 6), the centripetal force is inversely as $\dfrac{2BC^2 \cdot CA^2}{PC}$; that is (because 2BC²·CA² is given), inversely as $\dfrac{1}{PC}$; that is, directly as the distance PC.   Q.E.I.

The same otherwise.

In the right line PG on the other side of the point T, take the point u so that Tu may be equal to Tv; then take uV, such that uV : vG = DC² : PC². Since, by the conic sections, $Qv^2 : Pv \cdot vG = DC^2 : PC^2$, we have $Qv^2 = Pv \cdot uV$. Add Pu·Pv to both sides, and the square of the chord of the arc PQ will be equal to the rectangle PV·Pv; and therefore a circle which touches the conic section in P, and passes through the point Q, will pass also through the point V. Now let the points P and Q meet, and the ratio of uV to vG, which is the same with the ratio of DC² to PC², will become the ratio of PV to PG, or PV to 2PC; and therefore PV will be equal to $\dfrac{2DC^2}{PC}$. And therefore the force by which the body P revolves in the ellipse will be inversely as $\dfrac{2DC^2}{PC} \cdot PF^2$ (by Cor. III, Prop. 6); that is (because 2DC²·PF² is given), directly as PC.   Q.E.I.

COR. I. And therefore the force is as the distance of the body from the centre of the ellipse; and, *vice versa*, if the force is as the distance, the body will move in an ellipse whose centre coincides with the centre of force, or perhaps in a circle into which the ellipse may degenerate.

COR. II. And the periodic times of the revolutions made in all ellipses whatsoever about the same centre will be equal. For those times in similar ellipses will be equal (by Cor. III and VIII, Prop. 4); but in ellipses that have their greater axis common, they are to each other as the whole areas of the ellipses directly, and the parts of the areas described in the same time inversely; that is, as the lesser axes directly, and the velocities of the bodies in their principal vertices inversely; that is, as those lesser axes directly, and the ordinates to the same point of the common axes inversely; and therefore (because of the equality of the direct and inverse ratios) in the ratio of equality, 1 : 1.

SCHOLIUM

If the ellipse, by having its centre removed to an infinite distance, degenerates into a parabola, the body will move in this parabola; and the force, now tending to a centre infinitely remote, will become constant. This is Galileo's theorem. And if the parabolic section of the cone (by changing the inclination of the cutting plane to the cone) degenerates into an hyperbola, the body will move in the perimeter of this hyperbola, having its centripetal force changed into a centrifugal force. And in like manner as in the circle, or in the ellipse, if the forces are directed to the centre of the figure placed in the abscissa, those forces by increasing or diminishing the ordinates in any given ratio, or even by changing the angle of the inclination of the ordinates to the abscissa, are always augmented or diminished in the ratio of the distances from the centre; provided the periodic times remain equal; so also in all figures whatsoever, if the ordinates are augmented or diminished in any given ratio, or their inclination is any way changed, the periodic time remaining the same, the forces directed to any centre placed in the abscissa are in the several ordinates augmented or diminished in the ratio of the distances from the centre.

SECTION III

THE MOTION OF BODIES IN ECCENTRIC CONIC SECTIONS

PROPOSITION 11. PROBLEM 6

If a body revolves in an ellipse; it is required to find the law of the centripetal force tending to the focus of the ellipse.

Let S be the focus of the ellipse. Draw SP cutting the diameter DK of the ellipse in E, and the ordinate Qv in x; and complete the parallelogram QxPR. It is evident that EP is equal to the greater semiaxis AC: for drawing HI from the other focus H of the ellipse parallel to EC, because CS, CH are equal, ES, EI will also be equal; so that EP is the half-sum of PS, PI, that is (because of the parallels HI, PR, and the equal angles IPR, HPZ), of PS, PH, which taken together are equal to the whole axis 2AC. Draw QT perpendicular to SP, and putting L for the principal latus rectum of the ellipse (or for $\frac{2BC^2}{AC}$), we shall have

L·QR : L·Pv = QR : Pv = PE : PC = AC : PC,

also, L·Pv : Gv·Pv = L : Gv, and, Gv·Pv : Qv^2 = PC^2 : CD^2.

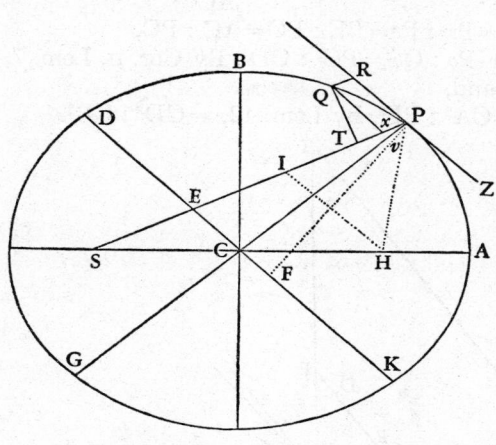

By Cor. II, Lem. 7, when the points P and Q coincide, Qv^2 = Qx^2, and Qx^2 or Qv^2 : QT^2 = EP^2 : PF^2 = CA^2 : PF^2, and (by Lem. 12) = CD^2 : CB^2. Multiplying together corresponding terms of the four proportions, and simplifying, we shall have L·QR : QT^2 = AC·L· PC^2·CD^2 : PC·Gv·CD^2·CB^2 = 2PC : Gv, since AC·L = 2BC^2. But the points Q and P coinciding, 2PC and Gv are equal. And therefore the quantities L·QR and QT^2, proportional to these, will be also equal. Let those equals be multiplied by $\dfrac{SP^2}{QR}$, and L·SP^2 will be-

come equal to $\dfrac{SP^2 \cdot QT^2}{QR}$. And therefore (by Cor. I and V, Prop. 6) the centripetal force is inversely as L·SP^2, that is, inversely as the square of the distance SP.   Q.E.I.

The same otherwise.

Since the force tending to the centre of the ellipse, by which the body P may revolve in that ellipse, is (by Cor. I, Prop. 10) as the distance CP of the body from the centre C of the ellipse, let CE be drawn parallel to the tangent PR of the ellipse; and the force by which the same body P may revolve about any other point S of the ellipse, if CE and PS intersect in E, will be as $\dfrac{PE^3}{SP^2}$ (by Cor. III, Prop. 7); that is, if the point S is the focus of the ellipse, and therefore PE be given as SP^2 reciprocally.   Q.E.I.

With the same brevity with which we reduced the fifth Problem to the parabola, and hyperbola, we might do the like here; but because of the dignity of the Problem and its use in what follows, I shall confirm the other cases by particular demonstrations.

PROPOSITION 12. PROBLEM 7

Suppose a body to move in an hyperbola; it is required to find the law of the centripetal force tending to the focus of that figure.

Let CA, CB be the semiaxes of the hyperbola; PG, KD other conjugate diameters; PF a perpendicular to the diameter KD; and Qv an ordinate to the diameter GP. Draw SP cutting the diameter DK in E, and the ordinate Qv in x, and complete the parallelogram QRPx. It is evident that EP is equal to the semitransverse axis AC; for drawing HI, from the other focus H of the hyperbola, parallel to EC, because CS, CH are equal, ES, EI will be also equal; so that EP is the half difference of PS, PI; that is (because of the parallels IH, PR, and the equal angles IPR, HPZ), of PS, PH, the difference of which is equal to the whole axis 2AC. Draw QT perpendicular to SP; and putting L for the principal latus rectum of the hyperbola (that is, for $\dfrac{2BC^2}{AC}$), we shall have

$$L \cdot QR : L \cdot Pv = QR : Pv = Px : Pv = PE : PC = AC : PC,$$

also, $L \cdot Pv : Gv \cdot Pv = L : Gv$, and $Gv \cdot Pv : Qv^2 = PC^2 : CD^2$. By Cor. II, Lem. 7, when P and Q coincide, $Qx^2 = Qv^2$, and,

$$Qx^2 \text{ or } Qv^2 : QT^2 = EP^2 : PF^2 = CA^2 : PF^2, \text{ by Lem. 12, } = CD^2 : CB^2.$$

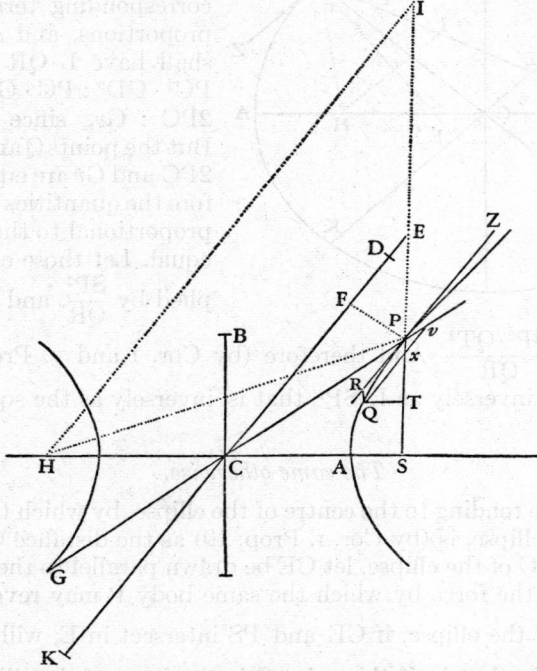

Multiplying together corresponding terms of the four proportions, and simplifying,

$$L \cdot QR : QT^2 = AC \cdot L \cdot PC^2 \cdot CD^2 : PC \cdot Gv \cdot CD^2 \cdot CB^2 = 2PC : Gv,$$

since $AC \cdot L = 2BC^2$. But the points P and Q coinciding, 2PC and Gv are equal. And therefore the quantities $L \cdot QR$ and QT^2, proportional to them, will also be equal. Let those equals be drawn into $\dfrac{SP^2}{QR}$, and we shall have $L \cdot SP^2$ equal to $\dfrac{SP^2 \cdot QT^2}{QR}$. And therefore (by Cor. I and V, Prop. 6) the centripetal force is inversely as $L \cdot SP^2$, that is, inversely as the square of the distance SP. Q.E.I.

The same otherwise.

Find out the force tending from the centre C of the hyperbola. This will be proportional to the distance CP. But from thence (by Cor. III, Prop. 7) the force tending to the focus S will be as $\dfrac{PE^3}{SP^2}$, that is, because PE is given reciprocally as SP^2. Q.E.I.

And the same way may it be demonstrated, that the body having its centripetal changed into a centrifugal force, will move in the conjugate hyperbola.

LEMMA 13

The latus rectum of a parabola belonging to any vertex is four times the distance of that vertex from the focus of the figure.

This is demonstrated by the writers on the conic sections.

LEMMA 14

The perpendicular, let fall from the focus of a parabola on its tangent, is a mean proportional between the distances of the focus from the point of contact, and from the principal vertex of the figure.

For, let AP be the parabola, S its focus, A its principal vertex, P the point of contact, PO an ordinate to the principal diameter, PM the tangent meeting the

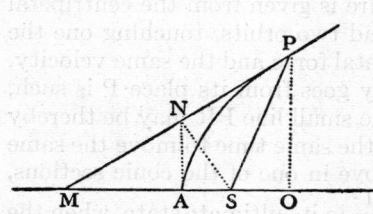

principal diameter in M, and SN the perpendicular from the focus on the tangent: join AN, and because of the equal lines MS and SP, MN and NP, MA and AO, the right lines AN, OP will be parallel; and thence the triangle SAN will be right-angled at A, and similar to the equal triangles SNM, SNP; therefore PS is to SN as SN is to SA.   Q.E.D.

COR. I. PS² is to SN² as PS is to SA.

COR. II. And because SA is given, SN² will vary as PS.

COR. III. And the intersection of any tangent PM, with the right line SN, drawn from the focus perpendicular on the tangent, falls in the right line AN that touches the parabola in the principal vertex.

PROPOSITION 13. PROBLEM 8

If a body moves in the perimeter of a parabola; it is required to find the law of the centripetal force tending to the focus of that figure.

Retaining the construction of the preceding Lemma, let P be the body in the perimeter of the parabola; and from the place Q, into which it is next to succeed, draw QR parallel and QT perpendicular to SP, as also Qv parallel to the tangent, and meeting the diameter PG in v, and the distance SP in x. Now because of the similar triangles Pxv, SPM, and of the equal sides SP, SM of the one, the sides Px or QR and Pv of the other will be also equal. But (by the conic sections) the square of the ordinate Qv is equal to the rectangle under the latus rectum

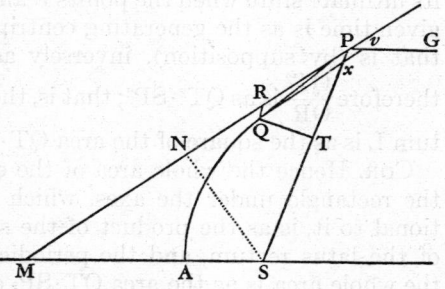

and the segment Pv of the diameter; that is (by Lem. 13), to the rectangle 4PS·Pv, or 4PS·QR; and the points P and Q coinciding, (by Cor. II, Lem. 7), Qx = Qv. And therefore Qx², in this case, becomes equal to the rectangle 4PS·QR. But (because of the similar triangles QxT, SPN),

$$Qx^2 : QT^2 = PS^2 : SN^2 = PS : SA \text{ (by Cor. I, Lem. 14)},$$
$$= 4PS \cdot QR : 4SA \cdot QR.$$

Therefore (by Prop. 9, Book v, *Elements of* Euclid), $QT^2 = 4SA \cdot QR$. Multiply these equals by $\dfrac{SP^2}{QR}$, and $\dfrac{SP^2 \cdot QT^2}{QR}$ will become equal to $SP^2 \cdot 4SA$: and therefore (by Cor. I and v, Prop. 6), the centripetal force is inversely as $SP^2 \cdot 4SA$; that is, because $4SA$ is given, inversely as the square of the distance SP.   Q.E.I.

COR. I. From the three last Propositions it follows, that if any body P goes from the place P with any velocity in the direction of any right line PR, and at the same time is urged by the action of a centripetal force that is inversely proportional to the square of the distance of the places from the centre, the body will move in one of the conic sections, having its focus in the centre of force; and conversely. For the focus, the point of contact, and the position of the tangent, being given, a conic section may be described, which at that point shall have a given curvature. But the curvature is given from the centripetal force and velocity of the body being given; and two orbits, touching one the other, cannot be described by the same centripetal force and the same velocity.

COR. II. If the velocity with which the body goes from its place P is such, that in any infinitely small moment of time the small line PR may be thereby described; and the centripetal force such as in the same time to move the same body through the space QR; the body will move in one of the conic sections, whose principal latus rectum is the quantity $\dfrac{QT^2}{QR}$ in its ultimate state, when the small lines PR, QR are diminished *in infinitum*. In these Corollaries I consider the circle as an ellipse; and I except the case where the body descends to the centre in a right line.

PROPOSITION 14. THEOREM 6

If several bodies revolve about one common centre, and the centripetal force is inversely as the square of the distance of places from the centre: I say, that the principal latera recta of their orbits are as the squares of the areas, which the bodies by radii drawn to the centre describe in the same time.

For (by Cor. II, Prop. 13) the latus rectum L is equal to the quantity $\dfrac{QT^2}{QR}$ in its ultimate state when the points P and Q coincide. But the small line QR in a given time is as the generating centripetal force; that is (by supposition), inversely as SP^2. and therefore $\dfrac{QT^2}{QR}$ is as $QT^2 \cdot SP^2$; that is, the latus rectum L is as the square of the area $QT \cdot SP$.   Q.E.D.

COR. Hence the whole area of the ellipse, and the rectangle under the axes, which is proportional to it, is as the product of the square root of the latus rectum, and the periodic time. For the whole area is as the area $QT \cdot SP$, described in a given time, multiplied by the periodic time.

PROPOSITION 15. THEOREM 7

The same things being supposed, I say, that the periodic times in ellipses are as the ³⁄₂th power (in ratione sesquiplicata) of their greater axes.

For the lesser axis is a mean proportional between the greater axis and the latus rectum; and, therefore, the product of the axes is equal to the product of the square root of the latus rectum and the $\frac{3}{2}$th power of the greater axis. But the product of the axes (by Cor., Prop. 14) varies as the product of the square root of the latus rectum, and the periodic time. Divide both sides by the square root of the latus rectum and it follows that the $\frac{3}{2}$th power of the greater axis varies as the periodic time.   Q.E.D.

Cor. Therefore the periodic times in ellipses are the same as in circles whose diameters are equal to the greater axes of the ellipses.

Proposition 16. Theorem 8

The same things being supposed, and right lines being drawn to the bodies that shall touch the orbits, and perpendiculars being let fall on those tangents from the common focus: I say, that the velocities of the bodies vary inversely as the perpendiculars and directly as the square roots of the principal latera recta.

From the focus S draw SY perpendicular to the tangent PR, and the velocity of the body P varies inversely as the square root of the quantity $\frac{SY^2}{L}$. For that velocity is as the infinitely small arc PQ described in a given moment of time,

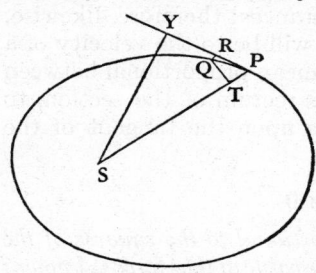

that is (by Lem. 7), as the tangent PR; that is (because of the proportion, PR : QT = SP : SY), as $\frac{SP \cdot QT}{SY}$; or inversely as SY, and directly as SP·QT; but SP·QT is as the area described in the given time, that is (by Prop. 14), as the square root of the latus rectum.   Q.E.D.

Cor. i. The principal latera recta vary as the squares of the perpendiculars and the squares of the velocities.

Cor. ii. The velocities of bodies, in their greatest and least distances from the common focus, are inversely as the distances and directly as the square root of the principal latera recta. For those perpendiculars are now the distances.

Cor. iii. And therefore the velocity in a conic section, at its greatest or least distance from the focus, is to the velocity in a circle, at the same distance from the centre, as the square root of the principal latus rectum is to the square root of double that distance.

Cor. iv. The velocities of the bodies revolving in ellipses, at their mean distances from the common focus, are the same as those of bodies revolving in circles, at the same distances; that is (by Cor. vi, Prop. 4), inversely as the square root of the distances. For the perpendiculars are now the lesser semi-axes, and these are as mean proportionals between the distances and the latera recta. Let the inverse of this ratio [of the minor semiaxes] be multiplied by the square root of the direct ratio of the latera recta, and we shall have the square root of the inverse ratio of the distances.

Cor. v. In the same figure, or even in different figures, whose principal latera recta are equal, the velocity of a body is inversely as the perpendicular let fall from the focus on the tangent.

Cor. vi. In a parabola, the velocity is inversely as the square root of the ratio of the distance of the body from the focus of the figure; it is more variable in the ellipse, and less in the hyperbola, than according to this ratio. For (by Cor. ii, Lem. 14) the perpendicular let fall from the focus on the tangent of a parabola is as the square root of the distance. In the hyperbola the perpendicular is less variable; in the ellipse, more.

Cor. VII. In a parabola, the velocity of a body at any distance from the focus is to the velocity of a body revolving in a circle, at the same distance from the centre, as the square root of the ratio of the number 2 to 1; in the ellipse it is less, and in the hyperbola greater, than according to this ratio. For (by Cor. II of this Prop.) the velocity at the vertex of a parabola is in this ratio, and (by Cor. VI of this Prop. and Prop. 4) the same proportion holds in all distances. And hence, also, in a parabola, the velocity is everywhere equal to the velocity of a body revolving in a circle at half the distance; in the ellipse it is less, and in the hyperbola greater.

Cor. VIII. The velocity of a body revolving in any conic section is to the velocity of a body revolving in a circle, at the distance of half the principal latus rectum of the section, as that distance to the perpendicular let fall from the focus on the tangent of the section. This appears from Cor. V.

Cor. IX. Wherefore, since (by Cor. VI, Prop. 4) the velocity of a body revolving in this circle is to the velocity of another body revolving in any other circle, inversely as the square root of the ratio of the distances; therefore, likewise, the velocity of a body revolving in a conic section will be to the velocity of a body revolving in a circle at the same distance as a mean proportional between that common distance, and half the principal latus rectum of the section, to the perpendicular let fall from the common focus upon the tangent of the section.

PROPOSITION 17. PROBLEM 9

Supposing the centripetal force to be inversely proportional to the squares of the distances of places from the centre, and that the absolute value of that force is known; it is required to determine the line which a body will describe that is let go from a given place with a given velocity in the direction of a given right line.

Let the centripetal force tending to the point S be such as will make the body p revolve in any given orbit pq; and suppose the velocity of this body in the

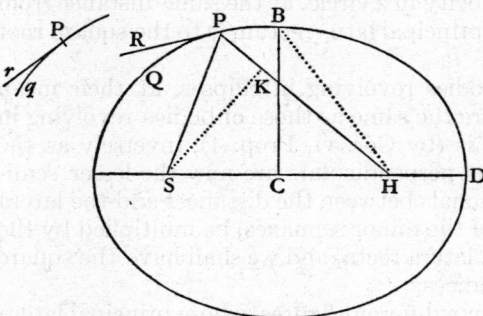

place p is known. Then from the place P suppose the body P to be let go with a given velocity in the direction of the line PR; but by virtue of a centripetal force to be immediately turned aside from that right line into the conic section PQ. This, the right line PR will therefore touch in P. Suppose likewise that the right line pr touches the orbit pq in p; and if from S you suppose perpendiculars let fall on those tangents, the principal latus rectum of the conic section (by Cor. I, Prop. 16) will be to the principal latus rectum of that orbit in a ratio compounded of the squared ratio of the perpendiculars, and the squared ratio of the velocities; and is therefore given. Let this latus rectum be L; the focus S of the conic section is also given. Let the angle RPH be the supplement of the angle RPS, and the line PH, in which the other focus H is placed, is given by position. Let fall SK perpendicular on PH, and erect the conjugate semiaxis BC; this done, we shall have

$$SP^2 - 2PH \cdot PK + PH^2 = SH^2 = 4CH^2 = 4(BH^2 - BC^2) =$$
$$(SP + PH)^2 - L(SP + PH) = SP^2 + 2PS \cdot PH + PH^2 - L(SP + PH).$$

Add on both sides

$$2PK \cdot PH - SP^2 - PH^2 + L(SP + PH),$$

and we shall have

$$L(SP + PH) = 2PS \cdot PH + 2PK \cdot PH, \text{ or}$$
$$(SP + PH) : PH = 2 (SP + KP) : L.$$

Hence PH is given both in length and position. That is, if the velocity of the body in P is such that the latus rectum L is less than $2SP + 2KP$, PH will lie on the same side of the tangent PR with the line SP; and therefore the figure will be an ellipse, which from the given foci S, H, and the principal axis $SP + PH$, is given also. But if the velocity of the body is so great, that the latus rectum L becomes equal to $2SP + 2KP$, the length PH will be infinite; and therefore, the figure will be a parabola, which has its axis SH parallel to the line PK, and is thence given. But if the body goes from its place P with a yet greater velocity, the length PH is to be taken on the other side the tangent; and so the tangent passing between the foci, the figure will be an hyperbola having its principal axis equal to the difference of the lines SP and PH, and thence is given. For if the body, in these cases, revolves in a conic section so found, it is demonstrated in Props. 11, 12, and 13, that the centripetal force will be inversely as the square of the distance of the body from the centre of force S; and therefore we have rightly determined the line PQ, which a body let go from a given place P with a given velocity, and in the direction of the right line PR given by position, would describe with such a force.   Q.E.F.

COR. I. Hence in every conic section, from the principal vertex D, the latus rectum L, and the focus S given, the other focus H is given, by taking DH to DS as the latus rectum to the difference between the latus rectum and 4DS. For the proportion

$$SP + PH : PH = 2SP + 2KP : L$$

becomes, in the case of this Corollary,

$$DS + DH : DH = 4DS : L,$$
$$\text{and } DS : DH = 4DS - L : L.$$

COR. II. Whence if the velocity of a body in the principal vertex D is given, the orbit may be readily found; namely, by taking its latus rectum to twice the distance DS, in the squared ratio of this given velocity to the velocity of a body revolving in a circle at the distance DS (by Cor. III, Prop. 16), and then taking DH to DS as the latus rectum to the difference between the latus rectum and 4DS.

COR. III. Hence also if a body move in any conic section, and if forced out of its orbit by any impulse, you may discover the orbit in which it will afterwards pursue its course. For by compounding the proper motion of the body with that motion, which the impulse alone would generate, you will have the motion with which the body will go off from a given place of impulse in the direction of a right line given in position.

COR. IV. And if that body is continually disturbed by the action of some foreign force, we may nearly know its course, by collecting the changes which that force introduces in some points, and estimating the continual changes it will undergo in the intermediate places, from the analogy that appears in the progress of the series.

If a body P, by means of a centripetal force tending to any given point R, move in the perimeter of any given conic section whose centre is C; and the law of the centripetal force is required: draw CG parallel to the radius RP, and meeting the tangent PG of the orbit in G; and the force required (by Cor. I and Schol., Prop. 10, and Cor. III, Prop. 7) will be as $\frac{CG^3}{RP^2}$.

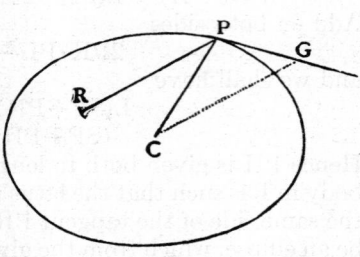

SECTION IV

THE FINDING OF ELLIPTIC, PARABOLIC, AND HYPERBOLIC ORBITS, FROM THE FOCUS GIVEN

LEMMA 15

If from the two foci S, H, *of any ellipse or hyperbola, we draw to any third point* V *the right lines* SV, HV, *whereof one* HV *is equal to the principal axis of the figure,*

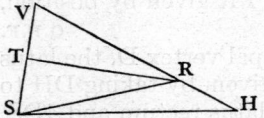

that is, to the axis in which the foci are situated, the other, SV, *is bisected in* T *by the perpendicular* TR *let fall upon it; that perpendicular* TR *will somewhere touch the conic section: and,* vice versa, *if it does touch it,* HV *will be equal to the principal axis of the figure.*

For, let the perpendicular TR cut the right line HV, produced, if need be, in R; and join SR. Because TS, TV are equal, therefore the right lines SR, VR, as well as the angles TRS, TRV, will be also equal. Whence the point R will be in the conic section, and the perpendicular TR will touch the same; and the contrary. Q.E.D.

PROPOSITION 18. PROBLEM 10

From a focus and the principal axes given, to describe elliptic and hyperbolic curves which shall pass through given points, and touch right lines given by position.

Let S be the common focus of the figures; AB the length of the principal axis of any conic; P a point through which the conic should pass; and TR a right line which it should touch. About the centre P, with the radius AB−SP, if the orbit is an ellipse, or AB+SP, if the orbit is an hyperbola, describe the circle HG. On the tangent TR let fall the perpendicular ST, and produce the same to V, so that TV may be equal to ST; and about V as a centre with the interval AB describe the circle FH. In this manner, whether two points P, *p*, are given, or two tangents TR, *tr*, or a point P and a tangent TR, we are to describe two circles. Let H be their

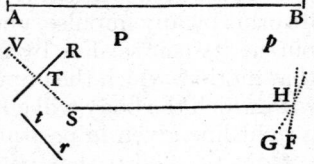

common intersection, and from the foci S, H, with the given axis describe the conic: I say, the thing is done. For (because PH+SP in the ellipse, and PH−SP in the hyperbola, is equal to the axis) the described conic will pass through the point P, and (by the preceding Lemma) will touch the right line TR. And by the same argument it will either pass through the two points P, *p*, or touch the two right lines TR, *tr*.   Q.E.F.

PROPOSITION 19. PROBLEM 11

About a given focus, to describe a parabola which shall pass through given points and touch right lines given by position.

Let S be the focus, P a point, and TR a tangent of the curve to be described. About P as a centre, with the radius PS, describe the circle FG. From the focus let fall ST perpendicular on the tangent, and produce the same to V, so as TV

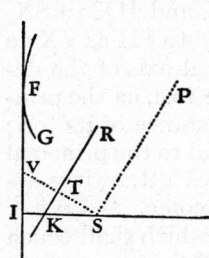

may be equal to ST. After the same manner another circle *fg* is to be described, if another point *p* is given; or another point *v* is to be found, if another tangent *tr* is given; then draw the right line IF, which shall touch the two circles FG, *fg*, if two points P, *p* are given; or pass through the two points V, *v*, if two tangents TR, *tr*, are given; or touch the circle FG, and pass through the point V, if the point P and the tangent TR are given. On FI let fall the perpendicular SI, and bisect the same in K; and with the axis SK and principal vertex K describe a parabola: I say, the thing is done. For this parabola (because SK is equal to IK, and SP to FP) will pass through the point P; and (by Cor. III, Lem. 14) because ST is equal to TV, and STR a right angle, it will touch the right line TR.   Q.E.F.

PROPOSITION 20. PROBLEM 12

About a given focus, to describe any given conic which shall pass through given points and touch right lines given by position.

CASE 1. About the focus S it is required to describe a conic ABC, passing through two points B, C. Because the conic is given in kind, the ratio of the principal axis to the distance of the foci will be given. In that ratio take KB to BS, and LC to CS. About the centres B, C, with the intervals BK, CL, describe two circles; and on the right line KL, that touches the same in K and L, let fall the perpendicular SG; which cut in A and *a*, so that GA may be to AS, and G*a* to *a*S, as KB to BS; and with the axis A*a*, and vertices A, *a*, describe a conic: I say, the thing is done. For let H be the other focus of the described figure, and seeing that GA : AS=G*a* : *a*S, we shall have

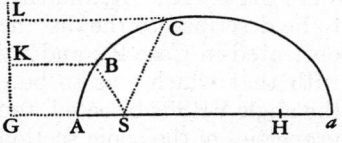

G*a*−GA : *a*S−AS=GA : AS, or A*a* : SH=GA : AS, and therefore GA and AS are in the ratio which the principal axis of the figure to be described has to the distance of its foci; and therefore the described figure is of the same kind with the figure which was to be described. And since KB to BS, and LC to CS, are in the same ratio, this figure will pass through the points B, C, as is manifest from the conic sections.

CASE 2. About the focus S it is required to describe a conic which shall somewhere touch two right lines TR, *tr*. From the focus on those tangents let fall the perpendiculars ST, S*t*, which produce to V, *v*, so that TV, *tv* may be equal to TS, *t*S. Bisect V*v* in O, and erect the indefinite perpendicular OH, and cut the right line VS infinitely produced in K and *k*, so that VK be to KS, and V*k* to *k*S, as the principal axis of the conic to be described is to the distance of its foci. On the diameter K*k* describe a circle cutting OH in H; and with the foci S, H, and principal axis equal to VH, describe a conic: I say, the thing is done. For bisecting K*k* in X, and joining HX, HS, HV, H*v*, because VK is to KS as V*k* to *k*S; and by composition, as VK+V*k* to KS+*k*S; and by subtraction, as V*k*−VK to *k*S−KS, that is, as 2VX to 2KX, and 2KX to 2SX, and therefore as VX to HX and HX to SX, the triangles VXH, HXS will be similar; therefore VH will be to SH as VX to XH; and therefore as VK to KS. Wherefore VH, the principal axis of the described conic, has the same ratio to SH, the distance of the foci, as the principal axis of the conic which was to be described has to the distance of its foci; and is therefore of the same kind. And seeing VH, *v*H are equal to the principal axis, and VS, *v*S are perpendicularly bisected by the right lines TR, *tr*, it is evident (by Lem. 15) that those right lines touch the described conic.   Q.E.F.

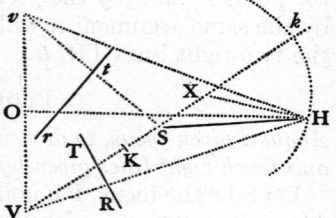

CASE 3. About the focus S it is required to describe a conic which shall touch a right line TR in a given point R. On the right line TR let fall the perpendicular ST, which produce to V, so that TV may be equal to ST; join VR, and cut the right line VS indefinitely produced in K and *k*, so that VK may be to SK, and V*k* to S*k*, as the principal axis of the ellipse to be described to the distance of its foci; and on the diameter K*k* describing a circle, cut the right line VR produced in H; then with the foci S, H, and principal axis equal to VH, describe a conic: I say, the thing is done. For VH : SH = VK : SK, and therefore as the principal axis of the conic which was to be described to the distance of its foci (as appears from what we have demonstrated in Case 2); and therefore the described conic is of the same kind with that which was to be described; but that the right line TR, by which the angle VRS is bisected, touches the conic in the point R, is certain from the properties of the conic sections.   Q.E.F.

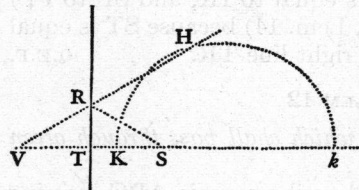

CASE 4. About the focus S it is required to describe a conic APB that shall touch a right line TR, and pass through any given point P without the tangent, and shall be similar to the figure *apb*, described with the principal axis *ab*, and foci *s*, *h*. On the tangent TR let fall the perpendicular ST, which produce to V, so that TV may be equal to ST; and making the angles *hsq*, *shq*, equal to the angles VSP, SVP, about *q* as a centre, and with a radius which shall be to *ab* as SP to VS, describe a circle cutting the figure *apb* in *p*. Join *sp*, and draw SH such that it may be to *sh* as SP is to *sp*, and may make the angle PSH equal to the angle *psh*, and the angle VSH equal to the angle *psq*. Then with the foci S, H, and principal axis AB, equal to the distance VH, describe a conic section: I say, the thing is done; for if *sv* is drawn so that it shall be to *sp* as *sh* is to *sq*,

and shall make the angle *vsp* equal to the angle *hsq*, and the angle *vsh* equal to the angle *psq*, the triangles *svh*, *spq*, will be similar, and therefore *vh* will be to *pq* as *sh* is to *sq*; that is (because of the similar triangles VSP, *hsq*), as VS is to SP, or as *ab* to *pq*. Wherefore *vh* and *ab* are equal. But, because of the similar

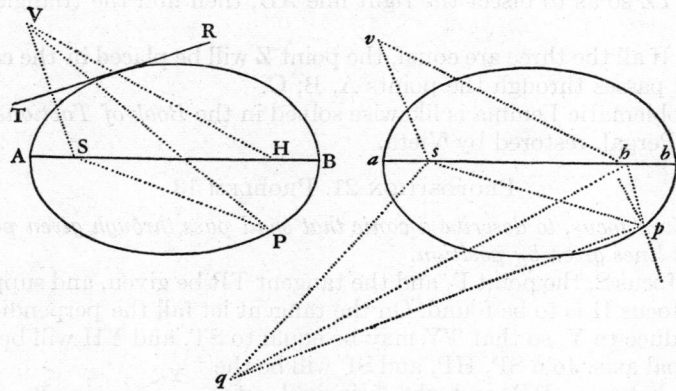

triangles VSH, *vsh*, VH is to SH as *vh* to *sh*; that is, the axis of the conic section now described is to the distance of its foci as the axis *ab* to the distance of the foci *sh*; and therefore the figure now described is similar to the figure *aph*. But, because the triangle PSH is similar to the triangle *psh*, this figure passes through the point P; and because VH is equal to its axis, and VS is perpendicularly bisected by the right line TR, the said figure touches the right line TR. Q.E.F.

LEMMA 16

From three given points to draw to a fourth point that is not given three right lines whose differences either shall be given or are zero.

CASE 1. Let the given points be A, B, C, and Z the fourth point which we are to find; because of the given difference of the lines AZ, BZ, the locus of the point Z will be an hyperbola whose foci are A and B, and whose principal axis

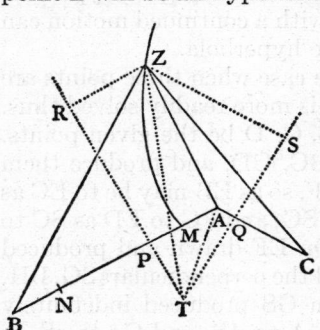

is the given difference. Let that axis be MN. Taking PM to MA as MN to AB, erect PR perpendicular to AB, and let fall ZR perpendicular to PR; then from the nature of the hyperbola, ZR : AZ = MN : AB. And by the like argument, the locus of the point Z will be another hyperbola, whose foci are A, C, and whose principal axis is the difference between AZ and CZ; and QS a perpendicular on AC may be drawn, to which (QS) if from any point Z of this hyperbola a perpendicular ZS is let fall, (this ZS) shall be to AZ as the difference between AZ and CZ is to AC.

Wherefore the ratios of ZR and ZS to AZ are given, and consequently the ratio of ZR to ZS one to the other; and therefore if the right lines RP, SQ, meet in T, and TZ and TA are drawn, the figure TRZS will be given in kind, and the right line TZ, in which the point Z is somewhere placed, will be given in position. There will be given also the right line TA, and the angle ATZ; and because the ratios of AZ and TZ to ZS are given, their ratio to each other is given also; and thence will be given likewise the triangle ATZ, whose vertex is the point Z.   Q.E.I.

CASE 2. If two of the three lines, for example AZ and BZ, are equal, draw the right line TZ so as to bisect the right line AB; then find the triangle ATZ as above.   Q.E.I.

CASE 3. If all the three are equal, the point Z will be placed in the centre of a circle that passes through the points A, B, C.   Q.E.I.

This problematic Lemma is likewise solved in the *Book of Tactions* of Apollonius [of Perga], restored by Vieta.

PROPOSITION 21. PROBLEM 13

About a given focus, to describe a conic that shall pass through given points and touch right lines given by position.

Let the focus S, the point P, and the tangent TR be given, and suppose that the other focus H is to be found. On the tangent let fall the perpendicular ST, which produce to Y, so that TY may be equal to ST, and YH will be equal to the principal axis. Join SP, HP, and SP will be the 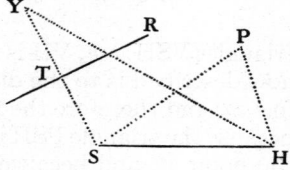 difference between HP and the principal axis. After this manner, if more tangents TR are given, or more points P, we shall always determine as many lines YH, or PH, drawn from the said points Y or P, to the focus H, which either shall be equal to the axes, or differ from the axes by given lengths SP; and therefore which shall either be equal among themselves, or shall have given differences; from whence (by the preceding Lemma), that other focus H is given. But having the foci and the length of the axis (which is either YH, or, if the conic be an ellipse, PH+SP; or PH−SP, if it be an hyperbola), the conic is given.   Q.E.I.

SCHOLIUM

When the conic is an hyperbola, I do not include its conjugate hyperbola under the name of this conic. For a body going on with a continued motion can never pass out of one hyperbola into its conjugate hyperbola.

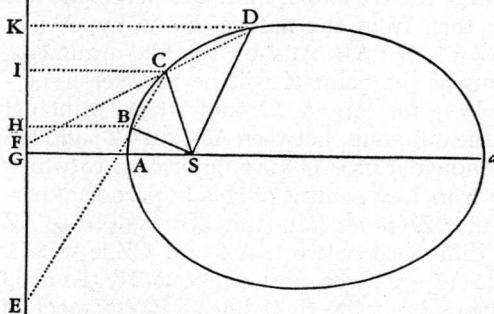

The case when three points are given is more readily solved thus. Let B, C, D be the given points. Join BC, CD, and produce them to E, F, so as EB may be to EC as SB to SC; and FC to FD as SC to SD. On EF drawn and produced let fall the perpendiculars SG, BH, and in GS produced indefinitely take GA to AS, and G*a* to *a*S, as HB is to BS: then A will be the vertex, and A*a* the principal axis of the conic; which, according as GA is greater than, equal to, or less than AS, will be either an ellipse, a parabola, or an hyperbola; the point *a* in the first case falling on the same side of the line GF as the point A; in the second, going off to an infinite distance; in the third, falling on the other side of the line GF. For if on GF the perpendiculars CI, DK are let fall, IC will be to HB as EC to EB; that is, as SC to SB; and by permutation, IC to SC as HB to SB, or as GA to SA. And, by the like argument, we may prove that KD is to SD in the same ratio. Wherefore the points B, C, D lie in a conic section described about the focus S, in such manner that all the right lines drawn from the focus S to the several points of the section, and the perpendiculars let fall from the same points on the right line GF, are in that given ratio.

That excellent geometer M. de la Hire has solved this **Problem** much after the same way, in his *Conics*, Prop. 25, Book VIII.

SECTION V

HOW THE ORBITS ARE TO BE FOUND WHEN NEITHER FOCUS IS GIVEN

LEMMA 17

If from any point P *of a given conic section, to the four produced sides* AB, CD, AC, DB *of any trapezium* ABDC *inscribed in that section, as many right lines* PQ, PR, PS, PT *are drawn in given angles, each line to each side; the rectangle* PQ·PR *of those on the opposite sides* AB, CD, *will be to the rectangle* PS·PT *of those on the other two opposite sides* AC, BD, *in a given ratio.*

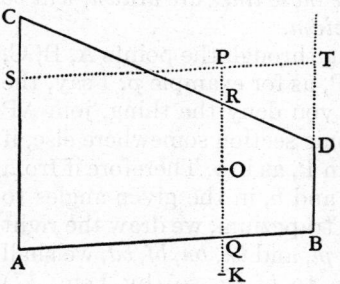

CASE 1. Let us suppose, first, that the lines drawn to one pair of opposite sides are parallel to either of the other sides; as PQ and PR to the side AC, and PS and PT to the side AB. And further, that one pair of the opposite sides, as AC and BD, are parallel between themselves; then the right line which bisects those parallel sides will be one of the diameters of the conic section, and will likewise bisect RQ. Let O be the point in which RQ is bisected, and PO will be an ordinate to that diameter. Produce PO to K, so that OK may be equal to PO, and OK will be an ordinate on the other side of that diameter. Since, therefore, the points A, B, P, and K are placed in the conic section, and PK cuts AB in a given angle, the rectangle PQ·QK (by Props. 17, 19, 21, and 23, Book III, *Conics* of Apollonius) will be to the rec-

tangle AQ·QB in a given ratio. But QK and PR are equal, as being the differences of the equal lines OK, OP, and OQ, OR; whence the rectangles PQ·QK and PQ·PR are equal; and therefore the rectangle PQ·PR is to the rectangle AQ·QB, that is, to the rectangle PS·PT, in a given ratio. Q.E.D.

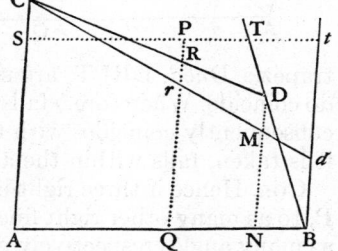

CASE 2. Let us next suppose that the opposite sides AC and BD of the trapezium are not parallel. Draw B*d* parallel to AC, and meeting as well the right line ST in *t*, as the conic section in *d*. Join C*d* cutting PQ in *r*, and draw DM parallel to PQ, cutting C*d* in M, and AB in N. Then (because of

the similar triangles BT*t*, DBN) B*t* or PQ : T*t* = DN : NB. And so R*r* : AQ or PS = DM : AN. Wherefore, by multiplying the antecedents by the antecedents, and the consequents by the consequents, as the rectangle PQ·R*r* is to the rectangle PS·T*t*, so will the rectangle DN·DM be to the rectangle NA·NB; and (by Case 1) so is the rectangle PQ·P*r* to the rectangle PS·P*t*, and, by division, so is the rectangle PQ·PR to the rectangle PS·PT.   Q.E.D.

CASE 3. Let us suppose, lastly, the four lines PQ, PR, PS, PT not to be parallel to the sides AC, AB, but any way inclined to them. In their place draw P*q*, P*r*, par-
allel to AC; and P*s*, P*t* parallel to AB; and because the angles of the triangles PQ*q*, PR*r*, PS*s*,
PT*t* are given, the ratios of PQ to P*q*, PR to P*r*,
PS to P*s*, PT to P*t* will be also given; and therefore the compounded ratios PQ·PR to P*q*·P*r*,
and PS·PT to P*s*·P*t* are given. But from what
we have demonstrated before, the ratio of P*q*·P*r*
to P*s*·P*t* is given; and therefore also the ratio of
PQ·PR to PS·PT.   Q.E.D.

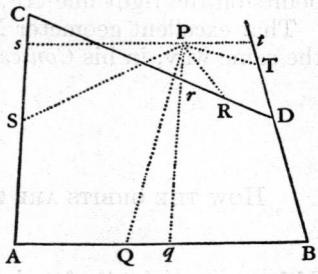

LEMMA 18

The same things supposed, if the rectangle PQ·PR *of the lines drawn to the two opposite sides of the trapezium is to the rectangle* PS·PT *of those drawn to the other two sides in a given ratio, the point* P, *from whence those lines are drawn, will be placed in a conic section described about the trapezium.*

Conceive a conic section to be described passing through the points A, B, C, D, and any one of the infinite number of points P, as for example *p*: I say, the point P will be always placed in this section. If you deny the thing, join AP

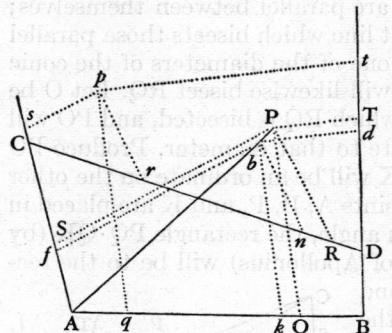

cutting this conic section somewhere else, if possible, than in P, as in *b*. Therefore if from those points *p* and *b*, in the given angles to the sides of the trapezium, we draw the right lines *pq, pr, ps, pt*, and *bk, bn, bf, bd*, we shall have, as *bk·bn* to *bf·bd*, so (by Lem. 17) *pq·pr* to *ps·pt*; and so (by supposition) PQ·PR to PS·PT. And because of the similar trapezia *bkAf*, PQAS, as *bk* to *bf*, so PQ to PS. Wherefore by dividing the terms of the preceding proportion by the correspond-
ent terms of this, we shall have *bn* to *bd* as PR to PT. And therefore the equiangular
trapezia D*nbd*, DRPT, are similar, and consequently their diagonals D*b*, DP do coincide. Wherefore *b* falls in the intersection of the right lines AP, DP, and consequently coincides with the point P. And therefore the point P, wherever it is taken, falls within the assigned conic section.   Q.E.D.

COR. Hence if three right lines PQ, PR, PS are drawn from a common point P, to as many other right lines given in position, AB, CD, AC, each to each, in as many angles respectively given, and the rectangle PQ·PR under any two of the lines drawn be to the square of the third PS in a given ratio; the point P, from which the right lines are drawn, will be placed in a conic section that touches the lines AB, CD in A and C; and the contrary. For the position of the three right lines AB, CD, AC remaining the same, let the line BD approach to and coincide with the line AC; then let the line PT come likewise to coincide with the line PS; and the rectangle PS·PT will become PS², and the right lines AB, CD, which before did cut the curve in the points A and B, C and D, can no longer cut, but only touch, the curve in those coinciding points.

SCHOLIUM

In this Lemma, the name of conic section is to be understood in a large sense, comprehending as well the rectilinear section through the vertex of the cone, as the circular one parallel to the base. For if the point p happens to be in a right line, by which the points A and D, or C and B are joined, the conic section will be changed into two right lines, one of which is that right line upon which the point p falls, and the other is a right line that joins the other two of the four points. If the two opposite angles of the trapezium taken together are equal to two right angles, and if the four lines PQ, PR, PS, PT are drawn to the sides thereof at right angles, or any other equal angles, and the rectangle PQ·PR under two of the lines drawn PQ and PR, is equal to the rectangle PS·PT under the other two PS and PT, the conic section will become a circle. And the same thing will happen if the four lines are drawn in any angles, and the rectangle PQ·PR, under one pair of the lines drawn, is to the rectangle PS·PT under the other pair as the rectangle under the sines of the angles S, T, in which the two last lines PS, PT are drawn, to the rectangle under the sines of the angles Q, R, in which the first two PQ, PR are drawn. In all other cases the locus of the point P will be one of the three figures which pass commonly by the name of the conic sections. But in place of the trapezium ABCD, we may substitute a quadrilateral figure whose two opposite sides cross one another like diagonals. And one or two of the four points A, B, C, D may be supposed to be removed to an infinite distance, by which means the sides of the figure which converge to those points, will become parallel; and in this case the conic section will pass through the other points, and will go the same way as the parallels *in infinitum*.

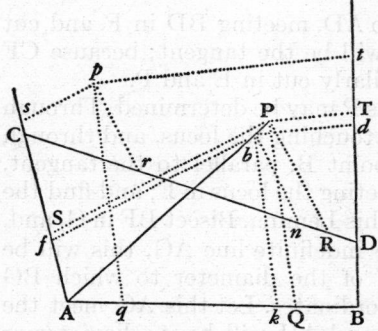

LEMMA 19

To find a point P from which if four right lines PQ, PR, PS, PT are drawn to as many other right lines AB, CD, AC, BD, given by position, each to each, at given angles, the rectangle PQ·PR, under any two of the lines drawn, shall be to the rectangle PS·PT, under the other two, in a given ratio.

Suppose the lines AB, CD, to which the two right lines PQ, PR, containing one of the rectangles, are drawn to meet two other lines, given by position, in the points A, B, C, D. From one of those, as A, draw any right line AH, in which you would find the point P. Let this cut the opposite lines BD, CD, in H and I; and, because all the angles of the figure are given, the ratio of PQ to PA, and PA to PS, and therefore of PQ to PS, will be also given. This ratio taken as a divisor of the given ratio of PQ·PR to PS·PT, gives the ratio of PR to PT; and multiplying the given ratios of PI to PR, and PT to PH, the ratio of PI to PH, and therefore the point P, will be given.

Q.E.I.

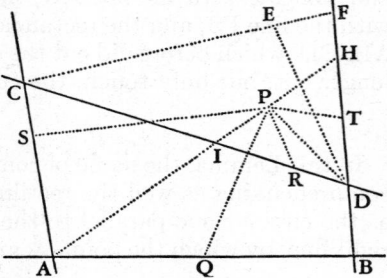

Cor. I. Hence also a tangent may be drawn to any point D of the locus of all the points P. For the chord PD, where the points P and D meet, that is, where AH is drawn through the point D, becomes a tangent. In which case the ultimate ratio of the evanescent lines IP and PH will be found as above. Therefore draw CF parallel to AD, meeting BD in F, and cut it in E in the same ultimate ratio, then DE will be the tangent; because CF and the evanescent IH are parallel, and similarly cut in E and P.

Cor. II. Hence also the locus of all the points P may be determined. Through any of the points A, B, C, D, as A, draw AE touching the locus, and through

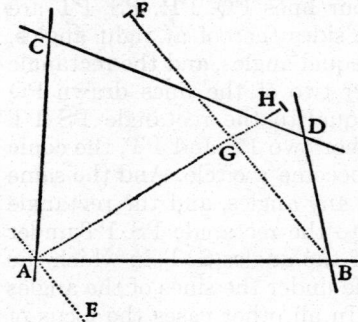

any other point B, parallel to the tangent, draw BF meeting the locus in F; and find the point F by this Lemma. Bisect BF in G, and, drawing the indefinite line AG, this will be the position of the diameter to which BG and FG are ordinates. Let this AG meet the locus in H, and AH will be its diameter or latus transversum, to which the latus rectum will be as BG² to AG·GH. If AG nowhere meets the locus, the line AH being infinite, the locus will be a parabola; and its latus rectum corresponding to the diameter AG

will be $\frac{BG^2}{AG}$. But if it does meet it anywhere, the locus will be an hyperbola, when the points A and H are placed on the same side of the point G; and an ellipse, if the point G falls between the points A and H; unless, perhaps, the angle AGB is a right angle, and at the same time BG² equal to the rectangle GA·GH, in which case the locus will be a circle.

And so we have given in this Corollary a solution of that famous Problem of the ancients concerning four lines, begun by Euclid, and carried on by Apollonius; and this not an analytical calculus but a geometrical composition, such as the ancients required.

Lemma 20

If the two opposite angular points A *and* P *of any parallelogram* ASPQ *touch any conic section in the points* A *and* P; *and the sides* AQ, AS *of one of those angles, indefinitely produced, meet the same conic section in* B *and* C; *and from the points of meeting* B *and* C *to any fifth point* D *of the conic section, two right lines* BD, CD *are drawn meeting the two other sides* PS, PQ *of the parallelogram, indefinitely produced in* T *and* R; *the parts* PR *and* PT, *cut off from the sides, will always be one to the other in a given ratio. And conversely, if those parts cut off are one to the other in a given ratio, the locus of the point* D *will be a conic section passing through the four points* A, B, C, P.

CASE 1. Join BP, CP, and from the point D draw the two right lines DG, DE, of which the first DG shall be parallel to AB, and meet PB, PQ, CA, in H,

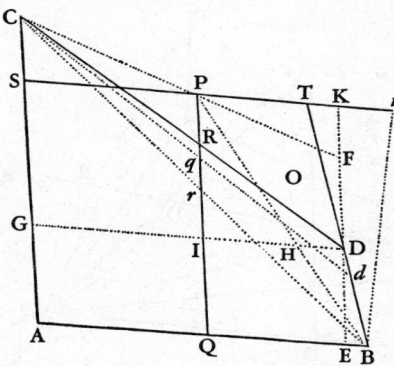

I, G; and the other DE shall be parallel to AC, and meet PC, PS, AB, in F, K, E; and (by Lem. 17) the rectangle DE·DF will be to the rectangle DG·DH in a given ratio. But PQ is to DE (or IQ) as PB to HB, and consequently as PT to DH; and by permutation PQ is to PT as DE to DH. Likewise PR is to DF as RC to DC, and therefore as (IG or) PS to DG; and by permutation PR is to PS as DF to DG; and, by compounding those ratios, the rectangle PQ·PR will be to the rectangle PS·PT as the rectangle DE·DF is to the rectangle DG·DH, and consequently in a given ratio. But PQ and PS are given, and therefore the ratio of PR to PT is given. Q.E.D.

CASE 2. But if PR and PT are supposed to be in a given ratio one to the other, then by going back again, by a like reasoning, it will follow that the rectangle DE·DF is to the rectangle DG·DH in a given ratio; and so the point D (by Lem. 18) will lie in a conic section passing through the points A, B, C, P, as its locus. Q.E.D.

COR. I. Hence if we draw BC cutting PQ in *r* and in PT take P*t* to P*r* in the same ratio which PT has to PR; then B*t* will touch the conic section in the point B. For suppose the point D to coalesce with the point B, so that the chord BD vanishing, BT shall become a tangent; and CD and BT will coincide with CB and B*t*.

COR. II. And, *vice versa*, if B*t* is a tangent, and the lines BD, CD meet in any point D of a conic section, PR will be to PT as P*r* to P*t*. And, on the contrary, if PR is to PT as P*r* to P*t*, then BD and CD will meet in some point D of a conic section.

COR. III. One conic section cannot cut another conic section in more than four points. For, if it is possible, let two conic sections pass through the five points A, B, C, P, O; and let the right line BD cut them in the points D, *d*, and the right line C*d* cut the right line PQ in *q*. Therefore PR is to PT as P*q* to PT: whence PR and P*q* are equal one to the other, against the supposition.

LEMMA 21

If two movable and indefinite right lines BM, CM *drawn through given points* B, C, *as poles, do by their point of meeting* M *describe a third right line* MN *given by position; and other two indefinite right lines* BD, CD *are drawn, making with the former two at those given points* B, C, *given angles*, MBD, MCD: *I say, that those two right lines* BD, CD *will by their point of meeting* D *describe a conic section passing through the points* B, C. *And conversely, if the right lines* BD, CD *do by their point of meeting* D *describe a conic section passing through the given points* B, C, A, *and the angle* DBM *is always equal to the given angle* ABC, *as well as the angle* DCM *always equal to the given angle* ACB, *the point* M *will lie in a right line given by position, as its locus.*

For in the right line MN let a point N be given, and when the movable point M falls on the immovable point N, let the movable point D fall on an immovable point P. Join CN, BN, CP, BP, and from the point P draw the right lines PT, PR meeting BD, CD in T and R, and making the angle BPT equal to the given angle BNM, and the angle CPR equal to the given angle CNM. Wherefore since (by supposition) the angles MBD, NBP are equal, as also the angles MCD, NCP, take away the angles NBD and NCD that are common, and there will remain the angles

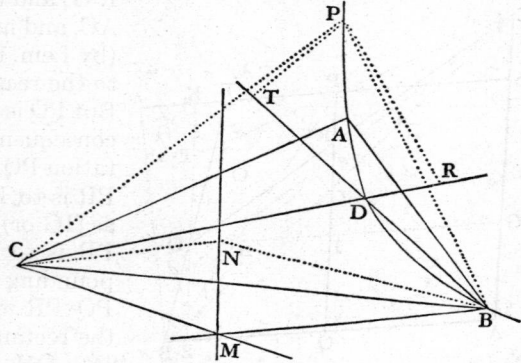

NBM and PBT, NCM and PCR equal; and therefore the triangles NBM, PBT are similar, as also the triangles NCM, PCR. Wherefore PT is to NM as PB to NB; and PR to NM as PC to NC. But the points B, C, N, P are immovable: wherefore PT and PR have a given ratio to NM, and consequently a given ratio between themselves; and therefore, (by Lem. 20) the point D wherein the movable right lines BT and CR continually concur, will be placed in a conic section passing through the points B, C, P.   Q.E.D.

And conversely, if the movable point D lies in a conic section passing through the given points B, C, A; and the angle DBM is always equal to the given angle ABC, and the angle DCM always equal to the given angle ACB, and when the point D falls successively on any two immovable points p, P, of the conic section, the movable point M falls successively on two immovable points n, N. Through these points n, N, draw the right line nN: this line nN will be the continual locus of that movable point M. For, if possible, let the point M be placed in any curved line. Therefore the point D will be placed in a conic section passing through the five

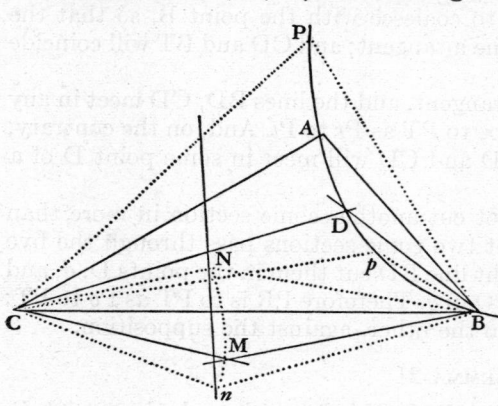

points B, C, A, p, P, when the point M is continually placed in a curved line. But from what was demonstrated before, the point D will be also placed in a conic section passing through the same five points B, C, A, p, P, when the point M is continually placed in a right line. Wherefore the two conic sections will both pass through the same five points, against Cor. III, Lem. 20. It is therefore absurd to suppose that the point M is placed in a curved line.   Q.E.D.

PROPOSITION 22. PROBLEM 14

To describe a conic that shall pass through five given points.

Let the five given points be A, B, C, P, D. From any one of them, as A, to any other two as B, C, which may be called the poles, draw the right lines AB,

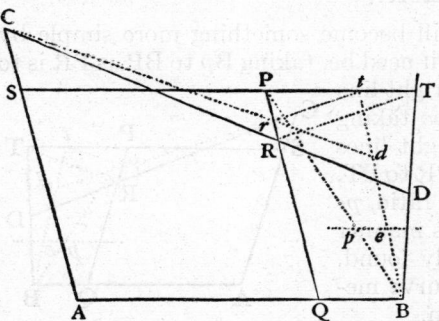

AC, and parallel to those the lines TPS, PRQ through the fourth point P. Then from the two poles B, C, draw through the fifth point D two indefinite lines BDT, CRD, meeting with the last drawn lines TPS, PRQ (the former with the former, and the latter with the latter) in T and R. And then draw the right line *tr* parallel to TR, cutting off from the right lines PT, PR, any segments P*t*,P*r*, proportional to PT, PR; and if through their extremities *t*, *r*, and the poles B, C, the right lines B*t*, C*r* are drawn, meeting in *d*, that point *d* will be placed in the conic required. For (by Lem. 20) that point *d* is placed in a conic section passing through the four points A, B, C, P; and the lines R*r*, T*t* vanishing, the point *d* comes to coincide with the point D. Wherefore the conic section passes through the five points A, B, C, P, D.

Q.E.D.

The same otherwise.

Of the given points join any three, as A, B, C; and about two of them B, C, as poles, making the angles ABC, ACB of a given magnitude to revolve, apply

the legs BA, CA, first to the point D, then to the point P, and mark the points M, N, in which the other legs BL, CL intersect each other in both cases. Draw the indefinite right line MN, and let those movable angles revolve about their poles B, C, in such manner that the intersection, which is now supposed to be *m*, of the legs BL, CL, or BM, CM, may always fall in that indefinite right line MN; and the intersection, which is now supposed to be *d*, of the legs BA, CA, or BD, CD, will describe the conic required, PAD*d*B. For (by Lem.

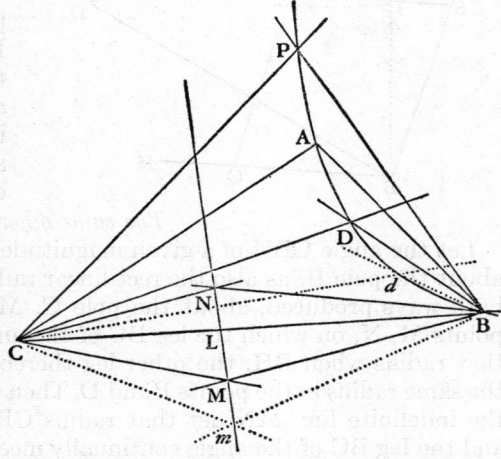

21) the point *d* will be placed in a conic section passing through the points B, C; and when the point *m* comes to coincide with the points L, M, N, the point *d* will (by construction) come to coincide with the points A, D, P. Wherefore a conic section will be described that shall pass through the five points A, B, C, P, D.

Q.E.F.

COR. I. Hence a right line may be readily drawn which shall be a tangent to the conic in any given point B. Let the point d come to coincide with the point B, and the right line Bd will become the tangent required.

Cor. II. Hence also may be found the centres, diameters, and latera recta of the conics, as in Cor. II, Lem. 19.

SCHOLIUM

The former of these constructions will become something more simple by joining B, P, and in that line, produced, if need be, taking Bp to BP as PR is to PT; and through p draw the indefinite right line pe parallel to SPT, and in that line pe taking always pe equal to Pr; and draw the right lines Be, Cr to meet in d. For since Pr to Pt, PR to PT, pB to PB, pe to Pt, are all in the same ratio, pe and Pr will be always equal. After this manner the points of the conic are most readily found, unless you would rather describe the curve mechanically, as in the second construction.

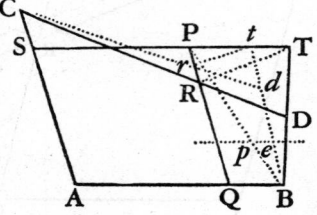

PROPOSITION 23. PROBLEM 15

To describe a conic that shall pass through four given points, and touch a given right line.

CASE 1. Suppose that HB is the given tangent, B the point of contact, and C, D, P, the three other given points. Join BC, and draw PS parallel to BH, and PQ parallel to BC; complete the parallelogram BSPQ. Draw BD cutting SP in T, and CD cutting PQ in R. Lastly, draw any line tr parallel to TR, cutting off from PQ, PS, the segments Pr, Pt proportional to PR, PT respectively, and draw Cr, Bt; their point of intersection d will (by Lem. 20) always fall on the conic to be described.

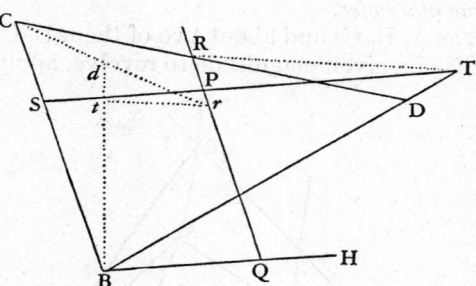

The same otherwise.

Let the angle CBH of a given magnitude revolve about the pole B, as also the rectilinear radius DC, both ways produced, about the pole C. Mark the points M, N, on which the leg BC of the angle cuts that radius when BH, the other leg thereof, meets the same radius in the points P and D. Then drawing the indefinite line MN, let that radius CP or CD and the leg BC of the angle continually meet in this line; and the point of meeting of the other leg BH with the radius will delineate the conic required.

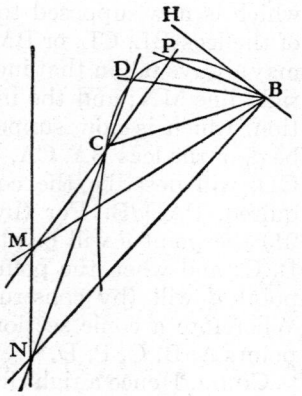

For if in the constructions of the preceding Problem the point A comes to a coincidence with the point B, the lines CA and CB will coincide, and the line AB, in its last situation, will become the tangent BH; and therefore the constructions there set down will become the same with the constructions here described. Wherefore the intersection of the leg BH with the radius will describe a conic section passing through the points C, D, P, and touching the line BH in the point B.   Q.E.F.

CASE 2. Suppose the four points B, C, D, P, given, being situated without the tangent HI. Join each two by the lines BD, CP meeting in G, and cutting the tangent in H and I. Cut the tangent in A in such manner that HA may be

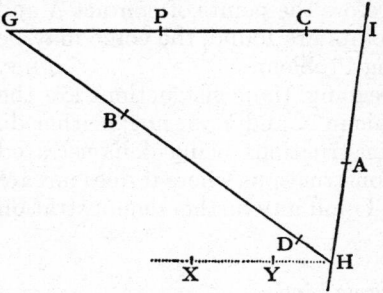

to IA as the product of the mean proportional between CG and GP, and the mean proportional between BH and HD is to the product of the mean proportional between GD and GB, and the mean proportional between PI and IC, and A will be the point of contact. For if HX, a parallel to the right line PI, cuts the conic in any points X and Y, the point A (by the properties of the conic sections) will come to be so placed, that HA² will become to AI² in a ratio that is compounded out of the ratio of the rectangle HX·HY to the rectangle BH·HD, or of the rectangle CG·GP to the rectangle DG·GB; and the ratio of the rectangle BH·HD to the rectangle PI·IC. But after the point of contact A is found, the conic will be described as in the first Case. Q.E.F. But the point A may be taken either between or without the points H and I, upon which account a two-fold conic may be described.

PROPOSITION 24. PROBLEM 16

To describe a conic that shall pass through three given points, and touch two given right lines.

Suppose HI, KL to be the given tangents and B, C, D the given points. Through any two of those points, as B, D, draw the indefinite right line BD meeting the tangents in the points H, K. Then likewise through any other two of these points, as C, D, draw the indefinite right line CD meeting the tangents in the points I, L. Cut the lines drawn in R and S, so that HR may be to KR as the mean proportional between BH and HD is to the mean proportional between BK and KD, and IS to LS as the mean proportional between CI and ID is to the mean proportional between CL and LD. But you may cut, at pleasure, either within or between the points K and H, I and L, or without them. Then draw RS cutting the tangents in A and P,

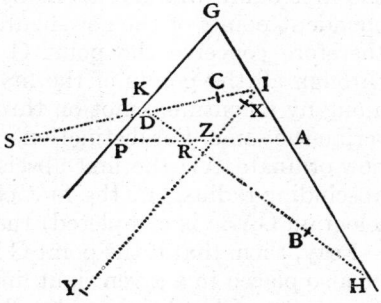

and A and P will be the points of contact. For if A and P are supposed to be the points of contact, situated anywhere else in the tangents, and through any of the points H, I, K, L, as I, situated in either tangent HI, a right line IY is drawn parallel to the other tangent KL, and meeting the curve in X and Y, and in that right line there be taken IZ equal to a mean proportional between IX and IY, the rectangle XI·IY or IZ² will (by the properties of the conic sections) be to LP² as the rectangle CI·ID is to the rectangle CL·LD; that is (by the construction), as SI is to SL², and therefore IZ : LP = SI : SL. Wherefore the points S, P, Z are in one right line. Moreover, since the tangents meet in G, the rectangle XI·IY or IZ² will (by the properties of the conic sections) be to IA² as GP² is to GA², and consequently IZ : IA = GP : GA. Wherefore the points P, Z, A lie in one right line, and therefore the points S, P, and A are in one right line. And the same argument will prove that the points R, P, and A are in one right line. Wherefore the points of contact A and P lie in the right line RS. But after these points are found, the conic may be described, as in the first Case of the preceding Problem.   Q.E.F.

In this Proposition, and Case 2 of the foregoing, the constructions are the same, whether the right line XY cuts the conic in X and Y, or not; neither do they depend upon that section. But the constructions being demonstrated where that right line does cut the conic, the constructions where it does not are also known; and therefore, for brevity's sake, I omit any further demonstration of them.

LEMMA 22

To transform figures into other figures of the same kind.

Suppose that any figure HGI is to be transformed. Draw, at pleasure, two parallel lines AO, BL, cutting any given third line AB in A and B, and from any point G of the figure, draw out any right line GD, parallel to OA, till it

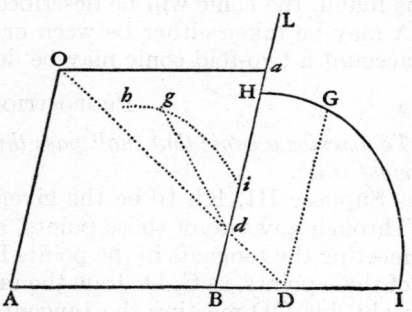

meets the right line AB. Then from any given point O in the line OA, draw to the point D the right line OD, meeting BL in d; and from the point of intersection raise the right line dg containing any given angle with the right line BL, and having such ratio to Od as DG has to OD; and g will be the point in the new figure hgi, corresponding to the point G. And in like manner the several points of the first figure will give as many correspondent points of the new figure. If we therefore conceive the point G to be carried along by a continual motion through all the points of the first figure, the point g will be likewise carried along by a continual motion through all the points of the new figure, and describe the same. For distinction's sake, let us call DG the first ordinate, dg the new ordinate, AD the first abscissa, ad the new abscissa, O the pole, OD the abscinding radius, OA the first ordinate radius, and Oa (by which the parallelogram OABa is completed) the new ordinate radius.

I say, then, that if the point G is placed in a given right line, the point g will be also placed in a given right line. If the point G is placed in a conic section, the point g will be likewise placed in a conic section. And here I understand the circle as one of the conic sections. But further, if the point G is placed in a line of the third analytical order, the point g will also be placed in a line of the third order, and so on in curved lines of higher orders. The two lines in which the points G, g are placed, will be always of the same analytical order. For as

$$ad : OA = Od : OD = dg : DG = AB : AD; \text{ and therefore AD is equal to } \frac{OA \cdot AB}{ad},$$

and DG equal to $\dfrac{OA \cdot dg}{ad}$. Now if the point G is placed in a right line, and there-fore, in any equation by which the relation between the abscissa AD and the ordinate GD is expressed, those indetermined lines AD and DG rise no higher than to one dimension, by writing this equation $\dfrac{OA \cdot AB}{ad}$ in place of AD, and $\dfrac{OA \cdot dg}{ad}$ in place of DG, a new equation will be produced, in which the new abscissa ad and new ordinate dg rise only to one dimension; and which therefore must denote a right line. But if AD and DG (or either of them) had risen to two dimensions in the first equation, ad and dg would likewise have risen to two dimensions in the second equation. And so on in three or more dimensions. The indetermined lines, ad, dg in the second equation, and AD, DG in the first, will always rise to the same number of dimensions; and therefore the lines in which the points G, g are placed are of the same analytical order.

I say, further, that if any right line touches the curved line in the first figure, the same right line transferred the same way with the curve into the new figure will touch that curved line in the new figure, and conversely. For if any two points of the curve in the first figure are supposed to approach one the other till they come to coincide, the same points transferred will approach one the other till they come to coincide in the new figure; and therefore the right lines with which those points are joined will become together tangents of the curves in both figures. I might have given demonstrations of these assertions in a more geometrical form; but I study to be brief.

Wherefore if one rectilinear figure is to be transformed into another, we need only transfer the intersections of the right lines of which the first figure con-sists, and through the transferred intersections to draw right lines in the new figure. But if a curvilinear figure is to be transformed, we must transfer the points, the tangents, and other right lines, by means of which the curved line is defined. This Lemma is of use in the solution of the more difficult Problems; for thereby we may transform the proposed figures, if they are intricate, into others that are more simple. Thus any right lines converging to a point are transformed into parallels, by taking for the first ordinate radius any right line that passes through the point of intersection of the converging lines, and that because their point of intersection is by this means made to go off *in infinitum;* and parallel lines are such as tend to a point infinitely remote. And after the problem is solved in the new figure, if by the inverse operations we transform the new into the first figure, we shall have the solution required.

This Lemma is also of use in the solution of solid problems. For as often as two conic sections occur, by the intersection of which a problem may be solved, any one of them may be transformed, if it is an hyperbola or a parabola, into an ellipse, and then this ellipse may be easily changed into a circle. So also a right line and a conic section, in the construction of plane problems, may be transformed into a right line and a circle.

PROPOSITION 25. PROBLEM 17

To describe a conic that shall pass through two given points, and touch three given right lines.

Through the intersection of any two of the tangents one with the other, and the intersection of the third tangent with the right line which passes through the two given points, draw an indefinite right line; and, taking this line for the first ordinate radius, transform the figure by the preceding Lemma into a new figure. In this figure those two tangents will be-

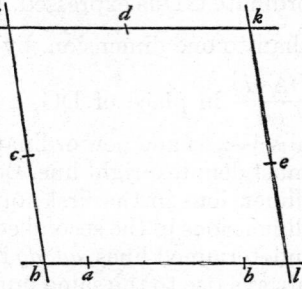

come parallel to each other, and the third tangent will be parallel to the right line that passes through the two given points. Suppose hi, kl to be those two parallel tangents, ik the third tangent, and hl a right line parallel thereto, passing through those points a, b, through which the conic section ought to pass in this new figure; and completing the parallelogram $hikl$, let the right lines hi, ik, kl be so cut in c, d, e, that hc may be to the square root of the rectangle ahb, ic to id, and ke to kd, as the sum of the right lines hi and kl is to the sum of the three lines, the first whereof is the right line ik, and the other two are the square roots of the rectangles ahb and alb; and c, d, e will be the points of contact. For by the properties of the conic sections,

$$hc^2 : ah \cdot hb = ic^2 : id^2 = ke^2 : kd^2 = el^2 : al \cdot lb.$$

Therefore,

$$hc : \sqrt{(ah \cdot hb)} = ic : id = ke : kd = el : \sqrt{(al \cdot lb)}$$
$$= hc + ic + ke + el : \sqrt{(ah \cdot hb)} + id + kd + \sqrt{al \cdot lb}$$
$$= hi + kl : \sqrt{(ah \cdot hb)} + ik + \sqrt{(al \cdot lb)}.$$

Wherefore from that given ratio we have the points of contact c, d, e, in the new figure. By the inverted operations of the last Lemma, let those points be transferred into the first figure, and the conic will be there described by Prob. 14. q.e.f. But according as the points a, b, fall between the points h, l, or without them, the points c, d, e must be taken either between the points h, i, k, l, or without them. If one of the points a, b falls between the points h, i, and the other without the points h, l, the Problem is impossible.

PROPOSITION 26. PROBLEM 18

To describe a conic that shall pass through a given point, and touch four given right lines.

From the common intersections of any two of the tangents to the common intersection of the other two, draw an indefinite right line; and taking this line

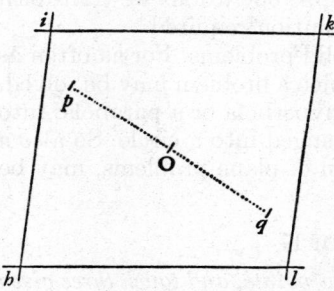

for the first ordinate radius, transform the figure (by Lem. 22) into a new figure, and the two pairs of tangents, each of which before concurred in the first ordinate radius, will now become parallel. Let hi and kl, ik and hl, be those pairs of parallels completing the parallelogram $hikl$. And let p be the point in this new figure corresponding to the given point in the first figure. Through O the centre of the figure draw pq: and Oq being equal to Op, q will be the other point through which the conic section must pass in this new figure. Let this point be transferred, by the inverse operation of Lem. 22, into the first figure, and there we shall have the two points through which the conic is to be described. But through those points that conic may be described by Prop. 17.

LEMMA 23

If two given right lines, as AC, BD, terminating in given points A, B, are in a given ratio one to the other, and the right line CD, by which the indetermined points C, D are joined is cut in K in a given ratio: I say, that the point K will be placed in a given right line.

For let the right lines AC, BD meet in E, and in BE take BG to AE as BD is to AC, and let FD be always equal to the given line EG; and, by construc-

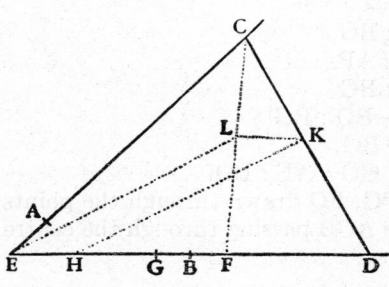

tion, EC will be to GD, that is, to EF, as AC to BD, and therefore in a given ratio; and therefore the triangle EFC will be given in kind. Let CF be cut in L so as CL may be to CF in the ratio of CK to CD; and because that is a given ratio, the triangle EFL will be given in kind, and therefore the point L will be placed in the given right line EL. Join LK, and the triangles CLK, CFD will be similar; and because FD is a given line, and LK is to FD in a given ratio, LK will be also given. To this let EH be taken equal, and ELKH will be always a parallelogram. And therefore the point K is always placed in the given side HK of that parallelogram. Q.E.D.

COR. Because the figure EFLC is given in kind, the three right lines EF, EL, and EC, that is, GD, HK, and EC, will have given ratios to each other.

LEMMA 24

If three right lines, two whereof are parallel, and given in position, touch any conic section: I say, that the semidiameter of the section which is parallel to those two is a mean proportional between the segments of those two that are intercepted between the points of contact and the third tangent.

Let AF, GB be the two parallels touching the conic section ADB in A and B; EF the third right line touching the conic section in I, and meeting the two former tangents in F and G, and let CD be the semidiameter of the figure parallel to those tangents: I say, that AF, CD, BG are continually proportional. For if the conjugate diameters AB, DM meet the tangent FG in E and H, and cut one the other in C, and the parallelogram IKCL be completed; from the nature of the conic sections,

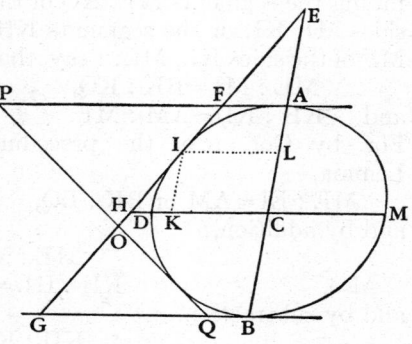

$$EC : CA = CA : CL;$$

thence, $$EC - CA : CA - CL = EC : CA$$

or $$EA : AL = EC : CA;$$

thence, $$EA : EA + AL = EC : EC + CA$$

or $$EA : EL = EC : EB.$$

Therefore, because of the similitude of the triangles EAF, ELI, ECH, EBG,

$$AF : LI = CH : BG.$$

Likewise, from the nature of the conic sections,

$$LI \text{ or } CK : CD = CD : CH.$$

Taking the products of corresponding terms in the last two proportions and simplifying,

$$AF : CD = CD : BG.$$ Q.E.D.

COR. I. Hence if two tangents FG, PQ meet two parallel tangents AF, BG in F and G, P and Q, and cut one the other in O; then by the Lemma applied to EG and PQ,

$$AF : CD = CD : BG,$$
$$BQ : CD = CD : AP.$$

Therefore, $\qquad AF : AP = BQ : BG$

and $\qquad AP - AF : AP = BG - BQ : BG$

or $\qquad PF : AP = GQ : BG,$

and $\qquad AP : BG = PF : GQ = FO : GO = AF : BQ.$

COR. II. Whence also the two right lines PG, FQ drawn through the points P and G, F and Q, will meet in the right line ACB passing through the centre of the figure and the points of contact A, B.

LEMMA 25

If four sides of a parallelogram indefinitely produced touch any conic section, and are cut by a fifth tangent: I say, that, taking those segments of any two conterminous sides that terminate in opposite angles of the parallelogram, either segment is to the side from which it is cut off as that part of the other conterminous side which is intercepted between the point of contact and the third side is to the other segment.

Let the four sides ML, IK, KL, MI of the parallelogram MLIK touch the conic section in A, B, C, D; and let the fifth tangent FQ cut those sides in F, Q, H, and E; and taking the segments ME, KQ of the sides MI, KI, or the segments KH, MF of the sides KL, ML: I say, that

$$ME : MI = BK : KQ,$$

and $\quad KH : KL = AM : MF.$

For, by Cor. I of the preceding Lemma,

$$ME : EI = AM \text{ or } BK : BQ,$$

and by addition,

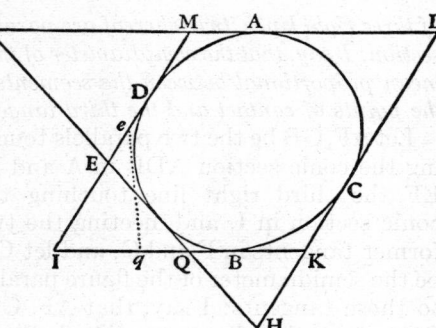

$$ME : MI = BK : KQ.$$ Q.E.D.

Also, $\qquad KH : HL = BK \text{ or } AM : AF,$

and by subtraction,

$$KH : KL = AM : MF.$$ Q.E.D.

COR. I. Hence if a parallelogram IKLM described about a given conic section is given, the rectangle KQ·ME, as also the rectangle KH·MF equal thereto, will be given. For, by reason of the similar triangles KQH, MFE, those rectangles are equal.

COR. II. And if a sixth tangent *eq* is drawn meeting the tangents KI, MI in *q*

and e, the rectangle KQ·ME will be equal to the rectangle Kq·Me, and
$$KQ : Me = Kq : ME,$$
and by subtraction
$$KQ : Me = Qq : Ee.$$

COR. III. Hence, also, if Eq, eQ are joined and bisected, and a right line is drawn through the points of bisection, this right line will pass through the centre of the conic section. For since Qq : Ee = KQ : Me, the same right line will pass through the middle of all the lines Eq, eQ, MK (by Lem. 23), and the middle point of the right line MK is the centre of the section.

PROPOSITION 27. PROBLEM 19

To describe a conic that may touch five right lines given in position.

Supposing ABG, BCF, GCD, FDE, EA to be the tangents given in position. Bisect in M and N, AF, BE, the diagonals of the quadrilateral figure ABFE contained under any four of them; and (by Cor. III, Lem. 25) the right line MN

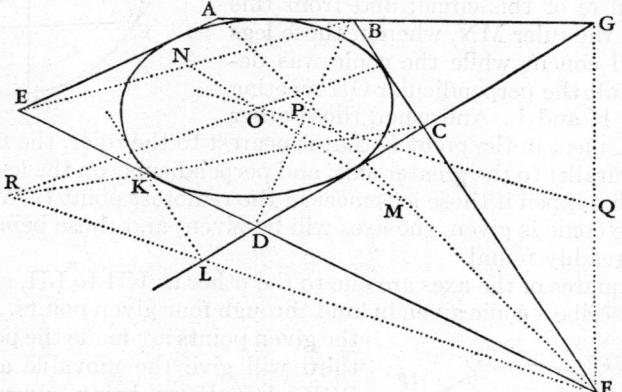

drawn through the points of bisection will pass through the centre of the conic. Again, bisect in P and Q the diagonals (if I may so call them) BD, GF of the quadrilateral figure BGDF contained under any other four tangents, and the right line PQ drawn through the points of bisection will pass through the centre of the conic; and therefore the centre will be given in the intersection of the bisecting lines. Suppose it to be O. Parallel to any tangent BC draw KL at such distance that the centre O may be placed in the middle between the parallels; this KL will touch the conic to be described. Let this cut any other two tangents GCD, FDE, in L and K. Through the points C and K, F and L, where the tangents not parallel, CL, FK, meet the parallel tangents CF, KL, draw CK, FL meeting in R; and the right line OR, drawn and produced, will cut the parallel tangents CF, KL, in the points of contact. This appears from Cor. II, Lem. 24. And by the same method the other points of contact may be found, and then the conic may be described by Prob. 14. Q.E.F.

SCHOLIUM

Under the preceding Propositions are comprehended those Problems wherein either the centres or asymptotes of the conics are given. For when points and tangents and the centre are given, as many other points and as many other tangents are given at an equal distance on the other side of the centre. And an asymptote is to be considered as a tangent, and its infinitely remote extremity (if we may say so) is a point of contact. Conceive the point of contact of any tangent removed *in infinitum,* and the tangent will degenerate into an asymptote, and the constructions of the preceding Problems will be changed into the constructions of those Problems wherein the asymptote is given.

After the conic is described, we may find its axes and foci in this manner. In the construction and figure of Lem. 21, let those legs BP, CP, of the movable

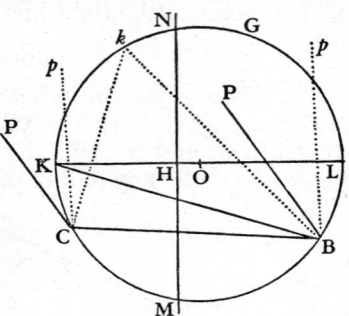

angles PBN, PCN, by the intersection of which the conic was described, be made parallel one to the other; and retaining that position, let them revolve about their poles B, C, in that figure. In the meanwhile let the other legs CN, BN, of those angles, by their intersection K or k, describe the circle BKGC. Let O be the centre of this circle; and from this centre upon the ruler MN, wherein those legs CN, BN did concur while the conic was described, let fall the perpendicular OH meeting the circle in K and L. And when those other legs CK, BK meet in the point K that is nearest to the ruler, the first legs CP, BP will be parallel to the greater axis, and perpendicular on the lesser; and the contrary will happen if those legs meet in the remotest point L. Whence if the centre of the conic is given, the axes will be given; and those being given, the foci will be readily found.

But the squares of the axes are one to the other as KH to LH, and thence it is easy to describe a conic given in kind through four given points. For if two of

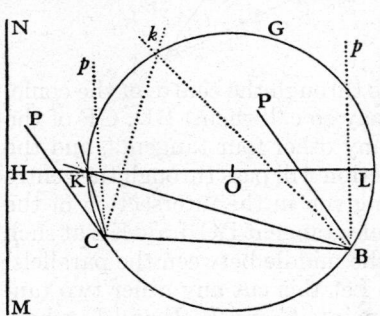

the given points are made the poles C, B, the third will give the movable angles PCK, PBK; but those being given, the circle BGKC may be described. Then, because the conic is given in kind, the ratio of OH to OK, and therefore OH itself, will be given. About the centre O, with the interval OH, describe another circle, and the right line that touches this circle, and passes through the intersection of the legs CK, BK, when the first legs CP, BP meet in the fourth given point, will be the ruler MN, by means of which the conic may be described. Whence also on the other hand a trapezium given in kind (excepting a few cases that are impossible) may be inscribed in a given conic section.

There are also other Lemmas, by the help of which conics given in kind may be described through given points, and touching given lines. Of such a sort is this, that if a right line is drawn through any point given in position, that may cut a given conic section in two points, and the distance of the intersections is bisected, the point of bisection will touch another conic section of the same kind with the former, and having its axes parallel to the axes of the former. But I hasten to things of greater use.

LEMMA 26

To place the three angles of a triangle, given both in kind and in magnitude, in respect to as many right lines given in position, provided they are not all parallel among themselves, in such manner that the several angles may touch the several lines.

Three indefinite right lines AB, AC, BC are given in position, and it is required so to place the triangle DEF that its angle D may touch the line AB, its

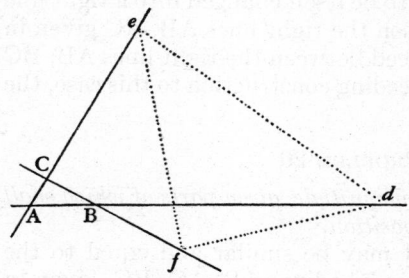

angle E the line AC, and its angle F the line BC. Upon DE, DF, and EF describe three segments of circles DRE, DGF, EMF, capable of angles equal to the angles BAC, ABC, ACB respectively. But those segments are to be described towards such sides of the lines DE, DF, EF, that the letters DRED may turn round about in the same order with the letters BACB; the letters DGFD in the same order with the letters ABCA; and the letters EMFE in the same order with the letters ACBA; then, completing those segments into entire circles, let the two former circles cut each other in G, and suppose P and Q to be their centres. Then joining GP, PQ, take

$$Ga : AB = GP : PQ;$$

and about the centre G, with the interval Ga, describe a circle that may cut the first circle DGE in a. Join aD cutting the second circle DFG in b, as well as aE cutting the third circle EMF in c. Complete the figure ABCdef similar and equal to the figure abcDEF: I say, the thing is done.

For drawing Fc meeting aD in n, and joining aG, bG, QG, QD, PD, by construction the angle EaD is equal to the angle CAB, and the angle acF equal to the angle ACB; and therefore the triangle anc equiangular to the triangle ABC. Wherefore the angle anc or FnD is equal to the angle ABC, and consequently to the angle FbD; and therefore the point n falls on the point b. Moreover the angle GPQ, which is half the angle GPD at the centre, is equal to the angle GaD at the circumference; and the angle GQP, which is half the angle GQD at the centre, is equal to the supplement of the angle GbD at the circumference, and therefore equal to the angle Gba. Upon which account the triangles GPQ, Gab are similar, and

$$Ga : ab = GP : PQ$$

and, by construction,

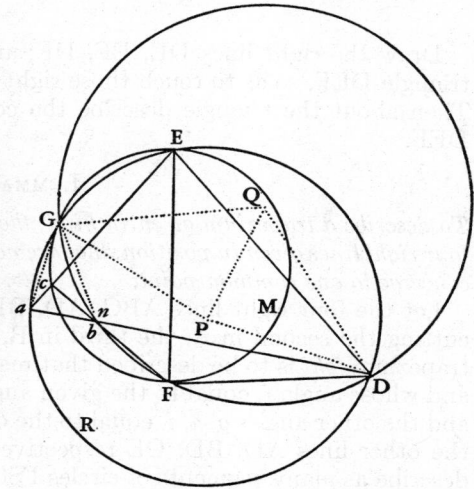

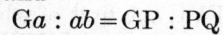

$$GP : PQ = Ga : AB.$$

Wherefore *ab* and AB are equal; and consequently the triangles *abc*, ABC, which we have now proved to be similar, are also equal. And therefore since the angles D, E, F of the triangle DEF do respectively touch the sides *ab*, *ac*, *bc* of the triangle *abc*, the figure ABC*def* may be completed similar and equal to the figure *abc*DEF, and by completing it the Problem will be solved.   Q.E.F.

COR. Hence a right line may be drawn whose parts given in length may be intercepted between three right lines given in position. Suppose the triangle DEF, by the approach of its point D to the side EF, and by having the sides DE, DF placed into the same straight line, to be itself changed into a right line whose given part DE is to be placed between the right lines AB, AC given in position; and its given part DF is to be placed between the right lines AB, BC given in position; then, by applying the preceding construction to this case, the Problem will be solved.

PROPOSITION 28. PROBLEM 20

To describe a conic given both in kind and in magnitude, given parts of which shall be placed between three right lines given in position.

Suppose a conic is to be described that may be similar and equal to the curved line DEF, and may be cut by three right lines AB, AC, BC, given in position, into parts DE and EF, similar and equal to the given parts of this curved line.

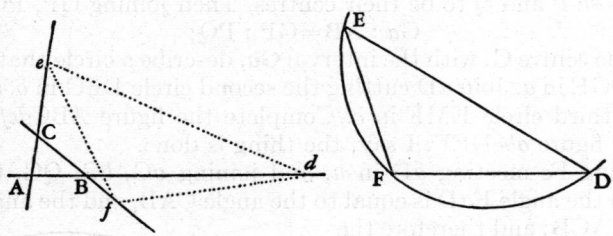

Draw the right lines DE, EF, DF; and place the angles D, E, F, of this triangle DEF, so as to touch those right lines given in position (by Lem. 26). Then about the triangle describe the conic, similar and equal to the curve DEF.   Q.E.F.

LEMMA 27

To describe a trapezium given in kind, the angles whereof may respectively touch four right lines given in position, that are neither all parallel among themselves, nor converge to one common point.

Let the four right lines ABC, AD, BD, CE be given in position; the first cutting the second in A, the third in B, and the fourth in C; and suppose a trapezium *fghi* is to be described that may be similar to the trapezium FGHI, and whose angle *f*, equal to the given angle F, may touch the right line ABC; and the other angles *g*, *h*, *i*, equal to the other given angles G, H, I, may touch the other lines AD, BD, CE respectively. Join FH, and upon FG, FH, FI describe as many segments of circles FSG, FTH, FVI, the first of which FSG may be capable of an angle equal to the angle BAD; the second FTH capable of an angle equal to the angle CBD; and the third FVI of an angle equal to the angle ACE. But the segments are to be described towards those sides of the lines FG, FH, FI, that the circular order of the letters FSGF may be the same as of the letters BADB, and that the letters FTHF may turn about in the same order as the letters CBDC, and the letters FVIF in the same order as the letters ACEA. Complete the segments into entire circles, and let P be the centre

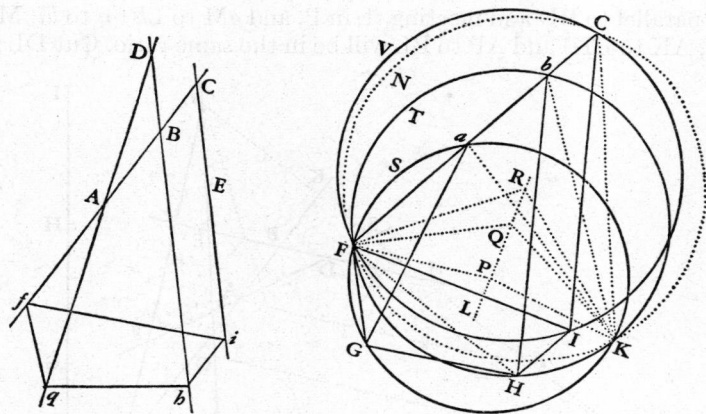

of the first circle FSG, Q the centre of the second FTH. Join and produce both ways the line PQ, and in it take QR so that QR : PQ=BC : AB. But QR is to be taken towards that side of the point Q, that the order of the letters P, Q, R may be the same as of the letters A, B, C; and about the centre R with the radius RF describe a fourth circle FN*c* cutting the third circle FVI in *c*. Join F*c* cutting the first circle in *a*, and the second in *b*. Draw *a*G, *b*H, *c*I, and let the figure ABC*fghi* be made similar to the figure *abc*FGHI; and the trapezium *fghi* will be that which was required to be described.

For let the two first circles FSG, FTH cut one the other in K; join PK, QK, RK, *a*K, *b*K, *c*K, and produce QP to L. The angles F*a*K, F*b*K, F*c*K at the circumferences are the halves of the angles FPK, FQK, FRK at the centres, and therefore equal to LPK, LQK, LRK, the halves of those angles. Therefore the figure PQRK is equiangular and similar to the figure *abc*K, and consequently *ab* is to *bc* as PQ to QR, that is, as AB to BC. But by construction the angles *f*A*g*, *f*B*h*, *f*C*i* are equal to the angles F*a*G, F*b*H, F*c*I. And therefore the figure ABC*fghi* may be completed similar to the figure *abc*FGHI. This done, a trapezium *fghi* will be constructed similar to the trapezium FGHI, and by its angles *f*, *g*, *h*, *i* will touch the right lines ABC, AD, BD, CE.   Q.E.F.

Cor. Hence a right line may be drawn whose parts intercepted in a given order, between four right lines given by position, shall have a given proportion among themselves. Let the angles FGH, GHI be so far increased that the right lines FG, GH, HI may lie in the same line; and by constructing the Problem in this case, a right line *fghi* will be drawn, whose parts *fg*, *gh*, *hi*, intercepted between the four right lines given in position, AB and AD, AD and BD, BD and CE, will be to each other as the lines FG, GH, HI, and will observe the same order among themselves. But the same thing may be more readily done in this manner:

Produce AB to K and BD to L, so as BK may be to AB as HI to GH; and DL to BD as GI to FG; and join KL meeting the right line CE in i. Produce iL to M, so as LM may be to iL as GH to HI; then draw MQ parallel to LB, and meeting the right line AD in g, and join gi cutting AB, BD in f, h: I say, the thing is done.

For let Mg cut the right line AB in Q, and AD the right line KL in S, and draw AP parallel to BD and meeting iL in P, and gM to Lh (gi to hi, Mi to Li, GI to HI, AK to BK) and AP to BL will be in the same ratio. Cut DL in R, so

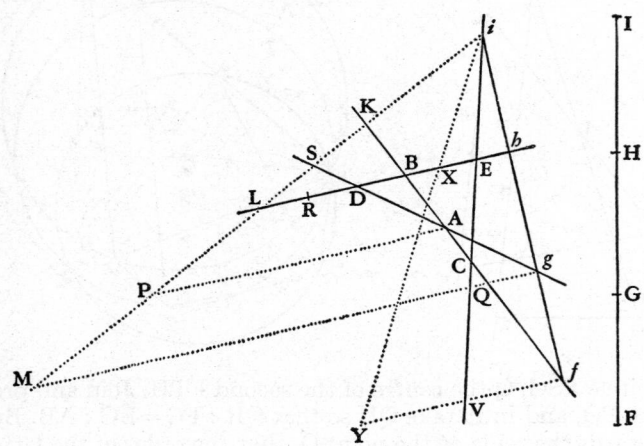

as DL to RL may be in that same ratio; and because gS to gM, AS to AP, and DS to DL are proportional; therefore, as gS to Lh, so will AS be to BL, and DS to RL; and mixtly, BL−RL to Lh−BL, as AS−DS to gS−AS. That is, BR is to Bh as AD is to Ag, and therefore as BD to gQ. And alternately BR is to BD as Bh to gQ, or as fh to fg. But by construction the line BL was cut in D and R in the same ratio as the line FI in G and H; and therefore BR is to BD as FH to FG. Therefore fh is to fg as FH to FG. Since, therefore, gi to hi likewise is as Mi to Li, that is, as GI to HI, it is manifest that the lines FI, fi are similarly cut in G and H, g and h.   Q.E.F.

In the construction of this Corollary, after the line LK is drawn cutting CE in i, we may produce iE to V, so as EV may be to Ei as FH to HI, and then draw Vf parallel to BD. It will come to the same, if about the centre i with an interval IH, we describe a circle cutting BD in X, and produce iX to Y so as iY may be equal to IF, and then draw Yf parallel to BD.

Sir Christopher Wren and Dr. Wallis have long ago given other solutions of this Problem.

Proposition 29. Problem 21

To describe a conic given in kind, that may be cut by four right lines given in position, into parts given in order, kind, and proportion.

Suppose a conic is to be described that may be similar to the curved line FGHI, and whose parts, similar and proportional to the parts FG, GH, HI of the other, may be intercepted between the right lines AB and AD, AD and BD, BD and CE given in position, viz., the first between the first pair of those lines, the second between the second, and the third between the third. Draw the right lines FG, GH, HI, FI; and (by Lem. 27) describe a trapezium *fghi* that may be similar to the trapezium FGHI, and whose angles *f*, *g*, *h*, *i* may touch the right lines given in position AB, AD, BD, CE, severally according to their order. And then about this trapezium describe a conic, that conic will be similar to the curved line FGHI.

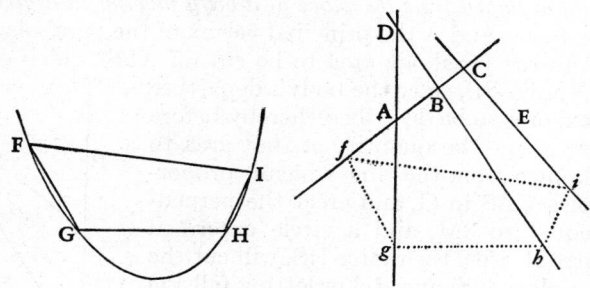

SCHOLIUM

This problem may be likewise constructed in the following manner. Joining FG, GH, HI, FI, produce GF to V, and join FH, IG, and make the angles CAK, DAL equal to the angles FGH, VFH. Let AK, AL meet the right line BD in K and L, and thence draw KM, LN, of which let KM make the angle AKM equal to the angle GHI, and be itself to AK as HI is to GH; and let LN make the angle ALN equal to the angle FHI, and be itself to AL as HI to FH. But AK, KM, AL, LN are to be drawn towards those sides of the lines AD,

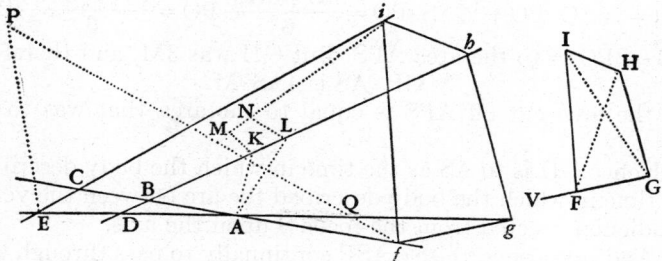

AK, AL, that the letters CAKMC, ALKA, DALND may be carried round in the same order as the letters FGHIF; and draw MN meeting the right line CE in *i*. Make the angle *i*EP equal to the angle IGF, and let PE be to E*i* as FG to GI; and through P draw PQ*f* that may with the right line ADE contain an angle PQE equal to the angle FIG, and may meet the right line AB in *f*, and join *fi*. But PE and PQ are to be drawn towards those sides of the lines CE, PE that the circular order of the letters PE*i*P and PEQP may be the same as of the letters FGHIF; and if upon the line *fi*, in the same order of letters, and similar to the trapezium FGHI, a trapezium *fghi* is constructed, and a conic given in kind is circumscribed about it, the Problem will be solved.

So far concerning the finding of the orbits. It remains that we determine the motions of bodies in the orbits so found.

SECTION VI

How the motions are to be found in given orbits

Proposition 30. Problem 22

To find at any assigned time the place of a body moving in a given parabola.

Let S be the focus, and A the principal vertex of the parabola; and suppose
4AS·M equal to the parabolic area to be cut off APS, which either was described by the radius SP, since the body's departure
from the vertex, or is to be described thereby before
its arrival there. Now the quantity of that area to
be cut off is known from the time which is proportional to it. Bisect AS in G, and erect the perpendicular GH equal to 3M, and a circle described
about the centre H, with the radius HS, will cut the
parabola in the place P required. For letting fall PO
perpendicular on the axis, and drawing PH, there
will be

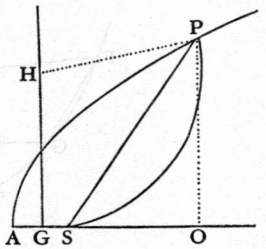

$$AG^2 + GH^2 (= HP^2 = (AO - AG)^2 + (PO - GH)^2)$$
$$= AO^2 + PO^2 - 2AO \cdot AG - 2GH \cdot PO + AG^2 + GH^2.$$

Whence
$$2GH \cdot PO (= AO^2 + PO^2 - 2AO \cdot AG) = AO^2 + \tfrac{3}{4}PO^2. \text{ For } AO^2$$
write $AO \cdot \dfrac{PO^2}{4AS}$; then dividing all the terms by 3PO, and multiplying them by
2AS, we shall have

$$\tfrac{4}{3}GH \cdot AS (= \tfrac{1}{6}AO \cdot PO + \tfrac{1}{2}AS \cdot PO = \frac{AO + 3AS}{6} \cdot PO = \frac{4AO - 3SO}{6} \cdot PO = \text{to the}$$

area, APO − SPO) = to the area APS. But GH was 3M, and therefore
$$\tfrac{4}{3}GH \cdot AS \text{ is } 4AS \cdot M.$$
Therefore the area cut off APS is equal to the area that was to be cut off
4AS·M.   Q.E.D.

Cor. i. Hence GH is to AS as the time in which the body described the arc
AP to the time in which the body described the arc between the vertex A and
the perpendicular erected from the focus S upon the axis.

Cor. ii. And supposing a circle ASP continually to pass through the moving
body P, the velocity of the point H is to the velocity which the body had in the
vertex A as 3 to 8; and therefore in the same ratio is the line GH to the right
line which the body, in the time of its moving from A to P, would describe with
that velocity which it had in the vertex A.

Cor. iii. Hence, also, on the other hand, the time may be found in which the
body has described any assigned arc AP. Join AP, and on its middle point erect
a perpendicular meeting the right line GH in H.

Lemma 28

*There is no oval figure whose area, cut off by right lines at pleasure, can be
universally found by means of equations of any number of finite terms and
dimensions.*

Suppose that within the oval any point is given, about which as a pole a
right line is continually revolving with an uniform motion, while in that right

line a movable point going out from the pole moves always forwards with a velocity proportional to the square of that right line within the oval. By this motion that point will describe a spiral with infinite circumgyrations. Now if a portion of the area of the oval cut off by that right line could be found by a finite equation, the distance of the point from the pole, which is proportional to this area, might be found by the same equation, and therefore all the points of the spiral might be found by a finite equation also; and therefore the intersection of a right line given in position with the spiral might also be found by a finite equation. But every right line infinitely produced cuts a spiral in an infinite number of points; and the equation by which any one intersection of two lines is found at the same time exhibits all their intersections by as many roots, and therefore rises to as many dimensions as there are intersections. Because two circles cut one another in two points, one of those intersections is not to be found but by an equation of two dimensions, by which the other intersection may be also found. Because there may be four intersections of two conic sections, any one of them is not to be found universally, but by an equation of four dimensions, by which they may be all found together. For if those intersections are severally sought, because the law and condition of all is the same, the calculus will be the same in every case, and therefore the conclusion always the same, which must therefore comprehend all those intersections at once within itself, and exhibit them all indifferently. Hence it is that the intersections of the conic sections with the curves of the third order, because they may amount to six, come out together by equations of six dimensions; and the intersections of two curves of the third order, because they may amount to nine, come out together by equations of nine dimensions. If this did not necessarily happen, we might reduce all solid to plane Problems, and those higher than solid to solid Problems. But here I speak of curves irreducible in power. For if the equation by which the curve is defined may be reduced to a lower power, the curve will not be one single curve, but composed of two, or more, whose intersections may be severally found by different calculi. After the same manner the two intersections of right lines with the conic sections come out always by equations of two dimensions; the three intersections of right lines with the irreducible curves of the third order, by equations of three dimensions; the four intersections of right lines with the irreducible curves of the fourth order, by equations of four dimensions; and so on *in infinitum*. Wherefore the innumerable intersections of a right line with a spiral, since this is but one simple curve, and not reducible to more curves, require equations infinite in number of dimensions and roots, by which they may be all exhibited together. For the law and calculus of all is the same. For if a perpendicular is let fall from the pole upon that intersecting right line, and that perpendicular together with the intersecting line revolves about the pole, the intersections of the spiral will mutually pass the one into the other; and that which was first or nearest, after one revolution, will be the second; after two, the third; and so on: nor will the equation in the meantime be changed but as the magnitudes of those quantities are changed, by which the position of the intersecting line is determined. Therefore since those quantities after every revolution return to their first magnitudes, the equation will return to its first form; and consequently one and the same equation will exhibit all the intersections, and will therefore have an infinite number of roots, by which they may be all exhibited. Therefore the intersection of a right line with a spiral cannot be universally found by any finite equation; and hence there is no oval figure whose area, cut off by right lines at pleasure, can be universally exhibited by any such equation.

By the same argument, if the interval of the pole and point by which the spiral is described is taken proportional to that part of the perimeter of the oval which is cut off, it may be proved that the length of the perimeter cannot be universally exhibited by any finite equation. But here I speak of ovals that are not touched by conjugate figures running out *in infinitum*.

Cor. Hence the area of an ellipse, described by a radius drawn from the focus to the moving body, is not to be found from the time given by a finite equation; and therefore cannot be determined by the description of curves geometrically rational. Those curves I call geometrically rational, all the points whereof may be determined by lengths that are definable by equations; that is, by the complicated ratios of lengths. Other curves (such as spirals, quadratrixes, and cycloids) I call geometrically irrational. For the lengths which are or are not as number to number (according to Book x, *Elements* of Euclid) are arithmetically rational or irrational. And therefore I cut off an area of an ellipse proportional to the time in which it is described by a curve geometrically irrational, in the following manner:

Proposition 31. Problem 23

To find the place of a body moving in a given ellipse at any assigned time.

Suppose A to be the principal vertex, S the focus, and O the centre of the ellipse APB; and let P be the place of the body to be found. Produce OA to G so that OG : OA = OA : OS. Erect the perpendicular GH; and about the centre

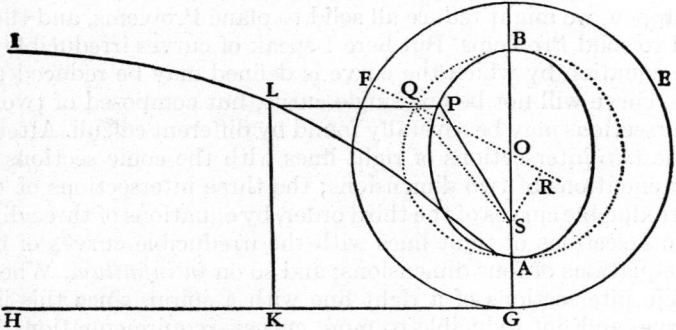

O, with the radius OG, describe the circle GEF; and on the ruler GH, as a base, suppose the wheel GEF to move forwards, revolving about its axis, and in the meantime by its point A describing the cycloid ALI. This done, take GK to the perimeter GEFG of the wheel, in the ratio of the time in which the body proceeding from A described the arc AP, to the time of a whole revolution in the ellipse. Erect the perpendicular KL meeting the cycloid in L; then LP drawn parallel to KG will meet the ellipse in P, the required place of the body.

For about the centre O with the radius OA describe the semicircle AQB, and let LP, produced, if need be, meet the arc AQ in Q, and join SQ, OQ. Let OQ meet the arc EFG in F, and upon OQ let fall the perpendicular SR. The area APS varies as the area AQS, that is, as the difference between the sector OQA and the triangle OQS, or as the difference of the rectangles ½OQ·AQ, and

½OQ·SR, that is, because ½OQ is given, as the difference between the arc AQ and the right line SR; and therefore (because of the equality of the given ratios SR to the sine of the arc AQ, OS to OA, OA to OG, AQ to GF; and by division, AQ−SR to GF−sine of the arc AQ) as GK, the difference between the arc GF and the sine of the arc AQ.   Q.E.D.

SCHOLIUM

But since the description of this curve is difficult, a solution by approximation will be preferable. First, then, let there be found a certain angle B which may be to an angle of 57.29578 degrees, which an arc equal to the radius subtends, as SH, the distance of the foci, to AB, the diameter of the ellipse.

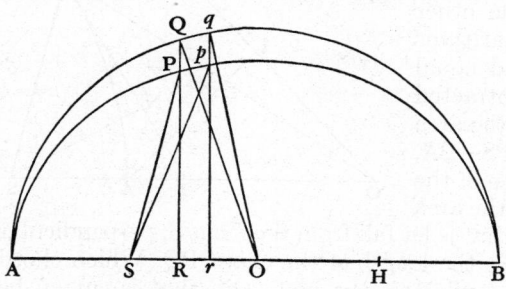

Secondly, a certain length L, which may be to the radius in the same ratio inversely. And these being found, the Problem may be solved by the following analysis. By any construction (or even by conjecture), suppose we know P the place of the body near its true place p. Then letting fall on the axis of the ellipse the ordinate PR from the proportion of the diameters of the ellipse, the ordinate RQ of the circumscribed circle AQB will be given; which ordinate is the sine of the angle AOQ, supposing AO to be the radius, and also cuts the ellipse in P. It will be sufficient if that angle is found by a rude calculus in numbers near the truth. Suppose we also know the angle proportional to the time, that is, which is to four right angles as the time in which the body described the arc Ap to the time of one revolution in the ellipse. Let this angle be N. Then take an angle D, which may be to the angle B as the sine of the angle AOQ to the radius; and an angle E which may be to the angle N−AOQ+D as the length L to the same length L diminished by the cosine of the angle AOQ, when that angle is less than a right angle, or increased thereby when greater. In the next place, take an angle F that may be to the angle B as the sine of the angle AOQ+E to the radius, and an angle G, that may be to the angle N −AOQ−E+F as the length L to the same length L diminished by the cosine of the angle AOQ+E, when that angle is less than a right angle, or increased thereby when greater. For the third time take an angle H, that may be to the angle B as the sine of the angle AOQ+E+G to the radius; and an angle I to the angle N−AOQ−E−G+H, as the length L is to the same length L diminished by the cosine of the angle AOQ+E+G, when that angle is less than a right angle, or increased thereby when greater. And so we may proceed *in infinitum*. Lastly, take the angle AOq equal to the angle AOQ+E+G+I+, &c., and from its cosine Or and the ordinate pr, which is to its sine qr as the lesser axis of the ellipse to the greater, we shall have p the correct place of the body. When the angle N− AOQ+D happens to be negative, the sign + of the angle E must be everywhere changed into −, and the sign − into +. And the same thing is to be understood of the signs of the angles G and I, when the angles N−AOQ−E+F, and N−AOQ−E−G+H come out negative. But the infinite series AOQ+

E+G+I+, &c., converges so very fast, that it will be scarcely ever needful to proceed beyond the second term E. And the calculus is founded upon this Theorem, that the area APS varies as the difference between the arc AQ and the right line let fall from the focus S perpendicularly upon the radius OQ.

And by a calculus not unlike, the Problem is solved in the hyperbola. Let its centre be O, its vertex A, its focus S, and asymptote OK; and suppose the amount of the area to be cut off is known, as being proportional to the time. Let that be A, and by conjecture suppose we know the position of a right line SP, that cuts off an area APS near the truth. Join OP, and from A and P to the asymptote draw AI, PK, parallel to the other asymptote; and by the table of logarithms the area AIKP will be given, and equal thereto the area OPA, which, subtracted from the triangle OPS, will leave the area cut off APS. And by applying 2APS−2A, or 2A−2APS, the double difference of the area A that was to be cut off, and the area

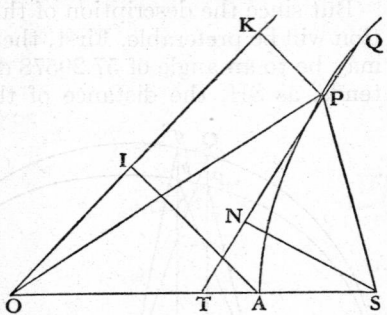

APS that is cut off, to the line SN that is let fall from the focus S, perpendicular upon the tangent TP, we shall have the length of the chord PQ. Which chord PQ is to be inscribed between A and P, if the area APS that is cut off be greater than the area A that was to be cut off, but towards the contrary side of the point P, if otherwise: and the point Q will be the place of the body more accurately. And by repeating the computation the place may be found continually to greater and greater accuracy.

And by such computations we have a general analytical resolution of the Problem. But the particular calculus that follows is better fitted for astronomical purposes. Supposing AO, OB, OD to be the semiaxes of the ellipse, and L its latus rectum, and D the difference between the lesser semiaxis OD, and

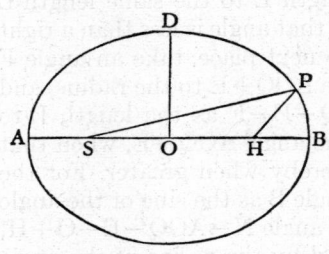

½L the half of the latus rectum: let an angle Y be found, whose sine may be to the radius as the rectangle under that difference D, and AO+OD the half sum of the axes, to the square of the greater axis AB. Find also an angle Z, whose sine may be to the radius as the double rectangle under the distance of the foci SH and that difference D, to triple the square of half the greater semiaxis AO. Those angles being once found, the place of the body may be thus determined.

Take the angle T proportional to the time in which the arc BP was described, or equal to what is called the mean motion; and take an angle V, the first equation of the mean motion, to the angle Y, the greatest first equation, as the sine of double the angle T is to the radius; and take an angle X, the second equation, to the angle Z, the second greatest equation, as the cube of the sine of the angle T is to the cube of the radius. Then take the angle BHP, the mean equated motion either equal to T+X+V, the sum of the angles T, V, X, if the angle T is less than a right angle, or equal to T+X−V, the difference of the same, if that angle T is greater than one and less than two right angles; and if HP meets the ellipse in P, draw SP, and it will cut off the area BSP, nearly proportional to the time.

This practice seems to be expeditious enough, because the angles V and X, taken in fractions of seconds, if you please, being very small, it will be sufficient to find two or three of their first figures. But it is likewise sufficiently accurate to answer to the theory of the planets' motions. For even in the orbit of Mars, where the greatest equation of the centre amounts to ten degrees, the error will scarcely exceed one second. But when the angle of the mean motion equated BHP is found, the angle of the true motion BSP, and the distance SP, are readily had by the known methods.

And so far concerning the motion of bodies in curved lines. But it may also come to pass that a moving body shall ascend or descend in a right line; and I shall now go on to explain what belongs to such kind of motions.

SECTION VII

The rectilinear ascent and descent of bodies

Proposition 32. Problem 24

Supposing that the centripetal force is inversely proportional to the square of the distance of the places from the centre; it is required to define the spaces which a body, falling directly, describes in given times.

Case 1. If the body does not fall perpendicularly, it will (by Cor. i, Prop. 13) describe some conic section whose focus is placed in the centre of force. Suppose that conic section to be ARPB and its focus S. And, first, if the figure be an ellipse, upon the greater axis thereof AB describe the semicircle ADB, and let the right line DPC pass through the falling body, making right angles with the axis; and drawing DS, PS, the area ASD will be proportional to the area ASP, and therefore also to the time. The axis AB still remaining the same, let the breadth of the ellipse be continually diminished, and the area ASD will always remain proportional to the time. Suppose that breadth to be diminished *in infinitum;* and the orbit APB in that case coinciding with the axis AB, and the focus S with the extreme point of the axis B, the body will descend in the right line AC, and the area ABD will become proportional to the time. Therefore the space AC will be given which the body describes in a given time by its perpendicular fall from the place A, if the area ABD is taken proportional to the time, and from the point D the right line DC is let fall perpendicularly on the right line AB.   Q.E.I.

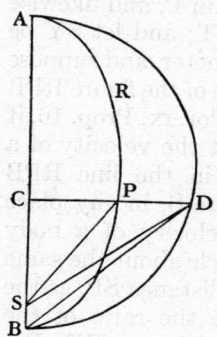

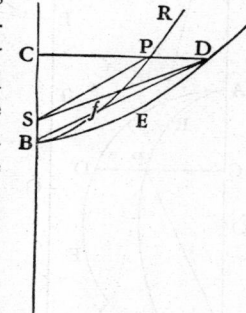

Case 2. If the figure RPB is an hyperbola, on the same principal diameter AB describe the rectangular hyperbola BED; and because there exist between the several areas and the heights CP and CD relations,

CSP : CSD = CBfP : CBED = SPfB : SDEB = CP : CD, and since the area SPfB varies as the time in which the body P will move through the arc PfB, the area SDEB will also vary as that time. Let the latus rectum of the hyperbola RPB be diminished *in infinitum*, the transverse axis remaining the same; and the arc PB will come to coincide with the right line CB, and the focus S with the vertex B, and the right line SD with the right line BD. And therefore the area BDEB will vary as the time in which the body C, by its perpendicular descent, describes the line CB. Q.E.I.

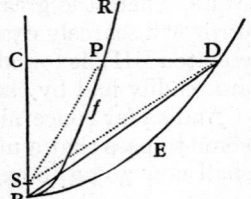

CASE 3. And by the like argument, if the figure RPB is a parabola, and to the same principal vertex B another parabola BED is described, that may always remain given while the former parabola in whose perimeter the body P moves, by having its latus rectum diminished and reduced to nothing, comes to coincide with the line CB, the parabolic segment BDEB will vary as the time in which that body P or C will descend to the centre S or B. Q.E.I.

PROPOSITION 33. THEOREM 9

The things above found being supposed, I say, that the velocity of a falling body in any place C is to the velocity of a body, describing a circle about the centre B at the distance BC, as the square root of the ratio of AC, the distance of the body from the remoter vertex A of the circle or rectangular hyperbola, to ½AB, the principal semi-diameter of the figure.

Let AB, the common diameter of both figures RPB, DEB, be bisected in O; and draw the right line PT that may touch the figure RPB in P, and likewise cut that common diameter AB (produced, if need be) in T; and let SY be perpendicular to this line, and BQ perpendicular to this diameter, and suppose the latus rectum of the figure RPB to be L. From Cor. IX, Prop. 16, it is manifest that the velocity of a body, moving in the line RPB about the centre S, in any place P, is to the velocity of a body describing a circle about the same centre, at the distance SP, as the square root of the ratio of the rectangle ½L·SP to SY². For by the properties of the conic sections AC·CB is to CP² as 2AO to L, and therefore $\dfrac{2CP^2 \cdot AO}{AC \cdot CB}$ is equal to L. Therefore those velocities are to each other as the square root of the ratio of $\dfrac{CP^2 \cdot AO \cdot SP}{AC \cdot CB}$ to SY². Moreover, by the properties of the conic sections,

$$CO : BO = BO : TO,$$

thence, $$CO + BO : BO = BO + TO : TO,$$

and $$CO : BO = CB : BT.$$

From this, $$BO - CO : BO = BT - CB : BT$$

and $$AC : AO = TC : BT = CP : BQ;$$

and, since $$CP = \frac{BQ \cdot AC}{AO},$$

one obtains $$\frac{CP^2 \cdot AO \cdot SP}{AC \cdot CB} \text{ equal to } \frac{BQ^2 \cdot AC \cdot SP}{AO \cdot BC}.$$

Now suppose CP, the breadth of the figure RPB, to be diminished *in infinitum*, so that the point P may come to coincide with the point C, and the point S with the point B, and the line SP with the line BC, and the line SY with the line BQ; and the velocity of the body now descending perpendicularly in the line CB will be to the velocity of a body describing a circle about the centre B, at the distance BC, as the square root of the ratio of $\frac{BQ^2 \cdot AC \cdot SP}{AO \cdot BC}$ to SY^2, that is (neglecting the ratios of equality of SP to BC, and BQ^2 to SY^2), as the square root of the ratio of AC to AO, or ½AB.   Q.E.D.

COR. I. When the points B and S come to coincide, TC will become to TS as AC to AO.

COR. II. A body revolving in any circle at a given distance from the centre, by its motion converted upwards, will ascend to double its distance from the centre.

PROPOSITION 34. THEOREM 10

If the figure BED is a parabola, I say, that the velocity of a falling body in any place C is equal to the velocity by which a body may uniformly describe a circle about the centre B at half the interval BC.

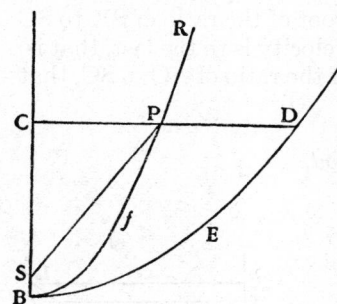

For (by Cor. VII, Prop. 16) the velocity of a body describing a parabola RPB about the centre S, in any place P, is equal to the velocity of a body uniformly describing a circle about the same centre S at half the interval SP. Let the breadth CP of the parabola be diminished *in infinitum*, so that the parabolic arc P*f*B may come to coincide with the right line CB, the centre S with the vertex B, and the interval SP with the interval BC, and the Proposition will be manifest.   Q.E.D.

PROPOSITION 35. THEOREM 11

The same things supposed, I say, that the area of the figure DES, described by the indefinite radius SD, is equal to the area which a body with a radius equal to half the latus rectum of the figure DES describes in the same time, by uniformly revolving about the centre S.

For suppose a body C in the smallest moment of time describes in falling the infinitely little line C*c*, while another body K, uniformly revolving about the centre S in the circle OK*k*, describes the arc K*k*. Erect the perpendiculars CD, *cd*, meeting the figure DES in D, *d*. Join SD, S*d*, SK, S*k*, and draw D*d* meeting the axis AS in T, and thereon let fall the perpendicular SY.

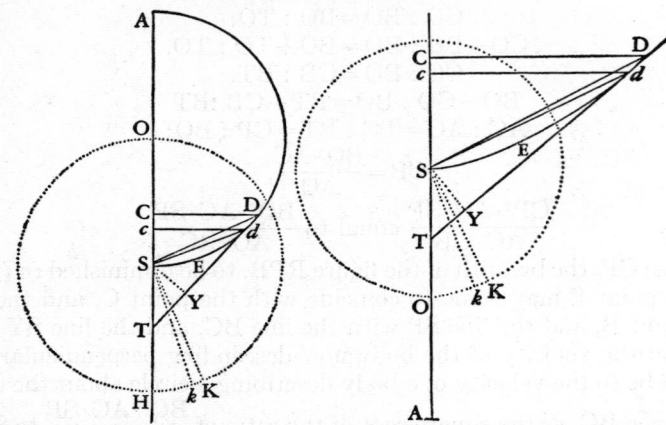

CASE 1. If the figure DES is a circle, or a rectangular hyperbola, bisect its transverse diameter AS in O, and SO will be half the latus rectum. And because
$$TC : TD = Cc : Dd,$$
and
$$TD : TS = CD : Sy,$$
there follows
$$TC : TS = CD \cdot Cc : SY \cdot Dd.$$
But (by Cor. I, Prop. 33)
$$TC : TS = AC : AO,$$
namely, if in the coalescence of the points D, d the ultimate ratios of the lines are taken. Therefore,
$$AC : AO \text{ or } SK = CD \cdot Cc : SY \cdot Dd.$$
Further, the velocity of the descending body in C is to the velocity of a body describing a circle about the centre S, at the interval SC, as the square root of the ratio of AC to AO or SK (by Prop. 33); and this velocity is to the velocity of a body describing the circle OKk as the square root of the ratio of SK to SC (by Cor. VI, Prop. 4); and, consequently, the first velocity is to the last, that is, the little line Cc to the arc Kk, as the square root of the ratio of AC to SC, that is, in the ratio of AC to CD. Therefore,
$$CD \cdot Cc = AC \cdot Kk,$$
hence,
$$AC : SK = AC \cdot Kk : SY \cdot Dd,$$
and
$$SK \cdot Kk = SY \cdot Dd,$$
and
$$\tfrac{1}{2}SK \cdot Kk = \tfrac{1}{2}SY \cdot Dd,$$
that is, the area KSk is equal to the area SDd. Therefore in every moment of time two equal particles, KSk and SDd, of areas are generated, which, if their magnitude is diminished, and their number increased *in infinitum*, obtain the ratio of equality, and consequently (by Cor., Lem. IV) the whole areas together generated are always equal.   Q.E.D.

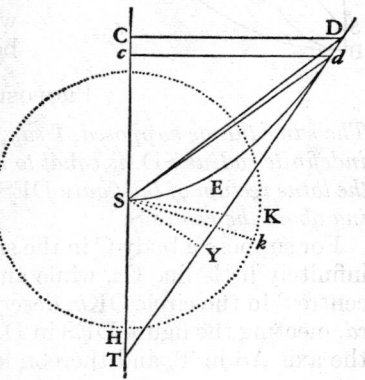

CASE 2. But if the figure DES is a parabola, we shall find, as above,
$$CD \cdot Cc : SY \cdot Dd = TC : TS,$$
that is, $= 2 : 1$; therefore,
$$\tfrac{1}{4}CD \cdot Cc = \tfrac{1}{2} SY \cdot Dd.$$
But the velocity of the falling body in C is

equal to the velocity with which a circle may be uniformly described at the interval ½SC (by Prop. 34). And this velocity to the velocity with which a circle may be described with the radius SK, that is, the little line Cc to the arc Kk, is (by Cor. VI, Prop. 4) as the square root of the ratio of SK to ½SC; that is, in the ratio of SK to ½CD. Therefore ½SK·Kk is equal to ¼CD·Cc, and therefore equal to ½SY·Dd; that is, the area KSk is equal to the area SDd, as above.

Q.E.D.

PROPOSITION 36. PROBLEM 25

To determine the times of the descent of a body falling from a given place A.

Upon the diameter AS, the distance of the body from the centre at the beginning, describe the semicircle ADS, as likewise the semicircle OKH equal thereto, about the centre S. From any place C of the body erect the ordinate CD. Join SD, and make the sector OSK equal to the area ASD. It is evident (by Prop. 35) that the body in falling will describe the space AC in the same time in which another body, uniformly revolving about the centre S, may describe the arc OK.

Q.E.F.

PROPOSITION 37. PROBLEM 26

To define the times of the ascent or descent of a body projected upwards or downwards from a given place.

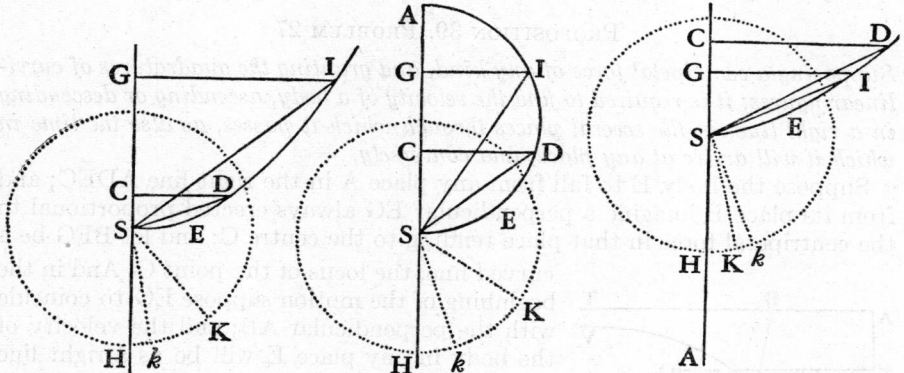

Suppose the body to go off from the given place G, in the direction of the line GS, with any velocity. Take GA to ½AS as the square of the ratio of this velocity to the uniform velocity in a circle, with which the body may revolve about the centre S at the given interval SG. If that ratio is the same as of the number 2 to 1, the point A is infinitely remote; in which case a parabola is to be described with any latus rectum to the vertex S, and axis SG; as appears by Prop. 34. But if that ratio is less or greater then the ratio of 2 to 1, in the former case a circle, in the latter a rectangular hyperbola, is to be described on the diameter SA; as appears by Prop. 33. Then about the centre S, with a radius equal to half the latus rectum, describe the circle HkK; and at the place G of the ascending or descending body, and at any other place C, erect the perpendiculars GI, CD, meeting the conic section or circle in I and D. Then joining SI, SD, let the sectors HSK, HS*k* be made equal to the segments SEIS,SEDS, and (by Prop. 35) the body G will describe the space GC in the same time in which the body K may describe the arc K*k*.   Q.E.F.

PROPOSITION 38. THEOREM 12

Supposing that the centripetal force is proportional to the altitude or distance of places from the centre, I say, that the times and velocities of falling bodies, and the spaces which they describe, are respectively proportional to the arcs, and the sines and versed sines of the arcs.

Suppose the body to fall from any place A in the right line AS; and about the centre of force S, with the radius AS, describe the quadrant of a circle AE; and let CD be the sine of any arc AD; and the body A will in the time AD in falling describe the space AC, and in the place C will acquire the velocity CD.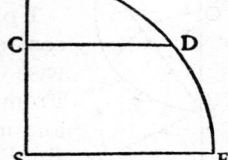

This is demonstrated the same way from Prop. 10, as Prop. 32 was demonstrated from Prop. 11.

Cor. i. Hence the times are equal in which one body falling from the place A arrives at the centre S, and another body revolving describes the quadrantal arc ADE.

Cor. ii. Therefore all the times are equal in which bodies falling from whatsoever places arrive at the centre. For all the periodic times of revolving bodies are equal (by Cor. iii, Prop. 4).

PROPOSITION 39. PROBLEM 27

Supposing a centripetal force of any kind, and granting the quadratures of curvilinear figures; it is required to find the velocity of a body, ascending or descending in a right line, in the several places through which it passes, as also the time in which it will arrive at any place; and conversely.

Suppose the body E to fall from any place A in the right line ADEC; and from its place E imagine a perpendicular EG always erected proportional to the centripetal force in that place tending to the centre C; and let BFG be a

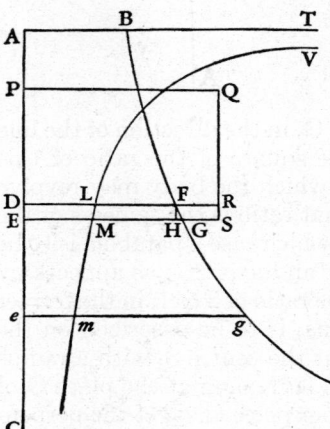

curved line, the locus of the point G. And in the beginning of the motion suppose EG to coincide with the perpendicular AB; and the velocity of the body in any place E will be as a right line whose square is equal to the curvilinear area ABGE.   Q.E.I.

In EG take EM inversely proportional to a right line whose square is equal to the area ABGE, and let VLM be a curved line wherein the point M is always placed, and to which the right line AB produced is an asymptote; and the time in which the body in falling describes the line AE, will be as the curvilinear area ABTVME.   Q.E.I.

For in the right line AE let there be taken the very small line DE of a given length, and let

DLF be the place of the line EMG, when the body was in D; and if the centripetal force be such, that a right line, whose square is equal to the area ABGE, is as the velocity of the descending body, the area itself will be as the square of that velocity; that is, if for the velocities in D and E we write V and V+I, the area ABFD will be as VV, and the area ABGE as VV+2VI+II; and by subtraction, the area DFGE as 2VI+II, and therefore $\frac{DFGE}{DE}$ will be as $\frac{2VI+II}{DE}$; that is, if we take the first ratios of those quantities when just nascent, the length DF is as the quantity $\frac{2VI}{DE}$, and therefore also as half that quantity $\frac{I \cdot V}{DE}$. But the time in which the body in falling describes the very small line DE, is directly as that line and inversely as the velocity V; and the force will be directly as the increment I of the velocity and inversely as the time; and therefore if we take the first ratios when those quantities are just nascent, as $\frac{I \cdot V}{DE}$, that is, as the length DF. Therefore a force proportional to DF or EG will cause the body to descend with a velocity that is as the right line whose square is equal to the area ABGE.   Q.E.D.

Moreover, since the time in which a very small line DE of a given length may be described is inversely as the velocity and therefore also inversely as a right line whose square is equal to the area ABFD; and since the line DL, and by consequence the nascent area DLME, will be inversely as the same right line, the time will be as the area DLME, and the sum of all the times will be as the sum of all the areas; that is (by Cor., Lem. 4), the whole time in which the line AE is described will be as the whole area ATVME.   Q.E.D.

COR. I. Let P be the place from whence a body ought to fall, so as that, when urged by any known uniform centripetal force (such as gravity is commonly supposed to be), it may acquire in the place D a velocity equal to the velocity which another body, falling by any force whatever, hath acquired in that place D. In the perpendicular DF let there be taken DR, which may be to DF as that uniform force to the other force in the place D. Complete the rectangle PDRQ, and cut off the area ABFD equal to that rectangle. Then A will be the place from whence the other body fell. For completing the rectangle DRSE, since the area ABFD is to the area DFGE as VV to 2VI, and therefore as ½V to I, that is, as half the whole velocity to the increment of the velocity of the body falling by the variable force; and in like manner the area PQRD to the area DRSE as half the whole velocity to the increment of the velocity of the body falling by the uniform force; and since those increments (by reason of the equality of the nascent times) are as the generating forces, that is, as the ordinates DF, DR, and consequently as the nascent areas DFGE, DRSE; therefore, the whole areas ABFD, PQRD will be to each other as the halves of the whole velocities; and therefore, because the velocities are equal, they become equal also.

COR. II. Whence if any body be projected either upwards or downwards with a given velocity from any place D, and there be given the law of centripetal force acting on it, its velocity will be found in any other place, as e, by erecting the ordinate eg, and taking that velocity to the velocity in the place D as a right line whose square is equal to the rectangle PQRD, either increased by the curvilinear area DF*ge*, if the place *e* is below the place D, or diminished by the same area DF*ge*, if it be higher, is to the right line whose square is equal to the rectangle PQRD alone.

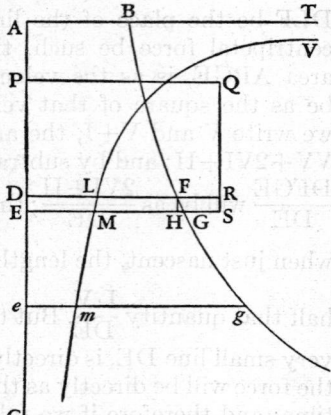

Cor. iii. The time is also known by erecting the ordinate *em* inversely proportional to the square root of PQRD+ or −DF*ge*, and taking the time in which the body has described the line D*e* to the time in which another body has fallen with an uniform force from P, and in falling arrived at D in the proportion of the curvilinear area DL*me* to the rectangle 2PD·DL. For the time in which a body falling with an uniform force hath described the line PD is to the time in which the same body hath described the line PE as the square root of the ratio of PD to PE; that is (the very small line DE being just nascent), in the ratio of PD to PD+½DE or 2PD to 2PD+DE, and, by subtraction, to the time in which the body hath described the small line DE, as 2PD to DE, and therefore as the rectangle 2PD·DL to the area DLME; and the time in which both the bodies described the very small line DE is to the time in which the body with the variable motion described the line D*e* as the area DLME to the area DL*me*; and therefore the first mentioned of these times is to the last as the rectangle 2PD·DL to the area DL*me*.

SECTION VIII

The determination of orbits in which bodies will revolve, being acted upon by any sort of centripetal force

Proposition 40. Theorem 13

If a body, acted upon by any centripetal force, is moved in any manner, and another body ascends or descends in a right line, and their velocities be equal in any one case of equal altitudes, their velocities will be also equal at all equal altitudes.

Let a body descend from A through D and E, to the centre C; and let another body move from V in the curved line VIK*k*. From the centre C, with any distances, describe the concentric circles DI, EK, meeting the right line AC in D and E, and the curve VIK in I and K. Draw IC meeting KE in N, and on IK let fall the perpendicular NT; and let the interval DE or IN between the circumferences of the circles be very small; and imagine the bodies in D and I to have equal velocities. Then because the distances CD and CI are equal, the centripetal forces in D and I will be also equal. Let those forces be expressed by the equal short lines DE and IN; and let the force IN (by Cor. ii of the Laws of Motion) be resolved into two others, NT and IT. Then the force NT acting in the direction of the line NT perpendicular to the path ITK of the body will not at all affect or change the velocity of the body in that path, but only draw it aside from a rectilinear course, and make it deflect continually from the tangent of the orbit, and proceed in the curvilinear path ITK*k*. That

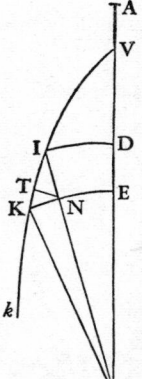

whole force, therefore, will be spent in producing this effect; but the other force IT, acting in the direction of the course of the body, will be all employed in accelerating it, and in the least given time will produce an acceleration proportional to itself. Therefore the accelerations of the bodies in D and I, produced in equal times, are as the lines DE, IT (if we take the first ratios of the nascent lines DE, IN, IK, IT, NT); and in unequal times as the product of those lines and the times. But the times in which DE and IK are described, are, by reason of the equal velocities (in D and I), as the spaces described DE and IK, and therefore the accelerations in the course of the bodies through the lines DE and IK are as DE and IT, and DE and IK conjointly; that is, as the square of DE to the rectangle IT·IK. But the rectangle IT·IK is equal to the square of IN, that is, equal to the square of DE; and therefore the accelerations generated in the passage of the bodies from D and I to E and K are equal. Therefore the velocities of the bodies in E and K are also equal: and by the same reasoning they will always be found equal in any subsequent equal distances. Q.E.D.

By the same reasoning, bodies of equal velocities and equal distances from the centre will be equally retarded in their ascent to equal distances. Q.E.D.

COR. I. Therefore if a body either oscillates by hanging to a string, or by any polished and perfectly smooth impediment is forced to move in a curved line; and another body ascends or descends in a right line, and their velocities be equal at any one equal altitude, their velocities will be also equal at all other equal altitudes. For by the string of the pendulous body, or by the impediment of a vessel perfectly smooth, the same thing will be effected as by the transverse force NT. The body is neither accelerated nor retarded by it, but only is obliged to leave its rectilinear course.

COR. II. Suppose the quantity P to be the greatest distance from the centre to which a body can ascend, whether it be oscillating, or revolving in a curve, and so the same projected upwards from any point of a curve with the velocity it has in that point. Let the quantity A be the distance of the body from the centre in any other point of the orbit; and let the centripetal force be always as the power A^{n-1}, of the quantity A, the index of which power $n-1$ is any number n diminished by unity. Then the velocity in every altitude A will be as $\sqrt{(P^n - A^n)}$, and therefore will be given. For by Prop. 39, the velocity of a body ascending and descending in a right line is in that very ratio.

PROPOSITION 41. PROBLEM 28

Supposing a centripetal force of any kind, and granting the quadratures of curvilinear figures; it is required to find as well the curves in which bodies will move, as the times of their motions in the curves found.

Let any centripetal force tend to the centre C, and let it be required to find the curve VIK*k*. Let there be given the circle VR, described from the centre C with any radius CV; and from the same centre describe any other circles ID, KE, cutting the curve in I and K, and the right line CV in D and E. Then draw the right line CNIX cutting the circles KE, VR in N and X, and the right line CKY meeting the circle VR in Y. Let the points I and K be indefinitely near; and let the body go on from V through I and K to *k*; and let the point A

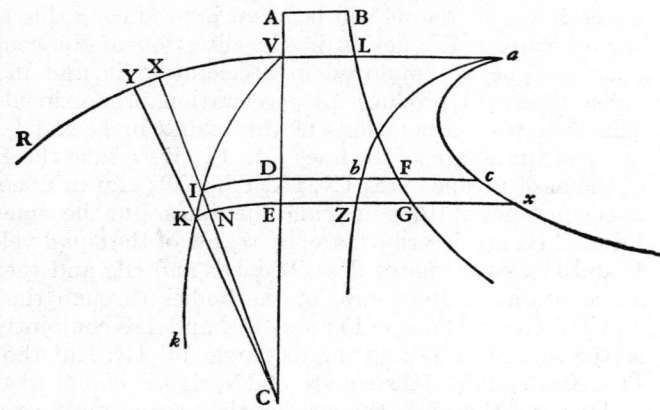

be the place from which another body is to fall, so as in the place D to acquire a velocity equal to the velocity of the first body in I. And things remaining as in Prop. 39, the short line IK, described in the least given time, will be as the velocity, and therefore as the right line whose square is equal to the area ABFD, and the triangle ICK proportional to the time will be given, and therefore KN will be inversely as the altitude IC; that is (if there be given any quantity Q, and the altitude IC be called A), as $\frac{Q}{A}$. This quantity $\frac{Q}{A}$ call Z, and suppose the magnitude of Q to be such that in some one case

$$\sqrt{\text{ABFD}} : Z = \text{IK} : \text{KN},$$

and then in all cases

$$\sqrt{\text{ABFD}} : Z = \text{IK} : \text{KN},$$

and

$$\text{ABFD} : \text{ZZ} = \text{IK}^2 : \text{KN}^2,$$

and by subtraction,

$$\text{ABFD} - \text{ZZ} : \text{ZZ} = \text{IN}^2 : \text{KN}^2,$$

and therefore

$$\sqrt{(\text{ABFD} - \text{ZZ})} : Z \text{ or } \frac{Q}{A} = \text{IN} : \text{KN},$$

and

$$\text{A} \cdot \text{KN} = \frac{Q \cdot \text{IN}}{\sqrt{(\text{ABFD} - \text{ZZ})}}.$$

Since

$$\text{YX} \cdot \text{XC} : \text{A} \cdot \text{KN} = \text{CX}^2 : \text{AA},$$

it follows that

$$\text{YX} \cdot \text{XC} = \frac{Q \cdot \text{IN} \cdot \text{CX}^2}{\text{AA}\sqrt{(\text{ABFD} - \text{ZZ})}}.$$

Therefore in the perpendicular DF let there be taken continually Db, Dc equal to $\dfrac{Q}{2\sqrt{(\text{ABFD} - \text{ZZ})}}$, $\dfrac{Q \cdot \text{CX}^2}{2\text{AA}\sqrt{(\text{ABFD} - \text{ZZ})}}$ respectively, and let the curved lines ab, ac, the foci of the points b and c, be described; and from the point V let the perpendicular Va be erected to the line AC, cutting off the curvilinear areas VDba, VDca, and let the ordinates Ez, Ex, be erected also. Then because the rectangle Db·IN or DbzE is equal to half the rectangle A·KN, or to the triangle ICK; and the rectangle Dc·IN or DcxE is equal to half the rectangle YX·XC, or to the triangle XCY; that is, because the nascent particles DbzE, ICK of the areas VDba, VIC are always equal; and the nascent particles DcxE,

XCY of the areas VD*ca*, VCX are always equal: therefore the generated area VD*ba* will be equal to the generated area VIC, and therefore proportional to the time; and the generated area VD*ca* is equal to the generated sector VCX. If, therefore, any time be given during which the body has been moving from V, there will be also given the area proportional to it VD*ba*; and thence will be given the altitude of the body CD or CI; and the area VD*ca*, and the sector VCX equal thereto, together with its angle VCI. But the angle VCI, and the altitude CI being given, there is also given the place I, in which the body will be found at the end of that time. Q.E.I.

Cor. I. Hence the greatest and least altitudes of the bodies, that is, the apsides of the curves, may be found very readily. For the apsides are those points in which a right line IC drawn through the centre falls perpendicularly upon the curves VIK; which comes to pass when the right lines IK and NK become equal; that is, when the area ABFD is equal to ZZ.

Cor. II. So also the angle KIN, in which the curve at any place cuts the line IC, may be readily found by the given altitude IC of the body; namely, by making the sine of that angle to the radius as KN to IK, that is, as Z to the square root of the area ABFD.

Cor. III. If to the centre C, and the principal vertex V, there be described a conic section VRS; and from any point thereof, as R, there be drawn the tangent RT meeting the axis CV indefinitely produced in the point T; and then

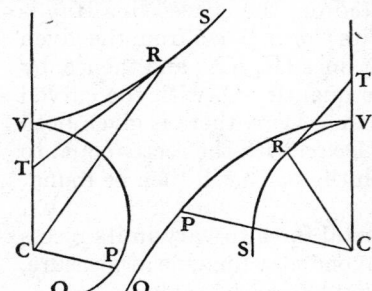

joining CR there be drawn the right line CP, equal to the abscissa CT, making an angle VCP proportional to the sector VCR; and if a centripetal force inversely proportional to the cubes of the distances of the places from the centre, tends to the centre C; and from the place V there sets out a body with a just velocity in the direction of a line perpendicular to the right line CV; that body will proceed in a curve VPQ, which the point P will always touch; and therefore if the conic section VRS be an hyperbola, the body will descend to the centre; but if it be an ellipse, it will ascend continually, and go farther and farther off *in infinitum*. And, on the contrary, if a body endued with any velocity goes off from the place V, and according as it begins either to descend obliquely to the centre, or to ascend obliquely from it, the figure VRS be either an hyperbola or an ellipse, the curve may be found by increasing or diminishing the angle VCP in a given ratio. And the centripetal force becoming centrifugal, the body will ascend obliquely in the curve VPQ, which is found by taking the angle VCP proportional to the elliptic sector VRC, and the length CP equal to the length CT, as before. All these things follow from the foregoing Proposition, by the quadrature of a certain curve, the invention of which, as being easy enough, for brevity's sake I omit.

PROPOSITION 42. PROBLEM 29

The law of centripetal force being given, it is required to find the motion of a body setting out from a given place, with a given velocity, in the direction of a given right line.

Suppose the same things as in the three preceding Propositions; and let the body go off from the place I in the direction of the little line IK, with the same velocity as another body, by falling with an uniform centripetal force from the place P, may acquire in D; and let this uniform force be to the force with which the body is at first urged in I, as DR to DF. Let the body go on towards k; and

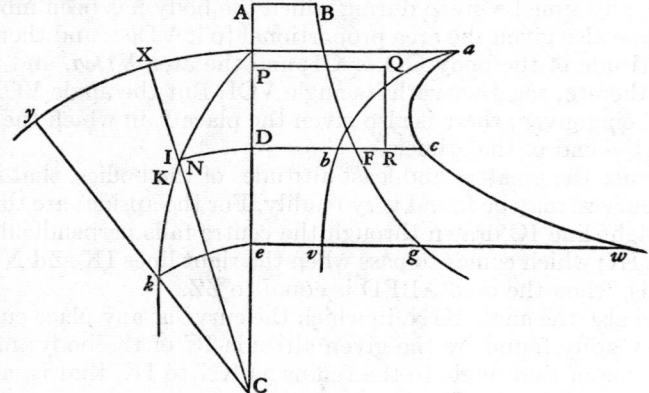

about the centre C, with the radius Ck, describe the circle ke, meeting the right line PD in e, and let there be erected the lines eg, ev, ew, ordinately applied to the curves BFg, abv, acw. From the given rectangle PDRQ and the given law of centripetal force, by which the first body is acted on, the curved line BFg is also given, by the construction of Prop. 27, and its Cor. I. Then from the given angle CIK is given the proportion of the nascent lines IK, KN; and thence, by the construction of Prob. 28, there is given the quantity Q, with the curved lines abv, acw; and therefore, at the end of any time Dbve, there is given both the altitude of the body Ce or Ck, and the area Dcwe, with the sector equal to it XCy, the angle ICk, and the place k, in which the body will then be found.

Q.E.I.

We suppose in these Propositions the centripetal force to vary in its recess from the centre according to some law, which anyone may imagine at pleasure, but at equal distances from the centre to be everywhere the same.

I have hitherto considered the motions of bodies in immovable orbits. It remains now to add something concerning their motions in orbits which revolve round the centres of force.

SECTION IX

THE MOTION OF BODIES IN MOVABLE ORBITS; AND THE MOTION OF THE APSIDES

PROPOSITION 43. PROBLEM 30

It is required to make a body move in a curve that revolves about the centre of force in the same manner as another body in the same curve at rest.

In the fixed orbit VPK, let the body P revolve, proceeding from V towards K. From the centre C let there be continually drawn Cp, equal to CP, making the angle VCp proportional to the angle VCP; and the area which the line Cp describes will be to the area VCP, which the line CP describes at the same time, as the velocity of the describing line Cp to the velocity of the describing line

CP; that is, as the angle VC*p* to the angle VCP, therefore in a given ratio, and therefore proportional to the time. Since, then, the area described by the line C*p* in a fixed plane is proportional to the time, it is manifest that a body, being

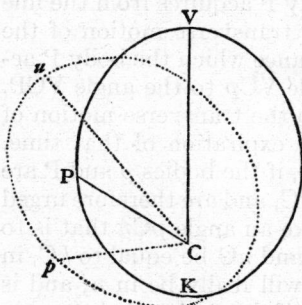

acted upon by a suitable centripetal force, may revolve with the point *p* in the curved line which the same point *p*, by the method just now explained, may be made to describe in a fixed plane. Make the angle VC*u* equal to the angle PC*p*, and the line C*u* equal to CV, and the figure *u*C*p* equal to the figure VCP, and the body being always in the point *p*, will move in the perimeter of the revolving figure *u*C*p*, and will describe its (revolving) arc *up* in the same time that the other body P describes the similar and equal arc VP in the fixed figure VPK. Find, then, by Cor. v, Prop. 6, the centripetal force by which the body may be made to revolve in the curved line which the point *p* describes in a fixed plane, and the Problem will be solved.   Q.E.F.

PROPOSITION 44. THEOREM 14

The difference of the forces, by which two bodies may be made to move equally, one in a fixed, the other in the same orbit revolving, varies inversely as the cube of their common altitudes.

Let the parts of the fixed orbit VP, PK be similar and equal to the parts of the revolving orbit *up*, *pk*; and let the distance of the points P and K be supposed of the utmost smallness. Let fall a perpendicular *kr* from the point *k* to

the right line *p*C, and produce it to *m*, so that *mr* may be to *kr* as the angle VC*p* to the angle VCP. Because the altitudes of the bodies PC and *p*C, KC and *k*C, are always equal, it is manifest that the increments or decrements of the lines PC and *p*C are always equal; and therefore if each of the several motions of the bodies in the places P and *p* be resolved into two (by Cor. II of the Laws of Motion), one of which is directed towards the centre, or according to the lines PC, *p*C, and the other, transverse to the former, hath a direction perpendicular to the lines PC and *p*C; the motions towards the centre will be equal, and the transverse motion of the body *p* will be to the trans-

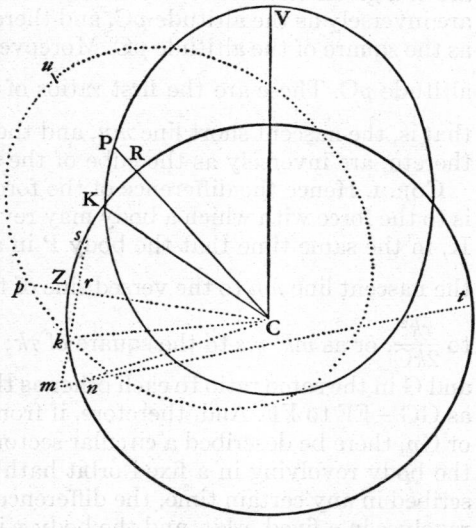

verse motion of the body P as the angular motion of the line *p*C to the angular motion of the line PC; that is, as the angle VC*p* to the angle VCP. Therefore, at the same time that the body P, by both its motions, comes to the point K, the body *p*, having an equal motion towards the centre, will be equally moved from p towards C; and therefore that time being expired, it will be found some-where in the line mkr, which, passing through the point k, is perpendicular to the line pC; and by its transverse motion will acquire a distance from the line pC, that will be to the distance which the other body P acquires from the line PC as the transverse motion of the body p to the transverse motion of the other body P. Therefore since kr is equal to the distance which the body P acquires from the line PC, and mr is to kr as the angle VCp to the angle VCP, that is, as the transverse motion of the body p to the transverse motion of the body P, it is manifest that the body p, at the expiration of that time, will be found in the place m. These things will be so, if the bodies p and P are equally moved in the directions of the lines pC and PC, and are therefore urged with equal forces in those directions. But if we take an angle pCn that is to the angle pCk as the angle VCp to the angle VCP, and nC be equal to kC, in that case the body p at the expiration of the time will really be in n; and is therefore urged with a greater force than the body P, if the angle nCp is greater than the angle kCp, that is, *if* the orbit upk moves either progressively, or in a retrograde direction, with a velocity greater than the double of that with which the line CP is carried forwards; and with a less force if the retrograde motion of the orbit is slower. And the difference of the forces will be as the interval mn of the places through which the body would be carried by the action of that difference in that given space of time. About the centre C with the interval Cn or Ck suppose a circle described cutting the lines mr, mn produced in s and t, and the rectangle $mn \cdot mt$ will be equal to the rectangle $mk \cdot ms$, and therefore mn will be equal to $\dfrac{mk \cdot ms}{mt}$. But since the triangles pCk, pCn, in a given time, are of a given magnitude, kr and mr, and their difference mk, and their sum ms, are inversely as the altitude pC, and therefore the rectangle $mk \cdot ms$ is inversely as the square of the altitude pC. Moreover, mt is directly as $\frac{1}{2}mt$, that is, as the altitude pC. These are the first ratios of the nascent lines; and hence $\dfrac{mk \cdot ms}{mt}$, that is, the nascent short line mn, and the difference of the forces proportional thereto, are inversely as the cube of the altitude pC.   Q.E.D.

COR. I. Hence the difference of the forces in the places P and p, or K and k, is to the force with which a body may revolve with a circular motion from R to K, in the same time that the body P in a fixed orbit describes the arc PK, as the nascent line mn to the versed sine of the nascent arc RK, that is, as $\dfrac{mk \cdot ms}{mt}$ to $\dfrac{rk^2}{2kC}$, or as $mk \cdot ms$ to the square of rk; that is, if we take given quantities F and G in the same ratio to each other as the angle VCP bears to the angle VCp, as GG−FF to FF. And, therefore, if from the centre C, with any distance CP or Cp, there be described a circular sector equal to the whole area VPC, which the body revolving in a fixed orbit hath by a radius drawn to the centre described in any certain time, the difference of the forces, with which the body P revolves in a fixed orbit, and the body p in a movable orbit, will be to the centripetal force, with which another body by a radius drawn to the centre can uniformly describe that sector in the same time as the area VPC is described, as GG−FF to FF. For that sector and the area pCk are to each other as the times in which they are described.

COR. II. If the orbit VPK be an ellipse, having its focus C, and its highest apse V, and we suppose the ellipse upk similar and equal to it, so that pC may be always equal to PC, and the angle VCp be to the angle VCP in the given ratio of G to F; and for the altitude PC or pC we put A, and 2R for the latus rectum of the ellipse, the force with which a body may be made to revolve in a movable ellipse will be as $\frac{FF}{AA} + \frac{RGG - RFF}{A^3}$, and conversely. Let the force with which a body may revolve in a fixed ellipse be expressed by the quantity $\frac{FF}{AA}$, and the force in V will be $\frac{FF}{CV^2}$. But the force with which a body may revolve in a circle at the distance CV, with the same velocity as a body revolving in an ellipse has in V, is to the force with which a body revolving in an ellipse is acted upon in the apse V, as half the latus rectum of the ellipse to the semidiameter CV of the circle, and therefore is as $\frac{RFF}{CV^3}$; and the force which is to this as GG − FF to FF, is as $\frac{RGG - RFF}{CV^3}$; and this force (by Cor. I of this Prop.) is the difference of the forces in V, with which the body P revolves in the fixed ellipse VPK, and the body p in the movable ellipse upk. Then since by this Proposition that difference at any other altitude A is to itself at the altitude CV as $\frac{1}{A^3}$ to $\frac{1}{CV^2}$, the same difference in every altitude A will be as $\frac{RGG - RFF}{A^3}$. Therefore to the force $\frac{FF}{AA}$, by which the body may revolve in a fixed ellipse VPK, add the excess $\frac{RGG - RFF}{A^3}$, and the sum will be the whole force $\frac{FF}{AA} + \frac{RGG - RFF}{A^3}$ by which a body may revolve in the same time in the movable ellipse upk.

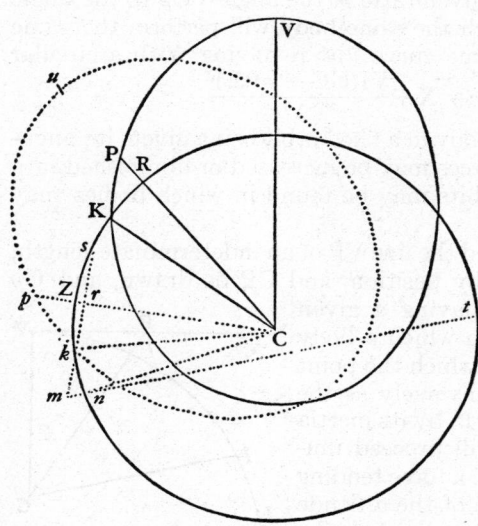

COR. III. In the same manner it will be found, that, if the fixed orbit VPK be an ellipse having its centre in the centre of the forces C, and there be supposed a movable ellipse upk, similar, equal, and concentric to it; and 2R be the principal latus rectum of that ellipse, and 2T the latus transversum, or greater axis; and the angle VCp be continually to the angle VCP as G to F; the forces with which bodies may revolve in the fixed and movable ellipse, in equal times, will be as $\frac{FFA}{T^3}$ and $\frac{FFA}{T^3} + \frac{RGG - RFF}{A^3}$ respectively.

COR. IV. And universally, if the greatest altitude CV of the body be called T, and the radius of the curvature which the orbit VPK has in V, that is, the radius of a circle equally curved, be called R, and the centripetal force with which a body may revolve in any fixed curve VPK at the place V be called $\frac{VFF}{TT}$, and in other places P be indefinitely styled X; and the altitude CP be called A, and G be taken to F in the given ratio of the angle VCp to the angle VCP; the centripetal force with which the same body will perform the same motions in the same time, in the same curve *upk* revolving with a circular motion, will be as the sum of the forces $X+\frac{VRGG-VRFF}{A^3}$.

Cor. v. Therefore the motion of a body in a fixed orbit being given, its angular motion round the centre of the forces may be increased or diminished in a given ratio; and thence new fixed orbits may be found in which bodies may revolve with new centripetal forces.

Cor. vi. Therefore if there be erected the line VP of an indeterminate length, perpendicular to the line CV given by position, and CP be drawn, and Cp equal to it, making the angle VCp having a given ratio to the angle VCP, the force with which a body may revolve in the curved line Vpk, which the point p is continually describing, will be inversely as the cube of the altitude Cp. For the body P, by its inertia alone, no other force impelling it, will proceed uniformly in the right line VP. Add, then, a force tending to the centre C inversely as the cube of the altitude CP or Cp, and (by what was just demonstrated) the

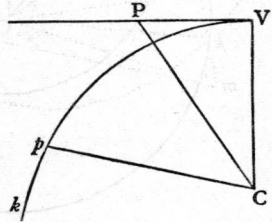

body will deflect from the rectilinear motion into the curved line Vpk. But this curve Vpk is the same with the curve VPQ found in Cor. iii, Prop. 41, in which, I said, bodies attracted with such forces would ascend obliquely.

Proposition 45. Problem 31

To find the motion of the apsides in orbits approaching very near to circles.

This problem is solved arithmetically by reducing the orbit, which a body revolving in a movable ellipse (as in Cor. ii and iii of the above Prop.) describes in a fixed plane, to the figure of the orbit whose apsides are required; and then seeking the apsides of the orbit which that body describes in a fixed plane. But orbits acquire the same figure, if the centripetal forces with which they are described, compared between themselves, are made proportional at equal altitudes. Let the point V be the highest apse, and write T for the greatest altitude CV, A for any other altitude CP or Cp, and X for the difference of the altitudes CV−CP; and the force with which a body moves in an ellipse revolving about its focus C (as in Cor. ii), and which in Cor. ii was as $\frac{FF}{AA}+\frac{RGG-RFF}{A^3}$, that is, as $\frac{FFA+RGG-RFF}{A^3}$, by substituting T−X for A, will become as $\frac{RGG-RFF+TFF-FFX}{A^3}$. In like manner any other centripetal force is to be reduced to a fraction whose denominator is A³, and the numerators are to be made analogous by collating together the homologous terms. This will be made plainer by Examples.

Exam. i. Let us suppose the centripetal force to be uniform, and therefore as

$\frac{A^3}{A^3}$, or, writing $T-X$ for A in the numerator, as $\frac{T^3-3TTX+3TXX-X^3}{A^3}$. Then collating together the correspondent terms of the numerators, that is, those that consist of given quantities with those of given quantities, and those of quantities not given with those of quantities not given, it will become

$$RGG-RFF+TFF : T^3 = -FFX : -3TTX+3TXX-X^3$$
$$= -FF : -3TT+3TX-XX.$$

Now since the orbit is supposed extremely near to a circle, let it coincide with a circle; and because in that case R and T become equal, and X is infinitely diminished, the last ratios will be

$$GG : T^2 = -FF : -3TT,$$

and again, $\qquad GG : FF = TT : 3TT = 1 : 3;$

and therefore G is to F, that is, the angle VCp to the angle VCP, as 1 to $\sqrt{3}$. Therefore since the body, in a fixed ellipse, in descending from the upper to the lower apse, describes an angle, if I may so speak, of 180°, the other body in a movable ellipse, and therefore in the fixed plane we are treating of, will in its descent from the upper to the lower apse, describe an angle VCp of $\frac{180°}{\sqrt{3}}$. And this comes to pass by reason of the likeness of this orbit which a body acted upon by an uniform centripetal force describes, and of that orbit which a body performing its circuits in a revolving ellipse will describe in a fixed plane. By this collation of the terms, these orbits are made similar; not universally, indeed, but then only when they approach very near to a circular figure. A body, therefore, revolving with an uniform centripetal force in an orbit nearly circular, will always describe an angle of $\frac{180°}{\sqrt{3}}$, or 103° 55′ 23″ at the centre; moving from the upper apse to the lower apse when it has once described that angle, and thence returning to the upper apse when it has described that angle again; and so on *in infinitum*.

EXAM. 2. Suppose the centripetal force to be as any power of the altitude A, as, for example, A^{n-3}, or $\frac{A^n}{A^3}$; where $n-3$ and n signify any indices of powers whatever, whether integers or fractions, rational or surd, affirmative or negative. That numerator A^n or $(T-X)^n$ being reduced to an indeterminate series by my method of converging series, will become

$$T^n - nXT^{n-1} + \frac{nn-n}{2} XXT^{n-2}, \&c.$$

And comparing these terms with the terms of the other numerator,

$$RGG-RFF+TFF-FFX,$$

it becomes

$$RGG-RFF+TFF : T^n = -FF : -nT^{n-1} + \frac{nn-n}{2} XT^{n-2}, \&c.$$

And taking the last ratios where the orbits approach to circles, it becomes

$$RGG : T^n = -FF : -nT^{n-1},$$

or, $\qquad GG : T^{n-1} = FF : nT^{n-1},$

and again, $\qquad GG : FF = T^{n-1} : nT^{n-1} = 1 : n;$

and therefore G is to F, that is, the angle VCp to the angle VCP, as 1 to $\sqrt{n}$. Therefore since the angle VCP, described in the descent of the body from the upper apse to the lower apse in an ellipse, is of 180°, the angle VCp, described in the descent of the body from the upper apse to the lower apse in an orbit nearly circular which a body describes with a centripetal force proportional to the power A^{n-3}, will be equal to an angle of $\dfrac{180°}{\sqrt{n}}$, and this angle being repeated, the body will return from the lower to the upper apse, and so on *in infinitum*. As if the centripetal force be as the distance of the body from the centre, that is, as A, or $\dfrac{A^4}{A^3}$, n will be equal to 4, and $\sqrt{n}$ equal to 2; and therefore the angle between the upper and the lower apse will be equal to $\dfrac{180°}{2}$, or 90°. Therefore the body having performed a fourth part of one revolution, will arrive at the lower apse, and having performed another fourth part, will arrive at the upper apse, and so on *in infinitum*. This appears also from Prop. x. For a body acted on by this centripetal force will revolve in a fixed ellipse, whose centre is the centre of force. If the centripetal force is inversely as the distance, that is, directly as $\dfrac{1}{A}$ or $\dfrac{A^2}{A^3}$, n will be equal to 2; and therefore the angle between the upper and the lower apse will be $\dfrac{180°}{\sqrt{2}}$, or 127° 16′ 45″; and hence a body revolving with such a force will, by a continual repetition of this angle, move alternately from the upper to the lower and from the lower to the upper apse forever. So, also, if the centripetal force be inversely as the fourth root of the eleventh power of the altitude, that is, inversely as $A^{1\frac{1}{4}}$, and therefore directly as $\dfrac{1}{A^{1\frac{1}{4}}}$, or as $\dfrac{A^{\frac{1}{4}}}{A^3}$, n will be equal to ¼, and $\dfrac{180°}{\sqrt{n}}$ will be equal to 360°; and therefore the body parting from the upper apse, and from thence continually descending, will arrive at the lower apse when it has completed one entire revolution; and thence ascending continually, when it has completed another entire revolution, it will arrive again at the upper apse; and so alternately forever.

EXAM. 3. Taking m and n for any indices of the powers of the altitude, and b and c for any given numbers, suppose the centripetal force to be as (bA^m+cA^n) $\div A^3$, that is, as $[b(T-X)^m \div c(T-X)^n]\div A^3$, or (by the method of converging series above mentioned) as

$$[bT^m+cT^n-mbXT^{m-1}-ncXT^{n-1}+\frac{mm-m}{2}\,bXXT^{m-2}+\frac{nn-n}{2}$$
$$-cXXT^{n-2}, \text{ \&c.}]\div A^3;$$

and comparing the terms of the numerators, there will arise,

$$RGG-RFF+TFF : bT^m+cT^n = -FF : -mbT^{m-1}-ncT^{n-1}+$$
$$\frac{mm-m}{2}\,bXT^{m-2}+\frac{nn-n}{2}\,cXT^{n-2}, \text{ \&c.}$$

And taking the last ratios that arise when the orbits come to a circular form, there will come forth

$$GG : bT^{m-1}+cT^{n-1}=FF : mbT^{m-1}+ncT^{n-1};$$

and again, $\quad GG : FF = bT^{m-1}+cT^{n-1} : mbT^{n-1}+ncT^{n-1}.$

This proportion, by expressing the greatest altitude CV or T arithmetically by unity, becomes, GG : FF $=b+c : mb+nc=1 : \dfrac{mb+nc}{b+c}$. Whence G becomes to F, that is, the angle VCp to the angle VCP, as 1 to $\sqrt{\dfrac{mb+nc}{b+c}}$. And therefore, since the angle VCP between the upper and the lower apse, in a fixed ellipse, is of 180°, the angle VCp between the same apsides in an orbit which a body describes with a centripetal force, that is, as $\dfrac{bA^m + cA^n}{A^3}$, will be equal to an angle of 180° $\sqrt{\dfrac{b+c}{mb+nc}}$. And by the same reasoning, if the centripetal force be as $\dfrac{bA^m - cA^n}{A^3}$, the angle between the apsides will be found equal to

$$180° \sqrt{\frac{b-c}{mb-nc}}.$$

After the same manner the Problem is solved in more difficult cases. The quantity to which the centripetal force is proportional must always be resolved into a converging series whose denominator is A^3. Then the given part of the numerator arising from that operation is to be supposed in the same ratio to that part of it which is not given, as the given part of this numerator RGG −RFF+TFF−FFX is to that part of the same numerator which is not given. And taking away the superfluous quantities, and writing unity for T, the proportion of G to F is obtained.

COR. I. Hence if the centripetal force be as any power of the altitude, that power may be found from the motion of the apsides; and conversely. That is, if the whole angular motion, with which the body returns to the same apse, be to the angular motion of one revolution, or 360°, as any number as m to another as n, and the altitude be called A; the force will be as the power $A^{\frac{nn}{mm}-3}$ of the altitude A; the index of which power is $\dfrac{nn}{mm}-3$. This appears by the second Example. Hence it is plain that the force in its recess from the centre cannot decrease in a greater than a cubed ratio of the altitude. A body revolving with such a force, and parting from the apse, if it once begins to descend, can never arrive at the lower apse or least altitude, but will descend to the centre, describing the curved line treated of in Cor. III, Prop. 41. But if it should, at its parting from the lower apse, begin to ascend ever so little, it will ascend *in infinitum*, and never come to the upper apse; but will describe the curved line spoken of in the same Cor., and Cor. VI, Prop. 45. So that where the force in its recess from the centre decreases in a greater than a cubed ratio of the altitude, the body at its parting from the apse, will either descend to the centre, or ascend *in infinitum*, according as it descends or ascends at the beginning of its motion. But if the force in its recess from the centre either decreases in a less than a cubed ratio of the altitude, or increases in any ratio of the altitude whatsoever, the body will never descend to the centre, but will at some time arrive at the lower apse; and, on the contrary, if the body alternately ascending and descending from one apse to another never comes to the centre, then either the force increases in the recess from the centre, or it decreases in a less than a cubed ratio of the altitude; and the sooner the body returns from one apse to another, the farther is the ratio of the forces from the cubed ratio. As if the body should return to and from the upper apse by an alternate descent and ascent in 8 revolutions, or in 4, or 2, or $1\frac{1}{2}$; that is, if m should be to n as 8, or 4, or 2, or $1\frac{1}{2}$ to 1, and therefore $\dfrac{nn}{mm}-3$, be $\frac{1}{64}-3$, or $\frac{1}{16}-3$, or $\frac{1}{4}-3$, or $\frac{4}{9}$ −3; then the force will be as $A^{\frac{1}{64}-3}$, or $A^{\frac{1}{16}-3}$, or $A^{\frac{1}{4}-3}$, or $A^{\frac{4}{9}-3}$; that is, it will be inversely as $A^{3-\frac{1}{64}}$, or $A^{3-\frac{1}{16}}$, or $A^{3-\frac{1}{4}}$, or $A^{3-\frac{4}{9}}$. If the body after each revolution returns to the same apse, and the apse remains unmoved, then m will be to n as 1 to 1, and therefore $A^{\frac{nn}{mm}-3}$ will be equal to A^{-2}, or $\dfrac{1}{AA}$; and therefore the decrease of the forces will be in a squared ratio of the altitude; as was demonstrated above. If the body in three fourth parts, or two thirds, or one third, or one fourth part of an entire revolution, return to the same apse; m will be to n as $\frac{3}{4}$ or $\frac{2}{3}$ or $\frac{1}{3}$ or $\frac{1}{4}$ to 1, and therefore $A^{\frac{nn}{mm}-3}$ is equal to $A^{\frac{16}{9}-3}$, or $A^{\frac{9}{4}-3}$, or A^{9-3}, or A^{16-3}; and therefore the force is either inversely as $A^{\frac{11}{9}}$ or $A^{\frac{3}{4}}$, or directly as A^6 or A^{13}. Lastly if the body in its progress from the upper apse to the same upper apse again, goes over one entire revolution and three degrees more, and therefore that apse in each revolution of the body moves forward three degrees, then m will be to n as 363° to 360°, or as 121 to 120, and therefore $A^{\frac{nn}{mm}-3}$ will be equal to $A^{-\frac{29523}{14641}}$, and therefore the centripetal force will be inversely as $A^{\frac{29523}{14641}}$, or inversely as $A^{2\frac{4}{243}}$ very nearly. Therefore the centripetal force decreases in a ratio something greater than the squared ratio; but approaching $59\frac{3}{4}$ times nearer to the squared than the cubed.

COR. II. Hence also if a body, urged by a centripetal force which is inversely as the square of the altitude, revolves in an ellipse whose focus is in the centre of the forces; and a new and foreign force should be added to or subtracted from this centripetal force, the motion of the apsides arising from that foreign force may (by the third Example) be known; and conversely: If the force with which the body revolves in the ellipse be as $\dfrac{1}{AA}$; and the foreign force as cA, and therefore the remaining force as $\dfrac{A-cA^4}{A^3}$; then (by the third Example) b will be equal to 1, m equal to 1, and n equal to 4; and therefore the angle of revolution between the apsides is equal to $180°\sqrt{\dfrac{1-c}{1-4c}}$. Suppose that foreign force to be 357.45 times less than the other force with which the body revolves in the ellipse; that is, c to be $\frac{100}{35745}$, A or T being equal to 1; and then $180°\sqrt{\dfrac{1-c}{1-4c}}$ will be 180° $\sqrt{\frac{35645}{35345}}$ or 180°·7623, that is, 180° 45′ 44″. Therefore the body, parting from the upper apse, will arrive at the lower apse with an angular motion of 180° 45′ 44″, and this angular motion being repeated, will return to the upper apse; and therefore the upper apse in each revolution will go forward 1° 31′ 28″. The apse of the moon is about twice as swift.

So much for the motion of bodies in orbits whose planes pass through the centre of force. It now remains to determine those motions in eccentric planes. For those authors who treat of the motion of heavy bodies used to consider the ascent and descent of such bodies, not only in a perpendicular direction, but at all degrees of obliquity upon any given planes; and for the same reason we are to consider in this place the motions of bodies tending to centres by means of any forces whatsoever, when those bodies move in eccentric planes. These planes are supposed to be perfectly smooth and polished, so as not to retard the motion of the bodies in the least. Moreover, in these demonstrations, instead of the planes upon which those bodies roll or slide, and which are therefore tangent planes to the bodies, I shall use planes parallel to them, in which the centres of the bodies move, and by that motion describe orbits. And by the same method I afterwards determine the motions of bodies performed in curved surfaces.

SECTION X

THE MOTION OF BODIES IN GIVEN SURFACES; AND THE OSCILLATING PENDULOUS MOTION OF BODIES

PROPOSITION 46. PROBLEM 32

Any kind of centripetal force being supposed, and the centre of force, and any plane whatsoever in which the body revolves, being given, and the quadratures of curvilinear figures being allowed; it is required to determine the motion of a body going off from a given plane with a given velocity, in the direction of a given right line in that plane.

Let S be the centre of force, SC the least distance of that centre from the given plane, P a body issuing from the place P in the direction of the right line PZ, Q the same body revolving in its curve, and PQR the curve itself which is required to be found, described in that given plane. Join CQ, QS, and if in QS

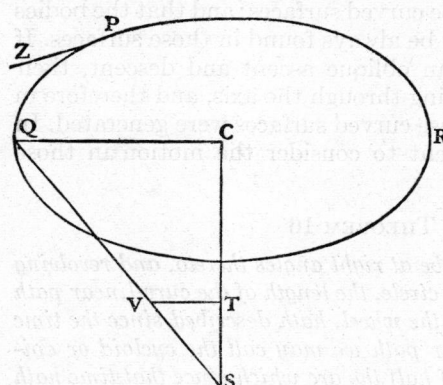

we take SV proportional to the centripetal force with which the body is attracted towards the centre S, and draw VT parallel to CQ, and meeting SC in T; then will the force SV be resolved into two (by Cor. II of the Laws of Motion), the force ST, and the force TV; of which ST attracting the body in the direction of a line perpendicular to that plane, does not at all change its motion in that plane. But the action of the other force TV, coinciding with the position of the plane itself, attracts the body directly towards the given

point C in that plane; and therefore causes the body to move in the plane in the same manner as if the force ST were taken away, and the body were to revolve in free space about the centre C by means of the force TV alone. But there being given the centripetal force TV with which the body Q revolves in free space about the given centre C, there is given (by Prop. 42) the curve PQR which the body describes; the place Q, in which the body will be found at any given time; and, lastly, the velocity of the body in that place Q. And conversely.   Q.E.I.

PROPOSITION 47. THEOREM 15

Supposing the centripetal force to be proportional to the distance of the body from the centre; all bodies revolving in any planes whatsoever will describe ellipses, and complete their revolutions in equal times; and those which move in right lines, running backwards and forwards alternately, will complete their several periods of going and returning in the same times.

For letting all things stand as in the foregoing Proposition, the force SV, with which the body Q revolving in any plane PQR is attracted towards the centre S, is as the distance SQ; and therefore because SV and SQ, TV and CQ are proportional, the force TV with which the body is attracted towards the given point C in the plane of the orbit, is as the distance CQ. Therefore the forces with which bodies found in the plane PQR are attracted towards the point C, are in proportion to the distances equal to the forces with which the same bodies are attracted every way towards the centre S; and therefore the bodies will move in the same times, and in the same figures, in any plane PQR about the point C, as they would do in free spaces about the centre S; and therefore (by Cor. II, Prop. 10, and Cor. II, Prop. 38) they will in equal times either describe ellipses in that plane about the centre C, or move to and fro in right lines passing through the centre C in that plane; completing the same periods of time in all cases.   Q.E.D.

SCHOLIUM

The ascent and descent of bodies in curved surfaces has a near relation to these motions we have been speaking of. Imagine curved lines to be described on any plane, and to revolve about any given axes passing through the centre of force, and by that revolution to describe curved surfaces; and that the bodies move in such sort that their centres may be always found in those surfaces. If those bodies oscillate to and fro with an oblique ascent and descent, their motions will be performed in planes passing through the axis, and therefore in the curved lines, by whose revolution those curved surfaces were generated. In those cases, therefore, it will be sufficient to consider the motion in those curved lines.

PROPOSITION 48. THEOREM 16

If a wheel stands upon the outside of a globe at right angles thereto, and revolving about its own axis goes forwards in a great circle, the length of the curvilinear path which any point, given in the perimeter of the wheel, hath described since the time that it touched the globe (which curvilinear path we may call the cycloid or epicycloid), will be to double the versed sine of half the arc which since that time hath touched the globe in passing over it, as the sum of the diameters of the globe and the wheel to the semidiameter of the globe.

PROPOSITION 49. THEOREM 17

If a wheel stands upon the inside of a concave globe at right angles thereto, and revolving about its own axis goes forwards in one of the great circles of the globe, the length of the curvilinear path which any point, given in the perimeter of the wheel, hath described since it touched the globe, will be to the double of the versed sine of half the arc which in all that time hath touched the globe in passing over it, as the difference of the diameters of the globe and the wheel to the semidiameter of the globe.

Let ABL be the globe, C its centre, BPV the wheel resting on it, E the centre of the wheel, B the point of contact, and P the given point in the perimeter of the wheel. Imagine this wheel to proceed in the great circle ABL from A through B towards L, and in its progress to revolve in such a manner that the arcs AB, PB may be always equal one to the other, and the given point P in the perimeter of the wheel may describe in the meantime the curvilinear path AP. Let AP be the whole curvilinear path described since the wheel touched the globe in A, and the length of this path AP will be to twice the versed sine of the arc ½PB as 2CE to CB. For let the right line CE (produced if need be) meet the wheel in V, and join CP, BP, EP, VP; produce CP, and let fall thereon the perpendicular VF. Let PH, VH, meeting in H, touch the circle in P and V, and let PH cut VF in G, and to VP let fall the perpendiculars GI, HK. From

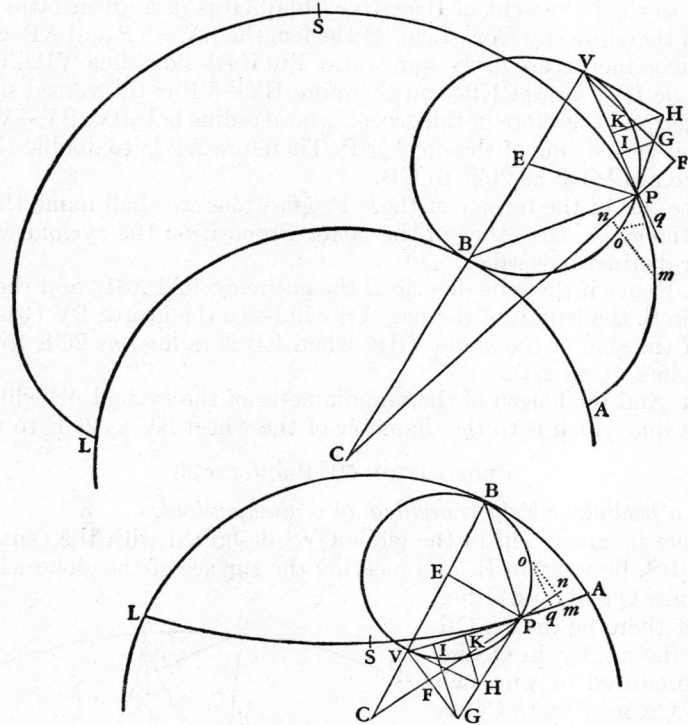

the centre C with any radius let there be described the circle *nom*, cutting the right line CP in *n*, the perimeter of the wheel BP in *o*, and the curvilinear path AP in *m*; and from the centre V with the radius V*o* let there be described a circle cutting VP produced in *q*.

Because the wheel in its progress always revolves about the point of contact B, it is manifest that the right line BP is perpendicular to that curved line AP which the point P of the wheel describes, and therefore that the right line VP will touch this curve in the point P. Let the radius of the circle *nom* be gradually increased or diminished so that at last it becomes equal to the distance CP; and by reason of the similitude of the evanescent figure P*nomq*, and the figure PFGVI, the ultimate ratio of the evanescent short lines P*m*, P*n*, P*o*, P*q*, that is, the ratio of the momentary increments of the curve AP, the right line CP, the circular arc BP, and the right line VP, will be the same as of the lines

PV, PF, PG, PI, respectively. But since VF is perpendicular to CF, and VH to CV, and therefore the angles HVG, VCF equal; and the angle VHG (because the angles of the quadrilateral HVEP are right in V and P) is equal to the angle CEP, the triangles VHG, CEP will be similar; and thence it will come to pass that   EP : CE = HG : HV or HP = KI : PK,
and by addition or subtraction,
$$CB : CE = PI : PK,$$
and $$CB : 2CE = PI : PV = Pq : Pm.$$
Therefore the decrement of the line VP, that is, the increment of the line BV−VP to the increment of the curved line AP is in a given ratio of CB to 2CE, and therefore (by Cor., Lem. 4) the lengths BV−VP and AP, generated by those increments, are in the same ratio. But if BV be radius, VP is the cosine of the angle BVP or ½BEP, and therefore BV−VP is the versed sine of the same angle, and therefore in this wheel, whose radius is ½BV, BV−VP will be double the versed sine of the arc ½BP. Therefore AP is to double the versed sine of the arc ½BP as 2CE to CB.   Q.E.D.

The line AP in the former of these Propositions we shall name the cycloid without the globe, the other in the latter Proposition the cycloid within the globe, for distinction's sake.

COR. I. Hence if there be described the entire cycloid ASL, and the same be bisected in S, the length of the part PS will be to the length PV (which is the double of the sine of the angle VBP, when EB is radius) as 2CE to CB, and therefore in a given ratio.

COR. II. And the length of the semidiameter of the cycloid AS will be equal to a right line which is to the diameter of the wheel BV as 2CE to CB.

PROPOSITION 50. PROBLEM 33

To cause a pendulous body to oscillate in a given cycloid.

Let there be given within the globe QVS described with the centre C, the cycloid QRS, bisected in R, and meeting the surface of the globe with its extreme points Q and S on either hand. Let there be drawn CR bisecting the arc QS in O, and let it be produced to A in such sort that CA may be to CO as CO to CR. About the centre C, with the radius CA, let there be described an exterior globe DAF; and within this globe, by a wheel whose diameter is AO, let there be described two semicycloids AQ, AS, touching the interior globe in Q and S, and meeting the exterior globe in A. From that point A, with a thread APT in length equal to the line AR, let the body T be suspended and oscillated in such manner between the two

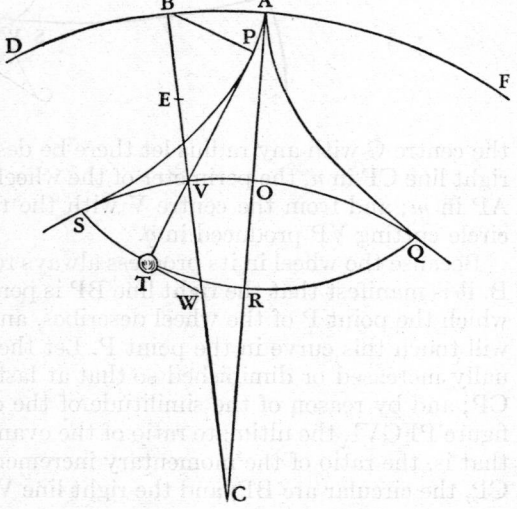

semicycloids AQ, AS, that, as often as the pendulum parts from the perpendicular AR, the upper part of the thread AP may be applied to that semicycloid APS towards which the motion tends, and fold itself round that curved
line, as if it were some solid obstacle, the remaining part of the same thread
PT which has not yet touched the semicycloid continuing straight. Then will
the weight T oscillate in the given cycloid QRS.   Q.E.F.

For let the thread PT meet the cycloid QRS in T, and the circle QOS in V,
and let CV be drawn; and to the rectilinear part of the thread PT from the extreme points P and T let there be erected the perpendiculars BP, TW, meeting
the right line CV in B and W. It is evident, from the construction and generation of the similar figures AS, SR, that those perpendiculars PB, TW, cut off
from CV the lengths VB, VW, equal the diameters of the wheels OA, OR.
Therefore TP is to VP (which is double the sine of the angle VBP when ½BV
is radius) as BW to BV, or AO+OR to AO, that is (since CA and CO, CO and
CR, and by division AO and OR are proportional), as CA+CO to CA, or, if
BV be bisected in E, as 2CE to CB. Therefore (by Cor. I, Prop. 49), the length
of the rectilinear part of the thread PT is always equal to the arc of the cycloid
PS, and the whole thread APT is always equal to half the cycloid APS, that is
(by Cor. II, Prop. 49), to the length AR. And conversely, if the string is always
equal to the length AR, the point T will always move in the given cycloid QRS.
                                                                    Q.E.D.

Cor. The string AR is equal to the semicycloid AS, and therefore has the
same ratio to AC, the semidiameter of the exterior globe, as the like semicycloid
SR has to CO, the semidiameter of the interior globe.

PROPOSITION 51. THEOREM 18

*If a centripetal force tending on all sides to the centre C of a globe, be in all places
as the distance of the place from the centre; and, by this force alone acting upon it,*

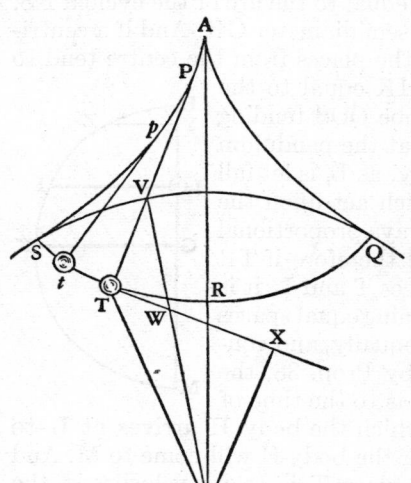

*the body T oscillate (in the manner above
described) in the perimeter of the cycloid
QRS: I say, that all the oscillations, howsoever unequal in themselves, will be performed in equal times.*

For upon the tangent TW indefinitely
produced let fall the perpendicular CX,
and join CT. Because the centripetal
force with which the body T is impelled
towards C is as the distance CT, let this
(by Cor. II of the Laws) be resolved into
the parts CX, TX, of which CX impelling
the body directly from P stretches the
thread PT, and by the resistance the
thread makes to it is totally employed,
producing no other effect; but the other
part TX, impelling the body transversely
or towards X, directly accelerates the
motion in the cycloid. Then it is plain
that the acceleration of the body, proportional to this accelerating force, will
be every moment as the length TX, that is (because CV, WV, and TX, TW

proportional to them are given), as the length TW, that is (by Cor. I, Prop. 39), as the length of the arc of the cycloid TR. If therefore two pendulums APT, A*pt*, be unequally drawn aside from the perpendicular AR, and let fall together, their accelerations will be always as the arcs to be described TR, *t*R. But the parts described at the beginning of the motion are as the accelerations, that is, as the whole spaces that are to be described at the beginning, and therefore the parts which remain to be described, and the subsequent accelerations proportional to those parts, are also as the whole, and so on. Therefore the accelerations, and consequently the velocities generated, and the parts described with those velocities, and the parts to be described, are always as the whole; and therefore the parts to be described preserving a given ratio to each other will vanish together, that is, the two bodies oscillating will arrive together at the perpendicular AR. And since on the other hand the ascent of the pendulums from the lowest place R through the same cycloidal arcs with a retrograde motion, is retarded in the several places they pass through by the same forces by which their descent was accelerated, it is plain that the velocities of their ascent and descent through the same arcs are equal, and consequently performed in equal times; and, therefore, since the two parts of the cycloid RS and RQ lying on either side of the perpendicular are similar and equal, the two pendulums will perform as well the whole as the half of their oscillations in the same times.   Q.E.D.

Cor. The force with which the body T is accelerated or retarded in any place T of the cycloid, is to the whole weight of the same body in the highest place S or Q as the arc of the cycloid TR is to the arc SR or QR.

PROPOSITION 52. PROBLEM 34

To define the velocities of pendulums in the several places, and the times in which both the entire oscillations and their several parts are performed.

About any centre G, with the radius GH equal to the arc of the cycloid RS, describe a semicircle HKM bisected by the semidiameter GK. And if a centripetal force proportional to the distance of the places from the centre tend to the centre G, and it be in the perimeter HIK equal to the centripetal force in the perimeter of the globe QOS tending towards its centre, and at the same time that the pendulum T is let fall from the highest place S, a body, as L, is let fall from H to G; then because the forces which act upon the bodies are equal at the beginning, and always proportional to the spaces to be described TR, LG, and therefore if TR and LG are equal, are also equal in the places T and L, it is plain that those bodies describe at the beginning equal spaces ST, HL, and therefore are still acted upon equally, and continue to describe equal spaces. Therefore by Prop. 38, the time in which the body describes the arc ST is to the time of

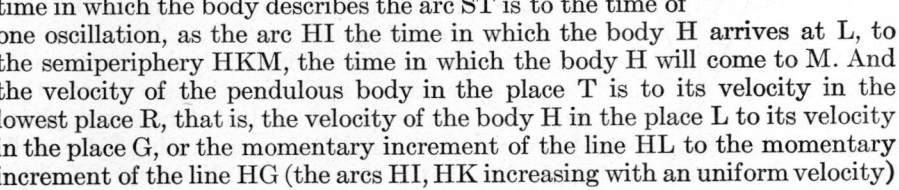

one oscillation, as the arc HI the time in which the body H arrives at L, to the semiperiphery HKM, the time in which the body H will come to M. And the velocity of the pendulous body in the place T is to its velocity in the lowest place R, that is, the velocity of the body H in the place L to its velocity in the place G, or the momentary increment of the line HL to the momentary increment of the line HG (the arcs HI, HK increasing with an uniform velocity) as the ordinate LI to the radius GK, or as $\sqrt{(SR^2 - TR^2)}$ to SR. Hence, since in unequal oscillations there are described in equal times arcs proportional to the entire arcs of the oscillations, there are obtained, from the times given, both the velocities and the arcs described in all the oscillations universally. Which was first required.

Let now any pendulous bodies oscillate in different cycloids described within different globes, whose absolute forces are also different; and if the absolute force of any globe QOS be called V, the accelerative force with which the pen-

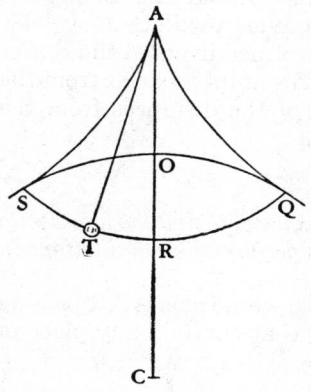

dulum is acted on in the circumference of this globe, when it begins to move directly towards its centre, will be as the distance of the pendulous body from that centre and the absolute force of the globe conjointly, that is, as CO·V. Therefore the short line HY, which is as this accelerated force CO·V, will be described in a given time; and if there be erected the perpendicular YZ meeting the circumference in Z, the nascent arc HZ will denote that given time. But that nascent arc HZ varies as the square root of the rectangle GH·HY, and therefore as $\sqrt{(GH·CO·V)}$. Whence the time of an entire oscillation in the cycloid QRS (it being as the semiperiphery HKM, which denotes that entire oscillation, directly; and as the arc HZ, which in like manner denotes a given time, inversely) will be as GH directly and $\sqrt{(GH·CO·V)}$ inversely; that is, because GH and SR are equal, as $\sqrt{\dfrac{SR}{CO·V}}$, or (by Cor., Prop. 50), as $\sqrt{\dfrac{AR}{AC·V}}$. Therefore the oscillations in all globes and cycloids, performed with any absolute forces whatever, vary directly as the square root of the length of the string, and inversely as the square root of the distance between the point of suspension and the centre of the globe, and also inversely as the square root of the absolute force of the globe.   Q.E.I.

COR. I. Hence also the times of oscillating, falling, and revolving bodies may be compared among themselves. For if the diameter of the wheel with which the cycloid is described within the globe is supposed equal to the semidiameter of the globe, the cycloid will become a right line passing through the centre of the globe, and the oscillation will be changed into a descent and subsequent ascent in that right line. Hence there is given both the time of the descent from any place to the centre, and the time equal to it in which the body revolving uniformly about the centre of the globe at any distance describes an arc of a quadrant. For this time (by Case 2) is to the time of half the oscillation in any cycloid QRS as 1 to $\sqrt{\dfrac{AR}{AC}}$.

COR. II. Hence also follow what Sir Christopher Wren and Mr. Huygens have discovered concerning the common cycloid. For if the diameter of the globe be infinitely increased, its spherical surface will be changed into a plane, and the centripetal force will act uniformly in the direction of lines perpendicular to that plane, and our cycloid will become the same with the common cycloid. But in that case the length of the arc of the cycloid between that plane and the describing point will become equal to four times the versed sine of half the arc of the wheel between the same plane and the describing point, as was discovered by Sir Christopher Wren. And a pendulum between two such cycloids will oscillate in a similar and equal cycloid in equal times, as Mr. Huygens demonstrated. The descent of heavy bodies also in the time of one oscillation will be the same as Mr. Huygens exhibited.

The Propositions here demonstrated are adapted to the true constitution of the earth, so far as wheels moving in any of its great circles will describe, by the motions of nails fixed in their perimeters, cycloids without the globe; and pendulums, in mines and deep caverns of the earth, must oscillate in cycloids within the globe, that those oscillations may be performed in equal times. For gravity (as will be shown in the third book) decreases in its progress from the surface of the earth; upwards as the square root of the distances from the centre of the earth; downwards as these distances.

PROPOSITION 53. PROBLEM 35

Granting the quadratures of curvilinear figures, it is required to find the forces with which bodies moving in given curved lines may always perform their oscillations in equal times.

Let the body T oscillate in any curved line STRQ, whose axis is AR passing through the centre of force C. Draw TX touching that curve in any place of the body T, and in that tangent TX take TY equal to the arc TR. The length of that arc is known from the common methods used for the quadratures of figures. From the point Y draw the right line YZ perpendicular to the tangent. Draw CT meeting YZ in Z, and the centripetal force will be proportional to the right line TZ. Q.E.I.

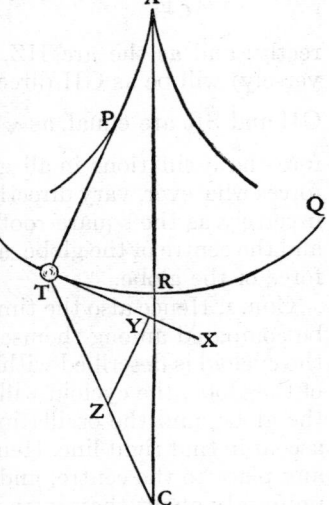

For if the force with which the body is attracted from T towards C be expressed by the right line TZ taken proportional to it, that force will be resolved into two forces TY, YZ, of which YZ, drawing the body in the direction of the length of the thread PT, does not at all change its motion; whereas the other force TY directly accelerates or retards its motion in the curve STRQ. Therefore since that force is as the space to be described TR, the accelerations or retardations of the body in describing two proportional parts (a greater and a less) of two oscillations, will be always as those parts, and therefore will cause those parts to be described together. But bodies which continually describe in the same time parts proportional to the whole, will describe the whole in the same time. Q.E.D.

COR. I. Hence if the body T, hanging by a rectilinear thread AT from the centre A, describe the circular arc STRQ, and in the meantime be acted on by any force tending downwards with parallel directions, which is to the uniform force of gravity as the arc TR to its sine TN, the times of the several oscillations will be equal. For because TZ, AR are parallel, the triangles ATN, ZTY

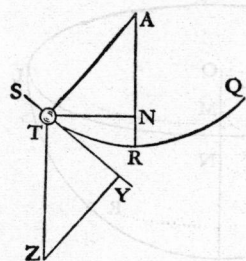

are similar; and therefore TZ will be to AT as TY to TN; that is, if the uniform force of gravity be expressed by the given length AT, the force TZ, by which the oscillations become isochronous, will be to the force of gravity AT, as the arc TR equal to TY is to TN the sine of that arc.

COR. II. And therefore in clocks, if forces are impressed by some machine upon the pendulum which continues the motion, and so compounded with the force of gravity that the whole force tending downwards will be always as a line which is obtained by dividing the product of the arc TR and the radius AR, by the sine TN, then all the oscillations will become isochronous.

PROPOSITION 54. PROBLEM 36

Granting the quadratures of curvilinear figures, it is required to find the times in which bodies by means of any centripetal force will descend or ascend in any curved lines in a plane passing through the centre of force.

Let the body descend from any place S, and move in any curve ST*t*R given in a plane passing through the centre of force C. Join CS, and let it be divided into innumerable equal parts, and let D*d* be one of those parts. From the centre C, with the radii CD, C*d*, let the circles DT, *dt* be described, meeting the curved line ST*t*R in T and *t*. And because the law of centripetal force is given, and also the altitude CS from which the body at first fell, there will be given the velocity of the body in any other altitude CT (by Prop. 39). But the time in which the body describes the short line T*t* is as the length of that short line, that is, directly as the secant of the angle *t*TC and inversely as the velocity. Let the ordinate DN, proportional to this time, be made perpendicular to the right line CS at the point D, and because D*d* is given, the rectangle D*d*·DN, that is, the area DN*nd*, will be proportional to the same time. Therefore if PN*n* be a

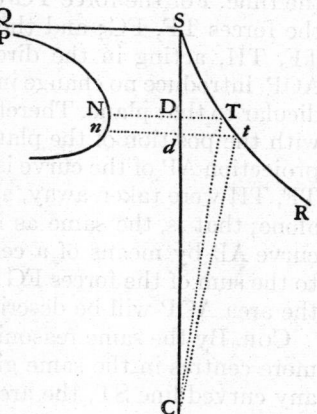

curved line which the point N continually touches, and its asymptote be the right line SQ standing upon the line CS at right angles, the area SQPND will be proportional to the time in which the body in its descent hath described the line ST; and therefore that area being found, the time is also given.   Q.E.I.

PROPOSITION 55. THEOREM 19

If a body move in any curved surface, whose axis passes through the centre of force, and from the body a perpendicular be let fall upon the axis; and a line parallel and equal thereto be drawn from any given point of the axis: I say, that this parallel line will describe an area proportional to the time.

Let BKL be a curved surface, T a body revolving in it, STR a curve which the body describes in the same, S the beginning of the curve, OMK the axis of the curved surface, TN a right line let fall perpendicularly from the body to the axis; OP a line parallel and equal thereto drawn from the given point O in the axis; AP the path described by the point P in the plane AOP in which the revolving line OP is found; A the beginning of that path answering to the point S; TC a right line drawn from the body to the centre; TG a part thereof proportional to the centripetal force with which the body tends towards the centre C; TM a right line perpendicular to the curved surface; TI a part thereof proportional to the force of pressure with which the body urges the surface, and therefore with which it is again repelled by the surface towards M; PTF a right line parallel to the axis and passing through the body, and GF, IH right lines let fall perpendicularly from the

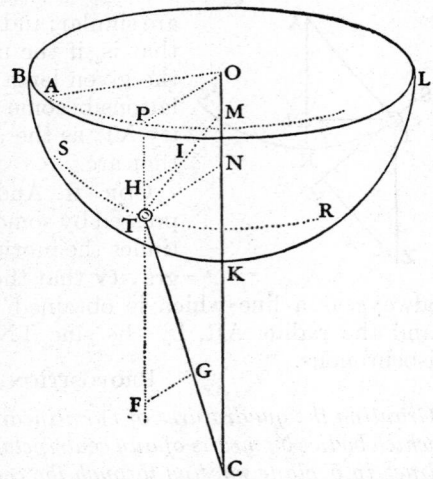

points G and I upon that parallel PHTF. I say, now, that the area AOP, described by the radius OP from the beginning of the motion, is proportional to the time. For the force TG (by Cor. II of the Laws of Motion) is resolved into the forces TF, FG; and the force TI into the forces TH, HI; but the forces TF, TH, acting in the direction of the line PF perpendicular to the plane AOP, introduce no change in the motion of the body but in a direction perpendicular to that plane. Therefore its motion, so far as it hath the same direction with the position of the plane, that is, the motion of the point P, by which the projection AP of the curve is described in that plane, is the same as if the forces TF, TH were taken away, and the body were acted on by the forces FG, HI alone; that is, the same as if the body were to describe in the plane AOP the curve AP by means of a centripetal force tending to the centre O, and equal to the sum of the forces FG and HI. But with such a force as that (by Prop.1) the area AOP will be described proportional to the time.   Q.E.D.

Cor. By the same reasoning, if a body, acted on by forces tending to two or more centres in the same given right line CO, should describe in a free space any curved line ST, the area AOP would be always proportional to the time.

PROPOSITION 56. PROBLEM 37

Granting the quadratures of curvilinear figures, and supposing that there are given both the law of centripetal force tending to a given centre, and the curved surface whose axis passes through that centre; it is required to find the curve which a body will describe in that surface, when going off from a given place with a given velocity, and in a given direction in that surface.

The last construction remaining, let the body T go from the given place S, in the direction of a line given by position, and turn into the curve sought STR, whose orthographic projection in the plane BDO is AP. And from the given velocity of the body in the altitude SC, its velocity in any other altitude TC will be also given. With that velocity, in a given moment of time, let the body describe the segment Tt of its curve and let Pp be the projection of that segment described in the plane AOP. Join Op, and a little circle being described upon the curved surface about the centre T with the radius Tt, let the pro-

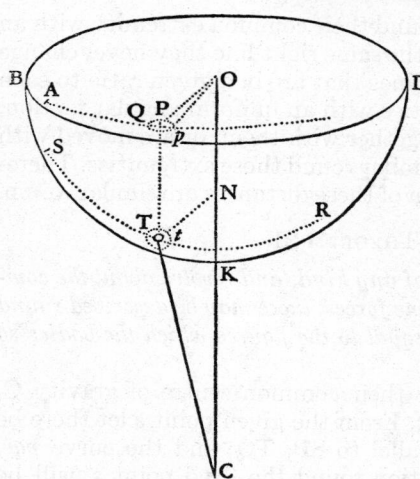

jection of that little circle in the plane AOP be the ellipse pQ. And because the magnitude of that little circle Tt, and TN or PO its distance from the axis CO is also given, the ellipse pQ will be given both in kind and magnitude, as also its position to the right line PO. And since the area POp is proportional to the time, and therefore given because the time is given, the angle POp will be given. And thence will be given p the common intersection of the ellipse and the right line Op, together with the angle OPp, in which the projection APp of the curve cuts the line OP. But from thence (by comparing Prop. 41, with its Cor. II) the manner of determining the curve APp easily appears. Then from the several points P of that projection erecting to the plane AOP, the perpendiculars PT meeting the curved surface in T, there will be given the several points T of the curve.   Q.E.I.

SECTION XI

The motions of bodies tending to each other with centripetal forces

I have hitherto been treating of the attractions of bodies towards an immovable centre; though very probably there is no such thing existent in nature. For attractions are made towards bodies, and the actions of the bodies attracted and attracting are always reciprocal and equal, by Law III; so that if there are two bodies, neither the attracted nor the attracting body is truly at rest, but both (by Cor. IV of the Laws of Motion), being as it were mutually attracted, revolve about a common centre of gravity. And if there be more bodies, which either are attracted by one body, which is attracted by them again, or which all attract each other mutually, these bodies will be so moved among themselves, that their common centre of gravity will either be at rest, or move uniformly forwards in a right line. I shall therefore at present go on to treat of the motion of bodies attracting each other; considering the centripetal forces as attractions; though perhaps in a physical strictness they may more truly be called impulses. But these Propositions are to be considered as purely mathematical; and therefore, laying aside all physical considerations, I make use of a familiar way of speaking, to make myself the more easily understood by a mathematical reader.

Proposition 57. Theorem 20

Two bodies attracting each other mutually describe similar figures about their common centre of gravity, and about each other mutually.

For the distances of the bodies from their common centre of gravity are inversely as the bodies; and therefore in a given ratio to each other; and thence, by composition of ratios, in a given ratio to the whole distance between the bodies. Now these distances are carried round their common extremity with an uniform angular motion, because lying in the same right line they never change their inclination to each other. But right lines that are in a given ratio to each other, and are carried round their extremities with an uniform angular motion, describe upon planes, which either rest together with them, or are moved with any motion not angular, figures entirely similar round those extremities. Therefore the figures described by the revolution of these distances are similar. Q.E.D.

Proposition 58. Theorem 21

If two bodies attract each other with forces of any kind, and revolve about the common centre of gravity: I say, that, by the same forces, there may be described round either body unmoved a figure similar and equal to the figures which the bodies so moving describe round each other.

Let the bodies S and P revolve about their common centre of gravity C, proceeding from S to T, and from P to Q. From the given point *s* let there be continually drawn *sp*, *sq*, equal and parallel to SP, TQ; and the curve *pqv*, which the point *p* describes in its revolution round the fixed point *s*, will be

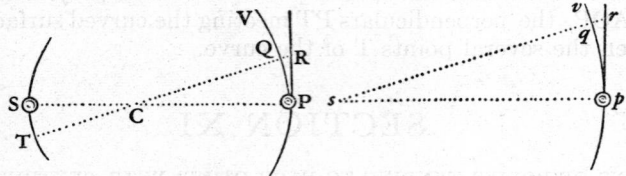

similar and equal to the curves which the bodies S and P describe about each other; and therefore, by Theor. 20, similar to the curves ST and PQV which the same bodies describe about their common centre of gravity C; and that because the proportions of the lines SC, CP, and SP or *sp*, to each other, are given.

Case 1. The common centre of gravity C (by Cor. IV of the Laws of Motion) is either at rest, or moves uniformly in a right line. Let us first suppose it at rest, and in *s* and *p* let there be placed two bodies, one immovable in *s*, the other movable in *p*, similar and equal to the bodies S and P. Then let the right lines PR and *pr* touch the curves PQ and *pq* in P and *p*, and produce CQ and *sq* to R and *r*. And because the figures CPRQ, *sprq* are similar, RQ will be to *rq* as CP to *sp*, and therefore in a given ratio. Hence if the force with which the body P is attracted towards the body S, and by consequence towards the intermediate centre C, were to the force with which the body *p* is attracted towards the centre *s*, in the same given ratio, these forces would in equal times attract the bodies from the tangents PR, *pr* to the arcs PQ, *pq*, through the intervals proportional to them RQ, *rq*; and therefore this last force (tending to *s*) would make the body *p* revolve in the curve *pqv*, which would become similar to the curve PQV, in which the first force obliges the body P to revolve; and their revolutions would be completed in the same times. But because those forces are not to each other in the ratio of CP to *sp*, but (by reason of the similarity and equality of the bodies S and *s*, P and *p*, and the equality of the distances SP, *sp*) mutually equal, the bodies in equal times will be equally drawn from the tangents; and therefore that the body *p* may be attracted through the greater interval *rq*, there is required a greater time, which will vary as the square root of the intervals; because, by Lem. 10, the spaces described at the beginning of the motion are as the square of the times. Suppose, then, the velocity of the body p to be to the velocity of the body P as the square root of the ratio of the distance sp to the distance CP, so that the arcs pq, PQ, which are in a simple proportion to each other, may be described in times that are as the square root of the distances; and the bodies P, p, always attracted by equal forces, will describe round the fixed centres C and s similar figures PQV, pqv, the latter of which pqv is similar and equal to the figure which the body P describes round the movable body S.   Q.E.D.

CASE 2. Suppose now that the common centre of gravity, together with the space in which the bodies are moved among themselves, proceeds uniformly in a right line; and (by Cor. VI of the Laws of Motion) all the motions in this space will be performed in the same manner as before; and therefore the bodies will describe about each other the same figures as before, which will be therefore similar and equal to the figure pqv.   Q.E.D.

COR. I. Hence two bodies attracting each other with forces proportional to their distance, describe (by Prop. 10), both round their common centre of gravity, and round each other, concentric ellipses; and, conversely, if such figures are described, the forces are proportional to the distances.

COR. II. And two bodies, whose forces are inversely proportional to the square of their distance, describe (by Props. 11, 12, 13), both round their common centre of gravity, and round each other, conic sections having their focus in the centre about which the figures are described. And, conversely, if such figures are described, the centripetal forces are inversely proportional to the square of the distance.

COR. III. Any two bodies revolving round their common centre of gravity describe areas proportional to the times, by radii drawn both to that centre and to each other.

PROPOSITION 59. THEOREM 22

The periodic time of two bodies S *and* P *revolving round their common centre of gravity* C, *is to the periodic time of one of the bodies* P *revolving round the other* S *remaining fixed, and describing a figure similar and equal to those which the bodies describe about each other, as* $\sqrt{S}$ *is to* $\sqrt{(S+P)}$.

For, by the demonstration of the last Proposition, the times in which any similar arcs PQ and pq are described are as $\sqrt{CP}$ is to $\sqrt{SP}$, or $\sqrt{sp}$, that is, as $\sqrt{S}$ is to $\sqrt{(S+P)}$. And by composition of ratios, the sums of the times in which all the similar arcs PQ and pq are described, that is, the whole times in which the whole similar figures are described, are in the same ratio, $\sqrt{S}$ to $\sqrt{(S+P)}$.   Q.E.D.

PROPOSITION 60. THEOREM 23

If two bodies S *and* P, *attracting each other with forces inversely proportional to the square of their distance, revolve about their common centre of gravity: I say, that the principal axis of the ellipse which either of the bodies, as* P, *describes by this motion about the other* S, *will be to the principal axis of the ellipse, which the same body* P *may describe in the same periodic time about the other body* S *fixed, as the sum of the two bodies* S+P *to the first of two mean proportionals between that sum and the other body* S.

For if the ellipses described were equal to each other, their periodic times by the last Theorem would be as the square root of the ratio of the body S to the sum of the bodies S+P. Let the periodic time in the latter ellipse be diminished in that ratio, and the periodic times will become equal; but, by Prop. 15, the principal axis of the ellipse will be diminished in a ratio which is the $^3\!/_2$th power of the former ratio; that is, in a ratio to which the ratio of S to S+P is the cube, and therefore that axis will be to the principal axis of the other ellipse as the first of two mean proportionals between S+P and S to S+P. And inversely the principal axis of the ellipse described about the movable body will be to the principal axis of that described round the immovable as S+P to the first of two mean proportionals between S+P and S.   Q.E.D.

PROPOSITION 61. THEOREM 24

If two bodies attracting each other with any kind of forces, and not otherwise agitated or obstructed, are moved in any manner whatsoever, those motions will be the same as if they did not at all attract each other, but were both attracted with the same forces by a third body placed in their common centre of gravity; and the law of the attracting forces will be the same in respect of the distance of the bodies from the common centre, as in respect of the distance between the two bodies.

For those forces with which the bodies attract each other, by tending to the bodies, tend also to the common centre of gravity lying directly between them; and therefore are the same as if they proceeded from an intermediate body.

                                                                 Q.E.D.

And because there is given the ratio of the distance of either body from that common centre to the distance between the two bodies, there is given, of course, the ratio of any power of one distance to the same power of the other distance; and also the ratio of any quantity derived in any manner from one of the distances compounded in any manner with given quantities, to another quantity derived in like manner from the other distance, and as many given quantities having that given ratio of the distances to the first. Therefore if the force with which one body is attracted by another be directly or inversely as the distance of the bodies from each other, or as any power of that distance; or, lastly, as any quantity derived after any manner from that distance compounded with given quantities; then will the same force with which the same body is attracted to the common centre of gravity be in like manner directly or inversely as the distance of the attracted body from the common centre, or as any power of that distance; or, lastly, as a quantity derived in like sort from that distance compounded with analogous given quantities. That is, the law of attracting force will be the same with respect to both distances.   Q.E.D.

PROPOSITION 62. PROBLEM 38

To determine the motions of two bodies which attract each other with forces inversely proportional to the squares of the distance between them, and are let fall from given places.

The bodies, by the last Theorem, will be moved in the same manner as if they were attracted by a third placed in the common centre of their gravity; and by the hypothesis that centre will be fixed at the beginning of their motion, and therefore (by Cor. IV of the Laws of Motion) will be always fixed. The motions of the bodies are therefore to be determined (by Prob. 25) in the same manner as if they were impelled by forces tending to that centre; and then we shall have the motions of the bodies attracting each other.   Q.E.I.

PROPOSITION 63. PROBLEM 39

To determine the motions of two bodies attracting each other with forces inversely proportional to the squares of their distance, and going off from given places in given directions with given velocities.

The motions of the bodies at the beginning being given, there is given also the uniform motion of the common centre of gravity, and the motion of the space which moves along with this centre uniformly in a right line, and also the very first, or beginning motions of the bodies in respect of this space. Then (by Cor. v of the Laws, and the last Theorem) the subsequent motions will be performed in the same manner in that space, as if that space together with the common centre of gravity were at rest, and as if the bodies did not attract each other, but were attracted by a third body placed in that centre. The motion therefore in this movable space of each body going off from a given place, in a given direction, with a given velocity, and acted upon by a centripetal force tending to that centre, is to be determined by Probs. 9 and 26, and at the same time will be obtained the motion of the other round the same centre. With this motion compound the uniform progressive motion of the entire system of the space and the bodies revolving in it, and there will be obtained the absolute motion of the bodies in immovable space.   Q.E.I.

PROPOSITION 64. PROBLEM 40

Supposing forces with which bodies attract each other to increase in a simple ratio of their distances from the centres; it is required to find the motions of several bodies among themselves.

Suppose the first two bodies T and L to have their common centre of gravity in D. These, by Cor. I, Theor. 21, will describe ellipses having their centres in D, the magnitudes of which ellipses are known by Prob. 5.

Let now a third body S attract the two former T and L with the accelerative forces ST, SL, and let it be attracted again by them. The force ST (by Cor. II of the Laws of Motion) is resolved into the forces SD, DT; and the force SL into the forces SD and DL. Now the forces DT, DL, which are as their sum

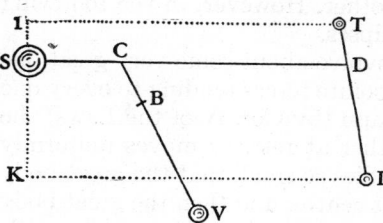

TL, and therefore as the accelerative forces with which the bodies T and L attract each other, added to the forces of the bodies T and L, the first to the first, and the last to the last, compose forces proportional to the distances DT and DL as before, but only greater than those former forces; and therefore (by Cor. I, Prop. 10, and Cor. I and VIII, Prop. 4) they will cause those bodies to describe ellipses as before, but with a swifter motion. The remaining accelerative forces SD and DL, by the motive forces SD·T and SD·L, which are as the bodies attracting those bodies equally and in the direction of the lines TI, LK parallel to DS, do not at all change their situations with respect to one another, but cause them equally to approach to the line IK; which must be imagined drawn through the middle of the body S, and perpendicular to the line DS. But that approach to the line IK will be hindered by causing the system of the bodies T and L on one side, and the body S on the other, with proper velocities, to revolve round the common centre of gravity C. With such a motion the body S, because the sum of the motive forces SD·T and SD·L is proportional to the distance CS, tends to the centre C, and will describe an ellipse round that centre; and the point D, because the lines CS and CD are proportional, will describe a like ellipse over against it. But the bodies T and L, attracted by the motive forces SD·T and SD·L, the first by the first, and the last by the last, equally and in the direction of the parallel lines TI and LK, as was said before, will (by Cor. v and vi of the Laws of Motion) continue to describe their ellipses round the movable centre D, as before.   q.e.i.

Let there be added a fourth body V, and, by the like reasoning, it will be demonstrated that this body and the point C will describe ellipses about the common centre of gravity B; the motions of the bodies T, L, and S round the centres D and C remaining the same as before, but accelerated. And by the same method one may add yet more bodies at pleasure.   q.e.i.

This would be the case, though the bodies T and L should attract each other with accelerative forces greater or less than those with which they attract the other bodies in proportion to their distance. Let all the accelerative attractions be to each other as the distances multiplied into the attracting bodies; and from what has gone before it will easily be concluded that all the bodies will describe different ellipses with equal periodic times about their common centre of gravity B, in an immovable plane.   q.e.i.

Proposition 65. Theorem 25

Bodies, whose forces decrease as the square of their distances from their centres, may move among themselves in ellipses; and by radii drawn to the foci may describe areas very nearly proportional to the times.

In the last Proposition we demonstrated that case in which the motions will be performed exactly in ellipses. The more distant the law of the forces is from the law in that case, the more will the bodies disturb each other's motions; neither is it possible that bodies attracting each other according to the law supposed in this Proposition should move exactly in ellipses, unless by keeping a certain proportion of distances from each other. However, in the following cases the orbits will not much differ from ellipses.

Case 1. Imagine several lesser bodies to revolve about some very great one at different distances from it, and suppose absolute forces tending to every one of the bodies proportional to each. And because (by Cor. iv of the Laws) the common centre of gravity of them all is either at rest, or moves uniformly forwards in a right line, suppose the lesser bodies so small that the great body may be never at a sensible distance from that centre; and then the great body will, without any sensible error, be either at rest, or move uniformly forwards in a right line; and the lesser will revolve about that great one in ellipses, and by radii drawn thereto will describe areas proportional to the times; if we except the errors that may be introduced by the receding of the great body from the common centre of gravity, or by the actions of the lesser bodies upon each other. But the lesser bodies may be so far diminished, as that this recess and the actions of the bodies on each other may become less than any assignable; and therefore so as that the orbits may become ellipses, and the areas answer to the times, without any error that is not less than any assignable.   q.e.o.

CASE 2. Let us imagine a system of lesser bodies revolving about a very great one in the manner just described, or any other system of two bodies revolving about each other, to be moving uniformly forwards in a right line, and in the meantime to be impelled sideways by the force of another vastly greater body situate at a great distance. And because the equal accelerative forces with which the bodies are impelled in parallel directions do not change the situation of the bodies with respect to each other, but only oblige the whole system to change its place while the parts still retain their motions among themselves, it is manifest that no change in those motions of the attracted bodies can arise from their attractions towards the greater, unless by the inequality of the accelerative attractions, or by the inclinations of the lines towards each other, in whose directions the attractions are made. Suppose, therefore, all the accelerative attractions made towards the great body to be among themselves inversely as the squares of the distances; and then, by increasing the distance of the great body till the differences of the right lines drawn from that to the others in respect of their length, and the inclinations of those lines to each other, be less than any given, the motions of the parts of the system will continue without errors that are not less than any given. And because, by the small distance of those parts from each other, the whole system is attracted as if it were but one body, it will therefore be moved by this attraction as if it were one body; that is, its centre of gravity will describe about the great body one of the conic sections (that is, a parabola or hyperbola when the attraction is but languid and an ellipse when it is more vigorous); and by radii drawn thereto, it will describe areas proportional to the times, without any errors but those which arise from the distances of the parts, and these are by the supposition exceedingly small, and may be diminished at pleasure. Q.E.O.

By a like reasoning one may proceed to more complicated cases *in infinitum*.

COR. I. In the second Case, the nearer the very great body approaches to the system of two or more revolving bodies, the greater will the perturbation be of the motions of the parts of the system among themselves; because the inclinations of the lines drawn from that great body to those parts become greater; and the inequality of the proportion is also greater.

COR. II. But the perturbation will be greatest of all, if we suppose the accelerative attractions of the parts of the system towards the greatest body of all are not to each other inversely as the squares of the distances from that great body; especially if the inequality of this proportion be greater than the inequality of the proportion of the distances from the great body. For if the accelerative force, acting in parallel directions and equally, causes no perturbation in the motions of the parts of the system, it must of course, when it acts unequally, cause a perturbation somewhere, which will be greater or less as the inequality is greater or less. The excess of the greater impulses acting upon some bodies, and not acting upon others, must necessarily change their situation among themselves. And this perturbation, added to the perturbation arising from the inequality and inclination of the lines, makes the whole perturbation greater.

COR. III. Hence if the parts of this system move in ellipses or circles without any remarkable perturbation, it is manifest that, if they are at all impelled by accelerative forces tending to any other bodies, the impulse is very weak, or else is impressed very near equally and in parallel directions upon all of them.

PROPOSITION 66. THEOREM 26

If three bodies, whose forces decrease as the square of the distances, attract each other; and the accelerative attractions of any two towards the third be between themselves inversely as the squares of the distances; and the two least revolve about the greatest: I say, that the interior of the two revolving bodies will, by radii drawn to the innermost and greatest, describe round that body areas more proportional to the times, and a figure more approaching to that of an ellipse having its focus in the point of intersection of the radii, if that great body be agitated by those attractions, than it would do if that great body were not attracted at all by the lesser, but remained at rest; or than it would do if that great body were very much more or very much less attracted, or very much more or very much less agitated, by the attractions.

This appears plainly enough from the demonstration of the second Corollary of the foregoing Proposition; but it may be made out after this manner by a way of reasoning more distinct and more universally convincing.

CASE 1. Let the lesser bodies P and S revolve in the same plane about the greatest body T, the body P describing the interior orbit PAB, and S the exterior orbit ESE. Let SK be the mean distance of the bodies P and S; and let the accelerative attraction of the body P towards S, at that mean distance, be expressed by that line SK. Make SL to SK as the square of SK to the square of SP, and SL will be the accelerative attraction of the body P towards S at any distance SP. Join PT, and draw LM parallel to it meeting ST in M; and

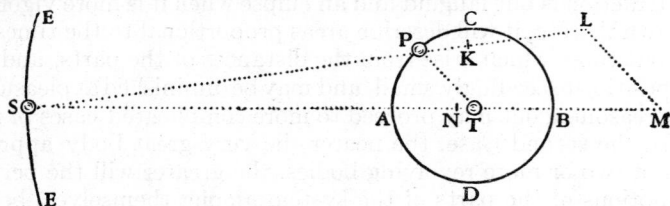

the attraction SL will be resolved (by Cor. II of the Laws of Motion) into the attractions SM, LM. And so the body P will be urged with a threefold accelerative force. One of these forces tends towards T, and arises from the mutual attraction of the bodies T and P. By this force alone the body P would describe round the body T, by the radius PT, areas proportional to the times, and an ellipse whose focus is in the centre of the body T; and this it would do whether the body T remained unmoved, or whether it were agitated by that attraction. This appears from Prop. 11, and Cor. II and III of Theor. 21. The other force is that of the attraction LM, which, because it tends from P to T, will be superadded to and coincide with the former force; and cause the areas to be still proportional to the times, by Cor. III, Theor. 21. But because it is not inversely proportional to the square of the distance PT, it will compose, when added to the former, a force varying from that proportion; this variation will be the greater by as much as the proportion of this force to the former is greater, other things remaining the same. Therefore, since by Prop. 11, and by Cor. II, Theor. 21, the force with which the ellipse is described about the focus T ought to be directed to that focus, and to be inversely proportional to the square of the distance PT, that compounded force varying from that proportion will make the orbit PAB vary from the figure of an ellipse that has its focus in the point T; and so much the more by as much as the variation from that proportion is greater; and in consequence by as much as the proportion of the second force LM to the first force is greater, other things remaining the same. But now the third force SM, attracting the body P in a direction parallel to ST, composes with the other forces a new force which is no longer directed from P to T; and this varies so much more from this direction by as much as the proportion of the third force to the other forces is greater, other things remaining the same; and therefore causes the body P to describe, by the radius TP, areas no longer proportional to the times; and therefore makes the variation from that proportionality so much greater by as much as the proportion of this force to the others is greater. But this third force will increase the variation of the orbit PAB from the elliptical figure before mentioned upon two accounts: first, because that force is not directed from P to T; and, secondly, because it is not inversely proportional to the square of the distance PT. These things being premised, it is manifest that the areas are then most nearly proportional to the times, when that third force is the least possible, the rest preserving their former quantity; and that the orbit PAB does then approach nearest to the elliptical figure above mentioned, when both the second and third, but especially the third force, is the least possible; the first force remaining in its former quantity.

Let the accelerative attraction of the body T towards S be expressed by the line SN; then if the accelerative attractions SM and SN were equal, these, attracting the bodies T and P equally and in parallel directions, would not at all change their situation with respect to each other. The motions of the bodies between themselves would be the same in that case as if those attractions did not act at all, by Cor. VI of the Laws of Motion. And, by a like reasoning, if the attraction SN is less than the attraction SM, it will take away out of the attraction SM the part SN, so that there will remain only the part (of the attraction) MN to disturb the proportionality of the areas and times, and the elliptical figure of the orbit. And in like manner if the attraction SN be greater than the attraction SM, the perturbation of the orbit and proportion will be produced by the difference MN alone. After this manner the attraction SN reduces always the attraction SM to the attraction MN, the first and second attractions remaining perfectly unchanged; and therefore the areas and times come then nearest to proportionality, and the orbit PAB to the above-mentioned elliptical figure, when the attraction MN is either none, or the least that is possible; that is, when the accelerative attractions of the bodies P and T approach as near as possible to equality; that is, when the attraction SN is neither none at all, nor less than the least of all the attractions SM, but is, as it were, a mean between the greatest and least of all those attractions SM, that is, not much greater nor much less than the attraction SK.   Q.E.D.

CASE 2. Let now the lesser bodies P, S revolve about a greater T in different planes; and the force LM, acting in the direction of the line PT situated in the plane of the orbit PAB, will have the same effect as before; neither will it draw the body P from the plane of its orbit. But the other force NM, acting in the direction of a line parallel to ST (and therefore, when the body S is without the line of the nodes, inclined to the plane of the orbit PAB), besides the perturbation of the motion just now spoken of as to longitude, introduces another perturbation also as to latitude, attracting the body P out of the plane of its orbit. And this perturbation, in any given situation of the bodies P and T to each other, will be as the generating force MN; and therefore becomes least when the force MN is least, that is (as was just now shown), where the attraction SN is not much greater nor much less than the attraction SK.   Q.E.D.

COR. I. Hence it may be easily inferred, that if several less bodies P, S, R, &c., revolve about a very great body T, the motion of the innermost revolving body P will be least disturbed by the attractions of the others, when the great body is as well attracted and agitated by the rest (according to the ratio of the accelerative forces) as the rest are by each other.

COR. II. In a system of three bodies T, P, S, if the accelerative attractions of any two of them towards a third be to each other inversely as the squares of the distances, the body P, by the radius PT, will describe its area about the body T swifter near the conjunction A and the opposition B than it will near the quadratures C and D. For every force with which the body P is acted on and the body T is not, and which does not act in the direction of the line PT, does either accelerate or retard the description of the area, according as its direction is the same as, or contrary to that of the motion of the body. Such is the force NM. This force in the passage of the body P from C to A tends in the direction in which the body is moving, and therefore accelerates it; then as far as D, it tends in the opposite direction, and retards the motion; then in the direction of the body, as far as B; and lastly in a contrary direction, as it moves from B to C.

COR. III. And from the same reasoning it appears that the body P, other things remaining the same, moves more swiftly in the conjunction and opposition than in the quadratures.

COR. IV. The orbit of the body P, other things remaining the same, is more curved at the quadratures than at the conjunction and opposition. For the swifter bodies move, the less they deflect from a rectilinear path. And besides, the force KL, or NM, at the conjunction and opposition, is contrary to the force with which the body T attracts the body P, and therefore diminishes that force; but the body P will deflect the less from a rectilinear path the less it is impelled towards the body T.

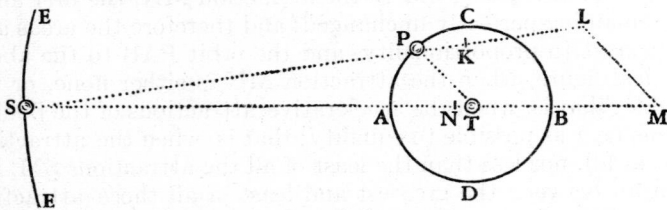

COR. V. Hence the body P, other things remaining the same, goes farther from the body T at the quadratures than at the conjunction and opposition. This is said, however, when no account is taken of the variable eccentricity. For if the orbit of the body P be eccentric, its eccentricity (as will be shown presently by Cor. IX) will be greatest when the apsides are in the syzygies; and thence it may sometimes come to pass that the body P, in its near approach to the farther apse, may go farther from the body T at the syzygies than at the quadratures.

COR. VI. Because the centripetal force of the central body T, by which the body P is retained in its orbit, is increased at the quadratures by the addition caused by the force LM, and diminished at the syzygies by the subtraction of the force KL, and, because the force KL is greater than LM, it is more diminished than increased; and, moreover, since that centripetal force (by Cor. II, Prop. 4) varies directly as the radius TP, and inversely as the square of the periodical time, it is plain that the resulting ratio is diminished by the action of the force KL; and therefore that the periodical time, supposing the radius of the orbit PT to remain the same, will be increased, and that as the square root of that ratio in which the centripetal force is diminished; and, therefore, supposing this radius increased or diminished, the periodical time will be increased more or diminished less than in the $\frac{3}{2}$th power of this radius, by Cor. VI, Prop. 4. If that force of the central body should gradually decay, the body P being less and less attracted would go farther and farther from the centre T; and, on the contrary, if it were increased, it would draw nearer to it. Therefore if the action of the distant body S, by which that force is diminished, were to increase and decrease by turns, the radius TP would be also increased and diminished by turns; and the periodical time would be increased and diminished in a ratio compounded of the $\frac{3}{2}$th power of the ratio of the radius, and of the square root of that ratio in which the centripetal force of the central body T was diminished or increased, by the increase or decrease of the action of the distant body S.

COR. VII. It also follows, from what was before laid down, that the axis of the ellipse described by the body P, or the line of the apsides, does as to its angular motion go forwards and backwards by turns, but more forwards than backwards, and by the excess of its direct motion is on the whole carried for-

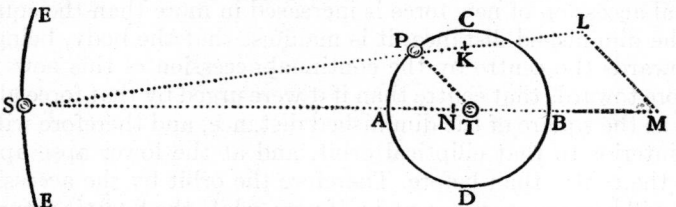

wards. For the force with which the body P is urged to the body T at the quadratures, where the force MN vanishes, is compounded of the force LM and the centripetal force with which the body T attracts the body P. The first force LM, if the distance PT be increased, is increased in nearly the same proportion with that distance, and the other force decreases as the square of the ratio of the distance; and therefore the sum of these two forces decreases in less than the square of the ratio of the distance PT; and therefore, by Cor. I, Prop. 45, will make the line of the apsides, or, which is the same thing, the upper apse, to go backwards. But at the conjunction and opposition the force with which the body P is urged towards the body T is the difference of the force KL, and of the force with which the body T attracts the body P; and that difference, because the force KL is very nearly increased in the ratio of the distance PT, decreases in more than the square of the ratio of the distance PT; and therefore, by Cor. I, Prop. 45, causes the line of the apsides to go forwards. In the places between the syzygies and the quadratures, the motion of the line of the apsides depends upon both of these causes conjointly, so that it either goes forwards or backwards in proportion to the excess of one of these causes above the other. Therefore since the force KL in the syzygies is almost twice as great as the force LM in the quadratures, the excess will be on the side of the force KL, and by consequence the line of the apsides will be carried forwards. The truth of this and the foregoing Corollary will be more easily understood by conceiving the system of the two bodies T and P to be surrounded on every side by several bodies S, S, S, &c., disposed about the orbit ESE. For by the actions of these bodies the action of the body T will be diminished on every side, and decrease in more than the square of the ratio of the distance.

Cor. viii. But since the direct or retrograde motion of the apsides depends upon the decrease of the centripetal force, that is, upon its being in a greater or less ratio than the square of the ratio of the distance TP, in the passage of the body from the lower apse to the upper; and upon a like increase in its return to the lower apse again; and therefore becomes greatest where the proportion of the force at the upper apse to the force at the lower apse recedes farthest from the inverse square of the ratio of the distances; it is plain that, when the apsides are in the syzygies, they will, by reason of the subtracted force KL or NM−LM, go forwards more swiftly; and in the quadratures by the additional force LM go backwards more slowly. Because the velocity of the progression or the slowness of the retrogression is continued for a long time, this inequality becomes exceedingly great.

Cor. ix. If a body is obliged, by a force inversely proportional to the square of its distance from any centre, to revolve in an ellipse round that centre; and afterwards in its descent from the upper apse to the lower apse, that force by a continual accession of new force is increased in more than the square of the ratio of the diminished distance; it is manifest that the body, being impelled always towards the centre by the continual accession of this new force, will incline more towards that centre than if it were urged by that force alone which decreases as the square of the diminished distance, and therefore will describe an orbit interior to that elliptical orbit, and at the lower apse approaching nearer to the centre than before. Therefore the orbit by the accession of this new force will become more eccentric. If now, while the body is returning from the lower to the upper apse, it should decrease by the same degrees by which it increased before, the body would return to its first distance; and therefore if the force decreases in a yet greater ratio, the body, being now less attracted than before, will ascend to a still greater distance, and so, the eccentricity of the orbit will be increased still more. Therefore if the ratio of the increase and decrease of the centripetal force be augmented with each revolution, the eccentricity will be augmented also; and, on the contrary, if that ratio decrease, it will be diminished.

Now, therefore, in the system of the bodies T, P, S, when the apsides of the orbit PAB are in the quadratures, the ratio of that increase and decrease is least of all, and becomes greatest when the apsides are in the syzygies. If the apsides are placed in the quadratures, the ratio near the apsides is less, and near the syzygies greater, than the square of the ratio of the distances; and from that greater ratio arises a direct motion of the line of the apsides, as was just now said. But if we consider the ratio of the whole increase or decrease in the progress between the apsides, this is less than the square of the ratio of the distances. The force in the lower is to that in the upper apse in less than the

square of the ratio of the distance of the upper apse from the focus of the ellipse
to the distance of the lower apse from the same focus; and conversely, when
the apsides are placed in the syzygies, the force in the lower apse is to the force
in the upper apse in a greater than the square of the ratio of the distances. For
the forces LM in the quadratures added to the forces of the body T, compose
forces in a less ratio; and the forces KL in the syzygies subtracted from the
forces of the body T, leave the forces in a greater ratio. Therefore the ratio of
the whole increase and decrease in the passage between the apsides is least at
the quadratures and greatest at the syzygies; and therefore in the passage of
the apsides from the quadratures to the syzygies it is continually augmented,
and increases the eccentricity of the ellipse; and in the passage from the syzygies
to the quadratures it is continually decreasing, and diminishes the eccentricity.

COR. X. That we may give an account of the errors of latitude, let us suppose
the plane of the orbit EST to remain immovable; and from the cause of the
errors above explained, it is manifest that, of the two forces NM, ML, which
are the only and entire cause of them, the force ML acting always in the plane
of the orbit PAB never disturbs the motions as to latitude; and that the force
NM, when the nodes are in the syzygies, acting also in the same plane of the
orbit, does not at that time affect those motions. But when the nodes are in the
quadratures, it disturbs them very much, and, attracting the body P continually out of the plane of its orbit, it diminishes the inclination of the plane in
the passage of the body from the quadratures to the syzygies, and again increases the same in the passage from the syzygies to the quadratures. Hence it
comes to pass that when the body is in the syzygies, the inclination is then
least of all, and returns to the first magnitude nearly, when the body arrives

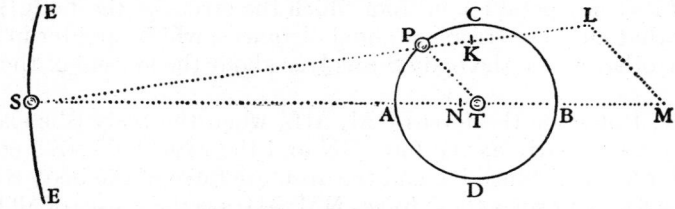

at the next node. But if the nodes are situated at the octants after the quadratures, that is, between C and A, D and B, it will appear, from what was just
now shown, that in the passage of the body P from either node to the ninetieth
degree from thence, the inclination of the plane is continually diminished;
then, in the passage through the next 45 degrees to the next quadrature, the
inclination is increased; and afterwards, again, in its passage through another
45 degrees to the next node, it is diminished. Therefore the inclination is more
diminished than increased, and is therefore always less in the subsequent node
than in the preceding one. And, by a like reasoning, the inclination is more
increased than diminished when the nodes are in the other octants between
A and D, B and C. The inclination, therefore, is the greatest of all when the
nodes are in the syzygies. In their passage from the syzygies to the quadratures
the inclination is diminished at each appulse of the body to the nodes; and
becomes least of all when the nodes are in the quadratures, and the body in the
syzygies; then it increases by the same degrees by which it decreased before; and,
when the nodes come to the next syzygies, returns to its former magnitude.

COR. XI. Because when the nodes are in the quadratures the body P is continually attracted from the plane of its orbit; and because this attraction is made towards S in its passage from the node C through the conjunction A to the node D; and in the opposite direction in its passage from the node D through the opposition B to the node C; it is manifest that, in its motion from the node C, the body recedes continually from the former plane CD of its orbit till it comes to the next node; and therefore at that node, being now at its greatest distance from the first plane CD, it will pass through the plane of the orbit EST not in D, the other node of that plane, but in a point that lies nearer to the body S, which therefore becomes a new place of the node behind its former place. And, by a like reasoning, the nodes will continue to recede in their passage from this node to the next. The nodes, therefore, when situated in the quadratures, recede continually; and at the syzygies, where no perturbation can be produced in the motion as to latitude, are quiescent; in the intermediate places they partake of both conditions, and recede more slowly; and, therefore, being always either retrograde or stationary, they will be carried backwards, or made to recede in each revolution.

COR. XII. All the errors described in these Corollaries are a little greater at the conjunction of the bodies P, S than at their opposition; because the generating forces NM and ML are greater.

COR. XIII. And since the causes and proportions of the errors and variations mentioned in these Corollaries do not depend upon the magnitude of the body S, it follows that all things before demonstrated will happen, if the magnitude of the body S be imagined so great that the system of the two bodies P and T may revolve about it. And from this increase of the body S, and the consequent increase of its centripetal force, from which the errors of the body P arise, it will follow that all these errors, at equal distances, will be greater in this case, than in the other where the body S revolves about the system of the bodies P and T.

COR. XIV. But since the forces NM, ML, when the body S is exceedingly distant, are very nearly as the force SK and the ratio PT to ST conjointly; that is, if both the distance PT and the absolute force of the body S be given, inversely as ST^3; and since those forces NM, ML are the causes of all the errors and effects treated of in the foregoing Corollaries; it is manifest that all those effects, if the system of bodies T and P continue as before, and only the distance ST and the absolute force of the body S be changed, will be very nearly in a ratio compounded of the direct ratio of the absolute force of the body S, and the cubed inverse ratio of the distance ST. Hence if the system of bodies T and P revolve about a distant body S, those forces NM, ML, and their effects, will be (by Cor. II and VI, Prop. 4) inversely as the square of the periodical time. And thence, also, if the magnitude of the body S be proportional to its absolute force, those forces NM, ML, and their effects, will be directly as the cube of the apparent diameter of the distant body S viewed from T; and conversely. For these ratios are the same as the compounded ratio above mentioned.

COR. XV. If the orbits ESE and PAB, retaining their figure, proportions, and inclination to each other, should alter their magnitude, and if the forces of the bodies S and T should either remain unaltered or be changed in any given ratio, then these forces (that is, the force of the body T, which obliges the body

P to deflect from a rectilinear course into the orbit PAB, and the force of the body S, which causes the body P to deviate from that orbit) will act always in the same manner, and in the same proportion. Consequently it follows, that all the effects will be similar and proportional, and the times of those effects will be proportional also; that is, that all the linear errors will be as the diameters of the orbits, the angular errors the same as before; and the times of similar linear errors, or equal angular errors, are as the periodical times of the orbits.

Cor. xvi. Therefore if the figures of the orbits and their inclination to each other be given, and the magnitudes, forces, and distances of the bodies be changed in any manner, we may, from the errors and times of those errors in one case, obtain very nearly the errors and times of the errors in any other case. But this may be done more expeditiously by the following method. The forces NM, ML, other things remaining unaltered, are as the radius TP; and their periodical effects (by Cor. ii, Lem. 10) are as the forces and the square of the periodical time of the body P jointly. These are the linear errors of the body P; and hence the angular errors as they appear from the centre T (that is, the motion of the apsides and of the nodes, and all the apparent errors of longitude and latitude) are in each revolution of the body P as the square of the time of the revolution, very nearly. Let these ratios be compounded with

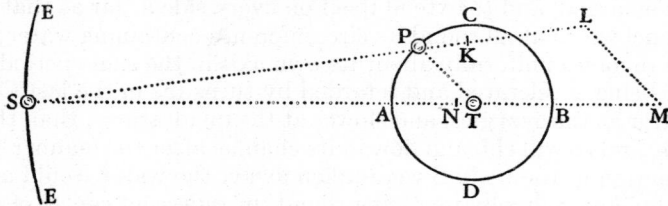

the ratios in Cor. xiv, and in any system of bodies T, P, S, where P revolves about T very near to it, and T revolves about S at a great distance, the angular errors of the body P, observed from the centre T, will be in each revolution of the body P directly as the square of the periodical time of the body P, and inversely as the square of the periodical time of the body T. And therefore the mean motion of the line of the apsides will be in a given ratio to the mean motion of the nodes; and both those motions will be directly as the periodical time of the body P, and inversely as the square of the periodical time of the body T. The increase or diminution of the eccentricity and inclination of the orbit PAB makes no sensible variation in the motions of the apsides and nodes, unless that increase or diminution be very great indeed.

Cor. xvii. Since the line LM becomes sometimes greater and sometimes less than the radius PT, let the mean quantity of the force LM be expressed by that radius PT; and then that mean force will be to the mean force SK or SN (which may be also expressed by ST) as the length PT to the length ST. But the mean force SN or ST, by which the body T is retained in the orbit it describes about S, is to the force with which the body P is retained in its orbit about T in a ratio compounded of the ratio of the radius ST to the radius PT, and the squared ratio of the periodical time of the body P about T to the periodical time of the body T about S. And, consequently, the mean force LM is to the force by which the body P is retained in its orbit about T (or by which the same body P might revolve at the distance PT in the same periodical time about any immovable point T) in the same squared ratio of the periodical times. The periodical times therefore being given, together with the distance PT, the mean force' LM is also given; and that force being given, there is given also the force MN, very nearly, by the analogy of the lines PT and MN.

COR. XVIII. By the same laws by which the body P revolves about the body T, let us suppose many fluid bodies to move round T at equal distances from it; and to be so numerous, that they may all become contiguous to each other, so as to form a fluid annulus, or ring, of a round figure, and concentric to the body T; and the several parts of this ring, performing their motions by the same law as the body P, will draw nearer to the body T, and move swifter in the conjunction and opposition of themselves and the body S, than in the quadratures. And the nodes of this ring or its intersections with the plane of the orbit of the body S or T, will rest at the syzygies; but out of the syzygies they will be carried backwards, or in a retrograde direction, with the greatest swiftness in the quadratures, and more slowly in other places. The inclination of this ring also will vary, and its axis will oscillate in each revolution, and when the revolution is completed will return to its former situation, except only that it will be carried round a little by the precession of the nodes.

COR. XIX. Suppose now the spherical body T, consisting of some matter not fluid, to be enlarged, and to extend itself on every side as far as that ring, and that a channel were cut all round its circumference containing water; and that this sphere revolves uniformly about its own axis in the same periodical time. This water being accelerated and retarded by turns (as in the last Corollary), will be swifter at the syzygies, and slower at the quadratures, than the surface of the globe, and so will ebb and flow in its channel after the manner of the sea. If the attraction of the body S were taken away, the water would acquire no motion of flux and reflux by revolving round the quiescent centre of the globe. The case is the same of a globe moving uniformly forwards in a right line, and in the meantime revolving about its centre (by Cor. V of the Laws of Motion), and of a globe uniformly attracted from its rectilinear course (by Cor. VI of the same Laws). But let the body S come to act upon it, and by its varying attraction the water will receive this new motion; for there will be a stronger attraction upon that part of the water that is nearest to the body, and a weaker upon that part which is more remote. And the force LM will attract the water downwards at the quadratures, and depress it as far as the syzygies; and the force KL will attract it upwards in the syzygies, and withhold its descent, and make it rise as far as the quadratures; except only so far as the motion of flux and reflux may be directed by the channel, and be a little retarded by friction.

COR. XX. If, now, the ring becomes hard, and the globe is diminished, the motion of flux and reflux will cease; but the oscillating motion of the inclination and the precession of the nodes will remain. Let the globe have the same axis with the ring, and perform its revolutions in the same times, and at its surface touch the ring within, and adhere to it; then the globe partaking of the motion of the ring, this whole body will oscillate, and the nodes will go backwards for the globe, as we shall show presently, is perfectly indifferent to the receiving of all impressions. The greatest angle of the inclination of the ring alone is when the nodes are in the syzygies. Thence in the progress of the nodes to the quadratures, it endeavors to diminish its inclination, and by that endeavor impresses a motion upon the whole globe. The globe retains this motion impressed, till the ring by a contrary endeavor destroys that motion, and impresses a new motion in a contrary direction. And by this means the greatest motion of the decreasing inclination happens when the nodes are in the quadratures, and the least angle of inclination in the octants after the quadratures; and, again, the greatest motion of the reclination happens when the nodes are in the syzygies; and the greatest angle of inclination in the octants following. And the case is the same of a globe without this ring, if it be a little higher or a little denser in the equatorial than in the polar regions; for the excess of that matter in the regions near the equator supplies the place of the ring. And al-

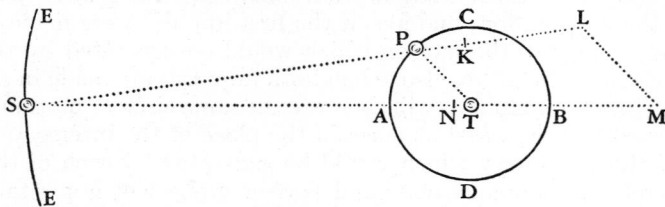

though we should suppose the centripetal force of this globe to be increased in any manner, so that all its parts tend downwards, as the parts of our earth gravitate to the centre, yet the phenomena of this and the preceding Corollary would scarce be altered; except that the places of the greatest and least height of the water will be different; for the water is now no longer sustained and kept in its orbit by its centrifugal force, but by the channel in which it flows. And, besides, the force LM attracts the water downwards most in the quadratures, and the force KL or NM−LM attracts it upwards most in the syzygies. And these forces conjoined cease to attract the water downwards, and begin to attract it upwards in the octants before the syzygies; and cease to attract the water upwards, and begin to attract the water downwards in the octants after the syzygies. And thence the greatest height of the water may happen about the octants after the syzygies; and the least height about the octants after the quadratures; excepting only so far as the motion of ascent or descent impressed by these forces may by the inertia of the water continue a little longer, or be stopped a little sooner by impediments in its channel.

COR. XXI. For the same reason that redundant matter in the equatorial regions of a globe causes the nodes to go backwards, and therefore by the increase of that matter that retrograde motion is increased, by the diminution is diminished, and by the removal quite ceases; it follows, that, if more than that redundant matter be taken away, that is, if the globe be either more depressed, or of a rarer consistence near the equator than near the poles, there will arise a direct motion of the nodes.

COR. XXII. And thence from the motion of the nodes is known the constitution of the globe. That is, if the globe retains unalterably the same poles, and the motion (of the nodes) is retrograde, there is a redundance of the matter near the equator; but if that motion is direct, a deficiency. Suppose a uniform and exactly spherical globe to be first at rest in a free space; then by some impulse made obliquely upon its surface to be driven from its place, and to receive a motion partly circular and partly straight forward. Since this globe is perfectly indifferent to all the axes that pass through its centre, nor has a greater propensity to one axis or to one situation of the axis than to any other, it is manifest that by its own force it will never change its axis, or the inclination of its axis. Let now this globe be impelled obliquely by a new impulse in the same part of its surface as before; and since the effect of an impulse is not at all changed by its coming sooner or later, it is manifest that these two impulses, successively impressed, will produce the same motion, as if they had been impressed at the same time; that is, the same motion, as if the globe had been impelled by a simple force compounded of them both (by Cor. II of the Laws), that is, a simple motion about an axis of a given inclination. And the case is the same if the second impulse were made upon any other place of the equator of the first motion; and also if the first impulse were made upon any place in the equator of the motion which would be generated by the second impulse alone; and therefore, also, when both impulses are made in any places whatsoever; for these impulses will generate the same circular motion as if they were impressed together, and at once, in the place of the intersections of the equators of those motions, which would be generated by each of them separately. Therefore, a homogeneous and perfect globe will not retain several motions distinct, but will unite all those that are impressed on it, and reduce them into one; revolving, as far as in it lies, always with a simple and uniform motion about one single given axis, with an inclination always invariable. And the inclination of the axis, or the velocity of the rotation, will not be changed by centripetal force. For if the globe be supposed to be divided into two hemispheres, by any plane whatsoever passing through its own centre, and the centre to which the force is directed, that force will always urge each hemisphere equally; and therefore will not incline the globe to any side with respect to its motion round its own axis. But let there be added anywhere between the pole and the equator a heap of new matter like a mountain, and this, by its continual endeavor to recede from the centre of its motion, will disturb the motion of the globe, and cause its poles to wander about its surface describing circles about themselves and the points opposite to them. Neither can this enormous deviation of the poles be corrected otherwise than by placing that mountain either in one of the poles, in which case, by Cor. XXI, the nodes of the equator will go forwards; or in the equatorial regions, in which case, by Cor. XX, the nodes will go backwards; or, lastly, by adding on the other side of the axis a new quantity of matter, by which the mountain may be balanced in its motion; and then the nodes will either go forwards or backwards, as the mountain and this newly added matter happen to be nearer to the pole or to the equator.

PROPOSITION 67. THEOREM 27

The same laws of attraction being supposed, I say, that the exterior body S does, by radii drawn to the point O, the common centre of gravity of the interior bodies P and T, describe round that centre areas more proportional to the times, and an orbit more approaching to the form of an ellipse having its focus in that centre, than it can describe round the innermost and greatest body T by radii drawn to that body.

For the attractions of the body S towards T and P compose its absolute attraction, which is more directed towards O, the common centre of gravity of the bodies T and P, than it is to the

greatest body T; and which approaches nearer to the inverse proportion of the
square of the distance SO, than of the square of the distance ST; as will easily
appear by a little consideration.

PROPOSITION 68. THEOREM 28

The same laws of attraction supposed, I say, that the exterior body S *will, by radii
drawn to* O, *the common centre of gravity of the interior bodies* P *and* T, *describe
round that centre areas more proportional to the times, and an orbit more approaching to the form of an ellipse having its focus in that centre, if the innermost and
greatest body be agitated by these attractions as well as the rest, than it would do if
that body either were at rest and not attracted at all, or were much more or much less
attracted, or were much more or much less agitated.*

This may be demonstrated after the same manner as Prop. 66, but by a
more prolix reasoning, which I therefore pass over. It will be sufficient to consider it after this manner. From the demonstration of the last Proposition it
is plain, that the centre, towards which the body S is urged by the two forces
conjointly, is very near to the common centre of gravity of those two other
bodies. If this centre were to coincide with that common centre, and moreover
the common centre of gravity of all the three bodies were at rest, the body S on

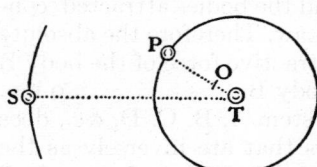

one side, and the common centre of gravity of the
other two bodies on the other side, would describe
true ellipses about that quiescent common centre.
This appears from Cor. II, Prop. 58, compared
with what was demonstrated in Props. 64 and 65.
Now this accurate elliptical motion will be disturbed a little by the distance of the centre of the
two bodies from the centre towards which the third body S is attracted. Let
there be added, moreover, a motion to the common centre of the three, and
the perturbation will be increased yet more. Therefore the perturbation is least
when the common centre of the three bodies is at rest; that is, when the innermost and greatest body T is attracted according to the same law as the rest
are; and is always greatest when the common centre of the three, by the diminution of the motion of the body T, begins to be moved, and is more and more
agitated.

COR. And hence if several smaller bodies revolve about the great one, it may
easily be inferred that the orbits described will approach nearer to ellipses; and
the descriptions of areas will be more nearly uniform, if all the bodies attract
and agitate each other with accelerative forces that are directly as their absolute forces, and inversely as the squares of the distances, and if the focus of
each orbit be placed in the common centre of gravity of all the interior bodies
(that is, if the focus of the first and innermost orbit be placed in the centre of
gravity of the greatest and innermost body; the focus of the second orbit in
the common centre of gravity of the two innermost bodies; the focus of the
third orbit in the common centre of gravity of the three innermost; and so on),
than if the innermost body were at rest, and was made the common focus of
all the orbits.

PROPOSITION 69. THEOREM 29

In a system of several bodies A, B, C, D, *&c., if any one of those bodies, as* A, *attract all the rest,* B, C, D, *&c., with accelerative forces that are inversely as the squares of the distances from the attracting body; and another body, as* B, *attracts also the rest,* A, C, D, *&c., with forces that are inversely as the squares of the distances from the attracting body; the absolute forces of the attracting bodies* A *and* B *will be to each other as those very bodies* A *and* B *to which those forces belong.*

For the accelerative attractions of all the bodies B, C, D, towards A, are by the supposition equal to each other at equal distances; and in like manner the accelerative attractions of all the bodies towards B are also equal to each other at equal distances. But the absolute attractive force of the body A is to the absolute attractive force of the body B as the accelerative attraction of all the bodies towards A is to the accelerative attraction of all the bodies towards B at equal distances; and so is also the accelerative attraction of the body B towards A to the accelerative attraction of the body A towards B. But the accelerative attraction of the body B towards A is to the accelerative attraction of the body A towards B as the mass of the body A is to the mass of the body B; because the motive forces which (by the second, seventh and eighth Definitions) are as the accelerative forces and the bodies attracted conjointly are here equal to one another by the third Law. Therefore the absolute attractive force of the body A is to the absolute attractive force of the body B as the mass of the body A is to the mass of the body B.   Q.E.D.

Cor. i. Therefore if each of the bodies of the system A, B, C, D, &c., does singly attract all the rest with accelerative forces that are inversely as the squares of the distances from the attracting body, the absolute forces of all those bodies will be to each other as the bodies themselves.

Cor. ii. By a like reasoning, if each of the bodies of the system A, B, C, D, &c., does singly attract all the rest with accelerative forces, which are either inversely or directly in the ratio of any power whatever of the distances from the attracting body; or which are defined by the distances from each of the attracting bodies according to any common law; it is plain that the absolute forces of those bodies are as the bodies themselves.

Cor. iii. In a system of bodies whose forces decrease as the square of the distances, if the lesser revolve about one very great one in ellipses, having their common focus in the centre of that great body, and of a figure exceedingly accurate; and moreover by radii drawn to that great body describe areas proportional to the times exactly; the absolute forces of those bodies to each other will be either accurately or very nearly in the ratio of the bodies. And so conversely. This appears from Cor. of Prop. 68, compared with the first Corollary of this Proposition.

SCHOLIUM

These Propositions naturally lead us to the analogy there is between centripetal forces and the central bodies to which those forces are usually directed; for it is reasonable to suppose that forces which are directed to bodies should depend upon the nature and quantity of those bodies, as we see they do in magnetical experiments. And when such cases occur, we are to compute the attractions of the bodies by assigning to each of their particles its proper force, and then finding the sum of them all. I here use the word *attraction* in general for any endeavor whatever, made by bodies to approach to each other, whether that endeavor arise from the action of the bodies themselves, as tending to each other or agitating each other by spirits emitted; or whether it arises from the action of the ether or of the air, or of any medium whatever, whether corporeal or incorporeal, in any manner impelling bodies placed therein towards each other. In the same general sense I use the word *impulse*, not defining in this treatise the species or physical qualities of forces, but investigating the quantities and mathematical proportions of them; as I observed before in the Definitions. In mathematics we are to investigate the quantities of forces with their proportions consequent upon any conditions supposed; then, when we enter upon physics, we compare those proportions with the phenomena of Nature, that we may know what conditions of those forces answer to the several kinds of attractive bodies. And this preparation being made, we argue more safely concerning the physical species, causes, and proportions of the forces. Let us see, then, with what forces spherical bodies consisting of particles endued with attractive powers in the manner above spoken of must act upon one another; and what kind of motions will follow from them.

SECTION XII

THE ATTRACTIVE FORCES OF SPHERICAL BODIES

PROPOSITION 70. THEOREM 30

If to every point of a spherical surface there tend equal centripetal forces decreasing as the square of the distances from those points, I say, that a corpuscle placed within that surface will not be attracted by those forces any way.

Let HIKL be that spherical surface, and P a corpuscle placed within. Through P let there be drawn to this surface two lines HK, IL, intercepting very small arcs HI, KL; and because (by Cor. III, Lem. 7) the triangles HPI,

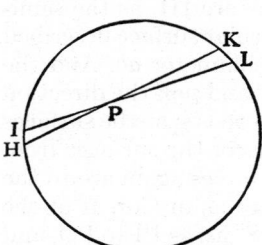

LPK are alike, those arcs will be proportional to the distances HP, LP; and any particles at HI and KL of the spherical surface, terminated by right lines passing through P, will be as the square of those distances. Therefore the forces of these particles exerted upon the body P are equal between themselves. For the forces are directly as the particles, and inversely as the square of the distances. And these two ratios compose the ratio of equality, 1 : 1. The attractions therefore, being equal, but exerted in opposite directions, destroy each other. And by a like reasoning all the attractions through the whole spherical surface are destroyed by contrary attractions. Therefore the body P will not be any way impelled by those attractions.   Q.E.D.

PROPOSITION 71. THEOREM 31

The same things supposed as above, I say, that a corpuscle placed without the spherical surface is attracted towards the centre of the sphere with a force inversely proportional to the square of its distance from that centre.

Let AHKB, *ahkb* be two equal spherical surfaces described about the centres S, *s;* their diameters AB, *ab;* and let P and *p* be two corpuscles situate without the spheres in those diameters produced. Let there be drawn from the corpuscles the lines PHK, PIL, *phk*, *pil*, cutting off from the great circles AHB, *ahb*, the equal arcs HK, *hk*, IL, *il*; and to those lines let fall the perpendiculars SD, *sd*, SE, *se*, IR, *ir*; of which let SD, *sd*, cut PL, *pl*, in F and *f*. Let fall also

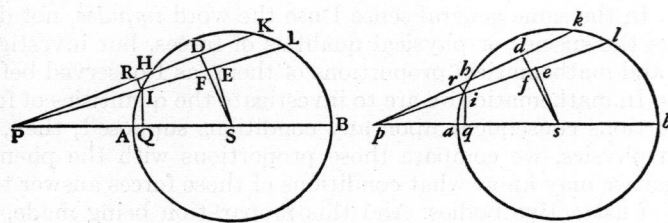

to the diameters the perpendiculars IQ, *iq*. Let now the angles DPE, *dpe* vanish; and because DS and *ds*, ES and *es* are equal, the lines PE, PF, and *pe*, *pf*, and the short lines DF, *df* may be taken for equal; because their last ratio, when the angles DPE, *dpe* vanish together, is the ratio of equality. These things being thus determined, it follows that

$$PI : PF = RI : DF$$

and $$pf : pi = df \text{ or } DF : ri.$$

Multiplying corresponding terms,

$$PI \cdot pf : PF \cdot pi = RI : ri = \text{arc IH} : \text{arc } ih \text{ (by Cor. III, Lem. VII)}.$$

Again, $$PI : PS = IQ : SE$$

and $$ps : pi = se \text{ or } SE : iq.$$

Hence, $$PI \cdot ps : PS \cdot pi = IQ : iq.$$

Multiplying together corresponding terms of this and the similarly derived preceding proportion,

$$PI^2 \cdot pf \cdot ps : pi^2 \cdot PF \cdot PS = HI \cdot IQ : ih \cdot iq,$$

that is, as the circular surface which is described by the arc IH, as the semicircle AKB revolves about the diameter AB, is to the circular surface described by the arc *ih* as the semicircle *akb* revolves about the diameter *ab*. And the forces with which these surfaces attract the corpuscles P and *p* in the direction of lines tending to those surfaces are directly, by the hypothesis, as the surfaces themselves, and inversely as the squares of the distances of the surfaces from those corpuscles; that is, as *pf·ps* to PF·PS. And these forces again are to the oblique parts of them which (by the resolution of forces as in Cor. II of the Laws) tend to the centres in the directions of the lines PS, *ps*, as PI to PQ, and *pi* to *pq*; that is (because of the like triangles PIQ and PSF, *piq* and *psf*), as PS to PF and *ps* to *pf*. Thence, the attraction of the corpuscle P towards S is to the attraction of the corpuscle *p* towards *s* as $\dfrac{PF \cdot pf \cdot ps}{PS}$ is to $\dfrac{pf \cdot PF \cdot PS}{ps}$, that is, as *ps*² to PS². And, by a like reasoning, the forces with which the surfaces described by the revolution of the arcs KL, *kl* attract those corpuscles, will be as *ps*² to PS². And in the same ratio will be the forces of all the circular surfaces into which each of the spherical surfaces may be divided by taking *sd* always equal to SD, and *se* equal to SE. And therefore, by composition, the forces of the entire spherical surfaces exerted upon those corpuscles will be in the same ratio.   Q.E.D.

PROPOSITION 72. THEOREM 32

If to the several points of a sphere there tend equal centripetal forces decreasing as the square of the distances from those points; and there be given both the density of the sphere and the ratio of the diameter of the sphere to the distance of the corpuscle from its centre: I say, that the force with which the corpuscle is attracted is proportional to the semidiameter of the sphere.

For conceive two corpuscles to be severally attracted by two spheres, one by one, the other by the other, and their distances from the centres of the spheres to be proportional to the diameters of the spheres respectively; and the spheres to be resolved into like particles, disposed in a like situation to the corpuscles. Then the attractions of one corpuscle towards the several particles of one sphere will be to the attractions of the other towards as many analogous particles of the other sphere in a ratio compounded of the ratio of the particles directly, and the square of the distances inversely. But the particles are as the spheres, that is, as the cubes of the diameters, and the distances are as the diameters; and the first ratio directly with the last ratio taken twice inversely, becomes the ratio of diameter to diameter.   Q.E.D.

COR. I. Hence if corpuscles revolve in circles about spheres composed of matter equally attracting, and the distances from the centres of the spheres be proportional to their diameters, the periodic times will be equal.

COR. II. And, *vice versa*, if the periodic times are equal, the distances will be proportional to the diameters. These two Corollaries appear from Cor. III, Prop. 4.

COR. III. If to the several points of any two solids whatever, of like figure and equal density, there tend equal centripetal forces decreasing as the square of the distances from those points, the forces, with which corpuscles placed in a like situation to those two solids will be attracted by them, will be to each other as the diameters of the solids.

PROPOSITION 73. THEOREM 33

If to the several points of a given sphere there tend equal centripetal forces decreasing as the square of the distances from the points, I say, that a corpuscle placed within the sphere is attracted by a force proportional to its distance from the centre.

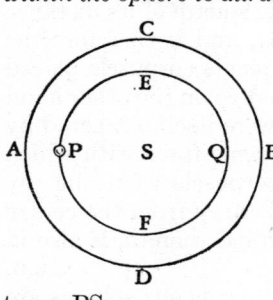

In the sphere ACBD, described about the centre S, let there be placed the corpuscle P; and about the same centre S, with the interval SP, conceive described an interior sphere PEQF. It is plain (by Prop. 70) that the concentric spherical surfaces of which the difference AEBF of the spheres is composed, have no effect at all upon the body P, their attractions being destroyed by contrary attractions. There remains, therefore, only the attraction of the interior sphere PEQF. And (by Prop. 72) this is as the distance PS.   Q.E.D.

SCHOLIUM

By the surfaces of which I here imagine the solids composed, I do not mean surfaces purely mathematical, but orbs so extremely thin, that their thickness is as nothing; that is, the evanescent orbs of which the sphere will at last consist, when the number of the orbs is increased, and their thickness diminished without end. In like manner, by the points of which lines, surfaces, and solids are said to be composed, are to be understood equal particles, whose magnitude is perfectly inconsiderable.

PROPOSITION 74. THEOREM 34

The same things supposed, I say, that a corpuscle situated without the sphere is attracted with a force inversely proportional to the square of its distance from the centre.

For suppose the sphere to be divided into innumerable concentric spherical surfaces, and the attractions of the corpuscle arising from the several surfaces will be inversely proportional to the square of the distance of the corpuscle from the centre of the sphere (by Prop. 71). And, by composition, the sum of those attractions, that is, the attraction of the corpuscle towards the entire sphere, will be in the same ratio.   Q.E.D.

COR. I. Hence the attractions of homogeneous spheres at equal distances from the centres will be as the spheres themselves. For (by Prop. 72) if the distances be proportional to the diameters of the spheres, the forces will be as the diameters. Let the greater distance be diminished in that ratio; and the distances now being equal, the attraction will be increased as the square of that ratio; and therefore will be to the other attraction as the cube of that ratio; that is, in the ratio of the spheres.

COR. II. At any distances whatever the attractions are as the spheres applied to the squares of the distances.

COR. III. If a corpuscle placed without an homogeneous sphere is attracted by a force inversely proportional to the square of its distance from the centre, and the sphere consists of attractive particles, the force of every particle will decrease as the square of the distance from each particle.

PROPOSITION 75. THEOREM 35

If to the several points of a given sphere there tend equal centripetal forces decreasing as the square of the distances from the point, I say, that another similar sphere will be attracted by it with a force inversely proportional to the square of the distance of the centres.

For the attraction of every particle is inversely as the square of its distance from the centre of the attracting sphere (by Prop. 74), and is therefore the same as if that whole attracting force issued from one single corpuscle placed in the centre of this sphere. But this attraction is as great as on the other hand the attraction of the same corpuscle would be, if that were itself attracted by the several particles of the attracted sphere with the same force with which they are attracted by it. But that attraction of the corpuscle would be (by Prop. 74) inversely proportional to the square of its distance from the centre of the sphere; therefore the attraction of the sphere, equal thereto, is also in the same ratio.   Q.E.D.

COR. I. The attractions of spheres towards other homogeneous spheres are as the attracting spheres applied to the squares of the distances of their centres from the centres of those which they attract.

COR. II. The case is the same when the attracted sphere does also attract. For the several points of the one attract the several points of the other with the same force with which they themselves are attracted by the others again; and therefore since in all attractions (by Law III) the attracted and attracting point are both equally acted on, the force will be doubled by their mutual attractions, the proportions remaining.

COR. III. Those several truths demonstrated above concerning the motion of bodies about the focus of the conic sections will take place when an attracting sphere is placed in the focus, and the bodies move without the sphere.

COR. IV. Those things which were demonstrated before of the motion of bodies about the centre of the conic sections take place when the motions are performed within the sphere.

PROPOSITION 76. THEOREM 36

If spheres be however dissimilar (as to density of matter and attractive force) in the same ratio onwards from the centre to the circumference; but everywhere similar, at every given distance from the centre, on all sides round about; and the attractive force of every point decreases as the square of the distance of the body attracted: I say, that the whole force with which one of these spheres attracts the other will be inversely proportional to the square of the distance of the centres.

Imagine several concentric similar spheres AB, CD, EF, &c., the innermost of which added to the outermost may compose a matter more dense towards the centre, or subtracted from them may leave the same more lax and rare.

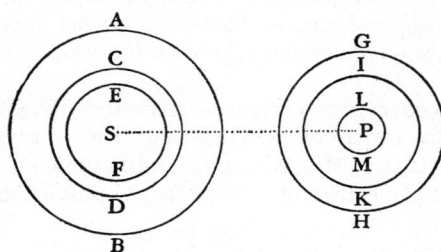

Then, by Prop. 75, these spheres will attract other similar concentric spheres GH, IK, LM, &c., each the other, with forces inversely proportional to the square of the distance SP. And, by addition or subtraction, the sum of all those forces, or the excess of any of them above the others; that is, the entire force with which the whole sphere AB (composed of any concentric spheres or of their differences) will attract the whole sphere GH (composed of any concentric spheres or their differences) in the same ratio. Let the number of the concentric spheres be increased *in infinitum*, so that the density of the matter together with the attractive force may, in the progress from the circumference to the centre, increase or decrease according to any given law; and by the addition of matter not attractive, let the deficient density be supplied, that so the spheres may acquire any form desired; and the force with which one of these attracts the other will be still, by the former reasoning, in the same inverse ratio of the square of the distance.   Q.E.D.

COR. I. Hence if many spheres of this kind, similar in all respects, attract each other, the accelerative attractions of each to each, at any equal distances of the centres, will be as the attracting spheres.

COR. II. And at any unequal distances, as the attracting spheres divided by the squares of the distances between the centres.

COR. III. The motive attractions, or the weights of the spheres towards one another, will be at equal distances of the centres conjointly as the attracting and attracted spheres; that is, as the products arising from multiplying the spheres into each other.

Cor. iv. And at unequal distances directly as those products and inversely as the squares of the distances between the centres.

Cor. v. These proportions hold true also when the attraction arises from the attractive power of both spheres exerted upon each other. For the attraction is only doubled by the conjunction of the forces, the proportions remaining as before.

Cor. vi. If spheres of this kind revolve about others at rest, each about each, and the distances between the centres of the quiescent and revolving bodies are proportional to the diameters of the quiescent bodies, the periodic times will be equal.

Cor. vii. And, again, if the periodic times are equal, the distances will be proportional to the diameters.

Cor. viii. All those truths above demonstrated, relating to the motions of bodies about the foci of conic sections, will take place when an attracting sphere, of any form and condition like that above described, is placed in the focus.

Cor. ix. And also when the revolving bodies are also attracting spheres of any condition like that above described.

PROPOSITION 77. THEOREM 37

If to the several points of spheres there tend centripetal forces proportional to the distances of the points from the attracted bodies, I say, that the compounded force with which two spheres attract each other is as the distance between the centres of the spheres.

Case 1. Let AEBF be a sphere; S its centre; P a corpuscle attracted; PASB the axis of the sphere passing through the centre of the corpuscle; EF, *ef* two planes cutting the sphere, and perpendicular to the axis, and equidistant, one on one side, the other on the other, from the centre of the sphere; G and *g* the

intersections of the planes and the axis; and H any point in the plane EF. The centripetal force of the point H upon the corpuscle P, exerted in the direction of the line PH, is as the distance PH; and (by Cor. ii of the Laws) the same exerted in the direction of the line PG, or towards the centre S, is as the length PG. Therefore the force of all the points in the plane EF

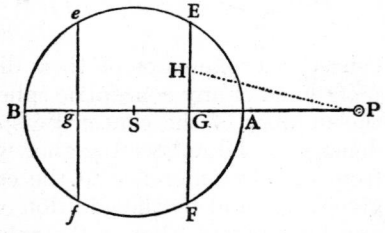

(that is, of that whole plane) by which the corpuscle P is attracted towards the centre S is as the distance PG multiplied by the number of those points, that is, as the solid contained under that plane EF and the distance PG. And in like manner the force of the plane *ef*, by which the corpuscle P is attracted towards the centre S, is as that plane multiplied by its distance P*g*, or as the equal plane EF multiplied by that distance P*g*; and the sum of the forces of both planes as the plane EF multiplied by the sum of the distances PG+P*g*, that is, as that plane multiplied by twice the distance PS of the centre and the corpuscle; that is, as twice the plane EF multiplied by the distance PS, or as the sum of the equal planes EF+*ef* multiplied by the same distance. And, by a like reasoning, the forces of all the planes in the whole sphere, equidistant on each side from the centre of the sphere, are as the sum of those planes multiplied by the distance PS, that is, as the whole sphere and the distance PS conjointly.   Q.E.D.

CASE 2. Let now the corpuscle P attract the sphere AEBF. And, by the same reasoning, it will appear that the force with which the sphere is attracted is as the distance PS.   Q.E.D.

CASE 3. Imagine another sphere composed of innumerable corpuscles P; and because the force with which every corpuscle is attracted is as the distance of the corpuscle from the centre of the first sphere, and as the same sphere conjointly, and is therefore the same as if it all proceeded from a single corpuscle situated in the centre of the sphere, the entire force with which all the corpuscles in the second sphere are attracted, that is, with which that whole sphere is attracted, will be the same as if that sphere were attracted by a force issuing from a single corpuscle in the centre of the first sphere; and is therefore proportional to the distance between the centres of the spheres.   Q.E.D.

CASE 4. Let the spheres attract each other, and the force will be doubled, but the proportion will remain.   Q.E.D.

CASE 5. Let the corpuscle p be placed within the sphere AEBF; and because the force of the plane ef upon the corpuscle is as the solid contained under that plane and the distance pg; and the contrary force of the plane EF as the solid

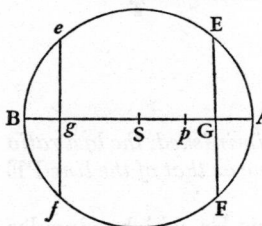

contained under that plane and the distance pG; the force compounded of both will be as the difference of the solids, that is, as the sum of the equal planes multiplied by half the difference of the distances; that is, as that sum multiplied by pS, the distance of the corpuscle from the centre of the sphere. And, by a like reasoning, the attraction of all the planes EF, ef, throughout the whole sphere, that is, the attraction of the whole sphere, is conjointly as the sum of all the planes, or as the whole sphere, and as pS, the distance of the corpuscle from the centre of the sphere.   Q.E.D.

CASE 6. And if there be composed a new sphere out of innumerable corpuscles such as p, situated within the first sphere AEBF, it may be proved, as before, that the attraction, whether single of one sphere towards the other, or mutual of both towards each other, will be as the distance pS of the centres.
                                                          Q.E.D.

PROPOSITION 78. THEOREM 38

If spheres in the progress from the centre to the circumference be however dissimilar and unequable, but similar on every side round about at all given distances from the centre; and the attractive force of every point be as the distance of the attracted body: I say, that the entire force with which two spheres of this kind attract each other mutually is proportional to the distance between the centres of the spheres.

This is demonstrated from the foregoing Proposition, in the same manner as Prop. 76 was demonstrated from Prop. 75.

COR. Those things that were above demonstrated in Props. 10 and 64, of the motion of bodies round the centres of conic sections, take place when all the attractions are made by the force of spherical bodies of the condition above described, and the attracted bodies are spheres of the same kind.

Scholium

I have now explained the two principal cases of attractions; to wit, when the centripetal forces decrease as the square of the ratio of the distances, or increase in a simple ratio of the distances, causing the bodies in both cases to revolve in conic sections, and composing spherical bodies whose centripetal forces observe the same law of increase or decrease in the recess from the centre as the forces of the particles themselves do; which is very remarkable. It would be tedious to run over the other cases, whose conclusions are less elegant and important, so particularly as I have done these. I choose rather to comprehend and determine them all by one general method as follows.

Lemma 29

If about the centre S *there be described any circle as* AEB, *and about the centre* P *there be also described two circles* EF, ef, *cutting the first in* E *and* e, *and the line* PS *in* F *and* f; *and there be let fall to* PS *the perpendiculars* ED, ed: *I say, that if*

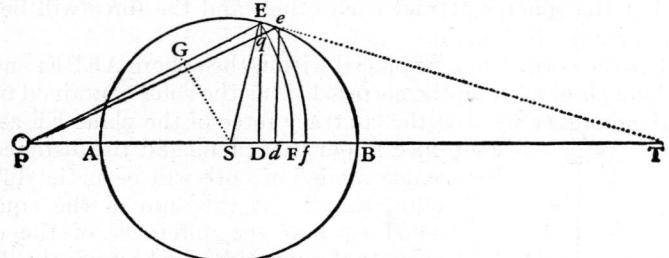

the distance of the arcs EF, ef *be supposed to be infinitely diminished, the last ratio of the evanescent line* Dd *to the evanescent line* Ff *is the same as that of the line* PE *to the line* PS.

For if the line Pe cut the arc EF in q; and the right line Ee, which coincides with the evanescent arc Ee, be produced, and meet the right line PS in T; and there be let fall from S to PE the perpendicular SG; then, because of the like triangles DTE, dTe, DES,

$$Dd : Ee = DT : TE = DE : ES;$$

and because the triangles, Eeq, ESG (by Lem. 8, and Cor. III, Lem. 7) are similar, $$Ee : eq \text{ or } Ff = Es : SG.$$

Multiplying together corresponding terms of the two proportions,

$$Dd : Ff = DE : SG = PE : PS$$

(because of the similar triangles PDE, PGS).   Q.E.D.

Proposition 79. Theorem 39

Suppose a surface as EFfe *to have its breadth infinitely diminished, and to be just vanishing; and that the same surface by its revolution round the axis* PS *describes a spherical concavoconvex solid, to the several equal particles of which there tend equal centripetal forces: I say, that the force with which that solid attracts a corpuscle situated in* P *is in a ratio compounded of the ratio of the solid* DE²·Ff *and the ratio of the force with which the given particle in the place* Ff *would attract the same corpuscle.*

For if we consider, first, the force of the spherical surface FE which is generated by the revolution of the arc FE, and is cut anywhere, as in r, by the line *de*, the annular part of the surface generated by the revolution of the arc *r*E will be as the short line D*d*, the radius of the sphere PE remaining the same; as Archimedes has demonstrated in his *Book on the Sphere and Cylinder*. And the force of this surface exerted in the direction of the lines PE or P*r* situated

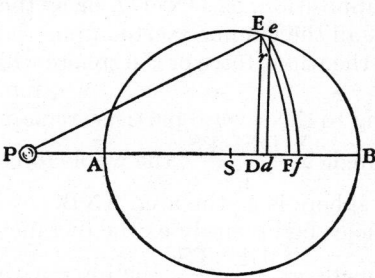

all round in the conical surface, will be as this annular surface itself; that is, as the short line D*d*, or, which is the same, as the rectangle under the given radius PE of the sphere and the short line D*d*; but that force, exerted in the direction of the line PS tending to the centre S, will be less in the ratio PD to PE, and therefore will be as PD·D*d*. Suppose now the line DF to be divided into innumerable little equal particles, each of which call D*d*, and then the surface FE will be divided into so many equal annuli, whose forces will be as the sum of all the rectangles PD·D*d*, that is, as $\frac{1}{2}$PF^2 − $\frac{1}{2}$PD^2, and therefore as DE^2. Let now the surface FE be multiplied by the altitude F*f*; and the force of the solid EF*fe* exerted upon the corpuscle P will be as DE^2·F*f*; that is, if the force be given which any given particle as F*f* exerts upon the corpuscle P at the distance PF. But if that force be not given, the force of the solid EF*fe* will be conjointly as the solid DE^2·F*f* and that force not given.   Q.E.D.

PROPOSITION 80. THEOREM 40

If to the several equal parts of a sphere ABE *described about the centre* S *there tend equal centripetal forces; and from the several points* D *in the axis of the sphere* AB *in which a corpuscle, as* P, *is placed, there be erected the perpendiculars* DE *meeting the sphere in* E, *and if in those perpendiculars the lengths* DN *be taken as the quantity* $\frac{\text{DE}^2 \cdot \text{PS}}{\text{PE}}$, *and as the force which a particle of the sphere situated in the axis exerts at the distance* PE *upon the corpuscle* P *conjointly: I say, that the whole force with which the corpuscle* P *is attracted towards the sphere is as the area* ANB, *comprehended under the axis of the sphere* AB, *and the curved line* ANB, *the locus of the point* N.

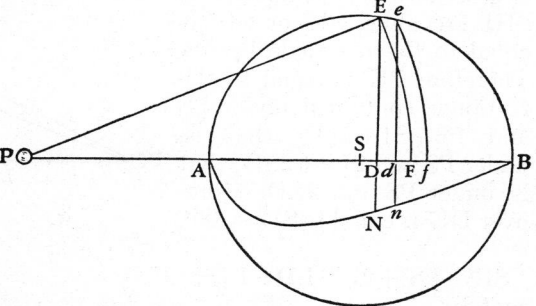

For supposing the construction in the last Lemma and Theorem to stand, conceive the axis of the sphere AB to be divided into innumerable equal particles D*d*, and the whole sphere to be divided into so many spherical concavoconvex laminæ EF*fe*; and erect the perpendicular *dn*. By the last Theorem, the force with which the laminæ EF*fe* attract the corpuscle P is as DE^2·F*f* and the force of one particle exerted at the distance PE or PF, conjointly. But (by the last Lemma) D*d* is to F*f* as PE to PS, and therefore F*f* is equal to $\dfrac{\text{PS}\cdot\text{D}d}{\text{PE}}$; and $\text{DE}^2\cdot\text{F}f$ is equal to $\text{D}d\cdot\dfrac{\text{DE}^2\cdot\text{PS}}{\text{PE}}$; and therefore the force

of the lamina EFfe is as $\text{D}d\cdot\dfrac{\text{DE}^2\cdot\text{PS}}{\text{PE}}$ and the force of a particle exerted at

the distance PF conjointly; that is, by the supposition, as $\text{DN}\cdot\text{D}d$, or as the evanescent area DNnd. Therefore the forces of all the laminæ exerted upon the corpuscle P are as all the areas DNnd, that is, the whole force of the sphere will be as the whole area ANB.   Q.E.D.

COR. I. Hence if the centripetal force tending to the several particles remain always the same at all distances, and DN be made as $\dfrac{\text{DE}^2\cdot\text{PS}}{\text{PE}}$, the whole force with which the corpuscle is attracted by the sphere is as the area ANB.

COR. II. If the centripetal force of the particles be inversely as the distance of the corpuscle attracted by it, and DN be made as $\dfrac{\text{DE}^2\cdot\text{PS}}{\text{PE}^2}$, the force with which the corpuscle P is attracted by the whole sphere will be as the area ANB.

COR. III. If the centripetal force of the particles be inversely as the cube of the distance of the corpuscle attracted by it, and DN be made as $\dfrac{\text{DE}^2\cdot\text{PS}}{\text{PE}^4}$, the force with which the corpuscle is attracted by the whole sphere will be as the area ANB.

COR. IV. And universally if the centripetal force tending to the several particles of the sphere be supposed to be inversely as the quantity V; and DN be made as $\dfrac{\text{DE}^2\cdot\text{PS}}{\text{PE}\cdot\text{V}}$; the force with which a corpuscle is attracted by the whole sphere will be as the area ANB.

PROPOSITION 81. PROBLEM 41

The things remaining as above, it is required to measure the area ANB.

From the point P let there be drawn the right line PH touching the sphere in H; and to the axis PAB, letting fall the perpendicular HI, bisect PI in L; and (by Prop. 12, Book II, *Elements* of Euclid) PE^2 is equal to $\text{PS}^2+\text{SE}^2+2\text{PS}\cdot\text{SD}$.

But because the triangles SPH, SHI are alike, SE^2 or SH^2 is equal to the rectangle $\text{PS}\cdot\text{IS}$. Therefore PE^2 is equal to the rectangle contained under PS and $\text{PS}+\text{SI}+2\text{SD}$; that is, under PS and $2\text{LS}+2\text{SD}$; that is, under PS and 2LD. Moreover DE^2 is equal to SE^2-SD^2, or

$$\text{SE}^2-\text{LS}^2+2\text{LS}\cdot\text{LD}-\text{LD}^2,$$

that is,

$$2\text{LS}\cdot\text{LD}-\text{LD}^2-\text{LA}\cdot\text{LB}.$$

For LS^2-SE^2 or LS^2-SA^2 (by Prop. 6, Book II, *Elements* of Euclid) is equal to the rectangle $\text{LA}\cdot\text{LB}$. Therefore if instead of DE^2 we write

$$2\text{LS}\cdot\text{LD}-\text{LD}^2-\text{LA}\cdot\text{LB},$$

the quantity $\dfrac{DE^2 \cdot PS}{PE \cdot V}$,which (by Cor. IV of the foregoing Prop.) is as the length

of the ordinate DN, will now resolve itself into three parts

$$\frac{2SLD \cdot PS}{PE \cdot V} - \frac{LD^2 \cdot PS}{PE \cdot V} - \frac{ALB \cdot PS}{PE \cdot V};$$

where if instead of V we write the inverse ratio of the centripetal force, and
instead of PE the mean proportional between PS and 2LD, those three parts
will become ordinates to so many curved lines, whose areas are discovered by
the common methods.   Q.E.D.

EXAM. 1. If the centripetal force tending to the several particles of the sphere
be inversely as the distance; instead of V write PE the distance, then $2PS \cdot LD$

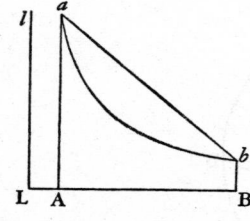

for PE^2; and DN will become as $SL - \tfrac{1}{2}LD - \dfrac{LA \cdot LB}{2LD}$.

Suppose DN equal to its double $2SL - LD - \dfrac{LA \cdot LB}{LD}$;

and 2SL the given part of the ordinate drawn into the
length AB will describe the rectangular area $2SL \cdot AB$;
and the indefinite part LD, drawn perpendicularly into
the same length with a continued motion, in such sort as
in its motion one way or another it may either by increasing or decreasing remain always equal to the length LD, will describe
the area $\dfrac{LB^2 - LA^2}{2}$, that is, the area $SL \cdot AB$; which taken from the former area

$2SL \cdot AB$, leaves the area $SL \cdot AB$. But the third part $\dfrac{LA \cdot LB}{LD}$, drawn after the
same manner with a continued motion perpendicularly into the same length,
will describe the area of an hyperbola, which subtracted from the area $SL \cdot AB$
will leave ANB the area sought. Whence arises this construction of the Problem. At the points L, A, B, erect the perpendiculars Ll, Aa, Bb; making Aa
equal to LB, and Bb equal to LA. Making Ll and LB asymptotes, describe
through the points a, b the hyperbolic curve ab. And the chord ba being drawn,
will inclose the area aba equal to the area sought ANB.

EXAM. 2. If the centripetal force tending to the several particles of the sphere
be inversely as the cube of the distance, or (which is the same thing) as that

cube applied to any given plane; write $\dfrac{PE^3}{2AS^2}$ for V,

and $2PS \cdot LD$ for PE^2; and DN will become as

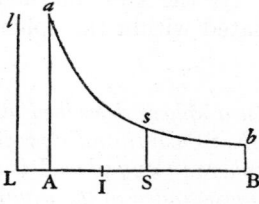

$$\frac{SL \cdot AS^2}{PS \cdot LD} - \frac{AS^2}{2PS} - \frac{LA \cdot LB \cdot AS^2}{2PS \cdot LD^2},$$

that is (because PS, AS, SI are continually proportional), as

$$\frac{LSI}{LD} - \tfrac{1}{2}SI - \frac{LA \cdot LB \cdot SI}{2LD^2}.$$

If we draw then these three parts into the length AB, the first $\dfrac{SL \cdot SI}{LD}$ will

generate the area of an hyperbola; the second $\tfrac{1}{2}$SI the area $\tfrac{1}{2}AB \cdot SI$; the third
$\dfrac{LA \cdot LB \cdot SI}{2LD^2}$ the area $\dfrac{LA \cdot LB \cdot SI}{2LA} - \dfrac{LA \cdot LB \cdot SI}{2LB}$, that is, $\tfrac{1}{2}AB \cdot SI$. From the first
subtract the sum of the second and third, and there will remain ANB the area

sought. Whence arises this construction of the Problem. At the points L, A, S, B, erect the perpendiculars Ll, Aa, Ss, Bb, of which suppose Ss equal to SI; and through the point s, to the asymptotes Ll, LB, describe the hyperbola asb meeting the perpendiculars Aa, Bb in a and b; and the rectangle 2SA·SI subtracted from the hyperbolic area AasbB, will leave ANB the area sought.

EXAM. 3. If the centripetal force tending to the several particles of the spheres decrease as the fourth power of the distance from the particles; write $\dfrac{\text{PE}^4}{2\text{AS}^3}$ for V, then $\sqrt{(2\text{PS}+\text{LD})}$ for PE, and DN will become as

$$\frac{\text{SI}^2\cdot\text{SL}}{\sqrt{2\text{SI}}}\cdot\frac{1}{\sqrt{\text{LD}^3}}-\frac{\text{SI}^2}{2\sqrt{2\text{SI}}}\cdot\frac{1}{\sqrt{\text{LD}}}-\frac{\text{SI}^2\cdot\text{LA}\cdot\text{LB}}{2\sqrt{2\text{SI}}}\cdot\frac{1}{\sqrt{\text{LD}^5}}.$$

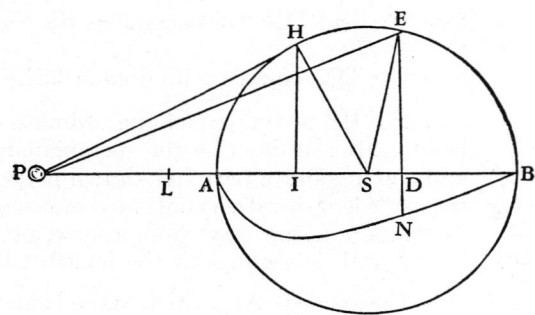

These three parts drawn into the length AB, produce so many areas, viz., $\dfrac{2\text{SI}^2\cdot\text{SL}}{\sqrt{2\text{SI}}}$ into $\left(\dfrac{1}{\sqrt{\text{LA}}}-\dfrac{1}{\sqrt{\text{LB}}}\right)$; $\dfrac{\text{SI}^2}{\sqrt{2\text{SI}}}$ into $\sqrt{(\text{LB}-\sqrt{\text{LA}})}$; and $\dfrac{\text{SI}^2\cdot\text{LA}\cdot\text{LB}}{3\sqrt{2\text{SI}}}$ into $\left(\dfrac{1}{\sqrt{\text{LA}^3}}-\dfrac{1}{\sqrt{\text{LB}^3}}\right)$. And these after due reduction come forth $\dfrac{2\text{SI}^2\cdot\text{SL}}{\text{LI}}$, SI^2, and SI$^2+\dfrac{2\text{SI}^3}{3\text{LI}}$. And these by subtracting the last from the first, become $\dfrac{4\text{SI}^3}{3\text{LI}}$. Therefore the entire force with which the corpuscle P is attracted towards the centre of the sphere is as $\dfrac{\text{SI}^3}{\text{PI}}$, that is, inversely as PS^3·PI. Q.E.I.

By the same method one may determine the attraction of a corpuscle situated within the sphere, but more expeditiously by the following Theorem.

PROPOSITION 82. THEOREM 41

In a sphere described about the centre S with the radius SA, if there be taken SI, SA, SP continually proportional: I say, that the attraction of a corpuscle within the sphere in any place I is to its attraction without the sphere in the place P in a ratio compounded of the square root of the ratio of IS, PS, the distances from the centre, and the square root of the ratio of the centripetal forces tending to the centre in those places P and I.

As, if the centripetal forces of the particles of the sphere be inversely as the distances of the corpuscle attracted by them, the force with which the corpuscle situated in I is attracted by the entire sphere will be to the force with which it is attracted in P in a ratio compounded of the square root of the ratio of the distance SI to the distance SP, and the square root of the ratio of the centripetal force in the place I arising from any particle in the centre to the centripetal force in the place P arising from the same particle in the centre; that is, inversely as the square root of the ratio of the distances SI, SP to each

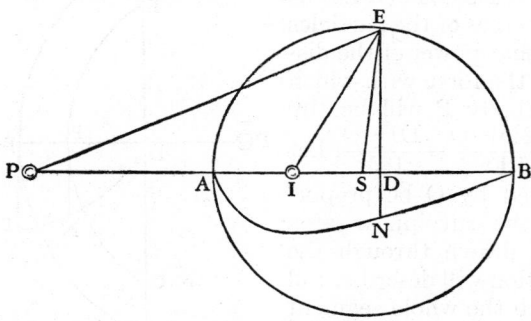

other. These two square roots of ratios compose the ratio of equality, and therefore the attractions in I and P produced by the whole sphere are equal. By the like calculation, if the forces of the particles of the sphere are inversely as the square of the ratio of the distances, it will be found that the attraction in I is to the attraction in P as the distance SP to the semidiameter SA of the sphere. If those forces are inversely as the cube of the ratio of the distances, the attractions in I and P will be to each other as SP^2 to SA^2; if as the fourth power of the ratio, as SP^3 to SA^3. Therefore since the attraction in P was found in this last case to be inversely as $PS^3 \cdot PI$, the attraction in I will be inversely as $SA^3 \cdot PI$, that is, because SA^3 is given, inversely as PI. And the progression is the same *in infinitum*. The demonstration of this Theorem is as follows:

The things remaining as above constructed, and a corpuscle being in any place P, the ordinate DN was found to be as $\dfrac{DE^2 \cdot PS}{PE \cdot V}$. Therefore if IE be drawn, that ordinate for any other place of the corpuscle, as I, will become (other things being equal) as $\dfrac{DE^2 \cdot IS}{IE \cdot V}$. Suppose the centripetal forces flowing from any point of the sphere, as E, to be to each other at the distances IE and PE as PE^n to IE^n (where the number n denotes the index of the powers of PE and IE), and those ordinates will become as $\dfrac{DE^2 \cdot PS}{PE \cdot PE^n}$ and $\dfrac{DE^2 \cdot IS}{IE \cdot IE^n}$, whose ratio to each other is as $PS \cdot IE \cdot IE^n$ to $IS \cdot PE \cdot PE^n$. Because SI, SE, SP are in continued proportion, the triangles SPE, SEI are alike; and thence IE is to PE as IS to SE or SA. For the ratio of IE to PE write the ratio of IS to SA; and the ratio of the ordinates becomes that of $PS \cdot IE^n$ to $SA \cdot PE^n$. But the ratio of PS to SA is the square root of that of the distances PS, SI; and the ratio of IE^n to PE^n (because IE is to PE as IS to SA) is the square root of that of the forces at the distances PS, IS. Therefore the ordinates, and consequently the areas which the ordinates describe, and the attractions proportional to them, are in a ratio compounded of the square root of those ratios. Q.E.D.

PROPOSITION 83. PROBLEM 42

To find the force with which a corpuscle placed in the centre of a sphere is attracted towards any segment of that sphere whatsoever.

Let P be a body in the centre of that sphere, and RBSD a segment thereof contained under the plane RDS and the spherical surface RBS. Let DB be cut in F by a spherical surface EFG described from the centre P, and let the seg-

ment be divided into the parts BREFGS, FEDG. Let us suppose that segment
to be not a purely mathematical but a physical surface, having some, but a
perfectly inconsiderable thickness. Let that thickness
be called O, and (by what Archimedes hath demonstrated) that surface will be as PF·DF·O. Let us
suppose, besides, the attractive forces of the particles
of the sphere to be inversely as that power of the distances, of which n is index; and the force with which
the surface EFG attracts the body P will be (by
Prop. 79) as $\dfrac{DE^2 \cdot O}{PF^n}$, that is, as $\dfrac{2DF \cdot O}{PF^{n-1}} - \dfrac{DF^2 \cdot O}{PF^n}$. Let

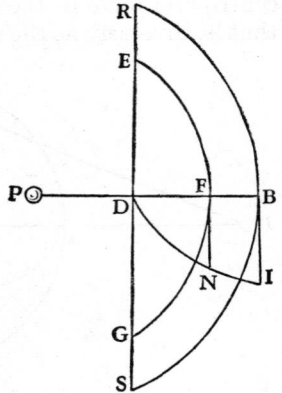

the perpendicular FN multiplied by O be proportional to this quantity; and the curvilinear area
BDI, which the ordinate FN, drawn through the
length DB with a continued motion will describe, will
be as the whole force with which the whole segment
RBSD attracts the body P.   Q.E.I.

PROPOSITION 84. PROBLEM 43

*To find the force with which a corpuscle, placed without the centre of a sphere in the
axis of any segment, is attracted by that segment.*

Let the body P placed in the axis ADB
of the segment EBK be attracted by that
segment. About the centre P, with the radius PE, let the spherical surface EFK be
described; and let it divide the segment
into two parts EBKFE and EFKDE.
Find the force of the first of those parts
by Prop. 81, and the force of the latter
part by Prop. 83, and the sum of the
forces will be the force of the whole segment EBKDE.   Q.E.I.

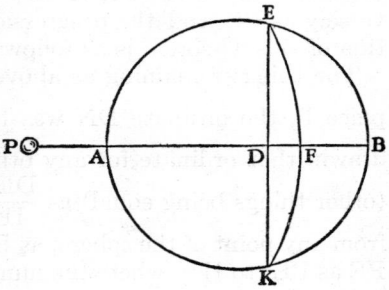

SCHOLIUM

The attractions of spherical bodies being now explained, it comes next in
order to treat of the laws of attraction in other bodies consisting in like manner of attractive particles; but to treat of them particularly is not necessary to
my design. It will be sufficient to add some general Propositions relating to the
forces of such bodies, and the motions thence arising, because the knowledge of
these will be of some little use in philosophical inquiries.

SECTION XIII

THE ATTRACTIVE FORCES OF BODIES WHICH ARE NOT SPHERICAL

PROPOSITION 85. THEOREM 42

*If a body be attracted by another, and its attraction be vastly stronger when it is
contiguous to the attracting body than when they are separated from each other by a*

very small interval; the forces of the particles of the attracting body decrease, in the recess of the body attracted, in more than the squared ratio of the distance of the particles.

For if the forces decrease as the square of the distances from the particles, the attraction towards a spherical body being (by Prop. 74) inversely as the square of the distance of the attracted body from the centre of the sphere, will not be sensibly increased by the contact, and it will be still less increased by it, if the attraction, in the recess of the body attracted, decreases in a still less proportion. The Proposition, therefore, is evident concerning attractive spheres. And the case is the same of concave spherical orbs attracting external bodies. And much more does it appear in orbs that attract bodies placed within them, because there the attractions diffused through the cavities of those orbs are (by Prop. 70) destroyed by contrary attractions, and therefore have no effect even in the place of contact. Now if from these spheres and spherical orbs we take away any parts remote from the place of contact, and add new parts anywhere at pleasure, we may change the figures of the attractive bodies at pleasure; but the parts added or taken away, being remote from the place of contact, will cause no remarkable excess of the attraction arising from the contact of the two bodies. Therefore the Proposition holds good in bodies of all figures. Q.E.D.

PROPOSITION 86. THEOREM 43

If the forces of the particles of which an attractive body is composed decrease, in the recession of the attractive body, as the third or more than the third power of the distance from the particles, the attraction will be vastly stronger in the point of contact than when the attracting and attracted bodies are separated from each other, though by ever so small an interval.

For that the attraction is infinitely increased when the attracted corpuscle comes to touch an attracting sphere of this kind, appears, by the solution of Problem 41, exhibited in the second and third Examples. The same will also appear (by comparing those Examples and Theor. 41 together) of attractions of bodies made towards concavoconvex orbs, whether the attracted bodies be placed without the orbs, or in the cavities within them. And by adding to or taking from those spheres and orbs any attractive matter anywhere without the place of contact, so that the attractive bodies may receive any assigned figure, the Proposition will hold good of all bodies universally.   Q.E.D.

PROPOSITION 87. THEOREM 44

If two bodies similar to each other, and consisting of matter equally attractive, attract separately two corpuscles proportional to those bodies, and in a like situation to them, the accelerative attractions of the corpuscles towards the entire bodies will be as the accelerative attractions of the corpuscles towards particles of the bodies proportional to the wholes, and similarly situated in them.

For if the bodies are divided into particles proportional to the wholes, and alike situated in them, it will be, as the attraction towards any particle of one of the bodies to the attraction towards the correspondent particle in the other body, so are the attractions towards the several particles of the first body, to the attractions towards the several correspondent particles of the other body; and, by composition, so is the attraction towards the first whole body to the attraction towards the second whole body.   Q.E.D.

COR. I. Therefore if, as the distances of the corpuscles attracted increase, the attractive forces of the particles decrease in the ratio of any power of the distances, the accelerative attractions towards the whole bodies will be directly as the bodies, and inversely as those powers of the distances. As if the forces of the particles decrease as the square of the distances from the corpuscles attracted, and the bodies are as A^3 and B^3, and therefore both the cubic sides of the bodies, and the distance of the attracted corpuscles from the bodies, are as A and B; the accelerative attractions towards the bodies will be as $\dfrac{A^3}{A^2}$ and $\dfrac{B^3}{B^2}$, that is, as A and B the cubic sides of those bodies. If the forces of the particles decrease as the cube of the distances from the attracted corpuscles, the accelerative attractions towards the whole bodies will be as $\dfrac{A^3}{A^3}$ and $\dfrac{B^3}{B^3}$, that is, equal. If the forces decrease as the fourth power, the attractions towards the bodies will be as $\dfrac{A^3}{A^4}$ and $\dfrac{B^3}{B^4}$, that is, inversely as the cubic sides A and B. And so in other cases.

COR. II. Hence, on the other hand, from the forces with which like bodies attract corpuscles similarly situated, may be obtained the ratio of the decrease of the attractive forces of the particles as the attracted corpuscle recedes from them; if only that decrease is directly or inversely in any ratio of the distances.

PROPOSITION 88. THEOREM 45

If the attractive forces of the equal particles of any body be as the distance of the places from the particles, the force of the whole body will tend to its centre of gravity; and will be the same with the force of a globe, consisting of similar and equal matter, and having its centre in the centre of gravity.

Let the particles A, B of the body RSTV attract any corpuscle Z with forces which, supposing the particles to be equal between themselves, are as the distances AZ, BZ; but, if they are supposed unequal, are as those particles and their distances AZ, BZ conjointly, or (if I may so speak) as those particles multiplied by their distances AZ, BZ respectively. And let those forces be expressed by the contents under A·AZ, and B·BZ. Join AB, and let it be cut in G, so that AG may be to BG as the particle B to the particle A; and G will be the common centre of gravity of the particles A and B. The force A·AZ will (by Cor. II of the Laws) be resolved into the forces A·GZ and A·AG; and the force B·BZ into the forces B·GZ and B·BG. Now

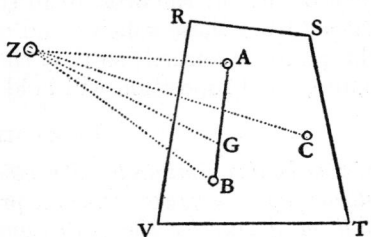

the forces A·AG and B·BG, because A is proportional to B, and BG to AG, are equal, and therefore having contrary directions destroy one another. There remain then the forces A·GZ and B·GZ. These tend from Z towards the centre G, and compose the force $(A+B)·GZ$; that is, the same force as if the attractive particles A and B were placed in their common centre of gravity G, composing there a little globe.

By the same reasoning, if there be added a third particle C, and the force of it be compounded with the force $(A+B)·GZ$ tending to the centre G, the force thence arising will tend to the common centre of gravity of that globe in G and of the particle C; that is, to the common centre of gravity of the three particles A, B, C; and will be the same as if that globe and the particle C were placed in that common centre composing a greater globe there; and so we may go on *in infinitum.* Therefore the whole force of all the particles of any body whatever RSTV is the same as if that body, without removing its centre of gravity, were to put on the form of a globe.   Q.E.D.

Cor. Hence the motion of the attracted body Z will be the same as if the attracting body RSTV were spherical; and therefore if that attracting body be either at rest, or proceed uniformly in a right line, the body attracted will move in an ellipse having its centre in the centre of gravity of the attracting body,

Proposition 89. Theorem 46

If there be several bodies consisting of equal particles whose forces are as the distances of the places from each, the force compounded of all the forces by which any corpuscle is attracted will tend to the common centre of gravity of the attracting bodies; and will be the same as if those attracting bodies, preserving their common centre of gravity, should unite there, and be formed into a globe.

This is demonstrated after the same manner as the foregoing Proposition.

Cor. Therefore the motion of the attracted body will be the same as if the attracting bodies, preserving their common centre of gravity, should unite there, and be formed into a globe. And, therefore, if the common centre of gravity of the attracting bodies be either at rest, or proceed uniformly in a right line, the attracted body will move in an ellipse having its centre in the common centre of gravity of the attracting bodies.

Proposition 90. Problem 44

If to the several points of any circle there tend equal centripetal forces, increasing or decreasing in any ratio of the distances; it is required to find the force with which a corpuscle is attracted, that is, situated anywhere in a right line which stands at right angles to the plane of the circle at its centre.

Suppose a circle to be described about the centre A with any radius AD in a plane to which the right line AP is perpendicular; and let it be required to find

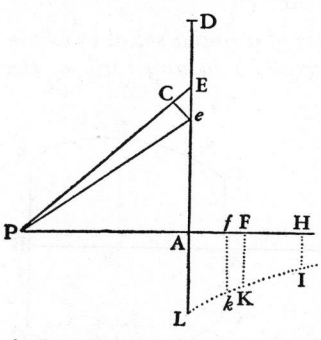

the force with which a corpuscle P is attracted towards the same. From any point E of the circle, to the attracted corpuscle P, let there be drawn the right line PE. In the right line PA take PF equal to PE, and make a perpendicular FK, erected at F, to be as the force with which the point E attracts the corpuscle P. And let the curved line IKL be the locus of the point K. Let that curve meet the plane of the circle in L. In PA take PH equal to PD, and erect the perpendicular HI meeting that curve in I; and the attraction of the corpuscle P towards the circle will be as the area AHIL multiplied by the altitude AP.   Q.E.I.

For let there be taken in AE a very small line E*e*. Join P*e*, and in PE, PA take PC, P*f*, both equal to P*e*. And because the force, with which any point E of the ring described about the centre A with the radius AE in the aforesaid plane attracts to itself the body P, is supposed to be as FK; and, therefore, the force with which that point attracts the body P towards A is as $\dfrac{AP \cdot FK}{PE}$; and the force with which the whole ring attracts the body P towards A is as the ring and $\dfrac{AP \cdot FK}{PE}$ conjointly; and that ring also is as the rectangle under the radius AE and the breadth Ee, and this rectangle (because PE and AE, Ee and CE are proportional) is equal to the rectangle PE $\cdot$ CE or PE $\cdot$ Ff; the force with which that ring attracts the body P towards A will be as PE $\cdot$ Ff and $\dfrac{AP \cdot FK}{PE}$ conjointly; that is, as the content under Ff $\cdot$ FK $\cdot$ AP, or as the area FKkf multiplied by AP. And therefore the sum of the forces with which all the rings, in the circle described about the centre A with the radius AD, attract the body P towards A, is as the whole area AHIKL multiplied by AP.   Q.E.D.

Cor. I. Hence if the forces of the points decrease as the square of the distances, that is, if FK be as $\dfrac{1}{PF^2}$, and therefore the area AHIKL as $\dfrac{1}{PA} - \dfrac{1}{PH}$; the attraction of the corpuscle P towards the circle will be as

$$1 - \frac{PA}{PH}; \text{ that is, as } \frac{AH}{PH}.$$

Cor. II. And universally if the forces of the points at the distances D be inversely as any power D^n of the distances; that is, if FK be as $\dfrac{1}{D^n}$, and therefore the area AHIKL as $\dfrac{1}{PA^{n-1}} - \dfrac{1}{PH^{n-1}}$; the attraction of the corpuscle P towards the circle will be as $\dfrac{1}{PA^{n-2}} - \dfrac{PA}{PH^{n-1}}$.

Cor. III. And if the diameter of the circle be increased *in infinitum*, and the number n be greater than unity; the attraction of the corpuscle P towards the whole infinite plane will be inversely as PA^{n-2}, because the other term $\dfrac{PA}{PH^{n-1}}$ vanishes.

PROPOSITION 91. PROBLEM 45

To find the attraction of a corpuscle situated in the axis of a round solid, to whose several points there tend equal centripetal forces decreasing in any ratio of the distances whatsoever.

Let the corpuscle P, situated in the axis AB of the solid DECG, be attracted towards that solid. Let the solid be cut by any circle as RFS, perpendicular to the axis; and in its semidiameter FS, in any plane PALKB passing through the axis, let there be taken (by Prop. 90) the length FK proportional to the force with which the corpuscle P is attracted towards that circle. Let the locus of the point K be the curved line LKI, meeting the planes

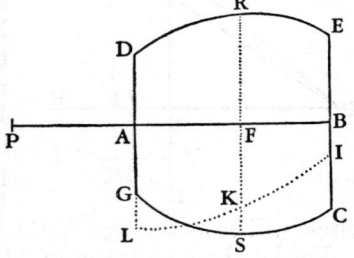

of the outermost circles AL and BI in L and I; and the attraction of the corpuscle P towards the solid will be as the area LABI.   Q.E.I.

COR. I. Hence if the solid be a cylinder described by the parallelogram ADEB revolved about the axis AB, and the centripetal forces tending to the several points be inversely as the squares of the distances from the points; the attraction of the corpuscle P towards this cylinder will be as AB−PE+PD. For the ordinate FK (by Cor. I, Prop. 90) will be as $1-\frac{PF}{PR}$. The part 1 of this quantity, multiplied by the length AB, describes the area $1 \cdot AB$; and the other part $\frac{PF}{PR}$, multiplied by the length PB, describes the area $1 \cdot (PE-$ AD) (as may be easily shown from the quadrature of the curve LKI); and, in like manner, the same part multiplied by the length PA describes the area $1 \cdot (PD-AD)$, and multiplied by AB, the difference of PB and PA, describes $1 \cdot (PE-PD)$, the difference of the areas. From the first content $1 \cdot AB$ take away the last content $1 \cdot (PE-PD)$, and there will remain the area LABI equal to $1 \cdot (AB-PE+PD)$. Therefore the force, being proportional to this area, is as AB−PE+PD.

COR. II. Hence also is known the force by which a spheroid AGBC attracts any body P situate externally in its axis AB. Let NKRM be a conic section whose ordinate ER perpendicular to PE may be always equal to the length of the line PD, continually drawn to the point D in which that ordinate cuts the spheroid. From the vertices A, B of the spheroid, let there be erected to its axis AB the perpendiculars AK, BM, respectively equal to AP, BP, and therefore meeting the conic section in K and M; and join KM cutting off from it the segment KMRK. Let S be the centre of the spheroid, and SC its

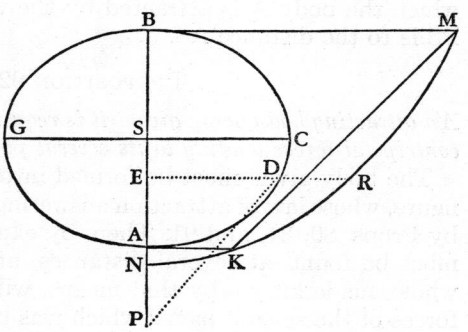

greatest semidiameter; and the force with which the spheroid attracts the body P will be to the force with which a sphere described with the diameter AB attracts the same body as $\frac{AS \cdot CS^2 - PS \cdot KMRK}{PS^2 + CS^2 - AS^2}$ is to $\frac{AS^3}{3PS^2}$. And by a calculation founded on the same principles may be found the forces of the segments of the spheroid.

COR. III. If the corpuscle be placed within the spheroid and in its axis, the attraction will be as its distance from the centre. This may be easily inferred from the following reasoning, whether the particle be in the axis or in any other given diameter. Let AGOF be an attracting spheroid, S its centre, and P the body attracted. Through the body P let there be drawn the semidiameter SPA, and two right lines DE, FG meeting the spheroid in D and E, F and G; and let PCM, HLN be the surfaces of two interior spheroids similar and concentric to the exterior, the first of which passes through the body P, and cuts the right lines DE, FG in B and C; the latter cuts the same right lines in H and I, K and

L. Let the spheroids have all one common axis, and the parts of the right lines intercepted on both sides DP and BE, FP and CG, DH and IE, FK and LG, will be mutually equal; because the right lines DE, PB, and HI are bisected in the same point, as are also the right lines FG, PC, and KL. Conceive now DPF, EPG to represent opposite cones described with the infinitely small vertical angles DPF, EPG, and the lines DH,

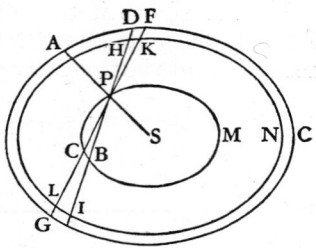

EI to be infinitely small also. Then the particles of the cones DHKF, GLIE, cut off by the spheroidal surfaces, by reason of the equality of the lines DH and EI, will be to one another as the squares of the distances from the body P, and will therefore attract that corpuscle equally. And by a like reasoning if the spaces DPF, EGCB be divided into particles by the surfaces of innumerable similar spheroids concentric to the former and having one common axis, all these particles will equally attract on both sides the body P towards contrary parts. Therefore the forces of the cone DPF, and of the conic segment EGCB, are equal, and by their opposed actions destroy each other. And the case is the same of the forces of all the matter that lies without the interior spheroid PCBM. Therefore the body P is attracted by the interior spheroid PCBM alone, and therefore (by Cor. III, Prop. 72) its attraction is to the force with which the body A is attracted by the whole spheroid AGOD as the distance PS is to the distance AS.   Q.E.D.

PROPOSITION 92. PROBLEM 46

An attracting body being given, it is required to find the ratio of the decrease of the centripetal forces tending to its several points.

The body given must be formed into a sphere, a cylinder, or some regular figure, whose law of attraction answering to any ratio of decrease may be found by Props. 80, 81, and 91. Then, by experiments, the force of the attractions must be found at several distances, and the law of attraction towards the whole, made known by that means, will give the ratio of the decrease of the forces of the several parts; which was to be found.

PROPOSITION 93. THEOREM 47

If a solid be plane on one side, and infinitely extended on all other sides, and consist of equal particles equally attractive, whose forces decrease, in receding from the solid, in the ratio of any power greater than the square of the distances; and a corpuscle placed towards either part of the plane is attracted by the force of the whole solid: I say, that the attractive force of the whole solid, in receding from its plane surface will decrease in the ratio of a power whose side is the distance of the corpuscle from the plane, and its index less by 3 than the index of the power of the distances.

CASE 1. Let LGl be the plane by which the solid is terminated. Let the solid lie on that side of the plane that is towards I, and let it be resolved into innumerable planes mHM, nIN, oKO, &c., parallel to GL. And first let the attracted body C be placed without the solid. Let there be drawn CGHI perpendicular to those innumerable planes, and let the attractive forces of the points of the solid decrease in the ratio of a power of the distances whose index is the number n

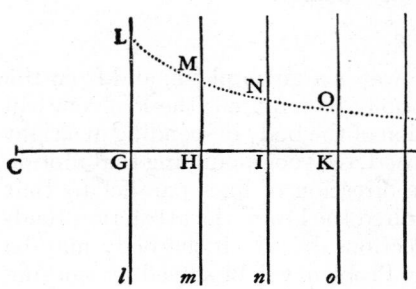

not less than 3. Therefore (by Cor. III, Prop. 90) the force with which any plane mHM attracts the point C is inversely as CH^{n-2}. In the plane mHM take the length HM inversely proportional to CH^{n-2}, and that force will be as HM. In like manner in the several planes lGL, nIN, oKO, &c., take the lengths GL, IN, KO, &c., inversely proportional to CG^{n-2}, CI^{n-2}, CK^{n-2}, &c., and the forces of those planes will be as the lengths so taken, and therefore the sum of the forces as the sum of the lengths, that is, the force of the whole solid as the area GLOK produced infinitely towards OK. But that area (by the known methods of quadratures) is inversely as CG^{n-3}, and therefore the force of the whole solid is inversely as CG^{n-3}.   Q.E.D.

CASE 2. Let the corpuscle C be now placed on that side of the plane lGL that is within the solid, and take the distance CK equal to the distance CG. And the part of the solid LGloKO terminated by the parallel planes lGL, oKO, will attract the corpuscle C, situated in the middle, neither one way nor another, the contrary actions of the opposite points destroying one another by reason of their equality. Therefore the corpuscle C is attracted by the force only of the solid situated beyond the plane OK. But this force (by Case 1) is inversely as CK^{n-3}, that is (because CG, CK are equal), inversely as CG^{n-3}.   Q.E.D.

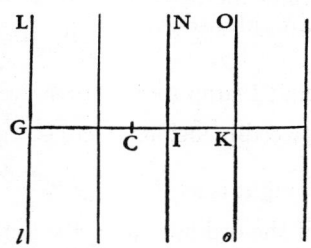

COR. I. Hence if the solid LGIN be terminated on each side by two infinite parallel planes LG, IN, its attractive force is known, subtracting from the attractive force of the whole infinite solid LGKO the attractive force of the more distant part NIKO infinitely produced towards KO.

COR. II. If the more distant part of this solid be rejected, because its attraction compared with the attraction of the nearer part is inconsiderable, the attraction of that nearer part will, as the distance increases, decrease nearly in the ratio of the power CG^{n-3}.

COR. III. And hence if any finite body, plane on one side, attract a corpuscle situated over against the middle of that plane, and the distance between the corpuscle and the plane compared with the dimensions of the attracting body be extremely small; and the attracting body consist of homogeneous particles, whose attractive forces decrease in the ratio of any power of the distances greater than the fourth; the attractive force of the whole body will decrease very nearly in the ratio of a power whose side is that very small distance, and the index less by 3 than the index of the former power. This assertion does not hold good, however, of a body consisting of particles whose attractive forces decrease in the ratio of the third power of the distances; because, in that case, the attraction of the remoter part of the infinite body in the second Corollary is always infinitely greater than the attraction of the nearer part.

SCHOLIUM

If a body is attracted perpendicularly towards a given plane, and from the law of attraction given, the motion of the body be required; the Problem will be solved by seeking (by Prop. 39) the motion of the body descending in a right line towards that plane, and (by Cor. II of the Laws) compounding that motion with an uniform motion performed in the direction of lines parallel to that plane. And, on the contrary, if there be required the law of the attraction tending towards the plane in perpendicular directions, by which the body may be caused to move in any given curved line, the Problem will be solved by working after the manner of the third Problem.

But the operations may be contracted by resolving the ordinates into converging series. As if to a base A the length B be ordinately applied in any given angle, and that length be as any power of the base $A^{\frac{m}{n}}$; and there be sought the force with which a body, either attracted towards the base or driven from it in the direction of that ordinate, may be caused to move in the curved line which that ordinate always describes with its superior extremity; I suppose the base to be increased by a very small part O, and I resolve the ordinate $(A+O)^{\frac{m}{n}}$ into an infinite series

$$A^{\frac{m}{n}}+\frac{m}{n}\,OA^{\frac{m-n}{n}}+\frac{mm-mn}{2nn}\,OOA^{\frac{m-2n}{n}}\ \&c.,$$

and I suppose the force proportional to the term of this series in which O is of two dimensions, that is, to the term $\frac{mm-mn}{2nn}OOA^{\frac{m-2n}{n}}.$ Therefore the force sought is as $\frac{mm-mn}{nn}A^{\frac{m-2n}{n}}$, or, which is the same thing, as $\frac{mm-mn}{nn}B^{\frac{m-2n}{n}}.$ As if the ordinate describe a parabola, m being $=2$, and $n=1$, the force will be as the given quantity $2B^{0}$, and therefore is given. Therefore with a given force the body will move in a parabola, as Galileo hath demonstrated. If the ordinate describe an hyperbola, m being $=0-1$, and $n=1$, the force will be as $2A^{-3}$ or $2B^{3}$; and therefore a force which is as the cube of the ordinate will cause the body to move in an hyperbola. But leaving Propositions of this kind, I shall go on to some others relating to motion which I have not yet touched upon.

SECTION XIV

THE MOTION OF VERY SMALL BODIES WHEN AGITATED BY CENTRIPETAL FORCES TENDING TO THE SEVERAL PARTS OF ANY VERY GREAT BODY

PROPOSITION 94. THEOREM 48

If two similar mediums be separated from each other by a space terminated on both sides by parallel planes, and a body in its passage through that space be attracted or impelled perpendicularly towards either of those mediums, and not agitated or hindered by any other force; and the attraction be everywhere the same at equal distances from either plane, taken towards the same side of the plane: I say, that the sine of incidence upon either plane will be to the sine of emergence from the other plane in a given ratio.

CASE 1. Let Aa and Bb be two parallel planes, and let the body light upon the first plane Aa in the direction of the line GH, and in its whole passage through

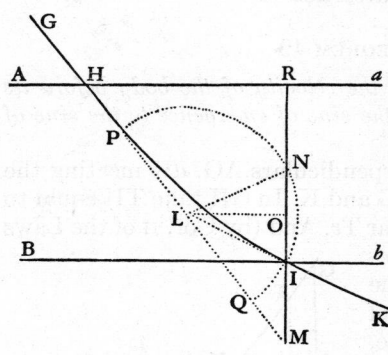

the intermediate space let it be attracted or impelled towards the medium of incidence, and by that action let it be made to describe a curved line HI, and let, it emerge in the direction of the line IK. Let there be erected IM perpendicular to B*b* the plane of emergence, and meeting the line of incidence GH prolonged in M, and the plane of incidence A*a* in R; and let the line of emergence KI be produced and meet HM in L. About the centre L, with the radius LI, let a circle be described cutting both HM in P and Q, and MI produced in N; and, first, if the attraction or impulse be supposed uniform, the curve HI (by what Galileo hath demonstrated) will be a parabola, whose property is that of a rectangle under its given latus rectum, and the line IM equal to the square of HM; and moreover the line HM will be bisected in L. Hence if to MI there be let fall the perpendicular LO, then MO, OR will be equal; and adding the equal lines ON, OI, the wholes MN, IR will be equal also. Therefore since IR is given, MN is also given, and the rectangle MI·MN is to the rectangle under the latus rectum and IM, that is, to HM^2 in a given ratio. But the rectangle MI·MN is equal to the rectangle MP·MQ, that is, to the difference of the squares ML^2, and PL^2 or LI^2; and HM^2 hath a given ratio to its fourth part ML^2; therefore the ratio of ML^2−LI^2 to ML^2 is given, and by conversion the ratio of LI^2 to ML^2, and its square root, the ratio of LI to ML. But in every triangle, as LMI, the sines of the angles are proportional to the opposite sides. Therefore the ratio of the sine of the angle of incidence LMR to the sine of the angle of emergence LIR is given.   Q.E.D.

CASE 2. Let now the body pass successively through several spaces terminated with parallel planes A*ab*B, B*bc*C, &c., and let it be acted on by a force which is uniform in each of them separately, but different in the different

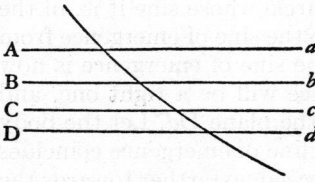

spaces; and by what was just demonstrated, the sine of the angle of incidence on the first plane A*a* is to the sine of emergence from the second plane B*b* in a given ratio; and this sine of incidence upon the second plane B*b* will be to the sine of emergence from the third plane C*c* in a given ratio; and this sine to the sine of emergence from the fourth plane D*d* in a given ratio; and so on *in infinitum;* and, by multiplication of equals, the sine of incidence on the first plane is to the sine of emergence from the last plane in a given ratio. Let now the intervals of the planes be diminished, and their number be infinitely increased, so that the action of attraction or impulse, exerted according to any assigned law, may become continual, and the ratio of the sine of incidence on the first plane to the sine of emergence from the last plane being all along given, will be given then also.   Q.E.D.

PROPOSITION 95. THEOREM 49

The same things being supposed, I say, that the velocity of the body before its incidence is to its velocity after emergence as the sine of emergence to the sine of incidence.

Make AH and I*d* equal, and erect the perpendiculars AG, *d*K meeting the lines of incidence and emergence GH, IK in G and K. In GH take TH equal to IK, and to the plane A*a* let fall a perpendicular T*v*. And (by Cor. II of the Laws of Motion) let the motion of the body be re-solved into two, one perpendicular to the planes A*a*, B*b*, C*c*, &c., and another parallel to them. The force of attraction or impulse, acting in directions perpendicular to those planes, does not at all alter the motion in par-allel directions; and therefore the body pro-ceeding with this motion will in equal times go through those equal parallel intervals that lie between the line AG and the point H, and between the point I and the line *d*K; that is, they will describe the lines GH, IK in equal times. Therefore the velocity before incidence is to the velocity after emergence as GH to IK or TH, that is, as AH or I*d* to *v*H, that is (suppo-sing TH or IK radius), as the sine of emergence to the sine of incidence.   Q.E.D.

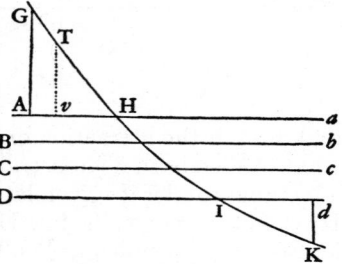

PROPOSITION 96. THEOREM 50

The same things being supposed, and that the motion before incidence is swifter than afterwards: I say, that if the line of incidence be inclined continually, the body will be at last reflected, and the angle of reflection will be equal to the angle of incidence.

For conceive the body passing between the parallel planes A*a*, B*b*, C*c*, &c., to describe parabolic arcs as above; and let those arcs be HP, PQ, QR, &c. And let the obliquity of the line of incidence GH to the first plane A*a* be such that the sine of incidence may be to the radius of the circle whose sine it is, in the same ratio which the same sine of incidence hath to the sine of emergence from the plane D*d* into the space D*deE*; and because the sine of emergence is now become equal to the radius, the angle of emergence will be a right one, and therefore the line of emergence will coincide with the plane D*d*. Let the body come to this plane in the point R; and because the line of emergence coincides with that plane, it is manifest that the body can proceed no farther towards the plane E*e*. But neither can it proceed in the line of emergence R*d*; because it is perpetually attracted or impelled to-wards the medium of incidence. It will return, therefore, between the planes C*c*, D*d*, describing an arc of a parabola

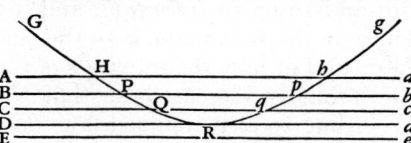

QR*q*, whose principal vertex (by what Galileo hath demonstrated) is in R, cutting the plane C*c* in the same angle at *q*, that it did before at Q; then going on in the parabolic arcs *qp*, *ph*, &c., similar and equal to the former arcs QP, PH, &c., it will cut the rest of the planes in the same angles at *p*, *h*, &c., as it did before in P, H, &c., and will emerge at last with the same obliquity at h with which it first impinged on that plane at H. Conceive now the intervals of the planes Aa, Bb, Cc, Dd, Ee, &c., to be infinitely diminished, and the number infinitely increased, so that the action of attraction or impulse, exerted according to any assigned law, may become continual; and, the angle of emergence remaining all along equal to the angle of incidence, will be equal to the same also at last.   Q.E.D.

SCHOLIUM

These attractions bear a great resemblance to the reflections and refractions of light made in a given ratio of the secants, as was discovered by Snell; and

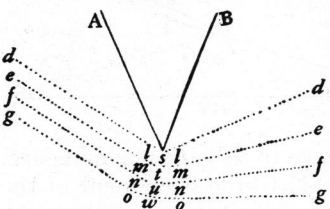

consequently in a given ratio of the sines, as was exhibited by Descartes. For it is now certain from the phenomena of Jupiter's satellites, confirmed by the observations of different astronomers, that light is propagated in succession, and requires about seven or eight minutes to travel from the sun to the earth. Moreover, the rays of light that are in our air (as lately was discovered by Grimaldi, by the admission of light into a dark room through a small hole, which I have also tried) in their passage near the angles of bodies, whether transparent or opaque (such as the circular and rectangular edges of gold, silver, and brass coins, or of knives, or broken pieces of stone or glass), are bent or inflected round those bodies as if they were attracted to them; and those rays which in their passage come nearest to the bodies are the most inflected, as if they were most attracted; which thing I myself have also carefully observed. And those which pass at greater distances are less inflected; and those at still greater distances are a little inflected the contrary way, and form three fringes of colors. In the figure s represents the edge of a knife, or any kind of wedge AsB; and *gowog, fnunf, emtme, dlsld* are rays inflected towards the knife in the arcs *owo, nun, mtm, lsl*; which inflection is greater or less according to their distance from the knife. Now since this inflection of the rays is performed in the air without the knife, it follows that the rays which fall upon the knife are first inflected in the air before they touch the knife. And the case is the same of the rays falling upon glass. The refraction, therefore, is made not in the point of incidence, but gradually, by a continual inflection of the rays; which is done partly in the air before they touch the glass, partly (if I mistake not) within the glass, after they have entered it; as is represented in the rays *ckzc, biyb, ahxa*, falling upon r, q, p, and inflected between k and z, i and y, h and x. Therefore because of the analogy there is between the propagation of the rays of light and the motion of bodies, I thought it not amiss to add the following Propositions for optical uses; not at all considering the nature of the rays of light, or inquiring whether they are bodies or not; but only determining the curves of bodies which are extremely like the curves of the rays.

Proposition 97. Problem 47

Supposing the sine of incidence upon any surface to be in a given ratio to the sine of emergence; and that the inflection of the paths of those bodies near that surface is performed in a very short space, which may be considered as a point; it is required to determine such a surface as may cause all the corpuscles issuing from any one given place to converge to another given place.

Let A be the place from whence the corpuscles diverge; B the place to which they should converge; CDE the curved line which by its revolution round the axis AB describes the surface sought; D, E any two points of that curve; and EF, EG perpendiculars let fall on the paths of the bodies AD, DB. Let the point D approach to and coalesce with the point E; and the ultimate ratio of the line DF by which AD is increased, to the line DG by which DB is dimin-

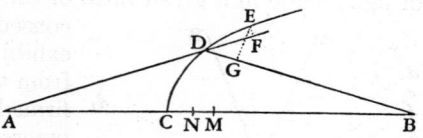

ished, will be the same as that of the sine of incidence to the sine of emergence. Therefore the ratio of the increment of the line AD to the decrement of the line DB is given; and therefore if in the axis AB there be taken anywhere the point C through which the curve CDE must pass, and CM the increment of AC be taken in that given ratio to CN the decrement of BC, and from the centres A, B, with the radii AM, BN, there be described two circles cutting each other in D; that point D will touch the curve sought CDE, and, by touching it anywhere at pleasure, will determine that curve.   Q.E.I.

Cor. I. By causing the point A or B to go off sometimes *in infinitum*, and sometimes to move towards other parts of the point C, will be obtained all those figures which Descartes has exhibited in his *Optics* and *Geometry* relating to refractions. The invention of which Descartes having thought fit to conceal is here laid open in this Proposition.

Cor. II. If a body lighting on any surface CD in the direction of a right line AD, drawn according to any law, should emerge in the direction of another right line DK; and from the point C there be drawn curved lines CP, CQ, always perpendicular to AD, DK; the increments of the lines PD, QD, and there-

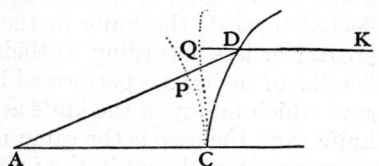

fore the lines themselves PD, QD, generated by those increments, will be as the sines of incidence and emergence to each other, and conversely.

Proposition 98. Problem 48

The same things supposed; if round the axis AB any attractive surface be described, as CD, regular or irregular, through which the bodies issuing from the given place A must pass; it is required to find a second attractive surface EF, which may make those bodies converge to a given place B.

Let a line joining AB cut the first surface in C and the second in E, the point D being taken in any manner at pleasure. And supposing the sine of incidence on the first surface to the sine of emergence from the same, and the sine of emergence from the second surface to the sine of incidence on the same, to be as any given quantity M to another given quantity N; then produce AB to G, so

that BG may be to CE as M − N to N; and AD to H, so that AH may be equal
to AG; and DF to K, so that DK may be to DH as N to M. Join KB, and about
the centre D with the radius DH describe a circle meeting KB produced in L,

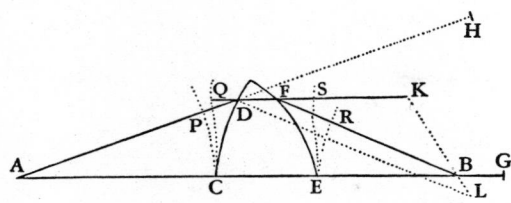

and draw BF parallel to DL; and the point F will touch the line EF, which,
being turned round the axis AB, will describe the surface sought.   Q.E.F.

For conceive the lines CP, CQ to be everywhere perpendicular to AD, DF,
and the lines ER, ES to FB, FD respectively, and therefore QS to be always
equal to CE; and (by Cor. II, Prop. 97) PD will be to QD as M to N, and therefore as DL to DK, or FB to FK; and by subtraction, as DL − FB or PH − PD −
FB to FD or FQ − QD; and by addition as PH − FB to FQ, that is (because
PH and CG, QS and CE, are equal), as CE + BG − FR to CE − FS. But (because BG is to CE as M − N to N) it comes to pass also that CE + BG is to CE
as M to N; and therefore, by subtraction, FR is to FS as M to N; and therefore
(by Cor. II, Prop. 97) the surface EF compels a body, falling upon it in the
direction DF, to go on in the line FR to the place B.   Q.E.D.

SCHOLIUM

In the same manner one may go on to three or more surfaces. But of all
figures the spherical is the most proper for optical uses. If the object glasses of
telescopes were made of two glasses of a spherical figure, containing water between them, it is not unlikely that the errors of the refractions made in the
extreme parts of the surfaces of the glasses may be accurately enough corrected
by the refractions of the water. Such object glasses are to be preferred before
elliptic and hyperbolic glasses, not only because they may be formed with more
ease and accuracy, but because the pencils of rays situated without the axis of
the glass would be more accurately refracted by them. But the different refrangibility of different rays is the real obstacle that hinders optics from being
made perfect by spherical or any other figures. Unless the errors thence arising
can be corrected, all the labor spent in correcting the others is quite thrown
away.

BOOK TWO

THE MOTION OF BODIES
IN RESISTING MEDIUMS

SECTION I

THE MOTION OF BODIES THAT ARE RESISTED IN THE RATIO OF THE VELOCITY

PROPOSITION 1. THEOREM 1

If a body is resisted in the ratio of its velocity, the motion lost by resistance is as the space gone over in its motion.

For since the motion lost in each equal interval of time is as the velocity, that is, as the small increment of space gone over, then, by composition, the motion lost in the whole time will be as the whole space gone over.   Q.E.D.

COR. Therefore if the body, destitute of all gravity, move by its innate force only in free spaces, and there be given both its whole motion at the beginning, and also the motion remaining after some part of the way is gone over, there will be given also the whole space which the body can describe in an infinite time. For that space will be to the space now described as the whole motion at the beginning is to the part lost of that motion.

LEMMA 1

Quantities proportional to their differences are continually proportional.

Let $\qquad A : A - B = B : B - C = C : C - D = \&c.;$

then, by subtraction,

$$A : B = B : C = C : D = \&c. \qquad \text{Q.E.D.}$$

PROPOSITION 2. THEOREM 2

If a body is resisted in the ratio of its velocity, and moves, by its inertia only, through an homogeneous medium, and the times be taken equal, the velocities in the beginning of each of the times are in a geometrical progression, and the spaces described in each of the times are as the velocities.

CASE 1. Let the time be divided into equal intervals; and if at the very beginning of each interval we suppose the resistance to act with one single impulse which is as the velocity, the decrement of the velocity in each of the intervals of time will be as the same velocity. Therefore the velocities are proportional to their differences, and therefore (by Lem. 1, Book II) continually proportional. Therefore if out of an equal number of intervals there be compounded any equal portions of time, the velocities at the beginning of those times will be as terms in a continued progression, which are taken by jumps, omitting everywhere an equal number of intermediate terms. But the ratios of these terms are compounded of the equal ratios of the intermediate terms equally repeated, and therefore are equal. Therefore the velocities, being proportional to those terms, are in geometrical progression. Let those equal intervals of time be diminished, and their number increased *in infinitum*, so that the impulse of resistance may become continual; and the velocities at the beginnings of equal times, always continually proportional, will be also in this case continually proportional.   Q.E.D.

CASE 2. And, by division, the differences of the velocities, that is, the parts of the velocities lost in each of the times, are as the wholes; but the spaces described in each of the times are as the lost parts of the velocities (by Prop. 1, Book I), and therefore are also as the wholes.   Q.E.D.

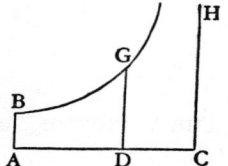

COR. Hence if to the rectangular asymptotes AC, CH, the hyperbola BG is described, and AB, DG be drawn perpendicular to the asymptote AC, and both the velocity of the body, and the resistance of the medium, at the very beginning of the motion, be expressed by any given line AC, and, after some time is elapsed, by the indefinite line DC; the time may be expressed by the area ABGD, and the space described in that time by the line AD. For if that area, by the motion of the point D, be uniformly increased in the same manner as the time, the right line DC will decrease in a geometrical ratio in the same manner as the velocity; and the parts of the right line AC, described in equal times, will decrease in the same ratio.

PROPOSITION 3. PROBLEM 1

To define the motion of a body which, in an homogeneous medium, ascends or descends in a right line, and is resisted in the ratio of its velocity, and acted upon by an uniform force of gravity.

The body ascending, let the gravity be represented by any given rectangle BACH; and the resistance of the medium, at the beginning of the ascent, by

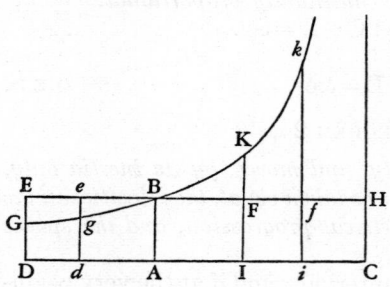

the rectangle BADE, taken on the contrary side of the right line AB. Through the point B, with the rectangular asymptotes AC, CH, describe an hyperbola, cutting the perpendiculars DE, *de* in G, *g*; and the body ascending will in the time DG*gd* describe the space EG*ge*; in the time DGBA, the space of the whole ascent EGB; in the time ABKI, the space of descent BFK; and in the time IK*ki* the space of descent KF*fk*; and the velocities of the bodies (proportional to the resistance of the medium) in these periods of time will be ABED, AB*ed*, o, ABFI, AB*fi* respectively; and the greatest velocity which the body can acquire by descending will be BACH.

For let the rectangle BACH be resolved into innumerable rectangles A*k*, K*l*, L*m*, M*n*, &c., which shall be as the increments of the velocities produced in so many equal times; then will o, A*k*, A*l*, A*m*, A*n*, &c., be as the whole velocities, and therefore (by supposition) as the resistances of the medium in the beginning of each of the equal times. Make AC to AK, or ABHC to AB*k*K, as the force of gravity to the resistance in the beginning of the second time; then from the force of gravity subtract the resistances, and ABHC, K*k*HC, L*l*HC, M*m*-HC, &c., will be as the absolute forces with which the body is acted upon in the beginning of each of the times, and therefore (by Law I) as the increments of the velocities, that is, as the rectangles A*k*, K*l*, L*m*, M*n*, &c., and therefore (by Lem. 1, Book II) in a geometrical progression. Therefore, if the right lines K*k*, L*l*, M*m*, N*n*, &c., are produced so as to meet the hyperbola in *q, r, s, t*, &c., the areas AB*q*K, K*qr*L, L*rs*M, M*st*N, &c., will be equal, and therefore analogous to

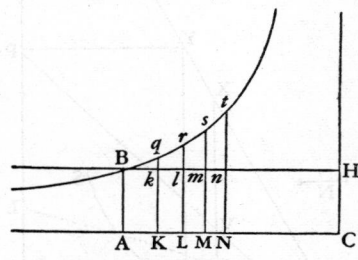

the equal times and equal gravitating forces. But the area AB*q*K (by Cor. III, Lems. 7 and 8, Book I) is to the area B*kq* as K*q* to ½*kq*, or AC to ½AK, that is, as the force of gravity to the resistance in the middle of the first time. And by the like reasoning, the areas *q*KL*r*, *r*LM*s*, *s*MN*t*, &c., are to the areas *qklr*, *rlms*, *smnt*, &c., as the gravitating forces to the resistances in the middle of the second, third, fourth time, and so on. Therefore since the equal areas BAK*q*, *q*KL*r*, *r*LM*s*, *s*MN*t*, &c., are analogous to the gravitating forces, the areas B*kq*, *qklr*, *rlms*, *smnt*, &c., will be analogous to the resistances in the middle of each of the times, that is (by supposition), to the velocities, and so to the spaces described. Take the sums of the analogous quantities, and the areas B*kq*, B*lr*, B*ms*, B*nt*, &c., will be analogous to the whole spaces described; and also the areas AB*q*K, AB*r*L, AB*s*M, AB*t*N, &c., to the times. Therefore the body, in descending, will in any time AB*r*L describe the space B*lr*, and in the time L*rt*N the space *rlnt*. Q.E.D. And the like demonstration holds in ascending motion.

COR. I. Therefore the greatest velocity that the body can acquire by falling is to the velocity acquired in any given time as the given force of gravity which continually acts upon it to the resisting force which opposes it at the end of that time.

COR. II. But the time being augmented in an arithmetical progression, the sum of that greatest velocity and the velocity in the ascent, and also their difference in the descent, decreases in a geometrical progression.

COR. III. Also the differences of the spaces, which are described in equal differences of the times, decrease in the same geometrical progression.

COR. IV. The space described by the body is the difference of two spaces, whereof one is as the time taken from the beginning of the descent, and the other as the velocity; which [spaces] also at the beginning of the descent are equal among themselves.

PROPOSITION 4. PROBLEM 2

Supposing the force of gravity in any homogeneous medium to be uniform, and to tend perpendicularly to the plane of the horizon: to define the motion of a projectile therein, which suffers resistance proportional to its velocity.

Let the projectile go from any place D in the direction of any right line DP, and let its velocity at the beginning of the motion be represented by the length DP. From the point P let fall the perpendicular PC on the horizontal line DC, and cut DC in A, so that DA may be to AC as the vertical component of the resistance of the medium arising from the motion upwards at the beginning, to the force of gravity; or (which comes to the same) so that the rectangle under DA and DP may be to that under AC and CP as the whole resistance at the beginning of the motion, to the force of gravity. With the asymptotes DC, CP describe any hyperbola GTBS cutting the perpendiculars DG, AB in G and B; complete the parallelogram DGKC, and let its side GK cut AB in Q. Take a line N in the same ratio to QB as DC is in to CP; and from any point R of the right line DC erect RT perpendicular to it, meeting the hyperbola in T, and the right lines EH, GK, DP in I, t, and V; in that perpendicular take Vr equal to $\dfrac{t\mathrm{GT}}{\mathrm{N}}$, or, which is the same thing, take Rr equal to $\dfrac{\mathrm{GTIE}}{\mathrm{N}}$; and the projectile in the

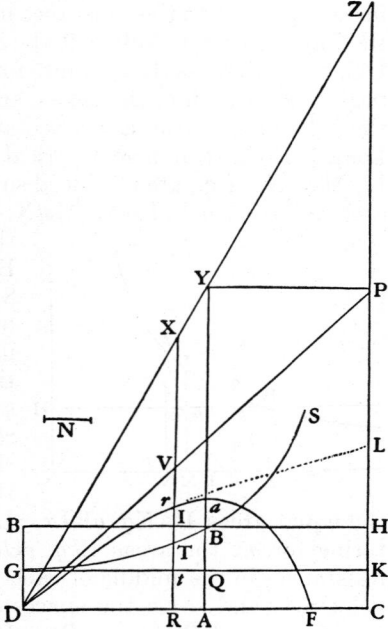

time DRTG will arrive at the point r, describing the curved line DraF, the locus of the point r; thence it will come to its greatest height a in the perpendicular AB; and afterwards ever approach to the asymptote PC. And its velocity in any point r will be as the tangent rL to the curve.   Q.E.I.

For $\mathrm{N} : \mathrm{QB} = \mathrm{DC} : \mathrm{CP} = \mathrm{DR} : \mathrm{RV}$,

and therefore RV is equal to $\dfrac{\mathrm{DR}\cdot\mathrm{QB}}{\mathrm{N}}$, and R$r$

$\left(\text{that is, RV}-\mathrm{V}r, \text{ or } \dfrac{\mathrm{DR}\cdot\mathrm{QB}-t\mathrm{GT}}{\mathrm{N}}\right)$ is equal to $\dfrac{\mathrm{DR}\cdot\mathrm{AB}-\mathrm{RDGT}}{\mathrm{N}}$. Now let

the time be represented by the area RDGT, and (by Laws, Cor. II) distinguish the motion of the body into two others, one of ascent, the other lateral. And since the resistance is as the motion, let that also be distinguished into two parts proportional and contrary to the parts of the motion: and therefore the length described by the lateral motion will be (by Prop. 2, Book II) as the line DR, and the height (by Prop. 3, Book II) as the area $\mathrm{DR}\cdot\mathrm{AB}-\mathrm{RDGT}$, that is, as the line R$r$. But in the very beginning of the motion the area RDGT is equal to the rectangle $\mathrm{DR}\cdot\mathrm{AQ}$, and therefore that line Rr $\left(\text{or } \dfrac{\mathrm{DR}\cdot\mathrm{AB}-\mathrm{DR}\cdot\mathrm{AQ}}{\mathrm{N}}\right)$

will then be to DR as $\mathrm{AB}-\mathrm{AQ}$ or QB to N, that is, as CP to DC; and therefore as the motion upwards to the motion lengthwise at the beginning. Since, therefore, Rr is always as the height, and DR always as the length, and Rr is to DR at the beginning as the height to the length, it follows, that Rr is always to DR as the height to the length; and therefore that the body will move in the line DraF, which is the locus of the point r.   Q.E.D.

Cor. I. Therefore Rr is equal to $\dfrac{\mathrm{DR}\cdot\mathrm{AB}}{\mathrm{N}} - \dfrac{\mathrm{RDGT}}{\mathrm{N}}$; and therefore if RT be produced to X so that RX may be equal to $\dfrac{DR \cdot AB}{N}$, that is, if the parallelogram ACPY be completed, and DY cutting CP in Z be drawn, and RT be produced till it meets DY in X; Xr will be equal to $\dfrac{RDGT}{N}$, and therefore proportional to the time.

COR. II. Whence if innumerable lines CR, or, which is the same, innumerable lines ZX, be taken in a geometrical progression ,there will be as many lines Xr in an arithmetical progression. And hence the curve DraF is easily delineated by the table of logarithms.

COR. III. If a parabola be constructed to the vertex D, and the diameter DG produced downwards, and its latus rectum is to 2DP as the whole resistance at the beginning of the motion to the gravitating force, the velocity with which the body ought to go from the place D, in the direction of the right line DP, so

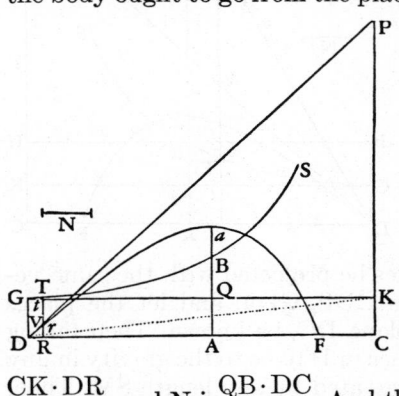

as in an uniform resisting medium to describe the curve DraF, will be the same as that with which it ought to go from the same place D in the direction of the same right line DP, so as to describe a parabola in a nonresisting medium. For the latus rectum of this parabola, at the very beginning of the motion, is $\dfrac{DV^2}{V r}$; and Vr is $\dfrac{t GT}{N}$ or $\dfrac{DR \cdot T t}{2N}$. But a right line which, if drawn, would touch the hyperbola GTS in G, is parallel to DK, and therefore Tt is $\dfrac{CK \cdot DR}{DC}$, and N is $\dfrac{QB \cdot DC}{CP}$. And therefore Vr is equal to $\dfrac{DR^2 \cdot CK \cdot CP}{2DC^2 \cdot QB}$, that is (because DR and DC, DV and DP are proportionals), to $\dfrac{DV^2 \cdot CK \cdot CP}{2DP^2 \cdot QB}$; and the latus rectum $\dfrac{DV^2}{V r}$ comes out $\dfrac{2DP^2 \cdot QB}{CK \cdot CP}$, that is (because QB and CK, DA and AC are proportionals), $\dfrac{2DP^2 \cdot DA}{AC \cdot CP}$, and therefore is to 2DP as DP$\cdot$DA to CP$\cdot$AC; that is, as the resistance to the gravity.   Q.E.D.

COR. IV. Hence if a body be projected from any place D with a given velocity, in the direction of a right line DP given by position, and the resistance of the medium, at the beginning of the motion, be given, the curve DraF, which that body will describe, may be found. For the velocity being given, the latus rectum of the parabola is given, as is well known. And taking 2DP to that latus rectum, as the force of gravity to the resisting force, DP is also given. Then cutting DC in A, so that CP$\cdot$AC may be to DP$\cdot$DA in the same ratio of the gravity to the resistance, the point A will be given. And hence the curve DraF is also given.

COR. V. And conversely, if the curve DraF be given, there will be given both the velocity of the body and the resistance of the medium in each of the places r. For the ratio of CP$\cdot$AC to DP$\cdot$DA being given, there is given both the resistance of the medium at the beginning of the motion, and the latus rectum of the parabola; and thence the velocity at the beginning of the motion is given also. Then from the length of the tangent rL there is given both the velocity proportional to it, and the resistance proportional to the velocity in any place r.

COR. VI. But since the length 2DP is to the latus rectum of the parabola as the gravity to the resistance in D, and, from the velocity augmented, the resistance is augmented in the same ratio, but the latus rectum of the parabola is augmented as the square of that ratio, it is plain that the length 2DP is augmented in that simple ratio only; and is therefore always proportional to the velocity; nor will it be augmented or diminished by the change of the angle CDP, unless the velocity be also changed.

COR. VII. Hence appears the method of determining the curve DraF nearly from the phenomena, and thence finding the resistance and velocity with which the body

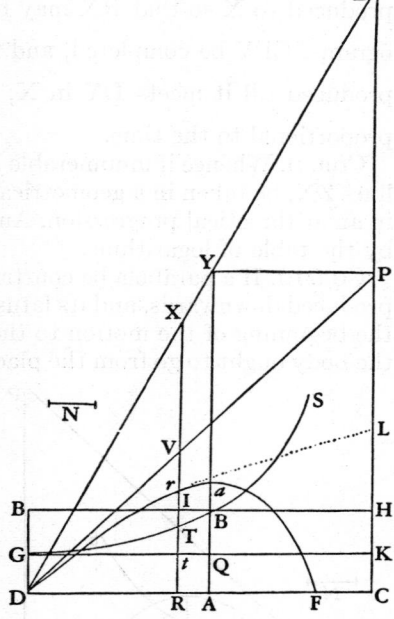

is projected. Let two similar and equal bodies be projected with the same velocity, from the place D, in different angles CDP, CDp; and let the places F, f, where they fall upon the horizontal plane DC, be known. Then taking any length for DP or Dp suppose the resistance in D to be to the gravity in any ratio whatsoever, and let that ratio be represented by any length SM. Then, by computation, from that assumed length DP, find the lengths DF, Df;

and from the ratio $\dfrac{Ff}{DF}$, found by calcu-lation, subtract the same ratio as found by experiment; and let the difference be represented by the perpendicular MN. Repeat the same a second and a third time, by assuming always a new ratio SM of the resistance to the gravity, and collecting a new difference MN. Draw the positive differences on one side of the right line SM, and the negative on the other side; and through the points N, N, N, draw a regular curve NNN, cutting the right line SMMM in X, and SX will be the true ratio of the resistance to the gravity, which was to be found. From this ratio the length DF is to be found by calculation; and a length, which is to the assumed length DP as the length DF known by experiment to the length DF just now found, will be the true length DP. This being known, you will have both the curved line D*ra*F which the body describes, and also the velocity and resistance of the body in each place.

SCHOLIUM

However, that the resistance of bodies is in the ratio of the velocity, is more a mathematical hypothesis than a physical one. In mediums void of all tenacity, the resistances made to bodies are as the square of the velocities. For by the action of a swifter body, a greater motion in proportion to a greater velocity is communicated to the same quantity of the medium in a less time; and in an equal time, by reason of a greater quantity of the disturbed medium, a motion is communicated as the square of the ratio greater; and the resistance (by Laws II and III) is as the motion communicated. Let us, therefore, see what motions arise from this law of resistance.

SECTION II

THE MOTION OF BODIES THAT ARE RESISTED AS THE SQUARE OF THEIR VELOCITIES

PROPOSITION 5. THEOREM 3

If a body is resisted as the square of its velocity, and moves by its innate force only through an homogeneous medium; and the times be taken in a geometrical progression, proceeding from less to greater terms: I say, that the velocities at the beginning of each of the times are in the same geometrical progression inversely; and that the spaces are equal, which are described in each of the times.

For since the resistance of the medium is proportional to the square of the velocity, and the decrement of the velocity is proportional to the resistance: if the time be divided into innumerable equal intervals, the squares of the velocities at the beginning of each of the times will be proportional to the dif-

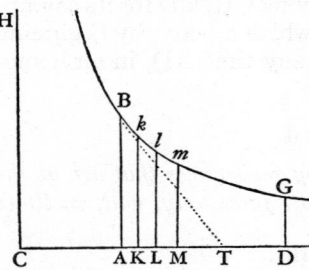

ferences of the same velocities. Let those intervals of time be AK, KL, LM, &c., taken in the right line CD; and erect the perpendiculars AB, K*k*, L*l*, M*m*, &c., meeting the hyperbola B*klm*G, described with the centre C, and the rectangular asymptotes CD, CH, in B, *k*, *l*, *m*, &c.; then AB will be to K*k* as CK to CA, and, by division, AB−K*k* to K*k* as AK to CA, and, alternately, AB−K*k* to AK as K*k* to CA; and therefore as AB·K*k* to AB·CA. Therefore since AK and AB·CA are given, AB−K*k* will be as AB·K*k*; and, lastly, when AB and K*k* coincide, as AB². And, by the like reasoning, K*k*−L*l*, L*l*−M*m*, &c., will be as K*k*², L*l*², &c. Therefore the squares of the lines AB, K*k*, L*l*, M*m*, &c., are as their differences; and, therefore, since the squares of the velocities were shown above to be as their differences, the progression of both will be alike. This being demonstrated it follows also that the areas described by these lines are in a like progression with the spaces described by these velocities. Therefore if the velocity at the beginning of the first time AK be represented by the line AB, and the velocity at the beginning of the second time KL by the line K*k*, and the length described in the first time by the area AK*k*B, all the following velocities will be represented by the following lines L*l*, M*m*, &c., and the lengths described by the areas K*l*, L*m*, &c. And, by composition, if the whole time be represented by AM, the sum of its parts, the whole length described will be represented by AM*m*B, the sum of its parts. Now conceive the time AM to be divided into the parts AK, KL, LM, &c., so that CA, CK, CL, CM, &c., may be in a geometrical progression; and those parts will be in the same progression, and the velocities AB, K*k*, L*l*, M*m*, &c., will be in the same progression inversely, and the spaces described A*k*, K*l*, L*m*, &c., will be equal.   Q.E.D.

COR. I. Hence it appears, that if the time be represented by any part AD of the asymptote, and the velocity in the beginning of the time by the ordinate AB, the velocity at the end of the time will be represented by the ordinate DG; and the whole space described by the adjacent hyperbolic area ABGD; and the space which any body can describe in the same time AD, with the first velocity AB, in a nonresisting medium, by the rectangle AB·AD.

COR. II. Hence the space described in a resisting medium is given, by taking it to the space described with the uniform velocity AB in a nonresisting medium, as the hyperbolic area ABGD to the rectangle AB·AD.

COR. III. The resistance of the medium is also given, by making it equal, in the very beginning of the motion, to an uniform centripetal force, which could generate, in a body falling through a nonresisting medium, the velocity AB in the time AC. For if BT be drawn touching the hyperbola in B, and meeting the asymptote in T, the right line AT will be equal to AC, and will express the time in which the first resistance, uniformly continued, may take away the whole velocity AB.

COR. IV. And thence is also given the proportion of this resistance to the force of gravity, or any other given centripetal force.

COR. V. And, conversely, if there is given the proportion of the resistance to any given centripetal force, the time AC is also given, in which a centripetal force equal to the resistance may generate any velocity as AB; and thence is given the point B, through which the hyperbola, having CH, CD for its asymptotes, is to be described; as also the space ABGD, which a body, by beginning its motion with that velocity AB, can describe in any time AD, in an homogeneous resisting medium.

PROPOSITION 6. THEOREM 4

Homogeneous and equal spherical bodies, opposed by resistances that are as the square of the velocities, and moving on by their innate force only, will, in times which are inversely as the velocities at the beginning, describe equal spaces, and lose parts of their velocities proportional to the wholes.

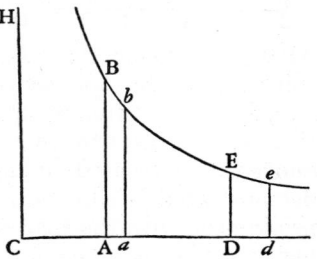

To the rectangular asymptotes CD, CH describe any hyperbola B*b*E*e*, cutting the perpendiculars AB, *ab*, DE, *de* in B, *b*, E, *e*; let the initial velocities be represented by the perpendiculars AB, DE, and the times by the lines A*a*, D*d*. Therefore as A*a* is to D*d*, so (by the hypothesis) is DE to AB, and so (from the nature of the hyperbola) is CA to CD; and, by composition, so is C*a* to C*d*. Therefore the areas AB*ba*, DE*ed*, that is, the spaces described, are equal among themselves, and the first velocities AB, DE are proportional to the last *ab*, *de*; and therefore, by subtraction, proportional to the parts of the velocities lost, AB−*ab*, DE−*de*. Q.E.D.

PROPOSITION 7. THEOREM 5

If spherical bodies are resisted as the squares of their velocities, in times which are directly as the first motions, and inversely as the first resistances, they will lose parts of their motions proportional to the wholes, and will describe spaces proportional to the product of those times and the first velocities.

For the parts of the motions lost are as the product of the resistances and times. Therefore, that those parts may be proportional to the wholes, the product of the resistance and time ought to be as the motion. Therefore the time will be as the motion directly and the resistance inversely. Therefore the intervals of the times being taken in that ratio, the bodies will always lose parts of their motions proportional to the wholes, and therefore will retain velocities always proportional to their first velocities. And because of the given ratio of the velocities, they will always describe spaces which are as the product of the first velocities and the times. Q.E.D.

COR. I. Therefore if bodies equally swift are resisted as the square of their diameters, homogeneous globes moving with any velocities whatsoever, by describing spaces proportional to their diameters, will lose parts of their motions proportional to the wholes. For the motion of each globe will be as the product of its velocity and mass, that is, as the product of the velocity and the cube of its diameter; the resistance (by supposition) will be as the product of the square of the diameter and the square of the velocity; and the time (by this Proposition) is in the former ratio directly, and in the latter inversely, that is, as the diameter directly and the velocity inversely; and therefore the space, which is proportional to the time and velocity, is as the diameter.

COR. II. If bodies equally swift are resisted as the $\frac{3}{2}$th power of their diameters, homogeneous globes, moving with any velocities whatsoever, by describing spaces that are as the $\frac{3}{2}$th power of the diameters, will lose parts of their motions proportional to the wholes.

COR. III. And universally, if equally swift bodies are resisted in the ratio of any power of the diameters, the spaces, in which homogeneous globes, moving with any velocity whatsoever, will lose parts of their motions proportional to the wholes, will be as the cubes of the diameters applied to that power. Let those diameters be D and E; and if the resistances, where the velocities are supposed equal, are as D^n and E^n; the spaces in which the globes, moving with any velocities whatsoever, will lose parts of their motions proportional to the wholes, will be as D^{3-n} and E^{3-n}. And therefore homogeneous globes, in describing spaces proportional to D^{3-n} and E^{3-n}, will retain their velocities in the same ratio to one another as at the beginning.

COR. IV. Now if the globes are not homogeneous, the space described by the denser globe must be augmented in the ratio of the density. For the motion, with an equal velocity, is greater in the ratio of the density, and the time (by this Proposition) is augmented in the ratio of motion directly, and the space described in the ratio of the time.

Cor. v. And if the globes move in different mediums, the space, in a medium which, other things being equal, resists the most, must be diminished in the ratio of the greater resistance. For the time (by this Proposition) will be diminished in the ratio of the augmented resistance, and the space in the ratio of the time.

Lemma 2

The moment of any genitum *is equal to the moments of each of the generating sides multiplied by the indices of the powers of those sides, and by their coefficients continually.*

I call any quantity a *genitum* which is not made by addition or subtraction of divers parts, but is generated or produced in arithmetic by the multiplication, division, or extraction of the root of any terms whatsoever; in geometry by the finding of contents and sides, or of the extremes and means of proportionals. Quantities of this kind are products, quotients, roots, rectangles, squares, cubes, square and cubic sides, and the like. These quantities I here consider as variable and indetermined, and increasing or decreasing, as it were, by a continual motion or flux; and I understand their momentary increments or decrements by the name of moments; so that the increments may be esteemed as added or affirmative moments; and the decrements as subtracted or negative ones. But take care not to look upon finite particles as such. Finite particles are not moments, but the very quantities generated by the moments. We are to conceive them as the just nascent principles of finite magnitudes. Nor do we in this Lemma regard the magnitude of the moments, but their first proportion, as nascent. It will be the same thing, if, instead of moments, we use either the velocities of the increments and decrements (which may also be called the motions, mutations, and fluxions of quantities), or any finite quantities proportional to those velocities. The coefficient of any generating side is the quantity which arises by applying the *genitum* to that side.

Wherefore the sense of the Lemma is, that if the moments of any quantities A, B, C, &c., increasing or decreasing by a continual flux, or the velocities of the mutations which are proportional to them, be called a, b, c, &c., the moment or mutation of the generated rectangle AB will be aB$+b$A; the moment of the generated content ABC will be aBC$+b$AC$+c$AB; and the moments of the generated powers A^2, A^3, A^4, $A^{1/2}$, $A^{3/2}$, $A^{1/3}$, $A^{2/3}$, A^{-1}, A^{-2}, $A^{-1/2}$ will be $2a$A, $3a$A^2, $4a$A^3, $\frac{1}{2}a$A$^{-1/2}$, $\frac{3}{2}a$A$^{1/2}$, $\frac{1}{3}a$A$^{-2/3}$, $\frac{2}{3}a$A$^{-1/3}$, $-a$A^{-2}, $-2a$A^{-3}, $-\frac{1}{2}a$A$^{-3/2}$ respectively; and, in general, that the moment of any power $A^{\frac{n}{m}}$ will be $\frac{n}{m} a$A$^{\frac{n-m}{m}}$. Also, that the moment of the generated quantity A^2B will be $2a$AB$+b$A^2; the moment of the generated quantity A^3B^{4}C^2 will be $3a$A^{2}B^{4}C$^2+$ $4b$A^{3}B^{3}C^2+2cA^{3}B^{4}C; and the moment of the generated quantity $\frac{A^3}{B^2}$ or A^3B^{-2} will be $3a$A^{2}B$^{-2}-2b$A^{3}B^{-3}; and so on. The Lemma is thus demonstrated.

Case 1. Any rectangle, as AB, augmented by a continual flux, when, as yet, there wanted of the sides A and B half their moments $\frac{1}{2}a$ and $\frac{1}{2}b$, was A$-\frac{1}{2}a$ into B$-\frac{1}{2}b$, or AB$-\frac{1}{2}a$ B$-\frac{1}{2}$b A$+\frac{1}{4}ab$; but as soon as the sides A and B are augmented by the other half-moments, the rectangle becomes A$+\frac{1}{2}a$ into B$+\frac{1}{2}b$, or AB$+\frac{1}{2}a$ B$+\frac{1}{2}$b A$+\frac{1}{4}ab$. From this rectangle subtract the former rectangle, and there will remain the excess aB$+b$A. Therefore with the whole increments a and b of the sides, the increment $a\text{B}+b\text{A}$ of the rectangle is generated.   Q.E.D.

CASE 2. Suppose AB always equal to G, and then the moment of the content ABC or GC (by CASE 1) will be $g\text{C}+c\text{G}$, that is (putting AB and $a\text{B}+b\text{A}$ for G and g), $a\text{BC}+b\text{AC}+c\text{AB}$. And the reasoning is the same for contents under ever so many sides.   Q.E.D.

CASE 3. Suppose the sides A, B, and C, to be always equal among themselves; and the moment $a\text{B}+b\text{A}$, of A^2, that is, of the rectangle AB, will be $2a\text{A}$; and the moment $a\text{BC}+b\text{AC}+c\text{AB}$ of A^3, that is, of the content ABC, will be $3a\text{A}^2$. And by the same reasoning the moment of any power A^n is $na\text{A}^{n-1}$.   Q.E.D.

CASE 4. Therefore since $\frac{1}{\text{A}}$ into A is 1, the moment of $\frac{1}{\text{A}}$ multiplied by A, together with $\frac{1}{\text{A}}$ multiplied by a, will be the moment of 1, that is, nothing. Therefore the moment of $\frac{1}{\text{A}}$, or of A^{-1}, is $\frac{-a}{\text{A}^2}$. And generally since $\frac{1}{\text{A}^n}$ into A^n is 1, the moment of $\frac{1}{\text{A}^n}$ multiplied by A^n together with $\frac{1}{\text{A}^n}$ into $na\text{A}^{n-1}$ will be nothing. And, therefore, the moment of $\frac{1}{\text{A}^n}$ or A^{-n} will be $-\frac{na}{\text{A}^{n+1}}$.   Q.E.D.

CASE 5. And since $\text{A}^{1/2}$ into $\text{A}^{1/2}$ is A, the moment of $\text{A}^{1/2}$ multiplied by $2\text{A}^{1/2}$ will be a (by Case 3); and, therefore, the moment of $\text{A}^{1/2}$ will be $\frac{a}{2\text{A}^{\frac{1}{2}}}$ or $\frac{1}{2}a\text{A}^{-1/2}$. And generally, putting $\text{A}^{\frac{m}{n}}$ equal to B, then A^m will be equal to B^n, and therefore $ma\text{A}^{m-1}$ equal to $nb\text{B}^{n-1}$, and $ma\text{A}^{-1}$ equal to $nb\text{B}^{-1}$, or $nb\text{A}^{-\frac{m}{n}}$; and therefore $\frac{m}{n}a\text{A}^{\frac{n-m}{n}}$ is equal to b, that is, equal to the moment of $\text{A}^{\frac{m}{n}}$.   Q.E.D.

CASE 6. Therefore the moment of any generated quantity A^mB^n is the moment of A^m multiplied by B^n, together with the moment of B^n multiplied by A^m, that is, $ma\text{A}^{m-1}\text{B}^n+nb\text{B}^{n-1}\text{A}^m$; and that whether the indices m and n of the powers be whole numbers or fractions, affirmative or negative. And the reasoning is the same for higher powers.   Q.E.D.

COR. I. Hence in quantities continually proportional, if one term is given, the moments of the rest of the terms will be as the same terms multiplied by the number of intervals between them and the given term. Let A, B, C, D, E, F be continually proportional; then if the term C is given, the moments of the rest of the terms will be among themselves as -2A, $-\text{B}$, D, 2E, 3F.

COR. II. And if in four proportionals the two means are given, the moments of the extremes will be as those extremes. The same is to be understood of the sides of any given rectangle.

COR. III. And if the sum or difference of two squares is given, the moments of the sides will be inversely as the sides.

SCHOLIUM

In a letter of mine to Mr. J. Collins, dated December 10, 1672, having described a method of tangents, which I suspected to be the same with Sluse's method, which at that time was not made public, I added these words: *This is one particular, or rather a Corollary, of a general method, which extends itself, without any troublesome calculation, not only to the drawing of tangents to any curved lines, whether geometrical or mechanical or in any manner respecting right lines or other curves, but also to the resolving other abstruser kinds of problems about the crookedness, areas, lengths, centres of gravity of curves, &c.; nor is it (as Hudden's method* de maximis et minimis) *limited to equations which are free from surd quantities. This method I have interwoven with that other of working in equations, by reducing them to infinite series.* So far that letter. And these last words relate to a treatise I composed on that subject in the year 1671. The foundation of that general method is contained in the preceding Lemma.

PROPOSITION 8. THEOREM 6

If a body in an uniform medium, being uniformly acted upon by the force of gravity, ascends or descends in a right line; and the whole space described be divided into equal parts, and in the beginning of each of the parts (by adding or subtracting the resisting force of the medium to or from the force of gravity, when the body ascends or descends) you derive the absolute forces: I say, that those absolute forces are in a geometrical progression.

Let the force of gravity be represented by the given line AC; the force of resistance by the indefinite line AK; the absolute force in the descent of the body by the difference KC; the velocity of the body by a line AP, which shall be a mean proportional between AK and AC, and therefore as the square root of the resistance; the increment of the resistance made in a given interval of time by the short line KL, and the contemporaneous increment of the velocity by the short line PQ; and with the centre C, and rectangular asymptotes CA, CH, describe any hyperbola BNS meeting the erected perpendiculars AB, KN, LO in B, N, and O. Because AK is as AP², the moment KL

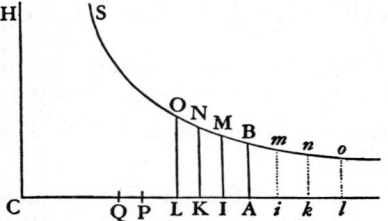

of the one will be as the moment 2AP·PQ of the other, that is, as AP·KC; for the increment PQ of the velocity is (by Law II) proportional to the generating force KC. Let the ratio of KL be multiplied by the ratio KN, and the rectangle KL·KN will become as AP·KC·KN; that is (because the rectangle KC·KN is given), as AP. But the ultimate ratio of the hyperbolic area KNOL to the rectangle KL·KN becomes, when the points K and L coincide, the ratio of equality. Therefore that hyperbolic evanescent area is as AP. Therefore the whole hyperbolic area ABOL is composed of intervals KNOL which are always proportional to the velocity AP; and therefore is itself proportional to the space described with that velocity. Let that area be now divided into equal parts, as ABMI, IMNK, KNOL, &c., and the absolute forces AC, IC, KC, LC, &c., will be in a geometrical progression. Q.E.D. And by a like reasoning, in the ascent of the body, taking, on the contrary side of the point A, the equal areas AB*mi*, *imnk, knol*, &c., it will appear that the absolute forces AC, *i*C, *k*C, *l*C, &c., are continually proportional. Therefore if all the spaces in the ascent and descent are taken equal, all the absolute forces *l*C, *k*C, *i*C, AC, IC, KC, LC, &c., will be continually proportional.   Q.E.D.

COR. I. Hence if the space described be represented by the hyperbolic area ABNK, the force of gravity, the velocity of the body, and the resistance of the medium, may be represented by the lines AC, AP, and AK respectively; and conversely.

COR. II. And the greatest velocity which the body can ever acquire in an infinite descent will be represented by the line AC.

COR. III. Therefore if the resistance of the medium answering to any given velocity be known, the greatest velocity will be found, by taking it to that given velocity, as the square root of the ratio which the force of gravity bears to that known resistance of the medium.

PROPOSITION 9. THEOREM 7

Supposing what is above demonstrated, I say, that if the tangents of the angles of the sector of a circle, and of an hyperbola, be taken proportional to the velocities, the radius being of a fit magnitude, all the time of the ascent to the highest place will be as the sector of the circle, and all the time of descending from the highest place as the sector of the hyperbola.

To the right line AC, which expresses the force of gravity, let AD be drawn perpendicular and equal. From the centre D, with the semidiameter AD describe as well the quadrant A*t*E of a circle, as the rectangular hyperbola AVZ, whose axis is AK, principal vertex A, and asymptote DC. Let D*p*, DP

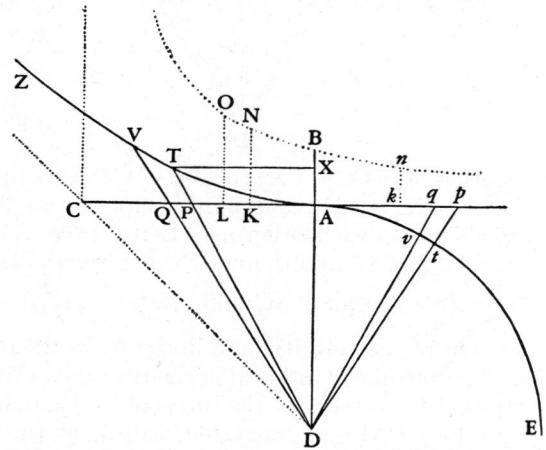

be drawn; and the circular sector A*t*D will be as all the time of the ascent to the highest place; and the hyperbolic sector ATD as all the time of descent from the highest place; if so be that the tangents A*p*, AP of those sectors be as the velocities.

CASE 1. Draw D*vq* cutting off the moments or least intervals *t*D*v* and *q*D*p*, described in the same time, of the sector AD*t* and of the triangle AD*p*. Since those intervals (because of the common angle D) are as the square of the sides, the interval *t*D*v* will be as $\frac{qDp \cdot tD^2}{pD^2}$, that is (because *t*D is given), as $\frac{qDp}{pD^2}$. But pD^2 is $AD^2 + Ap^2$, that is, $AD^2 + AD \cdot Ak$, or $AD \cdot Ck$; and qDp is $\frac{1}{2}AD \cdot pq$. Therefore *t*D*v*, the interval of the sector, is as $\frac{pq}{Ck}$; that is, directly as the least decrement *pq* of the velocity, and inversely as the force C*k* which diminishes the velocity; and therefore as the interval of time answering to the decrement of the velocity. And, by composition, the sum of all the intervals tDv in the sector ADt will be as the sum of the intervals of time answering to each of the lost intervals pq of the decreasing velocity Ap, till that velocity, being diminished into nothing, vanishes; that is, the whole sector ADt is as the whole time of ascent to the highest place.   Q.E.D.

CASE 2. Draw DQV cutting off the least intervals TDV and PDQ of the sector DAV, and of the triangle DAQ; and these intervals will be to each other as DT^2 to DP^2, that is (if TX and AP are parallel), as DX^2 to DA^2 or TX^2 to

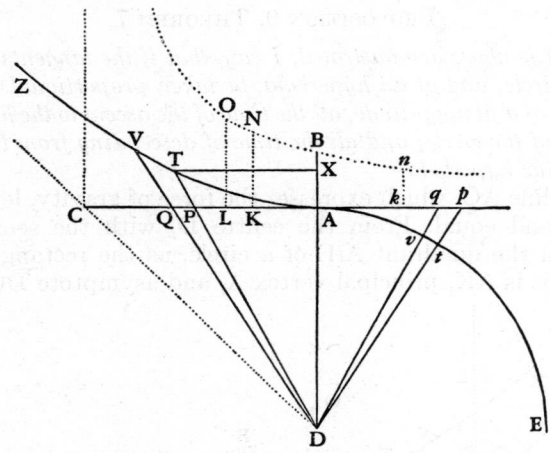

AP^2; and, by subtraction, as $DX^2 - TX^2$ to $DA^2 - AP^2$. But, from the nature of the hyperbola, $DX^2 - TX^2$ is AD^2; and, by the supposition, AP^2 is $AD \cdot AK$. Therefore the intervals are to each other as AD^2 to $AD^2 - AD \cdot AK$; that is, as AD to $AD - AK$ or AC to CK; and therefore the interval TDV of the sector is $\dfrac{PDQ \cdot AC}{CK}$; and therefore (because AC and AD are given) as $\dfrac{PQ}{CK}$; that is, directly as the increment of the velocity, and inversely as the force generating the increment; and therefore as the interval of the time answering to the increment. And, by composition, the sum of the intervals of time, in which all the intervals PQ of the velocity AP are generated, will be as the sum of the intervals of the sector ATD; that is, the whole time will be as the whole sector.
                    Q.E.D.

COR. I. Hence if AB be equal to a fourth part of AC, the space which a body will describe by falling in any time will be to the space which the body could describe, by moving uniformly on in the same time with its greatest velocity AC, as the area ABNK, which expresses the space described in falling to the area ATD, which expresses the time. For since
$$AC : AP = AP : AK,$$
and by Cor. I, Lem. 2, of this Book,
$$LK : PQ = 2AK : AP = 2AP : AC,$$
therefore $LK : \tfrac{1}{2}PQ = AP : \tfrac{1}{4}AC$ or AB,
and since $KN : AC$ or $AD = AD : CK$,
multiplying together corresponding terms,
$$LKNO : DPQ = AP : CK.$$

As shown above,

$$DPQ : DTV = CK : AC.$$

Hence, $$LKNO : DTV = AP : AC;$$

that is, as the velocity of the falling body to the greatest velocity which the body by falling can acquire. Since, therefore, the moments LKNO and DTV of the areas ABNK and ATD are as the velocities, all the parts of those areas generated in the same time will be as the spaces described in the same time; and therefore the whole areas ABNK and ADT, generated from the beginning, will be as the whole spaces described from the beginning of the descent. Q.E.D.

COR. II. The same is true also of the space described in the ascent. That is to say, that all that space is to the space described in the same time, with the uniform velocity AC, as the area AB*nk* is to the sector AD*t*.

COR. III. The velocity of the body, falling in the time ATD, is to the velocity which it would acquire in the same time in a nonresisting space, as the triangle APD to the hyperbolic sector ATD. For the velocity in a nonresisting medium would be as the time ATD, and in a resisting medium is as AP, that is, as the triangle APD. And those velocities, at the beginning of the descent, are equal among themselves, as well as those areas ATD, APD.

COR. IV. By the same argument, the velocity in the ascent is to the velocity with which the body in the same time, in a nonresisting space, would lose all its motion of ascent, as the triangle A*p*D to the circular sector A*t*D; or as the right line A*p* to the arc A*t*.

COR. V. Therefore the time in which a body, by falling in a resisting medium, would acquire the velocity AP, is to the time in which it would acquire its greatest velocity AC, by falling in a nonresisting space, as the sector ADT to the triangle ADC; and the time in which it would lose its velocity A*p*, by ascending in a resisting medium, is to the time in which it would lose the same velocity by ascending in a nonresisting space, as the arc A*t* to its tangent A*p*.

COR. VI. Hence from the given time there is given the space described in the ascent or descent. For the greatest velocity of a body descending *in infinitum* is given (by Cor. II and III, Theor. 6, of this book); and thence the time is given in which a body would acquire that velocity by falling in nonresisting space. Taking the sector ADT or AD*t* to the triangle ADC in the ratio of the given time to the time just found, there will be given both the velocity AP or A*p*, and the area ABNK or AB*nk*, which is to the sector ADT, or AD*t* as the space sought to that which would, in the given time, be uniformly described with that greatest velocity found just before.

COR. VII. And by going backwards, from the given space of ascent or descent AB*nk* or ABNK, there will be given the time AD*t* or ADT.

PROPOSITION 10. PROBLEM 3

Suppose the uniform force of gravity to tend directly to the plane of the horizon, and the resistance to be as the product of the density of the medium and the square of the velocity: it is proposed to find the density of the medium in each place, which shall make the body move in any given curved line, the velocity of the body, and the resistance of the medium in each place.

Let PQ be a plane perpendicular to the plane of the scheme itself; PFHQ a curved line meeting that plane in the points P and Q; G, H, I ,K four places of the body going on in this curve from F to Q; and GB, HC, ID, KE four parallel ordinates let fall from these points to the horizon, and standing on the horizontal line PQ at the points B, C, D, E; and let the distances BC, CD, DE of the ordinates be equal among themselves. From the points G and H let the right lines GL, HN be drawn touching the curve in G and H, and meeting the ordinates CH, DI, produced upwards, in L and N; and complete the parallelogram HCDM. And the times in which the body describes the arcs GH, HI, will be as the square root of the altitudes LH, NI, which the bodies would describe in those times, by falling from the tangents; and the velocities will be directly as the lengths described GH, HI, and inversely as the times. Let the times be represented by T and t,

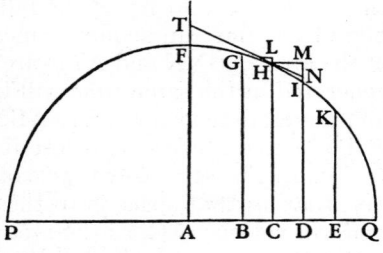

and the velocities by $\dfrac{GH}{T}$ and $\dfrac{HI}{t}$; and the decrement of the velocity produced

in the time t will be represented by $\dfrac{GH}{T} - \dfrac{HI}{t}$. This decrement arises from the

resistance which retards the body, and from the gravity which accelerates it. Gravity, in a falling body, which in its fall describes the space NI, produces a velocity with which it would be able to describe twice that space in the same

time, as Galileo hath demonstrated; that is, the velocity $\dfrac{2NI}{t}$: but if the body

describes the arc HI, it augments that arc only by the length HI−HN or

$\dfrac{MI \cdot NI}{HI}$; and therefore generates only the velocity $\dfrac{2MI \cdot NI}{t \cdot HI}$. Let this velocity

be added to the before-mentioned decrement, and we shall have the decrement

of the velocity arising from the resistance alone, that is, $\dfrac{GH}{T} - \dfrac{HI}{t} + \dfrac{2MI \cdot NI}{t \cdot HI}$.

Therefore since, in the same time, the action of gravity generates, in a falling

body, the velocity $\dfrac{2NI}{t}$, the resistance will be to the gravity as

$$\frac{GH}{T} - \frac{HI}{t} + \frac{2MI \cdot NI}{t \cdot HI} \text{ to } \frac{2NI}{t} \text{ or as } \frac{t \cdot GH}{T} - HI + \frac{2MI \cdot NI}{HI} \text{ to } 2NI.$$

Now, for the abscissas CB, CD, CE, put −o, o, 2o. For the ordinate CH put P; and for MI put any series $Qo+Ro^2+So^3+$, &c. And all the terms of the series after the first, that is, Ro^2+So^3+, &c., will be NI; and the ordinates DI, EK, and BG will be $P-Qo-Ro^2-So^3-$, &c., $P-2Qo-4Ro^2-8So^3-$, &c., and $P+Qo-Ro^2+So^3-$, &c., respectively. And by squaring the differences of the ordinates BG−CH and CH−DI, and to the squares thence produced adding the squares of BC and CD themselves, you will have $oo+QQoo-2QRo^3+$, &c., and $oo+QQoo+2QRo^3+$, &c., the squares of the arcs GH, HI;

whose roots $o\sqrt{(1+QQ)} - \dfrac{QRoo}{\sqrt{(1+QQ)}}$ and $o\sqrt{(1+QQ)} + \dfrac{QRoo}{\sqrt{(1+QQ)}}$ are the

arcs GH and HI. Moreover, if from the ordinate CH there be subtracted half the sum of the ordinates BG and DI, and from the ordinate DI there be subtracted half the sum of the ordinates CH and EK, there will remain Roo and $Roo+3So^3$, the versed sines of the arcs GI and HK. And these are proportional to the short lines LH and NI, and therefore are as the squares of the infinitely small times T and t: and thence the ratio $\frac{t}{T}$ varies as the square root of $\frac{R+3So}{R}$

or $\frac{R+\frac{3}{2}So}{R}$; and $\frac{t\times GH}{T}-HI+\frac{2MI\times NI}{HI}$ by substituting the values of $\frac{t}{T}$, GH,

HI, MI, and NI just found, becomes $\frac{3Soo}{2R}$. $\sqrt{(1+QQ)}$. And since 2NI is 2Roo,

the resistance will be now to the gravity as $\frac{3Soo}{2R}\sqrt{(1+QQ)}$ to 2Roo, that is, as

$3S\sqrt{(1+QQ)}$ to 4RR.

And the velocity will be such, that a body going off therewith from any place H, in the direction of the tangent HN, would describe, in a vacuum, a parabola, whose diameter is HC, and its latus rectum $\frac{HN^2}{NI}$ or $\frac{1+QQ}{R}$.

And the resistance is as the product of the density of the medium and the

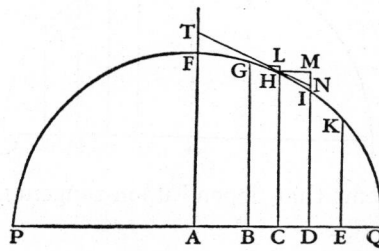

square of the velocity; and therefore the density of the medium is directly as the resistance, and inversely as the square of the velocity; that is, directly as $\frac{3S\sqrt{(1+QQ)}}{4RR}$ and inversely as $\frac{1+QQ}{R}$; that is, as $\frac{S}{R\sqrt{(1+QQ)}}$.   Q.E.I.

COR. I. If the tangent HN be produced both ways, so as to meet any ordinate AF in T, $\frac{HT}{AC}$ will be equal to $\sqrt{(1+QQ)}$, and therefore in what has gone before may be put for $\sqrt{(1+QQ)}$. By this means the resistance will be to the gravity as $3S\cdot HT$ to $4RR\cdot AC$; the velocity will be as $\frac{HT}{AC\sqrt{R}}$, and the density of the medium will be as $\frac{S\cdot AC}{R\cdot HT}$.

COR. II. And hence, if the curved line PFHQ be defined by the relation between the base or abscissa AC and the ordinate CH, as is usual, and the value of the ordinate be resolved into a converging series, the Problem will be expeditiously solved by the first terms of the series; as in the following Examples.

EXAM. 1. Let the line PFHQ be a semicircle described upon the diameter PQ; to find the density of the medium that shall make a projectile move in that line.

Bisect the diameter PQ in A; and call AQ, n; AC, a; CH, e; and CD, o; then DI^2 or $AQ^2-AD^2=nn-aa-2ao-oo$, or $ee-2ao-oo$; and the root being extracted by our method, will give

$$DI=e-\frac{ao}{e}-\frac{oo}{2e}-\frac{aaoo}{2e^3}-\frac{ao^3}{2e^3}-\frac{a^3o^3}{2e^5},\ \&c.$$

Here put nn for $ee+aa$, and DI will become $=ee-\frac{ao}{e}-\frac{nnoo}{2e^3}-\frac{anno^3}{2e^5}-,\&c.$

In such a series I distinguish the successive terms after this manner: I call that the first term in which the infinitely small quantity o is not found; the second, in which that quantity is of one dimension only; the third, in which it arises to two dimensions; the fourth, in which it is of three; and so *ad infinitum*. And the first term, which here is e, will always denote the length of the ordinate CH, erected at the starting point of the indefinite quantity o. The second term, which here is $\dfrac{ao}{e}$, will denote the difference between CH and DN; that is, the short line MN which is cut off by completing the parallelogram HCDM; and therefore always determines the position of the tangent HN; as, in this case, by taking $\text{MN} : \text{HM} = \dfrac{ao}{e} : o = a : e$. The third term, which here is $\dfrac{nnoo}{2e^3}$, will represent the short line IN, which lies between the tangent and the curve; and therefore determines the angle of contact IHN, or the curvature which the curved line has in H. If that short line IN is of a finite magnitude, it will be expressed by the third term, together with those that follow *in infinitum*. But if that short line be diminished *in infinitum*, the terms following become infinitely less than the third term, and therefore may be neglected. The fourth term determines the variation of the curvature; the fifth, the variation of the variation; and so on. From this, by the way, appears the use, not to be disdained, which may be

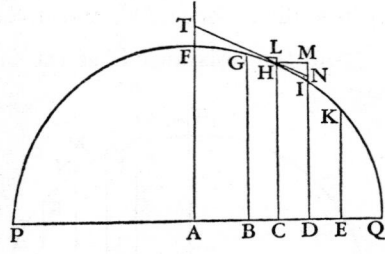

made of these series in the solution of problems that depend upon tangents, and the curvature of curves.

Now compare the series

$$e - \frac{ao}{e} - \frac{nnoo}{2e^3} - \frac{anno^3}{2e^5} - \&c.,$$

with the series

$$P - Qo - Roo - So^3 - \&c.,$$

and for P, Q, R and S, put $e, \dfrac{a}{e}, \dfrac{nn}{2e^3}$ and $\dfrac{ann}{2e^5}$, and for $\sqrt{(1+QQ)}$ put $\sqrt{\left(1 + \dfrac{aa}{ee}\right)}$ or $\dfrac{n}{e}$; and the density of the medium will come out as $\dfrac{a}{ne}$; that is (because n is given), as $\dfrac{a}{e}$ or $\dfrac{\text{AC}}{\text{CH}}$, that is, as that length of the tangent HT, which is terminated at the semidiameter AF standing perpendicularly on PQ: and the resistance will be to the gravity as $3a$ to $2n$, that is, as 3AC to the diameter PQ of the circle; and the velocity will be as $\sqrt{\text{CH}}$. Therefore if the body goes from the place F, with a due velocity, in the direction of a line parallel to PQ, and the density of the medium in each of the places H is as the length of the tangent HT, and the resistance also in any place H is to the force of gravity as 3AC to PQ, that body will describe the quadrant FHQ of a circle.   Q.E.I.

But if the same body should go from the place P, in the direction of a line perpendicular to PQ, and should begin to move in an arc of the semicircle PFQ, we must take AC or a on the contrary side of the centre A; and therefore its sign must be changed, and we must put $-a$ for $+a$. Then the density of the medium would come out as $-\dfrac{a}{e}$. But Nature does not admit of a negative density, that is, a density which accelerates the motion of bodies; and therefore it cannot naturally come to pass that a body by ascending from P should describe the quadrant PF of a circle. To produce such an effect, a body ought to be accelerated by an impelling medium, and not impeded by a resisting one.

EXAM. 2. Let the line PFQ be a parabola, having its axis AF perpendicular to the horizon PQ; to find the density of the medium, which will make a projectile move in that line.

From the nature of the parabola, the rectangle $-$PD·DQ is equal to the rectangle under the ordinate DI and some given right line; that is, if that right line be called b; PC, a; PQ, c; CH, e; and CD, o; the rectangle

$$(a+o)(c-a-o)=ac-aa-2ao+co-oo=b\cdot\text{DI};$$

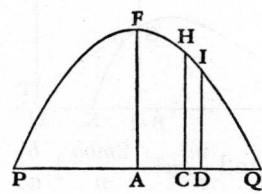

therefore
$$\text{DI}=\frac{ac-aa}{b}+\frac{c-2a}{b}\cdot o-\frac{oo}{b}.$$

Now the second term $\dfrac{c-2a}{b}o$ of this series is to be put for Qo, and the third term $\dfrac{oo}{b}$ for Roo. But since there are no more terms, the coefficient S of the fourth term will vanish; and therefore the quantity $\dfrac{\text{S}}{\text{R}\sqrt{(1+\text{QQ})}}$, to which the density of the medium is proportional, will be nothing. There-fore, where the medium is of no density, the projectile will move in a parabola; as Galileo hath heretofore demonstrated.   Q.E.I.

EXAM. 3. Let the line AGK be an hyperbola, having its asymptote NX per-pendicular to the horizontal plane AK: to find the density of the medium that will make a projectile move in that line.

Let MX be the other asymptote, meeting the ordinate DG produced in V; and from the nature of the hyperbola, the rectangle of XV into VG will be given. There is also given the ratio of DN to VX, and therefore the rectangle of DN into VG is given. Let that be bb; and, completing the parallelogram DNXZ, let BN be called a; BD, o; NX, c; and let the given ratio of VZ to ZX or DN be $\dfrac{m}{n}$. Then DN will be equal to $a-o$, VG equal to $\dfrac{bb}{a-o}$, VZ equal to $\dfrac{m}{n}\cdot(a-o)$ and GD or NX$-$VZ$-$VG equal to

$$c-\frac{m}{n}a+\frac{m}{n}o-\frac{bb}{a-o}.$$

Let the term $\dfrac{bb}{a-o}$ be resolved into the con-verging series

$$\frac{bb}{a}+\frac{bb}{aa}o+\frac{bb}{a^3}oo+\frac{bb}{a^4}o^3,\ \&c.,$$

and GD will become equal to

$$c-\frac{m}{n}a-\frac{bb}{a}+\frac{m}{n}o-\frac{bb}{aa}o-\frac{bb}{a^3}o^2-\frac{bb}{a^4}o^3,\ \&c.$$

The second term $\dfrac{m}{n}o-\dfrac{bb}{aa}o$ of this series is to be used for Qo; the third $\dfrac{bb}{a^3}o^2$, with its sign changed for Ro^2; and the fourth $\dfrac{bb}{a^4}o^3$, with

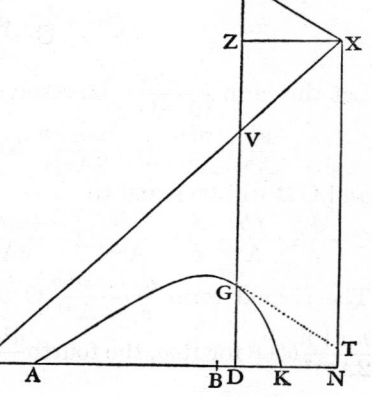

its sign changed also for So^3, and their coefficients $\dfrac{m}{n}-\dfrac{bb}{aa}$, $\dfrac{bb}{a^3}$, and $\dfrac{bb}{a^4}$ are to be put for Q, R, and S in the former rule. Which being done, the density of the medium will come out as

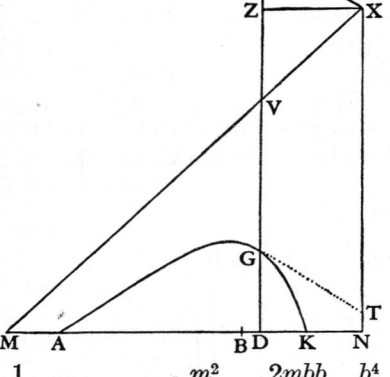

$$\frac{\dfrac{bb}{a^4}}{\dfrac{bb}{a^3}\sqrt{\left(1+\dfrac{mm}{nn}-\dfrac{2mbb}{naa}+\dfrac{b^4}{a^4}\right)}}$$

or

$$\frac{1}{\sqrt{\left(aa+\dfrac{mm}{nn}aa-\dfrac{2mbb}{n}+\dfrac{b^4}{aa}\right)}},$$

that is, if in VZ you take VY equal to VG, as $\dfrac{1}{XY}$. For aa and $\dfrac{m^2}{n^2}a^2-\dfrac{2mbb}{n}+\dfrac{b^4}{aa}$ are the squares of XZ and ZY. But the ratio of the resistance to gravity is found to be that of 3XY to 2YG; and the velocity is that with which the body would describe a parabola, whose vertex is G, diameter DG, latus rectum $\dfrac{XY^2}{VG}$. Suppose, therefore, that the densities of the medium in each of the places G are inversely as the distances XY, and that the resistance in any place G is to the gravity as 3XY to 2YG; and a body let go from the place A, with a due velocity, will describe that hyperbola AGK.   Q.E.I.

EXAM. 4. Suppose, indefinitely, the line AGK to be an hyperbola described with the centre X, and the asymptotes MX, NX, so that, having constructed the rectangle XZDN, whose side ZD cuts the hyperbola in G and its asymptote in V, VG may be inversely as any power DN^n of the line ZX or DN, whose index is the number n: to find the density of the medium in which a projected body will describe this curve.

For BN, BD, NX, put A, O, C, respectively, and let VZ be to XZ or DN as d to e, and VG be equal to $\dfrac{bb}{DN^n}$; then DN will be equal to A$-$O, VG$=\dfrac{bb}{(A-C)^n}$, VZ$=\dfrac{d}{e}(A-O)$ and GD or NX$-$VZ$-$VG equal to

$$C-\frac{d}{e}A+\frac{d}{e}O-\frac{bb}{(A-O)^n}.$$

Let the term $\dfrac{bb}{(A-O)^n}$ be resolved into an infinite series

$$\frac{bb}{A^n}+\frac{nbb}{A^{n+1}}\cdot O+\frac{nn+n}{2A^{n+2}}\cdot bbO^2+\frac{n^3+3nn+2n}{6A^{n+3}}\cdot bbO^3, \&c.,$$

and GD will be equal to

$$C-\frac{d}{e}A-\frac{bb}{A^n}+\frac{d}{e}O-\frac{nbb}{A^{n+1}}O-\frac{+nn+n}{2A^{n+2}}bbO^2-\frac{+n^3+3nn+2n}{6A^{n+3}}bbO^3, \&c.$$

The second term $\dfrac{d}{e}O-\dfrac{nbb}{A^{n+1}}O$ of this series is to be used for Qo, the third $\dfrac{nn+n}{2A^{n+2}}bbO^2$ for Roo, the fourth $\dfrac{n^3+3nn+2n}{6A^{n+3}}bbO$ for So^3. And thence the density of the medium $\dfrac{S}{R\sqrt{(1+QQ)}}$, in any place G, will be

$$\dfrac{n+2}{3\sqrt{\left(A^2+\dfrac{dd}{ee}A^2-\dfrac{2dnbb}{eA^n}A+\dfrac{nnb^4}{A^{2n}}\right)}},$$

and therefore if in VZ you take VY equal to $n\cdot VG$, that density is reciprocally as XY. For A^2 and $\dfrac{dd}{ee}A^2-\dfrac{2dnbb}{eA^n}A+\dfrac{nnb^4}{A^{2n}}$ are the squares of XZ and ZY. But

the resistance in the same place G is to the force of gravity as $3S\cdot\dfrac{XY}{A}$ to 4RR,

that is, as XY to $\dfrac{2nn+2n}{n+2}$ VG. And the velocity there is the same wherewith

the projected body would move in a parabola, whose vertex is G, diameter GD, and latus rectum $\dfrac{1+QQ}{R}$ or $\dfrac{2XY^2}{(nn+n)\cdot VG}$.   Q.E.I.

SCHOLIUM

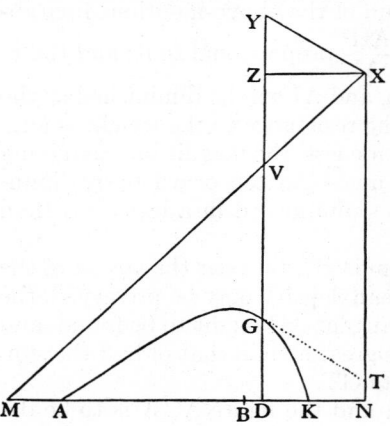

In the same manner that the density of the medium comes out to be as $\dfrac{S\cdot AC}{R\cdot HT}$, in Cor. I, if the resistance is put as any power V^n of the velocity V, the density of the medium will come out to be as

$$\dfrac{S}{R^{\frac{4-n}{2}}}\cdot\left(\dfrac{AC}{HT}\right)^{n-1}.$$

And therefore, if a curve can be found, such that the ratio of $\dfrac{S}{R^{\frac{4-n}{2}}}$ to $\left(\dfrac{HT}{AC}\right)^{n-1}$, or of $\dfrac{S^2}{R^{4-n}}$ to $(1+QQ)^{n-1}$ may be given; the

body, in an uniform medium, whose resistance is as the power V^n of the velocity V, will move in this curve. But let us return to more simple curves.

Since there can be no motion in a parabola except in a nonresisting medium, but in the hyperbolas here described it is produced by a continual resistance; it is evident that the line which a projectile describes in an uniformly resisting medium approaches nearer to these hyperbolas than to a parabola. That line is certainly of the hyperbolic kind, but about the vertex it is more distant from the asymptotes, and in the parts remote from the vertex draws nearer to them than these hyperbolas here described. The difference, however, is not so great between the one and the other but that these latter may be commodiously enough used in practice instead of the former. And perhaps these may prove more useful than an hyperbola that is more accurate, and at the same time more complex. They may be made use of, then, in this manner.

Complete the parallelogram XYGT, and the right line GT will touch the hyperbola in G, and therefore the density of the medium in G is inversely as the tangent GT, and the velocity there as $\sqrt{\dfrac{GT^2}{GV}}$; and the resistance is to the force of gravity as GT to $\dfrac{2nn+2n}{n+2} \cdot$ GV.

Therefore if a body projected from the place A, in the direction of the right line AH, describes the hyperbola AGK, and AH produced meets the asymptote NX in H, and AI drawn parallel to it meets the other asymptote MX in I; the density of the medium in A will be inversely as AH and the velocity of the body as $\sqrt{\dfrac{AH^2}{AI}}$, and the resistance there to the force of gravity as AH to $\dfrac{2nn+2n}{n+2} \cdot$ AI. Hence the following Rules are deduced.

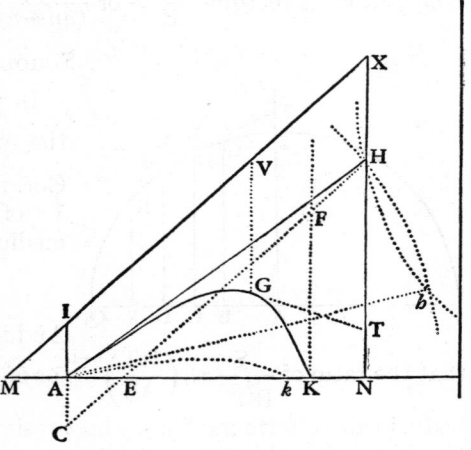

RULE 1. If the density of the medium at A, and the velocity with which the body is projected, remain the same, and the angle NAH be changed; the lengths AH, AI, HX will remain. Therefore if those lengths, in any one case, are found, the hyperbola may afterwards be easily determined from any given angle NAH.

RULE 2. If the angle NAH, and the density of the medium at A, remain the same, and the velocity with which the body is projected be changed, the length AH will continue the same; and AI will be changed inversely as the square of the velocity.

RULE 3. If the angle NAH, the velocity of the body at A, and the accelerative gravity remain the same, and the proportion of the resistance at A to the motive gravity be augmented in any ratio; the proportion of AH to AI will be augmented in the same ratio, the latus rectum of the above-mentioned parabola remaining the same, and also the length $\dfrac{AH^2}{AI}$ proportional to it; and therefore AH will be diminished in the same ratio, and AI will be diminished as the square of that ratio. But the proportion of the resistance to the weight is augmented, when either the specific gravity is made less, the magnitude remaining equal, or when the density of the medium is made greater, or when, by diminishing the magnitude, the resistance becomes diminished in a less ratio than the weight.

RULE 4. Because the density of the medium is greater near the vertex of the hyperbola than it is in the place A, that a mean density may be preserved, the ratio of the least of the tangents GT to the tangent AH ought to be found, and the density in A augmented in a ratio a little greater than that of half the sum of those tangents to the least of the tangents GT.

RULE 5. If the lengths AH, AI are given, and the figure AGK is to be de-

scribed, produce HN to X, so that HX may be to AI as $n+1$ to 1; and with
the centre X, and the asymptotes MX, NX, describe an hyperbola through the
point A, such that AI may be to any of the lines VG as XV^n to XI^n.

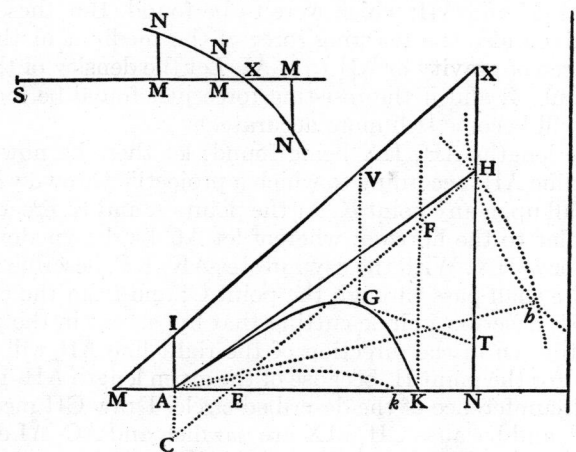

RULE 6. By how much the greater the number n is, so much the more accurate are these hyperbolas in the ascent of the body from A, and less accurate
in its descent to K; and conversely. The conic hyperbola keeps a mean ratio
between these, and is more simple than the rest. Therefore if the hyperbola be
of this kind, and you are to find the point K, where the projected body falls
upon any right line AN passing through the point A, let AN produced meet the
asymptotes MX, NX in M and N, and take NK equal to AM.

RULE 7. And hence appears an expeditious method of determining this hyperbola from the phenomena. Let two similar and equal bodies be projected
with the same velocity, in different angles HAK, hAk, and let them fall upon
the plane of the horizon in K and k; and note the proportion of AK to Ak. Let
it be as d to e. Then erecting a perpendicular AI of any length, assume any

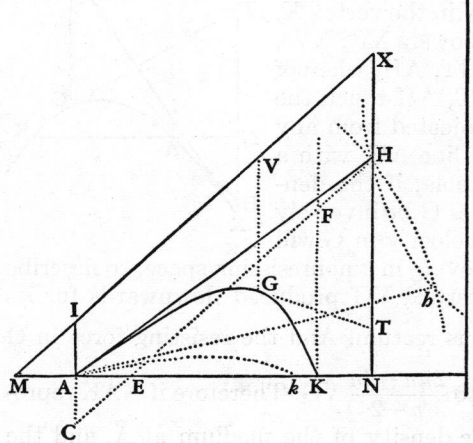

length AH or Ah, and thence graph-
ically, or by scale and compass,
collect the lengths AK, Ak (by Rule
6). If the ratio of AK to Ak be the
same with that of d to e, the length
of AH was rightly assumed. If not,
take on the indefinite right line SM,
the length SM equal to the assumed
AH; and erect a perpendicular MN
equal to the difference $\frac{AK}{Ak} - \frac{d}{e}$ of the
ratios multiplied by any given right
line. By the like method, from several
assumed lengths AH, you may find
several points N; and draw through
them all a regular curve NNXN,
cutting the right line SMMM in X.

Lastly, assume AH equal to the abscissa SX, and thence find again the length AK; and the lengths, which are to the assumed length AI, and this last AH, as the length AK known by experiment, to the length AK last found, will be the true lengths AI and AH, which were to be found. But these being given, there will be given also the resisting force of the medium in the place A, it being to the force of gravity as AH to $\frac{4}{3}$AI. Let the density of the medium be increased by Rule 4, and if the resisting force just found be increased in the same ratio, it will become still more accurate.

Rule 8. The lengths AH, HX being found; let there be now required the position of the line AH, according to which a projectile thrown with that given velocity shall fall upon any point K. At the points A and K, erect the lines AC, KF perpendicular to the horizon; whereof let AC be drawn downwards, and be equal to AI or $\frac{1}{2}$HX. With the asymptotes AK, KF, describe an hyperbola, whose conjugate shall pass through the point C; and from the centre A, with the interval AH, describe a circle cutting that hyperbola in the point H; then the projectile thrown in the direction of the right line AH will fall upon the point K. Q.E.I. For the point H, because of the given length AH, must be somewhere in the circumference of the described circle. Draw CH meeting AK and KF in E and F; and because CH, MX are parallel, and AC, AI equal, AE will be equal to AM, and therefore also equal to KN. But CE is to AE as FH to KN, and therefore CE and FH are equal. Therefore the point H falls upon the hyperbolic curve described with the asymptotes AK, KF whose conjugate passes through the point C; and is therefore found in the common intersection of this hyperbolic curve and the circumference of the described circle. Q.E.D. It is to be observed that this operation is the same, whether the right line AKN be parallel to the horizon, or inclined thereto in any angle; and that from two intersections H, h, there arise two angles NAH, NAh; and that in mechanical practice it is sufficient once to describe a circle, then to apply a ruler CH, of an indeterminate length, so to the point C, that its part FH, intercepted between the circle and the right line FK, may be equal to its part CE placed between the point C and the right line AK.

What has been said of hyperbolas may be easily applied to parabolas. For if a parabola be represented by XAGK, touched by a right line XV in the vertex X, and the ordinates IA, VG be as any powers XI^n, XV^n, of the abscissas XI, XV; draw XT, GT, AH, whereof let XT be parallel to VG, and let GT, AH touch the parabola in G and A: and a body projected from any place A, in the direction of the right line AH, with a due velocity, will describe this parabola, if the density of the medium in each of the places G be inversely as the tangent GT. In that case the velocity in G will be the same as would cause a body, moving in a nonresisting space, to describe a conic parabola, having G for its vertex, VG produced downwards for its diameter, and $\dfrac{2GT^2}{(nn-n)\cdot VG}$ for its latus rectum. And the resisting force in G will be to the force of gravity as GT to $\dfrac{2nn-2n}{n-2}$ VG. Therefore if NAK represent an horizontal line, and both the density of the medium at A, and the velocity with which the body is projected, remaining the same, the angle NAH be anyhow altered, the lengths AH, AI, HX will remain; and thence will be given the vertex X of the parabola, and the position of the right line XI; and by taking VG to IA as XV^n to XI^n, there will be given all the points G of the parabola, through which the projectile will pass.

SECTION III

THE MOTION OF BODIES THAT ARE RESISTED PARTLY IN THE RATIO OF THE VELOCITIES, AND PARTLY AS THE SQUARE OF THE SAME RATIO

PROPOSITION 11. THEOREM 8

If a body be resisted partly in the ratio and partly as the square of the ratio of its velocity, and moves in a similar medium by its innate force only; and the times be taken in arithmetical progression: then quantities inversely proportional to the velocities, increased by a certain given quantity, will be in geometrical progression.

With the centre C, and the rectangular asymptotes CAD*d* and CH, describe an hyperbola BE*e*, and let AB, DE, *de* be parallel to the asymptote CH. In

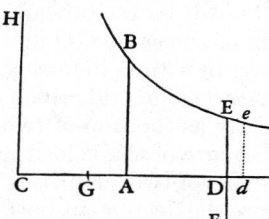

the asymptote CD let A, G be given points; and if the time be represented by the hyperbolic area ABED uniformly increasing, I say, that the velocity may be expressed by the length DF, whose reciprocal GD, together with the given line CG, compose the length CD increasing in a geometrical progression.

For let the small area DE*ed* be the least given increment of the time, and D*d* will be inversely as DE, and therefore directly as CD. Therefore the decrement of $\frac{1}{GD}$, which (by Lem. 2, Book II) is $\frac{Dd}{GD^2}$, will be also as $\frac{CD}{GD^2}$ or $\frac{CG+GD}{GD^2}$, that is, as $\frac{1}{GD} + \frac{CG}{GD^2}$. Therefore, the time ABED uniformly increasing by the addition of the given intervals ED*de*, it follows that $\frac{1}{GD}$ decreases in the same ratio with the velocity. For the decrement of the velocity is as the resistance, that is (by the supposition), as the sum of two quantities, whereof one is as the velocity, and the other as the square of the velocity; and the decrement of $\frac{1}{GD}$ is as the sum of the quantities $\frac{1}{GD}$ and $\frac{CG}{GD^2}$, whereof the first is $\frac{1}{GD}$ itself, and the last $\frac{CG}{GD^2}$ is as $\frac{1}{GD^2}$: therefore $\frac{1}{GD}$ is as the velocity, the decrements of both being analogous. And if the quantity GD inversely proportional to $\frac{1}{GD}$, be augmented by the given quantity CG; the sum CD, the time ABED uniformly increasing, will increase in a geometrical progression. Q.E.D.

COR. I. Therefore, if, having the points A and G given, the time be represented by the hyperbolic area ABED, the velocity may be represented by $\frac{1}{GD}$ the reciprocal of GD.

COR. II. And by taking GA to GD as the reciprocal of the velocity at the beginning to the reciprocal of the velocity at the end of any time ABED, the point G will be found. And that point being found, the velocity may be found from any other time given.

PROPOSITION 12. THEOREM 9

The same things being supposed, I say, that if the spaces described are taken in arithmetical progression, the velocities augmented by a certain given quantity will be in geometrical progression.

In the asymptote CD let there be given the point R, and, erecting the perpendicular RS meeting the hyperbola in S, let the space described be represented by the hyperbolic area RSED; and the velocity will be as the length GD, which, together with the given line CG, composes a length CD decreasing in a geometrical progression, while the space RSED increases in an arithmetical progression.

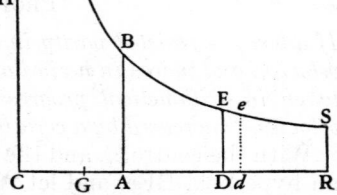

For, because the increment ED*de* of the space is given, the short line D*d*, which is the decrement of GD, will be reciprocally as ED, and therefore directly as CD; that is, as the sum of the same GD and the given length CG. But the decrement of the velocity, in a time inversely proportional thereto, in which the given interval of space D*de*E is described, is as the resistance and the time conjointly, that is, directly as the sum of two quantities, whereof one is as the velocity, the other as the square of the velocity, and inversely as the velocity; and therefore directly as the sum of two quantities, one of which is given, the other is as the velocity. Therefore the decrement both of the velocity and of the line GD is as a given quantity and a decreasing quantity conjointly; and, because the decrements are analogous, the decreasing quantities will always be analogous; viz., the velocity, and the line GD.   Q.E.D.

COR. I. If the velocity be represented by the length GD, the space described will be as the hyperbolic area DESR.

COR. II. And if the point R be assumed anywhere, the point G will be found, by taking GR to GD as the velocity at the beginning to the velocity after any space RSED is described. The point G being given, the space is given from the given velocity; and conversely.

COR. III. Whence since (by Prop. 11) the velocity is given from the given time, and (by this Proposition) the space is given from the given velocity, the space will be given from the given time; and conversely.

PROPOSITION 13. THEOREM 10

Supposing that a body attracted downwards by an uniform gravity ascends or descends in a right line; and that the same is resisted partly in the ratio of its velocity, and partly as the square of the ratio thereof: I say, that, if right lines parallel to the diameters of a circle and an hyperbola be drawn through the ends of the conjugate diameters, and the velocities be as some segments of those parallels drawn from a given point, the times will be as the sectors of the areas cut off by right lines drawn from the centre to the ends of the segments; and conversely.

CASE 1. Suppose first that the body is ascending, and from the centre D, with any semidiameter DB, describe a quadrant BETF of a circle, and through

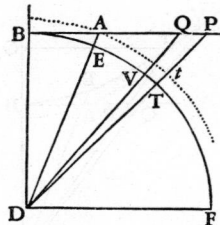

the end B of the semidiameter DB draw the indefinite line BAP, parallel to the semidiameter DF. In that line let there be given the point A, and take the segment AP proportional to the velocity. And since one part of the resistance is as the velocity, and another part as the square of the velocity, let the whole resistance be as $AP^2+2BA \cdot AP$. Join DA, DP, cutting the circle in E and T, and let the gravity be represented by DA^2, so that the gravity shall be to the resistance in P as DA^2 to $AP^2+2BA \cdot AP$; and the time of the whole ascent will be as the sector EDT of the circle.

For draw DVQ, cutting off the moment PQ of the velocity AP, and the moment DTV of the sector DET answering to a given moment of time; and that decrement PQ of the velocity will be as the sum of the forces of gravity DA^2 and of resistance $AP^2+2BA \cdot AP$; that is (by Prop. 12, Book II, *Elements* of Euclid), as DP^2. Then the area DPQ, proportional to PQ, is as DP^2, and the area DTV, which is to the area DPQ as DT^2 to DP^2, is as the given quantity DT^2. Therefore the area EDT decreases uniformly according to the rate of the future time, by subtraction of given intervals DTV, and is therefore proportional to the time of the whole ascent.   Q.E.D.

CASE 2. If the velocity in the ascent of the body be represented by the length AP as before, and the resistance be made as $AP^2+2BA \cdot AP$; and if the force of gravity be less than can be expressed by DA^2; take BD of such a length, that AB^2-BD^2 may be proportional to the gravity, and let DF be perpendicular and equal to DB, and through the vertex F describe the hyperbola FTVE, whose conjugate semidiameters are DB and DF, and which cuts DA in E, and DP, DQ in

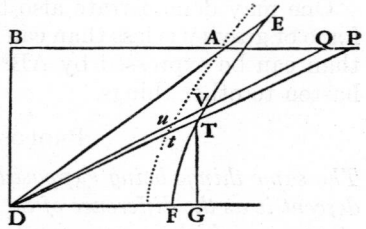

T and V; and the time of the whole ascent will be as the hyperbolic sector TDE.

For the decrement PQ of the velocity, produced in a given interval of time, is as the sum of the resistance $AP^2+2BA \cdot AP$ and of the gravity AB^2-BD^2, that is, as BP^2-BD^2. But the area DTV is to the area DPQ as DT^2 to DP^2; and, therefore, if GT be drawn perpendicular to DF, as GT^2 or GD^2-DF^2 to BD^2, and as GD^2 to BP^2, and, by subtraction, as DF^2 to BP^2-BD^2. Therefore since the area DPQ is as PQ, that is, as BP^2-BD^2, the area DTV will be as the given quantity DF^2. Therefore the area EDT decreases uniformly in each of the equal intervals of time, by the subtraction of so many given intervals DTV, and therefore is proportional to the time.   Q.E.D.

CASE 3. Let AP be the velocity in the descent of the body, and $AP^2+2BA \cdot AP$ the force of resistance, and BD^2-AB^2 the force of gravity, the angle DBA being a right one. And if with the centre D, and the principal vertex B, there be described a rectangular hyperbola BETV cutting DA, DP, and DQ produced in E, T, and V; the sector DET of this hyperbola will be as the whole time of descent.

For the increment PQ of the velocity, and the area DPQ proportional to it, is as the excess of the gravity above the resistance, that is, as

$$BD^2-AB^2-2BA \cdot AP-AP^2$$

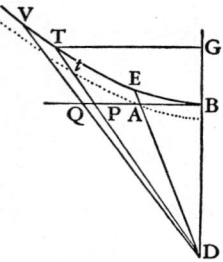

or BD^2-BP^2. And the area DTV is to the area DPQ as DT^2 to DP^2; and therefore as GT^2 or GD^2-BD^2 to BP^2; and as GD^2 to BD^2, and, by subtraction, as BD^2 to BD^2-BP^2. Therefore since the area DPQ is as BD^2-BP^2, the area DTV will be as the given quantity BD^2. Therefore the area EDT increases uniformly in the several equal intervals of time by the addition of as many given intervals DTV, and therefore is proportional to the time of the descent.   Q.E.D.

COR. If with the centre D and the semidiameter DA there be drawn through the vertex A an arc A*t* similar to the arc ET, and similarly subtending the angle ADT, the velocity AP will be to the velocity which the body in the time EDT, in a nonresisting space, can lose in its ascent, or acquire in its descent, as the area of the triangle DAP to the area of the sector DA*t*; and therefore is given from the time given. For the velocity in a nonresisting medium is proportional to the time, and therefore to this sector; in a resisting medium, it is as the triangle; and in both mediums, where it is least, it approaches to the ratio of equality, as the sector and triangle do.

SCHOLIUM

One may demonstrate also that case in the ascent of the body, where the force of gravity is less than can be expressed by DA^2 or AB^2+BD^2, and greater than can be expressed by AB^2-DB^2, and must be expressed by AB^2. But I hasten to other things.

PROPOSITION 14. THEOREM 11

The same things being supposed, I say, that the space described in the ascent or descent is as the difference of the area by which the time is expressed, and of some other area which is augmented or diminished in an arithmetical progression; if the forces compounded of the resistance and the gravity be taken in a geometrical progression.

Take AC (in these three figures) proportional to the gravity, and AK to the resistance; but take them on the same side of the point A, if the body is descending, otherwise on the contrary. Erect A*b*, which make to DB as DB^2 to $4BA \cdot CA$; and to the rectangular asymptotes CK, CH, describe the hyperbola *b*N; and, erecting KN perpendicular to CK, the area A*b*NK will be augmented or diminished in an arithmetical progression, while the forces CK are taken in a geometrical progression. I say, therefore, that the distance of the body from its greatest altitude is as the excess of the area A*b*NK above the area DET.

For since AK is as the resistance, that is, as $AP^2 \cdot 2BA \cdot AP$; assume any given quantity Z, and put AK equal to $\dfrac{AP^2+2BA \cdot AP}{Z}$; then (by Lem. 2 of this book) the moment KL of AK will be equal to $\dfrac{2PQ \cdot AP+2BA \cdot PQ}{Z}$ or $\dfrac{2PQ \cdot BP}{Z}$, and the moment KLON of the area A*b*NK will be equal to $\dfrac{2PQ \cdot BP \cdot LO}{Z}$ or $\dfrac{PQ \cdot BP \cdot BD^3}{2Z \cdot CK \cdot AB}$.

CASE 1. Now if the body ascends, and the gravity be as AB^2+BD^2, BET being a circle, the line AC, which is proportional to the gravity, will be $\frac{AB^2+BD^2}{Z}$, and DP^2 or $AP^2+2BA \cdot AP+AB^2+BD^2$ will be $AK \cdot Z+AC \cdot Z$ or $CK \cdot Z$; and therefore the area DTV will be to the area DPQ as DT^2 or DB^2 to $CK \cdot Z$.

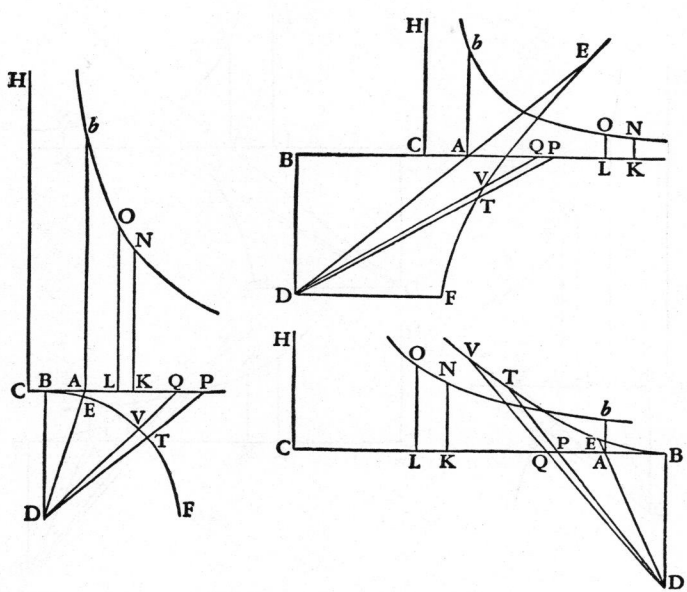

CASE 2. If the body ascends, and the gravity be as AB^2-BD^2, the line AC will be $\frac{AB^2-BD^2}{Z}$, and DT^2 will be to DP^2 as DF^2 or DB^2 to BP^2-BD^2 or $AP^2+2BA \cdot AP+AB^2-BD^2$, that is, to $AK \cdot Z+AC \cdot Z$ or $CK \cdot Z$. And therefore the area DTV will be to the area DPQ as DB^2 to $CK \cdot Z$.

CASE 3. And by the same reasoning, if the body descends, and therefore the gravity is as BD^2-AB^2, and the line AC becomes equal to $\frac{BD^2-AB^2}{Z}$; the area DTV will be to the area DPQ as DB^2 to $CK \cdot Z$: as above.

Since, therefore, these areas are always in this ratio, if for the area DTV, by which the moment of the time, always equal to itself, is expressed, there be put any determinate rectangle, as $BD \cdot m$, the area DPQ, that is, $\frac{1}{2}BD \cdot PQ$, will be to $BD \cdot m$ as $CK \cdot Z$ to BD^2. And thence $PQ \cdot BD^3$ becomes equal to $2BD \cdot m \cdot CK \cdot Z$, and the moment KLON of the area AbNK, found before, becomes $\frac{BP \cdot BD \cdot m}{AB}$. From the area DET subtract its moment DTV or $BD \cdot m$, and there will remain $\frac{AP \cdot BD \cdot m}{AB}$. Therefore the difference of the moments, that is, the moment of the difference of the areas, is equal to $\frac{AP \cdot BD \cdot m}{AB}$; and therefore (because of the given quantity $\dfrac{\text{BD} \cdot m}{\text{AB}}$) as the velocity AP; that is, as the moment of the space which the body describes in its ascent or descent. And therefore the difference of the areas, and that space, increasing or decreasing by proportional moments, and beginning together or vanishing together, are proportional.   Q.E.D

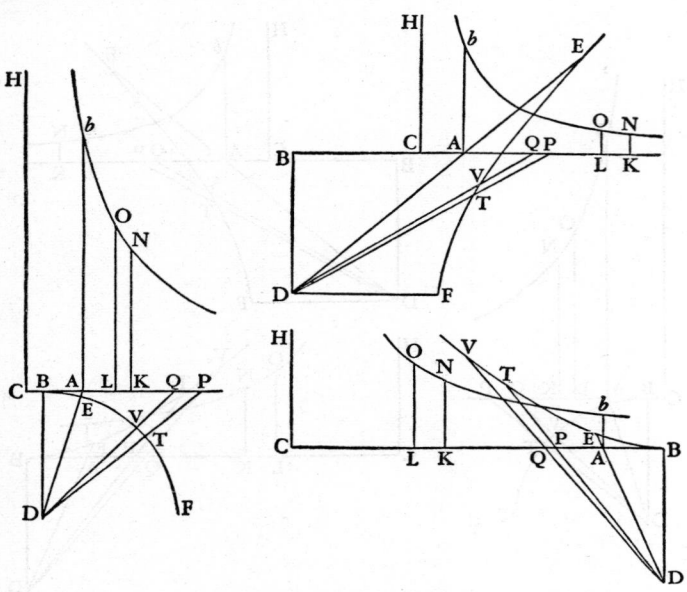

COR. If the length, which arises by applying the area DET to the line BD, be called M; and another length V be taken in that ratio to the length M, which the line DA has to the line DE; the space which a body, in a resisting medium, describes in its whole ascent or descent, will be to the space which a body, in a nonresisting medium, falling from rest, can describe in the same time, as the difference of the aforesaid areas to $\dfrac{\text{BD} \cdot \text{V}^2}{\text{AB}}$; and therefore is given from the time given. For the space in a nonresisting medium is as the square of the time, or as V^2; and, because BD and AB are given, as $\dfrac{\text{BD} \cdot \text{V}^2}{\text{AB}}$. This area is equal to the area $\dfrac{\text{DA}^2 \cdot \text{BD} \cdot \text{M}^2}{\text{DE}^2 \cdot \text{AB}}$ and the moment of M is m; and therefore the moment of this area is $\dfrac{\text{DA}^2 \cdot \text{BD} \cdot 2\text{M} \cdot m}{\text{DE}^2 \cdot \text{AB}}$. But this moment is to the moment of the difference of the aforesaid areas DET and AbNK, viz., to $\dfrac{\text{AP} \cdot \text{BD} \cdot m}{\text{AB}}$, as $\dfrac{\text{DA}^2 \cdot \text{BD} \cdot \text{M}}{\text{DE}^2}$ to ½BD·AP, or as $\dfrac{\text{DA}^2}{\text{DE}^2}$ into DET to DAP; and, therefore, when the areas DET and DAP are least, in the ratio of equality. Therefore the area $\dfrac{\text{BD} \cdot \text{V}^2}{\text{AB}}$ and the difference of the areas DET and AbNK, when all these areas are least, have equal moments; and are therefore equal. Therefore since the velocities, and therefore also the spaces in both mediums described together, in the beginning of the descent, or the end of the ascent, approach to equality, and therefore are then one to another as the area $\dfrac{\mathrm{BD}\cdot\mathrm{V}^2}{\mathrm{AB}}$, and the difference of the areas DET and A*b*NK; and moreover since the space, in a nonresisting medium, is continually as $\dfrac{\mathrm{BD}\cdot\mathrm{V}^2}{\mathrm{AB}}$, and the space, in a resisting medium, is continually as the difference of the areas DET and A*b*NK; it necessarily follows, that the spaces, in both mediums, described in any equal times, are one to another as that area $\dfrac{\mathrm{BD}\cdot\mathrm{V}^2}{\mathrm{AB}}$, and the difference of the areas DET and A*b*NK.   Q.E.D.

SCHOLIUM

The resistance of spherical bodies in fluids arises partly from the tenacity, partly from the attrition, and partly from the density of the medium. And that part of the resistance which arises from the density of the fluid is, as I said, as the square of the velocity; the other part, which arises from the tenacity of the fluid, is uniform, or as the moment of the time; and, therefore, we might now proceed to the motion of bodies, which are resisted partly by an uniform force, or in the ratio of the moments of the time, and partly as the square of the velocity. But it is sufficient to have cleared the way to this speculation in Props. 8 and 9 foregoing, and their Corollaries. For in those Propositions, instead of the uniform resistance made to an ascending body arising from its gravity, one may substitute the uniform resistance which arises from the tenacity of the medium, when the body moves by its inertia alone; and when the body ascends in a right line, add this uniform resistance to the force of gravity, and subtract it when the body descends in a right line. One might also go on to the motion of bodies which are resisted in part uniformly, in part in the ratio of the velocity, and in part as the square of the same velocity. And I have opened a way to this in Props. 13 and 14 foregoing, in which the uniform resistance arising from the tenacity of the medium may be substituted for the force of gravity, or be compounded with it as before. But I hasten to other things.

SECTION IV

THE CIRCULAR MOTION OF BODIES IN RESISTING MEDIUMS

LEMMA 3

Let PQR *be a spiral cutting all the radii* SP, SQ, SR, *&c., in equal angles. Draw the right line* PT *touching the spiral in any point* P, *and cutting the radius* SQ *in* T; *draw* PO, QO *perpendicular to the spiral, and meeting in* O, *and join* SO: *I say, that if the points* P *and* Q *approach and coincide, the angle* PSO *will become a right angle, and the ultimate ratio of the rectangle* TQ·2PS *to* PQ² *will be the ratio of equality.*

For, from the right angles OPQ, OQR, subtract the equal angles SPQ, SQR, and there will remain the equal angles OPS, OQS. Therefore a circle which passes through the points OSP will pass also through the point Q. Let the points P and Q coincide, and this circle will touch the spiral in the place of coincidence PQ, and will therefore cut the right line OP perpendicularly. Therefore OP will become a diameter of this circle, and the angle OSP, being in a semicircle, becomes a right one.   Q.E.D.

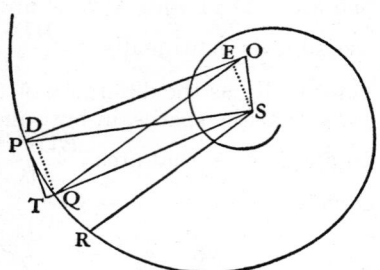

Draw QD, SE perpendicular to OP, and the ultimate ratios of the lines will be as follows:

TQ : PD = TS or PS : PE = 2PO : 2PS;

and   PD : PQ = PQ : 2PO;

multiplying together corresponding terms of equal ratios,

TQ : PQ = PQ : 2PS.

Whence PQ² becomes equal to TQ·2PS.

                    Q.E.D.

PROPOSITION 15. THEOREM 12

If the density of a medium in each place thereof be inversely as the distance of the places from an immovable centre, and the centripetal force be as the square of the density: I say, that a body may revolve in a spiral which cuts all the radii drawn from that centre in a given angle.

Suppose everything to be as in the foregoing Lemma, and produce SQ to V so that SV may be equal to SP. In any time let a body, in a resisting medium, describe the least arc PQ, and in double the time the least arc PR; and the decrements of those arcs arising from the resistance, or their differences from

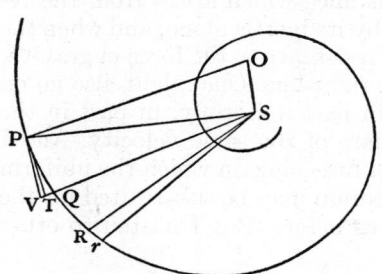

the arcs which would be described in a non-resisting medium in the same times, will be to each other as the squares of the times in which they are generated; therefore the decrement of the arc PQ is the fourth part of the decrement of the arc PR. Whence also if the area QS*r* be taken equal to the area PSQ, the decrement of the arc PQ will be equal to half the short line R*r*; and therefore the force of resistance and the centripetal force are to each other as the short line

½R*r* and TQ which they generate in the same time. Because the centripetal force with which the body is urged in P is inversely as SP², and (by Lem. 10, Book I) the short line TQ, which is generated by that force, is in a ratio compounded of the ratio of this force and the squared ratio of the time in which the arc PQ is described (for in this case I neglect the resistance, as being infinitely less than the centripetal force), it follows that TQ·SP², that is (by the last Lemma), ½PQ²·SP, will be as the square of the time, and therefore the time is as PQ·√SP; and the velocity of the body, with which the arc PQ is described

in that time, as $\dfrac{PQ}{PQ \cdot \sqrt{SP}}$ or $\dfrac{1}{\sqrt{SP}}$, that is, inversely as the square root of SP.

And, by a like reasoning, the velocity with which the arc QR is described, is inversely as the square root of SQ. Now those arcs PQ and QR are as the describing velocities to each other; that is, as the square root of the ratio of

SQ to SP, or as SQ to $\sqrt{(SP \cdot SQ)}$; and, because of the equal angles SPQ, SQr, and the equal areas PSQ, QSr, the arc PQ is to the arc Qr as SQ to SP. Take the differences of the proportional consequents, and the arc PQ will be to the arc Rr as SQ to $SP - \sqrt{(SP \cdot SQ)}$, or ½VQ. For, the points P and Q coinciding, the ultimate ratio of $SP - \sqrt{(SP \cdot SQ)}$ to ½VQ is the ratio of equality. Since the decrement of the arc PQ arising from the resistance, or its double Rr, is as the resistance and the square of the time conjointly, the resistance will be as $\frac{Rr}{PQ^2 \cdot SP}$. But PQ was to Rr as SQ to ½VQ, and thence $\frac{Rr}{PQ^2 \cdot SP}$ becomes as $\frac{\frac{1}{2}VQ}{PQ \cdot SP \cdot SQ}$, or as $\frac{\frac{1}{2}OS}{OP \cdot SP^2}$. For, the points P and Q coinciding, SP and SQ coincide also, and the angle PVQ becomes a right one; and, because of the similar triangles PVQ, PSO, PQ becomes to ½ VQ as OP to ½OS. Therefore $\frac{OS}{OP \cdot SP^2}$ is as the resistance, that is, in the ratio of the density of the medium in P and the squared ratio of the velocity conjointly. Subtract the squared ratio of the velocity, namely, the ratio $\frac{1}{SP}$, and there will remain the density of the medium in P, as $\frac{OS}{OP \cdot SP}$. Let the spiral be given, and, because of the given ratio of OS to OP, the density of the medium in P will be as $\frac{1}{SP}$. Therefore in a medium whose density is inversely as SP the distance from the centre, a body will revolve in this spiral.   Q.E.D.

COR. I. The velocity in any place P, is always the same wherewith a body in a nonresisting medium with the same centripetal force would revolve in a circle, at the same distance SP from the centre.

COR. II. The density of the medium, if the distance SP be given, is as $\frac{OS}{OP}$, but if that distance is not given, as $\frac{OS}{OP \cdot SP}$. And thence a spiral may be fitted to any density of the medium.

COR. III. The force of the resistance in any place P is to the centripetal force in the same place as ½OS to OP. For those forces are to each other as ½Rr and TQ, or as $\frac{\frac{1}{4}VQ \cdot PQ}{SQ}$ and $\frac{\frac{1}{2}PQ^2}{SP}$, that is, as ½VQ and PQ, or ½OS and OP. The

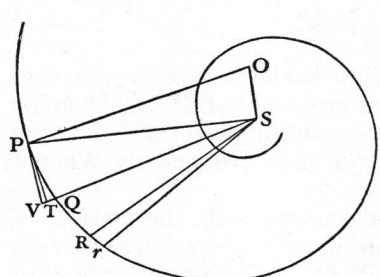

spiral therefore being given, there is given the proportion of the resistance to the centripetal force; and, conversely, from that proportion given the spiral is given.

COR. IV. Therefore the body cannot revolve in this spiral, except where the force of resistance is less than half the centripetal force. Let the resistance be made equal to half the centripetal force, and the spiral will coincide with the right line PS, and in that right line the body will descend to the centre with a velocity that is to the velocity with which it was proved before in the case of the parabola (Theor. 10, Book I) that the descent would be made in a nonresisting medium, as the square root of the ratio of unity to the number 2. And the times of the descent will be here inversely as the velocities, and therefore given.

COR. V. And because at equal distances from the centre the velocity is the same in the spiral PQR as it is in the right line SP, and the length of the spiral is to the length of the right line PS in a given ratio, namely, in the ratio of OP to OS; the time of the descent in the spiral will be to the time of the descent in the right line SP in the same given ratio, and therefore given.

COR. VI. If from the centre S, with any two given radii, two circles are described; and these circles remaining, the angle which the spiral makes with the radius PS be changed in any manner; the number of revolutions which the body can complete in the space between the circumferences of those circles, going round in the spiral from one circumference to another, will be as $\frac{PS}{OS}$, or as the tangent of the angle which the spiral makes with the radius PS; and the time of the same revolutions will be as $\frac{OP}{OS}$, that is, as the secant of the same angle, or inversely as the density of the medium.

COR. VII. If a body, in a medium whose density is inversely as the distances of places from the centre, revolves in any curve AEB about that centre, and cuts the first radius AS in the same angle in B as it did before in A, and that with a velocity that shall be to its first velocity in A inversely as the square root of the distances from the cen-

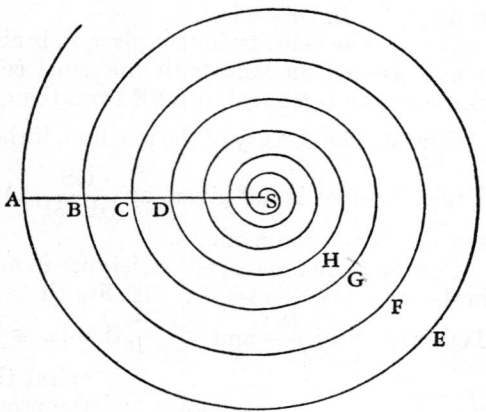

tre (that is, as AS to a mean proportional between AS and BS), that body will continue to describe innumerable similar revolutions BFC, CGD, &c., and by its intersections will divide the radius AS into parts AS, BS, CS, DS, &c., that are continually proportional. But the times of the revolutions will be directly as the perimeters of the orbits AEB, BFC, CGD, &c., and inversely as the velocities at the beginnings A, B, C of those orbits; that is, as $AS^{3/2}$, $BS^{3/2}$, $CS^{3/2}$. And the whole time in which the body will arrive at the centre, will be to the time of the first revolution as the sum of all the continued proportionals $AS^{3/2}$, $BS^{3/2}$, $CS^{3/2}$, going on *ad infinitum*, is to the first term $AS^{3/2}$; that is, as the first term $AS^{3/2}$ is to the difference of the two first $AS^{3/2}-BS^{3/2}$, or as ⅔AS is to AB, very nearly. Whence the whole time may be easily found.

COR. VIII. From hence also may be deduced, near enough, the motions of bodies in mediums whose density is either uniform, or observes any other assigned law. From the centre S, with radii SA, SB, SC, &c., continually proportional, describe as many circles; and suppose the time of the revolutions between the perimeters of any two of those circles, in the medium whereof we treated, to be to the time of the revolutions between the same in the medium

proposed as the mean density of the proposed medium between those circles is
to the mean density of the medium whereof we treated, between the same circles, nearly; and that the secant of the angle in which the spiral above determined, in the medium whereof we treated, cuts the radius AS, is in the same
ratio to the secant of the angle in which the new spiral, in the proposed medium, cuts the same radius; and also that the number of all the revolutions
between the same two circles is nearly as the tangents of those angles. If this
be done everywhere between every two circles, the motion will be continued
through all the circles. And by this means one may without difficulty ascertain
at what rate and in what time bodies ought to revolve in any regular medium.

COR. IX. And although these motions becoming eccentric should be performed in spirals approaching to an oval figure, yet, assuming the several
revolutions of those spirals to be at the same distances from each other, and to
approach to the centre by the same degrees as the spiral above described, we
may also understand how the motions of bodies may be performed in spirals of
that kind.

PROPOSITION 16. THEOREM 13

*If the density of the medium in each of the places be inversely as the distance of the
places from the immovable centre, and the centripetal force be inversely as any
power of the same distance: I say, that the body may revolve in a spiral intersecting
all the radii drawn from that centre in a given angle.*

This is demonstrated in the same manner as the foregoing Proposition. For
if the centripetal force in P be inversely as any power SP^{n+1} of the distance SP

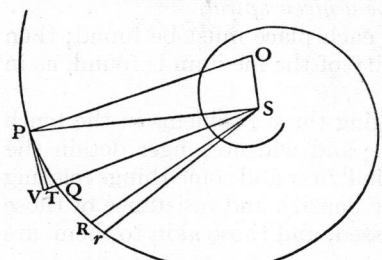

whose index is $n+1$; it will be concluded,
as above, that the time in which the body
describes any arc PQ, will be as $PQ \cdot PS^{1/2n}$;
and the resistance in P as $\dfrac{Rr}{PQ^2 \cdot SP^n}$, or as
$\dfrac{(1-\frac{1}{2}n) \cdot VQ}{PQ \cdot SP^n \cdot SQ}$, and therefore as $\dfrac{(1-\frac{1}{2}n) \cdot OS}{OP \cdot SP^{n+1}}$,
that is (because $\dfrac{(1-\frac{1}{2}n) \cdot OS}{OP}$ is a given

quantity), inversely as SP^{n+1}. And there-
fore, since the velocity is inversely as $SP^{1/2n}$, the density in P will be reciprocally as SP.

COR. I. The resistance is to the centripetal force as $(1-\frac{1}{2}n) \cdot OS$ to OP.

COR. II. If the centripetal force be inversely as SP^3, $1-\frac{1}{2}n$ will be $=0$; and
therefore the resistance and density of the medium will be nothing, as in Prop.
9, Book I.

COR. III. If the centripetal force be inversely as any power of the radius SP,
whose index is greater than the number 3, the positive resistance will be changed
into a negative.

SCHOLIUM

This Proposition and the former, which relate to mediums of unequal density, are to be understood as applying only to the motion of bodies that are so
small, that the greater density of the medium on one side of the body above
that on the other is not to be considered. I suppose also the resistance, other

things being equal, to be proportional to its density. Hence, in mediums whose force of resistance is not as the density, the density must be so much augmented or diminished, that either the excess of the resistance may be taken away, or the defect supplied.

PROPOSITION 17. PROBLEM 4

To find the centripetal force and the resisting force of the medium, by which a body, the law of the velocity being given, shall revolve in a given spiral.

Let that spiral be PQR. From the velocity, with which the body goes over the very small arc PQ, the time will be given; and from the altitude TQ, which is as the centripetal force, and the square of the time, that force will be given. Then from the difference RS*r* of the areas PSQ and QSR described in equal intervals of time, the retardation of the body will be given; and from the retardation will be found the resisting force and density of the medium.

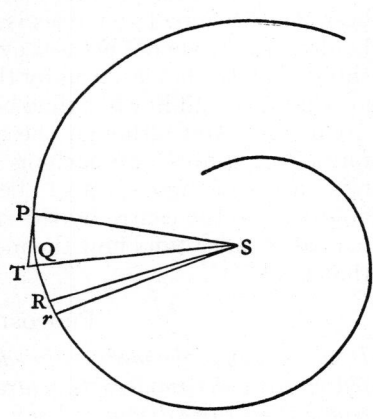

PROPOSITION 18. PROBLEM 5

The law of centripetal force being given, to find the density of the medium in each of the places thereof, by which a body may describe a given spiral.

From the centripetal force the velocity in each place must be found; then from the retardation of the velocity the density of the medium is found, as in the foregoing Proposition.

But I have explained the method of managing these Problems in the tenth Proposition and second Lemma of this book; and will no longer detain the reader in these complicated investigations. I shall now add some things relating to the forces of progressive bodies, and to the density and resistance of those mediums in which the motions hitherto discussed, and those akin to them, are performed.

SECTION V

THE DENSITY AND COMPRESSION OF FLUIDS; HYDROSTATICS.
THE DEFINITION OF A FLUID

A FLUID IS ANY BODY WHOSE PARTS YIELD TO ANY FORCE IMPRESSED ON IT, AND, BY YIELDING, ARE EASILY MOVED AMONG THEMSELVES

PROPOSITION 19. THEOREM 14

All the parts of an homogeneous and unmoved fluid included in any unmoved vessel, and compressed on every side (setting aside the consideration of condensation, gravity, and all centripetal forces), will be equally pressed on every side, and remain in their places without any motion arising from that pressure.

CASE 1. Let a fluid be included in the spherical vessel ABC, and uniformly compressed on every side: I say, that no part of it will be moved by that pressure. For if any part, as D, be moved, all such parts at the same distance from the centre on every side must necessarily be moved at the same time by a like

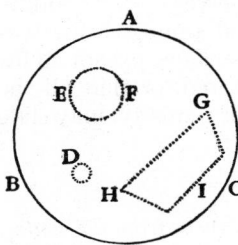

motion; because the pressure of them all is similar and equal; and all other motion is excluded that does not arise from that pressure. But if these parts come all of them nearer to the centre, the fluid must be condensed towards the centre, contrary to the supposition. If they recede from it, the fluid must be condensed towards the circumference; which is also contrary to the supposition. Neither can they move in any one direction retaining their distance from the centre, because, for the same reason, they may move in a contrary direction; but the same part cannot be moved contrary ways at the same time. Therefore no part of the fluid will be moved from its place.   Q.E.D.

CASE 2. I say now, that all the spherical parts of this fluid are equally pressed on every side. For let EF be a spherical part of the fluid; if this be not pressed equally on every side, augment the lesser pressure till it be pressed equally on every side; and its parts (by Case 1) will remain in their places. But before the increase of the pressure, they would remain in their places (by Case 1); and by the addition of a new pressure they will be moved, by the definition of a fluid, from those places. Now these two conclusions contradict each other. Therefore it was false to say that the sphere EF was not pressed equally on every side.   Q.E.D.

CASE 3. I say besides, that different spherical parts have equal pressures. For the contiguous spherical parts press each other mutually and equally in the point of contact (by Law III). But (by Case 2) they are pressed on every side with the same force. Therefore any two spherical parts not contiguous, since an intermediate spherical part can touch both, will be pressed with the same force.   Q.E.D.

CASE 4. I say now, that all the parts of the fluid are everywhere pressed equally. For any two parts may be touched by spherical parts in any points whatever; and there they will equally press those spherical parts (by Case 3), and are in reaction equally pressed by them (by Law III).   Q.E.D.

CASE 5. Since, therefore, any part GHI of the fluid is inclosed by the rest of the fluid as in a vessel, and is equally pressed on every side; and also its parts equally press one another, and are at rest among themselves; it is manifest that all the parts of any fluid as GHI, which is pressed equally on every side, do press each other mutually and equally, and are at rest among themselves.   Q.E.D.

CASE 6. Therefore if that fluid be included in a vessel of a yielding substance, or that is not rigid, and be not equally pressed on every side, the same will give way to a stronger pressure, by the definition of fluidity.

CASE 7. And therefore, in an inflexible or rigid vessel, a fluid will not sustain a stronger pressure on one side than on the other, but will give way to it, and that in a moment of time; because the rigid side of the vessel does not follow the yielding liquor. But the fluid, by thus yielding, will press against the opposite side, and so the pressure will tend on every side to equality. And because the fluid, as soon as it endeavors to recede from the part that is most pressed, is withstood by the resistance of the vessel on the opposite side, the pressure will on every side be reduced to equality, in a moment of time, without any local motion; and from thence the parts of the fluid (by Case 5) will press each other mutually and equally, and be at rest among themselves.   Q.E.D.

COR. Hence neither will a motion of the parts of the fluid among themselves be changed by a pressure communicated to the external surface, except so far as either the figure of the surface may be somewhere altered, or that all the parts of the fluid, by pressing one another more intensely or remissly, may slide with more or less difficulty among themselves.

PROPOSITION 20. THEOREM 15

If all the parts of a spherical fluid, homogeneous at equal distances from the centre, lying on a spherical concentric bottom, gravitate towards the centre of the whole, the bottom will sustain the weight of a cylinder, whose base is equal to the surface of the bottom, and whose altitude is the same with that of the incumbent fluid.

Let DHM be the surface of the bottom, and AEI the upper surface of the fluid. Let the fluid be divided into concentric orbs of equal thickness, by the innumerable spherical surfaces BFK, CGL; and conceive the force of gravity to act only in the upper surface of every orb, and the actions to be equal on the equal parts of the surfaces. Therefore the upper surface AE is pressed by the single force of its own gravity, by which all the parts of the upper orb, and the second surface BFK, will (by Prop. 19), according to its measure, be equally pressed. The second surface BFK is pressed likewise by the force of its own gravity, which, added to the former force, makes the pressure double. The third surface CGL is, according to its measure, acted on by this pressure and the force of its own gravity besides, which makes its pressure triple. And in like manner the fourth surface receives a quadruple pressure, the fifth surface a quintuple, and so on. Therefore the pressure acting on every surface is not as the solid quantity of the incumbent fluid, but as the number of the orbs reaching to the upper surface of the fluid; and is equal to the gravity of the lowest orb multiplied by the number of orbs; that is, to the gravity of a solid whose ultimate ratio to the cylinder above mentioned (when the number of the orbs is increased and their thickness diminished, *ad infinitum,* so that the action of gravity from the lowest surface to the uppermost may become continued) is the ratio of equality. Therefore the lowest surface sustains the weight of the cylinder above determined. Q.E.D. And by a like reasoning the Proposition will be evident, where the gravity of the fluid decreases in any assigned ratio of the distance from the centre, and also where the fluid is more rare above and denser below.   Q.E.D.

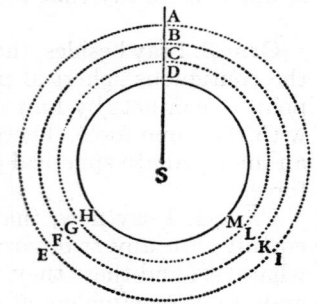

COR. I. Therefore the bottom is not pressed by the whole weight of the incumbent fluid, but only sustains that part of it which is described in the Proposition; the rest of the weight being sustained archwise by the spherical figure of the fluid.

COR. II. The quantity of the pressure is the same always at equal distances from the centre, whether the surface pressed be parallel to the horizon, or perpendicular, or oblique; or whether the fluid, continued upwards from the compressed surface, rises perpendicularly in a rectilinear direction, or creeps obliquely through crooked cavities and canals, whether those passages be regular or irregular, wide or narrow. That the pressure is not altered by any of these circumstances, may be inferred by applying the demonstration of this Theorem to the several cases of fluids.

Cor. iii. From the same demonstration it may also be concluded (by Prop. 19), that the parts of a heavy fluid acquire no motion among themselves by the pressure of the incumbent weight, except that motion which arises from condensation.

Cor. iv. And therefore if another body of the same specific gravity, incapable of condensation, be immersed in this fluid, it will acquire no motion by the pressure of the incumbent weight: it will neither descend nor ascend, nor change its figure. If it be spherical, it will remain so, notwithstanding the pressure; if it be square, it will remain square; and that, whether it be soft or fluid; whether it swims freely in the fluid, or lies at the bottom. For any internal part of a fluid is in the same state with the submersed body; and the case of all submersed bodies that have the same magnitude, figure, and specific gravity, is alike. If a submersed body, retaining its weight, should dissolve and put on the form of a fluid, this body, if before it should have ascended, descended, or from any pressure assumed a new figure, would now likewise ascend, descend, or put on a new figure; and that, because its gravity and the other causes of its motion remain. But (by Case 5, Prop. 19) it would now be at rest, and retain its figure. Therefore also in the former case.

Cor. v. Therefore a body that is specifically heavier than a fluid contiguous to it will sink; and that which is specifically lighter will ascend, and attain so much motion and change of figure as that excess or defect of gravity is able to produce. For that excess or defect is the same thing as an impulse, by which a body, otherwise in equilibrium with the parts of the fluid, is acted on; and may be compared with the excess or defect of a weight in one of the scales of a balance.

Cor. vi. Therefore bodies placed in fluids have a twofold gravity: the one true and absolute, the other apparent, common, and comparative. Absolute gravity is the whole force with which the body tends downwards; relative and common gravity is the excess of gravity with which the body tends downwards more than the ambient fluid. By the first kind of gravity the parts of all fluids and bodies gravitate in their proper places; and therefore their weights taken together compose the weight of the whole. For the whole taken together is heavy, as may be experienced in vessels full of liquor; and the weight of the whole is equal to the weights of all the parts, and is therefore composed of them. By the other kind of gravity bodies do not gravitate in their places; that is, compared with one another, they do not preponderate, but, hindering one another's endeavor to descend, remain in their proper places as if they were not heavy. Those things which are in the air, and do not preponderate, are commonly looked on as not heavy. Those which do preponderate are commonly reckoned heavy, inasmuch as they are not sustained by the weight of the air. The common weights are nothing else but the excess of the true weights above the weight of the air. Hence also, commonly, those things are called light which are less heavy, and, by yielding to the preponderating air, mount upwards. But these are only comparatively light, and not truly so, because they descend in a vacuum. Thus, in water, bodies which, by their greater or less gravity, descend or ascend, are comparatively and apparently heavy or light; and their comparative and apparent gravity or levity is the excess or defect by which their true gravity either exceeds the gravity of the water or is exceeded by it. But those things which neither by preponderating descend, nor, by yielding to the preponderating fluid, ascend, although by their true weight they do increase the weight of the whole, yet comparatively, and as commonly understood, they do not gravitate in the water. For these cases are alike demonstrated.

COR. VII. These things which have been demonstrated concerning gravity take place in any other centripetal forces.

COR. VIII. Therefore if the medium in which any body moves be acted on either by its own gravity, or by any other centripetal force, and the body be urged more powerfully by the same force; the difference of the forces is that very motive force, which, in the foregoing Proposition, I have considered as a centripetal force. But if the body be more lightly urged by that force, the difference of the forces becomes a centrifugal force, and is to be considered as such.

COR. IX. But since fluids by pressing the included bodies do not change their external figures, it appears also (by Cor., Prop. 19) that they will not change the situation of their internal parts in relation to one another; and therefore if animals were immersed therein, and if all sensation did arise from the motion of their parts, the fluid would neither hurt the immersed bodies, nor excite any sensation, unless so far as those bodies might be condensed by the compression. And the case is the same of any system of bodies encompassed with a compressing fluid. All the parts of the system will be agitated with the same motions as if they were placed in a vacuum, and would only retain their comparative gravity; unless so far as the fluid may somewhat resist their motions, or be requisite to unite them by compression.

PROPOSITION 21. THEOREM 16

Let the density of any fluid be proportional to the compression, and its parts be attracted downwards by a centripetal force inversely proportional to the distances from the centre: I say, that, if those distances be taken continually proportional, the densities of the fluid at the same distances will be also continually proportional.

Let ATV denote the spherical bottom of the fluid, S the centre, SA, SB, SC, SD, SE, SF, &c., distances continually proportional. Erect the perpendiculars AH, BI, CK, DL, EM, FN, &c., which shall be as the densities of the medium in the places A, B, C, D, E, F; and the specific gravities in those places will be as $\dfrac{AH}{AS}, \dfrac{BI}{BS}, \dfrac{CK}{CS}$, &c., or, which is all one, as $\dfrac{AH}{AB}, \dfrac{BI}{BC}, \dfrac{CK}{CD}$, &c. Suppose, first, these gravities to be uniformly continued from A to B, from B to C, from C to D, &c., the decrements in the points B, C, D, &c., being taken by steps. And these gravities multiplied by the altitudes AB, BC, CD, &c., will give the pressures AH, BI, CK, &c., by which the bottom ATV is acted on (by Theor. 15). Therefore the particle A sustains all the pressures AH, BI, CK, DL, &c., proceeding *in infinitum;* and the particle B sustains the pressures of all but the first AH; and the particle C all but the two first AH, BI; and so on: and therefore the density AH of the first particle A is to the density BI of the second

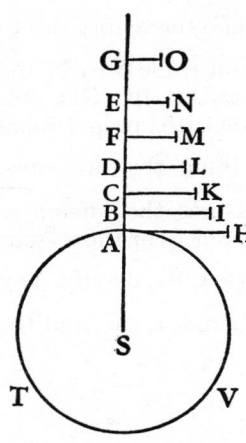

particle B as the sum of all AH+BI+CK+DL, *in infinitum*, to the sum of all BI+CK+DL, &c. And BI the density of the second particle B is to CK the density of the third C, as the sum of all BI+CK+DL, &c., to the sum of all CK+DL, &c. Therefore these sums are proportional to their differences AH, BI, CK, &c., and therefore continually proportional (by Lem. 1 of this book); and therefore the differences AH, BI, CK, &c., proportional to the sums, are also continually proportional. Therefore since the densities in the places A, B, C, &c., are as AH, BI, CK, &c., they will also be continually proportional. Proceed intermissively, and, at the distances SA, SC, SE, continually proportional, the densities AH, CK, EM will be continually proportional. And by the same reasoning, at any distances SA, SD, SG, continually proportional, the densities AH, DL, GO will be continually proportional. Let now the points A, B, C, D, E, &c., coincide, so that the progression of the specific gravities from the bottom A to the top of the fluid may be made continual; and at any distances SA, SD, SG, continually proportional, the densities AH, DL, GO, being all along continually proportional, will still remain continually proportional.

Q.E.D.

COR. Hence if the density of the fluid in two places, as A and E, be given, its density in any other place Q may be obtained. With the centre S, and the rectangular asymptotes SQ, SX, describe an hyperbola cutting the perpendiculars AH, EM, QT in *a*, *e*, and *q*, as also the perpendiculars HX, MY, TZ, let fall upon the asymptote SX, in *h*, *m*, and *t*. Make the area Y*mt*Z to the given area Y*mh*X as the given area E*eq*Q to the given area E*ea*A; and the line Z*t* produced will cut off the line QT proportional to the density. For if the lines SA, SE, SQ are continually proportional, the areas E*eq*Q, E*ea*A will be equal, and thence the areas Y*mt*Z, X*hm*Y, proportional to them, will be also equal; and the lines SX, SY, SZ, that is, AH, EM, QT continually proportional, as they ought to be. And if the lines SA, SE, SQ obtain any other order in the series of continued proportionals, the lines AH, EM, QT, because of the proportional hyperbolic areas, will obtain the same order in another series of quantities continually proportional.

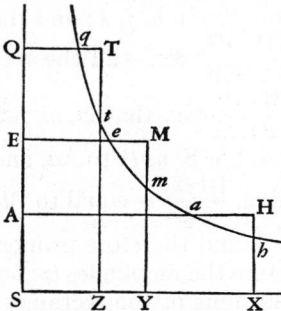

PROPOSITION 22. THEOREM 17

Let the density of any fluid be proportional to the compression, and its parts be attracted downwards by a gravitation inversely proportional to the squares of the distances from the centre: I say, that if the distances be taken in harmonic progression, the densities of the fluid at those distances will be in a geometrical progression.

Let S denote the centre, and SA, SB, SC, SD, SE the distances in geometrical progression. Erect the perpendiculars AH, BI, CK, &c., which shall be as the densities of the fluid in the places A, B, C, D, E, &c., and the specific gravities thereof in those places will be as $\dfrac{AH}{SA^2}$, $\dfrac{BI}{SB^2}$, $\dfrac{CK}{SC^2}$, &c. Suppose these gravities to be uniformly continued, the first from A to B, the second from B to C, the third from C to D, &c. And these multiplied by the altitudes AB, BC, CD, DE, &c., or, which is the same thing, by the distances SA, SB, SC, &c., proportional to those altitudes, will give $\dfrac{AH}{SA}$, $\dfrac{BI}{SB}$, $\dfrac{CK}{SC}$, &c., representing the pressures. Therefore since the densities are as the sums of those pressures, the differences AH−BI, BI−CK, &c., of the densities will be as the differences of those sums $\dfrac{AH}{SA}$, $\dfrac{BI}{SB}$, $\dfrac{CK}{SC}$, &c. With the centre S, and the asymptotes SA, Sx, describe any hyperbola, cutting the perpendiculars AH, BI, CK, &c., in a, b, c, &c., and the

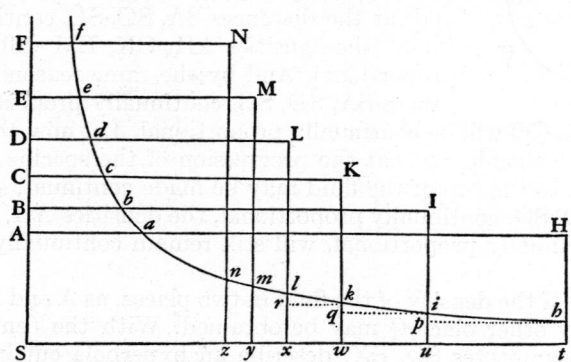

perpendiculars Ht, Iu, Kw, let fall upon the asymptote Sx, in h, i, k; and the differences of the densities, tu, uw, &c., will be as $\dfrac{AH}{SA}$, $\dfrac{BI}{SB}$, &c. And the rectangles $tu \cdot th$, $uw \cdot ui$, &c., or tp, uq, &c., as $\dfrac{AH \cdot th}{SA}$, $\dfrac{BI \cdot ui}{SB}$, &c., that is, as Aa, Bb, &c. For, by the nature of the hyperbola, SA is to AH or St as th to Aa, and therefore $\dfrac{AH \cdot th}{SA}$ is equal to Aa. And, by a like reasoning, $\dfrac{BI \cdot ui}{SB}$ is equal to Bb, &c. But Aa, Bb, Cc, &c., are continually proportional, and therefore proportional to their differences Aa−Bb, Bb−Cc, &c., therefore the rectangles tp, uq, &c., are proportional to those differences; as also the sums of the rectangles $tp+uq$ or $tp+uq+wr$ to the sums of the differences Aa−Cc or Aa−Dd. Suppose several of these terms, and the sum of all the differences, as Aa−Ff, will be proportional to the sum of all the rectangles, as $zthn$. Increase the number of terms, and diminish the distances of the points A, B, C, &c., *in infinitum*, and those rectangles will become equal to the hyperbolic area $zthn$, and therefore the difference Aa−Ff is proportional to this area. Take now any distances, as SA, SD, SF, in harmonic progression, and the differences Aa−Dd, Dd−Ff will be equal; and therefore the areas $thlx$, $xlnz$, proportional to those differences, will be equal among themselves, and the densities St, Sx, Sz, that is, AH, DL, FN, continually proportional.   Q.E.D.

COR. Hence if any two densities of the fluid, as AH and BI, be given, the area *thiu*, answering to their difference tu, will be given; and thence the density

FN will be found at any height SF, by taking the area *thnz* to that given area *thiu* as the difference A*a* − F*f* to the difference A*a* − B*b*.

Scholium

By a like reasoning it may be proved, that if the gravity of the particles of a fluid diminishes as the cube of the distances from the centre, and the reciprocals of the squares of the distances SA, SB, SC, &c., (namely, $\frac{SA^3}{SA^2}, \frac{SA^3}{SB^2}, \frac{SA^3}{SC^2}$) be taken in an arithmetical progression, the densities AH, BI, CK, &c., will be in a geometrical progression. And if the gravity be diminished as the fourth power of the distances, and the reciprocals of the cubes of the distances (as $\frac{SA^4}{SA^3}, \frac{SA^4}{SB^3}, \frac{SA^4}{SC^3}$, &c.) be taken in arithmetical progression, the densities AH, BI, CK, &c., will be in geometrical progression. And so *in infinitum*. Again; if the gravity of the particles of the fluid be the same at all distances, and the distances be in arithmetical progression, the densities will be in a geometrical progression, as Dr. Halley hath found. If the gravity be as the distance, and the squares of the distances be in arithmetical progression, the densities will be in geometrical progression. And so *in infinitum*. These things will be so, when the density of the fluid condensed by compression is as the force of compression; or, which is the same thing, when the space possessed by the fluid is inversely as this force. Other laws of condensation may be supposed, as that the cube of the compressing force may be as the fourth power of the density, or the cube of the ratio of the force the same with the fourth power of the ratio of the density: in which case, if the gravity be inversely as the square of the distance from the centre, the density will be inversely as the cube of the distance. Suppose that the cube of the compressing force be as the fifth power of the density; and if the gravity be inversely as the square of the distance, the density will be inversely as the $\frac{3}{2}$th power of the distance. Suppose the compressing force to be as the square of the density, and the gravity inversely as the square of the distance, then the density will be inversely as the distance. To run over all the cases that might be offered would be tedious. But as to our own air, this is certain from experiment, that its density is either accurately, or very nearly at least, as the compressing force; and therefore the density of the air in the atmosphere of the earth is as the weight of the whole incumbent air, that is, as the height of the mercury in the barometer.

Proposition 23. Theorem 18

If a fluid be composed of particles fleeing from each other, and the density be as the compression, the centrifugal forces of the particles will be inversely proportional to the distances of their centres. And, conversely, particles fleeing from each other, with forces that are inversely proportional to the distances of their centres, compose an elastic fluid, whose density is as the compression.

Let the fluid be supposed to be included in a cubic space ACE, and then to be reduced by compression into a lesser cubic space *ace*; and the distances of the particles retaining a like situation with respect to each other in both the spaces, will be as the sides AB, *ab* of the cubes; and the densities of the mediums will be inversely as the containing spaces AB³, *ab*³. In the plane side of the

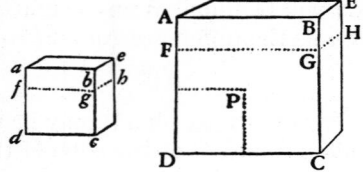

greater cube ABCD take the square DP equal to the plane side *db* of the lesser cube; and, by the supposition, the pressure with which the square DP urges the inclosed fluid will be to the pressure with which that square *db* urges the inclosed fluid as the densities of the mediums are to each other, that is, as ab^3 to AB^3. But the pressure with which the square DB urges the included fluid is to the pressure with which the square DP urges the same fluid as the square DB to the square DP, that is, as AB^2 to ab^2. Therefore, multiplying together corresponding terms of the proportions, the pressure with which the square DB urges the fluid is to the pressure with which the square *db* urges the fluid as *ab* to AB. Let the planes FGH, *fgh* be drawn through the interior of the two cubes, and divide the fluid into two parts. These parts will press each other with the same forces with which they are themselves pressed by the planes AC, *ac*, that is, in the proportion of *ab* to AB: and therefore the centrifugal forces by which these pressures are sustained are in the same ratio. The number of the particles being equal, and the situation alike, in both cubes, the forces which all the particles exert, according to the planes FGH, *fgh*, upon all, are as the forces which each exerts on each. Therefore the forces which each exerts on each, according to the plane FGH in the greater cube, are to the forces which each exerts on each, according to the plane *fgh* in the lesser cube, as *ab* to AB, that is, inversely as the distances of the particles from each other.   Q.E.D.

And, conversely, if the forces of the single particles are inversely as the distances, that is, inversely as the sides of the cubes AB, *ab*; the sums of the forces will be in the same ratio, and the pressures of the sides DB, *db* as the sums of the forces; and the pressure of the square DP to the pressure of the side DB as ab^2 to AB^2. And, multiplying together corresponding terms of the proportions, one obtains the pressure of the square DP to the pressure of the side *db* as ab^3 to AB^3; that is, the force of compression in the one is to the force of compression in the other as the density in the former to the density in the latter.   Q.E.D.

SCHOLIUM

By a like reasoning, if the centrifugal forces of the particles are inversely as the square of the distances between the centres, the cubes of the compressing forces will be as the fourth power of the densities. If the centrifugal forces be inversely as the third or fourth power of the distances, the cubes of the compressing forces will be as the fifth or sixth power of the densities. And universally, if D be put for the distance, and E for the density of the compressed fluid, and the centrifugal forces be inversely as any power D^n of the distance, whose index is the number n, the compressing forces will be as the cube roots of the power E^{n+2}, whose index is the number $n+2$; and conversely. All these things are to be understood of particles whose centrifugal forces terminate in those particles that are next them, or are diffused not much farther. We have an example of this in magnetic bodies. Their attractive force is terminated nearly in bodies of their own kind that are next them. The force of the magnet is reduced by the interposition of an iron plate, and is almost terminated at it: for bodies farther off are not attracted by the magnet so much as by the iron plate. If in this manner particles repel others of their own kind that lie next them, but do not exert their force on the more remote, particles of this kind will compose such fluids as are treated of in this Proposition. If the force of any particle diffuse itself every way *in infinitum*, there will be required a greater force to produce an equal condensation of a greater quantity of the fluid. But whether elastic fluids do really consist of particles so repelling each other, is a physical question. We have here demonstrated mathematically the property of fluids consisting of particles of this kind, that hence philosophers may take occasion to discuss that question.

SECTION VI

The motion and resistance of pendulous bodies

Proposition 24. Theorem 19

The quantities of matter in pendulous bodies, whose centres of oscillation are equally distant from the centre of suspension, are in a ratio compounded of the ratio of the weights and the squared ratio of the times of the oscillations in a vacuum.

For the velocity which a given force can generate in a given matter in a given time is directly as the force and the time, and inversely as the matter. The greater the force or the time is, or the less the matter, the greater the velocity generated. This is manifest from the second Law of Motion. Now if pendulums are of the same length, the motive forces in places equally distant from the perpendicular are as the weights: and therefore if two bodies by oscillating describe equal arcs, and those arcs are divided into equal parts; since the times in which the bodies describe each of the correspondent parts of the arcs are as the times of the whole oscillations, the velocities in the correspondent parts of the oscillations will be to each other directly as the motive forces and the whole times of the oscillations, and inversely as the quantities of matter: and therefore the quantities of matter are directly as the forces and the times of the oscillations, and inversely as the velocities. But the velocities are inversely as the times, and therefore the times are directly and the velocities inversely as the squares of the times; and therefore the quantities of matter are as the motive forces and the squares of the times, that is, as the weights and the squares of the times. Q.E.D.

Cor. i. Therefore if the times are equal, the quantities of matter in each of the bodies are as the weights.

Cor. ii. If the weights are equal, the quantities of matter will be as the squares of the times.

Cor. iii. If the quantities of matter are equal, the weights will be inversely as the squares of the times.

Cor. iv. Since the squares of the times, other things being equal, are as the lengths of the pendulums, therefore if both the times and the quantities of matter are equal, the weights will be as the lengths of the pendulums.

Cor. v. And, in general, the quantity of matter in the pendulous body is directly as the weight and the square of the time, and inversely as the length of the pendulum.

COR. VI. But in a nonresisting medium, the quantity of matter in the pendulous body is directly as the comparative weight and the square of the time, and inversely as the length of the pendulum. For the comparative weight is the motive force of the body in any heavy medium, as was shown above; and therefore does the same thing in such a nonresisting medium as the absolute weight does in a vacuum.

COR. VII. And hence appears a method both of comparing bodies one with another, as to the quantity of matter in each; and of comparing the weights of the same body in different places, to know the variation of its gravity. And by experiments made with the greatest accuracy, I have always found the quantity of matter in bodies to be proportional to their weight.

PROPOSITION 25. THEOREM 20

Pendulous bodies that are, in any medium, resisted in the ratio of the moments of time, and pendulous bodies that move in a nonresisting medium of the same specific gravity, perform their oscillations in a cycloid in the same time, and describe proportional parts of arcs together.

Let AB be an arc of a cycloid, which a body D, by vibrating in a nonresisting medium, shall describe in any time. Bisect that arc in C, so that C may be the lowest point thereof; and the accelerative force with which the body is urged in any place D, or d, or E, will be as the length of the arc CD, or Cd, or CE. Let that force be expressed by that same arc; and since the resistance is as the moment of the time, and therefore given, let it be expressed by the given part CO of the cycloidal arc, and take the arc Od in the same ratio to the arc CD that the arc OB has to the arc CB: and the force with which the body in d is urged in a resisting medium, being the excess of the force Cd above the resistance CO, will be expressed by the arc Od, and will therefore be to the force with

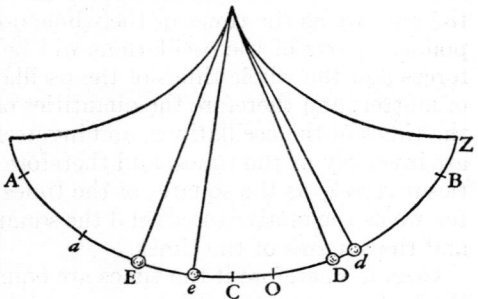

which the body D is urged in a nonresisting medium in the place D, as the arc Od to the arc CD; and therefore also in the place B, as the arc OB to the arc CB. Therefore if two bodies D, d go from the place B, and are urged by these forces; since the forces at the beginning are as the arcs CB and OB, the first velocities and arcs first described will be in the same ratio. Let those arcs be BD and Bd, and the remaining arcs CD, Od will be in the same ratio. Therefore the forces, being proportional to those arcs CD, Od, will remain in the same ratio as at the beginning, and therefore the bodies will continue describing together arcs in the same ratio. Therefore the forces and velocities and the remaining arcs CD, Od, will be always as the whole arcs CB, OB, and therefore those remaining arcs will be described together. Therefore the two bodies D and d will arrive together at the places C and O; that which moves in the nonresisting medium, at the place C, and the other, in the resisting medium, at the place O. Now since the velocities in C and O are as the arcs CB, OB, the arcs which the bodies describe when they go farther will be in the same ratio. Let those arcs be CE and Oe.

The force with which the body D in a nonresisting medium is retarded in E is as CE, and the force with which the body d in the resisting medium is retarded in e, is as the sum of the force Ce and the resistance CO, that is, as Oe; and therefore the forces with which the bodies are retarded are as the arcs CB, OB, proportional to the arcs CE, Oe; and therefore the velocities, retarded in that given ratio, remain in the same given ratio. Therefore the velocities and the arcs described with those velocities are always to each other in that given ratio of the arcs CB and OB; and therefore if the entire arcs AB, aB are taken in the same ratio, the bodies D and d will describe those arcs together, and in the places A and a will lose all their motion together. Therefore the whole oscillations are isochronal, or are performed in equal times; and any parts of the arcs, as BD, Bd, or BE, Be, that are described together, are proportional to the whole arcs BA, Ba.   Q.E.D.

Cor. Therefore the swiftest motion in a resisting medium does not fall upon the lowest point C, but is found in that point O, in which the whole arc described Ba is bisected. And the body, proceeding from thence to a, is retarded at the same rate with which it was accelerated before in its descent from B to O.

Proposition 26. Theorem 21

Pendulous bodies, that are resisted in the ratio of the velocity, have their oscillations in a cycloid isochronal.

For if two bodies, equally distant from their centres of suspension, describe, in oscillating, unequal arcs, and the velocities in the correspondent parts of the arcs be to each other as the whole arcs; the resistances, proportional to the velocities, will be also to each other as the same arcs. Therefore if these resistances be subtracted from or added to the motive forces arising from gravity which are as the same arcs, the differences or sums will be to each other in the same ratio of the arcs; and since the increments and decrements of the velocities are as these differences or sums, the velocities will be always as the whole arcs; therefore if the velocities are in any one case as the whole arcs, they will remain always in the same ratio. But at the beginning of the motion, when the bodies begin to descend and describe those arcs, the forces, which at that time are proportional to the arcs, will generate velocities proportional to the arcs. Therefore the velocities will be always as the whole arcs to be described, and therefore those arcs will be described in the same time.   Q.E.D.

Proposition 27. Theorem 22

If pendulous bodies are resisted as the square of their velocities, the differences between the times of the oscillations in a resisting medium, and the times of the oscillations in a nonresisting medium of the same specific gravity, will be proportional to the arcs described in oscillating, nearly.

For let equal pendulums in a resisting medium describe the unequal arcs A, B; and the resistance of the body in the arc A will be to the resistance of the body in the correspondent part of the arc B as the square of the velocities, that is, as AA to BB, nearly. If the resistance in the arc B were to the resistance in the arc A as AB to AA, the times in the arcs A and B would be equal (by the last Proposition). Therefore the resistance AA in the arc A, or AB in the arc B, causes the excess of the time in the arc A above the time in a nonresisting medium; and the resistance BB causes the excess of the time in the arc B above the time in a nonresisting medium. But those excesses are as the efficient forces AB and BB nearly, that is, as the arcs A and B.   Q.E.D.

COR. I. Hence from the times of the oscillations in unequal arcs in a resisting medium, may be known the times of the oscillations in a nonresisting medium of the same specific gravity. For the difference of the times will be to the excess of the time in the shorter arc above the time in a nonresisting medium as the difference of the arcs is to the shorter arc.

COR. II. The shorter oscillations are more isochronal, and very short ones are performed nearly in the same times as in a nonresisting medium. But the times of those which are performed in greater arcs are a little greater, because the resistance in the descent of the body, by which the time is prolonged, is greater, in proportion to the length described in the descent than the resistance in the subsequent ascent, by which the time is contracted. But the time of the oscillations, both short and long, seems to be prolonged in some measure by the motion of the medium. For retarded bodies are resisted somewhat less in proportion to the velocity, and accelerated bodies somewhat more than those that proceed uniformly forwards; because the medium, by the motion it has received from the bodies, going forwards the same way with them, is more agitated in the former case, and less in the latter; and so conspires more or less with the bodies moved. Therefore it resists the pendulums in their descent more, and in their ascent less, than in proportion to the velocity; and these two causes concurring prolong the time.

PROPOSITION 28. THEOREM 23

If a pendulous body, oscillating in a cycloid, be resisted in the ratio of the moments of the time, its resistance will be to the force of gravity, as the excess of the arc described in the whole descent above the arc described in the subsequent ascent is to twice the length of the pendulum.

Let BC represent the arc described in the descent, Ca the arc described in the ascent, and Aa the difference of the arcs: and things remaining as they were constructed and demonstrated in Prop. 25, the force with which the oscillating body is urged in any place D will be to the force of resistance as the arc CD to the arc CO, which is half of that difference Aa. Therefore the force with which the oscillating body is urged at the beginning or the highest point of the cycloid, that is, the force of gravity, will be to the resistance as the arc of the cycloid, between that highest point and the lowest point C, is to the arc CO; that is

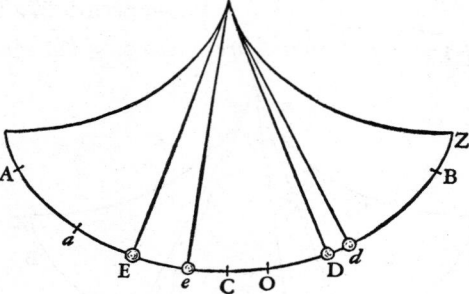

that is, the force of gravity, will be to the resistance as the arc of the cycloid, between that highest point and the lowest point C, is to the arc CO; that is (doubling those arcs), as the whole cycloidal arc, or twice the length of the pendulum, is to the arc Aa. Q.E.D.

PROPOSITION 29. PROBLEM 6

Supposing that a body oscillating in a cycloid is resisted as the square of the velocity; to find the resistance in each place.

Let Ba be an arc described in one entire oscillation, C the lowest point of the cycloid, and CZ half the whole cycloidal arc, equal to the length of the pendulum; and let it be required to find the resistance of the body in any place D. Cut the indefinite right line OQ in the points O, S, P, Q, so that (erecting the perpendiculars OK, ST, PI, QE, and with the centre O, and the asymptotes OK, OQ, describing the hyperbola TIGE cutting the perpendiculars ST, PI, QE in T, I, and E, and through the point I drawing KF, parallel to the asymptote, OQ, meeting the asymptote OK in K, and the perpendiculars ST and QE in L and F) the hyperbolic area PIEQ may be to the hyperbolic area PITS as the arc BC, described in the descent of the body, is to the arc Ca described in the ascent; and that the area IEF may be to the area ILT as OQ to OS. Then

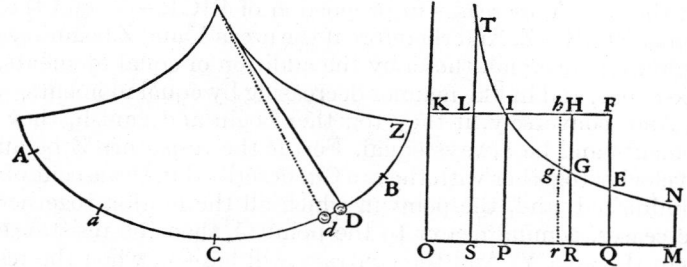

with the perpendicular MN cut off the hyperbolic area PINM, and let that area be to the hyperbolic area PIEQ as the arc CZ to the arc BC described in the descent. And if the perpendicular RG cuts off the hyperbolic area PIGR, which shall be to the area PIEQ as any arc CD is to the arc BC described in the whole descent, the resistance in any place D will be to the force of gravity as the area $\frac{OR}{OQ}$ IEF − IGH is to the area PINM.

For since the forces arising from gravity with which the body is urged in the places Z, B, D, a are as the arcs CZ, CB, CD, Ca, and those arcs are as the areas PINM, PIEQ, PIGR, PITS; let those areas represent both the arcs and the forces respectively. Let Dd be a very small space described by the body in its descent; and let it be expressed by the very small area RGgr, comprehended between the parallels RG, rg; and produce rg to h, so that GHhg and RGgr may be the contemporaneous decrements of the areas IGH, PIGR. And the increment GHhg − $\frac{Rr}{OQ}$ IEF, or Rr·HG − $\frac{Rr}{OQ}$ IEF, of the area $\frac{OR}{OQ}$ IEF − IGH will be to the decrement RGgr, or Rr·RG, of the area PIGR, as HG − $\frac{IEF}{OQ}$ is to RG; and therefore as OR·HG − $\frac{OR}{OQ}$ IEF is to OR·GR or OP·PI, that is (because of the equal quantities OR·HG, OR·HR − OR·GR, ORHK − OPIK,

PIHR and PIGR+IGH), as PIGR+IGH$-\dfrac{OR}{OQ}$ IEF is to OPIK. Therefore if

the area $\dfrac{OR}{OQ}$ IEF$-$IGH be called Y, and RGgr the decrement of the area

PIGR be given, the increment of the area Y will be as PIGR$-$Y.

Then if V represent the force arising from the gravity, proportional to the arc CD to be described, by which the body is acted upon in D, and R be put for the resistance, V$-$R will be the whole force with which the body is urged in D. Therefore the increment of the velocity is as V$-$R and the interval of time in which it is generated conjointly. But the velocity itself is directly as the contemporaneous increment of the space described and inversely as the same interval of time. Therefore, since the resistance is, by the supposition, as the square of the velocity, the increment of the resistance will (by Lem. 2) be as the velocity and the increment of the velocity conjointly, that is, as the moment of the space and V$-$R conjointly; and, therefore, if the moment of the space be given, as V$-$R; that is, if for the force V we put its expression PIGR, and the resistance R be expressed by any other area Z, as PIGR$-$Z.

Therefore the area PIGR uniformly decreasing by the subtraction of given moments, the area Y increases in proportion of PIGR$-$Y, and the area Z in proportion of PIGR$-$Z. And therefore if the areas Y and Z begin together, and at the beginning are equal, these, by the addition of equal moments, will continue to be equal; and in like manner decreasing by equal moments, will vanish together. And, conversely, if they together begin and vanish, they will have equal moments and be always equal. For, if the resistance Z be augmented, then the velocity together with the arc Ca, described in the ascent of the body, will be diminished; and, the point in which all the motion together with the resistance ceases, coming nearer to the point C, then the resistance vanishes sooner than the area Y. And the contrary will happen when the resistance is diminished.

Now the area Z begins and ends where the resistance is nothing, that is, at the beginning of the motion where the arc CD is equal to the arc CB, and the right line RG falls upon the right line QE; and at the end of the motion where the arc CD is equal to the arc Ca, and RG falls upon the right line ST. And the

area Y or $\dfrac{OR}{OQ}$ IEF$-$IGH begins and ends also where the resistance is nothing,

and therefore where $\dfrac{OR}{OQ}$ IEF and IGH are equal; that is (by the construction),

where the right line RG falls successively upon the right lines QE and ST. Therefore those areas begin and vanish together, and are therefore always

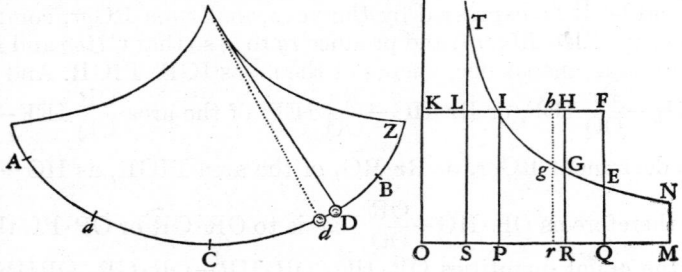

equal. Hence, the area $\dfrac{OR}{OQ}$ IEF$-$IGH is equal to the area Z, by which the resistance is expressed, and therefore is to the area PINM, by which the gravity is expressed, as the resistance is to the gravity. Q.E.D.

COR. I. Therefore the resistance in the lowest place C is to the force of gravity as the area $\dfrac{OP}{OQ}$ IEF is to the area PINM.

COR. II. But it becomes greatest where the area PIHR is to the area IEF as OR is to OQ. For in that case its moment (that is, PIGR$-$Y) becomes nothing.

COR. III. Hence also may be known the velocity in each place, as varying as the square root of the resistance, and at the beginning of the motion being equal to the velocity of the body oscillating in the same cycloid without any resistance.

However, by reason of the difficulty of the calculation by which the resistance and the velocity are found by this Proposition, we have thought fit to subjoin the Proposition following.

PROPOSITION 30. THEOREM 24

If a right line aB be equal to the arc of a cycloid which an oscillating body describes, and at each of its points D the perpendiculars DK be erected, which shall be to the length of the pendulum as the resistance of the body in the corresponding points of the arc is to the force of gravity: I say, that the difference between the arc described in the whole descent and the arc described in the whole subsequent ascent multiplied by half the sum of the same arcs will be equal to the area BKa which all those perpendiculars take up.

Let the arc of the cycloid, described in one entire oscillation, be expressed by the right line *a*B, equal to it, and the arc which would have been described in a vacuum by the length AB. Bisect AB in C, and the point C will represent the lowest point of the cycloid, and CD will be as the force arising from gravity, with which the body in D is urged in the direction of the tangent of the cycloid, and will have the same ratio to the length of the pendulum as the force in D has

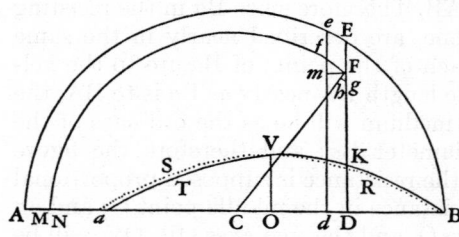

to the force of gravity. Let that force, therefore, be expressed by that length CD, and the force of gravity by the length of the pendulum; and if in DE you take DK in the same ratio to the length of the pendulum as the resistance is to the gravity, DK will be the exponent of the resistance.

From the centre C with the interval CA or CB describe a semicircle BE*e*A. Let the body describe, in the least time, the space D*d*; and, erecting the perpendiculars DE, *de*, meeting the circumference in E and *e*, they will be as the velocities which the body descending in a vacuum from the point B would acquire in the places D and *d*. This appears by Prop. 52, Book I. Let, therefore, these velocities be expressed by those perpendiculars DE, *de*; and let DF be the velocity which it acquires in D by falling from B in the resisting medium. And if from the centre C with the interval CF we describe the circle F*f*M meeting the right lines *de* and AB in *f* and M, then M will be the place to which it would thenceforward, without further resistance, ascend, and df the velocity it would acquire in d. Hence, also, if Fg represent the moment of the velocity which the body D, in describing the least space Dd, loses by the resistance of the medium; and CN be taken equal to Cg; then will N be the place to which the body, if it met no further resistance, would thenceforward ascend, and MN will be the decrement of the ascent arising from the loss of that velocity. Draw Fm perpendicular to df, and the decrement Fg of the velocity DF generated by the resistance DK will be to the increment fm of the same velocity, generated by the force CD, as the generating force DK to the generating force CD. But because of the similar triangles Fmf, Fhg, FDC, fm is to Fm or Dd as CD to DF; and, by multiplication of corresponding terms, Fg to Dd as DK to DF. Also Fh is to Fg as DF to CF; and, again by multiplication of corresponding terms, Fh or MN to Dd as DK to CF or CM; and therefore the sum of all the MN$\cdot$CM will be equal to the sum of all the D$d\cdot$DK. At the movable point M suppose always a rectangular ordinate erected equal to the indeterminate CM, which by a continual motion is multiplied by the whole length Aa; and the trapezium described by that motion, or its equal, the rectangle A$a\cdot\frac{1}{2}a$B, will be equal to the sum of all the MN$\cdot$CM, and therefore to the sum of all the D$d\cdot$DK, that is, to the area BKVTa.   Q.E.D.

COR. Hence from the law of resistance, and the difference Aa of the arcs Ca, CB, may be derived the proportion of the resistance to the gravity, nearly.

For if the resistance DK be uniform, the figure BKTa will be a rectangle under Ba and DK; and hence the rectangle under $\frac{1}{2}$Ba and Aa will be equal to the rectangle under Ba and DK, and DK will be equal to $\frac{1}{2}$Aa. Therefore since DK represents the resistance, and the length of the pendulum represents the gravity, the resistance will be to the gravity as $\frac{1}{2}$Aa is to the length of the pendulum; altogether as in Prop. 28 is demonstrated.

If the resistance be as the velocity, the figure BKTa will be nearly an ellipse. For if a body, in a nonresisting medium, by one entire oscillation, should describe the length BA, the velocity in any place D would be as the ordinate DE of the circle described on the diameter AB. Therefore since Ba in the resisting medium, and BA in the nonresisting one, are described nearly in the same times; and therefore the velocities in each of the points of Ba are to the velocities in the corresponding points of the length BA nearly as Ba is to BA, the velocity in the point D in the resisting medium will be as the ordinate of the circle or ellipse described upon the diameter Ba; and therefore the figure BKVTa will be nearly an ellipse. Since the resistance is supposed proportional to the velocity, let OV represent the resistance in the middle point O; and an ellipse BRVSa described with the centre O, and the semiaxes OB, OV, will be nearly equal to the figure BKVTa, and to its equal the rectangle A$a\cdot$BO. Therefore A$a\cdot$BO is to OV$\cdot$BO as the area of this ellipse to OV$\cdot$BO; that is, Aa is to OV as the area of the semicircle is to the square of the radius, or as 11 to 7 nearly; and, therefore, $\frac{7}{11}$Aa is to the length of the pendulum as the resistance of the oscillating body in O is to its gravity.

Now if the resistance DK varies as the square of the velocity, the figure BKVTa will be almost a parabola having V for its vertex and OV for its axis, and therefore will be nearly equal to the rectangle under $\frac{2}{3}$Ba and OV. Therefore the rectangle under $\frac{1}{2}$Ba and Aa is equal to the rectangle $\frac{2}{3}$B$a\cdot$OV, and therefore OV is equal to $\frac{3}{4}Aa$; and therefore the resistance in O made to the oscillating body is to its gravity as $\frac{3}{4}Aa$ is to the length of the pendulum.

And I take these conclusions to be accurate enough for practical uses. For since an ellipse or parabola BRVSa falls in with the figure BKVTa in the middle point V, that figure, if greater towards the part BRV or VSa, is less towards the contrary part, and is therefore nearly equal to it.

PROPOSITION 31. THEOREM 25

If the resistance made to an oscillating body in each of the proportional parts of the arcs described be augmented or diminished in a given ratio, the difference between the arc described in the descent and the arc described in the subsequent ascent will be augmented or diminished in the same ratio.

For that difference arises from the retardation of the pendulum by the resistance of the medium, and therefore is as the whole retardation and the retarding resistance proportional thereto. In the foregoing Proposition the rectangle under the right line $\frac{1}{2}aB$ and the difference Aa of the arcs CB, Ca, was equal to the area BKTa. And that area, if the length aB remains, is augmented or diminished in the ratio of the ordinates DK; that is, in the ratio of the resistance, and is therefore as the length aB and the resistance conjointly. And therefore the rectangle under Aa and $\frac{1}{2}aB$ is as aB and the resistance conjointly, and therefore Aa is as the resistance.   Q.E.D.

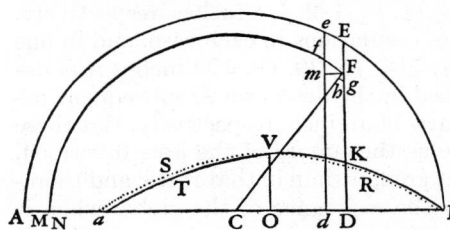

COR. I. Hence if the resistance be as the velocity, the difference of the arcs in the same medium will be as the whole arc described; and conversely.

COR. II. If the resistance varies as the square of the velocity, that difference will vary as the square of the whole arc; and conversely.

COR. III. And generally, if the resistance varies as the third or any other power of the velocity, the difference will vary as the same power of the whole arc; and conversely.

COR. IV. If the resistance varies partly as the first power of the velocity and partly as the square of the same, the difference will vary partly as the first power and partly as the square of the whole arc; and conversely. So that the law and ratio of the resistance will be the same for the velocity as the law and ratio of that difference for the length of the arc.

COR. V. And therefore if a pendulum describe successively unequal arcs, and we can find the ratio of the increment or decrement of this difference for the length of the arc described, there will be had also the ratio of the increment or decrement of the resistance for a greater or less velocity.

GENERAL SCHOLIUM

From these Propositions we may find the resistance of mediums by pendulums oscillating therein. I found the resistance of the air by the following experiments. I suspended a wooden globe or ball weighing $57\frac{7}{22}$ ounces troy, its diameter $6\frac{7}{8}$ London inches, by a fine thread on a firm hook, so that the distance between the hook and the centre of oscillation of the globe was $10\frac{1}{2}$

feet. I marked on the thread a point 10 feet and 1 inch distant from the centre of suspension; and even with that point I placed a ruler divided into inches, by the help of which I observed the lengths of the arcs described by the pendulum. Then I numbered the oscillations in which the globe would lose $\frac{1}{8}$ part of its motion. If the pendulum was drawn aside from the perpendicular to the distance of 2 inches, and then let go, so that in its whole descent it described an arc of 2 inches, and in the first whole oscillation, compounded of the descent and subsequent ascent, an arc of almost 4 inches, the pendulum in 164 oscillations lost $\frac{1}{8}$ part of its motion, so as in its last ascent to describe an arc of $1\frac{3}{4}$ inches. If in the first descent it described an arc of 4 inches, it lost $\frac{1}{8}$ part of its motion in 121 oscillations, so as in its last ascent to describe an arc of $3\frac{1}{2}$ inches. If in the first descent it described an arc of 8, 16, 32, or 64 inches, it lost $\frac{1}{8}$ part of its motion in 69, $35\frac{1}{2}$, $18\frac{1}{2}$, $9\frac{2}{3}$ oscillations, respectively. Therefore the difference between the arcs described in the first descent and the last ascent was in the 1st, 2d, 3d, 4th, 5th, 6th cases, $\frac{1}{4}$, $\frac{1}{2}$, 1, 2, 4, 8 inches, respectively. Divide those differences by the number of oscillations in each case, and in one mean oscillation, in which an arc of $3\frac{3}{4}$, $7\frac{1}{2}$, 15, 30, 60, 120 inches was described, the difference of the arcs described in the descent and subsequent ascent will be $\frac{1}{656}$, $\frac{1}{242}$, $\frac{1}{69}$, $\frac{4}{71}$, $\frac{8}{37}$, $\frac{24}{29}$ parts of an inch, respectively. But these differences in the greater oscillations are as the square of the arcs described, nearly, but in lesser oscillations somewhat greater than in that ratio; and therefore (by Cor. II, Prop. 31 of this Book) the resistance of the globe, when it moves very swiftly, varies as the square of the velocity, nearly; and when it moves slowly, in a somewhat greater ratio.

Now let V represent the greatest velocity in any oscillation, and let A, B, and C be given quantities, and let us suppose the difference of the arcs to be $AV + BV^{3/2} + CV^2$. Since the greatest velocities are in the cycloid as $\frac{1}{2}$ the arcs described in oscillating, and in the circle as $\frac{1}{2}$ the chords of those arcs; and therefore in equal arcs are greater in the cycloid than in the circle in the ratio of $\frac{1}{2}$ the arcs to their chords; but the times in the circle are greater than in the cycloid, in a ratio inversely as the velocity; it is plain that the differences of the arcs (which are as the resistance and the square of the time conjointly) are nearly the same in both curves: for in the cycloid those differences must be on the one hand augmented, with the resistance, in about the squared ratio of the arc to the chord, because of the velocity augmented in the simple ratio of the same; and on the other hand diminished, with the square of the time, in the same squared ratio. Therefore to reduce these observations to the cycloid, we must take the same differences of the arcs as were observed in the circle, and suppose the greatest velocities analogous to the half, or the whole arcs, that is, to the numbers $\frac{1}{2}$, 1, 2, 4, 8, 16. Therefore in the 2d, 4th, and 6th cases put 1, 4, and 16 for V; and the difference of the arcs in the 2d case will become $\frac{\frac{1}{2}}{121} = A + B + C$; in the 4th case, $\frac{2}{35\frac{1}{2}} = 4A + 8B + 16C$; in the 6th case, $\frac{8}{9\frac{2}{3}} = 16A + 64B + 256C$. These equations reduced give $A = 0.0000916$, $B = 0.0010847$, and $C = 0.0029558$. Therefore the difference of the arcs is as $0.0000916V + 0.0010847V^{3/2} + 0.0029558V^2$; and therefore since (by Cor., Prop. 30, applied to this case) the resistance of the globe in the middle of the arc described in oscillating, where the velocity is V, is to its weight as $\frac{7}{11}AV + \frac{7}{10}BV^{3/2} + \frac{3}{4}CV^2$ is to the length of the pendulum, if for A, B, and C you put the numbers found, the resistance of the globe will be to its weight as $0.0000583V + 0.0007593V^{3/2} + 0.0022169V^2$

is to the length of the pendulum between the centre of suspension and the ruler, that is, to 121 inches. Therefore since V in the second case represents 1, in the 4th case 4 and in the 6th case 16, the resistance will be to the weight of the globe, in the 2d case, as 0.0030345 is to 121; in the 4th, as 0.041748 is to 121; in the 6th, as 0.61705 is to 121.

The arc, which the point marked in the thread described in the 6th case, was $120 - \frac{8}{9\frac{2}{3}}$, or $119\frac{5}{29}$ inches. And therefore since the radius was 121 inches, and the length of the pendulum between the point of suspension and the centre of the globe was 126 inches, the arc which the centre of the globe described was $124\frac{3}{31}$ inches. Because the greatest velocity of the oscillating body, by reason of the resistance of the air, does not fall on the lowest point of the arc described, but near the middle place of the whole arc, this velocity will be nearly the same as if the globe in its whole descent in a nonresisting medium should describe $62\frac{3}{62}$ inches, the half of that arc, and that in a cycloid, to which we have above reduced the motion of the pendulum; and therefore that velocity will be equal to that which the globe would acquire by falling perpendicularly from a height equal to the versed sine of that arc. But that versed sine in the cycloid is to that arc $62\frac{3}{32}$ as the same arc to twice the length of the pendulum 252, and therefore equal to 15.278 inches. Therefore the velocity of the pendulum is the same which a body would acquire by falling, and in its fall describing a space of 15.278 inches. Therefore with such a velocity the globe meets with a resistance which is to its weight as 0.61705 is to 121, or (if we take that part only of the resistance which is in the squared ratio of the velocity) as 0.56752 to 121.

I found, by an hydrostatical experiment, that the weight of this wooden globe was to the weight of a globe of water of the same magnitude as 55 to 97; and therefore since 121 is to 213.4 in the same ratio, the resistance made to this globe of water, moving forwards with the above-mentioned velocity, will be to its weight as 0.56752 to 213.4, that is, as 1 to $376\frac{1}{50}$. Since the weight of a globe of water, in the time in which the globe with a velocity uniformly continued describes a length of 30.556 inches, will generate all that velocity in the falling globe, it is manifest that the force of resistance uniformly continued in the same time will take away a velocity, which will be less than the other in the ratio of 1 to $376\frac{1}{50}$, that is, the $\frac{1}{376\frac{1}{50}}$ part of the whole velocity. And therefore in the time that the globe, with the same velocity uniformly continued, would describe the length of its semidiameter, or $3\frac{7}{16}$ inches, it would lose the $\frac{1}{3342}$ part of its motion.

I also counted the oscillations in which the pendulum lost $\frac{1}{4}$ part of its motion. In the following table the upper numbers denote the length of the arc described in the first descent, expressed in inches and parts of an inch; the middle numbers denote the length of the arc described in the last ascent; and in the lowest place are the numbers of the oscillations. I give an account of this experiment, as being more accurate than that in which only $\frac{1}{8}$ part of the motion was lost. I leave the calculation to such as are disposed to make it.

First descent	2	4	8	16	32	64
Last ascent	$1\frac{1}{2}$	3	6	12	24	48
No. of oscillations	374	272	$162\frac{1}{2}$	$83\frac{1}{3}$	$41\frac{2}{3}$	$22\frac{2}{3}$

I afterwards suspended a leaden globe of 2 inches in diameter, weighing $26\frac{1}{4}$ ounces troy by the same thread, so that between the centre of the globe and the point of suspension there was an interval of $10\frac{1}{2}$ feet, and I counted the oscillations in which a given part of the motion was lost. The first of the following tables exhibits the number of oscillations in which $\frac{1}{8}$ part of the whole motion was lost; the second the number of oscillations in which there was lost $\frac{1}{4}$ part of the same.

First descent	1	2	4	8	16	32	64
Last ascent	$\frac{7}{8}$	$\frac{7}{4}$	$3\frac{1}{2}$	7	14	28	56
No. of oscillations	226	228	193	140	$90\frac{1}{2}$	53	30
First descent	1	2	4	8	16	32	64
Last ascent	$\frac{3}{4}$	$1\frac{1}{2}$	3	6	12	24	48
No. of oscillations	510	518	420	318	204	121	70

Selecting in the first table the 3d, 5th, and 7th observations, and expressing the greatest velocities in these observations particularly by the numbers 1, 4, 16, respectively, and generally by the quantity V as above, there will come out in the 3d observation $\frac{1}{193}=A+B+C$, in the 5th observation $\frac{2}{90\frac{1}{2}}=4A+8B+16C$, in the 7th observation $\frac{8}{30}=16A+64B+256C$. These equations reduced give A = 0.001414, B = 0.000297, C = 0.000879. And thence the resistance of the globe moving with the velocity V will be to its weight $26\frac{1}{4}$ ounces in the same ratio as $0.0009V+0.000208V^{3/2}+0.000659V^2$ to 121 inches, the length of the pendulum. And if we regard that part only of the resistance which is as the square of the velocity, it will be to the weight of the globe as $0.000659V^2$ to 121 inches. But this part of the resistance in the first experiment was to the weight of the wooden globe of $57\frac{7}{22}$ ounces as $0.002217V^2$ to 121; hence the resistance of the wooden globe is to the resistance of the leaden one (their velocities being equal) as $57\frac{7}{22}$ into 0.002217 to $26\frac{1}{4}$ into 0.000659, that is, as $7\frac{1}{3}$ to 1. The diameters of the two globes were $6\frac{7}{8}$ and 2 inches, and the squares of these are to each other as $47\frac{1}{4}$ and 4, or $11\frac{13}{16}$ and 1, nearly. Therefore the resistances of these equally swift globes were in less than a squared ratio of the diameters. But we have not yet considered the resistance of the thread, which was certainly very considerable, and ought to be subtracted from the resistance of the pendulums here found. I could not determine this accurately, but I found it greater than $\frac{1}{3}$ part of the whole resistance of the lesser pendulum; hence I gathered that the resistances of the globes, when the resistance of the thread is subtracted, are nearly in the squared ratio of their diameters. For the ratio of $7\frac{1}{2}-\frac{1}{3}$ to $1-\frac{1}{3}$, or $10\frac{1}{2}$ to 1 is not very different from the squared ratio of the diameters $11\frac{13}{16}$ to 1.

Since the resistance of the thread is of less moment in greater globes, I tried the experiment also with a globe whose diameter was $18\frac{3}{4}$ inches. The length of the pendulum between the point of suspension and the centre of oscillation was $122\frac{1}{2}$ inches, and between the point of suspension and the knot in the thread $109\frac{1}{2}$ inches. The arc described by the knot at the first descent of the pendulum was 32 inches. The arc described by the same knot in the last ascent after five oscillations was 28 inches. The sum of the arcs, or the whole arc described in one mean oscillation, was 60 inches; the difference of the arcs, 4 inches. The $\frac{1}{10}$ part of this, or the difference between the descent and ascent in one mean oscillation, is $\frac{2}{5}$ of an inch. Then as the radius $109\frac{1}{2}$ is to the radius $122\frac{1}{2}$, so is the whole arc of 60 inches described by the knot in one mean oscillation to the whole arc of $67\frac{1}{8}$ inches described by the centre of the globe in one mean oscillation; and so is the difference $\frac{2}{5}$ to a new difference 0.4475. If the length of the arc described were to remain, and the length of the pendulum should be augmented in the ratio of 126 to $122\frac{1}{2}$, the time of the oscillation would be augmented, and the velocity of the pendulum would be diminished as the square root of that ratio; so that the difference 0.4475 of the arcs described in the descent and subsequent ascent would remain. Then if the arc described be augmented in the ratio of $124\frac{3}{31}$ to $67\frac{1}{8}$, that difference 0.4475 would be augmented as the square of that ratio, and so would become 1.5295. These things would be so upon the supposition that the resistance of the pendulum were as the square of the velocity. Therefore if the pendulum describe the whole arc of $124\frac{3}{31}$ inches, and its length between the point of suspension and the centre of oscillation be 126 inches, the difference of the arcs described in the descent and subsequent ascent would be 1.5295 inches. And this difference multiplied by the weight of the pendulous globe, which was 208 ounces, produces 318.136. Again, in the pendulum above mentioned, made of a wooden globe, when its centre of oscillation, being 126 inches from the point of suspension, described the whole arc of $124\frac{3}{31}$ inches, the difference of the arcs described in the descent and ascent was $\frac{126}{121}$ into $\frac{8}{9\frac{3}{3}}$. This multiplied by the weight of the globe, which was $57\frac{7}{22}$ ounces, produces 49.396. But I multiply these differences by the weights of the globes, in order to find their resistances. For the differences arise from the resistances, and are as the resistances directly and the weights inversely. Therefore the resistances are as the numbers 318.136 and 49.396. But that part of the resistance of the lesser globe, which is as the square of the velocity, was to the whole resistance as 0.56752 to 0.61675, that is, as 45.453 to 49.396, whereas that part of the resistance of the greater globe is almost equal to its whole resistance, and so those parts are nearly as 318.136 and 45.453, that is, as 7 and 1. But the diameters of the globes are $18\frac{3}{4}$ and $6\frac{7}{8}$; and their squares $351\frac{9}{16}$ and $47\frac{17}{64}$ are as 7.438 and 1, that is, nearly as the resistances of the globes 7 and 1. The difference of these ratios is barely greater than may arise from the resistance of the thread. Therefore those parts of the resistances which are, when the globes are equal, as the squares of the velocities, are also, when the velocities are equal, as the squares of the diameters of the globes.

But the greatest of the globes I used in these experiments was not perfectly spherical, and therefore in this calculation I have, for brevity's sake, neglected some little niceties; being not very solicitous for an accurate calculus in an experiment that was not very accurate. So that I could wish that these experiments were tried again with other globes, of a larger size, more in number, and more accurately formed; since the demonstration of a vacuum depends thereon. If the globes be taken in a geometrical proportion, whose diameters, let us suppose, are 4, 8, 16, 32 inches; one may infer from the progression observed in the experiments what would happen if the globes were still larger.

In order to compare the resistances of different fluids with each other, I made the following trials. I procured a wooden vessel 4 feet long, 1 foot broad, and 1 foot high. This vessel, being uncovered, I filled with spring water, and, having immersed pendulums therein, I made them oscillate in the water. And I found that a leaden globe weighing $166\frac{1}{6}$ ounces, and in diameter $3\frac{5}{8}$ inches, moved therein as it is set down in the following table; the length of the pendulum from the point of suspension to a certain point marked in the thread being 126 inches, and to the centre of oscillation 134⅜ inches.

The arc described in the first descent, by a point marked in the thread was inches	64	32	16	8	4	2	1	½	¼
The arc described in the last ascent was inches	48	24	12	6	3	1½	¾	⅜	3/16
The difference of the arcs, proportional to the motion lost, was inches	16	8	4	2	1	½	¼	⅛	1/16
The number of the oscillations in water			29/60	1⅕	3	7	11¼	12⅔	13⅓
The number of the oscillations in air	85½	287	535						

In the experiments of the 4th column there were equal motions lost in 535 oscillations made in the air, and $1\frac{1}{5}$ in water. The oscillations in the air were indeed a little swifter than those in the water. But if the oscillations in the water were accelerated in such a ratio that the motions of the pendulums might be equally swift in both mediums, there would be still the same number of $1\frac{1}{5}$ oscillations in the water, and by these the same quantity of motion would be lost as before; because the resistance is increased, and the square of the time diminished in the same squared ratio. The pendulums, therefore, being of equal velocities, there were equal motions lost in 535 oscillations in the air, and $1\frac{1}{5}$ in the water; and therefore the resistance of the pendulum in the water is to its resistance in the air as 535 to $1\frac{1}{5}$. This is the proportion of the whole resistances in the case of the 4th column.

Now let $AV+CV^2$ represent the difference of the arcs described in the descent and subsequent ascent by the globe moving in air with the greatest velocity V; and since the greatest velocity is in the case of the 4th column to the greatest velocity in the case of the 1st column as 1 is to 8; and that difference of the arcs in the case of the 4th column to the difference in the case of the 1st column as $\frac{2}{535}$ to $\frac{16}{85\frac{1}{2}}$, or as 85½ to 4280; put in these cases 1 and 8 for the velocities, and 85½ and 4280 for the differences of the arcs, and $A+C$ will be $=85\frac{1}{2}$, and $8A+64C=4280$ or $A+8C=535$; and then, by reducing these equations, there will come out $7C=449\frac{1}{2}$ and $C=64\frac{3}{14}$ and $A=21\frac{2}{7}$; and therefore the resistance, which is as $\frac{7}{11}AV+\frac{3}{4}CV^2$, will become as $13\frac{6}{11}V$ $+48\frac{9}{56}V^2$. Therefore in the case of the 4th column, where the velocity was 1, the whole resistance is to its part proportional to the square of the velocity as $13\frac{6}{11}+48\frac{9}{56}$ or $61\frac{12}{17}$ to $48\frac{9}{56}$; and therefore the resistance of the pendulum in water is to that part of the resistance in air, which is proportional to the square of the velocity, and which in swift motions is the only part that deserves consideration, as $61\frac{12}{17}$ to $48\frac{9}{56}$ and 535 to $1\frac{1}{5}$ conjointly, that is, as 571 to 1. If the whole thread of the pendulum oscillating in the water had been immersed, its resistance would have been still greater; so that the resistance of the pendulum oscillating in the water, that is, that part which is proportional to the square of the velocity, and which only needs to be considered in swift bodies, is to the resistance of the same whole pendulum, oscillating in air with the same velocity, as about 850 to 1, that is, as the density of water is to the density of air, nearly.

In this calculation we ought also to have taken in that part of the resistance of the pendulum in the water which was as the square of the velocity; but I found (which will perhaps seem strange) that the resistance in the water was augmented in more than a squared ratio of the velocity. In searching after the cause, I thought upon this, that the vessel was too narrow for the magnitude of the pendulous globe, and by its narrowness obstructed the motion of the water as it yielded to the oscillating globe. For when I immersed a pendulous globe, whose diameter was one inch only, the resistance was augmented nearly as the square of the velocity. I tried this by making a pendulum of two globes, of which the lesser and lower oscillated in the water, and the greater and higher was fastened to the thread just above the water, and, by oscillating in the air, assisted the motion of the pendulum, and continued it longer. The experiments made by this contrivance resulted as shown in the following table.

Arc described in first descent	16 . 8 . 4 . 2 . 1 . $\frac{1}{2}$. $\frac{1}{4}$
Arc described in last ascent	12 . 6 . 3 . $1\frac{1}{2}$. $\frac{3}{4}$. $\frac{3}{8}$. $\frac{3}{16}$
Difference of arcs, proportional to motion lost	4 . 2 . 1 . $\frac{1}{2}$. $\frac{1}{4}$. $\frac{1}{8}$. $\frac{1}{16}$
Number of oscillations	$3\frac{3}{8}$. $6\frac{1}{2}$. $12\frac{1}{12}$. $21\frac{1}{5}$. 34 . 53 . $62\frac{1}{5}$

In comparing the resistances of the mediums with each other, I also caused iron pendulums to oscillate in quicksilver. The length of the iron wire was about 3 feet, and the diameter of the pendulous globe about $\frac{1}{3}$ of an inch. To the wire, just above the quicksilver, there was fixed another leaden globe of a bigness sufficient to continue the motion of the pendulum for some time. Then a vessel, that would hold about 3 pounds of quicksilver, was filled by turns with quicksilver and common water, so that, by making the pendulum oscillate successively in these two different fluids, I might find the proportion of their resistances; and the resistance of the quicksilver proved to be to the resistance of water as about 13 or 14 to 1; that is, as the density of quicksilver to the density of water. When I made use of a pendulous globe something bigger, as of one whose diameter was about $\frac{1}{2}$ or $\frac{2}{3}$ of an inch, the resistance of the quicksilver proved to be to the resistance of the water as about 12 or 10 to 1. But the former experiment is more to be relied on, because in the latter the vessel was too narrow in proportion to the magnitude of the immersed globe; for the vessel ought to have been enlarged together with the globe. I intended to repeat these experiments with larger vessels, and in melted metals, and other liquors both cold and hot; but I had not leisure to try all; and besides, from what is already described, it appears sufficiently that the resistance of bodies moving swiftly is nearly proportional to the densities of the fluids in which they move. I do not say accurately; for more tenacious fluids, of equal density, will undoubtedly resist more than those that are more liquid; as cold oil more than warm, warm oil more than rain water, and water more than spirit of wine. But in liquors, which are sensibly fluid enough, as in air, in salt and fresh water, in spirit of wine, of turpentine, and salts, in oil cleared of its feces by distillation and warmed, in oil of vitriol, and in mercury, and melted metals, and any other such like, that are fluid enough to retain for some time the motion impressed upon them by the agitation of the vessel, and which being poured out are easily resolved into drops, I doubt not that the rule already laid down may be accurate enough, especially if the experiments be made with larger pendulous bodies and more swiftly moved.

Lastly, since it is the opinion of some that there is a certain ethereal medium extremely rare and subtile, which freely pervades the pores of all bodies; and from such a medium, so pervading the pores of bodies, some resistance must needs arise; in order to try whether the resistance, which we experience in bodies in motion, be made upon their outward surfaces only, or whether their internal parts meet with any considerable resistance upon their surfaces, I thought of the following experiment. I suspended a round deal box by a thread 11 feet long, on a steel hook, by means of a ring of the same metal, so as to make a pendulum of the aforesaid length. The hook had a sharp hollow edge on its upper part, so that the upper arc of the ring pressing on the edge might move the more freely; and the thread was fastened to the lower arc of the ring. The pendulum being thus prepared, I drew it aside from the perpendicular to the distance of about 6 feet, and that in a plane perpendicular to the edge of the hook, lest the ring, while the pendulum oscillated, should slide to and fro on the edge of the hook; for the point of suspension, in which the ring touches the hook, ought to remain immovable. I therefore accurately noted the place to which the pendulum was brought, and letting it go, I marked three other places, to which it returned at the end of the 1st, 2d, and 3d oscillation. This I often repeated, that I might find those places as accurately as possible. Then I filled the box with lead and other heavy metals that were near at hand. But first, I weighed the box when empty, and that part of the thread that went round it, and half the remaining part, extended between the hook and the suspended box; for the thread so extended always acts upon the pendulum, when drawn aside from the perpendicular, with half its weight. To this weight I added the weight of the air contained in the box. And this whole weight was about $\frac{1}{78}$ of the weight of the box when filled with the metals. Then because the box when full of the metals, by extending the thread with its weight, increased the length of the pendulum, I shortened the thread so as to make the length of the pendulum, when oscillating, the same as before. Then drawing aside the pendulum to the place first marked, and letting it go, I reckoned about 77 oscillations before the box returned to the second mark, and as many afterwards before it came to the third mark, and as many after that before it came to the fourth mark. From this I conclude that the whole resistance of the box, when full, had not a greater proportion to the resistance of the box, when empty, than 78 to 77. For if their resistances were equal, the box, when full, by reason of its inertia, which was 78 times greater than the inertia of the same when empty, ought to have continued its oscillating motion so much the longer, and therefore to have returned to those marks at the end of 78 oscillations. But it returned to them at the end of 77 oscillations.

Let, therefore, A represent the resistance of the box upon its external surface, and B the resistance of the empty box on its internal surface, and if the resistances to the internal parts of bodies equally swift be as the matter, or the number of particles that are resisted, then 78B will be the resistance made to the internal parts of the box, when full; and therefore the whole resistance A+B of the empty box will be to the whole resistance A+78B of the full box as 77 to 78, and, by subtraction, A+B to 77B as 77 to 1; and thence A+B to

B as 77·77 to 1, and, by subtraction, again, A to B as 5928 to 1. Therefore the resistance of the empty box in its internal parts will be above 5000 times less than the resistance on its external surface. This reasoning depends upon the supposition that the greater resistance of the full box arises not from any other latent cause, but only from the action of some subtile fluid upon the included metal.

This experiment is related by memory, the paper being lost in which I had described it; so that I have been obliged to omit some fractional parts, which are slipped out of my memory; and I have no leisure to try it again. The first time I made it, the hook being weak, the full box was retarded sooner. The cause I found to be, that the hook was not strong enough to bear the weight of the box; so that, as it oscillated to and fro, the hook was bent sometimes this and sometimes that way. I therefore procured a hook of sufficient strength, so that the point of suspension might remain unmoved, and then all things happened as is above described.

SECTION VII

THE MOTION OF FLUIDS, AND THE RESISTANCE MADE TO PROJECTED BODIES

PROPOSITION 32. THEOREM 26

Suppose two similar systems of bodies consisting of an equal number of particles, and let the correspondent particles be similar and proportional, each in one system to each in the other, and have a like situation among themselves, and the same given ratio of density to each other; and let them begin to move among themselves in proportional times, and with like motions (that is, those in one system among one another, and those in the other among one another). And if the particles that are in the same system do not touch one another, except in the moments of reflection; nor attract, nor repel each other, except with accelerative forces that are inversely as the diameters of the correspondent particles, and directly as the squares of the velocities: I say, that the particles of those systems will continue to move among themselves with like motions and in proportional times.

Like bodies in like situations are said to be moved among themselves with like motions and in proportional times, when their situations at the end of those times are always found alike in respect of each other; as suppose we compare the particles in one system with the correspondent particles in the other. Hence the times will be proportional, in which similar and proportional parts of similar figures will be described by correspondent particles. Therefore if we suppose two systems of this kind, the correspondent particles, by reason of the similitude of the motions at their beginning, will continue to be moved with like motions, so long as they move without meeting one another; for if they are acted on by no forces, they will go on uniformly in right lines, by the first Law. But if they agitate one another with some certain forces, and those forces are inversely as the diameters of the correspondent particles and directly as the squares of the velocities, then, because the particles are in like situations, and their forces are proportional, the whole forces with which correspondent particles are agitated, and which are compounded of each of the agitating forces (by Cor. II of the Laws), will have like directions, and have the same effect as if they respected centres places alike among the particles; and those whole forces will be to each other as the several forces which compose them, that is, inversely as the diameters of the correspondent particles and directly as the squares of the velocities: and therefore will cause correspondent particles to continue to describe like figures. These things will be so (by Cor. I and VIII, Prop. 4, Book I), if those centres are at rest; but if they are moved, yet, by reason of the similitude of the translations, their situations among the particles of the system will remain similar, so that the changes introduced into the figures described by the particles will still be similar. So that the motions of correspondent and similar particles will continue similar till their first meeting with each other; and thence will arise similar collisions, and similar reflections; which will again beget similar motions of the particles among themselves (by what was just now shown), till they mutually fall upon one another again, and so on *ad infinitum*.   Q.E.D.

COR. I. Hence if any two bodies, which are similar and in like situations to the correspondent particles of the systems, begin to move amongst them in like manner and in proportional times, and their magnitudes and densities be to each other as the magnitudes and densities of the corresponding particles, these bodies will continue to be moved in like manner and in proportional times; for the case of the greater parts of both systems and of the particles is the very same.

COR. II. And if all the similar and similarly situated parts of both systems be at rest among themselves; and two of them, which are greater than the rest, and mutually correspondent in both systems, begin to move in lines alike posited, with any similar motion whatsoever, they will excite similar motions in the rest of the parts of the systems, and will continue to move among those parts in like manner and in proportional times; and will therefore describe spaces proportional to their diameters.

PROPOSITION 33. THEOREM 27

The same things being supposed, I say, that the greater parts of the systems are resisted in a ratio compounded of the squared ratio of their velocities, and the squared ratio of their diameters, and the simple ratio of the density of the parts of the systems.

For the resistance arises partly from the centripetal or centrifugal forces with which the particles of the system act on each other, partly from the collisions and reflections of the particles and the greater parts. The resistances of the first kind are to each other as the whole motive forces from which they arise, that is, as the whole accelerative forces and the quantities of matter in corresponding parts; that is (by the supposition), directly as the squares of the velocities and inversely as the distances of the corresponding particles, and directly as the quantities of matter in the correspondent parts: and therefore since the distances of the particles in one system are to the correspondent distances of the particles in the other, as the diameter of one particle or part in the former system to the diameter of the correspondent particle or part in the other, and since the quantities of matter are as the densities of the parts and the cubes of the diameters, the resistances are to each other as the squares of the velocities and the squares of the diameters and the densities of the parts of the systems. Q.E.D. The resistances of the latter sort are as the number of correspondent reflections and the forces of those reflections conjointly; but the number of the reflections are to each other directly as the velocities of the corresponding parts and inversely as the spaces between their reflections. And the forces of the reflections are as the velocities and the magnitudes and the densities of the corresponding parts conjointly; that is, as the velocities and the cubes of the diameters and the densities of the parts. And, joining all these ratios, the resistances of the corresponding parts are to each other as the squares of the velocities and the squares of the diameters and the densities of the parts conjointly.

Q.E.D.

Cor. i. Therefore if those systems are two elastic fluids, like our air, and their parts are at rest among themselves; and two similar bodies proportional in magnitude and density to the parts of the fluids, and similarly situated among those parts, be in any manner projected in the direction of lines similarly posited; and the accelerative forces with which the particles of the fluids act upon each other are inversely as the diameters of the bodies projected and directly as the squares of their velocities; those bodies will excite similar motions in the fluids in proportional times, and will describe similar spaces and proportional to their diameters.

Cor. ii. Therefore in the same fluid a projected body that moves swiftly meets with a resistance that is as the square of its velocity, nearly. For if the forces with which distant particles act upon one another should be augmented as the square of the velocity, the projected body would be resisted in the same squared ratio accurately; and therefore in a medium, whose parts when at a distance do not act with any force on one another, the resistance is as the square of the velocity, accurately. Let there be, therefore, three mediums A, B, C, consisting of similar and equal parts regularly disposed at equal distances. Let the parts of the mediums A and B recede from each other with forces that are among themselves as T and V; and let the parts of the medium C be entirely destitute of any such forces. And if four equal bodies D, E, F, G move in these mediums, the two first D and E in the two first A and B, and the other two F and G in the third C; and if the velocity of the body D be to the velocity of the body E, and the velocity of the body F to the velocity of the body G, as the square root of the ratio of the force T to the force V; then the resistance of the body D to the resistance of the body E, and the resistance of the body F to the resistance of the body G, will be as the square of the velocities; and therefore the resistance of the body D will be to the resistance of the body F as the resistance of the body E to the resistance of the body G. Let the bodies D and F be equally swift, as also the bodies E and G; and, augmenting the velocities of the bodies D and F in any ratio, and diminishing the forces of the particles of the medium B as the square of the same ratio, the medium B will approach to the form and condition of the medium C at pleasure; and therefore the resistances of the equal and equally swift bodies E and G in these mediums will continually approach to equality, so that their difference will at last become less than any given. Therefore since the resistances of the bodies D and F are to each other as the resistances of the bodies E and G, those will also in like manner approach to the ratio of equality. Therefore the bodies D and F, when they move with very great swiftness, meet with resistances very nearly equal; and therefore since the resistance of the body F is in a squared ratio of the velocity, the resistance of the body D will be nearly in the same ratio.

COR. III. Hence the resistance of a body moving very swiftly in an elastic fluid is almost the same as if the parts of the fluid were destitute of their centrifugal forces, and did not fly from each other; provided only that the elasticity of the fluid arise from the centrifugal forces of the particles, and the velocity be so great as not to allow the particles time enough to act.

COR. IV. Since the resistances of similar and equally swift bodies, in a medium whose distant parts do not fly from each other, are as the squares of the diameters, therefore the resistances made to bodies moving with very great and equal velocities in an elastic fluid will be as the squares of the diameters, nearly.

COR. V. And since similar, equal, and equally swift bodies, moving through mediums of the same density, whose particles do not fly from each other, will strike against an equal quantity of matter in equal times, whether the particles of which the medium consists be more and smaller, or fewer and greater, and therefore impress on that matter an equal quantity of motion, and in return (by the third Law of Motion) suffer an equal reaction from the same, that is, are equally resisted; it is manifest, also, that in elastic fluids of the same density, when the bodies move with extreme swiftness, their resistances are nearly equal, whether the fluids consist of gross parts, or of parts ever so subtile. For the resistance of projectiles moving with exceedingly great celerities is not much diminished by the subtilty of the medium.

COR. VI. All these things are so in fluids whose elastic force takes its rise from the centrifugal forces of the particles. But if that force arise from some other cause, as from the expansion of the particles after the manner of wool, or the boughs of trees, or any other cause, by which the particles are hindered from moving freely among themselves, the resistance, by reason of the lesser fluidity of the medium, will be greater than in the Corollaries above.

PROPOSITION 34. THEOREM 28

If in a rare medium, consisting of equal particles freely disposed at equal distances from each other, a globe and a cylinder described on equal diameters move with equal velocities in the direction of the axis of the cylinder, the resistance of the globe will be but half as great as that of the cylinder.

For since the action of the medium upon the body is the same (by Cor. v of the Laws) whether the body move in a quiescent medium, or whether the particles of the medium impinge with the same velocity upon the quiescent body, let us consider the body as if it were quiescent, and see with what force it would be impelled by the moving medium. Let, therefore, ABKI represent a spherical body described from the centre C with the semidiameter CA, and let the particles of the medium impinge with a given velocity upon that spherical body in the directions of right lines parallel to AC; and let FB be one of those right lines. In FB take LB equal to the semidiameter CB, and draw BD touching the sphere in B. Upon KC and BD let fall the

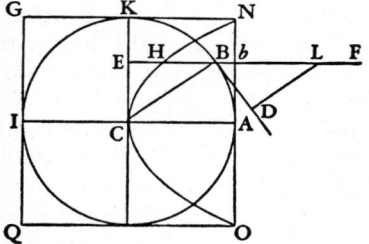

perpendiculars BE, LD; and the force with which a particle of the medium, impinging on the globe obliquely in the direction FB, would strike the globe in B, will be to the force with which the same particle, meeting the cylinder ONGQ described about the globe with the axis ACI, would strike it perpendicularly in *b*, as LD is to LB, or BE to BC. Again; the efficacy of this force to move the globe, according to the direction of its incidence FB or AC, is to the efficacy of the same to move the globe, according to the direction of its determination, that is, in the direction of the right line BC in which it impels the globe directly, as BE to BC. And, joining these ratios, the efficacy of a particle, falling upon the globe obliquely in the direction of the right line FB, to move the globe in the direction of its incidence, is to the efficacy of the same particle falling in the same line perpendicularly on the cylinder, to move it in the same direction, as BE² to BC². Therefore if in *b*E, which is perpendicular to the circular base of the cylinder NAO, and equal to the radius AC, we take *b*H equal to $\dfrac{BE^2}{CB}$; then *b*H will be to *b*E as the effect of the particle upon the globe to the effect of the particle upon the cylinder. And therefore the solid which is formed by all the right lines *b*H will be to the solid formed by all the right lines *b*E as the effect of all the particles upon the globe to the effect of all the particles upon the cylinder. But the former of these solids is a paraboloid whose vertex is C, its axis CA, and latus rectum CA, and the latter solid is a cylinder circumscribing the paraboloid; and it is known that a paraboloid is half its circumscribed cylinder. Therefore the whole force of the medium upon the globe is half the entire force of the same upon the cylinder. And therefore if the particles of the medium are at rest, and the cylinder and globe move with equal velocities, the resistance of the globe will be half the resistance of the cylinder.   Q.E.D.

SCHOLIUM

By the same method other figures may be compared together as to their resistance; and those may be found which are most apt to continue their motions in resisting mediums. As if upon the circular base CEBH from the centre O, with the radius OC, and the altitude OD, one would construct a frustum CBGF of a cone, which should meet with less resistance than any other frustum constructed with the same base and altitude, and going forwards towards D in the direction of its axis: bisect the altitude OD in Q, and produce OQ to S, so that QS may be equal to QC, and S will be the vertex of the cone whose frustum is sought.

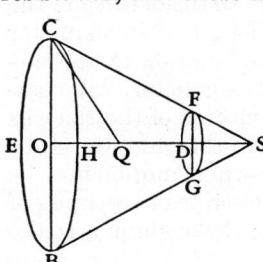

Incidentally, since the angle CSB is always acute, it follows from the above that, if the solid ADBE be generated by the convolution of an elliptical or oval figure ADBE about its axis AB, and the generating figure be touched by three right lines FG, GH, HI, in the points F, B, and I, so that GH shall be perpendicular to the axis in the point of contact B, and FG, HI may be inclined to GH in the angles FGB, BHI of 135 degrees: the solid arising from the convolution of the figure ADFGHIE about the same axis AB will be less resisted than the

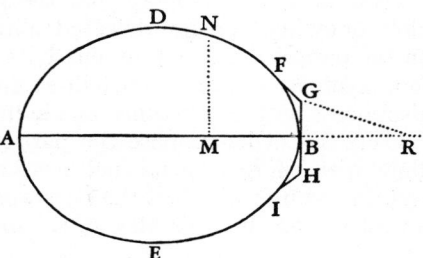

former solid, provided that both move forwards in the direction of their axis AB, and that the extremity B of each go foremost. This Proposition I conceive may be of use in the building of ships.

If the figure DNFG be such a curve, that if, from any point thereof, as N, the perpendicular NM be let fall on the axis AB, and from the given point G there be drawn the right line GR parallel to a right line touching the figure in N, and cutting the axis produced in R, MN becomes to GR as GR^3 to $4BR \cdot GB^2$, the solid described by the revolution of this figure about its axis AB, moving in the before-mentioned rare medium from A towards B, will be less resisted than any other circular solid whatsoever, described of the same length and breadth.

PROPOSITION 35. PROBLEM 7

If a rare medium consist of very small quiescent particles of equal magnitudes, and freely disposed at equal distances from one another: to find the resistance of a globe moving uniformly forwards in this medium.

CASE 1. Let a cylinder described with the same diameter and altitude be conceived to go forwards with the same velocity in the direction of its axis through the same medium; and let us suppose that the particles of the medium, on which the globe or cylinder falls, fly back with as great a force of reflection as possible. Then since the resistance of the globe (by the last Proposition) is but half the resistance of the cylinder, and since the globe is to the cylinder as 2 to 3, and since the cylinder by falling perpendicularly on the particles, and reflecting them with the utmost force, communicates to them a velocity double to its own: it follows that the cylinder in moving forwards uniformly half the length of its axis, will communicate a motion to the particles which is to the whole motion of the cylinder as the density of the medium to the density of the cylinder; and that the globe, in the time it describes one length of its diameter in moving uniformly forwards, will communicate the same motion to the particles; and, in the time that it describes two-thirds of its diameter, will communicate a motion to the particles which is to the whole motion of the globe as the density of the medium to the density of the globe. And therefore the globe meets with a resistance, which is to the force by which its whole motion may be either taken away or generated in the time in which it describes two-thirds of its diameter moving uniformly forwards, as the density of the medium is to the density of the globe.

CASE 2. Let us suppose that the particles of the medium incident on the globe or cylinder are not reflected; and then the cylinder falling perpendicularly on the particles will communicate its own simple velocity to them, and therefore meets a resistance but half so great as in the former case, and the globe also meets with a resistance but half so great.

CASE 3. Let us suppose the particles of the medium to fly back from the globe with a force which is neither the greatest, nor yet none at all, but with a certain mean force; then the resistance of the globe will be in the same mean ratio between the resistance in the first case and the resistance in the second.

Q.E.I.

COR. I. Hence if the globe and the particles are infinitely hard, and destitute of all elastic force, and therefore of all force of reflection, the resistance of the globe will be to the force by which its whole motion may be destroyed or generated, in the time that the globe describes four third parts of its diameter, as the density of the medium is to the density of the globe.

COR. II. The resistance of the globe, other things being equal, varies as the square of the velocity.

COR. III. The resistance of the globe, other things being equal, varies as the square of the diameter.

COR. IV. The resistance of the globe, other things being equal, varies as the density of the medium.

COR. V. The resistance of the globe varies jointly as the square of the velocity, as the square of the diameter, and as the density of the medium.

COR. VI. The motion of the globe and its resistance may be thus represented. Let AB be the time in which the globe may, by its resistance uniformly continued, lose its whole motion. Erect AD, BC perpendicular to AB. Let BC be that whole motion, and through the point C, the asymptotes being AD, AB,

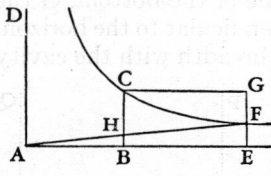 describe the hyperbola CF. Produce AB to any point E. Erect the perpendicular EF meeting the hyperbola in F. Complete the parallelogram CBEG, and draw AF meeting BC in H. Then if the globe in any time BE, with its first motion BC uniformly continued, describes in a nonresisting medium the space CBEG represented by the area of the parallelogram, the same in a resisting medium will describe the space CBEF, represented by the area of the hyperbola; and its motion at the end of that time will be represented by EF, the ordinate of the hyperbola, there being lost of its motion the part FG. And its resistance at the end of the same time will be represented by the length BH, there being lost of its resistance the part CH. All these things appear by Cor. I and III, Prop. 5, Book II.

COR. VII. Hence if the globe in the time T by the resistance R uniformly continued to lose its whole motion M, the same globe in the time t in a resisting medium, wherein the resistance R decreases as the square of the velocity, will lose out of its motion M the part $\frac{tM}{T+t}$, the part $\frac{TM}{T+t}$ remaining; and will describe a space which is to the space described in the same time t, with the uniform motion M, as the logarithm of the number $\frac{T+t}{T}$ multiplied by the number 2.302585092994 is to the number $\frac{t}{T}$, because the hyperbolic area BCFE is to the rectangle BCGE in that proportion.

SCHOLIUM

I have exhibited in this Proposition the resistance and retardation of spherical projectiles in mediums that are not continued, and shown that this resistance is to the force by which the whole motion of the globe may be destroyed or produced in the time in which the globe can describe two-thirds of its diameter, with a velocity uniformly continued, as the density of the medium is to the density of the globe, provided the globe and the particles of the medium be perfectly elastic, and are endued with the utmost force of reflection; and that this force, where the globe and particles of the medium are infinitely hard and void of any reflecting force, is diminished one-half. But in continued mediums, as water, hot oil, and quicksilver, the globe as it passes through them does not immediately strike against all the particles of the fluid that generate the resistance made to it, but presses only the particles that lie next to it, which press the particles beyond, which press other particles, and so on; and in these mediums the resistance is diminished one other half. A globe in these extremely fluid mediums meets with a resistance that is to the force by which its whole motion may be destroyed or generated in the time wherein it can describe, with that motion uniformly continued, eight third parts of its diameter, as the density of the medium is to the density of the globe. This I shall endeavor to show in what follows.

PROPOSITION 36. PROBLEM 8

To find the motion of water running out of a cylindrical vessel through a hole made at the bottom.

Let ACDB be a cylindrical vessel, AB the mouth of it, CD the bottom parallel to the horizon, EF a circular hole in the middle of the bottom, G the centre of the hole, and GH the axis of the cylinder perpendicular to the horizon. And suppose a cylinder of ice APQB to be of the same breadth with the cavity of the vessel, and to have the same axis, and to descend continually with an uniform motion, and that its parts, as soon as they touch the surface AB, dissolve into water, and flow down by their weight into the vessel, and in their fall compose the cataract or column of water ABNFEM, passing through the hole EF, and filling up the same exactly. Let the uniform velocity of the descending ice and of the contiguous water in the circle AB be that which the water would acquire by falling through the space IH; and let IH and HG lie in the same right line; and through the point I let there be drawn the right line KL parallel to the horizon, and meeting the ice on both the sides thereof in K and L. Then the velocity of the water running out at the hole EF will be the same that it would acquire by falling from I through the space IG. Therefore, by Galileo's Theorems, IG will be to IH as the square of the velocity of the water that runs out at the hole to the velocity of the water in the circle AB, that is, as the square of the ratio of the circle AB to the circle EF; those circles being inversely as the velocities of the water which in the same time and in equal quantities passes through each of them, and completely fills them both. We are now considering the velocity with which the water tends to the plane of the horizon. But the motion parallel to the same, by which the parts of the falling water approach to each other, is not here taken notice of; since it is neither produced by gravity, nor at all changes the motion perpendicular to the horizon which the gravity produces. We suppose, indeed, that the parts of the water cohere a little, that by their cohesion they may in falling approach to each other with motions parallel to the horizon in order to form one single cataract, and to prevent their being divided into several; but the motion parallel to the horizon arising from this cohesion does not come under our present consideration.

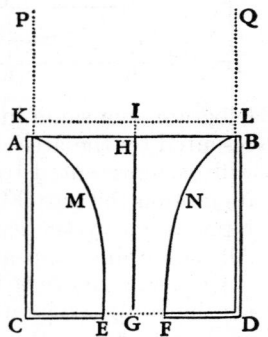

CASE 1. Conceive now the whole cavity in the vessel, which surrounds the falling water ABNFEM, to be full of ice, so that the water may pass through

the ice as through a funnel. Then if the water pass very near to the ice only, without touching it; or, which is the same thing, if by reason of the perfect smoothness of the surface of the ice, the water, though touching it, glides over it with the utmost freedom, and without the least resistance; the water will run through the hole EF with the same velocity as before, and the whole weight of the column of water ABNFEM will be taken up as before in forcing out the water, and the bottom of the vessel will sustain the weight of the ice surrounding that column.

Let now the ice in the vessel dissolve into water; but the efflux of the water will remain, as to its velocity, the same as before. It will not be less, because the ice now dissolved will endeavor to descend; it will not be greater, because the ice, now become water, cannot descend without hindering the descent of other water equal to its own descent. The same force ought always to generate the same velocity in the effluent water.

But the hole at the bottom of the vessel, by reason of the oblique motions of the particles of the effluent water, must be a little greater than before. For now the particles of the water do not all of them pass through the hole perpendicularly, but, flowing down on all parts from the sides of the vessel, and converging towards the hole, pass through it with oblique motions; and in tending downwards they meet in a stream whose diameter is a little smaller below the hole than at the hole itself; its diameter being to the diameter of the hole as 5 to 6, or as $5\frac{1}{2}$ to $6\frac{1}{2}$, very nearly, if I measured those diameters rightly. I procured a thin flat plate, having a hole pierced in the middle, the diameter of the circular hole being five eighth parts of an inch. And that the stream of running water might not be accelerated in falling, and by that acceleration become narrower, I fixed this plate not to the bottom, but to the side of the vessel, so as to make the water go out in the direction of a line parallel to the horizon. Then, when the vessel was full of water, I opened the hole to let it run out; and the diameter of the stream, measured with great accuracy at the distance of about half an inch from the hole, was $^{21}\!/_{40}$ of an inch. Therefore the diameter of this circular hole was to the diameter of the stream very nearly as 25 to 21. So that the water in passing through the hole converges on all sides, and, after it has run out of the vessel, becomes smaller by converging in that manner, and by becoming smaller is accelerated till it comes to the distance of half an inch from the hole, and at that distance flows in a smaller stream and with greater celerity than in the hole itself, and this in the ratio of $25 \cdot 25$ to $21 \cdot 21$, or 17 to 12, very nearly; that is, in about the ratio of $\sqrt{2}$ to 1. Now it is certain from experiments, that the quantity of water running out in a given time through a circular hole made in the bottom of a vessel is equal to the quantity, which, flowing freely with the aforesaid velocity, would run out in the same time through another circular hole, whose diameter is to the diameter of the former as 21 to 25. And therefore this running water in passing through the hole itself has a velocity downwards nearly equal to that which a heavy body would acquire in falling through half the height of the stagnant water in the vessel. But then, after it has run out, it is still accelerated by converging, till it arrives at a distance from the hole that is nearly equal to its diameter, and acquires a velocity greater than the other in about the ratio of $\sqrt{2}$ to 1; this velocity a heavy body would nearly acquire by falling freely through the whole height of the stagnant water in the vessel.

Therefore in what follows let the diameter of the stream be represented by that lesser hole which we shall call EF. And imagine another plane VW above the hole EF, and parallel to the plane thereof, to be placed at a distance equal to the diameter of the same hole, and to be pierced through with a greater hole ST, of such a magnitude that a stream which will exactly fill the lower hole EF may pass through it; the diameter of this hole will therefore be to the diameter of the lower hole nearly as 25 to 21. By this means the water will run perpendicularly out at the lower hole; and the quantity of the water running out will be, according to the magnitude of this last hole, very nearly the same as that which the solution of the Problem requires. The space included between the two planes and the falling stream may be con-

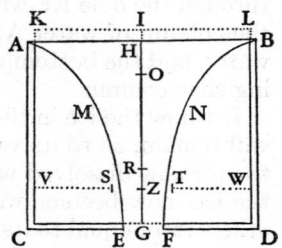

sidered as the bottom of the vessel. But to make the solution more simple and mathematical, it is better to take the lower plane alone for the bottom of the vessel, and to suppose that the water which flowed through the ice as through a funnel, and ran out of the vessel through the hole EF made in the lower plane, preserves its motion continually, and that the ice continues at rest. Therefore in what follows let ST be the diameter of a circular hole described from the centre Z, and let the stream run out of the vessel through that hole, when the water in the vessel is all fluid. And let EF be the diameter of the hole, which the stream, in falling through, exactly fills up, whether the water runs out of the vessel by that upper hole ST, or flows through the middle of the ice in the vessel, as through a funnel. And let the diameter of the upper hole ST be to the diameter of the lower EF as about 25 to 21, and let the perpendicular distance between the planes of the holes be equal to the diameter of the lesser hole EF. Then the velocity of the water downwards, in running out of the vessel through the hole ST, will be in that hole the same that a body may acquire by falling freely from half the height IZ; and the velocity of both the falling streams will be in the hole EF, the same which a body would acquire by falling freely from the whole height IG.

CASE 2. If the hole EF be not in the middle of the bottom of the vessel, but in some other part thereof, the water will still run out with the same velocity as before, if the magnitude of the hole be the same. For though a heavy body takes a longer time in descending to the same depth, by an oblique line, than by a perpendicular line, yet in both cases it acquires in its descent the same velocity; as Galileo hath demonstrated.

CASE 3. The velocity of the water is the same when it runs out through a hole in the side of the vessel. For if the hole be small, so that the interval between the surfaces AB and KL may vanish as to sense, and the stream of water horizontally issuing out may form a parabolic figure; from the latus rectum of this parabola one may see, that the velocity of the effluent water is that which a body may acquire by falling the height IG or HG of the stagnant water in the vessel. For, by making an experiment, I found that if the height of the stagnant water above the hole were 20 inches, and the height of the hole above a plane parallel to the horizon were also 20 inches, a stream of water springing out from thence would fall upon the plane, at the distance of very nearly 37 inches, from a perpendicular let fall upon that plane from the hole. For without resistance the stream would have fallen upon the plane at the distance of 40 inches, the latus rectum of the parabolic stream being 80 inches.

CASE 4. If the effluent water tend upwards, it will still issue forth with the same velocity. For the small stream of water springing upwards, ascends with a perpendicular motion to GH or GI, the height of the stagnant water in the vessel; except so far as its ascent is hindered a little by the resistance of the air; and therefore it springs out with the same velocity that it would acquire in falling from that height. Every particle of the stagnant water is equally pressed on all sides (by Prop. 19, Book II), and, yielding to the pressure, tends always with an equal force, whether it descends through the hole in the bottom of the vessel, or gushes out in an horizontal direction through a hole in the side, or passes into a canal, and springs up from thence through a little hole made in the upper part of the canal. And it may not only be inferred from reasoning, but is manifest also from the well-known experiments just mentioned, that the velocity with which the water runs out is the very same that is assigned in this Proposition.

CASE 5. The velocity of the effluent water is the same, whether the figure of the hole be circular, or square, or triangular, or of any other figure whatever equal to the circular; for the velocity of the effluent water does not depend upon the figure of the hole, but arises from such depth of the hole as it may have below the plane KL.

CASE 6. If the lower part of the vessel ABDC be immersed into stagnant water, and the height of the stagnant water above the bottom of the vessel be

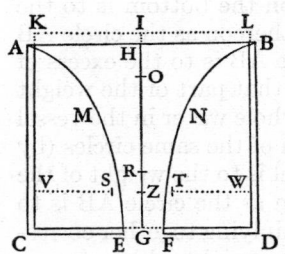

GR, the velocity with which the water that is in the vessel will run out at the hole EF into the stagnant water will be the same which the water would acquire by falling from the height IR; for the weight of all the water in the vessel that is below the surface of the stagnant water will be sustained in equilibrium by the weight of the stagnant water, and therefore does not at all accelerate the motion of the descending water in the vessel. This case will also become evident from experiments, measuring the times in which the water will run out.

COR. I. Hence if CA, the depth of the water, be produced to K, so that AK may be to CK as the square of the ratio of the area of a hole made in any part of the bottom to the area of the circle AB, the velocity of the effluent water will be equal to the velocity which the water would acquire by falling freely from the height KC.

COR. II. And the force with which the whole motion of the effluent water may be generated is equal to the weight of a cylindric column of water, whose base is the hole EF, and its altitude 2GI or 2CK. For the effluent water, in the time it becomes equal to this column, may acquire, by falling by its own weight from the height GI, a velocity equal to that with which it runs out.

COR. III. The weight of all the water in the vessel ABDC is to that part of the weight which is employed in forcing out the water as the sum of the circles AB and EF is to twice the circle EF. For let IO be a mean proportional between IH and IG, and the water running out at the hole EF will, in the time that a drop falling from I would describe the altitude IG, become equal to a cylinder whose base is the circle EF and its altitude 2IG, that is, to a cylinder whose base is the circle AB, and whose altitude is 2IO. For the circle EF is to the circle AB as the square root of the ratio of the altitude IH to the altitude IG; that is, in the simple ratio of the mean proportional IO to the altitude IG. Moreover, in the time that a drop falling from I can describe the altitude IH, the water that runs out will have become equal to a cylinder whose base is the circle AB, and its altitude 2IH; and in the time that a drop falling from I through H to G describes HG, the difference of the altitudes, the effluent water, that is, the water contained within the solid ABNFEM, will be equal to the difference of the cylinders, that is, to a cylinder whose base is AB, and its altitude 2HO. And therefore all the water contained in the vessel ABDC is to the whole falling water contained in the said solid ABNFEM as HG is to 2HO, that is, as HO+OG to 2HO, or IH+IO to 2IH. But the weight of all the water in the solid ABNFEM is employed in forcing out the water; and therefore the weight of all the water in the vessel is to that part of the weight that is employed in forcing out the water as IH+IO is to 2IH, and therefore as the sum of the circles EF and AB is to twice the circle EF.

Cor. iv. And hence the weight of all the water in the vessel ABDC is to the other part of the weight which is sustained by the bottom of the vessel as the sum of the circles AB and EF is to the difference of the same circles.

Cor. v. And that part of the weight which the bottom of the vessel sustains is to the other part of the weight employed in forcing out the water as the difference of the circles AB and EF is to twice the lesser circle EF, or as the area of the bottom to twice the hole.

Cor. vi. That part of the weight which presses upon the bottom is to the whole weight of the water perpendicularly incumbent thereon as the circle AB is to the sum of the circles AB and EF, or as the circle AB is to the excess of twice the circle AB above the area of the bottom. For that part of the weight which presses upon the bottom is to the weight of the whole water in the vessel as the difference of the circles AB and EF is to the sum of the same circles (by Cor. iv); and the weight of the whole water in the vessel is to the weight of the whole water perpendicularly incumbent on the bottom as the circle AB is to the difference of the circles AB and EF. Therefore, multiplying together corresponding terms of the two proportions, that part of the weight which presses upon the bottom is to the weight of the whole water perpendicularly incumbent thereon as the circle AB to the sum of the circles AB and EF, or the excess of twice the circle AB above the bottom.

Cor. vii. If in the middle of the hole EF there be placed the little circle PQ described about the centre G, and parallel to the horizon, the weight of water which that little circle sustains is greater than the weight of a third part of a cylinder of water whose base is that little circle and its height GH. For let ABNFEM be the cataract or column of falling water whose axis is GH, as above, and let all the water, whose fluidity is not requisite for the ready and quick descent of the water, be supposed to be congealed, as well round about the cataract, as above the little circle. And let PHQ be the column of water congealed above

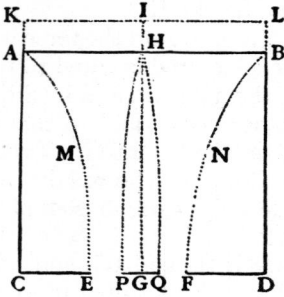

the little circle, whose vertex is H, and its altitude GH. And suppose this cataract to fall with its whole weight downwards, and not in the least to lie against or to press PHQ, but to glide freely by it without any friction, unless, perhaps, just at the very vertex of the ice, where the cataract at the beginning of its fall may tend to a concave figure. And as the congealed water AMEC, BNFD, lying round the cataract, is convex in its internal surfaces AME, BNF towards the falling cataract, so this column PHQ will be convex towards the cataract also, and will therefore be greater than a cone whose base is that little circle PQ and its altitude GH; that is, greater than a third part of a cylinder described with the same base and altitude. Now that little circle sustains the weight of this column, that is, a weight greater than the weight of the cone, or a third part of the cylinder.

COR. VIII. The weight of water which the circle PQ, when very small, sustains, seems to be less than the weight of two-thirds of a cylinder of water whose base is that little circle, and its altitude HG. For, things standing as above supposed, imagine the half of a spheroid described whose base is that little circle, and its semiaxis or altitude HG. This figure will be equal to two-thirds of that cylinder, and will comprehend within it the column of congealed water PHQ, the weight of which is sustained by that little circle. For though the motion of the water tends directly downwards, the external surfaces of that column must yet meet the base PQ in an angle somewhat acute, because the water in its fall is continually accelerated, and by reason of that acceleration becomes narrower. Therefore, since that angle is less than a right one, this column in the lower parts thereof will lie within the hemispheroid. In the upper parts also it will be acute or pointed; because to make it otherwise, the horizontal motion of the water must be at the vertex infinitely more swift than its motion towards the horizon. And the less this circle PQ is, the more acute will the vertex of this column be; and the circle being diminished *in infinitum*, the angle PHQ will be diminished *in infinitum*, and therefore the column will lie within the hemispheroid. Therefore that column is less than that hemispheroid, or than two third parts of the cylinder whose base is that little circle, and its altitude GH. Now the little circle sustains a force of water equal to the weight of this column, the weight of the ambient water being employed in causing its efflux out at the hole.

COR. IX. The weight of water which the little circle PQ sustains, when it is very small, is very nearly equal to the weight of a cylinder of water whose base is that little circle, and its altitude $\frac{1}{2}$GH; for this weight is an arithmetical mean between the weights of the cone and the hemispheroid above mentioned. But if that little circle be not very small, but on the contrary increased till it be equal to the hole EF, it will sustain the weight of all the water lying perpendicularly above it, that is, the weight of a cylinder of water whose base is that little circle, and its altitude GH.

COR. X. And (as far as I can judge) the weight which this little circle sustains is always to the weight of a cylinder of water whose base is that little circle, and its altitude $\frac{1}{2}$GH, as EF^2 is to $EF^2 - \frac{1}{2}PQ^2$, or as the circle EF is to the excess of this circle above half the little circle PQ, very nearly.

LEMMA 4

If a cylinder moves uniformly forwards in the direction of its length, the resistance made thereto is not at all changed by augmenting or diminishing that length; and is therefore the same with the resistance of a circle, described with the same diameter, and moving forwards with the same velocity in the direction of a right line perpendicular to its plane.

For the sides are not at all opposed to the motion; and a cylinder becomes a circle when its length is diminished *in infinitum*.

PROPOSITION 37. THEOREM 29

If a cylinder moves uniformly forwards in a compressed, infinite, and nonelastic fluid, in the direction of its length, the resistance arising from the magnitude of its transverse section is to the force by which its whole motion may be destroyed or generated, in the time that it moves four times its length, as the density of the medium is to the density of the cylinder, nearly.

For let the vessel ABDC touch the surface of stagnant water with its bottom CD, and let the water run out of this vessel into the stagnant water through the cylindric canal EFTS perpendicular to the horizon; and let the little circle PQ be placed parallel to the horizon anywhere in the middle of the canal; and produce CA to K, so that AK may be to CK as the square of the ratio, which the excess of the orifice of the canal EF above the little circle PQ bears to the circle AB. Then it is manifest (by Case 5, Case 6, and Cor. I, Prop. 36) that the velocity of the water passing through the annular space between the little circle and the sides of the vessel will be the very same as that which the water would acquire by falling, and in its fall describing the altitude KC or IG.

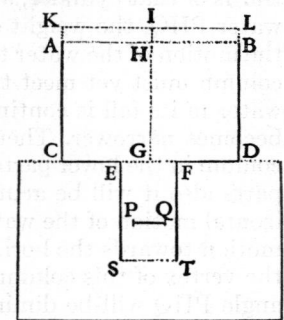

And (by Cor. x, Prop. 36) if the breadth of the vessel be infinite, so that the short line HI may vanish, and the altitudes IG, HG become equal; the force of the water that flows down and presses upon the circle will be to the weight of a cylinder whose base is that little circle, and the altitude $\frac{1}{2}$IG, as EF^2 is to $EF^2 - \frac{1}{2}PQ^2$, very nearly. For the force of the water flowing downwards uniformly through the whole canal will be the same upon the little circle PQ in whatsoever part of the canal it be placed.

Let now the orifices of the canal EF, ST be closed, and let the little circle ascend in the fluid compressed on every side, and by its ascent let it oblige the water that lies above it to descend through the annular space between the little circle and the sides of the canal. Then will the velocity of the ascending little circle be to the velocity of the descending water as the difference of the circles EF and PQ is to the circle PQ; and the velocity of the ascending little circle will be to the sum of the velocities, that is, to the relative velocity of the descending water with which it passes by the little circle in its ascent, as the difference of the circles EF and PQ is to the circle EF, or as $EF^2 - PQ^2$ to EF^2. Let that relative velocity be equal to the velocity with which it was shown above that the water would pass through the annular space, if the circle were to remain unmoved, that is, to the velocity which the water would acquire by falling, and in its fall describing the altitude IG; and the force of the water upon the ascending circle will be the same as before (by Cor. v of the Laws of Motion); that is, the resistance of the ascending little circle will be to the weight of a cylinder of water whose base is that little circle, and its altitude $\frac{1}{2}$IG, as EF^2 is to $EF^2 - \frac{1}{2}PQ^2$, nearly. But the velocity of the little circle will be to the velocity which the water acquires by falling, and in its fall describing the altitude IG, as $EF^2 - PQ^2$ is to EF^2.

Let the breadth of the canal be increased *in infinitum;* and the ratios between $EF^2 - PQ^2$ and EF^2, and between EF^2 and $EF^2 - \frac{1}{2}PQ^2$, will become at last ratios of equality. And therefore the velocity of the little circle will now be the same as that which the water would acquire in falling, and in its fall describing the altitude IG; and the resistance will become equal to the weight of a cylinder whose base is that little circle, and its altitude half the altitude IG, from which the cylinder must fall to acquire the velocity of the ascending circle; and with this velocity the cylinder in the time of its fall will describe four times its length. But the resistance of the cylinder moving forwards with this velocity in the direction of its length is the same with the resistance of the little circle (by Lem. 4), and is therefore nearly equal to the force by which its motion may be generated while it describes four times its length.

If the length of the cylinder be augmented or diminished, its motion, and the time in which it describes four times its length, will be augmented or diminished in the same ratio, and therefore the force by which the motion, so increased or diminished, may be destroyed or generated, will continue the same; because the time is increased or diminished in the same proportion; and therefore that force remains still equal to the resistance of the cylinder, because (by Lem. 4) that resistance will also remain the same.

If the density of the cylinder be augmented or diminished, its motion, and the force by which its motion may be generated or destroyed in the same time, will be augmented or diminished in the same ratio. Therefore the resistance of any cylinder whatsoever will be to the force by which its whole motion may be generated or destroyed, in the time during which it moves four times its length, as the density of the medium is to the density of the cylinder, nearly. Q.E.D.

A fluid must be compressed to become continued; it must be continued and nonelastic, that all the pressure arising from its compression may be propagated in an instant; and so, acting equally upon all parts of the body moved, may produce no change of the resistance. The pressure arising from the motion of the body is spent in generating a motion in the parts of the fluid, and this creates the resistance. But the pressure arising from the compression of the fluid, be it ever so forcible, if it be propagated in an instant, generates no motion in the parts of a continued fluid, produces no change at all of motion therein; and therefore neither augments nor lessens the resistance. This is certain, that the action of the fluid arising from the compression cannot be stronger on the hinder parts of the body moved than on its fore parts, and therefore cannot lessen the resistance described in this Proposition. And if its propagation be infinitely swifter than the motion of the body pressed, it will not be stronger on the fore parts than on the hinder parts. But that action will be infinitely swifter, and propagated in an instant, if the fluid be continued and nonelastic.

COR. I. The resistances, made to cylinders going uniformly forwards in the direction of their lengths through continued infinite mediums, are in a ratio compounded of the square of the ratio of the velocities and the square of the ratio of the diameters, and the ratio of the density of the mediums.

COR. II. If the breadth of the canal be not infinitely increased, but the cylinder go forwards in the direction of its length through an included quiescent medium, its axis all the while coinciding with the axis of the canal, its resistance

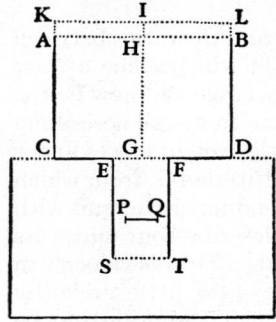

will be to the force by which its whole motion, in the time in which it describes four times its length, may be generated or destroyed, in a ratio compounded of the ratio of EF^2 to $EF^2 - \frac{1}{2}PQ^2$, and the square of the ratio of EF^2 to $EF^2 - PQ^2$, and the ratio of the density of the medium to the density of the cylinder.

COR. III. The same thing supposed, and that a length L is to four times the length of the cylinder in a ratio compounded of the ratio $EF^2 - \frac{1}{2}PQ^2$ to EF^2, and the square of the ratio of $EF^2 - PQ^2$ to EF^2: the resistance of the cylinder will be to the force by which its whole motion, in the time during which it describes the length L, may be destroyed or generated, as the density of the medium is to the density of the cylinder.

SCHOLIUM

In this Proposition we have investigated that resistance alone which arises from the magnitude of the transverse section of the cylinder, neglecting that part of the same which may arise from the obliquity of the motions. For as, in Case 1 of Prop. 36, the obliquity of the motions with which the parts of the water in the vessel converged on every side to the hole EF hindered the efflux of the water through the hole, so, in this Proposition, the obliquity of the motions, with which the parts of the water, pressed by the antecedent extremity of the cylinder, yield to the pressure, and diverge on all sides, retards their passage through the places that lie round that antecedent extremity, towards the hinder parts of the cylinder, and causes the fluid to be moved to a greater distance; which increases the resistance, and that in the same ratio almost in which it diminished the efflux of the water out of the vessel, that is, in the squared ratio of 25 to 21, nearly. And as, in Case 1 of that Proposition, we made the parts of the water pass through the hole EF perpendicularly and in the greatest plenty, by supposing all the water in the vessel lying round the cataract to be frozen, and that part of the water whose motion was oblique and useless to remain without motion, so in this Proposition, that the obliquity of the motions may be taken away, and the parts of the water may give the freest passage to the cylinder, by yielding to it with the most direct and quick motion possible, so that only so much resistance may remain as arises from the magnitude of the transverse section, and as is incapable of diminution, unless by diminishing the diameter of the cylinder; we must conceive those parts of the fluid whose motions are oblique and useless, and produce resistance, to be at rest among themselves at both extremities of the cylinder, and there to cohere, and be joined to the cylinder. Let ABCD be a rectangle, and let AE and BE be two parabolic arcs, described with the axis AB, and with a latus rectum that is to the space HG, which must be described by the cylinder in falling, in order to acquire the velocity with which it moves, as HG to ½AB. Let CF and DF be two other parabolic arcs described with the axis CD, and a latus rectum four times the former; and by the revolution of the figure about the axis EF let there be generated a solid, whose middle part ABDC is the cylinder we are here

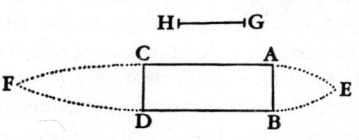

speaking of, and whose extreme parts ABE and CDF contain the parts of the fluid at rest among themselves, and concreted into two hard bodies, adhering to the cylinder at each end like a head and tail. Then if this solid EACFDB move in the direction of the length of its axis FE towards the parts beyond E, the resistance will be nearly the same as that which we have here determined in this Proposition; that is, it will have the same ratio to the force with which the whole motion of the cylinder may be destroyed or generated, in the time that it is describing the length 4AC with that motion uniformly continued, as the density of the fluid has to the density of the cylinder, nearly. And (by Cor. VII, Prop. 36) the resistance must be to this force in the ratio of 2 to 3, at the least.

Lemma 5

If a cylinder, a sphere, and a spheroid, of equal breadths be placed successively in the middle of a cylindric canal, so that their axes may coincide with the axis of the canal, these bodies will equally hinder the passage of the water through the canal.

For the spaces lying between the sides of the canal, and the cylinder, sphere, and spheroid, through which the water passes, are equal; and the water will pass equally through equal spaces.

This is true, upon the supposition that all the water above the cylinder, sphere, or spheroid, whose fluidity is not necessary to make the passage of the water the quickest possible, is congealed, as was explained above in Cor. VII, Prop. 36.

Lemma 6

The same supposition remaining, the fore-mentioned bodies are equally acted on by the water flowing through the canal.

This appears by Lem. 5 and the third Law. For the water and the bodies act upon each other mutually and equally.

Lemma 7

If the water be at rest in the canal, and these bodies move with equal velocity and in opposite directions through the canal, their resistances will be equal among themselves.

This appears from the last Lemma, for the relative motions remain the same among themselves.

Scholium

The case is the same for all convex and round bodies, whose axes coincide with the axis of the canal. Some difference may arise from a greater or less friction; but in these Lemmas we suppose the bodies to be perfectly smooth, and the medium to be void of all tenacity and friction; and that those parts of the fluid which by their oblique and superfluous motions may disturb, hinder, and retard the flux of the water through the canal, are at rest among themselves; being fixed like water by frost, and adhering to the force and hinder parts of the bodies in the manner explained in the Scholium of the last Proposition; for in what follows we consider the very least resistance that round bodies described with the greatest given transverse sections can possibly meet with.

Bodies swimming upon fluids, when they move straight forwards, cause the fluid to ascend at their fore parts and subside at their hinder parts, especially if they are of an obtuse figure; and hence they meet with a little more resistance than if they were acute at the head and tail. And bodies moving in elastic fluids, if they are obtuse behind and before, condense the fluid a little more at their fore parts, and relax the same at their hinder parts; and therefore meet also with a little more resistance than if they were acute at the head and tail. But in these Lemmas and Propositions we are not treating of elastic but nonelastic fluids; not of bodies floating on the surface of the fluid, but deeply immersed therein. And when the resistance of bodies in nonelastic fluids is once known, we may then augment this resistance a little in elastic fluids, as our air; and in the surfaces of stagnating fluids, as lakes and seas.

PROPOSITION 38. THEOREM 30

If a globe move uniformly forwards in a compressed, infinite, and nonelastic fluid, its resistance is to the force by which its whole motion may be destroyed or generated, in the time that it describes eight third parts of its diameter, as the density of the fluid is to the density of the globe, very nearly.

For the globe is to its circumscribed cylinder as 2 to 3; and therefore the force which can destroy all the motion of the cylinder, while the same cylinder is describing the length of four of its diameters, will destroy all the motion of the globe, while the globe is describing two-thirds of this length, that is, eight third parts of its own diameter. Now the resistance of the cylinder is to this force very nearly as the density of the fluid is to the density of the cylinder or globe (by Prop. 37), and the resistance of the globe is equal to the resistance of the cylinder (by Lems. 5, 6, 7).   Q.E.D.

COR. I. The resistances of globes in infinite compressed mediums are in a ratio compounded of the squared ratio of the velocity, and the squared ratio of the diameter, and the ratio of the density of the mediums.

COR. II. The greatest velocity, with which a globe can descend by its comparative weight through a resisting fluid, is the same as that which it may acquire by falling with the same weight, and without any resistance, and in its fall describing a space that is to four third parts of its diameter as the density of the globe is to the density of the fluid. For the globe in the time of its fall, moving with the velocity acquired in falling, will describe a space that will be to eight third parts of its diameter as the density of the globe is to the density of the fluid; and the force of its weight which generates this motion will be to the force that can generate the same motion, in the time that the globe describes eight third parts of its diameter, with the same velocity as the density of the fluid is to the density of the globe; and therefore (by this Proposition) the force of weight will be equal to the force of resistance, and therefore cannot accelerate the globe.

COR. III. If there be given both the density of the globe and its velocity at the beginning of the motion, and the density of the compressed quiescent fluid in which the globe moves, there is given at any time both the velocity of the globe and its resistance, and the space described by it (by Cor. VII, Prop. 35).

COR. IV. A globe moving in a compressed quiescent fluid of the same density with itself will lose half its motion before it can describe the length of two of its diameters (by the same Cor. VII).

PROPOSITION 39. THEOREM 31

If a globe move uniformly forwards through a fluid inclosed and compressed in a cylindric canal, its resistance is to the force by which its whole motion may be generated or destroyed, in the time in which it describes eight third parts of its diameter, in a ratio compounded of the ratio of the orifice of the canal to the excess of that orifice above half the greatest circle of the globe; and the squared ratio of the orifice of the canal to the excess of that orifice above the greatest circle of the globe; and the ratio of the density of the fluid to the density of the globe, nearly.

This appears by Cor. II, Prop. 37, and the demonstration proceeds in the same manner as in the foregoing Proposition.

SCHOLIUM

In the last two Propositions we suppose (as was done before in Lem. 5) that all the water which precedes the globe, and whose fluidity increases the resistance of the same, is congealed. Now if that water becomes fluid, it will somewhat increase the resistance. But in these Propositions that increase is so small, that it may be neglected, because the convex surface of the globe produces the very same effect almost as the congelation of the water.

PROPOSITION 40. PROBLEM 9

To find by experiment the resistance of a globe moving through a perfectly fluid compressed medium.

Let A be the weight of the globe in a vacuum, B its weight in the resisting medium, D the diameter of the globe, F a space which is to $\frac{4}{3}$D as the density of the globe is to the density of the medium, that is, as A is to A − B, G the time in which the globe falling with the weight B without resistance describes the space F, and H the velocity which the body acquires by that fall. Then H will be the greatest velocity with which the globe can possibly descend with the weight B in the resisting medium, by Cor. II, Prop. 38; and the resistance which the globe meets with, when descending with that velocity, will be equal to its weight B; and the resistance it meets with in any other velocity will be to the weight B as the square of the ratio of that velocity to the greatest velocity H, by Cor. I, Prop. 38.

This is the resistance that arises from the inactivity of the matter of the fluid. That resistance which arises from the elasticity, tenacity, and friction of its parts, may be thus investigated.

Let the globe be let fall so that it may descend in the fluid by the weight B; and let P be the time of falling, and let that time be expressed in seconds, if the time G be given in seconds. Find the absolute number N agreeing to the logarithm $0.4342944819 \frac{2P}{G}$, and let L be the logarithm of the number $\frac{N+1}{N}$; and the velocity acquired in falling will be $\dfrac{N-1}{N+1}H$, and the height described will be $\dfrac{2PF}{G} - 1.3862943611F + 4.605170186LF$. If the fluid be of a sufficient depth, we may neglect the term $4.605170186LF$; and $\dfrac{2PF}{G} - 1.3862943611F$ will be the altitude described, nearly. These things appear by Prop. 9, Book II, and its Corollaries, and are true upon this supposition, that the globe meets with no other resistance but that which arises from the inactivity of matter. Now if it really meet with any resistance of another kind, the descent will be slower, and from the amount of that retardation will be known the amount of this new resistance.

That the velocity and descent of a body falling in a fluid might more easily be known, I have composed the following table, the first column of which

The Times P	Velocities of the body falling in the fluid	The spaces described in falling in the fluid	The spaces described with the greatest motion	The spaces described by falling in a vacuum
0.001G	99999$^{29}/_{30}$	0.000001F	0.002F	0.000001F
0.01G	999967	0.0001F	0.02F	0.0001F
0.1G	9966799	0.0099834F	0.2F	0.01F
0.2G	19737532	0.0397361F	0.4F	0.04F
0.3G	29131261	0.0886815F	0.6F	0.09F
0.4G	37994896	0.1559070F	0.8F	0.16F
0.5G	46211716	0.2402290F	1.0F	0.25F
0.6G	53704957	0.3402706F	1.2F	0.36F
0.7G	60436778	0.4545405F	1.4F	0.49F
0.8G	66403677	0.5815071F	1.6F	0.64F
0.9G	71629787	0.7196609F	1.8F	0.81F
1G	76159416	0.8675617F	2F	1F
2G	96402758	2.6500055F	4F	4F
3G	99505475	4.6186570F	6F	9F
4G	99932930	6.6143765F	8F	16F
5G	99990920	8.6137964F	10F	25F
6G	99998771	10.6137179F	12F	36F
7G	99999834	12.6137073F	14F	49F
8G	99999980	14.6137059F	16F	64F
9G	99999997	16.6137057F	18F	81F
10G	99999999$^{3}/_{5}$	18.6137056F	20F	100F

denotes the times of descent; the second shows the velocities acquired in falling, the greatest velocity being 100,000,000; the third exhibits the spaces described by falling in those times, 2F being the space which the body describes in the time G with the greatest velocity; and the fourth gives the spaces described with the greatest velocity in the same times. The numbers in the fourth column are $\dfrac{2P}{G}$, and by subtracting the number $1.3862944 - 4.6051702L$, are found the numbers in the third column; and these numbers must be multiplied by the space F to obtain the spaces described in falling. A fifth column is added to all these, containing the spaces described in the same times by a body falling in a vacuum with the force of B its comparative weight.

SCHOLIUM

In order to investigate the resistances of fluids from experiments, I procured a square wooden vessel, whose length and breadth on the inside was 9 inches English measure, and its depth 9½ feet; this I filled with rain water; and having provided globes made up of wax, and lead included therein, I noted the times of the descents of these globes, the height through which they descended being 112 inches. A solid cubic foot of English measure contains 76 pounds troy weight of rain water; and a solid inch contains $^{19}\!/_{36}$ ounces troy weight, or 253⅓ grains; and a globe of water of one inch in diameter contains 132.645 grains in air, or 132.8 grains in a vacuum; and any other globe will be as the excess of its weight in a vacuum above its weight in water.

EXPER. 1. A globe whose weight was 156¼ grains in air, and 77 grains in water, described the whole height of 112 inches in 4 seconds. And, upon repeating the experiment, the globe spent again the very same time of 4 seconds in falling.

The weight of this globe in a vacuum is $156^{13}\!/_{38}$ grains; and the excess of this weight above the weight of the globe in water is $79^{13}\!/_{38}$ grains. Hence the diameter of the globe appears to be 0.84224 parts of an inch. Then it will be, as that excess to the weight of the globe in a vacuum, so is the density of the water to the density of the globe; and so is $^8\!/_3$ parts of the diameter of the globe (viz., 2.24597 inches) to the space 2F, which will be therefore 4.4256 inches. Now a globe falling in a vacuum with its whole weight of $156^{13}\!/_{38}$ grains in one second of time will describe 193⅓ inches; and falling in water in the same time with the weight of 77 grains without resistance, will describe 95.219 inches; and in the time G, which is to one second of time as the square root of the ratio of the space F, or of 2.2128 inches to 95.219 inches, will describe 2.2128 inches, and will acquire the greatest velocity H with which it is capable of descending in water. Therefore the time G is 0.15244 seconds. And in this time G, with that greatest velocity H, the globe will describe the space 2F, which is 4.4256 inches; and therefore in 4 seconds will describe a space of 116.1245 inches. Subtract the space 1.3862944·F, or 3.0676 inches, and there will remain a space of 113.0569 inches, which the globe falling through water in a very wide vessel will describe in 4 seconds. But this space, by reason of the narrowness of the wooden vessel before mentioned, ought to be diminished in a ratio compounded of the square root of the ratio of the orifice of the vessel to the excess of this orifice above half a great circle of the globe, and of the simple ratio of the same orifice to its excess above a great circle of the globe, that is, in a ratio of 1 to 0.9914. This done, we have a space of 112.08 inches, which a globe falling through the water in this wooden vessel in 4 seconds of time ought nearly to describe by this theory; but it described 112 inches by the experiment.

EXPER. 2. Three equal globes, whose weights were severally 76⅓ grains in air, and $5^1\!/_{16}$ grains in water, were let fall successively; and every one fell through the water in 15 seconds of time, describing in its fall a height of 112 inches.

By computation, the weight of each globe in a vacuum is $76^5\!/_{12}$ grains; the excess of this weight above the weight in water is $71^{17}\!/_{48}$ grains; the diameter of the globe 0.81296 of an inch; $^8\!/_3$ parts of this diameter 2.16789 inches; the space 2F is 2.3217 inches; the space which a globe of $5^1\!/_{16}$ grains in weight would describe in one second without resistance, 12.808 inches, and the time G

0.301056 seconds. Therefore the globe, with the greatest velocity it is capable of receiving from a weight of $5\frac{1}{16}$ grains in its descent through water, will describe in the time 0.301056 seconds the space 2.3217 inches; and in 15 seconds the space 115.678 inches. Subtract the space 1.3862944F, or 1.609 inches, and there remains the space 114.069 inches; which therefore the falling globe ought to describe in the same time, if the vessel were very wide. But because our vessel was narrow, the space ought to be diminished by about 0.895 of an inch. And so the space will remain 113.174 inches, which a globe falling in this vessel ought nearly to describe in 15 seconds. But by the experiment it described 112 inches. The difference is not sensible.

EXPER. 3. Three equal globes, whose weights were severally 121 grains in air, and 1 grain in water, were successively let fall; and they fell through the water in the times 46 seconds, 47 seconds, and 50 seconds, describing a height of 112 inches.

By the theory, these globes ought to have fallen in about 40 seconds. Now whether their falling more slowly were occasioned from the consideration that in slow motions the resistance arising from the force of inactivity does really bear a less proportion to the resistance arising from other causes; or whether it is to be attributed to little bubbles that might chance to stick to the globes, or to the rarefaction of the wax by the warmth of the weather, or of the hand that let them fall; or, lastly, whether it proceeded from some insensible errors in weighing the globes in the water, I am not certain. Therefore the weight of the globe in water should be of several grains, that the experiment may be certain, and to be depended on.

EXPER. 4. I began the foregoing Experiments to investigate the resistances of fluids, before I was acquainted with the theory laid down in the Propositions immediately preceding. Afterwards, in order to examine the theory after it was discovered, I procured a wooden vessel, whose breadth on the inside was $8\frac{2}{3}$ inches, and its depth $15\frac{1}{3}$ feet. Then I made four globes of wax, with lead included, each of which weighed $139\frac{1}{4}$ grains in air, and $7\frac{1}{8}$ grains in water. These I let fall, measuring the times of their falling in the water with a pendulum oscillating to half-seconds. The globes were cold, and had remained so some time, both when they were weighed and when they were let fall; because warmth rarefies the wax, and by rarefying it diminishes the weight of the globe in the water; and wax, when rarefied, is not instantly reduced by cold to its former density. Before they were let fall, they were totally immersed under water, lest, by the weight of any part of them that might chance to be above the water, their descent should be accelerated in its beginning. Then, when after their immersion they were perfectly at rest, they were let go with the greatest care, that they might not receive any impulse from the hand that let them down. And they fell successively in the times of $47\frac{1}{2}$, $48\frac{1}{2}$, 50, and 51 oscillations, describing a height of 15 feet and 2 inches. But the weather was now a little colder than when the globes were weighed, and therefore I repeated the experiment another day; and then the globes fell in the times of 49, $49\frac{1}{2}$, 50, and 53; and at a third trial in the times of $49\frac{1}{2}$, 50, 51, and 53 oscillations. And by making the experiment several times over, I found that the globes fell mostly in the times of $49\frac{1}{2}$ and 50 oscillations. When they fell slower, I suspect them to have been retarded by striking against the sides of the vessel.

Now, computing from the theory, the weight of the globe in a vacuum is $139\frac{2}{5}$ grains; the excess of this weight above the weight of the globe in water $132\frac{11}{40}$ grains; the diameter of the globe 0.99868 of an inch; $\frac{8}{3}$ parts of the diameter 2.66315 inches; the space 2F 2.8066 inches; the space which a globe weighing $7\frac{1}{8}$ grains falling without resistance describes in a second of time 9.88164 inches; and the time G 0.376843 seconds. Therefore the globe with the greatest velocity with which it is capable of descending through the water by the force of a weight of $7\frac{1}{8}$ grains, will in the time 0.376843 seconds describe a space of 2.8066 inches, and in one second of time a space of 7.44766 inches, and in the time 25 seconds, or in 50 oscillations, the space 186.1915 inches. Subtract the space 1.386294F, or 1.9454 inches, and there will remain the space 184.2461 inches which the globe will describe in that time in a very wide vessel. Because our vessel was narrow, let this space be diminished in a ratio compounded of the square root of the ratio of the orifice of the vessel to the excess of this orifice above half a great circle of the globe, and of the simple ratio of the same orifice to its excess above a great circle of the globe; and we shall have the space of 181.86 inches, which the globe ought by the theory to describe in this vessel in the time of 50 oscillations, nearly. But it described the space of 182 inches, by experiment, in $49\frac{1}{2}$ or 50 oscillations.

Exper. 5. Four globes weighing $154\frac{3}{8}$ grains in air, and $21\frac{1}{2}$ grains in water, being let fall several times, fell in the times of $28\frac{1}{2}$, 29, $29\frac{1}{2}$, and 30, and sometimes of 31, 32, and 33 oscillations, describing a height of 15 feet and 2 inches.

They ought by the theory to have fallen in the time of 29 oscillations, nearly.

Exper. 6. Five globes, weighing $212\frac{3}{8}$ grains in air, and $79\frac{1}{2}$ in water, being several times let fall, fell in the times of 15, $15\frac{1}{2}$, 16, 17, and 18 oscillations, describing a height of 15 feet and 2 inches.

By the theory they ought to have fallen in the time of 15 oscillations, nearly.

Exper. 7. Four globes, weighing $293\frac{3}{8}$ grains in air, and $35\frac{7}{8}$ grains in water, being let fall several times, fell in the times of $29\frac{1}{2}$, 30, $30\frac{1}{2}$, 31, 32, and 33 oscillations, describing a height of 15 feet and $1\frac{1}{2}$ inches.

By the theory they ought to have fallen in the time of 28 oscillations, nearly.

In searching for the cause that occasioned these globes of the same weight and magnitude to fall, some swifter and some slower, I hit upon this: that the globes, when they were first let go and began to fall, oscillated about their centres; that side which chanced to be the heavier descending first, and producing an oscillating motion. Now by oscillating thus, the globe communicates a greater motion to the water than if it descended without any oscillations; and by this communication loses part of its own motion with which it should descend; and therefore as this oscillation is greater or less, it will be more or less retarded. Besides, the globe always recedes from that side of itself which is descending in the oscillation, and by so receding comes nearer to the sides of the vessel, so as even to strike against them sometimes. And the heavier the globes are, the stronger this oscillation is; and the greater they are, the more is the water agitated by it. Therefore to diminish this oscillation of the globes, I made new ones of lead and wax, sticking the lead in one side of the globe very near its surface; and I let fall the globe in such a manner, that, as near as possible, the heavier side might be lowest at the beginning of the descent. By this means the oscillations became much less than before, and the times in which the globes fell were not so unequal: as in the following Experiments.

EXPER. 8. Four globes weighing 139 grains in air, and $6\frac{1}{2}$ in water, were let fall several times, and fell mostly in the time of 51 oscillations, never in more than 52, or in fewer than 50, describing a height of 182 inches.

By the theory they ought to fall in about the time of 52 oscillations.

EXPER. 9. Four globes weighing $273\frac{1}{4}$ grains in air, and $140\frac{3}{4}$ in water, being several times let fall, fell in never fewer than 12, and never more than 13 oscillations, describing a height of 182 inches.

These globes by the theory ought to have fallen in the time of $11\frac{1}{3}$ oscillations, nearly.

EXPER. 10. Four globes, weighing 384 grains in air, and $119\frac{1}{2}$ in water, being let fall several times, fell in the times of $17\frac{3}{4}$, 18, $18\frac{1}{2}$, and 19 oscillations, describing a height of $181\frac{1}{2}$ inches. And when they fell in the time of 19 oscillations, I sometimes heard them hit against the sides of the vessel before they reached the bottom.

By the theory they ought to have fallen in the time of $15\frac{5}{9}$ oscillations, nearly.

EXPER. 11. Three equal globes, weighing 48 grains in air, and $3\frac{29}{32}$ in water, being several times let fall, fell in the times of $43\frac{1}{2}$, 44, $44\frac{1}{2}$, 45, and 46 oscillations, and mostly in 44 and 45, describing a height of $182\frac{1}{2}$ inches, nearly.

By the theory they ought to have fallen in the time of $46\frac{5}{9}$ oscillations, nearly.

EXPER. 12. Three equal globes, weighing 141 grains in air, and $4\frac{3}{8}$ in water, being let fall several times, fell in the times of 61, 62, 63, 64, and 65 oscillations, describing a space of 182 inches.

And by the theory they ought to have fallen in $64\frac{1}{2}$ oscillations, nearly.

From these Experiments it is manifest, that when the globes fell slowly, as in the second, fourth, fifth, eighth, eleventh, and twelfth Experiments, the times of falling are rightly exhibited by the theory; but when the globes fell more swiftly, as in the sixth, ninth, and tenth Experiments, the resistance was somewhat greater than the square of the velocity. For the globes in falling oscillate a little; and this oscillation, in those globes that are light and fall slowly, soon ceases by the weakness of the motion; but in greater and heavier globes, the motion being strong, it continues longer, and is not to be checked by the ambient water till after several oscillations. Besides, the more swiftly the globes move, the less are they pressed by the fluid at their hinder parts; and if the velocity be continually increased, they will at last leave an empty space behind them, unless the compression of the fluid be increased at the same time. For the compression of the fluid ought to be increased (by Props. 32 and 33) as the square of the velocity, in order to maintain the resistance in the same squared ratio. But because this is not done, the globes that move swiftly are not so much pressed at their hinder parts as the others; and by the defect of this pressure it comes to pass that their resistance is a little greater than the square of their velocity.

So that the theory agrees with the experiments on bodies falling in water. It remains that we examine the observations of bodies falling in air.

EXPER. 13. From the top of St. Paul's Church in London, in June, 1710, there were let fall together two glass globes, one full of quicksilver, the other of air; and in their fall they described a height of 220 English feet. A wooden table was suspended upon iron hinges on one side, and the other side of the table was supported by a wooden pin. The two globes lying upon this table were let fall together by pulling out the pin by means of an iron wire reaching thence down to the ground; so that, the pin being removed, the table, which had then no support but the iron hinges, fell downwards, and turning round upon the hinges, gave leave to the globes to drop off from it. At the same instant, with the same pull of the iron wire that took out the pin, a pendulum oscillating to seconds was let go, and began to oscillate. The diameters and weights of the globes, and their times of falling, are exhibited in the accompanying table.

The globes filled with mercury			The globes full of air		
Weights	Diameters	Times in falling	Weights	Diameters	Times in falling
grains	inches	seconds	grains	inches	seconds
908	0.8	4	510	5.1	8½
983	0.8	4−	642	5.2	8
866	0.8	4	599	5.1	8
747	0.75	4+	515	5.0	8¼
808	0.75	4	483	5.0	8½
784	0.75	4+	641	5.2	8

But the times observed must be corrected; for the globes of mercury (by Galileo's theory), in 4 seconds of time, will describe 257 English feet, and 220 feet in only 3 seconds 42 thirds. So that the wooden table, when the pin was taken out, did not turn upon its hinges so quickly as it ought to have done; and the slowness of that revolution hindered the descent of the globes at the beginning. For the globes lay about the middle of the table, and indeed were rather nearer to the axis upon which it turned than to the pin. And hence the times of falling were prolonged about 18 thirds; and therefore ought to be corrected by subtracting that excess, especially in the larger globes, which, by reason of the largeness of their diameters, lay longer upon the revolving table than the others. This being done, the times in which the six larger globes fell will come forth 8 seconds 12 thirds, 7 seconds 42 thirds, 7 seconds 42 thirds, 7 seconds 57 thirds, 8 seconds 12 thirds, and 7 seconds 42 thirds.

Therefore the fifth in order among the globes that were full of air being 5 inches in diameter, and 483 grains in weight, fell in 8 seconds 12 thirds, describing a space of 220 feet. The weight of a bulk of water equal to this globe is 16,600 grains; and the weight of an equal bulk of air is $\frac{16600}{860}$ grains, or $19\frac{3}{10}$ grains; and therefore the weight of the globe in a vacuum is $502\frac{3}{10}$ grains; and this weight is to the weight of a bulk of air equal to the globe as $502\frac{3}{10}$ is to $19\frac{3}{10}$; and so is 2F to $\frac{8}{3}$ of the diameter of the globe, that is, to $13\frac{1}{3}$ inches. Hence 2F becomes 28 feet 11 inches. A globe, falling in a vacuum with its whole weight of $502\frac{3}{10}$ grains, will in one second of time describe $193\frac{1}{3}$ inches as above; and with the weight 483 grains will describe 185.905 inches; and with that weight 483 grains in a vacuum will describe the space F, or 14 feet 5½ inches, in the time of 57 thirds and 58 fourths, and acquire the greatest velocity it is capable of descending with in the air. With this velocity the globe in

8 seconds 12 thirds of time will describe 245 feet and $5\frac{1}{3}$ inches. Subtract $1.3863 \cdot F$, or 20 feet and $\frac{1}{2}$ an inch, and there remain 225 feet 5 inches. This space, therefore, the falling globe ought by the theory to describe in 8 seconds 12 thirds. But by the experiment it described a space of 220 feet. The difference is inappreciable.

By like calculations applied to the other globes full of air, I composed the following table.

The weights of the globes	The diameters	The times of falling from a height of 220 feet		The spaces which they would describe by the theory		The excesses	
grains	inches	seconds	thirds	feet	inches	feet	inches
510	5.1	8	12	226	11	6	11
642	5.2	7	42	230	9	10	9
599	5.1	7	42	227	10	7	0
515	5	7	57	224	5	4	5
483	5	8	12	225	5	5	5
641	5.2	7	42	230	7	10	7

Exper. 14. In the year 1719, in the month of July, Dr. Desaguliers made some experiments of this kind again, by forming hogs' bladders into spherical orbs; which was done by means of a concave wooden sphere, which the bladders, being wetted well first, were put into. After that, being blown full of air, they were obliged to fill up the spherical cavity that contained them; and then, when dry, were taken out. These were let fall from the lantern on the top of the cupola of the same church, namely, from a height of 272 feet; and at the same moment of time there was let fall a leaden globe, whose weight was about 2 pounds troy weight. And in the meantime some persons standing in the upper part of the church where the globes were let fall observed the whole times of falling; and others standing on the ground observed the differences of the times between the fall of the leaden weight and the fall of the bladder. The times were measured by pendulums oscillating to half-seconds. And one of those that stood upon the ground had a machine vibrating four times in one second; and another had another machine accurately made with a pendulum vibrating four times in a second also. One of those also who stood at the top of the church had a like machine; and these instruments were so contrived, that their motions could be stopped or renewed at pleasure. Now the leaden globe fell in about $4\frac{1}{4}$ seconds of time; and from the addition of this time to the difference of time above spoken of, was obtained the whole time in which the bladder was falling. The times which the five bladders spent in falling, after the leaden globe had reached the ground, were, the first time, $14\frac{3}{4}$ seconds, $12\frac{3}{4}$ seconds, $14\frac{5}{8}$ seconds, $17\frac{3}{4}$ seconds, and $16\frac{7}{8}$ seconds; and the second time, $14\frac{1}{2}$ seconds, $14\frac{1}{4}$ seconds, 14 seconds, 19 seconds, and $16\frac{3}{4}$ seconds. Add to these $4\frac{1}{4}$ seconds, the time in which the leaden globe was falling, and the whole times in which the five bladders fell were, the first time, 19 seconds, 17 seconds, $18\frac{7}{8}$ seconds, 22 seconds, and $21\frac{1}{8}$ seconds; and the second time, $18\frac{3}{4}$ seconds, $18\frac{1}{2}$ seconds, $18\frac{1}{4}$ seconds, $23\frac{1}{4}$ seconds, and 21 seconds. The times observed at the top of the church were, the first time, $19\frac{3}{8}$ seconds, $17\frac{1}{4}$ seconds, $18\frac{3}{4}$ seconds, $22\frac{1}{8}$ seconds, and $21\frac{5}{8}$ seconds; and the second time,

19 seconds, 18⅝ seconds, 18⅜ seconds, 24 seconds, and 21¼ seconds. But the bladders did not always fall directly down, but sometimes fluttered a little in the air, and waved to and fro, as they were descending. And by these motions the times of their falling were prolonged, and increased by half a second sometimes, and sometimes by a whole second. The second and fourth bladders fell most directly the first time, and the first and third the second time. The fifth bladder was wrinkled, and by its wrinkles was a little retarded. I found their diameters by their circumferences measured with a very fine thread wound about them twice. In the following table I have compared the experiments with the theory; making the density of air to be to the density of rain water as 1 to 860, and computing the spaces which by the theory the globes ought to describe in falling.

The weights of the bladders	The diameters	The times of falling from a height of 272 feet	The spaces which by the theory ought to have been described in those times		The difference between the theory and the experiments	
grains	inches	seconds	feet	inches	feet	inches
128	5.28	19	271	11	− 0	1
156	5.19	17	272	0½	+ 0	0½
137½	5.3	18	272	7	+ 0	7
97½	5.26	22	277	4	+ 5	4
99⅛	5	21⅛	282	0	+10	0

Our theory, therefore, exhibits rightly, within a very little, all the resistance that globes moving either in air or in water meet with; which appears to be proportional to the densities of the fluids in globes of equal velocities and magnitudes.

In the Scholium subjoined to the sixth Section, we showed, by experiments of pendulums, that the resistances of equal and equally swift globes moving in air, water, and quicksilver, are as the densities of the fluids. We here prove the same more accurately by experiments of bodies falling in air and water. For pendulums at each oscillation excite a motion in the fluid always contrary to the motion of the pendulum in its return; and the resistance arising from this motion, as also the resistance of the thread by which the pendulum is suspended, makes the whole resistance of a pendulum greater than the resistance deduced from the experiments of falling bodies. For by the experiments of pendulums described in that Scholium, a globe of the same density as water in describing the length of its semidiameter in air would lose the $\frac{1}{3342}$ part of its motion. But by the theory delivered in this seventh Section, and confirmed by experiments of falling bodies, the same globe in describing the same length would lose only a part of its motion equal to $\frac{1}{4586}$, supposing the density of water to be to the density of air as 860 to 1. Therefore the resistances were found greater by the experiments of pendulums (for the reasons just mentioned) than by the experiments of falling globes; and that in the ratio of about 4 to 3. But yet since the resistances of pendulums oscillating in air, water, and quicksilver, are alike increased by like causes, the proportion of the resistances in these mediums will be rightly enough exhibited by the experiments of pendulums, as well as by the experiments of falling bodies. And from all this it may be concluded, that the resistances of bodies, moving in any fluids whatsoever, though of the most extreme fluidity, are, other things being equal, as the densities of the fluids.

These things being thus established, we may now determine what part of its motion any globe projected in any fluid whatsoever would nearly lose in a given time. Let D be the diameter of the globe, and V its velocity at the beginning of its motion, and T the time in which a globe with the velocity V can describe in a vacuum a space that is to the space $\frac{8}{3}$D as the density of the globe to the density of the fluid; and the globe projected in that fluid will, in any other time t lose the part $\frac{tV}{T+t}$, the part $\frac{TV}{T+t}$ remaining; and will describe a space, which will be to that described in the same time in a vacuum with the uniform velocity V, as the logarithm of the number $\frac{T+t}{T}$ multiplied by the number 2.302585093 is to the number $\frac{t}{T}$ by Cor. VII, Prop. 35. In slow motions the resistance may be a little less, because the figure of a globe is more adapted to motion than the figure of a cylinder described with the same diameter. In swift motions the resistance may be a little greater, because the elasticity and compression of the fluid do not increase as the square of the velocity. But these little niceties I take no notice of.

And though air, water, quicksilver, and the like fluids, by the division of their parts *in infinitum,* should be subtilized, and become mediums infinitely fluid, nevertheless, the resistance they would make to projected globes would be the same. For the resistance considered in the preceding Propositions arises from the inactivity of the matter; and the inactivity of matter is essential to bodies, and always proportional to the quantity of matter. By the division of the parts of the fluid the resistance arising from the tenacity and friction of the parts may be indeed diminished; but the quantity of matter will not be at all diminished by this division; and if the quantity of matter be the same, its force of inactivity will be the same; and therefore the resistance here spoken of will be the same, as being always proportional to that force. To diminish this resistance, the quantity of matter in the spaces through which the bodies move must be diminished; and therefore the celestial spaces, through which the globes of the planets and comets are continually passing towards all parts, with the utmost freedom, and without the least sensible diminution of their motion, must be utterly void of any corporeal fluid, excepting, perhaps, some extremely rare vapors and the rays of light.

Projectiles excite a motion in fluids as they pass through them, and this motion arises from the excess of the pressure of the fluid at the fore parts of the projectile above the pressure of the same at the hinder parts; and cannot be less in mediums infinitely fluid than it is in air, water, and quicksilver, in proportion to the density of matter in each. Now this excess of pressure does, in proportion to its quantity, not only excite a motion in the fluid, but also acts upon the projectile so as to retard its motion; and therefore the resistance in every fluid is as the motion excited by the projectile in the fluid; and cannot be less in the most subtile ether in proportion to the density of that ether, than it is in air, water, and quicksilver, in proportion to the densities of those fluids.

SECTION VIII

The motion propagated through fluids

Proposition 41. Theorem 32

A pressure is not propagated through a fluid in rectilinear directions except where the particles of the fluid lie in a right line.

If the particles *a, b, c, d, e* lie in a right line, the pressure may be indeed directly propagated from *a* to *e*; but then the particle *e* will urge the obliquely posited particles *f* and *g* obliquely, and those particles *f* and *g* will not sustain

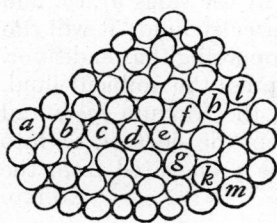

this pressure, unless they be supported by the particles *h* and *k* lying beyond them; but the particles that support them are also pressed by them; and those particles cannot sustain that pressure, without being supported by, and pressing upon, those particles that lie still farther, as *l* and *m*, and so on *in infinitum.* Therefore the pressure, as soon as it is propagated to particles that lie out of right lines, begins to deflect towards one hand and the other, and will be propagated obliquely *in infinitum;* and after it has begun to be propagated obliquely, if it reaches more distant particles lying out of the right line, it will deflect again on each hand; and this it will do as often as it lights on particles that do not lie exactly in a right line. Q.E.D.

Cor. If any part of a pressure, propagated through a fluid from a given point, be intercepted by any obstacle, the remaining part, which is not intercepted, will deflect into the spaces behind the obstacle. This may be demonstrated also after the following manner. Let a pressure be propagated from the point A towards any part, and, if it be possible, in rectilinear directions; and the obstacle NBCK being perforated in BC, let all the pressure be intercepted

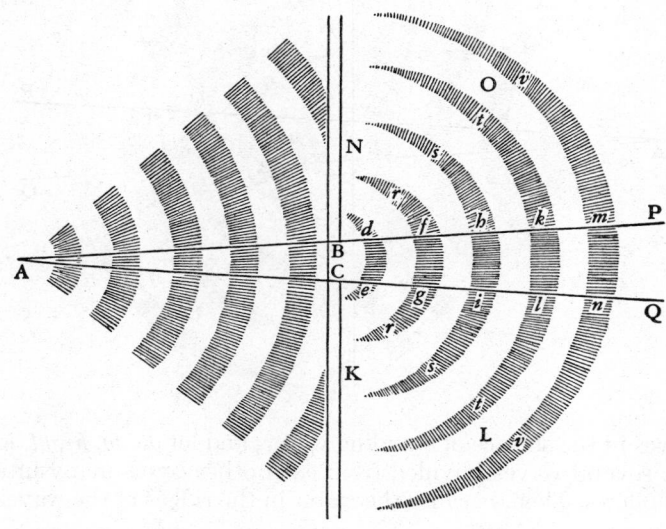

but the coniform part APQ passing through the circular hole BC. Let the cone APQ be divided into frustums by the transverse planes, *de*, *fg*, *hi*. Then while the cone ABC, propagating the pressure, urges the conic frustum *degf* beyond it on the surface *de*, and this frustum urges the next frustum *fgih* on the surface *fg*, and that frustum urges a third frustum, and so *in infinitum;* it is manifest (by the third Law) that the first frustum *defg* is, by the reaction of the second frustum *fghi*, as much urged and pressed on the surface *fg*, as it urges and presses that second frustum. Therefore the frustum *degf* is compressed on both sides, that is, between the cone A*de* and the frustum *fhig;* and therefore (by Case 6, Prop. 19) cannot preserve its figure, unless it be compressed with the same force on all sides. Therefore with the same force with which it is pressed on the surfaces *de*, *fg*, it will endeavor to break forth at the sides *df*, *eg;* and there (being not in the least tenacious or hard, but perfectly fluid) it will run out, expanding itself, unless there be an ambient fluid opposing that endeavor. Therefore, by the effort it makes to run out, it will press the ambient fluid, at its sides *df*, *eg*, with the same force that it does the frustum *fghi;* and therefore, the pressure will be propagated as much from the sides *df*, *eg*, into the spaces NO, KL this way and that way, as it is propagated from the surface *fg* towards PQ.   Q.E.D.

PROPOSITION 42. THEOREM 33

All motion propagated through a fluid diverges from a rectilinear progress into the unmoved spaces.

CASE 1. Let a motion be propagated from the point A through the hole BC, and, if it be possible, let it proceed in the conic space BCQP according to right lines diverging from the point A. And let us first suppose this motion to be

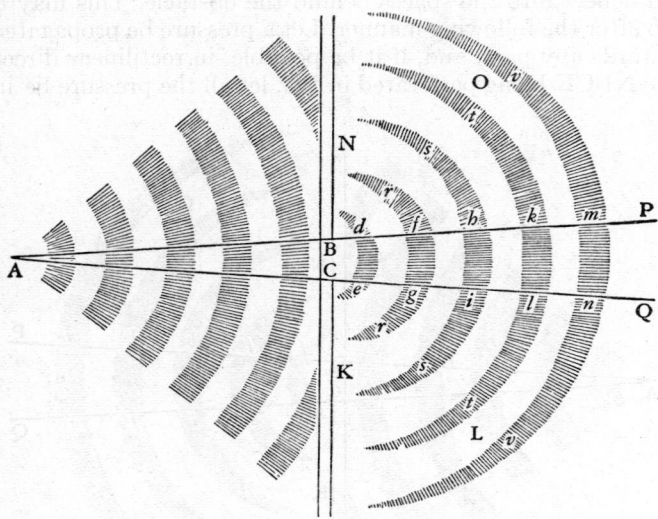

that of waves in the surface of standing water; and let *de*, *fg*, *hi*, *kl*, &c., be the tops of the several waves, divided from each other by as many intermediate valleys or hollows. Then, because the water in the ridges of the waves is higher than in the unmoved parts of the fluid KL, NO, it will run down from off the tops of those ridges, *e, g, i, l,* &c., *d, f, h, k,* &c., this way and that way towards KL and NO; and because the water is more depressed in the hollows of the waves than in the unmoved parts of the fluid KL, NO, it will run down into those hollows out of those unmoved parts. By the first deflux the ridges of the waves will dilate themselves this way and that way, and be propagated towards KL and NO. And because the motion of the waves from A towards PQ is carried on by a continual deflux from the ridges of the waves into the hollows next to them, and therefore cannot be swifter than in proportion to the celerity of the descent; and the descent of the water on each side towards KL and NO must be performed with the same velocity: it follows that the dilatation of the waves on each side towards KL and NO will be propagated with the same velocity as the waves themselves go forwards directly from A to PQ. And therefore the whole space this way and that way towards KL and NO will be filled by the dilated waves *rfgr, shis, tklt, vmnv,* &c. Q.E.D. That these things are so, anyone may find by making the experiment in still water.

CASE 2. Let us suppose that *de, fg, hi, kl, mn* represent pulses successively propagated from the point A through an elastic medium. Conceive the pulses to be propagated by successive condensations and rarefactions of the medium, so that the densest part of every pulse may occupy a spherical surface described about the centre A, and that equal intervals intervene between the successive pulses. Let the lines *de, fg, hi, kl,* &c., represent the densest parts of the pulses, propagated through the hole BC; and because the medium is denser there than in the spaces on either side towards KL and NO, it will dilate itself as well towards those spaces KL, NO, on each hand, as towards the rare intervals between the pulses; and hence the medium, becoming always more rare next the intervals, and more dense next the pulses, will partake of their motion. And because the progressive motion of the pulses arises from the continual relaxation of the denser parts towards the antecedent rare intervals; and since the pulses will relax themselves on each hand towards the quiescent parts of the medium KL, NO with very near the same celerity; therefore the pulses will dilate themselves on all sides into the unmoved parts KL, NO with almost the same celerity with which they are propagated directly from the centre A; and therefore will fill up the whole space KLON. Q.E.D. And we find the same by experience also in sounds which are heard through a mountain interposed; and, if they come into a chamber through the window, dilate themselves into all the parts of the room, and are heard in every corner; and not as reflected from the opposite walls, but directly propagated from the window, as far as our sense can judge.

CASE 3. Let us suppose, lastly, that a motion of any kind is propagated from A through the hole BC. Then since the cause of this propagation is that the parts of the medium that are near the centre A disturb and agitate those which lie farther from it; and since the parts which are urged are fluid, and therefore recede every way towards those spaces where they are less pressed: they will by consequence recede towards all the parts of the quiescent medium, as well to the parts on each hand, as KL and NO, as to those right before, as PQ; and by this means all the motion, as soon as it has passed through the hole BC, will begin to dilate itself, and from thence, as from its principle and centre, will be propagated directly every way. Q.E.D.

PROPOSITION 43. THEOREM 34

Every tremulous body in an elastic medium propagates the motion of the pulses on every side straight forwards; but in a nonelastic medium excites a circular motion.

CASE 1. The parts of the tremulous body, alternately going and returning, do in going urge and drive before them those parts of the medium that lie nearest, and by that impulse compress and condense them; and in returning suffer those compressed parts to recede again, and expand themselves. Therefore the parts of the medium that lie nearest to the tremulous body move to and fro by turns, in like manner as the parts of the tremulous body itself do; and for the same cause that the parts of this body agitate these parts of the medium, these parts, being agitated by like tremors, will in their turn agitate others next to themselves; and these others, agitated in like manner, will agitate those that lie beyond them, and so on *in infinitum.* And in the same manner as the first parts of the medium were condensed in going, and relaxed in returning, so will the other parts be condensed every time they go, and expand themselves every time they return. And therefore they will not be all going and all returning at the same instant (for in that case they would always maintain determined distances from each other, and there could be no alternate condensation and rarefaction); but since, in the places where they are condensed, they approach to, and, in the places where they are rarefied, recede from each other, therefore some of them will be going while others are returning; and so on *in infinitum.* The parts so going, and in their going condensed, are pulses, by reason of the progressive motion with which they strike obstacles in their way; and therefore the successive pulses produced by a tremulous body will be propagated in rectilinear directions; and that at nearly equal distances from each other, because of the equal intervals of time in which the body, by its several tremors, produces the several pulses. And though the parts of the tremulous body go and return in some certain and determinate direction, yet the pulses propagated from thence through the medium will dilate themselves towards the sides, by the foregoing Proposition; and will be propagated on all sides from that tremulous body, as from a common centre, in surfaces nearly spherical and concentric, as in waves excited by shaking a finger in water, which proceed not only forwards and backwards agreeably to the motion of the finger, but spread themselves in the manner of concentric circles all round the finger, and are propagated on every side. For the gravity of the water supplies the place of elastic force.

CASE 2. If the medium be not elastic, then, because its parts cannot be condensed by the pressure arising from the vibrating parts of the tremulous body, the motion will be propagated in an instant towards the parts where the medium yields most easily, that is, to the parts which the tremulous body would otherwise leave vacuous behind it. The case is the same with that of a body projected in any medium whatever. A medium yielding to projectiles does not recede *in infinitum,* but with a circular motion comes round to the spaces which the body leaves behind it. Therefore as often as a tremulous body tends to any part, the medium yielding to it comes round in a circle to the parts which the body leaves; and as often as the body returns to the first place, the medium will be driven from the place it came round to, and return to its original place. And though the tremulous body be not firm and hard, but every way flexible, yet if it continue of a given magnitude, since it cannot impel the medium by its tremors anywhere without yielding to it somewhere else, the medium receding from the parts of the body where it is pressed will always come round in a circle to the parts that yield to it.   q.e.d.

Cor. Hence it is a mistake to think that the agitation of the parts of flame conduces to the propagation of a pressure in rectilinear directions through an ambient medium. Such a pressure must be derived not from the agitation only of the parts of flame, but from the dilatation of the whole.

Proposition 44. Theorem 35

If water ascend and descend alternately in the erected legs KL, MN *of a canal or pipe; and a pendulum be constructed whose length between the point of suspension and the centre of oscillation is equal to half the length of the water in the canal: I say, that the water will ascend and descend in the same times in which the pendulum oscillates.*

I measure the length of the water along the axes of the canal and its legs, and make it equal to the sum of those axes; and take no notice of the resistance of the water arising from its attrition by the sides of the canal. Let, therefore, AB, CD represent the mean height of the water in both legs; and when the water in the leg KL ascends to the height EF, the water will descend in the

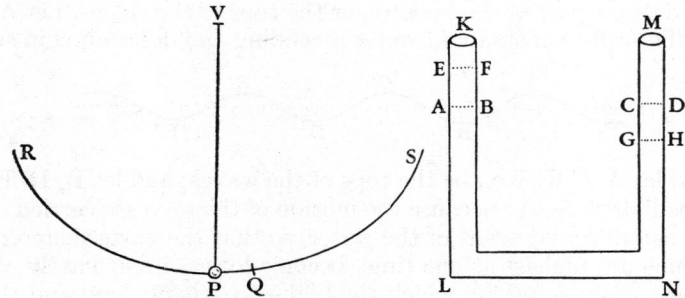

leg MN to the height GH. Let P be a pendulous body, VP the thread, V the point of suspension, RPQS the cycloid which the pendulum describes, P its lowest point, PQ an arc equal to the height AE. The force with which the motion of the water is accelerated and retarded alternately is the excess of the weight of the water in one leg above the weight in the other; and, therefore, when the water in the leg KL ascends to EF, and in the other leg descends to GH, that force is double the weight of the water EABF, and therefore is to the weight of the whole water as AE or PQ to VP or PR. The force also with which the body P is accelerated or retarded in any place, as Q, of a cycloid, is (by Cor., Prop. 51, Book I) to its whole weight as its distance PQ from the lowest place P to the length PR of the cycloid. Therefore the motive forces of the water and pendulum, describing the equal spaces AE, PQ, are as the weights to be moved; and therefore if the water and pendulum are quiescent at first, those forces will move them in equal times, and will cause them to go and return together with a reciprocal motion.   q.e.d.

Cor. i. Therefore the reciprocations of the water in ascending and descending are all performed in equal times, whether the motion be more or less intense or remiss.

COR. II. If the length of the whole water in the canal be of $6\frac{1}{9}$ feet of French measure, the water will descend in one second of time, and will ascend in another second, and so on by turns *in infinitum;* for a pendulum of $3\frac{1}{18}$ such feet in length will oscillate in one second of time.

COR. III. But if the length of the water be increased or diminished, the time of the reciprocation will be increased or diminished as the square root of the length.

PROPOSITION 45. THEOREM 36

The velocity of waves varies as the square root of the breadths.
This follows from the construction of the following Proposition.

PROPOSITION 46. PROBLEM 10

To find the velocity of waves.

Let a pendulum be constructed, whose length between the point of suspension and the centre of oscillation is equal to the breadth of the waves, and in the time that the pendulum will perform one single oscillation the waves will advance forwards nearly a space equal to their breadth.

That which I call the breadth of waves is the transverse measure lying between the deepest part of the hollows, or the tops of the ridges. Let ABCDEF represent the surface of stagnant water ascending and descending in successive

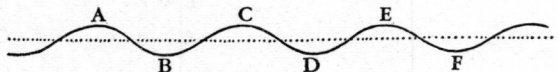

waves; and let A, C, E, &c., be the tops of the waves; and let B, D, F, &c., be the intermediate hollows. Because the motion of the waves is carried on by the successive ascent and descent of the water, so that the parts thereof, as A, C, E, &c., which are highest at one time, become lowest immediately after; and because the motive force, by which the highest parts descend and the lowest ascend, is the weight of the elevated water, that alternate ascent and descent will be analogous to the reciprocal motion of the water in the canal, and will observe the same laws as to the times of ascent and descent; and therefore (by Prop. 44) if the distances between the highest places of the waves A, C, E and the lowest B, D, F be equal to twice the length of any pendulum, the highest parts A, C, E will become the lowest in the time of one oscillation, and in the time of another oscillation will ascend again. Therefore with the passage of each wave, the time of two oscillations will occur; that is, the wave will describe its breadth in the time that pendulum will oscillate twice; but a pendulum of four times that length, and therefore equal to the breadth of the waves, will just oscillate once in that time.   Q.E.I.

COR. I. Therefore, waves whose breadth is equal to $3\frac{1}{18}$ French feet, will advance through a space equal to their breadth in one second of time; and therefore in one minute will go over a space of $183\frac{1}{3}$ feet; and in an hour, a space of 11,000 feet, nearly.

COR. II. And the velocity of greater or less waves will be augmented or diminished as the square root of their breadth.

These things are true upon the supposition that the parts of water ascend or descend in a straight line; but, in truth, that ascent and descent is rather performed in a circle; and therefore I give the time defined by this Proposition as only approximate.

PROPOSITION 47. THEOREM 37

If pulses are propagated through a fluid, the several particles of the fluid, going and returning with the shortest reciprocal motion, are always accelerated or retarded according to the law of the oscillating pendulum.

Let AB, BC, CD, &c., represent equal distances of successive pulses; ABC the line of direction of the motion of the successive pulses propagated from A to B; E, F, G three physical points of the quiescent medium situate in the right line AC at equal distances from each other; E*e*, F*f*, G*g* equal spaces of extreme shortness, through which those points go and return with a reciprocal motion in each vibration; ε, φ, γ any intermediate places of the same points; EF, FG physical short lines, or linear parts of the medium lying between those points, and successively transferred into the places εφ, φγ, and *ef*, *fg*. Let there be drawn the right line PS equal to the right line E*e*. Bisect the same in O, and from the centre O, with the radius OP, describe the circle SIP*i*. Let the whole time of one vibration, with its proportional parts, be represented by the whole circumference of this circle and its parts, in such sort, that, when any time PH or PHS*h* is completed, if there be let fall to PS the perpendicular HL or *hl*, and there be taken Eε equal to PL or P*l*, the physical point E may be found in ε. A point, as E, moving according to this law with a reciprocal motion, in its going from E through ε to *e*, and returning again through ε to E, will perform its several vibrations with the same degrees of acceleration and retardation with those of an oscillating pendulum. We are now to prove that the several physical points of the medium will be agitated with such a kind of motion. Let us suppose, then, that a medium hath such a motion excited in it from any cause whatsoever, and consider what will follow from thence.

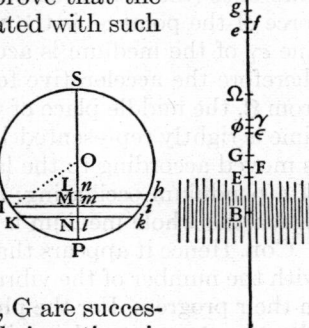

In the circumference PHS*h* let there be taken the equal arcs, HI, IK, or *hi*, *ik*, having the same ratio to the whole circumference as the equal right lines EF, FG have to BC, the whole interval of the pulses. Let fall the perpendiculars IM, KN, or *im*, *kn*; then because the points E, F, G are successively agitated with like motions, and perform their entire vibrations composed of their going and return, while the pulse is transferred from B to C; if PH or PHS*h* be the time elapsed since the beginning of the motion of the point E, then will PI or PHS*i* be the time elapsed since the beginning of the motion of the point F, and PK or PHS*k* the time elapsed since the beginning of the motion of the point G; and therefore Eε, Fφ, Gγ will be respectively equal to PL, PM, PN, while the points are going, and to P*l*, P*m*, P*n*, when the points are returning. Therefore $\epsilon\gamma$ or EG+Gγ−Eϵ will, when the points are going, be equal to EG−LN, and in their return equal to EG+*ln*. But $\epsilon\gamma$ is the breadth or expansion of the part EG of the medium in the place $\epsilon\gamma$; and therefore the expansion of that part in its going is to its mean expansion as EG−LN to EG; and in its return, as EG+*ln* or EG+LN is to EG. Therefore since LN is to KH as IM to the radius OP, and KH to EG as the circumference PHS*h*P to BC; that is, if we put V for the radius of a circle whose circumference is equal to BC, the interval of the pulses, as OP is to V; and, multiplying together corresponding terms of the proportions, we obtain LN to EG as IM to V; the expansion of the part EG, or of the physical point F in the place $\epsilon\gamma$, is to the mean expansion of the same part in its first place EG, as V−IM is to V in going, and as V+*im* is to V in its return. Hence the elastic force of the point F in the place $\epsilon\gamma$ is to its mean elastic force in the place EG as $\dfrac{1}{\text{V}-\text{IM}}$ is to $\dfrac{1}{\text{V}}$ in its going, and as $\dfrac{1}{\text{V}+im}$ is to $\dfrac{1}{\text{V}}$ in its return. And by the same reasoning the elastic forces of the physical points E and G in going are as $\dfrac{1}{\text{V}-\text{HL}}$ and $\dfrac{1}{\text{V}-\text{KN}}$ is to $\dfrac{1}{\text{V}}$; and the difference of the forces is to the mean elastic force of the medium as $\dfrac{\text{HL}-\text{KN}}{\text{VV}-\text{V}\cdot\text{HL}-\text{V}\cdot\text{KN}+\text{HL}\cdot\text{KN}}$ is to $\dfrac{1}{\text{V}}$; that is, as $\dfrac{\text{HL}-\text{KN}}{\text{VV}}$ is to $\dfrac{1}{\text{V}}$, or as HL−KN is to V; if we suppose (by reason of the very short extent of the vibrations) HL and KN to be indefinitely less than the quantity V. Therefore since the quantity V is given, the difference of the forces is as HL−KN; that is (because HL−KN is proportional to HK, and OM to OI or OP; and because HK and OP are given), as OM; that is, if F*f* be bisected in Ω, as $\Omega\phi$. And for the same reason the difference of the elastic forces of the physical points ϵ and γ, in the return of the physical short line $\epsilon\gamma$, is as $\Omega\phi$. But that difference (that is, the excess of the elastic force of the point ϵ above the elastic force of the point γ) is the very force by which the intervening physical short line $\epsilon\gamma$ of the medium is accelerated in going, and retarded in returning; and therefore the accelerative force of the physical short line $\epsilon\gamma$ is as its distance from Ω, the middle place of the vibration. Therefore (by Prop. 38, Book i) the time is rightly represented by the arc PI; and the linear part of the medium $\epsilon\gamma$ is moved according to the law above mentioned, that is, according to the law of a pendulum oscillating; and the case is the same of all the linear parts of which the whole medium is compounded.   q.e.d.

Cor. Hence it appears that the number of the pulses propagated is the same with the number of the vibrations of the tremulous body, and is not multiplied in their progress. For the physical short line $\epsilon\gamma$ as soon as it returns to its first place is at rest; neither will it move again, unless it receives a new motion either from the impulse of the tremulous body, or of the pulses propagated from that body. As soon, therefore, as the pulses cease to be propagated from the tremulous body, it will return to a state of rest, and move no more.

PROPOSITION 48. THEOREM 38

The velocities of pulses propagated in an elastic fluid are in a ratio compounded of the square root of the ratio of the elastic force directly, and the square root of the ratio of the density inversely; supposing the elastic force of the fluid to be proportional to its condensation.

CASE 1. If the mediums be homogeneous, and the distances of the pulses in those mediums be equal amongst themselves, but the motion in one medium is more intense than in the other, the contractions and dilatations of the corresponding parts will be as those motions; not that this proportion is perfectly accurate. However, if the contractions and dilatations are not exceedingly intense, the error will not be sensible; and therefore this proportion may be considered as physically exact. Now the motive elastic forces are as the contractions and dilatations; and the velocities generated in the same time in equal parts are as the forces. Therefore equal and corresponding parts of corresponding pulses will go and return together, through spaces proportional to their contractions and dilatations, with velocities that are as those spaces; and therefore the pulses, which in the time of one going and returning advance forwards a space equal to their breadth, and are always succeeding into the places of the pulses that immediately go before them, will, by reason of the equality of the distances, go forwards in both mediums with equal velocity.

CASE 2. If the distances of the pulses or their lengths are greater in one medium than in another, let us suppose that the correspondent parts describe spaces, in going and returning, each time proportional to the breadths of the pulses; then will their contractions and dilatations be equal; and therefore if the mediums are homogeneous, the motive elastic forces, which agitate them with a reciprocal motion, will be equal also. Now the matter to be moved by these forces is as the breadth of the pulses; and the space through which they move every time they go and return is in the same ratio. And, moreover, the time of one going and returning is in a ratio compounded of the square root of the matter and the square root of the space; and therefore is as the space. But the pulses advance a space equal to their breadths in the times of going once and returning once; that is, they go over spaces proportional to the times, and therefore are equally swift.

CASE 3. And therefore in mediums of equal density and elastic force, all the pulses are equally swift. Now if the density or the elastic force of the medium were augmented, then, because the motive force is increased in the ratio of the elastic force, and the matter to be moved is increased in the ratio of the density, the time which is necessary for producing the same motion as before will be increased as the square root of the ratio of the density, and will be diminished as the square root of the ratio of the elastic force. And therefore the velocity of the pulses will be in a ratio compounded of the square root of the inverse ratio of the density of the medium, and the square root of the direct ratio of the elastic force.   Q.E.D.

This Proposition will be made clearer from the construction of the following Problem.

Proposition 49. Problem 11

The density and elastic force of a medium being given, to find the velocity of the pulses.

Suppose the medium to be pressed by an incumbent weight after the manner of our air; and let A be the height of an homogeneous medium, whose weight is equal to the incumbent weight, and whose density is the same with the density of the compressed medium in which the pulses are propagated. Suppose a pendulum to be constructed whose length between the point of suspension and the centre of oscillation is A: and in the time in which that pendulum will perform one entire oscillation composed of its going and returning, the pulse will be propagated right onwards through a space equal to the circumference of a circle described with the radius A.

For, letting those things stand which were constructed in Prop. 47, if any physical line, as EF, describing the space PS in each vibration, be acted on in the extremities P and S of every going and return that it makes by an elastic force that is equal to its weight, it will perform its several vibrations in the time in which the same might oscillate in a cycloid whose whole perimeter is equal to the length PS; and that because equal forces will impel equal corpuscles through equal spaces in the same or equal times. Therefore since the times of the oscillations are as the square root of the lengths of the pendulums, and the length of the pendulum is equal to half the arc of the whole cycloid, the time of one vibration would be to the time of the oscillation of a pendulum whose length is A as the square root of the length ½PS or PO to the length A. But the elastic force with which the physical short line EG is urged, when it is found in its extreme places P, S, was (in the demonstration of Prop. 47) to its whole elastic force as HL − KN is to V, that is (since the point K now falls upon P), as HK to V; and all that force, or, which is the same thing, the incumbent weight by which the short line EG is compressed, is to the weight of the short line as the altitude of the incumbent weight is to EG the length of the short line; and therefore, taking the product of corresponding terms, the force with which the short line EG is urged in the places P and S is to the weight of that short line as HK·A is to V·EG; or as PO·A is to VV; because HK was to EG as PO to V. Therefore, since the times in which equal bodies are impelled through equal spaces are inversely as the square root of the forces, the time of one vibration, produced by the action of that elastic force, will be to the time of a vibration, produced by the impulse of the weight, as the square root of the ratio of VV to PO·A, and therefore to the time of the oscillation of a pendulum whose length is A as the square root of the ratio of VV to PO·A, and as the square root of the ratio of PO to A conjointly; that is, in the entire ratio of V to A. But in the time of one vibration composed of the going

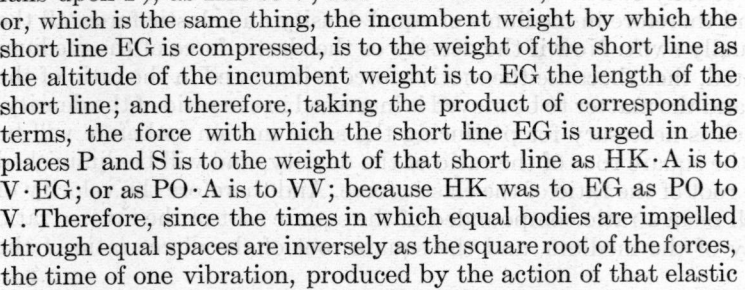

and returning of the pendulum, the pulse will be propagated right onwards through a space equal to its breadth BC. Therefore the time in which a pulse runs over the space BC is to the time of one oscillation composed of the going and returning of the pendulum as V is to A, that is, as BC is to the circumference of a circle whose radius is A. But the time in which the pulse will run over the space BC is to the time in which it will run over a length equal to that circumference in the same ratio; and therefore in the time of such an oscillation the pulse will run over a length equal to that circumference.   Q.E.D.

COR. I. The velocity of the pulses is equal to that which heavy bodies acquire by falling with an equally accelerated motion, and in their fall describing half the altitude A. For the pulse will, in the time of this fall, supposing it to move with the velocity acquired by that fall, run over a space that will be equal to the whole altitude A; and therefore in the time of one oscillation composed of one going and return, will go over a space equal to the circumference of a circle described with the radius A; for the time of the fall is to the time of oscillation as the radius of a circle to its circumference.

COR. II. Therefore since that altitude A is directly as the elastic force of the fluid, and inversely as the density of the same, the velocity of the pulses will be in a ratio compounded of the square root of the ratio of the density inversely, and the square root of the ratio of the elastic force directly.

PROPOSITION 50. PROBLEM 12

To find the distances of the pulses.

Let the number of the vibrations of the body, by whose tremor the pulses are produced, be found to any given time. By that number divide the space which a pulse can go over in the same time, and the part found will be the breadth of one pulse.   Q.E.I.

SCHOLIUM

The last Propositions respect the motions of light and sounds; for since light is propagated in right lines, it is certain that it cannot consist in action alone (by Props. 41 and 42). As to sounds, since they arise from tremulous bodies, they can be nothing else but pulses of the air propagated through it (by Prop. 43); and this is confirmed by the tremors which sounds, if they be loud and deep, excite in the bodies near them, as we experience in the sound of drums; for quick and short tremors are less easily excited. But it is well known that any sounds, falling upon strings in unison with the sonorous bodies, excite tremors in those strings. This is also confirmed from the velocity of sounds; for since the specific gravities of rain water and quicksilver are to one another as about 1 to 13⅔, and when the mercury in the barometer is at the height of 30 inches of our measure, the specific gravities of the air and of rain water are to one another as about 1 to 870, therefore the specific gravities of air and quicksilver are to each other as 1 to 11,890. Therefore when the height of the quicksilver is at 30 inches, a height of uniform air, whose weight would be sufficient to compress our air to the density we find it to be of, must be equal to 356,700 inches, or 29,725 feet of our measure; and this is that very height of the medium, which I have called A in the construction of the foregoing Proposition. A circle whose radius is 29,725 feet is 186,768 feet in circumference. And since a pendulum 39⅕ inches in length completes one oscillation, composed of its going and return, in two seconds of time, as is commonly known, it follows that a pendulum 29,725 feet, or 356,700 inches in length will perform a like oscillation in 190¾ seconds. Therefore in that time a sound will go right onwards 186,768 feet, and therefore in one second, 979 feet.

But in this computation we have made no allowance for the crassitude of the solid particles of the air, by which the sound is propagated instantaneously. Because the weight of air is to the weight of water as 1 to 870, and because salts are almost twice as dense as water; if the particles of air are supposed to be of about the same density as those of water or salt, and the rarity of the air arises from the intervals of the particles, the diameter of one particle of air will be to the interval between the centres of the particles as 1 to about 9 or 10, and to the interval between the particles themselves as 1 to 8 or 9. Therefore to 979 feet, which, according to the above calculation, a sound will advance forwards in one second of time, we may add $\frac{979}{9}$, or about 109 feet, to compensate for the crassitude of the particles of the air: and then a sound will go forwards about 1088 feet in one second of time.

Moreover, the vapors floating in the air being of another spring, and a different tone, will hardly, if at all, partake of the motion of the true air in which the sounds are propagated. Now if these vapors remain unmoved, that motion will be propagated the swifter through the true air alone, and that as the square root of the defect of the matter. So if the atmosphere consist of ten parts of true air and one part of vapors, the motion of sounds will be swifter as the square root of the ratio of 11 to 10, or very nearly in the entire ratio of 21 to 20 than if it were propagated through eleven parts of true air: and therefore the motion of sounds above discovered must be increased in that ratio. By this means the sound will pass through 1142 feet in one second of time.

These things will be found true in spring and autumn, when the air is rarefied by the gentle warmth of those seasons, and by that means its elastic force becomes somewhat more intense. But in winter, when the air is condensed by the cold, and its elastic force is somewhat remitted, the motion of sounds will be slower as the square root of the density; and, on the other hand, swifter in the summer.

Now by experiments it actually appears that sounds do really advance in one second of time about 1142 feet of English measure, or 1070 feet of French measure.

The velocity of sounds being known, the intervals of the pulses are known also. For M. Sauveur, by some experiments that he made, found that an open pipe about five Paris feet in length gives a sound of the same tone with a viol string that vibrates a hundred times in one second. Therefore there are near 100 pulses in a space of 1070 Paris feet, which a sound runs over in a second of time; and therefore one pulse fills up a space of about 10⁷⁄₁₀ Paris feet, that is, about twice the length of the pipe. From this it is probable that the breadths of the pulses, in all sounds made in open pipes, are equal to twice the length of the pipes.

Moreover, from the Corollary of Prop. 47 appears the reason why the sounds immediately cease with the motion of the sonorous body, and why they are heard no longer when we are at a great distance from the sonorous bodies than when we are very near them. And besides, from the foregoing principles, it plainly appears how it comes to pass that sounds are so mightily increased in speaking-trumpets; for all reciprocal motion tends to be increased by the generating cause at each return. And in tubes hindering the dilatation of the sounds, the motion decays more slowly, and recurs more forcibly; and therefore is the more increased by the new motion impressed at each return. And these are the principal phenomena of sounds.

SECTION IX

THE CIRCULAR MOTION OF FLUIDS

HYPOTHESIS

The resistance arising from the want of lubricity in the parts of a fluid, is, other things being equal, proportional to the velocity with which the parts of the fluid are separated from one another.

PROPOSITION 51. THEOREM 39

If a solid cylinder infinitely long, in an uniform and infinite fluid, revolves with an uniform motion about an axis given in position, and the fluid be forced round by only this impulse of the cylinder, and every part of the fluid continues uniformly in its motion: I say, that the periodic times of the parts of the fluid are as their distances from the axis of the cylinder.

Let AFL be a cylinder turning uniformly about the axis S, and let the concentric circles BGM, CHN, DIO, EKP, &c., divide the fluid into innumerable concentric cylindric solid orbs of the same thickness. Then, because the fluid is homogeneous, the impressions which the contiguous orbs make upon each

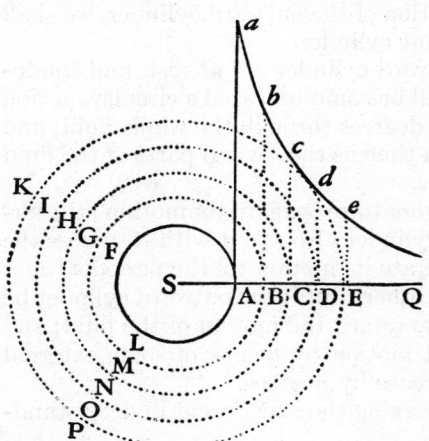

other will be (by the Hypothesis) as their translations from each other, and as the contiguous surfaces upon which the impressions are made. If the impression made upon any orb be greater or less on its concave than on its convex side, the stronger impression will prevail, and will either accelerate or retard the motion of the orb, according as it agrees with, or is contrary to, the motion of the same. Therefore, that every orb may continue uniformly in its motion, the impressions made on both sides must be equal and their directions contrary. Therefore since the impressions are as the contiguous surfaces, and as their translations from one another, the translations will be inversely as the surfaces, that is, inversely as the distances of the surfaces from the axis. But the differences of the angular motions about the axis are as those translations applied to the distances, or directly as the translations and inversely as the distances; that is, joining these ratios together, inversely as the squares of the distances. Therefore if there be erected the lines Aa, Bb, Cc, Dd, Ee, &c., perpendicular to the several parts of the infinite right line SABCDEQ, and inversely proportional to the squares of SA, SB, SC, SD, SE, &c., and through the extremities of those perpendiculars there be supposed to pass an hyperbolic curve, the sums of the differences, that is, the whole angular motions, will be as the correspondent sums of the lines A*a*, B*b*, C*c*, D*d*, E*e*, that is (if to constitute a medium uniformly fluid the number of the orbs be increased and their breadth diminished *in infinitum*), as the hyperbolic areas A*a*Q, B*b*Q, C*c*Q, D*d*Q, E*e*Q, &c., analogous to the sums; and the times, inversely proportional to the angular motions, will be also inversely proportional to those areas. Therefore the periodic time of any particle, as D, is inversely as the area D*d*Q, that is (as appears from the known methods of quadratures of curves), directly as the distance SD.   Q.E.D.

Cor. i. Hence the angular motions of the particles of the fluid are inversely as their distances from the axis of the cylinder, and the absolute velocities are equal.

Cor. ii. If a fluid be contained in a cylindric vessel of an infinite length, and contain another cylinder within, and both the cylinders revolve about one common axis, and the times of their revolutions be as their semidiameters, and every part of the fluid continues in its motion, the periodic times of the several parts will be as the distances from the axis of the cylinders.

Cor. iii. If there be added or taken away any common quantity of angular motion from the cylinder and fluid moving in this manner, yet because this new motion will not alter the mutual attrition of the parts of the fluid, the motion of the parts among themselves will not be changed; for the translations of the parts from one another depend upon the attrition. Any part will continue in that motion, which, by the attrition made on both sides with contrary directions, is no more accelerated than it is retarded.

Cor. vi. Therefore if there be taken away from this whole system of the cylinders and the fluid all the angular motion of the outward cylinder, we shall have the motion of the fluid in a quiescent cylinder.

Cor. v. Therefore if the fluid and outward cylinder are at rest, and the inward cylinder revolve uniformly, there will be communicated a circular motion to the fluid, which will be propagated by degrees through the whole fluid; and will go on continually increasing, till such time as the several parts of the fluid acquire the motion determined in Cor. iv.

Cor. vi. And because the fluid endeavors to propagate its motion still farther, its impulse will carry the outmost cylinder also about with it, unless the cylinder be forcibly held back; and accelerate its motion till the periodic times of both cylinders become equal with each other. But if the outward cylinder be forcibly held fast, it will make an effort to retard the motion of the fluid; and unless the inward cylinder preserve that motion by means of some external force impressed thereon, it will make it cease by degrees.

All these things will be found true by making the experiment in deep standing water.

Proposition 52. Theorem 40

If a solid sphere, in an uniform and infinite fluid, revolves about an axis given in position with an uniform motion, and the fluid be forced round by only this impulse of the sphere; and every part of the fluid continues uniformly in its motion: I say, that the periodic times of the parts of the fluid are as the squares of their distances from the centre of the sphere.

Case 1. Let AFL be a sphere turning uniformly about the axis S, and let the concentric circles BGM, CHN, DIO, EKP, &c., divide the fluid into innumerable concentric orbs of the same thickness. Suppose those orbs to be solid; and, because the fluid is homogeneous, the impressions which the contiguous orbs make one upon another will be (by the supposition) as their translations from one another, and the contiguous surfaces upon which the impressions are made. If the impression upon any orb be greater or less upon its concave than upon its convex side, the more forcible impression will prevail, and will either accelerate or retard the velocity of the orb, according as it is directed with a conspiring or contrary motion to that of the orb. Therefore that every orb may continue uniformly in its motion, it is necessary that the impressions made upon both sides of the orb should be equal, and have contrary directions. Therefore since the impressions are as the contiguous surfaces, and as their translations from one another, the translations will be inversely as the surfaces, that is, inversely as the squares of the distances of the surfaces from the centre. But the differences of the angular motions about the axis are as those translations applied to the distances, or directly as the translations and inversely as the distances; that is, by compounding those ratios, inversely as the cubes of the distances. Therefore, if upon the several parts of the infinite right line SABCDEQ there be erected the perpendiculars Aa, Bb, Cc, Dd, Ee, &c., inversely proportional to the cubes of SA, SB, SC, SD, SE, &c., the sums of the differences, that is, the whole angular motions, will be as the corresponding sums of the lines Aa, Bb, Cc, Dd, Ee, &c., that is (if to constitute an uniformly fluid medium the number of the orbs be increased and their thickness diminished *in infinitum*), as the hyperbolic areas AaQ, BbQ, CcQ, DdQ, EeQ, &c., analogous to the sums; and the periodic times being inversely proportional to the angular motions, will be also inversely proportional to those areas. Therefore the periodic time of any orb DIO is inversely as the area DdQ, that is (by the known methods of quadratures), directly as the square of the distance SD. Which was first to be demonstrated.

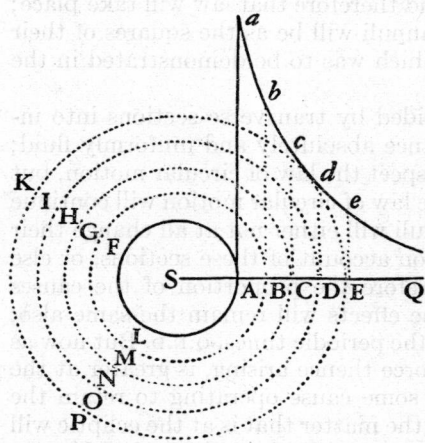

CASE 2. From the centre of the sphere let there be drawn a great number of indefinite right lines, making given angles with the axis, exceeding one another by equal differences; and, by these lines revolving about the axis, conceive the orbs to be cut into innumerable annuli; then will every annulus have four annuli contiguous to it, that is, one on its inside, one on its outside, and two on each hand. Now each of these annuli cannot be impelled equally and with contrary directions by the attrition of the interior and exterior annuli, unless the motion be communicated according to the law which we demonstrated in Case 1. This appears from that demonstration. And therefore any series of annuli, taken in any right line extending itself *in infinitum* from the globe, will move according to the law of Case 1, except we should imagine it hindered by the attrition of the annuli on each side of it. But now in a motion, according to

this law, no such is, and therefore cannot be, any obstacle to the motions continuing according to that law. If annuli at equal distances from the centre revolve either more swiftly or more slowly near the poles than near the ecliptic they will be accelerated if slow, and retarded if swift, by their mutual attrition; and so the periodic times will continually approach to equality, according to the law of Case 1. Therefore this attrition will not at all hinder the motion from going on according to the law of Case 1, and therefore that law will take place; that is, the periodic times of the several annuli will be as the squares of their distances from the centre of the globe. Which was to be demonstrated in the second place.

CASE 3. Let now every annulus be divided by transverse sections into innumerable particles constituting a substance absolutely and uniformly fluid; and because these sections do not at all respect the law of circular motion, but only serve to produce a fluid substance, the law of circular motion will continue the same as before. All the very small annuli will either not at all change their asperity and force of mutual attrition upon account of these sections, or else they will change the same equally. Therefore the proportion of the causes remaining the same, the proportion of the effects will remain the same also; that is, the proportion of the motions and the periodic times. Q.E.D. But now as the circular motion, and the centrifugal force thence arising, is greater at the ecliptic than at the poles, there must be some cause operating to retain the several particles in their circles; otherwise the matter that is at the ecliptic will always recede from the centre, and come round about to the poles by the outside of the vortex, and from thence return by the axis to the ecliptic with a continual circulation.

COR. I. Hence the angular motions of the parts of the fluid about the axis of the globe are inversely as the squares of the distances from the centre of the globe, and the absolute velocities are inversely as the same squares applied to the distances from the axis.

COR. II. If a globe revolve with an uniform motion about an axis of a given position in a similar and infinite quiescent fluid with an uniform motion, it will communicate a whirling motion to the fluid like that of a vortex, and that motion will by degrees be propagated onwards *in infinitum;* and this motion will be increased continually in every part of the fluid, till the periodical times of the several parts become as the squares of the distances from the centre of the globe.

COR. III. Because the inward parts of the vortex are by reason of their greater velocity continually pressing upon and driving forwards the external parts, and by that action are continually communicating motion to them, and at the same time those exterior parts communicate the same quantity of motion to those that lie still beyond them, and by this action preserve the quantity of their motion continually unchanged, it is plain that the motion is continually transferred from the centre to the circumference of the vortex, till it is quite swallowed up and lost in the boundless extent of that circumference. The matter between any two spherical surfaces concentric to the vortex will never be accelerated; because that matter will be always transferring the motion it receives from the matter nearer the centre to that matter which lies nearer the circumference.

COR. IV. Therefore, in order to continue a vortex in the same state of motion, some active principle is required from which the globe may receive continually the same quantity of motion which it is always communicating to the matter of the vortex. Without such a principle it will undoubtedly come to pass that the globe and the inward parts of the vortex, being always propagating their motion to the outward parts, and not receiving any new motion, will gradually move slower and slower, and at last be carried round no longer.

COR. V. If another globe should be swimming in the same vortex at a certain distance from its centre, and in the meantime by some force revolve constantly about an axis of a given inclination, the motion of this globe will drive the fluid round after the manner of a vortex; and at first this new and small vortex will revolve with its globe about the centre of the other; and in the meantime its motion will creep on farther and farther, and by degrees be propagated *in infinitum*, after the manner of the first vortex. And for the same reason that the globe of the new vortex was carried about before by the motion of the other vortex, the globe of this other will be carried about by the motion of this new vortex, so that the two globes will revolve about some intermediate point, and by reason of that circular motion mutually fly from each other, unless some force restrains them. Afterwards, if the constantly impressed forces, by which the globes continue in their motions, should cease, and everything be left to act according to the laws of mechanics, the motion of the globes will languish by degrees (for the reason assigned in Cor. III and IV), and the vortices at last will quite stand still.

COR. VI. If several globes in given places should constantly revolve with determined velocities about axes given in position, there would arise from them as many vortices going on *in infinitum*. For upon the same account that any one globe propagates its motion *in infinitum*, each globe apart will propagate its motion *in infinitum* also; so that every part of the infinite fluid will be agitated with a motion resulting from the actions of all the globes. Therefore the vortices will not be confined by any certain limits, but by degrees run into each other; and by the actions of the vortices on each other, the globes will be continually moved from their places, as was shown in the last Corollary; neither can they possibly keep any certain position among themselves, unless some force restrains them. But if those forces, which are constantly impressed upon the globes to continue these motions, should cease, the matter (for the reason assigned in Cor. III and IV) will gradually stop, and cease to move in vortices.

COR. VII. If a similar fluid be inclosed in a spherical vessel, and, by the uniform rotation of a globe in its centre, be driven round in a vortex; and the globe and vessel revolve the same way about the same axis, and their periodic times be as the squares of the semidiameters: the parts of the fluid will not go on in their motions without acceleration or retardation, till their periodical times are as the squares of their distances from the centre of the vortex. No constitution of a vortex can be permanent but this.

COR. VIII. If the vessel, the inclosed fluid, and the globe, retain this motion, and revolve besides with a common angular motion about any given axis, because the mutual attrition of the parts of the fluid is not changed by this motion, the motions of the parts among themselves will not be changed; for the translations of the parts among themselves depend upon this attrition. Any part will continue in that motion in which its attrition on one side retards it just as much as its attrition on the other side accelerates it.

Cor. ix. Therefore if the vessel be quiescent, and the motion of the globe be given, the motion of the fluid will be given. For conceive a plane to pass through the axis of the globe, and to revolve with a contrary motion; and suppose the sum of the time of this revolution and of the revolution of the globe to be to the time of the revolution of the globe as the square of the semidiameter of the vessel to the square of the semidiameter of the globe; and the periodic times of the parts of the fluid in respect of this plane will be as the squares of their distances from the centre of the globe.

Cor. x. Therefore if the vessel move about the same axis with the globe, or with a given velocity about a different one, the motion of the fluid will be given. For if from the whole system we take away the angular motion of the vessel, all the motions will remain the same among themselves as before, by Cor. viii, and those motions will be given by Cor. ix.

Cor. xi. If the vessel and the fluid are quiescent, and the globe revolves with an uniform motion, that motion will be propagated by degrees through the whole fluid to the vessel, and the vessel will be carried round by it, unless forcibly held back; and the fluid and the vessel will be continually accelerated till their periodic times become equal to the periodic times of the globe. If the vessel be either restrained by some force, or revolve with any constant and uniform motion, the medium will come little by little to the state of motion defined in Cor. viii, ix, x, nor will it ever continue in any other state. But if then the forces, by which the globe and vessel revolve with certain motions, should cease, and the whole system be left to act according to the mechanical laws, the vessel and globe, by means of the intervening fluid, will act upon each other, and will continue to propagate their motions through the fluid to each other, till their periodic times become equal among themselves, and the whole system revolves together like one solid body.

SCHOLIUM

In all these reasonings I suppose the fluid to consist of matter of uniform density and fluidity; I mean, that the fluid is such, that a globe placed anywhere therein may propagate with the same motion of its own, at distances from itself continually equal, similar and equal motions in the fluid in the same interval of time. The matter by its circular motion endeavors to recede from the axis of the vortex, and therefore presses all the matter that lies beyond. This pressure makes the attrition greater, and the separation of the parts more difficult; and by consequence diminishes the fluidity of the matter. Again; if the parts of the fluid are in any one place denser or larger than in the others, the fluidity will be less in that place, because there are fewer surfaces where the parts can be separated from each other. In these cases I suppose the defect of the fluidity to be supplied by the smoothness or softness of the parts, or some other condition; otherwise the matter where it is less fluid will cohere more, and be more sluggish, and therefore will receive the motion more slowly, and propagate it farther than agrees with the ratio above assigned. If the vessel be not spherical, the particles will move in lines not circular, but answering to the figure of the vessel; and the periodic times will be nearly as the squares of the mean distances from the centre. In the parts between the centre and the circumference the motions will be slower where the spaces are wide, and swifter where narrow; nevertheless, the particles will not tend to the circumference at all the more because of their greater swiftness; for they then describe arcs of less curvature, and the tendency to recede from the centre is as much diminished by the lessening of this curvature as it is augmented by the increase of the velocity. As they go out of narrow into wide spaces, they recede a little farther from the centre, but in doing so are retarded; and when they come out of wide into narrow spaces, they are again accelerated; and so each particle is retarded and accelerated by turns forever. These things will come to pass in a rigid vessel; for the state of vortices in an infinite fluid is known by Cor. VI of this Proposition.

I have endeavored in this Proposition to investigate the properties of vortices, that I might find whether the celestial phenomena can be explained by them; for the phenomenon is this, that the periodic times of the planets revolving about Jupiter are as the $\frac{3}{2}$th power of their distances from Jupiter's centre; and the same rule obtains also among the planets that revolve about the sun. And these rules obtain also with the greatest accuracy, as far as has been yet discovered by astronomical observation. Therefore if those planets are carried round in vortices revolving about Jupiter and the sun, the vortices must revolve according to that law. But here we found the periodic times of the parts of the vortex to be as the square of the distances from the centre of motion; and this ratio cannot be diminished and reduced to the $\frac{3}{2}$th power, unless either the matter of the vortex be more fluid the farther it is from the centre, or the resistance arising from the want of lubricity in the parts of the fluid should, as the velocity with which the parts of the fluid are separated goes on increasing, be augmented with it in a greater ratio than that in which the velocity increases. But neither of these suppositions seems reasonable. The more gross and less fluid parts will tend to the circumference, unless they are heavy towards the centre. And though, for the sake of demonstration, I proposed, at the beginning of this Section, an Hypothesis that the resistance is proportional to the velocity, nevertheless, it is in truth probable that the resistance is in a less ratio than that of the velocity; which granted, the periodic times of the parts of the vortex will be in a greater ratio than the square of the distances from its centre. If, as some think, the vortices move more swiftly near the centre, then slower to a certain limit, then again swifter near the circumference, certainly neither the $\frac{3}{2}$th power, nor any other certain and determinate power, can obtain in them. Let philosophers then see how that phenomenon of the $\frac{3}{2}$th power can be accounted for by vortices.

PROPOSITION 53. THEOREM 41

Bodies carried about in a vortex, and returning in the same orbit, are of the same density with the vortex, and are moved according to the same law with the parts of the vortex, as to velocity and direction of motion.

For if any small part of the vortex, whose particles or physical points continue a given situation among themselves, be supposed to be congealed, this particle will move according to the same law as before, since no change is made either in its density, inertia, or figure. And again; if a congealed or solid part of the vortex be of the same density with the rest of the vortex, and be resolved into a fluid, this will move according to the same law as before, except so far as its particles, now become fluid, may be moved among themselves. Neglect, therefore, the motion of the particles among themselves as not at all concerning the progressive motion of the whole, and the motion of the whole will be the same as before. But this motion will be the same with the motion of other parts of the vortex at equal distances from the centre; because the solid, now resolved into a fluid, is become exactly like the other parts of the vortex. Therefore a solid, if it be of the same density with the matter of the vortex, will move with the same motion as the parts thereof, being relatively at rest in the matter that surrounds it. If it be more dense, it will endeavor more than before to recede from the centre; and therefore overcoming that force of the vortex, by which, being, as it were, kept in equilibrium, it was retained in its orbit, it will recede from the centre, and in its revolution describe a spiral, returning no longer into the same orbit. And, by the same argument, if it be more rare, it will approach to the centre. Therefore it can never continually go round in the same orbit, unless it be of the same density with the fluid. But we have shown in that case that it would revolve according to the same law with those parts of the fluid that are at the same or equal distances from the centre of the vortex.

Cor. i. Therefore a solid revolving in a vortex, and continually going round in the same orbit, is relatively quiescent in the fluid that carries it.

Cor. ii. And if the vortex be of an uniform density, the same body may revolve at any distance from the centre of the vortex.

SCHOLIUM

Hence it is manifest that the planets are not carried round in corporeal vortices; for, according to the Copernican hypothesis, the planets going round the sun revolve in ellipses, having the sun in their common focus; and by radii drawn to the sun describe areas proportional to the times. But the parts of a vortex can never revolve with such a motion. For, let AD, BE, CF represent three orbits described about the sun S, of which let the outmost circle CF be concentric to the sun; let the aphelions of the two innermost be A, B; and their perihelions D, E. Hence a body revolving in the orb CF, describing, by a radius drawn to the sun, areas proportional to the times, will move with an uniform motion. And, according to the laws of astronomy, the body revolving in the orbit BE will move slower in its aphelian B, and swifter in its perihelion E; whereas, according to the laws of mechanics, the matter of the vortex ought to move more swiftly in the narrow space between A and C than in the wide space between D and F; that is, more swiftly in the aphelion than in the perihelion. Now these two conclusions contradict each other. So at the beginning of the sign of Virgo, where the aphelion of Mars is at present, the distance between the orbits of Mars and Venus is to the distance between the same orbits, at the beginning of the sign

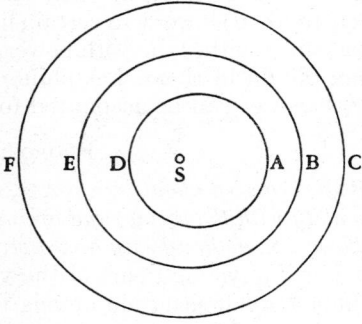

of Pisces, as about 3 to 2; and therefore the matter of the vortex between those orbits ought to be swifter at the beginning of Pisces than at the beginning of Virgo in the ratio of 3 to 2; for the narrower the space is through which the same quantity of matter passes in the same time of one revolution, the greater will be the velocity with which it passes through it. Therefore if the earth being relatively at rest in this celestial matter should be carried round by it, and revolve together with it about the sun, the velocity of the earth at the beginning of Pisces would be to its velocity at the beginning of Virgo in the ratio of 3 to 2. Therefore the sun's apparent diurnal motion at the beginning of Virgo ought to be above 70 minutes, and at the beginning of Pisces less than 48 minutes; whereas, on the contrary, that apparent motion of the sun is really greater at the beginning of Pisces than at the beginning of Virgo, as experience testifies; and therefore the earth is swifter at the beginning of Virgo than at the beginning of Pisces; so that the hypothesis of vortices is utterly irreconcilable with astronomical phenomena, and rather serves to perplex than explain the heavenly motions. How these motions are performed in free spaces without vortices, may be understood by the first book; and I shall now more fully treat of it in the following book.

BOOK THREE
SYSTEM OF THE WORLD
(IN MATHEMATICAL TREATMENT)

In the preceding books I have laid down the principles of philosophy; principles not philosophical but mathematical: such, namely, as we may build our reasonings upon in philosophical inquiries. These principles are the laws and conditions of certain motions, and powers or forces, which chiefly have respect to philosophy; but, lest they should have appeared of themselves dry and barren, I have illustrated them here and there with some philosophical scholiums, giving an account of such things as are of more general nature, and which philosophy seems chiefly to be founded on; such as the density and the resistance of bodies, spaces void of all bodies, and the motion of light and sounds. It remains that, from the same principles, I now demonstrate the frame of the System of the World. Upon this subject I had, indeed, composed the third book in a popular method, that it might be read by many; but afterwards, considering that such as had not sufficiently entered into the principles could not easily discern the strength of the consequences, nor lay aside the prejudices to which they had been many years accustomed, therefore, to prevent the disputes which might be raised upon such accounts, I chose to reduce the substance of this book into the form of Propositions (in the mathematical way), which should be read by those only who had first made themselves masters of the principles established in the preceding books: not that I would advise anyone to the previous study of every Proposition of those books; for they abound with such as might cost too much time, even to readers of good mathematical learning. It is enough if one carefully reads the Definitions, the Laws of Motion, and the first three sections of the first book. He may then pass on to this book, and consult such of the remaining Propositions of the first two books, as the references in this, and his occasions, shall require.

RULES OF REASONING IN PHILOSOPHY

RULE I

We are to admit no more causes of natural things than such as are both true and sufficient to explain their appearances.

To this purpose the philosophers say that Nature does nothing in vain, and more is in vain when less will serve; for Nature is pleased with simplicity, and affects not the pomp of superfluous causes.

RULE II

Therefore to the same natural effects we must, as far as possible, assign the same causes.

As to respiration in a man and in a beast; the descent of stones in Europe and in America; the light of our culinary fire and of the sun; the reflection of light in the earth, and in the planets.

RULE III

The qualities of bodies, which admit neither intensification nor remission of degrees, and which are found to belong to all bodies within the reach of our experiments, are to be esteemed the universal qualities of all bodies whatsoever.

For since the qualities of bodies are only known to us by experiments, we are to hold for universal all such as universally agree with experiments; and such as are not liable to diminution can never be quite taken away. We are certainly not to relinquish the evidence of experiments for the sake of dreams and vain fictions of our own devising; nor are we to recede from the analogy of Nature, which is wont to be simple, and always consonant to itself. We no other way know the extension of bodies than by our senses, nor do these reach it in all bodies; but because we perceive extension in all that are sensible, therefore we ascribe it universally to all others also. That abundance of bodies are hard, we learn by experience; and because the hardness of the whole arises from the hardness of the parts, we therefore justly infer the hardness of the undivided particles not only of the bodies we feel but of all others. That all bodies are impenetrable, we gather not from reason, but from sensation. The bodies which we handle we find impenetrable, and thence conclude impenetrability to be an universal property of all bodies whatsoever. That all bodies are movable, and endowed with certain powers (which we call the inertia) of persevering in their motion, or in their rest, we only infer from the like properties observed in the bodies which we have seen. The extension, hardness, impenetrability, mobility, and inertia of the whole, result from the extension, hardness, impenetrability, mobility, and inertia of the parts; and hence we conclude the least particles of all bodies to be also all extended, and hard and impenetrable, and movable, and endowed with their proper inertia. And this is the foundation of all philosophy. Moreover, that the divided but contiguous particles of bodies may be separated from one another, is matter of observation; and, in the particles that remain undivided, our minds are able to distinguish yet lesser parts, as is mathematically demonstrated. But whether the parts so distinguished, and not yet divided, may, by the powers of Nature, be actually divided and separated from one another, we cannot certainly determine. Yet, had we the proof of but one experiment that any undivided particle, in breaking a hard and solid body, suffered a division, we might by virtue of this rule conclude that the undivided as well as the divided particles may be divided and actually separated to infinity.

Lastly, if it universally appears, by experiments and astronomical observations, that all bodies about the earth gravitate towards the earth, and that in proportion to the quantity of matter which they severally contain; that the moon likewise, according to the quantity of its matter, gravitates towards the earth; that, on the other hand, our sea gravitates towards the moon; and all the planets one towards another; and the comets in like manner towards the sun; we must, in consequence of this rule, universally allow that all bodies whatsoever are endowed with a principle of mutual gravitation. For the argument from the appearances concludes with more force for the universal gravitation of all bodies than for their impenetrability; of which, among those in the celestial regions, we have no experiments, nor any manner of observation. Not that I affirm gravity to be essential to bodies: by their *vis insita* I mean nothing but their inertia. This is immutable. Their gravity is diminished as they recede from the earth.

RULE IV

In experimental philosophy we are to look upon propositions inferred by general induction from phenomena as accurately or very nearly true, notwithstanding any contrary hypotheses that may be imagined, till such time as other phenomena occur, by which they may either be made more accurate, or liable to exceptions.

This rule we must follow, that the argument of induction may not be evaded by hypotheses.

PHENOMENA[1]

PHENOMENON I

That the circumjovial planets, by radii drawn to Jupiter's centre, describe areas proportional to the times of description; and that their periodic times, the fixed stars being at rest, are as the $\frac{3}{2}$th power of their distances from its centre.

This we know from astronomical observations. For the orbits of these planets differ but insensibly from circles concentric to Jupiter; and their motions in those circles are found to be uniform. And all astronomers agree that their periodic times are as the $\frac{3}{2}$th power of the semidiameters of their orbits; and so it manifestly appears from the following table.

The periodic times of the satellites of Jupiter.

$1^d.\ 18^h.\ 27^m.\ 34^s.,\ 3^d.\ 13^h.\ 13^m.\ 42^s.,\ 7^d.\ 3^h.\ 42^m.\ 36^s.,\ 16^d.\ 16^h.\ 32^m.\ 9^s.$

The distances of the satellites from Jupiter's centre.

	1	2	3	4	
From the observations of:					
Borelli	$5\frac{2}{3}$	$8\frac{2}{3}$	14	$24\frac{2}{3}$	
Townly *by the micrometer*	5.52	8.78	13.47	24.72	*Semi-*
Cassini *by the telescope*	5	8	13	23	*diameter of*
Cassini *by the eclipse of the satellites*	$5\frac{2}{3}$	9	$14^{23}/_{60}$	$25^3/_{10}$	*Jupiter*
From the periodic times	5.667	9.017	14.384	25.299	

Mr. Pound hath determined, by the help of excellent micrometers, the diameters of Jupiter and the elongation of its satellites after the following manner. The greatest heliocentric elongation of the fourth satellite from Jupiter's centre was taken with a micrometer in a 15-foot telescope, and at the mean distance of Jupiter from the earth was found about 8′ 16″. The elongation of the third satellite was taken with a micrometer in a telescope of 123 feet, and at the same distance of Jupiter from the earth was found 4′ 42″. The greatest elongations of the other satellites, at the same distance of Jupiter from the earth, are found from the periodic times to be 2′ 56″ 47‴, and 1′ 51″ 6‴.

The diameter of Jupiter taken with the micrometer in a 123-foot telescope several times, and reduced to Jupiter's mean distance from the earth, proved always less than 40″, never less than 38″, generally 39″. This diameter in shorter telescopes is 40″, or 41″; for Jupiter's light is a little dilated by the unequal refrangibility of the rays, and this dilatation bears a less ratio to the diameter of Jupiter in the longer and more perfect telescopes than in those which are shorter and less perfect. The times in which two satellites, the first

[1][In the following parts of Book III, scattered words and phrases in italics (except in Latin expressions and in names of writings) are, in Motte's translation, interpolations of words and phrases not in the Latin text of the *Principles;* and a few are departures from a literal translation of the Latin].

and the third, passed over Jupiter's body, were observed, from the beginning of the ingress to the beginning of the egress, and from the complete ingress to the complete egress, with the long telescope. And from the transit of the first satellite, the diameter of Jupiter at its mean distance from the earth came forth $37\frac{1}{8}''$, and from the transit of the third $37\frac{3}{8}''$. There was observed also the time in which the shadow of the first satellite passed over Jupiter's body, and thence the diameter of Jupiter at its mean distance from the earth came out about $37''$. Let us suppose its diameter to be $37\frac{1}{4}''$, very nearly, and then the greatest elongations of the first, second, third, and fourth satellite will be respectively equal to 5.965, 9.494, 15.141, and 26.63 semidiameters of Jupiter.

PHENOMENON II

That the circumsaturnal planets, by radii drawn to Saturn's centre, describe areas proportional to the times of description; and that their periodic times, the fixed stars being at rest, are as the $\frac{3}{2}$th power of their distances from its centre.

For, as Cassini from his own observations hath determined, their distances from Saturn's centre and their periodic times are as follows:

The periodic times of the satellites of Saturn.

$1^d. 21^h. 18^m. 27^s.$, $2^d. 17^h. 41^m. 22^s.$, $4^d. 12^h. 25^m. 12^s.$, $15^d. 22^h. 41^m. 14^s.$, $79^d. 7^h. 48^m. 00^s.$

The distances of the satellites from Saturn's centre, in semidiameters of its ring.

From observations	$1\frac{19}{20}$	$2\frac{1}{2}$	$3\frac{1}{2}$	8	24
From the periodic times	1.93	2.47	3.45	8	23.35

The greatest elongation of the fourth satellite from Saturn's centre is commonly determined from the observations to be eight of those semidiameters, very nearly. But the greatest elongation of this satellite from Saturn's centre, when taken with an excellent micrometer in Mr. Huygens' telescope of 123 feet, appeared to be eight semidiameters and $\frac{7}{10}$ of a semidiameter. And from this observation and the periodic times the distances of the satellites from Saturn's centre in semidiameters of the ring are 2.1, 2.69, 3.75, 8.7, and 25.35. The diameter of Saturn observed in the same telescope was found to be to the diameter of the ring as 3 to 7; and the diameter of the ring, May 28-29, 1719, was found to be $43''$; and hence the diameter of the ring when Saturn is at its mean distance from the earth is $42''$, and the diameter of Saturn $18''$. These things appear so in very long and excellent telescopes, because in such telescopes the apparent magnitudes of the heavenly bodies bear a greater proportion to the dilatation of light in the extremities of those bodies than in shorter telescopes. If, then, we reject all the spurious light, the diameter of Saturn will not amount to more than $16''$.

PHENOMENON III

That the five primary planets, Mercury, Venus, Mars, Jupiter, and Saturn, with their several orbits, encompass the sun.

That Mercury and Venus revolve about the sun, is evident from their moonlike appearances. When they shine out with a full face, they are, in respect of us, beyond or above the sun; when they appear half full, they are about the same height on one side or other of the sun; when horned, they are below or between us and the sun; and they are sometimes, *when directly under*, seen like spots traversing the sun's disk. That Mars surrounds the sun, is as plain from its full face when near its conjunction with the sun, and from the gibbous figure which it shows in its quadratures. And the same thing is demonstrable of Jupiter and Saturn, from their appearing full in all situations; for the shadows of their satellites that appear sometimes upon their disks make it plain that the light they shine with is not their own, but borrowed from the sun.

PHENOMENON IV

That the fixed stars being at rest, the periodic times of the five primary planets, and (whether of the sun about the earth, or) of the earth about the sun, are as the ³⁄₂th power of their mean distances from the sun.

This proportion, first observed by Kepler, is now received by all astronomers; for the periodic times are the same, and the dimensions of the orbits are the same, whether the sun revolves about the earth, or the earth about the sun. And as to the measures of the periodic times, all astronomers are agreed about them. But for the dimensions of the orbits, Kepler and Boulliau, above all others, have determined them from observations with the greatest accuracy; and the mean distances corresponding to the periodic times differ but insensibly from those which they have assigned, and for the most part fall in between them; as we may see from the following table.

The periodic times, with respect to the fixed stars, of the planets and earth revolving about the sun, in days and decimal parts of a day.

♄	♃	♂	♁	♀	☿
10759.275	4332.514	686.9785	365.2565	224.6176	87.9692

The mean distances of the planets and of the earth from the sun.

	♄	♃	♂
According to Kepler	951,000	519,650	152,350
" " Boulliau	954,198	522,520	152,350
" " the periodic times	954,006	520,096	152,369

	♁	♀	☿
According to Kepler	100,000	72,400	38,806
" " Boulliau	100,000	72,398	38,585
" " the periodic times	100,000	72,333	38,710

As to Mercury and Venus, there can be no doubt about their distances from the sun; for they are determined by the elongations of those planets from the sun; and for the distances of the superior planets, all dispute is cut off by the eclipses of the satellites of Jupiter. For by those eclipses the position of the shadow which Jupiter projects is determined; from this we have the heliocentric longitude of Jupiter. And from its heliocentric and geocentric longitudes compared together, we determine its distance.

PHENOMENON V

Then the primary planets, by radii drawn to the earth, describe areas in no wise proportional to the times; but the areas which they describe by radii drawn to the sun are proportional to the times of description.

For to the earth they appear sometimes direct, sometimes stationary, nay, and sometimes retrograde. But from the sun they are always seen direct, and to proceed with a motion nearly uniform, that is to say, a little swifter in the perihelion and a little slower in the aphelion distances, so as to maintain an equality in the description of the areas. This is a noted proposition among astronomers, and particularly demonstrable in Jupiter, from the eclipses of his satellites; by the help of these eclipses, as we have said, the heliocentric longitudes of that planet, and its distances from the sun, are determined.

PHENOMENON VI

That the moon, by a radius drawn to the earth's centre, describes an area proportional to the time of description.

This we gather from the apparent motion of the moon, compared with its apparent diameter. It is true that the motion of the moon is a little disturbed by the action of the sun: but in laying down these Phenomena, I neglect those small and inconsiderable errors.

PROPOSITIONS

PROPOSITION 1. THEOREM 1

That the forces by which the circumjovial planets are continually drawn off from rectilinear motions, and retained in their proper orbits, tend to Jupiter's centre; and are inversely as the squares of the distances of the places of those planets from that centre.

The former part of this Proposition appears from Phen. I, and Prop. 2 or 3, Book I; the latter from Phen. I, and Cor. VI, Prop. 4, of the same book.

The same thing we are to understand of the planets which encompass Saturn, by Phen. II.

PROPOSITION 2. THEOREM 2

That the forces by which the primary planets are continually drawn off from rectilinear motions, and retained in their proper orbits, tend to the sun; and are inversely as the squares of the distances of the places of those planets from the sun's centre.

The former part of the Proposition is manifest from Phen. V, and Prop. 2, Book I; the latter from Phen. IV, and Cor. VI, Prop. 4, of the same book. But this part of the Proposition is, with great accuracy, demonstrable from the quiescence of the aphelion points; for a very small aberration from the proportion according to the inverse square of the distances would (by Cor. I, Prop. 45, Book I) produce a motion of the apsides sensible enough in every single revolution, and in many of them enormously great.

PROPOSITION 3. THEOREM 3

That the force by which the moon is retained in its orbit tends to the earth; and is inversely as the square of the distance of its place from the earth's centre.

The former part of the Proposition is evident from Phen. VI, and Prop. 2 or 3, Book I; the latter from the very slow motion of the moon's apogee; which in every single revolution amounting but to $3° 3'$ forwards, may be neglected. For (by Cor. I, Prop. 45, Book I) it appears that, if the distance of the moon from the earth's centre is to the semidiameter of the earth as D to 1, the force, from which such a motion will result, is inversely as $D^{2\frac{4}{243}}$, i.e., inversely as the power of D, whose exponent is $2^{4}/_{243}$; that is to say, in the proportion of the distance somewhat greater than the inverse square, but which comes $59\frac{3}{4}$ times nearer to the proportion according to the square than to the cube. But since this increase is due to the action of the sun (as we shall afterwards show), it is here to be neglected. The action of the sun, attracting the moon from the earth, is nearly as the moon's distance from the earth; and therefore (by what we have shown in Cor. II, Prop. 45, Book I) is to the centripetal force of the moon as 2 to 357.45, or nearly so; that is, as 1 to $178^{29}/_{40}$. And if we neglect so inconsiderable a force of the sun, the remaining force, by which the moon is retained in its orb, will be inversely as D^2. This will yet more fully appear from comparing this force with the force of gravity, as is done in the next Proposition.

COR. If we augment the mean centripetal force by which the moon is retained in its orb, first in the proportion of $177^{29}\!/_{40}$ to $178^{29}\!/_{40}$, and then in the proportion of the square of the semidiameter of the earth to the mean distance of the centres of the moon and earth, we shall have the centripetal force of the moon at the surface of the earth; supposing this force, in descending to the earth's surface, continually to increase inversely as the square of the height.

PROPOSITION 4. THEOREM 4

That the moon gravitates towards the earth, and by the force of gravity is continually drawn off from a rectilinear motion, and retained in its orbit.

The mean distance of the moon from the earth in the syzygies in semidiameters of the earth, is, according to Ptolemy and most astronomers, 59; according to Vendelin and Huygens, 60; to Copernicus, $60\frac{1}{3}$; to Street, $60\frac{2}{5}$; and to Tycho, $56\frac{1}{2}$. But Tycho, and all that follow his tables of refraction, making the refractions of the sun and moon (altogether against the nature of light) to exceed the refractions of the fixed stars, and that by four or five minutes *near the horizon*, did thereby increase the moon's *horizontal* parallax by a like number of minutes, that is, by a twelfth or fifteenth part of the whole parallax. Correct this error, and the distance will become about $60\frac{1}{2}$ semidiameters of the earth, near to what others have assigned. Let us assume the mean distance of 60 diameters in the syzygies; and suppose one revolution of the moon, in respect of the fixed stars, to be completed in $27^d \cdot 7^h \cdot 43^m$., as astronomers have determined; and the circumference of the earth to amount to 123,249,600 Paris feet, as the French have found by mensuration. And now if we imagine the moon, deprived of all motion, to be let go, so as to descend towards the earth with the impulse of all that force by which (by Cor. Prop. 3) it is retained in its orb, it will in the space of one minute of time, describe in its fall $15^1\!/_{12}$ Paris feet. This we gather by a calculus, founded either upon Prop. 36, Book I, or (which comes to the same thing) upon Cor. IX, Prop. 4, of the same book. For the versed sine of that arc, which the moon, in the space of one minute of time, would by its mean motion describe at the distance of 60 semidiameters of the earth, is nearly $15^1\!/_{12}$ Paris feet, or more accurately 15 feet, 1 inch, and 1 line $\frac{4}{9}$. Wherefore, since that force, in approaching to the earth, increases in the proportion of the inverse square of the distance, and, upon that account, at the surface of the earth, is $60 \cdot 60$ times greater than at the moon, a body in our regions, falling with that force, ought in the space of one minute of time, to describe $60 \cdot 60 \cdot 15^1\!/_{12}$ Paris feet; and, in the space of one second of time, to describe $15^1\!/_{12}$ of those feet; or more accurately 15 feet, 1 inch, and 1 line $\frac{4}{9}$. And with this very force we actually find that bodies here upon earth do really descend; for a pendulum oscillating seconds in the latitude of Paris will be 3 Paris feet, and 8 lines $\frac{1}{2}$ in length, as Mr. Huygens has observed. And the space which a heavy body describes by falling in one second of time is to half the length of this pendulum as the square of the ratio of the circumference of a circle to its diameter (as Mr. Huygens has also shown), and is therefore 15 Paris feet, 1 inch, 1 line $\frac{7}{9}$. And therefore the force by which the moon is retained in its orbit becomes, at the very surface of the earth, equal to the force of gravity which we observe in heavy bodies there. And therefore (by Rules 1 and 2) the force by which the moon is retained in its orbit is that very same force which we commonly call gravity; for, were gravity another force different from that, then bodies descending to the earth with the joint impulse of both forces would fall with a double velocity, and in the space of one second of time would describe $30\frac{1}{6}$ Paris feet; altogether against experience.

This calculus is founded on the hypothesis of the earth's standing still; for if both earth and moon move about the sun, and at the same time about their common centre of gravity, the distance of the centres of the moon and earth from one another will be $60\frac{1}{2}$ semidiameters of the earth; as may be found by a computation from Prop. 60, Book I.

SCHOLIUM

The demonstration of this Proposition may be more diffusely explained after the following manner. Suppose several moons to revolve about the earth, as in the system of Jupiter or Saturn; the periodic times of these moons (by the argument of induction) would observe the same law which Kepler found to obtain among the planets; and therefore their centripetal forces would be inversely as the squares of the distances from the centre of the earth, by Prop. 1, of this book. Now if the lowest of these were very small, and were so near the earth as almost to touch the tops of the highest mountains, the centripetal force thereof, retaining it in its orbit, would be nearly equal to the weights of any terrestrial bodies that should be found upon the tops of those mountains, as may be known by the foregoing computation. Therefore if the same little moon should be deserted by its centrifugal force that carries it through its orbit, and be disabled from going onward therein, it would descend to the earth; and that with the same velocity, with which heavy bodies actually fall upon the tops of those very mountains, because of the equality of the forces that oblige them both to descend. And if the force by which that lowest moon would descend were different from gravity, and if that moon were to gravitate towards the earth, as we find terrestrial bodies do upon the tops of mountains, it would then descend with twice the velocity, as being impelled by both these forces conspiring together. Therefore since both these forces, that is, the gravity of heavy bodies, and the centripetal forces of the moons, are directed to the centre of the earth, and are similar and equal between themselves, they will (by Rules 1 and 2) have one and the same cause. And therefore the force which retains the moon in its orbit is that very force which we commonly call gravity; because otherwise this little moon at the top of a mountain must either be without gravity, or fall twice as swiftly as heavy bodies are wont to do.

PROPOSITION 5. THEOREM 5

That the circumjovial planets gravitate towards Jupiter; the circumsaturnal towards Saturn; the circumsolar towards the sun; and by the forces of their gravity are drawn off from rectilinear motions, and retained in curvilinear orbits.

For the revolutions of the circumjovial planets about Jupiter, of the circumsaturnal about Saturn, and of Mercury and Venus, and the other circumsolar planets, about the sun, are appearances of the same sort with the revolution of the moon about the earth; and therefore, by Rule 2, must be owing to the same sort of causes; especially since it has been demonstrated, that the forces upon which those revolutions depend tend to the centres of Jupiter, of Saturn, and of the sun; and that those forces, in receding from Jupiter, from Saturn, and from the sun, decrease in the same proportion, and according to the same law, as the force of gravity does in receding from the earth.

Cor. i. There is, therefore, a power of gravity tending to all the planets; for, doubtless, Venus, Mercury, and the rest, are bodies of the same sort with Jupiter and Saturn. And since all attraction (by Law iii) is mutual, Jupiter will therefore gravitate towards all his own satellites, Saturn towards his, the earth towards the moon, and the sun towards all the primary planets.

Cor. ii. The force of gravity which tends to any one planet is inversely as the square of the distance of places from that planet's centre.

Cor. iii. All the planets do gravitate towards one another, by Cor. i and ii. And hence it is that Jupiter and Saturn, when near their conjunction, by their mutual attractions sensibly disturb each other's motions. So the sun disturbs the motions of the moon; and both sun and moon disturb our sea, as we shall hereafter explain.

Scholium

The force which retains the celestial bodies in their orbits has been hitherto called centripetal force; but it being now made plain that it can be no other than a gravitating force, we shall hereafter call it gravity. For the cause of that centripetal force which retains the moon in its orbit will extend itself to all the planets, by Rules 1, 2, and 4.

Proposition 6. Theorem 6

That all bodies gravitate towards every planet; and that the weights of bodies towards any one planet, at equal distances from the centre of the planet, are proportional to the quantities of matter which they severally contain.

It has been, now for a long time, observed by others, that all sorts of heavy bodies (allowance being made for the inequality of retardation which they suffer from a small power of resistance in the air) descend to the earth *from equal heights* in equal times; and that equality of times we may distinguish to a great accuracy, by the help of pendulums. I tried experiments with gold, silver, lead, glass, sand, common salt, wood, water, and wheat. I provided two wooden boxes, round and equal: I filled the one with wood, and suspended an equal weight of gold (as exactly as I could) in the centre of oscillation of the other. The boxes, hanging by equal threads of 11 feet, made a couple of pendulums perfectly equal in weight and figure, and equally receiving the resistance of the air. And, placing the one by the other, I observed them to play together forwards and backwards, for a long time, with equal vibrations. And therefore the quantity of matter in the gold (by Cor. i and vi, Prop. 24, Book ii) was to the quantity of matter in the wood as the action of the motive force (or *vis motrix*) upon all the gold to the action of the same upon all the wood; that is, as the weight of the one to the weight of the other: and the like happened in the other bodies. By these experiments, in bodies of the same weight, I could manifestly have discovered a difference of matter less than the thousandth part of the whole, had any such been. But, without all doubt, the nature of gravity towards the planets is the same as towards the earth. For, should we imagine our terrestrial bodies taken to the orbit of the moon, and there, together with the moon, deprived of all motion, to be let go, so as to fall together towards the earth, it is certain, from what we have demonstrated before, that, in equal times, they would describe equal spaces with the moon, and of consequence are to the moon, in quantity of matter, as their weights to its weight. Moreover, since the satellites of Jupiter perform their revolutions in times which observe the $\frac{3}{2}$th power of the proportion of their distances from Jupiter's centre, their accelerative gravities towards Jupiter will be inversely as the squares of their distances from Jupiter's centre; that is, equal, at equal distances. And, therefore, these satellites, if supposed to fall *towards Jupiter* from equal heights, would describe equal spaces in equal times, in like manner as heavy bodies do on our earth. And, by the same argument, if the circumsolar planets were supposed to be let fall at equal distances from the sun, they would, in their descent towards the sun, describe equal spaces in equal times. But forces which equally accelerate unequal bodies must be as those bodies: that is to say, the weights of the planets *towards the sun* must be as their quantities of matter. Further, that the weights of Jupiter and of his satellites towards the sun are proportional to the several quantities of their matter, appears from the exceedingly regular motions of the satellites (by Cor. iii, Prop. 65, Book i). For if some of those bodies were more strongly attracted to the sun in proportion to their quantity of matter than others, the motions of the satellites would be disturbed by that inequality of attraction (by Cor. ii, Prop. 65, Book i). If, at equal distances from the sun, any satellite, in proportion to the quantity of its matter, did gravitate towards the sun with a force greater than Jupiter in proportion to his, according to any given proportion, suppose of d to e; then the distance between the centres of the sun and of the satellite's orbit would be always greater than the distance between the centres of the sun and of Jupiter, nearly as the square root of that proportion: as by some computations I have found. And if the satellite did gravitate towards the sun with a force, less in the proportion of e to d, the distance of the centre of the satellite's orbit from the sun would be less than the distance of the centre of Jupiter from the sun as the square root of the same proportion. Therefore if, at equal distances from the sun, the accelerative gravity of any satellite towards the sun were greater or less than the accelerative gravity of Jupiter towards the sun but by one $\frac{1}{1000}$ part of the whole gravity, the distance of the centre of the satellite's orbit from the sun would be greater of less than the distance of Jupiter from the sun by one $\frac{1}{2000}$ part of the whole distance; that is, by a fifth part of the distance of the utmost satellite from the centre of Jupiter; an eccentricity of the orbit which would be very sensible. But the orbits of the satellites are concentric to Jupiter, and therefore the accelerative gravities of Jupiter, and of all its satellites towards the sun, are equal among themselves. And by the same argument, the weights of Saturn and of his satellites towards the sun, at equal distances from the sun, are as their several quantities of matter; and the weights of the moon and of the earth towards the sun are either none, or accurately proportional to the masses of matter which they contain. But some weight they have, by Cor. i and iii, Prop. 5.

But further; the weights of all the parts of every planet towards any other planet are one to another as the matter in the several parts; for if some parts did gravitate more, others less, than for the quantity of their matter, then the whole planet, according to the sort of parts with which it most abounds, would gravitate more or less than in proportion to the quantity of matter in the whole. Nor is it of any moment whether these parts are external or internal; for if, for example, we should imagine the terrestrial bodies with us to be raised to the orbit of the moon, to be there compared with its body; if the weights of such bodies were to the weights of the external parts of the moon as the quantities of matter in the one and in the other respectively, but to the weights of the internal parts in a greater or less proportion, then likewise the weights of those bodies would be to the weight of the whole moon in a greater or less proportion; against what we have shown above.

COR. I. Hence the weights of bodies do not depend upon their forms and textures; for if the weights could be altered with the forms, they would be greater or less, according to the variety of forms, in equal matter; altogether against experience.

COR. II. Universally, all bodies about the earth gravitate towards the earth; and the weights of all, at equal distances from the earth's centre, are as the quantities of matter which they severally contain. This is the quality of all bodies within the reach of our experiments; and therefore (by Rule 3) to be affirmed of all bodies whatsoever. If the ether, or any other body, were either altogether void of gravity, or were to gravitate less in proportion to its quantity of matter, then, because (according to Aristotle, Descartes, and others) there is no difference between that and other bodies but in *mere* form of matter, by a successive change from form to form, it might be changed at last into a body of the same condition with those which gravitate most in proportion to their quantity of matter; and, on the other hand, the heaviest bodies, acquiring the first form of that body, might by degrees quite lose their gravity. And therefore the weights would depend upon the forms of bodies, and with those forms, might be changed: contrary to what was proved in the preceding Corollary.

COR. III. All spaces are not equally full; for if all spaces were equally full, then the specific gravity of the fluid which fills the region of the air, on account of the extreme density of the matter, would fall nothing short of the specific gravity of quicksilver, or gold, or any other the most dense body; and, therefore, neither gold, nor any other body, could descend in air; for bodies do not descend in fluids, unless they are specifically heavier than the fluids. And if the quantity of matter in a given space can, by any rarefaction, be diminished, what should hinder a diminution to infinity?

COR. IV. If all the solid particles of all bodies are of the same density, and cannot be rarefied without pores, then a void, space, or vacuum must be granted. By bodies of the same density, I mean those whose inertias are in the proportion of their bulks.

COR. V. The power of gravity is of a different nature from the power of magnetism; for the magnetic attraction is not as the matter attracted. Some bodies are attracted more by the magnet; others less; most bodies not at all. The power of magnetism in one and the same body may be increased and diminished; and is sometimes far stronger, for the quantity of matter, than the power of gravity; and in receding from the magnet decreases not as the square but almost as the cube of the distance, as nearly as I could judge from some rude observations.

PROPOSITION 7. THEOREM 7

That there is a power of gravity pertaining to all bodies, proportional to the several quantities of matter which they contain.

That all the planets gravitate one towards another, we have proved before; as well as that the force of gravity towards every one of them, considered apart, is inversely as the square of the distance of places from the centre of the planet. And thence (by Prop. 69, Book I, and its Corollaries) it follows that the gravity tending towards all the planets is proportional to the matter which they contain.

Moreover, since all the parts of any planet A gravitate towards any other planet B; and the gravity of every part is to the gravity of the whole as the matter of the part to the matter of the whole; and (by Law III) to every action corresponds an equal reaction; therefore the planet B will, on the other hand, gravitate towards all the parts of the planet A; and its gravity towards any one part will be to the gravity towards the whole as the matter of the part to the matter of the whole.   Q.E.D.

COR. I. Therefore the force of gravity towards any whole planet arises from, and is compounded of, the forces of gravity towards all its parts. Magnetic and electric attractions afford us examples of this; for all attraction towards the whole arises from the attractions towards the several parts. The thing may be easily understood in gravity, if we consider a greater planet, as formed of a number of lesser planets, meeting together in one globe; for *hence it would appear* that the force of the whole must arise from the forces of the component parts. If it is objected that, according to this law, all bodies with us must gravitate one towards another, whereas no such gravitation anywhere appears, I answer, that since the gravitation towards these bodies is to the gravitation towards the whole earth as these bodies are to the whole earth, the gravitation towards them must be far less than to fall under the observation of our senses.

COR. II. The force of gravity towards the several equal particles of any body is inversely as the square of the distance of places from the particles; as appears from Cor. III, Prop. 74, Book I.

PROPOSITION 8. THEOREM 8

In two spheres gravitating each towards the other, if the matter in places on all sides round about and equidistant from the centres is similar, the weight of either sphere towards the other will be inversely as the square of the distance between their centres.

After I had found that the force of gravity towards a whole planet did arise from and was compounded of the forces of gravity towards all its parts, and towards every one part was in the inverse proportion of the squares of the distances from the part, I was yet in doubt whether that proportion inversely as the square of the distance did accurately hold, or but nearly so, in the total force compounded of so many partial ones; for it might be that the proportion which accurately enough took place in greater distances should be wide of the truth near the surface of the planet, where the distances of the particles are unequal, and their situation dissimilar. But by the help of Props. 75 and 76, Book I, and their Corollaries, I was at last satisfied of the truth of the Proposition, as it now lies before us.

COR. I. Hence we may find and compare together the weights of bodies towards different planets; for the weights of bodies revolving in circles about planets are (by Cor. II, Prop. 4, Book I) directly as the diameters of the circles and inversely as the squares of their periodic times; and their weights at the surfaces of the planets, or at any other distances from their centres, are (by this Proposition) greater or less inversely as the square of the distances. Thus from the periodic times of Venus, revolving about the sun, in $224^d \cdot 16\frac{3}{4}^h$.; of the utmost circumjovial satellite revolving about Jupiter, in 16^d., $16\frac{8}{15}^h$.; of the Huygenian satellite about Saturn, in 15^d. $22\frac{2}{3}^h$.; and of the moon about the earth, in 27^d. 7^h. 43^m.; compared with the mean distance of Venus from the sun, and with the greatest heliocentric elongations of the outmost circumjovial satellite from Jupiter's centre, $8'\ 16''$; of the Huygenian satellite from the centre of Saturn, $3'\ 4''$; and of the moon from the earth, $10'\ 33''$; by computation I found that the weight of equal bodies, at equal distances from the centres of the sun, of Jupiter, of Saturn, and of the earth, towards the sun, Jupiter, Saturn, and the earth, were one to another, as 1, $\frac{1}{1067}$, $\frac{1}{3021}$, and $\frac{1}{169282}$ respectively. Then because as the distances are increased or diminished, the weights are diminished or increased in a squared ratio, the weights of equal bodies towards the sun, Jupiter, Saturn, and the earth, at the distances $10{,}000$, 997, 791, and 109 from their centres, that is, at their very surfaces, will be as $10{,}000$, 943, 529, and 435 respectively. How much the weights of bodies are at the surface of the moon, will be shown hereafter.

Cor. ii. Hence likewise we discover the quantity of matter in the several planets; for their quantities of matter are as the forces of gravity at equal distances from their centres; that is, in the sun, Jupiter, Saturn, and the earth, as 1, $\frac{1}{1067}$, $\frac{1}{3021}$, and $\frac{1}{169282}$ respectively. If the parallax of the sun be taken greater or less than $10''\ 30'''$, the quantity of matter in the earth must be augmented or diminished as the cube of that proportion.

Cor. iii. Hence also we find the densities of the planets; for (by Prop. 72, Book i) the weights of equal and similar bodies towards similar spheres are, at the surfaces of those spheres, as the diameters of the spheres; and therefore the densities of dissimilar spheres are as those weights applied to the diameters of the spheres. But the true diameters of the sun, Jupiter, Saturn, and the earth, were one to another as $10{,}000$, 997, 791, and 109; and the weights towards the same as $10{,}000$, 943, 529, and 435 respectively; and therefore their densities are as 100, $94\frac{1}{2}$, 67, and 400. The density of the earth, which comes out by this computation, does not depend upon the parallax of the sun, but is determined by the parallax of the moon, and therefore is here truly defined. The sun, therefore, is a little denser than Jupiter, and Jupiter than Saturn, and the earth four times denser than the sun; for the sun, by its great heat, is kept in a sort of rarefied state. The moon is denser than the earth, as shall appear afterwards.

Cor. iv. The smaller the planets are, they are, other things being equal, of so much the greater density; for so the powers of gravity on their several surfaces come nearer to equality. They are likewise, other things being equal, of the greater density, as they are nearer to the sun. So Jupiter is more dense than Saturn, and the earth than Jupiter; for the planets were to be placed at different distances from the sun, that, according to their degrees of density, they might enjoy a greater or less proportion of the sun's heat. Our water, if it were removed as far as the orbit of Saturn, would be turned into ice, and in that of Mercury would quickly fly away in vapor; for the light of the sun, to which its heat is proportional, is seven times denser in the orb of Mercury than with us: and by the thermometer I have found that a sevenfold heat of our summer sun will make water boil. Nor are we to doubt that the matter of Mercury is adapted to its heat, and is therefore more dense than the matter of our earth; since, in a denser matter, the operations of Nature require a stronger heat.

PROPOSITION 9. THEOREM 9

*That the force of gravity, considered downwards from the surface of the planets,
decreases nearly in the proportion of the distances from the centre of the planets.*

If the matter of the planet were of an uniform density, this Proposition would
be accurately true (by Prop. 73, Book I). The error, therefore, can be no greater
than what may arise from the inequality of the density.

PROPOSITION 10. THEOREM 10

That the motions of the planets in the heavens may subsist an exceedingly long time.

In the Scholium of Prop. 40, Book II, I have shown that a globe of water
frozen into ice, and moving freely in our air, in the time that it would describe
the length of its semidiameter, would lose by the resistance of the air $\frac{1}{4586}$ part
of its motion; and the same proportion holds nearly in all globes, however
great, and moved with whatever velocity. But that our globe of earth is of
greater density than it would be if the whole consisted of water only, I thus
make out. If the whole consisted of water only, whatever was of less density
than water, because of its less specific gravity, would emerge and float above.
And upon this account, if a globe of terrestrial matter, covered on all sides with
water, was less dense than water, it would emerge somewhere; and, the subsiding water falling back, would be gathered to the opposite side. And such is the
condition of our earth, which in a great measure is covered with seas. The earth,
if it was not for its greater density, would emerge from the seas, and, according
to its degree of levity, would be raised more or less above their surface, the
water of the seas flowing backwards to the opposite side. By the same argument, the spots of the sun, which float upon the lucid matter thereof, are lighter
than that matter; and, however the planets have been formed while they were
yet in fluid masses, all the heavier matter subsided to the centre. Since, therefore, the common matter of our earth on the surface thereof is about twice as
heavy as water, and a little lower, in mines, is found about three, or four, or
even five times heavier, it is probable that the quantity of the whole matter of
the earth may be five or six times greater than if it consisted all of water;
especially since I have before shown that the earth is about four times more
dense than Jupiter. If, therefore, Jupiter is a little more dense than water, in
the space of thirty days, in which that planet describes the length of 459 of its
semidiameters, it would, in a medium of the same density with our air, lose
almost a tenth part of its motion. But since the resistance of mediums decreases
in proportion to their weight or density, so that water, which is $13\frac{3}{5}$ times
lighter than quicksilver, resists less in that proportion; and air, which is 860
times lighter than water, resists less in the same proportion; therefore in the
heavens, where the weight of the medium in which the planets move is immensely diminished, the resistance will almost vanish.

It is shown in the Scholium of Prop. 22, Book II, that at the height of 200
miles above the earth the air is more rare than it is at the surface of the earth in
the ratio of 30 to 0.0000000000003998, or as 75,000,000,000,000 to 1, nearly. And
hence the planet Jupiter, revolving in a medium of the same density with that
superior air, would not lose by the resistance of the medium the 1,000,000th part
of its motion in 1,000,000 years. In the spaces near the earth the resistance is
produced only by the air, exhalations, and vapors. When these are carefully

exhausted by the air pump from under the receiver, heavy bodies fall within the receiver with perfect freedom, and without the least sensible resistance: gold itself, and the lightest down, let fall together, will descend with equal velocity; and though they fall through a space of four, six, and eight feet, they will come to the bottom at the same time; as appears from experiments. And therefore, the celestial regions being perfectly void of air and exhalations, the planets and comets meeting no sensible resistance in those spaces will continue their motions through them for an immense tract of time.

HYPOTHESIS I

THAT THE CENTRE OF THE SYSTEM OF THE WORLD IS IMMOVABLE.

This is acknowledged by all, while some contend that the earth, others that the sun, is fixed in that centre. Let us see what may from hence follow.

PROPOSITION 11. THEOREM 11

That the common centre of gravity of the earth, the sun, and all the planets, is immovable.

For (by Cor. IV of the Laws) that centre either is at rest, or moves uniformly forwards in a right line; but if that centre moved, the centre of the world would move also, against the Hypothesis.

PROPOSITION 12. THEOREM 12

That the sun is agitated by a continual motion, but never recedes far from the common centre of gravity of all the planets.

For since (by Cor. II, Prop. 8) the quantity of matter in the sun is to the quantity of matter in Jupiter as 1067 to 1; and the distance of Jupiter from the sun is to the semidiameter of the sun in a proportion but a small matter greater, the common centre of gravity of Jupiter and the sun will fall upon a point a little without the surface of the sun. By the same argument, since the quantity of matter in the sun is to the quantity of matter in Saturn as 3021 to 1, and the distance of Saturn from the sun is to the semidiameter of the sun in a proportion but a small matter less, the common centre of gravity of Saturn and the sun will fall upon a point a little within the surface of the sun. And, pursuing the principles of this computation, we should find that though the earth and all the planets were placed on one side of the sun, the distance of the common centre of gravity of all from the centre of the sun would scarcely amount to one diameter of the sun. In other cases, the distances of those centres are always less; and therefore, since that centre of gravity is continually at rest, the sun, according to the various positions of the planets, must continually be moved every way, but will never recede far from that centre.

COR. Hence the common centre of gravity of the earth, the sun, and all the planets, is to be esteemed the centre of the world; for since the earth, the sun, and all the planets gravitate one towards another, and are, therefore, according to their powers of gravity, in continual agitation, as the Laws of Motion require, it is plain that their movable centres cannot be taken for the immovable centre of the world. If that body were to be placed in the centre, towards which other bodies gravitate most (according to common opinion), that privilege ought to be allowed to the sun; but since the sun itself is moved, a fixed point is to be chosen from which the centre of the sun recedes least, and from which it would recede yet less if the body of the sun were denser and greater, and therefore less apt to be moved.

PROPOSITION 13. THEOREM 13

The planets move in ellipses which have their common focus in the centre of the sun; and, by radii drawn to that centre, they describe areas proportional to the times of description.

We have discoursed above on these motions from the Phenomena. Now that we know the principles on which they depend, from those principles we deduce the motions of the heavens *a priori*. Because the weights of the planets towards the sun are inversely as the squares of their distances from the sun's centre, if the sun were at rest, and the other planets did not act one upon another, their orbits would be ellipses, having the sun in their common focus; and they would describe areas proportional to the times *of description*, by Props. 1 and 11, and Cor. ɪ, Prop. 13, Book ɪ. But the actions of the planets one upon another are so very small, that they may be neglected; and by Prop. 66, Book ɪ, they disturb the motions of the planets around the sun in motion, less than if those motions were performed about the sun at rest.

It is true, that the action of Jupiter upon Saturn is not to be neglected; for the force of gravity towards Jupiter is to the force of gravity towards the sun (at equal distances, Cor. ɪɪ, Prop. 8) as 1 to 1067; and therefore in the conjunction of Jupiter and Saturn, because the distance of Saturn from Jupiter is to the distance of Saturn from the sun almost as 4 to 9, the gravity of Saturn towards Jupiter will be to the gravity of Saturn towards the sun as 81 to $16 \cdot 1067$; or, as 1 to about 211. And hence arises a perturbation of the orbit of Saturn in every conjunction of this planet with Jupiter, so sensible, that astronomers are puzzled with it. As the planet is differently situated in these conjunctions, its eccentricity is sometimes augmented, sometimes diminished; its aphelion is sometimes carried forwards, sometimes backwards, and its mean motion is by turns accelerated and retarded; yet the whole error in its motion about the sun, though arising from so great a force, may be almost avoided (except in the mean motion) by placing the lower focus of its orbit in the common centre of gravity of Jupiter and the sun (according to Prop. 67, Book ɪ), and therefore that error, when it is greatest, scarcely exceeds two minutes; and the greatest error in the mean motion scarcely exceeds two minutes yearly. But in the conjunction of Jupiter and Saturn, the accelerative forces of gravity of the sun towards Saturn, of Jupiter towards Saturn, and of Jupiter towards the sun, are almost as 16, 81, and $\dfrac{16 \cdot 81 \cdot 3021}{25}$, or 156,609; and therefore the difference of the forces of gravity of the sun towards Saturn, and of Jupiter towards Saturn, is to the force of gravity of Jupiter towards the sun as 65 to 156,609, or as 1 to 2409. But the greatest power of Saturn to disturb the motion of Jupiter is proportional to this difference; and therefore the perturbation of the orbit of Jupiter is much less than that of Saturn's. The perturbations of the other orbits are yet far less, except that the orbit of the earth is sensibly disturbed by the moon. The common centre of gravity of the earth and moon moves in an ellipse about the sun in the focus thereof, and, by a radius drawn to the sun, describes areas proportional to the times of description. But the earth in the meantime by a menstrual motion is revolved about this common centre.

Proposition 14. Theorem 14

The aphelions and nodes of the orbits of the planets are fixed.

The aphelions are immovable by Prop. 11, Book I; and so are the planes of the orbits, by Prop. 1 of the same book. And if the planes are fixed, the nodes must be so too. It is true that some inequalities may arise from the mutual actions of the planets and comets in their revolutions, but these will be so small, that they may be here passed by.

Cor. I. The fixed stars are immovable, seeing they keep the same position to the aphelions and nodes of the planets.

Cor. II. And since these stars are liable to no sensible parallax from the annual motion of the earth, they can have no force, because of their immense distance, to produce any sensible effect in our system. Not to mention that the fixed stars, everywhere promiscuously dispersed in the heavens, by their contrary attractions destroy their mutual actions, by Prop. 70, Book I.

Scholium

Since the planets near the sun (viz., Mercury, Venus, the earth, and Mars) are so small that they can act with but little force upon one another, therefore their aphelions and nodes must be fixed, except so far as they are disturbed by the actions of Jupiter and Saturn, and other higher bodies. And hence we may find, by the theory of gravity, that their aphelions move forwards a little, in respect of the fixed stars, and that as the $\frac{3}{2}$th power of their several distances from the sun. So that if the aphelion of Mars, in the space of a hundred years, is carried forwards 33′ 20″, in respect of the fixed stars, the aphelions of the earth, of Venus, and of Mercury, will in a hundred years be carried forwards 17′ 40″, 10′ 53″, and 4′ 16″, respectively. But these motions are so inconsiderable, that we have neglected them in this Proposition.

Proposition 15. Problem 1

To find the principal diameters of the orbits of the planets.

They are to be taken as the $\frac{2}{3}$th power of the periodic times, by Prop. 15, Book I, and then to be severally augmented in the proportion of the sum of the masses of matter in the sun and each planet to the first of two mean proportionals between that sum and the quantity of matter in the sun, by Prop. 60, Book I.

Proposition 16. Problem 2

To find the eccentricities and aphelions of the planets.
This Problem is resolved by Prop. 18, Book I.

Proposition 17. Theorem 15

That the diurnal motions of the planets are uniform, and that the libration of the moon arises from its diurnal motion.

The Proposition is proved from the first Law of Motion, and Cor. XXII, Prop. 66, Book I. Jupiter, with respect to the fixed stars, revolves in 9ʰ. 56ᵐ.; Mars in 24ʰ. 39ᵐ.; Venus in about 23ʰ.; the earth in 23ʰ. 56ᵐ.; the sun in 25½ᵈ., and the moon in 27ᵈ. 7ʰ. 43ᵐ. These things appear by the Phenomena. The spots in the sun's body return to the same situation on the sun's disk, with respect to the earth, in 27½ days; and therefore with respect to the fixed stars the sun revolves in about 25½ days. But because the lunar day, arising from its uniform revolution about its axis, is menstrual, *that is, equal to the time of its periodic revolution in its orbit*, hence the same face of the moon will be always nearly turned to the upper focus of its orbit; but, as the situation of that focus requires, will deviate a little to one side and to the other from the earth in the lower focus; and this is the libration in longitude; for the libration in latitude arises from the moon's latitude, and the inclination of its axis to the plane of the ecliptic. This theory of the libration of the moon, Mr. N. Mercator, in his *Astronomy*, published at the beginning of the year 1676, explained more fully out of the letters I sent him. The utmost satellite of Saturn seems to revolve about its axis with a motion like this of the moon, respecting Saturn continually with the same face; for in its revolution round Saturn, as often as it comes to the eastern part of its orbit, it is scarcely visible, and generally quite disappears; this is probably occasioned by some spots in that part of its body, which is then turned towards the earth, as M. Cassini has observed. So also the utmost satellite of Jupiter seems to revolve about its axis with a like motion, because in that part of its body which is turned from Jupiter it has a spot, which always appears as if it were in Jupiter's own body, whenever the satellite passes between Jupiter and our eye.

PROPOSITION 18. THEOREM 16

That the axes of the planets are less than the diameters drawn perpendicular to the axes.

The equal gravitation of the parts on all sides would give a spherical figure to the planets, if it was not for their diurnal revolution in a circle. By that circular motion it comes to pass that the parts receding from the axis endeavor to ascend about the equator; and therefore if the matter is in a fluid state, by its ascent towards the equator it will enlarge the diameters there, and by its descent towards the poles it will shorten the axis. So the diameter of Jupiter (by the concurring observations of astronomers) is found shorter between pole and pole than from east to west. And, by the same argument, if our earth was not higher about the equator than at the poles, the seas would subside about the poles, and, rising towards the equator, would lay all things there under water.

PROPOSITION 19. PROBLEM 3

To find the proportion of the axis of a planet to the diameters perpendicular thereto.

Our countryman, Mr. Norwood, measuring a distance of 905,751 feet of London measure between London and York, in 1635, and observing the difference of latitudes to be 2° 28′, determined the measure of one degree to be 367,196 feet of London measure, that is, 57,300 Paris toises. M. Picard, measuring an arc of one degree, and 22′ 55″ of the meridian between Amiens and Malvoisine, found an arc of one degree to be 57,060 Paris toises. M. Cassini, the father, measured the distance upon the meridian from the town of Collioure in Roussillon to the Observatory of Paris; and his son added the distance from the Observatory to the Citadel of Dunkirk. The whole distance was 486156½ toises and the difference of the latitudes of Collioure and Dunkirk was 8 degrees, and 31′ 11⅚″. Hence an arc of one degree appears to be 57,061 Paris toises. And from these measures we conclude that the circumference of the earth is 123,249,600, and its semidiameter 19,615,800 Paris feet, upon the supposition that the earth is of a spherical figure.

In the latitude of Paris a heavy body falling in a second of time describes 15 Paris feet, 1 inch, $1\frac{7}{9}$ lines, as above, that is, $2173\frac{7}{9}$ lines. The weight of the body is diminished by the weight of the ambient air. Let us suppose the weight lost thereby to be $\frac{1}{11000}$ part of the whole weight; then that heavy body falling in a vacuum will describe a height of 2174 lines in one second of time.

A body in every sidereal day of 23^h. 56^m. 4^s. uniformly revolving in a circle at the distance of 19,615,800 feet from the centre, in one second of time describes an arc of 1433.46 feet; the versed sine of which is 0.05236561 feet, or 7.54064 lines. And therefore the force with which bodies descend in the latitude of Paris is to the centrifugal force of bodies in the equator arising from the diurnal motion of the earth as 2174 to 7.54064.

The centrifugal force of bodies in the equator is to the centrifugal force with which bodies recede directly from the earth in the latitude of Paris, 48° 50′ 10″, as the square of the ratio of the radius to the cosine of the latitude, that is, as 7.54064 to 3.267. Add this force to the force with which bodies descend by their weight in the latitude of Paris, and a body, in the latitude of Paris, falling by its whole undiminished force of gravity, in the time of one second, will describe 2177.267 lines, or 15 Paris feet, 1 inch, and 5.267 lines. And the total force of gravity in that latitude will be to the centrifugal force of bodies in the equator of the earth as 2177.267 to 7.54064, or as 289 to 1.

Therefore if APBQ represent the figure of the earth, now no longer spherical, but generated by the rotation of an ellipse about its lesser axis PQ; and ACQqca a canal full of water, reaching from the pole Qq to the centre Cc, and thence rising to the equator Aa; the weight of the water in the leg of the canal ACca will be to the weight of water in the other leg QCcq as

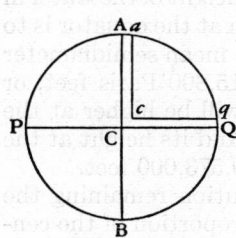

289 to 288, because the centrifugal force arising from the circular motion sustains and takes off one of the 289 parts of the weight (in the one leg), and the weight of 288 in the other sustains the rest. But by computation (from Cor. II, Prop. 91, Book I) I find, that, if the matter of the earth was all uniform, and without any motion, and its axis PQ were to the diameter AB as 100 to 101, the force of gravity in the place Q towards the earth would be to the force of gravity in the same place Q towards a sphere described about the centre C with the radius PC, or QC, as 126 to 125. And, by the same argument, the force of gravity in the place A towards the spheroid generated by the rotation of the ellipse APBQ about the axis AB is to the force of gravity in the same place A, towards the sphere described about the centre C with the radius AC, as 125 to 126. But the force of gravity in the place A towards the earth is a mean proportional between the forces of gravity towards the spheroid and this sphere; because the sphere, by having its diameter PQ diminished in the proportion of 101 to 100, is transformed into the figure of the earth; and this figure, by having a third diameter perpendicular to the two diameters AB and PQ diminished in the same proportion, is converted into the said spheroid; and the force of gravity in A, in either case, is diminished nearly in the same proportion. Therefore the force of gravity in A towards the sphere described about the centre C with the radius

AC, is to the force of gravity in A towards the earth as 126 is to $125\frac{1}{2}$. And the force of gravity in the place Q towards the sphere described about the centre C with the radius QC, is to the force of gravity in the place A towards the sphere described about the centre C with the radius AC, in the proportion of the diameters (by Prop. 72, Book I), that is, as 100 to 101. If, therefore, we compound those three proportions 126 to 125, 126 to $125\frac{1}{2}$, and 100 to 101, into one, the force of gravity in the place Q towards the earth will be to the force of gravity in the place A towards the earth as $126 \cdot 126 \cdot 100$ to $125 \cdot 125\frac{1}{2} \cdot 101$; or as 501 to 500.

Now since (by Cor. III, Prop. 91, Book I) the force of gravity in either leg of the canal ACca, or QCcq, is as the distance of the places from the centre of the earth, if those legs are conceived to be divided by transverse, parallel, and equidistant surfaces, into parts proportional to the wholes, the weights of any number of parts in the one leg ACca will be to the weights of the same number of parts in the other leg as their magnitudes and the accelerative forces of their gravity conjointly, that is, as 101 to 100, and 500 to 501, or as 505 to 501. And therefore if the centrifugal force of every part in the leg ACca, arising from the diurnal motion, was to the weight of the same part as 4 to 505, so that from the weight of every part, conceived to be divided into 505 parts, the centrifugal force might take off four of those parts, the weights would remain equal in each leg, and therefore the fluid would rest in an equilibrium. But the centrifugal force of every part is to the weight of the same part as 1 to 289; that is, the centrifugal force, which should be $\frac{4}{505}$ parts of the weight, is only $\frac{1}{289}$ part thereof. And, therefore, I say, by the rule of proportion, that if the centrifugal force $\frac{4}{505}$ make the height of the water in the leg ACca to exceed the height of the water in the leg QCcq by $\frac{1}{100}$ part of its whole height the centrifugal force $\frac{1}{289}$ will make the excess of the height in the leg ACca only $\frac{1}{289}$ part of the height of the water in the other leg QCcq; and therefore the diameter of the earth at the equator is to its diameter from pole to pole as 230 to 229. And since the mean semidiameter of the earth, according to Picard's mensuration, is 19,615,800 Paris feet, or 3923.16 miles (reckoning 5000 feet to a mile), the earth will be higher at the equator than at the poles by 85,472 feet, or $17\frac{1}{10}$ miles. And its height at the equator will be about 19,658,600 feet, and at the poles 19,573,000 feet.

If, the density and periodic time of the diurnal revolution remaining the same, the planet was greater or less than the earth, the proportion of the centrifugal force to that of gravity, and therefore also of the diameter between the poles to the diameter at the equator, would likewise remain the same. But if the diurnal motion was accelerated or retarded in any proportion, the centrifugal force would be augmented or diminished nearly in the same proportion squared; and therefore the difference of the diameters will be increased or diminished in the same squared ratio, very nearly. And if the density of the planet was augmented or diminished in any proportion, the force of gravity tending towards it would also be augmented or diminished in the same proportion: and the difference of the diameters on the contrary would be diminished in proportion as the force of gravity is augmented, and augmented in proportion as the force of gravity is diminished. Therefore, since the earth, in respect of the fixed stars, revolves in 23^h. 56^m., but Jupiter in 9^h. 56^m., and the squares of their periodic times are as 29 to 5, and their densities as 400 to $94\frac{1}{2}$, the difference of the diameters of Jupiter will be to its lesser diameter as

$\frac{29}{5} \cdot \frac{400}{94\frac{1}{4}} \cdot \frac{1}{229}$ to 1, or as 1 to $9\frac{1}{3}$, nearly. Therefore the diameter of Jupiter from east to west is to its diameter from pole to pole nearly as $10\frac{1}{3}$ to $9\frac{1}{3}$. Therefore, since its greatest diameter is $37''$, its lesser diameter lying between the poles will be $33'' 25'''$. Add thereto about $3''$ for the irregular refraction of light, and the apparent diameters of this planet will become $40''$ and $36'' 25'''$; which are to each other as $11\frac{1}{6}$ to $10\frac{1}{6}$, very nearly. These things are so upon the supposition that the body of Jupiter is uniformly dense. But now if its body be denser towards the plane of the equator than towards the poles, its diameters may be to each other as 12 to 11, or 13 to 12, or perhaps as 14 to 13.

And Cassini observed, in the year 1691, that the diameter of Jupiter reaching from east to west is greater by about a fifteenth part than the other diameter. Mr. Pound with his 123-foot telescope, and an excellent micrometer, measured the diameters of Jupiter in the year 1719, and found them as follows:

The times		Greatest diameter	Lesser diameter	The diameters to each other
	days	hours	Parts	Parts	
January	28	6	13.40	12.28	As 12 to 11
March	6	7	13.12	12.20	$13\frac{3}{4}$ to $12\frac{3}{4}$
March	9	7	13.12	12.08	$12\frac{2}{3}$ to $11\frac{2}{3}$
April	9	9	12.32	11.48	$14\frac{1}{2}$ to $13\frac{1}{2}$

So that the theory agrees with the phenomena; for the planets are more heated by the sun's rays towards their equators, and therefore are a little more condensed by that heat than towards their poles.

Moreover, that there is a diminution of gravity occasioned by the diurnal rotation of the earth, and therefore the earth rises higher there than it does at the poles (supposing that its matter is uniformly dense), will appear by the experiments of pendulums related under the following Proposition.

PROPOSITION 20. PROBLEM 4

To find and compare together the weights of bodies in the different regions of our earth.

Because the weights of the unequal legs of the canal of water ACQ*qca* are equal; and the weights of the parts proportional to the whole legs, and alike situated in them, are one to another as the weights of the wholes, and therefore equal between themselves; the weights of equal parts, and alike situated in the

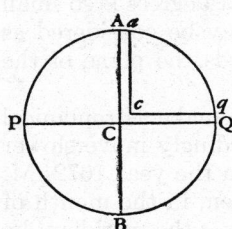

legs, will be inversely as the legs, that is, inversely as 230 to 229. And the case is the same in all homogeneous equal bodies alike situated in the legs of the canal. Their weights are inversely as the legs, that is, inversely as the distances of the bodies from the centre of the earth. Therefore if the bodies are situated in the uppermost parts of the canals, or on the surface of the earth, their weights will be one to another inversely as their distances from the centre. And, by the same argument, the weights in all other places round the whole surface of the earth are inversely as the distances of the places from the centre; and, therefore, on the hypothesis of the earth's being a spheroid, are given in proportion.

From this arises the theorem that the increase of weight in passing from the equator to the poles is nearly as the versed sine of double the latitude; or, which comes to the same thing, as the square of the sine of the latitude; and the arcs of the degrees of latitude in the meridian increase nearly in the same proportion. And, therefore, since the latitude of Paris is 48° 50′, that of places under the equator 00°00′, and that of places under the poles 90°; and the versed sines of double those arcs are 1,133,400,000 and 20,000, the radius being 10,000; and the force of gravity at the pole is to the force of gravity at the equator as 230 to 229; and the excess of the force of gravity at the pole to the force of gravity at the equator is as 1 to 229; the excess of the force of gravity in the latitude of Paris will be to the force of gravity at the equator as $1 \cdot \frac{11334}{20000}$ to 229, or as 5667 to 2,290,000. And therefore the whole forces of gravity in those places will be one to the other as 2,295,667 to 2,290,000. Therefore, since the lengths of pendulums vibrating in equal times are as the forces of gravity, and in the latitude of Paris the length of a pendulum vibrating seconds is 3 Paris feet and 8½ lines, or rather, because of the weight of the air, $8\frac{5}{9}$ lines, the length of a pendulum vibrating in the same time under the equator will be shorter by 1.087 lines. And by a like calculus the following table is made.

Latitude of the place	Length of the pendulum		Measure of one degree in the meridian	Latitude of the place	Length of the pendulum		Measure of one degree in the meridian
degrees	feet	lines	toises	degrees	feet	lines	toises
0	3 .	7.468	56637	6	3 .	8.461	57022
5	3 .	7.482	56642	7	3 .	8.494	57035
10	3 .	7.526	56659	8	3 .	8.528	57048
15	3 .	7.596	56687	9	3 .	8.561	57061
20	3 .	7.692	56724	50	3 .	8.594	57074
25	3 .	7.812	56769	55	3 .	8.756	57137
30	3 .	7.948	56823	60	3 .	8.907	57196
35	3 .	8.099	56882	65	3 .	9.044	57250
40	3 .	8.261	56945	70	3 .	9.162	57295
1	3 .	8.294	56958	75	3 .	9.258	57332
2	3 .	8.327	56971	80	3 .	9.329	57360
3	3 .	8.361	56984	85	3 .	9.372	57377
4	3 .	8.394	56997	90	3 .	9.387	57382
45	3 .	8.428	57010				

By this table, therefore, it appears that the inequality of degrees is so small that the figure of the earth, in geographical matters, may be considered as spherical; especially if the earth be a little denser towards the plane of the equator than towards the poles.

Now several astronomers, sent into remote countries to make astronomical observations, have found that pendulum clocks do accordingly move slower near the equator than in our climates. And, first of all, in the year 1672, M. Richer took notice of it in the island of Cayenne; for when, in the month of August, he was observing the transits of the fixed stars over the meridian, he found his clock to go slower than it ought in respect of the mean motion of the sun at the rate of 2ᵐ. 28ˢ. a day. Therefore, fitting up a simple pendulum to vibrate in seconds, which were measured by an excellent clock, he observed the length of that simple pendulum; and this he did over and over every week for ten months together. And upon his return to France, comparing the length of that pendulum with the length of the pendulum at Paris (which was 3 Paris feet and $8\frac{3}{5}$ lines), he found it shorter by $1\frac{1}{4}$ lines.

Afterwards, our friend Dr. Halley, about the year 1677, arriving at the island of St. Helena, found his pendulum clock to go slower there than at London without marking the difference. But he shortened the rod of his clock by more than $\frac{1}{8}$ of an inch, or $1\frac{1}{2}$ lines; and, to effect this, because the length of the screw at the lower end of the rod was not sufficient, he interposed a wooden ring between the nut and the ball.

Then, in the year 1682, M. Varin and M. des Hayes found the length of a simple pendulum vibrating in seconds at the Royal Observatory of Paris to be 3 feet and $8\frac{5}{9}$ lines. And by the same method in the island of Goree, they found the length of an isochronal pendulum to be 3 feet and $6\frac{5}{9}$ lines, differing from the former by two lines. And in the same year, going to the islands of Guadaloupe and Martinico, they found that the length of an isochronal pendulum in those islands was 3 feet and $6\frac{1}{2}$ lines.

After this, M. Couplet, the son, in the month of July, 1697, at the Royal Observatory of Paris, so fitted his pendulum clock to the mean motion of the sun, that for a considerable time together the clock agreed with the motion of the sun. In November following, upon his arrival at Lisbon, he found his clock to go slower than before at the rate of $2^{\mathrm{m}}.$ $13^{\mathrm{s}}.$ in 24 hours. And the following March, coming to Paraiba, he found his clock to go slower than at Paris, and at the rate $4^{\mathrm{m}}.$ $12^{\mathrm{s}}.$ in 24 hours; and he affirms that the pendulum vibrating in seconds was shorter at Lisbon by $2\frac{1}{2}$ lines, and at Paraiba by $3\frac{2}{3}$ lines, than at Paris. He would have done better to have reckoned those differences $1\frac{1}{3}$ and $2\frac{5}{9}$: for these differences correspond to the differences of the times $2^{\mathrm{m}}.$ $13^{\mathrm{s}}.$ and $4^{\mathrm{m}}.$ $12^{\mathrm{s}}.$ But this gentleman's observations are so gross, that we cannot confide in them.

In the following years, 1699 and 1700, M. des Hayes, making another voyage to America, determined that in the islands of Cayenne and Granada the length of the pendulum vibrating in seconds was a small matter less than 3 feet and $6\frac{1}{2}$ lines; that in the island of St. Christopher it was 3 feet and $6\frac{3}{4}$ lines; and in the island of St. Domingo 3 feet and 7 lines.

And, in the year 1704, Feuillé, at Puerto Bello in America, found that the length of the pendulum vibrating in seconds was 3 Paris feet and only $5\frac{7}{12}$ lines, that is, almost 3 lines shorter than at Paris; but the observation was faulty. For afterwards, going to the island of Martinico, he found the length of the isochronal pendulum there 3 Paris feet and $5^{10}\!/_{12}$ lines.

Now the latitude of Paraiba is 6° 38′ south; that of Puerto Bello, 9° 33′ north; and the latitudes of the islands Cayenne, Goree, Guadaloupe, Martinico, Granada, St. Christopher, and St. Domingo, are respectively 4° 55′, 14° 40″, 15° 00′, 14° 44′, 12° 06′, 17° 19′, and 19° 48′, north. And the excesses of the length of the pendulum at Paris above the lengths of the isochronal pendulums observed in those latitudes are a little greater than by the table of the lengths of the pendulum before computed. And therefore the earth is a little higher under the equator than by the preceding calculus, and a little denser at the centre than in mines near the surface, unless, perhaps, the heats of the torrid zone have a little extended the length of the pendulums.

For M. Picard has observed that a rod of iron, which in frosty weather in the winter season was one foot long, when heated by fire, was lengthened into one foot and $\frac{1}{4}$ line. Afterwards M. de la Hire found that a rod of iron, which in the like winter season was 6 feet long, when exposed to the heat of the summer sun, was extended into 6 feet and $\frac{2}{3}$ line. In the former case the heat was greater than in the latter; but in the latter it was greater than the heat of the external parts of a human body; for metals exposed to the summer sun acquire a very considerable degree of heat. But the rod of a pendulum clock is never exposed to the heat of the summer sun, nor ever acquires a heat equal to that of the external parts of a human body; and, therefore, though the 3-foot rod of a pendulum clock will indeed be a little longer in the summer than in the winter season, yet the difference will scarcely amount to $\frac{1}{4}$ line. Therefore the total difference of the lengths of isochronal pendulums in different climates cannot be ascribed to the difference of heat; nor indeed to the mistakes of the French astronomers. For although there is not a perfect agreement between their observations, yet the errors are so small that they may be neglected; and in this they all agree, that isochronal pendulums are shorter under the equator than at the Royal Observatory of Paris, by a difference not less than $1\frac{1}{4}$ lines, nor greater than $2\frac{2}{3}$ lines. By the observations of M. Richer, in the island of Cayenne, the difference was $1\frac{1}{4}$ lines. That difference being corrected by those of M. des Hayes, becomes $1\frac{1}{2}$ lines or $1\frac{3}{4}$ lines. By the less accurate observations of others, the same was made about 2 lines. And this disagreement might arise partly from the errors of the observations, partly from the dissimilitude of the internal parts of the earth, and the height of mountains; partly from the different temperatures of the air.

I take an iron rod 3 feet long to be shorter by a sixth part of one line in winter time with us here in England than in the summer. Because of the great heats under the equator, subtract this quantity from the difference of $1\frac{1}{4}$ lines observed by M. Richer, and there will remain $1\frac{1}{12}$ lines, which agrees very well with $1\frac{87}{1000}$ lines, obtained earlier by the theory. M. Richer repeated his observations, made in the island of Cayenne, every week for ten months together, and compared the lengths of the pendulum which he had there noted in the iron rods with the lengths thereof which he observed in France. This diligence and care seems to have been wanting to the other observers. If this gentleman's observations are to be depended on, the earth is higher under the equator than at the poles, and that by an excess of about 17 miles; as appeared above by the theory.

Proposition 21. Theorem 17

That the equinoctial points go backwards, and that the axis of the earth, by a nutation in every annual revolution, twice vibrates towards the ecliptic, and as often returns to its former position.

The Proposition appears from Cor. xx, Prop. 66, Book i; but that motion of nutation must be very small, and, indeed, scarcely perceptible.

Proposition 22. Theorem 18

That all the motions of the moon, and all the inequalities of those motions, follow from the principles which we have laid down.

That the greater planets, while they are carried about the sun, may in the meantime carry other lesser planets, revolving about them, and that those lesser planets must move in ellipses which have their foci in the centres of the greater, appears from Prop. 65, Book i. But then their motions will be in several ways disturbed by the action of the sun, and they will suffer such inequalities as are observed in our moon. Thus our moon (by Cor. ii, iii, iv, and v, Prop. 66, Book i) moves faster, and, by a radius drawn to the earth, describes an area greater for the time, and has its orbit less curved, and therefore approaches nearer to the earth in the syzygies than in the quadratures, excepting so far as these effects are hindered by the motion of eccentricity; for (by Cor. ix, Prop. 66, Book i) the eccentricity is greatest when the apogee of the moon is in the syzygies, and least when the same is in the quadratures; and upon this account the perigean moon is swifter, and nearer to us, but the apogean moon slower and farther from us, in the syzygies than in the quadratures. Moreover, the apogee goes forwards, and the nodes backwards; and this is done not with a regular but an unequal motion. For (by Cor. vii and viii, Prop. 66, Book i) the apogee goes more swiftly forwards in its syzygies, more slowly backwards in its quadratures; and, by the excess of its progress above its regress, advances yearly forwards. But the nodes, on the contrary (by Cor. xi, Prop. 66, Book i), are quiescent in their syzygies, and go fastest back in their quadratures. Further, the greatest latitude of the moon (by Cor. x, Prop. 66, Book i) is greater in the quadratures of the moon than in its syzygies. And (by Cor. vi, Prop. 66, Book i) the mean motion of the moon is slower in the perihelion of the earth than in its aphelion. And these are the principal inequalities (of the moon) taken notice of by astronomers.

But there are yet other inequalities not observed by former astronomers, by which the motions of the moon are so disturbed that to this day we have not been able to bring them under any certain rule. For the velocities or hourly motions of the apogee and nodes of the moon, and their equations, as well as the difference between the greatest eccentricity in the syzygies and the least eccentricity in the quadratures, and that inequality which we call the variation, are (by Cor. xiv, Prop. 66, Book i) in the course of the year augmented and diminished as the cube of the sun's apparent diameter. And besides (by Cor. i and ii, Lem. 10, and Cor. xvi, Prop. 66, Book i) the variation is augmented and diminished nearly as the square of the time between the quadratures. But, in astronomical calculations, this inequality is commonly thrown into and combined with the equation of the moon's centre.

Proposition 23. Problem 5

To derive the unequal motions of the satellites of Jupiter and Saturn from the motions of our moon.

From the motions of our moon we deduce the corresponding motions of the moons or satellites of Jupiter in this manner, by Cor. xvi, Prop. 66, Book i. The mean motion of the nodes of the outmost satellite of Jupiter is to the mean motion of the nodes of our moon in a proportion compounded of the squared ratio of the periodic times of the earth about the sun to the periodic times of Jupiter about the sun, and the simple ratio of the periodic time of the satellite about Jupiter to the periodic time of our moon about the earth; and therefore, those nodes, in the space of an hundred years, are carried 8° 24' backwards or forwards. The mean motions of the nodes of the inner satellites are to the mean motion of the nodes of the outmost as their periodic times are to the periodic time of the former, by the same Corollary, and are thence given. And

the forward motion of the apse of every satellite is to the backward motion of
its nodes as the motion of the apogee of our moon to the motion of its nodes (by
the same Corollary), and is thence given. But the motions of the apsides thus
found must be diminished in the proportion of 5 to 9, or of about 1 to 2, on
account of a cause which I cannot here stop to explain. The greatest equations
of the nodes, and of the apse of every satellite, are to the greatest equations of
the nodes, and apogee of our moon respectively, as the motions of the nodes
and apsides of the satellites, in the time of one revolution of the former equations, to the motions of the nodes and apogee of our moon, in the time of one
revolution of the latter equations. The variation of a satellite seen from Jupiter
is to the variation of our moon in the same proportion as the whole motions of
their nodes respectively during the times in which the satellite and our moon
(after parting from) are revolved (again) to the sun, by the same Corollary;
and therefore in the outmost satellite the variation does not exceed 5^s 12th.

PROPOSITION 24. THEOREM 19

That the flux and reflux of the sea arise from the actions of the sun and moon.
   By Cor. xix and xx, Prop. 66, Book i, it appears that the waters of the sea
ought twice to rise and twice to fall every day, as well lunar as solar; and that
the greatest height of the waters in the open and deep seas ought to follow the
approach of the luminaries to the meridian of the place by a less interval than
six hours; as happens in all that eastern tract of the Atlantic and Ethiopic seas
between *France* and the Cape of Good Hope; and on the coasts of Chile and
Peru in the South Sea; in all which shores the flood falls out about the second,
third, or fourth hour, unless where the motion propagated from the deep ocean
is by the shallowness of the channels, through which it passes to some particular places, retarded to the fifth, sixth, or seventh hour, and even later. The
hours I reckon from the approach of each luminary to the meridian of the
place, as well under as above the horizon; and by the hours of the lunar day I
understand the 24th parts of that time which the moon, by its apparent diurnal
motion, employs to come about again to the meridian of the place which it left
the day before. The force of the sun or moon in raising the sea is greatest in the
approach of the luminary to the meridian of the place; but the force impressed
upon the sea at that time continues a little while after the impression, and is
afterwards increased by a new though less force still acting upon it. This makes
the sea rise higher and higher, till, this new force becoming too weak to raise it
any more, the sea rises to its greatest height. And this will come to pass, perhaps, in one or two hours, but more frequently near the shores in about three
hours, or even more, where the sea is shallow.
   The two luminaries excite two motions, which will not appear distinctly, but
between them will arise one mixed motion compounded out of both. In the
conjunction or opposition of the luminaries their forces will be conjoined, and
bring on the greatest flood and ebb. In the quadratures the sun will raise the
waters which the moon depresses, and depress the waters which the moon
raises, and from the difference of their forces the smallest of all tides will follow.
And because (as experience tells us) the force of the moon is greater than that
of the sun, the greatest height of the waters will happen about the third lunar
hour. Out of the syzygies and quadratures, the greatest tide, which by the
single force of the moon ought to fall out at the third lunar hour, and by the

single force of the sun at the third solar hour, by the compounded forces of both must fall out in an intermediate time that approaches nearer to the third hour of the moon than to that of the sun. And, therefore, while the moon is passing from the syzygies to the quadratures, during which time the third hour of the sun precedes the third hour of the moon, the greatest height of the waters will also precede the third hour of the moon, and that, by the greatest interval, a little after the octants of the moon; and, by like intervals, the greatest tide will follow the third lunar hour, while the moon is passing from the quadratures to the syzygies. Thus it happens in the open sea; for in the mouths of rivers the greater tides come later to their height.

But the effects of the luminaries depend upon their distances from the earth; for when they are less distant, their effects are greater, and when more distant, their effects are less, and that as the cube of their apparent diameter. Therefore it is that the sun, in the winter time, being then in its perigee, has a greater effect, and makes the tides in the syzygies somewhat greater, and those in the quadratures somewhat less than in the summer season; and every month the moon, while in the perigee, raises greater tides than at the distance of fifteen days before or after, when it is in its apogee. From this it comes to pass that two highest tides do not follow one the other in two immediately succeeding syzygies.

The effect of either luminary doth likewise depend upon its declination or distance from the equator; for if the luminary was placed at the pole, it would constantly attract all the parts of the waters without any intensification or remission of its action, and could cause no reciprocation of motion. And, therefore, as the luminaries decline from the equator towards either pole they will, by degrees, lose their force, and on this account will excite lesser tides in the solstitial than in the equinoctial syzygies. But in the solstitial quadratures they will raise greater tides than in the quadratures about the equinoxes; because the force of the moon, then situated in the equator, most exceeds the force of the sun. Therefore the greatest tides occur in those syzygies, and the least in those quadratures, which happen about the time of both equinoxes; and the greatest tide in the syzygies is always succeeded by the least tide in the quadratures, as we find by experience. But, because the sun is less distant from the earth in winter than in summer, it comes to pass that the greatest and least tides more frequently appear before than after the vernal equinox, and more frequently after than before the autumnal.

Moreover, the effects of the luminaries depend upon the latitudes of places. Let ApEP represent the earth covered with deep waters; C its centre; P, p its poles; AE the equator; F any place without the equator; Ff the parallel of the

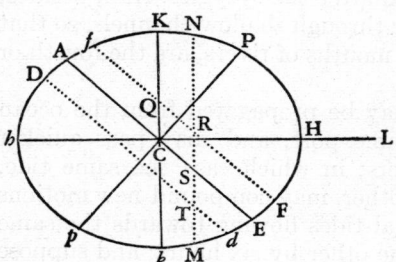

place; Dd the correspondent parallel on the other side of the equator; L the place of the moon three hours before; H the place of the earth directly under it; h the opposite place; K, k the places at 90 degrees distance; CH, Ch, the greatest heights of the sea from the centre of the earth; and CK, Ck its least heights: and if with the axes Hh, Kk, an ellipse is described, and by the revolution of that ellipse about its longer axis H*h* a spheroid HPK*hpk* is formed, this spheroid will nearly represent the figure of the sea; and CF, C*f*, CD, C*d*, will represent the heights of the sea in the places F*f*, D*d*. But further; in the said revolution of the ellipse any point N describes the circle NM cutting the parallels F*f*, D*d*, in any places RT, and the equator AE in S; CN will represent the height of the sea in all those places, R, S, T, situated in this circle. Therefore, in the diurnal revolution of any place F, the greatest flood will be in F, at the third hour after the appulse of the moon to the meridian above the horizon; and afterwards the greatest ebb in Q, at the third hour after the setting of the moon; and then the greatest flood in *f*, at the third hour after the appulse of the moon to the meridian under the horizon; and, lastly, the greatest ebb in Q, at the third hour after the rising of the moon; and the latter flood in *f* will be less than the preceding flood in F. For the whole sea is divided into two hemispherical floods, one in the hemisphere KH*k* on the north side, the other in the opposite hemisphere K*hk*, which we may therefore call the northern and the southern floods. These floods, being always opposite the one to the other, come by turns to the meridians of all places, after an interval of twelve lunar hours. And as the northern countries partake more of the northern flood, and the southern countries more of the southern flood, thence arise tides, alternately greater and less in all places without the equator, in which the luminaries rise and set. But the greatest tide will happen when the moon declines towards the vertex of the place, about the third hour after the appulse of the moon to the meridian above the horizon; and when the moon changes its declination *to the other side of the equator*, that which was the greater tide will be changed into a lesser. And the greatest difference of the floods will fall out about the times of the solstices; especially if the ascending node of the moon is about the first of Aries. So it is found by experience that the morning tides in winter exceed those of the evening, and the evening tides in summer exceed those of the morning; at Plymouth by the height of one foot, but at Bristol by the height of fifteen inches, according to the observations of Colepress and Sturmy.

But the motions which we have been describing suffer some alteration from that force of reciprocation, which the waters, being once moved, retain a little while *by their inertia*. Whence it comes to pass that the tides may continue for some time, though the actions of the luminaries should cease. This power of retaining the impressed motion lessens the difference of the alternate tides, and makes those tides which immediately succeed after the syzygies greater, and those which follow next after the quadratures less. And hence it is that the alternate tides at Plymouth and Bristol do not differ much more from each other than by the height of a foot or fifteen inches, and that the greatest tides at those ports are not the first but the third after the syzygies. And, besides, all the motions are retarded in their passage through shallow channels, so that the greatest tides of all, in some straits and mouths of rivers, are the fourth or even the fifth after the syzygies.

Further, it may happen that the tide may be propagated from the ocean through different channels towards the same port, and may pass quicker through some channels than through others; in which case the same tide, divided into two or more succeeding one another, may compound new motions of different kinds. Let us suppose two equal tides flowing towards the same port from different places, one preceding the other by six hours; and suppose the first tide to happen at the third hour of the approach of the moon to the meridian of the port. If the moon at the time of the approach to the meridian was in the equator, every six hours alternately there would arise equal floods, which, meeting with as many equal ebbs, would so balance each other that for that day the water would stagnate and be quiet. If the moon then declined from the equator, the tides in the ocean would be alternately greater and less, as was said; and from thence two greater and two less tides would be alternately propagated towards that port. But the two greater floods would make the greatest height of the waters to fall out in the middle time between both; and the greater and less floods would make the waters to rise to a mean height in the middle time between them, and in the middle time between the two less floods the waters would rise to their least height. Thus in the space of twenty-four hours the waters would come, not twice, as commonly, but once only to their greatest, and once only to their least height; and their greatest height, if the moon declined towards the elevated pole, would happen at the sixth or thirtieth hour after the approach of the moon to the meridian; and when the moon changed its declination, this flood would be changed into an ebb. An example of this Dr. Halley has given us, from the observations of seamen in the port of Batshaw, in the kingdom of Tunquin, in the latitude of 20° 50′ north. In that port, on the day which follows after the passage of the moon over the equator, the waters stagnate: when the moon declines to the north, they begin to flow and ebb, not twice, as in other ports, but once only every day; and the flood happens at the setting, and the greatest ebb at the rising of the moon. This tide increases with the declination of the moon till the seventh or eighth day; then for the seven or eight days following it decreases at the same rate as it had increased, and ceases when the moon changes its declination, crossing over the equator to the south. After which the flood is immediately changed into an ebb; and thenceforth the ebb happens at the setting and the flood at the rising of the moon; till the moon, again passing the equator, changes its declination. There are two inlets to this port and the neighboring channels, one from the seas of China, between the continent and the island of Leuconia; the other from the Indian Sea, between the continent and the island of Borneo. But whether there be really two tides propagated through the said channels, one from the Indian Sea in the space of twelve hours, and one from the sea of China in the space of six hours, which therefore happening at the third and ninth lunar hours, by being compounded together, produce those motions; or whether there be any other circumstances in the state of those seas, I leave to be determined by observations on the neighboring shores.

Thus I have explained the causes of the motions of the moon and of the sea. Now it is fit to subjoin something concerning the amount of those motions.

PROPOSITION 25. PROBLEM 6

To find the forces with which the sun disturbs the motions of the moon.

Let S represent the sun, T the earth, P the moon, CADB the moon's orbit. In SP take SK equal to ST; and let SL be to SK as the square of SK to SP: draw LM parallel to PT; and if ST or SK is supposed to represent the accelerated force of gravity of the earth towards the sun, SL will represent the accelerative force of gravity of the moon towards the sun. But that force is

compounded of the parts SM and LM, of which the force LM, and that part
of SM which is represented by TM, disturb the motion of the moon, as we have
shown in Prop. 66, Book I, and its Corollaries. Forasmuch as the earth and
moon are revolved about their common centre of gravity, the motion of the
earth about that centre will be also disturbed by the like forces; but we may
consider the sums both of the forces
and of the motions as in the moon,
and represent the sum of the forces
by the lines TM and ML, which are
analogous to them both. The force
ML (in its mean amount) is to the
centripetal force by which the moon
may be retained in its orbit revolving about the earth at rest, at the

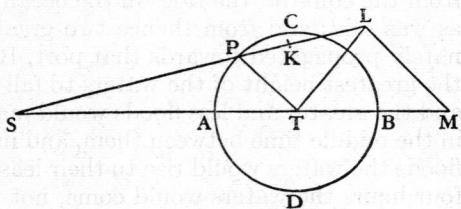

distance PT, as the square of the ratio of the periodic time of the moon about
the earth to the periodic time of the earth about the sun (by Cor. XVII, Prop.
66, Book I); that is, as the square of $27^d \cdot 7^h \cdot 43^m \cdot$ to $365^d \cdot 6^h \cdot 9^m \cdot$; or as 1000
to 178725; or as 1 to $178^{29}\!/_{40}$. But in Prop. 4 of this book we found that, if
both earth and moon were revolved about their common centre of gravity,
the mean distance of the one from the other would be nearly $60\frac{1}{2}$ mean semidiameters of the earth; and the force by which the moon may be kept revolving
in its orbit about the earth at rest at the distance PT of $60\frac{1}{2}$ semidiameters of
the earth, is to the force by which it may be revolved in the same time, at the
distance of 60 semidiameters, as $60\frac{1}{2}$ is to 60: and this force is to the force of
gravity with us very nearly as 1 is to $60 \cdot 60$. Therefore the mean force ML is
to the force of gravity on the surface of our earth as $1 \cdot 60\frac{1}{2}$ to $60 \cdot 60 \cdot 60 \cdot$
$178^{29}\!/_{40}$, or as 1 to 638092.6; hence, by the proportion of the lines TM, ML,
the force TM is also given; and these are the forces with which the sun disturbs
the motions of the moon.   Q.E.I.

PROPOSITION 26. PROBLEM 7

*To find the hourly increment of the area which the moon, by a radius drawn to
the earth, describes in a circular orbit.*

We have above shown that the area which the moon describes by a radius
drawn to the earth is proportional to the time of description, excepting so far
as the moon's motion is disturbed by the action of the sun; and here we propose
to investigate the inequality of the moment, or hourly increment *of that area or
motion so disturbed*. To render the calculus more easy, we shall suppose the
orbit of the moon to be circular, and neglect all inequalities but that only
which is now under consideration; and, because of the immense distance of the
sun, we shall further suppose that the lines SP and ST are parallel. By this
means, the force LM will be always reduced to its mean amount TP, as well as
the force TM to its mean amount 3PK. These forces (by Cor. II of the Laws of
Motion) compose the force TL; and this force, by letting fall the perpendicular
LE upon the radius TP, is resolved into the forces TE, EL; of which the force
TE, acting constantly in the direction of the radius TP, neither accelerates nor
retards the description of the area TPC made by that radius TP; but EL,
acting on the radius TP *in a perpendicular direction, accelerates or retards the
description of the area* in proportion as it accelerates or retards the moon. That

acceleration of the moon, in its passage from the quadrature C to the conjunction A, is in every moment of time as the *generating* accelerative force EL, that is, as $\dfrac{3PK \cdot TK}{TP}$. Let the time be represented by the mean motion of the moon, or (which comes to the same thing) by the angle CTP, or even by the arc CP. At right angles upon CT erect CG equal to CT; and, supposing the

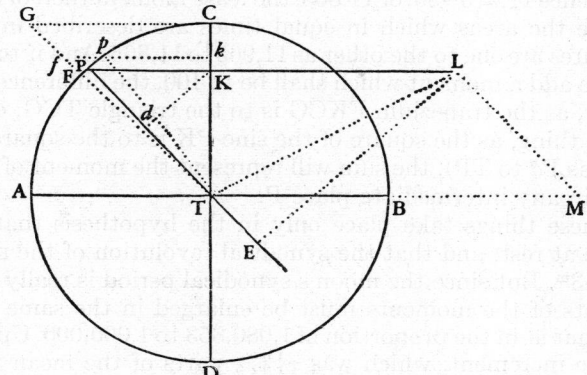

quadrantal arc AC to be divided into an infinite number of equal parts P*p*, &c., these *parts* may represent the like *infinite* number of the equal parts of time. Let fall *pk* perpendicular on CT, and draw TG meeting with KP, *kp* produced in F and *f*; then will FK be equal to TK, and K*k* be to PK as P*p* is to T*p*, that is, in a given proportion; and therefore FK·K*k*, or the area FK*kf*, will be as $\dfrac{3PK \cdot TK}{TP}$, that is, as EL; and, compounding, the whole area GCKF will vary as the sum of all the forces EL impressed upon the moon in the whole time CP; and therefore also as the velocity generated by that sum, that is, as the acceleration of the description of the area CTP, or as the increment of the moment *thereof*. The force by which the moon may in its periodic time CADB of 27^d. 7^h. 43^m. be retained revolving about the earth at rest at the distance TP, would cause a body falling in the time CT to describe the length ½CT, and at the same time to acquire a velocity equal to that with which the moon is moved in its orbit. This appears from Cor. IX, Prop. 4, Book I. But since K*d*, drawn perpendicular on TP, is *but* a third part of EL, and *equal* to the half of TP, or ML, in the octants, the force EL in the octants, where it is greatest, will exceed the force ML in the ratio of 3 to 2; and therefore will be to that force by which the moon in its periodic time may be retained revolving about the earth at rest as 100 is to ⅔·17872½, or 11915; and in the time CT will generate a velocity equal to $\frac{100}{11915}$ parts of the velocity of the moon; but in the time CPA will generate a greater velocity in the proportion of CA to CT or TP. Let the greatest EL force in the octants be represented by the area FK·K*k*, or by the rectangle ½TP·P*p*, which is equal thereto; and the velocity which that greatest force can generate in any time CP will be to the velocity which any other lesser force EL can generate in the same time as the rectangle ½TP·CP to the area KCGF; but the velocities generated in the whole time CPA will be one to the other as the rectangle ½TP·CA is to the triangle TCG, or as the quadrantal arc CA is to the radius TP; and therefore the latter velocity generated in the whole time will be $\frac{100}{11915}$ parts of the velocity of the moon. To this velocity of the moon, which is proportional to the mean moment of the area (supposing this mean moment to be represented by the number 11,915), we add and subtract the half of the other velocity; the sum 11,915+50, or 11,965, will represent the greatest moment of the area in the syzygy A; and the difference 11,915−50, or 11,865, the least moment thereof in the quadratures. Therefore the areas which in equal times are described in the syzygies and quadratures are one to the other as 11,965 to 11,865. And if to the least moment 11,865 we add a moment which shall be to 100, the difference of the two former moments, as the trapezium FKCG is to the triangle TCG, or, which comes to the same thing, as the square of the sine PK is to the square of the radius TP (that is, as Pd to TP), the sum will represent the moment of the area when the moon is in any intermediate place P.

But these things take place only in the hypothesis that the sun and the earth are at rest, and that the synodical revolution of the moon is finished in 27^{d}. 7^{h}. 43^{m}. But since the moon's synodical period is really 29^{d}. 12^{h}. 44^{m}., the increments of the moments must be enlarged in the same proportion as the time is, that is, in the proportion of 1,080,853 to 1,000,000. Upon which account, the whole increment, which was $\frac{100}{11915}$ parts of the mean moment, will now become $\frac{100}{11023}$ parts thereof; and therefore the moment of the area in the quadrature of the moon will be to the moment thereof in the syzygy as 11,023−50 to 11,023+50; or as 10,973 to 11,073; and to the moment thereof, when the moon is in any intermediate place P, as 10,973 to 10,973+Pd; that is, supposing TP = 100.

The area, therefore, which the moon, by a radius drawn to the earth, describes in the several little equal parts of time, is nearly as the sum of the number 219.46, and the versed sine of the double distance of the moon from the nearest quadrature, considered in a circle which hath unity for its radius. Thus it is when the variation in the octants is in its mean quantity. But if the variation there is greater or less, that versed sine must be augmented or diminished in the same proportion.

PROPOSITION 27. PROBLEM 8

From the hourly motion of the moon to find its distance from the earth.
The area which the moon, by a radius drawn to the earth, describes in every moment of time, is as the hourly motion of the moon and the square of the distance of the moon from the earth conjointly. And therefore the distance of the moon from the earth varies directly as the square root of the area and inversely as the square root of the hourly motion, taken jointly.   Q.E.I.

Cor. I. Hence the apparent diameter of the moon is given; for it is inversely as the distance of the moon from the earth. Let astronomers try how accurately this rule agrees with the phenomena.

Cor. II. Hence also the orbit of the moon may be more exactly defined from the phenomena than hitherto could be done.

PROPOSITION 28. PROBLEM 9

To find the diameters of the orbit, in which, without eccentricity, the moon would move.
The curvature of the orbit which a body describes, if attracted in lines perpendicular to the orbit, is directly as the force of attraction, and inversely as

the square of the velocity. I estimate the curvatures of lines compared one with another according to the evanescent ratio of the sines or tangents of their angles of contact to equal radii, supposing those radii to be infinitely diminished. But the attraction of the moon towards the earth in the syzygies is the excess of its gravity towards the earth above the force of the sun 2PK (see Fig., Prop. 25), by which force the accelerative gravity of the moon towards the sun exceeds the accelerative gravity of the earth towards the sun or is exceeded by it. But in the quadratures that attraction is the sum of the gravity of the moon towards the earth, and the sun's force KT, by which the moon is attracted towards the earth. And these attractions, putting N for $\dfrac{AT+CT}{2}$,

are nearly as $\dfrac{178725}{AT^2} - \dfrac{2000}{CT \cdot N}$ and $\dfrac{178725}{CT^2} + \dfrac{1000}{AT \cdot N}$, or as $178{,}725N \cdot CT^2 - 2000AT^2 \cdot CT$, and $178{,}725N \cdot AT^2 + 1000CT^2 \cdot AT$. For if the accelerative gravity of the moon towards the earth be represented by the number 178,725, the mean force ML, which in the quadratures is PT or TK, and draws the moon towards the earth, will be 1000, and the mean force TM in the syzygies will be 3000; from which, if we subtract the mean force ML, there will remain 2000, the force by which the moon in the syzygies is drawn from the earth, and which we above called 2PK. But the velocity of the moon in the syzygies A and B is to its velocity in the quadratures C and D as CT is to AT, and as the moment of the area, which the moon by a radius drawn to the earth describes in the syzygies, is to the moment of that area *described* in the quadratures conjointly; that is, as 11,073CT is to 10,973AT. Take the square of this ratio inversely, and the former ratio directly, and the curvature of the moon's orbit in the syzygies will be to the curvature thereof in the quadratures as $120{,}406{,}729 \cdot 178{,}725AT^2 \cdot CT^2 \cdot N - 120{,}406{,}729 \cdot 2000AT^4 \cdot CT$ is to $122{,}611{,}329 \cdot 178{,}725AT^2 \cdot CT^2 \cdot N + 122{,}611{,}329 \cdot 1000CT^4 \cdot AT$, that is, as $2{,}151{,}969AT \cdot CT \cdot N - 24{,}081AT^3$ is to $2{,}191{,}371AT \cdot CT \cdot N + 12{,}261CT^3$.

Because the figure of the moon's orbit is unknown, let us, in its stead, assume the ellipse DBCA, in the centre of which we suppose the earth to be situated, and the greater axis DC to lie between the quadratures as the lesser AB between the syzygies. But since the plane of this ellipse is revolved about the earth by an angular motion, and the orbit,

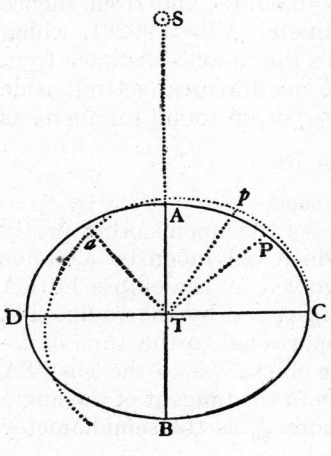

whose curvature we now examine, should be described in a plane void of such motion, we are to consider the figure which the moon, while it is revolved in that ellipse, describes in this plane, that is to say, the figure C*pa*, the several points *p* of which are found by assuming any point P in the ellipse, which may represent the place of the moon, and drawing T*p* equal to TP in such manner that the angle PT*p* may be equal to the apparent motion of the sun from the time of the last quadrature in C; or (which comes to the same thing) that the angle CT*p* may be to the angle CTP as the time of the synodic revolution of the moon to the time of the periodic revolution thereof, or as 29^d. 12^h. 44^m. to 27^d.

7^{h}. 43^{m}. If, therefore, in this proportion we take the angle CTa to the right angle CTA, and make Ta of equal length with TA, we shall have a the lower and C the upper apse of this orbit Cpa. But, by computation, I find that the difference between the curvature of this orbit Cpa at the vertex a, and the curvature of a circle described about the centre T with the interval TA, is to the difference between the curvature of the ellipse at the vertex A, and the curvature of the same circle, as the square of the ratio of the angle CTP to the angle CTp; and that the curvature of the ellipse in A is to the curvature of that circle as the square of the ratio of TA is to TC; and the curvature of that circle is to the curvature of a circle described about the centre T with the radius TC as TC is to TA; but that the curvature of this *last arch* is to the curvature of the ellipse in C as the square of the ratio of TA is to TC; and that the difference between the curvature of the ellipse in the vertex C, and the curvature of this last circle, is to the difference between the curvature of the figure Tpa, at the vertex C, and the curvature of this same *last* circle, as the square of the ratio of the angle CTp to the angle CTP. All these relations are easily derived from the sines of the angles of contact, and of the differences of those angles. But, by comparing those ratios, we find the curvature of the figure Cpa at a to be to its curvature at C as $AT^3 - \frac{16824}{100000} CT^2 \cdot AT$ is to $CT^3 + \frac{16824}{100000} AT^2 \cdot CT$; where the number $\frac{16824}{100000}$ represents the difference of the squares of the angles CTP and CTp, divided by the square of the lesser angle CTP; or (which is all one) the difference of the squares of the times 27^{d}. 7^{h}. 43^{m}. and 29^{d}. 12^{h}. 44^{m}. divided by the square of the time 27^{d}. 7^{h}. 43^{m}.

Since, therefore, a represents the syzygy of the moon, and C its quadrature, the ratio now found must be the same as the ratio of the curvature of the moon's orb in the syzygies to the curvature thereof in the quadratures, which we found above. Therefore, in order to find the ratio of CT to AT, let us multiply the extremes and the means of the resulting proportion, and the terms which come out, divided by AT·CT, yield the following equation: $2062.79CT^4 - 2,151,969N \cdot CT^3 + 368,676N \cdot AT \cdot CT^2 + 36,342AT^2 \cdot CT^2 - 362,047N \cdot AT^2 \cdot CT + 2,191,371N \cdot AT^3 + 4051.4AT^4 = 0$. Now if for the half sum N of the terms AT and CT we put 1, and x for their half difference, then CT will be $= 1 + x$, and $AT = 1 - x$. And substituting those values in the equation, after resolving thereof, we shall find $x = 0.00719$; and from thence the semidiameter $CT = 1.00719$, and the semidiameter $AT = 0.99281$, which numbers are nearly as $70\frac{1}{24}$, and $69\frac{1}{24}$. Therefore the moon's distance from the earth in the syzygies is to its distance in the quadratures (setting aside the consideration of eccentricity) as $69\frac{1}{24}$ to $70\frac{1}{24}$; or, in round numbers, as 69 to 70.

PROPOSITION 29. PROBLEM 10

To find the variation of the moon.

This inequality is due partly to the elliptic figure of the moon's orbit, partly to the inequality of the moments of the area which the moon by a radius drawn to the earth describes. If the moon P revolved in the ellipse DBCA about the earth quiescent in the centre of the ellipse, and by the radius TP, drawn to the earth, described the area CTP, proportional to the time *of description;* and the greatest semidiameter CT of the ellipse was to the least TA as 70 to 69; the tangent of the angle CTP would be to the tangent of the angle of the mean motion, computed from the quadrature C, as the semidiameter

TA of the ellipse to its semidiameter TC, or as 69 to 70. But the description of the area CTP as the moon advances from the quadrature to the syzygy, ought to be in such manner accelerated, that the moment of the area in the moon's syzygy may be to the moment thereof in its quadrature as 11,073 to 10,973; and that the excess of the moment in any intermediate place P above the moment in the quadrature may be as the square of the sine of the angle CTP; which we may effect with accuracy enough, if we diminish the tangent of the angle CTP in the ratio obtained from the square root of the ratio of the number 10,973 to the number 11,073, that is, in the ratio of the number 68.6877 to the number 69. On this account the tangent of the angle CTP will now be to the tangent of the mean motion as 68.6877 is to 70; and the angle CTP in the octants, where the mean motion is 45°, will be found 44° 27′ 28″, which subtracted from 45°, the angle of the mean motion, leaves the greatest variation 32′ 32″. Thus it would be, if the moon, in passing from the quadrature to the syzygy, described an angle CTA of 90° only. But because of the motion of the earth, by which the sun is apparently transferred forwards, the moon, before it overtakes the sun, describes an angle CT*a*, greater than a right angle, in the ratio of the time of the synodic revolution of the moon to the time of its periodic revolution, that is, in the ratio of 29ᵈ. 12ʰ. 44ᵐ. to 27ᵈ. 7ʰ. 43ᵐ. Whence it comes to pass that all the angles about the centre T are dilated in the same ratio; and the greatest variation, which otherwise would be *but* 32′ 32″, now augmented in the said proportion, becomes 35′ 10″.

And this is its magnitude in the mean distance of the sun from the earth, neglecting the differences which may arise from the curvature of the great orbit, and the stronger action of the sun upon the moon when horned and new, than when gibbous and full. In other distances of the sun from the earth, the greatest variation is in a ratio compounded, directly of the square of the ratio of the time of the synodic revolution of the moon (the time of the year being given), and inversely as the cube of the ratio of the distance of the sun from the earth. And, therefore, in the apogee of the sun, the greatest variation is 33′ 14″, and in its perigee 37′ 11″, if the eccentricity of the sun is to the transverse semidiameter of the great orbit as $16^{15}/_{16}$ to 1000.

Hitherto we have investigated the variation in an orbit not eccentric, in which, to wit, the moon in its octants is always in its mean distance from the earth. If the moon, on account of its eccentricity, is more or less removed from the earth than if placed in this orbit, the variation may be something greater, or something less, than according to this rule. But I leave the excess or defect to the determination of astronomers from the phenomena.

PROPOSITION 30. PROBLEM 11

To find the hourly motion of the nodes of the moon in a circular orbit.

Let S represent the sun, T the earth, P the moon, NP*n* the orbit of the moon, N*pn* the orthographic projection of the orbit upon the plane of the ecliptic; N, *n* the nodes, *n*TN*m* the line of the nodes produced indefinitely; PI, PK perpendiculars upon the lines ST, Q*q*; P*p* a perpendicular upon the plane of the ecliptic; A, B the moon's syzygies in the plane of the ecliptic; AZ a perpendicular let fall upon N*n*, the line of the nodes; Q, *q* the quadratures of the moon in the plane of the ecliptic, and *p*K a perpendicular on the line Q*q* lying between the quadratures. The force of the sun to disturb the motion of the moon

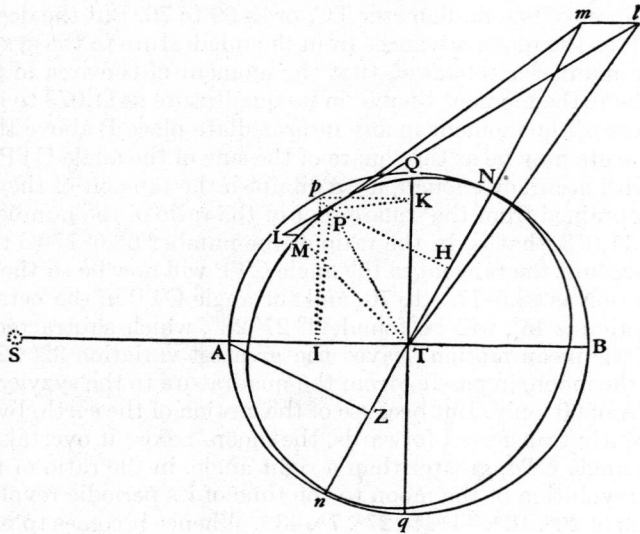

(by Prop. 25) is twofold, one proportional to the line LM, the other to the line
MT, in the scheme of that Proposition; and the moon by the former force is
drawn towards the earth, by the latter towards the sun, in a direction parallel
to the right line ST joining the earth and the sun. The former force LM acts in
the direction of the plane of the moon's orbit, and therefore makes no change
upon the situation thereof, and is upon that account to be neglected; the latter
force MT, by which the plane of the moon's orbit is disturbed, is the same with
the force 3PK or 3IT. And this force (by Prop. 25) is to the force by which the
moon may, in its periodic times, be uniformly revolved in a circle about the
earth at rest, as 3IT to the radius of the circle multiplied by the number
178.725, or as IT to the radius thereof multiplied by 59.575. But in this calculus, and all that follows, I consider all the lines drawn from the moon to the
sun as parallel to the line which joins the earth and the sun; because what
inclination there is almost as much diminishes all effects in some cases as it
augments them in others; and we are now inquiring after the mean motions
of the nodes, neglecting such niceties as are of no moment and would only serve
to render the calculus more complicated.

Now suppose PM to represent an arc which the moon describes in the least
moment of time, and ML a little line, the half of which the moon, by the impulse of the said force 3IT, would describe in the same time; and joining PL,
MP, let them be produced to m and l, where they cut the plane of the ecliptic,
and upon Tm let fall the perpendicular PH. Now, since the right line ML is
parallel to the plane of the ecliptic, and therefore can never meet with the right
line ml which lies in that plane, and yet both those right lines lie in one common
plane LMPml, they will be parallel, and upon that account the triangles LMP,
lmP will be similar. And seeing MPm lies in the plane of the orbit, in which the
moon did move while in the place P, the point m will fall upon the line Nn,
which passes through the nodes N, n, of that orbit. And because the force by
which the half of the little line LM is generated, if the whole had been together,

and at once impressed in the point P, would have generated that whole line, and caused the moon to move in the arc whose chord is LP; that is to say, would have transferred the moon from the plane MPmT into the plane LPlT; therefore the angular motion of the nodes generated by that force will be equal to the angle mTl. But ml is to mP as ML to MP; and since MP, because of the time given, is also given, ml will be as the rectangle ML$\cdot m$P, that is, as the rectangle IT$\cdot m$P. And if Tml is a right angle, the angle mTl will be as $\dfrac{ml}{\mathrm{T}m}$, and

therefore as $\dfrac{\mathrm{IT}\cdot\mathrm{P}m}{\mathrm{T}m}$, that is (because T$m$ and mP, TP and PH are propor-

tional), as $\dfrac{\mathrm{IT}\cdot\mathrm{PH}}{\mathrm{TP}}$; and, therefore, because TP is given, as IT$\cdot$PH. But if the

angle Tml or STN is oblique, the angle mTl will be yet less, in proportion of the sine of the angle STN to the radius, or AZ to AT. And therefore the velocity of the nodes is as IT$\cdot$PH$\cdot$AZ, or as the product of the sines of the three angles TPI, PTN, and STN.

If these are right angles, as happens when the nodes are in the quadratures, and the moon in the syzygy, the little line ml will be removed to an infinite distance, and the angle mTl will become equal to the angle mPl. But in this case the angle mPl is to the angle PTM, which the moon in the same time by its apparent motion describes about the earth, as 1 to 59.575. For the angle mPl is equal to the angle LPM, that is, to the angle of the moon's deflection from a rectilinear path; which angle, if the gravity of the moon should have then ceased, the said force of the sun 3IT would by itself have generated in that given time; and the angle PTM is equal to the angle of the moon's deflection from a rectilinear path; which angle, if the force of the sun 3IT should have then ceased, the force alone by which the moon is retained in its orbit would have generated in the same time. And these forces (as we have above shown) are the one to the other as 1 to 59.575. Since, therefore, the mean hourly motion of the moon (in respect of the fixed stars) is $32^{\mathrm{m}}\ 56^{\mathrm{s}}\ 27^{\mathrm{th}}\ 12\frac{1}{2}^{\mathrm{iv}}$ the hourly motion of the node in this case will be $33^{\mathrm{s}}\ 10^{\mathrm{th}}\ 33^{\mathrm{iv}}\ 12^{\mathrm{v}}$. But in other cases the hourly motion will be to $33^{\mathrm{s}}\ 10^{\mathrm{th}}\ 33^{\mathrm{iv}}\ 12^{\mathrm{v}}$ as the product of the sines of the three angles TPI, PTN, and STN (or of the distances of the moon from the quadrature, of the moon from the node, and of the node from the sun) to the cube of the radius. And as often as the sine of any angle is changed from positive to negative, and from negative to positive, so often must the regressive be changed into a progressive, and the progressive into a regressive motion. Whence it comes to pass that the nodes are progressive as often as the moon happens to be placed between either quadrature, and the node nearest to that quadrature. In other cases they are regressive, and by the excess of the regress above the progress, they are monthly transferred backwards.

Cor. i. Hence if from P and M, the extreme points of a least arc PM, on the line Qq joining the quadratures we let fall the perpendiculars PK, Mk, and produce the same till they cut the line of the nodes Nn in D and d, the hourly motion of the nodes will be as the area MPDd, and the square of the line AZ, conjointly. For let PK, PH, and AZ be the three said sines, viz., PK the sine of the distance of the moon from the quadrature, PH the sine of the distance of the moon from the node, and AZ the sine of the distance of the node from the sun; and the velocity of the node will be as the product PK$\cdot$PH$\cdot$AZ. But

PT is to PK as PM to Kk; and, therefore, because PT and PM are given, Kk will be as PK. Likewise AT is to PD as AZ is to PH, and therefore PH is as the rectangle PD·AZ; and, by compounding those proportions, PK·PH is as the solid content Kk·PD·AZ, and PK·PH·AZ as Kk·PD·AZ²; that is, as the area PDdM and AZ² conjointly.   Q.E.D.

Cor. II. In any given position of the nodes their mean hourly motion is half their hourly motion in the moon's syzygies; and therefore is to 16ˢ 35ᵗʰ 16ⁱᵛ 36ᵛ as the square of the sine of the distance of the nodes from the syzygies is to the square of the radius, or as AZ² to AT². For if the moon, by an uniform motion, describes the semicircle QAq, the sum of all the areas PDdM, during the time of the moon's passage from Q to M, will make up the area QMdE, terminating at the tangent QE of the circle; and by the time that the moon has arrived at the point n, that sum will make up the whole area EQAn described by the line PD: but when the moon proceeds from n to q, the line PD will fall without the circle, and describe the area nqe, terminating at the tangent qe of the circle, which area, because the nodes were before regressive, but are now progressive,

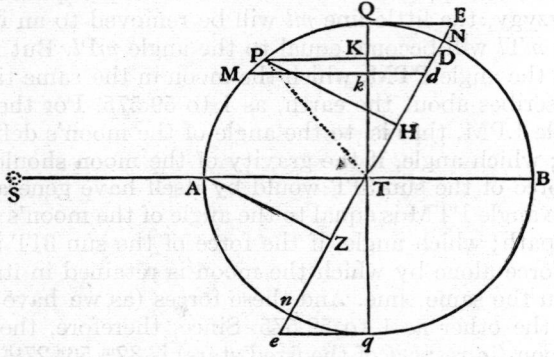

must be subtracted from the former area, and, being itself equal to the area QEN, will leave the semicircle NQAn. While, therefore, the moon describes a semicircle, the sum of all the areas PDdM will be the area of that semicircle; and while the moon describes a complete circle, the sum of those areas will be the area of the whole circle. But the area PDdM, when the moon is in the syzygies, is the rectangle of the arc PM into the radius PT; and the sum of all the areas, *every one* equal to this area, in the time that the moon describes a complete circle, is the rectangle of the whole circumference into the radius of the circle; and this rectangle, being double the area of the circle, will be double the former sum. If, therefore, the nodes went on with that velocity uniformly continued which they acquire in the moon's syzygies, they would describe a space double that which they describe in fact; and, therefore, the mean motion, by which, if uniformly continued, they would describe the same space with that which they do in fact describe by an unequal motion, is *but* one-half of that motion which they are possessed of in the moon's syzygies. Wherefore, since their greatest hourly motion, if the nodes are in the quadratures, is 33ˢ 10ᵗʰ 33ⁱᵛ 12ᵛ, their mean hourly motion in this case will be 16ˢ 35ᵗʰ 16ⁱᵛ 36ᵛ. And seeing the hourly motion of the nodes is everywhere as AZ² and the area PDdM conjointly, and, therefore, in the moon's syzygies, the hourly motion of the nodes is as AZ² and the area PDdM conjointly, that is (because the area PDdM described in the syzygies is given), as AZ², therefore the mean motion also will be as AZ²; and, therefore, when the nodes are without the quadratures, this motion will be to 16ˢ 35ᵗʰ 16ⁱᵛ 36ᵛ as AZ² to AT².   Q.E.D.

PROPOSITION 31. PROBLEM 12

To find the hourly motion of the nodes of the moon in an elliptic orbit.

Let Q$pmaq$ represent an ellipse described with the greater axis Qq and the less axis ab; QAqB a circle circumscribed; T the earth in the common centre of both; S the sun; p the moon moving in this ellipse; and pm an arc which it describes in the least moment of time; N and n the nodes joined by the line Nn; pK and mk perpendiculars upon the axis Qq, produced both ways till they meet the circle in P and M, and the line of the nodes in D and d. And if the moon, by a radius drawn to the earth, describes an area proportional to the time *of description*, the hourly motion of the node in the ellipse will be as the area pDdm and AZ² conjointly.

For let PF touch the circle in P, and produced meet TN in F; and pf touch the ellipse in p, and produced meet the same TN in f, and both tangents concur in the axis TQ at Y; and let ML represent the space which the moon, by the impulse of the above-mentioned force 3IT or 3PK, would describe with a transverse motion, in the meantime while revolving in the circle it describes the arc PM; and ml denote the space which the moon revolving in the ellipse would describe in the same time by the impulse of the same force 3IT or 3PK; and let LP and lp be produced till they meet the plane of the ecliptic in G and g, and FG and fg be joined, of which FG produced may cut pf, pg, and TQ, in

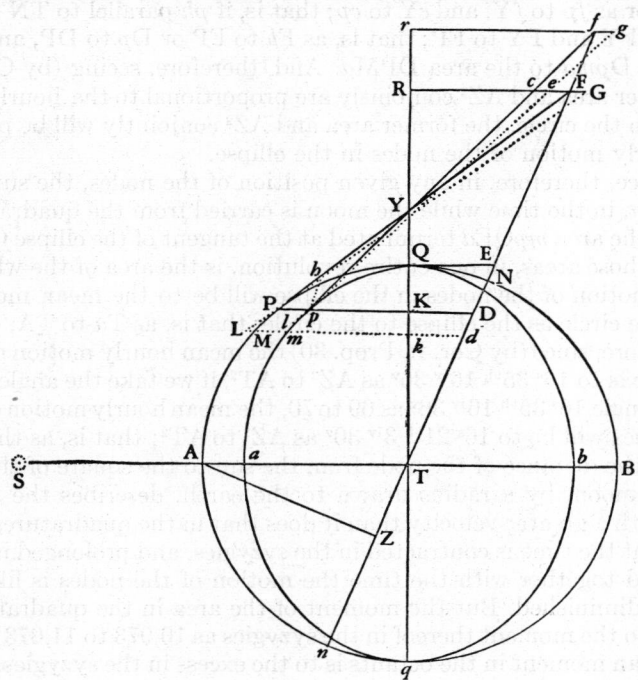

c, e, and R respectively; and fg produced may cut TQ in r. Because the force 3IT or 3PK in the circle is to the force 3IT or $3pK$ in the ellipse as PK to pK, or as AT to aT, the space ML generated by the former force will be to the space ml generated by the latter as PK to pK; that is, because of the similar figures PYKp and FYRc, as FR to cR. But (because of the similar triangles PLM, PGF) ML is to FG as PL is to PG, that is (on account of the parallels Lk, PK, GR), as pl is to pe, that is (because of the similar triangles plm, cpe), as lm is to ce; and inversely as LM is to lm, or as FR is to cR, so is FG to ce. And therefore if fg was to ce as fy to cY, that is, as fr to cR (that is, as fr to FR and FR to cR conjointly, that is, as fT to FT, and FG to ce conjointly), because the ratio of FG to ce, expunged on both sides, leaves the ratios fg to FG and fT to FT, fg would be to FG as fT to FT; and, therefore, the angles which FG and fg would subtend at the earth T would be equal to each other. But these angles (by what we have shown in the preceding Proposition) are the motions of the nodes, while the moon describes in the circle the arc PM, in the ellipse the arc pm; and therefore the motions of the nodes in the circle and in the ellipse would be equal to each other. Thus, I say, it would be, if fg was to ce as fY to cY, that is, if fg was equal to $\dfrac{ce \cdot f\text{Y}}{c\text{Y}}$. But because of the similar triangles fgp, cep, fg is to ce as fp to cp; and therefore fg is equal to $\dfrac{ce \cdot fp}{cp}$; and therefore the angle which fg subtends in fact is to the former angle which FG subtends, that is to say, the motion of the nodes in the ellipse is to the motion of the same in the circle as this fg or $\dfrac{ce \cdot fp}{cp}$ to the former fg or $\dfrac{ce \cdot f\text{Y}}{c\text{Y}}$, that is, as $fp \cdot c$Y to fY$\cdot cp$, or as fp to fY, and cY to cp; that is, if ph parallel to TN meet FP in h, as Fh to FY and FY to FP; that is, as Fh to FP or Dp to DP, and therefore as the area Dpmd to the area DPMd. And, therefore, seeing (by Cor. I, Prop. 30) the latter area and AZ² conjointly are proportional to the hourly motion of the nodes in the circle, the former area and AZ² conjointly will be proportional to the hourly motion of the nodes in the ellipse.   Q.E.D.

COR. Since, therefore, in any given position of the nodes, the sum of all the areas pDdm, in the time while the moon is carried from the quadrature to any place m, is the area mpQEd terminated at the tangent of the ellipse QE; and the sum of all those areas, in one entire revolution, is the area of the whole ellipse; the mean motion of the nodes in the ellipse will be to the mean motion of the nodes in the circle as the ellipse to the circle; that is, as Ta to TA, or 69 to 70. And, therefore, since (by Cor. II, Prop. 30) the mean hourly motion of the nodes in the circle is to 16^s 35th 16^{iv} 36^v as AZ² to AT², if we take the angle 16^s 21th 3^{iv} 30^v to the angle 16^s 35th 16^{iv} 36^v as 69 to 70, the mean hourly motion of the nodes in the ellipses will be to 16^s 21th 3^{iv} 30^v as AZ² to AT²; that is, as the square of the sine of the distance of the node from the sun to the square of the radius.

But the moon, by a radius drawn to the earth, describes the area in the syzygies with a greater velocity than it does that in the quadratures, and upon that account the time is contracted in the syzygies, and prolonged in the quadratures; and together with the time the motion of the nodes is likewise augmented or diminished. But the moment of the area in the quadratures of the moon was to the moment thereof in the syzygies as 10,973 to 11,073; and therefore the mean moment in the octants is to the excess in the syzygies, and to the defect in the quadratures, as 11,023, the half-sum of those numbers, is to their half-difference 50. Wherefore, since the time of the moon in the several little equal parts of its orbit is inversely as its velocity, the mean time in the octants will be to the excess of the time in the quadratures, and to the defect *of the time* in the syzygies arising from this cause, nearly as 11,023 to 50. But, reckoning from the quadratures to the syzygies, I find that the excess of the moments of the area, in the several places above the least moment in the quadratures, is nearly as the square of the sine of the moon's distance from the quadratures; and therefore the difference between the moment in any place, and the mean moment in the octants, is as the difference between the square of the sine of the moon's distance from the quadratures, and the square of the sine of 45 degrees, or half the square of the radius; and the increment of the time in the several places between the octants and quadratures, and the decrement thereof between the octants and syzygies, is in the same proportion. But the motion of the nodes, while the moon describes the several little equal parts of its orbit, is accelerated or retarded as the square of the time; for that motion, while the moon describes PM, is (other things being equal) as ML, and ML varies as the square of the time. Wherefore, the motion of the nodes in the syzygies, in the time while the moon describes given little parts of its orbit, is diminished as the square of the ratio of the number 11,073 to the number 11,023; and the decrement is to the remaining motion as 100 to 10,973; but to the whole motion is as 100 to 11,073, nearly. But the decrement in the places between the octants and syzygies, and the increment in the places between the octants and quadratures, is to this decrement nearly as the whole motion in these places to the whole motion in the syzygies, and the difference between the square of the sine of the moon's distance from the quadrature, and the half-square of the radius, is to the half-square of the radius conjointly. Wherefore, if the nodes are in the quadratures, and we take two places, one on one side, one on the other, equally distant from the octant and other two distant by the same interval, one from the syzygy, the other from the quadrature, and from the decrements of the motions in the two places between the syzygy and octant we subtract the increments of the motions in the two other places between the octant and the quadrature, the remaining decrement will be equal to the decrement in the syzygy, as will easily appear by computation; and therefore the mean decrement, which ought to be subtracted from the mean motion of the nodes, is the fourth part of the decrement in the syzygy. The whole hourly motion of the nodes in the syzygies (when the moon by a radius drawn to the earth was supposed to describe an area proportional to the time) was $32^s \, 42^{th} \, 7^{iv}$. And we have shown that the decrement of the motion of the nodes, in the time while the moon, now moving with greater velocity, describes the same space, was to this motion as 100 to 11,073; and therefore this decrement is $17^{th} \, 43^{iv} \, 11^v$. The fourth part of which $4^{th} \, 25^{iv} \, 48^v$ subtracted from the mean hourly motion above found, $16^s \, 21^{th} \, 3^{iv} \, 30^v$, leaves $16^s \, 16^{th} \, 37^{iv} \, 42^v$, their correct mean hourly motion.

If the nodes are without the quadratures, and two places are considered, one on one side, one on the other, equally distant from the syzygies, the sum of the motions of the nodes, when the moon is in those places, will be to the sum of their motions, when the moon is in the same places and the nodes in the quadratures, as AZ^2 to AT^2. And the decrements of the motions arising from the causes but now explained will be mutually as the motions themselves, and therefore the remaining motions will be mutually between themselves as AZ^2 to AT^2; and the mean motions will be as the remaining motions. And, therefore, in any given position of the nodes, their correct mean hourly motion is to 16^s 16th 37^{iv} 42^v as AZ^2 to AT^2; that is, as the square of the sine of the distance of the nodes from the syzygies to the square of the radius.

PROPOSITION 32. PROBLEM 13

To find the mean motion of the nodes of the moon.

The yearly mean motion is the sum of all the mean hourly motions throughout the course of the year. Suppose that the node is in N, and that, after every hour is elapsed, it is drawn back again to its former place; so that, notwithstanding its proper motion, it may constantly remain in the same situation with respect to the fixed stars; while in the meantime the sun S, by the motion of the earth, is seen to leave the node, and to proceed till it completes its apparent annual course by an uniform motion. Let A*a* represent a given least arc, which the right line TS always drawn to the sun, by its intersection with the circle NA*n*, describes in the least given moment of time; and the mean hourly motion (from what we have above shown) will be as AZ^2, that is (because AZ and ZY are proportional), as the rectangle of AZ into ZY, that is, as the area AZY*a*; and the sum of all the mean hourly motions from the beginning will be as the sum of all the areas *a*YZA, that is, as the area NAZ. But the greatest AZY*a* is equal to the rectangle of the arc A*a* into the radius of the circle; and therefore the sum of all these rectangles in the whole circle will be to the like sum of all the greatest rectangles as the area of the whole circle to the rectangle of the whole circumference into the radius, that is, as 1 to 2. But the hourly motion corresponding to that greatest rectangle was 16^s 16th 37^{iv} 42^v and this motion in the complete course of the sidereal year, 365^d. 6^h. 9^s., amounts to $39°$ $38'$ $7''$ $50'''$; and therefore the half thereof, $19°$ $49'$ $3''$ $55'''$, is the mean motion of the nodes corresponding to the whole circle. And the motion of the nodes, in the time while the sun is carried from N to A, is to $19°$ $49'$ $3''$ $55'''$ as the area NAZ to the whole circle.

Thus it would be if the node was after every hour drawn back again to its former place, that so, after a complete revolution, the sun at the year's end would be found again in the same node which it had left when the year began. But, because of the motion of the node in the meantime, the sun must needs meet the node sooner; and now it remains that we compute the abbreviation of the time. Since, then, the sun, in the course of the year, travels 360 degrees, and the node in the same time by its greatest motion would be carried $39°$ $38'$ $7''$ $50'''$, or 39.6355 degrees; and the mean motion of the node in any place N is to its mean motion in its quadratures as AZ^2 to AT^2; the motion of the sun will be to the motion of the node in N as 360 AT^2 to $39.6355AZ^2$; that is, as $9.0827646AT^2$ to AZ^2. Therefore, if we suppose the circumference NA*n* of the whole circle to be divided into little equal parts, such as A*a*, the time in which the sun would describe the little arc A*a*, if the circle was quiescent, will be to the time in which it would describe the same arc, supposing the circle together with the nodes to be revolved about the centre T, inversely as $9.0827646AT^2$ to $9.0827646AT^2+AZ^2$; for the time is inversely as the velocity with which the little arc is described, and this velocity is the sum of the velocities of both sun and node. If, therefore, the sector NTA represent the time in which the sun by itself, without the motion of the node, would describe the arc NA, and the indefinitely small part ATa of the sector represent the little moment of the

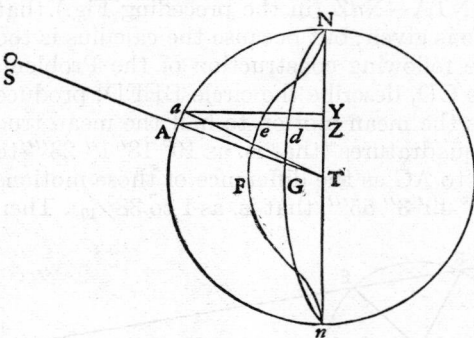

time in which it would describe the least arc Aa; and (letting fall aY perpendicular upon Nn) if in AZ we take dZ of such length that the rectangle of dZ into ZY may be to the least part ATa of the sector as AZ^2 to $9.0827646AT^2+AZ^2$; that is to say, that dZ may be to ½AZ as AT^2 to $9.0827646AT^2+AZ^2$; the rectangle of dZ into ZY will represent the decrement of the time arising from the motion of the node, while the arc Aa is described; and if the curve NdGn is the locus where the point d is always found, the curvilinear area NdZ will be as the whole decrement *of time* while the whole arc NA is described; and, therefore, the excess of the sector NAT above the area NdZ will be as the whole time. But because the motion of the node in a less time is less in proportion to the time, the area AaYZ must also be diminished in the same proportion; which may be done by taking in AZ the line eZ of such length, that it may be to the length of AZ as AZ^2 to $9.0827646AT^2+AZ^2$; for so the rectangle of eZ into ZY will be to the area AZYa as the decrement of the time in which the arc Aa is described to the whole time in which it would have been described, if the node had been quiescent; and, therefore, that rectangle will be as the decrement of the motion of the node. And if the curve NeFn is the locus of the point e, the whole area NeZ, which is the sum of all the decrements *of that motion*, will be as the whole decrement *thereof* during the time in which the arc AN is described; and the remaining area NAe will be as the remaining motion, which is the true motion of the node, during the time in which the whole arc NA is described by the joint motions of both sun and node. Now the area of the semicircle is to the area of the figure NeFn found by the method of infinite series nearly as 793 to 60. But the motion corresponding *or proportional* to the whole circle was 19° 49′ 3″ 55‴; and therefore the motion corresponding to double the figure NeFn is 1° 29′ 58″ 2‴, which taken from the former motion leaves 18° 19′ 5″ 53‴, the whole motion of the node with respect to the fixed stars in the interval between two of its conjunctions with the sun; and this motion subtracted from the annual motion of the sun, 360°, leaves 341° 40′ 54″ 7‴, the motion of the sun in the interval between the same conjunctions. But as this motion is to the annual motion 360°, so is the motion of the node but just now found 18° 19′ 5″ 53‴ to its annual motion, which will therefore be 19° 18′ 1″ 23‴; and this is the mean motion of the nodes in the sidereal year. By astronomical tables, it is 19° 21′ 21″ 50‴. The difference is less than $\frac{1}{300}$ part of the whole motion, and seems to arise from the eccentricity of the moon's orbit, and its inclination to the plane of the ecliptic. By the eccentricity of this orbit the motion of the nodes is too much accelerated; and, on the other hand, by the inclination of the orbit, the motion of the nodes is somewhat retarded, and reduced to its just velocity.

PROPOSITION 33. PROBLEM 14

To find the true motion of the nodes of the moon.

In the time which is as the area NTA−NdZ (in the preceding Fig.) that motion is as the area NAe, and hence is given; but because the calculus is too difficult, it will be better to use the following construction of the Problem. About the centre C, with any radius CD, describe the circle BEFD; produce DC to A so as AB may be to AC as the mean motion to half the mean true motion when the nodes are in their quadratures (that is, as 19° 18′ 1″ 23‴ to 19° 49′ 3″ 55‴; and therefore BC is to AC as the difference of those motions 0° 31′ 2″ 32‴ to the latter motion 19° 49′ 3″ 55‴, that is, as 1 to 38³⁄₁₀). Then through the point D draw the indefinite line Gg, touching the circle in D; and if we take the angle BCE, or BCF, equal to the double distance of the sun from the place of the node, as found by the mean motion, and drawing AE or AF cutting the perpendicular DG in G, we

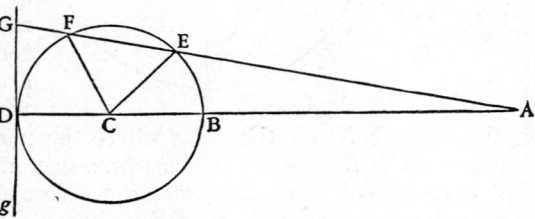

take another angle which shall be to the whole motion of the node in the interval between its syzygies (that is, to 9° 11′ 3″) as the tangent DG to the whole circumference of the circle BED, and add this *last* angle (for which the angle DAG may be used) to the mean motion of the nodes, while they are passing from the quadratures to the syzygies, and subtract it from their mean motion while they are passing from the syzygies to the quadratures, we shall have their true motion; for the true motion so found will nearly agree with the true motion which comes out from assuming the times as the area NTA−NdZ, and the motion of the node as the area NAe; as anyone who chooses to examine and make the computations will find: and this is the semimenstrual equation of the motion of the nodes. But there is also a menstrual equation, but which is by no means necessary for finding of the moon's latitude; for since the variation of the inclination of the moon's orbit to the plane of the ecliptic is liable to a twofold inequality, the one semimenstrual, the other menstrual, the menstrual inequality *of this variation*, and the menstrual equation of the nodes, so moderate and correct each other, that in computing the latitude of the moon both may be neglected.

COR. From this and the preceding Proposition it appears that the nodes are quiescent in their syzygies, but regressive in their quadratures, by an hourly motion of 16ˢ 19ᵗʰ 26ⁱᵛ; and that the equation of the motion of the nodes in the octants is 1° 30′; all of which exactly agree with the phenomena of the heavens.

SCHOLIUM

Mr. Machin, Professor Gresham, and Dr. Henry Pemberton, separately found out the motion of the nodes by a different method. Mention has been made of this method in another place. Their papers, which I have seen, contained two Propositions, and exactly agreed with each other in both of them. Mr. Machin's paper, coming first to my hands, I shall here insert.

THE MOTION OF THE MOON'S NODES

"PROPOSITION 1

"The mean motion of the sun from the node is defined by a geometric mean proportional between the mean motion of the sun and that mean motion with which the sun recedes with the greatest swiftness from the node in the quadratures.

"Let T be the earth's place, N*n* the line of the moon's nodes at any given time, KTM a perpendicular thereto, TA a right line revolving about the centre with the same angular velocity with which the sun and the node recede from each other, in such sort that the angle between the quiescent right line N*n* and the revolving line TA may be always equal to the distance of the places of the sun and node. Now if any right line TK be divided into parts TS and SK, and those parts be taken as the mean hourly motion of the sun to the mean hourly motion of the node in the quadratures, and there be taken the right line TH, a mean proportional between the part TS and the whole TK, this right line will be proportional to the sun's mean motion from the node.

"For let there be described the circle NK*n*M from the centre T and with the radius TK, and about the same centre, with the semiaxes TH and TN, let there be described an ellipse NH*n*L; and in the time in which the sun recedes from the node through the arc N*a*, if there be drawn the right line T*ba*, the area of the sector NT*a* will be the exponent of the sum of the motions of the sun and node in the same time. Let, therefore, the extremely small arc *a*A be that which the right line T*ba*, revolving according to the aforesaid law, will uniformly describe in a given interval of time, and the extremely small sector TA*a* will be as the sum of the velocities with which the sun and node are carried two different ways in that time. Now the sun's velocity is almost uniform, its inequality being so small as scarcely to produce the least inequality in the mean motion of the nodes. The other part of this sum, namely, the mean quantity of the velocity of the node, is increased in the recess from the syzygies in a squared ratio of the sine of its distance from the sun (by Cor., Prop. 31 of this book), and, being greatest in its quadratures with the sun in K, is in the same ratio to the sun's velocity as SK to TS, that is, as (the difference of the squares of TK and TH, or) the rectangle KHM to TH^2. But the ellipse NBH divides the sector AT*a*, the exponent of the sum of these two velocities, into two parts AB*ba* and BT*b*, proportional to the velocities. For, produce BT to the circle in β, and from the point B let fall upon the greater axis the perpendicular BG, which being produced both ways may meet the circle in the points F and *f*; and because the space AB*ba* is to the sector TB*b* as the rectangle ABβ is to BT^2 (that rectangle being equal to the difference of the squares of TA and TB, because the right line Aβ is equally cut in T, and unequally in B), therefore when the space AB*ba* is the greatest of all in K, this ratio will be the same as the ratio of the rectangle KHM to HT^2. But the greatest mean velocity of the node was shown above to be in that very ratio to the velocity of the sun; and therefore in

315

the quadratures the sector AT*a* is divided into parts proportional to the velocities. And because the rectangle KHM is to HT² as FB*f* to BG², and the rectangle ABβ is equal to the rectangle FB*f*, therefore the little area AB*ba*, where it is greatest, is to the remaining sector TB*b* as the rectangle ABβ is to BG². But the ratio of these little areas always was as the rectangle ABβ to BT²; and therefore the little area AB*ba* in the place A is less than its correspondent little area in the quadratures in the squared ratio of BG to BT, that is, in the squared

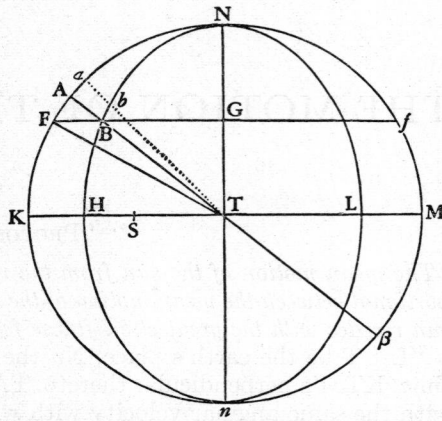

ratio of the sine of the sun's distance from the node. And therefore the sum of all the little areas AB*ba*, namely, the space ABN, will be as the motion of the node in the time in which the sun hath been going over the arc NA since he left the node; and the remaining space, namely, the elliptic sector NTB, will be as the sun's mean motion in the same time. And because the mean annual motion of the node is that motion which it performs in the time that the sun completes one period of its course, the mean motion of the node from the sun will be to the mean motion of the sun itself as the area of the circle is to the area of the ellipse; that is, as the right line TK to the right line TH, which is a mean proportional between TK and TS; or, which comes to the same, as the mean proportional TH to the right line TS.

"Proposition 2

"The mean motion of the moon's nodes being given, to find their true motion.

"Let the angle A be the distance of the sun from the mean place of the node,

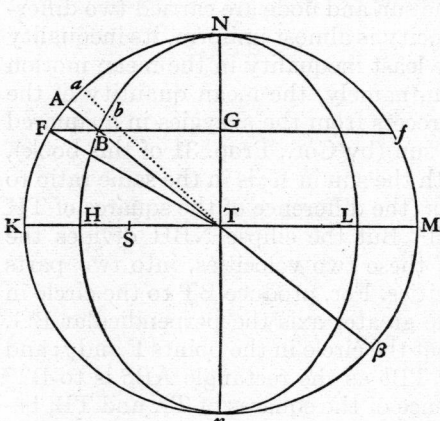

or the sun's mean motion from the node. Then if we take the angle B, whose tangent is to the tangent of the angle A as TH to TK, that is, as the square root of the ratio of the mean hourly motion of the sun to the mean hourly motion of the sun from the node, when the node is in the quadrature, that angle B will be the distance of the sun from the node's true place. For join FT, and, by the demonstration of the last Proposition, the angle FTN will be the distance of the sun from the mean place of the node, and the angle ATN the distance from the true place, and the tangents of these angles are between themselves as TK to TH.

"Cor. Hence the angle FTA is the equation of the moon's nodes; and the sine of this angle, where it is greatest in the octants, is to the radius as KH is to TK+TH. But the sine of this equation in any other place A is to the greatest sine as the sine of the sums of the angles FTN+ATN is to the radius; that is, nearly as the sine of double the distance of the sun from the mean place of the node (namely, 2FTN) to the radius.

"SCHOLIUM

"If the mean hourly motion of the nodes in the quadratures be 16″ 16‴ 37^{iv} 42^{v}, that is, in a whole sidereal year, 39° 38′ 7″ 50‴, TH will be to TK as the square root of the ratio of the number 9.0827646 to the number 10.0827646, that is, as 18.6524761 to 19.6524761. And, therefore, TH is to HK as 18.6524761 to 1; that is, as the motion of the sun in a sidereal year to the mean motion of the node 19° 18′ 1″ 23⅔‴.

"But if the mean motion of the moon's nodes in 20 Julian years is 386° 50′ 16″, as is obtained from the observations made use of in the theory of the moon, the mean motion of the nodes in one sidereal year will be 19° 20′ 31″ 58‴ and TH will be to HK as 360° to 19° 20′ 31″ 58‴; that is, as 18.61214 to 1: and from hence the mean hourly motion of the nodes in the quadratures will come out 16″ 18‴ 48^{iv}. And the greatest equation of the nodes in the octants will be 1° 29′ 57″."

PROPOSITION 34. PROBLEM 15

To find the hourly variation of the inclination of the moon's orbit to the plane of the ecliptic.

Let A and a represent the syzygies; Q and q the quadratures; N and n the nodes; P the place of the moon in its orbit; p the orthographic projection of that place upon the plane of the ecliptic; and mTl the momentary motion of the nodes as above. If upon Tm we let fall the perpendicular PG, and joining

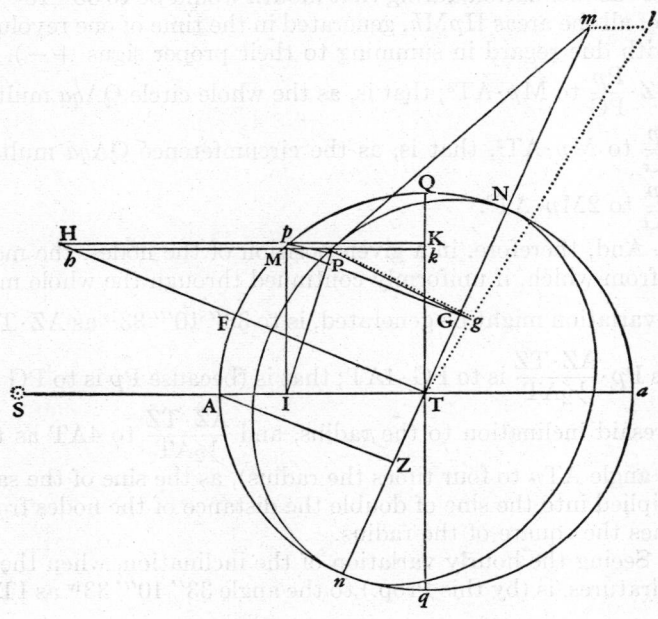

pG we produce it till it meet Tl in g, and join also Pg, the angle PGp will be the inclination of the moon's orbit to the plane of the ecliptic when the moon is in P; and the angle Pgp will be the inclination of the same after a small moment of time is elapsed; and therefore the angle GPg will be the momentary variation of the inclination. But this angle GPg is to the angle GTg as TG to PG and Pp to PG conjointly. And, therefore, if for the moment of time we assume an hour, since the angle GTg (by Prop. 30) is to the angle 33″ 10‴ 33^{iv} as IT·PG·AZ to AT^3, the angle GPg (or the hourly variation of the inclination) will be to the angle 33″ 10‴ 33^{iv} as IT·AZ·TG·$\dfrac{Pp}{PG}$ to AT^3.   Q.E.I.

And thus it would be if the moon were uniformly revolved in a circular orbit. But if the orbit is elliptical, the mean motion of the nodes will be diminished in proportion of the less axis to the greater, as we have shown above; and the variation of the inclination will be also diminished in the same proportion.

COR. I. Upon Nn erect the perpendicular TF, and let pM be the hourly motion of the moon in the plane of the ecliptic; upon QT let fall the perpendiculars pK, Mk, and produce them till they meet TF in H and h; then IT will be to AT as Kk to Mp; and TG to Hp as TZ to AT; and, therefore, IT·TG will be equal to $\dfrac{Kk \cdot Hp \cdot TZ}{Mp}$, that is, equal to the area HpMh multiplied into the ratio $\dfrac{TZ}{Mp}$: and therefore the hourly variation of the inclination will be to 33″ 10‴ 33^{iv} as the area HpMh multiplied into AZ·$\dfrac{TZ}{Mp} \cdot \dfrac{Pp}{PG}$ is to AT^3.

COR. II. And, therefore, if the earth and nodes were after every hour drawn back from their new and instantly restored to their old places, so that their situation might continue given for a whole periodic month together, the whole variation of the inclination during that month would be to 33″ 10‴ 33^{iv} as the aggregate of all the areas HpMh, generated in the time of one revolution of the point p (with due regard in summing to their proper signs $+ -$), multiplied into AZ·TZ·$\dfrac{Pp}{PG}$ to Mp·AT^3; that is, as the whole circle QAqa multiplied into AZ·TZ·$\dfrac{Pp}{PG}$ to Mp·AT^3, that is, as the circumference QAqa multiplied into AZ·TZ·$\dfrac{Pp}{PG}$ to 2Mp·AT^2.

COR. III. And, therefore, in a given position of the nodes, the mean hourly variation, from which, if uniformly continued through the whole month, that menstrual variation might be generated, is to 33″ 10‴ 33^{iv} as AZ·TZ $\dfrac{Pp}{PG}$ is to 2AT^2, or as Pp·$\dfrac{AZ·TZ}{\frac{1}{2}AT}$ is to PG·4AT; that is (because Pp is to PG as the sine of the aforesaid inclination to the radius, and $\dfrac{AZ·TZ}{\frac{1}{2}AT}$ to 4AT as the sine of double the angle ATn to four times the radius), as the sine of the same inclination multiplied into the sine of double the distance of the nodes from the sun to four times the square of the radius.

COR. IV. Seeing the hourly variation of the inclination, when the nodes are in the quadratures, is (by this Prop.) to the angle 33″ 10‴ 33^{iv} as IT·AZ·TG·

$\frac{Pp}{PG}$ is to AT³, that is, as $\frac{IT \cdot TG}{\frac{1}{2}AT} \cdot \frac{Pp}{PG}$ to 2AT, that is, as the sine of double the

distance of the moon from the quadratures multiplied into $\frac{Pp}{PG}$ is to twice the

radius, the sum of all the hourly variations during the time that the moon, in this situation of the nodes, passes from the quadrature to the syzygy (that is, in the space of 177⅙ hours) will be to the sum of as many angles 33″ 10‴ 33ⁱᵛ or 5878″, as the sum of all the sines of double the distance of the moon from the

quadratures multiplied into $\frac{Pp}{PG}$ is to the sum of as many diameters; that is, as

the diameter multiplied into $\frac{Pp}{PG}$ is to the circumference; that is, if the inclin-

ation be 5° 1′, as $7 \cdot \frac{874}{10000}$ is to 22, or as 278 to 10,000. And, therefore, the whole variation, composed out of the sum of all the hourly variations in the aforesaid time, is 163″, or 2′ 43″.

Proposition 35. Problem 16

To a given time to find the inclination of the moon's orbit to the plane of the ecliptic.

Let AD be the sine of the greatest inclination, and AB the sine of the least. Bisect BD in C; and round the centre C, with the radius BC, describe the circle

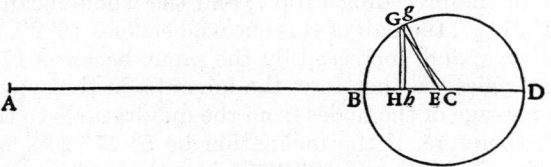

BGD. In AC take CE in the same proportion to EB as EB to twice BA. And if to the time given we set off the angle AEG equal to double the distance of the nodes from the quadratures, and upon AD let fall the perpendicular GH, AH will be the sine of the inclination required.

For GE² is equal to
$$GH^2 + HE^2 = BHD + HE^2 = HBD + HE^2 - BH^2 = HBD + BE^2 -$$
$$2BH \cdot BE = BE^2 + 2EC \cdot BH = 2EC \cdot AB + 2EC \cdot BH = 2EC \cdot AH;$$
wherefore, since 2EC is given, GE² will be as AH. Now let AEg represent double the distance of the nodes from the quadratures, in a given moment of time after, and the arc Gg, on account of the given angle GEg, will be as the distance GE. But Hh is to Gg as GH to GC, and, therefore, Hh is as the rec-

tangle GH·Gg, or GH·GE, that is, as $\frac{GH}{GE} \cdot GE^2$, or $\frac{GH}{GE} \cdot AH$; that is, as AH and

the sine of the angle AEG conjointly. If, therefore, in any one case, AH be the sine of inclination, it will increase by the same increments as the sine of inclination doth (by Cor. III of the preceding Prop.), and therefore will always continue equal to that sine. But when the point G falls upon either point B or D, AH is equal to this sine, and therefore remains always equal thereto.   Q.E.D.

In this demonstration I have supposed that the angle BEG, representing double the distance of the nodes from the quadratures, increaseth uniformly; for I cannot descend to every minute circumstance of inequality. Now suppose that BEG is a right angle, and that Gg is in this case the hourly increment of double the distance of the nodes from the sun; then (by Cor. III of the last Prop.) the hourly variation of the inclination in the same case will be to 33″ 10‴ 33^{iv} as the rectangle of AH, the sine of the inclination, into the sine of the right angle BEG, double the distance of the nodes from the sun, is to four times the square of the radius; that is, as AH, the sine of the mean inclination, is to four times the radius; that is, seeing the mean inclination is about 5° 8½′, as its sine 896 is to 40,000, the quadruple of the radius, or as 224 to 10,000. But the whole variation corresponding to BD, the difference of the sines, is to this hourly variation as the diameter BD is to the arc G*g*, that is, conjointly as the diameter BD to the semicircumference BGD, and as the time of 2079$\frac{7}{10}$ hours, in which the node proceeds from the quadratures to the syzygies, is to one hour, that is, as 7 to 11, and 2079$\frac{7}{10}$ to 1. Therefore compounding all these proportions, we shall have the whole variation BD to 33″ 10‴ 33^{iv} as 224·7· 2079$\frac{7}{10}$ is to 110,000, that is, as 29,645 to 1000; and from thence that variation BD will come out 16′ 23½″.

And this is the greatest variation of the inclination, abstracting from the situation of the moon in its orbit; for, if the nodes are in the syzygies, the inclination suffers no change from the various positions of the moon. But if the nodes are in the quadratures, the inclination is less when the moon is in the syzygies than when it is in the quadratures by a difference of 2′ 43″, as we showed (Cor. IV of the preceding Prop.); and the whole mean variation BD, diminished by 1′ 21½″, the half of this excess, becomes 15′ 2″, when the moon is in the quadratures; and, increased by the same, becomes 17′ 45″ when the moon is in the syzygies. If, therefore, the moon be in the syzygies, the whole variation in the passage of the nodes from the quadratures to the syzygies will be 17′ 45″; and, therefore, if the inclination be 5° 17′ 20″, when the nodes are in the syzygies, it will be 4° 59′ 35″ when the nodes are in the quadratures and the moon in the syzygies. The truth of all this is confirmed by observations.

Now if the inclination of the orbit should be required when the moon is in the syzygies, and the nodes anywhere between them and the quadratures, let AB be to AD as the sine of 4° 59′ 35″ is to the sine of 5° 17′ 20″, and take the angle AEG equal to double the distance of the nodes from the quadratures; and AH will be the sine of the inclination desired. To this inclination of the orbit the inclination of the same is equal, when the moon is 90° distant from the nodes. In other situations of the moon, this menstrual inequality, to which the variation of the inclination is subject in the calculus of the moon's latitude, is balanced, and in a manner taken off, by the menstrual inequality of the motion of the nodes (as we said before), and therefore may be neglected in the computation of the said latitude.

SCHOLIUM

By these computations of the lunar motions I was desirous of showing that by the theory of gravity the motions of the moon could be calculated from their physical causes. By the same theory I moreover found that the annual equation of the mean motion of the moon arises from the varying dilatation which the orbit of the moon suffers from the action of the sun according to Cor. VI, Prop. 66, Book I. The force of this action is greater in the perigean sun, and dilates the moon's orbit; in the apogean sun it is less, and permits the orbit to be again contracted. The moon moves slower in the dilated and faster in the contracted orbit; and the annual equation, by which this inequality is regulated, vanishes in the apogee and perigee of the sun. In the mean distance of the sun from the earth it rises to about 11′ 50″; in other distances of the sun it is proportional to the equation of the sun's centre, and is added to the mean motion of the moon, while the earth is passing from its aphelion to its perhelion, and subtracted while the earth is in the opposite semicircle. Taking for the radius of the great orbit 1000, and $16\frac{7}{8}$ for the earth's eccentricity, this equation, when of the greatest magnitude, by the theory of gravity comes out 11′ 49″. But the eccentricity of the earth seems to be somewhat greater, and with the eccentricity this equation will be augmented in the same proportion. Suppose the eccentricity $16\frac{11}{12}$, and the greatest equation will be 11′ 51″.

Further, I found that the apogee and nodes of the moon move faster in the perihelion of the earth, where the force of the sun's action is greater, than in the aphelion thereof, and that inversely as the cube of the ratio of the earth's distance from the sun; and hence arise annual equations of those motions proportional to the equation of the sun's centre. Now the motion of the sun varies inversely as the square of the earth's distance from the sun; and the greatest equation of the centre which this inequality generates is 1° 56′ 20″, corresponding to the above-mentioned eccentricity of the sun, $16\frac{11}{12}$. But if the motion of the sun had been inversely as the cube of the distance, this inequality would have generated the greatest equation 2° 54′ 30″; and therefore the greatest equations which the inequalities of the motions of the moon's apogee and nodes do generate are to 2° 54′ 30″ as the mean diurnal motion of the moon's apogee and the mean diurnal motion of its nodes are to the mean diurnal motion of the sun. Hence the greatest equation of the mean motion of the apogee comes out 19′ 43″, and the greatest equation of the mean motion of the nodes 9′ 24″. The former equation is added, and the latter subtracted, while the earth is passing from its perihelion to its aphelion, and contrariwise when the earth is in the opposite semicircle.

By the theory of gravity I likewise found that the action of the sun upon the moon is somewhat greater when the transverse diameter of the moon's orbit passes through the sun than when the same is perpendicular upon the line which joins the earth and the sun; and therefore the moon's orbit is somewhat larger in the former than in the latter case. And hence arises another equation of the moon's mean motion, depending upon the situation of the moon's apogee in respect of the sun, which is greatest when the moon's apogee is in the octants of the sun, and vanishes when the apogee arrives at the quadratures or syzygies; and it is added to the mean motion while the moon's apogee is passing from the quadrature of the sun to the syzygy, and subtracted while the apogee is passing from the syzygy to the quadrature. This equation, which I shall call the semiannual, when greatest in the octants of the apogee, arises to about 3′ 45″, so far as I could determine from the phenomena: and this is its quantity in the mean distance of the sun from the earth. But it is increased and diminished inversely as the cube of the sun's distance, and therefore is nearly 3′ 34″ when that distance is greatest, and 3′ 56″ when least. But when the moon's apogee is without the octants, it becomes less, and is to its greatest amount as the sine of double the distance of the moon's apogee from the nearest syzygy or quadrature is to the radius.

By the same theory of gravity, the action of the sun upon the moon is some-what greater when the line of the moon's nodes passes through the sun than when it is at right angles with the line which joins the sun and the earth; and hence arises another equation of the moon's mean motion, which I shall call the second semiannual; and this is greatest when the nodes are in the octants of the sun, and vanishes when they are in the syzygies or quadratures; and in other positions of the nodes is proportional to the sine of double the distance of either node from the nearest syzygy or quadrature. And it is added to the mean motion of the moon, if the sun is behind the node which is nearest to him, and is subtracted, if forward; and in the octants, where it is of the greatest magnitude, it arises to 47″ in the mean distance of the sun from the earth, as I find from the theory of gravity. In other distances of the sun, this equation, greatest in the octants of the nodes, is inversely as the cube of the sun's dis-tance from the earth; and therefore in the sun's perigee it comes to about 49″, and in its apogee to about 45″.

By the same theory of gravity, the moon's apogee goes forwards at the greatest rate when it is either in conjunction with or in opposition to the sun, but in its quadratures with the sun it goes backwards; and the eccentricity comes, in the former case, to its greatest quantity; in the latter, to its least, by Cor. vii, viii, and ix, Prop. 66, Book i. And those inequalities, by the Corol-laries we have named, are very great, and generate the principle which I call the semiannual equation of the apogee; and this semiannual equation in its greatest quantity comes to about 12° 18′, as nearly as I could determine from the phenomena. Our countryman, Horrox, was the first who advanced the theory of the moon's moving in an ellipse about the earth placed in its lower focus. Dr. Halley improved the notion, by putting the centre of the ellipse in an epicycle whose centre is uniformly revolved about the earth; and from the motion in this epicycle the mentioned inequalities in the progress and regress of the apogee, and in the quantity of eccentricity, do arise. Suppose the mean distance of the moon from the earth to be divided into 100,000 parts, and let T represent the earth, and TC the moon's mean eccentricity of 5505 such parts. Produce TC to B, so as CB may be the sine of the greatest semiannual equation 12° 18′ to the radius TC; and the circle BDA described about the centre C, with the radius CB, will be the epicycle spoken of, in which the centre of the moon's orbit is placed, and revolved according to the order of the letters BDA. Set off the angle BCD equal to twice the annual argument, or twice the distance of the sun's true place from the place of the moon's apogee once corrected, and CTD will be the semiannual 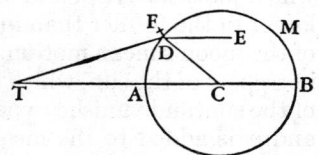 equation of the moon's apogee, and TD the eccentricity of its orbit, tending to the place of the apogee now twice corrected. But, having the moon's mean motion, the place of its apogee, and its eccentricity, as well as the longer axis of its orbit 200,000, from these data the true place of the moon in its orbit, to-gether with its distance from the earth, may be determined by the methods commonly known.

In the perihelion of the earth, where the force of the sun is greatest, the centre of the moon's orbit moves faster about the centre C than in the aphelion, and that inversely as the cube of the sun's distance from the earth. But, because the equation of the sun's centre is included in the annual argument, the centre of the moon's orbit moves faster in its epicycle BDA, inversely as the square of the sun's distance from the earth. Therefore, that it may move yet faster, inversely as the distance, suppose that from D, the centre of the orbit, a right line DE is drawn, tending towards the moon's apogee once corrected, that is, parallel to TC; and set off the angle EDF equal to the excess of the aforesaid annual argument above the distance of the moon's apogee from the sun's perigee forwards; or, which comes to the same thing, take the angle CDF equal to the complement of the sun's true anomaly to 360°; and let DF be to DC as twice the eccentricity of the great orbit to the sun's mean distance from the earth, and the sun's mean diurnal motion from the moon's apogee to the sun's mean diurnal motion from its own apogee conjointly, that is, as $33\frac{7}{8}$ to 1000, and $52'\ 27''\ 16'''$ to $59'\ 8''\ 10'''$ conjointly, or as 3 to 100; and imagine the centre of the moon's orbit placed in the point F to be revolved in an epicycle whose centre of the moon's orbit placed in the point F to be revolved in an epicycle whose centre is D, and radius DF, while the point D moves in the circumference of the circle DABD: for by this means the centre of the moon's orbit comes to describe a certain curved line about the centre C, with a velocity which will be almost inversely as the cube of the sun's distance from the earth, as it ought to be.

The calculus of this motion is difficult, but may be rendered easier by the following approximation. Assuming, as above, the moon's mean distance from the earth of 100,000 parts, and the eccentricity TC of 5505 such parts, the line CB or CD will be found $1172\frac{3}{4}$, and DF $35\frac{1}{5}$ of those parts; and this line DF at the distance TC subtends the angle at the earth, which the removal of the centre of the orbit from the place D to the place F generates in the motion of this centre; and double this line DF in a parallel position, at the distance of the upper focus of the moon's orbit from the earth, subtends at the earth the same angle as DF did before, which that removal generates in the motion of this upper focus; but at the distance of the moon from the earth this double line 2DF at the upper focus, in a parallel position to the first line DF, subtends an angle at the moon, which the said removal generates in the motion of the moon, which angle may be therefore called the second equation of the moon's centre; and this equation, in the mean distance of the moon from the earth, is nearly as the sine of the angle which that line DF contains with the line drawn from the point F to the moon, and when greatest amounts to $2'\ 25''$. But the angle which the line DF contains with the line drawn from the point F to the moon is found either by subtracting the angle EDF from the mean anomaly of the moon, or by adding the distance of the moon from the sun to the distance of the moon's apogee from the apogee of the sun; and as the radius is to the sine of the angle thus found, so is $2'\ 25''$ to the second equation of the centre: to be added, if the fore-mentioned sum be less than a semi-circle; to be subtracted, if greater. And from the moon's place in its orbit thus corrected, its longitude may be found in the syzygies of the luminaries.

The atmosphere of the earth to the height of 35 or 40 miles refracts the sun's light. This refraction scatters and spreads the light over the earth's shadow; and the dissipated light near the limits of the shadow dilates the shadow. On this account, to the diameter of the shadow, as it comes out by the parallax, I add 1 or $1\frac{1}{3}$ minutes in lunar eclipses.

But the theory of the moon ought to be examined and proved from the phenomena, first in the syzygies, then in the quadratures, and last of all in the octants; and whoever pleases to undertake the work will find it not amiss to assume the following mean motions of the sun and moon at the Royal Observatory of Greenwich, to the last day of December at noon, in the year 1700, o.s.: the mean motion of the sun ♏ 20° 43′ 40″, and of its apogee ♋ 7° 44′ 30″; the mean motion of the moon ♒ 15° 21′ 00″; of its apogee, ♓ 8° 20′ 00″; and of its ascending node ♌ 27° 24′ 20″; and the difference of meridians between the Observatory at Greenwich and the Royal Observatory at Paris, $0^h. 9^m. 20^s.$: but the mean motion of the moon and of its apogee are not yet obtained with sufficient accuracy.

PROPOSITION 36. PROBLEM 17

To find the force of the sun to move the sea.

The sun's force ML or PT to disturb the motions of the moon was (by Prop. 25), in the moon's quadratures, to the force of gravity with us, as 1 to 638092.6; and the force TM − LM or 2PK in the moon's syzygies is double that quantity. But, descending to the surface of the earth, these forces are diminished in proportion of the distances from the centre of the earth, that is, in the proportion of 60½ to 1; and therefore the former force on the earth's surface is to the force of gravity as 1 to 38,604,600; and by this force the sea is depressed in such places as are 90 degrees distant from the sun. But by the other force, which is twice as great, the sea is raised not only in the places directly under the sun, but in those also which are directly opposed to it; and the sum of these forces is to the force of gravity as 1 to 12,868,200. And because the same force excites the same motion, whether it depresses the waters in those places which are 90 degrees distant from the sun, or raises them in the places which are directly under and directly opposed to the sun, the aforesaid sum will be the total force of the sun to disturb the sea, and will have the same effect as if the whole was employed in raising the sea in the places directly under and directly opposed to the sun, and did not act at all in the places which are 90 degrees removed from the sun.

And this is the force of the sun to disturb the sea in any given place, where the sun is at the same time both vertical, and in its mean distance from the earth. In other positions of the sun, its force to raise the sea is directly as the versed sine of double its altitude above the horizon of the place, and inversely as the cube of the distance from the earth.

COR. Since the centrifugal force of the parts of the earth, arising from the earth's diurnal motion, which is to the force of gravity as 1 is to 289, raises the waters under the equator to a height exceeding that under the poles by 85,472 Paris feet, as above, in Prop. 19, the force of the sun, which we have now shown to be to the force of gravity as 1 is to 12,868,200, and therefore is to that centrifugal force as 289 to 12,868,200, or as 1 to 44,527, will be able to raise the waters in the places directly under and directly opposed to the sun to a height exceeding that in the places which are 90 degrees removed from the sun only by one Paris foot and 113 1/30 inches; for this measure is to the measure of 85,472 feet as 1 to 44,527.

PROPOSITION 37. PROBLEM 18

To find the force of the moon to move the sea.

The force of the moon to move the sea is to be deduced from its ratio to the force of the sun, and this ratio is to be determined from the ratio of the motions of the sea, which are the effects of those forces. Before the mouth of the river Avon, three miles below Bristol, the height of the ascent of the water in the vernal and autumnal syzygies of the luminaries (by the observations of Samuel Sturmy) amounts to about 45 feet, but in the quadratures to 25 only. The former of those heights arises from the sum of the aforesaid forces, the latter from their difference. If, therefore, S and L are supposed to represent respectively the forces of the sun and moon while they are in the equator, as well as in their mean distances from the earth, we shall have L+S to L−S as 45 to 25, or as 9 to 5.

At Plymouth (by the observations of Samuel Colepress) the tide in its mean height rises to about 16 feet, and in the spring and autumn the height thereof in the syzygies may exceed that in the quadratures by more than 7 or 8 feet. Suppose the greatest difference of those heights to be 9 feet, and L+S will be to L−S as 20½ to 11½, or as 41 to 23; a proportion that agrees well enough with the former. But because of the great tide at Bristol, we are rather to depend upon the observations of Sturmy; and, therefore, till we procure something that is more certain, we shall use the proportion of 9 to 5.

But because of the reciprocal motions of the waters, the greatest tides do not happen at the times of the syzygies of the luminaries, but, as we have said before, are the third in order after the syzygies; or (reckoning from the syzygies) follow next after the third approach of the moon to the meridian of the place after the syzygies; or rather (as Sturmy observes) are the third after the day of the new or full moon, or rather nearly after the twelfth hour from the new or full moon, and therefore fall nearly upon the forty-third hour after the new or full moon. But in this port they come to pass about the seventh hour after the approach of the moon to the meridian of the place; and therefore follow next after the approach of the moon to the meridian, when the moon is distant from the sun, or from opposition with the sun by about 18 or 19 degrees forwards. So the summer and winter seasons come not to their height in the solstices themselves, but when the sun is advanced beyond the solstices by about a tenth part of its whole course, that is, by about 36 or 37 degrees. In like manner, the greatest tide is raised after the approach of the moon to the meridian of the place, when the moon has passed by the sun, *or the opposition thereof*, by about a tenth part of the whole motion from *one greatest* tide to *the next following greatest* tide. Suppose that distance about 18½ degrees; and the sun's force in this distance of the moon from the syzygies and quadratures will be of less moment to augment and diminish that part of the motion of the sea which proceeds from the motion of the moon than in the syzygies and quadratures themselves in the proportion of the radius to the cosine of double this distance, or of an angle of 37 degrees; that is, in the ratio of 10,000,000 to 7,986,355; and, therefore, in the preceding analogy, in place of S we must put 0.7986355S.

But further, the force of the moon in the quadratures must be diminished, on account of its declination from the equator; for the moon in those quadratures, or rather in 18½ degrees past the quadratures, declines from the equator by about 23° 13′; and the force of either luminary to move the sea is diminished as it declines from the equator nearly as the square of the cosine of the declination; and therefore the force of the moon in those quadratures is only 0.8570327L; hence we have L+0.7986355S to 0.8570327L−0.7986355S as 9 to 5.

Further yet, the diameters of the orbit in which the moon should move, setting aside the consideration of eccentricity, are one to the other as 69 to 70; and therefore the moon's distance from the earth in the syzygies is to its distance in the quadratures, other things being equal, as 69 to 70; and its distances, when $18\frac{1}{2}$ degrees advanced beyond the syzygies, where the greatest tide was excited, and when $18\frac{1}{2}$ degrees passed by the quadratures, where the least tide was produced, are to its mean distance as 69.098747 and 69.897345 to $69\frac{1}{2}$. But the force of the moon to move the sea varies inversely as the cube of its distance; and therefore its forces, in the greatest and least of those distances, are to its force in its mean distance as 0.9830427 and 1.017522 is to 1. From this we have $1.017522L \cdot 0.7986355S$ to $0.9830427 \cdot 0.8570327L - 0.7986355S$ as 9 to 5; and S to L as 1 to 4.4815. Therefore, since the force of the sun is to the force of gravity as 1 to 12,868,200, the moon's force will be to the force of gravity as 1 to 2,871,400.

COR. I. Since the waters attracted by the sun's force rise to the height of 1 foot and $11\frac{1}{30}$ inches, the moon's force will raise the same to the height of 8 feet and $7\frac{5}{22}$ inches; and the joint forces of both will raise the same to the height of $10\frac{1}{2}$ feet; and when the moon is in its perigee to the height of $12\frac{1}{2}$ feet, and more, especially when the wind sets the same way as the tide. And a force of that amount is abundantly sufficient to produce all the motions of the sea, and agrees well with the ratio of those motions; for in such seas as lie free and open from east to west, as in the Pacific sea, and in those tracts of the Atlantic and Ethiopic seas which lie without the tropics, the waters commonly rise to 6, 9, 12, or 15 feet; but in the Pacific sea, which is of a greater depth, as well as of a larger extent, the tides are said to be greater than in the Atlantic and Ethiopic seas; for, to have a full tide raised, an extent of sea from east to west is required of no less than 90 degrees. In the Ethiopic sea, the waters rise to a less height within the tropics than in the temperate zones: because of the narrowness of the sea between Africa and the southern parts of America. In the middle of the open sea the waters cannot rise without falling together, and at the same time, upon both the eastern and western shores, when, notwithstanding, in our narrow seas, they ought to fall on those shores by alternate turns; upon this account there is commonly but a small flood and ebb in such islands as lie far distant from the continent. On the contrary, in some ports, where to fill and empty the bays alternately the waters are with great violence forced in and out through shallow channels, the flood and ebb must be greater than ordinary; as at Plymouth and Chepstow Bridge in England, at the mountains of St. Michael, and the town of Avranches, in Normandy, and at Cambaia and Pegu in the East Indies. In these places the sea is hurried in and out with such violence as sometimes to lay the shores under water, sometimes to leave them dry for many miles. Nor is this force of the influx and efflux to be stopped till it has raised and depressed the waters to 30, 40, or 50 feet and above. And a like account is to be given of long and shallow channels or straits, such as the Magellanic straits, and those channels which environ England. The tide in such ports and straits, by the violence of the influx and efflux, is augmented greatly. But on such shores as lie towards the deep and open sea with a steep descent, where the waters may freely rise and fall without that precipitation of influx and efflux, the ratio of the tides agrees with the forces of the sun and moon.

COR. II. Since the moon's force to move the sea is to the force of gravity as 1 to 2,871,400, it is evident that this force is inappreciable in statical or hydrostatical experiments, or even in those of pendulums. It is in the tides only that this force shows itself by any sensible effect.

COR. III. Because the force of the moon for moving the sea is to the like force of the sun as 4.4815 to 1, and those forces (by Cor. XIV, Prop. 66, Book I) are as the densities of the bodies of the sun and moon and the cubes of their apparent diameters conjointly, the density of the moon will be to the density of the sun directly as 4.4815 to 1, and inversely as the cube of the moon's diameter to the cube of the sun's diameter; that is (seeing the mean apparent diameters of the moon and sun are 31' 16½", and 32' 12"), as 4891 to 1000. But the density of the sun was to the density of the earth as 1000 to 4000; and therefore the density of the moon is to the density of the earth as 4891 is to 4000, or as 11 to 9. Therefore the body of the moon is more dense and more earthly than the earth itself.

COR. IV. And since the true diameter of the moon (from the observations of astronomers) is to the true diameter of the earth as 100 to 365, the mass of matter in the moon will be to the mass of matter in the earth as 1 to 39.788.

COR. V. And the accelerative gravity on the surface of the moon will be about three times less than the accelerative gravity on the surface of the earth.

COR. VI. And the distance of the moon's centre from the centre of the earth will be to the distance of the moon's centre from the common centre of gravity of the earth and moon as 40.788 to 39.788.

COR. VII. And the mean distance of the centre of the moon from the centre of the earth will be (in the moon's octants) nearly $60\frac{2}{5}$ of the greatest semidiameters of the earth; for the greatest semidiameter of the earth was 19,658,600 Paris feet, and the mean distance of the centres of the earth and moon, consisting of $60\frac{2}{5}$ such semidiameters, is equal to 1,187,379,440 feet. And this distance (by the preceding Cor.) is to the distance of the moon's centre from the common centre of gravity of the earth and moon as 40.788 to 39.788; which latter distance, therefore, is 1,158,268,534 feet. And since the moon, in respect of the fixed stars, performs its revolution in $27^{d}.$ $7^{h}.$ $43\frac{4}{9}^{m}.$, the versed sine of that angle which the moon in a minute of time describes is 12,752,341 to the radius 1,000,000,000,000,000; and as the radius is to this versed sine, so are 1,158,268,534 feet to 14.7706353 feet. The moon, therefore, falling towards the earth by that force which retains it in its orbit, would in one minute of time describe 14.7706353 feet; and, if we augment this force in the proportion of $178\frac{29}{40}$ to $177\frac{29}{40}$, we shall have the total force of gravity at the orbit of the moon, by Cor., Prop. 3; and the moon falling by this force, in one minute of time would describe 14.8538067 feet. And at the 60th part of the distance of the moon from the earth's centre, that is, at the distance of 197,896,573 feet from the centre of the earth, a body falling by its weight, would, in one second of time, likewise describe 14.8538067 feet. And, therefore, at the distance of 19,615,800, which compose one mean semidiameter of the earth, a heavy body would describe in falling 15.11175, or 15 feet, 1 inch, and $4\frac{1}{11}$ lines, in the same time. This will be the descent of bodies in the latitude of 45 degrees. And by the foregoing table, to be found under Prop. 20, the descent in the latitude of Paris will be a little greater by an excess of about $\frac{2}{3}$ parts of a line. Therefore, by this computation, heavy bodies in the latitude of Paris falling in a vacuum will describe

15 Paris feet, 1 inch, $4^{25}/_{33}$ lines, very nearly, in one second of time. And if the gravity be diminished by taking away a quantity equal to the centrifugal force arising in that latitude from the earth's diurnal motion, heavy bodies falling there will describe in one second of time 15 feet, 1 inch, and $1\frac{1}{2}$ lines. And with this velocity heavy bodies do really fall in the latitude of Paris, as we have shown above in Props. 4 and 19.

COR. VIII. The mean distance of the centres of the earth and moon in the syzygies of the moon is equal to 60 of the greatest semidiameters of the earth, subtracting only about one 30th part of a semidiameter; and in the moon's quadratures the mean distance of the same centres is $60^5/_6$ such semidiameters of the earth; for these two distances are to the mean distance of the moon in the octants as 69 and 70 to $69\frac{1}{2}$, by Prop. 28.

COR. IX. The mean distance of the centres of the earth and moon in the syzygies of the moon is 60 mean semidiameters of the earth, and a 10th part of one semidiameter; and in the moon's quadratures the mean distance of the same centres is 61 mean semidiameters of the earth, subtracting one 30th part of one semidiameter.

COR. X. In the moon's syzygies its mean horizontal parallax in the latitudes of 0, 30, 38, 45, 52, 60, 90 degrees is 57′ 20″, 57′ 16″, 57′ 14″, 57′ 12″, 57′ 10″, 57′ 8″, 57′ 4″, respectively.

In these computations I do not consider the magnetic attraction of the earth, whose quantity is very small and unknown: if this quantity should ever be found out, and the measures of degrees upon the meridian, the lengths of isochronous pendulums in different parallels, the laws of the motions of the sea, and the moon's parallax, with the apparent diameters of the sun and moon, should be more exactly determined from phenomena: we should then be enabled to bring this calculation to a greater accuracy.

PROPOSITION 38. PROBLEM 19

To find the figure of the moon's body.

If the moon's body were fluid like our sea, the force of the earth to raise that fluid in the nearest and remotest parts would be to the force of the moon by which our sea is raised in the places under and opposite to the moon as the accelerative gravity of the moon towards the earth is to the accelerative gravity of the earth towards the moon, and the diameter of the moon is to the diameter of the earth conjointly; that is, as 39.788 to 1, and 100 to 365 conjointly, or as 1081 to 100. Therefore, since our sea, by the force of the moon, is raised to $8^3/_5$ feet, the lunar fluid would be raised by the force of the earth to 93 feet; and upon this account the figure of the moon would be a spheroid, whose greatest diameter produced would pass through the centre of the earth, and exceed the diameters perpendicular thereto by 186 feet. Such a figure, therefore, the moon possesses, and must have had from the beginning.   Q.E.I.

COR. Hence it is that the same face of the moon always is turned toward the earth; nor can the body of the moon possibly rest in any other position, but would return always by a libratory motion to this situation; but those librations, however, must be exceedingly slow, because of the weakness of the forces which excite them; so that the face of the moon, which should be always directed to the earth, may, for the reason assigned in Prop. 17, be turned towards the other focus of the moon's orbit, without being immediately drawn back, and turned again towards the earth.

Lemma 1

If APEp represent the earth uniformly dense, marked with the centre C, the poles P, p, and the equator AE; and if about the centre C, with the radius CP, we suppose the sphere Pape to be described, and QR to denote the plane on which a right line, drawn from the centre of the sun to the centre of the earth, stands at right angles; and further suppose that the several particles of the whole exterior earth PapAPepE, without the height of the said sphere, endeavor to recede towards this side and that side from the plane QR, every particle by a force proportional to its distance from that plane; I say, in the first place, that the whole force and efficacy of all the particles that are situated in AE, the circle of the equator, and disposed uniformly without the globe, encompassing the same after the manner of a ring, to wheel the earth about its centre, is to the whole force and efficacy of as many particles in that point A of the equator which is at the greatest distance from the plane QR, to wheel the earth about its centre with a like circular motion as is 1 to 2. And that circular motion will be performed about an axis lying in the common section of the equator and the plane QR.

For let there be described from the centre K, with the diameter IL, the semicircle INL. Suppose the semicircumference INL to be divided into innumerable equal parts, and from the several parts N to the diameter IL let fall the sines NM. Then the sums of the squares of all the sines NM will be equal

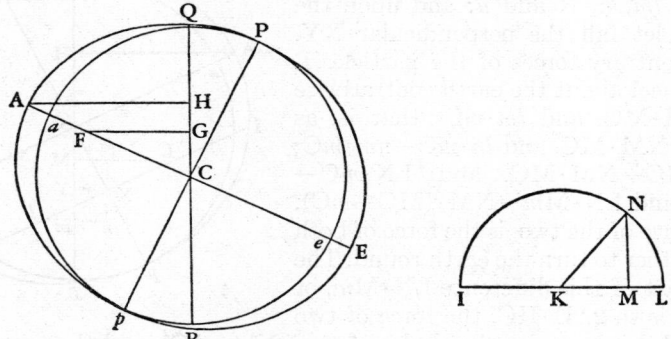

to the sums of the squares of the sines KM, and both sums together will be equal to the sums of the squares of as many semidiameters KN; and therefore the sum of the squares of all the sines NM will be but half so great as the sum of the squares of as many semidiameters KN.

Suppose now the circumference of the circle AE to be divided into the like number of little equal parts, and from every such part F a perpendicular FG to be let fall upon the plane QR, as well as the perpendicular AH from the point A. Then the force by which the particle F recedes from the plane QR will (by supposition) be as that perpendicular FG; and this force multiplied by the distance CG will represent the power of the particle F to turn the earth round its centre. And, therefore, the power of a particle in the place F will be to the power of a particle in the place A as FG·GC is to AH·HC; that is, as FC^2 to AC^2: and therefore the whole power of all the particles F, in their proper places

F, will be to the power of the like number of particles in the place **A** as the sum of all the FC² is to the sum of all the AC², that is (by what we have demonstrated before), as 1 to 2.   Q.E.D.

And because the action of those particles is exerted in the direction of lines perpendicularly receding from the plane QR, and that equally from each side of this plane, they will wheel about the circumference of the circle of the equator, together with the adherent body of the earth, round an axis which lies as well in the plane QR as in that of the equator.

LEMMA 2

The same things still supposed, I say, in the second place, that the total force or power of all the particles situated everywhere about the sphere to turn the earth about the said axis is to the whole force of the like number of particles, uniformly disposed round the whole circumference of the equator AE in the fashion of a ring, to turn the whole earth about with the like circular motion as is 2 to 5.

For let IK be any lesser circle parallel to the equator AE, and let L*l* be any two equal particles in this circle, situated without the sphere P*ape*; and if upon the plane QR, which is at right angles with a radius drawn to the sun, we let fall the perpendiculars LM, *lm*, the total forces by which these particles recede from the plane QR will be proportional to the perpendiculars LM, *lm*. Let the right line L*l* be drawn parallel to the plane P*ape*, and bisect the same in X; and

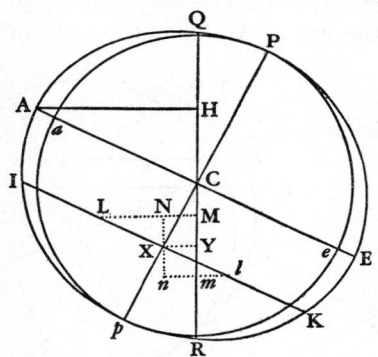

through the point X draw N*n* parallel to the plane QR, and meeting the perpendiculars LM, *lm*, in N and *n;* and upon the plane QR let fall the perpendicular XY. And the contrary forces of the particles L and *l* to wheel about the earth contrariwise are as LM·MC, and *lm·mC*; that is, as LN·MC+NM·MC, and *ln·mC−nm·mC*; or LN·MC+NM·MC, and LN·*mC*−NM·*mC*, and LN·M*m*−NM·(MC+*mC*), the difference of the two, is the force of both taken together to turn the earth round. The positive part of this difference LN·M*m*, or 2LN·NX, is to 2AH·HC, the force of two

particles of the same size situated in A, as LX² to AC²; and the negative part NM·(MC+*mC*), or 2XY·CY, is to 2AH·HC, the force of the same two particles situated in A, as CX² to AC². And therefore the difference of the parts, that is, the force of the two particles L and *l*, taken together, to wheel the earth about, is to the force of two particles, equal to the former and situated in the place A, to turn in like manner the earth round, as LX²−CX² is to AC². But if the circumference IK of the circle IK is supposed to be divided into an infinite number of little equal parts L, all the LX² will be to the like number of IX² as 1 to 2 (by Lem. 1); and to the same number of AC² as IX² is to 2AC²; and the same number of CX² to as many AC² as 2CX² is to 2AC². Therefore the united forces of all the particles in the circumference of the circle IK are to the joint forces of as many particles in the place A as IX²−2CX² is to 2AC²; and therefore (by Lem. 1) to the united forces of as many particles in the circumference of the circle AE as IX²−2CX² is to AC².

Now if Pp, the diameter of the sphere, is conceived to be divided into an infinite number of equal parts, upon which a like number of circles IK are supposed to stand, the matter in the circumference of every circle IK will be as IX^2; and therefore the force of that matter to turn the earth about will be as IX^2 into IX^2 − 2CX^2; and the force of the same matter, if it was situated in the circumference of the circle AE, would be as IX^2 into AC^2. And therefore the force of all the particles of the whole matter situated without the sphere in the circumferences of all the circles is to the force of the like number of particles situated in the circumference of the greatest circle AE as all the IX^2 into IX^2 − 2CX^2 is to as many IX^2 into AC^2; that is, as all the AC^2 − CX^2 into AC^2 − 3CX^2 to as many AC^2 − CX^2 into AC^2; that is, as all the AC^4 − 4AC^2 · CX^2 + 3CX^4 to as many AC^4 − AC^2 · CX^2; that is, as the whole fluent quantity whose fluxion is AC^4 − 4AC^2 · CX^2 + 3CX^4, is to the whole fluent quantity, whose fluxion is AC^4 − AC^2 · CX^2; and, therefore, by the method of fluxions, as AC^4 · CX − ⁴⁄₃AC^2 · CX^3 + ³⁄₅CX^5 is to AC^4 · CX − ⅓AC^2 · CX^3; that is, if for CX we write the whole Cp, or AC, as ⁴⁄₁₅AC^5 is to ⅔AC^5; that is, as 2 is to 5.   q.e.d.

LEMMA 3

The same things still supposed, I say, in the third place, that the motion of the whole earth about the axis above named arising from the motions of all the particles, will be to the motion of the aforesaid ring about the same axis in a ratio compounded of the ratio of the matter in the earth to the matter in the ring; and the ratio of three squares of the quadrantal arc of any circle to two squares of its diameter, that is, in the ratio of the matter to the matter, and of the number 925,275 to the number 1,000,000.

For the motion of a cylinder revolved about its quiescent axis is to the motion of the inscribed sphere revolved together with it as any four equal squares are to three circles inscribed in three of those squares, and the motion of this cylinder is to the motion of an exceedingly thin ring surrounding both sphere and cylinder in their common contact as double the matter in the cylinder is to triple the matter in the ring; and this motion of the ring, uniformly continued about the axis of the cylinder, is to the uniform motion of the same about its own diameter performed in the same periodic time as is the circumference of a circle to double its diameter.

HYPOTHESIS II

IF THE OTHER PARTS OF THE EARTH WERE TAKEN AWAY, AND THE REMAINING RING WAS CARRIED ALONE ABOUT THE SUN IN THE ORBIT OF THE EARTH BY THE ANNUAL MOTION, WHILE BY THE DIURNAL MOTION IT WAS IN THE MEANTIME REVOLVED ABOUT ITS OWN AXIS INCLINED TO THE PLANE OF THE ECLIPTIC BY AN ANGLE OF 23½ DEGREES, THE MOTION OF THE EQUINOCTIAL POINTS WOULD BE THE SAME, WHETHER THE RING WERE FLUID, OR WHETHER IT CONSISTED OF A HARD AND RIGID MATTER.

PROPOSITION 39. PROBLEM 20

To find the precession of the equinoxes.

The middle hourly motion of the moon's nodes in a circular orbit, when the nodes are in the quadratures, was 16″ 35‴ 16^{iv} 36^v; the half of which, 8″ 17‴ 38^{iv} 18^v (for the reasons above explained), is the mean hourly motion of the nodes in such an orbit, which motion in a whole sidereal year becomes 20° 11′ 46″.

Since, therefore, the nodes of the moon in such an orbit would be yearly transferred 20° 11′ 46″ backwards, and, if there were more moons, the motion of the nodes of every one (by Cor. xvi, Prop. 66, Book i) would be as its periodic time, if upon the surface of the earth a moon was revolved in the time of a sidereal day, the annual motion of the nodes of this moon would be to 20° 11′ 46″ as 23^h. 56^m., the sidereal day, is to 27^d. 7^h. 43^m., the periodic time of our moon, that is, as 1436 is to 39,343. And the same thing would happen to the nodes of a ring of moons encompassing the earth, whether these moons did not mutually touch each the other, or whether they were molten, and formed into a continued ring, or whether that ring should become rigid and inflexible.

Let us, then, suppose that this ring is in quantity of matter equal to the whole exterior earth PapAPepE, which lies without the sphere Pape (see Fig., Lem. 2); and because this sphere is to that exterior earth as aC^2 is to AC$^2 - a$C^2, that is (seeing PC or aC the least semidiameter of the earth is to AC the greatest semidiameter of the same as 229 is to 230), as 52,441 is to 459; if this ring encompassed the earth round the equator, and both together were revolved about the diameter of the ring, the motion of the ring (by Lem. 3) would be to the motion of the inner sphere as 459 to 52,441 and 1,000,000 to 925,275 conjointly, that is, as 4590 to 485,223; and therefore the motion of the ring would be to the sum of the motions of both ring and sphere as 4590 is to 489,813. Therefore, if the ring adheres to the sphere, and communicates its motion to the sphere, by which its nodes or equinoctial points recede, the motion remaining in the ring will be to its former motion as 4590 is to 489,813; on account of which the motion of the equinoctial points will be diminished in the same ratio. Therefore, the annual motion of the equinoctial points of the body, composed of both ring and sphere, will be to the motion 20° 11′ 46″ as 1436 to 39,343 and 4590 to 489,813 conjointly, that is, as 100 to 292,369. But the forces by which the nodes of a number of moons (as we explained above), and therefore by which the equinoctial points of the ring recede (that is, the forces 3IT, in Fig., Prop. 30), are in the several particles as the distances of those particles from the plane QR; and by these forces the particles recede from that plane: and therefore (by Lem. 2) if the matter of the ring was spread all over the surface of the sphere, after the fashion of the figure PapAPepE, in order to make up that exterior part of the earth, the total force or power of all the particles to wheel about the earth round any diameter of the equator, and therefore to move the equinoctial points, would become less than before in the proportion of 2 to 5. Therefore the annual regress of the equinoxes now would be to 20° 11′ 46″ as 10 is to 73,092; that is, would be 9″ 56‴ 50^{iv}.

But because the plane of the equator is inclined to that of the ecliptic, this motion is to be diminished in the ratio of the sine 91,706 (which is the cosine of 23½ degrees) to the radius 100,000; and the remaining motion will now be 9″ 7‴ 20^{iv}, which is the annual precession of the equinoxes arising from the force of the sun.

But the force of the moon to move the sea was to the force of the sun nearly as 4.4815 to 1; and the force of the moon to move the equinoxes is to that of the sun in the same proportion. Whence the annual precession of the equinoxes proceeding from the force of the moon comes out 40″ 52‴ 52^{iv}, and the total annual precession arising from the united forces of both will be 50″ 00‴ 12^{iv}, the amount of which motion agrees with the phenomena; for the precession of the equinoxes, by astronomical observations, is about 50″ yearly.

If the height of the earth at the equator exceeds its height at the poles by more than $17\frac{1}{6}$ miles, the matter thereof will be more rare near the surface than at the centre; and the precession of the equinoxes will be augmented by the excess of height, and diminished by the greater rarity.

And now we have described the system of the sun, the earth, moon, and planets, it remains that we add something about the comets.

LEMMA 4

The comets are more remote than the moon, and are in the regions of the planets.

As the comets were placed by astronomers beyond the moon, because they were found to have no diurnal parallax, so their annual parallax is a convincing proof of their descending into the regions of the planets; for all the comets which move in a direct course according to the order of the signs, about the end of their appearance become more than ordinarily slow or retrograde, if the earth is between them and the sun; and more than ordinarily swift, if the earth is approaching to a heliocentric opposition with them; on the other hand, those which move against the order of the signs, towards the end of their appearance appear swifter than they ought to be, if the earth is between them and the sun; and slower, and perhaps retrograde, if the earth is in the other side of its orbit. And these appearances proceed chiefly from the diverse situations which the earth acquires in the course of its motion, after the same manner as it happens to the planets, which appear sometimes retrograde, sometimes more slowly, and sometimes more swiftly, progressive, according as the motion of the earth falls in with that of the planet, or is directed in the contrary way. If the earth move the same way with the comet, but, by an angular motion about the sun, so much swifter that right lines drawn from the earth to the comet converge towards the parts beyond the comet, the comet seen from the earth, because of its slower motion, will appear retrograde; and even if the earth is slower than the comet, the motion of the earth being subtracted, the motion of the comet will at least appear retarded; but if the earth tends the contrary way to that of the comet, the motion of the comet will from thence appear accelerated; and from this apparent acceleration, or retardation, or regressive motion, the distance of the comet may be inferred in this manner.

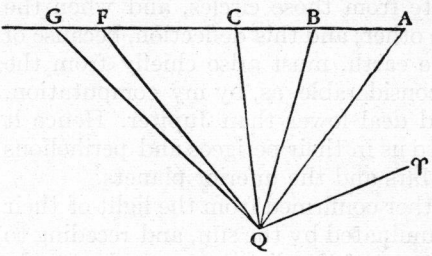

Let ♈QA, ♈QB, ♈QC be three observed longitudes of the comet about the time of its first appearing, and ♈QF its last observed longitude before its disappearing. Draw the right line ABC, whose parts AB, BC, intercepted between the right lines QA and QB, QB and QC, may be one to the other as the two times between the three first observations. Produce AC to G, so that AG may be to AB as the time between the first and last observations is to the time between the first and second; and join QG. Now if the comet did move uniformly in a right line, and the earth either stood still, or was likewise carried forwards in a right line by an uniform motion, the angle ♈QG would be the longitude of the comet at the time of the last observation. Therefore, the angle FQG, which is the difference of the longitude, proceeds from the inequality of the motions of the comet and the earth; and if the earth and comet move contrary ways, this angle is added to the angle ♈QG, and accelerates the apparent motion of the comet; but if the comet moves the same way with the earth, it is subtracted, and either retards the motion of the comet, or perhaps renders it retrograde, as we have just now explained. This angle, therefore, proceeding chiefly from the motion of the earth, is justly to be esteemed the parallax of the comet, there being neglected thereby some little increment or decrement that may arise from the unequal motion of the comet in its orbit. From this parallax we thus deduce the distance of the comet. Let S represent

the sun, *ac*T the great orbit, *a* the earth's place in the first observation, *c* the place of the earth in the third observation, T the place of the earth in the last observation, and T♈ a right line drawn to the beginning of Aries. Set off the angle ♈TV equal to the angle ♈QF, that is, equal to the longitude of the comet at the time when the earth is in T; join *ac*, and produce it to *g*, so that *ag* may be to *ac* as AG is to AC; and *g* will be the place at which the earth would have arrived in the time of the last observation, if it had continued to move uniformly in the right line *ac*. Therefore, if we draw *g*♈ parallel

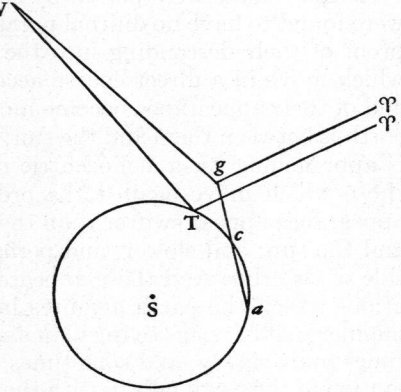

to T♈, and make the angle ♈*g*V equal to the angle ♈QG, this angle ♈*g*V will be equal to the longitude of the comet seen from the place *g*, and the angle TV*g* will be the parallax which arises from the earth's being transferred from the place *g* into the place T; and therefore V will be the place of the comet in the plane of the ecliptic. And this place V is commonly lower than the orbit of Jupiter.

The same thing may be deduced from the incurvation of the way of the comets; for these bodies move almost in great circles, while their velocity is great; but about the end of their course, when that part of their apparent motion which arises from the parallax bears a greater proportion to their whole apparent motion, they commonly deviate from those circles, and when the earth goes to one side, they deviate to the other; and this deflection, because of its corresponding with the motion of the earth, must arise chiefly from the parallax; and the quantity thereof is so considerable, as, by my computation, to place the disappearing comets a good deal lower than Jupiter. Hence it follows that when they approach nearer to us in their perigees and perihelions they often descend below the orbits of Mars and the inferior planets.

The near approach of the comets is further confirmed from the light of their heads; for the light of a celestial body, illuminated by the sun, and receding to remote parts, diminishes as the fourth power of the distance; namely, as the square, on account of the increase of the distance from the sun, and as another square, on account of the decrease of the apparent diameter. Therefore, if both the quantity of light and the apparent diameter of a comet are given, its distance will be given also, by taking the distance of the comet to the distance of a planet directly as their diameters and inversely as the square root of their lights. Thus, in the comet of the year 1682, Mr. Flamsteed observed with a telescope of 16 feet, and measured with a micrometer, the least diameter of its head, 2′ 00″; but the nucleus or star in the middle of the head scarcely amounted to the tenth part of this measure, and therefore its diameter was only 11″ or 12″; but in the light and splendor of its head it surpassed that of the comet in the year 1680, and might be compared with the stars of the first or second magnitude. Let us suppose that Saturn with its ring was about four times more lucid; and because the light of the ring was almost equal to the light of the globe within, and the apparent diameter of the globe is about 21″, and therefore the united light of both globe and ring would be equal to the light of a globe whose diameter is 30″, it follows that the distance of the comet was to the distance of Saturn inversely as 1 to $\sqrt{4}$, and directly as 12″ to 30″; that is, as 24 to 30, or 4 to 5. Again; the comet in the month of April, 1665, as Hewelcke informs us, excelled almost all the fixed stars in splendor, and even Saturn itself, as being of a much more vivid color; for this comet was more lucid than that other which had appeared about the end of the preceding year, and had been compared to the stars of the first magnitude. The diameter of its head was about 6′; but the nucleus, compared with the planets by means of a telescope, was plainly less than Jupiter; and sometimes judged less, sometimes judged equal, to the globe of Saturn within the ring. Since, then, the diameters of the heads of the comets seldom exceed 8′ or 12′, and the diameter of the nucleus or central star is but about a tenth or perhaps fifteenth part of the diameter of the head, it appears that these stars are generally of about the same apparent magnitude with the planets. But since their light may be often compared with the light of Saturn, yea, and sometimes exceeds it, it is evident that all comets in their perihelions must either be placed below or not far above Saturn; and they are much mistaken who remove them almost as far as the fixed stars; for if it were so, the comets could receive no more light from our sun than our planets do from the fixed stars.

So far we have gone, without considering the obscuration which comets suffer from that plenty of thick smoke which encompasses their heads, and through which the heads always show dull, as through a cloud. But the more a body is obscured by this smoke, the nearer must it be allowed to come to the sun, that it may vie with the planets in the quantity of light which it reflects. Hence it is probable that the comets descend far below the orbit of Saturn, as we proved before from their parallax. But, above all, the thing is evinced from their tails, which must be due either to the sun's light reflected by a smoke arising from them, and dispersing itself through the ether, or to the light of their own heads. In the former case, we must shorten the distance of the comets, lest we be obliged to allow that the smoke arising from their heads is propagated through such a vast extent of space, and with such a velocity and expansion as will seem altogether incredible; in the latter case, the whole light of both head and tail is to be ascribed to the central nucleus. But, then, if we suppose all this light to be united and condensed within the disk of the nucleus, certainly the nucleus will by far exceed Jupiter itself in splendor, especially when it emits a very large and lucid tail. If, therefore, under a less apparent diameter, it reflects more light, it must be much more illuminated by the sun, and therefore much nearer to it; and the same argument will bring down the heads of comets sometimes within the orbit of Venus, viz., when, being hid under the sun's rays, they emit such huge and splendid tails, like beams of fire, as sometimes they do; for if all that light was supposed to be gathered together into one star, it would some-times exceed not one Venus only, but a great many such united into one.

Lastly, the same thing is inferred from the light of the heads, which increases in the recess of the comets from the earth towards the sun, and decreases in their return from the sun towards the earth. Thus, the comet of the year 1665 (by the observations of Hewelcke), from the time that it was first seen, was always losing of its apparent motion, and therefore had already passed its perigee; but yet the splendor of its head was daily increasing, till, being hid under the sun's rays, the comet ceased to appear. The comet of the year 1683 (by the observations of the same Hewelcke), about the end of July, when it first appeared, moved at a very slow rate, advancing only about 40 or 45 minutes in its orbit in a day's time; but from that time its diurnal motion was continually upon the increase, till September 4, when it arose to about 5 de-grees; and therefore, in all this interval of time, the comet was approaching to the earth. This is likewise proved from the diameter of its head, measured with a micrometer; for, on August 6, Hewelcke found it only 6' 5", including the coma, which, on September 2, he observed to be 9' 7"; and therefore its head appeared far less about the beginning than towards the end of the motion, though about the beginning, because nearer to the sun, it appeared far more lucid than towards the end, as the same Hewelcke declares. Therefore in all this interval of time, on account of its recess from the sun, it decreased in splendor, notwithstanding its approach towards the earth. The comet of the year 1618, about the middle of December, and that of the year 1680, about the end of the same month, did both move with their greatest velocity, and were therefore then in their perigees, but the greatest splendor of their heads was seen two weeks before, when they had just got clear of the sun's rays, and the greatest splendor of their tails a little earlier, when yet nearer to the sun. The head of the former comet (according to the observations of Cysat), on December 1, appeared greater than the stars of the first magnitude; and, on December 16 (then in the perigee), it was diminished but little in magnitude, but much diminished in the splendor and brightness of its light. On January 7, Kepler, being uncertain about the head, left off observing. On December 12, the head of the latter comet was seen and observed by Mr. Flamsteed, when but 9 de-grees distant from the sun, which is scarcely to be done in a star of the third magnitude. On December 15 and 17, it appeared as a star of the third magni-tude, its luster being diminished by the brightness of the clouds near the setting sun. On December 26, when it moved with the greatest velocity, being almost in its perigee, it was less than the mouth of Pegasus, a star of the third magni-tude. On January 3, it appeared as a star of the fourth. On January 9, as one of the fifth. On January 13, it was hid by the splendor of the moon, then in her increase. On January 25, it was scarcely equal to the stars of the seventh magnitude. If we compare equal intervals of time, taken on one side of the perigee and then on the other, we shall find that the head of the comet, which at both intervals of time was far, but yet equally removed from the earth, and should therefore have shone with equal splendor, appeared brightest on the side of the perigee towards the sun, and disappeared on the other. Therefore, from the great difference of light in the one situation and in the other, we con-clude the great vicinity of the sun and comet in the former, for the light of comets tends to be regular, and to appear greatest when the heads move fastest, and are therefore in their perigees, except so far as it is increased by their nearness to the sun.

Cor. I. Therefore the comets shine by the sun's light, which they reflect.

Cor. II. From what has been said, we may likewise understand why comets are so frequently seen in that region in which the sun is, and so seldom in the other. If they were visible in the regions far above Saturn, they would appear more frequently in the parts opposite to the sun; for such as were in those parts would be nearer to the earth, whereas the presence of the sun must obscure and hide those that appear in the region in which he is. Yet, looking over the history of comets, I find that four or five times more have been seen in the hemisphere towards the sun than in the opposite hemisphere; besides, without doubt, not a few, which have been hid by the light of the sun: for comets descending into our parts neither emit tails, nor are so well illuminated by the sun as to reveal themselves to our naked eyes, until they have come nearer to us than Jupiter. But the far greater part of that spherical space, which is described about the sun with so small a radius, lies on that side of the earth which faces the sun; and the comets in that greater part are commonly more strongly illuminated, for they are for the most part nearer to the sun.

Cor. III. Hence also it is evident that the celestial spaces are void of resistance; for though the comets are carried in oblique paths, and sometimes contrary to the course of the planets, yet they move every way with the greatest freedom, and preserve their motions for an exceeding long time, even where contrary to the course of the planets. I am out in my judgment, if they are not a sort of planets revolving in orbits returning into themselves with a continual motion; for the opinion of some writers, that they are no other than meteors, an opinion based on the continual changes that happen to their heads, seems to have no foundation; for the heads of comets are encompassed with huge atmospheres, and the lowermost parts of these atmospheres must be the densest; and therefore it is in the clouds only, not in the bodies of the comets themselves, that these changes are seen. Thus the earth, if it were viewed from the planets, would, without all doubt, shine by the light of its clouds, and the solid body would scarcely appear through the surrounding clouds. Thus also the belts of Jupiter are formed in the clouds of that planet, for they change their position to each other, and the solid body of Jupiter is hardly to be seen through them; and much more must the bodies of comets be hid under their atmospheres, which are both deeper and thicker.

Proposition 40. Theorem 20

That the comets move in some of the conic sections, having their foci in the centre of the sun, and by radii drawn to the sun describe areas proportional to the times.

This Proposition appears from Cor. I, Prop. 13, Book I, compared with Props. 8, 12, and 13, Book III.

Cor. I. Hence if comets revolve in orbits returning into themselves, the orbits will be ellipses; and their periodic times will be to the periodic times of the planets as the $\frac{3}{2}$th power of their principal axes. And therefore the comets, which for the most part of their course are more remote than the planets, and upon that account describe orbits with greater axes, will require a longer time to finish their revolutions. Thus if the axis of a comet's orbit was four times greater than the axis of the orbit of Saturn, the time of the revolution of the comet would be to the time of the revolution of Saturn, that is, to 30 years, as $4\sqrt{4}$ (or 8) is to 1, and would therefore be 240 years.

COR. II. But their orbits will be so near to parabolas, that parabolas may be used for them without sensible error.

COR. III. And, therefore, by Cor. VII, Prop. 16, Book I, the velocity of every comet will always be to the velocity of any planet, supposed to be revolved at the same distance in a circle about the sun, nearly as the square root of double the distance of the planet from the centre of the sun to the distance of the comet from the sun's centre. Let us suppose the radius of the great orbit, or the greatest semidiameter of the ellipse which the earth describes, to consist of 100,000,000 parts; and then the earth by its mean diurnal motion will describe 1,720,212 of those parts, and 71,675½ by its hourly motion. And therefore the comet, at the same mean distance of the earth from the sun, with a velocity which is to the velocity of the earth as $\sqrt{2}$ to 1, would by its diurnal motion describe 2,432,747 parts, and 101,364½ parts by its hourly motion. But at greater or less distances both the diurnal and hourly motion will be to this diurnal and hourly motion inversely as the square root of the distances, and is therefore given.

COR. IV. Therefore if the latus rectum of the parabola is four times the radius of the great orbit, and the square of that radius is supposed to consist of 100,000,000 parts, the area which the comet will daily describe by a radius drawn to the sun will be 1,216,373½ parts, and the hourly area will be 50,682¼ parts. But, if the latus rectum is greater or less in any ratio, the diurnal and hourly area will be less or greater inversely as the square root of that ratio.

LEMMA 5

To find a curved line of the parabolic kind which shall pass through any given number of points.

Let those points be A, B, C, D, E, F, &c., and from the same to any right line HN, given in position, let fall as many perpendiculars AH, BI, CK, DL, EM, FN, &c.

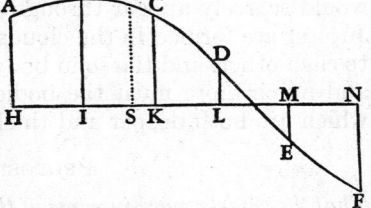

$$b \quad 2b \quad 3b \quad 4b \quad 5b$$
$$c \quad 2c \quad 3c \quad 4c$$
$$d \quad 2d \quad 3d$$
$$e \quad 2e$$
$$f$$

CASE 1. If HI, IK, KL, &c., the intervals of the points H, I, K, L, M, N, &c., are equal, take b, $2b$, $3b$, $4b$, $5b$, &c., the first differences of the perpendiculars AH, BI, CK, &c.; their second differences, c, $2c$, $3c$, $4c$, &c.; their third, d, $2d$, $3d$, &c., that is to say, so as $AH - BI$ may be $= b$, $BI - CK = 2b$, $CK - DL = 3b$, $DL + EM = 4b$, $-EM + FN = 5b$, &c.; then $b - 2b = c$, &c., and so on to the last difference, which is here f. Then, erecting any perpendicular RS, which may be considered as an ordinate of the curve required, in order to find the length of this ordinate, suppose the intervals HI, IK, KL, LM, &c., to be units, and let $AH = a$, $-HS = p$, $½p$ into $-IS = q$, $⅓q$ into $+SK = r$, $¼r$ into $+SL = s$, $⅕s$ nto $+SM = t$; proceeding in this manner, to ME, the last perpendicular but one, and prefixing negative signs before the terms HS, IS, &c., which lie from S towards A; and positive signs before the terms SK, SL, &c., which lie on the other side of the point S; and, observing well the signs, RS will be $= a + bp + cq + dr + es + ft, +$ &c.

CASE 2. But if HI, IK, &c., the intervals of the points H, I, K, L, &c., are unequal, take b, $2b$, $3b$, $4b$, $5b$, &c., the first differences of the perpendiculars AH, BI, CK, &c., divided by the intervals between those perpendiculars; c, $2c$, $3c$, $4c$, &c., their second differences, divided by the intervals between every two; d, $2d$, $3d$, &c., their third differences, divided by the intervals between every three; e, $2e$, &c., their fourth differences, divided by the intervals between every four; and so forth; that is, in such manner, that b may be $= \dfrac{\text{AH} - \text{BI}}{\text{HI}}$,

$$2b = \frac{\text{BI} - \text{CK}}{\text{IK}}, \ 3b = \frac{\text{CK} - \text{DL}}{\text{KL}}, \text{ \&c., then } c = \frac{b - 2b}{\text{HK}}, \ 2c = \frac{2b - 3b}{\text{IL}}, \ 3c = \frac{3b - 4b}{\text{KM}}, \text{ \&c.,}$$

then $d = \dfrac{c - 2c}{\text{HL}}$, $2d = \dfrac{2c - 3c}{\text{IM}}$, &c. And those differences being found, let AH be $= a$, $-\text{HS} = p$, p into $-\text{IS} = q$, q into $+\text{SK} = r$, r into $+\text{SL} = s$, s into $+\text{SM} = t$; proceeding in this manner to ME, the last perpendicular but one; and the ordinate RS will be $= a + bp + cq + dr + es + ft +$ &c.

COR. Hence the areas of all curves may be nearly found; for if some number of points of the curve to be squared are found, and a parabola be supposed to be drawn through those points, the area of this parabola will be nearly the same with the area of the curvilinear figure proposed to be squared: but the parabola can be always squared geometrically by methods generally known.

LEMMA 6

Certain observed places of a comet being given, to find the place of the same at any intermediate given time.

Let HI, IK, KL, LM (in the preceding Fig.) represent the times between the observations; HA, IB, KC, LD, ME, five observed longitudes of the comet; and HS the given time between the first observation and the longitude required. Then if a regular curve ABCDE is supposed to be drawn through the points A, B, C, D, E, and the ordinate RS is found out by the preceding Lemma, RS will be the longitude required.

By the same method, from five observed latitudes, we may find the latitude at a given time.

If the differences of the observed longitudes are small, let us say 4 or 5 degrees, then three or four observations will be sufficient to find a new longitude and latitude; but if the differences are greater, as of 10 or 20 degrees, five observations ought to be used.

LEMMA 7

Through a given point P to drawn a right line BC, whose parts PB, PC, cut off by two right lines AB, AC, given in position, may be one to the other in a given ratio.

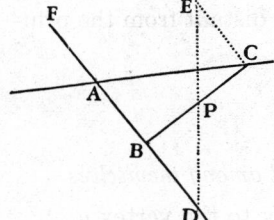

From the given point P suppose any right line PD to be drawn to either of the right lines given, as AB; and produce the same towards AC, the other given right line, as far as E, so as PE may be to PD in the given ratio. Let EC be parallel to AD. Draw CPB, and PC will be to PB as PE to PD.

Q.E.F.

Let ABC be a parabola, having its focus in S. *By the chord AC bisected in* I *cut off the segment ABCI, whose diameter is* Iμ *and vertex* μ. *In* Iμ *produced take* μO *equal to one-half of* Iμ. *Join OS, and produce it to* ξ, *so that* Sξ *may be equal to* 2SO. *Now, supposing a comet to revolve in the arc CBA, draw* ξB, *cutting AC in E:* I *say, the point E will cut off from the chord AC the segment AE, nearly proportional to the time.*

For if we join EO, cutting the parabolic arc ABC in Y, and draw μX touching the same arc in the vertex μ, and meeting EO in X, the curvilinear area AEXμA will be to the curvilinear area ACYμA as AE to AC; and, therefore,

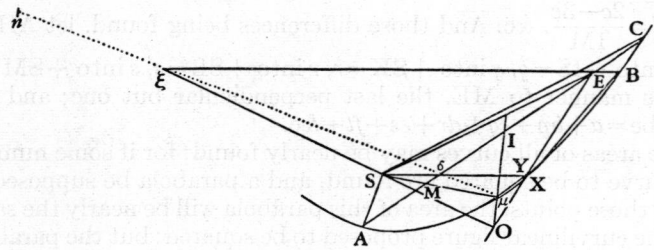

since the triangle ASE is to the triangle ASC in the same ratio, the whole area ASEXμA will be to the whole area ASCYμA as AE is to AC. But, because ξO is to SO as 3 to 1, and EO to XO in the same ratio, SX will be parallel to EB; and, therefore, joining BX, the triangle SEB will be equal to the triangle XEB. Therefore, if to the area ASEXμA we add the triangle EXB, and from the sum subtract the triangle SEB, there will remain the area ASBXμA, equal to the area ASEXμA, and therefore in the ratio to the area ASCYμA as AE to AC. But the area ASBYμA is nearly equal to the area ASBXμA; and this area ASBYμA is to the area ASCYμA as the time of description of the arc AB is to the time of description of the whole arc AC; and, therefore, AE is to AC nearly in the proportion of the times.   Q.E.D.

Cor. When the point B falls upon the vertex μ of the parabola, AE is to AC accurately in the proportion of the times.

If we join μξ cutting AC in δ, and in it take ξn in proportion to μB as 27MI to 16 Mμ, and draw Bn, this Bn will cut the chord AC, in the ratio of the times, more accurately than before; but the point n is to be taken beyond or on this side the point ξ, according as the point B is more or less distant from the principal vertex of the parabola than the point μ.

The right lines Iμ *and* μM, *and the length* $\dfrac{AI^2}{4S\mu}$, *are equal among themselves.*

For 4Sμ is the latus rectum of the parabola belonging to the vertex μ.

LEMMA 10

Produce Sμ *to* N *and* P, *so that* μN *may be one-third of* μI, *and* SP *may be to* SN *as* SN *to* Sμ; *and in the time that a comet would describe the arc* AμC, *if it was supposed to move always forwards with the velocity which it has in a height equal to* SP, *it would describe a length equal to the chord* AC.

For if the comet with the velocity which it hath in μ was in the said time supposed to move uniformly forwards in the right line which touches the parabola in μ, the area which it would describe by a radius drawn to the point S

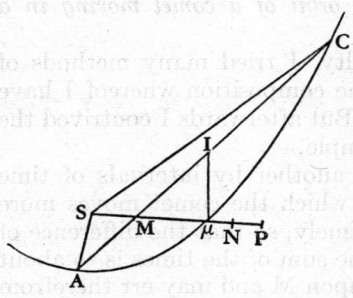

would be equal to the parabolic area ASCμA; and therefore the space contained under the length described in the tangent and the length Sμ would be to the space contained under the lengths AC and SM as the area ASCμA is to the triangle ASC, that is, as SN to SM. Therefore AC is to the length described in the tangent as Sμ to SN. But since the velocity of the comet in the height SP (by Cor. VI, Prop. 16, Book I) is to the velocity of the same in the height Sμ, inversely as the square root of SP to Sμ, that is, in the ratio of Sμ to SN, it follows that the length described with this velocity will be to the length in the same time described in the tangent, as Sμ to SN. Therefore, since AC, and the length described with this new velocity, are in the same proportion to the length described in the tangent, they must be equal between themselves.   Q.E.D.

COR. Therefore a comet, with that velocity which it hath in the height S$\mu+\frac{2}{3}$Iμ, would in the same time nearly describe the chord AC.

LEMMA 11

If a comet void of all motion was let fall from the height SN, *or* S$\mu+\frac{1}{3}$Iμ, *towards the sun, and was still impelled to the sun by the same force uniformly continued by which it was impelled at first, the same, in one-half of that time in which it might describe the arc* AC *in its own orbit, would in descending describe a space equal to the length* Iμ.

For in the same time that the comet would require to describe the parabolic arc AC, it would (by the last Lemma), with that velocity which it hath in the height SP, describe the chord AC; and, therefore (by Cor. VII, Prop. 16, Book I), if it was in the same time supposed to revolve by the force of its own gravity in a circle whose semidiameter was SP, it would describe an arc of that circle, the length of which would be to the chord of the parabolic arc AC in the ratio of 1 to $\sqrt{2}$. Therefore, if with that weight, which in the height SP it hath towards the sun, it should fall from that height towards the sun, it would (by Cor. IX, Prop. 16, Book

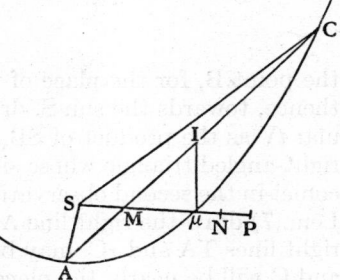

I) in half the said time describe a space equal to the square of half the said chord, divided by four times the height SP, that is, it would describe the space

$\dfrac{AI^2}{4SP}$. But since the weight of the comet towards the sun in the height SN is to the weight of the same towards the sun in the height SP as SP to $S\mu$, the comet, by the weight which it hath in the height SN, in falling from that height towards the sun, would in the same time describe the space $\dfrac{AI^2}{4S\mu}$; that is, a space equal to the length $I\mu$ or μM.   Q.E.D.

PROPOSITION 41. PROBLEM 21

From three given observations to determine the orbit of a comet moving in a parabola.

This being a Problem of very great difficulty, I tried many methods of resolving it; and several of those Problems, the composition whereof I have given in the first book, tended to this purpose. But afterwards I contrived the following solution, which is somewhat more simple.

Select three observations distant one from another by intervals of time nearly equal; but let that interval of time in which the comet moves more slowly be somewhat greater than the other; namely, so that the difference of the times may be to the sum of the times as the sum of the times is to about 600 days; or that the point E may fall nearly upon M and may err therefrom rather towards I than towards A. If such direct observations are not at hand, a new place of the comet must be found, by Lemma 6.

Let S represent the sun; T, t, τ three places of the earth in the earth's orbit; TA, tB, τC three observed longitudes of the comet; V the time between the first observation and the second; W the time between the second and the third; X the length which in the whole time V+W the comet might describe with that velocity which it has in the mean distance of the earth from the sun, which length is to be found by Cor. III, Prop. XL, Book III; and tV a perpendicular upon the chord Tτ. In the mean observed longitude tB take at pleasure

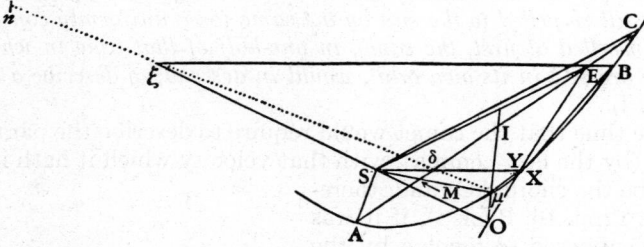

the point B, for the place of the comet in the plane of the ecliptic; and from thence, towards the sun S, draw the line BE, which may be to the perpendicular tV as the product of SB and St^2 is to the cube of the hypothenuse of the right-angled triangle whose sides are SB and the tangent of the latitude of the comet in the second observation to the radius tB. And through the point E (by Lem. 7) draw the right line AEC, whose parts AE and EC, terminating in the right lines TA and τC, may be one to the other as the times V and W: then A and C will be nearly the places of the comet in the plane of the ecliptic in the first and third observations, if B was its place rightly assumed in the second.

Upon AC, bisected in I, erect the perpendicular Ii. Through B imagine the

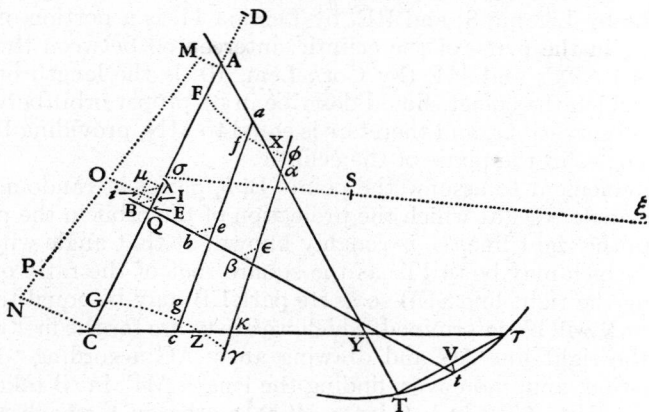

line Bi drawn parallel to AC. Imagine the line Si drawn, cutting AC in λ, and complete the parallelogram iIλμ. Take Iσ equal to 3Iλ; and through the sun S imagine the line σξ drawn equal to 3Sσ+3iλ. Then, canceling the letters A, E, C, I, from the point B towards the point ξ, imagine the new line BE drawn, which may be to the former BE as the square of the ratio of the distance BS to the quantity Sμ+⅓iλ. And through the point E draw again the right line AEC by the same rule as before; that is, so that its parts AE and EC may be one to the other as the times V and W between the observations. Thus A and C will be the places of the comet more accurately.

Upon AC, bisected in I, erect the perpendiculars AM, CN, IO, of which AM and CN may be the tangents of the latitudes in the first and third observations, to the radii TA and τC. Join MN, cutting IO and O. Draw the rectangular parallelogram iIλμ, as before. In IA produced take ID equal to Sμ+⅔iλ. Then in MN, towards N, take MP, which may be to the above-found length X as the square root of the ratio of the mean distance of the earth from the sun (or of the semidiameter of the earth's orbit) to the distance OD. If the point P fall upon the point N; A, B, and C will be three places of the comet, through which its orbit is to be described in the plane of the ecliptic. But if the point P falls not upon the point N, in the right line AC take CG equal to NP, so that the points G and P may lie on the same side of the line NC.

By the same method as the points E, A, C, G were found from the assumed point B, from other points b and $β$ assumed at pleasure, find out the new points e, a, c, g; and $ε$, a, $κ$, $γ$. Then through G, g, and $γ$ draw the circumference of a circle Ggγ, cutting the right line τC in Z: and Z will be one place of the comet in the plane of the ecliptic. And in AC, ac, $aκ$, taking AF, af, $a\phi$, equal respectively to CG, cg, $κγ$; through the points F, f, and ϕ, draw the circumference of a circle F$f\phi$, cutting the right line AT in X; and the point X will be another place of the comet in the plane of the ecliptic. And at the points X and Z, erecting the tangents of the latitudes of the comet to the radii TX and τZ, two places of the comet in its own orbit will be determined. Lastly, if (by Prop. 19, Book I) to the focus S a parabola is described passing through those two places, this parabola will be the orbit of the comet.   Q.E.I.

The demonstration of this construction follows from the preceding Lemmas, because the right line AC is cut in E in the proportion of the times, by Lemma

7, as it ought to be by Lemma 8; and BE, by Lemma 11, is a portion of the right line BS or Bξ in the plane of the ecliptic, intercepted between the arc ABC and the chord AEC; and MP (by Cor., Lem. 10) is the length of the chord of that arc, which the comet should describe in its proper orbit between the first and third observations, and therefore is equal to MN, providing B is a true place of the comet in the plane of the ecliptic.

But it will be convenient to assume the points B, b, β, not at random, but nearly true. If the angle AQt, at which the projection of the orbit in the plane of the ecliptic cuts the right line tB, is roughly known, at that angle with Bt draw the line AC, which may be to $\frac{4}{3}$Tτ as the square root of the ratio of SQ to St; and, drawing the right line SEB so as its part EB may be equal to the length Vt, the point B will be determined, which we are to use for the first time. Then, canceling the right line AC and drawing anew AC according to the preceding construction, and, moreover, finding the length MP, in tB take the point b, by this rule, that, if TA and τC intersect each other in Y, the distance Yb may be to the distance YB in a ratio compounded of the ratio of MP to MN, and the square root of the ratio of SB to Sb. And by the same method you may find the third point β, if you please to repeat the operation the third time; but if this method is followed, two operations generally will be sufficient; for if the distance Bb happens to be very small, after the points F, f, and G, g, are found, draw the right lines Ff and Gg, and they will cut TA and τC in the points required, X and Z.

EXAMPLE

Let the comet of the year 1680 be proposed. The following table shows the motion thereof, as observed by Flamsteed, and calculated afterwards by him from his observations, and corrected by Dr. Halley from the same observations.

| | Time | | Sun's longitude | Comet's | |
	Apparent	True		Longitude	Latitude north
	h m	h m s	° ′ ″	° ′ ″	° ′ ″
1680, *Dec.* 12	4.46	4.46. 0	♑ 1.51.23	♑ 6.32.30	8.28. 0
21	6.32½	6.36.59	11.06.44	♒ 5.08.12	21.42.13
24	6.12	6.17.52	14.09.26	18.49.23	25.23. 5
26	5.14	5.20.44	16.09.22	28.24.13	27.00.52
29	7.55	8.03.02	19.19.43	♓13.10.41	28.09.58
30	8.02	8.10.26	20.21.09	17.38.20	28.11.53
1681, *Jan.* 5	5.51	6.01.38	26.22.18	♈ 8.48.53	26.15. 7
9	6.49	7.00.53	♒ 0.29.02	18.44.04	24.11.56
10	5.54	6.06.10	1.27.43	20.40.50	23.43.52
13	6.56	7.08.55	4.33.20	25.59.48	22.17.28
25	7.44	7.58.42	16.45.36	♉ 9.35. 0	17.56.30
30	8.07	8.21.53	21.49.58	13.19.51	16.42.18
Feb. 2	6.20	6.34.51	24.46.59	15.13.53	16.04. 1
5	6.50	7.04.41	27.49.51	16.59.06	15.27. 3

To these you may add some observations of mine.

These observations were made by a telescope of 7 feet, with a micrometer and threads placed in the focus of the telescope; by these instruments we determined the positions both of the fixed stars among themselves, and of the

	Apparent time	Comet's	
		Longitude	Latitude north
	h m	° ′ ″	° ′ ″
1681, *Feb.* 25	8.30	♉26.18.35	12.46.46
27	8.15	27.04.30	12.36.12
Mar. 1	11. 0	27.52.42	12.23.40
2	8. 0	28.12.48	12.19.38
5	11.30	29.18. 0	12.03.16
7	9.30	♊ 0. 4. 0	11.57. 0
9	8.30	0.43. 4	11.45.52

comet in respect of the fixed stars. Let A represent the star of the fourth magnitude in the left heel of Perseus (Bayer's *o*), B the following star of the third magnitude in the left foot (Bayer's ʒ), C a star of the sixth magnitude (Bayer's

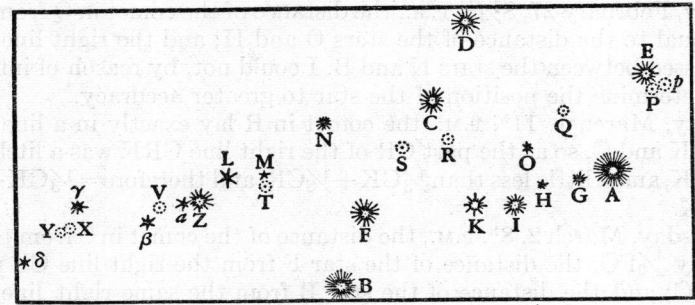

n) in the heel of the same foot, and D, E, F, G, H, I, K, L, M, N, O, Z, *a*, *β*, *γ*, *δ* other smaller stars in the same foot; and let *p*, P, Q, R, S, T, V, X represent the places of the comet in the observations above set down; and, reckoning the distance AB of 80⁷/₁₂ parts, AC was 52¼ of those parts; BC, 58⁵/₆; AD, 57⁵/₁₂; BD, 82⁶/₁₁; CD, 23⅔; AE, 29⁴/₇; CE, 57½; DE, 49¹¹/₁₂; AI, 27⁷/₁₂; BI, 52¹/₆; CI, 36⁷/₁₂; DI, 53⁵/₁₁; AK, 38⅔; BK, 43; CK, 31⁵/₉; FK, 29; FB, 23; FC, 36¼; AH, 18⁶/₇; DH, 50⅞; BN, 46⁵/₁₂; CN, 31⅓; BL, 45⁵/₁₂; NL, 31⁵/₇. HO was to HI as 7 to 6, and, produced, did pass between the stars D and E, so as the distance of the star D from this right line was ⅙CD. LM was to LN as 2 to 9, and, produced, did pass through the star H. Thus were the positions of the fixed stars determined in respect to one another.

The fixed stars	Their longitudes	Latitude north	The fixed stars	Their longitudes	Latitude north
	° ′ ″	° ′ ″		° ′ ″	° ′ ″
A	♉26.41.50	12. 8.36	L	♉29.33.34	12. 7.48
B	28.40.23	11.17.54	M	29.18.54	12. 7.20
C	27.58.30	12.40.25	N	28.48.29	12.31. 9
E	26.27.17	12.52. 7	Z	29.44.48	11.57.13
F	28.28.37	11.52.22	*a*	29.52. 3	11.55.48
G	26.56. 8	12. 4.58	*β*	♊ 0. 8.23	11.48.56
H	27.11.45	12. 2. 1	*γ*	0.40.10	11.55.18
I	27.25. 2	11.53.11	*δ*	1. 3.20	11.30.42
K	27.42. 7	11.53.26			

Mr. Pound has since observed a second time the positions of these fixed stars amongst themselves, and obtained their longitudes and latitudes according to the preceding table.

The positions of the comet to these fixed stars were observed to be as follows:

Friday, February 25, o.s., at $8\frac{1}{2}^h$. P.M., the distance of the comet in p from the star E was less than $\frac{3}{13}$ AE, and greater than $\frac{1}{5}$AE, and therefore nearly equal to $\frac{3}{14}$AE; and the angle ApE was a little obtuse, but almost right. For from A, letting fall a perpendicular on pE, the distance of the comet from that perpendicular was $\frac{1}{5}p$E.

The same night, at $9\frac{1}{2}^h$., the distance of the comet in P from the star E was greater than $\frac{1}{4\frac{1}{4}}$AE, and less than $\frac{1}{5\frac{1}{4}}$AE, and therefore nearly equal to $\frac{1}{4\frac{7}{8}}$ of AE, or $\frac{8}{39}$ AE. But the distance of the comet from the perpendicular let fall from the star A upon the right line PE was $\frac{4}{5}$PE.

Sunday, February 27, $8\frac{1}{4}^h$. P.M., the distance of the comet in Q from the star O was equal to the distance of the stars O and H; and the right line QO produced passed between the stars K and B. I could not, by reason of intervening clouds, determine the position of the star to greater accuracy.

Tuesday, March 1, 11^h. P.M., the comet in R lay exactly in a line between the stars K and C, so as the part CR of the right line CRK was a little greater than $\frac{1}{3}$CK, and a little less than $\frac{1}{3}$CK$+\frac{1}{8}$CR, and therefore $=\frac{1}{3}$CK$+\frac{1}{16}$CR, or $\frac{16}{45}$CK.

Wednesday, March 2, 8^h. P.M., the distance of the comet in S from the star C was nearly $\frac{4}{9}$FC; the distance of the star F from the right line CS produced was $\frac{1}{24}$FC; and the distance of the star B from the same right line was five times greater than the distance of the star F; and the right line NS produced passed between the stars H and I five or six times nearer to the star H than to the star I.

Saturday, March 5, $11\frac{1}{2}^h$. P.M., when the comet was in T, the right line MT was equal to $\frac{1}{2}$ML, and the right line LT produced passed between B and F four or five times nearer to F than to B, cutting off from BF a fifth or sixth part thereof towards F; and MT produced passed on the outside of the space BF towards the star B four times nearer to the star B than to the star F. M was a very small star, scarcely to be seen by the telescope; but the star L was greater, and of about the eighth magnitude.

Monday, March 7, $9\frac{1}{2}^h$. P.M., the comet being in V, the right line Va produced did pass between B and F, cutting off, from BF towards F, $\frac{1}{10}$ of BF, and was to the right line Vβ as 5 to 4. And the distance of the comet from the right line $a\beta$ was $\frac{1}{2}$Vβ.

Wednesday, March 9, $8\frac{1}{2}^h$. P.M., the comet being in X, the right line γX was equal to $\frac{1}{4}\gamma\delta$; and the perpendicular let fall from the star δ upon the right line γX was $\frac{2}{5}$ of $\gamma\delta$.

The same night, at 12^h., the comet being in Y, the right line γY was equal to $\frac{1}{3}$ of $\gamma\delta$, or a little less, as perhaps $\frac{5}{16}$ of $\gamma\delta$; and a perpendicular let fall from the star δ on the right line γY was equal to about $\frac{1}{6}$ or $\frac{1}{7}$ $\gamma\delta$. But the comet, being then extremely near the horizon, was scarcely discernible, and therefore its place could not be determined with the same certainty as in the foregoing observations.

From these observations, by constructions of figures and calculations, I deduced the longitudes and latitudes of the comet; and Mr. Pound, by correcting the places of the fixed stars, has determined more correctly the places of the comet, which correct places are set down above. Though my micrometer was none of the best, yet the errors in longitude and latitude (as derived from my observations) scarcely exceed one minute. The comet (according to my observations), about the end of its motion, began to decline sensibly towards the north, from the parallel which it described about the end of February.

Now, in order to determine the orbit of the comet from the observations above described, I selected those three which Flamsteed made (Dec. 21, Jan. 5, and Jan. 25); from which I found S*t* of 9842.1 parts, and V*t* of 455, supposing the semidiameter of the earth's orbit contains 10,000. Then, for the first observation, assuming *t*B of 5657 of those parts, I found SB 9747, BE for the first time 412, Sμ 9503, $i\lambda$413, BE for the second time 421, OD 10,186, X 8528.4, PM 8450, MN 8475, NP 25; from this, by the second operation, I obtained the distance *tb* 5640; and by this operation I at last deduced the distances TX 4775 and τZ 11,322. From these values, determining the orbit, I found its descending node in ♋, and ascending node in ♑ 1° 53′; the inclination of its plane to the plane of the ecliptic 61° 20⅓′, the vertex thereof (or the perihelion of the comet) distant from the node 8° 38′, and in ♐ 27° 43′, with latitude 7° 34′ south; its latus rectum 236.8; and the diurnal area described by a radius drawn to the sun 93,585, supposing the square of the semidiameter of the earth's orbit 100,000,000; that the comet in this orbit moved directly according to the order of the signs, and on Dec. 8ᵈ. 00ʰ. 04ᵐ. P.M. was in the vertex or perihelion of its orbit. All this I determined by scale and compass, and the chords of angles, taken from the table of natural sines, in a pretty large figure, in which, to wit, the radius of the earth's orbit (consisting of 10,000 parts) was equal to 16⅓ inches of an English foot.

Lastly, in order to discover whether the comet did truly move in the orbit so determined, I investigated its places in this orbit partly by arithmetical operations, and partly by scale and compass, to the times of some of the observations, as may be seen in the following table:

	The Comet's						
	Distance from sun	*Longitude computed*	*Latitude computed*	*Longitude observed*	*Latitude observed*	*Difference longitude*	*Difference latitude*
Dec. 12	2792	♑ 6° 32′	8° 18½	♑ 6° 31½	8° 26	+1	− 7½
29	8403	♓13.13⅔	28.00	♓13.11¾	28.10$\frac{1}{12}$	+2	−10$\frac{1}{12}$
Feb. 5	16669	♉17.00	15.29⅔	♉16.59⅞	15.27⅖	+0	+ 2¼
Mar. 5	21737	29.19¾	12. 4	29.20$\frac{6}{7}$	12. 3½	−1	+ ½

But afterwards Dr. Halley did determine the orbit to a greater accuracy by an arithmetical calculus than could be done by graphic operations; and, retaining the place of the nodes in ♋ and ♑ 1° 53′, and the inclination of the plane of the orbit to the ecliptic 61° 20⅓′, as well as the time of the comet's being in perihelion, Dec. 8ᵈ. 00ʰ. 04ᵐ. he found the distance of the perihelion from the ascending node measured in the comet's orbit 9° 20′, and the latus rectum of the parabola 2430 parts, supposing the mean distance of the sun from the earth to be 100,000 parts; and from these data by an accurate arithmetical calculus, he computed the places of the comet to the times of the observations as given in the table on page 348.

This comet also appeared in the November before, and at Coburg, in Saxony, was observed by Mr. Gottfried Kirch, on the 4th of that month, on the 6th and 11th, o.s.; from its positions to the nearest fixed stars observed with sufficient accuracy, sometimes with a two-foot, and sometimes with a ten-foot telescope; from the difference of longitudes of Coburg and London, 11°; and from the places of the fixed stars observed by Mr. Pound, Dr. Halley has determined the places of the comet as follows:

Nov. 3, 17^h. 2^m., apparent time at London, the comet was in ♌ 29° 51′, with 1° 17′ 45″ latitude north.

Nov. 5, 15^h. 58^m., the comet was in ♍ 3° 23′, with 1° 6′ latitude north.

Nov. 10, 16^h. 31^m., the comet was equally distant from two stars in ♌, which are designated σ and τ in Bayer; but it had not quite touched the right line that joins them, but was very little distant from it. In Flamsteed's cat-

True time			Distance from the sun	The Comet's Longitude computed	The Comet's Latitude computed	Errors in Longitude	Errors in Latitude
d	h	m		° ′ ″	° ′ ″	′ ″	′ ″
Dec. 12.	4.	46.	28028	♑ 6.29.25	8.26. 0 bor.	−3. 5	−2. 0
21.	6.	37.	61076	♒ 5. 6.30	21.43.20	−1.42	+1. 7
24.	6.	18.	70008	18.48.20	25.22.40	−1. 3	−0.25
26.	5.	20.	75576	28.22.45	27. 1.36	−1.28	+0.44
29.	8.	3.	84021	♓13.12.40	28.10.10	+1.59	+0.12
30.	8.	10.	86661	17.40. 5	28.11.20	+1.45	−0.33
Jan. 5.	6.	1.½	101440	♈ 8.49.49	26.15.15	+0.56	+0. 8
9.	7.	0.	110959	18.44.36	24.12.54	+0.32	+0.58
10.	6.	6.	113162	20.41. 0	23.44.10	+0.10	+0.18
13.	7.	9.	120000	26. 0.21	22.17.30	+0.33	+0. 2
25.	7.	59.	145370	♉ 9.33.40	17.57.55	−1.20	+1.25
30.	8.	22.	155303	13.17.41	16.42. 7	−2.10	−0.11
Feb. 2.	6.	35.	160951	15.11.11	16. 4.15	−2.42	+0.14
5.	7.	4.½	166686	16.58.55	15.29.13	−0.41	+2. 0
25.	8.	41.	202570	26.15.46	12.48. 0	−2.49	+1.10
Mar. 5.	11.	39.	216205	29.18.35	12. 5.40	+0.35	+2.14

alogue this star σ was then in ♍ 14° 15′, with 1° 41′ latitude north nearly, and τ in ♍17° 3½′ with 0° 34′ latitude south; and the middle point between those stars was ♍ 15° 39¼′, with 0° 33½′ latitude north. Let the distance of the comet from that right line be about 10′ or 12′; and the difference of the longitude of the comet and that middle point will be 7′; and the difference of the latitude nearly 7½′; and thence it follows that the comet was in ♍ 15° 32′, with about 26′ latitude north.

The first observation from the position of the comet with respect to certain small fixed stars had all the exactness that could be desired; the second also was accurate enough. In the third observation, which was the least accurate, there might be an error of 6′ or 7′, but hardly greater. The longitude of the comet, as found in the first and most accurate observation, being computed in the afore-said parabolic orbit, comes out ♌ 29° 30′ 32″, its latitude north 1° 25′ 7″, and its distance from the sun 115,546.

Moreover, Dr. Halley, observing that a remarkable comet had appeared four times at equal intervals of 575 years (that is, in the month of September after Julius Caesar was killed; [in A.D.] 531, in the consulate of Lampadius and Orestes; [in] 1106, in the month of February: and at the end of the year 1680; and that with a long and remarkable tail, except when it was seen after Caesar's death, at which time, by reason of the inconvenient situation of the earth, the tail was not so conspicuous), set himself to find out an elliptic orbit whose greater axis should be 1,382,957 parts, the mean distance of the earth from the sun containing 10,000 such; in this orbit a comet might revolve in 575 years; and, placing the ascending node in ♋ 2° 2′, the inclination of the plane of the orbit to the plane of the ecliptic in an angle of 61° 6′ 48″, the perihelion of the comet in this plane in ♐ 22° 44′ 25″, the equal time of the perihelion Dec. 7ᵈ. 23ʰ. 9ᵐ., the distance of the perihelion from the ascending node in the

True time	Longitude observed	Latitude N observed	Longitude computed	Latitude computed	Errors in longitude	Errors in latitude
d h m	° ′ ″	° ′ ″	° ′ ″	° ′ ″	′ ″	′ ″
Nov. 3.16.47	♌29.51. 0	1.17.45	♌29.51.22	1.17.32 N	+0.22	−0.13
5.15.37	♍ 3.23. 0	1. 6. 0	♍ 3.24.32	1. 6. 9	+1.32	+0. 9
10.16.18	15.32. 0	0.27. 0	15.33. 2	0.25. 7	+1. 2	−1.53
16.17.00			♎ 8.16.45	0.53. 7 S		
18.21.34			18.52.15	1.26.54		
20.17. 0			28.10.36	1.53.35		
23.17. 5			♏13.22.42	2.29. 0		
Dec. 12. 4.46	♑ 6.32.30	8.28. 0	♑ 6.31.20	8.29 .6 N	−1.10	+1. 6
21. 6.37	♒ 5. 8.12	21.42.13	♒ 5. 6.14	21.44.42	−1.58	+2.29
24. 6.18	18.49.23	25.23. 5	18.47.30	25.23.35	−1.53	+0.30
26. 5.21	28.24.13	27. 0.52	28.21.42	27. 2. 1	−2.31	+1. 9
29. 8. 3	♓13.11.41	28. 9.58	♓13.10.38	28.10.38	+0.33	+0.40
30. 8.10	17.38. 0	28.11.53	17.38.27	28.11.37	+0. 7	−0.16
Jan. 5. 6. 1½	♈ 8.48.53	26.15. 7	♈ 8.48.51	26.14.57	−0. 2	−0.10
9. 7. 1	18.44. 4	24.11.56	18.43.51	24.12.17	−0.13	+0.21
10. 6. 6	20.40.50	23.43.32	20.40.23	23.43.25	−0.27	−0. 7
13. 7. 9	25.59.48	22.17.28	26. 0. 8	22.16.32	+0.20	−0.56
25. 7.59	♉ 9.35. 0	17.56.30	♉ 9.34.11	17.56. 6	−0.49	−0.24
30. 8.22	13.19.51	16.42.18	13.18.28	16.40. 5	−1.23	−2.13
Feb. 2. 6.35	15.13.53	16. 4. 1	15.11.59	16. 2.17	−1.54	−1.54
5. 7. 4½	16.59. 6	15.27. 3	16.59.17	15.27. 0	+0.11	−0. 3
25. 8.41	26.18.35	12.46.46	26.16.59	12.45.22	−1.36	−1.24
Mar. 1.11.10	27.52.42	12.23.40	27.51.47	12.22.28	−0.55	−1.12
5.11.39	29.18. 0	12. 3.16	29.20.11	12. 2.50	+2.11	−0.26
9. 8.38	♊ 0.43. 4	11.45.52	♊0.42.43	11.45.35	−0.21	−0.17

plane of the ecliptic 9° 17′ 35″, and its conjugate axis 18,481.2, he computed the motions of the comet in this elliptic orbit. The places of the comet, as deduced from the observations, and as arising from computation made in this orbit, may be seen in the preceding table.

The observations of this comet from the beginning to the end agree as perfectly with the motion of the comet in the orbit just now described as the motions of the planets do with the theories from whence they are calculated, and by this agreement plainly evince that it was one and the same comet that appeared all that time, and also that the orbit of that comet is here rightly defined.

In the foregoing table we have omitted the observations of Nov. 16, 18, 20, and 23, as not sufficiently accurate, for at those times several persons had observed the comet. Nov. 17, o.s., Ponthio and his companions, at 6ʰ. in the morning at Rome (that is, 5^h. 10^m. at London), by threads directed to the fixed stars, observed the comet in $\simeq 8°\ 30'$, with latitude $0°\ 40'$ south. Their observations may be seen in a treatise which Ponthio published concerning this comet. Cellio, who was present, and communicated his observations in a letter to Cassini, saw the comet at the same hour in $\simeq 8°\ 30'$, with latitude $0°$ $30'$ south. It was likewise seen by Gallet at the same hour at Avignon (that is, at 5^h. 42^m. morning at London) in $\simeq 8°$ without latitude. But by the theory the comet was at that time in $\simeq 8°\ 16'\ 45''$, and its latitude was $0°\ 53'\ 7''$ south.

Nov. 18, at 6^h. 30^m. in the morning at Rome (that is, at 5^h. 40^m. at London), Ponthio observed the comet in $\simeq 13°\ 30'$, with latitude $1°\ 20'$ south; and Cellio in $\simeq 13°\ 30'$, with latitude $1°\ 00'$ south. But at 5^h. 30^m. in the morning at Avignon, Gallet saw it in $\simeq 13°\ 00'$, with latitude $1°\ 00'$ south. In the University of La Fleche, in France, at 5^h. in the morning (that is, at 5^h. 9^m. at London), it was seen by Ango, in the middle between two small stars, one of which is the middle of the three which lie in a right line in the southern hand of Virgo, Bayer's Ψ; and the other is the outmost of the wing, Bayer's θ. Hence, the comet was then in $\simeq 12°\ 46'$ with latitude $50'$ south. And I was informed by Dr. Halley, that on the same day at Boston in New England, in the latitude of $42\frac{1}{2}'$, at 5^h. in the morning (that is, at 9^h. 44^m. in the morning at London) the comet was seen near $\simeq 14°$, with latitude $1°\ 30'$ south.

Nov. 19, at $4\frac{1}{2}^h$. at Cambridge, the comet (by the observation of a young man) was distant from Spica ♍ about $2°$ towards the northwest. Now the Spike was at that time in $\simeq 19°\ 23'\ 47''$, with latitude $2°\ 1'\ 59''$ south. The same day, at 5^h. in the morning, at Boston in New England, the comet was distant from Spica ♍ $1°$, with the difference of $40'$ in latitude. The same day, in the island of Jamaica, it was about $1°$ distant from Spica ♍. The same day, Mr. Arthur Storer, at the river Patuxent, near Hunting Creek, in Maryland, in the confines of Virginia in latitude $38\frac{1}{2}°$, at 5^h. in the morning (that is, at 10^h. at London), saw the comet above Spica ♍, and very nearly joined with it, the distance between them being about $\frac{3}{4}$ of one degree. And from these observations compared, I conclude, that at 9^h. 44^m. at London the comet was in $\simeq 18°\ 50'$, with about $1°\ 25'$ latitude south. Now by the theory the comet was at that time in $\simeq 18°\ 52'\ 15''$, with $1°\ 26'\ 54''$ latitude south.

Nov. 20, Montenari, Professor of Astronomy at Padua, at 6^h. in the morning at Venice (that is, 5^h. 10^m. at London), saw the comet in $\simeq 23°$, with latitude $1°\ 30'$ south. The same day, at Boston, it was distant from Spica ♍ by about $4°$ of longitude east, and therefore was in $\simeq 23°\ 24'$, nearly.

Nov. 21, Ponthio and his companions, at $7\frac{1}{4}^h$. in the morning, observed the comet in $\simeq 27°\ 50'$, with latitude $1°\ 16'$ south; Cellio, in $\simeq 28°$; Ango at 5^h. in the morning, in $\simeq 27°\ 45'$; Montenari in $\simeq 27°\ 51'$. The same day, in the island of Jamaica, it was seen near the beginning of ♏, and of about the same latitude with Spica ♍, that is, $2°\ 2'$. The same day, at 5^h. morning, at Ballasore, in the East Indies (that is, at 11^h. 20^m. of the night preceding at London), the distance of the comet from Spica ♍ was taken $7°\ 35'$ to the east. It was in a right line between the Spike and the Balance, and therefore was then in $\simeq 26°\ 58'$, with about $1°\ 11'$ latitude south; and after 5^h. 40^m. (that is, at 5^h. in the morning at London), it was in $\simeq 28°\ 12'$ with $1°\ 16'$ latitude south. Now by the theory the comet was then in $\simeq 28°\ 10'\ 36''$, with $1°\ 53'\ 35''$ latitude south.

Nov. 22, the comet was seen by Montenari in ♏ 2° 33′; but at Boston in New England it was found in about ♏ 3°, and with almost the same latitude as before, that is, 1° 30′. The same day, at 5ʰ. morning at Ballasore, the comet was observed in ♏ 1° 50′; and therefore at 5ʰ. morning at London, the comet was in ♏ 3° 5′, nearly. The same day at 6½ʰ. in the morning at London, Dr. Hooke observed it in about ♏ 3° 30′, and that in the right line which passeth through Spica ♍ and Cor Leonis; not, indeed, exactly, but deviating a little from that line towards the north. Montenari likewise observed, that this day, and some days after, a right line drawn from the comet through Spica passed by the south side of Cor Leonis at a very small distance therefrom. The right line through Cor Leonis and Spica ♍ did cut the ecliptic in ♍ 3° 46′ at an angle of 2° 51′; and, if the comet had been in this line and in ♏ 3°, its latitude would have been 2° 26′; but since Hooke and Montenari agree that the comet was at some small distance from this line towards the north, its latitude must have been somewhat less. On the 20th, by the observation of Montenari, its latitude was almost the same with that of Spica ♍, that is, about 1° 30′. But by the agreement of Hooke, Montenari, and Ango, the latitude was continually increasing, and therefore must now, on the 22d, be sensibly greater than 1° 30′; and, taking a mean between the extreme limits but now stated, 2° 26′ and 1° 30′, the latitude will be about 1° 58′. Hooke and Montenari agree that the tail of the comet was directed towards Spica ♍, declining a little from that star towards the south according to Hooke, but towards the north according to Montenari; and, therefore, that declination was scarcely sensible; and the tail, lying nearly parallel to the equator, deviated a little from the opposition of the sun towards the north.

Nov. 23, o.s., at 5ʰ. morning, at Nuremberg (that is, at 4½ʰ. at London), Mr. Zimmerman saw the comet in ♏ 8° 8′, with 2° 31′ south latitude, its place being obtained by taking its distances from fixed stars.

Nov. 24, before sunrise, the comet was seen by Montenari in ♏ 12° 52′ on the north side of the right line through Cor Leonis and Spica ♍, and therefore its latitude was somewhat less than 2° 38′; and since the latitude, as we said, by the concurring observations of Montenari, Ango, and Hooke, was continually increasing, therefore, it was now, on the 24th, somewhat greater than 1° 58′; and, taking the mean quantity, may be reckoned 2° 18′, without any considerable error. Ponthio and Gallet will have it that the latitude was now decreasing; and Cellio, and the observer in New England, that it continued the same, viz., of about 1°, or 1½°. The observations of Ponthio and Cellio are rougher, especially those which were made by taking the azimuths and altitudes; as are also the observations of Gallet. Those are better which were made by taking the position of the comet to the fixed stars by Montenari, Hooke, Ango, and the observer in New England, and sometimes by Ponthio and Cellio. The same day, at 5ʰ. morning, at Ballasore, the comet was observed in ♏ 11° 45′; and, therefore, at 5ʰ. morning at London, was in ♏ 13°, nearly. And, by the theory, the comet was at that time in ♏ 13° 22′ 42″.

Nov. 25, before sunrise, Montenari observed the comet in ♏ 17¾°, nearly; and Cellio observed at the same time that the comet was in a right line between the bright star in the right thigh of Virgo and the southern scale of Libra; and this right line cuts the comet's way in ♏ 18° 36′. And, by the theory, the comet was in ♏ 18⅓°, nearly.

From all this it is plain that these observations agree with the theory, so far as they agree with one another; and by this agreement it is made clear that it was one and the same comet that appeared all the time from Nov. 4 to Mar. 9. The path of this comet did twice cut the plane of the ecliptic, and therefore was not a right line. It did cut the ecliptic not in opposite parts of the heavens, but in the end of Virgo and beginning of Capricorn, including an arc of about 98°; and therefore the way of the comet did very much deviate from the path of a great circle; for in the month of Nov. it declined at least 3° from the ecliptic towards the south; and in the month of Dec. following it declined 29° from the ecliptic towards the north; the two parts of the orbit in which the comet descended towards the sun, and ascended again from the sun, declining one from the other by an apparent angle of above 30°, as observed by Montenari. This comet traveled over nine signs, namely, from the last degree of ♌ to the beginning of ♐, beside the sign of ♌, through which it passed before it began to be seen; and there is no other theory by which a comet can go over so great a part of the heavens with a regular motion. The motion of this comet was very unequable; for about the 20th of Nov. it described about 5° a day. Then its motion being retarded between Nov. 26 and Dec. 12, to wit, in the space of 15½ days, it described only 40°. But the motion thereof being afterwards accelerated, it described near 5° a day, till its motion began to be again retarded. And the theory which justly corresponds with a motion so unequable, and through so great a part of the heavens, which observes the same laws with the theory of the planets, and which accurately agrees with accurate astronomical observations, cannot be otherwise than true.

And, thinking it would not be improper, I have given in the annexed figure, plotted in the plane of the curve, a true representation of the orbit which this comet described, and of the tail which it emitted in several places. In this drawing ABC represents the orbit of the comet, D the sun, DE the axis of the orbit, DF the line of the nodes, GH the intersection of the sphere of the earth's

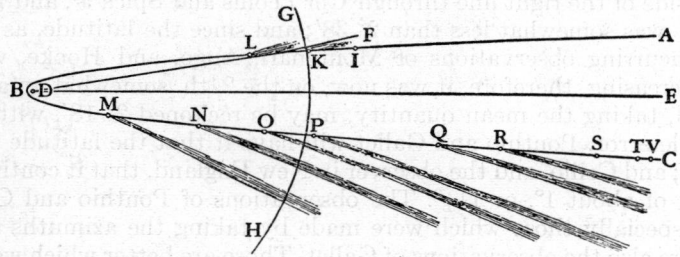

orbit with the plane of the comet's orbit, I the place of the comet Nov. 4, 1680; K the place of the same Nov. 11; L the place of the same Nov. 19; M its place Dec. 12; N its place Dec. 21; O its place Dec. 29; P its place Jan. 5 following; Q its place Jan. 25; R its place Feb. 5; S its place Feb. 25; T its place March 5; and V its place March 9. In determining the length of the tail, I made the following observations:

Nov. 4 and 6, the tail did not appear; Nov. 11, the tail just began to show itself, but did not appear above ½ degree long through a 10-foot telescope; Nov. 17, the tail was seen by Ponthio more than 15° long; Nov. 18, in New England, the tail appeared 30° long, and directly opposite to the sun, extending itself to the planet Mars, which was then in ♍, 9° 54'; Nov. 19, in Maryland, the tail was found 15° or 20° long; Dec. 10 (by the observation of Mr. Flamsteed), the tail passed through the middle of the distance intercepted between the tail of the serpent of Ophiuchus and the star δ in the south wing of Aquila, and did terminate near the stars A, ω, b in Bayer's tables. Therefore the end of the tail was in ♑ 19½°, with latitude about 34¼° north; Dec. 11, it ascended to the head of Sagitta (Bayer's α, β), terminating in ♑ 26° 43', with latitude 38° 34' north; Dec. 12, it passed through the middle of Sagitta, nor did it reach much farther; terminating in ♒ 4°, with latitude 42½° north, nearly. But these things are to be understood of the length of the brighter part of the tail; for, with a more faint light, observed, too, perhaps, in a serener sky, at Rome, Dec. 12, 5ʰ. 40ᵐ., by the observation of Ponthio, the tail arose to 10° above the rump of the Swan, and the side thereof towards the west and towards the north was 45' distant from this star. But about that time the tail was 3° broad towards the upper end; and therefore the middle thereof was 2° 15' distant from that star towards the south, and the upper end was in ♓ 22°, with latitude 61° north; and thence the tail was about 70° long; Dec. 21, it extended almost to Cassiopeia's Chair, equally distant from β and from Schedir, so as its distance from either of the two was equal to the distance of the one from the other, and therefore did terminate in ♈ 24°, with latitude 47½°; Dec. 29, it reached to a contact with Scheat on its left, and exactly filled up the space between the two stars in the northern foot of Andromeda, being 54° in length; and therefore terminated in ♉ 19°, with 35° of latitude; Jan. 5, it touched the star π in the breast of Andromeda on its right side, and the star μ of the girdle on its left; and, according to our observations, was 40° long; but it was curved, and the convex side thereof lay to the south; and near the head of the comet it made an angle of 4° with the circle which passed through the sun and the comet's head; but towards the other end it was inclined to that circle in an angle of about 10° or 11°; and the chord of the tail contained with that circle an angle of 8°. Jan. 13, the tail terminated between Alamech and Algol, with a light that was sensible enough; but with a faint light it ended over against the star κ in Perseus' side. The distance of the end of the tail from the circle passing through the sun and the comet was 3° 50'; and the inclination of the chord of the tail to that circle was 8½°. Jan. 25 and 26, it shone with a faint light to the length of 6° or 7°; and, for a night or two after, when there was a very clear sky, it extended to the length of 12°, or somewhat more, with a light that was very faint and very hardly to be seen; but the axis thereof was exactly directed to the bright star in the eastern shoulder of Auriga, and therefore deviated from the opposition of the sun towards the north by an angle of 10°. Lastly, Feb. 10, with a telescope I observed the tail 2° long; for that fainter light which I spoke of did not appear through the glasses. But Ponthio writes that, on Feb. 7, he saw the tail 12° long. Feb. 25, the comet was without a tail, and so continued till it disappeared.

Now if one reflects upon the orbit described, and duly considers the other appearances of this comet, he will be easily satisfied that the bodies of comets are solid, compact, fixed, and durable, like the bodies of the planets; for if they were nothing else but the vapors or exhalations of the earth, of the sun, and other planets, this comet, in its passage by the neighborhood of the sun, would have been immediately dissipated; for the heat of the sun is as the density of its rays, that is, inversely as the square of the distance of the places from the sun. Therefore, since on Dec. 8, when the comet was in its perihelion, the distance thereof from the centre of the sun was to the distance of the earth from the same as about 6 to 1000, the sun's heat on the comet was at that time to the heat of the summer-sun with us as 1,000,000 to 36, or as 28,000 to 1. But the heat of boiling water is about three times greater than the heat which dry earth acquires from the summer-sun, as I have tried; and the heat of red-hot iron (if my conjecture is right) is about three or four times greater than the heat of boiling water. And therefore the heat which dry earth on the comet, while in its perihelion, might have received from the rays of the sun, was about 2000 times greater than the heat of red-hot iron. But by so fierce a heat, vapors and exhalations, and every volatile matter, must have been immediately consumed and dissipated.

This comet, therefore, must have received an immense heat from the sun, and retained that heat for an exceeding long time; for a globe of iron of an inch in diameter, exposed red-hot to the open air, will scarcely lose all its heat in an hour's time; but a greater globe would retain its heat longer in the ratio of its diameter, because the surface (in proportion to which it is cooled by the contact of the ambient air) is in that ratio less in respect of the quantity of the included hot matter; and therefore a globe of red-hot iron equal to our earth, that is, about 40,000,000 feet in diameter, would scarcely cool in an equal number of days, or in above 50,000 years. But I suspect that the duration of heat may, on account of some latent causes, increase in a yet less ratio than that of the diameter; and I should be glad that the true ratio was investigated by experiments.

It is further to be observed, that the comet in the month of December, just after it had been heated by the sun, did emit a much longer tail, and much more splendid, than in the month of November before, when it had not yet arrived at its perihelion; and, universally, the greatest and most fulgent tails always arise from comets immediately after their passing by the neighborhood of the sun. Therefore the heat received by the comet conduces to the greatness of the tail: from this, I think I may infer, that the tail is nothing else but a very fine vapor, which the head or nucleus of the comet emits by its heat.

But we have had three several opinions about the tails of comets: for some will have it that they are nothing else but the beams of the sun's light transmitted through the comets' heads, which they suppose to be transparent; others, that they proceed from the refraction which light suffers in passing from the comet's head to the earth; and, lastly, others, that they are a sort of cloud or vapor constantly rising from the comets' heads, and tending towards the parts opposite to the sun. The first is the opinion of such as are yet unacquainted with optics; for the beams of the sun are seen in a darkened room only in consequence of the light that is reflected from them by the little particles of dust and smoke which are always flying about in the air; and, for that reason, in air impregnated with thick smoke, those beams appear with great brightness, and impress the eye more strongly; in a yet finer air they appear more faint, and are less easily discerned; but in the heavens, where there is no matter to reflect the light, they can never be seen at all. Light is not seen as it is in the beam, but as it is thence reflected to our eyes; for vision can be produced in no other way than by rays falling upon the eyes; and, therefore, there must be some reflecting matter in those parts where the tails of the comets are seen: for otherwise, since all the celestial spaces are equally illuminated by the sun's light, no part of the heavens could appear with more splendor than another. The second opinion is liable to many difficulties. The tails of comets are never seen variegated with those colors which commonly are inseparable from refraction; and the distinct transmission of the light of the fixed stars and planets to us is a demonstration that the ether or celestial medium is not endowed with any refractive power: for, as to what is alleged, that the fixed stars have been sometimes seen by the Egyptians environed with a coma, because that has but rarely happened, it is rather to be ascribed to a casual refraction of clouds; and so the radiation and scintillation of the fixed stars to the refractions both of the eyes and air; for, upon laying a telescope to the eye, those radiations and scintillations immediately disappear. By the tremulous agitation of the air and ascending vapors, it happens that the rays of light are alternately turned aside from the narrow space of the pupil of the eye; but no such thing can have place in the much wider aperture of the object glass of a telescope; and hence it is that a scintillation is occasioned in the former case, which ceases in the latter; and this cessation in the latter case is a demonstration of the regular transmission of light through the heavens, without any perceptible refraction. But, to obviate an objection that may be made from the appearing of no tail in such comets as shine but with a faint light, as if the secondary rays were then too weak to affect the eyes, and for that reason it is that the tails of the fixed stars do not appear, we are to consider, that by the means of telescopes the light of the fixed stars may be augmented above an hundredfold, and yet no tails are seen; that the light of the planets is yet more copious without any tail; but that comets are seen sometimes with huge tails, when the light of their heads is but faint and dull. For so it happened in the comet of the year 1680, when in the month of December it was scarcely equal in light to the stars of the second magnitude, and yet emitted a notable tail, extending to the length of 40°, 50°, 60°, or 70°, and upwards; and afterwards, on the 27th and 28th of January, when the head appeared but as a star of the 7th magnitude, yet the tail (as we said above), with a light that was clearly perceptible, though faint, was stretched out to 6° or 7° in length, and with a languishing light that was more difficult to see, even to 12°, and upwards. But on the 9th and 10th of February, when to the naked eye the head appeared no more, through a telescope I viewed the tail of 2° in length. But further: if the tail was due to the crumbling of the celestial matter, and did deviate from the opposition of the sun, according to the figure of the heavens, that deviation in the same places of the heavens should be always directed towards the same parts. But the comet of the year 1680, December 28^d. 8½^h. P.M. at London, was seen in ♓ 8° 41′, with latitude north 28° 6′; while the sun was in ♑ 18° 26′. And the comet of the year 1577, December 29^d., was in ♓ 8° 41′, with latitude north 28° 40′, and the sun, as before, in about ♑ 18° 26′. In both cases the situation of the earth was the same, and the comet appeared in the same place of the heavens; yet in the former case the tail of the comet (as well by my observations as by the observations of others) deviated from the opposition of the sun towards the north by an angle of 4½ degrees; whereas in the latter there was (according to the observations of Tycho) a deviation of 21 degrees towards the south. The crumbling, therefore, of the heavens being thus disproved, it remains that the phenomena of the tails of comets must be derived from some reflecting matter.

And that the tails of comets do arise from their heads, and tend towards the parts opposite to the sun, is further confirmed from the laws which the tails observe: As that, lying in the planes of the comets' orbits which pass through the sun, they constantly deviate from the opposition of the sun towards the parts which the comets' heads in their progress along these orbits have left. That to a spectator, placed in those planes, they appear in the parts directly opposite to the sun; but, as the spectator recedes from those planes, their deviation begins to appear, and daily becomes greater. That the deviation, other things being equal, appears less when the tail is more oblique to the orbit of the comet, as well as when the head of the comet approaches nearer to the sun, especially if the angle of deviation is estimated near the head of the comet. That the tails which have no deviation appear straight, but the tails which deviate are likewise bended into a certain curvature. That this curvature is greater when the deviation is greater; and is more sensible when the tail, other things being equal, is longer; for in the shorter tails the curvature is hardly to be perceived. That the angle of deviation is less near the comet's head, but greater towards the other end of the tail; and that because the convex side of the tail regards the parts from which the deviation is made, and which lie in a right line drawn out infinitely from the sun through the comet's head. And that the tails that are long and broad, and shine with a stronger light, appear more resplendent and more exactly defined on the convex than on the concave side. Upon these accounts it is plain that the phenomena of the tails of comets depend upon the motions of their heads, and by no means upon the places of the heavens in which their heads are seen; and that, therefore, the tails of comets do not proceed from the refraction of the heavens, but from their own heads, which furnish the matter that forms the tail. For, as in our air, the smoke of a heated body ascends either perpendicularly if the body is at rest, or obliquely if the body is moved obliquely, so in the heavens, where all bodies gravitate towards the sun, smoke and vapor must (as we have already said) ascend from the sun, and either rise perpendicularly if the smoking body is at rest, or obliquely if the body, in all the progress of its motion, is always leaving those places from which the upper or higher parts of the vapor had risen before; and that obliquity will be least where the vapor ascends with most velocity, namely, near the smoking body, when that is near the sun. But, because the obliquity varies, the column of vapor will be incurvated; and because the vapor in the preceding side is something more recent, *that is, has ascended something more late from the body*, it will therefore be somewhat more dense on that side, and must on that account reflect more light, as well as be better defined. I add nothing concerning the sudden uncertain agitation of the tails of comets, and their irregular figures, which authors sometimes describe, because they may arise from the mutations of our air, and the motions of our clouds, in part obscuring those tails; or, perhaps, from parts of the Milky Way which might have been confounded with and mistaken for parts of the tails of the comets as they passed by.

But that the atmospheres of comets may furnish a supply of vapor great enough to fill so immense spaces, we may easily understand from the rarity of our own air; for the air near the surface of our earth possesses a space 850

times greater than water of the same weight; and therefore a cylinder of air
850 feet high is of equal weight with a cylinder of water of the same breadth,
and but one foot high. But a cylinder of air reaching to the top of the atmosphere is of equal weight with a cylinder of water about 33 feet high: and, therefore, if from the whole cylinder of air the lower part of 850 feet high is taken
away, the remaining upper part will be of equal weight with a cylinder of
water 32 feet high: and from thence (and by the hypothesis, confirmed by
many experiments, that the compression of air is as the weight of the incumbent atmosphere, and that the force of gravity is inversely as the square of the
distance from the centre of the earth) proceeding by calculation, by Cor., Prop.
22, Book II, I found, that, at the height of one semidiameter of the earth,
reckoned from the earth's surface, the air is more rare than with us in a far
greater ratio than that of the whole space within the orbit of Saturn to a
spherical space one inch in diameter; and therefore, if a sphere of our air of
but one inch in thickness was equally rarefied with the air at the height of one
semidiameter of the earth from the earth's surface, it would fill all the regions
of the planets to the orb of Saturn, and far beyond it. Therefore, since the air
at greater distances is immensely rarefied, and the coma or atmosphere of
comets is ordinarily about ten times higher, reckoning from their centres, than
the surface of the nucleus, and the tails rise yet higher, they must therefore be
exceedingly rare; and though, on account of the much thicker atmospheres of
comets, and the great gravitation of their bodies towards the sun, as well as of
the particles of their air and vapors towards each other, it may happen that
the air in the celestial spaces and in the tails of comets is not so vastly rarefied,
yet from this computation it is plain that a very small quantity of air and
vapor is abundantly sufficient to produce all the appearances of the tails of
comets; for that they are, indeed, of a very notable rarity appears from the
shining of the stars through them. The atmosphere of the earth, illuminated by
the sun's light, though but of a few miles in thickness, quite obscures and ex-
tinguishes the light not only of all the stars, but even of the moon itself; whereas the smallest stars are seen to shine through the immense thickness of the
tails of comets, likewise illuminated by the sun, without the least diminution
of their splendor. Nor is the brightness of the tails of most comets ordinarily
greater than that of our air, an inch or two in thickness, reflecting in a darkened room the light of the sunbeams let in by a hole of the window shutter.

And we may pretty nearly determine the time spent during the ascent of the
vapor from the comet's head to the extremity of the tail, by drawing a right
line from the extremity of the tail to the sun, and marking the place where
that right line intersects the comet's orbit; for the vapor that is now in the
extremity of the tail, if it has ascended in a right line from the sun, must have
begun to rise from the head at the time when the head was in the point of
intersection. It is true, the vapor does not rise in a right line from the sun, but,
retaining the motion which it had from the comet before its ascent, and compounding that motion with its motion of ascent, arises obliquely; and, therefore, the solution of the Problem will be more exact, if we draw the line which
intersects the orbit parallel to the length of the tail; or rather (because of the
curvilinear motion of the comet) diverging a little from the line or length of
the tail. And by means of this principle I found that the vapor which, January
25, was in the extremity of the tail, had begun to rise from the head before

December 11, and therefore had spent in its whole ascent 45 days; but that the whole tail which appeared on December 10 had finished its ascent in the space of the two days then elapsed from the time of the comet's being in its perihelion. The vapor, therefore, about the beginning and in the neighborhood of the sun rose with the greatest velocity, and afterwards continued to ascend with a motion constantly retarded by its own gravity; and the higher it ascended, the more it added to the length of the tail; and while the tail continued to be seen, it was made up of almost all that vapor which had risen since the time of the comet's being in its perihelion; nor did that part of the vapor which had risen first, and which formed the extremity of the tail, cease to appear, till its too great distance, as well from the sun, from which it received its light, as from our eyes, rendered it invisible. Whence also it is that the tails of other comets which are short do not rise from their heads with a swift and continued motion, and soon after disappear, but are permanent and lasting columns of vapors and exhalations, which, ascending from the heads with a slow motion of many days, and partaking of the motion of the heads which they had from the beginning, continue to go along together with them through the heavens. From this again we have another argument proving the celestial spaces to be free, and without resistance, since in them not only the solid bodies of the planets and comets, but also the extremely rare vapors of comets' tails, maintain their rapid motions with great freedom, and for an exceeding long time.

Kepler ascribes the ascent of the tails of the comets to the atmospheres of their heads; and their direction towards the parts opposite to the sun to the action of the rays of light carrying along with them the matter of the comets' tails; and without any great incongruity we may suppose that, in so free spaces, so fine a matter as that of the ether may yield to the action of the rays of the sun's light, though those rays are not able sensibly to move the gross substances in our parts, which are clogged with so palpable a resistance. Another author thinks that there may be a sort of particles of matter endowed with a principle of levity, as well as others are with a power of gravity; that the matter of the tails of comets may be of the former sort, and that its ascent from the sun may be owing to its levity; but, considering that the gravity of terrestrial bodies is as the matter of the bodies, and therefore can be neither more nor less in the same quantity of matter, I am inclined to believe that this ascent may rather proceed from the rarefaction of the matter of the comets' tails. The ascent of smoke in a chimney is due to the impulse of the air with which it is entangled. The air rarefied by heat ascends, because its specific gravity is diminished, and in its ascent carries along with it the smoke which floats in it; and why may not the tail of a comet rise from the sun after the same manner? For the sun's rays do not act upon the mediums which they pervade otherwise than by reflection and refraction; and those reflecting particles heated by this action, heat the matter of the ether which is involved with them. That matter is rarefied by the heat which it acquires, and because, by this rarefaction, the specific gravity with which it tended towards the sun before is diminished, it will ascend therefrom, and carry along with it the reflecting particles of which the tail of the comet is composed. But the ascent of the vapors is further promoted by their circumgyration about the sun; in consequence thereof they endeavor to recede from the sun, while the sun's atmosphere and the other matter of the heavens are either altogether quiescent, or are only moved with a slower circumgyration derived from the rotation of the sun. And these are the causes of the ascent of the tails of the comets in the neighborhood of the sun, where their orbits are bent into a greater curvature, and the comets themselves are plunged into the denser and therefore heavier parts of the sun's atmosphere: upon which account they do then emit tails of an huge length; for the tails which then arise, retaining their own proper motion, and in the meantime gravitating towards the sun, must be revolved in ellipses about the sun in like manner as the heads are, and by that motion must always accompany the heads, and freely adhere to them. For the gravitation of the vapors towards the sun can no more force the tails to abandon the heads, and descend to the sun, than the gravitation of the heads can oblige them to fall from the tails. They must by their common gravity either fall together towards the sun, or be retarded together in their common ascent therefrom; and, therefore (whether from the causes already described, or from any others), the tails and heads of comets may easily acquire and freely retain any position one to the other, without disturbance or impediment from that common gravitation.

The tails, therefore, that rise in the perihelian positions of the comets will go along with their heads into far remote parts, and together with the heads will either return again from thence to us, after a long course of years, or rather will be there rarefied, and by degrees quite vanish away; for afterwards, in the descent of the heads towards the sun, new short tails will be emitted from the heads with a slow motion; and those tails by degrees will be augmented immensely, especially in such comets as in their perihelian distances descend as low as the sun's atmosphere; for all vapor in those free spaces is in a perpetual state of rarefaction and dilatation; and from hence it is that the tails of all comets are broader at their upper extremity than near their heads. And it is not unlikely but that the vapor, thus continually rarefied and dilated, may be at last dissipated and scattered through the whole heavens, and by little and little be attracted towards the planets by its gravity, and mixed with their atmosphere; for as the seas are absolutely necessary to the constitution of our earth, that from them, the sun, by its heat, may exhale a sufficient quantity of vapors, which, being gathered together into clouds, may drop down in rain, for watering of the earth, and for the production and nourishment of vegetables; or, being condensed with cold on the tops of mountains (as some philosophers with reason judge), may run down in springs and rivers; so for the conservation of the seas, and fluids of the planets, comets seem to be required, that, from their exhalations and vapors condensed, the wastes of the planetary fluids spent upon vegetation and putrefaction, and converted into dry earth, may be continually supplied and made up; for all vegetables entirely derive their growths from fluids, and afterwards, in great measure, are turned into dry earth by putrefaction; and a sort of slime is always found to settle at the bottom of putrefied fluids; and hence it is that the bulk of the solid earth is continually increased; and the fluids, if they are not supplied from without, must be in a continual decrease, and quite fail at last. I suspect, moreover, that it is chiefly from the comets that spirit comes, which is indeed the smallest but the most subtle and useful part of our air, and so much required to sustain the life of all things with us.

The atmospheres of comets, in their descent towards the sun, by running out into the tails, are spent and diminished, and become narrower, at least on that side which regards the sun; and in receding from the sun, when they less run out into the tails, they are again enlarged, if Hewelcke has justly marked their appearances. But they are seen least of all just after they have been most heated by the sun, and on that account then emit the longest and most resplendent tails; and, perhaps, at the same time, the nuclei are environed with a denser and blacker smoke in the lowermost parts of their atmosphere; for smoke that is raised by a great and intense heat is commonly the denser and blacker. Thus the head of that comet which we have been describing, at equal distances both from the sun and from the earth, appeared darker after it had passed by its perihelion than it did before; for in the month of December it was commonly compared with the stars of the third magnitude, but in November with those of the first or second; and such as saw both appearances have described the first as of another and greater comet than the second. For, November 19, this comet appeared to a young man at Cambridge, though with a pale and dull light, yet equal to Spica Virginis; and at that time it shone with greater brightness than it did afterwards. And Montenari, November 20, o.s., observed it larger than the stars of the first magnitude, its tail being then 2 degrees long. And Mr. Storer (by letters which have come into my hands) writes that in the month of December, when the tail appeared of the greatest bulk and splendor, the head was but small, and far less than that which was seen in the month of November before sun rising; and, conjecturing at the cause of the appearance, he judged it to proceed from the existence of a greater quantity of matter in the head at first, which was afterwards gradually spent.

And, for the same reason, I find, that the heads of other comets, which did put forth tails of the greatest bulk and splendor, have appeared but obscure and small. For in Brazil, March 5, 1668, N.S., 7^h. P.M., Valentin Estancel saw a comet near the horizon, and towards the southwest, with a head so small as scarcely to be discerned, but with a tail above measure splendid, so that the reflection thereof from the sea was easily seen by those who stood on the shore; it looked like a fiery beam extended 23 degrees in length from the west to south, almost parallel to the horizon. But this excessive splendor continued only three days, decreasing apace afterwards; and while the splendor was decreasing, the bulk of the tail increased: also in Portugal it is said to have taken up one-quarter of the heavens, that is, 45 degrees, extending from west to east with a very notable splendor, though the whole tail was not seen in those parts, because the head was always hid under the horizon: and from the increase of the bulk and decrease of the splendor of the tail, it appears that the head was then in its recess from the sun, and had been very near to it in its perihelion, as the comet of 1680 was. And we read, in the *Saxon Chronicle*, of a like comet appearing in the year 1106, *the star whereof was small and obscure* (as that of 1680), *but the splendor of its tail was very bright, and like a huge fiery beam stretched out in a direction between the east and north*, as Hewelcke has it also from Simeon, the monk of Durham. This comet appeared in the beginning of February, about the evening, and towards the southwest part of heaven; from this, and from the position of the tail, we infer that the head was near the sun. Matthew Paris says, *It was distant from the sun by about a cubit, from three o'clock* (rather six) *till nine, putting forth a long tail*. Such also was that resplendent comet described by Aristotle, *Meteorology*, i, 6. *The head whereof could not be seen, because it had set before the sun, or at least was hid under the sun's rays; but next day it was seen as well as might be; for, having left the sun but a very little way, it set immediately after it. And the scattered light of the head, obscured by the too great splendor* (of the tail) *did not yet appear. But afterwards* (as Aristotle says) *when the splendor* (of the tail) *had diminished,* (the head of) *the comet recovered its native brightness; and the splendor* (of its tail) *reached now to a third part of the heavens* (that is, to 60°). *This appearance was in the winter season* (the fourth year of the 101st Olympiad), *and, rising to Orion's girdle, it there vanished away.* It is true that the comet of 1618, which came out directly from under the sun's rays with a very large tail, seemed to equal, if not to exceed, the stars of the first magnitude; but then, abundance of other comets have appeared yet greater than this, that put forth shorter tails; some of which are said to have appeared as big as Jupiter, others as big as Venus, or even as the moon.

We have said that comets are a sort of planets revolved in very eccentric orbits about the sun; and as, in the planets which are without tails, those are commonly less which are revolved in lesser orbits, and nearer to the sun, so in comets it is probable that those which in their perihelion approach nearer to the sun are generally of less magnitude, that they may not agitate the sun too much by their attractions. But as to the transverse diameters of their orbits, and the periodic times of their revolutions, I leave them to be determined by comparing comets together which after long intervals of time return again in the same orbit. In the meantime, the following Proposition may give some light in that inquiry.

PROPOSITION 42. PROBLEM 22

To correct a comet's orbit found as above.

OPERATION 1. Assume that position of the plane of the orbit which was determined according to the preceding Proposition; and select three places of the comet, deduced from very accurate observations, and at great distances one from the other. Then suppose A to represent the time between the first observation and the second, and B the time between the second and the third; but it will be convenient that in one of those times the comet be in its perigee, or at least not far from it. From those apparent places find, by trigonometric operations, the three true places of the comet in that assumed plane of the orbit; then through the places found, and about the centre of the sun as the focus, describe a conic section by arithmetical operations, according to Prop. 21, Book I. Let the areas of this figure which are terminated by radii drawn from the sun to the places found be D and E; namely, D the area between the first observation and the second, and E the area between the second and third; and let T represent the whole time in which the whole area D+E should be described with the velocity of the comet found by Prop. 16, Book I.

OPER. 2. Retaining the inclination of the plane of the orbit to the plane of the ecliptic, let the longitude of the nodes of the plane of the orbit be increased by the addition of 20′ or 30′, which call P. Then from the aforesaid three observed places of the comet let the three true places be found (as before) in this new plane; as also the orbit passing through those places, and the two areas of the same described between the two observations, which call d and e; and let t be the whole time in which the whole area d+e should be described.

OPER. 3. Retaining the longitude of the nodes in the first operation, let the inclination of the plane of the orbit to the plane of the ecliptic be increased by adding thereto 20′ or 30′, which call Q. Then from the aforesaid three observed apparent places of the comet let the three true places be found in this new plane, as well as the orbit passing through them, and the two areas of the same described between the observation, which call δ and ε; and let τ be the whole time in which the whole area δ+ε should be described.

Then taking C to 1 as A to B; and G to 1 as D to E; and g to 1 as d to e; and γ to 1 as δ to ε; let S be the true time between the first observation and the third; and, observing well the signs + and −, let such numbers m and n be found out as will make $2G-2C=mG-mg+nG-n\gamma$; and $2T-2S=mT-mt+nT-n\tau$. And if, in the first operation, I represents the inclination of the plane of the orbit to the plane of the ecliptic, and K the longitude of either node, then $I+nQ$ will be the true inclination of the plane of the orbit to the plane of the ecliptic, and $K+mP$ the true longitude of the node. And, lastly, if in the first, second, and third operations, the quantities R, r, and ρ, represent the parameters of the orbit, and the quantities $\dfrac{1}{L}, \dfrac{1}{l}, \dfrac{1}{\gamma}$, the transverse diameters of the same, then $R+mr-mR+n\rho-nR$ will be the true parameter, and $\dfrac{1}{L+ml-mL+n\lambda-nL}$ will be the true transverse diameter of the orbit which the comet describes; and from the transverse diameter given the periodic time of the comet is also given. Q.E.I. But the periodic times of the revolutions of comets, and the transverse diameters of their orbits, cannot be accurately enough determined but by comparing comets together which appear at different times. If, after equal intervals of time, several comets are found to have described the same orbit, we may thence conclude that they are all but one and the same comet revolved in the same orbit; and then from the times of their revolutions the transverse diameters of their orbits will be given, and from those diameters the elliptic orbits themselves will be determined.

To this purpose the orbits of many comets ought to be computed, supposing those orbits to be parabolic; for such orbits will always nearly agree with the phenomena, as appears not only from the parabolic orbit of the comet of the year 1680, which I compared above with the observations, but likewise from that of the notable comet which appeared in the year 1664 and 1665, and was observed by Hewelcke, who, from his own observations, calculated the longitudes and latitudes thereof, though with little accuracy. But from the same observations Dr. Halley did again compute its places; and from those new places determined its orbit, finding its ascending node in ♓ 21° 13′ 55″; the inclination of the orbit to the plane of the ecliptic 21° 18′ 40″; the distance of its perihelion from the node, estimated in the comet's orbit, 49° 27′ 30″, its perihelion in ♌ 8° 40′ 30″, with heliocentric latitude south 16° 01′ 45″; the comet to have been in its perihelion November 24^d. 11^h. 52^m. P.M. equal time at London, or 13^h. 8^m. at Danzig, O.S.; and that the latus rectum of the parabola was 410,286 of such parts as the sun's mean distance from the earth is supposed to contain 100,000. And how nearly the places of the comet computed in this orbit agree with the observations, will appear from the table calculated by Dr. Halley (p 364).

In February, the beginning of the year 1665, the first star of Aries, which I shall hereafter call γ, was in ♈ 28° 30′ 15″, with 7° 8′ 58″ north latitude; the second star of Aries was in ♈ 29° 17′ 18″, with 8° 28′ 16″ north latitude; another star of the seventh magnitude, which I call A, was in ♈ 28° 24′ 45″, with 8° 28′ 33″ north latitude. The comet Feb. 7ᵈ. 7ʰ. 30ᵐ. at Paris (that is, Feb. 7ᵈ. 8ʰ. 37ᵐ. at Danzig), o.s., made a triangle with those stars γ and A, which was right-angled in γ; and the distance of the comet from the star γ was equal to the distance of the stars γ and A, that is, 1° 19′ 46″ of a great circle; and therefore in the parallel of the latitude of the star γ it was 1° 20′ 26″. Therefore if from the longitude of the star γ there be subtracted the longitude 1° 20′ 26″, there will remain the longitude of the comet ♈ 27° 9′ 49″. M. Auzout, from this observation of his, placed the comet in ♈ 27° 0′, nearly; and, by the drawing in which Dr. Hooke delineated its motion, it was then in ♈ 26° 59′ 24″. I place it in ♈ 27° 4′ 46″, taking the middle between the two extremes.

From the same observations, M. Auzout made the latitude of the comet at that time 7° and 4′ or 5′ to the north; but he had done better to have made it 7° 3′ 29″, the difference of the latitudes of the comet and the star γ being equal to the difference of the longitude of the stars γ and A.

February 22ᵈ. 7ʰ. 30ᵐ. at London, that is, February 22ᵈ. 8ʰ. 46ᵐ. at Danzig, the distance of the comet from the star A, according to Dr. Hooke's observation, as was delineated by himself in a scheme, and also by the observations of M. Auzout, delineated in like manner by M. Petit, was a fifth part of the distance between the star A and the first star of Aries, or 15′ 57″; and the distance of the comet from a right line joining the star A and the first of Aries was a fourth part of the same fifth part, that is, 4′; and therefore the comet was in ♈ 28° 29′ 46″, with 8° 12′ 36″ north latitude.

March 1, 7ʰ. 0ᵐ. at London, that is, March 1, 8ʰ. 16ᵐ. at Danzig, the comet was observed near the second star in Aries, the distance between them being to the distance between the first and second stars in Aries, that is, to 1° 33′, as 4 to 45 according to Dr. Hooke, or as 2 to 23 according to M. Gottignies. And, therefore, the distance of the comet from the second star in Aries was 8′ 16″ according to Dr. Hooke, or 8′ 5″ according to M. Gottignies; or, taking a mean between both, 8′ 10″. But, according to M. Gottignies, the comet had gone beyond the second star of Aries about a fourth or a fifth part of the space that it commonly went over in a day, to wit, about 1′ 35″ (in which he agrees very well with M. Auzout); or, according to Dr. Hooke, not quite so much, as perhaps only 1′. Therefore if to the longitude of the first star in Aries we add 1′, and 8′ 10″ to its latitude, we shall have the longitude of the comet ♈ 29° 18′, with 8° 36′ 26″ north latitude.

March 7, 7ʰ. 30ᵐ. at Paris, that is, March 7, 7ʰ. 37ᵐ. at Danzig, from the observations of M. Auzout, the distance of the comet from the second star in Aries was equal to the distance of that star from the star A, that is, 52′ 29″; and the difference of the longitude of the comet and the second star in Aries was 45′ or 46′, or, taking a mean quantity, 45′ 30″; and therefore the comet was in ♉ 0° 2′ 48″. From the drawing constructed by M. Petit, based on the observations of M. Auzout, Hewelcke determined the latitude of the comet 8° 54′. But the engraver did not rightly trace the curvature of the comet's way towards the end of the motion; and Hevelius, in the drawing of M. Auzout's observations which he constructed himself, corrected this irregular curvature,

Apparent time at Danzig	The observed distances of the comet from		The observed places		The places computed in the orbit
		° ′ ″		° ′ ″	° ′ ″
December d h m 3.18.29½	The Lion's heart The Virgin's spike	46.24.20 22.52.10	Long. ♎ 7.01.00 Lat. S. 21.39. 0		♎ 7. 1.29 21.38.50
4.18. 1½	The Lion's heart The Virgin's spike	46. 2.45 23.52.40	Long. ♎ 6.15. 0 Lat. S. 22.24. 0		♎ 6.16. 5 22.24. 0
7.17.48	The Lion's heart The Virgin's spike	44.48. 0 27.56.40	Long. ♎ 3. 6. 0 Lat. S. 25.22. 0		♎ 3. 7.33 25.21.40
17.14.43	The Lion's heart Orion's right shoulder	53.15.15 45.43.30	Long. ♌ 2.56. 0 Lat. S. 49.25. 0		♌ 2.56. 0 49.25. 0
19. 9.25	Procyon Bright star of Whale's jaw	35.13.50 52.56. 0	Long. ♊ 28.40.30 Lat. S. 45.48. 0		♊ 28.43. 0 45.46. 0
20. 9.53½	Procyon Bright star of Whale's jaw	40.49. 0 40.04. 0	Long. ♊ 13.03. 0 Lat. S. 39.54. 0		♊ 13. 5. 0 39.53. 0
21. 9. 9½	Orion's right shoulder Bright star of Whale's jaw	26.21.25 29.28. 0	Long. ♊ 2.16. 0 Lat. S. 33.41. 0		♊ 2.18.30 33.39.40
22. 9. 0	Orion's right shoulder Bright star of Whale's jaw	29.47. 0 20.29.30	Long. ♉ 24.24. 0 Lat. S. 27.45. 0		♉ 24.27. 0 27.46. 0
26. 7.58	The bright star of Aries Aldebaran	23.20. 0 26.44. 0	Long. ♉ 9. 0. 0 Lat. S. 12.36. 0		♉ 9. 2.28 12.34.13
27. 6.45	The bright star of Aries Aldebaran	20.45. 0 28.10. 0	Long. ♉ 7. 5.40 Lat. S. 10.23. 0		♉ 7. 8.45 10.23.13
28. 7.39	The bright star of Aries Palilicium	18.29. 0 29.37. 0	Long. ♉ 5.24.45 Lat. S. 8.22.50		♉ 5.27.52 8.23.37
31. 6.45	Andromeda's girdle Palilicium	30.48.10 32.53.30	Long. ♉ 2. 7.40 Lat. S. 4.13. 0		♉ 2. 8.20 4.16.25
Jan. 1665 7. 7.37½	Andromeda's girdle Palilicium	25.11. 0 37.12.25	Long. ♈ 28.24.47 Lat. N. 0.54. 0		♈ 28.24. 0 0.53. 0
13. 7. 0	Andromeda's head Palilicium	28. 7.10 38.55.20	Long. ♈ 27. 6.54 Lat. N. 3. 6.50		♈ 27. 6.39 3. 7.40
24. 7.29	Andromeda's girdle Palilicium	20.32.15 40. 5. 0	Long. ♈ 26.29.15 Lat. N. 5.25.50		♈ 26.28.50 5.26. 0
February 7. 8.37			Long. ♈ 27. 4.46 Lat. N. 7. 3.29		♈ 27.24.55 7. 3.15
22. 8.46			Long. ♈ 28.29.46 Lat. N. 8.12.36		♈ 28.29.58 8.10.25
March 1. 8.16			Long. ♈ 29.18.15 Lat. N. 8.36.26		♈ 29.18.20 8.36.12
7. 8.37			Long. ♉ 0. 2.48 Lat. N. 8.56.30		♉ 0. 2.42 8.56.56

and so made the latitude of the comet 8° 55′ 30″. And, by further correcting this irregularity, the latitude may become 8° 56′, or 8° 57′.

This comet was also seen March 9, and at that time its place must have been in ♉ 0° 18′, with 9° 3½′ north latitude, nearly.

This comet appeared for three months, in which space of time it traveled over almost six signs, and in one of the days described almost 20 degrees. Its course did very much deviate from a great circle, bending towards the north, and its motion towards the end from retrograde became direct; and, notwithstanding that its course was so uncommon, yet by the table it appears that the theory, from beginning to end, agrees with the observations no less accurately than the theories of the planets usually do with the observations of them; but we are to subtract about 2′ when the comet was swiftest, which we may effect by taking off 12″ from the angle between the ascending node and the perihelion, or by making that angle 49° 27′ 18″. The annual parallax of both these comets (this and the preceding) was very conspicuous, and by its quantity demonstrates the annual motion of the earth in the earth's orbit.

This theory is likewise confirmed by the motion of that comet, which in the year 1683 appeared retrograde, in an orbit whose plane contained almost a right angle with the plane of the ecliptic, and whose ascending node (by the computation of Dr. Halley) was in ♍ 23° 23′; the inclination of its orbit to the ecliptic 83° 11′; its perihelion in ♊ 25° 29′ 30″; its perihelian distance from the sun 56,020 of such parts as the radius of the earth's orbit contains 100,000; and the time of its perihelion was July 2ᵈ. 3ʰ. 50ᵐ. And the places thereof, computed by Dr. Halley in this orbit, are compared with the places observed by Mr. Flamsteed, in the following table.

This theory is yet further confirmed by the motion of that retrograde comet which appeared in the year 1682. The ascending node of this (by Dr. Halley's

1683 Equatorial time	Sun's place	Comet's longitude computed	Latitude north computed	Comet's longitude observed	Latitude north observed	Difference longitude	Difference latitude
d h m	° ′ ″	° ′ ″	° ′ ″	° ′ ″	° ′ ″	′ ″	′ ″
July 13.12.55	♌ 1.02.30	♋13.05.42	29.28.13	♋13. 6.42	29.28.20	+1.00	+0.07
15.11.15	2.53.12	11.37.48	29.34. 0	11.39.43	29.34.50	+1.55	+0.50
17.10.20	4.45.45	10. 7. 6	29.33.30	10. 8.40	29.34. 0	+1.34	+0.30
23.13.40	10.38.21	5.10.27	28.51.42	5.11.30	28.50.28	+1.03	−1.14
25.14. 5	12.35.28	3.27.53	24.24.47	3.27. 0	28.23.40	−0.53	−1. 7
31. 9.42	18.09.22	♊27.55. 3	26.22.52	♊27.54.24	26.22.25	−0.39	−0.27
31.14.55	18.21.53	27.41. 7	26.16.57	27.41. 8	26.14.50	+0. 1	−2. 7
Aug. 2.14.56	20.17.16	25.29.32	25.16.19	25.28.46	25.17.28	−0.46	+1. 9
4.10.49	22.02.50	23.18.20	24.10.49	23.16.55	24.12.19	−1.25	+1.30
6.10. 9	23.56.45	20.42.23	22.47. 5	20.40.32	22.49. 5	−1.51	+2. 0
9.10.26	26.50.52	16. 7.57	20. 6.37	16. 5.55	20. 6.10	−2. 2	−0.27
15.14. 1	♍ 2.47.13	3.30.48	11.37.33	3.26.18	11.32. 1	−4.30	−5.32
16.15.10	3.48. 2	0.43. 7	9.34.16	0.41.55	9.34.13	−1.12	−0. 3
18.15.44	5.45.33	♉24.52.53	5.11.15	♉24.49. 5	5. 9.11	−3.48	−2. 4
			South		South		
22.14.44	9.35.49	11. 7.14	5.16.58	11.07.12	5.16.58	−0. 2	−0. 3
23.15.52	10.36.48	7. 2.18	8.17. 9	7. 1.17	8.16.41	−1. 1	−0.28
26.16. 2	13.31.10	♈24.45.31	16.38. 0	♈24.44.00	16.38.20	−1.31	+0.20

computation) was in ♉ 21° 16′ 30″; the inclination of its orbit to the plane of the ecliptic 17° 56′ 00″; its perihelion in ♒ 2° 52′ 50″; its perihelian distance from the sun 58,328 parts, of which the radius of the earth's orbit contains 100,000; the equal time of the comet's being in its perihelion September 4^d. 7^h. 39^m. And its places determined from Mr. Flamsteed's observations, are compared with its places computed from our theory in the following table:

1682 App. time	Sun's place	Comet's longitude computed	Latitude north computed	Comet's longitude observed	Latitude north observed	Difference longitude	Difference latitude
d h m	° ′ ″	° ′ ″	° ′ ″	° ′ ″	° ′ ″	′ ″	′ ″
Aug. 19.16.38	♍ 7. 0. 7	♌18.14.28	25.50. 7	♌18.14.40	25.49.55	−0.12	+0.12
20.15.38	7.55.52	24.46.23	26.14.42	24.46.22	26.12.52	+0. 1	+1.50
21. 8.21	8.36.14	29.37.15	26.20. 3	29.38.02	26.17.37	−0.47	+2.26
22. 8. 8	9.33.55	♍ 6.29.53	26. 8.42	♍ 6.30. 3	26. 7.12	−0.10	+1.30
29.08.20	16.22.40	♎12.37.54	18.37.47	♎12.37.49	18.34. 5	+0. 5	+3.42
30. 7.45	17.19.41	15.36. 1	17.26.43	15.35.18	17.27.17	+0.43	−0.34
Sept. 1. 7.33	19.16. 9	20.30.53	15.13. 0	20.27. 4	15. 9.49	+3.49	+3.11
4. 7.22	22.11.28	25.42. 0	12.23.48	25.40.58	12.22. 0	+1. 2	+1.48
5. 7.32	23.10.29	27. 0.46	11.33.08	26.59.24	11.33.51	+1.22	−0.43
8. 7.16	26. 5.58	29.58.44	9.26.46	29.58.45	9.26.43	−0. 1	+0. 3
9. 7.26	27. 5. 9	♏ 0.44.10	8.49.10	♏ 0.44. 4	8.48.25	+0. 6	+0.45

This theory is also confirmed by the retrograde motion of the comet that appeared in the year 1723. The ascending node of this comet (according to the computation of Mr. Bradley, Savilian Professor of Astronomy at Oxford) was in ♈ 14° 16′, the inclination of the orbit to the plane of the ecliptic 49° 59′. Its perihelion was in ♉ 12° 15′ 20″, its perihelian distance from the sun 998,651 parts, of which the radius of the earth's orbit contains 1,000,000, and the equal time of its perihelion September 16^d. 16^h. 10^m. The places of this comet computed in this orbit by Mr. Bradley, and compared with the places observed by himself, his uncle Mr. Pound, and Dr. Halley, may be seen in the following table.

1723 Equatorial time	Comet's longitude observed	Latitude north observed	Comet's longitude computed	Latitude north computed	Difference longitude	Difference latitude
d h m	° ′ ″	° ′ ″	° ′ ″	° ′ ″	″	″
Oct. 9.8. 5	♒7.22.15	5. 2. 0	♒7.21.26	5. 2.47	+49	−47
10.6.21	6.41.12	7.44.13	6.41.42	7.43.18	−50	+55
12.7.22	5.39.58	11.55. 0	5.40.19	11.54.55	−21	+ 5
14.8.57	4.59.49	14.43.50	5. 0.37	14.44. 1	−48	−11
15.6.35	4.47.41	15.40.51	4.47.45	15.40.55	− 4	− 4
21.6.22	4. 2.32	19.41.49	4. 2.21	19.42. 3	+11	−14
22.6.24	3.59. 2	20. 8.12	3.59.10	20. 8.17	− 8	− 5
24.8. 2	3.55.29	20.55.18	3.55.11	20.55. 9	+18	+ 9
29.8.56	3.56.17	22.20.27	3.56.42	22.20.10	−25	+17
30.6.20	3.58. 9	22.32.28	3.58.17	22.32.12	− 8	+16
Nov. 5.5.53	4.16.30	23.38.33	4.16.23	23.38. 7	+ 7	+26
8.7. 6	4.29.36	24. 4.30	4.29.54	24. 4.40	−18	−10
14.6.20	5. 2.16	24.48.46	5. 2.51	24.48.16	−35	+30
20.7.45	5.42.20	25.24.45	5.43.13	25.25.17	−53	−32
Dec. 7.6.45	8. 4.13	26.54.18	8. 3.55	26.53.42	+18	+36

From these examples it is abundantly evident that the motions of comets are no less accurately represented by our theory than the motions of the planets commonly are by the theories of them; and, therefore, by means of this theory, we may enumerate the orbits of comets, and so discover the periodic time of a comet's revolution in any orbit; hence, at last, we shall have the transverse diameters of their elliptic orbits and their aphelian distances.

That retrograde comet which appeared in the year 1607 described an orbit whose ascending node (according to Dr. Halley's computation) was in ♉ 20° 21′; and the inclination of the plane of the orbit to the plane of the ecliptic 17° 2′; whose perihelion was in ♒ 2° 16′; and its perihelian distance from the sun 58,680 of such parts as the radius of the earth's orbit contains 100,000; and the comet was in its perihelion October 16^d. 3^h. 50^m.; which orbit agrees very nearly with the orbit of the comet which was seen in 1682. If these were not two different comets, but one and the same, that comet will finish one revolution in the space of 75 years; and the greater axis of its orbit will be to the greater axis of the earth's orbit as $\sqrt[3]{75^2}$ to 1, or as 1778 to 100, nearly. And the aphelian distance of this comet from the sun will be to the mean distance of the earth from the sun as about 35 to 1; from these data it will be no hard matter to determine the elliptic orbit of this comet. But these things are to be supposed on condition that, after the space of 75 years, the same comet shall return again in the same orbit. The other comets seem to ascend to greater heights, and to require a longer time to perform their revolutions.

But, because of the great number of comets, of the great distance of their aphelions from the sun, and of the slowness of their motions in the aphelions, they will, by their mutual gravitations, disturb each other; so that their eccentricities and the times of their revolutions will be sometimes a little increased, and sometimes diminished. Therefore, we are not to expect that the same comet will return exactly in the same orbit, and in the same periodic times: it will be sufficient if we find the changes no greater than may arise from the causes just spoken of.

And hence a reason may be assigned why comets are not comprehended within the limits of a zodiac, as the planets are; but, being confined to no bounds, are with various motions dispersed all over the heavens; namely, to this purpose, that in their aphelions, where their motions are exceedingly slow, receding to greater distances one from another, they may suffer less disturbance from their mutual gravitations: and hence it is that the comets which descend the lowest, and therefore move the slowest in their aphelions, ought also to ascend the highest.

The comet which appeared in the year 1680 was in its perihelion less distant from the sun than by a sixth part of the sun's diameter; and because of its extreme velocity in that proximity to the sun, and some density of the sun's atmosphere, it must have suffered some resistance and retardation; and therefore, being attracted somewhat nearer to the sun in every revolution, will at last fall down upon the body of the sun. Nay, in its aphelion, where it moves the slowest, it may sometimes happen to be yet further retarded by the attractions of other comets, and in consequence of this retardation descend to the sun. So fixed stars, that have been gradually wasted by the light and vapors emitted from them for a long time, may be recruited by comets that fall upon them; and from this fresh supply of new fuel those old stars, acquiring new splendor, may pass for new stars. Of this kind are such fixed stars as appear on a sudden, and shine with a wonderful brightness at first, and afterwards vanish by little and little. Such was that star which appeared in Cassiopeia's Chair; which Cornelis Gemma did not see upon the 8th of November, 1572, though he was observing that part of the heavens upon that very night, and the sky was perfectly serene; but the next night (November 9) he saw it shining much brighter than any of the fixed stars, and scarcely inferior to Venus in splendor. Tycho Brahe saw it upon the 11th of the same month, when it shone with the greatest lustre; and from that time he observed it to decay by little and little; and in 16 months' time it entirely disappeared. In the month of November, when it first appeared, its light was equal to that of Venus. In the month of December, its light was a little diminished, and was now become equal to that of Jupiter. In January, 1573, it was less than Jupiter, and greater than Sirius, and about the end of February and the beginning of March became equal to that star. In the months of April and May it was equal to a star of the second magnitude; in June, July, and August, to a star of the third magnitude; in September, October, and November, to those of the fourth magnitude; in December and January, 1574, to those of the fifth; in February to those of the sixth magnitude; and in March it entirely vanished. Its color at the beginning was clear, bright, and inclining to white; afterwards it turned a little yellow; and in March, 1573, it became ruddy, like Mars or Aldebaran; in May it turned to a kind of dusky whiteness, like that we observe in Saturn; and that color it retained ever after, but growing always more and more obscure. Such also was the star in the right foot of Serpentarius, which Kepler's scholars first observed September 30, o.s., 1604, with a light exceeding that of Jupiter, though the night before it was not to be seen; and from that time it decreased by little and little, and in 15 or 16 months entirely disappeared. Such a new star appearing with an unusual splendor is said to have moved Hipparchus to observe, and make a catalogue of, the fixed stars. As to those fixed stars that appear and disappear by turns, and increase slowly and by degrees, and scarcely ever exceed the stars of the third magnitude, they seem to be of another kind, which revolve about their axes, and, having a light and a dark side, show those two different sides by turns. The vapors which arise from the sun, the fixed stars, and the tails of the comets, may meet at last with, and fall into, the atmospheres of the planets by their gravity, and there be condensed and turned into water and humid spirits; and from thence, by a slow heat, pass gradually into the form of salts, and sulphurs, and tinctures, and mud, and clay, and sand, and stones, and coral, and other terrestrial substances.

GENERAL SCHOLIUM

THE hypothesis of vortices is pressed with many difficulties. That every planet by a radius drawn to the sun may describe areas proportional to the times of description, the periodic times of the several parts of the vortices should observe the square of their distances from the sun; but that the periodic times of the planets may obtain the $\frac{3}{2}$th power of their distances from the sun, the periodic times of the parts of the vortex ought to be as the $\frac{3}{2}$th power of their distances. That the smaller vortices may maintain their lesser revolutions about Saturn, Jupiter, and other planets, and swim quietly and undisturbed in the greater vortex of the sun, the periodic times of the parts of the sun's vortex should be equal; but the rotation of the sun and planets about their axes, which ought to correspond with the motions of their vortices, recede far from all these proportions. The motions of the comets are exceedingly regular, are governed by the same laws with the motions of the planets, and can by no means be accounted for by the hypothesis of vortices; for comets are carried with very eccentric motions through all parts of the heavens indifferently, with a freedom that is incompatible with the notion of a vortex.

Bodies projected in our air suffer no resistance but from the air. Withdraw the air, as is done in Mr. Boyle's vacuum, and the resistance ceases; for in this void a bit of fine down and a piece of solid gold descend with equal velocity. And the same argument must apply to the celestial spaces above the earth's atmosphere; in these spaces, where there is no air to resist their motions, all bodies will move with the greatest freedom; and the planets and comets will constantly pursue their revolutions in orbits given in kind and position, according to the laws above explained; but though these bodies may, indeed, continue in their orbits by the mere laws of gravity, yet they could by no means have at first derived the regular position of the orbits themselves from those laws.

The six primary planets are revolved about the sun in circles concentric with the sun, and with motions directed towards the same parts, and almost in the same plane. Ten moons are revolved about the earth, Jupiter, and Saturn, in circles concentric with them, with the same direction of motion, and nearly in the planes of the orbits of those planets; but it is not to be conceived that mere mechanical causes could give birth to so many regular motions, since the comets range over all parts of the heavens in very eccentric orbits; for by that kind of motion they pass easily through the orbs of the planets, and with great rapidity; and in their aphelions, where they move the slowest, and are detained the longest, they recede to the greatest distances from each other, and hence suffer the least disturbance from their mutual attractions. This most beautiful system of the sun, planets, and comets, could only proceed from the counsel and dominion of an intelligent and powerful Being. And if the fixed stars are the centres of other like systems, these, being formed by the like wise counsel, must be all subject to the dominion of One; especially since the light of the fixed stars is of the same nature with the light of the sun, and from every system light passes into all the other systems: and lest the systems of the fixed stars should, by their gravity, fall on each other, he hath placed those systems at immense distances from one another.

This Being governs all things, not as the soul of the world, but as Lord over all; and on account of his dominion he is wont to be called *Lord God* παντοκρά-τωρ, or *Universal Ruler;* for *God* is a relative word, and has a respect to servants; and *Deity* is the dominion of God not over his own body, as those imagine who fancy God to be the soul of the world, but over servants. The Supreme God is a Being eternal, infinite, absolutely perfect; but a being, however perfect, without dominion, cannot be said to be Lord God; for we say, my God, your God, the God of Israel, the God of Gods, and Lord of Lords; but we do not say, my Eternal, your Eternal, the Eternal of Israel, the Eternal of Gods; we do not say, my Infinite, or my Perfect: these are titles which have no respect to servants. The word *God*[1] usually signifies *Lord;* but every lord is not a God. It is the dominion of a spiritual being which constitutes a God: a true, supreme, or imaginary dominion makes a true, supreme, or imaginary God. And from his true dominion it follows that the true God is a living, intelligent, and powerful Being; and, from his other perfections, that he is supreme, or most perfect. He is eternal and infinite, omnipotent and omniscient; that is, his duration reaches from eternity to eternity; his presence from infinity to infinity; he governs all things, and knows all things that are or can be done. He is not eternity and infinity, but eternal and infinite; he is not duration or space, but he endures and is present. He endures forever, and is everywhere present; and, by existing always and everywhere, he constitutes duration and space. Since every particle of space is *always*, and every indivisible moment of duration is *everywhere*, certainly the Maker and Lord of all things cannot be *never* and *nowhere*. Every soul that has perception is, though in different times and in different organs of sense and motion, still the same indivisible person. There are given successive parts in duration, coexistent parts in space, but neither the one nor the other in the person of a man, or his thinking principle; and much less can they be found in the thinking substance of God. Every man, so far as he is a thing that has perception, is one and the same man during his whole life, in all and each of his organs of sense. God is the same God, always and everywhere. He is omnipresent not *virtually* only, but also *substantially;* for virtue cannot subsist without substance. In him[2] are all things contained and moved; yet neither affects the other: God suffers nothing from the motion of bodies; bodies find no resistance from the omnipresence of God. It is allowed by all that the Supreme God exists necessarily; and by the same necessity he

---

[1]Dr. Pocock derives the Latin word *Deus* from the Arabic *du* (in the oblique case *di*), which signifies *Lord*. And in this sense princes are called *gods*, Psalms, 82.6; and John, 10.35. And Moses is called a *god* to his brother Aaron, and a *god* to Pharaoh, Exodus, 4.16; and 7.1. And in the same sense the souls of dead princes were formerly, by the heathens, called *gods*, but falsely, because of their want of dominion.

[2]This was the opinion of the ancients. So Pythagoras, in Cicero *De natura deorum* i. Thales, Anaxagoras, Virgil, in *Georgics* iv. 220; and *Aeneid* vi. 721. Philo, *Allegories*, at the beginning of Book I. Aratus, in his *Phænomena*, at the beginning. So also the sacred writers: as St. Paul, in Acts, 17.27, 28. St. John's Gospel, 14.2. Moses, in Deuteronomy, 4.39; and 10.14. David, in Psalms, 139.7,8,9. Solomon, in I Kings, 8.27. Job, 22.12,13,14. Jeremiah, 23.23,24. The idolaters supposed the sun, moon, and stars, the souls of men, and other parts of the world, to be parts of the Supreme God, and therefore to be worshipped; but erroneously.

exists *always* and *everywhere*. Whence also he is all similar, all eye, all ear, all brain, all arm, all power to perceive, to understand, and to act; but in a manner not at all human, in a manner not at all corporeal, in a manner utterly unknown to us. As a blind man has no idea of colors, so have we no idea of the manner by which the all-wise God perceives and understands all things. He is utterly void of all body and bodily figure, and can therefore neither be seen, nor heard, nor touched; nor ought he to be worshiped under the representation of any corporeal thing. We have ideas of his attributes, but what the real substance of anything is we know not. In bodies, we see only their figures and colors, we hear only the sounds, we touch only their outward surfaces, we smell only the smells, and taste the savors; but their inward substances are not to be known either by our senses, or by any reflex act of our minds: much less, than, have we any idea of the substance of God. We know him only by his most wise and excellent contrivances of things, and final causes; we admire him for his perfections; but we reverence and adore him on account of his dominion: for we adore him as his servants; and a god without dominion, providence, and final causes, is nothing else but Fate and Nature. Blind metaphysical necessity, which is certainly the same always and everywhere, could produce no variety of things. All that diversity of natural things which we find suited to different times and places could arise from nothing but the ideas and will of a Being necessarily existing. But, by way of allegory, God is said to see, to speak, to laugh, to love, to hate, to desire, to give, to receive, to rejoice, to be angry, to fight, to frame, to work, to build; for all our notions of God are taken from the ways of mankind by a certain similitude, which, though not perfect, has some likeness, however. And thus much concerning God; to discourse of whom from the appearances of things, does certainly belong to natural philosophy.

Hitherto we have explained the phenomena of the heavens and of our sea by the power of gravity, but have not yet assigned the cause of this power. This is certain, that it must proceed from a cause that penetrates to the very centres of the sun and planets, without suffering the least diminution of its force; that operates not according to the quantity of the surfaces of the particles upon which it acts (as mechanical causes used to do), but according to the quantity of the solid matter which they contain, and propagates its virtue on all sides to immense distances, decreasing always as the inverse square of the distances. Gravitation towards the sun is made up out of the gravitations towards the several particles of which the body of the sun is composed; and in receding from the sun decreases accurately as the inverse square of the distances as far as the orbit of Saturn, as evidently appears from the quiescence of the aphelion of the planets; nay, and even to the remotest aphelion of the comets, if those aphelions are also quiescent. But hitherto I have not been able to discover the cause of those properties of gravity from phenomena, and I frame no hypotheses; for whatever is not deduced from the phenomena is to be called an hypothesis; and hypotheses, whether metaphysical or physical, whether of occult qualities or mechanical, have no place in experimental philosophy. In this philosophy particular propositions are inferred from the phenomena, and afterwards rendered general by induction. Thus it was that the impenetrability, the mobility, and the impulsive force of bodies, and the laws of motion and of gravitation, were discovered. And to us it is enough that gravity does really exist, and act according to the laws which we have explained, and abundantly serves to account for all the motions of the celestial bodies, and of our sea.

And now we might add something concerning a certain most subtle spirit which pervades and lies hid in all gross bodies; by the force and action of which spirit the particles of bodies attract one another at near distances, and cohere, if contiguous; and electric bodies operate to greater distances, as well repelling as attracting the neighboring corpuscles; and light is emitted, reflected, refracted, inflected, and heats bodies; and all sensation is excited, and the members of animal bodies move at the command of the will, namely, by the vibrations of this spirit, mutually propagated along the solid filaments of the nerves, from the outward organs of sense to the brain, and from the brain into the muscles. But these are things that cannot be explained in few words, nor are we furnished with that sufficiency of experiments which is required to an accurate determination and demonstration of the laws by which this electric and elastic spirit operates.

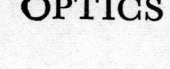

OPTICS

CONTENTS

CONTENTS

ADVERTISEMENT TO FIRST EDITION

PART of the ensuing discourse about light was written at the desire of some gentlemen of the Royal Society, in the year 1675, and then sent to their Secretary, and read at their meetings, and the rest was added about twelve years after to complete the theory; except the third book, and the last proposition of the second, which were since put together out of scattered papers. To avoid being engaged in disputes about these matters, I have hitherto delayed the printing, and should still have delayed it, had not the importunity of friends prevailed upon me. If any other papers writ on this subject are got out of my hands they are imperfect, and were perhaps written before I had tried all the experiments here set down, and fully satisfied myself about the laws of refractions and composition of colours. I have here published what I think proper to come abroad, wishing that it may not be translated into another language without my consent.

The crowns of colours, which sometimes appear about the Sun and Moon, I have endeavoured to give an account of; but for want of sufficient observations leave that matter to be further examined. The subject of the third book I have also left imperfect, not having tried all the experiments which I intended when I was about these matters, nor repeated some of those which I did try, until I had satisfied myself about all their circumstances. To communicate what I have tried, and leave the rest to others for further enquiry, is all my design in publishing these papers.

In a letter written to Mr. Leibnitz in the year 1679, and published by Dr. Wallis, I mentioned a method by which I had found some general theorems about squaring curvilinear figures, or comparing them with the conic sections, or other the simplest figures with which they may be compared. And some years ago I lent out a manuscript containing such theorems, and having since met with some things copied out of it, I have on this occasion made it public, prefixing to it an Introduction, and subjoining a Scholium concerning that method. And I have joined with it another small tract concerning the curvilinear figures of the second kind, which was also written many years ago, and made known to some friends, who have solicited the making it public.

I. N.

April 1, 1704.

ADVERTISEMENT TO SECOND EDITION

IN this Second Edition of these *Optics* I have omitted the mathematical tracts published at the end of the former edition, as not belonging to the subject. And at the end of the third book I have added some questions. And to shew that I do not take gravity for an essential property of bodies, I have added one question concerning its cause, choosing to propose it by way of a question, because I am not yet satisfied about it for want of experiments.

I. N.

July 16, 1717.

BOOK ONE

Part I

My design in this book is not to explain the properties of light by hypotheses, but to propose and prove them by reason and experiments: in order to which I shall premise the following definitions and axioms.

DEFINITIONS

DEFINITION I

By the rays of light I understand its least parts, and those as well successive in the same lines, as contemporary in several lines.

For it is manifest that light consists of parts, both successive and contemporary; because in the same place you may stop that which comes one moment, and let pass that which comes presently after; and in the same time you may stop it in any one place, and let it pass in any other. For that part of light which is stopped cannot be the same with that which is let pass. The least light or part of light, which may be stopped alone without the rest of the light, or propagated alone, or do or suffer any thing alone, which the rest of the light doth not or suffers not, I call a *ray* of light.

DEFINITION II

Refrangibility of the rays of light, is their disposition to be refracted or turned out of their way in passing out of one transparent body or medium into another. And a greater or less refrangibility of rays is their disposition to be turned more or less out of their way in like incidences on the same medium.

Mathematicians usually consider the rays of light to be lines reaching from the luminous body to the body illuminated, and the refraction of those rays to be the bending or breaking of those lines in their passing out of one medium into another. And thus may rays and refractions be considered, if light be propagated in an instant. But by an argument taken from the equations of the times of the eclipses of Jupiter's satellites, it seems that light is propagated in time, spending in its passage from the Sun to us about seven minutes of time: and, therefore, I have chosen to define rays and refractions in such general terms as may agree to light in both cases.

DEFINITION III

Reflexibility of rays is their disposition to be reflected or turned back into the same medium from any other medium upon whose surface they fall. And rays are more or less reflexible which are turned back more or less easily.

As if light pass out of a glass into air, and by being inclined more and more to the common surface of the glass and air, begins at length to be totally reflected by that surface; those sorts of rays which at like incidences are reflected most copiously, or by inclining the rays begin soonest to be totally reflected, are most reflexible.

DEFINITION IV

The angle of incidence is that angle which the line described by the incident ray contains with the perpendicular to the reflecting or refracting surface at the point of incidence.

DEFINITION V

The angle of reflexion or refraction is the angle which the line described by the reflected or refracted ray containeth with the perpendicular to the reflecting or refracting surface at the point of incidence.

DEFINITION VI

The sines of incidence, reflexion, and refraction are the sines of the angles of incidence, reflexion, and refraction.

DEFINITION VII

The light whose rays are all alike refrangible I call Simple, Homogeneal and Similar; and that whose rays are some more refrangible than others I call compound, heterogeneal *and* dissimilar.

The former light I call homogeneal, not because I would affirm it so in all respects, but because the rays which agree in refrangibility agree at least in all those their other properties which I consider in the following discourse.

DEFINITION VIII

The colours of homogeneal lights I call primary, homogeneal *and* simple; *and those of heterogeneal lights,* heterogeneal *and* compound.

For these are always compounded of the colours of homogeneal lights; as will appear in the following discourse.

AXIOMS

AXIOM I

The angles of reflexion and refraction lie in one and the same plane with the angle of incidence.

AXIOM II

The angle of reflexion is equal to the angle of incidence.

AXIOM III

If the refracted ray be returned directly back to the point of incidence, it shall be refracted into the line before described by the incident ray.

AXIOM IV

Refraction out of the rarer medium into the denser is made towards the perpendicular; that is, so that the angle of refraction be less than the angle of incidence.

AXIOM V

The sine of incidence is either accurately or very nearly in a given ratio to the sine of refraction.

Whence if that proportion be known in any one inclination of the incident ray, 'tis known in all the inclinations, and thereby the refraction in all cases of incidence on the same refracting body may be determined. Thus, if the refraction be made out of air into water, the sine of incidence of the red light is to the sine of its refraction as 4 to 3. If out of air into glass, the sines are as 17 to 11. In light of other colours the sines have other proportions: but the difference is so little that it need seldom be considered.

Suppose, therefore, that RS [Fig. 1] represents the surface of stagnating water, and that C is the point of incidence in which any ray coming in the air

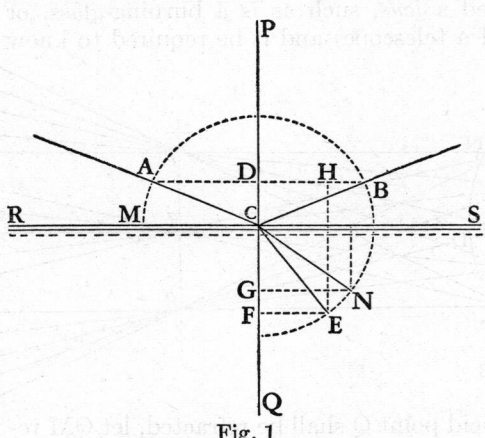

Fig. 1

from A in the line AC is reflected or refracted, and I would know whither this ray shall go after reflexion or refraction: I erect upon the surface of the water from the point of incidence the perpendicular CP and produce it downwards to Q, and conclude by the first Axiom that the ray after reflexion and refraction shall be found somewhere in the plane of the angle of incidence ACP produced. I let fall, therefore, upon the perpendicular CP the sine of incidence AD; and if the reflected ray be desired, I produce AD to B so that DB be equal to AD, and draw CB. For this line CB shall be the reflected ray; the angle of reflexion BCP and its sine BD being equal to the angle and sine of incidence, as they ought to be by the second Axiom. But if the refracted ray be desired, I produce AD to H, so that DH may be to AD as the sine of refraction to the sine of incidence, that is (if the light be red) as 3 to 4; and about the centre C and in the plane ACP, with the radius CA describing a circle ABE, I draw a parallel to the perpendicular CPQ, the line HE cutting the circumference in E and joining CE; this line CE shall be the line of the refracted ray. For if EF be let fall perpendicularly on the line PQ, this line EF shall be the sine of refraction of the ray CE, the angle of refraction being ECQ; and this sine EF is equal to DH, and consequently in proportion to the sine of incidence AD as 3 to 4.

In like manner, if there be a prism of glass (that is, a glass bounded with two equal and parallel triangular ends, and three plain and well polished sides, which meet in three parallel lines running from the three angles of one end to the

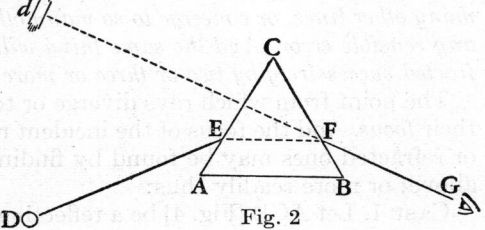

Fig. 2

three angles of the other end) and if the refraction of the light in passing cross this prism be desired: let ACB [Fig. 2] represent a plane cutting this prism transversely to its three parallel lines or edges there where the light passeth through it, and let DE be the ray incident upon the first side of the prism AC where the light goes into the glass; and by putting the proportion of the sine of incidence to the sine of refraction as 17 to 11 find EF the first refracted ray. Then, taking this ray for the incident ray upon the second side of the glass BC where the light goes out, find the next refracted ray FG by putting the proportion of the sine of incidence to the sine of refraction as 11 to 17. For if the sine of incidence out of air into glass be to the sine of refraction as 17 to 11, the sine of incidence out of glass into air must on the contrary be to the sine of refraction as 11 to 17, by the third Axiom.

Much after the same manner, if ACBD [Fig. 3] represent a glass spherically convex on both sides (usually called a *lens*, such as is a burning-glass, or spectacle-glass, or an object-glass of a telescope) and it be required to know

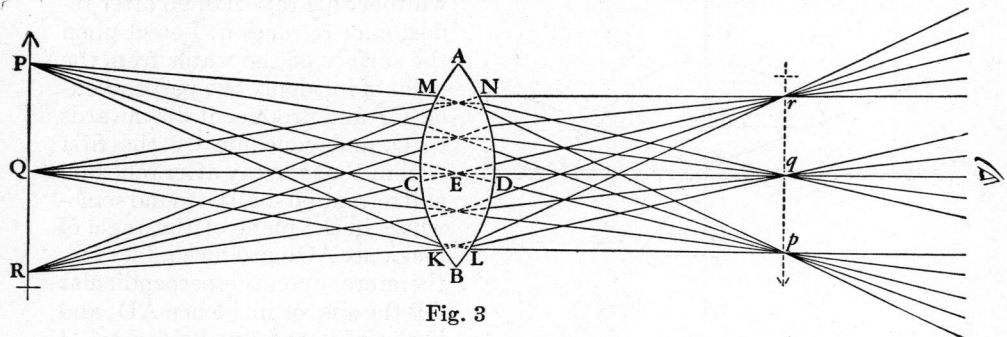

Fig. 3

how light falling upon it from any lucid point Q shall be refracted, let QM represent a ray falling upon any point M of its first spherical surface ACB, and by erecting a perpendicular to the glass at the point M, find the first refracted ray MN by the proportion of the sines 17 to 11. Let that ray in going out of the glass be incident upon N, and then find the second refracted ray Nq by the proportion of the sines 11 to 17. And after the same manner may the refraction be found when the lens is convex on one side and plane or concave on the other, or concave on both sides.

AXIOM VI

Homogeneal rays which flow from several points of any object, and fall perpendicularly or almost perpendicularly on any reflecting or refracting plane or spherical surface, shall afterwards diverge from so many other points, or be parallel to so many other lines, or converge to so many other points, either accurately or without any sensible error. And the same thing will happen if the rays be reflected or refracted successively by two or three or more plane or spherical surfaces.

The point from which rays diverge or to which they converge may be called their *focus*. And the focus of the incident rays being given, that of the reflected or refracted ones may be found by finding the refraction of any two rays, as above; or more readily thus:

CASE 1. Let ACB [Fig. 4] be a reflecting or refracting plane, and Q the focus of the incident rays, and Q*q*C a perpendicular to that plane. And if this perpendicular be produced to *q*, so that *q*C be equal to QC, the point *q* shall be the focus of the reflected rays; or if *q*C be taken on the same side of the plane with

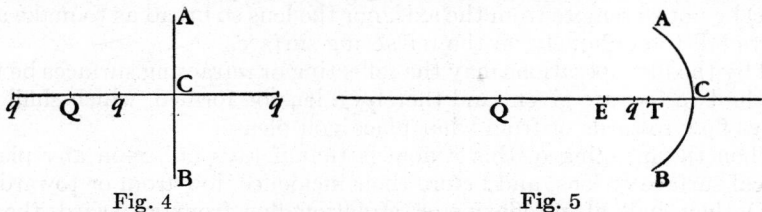

Fig. 4   Fig. 5

QC, and in proportion to QC as the sine of incidence to the sine of refraction, the point *q* shall be the focus of the refracted rays.

CASE 2. Let ACB [Fig. 5] be the reflecting surface of any sphere whose centre is E. Bisect any radius thereof, (suppose EC) in T, and if in that radius on the same side the point T you take the points Q and *q*, so that TQ, TE, and T*q* be continual proportionals, and the point Q be the focus of the incident rays, the point *q* shall be the focus of the reflected ones.

CASE 3. Let ACB [Fig. 6] be the refracting surface of any sphere whose centre is E. In any radius thereof EC produced both ways take ET and C*t* equal to one another and severally in such proportion to that radius as the lesser of the

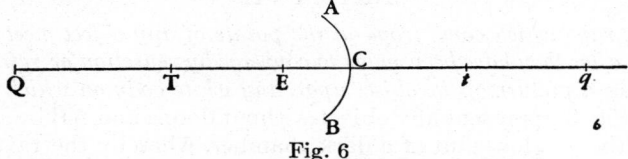

Fig. 6

sines of incidence and refraction hath to the difference of those sines. And then if in the same line you find any two points Q and *q*, so that TQ be to ET as E*t* to *tq*, taking *tq* the contrary way from *t* which TQ lieth from T, and if the point Q be the focus of any incident rays, the point *q* shall be the focus of the refracted ones.

And by the same means the focus of the rays after two or more reflexions or refractions may be found.

CASE 4. Let ACBD [Fig. 7] be any refracting lens, spherically convex or concave or plane on either side, and let CD be its axis (that is, the line which

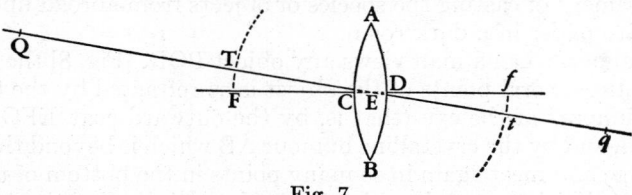

Fig. 7

cuts both its surfaces perpendicularly, and passes through the centres of the spheres), and in this axis produced let F and *f* be the foci of the refracted rays found as above, when the incident rays on both sides the lens are parallel to the same axis; and upon the diameter F*f* bisected in E, describe a circle. Suppose now that any point Q be the focus of any incident rays. Draw QE cutting the said circle in T and t, and therein take tq in such proportion to tE as tE or TE hath to TQ. Let tq lie the contrary way from t which TQ doth from T, and q shall be the focus of the refracted rays without any sensible error, provided the point Q be not so remote from the axis, nor the lens so broad as to make any of the rays fall too obliquely on the refracting surfaces.

And by the like operations may the reflecting or refracting surfaces be found when the two foci are given, and thereby a lens be formed, which shall make the rays flow towards or from what place you please.

So then the meaning of this Axiom is that if rays fall upon any plane or spherical surface or lens, and before their incidence flow from or towards any point Q, they shall, after reflexion or refraction, flow from or towards the point q found by the foregoing rules. And if the incident rays flow from or towards several points Q, the reflected or refracted rays shall flow from or towards so many other points q found by the same rules. Whether the reflected and refracted rays flow from or towards the point q is easily known by the situation of that point. For if that point be on the same side of the reflecting or refracting surface or lens with the point Q, and the incident rays flow from the point Q, the reflected flow towards the point q and the refracted from it; and if the incident rays flow towards Q, the reflected flow from q, and the refracted towards it. And the contrary happens when q is on the other side of the surface.

AXIOM VII

Wherever the rays which come from all the points of any object meet again in so many points after they have been made to converge by reflection or refraction, there they will make a picture of the object upon any white body on which they fall.

So if PR [Fig. 3] represent any object without doors, and AB be a lens placed at a hole in the window-shut of a dark chamber, whereby the rays that come from any point Q of that object are made to converge and meet again in the point q; and if a sheet of white paper be held at q for the light there to fall upon it, the picture of that object PR will appear upon the paper in its proper shape and colours. For as the light which comes from the point Q goes to the point q, so the light which comes from other points P and R of the object will go to so many other correspondent points p and r (as is manifest by the sixth Axiom); so that every point of the object shall illuminate a correspondent point of the picture, and thereby make a picture like the object in shape and colour, this only excepted, that the picture shall be inverted. And this is the reason of that vulgar experiment of casting the species of objects from abroad upon a wall or sheet of white paper in a dark room.

In like manner, when a man views any object PQR, [Fig. 8] the light which comes from the several points of the object is so refracted by the transparent skins and humours of the eye (that is, by the outward coat EFG, called the *tunica cornea*, and by the crystalline humour AB which is beyond the pupil mk) as to converge and meet again in so many points in the bottom of the eye, and there to paint the picture of the object upon that skin (called the *tunica retina*) with which the bottom of the eye is covered. For anatomists, when they have taken off from the bottom of the eye that outward and most thick coat called the *dura mater*, can then see through the thinner coats the pictures of objects lively painted thereon. And these pictures, propagated by motion along the fibres of the optic nerves into the brain, are the cause of vision. For accordingly

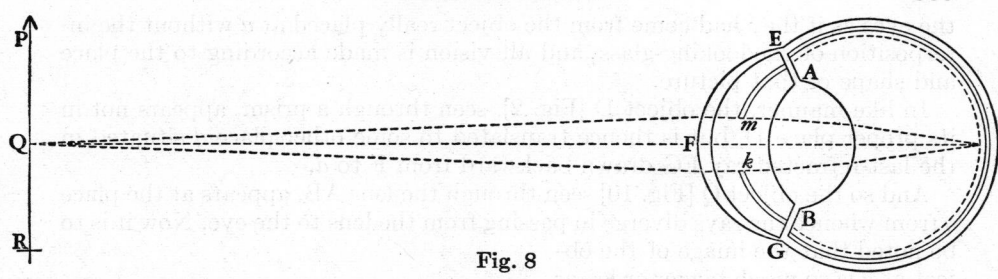

Fig. 8

as these pictures are perfect or imperfect, the object is seen perfectly or imperfectly. If the eye be tinged with any colour (as in the disease of the jaundice) so as to tinge the pictures in the bottom of the eye with that colour, then all objects appear tinged with the same colour. If the humours of the eye by old age decay, so as by shrinking to make the cornea and coat of the crystalline humour grow flatter than before, the light will not be refracted enough, and for want of a sufficient refraction will not converge to the bottom of the eye but to some place beyond it, and by consequence paint in the bottom of the eye a confused picture, and according to the indistinctness of this picture the object will appear confused. This is the reason of the decay of sight in old men, and shews why their sight is mended by spectacles. For those convex glasses supply the defect of plumpness in the eye, and by increasing the refraction make the rays converge sooner, so as to convene distinctly at the bottom of the eye if the glass have a due degree of convexity. And the contrary happens in short-sighted men whose eyes are too plump. For the refraction being now too great, the rays converge and convene in the eyes before they come at the bottom; and therefore the picture made in the bottom and the vision caused thereby will not be distinct, unless the object be brought so near the eye as that the place where the converging rays convene may be removed to the bottom, or that the plumpness of the eye be taken off and the refractions diminished by a concave-glass of a due degree of concavity, or lastly that by age the eye grow flatter till it come to a due figure: For short-sighted men see remote objects best in old age, and therefore they are accounted to have the most lasting eyes.

AXIOM VIII

An object seen by reflexion or refraction appears in that place from whence the rays after their last reflexion or refraction diverge in falling on the spectator's eye.

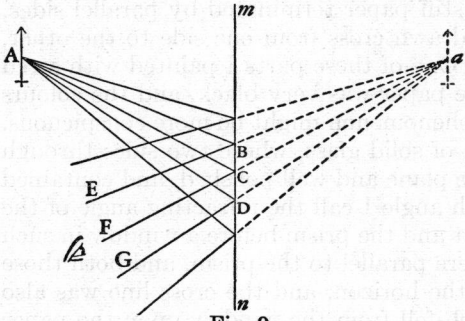

Fig. 9

If the object A [Fig. 9] be seen by reflexion of a looking-glass *mn*, it shall appear, not in its proper place A, but behind the glass at *a*, from whence any rays AB, AC, AD, which flow from one and the same point of the object, do, after their reflexion made in the points B, C, D, diverge in going from the glass to E, F, G, where they are incident on the spectator's eyes. For these rays do make the same picture in the bottom of the eyes as if they had come from the object really placed at *a* without the interposition of the looking-glass; and all vision is made according to the place and shape of that picture.

In like manner, the object D [Fig. 2], seen through a prism, appears not in its proper place D, but is thence translated to some other place *d* situated in the last refracted ray FG drawn backward from F to *d*.

And so the object Q [Fig. 10] seen through the lens AB, appears at the place *q* from whence the rays diverge in passing from the lens to the eye. Now it is to be noted that the image of the object at *q* is so much bigger or lesser than the object itself at Q, as the distance of the image at *q* from the lens AB is bigger or less than the distance of the object at Q from the same lens. And if the object be seen through two or more such convex or concave glasses, every glass shall

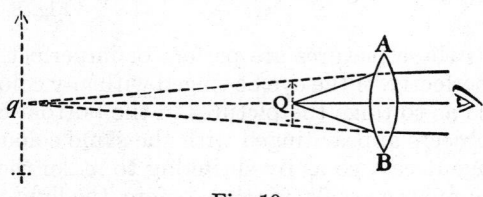

Fig. 10

make a new image, and the object shall appear in the place of the bigness of the last image. Which consideration unfolds the theory of microscopes and telescopes. For that theory consists in almost nothing else than the describing such glasses as shall make the last image of any object as distinct and large and luminous as it can conveniently be made.

I have now given in Axioms and their explications the sum of what hath hitherto been treated of in Optics. For what hath been generally agreed on I content myself to assume under the notion of Principles, in order to what I have further to write. And this may suffice for an Introduction to readers of quick wit and good understanding not yet versed in Optics: although those who are already acquainted with this science, and have handled glasses, will more readily apprehend what followeth.

PROPOSITIONS

PROPOSITION 1. THEOREM 1
Lights which differ in colour, differ also in degrees of refrangibility.

The Proof by Experiments

Experiment 1. I took a black oblong stiff paper terminated by parallel sides, and, with a perpendicular right line drawn cross from one side to the other, distinguished it into two equal parts. One of these parts I painted with a red colour and the other with a blue. The paper was very black, and the colours intense and thickly laid on, that the phenomenon might be more conspicuous. This paper I viewed through a prism of solid glass, whose two sides through which the light passed to the eye were plane and well polished, and contained an angle of about sixty degrees; which angle I call the refracting angle of the prism. And whilst I viewed it, I held it and the prism before a window in such manner that the sides of the paper were parallel to the prism, and both those sides and the prism were parallel to the horizon, and the cross line was also parallel to it: and that the light which fell from the window upon the paper made an angle with the paper equal to that angle which was made with the same paper by the light reflected from it to the eye. Beyond the prism was the wall of the chamber under the window covered over with black cloth, and the cloth was involved in darkness that no light might be reflected from thence, which in passing by the edges of the paper to the eye, might mingle itself with the light of the paper, and obscure the phenomenon thereof. These things being thus ordered, I found that if the refracting angle of the prism be turned upwards, so that the paper may seem to be lifted upwards by the refraction, its blue half will be lifted higher by the refraction than its red half. But if the refracting angle of the prism be turned downward, so that the paper may seem to be carried lower by the refraction, its blue half will be carried something lower thereby than its red half. Wherefore in both cases the light which comes from the blue half of the paper through the prism to the eye does in like circumstances suffer a greater refraction than the light which comes from the red half, and by consequence is more refrangible.

ILLUSTRATION. In the eleventh Figure, MN represents the window, and DE the paper terminated with parallel sides DJ and HE, and by the transverse line

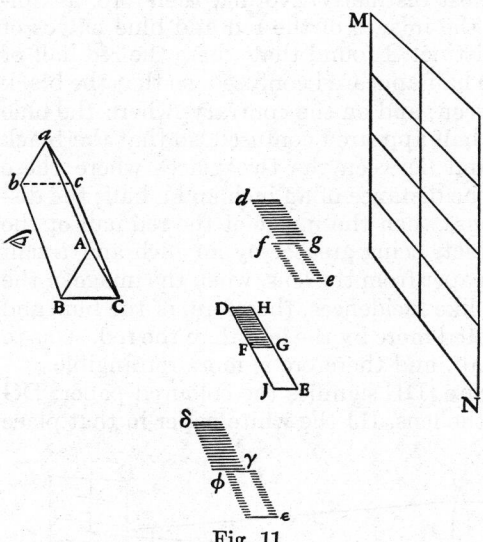

FG distinguished into two halves, the one DG of an intensely blue colour, the other FE of an intensely red. And BACcab represents the prism whose refracting planes ABba and ACca meet in the edge of the refracting angle Aa. This edge Aa, being upward, is parallel both to the horizon and to the parallel edges of the paper DJ and HE, and the transverse line FG is perpendicular to the plane of the window. And de represents the image of the paper seen by refraction upwards in such manner that the blue half DG is carried higher to dg than the red half FE is to fe, and therefore suffers a greater refraction. If the edge of the refracting angle be turned downward, the image of the paper

Fig. 11

will be refracted downward; suppose to δε, and the blue half will be refracted lower to δγ than the red half is to φε.

EXPER. 2. About the aforesaid paper, whose two halves were painted over with red and blue, and which was stiff like thin pasteboard, I lapped several times a slender thread of very black silk, in such manner that the several parts of the thread might appear upon the colours like so many black lines drawn over them, or like long and slender dark shadows cast upon them. I might have drawn black lines with a pen, but the threads were smaller and better defined. This paper thus coloured and lined I set against a wall perpendicularly to the horizon, so that one of the colours might stand to the right hand, and the other to the left. Close before the paper, at the confine of the colours below, I placed a candle to illuminate the paper strongly: for the experiment was tried in the night. The flame of the candle reached up to the lower edge of the paper, or a very little higher. Then at the distance of six feet, and one or two inches from the paper upon the floor I erected a glass lens four inches and a quarter broad, which might collect the rays coming from the several points of the paper, and make them converge towards so many other points at the same distance of six feet, and one or two inches on the other side of the lens, and so form the image of the coloured paper upon a white paper placed there, after the same manner that a lens at a hole in a window casts the images of objects abroad upon a sheet of white paper in a dark room. The aforesaid white paper, erected perpendicular to the horizon and to the rays which fell upon it from the lens, I moved sometimes towards the lens, sometimes from it, to find the places where the images of the blue and red parts of the coloured paper appeared most distinct. Those places I easily knew by the images of the black lines which I had made by winding the silk about the paper. For the images of those fine and slender lines (which by reason of their blackness were like shadows on the colours) were confused and scarce visible, unless when the colours on either side of each line were terminated most distinctly. Noting, therefore, as diligently as I could, the places where the images of the red and blue halves of the coloured paper appeared most distinct, I found that where the red half of the paper appeared distinct, the blue half appeared confused, so that the black lines drawn upon it could scarce be seen; and on the contrary, where the blue half appeared most distinct, the red half appeared confused, so that the black lines upon it were scarce visible. And between the two places where these images appeared distinct there was the distance of an inch and a half; the distance of the white paper from the lens, when the image of the red half of the coloured paper appeared most distinct, being greater by an inch and a half than the distance of the same white paper from the lens, when the image of the blue half appeared most distinct. In like incidences, therefore, of the blue and red upon the lens, the blue was refracted more by the lens than the red, so as to converge sooner by an inch and a half, and therefore is more refrangible.

ILLUSTRATION. In the twelfth Figure, DE signifies the coloured paper, DG the blue half, FE the red half, MN the lens, HJ the white paper in that place

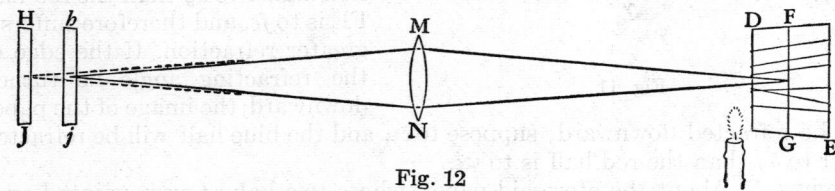

Fig. 12

where the red half with its black lines appeared distinct, and *hj* the same paper in that place where the blue half appeared distinct. The place *hj* was nearer to the lens MN than the place HJ by an inch and a half.

SCHOLIUM. The same things succeed, notwithstanding that some of the circumstances be varied; as in the first experiment when the prism and paper are any ways inclined to the horizon, and in both when coloured lines are drawn upon very black paper. But in the description of these experiments, I have set down such circumstances, by which either the phenomenon might be rendered more conspicuous, or a novice might more easily try them, or by which I did try them only. The same thing I have often done in the following experiments; concerning all which, this one admonition may suffice: now, from these experiments it follows not that all the light of the blue is more refrangible than all the light of the red; for both lights are mixed of rays differently refrangible, so that in the red there are some rays not less refrangible than those of the blue, and in the blue there are some rays not more refrangible than those of the red; but these rays, in proportion to the whole light, are but few, and serve to diminish the event of the experiment, but are not able to destroy it. For, if the red and blue colours were more dilute and weak, the distance of the images would be less than an inch and a half; and if they were more intense and full, that distance would be greater, as will appear hereafter. These experiments may suffice for the colours of natural bodies. For in the colours made by the refraction of prisms, this Proposition will appear by the experiments which are now to follow in the next Proposition.

PROPOSITION 2. THEOREM 2

The light of the Sun consists of rays differently refrangible.

The Proof by Experiments

EXPER. 3. In a very dark chamber, at a round hole, about one-third part of an inch broad, made in the shut of a window, I placed a glass prism, whereby the beam of the Sun's light, which came in at that hole, might be refracted upwards toward the opposite wall of the chamber, and there form a coloured image of the Sun. The axis of the prism (that is, the line passing through the middle of the prism from one end of it to the other end parallel to the edge of the refracting angle) was in this and the following experiments perpendicular to the incident rays. About this axis I turned the prism slowly, and saw the refracted light on the wall, or coloured image of the Sun, first to descend, and then to ascend. Between the descent and ascent, when the image seemed stationary, I stopped the prism, and fixed it in that posture, that it should be moved no more. For in that posture the refractions of the light at the two sides of the refracting angle, that is, at the entrance of the rays into the prism, and at their going out of it, were equal to one another. So also in other experiments, as often as I would have the refractions on both sides the prism to be equal to one another, I noted the place where the image of the Sun formed by the refracted light stood still between its two contrary motions, in the common period of its progress and regress; and when the image fell upon that place, I made fast the prism. And in this posture, as the most convenient, it is to be understood that all the prisms are placed in the following experiments, unless where some other posture is described. The prism, therefore, being placed in this posture, I let the refracted light fall perpendicularly upon a sheet of white paper at the opposite wall of the chamber, and observed the figure and dimensions of the solar image formed on the paper by that light. This image was oblong and not oval, but terminated with two rectilinear and parallel sides, and two semicircular ends. On its sides it was bounded pretty distinctly, but on its ends very confusedly and indistinctly, the light there decaying and vanishing by degrees. The breadth of this image answered to the Sun's diameter, and was about two inches and the eighth part of an inch, including the penumbra. For the image was eighteen feet and a half distant from the prism, and at this distance that breadth, if diminished by the diameter of the hole in the window-shut (that is, by a quarter of an inch), subtended an angle at the prism of about half a degree, which is the Sun's apparent diameter. But the length of the image was about ten inches and a quarter, and the length of the rectilinear sides about eight inches; and the refracting angle of the prism, whereby so great a length was made, was 64 degrees. With a less angle the length of the image was less, the breadth remaining the same. If the prism was turned about its axis that way which made the rays emerge more obliquely out of the second refracting surface of the prism, the image soon became an inch or two longer, or more; and if the prism was turned about the contrary way, so as to make the rays fall more obliquely on the first refracting surface, the image soon became an inch or two shorter. And, therefore, in trying this experiment, I was as curious as I could be in placing the prism, by the above-mentioned rule, exactly in such a posture that the refractions of the rays at their emergence out of the prism might be equal to that at their incidence on it. This prism had some veins running along within the glass from one end to the other, which scattered some of the sun's light irregularly, but had no sensible effect in increasing the length of the coloured spectrum. For I tried the same experiment with other prisms with the same success. And particularly with a prism which seemed free from such veins, and whose refracting angle was $62\frac{1}{2}$ degrees, I found the length of the image $9\frac{3}{4}$ or 10 inches at the distance of $18\frac{1}{2}$ feet from the prism, the breadth of the hole in the window-shut being one-quarter of an inch, as before. And because it is easy to commit a mistake in placing the prism in its due posture, I repeated the experiment four or five times, and always found the length of the image that which is set down above. With another prism of clearer glass and better polish, which seemed free from veins, and whose refracting angle was $63\frac{1}{2}$ degrees, the length of this image at the same distance of $18\frac{1}{2}$ feet was also about 10 inches, or $10\frac{1}{8}$. Beyond these measures for about $\frac{1}{4}$ or $\frac{1}{3}$ of an inch at either end of the spectrum the light of the clouds seemed to be a little tinged with red and violet, but so very faintly, that I suspected that tincture might either wholly, or in great measure, arise from some rays of the spectrum scattered irregularly by some inequalities in the substance and polish of the glass, and, therefore, I did not include it in these measures. Now, the different magnitude of the hole in the window-shut, and different thickness of the prism where the rays passed through it, and different inclinations of the prism to the horizon, made no sensible changes in the length of the image. Neither did the different matter of the prisms make any: for in a vessel made of polished plates of glass cemented together in the shape of a prism and filled with water, there is the like success of the experiment according to the quantity of the refraction. It is further to be observed, that the rays went on in right lines from the prism to the image, and, therefore, at their very going out of the prism, had all that inclination to one another from which the length of the image proceeded, that is, the inclination of more than two degrees and a half. And yet, according to the laws of Optics vulgarly received, they could not possibly be so much inclined to one another. For let EG [Fig. 13] represent the window-shut, F the hole made therein through which a beam of the Sun's light was transmitted into the darkened chamber, and ABC a triangular imaginary plane whereby the prism is feigned to be cut transversely through the middle of the light. Or if you please, let ABC represent the prism itself, looking directly towards the spectator's eye with its nearer end: and let XY be the Sun, MN the paper upon which the solar image or spectrum is cast, and PT the image itself whose sides towards v and w are rectilinear and parallel, and ends towards P and T semi-circular. YKHP and XLJT are two rays, the first of which comes from the lower part of the Sun to the higher part of the image, and is refracted in the prism at K and H, and the latter comes from the higher part of the Sun to the lower part of the image, and is refracted at L and J. Since the refractions on

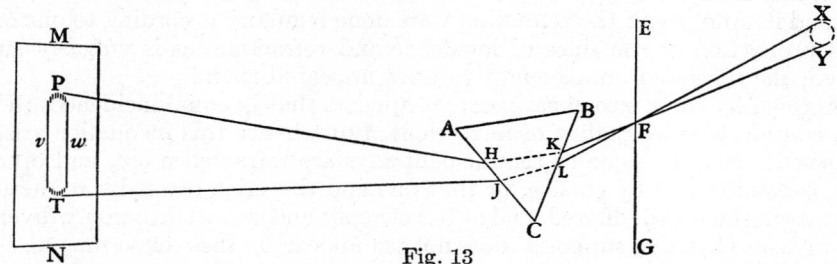

Fig. 13

both sides the prism are equal to one another, that is, the refraction at K equal to the refraction at J, and the refraction at L equal to the refraction at H, so that the refractions of the incident rays at K and L, taken together, are equal to the refractions of the emergent rays at H and J taken together: it follows, by adding equal things to equal things, that the refractions at K and H taken together are equal to the refractions at J and L taken together, and, therefore, the two rays being equally refracted, have the same inclination to one another after refraction which they had before; that is, the inclination of half a degree answering to the Sun's diameter. For so great was the inclination of the rays to one another before refraction. So then, the length of the image PT would by the rules of vulgar Optics subtend an angle of half a degree at the prism, and by consequence be equal to the breadth vw; and, therefore, the image would be round. Thus it would be were the two rays XLJT and YKHP, and all the rest which form the image PwTv, alike refrangible. And, therefore, seeing by experience it is found that the image is not round, but about five times longer than broad, the rays which, going to the upper end P of the image, suffer the greatest refraction must be more refrangible than those which go to the lower end T, unless the inequality of refraction be casual.

This image or spectrum PT was coloured, being red at its least refracted end T, and violet at its most refracted end P, and yellow, green and blue in the intermediate spaces. Which agrees with the first Proposition, that lights which differ in colour do also differ in refrangibility. The length of the image in the foregoing experiments I measured from the faintest and outmost red at one end, to the faintest and outmost blue at the other end, excepting only a little penumbra, whose breadth scarce exceeded a quarter of an inch, as was said above.

EXPER. 4. In the Sun's beam which was propagated into the room through the hole in the window-shut, at the distance of some feet from the hole, I held the prism in such a posture, that its axis might be perpendicular to that beam. Then I looked through the prism upon the hole, and turning the prism to and

fro about its axis to make the image of the hole ascend and descend, when
between its two contrary motions it seemed stationary, I stopped the prism,
that the refractions of both sides of the refracting angle might be equal to each
other, as in the former experiment. In this situation of the prism, viewing
through it the said hole, I observed the length of its refracted image to be
many times greater than its breadth, and that the most refracted part thereof
appeared violet, the least refracted red, the middle parts blue, green and yellow
in order. The same thing happened when I removed the prism out of the Sun's
light, and looked through it upon the hole shining by the light of the clouds
beyond it. And yet, if the refraction were done regularly according to one certain proportion of the sines of incidence and refraction, as is vulgarly supposed, the refracted image ought to have appeared round.

So then, by these two experiments it appears that in equal incidences there
is a considerable inequality of refractions. But whence this inequality arises,
whether it be that some of the incident rays are refracted more, and others
less, constantly, or by chance, or that one and the same ray is by refraction
disturbed, shattered, dilated, and as it were split and spread into many diverging rays, as Grimaldi supposes, does not yet appear by these experiments, but
will appear by those that follow.

EXPER. 5. Considering, therefore, that if in the third experiment the image
of the Sun should be drawn out into an oblong form, either by a dilatation of
every ray, or by any other casual inequality of the refractions, the same oblong
image would by a second refraction made sideways be drawn out as much in
breadth by the like dilatation of the rays, or other casual inequality of the
refractions sideways, I tried what would be the effects of such a second refraction. For this end I ordered all things as in the third experiment, and then
placed a second prism immediately after the first in a cross position to it, that
it might again refract the beam of the Sun's light which came to it through the
first prism. In the first prism this beam was refracted upwards, and in the
second sideways. And I found that by the refraction of the second prism, the
breadth of the image was not increased, but its superior part, which in the
first prism suffered the greater refraction, and appeared violet and blue, did
again in the second prism suffer a greater refraction than its inferior part,
which appeared red and yellow, and this without any dilatation of the image
in breadth.

ILLUSTRATION. Let S [Figs. 14, 15] represent the Sun, F the hole in the window,
ABC the first prism, DH the second prism, Y the round image of the Sun made
by a direct beam of light when the prisms are taken away, PT the oblong
image of the Sun made by that beam passing through the first prism alone,
when the second prism is taken away, and pt the image made by the cross
refractions of both prisms together. Now, if the rays which tend towards the
several points of the round image Y were dilated and spread by the refraction
of the first prism, so that they should not any longer go in single lines to single
points, but that every ray being split, shattered, and changed from a linear ray
to a superficies of rays diverging from the point of refraction, and lying in the
plane of the angles of incidence and refraction, they should go in those planes
to so many lines reaching almost from one end of the image PT to the other,
and if that image should thence become oblong, those rays and their several
parts tending towards the several points of the image PT ought to be again

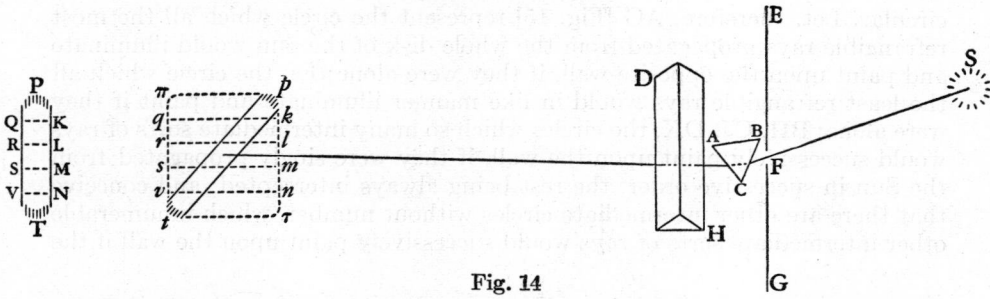

Fig. 14

dilated and spread sideways by the transverse refraction of the second prism, so as to compose a four square image, such as is represented at $\pi\tau$. For the better understanding of which, let the image PT be distinguished into five equal parts PQK, KQRL, LRSM, MSVN, NVT. And by the same irregularity that the orbicular light Y is by the refraction of the first prism dilated and drawn out into a long image PT, the light PQK which takes up a space of the same length and breadth with the light Y ought to be by the refraction of the second prism dilated and drawn out into the long image πqkp, and the light KQRL into the long image $kqrl$, and the lights LRSM, MSVN, NVT, into so many other long images $lrsm$, $msvn$, $nvt\tau$; and all these long images would compose the four square images $\pi\tau$. Thus it ought to be were every ray dilated by refraction, and spread into a triangular superficies of rays diverging from the point of refraction. For the second refraction would spread the rays one way as much as the first doth another, and so dilate the image in breadth as much as the first doth in length. And the same thing ought to happen were some rays casually refracted more than others. But the event is otherwise. The image PT was not made broader by the refraction of the second prism, but only became oblique, as 'tis represented at pt, its upper end P being by the refraction translated to a greater distance than its lower end T. So then the light which went towards the upper end P of the image was (at equal incidences) more refracted in the second prism than the light which tended towards the lower end T, that is, the blue and violet, than the red and yellow; and therefore was more refrangible. The same light was by the refraction of the first prism translated farther from the place Y to which it tended before refraction; and, therefore, suffered as well in the first prism as in the second a greater refraction than the rest of the light, and by consequence was more refrangible than the rest, even before its incidence on the first prism.

Sometimes I placed a third prism after the second, and sometimes also a fourth after the third, by all which the image might be often refracted sideways: but the rays which were more refracted than the rest in the first prism were also more refracted in all the rest, and that without any dilatation of the image sideways: and, therefore, those rays for their constancy of a greater refraction are deservedly reputed more refrangible.

But that the meaning of this experiment may more clearly appear, it is to be considered that the rays which are equally refrangible do fall upon a circle answering to the Sun's disk. For this was proved in the third experiment. By a circle I understand not here a perfect geometrical circle, but any orbicular figure whose length is equal to its breadth, and which, as to sense, may seem circular. Let, therefore, AG [Fig. 15] represent the circle which all the most refrangible rays propagated from the whole disk of the Sun would illuminate and paint upon the opposite wall, if they were alone; EL the circle which all the least refrangible rays would in like manner illuminate and paint if they were alone; BH, CJ, DK, the circles which so many intermediate sorts of rays would successively paint upon the wall, if they were singly propagated from the Sun in successive order, the rest being always intercepted; and conceive that there are other intermediate circles without number, which innumerable other intermediate sorts of rays would successively paint upon the wall if the

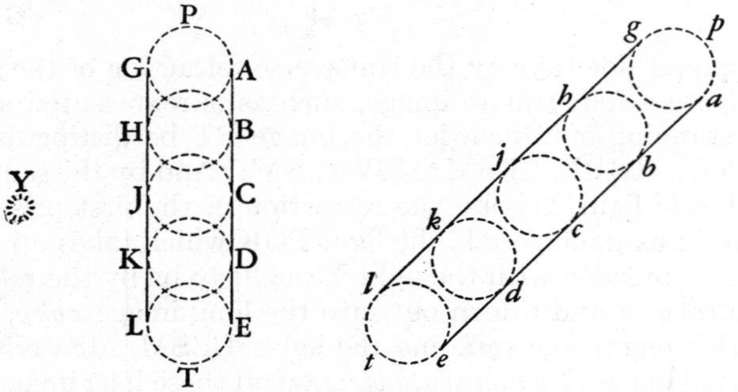

Fig. 15

Sun should successively emit every sort apart. And seeing the Sun emits all these sorts at once, they must all together illuminate and paint innumerable equal circles, of all which, being according to their degrees of refrangibility placed in order in a continual series, that oblong spectrum PT is composed which I described in the third experiment. Now, if the Sun's circular image Y [Fig. 15] which is made by an unrefracted beam of light was by any dilation of the single rays, or by any other irregularity in the refraction of the first prism, converted into the oblong spectrum, PT: then ought every circle AG, BH, CJ, &c. in that spectrum, by the cross refraction of the second prism again dilating or otherwise scattering the rays as before, to be in like manner drawn out and transformed into an oblong figure, and thereby the breadth of the image PT would be now as much augmented as the length of the image Y was before by the refraction of the first prism; and thus by the refractions of both prisms together would be formed a four square figure $p\pi t\tau$, as I described above. Wherefore, since the breadth of the spectrum PT is not increased by the re-fraction sideways, it is certain that the rays are not split or dilated, or other-ways irregularly scattered by that refraction, but that every circle is by a regular and uniform refraction translated entire into another place, as the circle AG by the greatest refraction into the place ag, the circle BH by a less refraction into the place bh, the circle CJ by a refraction still less into the place cj, and so of the rest; by which means a new spectrum pt inclined to the former PT is in like manner composed of circles lying in a right line; and these circles must be of the same bigness with the former, because the breadths of all the spectrums Y, PT, and pt at equal distances from the prisms are equal.

I considered, further, that by the breadth of the hole F through which the light enters into the dark chamber, there is a penumbra made in the circuit of the spectrum Y, and that penumbra remains in the rectilinear sides of the spectrums PT and *pt*. I placed, therefore, at that hole a lens or object-glass of a telescope which might cast the image of the Sun distinctly on Y without any penumbra at all, and found that the penumbra of the rectilinear sides of the oblong spectrums PT and *pt* was also thereby taken away, so that those sides appeared as distinctly defined as did the circumference of the first image Y. Thus it happens if the glass of the prisms be free from veins, and their sides be accurately plane and well polished without those numberless waves or curls which usually arise from sand-holes a little smoothed in polishing with putty. If the glass be only well polished and free from veins, and the sides not accurately plane, but a little convex or concave, as it frequently happens; yet may the three spectrums Y, PT, and *pt* want penumbras, but not in equal distances from the prisms. Now, from this want of penumbras I knew more certainly that every one of the circles was refracted according to some most regular, uniform, and constant law. For if there were any irregularity in the refraction, the right lines AE and GL, which all the circles in the spectrum PT do touch, could not by that refraction be translated into the lines *ae* and *gl* as distinct and straight as they were before, but there would arise in those translated lines some penumbra or crookedness or undulation, or other sensible perturbation contrary to what is found by experience. Whatsoever penumbra or perturbation should be made in the circles by the cross refraction of the second prism, all that penumbra or perturbation would be conspicuous in the right lines *ae* and *gl* which touch those circles. And, therefore, since there is no such penumbra or perturbation in those right lines, there must be none in the circles. Since the distance between those tangents or breadth of the spectrum is not increased by the refractions, the diameters of the circles are not increased thereby. Since those tangents continue to be right lines, every circle which in the first prism is more or less refracted is exactly in the same proportion more or less refracted in the second. And seeing all these things continue to succeed after the same manner when the rays are again in a third prism, and again in a fourth refracted sideways, it is evident that the rays of one and the same circle, as to their degree of refrangibility, continue always uniform and homogeneal to one another, and that those of several circles do differ in degree of refrangibility, and that in some certain and constant proportion. Which is the thing I was to prove.

There is yet another circumstance or two of this experiment by which it becomes still more plain and convincing. Let the second prism DH [Fig. 16] be placed not immediately after the first, but at some distance from it; suppose

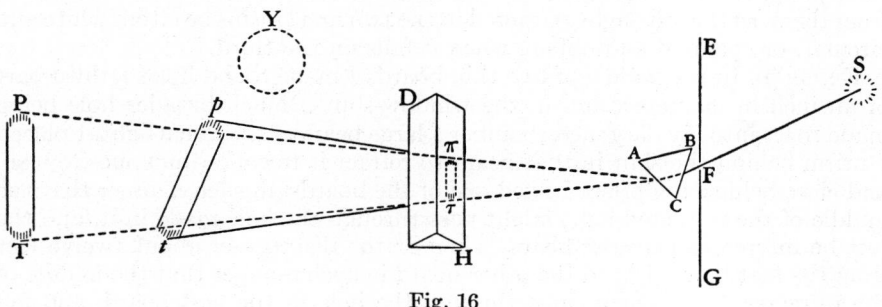

Fig. 16

in the mid-way between it and the wall on which the oblong spectrum PT is
cast, so that the light from the first prism may fall upon it in the form of an
oblong spectrum ττ parallel to this second prism, and be refracted sideways
to form the oblong spectrum pt upon the wall. And you will find, as before,
that this spectrum pt is inclined to that spectrum PT, which the first prism
forms alone without the second; the blue ends P and p being farther distant
from one another than the red ones T and t, and by consequence that the rays
which go to the blue end π of the image ττ, and which therefore suffer the greatest refraction in the first prism, are again in the second prism more refracted
than the rest.

The same thing I tried also by letting the Sun's light into a dark room
through two little round holes F and φ [Fig. 17] made in the window, and with
two parallel prisms ABC and αβγ placed at those holes (one at each) refracting

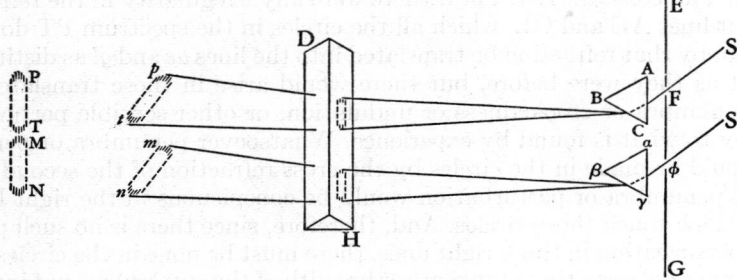

Fig. 17

those two beams of light to the opposite wall of the chamber, in such manner
that the two coloured images PT and MN which they there painted were joined
end to end and lay in one straight line, the red end T of the one touching the
blue end M of the other. For if these two refracted beams were again by a third
prism DH placed cross to the two first, refracted sideways, and the spectrums
thereby translated to some other part of the wall of the chamber, suppose the
spectrum PT to pt and the spectrum MN to mn, these translated spectrums
pt and mn would not lie in one straight line with their ends contiguous as
before, but be broken off from one another and become parallel, the blue end
m of the image mn being by a greater refraction translated farther from its
former place MT, than the red end t of the other image pt from the same place
MT; which puts the Proposition past dispute. And this happens whether the
third prism DH be placed immediately after the two first, or at a great distance
from them, so that the light refracted in the two first prisms be either white and
circular, or coloured and oblong when it falls on the third.

EXPER. 6. In the middle of two thin boards I made round holes a third part
of an inch in diameter, and in the window-shut a much broader hole being
made to let into my darkened chamber a large beam of the Sun's light, I placed
a prism behind the shut in that beam to refract it towards the opposite wall,
and close behind the prism I fixed one of the boards, in such manner that the
middle of the refracted light might pass through the hole made in it, and the
rest be intercepted by the board. Then at the distance of about twelve feet
from the first board I fixed the other board in such manner that the middle of
the refracted light which came through the hole in the first board, and fell

upon the opposite wall, might pass through the hole in this other board, and
the rest being intercepted by the board might paint upon it the coloured spectrum of the Sun. And close behind this board I fixed another prism to refract
the light which came through the hole. Then I returned speedily to the first
prism, and by turning it slowly to and fro about its axis, I caused the image
which fell upon the second board to move up and down upon that board, that
all its parts might successively pass through the hole in that board and fall
upon the prism behind it. And in the meantime I noted the places on the opposite wall to which that light after its refraction in the second prism did pass;
and by the difference of the places I found that the light which being most
refracted in the first prism did go the the blue end of the image, was again
more refracted in the second prism than the light which went to the red end
of that image, which proves as well the first Proposition as the second. And
this happened whether the axis of the two prisms were parallel, or inclined to
one another, and to the horizon in any given angles.

ILLUSTRATION. Let F [Fig. 18] be the wide hole in the window-shut, through
which the Sun shines upon the first prism ABC, and let the refracted light fall

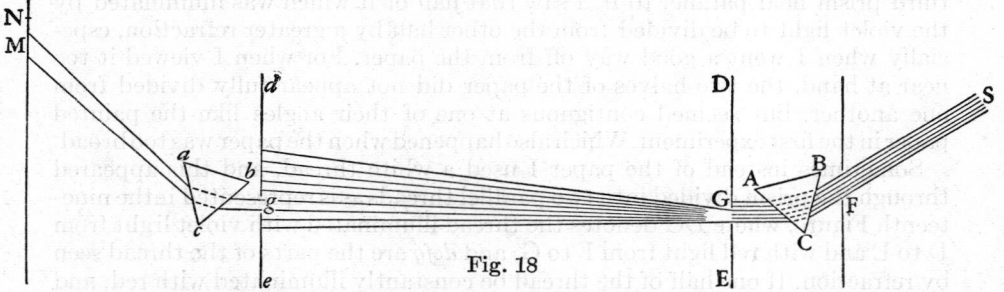

Fig. 18

upon the middle of the board DE, and the middle part of that light upon the
hole G made in the middle part of that board. Let this trajected part of that
light fall again upon the middle of the second board de, and there paint such
an oblong coloured image of the Sun as was described in the third experiment.
By turning the prism ABC slowly to and fro about its axis, this image will be
made to move up and down the board de, and by this means all its parts from
one end to the other may be made to pass successively through the hole g
which is made in the middle of that board. In the meanwhile, another prism
abc is to be fixed next after that hole g, to refract the trajected light a second
time. And these things being thus ordered, I marked the places M and N of the
opposite wall upon which the refracted light fell, and found that whilst the
two boards and second prism remained unmoved, those places, by turning the
first prism about its axis, were changed perpetually. For when the lower part
of the light which fell upon the second board de was cast through the hole g,
it went to a lower place M on the wall, and when the higher part of that light
was cast through the same hole g, it went to a higher place N on the wall, and
when any intermediate part of the light was cast through that hole, it went to
some place on the wall between M and N. The unchanged position of the holes
in the boards made the incidence of the rays upon the second prism to be the
same in all cases. And yet in that common incidence some of the rays were more
refracted, and others less. And those were more refracted in this prism, which

by a greater refraction in the first prism were more turned out of the way, and, therefore, for their constancy of being more refracted are deservedly called more refrangible.

EXPER. 7. At two holes made near one another in my window-shut I placed two prisms, one at each, which might cast upon the opposite wall (after the manner of the third experiment) two oblong coloured images of the Sun. And at a little distance from the wall I placed a long slender paper with straight and parallel edges, and ordered the prisms and paper so that the red colour of one image might fall directly upon one half of the paper, and the violet colour of the other image upon the other half of the same paper; so that the paper appeared of two colours, red and violet, much after the manner of the painted paper in the first and second experiments. Then with a black cloth I covered the wall behind the paper, that no light might be reflected from it to disturb the experiment, and viewing the paper through a third prism held parallel to it, I saw that half of it which was illuminated by the violet light to be divided from the other half by a greater refraction, especially when I went a good way off from the paper. For when I viewed it too near at hand, the two halves of the paper did not appear fully divided from one another, but seemed contiguous at one of their angles like the painted paper in the first experiment. Which also happened when the paper was too broad.

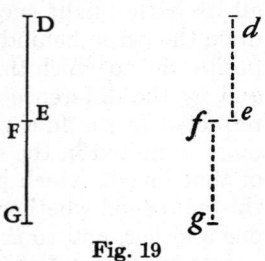

Fig. 19

Sometimes instead of the paper I used a white thread, and this appeared through the prism divided into two parallel threads as is represented in the nineteenth Figure, where DG denotes the thread illuminated with violet light from D to E and with red light from F to G, and *defg* are the parts of the thread seen by refraction. If one half of the thread be constantly illuminated with red, and the other half be illuminated with all the colours successively (which may be done by causing one of the prisms to be turned about its axis whilst the other remains unmoved), this other half, in viewing the thread through the prism, will appear in a continual right line with the first half when illuminated with red, and begin to be a little divided from it when illuminated with orange, and remove farther from it when illuminated with yellow, and still farther when with green, and farther when with blue, and go yet farther off when illuminated with indigo, and farthest when with deep violet. Which plainly shews that the lights of several colours are more and more refrangible one than another, in this order of their colours: red, orange, yellow, green, blue, indigo, deep violet; and so proves as well the first Proposition as the second.

I caused also the coloured spectrums PT [Fig. 17] and MN made in a dark chamber by the refractions of two prisms to lie in a right line end to end, as was described above in the fifth experiment, and viewing them through a third prism held parallel to their length, they appeared no longer in a right line, but became broken from one another, as they are represented at *pt* and *mn*, the violet end *m* of the spectrum *mn* being by a greater refraction translated farther from its former place MT than the red end *t* of the other spectrum *pt*.

I further caused those two spectrums PT [Fig. 20] and MN to become coincident in an inverted order of their colours, the red end of each falling on the violet end of the other, as they are represented in the oblong figure PTMN;

and then viewing them through a prism DH held parallel to their length, they
appeared not co-incident, as when viewed with the naked eye, but in the form

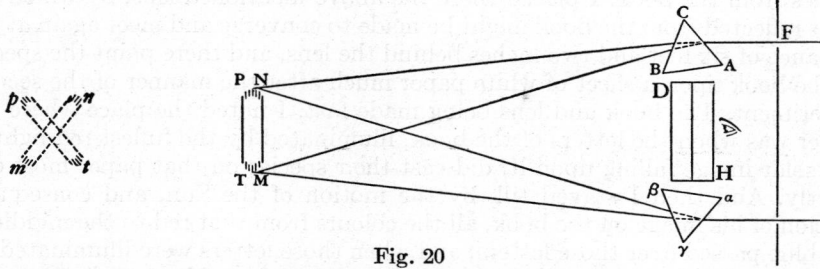

Fig. 20

of two distinct spectrums *pt* and *mn* crossing one another in the middle after
the manner of the letter X. Which shews that the red of the one spectrum and
violet of the other, which were co-incident at PN and MT, being parted from
one another by a greater refraction of the violet to *p* and *m* than of the red to
n and *t*, do differ in degrees of refrangibility.

I illuminated also a little circular piece of white paper all over with the
lights of both prisms intermixed, and when it was illuminated with the red of
one spectrum, and deep violet of the other, so as by the mixture of those
colours to appear all over purple, I viewed the paper, first at a less distance,
and then at a greater, through a third prism; and as I went from the paper, the
refracted image thereof became more and more divided by the unequal refraction of the two mixed colours, and at length parted into two distinct images,
a red one and a violet one, whereof the violet was farthest from the paper, and
therefore suffered the greatest refraction. And when that prism at the window,
which cast the violet on the paper, was taken away, the violet image disappeared; but when the other prism was taken away the red vanished; which
shews that these two images were nothing else than the lights of the two prisms,
which had been intermixed on the purple paper, but were parted again by their
unequal refractions made in the third prism, through which the paper was
viewed. This also was observable, that if one of the prisms at the window
(suppose that which cast the violet on the paper) was turned about its axis to
make all the colours, in this order: violet, indigo, blue, green, yellow, orange,
red, fall successively on the paper from that prism, the violet image changed
colour accordingly, turning successively to indigo, blue, green, yellow and red,
and in changing colour came nearer and nearer to the red image made by the
other prism, until when it was also red both images became fully co-incident.

I placed also two paper circles very near one another, the one in the red light
of one prism, and the other in the violet light of the other. The circles were
each of them an inch in diameter, and behind them the wall was dark, that the
experiment might not be disturbed by any light coming from thence. These
circles thus illuminated, I viewed through a prism so held that the refraction
might be made towards the red circle, and as I went from them they came
nearer and nearer together, and at length became co-incident; and afterwards
when I went still farther off, they parted again in a contrary order, the violet
by a greater refraction being carried beyond the red.

EXPER. 8. In summer, when the Sun's light uses to be strongest, I placed a
prism at the hole of the window-shut, as in the third experiment, yet so that

its axis might be parallel to the axis of the world, and at the opposite wall in the Sun's refracted light, I placed an open book. Then going six feet and two inches from the book, I placed there the above-mentioned lens, by which the light reflected from the book might be made to converge and meet again at the distance of six feet and two inches behind the lens, and there paint the species of the book upon a sheet of white paper much after the manner of the second experiment. The book and lens being made fast, I noted the place where the paper was when the letters of the book, illuminated by the fullest red light of the solar image falling upon it, did cast their species on that paper most distinctly. And then I stayed till, by the motion of the Sun, and consequent motion of his image on the book, all the colours from that red to the middle of the blue passed over those letters; and when those letters were illuminated by that blue, I noted again the place of the paper when they cast their species most distinctly upon it: And I found that this last place of the paper was nearer to the lens than its former place by about two inches and a half, or two and three quarters. So much sooner, therefore, did the light in the violet end of the image by a greater refraction converge and meet, than the light in the red end. But in trying this, the chamber was as dark as I could make it. For, if these colours be diluted and weakened by the mixture of any adventitious light, the distance between the places of the paper will not be so great. This distance in the second experiment, where the colours of natural bodies were made use of, was but an inch and a half, by reason of the imperfection of those colours. Here in the colours of the prism, which are manifestly more full, intense, and lively than those of natural bodies, the distance is two inches and three quarters. And were the colours still more full, I question not but that the distance would be considerably greater. For the coloured light of the prism, by the interfering of the circles described in the second figure of the fifth experiment [Fig. 15], and also by the light of the very bright clouds next the Sun's body intermixing with these colours, and by the light scattered by the inequalities in the polish of the prism, was so very much compounded, that the species which those faint and dark colours, the indigo and violet, cast upon the paper were not distinct enough to be well observed.

EXPER. 9. A prism, whose two angles at its base were equal to one another, and half right ones, and the third a right one, I placed in a beam of the Sun's light let into a dark chamber through a hole in the window-shut, as in the third experiment. And turning the prism slowly about its axis, until all the light which went through one of its angles, and was refracted by it began to be reflected by its base, at which till then it went out of the glass, I observed that those rays which had suffered the greatest refraction were sooner reflected than the rest. I conceived, therefore, that those rays of the reflected light, which were most refrangible, did first of all by a total reflexion become more copious in that light than the rest, and that afterwards the rest also, by a total reflexion, became as copious as these. To try this, I made the reflected light pass through another prism, and being refracted by it to fall afterwards upon a sheet of white paper placed at some distance behind it, and there by that refraction to paint the usual colours of the prism. And then causing the first prism to be turned about its axis as above, I observed that when those rays, which in this prism had suffered the greatest refraction, and appeared of a blue and violet colour, began to be totally reflected, the blue and violet light on the paper, which was most refracted in the second prism, received a sensible increase above that of the red and yellow, which was least refracted; and afterwards, when the rest of the light which was green, yellow, and red, began to be totally reflected in the first prism, the light of those colours on the paper received as great an increase as the violet and blue had done before. Whence 'tis manifest that the beam of light reflected by the base of the prism, being augmented first by the more refrangible rays, and afterwards by the less refrangible ones, is compounded of rays differently refrangible. And that all such reflected light is of the same nature with the Sun's light before its incidence on the base of the prism, no man ever doubted; it being generally allowed that light by such reflexions suffers no alteration in its modifications and properties. I do not here take notice of any refractions made in the sides of the first prism, because the light enters it perpendicularly at the first side, and goes out perpendicularly at the second side, and therefore suffers none. So then, the Sun's incident light being of the same temper and constitution with his emergent light, and the last being compounded of rays differently refrangible, the first must be in like manner compounded.

ILLUSTRATION. In the twenty-first Figure, ABC is the first prism, BC its base, B and C its equal angles at the base, each of 45 degrees, A its rectangular

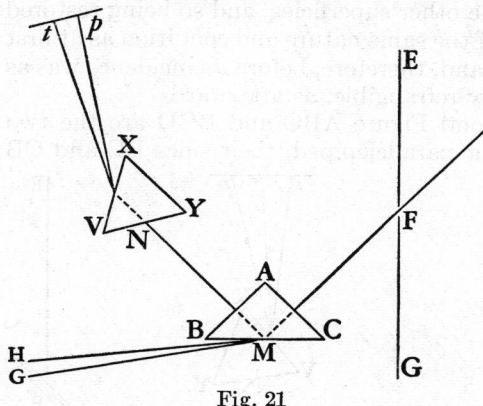

Fig. 21

vertex, FM a beam of the Sun's light let into a dark room through a hole F one third part of an inch broad, M its incidence on the base of the prism, MG a less refracted ray, MH a more refracted ray, MN the beam of light reflected from the base, VXY the second prism by which this beam in passing through it is refracted, N*t* the less refracted light of this beam, and N*p* the more refracted part thereof. When the first prism ABC is turned about its axis according to the order of the letters ABC, the rays MH emerge more and more obliquely out of that prism, and at length after their most oblique emergence are reflected towards N, and going on to *p* do increase the number of the rays N*p*. Afterwards, by continuing the motion of the first prism, the rays MG are also reflected to N and increase the number of the rays N*t*. And, therefore, the light MN admits into its composition, first the more refrangible rays, and then the less refrangible rays, and yet after this composition is of the same nature with the Sun's immediate light FM, the reflexion of the specular base BC causing no alteration therein.

EXPER. 10. Two prisms, which were alike in shape, I tied so together that, their axis and opposite sides being parallel, they composed a parallelepiped. And, the Sun shining into my dark chamber through a little hole in the window-shut, I placed that parallelepiped in his beam at some distance from the hole, in such a posture that the axes of the prisms might be perpendicular to the incident rays, and that those rays, being incident upon the first side of one prism, might go on through the two contiguous sides of both prisms, and emerge out of the last side of the second prism. This side, being parallel to the first side of the first prism, caused the emerging light to be parallel to the incident. Then, beyond these two prisms I placed a third, which might refract that emergent light, and by that refraction cast the usual colours of the prism upon the opposite wall, or upon a sheet of white paper held at a convenient distance behind the prism for that refracted light to fall upon it. After this I turned the parallelopiped about its axis, and found that when the contiguous sides of the two prisms became so oblique to the incident rays that those rays began all of them to be reflected, those rays which in the third prism had suffered the greatest refraction, and painted the paper with violet and blue, were first of all by a total reflexion taken out of the transmitted light, the rest remaining and on the paper painting their colours of green, yellow, orange and red, as before; and afterwards by continuing the motion of the two prisms, the rest of the rays also by a total reflexion vanished in order, according to their degrees of refrangibility. The light, therefore, which emerged out of the two prisms is compounded of rays differently refrangible, seeing the more refrangible rays may be taken out of it, while the less refrangible remain. But this light being trajected only through the parallel superficies of the two prisms, if it suffered any change by the refraction of one superficies it lost that impression by the contrary refraction of the other superficies, and so being restored to its pristine constitution, became of the same nature and condition as at first before its incidence on those prisms; and, therefore, before its incidence was as much compounded of rays differently refrangible, as afterwards.

ILLUSTRATION. In the twenty-second Figure ABC and BCD are the two prisms tied together in the form of a parallelepiped, their sides BC and CB

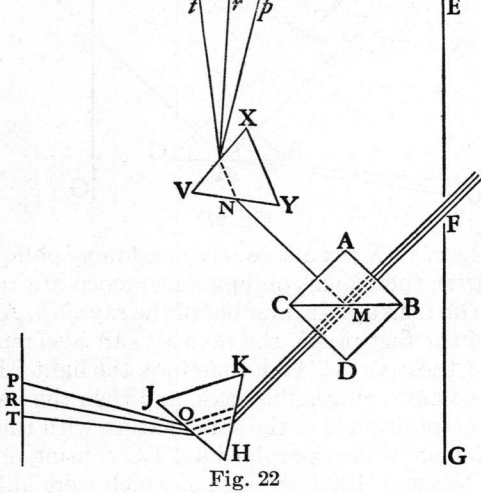

Fig. 22

being contiguous, and their sides AB and CD parallel. And HJK is the third prism, by which the Sun's light propagated through the hole F into the dark chamber, and there passing through those sides of the prisms AB, BC, CB and CD, is refracted at O to the white paper PT, falling there partly upon P by a greater refraction, partly upon T by a less refraction, and partly upon R and other intermediate places by intermediate refractions. By turning the parallelepiped ACBD about its axis, according to the order of the letters A, C, D, B, at length when the contiguous planes BC and CB become sufficiently oblique to the rays FM, which are incident upon them at M, there will vanish totally out of the refracted light OPT, first of all the most refracted rays OP (the rest OR and OT remaining as before), then the rays OR and other intermediate ones, and, lastly, the least refracted rays OT. For when the plane BC becomes sufficiently oblique to the rays incident upon it, those rays will begin to be totally reflected by it towards N; and first the most refrangible rays will be totally reflected (as was explained in the preceding experiment) and by consequence must first disappear at P, and afterwards the rest as they are in order totally reflected to N, they must disappear in the same order at R and T. So then the rays, which at O suffer the greatest refraction, may be taken out of the light MO whilst the rest of the rays remain in it, and therefore that light MO is compounded of rays differently refrangible. And because the planes AB and CD are parallel, and, therefore, by equal and contrary refractions destroy one another's effects, the incident light FM must be of the same kind and nature with the emergent light MO, and therefore doth also consist of rays differently refrangible. These two lights FM and MO, before the most refrangible rays are separated out of the emergent light MO, agree in colour and in all other properties so far as my observation reaches, and, therefore, are deservedly reputed of the same nature and constitution, and by consequence the one is compounded as well as the other. But after the most refrangible rays begin to be totally reflected, and thereby separated out of the emergent light MO, that light changes its colour from white to a dilute and faint yellow, a pretty good orange, a very full red successively, and then totally vanishes. For after the most refrangible rays, which paint the paper at P with a purple colour, are by a total reflexion taken out of the beam of light MO, the rest of the colours which appear on the paper at R and T being mixed in the light MO compound there a faint yellow, and after the blue and part of the green which appear on the paper between P and R are taken away, the rest which appear between R and T (that is, the yellow, orange, red and a little green) being mixed in the beam MO compound there an orange; and when all the rays are by reflexion taken out of the beam MO, except the least refrangible, which at T appear of a full red, their colour is the same in that beam MO as afterwards at T, the refraction of the prism HJK serving only to separate the differently refrangible rays, without making any alteration in their colours, as shall be more fully proved hereafter. All which confirms as well the first Proposition as the second.

SCHOLIUM. If this experiment and the former be conjoined and made one by applying a fourth prism VXY [Fig. 22] to refract the reflected beam MN towards *tp*, the conclusion will be clearer. For then the light N*p*, which in the fourth prism is more refracted, will become fuller and stronger when the light OP, which in the third prism HJK is more refracted, vanishes at P; and afterwards when the less refracted light OT vanishes at T, the less refracted light N*t* will become increased whilst the more refracted light at *p* receives no further increase. And as the trajected beam MO in vanishing is always of such a colour as ought to result from the mixture of the colours which fall upon the paper PT, so is the reflected beam MN always of such a colour as ought to result from the mixture of the colours which fall upon the paper *pt*. For when the most refrangible rays are by a total reflexion taken out of the beam MO, and leave that beam of an orange colour, the excess of those rays in the reflected light does not only make the violet, indigo and blue at *p* more full, but also makes the beam MN change from the yellowish colour of the Sun's light to a pale white inclining to blue, and afterward recover its yellowish colour again, so soon as all the rest of the transmitted light MOT is reflected.

Now, seeing that in all this variety of experiments, whether the trial be made in light reflected, and that either from natural bodies, as in the first and second experiment, or specular, as in the ninth; or in light refracted, and that either before the unequally refracted rays are by diverging separated from one another, and losing their whiteness which they have altogether, appear severally of several colours, as in the fifth experiment; or after they are separated from one another, and appear coloured as in the sixth, seventh, and eighth experiments; or in light trajected through parallel superficies, destroying each other's effects, as in the tenth experiment; there are always found rays, which at equal incidences on the same medium suffer unequal refractions, and that without any splitting or dilating of single rays, or contingence in the inequality of the refractions, as is proved in the fifth and sixth experiments. And seeing the rays which differ in refrangibility may be parted and sorted from one another, and that either by refraction as in the third experiment, or by reflexion as in the tenth, and then the several sorts apart at equal incidences suffer unequal refractions, and those sorts are more refracted than others after separation, which were more refracted before it, as in the sixth and following experiments, and if the Sun's light be trajected through three or more cross prisms successively, those rays which in the first prism are refracted more than others are in all the following prisms refracted more than others in the same rate and proportion, as appears by the fifth experiment; it's manifest that the Sun's light is an heterogeneous mixture of rays, some of which are constantly more refrangible than others, as was proposed.

PROPOSITION 3. THEOREM 3

The Sun's light consists of rays differing in reflexibility, and those rays are more reflexible than others which are more refrangible.

This is manifest by the ninth and tenth experiments: for in the ninth experiment, by turning the prism about its axis until the rays within it, which in going out into the air were refracted by its base, became so oblique to that base as to begin to be totally reflected thereby; those rays became first of all totally reflected, which before at equal incidences with the rest had suffered the greatest refraction. And the same thing happens in the reflexion made by the common base of the two prisms in the tenth experiment.

PROPOSITION 4. PROBLEM 1

To separate from one another the heterogeneous rays of compound light.

The heterogeneous rays are in some measure separated from one another by the refraction of the prism in the third experiment, and in the fifth experiment, by taking away the penumbra from the rectilinear sides of the coloured image, that separation in those very rectilinear sides or straight edges of the image becomes perfect. But in all places between those rectilinear edges, those innumerable circles there described, which are severally illuminated by homogeneal rays, by interfering with one another, and being everywhere commixed, do render the light sufficiently compound. But if these circles, whilst their centres keep their distances and positions, could be made less in diameter, their interfering one with another, and by consequence the mixture of the heterogeneous rays would be proportionally diminished. In the twenty-third Figure let AG, BH, CJ, DK, EL, FM be the circles which so many sorts of rays, flowing from the same disk of the Sun, do in the third experiment illuminate; of all which and innumerable other intermediate ones lying in a continual series between the two rectilinear and parallel edges of the Sun's oblong image

PT, that image is composed, as was explained in the fifth experiment. And let *ag, bh, cj, dk, el, fm* be so many less circles lying in a like continual series between two parallel right lines *af* and *gm* with the same distances between their centres, and illuminated by the same sorts of rays, that is, the circle *ag* with the same sort by which the corresponding circle AG was illuminated, and the

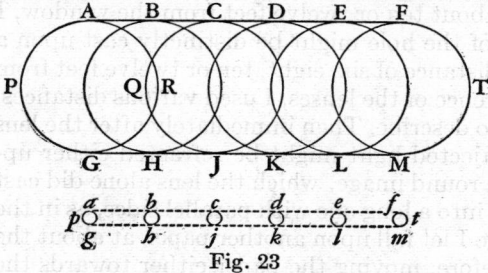

Fig. 23

circle *bh* with the same sort by which the corresponding circle BH was illuminated, and the rest of the circles *cj, dk, el, fm* respectively, with the same sorts of rays by which the several corresponding circles CJ, DK, EL, FM were illuminated. In the figure PT composed of the greater circles, three of those circles AG, BH, CJ, are so expanded into one another that the three sorts of rays by which those circles are illuminated, together with other innumerable sorts of intermediate rays, are mixed at QR in the middle of the circle BH. And the like mixture happens throughout almost the whole length of the figure PT. But in the figure *pt* composed of the less circles, the three less circles *ag, bh, cj*, which answer to those three greater, do not extend into one another; nor are there anywhere mingled so much as any two of the three sorts of rays by which those circles are illuminated, and which in the figure PT are all of them intermingled at BH.

Now, he that shall thus consider it will easily understand that the mixture is diminished in the same proportion with the diameters of the circles. If the diameters of the circles, whilst their centres remain the same, be made three times less than before, the mixture will be also three times less; if ten times less, the mixture will be ten times less, and so of other proportions. That is, the mixture of the rays in the greater figure PT will be to their mixture in the less *pt* as the latitude of the greater figure is to the latitude of the less. For the latitudes of these figures are equal to the diameters of their circles. And hence it easily follows that the mixture of the rays in the refracted spectrum *pt* is to the mixture of the rays in the direct and immediate light of the Sun as the breadth of that spectrum is to the difference between the length and breadth of the same spectrum.

So, then, if we would diminish the mixture of the rays, we are to diminish the diameters of the circles. Now, these would be diminished if the Sun's diameter to which they answer could be made less than it is, or (which comes to the same purpose) if without doors, at a great distance from the prism towards the sun, some opaque body were placed, with a round hole in the middle of it, to intercept all the Sun's light, excepting so much as coming from the middle of his body could pass through that hole to the prism. For so the circles AG, BH, and the rest would not any longer answer to the whole disk of the Sun, but only to that part of it which could be seen from the prism through that hole, that it is to the apparent magnitude of that hole viewed from the prism. But that these circles may answer more distinctly to that hole, a lens is to be placed by the prism to cast the image of the hole (that is, every one of the circles AG, BH, &c.) distinctly upon the paper at PT, after such a manner, as by a lens placed at a window, the species of objects abroad are cast distinctly upon a paper within the room, and the rectilinear sides of the oblong solar image in the fifth experiment became distinct without any penumbra. If this be done, it will not be necessary to place that hole very far off; no, not beyond the window. And, therefore, instead of that hole, I used the hole in the window-shut, as follows:

EXPER. 11. In the Sun's light let into my darkened chamber through a small round hole in my window-shut, at about ten or twelve feet from the window, I placed a lens, by which the image of the hole might be distinctly cast upon a sheet of white paper, placed at the distance of six, eight, ten or twelve feet from the lens. For, according to the difference of the lenses, I used various distances, which I think not worth the while to describe. Then immediately after the lens I placed a prism, by which the trajected light might be refracted either upwards or sideways, and thereby the round image, which the lens alone did cast upon the paper might be drawn out into a long one with parallel sides, as in the third experiment. This oblong image I let fall upon another paper at about the same distance from the prism as before, moving the paper either towards the prism or from it, until I found the just distance where the rectilinear sides of the image became most distinct. For in this case, the circular images of the hole, which compose that image after the same manner that the circles *ag*, *bh*, *cj*, &c. do the figure *pt* [Fig. 23] were terminated most distinctly without any penumbra, and therefore extended into one another the least that they could, and by consequence the mixture of the heterogeneous rays was now the least of all. By this means I used to form an oblong image (such as is *pt*) [Fig. 23 and 24] of circular images of the hole (such as are *ag*, *bh*, *cj*, &c.), and by using a greater or less hole in the window-shut I made the circular images *ag*, *bh*, *cj*, &c. of which it was formed to become greater or less at pleasure, and thereby the mixture of the rays in the image *pt* to be as much, or as little, as I desired.

ILLUSTRATION. In the twenty-fourth Figure, F represents the circular hole in the window-shut, MN the lens, whereby the image or species of that hole is

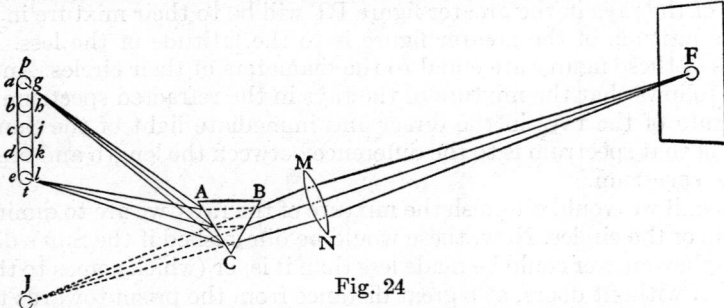

Fig. 24

cast distinctly upon a paper at J, ABC the prism, whereby the rays are at their emerging out of the lens refracted from J towards another paper at *pt*, and the round image at J is turned into an oblong image *pt* falling on that other paper. This image *pt* consists of circles placed one after another in a rectilinear order, as was sufficiently explained in the fifth experiment; and these circles are equal to the circle J, and consequently answer in magnitude to the hole F; and, therefore, by diminishing that hole they may be at pleasure diminished, whilst their centres remain in their places. By this means I made the breadth of the image *pt* to be forty times, and sometimes sixty or seventy times, less than its length. As, for instance, if the breadth of the hole F be one tenth of an inch, and MF

the distance of the lens from the hole be 12 feet; and if pB or pM the distance
of the image pt from the prism or lens be 10 feet, and the refracting angle of the
prism be 62 degrees, the breadth of the image pt will be one-twelfth of an inch,
and the length about six inches, and therefore the length to the breadth as 72
to 1, and by consequence the light of this image 71 times less compound than
the Sun's direct light. And light thus far simple and homogeneal is sufficient for
trying all the experiments in this book about simple light. For the composition
of heterogeneal rays is in this light so little that it is scarce to be discovered and
perceived by sense, except perhaps in the indigo and violet. For these being
dark colours do easily suffer a sensible allay by that little scattering light which
uses to be refracted irregularly by the inequalities of the prism.

Yet instead of the circular hole F, 'tis better to substitute an oblong hole
shaped like a long parallelogram with its length parallel to the prism ABC. For
if this hole be an inch or two long, and but a tenth or twentieth part of an inch
broad, or narrower, the light of the image pt will be as simple as before, or
simpler, and the image will become much broader, and therefore more fit to
have experiments tried in its light than before.

Instead of this parallelogram hole may be substituted a triangular one of
equal sides, whose base, for instance, is about the tenth part of an inch, and its
height an inch or more. For by this means, if the axis of the prism be parallel to
the perpendicular of the triangle, the image pt [Fig. 25] will now be formed of
equicrural triangles ag, bh, cj, dk, el, fm, &c. and innumerable other intermediate ones answering to the triangular hole in shape and bigness, and lying
one after another in a continual series between two parallel lines af and gm.

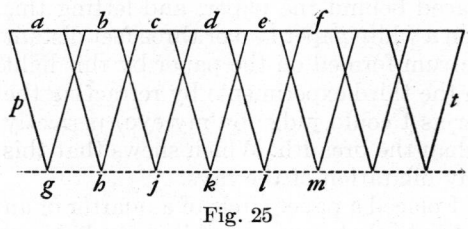

Fig. 25

These triangles are a little intermingled at their bases, but not at their
vertices; and, therefore, the light on
the brighter side af of the image,
where the bases of the triangles are,
is a little compounded, but on the
darker side gm is altogether uncompounded, and in all places between
the sides the composition is propor-
tional to the distances of the places from that obscurer side gm. And having
a spectrum pt of such a composition, we may try experiments either in its
stronger and less simple light near the side af, or in its weaker and simpler light
near the other side gm, as it shall seem most convenient.

But in making experiments of this kind the chamber ought to be made as
dark as can be, lest any foreign light mingle itself with the light of the spectrum
pt, and render it compound; especially if we would try experiments in the more
simple light next the side gm of the spectrum; which being fainter, will have a
less proportion to the foreign light; and so by the mixture of that light be more
troubled, and made more compound. The lens also ought to be good, such as
may serve for optical uses, and the prism ought to have a large angle, suppose
of 65 or 70 degrees, and to be well wrought, being made of glass free from
bubbles and veins, with its sides not a little convex or concave, as usually
happens, but truly plane, and its polish elaborate, as in working optic-glasses,
and not such as is usually wrought with putty, whereby the edges of the sand-
holes being worn away, there are left all over the glass a numberless company

of very little convex polite risings like waves. The edges also of the prism and lens, so far as they may make any irregular refraction, must be covered with a black paper glued on. And all the light of the Sun's beam let into the chamber, which is useless and unprofitable to the experiment, ought to be intercepted with black paper, or other black obstacles. For otherwise the useless light, being reflected every way in the chamber, will mix with the oblong spectrum, and help to disturb it. In trying these things, so much diligence is not altogether necessary, but it will promote the success of the experiments, and by a very scrupulous examiner of things deserves to be applied. It's difficult to get glass prisms fit for this purpose, and, therefore, I used sometimes prismatic vessels made with pieces of broken looking-glasses, and filled with rain water. And to increase the refraction, I sometimes impregnated the water strongly with *saccharum saturni*.

PROPOSITION 5. THEOREM 4

Homogeneal light is refracted regularly without any dilatation splitting or shattering of the rays, and the confused vision of objects seen through refracting bodies by heterogeneal light arises from the different refrangibility of several sorts of rays.

The first part of this Proposition has been already sufficiently proved in the fifth experiment, and will further appear by the experiments which follow.

EXPER. 12. In the middle of a black paper I made a round hole about a fifth or sixth part of an inch in diameter. Upon this paper I caused the spectrum of homogeneal light, described in the former Proposition, so to fall that some part of the light might pass through the hole of the paper. This transmitted part of the light I refracted with a prism placed behind the paper, and letting this refracted light fall perpendicularly upon a white paper two or three feet distant from the prism, I found that the spectrum formed on the paper by this light was not oblong, as when 'tis made (in the third experiment) by refracting the Sun's compound light, but was (so far as I could judge by my eye) perfectly circular, the length being no greater than the breadth. Which shews that this light is refracted regularly without any dilatation of the rays.

EXPER. 13. In the homogeneal light I placed a paper circle of a quarter of an inch in diameter, and in the Sun's unrefracted heterogeneal white light I placed another paper circle of the same bigness. And going from the papers to the distance of some feet, I viewed both circles through a prism. The circle illuminated by the Sun's heterogeneal light appeared very oblong, as in the fourth experiment, the length being many times greater than the breadth; but the other circle, illuminated with homogeneal light, appeared circular and distinctly defined, as when 'tis viewed with the naked eye. Which proves the whole Proposition.

EXPER. 14. In the homogeneal light I placed flies, and such-like minute objects, and viewing them through a prism, I saw their parts as distinctly defined as if I had viewed them with the naked eye. The same objects placed in the Sun's unrefracted heterogeneal light, which was white, I viewed also through a prism, and saw them most confusedly defined, so that I could not distinguish their smaller parts from one another. I placed also the letters of a small print, one while in the homogeneal light, and then in the heterogeneal, and viewing them through a prism, they appeared in the latter case so confused and indistinct that I could not read them; but, in the former, they appeared so distinct that I could read readily, and thought I saw them as distinct, as when I viewed them with my naked eye. In both cases I viewed the same objects through the same prism at the same distance from me, and in the same situation. There was no difference but in the light by which the objects were illuminated, and which in one case was simple, and in the other compound; and, therefore, the distinct vision in the former case, and confused in the latter, could arise from nothing else than from that difference of the lights. Which proves the whole Proposition.

And in these three experiments it is further very remarkable that the colour of homogeneal light was never changed by the refraction.

PROPOSITION 6. THEOREM 5

The sine of incidence of every ray considered apart, is to its sine of refraction in a given ratio.

That every ray, considered apart, is constant to itself in some degree of refrangibility is sufficiently manifest out of what has been said. Those rays, which in the first refraction are at equal incidences most refracted, are also in the following refractions at equal incidences most refracted; and so of the least refrangible, and the rest which have any mean degree of refrangibility, as is manifest by the fifth, sixth, seventh, eighth, and ninth experiments. And those which the first time at like incidences are equally refracted, are again at like incidences equally and uniformly refracted, and that whether they be refracted before they be separated from one another, as in the fifth experiment, or whether they be refracted apart, as in the twelfth, thirteenth and fourteenth experiments. The refraction, therefore, of every ray apart is regular, and what rule that refraction observes we are now to shew.

The late writers in Optics teach that the sines of incidence are in a given proportion to the sines of refraction, as was explained in the fifth Axiom; and some by instruments fitted for measuring of refractions, or otherwise experimentally examining this proportion, do acquaint us that they have found it accurate. But whilst they, not understanding the different refrangibility of several rays, conceived them all to be refracted according to one and the same proportion, 'tis to be presumed that they adapted their measures only to the middle of the refracted light; so that from their measures we may conclude only that the rays which have a mean degree of refrangibility (that is, those which when separated from the rest appear green) are refracted according to a given proportion of their sines. And, therefore, we are now to shew that the like given proportions obtain in all the rest. That it should be so is very reasonable, Nature being ever conformable to herself; but an experimental proof is desired. And such a proof will be had if we can shew that the sines of refraction of rays differently refrangible are one to another in a given proportion when their sines of incidence are equal. For, if the sines of refraction of all the rays are in given proportions to the sine of refractions of a ray which has a mean degree of refrangibility, and this sine is in a given proportion to the equal sines of incidence, those other sines of refraction will also be in given proportions to the equal sines of incidence. Now, when the sines of incidence are equal, it will appear by the following experiment that the sines of refraction are in a given proportion to one another.

EXPER. 15. The Sun shining into a dark chamber through a little round hole in the window-shut; let S [Fig. 26] represent his round white image painted on the opposite wall by his direct light, PT his oblong coloured image made by refracting that light with a prism placed at the window; and *pt*, or 2*p* 2*t*, 3*p* 3*t*, his oblong coloured image made by refracting again the same light sideways with a second prism placed immediately after the first in a cross position to it, as was explained in the fifth experiment; that is to say, *pt* when the refraction of the second prism is small, 2*p* 2*t* when its refraction is greater, and 3*p* 3*t* when it is greatest. For such will be the diversity of the refractions, if the refracting angle of the second prism be of various magnitudes; suppose of fifteen or twenty degrees to make the image *pt*, of thirty or forty to make the image 2*p* 2*t*, and of sixty to make the image 3*p* 3*t*. But, for want of solid glass prisms with angles of convenient bignesses, there may be vessels made of polished plates of glass cemented together in the form of prisms and filled with water. These things being thus ordered, I observed that all the solar images or coloured spectrums PT, *pt*, 2*p* 2*t*, 3*p* 3*t* did very nearly converge to the place S on which

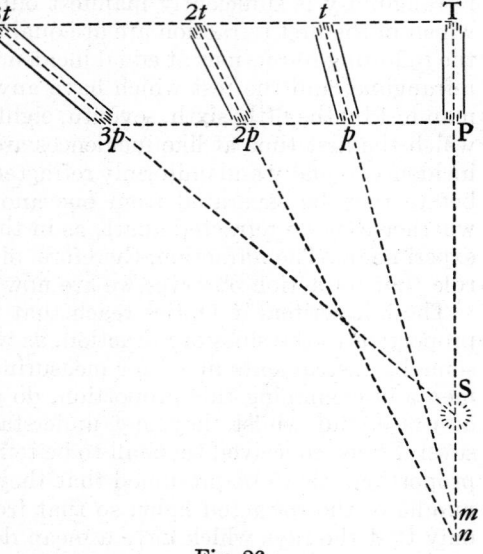

Fig. 26

the direct light of the Sun fell and painted his white round image when the prisms were taken away. The axis of the spectrum PT (that is, the line drawn through the middle of it parallel to its rectilinear sides) did, when produced, pass exactly through the middle of that white round image S. And when the refraction of the second prism was equal to the refraction of the first, the refracting angles of them both being about 60 degrees, the axis of the spectrum 3*p* 3*t* made by that refraction, did when produced pass also through the middle of the same white round image S. But when the refraction of the second prism was less than that of the first, the produced axes of the spectrums *tp* or 2*t* 2*p* made by that refraction did cut the produced axis of the spectrum TP in the points *m* and *n*, a little beyond the centre of that white round image S. Whence the proportion of the line 3*t*T to the line 3*p*P was a little greater than the proportion of 2*t*T or 2*p*P, and this proportion a little greater than that of *t*T to *p*P. Now, when the light of the spectrum PT falls perpendicularly upon the wall, those lines 3*t*T, 3*p*P, and 2*t*T, 2*p*P, and *t*T, *p*P, are the tangents of the refractions, and, therefore, by this experiment the proportions of the tangents of the refractions are obtained, from whence the proportions of the sines being derived, they come out equal, so far as by viewing the spectrums, and using some mathematical reasoning, I could estimate. For I did not make an accurate computation. So then the proposition holds true in every ray apart, so far as appears by experiment. And that it is accurately true may be demonstrated upon this supposition: *That bodies refract light by acting upon its rays in lines* *perpendicular to their surfaces.* But in order to this demonstration, I must distinguish the motion of every ray into two motions, the one perpendicular to the refracting surface, the other parallel to it, and concerning the perpendicular motion lay down the following Proposition:

If any motion or moving thing whatsoever be incident with any velocity on any broad and thin space terminated on both sides by two parallel planes, and in its passage through that space be urged perpendicularly towards the farther plane by any force which at given distances from the plane is of given quantities, the perpendicular velocity of that motion or thing, at its emerging out of that space, shall be always equal to the square root of the sum of the square of the perpendicular velocity of that motion or thing at its incidence on that space; and of the square of the perpendicular velocity which that motion or thing would have at its emergence, if at its incidence its perpendicular velocity was infinitely little.

And the same proposition holds true of any motion or thing perpendicularly retarded in its passage through that space, if instead of the sum of the two squares you take their difference. The demonstration mathematicians will easily find out, and therefore I shall not trouble the reader with it.

Suppose now that a ray coming most obliquely in the line MC [Fig. 1] be refracted at C by the plane RS into the line CN, and if it be required to find the line CE, into which any other ray AC shall be refracted; let MC, AD, be the sines of incidence of the two rays, and NG, EF, their sines of refraction, and let the equal motions of the incident rays be represented by the equal lines MC and AC, and the motion MC being considered as parallel to the refracting plane, let the other motion AC be distinguished into two motions AD and DC, one of which AD is parallel, and the other DC perpendicular to the refracting surface. In like manner, let the motions of the emerging rays be distinguished into two, whereof the perpendicular ones are $\frac{MC}{NG}$ CG and $\frac{AD}{EF}$ CF. And if the force of the refracting plane begins to act upon the rays either in that plane or at a certain distance from it on the one side, and ends at a certain distance from it on the other side, and in all places between those two limits acts upon the rays in lines perpendicular to that refracting plane, and the actions upon the rays at equal distances from the refracting plane be equal, and at unequal ones either equal or unequal according to any rate whatever; that motion of the ray which is parallel to the refracting plane, will suffer no alteration by that force; and that motion which is perpendicular to it will be altered according to the rule of the foregoing proposition. If, therefore, for the perpendicular velocity of the emerging ray CN you write $\frac{MC}{NG}$ CG as above, then the perpendicular velocity of any other emerging ray CE which was $\frac{AD}{EF}$ CF, will be equal to the square root of CD$q+\frac{MCq}{NGq}$ CGq. And by squaring these equals, and adding to them the equals ADq and MC$q-$CDq, and dividing the sums by the equals CF$q+$EFq and CG$q+$NGq, you will have $\frac{MCq}{NGq}$ equal to $\frac{MCq}{NGq}$. Whence AD, the sine of incidence, is to EF the sine of refraction, as MC to NG, that is, in a given ratio. And this demonstration being general, without determining what light is, or by what kind of force it is refracted, or assuming any thing further than that the refracting body acts upon the rays in lines perpendicular to its surface; I take it to be a very convincing argument of the full truth of this Proposition.

So then, if the ratio of the sines of incidence and refraction of any sort of rays be found in any one case, 'tis given in all cases; and this may be readily found by the method in the following Proposition.

PROPOSITION 7. THEOREM 6

The perfection of telescopes is impeded by the different refrangibility of the rays of light.

The imperfection of telescopes is vulgarly attributed to the spherical figures of the glasses, and, therefore, mathematicians have propounded to figure them by the conical sections. To shew that they are mistaken, I have inserted this proposition; the truth of which will appear by the measure of the refractions of the several sorts of rays; and these measures I thus determine.

In the third experiment of this first part, where the refracting angle of the prism was $62\frac{1}{2}$ degrees, the half of that angle 31 degrees 15 minutes is the angle of incidence of the rays at their going out of the glass into the air; and the sine of this angle is 5,188, the radius being 10,000. When the axis of this prism was parallel to the horizon, and the refraction of the rays at their incidence on this prism equal to that at their emergence out of it, I observed with a quadrant the angle which the mean refrangible rays, (that is, those which went to the middle of the Sun's coloured image) made with the horizon, and by this angle and the Sun's altitude observed at the same time, I found the angle which the emergent rays contained with the incident to be 44 degrees and 40 minutes and the half of this angle added to the angle of incidence 31 degrees 15 minutes makes the angle of refraction, which is, therefore, 53 degrees 35 minutes and its sine 8,047. These are the sines of incidence and refraction of the mean refrangible rays, and their proportion in round numbers is 20 to 31. This glass was of a colour inclining to green. The last of the prisms mentioned in the third experiment was of clear white glass; its refracting angle $63\frac{1}{2}$ degrees; the angle which the emergent rays contained, with the incident 45 degrees 50 minutes; the sine of half the first angle 5,262; the sine of half the sum of the angles 8,157; and their proportion in round numbers 20 to 31, as before.

From the length of the image, which was about $9\frac{3}{4}$ or 10 inches, subduct its breadth, which was $2\frac{1}{8}$ inches, and the remainder $7\frac{3}{4}$ inches would be the length of the image were the Sun but a point, and therefore subtends the angle which the most and least refrangible rays, when incident on the prism in the same lines, do contain with one another after their emergence. Whence this angle is 2 degrees 0′ 7″. For the distance between the image and the prism where this angle is made was $18\frac{1}{2}$ feet, and at that distance the chord $7\frac{3}{4}$ inches subtends an angle of 2 degrees 0′ 7″. Now, half this angle is the angle which these emergent rays contain with the emergent mean refrangible rays, and a quarter thereof (that is, 30′ 2″) may be accounted the angle which they would contain with the same emergent mean refrangible rays, were they coincident to them within the glass, and suffered no other refraction than that at their emergence. For, if two equal refractions, the one at the incidence of the rays on the prism, the other at their emergence, make half the angle 2 degrees

0′ 7″, then one of those refractions will make about a quarter of that angle, and this quarter added to and subducted from the angle of refraction of the mean refrangible rays, which was 53 degrees 35′, gives the angles of refraction of the most and least refrangible rays 54 degrees 5′ 2″, and 53 degrees 4′ 58″, whose sines are 8,099 and 7,995, the common angle of incidence being 31 degrees 15′, and its sine 5,188; and these sines in the least round numbers are in proportion to one another, as 78 and 77 to 50.

Now, if you subduct the common sine of incidence 50 from the sines of refraction 77 and 78, the remainders 27 and 28 shew that in small refractions the refraction of the least refrangible rays is to the refraction of the most refrangible ones as 27 to 28 very nearly, and that the difference of the refractions of the least refrangible and most refrangible rays is about the 27½th part of the whole refraction of the mean refrangible rays.

Whence they that are skilled in Optics will easily understand, that the breadth of the least circular space into which object-glasses of telescopes can collect all sorts of parallel rays, is about the 27½th part of half the aperture of the glass, or 55th part of the whole aperture; and that the focus of the most refrangible rays is nearer to the object-glass than the focus of the least refrangible ones, by about the 27½th part of the distance between the object-glass and the focus of the mean refrangible ones.

And if rays of all sorts, flowing from any one lucid point in the axis of any convex lens, be made by the refraction of the lens to converge to points not too remote from the lens, the focus of the most refrangible rays shall be nearer to the lens than the focus of the least refrangible ones, by a distance which is to the 27½th part of the distance of the focus of the mean refrangible rays from the lens, as the distance between that focus and the lucid point, from whence the rays flow, is to the distance between that lucid point and the lens very nearly.

Now, to examine whether the difference between the refractions, which the most refrangible and the least refrangible rays flowing from the same point suffer in the object-glasses of telescopes and suchlike glasses, be so great as is here described, I contrived the following experiment:

EXPER. 16. The lens which I used in the second and eighth Experiments, being placed six feet and an inch distant from any object, collected the species of that object by the mean refrangible rays at the distance of six feet and an inch from the lens on the other side. And, therefore, by the foregoing rule, it ought to collect the species of that object by the least refrangible rays at the distance of six feet and 3⅔ inches from the lens, and by the most refrangible ones at the distance of five feet and 10⅓ inches from it: So that between the two places, where these least and most refrangible rays collect the species, there may be the distance of about 5⅓ inches. For by that rule, as six feet and an inch (the distance of the lens from the lucid object) is to twelve feet and two inches (the distance of the lucid object from the focus of the mean refrangible rays) that is, as one is to two; so is the 27½th part of six feet and an inch (the distance between the lens and the same focus) to the distance between the focus of the most refrangible rays and the focus of the least refrangible ones, which is, therefore, 5$\frac{17}{55}$ inches; that is, very nearly 5⅓ inches. Now, to know whether this measure was true, I repeated the second and eighth experiment with coloured light, which was less compounded than that I there made use of.

For I now separated the heterogeneous rays from one another by the method I described in the eleventh experiment, so as to make a coloured spectrum about twelve or fifteen times longer than broad. This spectrum I cast on a printed book, and placing the above-mentioned lens at the distance of six feet and an inch from this spectrum to collect the species of the illuminated letters at the same distance on the other side, I found that the species of the letters illuminated with blue were nearer to the lens than those illuminated with deep red by about three inches, or three and a quarter; but the species of the letters illuminated with indigo and violet appeared so confused and indistinct that I could not read them; whereupon, viewing the prism, I found it was full of veins running from one end of the glass to the other; so that the refraction could not be regular. I took another prism, therefore, which was free from veins, and instead of the letters I used two or three parallel black lines a little broader than the strokes of the letters, and casting the colours upon these lines in such manner that the lines ran along the colours from one end of the spectrum to the other, I found that the focus where the indigo, or confine of this colour and violet, cast the species of the black lines most distinctly, to be about four inches, or 4¼ nearer to the lens than the focus, where the deepest red cast the species of the same black lines most distinctly. The violet was so faint and dark that I could not discern the species of the lines distinctly by that colour; and, therefore, considering that the prism was made of a dark-coloured glass inclining to green, I took another prism of clear white glass; but the spectrum of colours which this prism made had long white streams of faint light shooting out from both ends of the colours, which made me conclude that something was amiss; and viewing the prism, I found two or three little bubbles in the glass, which refracted the light irregularly. Wherefore I covered that part of the glass with black paper, and letting the light pass through another part of it which was free from such bubbles, the spectrum of colours became free from those irregular streams of light, and was now such as I desired. But still I found the violet so dark and faint that I could scarce see the species of the lines by the violet, and not at all by the deepest part of it, which was next the end of the spectrum. I suspected, therefore, that this faint and dark colour might be allayed by that scattering light which was refracted, and reflected irregularly, partly by some very small bubbles in the glasses, and partly by the inequalities of their polish; which light, tho' it was but little, yet it being of a white colour, might suffice to affect the sense so strongly as to disturb the phenomena of that weak and dark colour, the violet; and, therefore, I tried (as in the 12th, 13th, and 14th experiments) whether the light of this colour did not consist of a sensible mixture of heterogeneous rays, but found it did not. Nor did the refractions cause any other sensible colour than violet to emerge out of this light, as they would have done out of white light, and by consequence out of this violet light had it been sensibly compounded with white light. And, therefore, I concluded that the reason why I could not see the species of the lines distinctly by this colour was only the darkness of this colour and thinness of its light, and its distance from the axis of the lens; I divided, therefore, those parallel black lines into equal parts, by which I might readily know the distances of the colours in the spectrum from one another, and noted the distances of the lens from the foci of such colours, as cast the species of the lines distinctly, and then considered whether the difference of those distances bear such proportion to

$5\frac{1}{3}$ inches, the greatest difference of the distances, which the foci of the deepest red and violet ought to have from the lens, as the distance of the observed colours from one another in the spectrum bear to the greatest distance of the deepest red and violet measured in the rectilinear sides of the spectrum, (that is, to the length of those sides) or excess of the length of the spectrum above its breadth. And my observations were as follows:

When I observed and compared the deepest sensible red, and the colour in the confine of green and blue, which at the rectilinear sides of the spectrum was distant from it half the length of those sides, the focus where the confine of green and blue cast the species of the lines distinctly on the paper was nearer to the lens than the focus, where the red cast those lines distinctly on it by about $2\frac{1}{2}$ or $2\frac{3}{4}$ inches. For sometimes the measures were a little greater, sometimes a little less, but seldom varied from one another above one-third of an inch. For it was very difficult to define the places of the foci, without some little errors. Now, if the colours distant half the length of the image (measured at its recti-linear sides) give $2\frac{1}{2}$ or $2\frac{3}{4}$ difference of the distances of their foci from the lens, then the colours distant the whole length ought to give 5 or $5\frac{1}{2}$ inches difference of those distances.

But here it's to be noted that I could not see the red to the full end of the spectrum, but only to the centre of the semicircle which bounded that end, or a little farther; and, therefore, I compared this red, not with that colour which was exactly in the middle of the spectrum, or confine of green and blue, but with that which verged a little more to the blue than to the green. And as I reckoned the whole length of the colours not to be the whole length of the spectrum, but the length of its rectilinear sides, so completing the semicircular ends into circles, when either of the observed colours fell within those circles, I measured the distance of that colour from the semicircular end of the spectrum, and subducting half this distance from the measured distance of the two col-ours I took the remainder for their corrected distance; and in these observa-tions set down this corrected distance for the difference of the distances of their foci from the lens. For, as the length of the rectilinear sides of the spec-trum would be the whole length of all the colours, were the circles of which (as we shewed) that spectrum consists contracted and reduced to physical points, so in that case this corrected distance would be the real distance of the two observed colours.

When, therefore, I further observed the deepest sensible red, and that blue whose corrected distance from it was $\frac{7}{12}$ parts of the length of the rectilinear sides of the spectrum, the difference of the distances of their foci from the lens was about $3\frac{1}{4}$ inches; and as 7 to 12, so is $3\frac{1}{4}$ to $5\frac{4}{7}$.

When I observed the deepest sensible red, and that indigo whose corrected distance was $\frac{8}{12}$ or $\frac{2}{3}$ of the length of the rectilinear sides of the spectrum, the difference of the distances of their foci from the lens was about $3\frac{2}{3}$ inches; and as 2 to 3, so is $3\frac{2}{3}$ to $5\frac{1}{2}$.

When I observed the deepest sensible red, and that deep indigo whose cor-rected distance from one another was $\frac{9}{12}$ or $\frac{3}{4}$ of the length of the rectilinear sides of the spectrum, the difference of the distances of their foci from the lens was about 4 inches; and as 3 to 4, so is 4 to $5\frac{1}{3}$.

When I observed the deepest sensible red, and that part of the violet next the indigo, whose corrected distance from the red was $\frac{10}{12}$ or $\frac{5}{6}$ of the length of the rectilinear sides of the spectrum, the difference of the distances of their foci from the lens was about $4\frac{1}{2}$ inches; and as 5 to 6, so is $4\frac{1}{2}$ to $5\frac{2}{5}$. For sometimes, when the lens was advantageously placed, so that its axis respected the blue, and all things else were well ordered, and the Sun shone clear, and I held my eye very near to the paper on which the lens cast the species of the lines, I could see pretty distinctly the species of those lines by that part of the violet which was next the indigo; and sometimes I could see them by above half the violet. For in making these experiments I had observed that the species of those colours only appear distinct which were in or near the axis of the lens; so that if the blue or indigo were in the axis, I could see their species distinctly; and then the red appeared much less distinct than before. Wherefore I contrived to make the spectrum of colours shorter than before, so that both its ends might be nearer to the axis of the lens. And now its length was about $2\frac{1}{2}$ inches, and breadth about $\frac{1}{5}$ or $\frac{1}{6}$ of an inch. Also, instead of the black lines on which the spectrum was cast, I made one black line broader than those, that I might see its species more easily; and this line I divided by short cross lines into equal parts, for measuring the distances of the observed colours. And now I could sometimes see the species of this line with its divisions almost as far as the centre of the semicircular violet end of the spectrum, and made these farther observations:

When I observed the deepest sensible red, and that part of the violet, whose corrected distance from it was about $\frac{8}{9}$ parts of the rectilinear sides of the spectrum, the difference of the distances of the foci of those colours from the lens was one time $4\frac{2}{3}$, another time $4\frac{3}{4}$, another time $4\frac{7}{8}$ inches; and as 8 to 9, so are $4\frac{2}{3}$, $4\frac{3}{4}$, $4\frac{7}{8}$, to $5\frac{1}{4}$, $5\frac{11}{32}$, $5\frac{31}{64}$, respectively.

When I observed the deepest sensible red, and deepest sensible violet, (the corrected distance of which colours, when all things were ordered to the best advantage, and the Sun shone very clear, was about $\frac{11}{12}$ or $\frac{15}{16}$ parts of the length of the rectilinear sides of the coloured spectrum) I found the difference of the distances of their foci from the lens sometimes $4\frac{3}{4}$ sometimes $5\frac{1}{4}$, and for the most part 5 inches or thereabouts; and as 11 to 12, or 15 to 16, so is five inches to $5\frac{5}{11}$ or $5\frac{1}{3}$ inches.

And by this progression of experiments I satisfied myself that, had the light at the very ends of the spectrum been strong enough to make the species of the black lines appear plainly on the paper, the focus of the deepest violet would have been found nearer to the lens, than the focus of the deepest red, by about $5\frac{1}{3}$ inches at least. And this is a further evidence that the sines of incidence and refraction of the several sorts of rays hold the same proportion to one another in the smallest refractions which they do in the greatest.

My progress in making this nice and troublesome experiment I have set down more at large, that they that shall try it after me may be aware of the circumspection requisite to make it succeed well. And if they cannot make it succeed so well as I did, they may notwithstanding collect by the proportion of the distance of the colours of the spectrum, to the difference of the distances of their foci from the lens, what would be the success in the more distant colours by a better trial. And yet, if they use a broader lens than I did, and fix it to a long strait staff, by means of which it may be readily and truly directed to the colour whose focus is desired, I question not but the experiment will succeed

better with them than it did with me. For I directed the axis as nearly as I could
to the middle of the colours, and then the faint ends of the spectrum being remote from the axis, cast their species less distinctly on the paper than they
would have done had the axis been successively directed to them.

Now, by what has been said, it's certain that the rays which differ in refrangibility do not converge to the same focus; but if they flow from a lucid
point, as far from the lens on one side as their foci are on the other, the focus of
the most refrangible rays shall be nearer to the lens than that of the least
refrangible, by above the fourteenth part of the whole distance; and if they
flow from a lucid point, so very remote from the lens that before their incidence
they may be accounted parallel, the focus of the most refrangible rays shall be
nearer to the lens than the focus of the least refrangible by about the 27th or
28th part of their whole distance from it. And the diameter of the circle in the
middle space between those two foci which they illuminate, when they fall
there on any plane, perpendicular to the axis (which circle is the least into
which they can all be gathered) is about the 55th part of the diameter of the
aperture of the glass. So that 'tis a wonder that telescopes represent objects so
distinct as they do. But were all the rays of light equally refrangible, the error
arising only from the sphericalness of the figures of glasses would be many
hundred times less. For, if the object-glass of a telescope be plano-convex, and
the plane side be turned towards the object, and the diameter of the sphere,
whereof this glass is a segment, be called D, and the semidiameter of the aperture of the glass be called S, and the sine of incidence out of glass into air be to
the sine of refraction as I to R; the rays which come parallel to the axis of the
glass, shall in the place where the image of the object is most distinctly made
be scattered all over a little circle, whose diameter is $\dfrac{Rq \times S \ cub.}{Iq \times D \ quad.}$ very
nearly, as I gather by computing the errors of the rays by the method of in-
finite series, and rejecting the terms whose quantities are inconsiderable. As for
instance, if the sine of incidence I be to the sine of refraction R as 20 to 31, and
if D the diameter of the sphere, to which the convex-side of the glass is ground,
be 100 feet of 1200 inches, and S the semidiameter of the aperture be two
inches, the diameter of the little circle, $\left(\text{that is } \dfrac{Rq \times \ S \ cub.}{Iq \times D \ quad.}\right)$ will be
$\dfrac{31 \times 31 \times 8}{20 \times 20 \times 1200 \times 1200}$ (or $\frac{961}{72,000,000}$) parts of an inch. But the diameter of the
little circle, through which these rays are scattered by unequal refrangibility,
will be about the 55th part of the aperture of the object-glass, which here is
four inches. And, therefore, the error arising from the spherical figure of the
glass is to the error arising from the different refrangibility of the Rays as
$\frac{961}{72,000,000}$ to $\frac{4}{55}$; that is, as 1 to 5449; and, therefore, being in comparison so very
little, deserves not to be considered.

But you will say, if the errors caused by the different refrangibility be so
very great, how comes it to pass that objects appear through telescopes so
distinct as they do? I answer, 'tis because the erring rays are not scattered
uniformly over all that circular space, but collected infinitely more densely in
the centre than in any other part of the circle, and in the way from the centre
to the circumference, grow continually rarer and rarer, so as at the circumference to become infinitely rare; and by reason of their rarity are not strong

enough to be visible unless in the centre and very near it. Let ADE [Fig. 27] represent one of those circles described with the centre C, and semidiameter AC, and let BFG be a smaller circle concentric to the former, cutting with its circumference the diameter AC in B, and bisect AC in N; and by my reckoning the density of the light in any place B will be to its density in N as AB to BC; and the whole light within the lesser circle BFG will be to the whole light within the greater AED as the excess of the square of AC above the square of AB is to the square of AC. As if BC be the fifth part of AC, the light will be four times denser in B than in N, and the whole light within the less circle will be to the whole light within the greater as nine to twenty-five. Whence it's evident that the light within the less circle must strike the sense much more

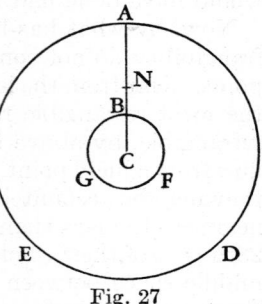

Fig. 27

strongly than that faint and dilated light round about between it and the circumference of the greater.

But it's further to be noted that the most luminous of the prismatic colours are the yellow and orange. These affect the senses more strongly than all the rest together, and next to these in strength are the red and green. The blue compared with these is a faint and dark colour, and the indigo and violet are much darker and fainter, so that these compared with the stronger colours are little to be regarded. The images of objects are therefore to be placed, not in the focus of the mean refrangible rays, which are in the confine of green and blue, but in the focus of those rays which are in the middle of the orange and yellow; there where the colour is most luminous and fulgent (that is, in the brightest yellow, that yellow which inclines more to orange than to green). And by the refraction of these rays (whose sines of incidence and refraction in glass are as 17 and 11) the refraction of glass and crystal for optical uses is to be measured. Let us, therefore, place the image of the object in the focus of these rays, and all the yellow and orange will fall within a circle whose diameter is about the 250th part of the diameter of the aperture of the glass. And if you add the brighter half of the red (that half which is next the orange) and the brighter half of the green (that half which is next the yellow), about three fifth parts of the light of these two colours will fall within the same circle, and two-fifth parts will fall without it round about; and that which falls without will be spread through almost as much more space as that which falls within, and so in the gross be almost three times rarer. Of the other half of the red and green, (that is, of the deep dark red and willow green), about one-quarter will fall within this circle, and three-quarters without, and that which falls without will be spread through about four or five times more space than that which falls within; and so in the gross be rarer, and if compared with the whole light within it, will be about 25 times rarer than all that taken in the gross; or rather more than 30 or 40 times rarer, because the deep red in the end of the spectrum of colours made by a prism is very thin and rare, and the willow green is something rarer than the orange and yellow. The light of these colours, therefore, being so very much rarer than that within the circle, will scarce affect the sense, especially since the deep red and willow green of this light are much darker colours than the rest. And for the same reason the blue and violet being much darker colours than these, and much more rarefied, may be neglected. For the dense and bright light of the circle will obscure the rare and weak light of these dark colours round about it, and render them almost insensible. The sensible image of a lucid point is, therefore, scarce broader than a circle, whose diameter is the 250th part of the diameter of the aperture of the object-glass of a good telescope, or not much broader, if you except a faint and dark misty light round about it, which a spectator will scarce regard. And, therefore, in a telescope whose aperture is four inches, and length an hundred feet, it exceeds not 2″ 45‴, or 3″. And in a telescope whose aperture is two inches, and length 20 or 30 feet, it may be 5″ or 6″, and scarce above. And this answers well to experience: for some astronomers have found the diameters of the fixed stars, in telescopes of between 20 and 60 feet in length, to be about 5″ or 6″, or at most 8 or 10 seconds. But if the eye-glass be tinted faintly with the smoke of a lamp or torch, to obscure the light of the star, the fainter light in the circumference of the star ceases to be visible, and the star (if the glass be sufficiently soiled with smoke) appears something more like a mathematical point. And, for the same reason, the enormous part of the light in the circumference of every lucid point ought to be less discernible in shorter telescopes than in longer, because the shorter transmit less light to the eye.

Now, that the fixed stars, by reason of their immense distance, appear like points, unless so far as their light is dilated by refraction, may appear from hence; that when the moon passes over them and eclipses them, their light vanishes, not gradually like that of the planets, but all at once; and in the end of the eclipse it returns into sight all at once, or certainly in less time than the second of a minute; the refraction of the moon's atmosphere a little protracting the time in which the light of the star first vanishes, and afterwards returns into sight.

Now, if we suppose the sensible image of a lucid point to be even 250 times narrower than the aperture of the glass, yet this image would be still much greater than if it were only from the spherical figure of the glass. For were it not for the different refrangibility of the rays, its breadth in a 100-foot telescope, whose aperture is 4 inches, would be but $\frac{961}{72,000,000}$ parts of an inch, as is manifest by the foregoing computation. And, therefore, in this case, the greatest errors arising from the spherical figure of the glass would be to the greatest sensible errors arising from the different refrangibility of the rays as $\frac{961}{72,000,000}$ to $\frac{4}{250}$ at most; that is, only as 1 to 1200. And this sufficiently shews that it is not the spherical figures of glasses, but the different refrangibility of the rays, which hinders the perfection of telescopes.

There is another argument by which it may appear that the different refrangibility of rays is the true cause of the imperfection of telescopes. For the errors of the rays, arising from the spherical figures of object-glasses are as the cubes of the apertures of the object-glasses; and thence to make telescopes of various lengths magnify with equal distinctness, the apertures of the object-glasses, and the charges or magnifying powers, ought to be as the cubes of the square roots of their lengths; which doth not answer to experience. But the errors of the rays, arising from the different refrangibility, are as the apertures of the object-glasses; and thence to make telescopes of various lengths magnify with equal distinctness, their apertures and charges ought to be as the square roots of their lengths; and this answers to experience, as is well known. For instance, a telescope of 64 feet in length, with an aperture of $2\frac{2}{3}$ inches, magnifies about 120 times, with as much distinctness as one of a foot in length, with $\frac{1}{3}$ of an inch aperture, magnifies 15 times.

Now, were it not for this different refrangibility of rays, telescopes might be brought to a greater perfection than we have yet described, by composing the object-glass of two glasses with water between them. Let ADFC [Fig. 28] represent the object-glass composed of two glasses ABED and BEFC, alike convex on the outsides AGD and CHF, and alike concave on the insides BME, BNE, with water in the concavity BMEN. Let the sine of incidence out of glass into air be as I to R, and out of water into air, as K to R, and by consequence out of glass into water, as I to K: and let the diameter of the sphere to which the convex sides AGD and CHF are ground be D, and the diameter of the sphere to which the concave sides BME and BNE are ground be to D as the cube root of KK—KI to the cube root of RK—RI: and the refractions on the concave sides of the glasses will very much correct the errors of the refractions on the convex sides, so far as they arise from the sphericalness of the figure. And by this means might telescopes be brought to sufficient perfection, were it not for the different refrangibility of

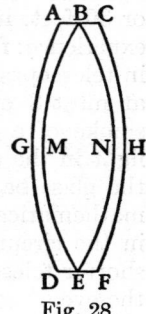

Fig. 28

several sorts of rays. But by reason of this different refrangibility, I do not yet see any other means of improving telescopes by refractions alone, than that of increasing their lengths, for which end the late contrivance of Huygens seems well accommodated. For very long tubes are cumbersome, and scarce to be readily managed, and by reason of their length are very apt to bend, and shake by bending, so as to cause a continual trembling in the objects, whereby it becomes difficult to see them distinctly; whereas by his contrivance the glasses are readily manageable, and the object-glass being fixed upon a strong upright pole becomes more steady.

Seeing, therefore, the improvement of telescopes of given lengths by refractions is desperate, I contrived heretofore a perspective by reflexion, using instead of an object-glass a concave metal. The diameter of the sphere to which the metal was ground concave was about 25 English inches, and by consequence the length of the instrument about six inches and a quarter. The eye-glass was plano-convex, and the diameter of the sphere to which the convex side was ground was about $\frac{1}{5}$ of an inch, or a little less, and by consequence it magnified between 30 and 40 times. By another way of measuring I found that it magnified about 35 times. The concave metal bore an aperture of an inch and a third part; but the aperture was limited, not by an opaque circle covering the limb of the metal round about, but by an opaque circle placed between the eye-glass and the eye, and perforated in the middle with a little round hole for the rays to pass through to the eye. For this circle by being placed here, stopped much of the erroneous light which otherwise would have disturbed the vision. By comparing it with a pretty good perspective of four feet in length, made with a concave eye-glass, I could read at a greater distance with my own instrument than with the glass. Yet objects appeared much darker in it than in the glass, and that partly because more light was lost by reflexion in the metal, than by refraction in the glass, and partly because my instrument was overcharged. Had it magnified but 30 or 25 times, it would have made the object appear more brisk and pleasant. Two of these I made about 16 years ago, and have one of them still by me, by which I can prove the truth of what I write. Yet it is not so good as at the first. For the concave has been divers times tarnished and cleared again, by rubbing it with very soft leather. When I made these an artist in London undertook to imitate it; but using another way of polishing them than I did, he fell much short of what I had attained to, as I afterwards understood by discoursing the under-workman he had employed. The polish I used was in this manner: I had two round copper plates, each six inches in diameter, the one convex, the other concave, ground very true to one another. On the convex I ground the object-metal or concave which was to be polished, till it had taken the figure of the convex and was ready for a polish. Then I pitched over the convex very thinly, by dropping melted pitch upon it, and warming it to keep the pitch soft, whilst I ground it with the concave copper wetted to make it spread evenly all over the convex. Thus by working it well I made it as thin as a groat, and after the convex was cold I ground it again to give it as true a figure as I could. Then I took putty which I had made very fine by washing it from all its grosser particles, and laying a little of this upon the pitch, I ground it upon the pitch with the concave copper, till it had done making a noise; and then upon the pitch I ground the object-metal with a brisk motion for about two or three minutes of time, leaning hard upon it. Then I put fresh putty upon the pitch, and ground it again till it had done making a noise, and afterwards ground the object-metal upon it as before. And this work I repeated till the metal was polished, grinding it the last time with all my strength for a good while together, and frequently breathing upon the pitch, to keep it moist without laying on any more fresh putty. The object-metal was two inches broad, and about one-third part of an inch thick, to keep it from bending. I had two of these metals, and when I had polished them both I tried which was best, and ground the other again, to see if I could make it better than that which I kept. And thus by many trials I learned the way of polishing, till I made those two reflecting perspectives I spake of above. For this art of polishing will be better learned by repeated practice than by my description. Before I ground the object-metal on the pitch, I always ground the putty on it with the concave copper, till it had done making a noise, because if the particles of the putty were not by this means made to stick fast in the pitch, they would by rolling up and down grate and fret the object-metal and fill it full of little holes.

But because metal is more difficult to polish than glass, and is afterwards very apt to be spoiled by tarnishing, and reflects not so much light as glass quick-silvered over does, I would propound to use instead of the metal a glass ground concave on the foreside, and as much convex on the backside, and quick-silvered over on the convex side. The glass must be everywhere of the same thickness exactly. Otherwise it will make objects look coloured and indistinct. By such a glass I tried about five or six years ago to make a reflecting telescope of four feet in length to magnify about 150 times, and I satisfied myself that there wants nothing but a good artist to bring the design to perfection. For the glass being wrought by one of our London artists after such a manner as they grind glasses for telescopes, though it seemed as well wrought as the object-glasses use to be, yet when it was quick-silvered, the reflexion discovered innumerable inequalities all over the glass. And by reason of these inequalities, objects appeared indistinct in this instrument. For the errors of reflected rays caused by any inequality of the glass are about six times greater than the errors of refracted rays caused by the like inequalities. Yet by this experiment I satisfied myself that the reflexion on the concave side of the glass, which I feared would disturb the vision, did no sensible prejudice to it, and by consequence that nothing is wanting to perfect these telescopes, but good workmen who can grind and polish glasses truly spherical. An object-glass of a fourteen foot telescope, made by an artificer at London, I once mended considerably by grinding it on pitch with putty, and leaning very easily on it in the grinding, lest the putty should scratch it. Whether this way may not do well enough for polishing these reflecting glasses, I have not yet tried. But he that shall try either this or any other way of polishing which he may think better, may do well to make his glasses ready for polishing by grinding them without that violence, wherewith our London workmen press their glasses in grinding. For by such violent pressure, glasses are apt to bend a little in the grinding, and such bending will certainly spoil their figure. To recommend, therefore, the consideration of these reflecting glasses to such artists as are curious in figuring glasses, I shall describe this optical instrument in the following Proposition.

PROPOSITION 8. PROBLEM 2

To shorten telescopes.

Let ABCD [Fig. 29] represent a glass spherically concave on the foreside AB, and as much convex on the backside CD, so that it be everywhere of an equal thickness. Let it not be thicker on one side than on the other, lest it make objects appear coloured and indistinct, and let it be very truly wrought and quick-silvered over on the backside, and set in the tube VXYZ which must be very black within. Let EFG represent a prism of glass or crystal placed near the other end of the tube, in the middle of it, by means of a handle of brass or iron FGK, to the end of which made flat it is cemented. Let this prism be rectangular at E, and let the other two angles at F and G be accurately equal to each other, and by consequence equal to half right ones, and let the plane sides FE and GE be square, and by consequence the third side FG a rectangular parallelogram, whose length is to its breadth in a subduplicate proportion of two to one. Let it be so placed in the tube that the axis of the speculum may pass through the middle of the square side EF perpendicularly, and by consequence through the middle of the side FG at an angle of 45 degrees, and let the side EF be turned towards the speculum, and the dis-

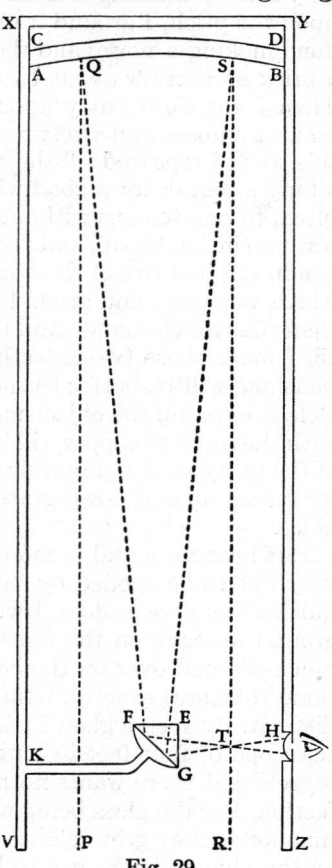

Fig. 29

tance of this prism from the speculum be such that the rays of the light PQ, RS, &c. which are incident upon the speculum in lines parallel to the axis thereof, may enter the prism at the side EF, and be reflected by the side FG, and thence go out of it through the side GE, to the point T, which must be the common focus of the speculum ABDC, and of a plano-convex eye-glass H, through which those rays must pass to the eye. And let the rays at their coming out of the glass pass through a small round hole, or aperture made in a little plate of lead, brass, or silver, wherewith the glass is to be covered, which hole must be no bigger than is necessary for light enough to pass through. For so it will render the object distinct, the plate in which 'tis made intercepting all the erroneous part of the light which comes from the verges of the speculum AB. Such an instrument well made, if it be six feet long (reckoning the length from the speculum to the prism, and thence to the focus T), will bear an aperture of six inches at the speculum, and magnify between two and three hundred times. But the hole H here limits the aperture with more advantage than if the aperture was placed at the speculum. If the instrument be made longer or shorter, the aperture must be in proportion as the cube of the square-square root of the length, and the magnifying as the aperture. But it's convenient that the speculum be an inch or two broader than the aperture at the least, and that the glass of the speculum be thick, that it bend not in the working. The prism EFG must be no bigger than is necessary, and its back-side FG must not be quick-silvered over. For, without quick-silver it will reflect all the light incident on it from the speculum.

In this instrument the object will be inverted, but may be erected by making the square sides FF and EG of the prism EFG not plane but spherically convex, that the rays may cross as well before they come at it as afterwards between it and the eye-glass. If it be desired that the instrument bear a larger aperture, that may be also done by composing the speculum of two glasses with water between them.

If the theory of making telescopes could at length be fully brought into practice, yet there would be certain bounds beyond which telescopes could not perform. For the air through which we look upon the stars is in a perpetual tremor; as may be seen by the tremulous motion of shadows cast from high towers, and by the twinkling of the fixed stars. But these stars do not twinkle when viewed through telescopes which have large apertures. For the rays of light, which pass through divers parts of the aperture, tremble each of them apart, and by means of their various and sometimes contrary tremors fall at one and the same time upon different points in the bottom of the eye, and their trembling motions are too quick and confused to be perceived severally. And all these illuminated points constitute one broad lucid point, composed of those many trembling points confusedly and insensibly mixed with one another by very short and swift tremors, and thereby cause the star to appear broader than it is and without any trembling of the whole. Long telescopes may cause objects to appear brighter and larger than short ones can do, but they cannot be so formed as to take away the confusion of the rays which arises from the tremors of the atmosphere. The only remedy is a most serene and quiet air, such as may perhaps be found on the tops of the highest mountains above the grosser clouds.

Part II

PROPOSITION 1. THEOREM 1

THE PHENOMENA OF COLOURS IN REFRACTED OR REFLECTED LIGHT ARE NOT
CAUSED BY NEW MODIFICATIONS OF THE LIGHT VARIOUSLY IMPRESSED, AC-
CORDING TO THE VARIOUS TERMINATIONS OF THE LIGHT AND SHADOW.

The Proof by Experiments

EXPERIMENT 1. For if the Sun shine into a very dark chamber through an oblong
hole F, [Fig. 1] whose breadth is the sixth or eighth part of an inch, or something less; and his beam FH do afterwards pass first through a very large prism
ABC, distant about 20 feet from the hole, and parallel to it, and then (with its
white part) through an oblong hole H, whose breadth is about the fortieth or
sixtieth part of an inch, and which is made in a black opaque body GI, and
placed at the distance of two or three feet from the prism, in a parallel situation
both to the prism and to the former hole; and if this white light thus transmitted through the hole H fall afterwards upon a white paper *pt*, placed after
that hole H at the distance of three or four feet from it, and there paint the

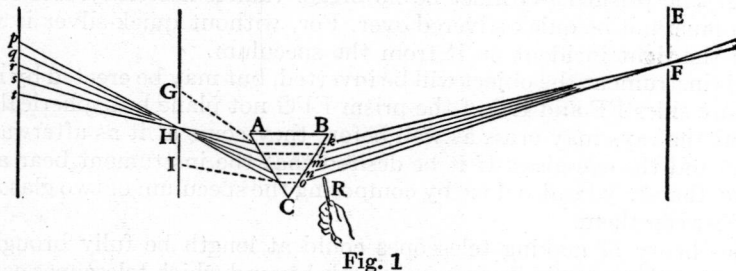

Fig. 1

usual colours of the prism, (suppose red at *t*, yellow at *s*, green at *r*, blue at *q*,
and violet at *p*) you may with an iron wire, or any such like slender opaque
body, whose breadth is about the tenth part of an inch, by intercepting the
rays at *k*, *l*, *m*, *n* or *o*, take away any one of the colours at *t*, *s*, *r*, *q* or *p*, whilst
the other colours remain upon the paper as before; or with an obstacle some-
thing bigger you may take away any two, or three, or four colours together, the
rest remaining: So that any one of the colours as well as violet may become outmost in the confine of the shadow towards *p*, and any one of them as well as red
may become outmost in the confine of the shadow towards *t*, and any one of
them may also border upon the shadow made within the colours by the obstacle
R intercepting some intermediate part of the light; and, lastly, any one of
them by being left alone may border upon the shadow on either hand. All the
colours have themselves indifferently to any confines of shadow, and therefore
the differences of these colours from one another do not arise from the different
confines of shadow, whereby light is variously modified, as has hitherto been
the opinion of philosophers. In trying these things 'tis to be observed that by
how much the holes F and H are narrower, and the intervals between them and
the prism greater, and the chamber darker, by so much the better doth the

experiment succeed; provided the light be not so far diminished but that the colours at *pt* be sufficiently visible. To procure a prism of solid glass large enough for this experiment will be difficult, and therefore a prismatic vessel must be made of polished glass plates cemented together, and filled with salt water or clear oil.

EXPER. 2. The Sun's light let into a dark chamber through the round hole F, [Fig. 2] half an inch wide, passed first through the prism ABC placed at the hole, and then through a lens PT something more than four inches broad, and about eight feet distant from the prism, and thence converged to O the focus of the lens distant from it about three feet, and there fell upon a white paper DE. If that paper was perpendicular to that light incident upon it, as 'tis

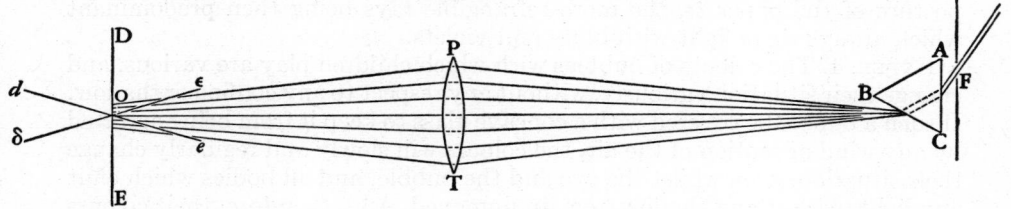

Fig. 2

represented in the posture DE, all the colours upon it at O appeared white. But if the paper being turned about an axis parallel to the prism, became very much inclined to the light, as 'tis represented in the positions *de* and δε, the same light in the one case appeared yellow and red, in the other blue. Here one and the same part of the light in one and the same place, according to the various inclinations of the paper, appeared in one case white, in another yellow or red, in a third blue, whilst the confine of light and shadow, and the refractions of the prism in all these cases remained the same.

EXPER. 3. Such another experiment may be more easily tried as follows: Let a broad beam of the Sun's light coming into a dark chamber through a hole in the window-shut be refracted by a large prism ABC, [Fig. 3] whose refracting angle C is more than 60 degrees, and so soon as it comes out of the prism, let it fall upon the white paper DE glued upon a stiff plane; and this light, when the paper is perpendicular to it, as 'tis represented in DE, will appear perfectly white upon the paper; but when the paper is very much inclined to it in such a manner as to keep always parallel to the axis of the prism, the whiteness of the

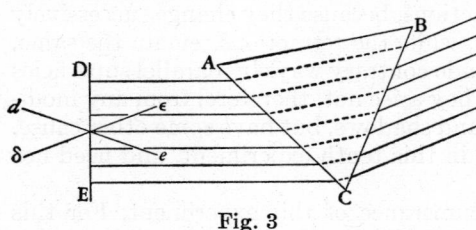

Fig. 3

whole light upon the paper will, according to the inclination of the paper this way or that way, change either into yellow and red, as in the posture *de*, or into blue and violet, as in the posture δε. And if the light before it fall upon the paper be twice refracted the same way by two parallel prisms, these colours will become the more conspicuous. Here all the middle parts of the broad beam of white light which fell upon the paper did, without any confine of shadow to modify it, become coloured all over with one uniform colour, the colour being always the same in the middle of the paper as at the edges, and this colour changed according to the various obliquity of the reflecting paper, without any change in the refractions or shadow, or in the light which fell upon the paper. And, therefore, these colours are to be derived from some other cause than the new modifications of light by refractions and shadows.

If it be asked, What then is their cause? I answer, That the paper in the posture *de,* being more oblique to the more refrangible rays than to the less refrangible ones, is more strongly illuminated by the latter than by the former, and, therefore, the less refrangible rays are predominant in the reflected light. And wherever they are predominant in any light, they tinge it with red or yellow, as may in some measure appear by the first Proposition of the first part of this book, and will more fully appear hereafter. And the contrary happens in the posture of the paper $\delta\epsilon$, the more refrangible rays being then predominant which always tinge light with blues and violets.

EXPER. 4. The colours of bubbles with which children play are various, and change their situation variously, without any respect to any confine or shadow. If such a bubble be covered with a concave glass to keep it from being agitated by any wind or motion of the air, the colours will slowly and regularly change their situation, even whilst the eye and the bubble, and all bodies which emit any light, or cast any shadow, remain unmoved. And, therefore, their colours arise from some regular cause which depends not on any confine of shadow. What this cause is will be shewed in the next book.

To these experiments may be added the tenth experiment of the first part of this first book, where the Sun's light in a dark room being trajected through the parallel superficies of two prisms tied together in the form of a parallelepiped, became totally of one uniform yellow or red colour, at its emerging out of the prisms. Here, in the production of these colours, the confine of shadow can have nothing to do. For the light changes from white to yellow, orange and red successively, without any alteration of the confine of shadow. And at both edges of the emerging light where the contrary confines of shadow ought to produce different effects, the colour is one and the same, whether it be white, yellow, orange or red. And in the middle of the emerging light, where there is no confine of shadow at all, the colour is the very same as at the edges, the whole light at its very first emergence being of one uniform colour, whether white, yellow, orange or red, and going on thence perpetually without any change of colour, such as the confine of shadow is vulgarly supposed to work in refracted light after its emergence. Neither can these colours arise from any new modifications of the light by refractions, because they change successively from white to yellow, orange and red, while the refractions remain the same, and also because the refractions are made contrary ways by parallel superficies which destroy one another's effects. They arise not, therefore, from any modifications of light made by refractions and shadows, but have some other cause. What that cause is we shewed above in this tenth experiment, and need not here repeat it.

There is yet another material circumstance of this experiment. For this emerging light being by a third prism HIK [Fig. 22 Part I.] refracted towards the paper PT, and there painting the usual colours of the prism, red, yellow, green, blue, violet: If these colours arose from the refractions of that prism modifying the light, they would not be in the light before its incidence on that prism. And yet in that experiment we found that when, by turning the two first prisms about their common axis all the colours were made to vanish but the red, the light, which makes that red being left alone, appeared of the very same red colour before its incidence on the third prism. And, in general, we find by other experiments that when the rays which differ in refrangibility are separated from one another, and any one sort of them is considered apart, the colour of the light which they compose cannot be changed by any refraction or reflexion whatever, as it ought to be were colours nothing else than modifications of light caused by refractions, and reflexions, and shadows. This unchangeableness of colour I am now to describe in the following Proposition.

PROPOSITION 2. THEOREM 2

All homogeneal light has its proper colour answering to its degree of refrangibility, and that colour cannot be changed by reflexions and refractions.

In the experiments of the fourth Proposition of the first part of this first book, when I had separated the heterogeneous rays from one another, the spectrum *pt* formed by the separated rays did in the progress from its end *p*, on which the most refrangible rays fell, unto its other end *t*, on which the least refrangible rays fell, appear tinged with this series of colours: violet, indigo, blue, green, yellow, orange, red, together with all their intermediate degrees in a continual succession perpetually varying. So that there appeared as many degrees of colours, as there were sorts of rays differing in refrangibility.

EXPER. 5. Now, that these colours could not be changed by refraction I knew by refracting with a prism sometimes one very little part of this light, sometimes another very little part, as is described in the twelfth experiment of the first part of this book. For by this refraction the colour of the light was never changed in the least. If any part of the red light was refracted, it remained totally of the same red colour as before. No orange, no yellow, no green or blue, no other new colour was produced by that refraction. Neither did the colour any way change by repeated refractions, but continued always the same red entirely as at first. The like constancy and immutability I found also in the blue, green, and other colours. So also, if I looked through a prism upon any body illuminated with any part of this homogeneal light, as in the fourteenth experiment of the first part of this book is described; I could not perceive any new colour generated this way. All bodies illuminated with compound light appear through prisms confused (as was said above) and tinged with various new colours, but those illuminated with homogeneal light appeared through prisms neither less distinct, nor otherwise coloured, than when viewed with the naked eyes. Their colours were not in the least changed by the refraction of the interposed prism. I speak here of a sensible change of colour: for the light which I here call homogeneal, being not absolutely homogeneal, there ought to arise some little change of colour from its heterogeneity. But, if that heterogeneity was so little as it might be made by the said experiments of the fourth Proposition, that change was not sensible, and therefore in experiments, where sense is judge, ought to be accounted none at all.

EXPER. 6. And as these colours were not changeable by refractions, so neither were they by reflexions. For all white, grey, red, yellow, green, blue, violet bodies, as paper, ashes, red lead, orpiment, indigo bice, gold, silver, copper, grass, blue flowers, violets, bubbles of water tinged with various colours, peacock's feathers, the tincture of *lignum nephriticum*, and such-like, in red homogeneal light appeared totally red, in blue light totally blue, in green light totally green, and so of other colours. In the homogeneal light of any colour they all appeared totally of that same colour, with this only difference: that some of them reflected that light more strongly, others more faintly. I never yet found any body, which by reflecting homogeneal light could sensibly change its colour.

From all which it is manifest that if the Sun's light consisted of but one sort of rays, there would be but one colour in the whole world, nor would it be possible to produce any new colour by reflexions and refractions, and, by consequence, that the variety of colours depends upon the composition of light.

DEFINITION

The homogeneal light and rays which appear red, or rather make objects appear so, I call rubrific or red-making; those which make objects appear yellow, green, blue, and violet, I call yellow-making, green-making, blue-making, violet-making, and so of the rest. And if at any time I speak of light and rays as coloured or endued with colours, I would be understood to speak not philosophically and properly, but grossly, and accordingly to such conceptions as vulgar people in seeing all these experiments would be apt to frame. For the rays, to speak properly, are not coloured. In them there is nothing else than a certain power and disposition to stir up a sensation of this or that colour. For as sound in a bell or musical string, or other sounding body, is nothing but a trembling motion, and in the air nothing but that motion propagated from the object, and in the sensorium 'tis a sense of that motion under the form of sound; so colours in the object are nothing but a disposition to reflect this or that sort of rays more copiously than the rest; in the rays they are nothing but their dispositions to propagate this or that motion into the sensorium, and in the sensorium they are sensations of those motions under the forms of colours.

PROPOSITION 3. PROBLEM 1

To define the refrangibility of the several sorts of homogeneal light answering to the several colours.

For determining this Problem I made the following experiment.

EXPER. 7. When I had caused the rectilinear sides AF, GM, [Fig. 4] of the spectrum of colours made by the prism to be distinctly defined, as in the fifth experiment of the first part of this book is described, there were found in it all

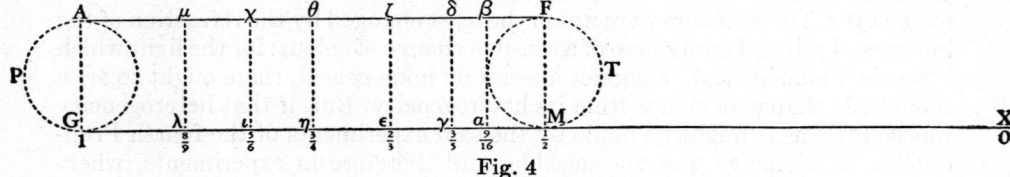

Fig. 4

the homogeneal colours in the same order and situation one among another as in the spectrum of simple light, described in the fourth Proposition of that part. For the circles of which the spectrum of compound light PT is composed, and which in the middle parts of the spectrum interfere, and are intermixed with one another, are not intermixed in their outmost parts where they touch those rectilinear sides AF and GM. And, therefore, in those rectilinear sides when distinctly defined, there is no new colour generated by refraction. I observed, also, that if anywhere between the two outmost circles TMF and PGA a right line, as $\gamma\delta$, was cross to the spectrum, so as both ends to fall perpendicularly upon its rectilinear sides, there appeared one and the same colour, and degree of colour from one end of this line to the other. I delineated, therefore, in a paper the perimeter of the spectrum FAP GMT, and, in trying the third experiment of the first part of this book, I held the paper so that the spectrum might fall upon this delineated figure, and agree with it exactly, whilst an assistant, whose eyes for distinguishing colours were more critical than mine, did by right lines $a\beta$, $\gamma\delta$, $\epsilon\zeta$, &c. drawn cross the spectrum, note the confines of the colours (that is, of the red M$a\beta$F, of the orange $a\gamma\delta\beta$, of the yellow $\gamma\epsilon\zeta\delta$, of the green $\epsilon\eta\theta\zeta$, of the blue $\eta\iota\kappa\theta$, of the indigo $\iota\lambda\mu\kappa$, and of the violet λGAμ). And this operation being divers times repeated both in the same and in several papers, I found that the observations agreed well enough with one another, and that the rectilinear sides MG and FA were by the said cross lines divided after the manner of a musical chord. Let GM be produced to X, that MX may be equal to GM, and conceive GX, λX, ιX, ηX, ϵX, γX, aX, MX, to be in proportion to one another, as the numbers, $1, \frac{8}{9}, \frac{5}{6}, \frac{3}{4}, \frac{2}{3}, \frac{3}{5}, \frac{9}{16}, \frac{1}{2}$, and so to represent the chords of the key, and of a tone, a third minor, a fourth, a fifth, a sixth major, a seventh and an eighth above that key. And the intervals Ma, $a\gamma$, $\gamma\epsilon$, $\epsilon\eta$, $\eta\iota$, $\iota\lambda$, and λG, will be the spaces which the several colours (red, orange, yellow, green, blue, indigo, violet) take up.

Now, these intervals or spaces subtending the differences of the refractions of the rays going to the limits of those colours (that is, to the Points M, a, γ, ϵ, η, ι, λ, G) may without any sensible error be accounted proportional to the differences of the sines of refraction of those rays having one common sine of incidence; and, therefore, since the common sine of incidence of the most and least refrangible rays out of glass into air was (by a method described above) found in proportion to their sines of refraction as 50 to 77 and 78, divide the difference between the sines of refraction 77 and 78, as the line GM is divided by those intervals, and you will have $77, 77\frac{1}{8}, 77\frac{1}{5}, 77\frac{1}{3}, 77\frac{1}{2}, 77\frac{2}{3}, 77\frac{7}{9}, 78$, the sines of refraction of those rays out of glass into air, their common sine of incidence being 50. So, then, the sines of the incidences of all the red-making rays out of glass into air were to the sines of their refractions not greater than 50 to 77, nor less than 50 to $77\frac{1}{8}$, but they varied from one another according to all intermediate proportions. And the sines of the incidences of the green-making rays were to the sines of their refractions in all proportions from that of 50 to $77\frac{1}{3}$, unto that of 50 to $77\frac{1}{2}$. And by the like limits above-mentioned were the refractions of the rays belonging to the rest of the colours defined, the sines of the red-making rays extending from 77 to $77\frac{1}{8}$, those of the orange-making from $77\frac{1}{8}$ to $77\frac{1}{5}$, those of the yellow-making from $77\frac{1}{5}$ to $77\frac{1}{3}$, those of the green-making from $77\frac{1}{3}$ to $77\frac{1}{2}$, those of the blue-making from $77\frac{1}{2}$ to $77\frac{2}{3}$, those of the indigo-making from $67\frac{2}{3}$ to $77\frac{7}{9}$, and those of the violet from $77\frac{7}{9}$ to 78.

These are the laws of the refractions made out of glass into air, and thence, by the third Axiom of the first part of this book, the laws of the refractions made out of air into glass are easily derived.

EXPER. 8. I found, moreover, that when light goes out of air through several contiguous refracting mediums as through water and glass, and thence goes out again into air, whether the refracting superficies be parallel or inclined to one another, that light as often as by contrary refractions 'tis so corrected, that it emergeth in lines parallel to those in which it was incident, continues ever after to be white. But if the emergent rays be inclined to the incident, the whiteness of the emerging light will by degrees in passing on from the place of emergence, become tinged in its edges with colours. This I tried by refracting light with prisms of glass placed within a prismatic vessel of water. Now, those colours argue a diverging and separation of the heterogeneous rays from one another by means of their unequal refractions, as in what follows will more fully appear. And, on the contrary, the permanent whiteness argues that in like incidences of the rays there is no such separation of the emerging rays, and by consequence no inequality of their whole refractions. Whence I seem to gather the two following theorems:

1. The excesses of the sines of refraction of several sorts of rays above their common sine of incidence when the refractions are made out of divers denser mediums immediately into one and the same rarer medium (suppose of air) are to one another in a given proportion.

2. The proportion of the sine of incidence to the sine of refraction of one and the same sort of rays out of one medium into another, is composed of the proportion of the sine of incidence to the sine of refraction out of the first medium into any third medium, and of the proportion of the sine of incidence to the sine of refraction out of that third medium into the second medium.

By the first theorem, the refractions of the rays of every sort made out of any medium into air are known by having the refraction of the rays of any one sort. As, for instance, if the refractions of the rays of every sort out of rain-water into air be desired, let the common sine of incidence out of glass into air be subducted from the sines of refraction, and the excesses will be 27, $27\frac{1}{8}$, $27\frac{1}{5}$, $27\frac{1}{3}$, $27\frac{1}{2}$, $27\frac{2}{3}$, $27\frac{7}{9}$, 28. Suppose, now, that the sine of incidence of the least refrangible rays be to their sine of refraction out of rain-water into air as 3 to 4, and say as 1 the difference of those sines is to 3 the sine of incidence, so is 27 the least of the excesses above-mentioned to a fourth number 81; and 81 will be the common sine of incidence out of rain-water into air, to which sine (if you add all the above-mentioned excesses) you will have the desired sines of the refractions 108, $108\frac{1}{8}$, $108\frac{1}{5}$, $108\overline{\frac{1}{3}}$, $108\frac{1}{2}$, $108\frac{2}{3}$, $108\frac{7}{9}$, 109.

By the latter theorem, the refraction out of one medium into another is gathered as often as you have the refractions out of them both into any third medium. As if the sine of incidence of any ray out of glass into air be to its sine of refraction as 20 to 31, and the sine of incidence of the same ray out of air into water be to its sine of refraction as 4 to 3; the sine of incidence of that ray out of glass into water will be to its sine of refraction as 20 to 31 and 4 to 3 jointly; that is, as the factum of 20 and 4 to the factum of 31 and 3, or as 80 to 93.

And these theorems being admitted into Optics, there would be scope enough of handling that science voluminously after a new manner, not only by teaching those things which tend to the perfection of vision, but also by determining mathematically all kinds of phenomena of colours which could be produced by refractions. For to do this, there is nothing else requisite than to find out the separations of heterogeneous rays, and their various mixtures and proportions in every mixture. By this way of arguing I invented almost all the phenomena described in these books, beside some others less necessary to the argument;

and by the successes I met with in the trials, I dare promise that to him who shall argue truly, and then try all things with good glasses and sufficient circumspection, the expected event will not be wanting. But he is first to know what colours will arise from any others mixed in any assigned proportion.

PROPOSITION 4. THEOREM 3

Colours may be produced by composition which shall be like to the colours of homogeneal light as to the appearance of colour, but not as to the immutability of colour and constitution of light. And those colours by how much they are more compounded by so much are they less full and intense, and by too much composition they may be diluted and weakened till they cease, and the mixture becomes white or grey. There may be also colours produced by composition, which are not fully like any of the colours of homogeneal light.

For a mixture of homogeneal red and yellow compounds an orange, like in appearance of colour to that orange which in the series of unmixed prismatic colours lies between them; but the light of one orange is homogeneal as to refrangibility, and that of the other is heterogeneal, and the colour of the one, if viewed through a prism, remains unchanged, that of the other is changed and resolved into its component colours, red and yellow. And after the same manner other neighbouring homogeneal colours may compound new colours, like the intermediate homogeneal ones, as yellow and green, the colour between them both; and afterwards, if blue be added, there will be made a green the middle colour of the three which enter the composition. For the yellow and blue on either hand, if they are equal in quantity they draw the intermediate green equally towards themselves in composition, and so keep it as it were in equilibrium, that it verge not more to the yellow on the one hand, and to the blue on the other, but by their mixed actions remain still a middle colour. To this mixed green there may be further added some red and violet, and yet the green will not presently cease, but only grow less full and vivid, and by increasing the red and violet, it will grow more and more dilute until, by the prevalence of the added colours, it be overcome and turned into whiteness or some other colour. So if to the colour of any homogeneal light the Sun's white light composed of all sorts of rays be added, that colour will not vanish or change its species, but be diluted; and by adding more and more white it will be diluted more and more, perpetually. Lastly, if red and violet be mingled, there will be generated according to their various proportions various purples, such as are not like in appearance to the colour of any homogeneal light, and of these purples mixed with yellow and blue may be made other new colours.

PROPOSITION 5. THEOREM 4

Whiteness, and all grey colours between white and black, may be compounded of colours, and the whiteness of the Sun's light is compounded of all the primary colours mixed in a due proportion.

The Proof by Experiments

EXPERIMENT 9. The Sun shining into a dark chamber through a little round hole in the window-shut, and his light being there refracted by a prism to cast his coloured image PT [Fig. 5] upon the opposite wall, I held a white paper V to that image in such manner that it might be illuminated by the coloured light reflected from thence, and yet not intercept any part of that light in its passage from the prism to the spectrum. And I found that when the paper was held nearer to any colour than to the rest, it appeared of that colour to which it approached nearest; but when it was equally or almost equally distant from all the colours, so that it might be equally illuminated by them all, it appeared white. And in this last situation of the paper, if some colours were intercepted the paper lost its white colour, and appeared of the colour of the rest of the light which was not intercepted. So, then, the paper was illuminated with lights of various colours (namely, red, yellow, green, blue and violet) and every part

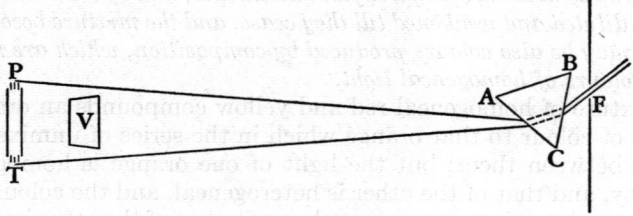

Fig. 5

of the light retained its proper colour until it was incident on the paper, and became reflected thence to the eye; so that if it had been either alone (the rest of the light being intercepted) or if it had abounded most, and been predominant in the light reflected from the paper, it would have tinged the paper with its own colour; and yet, being mixed with the rest of the colours in a due proportion, it made the paper look white, and therefore by a composition with the rest produced that colour. The several parts of the coloured light reflected from the spectrum, whilst they are propagated from thence through the air, do perpetually retain their proper colours, because wherever they fall upon the eyes of any spectator they make the several parts of the spectrum to appear under their proper colours. They retain, therefore, their proper colours when they fall upon the Paper V, and so by the confusion and perfect mixture of those colours compound the whiteness of the light reflected from thence.

EXPER. 10. Let that spectrum or solar image PT [Fig. 6] fall now upon the lens MN above four inches broad, and about six feet distant from the prism ABC and so figured that it may cause the coloured light which divergeth from the prism to converge and meet again at its focus G, about six or eight feet distant from the lens, and there to fall perpendicularly upon a white paper DE. And if you move this paper to and fro, you will perceive that near the lens, as at *de*, the whole solar image (suppose at *pt*) will appear upon it intensely

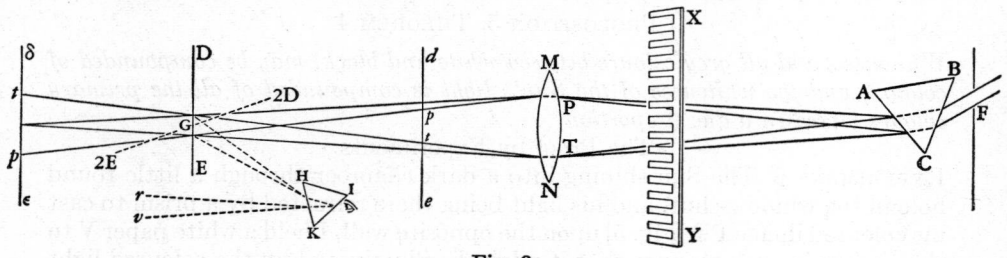

Fig. 6

coloured after the manner above-explained; and that by receding from the lens those colours will perpetually come towards one another, and, by mixing more and more, dilute one another continually until at length the paper come to the focus G, where by a perfect mixture they will wholly vanish and be converted into whiteness, the whole light appearing now upon the paper like a little white circle. And afterwards by receding farther from the lens, the rays which before converged will now cross one another in the focus G, and diverge from thence, and thereby make the colours to appear again, but yet in a contrary order; suppose at $\delta\epsilon$, where the red t is now above which before was below, and the violet p is below which before was above.

Let us now stop the paper at the focus G, where the light appears totally white and circular, and let us consider its whiteness. I say, that this is composed of the converging colours. For if any of those colours be intercepted at the lens, the whiteness will cease and degenerate into that colour which ariseth from the composition of the other colours which are not intercepted. And then if the intercepted colours be let pass and fall upon that compound colour, they mix with it, and by their mixture restore the whiteness. So if the violet, blue and green be intercepted, the remaining yellow, orange and red will compound upon the paper an orange, and then if the intercepted colours be let pass, they will fall upon this compounded orange, and together with it decompound a white. So also if the red and violet be intercepted, the remaining yellow, green and blue will compound a green upon the paper, and then the red and violet being let pass will fall upon this green, and together with it decompound a white. And that in this composition of white the several rays do not suffer any change in their colorific qualities by acting upon one another, but are only mixed, and by a mixture of their colours produce white, may further appear by these arguments.

If the paper be placed beyond the focus G, suppose at $\delta\epsilon$, and then the red colour at the lens be alternately intercepted, and let pass again, the violet colour on the paper will not suffer any change thereby, as it ought to do if the several sorts of rays acted upon one another in the focus G, where they cross. Neither will the red upon the paper be changed by any alternate stopping, and letting pass the violet which crosseth it.

And if the paper be placed at the focus G, and the white round image at G be viewed through the prism HIK, and by the refraction of that prism be translated to the place rv, and there appear tinged with various colours (namely, the violet at v and red at r, and others between) and then the red colours at the lens be often stopped and let pass by turns, the red at r will accordingly disappear, and return as often, but the violet at v will not thereby suffer any change. And so, by stopping and letting pass alternately the blue at the lens, the blue at v will accordingly disappear and return, without any change made in the red at r. The red, therefore, depends on one sort of rays, and the blue on another sort, which in the focus G, where they are commixed, do not act on one another. And there is the same reason of the other colours.

I considered, further, that when the most refrangible rays Pp, and the least refrangible ones Tt, are by converging inclined to one another, the paper, if held very oblique to those rays in the focus G, might reflect one sort of them more copiously than the other sort, and by that means the reflected light would be tinged in that focus with the colour of the predominant rays, provided those rays severally retained their colours, or colorific qualities in the composition of white made by them in that focus. But if they did not retain them in that white, but became all of them severally endued there with a disposition to strike the sense with the perception of white, then they could never lose their whiteness by such reflexions. I inclined, therefore, the paper to the rays very obliquely, as in the second experiment of this second part of the first book, that the most refrangible rays might be more copiously reflected than the rest, and the whiteness at length changed successively into blue, indigo, and violet. Then I inclined it the contrary way, that the least refrangible rays might be more copious in the reflected light than the rest, and the whiteness turned successively to yellow, orange, and red.

Lastly, I made an instrument XY in fashion of a comb whose teeth, being in number sixteen, were about an inch and a half broad, and the intervals of the teeth about two inches wide. Then by interposing successively the teeth of this instrument near the lens, I intercepted part of the colours by the interposed tooth, whilst the rest of them went on through the interval of the teeth to the paper DE, and there painted a round solar image. But the paper I had first placed so that the image might appear white as often as the comb was taken away; and then the Comb being as was said interposed, the whiteness by reason of the intercepted part of the colours at the lens did always change into the colour compounded of those colours which were not intercepted, and that colour was by the motion of the comb perpetually varied so that in the passing of every tooth over the lens all these colours (red, yellow, green, blue, and purple) did always succeed one another. I caused, therefore, all the teeth to pass successively over the lens, and when the motion was slow there appeared a perpetual succession of the colours upon the paper; but if I so much accelerated the motion that the colours by reason of their quick succession could not be distinguished from one another, the appearance of the single colours ceased. There was no red, no yellow, no green, no blue, nor purple to be seen any longer, but from a confusion of them all there arose one uniform white colour. Of the light which now by the mixture of all the colours appeared white, there was no part really white. One part was red, another yellow, a third green, a fourth blue, a fifth purple, and every part retains its proper colour till it strikes the sensorium. If the impressions follow one another slowly, so that they may be severally perceived, there is made a distinct sensation of all the colours one after another in a continual succession. But if the impressions follow one another so quickly that they cannot be severally perceived, there ariseth out of them all one common sensation, which is neither of this colour alone nor of that alone, but hath itself indifferently to them all, and this is a sensation of whiteness. By the quickness of the successions, the impressions of the several colours are confounded in the sensorium, and out of that confusion ariseth a mixed sensation. If a burning coal be nimbly moved round in a circle with gyrations continually repeated, the whole circle will apear like fire; the reason of which is that the sensation of the coal in the several places of that circle remains impressed on the sensorium until the coal return again to the same place. And so in a quick consecution of the colours the impression of every colour remains in the sensorium, until a revolution of all the colours be completed, and that first colour return again. The impressions, therefore, of all the successive colours are at once in the sensorium, and jointly stir up a sensation of them all; and so it is manifest by this experiment that the commixed impressions of all the colours do stir up and beget a sensation of white, that is, that whiteness is compounded of all the colours.

And if the comb be now taken away, that all the colours may at once pass from the lens to the paper, and be there intermixed, and together reflected thence to the spectator's eyes, their impressions on the sensorium being now more subtly and perfectly commixed there, ought much more to stir up a sensation of whiteness.

You may instead of the lens use two prisms HIK and LMN which, by refracting the coloured light the contrary way to that of the first refraction, may make the diverging rays converge and meet again in G, as you see represented in the seventh Figure. For where they meet and mix, they will compose a white light, as when a lens is used.

Exper. 11. Let the Sun's coloured image PT [Fig. 8] fall upon the wall of a dark chamber, as in the third experiment of the first book, and let the same be viewed through a prism abc, held parallel to the prism ABC, by whose refraction that image was made, and let it now appear lower than before, suppose in the place S over against the red colour T. And if you go near to the image PT,

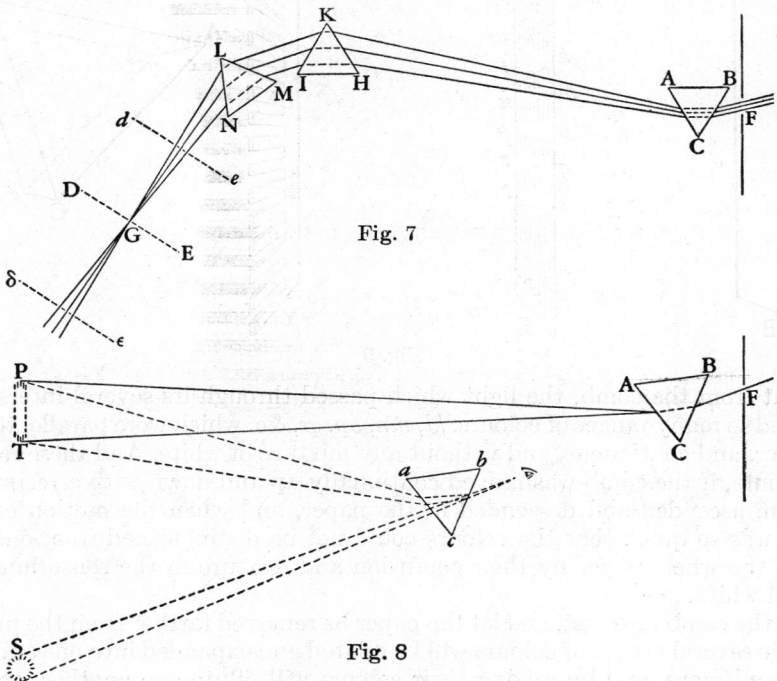

Fig. 7

Fig. 8

the spectrum S will appear oblong and coloured like the image PT; but if you recede from it the colours of the spectrum S will be contracted more and more, and at length vanish, that spectrum S becoming perfectly round and white; and if you recede yet farther, the colours will emerge again, but in a contrary order. Now that spectrum S appears white in that case, when the rays of several sorts which converge from the several parts of the image PT, to the prism abc, are so refracted unequally by it that in their passage from the prism to the eye they may diverge from one and the same point of the spectrum S, and so fall afterwards upon one and the same point in the bottom of the eye, and there be mingled.

And, further, if the comb be here made use of, by whose teeth the colours at the image PT may be successively intercepted, the spectrum S, when the comb is moved slowly, will be perpetually tinged with successive colours. But when, by accelerating the motion of the comb, the succession of the colours is so quick that they cannot be severally seen, that spectrum S, by a confused and mixed sensation of them all, will appear white.

EXPER. 12. The Sun shining through a large prism ABC [Fig. 9] upon a comb XY, placed immediately behind the prism, his light which passed through the interstices of the teeth fell upon a white paper DE. The breadths of the teeth were equal to their interstices, and seven teeth together with their interstices took up an inch in breadth. Now, when the paper was about two or three inches

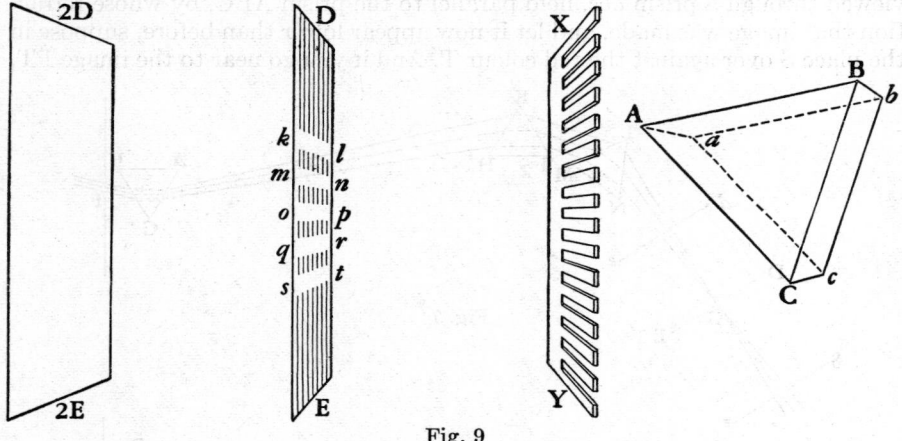

Fig. 9

distant from the comb, the light which passed through its several interstices painted so many ranges of colours, *kl, mn, op, qr,* &c. which were parallel to one another, and contiguous, and without any mixture of white. And these ranges of colours, if the comb was moved continually up and down with a reciprocal motion, ascended and descended in the paper, and when the motion of the comb was so quick that the colours could not be distinguished from one another, the whole paper by their confusion and mixture in the sensorium appeared white.

Let the comb now rest, and let the paper be removed farther from the prism, and the several ranges of colours will be dilated and expanded into one another more and more, and by mixing their colours will dilute one another, and at length, when the distance of the paper from the comb is about a foot, or a little more (suppose in the place 2D 2E) they will so far dilute one another as to become white.

With any obstacle, let all the light be now stopped which passes through any one interval of the teeth, so that the range of colours which comes from thence may be taken away, and you will see the light of the rest of the ranges to be expanded into the place of the range taken away, and there to be coloured. Let the intercepted range pass on as before, and its colours falling upon the colours of the other ranges, and mixing with them, will restore the whiteness.

Let the paper 2D 2E be now very much inclined to the rays, so that the most refrangible rays may be more copiously reflected than the rest, and the white colour of the paper through the excess of those rays will be changed into blue and violet. Let the paper be as much inclined the contrary way, that the least refrangible rays may be now more copiously reflected than the rest, and by their excess the whiteness will be changed into yellow and red. The several rays, therefore, in that white light do retain their colorific qualities, by which those of any sort, whenever they become more copious than the rest, do by their excess and predominance cause their proper colour to appear.

And by the same way of arguing, applied to the third experiment of this second part of the first book, it may be concluded that the white colour of all refracted light at its very first emergence, where it appears as white as before its incidence, is compounded of various colours.

EXPER. 13. In the foregoing experiment the several intervals of the teeth of the comb do the office of so many prisms, every interval producing the phenomenon of one prism. Whence instead of those intervals using several prisms, I tried to compound whiteness by mixing their colours, and did it by using only three prisms, as also by using only two as follows: Let two prisms ABC and abc, [Fig. 10] whose refracting angles B and b are equal, be so placed parallel to one

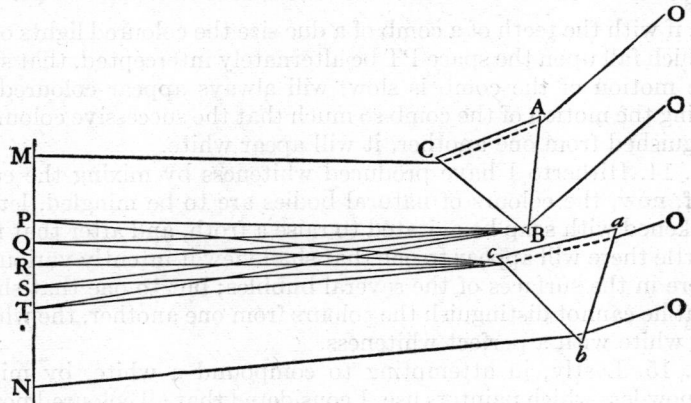

Fig. 10

another that the refracting angle B of the one may touch the angle c at the base of the other, and their planes CB and cb, at which the rays emerge, may lie in directum. Then let the light trajected through them fall upon the paper MN, distant about 8 or 12 inches from the prisms. And the colours generated by the interior limits B and c of the two prisms will be mingled at PT, and there compound white. For if either prism be taken away, the colours made by the other will appear in that place PT, and when the prism is restored to its place again, so that its colours may there fall upon the colours of the other, the mixture of them both will restore the whiteness.

This experiment succeeds also, as I have tried, when the angle b of the lower prism is a little greater than the angle B of the upper, and between the interior angles B and *c* there intercedes some space B*c*, as is represented in the figure, and the refracting planes BC and *bc* are neither in directum nor parallel to one another. For there is nothing more requisite to the success of this experiment than that the rays of all sorts may be uniformly mixed upon the paper in the place PT. If the most refrangible rays coming from the superior prism take up all the space from M to P, the rays of the same sort which come from the inferior prism ought to begin at P, and take up all the rest of the space from thence towards N. If the least refrangible rays coming from the superior prism take up the space MT, the rays of the same kind which come from the other prism ought to begin at T, and take up the remaining space TN. If one sort of the rays, which have intermediate degrees of refrangibility and come from the superior prism, be extended through the space MQ, and another sort of those rays through the space MR, and a third sort of them through the space MS, the same sorts of rays coming from the lower prism ought to illuminate the remaining spaces QN, RN, SN, respectively. And the same is to be understood of all the other sorts of rays. For thus the rays of every sort will be scattered uniformly and evenly through the whole space MN, and so, being everywhere mixed in the same proportion, they must everywhere produce the same colour. And, therefore, since by this mixture they produce white in the exterior spaces MP and TN, they must also produce white in the interior space PT. This is the reason of the composition by which whiteness was produced in this experiment, and by what other way soever I made the like composition, the result was whiteness.

Lastly, if with the teeth of a comb of a due size the coloured lights of the two prisms which fall upon the space PT be alternately intercepted, that space PT, when the motion of the comb is slow, will always appear coloured, but by accelerating the motion of the comb so much that the successive colours cannot be distinguished from one another, it will apear white.

EXPER. 14. Hitherto I have produced whiteness by mixing the colours of prisms. If, now, the colours of natural bodies are to be mingled, let water a little thickened with soap be agitated to raise a froth, and after that froth has stood a little there will appear to one that shall view it intently various colours everywhere in the surfaces of the several bubbles; but to one that shall go so far off that he cannot distinguish the colours from one another, the whole froth will grow white with a perfect whiteness.

EXPER. 15. Lastly, in attempting to compound a white, by mixing the coloured powders which painters use, I considered that all coloured powders do suppress and stop in them a very considerable part of the light by which they are illuminated. For they become coloured by reflecting the light of their own colours more copiously, and that of all other colours more sparingly, and yet they do not reflect the light of their own colours so copiously as white bodies do. If red lead, for instance, and a white paper be placed in the red light of the coloured spectrum made in a dark chamber by the refraction of a prism, as is described in the third experiment of the first part of this book, the paper will appear more lucid than the red lead, and therefore reflects the red-making rays more copiously than red lead doth. And if they be held in the light of any other colour, the light reflected by the paper will exceed the light reflected by the red lead in a much greater proportion. And the like happens in powders of other colours. And, therefore, by mixing such powders we are not to expect a strong and full white, such as is that of paper, but some dusky obscure one, such as might arise from a mixture of light and darkness, or from white and black; that is, a grey, or dun, or russet brown, such as are the colours of a man's nail, of a mouse, of ashes, of ordinary stones, of mortar, of dust and dirt in highways, and the like. And such a dark white I have often produced by mixing coloured powders. For thus one part of red lead, and five parts of *viride æris* composed a dun colour like that of a mouse. For these two colours were severally so compounded of others that in both together were a mixture of all colours; and there was less red lead used than *viride æris*, because of the fulness of its colour. Again, one part of red lead and four parts of blue bice composed a dun colour verging a little to purple, and by adding to this a certain mixture of orpiment and *viride æris* in a due proportion, the mixture lost its purple tincture and became perfectly dun. But the experiment succeeded best without minium thus: To orpiment I added by little and little a certain full bright purple, which painters use, until the orpiment ceased to be yellow, and became of a pale red. Then I diluted that red by adding a little *viride æris*, and a little more blue bice than *viride æris*, until it became of such a grey or pale white as verged to no one of the colours more than to another. For thus it became of a colour equal in whiteness to that of ashes, or of wood newly cut, or of a man's skin. The orpiment reflected more light than did any other of the powders, and therefore conduced more to the whiteness of the compounded colour than they. To assign the proportions accurately may be difficult, by reason of the different goodness of powders of the same kind. Accordingly, as the colour of any powder is more or less full and luminous, it ought to be used in a less or greater proportion.

Now, considering that these grey and dun colours may be also produced by mixing whites and blacks, and by consequence differ from perfect whites, not in species of colours but only in degree of luminousness, it is manifest that there is nothing more requisite to make them perfectly white than to increase their light sufficiently; and, on the contrary, if by increasing their light they can be brought to perfect whiteness, it will thence also follow that they are of the same species of colour with the best whites, and differ from them only in the quantity of light. And this I tried as follows: I took the third of the above-mentioned grey mixtures, (that which was compounded of orpiment, purple, bice, and *viride æris*) and rubbed it thickly upon the floor of my chamber where the Sun shone upon it through the opened casement; and by it, in the shadow, I laid a piece of white paper of the same bigness. Then, going from them to the distance of 12 or 18 feet, so that I could not discern the unevenness of the surface of the powder, nor the little shadows let fall from the gritty particles thereof, the powder appeared intensely white, so as to transcend even the paper itself in whiteness, especially if the paper were a little shaded from the light of the clouds, and then the paper compared with the powder appeared of such a grey colour as the powder had done before. But by laying the paper where the Sun shines through the glass of the window, or by shutting the window that the Sun might shine through the glass upon the powder, and by such other fit means of increasing or decreasing the lights wherewith the powder and paper were illuminated, the light wherewith the powder is illuminated may be made stronger in such a due proportion than the light wherewith the paper is illuminated that they shall both appear exactly alike in whiteness. For when I was trying this, a friend coming to visit me, I stopped him at the door, and before I told him what the colours were, or what I was doing, I asked him which of the two whites was the best, and wherein they differed. And after he had at that distance viewed them well, he answered that they were both good whites, and that he could not say which was best, nor wherein their colours differed. Now, if you consider that this white of the powder in the sunshine was compounded of the colours which the component powders (orpiment, purple, bice, and *viride æris*) have in the same sunshine, you must acknowledge by this experiment, as well as by the former, that perfect whiteness may be compounded of colours.

From what has been said it is also evident that the whiteness of the Sun's light is compounded of all the colours wherewith the several sorts of rays whereof that light consists, when by their several refrangibilities they are separated from one another, do tinge paper or any other white body whereon they fall. For those colours (by *Prop.* II. *Part* 2.) are unchangeable, and whenever all those rays with those their colours are mixed again, they reproduce the same white light as before.

PROPOSITION 6. PROBLEM 2

In a mixture of primary colours, the quantity and quality of each being given, to know the colour of the compound.

With the centre O [Fig. 11] and radius OD describe a circle ADF, and distinguish its circumference into seven parts DE, EF, FG, GA, AB, BC, CD, proportional to the seven musical tones or intervals of the eight sounds, *Sol, la, fa, sol, la, mi, fa, sol*, contained in an eight; that is, proportional to the number $\frac{1}{9}, \frac{1}{16}, \frac{1}{10}, \frac{1}{9}, \frac{1}{16}, \frac{1}{16}, \frac{1}{9}$. Let the first part DE represent a red colour, the second EF orange, the third FG yellow, the fourth CA green, the fifth AB blue, the sixth BC indigo, and the seventh CD violet. And conceive that these are all the colours of uncompounded light gradually passing into one another, as they do when made by prisms; the circumference DEFGABCD, representing the whole series of colours from one end of the Sun's coloured image to the other, so that from D to E be all degrees of red, at E the mean colour between red and orange, from E to F all degrees of orange, at F the mean between orange and yellow, from F to G all degrees of yellow, and so on. Let p be the centre of gravity of the arch DE, and q, r, s, t, u, x, the centres of gravity of the

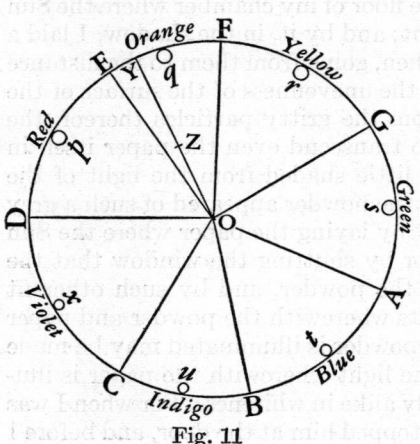

Fig. 11

arches EF, FG, GA, AB, BC, and CD, respectively, and about those centres of gravity let circles proportional to the number of rays of each colour in the given mixture be described: that is, the circle p proportional to the number of the red-making rays in the mixture, the circle q proportional to the number of the orange-making rays in the mixture, and so of the rest. Find the common centre of gravity of all those circles, p, q, r, s, t, u, x. Let that centre be Z; and from the centre of the circle ADF, through Z to the circumference, drawing the right line OY, the place of the point Y in the circumference shall shew the colour arising from the composition of all the colours in the given mixture, and the line OZ shall be proportional to the fulness or intenseness of the colour; that is, to its distance from whiteness. As if Y fall in the middle between F and G, the compounded colour shall be the best yellow; if Y verge from the middle towards F or G, the compound colour shall accordingly be a yellow, verging towards orange or green. If Z fall upon the circumference, the colour shall be intense and florid in the highest degree; if it fall in the midway between the circumference and centre, it shall be but half so intense; that is, it shall be such a colour as would be made by diluting the intensest yellow with an equal quantity of whiteness; and if it fall upon the centre O, the colour shall have lost all its intenseness, and become a white. But it is to be noted that if the point Z fall in or near the line OD, the main ingredients being the red and violet, the colour compounded shall not be any of the prismatic colours, but a purple, inclining to red or violet, accordingly as the point Z lieth on the side of the line DO towards E or towards C, and in general the compounded violet is more bright and more fiery than the uncompounded. Also, if only two of the primary colours which in the circle are opposite to one another be mixed in an equal proportion, the point Z shall fall upon the centre O, and yet the colour compounded of those two shall not be perfectly white, but some faint anonymous colour. For I could never yet by mixing only two primary colours produce a perfect white. Whether it may be compounded of a mixture of three taken at equal distances in the circumference I do not know, but of four or five I do not much question but it may. But these are curiosities of little or no moment to the understanding the phenomena of Nature. For in all whites produced by Nature, there uses to be a mixture of all sorts of rays, and by consequence a composition of all colours.

To give an instance of this rule, suppose a colour is compounded of these homogeneal colours: of violet one part, of indigo one part, of blue two parts, of green three parts, of yellow five parts, of orange six parts, and of red ten parts. Proportional to these parts describe the circles x, v, t, s, r, q, p, respectively, that is, so that if the circle x be one, the circle v may be one, the circle t two, the circle s three, and the circles r, q and p, five, six and ten. Then I find Z the common centre of gravity of these circles, and through Z drawing the line OY, the point Y falls upon the circumference between E and F, something nearer to E than to F; and thence I conclude that the colour compounded of these ingredients will be an orange, verging a little more to red than to yellow. Also I find that OZ is a little less than one half of OY, and thence I conclude that this orange hath a little less than half the fulness or intenseness of an uncompounded orange; that is to say, that it is such an orange as may be made by mixing an homogeneal orange with a good white in the proportion of the Line OZ to the Line ZY, this proportion being not of the quantities of mixed orange and white powders, but of the quantities of the lights reflected from them.

This rule I conceive accurate enough for practice, though not mathematically accurate; and the truth of it may be sufficiently proved to sense by stopping any of the colours at the lens in the tenth experiment of this book. For the rest of the colours which are not stopped, but pass on to the focus of the lens, will there compound either accurately or very nearly such a colour as by this rule ought to result from their mixture.

PROPOSITION 7. THEOREM 5

All the colours in the universe which are made by light, and depend not on the power of imagination, are either the colours of homogeneal lights, or compounded of these, and that either accurately or very nearly, according to the rule of the foregoing problem.

For it has been proved (Prop. 1, Part 2) that the changes of colours made by refractions do not arise from any new modifications of the rays impressed by those refractions, and by the various terminations of light and shadow, as has been the constant and general opinion of philosophers. It has also been proved that the several colours of the homogeneal rays do constantly answer to their degrees of refrangibility (Prop. 1, Part 1 and Prop. 2, Part 2) and that their degrees of refrangibility cannot be changed by refractions and reflexions (Prop. 2, Part 1) and by consequence that those their colours are likewise immutable. It has also been proved directly by refracting and reflecting homogeneal lights apart, that their colours cannot be changed (Prop. 2, Part 2). It has been proved, also, that when the several sorts of rays are mixed, and in crossing pass through the same space, they do not act on one another so as to change each other's colorific qualities (Exper. 10, Part 2) but by mixing their actions in the sensorium beget a sensation differing from what either would do apart (that is, a sensation of a mean colour between their proper colours); and particularly when by the concourse and mixtures of all sorts of rays a white colour is produced; the white is a mixture of all the colours which the rays would have apart (Prop. 5, Part 2). The rays in that mixture do not lose or alter their several colorific qualities, but by all their various kinds of actions, mixed in the sensorium, beget a sensation of a middling colour between all their colours, which is whiteness. For whiteness is a mean between all colours, having itself indifferently to them all, so as with equal facility to be tinged with any of them. A red powder mixed with a little blue, or a blue with a little red, doth not presently lose its colour, but a white powder mixed with any colour is presently tinged with that colour, and is equally capable of being tinged with any colour whatever. It has been shewed, also, that as the Sun's light is mixed of all sorts of rays, so its whiteness is a mixture of the colours of all sorts of rays; those rays having from the beginning their several colorific qualities as well as their several refrangibilities, and retaining them perpetually unchanged notwithstanding any refractions or reflexions they may at any time suffer, and that whenever any sort of the Sun's rays is by any means (as by reflexion in Expers. 9 and 10, Part 1 or by refraction as happens in all refractions) separated from the rest, they then manifest their proper colours. These things have been proved, and the sum of all this amounts to the proposition here to be proved. For if the Sun's light is mixed of several sorts of rays, each of which have originally their several refrangibilities and colorific qualities, and notwithstanding their refractions and reflexions, and their various separations or mixtures, keep those their original properties perpetually the same without alteration; then all the colours in the world must be such as constantly ought to arise from the original colorific qualities of the rays whereof the lights consist by which those colours are seen. And, therefore, if the reason of any colour whatever be required, we have nothing else to do than to consider how the rays in the Sun's light have by reflexions or refractions, or other causes, been parted from one another, or mixed together; or otherwise to find out what sorts of rays are in the light by which that colour is made, and in what proportion; and then, by the last problem, to learn the colour which ought to arise by mixing those rays (or their colours) in that proportion. I speak here of colours so far as they arise from light. For they appear sometimes by other causes, as when by the power of phantasy we see colours in a dream, or a madman sees things before him which are not there; or when we see fire by striking the eye, or see colours like the eye of a peacock's feather by pressing our eyes in either corner whilst we look the other way. Where these and such like causes interpose not, the colour always answers to the sort or sorts of the rays whereof the light consists, as I have constantly found in whatever phenomena of colours I have hitherto been able to examine. I shall in the following Propositions give instances of this in the phenomena of chiefest note.

PROPOSITION 8. PROBLEM 3

By the discovered properties of light, to explain the colours made by prisms.

Let ABC [Fig. 12] represent a prism refracting the light of the Sun, which comes into a dark chamber through a hole Fφ almost as broad as the prism, and let MN represent a white paper on which the refracted light is cast, and suppose the most refrangible or deepest violet-making rays fall upon the space Pπ, the least refrangible or deepest red-making rays upon the space Tτ, the middle sort between the indigo-making and blue-making rays upon the space Qχ, the middle sort of the green-making rays upon the space R, the middle sort between the yellow-making and orange-making rays upon the space Sσ, and

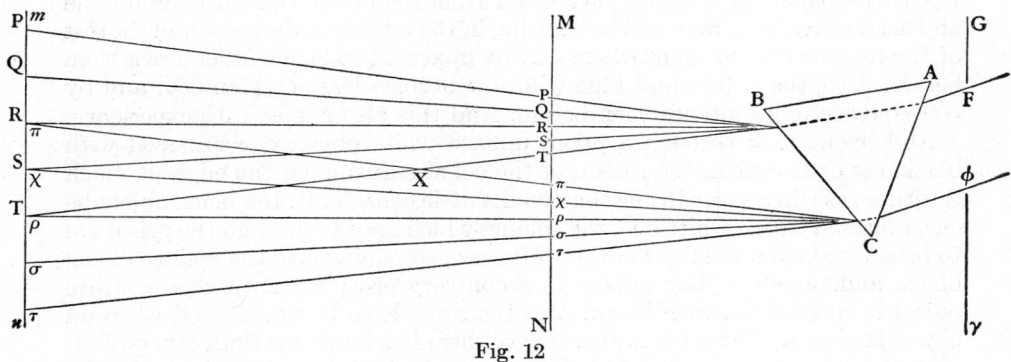

Fig. 12

other intermediate sorts upon intermediate spaces. For so the spaces upon which the several sorts adequately fall will, by reason of the different refrangibility of those sorts, be one lower than another. Now, if the paper MN be so near the prism that the spaces PT and ππ do not interfere with one another, the distance between them Tπ will be illuminated by all the sorts of rays in that proportion to one another which they have at their very first coming out of the prism, and consequently be white. But the spaces PT and ππ on either hand will not be illuminated by them all, and, therefore, will appear coloured. And particularly at P, where the outmost violet-making rays fall alone, the colour must be the deepest violet. At Q where the violet-making and indigo-making rays are mixed, it must be a violet inclining much to indigo. At R where the violet-making, indigo-making, blue-making, and one half of the green-making rays are mixed, their colours must (by the construction of the second problem) compound a middle colour between indigo and blue. At S where all the rays are mixed, except the red-making and orange-making, their colours ought by the same rule to compound a faint blue, verging more to green than indigo. And in the progress from S to T, this blue will grow more and more faint and dilute, till at T, where all the colours begin to be mixed, it ends in whiteness.

So again, on the other side of the white at τ, where the least refrangible or utmost red-making rays are alone, the colour must be the deepest red. At σ the mixture of red and orange will compound a red inclining to orange. At ρ the mixture of red, orange, yellow, and one half of the green must compound a middle colour between orange and yellow. At χ the mixture of all colours but violet and indigo will compound a faint yellow, verging more to green than to orange. And this yellow will grow more faint and dilute continually in its progress from χ to π, where by a mixture of all sorts of rays it will become white.

These colours ought to appear were the Sun's light perfectly white; but because it inclines to yellow, the excess of the yellow-making rays whereby 'tis tinged with that colour, being mixed with the faint blue between S and T, will draw it to a faint green. And so the colours in order from P to τ ought to be violet, indigo, blue, very faint green, white, faint yellow, orange, red. Thus it is by the computation; and they that please to view the colours made by a prism will find it so in Nature.

These are the colours on both sides the white when the paper is held between the prism and the point X where the colours meet, and the interjacent white vanishes. For if the paper be held still farther off from the prism, the most refrangible and least refrangible rays will be wanting in the middle of the light, and the rest of the rays which are found there will by mixture produce a fuller green than before. Also, the yellow and blue will now become less compounded, and by consequence more intense then before. And this also agrees with experience.

And if one look through a prism upon a white object encompassed with blackness or darkness, the reason of the colours arising on the edges is much the same, as will appear to one that shall a little consider it. If a black object be encompassed with a white one, the colours which appear through the prism are to be derived from the light of the white one, spreading into the regions of the black, and therefore they appear in a contrary order to that, when a white object is surrounded with black. And the same is to be understood when an object is viewed, whose parts are some of them less luminous than others. For, in the borders of the more and less luminous parts, colours ought always by the same principles to arise from the excess of the light of the more luminous, and to be of the same kind as if the darker parts were black, but yet to be more faint and dilute.

What is said of colours made by prisms may be easily applied to colours made by the glasses of telescopes or microscopes, or by the humours of the eye. For if the object-glass of a telescope be thicker on one side than on the other, or if one-half of the glass, or one-half of the pupil of the eye be covered with any opaque substance, the object-glass, or that part of it or of the eye which is not covered, may be considered as a wedge with crooked sides, and every wedge of glass or other pellucid substance has the effect of a prism in refracting the light which passes through it.

How the colours in the ninth and tenth experiments of the first part arise from the different reflexibility of light, is evident by what was there said. But it is observable in the ninth experiment that whilst the Sun's direct light is yellow, the excess of the blue-making rays in the reflected beam of light MN suffices only to bring that yellow to a pale white inclining to blue, and not to tinge it with a manifestly blue colour. To obtain, therefore, a better blue, I used instead of the yellow light of the Sun the white light of the clouds, by varying a little the experiment, as follows:

Exper. 16. Let HFG [Fig. 13] represent a prism in the open air, and S the eye of the spectator viewing the clouds by their light coming into the prism at the plane side FIGK, and reflected in it by its base HEIG, and thence going out through its plane side HEFK to the eye. And when the prism and eye are conveniently placed, so that the angles of incidence and reflexion at the base may be about 40 degrees, the spectator will see a bow MN of a blue colour running from one end of the base to the other, with the concave side towards him, and the part of the base IMNG beyond this bow will be brighter than the other part EMNH on the other side of it. This blue colour MN, being made by nothing else than by reflexion of a specular superficies, seems so odd a phenomenon, and so difficult to be explained by the vulgar hypothesis of philosophers, that I could not but think it deserved to be taken notice of. Now, for understanding the reason of it, suppose the plane ABC to cut the plane sides and base of the prism perpendicularly. From the eye to the line BC, wherein that

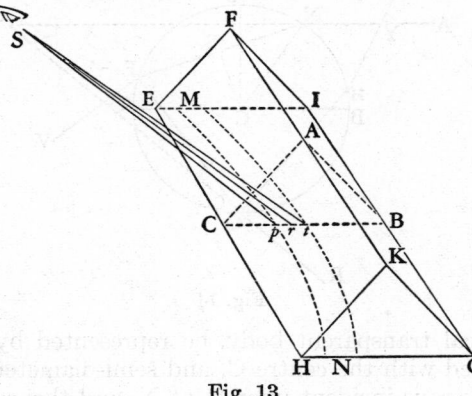

Fig. 13

plane cuts the base, draw the lines Sp and St, in the angles Spc 50 degrees $\frac{1}{9}$, and Stc 49 degrees $\frac{1}{28}$, and the point p will be the limit beyond which none of the most refrangible rays can pass through the base of the prism, and be refracted, whose incidence is such that they may be reflected to the eye; and the point t will be the like limit for the least refrangible rays (that is, beyond which none of them can pass through the base) whose incidence is such that by reflexion they may come to the eye. And the point r, taken in the middle way between p and t, will be the like limit for the meanly refrangible rays. And, therefore, all the least refrangible rays which fall upon the base beyond t, (that is, between t and B) and can come from thence to the eye, will be reflected thither; but on this side t (that is, between t and c) many of these rays will be transmitted through the base. And all the most refrangible rays which fall upon the base beyond p, (that is, between p and B) and can by reflexion come from thence to the eye will be reflected thither, but everywhere between p and c many of these rays will get through the base, and be refracted; and the same is to be understood of the meanly refrangible rays on either side of the point r. Whence it follows that the base of the prism must everywhere between t and B, by a total reflexion of all sorts of rays to the eye, look white and bright; and everywhere between p and C, by reason of the transmission of many rays of every sort, look more pale, obscure, and dark. But at r, and in other places between p and t, where all the more refrangible rays are reflected to the eye, and many of the less refrangible are transmitted, the excess of the most refrangible in the reflected light will tinge that light with their colour, which is violet and blue. And this happens by taking the line C prt B anywhere between the ends of the prism HG and EI.

PROPOSITION 9. PROBLEM 4

By the discovered properties of light, to explain the colours of the rainbow.

This bow never appears but where it rains in the sunshine, and may be made artificially by spouting up water which may break aloft, and scatter into drops, and fall down like rain. For the Sun shining upon these drops certainly causes the bow to appear to a spectator standing in a due position to the rain and Sun. And hence it is now agreed upon, that this bow is made by refraction of the Sun's light in drops of falling rain. This was understood by some of the ancients, and of late more fully discovered and explained by the famous Antonius de Dominis, Archbishop of Spalato in his book *De Radiis Visus & Lucis*, published by his friend Bartolus at Venice, in the year 1611, and written above 20 years before. For he teaches there how the interior bow is made in round drops of rain by two refractions of the Sun's light, and one reflexion between them, and the exterior by two refractions, and two sorts of reflexions between them in each drop of water, and proves his explications by experiments made with a phial full of water, and with globes of glass filled with water, and placed in the Sun to make the colours of the two bows appear in them. The same explication Descartes hath pursued in his *Meteors*, and mended that of the exterior bow. But whilst they understood not the true origin of colours, it's necessary to pursue it here a little farther. For understanding, therefore, how the bow is made, let

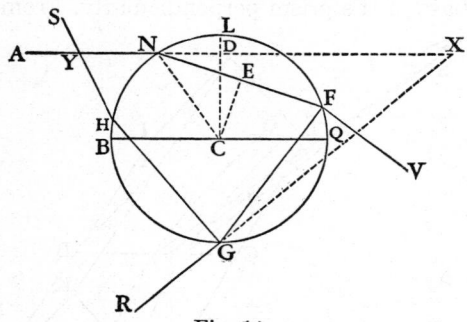

Fig. 14

a drop of rain, or any other spherical transparent body, be represented by the sphere BNFG, [Fig. 14] described with the centre C, and semi-diameter CN. And let AN be one of the Sun's rays incident upon it at N, and thence refracted to F, where let it either go out of the sphere by refraction towards V, or be reflected to G; and at G let it either go out by refraction to R, or be reflected to H; and at H let it go out by refraction towards S, cutting the incident ray in Y. Produce AN and RG, till they meet in X, and upon AX and NF, let fall the perpendiculars CD and CE, and produce CD till it fall upon the circumference at L. Parallel to the incident ray AN draw the diameter BQ, and let the sine of incidence out of air into water be to the sine of refraction as I to R. Now, if you suppose the point of incidence N to move from the point B continually till it come to L, the arch QF will first increase and then decrease, and so will the angle AXR which the rays AN and GR contain; and the arch QF and angle AXR will be biggest when ND is to CN as $\sqrt{\overline{II-RR}}$ to $\sqrt{3RR}$, in which case NE will be to ND as 2R to I. Also the angle AYS, which the rays

AN and HS contain, will first decrease and then increase and grow least when ND is to CN as $\sqrt{\mathrm{II-RR}}$ to $\sqrt{8RR}$, in which case NE will be to ND as 3R to I. And so the angle which the next emergent ray (that is, the emergent ray after three reflexions) contains with the incident ray AN will come to its limit when ND is to CN as $\sqrt{\mathrm{II-RR}}$ to $\sqrt{15RR}$, in which case NE will be to ND as 4R to I. And the angle which the ray next after that emergent (that is, the ray emergent after four reflexions) contains with the incident will come to its limit when ND is to CN as $\sqrt{\mathrm{II-RR}}$ to $\sqrt{24RR}$, in which case NE will be to ND as 5R to I; and so on infinitely, the numbers 3, 8, 15, 24, &c. being gathered by continual addition of the terms of the arithmetical progression 3, 5, 7, 9, &c. The truth of all this mathematicians will easily examine.

Now, it is to be observed that, as when the sun comes to his tropics, days increase and decrease but a very little for a great while together; so when by increasing the distance CD, these angles come to their limits, they vary their quantity but very little for some time together; and, therefore, a far greater number of the rays which fall upon all the points N in the quadrant BL shall emerge in the limits of these angles than in any other inclinations. And further it is to be observed that the rays which differ in refrangibility will have different limits of their angles of emergence, and by consequence according to their different degrees of refrangibility emerge most copiously in different angles, and being separated from one another appear each in their proper colours. And what those angles are may be easily gathered from the foregoing theorem by computation.

For in the least refrangible rays the sines I and R (as was found above) are 108 and 81, and thence by computation the greatest angle AXR will be found 42 degrees and 2 minutes, and the least angle AYS, 50 degrees and 57 minutes. And in the most refrangible rays the sines I and R are 109 and 81, and thence by computation the greatest angle AXR will be found 40 degrees and 17 minutes, and the least angle AYS 54 degrees and 7 minutes.

Suppose, now, that O [Fig. 15] is the spectator's eye, and OP a line drawn parallel to the Sun's rays; and let POE, POF, POG, POH, be angles of 40 degrees 17 minutes, 42 degrees 2 minutes, 50 degrees 57 minutes, and 54 degrees 7 minutes, respectively, and these angles turned about their common side OP, shall with their other sides OE, OF, OG, OH, describe the verges of two rain-

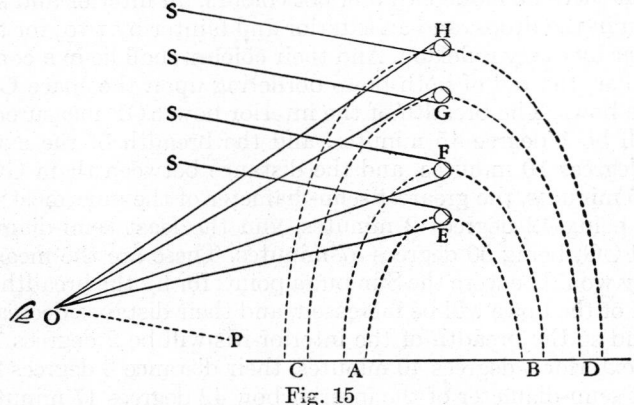

Fig. 15

bows AF, BE, and CHDG. For if E, F, G, H, be drops placed anywhere in the conical superficies described by OE, OF, OG, OH, and be illuminated by the Sun's rays SE, SF, SG, SH; the angle SEO being equal to the angle POE, or 40 degrees 17 minutes, shall be the greatest angle in which the most refrangible rays can after one reflexion be refracted to the eye; and, therefore, all the drops in the line OE shall send the most refrangible rays most copiously to the eye, and thereby strike the senses with the deepest violet colour in that region. And in like manner the angle SFO being equal to the angle POF, or 42 degrees 2 minutes, shall be the greatest in which the least refrangible rays after one reflexion can emerge out of the drops; and, therefore, those rays shall come most copiously to the eye from the drops in the line OF, and strike the senses with the deepest red colour in that region. And, by the same argument, the rays which have intermediate degrees of refrangibility shall come most copiously from drops between E and F, and strike the senses with the intermediate colours in the order which their degrees of refrangibility require; that is, in the progress from E to F, or from the inside of the bow to the outside, in this order: violet, indigo, blue, green, yellow, orange, red. But the violet, by the mixture of the white light of the clouds, will appear faint and incline to purple.

Again, the angle SGO being equal to the angle POG, or 50° 51', shall be the least angle in which the least refrangible rays can after two reflexions emerge out of the drops; and, therefore, the least refrangible rays shall come most copiously to the eye from the drops in the line OG, and strike the sense with the deepest red in that region. And the angle SHO being equal to the angle POH, or 54 degrees 7 minutes, shall be the least angle in which the most refrangible rays after two reflexions can emerge out of the drops; and, therefore, those rays shall come most copiously to the eye from the drops in the line OH, and strike the senses with the deepest violet in that region. And by the same argument, the drops in the regions between G and H shall strike the sense with the intermediate colours in the order which their degrees of refrangibility require; that is, in the progress from G to H, or from the inside of the bow to the outside, in this order: red, orange, yellow, green, blue, indigo, violet. And since these four lines OE, OF, OG, OH, may be situated anywhere in the above-mentioned conical superficies, what is said of the drops and colours in these lines is to be understood of the drops and colours everywhere in those superficies.

Thus shall there be made two bows of colours, an interior and stronger, by one reflexion in the drops, and an exterior and fainter by two; for the light becomes fainter by every reflexion. And their colours shall lie in a contrary order to one another, the red of both bows bordering upon the space GF, which is between the bows. The breadth of the interior bow EOF measured across the colours shall be 1 degree 45 minutes, and the breadth of the exterior GOH shall be 3 degrees 10 minutes, and the distance between them GOF shall be 8 degrees 15 minutes, the greatest semi-diameter of the innermost; that is, the angle POF being 42 degrees 2 minutes, and the least semi-diameter of the outermost POG, being 50 degrees 57 minutes. These are the measures of the bows as they would be were the Sun but a point; for by the breadth of his body the breadth of the bows will be increased, and their distance decreased by half a degree, and so the breadth of the interior iris will be 2 degrees 15 minutes, that of the exterior 3 degrees 40 minutes, their distance 8 degrees 25 minutes, the greatest semi-diameter of the interior bow 42 degrees 17 minutes, and the least of the exterior 50 degrees 42 minutes. And such are the dimensions of the bows in the heavens found to be very nearly, when their colours appear strong and perfect. For once, by such means as I then had, I measured the greatest semi-diameter of the interior iris about 42 degrees, and the breadth of the red, yellow and green in that iris 63 or 64 minutes, besides the outmost faint red obscured by the brightness of the clouds, for which we may allow 3 or 4 minutes more. The breadth of the blue was about 40 minutes more besides the violet, which was so much obscured by the brightness of the clouds that I could not measure its breadth. But supposing the breadth of the blue and violet together to equal that of the red, yellow and green together, the whole breadth of this iris will be about $2\frac{1}{4}$ degrees, as above. The least distance between this iris and the exterior iris was about 8 degrees and 30 minutes. The exterior iris was broader than the interior, but so faint, especially on the blue side, that I could not measure its breadth distinctly. At another time when both bows appeared more distinct, I measured the breadth of the interior iris 2 degrees 10 minutes, and the breadth of the red, yellow and green in the exterior iris was to the breadth of the same colours in the interior as 3 to 2.

This explication of the rainbow is yet further confirmed by the known experiment (made by Antonius de Dominis and Descartes) of hanging up anywhere in the sunshine a glass globe filled with water, and viewing it in such a posture that the rays which come from the globe to the eye may contain with the Sun's rays an angle of either 42 or 50 degrees. For if the angle be about 42 or 43 degrees, the spectator (suppose at O) shall see a full red colour in that side of the globe opposed to the Sun as 'tis represented at F, and if that angle become less (suppose by depressing the globe to E) there will appear other colours, yellow, green and blue successive in the same side of the globe. But if the angle be made about 50 degrees (suppose by lifting up the globe to G) there will appear a red colour in that side of the globe towards the Sun, and if the angle be made greater (suppose by lifting up the globe to H) the red will turn successively to the other colours, yellow, green and blue. The same thing I have tried by letting a globe rest, and raising or depressing the eye, or otherwise moving it to make the angle of a just magnitude.

I have heard it represented that if the light of a candle be refracted by a prism to the eye, when the blue colour falls upon the eye the spectator shall see red in the prism, and when the red falls upon the eye he shall see blue; and if this were certain the colours of the globe and rainbow ought to appear in a contrary order to what we find. But the colours of the candle being very faint, the mistake seems to arise from the difficulty of discerning what colours fall on the eye. For, on the contrary, I have sometimes had occasion to observe, in the Sun's light refracted by a prism, that the spectator always sees that colour in the prism which falls upon his eye. And the same I have found true also in candle-light. For when the prism is moved slowly from the line which is drawn directly from the candle to the eye, the red appears first in the prism and then the blue; and, therefore, each of them is seen when it falls upon the eye. For the red passes over the eye first, and then the blue.

The light which comes through drops of rain by two refractions without any reflexion ought to appear strongest at the distance of about 26 degrees from the Sun, and to decay gradually both ways as the distance from him increases and decreases. And the same is to be understood of light transmitted through spherical hailstones. And if the hail be a little flatted, as it often is, the light transmitted may grow so strong at a little less distance than that of 26 degrees, as to form a halo about the Sun or Moon; which halo, as often as the hailstones are duly figured, may be coloured, and then it must be red within by the least refrangible rays, and blue without by the most refrangible ones, especially if the hailstones have opaque globules of snow in their centre to intercept the light within the halo (as Huygens has observed) and make the inside thereof more distinctly defined than it would otherwise be. For such hailstones, though spherical, by terminating the light by the snow, may make a halo red within and colourless without, and darker in the red than without, as halos used to be. For of those rays which pass close by the snow the rubriform will be least refracted, and so come to the eye in the directest lines.

The light which passes through a drop of rain after two refractions, and three or more reflexions, is scarce strong enough to cause a sensible bow; but in those cylinders of ice by which Huygens explains the parhelia, it may perhaps be sensible.

PROPOSITION 10. PROBLEM 5

By the discovered properties of light, to explain the permanent colours of natural bodies.

These colours arise from hence, that some natural bodies reflect some sorts of rays, others other sorts more copiously than the rest. Minium reflects the least refrangible or red-making rays most copiously, and thence appears red. Violets reflect the most refrangible most copiously, and thence have their colour, and so of other bodies. Every body reflects the rays of its own colour more copiously than the rest, and from their excess and predominance in the reflected light has its colour.

EXPER. 17. For if, in the homogeneal lights obtained by the solution of the problem proposed in the fourth Proposition of the first part of this book, you place bodies of several colours, you will find, as I have done, that every body looks most splendid and luminous in the light of its own colour. Cinnabar in the homogeneal red light is most resplendent, in the green light it is manifestly less resplendent, and in the blue light still less. Indigo in the violet blue light is most resplendent, and its splendour is gradually diminished as it is removed thence by degrees through the green and yellow light to the red. By a leek the green light, and next that the blue and yellow which compound green, are more strongly reflected than the other colours red and violet, and so of the rest. But to make these experiments the more manifest, such bodies ought to be chosen as have the fullest and most vivid colours, and two of those bodies are to be compared together. Thus, for instance, if cinnabar and ultra-marine blue, or some other full blue be held together in the red homogeneal light, they will both appear red, but the cinnabar will appear of a strongly luminous and resplendent red, and the ultra-marine blue of a faint obscure and dark red; and if they be held together in the blue homogeneal light, they will both appear blue, but the ultra-marine will appear of a strongly luminous and resplendent blue, and the cinnabar of a faint and dark blue. Which puts it out of dispute that the cinnabar reflects the red light much more copiously than the ultra-marine doth, and the ultra-marine reflects the blue light much more copiously than the cinnabar doth. The same experiment may be tried successfully with red lead and indigo or with any other two coloured bodies, if due allowance be made for the different strength or weakness of their colour and light.

And as the reason of the colours of natural bodies is evident by these experiments, so it is further confirmed and put past dispute by the two first experiments of the first part, whereby 'twas proved in such bodies that the reflected lights which differ in colours do differ also in degrees of refrangibility. For thence it's certain that some bodies reflect the more refrangible, others the less refrangible rays more copiously.

And that this is not only a true reason of these colours, but even the only reason, may appear further from this consideration that the colour of homogeneal light cannot be changed by the reflexion of natural bodies.

For if bodies by reflexion cannot in the least change the colour of any one sort of rays, they cannot appear coloured by any other means than by reflecting those which either are of their own colour, or which by mixture must produce it.

But in trying experiments of this kind, care must be had that the light be sufficiently homogeneal. For if bodies be illuminated by the ordinary prismatic colours, they will appear neither of their own daylight colours, nor of the colour of the light cast on them, but of some middle colour between both, as I have found by experience. Thus, red lead (for instance) illuminated with the ordinary prismatic green, will not appear either red or green, but orange or yellow, or between yellow and green, accordingly as the green light by which 'tis illuminated is more or less compounded. For because red lead appears red when illuminated with white light, wherein all sorts of rays are equally mixed, and in the green light all sorts of rays are not equally mixed, the excess of the yellow-making, green-making and blue-making rays in the incident green light will cause those rays to abound so much in the reflected light as to draw the colour from red towards their colour. And because the red lead reflects the red-making rays most copiously in proportion to their number, and next after them the orange-making and yellow-making rays, these rays in the reflected light will be more in proportion to the light than they were in the incident green light, and thereby will draw the reflected light from green towards their colour. And, therefore, the red lead will appear neither red nor green, but of a colour between both.

In transparently coloured liquors, 'tis observable that their colour uses to vary with their thickness. Thus, for instance, a red liquor in a conical glass, held between the light and the eye, looks of a pale and dilute yellow at the bottom where 'tis thin, and a little higher where 'tis thicker grows orange, and where 'tis still thicker becomes red, and where 'tis thickest the red is deepest and darkest. For it is to be conceived that such a liquor stops the indigo-making and violet-making rays most easily, the blue-making rays more difficultly, the green-making rays still more difficultly, and the red-making most difficultly; and that if the thickness of the liquor be only so much as suffices to stop a competent number of the violet-making and indigo-making rays, without diminishing much the number of the rest, the rest must (by Prop. 6, Part 2) compound a pale yellow. But if the liquor be so much thicker as to stop also a great number of the blue-making rays, and some of the green-making, the rest must compound an orange; and where it is so thick as to stop also a great number of the green-making and a considerable number of the yellow-making, the rest must begin to compound a red, and this red must grow deeper and darker as the yellow-making and orange-making rays are more and more stopped by increasing the thickness of the liquor, so that few rays besides the red-making can get through.

Of this kind is an experiment lately related to me by Mr. Halley, who, in diving deep into the sea in a diving vessel, found in a clear sunshine day that when he was sunk many fathoms deep into the water the upper part of his hand on which the Sun shone directly through the water and through a small glass window in the vessel appeared of a red colour, like that of a damask rose, and the water below and the under part of his hand illuminated by light reflected from the water below looked green. For thence it may be gathered, that the sea water reflects back the violet and blue-making rays most easily, and lets the red-making rays pass most freely and copiously to great depths. For thereby the Sun's direct light at all great depths, by reason of the predominating red-making rays, must appear red; and the greater the depth is, the fuller and intenser must that red be. And at such depths as the violet-making rays scarce penetrate unto, the blue-making, green-making, and yellow-making rays, being reflected from below more copiously than the red-making ones, must compound a green.

Now, if there be two liquors of full colours, (suppose a red and blue) and both of them so thick as suffices to make their colours sufficiently full, though either liquor be sufficiently transparent apart, yet will you not be able to see through both together. For, if only the red-making rays pass through one liquor, and only the blue-making through the other, no rays can pass through both. This Mr. Hook tried casually with glass wedges filled with red and blue liquors, and was surprised at the unexpected event, the reason of it being then unknown; which makes me trust the more to his experiment, though I have not tried it myself. But he that would repeat it must take care the liquors be of very good and full colours.

Now, whilst bodies become coloured by reflecting or transmitting this or that sort of rays more copiously than the rest, it is to be conceived that they stop and stifle in themselves the rays which they do not reflect or transmit. For, if gold be foliated and held between your eye and the light, the light looks of a greenish-blue, and therefore massy gold lets into its body the blue-making rays to be reflected to and fro within it till they be stopped and stifled, whilst it reflects the yellow-making outwards, and thereby looks yellow, and much after the same manner that leaf gold is yellow by reflected, and blue by transmitted light, and massy gold is yellow in all positions of the eye; there are some liquors, as the tincture of *lignum nephriticum*, and some sorts of glass, which transmit one sort of light most copiously, and reflect another sort, and thereby look of several colours, according to the position of the eye to the light. But, if these liquors or glasses were so thick and massy that no light could get through them, I question not but they would, like all other opaque bodies, appear of one and the same colour in all positions of the eye, though this I cannot yet affirm by experience. For all coloured bodies, so far as my observation reaches, may be seen through if made sufficiently thin, and, therefore, are in some measure transparent, and differ only in degrees of transparency from tinged transparent liquors, these liquors as well as those bodies by a sufficient thickness becoming opaque. A transparent body which looks of any colour by transmitted light may also look of the same colour by reflected light, the light of that colour being reflected by the farther surface of the body, or by the air beyond it. And then the reflected colour will be diminished, and perhaps cease, by making the body very thick, and pitching it on the backside to diminish the reflexion of its farther surface, so that the light reflected from the tinging particles may predominate. In such cases, the colour of the reflected light will be apt to vary from that of the light transmitted. But whence it is that tinged bodies and liquors reflect some sort of rays, and intromit or transmit other sorts, shall be said in the next book. In this Proposition I content myself to have put it past dispute that bodies have such properties, and thence appear coloured.

PROPOSITION 11. PROBLEM 6

By mixing coloured lights, to compound a beam of light of the same colour and nature with a beam of the Sun's direct light, and therein to experience the truth of the foregoing Propositions.

Let ABC *abc* [Fig. 16] represent a prism, by which the Sun's light let into a dark chamber through the hole F, may be refracted towards the lens MN, and paint upon it at *p*, *q*, *r*, *s*, and *t*, the usual colours (violet, blue, green, yellow, and red) and let the diverging rays by the refraction of this lens converge again towards X, and there, by the mixture of all those their colours, compound a white according to what was shewn above. Then let another prism DEG *deg*, parallel to the former, be placed at X, to refract that white light upwards towards Y. Let the refracting angles of the prisms and their distances from the lens be equal so that the rays, which converged from the lens towards X, and without refraction, would there have crossed and diverged again, may by the refraction of the second prism be reduced into parallelism and diverge no more. For then those rays will recompose a beam of white light XY. If the refracting angle of either prism be the bigger, that prism must be so much the nearer to the lens. You will know when the prisms and the lens are well set together, by observing if the beam of light XY, which comes out of the second prism, be perfectly white to the very edges of the light, and at all distances from the prism continue perfectly and totally white like a beam of the Sun's light. For till this happens, the position of the prisms and lens to one another must be corrected; and then if by the help of a long beam of wood, as is represented in the Figure, or by a tube, or some other such instrument, made for that purpose, they be made fast in that situation, you may try all the same experiments in this compounded beam of light XY which have been made in the Sun's direct light.

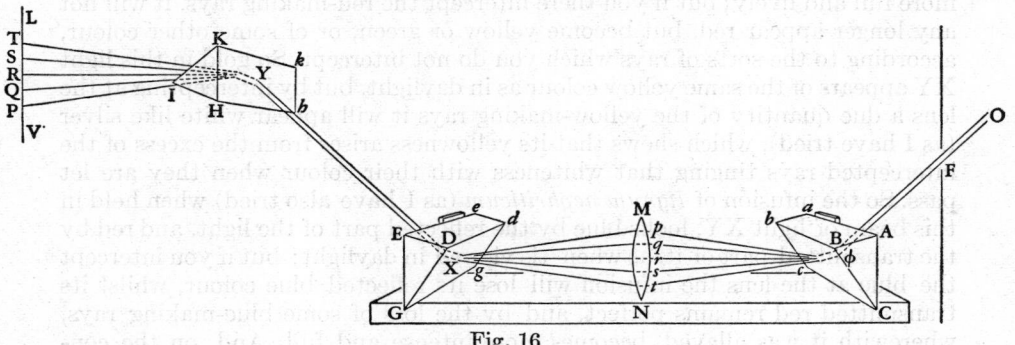

Fig. 16

For this compounded beam of light has the same appearance, and is endowed with all the same properties, with a direct beam of the Sun's light, so far as my observation reaches. And in trying experiments in this beam you may by stopping any of the colours, p, q, r, s, and t, at the lens, see how the colours produced in the experiments are no other than those which the rays had at the lens before they entered the composition of this beam; and, by consequence, that they arise not from any new modifications of the light by refractions and reflexions, but from the various separations and mixtures of the rays originally endowed with their colour-making qualities.

So, for instance, having with a lens $4\frac{1}{4}$ inches broad, and two prisms on either hand $6\frac{1}{4}$ feet distant from the lens, made such a beam of compounded light, to examine the reason of the colours made by prisms, I refracted this compounded beam of light XY with another prism HIK kh, and thereby cast the usual prismatic colours PQRST upon the paper LV placed behind. And then, by stopping any of the colours p, q, r, s, t, at the lens, I found that the same colour would vanish at the paper. So if the purple p was stopped at the lens, the purple P upon the paper would vanish, and the rest of the colours would remain unaltered, unless perhaps the blue, so far as some purple latent in it at the lens might be separated from it by the following refractions. And so by intercepting the green upon the lens, the green R upon the paper would vanish, and so of the rest; which plainly shews that as the white beam of light XY was compounded of several lights variously coloured at the lens, so the colours which afterwards emerge out of it by new refractions are no other than those of which its whiteness was compounded. The refraction of the prism HIK kh generates the colours PQRST upon the paper, not by changing the colorific qualities of the rays, but by separating the rays which had the very same colorific qualities before they entered the composition of the refracted beam of white light XY. For otherwise the rays which were of one colour at the lens might be of another upon the paper, contrary to what we find.

So again, to examine the reason of the colours of natural bodies, I placed such bodies in the beam of light XY, and found that they all appeared there of those their own colours which they have in daylight, and that those colours depend upon the rays which had the same colours at the lens before they entered the composition of that beam. Thus, for instance, cinnabar illuminated by this beam appears of the same red colour as in daylight; and if at the lens you intercept the green-making and blue-making rays, its redness will become more full and lively; but if you there intercept the red-making rays, it will not any longer appear red, but become yellow or green, or of some other colour, according to the sorts of rays which you do not intercept. So gold in this light XY appears of the same yellow colour as in daylight, but by intercepting at the lens a due quantity of the yellow-making rays it will appear white like silver (as I have tried), which shews that its yellowness arises from the excess of the intercepted rays tinging that whiteness with their colour when they are let pass. So the infusion of *lignum nephriticum* (as I have also tried) when held in this beam of light XY, looks blue by the reflected part of the light, and red by the transmitted part of it, as when 'tis viewed in daylight; but if you intercept the blue at the lens the infusion will lose its reflected blue colour, whilst its transmitted red remains perfect, and by the loss of some blue-making rays, wherewith it was allayed, becomes more intense and full. And, on the contrary, if the red and orange-making rays be intercepted at the lens, the infusion will lose its transmitted red, whilst its blue will remain and become more full and perfect. Which shews that the infusion does not tinge the rays with blue and red, but only transmits those most copiously which were red-making before, and reflects those most copiously which were blue-making before. And after the same manner may the reasons of other phenomena be examined, by trying them in this artificial beam of light XY.

BOOK TWO

Part I

Observations concerning the reflexions, refractions, and colours of thin transparent bodies.

IT has been observed by others that transparent substances (as glass, water, air, &c.) when made very thin by being blown into bubbles, or otherwise formed into plates, do exhibit various colours according to their various thinness, altho' at a greater thickness they appear very clear and colourless. In the former book I forbore to treat of these colours, because they seemed of a more difficult consideration, and were not necessary for establishing the properties of light there discoursed of. But because they may conduce to further discoveries for completing the theory of light, especially as to the constitution of the parts of natural bodies, on which their colours or transparency depend, I have here set down an account of them. To render this discourse short and distinct, I have first described the principal of my Observations, and then considered and made use of them. The Observations are these:

OBSERVATION 1. Compressing two prisms hard together that their sides (which by chance were a very little convex) might somewhere touch one another, I found the place in which they touched to become absolutely transparent, as if they had there been one continued piece of glass. For when the light fell so obliquely on the air, which in other places was between them, as to be all reflected, it seemed in that place of contact to be wholly transmitted, insomuch that when looked upon it appeared like a black or dark spot, by reason that little or no sensible light was reflected from thence, as from other places; and when looked through it seemed (as it were) a hole in that air which was formed into a thin plate, by being compressed between the glasses. And through this hole objects that were beyond might be seen distinctly, which could not at all be seen through other parts of the glasses where the air was interjacent. Although the glasses were a little convex, yet this transparent spot was of a considerable breadth, which breadth seemed principally to proceed from the yielding inwards of the parts of the glasses, by reason of their mutual pressure. For by pressing them very hard together it would become much broader than otherwise.

OBS. 2. When the plate of air, by turning the prisms about their common axis, became so little inclined to the incident rays that some of them began to be transmitted, there arose in it many slender arcs of colours which at first were shaped almost like the conchoid, as you see them delineated in the first Figure. And by continuing the

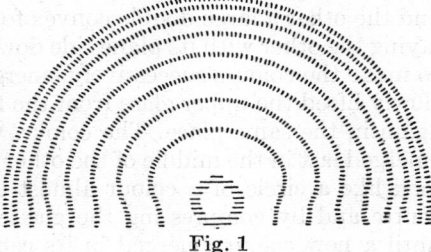

Fig. 1

457

motion of the prisms, these arcs increased and bended more and more about the said transparent spot, till they were completed into circles or rings encompassing it, and afterwards continually grew more and more contracted.

These arcs at their first appearance were of a violet and blue colour, and between them were white arcs of circles, which presently by continuing the motion of the prisms became a little tinged in their inward limbs with red and yellow, and to their outward limbs the blue was adjacent. So that the order of these colours from the central dark spot, was at that time white, blue, violet; black, red, orange, yellow, white, blue, violet, &c. But the yellow and red were much fainter than the blue and violet.

The motion of the prisms about their axis being continued, these colours contracted more and more, shrinking towards the whiteness on either side of it, until they totally vanished into it. And then the circles in those parts appeared black and white, without any other colours intermixed. But by further moving the prisms about, the colours again emerged out of the whiteness, the violet and blue at its inward limb, and at its outward limb the red and yellow. So that now their order from the central spot was white, yellow, red; black; violet, blue, white, yellow, red, &c., contrary to what it was before.

Obs. 3. When the rings or some parts of them appeared only black and white, they were very distinct and well-defined, and the blackness seemed as intense as that of the central spot. Also in the borders of the rings, where the colours began to emerge out of the whiteness, they were pretty distinct, which made them visible to a very great multitude. I have sometimes numbered above thirty successions (reckoning every black and white ring for one succession) and seen more of them, which by reason of their smallness I could not number. But in other positions of the prisms, at which the rings appeared of many colours, I could not distinguish above eight or nine of them, and the exterior of those were very confused and dilute.

In these two Observations to see the rings distinct, and without any other colour than black and white, I found it necessary to hold my eye at a good distance from them. For by approaching nearer, although in the same inclination of my eye to the plane of the rings, there emerged a bluish colour out of the white, which by dilating itself more and more into the black rendered the circles less distinct, and left the white a little tinged with red and yellow. I found also by looking through a slit or oblong hole, which was narrower than the pupil of my eye, and held close to it parallel to the prisms, I could see the circles much distincter and visible to a far greater number than otherwise.

Obs. 4. To observe more nicely the order of the colours which arose out of the white circles as the rays became less and less inclined to the plate of air, I took two object-glasses (the one a plano-convex for a fourteen-foot telescope, and the other a large double convex for one of about fifty-feet) and upon this, laying the other with its plane side downwards, I pressed them slowly together, to make the colours successively emerge in the middle of the circles, and then slowly lifted the upper glass from the lower to make them successively vanish again in the same place. The colour, which by pressing the glasses together, emerged last in the middle of the other colours, would upon its first appearance look like a circle of a colour almost uniform from the circumference to the centre and by compressing the glasses still more, grow continually broader until a new colour emerged in its centre, and thereby it became a ring encompassing that new colour. And by compressing the glasses still more, the diameter of this ring would increase, and the breadth of its orbit or perimeter decrease until another new colour emerged in the centre of the last. And so on until a third, a fourth, a fifth, and other following new colours successively emerged there, and became rings encompassing the innermost colour, the last of which was the black spot. And, on the contrary, by lifting up the upper glass from the lower, the diameter of the rings would decrease, and the breadth of their orbit increase, until their colours reached successively to the centre; and then, they being of a considerable breadth, I could more easily discern and distinguish their species than before. And by this means I observed their succession and quantity to be as followeth:

Next to the pellucid central spot made by the contact of the glasses succeeded blue, white, yellow, and red. The blue was so little in quantity that I could not discern it in the circles made by the prisms, nor could I well distinguish any violet in it, but the yellow and red were pretty copious, and seemed about as much in extent as the white, and four or five times more than the blue. The next circuit in order of colours immediately encompassing these were violet, blue, green, yellow, and red; and these were all of them copious and vivid, excepting the green, which was very little in quantity, and seemed much more faint and dilute than the other colours. Of the other four, the violet was the least in extent, and the blue less than the yellow or red. The third circuit or order was purple, blue, green, yellow, and red; in which the purple seemed more reddish than the violet in the former circuit, and the green was much more conspicuous, being as brisk and copious as any of the other colours, except the yellow, but the red began to be a little faded, inclining very much to purple. After this succeeded the fourth circuit of green and red. The green was very copious and lively, inclining on the one side to blue, and on the other side to yellow. But in this fourth circuit there was neither violet, blue, nor yellow, and the red was very imperfect and dirty. Also the succeeding colours became more and more imperfect and dilute, till after three or four revolutions they ended

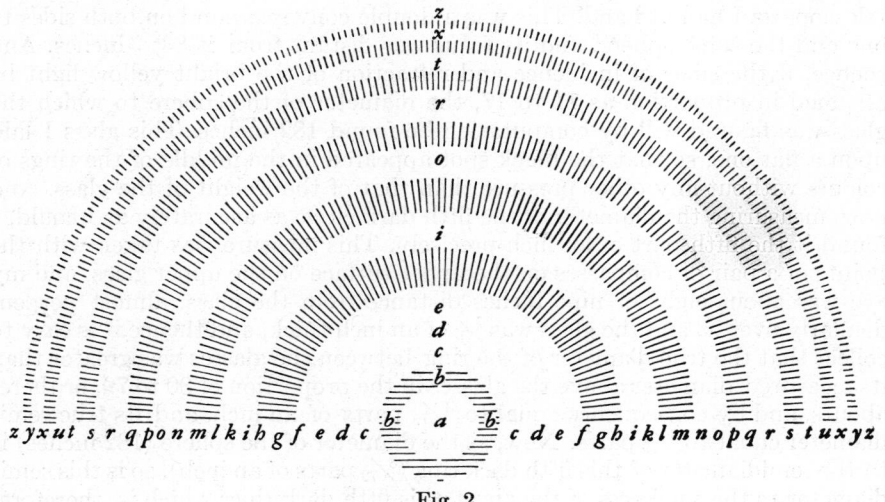

Fig. 2

in perfect whiteness. Their form, when the glasses were most compressed so as to make the black spot appear in the centre, is delineated in the second figure; where a, b, c, d, e: f, g, h, i, k: l, m, n, o, p: q, r: s, t: v, x: y, z, denote the colours reckoned in order from the center: black, blue, white, yellow, red; violet, blue, green, yellow, red; purple, blue, green, yellow, red; green, red; greenish blue, red; greenish blue, pale red; greenish blue, reddish white.

Obs. 5. To determine the interval of the glasses, or thickness of the interjacent air, by which each colour was produced, I measured the diameters of the first six rings at the most lucid part of their orbits, and, squaring them, I found their squares to be in the arithmetical progression of the odd numbers, 1, 3, 5, 7, 9, 11. And since one of these glasses was plane, and the other spherical, their intervals at those rings must be in the same progression. I measured also the diameters of the dark or faint rings between the more lucid colours, and found their squares to be in the arithmetical progression of the even numbers, 2, 4, 6, 8, 10, 12. And it being very nice and difficult to take these measures exactly, I repeated them divers times at divers parts of the glasses, that by their agreement I might be confirmed in them. And the same method I used in determining some others of the following observations.

Obs. 6. The diameter of the sixth ring at the most lucid part of its orbit was $\frac{58}{100}$ parts of an inch, and the diameter of the sphere on which the double convex object-glass was ground was about 102 feet, and hence I gathered the thickness of the air or aereal interval of the glasses at that ring. But some time after, suspecting that in making this observation I had not determined the diameter of the sphere with sufficient accurateness, and being uncertain whether the plano-convex glass was truly plane, and not something concave or convex on that side which I accounted plane; and whether I had not pressed the glasses together, as I often did, to make them touch (for by pressing such glasses together their parts easily yield inwards, and the rings thereby become sensibly broader than they would be, did the glasses keep their figures), I repeated the experiment, and found the diameter of the sixth lucid ring about $\frac{55}{100}$ parts of an inch. I repeated the experiment also with such an object-glass of another telescope as I had at hand. This was a double convex ground on both sides to one and the same sphere, and its focus was distant from it $83\frac{2}{5}$ inches. And thence, if the sines of incidence and refraction of the bright yellow light be assumed in proportion as 11 to 17, the diameter of the sphere to which the glass was figured will by computation be found 182 inches. This glass I laid upon a flat one, so that the black spot appeared in the middle of the rings of colours without any other pressure than that of the weight of the glass. And now, measuring the diameter of the fifth dark circle as accurately as I could, I found it the fifth part of an inch precisely. This measure was taken with the points of a pair of compasses on the upper surface on the upper glass, and my eye was about eight or nine inches distance from the glass, almost perpendicularly over it, and the glass was $\frac{1}{6}$ of an inch thick, and thence it is easy to collect that the true diameter of the ring between the glasses was greater than its measured diameter above the glasses in the proportion of 80 to 79, or thereabouts, and by consequence equal to $\frac{16}{79}$ parts of an inch, and its true semidiameter equal to $\frac{8}{79}$ parts. Now, as the diameter of the sphere (182 inches) is to the semidiameter of this fifth dark ring ($\frac{8}{79}$ parts of an inch), so is this semidiameter to the thickness of the air at this fifth dark ring; which is, therefore,

$\frac{32}{567,931}$ or $\frac{100}{1,774,784}$ parts of an inch; and the fifth part thereof (viz., the $\frac{1}{88,739}$th part of an inch) is the thickness of the air at the first of these dark rings.

The same experiment I repeated with another double convex object-glass ground on both sides to one and the same sphere. Its focus was distant from it 168½ inches, and, therefore, the diameter of that sphere was 184 inches. This glass being laid upon the same plain glass, the diameter of the fifth of the dark rings, when the black spot in their centre appeared plainly without pressing the glasses, was by the measure of the compasses upon the upper glass $\frac{121}{600}$ parts of an inch, and by consequence between the glasses it was $\frac{1.222}{6.000}$; for the upper glass was $\frac{1}{8}$ of an inch thick, and my eye was distant from it 8 inches. And a third proportional to half this from the diameter of the sphere is $\frac{5}{88,850}$ parts of an inch. This is, therefore, the thickness of the air at this ring, and a fifth part thereof (viz., the $\frac{1}{88,850}$th part of an inch) is the thickness thereof at the first of the rings, as above.

I tried the same thing by laying these object-glasses upon flat pieces of a broken looking-glass, and found the same measures of the rings; which makes me rely upon them till they can be determined more accurately by glasses ground to larger spheres, though in such glasses greater care must be taken of a true plane.

These dimensions were taken when my eye was placed almost perpendicularly over the glasses, being about an inch, or an inch and a quarter, distant from the incident rays, and eight inches distant from the glass; so that the rays were inclined to the glass in an angle of about four degrees. Whence, by the following Observation, you will understand that had the rays been perpendicular to the glasses, the thickness of the air at these rings would have been less in the proportion of the radius to the secant of four degrees (that is, of 10,000 to 10,024). Let the thicknesses found be, therefore, diminished in this proportion, and they will become $\frac{1}{88,952}$ and $\frac{1}{89,063}$, or (to use the nearest round number) the $\frac{1}{89,000}$th part of an inch. This is the thickness of the air at the darkest part of the first dark ring made by perpendicular rays; and half this thickness multiplied by the progression, 1, 3, 5, 7, 9, 11, &c. gives the thicknesses of the air at the most luminous parts of all the brightest rings, viz., $\frac{1}{178,000}$, $\frac{3}{178,000}$, $\frac{5}{178,000}$, $\frac{7}{178,000}$, &c., their arithmetical means $\frac{2}{178,000}$, $\frac{4}{178,000}$, $\frac{6}{178,000}$, &c. being its thicknesses at the darkest parts of all the dark ones.

OBS. 7. The rings were least when my eye was placed perpendicularly over the glasses in the axis of the rings; and when I viewed them obliquely they became bigger, continually swelling as I removed my eye farther from the axis. And partly by measuring the diameter of the same circle at several obliquities of my eye, partly by other means, as also by making use of the two prisms for very great obliquities, I found its diameter, and consequently the thickness of the air, at its perimeter in all those obliquities to be very nearly in the proportions expressed in the following Table:

Angle of incidence on the air		Angle of refraction into the air		Diameter of the ring	Thickness of the air
Deg.	Min.				
00	00	00	00	10	10
06	26	10	00	$10^1/_{13}$	$10^2/_{13}$
12	45	20	00	$10\frac{1}{3}$	$10\frac{2}{3}$
18	49	30	00	$10\frac{3}{4}$	$11\frac{1}{2}$
24	30	40	00	$11^2/_5$	13
29	37	50	00	$12\frac{1}{2}$	$15\frac{1}{2}$
33	58	60	00	14	20
35	47	65	00	$15\frac{1}{4}$	$23\frac{1}{4}$
37	19	70	00	$16^4/_5$	$28\frac{1}{4}$
38	33	75	00	$19\frac{1}{4}$	37
39	27	80	00	$22^6/_7$	$52\frac{1}{4}$
40	00	85	00	29	$84^1/_{12}$
40	11	90	00	35	$122\frac{1}{2}$

In the two first columns are expressed the obliquities of the incident and emergent rays to the plate of the air; that is, their angles of incidence and refraction. In the third column the diameter of any coloured ring at those obliquities is expressed in parts, of which ten constitute that diameter when the rays are perpendicular. And in the fourth column the thickness of the air at the circumference of that ring is expressed in parts, of which also ten constitute its thickness when the rays are perpendicular.

And from these measures I seem to gather this rule: that the thickness of the air is proportional to the secant of an angle, whose sine is a certain mean proportional between the sines of incidence and refraction. And that mean proportional, so far as by these measures I can determine it, is the first of a hundred and six arithmetical mean proportionals between those sines counted from the bigger sine; that is, from the sine of refraction when the refraction is made out of the glass into the plate of air, or from the sine of incidence when the refraction is made out of the plate of air into the glass.

OBS. 8. The dark spot in the middle of the rings increased also by the obliquation of the eye, although almost insensibly. But, if instead of the object-glasses the prisms were made use of, its increase was more manifest when viewed so obliquely that no colours appeared about it. It was least when the rays were incident most obliquely on the interjacent air, and as the obliquity decreased it increased more and more until the coloured rings appeared, and then decreased again, but not so much as it increased before. And hence it is evident that the transparency was not only at the absolute contact of the glasses, but also where they had some little interval. I have sometimes observed the diameter of that spot to be between half and two fifth parts of the diameter of the exterior circumference of the red in the first circuit or revolution of colours when viewed almost perpendicularly; whereas when viewed obliquely it hath wholly vanished and become opaque and white like the other parts of the glass; whence it may be collected that the glasses did then scarcely, or not at all, touch one another, and that their interval at the perimeter of that spot when viewed perpendicularly was about a fifth or sixth part of their interval at the circumference of the said red.

OBS. 9. By looking through the two contiguous object-glasses, I found that the interjacent air exhibited rings of colours, as well by transmitting light as by reflecting it. The central spot was now white, and from it the order of the colours were yellowish red; black, violet, blue, white, yellow, red; violet, blue, green, yellow, red, &c. But these colours were very faint and dilute, unless when the light was trajected very obliquely through the glasses; for by that means they became pretty vivid. Only the first yellowish red, like the blue in the fourth Observation, was so little and faint as scarcely to be discerned. Comparing the coloured rings made by reflexion, with these made by transmission of the light, I found that white was opposite to black, red to blue, yellow to violet, and green to a compound of red and violet. That is, those parts of the glass were black when looked through, which when looked upon appeared white, and on the contrary. And so those which in one case exhibited blue, did in the other case exhibit red. And the like of the other colours. The manner you have represented in the third Figure, where AB, CD, are the surfaces of the glasses contiguous at E, and the black lines between them are their distances in arithmetical progression, and the colours written above are seen by reflected light, and those below by light transmitted.

Obs. 10. Wetting the object-glasses a little at their edges, the water crept in slowly between them, and the circles thereby became less and the colours more faint, insomuch that as the water crept along, one half of them at which it first arrived would appear broken off from the other half, and contracted into a less room. By measuring them I found the proportions of their diameters to the diameters of the like circles made by air to be about seven to eight, and consequently the intervals of the glasses at like circles, caused by those two mediums (water and air) are as about three to four. Perhaps it may be a general rule that, if any other medium more or less dense than water be compressed between the glasses, their intervals at the rings caused thereby will be to their intervals caused by interjacent air, as the sines are which measure the refraction made out of that medium into air.

Obs. 11. When the water was between the glasses, if I pressed the upper glass variously at its edges to make the rings move nimbly from one place to another, a little white spot would immediately follow the centre of them, which upon creeping in of the ambient water into that place would presently vanish. Its appearance was such as interjacent air would have caused, and it exhibited the same colours. But it was not air, for where any bubbles of air were in the water they would not vanish. The reflexion must have rather been caused by a subtler medium which could recede through the glasses at the creeping in of the water.

Obs. 12. These observations were made in the open air. But farther to examine the effects of coloured light falling on the glasses, I darkened the room, and viewed them by reflexion of the colours of a prism cast on a sheet of white paper, my eye being so placed that I could see the coloured paper by reflexion in the glasses, as in a looking-glass. And by this means the rings became distincter and visible to a far greater number than in the open air. I have sometimes seen more than twenty of them, whereas in the open air I could not discern above eight or nine.

Obs. 13. Appointing an assistant to move the prism to and fro about its axis, that all the colours might successively fall on that part of the paper which I saw by reflexion from that part of the glasses, where the circles appeared, so that all the colours might be successively reflected from the circles to my eye, whilst I held it immovable, I found the circles which the red light made to be manifestly bigger than those which were made by the blue and violet. And it was very pleasant to see them gradually swell or contract accordingly as the colour of the light was changed. The interval of the glasses at any of the rings, when they were made by the utmost red light, was to their interval at the same ring when made by the utmost violet, greater than as 3 to 2, and less than as 13 to 8. By the most of my Observations it was as 14 to 9. And this proportion seemed very nearly the same in all obliquities of my eye, unless when two prisms were made use of instead of the object-glasses. For then at a certain great obliquity of my eye, the rings made by the several colours seemed equal, and at a greater obliquity those made by the violet would be greater than the same rings made by the red, the refraction of the prism in this case causing the most refrangible rays to fall more obliquely on that plate of the air than the least refrangible ones. Thus the experiment succeeded in the coloured light, which was sufficiently strong and copious to make the rings sensible. And thence it may be gathered that, if the most refrangible and least refrangible rays had been copious enough to make the rings sensible without the mixture of other rays, the proportion which here was 14 to 9 would have been a little greater, suppose 14¼ or 14⅓ to 9.

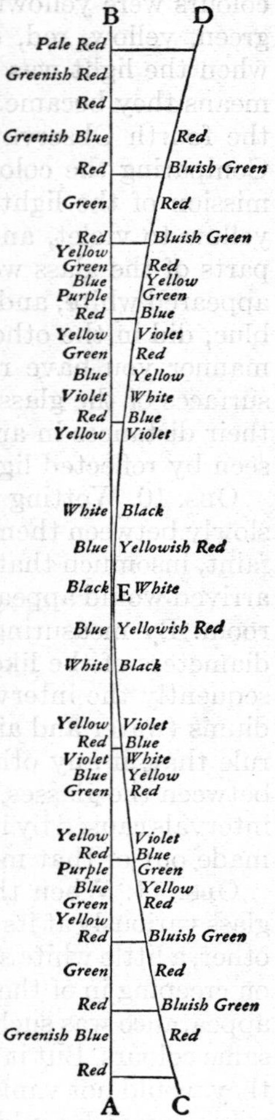

Obs. 14. Whilst the prism was turned about its axis with a uniform motion, to make all the several colours fall successively upon the object-glasses, and thereby to make the rings contract and dilate, the contraction or dilatation of each ring thus made by the variation of its colour was swiftest in the red, and slowest in the violet, and in the intermediate colours it had intermediate degrees of celerity. Comparing the quantity of contraction and dilatation made by all the degrees of each colour, I found that it was greatest in the red, less in the yellow, still less in the blue, and least in the violet. And to make as just an estimation as I could of the proportions of their contractions or dilatations, I observed that the whole contraction or dilatation of the diameter of any ring made by all the degrees of red was to that of the diameter of the same ring made by all the degrees of violet, as about four to three, or five to four, and that when the light was of the middle colour, between yellow and green, the diameter of the ring was very nearly an arithmetical mean between the greatest diameter of the same ring made by the outmost red, and the least diameter thereof made by the outmost violet—contrary to what happens in the colours of the oblong spectrum made by the refraction of a prism, where the red is most contracted, the violet most expanded, and in the midst of all the colours is the confine of green and blue. And hence I seem to collect that the thicknesses of the air between the glasses there, where the ring is successively made by the limits of the five

Fig. 3

Figure labels (left column): Pale Red, Greenish Red, Red, Greenish Blue, Red, Green, Red, Yellow, Green, Blue, Purple, Red, Yellow, Green, Blue, Violet, Red, Yellow; White, Blue, Black, Blue, White; Yellow, Red, Violet, Blue, Green; Yellow, Red, Purple, Blue, Green, Yellow, Red; Green; Red; Greenish Blue; Red

Figure labels (right column): Red, Bluish Green, Red, Bluish Green, Red, Yellow, Green, Blue, Violet, Red, Yellow, White, Blue, Violet; Black, Yellowish Red, White, Yellowish Red, Black; Violet, Blue, White, Yellow, Red; Violet, Blue, Green, Yellow, Red; Bluish Green; Red; Bluish Green; Red

Points: B, D (top); E (middle); A, C (bottom)

principal colours (red, yellow, green, blue, violet) in order (that is, by the extreme red, by the limit of red and yellow in the middle of the orange, by the limit of yellow and green, by the limit of green and blue, by the limit of blue and violet in the middle of the indigo, and by the extreme violet) are to one another very nearly as the sixth lengths of a chord which sound the notes in a sixth major, *sol, la, mi, fa, sol, la.* But it agrees something better with the Observation to say that the thicknesses of the air between the glasses there, where the rings are successively made by the limits of the seven colours (red, orange, yellow, green, blue, indigo, violet in order) are to one another as the cube roots of the squares of the eight lengths of a chord, which sound the notes in an eighth, *sol, la, fa, sol, la, mi, fa, sol;* that is, as the cube roots of the squares of the numbers, 1, $\frac{8}{9}$, $\frac{5}{6}$, $\frac{3}{4}$, $\frac{2}{3}$, $\frac{3}{5}$, $\frac{9}{16}$, $\frac{1}{2}$.

OBS. 15. These rings were not of various colours like those made in the open air, but appeared all over of that prismatic colour only with which they were illuminated. And by projecting the prismatic colours immediately upon the glasses, I found that the light which fell on the dark spaces which were between the coloured rings was transmitted through the glasses without any variation

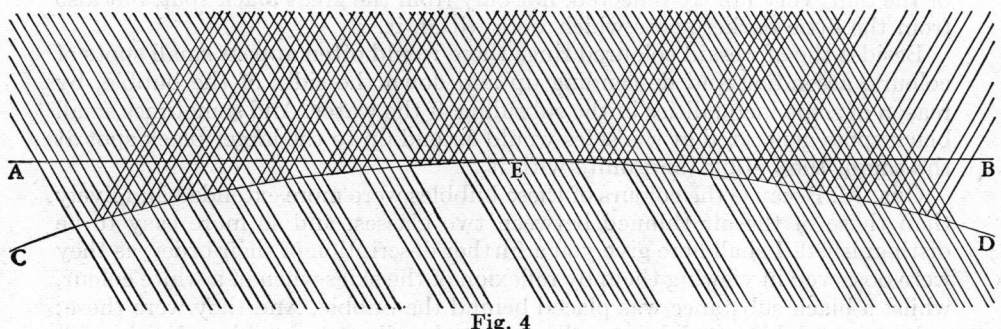

Fig. 4

of colour. For on a white paper placed behind, it would paint rings of the same colour with those which were reflected, and of the bigness of their immediate spaces. And from thence the origin of these rings is manifest; namely, that the air between the glasses, according to its various thickness, is disposed in some places to reflect, and in others to transmit, the light of any one colour (as you may see represented in the fourth Figure) and in the same place to reflect that of one colour where it transmits that of another.

OBS. 16. The squares of the diameters of these rings made by any prismatic colour were in arithmetical progression, as in the fifth Observation. And the diameter of the sixth circle, when made by the citrine yellow, and viewed almost perpendicularly, was about $\frac{58}{100}$ parts of an inch, or a little less, agreeable to the sixth Observation.

The precedent Observations were made with a rarer thin medium, terminated by a denser, such as was air or water compressed between two glasses. In those that follow are set down the appearances of a denser medium thinned within a rarer, such as are plates of Muscovy glass, bubbles of water, and some other thin substances terminated on all sides with air.

OBS. 17. If a bubble be blown with water first made tenacious by dissolving a little soap in it, 'tis a common observation that after a while it will appear tinged with a great variety of colours. To defend these bubbles from being agitated by the external air (whereby their colours are irregularly moved one among another, so that no accurate observation can be made of them), as soon as I had blown any of them I covered it with a clear glass, and by that means its colours emerged in a very regular order, like so many concentric rings encompassing the top of the bubble. And as the bubble grew thinner by the continual subsiding of the water, these rings dilated slowly and overspread the whole bubble, descending in order to the bottom of it, where they vanished successively. In the meanwhile, after all the colours were emerged at the top, there grew in the centre of the rings a small round black spot, like that in the first Observation, which continually dilated itself till it became sometimes more than ½ or ¾ of an inch in breadth before the bubble broke. At first I thought there had been no light reflected from the water in that place, but, observing it more curiously, I saw within it several smaller round spots which appeared much blacker and darker than the rest, whereby I knew that there was some reflexion at the other places which were not so dark as those spots. And by further trial I found that I could see the images of some things (as of a candle or the Sun) very faintly reflected, not only from the great black spot, but also from the little darker spots which were within it.

Besides the aforesaid coloured rings there would often appear small spots of colours, ascending and descending up and down the sides of the bubble, by reason of some inequalities in the subsiding of the water. And sometimes small black spots generated at the sides would ascend up to the larger black spot at the top of the bubble, and unite with it.

OBS. 18. Because the colours of these bubbles were more extended and lively than those of the air thinned between two glasses, and so more easy to be distinguished, I shall here give you a further description of their order, as they were observed in viewing them by reflexion of the skies when of a white colour, whilst a black substance was placed behind the bubble. And they were these: red, blue; red, blue; red, blue; red, green; red, yellow, green, blue, purple; red, yellow, green, blue, violet; red, yellow, white, blue, black.

The three first successions of red and blue were very dilute and dirty, especially the first, where the red seemed in a manner to be white. Among these there was scarce any other colour sensible besides red and blue, only the blues (and principally the second blue) inclined a little to green.

The fourth red was also dilute and dirty, but not so much as the former three; after that succeeded little or no yellow, but a copious green, which at first inclined a little to yellow, and then became a pretty brisk and good willow green, and afterwards changed to a bluish colour; but there succeeded neither blue nor violet.

The fifth red at first inclined very much to purple, and afterwards became more bright and brisk, but yet not very pure. This was succeeded with a very bright and intense yellow, which was but little in quantity, and soon changed to green; but that green was copious and something more pure, deep and lively, than the former green. After that followed an excellent blue of a bright sky colour, and then a purple, which was less in quantity than the blue, and much inclined to red.

The sixth red was at first of a very fair and lively scarlet, and soon after of a brighter colour, being very pure and brisk, and the best of all the reds. Then after a lively orange followed an intense bright and copious yellow, which was also the best of all the yellows, and this changed first to a greenish yellow, and then to a greenish blue; but the green between the yellow and the blue was very little and dilute, seeming rather a greenish white than a green. The blue which succeeded became very good, and of a very bright sky colour, but yet something inferior to the former blue; and the violet was intense and deep with little or no redness in it, and less in quantity than the blue.

In the last red appeared a tincture of scarlet next to violet, which soon changed to a brighter colour, inclining to an orange; and the yellow which followed was at first pretty good and lively, but afterwards it grew more dilute until by degrees it ended in perfect whiteness. And this whiteness, if the water was very tenacious and well-tempered, would slowly spread and dilate itself over the greater part of the bubble; continually growing paler at the top, where at length it would crack in many places, and those cracks, as they dilated, would appear of a pretty good, but yet obscure and dark, sky colour; the white between the blue spots diminishing, until it resembled the threads of an irregular network, and soon after vanished, and left all the upper part of the bubble of the said dark blue colour. And this colour, after the aforesaid manner, dilated itself downwards, until sometimes it hath overspread the whole bubble. In the mean while at the top, which was of a darker blue than the bottom, and appeared also full of many round blue spots (something darker than the rest) there would emerge one or more very black spots, and within those, other spots of an intenser blackness, which I mentioned in the former Observation; and these continually dilated themselves until the bubble broke.

If the water was not very tenacious, the black spots would break forth in the white, without any sensible intervention of the blue. And sometimes they would break forth within the precedent yellow, or red, or perhaps within the blue of the second order, before the intermediate colours had time to display themselves.

By this description you may perceive how great an affinity these colours have with those of air described in the fourth Observation, although set down in a contrary order, by reason that they begin to appear when the bubble is thickest, and are most conveniently reckoned from the lowest and thickest part of the bubble upwards.

OBS. 19. Viewing in several oblique positions of my eye the rings of colours emerging on the top of the bubble, I found that they were sensibly dilated by increasing the obliquity, but yet not so much by far as those made by thinned air in the seventh Observation. For there they were dilated so much as, when viewed most obliquely, to arrive at a part of the plate more than twelve times thicker than that where they appeared when viewed perpendicularly; whereas, in this case, the thickness of the water at which they arrived when viewed most obliquely was, to that thickness which exhibited them by perpendicular rays, something less than as 8 to 5. By the best of my observations it was between 15 and 15½ to 10; an increase about 24 times less than in the other case.

Sometimes the bubble would become of an uniform thickness all over, except at the top of it near the black spot, as I knew, because it would exhibit the same appearance of colours in all positions of the eye. And then the colours which were seen at its apparent circumference by the obliquest rays would be different from those that were seen in other places, by rays less oblique to it.

And divers spectators might see the same part of it of differing colours, by viewing it at very differing obliquities. Now, observing how much the colours at the same places of the bubble, or at divers places of equal thickness, were varied by the several obliquities of the rays, by the assistance of the 4th, 14th, 16th, and 18th Observations, as they are hereafter explained, I collect the thickness of the water requisite to exhibit any one and the same colour, at several obliquities, to be very nearly in the proportion expressed in this Table.

Incidence on the water		Refraction into the water		Thickness of the water
Deg.	Min.	Deg.	Min.	
00	00	00	00	10
15	00	11	11	$10\frac{1}{4}$
30	00	22	1	$10\frac{4}{5}$
45	00	32	2	$11\frac{4}{5}$
60	00	40	30	13
75	00	46	25	$14\frac{1}{2}$
90	00	48	35	$15\frac{1}{5}$

In the two first columns are expressed the obliquities of the rays to the superficies of the water (that is, their angles of incidence and refraction), where I suppose that the sines which measure them are in round numbers, as 3 to 4, though probably the dissolution of soap in the water may a little alter its refractive virtue. In the third column, the thickness of the bubble, at which any one colour is exhibited in those several obliquities, is expressed in parts, of which ten constitute its thickness when the rays are perpendicular. And the rule found by the seventh Observation agrees well with these measures, if duly applied; namely, that the thickness of a plate of water requisite to exhibit one and the same colour at several obliquities of the eye is proportional to the secant of an angle, whose sine is the first of a hundred and six arithmetical mean proportionals between the sines of incidence and refraction counted from the lesser sine; that is, from the sine of refraction when the refraction is made out of air into water, otherwise from the sine of incidence.

I have sometimes observed that the colours which arise on polished steel by heating it, or on bell-metal, and some other metalline substances, when melted and poured on the ground, where they may cool in the open air, have, like the colours of water-bubbles, been a little changed by viewing them at divers obliquities, and particularly that a deep blue, or violet, when viewed very obliquely, hath been changed to a deep red. But the changes of these colours are not so great and sensible as of those made by water. For the scoria, or vitrified part of the metal, which most metals when heated or melted do continually protrude and send out to their surface, and which by covering the metals in form of a thin glassy skin, causes these colours, is much denser than water; and I find that the change made by the obliquation of the eye is least in colours of the densest thin substances.

OBS. 20. As in the ninth Observation, so here, the bubble, by transmitted light, appeared of a contrary colour to that which it exhibited by reflexion. Thus, when the bubble being looked on by the light of the clouds reflected from it, seemed red at its apparent circumference, if the clouds at the same time, or immediately after, were viewed through it, the colour at its circumference would be blue. And, on the contrary, when by reflected light it appeared blue, it would appear red by transmitted light.

OBS. 21. By wetting very thin plates of Muscovy glass, whose thinness made the like colours appear, the colours became more faint and languid, especially by wetting the plates on that side opposite to the eye; but I could not perceive any variation of their species. So, then, the thickness of a plate requisite to produce any colour depends only on the density of the plate, and not on that of the ambient medium. And hence, by the 10th and 16th Observations, may be known the thickness which bubbles of water, or plates of Muscovy glass, or other substances, have at any colour produced by them.

OBS. 22. A thin transparent body, which is denser than its ambient medium, exhibits more brisk and vivid colours than that which is so much rarer; as I have particularly observed in the air and glass. For blowing glass very thin at a lamp furnace, those plates encompassed with air did exhibit colours much more vivid than those of air made thin between two glasses.

OBS. 23. Comparing the quantity of light reflected from the several rings, I found that it was most copious from the first or inmost, and in the exterior rings became gradually less and less. Also the whiteness of the first ring was stronger than that reflected from those parts of the thin medium or plate which were without the rings; as I could manifestly perceive by viewing at a distance the rings made by the two object-glasses; or by comparing two bubbles of water blown at distant times, in the first of which the whiteness appeared, which succeeded all the colours, and, in the other, the whiteness which preceded them all.

OBS. 24. When the two object-glasses were laid upon one another, so as to make the rings of the colours appear, though with my naked eye I could not discern above eight or nine of those rings, yet by viewing them through a prism I have seen a far greater multitude, insomuch that I could number more than forty, besides many others, that were so very small and close together that I could not keep my eye steady on them severally so as to number them, but by their extent I have sometimes estimated them to be more than a hundred. And I believe the experiment may be improved to the discovery of far greater numbers. For they seem to be really unlimited, though visible only so far as they can be separated by the refraction of the prism, as I shall hereafter explain.

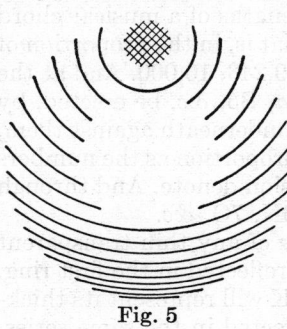

But it was but one side of these rings (namely, that towards which the refraction was made) which by that refraction was rendered distinct, and the other side became more confused than when viewed by the naked eye, insomuch that there I could not discern above one or two, and sometimes none of those rings, of which I could discern eight or nine with my naked eye. And their segments or arcs, which on the other side appeared so numerous, for the most part exceeded not the third part of a circle. If the refraction was very great, or the prism very distant from the object-glasses, the middle part of those arcs became also confused, so as to disappear and constitute an even whiteness, whilst on either side their ends, as also the whole arcs farthest from the centre, became distincter than before, appearing in the form as you see them designed in the fifth Figure.

Fig. 5

The arcs, where they seemed distinctest, were only white and black successively, without any other colours intermixed. But in other places there appeared colours whose order was inverted by the refraction in such manner that, if I first held the prism very near the object-glasses and then gradually removed it farther off towards my eye, the colours of the 2d, 3d, 4th and following rings, shrunk towards the white that emerged between them, until they wholly vanished into it at the middle of the arcs, and afterwards emerged again in a contrary order. But at the ends of the arcs they retained their order unchanged.

I have sometimes so laid one object-glass upon the other that, to the naked eye, they have all over seemed uniformly white, without the least appearance of any of the coloured rings; and yet, by viewing them through a prism, great multitudes of those rings have discovered themselves. And in like manner plates of Muscovy glass, and bubbles of glass blown at a lamp-furnace, which were not so thin as to exhibit any colours to the naked eye, have through the prism exhibited a great variety of them ranged irregularly up and down in the form of waves. And so bubbles of water, before they began to exhibit their colours to the naked eye of a bystander, have appeared through a prism, girded about with many parallel and horizontal rings; to produce which effect it was necessary to hold the prism parallel, or very nearly parallel, to the horizon, and to dispose it so that the rays might be refracted upwards.

Part II

Remarks upon the foregoing Observations.

HAVING given my Observations of these colours, before I make use of them to unfold the causes of the colours of natural bodies it is convenient that, by the simplest of them (such as are the 2d, 3d, 4th, 9th, 12th, 18th, 20th, and 24th) I first explain the more compounded. And first, to shew how the colours in the fourth and eighteenth Observations are produced, let there be taken in any right line from the point Y, [Fig. 6] the lengths YA, YB, YC, YD, YE, YF, YG, YH, in proportion to one another, as the cube roots of the squares of the numbers, $\frac{1}{2}$, $\frac{9}{16}$, $\frac{3}{5}$, $\frac{2}{3}$, $\frac{3}{4}$, $\frac{5}{6}$, $\frac{8}{9}$, 1, whereby the lengths of a musical chord to sound all the notes in an eighth are represented; that is, in the proportion of the numbers 6,300, 6,814, 7,114, 7,631, 8,255, 8,855, 9,243, 10,000. And at the points A, B, C, D, E, F, G, H, let perpendiculars Aa, Bβ, &c. be erected, by whose intervals the extent of the several colours, set underneath against them, is to be represented. Then divide the line Aa in such proportion as the numbers 1, 2, 3, 5, 6, 7, 9, 10, 11, &c. set at the points of division denote. And through those divisions from Y draw lines 1I, 2K, 3L, 5M, 6N, 7O, &c.

Now, if A2 be supposed to represent the thickness of any thin transparent body, at which the outmost violet is most copiously reflected in the first ring, or series of colours, then by the 13th Observation, HK will represent its thickness, at which the utmost red is most copiously reflected in the same series. Also, by the 5th and 16th Observations, A6 and HN will denote the thicknesses at which those extreme colours are most copiously reflected in the second series, and A10 and HQ the thicknesses at which they are most copiously reflected in the third series, and so on. And the thickness at which any of the intermediate colours are reflected most copiously, will, according to the 14th Observation, be defined by the distance of the line AH from the intermediate parts of the lines 2K, 6N, 10Q, &c. against which the names of those colours are written below.

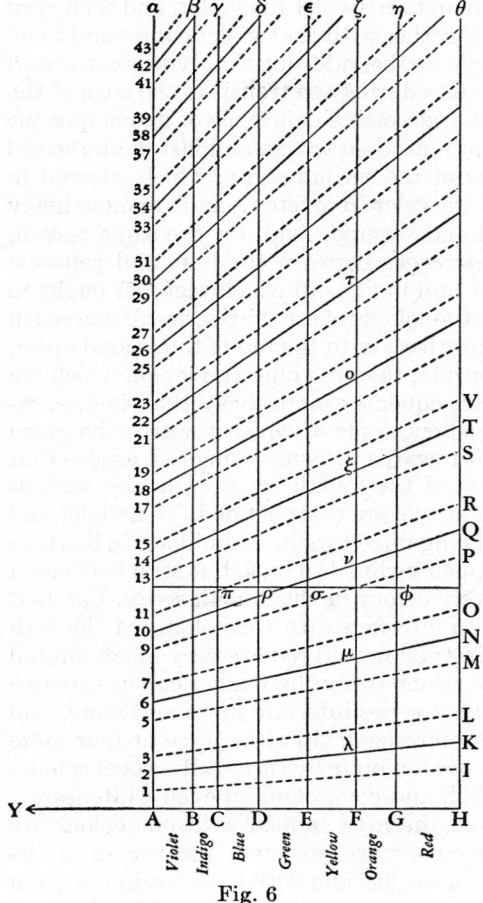

Fig. 6

But farther, to define the latitude of these colours in each ring or series, let A1 design the least thickness, and A3 the greatest thickness, at which the extreme violet in the first series is reflected, and let HI and HL design the like limits for the extreme red, and let the intermediate colours be limited by the intermediate parts of the lines 1I and 3L, against which the names of those colours are written, and so on; but yet with this caution: that the reflexions be supposed strongest at the intermediate spaces, 2K, 6N, 10Q, &c. and from thence to decrease gradually towards these limits, 1I, 3L, 5M, 7O, &c. on either side; where you must not conceive them to be precisely limited, but to decay indefinitely. And whereas I have assigned the same latitude to every series, I did it because, although the colours in the first series seem to be a little broader than the rest, by reason of a stronger reflexion there, yet that inequality is so insensible as scarcely to be determined by observation.

Now, according to this description, conceiving that the rays originally of several colours are by turns reflected at the spaces 1I, L3, 5M, O7, 9P, R11, &c. and transmitted at the spaces AHI1, 3LM5, 7OP9, &c. it is easy to know what colour must in the open air be exhibited at any thickness of a transparent thin body. For if a ruler be applied parallel to AH, at that distance from it by which the thickness of the body is represented, the alternate spaces 1IL3, 5MO7, &c. which it crosseth will denote the reflected original colours, of which the colour exhibited in the open air is compounded. Thus, if the constitution of the green in the third series of colours be desired, apply the ruler as you see at $\pi\rho\sigma\varphi$, and by its passing through some of the blue at π and yellow at σ, as well as through the green at ρ, you may conclude that the green exhibited at that thickness of the body is principally constituted of original green, but not without a mixture of some blue and yellow.

By this means you may know how the colours from the centre of the rings outward ought to succeed in order as they were described in the 4th and 18th

Observations. For if you move the ruler gradually from AH through all distances, having passed over the first space which denotes little or no reflexion to be made by thinnest substances, it will first arrive at 1 the violet, and then very quickly at the blue and green, which together with that violet compound blue, and then at the yellow and red, by whose further addition that blue is converted into whiteness, which whiteness continues during the transit of the edge of the ruler from I to 3, and after that by the successive deficience of its component colours, turns first to compound yellow, and then to red, and last of all the red ceaseth at L. Then begin the colours of the second series, which succeed in order during the transit of the edge of the ruler from 5 to O, and are more lively than before, because more expanded and severed. And, for the same reason, instead of the former white there intercedes between the blue and yellow a mixture of orange, yellow, green, blue and indigo, all which together ought to exhibit a dilute and imperfect green. So the colours of the third series all succeed in order; first, the violet, which a little interferes with the red of the second order, and is thereby inclined to a reddish purple; then the blue and green, which are less mixed with other colours, and consequently more lively than before, especially the green; then follows the yellow, some of which towards the green is distinct and good, but that part of it towards the succeeding red, as also that red is mixed with the violet and blue of the fourth series, whereby various degrees of red very much inclining to purple are compounded. This violet and blue, which should succeed this red, being mixed with, and hidden in it, there succeeds a green. And this at first is much inclined to blue, but soon becomes a good green, the only unmixed and lively colour in this fourth series. For as it verges towards the yellow, it begins to interfere with the colours of the fifth series, by whose mixture the succeeding yellow and red are very much diluted and made dirty, especially the yellow, which being the weaker colour is scarce able to shew itself. After this the several series interfere more and more, and their colours become more and more intermixed, till after three or four more revolutions (in which the red and blue predominate by turns) all sorts of colours are in all places pretty equally blended, and compound an even whiteness.

And since, by the 15th Observation, the rays endued with one colour are transmitted, where those of another colour are reflected, the reason of the colours made by the transmitted light in the 9th and 20th Observations is from hence evident.

If not only the order and species of these colours, but also the precise thickness of the plate, or thin body at which they are exhibited, be desired in parts of an inch, that may be also obtained by assistance of the 6th or 16th Observations. For according to those Observations the thickness of the thinned air, which between two glasses exhibited the most luminous parts of the first six rings were $\frac{1}{178,000}$, $\frac{3}{178,000}$, $\frac{5}{178,000}$, $\frac{7}{178,000}$, $\frac{9}{178,000}$, $\frac{11}{178,000}$, parts of an inch. Suppose the light reflected most copiously at these thicknesses be the bright citrine yellow, or confine of yellow and orange, and these thicknesses will be $F\lambda$, $F\mu$, $F\nu$, $F\xi$, Fo, $F\tau$. And this being known, it is easy to determine what thickness of air is represented by $G\varphi$, or by any other distance of the ruler from AH.

But further, since by the 10th Observation the thickness of air was to the thickness of water, which between the same glasses exhibited the same colour, as 4 to 3, and by the 21st Observation the colours of thin bodies are not varied by varying the ambient medium, the thickness of a bubble of water, exhibiting any colour will be ¾ of the thickness of air producing the same colour. And so, according to the same 10th and 21st Observations, the thickness of a plate of glass, whose refraction of the mean refrangible ray, is measured by the proportion of the sines 31 to 20, may be $\frac{20}{31}$ of the thickness of air producing the same colours; and the like of other mediums. I do not affirm that this proportion of 20 to 31 holds in all the rays; for the sines of other sorts of rays have other proportions. But the differences of those proportions are so little that I do not here consider them. On these grounds I have composed the following Table, wherein the thickness of air, water, and glass, at which each colour is most intense and specific, is expressed in parts of an inch divided into ten hundred thousand equal parts.

The thickness of coloured plates and particles

		of Air	Water	Glass
Their colours of the first order....	Very black	$\frac{1}{2}$	$\frac{3}{8}$	$\frac{10}{31}$
	Black	1	$\frac{3}{4}$	$\frac{20}{31}$
	Beginning of black	2	$1\frac{1}{2}$	$1\frac{2}{7}$
	Blue	$2\frac{2}{5}$	$1\frac{4}{5}$	$1\frac{11}{22}$
	White	$5\frac{1}{4}$	$3\frac{7}{8}$	$3\frac{2}{5}$
	Yellow	$7\frac{1}{9}$	$5\frac{1}{3}$	$4\frac{3}{5}$
	Orange	8	6	$5\frac{1}{5}$
	Red	9	$6\frac{3}{4}$	$5\frac{4}{5}$
Of the second order.............	Violet	$11\frac{1}{6}$	$8\frac{3}{8}$	$7\frac{1}{5}$
	Indigo	$12\frac{5}{6}$	$9\frac{5}{8}$	$8\frac{2}{11}$
	Blue	14	$10\frac{1}{2}$	9
	Green	$15\frac{1}{3}$	$11\frac{2}{3}$	$9\frac{5}{7}$
	Yellow	$16\frac{2}{7}$	$12\frac{1}{5}$	$10\frac{2}{5}$
	Orange	$17\frac{2}{9}$	13	$11\frac{1}{9}$
	Bright red	$18\frac{1}{3}$	$13\frac{3}{4}$	$11\frac{5}{6}$
	Scarlet	$19\frac{2}{3}$	$14\frac{3}{4}$	$12\frac{2}{3}$
Of the third order.........	Purple	21	$15\frac{3}{4}$	$13\frac{11}{20}$
	Indigo	$22\frac{1}{10}$	$16\frac{4}{7}$	$14\frac{1}{4}$
	Blue	$23\frac{2}{5}$	$17\frac{11}{20}$	$15\frac{1}{10}$
	Green	$25\frac{1}{5}$	$18\frac{9}{10}$	$16\frac{1}{4}$
	Yellow	$27\frac{1}{7}$	$20\frac{1}{3}$	$17\frac{1}{2}$
	Red	29	$21\frac{3}{4}$	$18\frac{5}{7}$
	Bluish-red	32	24	$20\frac{2}{3}$
Of the fourth order.............	Bluish-green	34	$25\frac{1}{2}$	22
	Green	$35\frac{2}{7}$	$26\frac{1}{2}$	$22\frac{3}{4}$
	Yellowish-green	36	27	$23\frac{2}{9}$
	Red	$40\frac{1}{3}$	$30\frac{1}{4}$	26
Of the fifth order...............	Greenish-blue	46	$34\frac{1}{2}$	$29\frac{2}{3}$
	Red	$52\frac{1}{2}$	$39\frac{3}{8}$	34
Of the sixth order...............	Greenish-blue	$58\frac{3}{4}$	44	38
	Red	65	$48\frac{3}{4}$	42
Of the seventh order	Greenish-blue	71	$53\frac{1}{4}$	$45\frac{4}{5}$
	Ruddy white	77	$57\frac{3}{4}$	$49\frac{2}{3}$

Now, if this Table be compared with the 6th scheme, you will there see the constitution of each colour, as to its ingredients, or the original colours of which it is compounded, and thence be enabled to judge of its intenseness or imperfection; which may suffice in explication of the 4th and 18th Observations, unless it be further desired to delineate the manner how the colours appear when the two object-glasses are laid upon one another. To do which, let there be described a large arc of a circle, and a straight line which may touch that arc, and parallel to that tangent several occult lines, at such distances from it as the numbers set against the several colours in the Table denote. For the arc and its tangent will represent the superficies of the glasses terminating the interjacent air; and the places where the occult lines cut the arc will show at what distances from the centre, or point of contact, each colour is reflected.

There are also other uses of this Table. For by its assistance the thickness of the bubble in the 19th Observation was determined by the colours which it exhibited. And so the bigness of the parts of natural bodies may be conjectured by their colours, as shall be hereafter shewn. Also, if two or more very thin plates be laid one upon another, so as to compose one plate equalling them all in thickness, the resulting colour may be hereby determined. For instance, Mr. Hook observed, as is mentioned in his *Micrographia*, that a faint yellow plate of Muscovy glass laid upon a blue one, constituted a very deep purple. The yellow of the first order is a faint one, and the thickness of the plate exhibiting it, according to the Table, is $4\frac{3}{5}$, to which add 9, the thickness exhibiting blue of the second order, and the sum will be $13\frac{3}{5}$, which is the thickness exhibiting the purple of the third order.

To explain, in the next place, the circumstances of the 2d and 3d Observations; that is, how the rings of the colours may (by turning the prisms about their common axis the contrary way to that expressed in those observations) be converted into white and black rings, and afterwards into rings of colours again, the colours of each ring lying now in an inverted order: it must be remembered that those rings of colours are dilated by the obliquation of the rays to the air which intercedes the glasses, and that according to the Table in the 7th Observation their dilatation or increase of their diameter is most manifest and speedy when they are obliquest. Now, the rays of yellow being more refracted by the first superficies of the said air than those of red, are thereby made more oblique to the second superficies, at which they are reflected to produce the coloured rings, and consequently the yellow circle in each ring will be more dilated than the red; and the excess of its dilatation will be so much the greater, by how much the greater is the obliquity of the rays, until at last it become of equal extent with the red of the same ring. And for the same reason the green, blue, and violet will be also so much dilated by the still greater obliquity of their rays, as to become all very nearly of equal extent with the red; that is, equally distant from the centre of the rings. And then all the colours of the same ring must be coincident, and by their mixture exhibit a white ring. And these white rings must have black and dark rings between them, because they do not spread and interfere with one another, as before. And for that reason also they must become distincter, and visible to far greater numbers. But yet the violet being obliquest will be something more dilated, in proportion to its extent, than the other colours, and so very apt to appear at the exterior verges of the white.

Afterwards, by a greater obliquity of the rays, the violet and blue become more sensibly dilated than the red and yellow, and so, being farther removed from the centre of the rings, the colours must emerge out of the white in an order contrary to that which they had before; the violet and blue at the exterior limbs of each ring, and the red and yellow at the interior. And the violet, by reason of the greatest obliquity of its rays, being in proportion most of all expanded, will soonest appear at the exterior limb of each white ring, and become more conspicuous than the rest. And the several series of colours belonging to the several rings, will, by their unfolding and spreading, begin again to interfere, and thereby render the rings less distinct, and not visible to so great numbers.

If instead of the prisms the object-glasses be made use of, the rings which they exhibit become not white and distinct by the obliquity of the eye, by reason that the rays in their passage through that air which intercedes the glasses are very nearly parallel to those lines in which they were first incident on the glasses, and consequently the rays endued with several colours are not inclined one more than another to that air, as it happens in the prisms.

There is yet another circumstance of these experiments to be considered, and that is why the black and white rings which, when viewed at a distance appear distinct, should not only become confused by viewing them near at hand, but also yield a violet colour at both the edges of every white ring. And the reason is that the rays which enter the eye at several parts of the pupil have several obliquities to the glasses, and those which are most oblique, if considered apart, would represent the rings bigger than those which are the least oblique. Whence the breadth of the perimeter of every white ring is expanded outwards by the obliquest rays, and inwards by the least oblique. And this expansion is so much the greater by how much the greater is the difference of the obliquity; that is, by how much the pupil is wider, or the eye nearer to the glasses. And the breadth of the violet must be most expanded, because the rays apt to excite a sensation of that colour are most oblique to a second or farther superficies of the thinned air at which they are reflected, and have also the greatest variation of obliquity, which makes that colour soonest emerge out of the edges of the white. And as the breadth of every ring is thus augmented, the dark intervals must be diminished, until the neighbouring rings become continuous, and are blended, the exterior first, and then those nearer the centre; so that they can no longer be distinguished apart, but seem to constitute an even and uniform whiteness.

Among all the Observations there is none accompanied with so odd circumstances as the twenty-fourth. Of those the principal are, that in thin plates, which to the naked eye seem of an even and uniform transparent whiteness, without any terminations of shadows, the refraction of a prism should make rings of colours appear, whereas it usually makes objects appear coloured only there where they are terminated with shadows, or have parts unequally luminous; and that it should make those rings exceedingly distinct and white, although it usually renders objects confused and coloured. The cause of these things you will understand by considering that all the rings of colours are really in the plate, when viewed with the naked eye, although by reason of the great breadth of their circumferences they so much interfere and are blended together that they seem to constitute an uniform whiteness. But when the rays pass through the prism to the eye, the orbits of the several colours in every ring are refracted, some more than others, according to their degrees of refrangibility; by which means the colours on one side of the ring (that is, in the circumference on one side of its centre) become more unfolded and dilated, and those on the other side more complicated and contracted. And where by a due refraction they are so much contracted that the several rings become narrower than to interfere with one another, they must appear distinct, and also white, if the constituent colours be so much contracted as to be wholly coincident. But on the other side, where the orbit of every ring is made broader by the farther unfolding of its colours, it must interfere more with other rings than before, and so become less distinct.

To explain this a little further, suppose the concentric circles AV, and BX, [Fig. 7] represent the red and violet of any order, which, together with the intermediate colours, constitute any one of these rings. Now, these being viewed through a prism, the violet circle BX, will, by a greater refraction, be farther translated from its place than the red AV, and so approach nearer to it on that side of the circles, towards which the refractions are made. For instance, if the red be translated to av, the violet may be translated to bx, so as to approach nearer to it at x than before; and if the red be farther translated to av, the violet may be so much farther translated to bx as to convene with it at x; and if the red be yet farther translated to $a\Upsilon$, the violet may be still so much farther translated to $\beta\xi$ as to pass beyond it at ξ, and convene with it at e and f. And this being understood not only of the red and violet, but of all the other intermediate colours, and also of every revolution of those colours, you will easily perceive how those of the same revolution or order, by their nearness at

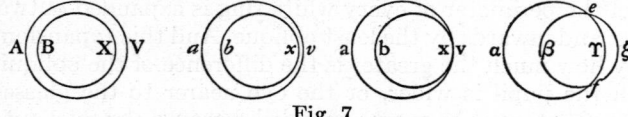

Fig. 7

xv and $\Upsilon\xi$, and their coincidence at xv, e and f, ought to constitute pretty distinct arcs of circles, especially at xv, or at e and f; and that they will appear severally at xv, and at xv exhibit whiteness by their coincidence, and again appear severally at $\Upsilon\xi$, but yet in a contrary order to that which they had before, and still retain beyond e and f. But on the other side, at ab, ab, or $a\beta$, these colours must become much more confused by being dilated and spread so as to interfere with those of other orders. And the same confusion will happen at $\Upsilon\xi$ between e and f, if the refraction be very great, or the prism very distant from the object-glasses; in which case no parts of the rings will be seen, save only two little arcs at e and f, whose distance from one another will be augmented by removing the prism still farther from the object-glasses. And these little arcs must be distinctest and whitest at their middle, and at their ends, where they begin to grow confused, they must be coloured. And the colours at one end of every arc must be in a contrary order to those at the other end, by reason that they cross in the intermediate white; namely, their ends, which verge towards $\Upsilon\xi$, will be red and yellow on that side next the centre, and blue and violet on the other side. But their other ends which verge from $\Upsilon\xi$, will on the contrary be blue and violet on that side towards the centre, and on the other side red and yellow.

Now, as all these things follow from the properties of light by a mathematical way of reasoning, so the truth of them may be manifested by experiments. For in a dark room, by viewing these rings through a prism, by reflexion of the several prismatic colours, which an assistant causes to move to and fro upon a wall or paper from whence they are reflected, whilst the spectator's eye, the prism, and the object-glasses (as in the 13th Observation) are placed steady;

the position of the circles made successively by the several colours, will be found such, in respect of one another, as I have described in the Figures *abxv*, or abxv, or *αβξτ*. And by the same method the truth of the explications of other Observations may be examined.

By what hath been said, the like phenomena of water and thin plates of glass may be understood. But in small fragments of those plates there is this further observable, that where they lie flat upon a table, and are turned about their centres whilst they are viewed through a prism, they will in some postures exhibit waves of various colours; and some of them exhibit these waves in one or two positions only, but the most of them do in all positions exhibit them, and make them for the most part appear almost all over the plates. The reason is that the superficies of such plates are not even, but have many cavities and swellings, which, how shallow soever, do a little vary the thickness of the plate. For at the several sides of those cavities, for the reasons newly described, there ought to be produced waves in several postures of the prism. Now, though it be but some very small and narrower parts of the glass by which these waves for the most part are caused, yet they may seem to extend themselves over the whole glass, because from the narrowest of those parts there are colours of several orders; that is, of several rings, confusedly reflected, which by refraction of the prism are unfolded, separated, and, according to their degrees of refraction, dispersed to several places, so as to constitute so many several waves, as there were divers orders of colours promiscuously reflected from that part of the glass.

These are the principal phenomena of thin plates or bubbles, whose explications depend on the properties of light, which I have heretofore delivered. And these you see do necessarily follow from them, and agree with them, even to their very least circumstances; and not only so, but do very much tend to their proof. Thus, by the 24th Observation it appears that the rays of several colours, made as well by thin plates or bubbles as by refractions of a prism, have several degrees of refrangibility; whereby those of each order, which at the reflexion from the plate or bubble are intermixed with those of other orders, are separated from them by refraction, and associated together so as to become visible by themselves like arcs of circles. For if the rays were all alike refrangible, 'tis impossible that the whiteness, which to the naked sense appears uniform, should by refraction have its parts transposed and ranged into those black and white arcs.

It appears also that the unequal refractions of difform rays proceed not from any contingent irregularities; such as are veins, an uneven polish, or fortuitous position of the pores of glass; unequal and casual motions in the air or ether, the spreading, breaking, or dividing the same ray into many diverging parts; or the like. For, admitting any such irregularities, it would be impossible for refractions to render those rings so very distinct and well defined as they do in the 24th Observation. It is necessary, therefore, that every ray have its proper and constant degree of refrangibility connate with it, according to which its refraction is ever justly and regularly performed; and that several rays have several of those degrees.

And what is said of their refrangibility may be also undersood of their reflexibility; that is, of their dispositions to be reflected, some at a greater and others at a less thickness of thin plates or bubbles; namely, that those dispositions are also connate with the rays, and immutable; as may appear by the

13th, 14th, and 15th Observations, compared with the fourth and eighteenth.

By the precedent Observations, it appears also that whiteness is a dissimilar mixture of all colours, and that light is a mixture of rays endued with all those colours. For, considering the multitude of the rings of colours in the 3d, 12th, and 24th Observations, it is manifest that although in the 4th and 18th Observations there appear no more than eight or nine of those rings, yet there are really a far greater number, which so much interfere and mingle with one another as, after those eight or nine revolutions, to dilute one another wholly, and constitute an even and sensibly uniform whiteness. And, consequently, that whiteness must be allowed a mixture of all colours, and the light which conveys it to the eye must be a mixture of rays endued with all those colours.

But further; by the 24th Observation it appears that there is a constant relation between colours and refrangibility; the most refrangible rays being violet, the least refrangible red, and those of intermediate colours having proportionably intermediate degrees of refrangibility. And by the 13th, 14th, and 15th Observations, compared with the 4th or 18th, there appears to be the same constant relation between colour and reflexibility; the violet being in like circumstances reflected at least thicknesses of any thin plate or bubble, the red at greatest thicknesses, and the intermediate colours at intermediate thicknesses. Whence it follows that the colorific dispositions of rays are also connate with them, and immutable; and, by consequence, that all the productions and appearances of colours in the world are derived, not from any physical change caused in light by refraction or reflexion, but only from the various mixtures or separations of rays, by virtue of their different refrangibility or reflexibility. And in this respect the science of colours becomes a speculation as truly mathematical as any other part of Optics. I mean, so far as they depend on the nature of light, and are not produced or altered by the power of imagination, or by striking or pressing the eye.

Part III

Of the permanent colours of natural bodies, and the analogy between them and the colours of thin transparent plates.

I AM now come to another part of this design, which is to consider how the phenomena of thin transparent plates stand related to those of all other natural bodies. Of these bodies I have already told you that they appear of divers colours, accordingly as they are disposed to reflect most copiously the rays originally endued with those colours. But their constitutions, whereby they reflect some rays more copiously than others, remain to be discovered; and these I shall endeavour to manifest in the following Propositions.

PROPOSITION 1

Those superficies of transparent bodies reflect the greatest quantity of light, which have the greatest refracting power; that is, which intercede mediums that differ most in their refractive densities. And in the confines of equally refracting mediums there is no reflexion.

The analogy between reflexion and refraction will appear by considering

that, when light passeth obliquely out of one medium into another which refracts from the perpendicular, the greater is the difference of their refractive
density, the less obliquity of incidence is requisite to cause a total reflexion.
For as the sines are which measure the refraction, so is the sine of incidence at
which the total reflexion begins, to the radius of the circle; and, consequently,
that angle of incidence is least where there is the greatest difference of the
sines. Thus, in the passing of light out of water into air, where the refraction
is measured by the ratio of the sines 3 to 4, the total reflexion begins when the
angle of incidence is about 48 degrees 35 minutes. In passing out of glass into
air, where the refraction is measured by the ratio of the sines 20 to 31, the total
reflexion begins when the angle of incidence is 40 degrees 10 minutes; and so in
passing out of crystal, or more strongly refracting mediums into air, there is
still a less obliquity requisite to cause a total reflexion. Superficies therefore
which refract most do soonest reflect all the light which is incident on them, and
so must be allowed most strongly reflexive.

But the truth of this Proposition will further appear by observing that, in
the superficies interceding two transparent mediums (such as are air, water, oil,
common glass, crystal, metalline glasses, island glasses, white transparent arsenic, diamonds, &c.), the reflexion is stronger or weaker accordingly as the
superficies hath a greater or less refracting power. For in the confine of air and
sal-gem 'tis stronger than in the confine of air and water, and still stronger in
the confine of air and common glass or crystal, and stronger in the confine of
air and a diamond. If any of these, and such like transparent solids, be immerged in water, its reflexion becomes much weaker than before; and still
weaker if they be immerged in the more strongly refracting liquors of well-
rectified oil of vitriol or spirit of turpentine. If water be distinguished into two
parts by any imaginary surface, the reflexion in the confine of those two parts
is none at all. In the confine of water and ice 'tis very little; in that of water and
oil 'tis something greater; in that of water and sal-gem still greater; and in
that of water and glass, or crystal or other denser substances still greater,
accordingly as those mediums differ more or less in their refracting powers.
Hence, in the confine of common glass and crystal, there ought to be a weak
reflexion, and a stronger reflexion in the confine of common and metalline
glass; though I have not yet tried this. But in the confine of two glasses of
equal density there is not any sensible reflexion, as was shewn in the first Observation. And the same may be understood of the superficies separating two
crystals, or two liquors, or any other substances in which no refraction is
caused. So, then, the reason why uniform pellucid mediums (such as water,
glass, or crystal) have no sensible reflexion but in their external superficies,
where they are adjacent to other mediums of a different density, is because all
their contiguous parts have one and the same degree of density.

PROPOSITION 2

*The least parts of almost all natural bodies are in some measure transparent: And
the opacity of those bodies ariseth from the multitude of reflexions caused in their
internal parts.*

That this is so has been observed by others, and will easily be granted by
them that have been conversant with microscopes. And it may be also tried
by applying any substance to a hole through which some light is immitted

into a dark room. For how opaque soever that substance may seem in the open air, it will by that means appear very manifestly transparent if it be of a sufficient thinness. Only white metalline bodies must be excepted, which by reason of their excessive density seem to reflect almost all the light incident on their first superficies; unless by solution in menstruums they be reduced into very small particles, and then they become transparent.

PROPOSITION 3

Between the parts of opaque and coloured bodies are many spaces, either empty, or replenished with mediums of other densities; as water between the tinging corpuscles wherewith any liquor is impregnated, air between the aqueous globules that constitute clouds or mists; and for the most part spaces void of both air and water, but yet perhaps not wholly void of all substance, between the parts of hard bodies.

The truth of this is evinced by the two precedent Propositions. For, by the second Proposition, there are many reflexions made by the internal parts of bodies, which, by the first Proposition, would not happen if the parts of those bodies were continued without any such interstices between them; because reflexions are caused only in superficies, which separate mediums of a differing density (Prop. 1).

But further, that this discontinuity of parts is the principal cause of the opacity of bodies will appear by considering that opaque substances become transparent by filling their pores with any substance of equal or almost equal density with their parts. Thus, paper dipped in water or oil, the *Oculus mundi* stone steeped in water, linen cloth oiled or varnished, and many other substances soaked in such liquors as will intimately pervade their little pores, become by that means more transparent than otherwise; so, on the contrary, the most transparent substances may, by evacuating their pores, or separating their parts, be rendered sufficiently opaque; as salts or wet paper, or the *Oculus mundi* stone by being dried, horn by being scraped, glass by being reduced to powder, or otherwise flawed; turpentine by being stirred about with water till they mix imperfectly, and water by being formed into many small bubbles, either alone in the form of froth, or by shaking it together with oil of turpentine, or olive oil, or with some other convenient liquor with which it will not perfectly incorporate. And to the increase of the opacity of these bodies, it conduces something, that by the 23d Observation the reflexions of very thin transparent substances are considerably stronger than those made by the same substances of a greater thickness.

PROPOSITION 4

The parts of bodies and their interstices must not be less than of some definite bigness, to render them opaque and coloured.

For the opaquest bodies, if their parts be subtly divided (as metals, by being dissolved in acid menstruums, &c.), become perfectly transparent. And you may also remember that in the eighth Observation there was no sensible reflexion at the superficies of the object-glasses, where they were very near one another, though they did not absolutely touch. And in the 17th Observation the reflexion of the water-bubble where it became thinnest was almost insensible, so as to cause very black spots to appear on the top of the bubble, by the want of reflected light.

On these grounds I perceive it is that water, salt, glass, stones, and such like substances are transparent. For, upon divers considerations, they seem to be as full of pores or interstices between their parts as other bodies are, but yet their parts and interstices to be too small to cause reflexions in their common surfaces.

PROPOSITION 5

The transparent parts of bodies, according to their several sizes, reflect rays of one colour, and transmit those of another, on the same grounds that thin plates or bubbles do reflect or transmit those rays. And this I take to be the ground of all their colours.

For if a thinned or plated body, which being of an even thickness appears all over of one uniform colour, should be slit into threads, or broken into fragments, of the same thickness with the plate, I see no reason why every thread or fragment should not keep its colour, and by consequence why a heap of those threads or fragments should not constitute a mass or powder of the same colour, which the plate exhibited before it was broken. And the parts of all natural bodies, being like so many fragments of a plate, must on the same grounds exhibit the same colours.

Now, that they do so will appear by the affinity of their properties. The finely coloured feathers of some birds, and particularly those of peacocks' tails, do, in the very same part of the feather, appear of several colours in several positions of the eye, after the very same manner that thin plates were found to do in the 7th and 19th Observations; and, therefore, their colours arise from the thinness of the transparent parts of the feathers; that is, from the slenderness of the very fine hairs, or *capillamenta*, which grow out of the sides of the grosser lateral branches or fibres of those feathers. And to the same purpose it is that the webs of some spiders, by being spun very fine, have appeared coloured, as some have observed, and that the coloured fibres of some silks, by varying the position of the eye, do vary their colour. Also the colours of silks, cloths, and other substances, which water or oil can intimately penetrate, become more faint and obscure by being immerged in those liquors, and recover their vigour again by being dried; much after the manner declared of thin bodies in the 10th and 21st Observations. Leaf-gold, some sorts of painted glass, the infusion of *lignum nephriticum*, and some other substances, reflect one colour, and transmit another, like thin bodies in the 9th and 20th Observations. And some of those coloured powders which painters use may have their colours a little changed by being very elaborately and finely ground. Where I see not what can be justly pretended for those changes, besides the breaking of their parts into less parts by that contrition, after the same manner that the colour of a thin plate is changed by varying its thickness. For which reason also it is that the coloured flowers of plants and vegetables, by being bruised, usually become more transparent than before, or at least in some degree or other change their colours. Nor is it much less to my purpose that, by mixing divers liquors, very odd and remarkable productions and changes of colours may be effected, of which no cause can be more obvious and rational than that the saline corpuscles of one liquor do variously act upon or unite with the tinging corpuscles of another, so as to make them swell, or shrink (whereby not only their bulk but their density also may be changed) or to divide them into smaller corpuscles (whereby a coloured liquor may become transparent), or to make many of them associate into one cluster, whereby two transparent liquors may compose a coloured one. For we see how apt those saline menstruums are to penetrate and dissolve substances to which they are applied, and some of them to precipitate what others dissolve. In like manner, if we consider the various phenomena of the atmosphere, we may observe that when vapours are first raised they hinder not the transparency of the air, being divided into parts too small to cause any reflexion in their superficies. But when in order to compose drops of rain they begin to coalesce and constitute globules of all intermediate sizes, those globules, when they become of convenient size to reflect some colours and transmit others, may constitute clouds of various colours, according to their sizes. And I see not what can be rationally conceived in so transparent a substance as water for the production of these colours, besides the various sizes of its fluid and globular parcels.

PROPOSITION 6

The parts of bodies on which their colours depend, are denser than the medium which pervades their interstices.

This will appear by considering that the colour of a body depends not only on the rays which are incident perpendicularly on its parts, but on those also which are incident at all other angles. And that, according to the 7th Observation, a very little variation of obliquity will change the reflected colour, where the thin body or small particles is rarer than the ambient medium, insomuch that such a small particle will at diversely oblique incidences reflect all sorts of colours, in so great a variety that the colour resulting from them all, confusedly reflected from a heap of such particles, must rather be a white or grey than any other colour, or at best it must be but a very imperfect and dirty colour. Whereas if the thin body or small particle be much denser than the ambient medium, the colours, according to the 19th Observation, are so little changed by the variation of obliquity, that the rays which are reflected least obliquely may predominate over the rest, so much as to cause a heap of such particles to appear very intensely of their colour.

It conduces also something to the confirmation of this Proposition that, according to the 22d Observation, the colours exhibited by the denser thin body within the rarer are more brisk than those exhibited by the rarer within the denser.

PROPOSITION 7

The bigness of the component parts of natural bodies may be conjectured by their colours.

For since the parts of these bodies (by Prop. 5), do most probably exhibit the same colours with a plate of equal thickness, provided they have the same refractive density; and since their parts seem for the most part to have much the same density with water or glass, as by many circumstances is obvious to collect; to determine the sizes of those parts, you need only have recourse to the precedent Tables, in which the thickness of water or glass exhibiting any colour is expressed. Thus, if it be desired to know the diameter of a corpuscle, which being of equal density with glass shall reflect green of the third order, the number $16\frac{1}{4}$ shews it to be $\frac{16\frac{1}{4}}{10,000}$ parts of an inch.

The greatest difficulty is here to know of what order the colour of any body is. And for this end we must have recourse to the 4th and 18th Observations; from whence may be collected these particulars.

Scarlets, and other *reds*, *oranges*, and *yellows*, if they be pure and intense, are most probably of the second order. Those of the first and third order also may be pretty good; only the yellow of the first order is faint, and the orange and red of the third order have a great mixture of violet and blue.

There may be good *greens* of the fourth order, but the purest are of the third. And of this order the green of all vegetables seems to be, partly by reason of the intenseness of their colours, and partly because when they wither some of them turn to a greenish yellow, and others to a more perfect yellow or orange, or perhaps to red, passing first through all the aforesaid intermediate colours. Which changes seem to be effected by the exhaling of the moisture which may leave the tinging corpuscles more dense, and something augmented by the accretion of the oily and earthy part of that moisture. Now the green, without doubt, is of the same order with those colours into which it changeth, because the changes are gradual, and those colours, though usually not very full, yet are often too full and lively to be of the fourth order.

Blues and *purples* may be either of the second or third order, but the best are of the third. Thus the colour of violets seems to be of that order, because their syrup by acid liquors turns red, and by urinous and alkalizate turns green. For since it is of the nature of acids to dissolve or attenuate, and of alkalies to precipitate or incrassate, if the purple colour of the syrup was of the second order an acid liquor, by attenuating its tinging corpuscles, would change it to a red of the first order, and an alkali by incrassating them would change it to a green of the second order; which red and green, especially the green, seem too imperfect to be the colours produced by these changes. But if the said purple be supposed of the third order, its change to red of the second, and green of the third, may without any inconvenience be allowed.

If there be found any body of a deeper and less reddish purple than that of the violets, its colour most probably is of the second order. But yet there being no body commonly known whose colour is constantly more deep than theirs, I have made use of their name to denote the deepest and least reddish purples, such as manifestly transcend their colour in purity.

The *blue* of the first order, though very faint and little, may possibly be the colour of some substances; and particularly the azure colour of the skies seems to be of this order. For all vapours when they begin to condense and coalesce into small parcels become first of that bigness, whereby such an azure must be reflected before they can constitute clouds of other colours. And so, this being the first colour which vapours begin to reflect, it ought to be the colour of the finest and most transparent skies, in which vapours are not arrived to that grossness requisite to reflect other colours, as we find it is by experience.

Whiteness, if most intense and luminous, is that of the first order, if less strong and luminous, a mixture of the colours of several orders. Of this last kind is the whiteness of froth, paper, linen, and most white substances; of the former I reckon that of white metals to be. For whilst the densest of metals, gold, if foliated, is transparent, and all metals become transparent if dissolved in menstruums or vitrified, the opacity of white metals ariseth not from their density alone. They, being less dense than gold, would be more transparent than it, did not some other cause concur with their density to make them opaque. And this cause I take to be such a bigness of their particles as fits them to reflect the white of the first order. For, if they be of other thicknesses, they may reflect other colours, as is manifest by the colours which appear upon hot steel in tempering it, and sometimes upon the surface of melted metals in the skin or scoria which arises upon them in their cooling. And as the white of the first order is the strongest which can be made by plates of transparent substances, so it ought to be stronger in the denser substances of metals than in the rarer of air, water, and glass. Nor do I see but that metallic substances of such a thickness as may fit them to reflect the white of the first order, may, by reason of their great density (according to the tenor of the first of these Propositions) reflect all the light incident upon them, and so be as opaque and splendent as it's possible for any body to be. Gold or copper mixed with less than half their weight of silver, or tin, or regulus of antimony, in fusion, or amalgamed with a very little mercury, become white; which shews both that the particles of white metals have much more superficies, and so are smaller, than those of gold and copper, and also that they are so opaque as not to suffer the particles of gold or copper to shine through them. Now, it is scarce to be doubted but that the colours of gold and copper are of the second and third order; and, therefore, the particles of white metals cannot be much bigger than is requisite to make them reflect the white of the first order. The volatility of mercury argues that they are not much bigger, nor may they be much less, lest they lose their opacity, and become either transparent as they do when attenuated by vitrification, or by solution in menstruums, or black as they do when ground smaller, by rubbing silver, or tin, or lead upon other substances to draw black lines. The first and only colour which white metals take by grinding their particles smaller is black, and therefore their white ought to be that which borders upon the black spot in the centre of the rings of colours; that is, the white of the first order. But, if you would hence gather the bigness of metallic particles, you must allow for their density. For were mercury transparent, its density is such that the sine of incidence upon it (by my computation) would be to the sine of its refraction as 71 to 20, or 7 to 2. And, therefore, the thickness of its particles, that they may exhibit the same colours with those of bubbles of water, ought to be less than the thickness of the skin of those bubbles in the proportion of 2 to 7. Whence it's possible that the particles of mercury may be as little as the particles of some transparent and volatile fluids, and yet reflect the white of the first order.

Lastly, for the production of *black*, the corpuscles must be less than any of those which exhibit colours. For at all greater sizes there is too much light reflected to constitute this colour. But if they be supposed a little less than is requisite to reflect the white and very faint blue of the first order, they will, according to the 4th, 8th, 17th and 18th Observations, reflect so very little light as to appear intensely black, and yet may perhaps variously refract it to and fro within themselves so long, until it happen to be stifled and lost, by which means they will appear black in all positions of the eye without any transparency. And from hence may be understood why fire, and the more subtle dissolver putrefaction, by dividing the particles of substances, turn them to black; why small quantities of black substances impart their colour very freely and intensely to other substances to which they are applied, the minute particles of these, by reason of their very great number, easily over-spreading the gross particles of others; why glass ground very elaborately with sand on a copper plate, till it be well polished, makes the sand, together with what is worn off from the glass and copper, become very black: why black substances do soonest of all others become hot in the Sun's light and burn (which effect may proceed partly from the multitude of refractions in a little room, and partly from the easy commotion of so very small corpuscles;) and why blacks are usually a little inclined to a bluish colour. For that they are so may be seen by illuminating white paper by light reflected from black sub-stances. For the paper will usually appear of a bluish-white; and the reason is that black borders in the obscure blue of the order described in the 18th Obser-vation, and, therefore, reflects more rays of that colour than of any other.

In these descriptions I have been the more particular, because it is not im-possible but that miscroscopes may at length be improved to the discovery of the particles of bodies on which their colours depend, if they are not already in some measure arrived to that degree of perfection. For if those instruments are or can be so far improved as with sufficient distinctness to represent objects five or six hundred times bigger than at a foot distance they appear to our naked eyes, I should hope that we might be able to discover some of the great-est of those corpuscles. And by one that would magnify three or four thousand times perhaps they might all be discovered, but those which produce blackness. In the meanwhile I see nothing material in this discourse that may rationally be doubted of, excepting this position: That transparent corpuscles of the same thickness and density with a plate do exhibit the same colour. And this I would have understood not without some latitude, as well because those corpuscles may be of irregular figures, and many rays must be obliquely incident on them, and so have a shorter way through them than the length of their diameters, as because the straitness of the medium put in on all sides within such corpuscles may a little alter its motions or other qualities on which the reflexion depends. But yet I cannot much suspect the last, because I have observed of some small plates of Muscovy glass, which were of an even thickness, that through a micro-scope they have appeared of the same colour at their edges and corners where the included medium was terminated, which they appeared of in other places. However, it will add much to our satisfaction if those corpuscles can be dis-covered with microscopes; which, if we shall at length attain to, I fear it will be the utmost improvement of this sense. For it seems impossible to see the more secret and noble works of Nature within the corpuscles by reason of their transparency.

PROPOSITION 8

The cause of reflexion is not the impinging of light on the solid or impervious parts of bodies, as is commonly believed.

This will appear by the following considerations: First, that in the passage of light out of glass into air there is a reflexion as strong as in its passage out of air into glass, or rather a little stronger, and by many degrees stronger than in its passage out of glass into water. And it seems not probable that air should have more strongly reflecting parts than water or glass. But if that should possibly be supposed, yet it will avail nothing; for the reflexion is as strong or stronger when the air is drawn away from the glass (suppose by the air-pump invented by Otto Gueriet, and improved and made useful by Mr. Boyle) as when it is adjacent to it. Secondly, if light in its passage out of glass into air be incident more obliquely than at an angle of 40 or 41 degrees it is wholly reflected, if less obliquely it is in great measure transmitted. Now, it is not to be imagined that light at one degree of obliquity should meet with pores enough in the air to transmit the greater part of it, and at another degree of obliquity should meet with nothing but parts to reflect it wholly, especially considering that in its passage out of air into glass, how oblique soever be its incidence, it finds pores enough in the glass to transmit a great part of it. If any man suppose that it is not reflected by the air, but by the outmost superficial parts of the glass, there is still the same difficulty; besides that, such a supposition is unintelligible, and will also appear to be false by applying water behind some part of the glass instead of air. For so in a convenient obliquity of the rays, (suppose of 45 or 46 degrees) at which they are all reflected where the air is adjacent to the glass, they shall be in great measure transmitted where the water is adjacent to it; which argues that their reflexion or transmission depends on the constitution of the air and water behind the glass, and not on the striking of the rays upon the parts of the glass. Thirdly, if the colours made by a prism placed at the entrance of a beam of light into a darkened room be successively cast on a second prism placed at a greater distance from the former, in such manner that they are all alike incident upon it, the second prism may be so inclined to the incident rays that those which are of a blue colour shall be all reflected by it, and yet those of a red colour pretty copiously transmitted. Now, if the reflexion be caused by the parts of air or glass, I would ask why at the same obliquity of incidence the blue should wholly impinge on those parts, so as to be all reflected, and yet the red find pores enough to be in a great measure transmitted. Fourthly, where two glasses touch one another, there is no sensible reflexion, as was declared in the first Observation; and yet I see no reason why the rays should not impinge on the parts of glass, as much when contiguous to other glass as when contiguous to air. Fifthly, when the top of a water-bubble (in the 17th Observation) by the continual subsiding and exhaling of the water grew very thin, there was such a little and almost insensible quantity of light reflected from it that it appeared intensely black; whereas round about that black spot, where the water was thicker, the reflexion was so strong as to make the water seem very white. Nor is it only at the least thickness of thin plates or bubbles that there is no manifest reflexion, but at many other thicknesses continually greater and greater. For in the 15th Observation the rays of the same colour were by turns transmitted at one thickness, and reflected at another thickness, for an indeterminate number of successions. And yet in the superficies of the thinned body, where it is of any one thickness, there are as many parts for the rays to impinge on as where it is of any other thickness. Sixthly, if reflexion were caused by the parts of reflecting bodies, it would be impossible for thin plates or bubbles, at one and the same place, to reflect the rays of one colour, and transmit those of another, as they do according to the 13th and 15th Observations. For it is not to be imagined that at one place the rays which, for instance, exhibit a blue colour, should have the fortune to dash upon the parts, and those which exhibit a red to hit upon the pores of the body; and then at another place, where the body is either a little thicker or a little thinner, that on the contrary the blue should hit upon its pores, and the red upon its parts. Lastly, were the rays of light reflected by impinging on the solid parts of bodies, their reflexions from polished bodies could not be so regular as they are. For in polishing glass with sand, putty, or tripoli, it is not to be imagined that those substances can, by grating and fretting the glass, bring all its least particles to an accurate polish; so that all their surfaces shall be truly plane or truly spherical, and look all the same way, so as together to compose one even surface. The smaller the particles of those substances are, the smaller will be the scratches by which they continually fret and wear away the glass until it be polished; but be they never so small they can wear away the glass no otherwise than by grating and scratching it, and breaking the protuberances; and, therefore, polish it no otherwise than by bringing its roughness to a very fine grain, so that the scratches and frettings of the surface become too small to be visible. And, therefore, if light were reflected by impinging upon the solid parts of the glass, it would be scattered as much by the most polished glass as by the roughest. So, then, it remains a problem how glass polished by fretting substances can reflect light so regularly as it does. And this problem is scarce otherwise to be solved than by saying that the reflexion of a ray is effected, not by a single point of the reflecting body, but by some power of the body which is evenly diffused all over its surface, and by which it acts upon the ray without immediate contact. For that the parts of bodies do act upon light at a distance shall be shewn hereafter.

Now, if light be reflected, not by impinging on the solid parts of bodies but by some other principle, it's probable that as many of its rays as impinge on the solid parts of bodies are not reflected but stifled and lost in the bodies. For otherwise we must allow two sorts of reflexions. Should all the rays be reflected which impinge on the internal parts of clear water or crystal, those substances would rather have a cloudy colour than a clear transparency. To make bodies look black, it's necessary that many rays be stopped, retained, and lost in them; and it seems not probable that any rays can be stopped and stifled in them which do not impinge on their parts.

And hence we may understand that bodies are much more rare and porous than is commonly believed. Water is nineteen times lighter, and by consequence nineteen times rarer, than gold; and gold is so rare as very readily and without the least opposition to transmit the magnetic effluvia, and easily to admit quick-silver into its pores, and to let water pass through it. For a concave sphere of gold filled with water, and soldered up, has, upon pressing the sphere with great force, let the water squeeze through it, and stand all over its outside in multitudes of small drops, like dew, without bursting or cracking the body of the gold, as I have been informed by an eye-witness. From all which we may conclude that gold has more pores than solid parts, and by consequence that water has above forty times more pores than parts. And he that shall find out an hypothesis by which water may be so rare, and yet not be capable of compression by force, may doubtless by the same hypothesis make gold, and water, and all other bodies, as much rarer as he pleases; so that light may find a ready passage through transparent substances.

The magnet acts upon iron through all dense bodies not magnetic nor red hot, without any diminution of its virtue; as for instance, through gold, silver, lead, glass, water. The gravitating power of the Sun is transmitted through the vast bodies of the planets without any diminution, so as to act upon all their parts to their very centres with the same force and according to the same laws, as if the part upon which it acts were not surrounded with the body of the planet. The rays of light, whether they be very small bodies projected, or only motion or force propagated, are moved in right lines; and whenever a ray of light is by any obstacle turned out of its rectilinear way, it will never return into the same rectilinear way, unless perhaps by very great accident. And yet light is transmitted through pellucid solid bodies in right lines to very great distances. How bodies can have a sufficient quantity of pores for producing these effects is very difficult to conceive, but perhaps not altogether impossible. For the colours of bodies arise from the magnitudes of the particles which reflect them, as was explained above. Now, if we conceive these particles of bodies to be so disposed amongst themselves that the intervals or empty spaces between them may be equal in magnitude to them all; and that these particles may be composed of other particles much smaller, which have as much empty space between them as equals all the magnitudes of these smaller particles; and that in like manner these smaller particles are again composed of others much smaller, all which together are equal to all the pores or empty spaces between them; and so on perpetually till you come to solid particles, such as have no pores or empty spaces within them; and if in any gross body there be, for instance, three such degrees of particles, the least of which are solid, this body will have seven times more pores than solid parts. But if there be four such degrees of particles, the least of which are solid, the body will have fifteen times more pores than solid parts. If there be five degrees, the body will have one and thirty times more pores than solid parts. If six degrees, the body will have sixty and three times more pores than solid parts. And so on perpetually. And there are other ways of conceiving how bodies may be exceeding porous. But what is really their inward frame is not yet known to us.

PROPOSITION 9

Bodies reflect and refract light by one and the same power, variously exercised in various circumstances.

This appears by several considerations. First, because when light goes out of glass into air, as obliquely as it can possibly do, if its incidence be made still more oblique, it becomes totally reflected. For the power of the glass after it has refracted the light as obliquely as is possible, if the incidence be still made more oblique, becomes too strong to let any of its rays go through, and by consequence causes total reflexions. Secondly, because light is alternately reflected and transmitted by thin plates of glass for many successions, accordingly as the thickness of the plate increases in an arithmetical progression. For here the thickness of the glass determines whether that power by which glass acts upon light shall cause it to be reflected, or suffer it to be transmitted. And, thirdly, because those surfaces of transparent bodies which have the greatest refracting power reflect the greatest quantity of light, as was shewn in the first Proposition.

PROPOSITION 10

If light be swifter in bodies than in vacuo, in the proportion of the sines which measure the refraction of the bodies the forces of the bodies to reflect and refract light are very nearly proportional to the densities of the same bodies; excepting that unctuous and sulphureous bodies refract more than others of this same density.

Let AB represent the refracting plane surface of any body, and IC a ray incident very obliquely upon the body in C, so that the angle ACI may be infinitely little, and let CR be the refracted ray. From a given point B perpendicular to the refracting surface erect BR meeting with the refracting ray CR in R, and if CR represent the motion of the refracted ray, and this motion be distinguished into two motions CB and BR, whereof CB is parallel to the refracting plane, and BR perpendicular to it: CB shall represent the motion of the incident ray, and BR the motion generated by the refraction, as opticians have of late explained.

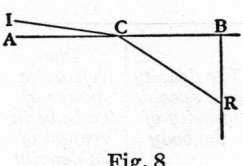

Fig. 8

Now, if any body or thing, in moving through any space of a given breadth terminated on both sides by two parallel planes, be urged forward in all parts of that space by forces tending directly forwards towards the last plane, and, before its incidence on the first plane, had no motion towards it, or but an infinitely little one; and if the forces in all parts of that space, between the planes, be at equal distances from the planes equal to one another, but at several distances be bigger or less in any given proportion, the motion generated by the forces in the whole passage of the body or thing through that space shall be in a subduplicate proportion of the forces, as mathematicians will easily understand. And, therefore, if the space of activity of the refracting superficies of the body be considered as such a space, the motion of the ray generated by the refracting force of the body, during its passage through that space (that is, the motion BR) must be in subduplicate proportion of that refracting force. I say, therefore, that the square of the line BR, and by consequence the refracting force of the body, is very nearly as the density of the same body. For this will appear by the following Table, wherein the proportion of the sines which measure the refractions of several bodies, the square of BR, supposing CB an unit, the densities of the bodies estimated by their specific gravities, and their refractive power in respect of their densities are set down in several columns.

The refraction of the air in this Table is determined by that of the atmosphere observed by astronomers. For, if light pass through many refracting substances or mediums gradually denser and denser, and terminated with parallel surfaces, the sum of all the refractions will be equal to the single refraction which it would have suffered in passing immediately out of the first medium into the last. And this holds true, though the number of the refracting substances be increased to infinity, and the distances from one another as much decreased, so that the light may be refracted in every point of its passage, and by continual refractions bent into a curve-line. And, therefore, the whole refraction of light, in passing through the atmosphere from the highest and rarest part thereof down to the lowest and densest part, must be equal to the refraction which it would suffer in passing at like obliquity out of a vacuum immediately into air of equal density with that in the lowest part of the atmosphere.

Now, although a pseudo-topaz, a selenitis, rock crystal, island crystal, vulgar glass (that is, sand melted together) and glass of antimony, which are terrestrial stony alkalizate concretes, and air which probably arises from such substances by fermentation, be substances very differing from one another in density, yet by this Table, they have their refractive powers almost in the same proportion to one another as their densities are, excepting that the refraction of that strange substance, island crystal, is a little bigger than the rest. And particularly air, which is 3,500 times rarer than the pseudo-topaz, and 4,400 times rarer than glass of antimony, and 2,000 times rarer than the selenitis, glass vulgar, or crystal of the rock, has notwithstanding its rarity the same refractive

The refracting bodies	The proportion of the sines of incidence and refraction of yellow light	The square of BR, to which the refracting force of the body is proportionate	The density and specific gravity of the body	The refractive power of the body in respect of its density
A pseudo-topazius, being a natural, pellucid, brittle, hairy stone, of a yellow colour....	23 to 14	1.699	4.27	3979
Air.....................	3201 to 3200	0.000625	0.0012	5208
Glass of antimony.........	17 to 9	2.568	5.28	4864
A selenitis...............	61 to 41	1.213	2.252	5386
Glass vulgar.............	31 to 20	1.4025	2.58	5436
Crystal of the rock........	25 to 16	1.445	2.65	5450
Island crystal............	5 to 3	1.778	2.72	6536
Sal gemmæ...............	17 to 11	1.388	2.143	6477
Alum....................	35 to 24	1.1267	1.714	6570
Borax...................	22 to 15	1.1511	1.714	6716
Nitre....................	32 to 21	1.345	1.9	7079
Danzig vitriol............	303 to 200	1.295	1.715	7551
Oil of vitriol.............	10 to 7	1.041	1.7	6124
Rain water...............	529 to 396	0.7845	1.	7845
Gum arabic..............	31 to 21	1.179	1.375	8574
Spirit of wine well rectified..	100 to 73	0.8765	0.866	10121
Camphor.................	3 to 2	1.25	0.996	12551
Olive oil.................	22 to 15	1.1511	0.913	12607
Linseed oil..............	40 to 27	1.1948	0.932	12819
Spirit of turpentine.......	25 to 17	1.1626	0.874	13222
Amber...................	14 to 9	1.42	1.04	13654
A diamond...............	100 to 41	4.949	3.4	14556

power in respect of its density which those very dense substances have in respect of theirs, excepting so far as those differ from one another.

Again, the refraction of camphor, olive oil, linseed oil, spirit of turpentine and amber, which are fat sulphureous unctuous bodies, and a diamond, which probably is an unctuous substance coagulated, have their refractive powers in proportion to one another as their densities without any considerable variation. But the refractive powers of these unctuous substances are two or three times greater in respect of their densities than the refractive powers of the former substances in respect of theirs.

Water has a refractive power in a middle degree between those two sorts of substances, and probably is of a middle nature. For out of it grow all vegetable and animal substances, which consist as well of sulphureous fat and inflammable parts, as of earthy lean and alkalizate ones.

Salts and vitriols have refractive powers in a middle degree between those of earthy substances and water, and accordingly are composed of those two sorts of substances. For by distillation and rectification of their spirits a great part of them goes into water, and a great part remains behind in the form of a dry fixed earth capable of vitrification.

Spirit of wine has a refractive power in a middle degree between those of water and oily substances, and accordingly seems to be composed of both, united by fermentation; the water, by means of some saline spirits with which 'tis impregnated, dissolving the oil, and volatizing it by the action. For spirit of wine is inflammable by means of its oily parts, and being distilled often from salt of tartar, grows by every distillation more and more aqueous and phlegmatic. And chemists observe that vegetables (as lavender, rue, marjoram, &c.) distilled per se, before fermentation yield oils without any burning spirits, but after fermentation yield ardent spirits without oils; which shews that their oil is by fermentation converted into spirit. They find also that if oils be poured in a small quantity upon fermentating vegetables, they distil over after fermentation in the form of spirits.

So then, by the foregoing Table, all bodies seem to have their refractive powers proportional to their densities (or very nearly); excepting so far as they partake more or less of sulphureous oily particles, and thereby have their refractive power made greater or less. Whence it seems rational to attribute the refractive power of all bodies chiefly, if not wholly, to the sulphureous parts with which they abound. For it's probable that all bodies abound more or less with sulphurs. And as light congregated by a burning-glass acts most upon sulphureous bodies, to turn them into fire and flame, so, since all action is mutual, sulphurs ought to act most upon light. For that the action between light and bodies is mutual may appear from this consideration: that the densest bodies which refract and reflect light most strongly grow hottest in the summer Sun, by the action of the refracted or reflected light.

I have hitherto explained the power of bodies to reflect and refract, and shewed that thin transparent plates, fibres, and particles do, according to their several thicknesses and densities, reflect several sorts of rays, and thereby appear of several colours; and by consequence that nothing more is requisite for producing all the colours of natural bodies than the several sizes and densities of their transparent particles. But whence it is that these plates, fibres, and particles do, according to their several thicknesses and densities, reflect several sorts of rays, I have not yet explained. To give some insight into this matter, and make way for understanding the next part of this book, I shall conclude this part with a few more Propositions. Those which preceded respect the nature of bodies, these the nature of light; for both must be understood before the reason of their actions upon one another can be known. And because the last Proposition depended upon the velocity of light, I will begin with a Proposition of that kind.

Proposition 11

Light is propagated from luminous bodies in time, and spends about seven or eight minutes of an hour in passing from the Sun to the Earth.

This was observed first by Römer, and then by others, by means of the eclipses of the satellites of Jupiter. For these eclipses, when the Earth is between the Sun and Jupiter, happen about seven or eight minutes sooner than they ought to do by the Tables, and when the Earth is beyond the Sun they happen about seven or eight minutes later than they ought to do; the reason being that the light of the satellites has farther to go in the latter case than in the former by the diameter of the Earth's orbit. Some inequalities of time may arise from the eccentricities of the orbs of the satellites; but those cannot answer in all the satellites, and at all times to the position and distance of the Earth from the Sun. The mean motions of Jupiter's satellites is also swifter in his descent from his aphelium to his perihelium, than in his ascent in the other half of his orb. But this inequality has no respect to the position of the Earth, and in the three interior satellites is insensible, as I find by computation from the theory of their gravity.

PROPOSITION 12

Every ray of light in its passage through any refracting surface is put into a certain transient constitution or state, which in the progress of the ray returns at equal intervals, and disposes the ray at every return to be easily transmitted through the next refracting surface, and between the returns to be easily reflected by it.

This is manifest by the 5th, 9th, 12th, and 15th Observations. For by those Observations it appears that one and the same sort of rays at equal angles of incidence on any thin transparent plate, is alternately reflected and transmitted for many successions accordingly as the thickness of the plate increases in arithmetical progression of the numbers, 0, 1, 2, 3, 4, 5, 6, 7, 8, &c. so that if the first reflexion (that which makes the first or innermost of the rings of colours there described) be made at the thickness 1, the rays shall be transmitted at the thicknesses 0, 2, 4, 6, 8, 10, 12, &c. and thereby make the central spot and rings of light, which appear by transmission, and be reflected at the thickness 1, 3, 5, 7, 9, 11, &c. and thereby make the rings which appear by reflexion. And this alternate reflexion and transmission, as I gather by the 24th Observation, continues for above a hundred vicissitudes, and by the Observations in the next part of this book, for many thousands, being propagated from one surface of a glass plate to the other, though the thickness of the plate be a quarter of an inch or above; so that this alternation seems to be propagated from every refracting surface to all distances without end or limitation.

This alternate reflexion and refraction depends on both the surfaces of every thin plate, because it depends on their distance. By the 21st Observation, if either surface of a thin plate of Muscovy glass be wetted, the colours caused by the alternate reflexion and refraction grow faint; and, therefore, it depends on them both.

It is therefore performed at the second surface; for if it were performed at the first, before the rays arrive at the second, it would not depend on the second.

It is also influenced by some action or disposition propagated from the first to the second, because otherwise at the second it would not depend on the first. And this action or disposition, in its propagation, intermits and returns by equal intervals, because in all its progress it inclines the ray at one distance from the first surface to be reflected by the second, at another to be transmitted by it, and that by equal intervals for innumerable vicissitudes. And because the ray is disposed to reflexion at the distances 1, 3, 5, 7, 9, &c. and to transmission at the distances 0, 2, 4, 6, 8, 10, &c. (for its transmission through the first surface is at the distance 0, and it is transmitted through both together, if their distance be infinitely little or much less than 1) the disposition to be transmitted at the distances 2, 4, 6, 8, 10, &c. is to be accounted a return of the same disposition which the ray first had at the distance 0; that is, at its transmission through the first refracting surface. All which is the thing I would prove.

What kind of action or disposition this is; whether it consists in a circulating or a vibrating motion of the ray, or of the medium, or something else, I do not here enquire. Those that are averse from assenting to any new discoveries, but such as they can explain by an hypothesis, may for the present suppose that as stones by falling upon water put the water into an undulating motion, and all bodies by percussion excite vibrations in the air, so the rays of light, by impinging on any refracting or reflecting surface, excite vibrations in the refracting or reflecting medium or substance, and by exciting them agitate the solid parts of the refracting or reflecting body, and by agitating them cause the body to grow warm or hot; that the vibrations thus excited are propagated in the refracting or reflecting medium or substance, much after the manner that vibrations are propagated in the air for causing sound, and move faster than the rays so as to overtake them; and that when any ray is in that part of the vibration which conspires with its motion, it easily breaks through a refracting surface, but when it is in the contrary part of the vibration which impedes its motion it is easily reflected; and, by consequence, that every ray is successively disposed to be easily reflected, or easily transmitted, by every vibration which overtakes it. But whether this hypothesis be true or false I do not here consider. I content myself with the bare discovery that the rays of light are, by some cause or other, alternately disposed to be reflected or refracted for many vicissitudes.

DEFINITION

The returns of the disposition of any ray to be reflected I will call its fits of easy reflexion, and those of its disposition to be transmitted its fits of easy transmisson, and the space it passes between every return and the next return, the interval of its fits.

PROPOSITION 13

The reason why the surfaces of all thick transparent bodies reflect part of the light incident on them, and refract the rest, is that some rays at their incidence are in fits of easy reflexion, and others in fits of easy transmission.

This may be gathered from the 24th Observation, where the light reflected by thin plates of air and glass, which to the naked eye appeared evenly white all over the plate, did through a prism appear waved with many successions of light and darkness made by alternate fits of easy reflexion and easy transmission, the prism severing and distinguishing the waves of which the white reflected light was composed, as was explained above.

And hence light is in fits of easy reflexion and easy transmission before its incidence on transparent bodies. And probably it is put into such fits at its first emission from luminous bodies, and continues in them during all its progress. For these fits are of a lasting nature, as will appear by the next part of this book.

In this Proposition I suppose the transparent bodies to be thick; because if the thickness of the body be much less than the interval of the fits of easy reflexion and transmission of the rays, the body loseth its reflecting power. For if the rays, which at their entering into the body are put into fits of easy transmission, arrive at the farthest surface of the body before they be out of those fits, they must be transmitted. And this is the reason why bubbles of water lose their reflecting power when they grow very thin; and why all opaque bodies, when reduced into very small parts, become transparent.

PROPOSITION 14

Those surfaces of transparent bodies, which if the ray be in a fit of refraction do refract it most strongly, if the ray be in a fit of reflexion do reflect it most easily.

For we shewed above, in Prop. 8, that the cause of reflexion is not the impinging of light on the solid impervious parts of bodies, but some other power by which those solid parts act on light at a distance. We shewed also, in Prop. 9, that bodies reflect and refract light by one and the same power, variously exercised in various circumstances; and in Prop. 1 that the most strongly refracting surfaces reflect the most light. All which compared together evince and rarify both this and the last Proposition.

PROPOSITION 15

In any one and the same sort of rays, emerging in any angle out of any refracting surface into one and the same medium, the interval of the following fits of easy reflexion and transmission are either accurately or very nearly as the rectangle of the secant of the angle of refraction, and of the secant of another angle, whose sine is the first of 106 arithmetical mean proportionals, between the sines of incidence and refraction, counted from the sine of refraction.

This is manifest by the 7th and 19th Observations.

PROPOSITION 16

In several sorts of rays emerging in equal angles out of any refracting surface into the same medium, the intervals of the following fits of easy reflexion and easy transmission are either accurately, or very nearly, as the cube roots of the squares of the lengths of a chord, which found the notes in an eight, sol, la, fa, sol, la, mi, fa, sol, with all their intermediate degrees answering to the colours of those rays, according to the analogy described in the seventh experiment of the second part of the first book.

This is manifest by the 13th and 14th Observations.

PROPOSITION 17

If rays of any sort pass perpendicularly into several mediums, the intervals of the fits of easy reflexion and transmission in any one medium are to those intervals in any other, as the sine of incidence to the sine of refraction, when the rays pass out of the first of those two mediums into the second.

This is manifest by the 10th Observation.

PROPOSITION 18

If the rays which paint the colour in the confine of yellow and orange pass perpendicularly out of any medium into air, the intervals of their fits of easy reflexion are the $\frac{1}{89,000}$th part of an inch. And of the same length are the intervals of their fits of easy transmission.

This is manifest by the 6th Observation.

From these Propositions it is easy to collect the intervals of the fits of easy reflexion and easy transmission of any sort of rays refracted in any angle into any medium; and thence to know whether the rays shall be reflected or transmitted at their subsequent incidence upon any other pellucid medium. Which thing, being useful for understanding the next part of this book, was here to be set down. And for the same reason I add the two following Propositions.

PROPOSITION 19

If any sort of rays falling on the polite surface of any pellucid medium be reflected back, the fits of easy reflexion, which they have at the point of reflexion, shall still continue to return; and the returns shall be at distances from the point of reflexion in the arithmetical progression of the numbers 2, 4, 6, 8, 10, 12, &c. and between these fits the rays shall be in fits of easy transmission.

For since the fits of easy reflexion and easy transmission are of a returning nature, there is no reason why these fits, which continued till the ray arrived at the reflecting medium and there inclined the ray to reflexion, should there cease. And if the ray at the point of reflexion was in a fit of easy reflexion, the progression of the distances of these fits from that point must begin from 0, and so be of the numbers 0, 2, 4, 6, 8, &c. And, therefore, the progression of the distances of the intermediate fits of easy transmission, reckoned from the same point, must be in the progression of the odd numbers 1, 3, 5, 7, 9, &c. contrary to what happens when the fits are propagated from points of refraction.

PROPOSITION 20

The intervals of the fits of easy reflexion and easy transmission, propagated from points of reflexion into any medium, are equal to the intervals of the like fits which the same rays would have if refracted into the same medium in angles of refraction equal to their angles of reflexion.

For when light is reflected by the second surface of thin plates, it goes out afterwards freely at the first surface to make the rings of colours which appear by reflexion; and, by the freedom of its egress, makes the colours of these rings more vivid and strong than those which appear on the other side of the plates by the transmitted light. The reflected rays are, therefore, in fits of easy transmission at their egress; which would not always happen if the intervals of the fits within the plate after reflexion were not equal, both in length and number, to their intervals before it. And this confirms also the proportions set down in the former Proposition. For if the rays both in going in and out at the first surface be in fits of easy transmission, and the intervals and numbers of those fits between the first and second surface, before and after reflexion, be equal, the distances of the fits of easy transmission from either surface must be in the same progression after reflexion as before; that is, from the first surface which transmitted them in the progression of the even numbers 0, 2, 4, 6, 8, &c. and from the second which reflected them, in that of the odd numbers 1, 3, 5, 7, &c. But these two Propositions will become much more evident by the Observations in the following part of this book.

Part IV

Observations concerning the reflexions and colours of thick transparent polished plates.

THERE is no glass or speculum how well soever polished but, besides the light which it refracts or reflects regularly, scatters every way irregularly a faint light, by means of which the polished surface, when illuminated in a dark room by a beam of the Sun's light, may be easily seen in all positions of the eye. There are certain phenomena of this scattered light, which when I first observed them, seemed very strange and surprising to me. My Observations were as follows.

OBS. 1. The Sun shining into my darkened chamber through a hole one-third of an inch wide, I let the intromitted beam of light fall perpendicularly upon a glass speculum ground concave on one side and convex on the other, to a sphere of five feet and eleven inches radius, and quick-silvered over on the convex side. And holding a white opaque chart or a quire of paper at the centre of the spheres to which the speculum was ground (that is, at the distance of about five feet and eleven inches from the speculum, in such manner that the beam of light might pass through a little hole made in the middle of the chart to the speculum, and thence be reflected back to the same hole) I observed upon the chart four or five concentric irises or rings of colours, like rainbows, encompassing the hole much after the manner that those, which in the fourth and following Observations of the first part of this book appeared between the object-glasses, encompassed the black spot, but yet larger and fainter than those. These rings as they grew larger and larger became diluter and fainter, so that the fifth was scarce visible. Yet sometimes, when the Sun shone very clear, there appeared faint lineaments of a sixth and seventh. If the distance of the chart from the speculum was much greater or much less than that of six feet, the rings became dilute and vanished. And if the distance of the speculum from the window was much greater than that of six feet, the reflected beam of light would be so broad, at the distance of six feet from the speculum where the rings appeared, as to obscure one or two of the innermost rings. And, therefore, I usually placed the speculum at about six feet from the window, so that its focus might there fall in with the centre of its concavity at the rings upon the chart. And this posture is always to be understood in the following Observations where no other is expressed.

OBS. 2. The colours of these rainbows succeeded one another from the centre outwards, in the same form and order with those which were made in the ninth Observation of the first part of this book, by light not reflected but transmitted through the two object-glasses. For, first, there was in their common centre a white round spot of faint light, something broader than the reflected beam of light, which beam sometimes fell upon the middle of the spot, and sometimes by a little inclination of the speculum receded from the middle, and left the spot white to the centre.

This white spot was immediately encompassed with a dark grey or russet, and that dark grey with the colours of the first iris; which colours on the inside next the dark grey were a little violet and indigo, and next to that a blue, which on the outside grew pale, and then succeeded a little greenish yellow, and after that a brighter yellow, and then on the outward edge of the iris a red which on the outside inclined to purple.

This iris was immediately encompassed with a second, whose colours were, in order from the inside outwards: purple, blue, green, yellow, light red, a red mixed with purple.

Then immediately followed the colours of the third iris, which were in order outwards a green inclining to purple, a good green, and a red more bright than that of the former iris.

The fourth and fifth iris seemed of a bluish-green within, and red without, but so faintly that it was difficult to discern the colours.

OBS. 3. Measuring the diameters of these rings upon the chart as accurately as I could, I found them also in the same proportion to one another with the rings made by light transmitted through the two object-glasses. For the diameters of the four first of the bright rings measured between the brightest parts of their orbits, at the distance of six feet from the speculum, were $1^{11}/_{16}$, $2\frac{3}{8}$, $2^{11}/_{12}$, $3\frac{3}{8}$ inches, whose squares are in arithmetical progression of the numbers 1, 2, 3, 4. If the white circular spot in the middle be reckoned amongst the rings, and its central light, where it seems to be most luminous, be put equipollent to an infinitely little ring, the squares of the diameters of the rings will be in the progression 0, 1, 2, 3, 4, &c. I measured also the diameters of the dark circles between these luminous ones, and found their squares in the progression of the numbers $\frac{1}{2}$, $1\frac{1}{2}$, $2\frac{1}{2}$, $3\frac{1}{2}$, &c. the diameters of the first four, at the distance of six feet from the speculum, being $1^{3}/_{16}$, $2^{1}/_{16}$, $2\frac{2}{3}$, $3^{3}/_{20}$ inches. If the distance of the chart from the speculum was increased or diminished, the diameters of the circles were increased or diminished proportionally.

OBS. 4. By the analogy between these rings and those described in the Observations of the first part of this book, I suspected that there were many more of them which spread into one another, and by interfering mixed their colours, and diluted one another so that they could not be seen apart. I viewed them, therefore, through a prism, as I did those in the 24th Observation of the first part of this book. And when the prism was so placed as by refracting the light of their mixed colours to separate them, and distinguish the rings from one another, as it did those in that Observation, I could then see them distincter than before, and easily number eight or nine of them, and sometimes twelve or thirteen. And had not their light been so very faint, I question not but that I might have seen many more.

OBS. 5. Placing a prism at the window to refract the intromitted beam of light, and cast the oblong spectrum of colours on the speculum, I covered the speculum with a black paper which had in the middle of it a hole to let any one of the colours pass through to the speculum, whilst the rest were intercepted by the paper. And now I found rings of that colour only which fell upon the speculum. If the speculum was illuminated with red, the rings were totally red with dark intervals; if with blue they were totally blue; and so of the other colours. And when they were illuminated with any one colour, the squares of their diameters, measured between their most luminous parts, were in the arithmetical progression of the numbers, 0, 1, 2, 3, 4 and the squares of the diameters of their dark intervals in the progression of the intermediate numbers

$\frac{1}{2}$, $1\frac{1}{2}$, $2\frac{1}{2}$, $3\frac{1}{2}$. But if the colour was varied, they varied their magnitude. In the red they were largest, in the indigo and violet least, and in the intermediate colours (yellow, green, and blue) they were of several intermediate bignesses answering to the colour; that is, greater in yellow than in green, and greater in green than in blue. And hence I knew that when the speculum was illuminated with white light, the red and yellow on the outside of the rings were produced by the least refrangible rays, and the blue and violet by the most refrangible, and that the colours of each ring spread into the colours of the neighbouring rings on either side, after the manner explained in the first and second parts of this book, and by mixing diluted one another so that they could not be distinguished, unless near the centre where they were least mixed. For in this Observation I could see the rings more distinctly, and to a greater number than before, being able in the yellow light to number eight or nine of them, besides a faint shadow of a tenth. To satisfy myself how much the colours of the several rings spread into one another, I measured the diameters of the second and third rings, and found them, when made by the confine of the red and orange, to be to the same diameters when made by the confine of blue and indigo, as 9 to 8, or thereabouts. For it was hard to determine this proportion accurately. Also the circles made successively by the red, yellow, and green differed more from one another than those made successively by the green, blue and indigo. For the circle made by the violet was too dark to be seen. To carry on the computation, let us therefore suppose that the differences of the diameters of circles made by the outmost red, the confine of red and orange, the confine of orange and yellow, the confine of yellow and green, the confine of green and blue, the confine of blue and indigo, the confine of indigo and violet, and outmost violet, are in proportion as the differences of the lengths of a monochord which sound the tones in an eight: *sol, la, fa, sol, la, mi, fa, sol;* that is, as the numbers $\frac{1}{9}$, $\frac{1}{18}$, $\frac{1}{12}$, $\frac{1}{12}$, $\frac{2}{27}$, $\frac{1}{27}$, $\frac{1}{18}$. And if the diameter of the circle made by the confine of red and orange be 9A, and that of the circle made by the confine of blue and indigo be 8A as above, their difference (9A−8A) will be to the difference of the diameters of the circles made by the outmost red, and by the confine of red and orange, as $\frac{1}{18}+\frac{1}{12}+\frac{1}{12}+\frac{2}{27}$ to $\frac{1}{9}$ (that is, as $\frac{8}{27}$ to $\frac{1}{9}$, or 8 to 3) and to the difference of the circles made by the outmost violet, and by the confine of blue and indigo, as $\frac{1}{18}+\frac{1}{12}+\frac{1}{12}+\frac{2}{27}$ to $\frac{1}{27}+\frac{1}{18}$ (that is, as $\frac{8}{27}$ to $\frac{5}{54}$, or as 16 to 5). And, therefore, these differences will be $\frac{3}{8}$A and $\frac{5}{16}$A. Add the first to 9A and subduct the last from 8A, and you will have the diameters of the circles made by the least and most refrangible rays $^{75}\!/_8$A and $^{61\frac{1}{2}}\!/_8$A. These diameters are, therefore, to one another as 75 to $61\frac{1}{2}$ or 50 to 41, and their squares as 2,500 to 1,681; that is, as 3 to 2 very nearly. Which proportion differs not much from the proportion of the diameters of the circles made by the outmost red and outmost violet, in the 13th Observation of the first part of this book.

Obs. 6. Placing my eye where these rings appeared plainest, I saw the speculum tinged all over with waves of colours (red, yellow, green, blue) like those which in the Observations of the first part of this book appeared between the object-glasses, and upon bubbles of water, but much larger. And after the manner of those, they were of various magnitudes in various positions of the eye, swelling and shrinking as I moved my eye this way and that way. They were formed like arcs of concentric circles, as those were; and when my eye was over against the centre of the concavity of the speculum, (that is, 5 feet and 10 inches distant from the speculum) their common centre was in a right line with that centre of concavity, and with the hole in the window. But in other postures of my eye their centre had other positions. They appeared by the light of the clouds propagated to the speculum through the hole in the window; and when the Sun shone through that hole upon the speculum, his light upon it was of the colour of the ring whereon it fell, but by its splendor obscured the rings made by the light of the clouds, unless when the speculum was removed to a great distance from the window so that his light upon it might be broad and faint. By varying the position of my eye, and moving it nearer to or farther from the direct beam of the Sun's light, the colour of the Sun's reflected light constantly varied upon the speculum, as it did upon my eye, the same colour always appearing to a bystander upon my eye which to me appeared upon the speculum. And thence I knew that the rings of colours upon the chart were made by these reflected colours, propagated thither from the speculum in several angles, and that their production depended not upon the termination of light and shadow.

Obs. 7. By the analogy of all these phenomena with those of the like rings of colours described in the first part of this book, it seemed to me that these colours were produced by this thick plate of glass, much after the manner that those were produced by very thin plates. For, upon trial, I found that if the quick-silver were rubbed off from the backside of the speculum, the glass alone would cause the same rings of colours, but much more faint than before; and, therefore, the phenomenon depends not upon the quick-silver, unless so far as the quick-silver, by increasing the reflexion of the backside of the glass, in-creases the light of the rings of colours. I found also that a speculum of metal without glass made some years since for optical uses, and very well wrought, produced none of those rings; and thence I understood that these rings arise not from one specular surface alone, but depend upon the two surfaces of the plate of glass whereof the speculum was made, and upon the thickness of the glass between them. For as in the 7th and 19th Observations of the first part of this book a thin plate of air, water, or glass of an even thickness appeared of one colour when the rays were perpendicular to it, of another when they were a little oblique, of another when more oblique, of another when still more oblique, and so on; so here, in the sixth Observation, the light which emerged out of the glass in several obliquities made the glass appear of several colours, and being propagated in those obliquities to the chart, there painted rings of those colours. And as the reason why a thin plate appeared of several colours in several obliquities of the rays was that the rays of one and the same sort are reflected by the thin plate at one obliquity and transmitted at another, and those of other sorts transmitted where these are reflected, and reflected where these are transmitted; so the reason why the thick plate of glass whereof the speculum was made did appear of various colours in various obliquities, and in those obliquities propagated those colours to the chart, was that the rays of one and the same sort did at one obliquity emerge out of the glass, at another did not emerge, but were reflected back towards the quick-silver by the hither surface of the glass, and accordingly as the obliquity became greater and greater, emerged and were reflected alternately for many successions; and that in one and the same obliquity the rays of one sort were reflected, and those of another transmitted. This is manifest by the fifth Observation of this part of this book. For in that Observation, when the speculum was illuminated by any one of the prismatic colours, that light made many rings of the same colour upon the chart with dark intervals, and, therefore, at its emergence out of the speculum was alternately transmitted and not transmitted from the speculum to the chart for many successions, according to the various obliquities of its emergence. And when the colour cast on the speculum by the prism was varied, the rings became of the colour cast on it, and varied their bigness with their colour; and, therefore, the light was now alternately transmitted and not transmitted from the speculum to the chart at other obliquities than before. It seemed to me, therefore, that these rings were of one and the same original with those of thin plates, but yet with this difference: that those of thin plates are made by the alternate reflexions and transmissions of the rays at the second surface of the plate, after one passage through it; but here the rays go twice through the plate before they are alternately reflected and transmitted. First, they go through it from the first surface to the quick-silver, and then return through it from the quick-silver to the first surface, and there are either transmitted to the chart or reflected back to the quick-silver, accordingly as they are in their fits of easy reflexion or transmission when they arrive at that surface. For the intervals of the fits of the rays which fall perpendicularly on the speculum, and are reflected back in the same perpendicular lines, by reason of the equality of these angles and lines, are of the same length and number within the glass after reflexion as before, by the 19th Proposition of the third part of this book. And, therefore, since all the rays that enter through the first surface are in their fits of easy transmission at their entrance, and as many of these as are reflected by the second are in their fits of easy reflexion there, all these must be again in their fits of easy transmission at their return to the first, and by consequence there go out of the glass to the chart, and form upon it the white spot of light in the centre of the rings. For the reason holds good in all sorts of rays, and, therefore, all sorts must go out promiscuously to that spot, and by their mixture cause it to be white. But the intervals of the fits of those rays which are reflected more obliquely than they enter, must be greater after reflexion than before, by the 15th and 20th Propositions. And thence it may happen that the rays at their return to the first surface may in certain obliquities be in fits of easy reflexion, and return back to the quick-silver, and in other intermediate obliquities be again in fits of easy transmission, and so go out to the chart, and paint on it the rings of colours about the white spot. And because the intervals of the fits at equal obliquities are greater and fewer in the less refrangible rays, and less and more numerous in the more refrangible, therefore the less refrangible at equal obliquities shall make fewer rings than the more refrangible, and the rings made by those shall be larger than the like number of rings made by these; that is, the red rings shall be larger than the yellow, the yellow than the green, the green than the blue, and the blue than the violet, as they were really found to be in the fifth Observation. And, therefore, the first ring of all colours encompassing the white spot of light shall be red without any violet within, and yellow, and green, and blue in the middle, as it was found in the second Observation; and these colours in the second ring, and those that follow, shall be more expanded, till they spread into one another, and blend one another by interfering.

These seem to be the reasons of these rings in general; and this put me upon observing the thickness of the glass, and considering whether the dimensions and proportions of the rings may be truly derived from it by computation.

Obs. 8. I measured, therefore, the thickness of this concavo-convex plate of glass, and found it everywhere one-quarter of an inch precisely. Now, by the sixth Observation of the first part of this book, a thin plate of air transmits the brightest light of the first ring (that is, the bright yellow) when its thickness is the $\frac{1}{89.000}$th part of an inch; and by the tenth Observation of the same part, a thin plate of glass transmits the same light of the same ring when its thickness is less in proportion of the sine of refraction to the sine of incidence (that is, when its thickness is the $\frac{11}{1.513.000}$th or $\frac{1}{137.545}$th part of an inch, supposing the sines are as 11 to 17). And if this thickness be doubled, it transmits the same bright light of the second ring; if tripled, it transmits that of the third, and so on; the bright yellow light in all these cases being in its fits of transmission. And, therefore, if its thickness be multiplied 34,386 times, so as to become one-quarter of an inch, it transmits the same bright light of the 34,386th ring. Suppose this be the bright yellow light transmitted perpendicularly from the reflecting convex side of the glass through the concave side to the white spot in the centre of the rings of colours on the chart; and by a rule in the 7th and 19th Observations in the first part of this book, and by the 15th and 20th Propositions of the third part of this book, if the rays be made oblique to the glass, the thickness of the glass requisite to transmit the same bright light of the same ring in any obliquity is to this thickness of one-quarter of an inch, as the secant of a certain angle to the radius, the sine of which angle is the first of a hundred and six arithmetical means between the sines of incidence and refraction, counted from the sine of incidence when the refraction is made out of any plated body into any medium encompassing it; that is, in this case, out of glass into air. Now, if the thickness of the glass be increased by degrees, so as to bear to its first thickness (viz., that of a quarter of an inch), the proportions which 34,386 (the number of fits of the perpendicular rays in going through the glass towards the white spot in the centre of the rings) hath to 34,385, 34,384, 34,383, and 34,382 (the numbers of the fits of the oblique rays in going through the glass towards the first, second, third, and fourth rings of colours); and if the first thickness be divided into 100,000,000 equal parts, the increased thicknesses will be 100,002,908, 100,005,816, 100,008,725, and 100,011,633, and the angles of which these thicknesses are secants will be 26′ 13″, 37′ 5″, 45′ 6″, and 52′ 26″, the radius being 100,000,000; and the sines of these angles are 762, 1,079, 1,321, and 1,525, and the proportional sines of refraction 1,172, 1,659, 2,031, and 2,345, the radius being 100,000. For since the sines of incidence out of glass into air are to the sines of refraction as 11 to 17, and to the above-mentioned secants as 11 to the first of 106 arithmetical means between 11 and 17 (that is, as 11 to $11\frac{6}{106}$), those secants will be to the sines of refraction as $11\frac{6}{106}$ to 17, and by this analogy will give these sines. So, then, if the obliquities of the rays to the concave surface of the glass be such that the sines of their refraction in passing out of the glass through that surface into the air be 1,172, 1,659, 2,031, 2,345, the bright light of the 34,386th ring shall emerge at the thicknesses of the glass, which are to one-quarter of an inch as 34,386 to 34,385, 34,384, 34,383, 34,382, respectively. And, therefore, if the thickness in all these cases be one-quarter of an inch (as it is in the glass of which the speculum was made) the bright light of the 34,385th ring shall emerge where the sine of refraction is 1,172, and that of the 34,384th, 34,383rd, and 34,382nd ring where the sine is 1,659, 2,031, and 2,345, respectively. And in these angles of refraction the light of these rings shall be propagated from the speculum to the chart, and there paint rings about the white central round spot of light which, we said, was the light of the 34,386th ring. And the semidiameters of these rings shall subtend the angles of refraction made at the concave surface of the speculum, and by consequence their diameters shall be to the distance of the chart from the speculum as those sines of refraction doubled are to the radius (that is, as 1,172, 1,659, 2,031, and 2,345, doubled, are to 100,000). And, therefore, if the distance of the chart from the concave surface of the speculum be six feet (as it was in the third of these Observations), the diameters of the rings of this bright yellow light upon the chart shall be 1.688, 2.389, 2.925, 3.375 inches; for these diameters are to six feet as the above-mentioned sines doubled are to the radius. Now, these diameters of the bright yellow rings, thus found by computation, are the very same with those found in the third of these Observations by measuring them, viz., with $1^{11}/_{16}$, $2\frac{3}{8}$, $2^{11}/_{12}$, and $3\frac{3}{8}$ inches; and, therefore, the theory of deriving these rings from the thickness of the plate of glass of which the speculum was made, and from the obliquity of the emerging rays, agrees with the Observation. In this computation I have equalled the diameters of the bright rings made by light of all colours, to the diameters of the rings made by the bright yellow. For this yellow makes the brightest part of the rings of all colours. If you desire the diameters of the rings made by the light of any other unmixed colour, you may find them readily by putting them to the diameters of the bright yellow ones in a subduplicate proportion of the intervals of the fits of the rays of those colours when equally inclined to the refracting or reflecting surface which caused those fits; that is, by putting the diameters of the rings made by the rays in the extremities and limits of the seven colours (red, orange, yellow, green, blue, indigo, violet) proportional to the cube roots of the numbers, 1, $\frac{8}{9}$, $\frac{5}{6}$, $\frac{3}{4}$, $\frac{2}{3}$, $\frac{3}{5}$, $\frac{9}{16}$, $\frac{1}{2}$, which express the lengths of a monochord sounding the notes in an eighth. For by this means the diameters of the rings of these colours will be found pretty nearly in the same proportion to one another which they ought to have by the fifth of these Observations.

And thus I satisfied myself that these rings were of the same kind and original with those of thin plates, and by consequence that the fits or alternate dispositions of the rays to be reflected and transmitted are propagated to great distances from every reflecting and refracting surface. But yet to put the matter out of doubt, I added the following Observation.

OBS. 9. If these rings thus depend on the thickness of the plate of glass, their diameters at equal distances from several speculums made of such concavo-convex plates of glass as are ground on the same sphere ought to be reciprocally in a subduplicate proportion of the thicknesses of the plates of glass. And if this proportion be found true by experience it will amount to a demonstration that these rings (like those formed in thin plates) do depend on the thickness of the glass. I procured, therefore, another concavo-convex plate of glass ground on both sides to the same sphere with the former plate. Its thickness was $\frac{5}{62}$ parts of an inch; and the diameters of the three first bright rings measured between the brightest parts of their orbits at the distance of six feet from the glass were 3, $4\frac{1}{6}$, $5\frac{1}{8}$ inches. Now, the thickness of the other glass being one-quarter of an inch was to the thickness of this glass as $\frac{1}{4}$ to $\frac{5}{62}$; that is, as 31 to 10, or 310,000,000 to 100,000,000; and the roots of these numbers are 17,607 and 10,000, and in the proportion of the first of these roots to the second are the diameters of the bright rings made in this Observation by the thinner glass, 3, $4\frac{1}{6}$, $5\frac{1}{8}$, to the diameters of the same rings made in the third of these Observations by the thicker glass $1\frac{11}{16}$, $2\frac{3}{8}$, $2\frac{11}{12}$; that is, the diameters of the rings are reciprocally in a subduplicate proportion of the thicknesses of the plates of glass.

So, then, in plates of glass which are alike concave on one side, and alike convex on the other side, and alike quick-silvered on the convex sides, and differ in nothing but their thickness, the diameters of the rings are reciprocally in a subduplicate proportion of the thicknesses of the plates. And this shews sufficiently that the rings depend on both the surfaces of the glass. They depend on the convex surface because they are more luminous when that surface is quick-silvered over than when it is without quick-silver. They depend also upon the concave surface, because without that surface a speculum makes them not. They depend on both surfaces, and on the distances between them, because their bigness is varied by varying only that distance. And this dependence is of the same kind with that which the colours of thin plates have on the distance of the surfaces of those plates, because the bigness of the rings, and their proportion to one another, and the variation of their bigness arising from the variation of the thickness of the glass, and the orders of their colours, is such as ought to result from the Propositions in the end of the third part of this book, derived from the phenomena of the colours of thin plates set down in the first part.

There are yet other phenomena of these rings of colours, but such as follow from the same Propositions, and therefore confirm both the truth of those Propositions, and the analogy between these rings and the rings of colours made by very thin plates. I shall subjoin some of them.

OBS. 10. When the beam of the Sun's light was reflected back from the speculum, not directly to the hole in the window but to a place a little distant from it, the common centre of that spot, and of all the rings of colours, fell in the middle way between the beam of the incident light and the beam of the reflected light, and by consequence in the centre of the spherical concavity of the speculum, whenever the chart on which the rings of colours fell was placed at that centre. And as the beam of reflected light by inclining the speculum receded more and more from the beam of incident light and from the common centre of the coloured rings between them, those rings grew bigger and bigger, and so also did the white round spot, and new rings of colours emerged successively out of their common centre, and the white spot became a white ring encompassing them; and the incident and reflected beams of light always fell upon the opposite parts of this white ring, illuminating its perimeter like two mock Suns in the opposite parts of an iris. So, then, the diameter of this ring, measured from the middle of its light on one side to the middle of its light on the other side, was always equal to the distance between the middle of the incident beam of light, and the middle of the reflected beam measured at the chart on which the rings appeared. And the rays which formed this ring were reflected by the speculum in angles equal to their angles of incidence, and by consequence to their angles of refraction at their entrance into the glass, but yet their angles of reflexion were not in the same planes with their angles of incidence.

Obs. 11. The colours of the new rings were in a contrary order to those of the former, and arose after this manner: the white round spot of light in the middle of the rings continued white to the centre till the distance of the incident and reflected beams at the chart was about $\frac{7}{8}$ parts of an inch, and then it began to grow dark in the middle. And when that distance was about $1\frac{3}{16}$ of an inch, the white spot was become a ring encompassing a dark round spot which in the middle inclined to violet and indigo. And the luminous rings encompassing it were grown equal to those dark ones which in the four first Observations encompassed them; that is to say, the white spot was grown a white ring equal to the first of those dark rings, and the first of those luminous rings was now grown equal to the second of those dark ones, and the second of those luminous ones to the third of those dark ones, and so on. For the diameters of the luminous rings were now $1\frac{3}{16}$, $2\frac{1}{16}$, $2\frac{2}{3}$, $3\frac{3}{20}$, &c. inches.

When the distance between the incident and reflected beams of light became a little bigger, there emerged out of the middle of the dark spot after the indigo a blue, and then out of that blue a pale green, and soon after a yellow and red. And when the colour at the centre was brightest (being between yellow and red) the bright rings were grown equal to those rings which in the four first Observations next encompassed them; that is to say, the white spot in the middle of those rings was now become a white ring equal to the first of those bright rings, and the first of those bright ones was now become equal to the second of those, and so on. For the diameters of the white ring, and of the other luminous rings encompassing it, were now $1\frac{11}{16}$, $2\frac{3}{8}$, $2\frac{11}{12}$, $3\frac{3}{8}$, &c. or thereabouts.

When the distance of the two beams of light at the chart was a little more increased, there emerged out of the middle, in order, after the red: a purple, a blue, a green, a yellow, and a red inclining much to purple; and when the colour was brightest (being between yellow and red) the former indigo, blue, green, yellow, and red were become an iris or ring of colours equal to the first of those luminous rings which appeared in the four first Observations, and the white ring which was now become the second of the luminous rings was grown equal to the second of those, and the first of those which was now become the third ring was become equal to the third of those, and so on. For their diameters were $1\frac{11}{16}$, $2\frac{3}{8}$, $2\frac{11}{12}$, $3\frac{3}{8}$ inches, the distance of the two beams of light, and the diameter of the white ring being $2\frac{3}{8}$ inches.

When these two beams became more distant there emerged out of the middle of the purplish red, first a darker round spot, and then out of the middle of that spot a brighter. And now the former colours (purple, blue, green, yellow, and purplish red) were become a ring equal to the first of the bright rings mentioned in the four first Observations, and the rings about this ring were grown equal to the rings about that, respectively; the distance between the two beams of light and the diameter of the white ring (which was now become the third ring) being about 3 inches.

The colours of the rings in the middle began now to grow very dilute, and if the distance between the two beams was increased half an inch, or an inch more, they vanished whilst the white ring, with one or two of the rings next it on either side, continued still visible. But if the distance of the two beams of light was still more increased, these also vanished; for the light which coming from several parts of the hole in the window fell upon the speculum in several angles of incidence, made rings of several bignesses, which diluted and blotted out one another, as I knew by intercepting some part of that light. For if I intercepted that part which was nearest to the axis of the speculum, the rings would be less; if the other part which was remotest from it, they would be bigger.

OBS. 12. When the colours of the prism were cast successively on the speculum, that ring which in the two last Observations was white, was of the same bigness in all the colours, but the rings without it were greater in the green than in the blue, and still greater in the yellow, and greatest in the red. And, on the contrary, the rings within that white circle were less in the green than in the blue, and still less in the yellow, and least in the red. For the angles of reflexion of those rays which made this ring, being equal to their angles of incidence, the fits of every reflected ray within the glass after reflexion are equal in length and number to the fits of the same ray within the glass before its incidence on the reflecting surface. And, therefore, since all the rays of all sorts at their entrance into the glass were in a fit of transmission, they were also in a fit of transmission at their returning to the same surface after reflexion; and by consequence were transmitted, and went out to the white ring on the chart. This is the reason why that ring was of the same bigness in all the colours, and why in a mixture of all it appears white. But in rays which are reflected in other angles, the intervals of the fits of the least refrangible being greatest, make the rings of their colour in their progress from this white ring, either outwards or inwards, increase or decrease by the greatest steps; so that the rings of this colour without are greatest, and within least. And this is the reason why in the last Observation, when the speculum was illuminated with white light, the exterior rings made by all colours appeared red without and blue within, and the interior blue without and red within.

These are the phenomena of thick convexo-concave plates of glass, which are everywhere of the same thickness. There are yet other phenomena when these plates are a little thicker on one side than on the other, and others when the plates are more or less concave than convex, or plano-convex, or double-convex. For in all these cases the plates make rings of colours, but after various manners; all which, so far as I have yet observed, follow from the Propositions in the end of the third part of this book, and so conspire to confirm the truth of those Propositions. But the phenomena are too various, and the calculations whereby they follow from those Propositions too intricate, to be here prosecuted. I content myself with having prosecuted this kind of phenomena so far as to discover their cause, and by discovering it to ratify the Propositions in the third Part of this book.

OBS. 13. As light reflected by a lens quick-silvered on the backside makes the rings of colours above described, so it ought to make the like rings of colours in passing through a drop of water. At the first reflexion of the rays within the drop, some colours ought to be transmitted, as in the case of a lens, and others to be reflected back to the eye. For instance, if the diameter of a small drop or globule of water be about the 500th part of an inch, so that a red-making ray in passing through the middle of this globule has 250 fits of easy transmission within the globule, and that all the red-making rays which are at a certain distance from this middle ray round about it have 249 fits within the globule, and all the like rays at a certain farther distance round about it have 248 fits, and all those at a certain farther distance 247 fits, and so on; these concentric circles of rays after their transmission, falling on a white paper, will make concentric rings of red upon the paper, supposing the light which passes through one single globule strong enough to be sensible. And, in like manner, the rays of other colours will make rings of other colours. Suppose, now, that in a fair day the Sun shines through a thin cloud of such globules of water or hail, and that the globules are all of the same bigness; and the Sun seen through this cloud shall appear encompassed with the like concentric rings of colours, and the diameter of the first ring of red shall be $7\frac{1}{4}°$, that of the second $10\frac{1}{4}°$, that of the third 12° 33'. And accordingly, as the globules of water are bigger or less, the rings shall be less or bigger. This is the theory, and experience answers it. For in June, 1692, I saw by reflexion in a vessel of stagnating water three halos, crowns, or rings of colours about the Sun, like three little rainbows, concentric to his body. The colours of the first or innermost crown were blue next the Sun, red without, and white in the middle between the blue and red. Those of the second crown were purple and blue within, and pale red without, and green in the middle. And those of the third were pale blue within, and pale red without; these crowns enclosed one another immediately, so that their colours proceeded in this continual order from the Sun outward: blue, white, red; purple, blue, green, pale yellow and red; pale blue, pale red. The diameter of the second crown measured from the middle of the yellow and red on one side of the Sun, to the middle of the same colour on the other side was $9\frac{1}{3}$ degrees, or thereabouts. The diameters of the first and third I had not time to measure, but that of the first seemed to be about five or six degrees, and that of the third about twelve. The like crowns appear sometimes about the Moon; for in the beginning of the year 1664, February 19th at night, I saw two such crowns about her. The diameter of the first or innermost was about three degrees, and that of the second about five degrees and a half. Next about the Moon was a circle of white, and next about that the inner crown, which was of a bluish-green within next the white, and of a yellow and red without, and next about these colours were blue and green on the inside of the outward crown, and red on the outside of it. At the same time there appeared a halo about 22 degrees 35' distant from the centre of the Moon. It was elliptical, and its long diameter was perpendicular to the horizon, verging below farthest from the Moon. I am told that the Moon has sometimes three or more concentric crowns of colours encompassing one another next about her body. The more equal the globules of water or ice are to one another, the more crowns of colours will appear, and the colours will be the more lively. The halo at the distance of $22\frac{1}{2}$ degrees from the Moon is of another sort. By its being oval and remoter from the Moon below than above, I conclude that it was made by refraction in some sort of hail or snow floating in the air in an horizontal posture, the refracting angle being about 58 or 60 degrees.

BOOK THREE
Part I

Observations concerning the inflexions of the rays of light, and the colours made thereby.

GRIMALDI has informed us that if a beam of the Sun's light be let into a dark room through a very small hole, the shadows of things in this light will be larger than they ought to be if the rays went on by the bodies in straight lines, and that these shadows have three parallel fringes, bands or ranks of coloured light adjacent to them. But if the hole be enlarged the fringes grow broad and run into one another, so that they cannot be distinguished. These broad shadows and fringes have been reckoned by some to proceed from the ordinary refraction of the air, but without due examination of the matter. For the circumstances of the phenomenon, so far as I have observed them, are as follows:

Obs. 1. I made in a piece of lead a small hole with a pin, whose breadth was the 42d part of an inch, for 21 of those pins laid together took up the breadth of half an inch. Through this hole I let into my darkened chamber a beam of the Sun's light, and found that the shadows of hairs, thread, pins, straws, and such like slender substances placed in this beam of light, were considerably broader than they ought to be, if the rays of light passed on by these bodies in right lines. And particularly a hair of a man's head, whose breadth was but the 280th part of an inch, being held in this light, at the distance of about twelve feet from the hole, did cast a shadow which at the distance of four inches from the hair was the sixtieth part of an inch broad (that is, above four times broader than the hair), and at the distance of two feet from the hair was about the eight and twentieth part of an inch broad (that is, ten times broader than the hair), and at the distance of ten feet was the eighth part of an inch broad (that is, 35 times broader).

Nor is it material whether the hair be encompassed with air, or with any other pellucid substance. For I wetted a polished plate of glass, and laid the hair in the water upon the glass, and then laying another polished plate of glass upon it, so that the water might fill up the space between the glasses, I held them in the aforesaid beam of light, so that the light might pass through them perpendicularly, and the shadow of the hair was at the same distances as big as before. The shadows of scratches made in polished plates of glass were also much broader than they ought to be, and the veins in polished plates of glass did also cast the like broad shadows. And, therefore, the great breadth of these shadows proceeds from some other cause than the refraction of the air.

Let the circle X [Fig. 1] represent the middle of the hair; ADG, BEH, CFI, three rays passing by one side of the hair at several distances; KNQ, LOR, MPS, three other rays passing by the other side of the hair at the like distances; D, E, F, and N, O, P, the places where the rays are bent in their passage by the hair; G, H, I, and Q, R, S, the places where the rays fall on a paper GQ; IS the

507

breadth of the shadow of the hair cast on the paper, and TI, VS, two rays passing to the points I and S without bending when the hair is taken away. And it's manifest that all the light between these two rays TI and VS is bent in passing by the hair, and turned aside from the shadow IS, because if any part of this light were not bent it would fall on the paper within the shadow, and there

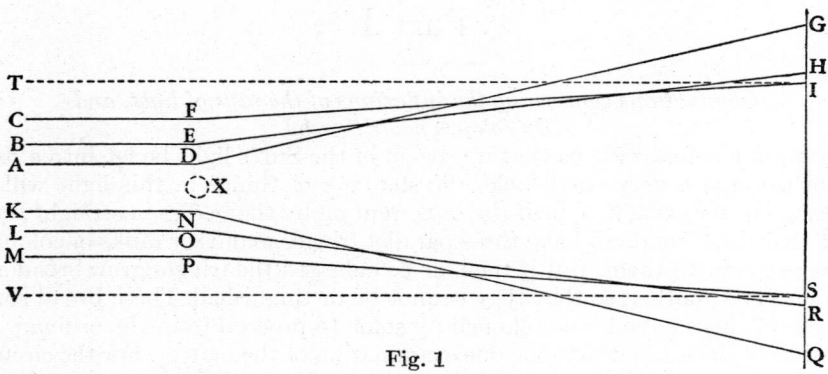

Fig. 1

illuminate the paper, contrary to experience. And because when the paper is at a great distance from the hair, the shadow is broad, and therefore the rays TI and VS are at a great distance from one another, it follows that the hair acts upon the rays of light at a good distance in their passing by it. But the action is strongest on the rays which pass by at least distances, and grows weaker and weaker accordingly as the rays pass by at distances greater and greater, as is represented in the scheme. For thence it comes to pass that the shadow of the hair is much broader in proportion to the distance of the paper from the hair, when the paper is nearer the hair, than when it is at a great distance from it.

OBS. 2. The shadows of all bodies (metals, stones, glass, wood, horn, ice, &c.) in this light were bordered with three parallel fringes or bands of coloured light, whereof that which was contiguous to the shadow was broadest and most luminous, and that which was remotest from it was narrowest, and so faint, as not easily to be visible. It was difficult to distinguish the colours, unless when the light fell very obliquely upon a smooth paper, or some other smooth white body, so as to make them appear much broader than they would otherwise do. And then the colours were plainly visible in this order: the first or innermost fringe was violet and deep blue next the shadow, and then light blue, green, and yellow in the middle, and red without. The second fringe was almost contiguous to the first, and the third to the second, and both were blue within, and yellow and red without, but their colours were very faint, especially those of the third. The colours, therefore, proceeded in this order from the shadow: violet, indigo, pale blue, green, yellow, red; blue, yellow, red; pale blue, pale yellow and red. The shadows made by scratches and bubbles in polished plates of glass were bordered with the like fringes of coloured light. And if plates of looking-glass, sloped off near the edges with a diamond-cut, be held in the same beam of light, the light which passes through the parallel planes of the glass will be bordered with the like fringes of colours where those planes meet with the diamond-cut, and by this means there will sometimes appear four or five fringes of colours. Let AB, CD [Fig. 2] represent the parallel planes of a looking-glass, and BD the plane of the diamond-cut, making at B a very obtuse angle with the plane AB. And let all the light between the rays ENI and FBM pass directly through the parallel planes of the glass, and fall upon the paper

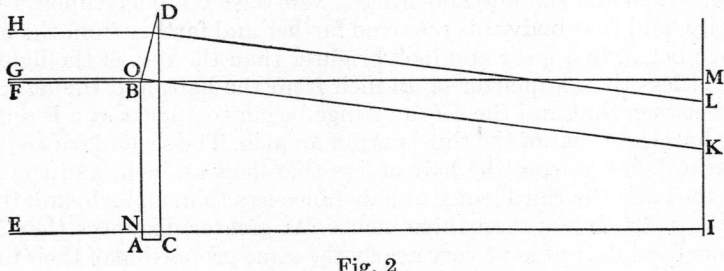

Fig. 2

between I and M, and all the light between the rays GO and HD be refracted by the oblique plane of the diamond-cut BD, and fall upon the paper between K and L; and the light which passes directly through the parallel planes of the glass, and falls upon the paper between I and M, will be bordered with three or more fringes at M.

So, by looking on the Sun through a feather or black ribband held close to the eye, several rainbows will appear; the shadows which the fibres or threads cast on the *tunica retina* being bordered with the like fringes of colours.

Obs. 3. When the hair was twelve feet distant from this hole, and its shadow fell obliquely upon a flat white scale of inches and parts of an inch placed half a foot beyond it, and also when the shadow fell perpendicularly upon the same scale placed nine feet beyond it, I measured the breadth of the shadow and fringes as accurately as I could, and found them in parts of an inch as follows:

At the distance of	Half a foot	Nine feet
The breadth of the shadow..............................	$\frac{1}{54}$	$\frac{1}{9}$
The breadth between the middles of the brightest light of the innermost fringes on either side the shadow..............	$\frac{1}{38}$ or $\frac{1}{39}$	$\frac{7}{50}$
The breadth between the middles of the brightest light of the middlemost fringes on either side the shadow............	$\frac{1}{23\frac{1}{2}}$	$\frac{4}{17}$
The breadth between the middles of the brightest light of the outmost fringes on either side the shadow...............	$\frac{1}{18}$ or $\frac{1}{18\frac{1}{2}}$	$\frac{3}{10}$
The distance between the middles of the brightest light of the first and second fringes.....................................	$\frac{1}{120}$	$\frac{1}{21}$
The distance between the middles of the brightest light of the second and third fringes................................	$\frac{1}{170}$	$\frac{1}{31}$
The breadth of the luminous part (green, white, yellow, and red) of the first fringe.....................................	$\frac{1}{170}$	$\frac{1}{32}$
The breadth of the darker space between the first and second fringes..	$\frac{1}{240}$	$\frac{1}{45}$
The breadth of the luminous part of the second fringe......	$\frac{1}{290}$	$\frac{1}{55}$
The breadth of the darker space between the second and third fringes..	$\frac{1}{340}$	$\frac{1}{63}$

These measures I took by letting the shadow of the hair, at half a foot distance, fall so obliquely on the scale as to appear twelve times broader than when it fell perpendicularly on it at the same distance, and setting down in this Table the twelfth part of the measures I then took.

Obs. 4. When the shadow and fringes were cast obliquely upon a smooth white body, and that body was removed farther and farther from the hair, the first fringe began to appear and look brighter than the rest of the light at the distance of less than a quarter of an inch from the hair, and the dark line or shadow between that and the second fringe began to appear at a less distance from the hair than that of the third part of an inch. The second fringe began to appear at a distance from the hair of less than half an inch, and the shadow between that and the third fringe at a distance less than an inch, and the third fringe at a distance less than three inches. At greater distances they became much more sensible, but kept very nearly the same proportion of their breadths and intervals which they had at their first appearing. For the distance between the middle of the first, and middle of the second fringe, was to the distance between the middle of the second and middle of the third fringe as three to two, or ten to seven. And the last of these two distances was equal to the breadth of the bright light or luminous part of the first fringe. And this breadth was to the breadth of the bright light of the second fringe as seven to four, and to the dark interval of the first and second fringe as three to two, and to the like dark interval between the second and third as two to one. For the breadths of the fringes seemed to be in the progression of the numbers $1, \sqrt{\frac{1}{3}}, \sqrt{\frac{1}{5}}$, and their intervals to be in the same progression with them; that is, the fringes and their intervals together to be in the continual progression of the numbers $1, \sqrt{\frac{1}{2}}$, $\sqrt{\frac{1}{3}}, \sqrt{\frac{1}{4}}, \sqrt{\frac{1}{5}}$, or thereabouts. And these proportions held the same very nearly at all distances from the hair; the dark intervals of the fringes being as broad in proportion to the breadth of the fringes at their first appearance as afterwards at great distances from the hair, though not so dark and distinct.

Obs. 5. The Sun shining into my darkened chamber through a hole a quarter of an inch broad, I placed at the distance of two or three feet from the hole a sheet of pasteboard, which was blacked all over on both sides, and in the middle of it had a hole about three-quarters of an inch square for the light to pass through. And behind the hole I fastened to the pasteboard with pitch the blade of a sharp knife, to intercept some part of the light which passed through the hole. The planes of the pasteboard and blade of the knife were parallel to one another, and perpendicular to the rays. And when they were so placed that none of the Sun's light fell on the pasteboard, but all of it passed through the hole to the knife, and there part of it fell upon the blade of the knife, and part of it passed by its edge, I let this part of the light which passed by, fall on a white paper two or three feet beyond the knife, and there saw two streams of faint light shoot out both ways from the beam of light into the shadow, like the tails of comets. But because the Sun's direct light by its brightness upon the paper obscured these faint streams, so that I could scarce see them, I made a little hole in the midst of the paper for that light to pass through and fall on a black cloth behind it; and then I saw the two streams plainly. They were like one another, and pretty nearly equal in length, and breadth, and quantity of light. Their light at that end next the Sun's direct light was pretty strong for the space of about a quarter of an inch, or half an inch, and in all its progress from that direct light decreased gradually till it became insensible. The whole length of either of these streams measured upon the paper at the distance of three feet from the knife was about six or eight inches; so that it subtended an angle at the edge of the knife of about 10 or 12, or at most 14 degrees. Yet sometimes I thought I saw it shoot three or four degrees farther, but with a light so very faint that I could scarce perceive it, and suspected it might (in some measure, at least) arise from some other cause than the two streams did. For, placing my eye in that light beyond the end of that stream which was behind the knife, and looking towards the knife, I could see a line of light upon its edge, and that not only when my eye was in the line of the streams, but also when it was without that line either towards the point of the knife, or towards the handle. This line of light appeared contiguous to the edge of the knife, and was narrower than the light of the innermost fringe, and narrowest when my eye was farthest from the direct light, and therefore seemed to pass between the light of that fringe and the edge of the knife, and that which passed nearest the edge to be most bent, though not all of it.

OBS. 6. I placed another knife by this, so that their edges might be parallel, and look towards one another, and that the beam of light might fall upon both the knives, and some part of it pass between their edges. And when the distance of their edges was about the 400th part of an inch, the stream parted in the middle, and left a shadow between the two parts. This shadow was so black and dark that all the light which passed between the knives seemed to be bent, and turned aside to the one hand or to the other. And as the knives still approached one another the shadow grew broader, and the streams shorter at their inward ends which were next the shadow, until upon the contact of the knives the whole light vanished, leaving its place to the shadow.

And hence I gather that the light which is least bent, and goes to the inward ends of the streams, passes by the edges of the knives at the greatest distance; and this distance, when the shadow begins to appear between the streams, is about the 800th part of an inch. And the light which passes by the edges of the knives at distances still less and less is more and more bent, and goes to those parts of the streams which are farther and farther from the direct light; because, when the knives approach one another till they touch, those parts of the streams vanish last which are farthest from the direct light.

OBS. 7. In the fifth Observation the fringes did not appear, but by reason of the breadth of the hole in the window became so broad as to run into one another, and, by joining, to make one continued light in the beginning of the streams. But in the sixth, as the knives approached one another a little before the shadow appeared between the two streams, the fringes began to appear on the inner ends of the streams on either side of the direct light; three on one side made by the edge of one knife, and three on the other side made by the edge of the other knife. They were distinctest when the knives were placed at the greatest distance from the hole in the window, and still became more distinct by making the hole less, insomuch that I could sometimes see a faint lineament of a fourth fringe beyond the three above mentioned. And as the knives continually approached one another, the fringes grew distincter and larger, until they vanished. The outmost fringe vanished first, and the middlemost next, and the innermost last. And after they were all vanished, and the line of light which was in the middle between them was grown very broad, enlarging itself on both sides into the streams of light described in the fifth Observation, the above-mentioned shadow began to appear in the middle of this line, and divide it along the middle into two lines of light, and increased until the whole light vanished. This enlargement of the fringes was so great that the rays which go to the innermost fringe seemed to be bent above twenty times more when this fringe was ready to vanish than when one of the knives was taken away.

And from this and the former Observation compared, I gather that the light of the first fringe passed by the edge of the knife at a distance greater than the 800th part of an inch, and the light of the second fringe passed by the edge of the knife at a greater distance than the light of the first fringe did, and that of the third at a greater distance than that of the second, and that of the streams of light described in the fifth and sixth Observations passed by the edges of the knives at less distances than that of any of the fringes.

OBS. 8. I caused the edges of two knives to be ground truly straight, and pricking their points into a board so that their edges might look towards one another, and meeting near their points contain a rectilinear angle, I fastened their handles together with pitch to make this angle invariable. The distance of the edges of the knives from one another at the distance of four inches from the angular point, where the edges of the knives met, was the eighth part of an inch; and, therefore, the angle contained by the edges was about 1 degree 54′. The knives thus fixed together I placed in a beam of the Sun's light, let into my darkened chamber through a hole the 42d part of an inch wide, at the distance of 10 or 15 feet from the hole, and let the light which passed between their edges fall very obliquely upon a smooth white ruler at the distance of half an inch, or an inch from the knives, and there saw the fringes by the two edges of the knives run along the edges of the shadows of the knives in lines parallel to those edges without growing sensibly broader, till they met in angles equal to the angle contained by the edges of the knives, and where they met and joined they ended without crossing one another. But if the ruler was held at a much greater distance from the knives, the fringes where they were farther from the place of their meeting were a little narrower, and became something broader and broader as they approached nearer and nearer to one another, and after they met they crossed one another, and then became much broader than before.

Whence I gather that the distances at which the fringes pass by the knives are not increased nor altered by the approach of the knives, but the angles in which the rays are there bent are much increased by that approach; and that the knife which is nearest any ray determines which way the ray shall be bent, and the other knife increases the bent.

OBS. 9. When the rays fell very obliquely upon the ruler at the distance of the third part of an inch from the knives, the dark line between the first and second fringe of the shadow of one knife, and the dark line between the first and second fringe of the shadow of the other knife met with one another, at the distance of the fifth part of an inch from the end of the light which passed between the knives at the concourse of their edges. And, therefore, the distance of the edges of the knives at the meeting of these dark lines was the 160th part of an inch. For as four inches to the eighth part of an inch, so is any length of the edges of the knives measured from the point of their concourse to the distance of the edges of the knives at the end of that length, and so is the fifth part of an inch to the 160th part. So, then, the dark lines above mentioned meet in the middle of the light which passes between the knives where they are distant the 160th part of an inch, and the one half of that light passes by the edge of one knife at a distance not greater than the 320th part of an inch, and falling upon the paper makes the fringes of the shadow of that knife, and the other half passes by the edge of the other knife, at a distance not greater than the 320th part of an inch, and falling upon the paper makes the fringes of the shadow of the other knife. But if the paper be held at a distance from the knives greater than the third part of an inch, the dark lines above mentioned meet at a greater distance than the fifth part of an inch from the end of the light which passed between the knives at the concourse of their edges; and, therefore, the light which falls upon the paper where those dark lines meet passes between the knives where the edges are distant above the 160th part of an inch.

For at another time, when the two knives were distant eight feet and five inches from the little hole in the window, made with a small pin as above, the light which fell upon the paper where the aforesaid dark lines met, passed between the knives, where the distance between their edges was as in the following Table, when the distance of the paper from the knives was also as follows:

Distances of the paper from the knives in inches	Distances between the edges of the knives in millesimal parts of an inch
$1\frac{1}{2}$	0.012
$3\frac{1}{3}$	0.020
$8\frac{3}{5}$	0.034
32	0.057
96	0.081
131	0.087

And hence I gather that the light which makes the fringes upon the paper is not the same light at all distances of the paper from the knives, but when the paper is held near the knives, the fringes are made by light which passes by the edges of the knives at a less distance, and is more bent than when the paper is held at a greater distance from the knives.

OBS. 10. When the fringes of the shadows of the knives fell perpendicularly upon a paper at a great distance from the knives, they were in the form of hyperbolas, and their dimensions were as follows: Let CA, CB [Fig. 3] represent lines drawn upon the paper parallel to the edges of the knives, and between which all the light would fall if it passed between the edges of the knives without inflexion; DE a right line drawn through C making the angles ACD, BCE, equal to one another, and terminating all the light which falls upon the paper from the point where the edges of the knives meet; *eis, fkt,* and *glv,* three hyperbolical lines representing the terminus of the shadow of one of the knives, the dark line between the first and second fringes of that shadow, and the dark line between the second and third fringes of the same shadow; *xip, ykq,* and *zlr,* three other hyperbolical lines representing the terminus of the shadow of the other knife, the dark line between the first and second fringes of that shadow, and the dark line between the second and third fringes of the same shadow.

And conceive that these three hyperbolas are like and equal to the former three, and cross them in the points i, k, and l, and that the shadows of the knives are terminated and distinguished from the first luminous fringes by the lines eis and xip, until the meeting and crossing of the fringes, and then those lines cross the fringes in the form of dark lines, terminating the first luminous fringes

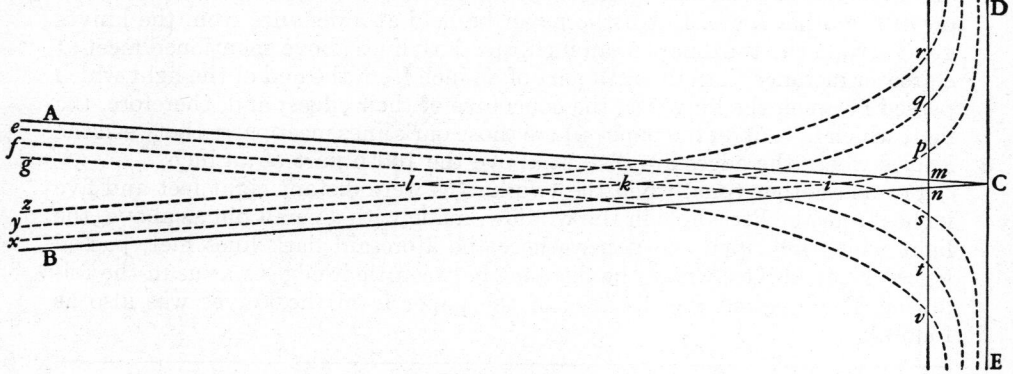

Fig. 3

within side, and distinguishing them from another light which begins to appear at i, and illuminates all the triangular space ipDEs comprehended by these dark lines, and the right line DE. Of these hyperbolas one asymptote is the line DE, and their other asymptotes are parallel to the lines CA and CB. Let rv represent a line drawn anywhere upon the paper parallel to the asymptote DE, and let this line cross the right lines AC in m, and BC in n, and the six dark hyperbolical lines in p, q, r; s, t, v; and by measuring the distances ps, qt, rv, and thence collecting the lengths of the ordinates np, nq, nr or ms, mt, mv, and doing this at several distances of the line rv from the asymptote DE, you may find as many points of these hyperbolas as you please, and thereby know that these curve lines are hyperbolas differing little from the conical hyperbola. And by measuring the lines Ci, Ck, Cl, you may find other points of these curves.

For instance, when the knives were distant from the hole in the window ten feet, and the paper from the knives nine feet, and the angle contained by the edges of the knives to which the angle ACB is equal was subtended by a chord which was to the radius as 1 to 32, and the distance of the line rv from the asymptote DE was half an inch, I measured the lines ps, qt, rv, and found them 0.35, 0.65, 0.98 inch, respectively; and by adding to their halves the line $\frac{1}{2}mn$ (which here was the 128th part of an inch, or 0.0078 inch), the sums np, nq, nr, were 0.1828, 0.3328, 0.4978 inch. I measured also the distances of the brightest parts of the fringes which run between pq and st, qr and tv, and next beyond r and v, and found them 0.5, 0.8, and 1.17 inches.

OBS. 11. The Sun shining into my darkened room through a small round hole made in a plate of lead with a slender pin, as above, I placed at the hole a prism to refract the light, and form on the opposite wall the spectrum of colours, described in the third experiment of the first book. And then I found that the shadows of all bodies held in the coloured light between the prism and the wall were bordered with fringes of the colour of that light in which they were held.

In the full red light they were totally red without any sensible blue or violet, and in the deep blue light they were totally blue without any sensible red or yellow; and so in the green light they were totally green, excepting a little yellow and blue, which were mixed in the green light of the prism. And comparing the fringes made in the several coloured lights, I found that those made in the red light were largest, those made in the violet were least, and those made in the green were of a middle bigness. For the fringes with which the shadow of a man's hair were bordered, being measured across the shadow at the distance of six inches from the hair, the distance between the middle and most luminous part of the first or innermost fringe on one side of the shadow, and that of the like fringe on the other side of the shadow, was in the full red light $\frac{1}{37\frac{1}{4}}$ of an inch, and in the full violet $\frac{7}{46}$. And the like distance between the middle and most luminous parts of the second fringes on either side the shadow was in the full red light $\frac{1}{22}$, and in the violet $\frac{1}{27}$ of an inch. And these distances of the fringes held the same proportion at all distances from the hair without any sensible variation.

So, then, the rays which made these fringes in the red light passed by the hair at a greater distance than those did which made the like fringes in the violet; and, therefore, the hair in causing these fringes acted alike upon the red light or least refrangible rays at a greater distance, and upon the violet or most refrangible rays at a less distance, and by those actions disposed the red light into larger fringes, and the violet into smaller, and the lights of intermediate colours into fringes of intermediate bignesses without changing the colour of any sort of light.

When, therefore, the hair in the first and second of these Observations was held in the white beam of the Sun's light, and cast a shadow which was bordered with three fringes of coloured light, those colours arose not from any new modifications impressed upon the rays of light by the hair, but only from the various inflexions whereby the several sorts of rays were separated from one another, which before separation, by the mixture of all their colours, composed the white beam of the Sun's light, but whenever separated compose lights of the several colours which they are originally disposed to exhibit. In this 11th Observation, where the colours are separated before the light passes by the hair, the least refrangible rays, which when separated from the rest make red, were inflected at a greater distance from the hair, so as to make three red fringes at a greater distance from the middle of the shadow of the hair; and the most refrangible rays which when separated make violet, were inflected at a less distance from the hair, so as to make three violet fringes at a less distance from the middle of the shadow of the hair. And other rays of intermediate degrees of refrangibility were inflected at intermediate distances from the hair, so as to make fringes of intermediate colours at intermediate distances from the middle of the shadow of the hair. And in the second Observation, where all the colours are mixed in the white light which passes by the hair, these colours are separated by the various inflexions of the rays, and the fringes which they make appear all together, and the innermost fringes being contiguous make one broad fringe composed of all the colours in due order, the violet lying on the inside of the fringe next the shadow, the red on the outside farthest from the shadow, and the blue, green, and yellow, in the middle. And, in like manner, the middlemost fringes of all the colours lying in order, and being contiguous, make another broad fringe composed of all the colours; and the outmost fringes of all the colours lying in order, and being contiguous, make a third broad fringe composed of all the colours. These are the three fringes of coloured light with which the shadows of all bodies are bordered in the second Observation.

When I made the foregoing Observations, I designed to repeat most of them with more care and exactness, and to make some new ones for determining the manner how the rays of light are bent in their passage by bodies, for making the fringes of colours with the dark lines between them. But I was then interrupted, and cannot now think of taking these things into further consideration. And since I have not finished this part of my design, I shall conclude with proposing only some queries, in order to a further search to be made by others.

QUERY 1. Do not bodies act upon light at a distance, and by their action bend its rays; and is not this action (*cæteris paribus*) strongest at the least distance?

QU. 2. Do not the rays which differ in refrangibility differ also in flexibility; and are they not by their different inflexions separated from one another, so as after separation to make the colours in the three fringes above described? And after what manner are they inflected to make those fringes?

QU. 3. Are not the rays of light, in passing by the edges and sides of bodies, bent several times backwards and forwards, with a motion like that of an eel? And do not the three fringes of coloured light above mentioned arise from three such bendings?

QU. 4. Do not the rays of light which fall upon bodies, and are reflected or refracted, begin to bend before they arrive at the bodies; and are they not reflected, refracted, and inflected, by one and the same principle, acting variously in various circumstances?

QU. 5. Do not bodies and light act mutually upon one another; that is to say, bodies upon light in emitting, reflecting, refracting and inflecting it, and light upon bodies for heating them, and putting their parts into a vibrating motion wherein heat consists?

QU. 6. Do not black bodies conceive heat more easily from light than those of other colours do, by reason that the light falling on them is not reflected outwards, but enters the bodies, and is often reflected and refracted within them, until it be stifled and lost?

QU. 7. Is not the strength and vigor of the action between light and sulphureous bodies observed above, one reason why sulphureous bodies take fire more readily, and burn more vehemently than other bodies do?

QU. 8. Do not all fixed bodies, when heated beyond a certain degree, emit light and shine; and is not this emission performed by the vibrating motions of their parts? And do not all bodies which abound with terrestrial parts, and especially with sulphureous ones, emit light as often as those parts are sufficiently agitated; whether that agitation be made by heat, or by friction, or percussion, or putrefaction, or by any vital motion, or any other cause? As for instance; sea-water in a raging storm; quick-silver agitated *in vacuo*; the back of a cat, or neck of a horse, obliquely struck or rubbed in a dark place; wood, flesh and fish while they putrefy; vapours arising from putrefied waters, usually called *ignes fatui;* stacks of moist hay or corn growing hot by fermentation; glow-worms and the eyes of some animals by vital motions; the vulgar phosphorus agitated by the attrition of any body, or by the acid particles of the air; amber and some diamonds by striking, pressing or rubbing them; scrapings of steel struck off with a flint; iron hammered very nimbly till it become so hot as to kindle sulphur thrown upon it; the axletrees of chariots taking fire by the rapid rotation of the wheels; and some liquors mixed with one another whose particles come together with an impetus, as oil of vitriol distilled from its weight of nitre, and then mixed with twice its weight of oil of anniseeds. So also a globe of glass about 8 or 10 inches in diameter, being put into a frame where it may be swiftly turned round its axis, will in turning shine where it rubs against the palm of one's hand applied to it. And if at the same time a piece of white paper or white cloth, or the end of one's finger be held at the distance of about a quarter of an inch or half an inch from that part of the glass where it is most in motion, the electric vapour which is excited by the friction of the glass against the hand will (by dashing against the white paper, cloth or finger) be put into such an agitation as to emit light, and make the white paper, cloth, or finger appear lucid like a glow-worm; and in rushing out of the glass will sometimes push against the finger so as to be felt. And the same things have been found by rubbing a long and large cylinder or glass or amber with a paper held in one's hand, and continuing the friction till the glass grew warm.

Qu. 9. Is not fire a body heated so hot as to emit light copiously? For what else is a red hot iron than fire? And what else is a burning coal than red hot wood?

Qu. 10. Is not flame a vapour, fume or exhalation heated red hot; that is, so hot as to shine? For bodies do not flame without emitting a copious fume, and this fume burns in the flame. The *ignis fatuus* is a vapour shining without heat, and is there not the same difference between this vapour and flame as between rotten wood shining without heat and burning coals of fire? In distilling hot spirits, if the head of the still be taken off, the vapour which ascends out of the still will take fire at the flame of a candle, and turn into flame, and the flame will run along the vapour from the candle to the still. Some bodies heated by motion, or fermentation, if the heat grow intense, fume copiously, and if the heat be great enough the fumes will shine and become flame. Metals in fusion do not flame for want of a copious fume, except spelter, which fumes copiously, and thereby flames. All flaming bodies, as oil, tallow, wax, wood, fossil coals, pitch, sulphur, by flaming waste and vanish into burning smoke, which smoke, if the flame be put out, is very thick and visible, and sometimes smells strongly, but in the flame loses its smell by burning, and according to the nature of the smoke the flame is of several colours, as that of sulphur blue, that of copper opened with sublimate green, that of tallow yellow, that of camphor white. Smoke passing through flame cannot but grow red-hot, and red-hot smoke can have no other appearance than that of flame. When gunpowder takes fire, it goes away into flaming smoke. For the charcoal and sulphur easily take fire, and set fire to the nitre, and the spirit of the nitre being thereby rarified into vapour, rushes out with explosion much after the manner that the vapour of water rushes out of an æolipile; the sulphur also being volatile is converted into vapour, and augments the explosion. And the acid vapour of the sulphur (namely, that which distils under a bell into oil of sulphur) entering violently into the fixed body of the nitre, sets loose the spirit of the nitre, and excites a great fermentation whereby the heat is further augmented, and the fixed body of the nitre is also rarified into fume, and the explosion is thereby made more vehement and quick. For if salt of tartar be mixed with gunpowder, and that mixture be warmed till it takes fire, the explosion will be more violent and quick than that of gunpowder alone; which cannot proceed from any other cause than the action of the vapour of the gunpowder upon the salt of tartar, whereby that salt is rarified. The explosion of gunpowder arises, therefore, from the violent action whereby all the mixture, being quickly and vehemently heated, is rarified and converted into fume and vapour: which vapour, by the violence of that action, becoming so hot as to shine, appears in the form of flame.

QU. 11. Do not great bodies conserve their heat the longest, their parts heating one another, and may not great dense and fixed bodies, when heated beyond a certain degree, emit light so copiously, as by the emission and reaction of its light, and the reflexions and refractions of its rays within its pores to grow still hotter, till it comes to a certain period of heat, such as is that of the Sun? And are not the Sun and fixed stars great earths vehemently hot, whose heat is conserved by the greatness of the bodies, and the mutual action and reaction between them, and the light which they emit, and whose parts are kept from fuming away, not only by their fixity, but also by the vast weight and density of the atmospheres incumbent upon them; and very strongly compressing them, and condensing the vapours and exhalations which arise from them? For if water be made warm in any pellucid vessel emptied of air, that water in the vacuum will bubble and boil as vehemently as it would in the open air in a vessel set upon the fire till it conceives a much greater heat. For the weight of the incumbent atmosphere keeps down the vapours, and hinders the water from boiling, until it grow much hotter than is requisite to make it boil *in vacuo*. Also a mixture of tin and lead being put upon a red-hot iron *in vacuo* emits a fume and flame, but the same mixture in the open air, by reason of the incumbent atmosphere, does not so much as emit any fume which can be perceived by sight. In like manner the great weight of the atmosphere which lies upon the globe of the Sun may hinder bodies there from rising up and going away from the Sun in the form of vapours and fumes, unless by means of a far greater heat than that which on the surface of our Earth would very easily turn them into vapours and fumes. And the same great weight may condense those vapours and exhalations as soon as they shall at any time begin to ascend from the Sun, and make them presently fall back again into him, and by that action increase his heat much after the manner that in our Earth the air increases the heat of a culinary fire. And the same weight may hinder the globe of the Sun from being diminished, unless by the emission of light, and a very small quantity of vapours and exhalations.

QU. 12. Do not the rays of light in falling upon the bottom of the eye excite vibrations in the *tunica retina?* Which vibrations, being propagated along the solid fibres of the optic nerves into the brain, cause the sense of seeing? For because dense bodies conserve their heat a long time, and the densest bodies conserve their heat the longest, the vibrations of their parts are of a lasting nature, and therefore may be propagated along solid fibres of uniform dense matter to a great distance, for conveying into the brain the impressions made upon all the organs of sense. For that motion which can continue long in one and the same part of a body, can be propagated a long way from one part to another, supposing the body homogeneal, so that the motion may not be reflected, refracted, interrupted or disordered by any unevenness of the body.

Qu. 13. Do not several sorts of rays make vibrations of several bignesses, which according to their bignesses excite sensations of several colours, much after the manner that the vibrations of the air, according to their several bignesses excite sensations of several sounds? And particularly do not the most refrangible rays excite the shortest vibrations for making a sensation of deep violet, the least refrangible the largest for making a sensation of deep red, and the several intermediate sorts of rays, vibrations of several intermediate bignesses to make sensations of the several intermediate colours?

Qu. 14. May not the harmony and discord of colours arise from the proportions of the vibrations propagated through the fibres of the optic nerves into the brain, as the harmony and discord of sounds arise from the proportions of the vibrations of the air? For some colours, if they be viewed together, are agreeable to one another, as those of gold and indigo, and others disagree.

Qu. 15. Are not the species of objects seen with both eyes united where the optic nerves meet before they come into the brain, the fibres on the right side of both nerves uniting there, and after union going thence into the brain in the nerve which is on the right side of the head, and the fibres on the left side of both nerves uniting in the same place, and after union going into the brain in the nerve which is on the left side of the head, and these two nerves meeting in the brain in such a manner that their fibres make but one entire species or picture, half of which on the right side of the sensorium comes from the right side of both eyes through the right side of both optic nerves to the place where the nerves meet, and from thence on the right side of the head into the brain, and the other half on the left side of the sensorium comes in like manner from the left side of both eyes? For the optic nerves of such animals as look the same way with both eyes (as of men, dogs, sheep, oxen, &c.) meet before they come into the brain, but the optic nerves of such animals as do not look the same way with both eyes (as of fishes, and of the chameleon) do not meet, if I am rightly informed.

Qu. 16. When a man in the dark presses either corner of his eye with his finger, and turns his eye away from his finger, he will see a circle of colours like those in the feather of a peacock's tail. If the eye and the finger remain quiet these colours vanish in a second minute of time, but if the finger be moved with a quavering motion they appear again. Do not these colours arise from such motions excited in the bottom of the eye by the pressure and motion of the finger as at other times are excited there by light for causing vision? And do not the motions once excited continue about a second of time before they cease? And when a man by a stroke upon his eye sees a flash of light, are not the like motions excited in the retina by the stroke? And when a coal of fire, moved nimbly in the circumference of a circle, makes the whole circumference appear like a circle of fire, is it not because the motions excited in the bottom of the eye by the rays of light are of a lasting nature, and continue till the coal of fire in going round returns to its former place? And considering the lastingness of the motions excited in the bottom of the eye by light, are they not of a vibrating nature?

Qu. 17. If a stone be thrown into stagnating water, the waves excited thereby continue some time to arise in the place where the stone fell into the water, and are propagated from thence in concentric circles upon the surface of the water to great distances. And the vibrations or tremors excited in the air by percussion continue a little time to move from the place of percussion in concentric spheres to great distances. And in like manner, when a ray of light falls upon the surface of any pellucid body, and is there refracted or reflected, may not waves of vibrations, or tremors, be thereby excited in the refracting or reflecting medium at the point of incidence, and continue to arise there, and to be propagated from thence as long as they continue to arise and be propagated, when they are excited in the bottom of the eye by the pressure or motion of the finger or by the light which comes from the coal of fire in the experiments above mentioned? And are not these vibrations propagated from the point of incidence to great distances? And do they not overtake the rays of light, and, by overtaking them successively, do they not put them into the fits of easy reflexion and easy transmission described above? For if the rays endeavour to recede from the densest part of the vibration, they may be alternately accelerated and retarded by the vibrations overtaking them.

Qu. 18. If in two large tall cylindrical vessels of glass inverted, two little thermometers be suspended so as not to touch the vessels, and the air be drawn out of one of these vessels, and these vessels thus prepared be carried out of a cold place into a warm one, the thermometer *in vacuo* will grow warm as much, and almost as soon, as the thermometer which is not *in vacuo*. And when the vessels are carried back into the cold place, the thermometer *in vacuo* will grow cold almost as soon as the other thermometer. Is not the heat of the warm room conveyed through the vacuum by the vibrations of a much subtiler medium than air, which after the air was drawn out remained in the vacuum? And is not this medium the same with that medium by which light is refracted and reflected, and by whose vibrations light communicates heat to bodies, and is put into fits of easy reflexion and easy transmission? And do not the vibrations of this medium in hot bodies contribute to the intenseness and duration of their heat? And do not hot bodies communicate their heat to contiguous cold ones, by the vibrations of this medium propagated from them into the cold ones? And is not this medium exceedingly more rare and subtile than the air, and exceedingly more elastic and active? And doth it not readily pervade all bodies? And is it not (by its elastic force) expanded through all the heavens?

Qu. 19. Doth not the refraction of light proceed from the different density of this æthereal medium in different places, the light receding always from the denser parts of the medium? And is not the density thereof greater in free and open spaces void of air and other grosser bodies, than within the pores of water, glass, crystal, gems, and other compact bodies? For when light passes through glass or crystal, and falling very obliquely upon the farther surface thereof is totally reflected, the total reflexion ought to proceed rather from the density and vigour of the medium without and beyond the glass, than from the rarity and weakness thereof.

Qu. 20. Doth not this æthereal medium in passing out of water, glass, crystal, and other compact and dense bodies into empty spaces, grow denser and denser by degrees, and by that means refract the rays of light not in a point, but by bending them gradually in curved lines? And doth not the gradual condensation of this medium extend to some distance from the bodies, and thereby cause the inflexions of the rays of light, which pass by the edges of dense bodies, at some distance from the bodies?

Qu. 21. Is not this medium much rarer within the dense bodies of the Sun, stars, planets and comets, than in the empty celestial spaces between them? And in passing from them to great distances, doth it not grow denser and denser perpetually, and thereby cause the gravity of those great bodies towards one another, and of their parts towards the bodies; every body endeavouring to go from the denser parts of the medium towards the rarer? For if this medium be rarer within the Sun's body than at its surface, and rarer there than at the hundredth part of an inch from its body, and rarer there than at the fiftieth part of an inch from its body, and rarer there than at the orb of Saturn, I see no reason why the increase of density should stop anywhere, and not rather be continued through all distances from the Sun to Saturn, and beyond. And though this increase of density may at great distances be exceeding slow, yet if the elastic force of this medium be exceeding great, it may suffice to impel bodies from the denser parts of the medium towards the rarer, with all that power which we call gravity. And that the elastic force of this medium is exceeding great, may be gathered from the swiftness of its vibrations. Sounds move about 1,140 English feet in a second minute of time, and in seven or eight minutes of time they move about one hundred English miles. Light moves from the Sun to us in about seven or eight minutes of time, which distance is about 7,000,000 English miles, supposing the horizontal parallax of the Sun to be about 12″. And the vibrations or pulses of this medium, that they may cause the alternate fits of easy transmission and easy reflexion, must be swifter than light, and by consequence above 700,000 times swifter than sounds. And, therefore, the elastic force of this medium, in proportion to its density, must be above $700,000 \times 700,000$ (that is, above 490,000,000,000) times greater than the elastic force of the air is in proportion to its density. For the velocities of the pulses of elastic mediums are in a subduplicate ratio of the elasticities and the rarities of the mediums taken together.

As attraction is stronger in small magnets than in great ones in proportion to their bulk, and gravity is greater in the surfaces of small planets than in those of great ones in proportion to their bulk, and small bodies are agitated much more by electric attraction than great ones; so the smallness of the rays of light may contribute very much to the power of the agent by which they are refracted. And so if any one should suppose that æther (like our air) may contain particles which endeavour to recede from one another (for I do not know what this æther is) and that its particles are exceedingly smaller than those of air, or even than those of light: the exceeding smallness of its particles may contribute to the greatness of the force by which those particles may recede from one another, and thereby make that medium exceedingly more rare and elastic than air, and by consequence exceedingly less able to resist the motions of projectiles, and exceedingly more able to press upon gross bodies, by endeavouring to expand itself.

Qu. 22. May not planets and comets, and all gross bodies, perform their motions more freely, and with less resistance in this æthereal medium than in any fluid, which fills all space adequately without leaving any pores, and by consequence is much denser than quick-silver or gold? And may not its resistance be so small, as to be inconsiderable? For instance: if this æther (for so I will call it) should be supposed 700,000 times more elastic than our air, and above 700,000 times more rare, its resistance would be above 600,000,000 times less than that of water. And so small a resistance would scarce make any sensible alteration in the motions of the planets in ten thousand years. If any one would ask how a medium can be so rare, let him tell me how the air, in the upper parts of the atmosphere, can be above a hundred thousand thousand times rarer than gold. Let him also tell me how an electric body can by friction emit an exhalation so rare and subtile, and yet so potent, as by its emission to cause no sensible diminution of the weight of the electric body, and to be expanded through a sphere, whose diameter is above two feet, and yet to be able to agitate and carry up leaf copper, or leaf gold, at the distance of above a foot from the electric body? And how the effluvia of a magnet can be so rare and subtile as to pass through a plate of glass without any resistance or diminution of their force, and yet so potent as to turn a magnetic needle beyond the glass?

Qu. 23. Is not vision performed chiefly by the vibrations of this medium, excited in the bottom of the eye by the rays of light, and propagated through the solid, pellucid and uniform capillamenta of the optic nerves into the place of sensation? And is not hearing performed by the vibrations either of this or some other medium, excited in the auditory nerves by the tremors of the air, and propagated through the solid, pellucid and uniform capillamenta of those nerves into the place of sensation? And so of the other senses.

Qu. 24. Is not animal motion performed by the vibrations of this medium, excited in the brain by the power of the will, and propagated from thence through the solid, pellucid and uniform capillamenta of the nerves into the muscles, for contracting and dilating them? I suppose that the capillamenta of the nerves are each of them solid and uniform, that the vibrating motion of the æthereal medium may be propagated along them from one end to the other uniformly, and without interruption, for obstructions in the nerves create palsies. And that they may be sufficiently uniform, I suppose them to be pellucid when viewed singly, tho' the reflexions in their cylindrical surfaces may make the whole nerve (composed of many capillamenta) appear opaque and white. For opacity arises from reflecting surfaces, such as may disturb and interrupt the motions of this medium.

Qu. 25. Are there not other original properties of the rays of light, besides those already described? An instance of another original property we have in the refraction of island crystal, described first by Erasmus Bartholinus, and afterwards more exactly by Huygens, in his book *De la Lumière*. This crystal is a pellucid, fissile stone, clear as water or crystal of the rock, and without colour; enduring a red heat without losing its transparency, and in a very strong heat calcining without fusion. Steeped a day or two in water, it loses its natural polish. Being rubbed on cloth, it attracts pieces of straws and other light things, like amber or glass; and with *aqua fortis* it makes an ebullition. It seems to be a sort of talc, and is found in form of an oblique parallelepiped, with six parallelogram sides and eight solid angles. The obtuse angles of the parallelograms are each of them 101 degrees and 52 minutes; the acute ones 78 degrees and 8 minutes. Two of the solid angles opposite to one another, as C and E, are compassed each of them with three of these obtuse angles, and each of the other six with one obtuse and two acute ones [Fig. 4]. It cleaves easily in planes parallel to any of its sides, and not in any other planes. It cleaves with a glossy polite surface not perfectly plane, but with some little unevenness. It is easily scratched, and by reason of its softness it takes a polish very difficultly. It polishes better upon polished looking-glass than upon metal,

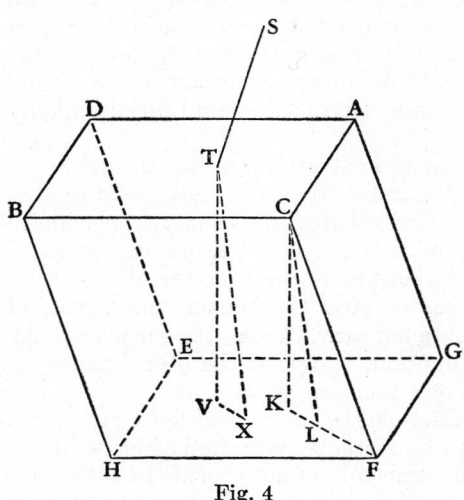

Fig. 4

and perhaps better upon pitch, leather or parchment. Afterwards it must be rubbed with a little oil or white of an egg to fill up its scratches; whereby it will become very transparent and polite. But for several experiments it is not necessary to polish it. If a piece of this crystalline stone be laid upon a book, every letter of the book seen through it will appear double, by means of a double refraction. And if any beam of light falls either perpendicularly, or in any oblique angle upon any surface of this crystal, it becomes divided into two beams by means of the same double refraction. Which beams are of the same colour with the incident beam of light, and seem equal to one another in the quantity of their light, or very nearly equal. One of these refractions is performed by the usual rule of Optics, the sine of incidence out of air into this crystal being to the sine of refraction as five to three. The other refraction, which may be called the unusual refraction, is performed by the following rule:

Let ADBC represent the refracting surface of the crystal, C the biggest solid angle at that surface, GEHF the opposite surface, and CK a perpendicular on that surface. This perpendicular makes with the edge of the crystal CF, an angle of 19 degrees 3'. Join KF, and in it take KL, so that the angle KCL be 6 degrees 40'. and the angle LCF 12 degrees 23'. And if ST represent any beam of light incident at T in any angle upon the refracting surface ADBC, let TV be the refracted beam determined by the given portion of the sines 5 to 3, according to the usual rule of Optics. Draw VX parallel and equal to KL. Draw it the same way from V in which L lieth from K; and joining TX, this line TX shall be the other refracted beam carried from T to X, by the unusual refraction.

If, therefore, the incident beam ST be perpendicular to the refracting surface, the two beams TV and TX, into which it shall become divided, shall be parallel to the lines CK and CL; one of those beams going through the crystal perpendicularly, as it ought to do by the usual laws of Optics, and the other TX by an unusual refraction diverging from the perpendicular, and making with it an angle VTX of about 6⅔ degrees, as is found by experience. And hence, the plane VTX, and such like planes which are parallel to the plane CFK, may be called the planes of perpendicular refraction. And the coast towards which the lines KL and VX are drawn, may be called the coast of unusual refraction.

In like manner, crystal of the rock has a double refraction; but the difference of the two refractions is not so great and manifest as in island crystal.

When the beam ST incident on island crystal is divided into two beams TV and TX, and these two beams arrive at the farther surface of the glass, the beam TV, which was refracted at the first surface after the usual manner, shall be again refracted entirely after the usual manner at the second surface; and the beam TX, which was refracted after the unusual manner in the first surface, shall be again refracted entirely after the unusual manner in the second surface; so that both these beams shall emerge out of the second surface in lines parallel to the first incident beam ST.

And if two pieces of island crystal be placed one after another, in such manner that all the surfaces of the latter be parallel to all the corresponding surfaces of the former, the rays which are refracted after the usual manner in the first surface of the first crystal, shall be refracted after the usual manner in all the following surfaces; and the rays which are refracted after the unusual manner in the first surface shall be refracted after the unusual manner in all the following surfaces. And the same thing happens, though the surfaces of the crystals be any ways inclined to one another, provided that their planes of perpendicular refraction be parallel to one another.

And, therefore, there is an original difference in the rays of light, by means of which some rays are in this experiment constantly refracted after the usual manner, and others constantly after the unusual manner; for if the difference be not original, but arises from new modifications impressed on the rays at their first refraction, it would be altered by new modifications in the three following refractions; whereas it suffers no alteration, but is constant, and has the same effect upon the rays in all the refractions. The unusual refraction is, therefore, performed by an original property of the rays. And it remains to be enquired whether the rays have not more original properties than are yet discovered.

Qu. 26. Have not the rays of light several sides, endued with several original properties? For if the planes of perpendicular refraction of the second crystal be at right angles with the planes of perpendicular refraction of the first crystal, the rays which are refracted after the usual manner in passing through the first crystal will be all of them refracted after the unusual manner in passing through the second crystal; and the rays which are refracted after the unusual manner in passing through the first crystal will be all of them refracted after the usual manner in passing through the second crystal. And, therefore, there are not two sorts of rays differing in their nature from one another, one of which is constantly and in all positions refracted after the usual manner, and the other constantly and in all positions after the unusual manner. The difference between the two sorts of rays, in the experiment mentioned in the 25th Question, was only in the positions of the sides of the rays to the planes of perpendicular refraction. For one and the same ray is here refracted, sometimes after the usual, and sometimes after the unusual manner, according to the position which its sides have to the crystals. If the sides of the ray are posited the same way to both crystals, it is refracted after the same manner in them both; but if that side of the ray which looks towards the coast of the unusual refraction of the first crystal be 90 degrees from that side of the same ray which looks toward the coast of the unusual refraction of the second crystal (which may be effected by varying the position of the second crystal to the first, and by consequence to the rays of light), the ray shall be refracted after several manners in the several crystals. There is nothing more required to determine whether the rays of light which fall upon the second crystal shall be refracted after the usual or after the unusual manner, but to turn about this crystal, so that the coast of this crystal's unusual refraction may be on this or on that side of the ray. And, therefore, every ray may be considered as having four sides or quarters, two of which opposite to one another incline the ray to be refracted after the unusual manner, as often as either of them are turned towards the coast of unusual refraction; and the other two, whenever either of them are turned towards the coast of unusual refraction, do not incline it to be otherwise refracted than after the usual manner. The two first may, therefore, be called the sides of unusual refraction. And since these dispositions were in the rays before their incidence on the second, third, and fourth surfaces of the two crystals, and suffered no alteration (so far as appears) by the refraction of the rays in their passage through those surfaces, and the rays were refracted by the same laws in all the four surfaces, it appears that those dispositions were in the rays originally, and suffered no alteration by the first refraction, and that by means of those dispositions the rays were refracted at their incidence on the first surface of the first crystal, some of them after the usual, and some of them after the unusual manner, accordingly as their sides of unusual refraction were then turned towards the coast of the unusual refraction of that crystal, or sideways from it.

Every ray of light has, therefore, two opposite sides, originally endued with a property on which the unusual refraction depends, and the other two opposite sides not endued with that property. And it remains to be enquired whether there are not more properties of light by which the sides of the rays differ, and are distinguished from one another.

In explaining the difference of the sides of the rays above mentioned, I have supposed that the rays fall perpendicularly on the first crystal. But if they fall obliquely on it, the success is the same. Those rays which are refracted after the usual manner in the first crystal will be refracted after the unusual manner in the second crystal, supposing the planes of perpendicular refraction to be at right angles with one another, as above; and on the contrary.

If the planes of the perpendicular refraction of the two crystals be neither parallel nor perpendicular to one another, but contain an acute angle, the two beams of light which emerge out of the first crystal will be each of them divided into two more at their incidence on the second crystal. For in this case the rays in each of the two beams will some of them have their sides of unusual refraction, and some of them their other sides turned towards the coast of the unusual refraction of the second crystal.

Qu. 27. Are not all hypotheses erroneous which have hitherto been invented for explaining the phenomena of light, by new modifications of the rays? For those phenomena depend not upon new modifications, as has been supposed, but upon the original and unchangeable properties of the rays.

Qu. 28. Are not all hypotheses erroneous in which light is supposed to consist in pression or motion, propagated through a fluid medium? For in all these hypotheses the phenomena of light have been hitherto explained by supposing that they arise from new modifications of the rays; which is an erroneous supposition.

If light consisted only in pression propagated without actual motion, it would not be able to agitate and heat the bodies which refract and reflect it. If it consisted in motion propagated to all distances in an instant, it would require an infinite force every moment, in every shining particle, to generate that motion. And if it consisted in pression or motion, propagated either in an instant or in time, it would bend into the shadow. For pression or motion cannot be propagated in a fluid in right lines, beyond an obstacle which stops part of the motion, but will bend and spread every way into the quiescent medium which lies beyond the obstacle. Gravity tends downwards, but the pressure of water arising from gravity tends every way with equal force, and is propagated as readily, and with as much force sideways as downwards, and through crooked passages as through straight ones. The waves on the surface of stagnating water, passing by the sides of a broad obstacle which stops part of them, bend afterwards and dilate themselves gradually into the quiet water behind the obstacle. The waves, pulses or vibrations of the air, wherein sounds consist, bend manifestly, though not so much as the waves of water. For a bell or a cannon may be heard beyond a hill which intercepts the sight of the sounding body, and sounds are propagated as readily through crooked pipes as through straight ones. But light is never known to follow crooked passages nor to bend into the shadow. For the fixed stars by the interposition of any of the planets cease to be seen. And so do the parts of the sun by the interposition of the Moon, Mercury or Venus. The rays which pass very near to the edges of any body are bent a little by the action of the body, as we shewed above; but this bending is not towards but from the shadow, and is performed only in the passage of the ray by the body, and at a very small distance from it. So soon as the ray is past the body, it goes right on.

To explain the unusual refraction of island crystal by pression or motion propagated, has not hitherto been attempted (to my knowledge) except by Huygens, who for that end supposed two several vibrating mediums within that crystal. But when he tried the refractions in two successive pieces of that crystal, and found them such as is mentioned above, he confessed himself at a loss for explaining them. For pressions or motions, propagated from a shining body through an uniform medium, must be on all sides alike; whereas by those experiments it appears that the rays of light have different properties in their different sides. He suspected that the pulses of æther in passing through the first crystal might receive certain new modifications, which might determine them to be propagated in this or that medium within the second crystal, according to the position of that crystal. But what modifications those might be he could not say, nor think of anything satisfactory in that point. And if he had known that the unusual refraction depends not on new modifications, but on the original and unchangeable dispositions of the rays, he would have found it as difficult to explain how those dispositions, which he supposed to be impressed on the rays by the first crystal, could be in them before their incidence on that crystal, and in general, how all rays emitted by shining bodies can have those dispositions in them from the beginning. To me, at least, this seems inexplicable, if light be nothing else than pression or motion propagated through æther.

And it is as difficult to explain by these hypotheses how rays can be alternately in fits of easy reflexion and easy transmission, unless perhaps one might suppose that there are in all space two æthereal vibrating mediums, and that the vibrations of one of them constitute light, and the vibrations of the other are swifter, and as often as they overtake the vibrations of the first, put them into those fits. But how two æthers can be diffused through all space, one of which acts upon the other, and by consequence is reacted upon, without retarding, shattering, dispersing and confounding one another's motions, is inconceivable. And against filling the heavens with fluid mediums, unless they be exceeding rare, a great objection arises from the regular and very lasting motions of the planets and comets in all manner of courses through the heavens. For thence it is manifest that the heavens are void of all sensible resistance, and by consequence of all sensible matter.

For the resisting power of fluid mediums arises partly from the attrition of the parts of the medium, and partly from the *vis inertiæ* of the matter. That part of the resistance of a spherical body which arises from the attrition of the parts of the medium is very nearly as the diameter, or, at the most, as the *factum* of the diameter, and the velocity of the spherical body together. And that part of the resistance which arises from the *vis inertiæ* of the matter is as the square of that *factum*. And by this difference the two sorts of resistance may be distinguished from one another in any medium; and these being distinguished, it will be found that almost all the resistance of bodies of a competent magnitude moving in air, water, quick-silver, and such like fluids with a competent velocity, arises from the *vis inertiæ* of the parts of the fluid.

Now, that part of the resisting power of any medium which arises from the tenacity, friction or attrition of the parts of the medium, may be diminished by dividing the matter into smaller parts, and making the parts more smooth and slippery; but that part of the resistance which arises from the *vis inertiæ* is proportional to the density of the matter, and cannot be diminished by dividing the matter into smaller parts, nor by any other means than by decreasing the density of the medium. And for these reasons the density of fluid mediums is very nearly proportional to their resistance. Liquors which differ not much in density as water, spirit of wine, spirit of turpentine, hot oil, differ not much in resistance. Water is thirteen or fourteen times lighter than quick-silver and by consequence thirteen or fourteen times rarer, and its resistance is less than that of quick-silver in the same proportion, or thereabouts, as I have found by experiments made with pendulums. The open air in which we breathe is eight or nine hundred times lighter than water, and by consequence eight or nine hundred times rarer, and accordingly its resistance is less than that of water in the same proportion, or thereabouts, as I have also found by experiments made with pendulums. And in thinner air the resistance is still less, and at length, by rarefying the air, becomes insensible. For small feathers falling in the open air meet with great resistance, but in a tall glass well emptied of air, they fall as fast as lead or gold, as I have seen tried several times. Whence the resistance seems still to decrease in proportion to the density of the fluid. For I do not find by any experiments that bodies moving in quick-silver, water, or air meet with any other sensible resistance than what arises from the density and tenacity of those sensible fluids, as they would do if the pores of those fluids, and all other spaces, were filled with a dense and subtile fluid. Now, if the resistance in a vessel well emptied of air was but a hundred times less than in the open air, it would be about a million of times less than in quick-silver. But it seems to be much less in such a vessel, and still much less in the heavens, at the height of three or four hundred miles from the Earth, or above. For Mr. Boyle has shewed that air may be rarified above ten thousand times in vessels of glass; and the heavens are much emptier of air than any vacuum we can make below. For since the air is compressed by the weight of the incumbent atmosphere, and the density of air is proportional to the force compressing it, it follows by computation that, at the height of about seven and a half English miles from the Earth, the air is four times rarer than at the surface of the Earth; and at the height of 15 miles it is sixteen times rarer than that at the surface of the Earth; and at the height of 22½, 30, or 38 miles, it is respectively 64, 256, or 1,024 times rarer, or thereabouts; and at the height of 76, 152, 228 miles, it is about 1,000,000, 1,000,000,000,000, or 1,000,000,000,000,000,000 times rarer; and so on.

Heat promotes fluidity very much by diminishing the tenacity of bodies. It makes many bodies fluid which are not fluid in cold, and increases the fluidity of tenacious liquids, as of oil, balsam, and honey, and thereby decreases their resistance. But it decreases not the resistance of water considerably, as it would do if any considerable part of the resistance of water arose from the attrition or tenacity of its parts. And, therefore, the resistance of water arises principally and almost entirely from the *vis inertiæ* of its matter; and by consequence, if the heavens were as dense as water, they would not have much less resistance than water; if as dense as quick-silver, they would not have much less resistance than quick-silver; if absolutely dense, or full of matter without any vacuum, let the matter be never so subtile and fluid, they would have a greater resistance than quick-silver. A solid globe in such a medium would lose above half its motion in moving three times the length of its diameter, and a globe not solid (such as are the planets), would be retarded sooner. And, therefore, to make way for the regular and lasting motions of the planets and comets, it's necessary to empty the heavens of all matter, except perhaps some very thin vapours, steams, or effluvia, arising from the atmospheres of the Earth, planets, and comets, and from such an exceedingly rare æthereal medium as we described above. A dense fluid can be of no use for explaining the phenomena of Nature, the motions of the planets and comets being better explained without it. It serves only to disturb and retard the motions of those great bodies, and make the frame of Nature languish; and in the pores of bodies it serves only to stop the vibrating motions of their parts, wherein their heat and activity consists. And as it is of no use, and hinders the operations of Nature, and makes her languish, so there is no evidence for its existence; and, therefore, it ought to be rejected. And if it be rejected, the hypotheses that light consists in pression or motion, propagated through such a medium, are rejected with it.

And, for rejecting such a medium, we have the authority of those the oldest and most celebrated philosophers of Greece and Phœnicia, who made a vacuum, and atoms, and the gravity of atoms, the first principles of their philosophy; tacitly attributing gravity to some other cause than dense matter. Later philosophers banish the consideration of such a cause out of natural philosophy, feigning hypotheses for explaining all things mechanically, and referring other causes to metaphysics; whereas the main business of natural philosophy is to argue from phenomena without feigning hypotheses, and to deduce causes from effects, till we come to the very first cause, which certainly is not mechanical; and not only to unfold the mechanism of the world, but chiefly to resolve these and such like questions. What is there in places almost empty of matter, and whence is it that the Sun and planets gravitate towards one another, without dense matter between them? Whence is it that Nature doth nothing in vain; and whence arises all that order and beauty which we see in the world? To what end are comets, and whence is it that planets move all one and the same way in orbs concentric, while comets move all manner of ways in orbs very eccentric; and what hinders the fixed stars from falling upon one another? How came the bodies of animals to be contrived with so much art, and for what ends were their several parts? Was the eye contrived without skill in Optics, and the ear without knowledge of sounds? How do the motions of the body follow from the will, and whence is the instinct in animals? Is not the sensory of animals that place to which the sensitive substance is present, and into which the sensible species of things are carried through the nerves and brain, that there they may be perceived by their immediate presence to that substance? And these things being rightly dispatched, does it not appear from phenomena that there is a Being incorporeal, living, intelligent, omnipresent, who in infinite space (as it were in his sensory) sees the things themselves intimately, and throughly perceives them, and comprehends them wholly by their immediate presence to himself? Of which things the images only carried through the organs of sense into our little sensoriums are there seen and beheld by that which in us perceives and thinks. And though every true step made in this philosophy brings us not immediately to the knowledge of the First Cause, yet it brings us nearer to it, and on that account is to be highly valued.

Qu. 29. Are not the rays of light very small bodies emitted from shining substances? For such bodies will pass through uniform mediums in right lines without bending into the shadow, which is the nature of the rays of light. They will also be capable of several properties, and be able to conserve their properties unchanged in passing through several mediums, which is another condition of the rays of light. Pellucid substances act upon the rays of light at a distance in refracting, reflecting, and inflecting them, and the rays mutually agitate the parts of those substances at a distance for heating them; and this action and reaction at a distance very much resembles an attractive force between bodies. If refraction be performed by attraction of the rays, the sines of incidence must be to the sines of refraction in a given proportion, as we shewed in our principles of philosophy. And this rule is true by experience. The rays of light in going out of glass into a vacuum, are bent towards the glass; and if they fall too obliquely on the vacuum, they are bent backwards into the glass, and totally reflected; and this reflexion cannot be ascribed to the resistance of an absolute vacuum, but must be caused by the power of the glass attracting the rays at their going out of it into the vacuum, and bringing them back. For if the farther surface of the glass be moistened with water or clear oil, or liquid and clear honey, the rays which would otherwise be reflected will go into the water, oil, or honey; and, therefore, are not reflected before they arrive at the farther surface of the glass, and begin to go out of it. If they go out of it into the water, oil, or honey, they go on, because the attraction of the glass is almost balanced and rendered ineffectual by the contrary attraction of the liquor. But if they go out of it into a vacuum which has no attraction to balance that of the glass, the attraction of the glass either bends and refracts them, or brings them back and reflects them.

And this is still more evident by laying together two prisms of glass, or two object-glasses of very long telescopes, the one plane, the other a little convex, and so compressing them that they do not fully touch, nor are too far asunder. For the light which falls upon the farther surface of the first glass where the interval between the glasses is not above the ten hundred thousandth part of an inch, will go through that surface, and through the air or vacuum between the glasses, and enter into the second glass, as was explained in the first, fourth, and eighth Observations of the first part of the second book. But, if the second glass be taken away, the light which goes out of the second surface of the first glass into the air or vacuum, will not go on forwards, but turns back into the first glass, and is reflected; and, therefore, it is drawn back by the power of the first glass, there being nothing else to turn it back. Nothing more is requisite for producing all the variety of colours, and degrees of refrangibility, than that the rays of light be bodies of different sizes, the least of which may take violet the weakest and darkest of the colours, and be more easily diverted by refracting surfaces from the right course; and the rest, as they are bigger and bigger, may make the stronger and more lucid colours (blue, green, yellow, and red) and be more and more difficultly diverted. Nothing more is requisite for putting the rays of light into fits of easy reflexion and easy transmission, than that they be small bodies which by their attractive powers, or some other force, stir up vibrations in what they act upon, which vibrations, being swifter than the rays, overtake them successively, and agitate them so as by turns to increase and decrease their velocities, and thereby put them into those fits. And, lastly, the unusual refraction of island crystal looks very much as if it were performed by some kind of attractive virtue lodged in certain sides both of the rays, and of the particles of the crystal. For were it not for some kind of disposition or virtue lodged in some sides of the particles of the crystal, and not in their other sides, and which inclines and bends the rays towards the coast of unusual refraction, the rays which fall perpendicularly on the crystal would not be refracted towards that coast rather than towards any other coast, both at their incidence and at their emergence, so as to emerge perpendicularly by a contrary situation of the coast of unusual refraction at the second surface; the crystal acting upon the rays after they have passed through it, and are emerging into the air; or, if you please, into a vacuum. And since the crystal by this disposition or virtue does not act upon the rays, unless when one of their sides of unusual refraction looks towards that coast, this argues a virtue or disposition in those sides of the rays which answers to, and sympathizes with, that virtue or disposition of the crystal as the poles of two magnets answer to one another. And as magnetism may be intended and remitted, and is found only in the magnet and in iron, so this virtue of refracting the perpendicular rays is greater in island crystal, less in crystal of the rock, and is not yet found in other bodies. I do not say that this virtue is magnetical: it seems to be of another kind. I only say that whatever it be, it's difficult to conceive how the rays of light, unless they be bodies, can have a permanent virtue in two of their sides which is not in their other sides, and this without any regard to their position to the space or medium through which they pass.

What I mean in this Question by a vacuum, and by the attractions of the rays of light towards glass or crystal, may be understood by what was said in the 18th, 19th, and 20th Questions.

QU. 30. Are not gross bodies and light convertible into one another, and may not bodies receive much of their activity from the particles of light which enter their composition? For all fixed bodies being heated emit light so long as they continue sufficiently hot, and light mutually stops in bodies as often as its rays strike upon their parts, as we shewed above. I know no body less apt to shine than water; and yet water, by frequent distillations, changes into fixed earth, as Mr. Boyle has tried, and then this earth being enabled to endure a sufficient heat, shines by heat like other bodies.

The changing of bodies into light, and light into bodies, is very conformable to the course of Nature, which seems delighted with transmutations. Water, which is a very fluid, tasteless salt she changes by heat into vapour, which is a sort of air, and by cold into ice, which is a hard, pellucid, brittle, fusible stone; and this stone returns into water by heat, and vapour returns into water by cold. Earth by heat becomes fire, and by cold returns into earth. Dense bodies by fermentation rarefy into several sorts of air, and this air by fermentation, and sometimes without it, returns into dense bodies. Mercury appears sometimes in the form of a fluid metal, sometimes in the form of a hard brittle metal, sometimes in the form of a corrosive pellucid salt called sublimate, sometimes in the form of a tasteless, pellucid, volatile white earth called *Mercurius dulcis;* or in that of a red opaque volatile earth called Cinnabar; or in that of a red or white precipitate, or in that of a fluid salt; and in distillation it turns into vapour, and being agitated *in vacuo,* it shines like fire. And after all these changes it returns again into its first form of mercury. Eggs grow from insensible magnitudes, and change into animals; tadpoles into frogs; and worms into flies. All birds, beasts and fishes, insects, trees, and other vegetables, with their several parts, grow out of water and watery tinctures and salts, and by putrefaction return again into watery substances. And water standing a few days in the open air, yields a tincture, which (like that of malt) by standing longer yields a sediment and a spirit, but before putrefaction is fit nourishment for animals and vegetables. And among such various and strange transmutations, why may not Nature change bodies into light, and light into bodies?

QU. 31. Have not the small particles of bodies certain powers, virtues, or forces, by which they act at a distance, not only upon the rays of light for reflecting, refracting, and inflecting them, but also upon one another for producing a great part of the phenomena of Nature? For it's well known that bodies act one upon another by the attractions of gravity, magnetism, and electricity; and these instances shew the tenor and course of Nature, and make it not improbable but that there may be more attractive powers than these. For Nature is very consonant and conformable to herself. How these attractions may be performed I do not here consider. What I call attraction may be performed by impulse, or by some other means unknown to me. I use that word here to signify only in general any force by which bodies tend towards one another, whatsoever be the cause. For we must learn from the phenomena of Nature what bodies attract one another, and what are the laws and properties of the attraction, before we enquire the cause by which the attraction is performed. The attractions of gravity, magnetism, and electricity reach to very sensible distances, and so have been observed by vulgar eyes, and there may be others which reach to so small distances as hitherto escape observation; and perhaps electrical attraction may reach to such small distances, even without being excited by friction.

For when salt of tartar runs *per deliquium*, is not this done by an attraction between the particles of the salt of tartar, and the particles of the water which float in the air in the form of vapours? And why does not common salt, or salt-petre, or vitriol, run *per deliquium*, but for want of such an attraction? Or why does not salt of tartar draw more water out of the air than in a certain proportion to its quantity, but for want of an attractive force after it is satiated with water? And whence is it but from this attractive power that water which alone distils with a gentle luke-warm heat, will not distil from salt of tartar without a great heat? And is it not from the like attractive power between the particles of oil of vitriol and the particles of water, that oil of vitriol draws to it a good quantity of water out of the air, and after it is satiated draws no more, and in distillation lets go the water very difficultly? And when water and oil of vitriol poured successively into the same vessel grow very hot in the mixing, does not this heat argue a great motion in the parts of the liquors? And does not this motion argue that the parts of the two liquors in mixing coalesce with violence, and by consequence rush towards one another with an accelerated motion? And when *aqua fortis*, or spirit of vitriol poured upon filings of iron dissolves the filings with a great heat and ebullition, is not this heat and ebullition effected by a violent motion of the parts, and does not that motion argue that the acid parts of the liquor rush towards the parts of the metal with violence, and run forcibly into its pores till they get between its outmost particles, and the main mass of the metal, and surrounding those particles loosen them from the main mass, and set them at liberty to float off into the water? And when the acid particles, which alone would distil with an easy heat, will not separate from the particles of the metal without a very violent heat, does not this confirm the attraction between them?

When spirit of vitriol poured upon common salt or saltpetre makes an ebullition with the salt, and unites with it, and in distillation the spirit of the common salt or saltpetre comes over much easier than it would do before, and the acid part of the spirit of vitriol stays behind, does not this argue that the fixed alkali of the salt attracts the acid spirit of the vitriol more strongly than its own spirit, and not being able to hold them both, lets go its own? And when oil of vitriol is drawn off from its weight of nitre, and from both the ingredients a compound spirit of nitre is distilled, and two parts of this spirit are poured on one part of oil of cloves or caraway seeds, or of any ponderous oil of vegetable or animal substances, or oil of turpentine thickened with a little balsam of sulphur, and the liquors grow so very hot in mixing, as presently to send up a burning flame—does not this very great and sudden heat argue that the two liquors mix with violence, and that their parts in mixing run towards one another with an accelerated motion, and clash with the greatest force? And is it not for the same reason that well-rectified spirit of wine poured on the same compound spirit flashes; and that the *pulvis fulminans*, composed of sulphur, nitre, and salt of tartar, goes off with a more sudden and violent explosion than gunpowder, the acid spirits of the sulphur and nitre rushing towards one another, and towards the salt of tartar, with so great a violence as by the shock to turn the whole at once into vapour and flame? Where the dissolution is slow, it makes a slow ebullition and a gentle heat; and where it is quicker, it makes a greater ebullition with more heat; and where it is done at once, the ebullition is contracted into a sudden blast or violent explosion, with a heat equal to that of fire and flame. So when a drachm of the above-mentioned compound spirit of nitre was poured upon half a drachm of oil of caraway seeds *in vacuo*, the mixture immediately made a flash like gunpowder, and burst the exhausted receiver, which was a glass six inches wide and eight inches deep. And even the gross body of sulphur powdered, and with an equal weight of iron filings and a little water made into paste, acts upon the iron, and in five or six hours grows too hot to be touched, and emits a flame. And by these experiments compared with the great quantity of sulphur with which the Earth abounds, and the warmth of the interior parts of the Earth, and hot springs, and burning mountains, and with damps, mineral coruscations, earthquakes, hot suffocating exhalations, hurricanes, and spouts, we may learn that sulphureous steams abound in the bowels of the Earth and ferment with minerals, and sometimes take fire with a sudden coruscation and explosion; and, if pent up in subterraneous caverns, burst the caverns with a great shaking of the Earth, as in springing of a mine. And then the vapour generated by the explosion, expiring through the pores of the Earth, feels hot and suffocates, and makes tempests and hurricanes, and sometimes causes the land to slide, or the sea to boil, and carries up the water thereof in drops, which by their weight fall down again in spouts. Also some sulphureous steams, at all times when the Earth is dry, ascending into the air, ferment there with nitrous acids, and sometimes taking fire cause lightning and thunder, and fiery meteors. For the air abounds with acid vapours fit to promote fermentations, as appears by the rusting of iron and copper in it, the kindling of fire by blowing, and the beating of the heart by means of respiration. Now, the above-mentioned motions are so great and violent as to shew that in fermentations the particles of bodies which almost rest are put into new motions by a very potent principle, which acts upon them only when they approach one another, and causes them to meet and clash with great violence, and grow hot with the motion, and dash one another into pieces, and vanish into air and vapour and flame.

When salt of tartar *per deliquium*, being poured into the solution of any metal, precipitates the metal and makes it fall down to the bottom of the liquor in the form of mud, does not this argue that the acid particles are attracted more strongly by the salt of tartar than by the metal, and by the stronger attraction go from the metal to the salt of tartar? And so when a solution of iron in *aqua fortis* dissolves the *lapis calaminaris*, and lets go the iron, or a solution of copper dissolves iron immersed in it and lets go the copper, or a solution of silver dissolves copper and lets go the silver, or a solution of mercury in *aqua fortis* being poured upon iron, copper, tin, or lead, dissolves the metal and lets go the mercury—does not this argue that the acid particles of the *aqua fortis* are attracted more strongly by the *lapis calaminaris* than by iron, and more strongly by iron than by copper, and more strongly by copper than by silver, and more strongly by iron, copper, tin, and lead, than by mercury? And is it not for the same reason that iron requires more *aqua fortis* to dissolve it than copper, and copper more than the other metals; and that, of all metals, iron is dissolved most easily, and is most apt to rust; and, next after iron, copper?

When oil of vitriol is mixed with a little water, or is run *per deliquium*, and in distillation the water ascends difficultly, and brings over with it some part of the oil of vitriol in the form of spirit of vitriol, and this spirit (being poured upon iron, copper, or salt of tartar) unites with the body and lets go the water

—doth not this shew that the acid spirit is attracted by the water, and more attracted by the fixed body than by the water, and therefore lets go the water to close with the fixed body? And is it not for the same reason that the water and acid spirits which are mixed together in vinegar, *aqua fortis*, and spirit of salt, cohere and rise together in distillation; but if the menstruum be poured on salt of tartar, or on lead, or iron, or any fixed body which it can dissolve, the acid by a stronger attraction adheres to the body, and lets go the water? And is it not also from a mutual attraction that the spirits of soot and sea-salt unite and compose the particles of sal-ammoniac, which are less volatile than before, because grosser and freer from water; and that the particles of sal-ammoniac in sublimation carry up the particles of antimony, which will not sublime alone; and that the particles of mercury uniting with the acid particles of spirit of salt compose mercury sublimate and with the particles of sulphur, compose cinnabar; and that the particles of spirit of wine and spirit of urine well rectified unite and, letting go the water which dissolved them, compose a consistent body; and that in subliming cinnabar from salt of tartar, or from quicklime, the sulphur by a stronger attraction of the salt or lime lets go the mercury, and stays with the fixed body; and that when mercury sublimate is sublimed from antimony, or from regulus of antimony, the spirit of salt lets go the mercury, and unites with the antimonial metal which attracts it more strongly, and stays with it till the heat be great enough to make them both ascend together, and then carries up the metal with it in the form of a very fusible salt called butter of antimony, although the spirit of salt alone be almost as volatile as water, and the antimony alone as fixed as lead?

When *aqua fortis* dissolves silver and not gold, and *aqua regia* dissolves gold and not silver, may it not be said that *aqua fortis* is subtile enough to penetrate gold as well as silver, but wants the attractive force to give it entrance; and that *aqua regia* is subtile enough to penetrate silver as well as gold, but wants the attractive force to give it entrance? For *aqua regia* is nothing else than *aqua fortis* mixed with some spirit of salt, or with sal-ammoniac; and even common salt dissolved in *aqua fortis* enables the menstruum to dissolve gold, though the salt be a gross body. When, therefore, spirit of salt precipitates silver out of *aqua fortis*, is it not done by attracting and mixing with the *aqua fortis*, and not attracting, or perhaps repelling silver? And when water precipitates antimony out of the sublimate of antimony and sal-ammoniac, or out of butter of antimony, is it not done by its dissolving, mixing with, and weakening the sal-armoniac or spirit of salt, and its not attracting, or perhaps repelling, the antimony? And is it not for want of an attractive virtue between the parts of water and oil, of quick-silver and antimony, of lead and iron, that these substances do not mix; and by a weak attraction, that quick-silver and copper mix difficultly; and from a strong one, that quick-silver and tin, antimony and iron, water and salts, mix readily? And, in general, is it not from the same principle that heat congregates homogeneal bodies, and separates heterogeneal ones?

When arsenic with soap gives a regulus, and with mercury sublimate a volatile fusible salt, like butter of antimony, doth not this shew that arsenic, which is a substance totally volatile, is compounded of fixed and volatile parts, strongly cohering by a mutual attraction, so that the volatile will not ascend without carrying up the fixed? And so, when an equal weight of spirit of wine and oil of vitriol are digested together, and in distillation yield two fragrant and volatile spirits which will not mix with one another, and a fixed black earth remains behind—doth not this shew that oil of vitriol is composed of volatile and fixed parts strongly united by attraction, so as to ascend together in form of a volatile, acid, fluid salt, until the spirit of wine attracts and separates the volatile parts from the fixed? And, therefore, since oil of sulphur *per campanam* is of the same nature with oil of vitriol, may it not be inferred that sulphur is also a mixture of volatile and fixed parts so strongly cohering by attraction as to ascend together in sublimation? By dissolving flowers of sulphur in oil of turpentine, and distilling the solution, it is found that sulphur is composed of an inflammable thick oil or fat bitumen, an acid salt, a very fixed earth, and a little metal. The three first were found not much unequal to one another, the fourth in so small a quantity as scarce to be worth considering. The acid salt, dissolved in water, is the same with oil of sulphur *per campanam*, and abounding much in the bowels of the Earth, and particularly in marcasites—unites itself to the other ingredients of the marcasite, which are, bitumen, iron, copper, and earth, and with them compounds alum, vitriol, and sulphur. With the earth alone it compounds alum; with the metal alone, or metal and earth together, it compounds vitriol; and with the bitumen and earth it compounds sulphur. Whence it comes to pass that marcasites abound with those three minerals. And is it not from the mutual attraction of the ingredients that they stick together for compounding these minerals, and that the bitumen carries up the other ingredients of the sulphur, which without it would not sublime? And the same question may be put concerning all, or almost all, the gross bodies in Nature. For all the parts of animals and vegetables are composed of substances volatile and fixed, fluid and solid, as appears by their analysis; and so are salts and minerals, so far as chemists have been hitherto able to examine their composition.

When mercury sublimate is re-sublimed with fresh mercury, and becomes *mercurius dulcis*, which is a white, tasteless earth scarce dissolvable in water, and *mercurius dulcis* re-sublimed with spirit of salt returns into mercury sublimate; and when metals corroded with a little acid turn into rust, which is an earth tasteless and indissolvable in water, and this earth imbibed with more acid becomes a metallic salt; and when some stones, as spar of lead, dissolved in proper menstruums become salts—do not these things shew that salts are dry earth and watery acid united by attraction, and that the earth will not become a salt without so much acid as makes it dissolvable in water? Do not the sharp and pungent tastes of acids arise from the strong attraction whereby the acid particles rush upon and agitate the particles of the tongue? And when metals are dissolved in acid menstruums, and the acids in conjunction with the metal act after a different manner, so that the compound has a different taste much milder than before, and sometimes a sweet one—is it not because the acids adhere to the metallic particles, and thereby lose much of their activity? And if the acid be in too small a proportion to make the compound dissolvable in water, will it not by adhering strongly to the metal become unactive and lose its taste, and the compound be a tasteless earth? For such things as are not dissolvable by the moisture of the tongue, act not upon the taste.

As gravity makes the sea flow round the denser and weightier parts of the globe of the Earth, so the attraction may make the watery acid flow round the denser and compacter particles of earth for composing the particles of salt. For otherwise the acid would not do the office of a medium between the earth and common water, for making salts dissolvable in the water; nor would salt of tartar readily draw off the acid from dissolved metals, nor metals the acid from mercury. Now, as in the great globe of the Earth and sea, the densest bodies by their gravity sink down in water, and always endeavour to go towards the centre of the globe; so in particles of salt the densest matter may always endeavour to approach the centre of the particle: so that a particle of salt may be compared to a chaos, being dense, hard, dry, and earthy in the centre; and rare, soft, moist, and watery in the circumference. And hence it seems to be that salts are of a lasting nature, being scarce destroyed unless by drawing away their watery parts by violence, or by letting them soak into the pores of the central earth by a gentle heat in putrefaction, until the earth be dissolved by the water, and separated into smaller particles, which by reason of their smallness make the rotten compound appear of a black colour. Hence also it may be that the parts of animals and vegetables preserve their several forms, and assimilate their nourishment; the soft and moist nourishment easily changing its texture by a gentle heat and motion till it becomes like the dense, hard, dry, and durable earth in the centre of each particle. But when the nourishment grows unfit to be assimilated, or the central earth grows too feeble to assimilate it, the motion ends in confusion, putrefaction, and death.

If a very small quantity of any salt or vitriol be dissolved in a great quantity of water, the particles of the salt or vitriol will not sink to the bottom, though they be heavier in species than the water, but will evenly diffuse themselves into all the water, so as to make it as saline at the top as at the bottom. And does not this imply that the parts of the salt or vitriol recede from one another, and endeavour to expand themselves, and get as far asunder as the quantity of water, in which they float, will allow? And does not this endeavour imply that they have a repulsive force by which they fly from one another, or, at least, that they attract the water more strongly than they do one another? For as all things ascend in water which are less attracted than water, by the gravitating power of the Earth; so all the particles of salt which float in water, and are less attracted than water by any one particle of salt, must recede from that particle, and give way to the more attracted water.

When any saline liquor is evaporated to a cuticle and let cool, the salt concretes in regular figures; which argues that the particles of the salt, before they concreted, floated in the liquor at equal distances in rank and file, and by consequence that they acted upon one another by some power which at equal distances is equal, at unequal distances unequal. For by such a power they will range themselves uniformly, and without it they will float irregularly, and come together as irregularly. And since the particles of island crystal act all the same way upon the rays of light for causing the unusual refraction, may it not be supposed that, in the formation of this crystal, the particles not only ranged themselves in rank and file for concreting in regular figures, but also by some kind of polar virtue turned their homogeneal sides the same way.

The parts of all homogeneal hard bodies which fully touch one another stick together very strongly. And for explaining how this may be, some have invented hooked atoms, which is begging the question; and others tell us that bodies are glued together by rest (that is, by an occult quality, or rather by nothing); and others, that they stick together by conspiring motions (that is, by relative rest amongst themselves). I had rather infer from their cohesion that their particles attract one another by some force, which in immediate contact is exceeding strong, at small distances performs the chemical operations above mentioned, and reaches not far from the particles with any sensible effect.

All bodies seem to be composed of hard particles, for otherwise fluids would not congeal; as water, oils, vinegar, and spirit or oil of vitriol do by freezing; mercury by fumes of lead; spirit of nitre and mercury by dissolving the mercury and evaporating the phlegm; spirit of wine and spirit of urine by dephlegming and mixing them; and spirit of urine and spirit of salt by subliming them together to make sal-ammoniac. Even the rays of light seem to be hard bodies; for otherwise they would not retain different properties in their different sides. And, therefore, hardness may be reckoned the property of all uncompounded matter. At least, this seems to be as evident as the universal impenetrability of matter. For all bodies, so far as experience reaches, are either hard, or may be hardened; and we have no other evidence of universal impenetrability, besides a large experience without an experimental exception. Now, if compound bodies are so very hard as we find some of them to be, and yet are very porous, and consist of parts which are only laid together, the simple particles which are void of pores, and were never yet divided, must be much harder. For such hard particles, being heaped up together, can scarce touch one another in more than a few points, and therefore must be separable by much less force than is requisite to break a solid particle whose parts touch in all the space between them, without any pores or interstices to weaken their cohesion. And how such very hard particles, which are only laid together and touch only in a few points, can stick together, and that so firmly as they do, without the assistance of something which causes them to be attracted or pressed towards one another, is very difficult to conceive.

The same thing I infer also from the cohering of two polished marbles *in vacuo*, and from the standing of quick-silver in the barometer at the height of 50, 60 or 70 inches, or above, whenever it is well-purged of air and carefully poured in, so that its parts be everywhere contiguous both to one another and to the glass. The atmosphere by its weight presses the quick-silver into the glass, to the height of 29 or 30 inches. And some other agent raises it higher, not by pressing it into the glass, but by making its parts stick to the glass, and to one another. For upon any discontinuation of parts, made either by bubbles or by shaking the glass, the whole mercury falls down to the height of 29 or 30 inches.

And of the same kind with these experiments are those that follow: If two plane polished plates of glass (suppose two pieces of a polished looking-glass) be laid together, so that their sides be parallel and at a very small distance from one another, and then their lower edges be dipped into water, the water will rise up between them. And the less the distance of the glasses is, the greater will be the height to which the water will rise. If the distance be about the hundredth part of an inch, the water will rise to the height of about an inch; and if the distance be greater or less in any proportion, the height will be reciprocally proportional to the distance very nearly. For the attractive force of the glasses is the same, whether the distance between them be greater or less; and the weight of the water drawn up is the same, if the height of it be reciprocally proportional to the distance of the glasses. And in like manner, water ascends between two marbles polished plane, when their polished sides are parallel, and at a very little distance from one another. And if slender pipes of glass be dipped at one end into stagnating water, the water will rise up within the pipe, and the height to which it rises will be reciprocally proportional to the diameter of the cavity of the pipe, and will equal the height to which it rises between two planes of glass, if the semi-diameter of the cavity of the pipe be equal to the distance between the planes, or thereabouts. And these experiments succeed after the same manner *in vacuo* as in the open air (as hath been tried before the Royal Society) and therefore are not influenced by the weight or pressure of the atmosphere.

And if a large pipe of glass be filled with sifted ashes well pressed together in the glass, and one end of the pipe be dipped into stagnating water, the water will rise up slowly in the ashes, so as in the space of a week or fortnight to reach up within the glass to the height of 30 or 40 inches above the stagnating water. And the water rises up to this height by the action only of those particles of the ashes which are upon the surface of the elevated water; the particles which are within the water attracting or repelling it as much downwards as upwards. And, therefore, the action of the particles is very strong. But the particles of the ashes being not so dense and close together as those of glass, their action is not so strong as that of glass, which keeps quick-silver suspended to the height of 60 or 70 inches, and, therefore, acts with a force which would keep water suspended to the height of above 60 feet.

By the same principle, a sponge sucks in water, and the glands in the bodies of animals, according to their several natures and dispositions, suck in various juices from the blood.

If two plane polished plates of glass three or four inches broad, and twenty or twenty-five long, be laid one of them parallel to the horizon, the other upon the first, so as at one of their ends to touch one another, and contain an angle of about 10 or 15 minutes, and the same be first moistened on their inward sides with a clean cloth dipped into oil of oranges or spirit of turpentine, and a drop or two of the oil or spirit be let fall upon the lower glass at the other; so soon as the upper glass is laid down upon the lower, so as to touch it at one end as above, and to touch the drop at the other end, making with the lower glass an angle of about 10 or 15 minutes, the drop will begin to move towards the concourse of the glasses, and will continue to move with an accelerated motion till it arrives at that concourse of the glasses. For the two glasses attract the drop, and make it run that way towards which the attractions incline. And if when the drop is in motion you lift up that end of the glasses where they meet, and towards which the drop moves, the drop will ascend between the glasses, and therefore is attracted. And as you lift up the glasses more and more, the drop will ascend slower and slower, and at length rest, being then carried downward by its weight, as much as upwards by the attraction. And by this means you may know the force by which the drop is attracted at all distances from the concourse of the glasses.

Now, by some experiments of this kind (made by Mr. Hauksbee), it has been found that the attraction is almost reciprocally in a duplicate proportion of the distance of the middle of the drop from the concourse of the glasses, viz., reciprocally in a simple proportion, by reason of the spreading of the drop, and its touching each glass in a larger surface; and again reciprocally in a simple proportion, by reason of the attractions growing stronger within the same quantity of attracting surface. The attraction, therefore, within the same quantity of attracting surface, is reciprocally as the distance between the glasses. And, therefore, where the distance is exceeding small, the attraction must be exceeding great. By the Table in the second part of the second book, wherein the thicknesses of coloured plates of water between two glasses are set down, the thickness of the plate where it appears very black is three-eighths of the ten hundred thousandth part of an inch. And where the oil of oranges between the glasses is of this thickness, the attraction collected by the foregoing rule seems to be so strong as, within a circle of an inch in diameter, to suffice to hold up a weight equal to that of a cylinder of water of an inch in diameter, and two or three furlongs in length. And where it is of a less thickness, the attraction may be proportionally greater, and continue to increase, until the thickness do not exceed that of a single particle of the oil. There are, therefore, agents in nature able to make the particles of bodies stick together by very strong attractions. And it is the business of experimental philosophy to find them out.

Now, the smallest particles of matter may cohere by the strongest attractions, and compose bigger particles of weaker virtue; and many of these may cohere and compose bigger particles whose virtue is still weaker, and so on for divers successions, until the progression end in the biggest particles on which the operations in chemistry, and the colours of natural bodies depend, and which by cohering compose bodies of a sensible magnitude. If the body is compact, and bends or yields inward to pression—without any sliding of its parts, it is hard and elastic, returning to its figure with a force rising from the mutual attraction of its parts. If the parts slide upon one another, the body is malleable or soft. If they slip easily, and are of a fit size to be agitated by heat, and the heat is big enough to keep them in agitation, the body is fluid; and if it be apt to stick to things, it is humid; and the drops of every fluid affect a round figure by the mutual attraction of their parts, as the globe of the Earth and sea affects a round figure by the mutual attraction of its parts by gravity.

Since metals dissolved in acids attract but a small quantity of the acid, their attractive force can reach but to a small distance from them. And as in algebra, where affirmative quantities vanish and cease, there negative ones begin; so in mechanics, where attraction ceases, there a repulsive virtue ought to succeed. And that there is such a virtue seems to follow from the reflexions and inflexions of the rays of light. For the rays are repelled by bodies in both these cases, without the immediate contact of the reflecting or inflecting body. It seems also to follow from the emission of light, the ray so soon as it is shaken off from a shining body by the vibrating motion of the parts of the body, and gets beyond the reach of attraction, being driven away with exceeding great velocity. For that force which is sufficient to turn it back in reflexion may be sufficient to emit it. It seems also to follow from the production of air and vapour. The particles when they are shaken off from bodies by heat or fermentation, so soon as they are beyond the reach of the attraction of the body, receding from it, and also from one another with great strength, and keeping at a distance, so as sometimes to take up above a million of times more space than they did before in the form of a dense body. Which vast contraction and expansion seems unintelligible, by feigning the particles of air to be springy and ramous, or rolled up like hoops, or by any other means than a repulsive power. The particles of fluids which do not cohere too strongly, and are of such a smallness as renders them most susceptible to those agitations which keep liquors in a Fluor, are most easily separated and rarefied into vapour, and in the language of the chemists they are volatile, rarefying with an easy heat, and condensing with cold. But those which are grosser, and so less susceptible of agitation, or cohere by a stronger attraction, are not separated without a stronger heat, or perhaps not without fermentation. And these last are the bodies which chemists call fixed, and being rarefied by fermentation become true, permanent air; those particles receding from one another with the greatest force, and being most difficultly brought together, which upon contact cohere most strongly. And because the particles of permanent air are grosser, and arise from denser substances than those of vapours, thence it is that true air is more ponderous than vapour, and that a moist atmosphere is lighter than a dry one, quantity for quantity. From the same repelling power it seems to be that flies walk upon the water without wetting their feet; and that the object-glasses of long telescopes lie upon one another without touching; and that dry powders are difficultly made to touch one another so as to stick together, unless by melting them, or wetting them with water, which by exhaling may bring them together; and that two polished marbles, which by immediate contact stick together, are difficultly brought so close together as to stick.

And thus Nature will be very conformable to herself and very simple, performing all the great motions of the heavenly bodies by the attraction of gravity which intercedes those bodies, and almost all the small ones of their particles by some other attractive and repelling powers which intercede the particles. The *vis inertiæ* is a passive principle by which bodies persist in their motion or rest, receive motion in proportion to the force impressing it, and resist as much as they are resisted. By this principle alone there never could have been any motion in the world. Some other principle was necessary for putting bodies into motion; and now they are in motion, some other principle is necessary for conserving the motion. For from the various composition of two motions, 'tis very certain that there is not always the same quantity of motion in the world. For if two globes, joined by a slender rod, revolve about their common centre of gravity with a uniform motion, while that centre moves on uniformly in a right line drawn in the plane of their circular motion, the sum of the motions of the two globes, as often as the globes are in the right line described by their common centre of gravity, will be bigger than the sum of their motions when they are in a line perpendicular to that right line. By this instance it appears that motion may be got or lost. But by reason of the tenacity of fluids, and attrition of their parts, and the weakness of elasticity in solids, motion is much more apt to be lost than got, and is always upon the decay. For bodies which are either absolutely hard, or so soft as to be void of elasticity, will not rebound from one another. Impenetrability makes them only stop. If two equal bodies meet directly *in vacuo*, they will by the laws of motion stop where they meet, and lose all their motion, and remain in rest, unless they be elastic, and receive new motion from their spring. If they have so much elasticity as suffices to make them re-bound with a quarter, or half, or three-quarters of the force with which they come together, they will lose three-quarters, or half, or a quarter of their motion. And this may be tried by letting two equal pendulums fall against one another from equal heights. If the pendulums be of lead or soft clay, they will lose all or almost all their motions; if of elastic bodies they will lose all but what they recover from their elasticity. If it be said that they can lose no motion but what they communicate to other bodies, the consequence is, that *in vacuo* they can lose no motion, but when they meet they must go on and penetrate one another's dimensions. If three equal round vessels be filled (the one with water, the other with oil, the third with molten pitch), and the liquors be stirred about alike to give them a vortical motion, the pitch by its tenacity will lose its motion quickly, the oil being less tenacious will keep it longer, and the water being less tenacious will keep it longest, but yet will lose it in a short time. Whence it is easy to understand that if many contiguous vortices of molten pitch were each of them as large as those which some suppose to revolve about the Sun and fixed stars, yet these and all their parts would, by their tenacity and stiffness, communicate their motion to one another till they all rested among themselves. Vortices of oil or water, or some fluider matter, might continue longer in motion; but unless the matter were void of all tenacity and attrition of parts, and communication of motion (which is not to be supposed), the motion would constantly decay. Seeing, therefore, the variety of motion which we find in the world is always decreasing, there is a necessity of conserving and recruiting it by active principles, such as are the cause of gravity, by which planets and comets keep their motions in their orbs, and bodies acquire great motion in falling; and the cause of fermentation, by which the heart and blood of animals are kept in perpetual motion and heat; the inward parts of the earth are constantly warmed, and in some places grow very hot; bodies burn and shine, mountains take fire, the caverns of the earth are blown up, and the Sun continues violently hot and lucid, and warms all things by his light. For we meet with very little motion in the world, besides what is owing to these active principles. And if it were not for these principles, the bodies of the earth, planets, comets, Sun, and all things in them, would grow cold and freeze, and become inactive masses; and all putrefaction, generation, vegetation and life would cease, and the planets and comets would not remain in their orbs.

All these things being considered, it seems probable to me that God in the beginning formed matter in solid, massy, hard, impenetrable, moveable particles, of such sizes and figures, and with such other properties, and in such proportion to space, as most conduced to the end for which he formed them; and that these primitive particles being solids, are incomparably harder than any porous bodies compounded of them; even so very hard as never to wear or break in pieces; no ordinary power being able to divide what God himself made one in the first creation. While the particles continue entire, they may compose bodies of one and the same nature and texture in all ages; but should they wear away, or break in pieces, the nature of things depending on them would be changed. Water and earth, composed of old worn particles and fragments of particles, would not be of the same nature and texture now, with water and earth composed of entire particles in the beginning. And, therefore, that Nature may be lasting, the changes of corporeal things are to be placed only in the various separations and new associations and motions of these permanent particles; compound bodies being apt to break, not in the midst of solid particles, but where those particles are laid together, and only touch in a few points.

It seems to me, further, that these particles have not only a *vis inertiæ*, accompanied with such passive laws of motion as naturally result from that force, but also that they are moved by certain active principles, such as is that of gravity, and that which causes fermentation, and the cohesion of bodies. These principles I consider, not as occult qualities, supposed to result from the specific forms of things, but as general laws of nature, by which the things themselves are formed; their truth appearing to us by phenomena, though their causes be not yet discovered. For these are manifest qualities, and their causes only are occult. And the Aristotelians gave the name of occult qualities, not to manifest qualities, but to such qualities only as they supposed to lie hid in bodies, and to be the unknown causes of manifest effects. Such as would be the causes of gravity, and of magnetic and electric attractions, and of fermentations, if we should suppose that these forces or actions arose from qualities unknown to us, and incapable of being discovered and made manifest. Such occult qualities put a stop to the improvement of natural philosophy, and therefore of late years have been rejected. To tell us that every species of things is endowed with an occult specific quality by which it acts and produces manifest effects, is to tell us nothing; but to derive two or three general principles of motion from phenomena, and afterwards to tell us how the properties and actions of all corporeal things follow from those manifest principles, would be a very great step in philosophy, though the causes of those principles were not yet discovered. And, therefore, I scruple not to propose the principles of motion above mentioned, they being of very general extent, and leave their causes to be found out.

Now, by the help of these principles, all material things seem to have been composed of the hard and solid particles above mentioned, variously associated in the first creation by the counsel of an intelligent agent. For it became Him who created them to set them in order. And if He did so, it's unphilosophical to seek for any other origin of the world, or to pretend that it might arise out of a chaos by the mere laws of Nature; though, being once formed, it may continue by those laws for many ages. For while comets move in very eccentric orbs in all manner of positions, blind fate could never make all the planets move one and the same way in orbs concentric, some inconsiderable irregularities excepted, which may have risen from the mutual actions of comets and planets upon one another, and which will be apt to increase, till this system wants a reformation. Such a wonderful uniformity in the planetary system must be allowed the effect of choice. And so must the uniformity in the bodies of animals, they having generally a right and a left side shaped alike, and on either side of their bodies two legs behind, and either two arms, or two legs, or two wings before upon their shoulders, and between their shoulders a neck running down into a backbone, and a head upon it; and in the head two ears, two eyes, a nose, a mouth, and a tongue, alike situated. Also the first contrivance of those very artificial parts of animals, the eyes, ears, brain, muscles, heart, lungs, midriff, glands, larynx, hands, wings, swimming bladders, natural spectacles, and other organs of sense and motion; and the instinct of brutes and insects can be the effect of nothing else than the wisdom and skill of a powerful, ever-living agent, who being in all places, is more able by His will to move the bodies within His boundless uniform sensorium, and thereby to form and reform the parts of the Universe, than we are by our will to move the parts of our own bodies. And yet we are not to consider the world as the body of God, or the several parts thereof as the parts of God. He is a uniform Being, void of organs, members or parts, and they are his creatures subordinate to him, and subservient to His will; and

He is no more the soul of them than the soul of man is the soul of the species of things carried through the organs of sense into the place of its sensation, where it perceives them by means of its immediate presence, without the intervention of any third thing. The organs of sense are not for enabling the soul to perceive the species of things in its sensorium, but only for conveying them thither; and God has no need of such organs, He being everywhere present to the things themselves. And since space is divisible *in infinitum*, and matter is not necessarily in all places, it may be also allowed that God is able to create particles of matter of several sizes and figures, and in several proportions to space, and perhaps of different densities and forces, and thereby to vary the laws of Nature, and make worlds of several sorts in several parts of the Universe. At least, I see nothing of contradiction in all this.

As in mathematics, so in natural philosophy, the investigation of difficult things by the method of analysis, ought ever to precede the method of composition. This analysis consists in making experiments and observations, and in drawing general conclusions from them by induction, and admitting of no objections against the conclusions but such as are taken from experiments, or other certain truths. For hypotheses are not to be regarded in experimental philosophy. And although the arguing from experiments and observations by induction be no demonstration of general conclusions, yet it is the best way of arguing which the nature of things admits of, and may be looked upon as so much the stronger, by how much the induction is more general. And if no exception occur from phenomena, the conclusion may be pronounced generally. But if at any time afterwards any exception shall occur from experiments, it may then begin to be pronounced with such exceptions as occur. By this way of analysis we may proceed from compounds to ingredients, and from motions to the forces producing them; and, in general, from effects to their causes, and from particular causes to more general ones, till the argument end in the most general. This is the method of analysis; and the synthesis consists in assuming the causes discovered, and established as principles, and by them explaining the phenomena proceeding from them, and proving the explanations.

In the two first books of these Optics, I proceeded by this analysis to discover and prove the original differences of the rays of light in respect of refrangibility, reflexibility, and colour, and their alternate fits of easy reflexion and easy transmission, and the properties of bodies, both opaque and pellucid, on which their reflexions and colours depend. And these discoveries, being proved, may be assumed in the method of composition for explaining the phenomena arising from them, an instance of which method I gave in the end of the first book. In this third book I have only begun the analysis of what remains to be discovered about light and its effects upon the frame of Nature, hinting several things about it, and leaving the hints to be examined and improved by the further experiments and observations of such as are inquisitive. And if natural philosophy in all its parts, by pursuing this method, shall at length be perfected, the bounds of moral philosophy will be also enlarged. For so far as we can know by natural philosophy what is the First Cause, what power He has over us, and what benefits we recieve from Him, so far our duty towards Him, as well as that towards one another, will appear to us by the light of Nature. And no doubt, if the worship of false gods had not blinded the heathen, their moral philosophy would have gone farther than to the four cardinal virtues;

and instead of teaching the transmigration of souls, and to worship the Sun and Moon, and dead heroes, they would have taught us to worship our true Author and Benefactor, as their ancestors did under the government of Noah and his sons before they corrupted themselves.

TREATISE ON LIGHT

BIOGRAPHICAL NOTE

CHRISTIAAN HUYGENS, 1629–1695

THE family into which Christiaan Huygens was born, April 14, 1629, at The Hague, was one of the most eminent in both the political and literary development of the Dutch Renaissance. The father of the scientist, Constantijn Huygens, Lord of Zuylichem, was secretary of state for three successive Princes of Orange; he carried out many diplomatic missions, particularly to England where he was knighted in 1621. While there he became the friend of Donne, whose poetry he began translating into Dutch. As one of the leaders of the Amsterdam school, he was the intimate friend of Vondel, the Dutch national poet, and was himself Holland's foremost classical poet.

Sir Constantijn, who was a distinguished Latinist, a musician, and a mathematician, took upon himself the preliminary instruction of his sons. Christiaan, the second son, was trained as a boy in languages, drawing, and music. At thirteen he began the study of mechanics, which together with mathematics soon became his chief interest. But before devoting his entire attention to these subjects he was sent to Leyden to study law with Vinnius, who later dedicated his famous commentary on the *Institutes* to him. In 1646 Huygens transferred to Breda, where his father directed the new university, and two years later he took his degree in law. In both places he continued his pursuit of mathematics, particularly with Van Schooten, who included some of Huygens' notes in his edition of Descartes' *Geometry*.

At seventeen Huygens communicated his first mathematical discovery to Mersenne, who introduced him to the learned world as "the Dutch Archimedes," and soon after, he was in correspondence with the leading scientists of Europe. Descartes, on being shown a mathematical paper of Huygens, declared his confidence that "he will excel in this science wherein I see hardly anyone who knows anything." Although Descartes frequented Sir Constantijn's house, it does not appear that he ever met his son. They exchanged letters, Descartes called Huygens "a son of his own blood," and when Huygens was traveling in Denmark in 1649 with the Count of Nassau, he regretted that time and weather did not permit his crossing over to Sweden to visit Descartes, who was then living there at the invitation of Queen Christina.

At the age of twenty-one Huygens published his first works on mathematics, dealing with the quadrature of conic sections, and in 1654, he made the closest approximation so far obtained of the area of the circle. Two years later he sent to Van Schooten his work on probability, which while recognizing the priority of Pascal's and Fermat's treatment, constituted the first treatise on the subject when published in a volume of Van Schooten's mathematical writings. At the same time Huygens was working with his elder brother on astronomy. They found a new method of grinding and polishing lenses which overcame the defects of spherical and chromatic aberration and enabled them to construct an improved telescope. Huygens' first observations yielded the discovery of the Orion nebula and of a new satellite to Saturn as well as a truer description of the rings about that planet. The need for an exact measure of time in observing the heavens led Huygens to the invention of the pendulum-clock, which was presented to the states-general in 1657 and was followed a year later by a description of the requisite mechanism.

Huygens' reputation now became international. As early as 1655 the University of Angers had distinguished him with an honorary degree of doctor of laws. In 1663, on the occasion of a visit to England, he was elected a fellow of the Royal Society. Two years later, on the establishment of the French Royal Academy of Sciences, Colbert invited him to be its first foreign resident, and for the next fifteen years Huygens made his home in France. He received a handsome pension from Louis XIV and lived at Paris in the Bibliothèque du Roi. Although Huygens disliked the world of rank, wealth, and fashion, he did not live the life of a recluse in Paris; he even wrote some verses to the celebrated Ninon de Lenclos. Yet the greater part of his efforts, despite delicate health, were spent in intense scientific research. His treatises on "Dioptrics" and the concussion of elastic bodies were hailed not only for their discoveries, but also for the style in which they were presented, and Newton claimed that among modern writers he had most closely approximated the style of the ancients. His greatest work, the *Horologium oscillatorium* (1673), dealt with the problems raised by the pendulum-clock, and contained original discoveries sufficient for several important treatises.

Twice during his residence in Paris, Huygens returned to Holland in the hope that his native air would restore his health, and in 1681, perhaps because of the revocation of the Edict of Nantes, he severed his connections and left France. Upon his return to Holland, Huygens took up again the study of optics, physics, and astronomy. He had always been interested in useful inventions and, in addition to the pendulum-clock, had already improved the air pump and the barometer, provided the first idea of the micrometer, and introduced the use of a spiral band for a watch-spring. In

Holland he turned again to the construction of telescopes. Using lenses of long focal distance mounted on poles, he produced what were called "aerial telescopes." He also succeeded in constructing an almost perfectly achromatic eye-piece, still known by his name. His researches in optics finally led him to publish in 1690 his *Treatise on Light*, which had been written in French in 1678 while at Paris. In response to the need for some means of representing the solar system, Huygens constructed a "planetary machine" capable of showing the motions of the planets. It was apparently also at this time that he wrote the imaginative work found among his posthumous papers called *Cosmotheoros*, and translated into English under the title, *"The celestial worlds discovered, or conjectures concerning the inhabitants, plants, and productions of the worlds in the planets."*

Worn out by his great and varied activity and the burden of an enormous correspondence, Huygens died at The Hague, June 8, 1695, at the age of sixty-six.

CONTENTS

CONTENTS

PREFACE

I WROTE this treatise during my sojourn in France twelve years ago, and I communicated it in the year 1678 to the learned persons who then composed the Royal Academy of Science, to the membership of which the King had done me the honour of calling me. Several of that body who are still alive will remember having been present when I read it, and above the rest those amongst them who applied themselves particularly to the study of mathematics; of whom I cannot cite more than the celebrated gentlemen, Cassini, Römer, and de la Hire. And, although I have since corrected and changed some parts, the copies which I had made of it at that time may serve for proof that I have yet added nothing to it save some conjectures touching the formation of Iceland crystal, and a novel observation on the refraction of rock crystal. I have desired to relate these particulars to make known how long I have meditated the things which now I publish, and not for the purpose of detracting from the merit of those who, without having seen anything that I have written, may be found to have treated of like matters: as has, in fact, occurred to two eminent geometricians, Messieurs Newton and Leibnitz, with respect to the problem of the figure of glasses for collecting rays when one of the surfaces is given.

One may ask why I have so long delayed to bring this work to the light. The reason is that I wrote it rather carelessly in the language in which it appears, with the intention of translating it into Latin, so doing in order to obtain greater attention to the thing. After which I proposed to myself to give it out along with another treatise on dioptrics, in which I explain the effects of telescopes and those things which belong more to that science. But the pleasure of novelty being past, I have put off from time to time the execution of this design, and I know not when I shall ever come to an end of it, being often turned aside either by business or by some new study. Considering which I have finally judged that it was better worth while to publish this writing, such as it is, than to let it run the risk, by waiting longer, of remaining lost.

There will be seen in it demonstrations of those kinds which do not produce as great a certitude as those of geometry, and which even differ much therefrom, since, whereas the geometers prove their propositions by fixed and incontestable principles, here the principles are verified by the conclusions to be drawn from them; the nature of these things not allowing of this being done otherwise. It is always possible to attain thereby to a degree of probability which very often is scarcely less than complete proof. To wit, when things which have been demonstrated by the principles that have been assumed correspond perfectly to the phenomena which experiment has brought under observation; especially when there are a great number of them, and further, principally, when one can imagine and foresee new phenomena which ought to follow from the hypotheses which one employs, and when one finds that therein the fact corresponds to our prevision. But if all these proofs of probability are met with in that which I propose to discuss, as it seems to me they are, this ought to be a very strong confirmation of the success of my inquiry; and it must be ill if the facts are not pretty much as I represent them. I would believe then that those who love to know the causes of things and who are able to admire the marvels of light, will find some satisfaction in these various speculations regarding it, and in the new explanation of its famous property which is the main foundation of the construction of our eyes, and of those great inventions which extend so vastly the use of them. I hope also that there will be some who, by following these beginnings, will penetrate much further into this question than I have been able to do, since the subject must be far from being exhausted. This appears from the passages which I have indicated where I leave certain difficulties without having resolved them, and still more from matters which I have not touched at all, such as luminous bodies of several sorts, and all that concerns colours; in which no one until now can boast of having succeeded. Finally, there remains much more to be investigated touching the nature of light which I do not pretend to have disclosed, and I shall owe much in return to him who shall be able to supplement that which is here lacking to me in knowledge.

The Hague, *January* 8, 1690

CHAPTER ONE
On Rays Propagated in Straight Lines

As happens in all the sciences in which geometry is applied to matter, the demonstrations concerning Optics are founded on truths drawn from experience. Such are: that the rays of light are propagated in straight lines; that the angles of reflexion and of incidence are equal; and that in refraction the ray is bent according to the law of sines, now so well-known, and which is no less certain than the preceding laws.

The majority of those who have written touching the various parts of Optics have contented themselves with presuming these truths. But some, more inquiring, have desired to investigate the origin and the causes, considering these to be in themselves wonderful effects of nature. In which they advanced some ingenious things, but not, however, such that the most intelligent folk do not wish for better and more satisfactory explanations. Wherefore I here desire to propound what I have meditated on the subject, so as to contribute as much as I can to the explanation of this department of natural science, which, not without reason, is reputed to be one of its most difficult parts. I recognize myself to be much indebted to those who were the first to begin to dissipate the strange obscurity in which these things were enveloped, and to give us hope that they might be explained by intelligible reasoning. But, on the other hand, I am astonished also that even here these have often been willing to offer, as assured and demonstrative, reasonings which were far from conclusive. For I do not find that any one has yet given a probable explanation of the first and most notable phenomena of light, namely, why it is not propagated except in straight lines, and how visible rays, coming from an infinitude of diverse places, cross one another without hindering one another in any way.

I shall therefore essay in this book, to give, in accordance with the principles accepted in the philosophy of the present day, some clearer and more probable reasons, firstly, of these properties of light propagated rectilinearly; secondly, of light which is reflected on meeting other bodies. Then I shall explain the phenomena of those rays which are said to suffer refraction on passing through transparent bodies of different sorts; and in this part I shall also explain the effects of the refraction of the air by the different densities of the atmosphere.

Thereafter, I shall examine the causes of the strange refraction of a certain kind of crystal which is brought from Iceland. And, finally, I shall treat of the various shapes of transparent and reflecting bodies by which rays are collected at a point or are turned aside in various ways. From this it will be seen with what facility, following our new theory, we find not only the ellipses, hyperbolas, and other curves which M. Descartes has ingeniously invented for this purpose; but also those which the surface of a glass lens ought to possess when its other surface is given as spherical or plane, or of any other figure that may be.

It is inconceivable to doubt that light consists in the motion of some sort of matter. For whether one considers its production, one sees that here upon the

553

earth it is chiefly engendered by fire and flame which contain without doubt bodies that are in rapid motion, since they dissolve and melt many other bodies, even the most solid; or whether one considers its effects, one sees that when light is collected, as by concave mirrors, it has the property of burning as a fire does, that is to say, it disunites the particles of bodies. This is assuredly the mark of motion, at least in the true philosophy, in which one conceives the causes of all natural effects in terms of mechanical motions. This, in my opinion, we must necessarily do, or else renounce all hopes of ever comprehending anything in physics.

And as, according to this philosophy, one holds as certain that the sensation of sight is excited only by the impression of some movement of a kind of matter which acts on the nerves at the back of our eyes, there is here yet one reason more for believing that light consists in a movement of the matter which exists between us and the luminous body.

Further, when one considers the extreme speed with which light spreads on every side, and how, when it comes from different regions, even from those directly opposite, the rays traverse one another without hindrance, one may well understand that when we see a luminous object, it cannot be by any transport of matter coming to us from this object, in the way in which a shot or an arrow traverses the air; for assuredly that would too greatly impugn these two properties of light, especially the second of them. It is then in some other way that light spreads; and that which can lead us to comprehend it is the knowledge which we have of the spreading of sound in the air.

We know that by means of the air, which is an invisible and impalpable body, sound spreads around the spot where it has been produced by a movement which is passed on successively from one part of the air to another; and that the spreading of this movement, taking place equally rapidly on all sides, ought to form spherical surfaces ever enlarging and which strike our ears. Now there is no doubt at all that light also comes from the luminous body to our eyes by some movement impressed on the matter which is between the two; since, as we have already seen, it cannot be by the transport of a body which passes from one to the other. If, in addition, light takes time for its passage— which we are now going to examine—it will follow that this movement, impressed on the intervening matter, is successive; and consequently it spreads, as sound does, by spherical surfaces and waves: for I call them waves from their resemblance to those which are seen to be formed in water when a stone is thrown into it, and which present a successive spreading as circles, though these arise from another cause, and are only in a flat surface.

To see then whether the spreading of light takes time, let us consider first whether there are any facts of experience which can convince us to the contrary. As to those which can be made here on the earth, by striking lights at great distances, although they prove that light takes no sensible time to pass over these distances, one may say with good reason that they are too small, and that the only conclusion to be drawn from them is that the passage of light is extremely rapid. M. Descartes, who was of opinion that it is instantaneous, founded his views, not without reason, upon a better basis of experience, drawn from the eclipses of the moon; which, nevertheless, as I shall show, is not at all convincing. I will set it forth, in a way a little different from his, in order to make the conclusion more comprehensible.

Let A be the place of the sun, BD a part of the orbit or annual path of the

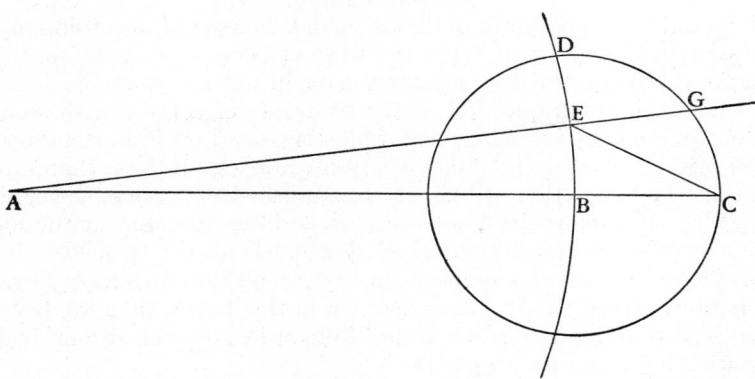

earth: ABC a straight line which I suppose to meet the orbit of the moon, which is represented by the circle CD, at C.

Now if light requires time, for example one hour, to traverse the space which is between the earth and the moon, it will follow that the earth having arrived at B, the shadow which it casts, or the interruption of the light, will not yet have arrived at the point C, but will only arrive there an hour after. It will then be one hour after, reckoning from the moment when the earth was at B, that the moon, arriving at C, will be obscured: but this obscuration or interruption of the light will not reach the earth till after another hour. Let us suppose that the earth in these two hours will have arrived at E. The earth then, being at E, will see the eclipsed moon at C, which it left an hour before, and at the same time will see the sun at A. For it being immovable, as I suppose with Copernicus, and the light moving always in straight lines, it must always appear where it is. But one has always observed, we are told, that the eclipsed moon appears at the point of the ecliptic opposite to the sun; and yet here it would appear in arrear of that point by an amount equal to the angle GEC, the supplement of AEC. This, however, is contrary to experience, since the angle GEC would be very sensible, and about 33 degrees. Now according to our computation, which is given in the treatise on the causes of the phenomena of Saturn, the distance BA between the earth and the sun is about twelve thousand diameters of the earth, and hence four hundred times greater than BC the distance of the moon, which is 30 diameters. Then the angle ECB will be nearly four hundred times greater than BAE, which is five minutes; namely, the path which the earth travels in two hours along its orbit; and thus the angle BCE will be nearly 33 degrees; and likewise the angle CEG, which is greater by five minutes.

But it must be noted that the speed of light in this argument has been assumed such that it takes a time of one hour to make the passage from here to the moon. If one supposes that for this it requires only one minute of time, then it is manifest that the angle CEG will only be 33 minutes; and if it requires only ten seconds of time, the angle will be less than six minutes. And then it will not be easy to perceive anything of it in observations of the eclipse; nor, consequently, will it be permissible to deduce from it that the movement of light is instantaneous.

It is true that we are here supposing a strange velocity that would be a hun-

dred thousand times greater than that of sound. For sound, according to what I
have observed, travels about 180 toises in the time of one second, or in about
one beat of the pulse. But this supposition ought not to seem to be an impossibility; since it is not a question of the transport of a body with so great a
speed, but of a successive movement which is passed on from some bodies to
others. I have then made no difficulty, in meditating on these things, in supposing that the emanation of light is accomplished with time, seeing that in
this way all its phenomena can be explained, and that in following the contrary
opinion everything is incomprehensible. For it has always seemed to me that
even M. Descartes, whose aim has been to treat all the subjects of physics intelligibly, and who assuredly has succeeded in this better than anyone before
him, has said nothing that is not full of difficulties, or even inconceivable, in
dealing with light and its properties.

But that which I employed only as a hypothesis, has recently received great
seemingness as an established truth by the ingenious proof of Mr. Römer
which I am going here to relate, expecting him himself to give all that is needed
for its confirmation. It is founded, as is the preceding argument, upon celestial
observations, and proves not only that light takes time for its passage, but also
demonstrates how much time it takes, and that its velocity is even at least six
times greater than that which I have just stated.

For this he makes use of the eclipses suffered by the little planets which
revolve around Jupiter, and which often enter his shadow: and see what is his
reasoning. Let A be the sun, BCDE the annual
orbit of the earth, F Jupiter, GN the orbit of the
nearest of his satellites, for it is this one which is
more apt for this investigation than any of the
other three because of the quickness of its revolution. Let G be this satellite entering into the
shadow of Jupiter, H the same satellite emerging
from the shadow.

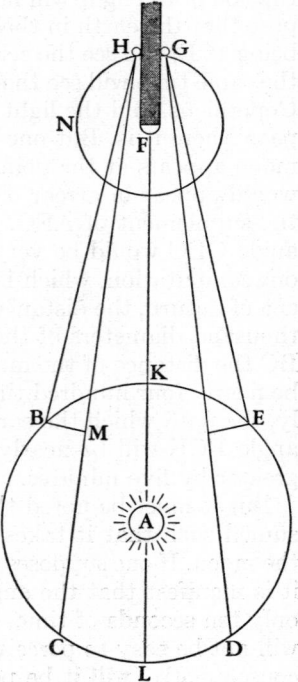

Let it be then supposed, the earth being at B
some time before the last quadrature, that one
has seen the said satellite emerge from the shadow;
it must needs be, if the earth remains at the same
place, that, after 42½ hours, one would again see
a similar emergence, because that is the time in
which it makes the round of its orbit, and when it
would come again into opposition to the sun. And
if the earth, for instance, were to remain always
at B during 30 revolutions of this satellite, one
would see it again emerge from the shadow after
30 times 42½ hours. But the earth having been
carried along during this time to C, increasing
thus its distance from Jupiter, it follows that if
light requires time for its passage the illumination
of the little planet will be perceived later at C
than it would have been at B, and that there must
be added to this time of 30 times 42½ hours that which the light has required
to traverse the space MC, the difference of the spaces CH, BH. Similarly, at

the other quadrature when the earth has come to E from D while approaching toward Jupiter, the immersions of the satellite ought to be observed at E earlier than they would have been seen if the earth had remained at D.

Now in quantities of observations of these eclipses, made during ten consecutive years, these differences have been found to be very considerable, such as ten minutes and more; and from them it has been concluded that in order to traverse the whole diameter of the annual orbit KL, which is double the distance from here to the sun, light requires about 22 minutes of time.

The movement of Jupiter in his orbit while the earth passed from B to C, or from D to E, is included in this calculation; and this makes it evident that one cannot attribute the retardation of these illuminations or the anticipation of the eclipses, either to any irregularity occurring in the movement of the little planet or to its eccentricity.

If one considers the vast size of the diameter KL, which according to me is some 24 thousand diameters of the earth, one will acknowledge the extreme velocity of light. For, supposing that KL is no more than 22 thousand of these diameters, it appears that being traversed in 22 minutes this makes the speed a thousand diameters in one minute, that is $16\frac{2}{3}$ diameters in one second or in one beat of the pulse, which makes more than 11 hundred times a hundred thousand toises; since the diameter of the earth contains 2,865 leagues, reckoned at 25 to the degree, and each league is 2,282 toises, according to the exact measurement which Mr. Picard made by order of the King in 1669. But sound, as I have said above, only travels 180 toises in the same time of one second: hence the velocity of light is more than six hundred thousand times greater than that of sound. This, however, is quite another thing from being instantaneous, since there is all the difference between a finite thing and an infinite. Now the successive movement of light being confirmed in this way, it follows, as I have said, that it spreads by spherical waves, like the movement of sound.

But if the one resembles the other in this respect, they differ in many other things; to wit, in the first production of the movement which causes them; in the matter in which the movement spreads; and in the manner in which it is propagated. As to that which occurs in the production of sound, one knows that it is occasioned by the agitation undergone by an entire body, or by a considerable part of one, which shakes all the contiguous air. But the movement of the light must originate as from each point of the luminous object, else we should not be able to perceive all the different parts of that object, as will be more evident in that which follows. And I do not believe that this movement can be better explained than by supposing that all those of the luminous bodies which are liquid, such as flames, and apparently the sun and the stars, are composed of particles which float in a much more subtle medium which agitates them with great rapidity, and makes them strike against the particles of the ether which surrounds them, and which are much smaller than they. But I hold also that in luminous solids such as charcoal or metal made red-hot in the fire, this same movement is caused by the violent agitation of the particles of the metal or of the wood; those of them which are on the surface striking similarly against the ethereal matter. The agitation, moreover, of the particles which engender the light ought to be much more prompt and more rapid than is that of the bodies which cause sound, since we do not see that the tremors of a body which is giving out a sound are capable of giving rise to light, even as the movement of the hand in the air is not capable of producing sound.

Now if one examines what this matter may be in which the movement coming from the luminous body is propagated, which I call ethereal matter, one will see that it is not the same that serves for the propagation of sound. For one finds that the latter is really that which we feel and which we breathe, and which being removed from any place still leaves there the other kind of matter that serves to convey light. This may be proved by shutting up a sounding body in a glass vessel from which the air is withdrawn by the machine which Mr. Boyle has given us, and with which he has performed so many beautiful experiments. But in doing this of which I speak, care must be taken to place the sounding body on cotton or on feathers, in such a way that it cannot communicate its tremors either to the glass vessel which encloses it, or to the machine; a precaution which has hitherto been neglected. For then after having exhausted all the air one hears no sound from the metal, though it is struck.

One sees here not only that our air, which does not penetrate through glass, is the matter by which sound spreads; but also that it is not the same air but another kind of matter in which light spreads; since if the air is removed from the vessel the light does not cease to traverse it as before.

And this last point is demonstrated even more clearly by the celebrated experiment of Torricelli, in which the tube of glass from which the quicksilver has withdrawn itself, remaining void of air, transmits light just the same as when air is in it. For this proves that a matter different from air exists in this tube, and that this matter must have penetrated the glass or the quicksilver, either one or the other, though they are both impenetrable to the air. And when, in the same experiment, one makes the vacuum after putting a little water above the quicksilver, one concludes equally that the said matter passes through glass or water, or through both.

As regards the different modes in which I have said the movements of sound and of light are communicated, one may sufficiently comprehend how this occurs in the case of sound if one considers that the air is of such a nature that it can be compressed and reduced to a much smaller space than that which it ordinarily occupies. And in proportion as it is compressed the more does it exert an effort to regain its volume; for this property along with its penetrability, which remains notwithstanding its compression, seems to prove that it is made up of small bodies which float about and which are agitated very rapidly in the ethereal matter composed of much smaller parts. So that the cause of the spreading of sound is the effort which these little bodies make in collisions with one another, to regain freedom when they are a little more squeezed together in the circuit of these waves than elsewhere.

But the extreme velocity of light, and other properties which it has, cannot admit of such a propagation of motion, and I am about to show here the way in which I conceive it must occur. For this, it is needful to explain the property which hard bodies must possess to transmit movement from one to another.

When one takes a number of spheres of equal size, made of some very hard substance, and arranges them in a straight line, so that they touch one another, one finds, on striking with a similar sphere against the first of these spheres, that the motion passes as in an instant to the last of them, which separates itself from the row, without one's being able to perceive that the others have been stirred. And even that one which was used to strike remains motionless with them. Whence one sees that the movement passes with an extreme velocity which is the greater, the greater the hardness of the substance of the spheres.

But it is still certain that this progression of motion is not instantaneous, but successive, and therefore must take time. For if the movement, or the disposition to movement, if you will have it so, did not pass successively through all these spheres, they would all acquire the movement at the same time, and hence would all advance together; which does not happen. For the last one leaves the whole row and acquires the speed of the one which was pushed. Moreover there are experiments which demonstrate that all the bodies which we reckon of the hardest kind, such as quenched steel, glass, and agate, act as springs and bend somehow, not only when extended as rods but also when they are in the form of spheres or of other shapes. That is to say, they yield a little in themselves at the place where they are struck, and immediately regain their former figure. For I have found that on striking with a ball of glass or of agate against a large and quite thick piece of the same substance which had a flat surface, slightly soiled with breath or in some other way, there remained round marks, of smaller or larger size according as the blow had been weak or strong. This makes it evident that these substances yield where they meet, and spring back: and for this time must be required.

Now in applying this kind of movement to that which produces light there is nothing to hinder us from estimating the particles of the ether to be of a substance as nearly approaching to perfect hardness and possessing a springiness as prompt as we choose. It is not necessary to examine here the causes of this hardness, or of that springiness, the consideration of which would lead us too far from our subject. I will say, however, in passing that we may conceive that the particles of the ether, notwithstanding their smallness, are in turn composed of other parts and that their springiness consists in the very rapid movement of a subtle matter which penetrates them from every side and constrains their structure to assume such a disposition as to give to this fluid matter the most overt and easy passage possible. This accords with the explanation which M. Descartes gives for the spring, though I do not, like him, suppose the pores to be in the form of round hollow canals. And it must not be thought that in this there is anything absurd or impossible, it being on the contrary quite credible that it is this infinite series of different sizes of corpuscles, having different degrees of velocity, of which Nature makes use to produce so many marvellous effects.

But though we shall ignore the true cause of springiness we still see that there are many bodies which possess this property; and thus there is nothing strange in supposing that it exists also in little invisible bodies like the particles of the ether. Also, if one wishes to seek for any other way in which the movement of light is successively communicated, one will find none which agrees better, with uniform progression, as seems to be necessary, than the property of springiness; because if this movement should grow slower in proportion as it is shared over a greater quantity of matter, in moving away from the source of the light, it could not conserve this great velocity over great distances. But by supposing springiness in the ethereal matter, its particles will have the property of equally rapid restitution whether they are pushed strongly or feebly; and thus the propagation of light will always go on with an equal velocity.

And it must be known that, although the particles of the ether are not ranged thus in straight lines, as in our row of spheres, but confusedly, so that one of them touches several others, this does not hinder them from transmitting their movement and from spreading it always forward. As to this, it is to

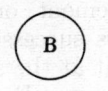
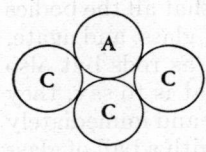

be remarked that there is a law of motion serving for this propagation, and verifiable by experiment. It is that when a sphere, such as A here, touches several other similar spheres CCC, if it is struck by another sphere B in such a way as to exert an impulse against all the spheres CCC which touch it, it transmits to them the whole of its movement, and remains after that motionless like the sphere B. And without supposing that the ethereal particles are of spherical form (for I see indeed no need to suppose them so) one may well understand that this property of communicating an impulse does not fail to contribute to the aforesaid propagation of movement.

Equality of size seems to be more necessary, because otherwise there ought to be some reflexion of movement backwards when it passes from a smaller particle to a larger one, according to the *Laws of Percussion* which I published some years ago.

However, one will see hereafter that we have to suppose such an equality not so much as a necessity for the propagation of light as for rendering that propagation easier and more powerful; for it is not beyond the limits of probability that the particles of the ether have been made equal for a purpose so important as that of light, at least in that vast space which is beyond the region of atmosphere and which seems to serve only to transmit the light of the sun and the stars.

I have then shown in what manner one may conceive light to spread successively, by spherical waves, and how it is possible that this spreading is accomplished with as great a velocity as that which experiments and celestial observations demand. Whence it may be further remarked that, although the particles are supposed to be in continual movement (for there are many reasons for this), the successive propagation of the waves cannot be hindered by this; because the propagation consists nowise in the transport of those particles but merely in a small agitation which they cannot help communicating to those surrounding, notwithstanding any movement which may act on them causing them to be changing positions amongst themselves.

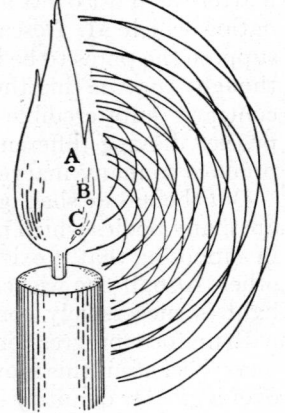

But we must consider still more particularly the origin of these waves, and the manner in which they spread. And, first, it follows from what has been said on the production of light, that each little region of a luminous body, such as the sun, a candle, or a burning coal, generates its own waves of which that region is the centre. Thus, in the flame of a candle, having distinguished the points A, B, C, concentric circles described about each of these points represent the waves which come from them. And one must imagine the same about every point of the surface and of the part within the flame.

But as the percussions at the centres of these waves possess no regular succession, it must not be supposed that the waves themselves follow one another at equal distances: and if the distances marked in the figure appear to be such, it is rather to mark the progression of one and the same wave at equal intervals of time than to represent several of them issuing from one and the same centre.

After all, this prodigious quantity of waves which traverse one another without confusion and without effacing one another must not be deemed inconceivable; it being certain that one and the same particle of matter can serve for many waves coming from different sides or even from contrary directions, not only if it is struck by blows which follow one another closely but even for those which act on it at the same instant. It can do so because the spreading of the movement is successive. This may be proved by the row of equal spheres

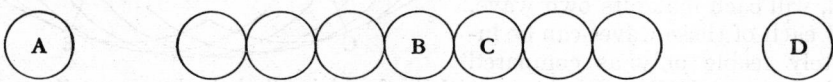

of hard matter, spoken of above. If against this row there are pushed from two opposite sides at the same time two similar spheres A and D, one will see each of them rebound with the same velocity which it had in striking, yet the whole row will remain in its place, although the movement has passed along its whole length twice over. And if these contrary movements happen to meet one another at the middle sphere, B, or at some other such as C, that sphere will yield and act as a spring at both sides, and so will serve at the same instant to transmit these two movements.

But what may at first appear full strange and even incredible is that the undulations produced by such small movements and corpuscles should spread to such immense distances; as for example, from the sun or from the stars to us. For the force of these waves must grow feeble in proportion as they move away from their origin, so that the action of each one in particular will without doubt become incapable of making itself felt to our sight. But one will cease to be astonished by considering how at a great distance from the luminous body an infinitude of waves, though they have issued from different points of this body, unite together in such a way that they sensibly compose one single wave only, which, consequently, ought to have enough force to make itself felt. Thus, this infinite number of waves which originate at the same instant from all points of a fixed star, big it may be as the sun, make practically only one single wave which may well have force enough to produce an impression on our eyes. Moreover, from each luminous point there may come many thousands of waves in the smallest imaginable time, by the frequent percussion of the corpuscles which strike the ether at these points: which further contributes to rendering their action more sensible.

There is the further consideration in the emanation of these waves, that each particle of matter, in which a wave spreads, ought not to communicate its motion only to the next particle which is in the straight line drawn from the luminous point, but that it also imparts some of it necessarily to all the others which touch it and which oppose themselves to its movement. So it arises that around each particle there is made a wave of which that particle is the centre. Thus, if DCF is a wave emanating from the luminous point A, which is its centre, the particle B, one of those comprised within the sphere DCF, will have made its particular

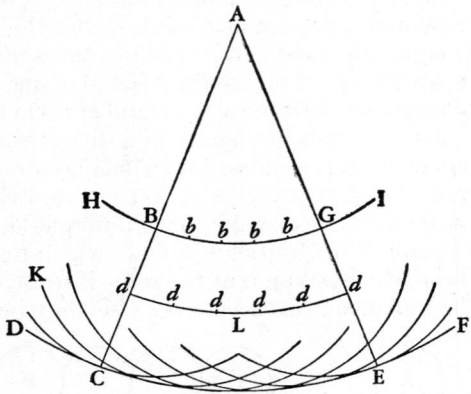

or partial wave KCL, which will touch the wave DCF at C at the same moment that the principal wave emanating from the point A has arrived at DCF; and it is clear that it will be only the region C of the wave KCL which will touch the wave DCF, to wit, that which is in the straight line drawn through AB. Similarly the other particles of the sphere DCF, such as *bb*, *dd*, etc., will each make its own wave. But each of these waves can be infinitely feeble only as compared with the wave DCF, to the composition of which all the others contribute by the part of their surface which is most distant from the centre A.

One sees, in addition, that the wave DCF is determined by the distance attained in a certain space of time by the movement which started from the point A; there being no movement beyond this wave, though there will be in the space which it encloses, namely, in parts of the particular waves, those parts which do not touch the sphere DCF. And all this ought not to seem fraught with too much minuteness or subtlety, since we shall see in the sequel that all the properties of light, and everything pertaining to its reflexion and its refraction, can be explained in principle by this means. This is a matter which has been quite unknown to those who hitherto have begun to consider the waves of light, amongst whom are Mr. Hooke in his *Micrographia*, and Father Pardies, who, in a treatise of which he let me see a portion, and which he was unable to complete as he died shortly afterward, had undertaken to prove by these waves the effects of reflexion and refraction. But the chief foundation, which consists in the remark I have just made, was lacking in his demonstrations; and for the rest he had opinions very different from mine, as may be will appear some day if his writing has been preserved.

To come to the properties of light. We remark first that each portion of a wave ought to spread in such a way that its extremities lie always between the same straight lines drawn from the luminous point. Thus, the portion BG of the wave, having the luminous point A as its centre, will spread into the arc CE bounded by the straight lines ABC, AGE. For although the particular waves produced by the particles comprised within the space CAE spread also outside this space, they yet do not concur at the same instant to compose a wave which terminates the movement, as they do precisely at the circumference CE, which is their common tangent.

And hence one sees the reason why light, at least if its rays are not reflected or broken, spreads only by straight lines, so that it illuminates no object except when the path from its source to that object is open along such lines. For if, for example, there were an opening BG, limited by opaque bodies BH, GI, the wave of light which issues from the point A will always be terminated by the straight lines AC, AE, as has just been shown; the parts of the partial waves which spread outside the space ACE being too feeble to produce light there.

Now, however small we make the opening BG, there is always the same reason causing the light there to pass between straight lines; since this opening is always large enough to contain a great number of particles of the ethereal matter, which are of an inconceivable smallness; so that it appears that each little portion of the wave necessarily advances following the straight line which comes from the luminous point. Thus, then, we may take the rays of light as if they were straight lines.

It appears, moreover, by what has been remarked touching the feebleness of the particular waves, that it is not needful that all the particles of the ether should be equal amongst themselves, though equality is more apt for the propagation of the movement. For it is true that inequality will cause a particle, by pushing against another larger one, to strive to recoil with a part of its movement; but it will thereby merely generate backwards towards the luminous point some partial waves incapable of causing light, and not a wave compounded of many as CE was.

Another property of waves of light, and one of the most marvellous, is that when some of them come from different or even from opposing sides, they produce their effect across one another without any hindrance. Whence also it comes about that a number of spectators may view different objects at the same time through the same opening, and that two persons can at the same time see one another's eyes. Now, according to the explanation which has been given of the action of light, how the waves do not destroy nor interrupt one another when they cross one another, these effects which I have just mentioned are easily conceived. But in my judgement they are not at all easy to explain according to the views of M. Descartes, who makes light to consist in a continuous pressure merely tending to movement. For this pressure not being able to act from two opposite sides at the same time against bodies which have no inclination to approach one another, it is impossible so to understand what I have been saying about two persons mutually seeing one another's eyes, or how two torches can illuminate one another.

CHAPTER TWO

On Reflexion

HAVING explained the effects of waves of light which spread in a homogeneous matter, we will examine next that which happens to them on encountering other bodies. We will first make evident how the reflexion of light is explained by these same waves, and why it preserves equality of angles.

Let there be a surface AB; plane and polished, of some metal, glass, or other body, which at first I will consider as perfectly uniform (reserving to myself to deal at the end of this demonstration with the inequalities from which it cannot be exempt), and let a line AC, inclined to AB, represent a portion of a wave of light, the centre of which is so distant that this portion AC may be considered as a straight line; for I consider all this as in one plane, imagining to myself that the plane in which this figure is cuts the sphere of the wave through its centre and intersects the plane AB at right angles. This explanation will suffice once for all.

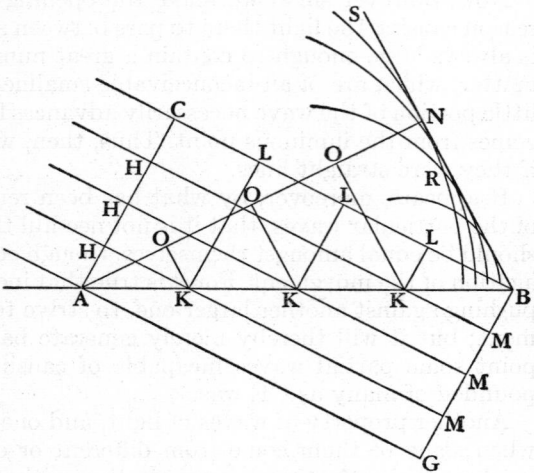

The piece C of the wave AC, will in a certain space of time advance as far as the plane AB at B, following the straight line CB, which may be supposed to come from the luminous centre, and which in consequence is perpendicular to AC. Now in this same space of time the portion A of the same wave, which has been hindered from communicating its movement beyond the plane AB, or at least partly so, ought to have continued its movement in the matter which is above this plane, and this along a distance equal to CB, making its own partial spherical wave, according to what has been said above. Which wave is here represented by the circumference SNR, the centre of which is A, and its semi-diameter AN equal to CB.

If one considers further the other pieces H of the wave AC, it appears that they will not only have reached the surface AB by straight lines HK parallel to CB, but that in addition they will have generated in the transparent air, from the centres K, K, K, particular spherical waves, represented here by circumferences the semi-diameters of which are equal to KM, that is to say, to the continuations of HK as far as the line BG parallel to AC. But all these circumferences have as a common tangent the straight line BN, namely, the same which is drawn from B as a tangent to the first of the circles, of which A is the centre, and AN the semi-diameter equal to BC, as is easy to see.

It is then the line BN (comprised between B and the point N where the perpendicular from the point A falls) which is, as it were, formed by all these circumferences, and which terminates the movement which is made by the reflexion of the wave AC; and it is also the place where the movement occurs in much greater quantity than anywhere else. Wherefore, according to that which has been explained, BN is the propagation of the wave AC at the moment when the piece C of it has arrived at B. For there is no other line which like BN is a common tangent to all the aforesaid circles, except BG below the plane AB; which line BG would be the propagation of the wave if the movement could have spread in a medium homogeneous with that which is above the plane. And if one wishes to see how the wave AC has come successively to BN, one has only to draw in the same figure the straight lines KO parallel to BN, and the straight lines KL parallel to AC. Thus one will see that the straight wave AC has become broken up into all the OKL parts successively, and that it has become straight again at NB.

Now it is apparent here that the angle of reflexion is made equal to the angle of incidence. For the triangles ACB, BNA, being rectangular and having the side AB common, and the side CB equal to NA, it follows that the angles opposite to these sides will be equal, and therefore also the angles CBA, NAB. But as CB, perpendicular to CA, marks the direction of the incident ray, so AN, perpendicular to the wave BN, marks the direction of the reflected ray; hence these rays are equally inclined to the plane AB.

But in considering the preceding demonstration, one might aver that it is indeed true that BN is the common tangent of the circular waves in the plane of this figure, but that these waves, being in truth spherical, have still an infinitude of similar tangents, namely, all the straight lines which are drawn from the point B in the surface generated by the straight line BN about the axis BA. It remains, therefore, to demonstrate that there is no difficulty herein: and by the same argument one will see why the incident ray and the reflected ray are always in one and the same plane perpendicular to the reflecting plane. I say then that the wave AC, being regarded only as a line, produces no light. For a visible ray of light, however narrow it may be, has always some width, and consequently it is necessary, in representing the wave whose progression constitutes the ray, to put instead of a line AC some plane figure such as the circle HC in the following figure, by supposing, as we have done, the luminous point to be infinitely distant. Now it is easy to see, following the preceding demonstration, that each small piece of this wave HC having arrived at the plane AB, and there generating each one its particular wave, these will all have, when C arrives at B, a common plane which will touch them, namely, a circle BN similar to CH; and this will be intersected at its middle and at right

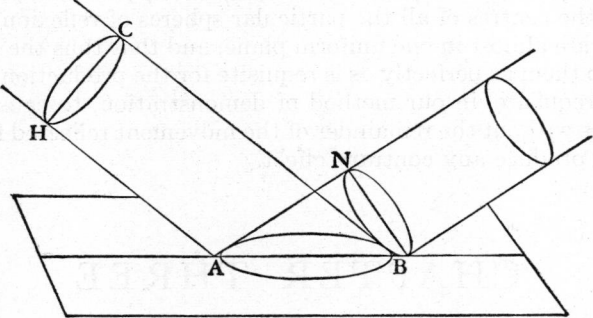

angles by the same plane which likewise intersects the circle CH and the ellipse AB.

One sees also that the said spheres of the partial waves cannot have any common tangent plane other than the circle BN; so that it will be this plane where there will be more reflected movement than anywhere else, and which will therefore carry on the light in continuance from the wave CH.

I have also stated in the preceding demonstration that the movement of the piece A of the incident wave is not able to communicate itself beyond the plane AB, or at least not wholly. Whence it is to be remarked that though the movement of the ethereal matter might communicate itself partly to that of the reflecting body, this could in nothing alter the velocity of progression of the waves on which the angle of reflexion depends. For a slight percussion ought to generate waves as rapid as strong percussion in the same matter. This comes about from the property of bodies which act as springs, of which we have spoken above; namely, that whether compressed little or much they recoil in equal times. Equally so in every reflexion of the light, against whatever body it may be, the angles of reflexion and incidence ought to be equal notwithstanding that the body might be of such a nature that it takes away a portion of the movement made by the incident light. And experiment shows that in fact there is no polished body the reflexion of which does not follow this rule.

But the thing to be above all remarked in our demonstration is that it does not require that the reflecting surface should be considered as a uniform plane, as has been supposed by all those who have tried to explain the effects of reflexion; but only an evenness such as may be attained by the particles of the matter of the reflecting body being set near to one another; which particles are larger than those of the ethereal matter, as will appear by what we shall say in treating of the transparency and opacity of bodies. For the surface consisting thus of particles put together, and the ethereal particles being above, and smaller, it is evident that one could not demonstrate the equality of the angles of incidence and reflexion by similitude to that which happens to a ball thrown against a wall, of which writers have always made use. In our way, on the other hand, the thing is explained without difficulty. For the smallness of the particles of quicksilver, for example, being such that one must conceive millions of them, in the smallest visible surface proposed, arranged like a heap of grains of sand which has been flattened as much as it is capable of being, this surface then becomes for our purpose as even as a polished glass is: and, although it always remains rough with respect to the particles of the ether it is evident that the centres of all the particular spheres of reflexion, of which we have spoken, are almost in one uniform plane, and that thus the common tangent can fit to them as perfectly as is requisite for the production of light. And this alone is requisite, in our method of demonstration, to cause equality of the said angles without the remainder of the movement reflected from all parts being able to produce any contrary effect.

CHAPTER THREE
On Refraction

IN the same way as the effects of reflexion have been explained by waves of light reflected at the surface of polished bodies, we will explain transparency and the phenomena of refraction by waves which spread within and across diaphanous bodies, both solids, such as glass, and liquids, such as water, oils, etc. But in order that it may not seem strange to suppose this passage of waves in the interior of these bodies, I will first show that one may conceive it possible in more than one mode.

First, then, if the ethereal matter cannot penetrate transparent bodies at all, their own particles would be able to communicate successively the movement of the waves, the same as do those of the ether, supposing that, like those, they are of a nature to act as a spring. And this is easy to conceive as regards water and other transparent liquids, they being composed of detached particles. But it may seem more difficult as regards glass and other transparent and hard bodies, because their solidity does not seem to permit them to receive movement except in their whole mass at the same time. This, however, is not necessary because this solidity is not such as it appears to us, it being probable rather that these bodies are composed of particles merely placed close to one another and held together by some pressure from without of some other matter, and by the irregularity of their shapes. For primarily their rarity is shown by the facility with which there passes through them the matter of the vortices of the magnet, and that which causes gravity. Further, one cannot say that these bodies are of a texture similar to that of a sponge or of light bread, because the heat of the fire makes them flow and thereby changes the situation of the particles amongst themselves. It remains then that they are, as has been said, assemblages of particles which touch one another without constituting a continuous solid. This being so, the movement which these particles receive to carry on the waves of light, being merely communicated from some of them to others, without their going for that purpose out of their places or without derangement, it may very well produce its effect without prejudicing in any way the apparent solidity of the compound.

By pressure from without, of which I have spoken, must not be understood that of the air, which would not be sufficient, but that of some other more subtle matter, a pressure which I chanced upon by experiment long ago, namely, in the case of water freed from air, which remains suspended in a tube open at its lower end, notwithstanding that the air has been removed from the vessel in which this tube is enclosed.

One can then in this way conceive of transparency in a solid without any necessity that the ethereal matter which serves for light should pass through it, or that it should find pores in which to insinuate itself. But the truth is that this matter not only passes through solids, but does so even with great facility; of which the experiment of Torricelli, above cited, is already a proof. Because on the quicksilver and the water quitting the upper part of the glass tube, it appears that it is immediately filled with ethereal matter, since light passes across it. But here is another argument which proves this ready penetrability, not only in transparent bodies but also in all others.

When light passes across a hollow sphere of glass, closed on all sides, it is certain that it is full of ethereal matter, as much as the spaces outside the sphere. And this ethereal matter, as has been shown above, consists of particles which just touch one another. If, then, it were enclosed in the sphere in such a way that it could not get out through the pores of the glass, it would be obliged to follow the movement of the sphere when one changes its place: and it would require, consequently, almost the same force to impress a certain velocity on this sphere, when placed on a horizontal plane, as if it were full of water or perhaps of quicksilver: because every body resists the velocity of the motion which one would give to it, in proportion to the quantity of matter which it contains, and which is obliged to follow this motion. But, on the contrary, one finds that the sphere resists the impress of movement only in proportion to the quantity of matter of the glass of which it is made. Then it must be that the ethereal matter which is inside is not shut up, but flows through it with very great freedom. We shall demonstrate hereafter that by this process the same penetrability may be inferred also as relating to opaque bodies.

The second mode, then, of explaining transparency, and one which appears more probably true, is by saying that the waves of light are carried on in the ethereal matter, which continuously occupies the interstices or pores of transparent bodies. For since it passes through them continuously and freely, it follows that they are always full of it. And one may even show that these interstices occupy much more space than the coherent particles which constitute the bodies. For if what we have just said is true: that force is required to impress a certain horizontal velocity on bodies in proportion as they contain coherent matter; and if the proportion of this force follows the law of weights, as is confirmed by experiment, then the quantity of the constituent matter of bodies also follows the proportion of their weights. Now we see that water weighs only one-fourteenth part as much as an equal portion of quicksilver: therefore, the matter of the water does not occupy the fourteenth part of the space which its mass obtains. It must even occupy much less of it, since quicksilver is less heavy than gold, and the matter of gold is by no means dense, as follows from the fact that the matter of the vortices of the magnet and of that which is the cause of gravity pass very freely through it.

But it may be objected here that if water is a body of so great rarity, and if its particles occupy so small a portion of the space of its apparent bulk, it is very strange how it yet resists compression so strongly without permitting itself to be condensed by any force which one has hitherto essayed to employ, preserving even its entire liquidity while subjected to this pressure.

This is no small difficulty. It may, however, be resolved by saying that the very violent and rapid motion of the subtle matter which renders water liquid, by agitating the particles of which it is composed, maintains this liquidity in spite of the pressure which hitherto any one has been minded to apply to it.

The rarity of transparent bodies being then such as we have said, one easily conceives that the waves might be carried on in the ethereal matter which fills the interstices of the particles. And, moreover, one may believe that the progression of these waves ought to be a little slower in the interior of bodies, by reason of the small detours which the same particles cause. In which different velocity of light I shall show the cause of refraction to consist.

Before doing so, I will indicate the third and last mode in which transparency may be conceived; which is by supposing that the movement of the waves of light is transmitted indifferently both in the particles of the ethereal matter which occupy the interstices of bodies, and in the particles which compose them, so that the movement passes from one to the other. And it will be seen hereafter that this hypothesis serves excellently to explain the double refraction of certain transparent bodies.

Should it be objected that if the particles of the ether are smaller than those of transparent bodies (since they pass through their intervals), it would follow that they can communicate to them but little of their movement, it may be replied that the particles of these bodies are in turn composed of still smaller particles, and so it will be these secondary particles which will receive the movement from those of the ether.

Furthermore, if the particles of transparent bodies have a recoil a little less prompt than that of the ethereal particles, which nothing hinders us from supposing, it will again follow that the progression of the waves of light will be slower in the interior of such bodies than it is outside in the ethereal matter.

All this I have found as most probable for the mode in which the waves of light pass across transparent bodies. To which it must further be added in what respect these bodies differ from those which are opaque; and the more so since it might seem because of the easy penetration of bodies by the ethereal matter, of which mention has been made, that there would not be any body that was not transparent. For by the same reasoning about the hollow sphere which I have employed to prove the smallness of the density of glass and its easy penetrability by the ethereal matter, one might also prove that the same penetrability obtains for metals and for every other sort of body. For this sphere being, for example, of silver, it is certain that it contains some of the ethereal matter which serves for light, since this was there as well as in the air when the opening of the sphere was closed. Yet, being closed and placed upon a horizontal plane, it resists the movement which one wishes to give to it, merely according to the quantity of silver of which it is made; so that one must conclude, as above, that the ethereal matter which is enclosed does not follow the movement of the sphere; and that, therefore, silver, as well as glass, is very easily penetrated by this matter. Some of it is therefore present continuously and in quantities between the particles of silver and of all other opaque bodies: and since it serves for the propagation of light it would seem that these bodies ought also to be transparent, which, however, is not the case.

Whence then, one will say, does their opacity come? Is it because the particles which compose them are soft; that is to say, these particles being composed of others that are smaller, are they capable of changing their figure on receiving the pressure of the ethereal particles, the motion of which they thereby damp, and so hinder the continuance of the waves of light? That cannot be: for if the particles of the metals are soft, how is it that polished silver and mercury reflect light so strongly? What I find to be most probable herein is to say that metallic bodies, which are almost the only really opaque ones, have mixed amongst their hard particles some soft ones; so that some serve to cause reflexion and the others to hinder transparency; while, on the other hand, transparent bodies contain only hard particles which have the faculty of recoil, and serve together with those of the ethereal matter for the propagation of the waves of light, as has been said.

Let us pass now to the explanation of the effects of refraction, assuming, as we have done, the passage of waves of light through transparent bodies, and the diminution of velocity which these same waves suffer in them.

The chief property of refraction is that a ray of light, such as AB, being in the air, and falling obliquely upon the polished surface of a transparent body, such as FG, is broken at the point of incidence B in such a way that, with the straight line DBE which cuts the surface perpendicularly, it makes an angle CBE less than ABD which it made with the same perpendicular when in the air. And the measure of these angles is found by describing, about the point B, a circle which cuts the radii AB, BC. For the perpendiculars AD, CE, let fall from the points of intersection upon the straight line DE, which are called the sines of the angles ABD, CBE, have a certain ratio between themselves; which

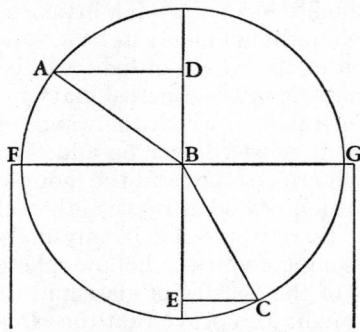

ratio is always the same for all inclinations of the incident ray, at least for a given transparent body. This ratio is, in glass, very nearly as 3 to 2; and in water very nearly as 4 to 3; and is likewise different in other diaphanous bodies.

Another property, similar to this, is that the refractions are reciprocal between the rays entering into a transparent body and those which are leaving it. That is to say, that if the ray AB in entering the transparent body is refracted into BC, then likewise CB being taken as a ray in the interior of this body will be refracted, on passing out, into BA.

To explain then the reasons of these phenomena according to our principles, let AB be the straight line which represents a plane surface bounding the transparent substances which lie towards C and towards N. When I say plane, that

does not signify a perfect evenness, but such as has been understood in treating of reflexion, and for the same reason. Let the line AC represent a portion of a wave of light, the centre of which is supposed so distant that this portion may be considered as a straight line. The piece C, then, of the wave AC, will in a certain space of time have advanced as far as the plane AB following the straight line CB, which may be imagined as coming from the luminous centre, and which

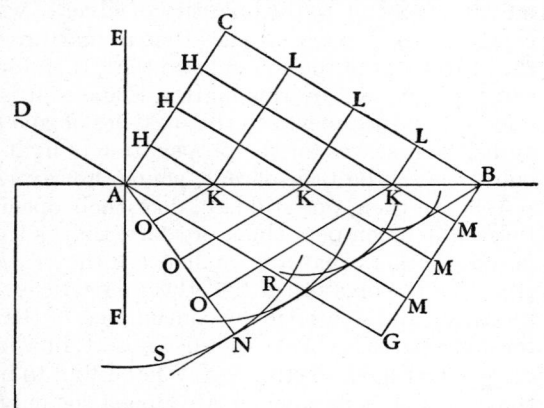

consequently will cut AC at right angles. Now in the same time the piece A would have come to G along the straight line AG, equal and parallel to CB; and all the portion of wave AC would be at GB if the matter of the transparent body transmitted the movement of the wave as quickly as the matter of the ether. But let us suppose that it transmits this movement less quickly, by one-third, for instance. Movement will then be spread from the point A, in the matter of the transparent body through a distance equal to two-thirds of CB, making its own particular spherical wave according to what has been said before. This wave is then represented by the circumference SNR, the centre of which is A, and its semi-diameter equal to two-thirds of CB. Then if one considers in order the other pieces H of the wave AC, it appears that in the same time that the piece C reaches B they will not only have arrived at the surface AB along the straight lines HK parallel to CB, but that, in addition, they will have generated in the diaphanous substance from the centres K, partial waves, represented here by circumferences the semi-diameters of which are equal to two-thirds of the lines KM, that is to say, to two-thirds of the prolongations of HK down to the straight line BG; for these semi-diameters would have been equal to entire lengths of KM if the two transparent substances had been of the same penetrability.

Now all these circumferences have for a common tangent the straight line BN; namely, the same line which is drawn as a tangent from the point B to the circumference SNR, which we considered first. For it is easy to see that all the other circumferences will touch the same BN, from B up to the point of contact N, which is the same point where AN falls perpendicularly on BN.

It is then BN, which is formed by small arcs of these circumferences, which terminates the movement that the wave AC has communicated within the transparent body, and where this movement occurs in much greater amount than anywhere else. And for that reason this line, in accordance with what has been said more than once, is the propagation of the wave AC at the moment when its piece C has reached B. For there is no other line below the plane AB which is, like BN, a common tangent to all these partial waves. And if one would know how the wave AC has come progressively to BN, it is necessary only to draw in the same figure the straight lines KO parallel to BN, and all the lines KL parallel to AC. Thus, one will see that the wave CA, from being a straight line, has become broken in all the positions LKO successively, and that it has again become a straight line at BN. This being evident by what has already been demonstrated, there is no need to explain it further.

Now, in the same figure, if one draws EAF, which cuts the plane AB at right angles at the point A, since AD is perpendicular to the wave AC, it will be DA which will mark the ray of incident light, and AN which was perpendicular to BN, the refracted ray: since the rays are nothing else than the straight lines along which the portions of the waves advance.

Whence it is easy to recognize this chief property of refraction, namely that the sine of the angle DAE has always the same ratio to the sine of the angle NAF, whatever be the inclination of the ray DA: and that this ratio is the same as that of the velocity of the waves in the transparent substance which is towards AE to their velocity in the transparent substance towards AF. For, considering AB as the radius of a circle, the sine of the angle BAC is BC, and the sine of the angle ABN is AN. But the angle BAC is equal to DAE, since each of them added to CAE makes a right angle. And the angle ABN is equal to NAF, since each of them with BAN makes a right angle. Then, also, the sine of the angle DAE is to the sine of NAF as BC is to AN. But the ratio of BC to AN was the same as that of the velocities of light in the substance which is towards AE and in that which is towards AF; therefore, also, the sine of the angle DAE will be to the sine of the angle NAF the same as the said velocities of light.

To see, consequently, what the refraction will be when the waves of light pass into a substance in which the movement travels more quickly than in that from which they emerge (let us again assume the ratio of 3 to 2), it is only necessary to repeat all the same construction and demonstration which we have just used, merely substituting everywhere $\frac{3}{2}$ instead of $\frac{2}{3}$. And it will be found by the same reasoning, in this other figure, that when the piece C of the wave AC shall have reached the surface AB at B, all the portions of the wave

AC will have advanced as far as BN, so that BC, the perpendicular on AC, is to AN, the perpendicular on BN, as 2 to 3. And there will finally be this same ratio of 2 to 3 between the sine of the angle EAD and the sine of the angle FAN.

Hence, one sees the reciprocal relation of the refractions of the ray on entering and on leaving one and the same transparent body: namely, that if NA

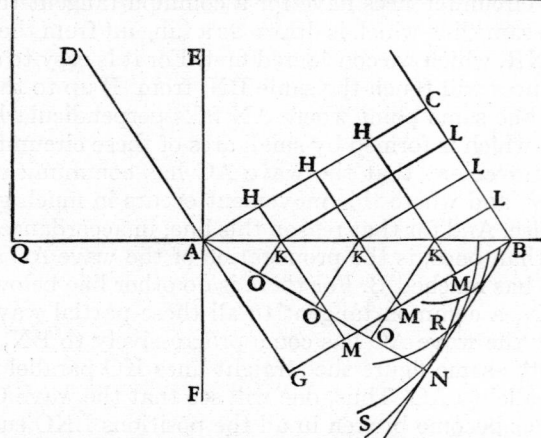

falling on the external surface AB is refracted into the direction AD, so the ray AD will be refracted on leaving the transparent body into the direction AN.

One sees also the reason for a noteworthy accident which happens in this refraction: which is this, that after a certain obliquity of the incident ray DA, it begins to be quite unable to penetrate into the other transparent substance. For if the angle DAQ or CBA is such that in the triangle ACB, CB is equal to ⅔ of AB, or is greater, then AN cannot form one side of the triangle ANB, since it becomes equal to or greater than AB: so that the portion of wave BN cannot be found anywhere, neither consequently can AN, which ought to be perpendicular to it. And thus the incident ray DA does not then pierce the surface AB.

When the ratio of the velocities of the waves is as 2 to 3, as in our example, which is that which obtains for glass and air, the angle DAQ must be more than 48 degrees 11 minutes in order that the ray DA may be able to pass by refraction. And when the ratio of the velocities is as 3 to 4, as it is very nearly in water and air, this angle DAQ must exceed 41 degrees 24 minutes. And this accords perfectly with experiment.

But it might here be asked: since the meeting of the wave AC against the surface AB ought to produce movement in the matter which is on the other side, why does no light pass there? To which the reply is easy if one remembers what has been said before. For although it generates an infinitude of partial waves in the matter which is at the other side of AB, these waves never have a common tangent line (either straight or curved) at the same moment; and so there is no line terminating the propagation of the wave AC beyond the plane AB, nor any place where the movement is gathered together in sufficiently great quantity to produce light. And one will easily see the truth of this, namely, that CB being larger than ⅔ of AB, the waves excited beyond the plane AB will have no common tangent if about the centres K one then draws circles having radii equal to $\frac{3}{2}$ of the lengths LB to which they correspond. For all these circles will be enclosed in one another and will all pass beyond the point B.

Now it is to be remarked that from the moment when the angle DAQ is smaller than is requisite to permit the refracted ray DA to pass into the other transparent substance, one finds that the interior reflexion which occurs at the surface AB is much augmented in brightness, as is easy to realize by experiment with a triangular prism; and for this our theory can afford this reason. When the angle DAQ is still large enough to enable the ray DA to pass, it is evident that the light from the portion AC of the wave is collected in a minimum space when it reaches BN. It appears also that the wave BN becomes so much the smaller as the angle CBA or DAQ is made less, until when the latter is diminished to the limit indicated a little previously, this wave BN is collected together always at one point. That is to say, that when the piece C of the wave AC has then arrived at B, the wave BN which is the propagation of AC is entirely reduced to the same point B. Similarly, when the piece H has reached K, the part AH is entirely reduced to the same point K. This makes it evident that in proportion as the wave CA comes to meet the surface AB, there occurs a great quantity of movement along that surface; which movement ought also to spread within the transparent body and ought to have much re-enforced the partial waves which produce the interior reflexion against the surface AB, according to the laws of reflexion previously explained.

And because a slight diminution of the angle of incidence DAQ causes the wave BN, however great it was, to be reduced to zero, (for this angle being 49 degrees 11 minutes in the glass, the angle BAN is still 11 degrees 21 minutes, and the same angle being reduced by one degree only the angle BAN is reduced to zero, and so the wave BN reduced to a point) thence it comes about that the interior reflexion from being obscure becomes suddenly bright, so soon as the angle of incidence is such that it no longer gives passage to the refraction.

Now as concerns ordinary external reflexion, that is to say which occurs when the angle of incidence DAQ is still large enough to enable the refracted ray to penetrate beyond the surface AB, this reflexion should occur against the particles of the substance which touches the transparent body on its outside. And it apparently occurs against the particles of the air or others mingled with the ethereal particles and larger than they. So, on the other hand, the external reflexion of these bodies occurs against the particles which compose them, and which are also larger than those of the ethereal matter, since the latter flows in their interstices. It is true that there remains here some difficulty in those experiments in which this interior reflexion occurs without the particles of air being able to contribute to it, as in vessels or tubes from which the air has been extracted.

Experience, moreover, teaches us that these two reflexions are of nearly equal force, and that in different transparent bodies they are so much the stronger as the refraction of these bodies is the greater. Thus, one sees manifestly that the reflexion of glass is stronger than that of water, and that of diamond stronger than that of glass.

I will finish this theory of refraction by demonstrating a remarkable proposition which depends on it; namely, that a ray of light in order to go from one point to another, when these points are in different media, is refracted in such wise at the plane surface which joins these two media that it employs the least possible time: and exactly the same happens in the case of reflexion against a plane surface. M. Fermat was the first to propound this property of refraction, holding with us, and directly counter to the opinion of M. Descartes, that light passes more slowly through glass and water than through air. But he assumed besides this a constant ratio of sines, which we have just proved by these different degrees of velocity alone: or rather, what is equivalent, he assumed not only that the velocities were different but that the light took the least time possible for its passage, and thence deduced the constant ratio of the sines. His demonstration, which may be seen in his printed works, and in the volume of letters of M. Descartes, is very long; wherefore I give here another which is simpler and easier.

Let KF be the plane surface; A the point in the medium which the light traverses more easily, as the air; C the point in the other which is more difficult to penetrate, as water. And suppose that a ray has come from A, by B, to C, having been refracted at B according to the law demonstrated a little before; that is to say that, having drawn PBQ, which cuts the plane at right angles, let the sine of the angle ABP have to the sine of the angle CBQ the same ratio as the velocity of light in the medium where A is to the velocity of light in the medium where C is. It is to be shown that the time of passage of light along AB and BC taken together is the shortest that can be. Let us assume that it may have come by other lines, and, in the first place, along AF, FC, 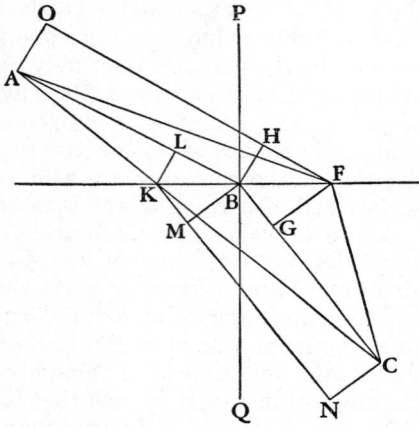 so that the point of refraction F may be farther from B than the point A; and let AO be a line perpendicular to AB, and FO parallel to AB; BH perpendicular to FO, and FG to BC.

Since then the angle HBF is equal to PBA, and the angle BFG equal to QBC, it follows that the sine of the angle HBF will also have the same ratio to the sine of BFG, as the velocity of light in the medium A is to its velocity in the medium C. But these sines are the straight lines HF, BG, if we take BF as the semi-diameter of a circle. Then these lines HF, BG, will bear to one another the said ratio of the velocities. And, therefore, the time of the light along HF, supposing that the ray had been OF, would be equal to the time along BG in the interior of the medium C. But the time along AB is equal to the time along OH; therefore, the time along OF is equal to the time along AB, BG. Again the time along FC is greater than that along GC; then the time along OFC will be longer than that along ABC. But AF is longer than OF, then the time along AFC will by just so much more exceed the time along ABC.

Now let us assume that the ray has come from A to C along AK, KC; the point of refraction K being nearer to A than the point B is; and let CN be the perpendicular upon BC, KN parallel to BC: BM perpendicular upon KN, and KL upon BA.

Here BL and KM are the sines of angles BKL, KBM; that is to say, of the angles PBA, QBC; and, therefore, they are to one another as the velocity of light in the medium A is to the velocity in the medium C. Then the time along LB is equal to the time along KM; and since the time along BC is equal to the time along MN, the time along LBC will be equal to the time along KMN. But the time along AK is longer than that along AL: hence, the time along AKN is longer than that along ABC. And KC being longer than KN, the time along AKC will exceed, by as much more, the time along ABC. Hence, it appears that the time along ABC is the shortest possible; which was to be proven.

CHAPTER FOUR
On the Refraction of the Air

WE have shown how the movement which constitutes light spreads by spherical waves in any homogeneous matter. And it is evident that when the matter is not homogeneous, but of such a constitution that the movement is communicated in it more rapidly toward one side than toward another, these waves cannot be spherical: but that they must acquire their figure according to the different distances over which the successive movement passes in equal times.

It is thus that we shall in the first place explain the refractions which occur in the air, which extends from here to the clouds and beyond. The effects of which refractions are very remarkable; for by them we often see objects which the rotundity of the earth ought otherwise to hide; such as islands, and the tops of mountains when one is at sea. Because also of them the sun and the moon appear as risen before in fact they have, and appear to set later: so that at times the moon has been seen eclipsed while the sun appeared still above the horizon. And so also the heights of the sun and of the moon, and those of all the stars, always appear a little greater than they are in reality, because of these same refractions, as astronomers know. But there is one experiment which renders this refraction very evident; which is that of fixing a telescope on some spot so that it views an object, such as a steeple or a house, at a distance of half a league or more. If then you look through it at different hours of the day, leaving it always fixed in the same way, you will see that the same spots of the object will not always appear at the middle of the aperture of the telescope, but that generally in the morning and in the evening, when there are more vapours near the earth, these objects seem to rise higher, so that the half or more of them will no longer be visible; and so that they seem lower toward mid-day when these vapours are dissipated.

Those who consider refraction to occur only in the surfaces which separate transparent bodies of different nature, would find it difficult to give a reason for all that I have just related; but according to our theory the thing is quite easy. It is known that the air which surrounds us, besides the particles which are proper to it and which float in the ethereal matter as has been explained, is full also of particles of water which are raised by the action of heat; and it has been ascertained further by some very definite experiments that as one mounts up higher the density of air diminishes in proportion. Now, whether the particles of water and those of air take part, by means of the particles of ethereal matter, in the movement which constitutes light, but have a less prompt recoil than these, or whether the encounter and hindrance which these particles of air and water offer to the propagation of movement of the ethereal progress retard the progression, it follows that both kinds of particles flying amidst the ethereal particles must render the air, from a great height down to the earth, gradually less easy for the spreading of the waves of light.

Whence the configuration of the waves ought to become nearly such as this

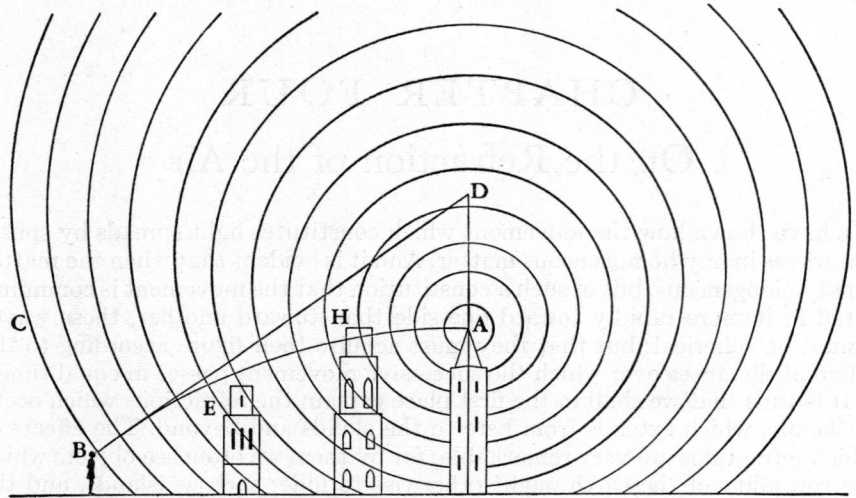

figure represents: namely, if A is a light, or the visible point of a steeple, the waves which start from it ought to spread more widely upwards and less widely downwards, but in other directions more or less as they approximate to these two extremes. This being so, it necessarily follows that every line intersecting one of these waves at right angles will pass above the point A, always excepting the one line which is perpendicular to the horizon.

Let BC be the wave which brings the light to the spectator who is at B, and let BD be the straight line which intersects this wave at right angles. Now because the ray or straight line by which we judge the spot where the object appears to us is nothing else than the perpendicular to the wave that reaches our eye, as will be understood by what was said above, it is manifest that the point A will be perceived as being in the line BD, and therefore higher than in fact it is.

Similarly if the earth be AB, and the top of the atmosphere CD, which probably is not a well defined spherical surface (since we know that the air becomes rare in proportion as one ascends, for above there is so much less of it to press down upon it), the waves of light from the sun coming, for instance, in such a way that so long as they have not reached the atmosphere CD the straight line AE intersects them perpendicularly, they ought, when they enter the atmosphere, to advance more quickly in elevated regions than in regions nearer to the earth. So that if CA is the wave which brings the light to the

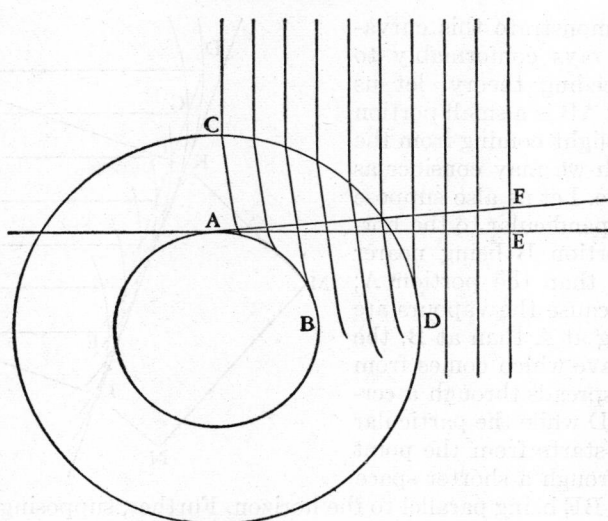

spectator at A, its region C will be the farthest advanced; and the straight line
AF, which intersects this wave at right angles, and which determines the apparent place of the sun, will pass above the real sun, which will be seen along the
line AE. And so it may occur that when it ought not to be visible in the absence
of vapours, because the line AE encounters the rotundity of the earth, it will
be perceived in the line AF by refraction. But this angle EAF is scarcely ever
more than half a degree because the attenuation of the vapours alters the
waves of light but little. Furthermore, these refractions are not altogether constant in all weathers, particularly at small elevations of 2 or 3 degrees; which
results from the different quantity of aqueous vapours rising above the earth.

And this same thing is the cause why at certain times a distant object will
be hidden behind another less distant one, and yet may at another time be able
to be seen, although the spot from which it is viewed is always the same. But
the reason for this effect will be still more evident from what we are going to
remark touching the curvature of rays. It appears from the things explained
above that the progression or propagation of a small part of a wave of light is
properly what one calls a ray. Now these rays, instead of being straight as they
are in homogeneous media, ought to be curved in an atmosphere of unequal
penetrability. For they necessarily follow from the object to the eye the line
which intersects at right angles all the progressions of the waves, as in the first
figure [p. 576] the line AEB does, as will be shown hereafter; and it is this line
which determines what interposed bodies would or would not hinder us from
seeing the object. For although the point of the steeple A appears raised to D,
it would yet not appear to the eye B if the tower H was between the two,
because it crosses the curve AEB. But the tower E, which is beneath this
curve, does not hinder the point A from being seen. Now according as the air
near the earth exceeds in density that which is higher, the curvature of the
ray AEB becomes greater: so that at certain times it passes above the summit
E, which allows the point A to be perceived by the eye at B; and at other times
it is intercepted by the same tower E which hides A from this same eye.

But to demonstrate this curvature of the rays conformably to
all our preceding theory, let us
imagine that AB is a small portion
of a wave of light coming from the
side C, which we may consider as
a straight line. Let us also suppose
that it is perpendicular to the horizon, the portion B being nearer
to the earth than the portion A;
and that, because the vapours are
less hindering at A than at B, the
particular wave which comes from
the point A spreads through a certain space AD while the particular
wave which starts from the point
B spreads through a shorter space

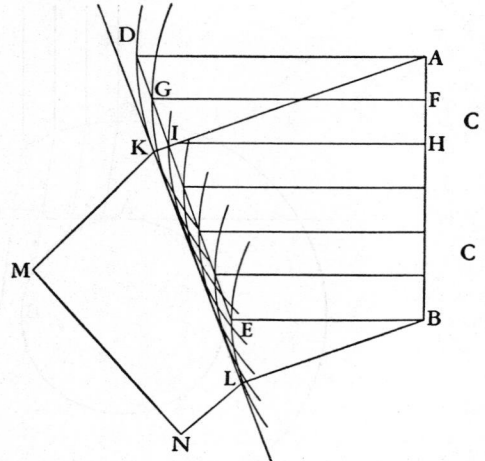

BE; AD and BE being parallel to the horizon. Further, supposing the straight
lines FG, HI, etc., to be drawn from an infinitude of points in the straight
line AB and to terminate on the line DE (which is straight or may be considered as such), let the different penetrabilities at the different heights in
the air between A and B be represented by all these lines; so that the particular wave, originating from the point F, will spread across the space FG,
and that from the point H across the space HI, while that from the point A
spreads across the space AD.

Now if about the centres A, B, one describes the circles DK, EL, which
represent the spreading of the waves which originate from these two points,
and if one draws the straight line KL which touches these two circles, it is easy
to see that this same line will be the common tangent to all the other circles
drawn about the centres F, H, etc.; and that all the points of contact will fall
within that part of this line which is comprised between the perpendiculars
AK, BL. Then it will be the line KL which will terminate the movement of the
particular waves originating from the points of the wave AB; and this movement will be stronger between the points KL, than anywhere else at the same
instant, since an infinitude of circumferences concur to form this straight line;
and consequently KL will be the propagation of the portion of wave AB, as
has been said in explaining reflexion and ordinary refraction. Now it appears
that AK and BL dip down toward the side where the air is less easy to penetrate: for AK being longer than BL, and parallel to it, it follows that the lines
AB and KL, being prolonged, would meet at the side L. But the angle K is a
right angle: hence KAB is necessarily acute, and consequently less than DAB.
If one investigates in the same way the progression of the portion of the wave
KL, one will find that after a further time it has arrived at MN in such a manner that the perpendiculars KM, LN dip down even more than do AK, BL.
And this suffices to show that the ray will continue along the curved line which
intersects all the waves at right angles, as has been said.

CHAPTER FIVE

On the Strange Refractions of Iceland Crystal

1. There is brought from Iceland, which is an island in the North Sea, in the latitude of 66 degrees, a kind of crystal or transparent stone, very remarkable for its figure and other qualities, but above all for its strange refractions. The causes of this have seemed to me to be worthy of being carefully investigated, the more so because amongst transparent bodies this one alone does not follow the ordinary rules with respect to rays of light. I have even been under some necessity to make this research, because the refractions of this crystal seemed to overturn our preceding explanation of regular refraction; which explanation, on the contrary, they strongly confirm, as will be seen after they have been brought under the same principle. In Iceland are found great lumps of this crystal, some of which I have seen of 4 or 5 pounds. But it occurs also in other countries, for I have had some of the same sort which had been found in France near the town of Troyes in Champagne, and some others which came from the island of Corsica, though both were less clear and only in little bits, scarcely capable of letting any effect of refraction be observed.

2. The first knowledge which the public has had about it is due to Mr. Erasmus Bartholinus, who has given a description of Iceland crystal and of its chief phenomena. But here I shall not desist from giving my own, both for the instruction of those who may not have seen his book, and because as respects some of these phenomena there is a slight difference between his observations and those which I have made: for I have applied myself with great exactitude to examine these properties of refraction, in order to be quite sure before undertaking to explain the causes of them.

3. As regards the hardness of this stone and the property which it has of being easily split, it must be considered rather as a species of talc than of crystal. For an iron spike effects an entrance into it as easily as into any other talc or alabaster, to which it is equal in gravity.

4. The pieces of it which are found have the figure of an oblique parallelepiped; each of the six faces being a parallelogram; and it admits of being split in three directions parallel to two of these opposed faces. Even in such wise, if you will, that all the six faces are equal and similar rhombuses. The figure here added represents a piece of this crystal. The obtuse angles of all the parallelograms, as C, D, here, are angles of 101 degrees 52 minutes, and consequently the acute angles, such as A and B, are of 78 degrees 8 minutes.

5. Of the solid angles, there are two opposite to one another, such as C and E, which are each composed of three equal obtuse plane angles. The other six are composed of two acute angles and one obtuse. All that I have just said has

been likewise remarked by Mr. Bartholinus in the aforesaid treatise; if we differ it is only slightly about the values of the angles. He recounts, moreover, some other properties of this crystal; to wit, that when rubbed against cloth it attracts straws and other light things as do amber, diamond, glass, and Spanish wax. Let a piece be covered with water for a day or more, the surface loses its natural polish. When aquafortis is poured on it, it produces ebullition, especially, as I have found, if the crystal has been pulverized. I have also found by experiment that it may be heated to redness in the fire without being in anywise altered or rendered less transparent; but a very violent fire calcines it, nevertheless. Its transparency is scarcely less than that of water or of rock crystal, and devoid of colour. But rays of light pass through it in another fashion and produce those marvellous refractions the causes of which I am now going to try to explain; reserving for the end of this treatise the statement of my conjectures touching the formation and extraordinary configuration of this crystal.

6. In all other transparent bodies that we know there is but one sole and simple refraction; but in this substance there are two different ones. The effect is that objects seen through it, especially such as are placed right against it, appear double; and that a ray of sunlight, falling on one of its surfaces, parts itself into two rays and traverses the crystal thus.

7. It is again a general law in all other transparent bodies that the ray which falls perpendicularly on their surface passes straight on without suffering refraction, and that an oblique ray is always refracted. But in this crystal the perpendicular ray suffers refraction, and there are oblique rays which pass through it quite straight.

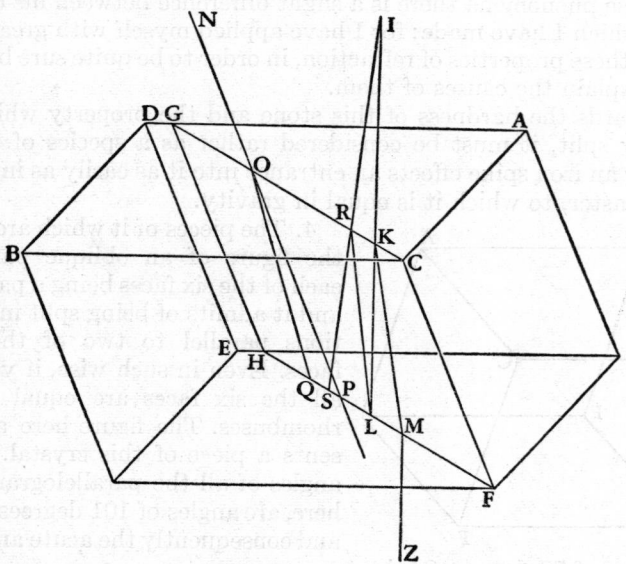

8. But in order to explain these phenomena more particularly, let there be, in the first place, a piece ABFE of the same crystal, and let the obtuse angle ACB, one of the three which constitute the equilateral solid angle C, be di-

vided into two equal parts by the straight line CG, and let it be conceived that the crystal is intersected by a plane which passes through this line and through the side CF, which plane will necessarily be perpendicular to the surface AB; and its section in the crystal will form a parallelogram GCFH. We will call this section the principal section of the crystal.

9. Now, if one covers the surface AB, leaving there only a small aperture at the point K, situated in the straight line CG, and if one exposes it to the sun, so that his rays face it perpendicularly above, then the ray IK will divide itself at the point K into two, one of which will continue to go on straight by KL, and the other will separate itself along the straight line KM, which is in the plane GCFH, and which makes with KL an angle of about 6 degrees 40 minutes, tending from the side of the solid angle C; and on emerging from the other side of the crystal it will turn again parallel to IK, along MZ. And as, in this extraordinary refraction, the point M is seen by the refracted ray MKI, which I consider as going to the eye at I, it necessarily follows that the point L, by virtue of the same refraction, will be seen by the refracted ray LRI, so that LR will be parallel to MK if the distance from the eye KI is supposed very great. The point L appears then as being in the straight line IRS; but the same point appears also, by ordinary refraction, to be in the straight line IK, hence, it is necessarily judged to be double. And, similarly, if L be a small hole in a sheet of paper or other substance which is laid against the crystal, it will appear when turned towards daylight as if there were two holes, which will seem the wider apart from one another the greater the thickness of the crystal.

10. Again, if one turns the crystal in such wise that an incident ray NO, of sunlight, which I suppose to be in the plane continued from GCFH, makes with GC an angle of 73 degrees and 20 minutes, and is consequently nearly parallel to the edge CF, which makes with FH an angle of 70 degrees 57 minutes, according to the calculation which I shall put at the end, it will divide itself at the point O into two rays, one of which will continue along OP in a straight line with NO, and will similarly pass out of the other side of the crystal without any refraction; but the other will be refracted and will go along OQ. And it must be noted that it is special to the plane through GCF and to those which are parallel to it, that all incident rays which are in one of these planes continue to be in it after they have entered the crystal and have become double; for it is quite otherwise for rays in all other planes which intersect the crystal, as we shall see afterwards.

11. I recognized at first by these experiments and by some others that of the two refractions which the ray suffers in this crystal, there is one which follows the ordinary rules; and it is this to which the rays KL and OQ belong. This is why I have distinguished this ordinary refraction from the other; and having measured it by exact observation, I found that its proportion, considered as to the sines of the angles which the incident and refracted rays make with the perpendicular, was very precisely that of 5 to 3, as was found also by Mr. Bartholinus, and consequently much greater than that of rock crystal, or of glass, which is nearly 3 to 2.

12. The mode of making these observations exactly is as follows. Upon a leaf of paper fixed on a thoroughly flat table there is traced a black line AB, and two others, CED and KML, which cut it at right angles and are more or less distant from one another according as it is desired to examine a ray that is

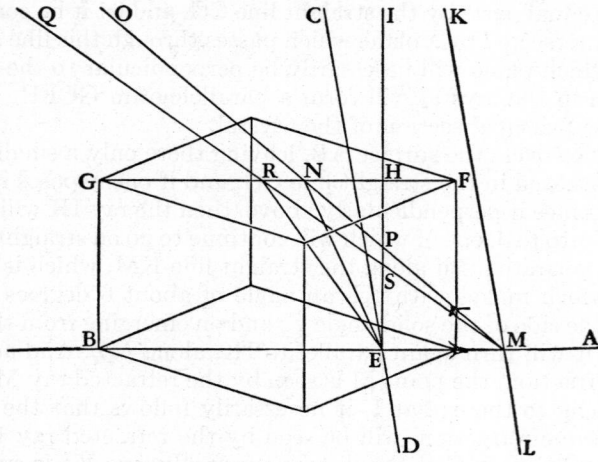

more or less oblique. Then place the crystal upon the intersection E so that the line AB concurs with that which bisects the obtuse angle of the lower surface, or with some line parallel to it. Then by placing the eye directly above the line AB it will appear single only; and one will see that the portion viewed through the crystal and the portions which appear outside it, meet together in a straight line: but the line CD will appear double, and one can distinguish the image which is due to regular refraction by the circumstance that when one views it with both eyes it seems raised up more than the other, or again by the circumstance that, when the crystal is turned around on the paper, this image remains stationary, whereas the other image shifts and moves entirely around. Afterwards let the eye be placed at I (remaining always in the plane perpendicular through AB) so that it views the image which is formed by regular refraction of the line CD making a straight line with the remainder of that line which is outside the crystal. And then, marking on the surface of the crystal the point H where the intersection E appears, this point will be directly above E. Then draw back the eye towards O, keeping always in the plane perpendicular through AB, so that the image of the line CD, which is formed by ordinary refraction, may appear in a straight line with the line KL viewed without refraction; and then mark on the crystal the point N where the point of intersection E appears.

13. Then one will know the length and position of the lines NH, EM, and of HE, which is the thickness of the crystal: which lines being traced separately upon a plan, and then joining NE and NM which cuts HE at P, the proportion of the refraction will be that of EN to NP, because these lines are to one another as the sines of the angles NPH, NEP, which are equal to those which the incident ray ON and its refraction NE make with the perpendicular to the surface. This proportion, as I have said, is sufficiently precisely as 5 to 3, and is always the same for all inclinations of the incident ray.

14. The same mode of observation has also served me for examining the extraordinary or irregular refraction of this crystal. For, the point H having been found and marked, as aforesaid, directly above the point E, I observed the appearance of the line CD, which is made by the extraordinary refraction;

and having placed the eye at Q, so that this appearance made a straight line with the line KL viewed without refraction, I ascertained the triangles REH, RES, and consequently the angles RSH, RES, which the incident and the refracted ray make with the perpendicular.

15. But I found in this refraction that the ratio of FR to RS was not constant, like the ordinary refraction, but that it varied with the varying obliquity of the incident ray.

16. I found also that when QRE made a straight line, that is, when the incident ray entered the crystal without being refracted (as I ascertained by the circumstance that then the point E viewed by the extraordinary refraction appeared in the line CD, as seen without refraction) I found, I say, then that the angle QRG was 73 degrees 20 minutes, as has been already remarked; and so it is not the ray parallel to the edge of the crystal which crosses it in a straight line without being refracted, as Mr. Bartholinus believed, since that inclination is only 70 degrees 57 minutes, as was stated above. And this is to be noted, in order that no one may search in vain for the cause of the singular property of this ray in its parallelism to the edges mentioned.

17. Finally, continuing my observations to discover the nature of this refraction, I learned that it obeyed the following remarkable rule. Let the parallelogram GCFH, made by the principal section of the crystal, as previously determined, be traced separately. I found then that always, when the inclinations of two rays which come from opposite sides, as VK, SK here, are equal, their refractions KX and KT meet the bottom line HF in such wise that points X and T are equally distant from the point M, where the refraction of the perpendicular ray IK falls; and this occurs also for refractions in other sections of this crystal. But before speaking of those, which have also other particular properties, we will investigate the causes of the phenomena which I have already reported.

It was after having explained the refraction of ordinary transparent bodies by means of the spherical emanations of light, as above, that I resumed my examination of the nature of this crystal, wherein I had previously been unable to discover anything.

18. As there were two different refractions, I conceived that there were also two different emanations of waves of light, and that one could occur in the ethereal matter extending through the body of the crystal. Which matter, being present in much larger quantity than is that of the particles which compose it, was alone capable of causing transparency, according to what has been explained heretofore. I attributed to this emanation of waves the regular re-

fraction which is observed in this stone, by supposing these waves to be ordinarily of spherical form, and having a slower progression within the crystal than they have outside it; whence proceeds refraction as I have demonstrated.

19. As to the other emanation which should produce the irregular refraction, I wished to try what elliptical waves, or rather spheroidal waves, would do; and these I supposed would spread indifferently both in the ethereal matter diffused throughout the crystal and in the particles of which it is composed, according to the last mode in which I have explained transparency. It seemed to me that the disposition or regular arrangement of these particles could contribute to form spheroidal waves (nothing more being required for this than that the successive movement of light should spread a little more quickly in one direction than in the other) and I scarcely doubted that there were in this crystal such an arrangement of equal and similar particles, because of its figure and of its angles with their determinate and invariable measure. Touching which particles, and their form and disposition, I shall, at the end of this treatise, propound my conjectures and some experiments which confirm them.

20. The double emission of waves of light, which I had imagined, became more probable to me after I had observed a certain phenomenon in the ordinary [rock] crystal, which occurs in hexagonal form, and which, because of this regularity, seems also to be composed of particles, of definite figure, and ranged in order. This was, that this crystal, as well as that from Iceland, has a double refraction, though less evident. For having had cut from it some well-polished prisms of different sections, I remarked in all, in viewing through them the flame of a candle or the lead of window panes, that everything appeared double, though with images not very distant from one another. Whence I understood the reason why this substance, though so transparent, is useless for telescopes, when they have ever so little length.

21. Now this double refraction, according to my theory hereinbefore established, seemed to demand a double emission of waves of light, both of them spherical (for both the refractions are regular) and those of one series a little slower only than the others. For thus the phenomenon is quite naturally explained, by postulating substances which serve as vehicle for these waves, as I have done in the case of Iceland crystal. I had then less trouble after that in admitting two emissions of waves in one and the same body. And since it might have been objected that in composing these two kinds of crystal of equal particles of a certain figure, regularly piled, the interstices which these particles leave and which contain the ethereal matter would scarcely suffice to transmit the waves of light which I have localized there, I removed this difficulty by regarding these particles as being of a very rare texture, or rather as composed of other much smaller particles, between which the ethereal matter passes quite freely. This, moreover, necessarily follows from that which has been already demonstrated touching the small quantity of matter of which the bodies are built up.

22. Supposing, then, these spheroidal waves besides the spherical ones, I began to examine whether they could serve to explain the phenomena of the irregular refraction, and how by these same phenomena I could determine the figure and position of the spheroids: as to which I obtained at last the desired success, by proceeding as follows.

23. I considered first the effect of waves so formed, as respects the ray which

falls perpendicularly on the flat surface of a transparent body in which they should spread in this manner. I took AB for the exposed region of the surface. And, since a ray perpendicular to a plane, and coming from a very distant

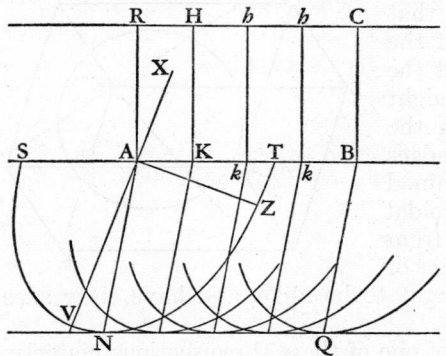

source of light, is nothing else, according to the precedent theory, than the incidence of a portion of the wave parallel to that plane, I supposed the straight line RC, parallel and equal to AB, to be a portion of a wave of light, in which an infinitude of points such as RH*h*C come to meet the surface AB at the points AK*k*B. Then instead of the hemispherical partial waves which in a body of ordinary refraction would spread from each of these last points, as we have above explained in treating of refraction, these must here be hemi-spheroids. The axes (or rather the major diameters) of these I supposed to be oblique to the plane AB, as is AV the semi-axis or semi-major diameter of the spheroid SVT, which represents the partial wave coming from the point A, after the wave RC has reached AB. I say axis or major diameter, because the same ellipse SVT may be considered as the section of a spheroid of which the axis is AZ perpendicular to AV. But, for the present, without yet deciding one or other, we will consider these spheroids only in those sections of them which make ellipses in the plane of this figure. Now taking a certain space of time during which the wave SVT has spread from A, it would needs be that from all the other points K*k*B there should proceed, in the same time, waves similar to SVT and similarly situated. And the common tangent NQ of all these semi-ellipses would be the propagation of the wave RC which fell on AB, and would be the place where this movement occurs in much greater amount than anywhere else, being made up of arcs of an infinity of ellipses, the centres of which are along the line AB.

24. Now it appeared that this common tangent NQ was parallel to AB, and of the same length, but that it was not directly opposite to it, since it was comprised between the lines AN, BQ, which are diameters of ellipses having A and B for centres, conjugate with respect to diameters which are not in the straight line AB. And in this way I comprehended, a matter which had seemed to me very difficult, how a ray perpendicular to a surface could suffer refraction on entering a transparent body; seeing that the wave RC, having come to the aperture AB, went on forward thence, spreading between the parallel lines AN, BQ, yet itself remaining always parallel to AB, so that here the light does not spread along lines perpendicular to its waves, as in ordinary refraction, but along lines cutting the waves obliquely.

25. Inquiring subsequently what might be the position and form of these spheroids in the crystal, I considered that all the six faces produced precisely the same refractions. Taking, then, the parallelepiped AFB, of which the obtuse solid angle C is contained between the three equal plane angles, and imagining in it the three principal sections, one of which is perpendicular to the face DC and passes through the edge CF, another perpendicular to the face BF passing through the edge CA, and the third perpendicular to the face AF

passing through the edge BC; I knew that the refractions of the incident rays belonging to these three planes were all similar. But there could be no position of the spheroid which would have the same relation to these three sections except that in which the axis was also the axis of the solid angle C. Consequently I saw that the axis of this angle, that is to say, the straight line which traversed the crystal from the point C with equal inclination to the edges CF, CA, CB was the line which determined the position of the axis of all the spheroidal waves which one imagined to originate from some point, taken within or on the surface of

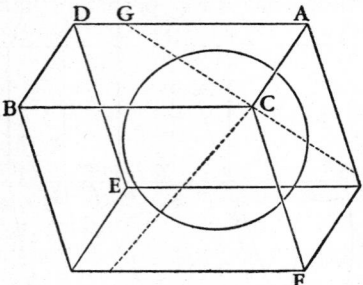

the crystal, since all these spheroids ought to be alike, and have their axes parallel to one another.

26. Considering after this the plane of one of these three sections, namely, that through GCF, the angle of which is 109 degrees 3 minutes, since the angle F was shown above to be 70 degrees 57 minutes; and, imagining a spheroidal wave about the centre C, I knew, because I have just explained it, that its axis must be in the same plane, the half of which axis I have marked CS in the next figure: and seeking by calculation (which will be given with others at the end of this discourse) the value of the angle CGS, I found it 45 degrees 20 minutes.

27. To know from this the form of this spheroid, that is to say, the proportion of the semi-diameters CS, CP, of its elliptical section, which are perpendicular to one another, I considered that the point M where the ellipse is touched by the straight line FH, parallel to CG, ought to be so situated that CM makes with the perpendicular CL an angle of 6 degrees 40 minutes; since, this being so, this ellipse satisfies what has been said about the refraction of the ray perpendicular to the surface CG, which is inclined to the perpendicular CL

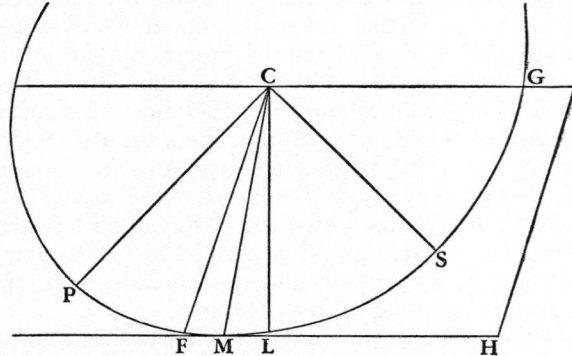

by the same angle. This, then, being thus disposed, and taking CM at 100,000 parts, I found by the calculation which will be given at the end, the semi-major diameter CP to be 105,032, and the semi-axis CS to be 93,410, the ratio of which numbers is very nearly 9 to 8; so that the spheroid was of the kind which resembles a compressed sphere, being generated by the revolution of an ellipse about its smaller diameter. I found also the value of CG the semi-diameter parallel to the tangent ML to be 98,779.

28. Now passing to the investigation of the refractions which obliquely incident rays must undergo, according to our hypothesis of spheroidal waves, I saw that these refractions depended on the ratio between the velocity of movement of the light outside the crystal in the ether, and that within the crystal. For supposing, for example, this proportion to be such that while the light in the crystal forms the spheroid GSP, as I have just said, it forms outside a sphere the semi-diameter of which is equal to the line N which will be determined hereafter, the following is the way of finding the refraction of the incident rays. Let there be such a ray RC falling upon the surface CK. Make CO perpendicular to RC, and across the angle KCO adjust OK, equal to N and perpendicular to CO; then draw KI, which touches the ellipse GSP, and from the point of contact I join IC, which will be the required refraction of the ray RC. The demonstration of this is, it will be seen, entirely similar to that of which we made use in explaining ordinary refraction. For the refraction of the ray RC is nothing else than the progression of the portion C of the wave CO, continued in the crystal. Now the portions H of this wave, during the time that O came to K, will have arrived at the surface CK along the straight lines Hx, and will, moreover, have produced in the crystal around the centres x some hemi-spheroidal partial waves similar to the hemi-spheroidal GSPg, and similarly disposed, and of which the major and minor diameters will bear the same

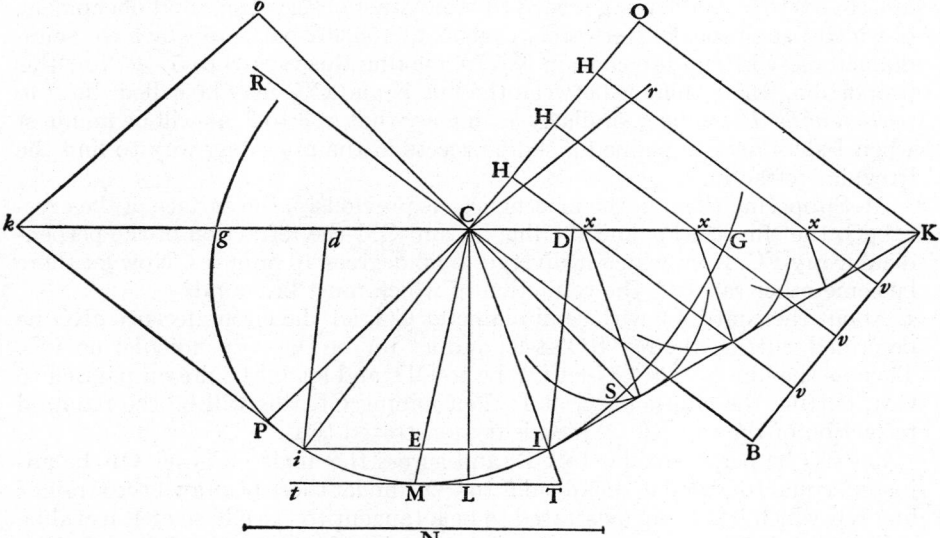

proportions to the lines xv (the continuations of the lines Hx up to KB parallel to CO) that the diameters of the spheroid GSPg bear to the line CB, or N. And it is quite easy to see that the common tangent of all these spheroids, which are here represented by ellipses, will be the straight line IK, which, consequently, will be the propagation of the wave CO; and the point I will be that of the point C, conformably with that which has been demonstrated in ordinary refraction.

Now as to finding the point of contact I, it is known that one must find CD a third proportional to the lines CK, CG, and draw DI parallel to CM, previously determined, which is the conjugate diameter to CG; for then, by drawing KI it touches the ellipse at I.

29. Now, as we have found CI the refraction of the ray RC, similarly, one will find C*i* the refraction of the ray *r*C, which comes from the opposite side, by making C*o* perpendicular to *r*C and following out the rest of the construction as before. Whence one sees that if the ray *r*C is inclined equally with RC, the line C*d* will necessarily be equal to CD, because C*k* is equal to CK, and C*g* to CG. And, in consequence, I*i* will be cut at E into equal parts by the line CM, to which DI and *di* are parallel. And because CM is the conjugate diameter to CG, it follows that *i*I will be parallel to *g*G. Therefore, if one prolongs the refracted rays CI, C*i*, until they meet the tangent ML at T and *t*, the distances MT, M*t*, will also be equal. And so, by our hypothesis, we explain perfectly the phenomenon mentioned above; to wit, that when there are two rays equally inclined, but coming from opposite sides, as here the rays RC, *rc*, their refractions diverge equally from the line followed by the refraction of the ray perpendicular to the surface, by considering these divergences in the direction parallel to the surface of the crystal.

30. To find the length of the line N, in proportion to CP, CS, CG, it must be determined by observations of the irregular refraction which occurs in this section of the crystal; and I find thus that the ratio of N to GC is just a little less than 8 to 5. And having regard to some other observations and phenomena of which I shall speak afterwards, I put N at 156,962 parts, of which the semi-diameter CG is found to contain 98,779, making this ratio 8 to $5\frac{1}{29}$. Now this proportion, which there is between the line N and CG, may be called the *Proportion of the Refraction;* similarly as in glass that of 3 to 2, as will be manifest when I shall have explained a short process in the preceding way to find the irregular refractions.

31. Supposing then, in the next figure, as previously, the surface of the crystal *g*G, the ellipse GP*g*, and the line N; and CM the refraction of the perpendicular ray FC, from which it diverges by 6 degrees 40 minutes. Now let there be some other ray RC, the refraction of which must be found.

About the centre C, with semi-diameter CG, let the circumference *g*RG be described, cutting the ray RC at R; and let RV be the perpendicular on CG. Then as the line N is to CG let CV be to CD, and let DI be drawn parallel to CM, cutting the ellipse *g*MG at I; then joining CI, this will be the required refraction of the ray RC. Which is demonstrated thus.

Let CO be perpendicular to CR, and across the angle OCG let OK be adjusted, equal to N and perpendicular to CO, and let there be drawn the straight line KI, which if it is demonstrated to be a tangent to the ellipse at I, it will be evident by the things heretofore explained that CI is the refraction of the ray RC. Now, since the angle RCO is a right angle, it is easy to see that the right-angled triangles RCV, KCO are similar. As then, CK is to KO, so also is RC to CV. But KO is equal to N, and RC to CG: then as CK is to N so will CG be to CV. But as N is to CG, so, by construction, is CV to CD. Then as CK is to CG so is CG to CD. And because DI is parallel to CM, the conjugate diameter to CG, it follows that KI touches the ellipse at I; which remained to be shown.

32. One sees, then, that as there is in the refraction of ordinary media a

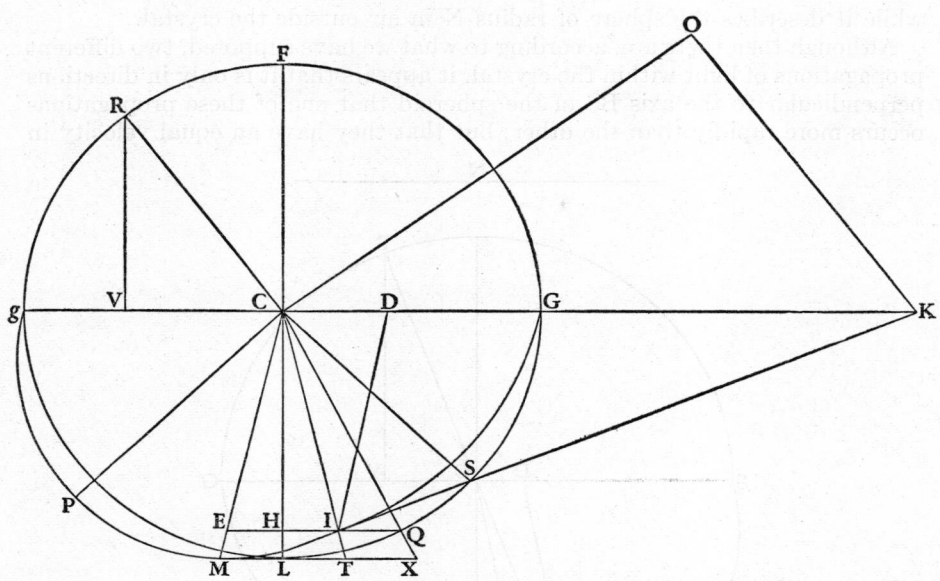

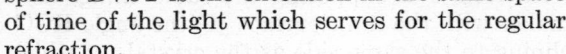

certain constant proportion between the sines of the angles which the incident ray and the refracted ray make with the perpendicular, so here there is such a proportion between CV and CD or IE; that is to say, between the sine of the angle which the incident ray makes with the perpendicular and the horizontal intercept, in the ellipse, between the refraction of this ray and the diameter CM. For the ratio of CV to CD is, as has been said, the same as that of N to the semi-diameter CG.

33. I will add here, before passing away, that in comparing together the regular and irregular refraction of this crystal, there is this remarkable fact, that if ABPS be the spheroid by which light spreads in the crystal in a certain space of time (which spreading, as has been said, serves for the irregular refraction), then the inscribed sphere BVST is the extension in the same space of time of the light which serves for the regular refraction.

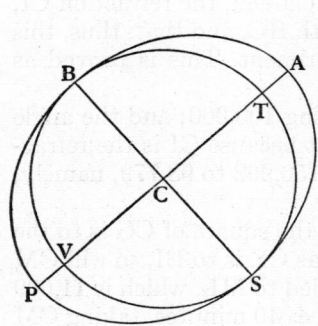

For we have stated before this that the line N being the radius of a spherical wave of light in air, while in the crystal it spread through the spheroid ABPS, the ratio of N to CS will be 156,962 to 93,410. But it has also been stated that the proportion of the regular refraction was 5 to 3; that is to say, that N being the radius of a spherical wave of light in air, its extension in the crystal would, in the same space of time, form a sphere the radius of which would be to N as 3 to 5. Now 156,962 is to 93,410 as 5 to 3 less $\frac{1}{41}$. So that it is sufficiently nearly, and may be exactly, the sphere BVST, which the light describes for the regular refraction in the crystal, while it describes the spheroid BPSA for the irregular refraction, and while it describes the sphere of radius N in air outside the crystal.

Although then there are, according to what we have supposed, two different propagations of light within the crystal, it appears that it is only in directions perpendicular to the axis BS of the spheroid that one of these propagations occurs more rapidly than the other; but that they have an equal velocity in

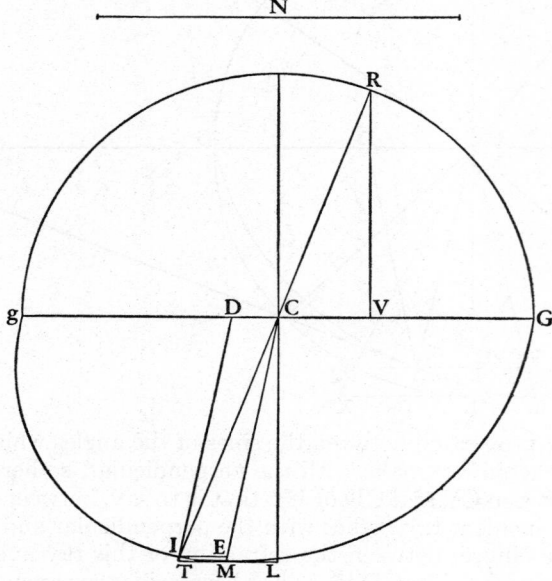

the other direction, namely, in that parallel to the same axis BS, which is also the axis of the obtuse angle of the crystal.

34. The proportion of the refraction being what we have just seen, I will now show that there necessarily follows thence that notable property of the ray which falling obliquely on the surface of the crystal enters it without suffering refraction. For supposing the same things as before, and that the ray RC makes with the same surface gG the angle RCG of 73 degrees 20 minutes, inclining to the same side as the crystal (of which ray mention has been made above); if one investigates, by the process above explained, the refraction CI, one will find that it makes exactly a straight line with RC, and that, thus, this ray is not deviated at all, conformably with experiment. This is proved as follows by calculation.

CG or CR being, as precedently, 98,779; CM being 100,000; and the angle RCV 73 degrees 20 minutes, CV will be 28,330. But because CI is the refraction of the ray RC, the proportion of CV to CD is 156,962 to 98,779, namely, that of N to CG; then CD is 17,828.

Now the rectangle gDC is to the square of DI as the square of CG is to the square of CM; hence DI or CE will be 98,353. But as CE is to EI, so will CM be to MT, which will then be 18,127. And being added to ML, which is 11,609 (namely the sine of the angle LCM, which is 6 degrees 40 minutes, taking CM

100,000 as radius) we get LT 27,936; and this is to LC 99,324 as CV to VR, that is to say, as 29,938, the tangent of the complement of the angle RCV, which is 73 degrees 20 minutes, is to the radius of the tables. Whence it appears that RCIT is a straight line; which was to be proved.

35. Further, it will be seen that the ray CI, in emerging through the opposite surface of the crystal, ought to pass out quite straight, according to the following demonstration, which proves that the reciprocal relation of refraction obtains in this crystal the same as in other transparent bodies; that is to say, that if a ray RC in meeting the surface of the crystal CG is refracted as CI, the ray CI emerging through the opposite parallel surface of the crystal which I suppose to be IB, will have its refraction IA parallel to the ray RC.

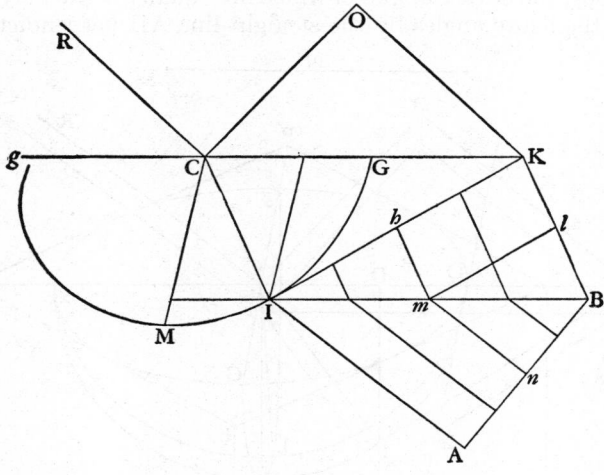

Let the same things be supposed as before; that is to say, let CO, perpendicular to CR, represent a portion of a wave, the continuation of which in the crystal is IK, so that the piece C will be continued on along the straight line CI, while O comes to K. Now, if one takes a second period of time equal to the first, the piece K of the wave IK will, in this second period, have advanced along the straight line KB, equal and parallel to CI, because every piece of the wave CO, on arriving at the surface CK, ought to go on in the crystal the same as the piece C; and in this same time there will be formed in the air from the point I a partial spherical wave having a semi-diameter IA equal to KO, since KO has been traversed in an equal time. Similarly, if one considers some other point of the wave IK, such as h, it will go along hm, parallel to CI, to meet the surface IB, while the point K traverses Kl equal to hm; and while this accomplishes the remainder lB, there will start from the point m a partial wave the semi-diameter of which, mn, will have the same ratio to lB as IA to KB. Whence it is evident that this wave of semi-diameter mn, and the other of semi-diameter IA will have the same tangent BA. And similarly for all the partial spherical waves which will be formed outside the crystal by the impact of all the points of the wave IK against the surface of the ether IB. It is then precisely the tangent BA which will be the continuation of the wave IK, outside the crystal, when the piece K has reached B. And in consequence IA, which is perpendicular to BA, will be the refraction of the ray CI on emerging from the crystal. Now it is clear that IA is parallel to the incident ray RC, since IB is equal to CK, and IA equal to KO, and the angles A and O are right angles.

It is seen then that, according to our hypothesis, the reciprocal relation of refraction holds good in this crystal as well as in ordinary transparent bodies; as is thus in fact found by observation.

36. I pass now to the consideration of other sections of the crystal, and of the refractions there produced, on which, as will be seen, some other very re-markable phenomena depend.

Let ABH be a parallelepiped of crystal, and let the top surface AEHF be a perfect rhombus, the obtuse angles of which are equally divided by the straight line EF, and the acute angles by the straight line AH perpendicular to FE.

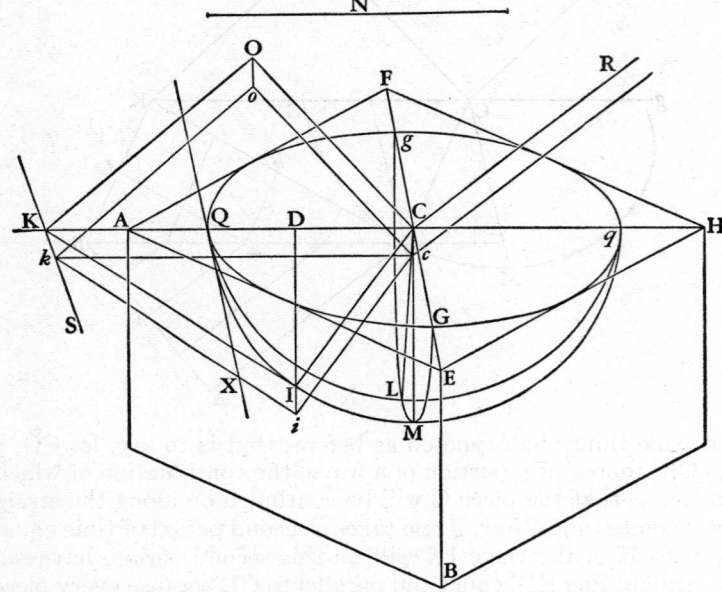

The section which we have hitherto considered is that which passes through the lines EF, EB, and which at the same time cuts the plane AEHF at right angles. Refractions in this section have this in common with the refractions in ordinary media: that the plane which is drawn through the incident ray and which also intersects the surface of the crystal at right angles is that in which the refracted ray also is found. But the refractions which appertain to every other section of this crystal have this strange property: that the refracted ray always quits the plane of the incident ray perpendicular to the surface, and turns away towards the side of the slope of the crystal. For which fact we shall show the reason, in the first place, for the section through AH; and we shall show at the same time how one can determine the refraction, according to our hypothesis. Let there be, then, in the plane which passes through AH, and which is perpendicular to the plane AFHE, the incident ray RC; it is required to find its refraction in the crystal.

37. About the centre C, which I suppose to be in the intersection of AH and FE, let there be imagined a hemi-spheroid QG*qg*M, such as the light would form in spreading in the crystal, and let its section by the plane AEHF form the ellipse QG*qg*, the major diameter of which Q*q*, which is in the line AH, will necessarily be one of the major diameters of the spheroid; because the axis of the spheroid being in the plane through FEB, to which QC is perpendicular, it follows that QC is also perpendicular to the axis of the spheroid, and, consequently, QC*q* one of its major diameters. But the minor diameter of this ellipse, G*g*, will bear to Q*q* the proportion which has been defined previously, Article 27, between CG and the major semi-diameter of the spheroid, CP, namely, that of 98,779 to 105,032.

Let the line N be the length of the travel of light in air during the time in which, within the crystal, it makes, from the centre C, the spheroid QG*qg*M. Then, having drawn CO perpendicular to the ray CR and situated in the plane through CR and AH, let there be adjusted, across the angle ACO, the straight line OK equal to N and perpendicular to CO, and let it meet the straight line AH at K. Supposing, consequently, that CL is perpendicular to the surface of the crystal AEHF, and that CM is the refraction of the ray which falls perpendicularly on this same surface, let there be drawn a plane through the line CM and through KCH, making in the spheroid the semi-ellipse QM*q*, which will be given, since the angle MCL is given of value 6 degrees 40 minutes. And it is certain, according to what has been explained above, Article 27, that a plane which would touch the spheroid at the point M, where I suppose the straight line CM to meet the surface, would be parallel to the plane QG*q*. If, then, through the point K one now draws KS parallel to G*g*, which will be parallel also to QX, the tangent to the ellipse QG*q* at Q; and if one conceives a plane passing through KS and touching the spheroid, the point of contact will necessarily be in the ellipse QM*q*, because this plane through KS, as well as the plane which touches the spheroid at the point M, are parallel to QX, the tangent of the spheroid: for this consequence will be demonstrated at the end of this treatise. Let this point of contact be at I, then making KC, QC, DC proportionals, draw DI parallel to CM; also join CI. I say that CI will be the required refraction of the ray RC. This will be manifest if, in considering CO, which is perpendicular to the ray RC, as a portion of the wave of light, we can demonstrate that the continuation of its piece C will be found in the crystal at I, when O has arrived at K.

38. Now as in the chapter on reflexion, in demonstrating that the incident and reflected rays are always in the same plane perpendicular to the reflecting surface, we considered the breadth of the wave of light, so, similarly, we must here consider the breadth of the wave CO in the diameter G*g*. Taking, then, the breadth C*c* on the side toward the angle E, let the parallelogram CO*oc* be taken as a portion of a wave, and let us complete the parallelograms CK*kc*, CI*ic*, KI*ik*, OK*ko*. In the time, then, that the line O*o* arrives at the surface of the crystal at K*k*, all the points of the wave CO*oc* will have arrived at the rectangle K*c* along lines parallel to OK; and from the points of their incidences there will originate, beyond that, in the crystal partial hemi-spheroids, similar to the hemi-spheroid QM*q*, and similarly disposed. These hemispheroids will necessarily all touch the plane of the parallelogram KI*ik* at the same instant that O*o* has reached K*k*. Which is easy to comprehend, since, of these hemi-

spheroids, all those which have their centres along the line CK, touch this plane in the line KI (for this is to be shown in the same way as we have demonstrated the refraction of the oblique ray in the principal section through EF) and all those which have their centres in the line Cc will touch the same plane KI in the line Ii; all these being similar to the hemi-spheroid QMq. Since, then, the parallelogram Ki is that which touches all these spheroids, this same parallelogram will be precisely the continuation of the wave COoc in the crystal, when Oo has arrived at Kk, because it forms the termination of the movement and because of the quantity of movement which occurs more there than anywhere else: and thus it appears that the piece C of the wave COoc has its continuation at I; that is to say, that the ray RC is refracted as CI.

From this it is to be noted that the proportion of the refraction for this section of the crystal is that of the line N to the semi-diameter CQ; by which one will easily find the refractions of all incident rays, in the same way as we have shown previously for the case of the section through FE; and the demonstration will be the same. But it appears that the said proportion of the refraction is less here than in the section through FEB; for it was there the same as the ratio of N to CG, that is to say, as 156,962 to 98,779, very nearly as 8 to 5; and here it is the ratio of N to CQ the major semi-diameter of the spheroid, that is to say, as 156,962 to 105,032, very nearly as 3 to 2, but just a little less. Which still agrees perfectly with what one finds by observation.

39. For the rest, this diversity of proportion of refraction produces a very singular effect in this crystal; which is that when it is placed upon a sheet of paper on which there are letters or anything else marked, if one views it from above with the two eyes situated in the plane of the section through EF, one sees the letters raised up by this irregular refraction more than when one puts one's eyes in the plane of section through AH: and the difference of these elevations appears by comparison with the other ordinary refraction of the crystal, the proportion of which is as 5 to 3, and which always raises the letters equally, and higher than the irregular refraction does. For one sees the letters and the paper on which they are written, as on two different stages at the same time; and in the first position of the eyes, namely, when they are in the plane through AH these two stages are four times more distant from one another than when the eyes are in the plane through EF.

We will show that this effect follows from the refractions; and it will enable us at the same time to ascertain the apparent place of a point of an object placed immediately under the crystal, according to the different situation of the eyes.

40. Let us see first by how much the irregular refraction of the plane through AH ought to lift the bottom of the crystal. Let the plane of this figure represent separately the section through Qq and CL, in which section there is also the ray RC, and let the semi-elliptic plane through Qq and CM be inclined to the former, as previously, by an angle of 6 degrees 40 minutes; and in this plane CI is then the refraction of the ray RC.

If now one considers the point I as at the bottom of the crystal, and that it is viewed by the rays ICR, Icr, refracted equally at the points Cc, which should be equally distant from D, and that these rays meet the two eyes at Rr; it is certain that the point I will appear raised to S where the straight lines RC, rc, meet; which point S is in DP, perpendicular to Qq. And if upon DP there is

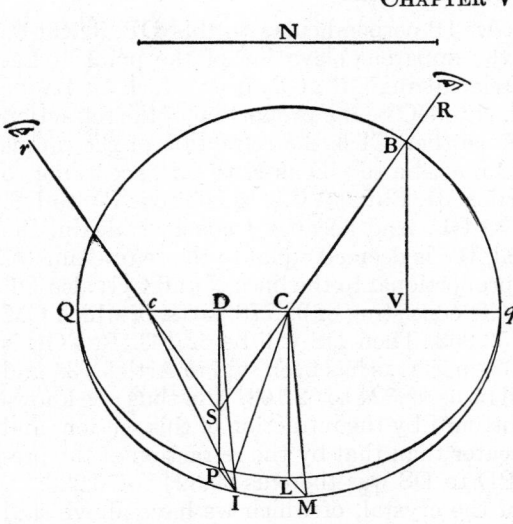

drawn the perpendicular IP, which will lie at the bottom of the crystal, the length SP will be the apparent elevation of the point I above the bottom.

Let there be described on Qq a semicircle cutting the ray CR at B, from which BV is drawn perpendicular to Qq; and let the proportion of the refraction for this section be, as before, that of the line N to the semi-diameter CQ.

Then as N is to CQ so is VC to CD, as appears by the method of finding the refraction which we have shown above, Article 31; but as VC is to CD, so is VB to DS. Then as N is to CQ, so is VB to DS. Let ML be perpendicular to CL. And because I suppose the eyes Rr to be distant about a foot or so from the crystal, and consequently the angle RSr very small, VB may be considered as equal to the semi-diameter CQ, and DP as equal to CL; then as N is to CQ so is CQ to DS. But N is valued at 156,962 parts, of which CM contains 100,000 and CQ 105,032. Then DS will have 70,283. But CL is 99,324, being the sine of the complement of the angle MCL which is 6 degrees 40 minutes; CM being supposed as radius. Then DP, considered as equal to CL, will be to DS as 99,324 to 70,283. And so the elevation of the point I by the refraction of this section is known.

41. Now let there be represented the other section through EF in the figure before the preceding one; and let CMg be the semi-ellipse, considered in Articles 27 and 28, which is made by cutting a spheroidal wave having centre C.

Let the point I, taken in this ellipse, be imagined again at the bottom of the crystal; and let it be viewed by the refracted rays ICR, Icr, which go to the two eyes; CR and cr being equally inclined to the surface of the crystal Gg. This being so, if one draws ID parallel to CM, which I suppose to be the refraction of the perpendicular ray incident at the point C, the distances DC, Dc, will be equal, as is easy to see by that which has been demonstrated in Article 28. Now it is certain that the point I should appear at S where the straight lines RC, rc meet when prolonged; and that this point will fall in the line

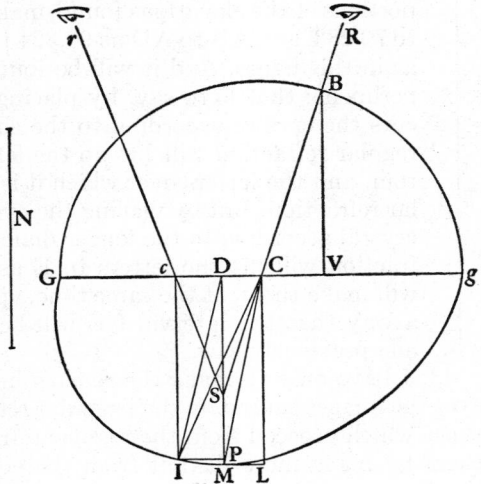

DP perpendicular to G*g*. If one draws IP perpendicular to this DP, it will be the distance PS which will mark the apparent elevation of the point I. Let there be described on G*g* a semicircle cutting CR at B, from which let BV be drawn perpendicular to G*g;* and let N to GC be the proportion of the refraction in this section, as in Article 28. Since then CI is the refraction of the radius BC, and DI is parallel to CM, VC must be to CD as N to GC, according to what has been demonstrated in Article 31. But as VC is to CD so is BV to DS. Let ML be drawn perpendicular to CL. And because I consider, again, the eyes to be distant above the crystal, BV is deemed equal to the semi-diameter CG; and hence DS will be a third proportional to the lines N and CG: also DP will be deemed equal to CL. Now CG consisting of 98,778 parts, of which CM contains 100,000, N is taken as 156,962. Then DS will be 62,163. But CL is also determined, and contains 99,324 parts, as has been said in Articles 34 and 40. Then the ratio of PD to DS will be as 99,324 to 62,163. And thus one knows the elevation of the point at the bottom I by the refraction of this section; and it appears that this elevation is greater than that by the refraction of the preceding section, since the ratio of PD to DS was there as 99,324 to 70,283.

But by the regular refraction of the crystal, of which we have above said that the proportion is 5 to 3, the elevation of the point I, or P, from the bottom, will be $\frac{2}{5}$ of the height DP; as appears by this figure, where the point P being viewed by the rays PCR, P*cr*, refracted equally at the surface C*c*, this point must needs appear to be at S, in the perpendicular PD where the lines RC, *rc* meet when prolonged: and one knows that the line PC is to CS as 5 to 3, since they are to one another as the sine of the angle CSP or DSC is to the sine of the angle SPC. And because the ratio of PD to DS is deemed the same as that of PC to CS, the two eyes R*r* being supposed very far above the crystal, the elevation PS will thus be $\frac{2}{5}$ of PD.

42. If one takes a straight line AB for the thickness of the crystal, its point B being at the bottom, and if one divides it at the points C, D, E, according to the proportions of the elevations found, making AE $\frac{3}{5}$ of AB, AB to AC as 99,324 to 70,283, and AB to AD as 99,324 to 62,163, these points will divide AB as in this figure. And it will be found that this agrees perfectly with experiment; that is to say, by placing the eyes above in the plane which cuts the crystal according to the shorter diameter of the rhombus, the regular refraction will lift up the letters to E; and one will see the bottom, and the letters over which it is placed, lifted up to D by the irregular refraction. But by placing the eyes above in the plane which cuts the crystal according to the longer diameter of the rhombus, the regular refraction will lift the letters to E as before; but the irregular refraction will make them, at the same time, appear lifted up only to C; and in such a way that the interval CE will be quadruple the interval ED, which one previously saw.

43. I have only to make the remark here that in both the positions of the eyes the images caused by the irregular refraction do not appear directly below those which proceed from the regular refraction, but they are separated from them by being more distant from the equilateral solid angle of the crystal.

That follows, indeed, from all that has been hitherto demonstrated about the irregular refraction; and it is particularly shown by these last demonstrations, from which one sees that the point I appears by irregular refraction at S in the perpendicular line DP, in which line also the image of the point P ought to appear by regular refraction, but not the image of the point I, which will be almost directly above the same point, and higher than S.

But as to the apparent elevation of the point I in other positions of the eyes above the crystal, besides the two positions which we have just examined, the image of that point by the irregular refraction will always appear between the two heights of D and C, passing from one to the other as one turns one's self around about the immovable crystal, while looking down from above. And all this is still found conformable to our hypothesis, as any one can assure himself after I shall have shown here the way of finding the irregular refractions which appear in all other sections of the crystal, besides the two which we have considered. Let us suppose one of the faces of the crystal, in which let there be the ellipse HDE, the centre C of which is also the centre of the spheroid HME in which the light spreads, and of which the said ellipse is the section. And let the incident ray be RC, the refraction of which it is required to find.

Let there be taken a plane passing through the ray RC and which is perpendicular to the plane of the ellipse HDE, cutting it along the straight line

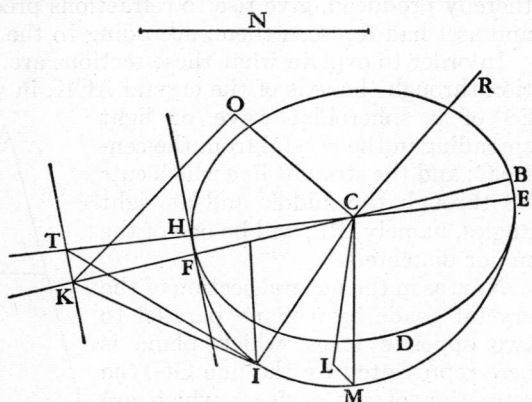

BCK; and having in the same plane through RC made CO perpendicular to CR, let OK be adjusted across the angle OCK, so as to be perpendicular to OC and equal to the line N, which I suppose to measure the travel of the light in air during the time that it spreads in the crystal through the spheroid HDEM. Then in the plane of the ellipse HDE let KT be drawn, through the point K, perpendicular to BCK. Now if one conceives a plane drawn through the straight line KT and touching the spheroid HME at I, the straight line CI will be the refraction of the ray RC, as is easy to deduce from that which has been demonstrated in Article 36.

But it must be shown how one can determine the point of contact I. Let there be drawn parallel to the line KT a line HF which touches the ellipse HDE, and let this point of contact be at H. And having drawn a straight line along CH to meet KT at T, let there be imagined a plane passing through the same CH and through CM (which I suppose to be the refraction of the perpendicular ray), which makes in the spheroid the elliptical section HME. It is certain that the plane which will pass through the straight line KT, and which will touch the spheroid, will touch it at a point in the ellipse HME, according to the Lemma which will be demonstrated at the end of the chapter. Now this point is necessarily the point I which is sought, since the plane drawn through TK can touch the spheroid at one point only. And this point I is easy to determine, since it is needful only to draw from the point T, which is in the plane of this ellipse, the tangent TI, in the way shown previously. For the ellipse HME is given, and its conjugate semi-diameters are CH and CM; because a straight line drawn through M, parallel to HE, touches the ellipse HME, as follows from the fact that a plane taken through M, and parallel to the plane HDE, touches the spheroid at that point M, as is seen from Articles 27 and 23. For the rest, the position of this ellipse, with respect to the plane through the ray RC and through CK, is also given; from which it will be easy to find the position of CI, the refraction corresponding to the ray RC.

Now it must be noted that the same ellipse HME serves to find the refractions of any other ray which may be in the plane through RC and CK. Because every plane, parallel to the straight line HF, or TK, which will touch the spheroid, will touch it in this ellipse, according to the Lemma quoted a little before.

I have investigated thus, in minute detail, the properties of the irregular refraction of this crystal, in order to see whether each phenomenon that is deduced from our hypothesis accords with that which is observed in fact. And this being so, it affords no slight proof of the truth of our suppositions and principles. But what I am going to add here confirms them again marvellously. It is this: that there are different sections of this crystal, the surfaces of which, thereby produced, give rise to refractions precisely such as they ought to be, and as I had foreseen them, according to the preceding theory.

In order to explain what these sections are, let ABKF be the principal section through the axis of the crystal ACK, in which there will also be the axis SS of a spheroidal wave of light spreading in the crystal from the centre C; and the straight line which cuts SS through the middle and at right angles, namely, PP, will be one of the major diameters.

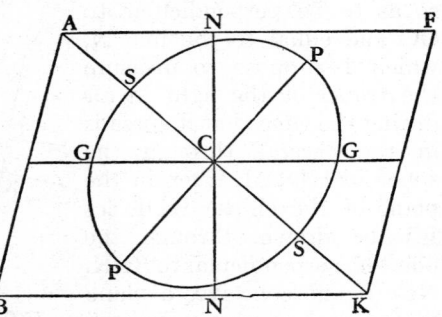

Now as in the natural section of the crystal, made by a plane parallel to two opposite faces, which plane is here represented by the line GG, the refraction of the surfaces which are produced by it will be governed by the hemi-spheroids GNG, according to what has been explained in the preceding theory. Similarly, cutting the crystal through NN, by a plane perpendicular to the parallelogram ABKF, the refraction of the surfaces will be governed by the hemi-spheroids NGN. And if one cuts it through PP, perpendicularly to the said parallelogram, the refraction of the surfaces ought to be governed by the hemi-spheroids PSP, and so for others. But I saw that if the plane NN was almost perpendicular to the plane GG, making the angle NCG, which is on the side A, an angle of 90 degrees 40 minutes, the hemi-spheroids NGN would become similar to the hemi-spheroids GNG, since the planes NN and GG were equally inclined by an angle of 45 degrees 20 minutes to the axis SS. In consequence it must needs be, if our theory is true, that the surfaces which the section through NN produces should effect the same refractions as the surfaces of the section through GG. And not only the surfaces of the section NN but all other sections produced by planes which might be inclined to the axis at an angle equal to 45 degrees 20 minutes. So that there are an infinitude of planes which ought to produce precisely the same refractions as the natural surfaces of the crystal, or as the section parallel to any one of those surfaces which are made by cleavage.

I saw also that by cutting it by a plane taken through PP, and perpendicular to the axis SS, the refraction of the surfaces ought to be such that the perpendicular ray should suffer thereby no deviation; and that for oblique rays there would always be an irregular refraction, differing from the regular, and by which objects placed beneath the crystal would be less elevated than by that other refraction.

That, similarly, by cutting the crystal by any plane through the axis SS, such as the plane of the figure is, the perpendicular ray ought to suffer no refraction; and that for oblique rays there were different measures for the irregular refraction according to the situation of the plane in which the incident ray was.

Now these things were found in fact so; and, after that, I could not doubt that a similar success could be met with everywhere. Whence I concluded that one might form from this crystal solids similar to those which are its natural forms, which should produce, at all their surfaces, the same regular and irregular refractions as the natural surfaces, and which, nevertheless, would cleave in quite other ways, and not in directions parallel to any of their faces. That out of it one would be able to fashion pyramids, having their base square, pentagonal, hexagonal, or with as many sides as one desired, all the surfaces of which should have the same refractions as the natural surfaces of the crystal, except the base, which will not refract the perpendicular ray. These surfaces will each make an angle of 45 degrees 20 minutes with the axis of the crystal, and the base will be the section perpendicular to the axis.

That, finally, one could also fashion out of it triangular prisms, or prisms with as many sides as one would, of which neither the sides nor the bases would refract the perpendicular ray, although they would yet all cause double refraction for oblique rays. The cube is included amongst these prisms, the bases of which are sections perpendicular to the axis of the crystal, and the sides are sections parallel to the same axis.

From all this it further appears that it is not at all in the disposition of the layers of which this crystal seems to be composed, and according to which it splits in three different senses, that the cause resides of its irregular refraction; and that it would be in vain to wish to seek it there.

But in order that any one who has some of this stone may be able to find, by his own experience, the truth of what I have just advanced, I will state here the process of which I have made use to cut it and to polish it. Cutting is easy by the slicing wheels of lapidaries, or in the way in which marble is sawn: but polishing is very difficult, and by employing the ordinary means one more often depolishes the surfaces than makes them lucent.

After many trials, I have at last found that for this service no plate of metal must be used, but a piece of mirror glass made matt and depolished. Upon this, with fine sand and water, one smooths the crystal little by little, in the same way as spectacle glasses, and polishes it simply by continuing the work, but ever reducing the material. I have not, however, been able to give it per-

fect clarity and transparency; but the evenness which the surfaces acquire enables one to observe in them the effects of refraction better than in those made
by cleaving the stone, which always have some inequality.

Even when the surface is only moderately smoothed, if one rubs it over with
a little oil or white of egg, it becomes quite transparent, so that the refraction
is discerned in it quite distinctly. And this aid is specially necessary when it is
wished to polish the natural surfaces to remove the inequalities; because one
cannot render them lucent equally with the surfaces of other sections, which
take a polish so much the better the less nearly they approximate to these
natural planes.

Before finishing the treatise on this crystal, I will add one more marvellous
phenomenon which I discovered after having written all the foregoing. For
though I have not been able till now to find its cause, I do not for that reason
wish to desist from describing it, in order to give opportunity to others to
investigate it. It seems that it will be necessary to make still further suppositions besides those which I have made; but these will not, for all that, cease to
keep their probability after having been confirmed by so many tests.

The phenomenon is, that by taking two pieces of this crystal and applying
them one over the other, or rather holding them with a space between the two,
if all the sides of one are parallel to those of the other, then a ray of light, such
as AB, is divided into two in the first piece, namely into BD and BC, following

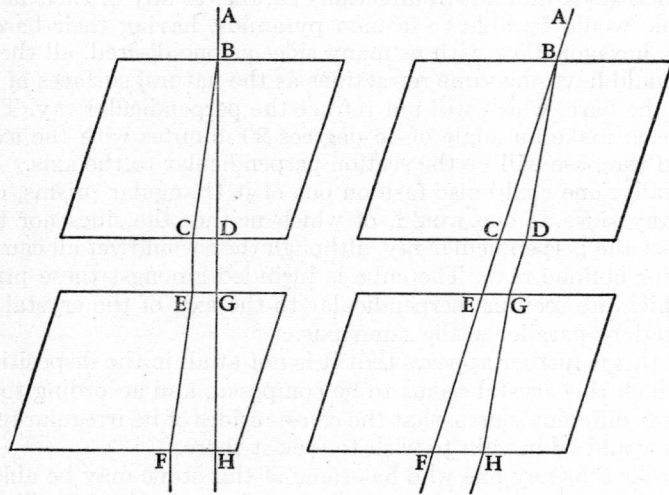

the two refractions, regular and irregular. On penetrating thence into the other
piece each ray will pass there without further dividing itself in two; but that
one which underwent the regular refraction, as here DG, will undergo again
only a regular refraction at GH; and the other, CE, an irregular refraction at
EF. And the same thing occurs not only in this disposition, but also in all those
cases in which the principal section of each of the pieces is situated in one and
the same plane, without it being needful for the two neighbouring surfaces to
be parallel. Now it is marvellous why the rays CE and DG, incident from the
air on the lower crystal, do not divide themselves the same as the first ray AB.

One would say that it must be that the ray DG in passing through the upper piece has lost something which is necessary to move the matter which serves for the irregular refraction; and that likewise CE has lost that which was necessary to move the matter which serves for regular refraction: but there is yet another thing which upsets this reasoning. It is that when one disposes the two crystals in such a way that the planes which constitute the principal sections intersect one another at right angles, whether the neighbouring surfaces are parallel or not, then the ray which has come by the regular refraction, as DG, undergoes only an irregular refraction in the lower piece; and on the contrary the ray which has come by the irregular refraction, as CE, undergoes only a regular refraction.

But in all the infinite other positions, besides those which I have just stated, the rays DG, CE, divide themselves anew each one into two, by refraction in the lower crystal, so that from the single ray AB there are four, sometimes of equal brightness, sometimes some much less bright than others, according to the varying agreement in the positions of the crystals: but they do not appear to have all together more light than the single ray AB.

When one considers here how, while the rays CE, DG remain the same, it depends on the position that one gives to the lower piece whether it divides them both in two, or whether it does not divide them, and yet how the ray AB above is always divided; it seems that one is obliged to conclude that the waves of light, after having passed through the first crystal, acquire a certain form or disposition in virtue of which, when meeting the texture of the second crystal, in certain positions, they can move the two different kinds of matter which serve for the two species of refraction; and when meeting the second crystal in another position are able to move only one of these kinds of matter. But to tell how this occurs, I have hitherto found nothing which satisfies me.

Leaving, then, to others this research, I pass to what I have to say touching the cause of the extraordinary figure of this crystal, and why it cleaves easily in three different senses, parallel to any one of its surfaces.

There are many bodies, vegetable, mineral, and congealed salts, which are formed with certain regular angles and figures. Thus, among flowers there are many which have their leaves disposed in ordered polygons, to the number of 3, 4, 5, or 6 sides, but not more. This well deserves to be investigated, both as to the polygonal figure, and as to why it does not exceed the number 6.

Rock crystal grows ordinarily in hexagonal bars, and diamonds are found which occur with a square point and polished surfaces. There is a species of small flat stones, piled up directly upon one another, which are all of pentagonal figure with rounded angles, and the sides a little folded inwards. The grains of gray salt which are formed from sea water affect the figure, or at least the angle, of the cube; and in the congelations of other salts, and in that of sugar, there are found other solid angles with perfectly flat faces. Small snowflakes almost always fall in little stars with 6 points, and sometimes in hexagons with straight sides. And I have often observed, in water which is beginning to freeze, a kind of flat and thin foliage of ice, the middle ray of which throws out branches inclined at an angle of 60 degrees. All these things are worthy of being carefully investigated to ascertain how and by what artifice Nature there operates. But it is not now my intention to treat fully of this matter. It seems that in general the regularity which occurs in these productions comes from the arrangement of the small invisible equal particles of which they are composed. And, coming to our Iceland crystal, I say that if there were a pyramid such as ABCD, composed of small rounded corpuscles, not spherical but flattened spheroids, such as would be made by the rotation of the ellipse GH around its lesser diameter EF (of which the ratio to the greater

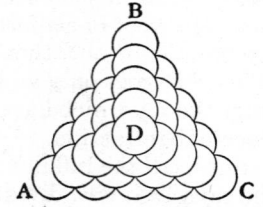

diameter is very nearly that of 1 to the square root of 8)—I say that then the solid angle of the point D would be equal to the obtuse and equilateral angle of this crystal. I say, further, that if these corpuscles were lightly stuck together, on breaking this pyramid it would break along faces parallel to those that make its point: and by this means, as it is easy to see, it would produce prisms similar to those of the same crystal as this other figure repre-

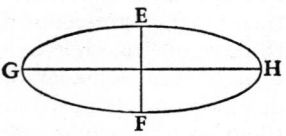

sents. The reason is that when broken in this fashion a whole layer separates easily from its neighbouring layer, since each spheroid has to be detached only from the three spheroids of the next layer; of which three there is but one which touches it on its flattened surface, and the other two at the edges. And the reason that the surfaces separate sharp and polished is that if any spheroid of the neighbouring surface would come out by attaching itself to the surface which is being separated, it would be needful for it to detach itself from six other spheroids which hold it locked, and four of which press it by these flattened surfaces. Since, then, not only the angles of our crystal but also the manner in which it splits agree precisely with what is observed in the assemblage composed of such spheroids, there is great reason to believe that the particles are shaped and ranged in the same way.

There is even probability enough that the prisms of this crystal are produced by the breaking up of pyramids, since Mr. Bartholinus relates that he occasionally found some pieces of triangularly pyramidal figure. But when a mass is composed interiorly only of these little spheroids thus piled up, whatever form it may have exteriorly, it is certain, by the same reasoning which I have just explained, that if broken it would produce similar prisms. It remains to be seen whether there are other reasons which confirm our conjecture, and whether there are none which are repugnant to it.

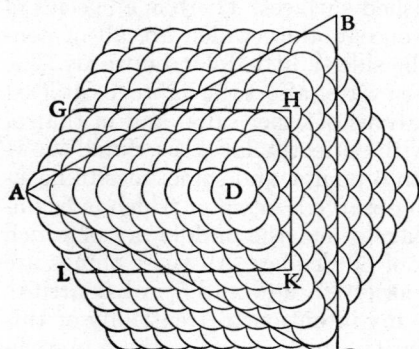

It may be objected that this crystal, being so composed, might be capable of cleavage in yet two more fashions; one of which would be along planes parallel to the base of the pyramid, that is to say to the triangle ABC; the other would be parallel to a plane the trace of which is marked by the lines GH, HK, KL. To which I say that both the one and the other, though practicable, are more difficult than those which were parallel to any one of the three planes of the pyramid; and that, therefore, when striking on the crystal in order to break it, it ought always to split rather along these three planes than along the two others. When one has a number of spheroids of the form above described, and ranges them in a pyramid, one sees why the two methods of division are more difficult. For in the case of that division which would be parallel to the base, each spheroid would be obliged to detach itself from three others which it touches upon their flattened surfaces, which hold more strongly than the contacts at the edges. And besides that, this division will not occur along entire layers, because each of the spheroids of a layer is scarcely held at all by the 6 of the same layer that surround it, since they only touch it at the edges; so that it adheres readily to the neighbouring layer, and the others to it, for the same reason; and this causes uneven surfaces. Also one sees by experiment that when grinding down the crystal on a rather rough stone, directly on the equilateral solid angle, one verily finds much facility in reducing it in this direction, but much difficulty afterwards in polishing the surface which has been flattened in this manner.

As for the other method of division along the plane GHKL, it will be seen that each spheroid would have to detach itself from four of the neighbouring layer, two of which touch it on the flattened surfaces, and two at the edges. So that this division is likewise more difficult than that which is made parallel to one of the surfaces of the crystal; where, as we have said, each spheroid is detached from only three of the neighbouring layer: of which three there is one only which touches it on the flattened surface, and the other two at the edges only.

However, that which has made me know that in the crystal there are layers in this last fashion is that in a piece weighing half a pound which I possess, one sees that it is split along its length, as is the above-mentioned prism by the plane GHKL; as appears by colours of the iris extending throughout this whole plane, although the two pieces still hold together. All this proves, then, that the composition of the crystal is such as we have stated. To which I again add this experiment; that if one passes a knife scraping along any one of the natural surfaces, and downwards as it were from the equilateral obtuse angle, that is to say, from the apex of the pyramid, one finds it quite hard; but by scraping in the opposite sense an incision is easily made. This follows manifestly from the situation of the small spheroids; over which, in the first manner, the knife glides; but in the other manner it seizes them from beneath almost as if they were the scales of a fish.

I will not undertake to say anything touching the way in which so many corpuscles all equal and similar are generated, nor how they are set in such beautiful order; whether they are formed first and then assembled, or whether they arrange themselves thus in coming into being and as fast as they are produced, which seems to me more probable. To develop truths so recondite there would be needed a knowledge of nature much greater than that which we have. I will add only that these little spheroids could well contribute to form the spheroids of the waves of light, here above supposed, these as well as those being similarly situated, and with their axes parallel.

Calculations which have been supposed in this chapter

Mr. Bartholinus, in his treatise of this crystal, puts at 101 degrees the obtuse angles of the faces, which I have stated to be 101 degrees 52 minutes. He states

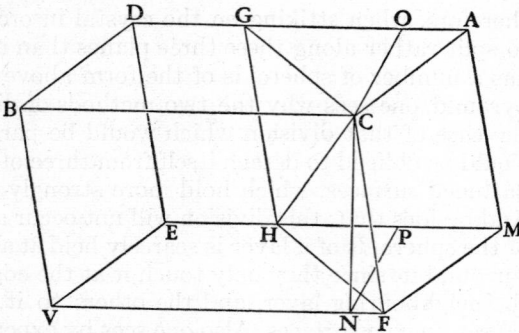

that he measured these angles directly on the crystal, which is difficult to do with ultimate exactitude, because the edges such as CA, CB, in this figure, are generally worn, and not quite straight. For more certainty, therefore, I preferred to measure actually the obtuse angle by which the faces CBDA, CBVF are inclined to one another, namely, the angle OCN formed by drawing CN perpendicular to FV, and CO perpendicular to DA. This angle OCN I found to be 105 degrees; and its supplement CNP to be 75 degrees, as it should be.

To find from this the obtuse angle BCA, I imagined a sphere having its centre at C, and on its surface a spherical triangle, formed by the intersection

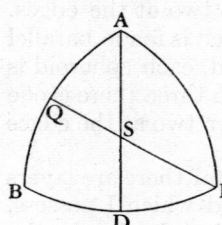

of three planes which enclose the solid angle C. In this equilateral triangle, which is ABF in this other figure, I see that each of the angles should be 105 degrees, namely, equal to the angle OCN; and that each of the sides should be of as many degrees as the angle ACB, or ACF, or BCF. Having then drawn the arc FQ perpendicular to the side AB, which it divides equally at Q, the triangle FQA has a right angle at Q, the angle A 105 degrees, and F half as much, namely 52 degrees 30 minutes; whence the hypotenuse AF is found to be 101 degrees 52 minutes. And this arc AF is the measure of the angle ACF in the figure of the crystal .

In the same figure, if the plane CGHF cuts the crystal so that it divides the obtuse angles ACB, MHV in the middle, it is stated, in Article 10, that the angle CFH is 70 degrees 57 minutes. This again is easily shown in the same spherical triangle ABF, in which it appears that the arc FQ is as many degrees as the angle GCF in the crystal, the supplement of which is the angle CFH. Now the arc FQ is found to be 109 degrees 3 minutes. Then its supplement, 70 degrees 57 minutes, is the angle CFH.

It was stated, in Article 26, that the straight line CS, which in the preceding figure is CH, being the axis of the crystal, that is to say, being equally inclined to the three sides CA, CB, CF, the angle GCH is 45 degrees 20 minutes. This is also easily calculated by the same spherical triangle. For by drawing the other arc AD which cuts BF equally, and intersects FQ at S, this point will be the centre of the triangle. And it is easy to see that the arc SQ is the measure of the angle GCH in the figure which represents the crystal. Now in the triangle QAS, which is right-angled, one knows also the angle A, which is 52 degrees 30 minutes, and the side AQ 50 degrees 56 minutes; whence the side SQ is found to be 45 degrees 20 minutes.

In Article 27 it was required to show that PMS, being an ellipse the centre of which is C, and which touches the straight line MD at M so that the angle MCL which CM makes with CL, perpendicular on DM, is 6 degrees 40 minutes, and its semi-minor axis CS making with CG (which is parallel to MD) an angle GCS of 45 degrees 20 minutes,—it was required to show, I say, that, CM being 100,000 parts, PC the semi-major diameter of this ellipse is 105,032 parts, and CS, the semi-minor diameter, 93,410.

Let CP and CS be prolonged and meet the tangent DM at D and Z; and from the point of contact M let MN and MO be drawn as perpendiculars to

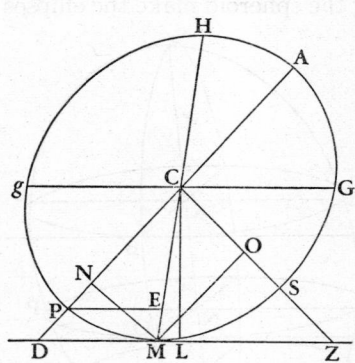

CP and CS. Now because the angles SCP, GCL, are right angles, the angle PCL will be equal to GCS which was 45 degrees 20 minutes. And deducting the angle LCM, which is 6 degrees 40 minutes, from LCP, which is 45 degrees 20 minutes, there remains MCP, 38 degrees 40 minutes. Considering, then, CM as a radius of 100,000 parts, MN, the sine of 38 degrees 40 minutes, will be 62,479. And in the right-angled triangle MND, MN will be to ND as the radius of the tables is to the tangent of 45 degrees 20 minutes (because the angle NMD is equal to DCL, or GCS); that is to say, as 100,000 to 101,170: whence results ND, 63,210. But NC is 78,079 of the same parts, CM being 100,000, because NC is the sine of the complement of the angle MCP, which was 38 degrees 40 minutes. Then the whole line DC is 141,289; and CP, which is a mean proportional between DC and CN, since MD touches the ellipse, will be 105,032.

Similarly, because the angle OMZ is equal to CDZ, or LCZ, which is 44 degrees 40 minutes, being the complement of GCS, it follows that, as the radius of the tables is to the tangent of 44 degrees 40 minutes, so will OM 78,079 be to OZ 77,176. But OC is 62,479 of these same parts of which CM is 100,000, because it is equal to MN, the sine of the angle MCP, which is 38 degrees 40 minutes. Then the whole line CZ is 139,655; and CS, which is a mean proportional between CZ and CO will be 93,410.

At the same place it was stated that GC was found to be 98,779 parts. To prove this, let PE be drawn in the same figure parallel to DM, and meeting CM at E. In the right-angled triangle CLD the side CL is 99,324 (CM being 100,000), because CL is the sine of the complement of the angle LCM, which is 6 degrees 40 minutes. And since the angle LCD is 45 degrees 20 minutes, being equal to GCS, the side LD is found to be 100,486: whence, deducting ML 11,609 there will remain MD 88,877. Now as CD (which was 141,289) is to DM 88,877, so will CP 105,032 be to PE 66,070. But as the rectangle MEH (or rather the difference of the squares on CM and CE) is to the square on MC, so is the square on PE to the square on Cg; then also as the difference of the squares on DC and CP to the square on CD, so also is the square on PE to the square on gC. But DP, CP, and PE are known; hence, also one knows GC, which is 98,779.

Lemma which has been supposed

If a spheroid is touched by a straight line, and also by two or more planes which are parallel to this line, though not parallel to one another, all the points of contact of the line, as well as of the planes, will be in one and the same ellipse made by a plane which passes through the centre of the spheroid.

Let LED be the spheroid touched by the line BM at the point B, and also
by the planes parallel to this line at the points O and A. It is required to demonstrate that the points B, O, and A are in one and the same ellipse made in
the spheroid by a plane which passes through its centre.

Through the line BM, and through the points O and A, let there be drawn
planes parallel to one another, which, in cutting the spheroid make the ellipses
LBD, POP, QAQ; which will all be similar
and similarly disposed, and will have their
centres K, N, R, in one and the same diameter of the spheroid, which will also be
the diameter of the ellipse made by the section of the plane that passes through the
centre of the spheroid, and which cuts the
planes of the three said ellipses at right
angles: for all this is manifest by Proposition 15 of the book of *Conoids and Spheroids*
of Archimedes. Further, the two latter
planes, which are drawn through the points
O and A, will also, by cutting the planes
which touch the spheroid in these same
points, generate straight lines, as OH and
AS, which will, as is easy to see, be parallel
to BM; and all three, BM, OH, AS, will

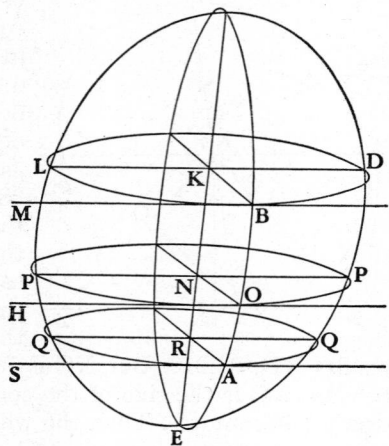

touch the ellipses LBD, POP, QAQ in these points, B, O, A; since they are in
the planes of these ellipses, and at the same time in the planes which touch the
spheroid. If now from these points B, O, A, there are drawn the straight lines
BK, ON, AR, through the centres of the same ellipses, and if through these
centres there are drawn also the diameters LD, PP, QQ, parallel to the tangents BM, OH, AS; these will be conjugate to the aforesaid BK, ON, AR. And
because the three ellipses are similar and similarly disposed, and have their diameters LD, PP, QQ parallel, it is certain that their conjugate diameters BK,
ON, AR, will also be parallel. And the centres K, N, R being, as has been
stated, in one and the same diameter of the spheroid, these parallels BK, ON,
AR will necessarily be in one and the same plane, which passes through this
diameter of the spheroid, and, in consequence, the points R, O, A are in one
and the same ellipse made by the intersection of this plane. Which was to be
proved. And it is manifest that the demonstration would be the same if,
besides the points O, A, there had been others in which the spheroid had been
touched by planes parallel to the straight line BM.

CHAPTER SIX

On the Figures of the Transparent Bodies

Which serve for refraction and for reflexion

AFTER having explained how the properties of reflexion and refraction follow from what we have supposed concerning the nature of light and of opaque bodies and of transparent media, I will here set forth a very easy and natural way of deducing, from the same principles, the true figures which serve, either by reflexion or by refraction, to collect or disperse the rays of light, as may be desired. For though I do not see yet that there are means of making use of these figures, so far as relates to refraction, not only because of the difficulty of shaping the glasses of telescopes with the requisite exactitude according to these figures, but also because there exists in refraction itself a property which hinders the perfect concurrence of the rays, as Mr. Newton has very well proved by experiment, I will yet not desist from relating the invention, since it offers itself, so to speak, of itself, and because it further confirms our theory of refraction, by the agreement which here is found between the refracted ray and the reflected ray. Besides, it may occur that some one in the future will discover in it utilities which at present are not seen.

To proceed, then, to these figures, let us suppose first that it is desired to find a surface CDE which shall reassemble at a point B rays coming from another point A; and that the summit of the surface shall be the given point D in the straight line AB. I say that, whether by reflexion or by refraction, it is

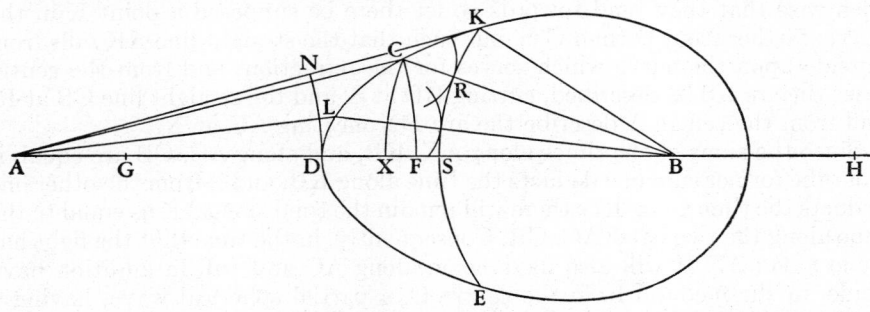

only necessary to make this surface such that the path of the light from the point A to all points of the curved line CDE, and from these to the point of concurrence (as here the path along the straight lines AC, CB, along AL, LB, and along AD, DB), shall be everywhere traversed in equal times: by which principle the finding of these curves becomes very easy.

So far as relates to the reflecting surface, since the sum of the lines AC, CB ought to be equal to that of AD, DB, it appears that DCE ought to be an ellipse; and for refraction, the ratio of the velocities of waves of light in the media A and B being supposed to be known, for example that of 3 to 2 (which is the same, as we have shown, as the ratio of the sines in the refraction), it is

only necessary to make DH equal to $\frac{3}{2}$
of DB; and having after that described
from the centre A some arc FC, cutting
DB at F, then describe another from
centre B with its semi-diameter BX
equal to $\frac{2}{3}$ of FH; and the point of intersection of the two arcs will be one
of the points required, through which
the curve should pass. For this point,
having been found in this fashion, it is
easy forthwith to demonstrate that the
time along AC, CB will be equal to the
time along AD, DB.

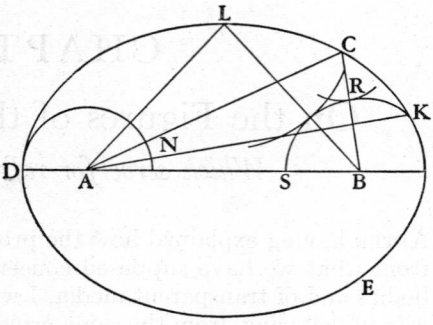

For, assuming that the line AD represents the time which the light takes to
traverse this same distance AD in air, it is evident that DH, equal to $\frac{3}{2}$ of DB,
will represent the time of the light along DB in the medium, because it needs
here more time in proportion as its speed is slower. Therefore, the whole line
AH will represent the time along AD, DB. Similarly, the line AC or AF will
represent the time along AC; and FH, being by construction equal to $\frac{3}{2}$ of CB,
it will represent the time along CB in the medium; and, in consequence, the
whole line AH will represent also the time along AC, CB. Whence it appears
that the time along AC, CB is equal to the time along AD, DB. And, similarly,
it can be shown, if L and K are other points in the curve CDE, that the times
along AL, LB, and along AK, KB, are always represented by the line AH, and,
therefore, equal to the said time along AD, DB.

In order to show further that the surfaces which these curves will generate
by revolution will direct all the rays which reach them from the point A in
such wise that they tend towards B, let there be supposed a point K in the
curve, farther from D than C is, but such that the straight line AK falls from
outside upon the curve which serves for the refraction; and from the centre
B let the arc KS be described, cutting BD at S, and the straight line CB at R;
and from the centre A describe the arc DN meeting AK at N.

Since the sums of the times along AK, KB, and along AC, CB are equal, if
from the former sum one deducts the time along KB, and if from the other one
deducts the time along RB, there will remain the time along AK as equal to the
time along the two parts AC, CR. Consequently, in the time that the light has
come along AK it will also have come along AC and will in addition have
made, in the medium from the centre C, a partial spherical wave, having a
semi-diameter equal to CR. And this wave will necessarily touch the circumference KS at R, since CB cuts this circumference at right angles. Similarly,
having taken any other point L in the curve, one can show that in the same
time as the light passes along AL it will also have come along AL and in addition will have made a partial wave, from the centre L, which will touch the
same circumference KS. And so with all other points of the curve CDE. Then,
at the moment that the light reaches K the arc KRS will be the termination
of the movement, which has spread from A through DCK. And thus this same
arc will constitute in the medium the propagation of the wave emanating from
A; which wave may be represented by the arc DN, or by any other nearer the
centre A. But all the pieces of the arc KRS are propagated successively along

straight lines which are perpendicular to them, that is to say, which tend to the centre B (for that can be demonstrated in the same way as we have proved above that the pieces of spherical waves are propagated along the straight lines coming from their centre), and these progressions of the pieces of the waves constitute the rays themselves of light. It appears, then, that all these rays tend here towards the point B.

One might also determine the point C, and all the others, in this curve which serves for the refraction, by dividing DA at G in such a way that DG is ⅔ of DA, and describing from the centre B any arc CX which cuts BD at X, and another from the centre A with its semi-diameter AF equal to ³⁄₂ of GX; or rather, having described, as before, the arc CX, it is only necessary to make DF equal to ³⁄₂ of DX, and from the centre A to strike the arc FC; for these two

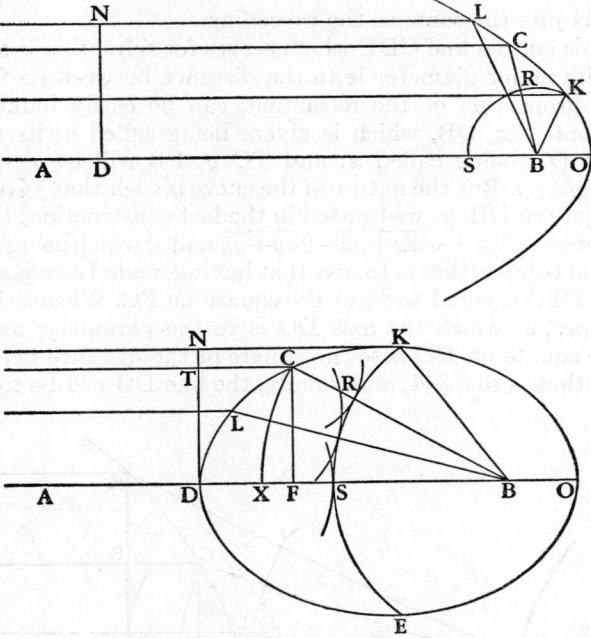

constructions, as may be easily known, come back to the first one which was shown before. And it is manifest by the last method that this curve is the same that M. Descartes has given in his *Geometry*, and which he calls the first of his Ovals.

It is only a part of this oval which serves for the refraction, namely, the part DK, ending at K, if AK is the tangent. As to the other part, Descartes has remarked that it could serve for reflexions, if there were some material of a mirror of such a nature that, by its means, the force of the rays (or, as we should say, the velocity of the light, which he could not say, since he held that the movement of light was instantaneous) could be augmented in the proportion of 3 to 2. But we have shown that in our way of explaining reflexion, such a thing could not arise from the matter of the mirror, and it is entirely impossible.

From what has been demonstrated about this oval, it will be easy to find
the figure which serves to collect to a point incident parallel rays. For by supposing just the same construction, but the point A infinitely distant, giving
parallel rays, our oval becomes a true ellipse, the construction of which differs
in no way from that of the oval, except that FC, which previously was an arc
of a circle, is here a straight line, perpendicular to DB. For the wave of light
DN, being likewise represented by a straight line, it will be seen that all the
points of this wave, travelling as far as the surface KD along lines parallel to
DB, will advance subsequently towards the point B, and will arrive there at
the same time. As for the ellipse which served for reflexion, it is evident that
it will here become a parabola, since its focus A may be regarded as infinitely
distant from the other, B, which is here the focus of the parabola, towards
which all the reflexions of rays parallel to AB tend. And the demonstration of
these effects is just the same as the preceding.

But that this curved line CDE which serves for refraction is an ellipse, and
is such that its major diameter is to the distance between its foci as 3 to 2,
which is the proportion of the refraction, can be easily found by the calculus of algebra. For, DB, which is given, being called a; its undetermined
perpendicular DT being called x; and TC y; FB will be $a-y$; CB will be
$\sqrt{xx+aa-2ay+yy}$. But the nature of the curve is such that $\frac{2}{3}$ of TC together
with CB is equal to DB, as was stated in the last construction: then the equation will be between $\frac{2}{3}y+\sqrt{xx+aa-2ay+yy}$ and a; which being reduced, gives
$\frac{6}{5}ay-yy$ equal to $\frac{9}{5}xx$; that is to say, that having made DO equal to $\frac{6}{5}$ of DB,
the rectangle DFO is equal to $\frac{9}{5}$ of the square on FC. Whence it is seen that
DC is an ellipse, of which the axis DO is to the parameter as 9 to 5; and,
therefore, the square on DO is to the square of the distance between the foci
as 9 to 9−5, that is to say 4; and, finally, the line DO will be to this distance
as 3 to 2.

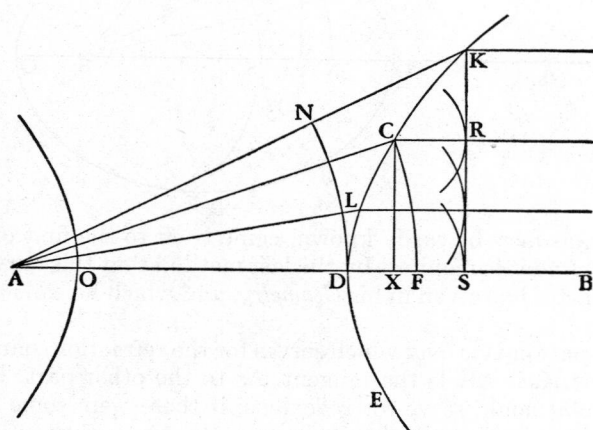

Again, if one supposes the point B to be infinitely distant, in lieu of our first
oval we shall find that CDE is a true hyperbola; which will make those rays
become parallel which come from the point A. And, in consequence also, those
which are parallel within the transparent body will be collected outside at the
point A. Now it must be remarked that CX and KS become straight lines per-

pendicular to BA, because they represent arcs of circles the centre of which is
infinitely distant. And the intersection of the perpendicular CX with the arc
FC will give the point C, one of those through which the curve ought to pass.
And this operates so that all the parts of the wave of light DN, coming to meet
the surface KDE, will advance thence along parallels to KS and will arrive at
this straight line at the same time; of which the proof is again the same as that
which served for the first oval. Besides, one finds by a calculation as easy as
the preceding one, that CDE is here a hyperbola of which the axis DO is $\frac{4}{5}$ of
AD, and the parameter equal to AD. Whence, it is easily proved that DO is to
the distance between the foci as 3 to 2.

These are the two cases in which conic sections serve for refraction, and are
the same which are explained, in his *Dioptrique*, by Descartes, who first found
out the use of these lines in relation to refraction, as also that of the ovals the

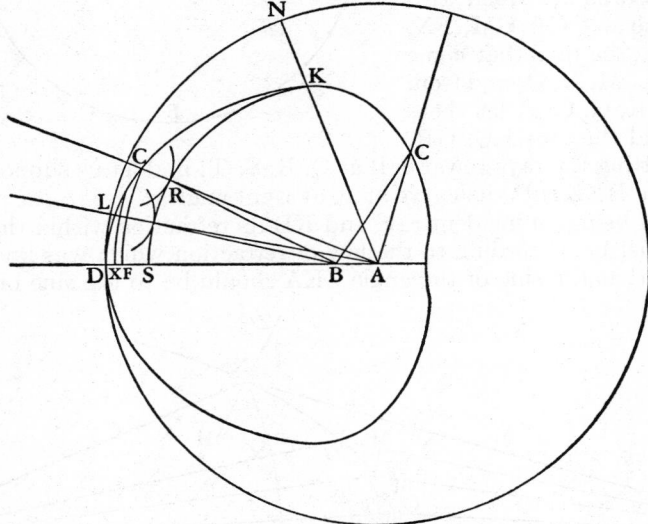

first of which we have already set forth. The second oval is that which serves
for rays that tend to a given point; in which oval, if the apex of the surface
which receives the rays is D, it will happen that the other apex will be situated
between B and A, or beyond A, according as the ratio of AD to DB is given of
greater or lesser value. And in this latter case it is the same as that which
Descartes calls his third oval.

Now the finding and construction of this second oval is the same as that of
the first, and the demonstration of its effect likewise. But it is worthy of remark
that in one case this oval becomes a perfect circle, namely when the ratio of
AD to DB is the same as the ratio of the refractions, here as 3 to 2, as I observed a long time ago. The fourth oval, serving only for impossible reflexions,
there is no need to set it forth.

As for the manner in which M. Descartes discovered these lines, since he has
given no explanation of it, nor anyone else since that I know of, I will say here,
in passing, what it seems to me it must have been. Let it be proposed to find
the surface generated by the revolution of the curve KDE, which, receiving

the incident rays coming to it
from the point A, shall deviate
them toward the point B. Then
considering this other curve as
already known, and that its
apex D is in the straight line
AB, let us divide it up into an
infinitude of small pieces by the
points G, C, F; and having
drawn from each of these points,
straight lines towards A to represent the incident rays, and
other straight lines towards B,
let there also be described with
centre A the arcs GL, CM, FN,
DO, cutting the rays that come
from A at L, M, N, O; and from
the points K, G, C, F, let there
be described the arcs KQ, GR,

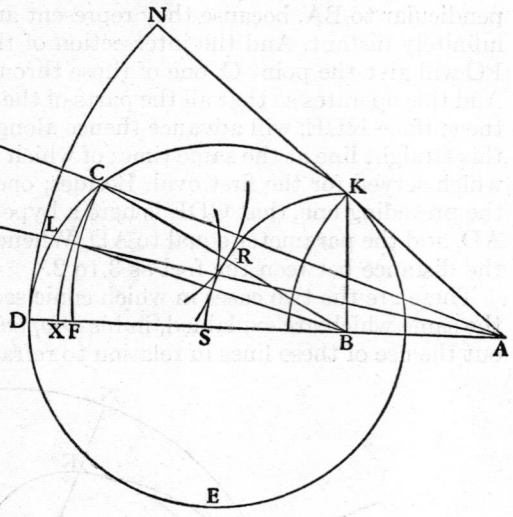

CS, FT cutting the rays towards B at Q, R, S, T; and let us suppose that the
straight line HKZ cuts the curve at K at right angles.

Then AK being an incident ray, and KB its refraction within the medium,
it needs must be, according to the law of refraction which was known to M.
Descartes, that the sine of the angle ZKA should be to the sine of the angle

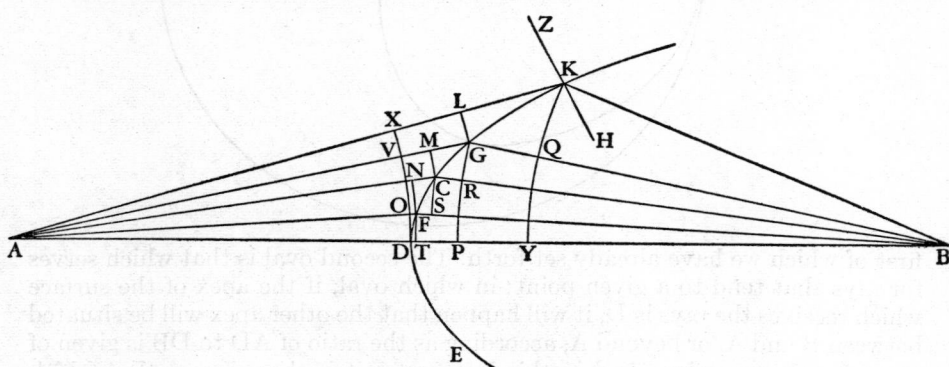

HKB as 3 to 2, supposing that this is the proportion of the refraction of glass;
or rather, that the sine of the angle KGL should have this same ratio to the
sine of the angle GKQ, considering KG, GL, KQ as straight lines because of
their smallness. But these sines are the lines KL and GQ, if GK is taken as the
radius of the circle. Then LK ought to be to GQ as 3 to 2; and in the same ratio
MG to CR, NC to FS, OF to DT. Then also the sum of all the antecedents to
all the consequents would be as 3 to 2. Now, by prolonging the arc DO until
it meets AK at X, KX is the sum of the antecedents. And by prolonging the
arc KQ till it meets AD at Y, the sum of the consequents is DY. Then KX
ought to be to DY as 3 to 2. Whence, it would appear that the curve KDE was
of such a nature that having drawn from some point which had been assumed,

such as K, the straight lines KA, KB, the excess by which AK surpasses AD should be to the excess of DB over KB, as 3 to 2. For it can similarly be demonstrated, by taking any other point in the curve, such as G, that the excess of AG over AD, namely VG, is to the excess of BD over DG, namely DP, in this same ratio of 3 to 2. And, following this principle, M. Descartes constructed these curves in his *Geometry;* and he easily recognized that in the case of parallel rays, these curves became hyperbolas and ellipses.

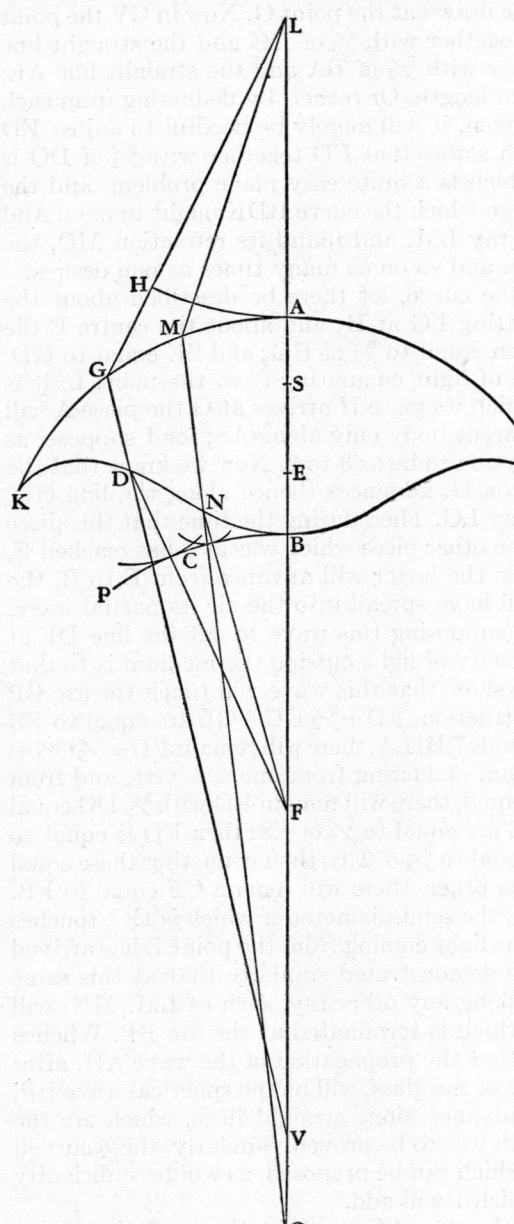

Let us now return to our method and let us see how it leads without difficulty to the finding of the curves which one side of the glass requires when the other side is of a given figure; a figure not only plane or spherical, or made by one of the conic sections (which is the restriction with which Descartes proposed this problem, leaving the solution to those who should come after him) but generally any figure whatever: that is to say, one made by the revolution of any given curved line to which one must merely know how to draw straight lines as tangents.

Let the given figure be that made by the revolution of some curve such as AK about the axis AV, and that this side of the glass receives rays coming from the point L. Furthermore, let the thickness AB of the middle of the glass be given, and the point F at which one desires the rays to be all perfectly reunited, whatever be the first refraction occurring at the surface AK.

I say that for this the sole requirement is that the outline BDK which constitutes the other surface shall be such that the path of the light from the point L to the surface AK, and from thence to the surface BDK, and from thence to the point F, shall be traversed everywhere in equal times, and in each case in a time equal to that which the light employs to pass along the straight line LF of which the part AB is within the glass.

Let LG be a ray falling on the arc AK. Its refraction GV will be given by means of the tangent which will be drawn at the point G. Now in GV the point D must be found such that FD together with $\frac{3}{2}$ of DG and the straight line GL, may be equal to FB together with $\frac{3}{2}$ of BA and the straight line AL; which, as is clear, make up a given length. Or rather, by deducting from each the length of LG, which is also given, it will merely be needful to adjust FD up to the straight line VG in such a way that FD together with $\frac{3}{2}$ of DG is equal to a given straight line, which is a quite easy plane problem: and the point D will be one of those through which the curve BDK ought to pass. And similarly, having drawn another ray LM, and found its refraction MO, the point N will be found in this line, and so on as many times as one desires.

To demonstrate the effect of the curve, let there be described about the centre L the circular arc AH, cutting LG at H; and about the centre F the arc BP; and in AB let AS be taken equal to $\frac{2}{3}$ of HG; and SE equal to GD. Then, considering AH as a wave of light emanating from the point L, it is certain that during the time in which its piece H arrives at G the piece A will have advanced within the transparent body only along AS; for I suppose, as above, the proportion of the refraction to be as 3 to 2. Now we know that the piece of wave, which is incident on G, advances thence along the line GD, since GV is the refraction of the ray LG. Then during the time that this piece of wave has taken from G to D, the other piece which was at S has reached E, since GD, SE are equal. But while the latter will advance from E to B, the piece of wave which was at D will have spread into the air its partial wave, the semi-diameter of which, DC (supposing this wave to cut the line DF at C), will be $\frac{3}{2}$ of EB, since the velocity of light outside the medium is to that inside as 3 to 2. Now it is easy to show that this wave will touch the arc BP at this point C. For since, by construction, FD+$\frac{3}{2}$DG+GL are equal to FB +$\frac{3}{2}$BA+AL; on deducting the equals LH, LA, there will remain FD+$\frac{3}{2}$DG+ GH equal to FB+$\frac{3}{2}$BA. And, again, deducting from one side GH, and from the other side $\frac{3}{2}$ of AS, which are equal, there will remain FD with $\frac{3}{2}$ DG equal to FB with $\frac{3}{2}$ of BS. But $\frac{3}{2}$ of DG are equal to $\frac{3}{2}$ of ES; then FD is equal to FB with $\frac{3}{2}$ of BE. But DC was equal to $\frac{3}{2}$ of EB; then deducting these equal lengths from one side and from the other, there will remain CF equal to FB. And thus it appears that the wave, the semi-diameter of which is DC, touches the arc BP at the moment when the light coming from the point L has arrived at B along the line LB. It can be demonstrated similarly that at this same moment the light that has come along any other ray, such as LM, MN, will have propagated the movement which is terminated at the arc BP. Whence it follows, as has been often said, that the propagation of the wave AH, after it has passed through the thickness of the glass, will be the spherical wave BP, all the pieces of which ought to advance along straight lines, which are the rays of light, to the centre F. Which was to be proved. Similarly, these curved lines can be found in all the cases which can be proposed, as will be sufficiently shown by one or two examples which I will add.

Let there be given the surface of the glass AK, made by the revolution about the axis BA of the line AK, which may be straight or curved. Let there be also given in the axis the point L and the thickness BA of the glass; and let it be required to find the other surface KDB, which receiving rays that are parallel to AB will direct them in such wise that after being again refracted at the given surface AK they will all be reassembled at the point L.

From the point L let there be drawn to some point of the given line AK the straight line LG, which, being considered as a ray of light, its refraction GD will then be found. And this line being then prolonged at one side or the other will meet the straight line BL, as here at V. Let there then be erected on AB the perpendicular BC, which will represent a wave of light coming from the infinitely distant point F, since we have supposed the rays to be parallel. Then all the parts of this wave BC must arrive at the same time at the point L; or

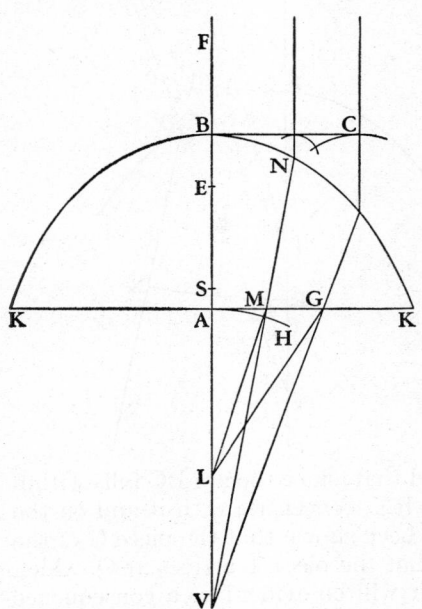

rather all the parts of a wave emanating from the point L must arrive at the same time at the straight line BC. And for that it is necessary to find in the line VGD the point D, such that having drawn DC parallel to AB, the sum of CD plus $\frac{3}{2}$ of DG, plus GL may be equal to $\frac{3}{2}$ of AB plus AL: or rather, on deducting from both sides GL, which is given, CD plus $\frac{3}{2}$ of DG must be equal to a given length; which is a still easier problem than the preceding construction. The point D thus found will be one of those through which the curve ought to pass; and the proof will be the same as before. And by this it will be proved that the waves which come from the point L, after having passed through the glass KAKB, will take the form of straight lines, as BC; which is the same thing as saying that the rays will become parallel. Whence it follows reciprocally that parallel rays falling on the surface KDB will be reassembled at the point L.

Again, let there be given the surface AK, of any desired form, generated by revolution about the axis AB, and let the thickness of the glass at the middle be AB. Also, let the point L be given in the axis behind the glass; and let it be supposed that the rays which fall on the surface AK tend to this point, and that it is required to find the surface BD, which on their emergence from the glass turns them as if they came from the point F in front of the glass.

Having taken any point G in the line AK, and drawing the straight line IGL, its part GI will represent one of the incident rays, the refraction of which, GV, will then be found: and it is in this line that we must find the point D, one of those through which the curve DG ought to pass. Let us suppose that it has been found: and about L as centre let there be described GT, the arc of a circle cutting the straight line AB at T, in case the distance LG is greater than LA; for otherwise the arc AH must be described about the same centre, cutting the straight line LG at H. This arc GT (or AH, in the other case) will represent an incident wave of light, the rays of which tend towards L. Similarly, about the centre F let there be described the circular arc DQ, which will represent a wave emanating from the point F.

Then the wave TG, after having passed through the glass, must form the wave QD; and for this I observe that the time taken by the light along GD in the glass must be equal to that taken along the three, TA, AB, and BQ, of which AB alone is within the glass. Or, rather, having taken AS equal to $\frac{2}{3}$ of AT, I observe that $\frac{3}{2}$ of GD ought to be equal to $\frac{3}{2}$ of SB, plus BQ; and, deducting both of them from FD or FQ, that FD less $\frac{3}{2}$ of GD ought to be equal to FB less $\frac{3}{2}$ of SB. And this last difference is a given length: and all that is required is to draw the straight line FD from the given point F to meet VG so that it may be thus. Which is a problem quite similar to that which served for the first of these constructions, where FD plus $\frac{3}{2}$ of GD had to be equal to a given length.

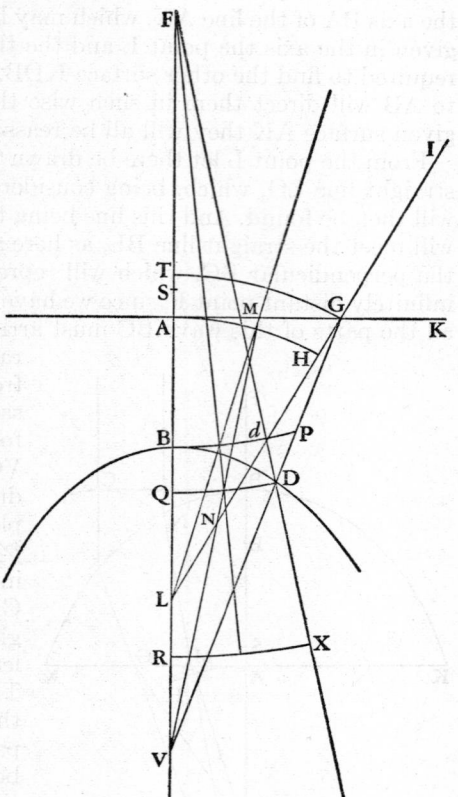

In the demonstration it is to be observed that, since the arc BC falls within the glass, there must be conceived an arc RX, concentric with it and on the other side of QD. Then, after it shall have been shown that the piece G of the wave GT arrives at D at the same time that the piece T arrives at Q, which is easily deduced from the construction, it will be evident as a consequence that the partial wave generated at the point D will touch the arc RX at the moment when the piece Q shall have come to R, and that thus this arc will at the same moment be the termination of the movement that comes from the wave TG; whence all the rest may be concluded.

Having shown the method of finding these curved lines which serve for the perfect concurrence of the rays, there remains to be explained a notable thing touching the uncoordinated refraction of spherical, plane, and other surfaces: an effect which if ignored might cause some doubt concerning what we have several times said, that rays of light are straight lines which intersect at right angles the waves which travel along them.

For in the case of rays which, for example, fall parallel upon a spherical surface AFE, intersecting one another, after refraction, at different points, as the figure [P. 617] represents; what can the waves of light be, in this transparent body, which are cut at right angles by the converging rays? For they can not be spherical. And what will these waves become after the said rays begin to inter-

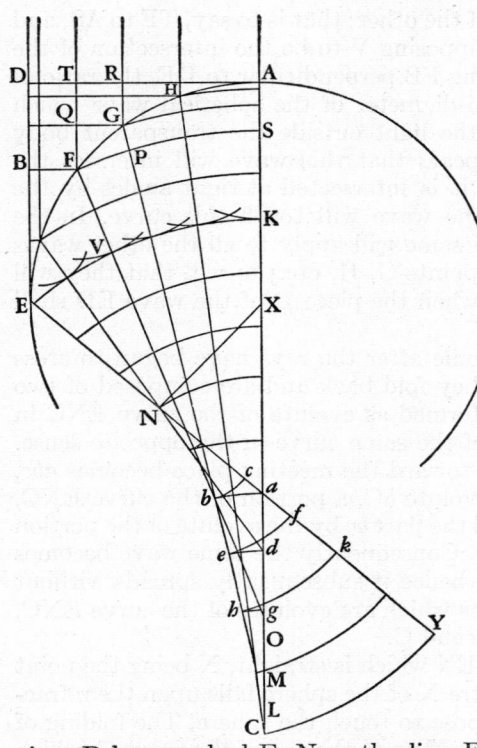

sect one another? It will be seen in the solution of this difficulty that something very remarkable comes to pass herein, and that the waves do not cease to persist though they do not continue entire, as when they cross the glasses designed according to the construction we have seen.

According to what has been shown above, the straight line AD, which has been drawn at the summit of the sphere, at right angles to the axis parallel to which the rays come, represents the wave of light; and in the time taken by its piece D to reach the spherical surface AGE at E, its other parts will have met the same surface at F, G, H, etc., and will have also formed spherical partial waves of which these points are the centres. And the surface EK which all those waves will touch, will be the continuation of the wave AD in the sphere at the moment when the piece D has reached E. Now the line EK is not an arc of a circle, but is a curved line formed as the evolute of another curve ENC, which touches all the rays HL, GM, FO, etc., that are the refractions of the parallel rays, if we imagine laid over the convexity ENC a thread which in unwinding describes at its end E the said curve EK. For, supposing that this curve has been thus described, we will show that the said waves formed from the centres F, G, H, etc., will all touch it.

It is certain that the curve EK and all the others described by the evolution of the curve ENC, with different lengths of thread, will cut all the rays HL, GM, FO, etc., at right angles, and in such wise that the parts of them intercepted between two such curves will all be equal; for this follows from what has been demonstrated in our treatise *de Motu Pendulorum*. Now imagining the incident rays as being infinitely near to one another, if we consider two of them, as RG, TF, and draw GQ perpendicular to RG, and if we suppose the curve FS which intersects GM at P to have been described by evolution from the curve NC, beginning at F, as far as which the thread is supposed to extend, we may assume the small piece FP as a straight line perpendicular to the ray GM, and similarly the arc GF as a straight line. But GM being the refraction of the ray RG, and FP being perpendicular to it, QF must be to GP as 3 to 2, that is to say in the proportion of the refraction; as was shown above in explaining the discovery of Descartes. And the same thing occurs in all the small arcs GH, HA, etc., namely that in the quadrilaterals which enclose them the side parallel to the axis is to the opposite side as 3 to 2. Then also as 3 to 2 will the sum of the one set be to the sum of the other; that is to say, TF to AS, and DE to AK, and BE to SK or DV, supposing V to be the intersection of the curve EK and the ray FO. But, making FB perpendicular to DE, the ratio of 3 to 2 is also that of BE to the semi-diameter of the spherical wave which emanated from the point F while the light outside the transparent body traversed the space BE. Then it appears that this wave will intersect the ray FM at the same point V where it is intersected at right angles by the curve EK, and consequently that the wave will touch this curve. In the same way it can be proved that the same will apply to all the other waves above mentioned, originating at the points G, H, etc.; to wit, that they will touch the curve EK at the moment when the piece D of the wave ED shall have reached E.

Now to say what these waves become after the rays have begun to cross one another: it is that from thence they fold back and are composed of two contiguous parts, one being a curve formed as evolute of the curve ENC in one sense, and the other as evolute of the same curve in the opposite sense. Thus the wave KE, while advancing toward the meeting place becomes *abc*, whereof the part *ab* is made by the evolute *b*C, a portion of the curve ENC, while the end C remains attached; and the part *bc* by the evolute of the portion *b*E while the end E remains attached. Consequently the same wave becomes *def*, then *ghk*, and finally CY, from whence it subsequently spreads without any fold, but always along curved lines which are evolutes of the curve ENC, increased by some straight line at the end C.

There is even, in this curve, a part EN which is straight, N being the point where the perpendicular from the centre X of the sphere falls upon the refraction of the ray DE, which I now suppose to touch the sphere. The folding of the waves of light begins from the point N up to the end of the curve C, which point is formed by taking AC to CX in the proportion of the refraction, as here 3 to 2.

As many other points as may be desired in the curve NC are found by a Theorem which Mr. Barrow has demonstrated in section 12 of his *Lectiones Opticæ*, though for another purpose. And it is to be noted that a straight line equal in length to this curve can be given. For since it together with the line NE is equal to the line CK, which is known, since DE is to AK in the proportion of the refraction, it appears that by deducting EN from CK the remainder will be equal to the curve NC.

Similarly the waves that are folded back in reflexion by a concave spherical mirror can be found. Let ABC be the section, through the axis, of a hollow hemisphere, the centre of which is D, its axis being DB, parallel to which I suppose the rays of light to come. All the reflexions of those rays which fall upon the quarter-circle AB will touch a curved line AFE, of which line the end E is at the focus of the hemisphere,

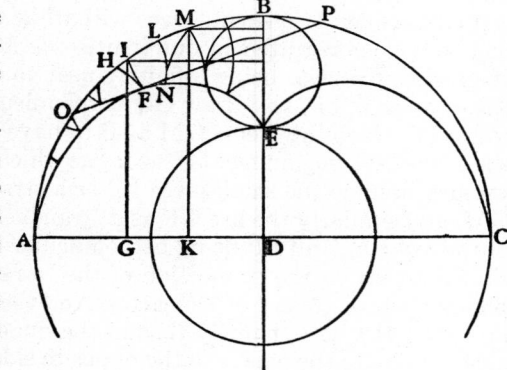

that is to say, at the point which divides the semi-diameter BD into two equal parts. The points through which this curve ought to pass are found by taking, beyond A, some arc AO, and making the arc OP double the length of it; then dividing the chord OP at F in such wise that the part FP is three times the part FO; for then F is one of the required points.

And as the parallel rays are merely perpendiculars to the waves which fall on the concave surface, which waves are parallel to AD, it will be found that as they come successively to encounter the surface AB, they form on reflexion folded waves composed of two curves which originate from two opposite evolutions of the parts of the curve AFE. So, taking AD as an incident wave, when the part AG shall have met the surface AI, that is to say when the piece G shall have reached I, it will be the curves HF, FI, generated as evolutes of the curves FA, FE, both beginning at F, which together constitute the propagation of the part AG. And a little afterwards, when the part AK has met the surface AM, the piece K having come to M, then the curves LN, NM, will together constitute the propagation of that part. And thus this folded wave will continue to advance until the point N has reached the focus E. The curve AFE can be seen in smoke, or in flying dust, when a concave mirror is held opposite the sun. And it should be known that it is none other than that curve which is described by the point E on the circumference of the circle EB, when that circle is made to roll within another whose semi-diameter is ED and whose centre is D. So that it is a kind of cycloid, of which, however, the points can be found geometrically.

Its length is exactly equal to ¾ of the diameter of the sphere, as can be found and demonstrated by means of these waves, nearly in the same way as the mensuration of the preceding curve; though it may also be demonstrated in other ways, which I omit as outside the subject. The area AOBEFA, comprised between the arc of the quarter-circle, the straight line BE, and the curve EFA, is equal to the fourth part of the quadrant DAB.

PRINTED IN THE U. S. A.